The Gramophone *Good* CD *Guide*

1994

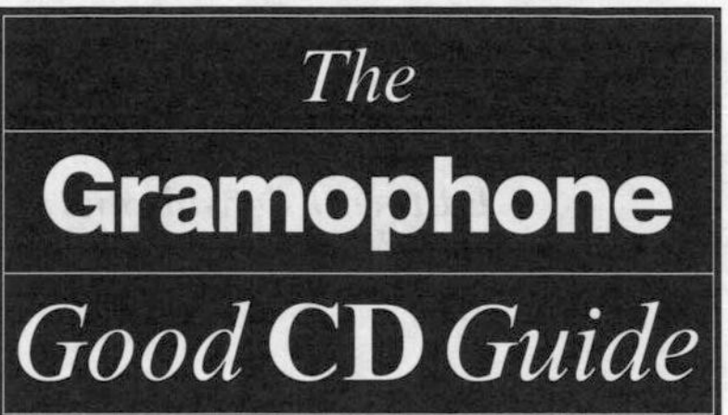

Published by

General Gramophone

Publications Ltd

177-179 Kenton Road

Harrow Middlesex HA3 0HA

Great Britain

in association with

Quad Electroacoustics Ltd

In a similar way to Gramophone magazine, which has been published monthly since 1923, Quad is practically an institution. Most audio-aware readers will know that Quad Electroacoustics Ltd (known worldwide simply as Quad, the name of their first amplifier), has always been the epitome of quality and of innovative, practical design. The publishers gratefully acknowledge their help with this publication which, for the seventh year in succession, benefits from their involvement.

Editorial Director	Christopher Pollard
Editor	Máire Taylor
Editorial Consultants	Nicholas Anderson, Quita Chavez, Michael Stewart, Jonathan Swain, Mark Wiggins
Production Editors	Dermot Jones, Ivor Humphreys, Christine Narain
Contributors	Andrew Achenbach, Nicholas Anderson, Mary Berry, Alan Blyth, Joan Chissell, Robert Cowan, Peter Dickinson, John Duarte, Jessica Duchen, David Fallows, David J. Fanning, Jonathan Freeman-Atwood, David Gutman, Douglas Hammond, Christopher Headington, Michael Jameson, James Jolly, Lindsay Kemp, Robert Kenchington, Michael Kennedy, Andrew Lamb, Robert Layton, Ivan March, John Milsom, Ivan Moody, Bryce Morrison, Patrick O'Connor, Michael Oliver, Richard Osborne, David Patmore, Marc Rochester, Julie-Anne Sadie, Stanley Sadie, Lionel Salter, Alan Sanders, Edward Seckerson, Robert Seeley, Harriet Smith, John Steane, Michael Stewart, Jonathan Swain, Arnold Whittall, Mark Wiggins and Richard Wigmore.

General Gramophone Publications Ltd 1993
UK ISBN 0-902470-40-X
USA ISBN 0-902470-45-O

Recording companies reserve the right to withdraw any Compact Disc without giving previous notice, and although every effort is made to obtain the latest information for inclusion in this book, no guarantee can be given that all the discs listed are immediately available. Any difficulties should be referred to the issuing company concerned. When ordering, purchasers are advised to quote all the relevant information in addition to the disc numbers. The publishers cannot accept responsibility for the consequences of any error.

Printed in Great Britain by William Clowes Ltd, Beccles, Suffolk, NR34 9QE.

Contents

Introduction by Sir Neville Marriner

[photo: EMI/Morrison

Since making my first record as a violinist in 1946, rarely has a month passed when I have not been in a recording studio; and whether it is in Abbey Road or Hollywood, the Concertgebouw or St Lukas Kirche in Dresden, as a conductor 50 years on, it is still supremely challenging to set down a permanent record of one's musical convictions. There is, above all, the striving to make the music sound as if it were for the first time and to convey the composer's message within one's own experience. I understand that I have made more records than any conductor extant — not all superlative! — but I can honestly say that the hours spent making those records have been immensely satisfying. The chemistry required to unify an orchestra, to integrate a soloist's conception, and to realize an unequivocal performance is extraordinary and inexplicable. The logistical circumstances surrounding the creation of such a performance are almost equally inconceivable. For the record critic, faced with over 20 versions of Elgar's Cello Concerto or nearly 100 CD recordings of Beethoven's Fifth Symphony, those intellectual and logistical circumstances are immaterial. It's what comes out of the loudspeakers that matters to them. To judge one recording against another is an unenviable task, and I am glad that it's not my profession. Nevertheless, it is a service the record collector needs if the business of buying a record is not to become too daunting. *The Gramophone Good CD Guide* aims to choose from a vast repertoire of music and select what is, in the opinion of its contributors, the best versions. If the *Guide* introduces even one more listener to great music then it has served its purpose. If it introduces listeners to new musicians it is doubly important, but if it chooses truly revelationary performances, then it has fully justified its publication.

How to use the Guide

In order to enhance the usefulness of this book and to cover as many 'good' CDs as possible from the huge range now available, this edition incorporates the following additional information: **Additional Recommendations:** Under a full review, which is generally the top recommendation for a particular work, single or multiple additional alternative recommendations will follow where appropriate. **Further listening:** Contains details of further musical works worthy of consideration from the same composer. **Suggested listening:** Contains details of musical works by composers for whom no full reviews exist or where few recordings are available.

Details are given of composer(s), work(s), instrument(s), voice range(s), record company or label (see the listing of Labels/Manufacturers and Distributors), disc number (and previous number when the newcomer is a reissue) and review date(s) in *Gramophone*. Addresses of distributing companies are provided at the rear of this book.

On the musical staves following a heading, information is provided by a system of symbols as follows:

The symbols

•••	② ②	lh 23m	DDD	6/88
Price	*Quantity/ availability*	*Timing*	*Mode*	*Review date*

Price

••• Full price: £10·00 and over

•• Medium price: £7·00–£9·99

•• Budget price: £5·00–£6·99

• Super-budget price: below £4·99

Quantity/availability

If there is more than one disc, the number involved is shown here. The first type of circle indicates sets in which the individual discs are not available separately. The second type indicates that the discs are *only* available separately.

Timing

Calculated to the nearest minute.

Mode

This three-letter code is now used by almost all manufacturers to indicate the type of processing employed during manufacture. The letters A or D are used to denote Analogue or Digital and the letter sequence represents chronological steps in the chain: the recording session itself; the editing and/or mixing routines; and finally the mastering or transcription used in preparation of the master tape which is sent to the factory.

Review date

The month and year in which the recording was reviewed in *Gramophone*.

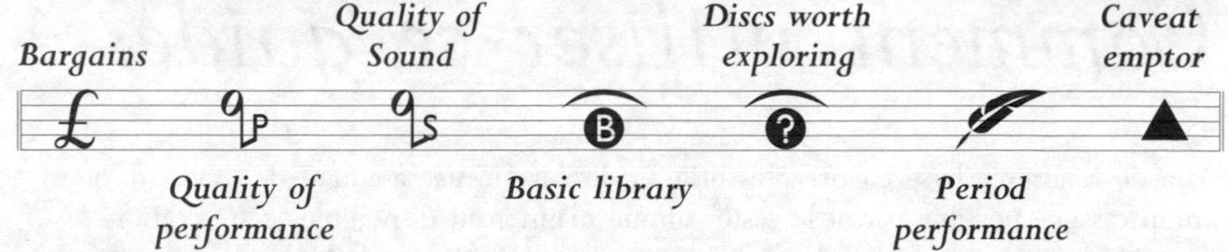

Bargains
Sometimes it is more than price alone which makes for a true bargain. A disc which involves some of the finest artists in a superlative performance and recording, for example, or possibly the sheer length in terms of playing time, will occasionally emerge at mid or bargain price. This symbol is the key to these special releases.

Quality of performance
Recordings which really brook no argument — 'musts' for the keen collector. Often the older recordings among these might well have won a *Gramophone* Award had the Awards existed when they first appeared.

Quality of sound
Those recordings which truly merit the epithet 'demonstration quality'.

Basic library
Recordings with which to begin building your CD collection.

Discs worth exploring
For the adventurous! Recordings which might easily be overlooked since they are not among the best-known works or by the better-known composers. But they could well provide some interesting surprises.

Period performance
Recordings in which some attempt is made at historical authenticity. Typically these involve the use of period instruments and/or original manuscript sources.

Caveat emptor
Performances which have stood the test of time but where the recording quality may not be up to the highest standards. This generally applies to pre-1960 recordings.

Two further symbols are used in the reviews:

Gramophone Award winners
The classical music world's most coveted accolades for recordings, these are awarded each year by *Gramophone* in categories ranging from Orchestral to Operatic, Baroque to Contemporary. One recording is also chosen from the overall list to be given the Award of Record of the Year.

Artists of the Year
Five artists whose qualities of musicianship and overall interpretation have consistently brought them to our attention.
See also the artist profiles beginning on page 17.

Comment utiliser ce guide?

Afin de rendre ce livre encore plus utile et de faire justice à autant de “bons” disques compacts que possible parmi la vaste gamme maintenant disponible, cette édition fournit les informations supplémentaires suivantes: **Recommandations supplémentaires:** Sous une critique complète, qui représente en général la plus haute recommandation pour une oeuvre donnée, une ou plusieurs autres oeuvres sont éventuellement conseillées. **A écouter également:** Des informations concernant d'autres oeuvres musicales du même compositeur, et qui méritent qu'on les écoute. **Conseils:** Des informations concernant des oeuvres musicales de compositeurs n'ayant pas fait l'objet de critiques complètes ou dont il existe peu d'enregistrements.

Compositeur(s), oeuvre(s), instrument(s), registre(s) de voix, maison de disques ou label (reportez-vous á la liste des labels/fabricants et sociétés de distribution), numéro de disque (et le numéro précédent lorsque le disque est ressorti) et date(s) de critique(s) dans *Gramophone* sont indiqués.

Les portées à la suite des titres vous fournissent des informations grâce au système de symboles suivant.

Les symboles

●●●	② ②	lh 23m	DDD	6/88
Prix	*Quantité/ disponibilité*	*Durée*	*Mode*	*Date de la critique*

Prix

●●● Prix normal

●● Prix moyen

●● Prix modique

● Prix très modique

Quantité/disponiblité

S'il y a plus d'un disque, le nombre est indiqué ici. Le premier type de cercle indique des séries dont les disques ne sont pas vendus séparément. Le second type indique que les disques ne sont disponibles *que* séparément.

Durée

Calculée à la minute près.

Mode

Ce code de trois lettres est maintenant utilisé par presque tous les fabricants pour indiquer le procédé utilisé lors de la fabrication. Les lettres A ou D signifient ‘analogique’ ou ‘numérique’ et l'ordre des lettres correspond aux étapes, par ordre chronologique, dans la chaîne: la séance d'enregistrement à proprement parler, le mixage et/ou le montage, et enfin la gravure pour la préparation de la bande maîtresse envoyée à l'usine.

Date de la critique

Le mois et l'année de publication de la critique de l'enregistrement dans *Gramophone*.

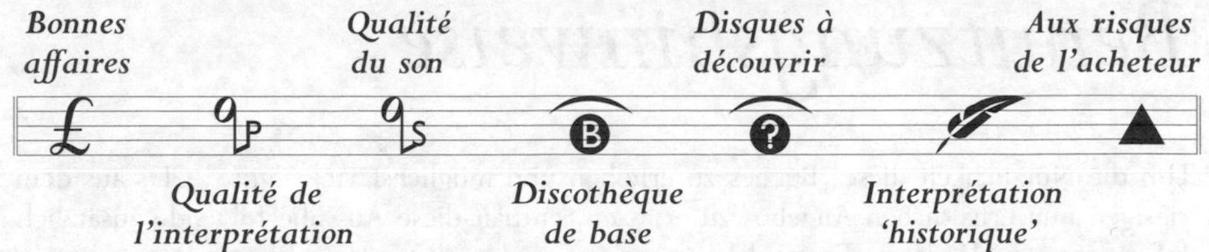

Bonnes affaires
Parfois, ce n'est pas le prix seul qui fait la bonne affaire. Un disque regroupant certains des meilleurs artistes dans une interprétation et un enregistrement excellents par exemple, ou peut-être même un enregistrement particulièrement long, est parfois vendu à un prix moyen ou très modique. Ce symbole indique ces disques spéciaux.

Qualité de l'interprétation
Des enregistrements dont la qualité est indiscutable – des 'musts' pour le collectionneur passionné. Les plus anciens parmi ceux-ci auraient souvent remporté le prix du disque *Gramophone* s'il avait existé à leur sortie.

Qualité du son
Des enregistrements dont on peut vraiment dire qu'ils sont de 'qualité démonstration'.

Discothèque de base
Des enregistrements qui constitueront les fondements de votre collection de disques compacts.

Disques à découvrir
Pour les touche-à-tout de la musique! Des enregistrements à côté desquels on aurait tendance à passer parce qu'on ne les doit pas aux compositeurs les plus célèbres, mais qui peuvent réserver de bien agréables surprises.

Interprétation 'historique'
Des enregistrements empreints de tentatives d'authenticité historique, généralement grâce à l'utilisation d'instruments d'époque et/ou de manuscrits d'origine.

Aux risques de l'acheteur
Des interprétations qui ont "bien vieilli", mais dont l'enregistrement n'est peut-être pas de la plus haute qualité. C'est généralement le cas des enregistrements datant d'avant 1960.

Deux autres symboles sont utilisés dans les critiques:

Lauréats du prix Gramophone
La distinction la plus convoitée dans le monde de la musique classique, décernée chaque année par le magazine dont nous sommes issus, par catégories allant d'Orchestral à Opéra en passant par Baroque et Contemporain. Un enregistrement est également sélectionné sur toute la liste pour le prix du disque de l'année.

Artistes de l'année
Cinq artistes qui se sont distingués par leurs qualités de musiciens et d'interprètes. Voir aussi les profils page 17 et suivantes.

Benutzungshinweise

Um die Nützlichkeit dieses Buches zu erhöhen und möglichst viele "gute" CDs aus dem riesigen nun erhältlichen Angebot zu erfassen, enthält diese Ausgabe folgende zusätzliche Informationen: **Weitere Empfehlungen:** Bei einer vollständigen Besprechung, die im allgemeinen die höchste Empfehlung für ein bestimmtes Werk ist, werden gegebenenfalls zusätzlich alternative Einzel- oder Mehrfachempfehlungen folgen. **Weitere Werke:** Einzelheiten über weitere beachtenswerte musikalische Werke desselben Komponisten. **Vorgeschlagene Werke:** Einzelheiten über musikalische Werke von Komponisten, für die keine vollständigen Besprechungen vorliegen oder wo wenige Aufnahmen verfügbar sind.

Die angegebenen Einzelheiten betreffen Komponist(en), Werk(e), Instrument(e), Stimmumfang, Plattenfirma oder Label (siehe die Auflistung der Labels/Hersteller und Händler), CD-Nummer (plus alter Nummer, falls es sich um eine Wiederveröffentlichung handelt) und Besprechungsdatum in *Gramophone*.
Auf den Notenlinien unter einer überschrift werden folgende Informationen durch Symbole wiedergegeben:

Symbole

•••	② ②	lh 23m	DDD	6/88
Preis	***Anzahl/ Verfügbarkeit***	***Dauer***	***Modus***	***Besprechungs-datum***

Preis

••• Normalpreis

•• Mittlere Preislage

•• Sparpreis

• Super-Sparpreis

Anzahl/Verfügbarkeit
Falls es sich um mehr als eine CD handelt, wird die entsprechende Zahl hier angegeben. Der erste Kreistyp zeigt Sets an, bei denen individuelle CDs nicht separat verfügbar sind. Der zweite Kreistyp zeigt an, daß die CDs *nur* separat verfügbar sind.

Dauer
Auf volle Minuten ab-oder aufgerundet.

Modus
Dieser Code aus drei Buchstaben wird heute von fast allen Herstellern verwendet, um Verfahren bei Aufnahme, Schnitt und Abmischung zu kennzeichnen. Die Buchstaben A und D stehen für Analog bzw Digital, und die Buchstabenfolge bezeichnet die chronologischen Schritte der Produktionskette: die Aufnahme selbst; das Schnitt- und/oder Abmischverfahren; und schließlich die Art der überspielung oder Transkription, die zur Vorbereitung des Originalbandes verwendet wird, welches dann die Vorlage für die Pressung bildet.

Besprechungsdatum
Monat und Jahr, in dem die Aufnahme in *Gramophone* besprochen wurde.

Sonderangebote
Manchmal ist es nicht der Preis allein, der ein wahres Sonderangebot ausmacht. Eine CD, die die besten Künstler zu einer unübertrefflichen Aufnahme bei bester Aufnahmetechnik vereint, oder die sich vielleicht einfach durch die außergewöhnliche Länge der Spielzeit auszeichnet, wird gelegentlich in der mittleren oder Sonderpreislage auftauchen. Dieses Symbol ist der Schlüssel zu diesen speziellen Veröffentlichungen.

Beste Interpretationen
Aufnahmen, die über jede Kritik erhaben sind – ein 'Muß' für jeden Sammler. Viele der älteren Aufnahmen hätten *Gramophone*-Preise gewonnen, hätte es diese Auszeichnung bei ihrem ersten Erscheinen bereits gegeben.

Beste Klangqualität
Aufnahmen, die wirklich die Bezeichnung "Vorspielqualität" verdienen.

Grundstock
Aufnahmen, die die Basis für Ihre CD-Sammlung bilden sollten.

Lohnende Aufnahmen
Nur für musikalisch Vielseitige! Diese Aufnahmen könnten leicht übersehen werden, da sie von weniger bekannten Komponisten stammen, sind jedoch oft für eine angenehme überraschung gut.

Historische Authentizität
Aufnahmen, bei denen der Versuch historischer Authentizität unternommen wurde, etwa durch Verwendung von zeitgenössischen Instrumenten und/oder Originalmanuskripten.

Achtung!
Interpretationen, die die Zeiten überdauert haben, deren Aufnahmequalität jedoch eventuell nicht dem höchsten Standard entspricht. Dies betrifft im allgemeinen Aufnahmen von vor 1960.

Zwei weitere Symbole werden in Besprechungen verwendet:

Gramophone-Preisträger
Die begehrtesten Auszeichnungen für Aufnahmen im Bereich der klassischen Musik. Sie werden jedes Jahr von unserer Mutterzeitschrift in verschiedenen Kategorien verliehen, die von Orchestermusik bis Oper, von Barock- bis zu zeitgenössischer Musik reichen. Aus dieser Liste wird ebenfalls eine Aufnahme ausgewählt, die den Titel Platte des Jahres erhält.

Musiker des Jahres
Fünf Künstler, die uns regelmäßig aufgrund ihrer Fähigkeiten als Musiker und Interpreten aufgefallen sind. Siehe auch die Künstlerprofile auf Seite 17.

Cómo valerse de esta Guía

A fin de aumentar la utilidad de este libro y de cubrir tantos CD "buenos" como sea posible de la amplia gama actualmente disponible, esta edición incorpora la siguiente información adicional: **Recomendaciones adicionales:** Dentro de una revisión completa, que generalmente constituye la recomendación principal de una obra en especial, cuando sea adecuado habrá una o múltiples recomendaciones alternativas adicionales. **Audiciones adicionales:** Contiene detalles de otras obras musicales del mismo compositor que sean merecedoras de consideración. **Audiciones sugeridas:** Contiene detalles de obras musicales de aquellos compositores para los cuales no existen revisiones completas o de los que hay disponibles pocas grabaciones.

Se ofrecen detalles de los compositores, obras, instrumentos, escala vocal, compañía o etiqueta productora de los discos (véase de Etiquetas/Fabricantes y Distribuidores), número de disco (y número anterior cuando el nuevo es una reedición), así como la fecha o fechas de la revisión en *Gramophone*.
En los pentagramas musicales que siguen el título se facilita un índice informativo con el sistema de símbolos siguiente:

Los símbolos

•⁄•⁄•⁄•	② ②	lh 23m	DDD	6/88
Precio	***Cantidad/ disponibilidad***	***Duración***	***Proceso***	***Fecha revisión***

Precio

••••	Precio completo	•••	Precio intermedio
••	Precio asequible	•	Precio módico

Cantidad/Disponibilidad
Si hubiese más de un disco, el número de que se trate se mostrará aquí. El primer tipo de círculo indica los álbumes en que no están disponibles los discos por separado. El segundo tipo indica que los discos *solamente* están disponibles por separado.

Duración
Cálculo redondeado hasta el minuto más próximo.

Proceso
Este es un código formado por tres letras, que usan en la actualidad casi todos los fabricantes para indicar el tipo de proceso empleado en la manufactura. Las letras A ó D se emplean como denotadoras de Análogo o Digital, y la secuencia de las letras representa los pasos cronológicos en la cadena: la misma sesión de grabación, los procesos de edición y/o mezcla y, por último, la preparación del disco maestro de la transcripción, según el método de preparación de la cinta maestra que se envía a la fábrica.

Fecha de revisión
El mes y el año en qué se revisó la grabación en *Gramophone*.

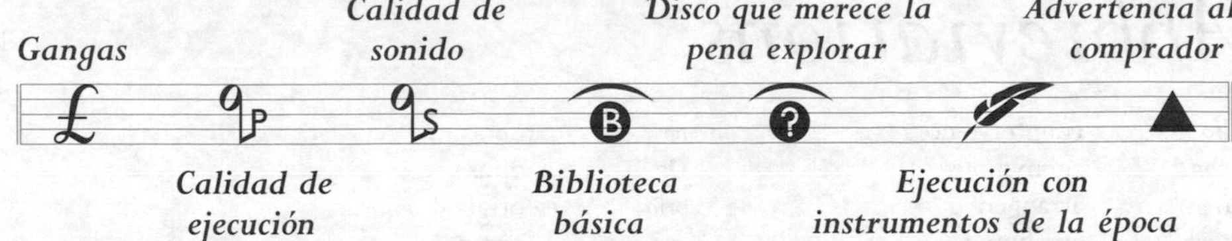

Gangas
A veces, hay otros elementos, aparte del precio, que hacen del disco una verdadera ganga. Un disco grabado por buenas artistas en una ejecución excepcional con una magnífica grabación, por ejemplo, o quizá la gran duración de la grabación, pueden a veces venderse a precios de ganga o intermedios. Este símbolo es el que denota tales ediciones.

Calidad de la Ejecución
Grabaciones indiscutibles – 'obligatorias' para el buen coleccionista. A veces, las ediciones más antiguas hubieran merecido un Premio al Disco de *Gramophone* si dicho Premio hubiese existido cuando aparecieron.

Calidad de Sonido
Estas grabaciones merecen verdaderamente el epíteto de 'parangones de buena calidad'.

Colección Fundamental
Grabaciones con que comenzar a coleccionar discos compactos.

Discos que merece la pena explorar
Para el musicalmente promiscuo! Grabaciones que podrían pasarse por alto con facilidad puesto que no pertenecen a los compositores más conocidos. Pero quizá encierran agradables sorpresas.

Ejecución con instrumentos de la época
Grabaciones en que se ha intentado una autenticidad histórica. Habitualmente se han ejecutado con instrumentos de la época y/o empleando los manuscritos originales.

Advertencia al comprador
Interpretaciones que han resistido al paso del tiempo, pero en las que la calidad de la grabación puede no ser del más alto nivel. Esto generalmente se aplica a las grabaciones anteriores a 1960.

Dos símbolos más que se emplean en estas revisiones:

Ganadores de Premios Gramophone
Los más ambicionados en el mundo de la música clásica; se conceden todos los años por nuestra revista matriz en categorías desde Orquestal hasta Opera, Barroco y Contemporánea. Una grabación se escoge también en la lista general para recibir el Premio al Disco del Año.

Artistas del Año
Cinco artistas, cuyas cualidades y maestría musical, junto con sus interpretaciones generales, les han dado, a nuestro juicio, la notoriedad. Véanse también las reseñas de los mismos, que comienzan en la página 17.

Abbreviations

alto	counter-tenor	*ob*	oboe
anon	anonymous	*Op*	opus
arr	arranged	*orig*	original
attrib	attributed	*org*	organ
bar	baritone	*perc*	percussion
bass-bar	bass-baritone	*pf*	piano
bn	bassoon	*picc*	piccolo
c.	circa (about)	*pub*	publisher/published
cl	clarinet	*rec*	recorder
clav	clavichord	*rev*	revised
cont	continuo	*sax*	saxophone
contr	contralto	*sngr*	singer
cor ang	cor anglais	*sop*	soprano
cpte(d)	complete(d)	*spkr*	speaker
db	double-bass	*stg*	string
dig pf	digital piano	*synth*	synthesizer
dir	director	*tbn*	trombone
ed	edited (by)/edition	*ten*	tenor
exc	excerpt	*timp*	timpani
fl	flute	*tpt*	trumpet
fp	fortepiano	*trad*	traditional
gtr	guitar	*trans*	transcribed
harm	harmonium	*treb*	treble
hn	horn	*va*	viola
hp	harp	*va da gamba*	viola da gamba
hpd	harpsichord	*vars*	variations
keybd	keyboard	*vc*	cello
lte	lute	*vib*	vibraphone
mez	mezzo-soprano	*vn*	violin
mndl	mandolin	*voc*	vocal/vocalist
narr	narrator	*wds*	words

Chamber Music Forms

string trio	violin, viola, cello
piano trio	violin, cello, piano
horn trio	horn, piano, violin
clarinet trio	clarinet, piano, cello
wind trio	oboe, clarinet, basssoon
baryton trio	baryton, viola, bass instrument
string quartet	2 violins, viola, cello
piano quartet	piano, string trio
wind quartet	flute, clarinet, horn, bassoon
string quintet	2 violins, 2 violas, cello
piano quintet	piano, string quartet
clarinet quintet	clarinet, string quartet
flute quartet	flute, string quartet
wind quintet	flute, oboe, clarinet, bassoon, horn
string sextet	piano, violin, 2 violas, cello, double bass

Artists of the Year

Pierre Boulez

by Robert Cowan

Pierre Boulez is a seminal force in modern music who, as an interpreter of standard repertory, often confounds expectations. His renditions of early Schoenberg have genuine warmth and romantic lustre, his Debussy and Ravel are full of beautifully tailored detail and his Stravinsky is always tellingly thought through. One might additionally consider his variegated readings of Beethoven, Wagner, Mahler and a whole host of twentieth-century composers, from Messiaen to Berio. Yet because of his undemonstrative podium stance, his preference for conducting without a baton, his less-than-popular repertoire preferences and his unstinting championing of the avant-garde, Boulez has all-too-frequently been misunderstood or, worse, misrepresented.

[photo: DG/Kalter]

He was born in Montbrison, France in 1925 and, while still in his teens, studied with Messiaen at the Paris Conservatoire. He also worked with the pioneering composer/conductor René Leibowitz, who espoused the Schoenberg tradition, thus greatly extending the range of Boulez's aural canvas. Early works included two striking piano sonatas, *Livre pour quatuor* for string quartet (revised as *Livre pour cordes* in 1968), and two works based on the poetry of René Char, *Le visage nuptial* and *Le soleil des eaux*. His association with Karlheinz Stockhausen during the early 1950s was highly significant: the two men were widely considered figureheads of the European musical avant-garde, and Boulez's fine-honed, serial *Le marteau sans maître* (again, settings of Char) preceded a 12-year period of teaching at Darmstadt (from 1955 to 1967). Boulez intensified his conducting work during the 1950s, most notably through the Domaine Musicale concert series, which again did much to promote the cause of new music. Midway between this and his directorship of the Institut de Recherche et Coordination Acoustique/Musique (IRCAM), he started a Third Piano Sonata, then completed (and subsequently revised) his *Pli selon pli* for soprano and orchestra (settings of poems by Mallarmé). A small number of pieces have since appeared, some of them attaining a wider audience than his earlier work; one thinks, in particular, of *Rituels in memoriam Bruno Maderna* (1974) and a

1978 revision of his first four *Notations*, originally conceived in the late 1940s and memorably recorded by both Abbado (DG) and Barenboim (Erato).

As a recording artist, Boulez shot into prominence in the early 1960s with a still-talked-about coupling of Stravinsky's *The Rite of Spring* and *Quatre Etudes*. His work as chief conductor of, respectively, the BBC Symphony Orchestra (1971-4) and the New York Philharmonic Orchestra (1971-7) is well documented on CD and recent recordings (for DG) include a spectacular coupling of Bartók's ballet *The wooden prince* and *Cantata profana*, a much-praised Debussy concert (including *Images* and *Printemps*), and a well considered re-recording of Stravinsky's *Rite* and *Petrushka*; both these last discs are with the Cleveland Orchestra. Boulez's legacy for Sony Classical has of late been reappearing at regular intervals, often at mid-price, and includes his epoch-making Webern series (a project in which the LSO plays a prominent part), Berg, Bartók, and Ravel from New York, Stravinsky with the Ensemble Intercontemporain and much Schoenberg. His Paris opera recording of Berg's *Wozzeck* is still considered one of the most compelling, and his première recording of Cerha's completion of *Lulu* (also with Paris Opera) was among the major operatic releases of the 1980s. Always the thinking interpreter, Boulez will continue to inspire extremes of critical opinion. His records, whether studio or live, unquestionably testify to a mind where no idea, no interpretation is ever set in stone. In that respect at least, he remains the perennial musical innovator.

Selected discography

Bartók. The wooden prince, Sz60. Cantata profana, Sz94[a]. [a]**John Aler** (ten); [a]**John Tomlinson** (bass); **Chicago Symphony** [a]**Chorus and Orchestra.** DG 435 863-2GH — 1h 13m DDD 3/93

Berg. Lulu Suite[a]. Der Wein[b]. Lyric Suite. [a]**Judith Blegen,** [b]**Jessye Norman** (sops); **New York Philharmonic Orchestra.** Sony Classical CD45838 — 59m ADD 12/90

Berg. LULU. **Teresa Stratas** (sop) Lulu; **Franz Mazura** (bar) Dr Schön, Jack; **Kenneth Riegel** (ten) Alwa; **Yvonne Minton** (mez) Countess Geschwitz; **Robert Tear** (ten) The Painter, A Negro; **Toni Blankenheim** (bar) Schigolch, Professor of Medicine, The Police Officer; **Gerd Nienstedt** (bass) An Animal-tamer, Rodrigo; **Helmut Pampuch** (ten) The Prince, The Manservant, The Marquis; **Jules Bastin** (bass) The Theatre Manager, The Banker; **Hanna Schwarz** (mez) A Dresser in the theatre, High School Boy, A Groom; **Jane Manning** (sop) A 15-year-old girl; **Ursula Boese** (mez) Her Mother; **Anna Ringart** (mez) A Lady Artist; **Claude Meloni** (bar) A Journalist; **Pierre-Yves Le Maigat** (bass) A Manservant; **Paris Opéra Orchestra.** DG 415 489-2GH3 — ③ 2h 52m 11/86

Boulez. Rituel in memoriam Bruno Maderna[a]. Eclat/Multiples[b]. [a]**BBC Symphony Orchestra,** [b]**Ensemble Intercontemporain.** Sony Classical CD45839 — 52m ADD/DDD 8/90

Debussy. Prélude à l'après-midi d'un faune. Images. Printemps. **Cleveland Orchestra.** DG 435 766-2GH — 1h DDD 9/92

Schoenberg. Variations for Orchestra, Op. 31. Pelleas und Melisande, Op. 5. **Chicago Symphony Orchestra.** Erato 2292-45827-2 — 1h 2m DDD 4/93

Stravinsky. Four Etudes. The Rite of Spring — ballet. **French National Orchestra.** Adès 13222 — 42m AAD

Stravinsky. Pulcinella — ballet[a]. Le chant du rossignol[b]. [a]**Ann Murray** (mez); [a]**Anthony Rolfe Johnson** (ten); [a]**Simon Estes** (bass); [a]**Ensemble Intercontemporain;** [b]**French National Orchestra.** Erato 2292-45382-2 — ADD 5/86

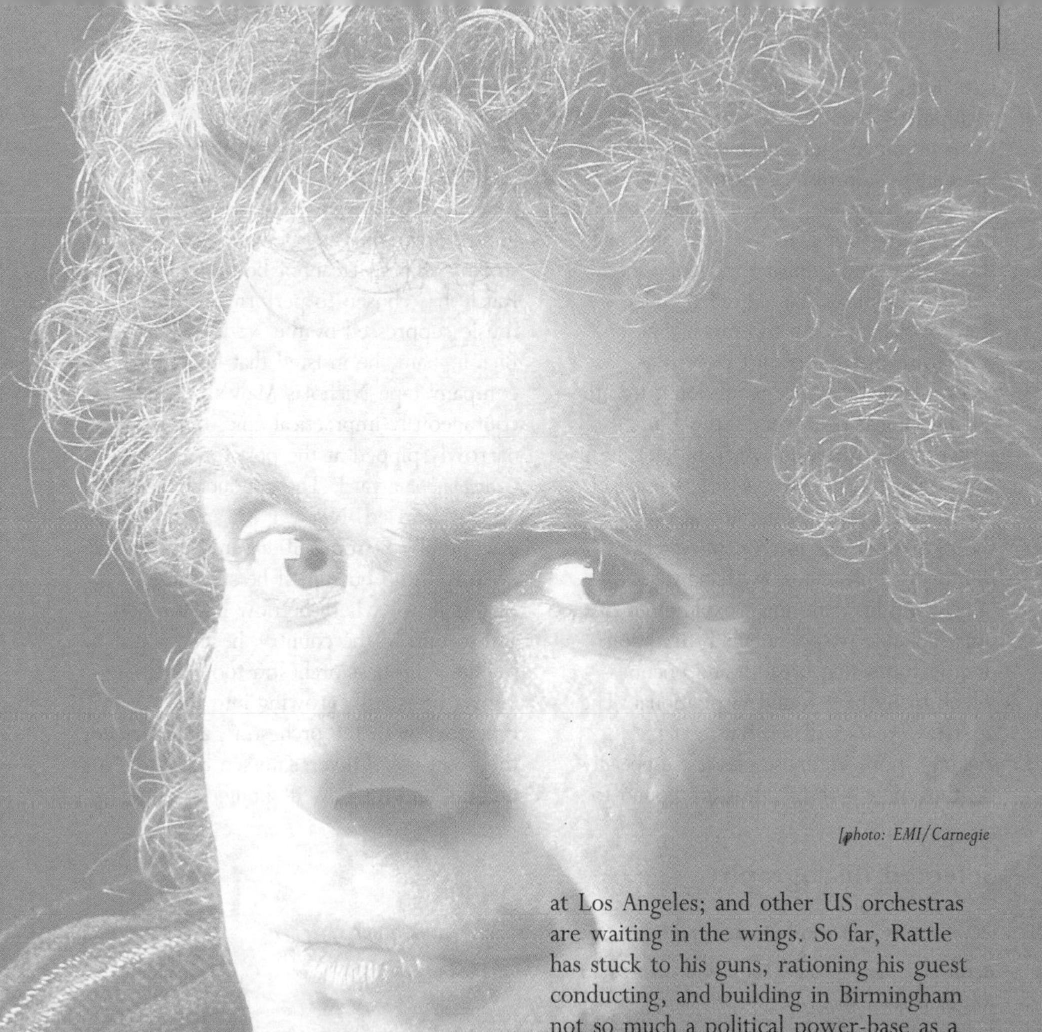

[photo: EMI/Carnegie

Simon Rattle

by David Gutman

Simon Rattle has not looked back since his victory at the 1974 John Player International Conducting Competition. His position as Britain's Number One conductor, established at an impossibly young age and with perhaps only conjectural evidence, now seems fully justified. Rumours persist that he is about to be lured away by a 'top' orchestral outfit: not Berlin — not yet anyhow — though Rattle is a regular guest of that orchestra. But there have been closer calls at Los Angeles; and other US orchestras are waiting in the wings. So far, Rattle has stuck to his guns, rationing his guest conducting, and building in Birmingham not so much a political power-base as a real artistic powerhouse.

In recent years, Rattle has sought to put music-making into its larger cultural context through the "Towards the Millennium" concert series, but expanding the repertoire has long been a preoccupation of his, along with older verities like proper orchestral training. Comparisons with Stokowski at Philadelphia, Barbirolli at the Hallé, Szell at Cleveland and Slatkin at St Louis are well made. Rattle's recordings convey an extraordinary depth of preparation quite as much as the more superficial excitement you might expect of a charismatic young firebrand. His Mahler *Resurrection* Symphony is one of several Rattle performances to have won a *Gramophone* award, but it divided critics elsewhere, particularly in America where its marmoreal qualities were not always appreciated. Even closer to home, some have found his unorthodox textural manipulations and preference for extreme dynamic range sounding not-quite-spontaneous on disc. Perhaps feeling that things were getting a bit too studied, Rattle has recently turned to live recording and the results are promising indeed.

For an admirer like Alfred Brendel, Rattle risks spending too much time on repertoire that the pianist regards as second-rate, but there is no doubt that the conductor has been very shrewd in targeting the music in which he feels he has something to say. Always one step ahead, his Nielsen cycle is emerging at precisely the right time; his interest in American minimalism pre-dates any bandwagon effect, and his continuing exploration of the unfashionable post-Schoenberg tradition demonstrates that breadth and openness which many have found inspirational. The next few years will see Rattle at last tackling more Viennese classics, especially Beethoven, where his ideas are bound to provoke controversy given his willingness to adopt elements of 'authentic' performance practice. With a conductor determined to strip away the ingrained perceptions of even the starriest band, guest conducting engagements can be stormy affairs. It cannot be coincidence that Rattle has chosen to perform so much music suppressed by the Nazis in Berlin. In Birmingham, he insisted that his record company tape Nicholas Maw's *Odyssey*, a courageously impractical epic, only to see it narrowly pipped at the post for a *Gramophone* award. The conductor need not be too worried. Not yet 40, and with a discography of some 50 albums, Rattle has no way to go but up. If he stays in Birmingham, where he now has the best auditorium in the country, he might just be building the best orchestra too. Rattle knows he is still "growing into the repertory with the orchestra", as his friend, the composer Oliver Knussen has said: "it's unique, and it's how it should be done."

Selected discography

(all with **City of Birmingham Symphony Orchestra** *unless otherwise stated)*

Berg. Lulu Suite[a]. ***Schoenberg.*** Five Orchestral Pieces, Op. 16. ***Webern.*** Six Pieces, Op. 6. [a]**Arleen Auger** (sop). EMI CDC7 49857-2 — ⁂ Ih 6m DDD 11/89

Britten. War Requiem, Op. 66. **Elisabeth Söderström** (sop); **Robert Tear** (ten); **Thomas Allen** (bar); **Mark Blatchly** (org); **Boys of Christ Church Cathedral, Oxford; City of Birmingham Symphony Chorus.** EMI CDS7 47034-8 — ⁂ ② 1h 23m DDD 2/84

Debussy. Jeux. Images. Musiques pour le Roi Lear (orch. Roger-Ducasse). EMI CDC7 49947 — ⁂ Ih 2m DDD 3/90

Gershwin. PORGY AND BESS. **Willard White** (bass) Porgy; **Cynthia Haymon** (sop) Bess; **Harolyn Blackwell** (sop) Clara; **Cynthia Clarey** (sop) Serena; **Damon Evans** (ten) Sportin' Life; **Marietta Simpson** (mez) Maria; **Gregg Baker** (bar) Crown; **Glyndebourne Chorus; London Philharmonic Orchestra.** EMI CDS7 49568-2 — ⁂ ③ 3h 9m DDD 6/89

Janáček. Sinfonietta, Op. 60[a]. Glagolitic Mass[b]. **Felicity Palmer** (sop); **Ameral Gunson** (mez); **John Mitchinson** (ten); **Malcolm King** (bass); **Jane Parker-Smith** (org); [a]**Philharmonia Orchestra;** [b]**City of Birmingham Symphony Chorus.** EMI CDC7 47504-2 — ⁂ Ih 2m DDD 10/88

Mahler. Symphony No. 2, "Resurrection". **Arleen Auger** (sop); **Dame Janet Baker** (mez); **City of Birmingham Symphony Chorus.** EMI CDS7 47962-2 — ⁂ Ih 26m DDD 12/87

Mahler. Symphony No. 7. EMI CDC7 54344-2 — ⁂ Ih 17m DDD 9/92

Mahler. Symphony No. 10 in F sharp major (ed. Cooke). **Bournemouth Symphony Orchestra.** EMI CDC7 54406-2 — ⁂ Ih 16m DDD 5/92

Maw. Odyssey. EMI CDS7 54277-2 — ⁂ ② Ih 35m DDD 9/91

Messiaen. Turangalîla-symphonie[a]. Quatuor pour la fin du temps[b]. [b]**Saschko Gawriloff** (vn); [b]**Siegfried Palm** (vc); [b]**Hans Deinzer** (cl); [b]**Aloys Kontarsky,** [a]**Peter Donohoe** (pfs); [a]**Tristan Murail** (ondes martenot); [a]**CBSO.** EMI CDS7 47463-2 — ⁂ ② 2h 10m DDD/ADD 12/87

Sibelius. Symphonies — No. 4 in A minor, Op. 63; No. 6 in D minor, Op. 104. EMI CDM7 64121-2 — ⁂ Ih 7m DDD 2/92

[photo: DG/Reichardt

Cheryl Studer

by Alan Blyth

Ebullient, full of American enthusiasm, willing to tackle every kind of repertory, Cheryl Studer is the epitome of the star singer of today. She is intelligent, amusing and keen to engage in conversation on all things operatic. She is also healthily ambitious, knowing her own mind, determined to fulfil every aspect of her huge talent — yet never at the expense of sincere artistry. She is one of those remarkable singers who can encompass and shine in Italian, German and French repertory, and can tackle the Queen of Night almost at the same time as she can sing taxing Wagner roles, taking in Rossini, Verdi and Gounod along the road. These things are possible for her providing she allows time between one style and another. In this respect she resembles two notable prima donnas of the past — Lilli Lehmann and Maria Callas.

Studer hails from Michigan, from where she surely has her generous, forthright nature, typical of the American Mid West. She began her singing lessons when she was 12, working on Italian vocalises and *arie antiche*, a sound source for learning technique. She studied on a scholarship for three years at the Berkshire Music Center at Tanglewood. In 1978 she won the Metropolitan Opera Competition for Young Singers after which she moved to Europe to gain experience. She was not initially interested in opera, rather in song. She studied Lieder in Vienna, won a competition there in 1979 and then went on to study with the great Hans Hotter in Munich. He persuaded her to consider opera as a main career. She auditioned for the Bavarian State Opera in Munich and was immediately awarded a contract. After taking small roles, she won acclaim as Irene in a revival of Wagner's *Rienzi* in 1981 and was immediately engaged by the Bayreuth Festival (début in 1985), where she sang Elisabeth followed by Elisa, also her début role at the Metropolitan and Covent Garden.

Violetta in Hamburg and Semiramide in Bonn presaged a move into a new field. Since then her Donna Anna (*Don Giovanni*), Mathilde (*Guillaume Tell*), Odabella (*Attila*), Elena (*I Vespri Siciliani*) and Lucia (*Lucia di Lammermoor*) have been acclaimed and recorded. She takes on Aida in a new production at Covent Garden in 1994. As this variety suggests, her voice is at once substantial, warm and flexible. But she has not neglected her German repertory with which she first found fame. Either in the theatre or on disc, Eva, Chrysothemis, Ariadne and Danae (in Strauss's *Die Liebe der Danae*) are in her sights. She has sung and recorded Sieglinde (in Wagner's *Die Walküre*). She has also recorded a memorable Salome with Sinopoli for DG and an equally arresting Empress in *Die Frau ohne Schatten* for EMI. Even then the sum of her achievements isn't told. Her Marguérite in EMI's excellent set of *Faust*, much praised, shows her accomplishments in the French field. She sang the taxing soprano part in Beethoven's *Missa solemnis* under Levine at the 1991 Salzburg Festival (recorded by DG) and she has not forsaken Lieder.

Her voice is a rich *lirico-spinto*. She has the technique and understanding to vary her colouring and dynamics to the needs of a specific role or a particular phrase. She is keen on characterization and is intent on thinking herself into every part and song she tackles. These attributes help towards her goal of complete mastery of her art.

Selected discography

Gounod. FAUST. **Richard Leech** (ten) Faust; **Cheryl Studer** (sop) Marguérite; **José van Dam** (bass-bar) Méphistophélès; **Thomas Hampson** (bass) Valentin; **Martine Mahé** (mez) Siebel; **Nadine Denize** (sop) Marthe; **Marc Barrard** (bar) Wagner; **French Army Chorus; Toulouse Capitole Choir and Orchestra/Michel Plasson.** EMI CDS7 54228-2 — ③ 3h 24m DDD 12/91

Mozart. OPERA ARIAS. **Cheryl Studer** (sop); **Academy of St Martin in the Fields/Sir Neville Marriner.** Philips 426 721-2PH — 55m DDD 5/91

R. Strauss. DIE FRAU OHNE SCHATTEN. **Cheryl Studer** (sop) Empress; **René Kollo** (ten) Emperor; **Ute Vinzing** (sop) Dyer's Wife; **Alfred Muff** (bass-bar) Barak the Dyer; **Hanna Schwarz** (mez) Nurse; **Andreas Schmidt** (bar) Spirit Messenger; **Julie Kaufmann** (sop) Voice of the Falcon; **Cyndia Sieden** (sop) Guardian of the threshold of the Temple; **Paul Frey** (ten) Voice of a young man; **Marjana Lipovšek** (sop) Voice from above; **Jan-Hendrick Rootering** (bass) One-eyed Brother; **Kurt Rydl** (bass) One-armed Brother; **Kenneth Garrison** (ten) Hunchback Brother; **Tölz Boys' Choir; Bavarian Radio Chorus and Symphony Orchestra/Wolfgang Sawallisch.** EMI CDS7 49074-2 — ③ 3h 11m DDD 9/88

R. Strauss. SALOME. **Cheryl Studer** (sop) Salome; **Bryn Terfel** (bar) Jokanaan; **Horst Hiestermann** (ten) Herod; **Leonie Rysanek** (sop) Herodias; **Clemens Bieber** (ten) Narraboth; **Marianne Rørholm** (contr) Page; **Friedrich Molsberger** (bass) First Nazarene; **Ralf Lukas** (bass) Second Nazarene; **William Murray** (bass) First Soldier; **Bengt Rundgren** (bass) Second Soldier; **Klaus Lang** (bar) Cappadocian; **Orchestra of the Deutsche Oper, Berlin/Giuseppe Sinopoli.** DG 431 810-2GH2 — ② 1h 42m DDD 9/91

Verdi. ATTILA. **Samuel Ramey** (bass) Attila; **Cheryl Studer** (sop) Odabella; **Giorgio Zancanaro** (bar) Ezio; **Neil Shicoff** (ten) Foresto; **Ernesto Gavazzi** (ten) Uldino; **Giorgio Surian** (bass) Leone; **Chorus and Orchestra of La Scala, Milan/Riccardo Muti.** EMI CDS7 49952-2 — ② 1h 49m DDD 5/90

Verdi. LA TRAVIATA. **Cheryl Studer** (sop) Violetta; **Luciano Pavarotti** (ten) Alfredo; **Juan Pons** (bar) Germont; **Wendy White** (mez) Flora; **Sondra Kelly** (contr) Annina; **Anthony Laciura** (ten) Gaston; **Bruno Pola** (bar) Baron; **Jeffrey Wells** (bass-bar) Marquis; **Julien Robbins** (bass) Doctor; **John Hanriot** (ten) Giuseppe; **Mitchell Sendrowitz** (bar) Messenger; **Ross Crolius** (bass) Servant; **Metropolitan Opera Chorus and Orchestra/James Levine.** DG 435 797-2GH2 — ② 2h 2m DDD 11/92

John Mark Ainsley

by James Jolly

For a singer who has only just turned 30 John Mark Ainsley has made a remarkable number of records, and over an even more remarkable range of music. From the title-role of Monteverdi's *Orfeo* to the romantic Charlie in Lerner and Loewe's *Brigadoon,* Ainsley's light, supple tenor has embraced a host of styles and characters. A student of Anthony Rolfe Johnson, Ainsley looks set to succeed his teacher in that peculiar niche in the repertoire occupied by British and American tenors which allows them to embrace a large diversity of idioms: one day, no doubt, we'll be hearing a Gerontius (something highly appropriate for someone raised in Worcester) and perhaps an Idomeneo from this most promising of singers (what better position to be in than having one of the leading exponents of the role as a teacher?). Ainsley first sang with an orchestra as a schoolboy in a production of *The bartered bride*, an experience he still describes as "pretty shattering. It was like having a bath rather than a wash". His move from amateur to professional came after university in Oxford when he started

[photo: Hyperion/Schillinger

singing with Gothic Voices. "It was the most nerve-wracking experience of my whole career; standing next to someone I thought of as a god in those days; I mean Rogers Covey-Crump, who was and is one of my favourite tenors and who exerted an enormous influence on my early days." This lead effortlessly into the recording studio and those early discs for Hyperion that have gathered such a following (Ainsley sang on four of them).

Since those early days in Gothic Voices, John Mark Ainsley has recorded the Monteverdi *Vespers* with Philip Pickett who later gave him the lead in *Orfeo*; it is a reading of great subtlety, beauty and intensity, characteristics that he brings to the music of Mozart whose music his voice fits so well. Glyndebourne audiences have been treated to his Ferrando in their shipboard *Così*, and EMI have recorded his Don Ottavio with Roger Norrington conducting — and we are sure to be sampling a Tamino before too long. For Decca he has certainly tackled a rarity — songs by the 90-year-old Berthold Goldschmidt. In the choral repertoire Mozart again features highly with recordings of the *Coronation* Mass and the Requiem appearing within the last year, Bach, Handel and Haydn are not far behind either. In song he prefers to tread warily; a *Schöne Müllerin* would be a thing of beauty, but we shall have to wait — Ainsley is not someone to tackle something so delicate without a complete and idiomatic grasp of the language involved. Songs by John Blow and Herbert Howells have recently been released but maybe some enterprising record company could tempt a disc of folksongs from him, since his feeling for words and his wonderful control of line would guarantee a de luxe treatment for some favourite songs.

The operatic stage calls frequently but Ainsley is not one to rush headlong into productions. A mellifluous Fenton for Scottish Opera was well-received and the Glyndebourne *Così* revealed a rare comic gift, aided by a true musician's sense of timing. Maybe a Lensky in *Eugene Onegin* will be forthcoming, preferably in a house that will allow the voice to blossom without being dwarfed. Whatever the repertoire, there is no doubt that it will receive the care and attention he brings to all he does, making him a tenor not just of style but of great variety and range.

Selected discography:

Handel. Joshua. **Emma Kirkby** (sop); **Aidan Oliver** (treb); **James Bowman** (alto); **John Mark Ainsley** (ten); **Michael George** (bass); **New College Choir, Oxford; The King's Consort/Robert King.** Hyperion CDA66461/2 — ⚬ ② 2h 5m DDD 7/91

Monteverdi. L'ORFEO. **John Mark Ainsley** (ten) Orfeo; **Julia Gooding** (sop) Euridice; **Catherine Bott** (sop) Music, Messenger, Prosperina; **Tessa Bonner** (sop) Nymph; **Christopher Robson** (alto) Hope, Shepherd II; **Andrew King** (ten) Shepherd I, Spirit I, Echo, Apollo; **Michael George** (bass) Plutone, Shepherd IV; **Simon Grant** (bass) Caronte, Spirit III; **Robert Evans** (bass) Shepherd III, Spirit II; **New London Consort/Philip Pickett.** L'Oiseau Lyre 433 545-2OH2 — ⚬ ② 1h 48m DDD 2/93

Mozart. Mass in C major, K317, "Coronation". Vesperae solennes de confessore in C major, K339. Epistle Sonata in C major, K278/271*e*[a]. **Emma Kirkby** (sop); **Catherine Robbin** (mez); **John Mark Ainsley** (ten); **Michael George** (bass); **Winchester Cathedral Choir; Winchester Quiristers; Academy of Ancient Music/Christopher Hogwood** with [a]**Alastair Ross** (org). L'Oiseau Lyre 436 585-2OH — ⚬ 54m DDD 4/93

Mozart. Mass in D minor, K626, "Requiem" (ed. Druce)[a]. Ave verum corpus, K618[b]. Maurerische Trauermusik, K477/479[a]. [a]**Nancy Argenta** (sop); [a]**Catherine Robbin** (mez); [a]**John Mark Ainsley** (ten); [a]**Alastair Miles** (bass); [a]**Schütz Choir of London;** [b]**Schütz Consort; London Classical Players/Roger Norrington.** EMI CDC7 54525-2 — ⚬ 58m DDD 11/92

BRIGADOON (Lerner/Loewe). **Brent Barrett** (ten) Tommy Albright; **Rebecca Luker** (sop) Fiona MacLaren; **Judy Kaye** (sop) Meg Brockie; **John Mark Ainsley** (ten) Charlie Dalrymple; **Ambrosian Chorus; London Sinfonietta/John McGlinn.** EMI CDC7 54481-2 — ⚬ 1h 20m DDD 1/93

Graham Johnson

by James Jolly

If there's one thing besides the song repertoire that the pianist Graham Johnson must know more about than any other musician it is airports: there can be few busier performers around today and fewer who work with so many others. The list of singers he collaborates with is like a role call of the most prominent artists of the day: Dame Margaret Price, Brigitte Fassbaender, Anthony Rolfe Johnson, Peter Schreier, Arleen Auger, Sarah Walker, Philip Langridge and Ann Murray to name but a few. And what links them all together is their participation in the huge task Johnson and Hyperion have set themselves, that of recording the complete songs of Franz Schubert in the years leading up to the bicentenary in 1997.

Johnson has matched song and singer with the eye for detail of a master couturier, the fabric of the text and line perfectly reflecting the personality and weave of the performer's character and voice. He has created a series of fascinating programmes, not artfully assembled but logically constructed. "When Schubert gathered his Lieder together for publication, he was clearly interested in programme building: he took songs from various periods and garlanded them together in a variety of ways." And it's a recipe that Johnson clearly approves and seeks to emulate. The pairing of song and singer has drawn some inspired performances to the series: Sarah Walker's *Erlkönig* is one particularly powerful reading that shows both performers at their most intense. It is also a reading of a familiar song that points up one of Johnson's most powerful qualities, his eye and ear for the dramatic intentions behind so many of the songs he accompanies. In his hands they become mini-operas, music dramas in minuscule that summon forth feelings of theatrical intensity.

But there is more to Graham Johnson's life than Schubert alone. His teaching and performing embraces music of many eras and nations. He brings style and power to the romantic composers of the

[photo: Hyperion/Crowthers

nineteenth century, to his Brahms and Schumann. Yet in the apparently artless folk-song he is equally at home, summoning up the wealth of performing the masters to these perfect little jewels of deceptive simplicity. And as a constructor of programmes Johnson has few peers. Followers of the Songmakers' Almanac — a performing 'company' of singers who work with Johnson, invariably at London's Wigmore Hall — will appreciate the skill with which he builds evenings of song that stay in the memory long after the happily endless encores and final bows are over. As the natural successor to Gerald Moore and Geoffrey Parsons, Graham Johnson has made an enormous contribution to the broadening of the appeal of the song, the *Lied* or the *mélodie,* and his loyal supporters (he must be one of a very few accompanists who can attract an audience regardless of whom he accompanies) know that they will not be disappointed. Thankfully for record collectors he is an avid studio performer and the favourite of too many singers not to be in constant demand — and it's no surprise why.

Selected discography:

Schubert. LIEDER, Volume 7. **Elly Ameling** (sop). Hyperion CDJ33007 — ⁘ 1h 11m DDD 8/90

Schubert. LIEDER, Volume 11. **Brigitte Fassbaender** (mez). Hyperion CDJ33011 — ⁘ 1h 5m DDD 8/91

Schubert. LIEDER, Volume 14. **Thomas Hampson** (bar). Hyperion CDJ33014 — ⁘ 1h 20m DDD 4/92

Schubert. LIEDER, Volume 17. **Lucia Popp** (sop). Hyperion CDJ33017 — ⁘ 1h 11m DDD 6/93

Schubert. LIEDER, Volume 18. **Peter Schreier** (ten). Hyperion CDJ33018 — ⁘ 1h 16m DDD 7/93

SOUVENIRS DE VENISE. The Songmakers' Almanac (Felicity Lott, sop; Ann Murray, mez; Anthony Rolfe Johnson, ten; Richard Jackson, bar). Works by ***Beethoven, Fauré, Glinka, Gounod, Hahn, Jensen, Massenet, Mendelssohn, Rossini, Schubert and Taneyev.*** Hyperion CDA66112 — ⁘ 49m DDD 3/88

SWEET POWER OF SONG. Felicity Lott (sop); **Ann Murray** (mez); **Galina Solodchin** (vn); **Jonathan Williams** (va). Works by ***Beethoven, Berlioz, Brahms, Chausson, Fauré, Gounod, Saint-Saëns and Schumann.*** EMI CDC7 49930-2 — ⁘ 1h 2m DDD 11/90

ON WINGS OF SONG. Felicity Lott (sop); **Ann Murray** (mez). Songs and Duets by ***Aubert, Balfe, Britten, Delibes, Gounod, Massenet, Mendelssohn, Paladilhe, Purcell, Quilter, Rossini and Sullivan.*** EMI CDC7 54411-2 — ⁘ 1h 16m DDD 7/92

Reviews

The variety and sheer quantity of classical music available on CD is quite astonishing, as a glance through *Gramophone*'s *Classical Catalogue* reveals. With this new edition of *The Gramophone Good CD Guide* a number of changes have taken place to take account of this fact and to cover as many recommendable CDs as possible.

The reviews

These indicate the best recordings available, in certain instances the only recording as in the case of Adolphe Adam's ballet, *Le corsaire*. This is a new review to the *Guide*, as is clearly indicated. There follows a review of the same composer's other ballet, *Giselle*, of which there are five complete CD recordings in the current *Catalogue*. Michael Tilson Thomas's 1986 Sony recording is the first choice.

Additional recommendations ...

These will include the same information as that provided on the staves following the main review headings, i.e. price category, number of discs, timing, original *Gramophone* review date and so on (full details are provided on page 8 onwards and a brief explanation is provided at regular intervals throughout the book). An example of such a recommendation is the Herbert von Karajan mid-price Decca Ovation recording of *Giselle*. In this case there is just one alternative recommendation — sometimes there will be several (see under J.S. Bach's *Brandenburg Concertos*, for example, on page 52).

Suggested listening ...

Full title details are given of recording/s of works by more obscure composers who deserve attention but not, perhaps, a full review. An example of this is the first entry for Carl Friedrich Abel. The date in brackets refers to the original *Gramophone* review date.

Further listening ...

As this heading implies, these are works (again with full title information) by the same composer, listed at the end of a composer entry, which should be considered as worthwhile additions to a classical CD collection. An example of this are the recordings listed at the end of the entry for John Adams on page 31. Again, the date in brackets refers to the original *Gramophone* review date.

These set the pattern for the rest of this book ... lots of reviews, single alternative recommendations, multiple additional recommendations, suggested listening, further listening ... it reflects what is available and 'good'.

Carl Friedrich Abel

German/British 1723-1787

Suggested listening ...

Symphonies, Op. 7 — No. 1 in G major; No. 2 in B flat major; No. 3 in D major; No. 4 in F major; No. 5 in C major; No. 6 in E flat major. **Cantilena/Adrian Shepherd.** Chandos CHAN8648 (6/89).

Adolphe Adam

French 1803-1856

NEW REVIEW

Adam. Le corsaire. **English Chamber Orchestra/Richard Bonynge.** Decca 430 286-2DH2. Recorded in 1990.

② 2h 11m DDD 10/92 S

That the name of Adolphe Adam is remembered at all today is due almost entirely to the continuing popularity of his best loved ballet score, *Giselle* (reviewed below). Fine as it is, *Giselle* serves as but a slender reminder of its composer; once revered as the most influential French musician writing for the ballet, the improbable fact is that today Adam's posthumous fame rests largely with this solitary work. Two of his operas, *Le postillon de Lonjumeau* and *La poupée de Nuremberg* are occasionally revived today, but Decca's splendid recording of Adam's score for *Le corsaire* should do much to revive interest in this unjustly neglected composer. It was first heard during the 1856 season at the Paris Opéra, crowning a period of unparalleled artistic endeavour under the patronage of the Empress Eugenie. No expense was spared in any aspect of the production, but despite a triumphant initial reception, *Le corsaire* was abandoned in Paris, although sets and costumes still survive in St Petersburg, where rare revivals have occasionally been staged. The initial enthusiasm of Parisian audiences secured 43 performances during the 1856 season, prompting Delibes to revise and enlarge the score for a new production planned for the following year, and this version is used here by Richard Bonynge. True to form, the plot is convoluted, even absurd at times, as the pirate Conrad and his vagabond crew plan the rescue of the beautiful Medora, imprisoned at Adrianople by an evil Pasha. Predictably, Conrad is betrayed by one of his henchmen, leaving him stranded (though now reunited with Medora) upon a rock. The vessel is destroyed and the pair reach safety just as the final curtain falls. Bonynge draws superior playing from the English Chamber Orchestra and the performance has great poise and inner clarity, allowing the listener to follow the plot with ease. The music is engaging, if not always memorable, but with a lifetime of experience with scores intended for the stage, Bonynge knows just how to sustain dramatic impetus, so that nothing appears fabricated or meaningless in the absence of a visual dimension. Demonstration quality sound enhances the appeal of this unfamiliar but very engaging music.

Adam. Giselle (abridged). **London Symphony Orchestra/Michael Tilson Thomas.** Sony Classical SK42450. Recorded in 1986.

1h 17m DDD 3/92 P

Adam's ballet *Giselle* is a typically romantic work and tells of the Wilis, affianced maidens who die before their wedding. Unable to rest they rise from their graves at night and enjoy the dancing that they were unable to indulge in whilst living. Anyone who comes across them as they dance is forced to join them until he drops dead. Set into this framework is the love between Giselle and Prince Albrecht. Like the Karajan recording, Tilson Thomas gives an abridged version of the score, but the cuts in transitions and repeats are just that bit less severe, thereby giving us an extra quarter of an hour or so of music. Tilson Thomas resists any temptation to force upon the music an intensity that is alien to it. His feel for characterization and atmosphere is readily apparent. Where Karajan is perhaps more magical in one place, Tilson

Thomas is that bit more elegant in another. The recorded sound is obviously that bit more vivid than the Karajan — good though the latter still sounds. For all but the specialist ballet collector who insists on *Giselle* absolutely complete, this version is the clear first choice among modern recordings.

Additional recommendation ...

Vienna Philharmonic Orchestra/Herbert von Karajan. Decca Ovation 417 738-2DM — ∴ Ih ADD 𝄢P £

John Adams

American 1947-

Adams. ORCHESTRAL WORKS. **San Francisco Symphony Orchestra/Edo de Waart.** Elektra Nonesuch 7559-79144-2.
The Chairman Dances — foxtrot for orchestra (1985). Christian Zeal and Activity (1973). Two Fanfares for Orchestra — Tromba lontana (1986); Short Ride in a Fast Machine (1986). Common Tones in Simple Time (1980).

∴ 52m DDD 8/88

There is no better way of sampling the music of John Adams than through this attractive compilation. His descriptive scores combine pastiche or parody with glossy orchestration and also set out to shrewdly scrutinize his own nationality. Thus the earliest piece, *Christian Zeal and Activity*, is a variation on *Onward, Christian Soldiers*, not sung with upstanding confidence but rather played *pianissimo* by a small body of strings, naked and vulnerable. In similar but more flamboyant vein, *The Chairman Dances* enters the world of American politics, drawing on the same events as Adams's opera *Nixon in China*. It's a Hollywood-like fantasy, part slick, part sleazy, that evokes a bygone age of glamour and style. Even the works that have no obvious story to tell have a sensuality that makes them instantly alluring. Both orchestra and conductor have long-standing connections with Adams, and the performances are as full of life as they are authoritative.

Adams. The Wound-dresser[a]. Fearful symmetries. [a]**Sanford Sylvan** (bar); **St Luke's Orchestra/John Adams.** Elektra Nonesuch 7559-79218-2. Text included.

∴ 47m DDD 6/90 

This disc displays particularly well the two "opposing polarities" (the composer's words) of Adams's creativity. *The Wound-dresser* is a setting of Walt Whitman's poem of the same name, recounting Whitman's own experience of nursing the wounded and dying soldiers during the American Civil War. Though the poem is graphic in its description of the atrocities of war, it is also a profoundly moving testament of compassion and humanity. Adams's elegiac and atmospheric setting is one of his most accessible and luminously scored pieces — its strong triadic harmonies and lyrical, melodic beauty underpinning and elevating the compassionate overtones of the text. *Fearful symmetries* on the other hand is an example of what Adams calls his "trickster" pieces — irreverent and hugely entertaining. More overtly minimalist in its language, its relatively slender material sometimes comes close to outstaying it welcome, but the work's propulsive energy seem to keep the listener riveted and fascinated until the very last note. Performances and recording are excellent.

Adams. NIXON IN CHINA. **Sanford Sylvan** (bar) Chou en-Lai; **James Maddalena** (bar) Richard Nixon; **Thomas Hammons** (bar) Henry Kissinger; **Mari Opatz** (mez) Nancy T'ang (First Secretary to Mao); **Stephanie Friedman** (mez) Second Secretary to Mao; **Marion Dry** (mez) Third Secretary to Mao; **John Duykers** (ten) Mao Tse-Tung; **Carolann Page** (sop) Pat

Nixon; **Trudy Ellen Craney** (sop) Chiang Ch'ing; **St Luke's Chorus and Orchestra/Edo de Waart.** Elektra Nonesuch 7559-79177-2. Notes and text included.

If few operas deal with current affairs and even fewer address political issues, then *Nixon in China* takes the unusual risk of bordering on the documentary. But it is also a study in the psychology of its principal characters, and by peering into the personalities it goes well beyond fact alone, revealing instead a truly human drama. Alice Goodman's libretto is structured around the American presidential visit to Beijing in February 1972. At first all is a whirl of formalities, functions and fervent debate, but as the energy begins to flag so human vulnerabilities show through, and the opera ends in a state of lassitude, a strange super-imposition of bedroom scenes in which the protagonists share with one another their various reminiscences and dreams. Adams's score is particularly strong when the action is fast-moving: he is a master of energetic, sonorous music, and his minimalist leanings serve him well in those parts of the story that require movement or depend upon quick-fire exchanges. Less dynamic moments — and Goodman's libretto is rich in poetical soliloquies and dialogues — he perhaps handles less elegantly, though in the long final act the mood of intimacy and soul-searching is cleverly caught. Best of all, however, is the music that captures the mood of the public scenes. Adams revels in evoking tawdry glamour, and a hint of fox-trot often hangs deliciously in the air. The cast is a strong one; James Maddalena in particular faces us with a life-like Richard Nixon, and Trudy Ellen Craney is memorable in Adams's most exaggerated character, the coloratura Madame Mao. So familiar are the faces behind the names that *Nixon in China* cannot be an easy work to watch on stage. On disc, with a few photographs provided in the insert booklet to jog the memory, it's perhaps easier to reconcile historical truth with the fantasy-world of this curious opera.

Further listening ...

Shaker Loops. *Coupled with* **Reich.** Variations. **San Francisco Symphony Orchestra/Edo de Waart.** Philips 412 214-2PH (9/86).

Harmonium. **San Francisco Symphony Chorus and Orchestra/Edo de Waart.** ECM New Series 821 465-2.

THE DEATH OF KLINGHOFFER. **Soloists; London Opera Chorus; Lyon Opera Orchestra/Kent Nagano.** Elektra Nonesuch 7559-79281-2 (3/93).

Key to Symbols

	2 2	1h 23m	DDD	6/88
Price	***Quantity/ availability***	***Timing***	***Mode***	***Review date***

Richard Addinsell

British 1904-1977

Suggested listening ...

Warsaw Concerto. *Coupled with* **Gottschalk.** Grande fantaisie triomphale sur l'hymne national brésilien, RO108. ***Litolff.*** Concerto symphonique No. 4 in D minor, Op. 102 — Scherzo. ***Rachmaninov.*** Piano Concerto No. 2 in C minor, Op. 18. **Cristina Ortiz** (pf). **Royal Philharmonic Orchestra/Moshe Atzmon.** Decca 414 348-2DH (9/86).
Reviewed in Collections section; refer to Index to Reviews.

Vladimir Agopov

Armenian 1953-

NEW REVIEW

Agopov. Cello Concerto, Op. 10, "Tres Viae"[a].
Dutilleux. Cello Concerto, "Tout un monde lointain"[b]. **Arto Noras** (vc); **Finnish Radio Symphony Orchestra/Jukka-Pekka Saraste.** Finlandia FACD401. Item marked [a] recorded in 1988, [b] 1991.

50m DDD 10/92

Resident in Finland since 1978, the Armenian-born composer Vladimir Agopov — a pupil of Khachaturian and Denisov – completed his Cello Concerto in 1984: the severity of its countenance lends it a certain stoic defiance, though a lack of real incident will prove a stumbling block for many. No, the real reason for investing in this Finlandia CD is the marvellous Dutilleux concerto. Taking as its inspiration the verse of the great metaphysical poet Charles Baudelaire (whence comes the evocative subtitle "Tout un monde lointain"), this is a 27-minute essay of great imagination and wondrous, other-worldly beauty. Dutilleux's richly evocative idiom is readily approachable; indeed, this is a work which can be urgently commended even to those listeners who normally fight shy of contemporary music. Both works receive passionately dedicated performances from that fine Finnish cellist Arto Noras, and he is backed to a man by Jukka-Pekka Saraste and the highly responsive Finnish Radio Symphony Orchestra. Of course, Rostropovich's now-deleted world première recording for EMI of the Dutilleux had a very special intensity not quite matched here (and a rather more desirable coupling in the form of the Lutoslawski Cello Concerto – in another definitive rendering), but this impressive newcomer certainly fills a valuable gap in the catalogue. Helpfully analytical sound, too, if a touch on the dry side.

Alexander Agricola

Flanders c.1446-1506

NEW REVIEW

Agricola. VOCAL AND INSTRUMENTAL WORKS. **Ferrara Ensemble; Ensemble Este of the Schola Cantorum Basiliensis/Crawford Young.** Deutsche Harmonia Mundi RD77038. Texts and translations included.
Vocal Works — Virgo sub ethereis. Je n'ay dueil. Revenez tous regretz. En actendant. Jam fulsit sol de sidere. Gardez voz bien. A la mignonne de fortune. In mijnen sin. *Instrumental Works* — De tous bien playne (two versions). Tandernaken al op den rijn. Pater meus agricola est. Dictes moi toutes. Cecus non judicat de coloribus. Helas madame. Fortuna desperata.

57m ADD 7/90

Agricola's name is little-known today, and his music almost never appears in concert programmes and recordings. This disc from the Ferrara Ensemble makes one wonder why. Even allowing for the conventional exaggerations of the time, it is clear that Agricola was held in the highest esteem by his contemporaries: anyone who is spoken of in the same breath as Obrecht, Josquin and Isaac is surely worthy of at least one recording of his works. The songs and instrumental pieces here recorded show not only an impressive melodic gift (almost any item on the disc will serve as an example of this, but the two settings of *De tous bien playne* perhaps deserve the laurel), but also an imaginative and idiosyncratic contrapuntal sense. In his tantalizingly brief note Crawford Young draws attention to an attraction to "the unexpected, the irrational, the rare" which Agricola would seem to have in common with Hieronymus Bosch — they both enjoyed the patronage of Philip the Fair — and which finds expression in quirky sequential writing and obsessively repeating fragments (particularly evident in *Tandernaken al op den rijn*, for example). All this is reminiscent of Obrecht, and what is urgently needed now is a recording of Agricola's sacred music in order to make a fuller comparison. Meanwhile, there is vast pleasure to be derived from these sensitive performances of the secular works.

Jehan Alain

French 1911-1940

Alain. ORGAN WORKS. **Thomas Trotter.** Argo 430 833-2ZH. Played on the Het Van den Heuvel organ, Nieuwe Kerk te Katwijk aan Zee, Holland.
Trois danses. Fantasmagorie. Première fantasie. Deuxième fantasie. Suite. Deux danses à Agni Yavishta. Trois pièces.

1h 16m DDD 7/91

No doubt Jehan Alain would have become one of the most significant composers of his generation had he not been killed in action during World War II. As it is, though, he left sufficient music of considerable genius and originality to earn him a lasting place among this century's major French composers of organ music. A strong impression left after listening through this generously-filled disc is of electrifying rhythmic intensity reaching a climax, as it were, with his most enduringly popular piece, "Litanies". The *Trois danses* and the two dances to the Hindu God of fire, Agni Yavishta, have an equally hypnotic effect which Thomas Trotter's compelling playing underlines superbly. This splendid Dutch organ helps matters immeasurably as does Argo's close recording. Particularly successful is the delightful set of ornate variations Alain based on a charming melody attributed to the sixteenth-century composer, Clément Jannequin. Perhaps in the few more reflective moments which this programme offers (such as the evocation of the Hanging Gardens of Babylon, "Le jardin suspendu") the very directness of the organ sound, not to mention some rather obvious action noise detracts from the atmosphere. But against this the organ possesses some magical colours and produces some captivating sounds which suit this somewhat other-worldly music.

Further listening ...

Intermezzo. Litanies, Op. 79. *Coupled with* ***Dupré.*** Preludes and Fugues, Op. 7. ***Franck.*** Prélude, fugue et variation in B minor, Op. 18. Fantaisie in A major. ***Tournemire.*** Petite rapsodie improvisée. Cantilène improvisée. Improvisation sur le Te Deum. **Jane Watts** (org). Priory PRCD286 (9/90).

Isaac Albéniz

Spanish 1860-1909

Albéniz (orch. Halffter). Rapsodia española, Op. 70.
Falla. Nights in the gardens of Spain (1915).
Turina. Rapsodia sinfónica, Op. 66. **Alicia de Larrocha** (pf); **London Philharmonic Orchestra/Rafael Frühbeck de Burgos.** Decca 410 289-2DH. From 410 289-1DH (6/84).

52m DDD 10/84 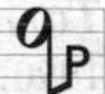

The three magically beautiful nocturnes which make up Falla's *Nights in the gardens of Spain* express the feelings and emotions evoked by contrasted surroundings, whilst Albéniz's enjoyably colourful *Rapsodia española* is a loosely assembled sequence of Spanish dances such as the *jota* and the *malagueña*. Like Falla's *Nights* the work was conceived as a piano solo, but this disc contains a version with orchestra arranged by Cristobal Halffter. The disc is completed by Turina's short, two-part work for piano and strings. All three pieces are excellently performed, but it is the Falla work which brings out the quality of Larrocha's artistry; her ability to evoke the colour of the Spanish atmosphere is remarkable. Frühbeck de Burgos supports her magnificently and persuades the LPO to some very Latin-sounding playing. The recording is suitably atmospheric.

Albéniz. Iberia[a] (arr. Gray) — El Albaicín; Triana; Rondeña.
Granados. Seven Valses poéticos (trans. Williams).
Rodrigo. Invocación y Danza. En los trigales.
Anonymous (arr. Llobet): Ten Catalan Folk-songs — Canço del lladre; El testament d'Amelia;

La filadora; El mestre; La nit de Nadal; L'hereu Riera; Lo fill del Ré; La Pastoreta; El Noi de la Mare. **John Williams** (gtr); [a]**London Symphony Orchestra/Paul Daniels.** Sony Classical SK48480.

1h 11m DDD 7/92 

The amalgam of technical guitaristic perfection in the face of daunting demands, fluid musicality and exemplary tone-production, caught in this exceptionally lifelife recording, represents a landmark in the instrument's march towards true parity with other instruments. Granados's *Valses* are unabridged, Rodrigo's moody *Invocación y Danza* comes in its original and more effective form, and two of the charming settings of Catalan folk-songs arranged by Llobet have no other recording. Nothing in Albéniz's virtuosic *Iberia* is accessible to the solo guitar, but with the aid of the London Symphony Orchestra and Gray's enchantingly evocative arrangements, Williams shows three of its movements in a new and colourful light. To anyone with the slightest interest in the guitar or Spanish romantic music this disc is a required purchase.

Albéniz. Iberia. Navarra (compl. de Séverac). Suite española, Op. 47. **Alicia de Larrocha** (pf). Decca 417 887-2DH2. Recorded in 1986.

② 2h 6m DDD 6/88 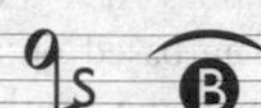

The *Iberia* suite is the greatest piano work in all Spanish musical literature and when played by Spain's leading pianist and recorded with warm but superlatively clean sound-quality is pure joy. A Catalan like Albéniz himself, Larrocha revels in the colour of these 12 highly picturesque and mostly Andalusian impressions, such as the quiet reverie of "Evocación", the lively bustle of "El puerto", the tense religious fervour of "El Corpus Christi en Sevilla", the swirling gaiety of "Triana", the brooding melancholy of "El Albaicín" and the exuberant bravura of *Navarra*. The Albéniz of 20 years earlier is illustrated by the 1886 *Suite española*, which Larrocha presents with winningly natural ease and charm.

Additional recommendations ...

Suite española. ***Granados.*** *Goyescas — excerpts.* ***Falla.*** *El amor brujo.* **New Philharmonia Orchestra/Rafael Frühbeck de Burgos.** Decca 417 786-2DM — 1h 9m ADD 10/89 (B)

Iberia. Cantos de España, Op. 232. **Rafael Orozco** (pf). Auvidis Valois V4663 — ② 1h 2m DDD 11/92 (B)

Iberia. Navarra. Suite española — Granada. Pavana-capricho, Op. 12. España, Op. 165 — Tango. Recuerdos de viaje, Op. 71 — Puerta de tierra (Bolero); Rumores de la caleta (Malagueña). **Alicia de Larrocha** (pf). EMI CMS7 64504-2 — ② 1h 56m ADD 11/92 (B)

NEW REVIEW

Albéniz (arr. Barrueco). Suite española, Op. 47.
Turina. GUITAR WORKS. **Manuel Barrueco** (gtr). EMI CDC7 54382-2. Recorded in 1990.

Fandanguillo, Op. 36. Sevillana, Op. 29. Ráfaga, Op. 53. Hommage à Tárrega, Op. 69. Sonata, Op. 61.

1h 5m DDD 3/93

Albéniz's enthusiastic approval of Tárrega's arrangements of some of his piano pieces is an oft-quoted justification for such exercises, to which Manuel Barrueco and others have added that of their success in that field. Whilst many have selected the items from the *Suite española* which are easier to handle, leaving the harder ones to ensembles of two or more guitars, Barrueco does not flinch from facing the Suite in its entirety — and he is well equipped in every respect to do so. In presenting these highly attractive 'portraits' of Spain (and one of Cuba, Barrueco's birthplace) the guitar adds expressive elements of tonal variety and vibrato that are beyond the capability of the piano. Turina was one of the first non-guitarist composers to provide Segovia with new repertory in the post-World War I years, taking full advantage of his co-operation in learning to write for an idiomatic instrument that he knew only through the sounds it produced. The recording contains everything that Turina wrote for the guitar, unmistakably Spanish to the final cadence — even in the formal dress of sonata-form, as in Op. 61. Barrueco's complete technical mastery is complemented by warmly aristocratic musicality and transmitted with great beauty of tone.

Eugen d'Albert

British/German 1864-1932

Suggested listening ...

TIEFLAND. **Gerd Feldhoff** (bar) Sebastiano; **Ivan Sardi** (bass) Tommaso; **Ernst Krikowski** (bar) Moruccio; **Isabel Strauss** (sop) Marta; **Martha Musial** (sop) Pepa; **Alice Oelke** (contr) Antonia; **Margarete Klose** (contr) Rosalia; **Angelika Fischer** (sop) Nuri; **Rudolf Schock** (ten) Pedro; **Karl-Ernst Mercker** (ten) Nando; **Berlin RIAS Chorus; Berlin Symphony Orchestra/Hans Zanotelli.** Eurodisc 353 240 (2/89).

Tomaso Albinoni

Italian 1671-1751

Albinoni. WIND CONCERTOS.
Vivaldi. WIND CONCERTOS. **Paul Goodwin** (ob); **King's Consort/Robert King.** Hyperion CDA66383. Recorded in 1990.
Albinoni: Concertos, Op. 9 — No. 2 in D minor; No. 6 in G major; No. 9 in C major. Concerto in C major. ***Vivaldi:*** Concertos — C major, RV560; F major, RV457; C major, RV559.

lh 10m DDD 6/91 

Few lovers of baroque concertos will be disappointed by this anthology. For the most part the programme has been well chosen both for the quality of the music and for the variety of instrumental colour which it affords. One piece, though, for trumpet, three oboes and a bassoon, for whom Albinoni's authorship is claimed is spurious and musically of a lower order than the remainder of the concertos. Albinoni was, if not the first, one of the first to write concertos for one and two solo oboes. They are without exception appealing for their warm colours and alluring conviviality. Happily, the disc includes one of Albinoni's most impressive compositions, the Oboe Concerto in D minor (Op. 9 No. 2) with its lyrical, aria-like *Adagio*; thankfully, not *the Adagio* but a genuine product from the composer's pen and an incomparably superior creation. The Vivaldi concertos are immediately engaging for their rhythmic energy and their varied colours. Two of the works are for pairs of oboes and clarinets, the latter very much in their infancy; the third is a piece for oboe and strings which the composer adapted from an earlier bassoon concerto. It has an especially effective opening movement, sensitively played by Paul Goodwin.

NEW REVIEW

Albinoni. Concerti a cinque, Op. 7. Sinfonie e concerti a cinque, Op. 2 — No. 5 in D major; No. 6 in G minor. **Heinz Holliger, Maurice Bourgue** (obs); **I Musici.** Philips 432 115-2PH2. Recorded 1990-91.
No. 1 in D major; No. 2 in C major; No. 3 in B flat major; No. 4 in G major; No. 5 in C major; No. 6 in D major; No. 7 in A major; No. 8 in D major; No. 9 in F major; No. 10 in B flat major; No. 11 in C major; No. 12 in C major

② lh 34m DDD 1/93

Albinoni's 12 Concertos, Op. 7 fall into three distinct types: four of them are for strings alone, four for strings with a single oboe and four for strings with two oboes. More than in Vivaldi's oboe concertos, Albinoni's earlier examples of the form contain a greater interaction between the oboes and the violins. This repertory has been a stock-in-trade for I Musici for well over 30 years so, as we might expect, the performances are lively, well polished and, within certain boundaries, stylish. But it is above all the oboists on whom the success or failure of this set ultimately depends. In the partnership of Heinz Holliger and Maurice Bourgue we could hardly find stronger advocates. They phrase eloquently, shade effectively, ornament tastefully and unfailingly play in tune. Holliger also plays the four concertos for one oboe, bringing a wonderful sense of poetry to the music, wistful in slow movements, athletic in faster ones. I Musici are perhaps on occasion a little weighty in their accompaniments but clean ensemble and clear articulation are positive virtues. Two additional pieces in this release come from Albinoni's Op. 2. Both of them are attractive sonatas in five parts for strings only. In short an enjoyable issue, affectionately realized.

Additional recommendations ...

Op. 7, Nos. 2, 3, 5, 6, 8, 9, 11 and 12. **Heinz Holliger, Hans Elhorst** (obs); **Berne Camerata.** Archiv Produktion Galleria 427 111-2AGA — 57m ADD 4/89

Op. 7, Nos. 3, 6, 9 and 12. Op. 9, No. 2 in D minor; No. 5 in C major; No. 8 in G minor; No. 11 in B flat major. **London Harpsichord Ensemble/Sarah Francis** (ob). Unicorn-Kanchana DKPCD9088 — lh 14m DDD 3/90

Hugo Alfvén

Swedish 1872-1960

Alfvén. Symphony No. 2 in D major, R28. Midsummer Vigil — Swedish Rhapsody No. 1, R45. **Stockholm Philharmonic Orchestra/Neeme Järvi.** BIS CD385.

lh 8m DDD 7/88 

Hugo Alfvén was one of Sweden's major symphonists, but also wrote several melodies that are popular the world over. Best known of all is the dance theme of *Midsummer Vigil*, the first of three Swedish Rhapsodies and the one that is generally known as *the* Swedish Rhapsody. The piece as a whole is a charming tone poem depicting youthful, high-spirited revelry during a midsummer Scandinavian night. Of Alfvén's four symphonies, the Second is the one that put him on the map in 1899. Its idiom is rooted in the music of Dvořák, with a touch of the freshness of Svendsen. Perhaps the best music is to be found in the first three movements, which Alfvén said were sketched beside the sea. The first (*moderato*) is bubbling over with freshness and melody, and is followed by sounds of grim foreboding from the lower brass in the *andante* second movement. The *scherzo* is followed by a final movement in the form of a prelude and fugue. Neeme Järvi brings to the works his feel for Scandinavian music, and the recording lives up to BIS's regular high standards.

NEW REVIEW

Alfvén. Symphony No. 4, Op. 39, "From the Outermost Skerries"[a]. A legend of the Skerries, Op. 20. [a]**Christina Högman** (sop); [a]**Claes-Håkan Ahnsjö** (ten); [a]**Per-Olof Gillblad** (cor ang); [a]**Karl-Ove Mannberg** (vn); [a]**Elemér Lavotha** (vc); [a]**Lucia Negro** (pf); **Stockholm Philharmonic Orchestra/Neeme Järvi.** BIS CD505. Recorded in 1990.

lh 4m DDD 8/92

The Fourth Symphony occupied Alfvén for the best part of a decade; the first ideas come from 1908 and he returned to the score in 1913. He put it into its final shape during 1918-19 after spending a great deal of time in the outer archipelago of Stockholm, that stretches out far into the Baltic. Anyone who has spent any time there will know just how magical it is. This is a highly romantic programme. Its opulence of colour and sumptuousness of texture has won it many admirers: there is a lot of Strauss in it, and a touch of Reger and even Debussy. There is a wordless vocalise, inspired no doubt by Nielsen's *Sinfonia Espansiva* (1912). The soloists in this performance are excellent and the orchestral playing under Neeme Järvi is very responsive. The recording is beautifully balanced with detail perfectly placed and plenty of air round the sound.

A legend of the Skerries is an earlier piece, which comes from the same period as his *Midsummer Vigil* but does not have its independence of outlook. There is a lot of Wagner in this piece. Eminently recommendable to those who like to wallow in lush romantic sonorities.

Charles-Valentin Alkan

French 1813-1888

Alkan. 25 Préludes dans les tons majeurs et mineur, Op. 31.
Shostakovich. 24 Preludes, Op. 34. **Olli Mustonen** (pf). Decca 433 055-2DH. Recorded in 1990.

1h 16m DDD 10/91

It was brave of Decca to launch the career of their latest star pianist with a disc of miniatures few people actually know. Despite the sterling efforts of Ronald Smith, the *oeuvre* of Charles-Valentin Alkan is usually confined to specialist labels and second-rate executants. The 25 Preludes are a reasonably benign introduction to Alkan's idiosyncratic world — elusive and quirky to be sure but less ruthlessly barnstorming than much of his output. They are by no means easy pieces to bring off, but you wouldn't know it from Mustonen's exceptionally assured, brilliantly poised readings. Where rival versions are content to offer the 25 Preludes without coupling, Mustonen adds deft and sparkling performances of Shostakovich's not exactly insubstantial Op. 34 Preludes. Exceptional pianism, excellent, bright recording and helpful notes.

Further listening ...

Grand Duo Concertant in F sharp minor, Op. 21[a]. Sonate de Concert in E major, Op. 47[b]. Trio in G minor, Op. 30[c]. [ab]**Rainer M. Klaas,** [a]**Kolja Lessing** (pfs); [b]**Bernhard Schwarz** (vc); [c]**Alkan Trio.** Marco Polo 8 223383.

12 Etudes, Op. 35 — Allegro barbaro. 12 Etudes dans les ton mineurs, Op. 39 — Nos. 1-3. Grande sonate — Les quatre âges, Op. 33. 24 Préludes, Op. 31 — La chanson de la folle au bord de la mer. **Ronald Smith** (pf). EMI CDM7 64280-2.

Sonatine, Op. 61. Zorcico. Scherzo diabolico, Op. 39 No. 3. Nocturne No. 2, Op. 57 No. 1. Gigue, Op. 24. Marche, Op. 37 No. 1. Barcarolle, Op. 67 No. 6. Saltarelle, Op. 23. **Bernard Ringeissen** (pf). Harmonia Mundi HMA190 927 (11/88).

12 Etudes dans les ton mineurs, Op. 39 — Concerto for Solo Piano (Nos. 8-10). **Marc-Andre Hamelin** (pf). Music and Arts CD-724.

Gregorio Allegri

Italian c.1582-1652

NEW REVIEW

Allegri. Miserere mei.
Palestrina. MOTETS. **Roy Goodman** (treb); **King's College Choir, Cambridge / Sir David Willcocks.** Decca Ovation 421 147-2DM.
Palestrina: Stabat mater a 8. Hodie beata virgo. Senex puerum portabat. Magnificat a 8. Litaniae de Beata Vergine Mariae I a 8.

56m ADD 5/89

Thirty years have passed since this recording of Allegri's *Miserere* was made yet it still has the power to enchant: it was one of the glories of Sir David Willcocks's influential tenure at King's, the days of a uniform sound of voices which blended seamlessly with each other, making here the perfect aural backdrop for the voice of a boy treble. Here it is Roy Goodman (who has gone on to become a successful violinist and director) whose clear tones soar effortlessly into the vaults of the College Chapel, creating arches of sound that mirror the architecture of the Chapel. It is recordings like this that draw visitors to the Chapel in Cambridge and listeners to the radio to hear the choir sing in the Service of Nine Lessons and Carols each Christmas and yet it is still regrettably the only piece generally known by this grand-pupil of Palestrina (and from Palestrina we have some superbly sung and well-chosen motets). In short, for an endearing selection of Palestrina's art and Allegri's gem, both allied to the timeless quality of King's, this mid-price disc cannot be beaten.

Additional recommendations ...
Miserere (with Nicholas Thompson, treb; Wilfred Swansborough, alto; Timothy Jones, bass). *Coupled with* ***B. Rose.*** *Feast Song for St Cecilia* (with Simon Hill, alto; Alan Green, ten). ***Brahms.*** *Ein deutsches Requiem — Ich hab nun Traurigkeit.* ***Britten.*** *Festival Te Deum, Op. 32.* ***Harvey.*** *Come, Holy Ghost* (with Andrew Burden, ten; Nigel Beaven, bass). ***Mendelssohn.*** *Hear my prayer.* ***Stanford.*** *Evening Canticles in G major* (with Timothy Jones). ***Tavener.*** *I will lift up mine eyes.* ***Wise.*** *The way of Zion do mourn* (with Charles Gibbs, bass). **Jeremy Budd** (treb); **St Paul's Cathedral Choir/John Scott** with **Andrew Lucas** (org). Hyperion CDA66439 — 1h 16m DDD 10/91 (B)

Miserere. Coupled with ***Lotti.*** *Crucifixus.* ***Palestrina.*** *Missa Papae Marcelli. Stabat mater a 8.* **The Sixteen/Harry Christophers.** Collins Classics 5009-2 — 56m DDD 10/90 (B)

For further recommendations for Allegri's Miserere, refer to Index to Reviews.

Key to Symbols

Bargains — £
Quality of Sound
Quality of performance
Basic library — (B)
Discs worth exploring — (?)
Period performance
Caveat emptor — ▲

Francisco António de Almeida

Portuguese c. 1702-1755

NEW REVIEW

Almeida. La Giuditta. **Lena Lootens, Francesca Congiu** (sops); **Axel Köhler** (alto); **Martyn Hill** (ten); **Cologne Concerto/René Jacobs.** Harmonia Mundi HMC90 1411/2. Text and translation included. Recorded in 1992.

② 2h 1m DDD 11/92

Francisco António de Almeida is a name that will be unfamiliar to all but the most ardent aficionados of baroque music. Born in Portugal, he spent some time in Rome which led to the composition of several comic operas and a large amount of sacred music, most of which has been lost. *La Giuditta*, based on the biblical story of Judith's victory over Holofernes, is his only surviving oratorio. Stylistically he is closest to Handel, with those characteristic Handelian harmonies in "Quella fiamma" on track 3, though *Giuditta* was written before any of Handel's oratorios except *La Resurrezione*. But Almeida establishes a style very much his own from the very first chord, here brilliantly brought to life by René Jacobs and his Cologne Concerto. Martyn Hill as Holofernes is appropriately war-like, though he is occasionally choppy, notably in "Invitti miei guerrieri". Axel Köhler as Ozia, beseiged by Holofernes's armies, is, however, superb, with a fine dramatic range: the gentleness of his "Tortorella, se rimira" is particularly moving. Lena Lootens in the title-role is wonderfully stylish, pure of voice throughout "Sento che dice al cor", with great strength and clean *fioriture* in her plea to God to defeat her enemies, "Dalla destra onnipotente". It is perhaps a pity that the part of Achiorre should have been written for a soprano: Francesca Congiu has a hard time convincing listeners that she is indeed

Commander of the Ammonites, though this illusion would probably be easier to sustain on stage. René Jacobs guides the work with an unerring sense of pace and drama. From the attention-grabbing Overture through to the final notes, this is a totally committed, totally compelling performance of a newly discovered masterpiece.

William Alwyn

British 1905-1985

NEW REVIEW

Alwyn. Symphonies — No. 1 in D major; No. 4. **London Philharmonic Orchestra/William Alwyn.** Lyrita SRCD227. Item marked [a] from SRCS86 (4/77), [b] SRCS76 (5/75).

lh 17m ADD 7/92

At 45, William Alwyn was a comparative latecomer to the symphony, but in previous years he had garnered an extraordinarily intimate knowledge of the orchestra through a great many film and documentary assignments (his output includes over 60 film scores). Not surprisingly, then, much of the scoring in the First Symphony (premièred by Sir John Barbirolli and the Hallé at the 1950 Cheltenham Festival) is thrilling in its beauty and physical impact, and the work's gloriously affirmative character went down exceedingly well with that first-night audience, even if, truth to tell, Alwyn does rather overdo the rhetoric in the jubilant finale. By the time of the Fourth Symphony (1959), however, Alwyn was developing his ideas with a cogency and fluency which would be the envy of any symphonic master. This is a passionate, noble utterance, once again magnificently orchestrated, and encompassing an enormous emotional range during its 35-minute duration. The composer himself draws playing of generally high quality from the LPO and, as ever from this pioneering label, production values are stunningly high; indeed, much of this material remains demonstration-worthy in its naturalness and sheen. A valuable document which all devoted Anglophiles will not want to miss.

NEW REVIEW

Alwyn. Symphonies — No. 2[a]; No. 3[b]; No. 5, "Hydriotaphia"[c]. **London Philharmonic Orchestra/William Alwyn.** Lyrita SRCD228. Item marked [a] from SRCS85 (11/75), [b] SRCS63 (10/72), [c] SRCS76 (5/75).

lh 17m ADD 10/92

An impressive symphonic triptych, outstandingly well recorded. The technical quality of these Lyrita productions drew many an admiring comment when they first appeared during the 1970s, and these superb remasterings for CD certainly preserve all the glorious warmth and lustrous transparency of the vinyl originals. Alwyn completed his powerful two-movement Second Symphony in 1953: its satisfying organic unity and fluent, natural progress proclaim a true symphonist, and Alwyn's rich-hued, never clotted orchestration is always masterly — lovers of Bax will surely recognise a kindred spirit. If anything, though, the Third (1956) is an even more distinguished achievement: there's an almost Sibelian scope and inevitability here about Alwyn's driven inspiration, and one is inclined to agree with those admirers of the composer who have hailed it as his masterpiece. The single-movement Fifth from 1973, inspired by lines from an elegiac discourse by the seventeenth-century writer Sir Thomas Browne entitled *Hydriotaphia*, is another concise structure, full of colourful orchestral incident and memorable invention. With the composer in charge of proceedings, these can all be regarded as authoritative readings, and the LPO respond to his clear-headed direction with commendable discipline and no little enthusiasm. Generous measure, too!

Additional recommendation ...

No. 2. Overture to a Masque. The Magic Island — symphonic prelude. Overture, "Derby Day". Fanfare for a Joyful Occasion. **London Symphony Orchestra/Richard Hickox.** Chandos CHAN9093 — lh 2m DDD 2/93

NEW REVIEW

Alwyn. Lyra Angelica[a]. Autumn Legend[b]. Pastoral fantasia[c]. Tragic Interlude. [a]**Rachel Masters** (hp); [b]**Nicholas Daniel** (cor ang); [c]**Stephen Tees** (va); **City of London Sinfonia/Richard Hickox.** Chandos CHAN9065. Recorded in 1991.

lh 4m DDD 10/92

Richard Hickox and Chandos are really doing Alwyn proud these days. Two of the works on this latest compilation, namely the *Autumn Legend* for cor anglais and string orchestra (veritably an English *Swan of Tuonela*) and the ravishing Harp Concerto entitled *Lyra Angelica*, have been recorded before (and most beautifully, too) under the composer's own direction on Lyrita (see below), but if anything these new versions are even more succulently characterful, aided by unimpeachably natural Chandos sonics (balance is impeccable throughout). Two première recordings complete this survey: the appealing *Pastoral fantasia* (1939) inhabits a bitter-sweet harmonic world not far removed from that of, say, Warlock or Bax, and the writing for solo viola has both poetry and flair; the *Tragic Interlude* (1936) is another darkly atmospheric essay, reflecting the anxious times in which it was conceived. If you don't already know Alwyn's haunting, gorgeously-textured *Lyra Angelica*, let us urge you to repair that omission without delay. The composer himself thought it his finest work, and the present account is acutely sensitive to every nuance of Alwyn's marvellously-judged scoring. Lovely music, radiantly presented.

Additional recommendation ...

Lyra Angelica. Autumn Legend. Concerto Grosso No. 2 in G major. **Osian Ellis** (hp); **Geoffrey Browne** (cor ang); **London Philharmonic Orchestra/William Alwyn.** Lyrita SRCD230 — 59m ADD 12/92

NEW REVIEW

Alwyn. MISS JULIE. **Jill Gomez** (sop) Miss Julie; **Benjamin Luxon** (bar) Jean; **Della Jones** (mez) Kristin; **John Mitchinson** (ten) Ulrik; **Philharmonia Orchestra/Vilem Tausky.** Lyrita SRCD2218. Notes and text included. From SRCS121/2 (12/83). Recorded in 1979.

② lh 58m ADD 3/93 

A magnificent recorded presentation of an (as yet) unstaged opera. William Alwyn's strong and characterful adaptation of August Strindberg's drama was three years in the making and first performed in February 1977 for a BBC Radio 3 broadcast some five months later. The composer himself wrote the fluent (if somewhat over-sanitized) libretto, creating in the process an extra character in the personage of Ulrik, the gamekeeper; in the opera, Ulrik (off-stage) shoots the lap-dog Miss Julie wants to take with her when she elopes with her manservant Jean, whereas in Strindberg's original it is Jean who (on on-stage) horrifically kills Miss Julie's pet finch — both dramatically and symbolically a far more pungent gesture. As ever, Alwyn's idiom is approachable (there are strong echoes of Puccini and Walton) and impeccably crafted; certainly the Philharmonia seem to revel in the confident orchestral writing, and Vilem Tausky directs proceedings with real passion and conviction. The cast, too, is uniformly excellent: Benjamin Luxon is on commanding form as Jean, whilst Jill Gomez in the title-role produces the most ravishing sounds throughout (try sampling her gorgeous delivery of the Midsummer Night aria at the end of Act 1 Scene 1). The Kingsway Hall sessions (supervised by the Decca team of producer Andrew Cornall and sound engineer Kenneth Wilkinson) took place over a four-day period in January 1979. The expertly-annotated booklet may say "ADD", but this is, technically speaking, as realistic a recording as you will ever hear, with soloists set in perfect relief against an impeccably balanced orchestral backdrop. From every conceivable point of view, then, this welcome CD reissue represents an unqualified success.

Further listening ...

 Fantasy-Waltzes. Preludes. **John Ogdon** (pf). Chandos CHAN8399 (7/86).

George Antheil

American 1900-1959

Suggested listening ...

String Quartets Nos. 1-3. **Mondriaan Quartet.** Etcetera KTC1093 (6/91).

Hans Erich Apostel

Austrian 1901-1972

Apostel. String Quartet No. 1, Op. 7[a].
Zemlinsky. String Quartets — No. 1 in A major, Op. 4[a]; No. 2, Op. 15[b]; No. 3, Op. 19[a]; No. 4, Op. 25[a]. **LaSalle Quartet** (Walter Levin, Henry Meyer, vns; Peter Kamnitzer, va; Lee Fiser, vc). DG 427 421-2GC2. Items marked [a] from 2741 016 (2/84), [b] 2530 082 (4/79). Recorded 1977-1981.

② 2h 18m DDD/ADD 8/89

When the LaSalle Quartet's pioneering recording of Zemlinsky's Second Quartet was first issued, the composer — the *Lyric Symphony* apart — was still a relatively unknown quantity. Today his strengths and weaknesses (especially in opera) can be more completely and realistically evaluated, and alternative performances of various works have begun to appear. Just occasionally the LaSalle Quartet may seem to press the music too hard, and the sound to lack that last degree of bloom and warmth which present-day techniques can ensure. But these are minor quibbles compared with the confidence and conviction of the enterprise as a whole. The Second Quartet remains the jewel in the crown, a powerful, large-scale conception far from dwarfed by comparison with the Schoenberg First Quartet that was its evident model. From the Brahmsian late-romanticism of No. 1 to the well-balanced tensions of the later pieces, the LaSalle players are persuasive advocates. With the bonus of a well-crafted, pithily-argued piece by the Schoenberg pupil, Hans Erich Apostel, this medium-priced issue is highly attractive.

Anton Arensky

Russian 1861-1906

Suggested listening ...

Symphonies — No. 1 in B minor, Op. 4; No. 2 in A major, Op. 22. **USSR Academy Symphony Orchestra/Evgeni Svetlanov.** Olympia OCD167 (7/89).

Harold Arlen

American 1905-1986

Suggested listening ...

THE WIZARD OF OZ — *Musical Show.* **1988 Royal Shakespeare Company cast.** That's Entertainment CDTER1165 (12/89).

Thomas Arne

British 1710-1778

NEW REVIEW

Arne. FAVOURITE CONCERTOS. **The Parley of Instruments/Paul Nicholson** ([a]hpd, [b]org, [c]fp). Hyperion CDA66509. Recorded in 1991.

No. 1 in C major[a]; No. 2 in G major[b]; No. 3 in A major[c]; No. 4 in B flat major[b]; No. 5 in G minor[a]; No. 6 in B flat major[c].

1h 18m DDD 9/92

Arne's "Six Favourite Concertos" for organ, harpsichord or fortepiano, though posthumously published in 1793, were written at different times in the composer's life. In this recording the soloist, Paul Nicholson rings the changes between the three solo instruments. He is a stylish player and an accurate one too, with a technique that allows him to indulge in nimble fingerwork without mishap. Nicholson furthermore approaches the music with a pleasing rhythmic suppleness and an intuitive feeling for expressive punctuation. In the bad old days such elasticity might have been censored for its unsteadiness but it is this, above all, which breathes life into the music and which turns unpunctuated speech into eloquent conversation. All but one of the Concertos is scored for keyboard solo with oboes, bassoon, strings and continuo; the odd man out, so-to-speak, is the First Concerto of the set where Arne, in a startlingly unexpected way introduces two trumpets, two horns and timpani at the end of the concluding Minuet. Here and throughout Arne beguiles the senses with his melodic gift with its occasional Handelian echo as, for instance, in the gigue finale of the Second Concerto. Not everything is quite as tidy as it should be in the orchestra but the music and the spirit of its performance should win many friends.

Arne. INSTRUMENTAL WORKS. **Le Nouveau Quatuor** (Utako Ikeda, fl; Catherine Weiss, vn; Mark Caudle, vc; [a]Paul Nicholson, hpd). Amon Ra CDSAR-42. Recorded in 1989.
Favourite Concertos — No. 1 in C major (solo hpd version)[a]. Keyboard Sonatas (1756) — No. 1 in F major[a]. Trio Sonatas (1757) — No. 2 in G major; No. 5; No. 6 in B minor; No. 7 in E minor.

58m DDD 5/90

If the music history books offer little more than a passing reference to the slim repertoire of enchanting chamber music by Thomas Arne, the ordinary man in the street, who can at least whistle *Rule Britannia*, is unlikely even to have heard that any exists. This disc comes therefore as something of a revelation. The members of the Nouveau Quatuor perform on instruments dating from the composer's lifetime, tuned down a semitone. The trio sonatas, originally published for two violins and continuo, are played here by a mixed quartet: flute, violin, cello and harpsichord, which is believed to have been what the composer really intended. The introduction of the flute adds colour, brightness and definition to these charming pieces and gives the listener a chance to savour the admirable tone and phrasing of the flautist, Utako Ikeda. Paul Nicholson's harpsichord solos are distinguished as much by their elegance as by their extraordinary power and brilliance. A word, finally, in praise of Peter Holman's excellent sleeve-notes: they are both scholarly and extremely readable.

Further listening ...

Symphonies — No. 1 in C major; No. 2 in F major; No. 3 in E flat major; No. 4 in C minor. **Cantilena/Adrian Shepherd.** Chandos CHAN8403 (6/87).

Sir Malcolm Arnold

British 1921-

Arnold. CONCERTOS. [a]**Karen Jones** (fl); [b]**Michael Collins** (cl); [c]**Richard Watkins** (hn); [d]**Kenneth Sillito,** [d]**Lyn Fletcher** (vns); **London Musici/Mark Stephenson.** Conifer CDCF172. Recorded in 1988.
Concerto for two violins and orchestra, Op. 77[d]. Concerto No. 1 for clarinet and strings, Op. 20[b]. Concerto No. 1 for flute and strings, Op. 45[a]. Concerto No. 2 for horn and strings, Op. 58[c].

56m DDD 8/89

The four concertos presented on this disc provide an excellent opportunity to sample Arnold's wonderful gift for concertante writing. Each was written for or commissioned by an outstanding British virtuoso, which in turn reflects the admiration and respect with which Sir Malcolm is held by his musical colleagues. Listening to these concertos it's easy to see why he is so frequently commissioned by soloists for new works, as his ability to bring out the natural characteristics of each instrument as well as capture something of the style and personality for whom he writes is quite extraordinary. The Clarinet Concerto dates from 1948 and is a work full of contrast and contradictions, sometimes introspective and serious (slow movement), sometimes humorous and light-hearted, but always extremely approachable and lyrical. The exuberant and extrovert outer movements of the Flute Concerto capture the mercurial qualities of the instrument very well, and these are contrasted by a slow movement of great beauty and simplicity. Not surprisingly the Horn Concerto reflects the considerable virtuosity of its dedicatee, Dennis Brain, who died so tragically only a few weeks after its first performance in 1957. The Double Violin Concerto of 1964 surprisingly finds its way on to CD for the first time, and a most welcome addition to the catalogue it is too. Though it has a rather more serious, neo-classical approach than the other concertos its immediacy and charm are evident from the very beginning, and one is left wondering why this work is not heard or recorded more frequently. The superb performances from all concerned, not least the beautifully rich string tone of the London Musici, make this a highly recommendable introduction to Arnold's music.

Arnold. ORCHESTRAL WORKS. [a]**Phyllis Sellick,** [a]**Cyril Smith** (pfs); [b]**Bournemouth Symphony Orchestra,** [c]**City of Birmingham Symphony Orchestra,** [d]**Phiharmonia Orchestra/Malcolm Arnold.** EMI British Composers [abc]stereo/[d]mono CDM7 64044-2. Items marked [abc] recorded 1970-1979, [d] 1955.
Concerto for two pianos (three hands), Op. 101[ac] (from HMV ASD2612, 10/70). Symphony No. 1, Op. 22[b]. Solitaire[b] — Sarabande; Polka (all from ASD3823, 6/80). Tam O'Shanter — Overture, Op. 51[d]. English Dances[d] — No. 3, Op. 27 No. 3; No. 5, Op. 33 No. 1 (Columbia SED5529, 2/56).

1h 16m ADD 10/91 

When Sir Malcolm celebrated his seventieth birthday in 1991, many people realized how badly he had been neglected by the stiff British establishment as too tuneful, uninhibited and (worst of all!) communicative to be 'serious'. These recordings under his own baton were ripe for this mid-price reissue, for although the sound is not new — the *Tam O'Shanter* Overture and *English Dances* are in mono and date from 1955 — it is surprisingly good. Newcomers to Arnold's music (or who think they are, for they've probably heard it in several famous British films) could well start with *Tam O'Shanter*, which was inspired by a Robert Burns poem about a Scotsman's wild night ride with the devil in pursuit. The boisterous and brilliant scoring here is a delight, as is the marvellous sense of atmosphere. The Two Piano Concerto was commissioned for the 1969 Proms and the duo of Phyllis Sellick and Cyril Smith, the "three hands" being because Smith had lost the use of his left hand after a stroke a decade before. Such is Arnold's skill that one's not conscious of a limitation, although his keyboard writing is more as if laid out for one three-handed pianist than for two players of whom one is at a disadvantage. As usual with him, there are contrasts of noisy high spirits and gentle lyricism, and no shortage of tunes, as in the cool, slow movement in slow waltz time. This concerto makes us realize that Arnold is the nearest British equivalent to Poulenc. But like Poulenc, he also had a darker and tougher side, and it comes across in the First Symphony which, for all its vigour, contains real bitterness too. One sometimes thinks of Sibelius and Nielsen as it unfolds, but the voice is still Arnold's and this is fine music if not by any means cosy listening (the end of the finale reaches unmistakable tragedy). The other, lighter pieces make up a valuable issue, with unfailingly strong, authentic-sounding performances.

Arnold. ORCHESTRAL WORKS. **London Philharmonic Orchestra/Malcolm Arnold.** Lyrita SRCD201. Item marked [a] from SRCS109 (3/79).
Four Cornish Dances, Op. 91[a]. English Dances, Op. 27; Op. 33[a]. Irish Dances, Op. 126. Four Scottish Dances, Op. 59[a]. Solitaire — Sarabande; Polka.

1h 1m ADD/DDD 12/90 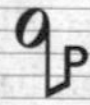

The arrival of Malcolm Arnold as a composer in the 1940s blew a gust of fresh air through English music, as William Walton's had some decades earlier. His training was as a composer and a trumpet player, in which latter capacity he first achieved prominence; his experience as a "rude mechanical" both gave him the insight that contributed to his remarkable skill in orchestration, and helped him to keep his aesthetic feet on the ground. Arnold has never lost faith in tonality, has never hesitated to write tunes that, despite their subtle craftsmanship, sound 'popular', and has not remained aloof from the influences of jazz and rock; he is in the best sense 'Everyman's composer'. The regional characters of his dances (1950-86) are as he perceives them to be, for he makes no use of folk material, and they are reinforced by the versatility of his orchestration. This is music that speaks directly, but does not talk down to the common man, and here it has the benefit of joyous performances conducted by the composer himself, and recorded sound that is as clear as Arnold's orchestral textures. One might describe it as 'Music for Pleasure'.

Additional recommendation ...
As above. **Philharmonia Orchestra/Bryden Thomson.** Chandos CHAN8867 — ·:·
48m DDD 10/90

Arnold. Guitar Concerto, Op. 67.
Brouwer. Retrats Catalans.
Chappell. Guitar Concerto No. 1, "Caribbean Concerto". **Eduardo Fernández** (gtr); **English Chamber Orchestra/Barry Wordsworth.** Decca 430 233-2DH. Recorded in 1989.

·:· lh DDD 4/91

In a world swamped by Rodrigo's *Concierto de Aranjuez*, Malcolm Arnold's Guitar Concerto has been heard much less often than it deserves. His musical roots spread in many directions, here toward lighter soil; the first movement's second subject might make a very popular song (if someone provided it with lyrics), the second movement, a lament for Django Reinhardt, breathes the late-night air of a jazz club, and the one-octave glissando that ends the third is the last of the many demands placed on the soloist in this joyous romp. Brouwer's *Retrats* (portraits) are of Federico Mompou and Antoni Gaudi, painted in fresh colours to which the guitar (and, unusually, the piano) contributes; the guitar here acts as an orchestral 'voice', rather than a concerto-status soloist, and, like Arnold, Brouwer is a master of the orchestral medium. Herbert Chappell, avoiding the cliché of 'Spanishry', enters the guitarist's domain via the Caribbean door; his Concerto is a stunning *tour de force*, a kaleidoscope of colour and movement, and no less a vehicle for the virtuosity of anyone bold enough to approach it. If *Aranjuez* is to have a successor, this could well be it; if so, this recording will long remain a touchstone. Fernández plays brilliantly — and stimulates the ECO to do likewise.

Arnold. OVERTURES. **London Philharmonic Orchestra/Malcolm Arnold.** Reference Recordings RRCD48.
A Sussex Overture, Op. 31. Beckus the Dandipratt, Op. 5. The Smoke, Op. 21. The Fair Field, Op. 110. Commonwealth Christmas Overture, Op. 64. Recorded in 1991.

·:· lh 3m DDD 6/92 

Four of the overtures here are early pieces com-posed before 1960, while *The Fair Field* (written for the Fairfield Halls in Croydon, Surrey) dates from 1972. All have recognizably and affectionately British origins, and their brilliant colour reminds us of Arnold's many outstanding film scores. The earliest piece is *Beckus the Dandipratt* — a dandipratt was an Elizabethan coin, but the word was also used for a cheeky small boy — and was inspired by a youngster that the composer and his wife befriended on a wartime Cornish holiday. *The Smoke* (a Cockney term for London) has raucous jazz elements, while the *Commonwealth Christmas Overture* places cosy English chimes alongside the more urgent Christmas music of a Caribbean pop group. Though much of this music is cheerfully extrovert, by no means all of it is, and for all its tunefulness it is not easy-listening music in the usual sense. Under the composer, the London Philharmonic play it brilliantly and lovingly, and the recording is rich and detailed. The booklet note by the producer, Christopher Palmer, is a model of information, enthusiasm and style and complements a splendid issue.

Arnold. Symphonies — No. 7, Op. 113; No. 8, Op. 124. **Royal Philharmonic Orchestra/Vernon Handley.** Conifer CDCF177.

lh 4m DDD 3/91

When we consider the music of Malcolm Arnold we generally conjure up his marvellously ebullient and good humoured works such as his Suites of English and Scottish Dances, his Overtures *Tam O'Shanter* and *Beckus the Dandipratt* or one of his many brilliant and lyrical concertos. But there is a darker, more serious side too, to this versatile and much misunderstood composer. Here we are presented with two of his most fierce and dissonant works — the Seventh and Eighth Symphonies. The Seventh was written in 1973 and is one of his longest and darkest symphonic utterances. The Symphony is dedicated to Arnold's three children — Katherine, Robert and Edward, and the composer explains that each are loosely portrayed in one of the three movements. Quite why they should be linked with such bleak and ferocious music remains something of an enigma. However, what we do have is a fascinating and compelling work that gives us a deeper insight into Arnold's creative personality. The dissonance and savagery of the first movement is heightened by the movement's disturbing and restless spirit and builds to an impressive, well-calculated climax. The second movement is a dark and melancholy landscape that, as the sleeve notes point out, is conceivably an evocation of the world of Arnold's autistic son Edward. The last movement returns to the unsettled, restless nature of the first, and includes a folksy Irish episode that imitates the style of the Irish folk band, The Chieftains — a particular favourite of Arnold's son Robert. The Eighth Symphony shares with the Seventh a quixotic and dissonant nature, if perhaps somewhat less pessimistic in its overall mood. Arnold's fondness for Irish whimsy makes another appearance with the inclusion in the first movement of a marching tune first used in his score to the film *The Reckoning*. The final movement recalls the high spirits of Arnold's earlier symphonies, though one is constantly aware of sobering and more dramatic undercurrents at work. Vernon Handley's affection for and commitment to these symphonies is evident from these powerful and persuasive performances. Recordings are first-class. Well worth investigating.

NEW REVIEW

Arnold. FILM MUSIC. **London Symphony Orchestra/Richard Hickox.** Chandos CHAN9100. Recorded in 1992.

Film Suites (arr. Palmer) — The Bridge on the River Kwai; The Inn of the Sixth Happiness; Hobson's Choice; Whistle down the Wind. The Sound Barrier, Op. 38.

lh 18m DDD 2/93 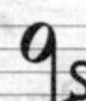

Arnold's vibrant, larger-than-life scoring and quirky, ebullient humour was tailor-made for the cinema and it is easy to appreciate why his career in the movies has spanned well over two decades. What is harder to understand is why so little of this output (with the exception of *The Sound Barrier* Rhapsody, reworked by the composer himself into a convincing concert piece) has been revived on disc in recent years. However, this thrilling collection of suites from five of his most popular scores was well worth waiting for. *The Bridge on the River Kwai*, written in only ten days, won Arnold an Oscar and gave Kenneth Alford's "Colonel Bogey" a completely new lease of life. (Although used to rousing effect in the film as a counter-melody to Arnold's own "River Kwai" March, a bizarre copyright restriction decrees that the two pieces can now only be performed separately.) The music was ill-served by the soundtrack album issued at the time, but here Arnold's expansive set-pieces come across with tremendous impact. On a much smaller scale is his enchanting music for *Whistle Down the Wind*, with its lovely, innocent main theme and piquant, chamber-like scoring. *Hobson's Choice* also uses a reduced orchestra, but here the effect is distinctly more boisterous as Arnold lets rip with the tuba and trombone to portray the portly, stubborn character of Henry Hobson. In direct contrast, the unconventional courtship of Willie and Maggie blossoms with great warmth and is another display of Arnold's gift for intimate scoring. More openly romantic is *The Inn of the Sixth Happiness*, chiefly remembered for its emotional finale as Ingrid Bergman (portraying Gladys Aylward) leads an army of Chinese war orphans to safety over the mountains. Here Arnold once again employs a march (this time the children's nursery rhyme, *This old man*) to counterpoint his own heroic main theme and so bring the score (and the disc) to a gloriously triumphant conclusion. Throughout this brilliant, spectacularly-recorded disc, Richard Hickox and the LSO capture the full flavour of Arnold's characteristic style and bring off each piece with aplomb. Authoratitive notes by the ever-reliable Christopher Palmer complete a most rewarding issue.

NEW REVIEW

Arnold. String Quartets — No. 1, Op. 23; No. 2, Op. 118. **McCapra Quartet** (Fiona McCapra, Jake Rea, vns; Ania Ullmann, va; Ben Chapell, vc). Chandos CHAN9112.

46m DDD 10/92

As his symphonies have consistently shown us, Sir Malcolm Arnold is a far more serious composer than you would ever guess from, say, his marvellously colourful (and justly popular) set of *English Dances*. Both the quartets recorded here command the utmost respect for their superb craft and terseness of argument. Like the First Symphony, which Arnold had only completed a few months earlier, the First Quartet from 1949 is an unremittingly anxious, questing utterance: its bleak demeanour and formidable concentration certainly make for challenging listening. If anything, though, its successor of 26 years later is an even more enigmatic beast: like so many of Arnold's provocative creations from this period (the deeply unsettling Seventh Symphony, for example), it raises far more questions than can be answered, and its bafflingly unpredictable nature can be unnerving to say the least. And yet, as producer Christopher Palmer rightly reminds us in his eloquent booklet-notes: "Arnold's quartets are not 'comfortable' music; but then, he is telling us, life is not always 'comfortable' either". These are exemplary, passionately disciplined performances from the McCapra Quartet, a talented young group of whom we'll surely be hearing a great deal more. Really excellent, intimate results from the Chandos sound engineers, too.

Further listening ...

Sinfoniettas — No. 1, Op. 48; No. 2, Op. 65; No. 3, Op. 81. Flute Concerto No. 1, Op. 45[a]. Oboe Concerto, Op. 39[b]. [a]**Edward Beckett** (fl); [b]**Malcolm Messiter** (ob); **London Festival Orchestra/Ross Pople.** Hyperion CDA66332 (3/90).

Key to Symbols

	② ②	lh 23m	DDD	6/88
Price	***Quantity/ availability***	***Timing***	***Mode***	***Review date***

Bargains — ***Quality of Sound*** — ***Discs worth exploring*** — ***Caveat emptor***

£   P   S   B   ?   ▲

Quality of performance — ***Basic library*** — ***Period performance***

Carl Philipp Emanuel Bach

German 1714-1788

C.P.E. Bach. Cello Concertos — A minor, Wq170; B flat major, Wq171; A major, Wq172. **Anner Bylsma** (vc); **Orchestra of the Age of Enlightenment/Gustav Leonhardt.** Virgin Classics Veritas VC7 59541-2.

lh 10m DDD 2/90

During his many years at the court of Frederick the Great, C.P.E. Bach composed these three cello concertos. The fact that they also exist in his transcriptions for harpsichord and flute hardly suggests very idiomatic writing for the cello and in a way the implied comment is true; nevertheless, they go very well on the tenor instrument and Anner Bylsma brings out their quirky charm (a quality never in short supply with this composer) while coping adequately with some tricky figuration in the quicker movements; he's also eloquent in the highly expressive slower ones that are especially characteristic of this Bach. This is perhaps not a CD for a basic collection, even of cello music, but it should give the pleasure which is itself audible in the music-making by players completely at home in the idiom. The recording was made in the well-tried location of All Saints' Church in Petersham in the UK; it places the cello rather far back, but convincingly, and has an agreeably warm sound. The period pitch is about a quarter of a tone lower than a modern one and the booklet gives the date and maker's name of the orchestra's 23 instruments, though, oddly, not those of the soloist's baroque cello.

Additional recommendations ...

Miklós Perényi (vc); **Franz Liszt Chamber Orchestra/János Rolla.** Quintana QU190 3026 — ⁘ lh 10m DDD 9/92

Balázs Máté (vc); **Concerto Armonico/Péter Szüts, Miklós Spányi.** Hungaroton HCD31337 — ⁘ lh 9m DDD 11/92

C.P.E. Bach. Harpsichord Concertos — D minor, Wq23; C minor, Wq31; F major, Wq33. **Miklós Spányi** (hpd); **Budapest Concerto Armonico.** Hungaroton Antiqua HCD31159.

⁘ lh 12m DDD 10/90

C.P.E. Bach, in keeping with family tradition, was both original composer and skilful keyboard player. His legacy of music for harpsichord and clavichord is large and varied and includes some 50 harpsichord concertos. This disc contains three of them, well-chosen for their contrasting features, imaginatively played and vividly recorded. These and indeed the majority of the others date from Bach's long period of employment as court harpsichordist to Frederick the Great. Each contains qualities which reflect the north German *empfindsamer Stil* or 'sensitive style' of which this member of the Bach family was a noted exponent. Emotions are projected in a powerful musical language whose idiom resists definition but has recognizable features; among these are short-winded phrases, strong dynamic contrasts, abrupt rhythmic disturbances and an abstracted intimacy. In short, temperamental unpredictability is of the essence. Miklós Spányi and the period-instrument ensemble enter wholeheartedly into this world of turbulent emotions and passionate gestures with vigour, insight and, especially where slow movements are concerned, affecting sensibility. These are vivid accounts of three strong compositions and should make an impact on any listener.

C.P.E. Bach. Oboe Concerto in E flat major, H468.
Lebrun. Oboe Concerto No. 1 in D minor.
Mozart. Oboe Concerto in C major, K314/285*d*. **Paul Goodwin** (ob); **The English Concert/Trevor Pinnock.** Archiv Produktion 431 821-2AH. Recorded 1989-1990.

⁘ lh 2m DDD 7/91

The oboe is supposed to have been Handel's favourite instrument, and with the move away from baroque to classical styles in the later eighteenth century, it still continued to attract composers, not least because there were fine players to inspire them. Of the three concertos here, Mozart's is the most familiar and arguably the finest, but the others are also well worth getting to know. Mozart himself admired C.P.E. Bach for his originality and expressive force, and his individuality comes out at once here: the vigorous first movement of his concerto has an unusual opening theme with repeated notes, and the *Adagio* a depth of feeling that looks forward to Beethoven, while a bouncily *galant* finale in triple time rounds things off well. Paul Goodwin's cadenzas are imaginative and appropriate, and the tone of his two-keyed modern replica of an old instrument is entirely convincing as well as pleasingly rounded. Lebrun is an almost forgotten figure today, but on the evidence of this piece this oboist-composer had plenty to say and his Concerto in D minor has an urgently dramatic first movement with trumpets and timpani often to the fore; in fact, there seems to be an operatic influence here and the slow movement is like a graceful aria. A finely textured recording complements the skilful playing of the soloist and Trevor Pinnock's orchestra.

C.P.E. Bach. Symphonies, Wq 182. **The English Concert/Trevor Pinnock.** Archiv Produktion 415 300-2AH. From 2533 499 (10/80).
No. 1 in G major; No. 2 in B flat major; No. 3 in C major; No. 4 in A major; No. 5 in B minor; No. 6 in E major.

lh 5m ADD 5/86

Carl Philipp Emanuel worked for 28 years at the Potsdam Court of Frederick the Great and although the post provided secure employment, Frederick's dictatorial attitude did nothing to encourage Bach's aspirations to break new ground. His 'imprisonment' ended when Frederick reluctantly released him to succeed Telemann, his godfather, as Music Director at Hamburg. Now he was able to give free rein to his imagination and these symphonies are as remarkable as they are stimulating, with abrupt, even wild changes of mood, dynamics and key. They are required listening, not least when they are played with so much vitality and vivid response to their wayward changeability as they are here by The English Concert, using period instruments. The engineers use theirs, of a much later period, in securing the cleanest of recordings.

Additional recommendation ...
As above. **Academy of Ancient Music/Christopher Hogwood.** L'Oiseau-Lyre Florilegium 417 124-2OH — lh 7m ADD 10/86

C.P.E. Bach. Symphonies, Wq183. **Orchestra of the Age of Enlightenment/Gustav Leonhardt.** Virgin Classics Veritas VC7 59543-2.
No. 1 in D major; No. 2 in E flat major; No. 3 in F major; No. 4 in G major. Wq182 — No. 5 in B minor.

54m DDD 8/90

During his period as Hamburg city's Music Director C.P.E. Bach wrote two sets of symphonies. This disc contains all four works from the second set (*c.*1776) and one from the earlier collection (1773). At least in terms of orchestration the later set, with its parts for horns, flutes, oboes, bassoon and strings, is more ambitious than the other providing an excellent showcase for the wind players of the Orchestra of the Age of Enlightenment. Gustav Leonhardt enjoys a warm rapport both with the Orchestra and the repertory and his interpretation of these symphonies is perceptive and spirited. Rhythms are taut yet with an effective elasticity well-suited to Bach's individual, sometimes quirky temperament. Leonhardt prefers a somewhat larger band than some of his competitors and this too, has positive advantages in as much as it allows for more telling contrasts between strings and wind; it is recorded that Emanuel Bach himself fielded an ensemble of 40 instrumentalists, no less. For good measure, he gives us an additional symphony from Bach's earlier Hamburg set of six, Wq182 (1773). Perhaps the performance of this does not quite match the others in vigour and finesse, but its phrases are beautifully shaped and well articulated. The recorded sound is bright, clear and ideally resonant.

Symphonies, Wq183. **Carl Philipp Emanuel Bach Chamber Orchestra/Hartmut Haenchen.** Capriccio 10 175 — 40m DDD 10/88

NEW REVIEW

C.P.E. Bach. SONATAS. **London Baroque** ([a]Charles Medlam, William Hunt, va da gambas; [b]Richard Egarr, hpd). Harmonia Mundi HMC90 1410. Recorded in 1991.
Viola da gamba Sonatas — C major, Wq136; D major, Wq137. Sonata for Viola da gamba and Harpsichord in G minor, Wq88[ab]. Keyboard Sonatas — E major, H26[b]; A minor, H30[b].

lh 8m DDD 1/93

Carl Philipp Emanuel Bach's three sonatas for viola da gamba must be among the very last solo pieces outside France for an instrument which had gradually been supplanted by the cello. Two of the sontatas (Wq136/137) are of the continuo accompaniment type and date from the mid-1740s. The third (Wq88) written in 1759 is, by contrast more up-to-date in style with a fully written out harpsichord part on an equal footing with the gamba. From the gambist's viewpoint all three works are virtuoso pieces which explore pretty widely the expressive and technical range of the instrument. The partnership of Charles Medlam and Richard Egarr, with William Hunt in the two continuo sonatas, is an effective one. Medlam's tone is well-focused, he articulates clearly and has a lively rapport with the north German *Empfindsamer Stil*, present to a greater or lesser extent in almost all C.P.E. Bach's music after 1740 or so. Medlam responds to the music with a happy blend of head and heart, realizing at the same time one of Bach's own tenets for a good performance, "the ability through singing or playing to make the ear conscious of the true content and affect of a composition". Two keyboard sonatas complete this entertaining programme, one from the *Prussian* set, the other from the *Württemberg*. Richard Egarr plays them stylishly with a lively response to ornaments. Some listeners may find the interpretations understate Bach's characteristically temperamental gestures but the virtuosity of the playing is admirable.

Additional recommendation ...

Sonatas — Wq88; Wq136; Wq137. Fantasia in C major, Wq59 No. 6. **Siegfried Pank** (va da gamba); **Christiane Jaccottet** (clav, fp). Capriccio 10 102 — 56m DDD 10/88

NEW REVIEW

C.P.E. Bach. Three Quartets, H537-9[a]. Fantasia in C major, H291. [a]**Nicholas McGegan** (fl); [a]**Catherine Mackintosh** (va); [a]**Anthony Pleeth** (vc); **Christopher Hogwood** (fp). L'Oiseau-Lyre 433 189-2OH. From DSLO520 (7/78). Recorded in 1976.

53m ADD 9/92

This recording of C.P.E. Bach's three Quartets for flute, viola and keyboard dates from 1978 but retains its initial sparkle. The pieces were written in 1788, the last year of Bach's life. He did not specify the type of keyboard instrument, doubtless recognizing that, from a practical viewpoint, the music was suited both to harpsichord and fortepiano; nor did he leave a cello part as such, though his designation of the Quartets for keyboard, flute, viola and bass strongly suggest that he envisaged a cello as a component of the ensemble. But the four strands making up quartet texture are present without it since it merely doubles the keyboard left hand. Christopher Hogwood opts for a fortepiano and makes provision for a cello. These are decisions which, on balance, are sound ones which serve well the character of Bach's writing: The performances are crisply articulated and gracefully phrased. Bach's music, as usual, is adorned with considerable fantasy and this, together with a lighthearted caprice by no means always present in his style is sensitively realized by these artists. In addition to the Quartets, Hogwood includes the second of two *Fantasias* from the 1785 collection for keyboard. This is an accomplished performance, once again on the fortepiano, of a piece full of bold ideas, telling contrasts and unexpected juxtapositions.

NEW REVIEW

C.P.E. Bach. ORGAN WORKS. **Nicholas Danby** (org). Virgin Classics VC7 59277-2. Played on an organ of Kloster Neresheim, Germany. Recorded in 1990.

Fantasia and Fugue a 4 in C minor, H103. Sonatas — F major, H84; A minor, H85; D major, H86; G minor, H87; B flat major, H134. Adagio per il organo a 2 claviere e pedal, H352.

lh 16m DDD 5/93

NEW REVIEW

C.P.E. Bach. ORGAN WORKS. **Jacques van Oortmerssen** (org). BIS CD569. Played on the Bätz organ of the Onze Lieve Vrouwe Kerk, Harderwijk, The Netherlands. Recorded in 1992.

Fantasia and Fugue a 4 in C minor, H103. Prelude in D major, H107. Sonatas — F major, H84; A minor, H85; D major, H86; G minor, H87.

lh 10m DDD 5/93

It may have been a deliberate decision, a subconscious reaction or just simple coincidence, but the most famous of Bach's sons established his reputation as a composer without ever really trespassing on his father's territory. Thus while the complete organ works of J.S. Bach cover anything up to 20 CDs, Carl Philipp Emanuel's can be accommodated on just one. Moreover with the exception of the grand *Fantasia and Fugue* in C minor there's little hint of Bach-the-elder's influence in these undeniably fine and distinctive pieces. C.P.E. Bach's keyboard *métier* was the sonata; for the organ he wrote four with a question mark hanging over several others. These are well-crafted, tuneful three-movement works for manuals only which thrive in the hands of an alert player and on a bright, colourful instrument. Both these discs provide first-rate interpretations of the Sonatas and the *Fantasia and Fugue* with a few spurious pieces thrown in for good measure. There's very little to choose between them and either would make a worthwhile addition to any CD collection. Nicholas Danby plays with wit and vitality while Jacques van Oortmerssen has rather more authority and seriousness of purpose. Similarly the recordings are exemplary and both instruments make a wonderful sound. The German organ on the Virgin Classics disc is wrapped up in a stunning eight-seconds' reverberation (for the real organ enthusiast, the choice of instrument is every bit as important as the music or the player).

NEW REVIEW

C.P.E. Bach. Die Auferstehung und Himmelfahrt Jesu, H777. **Hillevi Martinpelto** (sop); **Christoph Prégardien** (ten); **Peter Harvey** (bass); **Ghent Collegium Vocale Choir; Orchestra of the Age of Enlightenment/Philippe Herreweghe.** Virgin Classics Veritas VC7 59069-2. Text and translation included. Recorded in 1991.

1h 16m DDD 9/92

Carl Philipp Emanuel Bach considered his cantata *Die Auferstehung und Himmelfahrt Jesu* as "pre-eminent among all my vocal works in expression and in the composition". The author of the text was the German Enlightenment poet Karl Wilhelm Ramler with whom Bach closely collaborated over the piece. The first performance took place in Hamburg in 1778 when it was warmly received. Many subsequent performances were given, culminating in three directed by Mozart in Vienna. Philippe Herreweghe has chosen a fine group of soloists in Hillevi Martinpelto, Christoph Prégardien and Peter Harvey; his Ghent Collegium Vocale Choir with the Orchestra of the Age of Enlightenment make a fine showing, too. If Herreweghe perhaps never quite reaches the heart of the music (whose idiom, admittedly, is often elusive) the soloists, choir and orchestra are of a calibre to hold our attention throughout a fascinating and strikingly original score. The recorded sound is spacious and effective. A rarity well worth exploring.

Additional recommendation ...

Die Auferstehung und Himmelfahrt Jesu. Gott hat den Hern auferwecket — Easter Cantata, H803. **Barbara Schlick, Marina Lins** (sops); **Christoph Prégardien, Paul Elliott** (tens); **Stephen Varcoe** (bar); **Gotthold Schwarz** (bass); **Rheinische Kantorei; Das Kleine Konzert/Hermann Max.** Capriccio 10 206/07 — ② 1h 39m DDD 10/88

Further listening ...

Concerto in E flat major for harpsichord and fortepiano, Wq47. Organ Concerto in G major, Wq34. Sonatina in D major for two harpsichords, Wq109. **Richard Fuller** (fp); **Ingomar Rainer** (hpd); **Vienna Akademie/Martin Haselböck** (hpd, org). Novalis 150 025-2 (2/89).

Flute Concertos — D minor (original version of Harpsichord Concerto, Wq22); A major, Wq168; B flat major, Wq167; G major, Wq169; A minor, Wq166. **Konrad Hünteler** (fl); **Amsterdam Baroque Orchestra/Ton Koopman.** Erato 2292-45353-2 (7/89).

Johann Christian Bach

German 1735-1782

J.C. Bach. CHAMBER WORKS. **The English Concert** (Lisa Beznosiuk, fl; David Reichenberg, ob; Anthony Halstead, David Cox, hns; Simon Standage, vn; Trevor Jones, va; Anthony Pleeth, vc; Trevor Pinnock, hpd, fp, square pf). Archiv Produktion 423 385-2AH. Recorded in 1987.

Quintet in D major for flute, oboe, violin, cello and keyboard, Op. 22 No. 1. Sextet in C major for oboe, two horns, violin, cello and keyboard. Quintets for flute, oboe, violin, viola and continuo, Op. 11 — No. 1 in C major; No. 6 in D major.

lh 9m DDD 5/88

Johann Christian Bach was the youngest of J.S. Bach's sons and the most widely travelled of them. After studying with his father and with his half-brother C.P.E. Bach, Johann Christian worked in Italy and in England where he settled in 1762. For the remaining 20 years of his life J.C. Bach played a central role in London musical circles composing, playing and teaching. As well as operas, sacred music, symphonies and concertos the "London Bach" as he became affectionately known, composed various types of chamber music. Among the most engaging of these are the six Quintets, Op. 11, those of Op. 22 and the Sextet in C major once thought to be the work of his elder brother J.C.F. Bach. Trevor Pinnock and members of The English Concert give sparkling performances of music conspicuous for its abundance of captivating melodies, transparent textures and fine craftsmanship. Slow movements are especially beguiling and the subtly shaded dynamics, delicately contrived instrumental sonorities and informed sense of style with which these artists bring the music to life give the performances a rare delicacy and refinement. Pinnock himself plays a variety of keyboard instruments whose contrasting sound adds another pleasing dimension to the interpretations. Each of the artists makes a strong contribution but special praise, perhaps, should be given to the artistry of the late David Reichenberg, an oboist with outstanding lyrical gifts. Good recorded sound.

Further listening ...

Symphonies — Op. 3 Nos. 1 and 2; Op. 6 Nos. 1 and 6; Op. 9 No. 2. **Concerto Armonico/Péter Szüts, Miklós Spányi.** Hungaroton HCD31448 (9/92).

Symphonies — Op. 6 No. 3; Op. 9 No. 2; Op. 18 Nos. 2 and 4. **Bournemouth Sinfonietta/Kenneth Montgomery.** Classics for Pleasure CD-CFP4550 (3/89).

Sinfonias concertante — G major for two violins and cello, T.284/1; E flat major for two clarinets and bassoon, T290/9; A major for violin and cello, T284/4; E flat major for two violins, T288/4. **Soloists; London Festival Orchestra/Ross Pople.** ASV CDDCA651 (10/89).

Keyboard Sonatas — Op. 5 Nos. 5 and 6; Op. 17 Nos. 2, 3 and 5. **Virginia Black** (hpd). CRD CRD3453 (2/90).

Johann Sebastian Bach

German 1685-1750

NEW REVIEW

Bach. Violin Concertos — No. 1 in A minor, BWV1041; No. 2 in E major, BWV1042. Double Violin Concerto in D minor, BWV1043[a]. Violin and Oboe Concerto in C minor, BWV1060[b]. [a]**John Tunnell** (vn); [b]**Robin Miller** (ob); **Scottish Chamber Orchestra/Oscar Shumsky** (vn). Nimbus NI5325.

lh 3m DDD 9/92

The three basic concertos BWV1041-43 are models of what a good baroque violin concert should be — and raised to the 'peerage' by Bach's genius, with eloquent slow movements framed by sturdy faster ones that are full of energy and unflagging invention. The two notes that begin the A minor Concerto are an unmistakable gesture of confidence and purpose, and who could invest a descending scale with more sublimity than does Bach in the *Largo, ma non tanto* of the Double Concerto? These are essential works in any collection that does not turn its back on baroque music. Together they take less than 45 minutes to play, and the Violin and Oboe Concerto BWV1060, another gem, is perhaps their best helpmate in completing a well-filled

CD. Shumsky and his well-matched partners in the double concertos, John Tunnell and Robin Miller, are most successful in satisfying those who are comfortable with neither the sound of period instruments nor the excesses (no matter how slight) of romanticized performances, and period-instrument lovers who can happily accept outstandingly sensitive and stylish versions on modern instruments. Shumsky's is the view of one who has enjoyed a long love-affair with these works and, in the matters of ornamentation and use of vibrato (another form of ornamentation), has given thought to the status of every note. If this seems to suggest a studied, even dry, approach, you may rest assured that such is not the case; these performances are illuminated by serene love, expressed with singing tone. The Scottish Chamber Orchestra and those responsible for the recording itself have done their part in making this the memorable issue that it is.

Additional recommendations ...
As Nimbus. **Jaap Schröder, Christopher Hirons** (vns); **Academy of Ancient Music/Christopher Hogwood.** L'Oiseau-Lyre 400 080-2OH — 45m DDD 3/83
As Nimbus. **Anne-Sophie Mutter** (vn); **English Chamber Orchestra/Salvatore Accardo** (vn). EMI CDC7 47005-2 — 53m DDD 2/84
As Nimbus. **José-Luis Garcia** (vn); **Neil Black** (ob); **English Chamber Orchestra/Dimitri Sitkovetsky** (vn). Novalis 150 017-2 — 1h 5m DDD 5/88
Violin Concertos. Double Violin Concerto. **Simon Standage, Elizabeth Wilcock** (vns); **The English Concert/Trevor Pinnock** (hpd). Archiv Produktion 410 646-2AH — 46m DDD 8/84
No. 2. Double Violin Concerto. Harpsichord Concerto in F minor, BWV1056. **C.P.E. Bach.** *Cello Concerto in A major, Wq172.* **Jane Murdoch** (vn); **Caroline Dale** (vc); **Scottish Ensemble/Jonathan Rees.** Virgin Classics Virgo VJ7 59641-2 — 1h 6m DDD 12/91 £

Bach. Brandenburg Concertos, BWV1046-51[a]. Four Orchestral Suites, BWV1066-9[b]. **The English Concert/Trevor Pinnock.** Archiv Produktion 423 492-2AX3. Items marked [a] from 2742 003 (2/83), [b] 2533 410/1 (5/79).
Brandenburg Concertos — No. 1 in F major; No. 2 in F major; No. 3 in G major; No. 4 in G major; No. 5 in D major; No. 6 in B flat major. *Orchestral Suites* — No. 1 in C major; No. 2 in B minor; No. 3 in D major; No. 4 in F major.

③ 2h 53m DDD/ADD 10/88 £

These concertos, written in 1721, were Bach's response to a request from the Margrave of Brandenburg, whose name they now bear, but despite the dedication we do not know whether the Margrave acknowledged their receipt or ever heard them. Two, Concertos Nos. 3 and 6, are written for strings only, the latter without violins, but the others call for different combinations of other instrumental soloists. The music itself displays an amazing variety of form and use of instrumental colour, and since The English Concert use period instruments their performances must closely approach those which Bach may have heard, in both colour and balance — but he is unlikely to have heard them to greater advantage than we can through these excellent recordings.

Additional recommendations ...
Brandenburg Concertos. **English Chamber Orchestra/Raymond Leppard** (hpd). Philips Silver Line. *Nos. 1-3*: 420 345-2PM. *Nos. 4-6*: 420 346-2PM — ② 54m 46m ADD 6/87 £
Brandenburg Concertos. **Orchestra of the Age of Enlightenment.** Virgin Classics Veritas VCD7 59260-2 — ② 1h 33m DDD 7/89
Brandenburg Concertos. Overture in B flat major (from BWV194). Viola de gamba Sonata in C minor, BWV1029. **Taverner Players/Andrew Parrott.** EMI Reflexe CDS7 49806-2 — ② 1h 50m DDD 1/90 £
Brandenburg Concertos. **Chamber Orchestra of Europe.** DG 431 660-2GH2 — ② 1h 35m DDD 5/91
Brandenburg Concertos. Orchestral Suites. **Adolf Busch Chamber Players/A. Busch.** EMI Références mono CHS7 64047-2 — ③ 3h 15m ADD 12/91 £ ▲
Brandenburg Concertos. **Le Concert des Nations; La Capella Reial de Catalunya/Jordi Savall.** Astrée Auvidis E8737 — ② 1h 38m DDD 2/92 £

Brandenburg Concertos. **Hanover Band/Anthony Halstead** (hpd). EMI Eminence. *Nos. 1, 3 and 4:* CD-EMX2200. *Nos. 2, 5 and 6:* CD-EMX2201 — ② 44m 49m DDD 2/92 £

Brandenburg Concertos Nos. 1, 2 and 4. Orchestral Suite No. 2. **Vienna Concentus Musicus/Nikolaus Harnoncourt.** Teldec Digital Experience 9031-75858-2 — lh 13m DDD 9/92

Brandenburg Concertos Nos. 3, 5 and 6. Orchestral Suite No. 3. **Vienna Concentus Musicus/Nikolaus Harnoncourt.** Teldec Digital Experience 9031-75859-2 — lh 15m DDD 9/92

See also additional recommendations for the Orchestral Suites elsewhere in this section.

Bach. Keyboard Concertos, BWV1052-58. **Chamber Orchestra of Europe/András Schiff** (pf). Decca 425 676-2DH2. Recorded in 1989.

② lh 48m DDD 11/90

Although Bach's duties in Leipzig centred on the church he also wrote secular music for a series of coffee-house concerts, at which his keyboard concertos were probably first performed. The *Brandenburgs* were *concerti grossi*, in which the keyboard shares the limelight with other instruments; BWV1052-58 were the first-ever true keyboard concertos, a genre of which Bach was the 'father'. Practically all the music of the concertos was adapted from existing works of various kinds — cantatas and concertos (mostly for the violin) and the Fourth *Brandenburg* Concerto, a time-saving expedient for a hard-pressed composer. The instrument for which they were written was of course the harpsichord, but only the most rabid purist would now object to their presentation on the piano — providing that it embodies no stylistic anachronism. Schiff, with the attentive support of both the COE and the recording engineers, comes the closest yet to achieving that elusive goal.

Additional recommendations ...

BWV1052, 1057 and 1059. **Amsterdam Baroque Orchestra/Ton Koopman** (hpd). Erato 2292-45545-2 — 51m DDD

BWV1053, 1054, 1056 and 1058. **Amsterdam Baroque Orchestra/Ton Koopman** (hpd). Erato 2292-45644-2 — 57m DDD

Bach. DOUBLE CONCERTOS. [a]**Jaap Schröder,** [a]**Christopher Hirons,** [b]**Catherine Mackintosh** (vns); [b]**Stephen Hammer** (ob); [c]**Christophe Rousset** (hpd); **Academy of Ancient Music/Christopher Hogwood** ([c]hpd). L'Oiseau-Lyre Florilegium 421 500-2OH. Item marked [a] from DSDL702 (8/82), [b] and [c] new to UK.

D minor for two violins, BWV1043[a]; C minor for violin and oboe, BWV1060[b]; C minor for two harpsichords, BWV1060[c]; C minor for two harpsichords, BWV1062[c].

58m DDD 9/89 

The concept of a concerto with two or more soloists grew naturally out of the *concerto grosso*, and Bach was among those baroque composers who explored its possibilities. The Concerto in D minor, BWV1043, for two violins is perhaps the best known of his works in the *genre*, which Bach himself reworked as a Concerto for two harpsichords, BWV1062, in the key of C minor. No alternative version has survived in the case of the two-harpsichord Concerto BWV1060, also in C minor, but musicological evidence suggests that it was originally intended for two single-line instruments — two violins or one violin and an oboe. The work has thus been notionally reconstructed in the latter form and, unlike the other three concertos in this recording, it has at present no other version on CD; neither are these two revealing comparisons available on any other single disc. Baroque music never sounds better than when it is played on period instruments, in proper style, and by performers of the quality of those in this recording, not least the well matched soloists. The famous slow movement of BWV1043 is taken a little faster than usual, convincingly stripped of the specious sentimentality with which it is often invested. The recording is of suitably high quality.

See also additional recommendation for Double Concertos elsewhere in this section.

Bach. OBOE CONCERTOS — F major, BWV1053; A major, BWV1055; D minor, BWV1059. **Chamber Orchestra of Europe/Douglas Boyd** (ob, ob d'amore). DG 429 225-2GH. Recorded in 1989.

46m DDD 4/90

Although Bach is not known to have written any concerto for the oboe he did entrust it with some beautiful *obbligato* parts, so he clearly did not underrate its expressive capacities. He did however rearrange many of his works for different instrumental media and there is musicological evidence that original oboe concertos were the (lost) sources from which other works were derived. The Harpsichord Concerto in A major, BWV1055, is believed originally to have been written for the oboe d'amore, whilst the other two Oboe Concertos have been reassembled from movements found in various cantatas. Whatever the validity of the academic reasoning, the results sound very convincing. Douglas Boyd is a superb oboist, with a clear sound that is free from stridency, and a fluency that belies the instrument's technical difficulty. He plays the faster, outer movements with winsome lightness of tongue and spirit, and with alertness to dynamic nuance; the slow ones, the hearts of these works, are given with sensitivity but without sentimentality — which can easily invade that of BWV1059, taken from Cantata No. 156, *Ich steh mit einem Fuss im Grabe*. The Chamber Orchestra of Europe partners him to perfection in this crisp recording.

Key to Symbols

Price	Quantity/ availability	Timing	Mode	Review date
	② ②	lh 23m	DDD	6/88

NEW REVIEW

Bach. Orchestral Suites Nos. 1-4, BWV1066-69. Concerto for Flute, Violin, Harpsichord and Strings in A minor, BWV1044[a]. [a]**Christopher Krueger** (fl); [a]**Daniel Stepner** (vn); [a]**John Gibbons** (hpd); **Boston Early Music Festival Orchestra/Andrew Parrott.** EMI Reflexe CDS7 54653-2. Recorded in 1992.

② lh 5lm DDD 5/93 B

In these effectively light-textured performances of Bach's four Orchestral Suites courtly ceremony takes second place to an altogether more intimate, chamber music ethos. There is an airiness and a light tread in this playing, and an effectively balanced ensemble which enables the listener to follow what is going on in every strand of Bach's score. In the Suite No. 1 in C major, the director Andrew Parrott adopts recent thinking and employs a harpsichord alone as continuo, omitting the more usually heard cello and double-bass. Strings and woodwind are strong and such accomplished playing as we have here is a feature of the set as a whole. Parrott's performances of the Suites are crisply articulated, lively in spirit and infectiously enjoyable. That also goes for the less often heard Triple Concerto in A minor. As in the Suites, Parrott fields an orchestra of one instrument to a part though here the bass playing seemed on occasion a little too heavy. The solo group of violin, flute and harpsichord is an excellent one and, together with the vital ripieno playing of the Boston orchestra, they turn in thoughtful and musicianly performances.

Additional recommendations ...

Suites. **Cologne Musica Antiqua/Reinhard Goebel.** Archiv Produktion 415 671-2AH2 — ② lh 5lm DDD 10/86 B

Suites. **Amsterdam Baroque Orchestra/Ton Koopman.** Deutsche Harmonia Mundi RD77864 — ② lh 19m DDD 1/90 B

Suites. **Le Concert des Nations, Capella Reial de Catalunya/Jordi Savall.** Astrée Auvidis E8727/8 — ② lh 45 DDD 6/91 B

Suites. **Academy of St Martin in the Fields/Sir Neville Marriner.** Decca Serenata 430 378-2DM — lh 18m ADD 7/91 B

Suites. Double Concertos, BWV1043 and BWV1060. **Heinz Holliger** (ob); **Gidon Kremer,**

Henryk Szeryng, Maurice Hasson (vns); **Academy of St Martin in the Fields/Sir Neville Marriner.** Philips Baroque Classics 426 462-2PBQ2 — ② lh 54m ADD/DDD 11/91

Bach. The Art of Fugue, BWV1080[a]. A Musical Offering, BWV1079[b]. Canons, BWV1072-8; 1086-7[a]. **Cologne Musica Antiqua/Reinhard Goebel.** Archiv Produktion 413 642-2AH3. Booklet included. Items marked [a] from 413 728-1AH2 (4/85); [b] 2533 422 (11/79).

③ 2h 20m ADD 4/85

The great compilation of fugues, canons and a trio sonata which Bach dedicated to King Frederick the Great is one of the monuments of baroque instrumental music. Every contrapuntal device of canon at various intervals, augmentation, inversion, retrograde motion and so on is displayed here, and the performances are splendidly alive and authentic-sounding. It goes without saying that period instruments or modern replicas are used. The intellectually staggering *Art of Fugue* is a kind of testament to Bach's art and for this recording the instrumentation, unspecified by the composer, has been well chosen. The 14 miniature Canons which close this issue are for the most part a recent discovery and were written on a page of Bach's own copy of the *Goldberg Variations*; of curiosity value certainly but not much more than that. Excellent recording for these performances which have great authority.

Additional recommendations ...

The Art of Fugue. **Hespèrion XX/Jordi Savall.** Astrée Auvidis E2001 — ② lh 32m ADD 11/88
The Art of Fugue. **Amsterdam Bach Soloists.** Ottavo OTRC48503 — lh 12m DDD 8/89
The Art of Fugue. **Juilliard Quartet.** Sony Classical SK45937 — ② lh 30m DDD 6/92

See further on in this section for The Art of Fugue (harpsichord version).

Bach. VIOLIN SONATAS. **Monica Huggett** (vn); **Ton Koopman** (hpd). Philips 410 401-2PH2. From 410 401-1PH2 (8/84).
B minor, BWV1014; A major, BWV1015; E major, BWV1016; C minor, BWV1017; F minor, BWV1018; G major, BWV1019. Cantabile, ma un poco adagio, BWV1019*a*/1. Adagio, BWV1019*a*/2.

② lh 4lm DDD 3/86

These six Sonatas were preserved only in the form of copies made by Bach's pupils and the date of their composition is unknown. Fortunately several copies were made and except in the case of the Sixth Sonata all the versions correspond. The works are of great importance in the historical development of the violin sonata. For the first time the keyboard instrument has a fully written-out part and is treated as an equal and not merely as an obbligato instrument — indeed it is in many ways the senior partner. Huggett and Koopman have worked together for several years, and this is apparent in their confident and secure performances. Sometimes Huggett inclines towards blandness of expression, and Koopman seems the livelier musical personality, but these two discs will give great pleasure to those who like Bach played on period instruments. The recording leaves nothing to be desired.

Additional recommendations ...

BWV1014-9. **Susanne Lautenbacher** (vn); **Leonore Klinckerfuss** (hpd). Bayer BR100086/7 — ② lh 38m DDD 10/90
BWV1014-9. **Sigiswald Kuijken** (vn); **Gustav Leonhardt** (hpd). Deutsche Harmonia Mundi GD77170 — ② lh 34m ADD 10/90

Bach. FLUTE SONATAS. **Stephen Preston** (fl); [a]**Trevor Pinnock** (hpd); [b]**Jordi Savall** (va da gamba). CRD CRD3314/5. From CRD1014/5 (8/75).
Sonatas — B minor, BWV1030[a]; E flat major, BWV1031[a]; A major, BWV1032[a]; C major, BWV1033[ab]; E minor, BWV1034[ab]; E major, BWV1035[ab]. Partita in A minor, BWV1013.

② lh 38m ADD 1/90 

NEW REVIEW

Bach. FLUTE SONATAS. **Michala Petri** (rec); **Keith Jarrett** (hpd). RCA Victor Red Seal 09026 61274-2. Recorded in 1992.

Sonatas — B minor, BWV1030; E flat major, BWV1031; A major, BWV1032; C major, BWV1033; E minor, BWV1034; E major, BWV1035.

1h 11m DDD 2/93

Eight Flute Sonatas have at various times been attributed to Bach. Five of these are certainly from his hand: BWV1030, 1032, 1034-5 and 1013. The first two are for flute and 'concertante' harpsichord (true duos in which the keyboard part is fully notated), the second are for flute and continuo (the keyboard player is left to fill out his part from the figured bass), and the last, a Partita, is for flute alone. The authenticity of two, BWV1031 and 1033 (both for flute and continuo), is questionable but their musical quality is sufficient to make doubts almost irrelevant; the remaining Sonata, BWV1020, is now recognized to have been misattributed. These were not the earliest works of their kind but they are by far the most adventurous and substantial of their time, and the best of them have rightly been described as masterpieces; BWV1013 is a *tour de force* in which the single-line instrument clothes its melody with implied harmony — and even counterpoint. The baroque flute is a gentle instrument that caresses the sound and pitch of its notes, an art of which Preston is a master. Pinnock is the perfect partner, as too is Savall in the items with continuo, and the recording captures the warm intimacy of these wonderful works. Although Bach specified the transverse flute in these works, the recorder was still very much in use at that time and might be regarded as a viable alternative, as Michala Petri demonstrates, albeit using (for her own good reasons) instruments at modern pitch. Stimulated by her partner she has developed a freer approach to baroque music and is able and willing to add her own embellishments where they are fitting — and to avoid them where they are not. She has total mastery of her instrument and in Keith Jarrett she has a tailor-made partner; in all respects this is a strongly recommended alternative version.

Additional recommendation ...

BWV1030-5. G minor, BWV1020. **Janet See** (fl); **Davitt Moroney** (hpd); **Mary Springfels** (va da gamba). Harmonia Mundi HMU90 7024/5 — ② 1h 54m DDD 11/91

Bach. Sonatas and Partitas for Solo Violin, BWV1001-06. **Oscar Shumsky** (vn). ASV CDDCD454.

Sonatas: No. 1 in G minor, BWV1001; No. 2 in A minor, BWV1003; No. 3 in C major, BWV1005. *Partitas:* No. 1 in B minor, BWV1002; No. 2 in D minor, BWV1004; No. 3 in E major, BWV1006.

② 2h 27m ADD 9/87 

It was during his employment at the Court of Prince Leopold of Cöthen that Bach was able to devote himself to writing secular music. His six innovatory Suites for the cello and the six works for solo violin date from this period (*c.*1720) and could have been written only by someone with an intimate practical knowledge of the instrument. As the small fingerboard of the violin enables the player's left hand to encompass complex textures, Bach took full advantage of this. It remains difficult, even in the hi-tech state of today's violinistic art, simply to produce the notes with accurate intonation and without making heavy weather of the three- and four-note chords, but that is only the beginning. The player still has to realize the part-writing and to absorb and project the style and spirit of the immensely varied movements. All these parameters, and more, are admirably met by Oscar Shumsky; with his excellent recording one is able to fully appreciate the richness of the music, with little consciousness of the immense technical skill that makes the performances possible.

Additional recommendations ...

Jascha Heifetz. RCA Victor Gold Seal GD87708 — ② 2h 5m ADD 9/88

Henryk Szeryng. CBS Masterworks Portrait mono CD46721 — ② 2h 8m ADD 12/91

Sigiswald Kuijken. Deutsche Harmonia Mundi GD77043 — ② 2h 8m ADD

NEW REVIEW

Bach. SOLO CELLO SUITES, BWV1007-12. **Anner Bylsma** (vc). Sony Classical Vivarte SK48047. Recorded in 1992.

No. 1 in G major; No. 2 in D minor; No. 3 in C major; No. 4 in E flat major; No. 5 in C minor; No. 6 in D major.

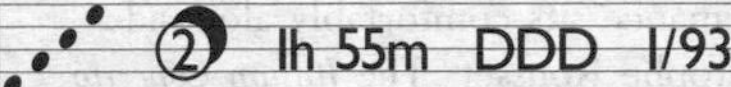

NEW REVIEW

Bach (arr. Söllscher). SOLO CELLO SUITES, BWV1007-8 and BWV1012. Sonata for Solo Violin No. 3 in C major, BWV1005. **Göran Söllscher** (gtr). DG 435 471-2GH. Recorded in 1991.

No. 1 in G major; No. 2 in D minor; No. 6 in D major — Sarabande; Gigue.

lh DDD 8/92
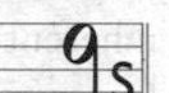

This is the second complete version of Bach's six Cello Suites recorded by the Dutch virtuoso Anner Bylsma (the first is listed below). In a period of some 13 years between the first and second recordings, Bylsma's concept of these works has not undergone any fundamental changes. The difference between them is rather one of degree for, as Byslma himself says in a lively note accompanying the discs, "one keeps finding new relationships between the notes and every motif can be played in so many different ways — and always with meaning, too". In the new version Bylsma intensifies the musical gestures which characterized the earlier one. He is, if anything, more spontaneous in his playing here and he takes greater risks. What we have, in fact, are 'performances' as opposed to studio-correct readings; and so listeners concerned with niceties of intonation, for instance, may sometimes be mildly disconcerted by what they hear. But from a purely interpretative standpoint the new set is bolder, more relaxed and more broadly expressive. Indeed, were it not for his impeccable 'early music' credentials Bylsma might be targeted by critics for excessive romanticism. The late Pierre Fournier was thus condemned for his Bach playing, yet his performances of the *Preludes* of these Suites, made three decades ago (listed below), were in many respects far stricter than those of Bylsma. All this and much else make it clear that convenient generalizations and tidy compart-ments are less acceptable than ever before. Bylsma is an artist who is not afraid to express himself individually, intensely and even, at times audaciously. Open-minded readers will find much to admire and much that is satisfying in these passionate, warmly expressive performances. But neither the noble Fournier nor Bylsma's earlier recording is lightly to be cast aside.

Bach was a prolific arranger of his own music for different instrumental (or vocal) media, as was the thrifty practice of his time. For those who have later adapted his solo violin or cello works for the lute or guitar, Bach's own reworkings of BWV1006 (BWV1006*a*) and BWV1011 (BWV995), often questionably said to be for the lute, have provided procedural models. The guitar lacks the sustaining power of the bowed strings but, with its greater harmonic and contrapuntal resources, it can overcome some of the limitations they impose. Chords do not *have* to be arpeggiated, important chords can be reinforced, some notes in one register do not have to be relinquished while those in another are played, and bass lines that are implied, but impossible to play on a bowed instrument, may be added. Such arrangements show the music in a new and satisfying light. The Swedish guitarist Göran Söllscher uses an instrument with 11 strings (five more than the standard guitar) which widens the pitch-range and allows the bass lines to be played with greater technical freedom. Söllscher brings scholarship and dignity (but not stiffness) to his interpretations, and the flawless beauty of his sound is perfectly caught by the recording.

Additional recommendations ...

Nos. 1-6. **Pierre Fournier.** DG 419 359-2GCM2 — 2 2h 19m ADD 3/89

Nos. 1-6. **Anner Bylsma.** RCA RD70950 — 2 2h 6m DDD

Nos. 1-6. **Robert Cohen.** Collins Classics 1081-2 — 2 2h 26m DDD 5/90

Nos. 1-6. **Paul Tortelier.** EMI CMS7 69431-2 — 2 2h 5m ADD 3/92 ▲

NEW REVIEW

Bach. HARPSICHORD WORKS. **Davitt Moroney.** Virgin Classics Veritas VC7 59272-2. Recorded in 1990.

Four Duets, BWV802-05. Overture in the French style in B minor, BWV831. Italian Concerto in F major, BWV971. Prelude, Fugue and Allegro in E flat major, BWV998.

1h 11m DDD 9/92 

Davitt Moroney has established a reputation both for his stylish Bach playing and his lively interest in background scholarship. In this recital his performance sits comfortably alongside those of his rivals Maggie Cole, Kenneth Gilbert and Christophe Rousset. The *Italian Concerto* and the Overture (Partita) in B minor come from the Second Part of Bach's *Clavier-Ubung* in which he provided the performer with contrasting examples of his skill in transferring orchestral forms — concerto and suite — to the keyboard. Moroney's interpretations are vivacious without being frenetic and he allows the music to breathe naturally. He is also conscious of the inherent poetry of Bach's keyboard genius, though the close recording balance favouring the lower register of the instrument sometimes threatens both the evenness of sound and the eloquence of Moroney's approach. But this in itself hardly deflects attention from disciplined, often passionate, and personally involved playing which is sensitive to the nobility of Bach's writing. This is apparent, above all, in the great French Overture itself which prefaces the B minor Suite. A musically satisfying disc.

Additional recommendations ...

Italian Concerto. French Overture. Four Duets. **Kenneth Gilbert.** Harmonia Mundi HMA190 1278 — 56m DDD 2/90

Italian Concerto. French Overture. Four Duets. Chromatic Fantasia. **Christophe Rousset.** L'Oiseau-Lyre 433 054-2OH — 1h 8m DDD 5/92

NEW REVIEW

Bach. HARPSICHORD WORKS. **Wanda Landowska** (hpd). RCA Victor Gold Seal mono GD60919. Recorded in 1945-57.

Goldberg Variations, BWV988 (from HMV ALP1139, 5/54). Concerto in D major, BWV972 (HMV DB6819, 12/48). Fantasias — C minor, BWV906 (RB16068, 9/58); C minor, BWV919. Prelude, Fugue and Allegro in E flat major, BWV998 (both from ALP1246, 6/55). Two-Part Inventions, BWV772-86. Three-Part Inventions, BWV787-801 — No. 1 in C major; No. 2 in C minor; No. 5 in E flat major; No. 11 in G minor; No. 13 in A minor; No. 14 in B flat major; No. 15 in B minor (all from RB16193, 7/60). Capriccio sopra la lontananza del suo fratello dilettissimo in B flat major, BWV992. Partita No. 2 in C minor, BWV826 (RB16068).

② 2h 30m ADD 3/93 

The lady who played for Tolstoy, who rediscovered the harpsichord for a modern listening audience and who enchanted generations of music-lovers with her engaging personality, was also one of the century's great Bach interpreters. But her grand, flamboyant and highly demonstrative style is largely out of step with modern theories on Bach performance, so these two discs — which are beautifully transferred from late 78s and early tape originals — are likely to annoy as well as inspire. However, the *Goldberg Variations* (the second of Landowska's two recordings of the work) are deeply poetic and chock-full of imagination, while few keyboard players since have injected quite so much pathos and personality into Bach's autobiographical *Capriccio sopra la lontananza del suo fratello dilettissimo* ("Capriccio on the Departure of His Beloved Brother") — his "departure" being *a* journey, as opposed to *the* journey! — or the Concerto in D major "After Vivaldi". Landowska's 'harpsichord Pleyel' makes a big, exciting sound, very unlike the softer, less dynamic sonority of a genuine period instrument. Few apologies need be made for the later recordings on the album, which come across with considerable presence, albeit in mono. One woman's Bach, perhaps ... but very much worth listening to.

Additional recommendation ...

Prelude and Fugue in A minor, BWV894. Toccatas — F sharp minor, BWV910; C minor, BWV911; G minor, BWV915. Aria variata in A minor, BWV989. Capriccio sopra .... **Kenneth Gilbert** (hpd). Archiv Produktion 437 555-2AH — 1h 10m DDD 6/93

Bach. The Well-tempered Clavier, Books 1 and 2, BWV846-93. **Davitt Moroney** (hpd). Harmonia Mundi HMC90 1285/8.

④ 4h 32m DDD 4/89 B

For those wanting both books of the *48*, the choice is wide. With some 16 or more versions currently available on CD the listener is confronted by a daunting process of selection. Davitt Moroney is a gifted and serious-minded artist whose performances are technically secure, stylistically informed and thoughtful. Empty rhetoric, uncalled-for flamboyance or superfluous gesture are not for him; indeed, on occasion listeners might feel that a degree of spontaneity is lacking. Yet where this playing is constantly impressive is in the successful marriage of virtuosity with the poetic content of the music. In short Moroney makes the music sing with carefully shaped phrases, admirable rhythmic suppleness and well-defined articulation. No listener will find all he wants from any one performance of these masterpieces since different registrations, tempos and indeed instruments bring out different colours and induce in us different responses. Moroney highlights many of the almost infinite contrasts which exist in the music with sensibility and affection. The instrument is effectively balanced, if a shade too closely, allowing listeners to discern subtle details in Bach's writing.

Additional recommendations ...

Books 1 and 2. **Kenneth Gilbert** (hpd). Archiv Produktion 413 439-2AH4 — ④ 4h 16m 2/87 B
Books 1 and 2. **Edwin Fischer** (pf). EMI Références mono CHS7 63188-2 — ③ 3h 57m ADD 3/90 B ▲
Book 1. **András Schiff** (pf). Decca 414 388-2DH2 — ② 1h 50m DDD 9/86 B
Book 2. **András Schiff** (pf). Decca 417 236-2DH2 — ② 2h 24m DDD 3/87 B
Books 1 and 2. **Colin Tilney** (clav/hpd). Hyperion CDA66351/4 ④ 5h 4m DDD 10/90 B

Bach. French Suites, BWV812-7. Suite in A minor, BWV818*a*. Suite in E flat major, BWV819*a*. **Davitt Moroney** (hpd). Virgin Classics Veritas VCD7 59011-2.

② 2h 24m DDD 4/91

Bach compiled his *French Suites*, so-called — the composer himself did not give them this title — towards the end of his Cöthen period and at the beginning of his final appointment at Leipzig. As well as performing the customary six suites, five of which have survived in Bach's own hand, Davitt Moroney includes two further suites prepared by Bach's pupil, Heinrich Nikolaus Gerber, in 1725. These and extra movements to the well-known six suites belong to various surviving sources and though we can be sure that Bach himself had good reason to discard them from his final thoughts, so-to-speak, their presence in this album is nonetheless welcome. Moroney has given careful thought and preparation to the project and the results are often illuminating. His interpretations are relaxed, articulate and show a lively awareness of the music's poetic content. There is a clarity in these performances which stems from lucid punctuation highlighting the significance of every phrase. Shorter dance movements have poise and are allowed to breathe while longer ones, notably *allemandes,* have a taut rhythmic elasticity which enable the listener to savour their eloquent often pensive inflexions. Perhaps *sarabandes* are sometimes a little too weighty, but this is to some extent a matter of taste and few will be disappointed by Moroney's stylistically informed and technically fluent playing. The recording is excellent.

Additional recommendation ...

French Suites. **Gustav Leonhardt** (hpd). RCA Victor Seon GD71963 — ② 1h 18m ADD 5/90

NEW REVIEW

Bach. Goldberg Variations, BWV988. **Kenneth Gilbert** (hpd) Harmonia Mundi HMC90 1240.

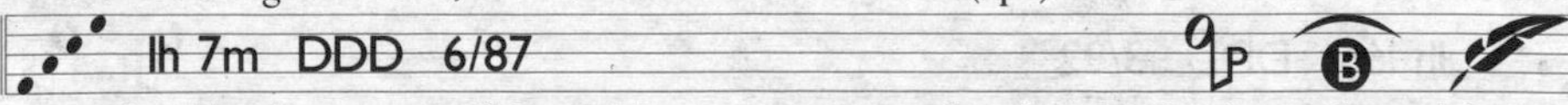

Kenneth Gilbert's account of the *Goldberg Variations* is relaxed and refined, gentler and less impulsive than some others and, partly for these reasons, less overtly virtuosic. He explains in a helpful sleeve-note how and why he set about omitting several of the repeats in the variations. He observes them in the Canons, for example, so that listeners can follow the lead melody first time round and concentrate on the canonic answer in the repeats. He also observes them where the first and second time bars differ, thus ensuring that not a single note of Bach's music is omitted; and he plays repeats in several shorter variations where their omission might appear almost dismissive. One of the particularly attractive features of this performance is Gilbert's emphasis on the dance element in the music and the natural grace with which he applies appoggiaturas. There is a remarkable agility, both technical and intellectual, in Gilbert's playing of the *Goldberg Variations* and he succeeds in communicating with his audience in a notably informed manner. The harpsichord which he plays was built after a Ruckers-Taskin housed in Paris. Although the sound is noticeably warm, Harmonia Mundi seem to have ended up with a slightly muffled element to it which takes a little getting used to. The detail is there and it has a very natural perspective, but it requires some aural adjustment and some listeners may regret a lack of immediate clarity. But they will almost certainly not regret anything else. Warmly recommended.

Additional recommendations ...

Goldberg Variations. **Trevor Pinnock** (hpd). Archiv Produktion 415 130-2AH — lh lm ADD 8/85

Goldberg Variations. **András Schiff** (pf). Decca 417 116-2DH — lh 13m DDD 12/86

Goldberg Variations. Prelude in G major, BWV902/1. Fantasia in C minor, BWV906/1. Adagio in G major, BWV968. Chromatic Fantasia and Fugue in D minor, BWV903. **Virginia Black** (hpd). Collins Classics 7003-2 — ② lh 50m DDD 2/92

Goldberg Variations. **Maggie Cole** (hpd). Virgin Classics Veritas VC7 59045-2 — lh 19m DDD 2/92

Goldberg Variations. **Glenn Gould** (pf). Sony Classical Glenn Gould Edition mono SMK52594 — 46m ADD 4/93

NEW REVIEW

Bach. Suite in G minor, BWV995.
Weiss. Suites — No. 3 in C major; D minor. **Stephen Stubbs** (lte). EMI CDC7 54519-2. Recorded in 1991.

lh 19m DDD 3/93

Bach knew and admired Leopold Weiss, the greatest lutenist of that time, and he also loved the sound of the lute — imitated by the lute-harpsichord — of which he owned two at the time of his death; the evidence that he intended any of his so-called 'lute works' for that instrument (rather than the lute-harpsichord) is both circumstantial and shaky. An adaptation of the Suite BWV995 (another form of what is the Cello Suite No. 5, BWV1011) by a contemporary lutenist suggests that Bach knew far more about writing fine music than he did of the basic workings of the lute. Weiss understood *both* very well. The magnificent Suite BWV995 (in 'standard' form) survives its minor surgery unscathed. The abundant music of Weiss is preserved mainly in manuscripts in London and Dresden, from which latter source the splendid Suite in C major comes, whilst that in D minor is compiled from some of the 48 pieces in a manuscript found in Moscow! Weiss's style is more *galant* than baroque, and his powers of invention are both attractive and impressive — as is Stephen Stubbs's ability to bring all the music on this cleanly recorded disc to life.

For details of availability of Complete Organ Works see the end of this section.

Bach. Orgelbüchlein, BWV599-644. **Simon Preston** (org). DG 431 816-2GH. Played on the Lorentz organ of Sorø Abbey, Denmark. Recorded in 1989.

lh 16m DDD 3/92

Bach's *Orgelbüchlein* ("Little Organ Book") contains 46 short preludes based on the chorale melodies used in the Lutheran church. It is arranged to follow the course of the church's year, beginning in Advent, passing through Christmas, Lent, Easter, Ascension, Pentecost and Trinity and ending with those miscellaneous areas classified in most hymn-books as "General". But Bach was not merely providing the church organist with something useful (although its enduring usefulness is still evident today — walk into almost any church and at some point you are likely to find the organist delving into a copy of Bach's *Orgelbüchlein*), he also intended these as teaching pieces. The title page describes them as offering "instruction in the various ways of working out a chorale, and also practice in the use of the pedals". What wonderful teaching pieces these are for any organ student — training exercises of this calibre would surely be enough to tempt anyone into learning how to play the organ! Here with that accomplished organist, Simon Preston, playing a ravishing Danish instrument sumptuously recorded by DG, the full genius of Bach is revealed. At just over an hour and a quarter, this CD represents astonishing value not just in playing time, but also in the quality of the playing, the magnificent recorded sound and, above all, the wealth of truly great music.

Bach. ORGAN PARTITAS. **Simon Preston.** DG 429 775-2GH. Played on the Lorentz organ of Sorø Abbey, Denmark. Recorded in 1989.
Christ, der du bist der helle Tag, BWV766; O Gott, du frommer Gott, BWV767; Sei gegrüsset, Jesu gütig, BWV768; Ach, was soll ich Sünder machen?, BWV770.

54m DDD 3/91 9s

At the last count the number of chorale preludes for organ believed to be by Bach was 239. In addition there are six Chorale Preludes — more extended sets of variations on the Lutheran chorales. These continue a tradition some of the greatest masters of which were Bach's immediate predecessors Böhm, Buxtehude and Pachelbel. While Bach's magnificent set on *Vom Himmel hoch, da komm ich her* (not included on this disc) is generally regarded as the pinnacle of the genre, the other partitas are all early works and with the exception of that based on *Sei gegrüsset* do not call for pedals. It seems that these pieces could just as easily have been intended for domestic consumption by harpsichordists as for church use by organists. As such, they have perhaps been somewhat overlooked by present-day organists, yet as this captivating disc shows most convincingly, the music contains an abundant wealth of variety, interest and charm. Simon Preston is on excellent form, showing his customary formidable technical mastery. His performances bring this music vividly to life and he unearths an astonishing variety of tone colours from a famous and historic organ. All of this is recorded with outstanding clarity and the overall sound is simply delicious.

Bach. ORGAN WORKS. **Christopher Herrick.** Hyperion CDA66434. Played on the Metzler organ of the Stadtkirche, Zofingen, Switzerland. Recorded in 1990.
Toccatas and Fugues — D minor, BWV565; F major, BWV540; D minor, BWV538, "Dorian". Toccata, Adagio and Fugue in C major, BWV564. Passacaglia and Fugue in C minor, BWV582.

1h 4m DDD 4/91  9s B

If you only have one disc of organ music in your collection, this must be it. It more than fulfils all the basic criteria which combine to make a 'Good CD'. First the music. Here are the five most important and impressive organ works by the indisputable king of organ music. Everyone knows Bach's *Toccata and Fugue* in D minor and such is its popularity that it is currently the most widely available piece of organ music on CD. Of the others, many would consider the *Passacaglia and Fugue* as the finest piece of organ music ever written while the *Adagio* from the *Toccata, Adagio and Fugue* is as beautiful a melody as can ever have been composed for the instrument. Second the performances. Christopher Herrick's playing is simply outstanding. He has just the right blend of dramatic flair, technical virtuosity and musical sensitivity. He avoids personal idiosyncrasies (rare indeed in such an old war-horse as the D minor) and maintains a bright, lively approach throughout the entire programme, giving it all a wonderful lift. Finally the recording. Hyperion have found the ideal organ set in the most magnificent of acoustics. Their recording has caught the finest detail with total clarity while the overall opulence of sound is a sheer aural delight.

NEW REVIEW

Bach. ORGAN WORKS, Volume 1. **Kevin Bowyer.** Nimbus NI5280. Played on the Marcussen organ of St Hans Kirke, Odense, Denmark. Recorded in 1991.
Fantasia and Fugue in G minor, BWV542. Trio Sonata No. 1 in E flat major, BWV525. Toccata and Fugue in D minor, BWV565. Pastorale in F major, BWV590. Organ Concerto No. 1 in G major, BWV592. Chorale Prelude — Erbarm' dich mein, O Herre Gott, BWV721. Organ Chorale — Aus tiefer Not schrei ich zu dir, BWV1099.

Ih 7m DDD 10/92

Organist Kevin Bowyer and record company Nimbus have set out to record every note Bach wrote for the organ, is believed to have written or is now known not to but in the past was thought to have written. It is a mammoth project planned to take several years. The first disc, perhaps inevitably, includes the best-known of all Bach's organ pieces — although some would dispute that it is an organ piece or even that Bach wrote it; Bowyer's account of the *Toccata and Fugue* in D minor is invigorating, exciting and very fast. It sets the scene for a CD of virtuoso performances and sound musicianship. The whole is a well-chosen, self-contained programme which also includes an indisputably 'great' organ work, a Trio Sonata, a transcription Bach made of an effervescent concerto by Ernst, a youthful chorale prelude as well as one from a collection only discovered in 1985 and one real oddity. Much thought has gone into the choice of organ and this instrument serves its purpose admirably; roaring magnificently in the *Fantasia* and emulating the tranquil sounds so characteristic of the *Pastorale*. If the remaining discs are going to be this good then it's a series well worth collecting.

Key to Symbols

Gramophone Award winners

Artists of the Year

Bach. ORGAN WORKS. Volume 3. **Peter Hurford.** Decca Ovation 421 617-2DM3. From Argo D150D3 (7/79). Recorded 1974-1979.
Chorale Variations and Partitas, BWV766-71. The Schübler Chorale Preludes, BWV645-50. Chorale Preludes — Herr Jesu Christ, dich zu uns wend', BWV726; Herzlich tut mich verlangen, BWV727; Jesus, meine Zuversicht, BWV728; In dulci jubilo, BWV729; Liebster Jesu, wir sind hier, BWV730; Liebster Jesu, wir sind hier, BWV731; Lobt Gott, ihr Christen, allzugleich, BWV732; Meine Seele erhebt den Herrn, BWV733; Nun freut euch, lieben Christen g'mein, BWV734; Valet will ich dir geben, BWV735; Valet will ich dir geben, BWV736; Vater unser im Himmelreich, BWV737; Vom Himmel hoch, da komm'ich her, BWV738; Wie schön leuchtet der Morgenstern, BWV739; Wir glauben all' an einen Gott, BWV740. Concertos — No. 1 in G major, BWV592; No. 2 in A minor, BWV593; No. 3 in C major, BWV594; No. 4 in C major, BWV595; No. 5 in D minor, BWV596; No. 6 in E flat, BWV597.

3 3h 3lm ADD 6/90 

Most record collectors will be familiar with Bach's great organ works; not least the ubiquitous *Toccata and Fugue* in D minor. While these are undeniably essential ingredients in any CD collection they represent only a tiny fraction of Bach's enormous output for the instrument. Generally these are what are known as chorale preludes; miniature pieces reflecting both the chorale's melody and the character of its words. Here are some of Bach's most ingenious and personal creations. In more extended form are the six Chorale Partitas which provide variations for each of the verses of the original chorale. Unique among his organ works are the secular concertos, transcriptions of string concertos by Vivaldi and Ernst. While Bach made few changes to the original, his unique genius has turned typically Italianate violin writing (in the third even the violin cadenzas have been retained) into something utterly at ease on the organ. Here is some of the most charming and effervescent music in the entire repertoire. Peter Hurford's playing, Decca's superlative recordings and a selection of top-rate organs from around the world provide the best realization imaginable of these works. If a three-disc set of lesser-known Bach organ works (even at mid-price) seems a tall order, rest assured you are buying some of the finest organ music, organ playing and organ recordings available. Here is a recording to be dipped into time and time again; it never loses its freshness or ability to captivate.

Bach. ORGAN WORKS. Volume 4. **Peter Hurford.** Decca Ovation 421 621-2DM3. Recorded 1975-1986.
Chorales from the Neumeister Collection Nos. 1-35. Chorale Preludes, BWV651-668, The "Eighteen". Chorale Preludes — O Lamm Gottes unschuldig, NBA; Ach Gott und Herr, BWV714; Allein Gott in der Höh' sei Ehr', BWV715; Allein Gott in der Höh' sei Ehr', BWV716; Allein Gott in der Höh', BWV717; Christ lag in Todesbanden, BWV718; Der Tag, der ist so freudenrich, BWV719; Ein' feste Burg ist unser Gott, BWV720; Erbarm' dich mein, o Herre Gott, BWV721; Gelobet seist du, Jesu Christ, BWV722; Gelobet seist du, Jesu Christ, BWV723; Gottes Sohn ist kommen, BWV724; Herr Gott, dich loben wir, BWV725.

③ 3h 50m ADD/DDD 6/90 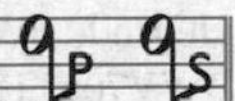

It's tantalizing to think that there is still music written by the great composers lying untouched and unrecognized by past generations just waiting to be discovered. That such major finds are still cropping up was evidenced in 1984, fortuitously timed for the tercentenary celebration of Bach's birth, when two scholars working independently in Yale University library came across a substantial manuscript put together in the early nineteenth century by J.G. Neumeister. Here they unearthed no less than 38 chorales for organ by Bach, most of which were not previously known to exist. Most experts accept them as genuine, although some doubts still exist. But for the CD collector such doubts should be irrelevant, for regardless of the music's origins, here is the fourth (and final) boxed set of Peter Hurford's landmark recordings of Bach's complete organ music; recordings no serious collector should be without. The music is wonderful; included here are, in addition to the 'Neumeister' chorales, some of Bach's greatest chorale-based organ works. Hurford's playing is a delight to behold. Every piece, no matter how small or simple, is treated as the gem it is; with loving care and an unerring sensitivity towards the finest detail. As with the other discs in the series, Decca have taken their microphones quite literally around the world to find the best instruments for the music — here organs from England, Germany, Austria, America and Australia are featured. The results from both a musical and technical point of view are superlative. Discs two and three were originally issued on LP and it goes almost without saying, given the emphasis on excellence with this entire venture, that the transfers to CD are magnificent.

Bach. ORGAN WORKS. Volume 3. **Ton Koopman.** Novalis 150036-2. Played on the organ of the Great Church, Leeuwarden, Holland. Recorded in 1988.
Toccata and Fugue in D minor, BWV538, "Dorian". Partita on "Sei gegrüsset, Jesu gutig", BWV768. Fantasia in G major, BWV572. Trio Sonata No. 6 in G major, BWV530. Chorale Preludes — "Vater Unser im Himmelreich", BWV682; "Jesu Christus unser Heiland", BWV688. Prelude and Fugue in A minor, BWV543.

1h 10m DDD 8/89 

Bach. ORGAN WORKS. **Michael Murray.** Telarc CD80179. Played on the organ of the College of St Thomas, St Paul, Minnesota, USA.
Prelude and Fugues — C major, BWV531; G minor, BWV535; D minor, BWV539. Concerto No. 1 in G major, BWV592. Fantasia in G major, BWV572. Prelude in C major, BWV567. "Little" Fugue in G minor, BWV578. Canzona in D minor, BWV588. Chorale Prelude "In dulci jubilo", BWV751.

58m DDD 8/89 

These two constitute 'Good CDs' from any standpoint. The playing is unwavering in its excellence, the instruments are well chosen, the combined programmes present a good cross-section of some of Bach's finest (if not exactly his best-known) organ compositions and the recordings are superlative (indeed Telarc's sound is nothing short of stunning). The one work common to both (the *Fantasia* in G) receives such utterly different interpretations that it is well worth having in both versions. Ton Koopman (playing on an instrument built when Bach was 42) is an acknowledged Bach expert and whilst his performances undoubtedly show scholarship and a keen appreciation of style, they are also exceedingly enjoyable in their own right. In fact, Koopman's playing is so compelling and vivacious that he manages to make accessible works which in lesser hands come across as dull and academic. Michael Murray uses a much more modern instrument. It has a bright, forthright tone which is ideally suited to this joyous and energetic music. Murray, too, plays with an infectious enthusiasm and allows the music to speak for itself, never allowing fussiness of detail or extravagant use of the organ to obscure the sheer ebullience of the writing.

Bach. ORGAN WORKS. **Nicholas Danby.** CBS Digital Masters CD45807. Played on the organ of Lübeck Cathedral, Germany. Recorded in 1989.
Chorale Preludes — Wachet auf, ruft uns die stimme, BWV645; Nun komm' der Heiden Heiland, BWV659; Dies sind die Heil'gen zehn gebot', BWV678; Liebster Jesu, wir sind hier, BWV706; Herr Jesu Christ, dich zu uns wend', BWV709; Erbarm' dich mein, O Herre Gott, BWV721; Herzlich thut mich verlangen, BWV727; Vater unser im Himmelreich, BWV737; Aus der tiefe rufe ich, BWV745. Fantasia in G major, BWV572. Prelude and Fugues — A minor, BWV543; C minor, BWV546. Toccata and Fugue in D minor, BWV565.

1h 10m DDD 6/90 

This is an excellent CD on every count. The music is wonderful, Bach at his most varied and interesting. The playing is sympathetic, tasteful, elegant and persuasive, with the organ making a really sumptuous sound. And the recording is exemplary, perfectly realizing the cathedral's warm atmosphere and the organ's splendid array of charms, but without any disturbing background thuds or clatters. Add to all this a generous playing time (forget about the useless accompanying booklet) and here is a disc for everyone's collection. Nicholas Danby has planned his programme with commendable good sense. It begins and ends with quiet reflective Chorale Preludes and passes through the powerful, quasi-orchestral C minor Prelude and Fugue, the exciting A minor Prelude and Fugue, the colourful Fantasia (one of the best performances of all, this) and numerous Chorale Preludes of widely differing moods before launching into everybody's favourite, the Toccata and Fugue in D minor. It makes compelling listening. This is not a disc from which to pick out your favourites; sit down, press 'play' and enjoy an hour and ten minutes' worth of unfettered pleasure.

NEW REVIEW

Bach. Six Trio Sonatas, BWV525-30. **Christopher Herrick** (org). Hyperion CDA66390. Played on the Metzler organ of the Parish Church of St Nikolaus, Bremgarten, Switzerland. Recorded in 1989.
No. 1 in E flat major; No. 2 in C minor; No. 3 in D minor; No. 4 in E minor; No. 5 in C major; No. 6 in G major.

1h 12m DDD 11/90 

The common assumption is that Bach wrote his six Trio Sonatas as training studies for his son Wilhelm Friedmann, and certainly to this day young organists regard the ability to play these pieces as a prerequisite in establishing proper organ technique. But if ever the notion that this is music "first to practise and secondly to admire" was shown to be false, this stunning disc presents an unanswerable argument. Christopher Herrick's performances are immense fun, brimming over with real affection for the music. He allows himself occasional displays of enthusiasm (adding a few exuberant glissandos in the last movement of the E flat major Sonata, for example) and he chooses his stops both to enhance the vitality of the quick movements and to underline the sheer beauty of the slower ones. Never has this music sounded less like a training study! The Hyperion recording of the sumptuous Swiss instrument makes this disc a worthwhile buy if only for its glorious sound; the organ speaks into a rich, opulent acoustic which treats each note as a priceless jewel, to be enhanced by its setting but not in any way to be obscured. A disc of rare beauty and a real gem in any collection.

Bach. The Art of Fugue, BWV1080. **Davitt Moroney** (hpd). Harmonia Mundi HMC90 1169/70.

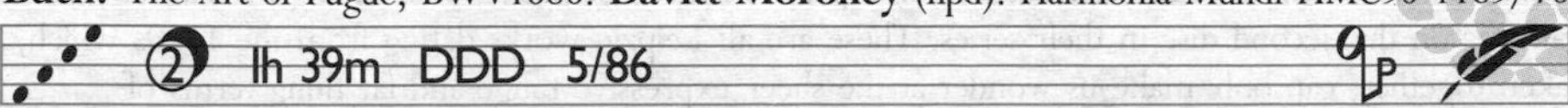

Bach died before the process of engraving his last great work had been completed, thus leaving a number of issues concerning performance in some doubt. However, Davitt Moroney is a performer-scholar who has a mature understanding of the complexity of Bach's work; in a lucid essay in the booklet, he discusses the problems of presenting *The Art of Fugue* whilst at the same time explaining his approach to performing it. Certain aspects of this version will be of particular importance to prospective buyers: Moroney, himself, has completed Contrapunctus 14 but he also plays the same Contrapunctus in its unfinished state as a fugue on three subjects. He omits Bach's own reworkings for two harpsichords of Contrapunctus 13 on the grounds that they do not play a part in the composer's logically-constructed fugue cycle; and he omits the Chorale Prelude in G major (BWV668*a*) which certainly had nothing to do with Bach's scheme but was added in the edition of 1751 so that the work should not end in an incomplete state. Moroney's performing technique is of a high order, placing emphasis on the beauty of the music which he reveals with passionate conviction. Exemplary presentation and an appropriate recorded sound enhance this fine achievement.

The Art of Fugue (earlier version). **Kenneth Gilbert** (hpd). Archiv Produktion 427 673-2AH — 59m DDD 4/90

The Art of Fugue. Overture in the French style in B minor, BWV831. Italian Concerto in F major, BWV971. Prelude, Fugue and Allegro in E flat major, BWV998. **Gustav Leonhardt, Bob van Asperen** (*Art of Fugue*) (hpds). Deutsche Harmonia Mundi GD77013 — 2 2h 12m ADD 12/90

Bach. Cantatas — Nos. 5-8. **Paul Esswood** (alto); **Kurt Equiluz** (ten); **Max van Egmond** (bass); **Vienna Boys' Choir; Chorus Viennensis; Vienna Concentus Musicus/Nikolaus Harnoncourt; Regensburger Domspatzen; King's College Choir, Cambridge; Leonhardt Consort/Gustav Leonhardt.** Teldec 2292-42498-2. Texts and translations included. From Telefunken SKW2 (2/72).

No. 5, Wo soll ich fliehen hin; No. 6, Bleib bei uns, denn ens will Abend werden; No. 7, Christ unser Herr zum Jordan kam; No. 8, Liebster Gott, wann werd' ich sterben.

2 lh 27m ADD 9/85

It was during Bach's final period of employment as Cantor at the Leipzig Thomass that he wrote his great series of church cantatas. His powerful Lutheran beliefs here fuse with his musical genius to create a series of beautifully integrated works. *Wo soll ich fliehen hin* follows the typical pattern: opening chorale; bass recitative; tenor aria (with a lovely viola obbligato); alto recitative; bass aria (with a characterful rhythm); soprano recitative; final chorale (in a stately measured gait). The effect is to illustrate with the greatest possible variety the religious measure of the service. This set is an excellent introduction to Bach's cantata writing with four uniformly accomplished and varied works. Harnoncourt and Leonhardt's cantata series is one of the monuments of the recorded age, a magnificent achievement that still continues. The soloists are excellent and the orchestras and choirs perform with imagination.

Additional recommendation ...

No. 8. No. 78, Jesu, der du meine Seele; No. 99, Was Gott tut, das ist wohlgetan. **Julianne Baird** (sop); **Allan Fast** (alto); **Frank Kelley** (ten); **Jan Opalach** (bass); **Bach Ensemble/Joshua Rifkin.** L'Oiseau-Lyre 421 728-2OH — 58m DDD 10/89

NEW REVIEW

Bach. Cantatas — No. 8, Liebster Gott, wann werd ich sterben?[a]; No. 156, Ich steh mit einem Fuss im Grabe[b]; No. 198, Lass, Fürstin, lass noch einen Strahl, "Trauer-Ode". [a]**Julianne Baird,** [c]**Judith Nelson** (sops); [c]**Judith Malafronte** (mez); [ab]**Steven Rickards** (alto);

[c]**William Sharp** (bar); [ab]**James Weaver** (bass); **American Bach Soloists/Jeffrey Thomas** (ten). Koch International Classics 37163-2. Texts and translations included. Recorded in 1992.

Ih 8m DDD 4/93

Jeffrey Thomas and his American Bach Soloists perform three of Bach's outstandingly beautiful sacred cantatas on this second disc in their series. These are all Leipzig works dating from the 1720s which, taken together, can only make us wonder at the sheer expressive range and far-flung terms of reference which Bach had at his disposal. Cantata No. 156 opens with a ravishing sinfonia for oboe and strings, better known in its version for harpsichord and strings in the Concerto in F minor (BWV1056); and the remainder of the work is of comparable expressive intensity. Cantata No. 8 begins with one of Bach's most miraculous poetic fantasies in which the composer's free-ranging imagination is cause for wonder. Cantata No. 198, the *Trauer-Ode* is no less impressive for its profoundly expressive qualities. Bach performed it in 1727 at the memorial service for the much loved and staunchly Protestant Christiane Eberhardine, Queen of Poland, Electoral Princess of Saxony and wife of Augustus the Strong. Each cantata is stylishly performed by these gifted artists and though there are a few weak moments the many instances of sensitive singing and playing far outweigh them. Thomas himself is an eloquent tenor and the sopranos Julianne Baird and Judith Nelson are both on strong form. The counter-tenor Steven Rickards sounds slightly less secure but the bass, James Weaver, gives a fine account of his robust aria in Cantata No. 8. Not only is this disc a marvellous introduction to Bach's cantatas but one which all Bach lovers will find very stimulating.

NEW REVIEW

Bach. Cantatas — No. 36, Schwingt freudig euch empor[a]; No. 61, Nun komm, der Heiden Heiland; No. 62, Nun komm, der Heiden Heiland[a]. **Nancy Argenta** (sop); [a]**Petra Lang** (mez); **Anthony Rolfe Johnson** (ten); **Olaf Bär** (bar); **Monteverdi Choir; English Baroque Soloists/John Eliot Gardiner.** Archiv Produktion 437 327-2AH. Texts and translations included. Recorded in 1992.

Ih Im DDD 2/93

This disc, the third in John Eliot Gardiner's series for DG, contains three of Bach's *Advent* Cantatas. Two of them, *Nun komm, der Heiden Heiland* (BWV61 and 62) are linked to Luther's metrical version of the fourth-century *Veni redemptor gentium*, while the third, *Schwingt freudig euch empor* (BWV36) is an adaptation of birthday music which Bach performed on several occasions during the mid- to late-1720s. The earliest and best known of them is Cantata No. 61, a masterpiece of Bach's Weimar years. None of its drama is lost on Gardiner who performs the work with affection and a lively sense of theatre. Were it not for the masterly nature of No. 61, its namesake of ten years later (Leipzig, 1724) would undoubtedly enjoy a higher profile. Gardiner brings to life the beautifully constructed, joyful opening chorus with crisply articulated phrasing and a feeling for the music's restless vivacity. The reverse side of this expressive coin is represented by an accompanied recitative for soprano and alto of affecting tenderness and intimacy. Cantata No. 36 is the most extended of the three and, perhaps, the least consistent in performance. Among the strongest features is the partnership of Nancy Argenta and the violinist Alison Bury in the aria "Auch mit gedämpften, schwachen Stimmen", though Gardiner sets a tempo which is dangerously slow. This is a captivating disc with many strong contributions from soloists and obbligato players. The recorded sound is warm and spacious.

NEW REVIEW

Bach. Cantatas — No. 51, Jauchzet Gott in allen Landen![a]; No. 54, Widerstehe doch der Sünde[b]. No. 55, Ich armer Mensch, ich Sündenknecht[c]; No. 82, Ich habe genug[d]. [a]**Julianne Baird** (sop); [b]**Drew Minter** (alto); [d]**William Sharp** (bar); [c]**Kathleen Kraft** (fl); [cd]**John Abberger** (ob); [a]**Barry Baugess** (tpt); **American Bach Soloists/Jeffrey Thomas** ([c]ten). Koch International Classics 37138-2. Texts and translations included. Recorded in 1990.

Ih 2m DDD 12/92

Jeffrey Thomas, the director of the American Bach Soloists is himself the excellent tenor in Bach's only solo cantata for tenor voice (BWV55). The remaining cantatas on the disc are for solo soprano (BWV51), solo alto (BWV54) and solo bass (BWV82). Readers may be startled initially by the brisk tempo set for the poignant opening aria of *Widerstehe doch der Sünde*; but musically it makes sense though at such a pace some may feel that Bach's searing and insistent dissonant sevenths above a tonic organ point do not make their full impact in their illustration of the text. The counter-tenor Drew Minter shapes the vocal line sensitively and with tonal precision. The soprano Julianne Baird and the baritone William Sharp are both appealing in their respective cantatas, *Jauchzet Gott in allen Landen!* and *Ich habe genug*, though there are occasional vocal insecurities. Throughout the programme the singers are sympathetically accompanied by the period instrumentalists of the American Bach Soloists; and there is some fine oboe obbligato playing from John Abberger.

Additional recommendation ...
No. 51. No. 140, Wachet auf, ruft uns die Stimme. **Julianne Baird** (sop); **Drew Minter** (alto); **Jeffrey Thomas** (ten); **Jan Opalach** (bass); **Fred Holmgren** (tpt); **Bach Ensemble/Joshua Rifkin.** L'Oiseau-Lyre 417 616-2OH — ∴ 43m DDD 11/87

NEW REVIEW

Bach. Cantatas — Nos. 51, 80, 147 and 208. **Ingrid Kertesi, [c]Julia Pászthy** (sops); **[ab]Judit Nemeth** (mez); **[abc]Jozsef Mukk** (ten); **[abc]István Gáti** (bar); **[abc]Hungarian Radio Chorus; Failoni Chamber Orchestra, Budapest/Mátyás Antál.** Naxos 8 550642/3. Recorded in 1992.
8 550642 — No. 80, Ein feste Burg ist unser Gott[a]; No. 147, Herz und Mund und Tat und Leben[b]. *8 550643* — No. 51, Jauchzet Gott in allen Landen!; No. 208, Was mir behagt, ist nur die muntre Jagd[c].

② 54m 50m DDD 12/92

On two separately available discs Naxos have included Bach's most celebrated and accessible cantatas. The performances are far removed in character and resources from the complete Teldec edition with Nikolaus Harnoncourt and Gustav Leonhardt: women rather than boys or male altos sing the soprano and alto solos, the Hungarian Radio Chorus is a mixed male and female ensemble and the Failoni Chamber Orchestra of Budapest plays modern instruments at today's concert pitch rather than period instruments at a lower baroque pitch. This is spirited music-making which, in its choice of tempos, its understanding of recitative and its feeling for lyricism in Bach's writing compares favourably with some rival versions. The general standard of executancy is seldom less than adequate and some of the solo vocal contributions are first-rate, but there are disappointments in store for enthusiasts who like to hear the instruments for which Bach wrote and who feel particular about performing texts. The celebrated aria from BWV208, "Sheep may safely graze", for instance is accompanied here by flutes rather than the recorders which Bach specified; and in the case of BWV80 the inflated version with brass and timpani of the first and fifth movements is preferred to Bach's own modest but no less effective scoring for woodwind and strings. This was, in fact, the work of his eldest son, Wilhelm Friedemann who undertook the revision shortly after his father's death. Much else comes across extremely well, however, and there is an outstandingly successful performance by the soprano, Ingrid Kertesi, of the brilliantly coloured *Jauchzet Gott in allen Landen* (BWV51). To sum up, here are two mainly very enjoyable discs which can be confidently recommended, though the absence of texts is regrettable.

Bach. Cantatas — No. 56, Ich will den Kreuzstab gerne tragen; No. 82, Ich habe genug; No. 158, Der Friede sei mit dir[a]. **[a]Laurie Monahan** (sop); **[a]Douglas Stevens** (alto); **[a]William Hite** (ten); **Jan Opalach** (bass); **The Bach Ensemble/Joshua Rifkin** (org). L'Oiseau-Lyre 425 822-2OH. Texts and translations included. Recorded in 1989.

∴ 51m DDD 9/91 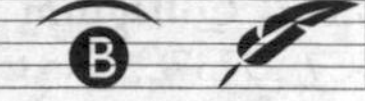

The three cantatas on this disc are for solo bass voice with an additional concluding four-voice chorale in two of them. *Ich habe genug* and *Ich will den Kreuzstab* are among Bach's best-known cantatas, the former containing the sublime aria "Schlummert ein, ihr matten Augen". Bach penned several versions of this tender lullaby and, in the present one the director Joshua Rifkin opts for that which the composer used for his last known performance in the late 1740s. It includes an oboe de caccia which reinforces the first violin part — an inspired, deeply affecting masterstroke. The bass, Jan Opalach, is a thoughtful singer whose close attention to the texts results in subtly coloured declamation. The performances are not without occasional weak moments felt mainly in ensemble but also occasionally in rhythm. The fine oboe playing of Stephen Hammer — his role is prominent in Cantatas 56 and 82 — provides a rewarding partnership with the voice though he cannot always conceal fatigue induced by the heavy demands made upon him by the music. But all-in-all this is a satisfying disc well recorded and well documented.

Additional recommendations ...

Nos. 56 and 82. **Max van Egmond** (bar); **St Bavo's Cathedral Boys' Choir; Baroque Instrumental Ensemble/Franz Brüggen.** RCA Seon GD71956 — 40m ADD 10/89

Nos. 56 and 82. **Harry van der Kemp** (bass); **Bremen Vocal Ensemble; Fiori Musicali/Thomas Albert.** Dabringhaus und Grimm L3297 — 42m DDD 10/89

Nos. 56, 82 and 158. **Peter Kooy** (bass); **La Chapelle Royale Choir and Orchestra/ Philippe Herreweghe.** Harmonia Mundi HMC90 1365 — 52m DDD 10/92

Nos. 56, 82 and 158. **Olaf Bär** (bar); **Scottish Chamber Orchestra/Peter Schreier.** EMI CDC7 54453-2 — 48m DDD 6/93

NEW REVIEW

Bach. Cantatas — No. 67, "Halt im Gedächtnis Jesum Christ"[a]; No. 108, "Es ist euch gut, dass ich hingehe"[a]; No. 127, "Herr Jesu Christ, wahr' Mensch und Gott"[b]. [b]**Antonia Fahberg** (sop); [a]**Lilian Benningsen** (contr); **Sir Peter Pears** (ten); **Keith Engen** (bass); **Munich Bach Choir; Munich State Opera Orchestra/Karl Richter.** Teldec Das Alte Werk 9031-77614-2. Texts and translations included. Recorded in 1958. New to UK.

1h 1m ADD 5/93

Collectors of Bach's choral music have strong views on Richter's performances, especially the church cantatas which represented the majority of his recorded output for Archiv. Most would agree that Richter's special affinity with Bach's music found its mark most persuasively in the 1960s before his mysterious adoption of the cloudy neo-romantic sound which did little to project his profound understanding of Bach's inner strength. Here we have a rarity from the late 1950s (a 'one-off' from Teldec not available in this country before) which forces us to revise our opinions about Richter's rigidity. These three cantatas were caught before the Munich Bach Orchestra had been formed though you would not know that they were not Bachians to the core; this is a state opera orchestra inspired by invigorating musical expression, blessed with an ignorance of self-conscious fashion. Certainly there are a few distracting mannerisms and a voice, notably Lilian Benningsen, which in hindsight seem somewhat out of place but they never detract from the prevailing conviction of the performances. In Cantata No. 67 the spirit of the text is directly and lucidly communicated by a spruce and well-balanced choral group, supported by the inimitable Peter Pears (a treasure or two here for his fans). The bass Keith Engen is also a Bach singer out of the top drawer; the opening aria of Cantata No. 108 is lovingly sung and the legendary Edgar Shann delivers an obbligato oboe line which is worth the cost of the disc alone, even without the other priceless revelations here.

NEW REVIEW

Bach. Cantatas — No. 73, "Herr, wie du willt, so schicks mit mir"; No. 105, "Herr, gehe nicht ins Gericht mit deinem Knecht"; No. 131, "Aus der Tiefen rufe ich, Herr, zu dir". **Barbara Schlick** (sop); **Gérard Lesne** (alto); **Howard Crook** (ten); **Peter Kooy** (bass); **Ghent Collegium Vocale Chorus and Orchestra/Philippe Herreweghe.** Virgin Classics VC7 59237-2. Texts and translation included. Recorded in 1990.

58m DDD 5/93

The three sacred cantatas on this disc reflect something of the wide stylistic range at Bach's command. All of them are masterpieces — which of us would dare to point a finger at one which is not? — and all of them profound examples of Bach's colossal expressive powers. Cantata No. 131 is very possibly Bach's earliest surviving cantata; it dates from 1707 while the remaining two are products of the almost unbelievably fertile early Leipzig years. Philippe Herreweghe has assembled a fine group of soloists for his recording and their contributions are outstanding. Most alluring of all, perhaps is the soprano Barbara Schlick's interpretation of the poignant canonic aria in Cantata No. 105. Here her partnership with the obbligato oboe playing of Marc Ponseele achieves one of the expressive high points of the programme. But much else is of a comparably high order, only the occasional astringent upper string tuning sounding less than ideal. The Ghent Collegium Vocale Chorus consisting of 16 voices makes a lively contribution and Herreweghe's overall direction has sensitivity and insight to the subtleties of the music. Well documented with effective recorded sound.

Key to Symbols

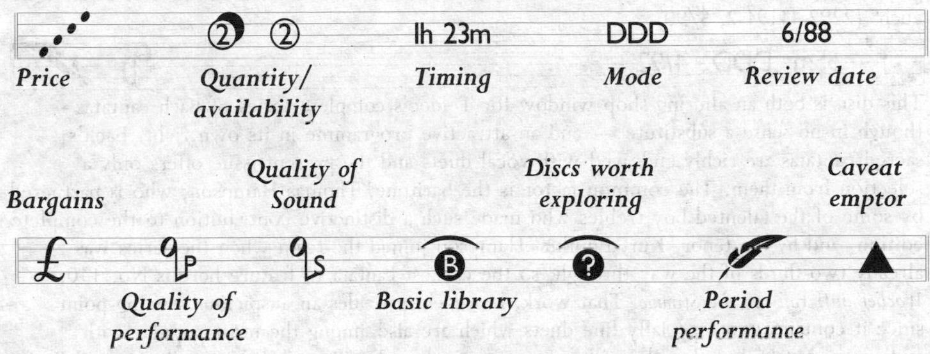

Bach. Cantatas — No. 140, Wachet auf! ruft uns die Stimme; No. 147, Herz und Mund und Tat und Leben. **Thomas Hampson** (bar); **Allan Bergius** (treb); **Kurt Equiluz** (ten); **Tolz Boys' Choir; Vienna Concentus Musicus/Nikolaus Harnoncourt.** Teldec 2292-43109-2.

This is another disc drawn from Teldec's pioneering Bach Cantata series shared by Harnoncourt and Leonhardt. Harnoncourt directs both cantatas here with a strong team of soloists, the Tolz Boys' Choir and the Vienna Concentus Musicus. Cantata No. 140 *Wachet auf!,* which includes the famous 'Sleepers wake', is variously charged with excitement, anticipation and tenderness. There are strong contributions from the solo treble, Allan Bergius, Kurt Equiluz, the oboist Jürg Schaeftlein and Alice Harnoncourt who gives a lyrical account of the violino piccolo solo in the first duet. Cantata No. 147 *Herz und Mund und Tat und Leben* includes the much loved chorale verses which conclude the first and second parts of the work, popularly known as "Jesu, joy of man's desiring", with a colourful assembly of instruments underlining the joyful nature of the Feast of the Visitation of Mary the Virgin. The four solo vocalists are impressive and the Vienna Concentus Musicus is on characteristically fine form in these brisk, joyful performances.

Additional recommendations ...

No. 80, Ein feste Burg ist unser Gott. No. 140. **Gabriele Fontana** (sop); **Júlia Hamari** (contr); **Gösta Winbergh** (ten); **Tom Krause** (bar); **Stuttgart Hymnus Boys' Choir; Stuttgart Chamber Orchestra/Karl Münchinger.** Decca Ovation 436 226-2DM— 58m DDD 11/85

Nos. 80 and 147. **Jane Bryden** (sop); **Drew Minter** (alto); **Jeffrey Thomas** (ten); **Jap Opalach** (bass); **Bach Ensemble/Joshua Rifkin.** L'Oiseau-Lyre 417 250-2OH — DDD 2/87

No. 51, Jauchzet Gott in allen landen. No. 140. **Julianne Baird** (sop); **Drew Minter** (alto); **Jeffrey Thomas** (ten); **Jan Opalach** (bass); **Fred Holmgren** (tpt); **Bach Ensemble/ Joshua Rifkin.** L'Oiseau-Lyre 417 616-2OH — 43m DDD 11/87

Nos. 140 and 147. **Ruth Holton** (sop); **Michael Chance** (alto); **Anthony Rolfe Johnson** (ten); **Stephen Varcoe** (bar); **Monteverdi Choir; English Baroque Soloists/John Eliot Gardiner.** Archiv Produktion 431 809-2AH — 53m DDD 6/92

Bach. CANTATAS. **Thomas Hampson** (bar); [a]**Allan Bergius,** [b]**Christoph Wegmann,** [a]**Helmut Wittek,** [d]**Stefan Gienger** (trebs); [e]**Kurt Equiluz** (ten); **Vienna Concentus Musicus/Nikolaus Harnoncourt.** Teldec 9031-74798-2. Recorded 1983-1987.
Cantata No. 140, Wachet auf! ruft uns die Stimme — Wann kommst du, mein Heil?[a]; Mein Freund ist mein![a]. Cantata No. 146, Wir müssen durch viel Trübsal in das Reich Gottes eingehen — Wie will ich mich freuen[e] (all from 6 35653, 1/85). Cantata No. 147, Herz und Mund und Tat und Leben — Ich will von Jesu Wundern singen (6 35654, 7/85). Cantata No. 152, Tritt auf die Glaubensahn — Tritt auf die Glaubensbahn; Wie soll ich dich, Liebster der Seelen[b]. Cantata No. 153, Schau, lieber Gott, wie meine Feind — Fürchte dich nicht, ich bin bei dir. Cantata No. 154, Mein liebster Jesus ist verloren — Wisset ihr nicht (6 35656, 4/86). Cantata No. 185, Barmherziges Herze der ewigen Liebes — Das ist der Christen Kunst (2292-44179-2, 9/89). Cantata No. 192, Nun danket alle Gott — Der ewig reiche Gott[c]. Cantata No. 194, Höchsterwünschtes Freudenfest — Was des Höchsten Glanz erfüllt; O wie wohl ist uns geschehn[d] (2292-44193-2, 5/90). Cantata No. 196, Der Herr denket an uns — Der Herr segne euch[e] (2292-44194-2, 5/90).

55m DDD 4/92 

This disc is both an alluring shop window for Teldec's complete series of Bach cantatas — though in no sense a substitute — and an attractive programme in its own right. Bach's sacred cantatas are richly endowed with vocal duets and the present issue offers only a selection from them. The common factor is the baritone, Thomas Hampson, who is partnered by some of the talented boy trebles who made such a distinctive contribution to the complete edition, and by the tenor, Kurt Equiluz. Hampson joined the team when the series was already two-thirds of the way through, so the earliest cantata to feature here is No. 140, *Wachet auf! ruft uns die Stimme.* That work, however, provides an auspicious starting-point since it contains two especially fine duets which are also among the most popular with audiences. Much else, though, will be comparatively unfamiliar to all but well-seasoned Bach cantata enthusiasts. In short, a very attractive compilation which, if it draws unsuspecting listeners into Bach's sacred dramatic wonderland will have more than fulfilled its purpose. Texts are not included, alas, but an accompanying note provides useful signposts to travellers in a strange land.

Bach. Cantatas — No. 206, Schleicht, spielende Wellen; No. 207a, Auf, schmetternde Töne der muntern Trompeten. **Ruth Ziesak** (sop); **Michael Chance** (alto); **Christoph Prégardien** (ten); **Peter Kooy** (bass); **Stuttgart Chamber Choir; Cologne Concerto/Frieder Bernius.** Sony Classical Vivarte SK46492. Texts and translation included. Recorded in 1990.

lh 7m DDD 9/91 

This disc contains two splendid examples of Bach's secular occasional style. *Auf, schmetternde Töne* dates from 1735 when it was performed in honour of the name day of Elector Frederick Augustus II. Lovers of the Brandenburg Concertos will be enchanted by two dazzling instances of Bach's art of parody contained in this colourfully scored work. The other cantata, *Schleicht, spielende Wellen* dates from 1736 when it was performed on the birthday of the selfsame Augustus. Here each of the principal rivers flowing through the countries united under Augustus's rule competes for the monarch's special affection. Inconsequential as the text may be, the music certainly is not; as well as two vigorous choruses there are four beautifully contrasted arias, pride-of-place to which might understandably be given the robust polonaise. This is the piece with which the Polish river Vistula (bass) serenades his ruler, and its rhythm and melody once heard, haunt the memory evermore. The performances are among the strongest to have emerged in this repertoire in recent years. Soloists and choir are first-rate and the orchestral playing on period instruments, comparably so. Full texts with translations are included.

Bach. Cantatas — No. 211, Schweigt stille, plaudert nicht, "Coffee"; No. 212, Mer hahn en neue Oberkeet, "Peasant". **Emma Kirkby** (sop); **Rogers Covey-Crump** (ten); **David**

Thomas (bass); **Academy of Ancient Music/Christopher Hogwood.** L'Oiseau-Lyre 417 621-2OH. Texts and translation included.

52m DDD 10/89

These two most delightful of Bach's secular cantatas here receive sparkling performances fully alive to the humour and invention of the music. The *Coffee* Cantata illustrates a family altercation over a current enthusiasm, the drinking of coffee. A narrator tells the story whilst the soprano and bass soloists confront each other in a series of delightful arias. Thomas brings out the crabby dyspeptic side of Schlendrian's character imaginatively and Kirkby makes a charming minx-like Lieschen. Covey-Crump's sweet light tenor acts as a good foil. The *Peasant* Cantata also takes the form of a dialogue, here between a somewhat dull and simple young man and his sweetheart Mieke, a girl who intends to better herself. Through the 24 short movements Bach conjures up a wonderfully rustic picture with some vivid dance numbers and rumbustious ritornellos. The soloists' nicely rounded characterizations emerge with great humour and Hogwood directs with vitality and sprightly rhythmic control. The recording is excellent.

Additional recommendation ...

No. 202, Weichet nur, betrübte Schatten, "Wedding Cantata"[a]. *No. 209, Non sa che sia dolore*[a]. *Nos. 211 and 212*[abc]. [a]**Elly Ameling** (sop); [b]**Gerald English** (ten); [c]**Siegmund Nimsgern** (bass); **Collegium Aureum.** Deutsche Harmonia Mundi Editio Classica GD77151 — ② 1h 46m ADD 10/90

NEW REVIEW

Bach. Motets, BWV225-30. **Greta de Reyghere, Katelijne van Laetham** (sops); **Martin van der Zeijst, Sytse Buwalda** (altos); **Hans Hermann Jansen** (ten); **Johannes-Christoph Happel** (bar); **La Petite Bande Choir; La Petite Bande/Sigiswald Kuijken.** Accent ACC9287D. Texts and translations included. Recorded in 1992.

Singet dem Herren, BWV225; Der Geist hilft unsrer Schwachheit auf, BWV226; Jesu meine Freude, BWV227; Fürchte dich nicht, BWV228; Komm, Jesu, komm, BWV229; Lobet den Herren, BWV230.

1h 5m DDD 5/93 

NEW REVIEW

Bach. Motets, BWV225-30. **Netherlands Chamber Choir/Ton Koopman.** Philips 434 165-2PH. Texts and translations included. Recorded 1986-87.

Singet dem Herren, BWV225; Der Geist hilft unsrer Schwachheit auf, BWV226; Jesu meine Freude, BWV227; Fürchte dich nicht, BWV228; Komm, Jesu, komm, BWV229; Lobet den Herren, BWV230.

1h 3m DDD 5/93 

These two approaches to Bach's Motets differ strongly from one another. Sigiswald Kuijken directs performances with *colla parte* instrumental support, that is to say with instruments doubling each of the vocal strands. Ton Koopman, on the other hand, prefers the vocal strands *a cappella* with instruments providing only the basso continuo. The choir in each version is made up of women sopranos and countertenors with the men's voices. Choosing between the versions is difficult and, to a large extent must be a matter of which approach you prefer. Kuijken's performances are more relaxed than those of Koopman. He avoids anything in the nature of over-direction and, while neither singing nor playing is always quite as tidy as it might be, there is a lively spontaneity, especially rewarding in the radiant performance of *Singet dem Herren*. Koopman draws more sharply articulated singing than Kuijken from the Netherlands Chamber Choir though sometimes at the expense of natural declamation and spontaneity. But there is greater linear clarity here than in the other and it pays off handsomely in *Komm, Jesu, komm*. It is a pity that Koopman does not avail himself of the surviving instrumental parts for *Der Geist hilft* but, in other respects, the strengths and weaknesses of the two performances are fairly evenly distributed and both are highly recommended.

Additional recommendations ...

As above. O Jesu Christ, meins Lebens Licht, BWV118. **Agnès Mellon, Greta de Reyghere** (sops); **Vincent Darras** (alto); **Howard Crook** (ten); **Peter Kooy** (bass); **Collegium Vocale; La**

Chapelle Royale Chorus and Orchestra/Philippe Herreweghe. Harmonia Mundi HMC90 1231 — lh 7m DDD 12/86

As above. **Trinity College Choir, Cambridge/Richard Marlow** with **Graham Jackson** and **Richard Pearce** (orgs). Conifer CDCF158 — lh 6m DDD 12/88

NEW REVIEW

Bach. Musicalisches Gesangbuch, BWV439-507 — excerpts[a]. Clavier-Ubung, Part 3, BWV669-89, "Orgelmesse". [a]**Peter Schreier** (ten); [a]**Jaap ter Linden** (vc); **Ton Koopman** (org). Philips 434 083-2PH. Texts and translations included. Recorded in 1991.

lh 6m DDD 4/93

Georg Christian Schemelli published his *Musicalisches Gesangbuch* in Leipzig in 1736. It was a collection of 954 hymns and airs, apparently intended for use by congregations at Zeitz where Schemelli was court cantor. Bach was invited to provide figured basses for 69 of the melodies, only two or three of which were by Bach himself. "Dir, dir Jehova, will ich singen" (BWV452) is one of them and that is included in this discerning selection made by Peter Schreier. The performances are stylish with a continuo of keyboard and cello. Sensibly, the programme has been devised in such a way that groups of songs are interspersed with pieces for organ without pedals from Part 3 of Bach's *Clavier-Ubung*. These, ten in all, are played with characteristic *élan* by the Dutch virtuoso Ton Koopman on the organ of the Raphaëlkirk in Amsterdam. Schreier himself is on excellent form, giving purpose, shape and clarity of diction to each of these beautiful songs. Voice and organ are effectively balanced and Koopman explores a wide variety of registration on the latter. Praise too, for the tasteful playing of the continuo cellist, Jaap ter Linden whose support is as dependable as it is discreet.

Bach. Magnificat in D major, BWV243[a].
Vivaldi. Ostro picta, RV642[b]. Gloria in D major, RV589[c]. [abc]**Emma Kirkby,** [ac]**Tessa Banner** (sops); [ac]**Michael Chance** (alto); [a]**John Mark Ainsley** (ten); [a]**Stephen Varcoe** (bar); **Collegium Musicum 90 Chorus and Orchestra/Richard Hickox.** Chandos Chaconne CHAN0518. Texts and translations included. Recorded in 1990.

lh 4m DDD 7/91 B

The Chandos issue was the first CD release featuring the then newly founded Collegium Musicum 90 under its directors Richard Hickox and Simon Standage. The Collegium embraces both choir and orchestra who are joined in this programme of Bach and Vivaldi by a comparably fine team of soloists. Hickox sets effective tempos in Bach's *Magnificat* and points up the many striking contrasts in colour and texture with which the piece abounds. From among the many successful features of the recording Stephen Varcoe's "Quia fecit mihi magna" and the "Et misericordia" sung by Michael Chance and John Mark Ainsley stand out. Vivaldi's *Gloria*, RV589 is the better known of two settings by the composer in D major. In this programme it is prefaced by an introductory motet *Ostro picta*, which may well in fact belong to the *Gloria* and here sung with warmth and radiance by Emma Kirkby. Hickox's performance of this evergreen vocal masterpiece comes over with conviction. It is gracefully phrased, sensitively sung and affectingly paced with an admirable rapport between vocalists and instrumentalists. The recorded sound is first-rate.

Additional recommendations ...

Magnificat. Cantata No. 51, Jauchzet Gott in allen Landen!. **Soloists; English Baroque Soloists/John Eliot Gardiner.** Philips 411 458-2PH — 41m DDD 9/85

Magnificat. Cantata No. 21, Ich hatte viel Bekümmernis". **Soloists; Netherland Chamber Choir; La Petite Bande/Sigiswald Kuijken.** Virgin Classics Veritas VC7 59528-2 — lh 13m DDD 2/90 B

Magnificat. ***Vivaldi.*** *Gloria in D major, RV589.* **Soloists; Academy of St Martin in the Fields Chorus and Orchestra/Sir Neville Marriner.** EMI CDC7 54283-2 — 56m DDD 3/92 B

Magnificat[a]. *Cantatas*[b] — *No. 67, Halt im Gedächtnis Jssum Christ; No. 130, Herr Gott, dich loben alle wir.* **Soloists; [a]Vienna Academy Choir; [a]Stuttgart Chamber Orchestra/Karl Münchinger; [b]Lausanne Pro Arte Choir; [b]Suisse Romande Orchestra/Ernest Ansermet.** Decca Serenata 433 175-2DM — lh 5m ADD 5/92

NEW REVIEW

Bach. Mass in B minor, BWV232. **Nancy Argenta** (sop); **Catherine Denley** (mez); **Mark Tucker** (ten); **Stephen Varcoe** (bar); **Collegium Musicum 90 Chorus and Orchestra/Richard Hickox.** Chandos Chanconne CHAN0533/4. Texts and translation included. Recorded in 1992.

② lh 48m DDD 1/93 

Chandos's early music label Chaconne is still, comparatively speaking in its infancy but, with recordings such as this in its catalogue its reputation for excellence is quickly being established. Richard Hickox, his soloists and the Collegium Musicum 90 Chorus and Orchestra deliver a performance which is satisfying on many levels. Hickox has a proven track-record with choirs and here he comes across as an effective disciplinarian in his firm control both of voices and instruments. Yet he avoids imposing that autocratic will on his forces which sometimes lessens the spontaneity of rival performances. Perhaps Hickox's strength lies more in the handling of the extrovert and most joyful sections of the Mass than in the deeply contemplative ones. Thus the *Et in terra pax*, for instance comes over especially well with articulate and transparently textured choral singing supported by robust but none the less sympathetic orchestral playing. The solo vocalists make a strong, even team and the use of a mezzo-soprano offers a welcome alternative in the *Agnus Dei* which, in most period instrument performances has unjustly become the sole preserve of counter-tenors. It may be that some other versions intermittently achieve greater heights of intensity but, taken as a whole this lively, spontaneous and consistently accomplished version is a fine achievement.

Additional recommendations ...

Soloists; Taverner Consort; Taverner Players/Andrew Parrott. EMI Reflexe CDS7 47293-8 — ② lh 43m DDD 8/86

Monteverdi Choir; English Baroque Soloists/John Eliot Gardiner. Archiv Produktion 415 514-2AH2 — ② DDD 2/86

Soloists; Netherlands Bach Society Collegium Musicum; La Petite Bande/Gustav Leonhardt. Deutsche Harmonia Mundi Editio Classica GD77040 — ② lh 5lm ADD 6/90

NEW REVIEW

Bach. St John Passion. **Nico van der Meel** (ten) Evangelist; **Kristin Sigmundsson** (bass) Jesus; **Annegeer Stumphius** (sop); **James Bowman** (alto); **Christoph Prégardien** (ten); **Peter Kooy** (bass); **Netherlands Chamber Choir; Orchestra of the Eighteenth Century/Frans Brüggen.** Philips 434 905-2PH2. Text and translation included. Recorded in 1992.

② lh 48m DDD 5/93 

At once striking in this thought-provoking performance of Bach's *St John Passion* is the softly spoken, lightly articulated continuo playing whose sensibility permeates all the remaining strands of the texture, instrumental and choral. The result is enlivening, especially in large choral movements where the director, Frans Brüggen, shapes the music expressively, introducing quite a wide dynamic range. A wonderfully affecting instance of this is demonstrated by the singing and playing of the opening chorus with its clear-textured, eloquent phrasing and its freedom from ponderous continuo gestures, symptomatic of excessive sentiment and laboured declamation. The solo vocal cast is strong with Nico van der Meel as an articulate and engaging Evangelist. No less impressive are contributions from James Bowman, Christoph Prégardien and Peter Kooy. The Netherlands Chamber Choir makes a more favourable impression here than on some previously issued recordings and the Orchestra of the Eighteenth Century is warmly and sensitively supportive of the voices. Choosing a *St John Passion* is a difficult proposition but Brüggen's version is a front-runner in the full-price bracket. At mid-price, versions by Harnoncourt and Kuijken are outstanding value.

Additional recommendations ...

Soloists; Monteverdi Choir; English Baroque Soloists/John Eliot Gardiner. Archiv Produktion 419 324-2AH2 — ② lh 47m DDD 2/87

Soloists; Vienna Boys' Choir; Chorus Viennensis; Vienna Concentus Musicus/Nikolaus Harnoncourt. Teldec 2292-42492-2 — ② lh 57m DDD 9/87

Soloists; Ghent Collegium Vocale; La Chapelle Royale Orchestra/Philippe Herreweghe. Harmonia Mundi HMC90 1264/5 — ② lh 55m DDD 5/88

Soloists; La Petite Bande Choir and Orchestra/Sigiswald Kuijken. Deutsche Harmonia Mundi Editio Classica GD77041 — ② 2h 2m ADD 6/90

Soloists; Taverner Consort and Players/Andrew Parrott. EMI Reflexe CDS7 54083-2 — ② lh 49m DDD 5/91

Bach. St Matthew Passion, BWV244. **Anthony Rolfe Johnson** (ten) Evangelist; **Andreas Schmidt** (bar) Jesus; **Barbara Bonney, Anne Monoyios** (sops); **Anne Sofie von Otter** (mez); **Michael Chance** (alto); **Howard Crook** (ten); **Olaf Bär** (bar); **Cornelius Hauptmann** (bass); **London Oratory Junior Choir; Monteverdi Choir; English Baroque Soloists/John Eliot Gardiner.** Archiv Produktion 427 648-2AH3. Text and translation included.

③ 2h 47m DDD 10/89

What makes John Eliot Gardiner's *St Matthew Passion* stand out in the face of stiff competition is perhaps more than anything his vivid sense of theatre. Bach's score is, after all, a sacred drama and Gardiner interprets this aspect of the work with lively and colourful conviction. That in itself, of course, is not sufficient to ensure a fine performance but here we have a first-rate group of solo voices, immediately responsive choral groups in the Monteverdi Choir and the London Oratory Junior Choir — a distinctive element this — and refined obbligato and orchestral playing from the English Baroque Soloists. Anthony Rolfe Johnson declaims the Evangelist's role with clarity, authority and the subtle inflexion of an accomplished story-teller. Ann Monoyios, Howard Crook and Olaf Bär also make strong contributions but it is Michael Chance's "Erbarme dich", tenderly accompanied by the violin obbligato which sets the seal of distinction on the performance. Singing and playing of this calibre deserve to win many friends and Gardiner's deeply-felt account of Bach's great Passion does the music considerable justice. Clear recorded sound.

Soloists; Ghent Collegium Vocale; Chapelle Royale Chorus and Orchestra/Philippe Herreweghe. Harmonia Mundi HMC90 1155/7 — ③ 2h 5lm DDD 11/85

Soloists; Berlin State and Cathedral Choirs; Vienna Singverein; Deutsche Oper Chorus; Berlin Philharmonic Orchestra/Herbert von Karajan. DG 419 789-2GH3 — ③ 3h 24m ADD 3/88

Soloists; Tölz Boys' Choir; La Petite Bande Men's Chorus and Orchestra/Gustav Leonhardt. Deutsche Harmonia Mundi RD77848 — ③ 2h 52m DDD 5/90

Soloists; Breda Sacraments Choir; Netherlands Bach Society Choir; Amsterdam Baroque Orchestra/Ton Koopman. Erato 2292-45814-2 — ③ DDD 5/93

Bach. Christmas Oratorio, BWV248. **Theo Altmeyer** (ten) Evangelist and arias; **Hans Buchhierl** (treb); **Andreas Stein** (boy alto); **Barry McDaniel** (bar); **Tölz Boys' Choir; Collegium Aureum/Gerhard Schmidt-Gaden.** Deutsche Harmonia Mundi GD77046. Notes, text and translation included. From EMI CDS7 49119-8 (4/88). Recorded in 1973.

③ 2h 43m 4/88

This performance of Bach's *Christmas Oratorio* possesses a radiance and a spontaneity perhaps unrivalled by more modern and carefully contrived versions. It is not without its weaknesses, which lie mainly in passages of insecure instrumental playing; but these are outweighed by its merits chief among which, perhaps, are the contributions, both solo and choral, of the Tölz Boys' Choir. All the soprano and alto solos are sung by boys and in the choruses it is boys rather than countertenors who sing the alto line. Gerhard Schmidt-Gaden, the chorusmaster and conductor, effectively relaxed tempos which may at first sound too leisurely to ears accustomed to the frenetic pace chosen by some rival versions. Occasionally, he is a little too slow as, for instance, in the opening chorus of Part Four but for the most part he directs a performance free from intrusive mannerisms which bedevil too many performances of baroque music today. The treble, Hans Buchhierl and the alto, Andreas Stein, are outstanding, and the tenor Theo Altmeyer and the bass, Barry McDaniel, are hardly less impressive. With its ingenuousness, its spirit of innocent joy and in its simple but sensitive response to the music this performance comes closer than most to the contemplative heart of Bach's Christmas masterpiece.

Additional recommendations ...

Soloists; Vienna Boys' Choir; Chorus Viennensis; Vienna Concentus Musicus/Nikolaus Harnoncourt. Teldec 9031-77610-2 — ② 2h 35m 12/86 Ⓑ
Soloists; Monteverdi Choir; English Baroque Soloists/John Eliot Gardiner. Archiv Produktion 423 232-2AH — ② 2h 20m DDD 12/87 Ⓑ
Soloists; Munich Bach Choir and Orchestra/Karl Richter. Archiv Produktion 427 236-2AX3 — ③ 2h 44m ADD 3/89 Ⓑ
Soloists; Ghent Collegium Vocale Chorus and Orchestra/Philippe Herreweghe. Virgin Classics Veritas VCD7 59530-2 — ② 2h 30m DDD 12/89 Ⓑ
Soloists; Frankfurt Vocal Ensemble; Cologne Concerto/Ralf Otto. Capriccio 60 025-2 — ② 2h 21m DDD 4/92 Ⓑ

Further listening ...

Trio Sonatas — D minor, BWV1036; C major, BWV1037; G major, BWV1038; G major, BWV1039. **London Baroque.** Harmonia Mundi HMC90 1173 (6/86).

Sacred Cantatas, Volumes. 1-41 on Teldec (some of the items listed below receive full reviews above, with different catalogue numbers). **Soloists; Choruses; Vienna Concentus Musicus/Nikolaus Harnoncourt; Leonhardt Consort/Gustav Leonhardt.** *1:* ***Nos. 1-4,*** 2292-42497-2; *2:* ***Nos. 5-8,*** 2292-42498-2; *3:* ***Nos. 9-11,*** 2292-42499-2; *4:* ***Nos. 12-14, 16,*** 2292-42500-2; *5:* ***Nos. 17-20,*** 2292-42501-2 (all reviewed in *Gramophone,* 9/85); *6:* ***Nos. 21-23,*** 2292-42502-2; *7:* ***Nos. 24-27,*** 2292-42503-2; *8:* ***Nos. 28-30,*** 2292-42504-2 (all reviewed 1/86); *9:* ***Nos. 31-34,*** 2292-42505-2; *10:* ***Nos. 35-38,*** 2292-42506-2; *11:* ***Nos. 39-42,*** 2292-42556-2; *12:* ***Nos. 43-46,*** 2292-42599-2; *13:* ***Nos. 47-50,*** 2292-42560-2 (all reviewed 1/88); *14:* ***Nos. 51, 52, 54-56,*** 2292-42422-2; *15:* ***Nos. 57-60,*** 2292-42423-2 (all reviewed 11/88); *16:* ***Nos. 61-64,*** 2292-42465-2; *17:* ***Nos. 65-68,*** 2292-42571-2 (all reviewed 2/89); *18:* ***Nos. 69, 69a-72,*** 2292-42572-2; *19:* ***Nos. 73-75,*** 2292-42573-2; *20:* ***Nos. 76-79,*** 2292-42576-2 (all reviewed 9/89); *21:* ***Nos. 80-83,*** 2292-42577-2; *22:* ***Nos. 84-90,*** 2292-42578-2; *23:* ***Nos. 91-94,*** 2292-42582-2; *24:* ***Nos. 95-98,*** 2292-42583-2; *25:* ***Nos. 99-102,*** 2292-42584-2 (all reviewed 12/89); *26:* ***Nos. 103-106,*** 2292-42602-2; *27:* ***Nos. 107-110,*** 2292-42603-2; *28:* ***Nos. 111-114,*** 2292-42606-2; *29:* ***Nos. 115-117, 119,*** 2292-42608-2 (all reviewed 2/90); *30:* ***Nos. 120-123,*** 2292-42609-2; *31:* ***Nos. 124-127,*** 2292-42615-2; *32:* ***Nos. 128-131,*** 2292-42617-2; *33:* ***Nos. 132-135,*** 2292-42618-2 (all reviewed 3/90); *34:* ***Nos. 136-139,*** 2292-42619-2; *35:* ***Nos. 140, 143, 144-146,*** 2292-42630-2; *36:* ***Nos. 147-151,*** 2292-42631-2 (2/86); *37:* ***Nos. 152-156,*** 2292-42632-2 (4/86); *38:* ***Nos. 157-159, 161-163,*** 2292-42633-2 (4/87); *39:* ***Nos. 164-169,*** 2292-42634-2 (9/87); *40:* ***Nos. 170-174,*** 2292-426635-2 (1/88); *41:* ***Nos. 175-179,*** 2292-42428-2 (10/88).

Complete Organ Works:

Marie-Claire Alain — Erato 2292-45732-2 (parts 1-4).
Kevin Boyer — *Volume 1* (reviewed above). *Volume 2,* Nimbus NI5289.
Michel Chapuis — Auvidis Valois V4425 (1-4). *Also available separately.*

Hans Fagius — *Volume 1,* BIS CD235/6 (11/86). *Volume 2,* BIS CD308/9. *Volume 3,* BIS CD329/30. *Volume 4,* BIS CD343/4 (10/91). *Volume 5,* BIS CD379/80. *Volume 6,* BIS CD397/8. *Volume 7,* BIS CD439/40 (10/91). *Volume 8,* BIS CD443/4. *Volume 9,* BIS CD445 (10/91).
Bernard Foccroulle — *Volume 4,* Ricercar RIC015030. *Volume 5,* Ricercar RIC064042 (3/90). *Volume 6,* Ricercar RIC085068 (10/91). *Volume 7,* Ricercar RIC086069 (10/91).
Peter Hurford — *Volume 1,* Decca Ovation 421 337-2DM3 (2/90). *Volume 2,* Decca Ovation 421 341-2DM3. *Volumes 3 and 4* (reviewed above).
André Isoir — Calliope CAL9703/17 (*Volumes 1-5*). *Volume 6,* CCAL9708. *Volume 7,* CAL9709. *Volume 8,* CAL9710 (8/89). *Volume 9,* CAL9711 (4/88). *Volume 10,* CAL9712. *Volume 12,* CAL9714. *Volume 13,* CAL9715. *Volume 14,* CAL9716. *Volume 15,* CAL9717.
Ton Koopman — *Volume 1,* Novalis 150 005-2 (4/88). *Volume 2,* Novalis 150 020-2. *Volume 3* (reviewed above). *Volume 4,* Novalis 150 052-2 (10/91). *Volume 5,* Novalis 150 066-2.

Heinrich Baermann

German 1784-1847

Suggested listening ...

Quintet in E flat major, Op. 23 — Adagio. *Coupled with* ***Brahms.*** Clarinet Quintet in B minor, Op. 115. ***Mozart.*** Clarinet Quintet in A major, K581. **Alfred Boskovsky** (cl); **Vienna Octet.** Decca Ovation 417 643-2DM (9/88).

Key to Symbols

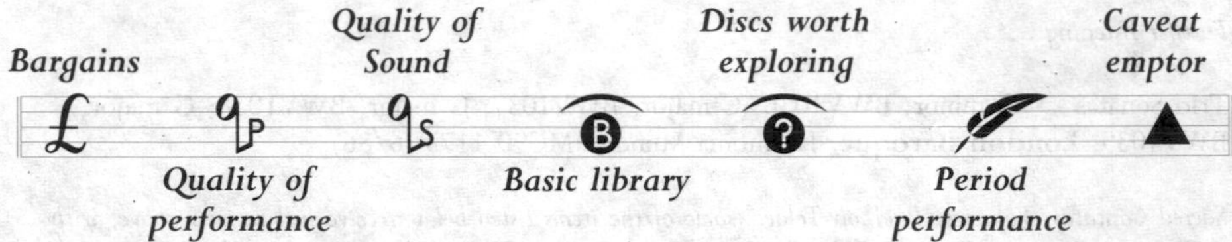

Simon Bainbridge

British 1952-

Bainbridge. Viola Concerto (1976)[a]. Fantasia for Double Orchestra (1983-4)[b]. Concertante in Moto Perpetuo (1979, rev. 1983)[c]. [a]**Walter Trampler** (va); **London Symphony Orchestra/Michael Tilson Thomas;** [b]**BBC Symphony Orchestra;** [c]**The Composers Ensemble/**[bc]**Simon Bainbridge.** Continuum CCD1020. Item marked [a] from Unicorn RHD400 (2/82), [bc] new to UK. Recorded 1982-1990.

54m DDD 5/91

When the recording of Simon Bainbridge's early Viola Concerto was first issued, it was rather overshadowed by the more outgoing, brightly-coloured music of Oliver Knussen with which it was coupled. Now the more outgoing, brightly-coloured coupling has been provided by Bainbridge himself, and the result is a disc as distinctive as it is distinguished. Bainbridge's music is modern in tone, romantic in temperament, and the most recent work on the disc, the *Fantasia for Double Orchestra*, presents a wide-ranging tapestry of moods and textures with an air of complete and justified confidence. There is a boldness, a directness that enables Bainbridge to evoke the opening of Wagner's *Das Rheingold* at the start without either irony or inappropriateness. His intention is evidently not to parody, but to build his own edifice on archetypically striking and substantial foundations. Structurally, the *Fantasia* works extremely well: expressively, it can be enjoyed even if the structure passes you by. The Viola Concerto is more introspective and more intense, but no less cogent. It may take longer to get the hang of than the *Fantasia*, but the results will be no less rewarding. The brief *Concertante in Moto Perpetuo* is an uncomplicated delight, and the whole disc has excellent sound and first-rate performance.

Sir Edward Bairstow

British 1874-1946

Suggested listening ...

Prelude in C major. Evening Song. Scherzo in A flat major. Nocturne. Prelude on "Vexilla Regis". Elegy. Toccata and Prelude on "Pange Lingua". Meditation. Three Short Preludes. Legend. Organ Sonata in E flat major. **Francis Jackson** (org). Mirabilis MRCD902 (4/91).

Mily Balakirev

Russian 1837-1910

Balakirev. Symphony No. 1 in C major. Russia — symphonic poem. **Philharmonia Orchestra/Evgeni Svetlanov.** Hyperion CDA66493. Recorded in 1991.

lh DDD 12/91

Balakirev was a major figure of Russian nationalism and one of the group of composers called "The Five", and he also gave useful advice and encouragement to Tchaikovsky. In some ways the most intellectual of these artists, he was also highly self-critical and this meant that his output was all too small, though of high quality. The spacious and sombre beginning of the First Symphony tells us at once that this is a work of epic proportions, imbued with the kind of Russianness that is hard to describe but easy to recognize. It is not surprising to find that Evgeni Svetlanov's view of Balakirev's First Symphony is very Russian in its power and whole-hearted commitment. In the first movement his pacing of the introductory *Largo* section is somewhat deliberate, in a manner which creates tension and very much whets the appetite. The main *Allegro vivo* part of the movement is played with a good deal of vigour and wit, and Svetlanov varies the basic pulse to bring out the music's changing moods very effectively. In the second movement he adopts quite a slow tempo and phrases the music with much care and delicacy. The *Andante* is shaped in a very appealing fashion, and in the finale Svetlanov's feather-light, bright-eyed manner is very attractive, though the work's ending is played strongly by the excellent Philharmonia Orchestra. *Russia*, an attractive, very well-written symphonic poem, is also played in a virile, vivacious fashion. Hyperion's recording has neither optimum clarity nor the greatest degree of atmosphere, but it serves well enough.

Additional recommendation ...
Tamara — symphonic poem. **Royal Philharmonic Orchestra/Sir Thomas Beecham.** EMI Beecham Edition CDM7 63375-2 — lh lm ADD 7/90 ▲

NEW REVIEW

Balakirev. Symphony No. 2 in D minor. Tamara — symphonic poem. Overture on the themes of three Russian songs. **Philharmonia Orchestra/Evgeni Svetlanov.** Hyperion CDA66586. Recorded in 1991.

lh 8m DDD 9/92

Balakirev's Second Symphony has never enjoyed the justly-deserved popularity of his First, yet in many respects it actually outstrips its predecessor, certainly in terms of creative originality. With a sure sense of structure in its outer movements, a colourful and refreshingly off-beat *Scherzo* at its core, and a delightful *Romanza* slow movement, it rivals the better-known 'second rung' symphonic essays of Borodin, Glazunov and Rimsky-Korsakov — in fact, its sure design probably places it a notch or two above even those. If the Second Symphony is precious metal within its genre, *Tamara* — inspired by Liszt and palpably superior to at least some of Liszt's own works in a similar vein — is a veritable diamond amongst symphonic poems. Based on verses by the romantic Russian poet Mikhail Lermontov, it tells of the evil and cunning Princess Tamara who lures passers-by to sleep with her. In this, it harbours a distant thematic resemblance to Bartók's *Miraculous Mandarin* except that, placed beside Balakirev's scheming temptress, Bartók's prostitute seems the very embodiment of innocence. The music, though, is quintessentially Russian, inhabiting as it does a deeply sensuous, vaguely sinister sound-world, and orchestrated by a master whose muse is at least as cunning and imaginative as the work's main protagonist. Heard after *Tamara*, the *Overture on the themes of three Russian songs* sounds comparatively conventional, although in truth it too is full of novel invention. It also happens to feature two folk-tunes that were shortly to re-emerge within the context of two separate masterpieces, Tchaikovsky's Fourth Symphony and Stravinsky's *Petrushka*. It is beautifully played by Svetlanov and the Philharmonia and superbly recorded, sterling virtues that apply in equal measure to the other two items on this excellent CD.

Michael William Balfe

Irish 1808-1870

Suggested listening ...

THE BOHEMIAN GIRL. **Nova Thomas** (sop) Arline (Cathryn Brennan); **Patrick Power** (ten) Thaddeus (Michael Grennell); **Jonathan Summers** (bar) Count Arnheim (Conor Farrington); **Bernadette Cullen** (contr) Queen of the Gipsies (Barbara McCaughey); **John Del Carlo** (bass) Devilshoof (Brendan O'Duill); **Timothy German** (ten) Florestein (Daniel Reardon); **Radio Telefis Eireann Philharmonic Choir; National Symphony Orchestra of Ireland/Richard Bonynge.** Argo 433 324-2ZH2 (8/92).

Sir Granville Bantock

British 1868-1946

NEW REVIEW

Bantock. Pagan Symphony. Fifine at the Fair. Two Heroic Ballads. **Royal Philharmonic Orchestra/Vernon Handley.** Hyperion CDA66630. Recorded in 1992.

lh 20m DDD 3/93

Granville Bantock was a man born at the wrong time. He wrote colourful, hedonistic late-romantic music well into the second quarter of the twentieth century, and has been neglected for many years as an anachronism. At times he recalls Strauss, at others Bax, but if he lacks that personal utterance that would stamp every page with his name and no other, there's plenty of compensation in his sheer craftsmanship. With some composers that word means a worthy but rather dull demonstration of technical facility, but Bantock has the gift of communicating his own pleasure in his craft. He will take a scale, twist it, bend it slightly, and we are not only delighted by the fine melody that he has made (and there are many of them) but also by the cleverness of the process. This could lead to mere garrulousness, an endless succession of pretty tricks, but Bantock's resource also ensures that the impulse of the two big pieces here (and they are both very big, single movement structures lasting half-an-hour) never flags. His scoring is particularly beautiful, sumptuous yet clean throughout, with many ingeniously original sonorities that work perfectly in such fine performances as these. The recordings are clear and spacious.

Further listening ...

The Pierrot of the Minute — comedy overture. *Coupled with* ***Bridge.*** Suite for strings, H93. Summer. There is a willow Grows Aslant a Brook, H174. ***Butterworth.*** The Banks of Green Willow (1913). **Bournemouth Sinfonietta/Norman Del Mar.** Chandos CHAN8373 (8/85).

Celtic Symphony. Tone Poems 5 — The Witch of Atlas. The Sea Reivers. Hebridean Symphony. **Royal Philharmonic Orchestra/Vernon Handley.** Hyperion CDA66450 (5/91).

Samuel Barber

American 1910-1981

Barber. Cello Concerto, Op. 22.
Britten. Symphony for cello and orchestra, Op. 68. **Yo-Yo Ma** (vc); **Baltimore Symphony Orchestra/David Zinman.** CBS Masterworks CD44900.

lh 2m DDD 6/89

This recording is highly recommended. The acoustic is warm, balance ideal and there is sufficient resonance. On this evidence, the Baltimore is a splendid orchestra, responding alertly and intelligently to David Zinman's very positive interpretation. How enterprising, too, to record two works which are not in the main repertoire of cello concertos, excellent though they are. Barber's dates from 1945 and has something of the late-romanticism of the Violin Concerto, but with a more classical approach. It makes large demands on the virtuosity of the soloist, which are met with apparent ease and relish by Yo-Yo Ma. Britten's Cello Symphony is more problematical. Its predominantly dark and brooding mood, with a savage *scherzo* followed by an almost jaunty finale, disconcerts some listeners, but the clue lies in the dedication to Rostropovich, for the music seems also to be an act of homage to the composer's friend Shostakovich and emulates the Russian master's ability to combine the tragic and the bizarre within one framework. Once the listener has penetrated the rather forbidding outer shell of this work, the rewards are great. Ma and Zinman obviously agree on the music's stature, for this is a compelling performance.

Barber. Essays for orchestra — No. 1, Op. 12; No. 2, Op. 17; No. 3, Op. 47.
Ives. Symphony No. 1. **Detroit Symphony Orchestra/Neeme Järvi.** Chandos CHAN9053. Recorded in 1991.

lh 10m DDD 3/92

This issue comes with a booklet celebrating Neeme Järvi's 100th disc for Chandos and a remarkable joint achievement by this conductor and company. Järvi's wide-ranging sympathies are proved yet again in the music of these two American composers, but there is a paradox here in that it is the innovator Ives who is the more conventional and the conservative Barber who challenges the ear. The explanation is that Ives's First Symphony is a graduation work from his years at Yale University, representing a compromise between his natural boldness and the discipline that he grudgingly accepted from his teacher Horatio Parker. The result is romantically expansive, often fascinating and occasionally beautiful, with influences including Brahms and Dvořák (there are echoes of the *New World* Symphony in the slow movement) but also a bold homespun element in places suggesting the Ivesian innovations that were yet to come. Samuel Barber seemed unhappy with the symphony as a form, writing a one-movement First Symphony in 1936 and eventually destroying all but one movement of his wartime Second (1944). Instead he wrote three impressive *Essays for orchestra* that have been called "surrogate symphonies" and of which No. 3 was his final work before his death. Each has a sequence of moods and tempos, the *First Essay* being partly elegiac (recalling his *Adagio for Strings*), the Second having some vigorously busy music and the Third being the most enigmatic. While none of these works sound especially American, the performances are convincing and the recording offers rich sound.

NEW REVIEW
Barber. Adagio for Strings, Op. 11.
Janáček (arr. Tognetti). String Quartet No. 1, "Kreutzer Sonata".
Walton. Sonata for Strings. **Australian Chamber Orchestra/Richard Tognetti.** Sony Classical SK48252. Recorded in 1991.

55m DDD 8/92

Three compelling and atmospheric essays for string orchestra, all of them outgrowths of string quartet originals — the Barber *Adagio* from his Quartet, Op. 11, the Janáček from his First Quartet (*Kreutzer Sonata*) and the Walton *Sonata* from his Quartet of 1947. That Barber's *Adagio* was part of a structured original hardly seems to matter, so popular has it become as a single movement. Yet if ever a sustained musical climax cried out for full-bodied augmentation, this is surely it — and its effective use in the films *Platoon* and *The Elephant Man* confirms it as one of the century's most enduring 'pop' classics. The beauty of Richard Tognetti's arrangement of the Janáček is in its obvious respect for the precise nature of its source. Rather than merely flesh out existing textures, Tognetti contrasts *tutti* and *concertante* (full band and soloists) and in doing so achieves a world of variegated tonal colours. Of course, he's prompted by the constantly shifting hues of an original that seems to run the gamut of its composer's complex emotional state: the First Quartet is in fact one of many works that Janáček wrote under the influence of Kamila Stösslová, the young woman who served as a sexual *idée fixée* during his later years. He was 63 at the time, she 25 — and the full impact of his infatuation burns from every bar. The title, by the way, mirrors a Tolstoy novel that roughly approximates the theme of Janáček's own inner turmoil. Walton himself was responsible for the transcription of his 1947 Quartet (a venture undertaken at the suggestion of Sir Neville Marriner) and he too succeeds in presenting something new without betraying the original's best qualities. It's a beautiful piece, wistful and restless in the first movement, mercurial in the *Scherzo* and with one of Walton's inimitably lyrical slow movements at its core. All three works are very well played and richly recorded.

Barber. Adagio for Strings, Op. 11.
Copland. Appalachian Spring — suite.
Gershwin. Rhapsody in Blue. **Los Angeles Philharmonic Orchestra/Leonard Bernstein** (pf). DG 431 048-2GBE. Recorded at a performance in Davies Symphony Hall, San Francisco in July 1982.

54m DDD

This disc shows Bernstein on home ground: American music played by an American orchestra. It captures, too, the most enduring elements of his music-making — the ryhthmic vitality and the sense of poise that he could so winningly embrace in music with a strong melody. This is Bernstein at his most engaging, his piano-playing as impressive as always, his feeling for the ebb and flow of this most elusive music beautifully judged. The 'big-band' version of the piece is used but with such a vital response from soloist and orchestra alike — the sense of real interplay between the musicians is almost palpable. Copland's lyrical *Appalachian Spring* is gloriously unfolded, the tempos are nicely judged and the Los Angeles orchestra clearly revels in the melodic weave of the piece. Similarly, the serene *Adagio* by Barber finds the strings rapt, unhurried and poised, the tempo dangerously slow but carried along by the commitment of the inspirational conductor. The live recordings are well handled, with virtually no evidence of the audience to be heard.

Barber. Symphony No. 1, Op. 9. The School for Scandal Overture, Op. 5.
Beach. Symphony in E minor, Op. 32, "Gaelic". **Detroit Symphony Orchestra/Neeme Järvi.** Chandos CHAN8958. Recorded in 1991.

lh l2m DDD l0/9l

Amy Beach (or Mrs H.H.A. Beach, as she was known professionally in her lifetime) was born in Henniker, New Hampshire in 1867. By all accounts she was a prodigiously talented youngster — she could sing 40 tunes by the age of two, and at four she was composing small pieces for the piano. She made her 'official' début as a pianist at the age of 16 playing Chopin's Rondo in E flat and Moscheles's G minor Piano Concerto, but after her marriage to a noted Boston surgeon in 1885 she abandoned her concert career and devoted her time exclusively to composition. The *Gaelic* Symphony (her only work in the genre) dates from 1896. Like Dvořák's *New World* Symphony, which had received its American première just a few years earlier, it draws its inspiration from folk material; though Beach's sources are drawn not from native America but rather from her Gaelic forebears. The writing reveals a remarkable degree of craftsmanship and maturity, and although the music contains perhaps more imitation than originality (Brahms, Tchaikovsky and Parry spring to mind) there is nevertheless plenty of enjoyment to be had from this fresh and engaging work. The music of Samuel Barber needs less introduction, though his First Symphony makes a welcome return after a protracted absence from the catalogue. Slatkin's account of the symphony might in some ways be more satisfactory as his orchestra seems more comfortable, and the American conductor clearly has an innate grasp of the music's style.This one-movement, highly compact work deserves to be much better known as it contains some of Barber's most invigorating and memorable material. Stylistically it finds allegiance with the post-romanticism of symphonies such as Walton's First and Howard Hanson's Second (*Romantic*). The disc also includes Barber's equally engaging Overture to *The School for Scandal*. Committed performances.

Additional recommendations ...
No. 1. Adagio for Strings. Essays for Orchestra, Opp. 12 and 17. Music for a scene from Shelley, Op. 7. The School for Scandal Overture. **Baltimore Symphony Orchestra/David Zinman.** Argo 436 288-2ZH — .:· lh 4m DDD 1/93
No. 1[a]. Piano Concerto, Op. 38[b]. Souvenirs, Op. 28[c]. [bc]**John Browning** (pf); [ab]**St Louis Symphony Orchestra/Leonard Slatkin** ([c]pf). RCA Victor Red Seal RD60732 — .:· lh 10m DDD 11/91

Barber. Prayers of Kierkegaard, Op. 30. The lovers, Op. 43. **Sarah Reese** (sop); **Dale Duesing** (bar); **Chicago Symphony Chorus and Orchestra/Andrew Schenck.** Koch Classics International 37125-2. Texts included. Recorded live in 1991.

.:· 52m DDD 3/92 

Barber never earned the popularity of Copland or Bernstein, nor their status as great American figures. Yet one of his pieces, the *Adagio for Strings* (originally the slow movement of a string quartet) has touched people's hearts for half a century. This disc is one to win him more admirers, and he could not be in better hands than those of the late Andrew Schenck, a Barber specialist. It also reminds us that this composer was a trained singer who cared deeply about words and said that when setting them he "let the music flow". *The lovers* is a late work, commissioned in 1971 by a Philadelphia bank whose committee was at first shocked by the eroticism of these poems by Pablo Neruda. Barber's music has personality and sensual power without in any way following the atonal path laid down by the Second Viennese School, and the toughly lyrical baritone soloist Dale Duesing is perfectly suited to these poems of Chilean peasant love and receives excellent support from the chorus and orchestra. *Prayers of Kierkegaard* is earlier (1954) and also comes across strongly, but its passions are of a more spiritual kind and Barber himself called this Danish philosopher "an exciting and enigmatic intellectual force". It begins with a plea for peace that soon rises to a fervent climax, and goes on to maintain considerable emotional force. Both of these works are beautifully laid out for the voices and orchestra. The live Chicago recording could ideally be better balanced, and there is a little audience noise, but it is effective and this issue should not be missed if you care about the music of this fine twentieth-century composer who dared to go his own way.

Barber. Piano Sonata in E flat major, Op. 26. Excursions, Op. 20.
Ives. Piano Sonata No. 1. **Joanna MacGregor** (pf). Collins Classics 1107-2.

.:· lh 8m DDD 3/92 

There are other fine recordings of the Barber Sonata, including Peter Lawson's which is reviewed in the "Collections" section of this book (refer to the Index to Reviews). It is a work which has attracted well-equipped players right from the start. MacGregor stands up well, but the greater attraction is her Ives Sonata No. 1, which ought to sweep the board on both sides of the Atlantic now. The work, which waited 45 years for a first performance, is just as characteristic of Ives as the Second Sonata (refer to the Index to Reviews), and in some ways its mixture of hymn-tunes and ragtime makes a more coherent impact. The ragtime aspects are based on what Ives heard improvised or played that way himself: he went to a lot of trouble to catch the difference between playing the dots and swinging away. This informality is superbly caught by MacGregor, who risks all in truly Ivesian fashion in one or two places. She thoroughly understands the driving rhythms as well as the transcendental calm. By comparison anything by Barber is more polite. But the four *Excursions* come off well and show a different approach to popular idioms — more that of a tourist than an insider. But both composers know how to make use of sonata structure in these two American classics, vividly played and recorded.

Additional recommendation ...
Piano Sonata. **Copland.** *Piano Sonata.* **Ives.** *Three-page Sonata (ed. Cowell).* **Carter.** *Piano Sonata.* **Peter Lawson.** Virgin Classics VC7 59008-2 — ·· lh 16m DDD 5/91

Barber. SONGS. **Roberta Alexander** (sop); **Tan Crone** (pf). Etcetera KTC1055. Texts included. Three Songs, Op. 2. Three Songs, Op. 10. Four Songs, Op. 13. Two Songs, Op. 18. Nuvoletta, Op. 25. Hermit Songs, Op. 29. Despite and Still, Op. 41.

··· lh lm DDD 9/88

If Samuel Barber had not been a composer he could have had a very respectable career as a baritone; he made a beautiful recording of his own *Dover Beach* many years ago. He also confessed to having "sometimes thought that I'd rather write words than music". Good qualifications for writing songs, both of them; so is his individual and discriminating taste in poetry. The average length of the ten *Hermit Songs* (settings of medieval Irish texts) is less than two minutes, but they often distil big images from tiny ones: the ringing of a little bell amid silence evokes a longing for the solitary life and the tranquil solitude of death, the cry of a bird is the starting point for a pitying description of the crucified Christ and his mother, a lazy rocking in the piano serves as metaphor for the simple contentment of an old scholar-monk and the purring of his companionable cat. Simplicity of imagery plus economy of means equals intensity of utterance is often Barber's equation, but there is humour here as well (lines from James Joyce's *Finnegan's Wake* are set as a brilliant, slightly dizzy waltz-song) and suave melodiousness ("Sure on this shining night") and bold, almost operatic declamation ("I hear an army"). There is scarcely a weak song among them. They need a singer with quite a range, and Roberta Alexander has it; her bright, vibrant but precise singing is as sensitive to words as Barber himself, and she never allows her expressiveness to break the poised elegance of his lines. Her pianist is excellent and the recording is clean, though rather close.

NEW REVIEW

Barber. A HAND OF BRIDGE[ae]. VOCAL AND ORCHESTRAL WORKS. [a]**Patricia Neway** (sop) Geraldine; [a]**Eunice Alberts** (contr) Sally; [a]**William Lewis** (ten) Bill; [a]**Philip Maero** (bar) David; [b]**Robert De Cormier Chorale;** [c]**Washington DC Cathedral Choir;** [d]**Zagreb Soloists/Antonio Janigro;** [e]**Symphony of the Air, New York/Vladimir Golschmann.** Vanguard Classics 084016 71. Texts included.
Second Essay for orchestra, Op. 17[e]. Music for a Scene from Shelley, Op. 7[e]. A Stopwatch and an Ordnance map, Op. 15[be]. Serenade for string orchestra, Op. 1[e] (all from VSL11019, 8/68). Adagio for Strings, Op. 11[d] (VSD2126, 4/72). Let Down the Bars, O Death![c] (new to UK).

·· 52m ADD 8/92

Anyone wishing to explore some lesser known works by this still under-rated composer will find plenty to enjoy in Vladimir Golschmann's splendid collection, augmented here with more recent recordings of the inevitable *Adagio* and a poignant Emily Dickinson setting, *Let Down the Bars, O Death!*. Much of the Golschmann material, taped over 30 years ago in smooth, slightly exaggerated stereo, is not otherwise available. *A Stopwatch and an Ordnance map* sets out Stephen Spender's text for the unusual combination of male chorus, kettledrums and brass, deliberately appropriating B-movie adventure clichés in a timely lament for the fallen *circa* 1940. *A Hand of Bridge* is unusual too, a sort of pocket (soap?) opera a little like Leonard Bernstein's *Trouble in Tahiti* seen throughout the wrong end of the telescope. Barber scrutinizes the bourgeoisie of 1950s America with a similar ironic edge and perhaps a more delicate sensibility. Of the orchestral works, only the very early *Serenade*, written when the composer was still in his teens, seems of primarily academic interest. There are helpful notes and full texts.

Barber. VOCAL WORKS. Various artists. CBS Masterworks Portrait CD46727. Knoxville: Summer of 1915 (Eleanor Steber, sop; Dumbarton Oaks Orchestra/William Strickland. New to UK. Recorded in mono in 1950). Dover Beach, Op. 3 (Dietrich Fischer-Dieskau, bar; Juilliard Quartet — Robert Mann, Earl Carlyss, vns; Raphael Hillyer, va; Claus Adam vc. From 72687, 11/68). Hermit Songs, Op. 29 (Leontyne Price, sop; Samuel Barber, pf. New to UK. Recorded in mono in 1954). Andromache's Farewell, Op. 39 (Martina Arroyo, sop; New York Philharmonic Orchestra/Thomas Schippers. New to UK. 1963).

5lm AAD 10/91 

This is a fascinating collection of Barber performances from the CBS vaults. Eleanor Steber, a familiar figure at New York's Metropolitan Opera, commissioned *Knoxville*, so her authoritative account, made as early as 1950, has special status. Her reading of this enchanting music is fresh and straightforward: *Knoxville* is, after all, supposed to be sung by a child, or rather by a man reliving his childhood so intensely that the child's voice speaks through him. *Dover Beach*, a much earlier work, is no less exquisite. Here, Fischer-Dieskau sings most beautifully, but Matthew Arnold's words are less well-served — and there are no texts provided. The high point of the anthology comes with Leontyne Price's moving account of the *Hermit Songs*. She premièred the cycle with the composer in 1953, taking time out from the celebrated run of *Porgy and Bess* which made her name. Barber again accompanies, and Price's lovely timbre and faultless diction are well preserved in the 1954 recording. Martina Arroyo is at *her* very best in *Andromache's Farewell*, a highly dramatic scene based on Euripides. Unfortunately, the music is reminiscent of a Hollywood sand and sandal epic, with Thomas Schippers and the New York Philharmonic working themselves up into a rare old sweat. All the same, this is an attractive way of exploring unfamiliar Barber, never less than decently recorded and often quite superbly performed. Robert Cushman's insert-notes are helpful too.

Further listening ...

Piano Concerto[a]. Medea — Media's Meditation and Dance of Vengeance. Adagio for Strings. [a]**Tedd Joselson** (pf); **London Symphony Orchestra/Andrew Schenck.** ASV CDDCA534 (6/86).

Agnus Dei, Op. 11. ***Bernstein.*** Chichester Psalms[a]. ***Copland.*** In the Beginning[b]. Four Motets. [a]**Dominic Martelli** (treb); [b]**Catherine Denley** (mez); [a]**Rachel Masters** (hp); [a]**Gary Kettel** (perc); [a]**Thomas Trotter** (org); **Corydon Singers/Matthew Best.** Hyperion CDA66219 (9/87).

John Barry

British 1933-

Suggested listening ...

MOVIOLA — *Film Scores:* Out of Africa. Midnight Cowboy. Body Heat. Somewhere in Time. Mary, Queen of Scots; Born Free. Dances with Wolves. Chaplin. The Cotton Club. Walkabout. Frances. On Her Majesty's Secret Service — We have all the time in the world. Moviola. **Royal Philharmonic Orchestra/John Barry.** Epic 472 490-2.

Lionel Bart

British 1930-

Suggested listening ...

OLIVER! **Soloists; National Symphony Orchestra/John Owen Edwards.** TER Classics CDTER1184 (10/92).

Key to Symbols

Price	Quantity/ availability	Timing	Mode	Review date
•••	② ②	1h 23m	DDD	6/88

Bargains — £

Quality of performance — 9_P

Quality of Sound — 9_S

Basic library — B

Discs worth exploring — ?

Period performance — (quill)

Caveat emptor — ▲

Béla Bartók

Hungarian 1881-1945

Bartók. Piano Concertos — No. 1, Sz83; No. 2, Sz95. **Maurizio Pollini** (pf); **Chicago Symphony Orchestra/Claudio Abbado.** DG 415 371-2GH. From 2530 901 (7/79).

••• 52m ADD 9/86 

The First Piano Concerto of 1926 was one of the first fruits of a new-found confidence in Bartók — a totally serious, uncompromisingly aggressive assertion that the future could be faced and shaped by human will-power. It is tough listening, and Bartók admitted as much, promising that the Second Concerto would be easier to play and to take in. Certainly the themes here tend to be a little more folk-like, but in no other respect could Bartók be said to have realized that aim. The pianist has to cope with one of the most fearsome cadenzas in the repertoire on top of an unrelenting complexity of argument which draws the orchestra into its maelstrom. Not surprisingly these concertos can sound dauntingly abstract and nothing more. Pollini's pianistic mastery is so complete, however, that he can find all sorts of shades and perspectives which turn apparently abstract geometry into a three-dimensional experience. Abbado and the Chicago orchestra are the perfect partners for his diamond-edged virtuosity, and the faithful recording provides an admirable vehicle for communication.

Additional recommendations ...

Nos. 1 and 2. Music for strings, percussion and celesta. Rhapsody for piano and orchestra. Scherzo for piano and orchestra. **Zoltán Kocsis** (pf); **Budapest Festival Orchestra/Iván Fischer.** Philips 416 831-2PH3 — ••• ③ 2h 37m 1/88 B

Nos. 1 and 2. No. 3, Sz119[a]. **Stephen Kovacevich** (pf); [a]**London Symphony Orchestra; BBC Symphony Orchestra/Sir Colin Davis.** Philips 426 660-2PSL — •• 1h 17m ADD 5/91 B

Bartók. Violin Concertos — No. 1, Sz36[a]; No. 2, Sz112[b]. **Kyung-Wha Chung** (vn); [a]**Chicago Symphony Orchestra;** [b]**London Philharmonic Orchestra/Sir Georg Solti.** Decca Ovation 425 015-2DM. Item marked [a] from 411 804-1DH (10/84), [b] SXL6212 (4/78).

••• 59m ADD/DDD 2/91 

Long gone are the times when Bartók was thought of as an arch-modernist incapable of writing a melody and the young Yehudi Menuhin was considered daring in championing his Violin Concerto. Today this work is listed as his second in this form, but four decades ago it stood alone because the composer had suppressed an earlier one dating from 1908, or more precisely reshaped it into another work called *Two Portraits*. When this earlier piece was finally published in its original form some 30 years ago, it became his First Concerto and the more familiar one of 1938 his Second. The First was inspired by a beloved woman friend, but it does not by any means wear its heart on its sleeve, being a complex and edgy work to which Kyung-Wha Chung brings a passionate lyricism. Her conductor Sir Georg Solti is the composer's compatriot and was actually his piano pupil as well, so that he too knows how to make this music breathe and sing. Chung and Solti are equally at home in the more obviously colourful and dramatic Second Concerto, giving it all the range, expressive force and occasional violence, driving momentum and sheer Hungarian charm that one could desire. The London Philharmonic Orchestra play as if inspired and the recordings (in two locations, seven years apart) are subtle yet lit with the right brilliance.

Additional recommendations ...

Nos. 1 and 2. **Nell Gotkovsky** (vn); **National Philharmonic Orchestra/Charles Gerhardt.** Pyramid PYR13486 — 1h DDD 3/87

No. 2. Sonata for solo violin, Sz117[a]. [a]**Christian Tetzlaff** (vn); **London Philharmonic Orchestra/Michael Gielen.** Virgin Classics VC7 59062-2 — 1h 3m DDD 11/91

No. 2. ***Moret.*** *En rêve.* **Anne-Sophie Mutter** (vn); **Boston Symphony Orchestra/Seiji Ozawa.** DG 431 626-2GH — 58m DDD 11/91

Bartók. ORCHESTRAL WORKS. [bc]**Géza Anda** (pf); **Berlin RIAS Symphony Orchestra/Ferenc Fricsay.** DG Dokumente 427 410-2GDO2. Item marked [a] from DGM18377 (1/58), [b] SLPM138708 (1/62), [c] SLPM138111 (5/61). Items marked [a] recorded in 1957, [b] 1960, [c] 1959.

Concerto for Orchestra, Sz116[a]. Rhapsody for piano and orchestra, Op. 1[b]. Piano Concertos — No. 1, Sz83[b]; No. 2, Sz95[c]; No. 3, Sz119[c].

② 2h 19m ADD 5/89  

This very useful compilation gathers together all of Bartók's *concertante* works for piano and orchestra as well as a simply magnificent account of the *Concerto for Orchestra*. Ferenc Fricsay was a pupil of Bartók in Hungary and the experience clearly gave him some very special insights into the composer's music. He discerns better than the majority of conductors the darker elements of the music, the subtle undertones. He phrases the music with great breadth which is perhaps his secret for capturing and sustaining a sense of atmosphere. Géza Anda, too, brings to the piano works a zest and unsophisticated directness that the music often fails to receive. Like Fricsay, Anda speaks the right language and the performances are the better for it. The Third Concerto, written as an insurance policy for his wife Ditta in the face of his inevitable death, is a very fine reading. The recordings sound well and the attractive price of these two well-filled discs makes this a set worth exploring.

Bartók. Concerto for Orchestra, Sz116[a]. Music for Strings, Percussion and Celesta, Sz106[b]. **Chicago Symphony Orchestra/Fritz Reiner.** RCA GD60175. From VICS1110 (12/65). Item marked [a] recorded in 1955, [b] 1958.

1h 5m ADD 1/90

These famous performances are by a compatriot of Bartók who was born in 1888, just seven years after the composer himself. Although they come from 1955 and 1958 respectively, the recorded sound has tremendous presence and only the lack of the fullest dynamic range and really soft sound in the *Music for Strings, Percussion and Celesta* betrays its age, along with a certain residual tape hiss. As for the performances, they have long been praised for their superb orchestral playing and above all for the sheer atmosphere that Reiner conjures up. The music itself is of monumental quality, demonstrating Bartók's stature as one of the great composers of the early twentieth century. The *Concerto for Orchestra* is the more obviously approachable work, for here the composer, in response to a commission near the end of his life, displayed a joy in writing a superbly Hungarian-sounding piece for a first-class American orchestra — incidentally, Fritz Reiner was partly responsible for Koussevitzky offering the commission and thus for the existence of the work itself. The other work, however, is no less rewarding and maybe more so, for it shows Bartók's extraordinary aural imagination — no one before or since has dared to write for this particular combination of instruments — and it, too, has a strange yet unforgettable beauty as well as an elemental strength.

Additional recommendations ...
Concerto for Orchestra. **Lutoslawski.** *Concerto for Orchestra.* **Cleveland Orchestra/Christoph von Dohnányi.** Decca 425 694-2DH — 1h 6m DDD 3/90 Ⓑ
Concerto for Orchestra[a]. Dance Suite, Sz77. Two Portraits, Sz37. Mikrokosmos — From the diary of a fly. [a]**London Symphony Orchestra; Philharmonia Hungarica/Antál Dorati.** Philips Mercury 432 017-2MM — 1h 12m ADD 11/91 Ⓑ ▲
Concerto for Orchestra[a]. The miraculous mandarin, Sz73 — suite[b]. [a]**Boston Symphony Orchestra/Rafael Kubelík;** [b]**Boston Symphony Orchestra/Seiji Ozawa.** DG 437 247-2GGA — 58m ADD 11/93 Ⓑ
Concerto for Orchestra. **Enescu.** *Romanian Rhapsodies, Op. 11 — No. 1 in A major; No. 2 in D major.* **Royal Scottish Orchestra/Neeme Järvi.** Chandos CHAN8947 — 1h 6m DDD 2/92 Ⓑ
Concerto for Orchestra. **Mussorgsky.** *Pictures at an exhibition.* **Chicago Symphony Orchestra/Sir Georg Solti.** Decca 417 754-2DM — 1h 9m DDD Ⓑ

Bartók. The wooden prince — ballet, Sz60. Hungarian sketches, Sz97. **Philharmonia Orchestra/Neeme Järvi.** Chandos CHAN8895. Recorded in 1990.

1h 6m DDD 10/91

The wooden prince is a sumptuous dance-pantomime with an unlikely story-line: a Princess finds a Prince's wooden staff more desirable than the Prince himself. In time the roles are reversed: the Princess changes her mind but now the Prince resists her, and only when she cuts off her hair does he relent and allow a happy ending. Neeme Järvi reveals the full beauty of the score — the only complaint a collector might have is that such rich beauty is not what we expect from Bartók! But though it starts with a plain chord of C major, the way it grows to a mighty climax after nearly four minutes is typically Bartókian in its power. Chandos's recording was made in the London venue of St Jude's Church and has tremendous atmosphere which is as it should be since the score is brimful of colour as well as being extremely elaborate. The Philharmonia Orchestra rise splendidly to this challenge and play most idiomatically although the work must have been unfamiliar as well as difficult. As with most ballets, the score is loosely constructed, but the music is so imaginative that it holds the attention, especially since the booklet note gives a detailed synopsis. The "Dance of the Waves" and the colossal climax near the end of the fourth (and longest) dance of the seven, where Nature herself bows to the Prince, are just two examples of the sonorous orchestral writing. The *Hungarian sketches* are Bartók's transcriptions of five short and fairly simple piano pieces (three of them written for children) which draw on Hungarian folk style and make flavoursome listening.

Additional recommendation ...
The wooden prince. Cantata profana[a]. [a]**John Aler** (ten); [a]**John Tomlinson** (bass); **Chicago Symphony** [a]**Chorus and Orchestra.** DG 435 863-2GH — 1h 13m DDD 3/93

Bartók. The miraculous mandarin, Sz73 — ballet[a].
L. Weiner. Suite on Hungarian Folk-tunes, Op. 18. [a]**London Voices; Philharmonia Orchestra/Neeme Järvi.** Chandos CHAN9029. Recorded in 1990.

1h 2m DDD 3/92 9p 9s

It is scarcely surprising that *The miraculous mandarin* failed to reach the stage for some years after it was composed, for the plot concerns three ruffians who force a girl into luring men from the street up to a shabby garret where they rob them. Bartók's music matches the savagery of the subject, with wild pounding rhythms and jagged outbursts. Järvi may not manage Abbado's precise control in the *Mandarin* (quite as miraculous as the subject matter itself), but is more flexible in the early scenes. These are slower and even more characterfully drawn, bringing, at times a welcome touch of humanity to the score. And the benefit of this holding back of tempo is felt immediately the Mandarin's passion explodes and he begins his frenzied pursuit of the girl; not one opportunity is missed to deliver the violence of the succeeding scenes (suffocation, stabbing and electrocution) with a graphic impact that renders the visual element completely unnecessary. Chandos are on hand to supply wide-screened sound that is literally stunning. Weiner's *Suite* comprises four short tone poems which draw on phonographic collections of original Hungarian folk-music. But there the parallels with his contemporary, Bartók, cease. The idiom is most definitely nineteenth rather than twentieth century, and the orchestration has a Respighian richness and colour. On this showing Järvi and the Philharmonia must surely be born, bred and proud Hungarians.

Additional recommendation ...
The miraculous mandarin[a]. *Two portraits, Sz37*[b]. ***Prokofiev.*** *Scythian Suite, Op. 20*[c]. [b]**Shlomo Mintz** (vn); [a]**Ambrosian Singers;** [ab]**London Symphony Orchestra,** [c]**Chicago Symphony Orchestra/Claudio Abbado.** DG 410 598-2GH — lh 3m ADD/DDD 6/87

Bartók. Music for Strings, Percussion and Celesta, Sz106. Divertimento, Sz113. The miraculous mandarin, Sz73 — suite. **Chicago Symphony Orchestra/Sir Georg Solti.** Decca 430 352-2DH. Recorded 1989-1990.

lh 9m DDD 5/91

Two generations ago, Bartók's *Music for Strings, Percussion and Celesta* was considered the height of modernity, and people saw eccentricity in such things as the glacial xylophone tappings on a high note at the start of the slow movement. Nowadays, the work is perfectly approachable (after all, it owes much to folk music) although still boldly imaginative. Solti takes the opening *Andante tranquillo* fast, and the recording is close and brightly lit, but we still feel some of the mystery which is so important in this composer. The conductor comes into his own in the rhythmically exciting *Allegro* that follows and in the marvellously dancelike finale, and he also brings plenty of atmosphere to the *Adagio* with its wondrously strange sounds. The *Divertimento* is gentler, at least by the standards of this composer whose music always shows nervous tension. Though one can imagine Count Dracula approaching in the inexorable slow *crescendo* of the slow movement, much of it bubbles over with melody and, as always, rhythms invigorate. Solti's gusto makes this music irresistible. *The miraculous mandarin* is the earliest and toughest music here, written in 1918-19 for a ballet with an erotic and gruesome story of a Chinese man who is lured into a prostitute's room and attacked by three male accomplices; but although in turn strangled, stabbed and hanged he cannot die until she embraces him. It makes for uncomfortable but compelling listening, not least in this gutsy performance which pulls no punches. A thrilling disc, with sound that leaps out of your speakers.

Bartók. CHAMBER WORKS. [a]**Michael Collins** (cl); **Krysia Osostowicz** (vn); [b]**Susan Tomes** (pf). Hyperion CDA66415. Recorded in 1990.
Contrasts, Sz111[ab]. Rhapsodies — No. 1, Sz86; No. 2, Sz89[b]. Romanian folk-dances, Sz56 (arr. Székely)[b]. Sonata for solo violin, Sz117 (original version).

lh 12m DDD 4/91

Unusually for a composer who wrote so much fine chamber music Bartók was not himself a string player. But he did enjoy close artistic understanding with a succession of prominent violin virtuosos, including the Hungarians Jelly d'Arányi, Joseph Szigeti and Zoltán Székely, and, towards the end of his life, Yehudi Menuhin. It was Menuhin who commissioned the Sonata for solo violin, but Bartók died before he could hear him play it — Menuhin was unhappy with the occasional passages in quarter-tones and the composer had reserved judgement on his proposal to omit them. It was Menuhin's edition which was later printed and which has been most often played and recorded; but Krysia Osostowicz returns to the original and, more importantly, plays the whole work with intelligence, imaginative flair and consummate skill. The Sonata is the most substantial work on this disc, but the rest of the programme is no less thoughtfully prepared or idiomatically delivered. There is the additional attraction of an extremely well balanced and natural-sounding recording. As a complement to the string quartets, which are at the very heart of Bartók's output, this is a most recommendable disc.

Bartók. STRING QUARTETS. **Emerson Quartet** (Eugene Drucker, Philip Setzer, vns; Lawrence Dutton, va; David Finckel, vc). DG 423 657-2GH2. Recorded in 1988.

No. 1 in A minor; No. 2 in A minor; No. 3 in C sharp minor; No. 4 in C major; No. 5 in B flat major; No. 6 in D major.

② 2h 29m DDD 12/88

It has long been recognized that this series of string quartets written over three decades has been one of the major contributions to Western music. The Emerson Quartet does not play them all the same way, for as its first violinist Eugene Drucker rightly says, "each has its own style". The Quartet has a fine unanimity and is equally good in the tense melodic lines and harmony of slower movements and the infectious rhythmic drive of quicker ones; and it also copes extremely well with Bartók's frequent changes of dynamics, texture and tempo. Here is not only striking virtuosity — to be convinced, listen to the wildly exciting *Allegro molto* finale of No. 4 — and yet great subtlety too. The recording is excellent, with good detail yet without harshness. Where most Bartók cycles take three discs, here 149 minutes are accommodated on two CDs. One readily concurs with the critic who called this "one of the most exciting chamber music recordings of recent years".

Additional recommendations ...
Nos. 1-6. **Végh Quartet.** Astrée Auvidis. *Nos. 1 and 2:* E7717. *Nos. 3 and 4:* E7718. *Nos. 5 and 6:* E7719 — ③ 57m 38m 60m DDD 3/87
Nos. 3-5. **Chilingirian Quartet.** Chandos CHAN8634 — 1h 8m DDD 6/89

NEW REVIEW

Bartók. Sonata for Two Pianos and Percussion, Sz110[a]. Suite for Two Pianos, Sz115a. **Jean-François Heisser, Georges Pludermacher** (pfs); **[a]Guy-Joel Cipriani, [a]Gérard Perotin** (perc). Erato 2292-45861-2. Recorded in 1992.

58m DDD 4/93

Composed in 1937, Bartók's Sonata for Two Pianos and Percussion is comparatively unusual among twentieth-century classics in that it appeals equally to the general concert audience (by its rhythmic excitement and range of character) and to the specialist musician (by the intricacy of its compositional processes). But the unprecedented scoring which makes its effect so special also creates severe problems for its interpreters, and it is rare to find four players who all feel the rhythmic interplay in precisely the same way. The Frenchmen on this Erato disc are perfectly attuned to one another, however. They are never tempted to go for unnecessary cheap effects, and the recording handles all the tricky balance problems admirably. The coupling is Bartók's 1941 arrangement of an orchestral suite composed in 1905-7, when it represented a turning-point in his output by virtue of its "freshening up of art music with elements of peasant art" — another fine performance and close, but not overbearing recorded sound.

Bartók. 44 Duos for two violins, Sz98. **Sándor Végh, Albert Lysy** (vns). Astrée Auvidis E7720. From AS70 (4/82).

50m AAD 3/88

Sándor Végh and Albert Lysy offer an unquestionably definitive version of Bartók's 44 *Duos* for two violins on this Astrée CD, which originally appeared over 20 years ago when complete performances of this set would have attracted very little interest from the majority of collectors. Today, however, Bartók's ostensibly educational miniatures are recognized as musically significant too, given that he devoted so much of his life to collecting and editing traditional central European folk-music, examples of which figure prominently here. Végh and Lysy do not follow Bartók's original sequence, and add endless variety and interest by juxtaposing differing idioms, but the composer himself sanctioned regrouping for concert performances and on this occasion the ear is constantly stimulated and captivated by the diversity and range of expression drawn from two string voices. Végh knew the composer personally, and so this performance has special historical significance; he and Lysy are ideally matched and their unique account of *Mikrokosmos* for violinists is unlikely to be surpassed as an enriching musical experience. The recorded sound is clear and well balanced, and the players are heard in an ideal acoustic setting.

NEW REVIEW

Bartók. SONGS. **Júlia Hamari** (contr); **[a]Ilona Prunyi** (pf); **[b]Hungarian State Orchestra/János Kovacs.** Hungaroton HCD31535. Texts and translations included. Recorded in 1992.

Five Songs, Sz61[a]. Five Songs, Sz63[a]. Hungarian Folksongs, Sz64 — Black is the earth; My God, my God; Wives, let me be one of your company; So much sorrow; If I climb the rocky mountains. Five Songs, Sz61 (orch. Kodály)[b]. Five Hungarian Folksongs, Sz101[b].

lh 7m DDD

Although often thought of as a fairly aggressive 'contemporary' composer whose heart was ruled by his head, Béla Bartók was in fact a passionate, deeply emotional individual with a romantic disposition towards women, especially young ones. His works are full of erotic references, conveyed either via written texts (the Op. 15 songs included on the present disc being a fair case in point) or through the textures and rhythms of his music — one thinks of *The miraculous mandarin* ballet, or the opera *Bluebeard's Castle,* or, indeed, the purely orchestral *Dance Suite.* The songs programmed by Júlia Hamari include both versions of Op. 15 (the texts are by a young recipient of Bartók's considerable affections) — that is, the originals (for voice and piano), and an orchestral setting, made many years after the songs were composed by Bartók's long-term friend and musical collaborator, Zoltán Kodály. Readers allergic to the harsh realities of Bartók's bare, uncompromising piano writing will probably enjoy the softer contours of Kodály's almost impressionistic reworkings, although (to be fair) some of the songs do retain their hot-house atmosphere. The settings of poems by Endre Ady are also deeply atmospheric, while the varied folk-song arrangements provide an effective contrast with the rest of the prgramme. Júlia Hamari sings with the sort of impassioned sincerity that Bartók's more perceptive contemporaries conveyed (one thinks, in particular, of the great Hungarian mezzo-soprano Maria Basilides), while her pianist, Ilona Prunyi, has an authentic feel for this challenging yet rewarding idiom. The Hungarian State Orchestra copes reasonably well with the orchestral items, although a more precise tang might have enlivened the proceedings, and the strings occasionally sound rather feeble. Hungaroton's recordings are clear and warm-textured, and the CD comes complete with full texts and translations, as well as usefully comprehensive annotations.

Further listening ...

For Children, Sz42 — 85 pieces for piano. Mikrokosmos, Sz107 — progressive pieces for piano in six volumes (complete, Books 1-6). **Dezsö Ránki** (pf). Teldec 9031-76139-2 (3-CD set), (10/92).

DUKE BLUEBEARD'S CASTLE. **Soloists; Hungarian State Opera Chorus and Orchestra/János Ferencsik.** Hungaroton HCD12254 (7/86).

Sir Arnold Bax

British 1883-1953

Bax. ORCHESTRAL WORKS. **[a]Lydia Mordkovitch** (vn); **London Philharmonic Orchestra/Bryden Thomson.** Chandos CHAN9003. Recorded in 1991.

Violin Concerto. Legend. Romantic Overture. Golden Eagle — incidental music.

lh 15m DDD 4/92

The rehabilitation of Bax's music after long neglect has been largely due to the zeal of the record companies, not least Chandos and the late Bryden Thomson, who brought to it commitment and insight. Now that most of his major works are available on disc, new issues can be bolder in programming and much of the music here will be unfamiliar save to specialists. The Violin Concerto is a substantial work (lasting 35 minutes) with a chequered history. It was written in 1937-38 for Jascha Heifetz, but he did not like it enough to perform and it did not reach the public until the British violinist Eda Kersey played it in

1943. When she died, aged 40, a few months later, the work was largely forgotten. One can see what might have worried Heifetz, for Bax does not always place the soloist centre stage and virtuosity is in short supply. But there are many lovely things, such as the Celtic-sounding melody in the slower middle part (called "Ballad") of the first movement. Lydia Mordkovitch's playing here is not only beautiful but gives us some idea of how Heifetz himself might have performed the work. Not all the music is equally inspired, but this concerto is a must for Bax enthusiasts. The other pieces are also worth getting to know. The somewhat Sibelian *Legend* (1943) is music intended to evoke "the tales of some northern land"; while the *Romantic Overture* (1926) was written in homage to Delius. The *Golden Eagle* music was devised for a play about Mary, Queen of Scots, by Clifford Bax, the composer's brother, and has a pleasant period flavour. The fine recording copes well with Bax's characteristically dense scoring.

NEW REVIEW

Bax. On the sea-shore (ed./orch. Parlett).
Bridge. The Sea.
Britten. PETER GRIMES — Four Sea Interludes; Passacaglia. **Ulster Orchestra/Vernon Handley.** Chandos CHAN8473.

52m DDD 3/87

One of Vernon Handley's finest recorded achievements to date, and certainly the pinnacle of all his Chandos collaborations with the Ulster Orchestra. As the ravishing string cantilena at the start of "Dawn" (the first of Britten's *Four Sea Interludes*) readily shows, the orchestral playing in Belfast combines telling refinement with the most sensitive feeling for atmosphere. Indeed, Handley's conception is one of the most evocative and deeply-felt renderings of this magical score we have yet encountered, and the Ulster Hall recording offers sound of truly demonstration standard, with textures superbly sumptuous yet well-defined. The powerful *Grimes* "Passacaglia" is also included here (a most welcome addition), whilst the windswept sonorities of Graham Parlett's uncannily authentic realization of Sir Arnold Bax's *On the sea-shore* (a seven-minute essay derived from sketches for an operatic project on the subject of the Irish heroine, Deirdre) resonate in the mind for long afterwards. But the highlight of this maritime collection comes in the shape of Frank Bridge's gorgeous suite from 1911, *The Sea*. The ten-year-old Benjamin Britten was "knocked sideways" by this ravishing, iridescently orchestrated score when he heard it at the 1924 Norwich Festival, and Bridge was subsequently to become Britten's most influential mentor. Sir Charles Groves's 1975 RLPO account has given good service over the years, but Handley's is in every way superior — a glowing, supremely affectionate rendering, superlatively well engineered.

NEW REVIEW

Bax. TONE POEMS. **London Philharmonic Orchestra/Sir Adrian Boult.** Lyrita SRCD231. Items marked [a] from SRCS62 (10/72), [b] SRCS37 (10/68).
Northern Ballad No. 1[a]. Mediterranean[a]. The Garden of Fand[a]. Tintagel[a]. November Woods[b].

lh 2m ADD 9/92 

The highlight of this disc, which brings together all of Sir Adrian Boult's Bax recordings for Lyrita, has to be without doubt the performance of the symphonic poem, *November Woods*. Beautifully paced, superbly balanced, and full of atmosphere and magical shimmer it must surely rank amongst the finest recordings of Bax on disc. The stirring, outer sections are here exquisitely drawn, successfully capturing not only Bax's marvellously atmospheric evocation of a windswept autumnal day, but perhaps also something of the emotional turmoil that Bax was experiencing at the time of composition (the break-up of his marrige and his love-affair with pianist Harriet Cohen). The more familiar tone-poems, *Tintagel* and the sumptuous *The Garden of Fand* also receive warm and suitably romantically charged performances (though *Fand* is more objectively portrayed here than in most readings), and in the later *Northern Ballad* No. 1 (1927) Boult brings out particularly well the chillier, darker side of the composer's creativity. The London Philharmonic Orchestra (particularly noted for their performances of Bax's music) are in fine fettle here and the recordings, which date from 1968 and 1972, still sound exceptionally fresh and vital. A classic disc.

Additional recommendation ...
November Woods. The Happy Forest. The Garden of Fand. Summer Music. **Ulster Orchestra/Bryden Thomson.** Chandos CHAN8307 — 57m DDD 1/84

NEW REVIEW

Bax. Symphonies — No. 1 in E flat major[a]; No. 7[b]. **London Philharmonic Orchestra/[a]Myer Fredman, [b]Raymond Leppard.** Lyrita SRCD232. Item marked [a] from SRCS53 (8/71), [b] SRCS83 (11/75).

1h 18m ADD 12/92

Few English composers have expressed such intense and fiercely passionate emotions as Bax has in the first two movements of his First Symphony. Such rage and grief as can be found there seem to suggest a psycho-drama being played out, and when we learn that at the time of its composition (1921) Bax may still have been coming to terms with the aftermath of the Great War, the loss of friends in the Easter Rising in Ireland and the irretrievable breakdown of his marriage, it is tempting to imagine that the symphony is indeed exercising some kind of personal exorcism on these events. Bax himself, however, was always reluctant to admit the existence of such a 'programme' behind the symphony, and in many ways he was probably right to do so. Whatever personal experiences Bax had poured into it, the end result is unquestionably a powerful, cogent symphony of universal appeal. The Seventh and last of Bax's symphonies makes an intelligent and well contrasted coupling. The first movement, though not without tension and some storm tossed passages (very much a Baxian seascape this) has a prevailing mood of hope and expectation — as though embarking on some adventurous seaward journey to new lands, whilst the second movement finds Bax in wistful 'legendary' mood so evocative of the early tone-poems. The last movement begins by echoing the optimism of the first movement, but finally gives way, in the long and beautiful epilogue, to a mood of autumnal nostalgia and sad farewell. These are classic Lyrita recordings, with exceptionally fine performances from Fredman and Leppard and superb digital transfers.

Bax. Symphony No. 3 in C major. Four Orchestral Sketches — Dance of Wild Irravel. Paean. **London Philharmonic Orchestra/Bryden Thomson.** Chandos CHAN8454.

59m DDD 12/86

Bax's Third Symphony has a long and gravely beautiful epilogue, one of the most magical things he ever wrote: a noble processional with a disturbing, motionless glitter at its centre and, just before the very end, a sudden bitter chill. It is pure Bax, and will haunt you for days. We may associate some of the Symphony with the lonely sands and the shining sea of Morar in Invernessshire (where the work was written), the impassioned string music that rises from that sea in the centre of the slow movement with deep emotion, the war-like dance of the finale with conflict or war and the frequent violent intercuttings of lyricism and darkness with what we know about Bax's temperament. But it is harder to explain in programmatic terms why lyric can become dark or vigour become brooding within startlingly few bars, why that epilogue seems so inevitable, why the Symphony for all its wild juxtapositions does not sound like a random sequence of vivid memories and passionate exclamations. That it is a real symphony after all, powered by purely musical imperatives, is suggested by this finely paced and tautly controlled performance, one of the finest in Thomson's Bax cycle. The enjoyable racket of *Paean* and the glittering colour of *Irravel* respond no less gratefully to the sumptuousness of the recording.

Additional recommendation ...
Symphony No. 3. ***Ireland.*** *These Things Shall Be. The Forgotten Rite. April.* **Parry Jones** (ten); **John Ireland** (pf); **Hallé Choir and Orchestra/Sir John Barbirolli.** EMI Great Recordings of the Century mono CDH7 63910-2 — 1h 14m ADD 4/92 ▲

Bax. Symphony No. 4. Tintagel — tone-poem. **Ulster Orchestra/Bryden Thomson.** Chandos CHAN8312. From ABRD1091 (1/84).

57m DDD 8/84

Bax's Fourth Symphony is less well regarded than most of his others, yet after several hearings it is still deeply affecting. The opening *Allegro moderato* movement has a dark, brooding eloquence typical of the composer, but it is well-argued and coherent in form. There follows a *Lento* movement, full of sad passion and poetry, and then the mood lightens a little in the last movement with a defiant *Allegro*, sub-titled *Tempo di marcia trionfale*. Thomson directs a performance which is lucid, extremely well played by the orchestra, and objective in style. The more familiar *Tintagel* is from an earlier, more rhapsodic phase of Bax's development. It portrays not only the Cornish seascape but also more intimate feelings arising from a romantic relationship. Here Thomson responds more to the ardent romanticism of the score. Both works are written for a very large orchestra and benefit from an outstanding recording which reproduces the heaviest passages with richness as well as clarity.

Bax. Oboe Quintet.
Bliss. Oboe Quintet.
Britten. Phantasy for oboe quartet, Op. 2. **Pamela Woods** (ob); **Audubon Quartet** (David Ehrlich, David Salness, vns; Doris Lederer, va; Thomas Shaw, vc). Telarc CD80205. Recorded in 1988.

55m DDD 10/89

The wealth of British chamber music composed during the first half of this century is now enjoying a richly-deserved boom, with the release of a number of first-class discs that revitalize pieces neglected for over 60 years. This disc is a prime example, effectively coupling works from the 1920s and early 1930s in deliciously idiomatic performances from these American players. The three-movement Bax Quintet dates from the time of his First Symphony and finds him in fine humour, characteristically infiltrating his rhapsodic style with Irish idioms and ending up with a spirited jig. The Bliss, composed in response to a Coolidge commission, still has much of the flame of adventure and innovation that was a feature of his early music, but which tended to spark less frequently in his later career. The better-known *Phantasy* Quartet of Benjamin Britten, with its satisfying, one-movement arch shape, brilliantly shows a major composer at the outset of his career already displaying those main features of his genius that were to bear such marvellous fruit later. All these works are played with vibrant involvement, the rounded, open sounds of Pamela Wood's timbre set in balanced contrast with the more effulgent warmth of the Audubon Quartet. Only a touch of plumpness in the loudest sections mars an otherwise exemplary recording.

NEW REVIEW

Bax. Symphony No. 1 (orig. version). Piano Sonata No. 2. Legend. **John McCabe** (pf). Continuum CCD1045. Recorded in 1992.

1h 7m DDD 11/92 

It was Arthur Alexander and Harriet Cohen who, on hearing Bax play through his Sonata in E flat, realized that amid the volatile, virtuoso and densely harmonic writing there was indeed a symphony trying to break free. Bax took wise council and immediately set about orchestrating it (as well as completely rewriting the slow movement). The end product, his First Symphony, resulted in one of the most thrilling symphonic experiences to have emerged during the 1920s (though the symphony is still widely undervalued to this day). The original piano sonata, however, deserves to be heard; partly because in its own right it is a powerfully convincing essay, but also because it affords us an opportunity to glimpse the creative processes of its composer. What we lose in the way of orchestral detail and colour in the first movement, for example, we more than recoup through the privilege of experiencing its raw originality and its stark clarity of invention. The heroic-tragic Second Piano Sonata is cast in a single arch-like movement and is the most frequently heard of Bax's piano sonatas. Like the First Symphony, much of the musical argument centres around conflict — light and dark, tragic and heroic — and indeed the Sonata's dedicatee, Harriet Cohen, described it as "a battle between good and evil" from which 'good' emerges victorious. There is very much a feeling of the 'heroic', too, in the short but atmospheric piano piece entitled *Legend*, which remained unperformed until 16 years after Bax's death. John McCabe's excellent performances reflect not only his considerable technical and interpretative powers but also his long standing commitment to the music of Bax. Excellent recorded sound. An indispensable disc for Bax enthusiasts.

Bax. PIANO WORKS. **Eric Parkin** (pf). Chandos CHAN8732. Recorded in 1988.
Two Russian Tone Pictures — Nocturne, "May Night in the Ukraine"; Gopak, "National Dance". The Maiden with the Daffodil — Idyll. The Princess's Rose Garden — Nocturne. Apple Blossom Time. On a May Evening. O Dame get up and bake your pies — Variations on a North Country Christmas carol. Nereid. Sleepy Head. A romance. Burlesque.

59m DDD 7/90

These are ideal performances of Bax's piano music, recorded by Chandos in the Snape Maltings in very true sound. It is the third volume of Eric Parkin's series and covers mainly the years 1912 to 1916, a crucial period in the composer's life. The works on this disc were inspired by his visit to Russia at the height of a love affair, then the beginning of his long association with the pianist Harriet Cohen, and the Easter Rising in Dublin. *May Night in the Ukraine* is a nocturnal tone-poem, evoking the heat of summer in languorous, shifting harmonies, and is perhaps the finest music in the selection. Bax's first meeting with Harriet Cohen is preserved in *The Maiden with the Daffodil*, a most touching piece. His gift for suggesting a wide range of colour on the keyboard rivals that displayed in his scoring for orchestra, while in these shorter forms his tendency to sprawl is curbed. In Parkin he has a sympathetic and persuasive interpreter.

NEW REVIEW

Bax. CHORAL WORKS.
Howells. CHORAL WORKS. **Finzi Singers/Paul Spicer.** Chandos CHAN9139. Texts included. Recorded in 1991.
Bax: This worldes joie. Mater ora filium. Five Greek Folk-Songs. I sing of a maiden.
Howells: Two Madrigals. Long, long ago. The summer is coming. Take him, earth, for cherishing.

lh 3m DDD 6/93 P

Under Paul Spicer's direction and working within a rich but limited area, the Finzi Singers have given us some of the most delightful programmes on record. After Finzi himself, they have taken a special interest in the choral music of Herbert Howells, and this is the third recital in which they have paired him with one of his contemporaries (the others being Vaughan Williams and Bernard Stevens). Bax is a companion from a rather different school, and perhaps therefore more stimulating. They had much in common, notably a feeling for word-setting and for choral textures, which may be what Howells had in mind when he wrote *The summer is coming* in memory of Bax in 1965. There are long, broadly arching phrases for the sopranos, of whom Bax asked so much in his own compositions. That is one of the differences between the two: Howells is always a considerate writer for voices, whereas Bax, especially in his *Mater ora filium*, will take his singers to the top of the precipice and dare them to look down. He will sometimes risk a bold reiteration (as in *This worldes joie*), and his harmonies sometimes employ a chromaticism that is not in Howells's normal vocabulary. All but Howells's elegy on the death of President Kennedy (*Take him, earth, for cherishing*) are otherwise unrepresented in the current catalogues, and all thoroughly deserve their place.

Further listening ...

Spring Fire. Symphonic Scherzo. Northern Ballad No. 2. **Royal Philharmonic Orchestra/Vernon Handley.** Chandos CHAN8464 (9/86).

Winter Legends. Saga Fragment. **Margaret Fingerhut** (pf); **London Philharmonic Orchestra/Bryden Thomson.** Chandos CHAN8484 (2/87).

Cello Concerto[a]. Northern Ballad No. 3 — Prelude for a Solemn Occasion. Cortège. Mediterranean. Overture to a Picaresque Comedy. [a]**Raphael Wallfisch** (vc); **London Philharmonic Orchestra/Bryden Thomson.** Chandos CHAN8494 (11/87).

Enchanted Summer[a]. Walsinghame[b]. Fatherland[c]. [a]**Anne Williams-King,** [ab]**Lynore McWhirter** (sops); [bc]**Martyn Hill** (ten); **Brighton Festival Chorus; Royal Philharmonic Orchestra/Vernon Handley.** Chandos CHAN8625 (10/89).

Oliver Twist — excerpts. Malta GC — suite. The Sound Barrier — Rhapsody for Orchestra. **Royal Philharmonic Orchestra/Kenneth Alwyn.** ASV White Line CDWHL2058.

Amy Beach

American 1867-1944

NEW REVIEW

Beach. Piano Concerto in C sharp minor, Op. 45[a].
MacDowell. Piano Concerto No. 2 in D minor, Op. 23[b]. [a]**Mary Louise Boehm,** [b]**Eugene List** (pfs); **Westphalian Symphony Orchestra/Siegfried Landau.** Vox 115718-2. Item marked [a] new to UK, [b] TV34535S (3/75).

59m ADD 5/93

"The weakness of our music is in its borrowing", declared Edward MacDowell of North American music, including his own. This gifted composer, who trained in Paris and Frankfurt and made his home for some years in Germany, was doubtless partially right, and for that reason his near-contemporary Charles Ives seems a stronger figure, if at the same time a more controversial one. Yet although MacDowell's debt to Grieg and Tchaikovsky is all too evident in his Second Piano Concerto, his creative talent was such that the work deserves to survive and this committed performance by the Philadelphia-born pianist Eugene List and a German conductor and orchestra should win it friends. The recording is far from new, and frankly its quality is both boxy and edgy, but once one is caught up in the music one can forgive that. The composer himself was an excellent pianist who performed in the première, and the keyboard writing is both vivid and idiomatic. Mrs Amy Beach (née Amy Marcy Cheney in New Hampshire) was also an expert pianist and indeed took part in the American première of Brahms's Piano Quintet for which the composer rewarded her with a signed photograph. Frankly, the invention in this Concerto is a touch homespun but the work, written 14 years after MacDowell's Concerto, has distinct charm, to say nothing of the valuable quality (nowadays sometimes underrated) of sheer sincerity. This is another attractive performance, with a soloist who has successfully championed this concerto in a number of venues, and again we can willingly make allowances for the dated recording.

Ludwig van Beethoven

German 1770-1827

NEW REVIEW

Beethoven. Violin Concerto in D major, Op. 61. Two Romances — No. 2 in F major, Op. 50. **Oscar Shumsky** (vn); **Philharmonia Orchestra/Andrew Davis.** ASV Quicksilva CDQS6080. Recorded in 1988.

54m ADD 12/92 £ 9P B

Beethoven's lone Violin Concerto is generally thought of as the most 'Olympian' in the repertory and although many great violinists have recorded it, few have had the good fortune to receive the support of a wholly sympathetic conductor. And as the work is weighted equally between soloist and orchestra, any such imbalance is immediately conspicuous. Oscar Shumsky has a style of playing which harks back to the expressive worlds of Fritz Kreisler and Jascha Heifetz; in fact his handling of Kreisler's magnificent cadenzas is so innately musical that one can easily forgive a handful of minor imperfections that crop up elsewhere. Shumsky's tone is clean and his phrasing pure, yet time and again he exhibits the sort of intuitive lyricism that one usually hears only through a barrage of 78rpm surface noise. What's more, he is treated to broad, imposing orchestral support, with Andrew Davis on top form and the Philharmonia Orchestra responding to him with obvious commitment. The charming *Romance* in F minor makes an apt, if hardly generous, makeweight; but as the asking price for this CD is so low, relatively short playing time is less of a disadvantage. ASV's recording is full-bodied and sumptuous, with a securely focused solo image. Shumsky is one of the very few digital-era violinists whose rendition of the Beethoven Concerto probes as deeply as Heifetz, Kreisler and Szigeti, all of whom made their greatest recordings of it on 78s.

Additional recommendations ...

Violin Concerto. **Itzhak Perlman** (vn); **Philharmonia Orchestra/Carlo Maria Giulini.** EMI CDC7 47002-2 — 44m DDD 2/84

Violin Concerto. **Erich Gruenberg** (vn); **New Philharmonia Orchestra/Jascha Horenstein.** Chandos Premium CHAN6521 — 58m DDD 1/85

Violin Concerto[a]. ***Mendelssohn.*** *Violin Concerto in E minor, Op. 64*[b]. **Yehudi Menuhin** (vn); [a]**Philharmonia Orchestra;** [b]**Berlin Philharmonic Orchestra/Wilhelm Furtwängler.** EMI Références CDH7 69799-2 — 1h 11m ADD 6/85 ▲

Violin Concerto. ***Brahms.*** *Violin Concerto in D major, Op. 77.* **Jascha Heifetz** (vn); **Boston Symphony Orchestra/Charles Munch.** RCA RD85402 — ADD 10/87

Violin Concerto. Two Romances[b] *— No. 1 in G major, Op. 40; No. 2.* **Wolfgang Schneiderhan,** [b]**David Oistrakh** (vns); **Berlin Philharmonic Orchestra/Eugen Jochum;** [b]**Royal Philharmonic Orchestra/Sir Eugene Goossens.** DG Privilege 427 197-2GR — 1h 3m AAD 10/89 £ ▲

Violin Concerto. ***Mendelssohn.*** *Violin Concerto.* **Sir Yehudi Menuhin** (vn); **Philharmonia Orchestra, Berlin Philharmonic Orchestra/Wilhelm Furtwängler.** EMI Références mono CDH7 69799-2 — 1h 11m ADD 10/89 ▲

Violin Concerto. Two Romances. **Itzhak Perlman** (vn); **Berlin Philharmonic Orchestra/Daniel Barenboim.** EMI CDC7 49567-2 — 1h 1m DDD 11/89

Violin Concerto. Two Romances[a]. **Arthur Grumiaux** (vn); **New Philharmonia Orchestra/Alceo Galliera;** [a]**Concertgebouw Orchestra/Bernard Haitink.** Philips Concert Classics 426 064-2PCC — 57m ADD 11/89 £ ▲

Violin Concerto. Egmont, Op. 84 — Overture[a]. **Herman Krebbers** (vn); **Concertgebouw Orchestra;** [a]**London Philharmonic Orchestra/Bernard Haitink.** Philips Concert Classics 422 971-2PCC — 54m ADD 3/91 £

Violin Concerto. ***Bruch.*** *Violin Concerto No. 1 in G minor, Op. 26*[a]. **Kyung Whah Chung** (vn); **Royal Concertgebouw Orchestra;** [a]**London Philharmonic Orchestra/Klaus Tennstedt.** EMI CDC7 54072-2 — 1h 10m DDD 6/92

Violin Concerto. Piano Sonata No. 10 in G major, Op. 96[a]. [a]**Marc Neikrug** (pf); **Pinchas Zukerman** (vn); **Los Angeles Philharmonic Orchestra/Zubin Mehta.** RCA Victor 09026-61219-2 — 1h 13m DDD 11/92

Piano Concerto in D major, Op. 61 (transcribed by the composer from the Violin Concerto)[a]. *Two Romances*[b]. [a]**Daniel Barenboim** (pf); [b]**Pinchas Zukerman** (vn); [a]**English Chamber Orchestra,** [b]**London Philharmonic Orchestra/Daniel Barenboim.** DG Galleria 429 179-2GGA — 1h 1m ADD 4/90

NEW REVIEW

Beethoven. Triple Concerto in C major, Op. 56[a].

Brahms. Double Concerto in A minor, Op. 102[b]. [a]**Rudolf Serkin** (pf); [a]**Jaime Laredo,** [b]**Isaac Stern** (vns); [a]**Leslie Parnas,** [b]**Leonard Rose** (vcs); [a]**Marlboro Festival**

Orchestra/Alexander Schneider; [b]Philadelphia Orchestra/Eugene Ormandy. Sony Portrait MK44842.

lh llm ADD 11/89

Beethoven made at least one early attempt at writing a Triple Concerto, but was dissatisfied with it and directed his energies elsewhere. His mature Triple Op. 56 was composed two years later (1804) for Archduke Rudolf, violinist Carl August Seidler and cellist Anton Kraft. As to its chronology, the Triple came after the first three piano concertos, but before the last two and the Violin Concerto. It is, like them, cast in three movements: a healthily ebullient opening *Allegro*, a touching but brief *Largo*, and a rumbustious Polonaise to finish. Many commentators have complained that the Triple suffers from a paucity of distinguished musical material, but in the hands of dedicated musicians it can sound hale and hearty, a sturdy but good-humoured vehicle for collaborative musical enjoyment. Because of its instrumentation for violin, cello, piano and orchestra, many chamber music ensembles (piano trios especially) gravitate to the work as a sort of concerto-cum-chamber-music showpiece, and the Sony Portrait CD is indeed very much an intimate meeting of minds. With Serkin and Schneider the benevolent elder statesmen, and two splendid young string soloists, it generates real *frisson* between the players and sounds good-as-new in this splendid transfer. It also has the benefit of a high-quality coupling, a big, bold account of Brahms's concerto swan-song, his Double Concerto for violin, cello and orchestra, featuring Isaac Stern and Leonard Rose as its rich-toned soloists, backed by an opulent Philadelphia Orchestra, spaciously (but rather hissily) recorded.

Additional recommendations ...
Triple Concerto. Piano Sonata No. 17 in D minor, Op. 31 No. 2, "Tempest". **Sviatoslav Richter** (pf); **David Oistrakh** (vn); **Mstislav Rostropovich** (vc); **Berlin Philharmonic Orchestra/Herbert von Karajan.** EMI Studio CDM7 69032-2 — lh ADD 4/88
Triple Concerto[a]. Choral Fantasia in C minor, Op. 80[b]. **[a]Christian Funke** (vn); **[a]Jürnjakob Timm** (vc); **[a]Peter Rösel, [b]Jörg-Peter Weigle** (pfs); **[b]Leipzig Radio Chorus; Dresden Philharmonic Orchestra/Herbert Kegel.** Capriccio 10 150 — 54m DDD 9/87

Beethoven. Piano Concertos — No. 1 in C major, Op. 15[a]; No. 2 in B flat major, Op. 19[b] **Wilhelm Kempff** (pf); **Berlin Philharmonic Orchestra/Ferdinand Leitner.** DG Galleria 419 856-2GGA. Item marked [a] from SLPM138774 (6/62), [b] SLPM138775 (9/62).

lh 5m ADD 9/88

The Second Piano Concerto was in fact written before the First, and recent research suggests that an initial version of the so-called Second Concerto dates back to Beethoven's teenage years. If the Second Concerto inevitably reflects eighteenth-century classical style, it has Beethoven's familiar drive and energy and a radical use of form and technique. The First Concerto pre-dates the revolutionary *Eroica* Symphony by some eight years and still shows classical influences, but it is on a larger scale than the Second Concerto, and has greater powers of invention. Kempff's recording of these two works dates from the early 1960s, but the sound quality is pleasingly open and full-bodied, so that the soloist's pearly, immaculate tone quality is heard to good effect. Kempff and Leitner enjoy what is obviously a close rapport and their aristocratic, Olympian but poetic music-making suits both works admirably.

Additional recommendations ...
Nos. 1-5. **Steven Lubin** (fp); **Academy of Ancient Music/Christopher Hogwood.** L'Oiseau-Lyre Florilegium 421 408-2OH3 — 3 2h 44m DDD 5/88
Nos. 1-5. **Murray Perahia** (pf); **Concertgebouw Orchestra/Bernard Haitink.** CBS Masterworks CD44575. *The Gramophone Award-winning disc containing Nos. 3 and 4 are available separately and are reviewed in full below* — 3 2h 58m DDD 1/89
Nos. 1-5. **Claudio Arrau** (pf); **Staatskapelle Dresden/Sir Colin Davis.** Philips 422 149-2PH3 — 3 3h 9m DDD 1/89
Nos. 1-5. Choral Fantasia in C minor, Op. 80[a]. **Cleveland [a]Chorus and Orchestra/Vladimir Ashkenazy** (pf). Decca 421 718-2DH3 — 3 3h 19m DDD 3/89
Nos. 1-5. Choral Fantasia[a]. **Daniel Barenboim** (pf); **[a]John Alldis Choir; New Philharmonia Orchestra/Otto Klemperer.** EMI CMS7 63360-2 — 3 3h 31m ADD 3/90

Nos. 1-5. Rondos, Op. 51. **Wilhelm Kempff** (pf); **Berlin Philharmonic Orchestra/Paul van Kempen.** DG Dokumente mono 435 744-2GDO3 — ③ 3h 9m ADD 4/93 ▲
Nos. 1 and 2. **Martha Argerich** (pf); **Philharmonia/Giuseppe Sinopoli.** DG 415 682-2GH — 1h 5m DDD 9/86
Nos. 1 and 2. **Murray Perahia** (pf); **Concertgebouw Orchestra/Bernard Haitink.** CBS CD42177 — 1h 10m DDD 4/87

Beethoven. Piano Concertos — No. 3 in C minor, Op. 37; No. 4 in G major, Op. 58. **Murray Perahia** (pf); **Concertgebouw Orchestra/Bernard Haitink.** CBS Masterworks CD39814. From IM39814 (7/86).

1h 10m DDD 10/86

This is an outstanding disc, containing two of the finest Beethoven performances to appear in recent years. In both works one feels that there is no conscious striving to interpret the music, rather that Perahia is allowing it simply to flow through him — an illusion, of course, but one which he is able to sustain with almost miraculous consistency. But the honours do not belong solely to Perahia: the contributions of Haitink and the Concertgebouw cannot be praised too highly, and the extraordinary sense of rapport and shared purpose that exist between these two fine musical minds is perhaps the most impressive aspect of the performances. The recordings, made by Decca engineers, are unusually sensitive, both to the sound of the piano and to the need for an overall balance that is homogeneous and clearly detailed.

Additional recommendations ...

Vladimir Ashkenazy (pf); **Chicago Symphony Orchestra/Sir Georg Solti.** Decca Ovation 417 740-2DM — 1h 11m ADD 5/88 £ ▲
Melvyn Tan (fp); **London Classical Players/Roger Norrington.** EMI CDC7 49815-2 — 1h 5m DDD 11/89
Stephen Kovacevich (pf); **BBC Symphony Orchestra/Sir Colin Davis.** Philips Concert Classics 426 062-2PCC — 1h 9m ADD 12/89 £

Beethoven. Piano Concerto No. 5 in E flat major, Op. 73, "Emperor". **Claudio Arrau** (pf); **Staatskapelle Dresden/Sir Colin Davis.** Philips 416 215-2PH. From 416 215-1PH (4/86).

41m DDD 8/86

By the time he wrote his Fifth Concerto, Beethoven was too deaf to continue playing in public and though he was still only 39 years old he wrote no more concertos. So the *Emperor* has a particular heroic quality, as if the composer was making a final, defiant contribution to a medium in which he could no longer physically participate. Arrau's is a highly personal and obviously deeply considered reading which appears to have gained in depth and insight over the years. The *Adagio* and *Rondo* come over particularly well: the slow movement sounds very relaxed, but there is actually considerable tension in Arrau's playing, as when he arrives at the astonishing transitional passage from which the finale suddenly erupts; it's as if a store of accumulated energy were suddenly translated into action, though once again there's a wonderful leisurely quality here, for all the purposefulness of the playing. Davis and the orchestra provide firm and dynamic support in a recording whose aural perspective is entirely plausible.

Additional recommendations ...

No. 5. Piano Sonata No. 32 in C minor, Op. 111. **Wilhelm Kempff** (pf); **Berlin Philharmonic Orchestra/Ferdinand Leitner.** DG Galleria 419 468-2GGA — 1h 3m ADD 12/87
No. 5. Piano Sonata in E major, Op. 109. **Stephen Kovacevich** (pf); **BBC Symphony Orchestra/Sir Colin Davies.** Philips Concert Classics 422 482-2PCC — 59m ADD 12/89 £
No. 5. **Arturo Benedetti Michelangeli** (pf); **Vienna Symphony Orchestra/Carlo Maria Giulini.** DG 419 249-2GH — 42m ADD 2/88
No. 5. Choral Fantasia in C minor, Op. 80[a]. **Melvyn Tan** (fp); [a]**Schütz Choir of London; London Classical Players/Roger Norrington.** EMI Reflexe CDC7 49965-2 — 52m DDD 4/90

No. 5. Triple Concerto in C major, Op. 56[a]. **Leon Fleisher** (pf); **Cleveland Orchestra/George Szell;** [a]**Eugene Istomin** (pf); [a]**Isaac Stern** (vn); [a]**Leonard Rose** (vc); [a]**Philadelphia Orchestra/Eugene Ormandy.** Sony Classics Essential Classics MK46549 — 1h 14m ADD 8/91 £ B

No. 5. Choral Fantasia[a]. **Alfred Brendel** (pf); **London Philharmonic** [a]**Choir and Orchestra/Bernard Haitink.** Philips Insignia 434 148-2PM — 1h 1m ADD 7/92 B

Beethoven. SYMPHONIES. [a]**Charlotte Margiono** (sop); [a]**Birgit Remmert** (mez); [a]**Rudolf Schasching** (ten); [a]**Robert Holl** (bass); [a]**Arnold Schönberg Choir; Chamber Orchestra of Europe/Nikolaus Harnoncourt.** Teldec 2292-46452-2. Recorded 1990-1991.

No. 1 in C major, Op. 21. No. 2 in D major, Op. 36. No. 3 in E flat major, Op. 55, "Eroica". No. 4 in B flat major, Op. 60. No. 5 in C minor, Op. 67. No. 6 in F major, Op. 68, "Pastoral". No. 7 in A major, Op. 92. No. 8 in F major, Op. 93. No. 9 in D minor, Op. 125, "Choral"[a].

5 5h 58m DDD 11/91 B

Brimful of intrepid character and interpretative incident, Nikolaus Harnoncourt and the splendid Chamber Orchestra of Europe give us what is surely the most stimulating Beethoven symphony cycle of recent times. As Harnoncourt himself states in a lively interview for the accompanying booklet to this set: "It has always been my conviction that music is not there to soothe people's nerves … but rather to open their eyes, to give them a good shaking, even to frighten them". So it transpires that there's a re-creative daring about his conducting — in essence an embracement of recent scholarly developments and Harnoncourt's own pungent sense of characterization — which is consistently illuminating, thus leaving the listener with the uncanny sensation that he or she is in fact encountering this great music for the very first time. In all of this Harnoncourt is backed to the hilt by some superbly responsive, miraculously assured playing from the COE: their personable, unforced assimilation of Harnoncourt's specific demands (complete with period-style lean-textured strings and bracingly cutting brass and timpani), allied to this conductor's intimate knowledge of the inner workings of these scores, make for wonderfully fresh, punchy results. In this respect Symphonies Nos. 6-8 in particular prove immensely rewarding, but the *Eroica* and (especially) the Fourth, too, are little short of superb. In sum, it's a cycle which excitingly reaffirms the life-enhancing mastery of Beethoven's vision for the 1990s and into the next century beyond: a more thought-provoking, unimpeachably eloquent achievement one does not expect to encounter for many moons to come.

Additional recommendations …

Nos. 1-9. Overtures — Coriolan, Op. 62; Leonore No. 3, Op. 72b; Fidelio, Op. 72c; Egmont, Op. 84. **Leipzig Gewandhaus Orchestra/Kurt Masur.** Philips 416 274-2PH6 — 6 6h 38m ADD 2/86 B

Nos. 1-9. Egmont Overture. **Royal Concertgebouw Orchestra/Bernard Haitink.** Philips 416 822-2PH6 — 6 6h 5m DDD 6/88 B

Nos. 1-9. Overtures — Die Geschöpfe des Prometheus, Op. 43. Coriolan. Egmont. **London Classical Players/Roger Norrington.** EMI Reflexe CDS7 49852-2 — 6 5h 53m DDD 11/89 b

Nos. 1-9. **Berlin Philharmonic Orchestra/Herbert von Karajan.** DG 429 036-2GX5 — 5 5h 32m ADD 1/90 B

Nos. 1-9. Overture — Leonore No. 3, Op. 62a. **NBC Symphony Orchesta/Arturo Toscanini.** RCA Gold Seal mono GD60324 — 5 5h 37m ADD 5/90 B ▲

Nos. 1-9. **Leipzig Radio Chorus; Leipzig Gewandhaus Orchestra/Kurt Masur.** Philips 426 290-2PH5 (*also available separately*): *Nos. 1 and 5:* 426 782-2PH (*reviewed below*); *Nos. 2 and 7:* 432 994-2PH; *Nos. 3 and 8:* 434 913-2PH; *Nos. 4 and 6:* 434 919-2PH; *No. 9:* 432 995-2PH — 5 1h 3m 1h 13m 1h 16m 1h 17m 1h 6m DDD 5/93 B

Beethoven. Symphonies — No. 1 in C major, Op. 21; No. 5 in C minor, Op. 67. **Leipzig Gewandhaus Orchestra/Kurt Masur.** Philips 426 782-2PH. Recorded in 1987-1989.

1h 3m DDD 7/90 B

So many loud partisan claims are made about Beethoven performances these days that you must use the instruments of the composer's own time, or that it's hopeless trying to equal past giants like Furtwängler, Toscanini or Klemperer — that it's very refreshing indeed to discover a conductor who pursues his own course, and argues for it so convincingly. Kurt Masur always gives the impression of having gone back to the score and thought it all through afresh. He not only adopts the recent innovation of restoring the scherzo-trio repeat in No. 5, he shows deep understanding of how this affects the finale's thunderous self-assertion. And while he avoids the old-fashioned wallowing of a Leonard Bernstein, the *Andantes* of both symphonies show that classicism doesn't mean coldness; far from it and the dancing energy of the First Symphony's *Scherzo* and finale make some revered older versions sound stodgy. There is a slight snag: the recording in the Fifth Symphony pushes the trumpets and drums back and the piccolo in the finale isn't the glittering presence it should be, but don't let that put you off buying these refreshing and authoritative Beethoven performances.

Additional recommendations ...
Nos. 1 and 4. Egmont Overture. **Berlin Philharmonic Orchestra/Herbert von Karajan.** DG Galleria 419 048-2GGA — lh 4m ADD 4/88 £
Nos. 1 and 6. **London Classical Players/Roger Norrington.** EMI Reflexe CDC7 49746-2 — lh 6m DDD 9/88
Nos. 1 and 2. **Cleveland Orchestra/Christoph von Dohnányi.** Telarc CD80187 — 59m DDD 6/89
Nos. 1 and 4. **Vienna Philharmonic Orchestra/Karl Böhm.** DG Resonance 429 152-2GR — lh 4m ADD 4/90 £
Nos. 1 and 5. **Leipzig Gewandhaus Orchestra/Kurt Masur.** Philips 426 782-2PH — lh 3m DDD 7/90

Key to Symbols

Beethoven Symphonies — No. 2 in D major, Op. 36; No. 4 in B flat major, Op. 60. **North German Radio Symphony Orchestra/Günter Wand.** RCA Victor Red Seal RD60058. Recorded in 1988.

lh 8m DDD 9/89

Seldom has Beethoven's Second Symphony sounded as fresh, dynamic or persuasive as this. The work occupies a transitional place in the symphonic line as begun by Mozart and Haydn; on the one hand it forms the climax of that line, on the other it looks forward to new beginnings. Günter Wand's stance clearly leans towards those new beginnings, with a reading that is more 'Beethovian' in approach than most, highlighting the fingerprints of his future symphonic style. The Fourth Symphony has always tended to be eclipsed by the towering edifices of the Third and Fifth Symphonies, but the Fourth takes stock, and with the maturity gained in the writing of the Third, looks back once more in an act of homage to the triumphs of the past. Wand's performances are inspired; he is a conductor who never imposes his own ego and never does anything for the sake of effect, resulting in performances that are honest, direct and unpretentious. His tempos are superbly judged; brisk, but not hurried, allowing the pristine articulation of the strings to come shining through (this needs to be heard to be believed; orchestral playing such as this is rare indeed). The orchestral balance is ideal, with woodwind textures nicely integrated into the orchestral sound, and this is supported by the excellent recorded sound which approaches demonstration quality. A very fine issue indeed.

Additional recommendations ...
Nos. 2 and 8. **London Classical Players/Roger Norrington.** EMI CDC7 47698-2 — 59m DDD 3/87

Nos. 4 and 5. **London Symphony Orchestra/Wyn Morris.** Pickwick IMP Classics PCD869 — 1h 7m DDD 11/87 £ B

Nos. 2 and 4. **Philharmonia Orchestra/Otto Klemperer.** EMI Studio CDM7 63355-2 — 1h 13m ADD 8/90 B ▲

Beethoven. Symphony No. 3 in E flat major, Op. 55, "Eroica"[a]. Overture — Leonora No. 3, Op. 72*a*[b]. **North German Radio Symphony Orchestra/Günter Wand.** RCA Victor RD60755. Recorded live in [a] 1989, [b] June 1990.

1h 5m DDD 10/91 B

Günter Wand's live performance of the *Eroica* represents a worthy alternative to Klemperer's 1955 landmark recording. In many ways Wand stands as a legitimate successor to Klemperer as one of the holders of the great Teutonic tradition of interpreting Beethoven in terms of struggle and triumph. Certainly he launches into the symphony with tremendous vigour and power and he sustains these characteristics throughout. Following an opening movement in which the tension never relaxes at all, Wand leads a reading of the Funeral March which is deeply felt but without self-indulgence. The scherzo and trio provide well-pointed relief prior to an epic reading of the triumphant final movement, which carries all before it. The fill-up, an equally powerful reading of the *Leonora* Overture No. 3, precedes the performance of the *Eroica* and acts as an excellent curtain-raiser and introduction to Wand's interpretative style: genuine and powerful and wholly without self-indulgence. The North German Radio recording is excellent, capturing the involved atmosphere of a live performance without any of the distractions normally encountered. Highly recommended.

Additional recommendations ...

No. 3. **Academy of Ancient Music/Christopher Hogwood.** L'Oiseau-Lyre 417 235-2OH — 51m DDD 11/86 B

No. 3. **Orchestra of the Eighteenth Century/Frans Brüggen.** Philips 422 052-2PH — 49m DDD 11/88 B

No. 3. Die Geschöpfe des Prometheus. **London Classical Players/Roger Norrington.** EMI Reflexe CDC7 49101-2 — 49m DDD 4/89 B

No. 3. Leonore No. 2. **Philharmonia Orchestra/Otto Klemperer.** EMI mono CDM7 63855-2 — 1h 16m ADD 4/92 B ▲

No. 3. Egmont Overture. **Staatskapelle Dresden/Sir Colin Davis.** Philips 434 120-2PH — 1h 5m DDD 3/93 B

Beethoven. Symphony No. 5 in C minor, Op. 67. **Vienna Philharmonic Orchestra/Carlos Kleiber.** DG 415 861-2GH. From 2530 516 (6/75).

33m ADD 11/85 B

Rarely, if ever, has the spirit of revolutionary turbulence been better expressed in music than in the first movement of the Fifth Symphony; and no musical transformation is more likely to lift the spirits than the transition from scherzo to finale over which Beethoven laboured so hard and pondered so long. Even if our century cannot always share Beethoven's unshakeable sense of optimism, the visionary goal he proposes is one which we abandon at our peril. The trouble with the Fifth Symphony is that it is, for all its apparent familiarity, a brute of a piece to conduct. The opening bars have unseated many a conductor, and it must be admitted that even Carlos Kleiber comes perilously close to allowing the famous motto to be played as a fast triplet. Thereafter, he barely puts a foot wrong. There are many other distinguished interpreters of this symphony but Kleiber's reading has an electricity, a sense of urgency and fresh discovery which puts it in a class of its own. The DG recording is rather dry and immediate, but the lean texturing is an aspect of Kleiber's radicalism without which the reading would not be the astounding thing it is. The timing of 33 minutes may seem short measure, but when the performance is of this revealing quality, the duration of the experience is of relatively little importance.

Additional recommendations ...
Nos. 5 and 7. **Concertgebouw Orchestra/Bernard Haitink.** Philips 420 540-2PH — lh 12m DDD 10/87
Nos. 5 and 6. **Vienna Philharmonic Orchestra/Karl Böhm.** *Overtures — Egmont; Name-Day, Op. 115; The Consecration of the House, Op. 124* (**Orchestre Lamoureux, Paris/Igor Markevitch**); *The Ruins of Athens, Op. 133* (**Bavarian Radio Symphony Orchestra/Eugen Jochum**). DG Compact Classics 413 144-2GW2 — 2 lh 54m ADD 12/91 £
Nos. 5 and 7. **Philharmonia Orchestra/Vladimir Ashkenazy.** Decca Ovation 430 701-2DM — lh 17m DDD 8/91

NEW REVIEW

Beethoven. Symphony No. 6 in F major, Op. 68, "Pastoral"[a]. ORCHESTRAL WORKS. [c]**Birgit Nilsson** (sop); [abc]**Philharmonia Orchestra;** [d]**New Philharmonia Orchestra/Otto Klemperer.** EMI Studio CDM7 63358-2. Items marked [a] from SAX2260 (10/58), [bc] 33CX1575 (11/58), [d] HMV SXDW3032 (6/77).
Egmont, Op. 84 — Overture[b]; Die Trommel gerühret[b]; Freudvoll und leidvoll[c]; Klärchens Tod bezeichnend[b]. Der Geschöpfe des Prometheus, Op. 43 — Overture[d].

lh 9m ADD 8/90 

Klemperer's most revered Beethoven recordings date from the middle and late 1950s. In its day, his account of the *Pastoral* was notorious for the slow *Scherzo* — "it's a Ländler" — he is said to have retorted grumpily — but once again the performance as a whole offers a wonderful example of Klemperer's ability to sustain dramatic interest within generously conceived spaces. The result is an overwhelming sense of vital but unhurrying reflection. The *Egmont* numbers on this disc are also very fine. Birgit Nilsson is wonderfully fresh in the two arias, and the rarely recorded "Klärchens Tod bezeichnend" is very affecting. As for the famous overture, Klemperer's account is steadily paced, and as cogent and gauntly explicit a reading of this symphonic music-drama as any on disc. It is a reading of great power and nobility in which nothing is overdone; in this respect the coda is a particular success.

Additional recommendations ...
Nos. 5 and 6. **Concertgebouw Orchestra/Erich Kleiber.** Decca mono 417 637-2DH — lh 13m ADD 9/87
Nos. 1 and 6. **Chicago Symphony Orchestra/Fritz Reiner.** RCA GD60002 — lh 4m ADD 9/90 £

Beethoven. Symphony No. 7 in A major, Op. 92. **Vienna Philharmonic Orchestra/Carlos Kleiber.** DG 415 862-2GH. From 2530 706 (9/76).

39m ADD 2/86 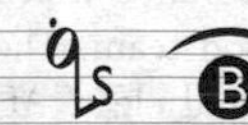

This may also seem short measure but as pointed out when discussing Kleiber's recording of the Fifth, the duration must be seen to be of relatively little importance. Kleiber's performance fairly bristles with electricity, but at all times one is aware of a tight control which never lets the exuberance get out of hand; moreover, he shows a scrupulous regard for the composer's instructions: all repeats are observed (to thrilling effect in the scherzo and finale) and tempo relationships are carefully calculated. It is Kleiber's feeling for the overall shape of each movement that is most impressive: how else could there be such a powerful sense of cumulative excitement in the finale? The recording is pre-digital, but it hardly seems to matter when given such a high-quality CD transfer.

Additional recommendations ...
No. 7. Die Geschöpfe des Prometheus — Overture. **Philharmonia Orchestra/Otto Klemperer.** EMI Studio CDM7 69183-2 — 44m ADD 4/88 £
Nos. 7 and 8. **Academy of Ancient Music/Christopher Hogwood.** L'Oiseau-Lyre Florilegium 425 695-2OH — lh 3m DDD 2/90
Nos. 7 and 8. **London Symphony Orchestra/Wyn Morris.** Pickwick IMP Classics PCD918 — lh 6m DDD 2/90 £

No. 7. **Haydn.** *Symphony No. 101 in D major, "Clock".* **Mendelssohn.** *A Midsummer Night's Dream — incidental music, Op. 61: Scherzo.* **New York Philharmonic Orchestra/Arturo Toscanini.** RCA Gold Seal mono GD60316 — lh 6m ADD 11/92

Beethoven. Symphony No. 8 in F major, Op. 93. Overtures — Coriolan; Fidelio; Leonore No. 3. **Berlin Philharmonic Orchestra/Herbert von Karajan.** DG 415 507-2GH.

56m DDD 6/86

The Eighth, for all its apparent brevity, lean athleticism and snapping vitality is at times generously expansive. The Trio of the steadily treading scherzo is as leisurely and countrified as anything you will find in the *Pastoral*; and even the finale, full of joy and abrupt changes of direction and mood, was expanded by Beethoven from material that was too dry, too laconic even for his taste. Following in Toscanini's footsteps, Karajan has always been a gifted exponent of this symphony, treating it as a vibrant and witty successor to the great Seventh rather than a throwback to the style of the First. His 1962 Berlin performance was more careful and keener-eared than this later CD version, but the performance here is a distinguished one still and the overtures are played and recorded with a great deal of power.

Beethoven. Symphony No. 9 in D minor, Op. 125, "Choral". **Anna Tomowa-Sintow** (sop); **Agnes Baltsa** (mez); **Peter Schreier** (ten); **José van Dam** (bass-bar); **Vienna Singverein; Berlin Philharmonic Orchestra/Herbert von Karajan.** DG Galleria 415 832-2GGA. Text and translation included. From 2740 172 (10/77).

lh 7m ADD 4/87 

All collections need Beethoven's *Choral* Symphony as one of the works at the very core of the nineteenth-century romantic movement. Within its remarkable span, Beethoven celebrates both the breadth and power of man's conception of his position in relation to the Universe; his sense of spirituality — especially in the great slow movement — and in the finale the essential life-enhancing optimism emerges, which makes human existence philosophically possible against all odds. Karajan lived alongside the Beethoven symphonies throughout his long and very distinguished recording career, and he recorded the Ninth three times in stereo. Sadly the most recent digital version, in spite of glorious playing in the *Adagio*, is flawed, but both analogue versions are very impressive indeed. His 1977 version is the best of the three. The slow movement has great intensity, and the finale brings a surge of incandescent energy and exuberance which is hard to resist. All four soloists are excellent individually and they also make a good team. The reading as a whole has the inevitability of greatness and the recording is vivid, full and clear. At mid-price this is very recommendable indeed.

Additional recommendations ...

No. 9. Coriolan Overture. **Gundula Janowitz** (sop); **Hilde Rössi-Majdan** (mez); **Waldemar Kmentt** (ten); **Walter Berry** (bass); **Vienna Singverein; Berlin Philharmonic Orchestra/Herbert von Karajan.** DG 435 095-2GCE — DDD

No. 9. **Anna Tomowa-Sintow** (sop); **Annelies Burmeister** (mez); **Peter Schreier** (ten); **Theo Adam** (bass); **Dresden Philharmonic Children's Choir; Berlin and Leipzig Radio Choruses; Leipzig Gewandhaus Orchestra/Kurt Masur.** Philips Silver Line 420 701-2PSL — lh 9m 12/87

No. 9. **Yvonne Kenny** (sop); **Sarah Walker** (mez); **Patrick Power** (ten); **Petteri Salomaa** (bass); **Schütz Choir; London Classical Players/Roger Norrington.** EMI CDC7 49221 — 10/87 DDD

No. 9. **Eileen Farrell** (sop); **Nan Merriman** (mez); **Jan Peerce** (ten); **Norman Scott** (bass); **Robert Shaw Chorale; NBC Symphony Orchestra/Arturo Toscanini.** RCA Gold Seal mono GD60256 — lh 5m ADD 3/88

No. 9. **Arleen Auger** (sop); **Catherine Robbin** (mez); **Anthony Rolfe Johnson** (ten);

Gregory Reinhart (bass); **London Symphony Chorus; Academy of Ancient Music/ Christopher Hogwood.** L'Oiseau-Lyre 425 517-2OH — lh 3m DDD 11/89
No. 9. **Aase Nordmo-Lövberg** (sop); **Christa Ludwig** (mez); **Waldemar Kmentt** (ten); **Hans Hotter** (bass); **Philharmonia Chorus and Orchestra/Otto Klemperer.** EMI Studio CDM7 63359-2 — lh 12m ADD 8/90
No. 9. **Brigitte Poschner-Klebel** (sop); **Margareta Hintermeier** (contr); **Robert Tear** (ten); **Robert Lloyd** (bass); **Vienna Singakademie; Vienna Symphony Orchestra/Eliahu Inbal.** Denon CO-76646 — lh 8m DDD 3/91
No. 9. **Joan Rodgers** (sop); **Della Jones** (mez); **Peter Bronder** (ten); **Bryn Terfel** (bass); **Royal Liverpool Philharmonic Choir and Orchestra/Sir Charles Mackerras.** EMI Eminence CD-EMX2186 — lh lm DDD 12/91 £

Beethoven. OVERTURES. **Bavarian Radio Symphony Orchestra/Sir Colin Davis.** CBS Masterworks CD44790. From MK12103 (9/86).
The Ruins of Athens, Op. 113. Coriolan, Op. 62. Leonore Nos. 1 and 3. The Creatures of Prometheus, Op. 43. Egmont, Op. 84. Fidelio, Op. 72*b*.

lh 3m DDD 9/89 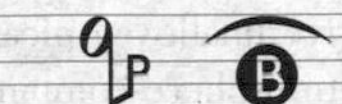

A collection of overtures must offer more than just a series of good performances: the juxtaposition of the works must provide contrast and variety, and the whole should progress so that some sense of climax and finality is reached at the end of the CD. Of course, it is possible for the listener to program the items in any order, but that shouldn't be necessary. Sir Colin Davis has here ordered the overtures in a way that could hardly be bettered, with the programme building through light and shade until the exultant finale of the *Fidelio* Overture is reached. In a full-bodied recording that allows the bloom of the strings to develop their richness, each overture receives a thoughtful, well-prepared reading that might not outrank the best of the competition, but which fits exactly in place in this Beethoven concert. *Coriolan* and *Egmont* make the most substantial individual effect here, Davis obviously warming to their expressive weight and the power with which Beethoven moves inexorably to their dramatic conclusions, yet the lighter works, the *Ruins of Athens* and *Prometheus* for example, are done with no less commitment, and the smoothness of approach adds a new dimension to their interpretation. In all, then, probably the most convincing collection of its kind in the catalogue.
See preceding reviews and listings for additional recommendations.

Beethoven. Quintet in E flat major for piano and wind, Op. 16.
Mozart. Quintet in E flat major for piano and wind, K452. **Murray Perahia** (pf); members of the **English Chamber Orchestra** (Neil Black, ob; Thea King, cl; Antony Halstead, hn; Graham Sheen, bn). CBS Masterworks CD42099. From IM42099 (8/86).

53m DDD 12/86 

"I myself consider it to be the finest work I have ever composed", stated Mozart on his Piano Quintet in a letter to his father in April 1784. The Quintet had in fact been composed at great speed but, dating as it does from the beginning of the composer's most impressive creative period, there are no signs of hasty work — indeed, it is written on quite an ambitious scale. Beethoven obviously knew the Mozart work when he came to write a quintet for the same combination of instruments and in the same key of E flat some 12 years later. There is but one difference in style. Mozart wrote the piano part as an integral part of the ensemble, whereas Beethoven wrote a piano part which was more soloistic. It is a delight to hear such immaculate ensemble and understanding between the players in these recordings. The clean and clear tone of the wind players, particularly that of the oboist Neil Black, is also a source of pleasure, as is Perahia's elegant pianism. Tempos are predominantly expansive and occasionally both works could have benefited from a little more thrust and brio, but the performances are most accomplished. The recording is pure in tone and well balanced.

NEW REVIEW

Beethoven. Duets, WoO27 — No. 1 in C major[a]. Trio in G major, WoO37[b]. Serenade in D major, Op. 25[c]. **Susan Milan** (fl); [ab]**Sergio Azzolini** (bn); [c]**Levon Chilingirian** (vn); [c]**Louise Williams** (va); [b]**Ian Brown** (pf). Chandos CHAN9108.

lh lm DDD 4/93

The grandeur of Beethoven's more mature works tend to overshadow his earlier compositions: and as this CD admirably demonstrates, there is much to enjoy in the music Beethoven composed prior to his thirtieth birthday in 1800. Not only does this programme contain three such diverting works, it also showcases the flawless musicianship and virtuosity of flautist Susan Milan, so there is much to commend this release. The centrepiece is the Serenade, Op. 25 for flute, violin and viola: published in 1802 it was probably written a few years earlier. In it Beethoven pays homage to the eighteenth-century *divertimento*, with six varied movements. Throughout the music is brilliant and engaging. The other two works, the trio for flute, bassoon and piano and the duo for flute and bassoon, date from the late 1780s and are equally delightful, if slightly less inspired. All the instrumentalists featured in these three works play with complete understanding of the style required, balancing the elegance of the eighteenth century, with the sense of freedom which was emerging at the time of this music's composition. Susan Milan's phrasing and tone give unalloyed pleasure throughout. Chandos's recorded sound is excellent: there is plenty of atmosphere combined with exactly the right degree of intimacy. Well worth investigating.

Beethoven. Septet in E flat major, Op. 20[a].
Mendelssohn. Octet in E flat major, Op. 20[b]. Members of the **Vienna Octet.** Decca 421 093-2DM. Item marked [a] from SXL2157 (3/60), [b] SDD389 (12/73). Item marked [a] recorded in 1959, [b] 1972.

lh l4m ADD 5/88 

Beethoven's Septet is a happy, relaxed divertimento-like work in six movements, scored for string trio with double-bass, clarinet, horn and bassoon. After its highly successful first performance in 1800 the work became very popular, and was arranged for many different instrumental combinations. Mendelssohn's Octet was written when the composer was only 16 years old. Scored for double string quartet, it is his first work to show individuality of expression and mastery of form and its mood is outgoing and high-spirited. Though the Decca recording of the Beethoven work dates from 1959 the sound is warm and attractive, to complement a delightfully unhurried, spontaneous yet relaxed performance which has a good deal of old-fashioned Viennese charm. The Octet performance dates from 1972, and has a less atmospheric, rather clean quality of sound. But the playing has just the right degree of delicacy and buoyancy, with textures very light and clear.

Additional recommendation ...
Septet. String Quintet in C major, Op. 29. **Hausmusik.** EMI Reflexe CDC7 54656-2 — lh l2m DDD 6/93

Beethoven. String Quartet in F major, Op. 59 No. 1, "Rasumovsky". String Quintet in C major, Op. 29[a]. **Medici Quartet** (Paul Robertson, David Matthews, vns; Ivo-Jan van der Werff, va; Anthony Lewis, vc); [a]**Simon Rowland-Jones** (va). Nimbus NI5207. Recorded in 1989.

lh l4m DDD 3/90

Beethoven. String Quartets — E minor, Op. 59 No. 2, "Rasumovsky"; C major, Op. 59 No. 3, "Rasumovsky". **Lindsay Quartet** (Peter Cropper, Ronald Birks, vns; Roger Bigley, va; Bernard Gregor-Smith, vc). ASV CDDCA554. From ALHB307 (10/84).

lh llm DDD l/89 9P

In the few years that separate the Op. 18 from the Op. 59 quartets, Beethoven's world was shattered by the oncoming approach of deafness and the threat of growing isolation. The Op. 59 consequently inhabit a totally different plane, one in which the boundaries of sensibility had been extended in much the same way as the map of Europe was being redrawn. Each of the three quartets alludes to a Russian theme by way of compliment to Count Rasumovsky, who had commissioned the set. The immediate impression the F major Quartet conveys is of great space, breadth and vision; this is to the quartet what the *Eroica* is to the symphony. The neglect of Beethoven's C major Quintet is unaccountable for it is a rewarding and remarkable score, written only a year before the First Symphony. At one time the presto finale earned it the nickname "Der Sturm", doubtless on account of the similarity, or rather anticipation of the storm in the *Pastoral* Symphony. The Medici Quartet with Simon Rowland-Jones give an eminently faithful and musical reading, free from any egocentric posturing. Tempos are sensible and the performance has all the spontaneity of live music-making: nothing is glamorized, yet there is no lack of polish. The first *Rasumovsky*, on the other hand, is not quite as successful: it is well played and there are some felicitous touches of phrasing and colour. Their first movement is on the fast side — not unacceptably so, but the slow movement is far too brisk and this may pose problems for some collectors. All the same the String Quintet alone is worth the price of the disc.

Although the Lindsays may be rivalled (and even surpassed) in some of their insights by the Végh and the Talich, taken by and large, they are second to none and superior to most. In each movement of the E minor they find the *tempo giusto* and all that they do as a result has the ring of complete conviction. The development and reprise of the first movement are repeated as well as the exposition and how imaginatively they play it too! The *pp* markings are scrupulously observed but are not obtrusively pasted on as they are in some sets. The C major is not quite in the same class though the opening has real mystery and awe and some listeners might legitimately feel that the whole movement could do with a little more momentum. On the other hand, they move the second movement on rather too smartly. Yet how splendidly they convey the pent-up torrent of energy unleashed in this fugal onrush. Even if it does not command quite the same elevation of feeling or quality of inspiration that distinguishes their F major and E minor quartets, it is still pretty impressive.

Additional recommendations ...

Op. 18: No. 1 in F major; No. 2 in G major; No. 3 in D major; No. 4 in C minor; No. 5 in A major; No. 6 in B flat major. **Quartetto Italiano.** Philips 426 046-2PM3 — ③ 2h 43m ADD 2/90

Op. 59, "Rasumovsky": No. 1 in F major; No. 2 in E minor; No. 3 in C major. E flat major, Op. 74, "Harp". F minor, Op. 95. **Quartetto Italiano.** Philips 420 797-2PM3 — ③ 2h 45m ADD 2/90

E flat major, Op. 127. B flat major, Op. 130. C sharp minor, Op. 131. A minor, Op. 132. F major, Op. 135. Grosse Fuge in B flat major, Op. 133. **Quartetto Italiano.** Philips 426 050-2PM4 — ④ 3h 36m ADD 2/90

Op. 18 Nos. 3, 4 and 6. **New Budapest Quartet.** Hyperion CDA66402 — 1h 15m DDD 10/90

Complete Quartets. **Talich Quartet.** Calliope CAL9633/9 — ⑦ 8h 22m AAD 1/89

Op. 18 Nos. 1-6. **Smithson Quartet.** Deutsche Harmonia Mundi RD77029 ② 2h 39m DDD 1/90

Op. 59 Nos. 1 and 2. **Budapest Quartet.** Sony Classical Essential Classics MK46545 — 1h 10m ADD 8/91 ▲

Beethoven. String Quartets — F minor, Op. 95, "Serioso"[a]; A minor, Op. 132[b]. **Végh Quartet** (Sándor Végh, Sándor Zöldy, vns; Georges Janzer, va; Paul Szabó, vc). Auvidis Valois V4406. Item marked [a] from Telefunken EX6 35041 (8/76); [b] EX6 35040 (10/74).

1h 8m ADD 4/88

Beethoven. String Quartets — A minor, Op. 132[a]; F major, Op. 135[b]. **Talich Quartet** (Petr Messiereur, Jan Kvapil, vns; Jan Talich, va; Evzen Rattai, vc). Calliope CAL9639. Item marked [a] from CAL1639, (6/80), [b] CAL1640 (6/80).

1h 8m ADD 12/86

After the expansive canvas of the Op. 59 Quartets and the *Eroica*, Beethoven's F minor Quartet, Op. 95, displays musical thinking of the utmost compression. The first movement is a highly concentrated sonata design, which encompasses in its four minutes almost as much drama as a full-scale opera. With it comes one of the greatest masterpieces of his last years, the A minor, Op. 132. The isolation wrought first by his deafness and secondly, by the change in fashion of which he complained in the early 1820s, forced Beethoven in on himself. Op. 132 with its other-worldly *Heiliger Dankgesang*, written on his recovery from an illness, is music neither of the 1820s nor of Vienna, it belongs to that art which transcends time and place. Though other performances may be technically more perfect, these are interpretations that come closer to the spirit of this great music than any other on CD. Collectors need have no doubts as to the depth and intelligence of the Talich Quartet's readings for they bring a total dedication to this music: their performances are innocent of artifice and completely selfless. There is no attempt to impress the listener with their own virtuosity or to draw attention to themselves in any way. The recordings are eminently faithful and natural, not 'hi-fi' or overbright but the overall effect is thoroughly pleasing.

Beethoven. STRING QUARTETS. **Végh Quartet** (Sándor Végh, Sándor Zöldy, vns; Georges Janzer, va; Paul Szabó, vc). Auvidis Valois V4405, V4408. Items marked [a] from Telefunken EX6 35041 (8/76), [b] Telefunken SKA25113T/1-4 (10/74).
V4405 — E flat major, Op. 74, "Harp"[a]; E flat major, Op. 127[b]. *V4408* — C sharp minor, Op. 131[b]; F major, Op. 135[b].

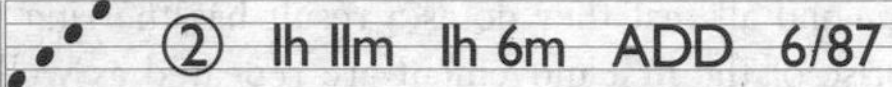
② lh 11m lh 6m ADD 6/87

NEW REVIEW

Beethoven (orch. Mitropoulos/Bernstein). String Quartets — C sharp minor, Op. 131[a]; F major, Op. 135[b]. **Vienna Phiharmonic Orchestra/Leonard Bernstein.** DG 435 779-2GH. Item marked [a] recorded in 1977, from 2531 077 (1/80), [b] 1989, new to UK.

lh 17m ADD/DDD 11/92
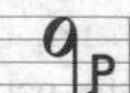

Beethoven stepped both outside and beyond his period nowhere more so than in the late quartets and the last five piano sonatas. The Op. 127 has been called Beethoven's "crowning monument to lyricism", whilst the Op. 131 is more inward-looking. Every ensemble brings a different set of insights to this great music so that it is not possible to hail any single quartet as offering the whole truth — yet these are as near to the whole truth as we are ever likely to come. The Végh give us music-making that has a profundity and spirituality that completely outweigh any tiny blemishes of intonation or ensemble. One does not get the feeling of four professional quartet players performing publicly for an audience but four thoughtful musicians sharing their thoughts about this music in the privacy of their own home. They bring us closer to this music than do any of their high-powered rivals.

Fifty or so years ago, there was something of a vogue for performing Beethoven's late quartets (either *in toto* or just selected movements) with a full complement of orchestral strings. In 1936, the young Leonard Bernstein, then an undergraduate at Harvard, heard Dmitri Mitropoulos present Beethoven's great Op. 131 with the strings of the Boston Symphony, later recalling: "I went out of my mind and have been ever since". Any understandable reservations one might have about the prospect of hearing such profoundly intimate music thus transformed are swept into insignificance by the huge eloquence of these live performances, both of which feature playing of extraordinary accomplishment and dedication from the incomparable VPO string section. Small wonder, then, that Bernstein himself rated the account of Op. 131 as the culmination of his long-standing relationship with this distinguished orchestra.

Beethoven. String Quartets — B flat major, Op. 130[a]; E minor, Op. 59 No. 2, "Rasumovsky"[b]. **Talich Quartet** (Petr Messiereur, Jan Kvapil, vns; Jan Talich, va; Evzen Rattai, vc). Calliope CAL9637. Item marked [a] from CAL1637/40, [b] CAL1634/6.

lh 13m ADD 3/87

The Beethoven quartets are one of the greatest musical expressions of the human spirit and they must be represented in any collection. The advantage of this Talich recording is that it couples a masterpiece from Beethoven's middle period, the great E minor Quartet, with one of the greatest of his last years. The B flat was the third of the late quartets to be composed and at its first performance in 1826 its last movement, the *Grosse Fuge*, baffled his contemporaries. Later that same year, he substituted the present finale, publishing the *Grosse Fuge* separately. The Talich Quartet have a no less impressive technical command than other ensembles but theirs are essentially private performances, which one is privileged to overhear rather than the over-projected 'public' accounts we so often hear on record nowadays. At 73 minutes this is marvellous value too.

Beethoven. Clarinet Trio in B flat major, Op. 11.
Brahms. Clarinet Trio in A minor, Op. 114. **Musicfest Trio** (David Campbell, cl; Lionel Handy, vc; Iwan Llewelyn-Jones, pf). Pickwick IMP Classics PCD959. Recorded in 1991.

44m DDD 11/91

With the possible exception of Mozart's *Kegelstatt* Trio, clarinet trios are a rarity in concerts and on collectors' shelves, and not all enthusiasts for Beethoven and Brahms know that these composers wrote one work each for the combination of clarinet, cello and piano. The Brahms was a late work of 1891, written after a year in which he had composed nothing and had confessed to his publisher that he was thinking of retiring — but then, fortunately for us, he heard the clarinettist Richard Mühlfeld and changed his mind. His trio has a quiet beauty which does not reveal itself all at once to the listener but is all the more rewarding for its depth, and this thoughtful performance offers fine tone and shapely phrasing, with each of the three artists playing with affection as well as skill. By contrast, Beethoven's Clarinet Trio is an early work, written in 1797 before his first string quartets. It bubbles over with youthful vigour and invention and has a particularly fetching finale in variation form on a theme by Joseph Weigl, a minor operatic composer of the day. All three instruments are given plenty to do, and the playing generally has a fine freshness with the pianist as well as the clarinettist sharing the melodic honours. The recording, though a touch over-reverberant, is perfectly acceptable. A pity, though, that room wasn't found for another work to go with these agreeable 44 minutes of attractively played music.

Beethoven. Piano Trios — E flat major, Op. 1 No. 1; B flat major, Op. 97, "Archduke". **Trio Zingara** (Elizabeth Layton, vn; Felix Schmidt, vc; Annette Cole, pf). Collins Classics 1057-2.

1h 13m DDD 5/90 9p

The young Trio Zingara's performance of Beethoven's great *Archduke* Trio is one of the most impressive versions in the current catalogue. It's a performance that flows, sometimes slowly and thoughtfully, sometimes with elegant quickness. Despite a slightly hesitant start, the *Andante* third movement grows steadily in intensity, and its quietly rippling fourth variation is revealed as the heart of the work. Impressive too is the way Trio Zingara manage the transition to the genial finale: all too often this can seem like a let-down — not here. The early E flat Trio makes a fine foil for the *Archduke*, and Zingara wisely don't try to find intimations of later profundity here, but then neither is there any twee 'classicizing' the tone seems just right throughout. Balancing a grand piano with two solo strings is a nightmare for any recording producer, but the Collins team seem to have got it about right: the strings are clearly audible, the piano doesn't sound over-restrained. One minor word of warning though: the insert note refers to the wrong E flat trio — Op. 70/2, instead of Op. 1/1.

Additional recommendations ...

E flat major, Op. 1 No. 1. G major, Op. 1 No. 2. C minor, Op. 1 No. 3. B flat major, Op. 11. D major after Symphony No. 2, Op. 36. E flat major, Op. 44. E flat major, Op. 38 (after Septet, Op. 20). D major, Op. 70 No. 1, "Ghost". E flat major, Op. 70 No. 2. B flat major, Op. 97, "Archduke". G major, Op. 121a. E flat major, WoO38. B flat major, WoO39. Trio-movement in E flat major, Hess No. 48. **Beaux Arts Trio.** Philips 432 381-2PM5 — ⑤ 5h 59m ADD/DDD 3/92

"Archduke". Variations in G major on Müller's "Ich bin der Schneider Kakadu", Op. 121a. **Robinson Trio.** Pickwick IMP Classics PCD874 — 1h 3m DDD 1/88

"Ghost"[a]. ***Schubert.*** *Piano Quintet in A major, D667, "Trout"*[b]. [b]**Samuel Rhodes** (va); [b]**Georg Hörtnagel** (db); [a]**Beaux Arts Trio.** Philips Silver Line Classics 420 716-2PSL — 1h 2m ADD 6/88

Op. 1 Nos. 1-3. "Ghost". "Archduke". Variations in G major on Müller's "Ich bin der Schneider Kakadu". 14 Variations in E flat major, Op. 44. Allegretto in E flat major, Hess 48. **Pinchas Zukerman** (vn); **Jacqueline du Pré** (vc); **Daniel Barenboim** (pf). EMI Studio CMS7 63124-2 — ③ 3h 50m ADD 8/89

"Archduke". "Ghost". **Henryk Szeryng** (vn); **Pierre Fournier** (vc); **Wilhelm Kempff** (pf). DG 429 712-2GGA — 1h 11m ADD 9/90

Op. 1 — Nos. 1 and 3. Variations in E flat major on an original theme, Op. 44. **Castle Trio.** Virgin Classics Veritas VC7 59590-2 — 1h 16 DDD 4/91

"Archduke". B flat major, WoO39. Variations in G major on Müller's "Ich bin der Schneider Kakadu". **Castle Trio.** Virgin Classics Veritas VC7 59044-2 — 1h 7m DDD 3/92

NEW REVIEW

Beethoven. STRING TRIOS. **Itzhak Perlman** (vn); **Pinchas Zukerman** (va); **Lynn Harrell** (vc). EMI CDS7 54198-2. Recorded live in 1989 and 1990.

String Trios: E flat major, Op. 3; Op. 9 — No. 1 in G major; No. 2 in D major; No. 3 in C minor. Serenade in D major, Op. 8.

② 2h 23m DDD 2/93

NEW REVIEW

Beethoven. String Trios, Op. 9 — No. 1 in G major; No. 2 in D major; No. 3 in C minor. **Archibudelli** (Vera Beths, vn; Jürgen Kussmaul, va; Anner Bylsma, vc). Sony Classical Vivarte SK48190. Recorded in 1991. Recorded in 1991.

1h 8m DDD 9/92 

Whereas the last of Beethoven's six Piano Trios, the *Archduke*, was not written until he was 41, all five of his String Trios date from his twenties, with the six-movement E flat Trio, Op. 3 appearing in 1792, to be followed by the *Serenade* in D, Op. 8, some five years later. But after banishing all such eighteenth-century entertainment connotations in his three next classically designed, four-movement String Trios (Op. 9) of 1798, he thereafter preferred to write not for three but rather, four strings in what grew into a legendary, life-long cycle of string quartets. The double-stopping in the noble slow movement of the high-powered C minor String Trio already portends pursuit of richer textures. So it is essentially the artist as a young man that we meet on the EMI set, and what a revelation of youthful genius they offer in imaginative range. Recorded live in New York, the playing is eloquent testimony to that little extra piquancy and boldness of characterization that an audience can draw from artists even as studio-friendly as Perlman, Zukerman and Harrell — perhaps all the more fresh in their approach because not in daily harness as an ensemble. Tone is splendidly vibrant. And incidentally they score over their also excellent, but less succulently reproduced DG rivals (see below), by including the arresting extra trio Beethoven subsequently provided for the *Scherzo* of the G major Trio.

A group with "a special love for historical stringed instruments" is how Archibudelli is described, as might be gleaned from their name (an Italian compilation of bows and strings) plus the fact that Anner Bylsma plays a 1835 Gianfrancesco Pressenda cello, Vera Bath a 1727 Stradivari violin and Jürgen Kussmaul a 1785 William Forster viola. But though striving for a special period quality of sound they are anything but antiquarian in their approach to these works, all of them striking enough to have placed Beethoven among the immortals even if he had written nothing else. With their brisk tempo, strong dynamic contrast and piquant accentuation, they leave no doubt of the urgency inherent in the key of C minor for this composer. The other two Trios in major keys are equally imaginatively characterized and contrasted. Some listeners might even feel they are over-volatile in their response to every detailed innuendo, at the expense of firmly drawn, classical line. But their relish of the music wins the day. Once or twice busy figuration in the lower strings emerge a bit bottom-heavy. The recording is true to life.

Additional recommendation ...

As EMI. **Anne-Sophie Mutter** (vn); **Bruno Giuranna** (va); **Mstislav Rostropovich** (vc). DG 427 687-2GH2 — ② 2h 19m DDD 7/89

Beethoven. Cello Sonatas, Op. 5 No. 1 in F major; No. 2 in G minor. 12 Variations in F major on "Ein Mädchen oder Weibchen" from "Die Zauberflöte", Op. 66. Seven Variations in E

flat major on Mozart's "Bei Männern, welche Liebe fühlen" from "Die Zauberflöte", WoO46.
Mischa Maisky (vc); **Martha Argerich** (pf). DG 431 801-2GH.

lh 6m DDD 2/92

Beethoven wrote five cello sonatas in all, and this disc, which concentrates on his earlier music for the instrument, has Nos. 1 and 2 (which date from 1796) flanked by two melodious sets of variations on themes from Mozart's *Die Zauberflöte* ("The Magic Flute"). This makes for an attractive programme that is on the light and playful side. The playing of Mischa Maisky and Martha Argerich is so vivid that we feel no monotony even though the *Ein Mädchen oder Weibchen* Variations (which are a bit conventional but make for very pleasant listening) and the First Sonata are in the same key of F major. Above all, it has a freshness that reminds us that we are listening to a young man's music. Maisky's cello tone has plenty of glow and warmth, and Argerich is a sensitive partner, her piano being placed a little backwardly but for that reason never threatening to overpower the cello as might otherwise happen with this gifted and passionate artist. Here, in sum, is impeccable ensemble, agility and wit, together with the broader style of utterance that we require in the slower music of the two sonatas. The special strength of the whole disc is that it conveys an infectious feeling of sheer enjoyment that was undoubtedly felt by Beethoven himself and then communicates in turn to the artists and, finally, ourselves as listeners.

Additional recommendations ...
Nos. 1 and 2. No. 3 in A major, Op. 69. No. 4 in C major, Op. 102 No. 1. No. 5 in D major, Op. 102 No. 2. **Mstislav Rostropovich** (vc); **Sviatoslav Richter** (pf). Philips 412 256-2PH2 — ② lh 49m ADD 1/85
Nos. 1 and 2. **Yo-Yo Ma** (vc); **Emmanuel Ax** (pf). CBS Masterworks CD37251 — DDD 11/85
Nos. 3 and 5. **Jacqueline du Pré** (vc); **Stephen Kovacevich** (pf). EMI Studio CDM7 69179-2 — 49m ADD 6/89

NEW REVIEW

Beethoven (trans. Liszt). Symphonies, S464 — No. 5[a]; No. 6: first movement[b]. **Glenn Gould** (pf). Sony Classical Glenn Gould Edition SMK52636. Item marked [a] from 72864 (11/70), [b] 76983 (6/81).

49m ADD 12/92

Liszt's transcriptions of the Beethoven symphonies are full-sized concert versions, at the opposite extreme from simplified, play-at-home versions, but still faithful to the letter of the original scores — that is to say, they are all substance and no added fripperies. Their pianistic demands are certainly not for the faint-hearted, since the aim is to reproduce the power and solidity of the full orchestra. Nothing daunted, Glenn Gould offers an account of the Fifth Symphony rock-like in its rhythmic stability and defiant willpower. Steadier in tempo than the average orchestral renditions it nevertheless generates far more electricity, and the finale is nothing short of an object lesson in sustained Beethoven intensity (for connoisseurs of studio trickery the insert-note owns up to Gould having faked a few bars near the end). The first movement of the *Pastoral* is comparably austere and might initially be off-putting for anyone expecting gentle bucolic descriptiveness; the close-miked recording quality tends to reinforce that impression. But adaptation is easy when the sense of conviction is this strong. Beethoven/Liszt/Gould is a true meeting of minds and as such it sets its terms of reference. Gould was a unique phenomenon; there is no finer monument to that uniqueness than this disc.

Beethoven. VARIATIONS.
Schumann. Etudes symphoniques, Op. 13 and posth. **Alfred Brendel** (pf). Philips 432 093-2PH. Recorded in 1990.
Variations — Six in F major on an Original Theme, Op. 34; Five in D major on "Rule Britannia", WoO79; Six in G major on "Nel cor più non mi sento" from Paisiello's "La mollinara", WoO70.

59m DDD 3/92

Throughout his life Beethoven was scarcely less drawn to variations than sonata form. Brendel includes the early Paisiello set as an example of the inherited classical tradition, but clearly enjoys himself most in the surprises of the composer's early thirties. "Worked out in quite a new manner" was Beethoven's own description of his Op. 34, in which he changes tempo, time-signature and even key for each successive number. In the *Rule Britannia* set we're not only given a "stylization of the sea in its various ruffles and wind speeds" but also racy humour, for "Beethoven treats the imperial folk-song with a broad wink" as Brendel himself puts it in insert-notes as stimulating and fresh as his own playing. The disc's main interest nevertheless centres in Schumann's *Etudes symphoniques* (or *Etudes en forme de variations* as he renamed his later revision) in a performance including the five posthumously published Eusebius-like variations rejected by the composer from both versions. Admitting to no longer being able to do without them ("since it is their inclusion that makes Schumann's Op. 13 one of his finest compositions") Brendel in fact inserts them so judiciously and imparts so splendid a romantic fervour and continuity to the performance as a whole that all doubts about defiance of Schumann's own wishes are silenced — at least temporarily! Made at The Maltings, Snape, the recording is wholly truthful.

NEW REVIEW

Beethoven. THE BEETHOVEN BROADWOOD FORTEPIANO. **Melvyn Tan** (fp). EMI CDC7 54526-2. Recorded in 1992.

Seven Bagatelles, Op. 33. Eleven Bagatelles, Op. 119. Fantasia in G minor, Op. 77. Seven Variations in C major on "God save the King", WoO78. Five Variations in D major on "Rule Britannia", WoO79.

1h 11m DDD 12/92 

A collector's piece, this, and primarily because of the fortepiano itself — none other than Beethoven's own six-octave Broadwood (then the world's most 'modern' keyboard) presented to him by its renowned English manufacturers in 1817. Much the worse for wear it was subsequently acquired by Liszt, who in his turn passed it on to the Hungarian National Museum where only two years ago it was restored (by the American-born David Winston) to a playable condition. Entrusted with it on a brief tour, Melvyn Tan recorded this recital in May 1992, at Forde Abbey in Dorset. Nothing in his discerningly chosen programme better demonstrates what warmth, strength, range and bravura can be drawn from it than the wholly unpredictable, improvisatory G minor *Fantasia,* which but for its date (1809) might be thought to have been written for that very purpose. In view of the instrument's country of origin it was a happy thought to begin and end with the pungent *God save the King* and *Rule Britannia*, both of 1803. The main musical substance nevertheless comes in the Bagatelles, miniatures yes, but as revealing of the composer's kaleidoscopic daily mood-changes as the pages of a diary. Characteristically, Tan slightly hurries one or two slower numbers which need more time to sing or speak, and just now and again he adds to the music's in-built caprice with a few little rhythmic idiosyncrasies of his own. But his playing remains a constant delight for its spontaneity, colour and spirit. The recording cannot be faulted.

NEW REVIEW

Beethoven. 33 Variations on a Waltz by Diabelli, Op. 120. **Alfred Brendel** (pf). Philips 426 232-2PH. Recorded in 1988.

53m DDD 8/90 

Beethoven's *Diabelli Variations* respond better to pianists who think between the notes than to those who take them at face value. Alfred Brendel's achievement is twofold: on the one hand he produces a refined, beautifully integrated body of tone, while on the other, he manages to quietly underline the very different character of each individual variation while keeping a watchful eye on the structural 'long view'. The result is a consistently compelling trip through one of Beethoven's most testing obstacle courses, and by the time we reach the far end — a satisfied, almost tongue-in-cheek *Tempo di minuetto moderato* — we doubly appreciate everything that went before. This is wholly magnificent music: playful, angry, profound, searching (Variations 29-31), sublime (try Variation 24, the Fughetta, more beautifully played here than anywhere else on disc) and cumulatively immense. It's also one of the most far-reaching of Beethoven's late works (although sketches for it date from as early as 1819), and is often prophetic of Liszt, Schumann, and even the music of our own century in its harmonic boldness. The recording is close but clear, and my only regret is that Brendel's own fascinating study on the work — which is printed in the booklet in French, German and Italian — is not printed in English, although William Kinderman's essay (included in the place of Brendel's) is both useful and informative.

Additional recommendations ...
Diabelli Variations. **Stephen Kovacevich** (pf). Philips Concert Classics 422 969-2PCC — 54m ADD 8/90 £ B
Diabelli Variations. 11 Bagatelles, Op. 119. **Rudolf Serkin** (pf). CBS Masterworks Portrait CD44837 — lh 6m ADD 8/90 £ B
Diabelli Variations. 2 Variations on an Original Theme in C minor, WoO80. **Benjamin Frith** (pf). ASV CDDCA715 — lh lm DDD 11/91 B

NEW REVIEW

Beethoven. COMPLETE PIANO SONATAS. **Wilhelm Kempff.** DG 429 306-2GX9. From SKL901/11 (12/66). Recorded 1964-65.
No. 1 in F minor, Op. 2 No. 1. No. 2 in A major, Op. 2 No. 2. No. 3 in C major, Op. 2 No. 3. No. 4 in E flat major, Op. 7. No. 5 in C minor, Op. 10 No. 1. No. 6 in F major, Op. 10 No. 2. No. 7 in D major, Op. 10 No. 3. No. 8 in C minor, Op. 13, "Pathétique". No. 9 in E major, Op. 14 No. 1. No. 10 in G major, Op. 14 No. 2. No. 11 in B flat major, Op. 22. No. 12 in A flat major, Op. 26. No. 13 in E flat major, Op. 27 No. 1, "Quasi una fantasia". No. 14 in C sharp minor, Op. 27 No. 2, "Moonlight". No. 15 in D major, Op. 28, "Pastoral". No. 16 in G major, Op. 31 No. 1. No. 17 in D minor, Op. 31 No. 2, "Tempest". No. 18 in E flat major, Op. 31 No. 3. No. 19 in G minor, Op. 49 No. 1. No. 20 in G major, Op. 49 No. 2. No. 21 in C major, Op. 53, "Waldstein". No. 22 in F major, Op. 54. No. 23 in F minor, Op. 57, "Appassionata". No. 24 in F sharp major, Op. 78. No. 25 in G major, Op. 79. No. 26 in E flat major, Op. 81*a*, "Les Adieux". No. 27 in E minor, Op. 90. No. 28 in A major, Op. 101. No. 29 in B flat major, Op. 106, "Hammerklavier". No. 30 in E major, Op. 109. No. 31 in A flat major, Op. 110. No. 32 in C minor, Op. 111.

9 9h 54m ADD 3/91 

When this set of the complete Beethoven Sonatas was reissued, Richard Osborne said in "Gramophone":
"Buying boxed sets of central repertory is often a lazy way of collecting, fraught with danger for the discriminating listener. But there are exceptional cases, and the case of the 32 Beethoven piano sonatas is certainly one of them. The sonatas make up a wonderfully diverse yet utterly cogent and self-contained body of work. There isn't a single sonata that it is safe to ignore (even the Op. 49 sonatas have their merits) yet try to collect them separately and you will have the devil's own job over couplings and availability. Having the complete opus played by a single great artist is also surprisingly satisfying ... It is a wonderful set, one of the finest things the gramophone has ever given us, not simply because it offers great music and great music-making, but because it is, over its ten-hour span, a thing of such unquenchable vitality. The LPs were very fine. On CD they come up superbly, with only minimal tape background ... it is astonishing value ... this set will always look well on your shelves, and in its new durable format it could go on giving pleasure and insight for generations to come."

Additional recommendations ...
Complete Piano Sonatas. **Alfred Brendel.** Philips 412 575-2PH11 — 11 10h 59m ADD 1/85 B
Complete Piano Sonatas. **Daniel Barenboim.** EMI CZS7 62863-2 — 10 11h 27m ADD 10/90 B
Complete Piano Sonatas. **Artur Schnabel.** EMI Références mono CHS7 63765-2 — 8 10h 5m ADD 7/91 B
Complete Piano Sonatas. Piano Variations. **Claudio Arrau.** Philips 432 301-2PM11 — 11 12h 19m ADD 1/92 B
Nos. 28-32. **Maurizio Pollini** (pf). DG 419 199-2GH2 — 2 2h 6m DDD 12/86 B
Nos. 8, 14, 15 and 24. **Wilhelm Kempff** (pf). DG Galleria 415 834-2GGA — ADD lh 8/87 B
Nos. 14, 21 and 23. **Vladimir Ashkenazy** (pf). Decca Ovation 417 732-2DM — lh 6m ADD 12/87 B

Nos. 17, 18 and 26. **Murray Perahia** (pf). CBS Masterworks CD43419 — ⁘ lh lm DDD 2/88 Ⓑ
Nos. 16-18. **Richard Goode** (pf). Elektra Nonesuch 979 212-2 — ⁘ lh 8m DDD 9/90 Ⓑ

Jenö Jandó's excellent complete super-bargain set of the sonatas are available on Naxos on two sets comprising five CDs each (8 505002 and 8 505003). They are also available on ten separate CDs, the details of which follow (the volume numbers do not indicate the numerical order of the sonatas).

(Vol. 3) *Nos. 1-3.* Naxos 8 550150 — . lh 7m DDD 12/90 Ⓑ
(Vol. 5) *Nos. 5, 6, 7 and 25.* Naxos 8 550161 — . lh 3m DDD 12/90 Ⓑ
(Vol. 8) *Nos. 4, 13, 19, 20 and 22.* Naxos 8 550167 — . lh 8m DDD 12/90 Ⓑ
(Vol. 6) *Nos. 9, 10, 24, 27 and 28.* Naxos 8 550162 — . lh 12m DDD 12/90 Ⓑ
(Vol. 1) *Nos. 8, 14 and 23.* Naxos 8 550045 — . 56m DDD 2/91 Ⓑ
(Vol. 10). *Nos. 15 and 33-38.* Naxos 8 550255 — . lh 9m DDD 2/91 Ⓑ
(Vol. 2) *Nos. 17, 21 and 26.* Naxos 8 550054 — . lh 3m DDD 2/91 Ⓑ
(Vol. 7) *Nos. 12, 16 and 18.* Naxos 8 550166 — . lh 4m DDD 6/91 Ⓑ
(Vol. 9) *Nos. 11 and 29.* Naxos 8 550234 — . lh 4m DDD 6/91 Ⓑ
(Vol. 4) *Nos. 30, 31 and 32.* Naxos 8 550151 — . lh 4m DDD 6/91 Ⓑ

NEW REVIEW

Beethoven. Piano Sonatas — No. 1 in F minor, Op. 2 No. 1; No. 2 in A major, Op. 2 No. 2; No. 3 in C major, Op. 2 No. 3. **Melvyn Tan** (fp). EMI Reflexe CDC7 54657-2. Recorded in 1992.

⁘ lh 13m DDD 5/93

Only after launching his Beethoven cycle with three of the most popular middle period sonatas (the *Waldstein, Appassionata* and *Les Adieux*) and following them with the three of Op. 31 and Op. 10 does Melvyn Tan allow us to hear how the great series of 32 actually began. As with previous releases in the cycle he plays not Beethoven's recently restored Broadwood but a Derek Adlam fortepiano modelled on an early nineteenth-century instrument of Anton Walter. And nothing better reveals the richness and variety of sonority he draws from it, in the very favourable recording venue of Forde Abbey in Dorset, than the *Adagio* of Op. 2 No. 3. If his tempo here might be thought just a little too fast to convey the full impact of Beethoven's plunge from the home key of C into the brave new world of E, the other two slow movements are judiciously paced, with a splendid inexorability of rhythmic tread in the *Largo appassionato* of Op. 2 No. 2 in A. For the rest he captures the 25-year-old composer's exploratory *élan* with an imaginative freshness and vitality all his own, only occasionally causing a raised eyebrow when underlining *sforzando* markings with a momentary disruption of pulse.

Additional recommendation ...
Nos. 1-3. **John O'Conor** (pf). Telarc CD80214 — ⁘ lh 7m DDD 9/90 Ⓑ

NEW REVIEW

Beethoven. Piano Sonatas — No. 5 in C minor, Op. 10 No. 1; No. 6 in F major, Op. 10 No. 2; No. 7 in D major, Op. 10 No. 3. **Louis Lortie** (pf). Chandos CHAN9101. Recorded in 1991.

⁘ 56m DDD 3/93

Written in his late twenties, Beethoven's three piano sonatas of Op. 10 point firmly forward towards romanticism in their sheer energy, drama and pathos, the latter quality being clearly exemplified in the *Largo e mesto* movement of the final D major work, with which Beethoven himself moved listeners to tears. In this famous slow movement, the Quebec-born pianist Louis Lortie does not let the music sink under excessive weight and solemnity (he takes less than eight minutes here where one British pianist on record requires more than 11), but is none the less powerfully expressive and moving. In general, this fine young artist brings a splendid crispness and energy to all three of these pieces, to say nothing of the dexterity he gives us in the *Presto* finale of the F major Sonata. He can be unusually forceful and brusque tonally, and although he never quite pushes his piano beyond what it will accept without protest, there are places where he gets dangerously close to that point. However, elsewhere his playing also shows the sensitivity of his ear, while even in quick and vigorous outer movements, such as those of the C minor work which comes first in the set, he will sometimes linger tellingly over an expressive detail so that the music never becomes merely well-drilled and indeed has a real feeling of spontaneity. Thus vitality and eloquence go hand-in-hand in these performances, and gives them much freshness. Since the booklet bears the title "Beethoven: The Piano Sonatas", and tells us that Lortie's recording plans "place special emphasis on Beethoven", we may hope that he will go on to give us all 32 of the sonatas. Not for the first time, Chandos have used the Maltings Concert Hall at Snape in Suffolk for the piano recording, and with great success. The sound of Lortie's modern grand may at first seem brittle and reverberant in the space of this large concert-hall, but the ear does become accustomed to it and one may well feel that it suits these early Beethoven sonatas better than the more cushioned and enclosed studio sound that we often hear.

Additional recommendation ...
Nos. 5-7 and 25. **Melvyn Tan** (fp). EMI CDC7 54207-2 — lh 5m DDD 6/92

Beethoven. Piano Sonatas — No. 17 in D minor, Op. 31 No. 2, "Tempest"; No. 18 in E flat major, Op. 31 No. 3; No. 26 in E flat major, Op. 81*a*, "Les Adieux". **Murray Perahia** (pf). CBS Masterworks CD42319.

lh lm DDD 2/88

"I am by no means satisfied with my works hitherto, and I intend to make a fresh start", so Beethoven is reputed to have remarked before embarking on the three sonatas comprising his Op. 31 in 1802. Ominous symptoms of deafness were already overshadowing his private life, as the flanking movements of the D minor Sonata betray even if feeling runs too deep to ruffle the tranquil surface of the central *Adagio*. Perahia's texture is crystalline (with skilful half-pedalling in the problematical recitatives in the opening movement of the D minor work) and even amidst the *con fuoco* of the E flat Sonata's finale rhythm is held on a tautly controlled rein. Whereas these two sonatas were studio recordings, the venue for *Les Adieux* was a warmer, more reverberant concert hall. Here we rightly meet a more impressionably romantic Perahia making every passing innuendo wholly his own in response to Beethoven's overtly expressed sadness, yearning and joy at the departure from — and return to — Vienna at the time of the Napoleonic invasion. Ingratiating in tone throughout a wide dynamic range, perfectly proportioned and finally excitingly brilliant, this performance has with good reason been widely hailed as "one of the most complete realizations of this work that has appeared in recent years".

Beethoven. Piano Sonatas — No. 21 in C major, Op. 53, "Waldstein"; No. 23 in F minor, Op. 57, "Appassionata"; No. 26 in E flat major, Op. 81*a*, "Les adieux". **Melvyn Tan** (fp). EMI Reflexe CDC7 49330-2.

lh 3m DDD 5/88

Here are three of Beethoven's most popular sonatas, played on the kind of instrument the composer himself would have used. Tan is a very brilliant player; the outer movements of the *Waldstein* are dazzlingly done, yet carefully too and with due attention to detail. But both here and in *Les adieux*, where the quick music again abounds in vitality, one sometimes wonders whether Tan is fully in command of the music's structure, for he does not always manage to convey just where it is going. A little more intellectual weight occasionally seems to be needed. It is more in evidence in the *Appassionata*, which is the most successful performance of the three works. Nevertheless, this is an impressive disc, with much brilliance and immediacy making the music seem just a little unnerving, which perhaps is what it should be.

Additional recommendation ...
Nos. 8, 14 and 23. **Daniel Barenboim.** EMI CDC7 47345-2 — lh 2m ADD 9/86

Beethoven. Piano Sonata No. 29 in B flat major, Op. 106, "Hammerklavier". **Emil Gilels** (pf). DG 410 527-2GH. From 410 527-1GH (12/83).

49m DDD 2/84

The great Soviet pianist Emil Gilels died in 1986, not many months before his seventieth birthday, and left behind him a major legacy of recorded performances. This account of the *Hammerklavier* is a fine memorial. The work is very long and exceedingly taxing technically and the pianist must plumb its often turbulent emotional depth, not least in the enormous 20-minute slow movement which requires deep concentration from player and listener alike. After the recording was made in 1983, the pianist told his producer: "I feel that the weight has been lifted, but I feel very empty." Gilels manages to give it more tonal beauty and warmth than most pianists, without any loss of strength or momentum. His is measured and beautiful playing, and finely recorded too.

Beethoven. PIANO SONATAS. **Maurizio Pollini** (pf). DG 429 569/70-2GH. From 419 199-2GH2 (12/86). Recorded 1975-7.
429 569-2GH — No. 28 in A major, Op. 101; No. 29 in B flat major, Op. 106, "Hammerklavier". *429 570-2GH* — No. 30 in E major, Op. 109; No. 31 in A flat major, Op. 110; No. 32 in C minor, Op. 111.

② lh 3m lh 2 AAD 7/90 

If Beethoven's 32 piano sonatas may be likened to a range of foothills and mountains, then these five sonatas are the last lofty pinnacles, difficult of access but offering great rewards to both pianist and listener. No library is complete without them. Pollini's playing must be praised for its interpretative mastery as well as its exemplary keyboard skill. These are prizewinning issues which have been widely admired, not least for the magnificent last sonata of all, Op. 111, and the recordings hardly show their age.

Additional recommendations ...
Nos. 30-32. **John O'Conor.** Telarc CD80261 — lh 5m DDD 11/92
Nos. 27-32. **Solomon.** EMI Références mono/stereo CHS7 64708-2 — ② 2h 21m ADD 7/93 ▲

Beethoven. COMPLETE VIOLIN SONATAS — No. 1 in D major, Op. 12 No. 1; No. 2 in A major, Op. 12 No. 2; No. 3 in E flat major, Op. 12 No. 3; No. 4 in A minor, Op. 23; No. 5 in F major, Op. 24, "Spring"; No. 6 in A major, Op. 30 No. 1; No. 7 in C minor, Op. 30 No. 2; No. 8 in G major, Op. 30 No. 3; No. 9 in A major, Op. 47, "Kreutzer"; No. 10 in G major, Op. 96.

Recommendations ...
Sir Yehudi Menuhin (vn); **Wilhelm Kempff** (pf). DG 415 874-2GCM4 — ④ 4h 32m ADD 6/87
Arthur Grumiaux (vn); **Clara Haskil** (pf). Philips Legendary Classics mono 422 140-2PLC3 — ③ 3h 34m ADD 1/89 ▲
Itzhak Perlman (vn); **Vladimir Ashkenazy** (pf). Decca Ovation 421 453-2DM4 — ④ 3h 59m ADD 1/89

NEW REVIEW

Beethoven. Violin Sonatas — No. 5 in F major, Op. 24, "Spring"; No. 8 in G major, Op. 30 No. 3; No. 9 in A major, Op. 47, "Kreuzer". **Pinchas Zukerman** (vn); **Daniel Barenboim** (pf). EMI Studio Plus CDM7 64631-2. Recorded in 1971-73.

lh 18m ADD 3/93 

This generously filled mid-price disc is a winner, for although the recordings date from the early 1970s, the sound has come up well in its digital transfer. The only reservation is that Barenboim's piano in the *Spring* Sonata seems more closely balanced than Zukerman's violin:

although Beethoven described these sonatas as being "for piano and violin", we think of them nowadays as for equal partners — which is, in fact, how they are written. But we can hear every detail of the violin part; it is only the balance which gives grounds for doubt, and one soon gets used to it. There is no doubt, though, about the quality of the performances of these three works, of which the ones with nicknames are deservedly the most popular among the ten that Beethoven wrote for these instruments. Zukerman and Barenboim do not hurry the music or force it expressively, so that all sounds natural. Not only that, their playing is also in scale and even intimate, as chamber music should be — in contrast to the over-projected performances offered by some of today's players. This, of course, is ideal for listening in one's own living room, in other words in much the same circumstances as prevailed when these works were written. We might like the Minuet middle movement of the G major Sonata to dance along a bit more freely, but such is the elegance of the playing that we are persuaded of the viability of the tempo, at least on this occasion, and it does bring a good contrast with the rapid (but unrushed) finale that follows. The performance of the *Kreutzer* Sonata is as noble as the music itself, something which one guesses will be the case as soon as one hears Zukerman's aristocratic delivery of the difficult double-stopped opening, played with impeccable intonation. This is not the most fiery account of the first movement and finale, but its warmth is still tempered by authority, and the variation-form slow movement is beautifully shaped.

Additional recommendations ...
Nos. 5 and 9. **Itzhak Perlman** (vn); **Vladimir Ashkenazy** (pf). Decca 410 554-2DH — lh 2m ADD 11/83
Nos. 5 and 9. **Thomas Zehetmair** (vn); **Malcolm Frager** (fp). Teldec Digital Experience 9031-75856-2 — 59m DDD 6/92
Nos. 5, 9 and 10. **Zino Francescatti** (vn); **Robert Casadesus** (pf). Sony Classical Essential Classics MK46342 — lh 16m ADD 3/91
Nos. 5 and 9. **Takako Nishizaki** (vn); **Jenö Jandó** (pf). Naxos 8 550283-2 — 56m DDD 3/91

Key to Symbols

Gramophone Award winners

Artists of the Year

Beethoven. CHORAL WORKS. **Ambrosian Singers; London Symphony Orchestra/Michael Tilson Thomas.** CBS Masterworks CD76404. Texts and translations included. From 76404 (11/75).
König Stephan — incidental music, Op. 117. Elegischer Gesang, Op. 118. Opferlied, Op. 121*b* (with Lorna Haywood, sop). Bundeslied, Op. 122. Meeresstille und glückliche Fahrt, Op. 112.

52m ADD 11/88

Astonishing as it may seem, none of the choral works here, with the exception of the imaginative setting of Goethe's *Meeresstille und glückliche Fahrt*, appears to have been recorded before. This disc is therefore warmly to be welcomed because of its first-class orchestral playing (heard on its own in the curious but lively *King Stephan* overture) and splendid choral singing, with a recording quality to match. The tender orchestral introduction to the elegy for the wife of Beethoven's sympathetic landlord Baron Pasqualati is a real gem (and is beautifully played); and two of the other works are of particular interest for their unusual scoring. The light-hearted convivial *Bundeslied* was mulled over in the composer's mind for a quarter of a century before emerging in 1822; and Beethoven was so fascinated by the poem of the *Opferlied* that he made no fewer than three settings of it before this last one.

Beethoven. LIEDER.
Brahms. LIEDER. **Dietrich Fischer-Dieskau** (bar); **Jörg Demus** (pf). DG 415 189-2GH. Text and translations included.
Beethoven: An die ferne Geliebte. Op 98. Adelaide, Op. 46. Zärtliche Liebe, WoO123. L'amante impaziente, Op. 82 Nos. 3 and 4. In questa tomba oscura, WoO133. Maigesang, Op. 52 No. 4. Es war einmal ein König, Op. 75 No. 3 (all from SLPM139216/18, 2/67).
Brahms: Vier ernste Gesänge, Op. 121[a]. O wüsst' ich doch den Weg zurück, Op. 63 No. 8[b]. Auf dem Kirchhofe, Op. 105 No. 4[b]. Alte Liebe, Op. 72 No. 1[b]. Verzagen, Op. 72 No. 4.[b] Nachklang, Op. 59 No. 4[b]. Feldeinsamkeit, Op. 86 No. 2[b] ([a] from SLPM138644, 10/61; [b] SLPM138011 (5/59).

1h 11m ADD 9/85

Beethoven's small oeuvre of songs is rich and varied. The six songs of *An die ferne Geliebte* follow the unrequited lover's reflections on his beloved, with the piano weaving its way between the individual songs setting the mood and gently assisting the narrative; indeed, it even has the last word. Fischer-Dieskau's intelligent and intense delivery are assisted by his warm tone and easy legato. He adds Beethoven's great song *Adelaide* and, among others, three Italian settings, lightening the tone and raising the spirits for the second half of the programme. Brahms's *Vier ernste Gesänge*, drawn from the image-laden texts of the Old Testament, reflect on man's fate in the great order of life and more particularly on death. The songs have a solemn character and settle in the lower register of the baritone's vocal range, a range that finds a particularly appropriate tone-colour in Fischer-Dieskau's expressive voice. The remainder of the recital draws on similarly severe songs, making for a well-devised programme with a consistent theme. Jörg Demus accompanies sensitively and the elderly recordings sound well.

NEW REVIEW

Beethoven. An die ferne Geliebte, Op. 98[a].
Schubert. Die schöne Müllerin, D795[b]. Winterreise, D911[c]. **Gerhard Hüsch** (bar); **Hanns Udo Müller** (pf). Preiser Lebendige Vergangenheit mono 89202. Item marked [a] from HMV DB4496/7 (3/50), [b] DB2429/36 (9/35), [c] DB2039/44 and HMV DA1344/6 (5/34). Recorded 1933-36.

② 2h 17m AAD 12/92 

These recordings by the German baritone Gerhard Hüsch were made for HMV in the mid-1930s, and through their superb quality, helped to establish the full performance of Schubert's song cycles on record. Hüsch was extraordinarily well-equipped as a singer: he possessed considerable musical insight, and a most beautiful mellow baritone voice. His diction was exemplary, having trained as an actor, and his overall approach to interpretation was restrained rather than demonstrative. The performances of the two Schubert song cycles possess an insight rare in recordings of these master pieces: while investing each song with its own individual character, Hüsch also creates throughout each cycle an appropriate atmosphere: of innocent joy in *Die schöne Müllerin*, and of more intense melancholy in *Winterreise*. In both instances the sense of a psychological as well as a physical journey is very strong. Beethoven's *An die ferne Geliebte* does not plumb such profound depths as the two Schubert cycles, but as one would expect, Hüsch provides a well-turned performance, full of subtlety. His accompanist throughout is the pianist/conductor Hanns Udo Müller whose piano playing is technically immaculate and who supports Hüsch with perfectly judged phrasing and timing. HMV's recordings stand the test of time, and the transcriptions, by the Austrian company Preiser, are most sympathetic. Prospective purchasers can be assured of a musically first rate set of performances which, despite their age, have worn extraordinarily well. Sadly, there are no texts or translations.

NEW REVIEW

Beethoven. Mass in C major, Op. 86[a]. Ah perfido!, Op. 65[b]. Meeresstille und glückliche Fahrt, Op. 112[c]. [ab]**Charlotte Margiono** (sop); [a]**Catherine Robbin** (mez); [a]**William Kendall** (ten); [a]**Alistair Miles** (bass); [ac]**Monteverdi Choir; Orchestre Révolutionnaire**

et Romantique/John Eliot Gardiner. Archiv Produktion 435 391-2AH. Texts and translations included. Items marked [a] recorded in 1989, [b] 1991.

1h 2m DDD 11/92 

The distinctive genius of this Mass would have been recognized much more widely if it had not been overshadowed by the supreme masterpiece, the *Missa solemnis*. That was written in 1820, and the C major Mass dates from 1808, so that not surprisingly it has a freshness of spirit about it as well as an innovative challenge caught in Beethoven's words to his publishers: "I believe I have treated the text as it has seldom been treated before". One feature that startled his contemporaries was a responsiveness to words, almost as though as to a dramatic text. Another is the characteristic unpredictability, a quality well brought out in this recording. Gardiner came to it in the studio *after* the *Missa solemnis*, in which his way of making familiar things new had almost limitless scope. It is manifest here too: details of the score repeatedly spring to a life which has specific character and purpose in it. The rhythms dance in the fine orchestral playing, and the Monteverdi Choir have always had the happy knack of making their discipline sound like spontaneity, and vice versa. There is also an excellent performance by Charlotte Margiono of the dramatic *scena, Ah perfido!*, marked equally by variety of expression and beauty of tone. The choral *Meeresstille* ("Sea-calm") has been used before now as a fill-up: a marvellously descriptive piece, imaginatively performed here and recorded with a finely-achieved balance between chorus and orchestra.

Beethoven. Mass in D major, Op. 123, "Missa solemnis". **Charlotte Margiono** (sop); **Catherine Robbin** (mez); **William Kendall** (ten); **Alastair Miles** (bass); **Monteverdi Choir; English Baroque Soloists/John Eliot Gardiner.** Archiv Produktion 429 779-2AH. Text and translation included. Recorded in 1989.

1h 12m DDD 3/91 

NEW REVIEW

Beethoven. Mass in D major, Op. 123, "Missa solemnis". **Cheryl Studer, Jessye Norman** (sops); **Plácido Domingo** (ten) **Kurt Moll** (bass); **Leipzig Radio Chorus; Swedish Radio Chorus; Eric Ericson Chamber Choir; Vienna Philharmonic Orchestra/James Levine.** DG 435 770-2GH2. Text and translation included. Recorded in 1991.

(2) 1h 23m DDD 11/92 

NEW REVIEW

Beethoven. Mass in D major, Op. 123, "Missa solemnis". **Eva Mei** (sop); **Marjana Lipovšek** (contr); **Anthony Rolfe Johnson** (ten); **Robert Holl** (bass); **Arnold Schöenberg Choir; Chamber Orchestra of Europe/Nikolaus Harnoncourt.** Teldec 9031-74884-2. Text and translation included. Recorded in 1992.

(2) 1h 21m DDD 4/93 

The *Missa solemnis* is generally agreed to be one of the supreme masterpieces of the nineteenth century, but attempts to record a genuinely great performance have over many years run into difficulties. Usually the greatness itself is flawed, perhaps in the quality of the solo singers or in some particular passages where the conductor's approach is too idiosyncratic or momentarily not up to the challenge of Beethoven's inspiration (an example is Klemperer's heavy-handedness in the fugues). The strain upon the choir, especially its sopranos, is notorious; similarly the technical problems of balance by producer and engineers. But suddenly in the last three years there have appeared three recordings, all of which rank with the best as performances, and at least two of which can be recommended as recorded sound. The version under John Eliot Gardiner came first, and it remains a very probable first choice. It combines discipline and spontaneous creativity, the rhythms are magically alive and the intricate texture of sound is made wonderfully clear. The great fugues of the *Gloria* and *Credo* achieve at the right points their proper Dionysiac sense of exalted liberation. These are qualities which the Levine recording shares, but the means are sharply contrasted. Gardiner uses a choir of 36 and an orchestra of 60 playing on period instruments, aiming at a "leaner and fitter" sound. Levine has the traditional large forces of singers and players. Gardiner's soloists are admirable but they are not 'names', whereas Levine has a quartet that constitutes what the record's promoters claimed as "the most luxurious of our time". That may create more suspicion than confidence, for singers who are at home in *Aida* do not necessarily fit the bill in the *Missa solemnis*. These four, however, sing magnificently and their opulence of tone proves a genuine enrichment. In some respects, Harnoncourt's performance is still finer. Though he, like Levine, is working in the Grosses Festspielhaus at Salzburg and is recorded live, his performance has the greater clarity, partly because of the forces used: his period timpani, for instance, do not boom like Levine's later ones. Then, in comparison with Gardiner, Harnoncourt's way sometimes has more humanity about it: the march of his *Credo*, for instance, is less military than Gardiner's. The drawback is in the quality of recorded sound, which lacks the bloom of Levine's and the sharp immediacy of the Gardiner, which, to that extent and in their contrasting ways, may be found preferable.

Additional recommendations ...

Soloists; Vienna Singverein; Berlin Philharmonic Orchestra/Herbert von Karajan. DG 419 166-2GH2 — ② 2h 21m DDD 10/86 Ⓑ

Soloists; Atlanta Symphony Chorus and Orchestra/Robert Shaw. Telarc CD80150 — ② 2h 19m DDD 11/88 Ⓑ

Mass[a]. *Choral Fantasia in C minor, Op. 80*[b]. **Soloists;** [a]**New Philharmonia Chorus;** [b]**John Alldis Choir; New Philharmonia Orchestra/Otto Klemperer.** EMI CMS7 69538-2 — ② 1h 40m ADD 12/88 Ⓑ

Beethoven. FIDELIO. **Christa Ludwig** (mez) Leonore; **Jon Vickers** (ten) Florestan; **Walter Berry** (bass) Don Pizarro; **Gottlob Frick** (bass) Rocco; **Ingeborg Hallstein** (sop) Marzelline; **Gerhard Unger** (ten) Jacquino; **Franz Crass** (bass) Don Fernando; **Kurt Wehofschitz** (ten) First Prisoner; **Raymond Wolansky** (bar) Second Prisoner; **Philharmonia Chorus and Orchestra/Otto Klemperer.** EMI CMS7 69324-2. Notes, text and translation included. From Columbia SAX2451/3 (6/62). Recorded in 1962.

② 2h 8m ADD 1/90 £ Ⓑ

Fidelio teems with emotional overtones and from the arresting nature of the Overture, through the eloquence of the quartet, through the mounting tension of the prison scene to the moment of release when the wrongly imprisoned Florestan is freed, Beethoven unerringly finds the right music for his subject. Klemperer's set has been a classic since it first appeared on LP way back in 1962. The performance draws its strength from his conducting: he shapes the whole work with a granite-like strength and a sense of forward movement that is unerring, while paying very deliberate attention to instrumental detail, particularly as regards the contribution of the woodwind. With the authoritative help of producer Walter Legge, the balance between voices and orchestra is faultlessly managed. The cumulative effect of the whole reading is something to wonder at and shows great dedication on all sides. Most remarkable among the singers is the soul and intensity of Christa Ludwig's Leonore. In her dialogue as much as in her singing she conveys the single-minded conviction in her mission of rescuing her beleaguered and much-loved husband. Phrase after phrase is given a frisson that has the ring of truth to it. As her Florestan, Jon Vickers conveys the anguish of his predicament. One or two moments of exaggeration apart this is another memorable assumption. Walter Berry, as Pizarro, suggests a small man given too much power. Gottlob Frick is a warm, touching Rocco, Ingeborg Hallstein a fresh, eager Marzelline, Gerhard Unger a youthful Jacquino, Franz Crass a noble Don Fernando. This is a set that should be in any worthwhile collection of opera.

Additional recommendations ...

Fidelio. **Soloists; Vienna State Opera Chorus; Vienna Philharmonic Orchestra/Leonard Bernstein.** DG 419 436-2GH2 — ② 2h 15m ADD 6/87 Ⓑ

Fidelio. **Soloists; Chorus of the Deutsche Oper, Berlin; Berlin Philharmonic Orchestra/Herbert von Karajan.** EMI CMS7 69290-2 — ② 1h 59m ADD 4/88 Ⓑ

Fidelio. **Soloists; Dresden State Opera Chorus; Staatskapelle Dresden/Bernard Haitink.** Philips 426 308-2PH2 — ② 2h 13m DDD 1/91 Ⓑ

Fidelio. **Soloists; Chorus; NBC Symphony Orchestra/Arturo Toscanini.** RCA Victor Gold Seal mono GD60273 — ② 1h 52m ADD 10/92 Ⓑ ▲

Fidelio. Leonore Overture No. 3, Op. 72[a]. **Soloists; Bavarian State Opera Chorus; Bavarian State Orchestra; [a]Berlin Philharmonic Orchestra/Ferenc Fricsay.** DG Dokumente 437 345-2GDO2 — ② 2h 8m ADD 5/93 Ⓑ ▲
Fidelio. **Soloists; Vienna State Opera Chorus; Vienna Philharmonic Orchestra/Wilhelm Furtwängler.** EMI Références mono CHS7 64496-2 — ② 2h 13m ADD 5/93 Ⓑ ▲

Vincenzo Bellini

Italian 1801-183

Bellini. OPERATIC ARIAS.
Puccini. OPERATIC ARIAS. **Maria Callas** (sop); [a]**Philharmonia Orchestra;** [b]**Orchestra of La Scala, Milan/Tullio Serafin.** EMI mono CDC7 47966-2. Texts and translations included. Items marked [a] from Columbia mono 33CX1204 (12/54), [b] HMV mono ASD3535 (8/78). Items marked [a] recorded in 1954, [b] 1955.
Puccini: MANON LESCAUT[a] — In quelle trine morbide; Sola, perduta, abbandonata. MADAMA BUTTERFLY[a] — Un bel dì vedremo; Con onor muore. LA BOHEME[a] — Sì, mi chiamano Mimì; Donde lieta uscì. SUOR ANGELICA[a] — Senza mamma. GIANNI SCHICCHI[a] — O mio babbino caro. TURANDOT[a] — Signore, ascolta!; In questa reggia; Tu che di gel sei cinta. ***Bellini:*** LA SONNAMBULA[b] — Compagne, teneri amici ... Come per me sereno; Oh, se una volta sola ... Ah, non credea mirarti ... Ah, non giunge.

1h 5m ADD 12/87 ▲

This coupling gives a fine insight into Maria Callas's unparalleled interpretative powers. The Puccini arias are all much-loved favourites. As Mimì, the heroine of *La bohème*, Callas softens the voice, seeking out the character's gloriously wide-eyed view of life as well as the vulnerability, whilst as Butterfly she displays a nobility and powerful optimism that holds our attention quite as powerfully as our obvious sympathy for her plight. Those two most beautiful melodies "Senza mamma" and "O mio babbino caro" are gently shaded and masterfully accompanied by Tullio Serafin, one of Callas's most sensitive accompanists. The sound dates from 1954-5 but is clear, well balanced and atmospheric. The two Bellini arias elicit a different response from singer and conductor. The character is carried totally in the voice, the shaping of a line, the shading of a word. The great Sleepwalking scene with which the disc closes is one of Callas's greatest assumptions and shows an insight into the psychology of the opera's central character that has never been equalled.

NEW REVIEW

Bellini. IL PIRATA. **Piero Cappuccilli** (bar) Ernesto; **Montserrat Caballé** (sop) Imogene; **Bernabé Martí** (ten) Gualtiero; **Giuseppe Baratti** (ten) Itulbo; **Ruggero Raimondi** (bass) Goffredo; **Flora Raffanelli** (sop) Adele; **Rome RAI Chorus and Orchestra/Gianandrea Gavazzeni.** EMI CMS7 64169-2. Notes, text and translation included. From HMV SLS953 (9/71). Recorded in 1970.

② 2h 22m ADD 2/93

Bellini's third opera had its première in 1827, in the heyday of Rossini whose influence is clearly discernible. Where the composer's own special qualities find best scope is often in the duets and ensembles, some of which rise to the needs of the dramatic situation with great power and beauty. The story tells of Gualtiero and his pirate band shipwrecked and thrown on the mercy of the noble lady Imogene who turns out to be the lost love of Gualtiero and subsequently married through cruel necessity to Ernesto. There is also a role for a hermit (Goffredo), so everybody is well provided, and the scenario yields many a dire event, signalled in the English translation by cries such as "What a moment to arrive!". In 1971 when the recording itself first arrived it was more of a novelty in kind than it is now and was warmly welcomed, both for the opportunity to hear an operatic rarity and for the singing of Montserrat Caballé, then at the height of her powers. She does indeed give a lovely performance, unmatched however by Bernabé Martí, who at least deserves credit for grappling with such a daunting role, or Piero Cappuccilli, who is simply dull. Fine singing comes from the young Raimondi as the hermit, and the Rome chorus and orchestra respond well to Gavazzeni's often inspired conducting.

Bellini. NORMA. **Maria Callas** (sop) Norma; **Ebe Stignani** (mez) Adalgisa; **Mario Filippeschi** (ten) Pollione; **Nicola Rossi-Lemeni** (bass) Orovesco; **Paolo Caroli** (ten) Flavio; **Rina Cavallari** (sop) Clotilde; **Chorus and Orchestra of La Scala, Milan/Tullio Serafin.** EMI mono CDS7 47304-8. Notes, text and translation included. From Columbia mono 33CX1179/80 (11/54). Recorded in 1954.

③ 2h 40m ADD 3/86 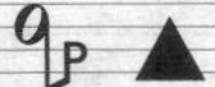

Norma may be considered the most potent of Bellini's operas, both in terms of its subject — the secret love of a Druid priestess for a Roman general — and its musical content. It has some of the most eloquent music ever written for the soprano voice and two duets that show Bellini's gift for liquid melody. The title-role has always been coveted by dramatic sopranos, but there have been few in the history of the opera who have completely fulfilled its considerable vocal and histrionic demands: in recent times the leading exponent has been Maria Callas. The mono recording comes up sounding remarkably forward and immediate on CD, and it captures Callas's commanding and moving assumption of the title part, the vocal line etched with deep feeling, the treatment of the recitative enlivening the text. Stignani is a worthy partner whilst Filippeschi is rough but quite effective. Serafin knew better than anyone since how to mould a Bellinian line to best effect.

Additional recommendations ...

Soloists; London Symphony Chorus and Orchestra/Richard Bonynge. Decca 425 488-2DM3 — ③ 2h 5lm ADD

Soloists; Chorus and Orchestra of La Scala, Milan/Tullio Serafin. EMI CMS7 63000-2 — ③ 2h 4lm ADD 7/89

Highlights from the above recording are also available separately. Details are as follows:
Casta diva; Va, crudele; O rimembranza; O non tremare; Introduction, Act 2; Mira, o Norma; Guerra, guerra; In mia man' alfin tu sei; Taci, ne ascolta appena. EMI CDM7 63091-2 — lh 4m ADD 7/89

Bellini. LA SONNAMBULA. **Maria Callas** (sop) Amina; **Nicola Monti** (ten) Elvino; **Nicola Zaccaria** (bass) Count Rodolfo; **Fiorenza Cossotto** (Mez) Teresa; **Eugenia Ratti** (sop) Lisa; **Giuseppe Morresi** (bass) Alessio; **Franco Ricciardi** (ten) Notary. **Chorus and Orchestra of La Scala, Milan/Antonino Votto.** EMI mono CDS7 47378-8. Notes text and translation included. From Columbia 33CX51469, 33CX1470/1 (10/57). Recorded in 1957.

② 2h lm ADD 9/86 

Dramatically this opera is a tepid little mix which might be subtitled *The mistakes of a night* if that did not suggest something more amusing than what actually takes place. Musically, the promise of a brilliant finale keeps most people in their seats until the end, and there are half-a-dozen charming, sometimes exquisite items on the way. But it is all a little insubstantial, and much depends upon the performance, especially that of the soprano. The name of Maria Callas is sufficient to guarantee that there will be a particular interest in the work of the heroine. As usual, her individuality is apparent from the moment of her arrival. Immediately a character is established, not an insipid little miss but a woman in whom lurks a potential for tragedy. This is the pattern throughout and much has exceptional beauty of voice and spirit. Nicola Monti has all the sweetness of the traditional lyric tenor; the pity is that what might have been a most elegant performance is marred by the intrusion of unwanted aspirates. Nicola Zaccaria sings the bass aria gracefully, and carrying off her small role with distinction is Fiorenza Cossotto, at the start of her career. The orchestral playing is neat, the conducting sensible and the recording clear.

Additional recommendation ...

Soloists; London Opera Chorus; National Philharmonic Orchestra/Richard Bonynge. Decca 417 424-2DH2 — ② 2h 2lm DDD 4/87

Bellini. I PURITANI. **Montserrat Caballé** (sop) Elvira; **Alfredo Kraus** (ten) Arturo; **Matteo Manuguerra** (bar) Riccardo; **Agostino Ferrin** (bass) Giorgio; **Júlia Hamari** (mez) Enrichetta; **Stefan Elenkov** (bass) Gualtiero; **Dennis O'Neill** (ten) Bruno; **Ambrosian Opera Chorus; Philharmonia Orchestra/Riccardo Muti.** EMI CMS7 69663-2. Notes, text and translation included. From SLS5201 (1/81). Recorded in 1979.

③ 2h 52m ADD 4/89

Bellini's opera of the English Civil War is probably his most readily attractive score, for its moods encompass a gaiety unknown to *Norma* and the writing is much more robust than *La sonnambula*. As in all of his work, a great deal depends upon the singers and it is to them that one normally looks first. Here, however, Riccardo Muti is in charge, a conductor with strong ideas about what may be allowed the singers by way of traditional license: on the whole he keeps a tight rein but compensates by taking slow speeds so that the melodies may never pass by with their beauties unobserved. The refinement is notable in the introduction to the bass aria near the start of Act 2, and there is no lack of strength and rhythmic excitement in the surging melody of the Finale to Act 1. The performance also benefits from particularly alert choral work by the Ambrosians, and from imaginative production. The spotlight is on the singers even so. As the sorely tried heroine Caballé is ideal as long as nothing too strenuous arises to put pressure on her exceptionally lovely voice. Her ethereal tones have a fine effect in the off-stage prayer, and her "Qui la voce" is deeply felt as well as beautifully sung. Kraus is perhaps the best tenor of recent times in this repertoire and there is nearly always a personal character about his singing that gives it distinction. This is a quality somewhat lacking in the baritone, Matteo Manuguerra; all the same there is some good solid tone and he makes an honest job of his cadenzas.

Additional recommendations ...

Soloists; Chorus and Orchestra of La Scala, Milan/Tullio Serafin. EMI mono CDS7 47308-8 — ② 2h 22m ADD 4/89

Soloists; Chorus and Orchestra of the Teatro Massimo, Catania/Richard Bonynge. Nuova Era 6842/44 — ③ 2h 30m DDD 10/91

Paul Ben-Haim

Israel 1897-1974

NEW REVIEW

Ben-Haim. Violin Concerto.

Castelnuovo-Tedesco. Violin Concerto No. 2, Op. 66, "I profeti". **Itzhak Perlman** (vn); **Israel Philharmonic Orchestra/Zubin Mehta.** EMI CDC7 54296-2. Recorded in 1990.

50m DDD 5/93 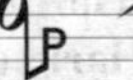 

Itzhak Perlman returns to his roots in this all-Jewish experience recorded live in Israel with the Israel Philharmonic under Zubin Mehta. Castelnuovo-Tedesco wrote three concertos of which this is the best-known, largely thanks to its ardent advocacy by no less a figure than Jascha Heifetz, who commissioned it. Stylistically it is reminiscent of Bloch and it would be difficult to imagine a more ideal soloist than Perlman, with his glowing tone and warm lyricism. Each movement takes the name of a prophet — thus the first is entitled "Isaiah", the second, an aptly long drawn-out lament is "Jeremiah" and the third, "Elijah", though here the connection between the thundering prophet and the opulent brilliance of the solo writing is more tenuous. At any rate, it proves an excellent vehicle for Perlman's lush brand of virtuosity. The second concerto is by Paul Ben-Haim, a German Jew who was born Paul Frankenburger but changed his name after settling in Palestine. Rather like Bartók, he has been heavily influenced by the folk music of his culture, though he is quick to point out that his language is influenced by his surroundings without borrowing melodies directly from other sources. Sound-wise, the sharply-etched rhythms of the first movement are reminiscent of Stravinsky's brand of neo-classicism while in the second movement the solo violin sings a cantorial-type melody high above the orchestra, culminating in a sparkling finale. This is surely one of Perlman's finest recordings and the live recording adds an extra *frisson* of excitement to the occasion.

George Benjamin

British 1960-

G. Benjamin. Antara.
Boulez. Dérive. Memoriale[a].
J. Harvey. Song Offerings[b]. [b]**Penelope Walmsley-Clark** (sop); [a]**Sebastian Bell** (fl); **London Sinfonietta/George Benjamin.** Nimbus NI5167. Text included. Recorded 1988-1989.

50m DDD 10/89

Well before reaching his thirtieth birthday in 1990 George Benjamin achieved a high reputation as a promising young composer and conductor. This disc sees that promise abundantly fulfilled with a well-balanced, satisfying programme of modern music. Benjamin's own work takes its titles from the Inca word for the panpipe and *Antara*'s scoring includes two synthesizer keyboards, linked to a sophisticated computer system, which enrich and transform the music's fascinating exploration of panpipe sound. Jonathan Harvey's inspiration is Indian rather than South American. In *Song Offerings* he sets a group of mystical love poems by Rabindranath Tagore in English, the music lacking nothing in immediacy of mood and exotic variety of vocal and instrumental colour. The two short pieces by Pierre Boulez are characteristically refined tributes: *Dérive* for Sir William Glock, who brought Boulez to the BBC in the 1960s, *Memoriale* for the French flautist Lawrence Beauregard, who died in 1985. They complete an excellently performed, atmospherically recorded disc: a cross-section of contemporary European music at its best.

Further listening ...

At first light[a]. Ringed by the flat horizon[b]. A Mind of Winter[c]. [c]**Penelope Walmsley-Clark** (sop); [a]**Gareth Hulse** (ob); [b]**Ross Pople** (vc); [c]**P. Archibald** (cl); [ac]**London Sinfonietta/George Benjamin;** [b]**BBC Symphony Orchestra/Mark Elder.** Nimbus NI5075.

Piano Sonata. **George Benjamin.** Nimbus NI1415 (CD single).

Richard Rodney Bennett

British 1936-

Suggested listening ...

Saxophone Concerto. *Coupled with* ***Debussy.*** Rapsodie. ***Glazunov.*** Saxophone Concerto in E flat major, Op. 109. ***Heath.*** Out of the Cool. ***Ibert.*** Concertino da camera. ***Villa-Lobos.*** Fantasia. **John Harle** (sax); **Academy of St Martin in the Fields/Sir Neville Marriner.** EMI CDC7 54301-2 (1/92).
See review in the Collections section; refer to the Index to Reviews.

Alban Berg

Austrian 1885-1935

NEW REVIEW

Berg. Violin Concerto.
Rihm. Gesungene Zeit. **Anne-Sophie Mutter** (vn); **Chicago Symphony Orchestra/James Levine.** DG 437 093-2GH. Recorded in 1992.

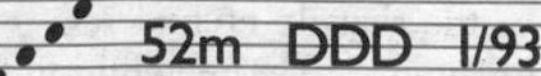

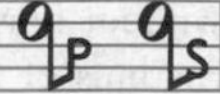

NEW REVIEW

Berg. Violin Concerto[a].
Janáček. Violin Concerto, "Pilgrimage of the soul"[a].

Hartmann. Concerto funebre[b]. **Thomas Zehetmair** (vn/[b]dir); [a]**Philharmonia Orchestra/Heinz Holliger;** [b]**Deutsche Kammerphilharmonie.** Teldec 2292-46449-2. Recorded 1990-91.

lh DDD 3/93

One of the very few 12-note pieces to have retained a place in the repertory, Berg's Violin Concerto is in fact a work on many levels. Behind the complex intellectual facade of the construction is a poignant sense of loss, ostensibly for Alma Mahler's daughter, Manon Gropius, but also for Berg's own youth; and behind that is a thoroughly disconcerting mixture of styles which resists interpretation as straightforward Romantic consolation. Not that performers need to go out of their way to project these layers; given a soloist as comprehensively equipped as Anne-Sophie Mutter and orchestral support as vivid as the Chicago Symphony's they simply cannot fail to register. This then makes a fine demonstration-quality recording alternative to the even more idiomatically insightful historic version of Krasner and Webern. And in their less flamboyant but equally persuasive way, Zehetmair and Holliger are very much in the same class; the Teldec recording is not quite so brightly lit as DG's, but if anything it is more realistically balanced. In other words, choice can safely be left to coupling; in which respect honours are again fairly even. In recent years Mutter has made a point of seeking out effective new *concertante* pieces as couplings to established repertoire concertos. The latest of these, by the 40-year-old German composer Wolfgang Rihm, is more or less in a historical line from Berg and his fellow-expressionists. *Gesungene Zeit* means "Time Chanted", and the music reflects the mystical implications of the title. It steers clear of the extremes of avant-garde hermeticism and post-modernist opportunism and should prove rewarding to anyone who can take Berg in their stride and is curious to discover what lies beyond. Zehetmair's choice is adventurous in a different way. Janáček's 12-minute Concerto, recently reconstructed from the fragmentary state in which he abandoned it in 1926, is related to his opera *From the House of the Dead*. Not a major addition to the repertory, it nevertheless has enough authentic late-Janáčekian passion to merit occasional performances. No less worthy of preservation is the 1959 Concerto by the Webern-pupil Karl Amadeus Hartmann. This is an energetic and assertive work, rather like radically intellectualized Prokofiev; performances and recording are again fine.

Additional recommendations ...

Violin Concerto. ***Stravinsky.*** *Violin Concerto in D minor.* **Itzhak Perlman** (vn); **Boston Symphony Orchestra/Seiji Ozawa.** DG 413 725-2GH — 48m ADD 12/84

Violin Concerto[a]. ***Stravinsky.*** *Violin Concerto in D minor*[b]. **Arthur Grumiaux** (vn); **Concertgebouw Orchestra/**[a]**Igor Markevitch,** [b]**Ernest Bour.** Philips Legendary Classics 422 136-2PLC — 45m ADD 10/88

Violin Concerto[a]. *Lyric Suite*[b]. [a]**Louis Krasner** (vn); [b]**Galimir Quartet;** [a]**BBC Symphony Orchestra/Anton Webern.** Testament SBT1004 — 57m ADD 6/91 ▲

Berg. Lyric Suite — arr. string orchestra (1929).
Schoenberg. Pelleas und Melisande, Op. 5. **Berlin Philharmonic Orchestra/Herbert von Karajan.** DG 423 132-2GH. From 2711 014 (3/75). Recorded 1973-1974.

lh lm ADD 5/88

If you thought Schoenberg's music was dominated by a singular distrust of harmony and other a-traditional beliefs then his vast tone-poem *Pelleas und Melisande* should restore the balance. Dating from 1903, *Pelleas* employs all the resources of the late-romantic symphony orchestra and the magnificent wash of colour Schoenberg conjures from these forces receives magnificent advocacy from Karajan and his Berliners. The music evocatively delineates the psychological contours of Maeterlinck's mysterious and emotionally-laden plot. Berg's *Lyric Suite* was composed as a six-movement chamber work but in 1927 his publisher suggested a string transcription. Berg chose the second, third and fourth movements as a suite for strings. Sparer and more advanced in sound than *Pelleas* these pieces have a shimmering beauty that is very intoxicating. Karajan obviously has great sympathy with this music and it receives a tender performance from him. The recordings are good if a trifle hazy.

Berg. Lulu Suite (1935)[a]. Three Orchestral Pieces, Op. 6 (rev. 1929). Altenberg Lieder, Op. 4[a]. [a]**Dame Margaret Price** (sop); **London Symphony Orchestra/Claudio Abbado.** DG 20th Century Classics 423 238-2GC. Texts and translations included. From 2530 146 (4/72).

1h 7m ADD 8/88

For all its subtlety and calculation, this is music that constantly spills over into raw, uninhibited aggressiveness, and Abbado's interpretations convey this quality magnificently. Berg's destiny as an opera composer is already discernible in the poised, arching vocal lines of the *Altenberg Lieder*, whose intricate accompaniments seem extravagantly detailed, given the brevity of the structures. Here, and even more clearly in the Three Orchestral Pieces, we can hear the sound-world and thematic characteristics of Mahler's later works carried to a still higher power, the music veering from frozen calm to frenzy in an instant. Berg's last years were dominated by his two great operas *Wozzeck* and *Lulu*, complementary studies in the psychopathology of degradation and despair that work the aesthetic miracle of drawing sublime music from the most sordid subject-matter. Although *Lulu* can now be heard complete, there is still a place for this suite of extracts that draws together some of the opera's most gripping and poignant music. Here, as in the *Altenberg Lieder*, the young Margaret Price is ideally flexible and full-toned. Although the digital remastering has produced an almost harshly immediate sound, the glare is tameable to a degree and is not inappropriate, given performances that vividly convey the barely-controlled violence of Berg's emotions.

Berg. Lulu Suite (1935)[a].
Schoenberg. Five Orchestral Pieces, Op. 16.
Webern. Six Pieces, Op. 6. [a]**Arleen Auger** (sop); **City of Birmingham Symphony Orchestra/Simon Rattle.** EMI CDC7 49857-2.

1h 6m DDD 11/89

Simon Rattle doesn't go to ostentatious lengths to demonstrate the different sound worlds these three composers inhabit (Schoenberg equals sinewy and Brahmsian, Berg equals lusciously Mahleresque, Webern equals coolly crystalline, would be an over-simple set of equations anyway) but he is good at recognizing each composer's tone of voice and his particular preoccupations; Berg's for a sort of sumptuous but ordered complexity, for instance, or Schoenberg's for an urgent forward impulse. All three have a refined lyricism in common, but Rattle's is a lighter, somewhat cooler lyricism than the polished but rather heavy-featured manner offered by many conductors in this repertory, and he reaches subtle or poignant areas of expression with greater ease. With the exception of a slight recessing of the soloist in the Berg, the recordings are excellent, their clarity revealing much beautifully moulded playing and precisely calculated internal balance.

Additional recommendation ...
Lulu Suite. Three Orchestral Pieces, Op. 6. **Schoenberg.** *Five Orchestral Pieces, Op. 16.* **Webern.** *Five Pieces for Orchestra, Op. 10.* **Helga Pilarczyk** (sop); **London Symphony Orchestra/Antal Dorati.** Mercury Living Presence 432 006-2MM — 1h 15m ADD 3/91

NEW REVIEW
Berg. Piano Sonata, Op. 1.
Liszt. Piano Works.
Webern. Variations, Op. 27. **Barry Douglas** (pf). RCA Victor Red Seal 09026 61221-2. Recorded in 1991.
Liszt: Piano Sonata in B minor, S178. Nuages gris, S199. R.W. — Venezia, S201. Schlaflos, Frage und Antwort, S203. Elegie No. 2, S197.

1h 1m DDD 12/92

Liszt's Piano Sonata leads something of a double life in the musical world. First of all it is a calling card for virtually every young virtuoso seeking to make a big impression; secondly it is recognized as one of the great path-breaking achievements in terms of compositional innovation, since its four movements-in-one structure is a source of inspiration for the early works of Schoenberg. Even more strikingly, the near-atonal intensity of the late piano works prepares for the harmonic explorations of Schoenberg, Berg and Webern. So Barry Douglas has been extremely astute in planning this recital. Berg's single-movement Sonata shares its home tonality with the Liszt Sonata and its main motif with that of *Nuages gris*, while the Webern *Variations* show the distant consequences of essentially the same line of thought. The outstanding performance is of the Berg, where Douglas is more responsive to the expressive ebb and flow than any current rival. His Liszt Sonata does not approach the heights of a Zimerman or a Brendel, but it is still an impressive achievement and the other works give much satisfaction too. The warm acoustic of Watford Town Hall lends a welcome glow to the recorded sound.

Berg. WOZZECK. **Franz Grundheber** (bar) Wozzeck; **Hildegard Behrens** (sop) Marie; **Heinz Zednik** (ten) Captain; **Aage Haugland** (bass) Doctor; **Philip Langridge** (ten) Andres; **Walter Raffeiner** (ten) Drum-Major; **Anna Gonda** (mez) Margret; **Alfred Sramek** (bass) First Apprentice; **Alexander Maly** (bar) Second Apprentice; **Peter Jelosits** (ten) Idiot; **Vienna Boys' Choir; Vienna State Opera Chorus; Vienna Philharmonic Orchestra/Claudio Abbado.** DG 423 587-2GH2. Notes, text and translation included. Recorded live in 1987.

② 1h 29m DDD 2/89

A live recording, in every sense of the word. The cast is uniformly excellent, with Grundheber, good both at the wretched pathos of Wozzeck's predicament and his helpless bitterness, and Behrens as an outstandingly intelligent and involving Marie, even the occasional touch of strain in her voice heightening her characterization. The Vienna Philharmonic respond superbly to Abbado's ferociously close-to-the-edge direction. It is a live recording with a bit of a difference, mark you: the perspectives are those of a theatre, not a recording studio. The orchestra is laid out as it would be in an opera house pit and the movement of singers on stage means that voices are occasionally overwhelmed. The result is effective: the crowded inn-scenes, the arrival and departure of the military band, the sense of characters actually reacting to each other, not to a microphone, makes for a grippingly theatrical experience. Audiences no longer think of *Wozzeck* as a 'difficult' work, but recordings have sometimes treated it as one, with a clinical precision either to the performance or the recorded perspective. This version has a raw urgency, a sense of bitter protest and angry pity that are quite compelling and uncomfortably eloquent.

Additional recommendations ...

Soloists; Chorus and Orchestra of the Deutsche Oper, Berlin/Karl Böhm. *Lulu (two-act version).* **Soloists; Chorus and Orchestra of the Deutsche Oper, Berlin/Karl Böhm.** DG 435 705-2GX3 — ③ ADD 3h 37m 1/93

Soloists; Vienna State Opera Chorus. ***Schoenberg.*** *Erwartung, Op. 17.* **Anja Silja** (sop); **Vienna Philharmonic Orchestra/Christoph von Dohnányi.** Decca 417 348-2DH2 — ② 2h 3m DDD 2/89

NEW REVIEW

Berg. LULU (orchestration of Act 3 completed by Friedrich Cerha). **Teresa Stratas** (sop) Lulu; **Franz Mazura** (bar) Dr Schön, Jack; **Kenneth Riegel** (ten) Alwa; **Yvonne Minton** (mez) Countess Geschwitz; **Robert Tear** (ten) The Painter, A Negro; **Toni Blankenheim** (bar) Schigolch, Professor of Medicine, The Police Officer; **Gerd Nienstedt** (bass) An Animal-tamer, Rodrigo; **Helmut Pampuch** (ten) The Prince, The Manservant, The Marquis; **Jules Bastin** (bass) The Theatre Manager, The Banker; **Hanna Schwarz** (mez) A Dresser in the theatre, High School Boy, A Groom; **Jane Manning** (sop) A 15-year-old girl; **Ursula Boese** (mez) Her Mother; **Anna Ringart** (mez) A Ldy Artist; **Claude Meloni** (bar) A Journalist; **Pierre-Yves Le Maigat** (bass) A Manservant; **Paris Opéra Orchestra/Pierre Boulez.** DG 415 489-2GH3. Notes, text and translation included. From 2740 213 (10/79).

③ 2h 52m ADD 11/86

Now here's a masterpiece that fulfils all the requirements needed for a commercial smash hit — it's sexy, violent, cunning, sophisticated, hopelessly complicated and leaves you emotionally drained. *Lulu* was Berg's second opera and easily matches his first — *Wozzeck* — for pathos and dramatic impact. The meaningful but gloriously over-the-top story-line, after two tragedies by Frank Wedekind, deserves acknowledgement. Lulu, mistress of Dr Schön, is married to a medical professor. An artist also has the hots for her, but just as his passion gets interestingly out of hand, her husband walks in, catches them approaching the act and dies of shock. She marries the artist, who learns about Dr Schön and kills himself; then she marries the jealous Dr Schön, and eventually kills *him*. Smuggled out of prison by an adoring lesbian, she sets up home in Paris with Schön's son, gets blackmailed and ends up in London as one of Jack the Ripper's victims! And that's not the half of it — but we'll spare you the rest. What matters is that Berg's music is magnificent, romantic enough to engage the passions of listeners normally repelled by 12-tone music, and cerebral enough to keep eggheads fully employed. It's opulent yet subtle (saxophone and piano lend the score a hint of jazz-tinted decadence), with countless telling thematic inter-relations and much vivid tonal character-painting. Berg left it incomplete (only 390 of the Third Act's 1,326 bars were orchestrated by him), but Friedrich Cerha's painstaking reconstruction is a major achievement, especially considering the complicated web of Berg's musical tapestry. This particular recording first opened our ears to the 'real' Lulu in 1979, and has transferred extremely well to CD. The booklet contains a superb essay by Boulez which in itself is enough to stimulate the interest of a potential listener. Performance-wise, it is highly distinguished. Teresa Stratas is an insinuating yet vulnerable Lulu, Yvonne Minton a sensuous Gräfin Geschwitz and Robert Tear an ardent artist. Dr Schön is tellingly portrayed by Franz Mazura (who also turns up as Jack the Ripper), Kenneth Riegel is highly creditable as Schön's son and that Boulez himself is both watchful of detail and responsive to the drama, hardly needs saying. It's not an easy listen, but it'll certainly keep you on your toes for a stimulating, even exasperating evening.

Erik Bergman

Finnish 1911-

Suggested listening ...

Nox, Op. 65. Bim Bam Boom, Op. 80. (The Birds) Fåglarna, Op. 56*a*. Hathor Suite, Op. 70. **Penelope Walmsley-Clark** (sop); **Stephen Varcoe** (bar); **John Potter** (ten); **New London Chamber Choir; Endymion Ensemble/James Wood.** Chandos CHAN8478 (1/88).

Auch so (myös näin). Came a letter (Det kom ett brev). Dreams. 4 Gallow Songs (Galgenlieder). Hathor Suite. The Lasses (Tyttöset). My tree is the stone-pine (Mitt träd är pinjen). Rain (Regn). Samothrake. The Single Moment (Den enda studen). Such an evening (En såda kväll). Watercolour (Akvarell). **Finnish Chamber Choir/Eric-Olof Söderström.** Finlandia FACD371 (12/89).

THE SINGING TREE. **Soloists; Dominante Choir; Tapiola Chamber Choir; Finnish National Opera Orchestra/Ulf Söderblom.** Ondine ODE794-2D (5/93).

Luciano Berio

Italian 1925-

Berio. Sinfonia[a]. Eindrücke. [a]**Regis Pasquier** (vn); [a]**New Swingle Singers; French National Orchestra/Pierre Boulez.** Erato 2292-45228-2. From NUM75198 (2/86).

45m DDD 7/88

Berio. Formazioni. 11 Folk Songs[a]. Sinfonia[b]. [a]**Jard van Nes** (mez); [b]**Electric Phoenix; Royal Concertgebouw Orchestra/Riccardo Chailly.** Decca 425 832-2DH. Texts and translations included.

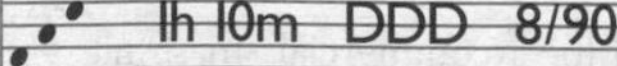

It's now far easier to distinguish avant-garde pieces of lasting value from ones that stand rather as historical curiosities and without question the music of Berio lives on, and his audience grows rather than dwindles. It says much for Berio's craftsmanship that his works still have a freshness about them where others today sound impossibly dated. Even *Sinfonia*, with its reference to Lévi-Strauss, Samuel Beckett and the death of Martin Luther King, transcends its original context and challenges us with extraordinary riches. Especially striking is the third movement, a weird collage of quotations from all manner of composers from Bach to Berg and from Beethoven to Boulez, carried out in stream-of-consciousness fashion against the ever-present background of the scherzo from Mahler's Second Symphony. Nor is it easy to forget the haunting second movement, in which a cloud of isolated floating syllables gradually coalesce into the words "Martin Luther King". Even in the movements that lack such a neat framework, the sheer energy of Berio's sound-world and the logic of his invention is utterly fascinating. This Boulez recording is authoritative and supersedes Berio's own. It is nicely complemented by the short but imposing orchestral score *Eindrücke*.

Riccardo Chailly's performance offers an innovative though still valid perspective of the *Sinfonia*. This is particularly noticeable in the now famous 'Mahler' movement, where Chailly tends to favour a more veiled and recessed balancing of the voices. This may seem rather an odd preference at first but it should be remembered that Berio himself asks for the voices to be only half-heard throughout the orchestral web of sound — an approach that is intended to encourage the listener to re-explore the music on each successive hearing. Chailly's performance certainly reveals more of the orchestral detail, and whereas Boulez brings to the surface the more menacing aspects of the work, in this recording they become submerged into an uneasy, subterranean undercurrent. The inclusion of the splendid *Formazioni* (Formations) of 1987 make this disc all the more desirable. The title reflects Berio's fascination for unusual displacements and groupings of instruments; in this case the dramatic deployment of antiphonal brass sections seated on either side of the orchestra, with strings occupying centre stage (the spatial qualities of this work are particularly effective in this recording). The result is a marvellously compelling and sonically spectacular piece of music which surely ranks as one of his most cogently structured and impressive works. The Decca recording is excellent.

Further listening ...

Coro for voices and instruments. **Cologne Radio Chorus and Symphony Orchestra/Luciano Berio.** DG 423 902-2GC (10/88).

Laborintus II. **Soloists; Chorale Expérimentale; Ensemble Musique Vivante/Luciano Berio.** Harmonia Mundi HMA190 764 (12/87).

Key to Symbols

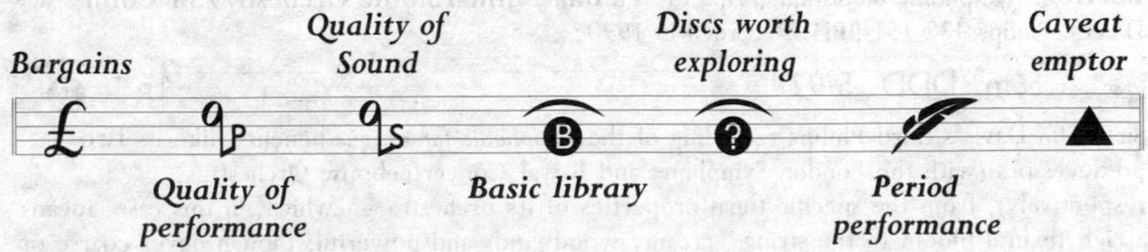

Sir Lennox Berkeley

British 1903-1989

Suggested listening ...

Five Short Pieces, Op. 4. Three Pieces, Op. 2. Polka, Op. 5*a*. Three Mazurkas, Op. 32 No. 1. Paysage. Improvisation on a Theme of Falla, Op. 55 No. 2. Mazurka, Op. 101 No. 2. Six Preludes, Op. 23. Piano Sonata, Op. 20. **Christopher Headington** (pf). Kingdom KCLCD2012 (6/89).

Irving Berlin

American 1888-1989

Suggested listening ...

ANNIE GET YOUR GUN. **Soloists; Ambrosian Chorus; London Sinfonietta/John McGlinn.** EMI CDC7 54206-2 (11/91).

Hector Berlioz

French 1803-1869

Berlioz. Harold in Italy, Op. 14[a]. Tristia, Op. 18[b]. Les troyens à Carthage – Act 2, Prelude[c]. [a]**Nobuko Imai** (va); [b]**John Alldis Choir; London Symphony Orchestra/Sir Colin Davis.** Philips 416 431-2PH. Texts and translations included. Item marked [a] from 9500 026 (3/76), [b] 9500 944 (6/83), [c] SAL3788 (3/70).

1h 10m ADD 12/86

Berlioz was much influenced by the British romantic poet, Byron, and his travels in Italy – where he went in 1831 as the winner of the Prix de Rome – led him to conceive a big orchestral work based on one of Byron's most popular works, *Childe Harold's Pilgrimage*. Like Berlioz's earlier *Symphonie fantastique*, *Harold in Italy* was not only a programme work but brilliantly unconventional and imaginative in its structure and argument. A commission from the great virtuoso, Paganini, led him to conceive a big viola concerto, but the idea of a Byronic symphony got in the way of that. Though there is an important viola solo in the symphony as we know it – richly and warmly played on this recording by Nobuko Imai – it is far from being the vehicle for solo display that Paganini was wanting. Sir Colin Davis's 1975 performance, beautifully transferred to CD, emphasizes the symphonic strength of the writing without losing the bite of the story-telling. The shorter works are also all valuable in illustrating Berlioz's extraordinary imagination. Excellent sound on all the different vintage recordings.

Additional recommendation ...
Harold in Italy. **Yuri Bashmet** (va); **Frankfurt Radio Symphony Orchestra/Eliahu Inbal.** Denon CO-73207 — 40m DDD 12/89

NEW REVIEW

Berlioz. Symphonie fantastique, Op. 14. **Vienna Philharmonic Orchestra/Sir Colin Davis.** Philips 432 151-2PH. Recorded in 1990.

56m DDD 5/92 

Sir Colin Davis's third Philips recording of the *Symphonie fantastique* benefits, like its two predecessors (with the London Symphony and Royal Concertgebouw Orchestras, respectively), from the specific tonal properties of its orchestra — which, in this case, means a rich texural bloom to the strings, creamy woodwinds and powerful, though never coarse or ungainly, brass. Davis has the VPO responding to him with absolute naturalness: barlines may as well not exist, and subtle rubato nudges salient passages with just the right degree of expressive emphasis. Repeats are observed in the first and fourth moments, while the second includes the rarely-heard solo cornet part which Berlioz added later and the fifth has tubular bells rather than electronic sound-alikes. The recording has immense impact, capturing as it does the orchestra's sweet violin tone, even at *pianissimo* and less, while allowing full impact at climaxes. The timpani, in particular, have great presence. As a composition, the *Symphonie fantastique* is a notoriously difficult synthesis of classical and romantic elements, a real stylistic crossroads. But Davis has the measure of its parts and fully undertands its musical tensions; his is the nearest we have to a thorough, all-embracing oveview, and it is to be enthusiastically recommended.

Additional recommendations ...
Symphonie fantastique. **London Classical Players/Roger Norrington.** EMI Reflexe CDC7 49541-2 — 53m DDD 4/89
Symphonie fantastique. Lélio, Op. 14b[a]. [a]**Nicolai Gedda,** [a]**Charles Burles** (tens); [a]**Jean van Gorp** (bar); [a]**Michel Sendrez** (pf); [a]**Jean Topart** (spkr); **Radio France** [a]**Chorus and Orchestra/Jean Martinon.** EMI CZS7 62739-2 — ② 1h 49m AAD 12/89
Symphonie fantastique[a]. *Overtures — King Lear, Op. 4*[b]. *Le carnaval romain, Op. 9*[c]. [a]**French Radio National Orchestra,** [b]**Royal Philharmonic Orchestra,** [c]**London Philharmonic Orchestra/Sir Thomas Beecham.** EMI Beecham Edition mono CDM7 64032-2 — 1h 11m ADD 8/92 ▲
Symphonie fantastique. **Orchestre Révolutionnaire et Romantique/John Eliot Gardiner.** Philips 434 402-2PH — 53m DDD 6/93

Berlioz. SONGS. [a]**Brigitte Fournier** (sop); [b]**Diana Montague,** [c]**Catherine Robbin** (mezs); [d]**Howard Crook** (ten); [e]**Gilles Cachemaille** (bar); **Lyon Opéra Orchestra/John Eliot Gardiner.** Erato MusiFrance 2292-45517-2. Texts and translations included. Recorded in 1989.
Le jeune pâtre breton, Op. 13 No. 4[d]. La captive, Op. 12[c]. Le chasseur danois, Op. 19 No. 6[e]. Zaïde, Op. 19 No. 1[a]. La belle voyageuse, Op. 2 No. 4[b]. Les nuits d'été, Op. 7 – Villanelle[d]; Le spectre de la rose[c]; Sur les lagunnes[e]; Absence[b]; Au cimetière[d]; L'île inconnue[b]. Aubade[d]. Tristia, Op. 18 – No. 2, La mort d'Ophélie[c].

1h 5m DDD 2/91

Berlioz intended the songs in his cycle *Les nuits d'eté* to be assigned to different types of singers. This excellent issue fulfils his wishes, and each of the performers has been carefully chosen to fit his or her particular offering. In turn, Montague, Robbin, Crook and Cachemaille ideally catches the mood and feeling of his or her piece, and each has the kind of tone that seems perfectly suited to Berlioz's idiom. In support, Gardiner finds just the right tempo for each song, never indulging in the over-deliberate speed that can kill the slower songs with kindness. He and his orchestra play Berlioz's wonderfully atmospheric accompaniments with beauty and sensitivity. To add to one's pleasure there is a generous selection of Berlioz's other songs with orchestra, equally well interpreted. Robbin's account of the marvellous *La captive*, the very essence of this composer's brand of romanticism, is a particular joy.

Berlioz. Grande messe des morts[a]. Symphonie funèbre et triomphale[b]. [a]**Ronald Dowd** (ten); [b]**Dennis Wick** (tb); [a]**Wandsworth School Boys' Choir;** [b]**John Alldis Choir; London Symphony Chorus**[a] **and Orchestra/Sir Colin Davis.** Philips 416 283-2PH2. Notes, texts and translations included. Item marked [a] from 6700 019 (9/70), [b] SAL3788 (3/70).

② 2h 7m 4/86

Berlioz's Requiem is not a liturgical work, any more than the *Symphonie funèbre* is really for the concert hall; but both are pieces of high originality, composed as ceremonials for the fallen, and standing as two of the noblest musical monuments to the French ideal of a *gloire*. The Requiem is most famous for its apocalyptic moment when, after screwing the key up stage by stage, Berlioz's four brass bands blaze forth "at the round earth's imagin'd corners"; this has challenged the engineers of various companies, but the Philips recording for Colin Davis remains as fine as any, not least since Davis directs the bands with such a strong sense of character. He also gives the troubled rhythms of the *Lacrymosa* a stronger, more disturbing emphasis than any other conductor, and time and again finds out the expressive counterpoint, the emphatic rhythm, the telling few notes within the texture, that reveal so much about Berlioz's intentions. The notorious flute and trombone chords of the *Hostias* work admirably. Ronald Dowd is a little strained in the *Sanctus*, but the whole performance continues to stand the test of time and of other competing versions. The same is true of the *Symphonie funèbre et triomphale*, which moves at a magisterial tread and is given a recording that does well by its difficult textures. A fine coupling of two remarkable works.

Additional recommendation ...
Grande messe[a]. *Te Deum, Op. 22*[b]. [a]**Stuart Burrows** (ten); [b]**Jean Dupouy** (ten); [b]**Jean Guillou** (org); [a]**French Radio Chorus;** [b]**Paris Orchestra Chorus;** [b]**Paris Enfante Choir;**

[b]Maîtrise de la Résurrection; [a]French National Orchestra; [a]French Radio Philharmonic Orchestra/Leonard Bernstein; [b]Paris Orchestra/Daniel Barenboim. CBS Maestro CD46461 — ② 2h 7m ADD 9/91

Berlioz. Roméo et Juliette – dramatic symphony, Op. 16. **Patricia Kern** (contr); **Robert Tear** (ten); **John Shirley-Quirk** (bar); **John Alldis Choir; London Symphony Chorus and Orchestra/Sir Colin Davis.** Philips 416 962-2PH2. Notes, text and translation included. From SAL3695/6 (12/68). Recorded in 1968.

② lh 37m ADD 6/88

Berlioz's 'dramatic symphony' of 1839 is a prime example of early and full-blooded romanticism. The impulsive young composer adored Shakespeare and here he took the English playwright's celebrated love story and set it to music, not as an opera but a symphony with voices, partly because he felt that the language of instrumental music was "richer, more varied and free of limitations and ... incomparably more powerful". This music is, nevertheless, sometimes inspired and sometimes simply naïve, but always spontaneous and Sir Colin Davis, a great Berlioz champion, plays it as if he believed passionately and urgently in every note. He is well supported by his three vocal soloists and the London Symphony Chorus and Orchestra plus the John Alldis Choir, and although the recording is now over 25 years old it does not show its age to any significant extent and indeed may be regarded as a classic Berlioz performance although the total length of 97 minutes for two full-priced discs is not generous by CD standards.

Additional recommendations ...

Roméo et Juliette[a]. *Les nuits d'été, Op.* 7. **Anne Sofie von Otter** (mez); **[a]Philip Langridge** (ten); **[a]James Morris** (bass); **[a]Berlin RIAS Chamber Choir; [a]Ernst Senff Chorus; Berlin Philharmonic Orchestra/James Levine.** DG 427 665-2GH2 — ② lh 43m DDD 8/90

Roméo et Juliette[a]. ***Franck.*** *Le Chasseur maudit*[b]. *Rédemption — Morceau symphonique*[b]. *Nocturne*[c]. **[a]Yvonne Minton, [c]Christa Ludwig** (mezs); **[a]Francisco Araiza** (ten); **[a]Jules Bastin** (bass); **[a]Orchestre de Paris Chorus; [abc]Orchestre de Paris/Daniel Barenboim.** DG Galleria 437 244-2GGA2 — ② 2h 9m ADD 1/93 £

Berlioz. Les nuits d'été, Op. 7[a]. La mort de Cléopâtre[b]. Les troyens – Act 5, scenes 2 and 3[c]. **Dame Janet Baker** (mez); **[c]Bernadette Greevy** (contr); **[c]Keith Erwen** (ten); **[c]Gwynne Howell** (bass); **[c]Ambrosian Opera Chorus; [a]New Philharmonia Orchestra/Sir John Barbirolli; [bc]London Symphony Orchestra/Sir Alexander Gibson.** EMI Studio CDM7 69544-2. Item marked [a] from ASD2444 (2/69), [b] and [c] ASD2516 (12/69).

lh 18m ADD 11/88 £ 

These performances can be recommended without hesitation, but unfortunately the presentation provides no texts and little information about the music. This is all very well if the listener has access to scores or librettos, but except for the laziest kind of enjoyment there is a real need here to know what the soloist is singing about. The words of *Les nuits d'été* are not too difficult to find, but with the deaths of Cleopatra and Dido you need to have more than a broad knowledge of the general situation. In mitigation it might be said that if any singer can be relied on to convey the sense of the words purely by her expression, and if any composer has a power of communication so vivid that words can almost be dispensed with, these are surely Baker and Berlioz respectively. The yearning and desperation of Cleopatra live in the singer's tone, just as surely as her pulse weirdly beats and then dies in the music. Similarly, Dido's changes of mood, her passionate intensity, her tender farewell to Carthage, are all imaginatively realized and deeply felt. *Les nuits d'été,* too, is wonderfully well caught in the whole range of its moods, with Barbirolli handling the orchestral score with unsurpassed sensitivity and care for detail.

Additional recommendations ...

Les nuits d'été[a]. ***Ravel.*** *Shéhérazade*[a]. ***Debussy.*** *Trois chansons de Bilitis*[b]. ***Poulenc***[b]. *Banalities — Chansons d'Orkenise; Hôtel. La courte paille — Le carafon; La reine de coeur. Chansons villageoises — Les gars qui vont à la fête. Deux poémes de Louis Aragon.* **Régine Crespin** (sop); **[b]John Wustman** (pf); [a]**Suisse Romande Orchestra/Ernest Ansermet.** Decca 417 813-2DH — lh 8m ADD 11/88

Les nuits d'été. **Duparc.** *Chanson triste. La manoir de Rosemonde. L'invitation au voyage. Soupir. Phidylé. La vie anterieure. Sérénade florentine.* **Bernadette Greevy** (mez); **Ulster Orchestra/Yan Pascal Tortelier.** Chandos CHAN8735 — 56m DDD 1/90

See also under "SONGS" earlier in this section.

Berlioz. L'enfance du Christ, Op. 25. **Robert Tear** (ten) Narrator; **David Wilson-Johnson** (bar) Herod; **Ann Murray** (mez) Mary; **Thomas Allen** (bar) Joseph; **Matthew Best** (bass) Ishmaelite Father; **Gerald Finley** (bar) Polydorus; **William Kendall** (ten) Centurion; **Choir of King's College, Cambridge; Royal Philharmonic Orchestra/Stephen Cleobury.** EMI CDS7 49935-2. Notes, text and translation included. Recorded in 1989.

② lh 37m DDD 12/90

The Choir of King's College, Cambridge has made this splendid recording of *L'enfance du Christ* with a strong, well-chosen all-English cast. The important role of Narrator falls to Robert Tear, who assumes it with warmth and sympathy and a good sense of the drama as it unfolds. David Wilson-Johnson makes a superb Herod, tortured and anguished in his mind before delivering his half-demented sentence of death upon the Holy Innocents. Ann Murray, as Mary, is tender and gentle, particularly in the quiet, idyllic stable scene. Thomas Allen portrays a convincing Joseph, firm and decisive in his singing, well able to face up to his responsibilities as head of the Holy Family. Matthew Best sings a rich and heart-warming welcome to them on their arrival in Egypt. The King's Choir, amply assisted by the chapel acoustics, are able to make the choir of angelic voices sound truly other-worldly, their repeated "Hosannas" fading gently upwards and away into the fan-vaulting – like clouds of incense – with magical effect. The acoustics also play an important part at the close of the oratorio, enabling the choir to bring it almost inevitably to its breathtaking conclusion of peace and quiet contemplation. Even if you've never heard any of this music before, except the famous "Shepherds' farewell" chorus, this really is compulsory Christmas listening!

Additional recommendations ...

L'enfance du Christ. **Soloists; Monteverdi Choir; Lyons Opera Orchestra/John Eliot Gardiner.** Erato 2292-45275-2 — ② lh 36m 1/88

L'enfance du Christ[a]. *Tristia, Op. 18 — excerpts*[b]. *Sara la baigneuse, Op. 11*[b]. *La mort de Cléopâtre*[b]. [a]**Soloists;** [ab]**St Anthony Singers;** [b]**English Chamber Orchestra,** [a]**Goldsbrough Orchestra, Sir Colin Davis.** Decca 425 445-2DM2 — ② 2h 22m ADD

Berlioz. La damnation de Faust. **Nicolai Gedda** (ten) Faust; **Jules Bastin** (bass) Méphistophélès; **Josephine Veasey** (mez) Marguérite; **Richard Van Allan** (bass) Brander; **Gillian Knight** (mez) Celestial Voice; **Wandsworth School Boys' Choir; Ambrosian Singers; London Symphony Chorus and Orchestra/Sir Colin Davis.** Philips 416 395-2PH2. Notes, text and translation included. From 6703 042 (1/74). Recorded in 1973.

② 2h 11m ADD 1/87

Sir Colin Davis's performance of *La damnation* reveals the colour and excitement of a work that has never found a true home in the opera house. No other of Berlioz's scores excels it in the subtle and telling use of detail, from the whole orchestra in full cry to the subtly judged chamber music combinations and to details of instrumental choice (as when the husky viola for Marguérite's touching little song about the bereft King of Thule yields to the mournful cor anglais for her abandonment by Faust). Davis's performance has the grandeur and excitement of Berlioz's vision of romantic man compassing his own damnation by being led to test and reject the consolations maliciously offered by Méphistophélès. No other conductor has made the "Hungarian March" turn so chillingly from its brave panoply to a menacing emptiness. The sylphs and will-o'-the-wisps flit and hover delicately. The transformation from the raucous boozers in Auerbach's cellar to Faust's dream of love on the banks of the Elbe is beautifully done, as the hurtling pace slows and the textures soften, Méphistophélès's sweet melodic line betrayed by the snarling brass accompaniment. The arrival of CD gave an extra edge to all this vivid and expressive detail. The singers are very much within this fine and faithful concept of the work. Gedda is an incomparably elegant, noble Faust, whose very gentleness is turned against him by the cold, sneering, ironic Méphistophélès of Jules Bastin. Josephine Veasey is a touching Marguérite who is not afraid to be simple; and Richard Van Allan knocks off a jovial Brander. Chorus and orchestra clearly enjoy the whole occasion, and rise to it.

Additional recommendation ...

Soloists; Cologne Radio Chorus; Stuttgart Radio Chorus; North German Radio Chorus, Hamburg; Frankfurt Radio Symphony Orchestra/Eliahu Inbal. Denon CO-77200/01 — ② 2h 7m DDD 7/91

Berlioz. BEATRICE ET BENEDICT. **Susan Graham** (sop) Béatrice; **Jean-Luc Viala** (ten) Bénédict; **Sylvia McNair** (sop) Héro; **Catherine Robbin** (mez) Ursule; **Gilles Cachemaille** (bar) Claudio; **Gabriel Bacquier** (bar) Somarone; **Vincent Le Texier** (bass) Don Pedro; **Philippe Magnant** (spkr) Léonato; **Lyon Opera Chorus and Orchestra/John Nelson.** Erato MusiFrance 2292-45773-2. Notes, text and translation included. Recorded in 1991.

② 1h 51m DDD 6/92

We have to note that the title is not a French version of *Much Ado about Nothing*, but that it takes the two principal characters of Shakespeare's play and constructs an opera around them. The comedy centres on the trick which is played upon the protagonists by their friends, producing love out of apparent antipathy. Much of the charm lies in the more incidental matters of choruses, dances, the magical "Nocturne" duet for Béatrice and Héro, and the curious addition of the character Somarone, a music-master who rehearses the choir in one of his own compositions. There is also a good deal of spoken dialogue, the present recording having more of it than did its closest rival, a version made in 1977 with Sir Colin Davis conducting and Dame Janet Baker and Robert Tear in the title-roles (see below). Perhaps surprisingly, the extra dialogue is a point in favour of the new set, for it is done very effectively by good French actors and it makes for a more cohesive, Shakespearian entertainment. John Nelson secures a well-pointed performance of the score, comparing well with Davis's, and with excellent playing by the Lyon Orchestra. Susan Graham and Jean-Luc Viala are attractively vivid and nimble in style, and Sylvia McNair makes a lovely impression in Héro's big solo. The veteran Gabriel Bacquier plays the music-master with genuine panache and without overmuch clownage. There is good work by the supporting cast and the chorus and the recording is finely produced and well recorded.

Additional recommendation ...

Soloists; John Alldis Choir; London Symphony Orchestra/Sir Colin Davis. Philips 416 952-2PH2 — ② 1h 38m DDD 9/87

Berlioz. LES TROYENS. **Jon Vickers** (ten) Aeneas; **Josephine Veasey** (mez) Dido; **Berit Lindholm** (sop) Cassandra; **Peter Glossop** (bar) Corebus, Ghost of Corebus; **Heather Begg** (sop) Anna; **Roger Soyer** (bar) Narbal, Spirit of Hector; **Anne Howells** (mez) Ascanius; **Anthony Raffell** (bass) Panthus; **Ian Partridge** (ten) Iopas; **Pierre Thau** (bass) Priam, Mercury, a Trojan soldier; **Elizabeth Bainbridge** (mez) Hecuba, Ghost of Cassandra; **Ryland Davies** (ten) Hylas; **David Lennox** (ten) Helenus; **Raimund Herincx** (bass) Ghost of Priam, First Sentry; **Dennis Wicks** (bar) Ghost of Hector, Second Sentry, Greek Chieftain; **Wandsworth School Boys' Choir; Royal Opera House, Covent Garden Chorus and Orchestra/Sir Colin Davis.** Philips 416 432-2PH4. Notes, text and translation included. From 6709 002 (5/70). Recorded in 1969.

④ 4h 1m ADD 12/86

One of the largest canvases in the whole genre of opera, *Les troyens* was for long considered unperformable. Yet it is no longer than some of Wagner's scores and certainly no more difficult to encompass in one evening. That has been proved conclusively in a succession of productions at Covent Garden, this one recorded not actually 'live' but immediately after stage performances. Sir Colin Davis, the leading Berlioz conductor of the day, fired his forces to give the kind of reading that could only have emerged from experience of the work in the opera house. He is fully aware of the epic quality of the story and no one else has quite so successfully conveyed the score's dramatic stature, its nobility and its tragic consequences. There are many splendid performances on this set, but in the end it is the sense of a team effort, of a cast, chorus and orchestra utterly devoted to the task in hand that is so boldly declared. The recording matches the quality of the music-making.

Additional recommendation ...

Act 5, scenes 2 and 3[c]. *Les nuits d'été, Op. 7*[a]. *La mort de Cléopâtre*[b]. **Dame Janet Baker** (mez); [c]**Bernadette Greevy** (contr); [c]**Keith Erwen** (ten); [c]**Gwynne Howell** (bass); [c]**Ambrosian Opera Chorus;** [a]**New Philharmonia Orchestra/Sir John Barbirolli;** [bc]**London Symphony Orchestra/Sir Alexander Gibson.** EMI Studio CDM7 69544-2 *(reviewed earlier in this section)* — 1h 18m ADD 11/88 £

Further listening ...

Rêverie et caprice, Op. 8. *Coupled with* ***Lalo.*** Symphonie espagnole, Op. 21. **Itzhak Perlman** (vn); **Orchestre de Paris/Daniel Barenboim.** DG 400 032-2GH (3/83).

BENVENUTO CELLINI. **Soloists; Royal Opera House Chorus, Covent Garden; BBC Symphony Orchestra/Sir Colin Davis.** Philips 416 955-2PH3 (1/89).

Baronet Lord Berners

British 1883-1950

Suggested listening ...

Berners. The Triumph of Neptune[a] — Schottische; Hornpipe; Polka; Harlequinade; Dance of the Fairy Princess; Intermezzo; Apotheosis of Neptune. *Coupled with* ***Bantock.*** Fifine at the Fair[b]. ***Bax.*** The Garden of Fand[b]. [a]**Robert Alva** (bar); [a]**London Philharmonic Orchestra,** [b]**Royal Philharmonic Orchestra/Sir Thomas Beecham.** EMI Beecham Edition mono CDM7 63405-2 (6/92).

Elmer Bernstein

American 1922-

Suggested listening ...

The Great Escape — *film score.* **Orchestra/Elmer Bernstein.** Intrada MAF7025D (5/93).

Kings Go Forth. Some Came Running — *Original film soundtracks.* Cloud Nine CNS5004 (5/93).

Leonard Bernstein

American 1918-1990

Bernstein. ORCHESTRAL WORKS. **New York Philharmonic Orchestra/Leonard Bernstein.** CBS Maestro CD44773. Items marked [a] from 72405 (5/66), [b] Philips SBBL652 (2/62). Candide – Overture[a]. West Side Story – Symphonic dances[b]. On the Town – Three dance episodes[a]. On the Waterfront – Symphonic suite[b].

55m ADD 2/91

Broadway and Hollywood form a backcloth to all the music on this disc. A maniacally driven Overture to Bernstein's third Broadway musical, *Candide*, sets the style from the outset with the conductor intent on squeezing every last ounce from both his music and players. The orchestra can sound hard-pressed at times and details get smudged, especially so in the cavernous acoustic, but the dazzling zest of this approach is totally winning and, when the music does relax into more tender moments, the pathos is overwhelming. In the Symphonic dances from *West Side Story*, few orchestras could better the NYPO's intuitive feel for the dance rhythms and cross accents, the rampaging Latin percussion barrage, the screaming trumpet writing, or the theatre-pit instrumental balance. The "Three Dance Episodes" from Bernstein's first musical, *On the Town*, are more overtly eclectic, with hints of Gershwin alongside allusions to Stravinsky, whilst the magnificent score for the film, *On the Waterfront*, finds Bernstein inventively complementing the highlights and deep shadows of Elia Kazan's visual style, and the savagery of the plot. As his own best interpreter, Bernstein goes straight for the key features of all these scores and inspires his orchestra to produce its best.

Bernstein. Concerto for Orchestra, "Jubilee Games" (1986-9)[a].
Del Tredici. Tattoo (1986)[b].
Rorem. Violin Concerto (1984)[bc]. [c]**Gidon Kremer** (vn); [a]**José Eduardo Chama** (bar); [a]**Israel Philharmonic Orchestra,** [b]**New York Philharmonic Orchestra/Leonard Bernstein.** DG 429 231-2GH. Recorded live in 1988-1989.

lh 12m DDD 1/92 

Leonard Bernstein was an ardent advocate of American music and this generous programme of live recordings show him exploring new repertoire at an age when most conductors are content to recycle their old favourites. David Del Tredici will be familiar to some record-buyers as the composer of an extraordinary sequence of large-scale, lushly romantic works based on *Alice in Wonderland*. "*Tatoo* is not *Alice*", the composer warns in the excellent booklet; and yet it's hard to take the proceedings too seriously as Mahler, Varèse, Paganini *et al* battle for allusive supremacy in a noisy postmodernist extravaganza. The music of Ned Rorem is barely known in the UK, but his elegiac lyrical invention should hold no terrors for admirers of Samuel Barber or Virgil Thomson. Under an enthusiastic Bernstein (who sings along in the most passionate sections) Gidon Kremer and the New York Philharmonic have you convinced that, in its unpretentious way – more suite than conventional concerto the work is a small masterpiece. Bernstein's own *Concerto for Orchestra* is a characteristically uneven piece, aping Lutoslawski and even Bartók before settling into that familiar *West Side Story* vein for some infectious "Diaspora Dances". The closing "Benediction" goes deeper and Bernstein's final plea for peace is beautifully intoned by baritone José Eduarda Chama. The Israel Philharmonic play less well than their American rivals but there are few major disasters and the sound throughout, though necessarily close-miked, gives the music plenty of room to breathe.

Bernstein. Candide – Overture. Symphony No. 2, "The Age of Anxiety"[a]. Fancy Free – ballet[b]. [b]**Billie Holiday** (sngr); [a]**Jeffrey Kahane** (pf); **Bournemouth Symphony Orchestra/Andrew Litton.** Virgin Classics VC7 59038-2. Item marked [b] recorded in mono in 1944.

lh 7m DDD 9/91 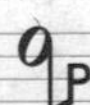

Stunning performances of three of Bernstein's most popular orchestral works. *The Age of Anxiety* (the second of his three symphonies) takes its inspiration from a W.H. Auden poem concerning four lonely characters on a journey of self-discovery, whose collective consciousness is represented in the symphony by a solo piano. Bernstein identified strongly with the theme of the poem, though on hearing it Auden is said to have disliked his treatment of it. It has, however, won many admirers and is by far the most frequently performed of Bernstein's symphonies. On a purely musical level it is a fascinating blend of Brahmsian romanticism, quasi-serial writing and jazz. The Overture to *Candide* hardly needs any introduction – a case of once heard never forgotten. Litton's performance is a real *tour de force* (by far the fastest on disc) with plenty of explosive vitality and an astonishing attention to minor detail. The ballet *Fancy Free* is another firm favourite, and here again Litton and the Bournemouth Symphony Orchestra pull out all the stops out in a suitably brash and raunchy performance – the inclusion of Billie Holiday's original recording of *Big Stuff* at the opening is inspired. Excellent sound, though an extra touch of volume is required for maximum enjoyment.

Bernstein. Songfest[a]. Chichester Psalms[b]. [a]**Clamma Dale** (sop); [a]**Rosalind Elias,** [a]**Nancy Williams** (mezs); [a]**Neil Rosenshein** (ten); [a]**John Reardon** (bar); [a]**Donald Gramm** (bass); [b]soloist from the **Vienna Boys' Choir;** [b]**Vienna Jeunesse Choir;** [a]**National Symphony Orchestra of Washington,** [b]**Israel Philharmonic Orchestra/Leonard Bernstein.** DG 415 965-2GH. Texts and, where appropriate, translations included. Item marked [a] from 2531 044 (11/78), [b] 2709 077 (9/78) which was recorded in 1977.

lh 2m ADD 5/86

"I, too, am America", is the message of Leonard Bernstein's orchestral song-cycle *Songfest*. The subject of the work is the American artist's emotional, spiritual and intellectual response to life in an essentially Puritan society, and, more specifically, to the eclecticism of American society and its many problems of social integration (blacks, women, homosexuals and expatriates). As expected from a composer/conductor equally at home on Broadway or in Vienna's Musikverein, the styles range widely. The scoring is colourful, occasionally pungent, always tuneful. Bernstein's soloists are well chosen and sing with feeling. This vivid live recording of the *Chichester Psalms* offers the full orchestral version and the performers all give their utmost.

Bernstein. SONGS AND DUETS. **Judy Kaye** (sop); **William Sharp** (bar); [a]**Sara Sant'Ambrogio** (vc); **Michael Barrett, Steven Blier** (pfs). Koch International Classics 37000-2. Texts included. Recorded in 1989.

Arias and Barcarolles. ON THE TOWN – Some other time; Lonely town; Carried away; I can cook. WONDERFUL TOWN – A little bit in love. PETER PAN – Dream with me[a]. Songfest – Storyette, H.M.; To what you said[a].

59m DDD 6/90

One of Bernstein's last compositions was the song-cycle *Arias and Barcarolles*, a work that gets its title from a remark made by President Eisenhower after hearing the composer play Mozart and Gershwin at the White House in 1960. "You know, I liked that last piece – it's got a *theme*. I like music with a theme, not all them arias and barcarolles." Well, Bernstein may have enjoyed a reputation as a conductor quite at home amongst the 'arias and barcarolles' of the repertoire, but as a composer his language would have surely spoken directly to Eisenhower. Tunes were his meat and drink, and he certainly knew how to write them. *Arias and Barcarolles* is about irony, capturing head-on clashes of emotion experienced in childhood, growing-up and everyday life. Bernstein draws on his own experiences – Jewish weddings, boyhood, bringing up children and so on. The two soloists interweave with different levels of consciousness and different outlooks. Initially difficult to grasp, these little vignettes, skilfully developed and harnessing the quintessential Bernstein, repay acquaintance. The remainder of the disc speaks directly to the heart and senses; here are a stream of Bernstein's most delicious melodies performed with style, wit and a great deal of elegance. This is the part of the record that speaks directly to the senses. Judy Kaye and William Sharp are nicely matched, and the piano duo team supply ideal accompaniments. It is no wonder that this enchanting record has garnered so many plaudits.

Bernstein. WEST SIDE STORY. **Dame Kiri Te Kanawa** (sop) Maria (Nina Bernstein); **José Carreras** (ten) Tony (Alexander Bernstein); **Tatiana Troyanos** (mez) Anita; **Kurt Ollmann** (bar) Riff; composite chorus and orchestra from 'on and off' Broadway/**Leonard Bernstein** with **Marilyn Horne** (mez). DG 415 253-2GH2. Including "On the Waterfront" – Israel Philharmonic Orchestra/Bernstein (recorded in 1984). From 2532 051 (7/82) and recorded live in 1981. Notes and text included.

 lh 38m DDD 4/85 

A complete recording of a full-blooded musical with five leading operatic stars? Here's 'crossover' with a vengeance! Before this recording Bernstein had not conducted the original full-length score. To have his presence at the sessions was clearly an enormous benefit – not only in his authoritative conducting but in his influence over the starry cast, all of whom respond with zest to his direction. The recording quality is dry and immediate, to enhance the dramatic impact of the score, but there is plenty of bloom on the voices. The suite from Bernstein's music for the 1954 film *On the Waterfront* is terse and powerful and provides an appropriate make-weight.

Bernstein. CANDIDE (1988 final version). **Jerry Hadley** (ten) Candide; **June Anderson** (sop) Cunegonde; **Adolph Green** (ten) Dr Pangloss, Martin; **Christa Ludwig** (mez) Old lady; **Nicolai Gedda** (ten) Governor, Vanderdendur, Ragotski; **Della Jones** (mez) Paquette; **Kurt Ollmann** (bar) Maximilian, Captain, Jesuit father; **Neil Jenkins** (ten) Merchant, Inquisitor, Prince Charles Edward; **Richard Suart** (bass) Junkman, Inquisitor, King Hermann Augustus; **John Treleaven** (ten) Alchemist, Inquisitor, Sultan Achmet, Crook; **Lindsay Benson** (bar) Doctor, Inquisitor, King Stanislaus; **Clive Bayley** (bar) Bear-Keeper, Inquisitor, Tsar Ivan; **London Symphony Chorus and Orchestra/Leonard Bernstein.** DG 429 734-2GH2. Notes and text included.

② lh 52m DDD 8/91 £ 9P

Here it is – all of it – musical comedy, grand opera, operetta, satire, melodrama, all rolled into one. We can thank John Mauceri for much of the restoration work: his 1988 Scottish Opera production was the spur for this recording and prompted exhaustive reappraisal. Numbers like "We Are Women", "Martin's Laughing Song" and "Nothing More Than This" have rarely been heard, if at all. The last mentioned, Candide's 'aria of disillusionment', is one of the enduring glories of the score, reinstated where Bernstein always wanted it (but where no producer would have it), near the very end of the show. Bernstein called it his "Puccini aria", and that it is – bitter-sweet, long-breathed, supported, enriched and ennobled by its inspiring string counterpoint. And this is but one of many forgotten gems. It was an inspiration on someone's part (probably Bernstein's) to persuade the great and versatile Christa Ludwig and Nicolai Gedda (in his sixties and still hurling out the top Bs) to fill the principal character roles. To say they do so ripely is to do them scant justice. Bernstein's old sparring partner Adolph Green braves the tongue-twisting and many-hatted Dr Pangloss with his own highly individual form of *sprechstimme*, Jerry Hadley sings the title role most beautifully, *con amore*, and June Anderson has all the notes, and more, for the faithless, air-headed Cunegonde. It is just a pity that someone didn't tell her that discretion is the better part of comedy. "Glitter and Be Gay" is much funnier for being played straighter, odd as it may sound. Otherwise, the supporting roles are all well taken and the London Symphony Chorus have a field-day in each of their collective guises. Having waited so long to commit every last note (or thereabouts) of his cherished score to disc, there are moments here where Bernstein seems almost reluctant to move on. His tempos are measured, to say the least, the score fleshier now in every respect: even that raciest of Overtures has now acquired a more deliberate gait, a more opulent tone. But Bernstein would be Bernstein, and there are moments where one is more than grateful for his indulgence: the grandiose chorales, the panoramic orchestrascapes (sumptuously recorded), and of course, that thrilling finale – the best of all possible Bernstein anthems at the slowest of all possible speeds – and why not (prepare to hold your breath at the choral *a capella*). It's true, perhaps, that somewhere in the midst of this glossy package there is a more modest show trying to get out, but let's not look gift horses in the mouth.

Additional recommendation ...

(Revised 1982 version). **Soloists; New York City Opera Chorus and Orchestra/John Mauceri.** New World NW340/41-2 — ② lh 33m DDD 10/86

Further listening ...

Serenade after Plato's Symposium. Fancy Free — ballet. **Gidon Kremer** (vn); **Israel Philharmonic Orchestra/Leonard Bernstein.** DG 423 583-2GH (1/89).

Symphonies — No. 1, "Jeremiah"; No. 2, "The Age of Anxiety"; No. 3, "Kaddish". Chichester Psalms. Serenade after Plato's Symposium. Prelude, Fugue and Riffs. **Soloists; Camerata**

Singers; Columbus Boy Choir; New York Philharmonic Orchestra; Columbia Jazz Combo/Leonard Bernstein. Sony Classical CD47162 (3-CD set) (3/92).

ON THE TOWN. TROUBLE IN TAHITI. On the Town — three dance episodes. Candide — Overture. Fancy Free. West Side Story — symphonic dances. On the Waterfront — symphonic suite. Facsimile choreographic essay. **Soloists; Columbia Wind Ensemble; New York Philharmonic Orchestra/Leonard Bernstein.** Sony Classical Portrait CD47154 (3-CD set) (5/92).

A QUIET PLACE. **Soloists; Austrian Radio Symphony Orchestra/Leonard Bernstein.** DG 419 761-2GH2 (10/87).

WEST SIDE STORY. *Original film soundtrack.* Sony CD48211.

WONDERFUL TOWN. **Original TV cast.** Sony Broadway CD48021.

Franz Adolf Berwald

Swedish 1796-1868

Berwald. SYMPHONIES. **Gothenburg Symphony Orchestra/Neeme Järvi.** DG 415 502-2GH2.
No. 1 in G minor, "Sinfonie sérieuse"; No. 2 in D major, "Sinfonie capricieuse"; No. 3 in C major, "Sinfonie Singulière"; No. 4 in E flat major.

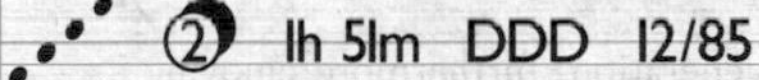

NEW REVIEW

Berwald. Symphonies — No. 3 in C major, "Sinfonie singulière"; No. 4 in E flat major. **London Symphony Orchestra/Sixten Ehrling.** Bluebell ABCD037. From Decca SXL6374 (11/68). Recorded in 1968.

57m ADD 8/92

Franz Berwald is certainly not an everyday name and his discovery was a twentieth-century phenomenon. His best music is fresh, original and appealing, and a refreshing change from the more familiar symphonies of Mendelssohn and Schumann. The *Singulière,* composed in 1845, had its first performance in 1905!. The opening is simple in technique but provides a rich germ for development. The *Sinfonie capricieuse* has momentary whiffs of Mendelssohn but, as with all of Berwald's music, parallels are not made easily. The smiling world of the last symphony, the E flat, finds Berwald in light-hearted mood, proffering a particularly charming and classical *Scherzo*. Paired on the second disc with the earlier *Sinfonie sérieuse* the darker hues of that work seem to glow more impressively. Järvi's advocacy of these works is totally committed and the Gothenburg Symphony Orchestra play splendidly with some fine wind articulation. The recording is well-detailed and crisp. Why the two symphonies recorded on the Bluebell CD are not standard repertory pieces remains baffling. Sixten Ehrling's versions of the *Singulière* and the E flat Symphony were made in London in 1967 and the former is arguably the best all-round performance on CD. Järvi's excellent set is just a bit too brisk. The Fourth Symphony, one of the sunniest of Berwald's scores gets a spirited and vital reading and the digital transfer is altogether excellent with no loss of warmth and a greater richness at the bottom end of the range. A viable alternative to the DG set.

Further listening ...

Piano Quintet No. 1 in C minor. Piano Trios — No. 1 in E flat major; No. 3 in D minor. **Stefan Lindgren** (pf); **Berwald Quartet.** Musica Sveciae MSCD521.

String Quartets — [ab]No. 2 in A minor; [c]No. 3 in E flat major. **[a]Skåne Quartet; [b]Ericson Quartet; [c]Kyndel Quartet.** Caprice CAP21506. Items marked [a]recorded in 1941, [b]1948, [c]1943.

Antonio Bibalo

Norwegian/Italian 1922-

Suggested listening ...

Sinfonia notturna. Sonatina 2A, Astrale. Autumnale. **Soloists; Norwegian Wind Quintet; Bergen Philharmonic Orchestra/Karsten Andersen.** Aurora NCD-B4943.

Key to Symbols

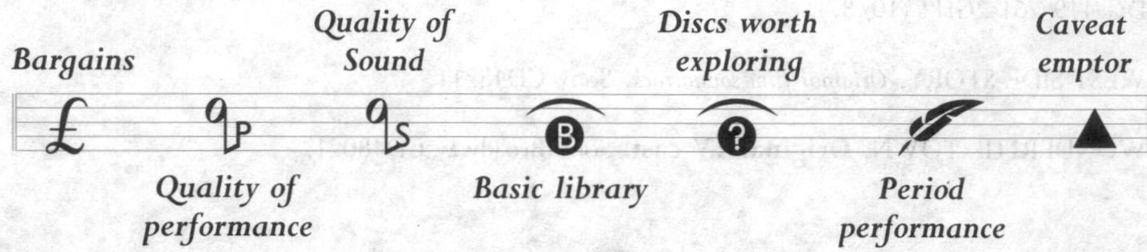

Heinrich Biber

Bohemian 1644-1704

Biber. Mensa sonora. Sonata violino solo representativa in A major[a]. **Cologne Musica Antiqua/Reinhard Goebel** ([a]vn). Archiv Produktion 423 701-2AH.

1h 2m DDD 11/89

Biber was one of the greatest German composers of his generation, furthermore enjoying a reputation as a virtuoso violinist of the first rank. This invigorating and stylish disc embraces both aspects of Biber's talent. *Mensa sonora* is a six-part anthology of music which occupies territory belonging to the chamber sonata and the suite. This is delightful music, strongly dance-orientated and with a marked feeling for gesture. These qualities, and others too, are affectingly realized by Reinhard Goebel and his impeccably drilled ensemble in such a way that a listener might be excused for leaving the comfort of an armchair and taking to the floor. By way of an entr'acte between the first three and the last three parts of the anthology, Goebel gives a virtuoso performance of Biber's *Sonata violino solo representativa* in which a nightingale, cuckoo, cockerel, frog, and other creatures make themselves heard; a cat wreaks havoc with them but is in turn sent packing by a musketeer. Many tricks of the violinist's trade are on display and Goebel revels in them all. A splendid achievement by all concerned.

Biber. Mystery Sonatas. **John Holloway** (vn); **Davitt Moroney** (org/hpd); **Tragicomedia** (Stephen Stubbs, lte/chitarrone; Erin Headley, va da gamba/lirone; Andrew Lawrence-King, hp/regal). Virgin Classics Veritas VCD7 59551-2.

② 2h 11m DDD 5/91

Biber was among the most talented musicians of the late seventeenth century. He was a renowned violinist and his compositions, above all for the violin, are technically advanced and strikingly individual. The 15 *Mystery Sonatas* with their additional *Passacaglia* for unaccompanied violin were written in about 1678 and dedicated to Biber's employer, the Archbishop of Salzburg. Each Sonata is inspired by a section of the Rosary devotion of the Catholic Church which offered a system of meditation on 15 Mysteries from the lives of Jesus and His mother. The music is not, strictly speaking, programmatic though often vividly illustrative of events which took place in the life of Christ. All but two of the 16 pieces require *scordatura* or retuning of the violin strings; in this way Biber not only facilitated some of the fingerings but also achieved sounds otherwise unavailable to him. The Sonatas are disposed into three groups of five: Joyful, Sorrowful and Glorious Mysteries whose contrasting states are affectingly evoked in music ranging from a spirit reflecting South German baroque exuberance to one of profound contemplation. John Holloway plays with imaginative sensibility and he is supported by a first-rate continuo group whose instruments include baroque lute, chitarrone, viola da gamba, a 15-string lirone, double harp and regal.

Additional recommendation ...

Cologne Musica Antiqua/Reinhard Goebel (vn). Archiv Produktion 431 656-2AH2 — ② lh 54m DDD 10/91

Further listening ...

Trumpet music — Sonata à 7. Sonata pro tabula. Sonata VII à 5. Sonata à 3. Sonata à 6. Sonata I à 8. Sonata Sancti Polycarpi à 9. *Coupled with* **Schmelzer**: Trumpet music — Sonata con arie zu der kaiserlichen Serenada. Sonata à 7 flauti. Balletto di spiritelli. Sonata I à 8. Balletto di centauri, ninfe e salvatici. **New London Consort/Philip Pickett.** L'Oiseau-Lyre 425 834-2OH (9/91).

William Billings

American 1746-1800

Suggested listening ...

The New-England Psalm-Singer. The Singing Master's Assistant. The Psalm-Singer's Amusement. The Suffolk Harmony. The Continental Harmony. The Lord is ris'n indeed. **His Majesties Clerkes/Paul Hillier.** Harmonia Mundi HMU90 7048 (10/92).

Gilles Binchois

French c.1400-1460

Suggested listening ...

"Triste plaisir et douleureuse joye" — Rondos and Ballades. *Coupled with* **Dufay.** Rondeaux, Ballades and Lamentations. **Ensemble Gilles Binchois/Dominique Vellard.** Virgin Classics Veritas VC7 59043-2.

Sir Harrison Birtwistle

British 1934-

Birtwistle. Carmen Arcadiae Mechanicae Perpetuum (1978). Silbury Air (1977). Secret Theatre (1984). **London Sinfonietta/Elgar Howarth.** Etcetera KTC1052. Recorded in 1987.

58m DDD 4/88 

Birtwistle is only 'difficult' if you are convinced in advance that he is going to be, or if you have read somewhere about the obscure numerical techniques that he uses to help him compose. Forget them: they're his concern, not the listener's; you don't get to understand Bach by reading textbooks on counterpoint. Jump straight in, with ears and mind open, and the sheer exhilaration of his music, its alluringly strange patterns and textures, its suggestions of mysterious ritual, above all the unmistakable sense of a composer in total control of a rich and resourceful language, will soon draw you in. The fact that it cannot be wholly comprehended at a single hearing is no drawback, but a positive bonus: this is music that changes each time you hear it, as a landscape changes when you explore different paths through it. The performances throughout are vividly virtuosic and the recording has tremendous impact.

NEW REVIEW

Birtwistle. For O, for O, the Hobby-horse is Forgot[a]. Refrains and Choruses[b]. Verses for Ensembles. [b]**Netherlands Wind Ensemble; [a]The Hague Percussion Ensemble/James Wood.** Etcetera KTC1130. Recorded live in 1991.

52m DDD 7/92

The Birtwistle discography will be seriously incomplete as long as so many of his major theatrical works remain unrecorded. The great value of this issue is that it lets you hear three important compositions in which Birtwistle tries out dramatic ideas in concert form. As their titles indicate, *Refrains and Choruses* and *Verses for Ensembles* both set up analogies with literary forms. Neither relate to specific literary subject-matter, although *Verses* has a strength and energy that evokes the dramatic world of Shakespeare's history plays. *For O, for O, the Hobby-horse is Forgot* is actually a line from *Hamlet*, expressing the Prince of Denmark's bitterness at the rapidity with which his mother has forgotten his dead father. Birtwistle calls the work a ceremony, and it relates to the play's dumb show, two of the six percussionists representing the Player King and Queen. A work for percussion alone may not have the purely musical riches of the other pieces on the disc, but it is still absorbing listening. The performances are notable for their precision and strength of character, and the recordings are no less effective.

Birtwistle. PUNCH AND JUDY. **Stephen Roberts** (bar) Punch; **Jan DeGaetani** (mez) Judy, Fortune-teller; **Phyllis Bryn-Julson** (sop) Pretty Polly, Witch; **Philip Langridge** (ten) Lawyer; **David Wilson-Johnson** (bar) Choregos, Jack Ketch; **John Tomlinson** (bass) Doctor; **London Sinfonietta/David Atherton.** Etcetera KTC2014. Notes and text included. From Decca Headline HEAD24/5 (9/80).

② 1h 43m ADD 12/89

In *Punch and Judy* Sir Harrison Birtwistle and his inspired librettist Stephen Pruslin succeeded in giving characters normally presented as simple caricatures an almost mythic power and substance. As opera *Punch and Judy* may owe more to such Stravinskian fables as *Renard* than to the great lyric tragedies of the Monteverdi/Wagner tradition, yet even in *Punch and Judy* the music is most memorable in moments of reflection – sinister, poignant, or both. Though different performers have presented the work brilliantly in the theatre since this recording was made, it is hard to imagine a more effective account of the opera on disc. The singers are expert and well contrasted, with none of the ranting and approximation that this kind of expressionistic vocal writing often elicits. Moreover, the London Sinfonietta are at their most responsive, as well they might be given the outstandingly musical direction of David Atherton, who conducted the opera's première at Aldeburgh in 1968. The analogue recording may sound a trifle shallow by the latest standards, but it leaves you in no doubt as to the brilliance and resourcefulness of Birtwistle's vocal and instrumental design.

Further listening ...

Endless Parade[a]. *Coupled with* ***Blake Watkins.*** Trumpet Concerto. ***Maxwell Davies.*** Trumpet Concerto. **Håkan Hardenberger** (tpt); [a]**Paul Patrick** (vib); **BBC Philharmonic Orchestra/Elgar Howarth.** Philips 432 075-2PH (6/91).

Cesare Andrea Bixio

Italian 1898-1978

Suggested listening ...

Mamma. Vivere. Parlami d'amore, Mariù. La mia canzone al vento, with a selection of Italian songs. **Luciano Pavarotti** (ten); **Andrea Griminelli** (fte); **Chorus and Orchestra/Henry Mancini.** Decca 411 959-2DH (8/84).

Georges Bizet

French 1838-1875

Bizet. Symphony in C major[a]. L'Arlésienne – Suite No. 1[b]; Suite No. 2 (arr. Guiraud)[b]. [a]**French Radio National Symphony Orchestra,** [b]**Royal Philharmonic Orchestra/Sir Thomas Beecham.** EMI CDC7 47794-2. Item marked [a] from ASD388 (4/61), [b] ASD252 (2/59).

lh 5m ADD 11/87

Bizet's only symphony was written within the space of a month just after his seventeenth birthday. It is an easy piece to listen to, fairly light-weight and with a hint of the mature composer-to-be in a long and beautiful oboe solo. But it has many conventional, immature features too, and needs special advocacy in performance. Beecham had a genius for making second-rate works seem masterpieces and his recording has tremendous flair, imagination and affection. From the incidental music for *L'Arlésienne* Bizet salvaged four pieces and re-orchestrated them for full orchestra in the form of what we know now as Suite No. 1. After his death Bizet's friend Ernest Guiraud re-scored four more numbers to make up Suite No. 2. The music has a marvellous sense of colour and atmosphere and Bizet's inspired invention reaches great heights of expression. It is difficult to imagine a more inspired, more sympathetic and beautifully played performance, for Beecham makes the music live and breathe in a way that is head and shoulders above any other conductor. The recordings were made in 1959 and 1956 respectively but both sound rich and clear.

Additional recommendations ...

Symphony. Jeux d'enfants — petite suite. ***Debussy.*** *Danse sacrée et danse profane.* **Vera Badings** (hp); **Concertgebouw Orchestra/Bernard Haitink.** Philips 416 437-2PH — 50m ADD 10/86

L'Arlésienne— Suites. Carmen – Suites Nos. 1 and 2. **Montreal Symphony Orchestra/Charles Dutoit.** Decca 417 839-2DH — lh 13m DDD 6/88

Symphony. ***Britten.*** *Simple Symphony, Op. 4.* ***Prokofiev.*** *Symphony No. 1 in D major, Op. 25, "Classical".* **Orpheus Chamber Orchestra.** DG 423 624-2GH — lh 4m DDD 1/89

L'Arlésienne – Suites. Carmen — Suite. ***Offenbach.*** *Orphée aux enfers — Overture. Les contes d'Hoffmann — Barcarolle.* **Berlin Philharmonic Orchestra/Herbert von Karajan.** DG Privilege 431 160-2GR — 59m ADD 8/91

L'Arlésienne – Suites. Carmen — Suite. Jeux d'enfants. **Orchestre de la Bastille/Myung-Whun Chung.** DG 431 778-2GH — lh 9m DDD 11/91 *Symphony.* ***Ravel.*** *Ma mère l'oye.* **Scottish Chamber Orchestra/Jukka-Pekka Saraste.** Virgin Classics Virgo VJ7 59657-2 — lh 4m DDD 12/91 £

Bizet. Jeux d'enfants — petite suite.
Ravel. Ma mère l'oye – ballet.
Saint-Saëns. Le carnaval des animaux[a]. [a]**Julian Jacobson,** [a]**Nigel Hutchinson** (pfs); members of **London Symphony Orchestra/Barry Wordsworth.** Pickwick IMP Classics PCD932.

lh 3m DDD 4/90 £

These three works make a very attractive programme and as a mid-price issue this CD is desirable indeed. No attempt is made to sensationalize *Le carnaval des animaux*, which is played with just ten instrumentalists as the composer intended, but there is plenty of wit and brilliance from the pianists Julian Jacobson and Nigel Hutchinson, not only in their charmingly droll own number (No. 11) which relegates them firmly to the animal kingdom but also in the work as a whole. The violinists' donkeys (No. 8) are no less amusing, and the cello 'swan' in No. 13 is serenely touching, but all the players are good and the finale is rightly uproarious. Barry Wordsworth's sense of style in this French repertory is no less evident in the Bizet *Jeux d'enfants* and Ravel's *Ma mère l'oye*, which in the latter case is the entire score of the ballet and not just the more familiar suite taken from it. We may single out such pleasures as the gently stated and lovingly shaped "Berceuse" and "Petit mari, petite femme" in the Bizet, but all is charmingly done and then in the Ravel we are transported at once into a child's fairyland of infinite delicacy, wit and tenderness which is crowned unforgettably by the inspired final number, *The*

Fairy Garden. A special word of praise to the LSO's oboists, so important in Ravel's score. EMI's Studio No. 1 in Abbey Road provides a beautifully atmospheric recording, close but not glaring. *See additional recommendations listed above for Jeux d'enfants.*

Bizet. CARMEN. **Julia Migenes** (mez) Carmen; **Plácido Domingo** (ten) Don José; **Faith Esham** (sop) Micaëla; **Ruggero Raimondi** (bass) Escamillo; **Lilian Watson** (sop) Frasquita; **Susan Daniel** (mez) Mercédès; **Jean-Philippe Lafont** (bar) Dancairo; **Gérard Garino** (ten) Remendado; **François Le Roux** (bar) Moralès; **John Paul Bogart** (bass) Zuniga; **French Radio Chorus; French Radio Children's Chorus; French National Orchestra/Lorin Maazel.** Erato 2292-45207-2. Notes, text and translation included. From NUM75113 (3/84).

③ 2h 31m DDD 9/85 P B

With some justification, *Carmen* is reckoned to be the world's most popular opera. Its score is irresistible, its dramatic realism riveting, its sense of *milieu* unerring, though it has to be remembered that the work was not an immediate triumph. Too many recordings have blown up the work to proportions beyond its author's intentions but here Maazel adopts a brisk, lightweight approach that seems to come close to what Bizet wanted. Similarly Julia Migenes approaches the title part in an immediate, vivid way, exuding the gipsy's allure in a performance that suggests Carmen's fierce temper and smouldering eroticism, and she develops the character intelligently into the fatalistic person of the card scene and finale. Her singing isn't conventionally smooth but it is compelling from start to finish. Plácido Domingo has made the part of Don José very much his own, and here he sings with unstinting involvement and a good deal of finesse. Ruggero Raimondi is a macho Toreador though Faith Esham is a somewhat pallid Micaëla.

Additional recommendations ...

Soloists; Les Petits Chanteurs de Versailles; French National Radio Chorus and Orchestra/Sir Thomas Beecham. EMI CDS7 49240-2 — ③ 2h 41m ADD 6/88 P B ▲
Soloists; Ambrosian Singers; London Symphony Orchestra/Claudio Abbado. DG 419 636-2GH3 — ③ 2h 37m 2/88 P B
Soloists; Radio France Maîtrise and Chorus; French National Orchestra/Seiji Ozawa. Philips 422 366-2PH3 — ③ 2h 39m DDD 8/89 P B
Soloists; Manhattan Opera Chorus; Metropolitan Opera Children's Chorus and Orchestra/Leonard Bernstein. DG 427 440-2GX3 — ③ 2h 40m ADD 9/91 P B
Soloists; René Duclos Choir; Jean Pesneaud Children's Choir; Paris Opera Orchestra/Georges Prêtre. EMI CDS7 54368-2 — ② 2h 26m ADD 5/92 P B

Bizet. LES PECHEURS DE PERLES. **Barbara Hendricks** (sop) Leïla; **John Aler** (ten) Nadir; **Gino Quilico** (bar) Zurga; **Jean-Philippe Courtis** (bass) Nourabad; **Chorus and Orchestra of the Capitole, Toulouse/Michel Plasson.** EMI CDS7 49837-2. Notes, text and translation included.

② 2h 7m DDD 1/90

Let a tenor and a baritone signify that they are willing to oblige with a duet, and the cry will go up for *The Pearl Fishers*. It's highly unlikely that many of the company present will know what the duet is about – it recalls the past, proclaims eternal friendship and nearly ends up in a quarrel – but the melody and the sound of two fine voices blending in its harmonies will be quite sufficient. In fact there is much more to the opera than the duet, or even than the three or four solos which are sometimes sung in isolation; and the EMI recording goes further than previous versions in giving a complete account of a score remarkable for its unity as well as for the attractiveness of individual numbers. It is a lyrical opera, and the voices need to be young and graceful. Barbara Hendricks and John Aler certainly fulfil those requirements, she with a light, silvery timbre, he with a high tenor admirably suited to the tessitura of his solos. The third main character, the baritone whose role is central to the drama, assumes his rightful place here: Gino Quilico brings genuine distinction to the part, and his aria in Act 3 is one of the highlights. Though Plasson's direction at first is rather square, the performance grows in responsiveness act by act. It is a pity that the accompanying notes are not stronger in textual detail, for the full score given here stimulates interest in its history. One of the changes made in the original score of 1863 concerns the celebrated duet itself, the first version of which is given in an appendix. It ends in a style that one would swear owed much to the 'friendship' duet in Verdi's *Don Carlos* – except that Bizet came first.

Additional recommendation ...

Soloists; Paris Opéra Chorus and Orchestra/Georges Prêtre. Classics for Pleasure CD-CFPD4721 — ② lh 44m ADD 10/91 £

Further listening ...

DJAMILEH. **Soloists; Bavarian Radio Chorus; Munich Radio Orchestra/Lamberto Gardelli.** Orfeo C174881A (4/89).

Michael Blake Watkins

British 1948-

Suggested listening ...

Trumpet Concerto. *Coupled with* ***Birtwistle.*** Endless Parade[a]. ***Maxwell Davies.*** Trumpet Concerto. **Håkan Hardenberger** (tpt); [a]**Paul Patrick** (vib); **BBC Philharmonic Orchestra/Elgar Howarth.** Philips 432 075-2PH (6/91).

Michel Blavet

French 1700-1768

NEW REVIEW

Blavet. FLUTE SONATAS. **Masahiro Arita** (fl); **Wieland Kuijken** (bass viol); **Chiyoko Arita** (hpd). Denon Aliare CO-79550. Recorded in 1991.

Op. 2 — No. 2 in D minor; No. 4 in G minor, "La lumague"; No. 5 in D major, "Lachauvet". Op. 3 — No. 2 in B minor; No. 6 in D major.

lh 4m DDD 9/92 

Michel Blavet was the most celebrated French flautist during the first half of the eighteenth century. A younger contemporary of Rameau, he appeared frequently at the Paris Concert Spirituel during the 1720s, 1730s and 1740s where his performances were admired both by his fellow countrymen and by connoisseurs further afield. Telemann named him as the flautist who took part in the first performances of his 1738 *Paris* Quartets: "if only words were enough to describe the wonderful way in which the quartets were played by Herr Blavet ...". The Japanese flautist Masahiro Arita plays five of Blavet's Sonatas, three from the composer's Op. 2 (1732), and two from Op. 3 (1740). He uses a baroque flute and appropriately includes a bass viol for the continuo together with harpsichord. Listeners may feel that the continuo group is a shade too prominent in relation to the soft-spoken inflexions of an eighteenth-century flute. But the recital holds attention with its technical fluency and lively responses to music which is often inventive and always pleasing. Arita is stylishly supported throughout by Kuijken and Arita.

Sir Arthur Bliss

British 1891-1975

Bliss. Piano Concerto, Op. 58[a]. March, Op. 99, "Homage to a Great Man". [a]**Philip Fowke** (pf); **Royal Liverpool Philharmonic Orchestra/David Atherton.** Unicorn-Kanchana Souvenir UKCD2029. From DKP9006 (9/81).

44m DDD 8/90 

Bliss's Piano Concerto, written for the New York World Fair in 1939, is a deliberate essay in the grand manner, full of big, rhetorical gestures and opulent Rachmaninovian melodies. This performance does it full justice in a recording that has transferred well from LP, though some may find the sound rather unreverberant in places. Bliss was half-American and the music seems to reflect also the exuberance of the United States. It is romantic music in the best sense, not only in its richness of orchestration and the Lisztian virtuosity of the solo part, commandingly played by Philip Fowke – listen to the double octaves at the start – but in the sheer beauty of the meditative quieter passages, as when flute and oboe accompany the soloist's musings in the recapitulation section of the first movement. The *March of Homage* is a reminder of how splendidly Bliss fulfilled the role of Master of the Queen's Music. The homage is to Churchill and the work was broadcast just before the great man's funeral in 1965. In a short time, it goes to the heart of the matter. David Atherton and the RLPO are completely at home in these two fine works.

NEW REVIEW

Bliss. Music for Strings. Pastoral: Lie Strewn the White Flocks[a]. [a]**Della Jones** (mez); [a]**Sinfonia Chorus; Northern Sinfonia/Richard Hickox.** Chandos CHAN8886. Text included. Recorded in 1990.

lh lm DDD 7/91 

Surely *the* disc with which to start a Bliss collection. Here is a pairing of two of the composer's very strongest works in sensitive, ideally disciplined accounts from the ever-responsive Northern Sinfonia under Richard Hickox. Brimful of fine invention as well as the most swaggeringly idiomatic (and technically demanding) writing, Bliss's athletic *Music for Strings* is a mightily impressive achievement: its enviable fluency and consummately argued progress mark it out as another in the long line of superb string works British composers have produced this century. It was first performed in 1935 at the Salzburg Festival by the strings of the Vienna Philharmonic (no less) under Sir Adrian Boult; suffice to report, Hickox draws playing of splendidly full-blooded tone and unanimous skill from his Tyneside group that would not disgrace even the string section of that same great orchestra. The classically-inspired idyll *Pastoral: Lie Strewn the White Flocks* dates from seven years earlier and constitutes perhaps the first fully characteristic example of Bliss's mature style. It's a most beguiling song-cycle, limpidly scored for small choir, mezzo-soprano, flute, strings and timpani, and some of the individual numbers are hauntingly lovely, not least that ravishing setting of Robert Nichols's "The Pigeon Song" (with Della Jones a touchingly tender soloist). A valuable coupling, then, complemented by ideally warm-toned, transparent Chandos sonics throughout.

NEW REVIEW

Bliss. Morning Heroes[a]. Investiture Antiphonal Fanfares[b]. Prayer of St Francis of Assisi[c]. [a]**Brian Blessed** (narr); [ac]**East London Chorus;** [a]**Harlow Chorus;** [a]**East Hertfordshire Chorus;** [ab]**London Philharmonic Orchestra/Michael Kibblewhite.** Cala CACD1010. Recorded 1991-92.

lh 5m DDD 2/93

Sir Charles Groves's première 1974 recording of *Morning Heroes* served the work well, and has been successfully transferred to a mid-price CD (see below). Michael Kibblewhite's new version is on balance a better proposition, both in terms of a slightly more vivid recording, and a more dramatic performance. Bliss wrote the work as a tribute to his elder brother, who had been killed in the First World War, and in memory of all who died in the conflict. There are five parts, each of which deals with the subject of war and the suffering it causes, with diverse texts by Walt Whitman, Wilfred Owen, Robert Nicholls, and from *The Iliad*. There is an important part for narrator, and in this case Groves's strikingly dramatic John Westbrook is superior to Kibblewhite's more conversational Brian Blessed. On the other hand Kibblewhite's choral forces are slightly superior to the Liverpool chorus, and generally speaking the younger conductor shapes his work with rather more flair than did Groves. The Cala disc is at full-price, but has the bonus of a splendid fanfare and a touching little *Prayer*.

Additional recommendation ...

Morning Heroes. **John Westbrook** (narr); **Liverpool Philharmonic Choir; Royal Liverpool Philharmonic Orchestra/Sir Charles Groves.** EMI British Composers CDM7 63906-2 — lh ADD 10/91

Further listening ...

Cello Concerto[a]. The Enchantress[b]. Hymn to Apollo. [b]**Linda Finnie** (mez); [a]**Raphael Wallfisch** (vc); **Ulster Orchestra/Vernon Handley.** Chandos CHAN8818 (7/91).

String Quartets — No. 1 in B flat major; No. 2. **Delmé Quartet.** Hyperion CDA66178 (11/89).

Miniature Scherzo. Sonata. The Rout Trot. Study. Suite. Triptych. *Coupled with* **Bach** (arr. Bliss): Das alte Jahr vergangen ist BWV614. **Philip Fowke** (pf). Chandos CHAN8979 (1/92).

Checkmate – suite. *Coupled with* **Lambert.** Horoscope – suite. **Walton.** Façade – Suites Nos. 1 and 2. **English Northern Philharmonia/David Lloyd-Jones.** Hyperion CDA66436 (3/91).

Key to Symbols

Price	Quantity/ availability	Timing	Mode	Review date
•••	② ②	lh 23m	DDD	6/88

Marc Blitzstein

American 1905-1964

NEW REVIEW

Blitzstein. REGINA. **Katherine Ciesinski** (mez) Regina Giddens; **Angelina Réaux** (sop) Alexandra Giddens; **Sheri Greenawald** (sop) Birdie Hubbard; **Theresa Merritt** (sngr) Addie; **Samuel Ramey** (bass) Horace Giddens; **Timothy Noble** (sngr) Benjamin Hubbard; **James Maddalena** (bar) Oscar Hubbard; **David Kuebler** (ten) Leo Hubbard; **Bruce Hubbard** (bar) Cal; **David Morrison** (sngr) William Marshall; **Tim Johnson** (sngr) Jazz; **Scott Cooper** (bar) John Bagty; **Jeanette Wilson** (sop) Cordelia Adair; **Kate Morrell** (sngr) Ethelinda Horns; **William Peel** (sngr) Joe Horns; **John Beazley** (sngr) Miles Maury; **Graeme Danby** (sngr) Mr Manders; **John Mauceri** (narr) Maestro; **Scottish Opera Chorus and Orchestra/John Mauceri.** Decca 433 812-2DH2. Notes and text included. Recorded in 1991.

••• ② 2h 32m DDD 3/93

The most successful of all Marc Blitzstein's music-theatre pieces, *Regina* is based on Lillian Hellman's play *The little foxes.* Conceived as a 'Broadway opera', in the manner of *Porgy and Bess* and *Street Scene*, and based on an existing famous drama, it does not — like the Gershwin and Weill works — make any concessions to the hit-parade. The original version had to have numerous changes and cuts imposed upon it, and subsequent productions in opera houses used these. In recent years the revival of interest in Blitzstein's work has led to a new critical edition, made by Mauceri and Tommy Krasker, which restores the 'Chinkypin' jazz music as well as making Regina a mezzo-soprano. Ciesinski is wonderfully bitchy as Regina, singing her waltz-song "The best thing of all" with plenty of glitter. Her dying husband Horace is more an acting part but Samuel Ramey makes the most of it, and takes his part in the quartet, "Make a quiet day", the only soft moment in the action when the four 'good' characters are left alone for a moment, while the 'little foxes' — Regina and her brothers — are out of the way. Sheri Greenawald is a splendid Birdie — her aria is the biggest, most overtly operatic piece in the score, and Réaux is fine as the rebellious daughter whose confrontation with her mother played out with the sound of the chorus singing "A new day's a comin'" brings the piece to its melodramatic close. The Scottish forces, fresh from the 1991 Glasgow production, do the piece proud and Mauceri conducts with obvious affection. *Regina* is one of the pinnacles of mid-twentieth-century American opera and the best possible introduction to Blitzstein's music.

Ernest Bloch

Swiss/American 1880-1959

NEW REVIEW

Bloch. Symphony in C sharp minor. Schelomo[a]. [a]**Torleif Thedéen** (vc); **Malmö Symphony Orchestra/Lev Markiz.** BIS CD576. Recorded in 1990.

1h 18m DDD 5/93

Ernest Bloch's early symphony is an endearing and at times impressive showcase for a young composer (he was 23) endowed by nature and nurture with all the gifts save individuality (though there are hints in the later movements that that too is on the way). He can write impressively strong, expansive melodies, develop them with real ingenuity and build them into monumental climaxes. Climax-building, indeed, is what young Bloch seems most interested in at this stage of his career, that and a love for all the rich contrasts of colour and texture that a big orchestra, imaginatively used, can provide. He is so very good at his craft, so adept at pulling out still more stops when you thought there could hardly be any left, so sheerly and likeably clever that one is scarcely ever made impatient by the occasional feeling that this or that movement could have ended two or three minutes earlier. It's a pleasure, too, to listen for fulfilled echoes of that youthful exuberance in the mature 'biblical rhapsody' *Schelomo*. Just as Lev Markiz adroitly avoids any impression of over-padded grossness in the symphony, so he and his fine soloist find more than richly embroidered oriental voluptuousness in this portrait of King Solomon; there is gravity and even poignancy to the music as well, and Thedéen's subtle variety of tone colour gives the work shadow and delicacy as well as richness. Typically BIS reproduce a truthful aural equivalent of the modern concert hall experience.

Additional recommendation ...

Schelomo. Concerti grossi – No. 1; No. 2. **Georges Miquelle** (vc); **Eastman Rochester Orchestra/Howard Hanson.** Mercury 432 718-2MM — 1h 3m ADD 11/91

Further listening ...

Concerto grosso No. 1[a]. *Coupled with* ***Barber.*** Adagio for strings, Op. 11. ***Grieg.*** Holberg Suite, Op. 40. ***Puccini.*** Crisantemi (arr. string orchestra). [a]**Irit Rob** (pf); **Israel Chamber Orchestra/Yoav Talmi.** Chandos CHAN8593 (8/88).

America — epic rhapsody. **American Concert Choir; Symphony of the Air/Leopold Stokowski.** Vanguard Classics 08.8014.71.

Piano Quintets Nos. 1 and 2. **American Chamber Players.** Koch International 37041-2.

John Blow

British 1649-1708

Blow. VENUS AND ADONIS. **Nancy Argenta** (sop) Cupid; **Lynne Dawson** (sop) Venus; **Stephen Varcoe** (bar) Adonis; **Emily Van Evera** (sop) Shepherdess; **John Mark Ainsley, Charles Daniel** (tens), **Gordon Jones** (bass) Shepherds; **Rogers Covey-Crump** (ten) Huntsman; **Chorus; London Baroque/Charles Medlam.** Harmonia Mundi Musique d'abord HMA190 1276. Notes and text included.

50m DDD 9/88 

This is seventeenth-century court entertainment with nothing lacking in its charm and elegance. We know that Blow's mini opera was first performed in Oxford in 1681, with Moll Davies, the mistress of Charles II in the role of Venus. Her nine-year-old daughter, Lady Mary Tudor, must have been a particularly gifted child to have been able to sing and act the part of Cupid, and we can well imagine the delight of the court at such scenes as the spelling lesson with the infant Cupids. As for us, we can enjoy the accomplished performance of an expert cast, with the sprightliness of Nancy Argenta as Cupid matched only by the gently dramatic flexibility of Lynne Dawson and Stephen Varcoe in the title roles. Even the members of the chorus and those with lesser parts have all been hand-picked, and London Baroque are in their element. Yet nothing is exaggerated or overdone. What is outstanding in this performance is the fact that although we have sound alone, it is so cleverly recorded that we have the delightful illusion that the opera is actually taking place before our very eyes.

Luigi Boccherini

Italian 1743-1805

Boccherini. Symphonies – D minor, Op. 12 No. 4, G506, "La casa del Diavolo"; A major, Op. 12 No. 6, G508; A major, Op. 21 No. 6, G498. **London Festival Orchestra/Ross Pople.** Hyperion CDA66236.

54m DDD 9/87

Boccherini may not have been the most purposeful of composers of his time, but he was certainly one of the most endearing. Not for him the sturdy, strongly argued symphonic structures of a Haydn, in which each note has its place and its meaning, but rather pieces, coloured by the relaxed and sunny south, that indulge in graceful lines and tellingly manipulated detail. Boccherini loved playing with textures and producing sounds that are pleasurable in themselves; he also liked experimenting with musical forms, and one of the three symphonies here has as its finale just a slow introduction followed by a replay of part of the first movement. The symphony here from Op. 21 is a slight piece, with playful themes in its first movement, a refined little *Andantino* to follow and a cheerful minuet. The other two are on a larger scale, with quite expansive opening movements and in one case a wistful minor-key *Larghetto*, the other a charming minor-key gavotte, to follow. The D minor symphony ends with a reworking of the movement we know as the "Dance of the Furies" from Gluck's *Orphée*. The spirit of the music is happily captured in these performances even though modern instruments are used. The articulation is delightfully clear, light and rhythmic, and the tempos are lively; clearly Ross Pople has a sympathetic feeling for Boccherini.

Boccherini. CELLO CONCERTOS. **David Geringas** (vc); **Orchestra da Camera di Padova e del Veneto/Bruno Giuranna.** Claves CD50-8814/16.

No. 1 in E flat major, G474; No. 2 in A major, G475; No. 3 in D major, G476; No. 4 in C major, G477; No. 5 in D major, G478; No. 6 in D major, G479; No. 7 in G major, G480; No. 8 in C major, G481; No. 9 in B flat major, G482; No. 10 in D major, G483; No. 11 in G major, G573; No. 12 in E flat major.

③ 3h 24m DDD 7/89

"Boccherini: 12 Concerti per il Violoncello" proclaims the cover, a little ambitiously, perhaps – for Boccherini probably didn't compose that many. David Geringas has had to exercise a little ingenuity to reach this figure (two of the concertos are almost certainly spurious), but it was probably worth the effort, and the set is a thoroughly enjoyable one in its undemanding way. His intonation is virtually perfect, even high up on the A string, his passage-work is clean, his rhythms are crisp, and he produces (not using a period instrument) a light but pleasingly resonant tone. Listen in particular to the slow movements (such as those of G477 or G483) for eloquence and neatly timed detail. Geringas provides his own cadenzas, including one that quotes Mozart. A very pleasing release. The recording quality and balance are exemplary.

Additional recommendation ...

Julius Berger (vc); **South-West German Chamber Orchestra/Vladislav Czarnecki.** EBS EBS6058 — ③ 3h 31m DDD 9/92

NEW REVIEW

Boccherini. CELLO CONCERTOS AND SONATAS. **Steven Isserlis** (vc); [a]**Maggie Cole** (hpd); [b]**Ostrobothnian Chamber Orchestra/Juha Kangas.** Virgin Classics VC7 59015-2. Items marked [a] recorded in 1988, [b] 1990.

Concertos[b] — No. 7 in G major, G480; No. 9 in B flat major, G482. Sonatas[a] — C minor, G2*b*; G major, G5; A major, G6.

Ih Im DDD 7/92 9P 9S

The Boccherini Cello Concerto — the B flat major, as recorded by the likes of Pablo Casals, Pierre Fournier and János Starker — is in fact a composite made up of two concertos, one in B flat major (or, rather, its outer movements), the other in G major (its slow movement). The Dresden cellist, Friedrich Grützmacher, was responsible for refashioning the 'old' into the 'new' but on this splendidly engineered CD, Steven Isserlis offers us the two original works, so that we can now hear familiar music in an unfamiliar — but indisputably authentic — context. Both works are cheerful and decorative, with pleasing thematic material and plenty of opportunity for discreet shows of virtuosity from the soloist. The performances are suave and elegant, with Isserlis himself weaving a warm and agile thread of tone in and around a stylish orchestral accompaniment. Nothing could be further removed from the decidedly nineteenth-century flavour of Grützmacher's re-working nor, come to think of it, from the apparent 'harshness' of Boccherini's own playing. The scholars tell us that Boccherini wrote upwards to a dozen cello concertos, but his chamber output is better documented and the three sonatas included on this CD come from a family of around 30 similar works. Again, the music calls on the soloist to display his or her skills (which Isserlis does, of course — and to great effect) and has a chirpy, extrovert countenance, the C major especially. Maggie Cole's accompaniment in the sonatas is as on-the-ball as Juha Kangas's Ostrobothnian players are in the concertos.

Boccherini. Guitar Quintets – No. 3 in B flat, G447; No. 9 in C major, G453, "La ritirata di Madrid". **Pepe Romero** (gtr); **Academy of St Martin in the Fields Chamber Ensemble** (Iona Brown, Malcolm Latchem, vns; Stephen Shingles, va; Denis Vigay, vc). Philips Musica da Camera 426 092-2PC. From 9500 789 (10/81).

5lm ADD 6/90

Boccherini was asked by his friend and patron, the Marquis of Benavente, for some chamber music in which he, a guitarist of now-unknown ability – as was Boccherini, might take part. He responded by adapting a number of his existing works (mostly piano quintets) as guitar quintets, of which eight are known; in his catalogue of Boccherini's works Gérard assigns the numbers G445-53 to these works, but G452 represents four 'lost' quintets – which explains why one of eight is labelled No. 9. The Quintet G447 is based on the Piano Quintet, Op. 57/2, but G453 is of mixed parentage: the first three movements are derived from the Piano Quintet, Op. 56/3, but the fourth is adapted from a String Quintet (Op. 30/6), *La musica notturna delle strade di Madrid*. In this last, a military parade (in the form of a theme and 12 variations) approaches, passes and disappears into the distance via dynamic 'hairpins'. The original forms of these works, long on charm, grace and refined craftsmanship, are now rarely heard, but their survival as guitar quintets is fully justified in superb (and superbly recorded) performances such as those in this recording.

Boccherini. Guitar Quintets – No. 4 in D major, G448; No. 6 in G major, G450. ***Castelnuovo-Tedesco.*** Guitar Quintet, Op. 143. **Kazuhito Yamashita** (gtr); **Tokyo Quartet** (Peter Oundjian, Kikuei Ikeda, vns; Kazuhide Isomura, va; Sadao Harada, vc). RCA Victor Red Seal RD60421.

Ih Im DDD I/92

As explained above, Boccherini's Guitar Quintets are mostly revampings of movements from pre-existing chamber works, an exercise in which the French guitarist François de Fossa lent a helping hand that is seldom acknowledged. Castelnuovo-Tedesco was never stuck for a winsome tune, nor did he ever waver in his loyalty to traditional musical forms; written specifically as a with-guitar work and at a much later time, when guitar techniques had advanced beyond the bounds of Boccherini's day, his Quintet makes much more telling use of the instrument and elevates it to *concertante* status. Neither he nor Boccherini presents the listener with any problem, intellectual or emotional, but both provide exceptionally skilfully written and immediately appealing music. Yamashita, long associated with smash-and-grab displays of hard dexterity, plays with the utmost sensitivity and respect for good sound, as befits the company he keeps here, and the recording is managed with equal fidelity.

NEW REVIEW

Boccherini. Guitar Quintets — No. 5 in D major, G449[a]; No. 7 in E minor, G451[b]. String Quintet in A major, G308 (Op. 20 No. 2)[c]. [ab]**David Starobin** (gtr); **Pina Carmirelli,** [a]**Joseph Genualdi,** [b]**Philip Setzer,** [c]**Michaela Paetsch** (vns); [ab]**Philipp Naegele,** [c]**Toby Hoffman** (vas); [a]**Marcy Rosen,** [b]**Peter Wiley,** [c]**Ramon Bolipata,** [c]**Gary Hoffman** (vcs). Sony Classical SBK47298. Item marked [a] recorded in 1979, [b] 1981, [c] July 1974. New to UK.

lh lm AAD 9/92

If Boccherini was grateful for the money he received from the Marquis de Benavente for writing his Guitar Quintets, he would have been even happier to have had the royalties that their success would have brought more than a century later. Much attention has naturally focused on those with colourful titles and those in which the guitar has a prominent part, but the others are no less worthy and enjoyable. The Quintets G449 and G451, in which the guitar plays a mainly supporting role, derive variously from String Quartets (Opp. 52/1 and 53/2) and Piano Quintets (Opp. 56/1 and 56/5), of which *The Classical Catalogue* lists a recording of only Op. 56/1 in its original form; the delightful (guitar-less) String Quintet, G308 also lacks any other recording. This disc is one of several that were issued to celebrate the fortieth anniversary of the Marlboro Festival, which it does with great spirit and warmth. David Starobin is a fine musician who is equally effective both in and out of the limelight, and the varying string contingent — the personnel is different for each work — is firmly 'anchored' by Pina Carmirelli. Boccherini is never less than winsome, and these players know how to show it.

NEW REVIEW

Boccherini. Piano Quintets, Op. 57 — No. 2 in B flat major, G414; No. 3 in E minor, G415; No. 6 in C major, G418. **Patrick Cohen** (fp); **Mosaïques Quartet** (Erich Höbarth, Andrea Bischof, vns; Anita Mitterer, va; Christophe Coin, vc). Astrée Auvidis E8721. Recorded in 1989.

lh lm DDD 12/92

Boccherini was Italian by birth, but spent many years in Spain and mostly wrote instrumental music in the Viennese tradition, and he has perhaps suffered by not belonging to a particular stream of history. But this is hardly fair to a composer who possessed much skill, and whose music reflects a nature which one of his contemporaries called "gentle, patient and polite". These Piano Quintets come from a set of six dating from 1799 and dedicated "to the French Nation". Someone once paid a back-handed compliment to this composer's chamber music by saying that it was as if written "by Haydn's wife", and on listening to a movement such as the *Allegretto moderato* that begins the B flat major Quintet, one does see that Boccherini was no genius. There is a somewhat mannered politeness about it all, and nothing leads us to expect any drama beyond the drawing-room variety or any musical storm greater than might occur in a teacup. We may feel, too, that the four movements of this work are too alike, too similarly moderate in pace and emotion. The E minor Quintet goes a bit deeper, but here again one is never really disturbed by its little outbursts. However, the very gentility of this music is part of its charm, and at times one sees an affinity with the early romantic composers, not least Mendelssohn. One hears the composer at his attractive best in the "Provensal" music in the E minor Quintet and its fourth movement *Andante lento*: these have a wayward lilt and charm that is distinctly captivating. The C major Quintet also has its share of imagination and individuality and ends with a polonaise. Patrick Cohen and the Mosaïques Quartet play these three piano quintets with skill and affection on period instruments that sound well together and suit the music. The recording has a tendency to thicken in louder passages but is otherwise satisfying.

Boccherini. String Quintets – F minor, G274 (Op. 11 No. 4); E major, G275 (Op. 11 No. 5); D major, G276 (Op. 11 No. 6). **Smithsonian Chamber Players** (Marilyn MacDonald, Jorie Garrigue, vns; Anthony Martin, va; Anner Bylsma, Kenneth Slowik, vcs). Deutsche Harmonia Mundi RD77159.

lh 7m DDD 4/92

Boccherini was a virtuoso cellist and often played together with a family string quartet in Madrid and the experience was obviously a very pleasant one, for he wrote 100 quintets for two violins, viola and two cellos. He was never at a loss for ideas: the quintets are richly varied in form and texture, the latter enhanced by Boccherini's intimate knowledge of the techniques and sound-qualities of the bowed-string instruments. Many of us know the famous Minuet – but how many are familiar with the work from which it comes? The Quintet in E, the fifth of the six Quintets of his Op. 11 (1775), of which it is the third movement, is one of those in this recording. The bucolic Quintet in D, *dello l'ucceleria*, ("The aviary") is a cyclic work with bird-song, shepherd's pipes and hunting sounds. If Boccherini was, as Giuseppe Pupo described him, "the wife of Haydn", his music has the charm, grace and poise of the best wives, and there is nothing wrong with that"! The Smithsonian Players, using original Stradivarius instruments (1688-1787), play like good Italians, which none of them is, and are superbly recorded in this irresistibly attractive album.

NEW REVIEW

Boccherini. Stabat mater, G532 (1781 version)[a]. String Quintet in C minor, G328 (Op. 31 No. 4). [a]**Agnès Mellon** (sop); **Ensemble 415** (Chiara Banchini, Enrico Gatti, vns; Emilio Moreno, va; Roel Dieltiens, Hendrike ter Brugge, vcs). Harmonia Mundi HMC90 1378. Text and translation included. Recorded in 1991.

59m DDD 9/92 

The text of the *Stabat mater* dates from the thirteenth century and tells of Mary's sorrow as she keeps watch at the foot of the Cross. Her desolation as she waits for her son to die provides one of the most moving of religious texts and has inspired composers from Palestrina and Lassus through Haydn and Dvořák to, in more modern times, Sir Lennox Berkeley and Penderecki. Boccherini's is probably best known to audiences in its version for three voices and orchestra but the original scoring for a single soprano and string quintet certainly has a greater sense of intimacy and directness of expression which this beautifully clear recording captures admirably. The sweet-voiced Agnès Mellon sings with superb restraint and delicacy while the splendidly crisp and sensitive string playing of Ensemble 415 provides the ideal backdrop. In addition to being a devout Christian, Boccherini was also a most accomplished cellist and his profound understanding in writing for strings is never better displayed than in the Quintet which provides the fill-up for this disc. It's an inspired piece of programme-planning, for the Quintet begins where the *Stabat mater* left off — in reflective, sorrowful mood — before turning, almost imperceptibly, into a most gloriously vibrant piece of chamber music.

Further listening ...

BOCCHERINI EDITION, Volumes 1-5. **Soloists; Petersen Quartet; New Berlin Chamber Orchestra/Michael Erxleben** (vn). Capriccio (5/93) available as follows: *Volume 1 — 10 450:* String Sextets, Op. 23 — No. 1 in E flat major, G454; No. 3 in E major, G456; No. 4 in F minor, G457; No. 6 in F major, G459. *Volume 2 — 10 456:* Sextets (Divertimentos), Op. 16 — No. 1 in D major, G461; No. 4 in E flat major, G464; No. 5 in A major, G465; No. 6 in C major, G466. *Volume 3 — 10 457:* Symphonies, Op. 37 — No. 1 in C major, G515; No. 3 in D minor, G517; No. 4 in A major, G518. *Volume 4 — 10 458:* Symphonies — C minor, Op. 41, G519; D major, Op. 42, G520; D major, Op. 43, G521; D minor, Op. 45, G522. *Volume 5 — 10 451:* String Quartets — D major, Op. 15 No. 1, G177; G minor, Op. 24 No. 6, G194; A major, Op. 39, G213; F major, Op. 64 No. 1, G248.

Léon Boëllmann

French 1862-1897

Suggested listening ...

Deuxième Suite, Op. 27. 12 Pièces, Op. 16. Suite gothique, Op. 25. **Patrice Caire** (org). Rem REM311053 (7/89).

François Boïeldieu

French 1775-1834

Suggested listening ...

LES VOITURES VERSEES — opéra-comique. **Soloists; French Radio Lyric Orchestra/Jean Brebion.** Musidisc 20152-2 (3/92).

Arrigo Boito

Italian 1842-1918

Suggested listening ...

MEFISTOFELE. **Soloists; Trinity Boys' Choir; National Philharmonic Orchestra/Oliviero de Fabritiis.** Decca 410 175-2DH3 (12/85).

Alexander Borodin

Russian 1833-1887

NEW REVIEW

Borodin. ORCHESTRAL WORKS. [a]**Torgny Sporsén** (bass); **Gothenburg Symphony** [a]**Chorus and Orchestra/Neeme Järvi.** DG 435 757-2GH2. Items marked [b] from 429 984-2GH (3/91), others new to UK. Recorded 1989-91.

Symphonies — No. 1 in E flat major; No. 2 in B minor; No. 3 in A minor. Prince Igor — Overture; Dance of the Polovtsian Maidens; Polovtsian Dances[ab]. String Quartet No. 2 in D major — Nocturne (orch. N. Tcherepnin). In the Steppes of Central Asia[b]. Petite Suite (orch. Glazunov).

② 2h 28m DDD 9/92

While it is possible to imagine performances of even greater power and finesse in this strangely unfashionable repertoire, Järvi's Borodin set is by far the best to have appeared in recent years. The extravagant lay-out means we get not just the symphonies but a rich supplement or orchestral works, including even the *Petite Suite* as arranged by Glazunov. Another rarity, Nikolay Tcherepnin's orchestration of the famous *Nocturne* will astonish those familiar with the chaste original: Tcherepnin transforms it into an exotic Scriabin-like tableau, almost as remote from Borodin as its kitschy *Kismet* mutation. The more recognizable *Steppes* are negotiated with ample eloquence and the *Prince Igor* excerpts score by including a brief contribution from the great Khan himself, reminding us of the music's original operatic context. The main works are equally persuasive. The First Symphony emerges here as far more than a dry-run for the Second. Järvi plays the music for all its worth, with DG's big, resonant sound serving to boost the symphonic credentials of the piece. The unfinished Third is also tougher and more dramatic than usual, no mere pastoral reverie in Järvi's interventionist view. The Second Symphony is rather different, suitably epic and yet unusually long-drawn and thoughtful. Thus, the *Scherzo* is bubbling but sensibly articulate, while the *Andante* is daringly broad with a superbly sensitive horn solo.

Additional recommendations ...
Nos. 1-3. **CSR Symphony Orchestra, Bratislava/Stephen Gunzenhauser.** Naxos 8 550238 — 1h 16m DDD 8/91
No. 3. Petite Suite. In the Steppes. Prince Igor — Overture. **USSR Symphony Orchestra/Evgeni Svetlanov.** Melodiya SUCD10-00155 — 1h 8m AAD 5/93

Borodin. Symphony No. 2 in B minor. In the Steppes of Central Asia. Prince Igor – Overture; March; Dance of the Polovtsian Maidens; Polovtsian Dances. **John Alldis Choir; National Philharmonic Orchestra/Loris Tjeknavorian.** RCA Victor Silver Seal VD60535. From RL25098 (8/77).

1h 4m ADD 8/77

A nicely turned, sumptuously recorded concert comprising Borodin's most popular symphony in harness with the familiar orchestral items from his only opera, *Prince Igor*. Tjeknavorian revels in the Symphony's frequent dramatic outburst and opulent tunes (sampling the first movement should convince anyone), while the hand-picked National Philharmonic – well known for their virtuoso performances of classic film scores under this disc's producer, Charles Gerhardt – is enthusiastically assisted by the John Alldis Choir in the March and Dances from *Prince Igor*. Add a warmly played account of the appealing *In the Steppes of Central Asia* and you hav e a most attractive selection, expertly transferred from fine-sounding tapes. One hopes that it will soon be joined by the remaining two symphonies in Tjeknavorian's Borodin cycle.

Borodin. String Quartets – No. 1 in A major; No. 2 in D major. **Borodin Quartet** (Mikhail Kopelman, Andrei Abramenkov, vns; Dmitri Shebalin, va; Valentin Berlinsky, vc). EMI CDC7 47795-2. From EMI Melodiya ASD4100 (3/82).

1h 6m DDD 5/88 

These quartets are delightful music, and they are played here by the aptly-named Borodin Quartet with a conviction and authority that in no way inhibits panache, spontaneity and sheer charm. Doubtless the most popular music of Borodin and the other members of the Russian 'Five' will always be their colourful orchestral and stage music, but no CD collector should ignore these chamber works. Their style derives from a mid-nineteenth-century Russian tradition of spending happy hours in music-making at home and also from the refreshing musical springs of folk-song. This performance offers not only first-rate playing from artists who 'have the music in their blood' but also a warm and convincing recorded sound.

Borodin. String Quartet No. 2 in D major[a].
Shostakovich. String Quartet No. 8 in C minor, Op. 110[a].
Tchaikovsky. String Quartet No. 1 in D major, Op.11[b]. [a]**Borodin Quartet** (Rostislav Dubinsky, Jaroslav Alexandrov, vns; Dmitri Shebalin, va; Valentin Berlinsky, vc); [b]**Gabrieli Quartet** (Kenneth Sillito, Brendan O'Reilly, vns; Ian Jewel, va; Keith Harvey, vc). Decca 425 541-2DM. Items marked [a] from SXL6036 (2/63), [b] SDD524/5 (10/77).

1h 16m ADD 5/90 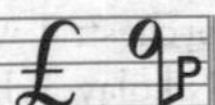

The programme adopted here deserves wide emulation: take the contents of a highly reissue-worthy LP and hunt for something appropriate to supplement it. The Borodin Quartet's affection for the composer after whom they named themselves was evidently still warmly fresh when this performance was recorded. The quiet charm of the piece (it was fondly dedicated to Borodin's wife) comes over beautifully. They are Shostakovich specialists, too, and their account of his most famous quartet is one of the noblest and most vehement it has ever received: superbly virtuoso and hair-raisingly expressive. But what should preface these two performances? An English quartet in Tchaikovsky might not seem the obvious choice, but it works very well, with the Gabrieli showing a fine responsiveness to the work's singing qualities and its refined colour, even in passages which can seem as though Tchaikovsky would just as soon have been writing for string orchestra. They (recorded in 1976) receive a rather closer recorded sound than the Borodin (whose performances date from 1962) but all three still sound very well.

Additional recommendations ...

As above. **Talich Quartet.** Calliope CAL9202 — 57m DDD 5/88

As above. **Alberni Quartet.** Collins Classics 1237-2 — 59m DDD 4/91

Borodin. PRINCE IGOR. **Boris Martinovich** (bar) Igor; **Nicolai Ghiuselev** (bass) Galitsky; **Nicolai Ghiaurov** (bass) Konchak; **Kaludi Kaludov** (ten) Vladimir; **Angel Petkov** (ten) Eroshka; **Stoil Georgiev** (bass) Skula; **Mincho Popov** (ten) Ovlur; **Stefka Evstatiev** (sop) Yaroslavna; **Alexandrina Milcheva** (contr) Konchakovna; **Elena Stoyanova** (sop) Nurse, Polovtsian Girl; **Sofia National Opera Chorus; Sofia Festival Orchestra/Emil Tchakarov.** Sony Classical SK44878. Notes, text and translation included.

③ 3h 30m DDD 6/90

Borodin's limited time to devote to composition meant that many of his works often took years to complete. *Prince Igor* was no exception; even after 18 years of work it remained unfinished at his death in 1887, and it was finally completed by Rimsky-Korsakov and Glazunov. Borodin's main problem with *Prince Igor* was the daunting task of turning what was principally an undramatic subject into a convincing stage work. In many ways he never really succeeded in this and the end result comes over more as a series of epic scenes rather than a musical drama. Despite this, however, one is nevertheless left with an impression of a rounded whole, and it contains some of Borodin's most poignant and moving music, rich in oriental imagery and full of vitality. Tchakarov conducts a performance that is both vigorous and refined, and there are some excellent performances from the principal singers too – Boris Martinovich makes a particularly strong Igor and Nicolai Ghiuselev and Nicolai Ghiaurov in the roles of Prince Galitsky and the Polovtsian Khan Konchak deserve special mention also. This Sony issue is a particularly welcome addition to the catalogue as it represents the only *complete* version of the opera on disc.

Additional recommendation ...

Prince Igor (Act 3 omitted). SONGS[a]. **Boris Christoff**[a] (bass) Galitsky, Konchak; **Soloists; Chorus and Orchestra of the National Opera Theatre, Sofia/Jerzy Semkov;** [b]**Lamoureux Concerts Orchestra/Georges Tzipine.** *Songs — Those people*[b]*; Song of the dark forest; From my tears; The queen of the sea; The beauty no loves me; The magic garden; Arabian melody; The Fishermaiden; Listen to my song, little friend; The sleeping princess; Arrogance; The sea; Why art thou so early, dawn? There is poison in my songs; The false note; For the shores of thy far native land*[b]. EMI Studio CMS7 63386-2 — ③ 3h 23m ADD 6/90

Key to Symbols

Bargains	Quality of performance	Quality of Sound	Basic library	Discs worth exploring	Period performance	Caveat emptor
£	P	S	B	?		▲

Rutland Boughton

British 1878-1960

Suggested listening ...

Symphony No. 3 in B minor. Oboe Concerto No. 1. **Sarah Francis** (ob); **Royal Philharmonic Orchestra/Vernon Handley.** Hyperion CDA66343 (1/90).

THE IMMORTAL HOUR. **Soloists; George Mitchell Choir; English Chamber Orchestra/Alan G. Melville.** Hyperion CDA66101/2 (8/87).

Lili Boulanger
French 1893-1918

Suggested listening ...

Les sirènes. Renouveau. Hymne au soleil. Soir sur la plaine. Dans l'immense tristesse. Attente. Reflets. Le retour. *Coupled with* ***Mendelssohn-Hensel.*** Gartenlieder, Op. 3. Nachtreigen; ***C. Schumann.*** Three Geibel Part-songs. **Christine Friedek** (sop); **Mitsuko Shirai, Regine Böhm** (mezs); **Bernhard Gärtner** (ten); **Hartmut Höll, Sabine Eberspächer** (pfs); **Heidelberg Madrigal Choir/Gerald Kegelmann.** Bayer BR100041 (4/90).

Pierre Boulez
French 1925-

Boulez. MISCELLANEOUS WORKS. [ad]**Sophie Cherrier** (fl); [e]**Alain Damiens** (cl); [ab]**Pierre-Laurent Aimard** (pf); [e]**Andrew Gerzo** (musical assistant); [f]**BBC Singers;** [cdf]**Ensemble Intercontemporain/Pierre Boulez.** Erato 2292-45648-2.
Flute Sonatine[a]. Piano Sonata No. 1[b]. Dérive[c]. Mémoriale (... explosante-fixe ... originel)[d]. Dialogue de l'ombre double[e]. Cummings ist der Dichter[f].

1h 3m DDD 2/92

The conjunction of early and relatively recent Boulez on this valuable disc is likely to inspire mixed feelings: admiration for his integrity, and regret at his reluctance to complete certain works and compose more new ones. The early sonatas (for the Flute Sonatine is as much a fully-fledged, substantial composition as the Piano Sonata No. 1) have confidence in their handling of form and a control of the way the thematic ideas evolve that seem both supremely cogent and remarkably spontaneous. Alongside the sonatas, short essays in expanding sonority like *Dérive* and *Mémoriale*, for all their refinement of tone colour, may seem almost wilfully unpretentious, while the reworked version of *Cummings ist der Dichter*, fascinating and convincing though it is on its own terms, is fussier than the original – less direct rather than more intense. What is beyond doubt is that in *Dialogue de l'ombre double* (1985) Boulez proves that he is still a master, not just of the memorable single line (a solo clarinet) but of the polyphony that results when that line is combined with a subtly varied electronic 'shadow' of itself. The quality of invention here is well-matched by Alain Damiens's superb performance, though all the playing is excellent, and the recordings are generally very good.

Boulez. Rituel (1974-75). Messagesquisse (1976). Notations 1-4 (1978). **Orchestre de Paris/Daniel Barenboim.** Erato 2292-45493-2.

41m DDD 10/90 

Obviously enough, this disc wins no prizes for length. It is nevertheless important in several significant respects. Only rarely do we have the chance to hear Boulez's music, not only under a conductor other than the composer, but a conductor whose whole artistic background is so different to Boulez's own. Barenboim clearly has his own point of view, and the technical skill to realize it convincingly with a first-class French orchestra. Boulez himself now tends to underline the public ceremonial of *Rituel* (a tribute to the Italian composer and conductor Bruno Maderna), whereas Barenboim, restraining the cumulative clangour of the music's dialogues between the implacable reiterations of gongs and tamtams and the seven other instrumental groups, preserves more of the intimacy of personal regret and loss. *Rituel* is unusual for Boulez in the clear-cut logic of its gradually evolving form, and Barenboim does well to convey that logic without making the whole design seem too predictable for its own good. He is equally attentive to the need to balance striking details with a feeling for overall shape in the shorter but no less personal structures of *Notations* and *Messagesquisse*. The recording is outstanding in its spaciousness and tonal range.

Boulez. Pli selon pli. **Phyllis Bryn-Julson** (sop); **BBC Symphony Orchestra/Pierre Boulez.** Erato 2292-45376-2. From NUM75050 (5/83).

1h 8m DDD 3/89 

Pli selon pli (1957-62) is one of the great pillars of post-war musical modernism. If that proclamation merely makes it sound forbidding, then it could scarcely be less appropriate. 'Pillar' it may be, but as exciting in its moment-to-moment shifts of colour and contour, and as compelling in its command of large-scale dramatic design as anything composed since the great years of Schoenberg and Stravinsky. Easy, no: enthralling and rewarding – yes. This is no grand, single-minded work in the great Germanic symphonic tradition, but a sequence of distinct yet balanced responses to aspects of the great symbolist poet Mallarmé. In this his second recording of the piece Boulez is prepared to let the music expand and resonate, the two large orchestral tapestries enclosing three "Improvisations", smaller-scale vocal movements in which the authority and expressiveness of Phyllis Bryn-Julson is heard to great advantage. The sound is brilliantly wide-ranging and well-balanced, and while the contrast between delicacy and almost delirious density embodied in *Pli selon pli* does take some getting used to, to miss it is to miss one of modern music's most original masterworks.

Boulez. Le visage nuptial[a]. Le soleil des eaux[b]. Figures, Doubles, Prismes. [ab]**Phyllis Bryn-Julson** (sop); [a]**Elizabeth Laurence** (mez); [ab]**BBC Singers; BBC Symphony Orchestra/Pierre Boulez.** Erato 2292-45494-2. Texts and translations included.

1h 2m DDD 12/90 

Anyone approaching Boulez the composer for the first time would do well to start with his short cantata *Le soleil des eaux* which, like everything on this disc, is expertly performed and effectively recorded. Here is lyricism and drama, refinement and prodigious energy, in a style that acknowledges a Debussian delicacy as well as a complementary expressionist vehemence. It is certainly rare to find Boulez choosing a text which celebrates the natural world so directly. In *Le visage nuptial* it is human love and loss to which René Char's complex, surrealist word-patterns allude, and the music (begun in the mid-1940s but revised as recently as the late 1980s) is imposingly resourceful in its response. Even if you conclude that in this case the mixture simply doesn't work, the confrontation of poet and composer, which reached its fullest expression in *Le marteau sans maitre*, is endlessly absorbing. *Figures, Doubles, Prismes* is a characteristic Boulez title suggesting a subtle process of reflection and variation. Variety is abundant in this purely orchestral score, yet a sense of the larger span also comes through – so much so that the forceful ending can seem like a disconcerting contradiction. If so, it is all the more authentically Boulezian for that.

Boulez. Le soleil des eaux[a].
Koechlin. Les Bandar-Log, Op. 176[b].
Messiaen. Chronochromie[c]. Et exspecto resurrectionem mortuorum[d]. [a]**Josephine Nendick** (sop); [a]**Barry McDaniel** (ten); [a]**Louis Devos** (bass); [a]**BBC Chorus**; [abc]**BBC Symphony Orchestra/Pierre Boulez,** [bc]**Antal Dorati**; [d]**Paris Orchestra/Serge Baudo.** EMI CDM7 63948-2. Items marked [abc] from ASD639 (7/65), [d] ASD2467 (12/69).

1h 12m ADD 3/92 

Koechlin's symphonic poem *Les Bandar-Log*, written in 1940, is part of a monumental work, *Livre de la Jungle*, which he had started over 40 years before. In the work played here he evokes the behaviour of monkey tribes and equates them satirically with musicians who wish to be in fashion but who are merely imitators of trends. Caricatures of various styles are woven into

Koechlin's own highly individual and expressive style, which after over half a century still sounds very modern. Boulez has produced four versions of *Le soleil des eaux*, and the third is performed here. This short work is in two contrasted sections, which are based on two poems by René Char, *Lament of the Love-Sick Lizard* and *Night-time*. Though Boulez's writing is highly complex, there is still a very French preoccupation with beauty of sound, and the result is an attractive composition. The two Messiaen works explore subjects which have continually exercised the composer. In *Chronochromie* we are taken into the world of nature, and birdsong in particular. *Et exspecto resurrectionem mortuorem* is inspired by meditation on the resurrection of Christ and the prospect of life everlasting. In this last work the Paris Orchestra acquits itself well under Baudo (the composer was also present at the sessions), and the sound is very good. The BBC Symphony Orchestra performances were recorded at a time when Dorati was its chief conductor, and when Boulez was just commencing his relationship with the orchestra. Their performances are strikingly brilliant, and the recordings have amazing presence for the mid-1960s.

Further listening ...

Rituel in memoriam Bruno Maderna[a]. Eclat/Multiples[b]. [a]**BBC Symphony Orchestra,** [b]**Ensemble Intercontemporain/Pierre Boulez.** Sony Classical SK45839 (8/90).

William Boyce

British 1711-1779

Boyce. SYMPHONIES. **The English Concert/Trevor Pinnock** (hpd). Archiv Produktion 419 631-2AH.

No. 1 in B flat major; No. 2 in A major; No. 3 in C major; No. 4 in F major; No. 5 in D major; No. 6 in F major; No. 7 in B flat major; No. 8 in D minor.

lh DDD 9/87 

Boyce's *Eight Symphonys* (to follow his own spelling) were written over a period of some 20 years, as overtures for court odes and theatre pieces; later he collected them for publication and use as concert music. They are typically English, in a variety of ways: their tunefulness, their eccentricities of melody and rhythm, their refusal to obey any of the rules about style. And if you think, on hearing the trumpets and drums of No. 5, that Boyce is giving way to Handel's influence (it's very like the *Fireworks Music*), pause a moment: this piece dates from 1739, ten years earlier than the Handel work. The freshness and the vivacity of Boyce's invention are beautifully caught in these performances by Trevor Pinnock and The English Concert, with their sure feeling for tempo, their sprightly dance rhythms, and indeed their understanding of the gentle vein of melancholy.

Additional recommendation ...

Bournemouth Sinfoneitta/Ronald Thomas. CRD CRD3356 — lh ADD 5/86

NEW REVIEW

Boyce. SELECT ANTHEMS. **New College Choir, Oxford/Edward Higginbottom** with [a]**Gary Cooper** (org). CRD CRD3483. Texts included. Recorded in 1991.

O where shall widom be found? Wherewithal shall a young man. I have surely built thee an house. O praise the Lord. Turn thee unto me. O give thanks. By the waters of Babylon. The Lord is King be the people never so impatient. Voluntaries[a] — Nos. 1, 4 and 7.

lh 16m DDD 10/92

Boyce was a younger contemporary of Handel and one of England's most gifted baroque composers. Nowadays Boyce is remembered chiefly for a set of eight Symphonies but in his own time he was highly regarded for his vocal music. Five of the pieces on this disc are verse anthems which essentially belong to the tradition established by Restoration composers in the previous century. Three others are full anthems consisting of outer choral movements framing one for a smaller group of voices. Additionally, the programme includes three organ solos from Boyce's *Ten*

Voluntaries for Organ and Harpsichord. The authenticity of some of these has been questioned but they sound well in the present context. The choir of New College, Oxford under Edward Higginbottom's direction is on characteristically strong form with carefully balanced vocal strands, clear textures, secure pitch and a pleasing radiance in the upper voices. The verse anthem, *I have surely built thee an house* comes over splendidly, providing the listener with a satisfying account of a fine piece. No less impressive is *By the waters of Babylon* in which Boyce's skill in the marriage of words with music is especially affecting. In this piece Higginbottom brings lucidity to the vocal ensemble while suffusing the whole with a soft radiance.

Boyce. Solomon – serenata. **Bronwen Mills** (sop) She; **Howard Crook** (ten) He; **The Parley of Instruments/Roy Goodman.** Hyperion CDA66378. Text included.

lh 16m DDD 11/90

Boyce's *Solomon* is not a biblical oratorio, like Handel's, but an extremely secular serenata based on *The Song of Solomon* – in short, a celebration of nature and of erotic love. It has just two 'characters', He and She, and most of their music is amorous – all of it gracefully written, some of it unsophisticatedly jolly, some markedly sensual. The most famous number is "Softly arise, O southern breeze!", for tenor with an eloquent bassoon obbligato and throbbing strings. For the most part the listener will be reminded of Handel's *Acis and Galatea*, with its typically pastoral features such as nature imitations (there are trilling birds and Purcellian frosty shivers); no one could fail to be charmed by this appealing, very English work. The singers here, Bronwen Mills and Howard Crook, are both good stylists, not perhaps as naturally sensuous in tone or phrasing as they might be but natural and fluent and showing an instinctive feeling for the shape of Boyce's lines, and they give due weight to the words. Roy Goodman conducts expertly with a period-instrument band, and the result is a gently beguiling performance.

Johannes Brahms

German 1833-1897

Brahms. Piano Concertos[a] – Nos. 1 and 2. Fantasias, Op. 116[b]. **Emil Gilels** (pf); [a]**Berlin Philharmonic Orchestra/Eugen Jochum.** DG 419 158-2GH2. Items marked [a] from 2707 064 (12/72), [b]2530 655 (7/76). Items marked [a] recorded in 1972, [b] 1975.

② 2h 6m ADD 9/86 

Emil Gilels was an ideal Brahms interpreter and his account of the two concertos with Eugen Jochum, another great Brahmsian, is one of the inspired classics of the gramophone. The youthful, leonine First Concerto and the expansive, lyrical Second were both played for the first time by Brahms himself, and it would be difficult to imagine any performances coming closer to the spirit of his music than these. They should not be missed and their value is further enhanced by the addition of the autumnal Fantasias, Op. 116. The recording, too, is natural and has plenty of concert hall ambience and an ideal balance between soloist and orchestra. This set cannot be too strongly recommended. We now also have them available separately at mid-price (see listings below).

Additional recommendations ...

No. 1. **Claudio Arrau** (pf); **Concertgebouw Orchestra/Bernard Haitink.** Philips Silver Line 420 702-2PSL — 53m ADD 11/87

No. 1. **Alfred Brendel** (pf); **Berlin Philharmonic Orchestra/Claudio Abbado.** Philips 420 071-2PH — 49m DDD 11/87

No. 1[a]. Variations on a Theme by Haydn, Op. 56a[b]. **Daniel Barenboim** (pf); [a]**Philharmonia Orchestra,** [b]**Vienna Philharmonic Orchestra/Sir John Barbirolli.** EMI Studio CDM7 63536-2 — lh 10m ADD 11/90

No. 1. Four Ballades, Op. 10. **Emil Gilels** (pf); **Berlin Philharmonic Orchestra/Eugen Jochum.** DG Brahms Edition 431 595-2GCE (*coupled with No. 2 and reviewed above*) — lh 17m ADD 8/91

No. 1[a]. *Zwei Gesänge, Op. 91*[b]. **Stephen Kovacevich** (pf); [b]**Ann Murray** (mez); [b]**Nobuko Imai** (va); [a]**London Philharmonic Orchestra/Wolfgang Sawallisch.** EMI CDC7 54578-2 — 59m DDD 10/92

No. 2[a]. *Academic Festival Overture, Op. 80*[b]. *Tragic Overture, Op. 81*[b]. **Daniel Barenboim** (pf); [a]**Philharmonia Orchestra,** [b]**Vienna Philharmonic Orchestra/Sir John Barbirolli.** EMI Studio CDM7 63537-2 — lh 16m ADD 11/90

No. 2. **Alfred Brendel** (pf); **Berlin Philharmonic Orchestra/Claudio Abbado.** Philips 432 975-2PH — 49m DDD 6/92

No. 2. Fantasias. **Emil Gilels** (pf); **Berlin Philharmonic Orchestra/Eugen Jochum.** DG Galleria 435 588-2GGA (*coupled with No. 1 and reviewed above*) — lh 14m ADD 9/92

Brahms. Violin Concerto in D major, Op. 77. **Itzhak Perlman** (vn); **Chicago Symphony Orchestra/Carlo Maria Giulini.** EMI CDC7 47166-2. From ASD3385 (11/77).

43m ADD 1/87

NEW REVIEW

Brahms. Violin Concerto in D major, Op. 77.
Sibelius. Violin Concerto in D minor, Op. 47. **Tasmin Little** (vn); **Royal Liverpool Philharmonic Orchestra/Vernon Handley.** EMI Eminence CD-EMX2203. Recorded in 1991.

lh 12m DDD 2/93 

Giulini conducts the opening of this work in a strong and serious fashion, and at a moderate tempo. The unhurried pace indeed seems dangerously slow for the soloist, but then Perlman enters the scene and all is found to be well. His magisterial playing, ardent, powerful, and with magnificent breadth of phrase and tone makes for a very satisfying first movement. The *Adagio* has a good solo oboe from Ray Still; here Perlman's playing is reflective at first and then it becomes more overtly passionate as the movement develops. The last movement's 'gipsy' rondo finale makes an effective contrast, with plenty of sharp attack and rhythmic bite. The late 1970s recording is of good tonal quality and well balanced. The talented young British violinist Tasmin Little admits that she prefers not to commit her interpretations to disc until she has "something to say and the means with which to say it". That is certainly the case with the Brahms Concerto, a clear, considered reading (much aided in the slow movement by Jonathan Small's excellent oboe solo), quite without mannerism and beautifully accompanied by Vernon Handley and the Royal Liverpool Philharmonic. The Sibelius has even more character, and here Little adds to an impressive roster of the work's many great female interpreters (Neveu, Wicks, Bustabo, Ignatius, etc). Handley is an impressive Sibelian whose feel for the idiom is apparent in every bar, and both recordings are excellent. As a coupling the two performances are irresistible.

Additional recommendations ...

Violin Concerto. ***Brahms.*** *Violin Concerto in D major, Op.* 77. **Jascha Heifetz** (vn); **Boston Symphony Orchestra/Charles Munch.** RCA RD85402 — ADD 10/87

Violin Concerto. ***Mendelssohn.*** *Violin Concerto in E minor, Op. 64.* **Xue-Wei** (vn); **London Philharmonic Orchestra/Ivor Bolton.** ASV CDDCA748 — lh 7m DDD 4/91

Violin Concerto. **Itzhak Perlman** (vn); **Berlin Philharmonic Orchestra/Daniel Barenboim.** EMI CDC7 54580-2 — 40m DDD 2/93

Violin Concerto. ***Tchaikovsky.*** *Violin Concerto in D major, Op. 35.* **Jascha Heifetz** (vn); **Chicago Symphony Orchestra/Fritz Reiner.** RCA Living Stereo 09026 61495-2 — lh 4m ADD 4/93

Brahms. Double Concerto in A minor, Op. 102[a]. Piano Quartet No. 3 in C minor, Op. 60[b]. **Isaac Stern** (vn); [b]**Jaime Laredo** (va); **Yo-Yo Ma** (vc); [b]**Emmanuel Ax** (pf); [a]**Chicago Symphony Orchestra/Claudio Abbado.** CBS Masterworks CD42387.

lh 8m DDD 6/88

The grave, declamatory utterances at the beginning of the Double Concerto tell us much about the nature of what will follow. They can also reveal a great deal about the two soloists who enter in turn with solo cadenzas separated by thematic orchestral material. Perhaps surprisingly it is the much younger man, Yo-Yo Ma, who brings out most strongly the noble gravity of the composer's inspiration, while the relatively veteran Isaac Stern is more melodious and spontaneous-sounding. The music's steady but unhurried paragraphs are very well handled by Claudio Abbado and the excellent Chicago Symphony Orchestra is responsive and pretty faithfully balanced with the soloists. This is a performance to satisfy rather than to thrill, perhaps, but satisfy it does. The recording is rich and rather reverberant, notably in orchestral tuttis. The powerful C minor Piano Quartet is also well played and provides a substantial partner to the concerto. Apparently Brahms once said that it had the mood of a man thinking of suicide, but one hastens to say that it is nothing like as gloomy as that would suggest.

NEW REVIEW

Brahms. Serenades — No. 1 in D major, Op. 11; No. 2 in A major, Op. 16. **West German Sinfonia/Dirk Joeres.** Pickwick IMP Classics PCD1024. Recorded in 1992.

lh 19m DDD 5/93 £

If the term serenade suggests something which is open-hearted and uncomplicated then Brahms's two compositions in this form follow classical conventions up to a point. Each work has an appealing geniality and mellow warmth, but Brahms had a perpetually serious side to his nature, and there's always a nearby cloud threatening to move over the sun. Such mixed characteristics are particularly evident in the Second Serenade, which is scored without violins, and lacks the brightness which upper strings bring to orchestral textures. It is no easy task for a conductor to balance the opposing elements in either work, but Dirk Joeres manages this very successfully. He has at his disposal a very fine body of players, who are given clear, high-quality recordings. In the faster, more outgoing sections of each score he points the rhythms very skilfully, and he shapes the slower, more inward movements in a highly sympathetic, attentive fashion. Even the First Serenade's long *Adagio no troppo* movement, which so easily loses direction, is kept on course through Joeres's subtle use of phrase and pulse.

Additional recommendation ...

Vienna Symphony Orchestra/Gary Bertini. Orfeo C008101A — lh 16m ADD 6/90

Brahms. Hungarian Dances Nos. 1-21 – orchestrations. **Vienna Philharmonic Orchestra/Claudio Abbado**. DG 410 615-2GH. From 2560 100 (3/83).
Brahms: Nos. 1, 3 and 10. ***Hallén:*** No. 2. ***Juon:*** No. 4. ***Schmeling:*** Nos. 5 and 6. ***Gál:*** Nos. 7, 8 and 9. ***Parlow:*** Nos. 11-16. ***Dvořák:*** Nos. 17-21.

48m DDD 9/84

To play the 21 *Hungarian Dances* through at one sitting is not recommended: far better for the CD user to choose a group of four or five and then just sit back and enjoy some charming and vivacious music, full of good tunes. High spirits predominate in the first set; in the second set there is more a mixture of liveliness and minor key 'gipsy' melancholy, though the introspection never becomes more than skin-deep. Abbado persuades the VPO to play with much brilliance and an engaging rhythmic lift and lightness of touch. These are highly enjoyable performances and the sound-quality emphasizes the nature of the playing, clear and brilliant, if a little lacking in warmth.

Additional recommendation ...

Leipzig Gewandhaus Orchestra/Kurt Masur. Philips 411 426-2PH — DDD 9/84

Brahms. ORCHESTRAL AND VOCAL WORKS. **NBC Symphony Orchestra/Arturo Toscanini.** RCA Gold Seal mono GD60325. Texts and translations included.
Symphonies – No. 1 in C minor, Op. 68 (from HMV ALP1012, 11/52); No. 2 in D major, Op. 73 (ALP1013, 11/52); No. 3 in F major, Op. 90 (ALP1166, 10/54); No. 4 in E minor, Op. 98 (ALP1029, 6/53). Double Concerto in A minor, Op. 102 (with Mischa Mischakoff, vn;

Frank Miller, vc. RB16066, 7/58). Variations on a Theme by Haydn, Op. 56*a* (ALP1204, 12/54). Tragic Overture, Op. 81 (VCM3, 4/67). Academic Festival Overture, Op. 80 (VCM3, 4/67). *Hungarian Dances* – No. 1 in G minor; No. 17 in F sharp minor; No. 20 in E minor; No. 21 in E minor (ALP1235, 5/55). Gesang der Parzen, Op. 89 (Robert Shaw Chorale. AT125, 4/74). Liebeslieder-Walzer, Op. 52 (Chorus; Artur Balsam, Joseph Kahn, pfs. Recorded in 1948. New to UK).

④ 4h 27m ADD 5/90

Despite many reissues, technical tinkerings, and critical re-evaluations, the recordings of the great Italian maestro Arturo Toscanini still stand head and shoulders above those which have the unenviable task of rivalling his genius as conductor and interpreter. This generous Brahms set is an excellent example of why Toscanini's recordings are still essential. The readings of the four symphonies must stand as benchmarks against which others are compared, and generally are found wanting. Toscanini's command of this music is total: his sense of architecture is unfailing, his control of tempos and rubato are masterly, and his ability to persuade the NBC Symphony Orchestra to play with extraordinary dynamic variety and tonal beauty is proof of his genius. In addition to the symphonies the set contains a fiery performance of the Double Concerto with the orchestra's principals as eloquent, if occasionally overshadowed, soloists and excellent readings of the essential shorter works of Brahms: the *Haydn Variations, Academic* and *Tragic* Overtures and *Hungarian Dances*. And to round off the set there are good, if not perfect, performances of two choral works, the rarely performed *Song of the Fates* and the *Liebeslieder Waltzes,* Op. 52. The transfer to CD of the original tapes has been handled particularly well: the worst tonal excesses have been successfully tamed, and there is a fine sense of balance throughout (the recordings range from 1948 to 1963). With such a giant as Toscanini recommendation really becomes superfluous. Suffice it to say that these recordings are testimony to the genius of one of the greatest conductors this century has ever known.

NEW REVIEW

Brahms. Symphony No. 1 in C minor, Op. 68. Gesang der Parzen, Op. 89[a]. [a]**Berlin Radio Chorus; Berlin Philharmonic Orchestra/Claudio Abbado.** DG 431 790-2GH. Recorded in 1990.

58m DDD 10/91

NEW REVIEW

Brahms. Symphony No. 1 in C minor, Op. 68[a].
Wagner. Siegfried Idyll[bc]. Siegfried — Siegfried's horn-call[c]. [c]**Dennis Brain** (hn); [ab]**Philharmonia Orchestra/Guido Cantelli.** Testament mono SBT1012. Item marked [a] from HMV ALP1152 (7/54), [b] HMV DB9746/7 (4/52), [c] HMV C3622 (11/47). Recorded 1947-53.

1h 2m ADD 2/93

Claudio Abbado's 1990 recording of Brahms's First Symphony achieves the sort of musical and sonic impact that Karajan's first DG version did in the mid-1960s. That too was with the Berlin Philharmonic, a rich, grandly imposing performance that sung and stamped, culminating in a massively jubilant finale. Abbado's tempos are generally broad — his first movement (without its repeat) is as boldly emphatic as Klemperer's — but he never stints on affection, and few would find fault with his warm, lyrical handling of the beautiful *Andante*, 'sostenuto', indeed! Abbado ventures between the score's little nooks and crannies (in that respect at least, he's Karajan's superior), highlighting small details without impeding the music's flow or weakening the performance's overall structure. When the finale breaks from *Più Andante* to *Allegro non troppo, ma con brio* (not *too* fast, but with plenty of spirit), Abbado really goes for the burn, very much as Furtwängler did before him. It's a truly inspired reading, grand but never grandiose; appreciative of Brahms's thick-set orchestration, but never stodgy. The fill-up is of enormous import, and opens with one of the composer's most inspired musical gestures: a bold, burgeoning *Maestoso*, anticipating the words "The gods should be feared/by the human race ...". *Gesang der Parzen*, or "Song of the Fates" is a setting of a particularly unsettling poem by Goethe, one that warns how the uplifted have particular reason to fear the gods, those who "turn their beneficent eyes away from whole races." Abbado surely sensed the terrible truth of that prophesy, and his reading of Op. 89 breathes a deeply disquieting air.

Cantelli conducts an interpretation of the Symphony which is free of any idiosyncrasy. Yet there is an extraordinary electricity in his conducting, a sense of concentration and conviction which lifts the performance into one of the greatest ever set down on record. The fiery young Italian makes the vintage Philharmonia play in an inspired fashion, and the 1953 mono recording is very acceptable. A slightly edgy string sound betrays the 1951 origin of the *Siegfried Idyll* recording, but the performance has a tenderness, warmth and eloquence which has never been surpassed. Dennis Brain's exuberant horn-call completes a very desirable Testament disc.

Additional recommendations ...

Nos. 1-4. **North German Radio Symphony Orchestra/Günter Wand.** RCA GD60085 — ③ 2h 38m ADD

Nos. 1-4. Variations on a Theme by Haydn, Op. 56a, "St Antoni". Academic Festival Overture, Op. 80. Hungarian Dances Nos. 17-21. Tragic Overture, Op. 81. **Cleveland Orchestra/George Szell.** Sony Classical SK48398 — ③ 3h 34m ADD

Nos. 1-4. Tragic Overture. Academic Festival Overture. **Chicago Symphony Orchestra/Sir Georg Solti.** Decca 430 799-2DC4 — ④ 3h 19m ADD 4/92

No. 1. Academic Festival Overture. **Concertgebouw Orchestra/Riccardo Chailly.** Decca 421 295-2DH — 59m DDD 9/88

No. 1. Tragic Overture. Academic Festival Overture. **Philharmonia Orchestra/Otto Klemperer.** EMI Studio CDM7 69651-2 — 1h 7m ADD 1/90

No. 1. **Schumann.** *Overture, Scherzo and Finale, Op. 52.* **Berlin Philharmonic Orchestra/Herbert von Karajan.** DG Privilege 431 161-2GR — 1h 3m ADD 8/91

No. 1. Variations on a Theme by Haydn. **London Classical Players/Roger Norrington.** EMI CDC7 54286-2 — 1h 1m DDD 10/91

NEW REVIEW

Brahms. Symphony No. 2 in D major, Op. 73. Tragic Overture, Op. 81. **Boston Symphony Orchestra/Bernard Haitink.** Philips 432 094-2PH. Recorded in 1990.

1h 2m DDD 10/92 

NEW REVIEW

Brahms. Symphony No. 2 in D major, Op. 73. Academic Festival Overture, Op. 80. **New York Philharmonic Orchestra/Kurt Masur.** Teldec 9031-77291-2. Recorded in 1992.

50m DDD 5/93  

Brahms's Second Symphony is the warmest, most lyrical of the four, and on the Philips disc it receives a performance which brings out those qualities to the full. Haitink's reading is very straightforward and unselfconscious: he allows the first movement to blossom attractively, but he ensures that this process is achieved within a string framework — one is always aware that detail has its secure place within the musical argument. The second movement's basic pulse is on the slow side, but Haitink's affectionate, watchful conducting ensures that the music flows naturally. The third movement is brought to life quite gently too, but accents are light and rhythms are sharp enough to ensure that the mood is still outgoing. In the finale Haitink sets a fast initial tempo, but he allows the music to breathe through the use of subtle inflexions and changes of pulse. There's plenty of excitement, but nothing is too hectic. In the Overture Haitink's basic tempo is quite measured, but again accents are sharp, and the score's dramatic element is well brought out. Throughout both works the playing of the Boston Symphony Orchestra is superlative, and the recording is excellent, with just a slight reservation that there is an occasional moment of slightly acid string tone.

Masur also brings warmth and affection to the Symphony in his performance. In the first movement he maintains a strong sense of line, and paces the music more objectively and straightforwardly than Haitink. The structure is clearer, but there's also a natural, unforced lyricism. The *Adagio* has a natural ebb and flow, and once again Masur makes the listener aware of the music's shape and argument very clearly. After a neatly pointed *Allegretto* the finale is given a beautifully balanced, strongly argued reading which eschews superficial excitement, but satisfies through the feeling of a symphonic argument brought to a logical conclusion. To sum up, Haitink caresses the music with more subjective warmth than Masur, whose reading by no means lacks affection, but is more architectural and objective. The New York Philharmonic responds to its musical director with highly sensitive, very accomplished playing, and Teldec's attractively warm but clearly recorded disc is completed by a genial, uplifting *Academic Festival Overture*.

Additional recommendations ...

No. 2. Alto Rhapsody, Op. 53[a]. [a]**Christa Ludwig** (mez); [a]**Philharmonia Chorus; Philharmonia Orchestra/Otto Klemperer.** EMI Studio CDM7 69650-2 — 51m ADD 1/90

No. 2. Alto Rhapsody[a]. [a]**Marjana Lipovšek** (contr); [a]**Ernst Senff Choir; Berlin Philharmonic Orchestra/Claudio Abbado.** DG 427 643-2GH — 1h DDD 2/90

No. 2. Academic Festival Overture. **Columbia Symphony Orchestra/Bruno Walter.** CBS Maestro CD44870 — 51m ADD 7/90

No. 2. ***Webern.*** *Im Sommerwind.* **Royal Concertgebouw Orchestra/Riccardo Chailly.** Decca 430 324-2DH — 56m DDD 12/90

No. 2. **Vienna Philharmonic Orchestra/Carlo Maria Giulini.** DG 435 348-2GH 47m DDD 5/92

Brahms. Symphony No. 3 in F major, Op. 90. Tragic Overture, Op. 81. Schicksalslied, Op. 54[a]. [a]**Ernst-Senff Choir; Berlin Philharmonic Orchestra/Claudio Abbado.** DG 429 765-2GH.

1h 8m DDD 1/91 

This disc is gloriously programmed for straight-through listening. Abbado gets off to a cracking start with an urgently impassioned *Tragic Overture* in which the credentials of the Berlin Philharmonic to make a richly idiomatic, Brahmsian sound – already well accepted – are substantially reaffirmed. A wide-eyed, breathtaking account of the *Schicksalslied* ("Song of Destiny") follows to provide sound contrast before the wonders of the Third Symphony are freshly explored. This is a reading of the Symphony to be savoured; it is underpinned throughout by a rhythmic vitality which binds the four movements together with a forward thrust, making the end inevitable right from the opening bars. Even in the moments of repose and, especially, the warmly-felt *Andante*, Abbado never lets the music forget its ultimate goal. Despite this, there are many moments of wonderful solo and orchestral playing along the way in which there is time to delight, and Abbado seems to bring out that affable, Bohemian-woods, Dvořák-like element in Brahms's music to a peculiar degree in this performance. The Symphony is recorded with a particular richness and some may find the heady waltz of the third movement done too lushly, emphasized by Abbado's lingering tempo. Nevertheless, this is splendid stuff, and not to be missed.

Additional recommendations ...

No. 3. Variations on a Theme by Haydn. **Columbia Symphony Orchestra/Bruno Walter.** CBS Masterworks CD42531 — 52m ADD 9/86

Nos. 3 and 4. **Berlin Philharmonic Orchestra/Herbert von Karajan.** DG Brahms Edition 431 593-2GCE — 1h 12m ADD 8/91

No. 3. Serenade No. 1 in D major, Op. 11. **Belgian Radio and Television Philharmonic Orchestra, Brussels/Alexander Rahbari.** Naxos 8 550280 — 1h 17m DDD 1/92 £

Brahms. Symphony No. 4 in E minor, Op. 98. **Vienna Philharmonic Orchestra/Carlos Kleiber.** DG 400 037-2GH. From 2532 003 (4/81).

39m DDD 9/85 

Carlos Kleiber's reading of Brahms's Fourth Symphony is highly individual and thought-provoking but those listeners who know Kleiber from his thrilling recordings of Beethoven's Fifth and Seventh Symphonies and are expecting similarly uncompromising, high-tension performances with enormous muscular energy are in for a surprise! His reading certainly has plenty of muscle, but he shows considerable patience and generosity in his handling of Brahms's long, constantly developing melodic lines. Sound is generally good, though the bass may need assistance on some equipment.

Additional recommendations ...
No. 4. Variations on a Theme by Haydn. **Chicago Symphony Orchestra/Sir Georg Solti.** Decca 430 440-2DM — ·· 1h 2m ADD 4/92 (B)
No. 4. Variations on a Theme by Haydn. **Hallé Orchestra/James Loughran.** EMI Eminence CD-CFP4614 — · 59m ADD 3/93 (B)

Brahms. String Sextets – No. 1 in B flat major, Op. 18; No. 2 in G major, Op. 36. **Raphael Ensemble** (James Clarke, Elizabeth Wexler, vns; Sally Beamish, Roger Tapping, vas; Andrea Hess, Rhydian Shaxson, vcs). Hyperion CDA66276.

··· 1h 14m DDD 1/89 9p

Completed after the First Piano Concerto, but still comparatively early works, the Sextets are typified by lush textures, ardent emotion, and wonderfully memorable melodic lines. The first is the warmer, more heart-on-the-sleeve piece, balancing with complete naturalness a splendidly lyrical first movement, an urgent, dark set of intricate variations, a lively rustic dance of a *Scherzo*, and a placidly flowing finale. The Second Sextet inhabits at first a more mysterious world of half-shadows, occasionally rent by glorious moments of sunlight. The finale, however, casts off doubt and ends with affirmation. Both works are very susceptible to differing modes of interpretation, and the Raphael Ensemble has established very distinctive views of each, allowing the richness of the texture its head without obscuring the lines, and selecting characteristically distinct tone qualities to typify the two works. The recording is clear and analytic without robbing the sound of its warmth and depth. Altogether an impressive recording début for this ensemble.

Brahms. Clarinet Quintet in B minor, Op. 115[a].
Mozart. Clarinet Quintet in A major, K581[b]. **Gervase de Peyer** (cl); Members of the **Melos Ensemble** (Emanuel Hurwitz, Ivor McMahon, vns; Cecil Aronowitz, va; Terence Weill, vc). EMI CDM7 63116-2. Item marked [a] from ASD620 (3/65), [b] ASD605 (9/64).

·· 1h 5m ADD 11/89 £ 9p

There can be few who hear the opening to Brahms's Clarinet Quintet who fail to succumb to the main subject's tender and haunting melancholy – surely one of Brahms's most poignant utterances and certainly one guaranteed to send tingles down the spine. Gervase de Peyer's warm, full-bodied tone and liquid playing is a delight to the ear, and the autumnal beauty of the work is captured particularly well in this affectionate and thoughtful performance. Unlike the Mozart Quintet, which treats the clarinet very much as a concertante instrument, Brahms integrates the clarinet into the overall texture, skilfully blending and juxtaposing the characteristic timbre with that of the strings into an homogeneous whole, a quality that comes over exceptionally well in this performance. The Mozart Quintet makes an ideal contrast to the autumnal glow of the Brahms, and receives an equally fine and engaging performance, if perhaps lacking just that extra bit of magic that makes the Brahms so irresistible. The Melos Ensemble convey the work's geniality and freshness from beginning to end, and the slow movement is imbued with great serenity and beauty. The 1964 recordings have retained a remarkable freshness, and are both naturally balanced and beautifully clear. At mid-price this reissue should not be missed.

Additional recommendation ...
Clarinet Quintet. Clarinet Trio in A minor, Op. 114. **Thea King** (cl); **Gabrieli Quartet; Karina Georgian** (vc); **Clifford Benson** (pf). Hyperion CDA66107 — ··· 1h 5m DDD 2/87

Brahms. Piano Quintet in F minor, Op. 34. **Maurizio Pollini** (pf); **Quartetto Italiano** (Paolo Borciani, Elisa Pegreffi, vns; Dino Asciolla, va; Franco Rossi, vc). DG 419 673-2GH. From 2531 197 (9/80).

··· 43m AAD 6/87 9p

This work was originally composed as a string quintet with two cellos. Brahms's influential friend Joseph Joachim then subjected the composition to a good deal of criticism, and Brahms took this to heart so much that he converted the quintet into a sonata for two pianos. As this version also was not well received Brahms turned to another friend, Clara Schumann, and as a result of her advice the work emerged in a third form, for piano quintet. This powerfully argued work gives little indication of its varied origins. The long first movement has a particularly strong yet highly romantic vein of expression, and in their performance Pollini and his colleagues bring out particularly well its stormy, dramatic nature. In the slow movement the performers bring a certain restless, questing quality to Brahms's rich lyricism and the *Scherzo*, perhaps the most inventive movement, is quickly and urgently expressed. The rondo-finale is a very substantial movement in its own right and is given its full weight by the five excellent players. The recording is clear and very immediate.

Additional recommendations ...
Piano Quintet. **Schumann.** *Piano Quintet in E flat major, Op. 44.* **Jenö Jandó** (pf); **Kodály Quartet.** Naxos 8 550406 — . lh 7m DDD 2/91 £
Piano Quintet[a]. *String Quartet No. 3 in B flat major, Op. 67.* [a]**Piers Lane** (pf); **Budapest Quartet.** Hyperion CDA66632 — ∴ lh 18m DDD 4/93

Brahms. Piano Quartets – No. 1 in G minor, Op. 25; No. 2 in A major, Op. 26; No. 3 in C minor, Op. 60. **Isaac Stern** (vn); **Jaime Laredo** (va); **Yo-Yo Ma** (vc); **Emanuel Ax** (pf). Sony Classical SK45846.

∴ ② 2h 8m DDD 3/91

These three piano quartets belong to the middle of Brahms's life. They have all the power and lyricism that we associate with his music, as well as the fine craftsmanship that he acquired when young and, with the high standards he set himself, demonstrated in every work thereafter. The mood of the music is again Brahmsian in that alongside a wealth of melodic and harmonic invention there are some shadows: all we know of Brahms's life suggests that he was never a happy man. But if this is reflected in the music, and especially the C minor Quartet, we can recognize the strength of intellect and will that keeps all in proportion so that there is no overt soul-bearing. These quartets are big pieces which often employ a grand manner, though less so in No. 2 than the others. For this reason, the present performances with their exuberant sweep are particularly telling, and although no detail is missed the players offer an overall strength. Top soloists in their own right, they combine their individual gifts with the ability to play as a well integrated team. The recording is close but not overwhelmingly so. Only the booklet, with notes in four languages, mars at least some copies of this issue, for it has some blank pages and details of the movements are missing, as are parts of the English and Italian notes.

Additional recommendations ...
Nos. 1 and 3. **Domus.** Virgin Classics VC7 59248-2 — ∴ lh 16m DDD 6/88
No. 2. ***Mahler.*** *Movement for piano quartet.* **Domus.** Virgin Classics VC7 59144-2 — ∴ lh lm DDD 1/89
No. 1. Variations and Fugue on a Theme by Handel, Op. 24 (orch. Rubbra). **London Symphony Orchestra/Neeme Järvi.** Chandos CHAN 8825 — ∴ lh llm DDD 2/91

Brahms. String Quartets – No. 1 in C minor, Op. 51 No. 1; No. 2 in A minor, Op. 51 No. 2. **Takács Quartet** (Gábor Takács-Nagy, Károly Schranz, vns; Gábor Ormai, va; András Fejer, vc). Decca 425 526-2DH.

∴ lh 6m DDD 9/90 

Few composers have ever been more self-critical than Brahms. He is said to have suppressed some 20 string quartets before writing one he deemed worthy of publication, and by then he was 40 years old. The C minor work was quickly followed by a second in A minor in the same year of 1873, and just two years later he produced his third and last in the major key of B flat. Though these four artists have now been together long enough to play as one, they are in fact still young enough to bring up every phrase with the immediacy of a new discovery. The two powerfully challenging flanking movements of the C minor work are sustained with splendid strength and drive. Yet how sensitively and subtly they convey the vulnerable heart concealed behind the classical façade in the second subject of the opening *Allegro*, for instance, and again, of course, in the work's two gentler central movements. They at once enter the more lyrical world of the first two movements of the A minor work, with its reminders of the motto themes adopted by both the composer himself and his great friend, the half-Hungarian violinist, Joachim. And how they relish the zest of the Hungarian-spiced finale.

Additional recommendations ...

No. 2. No. 3 in B flat major, Op. 67. **Orlando Quartet** . Ottavo OTRC68819 — 1h 15m DDD 6/90

Nos. 1 and 2. **New Budapest Quartet.** Hyperion CDA66651 — 1h 7m DDD 4/93

No. 3. Piano Quintet in F minor, Op. 34[a]. [a]**Piers Lane** (pf); **Budapest Quartet.** Hyperion CDA66632 — 1h 18m DDD 4/93

Brahms. Cello Sonatas — No. 1 in E minor, Op. 38; No. 2 in F major, Op. 99. **Steven Isserlis** (vc); **Peter Evans** (pf). Hyperion CDA66159. From A66159 (10/85).

50m DDD 4/86

Brahms worked on his Cello Sonata No. 1 over a period of three years, from 1862 to 1865. Originally the work included an *Adagio*, but this was destroyed by the composer before publication, and as a result we have a three-movement sonata consisting of a somewhat dark-hued, questing *Allegro non troppo*, a central *Allegretto quasi menuetto*, which has a slight eighteenth-century pastiche flavour, and a bold, tautly argued *Allegro* finale. The F major Sonata of 1886 is a bigger work in every way. It was one of three chamber works written during a summer stay in Switzerland, and the glorious scenery stimulated Brahms to compose in a warm, open-hearted fashion. Steven Isserlis plays throughout both works with an impressive tone-quality and an immaculate technique. Though his sympathy for the music is everywhere evident, he does lack the last ounce of interpretative insight. But with fine playing from the pianist Peter Evans, and a very good, natural sounding recording, this is a disc which will give much pleasure.

Additional recommendations ...

Nos. 1 and 2. **Mstislav Rostropovich** (vc); **Rudolf Serkin** (pf). DG 410 510-2GH — 58m DDD 9/83

Nos. 1 and 2. **Lynn Harrell** (vc); **Vladimir Ashkenazy** (pf). Decca 414 558-2DH — 52m ADD 10/85

Nos. 1 and 2. Violin Sonata No. 3 in D minor, Op. 108 (trans. cello). **Yo-Yo Ma** (vc); **Emanuel Ax** (pf). Sony Classical SK48191 — 1h 15m DDD 11/92

NEW REVIEW

Brahms. Piano Trios[a] — No. 1 in B major, Op. 8; No. 2 in C major, Op. 87; No. 3 in C minor, Op. 101.

Mendelssohn. Piano Trio No. 1 in D minor, Op 49[b].

Schubert. Piano Trios — No. 1 in B flat major, D898[c]; No. 2 in E flat major, D929[d]. **Isaac Stern** (vn); **Leonard Rose** (vc); **Eugene Istomin** (pf). Sony Classical SK46425. Items marked [a] from CBS SBRG72596/7 (1/68), [b] 73667 (9/68), [c] SBRG72344 (10/65), [d] 72858 (1/73).

(3) 3h 19m ADD 5/91 

Brahms's three published piano trios, which are among his greatest chamber works, combine the resonant lyricism that was such a distinctive aspect of his mature style with an engaging sense of mystery and, in the faster movements, a muscular ruggedness. The Op. 8 Trio (substantially revised from an earlier version) is the most expansively romantic, whereas the other two are more elusively argued, tightly constructed and less willing to reveal their secrets at a first hearing. The Stern/Rose/Istomin set of the trios was recorded in 1964-6, when America was producing a veritable plethora of great chamber music recordings. Isaac Stern was at the very height of his powers, producing a warm, strong body of tone and phrasing with endless reserves of imagination, while Leonard Rose achieved parallel distinction on cello, and Eugene Istomin — ever under-rated in Britain — leavened the mix with clean, thoughtful pianism. The overall blend is one of secure and perceptive musicianship, captured in sound that, although subject to some exaggerated channel separation, emerges on CD with far more warmth and presence than it did on LP. But that's not all Sony offer us: in addition to the Brahms, we're given Schubert's two great Trios and the first, and more immediately appealing, of Mendelssohn's two. These recordings date from roughly the same period as the Brahms set and are similarly direct, considered and sonically fresh.

Additional recommendations ...

Nos. 1-3; A major, Op. posth. (attrib. Brahms). **Beaux Arts Trio.** Philips Duo 438 365-2PM2 — ② 1h 59m DDD 1/88

No. 1. ***Ives.*** *Piano Trio.* **Trio Fontenay.** Teldec 2292-44924-2 — 57m DDD 4/90

Op. posth. ***Schumann.*** *Piano Trio No. 1 in D minor, Op. 63.* **Trio Fontenay.** Teldec 2292-44927-2 — 1h 5m DDD 3/92

Brahms. Piano Trio No. 2 in C major, Op. 87.
Dvořák. Piano Trio No. 1 in B flat major, B51. **Trio Fontenay** (Michael Mücke, vn; Niklas Schmidt, vc; Wolf Harden, pf). Teldec 2292-44177-2

1h 4m DDD 2/90 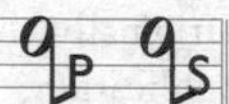

These two works were written within a few years of each other. In 1875, when Dvořák wrote his Piano Trio No. 1 (he revised it a little later), he was still an emerging talent. Brahms, the older composer by eight years, was very much an established figure when he completed his Second Piano Trio in 1882. The Dvořák work still has a spirit of youthfulness, which is reflected faithfully in the Fontenay Trio's spontaneous-seeming, beautifully poised and generously phrased performance. There is an unhurried, affectionate quality in their playing which is highly attractive and they seem to be enjoying the recording process greatly. In the mature, masterful Brahms work the Fontenay's playing has similar virtues. They project the music with great understanding and a superb sense of style. The tonal quality of the two string players is warm and sonorous and all three artists are technically immaculate. Teldec have crowned this disc with an excellent recording which clearly has taken place in an appropriately small chamber, but one which possesses plenty of resonance.

Brahms. Horn Trio in E flat major, Op. 40[a].
Franck. Violin Sonata in A major. **Itzhak Perlman** (vn); [a]**Barry Tuckwell** (hn); **Vladimir Ashkenazy** (pf). Decca 414 128-2DH. From SXL6408 (5/69).

56m AAD 4/85 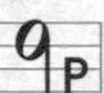

Anyone who thinks of chamber music as predominantly an intellectual medium should easily be persuaded otherwise by these two mellow works of the late nineteenth century. Brahms is the more classically shaped of the two, while the third movement of the Franck Sonata is a "recitative-fantasia" whose quiet eloquence seems more than a little to foreshadow Debussy. Here, as in the strictly canonic theme of the finale, Franck shows us that even baroque techniques can be turned with no apparent effort to romantic ends. In the Brahms Horn Trio, Perlman and Ashkenazy are joined by another virtuoso in the person of Barry Tuckwell; but it is not their dazzling technical command that we notice so much as their musicianly subtlety. In the rich textures of this work we are reminded of the composer's inspiration by the beauty of the Black Forest and also of his grief at the recent loss of his beloved mother. The combination of these three instruments is rare to say the least, but the engineer has balanced them satisfactorily.

Additional recommendation ...

Horn Trio[a]. ***Beethoven.*** *Sonata for horn and piano in F major, Op. 17.* ***Krufft.*** *Sonata for horn and piano in F major.* **Lowell Greer** (hn); [a]**Stephanie Chase** (vn); **Steven Lubin** (pf). Harmonia Mundi HMU90 7037 — 1h 5m DDD 9/92

NEW REVIEW

Brahms. Clarinet Sonatas, Op. 120 — No. 1 in F minor; No. 2 in E flat major. Clarinet Trio in A minor, Op. 114[a]. **Michel Portal** (cl); [a]**Boris Pergamenschikow** (vc); **Mikhail Rudy** (pf). EMI CDC7 54466-2. Recorded in 1991.

lh 10m DDD 5/93

It was late in his life, just when thinking the time had almost come to lay down his pen, that Brahms's creative flame was rekindled by the playing of Richard Mühlfeld, principal clarinettist of the Meiningen Court Orchestra. The outcome was a hauntingly nostalgic Clarinet Quintet as well as the two Sonatas and Trio offered on this excellently recorded disc. We're told that what Brahms so much admired in Mühlfeld's playing was its "polish and almost feminine sensitivity". And it is with these same qualities that the French clarinettist, Michel Portal, so persuasively woos the ear. His tone has a seductive liquidity and his phrasing a finely nuanced pliability totally banishing all misconceptions of the composer — such as harboured by the ruthlessly critical Hugo Wolf — as a gruff, antediluvian academic. Portal could scarcely have found more sensitively attuned partners than Mikhail Rudy and in the Trio Boris Pergamenschikow. Though not lacking strength of tone or direction, all three players leave you in no doubt as to the acutely vulnerable heart hidden behind Brahms's bushy beard, and equally, of his (sometimes questioned) ear for sonority *per se* — as is so magically proved at the end of the Trio's opening movement.

Additional recommendation ...

Clarinet Sonatas. **Thea King** (cl); **Clifford Benson** (pf). Hyperion CDA66202 — 43m DDD 10/87

Clarinet Sonatas. **Gervase de Peyer** (cl); **Gwenneth Pryor** (pf). Chandos CHAN8563 — 43m DDD 3/88

Clarinet Sonatas. ***Weber.*** *Grand duo concertant, J204.* **Paul Meyer** (cl); **François-René Duchable** (pf). Erato 2292-45480-2 — lh 6m DDD 9/90

Key to Symbols

		lh 23m	DDD	6/88
Price	***Quantity/ availability***	***Timing***	***Mode***	***Review date***

NEW REVIEW

Brahms. Viola Sonatas, Op. 120 — No. 1 in F minor; No. 2 in E flat major. ***Joachim.*** Variations on an Original Theme in E major, Op. 10. **Rivka Golani** (va); **Konstantin Bogino** (pf). Conifer CDCF199. Recorded in 1991.

lh 11m DDD 9/92

The Brahms Viola Sonatas belong to the last years of his life and were originally written for clarinet. But the composer always saw them as alternatively for viola and this version goes further than just transposing notes as necessary: for example, some figuration is different, there is double-stopping, and sometimes the viola even plays where the clarinet does not. Rivka Golani brings plenty of tonal flexibility to the music and demonstrates her understanding of Brahms's autumnal style, with its smouldering passions and hints of regret. So does her pianist Konstantin Bogino. The recording successfully balances the two players and instruments, and if the piano bass has a heavyish sound, that suits the music quite well. Golani comes across here as an essentially serious artist, which is perhaps right, although she might have brought more pace to the opening *Allegro appassionato* of the F minor Sonata and more of a smile to its *grazioso* third movement. She is also a little deliberate in the two *allegro* movements in the E flat major Sonata although its finale has fine vigour. But in compensation she offers much tonal beauty. Joachim was a friend of Brahms and the first interpreter of his Violin Concerto, and his Variations are here recorded for the first time. Their style suggests something between Schumann and Elgar and no very strong individuality emerges, but he wrote beautifully for the instrument and Golani's playing is as refined and expressive as one could wish for.

Additional recommendation ...
Viola Sonatas[a]*. Trio in A minor for viola, cello and piano, Op. 114*[b]*.* [ab]**Yuri Bashmet** (va); [b]**Valentin Berlinsky** (vc); [ab]**Mikhail Muntyan** (pf). Olympia OCD175 — 1h 7m DDD 5/88

Brahms. Violin Sonatas — No. 1 in G major, Op. 78; No. 2 in A major, Op. 100; No. 3 in D minor, Op. 108. **Josef Suk** (vn); **Julius Katchen** (pf). Decca Ovation 421 092-2DM. From SXL6321 (1/68).

1h 8m ADD 5/88 £ 

NEW REVIEW

Brahms. Violin Sonatas — No. 1 in G major, Op. 78; No. 2 in A major, Op. 100; No. 3 in D minor, Op. 108. **Augustin Dumay** (vn); **Maria-João Pires** (pf). DG 435 800-2GH.

1h 12m DDD 3/93

Brahms was 45 when he began to work on the first of these sonatas and he completed the final one some ten years later. These products of his mature genius are certainly the greatest works written in this form since Beethoven's. Though they are lovingly crafted and have a predominant air of lyricism, there is great variety of melody and of mood. The invention always sounds spontaneously conceived and they fit the CD format like a kid glove. Suk's control over nuance is magical whilst Katchen has a complete understanding of the style. In every way these are performances that truly deserve to be labelled as classics and the naturally vivid recorded sound brings them to life with magnificent immediacy. Collectors who seek a fully digital version of these sonatas, although coming at full price, will do well to consider the much more recent one by Augustin Dumay and Maria-João Pires. Again, these works, which could not have fitted on to a single disc in the days of LP, do so comfortably on CD and make a splendid triptych. Like Suk and Katchen, these younger artists recognize that, for all its technical challenges and occasional fiery outbursts, this is still predominantly lyrical music; and although they miss no special points and offer much interpretative refinement, their delivery is pleasingly unfussy, with the degree of simplicity and directness that was always characteristic of this composer. Though each sonata is finely performed, the G major, with its expansive eloquence, suits Dumay and Pires especially well. Some collectors will wish that they had brought a little more momentum to the A major Sonata, but there is an adequate *Sturm und Drang* content in the D minor which is the most dramatic of the three works, and as with Suk and Katchen, both artists are of distinction and at no time does the piano merely accompany. The recording is a good one, although ideally the piano sound could have a touch more immediacy.

Additional recommendations ...
Sonatas. **Itzhak Perlman** (vn); **Vladimir Ashkenazy** (pf). EMI CDC7 47403-2 — 1h 10m DDD 2/87
Sonatas. **Krysia Osostowicz** (vn); **Susan Tomes** (pf). Hyperion CDA66465 — 1h 8m DDD 11/91
Sonatas. Scherzo in C minor. **Pierre Amoyal** (vn); **Pascal Rogé** (pf). Decca 430 555-2DH — 1h 15m DDD 11/91

NEW REVIEW

Brahms. COMPLETE PIANO WORKS. **Gerhard Oppitz.** Eurodisc RD69245 (also available separately on the numbers listed below).
RD69246 — Piano Sonata No. 1 in C major, Op. 1. Four Piano Pieces, Op. 119. Variations and Fugue on a Theme by Handel, Op. 24. *RD69247* — Four Ballades, Op. 10. Variations on an Original Theme, Op. 21 No. 1. Variations on a Hungarian Song, Op. 21 No. 2. Six Piano Pieces, Op. 118. *RD69248* — Three Intermezzos, Op. 117. Piano Sonata No. 2 in F sharp minor, Op. 2. Eight Piano Pieces, Op. 76. *RD69249* — Two Rhapsodies, Op. 79. Scherzo in E flat minor, Op. 4. Seven Fantasias, Op. 116. Variations on a Theme by Paganini, Op. 35. *RD69250* — Variations on a Theme by Robert Schumann, Op. 9. 16 Waltzes, Op. 39. Piano Sonata No. 3 in F minor, Op. 5.

(5) 1h 14m 1h 13m 1h 13m 1h 16m 1h 16m DDD 10/90

To follow the creative development of these piano works is to trace the grand but darkening curve of the Brahms's spirit, rather like reading the diaries of a maturing writer or philosopher.

We start, appropriately enough, at Op. 1 — the First Sonata, a big, unkempt structure, full of confessional lyricism and imaginative piano writing (such as the *Scherzo*'s central section). Then there are the other two sonatas, the Second dark and rhetorical, the Third combining exuberance with a newly-won sense of poetry. From there on, the reins are tightened, faltering steps corrected, and inspiration is equalled by craftsmanship. The Variations — five sets of them — are masterpieces of tonal and contrapuntal invention, the Handel sequence in particular being on an almost symphonic scale (the English composer Edmund Rubbra made a fine orchestration of them), although the *Paganini Variations* offer the richer poetic yield. There are the *Ballades, Rhapsodies,* and miscellaneous shorter pieces, all of them significant statements condensed into relatively short time-spans: dark, questioning, mysterious and combining an orchestral range of colour with a sure sense of the instrument's strengths and limitations. Brahms was himself a fine pianist and knew well how to shape and shade his ideas in pianistic terms, a skill that was never better employed than in his four sets of late pieces, 20 testimonies of regret, anger and exaltation, chiselled with a breathtaking precision.

It goes without saying that any survey of Brahms's solo piano *oeuvre* is going to tax the imaginative resources of its interpreter. Gerhard Oppitz, a Wilhelm Kempff pupil, made his recordings under almost ideal conditions, with a producer whom he knew well and who understood his working methods. The result is a considered and accurate distillation of Oppitz's deepest thoughts on the music, be they on the sonatas' youthful flexing of muscles or on the deeply personal musings of Brahms's last years. This extra spontaneity, coupled with Oppitz's cerebral approach to the music, helps us focus on what is often an elusive musical spirit. Julius Katchen remains especially convincing in the Sonatas and earlier pieces, but Oppitz probes deeper into the later works and his instrument, a brightly-recorded, mahogany-toned Bösendorfer with a ringing treble, allows for extra clarity and more subtle colouring. Katchen's Steinway sounds bigger, more resilient and will please those readers who favour physical presence above presence of mind.

Additional recommendation ...
Julius Katchen. Decca 430 053-2DM6 — ⑥ 6h 28m ADD 2/91 ▲

Brahms. Piano Sonata No. 1 in C major, Op. 1.
Liszt. PIANO WORKS. **Sviatoslav Richter.** RCA Victor Red Seal RD60859. Recorded in 1988. Consolation S172 No. 6. Hungarian Rhapsody in D minor, S244 No. 17. Scherzo and March, S177. Etudes d'exécution transcendante, S139 — No. 11, Harmonies du soir.

1h 3m DDD 4/92

Sviatoslav Richter was born in 1915 and has been a part of the pianistic scene for as long as most people can remember. Even so, it is difficult to believe that this Russian pianist who gave the première of Prokofiev's Sixth Sonata in 1942 is still very much with us and, as this disc demonstrates, still a master of his instrument. The septuagenarian pianist plays a Brahms sonata written when the composer was 20, but the finest art knows no generation gaps and he brings great authority to a work which in lesser hands can seem naïve with its youthfully grandiloquent gestures. The first movement has an unforced strength, but essentially Richter's is a thoughtful reading rather than a virtuoso one, and there are delicate textures to admire along with the necessary dexterity. The Liszt pieces include two rarities that are well worth hearing (the second and third of the four listed above) flanked by the popular Sixth *Consolation* and the celebrated *Harmonies du soir*: the last of these is a magnificent example of pre-Debussian impressionism to which Richter brings both passion and nobility. The live recording could be richer and has a few creaks and clatterings, but not enough to disturb.

Brahms. PIANO WORKS. **Murray Perahia.** Sony Classical SK47181.
Piano Sonata No. 3 in F minor, Op. 5. Capriccio in B minor, Op. 76 No. 2. Intermezzo in E flat minor, Op. 118 No. 6. Two Rhapsodies, Op. 79 — No. 1 in B minor. Four Piano Pieces, Op. 119 — No. 4 in E flat major.

1h DDD 10/91 

Brahms composed his three piano sonatas early in life, completing the Third during his important friendship with Robert Schumann. It is a work of colossal scale and dimension, possessing a grandeur that seems to cry out for comparison with Beethoven's last compositions. Murray Perahia leads the field in his performance of this masterwork but Kocsis, Ashkenazy and the super-bargain Biret should also give great satisfaction to collectors who savour different approaches. Perahia's playing is riper and less youthfully impetuous and ardent, yet this too yields its rewards and makes him all the more capable of encompassing the many changes from virtuoso vigour to quiet lyricism in the first movement. He reminds us that Brahms was naturally introspective even when he was 20 and writing a virtuoso, leonine work such as this one — yet such is his pianistic intelligence and sensitivity that he does so without sacrificing vigour and forward movement, essential qualities in this big five-movement work. Needless to say, he is in his element in the songful twilight musings of the *Andante* and Intermezzo, but the big *Scherzo* and fleet finale (with a whirling, triumphant coda) are just as effective. The other four pieces are also satisfying, with tremendous vigour in the Rhapsody and all the brooding drama one could wish for in the tragic E flat minor Intermezzo. The recorded sound is faithful and enjoyable in all sound levels and textures — and that last word reminds me to praise his finely judged use of the sustaining pedal, so important in this composer.

Additional recommendations ...
Piano Sonata No. 3. **Zoltán Kocsis**. Hungaroton HCD12601 — 40m DDD 1/85 B
Piano Sonata No. 3. Variations and Fugue on a Theme by Handel, Op. 24. **Vladimir Ashkenazy** (pf). Decca 430 771-2DH — lh 4m DDD 7/92 B
Piano Sonata No. 3. Four Ballades, Op. 10. **Idil Biret** (pf). Naxos 8 550352 — lh 3m DDD 12/92 £ B

NEW REVIEW

Brahms. Four Ballades, Op. 10. Variations and Fugue on a Theme by Handel, Op. 24. Two Rhapsodies, Op. 79 — No. 1 in B minor; No. 2 in G minor. **Pascal Rogé** (pf). Decca 433 849-2DH. Recorded in 1991.

lh 8m DDD 4/93 

We may still think of Pascal Rogé as a young pianist, but this Paris-born artist passed his fortieth birthday three years ago and has in fact recorded Brahms's Handel Variations before, back in the 1970s. Clearly this work means much to him, and he brings the right clean and crisp baroque quality to the theme itself and to those of the succeeding variations which call for it, while opening out into a richer romanticism as and when Brahms demands. As regards tone and tempo, he avoids extremes as the *Variations* progress and his civilized playing style, which includes an admirably judged use of the sustaining pedal, is matched by a refined recording that in the bigger passages offers weight without harshness. In the two *Rhapsodies*, Rogé again gives us both strength and sensitivity, for, here as elsewhere, he understands that Brahms's northern dourness, central though it is to his music and its performance, was always tempered by gentleness and tenderness. The interpretative challenge for the pianist is perhaps greater in the Four *Ballades*, early works that are predominantly quiet and introspective although No. 1, based on a grim Scottish ballad, is a powerful tone-poem and No. 3 is a quirky, scherzo-like piece. Here, too, Rogé blends sternness with affection and these are likeable performances, refreshingly eschewing the heavy and ultimately self-conscious profundity that some German pianists bring to this repertory. Warmly recommended.

Additional recommendations ...
Ballades. ***Weber.*** *Piano Sonata No. 2 in A flat major, J199.* **Alfred Brendel** (pf). Philips 426 439-2PH — 53m DDD 6/91 B
Variations and Fugue. ***Reger.*** *Variations and Fugue on a Theme by Telemann, Op. 134.* **Jorge Bolet** (pf). Decca Ovation 417 791-2DM — 59m ADD 2/90 £ B
Ballades. Variations and Fugue. Variations on a Theme by Schumann, Op. 9. **Jorge Federico Osorio** (pf). ASV CDDCA616 — lh 8m DDD 11/88 B
Variations and Fugue. Rhapsodies. Six Piano Pieces, Op. 118. **Emanuel Ax** (pf). Sony Classical SK48046 — lh 8m DDD 10/92 B

Brahms. Two Rhapsodies, Op. 79 – No. 1 in B minor; No. 2 in G minor. 16 Waltzes, Op. 39. Six Piano Pieces, Op. 118. **Stephen Kovacevich** (pf). Philips 420 750-2PH. From 6514 229 (4/83).

53m DDD 4/88

NEW REVIEW

Brahms. 16 Waltzes, Op. 39. Eight Piano Pieces, Op. 76. Two Rhapsodies, Op. 79 — No. 1 in B minor; No. 2 in G minor. **Mikhail Rudy** (pf). EMI CDC7 54233-2. Recorded 1991-92.

59m DDD 5/93 

The Op. 79 *Rhapsodies* have been described as the "most temperamental" of all Brahms's later keyboard works. It would certainly be hard to imagine more vehement performances than those given by Kovacevich, thanks to his robust tone, trenchant attack and urgent tempos – perhaps even a shade too fast for the *Molto passionato, ma non troppo allegro* of the Second. But the pleading second subject of No. 1 in B minor brings all the requisite lyrical contrast. The Waltzes, too, have their tenderer moments of *Ländler*-like sentiment and charm. However, they emerge faster and more excitable than usual, as if Kovacevich were trying to remind us of Brahms's old love of Hungary no less than his new love of Vienna. "It is wonderful how he combines passion and tenderness in the smallest of spaces" was Clara Schumann's comment on the miniatures and the phrase fits Kovacevich's warmly responsive account of the Op. 118 set just as well. The piano is faithfully and fearlessly reproduced in what sounds like a ripely reverberant venue.

Mikhail Rudy's account of the Two *Rhapsodies* and the 16 Waltzes makes a pleasing alternative to Stephen Kovacevich's disc. For a start, the younger pianist has been exceptionally well recorded in the Salle Wagram in Paris, and he also plays a fine instrument that is in perfect condition. Of course that is not all: Rudy brings great character to the Eight Pieces, Op 76, with each one fully (but not exaggeratedly) characterized, not least in matters of texture, dynamics and pedalling. Similarly, this pianist effortlessly encompasses the blend of passion and gentler poetry that we find in the *Rhapsodies*. As for the Waltzes, this golden chain of Viennese melody and lilting charm comes across with affection and panache, as well as idiomatic rubato, not least in the famous A flat major Waltz which is the penultimate number. Repeats, too, are never mechanical, but often reveal something subtly new about the music which we could not have with a single playing. Finally, the frequent difficulty of Brahms's idiosyncratic piano writing, both here and in the other pieces, presents no more than a pleasing challenge to this intelligent and sensitive artist and all proceeds fluently, though never in a routine way.

Brahms. PIANO WORKS. **Radu Lupu.** Decca 417 599-2DH. Items marked [a] from SXL6504 (5/71), [b] SXL6831 (11/78).

Two Rhapsodies, Op. 79 — No. 1 in B minor[a]; No. 2 in G minor[b]. Three Intermezzos, Op. 117[a]. Six Piano Pieces, Op. 118[b]. Four Piano Pieces, Op. 119[b].

lh llm ADD 8/87 

Brahms's late piano music inhabits a very special world, equally appealing to the sentimental as to the intellectually inclined listener. A poignant sense of resignation, of autumnal wistfulness, is allied to consummate mystery of compositional technique, and these elements are mutually transformed, producing an effect impossible to capture in words. Radu Lupu's playing captures it, though. Listen to the quiet rapture as he sleepwalks into the last section of Op. 117 No. 3 or the revelation in Op. 118 No. 2 that the inversion of the theme is even more beautiful than its original statement. One senses a complete identity with the composer's thoughts, and it is to be doubted whether any finer recording of these works has ever been made.

Additional recommendation ...

Two Rhapsodies. Three Intermezzos. Theme and Variations in D minor. Variations on a Theme by Paganini, Op. 35. **François-René Duchable.** Erato 2292-45477-2 — lh 3m DDD 3/91

NEW REVIEW

Brahms. Rinaldo, Op. 50[a]. Schicksalslied, Op. 54[b]. Nänie, Op. 82[c]. [a]**James King** (ten); [ab]**Ambrosian Chorus;** [ab]**New Philharmonia Orchestra/Claudio Abbado;** [c]**Lausanne Pro Arte Choir;** [c]**Suisse Romande Radio Chorus and Orchestra/Ernest Ansermet.** Decca Ovation 425 030-2DM. Texts and translations included. Items marked [ab] from SXL6386 (1/70), recorded in 1968, [c] SET333/4 (7/67), recorded in 1966.

lh 8m ADD 9/92

Blomstedt's excellent full-price disc (reviewed below) remains first choice for those seeking a collection of Brahms choral works, but Decca's medium-price reissue is valuable for the inclusion of the rarely-heard cantata *Rinaldo*. This work has not always been highly praised, but Abbado clearly believes in it, and his fresh, eager conducting reveals some inspired invention, a sense of typically Brahmsian strength, and considerable depth of feeling. The choral singing and orchestral playing are both excellent, but though James King sings wholeheartedly he seems under some pressure in the solo part. Performances of the other two works are good, but Blomstedt's readings are better, for he phrases and paces the *Schicksalslied* with more maturity than did the youthful Abbado in 1968, and his American chorus and orchestra is superior to the Swiss forces in *Nänie*. In the latter work Ansermet's wise and experienced conducting makes for a satisfying alternative interpretation, however. During the 1960s Decca's engineering frequently reached very high standards, and this disc suffers little when compared with modern productions in terms of sound quality.

Brahms. CHORAL WORKS. [a]**Jard van Nes** (mez); **San Francisco Symphony Chorus and Orchestra/Herbert Blomstedt.** Decca 430 281-2DH. Texts and translations included. Gesang der Parzen, Op. 89. Nänie, Op. 82. Schicksalslied, Op. 54. Begräbnisgesang, Op. 13. Alto Rhapsody, Op. 53[a].

lh 3m DDD 8/90

Brahms is such a familiar figure that it is salutary to be reminded that one area of his work, choral music, remains mostly unknown to collectors save for the *German Requiem* and *Alto Rhapsody*. This is a pity, for this composer who was also a distinguished choral conductor drew some of his finest inspiration from this medium. This issue includes the *Rhapsody*, warmly and movingly sung by Jard van Nes, but its importance lies in the fact that it also does much to give us a better knowledge of other big pieces too. Don't be put off by the sombre subject mater — including *Begräbnisgesang,* "A Song of the Fates" (a tremendous piece), another work about fate itself and not one but two funeral hymns! — but listen instead to thrilling choral singing and orchestral playing under the direction of a conductor who believes passionately in the music. "Plenty of strength, light and drama" is what *Gramophone*'s critic found in this programme when it first came out, and to that one would add that the San Francisco Symphony Chorus sing the German texts with complete conviction. If this music makes us regret that Brahms wrote no opera, we may at least feel that here is something not far short of it even though it was not intended for the stage; to see this, listen only to the *Schicksalslied* which is the first work performed. A good recording complements the quality of performance, though ideally the choral textures could be clearer.

Additional recommendations ...

Marienlieder, Op. 22. Schicksalslied. Alto Rhapsody[a]*. Nänie. Gesang der Parzen.* [a]**Nathalie Stutzmann** (contr); **Bavarian Radio Chorus and Symphony Orchestra/Sir Colin Davis.** RCA Victor Red Seal 09026 61201-2 — lh 7m DDD 5/93

Triumphlied, Op. 55. Schicksalslied. Nänie. Alto Rhapsody[a]. [a]**Brigitte Fassbaender** (mez); **Prague Philharmonic Choir; Czech Philharmonic Orchestra/Giuseppe Sinopoli.** DG Galleria 435 066-2GGA — lh 10m DDD 11/91

Brahms. MOTETS. **Trinity College Choir, Cambridge/Richard Marlow.** Conifer CDCF178. Texts and translations included.

Op. 29 — Es ist das Heil uns kommen her; Schaffe in mir, Gott. Psalm 13, Op. 27 (with

Richard Pearce, org). Op. 110 — Ich aber bin elend; Ach, arme Welt, du trügest mich; Wenn wir in höchsten Nöten sein. Ave Maria, Op. 12 (Pearce). Op. 109 — Unsere Väter; Wenn ein starker Gewappneter; Wo ist ein so herrlich Volk. Geistliches Lied, Op. 30 (James Morgan, org). Op. 37 — O bone Jesu; Adoramus te Christe; Regina coeli, Op. 74 — Warum ist das licht gegeben dem Mühseligen?; O Heiland, reiss die Himmel auf.

lh 5m DDD 2/90 

The Choir of Trinity College, Cambridge have the remarkable gift of making music heavily overladen with contrapuntal wizardry sound, not only inevitable, but extraordinarily lovely. This recording of the complete set of Brahms's motets may be recommended unreservedly. The singing is of a high quality and the acoustic of the chapel serve to enhance both the clarity and the blend. The motets range from a fairly straightforward chorale style of writing to some very substantial double-choir composition. A few pieces are written for female voices only — not for nothing was Brahms conductor of the Hamburg Frauenchor and thus well-acquainted with that medium — the performance of these pieces by the high voices of the Trinity Choir is a model of lightness, lucidity and skill. The ingenious *Regina coeli* comes across with something of the sprightliness of an Elizabethan ballet (albeit with alleluias instead of Fa-la-la-ing!). This is a disc calculated to delight both the Brahms specialist and all music lovers.

Brahms. LIEDER. **Thomas Allen** (bar); **Geoffrey Parsons** (pf). Virgin Classics VC7 59593-2. Texts and translations included.

Wir wandelten, Op. 96 No. 2. Der Gang zum Liebchen, Op. 48 No. 1. Komm bald, Op. 97 No. 5. Salamander, Op. 107 No. 2. Nachtigall, Op. 97 No. 1. Serenade, Op. 70 No. 3. Geheimnis, Op. 71 No. 3. Von waldbekränzter Höhe, Op. 57 No. 1. Dein blaues Auge hält so still, Op. 59 No. 8. Wie bist du, meine Königin, Op. 32 No. 9. Junge Lieder I, Op. 63 No. 5. Die Kränze, Op. 46 No. 1. Sah dem edlen Bildnis, Op. 46 No. 2. An die Nachtigall, Op. 46 No. 4. Die Schale der Vergessenheit, Op. 46 No. 3. In Waldeseinsamkeit, Op. 85 No. 6. Wiegenlied, Op. 49 No. 4. Sonntag, Op. 47 No. 3. Heimweh II, Op. 63 No. 8. Minnelied, Op. 71 No. 5. Feldeinsamkeit, Op. 86 No. 2. Ständchen, Op. 106 No. 1. Von ewiger Liebe, Op. 43 No. 1. Die Mainacht, Op. 43 No. 2. Botschaft, Op. 47 No. 1.

lh 2m DDD 9/90 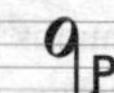

Brahms's songs are, on the whole, intimate, one-to-one statements. They rarely approach the nature of public announcements and thus only occasionally explore extreme loudness: they are ideally suited to home listening. The darkening timbre of Thomas Allen's voice makes it increasingly suited to Brahms, and his characteristic, though far from common, qualities of heroic breath control and vital, lissom phrasing compound his affinity with this music. The songs make best use of the distinctive parts of his range and this, wedded to Allen's innate musicianship, sets a solid foundation for an engrossing recital. Geoffrey Parsons picks up these features and mirrors them in the searching piano parts, bringing light and shade, clarity and mist to support the voice. The recital as a whole is well thought out: the songs have clear, unifying links in terms of mood and gesture, but there is enough variety here to retain interest throughout. A pleasantly close recording of the voice emphasizes subtleties of tonal shading, and the more subdued setting of the piano allows it to make its effect without overpowering the singer. This is a disc to delight both novice and seasoned listener alike.

Brahms. LIEDER. **Anne Sofie von Otter** (mez); **Bengt Forsberg** (pf). DG 429 727-2GH. Texts and translations included.

Zigeunerlieder, Op. 103 — No. 1-7 and 11. Dort in den Weiden, Op. 97 No. 4. Vergebliches Ständchen, Op. 84 No. 4. Die Mainacht, Op. 43 No. 2. Ach, wende diesen Blick, Op. 57 No. 4. O kühler Wald, Op. 72 No. 3. Von ewiger Liebe, Op. 43 No. 1. Junge Lieder I, Op. 63 No. 5. Wie rafft' ich mich auf in der Nacht, Op. 32 No. 1. Unbewegte laue Luft, Op. 57 No. 8. Heimweh II, Op. 63 No. 8. Mädchenlied, Op. 107 No. 5. Ständchen, Op. 106 No. 1. Sonntag, Op. 47 No. 3. Wiegenlied, Op. 49 No. 4. Zwei Gesänge, Op. 91 (with Nils-Erik Sparf, va).

lh lm DDD 4/91 

Many of the Lieder here are but meagrely represented in current catalogues, so that this recital is all the more welcome, particularly in view of the perceptive musicality of both singer and pianist. They show a fine free (but unanimous!) flexibility in the *Zigeunerlieder*, with a dashing "Brauner Bursche" and "Röslein dreie" and a passionate "Rote Abendwolken"; but there is also lightness, happy in "Wisst ihr, wann mein Kindchen", troubled in "Lieber Gott, du weisst"; and Otter's coolly tender tone in "Kommt dir manchmal in den Sinn" touches the heart. Also deeply moving are the profound yearning and the loving but anxious lullaby in the two songs with viola obbligato (most sensitively played). Elsewhere, connoisseurs of vocal technique will admire Otter's command of colour and legato line in the gravity of *O kühler Wald*, the stillness of *Die Mainacht* and the intensity of *Von ewiger Liebe*, and her lovely *mezza voce* in the *Wiegenlied* and the partly repressed fervour of *Unbewegte laue Luft*; but to any listener her remarkable control, her responsiveness to words and, not least, the sheer beauty of her voice make this a most rewarding disc, aided as she is by Forsberg's characterful playing.

Brahms. Ein deutsches Requiem, Op. 45. **Dame Elisabeth Schwarzkopf** (sop); **Dietrich Fischer-Dieskau** (bar); **Philharmonia Chorus and Orchestra/Otto Klemperer.** EMI CDC7 47238-2. Notes, text and translation included. From Columbia SAX2430/31 (2/62).

lh 9m ADD 6/87 

Brahms. Ein deutsches Requiem, Op. 45. **Charlotte Margiono** (sop); **Rodney Gilfry** (bar); **Monteverdi Choir; Orchestre Révolutionnaire et Romantique/John Eliot Gardiner.** Philips 432 140-2PH. Text and translation included.

lh 6m DDD 4/91 

Brahms's *German Requiem*, a work of great concentration and spiritual intensity, is, rather surprisingly, the creation of a man barely 30 years old. He turned for his text not to the liturgical Mass but to the German translations of the Old Testament. It is decidedly *not* a Requiem of 'fire and brimstone' overshadowed by the Day of Wrath; instead it is a work for those who mourn, those who remain in sorrow ("As one whom his mother comforteth, so I will comfort you", sings the soprano in a soaring hymn of grief-assuaging beauty). The texture is sinuous and Brahms employs the orchestra with great delicacy as well as enormous muscular energy. Klemperer's reading of this mighty work has long been famous: rugged, at times surprisingly fleet and with a juggernaut power. The superb Philharmonia are joined by their excellent Chorus and two magnificent soloists — Elisabeth Schwarzkopf offering comfort in an endless stream of pure tone and Fischer-Dieskau, still unequalled, singing with total absorption. A great performance, beautifully enhanced on CD.

The pungency of a small chorus and the incisive edge provided by the orchestra of period instruments, the Orchestre Révolutionnaire et Romantique, makes for a fresh reappraisal of a work that can all too often sound turgid and dull. Gardiner has written of the work's radiance, optimism and full-bloodedness and he instils these characteristics into his performance. The reduced forces employed mean that great subtlety can be drawn out of the score — words are meticulously cared for, dynamic nuances observed and, above all, strong and secure attack ensure a genuine intensity of expression. The soloists are good too, with the young American baritone Rodney Gilfry quite outstanding, offering firm, warm and beautifully rounded tone throughout. Charlotte Margiono, set a little far back in the aural perspective, is a sweet and suitably conciliatory soprano soloist. For anyone who has in the past found Brahms's *Ein deutsches Requiem* difficult to come to terms with then this pioneering period instrument set is probably the one to win the most converts.

Additional recommendations ...

Barbara Bonney (sop); **Andreas Schmidt** (bar); **Vienna State Opera Concert Choir; Vienna Philharmonic Orchestra/Carlo Maria Giulini.** DG 423 574-2GH — lh 14m DDD 9/88 B

Felicity Lott (sop); **David Wilson-Johnson** (bar); **London Symphony Chorus and Orchestra/Richard Hickox.** Chandos CHAN8942 — lh 14m DDD 1/92 B

Angela Maria Blasi (sop); **Bryn Terfel** (bass-bar); **Bavarian Radio Chorus and Symphony Orchestra/Sir Colin Davis.** RCA Victor Red Seal 09026 60868 — lh 13m DDD 5/93 B

Havergal Brian

British 1876-1972

NEW REVIEW

Brian. Symphony No. 1, "Gothic". **Eva Jenisová** (sop); **Dagmar Pecková** (contr); **Vladimir Dolezal** (ten); **Peter Mikulás** (bass); **Slovak Philharmonic Choir; Slovak National Theatre Opera Chorus; Slovak Folk Ensemble Chorus; Lucnica Chorus; Bratislava Chamber Choir; Bratislava Children's Choir; Youth Echo Choir; Czechoslovak Radio Symphony Orchestra, Bratislava; Slovak Philharmonic Orchestra/Ondrej Lenárd.** Marco Polo 8 223280/1. Text and translation included. Recorded in 1989.

② lh 4lm DDD 7/90

Left unperformed for 30-odd years and unrecorded for a further 40, the legendary *Gothic* makes superhuman demands of its performers: a passage where four four-part choirs sing in four adjacent keys simultaneously; another in which the music is designed to 'rotate' before the listener's ears, through a semicircle of four choirs and four brass bands. This first-ever recorded performance is amazingly good: such prodigies of choral virtuosity can only have been achieved at the cost of months of preparation (the spacious recording is a remarkable achievement, too). It is a performance also of radiant enthusiasm: everyone involved seems gripped, intent on communicating a true vision. For the work is visionary: a vision of an age of faith, the age that produced the complex majesty of the gothic cathedrals. The vision is that of a modern man, seeing gothic through the expressive resources of the intervening centuries; seeing, too, that the age of faith was also an age gripped with fear of judgement, wracked by guilt. All that is present in, and justification for, the symphony's vast structure. Huge, multi-part choruses to represent sorrowing, panic-stricken, jubilant humanity not as a monolithic mass but as individuals in all their variety. An enormous orchestra is employed (sextuple woodwind, octuple brass) to support this choral weight and also to provide a range of sonorities as wide as the contrasts, from brilliant windows to deep shadow, from massive piers to delicate tracery, of Lichfield Cathedral, a visit to which as a young man so moved Brian that it became one of the formative events of his life. There are flaws in the vision: the first movement has something of hesitancy to it, the eloquence of the choral pages sometimes stammers. But the tremendous second movement, with its Berliozian grandeur of utterance, is a genuine masterpiece, and the tripartite choral finale often reaches a comparably lofty nobility. And this was Havergal Brian's *first* symphony!

NEW REVIEW

Brian. SYMPHONIES AND ORCHESTRAL WORKS. [a]**Jana Valásková** (sop); [a]**Slovak Philharmonic Chorus;** [a]**Brno Philharmonic Chorus;** [a]**Cantus Choir;** [a]**Slovak Opera Chorus;** [a]**Youth Echo Choir;** [ab]**Bratislava Radio Symphony Orchestra/**[c]**Ireland National Symphony Orchestra/Adrian Leaper.** Marco Polo 8 223447 and 8 223481. Recorded in 1992.

8 223447: Symphonies — No. 4, "The Song of Victory"[a]; No. 12[b]. *8 223481*[c]: Symphonies — No. 17; No. 32 in A flat major. In Memoriam. Festal dance.

② lh lm lh DDD 2/93

Marco Polo have bravely announced their intention of recording a Havergal Brian cycle. After the success of their account of the mind-boggling *Gothic* symphony they could hardly have chosen a more comprehensive cross-section of his work to continue the project. The *Song of Victory*, though much shorter, comes from the same stable as the *Gothic*, with its extraordinarily dense choral writing and its sheer feverish energy. It is also a puzzling work, a denunciation of military might (written — to a German text — as rising Nazi power threatened Europe) that understands the allure of violence so well that it can seem to exult in it. The disturbing, exhausting power of this work is well contrasted with the almost Elgarian nobility of *In Memoriam* (a grand 'funeral symphony' in all but name), but the three other symphonies here provide opportunities to come to terms with the enigma of 'late Brian'. Retreating from the hyper-Brucknerian splendours of his earlier style, the aged, by now obscure and ignored Brian did something even more remarkable than writing 20 symphonies after reaching the age of 80. He seems to have subjected the whole concept of 'symphony' to a radical re-examination. The

Twelfth is crucial in this process, an epigrammatic single movement in which he searches for means other than conventional thematic transformation and development to unify and propel a large-scale structure (and it is on a very large scale, despite its brevity). Statement and counter-statement, fierce juxtaposition, balances and symmetries that the listener must work hard to identify. The Seventeenth refines this process still further. The Thirty-Second is by a composer of 92, writing what he half knows will be his last symphony, refusing to write an autumnal farewell, continuing to question. The ideas themselves aren't hard to listen to — they are often of great boldness or beauty, with recurring veins of elegiac mourning and craggy splendour — but the relationships between them (kinships of colour, texture, emotional temperature) do take repeated hearings for their logic to register. It is an absorbing process, though, and Marco Polo's complete survey will be an exciting journey. Decent performances, sometimes a little ragged at the edges, but finely recorded.

Frank Bridge

British 1879-1941

Bridge. Oration — Concerto elegiaco, H180.
Britten. Cello Symphony, Op. 68. **Steven Isserlis** (vc); **City of London Sinfonia/Richard Hickox.** EMI CDM7 63909-2. From CDC7 49716-2 (5/88).

lh 8m DDD 2/92 £ 9p

Steven Isserlis's decision to couple these two English masterpieces on one disc was a particularly intelligent one: not only because Frank Bridge was one of Britten's most influential teachers and mentors, but also because both works reflect, in their different ways, the two composers' strong pacifist beliefs and their deep concern at man's inhumanity to man. *Oration* (subtitled *Concerto elegiaco*) dates from 1930 and is both an explicit outcry against the futility of war and a vast lament for the many friends and colleagues that Bridge had lost as a result of the Great War. Indeed, throughout its 30-minute span the work is constantly haunted by images of war — sometimes in mocking parody (as in the central march section, or the martial fanfares that erupt violently into orchestral climaxes), and sometimes in sombre, grief-stricken episodes of moving intensity. Isserlis gives us an exceptionally fine performance that fully captures the intensity and vision of this richly rewarding and shamefully neglected masterpiece. Britten's own masterpiece in the idiom — the Cello Symphony — was composed some 30 years later, but the influence of *Oration* can be clearly discerned both in its emotional content (if perhaps less overtly displayed than in the former) and in the similar way that it eschews the conventions of a formal concerto. Again both soloist and conductor deserve the highest praise for a performance that matches the profundity and vision of the music. Well recorded.

Additional recommendation ...
Oration. Enter Spring, H174. **Alexander Baillie** (vc); **Cologne Radio Symphony Orchestra/John Carewe.** Pearl SHECD9601 — 52m ADD 1/88

Bridge. Piano Quintet in D minor.
Elgar. Piano Quintet in A minor, Op. 84. **Coull Quartet** (Roger Coull, Philip Gallaway, vns; David Curtis, va; John Todd, vc); **Allan Schiller** (pf). ASV CDDCA678.

lh 10m DDD 1/90

These two endearingly evocative works are clearly linked by their characteristic tendency to refer to something unnamed outside of themselves. This was typical of Bridge's style at the time (the Quintet was composed in 1905, revised in 1912) but for Elgar in 1919 it represented a culmination of the inner doubts and public sorrows that virtually ended his compositional career. Much of Bridge's finest music is to be found in his chamber works and, besides an enormous inventiveness, he always displays in them a keen sense of just proportion. In revising the Piano Quintet, hc took the opportunity to integrate the Scherzo into the slow movement, producing a more balanced structure, and resolving many of the inadequacies inherent in the work in its earlier guise. The performers here bring out that elegant shape most skilfully without undermining the passing delights to be savoured along the way. Elgar's Quintet is, for the most part, treated to a lighter touch than usual, emotional intensity being focused towards the central slow movement, and Allan Schiller's less dominating contribution allows the engineers to attain a subtle balance of strings and piano often missing in other recordings. Such an apt coupling is worth trying.

Bridge. STRING QUARTETS. **Brindisi Quartet** (Jacqueline Shave, Patrick Kiernan, vns; Katie Wilkinson, va; Jonathan Tunnell, vc). Continuum CCD1035/6.
CCD1035 — No. 1 in E minor, H70; No. 3, H175. *CCD1036* — No. 2 in G minor, H115; No. 4, H188.

② 59m 46m DDD 5/92

Belonging to the same generation as Bax and Ireland, Bridge latterly became more adventurous stylistically than either and paid the penalty by coming to be regarded askance by the British musical establishment. Indeed, his publisher refused to take his 1928 piano piece *Gargoyle* on account of its modernity. The same suspicion caused the neglect of his Third and Fourth String Quartets, works of 1926 and 1937 in which he has been said to have "approached the early works of the Second Viennese School" with all that this implies in terms of atonality. The truth is perhaps both more complex and more interesting, namely that the extreme chromaticism of his language in these works represents a new way of looking at tonality, just as a personal use of tonality is a stylistic feature of his only pupil, Britten. In any case, Bridge's music is always 'musical' and never just theoretical, and although it can be severe there is also melodic and harmonic charm (most obviously in the two earlier quartets of 1906 and 1915) as well as an individual Englishness that is highly rewarding in its own way. Furthermore, since he was a fine viola player and professionally experienced in chamber music, as a member for some years of the English String Quartet, the writing for the four instruments is always grateful. Despite its Italian-sounding name, the Brindisi Quartet is British and they play this music with skill and understanding, while the recording brings lucidity to the often subtle textures. The two discs are accompanied by informative booklet material and are obtainable separately, but one really wants them both for a proper survey of this repertory.

Bridge. Phantasie Trio in C minor.
R. Clarke. Piano Trio.
Ireland. Phantasie Trio in A minor. **Hartley Trio** (Jacqueline Hartley, vn; Martin Loveday, vc; Caroline Clemmow, pf). Gamut Classics GAMCD518.

50m DDD 9/91

The 'innocent ear' test of music is usually a good one, and this writer remembers once switching on the car radio and immediately being intrigued by the unfamiliar music being played. It was the Piano Trio by Rebecca Clarke who, like Ireland and Bridge, studied with Stanford at the Royal College of Music in London. She is less known than they, but had a personal voice, although the booklet note rightly points out her affinity with Ernest Bloch, a composer she admired and whose music also betokens a burning sincerity — incidentally, the beginning of the finale in her Trio does not sound at all British. Although she was also a professional viola player, her passionate Trio sometimes strains at the boundaries of chamber music, but for all its power it does not get out of proportion. Nor does it lack memorable ideas. One wonders whether there is any European country other than philistine Britain where such a good composer could have been ignored — she does not even rate an entry in *Grove* — and can only regret the loss of the other works that she might have given us if she had received recognition. Though better known than Clarke, Frank Bridge also never had quite the standing that he deserved, particularly after he developed a challengingly advanced harmonic language in the 1920s. His *Phantasie Trio* is an earlier piece, though, and is dramatic and well wrought. So is Ireland's attractive work of the same name, also cast in a single biggish movement. The Hartley Trio play all three of these works with love and understanding, and the recording is well balanced and faithful.

NEW REVIEW

Bridge. Cello Sonata in D minor, H125. Four Short Pieces, H104 — Meditation; Spring song.
Debussy. Cello Sonata.
E. Dohnányi. Cello Sonata in B flat minor, Op. 8. **Bernard Gregor-Smith** (vc); **Yolande Wrigley** (pf). ASV CDDCA796.

lh 8m DDD 9/92

The centrepiece of this superb recital disc from Bernard Gregor-Smith (long-standing cellist of the Lindsay Quartet) and the pianist Yolande Wrigley is the sumptuously expansive Sonata in B flat minor by Ernö Dohnányi. This vital and often heroic work dates from 1899, and despite its obvious lyric and virtuoso appeal, it has yet to attain any real foothold in the regular repertoire. It is lavishly conceived, owing much to the Lisztian pattern of juxtaposing virtuoso material with passages of affecting lyricism. Gregor-Smith's performance could scarcely be more persuasive or rewarding; his dextrous, fine-toned playing should do much to ensure that this splendid Sonata gains wider acceptance. This excellent husband and wife team are also heard to advantage in the Debussy Cello Sonata, never easy to bring off with its *commedia dell'arte* transparency and specialized effects. Gregor-Smith plays with refinement and tremendous *élan* in the finale particularly, and this is certainly a reading of great distinction. He is an ardent and confident exponent of the Bridge items too, and there have been few finer recorded versions of the Cello Sonata in D minor: a personal testament of grief and outrage following the atrocities of the First World War. Its broad paragraphs and obviously questioning language dictates, to a large extent, the most natural performing approach here. This is a most moving and dignified reading of another sadly undervalued composition. Gregor-Smith and Wrigley are splendid throughout this disc; their skills are eloquently supported by interpretations of unusual insight and perception, and they have been faithfully served by clear yet never unduly brilliant recorded sound.

Bridge. PIANO WORKS. **Kathryn Stott.** Conifer CDCF186.
A Sea Idyll, H54*a*. Capriccios — No. 1 in A minor, H52; No. 2 in F sharp minor, H54*b*. Three poems — Ecstasy, H112*b*. The Hour Glass, H148. Piano Sonata, H160. Vignettes de Marseille, H166.

lh 12m DDD 9/91 

Kathryn Stott's main work is the Piano Sonata, written in the early 1920s in memory of a composer friend killed in World War I: Bridge, a convinced pacifist, took three years over the writing of it and it is deeply felt music, surprisingly bold in harmonic language and with an element of angry protest as well as an elegiac mood most clearly felt in the central slow movement. It has been called "a work to be respected rather than loved" and one may feel that there are more gestures than substance, missing really memorable melody. But it makes a strong impression none the less and Stott's committed and intense playing provides very persuasive advocacy. The other pieces are no less idiomatically done, and the early ones like the capriccios and the *Sea Idyll* show Bridge as a master like Fauré, who can say much in a short piece and whose piano writing is unfailingly graceful. The crisply drawn *Vignettes de Marseille* are no less attractive, and *The Hour Glass* adds to these qualities a freedom of language that in the 1920s placed the composer among the avant-garde in British music. The recording of the shorter pieces is a fine one and, although rather resonant, it also satisfies in the Sonata. Peter Jacobs provides a useful complement to that of Kathryn Stott for only three short pieces are duplicated.

Additional recommendation ...
Arabesque. Capriccios Nos. 1 and 2. A Dedication. A Fairy Tale Suite. Gargoyle. Hidden Fires. In Autumn. Three Miniature Pastorals — Set 1; Set 2. A Sea Idyll. Three Improvisations for the Left Hand. Winter Pastoral. **Peter Jacobs.** Continuum CCD1016 — lh 13m DDD 9/90

Further listening ...

Elegy, H47. Scherzetto, H19. *Coupled with* ***Ireland.*** Cello Sonata in G minor; ***Stanford.*** Cello Sonata No. 2 in D minor, Op. 39. **Julian Lloyd-Webber** (vc); **John McCabe** (pf). ASV CDDCA807 (2/93).

Phantasm. *Coupled with* **Ireland.** Piano Concerto; **Walton.** Sinfonia concertante (original version). **Kathryn Stott** (pf); **Royal Philharmonic Orchestra/Vernon Handley.** Conifer CDCF175 (1/90).

Benjamin Britten (Lord Britten of Aldeburgh) *British 1913-1976*

Britten. Piano Concerto, Op. 13[a]. Violin Concerto, Op. 15[b]. [b]**Mark Lubotsky** (vn); [a]**Sviatoslav Richter** (pf); **English Chamber Orchestra/Benjamin Britten.** Decca London 417 308-2LM. From SXL6512 (8/71).

lh 7m ADD 10/89 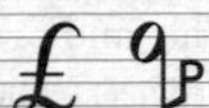

Just after Britten's performances were released on LP in 1971, the composer admitted with some pride that Sviatoslav Richter had learned his Piano Concerto "entirely off his own bat", and had revealed a Russianness that was in the score. Britten was attracted to Shostakovich during the late 1930s, when it was written, and the bravado, brittleness and flashy virtuosity of the writing, in the march-like finale most of all, at first caused many people (including Lennox Berkeley, to whom it is dedicated) to be wary of it, even to think it somehow outside the composer's style. Now we know his music better, it is easier to accept, particularly in this sparkling yet sensitive performance. The Violin Concerto dates from the following year, 1939, when Britten was in Canada, and it too has its self-conscious virtuosity, but it is its rich nostalgic lyricism which strikes to the heart and the quiet elegiac ending is unforgettable. Compared to Richter in the other work, Mark Lubotsky is not always the master of its hair-raising difficulties, notably in the scherzo, which has passages of double artificial harmonics that even Heifetz wanted simplified before he would play it (Britten refused), but this is still a lovely account. Fine recordings, made in The Maltings at Snape.

Additional recommendations ...

Piano Concerto[a]. *Violin Concerto*[b]. [a]**Joanna MacGregor** (pf); [b]**Lorrainse McAslan** (vn); **English Chamber Orchestra/Steuart Bedford.** Collins Classics 1301-2 — lh 6m DDD 9/92 9p

Violin Concerto[a]. *Canadian Carnival, Op. 19.* ***Britten/Berkeley.*** *Mont Juic, Op. 12.* [a]**Lorraine McAslan** (vn); **English Chamber Orchestra/Steuart Bedford.** Collins Classics 1123-2 — 58m DDD 12/90 9p 9s

Piano Concerto. ***Copland.*** *Piano Concerto.* **Gillian Lin** (pf); **Melbourne Symphony Orchestra/John Hopkins.** Chandos Collect CHAN6580 — 51m ADD 3/93 £

NEW REVIEW

Britten. Diversions for Piano (left-hand) and Orchestra, Op. 21.
Prokofiev. Piano Concerto No. 4 for the left hand in B flat major, Op. 53.
Ravel. Piano Concerto for the left hand. **Leon Fleisher** (pf); **Boston Symphony Orchetra/Seiji Ozawa.** Sony Classical SK47188.

lh 8m DDD 4/93 

Brother of the famous philosopher Ludwig, Paul Wittgenstein was a Leschetitzky pupil who lost his right arm in the First World War. Thereafter he devoted himself to the left-hand repertoire, commissioning *concertante* works from many of his most famous composer contemporaries. Not one to conceal his reactions, he upbraided Ravel for the latter's lengthy cadenzas ("Had I wanted to play alone, I wouldn't have commissioned a concerto with orchestra!") and he flatly refused to play Prokofiev's B flat Concerto ("I don't understand a single note of it"). Britten's *Diversions*, composed in the United States in 1940, pleased him more than any of his other commissions. These three works make a well-contrasted programme and may well fill a gap in many people's collections. The Ravel is an undoubted masterpiece, and Leon Fleisher, himself a victim of carpal tunnel syndrome in his right hand, plays it with virtuosity and a fine sense of idiomatic colour. He is a fraction less successful in the Prokofiev — a curious piece in some ways, and one which needs an extraordinary range of dynamic and accent to bring off. The Britten is again top-notch, however, and first-rate orchestral support and recording quality help to win this issue a warm recommendation.

Britten. Cello Symphony, Op. 68[a]. Sinfonia da Requiem, Op. 20[b]. Cantata misericordium, Op. 69[c]. [a]**Mstislav Rostropovich** (vc); [c]**Sir Peter Pears** (ten); [c]**Dietrich Fischer-Dieskau** (bar); [c]**London Symphony Chorus and Orchestra**, [a]**English Chamber Orchestra**, [b]**New Philharmonia Orchestra/Benjamin Britten.** Decca London 425 100-2LM. Text and translation included. Item marked [a] from SXL6138 (12/64), [bc] SXL6175 (9/65).

1h 15m ADD 9/89 

This mid-price disc offers two of Britten's finest works, the *Cello Symphony* and the *Sinfonia da Requiem*. The latter was written in 1940 and is one of the composer's most powerful orchestral works, harnessing opposing forces in a frighteningly intense way. From the opening drumbeat the *Sinfonia* employs sonata form in a dramatically powerful way, though the tone is never fierce or savage; it has an implacable tread and momentum. The central movement, "Dies irae", however, has a real sense of fury, satirical in its biting comment — the flutter-tongued wind writing rattling its defiance. The closing "Requiem aeternam" is a movement of restrained beauty. On this recording from 1964 the New Philharmonia play superbly. The Cello Symphony, written in 1963 as part of a series for the great Russian cellist Mstislav Rostropovich, was the first major sonata-form work written since the *Sinfonia*. The idea of a struggle between soloist and orchestra, implicit in the traditional concerto, has no part here; it is a conversation between the two. Rostropovich plays with a depth of feeling that has never quite been equalled in other recordings and the playing of the ECO has great bite. The recording too is extraordinarily fine for its years. The *Cantata misericordium*, one of Britten's lesser known works, was written in 1962 as a commission from the Red Cross. It takes the story of the Good Samaritan and is scored for tenor and baritone soloists, chorus, string quartet and orchestra. It is a universal plea for charity and here receives a powerful reading. This is a must for any collector of Britten's music.

Additional recommendations ...
Sinfonia da Requiem. The Young Person's Guide to the Orchestra, Op. 34. PETER GRIMES — Four Sea Interludes; Passacaglia. **Royal Liverpool Philharmonic Orchestra/Libor Pešek.** Virgin Classics VC7 59550-2 — 1h 3m DDD 4/90
Cello Symphony. ***Bridge.*** *Oration — Concerto elegiaco, H180.* **Steven Isserlis** (vc); **City of London Sinfonia/Richard Hickox.** EMI CDM7 63909-2 — 1h 8m DDD 2/92

Britten. The Young Person's Guide to the Orchestra, Op. 34[a]. Simple Symphony, Op. 4[b]. Variations on a Theme of Frank Bridge, Op. 10[c]. [a]**London Symphony Orchestra;** [bc]**English Chamber Orchestra/Benjamin Britten.** Decca 417 509-2DH. Item marked [a] from SXL6110 (9/64), [b] SXL6405 (6/69), [c] SXL6316 (11/67).

1h 1m ADD 1/87 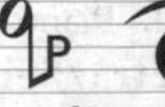

Britten's *Young Person's Guide to the Orchestra,* adapted from a theme by Purcell, came about through a film which would demonstrate to children the instruments of the orchestra. Britten's performance of his *Young Person's Guide* wisely omits the now rather dated text. He adopts quick tempos that must be demanding even for the LSO players, along with more spacious ones for the more introspective sections. This is beautiful playing, with all kinds of memorable touches. Britten's own childhood music is also here, in the shape of the delightfully fresh *Simple Symphony*. This fine CD then ends with more variations, the young composer's tribute to his teacher Frank Bridge. It is marvellous music, of astonishing wit and often intensely serious too, and the composer's own performance with the ECO is uniquely authoritative.

Additional recommendations ...
Simple Symphony. ***Bizet.*** *Symphony in C major.* ***Prokofiev.*** *Symphony No. 1 in D major, Op. 25, "Classical".* **Orpheus Chamber Orchestra.** DG 423 624-2GH — 1h 4m DDD 1/89

The Young Person's Guide to the Orchestra. Cello Symphony, Op. 68[a]. *PETER GRIMES — Four Sea Interludes, Op. 33a.* **Pärt.** *Cantus in memory of Benjamin Britten.* [a]**Truls Mørk** (vc); **Bergen Philharmonic Orchestra/Neeme Järvi.** BIS CD420 — lh 15m DDD 6/89 (B)

The Young Person's Guide to the Orchestra. Variations on a Theme of Frank Bridge. Peter Grimes — Four Sea Interludes; Passacaglia. **BBC Symphony Orchestra/Andrew Davis.** Teldec British Line 9031-73126-2 — lh 8m DDD 8/91 (B)

Britten. The Prince of the Pagodas, Op. 57. **London Sinfonietta/Oliver Knussen.** Virgin Classics VCD7 59578-2.

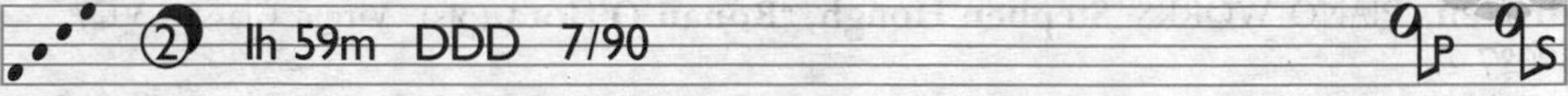

It is not surprising that this two-disc set won the 1990 *Gramophone* award in the Engineering category, for it is technically superlative (recorded in St Augustine's Church, Kilburn). But its primary importance is that Oliver Knussen has recorded the complete score of Britten's only ballet, restoring 20 minutes of music that had not previously been heard. Britten's 1957 recording for Decca had over 40 cuts, including four entire dances. It is extraordinary that the inclusion of this extra music should drastically alter the perspective of the whole work, but it does — it seems a better piece altogether, its debt to Tchaikovsky, Prokofiev and Stravinsky less obvious. Much connected with the production of the ballet at Covent Garden turned sour for Britten and this may have been reflected in his conducting of the recording. Knussen's interpretation is far more loving and effective and the playing of the London Sinfonietta is outstanding for individual virtuosity and for the richness and sparkle of the ensemble. This is that rare commodity, a disc that sheds entirely new light on a composition, and it should be in the collection of everyone who values Britten's — and British — music.

Key to Symbols

Price	Quantity/ availability	Timing	Mode	Review date
	2 2	lh 23m	DDD	6/88

Bargains · *Quality of Sound* · *Discs worth exploring* · *Caveat emptor*

Quality of performance · *Basic library* · *Period performance*

Britten. String Quartet No. 3, Op. 94.
Tippett. String Quartet No. 4 (1978). **Lindsay Quartet** (Peter Cropper, Ronald Birks, vns; Robin Ireland, va; Bernard Gregor-Smith, vc). ASV CDDCA608.

Neither Britten nor Tippett had written a string quartet for over 30 years when they returned to the medium in the 1970s. Both composed a masterpiece. In Britten's case there was the poignancy of its being the last major work he completed, yet there is no sign of declining powers in a work that pays homage to Shostakovich as well as to the special qualities of the Amadeus Quartet for whom it was written. The Lindsay Quartet's interpretation is very different; it is emotionally more intense and one can rarely be unaware of the shadow over the score, with its thematic references to Britten's last opera, *Death in Venice*. The last movement, a Passacaglia from which all passion has been drained to leave a serene air of resignation, is played very slowly. Tippett's Fourth Quartet has a lyrical and impassioned slow movement at its core and the predominant impression is one of energy and vigour. The music has such abundance that it seems to be bursting the confines of the medium and it is no surprise to learn that Tippett authorized an arrangement for string orchestra, not that the Lindsays sound at all strained by this vibrant score. The playing is masterful and the recording is admirably clear.

Additional recommendations ...
String Quartet No. 2 in C major, Op. 36. No. 3. **Alberni Quartet.** CRD CRD3395 — 55m ADD 3/89
No. 3. ***Tippett.*** *String Quartet No. 4.* **Lindsay Quartet.** ASV CDDCA608 — 53m DDD 5/88

Britten. PIANO WORKS. **Stephen Hough, [a]Ronan O'Hora** (pfs). Virgin Classics VC7 59027-2.
Holiday Diary, Op. 5. Three Character Pieces. Night Piece. Sonatina romantica — Moderato; Nocturne. 12 Variations on a Theme. Five Waltzes. Two Lullabies[a]. Mazurka elegiaca Op. 23 No. 2[a]. Introduction and Rondo alla burlesca, Op. 23 No. 1[a].

lh 20m DDD 8/91

Though a fine pianist, Britten wrote surprisingly little for his own instrument, admitting in later life that he found it unsatisfying. Thus even with the inclusion of boyhood pieces unpublished in his lifetime there is not enough solo piano music to fill a single disc, and Stephen Hough is joined by Ronan O'Hora for three two-piano works. The biggest item here is the one that comes first, the *Holiday Diary* of 1934, four pieces of which Britten wrote to a friend a decade later, "I have an awfully soft spot for them still — they just recreate that unpleasant young thing BB in 1934 — but who enjoyed being BB all the same!!" They have schoolboyish titles like "Early morning bathe" and "Funfair", and show an attractive youthful energy, but the final piece called "Night" is unusual in being slow and mysterious instead of a conventional brilliant finale. Stephen Hough has a coolly sharp way with this music, which is perhaps right for the buttoned-up young Britten that was revealed in the collection of his letters and diaries published in 1990. Not all the music here is distinguished, but it is well written; it is enlightening, too, to hear the influence of the composer's teacher, Ireland, in the *Three Character Pieces* and of Hindemith in the athletic *12 Variations*. Hough's playing has exemplary clarity and poise throughout, and the *Night Piece* of 1963 is beautifully atmospheric, while the two-piano music is also well delivered by thoughtful artists working well together. A clear and faithful recording complements this valuable issue.

Britten. Les illuminations, Op. 18[a]. Simple Symphony, Op. 4. Phaedra, Op. 93[a]. **[a]Christiane Eda-Pierre** (sop); **Jean-Walter Audoli Instrumental Ensemble/Jean-Walter Audoli.** Arion ARN68035.

56m DDD 6/89

It is good to have a recording of Britten's *Les illuminations* that is sung by a French singer and played by a French orchestra under a conductor from the same country. She and her colleagues bring a clean refinement to this score, and although other performances may have more excitement and sensuous charm this is one to appreciate for its sharp intelligence and Gallic clarity of judgement. Having written that Christiane Eda-Pierre is French-speaking, one must at once add that her English in *Phaedra* is also very good. Oddly enough, Britten here set a text which was originally in French (the translation is by the American poet Robert Lowell), and his music powerfully conveys the classical intensity of Racine's play on the subject of the Greek queen who falls into a forbidden love for her stepson Hippolythus and takes poison to escape a guilt that has become intolerable. Though called a cantata, *Phaedra* is really a miniature opera for a single singer (it was written for Dame Janet Baker) and it contains some of Britten's most effective writing for the female voice. The *Simple Symphony* which separates these two vocal works is altogether different, being based on music dating from the composer's happy childhood and having a fresh and often touching quality. The recording is as crisp as the performances.

Britten. Serenade for tenor, horn and strings, Op. 317[a]. Les illuminations, Op. 18[b]. Nocturne, Op. 60[c]. **[abc]Sir Peter Pears** (ten); **[c]Alexander Murray** (fl); **[c]Roger Lord** (cor a);

[c]**Gervase de Peyer** (cl); [c]**William Waterhouse** (bn); [ac]**Barry Tuckwell** (hn); [c]**Dennis Blyth** (timp); [c]**Osian Ellis** (hp); [ac]strings of the **London Symphony Orchestra,** [b]**English Chamber Orchestra/**[abc]**Benjamin Britten.** Decca 417 153-2DH. Texts included. Item marked [a] from SXL6110 (9/64), [b] SXL6316 (11/67), [c] SXL2189 (5/60).

1h 13m ADD 8/86

No instrument was more important to Britten than the human voice and, inspired by the musicianship and superb vocal craftsmanship of his closest friend, he produced an unbroken stream of vocal works of a quality akin to those of Purcell. Three of his most haunting vocal pieces are featured on this wonderful CD. The performances date from between 1959 and 1966 with Pears in penetratingly musical form, even if the voice itself was by now a little thin and occasionally unsteady. The ECO and LSO are superb in every way and of course Britten was his own ideal interpreter. The recordings are vintage Decca and excellent for their time.

NEW REVIEW

Britten. SONGS.
Poulenc. SONGS. [a]**Sir Peter Pears** (ten); [b]**Pierre Bernac** (bar); [a]**Benjamin Britten,** [b]**Francis Poulenc** (pfs). EMI Composers in Person mono CDC7 54605-2. Texts and translation included. Recorded 1936-47.

Britten[a]**:** Seven Sonnets of Michelangelo, Op. 22 (from HMV C3312 and B9302, 1/43). The Holy Sonnets of John Donne, Op. 35 (HMV DB6689/91, 3/49). ***Poulenc***[b]: Le bestiaire. Montparnasse (both from DB6299, 8/46). Chansons gaillardes — No. 4, Invocation aux parques; No. 7, La belle jeunesse (HMV DA4894. Recorded in 1936). Tel jour, telle nuit (DB6383/4, 12/48). Dans le jardin d'Anna (DB6384). Métamorphoses. Deux poèmes de Louis Aragon (DB6267, 4/46).

1h 16m ADD 4/93 

Here is an interesting juxtaposition, where each composer accompanies an artist for whom most of his songs were written. The Pears/Britten partnership was celebrated in many Decca recordings, of course, but here we have the very first collaboration on record, in a version of the *Michelangelo Sonnets* captured just two months after the two artists had given the work its première. There is an appealingly fresh, eager quality in the performance, and Pears's voice has an attractively youthful timbre. The recording of the *Donne Sonnets* was made just two years after the cycle had been written, and here again there is a particular vitality in the playing and singing not always present in the duo's later performances. Bernac and Poulenc made LP recordings of most of the songs here, and they are already available on CD, but by the late-1950s Bernac was almost 60 years old, and his voice had deteriorated. In these earlier versions he was in good vocal state, and he and Poulenc bring unrivalled qualities of elegance, wit and pathos to some finely crafted *mélodies*. All these highly authoritative performances are preserved in very acceptable sound.

NEW REVIEW

Britten. CHORAL WORKS, Volume 2. **The Sixteen/Harry Christophers** with [a]**Stephen Westrop** (pf); [b]**Margaret Phillips** (org). Collins Classics 1343-2. Texts and translations included.

Antiphon, Op. 56*b*[b]. Te Deum in C major[b]. A Wedding Anthem, Op. 46[b]. Rejoice in the Lamb, Op. 30[b]. The Sycamore tree. The Ballad of Little Musgrave and Lady Barnard[a]. Advance Democracy. Sacred and Profane, Op. 91.

1h 10m DDD 6/93 

Part of a composer's job is to write music for specific occasions and for particular performers. While many have clearly found this an irksome chore, Britten invariably responded to such commissions with alacrity. British prisoners-of-war languishing in a Nazi camp during 1943 formed a choir and for them Britten sent out, page-by-page in microfilm, *The Ballad of Little Musgrave and Lady Barnard* which must have raised their spirits as much for the quality of its writing as for its exuberant character. He expected no great technical prowess from the church choir (and organist) for whom he wrote the C major *Te Deum,* but nevertheless turned out a most distinctive setting of this familiar text, giving the choir simple but highly effective music (with a charming soprano solo gloriously sung here by Libby Crabtree) above an unusual organ accompaniment imitating the sound of pizzicato cellos. His astute response to texts, be they the naïvely idealistic *Advance Democracy* or the eccentric *Rejoice in the Lamb*, gives an added dimension to these small-scale choral pieces as do these outstanding performances from The Sixteen who, under the intuitive direction of Harry Christophers, undoubtedly rank as one of the finest British choral groups of our time.

Britten. SACRED CHORAL MUSIC. [a]**Sioned Williams** (hp); **Westminster Cathedral Choir/David Hill** with [b]**James O'Donnell** (org). Hyperion CDA66220. From A66220 (12/86). Texts included.

A Ceremony of Carols, Op. 28[a]. Missa brevis, Op. 63[b]. A Hymn to the Virgin (1934). A Hymn of St Columba (1962)[b]. Jubilate Deo in E flat major (1961)[b]. Deus in adjutorum meum (1945).

49m DDD 2/88

A Ceremony of Carols sets nine medieval and sixteenth-century poems between the "Hodie" of the plainsong Vespers. The sole accompanying instrument is a harp, but given the right acoustic, sensitive attention to the words and fine rhythmic control the piece has a remarkable richness and depth. The Westminster Cathedral Choir perform this work beautifully; diction is immaculate and the acoustic halo surrounding the voices gives a festive glow to the performance. A fascinating *Jubilate* and *A Hymn to the Virgin*, whilst lacking the invention and subtlety of *A Ceremony*, intrigue with some particularly felicitous use of harmony and rhythm. *Deus in adjutorum meum* employs the choir without accompaniment and has an initial purity that gradually builds up in texture as the psalm (No. 70) gathers momentum. The *Missa brevis* was written for this very choir and George Malcolm's nurturing of a tonal brightness in the choir allowed Britten to use the voices in a more flexibile and instrumental manner than usual. The effect is glorious. St Columba founded the monastery on the Scottish island of Iona and Britten's hymn sets his simple and forthright prayer with deceptive simplicity and directness. The choir sing this music beautifully and the recording is first rate.

Additional recommendation ...

Hymn to St Cecilia, Op. 27. Sacred and Profane, Op. 91. Rejoice in the Lamb, Op. 30. A Ceremony of Carols. **Soloists; Vasari Singers/Jeremy Backhouse.** EMI Eminence CD-EMX2204 —
lh 6m DDD 5/93

Britten. Deus in adjutorium meum[f]. Chorale on an old French carol[f]. Cantata misericordium, Op. 69[bdfg].
Finzi. Requiem da camera[acdfg].
Holst. Psalms, H117 — No. 86[aefg]; No. 148[efg]. [a]**Alison Barlow** (sop); [b]**John Mark Ainsley** (ten); [c]**David Hoult,** [d]**Stephen Varcoe** (bars); [e]**John Alley** (org); [f]**Britten Singers;** [g]**City of London Sinfonia/Richard Hickox.** Chandos CHAN8997. Texts included.

lh 7m DDD 3/92

Each in his own way, all of these composers bring comfort, but first they face a world of warfare, loss, affliction, where comfort is needed. Finzi dedicated his *Requiem* to his teacher and friend, Ernest Farrar, killed in 1918 and, as its editor, Philip Thomas, writes, it is "also a meditation on the achievement of all musicians killed or blighted by the Great War". The Prelude is music of the greatest beauty, and the choral and solo settings of words by Mansfield, Hardy and W.W. Gibson are all heartfelt, the restraint of their expression being all the more moving because there is clearly such a fund of emotion to draw upon. This is a fine performance, too, interesting historically because it includes for the first time the "Time of the Breaking of Nations" completed by Thomas from a draft found in the Bodleian Library. Britten's *Deus in adjutorium meum* makes a contrast in its boldness of rhythmic and harmonic invention, yet it also brings beauty out of affliction, as Britten does again with the parable of the Good Samaritan in the *Cantata misericordium.* Holst's Psalm settings similarly turn from sombre prayer to praise. All are performed with the utmost skill and sensitivity by soloists, chorus and orchestra under Richard Hickox's always perceptive direction, and the only regrettable feature of this valuable disc is the all too common one of an insufficiently forward presence allowed the choir in the recording balance.

Britten. Saint Nicolas, Op. 42[a]. Rejoice in the Lamb, Op. 30[b]. [a]**David Hemmings,** [b]**Michael Hartnett** (trebs); [b]**Jonathan Steele** (alto); [a]**Sir Peter Pears,** [b]**Philip Todd** (tens); [b]**Donald Francke** (bass); [a]**Girls' Choir of Sir John Leman School, Beccles;** [a]**Boys' Choir of Ipswich School Preparatory Department;** [b]**Purcell Singers;** [a]**Aldeburgh Festival Choir and Orchestra/Benjamin Britten** with [a]**Ralph Downes,** [b]**George Malcolm** (orgs). Decca London mono 425 714-2LM. Texts included. Item marked [a] from LXT5060 (7/55), [b] LXT5416 (5/58).

1h 4m ADD 9/90

This disc is a further example of Decca's wisdom in transferring to CD its historic collection of Britten/Pears performances of the former's music; and, incidentally, it shows how extremely good the recordings were in the first place. The performance of the cantata *Rejoice in the Lamb*, composed just after Britten returned to England from America during the war, was made in 1957 and remains unsurpassed. The mood of the work's touching setting of Christopher Smart's innocent but soul-searching poem is perfectly caught by the performers, who include George Malcolm as the organist. Britten's writing for the organ here is full of invention, whether he is illustrating Smart's cat Jeoffry "wreathing his body seven times round with elegant quickness" or the "great personal valour" of the mouse who defies Jeoffry. The Purcell Singers, impeccable in clarity of diction, and the soloists, are first-rate. *Saint Nicolas* was recorded even earlier, in Aldeburgh Church in 1955. The treble soloist is David Hemmings who had created Miles in *The Turn of the Screw* the previous year, and Pears sings the role he had created at the first Aldeburgh Festival in 1948. This disc is indispensable for the quality of the performance and as documentary evidence of the standard of the festival in its early years.

Britten. War Requiem, Op. 66[a]. Sinfonia da Requiem, Op. 20. Ballad of Heroes, Op. 14[b]. [a]**Heather Harper** (sop); [a]**Philip Langridge,** [b]**Martyn Hill** (tens); [a]**John Shirley-Quirk** (bar); [a]**St Paul's Cathedral Choir; London Symphony** [ab]**Chorus and Orchestra/Richard Hickox.** Chandos CHAN8983/4. Texts and translations included.

2 2h 5m DDD 11/91  

Britten's *War Requiem* is the composer's most public statement of his pacifism. The work is cast in six movements and calls for massive forces: full chorus, soprano soloist and full orchestra evoke mourning, supplication and guilty apprehension; boys' voices with chamber organ, the passive calm of a liturgy which points beyond death; tenor and baritone soloists with chamber orchestra, the passionate outcry of the doomed victims of war. The most recent challenger to the composer's classic Decca version offers up-to-date recording, excellently managed to suggest the various perspectives of the vast work, and possibly the most convincing execution of the choral writing to date under the direction of a conductor, Richard Hickox, who is a past master at obtaining the best from a choir in terms of dynamic contrast and vocal emphasis. Add to that his empathy with all that the work has to say and you have a cogent reason for acquiring this version even before you come to the excellent work of the soloists. In her recording swan song, Harper at last commits to disc a part she created. It is right that her special accents and impeccable shaping of the soprano's contribution have been preserved for posterity. Shirley-Quirk, always closely associated with the piece, sings the three baritone solos and duets with rugged strength and dedicated intensity. He is matched by Langridge's compelling and insightful reading, with his notes and words more dramatic than Pears's approach. The inclusion of two additional pieces, neither of them short, gives this version an added advantage even if the *Ballad of Heroes* is one of Britten's slighter works.

Additional recommendations ...

War Requiem. **Soloists; Christ Church Cathedral Choir, Oxford; City of Birmingham Symphony Chorus and Orchestra/Simon Rattle.** EMI CDS7 47034-8 — 2 DDD 12/84 B

War Requiem. **Soloists; Bach Choir; Highgate School Choir; London Symphony Chorus; Melos Ensemble; London Symphony Orchestra/Benjamin Britten.** Decca 414 383-2DH2 — ② 1h 21m ADD 4/85

Britten. CURLEW RIVER. **Sir Peter Pears** (ten) Madwoman; **John Shirley-Quirk** (bar) Ferryman; **Harold Blackburn** (bass) Abbot; **Bryan Drake** (bar) Traveller; **Bruce Webb** (treb) Voice of the Spirit; **English Opera Group/Benjamin Britten** and **Viola Tunnard.** Decca London 421 858-2LM. Text included. From Decca SET301 (1/66). Recorded in 1965.

1h 9m ADD 9/89

This "parable for church performance" is the first of three such works that Britten wrote in the 1960s, not long after the *War Requiem*, and it too breathes a strongly religious spirit while being far removed from conventional church music. Set in the fenland of East Anglia as a medieval Christian mystery play, it tells the story of a madwoman who, seeking the young son stolen from her, comes to, and finally crosses, the Curlew River, only to meet with the spirit of the dead boy who gives her his blessing. The story derives from a classical *Noh* play that the composer had seen in Tokyo a few years before, and following the Japanese tradition he used an all-male cast, a bold step that proved successful since he had an exceptional artist to play the Madwoman in the shape of Peter Pears. Sir Peter brings great dignity and depth to this role, one of his favourites among the many by Britten that he created, and the other principals are fine too, notably John Shirley-Quirk as the Ferryman and Bruce Webb as the Boy, both also from the original cast. The seven instrumentalists who participate are first rate, and under the composer's direction this is a moving experience and a recording of historic importance, made most atmospherically in Orford Church in Suffolk, where the work had its first performance.

NEW REVIEW

Britten. THE BURNING FIERY FURNACE. **Sir Peter Pears** (ten) Nebuchadnezzar; **Bryan Drake** (bar) Astrologer; **John Shirley-Quirk** (bar) Shadrach (Ananias); **Robert Tear** (ten) Meshach (Misael); **Stafford Dean** (bass) Abednego (Azarias); **Peter Leeming** (bass) Herald; **English Opera Group/Benjamin Britten.** Decca 414 663-2LM. Text included. From SET356 (12/67). Recorded in 1967.

1h 4m ADD 10/90

NEW REVIEW

Britten. THE PRODIGAL SON. **Sir Peter Pears** (ten) Tempter, Abbot; **John Shirley-Quirk** (bar) Father; **Bryan Drake** (bar) Elder Son; **Robert Tear** (ten) Younger Son; **English Opera Group/Benjamin Britten.** Decca 425 713-2LM. Text included. From SET438 (6/70). Recorded in 1969.

1h 9m ADD 9/90

For his second and third church parables, Britten and his librettist William Plomer turned to the Old and New Testaments respectively. The casts are again all male, but for *The Burning Fiery Furnace*, like *Curlew River*, Britten achieves the concluding miracle with the use of a boy's purest treble voice for a visit from the spirit world, in this case the angel that protects our three Israelites from the flames of the furnace. And the treble's floated vocalise over the Israelites' *Benedicite* at this point is further proof of Britten's ability to find a musical image that exactly matches and enhances the dramatic situation. Another is the 'constant' of a B flat major for *The Prodigal Son*'s father and family; its tender, reassuring radiance at the son's return is quite as miraculous as anything else in these three parables. That these recordings must remain definitive can be shown with one simple example: the close canon for the Prodigal and his alter ago the Tempter, where Britten must have had in mind the extraordinary similarity in timbre of the voices of Peter Pears and Robert Tear. In sum, the achievement here (by Britten, his performers and his producer, John Culshaw) is a full and wide-ranging projection of ideas and images, despite the small forces involved. This is theatre of the mind and heart at its most richly communicative, and the recorded sound is superb.

Britten. PAUL BUNYAN. **Pop Wagner** (bar) Narrator; **James Lawless** (spkr) Paul Bunyan; **Dan Dressen** (ten) Johnny Inkslinger; **Elisabeth Comeaux Nelson** (sop) Tiny; **Clifton Ware** (ten) Slim; **Vern Sutton** (ten), **Merle Fristad** (bass) Two Bad Cooks; **James Bohn** (bar) Hel Helson; **Phil Jorgenson, Tim Dahl, Thomas Shaffer, Lawrence Weller** (tens/bars) Four Swedes; **James McKeel** (bar) John Shears; **James Westbrock** (ten) Western Union Boy; **Maria Jette** (sop) Fido; **Sue Herber** (mez) Moppet; **Janis Hardy** (mez) Poppet; **Plymouth Music Series Chorus and Orchestra/Philip Brunelle.** Virgin Classics VC7 59249-2. Notes and text included.

② 1h 53m DDD 8/88 

Paul Bunyan was Britten's first opera and the libretto, characteristically witty, allusive and coruscating in its dexterity, is by W.H. Auden. By an extraordinary feat of creative imagination, these two exiled young Englishmen wrote an opera that is idiomatically American. Britten's score is a dazzling achievement, with songs in the form of blues, parodies of spirituals and Cole Porter, and remarkable anticipations of his own later works. Paul Bunyan is a mythical American folk-hero, never seen on-stage and whose part is spoken. The principal singing roles are those of his assistant Johnny Inkslinger, his Swedish foreman Hel Helson, a "man of brawn but no brains", his daughter Tiny, and a collection of cooks, farmers, cats and dogs. The work was none too favourably reviewed by the Americans in 1941 and Britten was only persuaded to look at it again in 1974 as a therapeutic exercise after his serious heart operation. This is its first recording and it is an unqualified success. It is not a work that requires star voices; teamwork and a generally good standard are the chief requirements and these are forthcoming. Each individual performance is neatly characterized and there is just enough homespun quality to remind us of the work's origins. Diction is exemplary and the American accents are genuine. Philip Brunelle conducts with real affection and understanding and the booklet is a superb piece of documentation. It is difficult to imagine a better performance.

Britten. PETER GRIMES. **Sir Peter Pears** (ten) Peter Grimes; **Claire Watson** (sop) Ellen Orford; **James Pease** (bass) Captain Balstrode; **Jean Watson** (contr) Auntie; **Raymond Nilsson** (ten) Bob Boles; **Owen Brannigan** (bass) Swallow; **Lauris Elms** (mez) Mrs Sedley; **Sir Geraint Evans** (bar) Ned Keene; **John Lanigan** (ten) Rector; **David Kelly** (bass) Hobson; **Marion Studholme** (sop) First Niece; **Iris Kells** (sop) Second Niece; **Chorus and Orchestra of the Royal Opera House, Covent Garden/Benjamin Britten**. Decca 414 577-2DH3. Notes and text included. From SXL2150/52 (10/59). Recorded in 1958.

② 2h 22m ADD 4/86 

The Decca set has long been regarded as the definitive recording which, in 1958, introduced the opera to many listeners and one which has never been superseded in its refinement or insight. Britten's conducting, lithe, lucid and as inexorable as "the tide that waits for no man", reveals his work as the complex, ambiguous drama that it is. Sir Peter Pears, in the title-role which was written for him, brings unsurpassed detail of nuance to Grimes's words while never losing sight of the essential plainness of the man's speech. The rest of the cast form a vivid portrait gallery. The recording is as live and clear as if it had been made yesterday and takes the listener right on to the stage. The bustle of activity and sound effects realize nicely Britten's own masterly painting of dramatic foreground and background.

Additional recommendations ...

Soloists; Chorus and Orchestra of the Royal Opera House, Covent Garden/Sir Colin Davis. Philips 432 578-2PM2 — ② 2h 26m ADD 11/91 B

Soloists; Chorus and Orchestra of the Royal Opera House, Covent Garden/Bernard Haitink. EMI CDS7 54832-2 — ② 2h 25m DDD 7/93 B

Britten. THE RAPE OF LUCRETIA[a]. Phaedra, Op. 93[b]. [a]**Sir Peter Pears** (ten) Male Chorus; [a]**Heather Harper** (sop) Female Chorus; [ab]**Dame Janet Baker** (mez) Lucretia; [a]**John Shirley-Quirk** (bar) Collatinus; [a]**Benjamin Luxon** (bar) Tarquinius; [a]**Bryan Drake** (bar)

Junius; [a]**Elizabeth Bainbridge** (mez) Bianca; [a]**Jenny Hill** (sop) Lucia; **English Chamber Orchestra/**[a]**Benjamin Britten,** [b]**Steuart Bedford.** Decca London 425 666-2LH2. Notes and texts included. Item marked [a] from SET492/3 (6/71); [b] SXL6847 (7/77). Item marked [a] recorded in 1970, [b] 1977.

② 2h 4m ADD 5/90

Other transfers in this series represent a celebration of the art of Peter Pears as well as that of Benjamin Britten, but this set brings Janet Baker into the limelight. She takes the title roles in two works that, though divided by nearly 30 years, are still closely linked. Dame Janet gives of her best in strongly drawn, sympathetic portrayals of the two classical 'heroines', Phaedra and Lucretia, but, despite this, neither lady becomes particularly endearing and Britten describes their fates with an underlying coolness that countermands the immediate brilliance of the sounds he creates. Nevertheless, there is so much in both works that is typical of Britten's genius that, coupled together, they form a very significant facet of his work. *The Rape of Lucretia* was Britten's first chamber opera. *Phaedra*, based on Racine's *Phêdre*, was one of the composer's final works and capped his long-time empathy with French culture. Both receive performances that do them full justice, though the recording of the latter could be a shade more lucid for its date. Steuart Bedford's conducting matches that of Britten in the earlier recording remarkably well and the whole now presents a particularly attractive package.

Britten. ALBERT HERRING. **Sir Peter Pears** (ten) Albert Herring; **Sylvia Fisher** (sop) Lady Billows; **Johanna Peters** (contr) Florence Pike; **April Cantelo** (sop) Miss Wordsworth; **John Noble** (bar) Mr George; **Edgar Evans** (ten) Mr Upfold; **Owen Brannigan** (bass) Mr Budd; **Joseph Ward** (ten) Sid; **Catherine Wilson** (mez) Nancy; **Sheila Rex** (mez) Mrs Herring; **Sheila Amit** (sop) Emmie; **Anne Pashley** (sop) Cis; **Stephen Terry** (treb) Harry; **English Chamber Orchestra/Benjamin Britten.** Decca London 421 849-2LH2. Notes and text included. From SET274/6 (10/64). Recorded in 1964.

② 2h 18m ADD 6/89 

Britten's chamber-opera has found a renewed place in the public's affection since Sir Peter Hall's celebrated production at Glyndebourne in 1985. The audience was once again charmed by the freshness and joyfulness of this delightful piece, an English ensemble work if ever there was one. Based on a Maupassant short story *Le rosier de Madame Husson*, Eric Crozier's libretto transports the story from France to Britten's native East Anglia. It tells of a market town's hunt for a May Queen to be crowned at the annual May Festival. None of the female candidates pass muster, leaving the honour to a boy, Albert Herring. This hand-picked cast, directed with evident affection and incomparable skill by the composer, could hardly be bettered. Peter Pears makes a perfect Albert, hesitant, callow but ultimately dignified; Sylvia Fisher is a domineering Lady Billows; April Cantelo twitters engagingly as Miss Wordworth; Owen Brannigan is splendid as the local policeman, Superintendent Budd. Indeed there isn't a weak link. The English Chamber Orchestra play superbly and the recording sounds quite superb for its years. All in all, this is a classic performance of an enchanting piece.

NEW REVIEW

Britten. BILLY BUDD[a]. **Peter Glossop** (bar) Billy Budd; **Sir Peter Pears** (ten) Captain Vere; **Michael Langdon** (bass) John Claggart; **John Shirley-Quirk** (bar) Mr Redburn; **Bryan Drake** (bar) Mr Flint; **David Kelly** (bass) Mr Ratcliffe; **Gregory Dempsey** (ten) Red Whiskers; **David Bowman** (bar) Donald; **Owen Brannigan** (bass) Dansker; **Robert Tear** (ten) Novice; **Robert Bowman** (ten) Squeak; **Delme Bryn-Jones** (bar) Bosun; **Eric Garrett** (bar) First Mate; **Nigel Rogers** (ten) Maintop; **Benjamin Luxon** (bar) Novice's Friend; **Geoffrey Coleby** (bar) Arthur Jones; **Ambrosian Opera Chorus; London Symphony Orchestra/Benjamin Britten.**

The Holy Sonnets of John Donne, Op. 35[b]. Songs and Proverbs of William Blake, Op. 74[c]. [b]**Sir Peter Pears** (ten); [c]**Dietrich Fischer-Dieskau** (bar); **Benjamin Britten** (pf). Decca 417

428-2LH3. Notes and text included. Item marked [a] from SET379/81 (9/68), [bc]SXL6391 (5/69). Recorded in 1967.

③ 3h 25m ADD 6/89

First performed in 1951, *Billy Budd*, like the later church parables uses an all-male cast (with never a hint of monotony of vocal tone). *Budd* is itself a parable: the claustrophobic atmosphere aboard a man-o'-war in Napoleonic times, and the pitiable lot of the ship's 'impressed' sailors set the scene for a direct confrontation between good and evil. It is arguably Britten's operatic masterpiece; his exploitation of the colour and potential of his largest opera orchestra is no less masterly than the opera's motivic concentration, or his handling of the Christian symbolism. And dramatically Britten shirks nothing: Billy's hanging in the final scene is surely Opera's most horrifying and heart-rending spectacle. No brief resumé can do justice to the corporate achievement here, but mention must be made of Glossop's Billy, strong, heroic and never merely virtuous; and Langdon's black-voiced Claggart, the very embodiment of malevolence (his every entry, accompanied by trombones and tuba, sends a shiver down the spine). The power and finesse of the orchestra's playing for the composer confirm that this was a vintage period for the LSO; and John Culshaw, in his last production for Decca, rightly opted for a dry, immediate sound stage, but one that uses width and depth with an imagination and accomplishment that few producers today can rival. The dark and dramatic song cycles make an ideal coupling.

Britten. THE TURN OF THE SCREW. **Sir Peter Pears** (ten) Prologue, Quint; **Joan Cross** (sop) Mrs Grose; **Arda Mandikian** (sop) Miss Jessel; **Jennifer Vyvyan** (sop) Governess; **David Hemmings** (treb) Miles; **Olive Dyer** (sop) Flora; **English Opera Group Orchestra/Benjamin Britten.** Decca London mono 425 672-2LH2. Notes and text included. From LXT5038/9 (8/55). Recorded in 1955.

② 1h 45m ADD 5/90 

Sir Colin Davis's magnificent Philips recording of *The Turn of the Screw* has yet to be transferred to CD, but Britten's own 1954 version, made with the original cast not long after the work's first performance, wants for virtually nothing — even the mono sound has a vigour and clarity that many a modern stereo recording would do well to match. Part of the lasting success of this recording is a result of Britten's use of a chamber ensemble to provide the orchestral background to the singers — this could be captured with much greater space and accuracy than would have been possible at that time with a full orchestra, and provided the opportunity to push farther the expressive potential of the chamber opera genre. Britten paces the work's chilling, insidious tale of good and evil so that it compounds, variation by variation, towards the tragic triumph of its conclusion. The key roles of Quint and the Governess, which subtly explore so many ramifications of male/female relationships, are definitively portrayed by Peter Pears and Jennifer Vyvyan, and the rest of the cast emulate the same high standard of musical distinction allied to sensitive characterization. This is, then, much more than an issue of only documentary interest.

Britten. A MIDSUMMER NIGHT'S DREAM. **Alfred Deller** (alto) Oberon; **Elizabeth Harwood** (sop) Tytania; **Sir Peter Pears** (ten) Lysander; **Thomas Hemsley** (bar) Demetrius; **Josephine Veasey** (mez) Hermia; **Heather Harper** (sop) Helena; **Stephen Terry** (spkr) Puck; **John Shirley-Quirk** (bar) Theseus; **Helen Watts** (contr) Hippolyta; **Owen Brannigan** (bass) Bottom; **Norman Lumsden** (bass) Quince; **Kenneth Macdonald** (ten) Flute; **David Kelly** (bass) Snug; **Robert Tear** (ten) Snout; **Keith Raggett** (ten) Starveling; **Richard Dakin** (treb) Cobweb; **John Prior** (treb) Peaseblossom; **Ian Wodehouse** (treb) Mustardseed; **Gordon Clark** (treb) Moth; **Choirs of Downside and Emanuel Schools; London Symphony Orchestra/Benjamin Britten.** Decca London 425 663-2LH2. Notes and text included. From SET338/40 (5/67).

② 2h 24m ADD 5/90 

From the first groanings of the Athenian wood, marvellously conjured by glissando strings, through to Puck's final adieu to the audience, Britten's adaptation of *A Midsummer Night's Dream* is a cascade of insight and invention, married to a clear and memorable tunefulness. Although this 1966 performance in many ways represents a definitive account of the opera, the work allows for a wide variety of interpretation. The role of Oberon, for example, is here filled with an other-worldly detachment by Alfred Deller, yet the fairy king's threatening and ambiguous sexuality has been strongly drawn by others in the opera house. A recording of the strength of this present issue does tend to inhibit the introduction on disc of other, equally viable, alternative views. Nevertheless, the transfer to CD of this performance was imperative and although the original vinyl set was splendidly vital, the recording now shines even brighter and the performance is still more lovable. There's not a weak link to be found, and the final ensemble, "Now until the break of day", retains the same power to move with its breathtaking beauty as it did when it was first recorded.

Britten. DEATH IN VENICE. **Sir Peter Pears** (ten) Gustav von Aschenbach; **John Shirley-Quirk** (bar) Traveller, Elderly Fop, Old Gondolier, Hotel Manager, Hotel Barber, Leader of the Players, Voice of Dionysus; **James Bowman** (alto) Voice of Apollo; **Kenneth Bowen** (ten) Hotel Porter; **Peter Leeming** (bass) Travel Clerk; **Iris Saunders** (sop) Strawberry-seller; **English Opera Group Chorus; English Chamber Orchestra/Steuart Bedford.** Decca London 425 669-2LH2. Notes and text included. From SET581-3 Recorded in 1974. (11/74).

② 2h 25m ADD 5/90

A special place is reserved for *Death in Venice* in the affections of most Britten aficionados, for not only is it one of his finest works but it also contains strong autobiographical associations. With his heart condition worsening as he composed, Britten feared that he might not live to complete the opera. Those troubles, coupled with his doubts about the value of what he had achieved in his life and career, found intense resonances in the plot and words of Myfanwy Piper's libretto. To us lesser mortals, his doubts might seem incomprehensible, yet they served to deepen and enrich the many layers of meaning that the music of *Death in Venice* encompasses. Recorded in The Maltings at Snape in 1974, this performance, so imaginatively and accurately directed by Steuart Bedford, brings the listener quickly to the work's chief themes. Pears's dominating presence as Aschenbach inevitably helps this process, yet much of the praise may go to the recording, which gives the singers an immediacy that, though rare in the opera house, is ideal for home listening. With magnificent support from the rest of the cast and the ECO, Pears, more than ever, seems Britten's alter ego here and the whole production a direct projection of the composer's mind.

Further listening ...

Nocturnal after John Dowland, Op. 70. *Coupled with* ***Schafer.*** Le cri de Merlin; ***Tippett.*** The blue guitar. **Norbert Kraft** (gtr). Chandos CHAN8784 (1/90).

GLORIANA. **Soloists; Welsh National Opera Chorus and Orchestra/Sir Charles Mackerras.** Argo 440 213-2ZHO2 (7/93).

František Brixi

Bohemian 1732-1771

NEW REVIEW

Brixi. Organ Concertos — No. 2 in D major; No. 4 in C major; No. 5 in C major. **Jan Hora** (org); **Prague Chamber Orchestra/František Vajnar.** Supraphon 10 3029-2. Played on the organ of the Union of Brethren, Prague. Recorded in 1982.

47m AAD 9/92

Brixi wrote five organ concertos — a tiny drop in the ocean of a vast output numbering some 500 works (including 105 Masses and 11 settings of the Requiem). His music has a direct appeal, full of delightful melodies and vivacious rhythms, and it's easy to hear why he was one of the most popular composers of his day. It is particularly appropriate that the three concertos on this disc should have been recorded in Prague and played by Prague musicians, for Brixi achieved at the remarkably early age of 27 the highest position in that city's musical life, Kapellmeister of St Vitus's Cathedral, and became a leading figure in Prague musical life in the middle years of the eighteenth century. These are well-prepared, neat performances full of vitality and with the kind of infectious enthusiasm which can only come from a team of players who are thoroughly enjoying their music-making. František Vajnar directs the orchestra with a wonderfully buoyant touch, providing splendid support for Jan Hora who finds plenty of colour and variety from this charming instrument and whose nimble fingers dance effortlessly over the athletic solo passagework of the concertos. The clear recordings do ample justice to these cheerful performances.

Leo Brouwer

Cuban 1939-

Suggested listening ...

Brouwer. Retrats Catalans. *Coupled with* ***Arnold.*** Guitar Concerto, Op. 67; ***Chappell.*** Guitar Concerto No. 1, "Caribbean Concerto". **Eduardo Fernández** (gtr); **English Chamber Orchestra/Barry Wordsworth.** Decca 430 233-2DH (4/91).

See full review under Arnold; refer to the Index to Reviews.

Max Bruch

German 1838-1920

Bruch. Violin Concerto No. 1 in G minor, Op. 26. Scottish Fantasy, Op. 46. **Cho-Liang Lin** (vn); **Chicago Symphony Orchestra/Leonard Slatkin.** CBS Masterworks CD42315. From IM42315 (3/87).

53m DDD 7/87  

When the CBS disc first appeared in 1987 Edward Greenfield was moved to write in *Gramophone*: "this is one of the most radiantly beautiful violin records I have heard for a long time". This seems to say it all. Cho-Liang Lin's playing is of the highest order here, with technically flawless performances of both works performed with such consummate ease that it leaves one with a sense of amazement. His handling of the first main subject in the Concerto's first movement has passion and intensity without resorting to sentimentality or over-indulgence, and a real feeling of excitement and momentum is generated as it leads to a truly magical account of the *Adagio*, where Lin's silky smooth tone is heard to its full advantage in the beautifully rapt and sustained melodic line. Bravura excitement returns in the finale which couples nobility and strength with warmth and tenderness. The *Scottish* Fantasy makes a welcome alternative to the normal Mendelssohn Concerto coupling. This is a less known and rarely recorded work, but is no less attractive or rewarding, especially in so persuasive and brilliant a performance as this. Leonard Slatkin and the Chicago Symphony Orchestra provide excellent and sympathetic support throughout. The recording is well balanced.

Additional recommendations ...

Violin Concerto. ***Mendelssohn.*** *Violin Concerto in E minor, Op. 64* **Anne-Sophie Mutter** (vn); **Berlin Philharmonic Orchestra/Herbert von Karajan.** DG 400 031-2GH — 57m DDD 3/83

Violin Concerto. ***Mendelssohn.*** *Violin Concerto.* **Scottish Chamber Orchestra/Jaime Laredo** (vn). Pickwick IMP Red Label PCD829 — 53m DDD 1/87

Violin Concerto. ***Mendelssohn.*** *Violin Concerto.* **Joshua Bell** (vn); **Academy of St Martin in the Fields/Sir Neville Marriner.** Decca 421 145-2DH — 54m DDD 5/88

Violin Concerto. **Mendelssohn.** *Violin Concerto.* **Schubert.** *Rondo in A major, D438.* **Nigel Kennedy** (vn); **English Chamber Orchestra/Jeffrey Tate.** EMI CDC7 49663-2 — 1h 11m DDD 1/89

Violin Concerto. **Dvořák.** Violin Concerto in A minor, Op. 53. **Tasmin Little** (vn); **Royal Liverpool Philharmonic Orchestra/Vernon Handley.** Classics for Pleasure CD-CFP4566 — 1h DDD 7/90

Violin Concerto. **Mendelssohn.** *Violin Concerto.* **Nathan Milstein** (vn); **Philharmonia Orchestra/Leon Barzin.** Classics for Pleasure CD-CFP4374 — 48m ADD

Violin Concerto[c]. **Mendelssohn.** *Violin Concerto*[b]. **Sarasate.** *Introduction et Tarantelle, Op. 43*[a]. **Kreisler.** *Liebesfreud*[a]. **Cho-Liang Lin** (vn); [a]**Sandra Rivers** (pf); [b]**Philharmonia Orchestra/Michael Tilson Thomas;** [c]**Chicago Symphony Orchestra/Leonard Slatkin.** CBS Masterworks CD44902 — 1h 1m DDD 3/91 £

Complete Works for Violin and Orchestra: Violin Concertos — No. 1; No. 2 in D minor, Op. 44; No. 3 in D minor, Op. 58. Adagio Appassionato, Op. 57. Romance, Op. 42. Scottish Fantasy[a]. *Konzertstück, Op. 84. Serenade, Op. 75. In Memoriam, Op. 65.* [a]**Elizabeth Unger** (hp); **Salvatore Accardo** (vn); **Leipzig Gewandhaus Orchestra/Kurt Masur.** Philips Silver Line 432 282-2PSL3 — ③ 3h 34m ADD 7/91 £

Violin Concerto. Scottish Fantasy. **Lalo.** *Symphonie espagnole, Op. 21.* **Anne Akiko Meyers** (vn); **Royal Philharmonic Orchestra/Jesús López-Cobos.** RCA Victor Red Seal RD60942 — 1h DDD 9/92

Bruch. Kol Nidrei, Op. 47. Canzone, Op. 55. Adagio on Celtic Themes, Op. 56. Ave Maria, Op. 61.
Bloch. Schelomo. **Ofra Harnoy** (vc); **London Philharmonic Orchestra/Sir Charles Mackerras.** RCA Victor Red Seal RD60757.

58m DDD 12/91

Bloch's passionate, improvisatory rhapsody, *Schelomo,* with its hebraic intensity, certainly makes a powerful impression. Harnoy's performance is outstanding and Mackerras matches her imaginative intensity with a central climax of great fervour; throughout, the changing moods and colours are imaginatively caught by soloist and orchestra alike. Bruch's *Kol Nidrei* also has a noble, Hebrew theme (though Bruch was not Jewish) and its sombre, ruminative character brings an equally sympathetic response from both soloist and orchestra. The mood lightens in the *Adagio on Celtic Themes*, a work as tuneful as it is charming, yet Mackerras's strong introduction again emphasizes his commitment to what proves a real musical partnership. Bruch's *Ave Maria* is less simply melismatic than more familiar settings, and there is finespun embroidery from the soloist before the tender reprise of the tune. Very good, expansive recording, with the acoustics providing spaciousness and breadth for these warm yet often poignant melodies.

Further listening ...

Clarinet and Viola Concerto in E minor, Op. 88[a]. *Coupled with* **Crusell.** Introduction, Theme and Variations on a Swedish air, Op. 12[b]; ***Mendelssohn.*** Two Concert Pieces[c] — F major, Op. 113; D minor, Op. 114. [abc]**Thea King** (cl); [a]**Nobuko Imai** (va); [c]**Georgina Dobrée** (basset-hn); **London Symphony Orchestra/Alun Francis.** Hyperion CDA66022 (1/88).

Symphonies — No. 1 in E flat major, Op. 28; No. 2 in F minor, Op. 36. No. 3 in E major, Op. 51. Swedish Dances, Op. 63. **Leipzig Gewandhaus Orchestra/Kurt Masur.** Philips 420 932-2PH2 (3/89).

Anton Bruckner

Austrian 1824-1896

Bruckner. SYMPHONIES. **Berlin Philharmonic Orchestra/Herbert von Karajan.** DG Karajan Symphony Edition 429 648-2GSE9. Recorded 1974-1981.

No. 1 in C minor (Linz version)[b]; No. 2 in C minor (ed. Nowak[b]. Both 2740 264, 6/82); No. 3 in D minor (1889 version, ed. Nowak[b]. 2532 007, 7/81); No. 4 in E flat major, "Romantic"[a] (2530 674, 10/76); No. 5 in B flat major[a] (2702 101, 10/78); No. 6 in A major[a] (2531 295, 11/80); No. 7 in E major[a] (2707 102, 4/78); No. 8 in C minor (ed. Haas[a]. 2707 085, 5/76); No. 9 in D minor[a] (2530 828, 6/77).

⑨ 8h 40m ADD/DDD 3/91 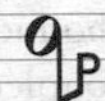

It is often said that the essence of good Bruckner conducting is a firm grasp of structure. In fact that's only a half-truth. Of course one must understand how Bruckner's massive statements and counterstatements are fused together, but a performance that was nothing but architecture would be a pretty depressing experience. Karajan's understanding of the slow but powerful currents that flow beneath the surfaces of symphonies like the Fifth or Nos. 7-9 has never been bettered, but at the same time he shows how much more there is to be reckoned with: strong emotions, a deep poetic sensitivity (a Bruckner symphony can evoke landscapes as vividly as Mahler or Vaughan Williams) and a gift for singing melody that at times rivals even Schubert. It hardly needs saying that there's no such thing as a perfect record cycle, and this collection of the numbered Bruckner symphonies (unfortunately Karajan never recorded "No. 0") has its weaknesses. The early First and Second Symphonies can be a little heavy-footed and, as with so many Bruckner sets, there's a suspicion that more time might have been spent getting to know the fine but elusive Sixth — and there's an irritating throwback to the days of corrupt Bruckner editions in the first big crescendo of the Fourth Symphony (high swooping violins — nasty!) — but none of these performances is without its major insights, and in the best of them — particularly Nos. 3, 5, 7, 8 and 9 — those who haven't stopped their ears to Karajan will find that whatever else he may have been, there was a side to him that could only be described as 'visionary'. As for the recordings: climaxes can sound a touch overblown in some of the earlier symphonies, but on the whole the image is well-focused and atmospheric. A valuable set, and a landmark in the history of Bruckner recording.

Additional recommendations ...

Nos. 1, 4 and 7-9 — **Berlin Philharmonic Orchestra;** *Nos. 2, 3, 5 and 6* — **Bavarian Radio Symphony Orchestra/Eugen Jochum.** DG 429 079-2GX9 — ⑨ 9h 12m ADD 2/90

Nos. 1-9. **Cologne Radio Symphony Orchestra/Günter Wand.** Deutsche Harmonia Mundi GD60075 — ⑩ 9h 19m ADD/DDD 2/90

Bruckner. Symphony No. 0 in D minor, "Die Nullte" (rev. 1869). Overture in G minor. **Berlin Radio Symphony Orchestra/Riccardo Chailly.** Decca 421 593-2DH.

58m DDD 1/90

It should be remembered that Bruckner wrote all his symphonies (including this one) after he was 40, indeed the bulk of *Die Nullte* that we encounter here was written after his official No. 1, and can be regarded as the progenitor of much that was to come in Bruckner's symphonic output: many of the motives can be found in later symphonies, the obvious example being the opening ostinato which later provided the underlay to the opening of the Third Symphony. Chailly's thoroughly convincing performance takes a fairly spacious view of the work, with much emphasis on nobility, poise and dynamic shaping. And if at times he comes dangerously close to sentimentality in the Andante, in the end it is his feeling of serenity and warmth that win us over. This is superbly contrasted with the exuberance and urgency that he conveys in the dance-like Scherzo. At times the strings have a tendency to sound a little thin in the trio section, but this is more than compensated for in the lyrical and graceful playing of the Berlin RSO. The Overture in G minor, dating from 1862, makes a welcome filler and receives a similarly warm and persuasive performance. The recording is warm and well balanced.

Bruckner. Symphony No. 1 in C minor (1866 version)[a]. Te Deum[b]. [a]**Jessye Norman** (sop); [b]**Yvonne Minton** (mez); [b]**David Rendall** (ten); [b]**Samuel Ramey** (bass); **Chicago Symphony** [b]**Chorus and Orchestra/Daniel Barenboim.** DG Galleria 435 068-2GGA.

Text and translation included. Item marked [a] from 2740 253 (10/81), [b] 2741 007 (10/81). Recorded 1980-1981.

lh 10m DDD 12/91 £ 9P

A Schubertian grace informs the first part of Bruckner's mighty First Symphony and this quality abounds in Barenboim's outstanding performance. His attention to detail and rhythmic accuracy, coupled with the Chicago Symphony Orchestra at their most brilliant and incisive, produces a fiery account of the work. Barenboim may lack the sweep and architectural control of Karajan (listed below) but he brings a compensating wit and enthusiasm to the score — his view of the delightful scherzo, for example, is deft and appropriately capricious. The rousing finale rips along as Barenboim and his orchestra pile on the power. To further enhance this mid-price recording, Barenboim's urgent, heroic and gloriously spontaneous version of the *Te Deum* is the substantial coupling. The superb diction, dynamic discipline and overall alertness of the Chicago Symphony Chorus brings refreshing vigour to this potentially turgid work. The soloists make a superb team, blending in with the glittering array of choral and orchestral colours. The 1981 recordings shine with rich, full-bodied balance. All in all, this is a Brucknerian bargain not to be missed.

NEW REVIEW

Bruckner. Symphony No. 3 in D minor (1889 version). **Vienna Philharmonic Orchestra/Karl Böhm.** Decca Ovation 425 032-2DM. From SXL6505 (10/71). Recorded in 1970.

57m ADD 3/93 

Karl Böhm's impressive account of Bruckner's Third Symphony re-emerges with startling clarity and body on this mid-price Ovation CD. Sonically speaking, of course, this was a peak period for the Decca technicians, and the exemplary focus and spectacular dynamic range of this Sofiensaal production really does take the breath away. As on Böhm's indispensable companion CD of the *Romantic* (see below), the VPO respond splendidly throughout (Bruckner's rustic trio section is inimitably Viennese in its earthy gait), though, perhaps inevitably, there isn't quite the same degree of electricity or concentration on show here that this conductor was later to achieve in that legendary traversal of the Fourth. At the price, though, this is undoubtedly worth investigating and must now be considered one of the front-runners. Incidentally, DG could do us all a great favour and transfer to the Privilege label Eugen Jochum's superb 1967 Munich account of this wonderful work (at present only available as part of a 9-CD set, details of which are listed above) — now, that really *would* sweep the board!

Additional recommendations ...
(1889 version). **Berlin Philharmonic Orchestra/Herbert von Karajan.** DG 413 362-2GH — 54m DDD 8/84 9S B
(1877 version). **Vienna Philharmonic Orchestra/Bernard Haitink.** Philips 422 411-2PH — lh 2m DDD 3/91 9S B

NEW REVIEW

Bruckner. Symphony No. 4 in E flat major, "Romantic" (1888 version). **Vienna Philharmonic Orchestra/Karl Böhm.** Decca Ovation 425 036-2DM. From 6BB171/2 (10/74). Recorded in 1973.

lh 8m ADD 3/93 9P 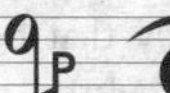

Did Karl Böhm ever make a finer disc? Here's a welcome mid-price resuscitation for this distinguished Bruckner *Romantic* set down in 1973. With glorious VPO playing (such fabulous, golden-toned horns — try the end of the first movement or the thrilling 'Hunting' *Scherzo*) and superbly ripe, effortlessly transparent engineering (Vienna's Sofiensaal, one of Decca's favourite haunts, was the recording location), Böhm's magnificently lucid conception could not have been better served than here. Imposing yet affectionate, he conveys the awesome mystery and architectural splendour of Bruckner's score with unerring mastery; even more strikingly, there's a totally disarming spontaneity and real sense of occasion about the finished article which was by no means always the case with this fine conductor in the recording studio. Make no mistake, this is a great and uplifting performance, and a mandatory acquisition for all Brucknerians.

Additional recommendations ...
(1874 version). **Staatskapelle Dresden/Herbert Blomstedt.** Denon C37-7126 — ⁂ 1h 7m DDD 2/85 Ⓑ
(1874 version) **Berlin Philharmonic Orchestra/Eugen Jochum.** DG Privilege 427 200-2GR — ⁂ 1h 5m ADD 9/89 £ 𝄢P Ⓑ
(1874 version). **Frankfurt Radio Symphony Orchestra/Eliahu Inbal.** Teldec Digital Experience 9031 77597-2 — ⁂ 1h 8m DDD 12/92 𝄢P Ⓑ
(1888 version). **Bavarian Radio Symphony Orchestra/Rafael Kubelík.** CBS CD46505 — 𝄢P Ⓑ
(1888 version). **Philharmonia Orchestra/Otto Klemperer.** EMI Studio CDM7 69127-2 — ⁂ 1h 1m ADD 12/88 𝄢P Ⓑ

Bruckner. Symphonies — No. 5 in B flat major (orig. version)[b]; No. 1 in C minor (1866 version)[a]. **Berlin Philharmonic Orchestra/Herbert von Karajan.** DG 415 985-2GH2. Item marked [a] from 2740 264 (6/82), [b] 2702 101 (10/78).

⁂ ② 2h 12m ADD/DDD 6/87 𝄢P

By the time Bruckner completed the Fifth Symphony, his style had become more complex and he allowed his ideas to develop at considerable length. This monumental work is handled superbly by Karajan. He has an unerring grasp of the work's structure, so that it seems to flow naturally and inevitably from beginning to end. The BPO's playing is superlative, and the 1977 analogue recording is rather better than that of the First Symphony. This work is a fully mature example of Bruckner's symphonic style. The very start, with its sturdy onward treading March, broken into by a chirpy little theme, was a startling innovation and the work contains other now familiar Brucknerian trademarks. Karajan projects it in a vital, ebullient fashion with a fine control of the music's ebb and flow.

Additional recommendations ...
No. 5. Te Deum[a]. [a]**Karita Mattila** (sop); [a]**Susanne Mentzer** (mez); [a]**Vinson Cole** (ten); [a]**Robert Holl** (bass); [a]**Bavarian Radio Chorus; Vienna Philharmonic Orchestra/Bernard Haitink.** Philips 422 342-2PH2 — ⁂ ② 1h 40m DDD 11/89 𝄢P 𝄢S
No. 5. **Berlin Philharmonic Orchestra/Daniel Barenboim.** Teldec 9031-73271-2 — ⁂ 1h 12m DDD 3/93 𝄢P 𝄢S

Bruckner (ed. Haas). Symphony No. 6 in A major. **New Philharmonia Orchestra/Otto Klemperer.** EMI Studio CDM7 63351-2. From Columbia SAX2582 (9/65). Recorded in 1964.

⁂ 55m ADD 3/90 𝄢P

No Brucknerian will want to be without Klemperer's legendary performance, indeed it has long been regarded as perhaps the finest recorded interpretation of this symphony. Part of Klemperer's success lies in his unerring ability to project the symphony's architectural and organic content through Bruckner's ever changing terrain. His vigorous and resolute approach is apparent from the outset, where the opening ostinato string figure, crisp and rhythmically assured, tell us that this is no routine performance. His handling of Bruckner's frequent *fortissimo* 'blaze ups' is always dramatic, exhilarating and sonorous, whilst never destroying the beautifully clear and lucid textures he achieves throughout the symphony. The adagio is one of Bruckner's most sublime creations. Klemperer's choice of tempo may seem fast here, but is entirely justified by the resulting sense of momentum and forward drive: and you will be hard pressed to find a better rendering of the tender and expansive second theme as it burgeons out of the sombre introduction. The Scherzo, with its incessant bass and cello ostinato tread is given a subtle and evocative reading, building the tension superbly before resolving into the haunting and mysterious trio section with its Tristanesque horn calls. The recording, made in the Kingsway Hall in 1964, is excellent.

Additional recommendation ...
Berlin Philharmonic Orchestra/Herbert von Karajan. DG 419 194-2GH — 58m ADD 4/87
North German Radio Symphony Orchestra/Günter Wand. RCA Victor Red Seal RD60061 — 55m DDD 2/91

Bruckner. Symphony No. 7. **Staatskapelle Dresden/Herbert Blomstedt.** Denon C37-7286. Recorded in 1980.

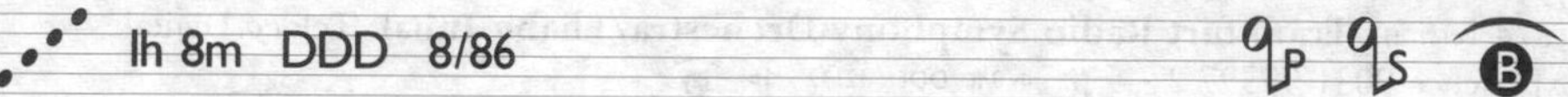

Bruckner's gloriously long-breathed Seventh Symphony is, of all his works, the one most indebted to the music of Wagner. Although the Third was dedicated to this composer, it is the Seventh which is closer in spirit and tonal colour to that of Wagner. Bruckner worked on this symphony for some two years, and after a play-through on two pianos in Vienna, it received its first performance in Leipzig late in 1884 under the baton of the great Artur Nikisch. The symphony is constructed in the usual four movements, the *Adagio* second movement being the powerful core of the work — a long, richly-scored meditation that carries solemn, even funereal overtones. Herbert Blomstedt's performance of this great work is glorious — well judged, beautifully played and with just the right blend of eloquence and tension. The recording is excellent.

Additional recommendations ...
Berlin Philharmonic Orchestra/Herbert von Karajan. EMI Studio CDM7 69923-2 — lh 8m ADD 6/89
Vienna Philharmonic Orchestra/Herbert von Karajan. DG 429 226-2GH — lh 6m DDD 5/90
Cleveland Orchestra/Christoph von Dohnányi. Decca 430 841-2DH — lh 4m DDD 10/92

Key to Symbols

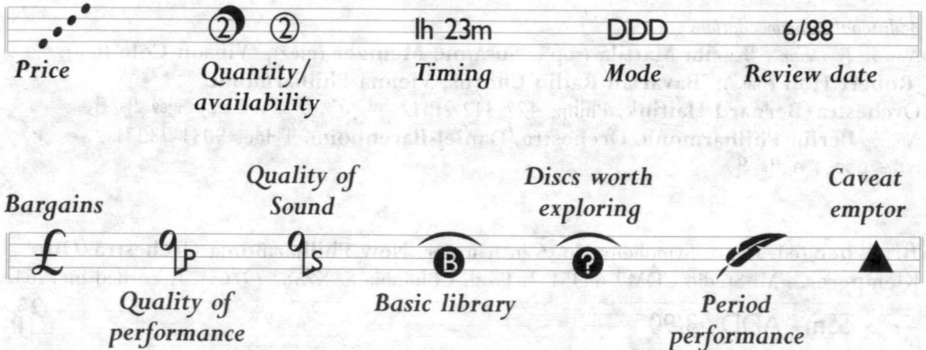

Bruckner. Symphony No. 8 in C minor. **Vienna Philharmonic Orchestra/Herbert von Karajan.** DG 427 611-2GH2. Recorded in 1988.

As if by some strange act of providence, great conductors have often been remembered by the immediate posthumous release of some fine and representative recording. With Karajan it is the Eighth Symphony of Bruckner, perhaps the symphony he loved and revered above all others. It is the sense of the music being in the hearts and minds and collective unconscious of Karajan and every one of the 100 and more players of the Vienna Philharmonic that gives this performances its particular charisma and appeal. It is a wonderful reading, every bit as authoritative as its many predecessors and every bit as well played but somehow more profound, more humane, more lovable if that is a permissible attribute of an interpretation of this Everest among symphonies. The end of the work, always astonishing and uplifting, is especially fine here and very moving. Fortunately, it has been recorded with plenty of weight and space and warmth and clarity, with the additional benefit of the added vibrancy of the Viennese playing. The sessions were obviously sufficiently happy for there to shine through moments of spontaneous power and eloquence that were commonplace in the concert hall in Karajan's later years, but which recordings can't always be relied upon to catch.

Additional recommendations ...
No. 8. **Vienna Philharmonic Orchestra/Carlo Maria Giulini.** DG 415 124-2GH2 — ② DDD 7/85
No. 8. ***Wagner.*** *Siegfried Idyll.* **Royal Concertgebouw Orchestra/Bernard Haitink.** Philips 412 465-2PH2 — ② 1h 44m DDD 7/86

Bruckner. Symphony No. 9 in D minor. **Berlin Philharmonic Orchestra/Herbert von Karajan.** DG 419 083-2GH. From 2530 828 (6/77). Recorded in 1976.

1h 2m ADD 9/86 

Karajan's 1976 recording has long been something of a classic, capturing the conductor and the Berlin Philharmonic on top form. From the opening of the titanic first movement to the final grinding dissonance of the lofty *Adagio* Karajan's control of phrase lengths, tempo and rhythmic swing are gloriously apparent. Compared with many more recent accounts of this solemn work, Karajan's beautifully recorded performance seems refreshingly urgent, cohesive and properly threatening. Exceptionally vivid, it was sometimes difficult to tame on LP, but the CD version gives unalloyed pleasure.

Additional recommendations ...
Cleveland Orchestra/Christoph von Dohnányi. Decca 425 405-2DH — 58m DDD 6/89
Vienna Philharmonic Orchestra/Carlo Maria Giulini. DG 427 345-2GH — 1h 8m DDD 8/89
Berlin Philharmonic Orchestra/Daniel Barenboim. Teldec 9031 72140-2 — 1h 3m DDD 10/91
Vienna Philharmonic Orchestra/Herbert von Karajan. DG 435 326-2GWP — ADD 2/92

Bruckner. CHORAL WORKS. **Corydon Singers; English Chamber Orchestra Wind Ensemble/Matthew Best.** Hyperion CDA66177. Texts and translations included. From A66177 (2/86).
Mass No. 2 in E minor. Libera me in F minor (Colin Sheen, Roger Brenner, Philip Brown, tbns). Aequali for three trombones, Nos. 1 and 2 (Sheen, Brenner, Brown).

53m DDD 9/86 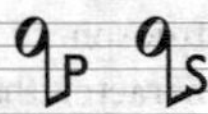

Bruckner's E minor Mass, unlike its two companions in D minor and F minor, employs a wind band as its instrumental base. By dispensing with the orchestra and concentrating purely on expression through human breath control Bruckner achieved a purity and translucence of texture that relate it most closely to the writing of Palestrina. The clarity of the writing and the easy unfolding of long contrapuntal lines gives the work a grandeur and feeling of architectural stability more often encountered in mightier structures. The rich accompaniment of the wind instruments creates a powerful foundation to the spaciously conceived vocal parts. The Mass is prefaced with the *Aequali* for three trombones which date from 1847. They have a stately and somewhat sombre quality ideally suited to the work they frame, the motet, *Libera me*. This is a gentle and beautifully wrought piece using an accompaniment of three trombones, cello, double-bass and organ. The performances are extremely good, matched by a recording of the kind at which Hyperion excel.

Bruckner. SACRED CHORAL WORKS. **Bavarian Radio [a]Chorus and [b]Symphony Orchestra; [c]Chorus of the Deutsche Oper, Berlin; [c]Berlin Philharmonic**

Orchestra/Eugen Jochum. DG 423 127-2GX4. Texts and translations included. Recorded 1963-72.

Masses[ab] — No. 1 in D minor (with Edith Mathis, sop; Marga Schiml, contr; Wieslaw Ochman, ten; Karl Ridderbusch, bass; Elmar Schloter, org. From 2720 054, 3/73); No. 2 in E minor (2720 054, 3/73); No. 3 in F minor (Maria Stader, sop; Claudia Hellmann, contr; Ernst Haefliger, ten; Kim Borg, bass; Anton Nowakowski, org. SLPM138829, 3/63). Te Deum[c] (Stader; Sieglinde Wagner, contr; Haefliger; Peter Lagger, bass; Wolfgang Meyer, org. SLPM139117/18, 5/66). Psalm 150[c] (Stader. SLPM139399, 5/69). Motets[a] — Virga Jesse; Ave Maria; Locus iste; Tota pulchra es (Richard Holm, ten; Nowakowski); Ecce sacerdos magnus (Ludwig Laberer, Josef Hahn, Alfons Hartenstein, tbns; Hedwig Bilgram, org. All from SLPM139135, 5/67); Os justi; Christus factus est; Vexilla regis (SLPM139138, 5/69); Affrentur regi (Laberer, Hahn, Hartenstein); Pange lingua (both from 2720 054).

④ 3h 47m ADD 9/88

Bruckner's first notable composition was a Requiem in D minor and is important because it contains fingerprints of Bruckner's symphonic style, as does the Mass No. 3 in F minor. But undoubtedly the *Te Deum* is Bruckner's greatest choral work, a mighty affirmation of faith in C major but with interludes of tenderness and warmth in which a solo violin is used expressively. The performances on this disc are a notable tribute to the art of the conductor Eugen Jochum and were made between 1963 and 1972. They have been transferred to CD with total success and the singing of the respective choirs is thrilling. Maria Stader and Kim Borg are the best of the soloists in the F minor Mass, with Stader also outstanding in the *Te Deum.* The discs are invaluable, too, for containing 10 short motets, most of which will be unfamiliar to many listeners. The seraphic *Ave Maria* and a particularly touching *Pange lingua* are typical of the quality of music and performance enshrined here.

Bruckner. SACRED CHORAL WORKS. [a]**Anne-Marie Owens** (mez); [b]**City of Birmingham Symphony Chorus;** [c]**Birmingham Symphony Orchestra Wind Ensemble/**[d]**Simon Halsey.** Conifer CDCF192. Texts and translations included.

Mass No. 2 in E minor[bcd]. Afferentur regi[bcd]. Ave Maria (1861)[bd]. Ave Maria (1882, with Peter King, org)[a]. Ecce sacerdos magnus[bcd]. Locus iste[bd]. Aequali for three trombones, No. 1 and 2[c].

1h 4m DDD 1/91 

Bruckner's religious works require for their full realization an elusive combination of classical restraint and romantic fervour. In this excellent recording by the City of Birmingham Symphony Chorus and Wind Ensemble this style is captured perfectly. Under conductor Simon Halsey the chorus's finely tuned singing and rich tone is ideally suited both to the E minor Mass of 1866 and the four brief but intense motets which provide an excellent makeweight. The CBSO Wind Ensemble's accompaniment in the Mass, and solo playing in the two *Aequali* for three trombones, is well-balanced and sonorous, qualities which are also shared by Conifer's atmospheric recorded sound. These choral works display a more personal side to Bruckner's character than the mighty symphonies, and so help to round out in a unique way the musical portrait of this great composer. Thus this finely prepared CD, completed by the first-ever recording of the *Ave Maria,* is an essential complement to the more well-known, and more public, works.

NEW REVIEW

Bruckner. Mass No. 3 in F minor. Psalm 150 in C major. **Juliet Booth** (sop); **Jean Rigby** (mez); **John Mark Ainsley** (ten); **Gwynne Howell** (bass); **Corydon Singers and Orchestra/Matthew Best.** Hyperion CDA66599. Texts and translations included. Recorded in 1992.

1h 8m DDD 3/93 

Bruckner, the devout Catholic who poured his very soul into his devotional, liturgical choral pieces often seems a very different being from Bruckner, the composer of gargantuan, almost self-indulgent symphonies rich in luscious orchestral colour and sensuous harmony. Where the two combine the result can be something almost other-worldly. The F minor Mass is certainly his finest choral work, if not the finest music he ever created. The intensity of religious feeling is heightened rather than diminished by the sumptuous orchestral support, and the soaring melodies and opulent harmonies are somehow purified and enriched by the devotional character of these familiar texts. Here is a performance which by understating the music's abundant richness gives tremendous point to the inner conviction of Bruckner's faith. This orchestra, brought together for this recording but sounding as if they have been playing this music all their days, plays with commendable discretion balancing admirably with a relatively small choral body. As with everything the Corydon Singers and Matthew Best turn their hands to, it is an impeccable performance, infused with real artistry and sensitive musicianship. Enhanced by the glorious solo voices from a high-powered team this is a CD of rare depth and conviction.

Nicolaus Bruhns

German 1665-1697

Suggested listening ...

Cantatas. Organ Works — Preludes and Fugues: No. 1 in E minor; No. 2 in E minor; G major; G minor. Nun komm der Heiden Heiland. **Greta de Reyghere, Jill Feldman** (sops); **James Bowman** (alto); **Guy de Mey, Ian Honeyman** (tens); **Max van Egmond** (bass); **Bernard Foccroulle** (org); **Ricercar Consort.** Ricercar RIC048035/7 (1/90).

Antoine Brumel

French c.1460-c.1515

NEW REVIEW

Brumel. Missa “Et ecce terrae motus”. Lamentations. Magnificat Secundi toni. **The Tallis Scholars/Peter Phillips.** Gimell CDGIM026. Texts and translations included.

lh 13m DDD 9/92

Antoine Brumel was one of the French members of the great Franco-Flemish school of composers which flourished during the fifteenth and sixteenth centuries. His 12-part *Earthquake Mass* is one of the most glorious, if little-known products of this school — a work of colossal power whose rhythmic complexities and virtuoso vocal writing are exceptionally demanding. It is a great tribute to the excellent Tallis Scholars and their fine conductor Peter Phillips that their performance of this masterpiece leaves nothing to be desired. The choir enters fully into the spirit of this visionary work — balancing vocal ecstasy with musical discipline in equal parts. The recording was made in the warm but clear acoustic of the parish church of Salle in Norfolk, an ideal setting for music of this period. The most sympathetic recorded sound captures perfectly the atmosphere of this location. Two more restrained works by Brumel, a set of *Lamentations* and a *Magnificat*, complete a disc of great interest. The comparison of the *Earthquake Mass* with another work of great complexity, Thomas Tallis's 40-part motet *Spem in alium*, is unavoidable. For those who enjoy the grandeur of such choral music performed in a completely authentic style this disc can be strongly recommended.

NEW REVIEW

Brumel. Missa “Et ecce terrae motus”. Dies irae. **Huelgas Ensemble/Paul van Nevel.** Sony Classical Vivarte SK46348. Texts and translations included. Recorded in 1990.

lh 7m DDD 5/91

The Huelgas Ensemble's recording of Brumel's *Earthquake* Mass was the first to introduce it to the CD catalogue, and it has a number of points of interest. The performance of the group, under the expert guidance of Paul van Nevel, is extremely good. It manages the extended counterpoint of Brumel's complex vocal writing with ease, and avoids the dangers of monotony setting in as a result of Brumel's stately, slow-moving harmonies. The actual tone produced by the ensemble seems highly authentic: it has a robust, reedy quality which is suitably continental, and the relatively close miking of the recording carries the listener into the heart of the performance. On stylistic grounds alone this reading has much to commend it. Unlike the other very different performance in the catalogue from The Tallis Scholars (see above), Paul van Nevel makes good the absence of the concluding *Agnus Dei* in the only surviving manuscript of the work (commissioned by Lassus for a performance some 50 years after Brumel's death) with the inclusion of a six part section from a contemporaneous Danish manuscript, and various canonic imitations. This substitution works well, and brings the performance as a whole to a powerful close. Van Nevel concludes the disc with the *Dies irae* from Brumel's Requiem Mass: an eloquent, if sombre, reading notable for the powerful effect made by a well-balanced accompaniment of brass instruments.

Gavin Bryars

British 1943-

Suggested listening ...

Prologue. String Quartet No. 1, "Between the National and the Bristol". First Viennese Dance. Epilogue. **Pascal Pongy** (hn); **Charles Fullbrook, Gavin Bryars** (perc); **Arditti Quartet.** ECM New Series 8829 484-2 (3/87).

Geoffrey Burgon

British 1941-

Suggested listening ...

Magnificat. Nunc dimittis. Two hymns to Mary. This world from. But have been found again. Short Mass. At the round earth's imagined corners. A prayer to the Trinity. Laudate Dominum. **Michael Laird** (tpt); **Jeremy Suter** (org); **Chichester Cathedral Choir/Alan Thurlow.** Hyperion CDA66123 (9/84).

Television Scores — Brideshead Revisited; Testament of Youth; Bleak House; Tinker, Tailor, Soldier, Spy[a]; The Chronicles of Narnia. [a]**Lesley Garrett** (sop); **Philharmonia Orchestra/Geoffrey Burgon.** Silva Screen FILMCD117 (5/93).

Ferruccio Busoni

Italian/German 1866-1924

Busoni. Piano Concerto, Op. 39. **Peter Donohoe** (pf); men's voices of the **BBC Singers; BBC Symphony Orchestra/Mark Elder.** EMI CDC7 49996-2. Recorded live in 1988.

1h 14m DDD 1/91 

Busoni's must be the longest piano concerto every written. Because of its length and its unusual proportions it can easily seem sprawling. Busoni gave a clue to avoiding this impression by describing the concerto in architectural terms: the central movement as a huge nave or dome, buttressed by the introduction and finale, with the scherzos envisaged as 'scenes from life', played out in the open air between the three great buildings. The sense of adventure and discovery inherent in this work is nowhere better realized than in the mould-breaking 1988 Proms reading from Donohoe and Elder. Their devotion to the work is evident in every bar, and the concentration that they apply to it does not waver from start to finish: the enrapt attention of the audience bears eloquent testament to this. The price you pay for this degree of integrity, typical of live performance, is relatively slight — balance is not always ideal, especially with the mens' voices in the final movement, and the orchestral sound has a certain fullness that a studio would probably have mitigated. But be warned: this is not a performance to be sampled — it works wonderfully as a whole and once begun it seems impossible not to see it through to the end.

Additional recommendations ...

Piano Concerto. **Volker Banfield** (pf); **Bavarian Radio Chorus; Bavarian Radio Symphony Orchestra/Lutz Herbig.** CPO CPO999 017-2 — lh 13m AAD 7/89

Piano Concerto. **Garrick Ohlsson** (pf); Men's voices of the **Cleveland Orchestra Chorus; Cleveland Symphony Orchestra/Christoph von Dohnányi.** Telarc CD80207 — lh 12m DDD 4/90

Busoni. Fantasia contrappuntistica (1910)[a]. Fantasia nach J. S. Bach (1909)[a]. Toccata[b]. **John Ogdon** (pf). Continuum CCD1006. Items marked [a] from Altarus AIR-2-9074 (10/88), [b] new to UK.

lh AAD 7/89 

Busoni's *Fantasia contrappuntistica* is of legendary difficulty, density and length and pianists seem very reluctant to learn it. Ogdon plays it with consummate virtuosity, clarity and sustained concentration, and alongside the technical assurance there is a firm intellectual grasp of Busoni's prodigious structure and a lofty eloquence in expressing his faith. It is a formidable feat of musicianship as well as pianism. The two other pieces are more personal; many may find them even more moving. The *Fantasia nach J.S. Bach* is freer in structure than the *Fantasia contrappuntistica* and with its dedication to his father's memory it is as though Busoni has chosen particularly beloved and appropriate pages for his tribute, adding his own meditations on them. The very late *Toccata* is a resurgence of the Faustian vein that runs throughout Busoni's work, but now dark and pessimistic. The three works add up to a sort of triple self-portrait and Ogdon characterizes them finely. Busoni's piano-writing demands a huge range of sonority as well as endurance and sheer dexterity; in these performances (and this superb recording) Busoni's piano is rendered full-size.

Further listening ...

Violin Concerto in D major, Op. 35*a*[a]. Violin Sonata No. 2 in E minor, Op. 36*a*[b]. [ab]**Joseph Szigeti** (vn); [b]**Mieczyslaw Horszowski** (pf); [a]**Little Orchestra Society/Thomas Scherman.** Sony Classical mono SK52537 (5/93).

Violin Sonatas — No. 1 in E minor, Op. 29; No. 2 in E minor, Op. 36*a*. **Lydia Mordkovitch** (vn); **Victoria Postnikova** (pf). Chandos CHAN8868.

DOKTOR FAUST. **Soloists; Bavarian Radio Chorus and Symphony Orchestra/Ferdinand Leitner.** DG 20th Century Classics 427 413-2GC3 (8/89).

George Butterworth

British 1885-1916

Suggested listening ...

The Banks of Green Willow. *Coupled with* ***Bantock.*** The Pierrot of the Minute — comedy overture; ***Bridge.*** Suite for strings, H93. Summer. There is a willow Grows Aslant a Brook, H174. **Bournemouth Sinfonietta/Norman Del Mar.** Chandos CHAN8373 (8/85).

Dietrich Buxtehude

Danish 1637-1707

Buxtehude. ORGAN WORKS. **Ton Koopman.** Novalis 150 048-2. Played on the Arp-Schnitger organ of St Ludgeri's, Norden.
Prelude and Ciacona in C major, BuxWV137. Eine feste Burg ist unser Gott, BuxWV184. Passacaglia in D minor, BuxWV161. Nun komm, der Heiden Heiland, BuxWV211. In dulci jubilo, BuxWV197. Fuga in C major, BuxWV174. Puer natus in Bethlehem, BuxWV217. Prelude in D major, BuxWV139. Nun lob, mein Seel, den Herren, BuxWV212. Prelude in G minor, BuxWV163. Wie schön leuchtet der Moregenstern, BuxWV223. Prelude in G minor, BuxWV149.

57m DDD 6/90 

A most welcome by-product of the CD revolution has been the generous exposure given to those composers whose music, if not their names, has been familiar only to those with specialized interest. For readers of potted histories of music Buxtehude will be known primarily as the man whose organ playing was considered sufficiently impressive for the young J.S. Bach to walk 400 miles to hear. But as for his music, even organists are largely unaware of the vast amount he wrote for that instrument. Yet there are those who would claim that, had it not been for the towering genius of Bach, Buxtehude would today be considered as one of the 'great' composers of the baroque age. Those of an inquisitive disposition who would like a representative cross-section of Buxtehude's organ music on a single disc will find this one ideal. From the big, flamboyant, virtuoso works (such as the Prelude in G minor) to the delightful miniatures which had a particularly strong influence on the young Bach (including a frivolous Gigue Fugue) here is Buxtehude on top form. Ton Koopman gives them all sturdy, no-nonsense performances on a full-blooded, earthy instrument dating from Buxtehude's time, and the recording has great presence.

Further listening ...

Trio Sonatas — C major, BuxWV266; G major, BuxWV271; B flat major, BuxWV273. *Coupled with* ***Pachelbel.*** Suite in G major. Musicalische Ergotzung — Suite No. 4 in E minor. Aria con variazoni in A major. Canon and Gigue in D major. **Cologne Musica Antiqua/Reinhard Goebel.** Archiv Produktion Galleria 427 118-2AGA (6/89).

Organ Works — Ach Gott und Herr, BuxWV177. Ach Herr mich armen Sünder, BuxWV178. Canzona in C major, BuxWV166. Canzonetta in C major, BuxWV167. Canzonetta in D minor, BuxWV168. Canzonetta in E minor, BuxWV168. Ciacona in C minor, BuxWV159. Jesus Christus, unser Heiland, BuxWV198. Komm, heiliiger Geist, Herre Gott, BuxWV199. Komm heiliger Geist, Herre Gott, BuxWV200. Prelude and Fugue in F major, BuxWV144. Prelude and Fugue in F major, BuxWV145. Prelude and Fugue in F sharp minor, BuxWV146. Prelude and Fugue in G minor, BuxWV150. Te Deum laudamus, Phrygian, BuxWV218. **Michel Chapuis** (org). Auvidis Valois V4431 (12/89).

Cantatas — Herr, ich lasse dich nicht, BuxWV36. Wo ist doch mei Freund geblieben, "Dialogus inter Christum et fidelium animam", BuxWV111. Nichts soll uns scheiden, BuxWV77. Ich halte es dafür, BuxWV48. Ich suchte des Nachtes, BuxWV50. Das neugeborne Kinderleine, BuxWV13. **Greta de Reyghere, Agnès Mellon** (sops); **Henri Ledroit** (alto); **Guy de Mey** (ten); **Max van Egmond** (bass); **Ricercar Consort.** Ricercar RIC041016 (1/90).

William Byrd

British 1543-1623

Byrd. MASSES AND MOTETS. **The Tallis Scholars/Peter Phillips.** Gimell CDGIM345. From BYRD345 (5/84).

Mass for five voices. Mass for four voices. Mass for three voices. Motet — Ave verum corpus a 4.

1h 7m DDD 3/86

Byrd was a fervently committed Roman Catholic and he helped enormously to enrich the music of the English Church. His Mass settings were made for the many recusant Catholic worshippers who held services in private. They were published between 1593 and 1595 and are creations of great feeling. The contrapuntal writing has a much closer texture and fibre than the Masses of Palestrina and there is an austerity and rigour that is allowed to blossom and expand with the text. The beautifully restrained and mellow recording, made in Merton College Chapel, Oxford, fully captures the measure of the music and restores the awe and mystery of music that familiarity has sometimes dimmed.

Additional recommendations ...
Masses. **The Hilliard Ensemble/Paul Hillier.** EMI Reflexe CDM7 63441-2 — 1h 17m DDD 5/85
Masses. **Winchester Cathedral Choir/David Hill.** Argo 430 164-2ZH — 1h 6m DDD 12/90
Mass for five voices. Mass Propers for the Feast of All Saints. Motets. **Christ Church Cathedral Choir, Oxford/Stephen Darlington** Nimbus NI5237 — 52m DDD 12/90

Byrd. GRADUALIA — THE MARIAN MASSES. **William Byrd Choir/Gavin Turner.** Hyperion CDA66451. Texts and translations included. Recorded in 1990.
Mass Propers — Feasts of the Purification of the BVM, the Nativity of the BVM, the Annunciation of the BVM, the Assumption of the BVM; Votive Masses of the BVM: Advent, Christmas to the Purification, Purification to Easter, Easter to Pentecost and Pentecost to Advent.

1h 20m DDD 11/91 

For sheer productivity and versatility William Byrd is unrivalled among Tudor composers, and much of his impressive output is still poorly represented in the catalogue. This useful recording explores one of those shadowy corners: *Gradualia*, the cycle of motets Byrd composed for English Roman Catholics to sing in their clandestine services. He began the project soon after writing the three Masses (which date from the mid 1590s), and took ten years to bring it to completion. Like so much of Byrd's late music, the *Gradualia* motets are compact and economical in expression: miniature masterpieces that glow with the warmth of the composer's personal religious convictions, and miraculously balance exquisite musical design with the most intelligent word-setting. Their chamber-music scale is nicely captured in these performances by the William Byrd Choir, headed by a superb team of five solo voices. Everything on the disc belongs to feasts of the Blessed Virgin, many of which share texts with one another. Byrd economized by setting each text once only, and to play them in their correct liturgical order the various tracks of the CD have to be pre-selected. This is great fun to do; but the disc also makes perfectly satisfying listening when played straight through from start to finish.

Further listening ...

Keyboard Works: Fantasias — No. 2 in C major; No. 2 in G major. Pavans and Galliards — No. 2 in F major, "Ph. Tregian"; No. 2 in G major; No. 3 in G minor. The Carman's Whistle; The Woods so Wild; Walsingham; All in a garden green. The Queen's Alman. The Bells. Ut re mi fa sol la. La volta — No. 1 in G major. **Ursula Duetschler** (hpd). Claves CD50-9001 (10/90).

Keyboard Works: My Lady Nevell's Ground. O mistress mine I must. John must come kiss me now. Passamezzo Pavan and Galliard. The Carman's Whistle. Walsingham. Hugh Ashton's Ground. Fortune my foe. Sellinger's Round. **Elaine Thornburgh** (hpd). Koch International Classics 37057-2 (4/92).

The Great Service: Morning Service — Venite; Te Deum; Benedictus; Creed. Evening Service — Magnificat; Nunc dimittis. Anthems — O God, the proud are risen against me; O Lord make thy servants. Sing joyfully unto God our strength. **The Tallis Scholars/Peter Phillips.** Gimell CDGIM011 (6/87).

Motets: In resurrectione tua. Aspice Domine de sede. Vide Domine afflictionem. Domine tu iurasti. Vigilate. Domine secundum multitudinem. Tristitia et anxietas. Ne irascaris Domine. O quam gloriosum. **New College Choir, Oxford/Edward Higginbottom.** CRD CRD3420 (12/91).

John Cage

American 1912-1992

Cage. Sonatas and Interludes for prepared piano. **Gérard Frémy** (prepared pf). Etcetera KTC2001. From ETC2001 (12/83).

1h 10m DDD 9/88 

John Cage made two major discoveries when he invented the 'prepared piano' in 1946. The first was that to insert nuts, bolts, rubber wedges and bits of plastic between the strings of a piano does not make it sound hideously nasty but, if done with care and precision, turns it into an orchestra of delicately chiming, bright, fragile and gamelan-like sounds. The second discovery was that this 'new' instrument had to be treated with great subtlety. The result is the most mysteriously lucid score he has ever written, a sequence of quiet rituals and arabesque gestures, of silences in which hazes of resonance die away. Transparent textures and low dynamic levels predominate, but the work is by no means incidentless. There is a fairly clear progress from the briefer, quieter, more hesitant earlier Sonatas to the bigger and more dramatic gestures of Sonatas 9 to 12. To hear the Sonatas and Interludes complete and in sequence, at least once in a while, is a wonderfully ear-cleansing experience, a demonstration of how potent, beautiful and startlingly fresh the simplest of musical events can be. The discovery led Cage into an entranced contemplation of the sounds around us that we cannot accept as 'music', and these pieces raise questions about how we listen and how we hear that will not go away. Frémy's absorbed and absorbing performance has the composer's approval and the transparent clarity of the recording is ideal.

Additional recommendation ...

Yuji Takahashi (prepared pf). Denon C37-7673 DDD 5/86

Cage. VOCAL WORKS. **Joan La Barbara** ([a]voc/[b]perc); [c]**Scott Evans** (perc); **William Winant** ([d]pf/[e]perc); [f]**Leonard Stein** (pf). New Albion NA035CD. Texts included. Recorded in 1990.

A flower[ad]. Mirakus[a]. Eight Whiskus[a]. The Wonderful Widow of Eighteen Springs[ad]. Nowth Upon Nacht[ad]. Sonnekus[f]. Forever and Sunsmell[ace]. Solo for Voice 49[a]. Solo for Voice 52[b]. Solo for Voice 67[a]. Music for Two (by One)[a].

56m DDD 9/91 

There was a time when Cage's impertinent theatrics and anti-art gestures served to obscure the beauty and delicacy of much of his own music. We were enjoined to experience his sound-constructions without the customary intervention of memory, taste or desire; the external noises occurring spontaneously during the performances of *his* sounds (and, notoriously, silences) had equal validity, were part of the spectacle. And yet it is possible to enjoy Joan La Barbara's carefully balanced selection — and Cage's sensitive, if unconventional, response to text — without philosophical baggage. La Barbara wants us to focus on particular aspects of Cage: "the sense of wonder, the feeling for beauty, the love of theatre, the fascination with words and sounds of all sorts and, of course, silence". The New Albion engineers surmount the various problems of balance with great skill, attempting to give each song an acoustic space appropriate to its content. And the booklet provides full texts, though it's not always easy to tell where you are as the tracks are wrongly listed on the CD itself! A pioneer of extended vocal techniques (which sounds a mite daunting), Joan La Barbara is in fact blessed with a voice of great beauty and strength. Many of the items here are for unaccompanied voice; others call for percussive or electronic effects; there is birdsong (apparently real) and piano (both the keys and the wooden case are struck). *Sonnekus* incorporates three Satie café songs. *Solo for Voice* 67 is the one to shock the neighbours, with La Barbara's virtuoso grunts and squeaks punctuated by an electronic pile driver!

Cage. The Perilous Night (1944)[a]. Four walls (1944)[b]. [b]**Joan La Barbara** (sop); **Margaret Leng Tan** ([a]prepared pf; [b]pf). New Albion NA037CD. Recorded in 1990.

1h 11m DDD 1/91 

The back of the CD shows a picture of Cage beaming and congratulating Margaret Leng Tan, who is crouching on a concert platform which looks rather like a large marimba. Well might Cage look pleased — this is some of his most accessible music. No tricks, no indeterminacy, no happenings. None of the things which tend to confuse people about his intentions, when he has them. Just music. Unless, that is, you think the prepared piano is a trick? Surely not, when the Sonatas and Interludes, written shortly after the works here and recorded several times have rightly achieved the status of classics. Two strands in Cage's earlier work are concerned with his pioneering development of percussion and his invention of the prepared piano. He used both media in a particularly original way to escape from convention and find new sounds. He succeeded, and that is the joy of *The Perilous Night* and *Four walls*. *The Perilous Night* is a highly personal set of movements concerned with unhappy love, presumably reflecting Cage's own crisis. *Four walls* was written for the dancer Merce Cunningham, whose choreographic approach to measured lengths of time has influenced Cage through most of his career and gives a certain classical charm to the prepared piano music. Another important influence on Cage is Erik Satie. Anyone who enjoys the detached calm of Satie's Rosicrucian music will recognize this and respond to the meditative tranquility, the repetitions and the silences in these unfamiliar Cage works. As Cage said: "This space of time is organized. We need not fear these silences — we may love them." And he has a fine advocate in Margaret Leng Tan along with the cool, chaste tones of Joan La Barbara.

Further listening ...

Etudes borealis. 26'1.1449". Concert for Piano and Orchestra — solo for cello. Variations — I-III. A Dip in the Lake. Lecture on nothing. **Frances-Marie Uitti** (vc, voice, various instruments). Etcetera KTC2016 (3/92).

Antonio Caldara

Italian c.1670-1736

Caldara. SOLO CANTATAS[a]. 12 Suonate da camera, Op. 2 — No. 3 in D major. 12 Suonate a 3, Op. 1 — No. 5 in E minor. [a]**Gérard Lesne** (alto); **Il Seminario Musicale.** Virgin Classics Veritas VC7 59058-2. Texts and translations included.
Cantatas: Medea in Corinto. Soffri, mio caro Alcino. D'improvviso. Vicino a un rivoletto.

1h 8m DDD 11/91 

The late baroque Venetian composer Caldara has fared much less well on disc than his more fashionable contemporaries Albinoni and Vivaldi. Yet Caldara was hardly less successful in his own lifetime which he divided between Venice, Rome and Vienna. This disc offers a glimpse of his chamber music, with four cantatas and two trio sonatas. The most impressive piece is the cantata *Medea in Corinto* whose text picks up the famous legend at that point in the story where Medea realizes that Jason intends to abandon her, and it follows through to the moment where she summons the Furies to assist her in her revenge. Caldara vividly colours this dramatic episode, effectively contrasting the moods of the Sorceress and enlivening the narrative with some splendidly declamatory recitative. The remaining cantatas, though attractive, are more modest in their expressive range and more conventional in their lovelorn Arcadian surroundings. The French countertenor, Gérard Lesne, gives technically accomplished and musical performances with dependable intonation and a fluent grasp of style. His interpretation of Medea is vividly conceived and skilfully projected with many pleasing nuances of expression. Il Seminario Musicale is a lively group which gives Lesne the necessary support though perhaps the trio-sonatas lack that finesse which Lesne unfailingly brings to his own performances. Fine recorded sound and full texts with translations are provided.

Further listening ...

Madrigals — Fra pioggie, nevi e gelo. Dell'uom la vita. Fugge di Lot a moglie. Vedi co'l crine sciolto. Là su morbide. De piacari. *Cantatas* — Lungi dall'idol mio. Il Dario. La forriera del giorno. Stella ria. Il Gelsomino. **Wren Baroque Soloists/Martin Elliott.** Unicorn-Kanchana DKPCD9130 (2/93).

Thomas Campion

British 1567-1620

Campion. AYRES. **Drew Minter** (alto); **Paul O'Dette** (lute). Harmonia Mundi HMU90 7023. Texts included. Recorded in 1989.

Beauty, since you so much desire. Love me or not. Your faire lookes. Never love unlesse you can. O never to be moved. The sypres curten of the night is spread. Awake thou spring of speaking grace. Come you pretty false-ey'd wanton. So tyr'd are all my thoughts. Fire, fire. Pin'd I am and like to dye. Author of light. See where she flies. Faire if you expect admiring. Shall I come sweet love to thee? It fell on a sommers daie. Kinde are her answers. Beauty is but a painted hell. Sweet exclude me not. Are you what your faire lookes expresse? I care not for these ladies. Never weather-beaten saile.

58m DDD 6/91 

Thomas Campion wrote even more lute songs than John Dowland, though it must be said that, unlike Dowland, he composed nothing else. His songs are marked by a careful marriage of music with speech-rhythms but they are less demonstrative than those of Dowland, whose penchant for dramatic harmonic underlining he did not share. They are nevertheless very rewarding, beautiful in their individual way, and often catchy; another respect in which Campion differed from Dowland (and others) was that he wrote both the music and the lyrics. This recording contains a selection from Campion's published books of 1601, 1613 and 1617, and their texts range from the devout (*Never weather-beaten saile; Author of light*) to the bawdy — but subtle enough to give Mary Whitehouse no offence (*Beauty, since you so much desire; It fell on a sommers daie*), with an extensive middle ground of songs concerning the pleasure and pains of love. Drew Minter's vocal quality is excellent and Paul O'Dette's lute accompaniments are exemplary; if Campion could do as well single-handed, he was indeed talented. Full texts are given (also in French and German) in the booklet, together with concisely informative annotation by Robert Spencer.

André Campra

French 1660-1744

Campra. Messe de Requiem. **Elisabeth Baudry, Monique Zanetti** (sops); **Josep Benet** (alto); **John Elwes** (ten); **Stephen Varcoe** (bar); **La Chapelle Royale Chorus and Orchestra/Philippe Herreweghe.** Harmonia Mundi HMC90 1251.

43m DDD 9/87 

Two outstandingly beautiful *Messes des Morts* were composed in France during the late baroque period. The earlier was by Jean Gilles, the later by André Campra. Both were Provençal composers and both were connected at least by the fact that Campra directed a performance of the other's Mass at Gilles's funeral in 1705. As well as being a gifted composer of sacred music — he succeeded Lalande as composer to the Chapelle Royale — Campra was a successful and innovative theatre composer. This is reflected in his ability to handle the components of an elaborate sacred work such as this Requiem Mass in a colourful and dramatic manner. But it is the quiet intensity and profoundly contemplative character of the Requiem which more deeply affect our senses. Listeners, too, may be struck by the music's individuality which almost, perhaps, forges a link with Fauré's *Requiem* some two hundred years later. Philippe Herreweghe is attentive to points of style and has assembled a strong cast of singers among whom John Elwes and Stephen Varcoe are outstanding. The voices of La Chapelle Royale are clear in texture and pleasantly blended and the Orchestra, too, makes an effective contribution. The work is well recorded and, by-and-large, eloquently performed.

Additional recommendation ...
Soloists; Monteverdi Choir; English Baroque Soloists/John Eliot Gardiner. Erato 2292-45993-2 — 52m ADD

Campra. IDOMENEE. **Bernard Deletré** (bass) Idoménée; **Sandrine Piau** (sop) Electre; **Monique Zanetti** (sop) Ilione; **Jean-Paul Fouchécourt** (bass) Idamante; **Marie Boyer** (mez) Venus; **Jérôme Correas** (bass) Eole, Neptune, Jealousy, Nemesis; **Richard Dugay** (ten) Arcas; **Jean-Claude Sarragosse** (bass) Arbas, Protée; **Mary Saint-Palais** (sop) Cretan Girl; **Anne Pichard** (sop) First Shepherd; **Anne Mopin** (sop) Second Shepherd, Trojan Girl; **Les Arts Florissants Chorus and Orchestra/William Christie.** Harmonia Mundi HMC90 1396/8. Notes, text and translation included. Recorded in 1991.

③ 2h 46m DDD 9/92 P

André Campra was one of the leading lights on the French musical scene between Lully's death in 1687 and Rameau's operatic début in 1733. He was a pioneer of opéra-ballet and wrote a significant corpus of sacred music and several successful *tragédies en musiques*. One of these was *Idoménée* which was first staged in 1712 and revived in 1731 in a reworked version. This later version has been chosen by William Christie for his recording. Campra's librettist was Antoine Danchet whose text was later to serve as a prime source for Mozart's *opera seria, Idomeneo*. Campra's score is an attractive one with few weak moments and the same may be said of Danchet's adaptation of Crébillon's contemporaneous play of the same name. Campra shows much skill in his writing for the human voice and a greater degree of sympathy, perhaps, than some of his fellow French composers. There are passages of finely sustained dialogue, notably between Idoménée and his son Idamante (Act 2, Scene 4), and Idoménée and Priam's daughter, Ilione. The instrumental writing, which plays a prominent part in the texture throughout the opera is also very effective; Act 3, for instance, contains a captivating sailors' dance for piccolos, drums and strings. Here is an opera which quickly proves itself deserving of the loving attention paid it by Christie and Les Arts Florissants. Supple choruses, colourful divertissements and a profusion of beguiling airs sung by a strong cast of soloists set the seal on a fine issue.

Campra. TANCREDE. **François Le Roux** (bar) Tancred; **Daphné Evangelatos** (contr) Clorinda; **Catherine Dubosc** (sop) Herminie; **Pierre-Yves Le Maigat** (bass-bar) Argant; **Gregory Reinhart** (bass) Ismenor; **Colette Alliot-Lugaz** (sop) Peace, Female Warrior, Dryad; **Dominique Visse** (alto) Wood-nymph; **Alison Wells** (sop) Shepherdess; **Andrew Murgatroyd** (ten) Warrior, Magician; **Christopher Royall** (alto), **Jeremy White** (bass) Magicians; **The Sixteen; Grande Ecurie et la Chambre du Roy/Jean-Claude Malgoire.** Erato Musifrance 2292-45001-2. Notes, text and translation included. Recorded live in 1986.

② 2h 2m DDD 6/90

André Campra carried on the Lullian tradition of *tragédies en musique* but made his own distinctive contribution to the development of dramatic forms with *opéra-ballet*. *Tancrède*, however, is a *tragédie* and proved to be one of Campra's most successful serious operas. It was first performed in 1702 and held the stage at frequent intervals until 1764. The story is loosely based on the legend of Tancred and Clorinda in Tasso's epic poem *Gerusalemme Liberata*. In its overture, prologue and five acts and its generous assortment of instrumental movements, *Tancrède* follows the pattern set by Lully. The present recording, made from a production of the work which took place during the 1986 Aix-en-Provence Festival, does not include all of Campra's music but is trimmed to a two-hour entertainment. The performance is enjoyable notwithstanding a few disappointments both in the singing and playing. Catherine Dubosc, François Le Roux and Gregory Reinhart are the most impressive of the principal soloists but some of the minor roles are well sung, too. Jean-Claude Malgoire's direction is more sharply focused than in some other of his recordings and the project as a whole gives a fair account of an appealing work.

Joseph Canteloube

French 1879-1957

Canteloube. CHANTS D'AUVERGNE, Volume 2. Triptyque. **Frederica von Stade** (mez); **Royal Philharmonic Orchestra/Antonio de Almeida.** Sony Classical SK37837. Texts and translations included. From IM37837 (7/86).
Là-haut, sur le rocher. Jou l'pount d'o Mirabel. Hé beyla-z-y-dau fé. Lou boussou. Pastourelle. Malurous qu'o uno fenno. Obal, din lo coumbèlo. La pastrouletta è lou chibaliè. Quand z'eyro petitoune. Pastouro sé tu m'aymo. Pastorale. La pastoura al camps. Lou diziou bé.

1h 1m DDD 10/86 

The intriguing combination of innocence and sophistication, a favourite feature in several of the arts, is alluringly exemplified in Canteloube's now famous settings of folk-songs from his native corner of France — lusciously ornate, beautifully and ingeniously scored free arrangements of basically simple material. Von Stade's purity of tone is ideally suited to this: she tells the little tales (mostly of shepherdesses) with an engaging directness, entering with spirit into the gaiety of the song about feeding the donkey or the rollicking irony of "Unhappy he who has a wife", and providing some characterization for the mixed pathos and humour of the dialogue between Jeanneton and the hunchback. Canteloube's remarkable invention gives the RPO a real outing, providing elaborate washes of sound in the *Pastorale* (which is cognate with the celebrated *Bailèro*) and dizzy chromaticisms in "At the Mirabel bridge". For sheer sensuous beauty, however, the prize should surely go to *Là-haut, sur le rocher* (the only one here in French: the rest are in the original *langue d'oc*). Canteloube also made various other collections of Auvergnat songs, besides composing symphonic works and two operas — none of which we ever hear. But von Stade does include here, besides 16 of the *Chants d'Auvergne*, his remarkable *Triptyque*, composed a decade earlier, ecstatic rhapsodies on pantheistic poems by Roger Frène (who ought to have been credited): the rapturous romanticism of these, sung with passion by von Stade, whets an appetite to know more of Canteloube's music.

Additional recommendation ...
La pastoura al camps. Bailèro. L'ïo dè rotso; Ound' onorèn gorda? Obal, din lou limouzi. Pastourelle. L'Antouèno. La pastrouletta è lo chibaliè. La delaïssádo. N'aï pas iéu de mîo. Lo calhé. Lo fiolairé. Passo pel prat. Lou boussu. Brezairola. Malurous qu'o uno fenno. **Dame Kiri Te Kanawa** (sop); **English Chamber Orchestra/Jeffrey Tate.** Decca 410 004-2DH — 50m DDD 7/83 B

André Caplet

French 1878-1925

NEW REVIEW

Caplet. Conte fantastique[a]. Two divertissements[b]. Les prières[c]. Two sonnets[d]. Septet[e]. [ce]**Sharon Coste,** [de]**Sandrine Piau** (sops); [e]**Sylvie Deguy** (mez); [abcd]**Laurence Cabel** (hp); [ace]**Musique Oblique Ensemble.** Harmonia Mundi HMC90 1417. Texts and translations included. Recorded in 1992.

55m DDD 2/93

Perhaps best known as a most promising conductor as well as the expert orchestrator of his friend Debussy's mystical *Le martyre de Saint-Sébastien*, André Caplet was, before his untimely death in 1925 at the age of 46, a notably imaginative composer in his own right, a fact readily borne out by this valuable Harmonia Mundi compilation. In many respects, it's the earliest work here, the *Conte fantastique* of 1908, which is the most forward-looking: this intrepid essay for harp and string quartet (based on Edgar Allen Poe's chilling tale, *The Masque of the Red Death*) employs an audacious range of instrumental effects, including, at one point, instructions for some theatrical knocking on the harp's sound-board. The Septet of a year later is a scarcely less haunting creation, ravishingly scored for the unusual combination of three wordless female voices and string quartet. During the First World War, whilst serving at the front (where he sustained the lung damage that eventually killed him), he composed *Les prières* (three settings for soprano and harp quintet of *The Lord's Prayer, Hail Mary* and *Creed* respectively) and the brief, but intensely nostalgic Du Bellay setting "Quand reverrai-je, hélas!...". A second sonnet setting (of Ronsard's "Doux fut le trait") followed in 1924, a year that also saw the appearance of the dazzlingly idiomatic *Divertissements* for solo harp. This fascinating cross-section of Caplet's exquisite, fastidious art is blessed with some beautifully prepared performances from all involved, not least an outstandingly sensitive contribution from harpist, Laurence Cabel. Admirably real sound, too. An excellent, enterprising collection.

Manuel Cardoso

Portuguese 1566-1650

Suggested listening ...

Requiem. Non mortui. Sitivit anima mea. Mulier quae erat. Nos autem gloriari. Magnificat Secundi Toni a 5. **The Tallis Scholars/Peter Phillips.** Gimell CDGIM021 (10/90).

Giacomo Carissimi

Italian 1605-1674

Suggested listening ...

Oratorios — Jepthe; Judicium Salomonis; Jonas. **Gabrieli Consort and Players/Paul McCreesh** (bass vn). Meridian CDE84132 (7/87).

John Alden Carpenter

American 1876-1951

Suggested listening ...

Piano Sonata No. 1 in G minor. Diversions. Nocturne. Polonaise américaine. Impromptu. Tango américain. Minuet. Litle Dancer. Little Indian. Twilight Reverie. Danza. **Denver Oldham** (pf). New World NW328/9-2 (7/88).

Elliott Carter

American 1908-

Carter. Piano Concerto (1964-5)[a]. Variations for Orchestra (1954-5). [a]**Ursula Oppens** (pf); **Cincinnati Symphony Orchestra/Michael Gielen.** New World NW347-2. Recorded at performances in the Music Hall, Cincinnati, Ohio in October 1984 and October 1985.

45m DDD/ADD 4/87

Live recordings of complex contemporary works are a risky enterprise and there are certainly a few rough and ready aspects to be heard in these performances. But they are trivial in the extreme beside the excitement and commitment of artists who have read beyond the notes into the spirit of this tough but exhilarating music. Carter is so important because, while a radical in the sense of moving well beyond transitional ideas of melody and harmony, he uses his new techniques to achieve an amazing directness of expression. The Variations and the Piano Concerto complement each other very well. In the Variations, echoes of the past can still be heard, and the moods are playful and aspiring, predominantly optimistic. The Concerto is darker, with elements of the tragic represented by the tension between the soloist and the orchestral mass. The result is far from negative, even so, since the soloist's material has all the delicacy and flamboyance of Carter at his most imaginative. This music is the perfect antidote to an overdose of Philip Glass or John Adams, and the recordings, despite the occasional contributions from the audience, are perfectly adequate.

Carter. Concerto for orchestra. Three Occasions for orchestra. Concerto for violin and orchestra[a]. [a]**Ole Böhn** (vn); **London Sinfonietta/Oliver Knussen.** Virgin Classics VC7 59271-2.

lh 3m DDD 7/92 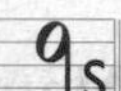

This disc is a first-class *recording*, the sound doing as much as is technically possible to ensure that the multiple, superimposed strata of Elliott Carter's characteristically complex textures are spaced and focused to make maximum aural sense. But there is also first-class music-making to be heard here. It would be an exaggeration to say that Oliver Knussen and the London Sinfonietta play Carter's *Concerto for orchestra* (1969) as effortlessly as if it were Mozart: but the effort it takes to get this music right, and to convey its full measure of exhilarating drama, has been transformed into a marvellously positive reading of the score. Comparison with Leonard Bernstein's LP recording of the *Concerto* with the New York Philharmonic Orchestra for CBS, first issued in 1973 (currently unavailable), gives graphic evidence of how far Carter interpretation has advanced in two decades. The more recent *Occasions for orchestra* are no less characterful: music of celebration and lament showing that the originality and intensity of Carter's vision have not faded as he moves into his eighties. The Violin Concerto (1990) may not be on the same high level of inspiration as the other works on this disc but it is still an absorbing demonstration of how to 'Carterize' the solo instrument's essential lyricism and capacity for fantasy, while ensuring that it remains bracingly at odds with the orchestra.

Key to Symbols

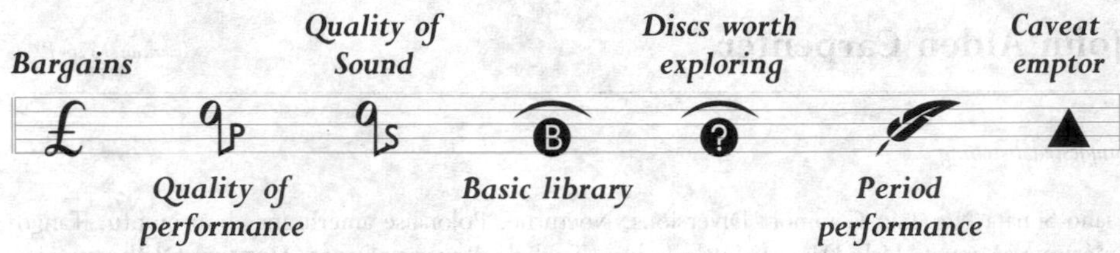

Carter. STRING QUARTETS. **Arditti Quartet** (Irvine Arditti, David Alberman, vns; Levine Andrade, va; Rohan de Saram, vc). Etcetera KTC1065/6. Recorded in 1988.
KTC1065: String Quartets — No. 1; No. 4. *KTC1066:* String Quartets — No. 2; No. 3. Elegy.

The Arditti Quartet can play the most complex modern music with confidence as well as accuracy. Their performances radiate enjoyment and enthusiasm, not just a dour determination to convey what is on the printed page with maximum precision. Carter's four quartets span 35 years (1951-86) and, with the early *Elegy* of 1943, chart with exemplary clarity his spiritual and stylistic odyssey. Starting with a shapely neoclassicism quite close to that of Copland, he moved around 1950 into a world nearer that of early twentieth-century Viennese expressionism, whilst retaining an cxpansive form and rhythmic buoyancy which is characteristically American. In the Third Quartet you sense a kind of crisis within this expressionism, overwhelming in its unsparing vehemence and stretching the medium to breaking point. In his later works the crisis recedes and the Fourth Quartet finds room for lighter moods and calmer considerations. The Second Quartet is perhaps the jewel of the collection, but all four quartets in this finely-recorded set, performed as they are with such authority and commitment, repay repeated as well as concentrated listening.

Robert Carver

British c.1490-1550

Suggested listening ...

Missa Dum sacrum mysterium. O bone Jesu. Gaude flore virginali. **Cappella Nova/Alan Tavener.** ASV Gaudeamus CDGAU124 (10/91).

Missa L'Homme armé. Mass for six voices. **Cappella Nova/Alan Tavener.** ASV Gaudeamus CDGAU126 (10/91).

Missa Fera pessima. Missa Pater creator omnium. **Cappella Nova/Alan Tavener.** ASV Gaudeamus CDGAU127 (5/92).

Pablo Casals

Spanish 1876-1973

Suggested listening ...

Sacred Choral Music — Nigra sum. Tota pulchra es. Cançó a la verge. Rosari. O vos omnes. Eucaristica. Recordare, virgo mater. Oració a la verge de Montserrat. Salve regina. **Montserrat Escolania/Ireneu Segarra.** Koch-Schwann Musica Sacra 313062 (1/92).

Philip Cashian

British 1963-

NEW REVIEW

Cashian. String Quartet No. 1.
Butler. Songs and Dances from a Haunted Place.
Nicholls. String Quartet, "Winter Landscape with Skaters and Birdtrap". **Bingham Quartet** (Stephen Bingham, Mark Messenger, vns; Brenda Stewart, va; Miriam Lowbury, vc). NMCD006. Recorded in 1991.

49m DDD II/92

A cynic might conclude that the safety-in-numbers principle is operating with this disc: three little-known British composers lumped together, and not subjected to the trauma of comparison with established masters. Yet even the most seasoned cynics should find that they can hear and enjoy the disc as a concert: the three pieces are satisfyingly different, but they share a high degree of technical accomplishment. David Nicholls (b. 1955) is the senior member of the trio, and his Quartet, whose title refers to a Breugel painting, is ambitious and closely-argued, balancing the claims of the modernist tradition against the more openly poetic concerns of those who seek alternative paths. As his title suggests, Martin Butler (born in 1960) may appear to be haunted by the pluralistic past of twentieth-century music, but the warmth and vitality of his writing make plain that this is not music built on the ruins of a rejected tradition. It's a clear-sighted statement of how it is possible to be positive without recourse to extremes. Something similar can be said of Philip Cashian, whose relish for lively and expressive pattern-making reveals a deep musicality. This relatively new music is expertly performed by a young quartet in well-balanced recordings.

John Casken

British 1949-

Casken. GOLEM. **Adrian Clarke** (bar) Maharal; **John Hall** (bass-bar) Golem; **Patricia Rozario** (sop) Miriam; **Christopher Robson** (alto) Ometh; **Paul Wilson** (ten) Stoikus; **Richard Morris** (bar) Jadek; **Paul Harrhy** (ten) Stump; **Mary Thomas** (sop) Gerty; **Music Projects London/Richard Bernas.** Virgin Classics VCD7 59028-2. Notes, text and translation included.

② Ih 39m ADD 8/91

It is fitting that *Golem* should have won for its composer the first Britten Award for composition in 1990 — not because John Casken's music sounds remotely like Britten's, but because the spirit of his opera does have things in common with the humanly focused rituals of Britten's own Parables for church performance. The story of *Golem* specifically shuns a Christian context, and although it deals with some of the same issues as, for example, the parable of the prodigal son, it has a tragic outcome: no happy ending here. Even so, the need for human beings to achieve a positive balance between thought and feeling is as important in *Golem* as it is in *Curlew River*. Maharal, the embodiment of human authority, creates a Golem — a man from clay — to serve him and society. But he fails to anticipate or control the consequences of his action, and in the end is driven to destroy his wayward but willing creation. As with all such symbolic tales, the dangers of falling into alienatingly schematic formulae are considerable. But Casken is remarkably successful in ensuring that, through his music, the story has a convincing social context and a strong basis in human feeling. If you are so inclined, you can approach the music by way of its associations with more familiar idioms: here with Birtwistle, there with Maxwell Davies, sometimes with Ligeti, Lutoslawski or Berio. But it soon becomes clear that Casken has evolved a distinctively personal 'brew' from the rich mix of mainly expressionist source-materials that underpin his style, and the result is a first opera — performed and recorded with admirable conviction — that is also a major achievement.

Mario Castelnuovo-Tedesco

Italian/American 1895-1968

Suggested listening ...

Guitar Concertos — No. 1 in D major, Op. 99; No. 2 in C major, Op. 160. Concerto for two guitars, Op. 201. **Kazuhito Yamashita, Naoko Yamashita** (gtrs); **London Philharmonic Orchestra/Leonard Slatkin.** RCA Victor Red Seal RD60355 (12/90).

Violin Concerto No. 2, "I profeti". *Coupled with* ***Ferguson.*** Violin Sonata No. 1, Op. 2; ***Françaix.*** String Trio in C major; ***K. Khachaturian.*** Violin Sonata in G minor, Op. 1. **Jascha Heifetz** (vn); **Joseph de Pasquale** (va); **Gregor Piatigorsky** (vc); **Lilian Steuber** (pf); **Los Angeles Philharmonic Orchestra/Alfred Wallenstein.** RCA Victor Gold Seal GD87872 (9/90).

Alfredo Catalani

Italian 1854-1893

Suggested listening ...

LA WALLY. **Soloists; Turin Lyric Chorus; Monte Carlo National Opera Orchestra/Fausto Cleva.** Decca 425 417-2DM2 (2/90).

Emmanuel Chabrier

French 1841-1894

NEW REVIEW

Chabrier. ORCHESTRAL WORKS.
Roussel. Suite in F major, Op. 33. **Detroit Symphony Orchestra/Paul Paray.** Mercury 434 303-2MM. Recorded 1957-60.
España. Suite pastorale. Joyeuse marche. Bourrée fantasque. Le Roi malgré lui — Fête polonaise; Danse slave. Gwendoline — Overture.

lh 8m ADD £ 9p

An irresistible confection. Paray's classic Chabrier collection radiates a truly life-enhancing spontaneity, an all-too-rare commodity in this day and age. His *España* has to be one of the most twinklingly good-humoured ever committed to disc — an account overflowing with rhythmic panache and unbuttoned exuberance — whilst the adorable *Suite pastorale* has rarely sounded so fresh-faced and sheerly disarming, even though Paray's very swift "Sous bois" does admittedly take some getting use to. Both the swaggering "Fête polonaise" and "Danse slave" from *Le Roi malgré lui* are despatched with memorable theatrical charisma and huge gusto, qualities which extend to a blistering rendition of the remarkable, almost feverish overture to *Gwendoline*. But Paray reserves perhaps his finest achievement for the uproarious *Joyeuse marche* and *Bourrée fantasque* (an astonishingly quick-witted, vital conception). Throughout, the Detroit SO respond with irrepressible spirit and characteristic Gallic poise, and the Mercury engineering continues to astonish in its intrepidly wide range of dynamic and full-blooded brilliance (just sample those wonderfully hefty bass-drum thwacks towards the end of *España*). All this and Roussel's bustling, neo-classical *Suite* too! An unmissable CD and make no mistake.

Additional recommendation ...
España. Suite pastorale. **Dukas.** *L'apprenti sorcier. La péri.* **Ulster Orchestra/Yan Pascal Tortelier.** Chandos CHAN8852 — 57m DDD 2/91 9s

NEW REVIEW

Chabrier. Bourrée fantasque. Impromptu in C major. Dix pièces pittoresques. **Richard McMahon** (pf). Pianissimo PP10792. From Oriana ONA0002 (9/84). Recorded in 1982.

52m DDD 8/92

Gaiety and sentiment, allied to a certain formality, sit at the heart of Chabrier's charming and largely neglected piano *oeuvre*. Various of the *Dix pièces pittoresques* are more familiar in their orchestral guise, but they work even better as piano pieces: the celebrated "Idylle", with its balletic staccato accompaniment and wistful melodic line, is on a par with late Brahms, while the joyous "Scherzo-valse" trips around the corners of your memory long after it has left the keys. Other notable movements include an atmospheric "Sous bois" and a consolatory, somewhat Schumanesque Improvisation. But were one to single out a highlight on this rewarding CD, it would unquestionably be the *Bourrée fantasque*, a miraculous six-minute tone-poem, rich in contrasts and harbouring one of Chabrier's inimitable, long-breathed melodies. In this instance, Felix Mottl's orchestration also has a special magic, but the original is just as appealing in its own way. As with the "Scherzo-valse", Richard McMahon takes on the work with manly resolve, yet remains sensitive to its poetry. Elsewhere, he negotiates the music's myriad interpretative stumbling blocks (elegance is called for as well as considerable reserves of virtuosity) with great facility, and his instrument is clearly, albeit rather dryly, recorded. Anyone seeking a full understanding of late nineteenth-century French piano music will have to hear this disc.

Further listening ...

L'ETOILE — *opéra bouffe.* **Soloists; Lyon Opera Chorus and Orchestra/John Eliot Gardiner.** EMI CDS7 47889-8 (8/88).

LE ROI MALGRE LUI — *opéra-comique.* **Soloists; French Radio Chorus; French Radio New Philharmonic Orchestra/Charles Dutoit.** Erato 2292-45792-2.

UNE EDUCATION MANQUEE — *operetta.* **Soloists; orchestra/Charles Bruck.** LE ROI MALGRE LUI — Hélas, à l'esclavage. Chanson pour Jeanne. L'île heureuse. GWENDOLINE — Blonde aux yeux de pervenche. Ballade des gros dindons. Pastorale des cochons roses. **Christiane Castelli** (sop); **Hélène Boschi** (pf). Le Chant du Monde mono LDC278 1068 (8/92).

Jacques Champion de Chambonnières

French 1601-1672

NEW REVIEW

Chambonnières. Harpsichord Suites[a] — C major; G major; A major; D major. ***d'Anglebert.*** Tombeau de M. de Chambonnières. **Skip Sempé** (hpd) with [a]**Brian Feehan** (theorbo). Deutsche Harmonia Mundi 05472 77210-2. Recorded in 1992.

lh 12m DDD 4/93 

Chambonnières is generally recognized as being the founder of the French harpsichord school. He cultivated and developed a style in harpsichord writing akin to that of the lutenist's *style brisé* creating an illusion of linear, horizontal writing. The young American harpsichordist Skip Sempé has mastered this style admirably. He plays with authority and insight to the subtle resonances of Chambonnières's craft. This is richly expressive music by a composer with a finely developed feeling for melody. Compared to his pupil, Louis Couperin, Chambonnières is less harmonically adventurous, but he is Couperin's equal where warmth of feeling and nobility of sentiment are concerned. Sempé has chosen his programme thoughtfully, intent in showing off the formal and expressive variety of which this gifted composer was capable. In five of the pieces he is supported by a theorbo, an effective idea which achieves beautiful results. An affectionate and apposite gesture is made in the concluding item of the programme; here Sempé performs what is, perhaps, the finest tribute to the composer, the *Tombeau de M. de Chambonnières* by another of his pupils, d'Anglebert. The late seventeenth-century harpsichord is recorded very closely, but the balance is sympathetic, picking up the radiant character of the instrument.

Cécile Chaminade

French 1857-1944

Chaminade. PIANO WORKS. **Eric Parkin.** Chandos CHAN8888. Recorded in 1990.
Air à danser, Op. 164. Air de ballet, Op. 30. Contes bleus No. 2, Op. 122. Danse créole, Op. 94. Etudes de concert, Op. 35 — No. 2, Automne. Feuillets d'album, Op. 98 — No. 4, Valse arabesque. Guitare, Op. 32. La lisonjera, Op. 50. Lolita, Op. 54. Minuetto, Op. 23. Pas des écharpes, Op. 37. Pas des sylphes: Intermezzo. Pièces humoristiques, Op. 87 — No. 4, Autrefois. Pierette, Op. 41. Romances sans paroles, Op. 76 — No. 1, Souvenance; No. 3, Idyll; No. 6, Méditation. Sérénade, Op. 29. Sous le masque, Op. 116. Toccata, Op. 39.

lh 5m DDD 8/91 

One doesn't have to be a feminist to regret that there have been all too few women composers compared to, say, women novelists, at least up to the late twentieth century. However, Cécile Chaminade was one of them and, as a fine pianist herself, a very skilful and attractive writer of piano music who numbered Bizet among her admirers. As Peter Dickinson rightly says in his booklet note, writing first-class salon music is a greater achievement than producing inadequate symphonies and sonatas, and less boring! No pianist could be a better advocate for this music than Eric Parkin, who knows how to bring out its strength as well as its charm and zest; readers of this *Guide* may already know his fine recordings of piano music by Bax and Mayerl. Tempos, tone, textures, pedalling and rubato are all splendidly judged, and one may simply say that this is music to be enjoyed, unfailingly tuneful and telling and with plenty of variety to avoid any tendency toward the *déjà vu* in the course of the 20 well-chosen tracks. Among the distinguished ancestors of this music are, no doubt, Schumann, Chopin and Fauré — no composer need be ashamed of such a lineage! — but there is a Chaminade personality here, too, as the lilting *Sérénade*, the teasing *Guitare*, the well-known *Automne* (a bravura concert study rather than an amateur's drawing-room piece) and the wittily understated, neo-baroque Toccata all remind us. The recording, made in The Maltings, Snape, offers fresh sound and a natural degree of reverberation.

Herbert Chappell

British 1934-

Suggested listening ...

Guitar Concerto No. 1, "Caribbean Concerto". *Coupled with* **Arnold.** Guitar Concerto, Op. 67. ***Brouwer.*** Retrats Catalans. **Eduardo Fernández** (gtr); **English Chamber Orchestra/Barry Wordsworth.** Decca 430 233-2DH (4/91).
See review under Arnold; refer to the Index to Reviews.

Gustave Charpentier

French 1860-1956

Charpentier. LOUISE. **Ileana Cotrubas** (sop) Louise; **Plácido Domingo** (ten) Julien; **Gabriel Bacquier** (bar) Father; **Jane Berbié** (sop) Mother; **Michel Sénéchal** (ten) Noctambulist, King of the Fools; **Lyliane Guitton** (mez) Irma; **Ambrosian Opera Chorus; New Philharmonia Orchestra/Georges Prêtre.** Sony Classical S2K46429. Text and translation included. From CBS 79302 (10/76). Recorded in 1976.

 ③ 2h 52m ADD 6/91

The generation gap, headstrong youth and 'free love', the pillars of the plot of *Louise*, could suggest a subject of contemporary relevance; but the scene here is Paris in 1900, where a naïve little seamstress (a lot more realistic than Mimì) becomes besotted with a handsome but feckless young poet (a great deal less sentimental than Rodolfo) with whom she goes to live, despite her parents' opposition. Her mother, worn out by poverty, treats her sternly, but her hard-working, respectable father has so deep an affection for her that, when she decides to remain with her lover although her father is ill, his final outburst against Parisian loose morals is all the more bitter. His is the most fully drawn character in this unromanticized story of ordinary working-class people (curiously, only the authentic street-vendors' cries seem contrived), and Bacquier is an almost ideal interpreter of it, capturing every nuance of the tormented father's emotions. Berbié brings distinction to her much smaller role as the mother. Cotrubas is extremely appealing, both in her tonal purity (in a technically very exacting part) and her sensitivity to words, and vividly depicts Louise's innocent charm. Julien is an entirely two-dimensional figure, but that really does not excuse his role being sung most of the time at an ardent, open-throated *forte* (thrilling as the sound is that Domingo produces). He creates several problems of balance for which the producer must shoulder some of the blame, as he should also for some ill-judged perspectives and some slips in the French. There is a vast array of small parts, on the whole very ably taken by members of the 1976 Ambrosian Opera Chorus (several of whom have since become well known in their own right), and Prêtre conducts sympathetically.

Marc-Antoine Charpentier

French 1643-1704

Charpentier. Quatuor anni tempestatis, H335-8. PSALMS. **Françoise Semellaz, Noémi Rime** (sops); **Bernard Délétré** (bass); **Le Parlement de Musique** (Christoph Ehrsam, Patrick Blanc, recs; Eunice Brandao, Laurence Bonnal, treble viols; Sylvia Abramowicz, bass viol; Yasunori Imamura, theorbo)/**Martin Gester.** Opus 111 OPS30-9005. Texts and translations included. Recorded in 1990.

Psalms — Quemadmodum desiderat cervus, H174. Nisi Dominus, H231. Notus in Judea, H179.

lh DDD 9/91

The main work in an attractive programme which wanders well away from the beaten track is Charpentier's *Quatuor anni tempestatis* ("The four seasons of the year"). When, or for whom Charpentier wrote these engaging little motets — there are four in all, one for each season — is not known. They draw their inspiration from the "Song of Solomon" and are scored for two sopranos and continuo. In addition "Aestas" ("Summer") has a short instrumental prelude for three recorders and continuo. Perhaps the music is not vintage Charpentier but it is none the less appealing with frequent instances of those affecting melismatic passages of which Charpentier was a distinctive master. The sopranos Françoise Semellaz and Noémi Rime are evenly matched in sound and convey a good sense of style. Not everything is immaculate but the character of the music is projected with warmth and authority. The remaining pieces are modestly scored psalms for one or two melody instruments with continuo. Of these the *Nisi Dominus* (Psalm 127) is the most striking and, perhaps the most confidently performed. The recording is clear and sympathetic and the repertoire well worth exploring. Full texts with translations included.

Charpentier. SACRED CHORAL WORKS: Canticum ad Beatam Virginem Mariam. **Le Concert des Nations/Jordi Savall.** Astrée Auvidis E8713. Texts and translations included.
Canticum in honorem Beatae Virginis Mariae inter homines et angelos, H400. Prélude a 3, H509. Pour la conception de la Vierge, H313. Nativité de la Vierge, H309. Prélude pour Salve regina a 3, H23*a*. Salve regina a 3, H23. Pour la fête de l'Epiphanie, H395. Prélude pour le Magnificat a 4, H533. Magnificat a 4, H80. Stabat mater pour des religieuses, H15. Litanies de la vierge, H83.

lh 15m DDD 2/90 

The music on this disc is a skilful compilation of disparate pieces by Charpentier all connected with Marian devotion. The two most extended works are the *Canticum in honorem Beatae Virginis Mariae* and the *Litanies de la vierge*; the first is intimate yet ardent in expression and takes the form of a dialogue between man and angels. Charpentier was a master of small-scale dramatic forms such as these and Jordi Savall brings passion and a lively sense of theatre to this one. The *Litanies* are more contemplative, sometimes profoundly so, but they are not without a quiet radiance and Savall convincingly explores their expressive vocabulary. Hardly less appealing is the beautiful *Stabat mater pour des religieuses*, written for soprano soloist with unison soprano chorus. Charpentier may well have composed it for the nuns of the convent of Port Royal, though Savall in fact uses male voices for the refrains retaining the soprano for the serene and ethereal solos. The remaining pieces are more modestly conceived but extremely effective in this thoughtfully constructed context. Savall creates a marvellous sense of occasion, bringing the music to life with Mediterranean verve. Lively continuo realizations, in which a theorbo plays a prominent part, are a constant delight as indeed is so much else in this captivating performance. Small vocal and instrumental insecurities matter little when interpretative skill is on such a level as this. Faithful and vibrant recorded sound set the seal on a distinguished project.

Charpentier. SACRED CHORAL WORKS. [a]**Greta de Reyghere,** [b]**Isabelle Poulenard,** [b]**Jill Feldman** (sops); [c]**Ludwig van Gijsegem** (ten); [d]**Capella Ricercar/Jerome Léjeune** with [e]**Bernard Foccroulle,** [f]**Benoit Mernier** (orgs). Ricercar RIC052034.
Magnificat pour le Port Royal, H81[abde]. Messe pour le Port Royal, H5[abcde]. O clementissime Domine Jesu, H256[abe]. Dixit Dominus pour le Port Royal[abdf]. Laudate Dominum pour le Port Royal, H227[abdf]. Stabat mater pour les religieuses, H15[bdf]. *Raison:* Pièces d'orgue[d].

lh 7m DDD 1/89

There are several distinctive features about the music (composed for the nuns of Port Royal) included on this delightful disc, the most striking of them being that the vocal writing is, of course, for female voices only. That may seem a confining discipline but is anything but that in the hands of a composer as resourceful as Charpentier. What is lacking in complexity and textural richness is more than compensated for by subtle inflexion, warm fervour and a radiance of sound. This is especially so in the *Magnificat*, a ravishingly beautiful setting for three voices. Here the solo sections are interspersed with a vocal ensemble refrain whose affecting suspensions haunt the memory. The most elaborate work is the *Messe pour le Port Royal* where the voices are deployed in a masterly fashion, ringing the changes between varying ensembles and vocal dispositions. Short organ solos which would have played a part in the 'Mass' were not included in Charpentier's original score since they would have probably been improvised. Sensibly, organ music by his contemporary, André Raison has been inserted at the appropriate places and very fine it sounds, too.

Charpentier. LE MALADE IMAGINAIRE. **Isabelle Poulenard, Jill Feldman** (sops); **Guillemette Laurens** (mez); **Gilles Ragon** (ten); **Michel Verschaeve, Bernard Deletré, Jean-Louis Bindi, Jean-Paul Fouchécourt** (basses); **Les Musiciens du Louvre/Marc Minkowski.** Erato MusiFrance 2292-45002-2. Notes, text and translation included. Recorded in 1988.

1h 13m DDD 6/90 

Comédie-ballet was a dramatic form developed by Molière in which music played both an integral and incidental part. Lully was his earliest collaborator but, following a quarrel Molière turned to Charpentier to provide music. *Le malade imaginaire*, first performed in 1673, was the playwright's last *comédie-ballet* and the one to which Charpentier made his most substantial contribution. Here it is the medical profession which comes under Molière's merciless scrutiny with a hypochondriac, his deceitful wife and doctors who know everything about disease except the cure of it. This recording omits the spoken dialogue but includes almost all of Charpentier's music; and delightful it is, too, in its engaging variety of airs and dances. The orchestra is colourful, consisting of flutes, recorders, oboes and strings together with some surprising sounds in the third of three *intermèdes* which follow the prologue. Here, besides castanets, drums and tambourines, Charpentier calls for apothecary's mortars, once cast in a bell foundry and for this recording lent by a Paris antiquarian: such is the lure of authenticity these days! Marc Minkowski, Les Musiciens du Louvre and a strong ensemble of solo voices combine to give a refreshingly unbuttoned performance of the music, little of which has previously been available to record collectors. The recording is excellent.

Additional recommendation ...

Soloists; Les Arts Florissants Chorus and Orchestra/William Christie. Harmonia Mundi HMC90 1336 — 1h 19m DDD 4/91

Included with this CD is a complementary CD (41m) containing Charpentier's "'O' Anthems for Advent", H36-43; "In nativatem Domini nostri Jesus Christi canticum", H414; "Noëls dur les instruments", H534.

Charpentier. ACTEON. **Dominique Visse** (alto) Actéon; **Agnès Mellon** (sop) Diane; **Guillemette Laurens** (mez) Junon; **Jill Feldman** (sop) Arthébuze; **Françoise Paut** (sop) Hyale; **Les Arts Florissants Vocal and Instrumental Ensemble/William Christie.** Harmonia Mundi Musique d'abord HMA190 1095. From HM1095 (5/83).

47m AAD 

Poor old Actaeon; if you recall, he was discovered hiding in the bushes while the goddess Diana and her followers were bathing. Without being given a chance to explain himself properly Diana turns him into a stag, whereupon he is torn to pieces by his own hounds. That is the version of the legend followed in Charpentier's opera. The score contains many ingredients of Lullian *tragédie-lyrique*, with a profusion of fine choruses and dances. William Christie and Les Arts Florissants bring stylistic unity, lively temperament and a sharp awareness of rhythmic and harmonic nuances to this music. The soloists make distinctive and accomplished contributions and the whole opera is performed with a fervour and intensity which emphasizes the poignant plot. No French text or translation are included in the CD booklet, but a useful synopsis takes their place. The recording is excellent.

Charpentier. MEDEE. **Jill Feldman** (sop) Médée; **Gilles Ragon** (ten) Jason; **Agnès Mellon** (sop) Creuse; **Jacques Bona** (bass) Créon; **Sophie Boulin** (sop) Nérine; **Philippe Contor** (bass) Oronte; **Les Arts Florissants Chorus and Orchestra/William Christie.** Harmonia Mundi HMC90 1139/41. Notes, text and translation included. From HM1139/41 (11/84).

③ 3h 2m AAD 3/85

Médée is Charpentier's dramatic masterpiece in the conventional French baroque form of a prologue and five acts and was first performed in 1693. Thomas Corneille based his libretto on the story of the sorceress Medea as told by Euripides and the opera begins after the arrival of Jason and Medea at Corinth in the "Argo"; thus the adventure of the Golden Fleece has already taken place. Charpentier's music is well able to rise to the occasion and does so with chilling effect in the memorable witchcraft scenes of Act 3. Jill Feldman's Medea contains many layers of expressive subtlety and her command of French declamation is impressive. Agnès Mellon is affecting as the innocent and sincere Creuse and Gilles Ragon an articulate and suitably complacent Jason. The chorus and orchestra of Les Arts Florissants have their rough patches but William Christie directs a thrilling performance of a work representing one of the finest achievements of French baroque musical drama. The recording was made in a lively and sympathetic acoustic but you will need a magnifying glass to read the libretto.

Further listening ...

Office de ténèbres — Incipit oratio Jeremiae, H95. Leçons de ténèbres — Manum suam, H92; Ego vir videns, H93. Responsories — Eram quasi agnus, H116; O Juda, H119; O vos omnes, H134. Miserere, H157. **Le Parlement de Musique/Martin Gester** (org, hpd). Opus 111 OPS55-9119 (9/92).

Ernest Chausson

French 1855-1899

NEW REVIEW

Chausson. Symphony, Op. 20[a]. Poème, Op. 25[b]. ***Saint-Saëns.*** Introduction and Rondo capriccioso, Op. 28[b]. [b]**David Oistrakh** (vn); **Boston Symphony Orchestra/Charles Munch.** RCA Gold Seal GD60683. Item marked [a] recorded in 1962, [b] 1955.

56m ADD

Chausson was haunted by "the red spectre of Wagner" when working on his opera *Le Roi Arthus.* Hardly surprising, given the choice of subject; and the fact that he spent his honeymoon at Bayreuth in 1883 in order to hear *Parsifal*! One of the differences between the Symphony (1890) and the *Poème* (1896) is that the former imitates and incorporates many of Wagner's specific ideas and techniques with the cyclical form of his teacher, Franck; whereas the latter shows Chausson having absorbed Wagner's sound-world into a language of his own. It was his young friend Debussy who encouraged Chausson to purge himself of external influences, though it was also Debussy's output that eventually left in the shade the post-Wagnerian utterances of the so-called "bande à Franck" of Chausson, d'Indy, Duparc and others. The tragedy of Chausson is that the new dawn was cut short — whilst bicycling on holiday in 1899, he lost control, crashed into a wall and was killed. The Symphony, for all its abundance of Wagner, and Franckian highmindedness, is underestimated; indeed, Wilfrid Mellers wrote that "one only has to compare his Symphony with Franck's to appreciate the difference between true nobility and grandiose intention". And it has surely never had a more passionate interpreter than Charles Munch. Sleek and powerful in the outer movements (the finale is thrillingly impetuous), it is never excessively serious, or seriously overblown. Oistrakh brings his full, vibrant tone to the *Poème*, another reading with faster tempos than we are used to today. Perhaps some of the work's dark, dreamy melancholic floating is compromised in this account; but the gains are an identifiable shape to the melody and a sense of direction. And the Saint-Saëns *Introduction and Rondo capriccioso*

impresses by not trying to impress. All this gloriously direct music-making is matched by forward and clear stereo sound, remarkable for its age.

Chausson. Poème de l'amour et de la mer, Op. 19[a]. Poème, Op. 25[b].
Fauré. Pelléas et Mélisande — suite, Op. 80. Pavane, Op. 50[c]. [a]**Linda Finnie** (contr); [c]**Renaissance Singers; Ulster Orchestra/Yan Pascal Tortelier** ([b]vn). Chandos CHAN8952. Texts and translations included. Recorded 1989-1990.

lh 9m DDD 12/91 

Belfast's Ulster Hall may seem an unlikely source for nearly 70 minutes worth of demure *fin de siècle* melancholia, but the Chandos engineers have secured just that from Yan Pascal Tortelier and the Ulster Orchestra, who show just how convincing they can sound in this refined and evocative music by Chausson and Fauré. They are joined by Linda Finnie in a voluptuous and often tenderly seductive reading of Chausson's *Poème de l'amour et de la mer* — a performance of clarity and winning understatement. The rich, dark-hued violin tone of Yan Pascal Tortelier, in the enigmatic *Poème* by Chausson, is an ideal foil to Finnie's crystalline vocalization of the earlier work, and the accompaniment of both soloists reveals the Ulster Orchestra to be as sympathetic and sensitive to their needs as one could possibly wish in this music. Fauré, like Debussy, Sibelius and even Schoenberg, perceived the musical possibilities of Maeterlinck's symbolist play *Pelléas et Mélisande*, and Tortelier and his orchestra offer a memorable performance of the suite from Fauré's complete incidental music of 1898. Again, a degree of reticence and understatement allows the elusive simplicity of expression to come to the fore, particularly in the contributions of the Ulster wind players. The orchestra are joined by the Renaissance Singers in the popular *Pavane* although it has to be said that the actual text by Robert de Montesquiou makes little impression here. With first-class sound and affecting, richly idiomatic performances, however, this admirable recording could hardly be more inviting.

Further listening ...

LE ROI ARTHUS. **Soloists; French Radio Chorus and New Philharmonic Orchestra/Armin Jordan.** Erato Libretto 2292-45407-2 (10/91).

Carlos Chávez (Y Ramírez)

Mexican 1899-1978

Suggested listening ...

Sinfonia de Antigona[a]. Symphony No. 4, "Sinfonia romantica"[a]. *Coupled with* ***Revueltas.*** Caminos[b]. Musica para charlar[b]. Ventanas[b]. [a]**Royal Philharmonic Orchestra,** [b]**Mexican State Philharmonic Orchestra/Enrique Bátiz.** ASV CDDCA653 (8/89).

Luigi Cherubini

Italian 1760-1842

NEW REVIEW

Cherubini. OVERTURES. **Academy of St Martin in the Fields/Sir Neville Marriner.** EMI CDC7 54438-2. Recorded in 1991.
Eliza. Médée. L'hôtellerie portugaise. Les deux journées. Anacréon. Faniska. Les abendcérages. Concert Overture.

lh 7m DDD 9/92

No one was a bigger fan of Luigi Cherubini than Beethoven. Later, the Florence-born figure was similarly adulated by Weber, Mendelssohn and Spohr who, on attending a performance of

Cherubini's opera *Les deux journées,* was inspired to become a composer himself. The superb overture to that same opera is one of the eight items on this very welcome CD from Marriner and his sparklingly accomplished Academy players, and one only has to sample its magical introduction (with its evocative orchestration and probing harmonic sense) to readily appreciate just why this music so captured the young Spohr's imagination. First heard in January 1800, *Les deux journées* proved to be Cherubini's single greatest operatic success, and this collection spans the period from *Eliza* (dating from 1794, and the second of his Parisian 'rescue' operas — a naïve form much favoured by newly-installed political powers since the 1789 Revolution) to the ambitious *Concert Overture* written in 1815 for the London Philharmonic Society. That latter work proves just a mite disappointing, though the finest offerings here (*Médée, Les deux journées, Faniska* and *Anacréon*) certainly all display, in the words of Basil Deane (the excellent annotator here), "a dramatic awareness and a wealth of thematic, harmonic and formal invention, combined with a vivid sense of orchestral colour and texture, which make them a group of compositions worthy to stand beside the overtures of his great contemporary, and admirer, Beethoven". An excellent recording complements the polished, sprightly performances.

Further listening ...

MEDEA. **Soloists; Hungarian Radio and Television Chorus; Budapest Symphony Orchestra/Lamberto Gardelli.** Hungaroton HCD11904/05-2 (4/87).

Fryderyk Chopin

Polish 1810-1849

Chopin. Piano Concertos — No. 1 in E minor, Op. 11; No. 2 in F minor, Op. 21. **Murray Perahia** (pf); **Israel Philharmonic Orchestra/Zubin Mehta.** Sony Classical SK44922. Recorded live in 1989.

1h 16m DDD 6/90

Warm applause from the audience is not the only pointer to the fact that Perahia's are live concert recordings. The playing itself is full of that "inspirational heat-of-the-moment" long known to mean more to Perahia than mere streamlined studio correctness. The miracle is the way his urgency of feeling finds an outlet in playing of such super-sensitive finesse. Nearly always he favours slightly faster tempo than many of his rivals on disc, giving the first movements of both works a strong sense of direction in response to their *risoluto* markings. Mehta and the Israel Philharmonic might even be thought over-resolute, at the cost of a measure of the music's aristocratic elegance. But tonal balance is good, and progressively in each work a close-tuned partnership is achieved. Both rapt slow movements are sung with an exquisite tonal purity as well as embellished with magical delicacy. Their contrasting middle sections nevertheless bring eruptions of burning intensity. The dance-inspired finales have a scintillating lightness and charm recalling Perahia, the fingertip magician, in Mendelssohn. Even if not in the five-star class, the recorded sound is the equal of anything to be heard in rival CD versions of these two endearing reminders of the young Chopin's last year in Warsaw before leaving his homeland for ever.

Additional recommendations ...

Nos. 1 and 2. **Krystian Zimerman** (pf). **Los Angeles Philharmonic Orchestra/Carlo Maria Giulini.** DG 415 970-2GH — 1h 12m ADD 9/86

No. 2[a]. ***Tchaikovsky.*** *Piano Concerto No. 1 in B flat minor, Op. 23*[b]. **Vladimir Ashkenazy** (pf); **London Symphony Orchestra/**[a]**David Zinman,** [b]**Lorin Maazel.** Decca Ovation 417 750-2DM — 1h 6m ADD 1/89

No. 1[a]. *No. 2*[b]. **Tamás Vásáry** (pf). **Berlin Philharmonic Orchestra/**[a]**Jerszy Semkow,** [b]**János Kulka.** DG Privilege 429 515-2GR — 1h 15m ADD 6/90 £

Nos. 1 and 2. Concerto Rondo in F major, Op. 14, "Krakowiak". Variations in B flat major on "Là ci darem la mano", Op. 2. Andante spianato and Grande Polonaise brillante in E flat major, Op. 22. Fantaisie-impromptu in C sharp minor, Op. 66. Barcarolle in F sharp major, Op. 60. Nocturnes — No. 2 in E flat major, Op. 9 No. 2; No. 5 in F sharp major, Op. 15 No. 2. Waltzes — No. 7 in C sharp minor, Op. 64 No. 2; No. 9 in A flat major, Op. 69 No. 1. Prelude in D flat major, Op. 28 No. 15. Ballade No. 3 in A flat major, Op. 47. Fantaisie in F minor, Op. 49. **Claudio Arrau** (pf); **London Philharmonic Orchestra/Eliahu Inbal.** Philips 426 147-2PS3 — ③ 3h 5m ADD 6/90 £ B

No. 1. Fantasia on Polish Airs, Op. 13. Andante spianato and Grande polonaise brillante in E flat major, Op. 22. **Idil Biret** (pf). **Czecho-Slovak State Philharmonic Orchestra, Košice/Robert Stankovsky.** Naxos 8 550368 — 1h 14m DDD 4/92 £ B

No. 2. Variations on "Là ci darem le mano", Op. 2. Concerto Rondo in F major, Op. 14, "Krakowiak". **Idil Biret** (pf). **Czecho-Slovak State Philharmonic Orchestra, Košice/Robert Stankovsky.** Naxos 8 550369 — 1h 7m DDD 4/92 £ B

Nos. 1 and 2. Waltz in C sharp minor, Op. 64 No. 2. Nocturnes — Nos. 1-19. **Artur Rubinstein** (pf); **London Symphony Orchestra/Sir John Barbirolli.** EMI Références mono CHS7 64491-2 — ② 2h 41m ADD 7/93 B ▲

Chopin. PIANO WORKS. **Maurizio Pollini** (pf); [a]**Philharmonia Orchestra/Paul Kletzki.** EMI Studio Plus CDM7 64354-2. Item marked [a] from ASD370 (11/60), [b] ASD2577 (8/70).
Piano Concerto No. 1 in E minor, Op. 11[a]. Ballade in G minor, Op. 23[b]. Nocturnes, Op. 15 — No. 1 in F major[b]; No. 2 in F sharp minor[b]. Nocturnes, Op. 27 — No. 1 in C sharp minor; No. 2 in D flat major. Polonaise in A flat major, Op. 53[b].

1h 13m ADD 11/92

Pollini's disc is a classic. The concerto was recorded shortly after the 18-year-old pianist's victory at the Warsaw competition in 1959. Nowadays we might expect a wider dynamic range to allow greater power in the first movement's tuttis, but in all other respects the recording completely belies its age, with a near perfect balance between soloist and orchestra. This is, of course, very much Pollini's disc, just as the First Concerto is very much the soloist's show, but effacing as the accompaniment is, Pollini's keyboard miracles of poetry and refinement could not have been achieved without one of the most characterful and responsive accounts of that accompaniment ever committed to tape. The expressive range of the Philharmonia on top form under Kletzki is at once, and continuously, exceptional, as is the accord between soloist and conductor in matters of phrasing and shading. The solo items, recorded in 1968, are a further reminder of Pollini's effortless bravura and aristocratic poise.

Chopin. PIANO WORKS. Volume 8. **Vladimir Ashkenazy** (pf). Decca 410 122-2DH. From 410 122-1DH (7/84).
Mazurkas, Op. 30 — No. 1 in C minor; No. 2 in B minor; No. 3 in D flat major; No. 4 in C sharp minor. Op. 33 — No. 1 in G sharp minor; No. 2 in D major; No. 3 in C major; No. 4 in B minor. *Nocturnes,* Op. 32 — No. 1 in B major; No. 2 in A flat major; C minor, Op. posth. Impromptu in A flat major, Op. 29. Largo in E flat major, Op. posth. Scherzo in B flat minor, Op. 31. Waltz in F major, Op. 34 No. 3. Variation No. 6 in E major, "Hexameron".

52m DDD 7/84

Though Ashkenazy's decision to offer a mix of genres on a disc instead of a chronological sequence may be questioned, the result is probably more satisfactory for listening, since one has here a real recital of varied music. It ranges from the extrovert brilliance of the B flat minor Scherzo and the F major *Grande valse brillante*, Op. 34 No. 3, through the elegantly wistful 'salon' mood of the A flat major Nocturne and the surprisingly varied and dramatic Mazurkas, to mere chips from the composer's workbench like the *Largo* in E flat major and the C minor Nocturne which were both unpublished until 1938. Ashkenazy's affinity with Chopin in all his moods is the justification for such a complete survey as this and only very occasionally might one feel a need for even more mystery and spontaneity. As for the sound-quality, it is bright but very faithful and never approaches harshness even in the most powerful passages. This is a noble recording.

Chopin. PIANO WORKS. **Peter Katin** (pf). Olympia OCD254.
Nocturnes — E minor, Op. 72 No. 1; C sharp minor, Op. posth. Op. 9 — No. 1 in B flat

minor; No. 2 in E flat major; No. 3 in B major. Op. 15 — No. 1 in F major; No. 2 in F sharp major; No. 3 in G minor. Op. 27 — No. 1 in C sharp minor; No. 2 in D flat major. Op. 32 — No. 1 in B major; No. 2 in A flat major; C minor. Op. 37 — No. 1 in G minor; No. 2 in G major. Op. 48 — No. 1 in C minor; No. 2 in F sharp minor. Op. 55 — No. 1 in F minor; No. 2 in E flat major. Op. 62 — No. 1 in B major; No. 2 in E major. *Impromptus* — No. 1 in A flat major, Op. 29; No. 2 in F sharp major, Op. 35; No. 3 in G flat major, Op. 51. Fantaisie-impromptu in C sharp minor, Op. 66.

② 2h 20m DDD 12/89

Here at medium price are 140 minutes of great piano music finely played. Katin is a quietly persuasive artist rather than a virtuoso and he brings an entirely appropriate sense of intimacy to this Chopin recital of nocturnes and impromptus. The approach is chronological and complete, so that in the nocturnes the E minor and the *Lento con gran espressione* in C sharp minor come first, although they were published posthumously, and we also hear the rarely played C minor (without opus number) which only came to light in 1937, a century after its composition. Rubato is used freely but tastefully and melodies really sing, so that a good balance is achieved between emotional richness and the fastidiousness that was also part of Chopin's musical nature. The impromptus are well done too, with the famous *Fantaisie-impromptu* played according to a manuscript source and so with rather fewer ornaments than usual. The recording was made in an Oslo church with a fine acoustic and an instrument that the pianist finds "exceptionally sympathetic", as the booklet tells us and his own programme notes are almost as poetic as the music itself, as when he writes of the E flat major Nocturne, Op. 55/2, that "a coda of sheer magic seems to descend from a height and passes into infinity" — which is not purple prose but a statement demonstrably true of the music and the performance.

Chopin. PIANO WORKS. **Nikolai Demidenko**. Hyperion CDA66514. Recorded 1989-1990.

Introduction and Variations in E major on a German air ("Der Schweizerbub"). *Scherzos* — No. 1 in B minor, Op. 20; No. 2 in B flat minor, Op. 31; No. 3 in C sharp minor, Op. 39; No. 4 in E major, Op. 54. Variations in B flat major on "Là ci darem la mano", Op. 2.

1h 3m DDD 1/92

"Off with your hats, gentlemen — a genius" were the percipient words of the 21-year-old Schumann on first discovering the *Là ci darem* Variations composed by Chopin when still only 17. Though well represented as originally conceived for piano and orchestra, it was left to the young Russian, Nikolai Demidenko (currently on the staff of the UK's Yehudi Menuhin School) to introduce the work to the CD catalogue as recast for solo piano. Serving as a grand finale to a recital opening with Chopin's still earlier, charmingly innocent *Swiss Boy* Variations, Demidenko's performance confirms him as a pianist of outstanding imaginative vitality as well as technical brilliance, moreover a player really able to make the piano sing throughout a wide and varied tonal range. The main musical tests nevertheless come in the four *Scherzos*, where again he surmounts all hurdles with effortless ease and poetic grace while extracting the loveliest sound from his instrument. But Chopin devotees should be warned that in making this music wholly his own he is sometimes a little idiosyncratically self-indulgent, notably in matters of lyrical relaxation, though also in No. 1, in choosing to remove the sting from Chopin's challenging opening chords. An artist to be watched none the less, here very well recorded.

NEW REVIEW

Chopin. PIANO WORKS. **Nikolai Demidenko.** Hyperion CDA66597. Recorded in 1992.

Polonaises — A flat major, Op. 61, "Polonaise-fantaisie"; G minor; B flat major; A flat major; G sharp minor; G flat major. Bolero in A minor, Op. 19. Allegro de concert, Op. 46. Berceuse in D flat major, Op. 57. Tarantelle in A flat major, Op. 43.

1h 6m DDD 11/92 

Nikolai Demidenko's first Chopin recital for Hyperion (see above) coloured familiarity with novelty, coupling the four *Scherzos* with lesser known sets of *Variations*. Here he takes such enterprise a stage further, alternating Chopin's earliest *Polonaises* (elegant and scintillating juvenilia) with mature examples of his poetic genius, and with the *Bolero* and *Tarantelle* as racy and exotic additions. Even more importantly, Demidenko's playing, while maintaining its former finesse and precision, is altogether more poised, less arbitrary in its musical thinking. The *Allegro de concert* may be among the most daunting examples of Chopin's virtuosity — some of its more outrageous demands suggest the influence of his next door neighbour, the reclusive and quixotic Charles-Valentin Alkan — but for Demidenko such difficulties hardly exist; the greater the challenge the cooler and more nonchalant the response. The *Polonaise-fantaisie* and *Berceuse*, too, are both given with great individuality, challenging convention in one detail after another yet remaining meticulously close to the score. Such exceptional lucidity and clarity of line combine with recordings of the finest quality to make further discs from this source eagerly anticipated occasions.

Chopin. PIANO WORKS. **Ivan Moravec.** Dorian DOR90140.
Scherzos — No. 1 in B minor, Op. 20; No. 2 in B flat minor, Op. 31; No. 3 in C sharp minor, Op. 39; No. 4 in E major, Op. 54. *Etudes,* Op. 25 — No. 1 in A flat major; No. 7 in C sharp minor. *Mazurkas* — C major, Op. 7 No. 5; C sharp minor, Op. 41 No. 1; C major, Op. 56 No. 2; F minor, Op. 68 No. 4.

57m DDD 2/92 

Here it is the shorter works that do most to explain this 62-year-old Czech pianist's enviable reputation as a Chopin player. The exquisite delicacy and finesse he brings to his concluding group of mazurkas while at the same time conveying the full potency of their folk-spirit, not least the rusticity of the last two in C, makes you long for a complete set from him. The A flat Etude is sheer magic as sound *per se*, while his intimately inflected melodic line in the laden C sharp minor Etude takes you to the innermost places of the composer's heart. Moravec plays the four scherzos with a light-fingered, mercurial, mood-of-the-moment impulse as if trying to recapture the unpredictable spontaneity and impressionability of Chopin's own playing, allegedly never the same twice. In the heat of excitement there is momentary loss of finesse in No. 2. And if copied by the younger generation, some of his rubato (especially in the more ruminative trio sections of all but No. 3) might sound mannered. So these four works are perhaps better recommended for occasional rather than everyday listening. A suspicion of boxiness in the otherwise mellow recording lessens as your ear tunes in.

NEW REVIEW

Chopin. PIANO WORKS. **Artur Rubinstein** (pf). EMI Références mono CHS7 64697-2. Recorded 1928-39.
Waltz in A flat major, Op. 34 No. 1 (from HMV DB1168, 2/30). Mazurkas — Nos. 1-51 (DB3802/8, 9/39 and DB3839/45, 2/42). Four Scherzos (DB1915/8, 11/33). Barcarolle in F sharp major, Op. 60 (DB1161, 8/28). Berceuse in D flat major, Op. 57 (DB2149, 7/34). Polonaises — Nos. 1-7 (DB2493/6, 7/36 and DB2497/9, 8/36). Andante spianato and Grand polonaise in E flat major, Op. 22 (DB2499/500, 8/36).

③ 3h 53m ADD 

Artur Rubinstein is popularly remembered as Chopin's genial, sparkling elder statesman; but, up until now, only seasoned collectors have been aware of his many pre-war recordings — where "aristocratic poise" (Rubinstein's best-known interpretative attribute) went hand-in-hand with impulsiveness, spontaneity and dazzling virtuosity. To compare these 1932-5 versions of the *Scherzos* and Polonaises with Rubinstein's wise, elegant (and extremely musical) post-war recordings for RCA is to pit "emotion recollected in tranquillity" against the hot-headed impact of immediate experience. There's less of a contrast with the Mazurkas, although — again — these first recordings (Rubinstein made two subsequent sets) have that extra degree of 'lift' and tension. Readers will of course ask themselves whether transfers from old 78s really can deliver as much musical pleasure as modern recordings. But in this case, so-called 'surface noise' is never intrusive and the quality of the playing is so exceptional that the mono sound and relative lack of dynamic range soon cease to pose a problem.

Chopin. PIANO WORKS. **Martha Argerich.** DG Galleria 415 836-2GGA.
24 Preludes, Op. 28. *Preludes* — C sharp minor, Op. 45; A flat major, Op. posth. (all from 2530 721, 2/78). Barcarolle in F sharp major, Op. 60 (SLPM138672, 1/68). Polonaise in A flat major, Op. 53 (SLPM139317, 5/68). Scherzo in B flat minor, Op. 31 (2530 530, 6/75).

lh 2m ADD 4/88 

Professor Zurawlew, the founder of the Chopin Competition in Warsaw was once asked which one of the prizewinners he would pick as having been his favourite. Looking back over the period 1927-75, the answer came back immediately: "Martha Argerich". This CD could explain why. There are very few recordings of the 24 Preludes that have such a perfect combination of temperamental virtuosity and compelling artistic insight. Argerich has the technical equipment to do whatever she wishes with the music. Whether it is in the haunting, dark melancholy of No. 2 in A minor or the lightning turmoil of No. 16 in B flat minor, she is profoundly impressive. It is these sharp changes of mood that make the performance scintillatingly unpredictable. In the *Barcarolle* there is no relaxed base on which the melodies of the right hand are constructed, as is conventional, but more the piece emerges as a stormy odyssey through life, with moments of visionary awareness. Argerich, it must be said, is on firmer ground in the *Polonaise*, where her power and technical security reign triumphant. The CD ends with a rippling and yet slightly aggressive reading of the second Scherzo. This is very much the playing of a pianist who lives in the 'fast lane' of life. The sound quality is a bit reverberant, an effect heightened by the fact that Argerich has a tendency to over-pedal.

Chopin. PIANO WORKS. **Krystian Zimerman.** (pf). DG 423 090-2GH.
Ballades — No. 1 in G minor, Op. 23; No. 2 in F major, Op. 38; No. 3 in A flat major, Op. 47; No. 4 in F minor, Op. 52. Barcarolle in F sharp major, Op. 60. Fantasie in F minor, Op. 49.

lh DDD 10/88 

Chopin's choice of the previously unused literary title of "ballade" for the four great works with which this recital begins suggests that they may well have been inspired by tales of his country's past. Certainly Krystian Zimerman, a Pole himself, unfolds all four with a rare appreciation of their freely self-evolving narrative style, almost as if he were composing the music himself while going along. His timing here and there might be thought a little self-indulgent in its lingerings but he never rushes his fences. The overall impression left by his playing is one of uncommon expansiveness, upheld by a splendidly full, warm, rich recording. Despite his very slow tempo in the F minor Fantasie he still manages to suggest that patriotic fires were very much aflame in the composer at the time. The *Barcarolle* is as seductively sensuous as it is passionate.

Additional recommendation ...
Ballades. Piano Sonata No. 2 in B flat minor, Op. 35. **Andrei Gavrilov** (pf). DG 435 622-2GH — 57m DDD 6/92

NEW REVIEW

Chopin. PIANO WORKS. **Cyril Huvé** (fp). EMI CDC7 54480-2. Recorded in 1991.
Ballades — No. 1 in G minor, Op. 23; No. 2 in F major, Op. 38; No. 3 in A flat major, Op. 47; No. 4 in F minor, Op. 52. *Scherzos* — No. 1 in B minor, Op. 20; No. 2 in B flat minor, Op. 31; No. 3 in C sharp minor, Op. 39; No. 4 in E major, Op. 54.

lh 14m DDD 12/92 

"When I feel out of sorts I use an Erard and quite easily find a sound which is there ready-made for me. But when I am on top form and feel strong enough to seek out a sound of my own, then what I need is a Pleyel." Chopin's own comments about his two favourite piano manufacturers are borne out by this unusual recording where Cyril Huvé (pupil of the late, great Claudio Arrau) performs the *Ballades* and *Scherzos* on two such instruments, both original, beautifully restored and both approximately a semitone below modern pitch (though the ear soon adjusts). Huvé is such a sensitive and technically brilliant musician that even non-devotees of the fortepiano should be delighted with the results. Of the two instruments, the Pleyel is the lighter and therefore better suited to the earlier works — in the First *Ballade* the inner voices are for once clearly audible, particularly in the lower range. It is also a much rawer sound — the final crashing dissonances of the same work are stark and shocking when heard without the fuller resonance of a modern-day piano we have become used to. Huvé moulds a beautiful *cantabile* tone, particularly in the middle section of the First *Scherzo* and the opening of the Second *Ballade*. The only minus point is perhaps a more restricted dynamic range than on a modern piano, felt particularly keenly at the dramatic opening of the Second *Scherzo*. However, this cannot be said of the Erard (on which Huvé plays the Third and Fourth *Scherzos* and *Ballades*), which sounds closer to a modern piano without losing the clarity of a fortepiano (listen, for example, to Huvé's filigree passages in the Third *Scherzo* — 1'36" onwards). And again in the Third *Ballade*, there is much greater lightness than in comparable modern performances. A pertinent essay on the instruments and the music by Huvé and clear, believable sound add to the allure of this fine disc.

Chopin. Etudes, Opp. 10 and 25. **Maurizio Pollini** (pf). DG 413 794-2GH. From 2530 291 (11/72).

56m ADD 5/85 p B

The 24 *Etudes* of Chopin's Opp. 10 and 25, although dating from his twenties, remain among the most perfect specimens of the genre ever known, with all technical challenges — and they are formidable — dissolved into the purest poetry. With his own transcendental technique (and there are few living pianists who can rival it) Pollini makes you unaware that problems even exist — as for instance in Op. 10 No. 10 in A flat, where the listener is swept along in an effortless stream of melody. The first and last of the same set in C major and C minor have an imperious strength and drive, likewise the last three impassioned outpourings of Op. 25. Lifelong dislike of a heart worn on the sleeve makes him less than intimately confiding in more personal contexts such as No. 3 in E and No. 6 in E flat minor from Op. 10, or the nostalgic middle section of No. 5 in E minor and the searing No. 7 in C sharp minor from Op. 25. Like the playing, so the recording itself could profitably be a little warmer from time to time, but it is a princely disc all the same, which all keyboard *aficionados* will covet.

Additional recommendations ...

Etudes. **Vladimir Ashkenazy** (pf). Decca 414 127-2DH — DDD 1/85 p B

Etudes. Trois nouvelles études, Op. posth. **Boris Berezovsky** (pf). Teldec 9031-73129-2 — 1h 8m DDD 4/92 p B

Etudes. **John Bingham** (pf). Meridian CDE84221 — 1h 7m DDD 5/93 p B

Chopin. Piano Sonatas — No. 2 in B flat minor, Op. 35; No. 3 in B minor, Op. 58. **Maurizio Pollini** (pf). DG 415 346-2GH.

52m DDD 8/86 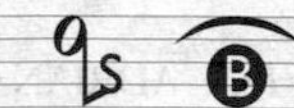

These two magnificent romantic sonatas are Chopin's longest works for solo piano. The passion of the B flat minor Sonata is evident throughout, as is its compression (despite the overall length) — for example, the urgent first subject of its first movement is omitted in the recapitulation. As for its mysterious finale, once likened to "a pursuit in utter darkness", it puzzled Chopin's contemporaries but now seems totally right. The B minor Sonata is more glowing and spacious, with a wonderful *Largo* third movement, but its finale is even more exhilarating than that of the B flat minor, and on a bigger scale. Pollini plays this music with overwhelming power and depth of feeling; the expressive intensity is rightly often disturbing. Magisterial technique is evident throughout and the recording is sharp-edged but thrilling.

Additional recommendations ...

Nos. 2 and 3. Fantaisie in F minor. **Artur Rubinstein** (pf). RCA Red Seal RD89812 — 1h 1m ADD 2/87 B

Nos. 2 and 3. **Murray Perahia** (pf). CBS CD76242 — 50m ADD 3/89 B

Nos. 2 and 3. No. 1 in C minor, Op. 4. Etudes, Op. 10 — No. 6 in E flat minor. Etudes, Op. 25 — No. 3 in F major; No. 4 in A minor; No. 10 in B minor; No. 11 in A minor. Mazurkas, Op. 17 — No. 1 in B flat major; No. 2 in E minor; No. 3 in A flat major; No. 4 in A minor. **Leif Ove Andsnes** (pf). Virgin Classics Duo VCK7 59072-2 — ② 1h 51m DDD 6/92 Ⓑ

Further listening ...

Rondo in C minor, Op. 1. Rondo "à la Mazur" in F major, Op. 5. Introduction and Rondo in C minor/E flat major, Op. 16. Rondo in C major, Op. 73. *Mazurkas, Op. posth.* — G major; B flat major; C major; A flat major; D major. Introduction and Variations in E major on "Der Schweizerbub". Introduction and Variations in B flat major on a theme from Hérold's "Ludovic", Op. 12. Souvenir de Paganini (Variations in A major). Variations No. 6 in E major on a march from Bellini's "I Puritani". Introduction, theme and variations (with Martin Sauer, pf). **Idil Biret** (pf). Naxos 8 550508 (5/93).

Preludes Nos. 1-26. Three Impromptus. Fantaisie-impromptu in C sharp minor, Op. 66. Waltzes Nos. 1-19. Four Ballades. Barcarolle in F sharp major, Op. 60. Fantasie in F minor, Op. 49. Four Scherzos. Polonaises — No. 7 in A flat major, Op. 61, "Polonaise-fantaisie". Nocturnes Nos. 1-21. **Claudio Arrau** (pf). Philips 422 038-2PH6 (6-disc set).

Complete Piano Works. **Vladimir Ashkenazy** (pf). Decca 421 185-2DH13 (13-disc set).

Johannes Ciconia

French/Italian c.1335-1411

Suggested listening ...

Amor por ti sempre. Caçando un giorno. O Padua, sidus praeclarum. Regina gloriosa. Aler m'en veus. Io crido amor. O rosa bella. Poy che morir. Ben che va dui donna. Le ray au soleyl (three versions). Pertrum Marcello Venetum/O petre antistes inclite. Chi nel servir antico. Per quella strada. Una panthera. Gli atti col dançar. Sus une fontayne. O Petre, Christe discipule. Doctorem principem/Melodia suavissima/Vir mitis. O virum omnimoda/O Lux et decus/O beate Nicholae. **Project Ars Nova Ensemble.** New Albion NA048CD (5/93).

Francesco Cilea

Italian 1866-1950

NEW REVIEW

Cilea. ADRIANA LECOUVREUR. **Renata Scotto** (sop) Adriana Lecouvreur; **Plácido Domingo** (ten) Maurizio; **Sherrill Milnes** (bar) Michonnet; **Elena Obraztsova** (mez) Princesse de Bouillon; **Giancarlo Luccardi** (bass) Prince de Bouillon; **Florindo Andreolli** (ten) Abbe de Chazeuil; **Lillian Watson** (sop) Jouvenot; **Ann Murray** (mez) Dangeville; **Paul Crook** (ten) Poisson; Major-domo; **Paul Hudson** (bass) Quinault; **Ambrosian Opera Chorus; Philharmonia Orchestra/James Levine.** CBS CD79310. Notes, text and translation included. From 79310 (6/78). Recorded in 1977.

② 2h 15m ADD 3/90

Adriana Lecouvreur is an archetypal prima donna vehicle. Look at the plot coldly, without reference to the music, and it's costumed hokum of an improbability that takes the breath away (of course there's jealousy, of course there's a death-scene, but what do you say to a bunch of poisoned violets as a murder weapon?). Even with the music, even allowing that Cilea was a much shrewder man of the theatre and a much more able musician than his detractors can bear to allow, it is still ... well, hokum with some damned good tunes. But Cilea wrote his opera in the full knowledge that an essential five per cent of its appeal would be added by the prima donna. Not with faultless vocalism, though that's a prerequisite too, but with the sort of allure of vocal personality that elsewhere would be called "star quality". With that extra five per cent, arguments about the artifice of the plot and the occasional thinness of the score fall away as the irrelevancies that they are. And you can tell very soon whether the soprano in question has that quality: after Cilea's brief but evocative scene-setting (telling us that we're back-stage at the Comédie Française in the eighteenth century, a world of glamour and intrigue), she enters, a prima donna portraying a prima donna, and tells us, to a sumptuous melody, that star though she is she's but the humble handmaid of her art. If you are not moved despite yourself, despite the obvious artifice (is it Adriana or the soprano herself speaking?) proceed no further; either this opera or this performance is not for you. Scotto has that magic quality, in abundance. That Domingo is an ardent hero, Milnes a touching elderly admirer, Obraztsova a baleful rival and Levine an enthusiastic exponent of the subtleties and ingenuities of a composer often despised for having written prima donna vehicles is all bonus, making this a performance that you can return to again and again. But the centre of its allure, its *raison d'être,* is Renata Scotto, glamour personified. Her entrance is electrifying, her death moving and everything between is more than life size.

Mikolajus Ciurlionis

Lithuanian 1875-1911

Ciurlionis. Symphonic poems — The sea; In the forest. Five preludes for string orchestra. **Slovak Philharmonic Orchestra/Juozas Domarkas.** Marco Polo 8 223323. Recorded in 1990.

51m DDD 6/91 

Mikolajus Ciurlionis was a Lithuanian composer who studied in Warsaw and Leipzig and became deeply involved in his country's history and folk-heritage. He was also a talented visual artist, and one of his paintings, a somewhat dark and forbidding landscape, is reproduced on the cover of this CD. As a composer he was clearly influenced by the great late romantics, but he has a distinctly individual musical personality, and he handles a big orchestra with much skill and imagination. *The sea,* a tone poem completed in 1907, is cast on a very ambitious scale, and over the course of nearly half an hour maintains a high level of inspiration and concentration. The slightly earlier and shorter piece *In the forest* is a little less distinguished in invention, but still attracts through the colour of its orchestration. Ciurlionis himself transcribed the brief *Five prèludes* from piano originals, and these wispy, atmospheric, and contrasted sketches show that he could work effectively on a smaller scale. The Slovak Philharmonic Orchestra's playing on this disc is efficient, but not particularly polished. Juozas Domarkas is regarded as Lithuania's leading conductor, and his performances certainly sound authoritative. The recording is very good.

Rebecca Clarke

British 1886-1979

NEW REVIEW

R. Clarke. VOCAL AND CHAMBER WORKS. [a]**Patricia Wright** (sop); [b]**Jonathan Rees** (vn); [c]**Kathron Sturrock** (pf). Gamut Classics GAMCD534. Texts included. Recorded in 1992. June Twilight[ac]. A Dream[ac]. The Cherry Blossom Wand[ac]. The Cloths of Heaven[ac]. Shy one[ac]. The Seal Man[ac]. Down by the Salley Gardens[ac]. Infant Joy[ac]. Lethe[ac]. Tiger tiger[ac]. Tears[ac]. God made a tree[ac]. Come, oh come, my Life's Delight[ac]. Greeting[ac]. The Donkey[ac]. Cradle Song[ac]. Eight o'clock[ac]. Psalm of David when he was in the wilderness of Judah[ac]. The Aspidistra[ac]. Three Old English Songs[ab]. Three Irish Country Songs[ab]. Midsummer Moon[bc]. Chinese Puzzle[bc]. Lullaby[bc].

1h 15m DDD 5/93

Rebecca Clarke, Stanford's only female composition pupil, has never been given the recognition she deserves — although she is better represented in concert halls and recordings than certain other British women composers who should receive more attention than they do. She is well served by this collection of 28 songs and violin pieces. Her style is paradoxically both rhapsodic and restrained; the settings use the voice economically, usually presenting one note per word and avoiding melismas, while the emotional climate tends to be atmospheric yet understated. But this very understatement means that when the moments of passion do arrive, they are all the more powerful. Sometimes the harmonic language resembles Debussy (as in The *Cherry Blossom Wand*), and at other times her fondness for exotic colours, often semitones strung out at intervals along the keyboard in accompaniments, even makes you think of Szymanowski, especially in the violin and piano miniature *Midsummer Moon*. Although tempos often tend to the medium rather than to extremes of fast and slow, there is plenty of subtle emotional variety within the settings, which show a wonderful sensitivity and imagination in responding to the poems of Yeats, Housman, Blake and John Masefield, among others. (It is unfortunate that several song texts could not be reproduced because of copyright complications.) Patricia Wright gives sensitive and beautiful performances, with a lovely clarity in both tone and strong characterization (especially in the supernatural narrative *The Seal Man*). Jonathan Rees's violin playing — which serves sometimes as obbligato, sometimes as the sole accompaniment — matches her style almost ideally, while Kathron Sturrock's piano playing captures and recreates the subtlety of Clarke's atmospheres.

Clemens non Papa

French/Flemish c.1510-c.1556

Clemens Non Papa. Missa Pastores quidnam vidistis. MOTETS. **The Tallis Scholars/Peter Phillips.** Gimell CDGIM013.

Motets — Pastores quidnam vidistis; Tribulationes civitatum; Pater peccavi; Ego flos campi.

54m DDD 12/87 

This recording is a feast for the ear. Thanks to the Tallis Scholars a great and prolific sixteenth-century Flemish master has been rescued from almost total oblivion. Peter Phillips once pinpointed two major requirements for the performance of polyphonic music, namely, tuning and sonority. From that standpoint one can, indeed, just lean back and enjoy every moment of this recording, because it fulfils amply both requirements. One is particularly impressed by the perfection of its implementation in the long extended eight-part motet *Pater, peccavi*, which describes the confession to his father of the Prodigal Son on his return to the family home. The eight voices are so well controlled and in such perfect accord that they generate an atmosphere of total serenity and confidence consistent with the theme of the text. Similar qualities are displayed in the Scholars' performance of the parody Mass *Pastores quidnam vidistis* and of its parent motet. The crafting of the performance is matched only by the carefully-wrought structuring of the music itself. In the Mass, the tuning and the rich sonority are bound together by a series of strong, interweaving arching phrases and by a slowly descending scale passing from voice to voice towards the end of certain movements.

Muzio Clementi

Italian/British 1752-1832

Suggested listening ...

Symphonies, Op. 18 — No. 1 in B flat major; No. 2 in D major. Minuetto poastorale in D major. Piano Concerto in C major. **Pietro Spada** (pf). **Philharmonia Orchestra/Francesco D'Avalos.** ASV CDDCA802 (2/93).

Symphonies — No. 1 in C major; No. 3 in G major, "Great National Symphony". Overture in C major. **Philharmonia Orchestra/Francesco D'Avalos.** ASV CDDCA803 (2/93).

Symphonies — No. 2 in D major; No. 4 in D major. Overture in D major. **Philharmonia Orchestra/Francesco D'Avalos.** ASV CDDCA804 (2/93).
The three recordings listed above are also available as part of a 3-disc mid-price set (ASV CDDCS322).

Louis-Nicolas Clérambault

French 1676-1749

Clérambault. DRAMATIC CANTATAS[a] — Orphée; Zéphire et Flore; Léandre et Héro. Sonata, "La Magnifique". [a]**Julianne Baird** (sop); **Music's Re-creation.** Meridian CDE84182. Texts and translations included.

lh 5m DDD 1/91

The *cantate française* was vigorously cultivated in France during the first three decades of the eighteenth century. A master, indeed *the* master of the form was Louis Nicolas Clérambault. Like his contemporary , he was skilful in blending features of the Italian style with those of his native France. Clérambault published five books of chamber cantatas between 1710 and 1726 as well as composing some half dozen others. Julianne Baird and Music's Re-creation have chosen a captivating programme which includes Clérambault's masterpiece, *Orphée*. Baird's declamation is stylish, her diction clear and her intonation dependable. She breathes life into each of the cantatas and, notwithstanding a somewhat harsh violin tone, is sympathetically accompanied by the instruments. This is a disc which explores an important and engaging area of French baroque musical life. The performances have strengths and weaknesses but it is the former which prevail, and the music emerges with bright colours and graceful gestures. Additionally, the programme includes Clérambault's attractive but seldom-performed trio sonata *La Magnifique*. Recorded sound is effective.

Further listening ...

Cantatas — Orphée; Médée. Harpsichord Suites — No. 1 in C major; No. 2 in C minor. **Rachel Yakar** (sop); **Wilbert Hazelzet** (fl); **Reinhard Goebel** (vn); **Charles Medlam** (va da gamba); **Alan Curtis, Kenneth Gilbert** (hpds). Archiv Produktion Collectio Argenta 437 085-2AT (1/93).

Eric Coates

British 1886-1957

Coates. ORCHESTRAL WORKS. [a]**Royal Liverpool Philharmonic Orchestra/Sir Charles Groves;** [b]**London Symphony Orchestra/Sir Charles Mackerras;** [c]**City of Birmingham Symphony Orchestra/Reginald Kilbey.** Classics for Pleasure CD-CFPD4456. From CFPD414456-3 (11/86). Recorded 1956-1971.
Saxo-Rhapsody. Wood Nymphs. Music Everywhere (Rediffusion March). From Meadow to Mayfair. The Dam Busters — march ([a] all from Columbia TWO226, 12/68); London. Cinderella — phantasy. London Again ([a] TWO321, 12/70). The Merrymakers — miniature overture. Summer Days — At the dance. By the Sleepy Lagoon. The Three Men — Man from the sea. The Three Bears — phantasy ([b] CFP40279, 3/78). Calling all Workers — march. The Three Elizabeths ([c] TWO361, 12/71).

② 2h 9m ADD 9/89

Eric Coates reached a vast public through the use of his music as signature tunes for radio programmes such as "In Town Tonight" ("Knightsbridge" from the *London Suite*), "Music While You Work" (*Calling all Workers*) and "Desert Island Discs" (*By the Sleepy Lagoon*). The cinema furthered the cause with the huge success of *The Dam Busters* march. There is much more to his music, though, than mere hit themes. Suites such as *London, London Again, From Meadow to Mayfair* and *The Three Elizabeths* offer a wealth of delights and are all the better for the juxtaposition of their contrasted movements. The two tone-poems for children, *Cinderella* and *The Three Bears* are splendidly apt pieces of programme music — simple to follow, ever charming, never trite. The miniature overture *The Merrymakers* and the elegant waltz "At the dance" (from the suite *Summer Days* are other superb pieces of light music, whilst the *Saxo-Rhapsody* shows Coates in somewhat more serious mood. Throughout there is a rich vein of melody, and an elegance and grace of orchestration that makes this music to listen to over and over again with ever increasing admiration. The three conductors and orchestras featured adopt a no-nonsense approach that modestly suggests that his music should not be lingered over, never taken too seriously. Considering that the Mackerras items were first issued in 1956 (the rest being from 1968-71), the sound is of astonishingly good and remarkably uniform quality. This is a veritable feast of delightful music and, at its low price, a remarkable bargain.

Samuel Coleridge-Taylor

British 1875-1912

NEW REVIEW

Coleridge-Taylor. CHAMBER WORKS. [a]**Harold Wright** (cl); [b]**Michael Ludwig** (vn); [c]**Hawthorne Quartet** (Ronan Lefkowitz, Si-Jing Huang, vns; Mark Ludwig, va; Sato Knudson, vc); [d]**Virginia Eskin** (pf). Koch International Classics 37056-2. Recorded in 1990.
Petite suite de concert, Op. 77[d]. Ballade in D minor, Op. 4[bd]. 24 Negro Melodies, Op. 59[d] — Take Nabandji; Going Up; Deep River; Run, Mary, run; Sometimes I feel like a motherless child; The Bamboula. Clarinet Quintet in F sharp minor, Op. 10[ac].

lh 20m DDD 10/92

The London-born Anglo-Negro composer Samuel Coleridge-Taylor is most commonly remembered nowadays for two works: the *Hiawatha* Oratorio and, perhaps, just one of the items on this CD — "Demande et Repose" from the once-popular *Petite suite de concert*, a delightful chunk of honeyed nostalgia that many of you will recognize, if not by name. However, Coleridge-Taylor's compositional skills were more varied than his reputation would have us believe: in addition to the pieces gathered here, he produced no less than 100 vocal and choral pieces, plus a number of operas, chamber and orchestral works. Virginia Eskin, who has long championed the farther reaches of romantic repertory, here comes up trumps with the piano version of the *Petite suite de concert* (it is somewhat better known as an orchestral work), a lively and engaging sequence of four movements, full of bland but evocative melodic invention. If the Dvořákian *Ballade* for violin and piano is sustained just a little longer than its material will comfortably bear, the *Negro Melodies* — more Brahmsian than Dvořákian this time — are spectacularly effective and should promptly be taken up by all discerning pianists in search of popular 'encore' pieces. The most ambitious work here, however, is the Clarinet Quintet, a 36-minute piece, essentially post-romantic in style, but purposefully argued and richly poetic, especially in a memorable and eminently repeatable *Larghetto affetuoso*. The rest of the work again betrays Dvořák's strong influence, but it is none the less well worth hearing and is played, like its appealing programme companions, in a way that communicates a refreshing level of commitment and enthusiasm. The recordings are generally excellent.

Coleridge-Taylor. Scenes from "The Song of Hiawatha". **Helen Field** (sop); **Arthur Davies** (ten); **Bryn Terfel** (bar); **Welsh National Opera Chorus and Orchestra/Kenneth Alwyn.** Argo 430 356-2ZH2. Notes and text included. Recorded in 1990.

② lh 59m DDD 9/91

Hiawatha's best days probably lie irrevocably in the past when the choral societies kept its publishers going with orders for copies and every year at the Albert Hall the tribes would gather for a performance in costume under Great Chief Malcolm Sargent. This new recording is at the very least an honourable reminder of those times, with choral forces that make it very clear why it was so beloved of choirs throughout the land, and orchestral playing that brings out the attractions of rhythm and colour that are also characteristic. There is an appropriately limpid, sparkling Laughing Waters in Helen Field, Arthur Davies sings the famous "Onaway, awake beloved" in fine lyrical style and Bryn Terfel makes a splendidly dramatic impression as he laments the death of Minnehaha. In short, it is a fully worthy performance under Kenneth Alwyn, and the recording is fine too. A question mark still hangs over the work itself. So often it seems to be on the verge of adventurous exploration and then to withdraw so as to remain within sound of the matinée teacups. Yet it has a genuine impulse behind it, and at times (particularly in Hiawatha's farewell) it generates emotion which one can well imagine might be almost alarmingly powerful on a grand occasion in the Albert Hall, if rather less so on an evening with the compact disc player at home.

Aaron Copland

American 1900-1990

Copland. ORCHESTRAL WORKS. [a]**Stanley Drucker** (cl); **New York Philharmonic Orchestra/Leonard Bernstein.** DG 431 672-2GH. Recorded live in 1989.
Clarinet Concerto[a]. Connotations. El salón México. Music for the Theatre.

lh 14m DDD 8/91

An excellent collection of music spanning much of Aaron Copland's career as a composer, with the added bonus of Bernstein's authoritative conducting. *El salón México* gives the disc a vigorous start with the New York Philharmonic playing with plenty of character and panache. Dating from the middle 1930s this is one of Copland's most attractive works, brilliantly evoking from simple means a sound portrait of Mexico. South America also played a part in the composition of the Clarinet Concerto, which Copland started writing for Benny Goodman in Rio de Janeiro in 1947. This great twentieth-century concerto receives the finest performance on the disc, with a deeply felt interpretation of the solo part from Stanley Drucker whose command of tone, phrasing and dynamics cannot be praised too highly. This is more than a match even for the rival Benny Goodman version (CBS CD42227). The remaining works, *Music for the Theatre* and *Connotations* stand at the opposite ends of Copland's career: the first dates from 1925 and the latter from 1962. Despite this, both works have a spiky character instantly identifiable as Copland. Bernstein, who both commissioned and premièred *Connotations*, gives it a particularly strong and committed reading, and clearly enjoys the jazz influence of *Music for the Theatre*. All the recordings were taken from live performances given in 1989, but sound balance and perspective are excellent, as is the playing of the New York Philharmonic at its peak.

Additional recommendation ...
El salón México[c]*. Danzón cubano*[e]*. An Outdoor Overture*[e]*. Quiet City*[e]*. Our Town*[e]*. Las agachadas*[c]*. Fanfare for the Common Man*[e]*. Lincoln Portrait*[be]*. Appalachian Spring — suite*[e]*. Rodeo — four dance episodes*[e]*. Billy the Kid — orchestral suite*[e]*. Music for Movies*[d]*. Letter from Home*[e]*. John Henry*[e]*. Symphony No. 3*[d]*. Clarinet Concerto*[af]. [a]**Benny Goodman** (cl); [b]**Henry Fonda** (narr); [c]**New England Conservatory Chorus;** [d]**New Philharmonia Orchestra;** [e]**London Symphony Orchestra;** [f]**Columbia Symphony Orchestra/Aaron Copland.** Sony Classical M3K46559 — ③ 3h 46m ADD 7/91

Copland. ORCHESTRAL WORKS. **Detroit Symphony Orchestra/Antál Dorati.** Decca Ovation 430 705-2DM. Items marked [a] from SXDL7547 (10/82), [b] 414 457-2DH (6/86). Recorded 1981-1984.
El salón México[a]. Dance Symphony[a]. Fanfare for the Common Man[a]. Rodeo — Four Dance Episodes[a]. Appalachian Spring — suite[b].

lh 14m DDD 8/91 £ B

This glorious disc shows how well Antál Dorati assimilated the music of Aaron Copland. The big-boned swagger of "Buckaroo Holiday" from *Rodeo* with its vision of open spaces and clear blue skies is established straightaway in Dorati's performance with keen rhythmic drive and fine orchestral articulation. The "Hoe Down" is properly exciting while the other two dance episodes are wonderfully expressive. In the 1945 suite of *Appalachian Spring* Dorati secures marvellous phrasing and dynamics but tends to understate the poetic elements of the score. Decca's sound quality is exemplary and is of demonstration standard in *Fanfare for the Common Man*, as it is in the enjoyable curtain-raiser, the sturdy, big-hearted *El salón México*. Dorati's vast experience as an interpreter of Stravinsky and Bartók pays fine dividends in Copland's gruesome *Dance Symphony*, music inspired by the vampire film fantasy, *Nosferatu*. This survey of Copland's most popular orchestral works is a welcome addition to the mid-price catalogue.

Additional recommendation ...
Appalachian Spring. Billy the Kid — Suite. Rodeo. Fanfare for the Common Man. **New York Philharmonic Orchestra/Leonard Bernstein.** Sony Classical Bernstein Royal Edition SMK47543 — ⁘ lh 3m ADD 5/93

NEW REVIEW

Copland. ORCHESTRAL WORKS.
R. Harris. American Creed. When Johnny comes marching home. [a]**James Earl Jones** (spkr); **Seattle** [b]**Chorale and Symphony Orchestra/Gerard Schwarz.** Delos DE3140. Texts included. Recorded in 1992.
Copland: Fanfare for the Common Man. Lincoln Portrait[a]. Canticle of Freedom[b]. An Outdoor Overture.

⁘ lh lm DDD

Recordings of Copland's music are legion, but not many are as well done as this and few are as imaginatively coupled. The familiar *Fanfare for the Common Man* makes an obvious enough prelude, followed by the rousing *Lincoln Portrait* but the *Canticle of Freedom*, not otherwise available on record, is something of a Copland discovery: strong, stirring and simple of outline. The lively *Outdoor Overture* reminds us how close wide open spaces are to the American idea of freedom, and this is taken up in the splendid *American Creed* of Roy Harris, which evokes the freedom to dream and the freedom to build as fundamentals: cues, respectively, for one of Harris's nobly plangent melodies and for a grandiose display of his contrapuntal skill. Even the overture on *When Johnny comes marching home* is more than a filler: finding contrasting characters within a single melody was another of Harris's gifts. The orchestra and choir are on excellent form, and Schwarz is as good at distilling Copland's and Harris's quiet lyricism as he is their pages of sonorous grandeur. James Earl Jones brings an actor's care to the projection and expression of Lincoln's words, in a work that is too often used as a vehicle by less vocally gifted politicians. He effortlessly dwarfs the orchestra, even when hardly raising his voice: the only flaw on an otherwise clear and natural recording.

Copland. ORCHESTRAL WORKS. [a]**Raymond Mase** (tpt); [a]**Stephen Taylor** (cor ang); **Orpheus Chamber Orchestra.** DG 427 335-2GH. Recorded in 1988.
Appalachian Spring — suite. Quiet city[a]. Short Symphony (No. 2). Three Latin-American Sketches.

⁘ lh lm DDD 8/89 9s

This disc will be of value to devotees of and newcomers to Copland's music alike. For the devotee, interest will be aroused not only by the *Three Latin-American Sketches*, but also by the inclusion of the 1958 version of the *Appalachian Spring* suite which uses the chamber orchestra scoring of the original ballet in place of the more frequently heard version for full orchestra. The lighter scoring gives the music a greater degree of luminosity and transparency, and also serves to highlight the crispness and buoyancy of Copland's rhythmic invention, especially when the performance is as fine as it is here; string textures are beautifully clear, and there are some wonderful solo performances from the woodwind players. The *Short* Symphony, with its obvious influences of Stravinsky (Symphony in Three Movements) and jazz is given a very rhythmically alert and vital performance, with much attention paid to subtle dynamic shading. Special mention must also be made to the solo playing of Raymond Mase and Stephen Taylor in *Quiet city* whose first-class performances create a very evocative and elegiac soundscape. With the *Three Latin-American Sketches* we return once more to the rhythmic drive that so often pervades Copland's music. The second and third dances were written in 1959; the first was added in 1971, presumably to give a more formal balance to the set, resulting in a fast-slow-fast sequence. The recorded sound is of the highest quality.

Copland. ORCHESTRAL WORKS. **St Paul Chamber Orchestra/Hugh Wolff.** Teldec 2292-46314-2. Recorded in 1990.
Appalachian Spring (orig. version). Music for the Theatre. Quiet City. Three Latin American Sketches.

1h 16m DDD 7/91 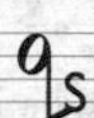

Much of what is best about Copland's vernacular music is encapsulated on this well-filled disc. Invigorating rhythms (derived from jazz, Latin-American dance, or American folk-music) and soulful musings, scored with painstaking delicacy, sit happily side-by-side in these works. *Music for the Theatre* is the earliest piece, premièred by Koussevitzky and the Boston Symphony Orchestra in 1925; its toe-tapping jauntiness reflects Copland's delight in jazz at that time, and his sidelong glances at Stravinsky and Satie. *Quiet City*, of 1940, with its effective coupling of trumpet and cor anglais, provides a reposeful heart to the programme, reflected in the simply beautiful "Paisaje mexicana", the second of the *Latin American Sketches*, finished in 1971. The original, chamber version of *Appalachian Spring* (1944) completes the disc with more dance rhythms, made all the more immediate by the use of smaller forces. The performances tie the works together through a keen sense of idiom: rhythmic lift and vitality drive the faster movements and the more meditative are either allowed to be peacefully simple or enriched by a finely poised degree of pathos that never cloys. A recording that manages to combine brightness with intimate warmth is a special bonus.

Copland. Symphony No. 3. Music for a Great City. **Saint Louis Symphony Orchestra/Leonard Slatkin.** RCA Victor Red Seal RD60149. Recorded in 1989.

1h 7m DDD 2/91 

Copland intended this symphony as a 'grand gesture' and there is no doubt at any point in Slatkin's performance that a big statement is being made. He is totally inside the music, and he secures playing of great precision and refinement from an orchestra which has exactly the right timbre and style. In 1964 the London Symphony Orchestra asked Copland for a work to celebrate its sixtieth season. *Music for a Great City* refers to New York, however, not London, for instead of a new work Copland adapted music from the 1961 Carroll Baker film *Something Wild*, shot on location in New York, and he fashioned four episodes roughly in the shape of a symphony. Each 'movement' bears a descriptive title such as "Skyline" or "Subway Jam". Leonard Slatkin obviously revels in Copland's highly expressive writing, sometimes sentimental, sometimes tense or jaggedly aggressive, and he conducts a brilliantly effective account of the score, with virtuoso playing from his Saint Louis orchestra. The recording has impressive range and sonority, yet detail is beautifully clear.

Additional recommendation ...
No. 3. Quiet City[a]. [a]**Philip Smith** (tpt); [a]**Thomas Stacy** (cor ang); **New York Philharmonic Orchestra/Leonard Bernstein.** DG 419 170-2GH — 54m DDD 11/86

Copland. Billy the Kid — ballet. Rodeo — ballet. **St Louis Symphony Orchestra/Leonard Slatkin.** EMI CDC7 47382-2. From EL270398-1 (7/86).

56m DDD 11/87 

Between 1938 and 1944 Copland wrote the three ballet scores which somehow managed to epitomize the American character in music: *Billy the Kid, Rodeo* and *Appalachian Spring*. Here we have the complete scores of the two 'Westerns', which are usually given in somewhat abridged form. *Billy* is built around a collection of cowboy ballads and is the more obviously symphonic, whilst *Rodeo* is closer to a dance suite. Slatkin and the St Louis Symphony Orchestra give spirited performances of these works, refined as well as brilliant and the recording, transferred at a rather lower level than usual, is very well defined and atmospheric, conveying both the broad horizons of the prairie and the violent exchanges to marvellous effect.

Copland. SONGS. **Roberta Alexander** (sop); **Roger Vignoles** (pf). Etcetera KTC1100. Texts included. Recorded in 1990.
A Summer Vacation. Alone. My heart is in the East. Night. Old American Songs, Sets 1 and 2. Old Poem. Pastorale. Poet's Song. 12 Poems of Emily Dickinson.

lh 12m DDD 3/92

It's a joy to have one of the greatest song-cycles to an English text back in the record catalogue — and performed by such a polished team as Alexander and Vignoles. The *12 Poems of Emily Dickinson* (1950) come from Copland's finest period — after the acknowledged successes of the three folk ballets and before he began to take on aspects of serial technique, after which he composed less and less. The cycle is a wonderful match between America's great New England nineteenth-century poet and one of her greatest composers. Warm lyricism, drama, and a continuously sensitive response to the poems make this work a landmark comparable to the best of Britten's cycles. The texts (the edited versions available at the time) are provided for all the songs. The performances, in a few details, are not quite flawless but Alexander has grown in stature and vocal control since her earliest recordings. Just as delightful, if not more so, are the early Copland songs — wistful, sad, nostalgic and beautifully wrought in every way. They demonstrate an instinctive musicianship of the highest order even before Copland went to study with Boulanger in Paris. And they get superb performances worthy of the finest Lieder. The *Old American Songs* are simply some of Copland's favourite tunes, some of which he used in other works and which he often performed himself as pianist or conductor. Alexander has plenty of zip, Vignoles is perhaps a little staid, but these songs complete an excellent and well-recorded vocal anthology.

Copland. THE TENDER LAND. **Elisabeth Comeaux** (sop) Laurie; **Janis Hardy** (mez) Ma Moss; **Maria Jette** (sop) Beth; **LeRoy Lehr** (bass) Grandpa Moss; **Dan Dressen** (ten) Martin; **James Bohn** (bar) Top; **Vern Sutton** (ten) Mr Splinters; **Agnes Smuda** (sop) Mrs Splinters; **Merle Fristad** (bass) Mr Jenks; **Sue Herber** (mez) Mrs Jenks; **Chorus and Orchestra of The Plymouth Music Series, Minnesota/Philip Brunelle.** Virgin Classics VCD7 59253-2. Notes and text included.

② lh 47m DDD 8/90

Aaron Copland was a father figure of American music, and Leonard Bernstein expressed a lifelong admiration when he called him "the best we have". Yet though a generation separates them, *The Tender Land* had its première in 1954 just three years before *West Side Story*. Both opened in New York, but while Bernstein's piece is set there and portrays a violent urban America, Copland's belongs to the wide Midwest and the quiet of a farming home. It was written for young singers and has a wonderful freshness, a clean 'plainness' which Copland compared to that of his ballet *Appalachian Spring*. The story tells how the young girl Laurie Moss falls in love with Martin, a travelling harvester who visits her mother's farm, and after being left by him still decides to leave home and make her own way in the world. It has been criticized as undramatic, and its partly spoken dialogue and small cast have also gone against it — Copland later wryly called opera "la forme fatale" and never wrote another — but whatever its viability on stage, on record it provides a satisfying experience and this Minnesota performance has just the right flavour, offering simplicity and sensitivity without affectation. The conductor is himself a Midwesterner who writes that his young cast "have their roots in this particular soil" which is the heartland of America. The recording is every bit as fresh as the music.

Further listening ...

Piano Concerto. *Coupled with* ***Britten.*** Piano Concerto. **Gillian Lin** (pf); **Melbourne Symphony Orchestra/John Hopkins.** Chandos Collect CHAN6580 (3/93).

Key to Symbols

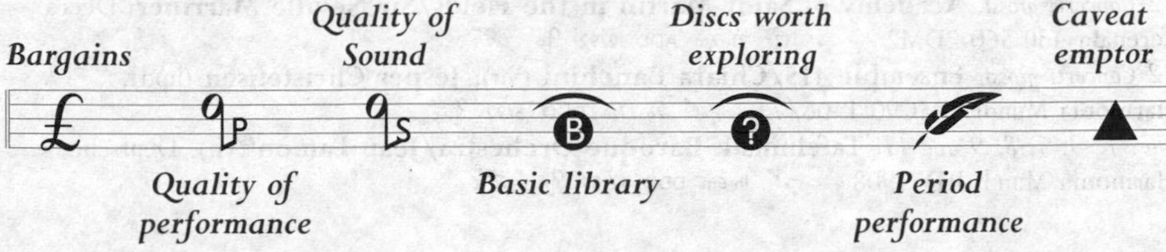

Arcangelo Corelli

Italian 1653-1713

Corelli. 12 Concerti grossi, Op. 6. **The English Concert/Trevor Pinnock.** Archiv Produktion 423 626-2AH2.

No. 1 in D major; No. 2 in F major; No. 3 in C minor; No. 4 in D major; No. 5 in B flat major; No. 6 in F major; No. 7 in D major; No. 8 in G minor; No. 9 in F major; No. 10 in C major; No. 11 in B flat major; No. 12 in F major.

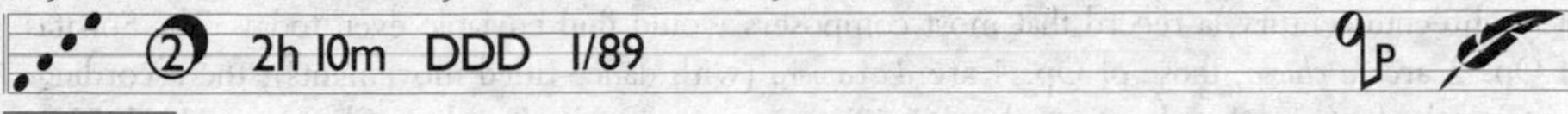

NEW REVIEW

Corelli. 12 Concerti grossi, Op. 6. **Guildhall String Ensemble/Robert Salter** (vn). RCA Victor Red Seal RD60071. Recorded 1988-89.

No. 1 in D major; No. 2 in F major; No. 3 in C minor; No. 4 in D major; No. 5 in B flat major; No. 6 in F major; No. 7 in D major; No. 8 in G minor; No. 9 in F major; No. 10 in C major; No. 11 in B flat major; No. 12 in F major.

2h 8m DDD 9/92

In his working life of about 40 years Corelli must have produced a great deal of orchestral music, yet the 12 Concerti grossi, Op. 6 form the bulk of what is known to have survived. Their original forms are mostly lost but we know that those in which they were published in Amsterdam by Estienne Roger had been carefully polished and revised by the composer — and that they were assembled from movements that had been written at various times. The first eight are in *da chiesa* form, the last four in *da camera* form — without and with named dance movements respectively, and the number of their movements varies from four to seven. Each features the interplay of a group of soloists, the *concertino* (two violins and a cello) and the orchestra, the *ripieno*, the size of which Corelli stated to be flexible. These are masterpieces of their genre, one that was later developed by, notably, Bach and Handel, and they are rich in variety. The scores leaves scope for embellishment, not least in cadential and lining passages, and the players of The English Concert take full advantage of them. Regarding the overall performances, suffice it to say that this recording won a *Gramophone* Award in 1990.

Recordings of these concertos have been a growth industry over the past five years or so. Now there are at least 12 versions for the prospective buyer to consider, and these reflect many differing shades of interpretative opinion. Following their excellent recordings of Handel's *Concerti grossi*, Op. 6, the Guildhall String Ensemble, playing modern instruments at today's pitch, have now turned their attention to Corelli. There is no one correct way of performing these concertos since it is evident that groups both large and small played them in Corelli's own lifetime. The Guildhall group field one of the smallest ensembles of all, consisting of five violins, two violas, two cellos and bass. From these players Corelli's two *concertino* violins and cello emerge for their solos in the customary way. Some listeners may feel the need, from time to time, for a slightly stronger upper string body than is provided here. Yet, on the other hand the playing is so full of character and vitality, so free from overstatement and exaggerated gesture that matters of weight are soon forgotten. A larger band, however, might achieve a greater sense of occasion, and this is needed, perhaps, in the resonant slow sections of the concertos *da chiesa*; but few will be other than delighted by the spontaneous, athletic playing of these artists.

Additional recommendations ...

12 Concerti grossi. **La Petite Bande/Sigiswald Kuijken.** Deutsche Harmonia Editio Classica

GD77007 — 2h 16m ADD 9/90

12 Concerti grossi. **Academy of Saint Martin in the Fields/Sir Neville Marriner.** Decca Serenata 430 560-2DM2 — 2h 7m ADD 2/92

12 Concerti grossi. **Ensemble 415/Chiara Banchini** (vn); **Jesper Christensen** (hpd). Harmonia Mundi HMC90 1406/7 — 2h 27m DDD 6/92

Nos. 1, 3, 7, 8, 9 and 11. **Tafelmusik Baroque Orchestra/Jean Lamon** (vn). Deutsche Harmonia Mundi RD77908 — 1h 6m DDD 12/89

NEW REVIEW

Corelli. TRIO SONATAS. [c]**Jakob Lindberg** (theorbo); **Purcell Quartet** (Catherine Mackintosh, [a]Elizabeth Wallfisch, [b]Catherine Weiss, vns; Richard Boothby, vc); **Robert Wooley** ([a]hpd/[b]org). Chandos Chaconne CHAN0526. Recorded (Op. 3) 1990, (Op. 4) 1992. 12 Trio Sonatas, Op. 3[a] — F major; D major[c]; B flat major; B minor; D minor[c]; G major. 12 Trio Sonatas, Op. 4[b] — C major; G minor; A major; D major; A minor; E major.

1h 16m DDD 12/92

Corelli's chamber music was reprinted 84 times during his lifetime and 31 more during the rest of the eighteenth century, a record that most composers would find enviable even today. The Sonatas of Op. 3 are *da chiesa*, those of Op. 4 are *da camera* (with dance-titled movements); the recording contains the first six of each set — the remaining ones are on another disc (Chandos CHAN0532), should you (as is probable) be tempted to add them to your collection. They are small gems: most have four movements and their durations range from five-and-a-half to seven-and-a-half minutes, within which they pack a wealth of invention, pure beauty and variety of pace and mood. Surviving evidence suggests that they were played at a much lower pitch than today's standard, the lower string tension adding warmth and opulence to the sound. Catherine Mackintosh takes full advantage of the works' opportunities for pliant phrasing and added embellishments; Elizabeth Wallfisch 'converses' with her in her own characteristic way, whilst Catherine Weiss (Wallfisch's replacement in Op. 4) follows her example more closely. The Purcell Quartet's oneness of thought and timing in these landmark works is a joy to hear and the recording is superb in all respects.

Additional recommendation ...

Complete Works: 12 Trio Sonatas, Op. 1. 12 Trio Sonatas, Op. 2. 12 Trio Sonatas, Op. 3. 12 Trio Sonatas, Op. 4. 12 Violin Sonatas, Op. 5. Violin Sonatas — A major; D major (3); A minor. 12 Concerti grossi, Op. 6. Sinfonia in D minor. Sonata a quattro in D major. Fuga a quattro in D major. 6 Trio Sonatas, Op. posth. —A major; D major (3); G minor (2). Sonata a quattro in G minor. **Bizantina Accademia/Carlo Chiarappa.** Europa Musica 350 202 — 9 9h 56m DDD 5/91

John Corigliano

American 1938-

Further listening ...

Clarinet Concerto[a]. *Coupled with* ***Barber.*** Third Essay for Orchestra, Op. 47. [a]**Stanley Drucker** (cl); **New York Philharmonic Orchestra/Zubin Mehta.** New World NW309-2 (5/88).

Oboe Concerto[a]. Three Irish Folk-song Settings[b] — The Salley Gardens; The Foggy, foggy dew; She moved thro' the fair. Poem in October[c]. [bc]**Robert White** (ten); [b]**Ransom Wilson,** [c]**Thomas Nyfenger** (fls); [ac]**Humbert Lucarelli** (ob); [c]**Joseph Rabbai** (cl); [c]**American Quartet/Maurice Peress** (hpd); [a]**American Symphony Orchestra/Kazuyoshi Akiyama.** RCA Victor Gold Seal GD60395 (5/91).

Symphony No. 1. **Chicago Symphony Orchestra/Daniel Barenboim.** Erato 2292 45601-2 (7/91).

Carl August Cornelius

German 1824-1874

Suggested listening ...

Stabat mater. Requiem. **Soloists; Cannes-Provence-Alpes-Côte d'Azur Chorus and Orchestra/Michel Piquemal.** Harmonia Mundi HMC90 5206 (4/90).

William Cornysh

British 1468-1523

Cornysh. CHORAL WORKS. **The Tallis Scholars/Peter Phillips.** Gimell CDGIM014. Texts and translations included.
Salve regina. Ave Maria, mater Dei. Gaude virgo mater Christi. Magnificat. Ah, Robin. Adieu, adieu, my heartes lust. Adieu courage. Woefully arrayed. Stabat mater.

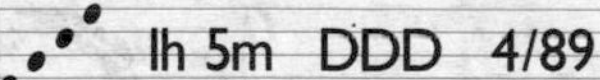

William Cornysh, the leading English composer of his generation, was creative, original to a degree of waywardness, sometimes tender, often ecstatic and he served both Henry VII and Henry VIII, holding the post of Master of the Children of the Chapel Royal. The highly skilled trebles he trained to tackle his own most exacting music are replaced, here, by two of the Scholars' most agile, boyish sopranos. The musical pyrotechnics they throw off with such apparent ease give one a good idea of what so delighted the ears of sixteenth-century audiences. The varied programme includes the magnificent *Salve regina*, which unfolds in never-ending volutes of melody, whilst the *Stabat mater*, depicting the sufferings of Mary, reveals Cornysh at his most powerfully imaginative. The relish with which The Scholars understand Cornysh's music makes this a disc of quite exceptional beauty.

François Couperin

French 1668-1733

F. Couperin. HARPSICHORD WORKS. **Kenneth Gilbert.** Harmonia Mundi Musique d'abord HMA190 351/60 (two triple- and two double-disc sets).
HMA 190 351/3 (2h 32m) — Premier livre de clavecin: Ordres — 1 (from RCA LSB4067, 9/72); 2 (LSB4077, 2/73); 3 and 4 (LSB4087, 5/73); 5 (LSB4098, 8/73). *HMA190 354/6* (3h 11m) Deuxième livre de clavecin: Ordres — 6 and 7 (RCA LHL1 5048, 1/75); 8. L'art de toucher le clavecin (LHL1 5049, 1/75). Ordres — 9 and 10 (LHL1 5050, 2/75); 11 and 12 (LHL1 5051, 2/75). *HMA190 357/8* (2h 30m) — Troisième livre de clavecin: Ordres — 13 (new to UK); 14 to 19 (all from RCA SER5720/23, 4/75). *HMA190 359/60* (2h 32m) — Quatrième livre de clavecin: Ordres — 20 to 27 (LHL4 5096, 12/75).

④ ADD 10/89

Couperin's solo harpsichord music, collected in four volumes and published between 1713 and 1730, represents one of the highest peaks of baroque keyboard repertory. Its elusive and, indeed allusive style, however, frequently gets the better of would-be performers and it is doubtless partly for this reason that only five complete versions of this music have been issued commercially. Kenneth Gilbert has long been acknowledged a master of French baroque interpretation and his performance of Couperin's 27 *Ordres* — the word implies something between a suite and an anthology — though now 21 years old, has not been surpassed. Indeed, it is no mean tribute to his informed approach that these interpretations strike today's audiences as being as stylish as when they were first issued in 1971. Gilbert scrupulously adheres to aspects of performance by which the composer himself set such store. Couperin was precise about ornamentation and related matters and Gilbert is meticulous in his observance of them. Unequal rhythms are applied discerningly but with a natural ease that variously brings out the nobility, the grandeur, and the tenderness of the music. There is, in short, a wonderful variety of affects to be found in these pieces and Gilbert seldom if ever disappoints us in his feeling for them. From among the most infinite delights to be found in this impressive and satisfying project we may, perhaps, mention the *Ordres* Nos. 6, 7, 8 and 26 in their entirety, and the exquisitely shaped seventh prelude from *L'art de toucher le clavecin* are outstanding examples of Gilbert's artistry. Small technical deficiencies in the remastering appear almost negligible in the face of so much that is rewarding. These are performances to treasure for a lifetime.

F. Couperin. HARPSICHORD WORKS. **Skip Sempé.** Deutsche Harmonia Mundi RD77219. Recorded in 1990.
L'art de toucher le clavecin: Préludes — C major; D minor; G minor; B flat major; F minor; A major. *Premier livre:* Troisième ordre — Allemande La ténébreuse; Courantes I and II; Sarabande La lugubre; L'espagnolète; Chaconne La favorite. Cinquième ordre — Sarabande La dangereuse; Les ordes. *Dieuxième livre:* Sixième ordre — Les baricades mistérieuses. Huitième ordre — La Raphaéle; Allemande L'Ausoniène; Courantes I and II. Sarabande L'unique; Gavotte; Rondeau; Gigue; Passacaille. *Troisième livre:* Quinzième ordre — Le dodo ou L'amour au berçeau. *Quatrième livre:* Vingt-troisième ordre — L'arlequine. Vingtquatrième ordre — Les vieux seigneurs.

1h 12m DDD 1/91 9p

Couperin's subtly expressive harpsichord music is amongst the most elusive in the French baroque repertory to the performer. The American, Skip Sempé, has an intuitive understanding of it and conveys to the listener the grandeur, the wit and metaphor variously present in Couperin's dances and delicately coloured character pieces. Sempé's programme is thoughtfully chosen both for its capacity to show off the composer's considerable if restrained emotional range, and in its inclusion of pieces which have helped to bring his music to a wide audience. So we find the enigmatically titled rondeau *Les baricades mistérieuses*, an enchanting pastoral "Rondeau in B flat" which Bach could not resist including in the *Music Book* for his wife Anna Magdalena, the great B minor *Passacaille* and *L'arlequine*, evoking the spirit of *commedia dell'arte* together with pieces which may be less familiar but no less rewarding on acquaintance. This is a delightful programme and an ideal introduction to Couperin's music for anyone not yet familiar with a veritable poet of the harpsichord. Sympathetically recorded and imaginatively presented.

F. Couperin. ORGAN MASSES. **Jean-Charles Ablitzer** (org). Harmonic Records H/CD8613 and H/CD8615. Played on the organs of [a]La Basilique Saint-Nazaire et Saint-Celse de Carcassone and [b]L'église Saint-Julien et Sainte-Basilisse de Vinça.
H/CD8613 — Messe à l'usage ordinaire des paroisses[a]. *Plainchant:* Liturgy for Easter Day (Ensemble Organum/Marcel Pérès). *H/CD8615* — Messe pour les couvents de religieux et religieuses. *Du Mage:* Livre d'orgue[b].

② 2h 12m DDD 9/91 9s

François Couperin wrote and published his two organ masses early on in life. They comprise his complete *Pièces d'orgue* and were issued in 1689. The Masses consist of organ music for the liturgy; the *Messe à l'usage ordinaire des paroisses* (the Parish Mass) is the grander of the two and was intended for use on important church feast days. The *Messe pour les couvents* (the Convent Mass) as its title implies, is more intimate in character and shorter in length. In this recording plainchant interpolations indicated for use in conjunction with the *Parish Mass* have been included as well as a substantial Easter introit which introduces the Mass. Couperin's music does not intrinsically suffer if the plainchant is missing but its eloquence is greatly enhanced by the punctuation imposed by its presence. Jean-Charles Ablitzer, an organist with a feeling for the elusive qualities of French baroque style, plays two magnificent instruments. For the *Parish Mass* he has chosen the famous organ in the Basilica at Carcassonne, for the other an organ at Vinça in the Pyrenees. It is on this last-mentioned instrument that Ablitzer performs the *Livre d'orgue* of Couperin's contemporary Pierre du Mage. The recording is thrillingly resonant, capturing the distinctive idiom and colours of the French baroque organ school.

F. Couperin. Trois leçons de ténèbres[a]. Motet — Victoria! Christo resurgenti. **Judith Nelson** [a]**Emma Kirkby** (sops); **Jane Ryan** (va da gamba); **Christopher Hogwood**

(chamber org). L'Oiseau-Lyre 430 283-2OH. Notes, texts and translations included. From DSLO536 (6/78). Recorded in 1977.

43m ADD 12/91

Couperin's three *Leçons de ténèbres*, dating from the second decade of the eighteenth century, are masterly examples of a peculiarly French sacred musical idiom. Sung during Holy Week, their texts are drawn from the *Lamentations of Jeremiah* interspersed with ornamental melismatic phrases inspired by ritualistic Hebrew letters. The subtle blend of Italian monody with French court air, which characterizes Couperin's *Leçons* and those of his predecessor Charpentier, seems to have been appearing both at court and wider afield. Several recordings of these beautiful pieces have been made and the competition is very strong. That being said, the lightly articulated and fresh-sounding performances of the sopranos Emma Kirkby and Judith Nelson have lost little or nothing of their charm over the intervening years. Nelson sings the first *Leçon* and Kirkby the second, by the way. These are cooler readings than some others and, one might perhaps say, more *da chiesa* in their approach than other sensuous performances. It is well recorded and includes the radiant Easter motet, *Victoria! Christo resurgenti*. Attention to stylistic details is a major feature here; the continuo realizations are discreet, tasteful and assured.

Additional recommendation ...
As above. Magnificat. **Mieke van der Sluis** (sop); **Guillemette Laurens** (mez); **Pascal Monteilhet** (lute); **Marianne Muller** (va da gamba); **Laurence Boulay** (hpd, org). Erato Musifrance 2292-45012-2 — Ih Im DDD 8/90

Key to Symbols

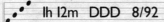

Bargains — ***Quality of performance*** — ***Quality of Sound*** — ***Basic library*** — ***Discs worth exploring*** — ***Period performance*** — ***Caveat emptor***

Louis Couperin

French c.1626-1661

NEW REVIEW

L. Couperin. HARPSICHORD WORKS. **Bob van Asperen** (hpd). EMI Reflexe CDC7 54340-2. Recorded in 1991.
Suites — D minor; F major; G minor. Pavanne in F sharp minor. Passacaille in C major.

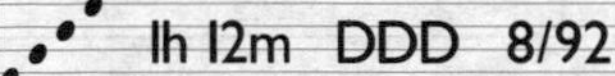

Ih 12m DDD 8/92

Louis Couperin — uncle of the more celebrated François Couperin "le grand" — was one of the greatest harpsichord composers of the seventeenth century. This recital of *Pièces de clavecin* may well appeal to those who feel that a complete survey on four discs by Davitt Moroney is more than they want. The Dutch harpsichordist, Bob van Asperen has a fine technique and a lively sense of style; and in this recording these qualities are complemented by the skilfully captured sound of an especially fine seventeenth-century instrument in the Unterlinden Museum at Colmar in France. Couperin did not write suites as such but rather grouped pieces according to key, leaving the performer to make his or her own selection. Van Asperen has chosen discerningly, including in his recital a deeply-felt tribute to the lutenist Monsieur de Blancrocher, three Chaconnes and two Passacailles, forms in which Couperin excelled. But there are lighter pieces, too, providing effective contrast with these more substantial compositions.

Additional recommendation ...
Suites — C major; C minor; F major; E minor; A major; F major; C major; D minor; A minor; B minor; D

minor; A minor; D major; G minor; C major; A minor; G major. Pavanne in F sharp minor. Prelude and Chaconne in G minor; Two Pieces in B flat major. Three Pieces in G minor. Four Pieces in G major. **Davitt Moroney** (hpd). Harmonia Mundi Musique d'abord HMA190 1124/7 — ④ 5h 15m ADD 4/90

Sir Noël Coward

British 1899-1973

Suggested listening ...

BITTER SWEET — *operetta.* **Soloists; New Sadler's Wells Opera Chorus and Orchestra/Michael Reed.** That's Entertainment Records CDTER2 1160 (11/89).

Sir Frederic Cowen

British 1852-1935

Suggested listening ...

Symphony No. 3 in C minor, "Scandinavian". Indian Rhapsody. The Butterfly's Ball. **Košice State Philharmonic Orchestra/Adrian Leaper.** Marco Polo 8 223273 (2/91).

Paul Creston

American 1906-1985

Suggested listening ...

Symphony No. 3, Op. 48, "Three Mysteries". Invocation and Dance, Op. 58. Out of the Cradle. Partita for flute, violin and string orchestra, Op. 12. **Iikka Talvi** (vn); **Scott Goff** (fl); **Seattle Symphony Orchestra, Gerald Schwarz.** Delos DE3114 (12/92).

William Crotch

British 1775-1847

Suggested listening ...

Organ Concerto No. 2 in A major. Overture in G major. Sinfonias — E flat major; F major. **Andrew Lumsden** (org); **Milton Keynes Chamber Orchestra/Hilary Davan Wetton.** Unicorn-Kanchana DKPCD9126 (1/93).

George Crumb

American 1929-

Suggested listening ...

 Five Pieces. Gnomic Variations. Makrokosmos I. **Jeffrey Jacob** (pf). Centaur CRC2050 (4/91).

Bernhard Crusell

Finnish 1775-1839

Crusell. Clarinet Concerto No. 1 in E flat major, Op. 1.
L. Koželuch. Clarinet Concerto in E flat major.
Krommer. Clarinet Concerto in E flat major, Op. 36. **Emma Johnson** (cl); **Royal Philharmonic Orchestra/Günther Herbig.** ASV CDDCA763.

lh 7m DDD 9/91

The idiom of Stockholm-based composer Bernhard Crusell embraces elements of Mozart, Spohr, Weber, Rossini and even Beethoven. But in the hands of the young woodwind virtuoso, Emma Johnson, his music has a personality all its own. Here she turns her attention to his First Clarinet Concerto which is full of engaging ideas. The slow movement is beautifully done and in the finale the soloist is at her very best — full of impulsive charm and swagger. Although the Koželuch concerto, a recent discovery, seems less distinctive, the slow movement of the Krommer is undeniably affecting and its finale bounces along in fine style. Emma Johnson plays throughout with a winning spontaneity and the RPO, arguably just a shade tubby of timbre for such music, back her up with distinction. The generous acoustic is effectively caught.

Carl Czerny

Austrian 1791-1857

Suggested listening ...

Fantasie in F minor, Op. 226. Grande Sonate in F minor, Op. 178. Grande Sonate brillante in C minor, Op. 10. Ouverture characteristique et brillante in B minor, Op. 54. **Yaara Tal, Andreas Groethuysen** (pf, four hands). Sony Classical SK45936 (5/91).

Benjamin Dale

British 1885-1943

NEW REVIEW

Dale. Piano Sonata in D minor. Night Fancies. Prunella. **Peter Jacobs** (pf). Continuum CCD1044. Recorded in 1991.

58m DDD 5/93 

Benjamin Dale is one of those composers who despite the huge revival in interest in English music has remained largely undiscovered. And yet during his lifetime, and in particular his student years and early career, he forged for himself something of a formidable reputation as a composer. The large-scale Piano Sonata in D minor dates from 1902-5 when Dale was still in his early teens, and was championed by fellow students Myra Hess and Irene Scharrer and, a little later, by Benno Moiseiwitsch. It was considered something of a landmark among British sonatas when it first appeared; primarily because there had been few examples of such virtuosic writing in British piano music prior to this date, but also because of the remarkable talent it displayed from so young a composer. The sonata is Lisztian in breadth and language, but despite the late nineteenth-century style of keyboard rhetoric contains much that is new and fresh, not least an elusive 'English' quality that sets it apart from other sonatas of the period. The small fill-ups, *Night Fancies* and *Prunella* are slighter fare compared to the epic sonata, but are attractive examples of their genre and no less worthy of exploration. No pianist could be a better choice for this recording than Peter Jacobs. He has the technique, poetry and persuasive advocacy to do full justice to this music, and this has been admirably projected by Continuum's warm and atmospheric recording. A valuable addition to recordings of British music.

Further listening ...

Phantasy in D minor, Op. 4. Suite in D minor, Op. 2. Night Fancies. **Simon Rowland Jones** (va); **Niel Immelman** (pf) Etcetera KTC1105.

Franz Danzi

German 1763-1826

Suggested listening ...

Flute Concertos — No. 1 in G major, Op. 30; No. 2 in D minor, Op. 31; No. 3 in D minor, Op. 42; No. 4 in D major, Op. 43. **András Adorján** (fl); **Munich Chamber Orchestra/Hans Stadlmair.** Orfeo C003812H (8/88).

Claude Debussy

French 1862-1918

NEW REVIEW

Debussy. Nocturnes[a]. Prélude à l'après-midi d'un faune. La mer. [a]**women's voices of the Chicago Symphony Chorus; Chicago Symphony Orchestra/Sir Georg Solti.** Decca 436 468-2DH. Recorded 1990-91.

55m DDD 10/92 

NEW REVIEW

Debussy. La mer[a]. Prélude à l'après-midi d'un faune[a].
Ravel. Daphnis et Chloé — Suite No. 2[a]. Boléro[b]. **Berlin Philharmonic Orchestra/Herbert von Karajan.** DG Galleria 427 250-2GGA. Items marked [a] from SLPM138 923 (3/65), [b] SLPM139 010 (11/66). Recorded 1964-66.

lh 4m ADD 7/89 

NEW REVIEW

Debussy. ORCHESTRAL WORKS. **Philharmonia Orchestra/Guido Cantelli.** Testament mono SBT1011. Item marked [a] from HMV BLP1089 (2/57), [b] ALP1207 (9/55), [c] ALP1228 (3/55). Recorded in 1954-55.
Nocturnes[a] — Nuages; Fêtes. Prélude à l'après-midi d'un faune[b]. Le martyre de Saint Sébastien[c] — symphonic fragments. La mer[c].

lh 7m ADD 10/92 

The sensation of the moment, very French we are told, is combined in *La mer* with a longer term — what one might call 'symphonic' — sense of direction. Debussy himself found the title 'Symphony' inhibiting, and preferred to call his seascape "Three Symphonic Sketches". His knowledge of, and reaction to, the sea — "I love the sea and have listened to it with the passionate respect it deserves" — and formal concerns are relayed in the score by the most precise details, and deviation from these yields a distortion of his imagery and 'symphonic' intent. Solti, and particularly Karajan, interpret *La mer*'s text "with the passionate respect it deserves". In 1964, Karajan's feeling for the sheer beauty of sound was never more acute (his later recordings of *La mer* were relatively disappointing), and the textures (when to separate and when to blend), their delicacy, subtlety, and the richness of colour is all quite breathtaking. The waves that sport in the middle movement do so in a marine Arcadia, and yet, in this movement's second half, the physical thrill of being borne along on the crest of a single gathering wave has rarely been more intense. Solti doesn't match this, though elsewhere he is equally rigorous in observing Debussy's carefully planned tempo relationships. Solti's is a magnificently grand impressionism, with a 1991 recording to ensure maximum impact for the climaxes, and an acoustic that comes closer to Debussy's ideal for music that "would resound through the open spaces".

Karajan's disc also contains a justly legendary Second *Daphnis* Suite: the way the birdsong emerges from within the texture to hover above the unfolding crescendo of "Lever du jour", the seductive allure of the solo flute in the "Pantomime" (as in the *Prélude*), the precise yet 'possessed' woodwind in the final "Danse générale" — all these have yet to meet their match on record. Only the *Boléro*, with its limited dynamic range, and stereophonic side-drums as masters of the rest of the orchestra in the latter half, brings doubts. Some may find Solti too fast in "Fêtes" from *Nocturnes*, but his manner exactly fits Debussy's description of this movement as "vibrating, dancing ... luminous dust participating in the cosmic rhythm", and his gradual approach of the central procession — "a dazzling, fantastic vision" — is a far more effective piece of stage-management than Haitink's (see below). And how marvellous to hear the sirens (the ladies of the Chicago Chorus) of the last movement pitch their difficult parts so accurately. A handsome disc, recorded live, and a basic recommendation for the start of a Debussy library.

Cantelli's disc is in mono only, but this need not deter lovers of orchestral colour, for the recordings have come up remarkably well in Testament's new transfers. Collectors will not acquire this reissue for its sound quality, but for the sake of some very remarkable conducting by a master whose death at the age of 36 in 1956 was one of the great post-war musical tragedies. The *Saint Sébastien* pieces have a quite extraordinary atmosphere and fervour in Cantelli's hands, and he captures the religious cum exotic flavour of the writing marvellously well. He treats *La mer* not as an orchestral showpiece, but as a highly evocative series of sound-pictures. The Philharmonia's playing is brilliant but also hypersensitive. Textures are very clear, and every phrase is perfectly in scale. In the two *Nocturnes* Cantelli persuades "Nuages" to flow gently but firmly onwards, so that its refined but expressive nature is perfectly revealed. "Fêtes" is for once not pressed too hard and the piece's colour and rhythms are allowed to blossom naturally. A beautifully shaped, very eloquent *L'après-midi* completes an extraordinarily distinguished disc.

Additional recommendations ...

La mer. Prélude. Jeux — poème dansé. **London Philharmonic Orchestra/Serge Baudo.** EMI Eminence CD-EMX9502 — 52m DDD 10/87 £ B

La mer. Prélude. Jeux. Le martyre de Saint Sébastien. **Montreal Symphony Orchestra/Charles Dutoit.** Decca 430 240-2DH — 1h 15m DDD 2/91 B

La mer[a]*. Nocturnes*[a]*.* ***Ravel.*** *Alborada del gracioso*[b]*. Valses nobles et sentimentales*[b]. [a]**Ambrosian Singers;** [a]**London Symphony Orchestra,** [b]**Royal Philharmonic Orchestra/André Previn.** EMI CDD7 64056-2 — 1h 17m DDD 1/92 B

La mer. Prélude. Jeux. Rapsodie[a]*. Suite bergamasque — Clair de lune. Petite Suite — Menuet.* [a]**Robert Gugholz** (cl); **Suisse Romande Orchestra/Ernest Ansermet.** Decca 433 711-2DM — 1h 14m ADD B

NEW REVIEW

Debussy. La boîte a joujoux — ballet. Prélude à l'après-midi d'un faune. Jeux. **London Symphony Orchestra/Michael Tilson Thomas.** Sony Classical SK48231. Recorded in 1991.

1h 3m DDD 11/92

"Something to amuse the children, nothing more" wrote Debussy about his ballet score for *La boîte à joujoux* (mostly written in 1913, but completed after his death by André Caplet). The children would have been a lot more amused by the goings-on of the occupants of Tilson Thomas's toy box had Sony provided a decent synopsis, but his characterization, storytelling and evocation of atmosphere are so vivid that foreknowledge of events is almost unnecessary. Strictly adult entertainment is provided by this languorous *Prélude*, with particularly lovely, long-breathed playing from the LSO's principal flute; and the suspect shenanigans of *Jeux*, where Tilson Thomas eschews some of Haitink's miraculous acuity of rhythm and texture (reviewed below), and Rattle's rich romanticism (listed below), in favour of greater urgency and spontaneity. Recorded levels are higher for the *Prélude* than the rest of the programme, but this disc is superbly engineered: the sound has both a fine bloom and a tactile presence.

Debussy. Nocturnes[a]. Jeux — poème dansé. [a]**Collegium Musicum Amstelodamense; Concertgebouw Orchestra/Bernard Haitink.** Philips 400 023-2PH. From 9500 674 (11/80).

43m ADD 6/83

Debussy wrote *Jeux* in 1913 for Diaghilev's Ballets Russes and, in particular, their star dancer Nijinsky, who choreographed it as well as dancing in it. The scenario was also Nijinsky's and has a sophisticated but flimsy story of a boy and two girls, tennis players in a park at dusk who flirt, quarrel and search for a lost ball. Unfortunately, the première in May 1913 was eclipsed by that of Stravinsky's *Le sacre du printemps*, given by the same company just two weeks later, but (as the booklet says) whereas that work seems like a great statement of modern music, Debussy's elusive and far less popular score poses an immense question with its fleeting melodies, changing tempos and iridescent orchestral colour. Debussy called his *Nocturnes* an experiment with a single colour — like the study of grey in painting. In their definitive form (1899) they must be numbered among his most perfect works and whether in the "Nuages", which portrays the "unchanging aspect of the sky and the slow, solemn motion of the clouds" or the vibrating, dancing rhythms of "Fêtes", Haitink succeeds in projecting their colourful atmosphere to masterly effect. Again, in *Jeux* he captures its sense of mystery and the playing of the Concertgebouw Orchestra is incomparable. This release won a *Gramophone* Award, both for the realism and naturalness of the recording and the artistry of the performance. It is one of those issues that sets a standard by which subsequent versions will be judged.

Additional recommendation ...

Jeux. Images. Musiques pour le Roi Lear. **City of Birmingham Symphony Orchestra/Simon Rattle.** EMI CDC7 49947-2 — lh 2m DDD 3/90

NEW REVIEW

Debussy. Images — Ibéria.

Ravel. Rapsodie espagnole. Pavane pour une infante défunte. Valses nobles et sentimentales. Alborada del gracioso. **Chicago Symphony Orchestra/Fritz Reiner.** RCA Gold Seal GD60179. Recorded 1956-57.

lh 8m ADD 1/90

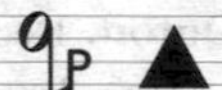

These performances are seldom less than mesmeric. The extremes of tempo and dynamics are exploited to the full in the Spanish night/day pieces: has any other conductor managed the gradual transition from *Ibéria*'s "perfumes of the night" to the gathering brilliance of the succeeding morning's holiday festivities, with such a delicate, yet precisely focused tracery of sounds? This is the very stuff of a waking dream. And the disc opens with what has to be the slowest, most languid account of the "Prélude" from the *Rapsodie espagnole* ever recorded; the resulting total concentration of the players on their conductor for control of rhythm and dynamics can be felt in every bar; it's not just a musical stunt, it creates a unique tension and atmosphere. Just listen to the finesse of the playing throughout, particularly the percussion, and marvel at how Reiner balances the textures in even the most riotous outbursts of the *Rapsodie*'s explosive "Feria". And the sound? Normally this *Guide* carries caveats for discs recorded in the mid-1950s, and audio boffins might nod their heads at a minuscule degree of tape saturation and hiss, but this writer can't think of any modern recording that renders the spectacle, colour and refinement of these scores with more clarity and atmosphere.

Debussy. CHAMBER WORKS. [cd]**Roger Bourdin** (fl); [a]**Arthur Grumiaux** (vn); [d]**Colette Lequien** (va); [b]**Maurice Gendron** (vc); [d]**Annie Challan** (hp); [a]**István Hajdu,** [b]**Jean Françaix** (pfs). Philips Musica da Camera 422 839-2PC. From SAL3644 (4/68). Recorded 1962-1966.

Violin Sonata[a]. Cello Sonata[b]. Syrinx[c]. Sonata for Flute, Viola and Harp[d].

45m ADD 10/89

The mystique that surrounds Debussy's late sonatas (six were intended but only three were completed before death intervened) sometimes inhibits performers from taking the music at its face value. These are direct, clean-boned compositions that benefit immeasurably from the sort of straightforward treatment they receive here from Philips. The Cello Sonata was written first, in 1915, and was followed later that year by the Sonata for Flute, Viola and Harp. The Violin Sonata was added, after a creative hiatus, in 1917 and, to some extent, it looks back to the clarity and single-mindedness that Debussy's earlier music exhibited. The flute solo, *Syrinx*, is an interloper, written in 1913 to illustrate Gabriel Mourey's *Psyche*. The playing on the Philips disc in all these works is a delight, never forced nor understated, but finding an easy balance of form and expression. The recording tidily defines the placing of the instruments across the soundstage whilst allowing just enough blending to provide a real sense of ensemble. If you've had trouble coming to terms with these works before, this disc should set you on the right path.

Additional recommendation ...
Violin Sonata. Sonata for Flute, Viola and Harp. Syrinx. Cello Sonata. Première Rapsodie for clarinet and piano. Petite pièce for clarinet and piano. **Athena Ensemble.** Chandos CHAN8385 — 55m ADD 5/87
Violin Sonata. Sonata for Flute, Viola and Harp. Syrinx. Cello Sonata. Chansons de Bilitis. **Nash Ensemble/Lionel Friend.** Virgin Classics VC7 59604-2 — 1h 8m DDD 4/91

Debussy. String Quartet in G minor, Op. 10.
Ravel. String Quartet in F major. **Quartetto Italiano** (Paolo Borciani; Elisa Pegreffi, vns; Piero Farulli, va; Franco Rossi, vc). Philips Silver Line 420 894-2PSL. From SAL3643 (5/68). Recorded in 1965.

57m ADD 10/88

Coupling the Debussy and Ravel string quartets has become something of a cliché in the record industry, but these two masterpieces do make a very satisfying pair in which similarities and differences complement each other to advantage. Both composers were around 30 when they wrote them and the medium seems to have drawn from them something unusually personal and expressive which is especially intense in the slow movements, although there is ample colour and vitality in the scherzos and the brilliant finales. These performances by the Quartetto Italiano were hailed as superlative when they first appeared and although there have been others of comparable quality since then, this is still one of the finest of chamber music records and especially desirable at medium price. The CD transfer is excellent and catches all the nuances of the playing.

Additional recommendations ...
Melos Quartet. DG 419 750 2GH 53m ADD 10/87
Chilingirian Quartet. EMI Eminence CD-EMX2156 — 55m DDD 3/91 £
LaSalle Quartet. DG Galleria 435 589-2GGA — 52m ADD 9/92 £
Carmina Quartet. Denon CO-75164 — 53m DDD 3/93

Debussy. Violin Sonata in G minor[a]. Sonata for flute, viola and harp[b].
Franck. Violin Sonata in A major[a].
Ravel. Introduction and Allegro[b]. [a]**Kyung Wha Chung** (vn); [b]**Osian Ellis** (hp); [a]**Radu Lupu** (pf); [b]**Melos Ensemble.** Decca 421 154-2DM. Items marked [a] from SXL6944 (9/80), [b] SOL60048 (9/62). Items marked [a] recorded in 1977, [b] 1962.

1h 7m ADD 1/89 £

This must be one of the best CD bargains around, with three masterpieces from the French tradition in excellent performances that have won the status of recording classics. Kyung Wha Chung and Radu Lupu are a fine duo who capture and convey the delicacy and poetry of the Franck Sonata as well as its rapturous grandeur, and never can the strict canonic treatment of the great tune in the finale have sounded more spontaneous and joyful. They are no less successful in the different world of the elusive Sonata which was Debussy's last work, with its smiles through tears and, in the finale, its echoes of a Neapolitan tarantella. The 1977 recording is beautifully balanced, with a natural sound given to both the violin and piano. The Melos Ensemble recorded the Ravel *Introduction and Allegro* 15 years before, but here too the recording is a fine one for which no allowances have to be made even by ears accustomed to good digital sound; as for the work itself, this has an ethereal beauty that is nothing short of magical and Osian Ellis and his colleagues give it the most skilful and loving performance. To talk about this disc as one for every collection savours of cliché, but anyone who does not have it may safely be urged to make its acquisition.

Additional recommendation ...
Violin Sonata. **Fauré.** *Violin Sonata No. 1 in A major, Op. 13.* **Franck.** *Violin Sonata in A major.* **Maurice Hasson** (vn); **Christian Ivaldi** (pf). Pickwick IMP Masters MCD37 — 1h 7m DDD 6/92

Debussy. Cello Sonata[a].
Schubert. Sonata in A minor, D821, "Arpeggione"[b].
Schumann. Fünf Stücke im Volkston, Op. 102[a]. **Mstislav Rostropovich** (vc); **Benjamin Britten** (pf). Decca 417 833-2DH. Items marked [a] from SXL6426 (10/70), [b] SXL2298 (1/62).

59m ADD 9/87 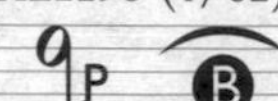

Britten was supremely gifted as conductor and pianist and here we hear him interpreting the music of others. The bewildering concentration of mood and imagery in Debussy's avowedly classical temperamental 15-minute Sonata presents special challenges to the players and its subtleties reveal themselves only after many hearings. Britten and Rostropovich bring to it and the other works a depth of understanding which is quite extraordinary. The Schubert Sonata is an engaging work, whilst the five Schumann pieces have a rustic simplicity and strength which these performers turn entirely to Schumann's advantage. Certainly a collector's item, this CD ought to be part of every chamber music collection. The analogue recordings have transferred extremely well.

Additional recommendations ...
Cello Sonata. **Martin.** *Ballade.* **Poulenc.** *Cello Sonata.* **William Conway** (vc); **Peter Evans** (pf). Linn Records CKD002 — 51m DDD 11/91
Cello Sonata. **Bridge.** *Cello Sonata in D minor, H125. Four Short Pieces, H104 — Meditation; Spring song.* **E. Dohnányi.** *Cello Sonata in B flat minor, Op. 8.* **Bernard Gregor-Smith** (vc); **Yolande Wrigley** (pf). ASV CDDCA796 — 1h 8m DDD 9/92

Debussy. MUSIC FOR TWO PIANOS. **Stephen Coombs, Christopher Scott.** Hyperion CDA66468. Recorded in 1989.
En blanc et noir. Prélude à l'après-midi d'un faune. Lindaraja. Trois nocturnes (trans. Ravel). Danse sacrée et danse profane.

59m DDDD 1/90

The number of works written for two pianos is small, perhaps because not many concert venues past or present possess two good, well-matched instruments, and masterpieces written for this combination of instruments is still smaller. But Debussy's suite *En blanc et noir* is certainly among them. Written in 1915 during the First World War, it is one of his last works and its second movement evokes the grimness of a battle scene and is dedicated to the memory of a young friend recently killed in action. The other two movements sparkle with mysterious life, their mood elusive but compelling. Stephen Coombs and Christopher Scott are young artists who joined forces as duo pianists in 1985, and on the evidence of this playing they are extremely skilful and sensitive. This is a lovely performance, alert to every nuance of Debussy's thought. The other works are no less well done, and although with the exception of the brief Spanish-style *Lindaraja* they are all transcriptions rather than pieces originally written for two pianos, the playing is so good that we are able to forget the lack of an orchestra and enjoy them in this format. The recorded sound is admirable and atmospheric.

Debussy. Préludes — Books 1[a] and 2[b]. **Walter Gieseking** (pf). EMI Références mono CDH7 61004-2. Item marked [a] from Columbia 33CX1098 (1/54), [b] 33CX1304 (11/55). Recorded 1953-1954.

1h 10m ADD 4/88

The Debussy *Préludes* have the rare distinction of appealing equally to the amateur and to the most sophisticated professional. And pianistic difficulty apart, their immediate charm as impressionistic evocations is as strong as the lasting fascination of their constructional intricacies. As repertoire pieces the technically more straightforward pieces demand considerable imaginative resources and tonal refinement, and Walter Gieseking was the epitome of this kind of artistry. His recordings of the *Préludes* have rightly remained touchstones for impressionist pianism. The subtlety of Gieseking's soft playing, his hypersensitive pedalling, his ability to separate textural strands and yet achieve an overall blended effect, are unsurpassed. Since the piano on these mid-1950s recordings is ideally regulated, since the recording quality is wholly acceptable and since both books of *Préludes* are accommodated on a single mid-price CD, it goes without saying that this is an exceptionally desirable issue.

Préludes. Images — Sets 1 and 2. Estampes. **Claudio Arrau.** Philips 432 304-2PM2 — ② 2h 14m ADD 2/92

Debussy. PIANO WORKS. **Zoltán Kocsis.** Philips 412 118-2PH.
Suite bergamasque. Images oubliées. Pour le piano. Estampes.

55m DDD 4/85

Debussy. PIANO WORKS. **Zoltán Kocsis.** Philips 422 404-2PH. Recorded in 1988.
Images, Sets 1 and 2. D'un cahier d'esquisses. L'isle joyeuse. Deux arabesques. Hommage à Haydn. Rêverie. Page d'album. Berceuse héroïque.

1h 2m DDD 2/90

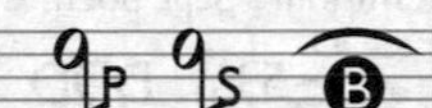

Three decades ago you could have counted on the fingers of one hand the performers who really had the measure of Debussy's piano style. Today there are many, but even so the Hungarian pianist Zoltán Kocsis stands out as especially idiomatic. On the first disc here, he plays four earlyish sets of pieces of which all but the *Suite bergamasque* are in the composer's favourite triptych form that he also used in *La mer*. The most 'classical' of them are the oddly titled *Pour le piano*, in which the Prelude echoes Bach's keyboard writing, and the *Suite bergamasque* with its eighteenth-century dances, but even in the latter work we find the composer's popular "Clair de lune" memorably impressionistic in its evocation of moonlight. In the *Estampes*, the last pieces played, he displayed a still more fully developed impressionism in musical pictures of the Far East, Moorish Spain and lastly a mysteriously rainswept urban garden. The rarity here is the *Images oubliées*, pieces dating from 1894 that Debussy left unpublished, doubtless because he reworked material from them in the *Estampes* and very obviously in the Sarabande of *Pour le piano*, but they are fine in their own right and here we can compare the different treatments of the similar ideas. Zoltán Kocsis brings refinement and brilliance to all this music and the piano sound is exceptionally rich and faithful.

The second Debussy recital by the same artist can be welcomed as a revealing portrait of the composer, its items discerningly offsetting the familiar with the less-known. It also brings playing not only of exceptional finesse, but at times of exceptional brilliance and fire. The main work is of course *Images*, its two sets completed in 1905 and 1907 respectively, by which time the composer was already master of that impressionistic style of keyboard writing so different from anything known before. For superfine sensitivity to details of textural shading Kocsis is at his most spellbinding in the first two numbers of the second set, "Cloches à travers les feuilles" and "Et la lune descend sur le temple qui fût". He is equally successful in reminding us of Debussy's wish to "forget that the piano has hammers" in the atmospheric washes of sound that he conjures (through his pedalling no less than his fingers) in *D'un cahier d'esquisses*. The sharp, clear daylight world of *L'isle joyeuse* reveals a Kocsis exulting in his own virtuosity and strength as he also does in the last piece of each set of *Images*, and even in the second of the two familiar, early *Arabesques*, neither of them mere vapid drawing-room charmers here. The recording is first rate. Both discs are highly recommendable.

Additional recommendation ...
Images, Sets 1 and 2. Berceuse héroïque. Mazurka. La plus que lente. Masques. Elégie. La petit nègre. Page d'album. Morceau de concours. Hommage à Haydn. D'un cahier d'esquisses. Children's Corner. **Martino Tirimo** (pf). Pickwick IMP Masters MCD32 — lh 17m DDD 10/92

Debussy. Etudes, Books 1 and 2. **Mitsuko Uchida** (pf). Philips 422 412-2PH. Recorded in 1989.

47m DDD 7/90 9P 9S

Near the beginning of his career, Debussy's *Prélude à l'après-midi d'un faune* (1894) opened the door (so it is often said) for modern music. His late works, including three chamber sonatas and the set of twelve piano studies (1915), opened another door, through which perhaps only he could have stepped. But his death from cancer in 1918 at the age of 56 put paid to that prospect. The harmonic language and continuity of the *Studies* is elusive even by Debussy's standards, and it takes an artist of rare gifts to play them 'from within', at the same time as negotiating their finger-knotting intricacies. Mitsuko Uchida is such an artist. On first hearing perhaps rather hyperactive, her playing wins you over by its bravura and sheer relish, eventually disarming criticism altogether. This is not just the finest-ever recorded version of the *Studies*; it is also one of the finest examples of recorded piano playing in modern times, matched by sound quality of outstanding clarity and ambient warmth.

Debussy. MELODIES. **Anne-Marie Rodde** (sop); **Noël Lee** (pf). Etcetera KTC1048. Texts and translations included.
Jane. Caprice. Rondeau. Aimons-nous et dormons. La fille aux cheveux de lin. Calmes dans le demi-jour. Sept poèmes de Banville. Proses lyriques. Trois Poèmes de Stéphane Mallarmé.

53m DDD 4/88

Very few CDs so far have been devoted to Debussy's songs, but in any case this one is exceptional in that it includes six that he composed before the age of 20 and seven to poems by Thédore de Banville, of which this is the first recording. The sweetness and freshness of Anne-Marie Rodde's voice, her purity of intonation, her security in the high register, and not least her understanding of style and the exemplary clarity of her enunciation make her a near-ideal interpreter of this repertoire, and she is sympathetically and ably partnered by Noël Lee. In a few places the piano is on the loud side, but otherwise the recording is excellent.

NEW REVIEW

Debussy. Le martyre de Saint-Sébastien. **Sylvia McNair** (sop); **Ann Murray** (mez); **Nathalie Stutzmann** (contr); **Leslie Caron** (narr); **London Symphony Chorus and Orchestra/Michael Tilson Thomas.** Sony Classical SK48240. Text and translation included. Recorded in 1991.

lh 6m DDD 3/93

"Archers aim closely, I am the target; whoever wounds me the most deeply, loves me the most. From the depths I call forth your terrible love ... again ... again! ...AGAIN!" cries the Saint in ecstasy. What Oscar Wilde did to the story of Salome, so the Italian writer D'Annunzio did to the story of Saint Sebastian (a young Roman officer ordered to be killed by his own archers because of his sympathy for persecuted Christians). This is the first recording for 30 years, not of the complete play (which lasted five hours!), but of an intelligent and effective reduction of the written text using the Saint as narrator, and incorporating all of an hour's worth of Debussy's incidental music. And it must be deemed a triumph. Leslie Caron's Saint is quietly intense and a model of restraint; Sylvia McNair's *vox coelestis* is just that, a gift from God; and the chorus and orchestra respond with total conviction to what is evidently, from Tilson Thomas, direction with a mission. The sheer sorcery of Debussy's music, as strongly imbued as his *Pélleas* with Wagner's *Parsifal*, benefits enormously from the acoustic of, appropriately, All Saints' Church in Tooting, London.

Additional recommendation ...
Le martyre de Saint-Sébastien. Ibéria. **Boston Symphony Orchestra/Charles Munch.** RCA GD60684 — lh 13m ADD ▲

Debussy. Ariettes oubliées. Cinq poèmes de Charles Baudelaire. Chansons de Bilitis.
Ravel. Histoires naturelles. **Nathalie Stutzmann** (contr); **Catherine Collard** (pf). RCA Victor Red Seal RD60899. Texts and translations included. Recorded in 1991.

lh 7m DDD 7/92 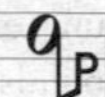

Debussy's songs rarely insist: they suggest, sometimes with happiness, sometimes sorrow, and most often with something in between. The voice uses notes to express the meaning of words, and the pianist too must reflect the delicate nuances of the poem. Both shun exaggeration or anything conventionally operatic. All of this implies such skill, sensitivity and discipline in performance that it is not surprising to find complete success elusive. Nathalie Stutzmann and her pianist Cathérine Collard now join the select ranks, the singer's place among them being distinguished from the start by the richness and depth of her voice. Here is a rarity these days, a genuine contralto, and one who sings with all due restraint both in the deployment of her tone and in the force of her utterance. The deep voice gives unusual colouring to the *Ariettes oubliées*, while the Baudelaire settings are subtly varied and the sublimely erotic *Chansons de Bilitis* sung responsively but without self-conscious characterization. The recital ends with Ravel's witty settings of prose-sketches by Jules Renard: peacock, cricket, swan, kingfisher and guinea-fowl are depicted in turn, in performances that are vivid if perhaps a little too 'straight'. Altogether a most attractive programme, well presented and admirable in the quality of recorded sound.

Debussy. La damoiselle élue[a]. Prélude à l'après-midi d'un faune. Images (1905-12) — No. 2, Ibéria. [a]**Maria Ewing** (sop) Damoiselle; [a]**Brigitte Balleys** (contr) Narrator; **London Symphony** [a]**Chorus and Orchestra/Claudio Abbado.** DG 423 103-2GH. Text and translation included.

49m DDD 3/88 

La damoiselle élue is scored for soprano, women's chorus and orchestra and sets verses from Dante Gabriel Rossetti's *The Blessed Damozel*. It is cast into four short movements and owes a clear debt to Wagner's *Parsifal*. The *Prélude à l'après-midi d'un faune* was Debussy's first real masterpiece and this evocation of Mallarmé's poem introduced a whole palette of new, supremely beautiful sounds, combining them into a musical structure both concise and subtly complex. Once heard it can never be forgotten. "Ibéria" is the central component of the orchestral set of *Images* and its three movements employ the rhythms and harmonies of Spanish music to conjure up a perfect picture of the Spanish/Mediterranean climate in its various moods. A fine Debussyan, Abbado penetrates to the heart of all these works and is given fine orchestral support throughout. Maria Ewing is an impressive Damoiselle and the women of the LSO chorus are in excellent voice. The recording is most successful, with good atmosphere and clarity.

Debussy. PELLEAS ET MELISANDE. **Eric Tappy** (ten) Pelléas; **Rachel Yakar** (sop) Mélisande; **Philippe Huttenlocher** (bar) Golaud; **Jocelyne Taillon** (mez) Geneviève; **Colette Alliot-Lugaz** (sop) Yniold; **François Loup** (bass) Arkel; **Michel Brodard** (bass) Doctor, Shepherd; **Monte-Carlo National Opera Orchestra/Armin Jordan.** Erato Libretto 2292-45684-2. Notes, text and translation included. From STU71296 (10/80). Recorded in 1979.

③ 2h 40m ADD 12/91 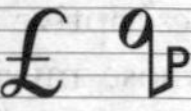

Maeterlinck's play was the inspiration for Debussy's sole masterpiece in the operatic genre. *Pelléas et Mélisande* tells of a medieval princess who falls in love with her husband Golaud's younger half-brother Pelléas, who is then killed by Golaud before Mélisande herself dies in childbirth. The story has a Wagnerian parallel in *Tristan und Isolde*, but the music is very different, being more restrained on the surface while suggesting no less powerful passions beneath. No modern performances have really succeeded in replacing the classic versions conducted by Roger Desormière and Ernest Ansermet, both of which preserve a tradition of performing this elusive piece that has since been lost. Armin Jordan's performance at once conjures up and then sustains the strange half-lit world of Maeterlinck's tale. Despite the title, in some ways the chief role is that of Golaud, and Philippe Huttenlocher, who is a superb singer-actor, makes us believe in and feel for him. Rachel Yakar is mysterious, delicate and wholly feminine as Mélisande — indeed, sometimes maddeningly so, for in her passivity and reluctance to explain herself she positively invites Golaud's jealous suspicions. The role of Pelléas can be sung either by a high baritone or by a tenor: again it is the latter and Eric Tappy therefore sounds all the more youthful and innocent compared with the dark baritone quality of Golaud (he's supposed to be 20 years younger). The other principals have less to do but are also satisfying, not least the bass François Loup as the kindly old king, Arkel. The orchestra under Armin Jordan play as if inspired and the clear recording allows every word to be heard, which is what Debussy wanted but is hard to achieve in the theatre. One gladly agrees with the original *Gramophone* review which found this performance "profoundly moving" and it offers us a considerable and very agreeable mid-price bargain.

Additional recommendations ...

Soloists; Montreal Symphony Chorus and Orchestra/Charles Dutoit. Decca 430 502-2DH2 — ③ 2h 3lm DDD 3/91
Soloists; Vienna State Opera Chorus; Vienna Philharmonic Orchestra/Claudio Abbado. DG 435 344-2GH2 — ② 2h 28m DDD 3/92
Soloists; Suisse Romande Orchestra/Ernest Ansermet. Decca Historic mono 425 965-2DM2 — ② 2h 28m ADD 4/93 ▲

Further listening ...

Mélodies — Ariettes oubliées — L'ombre de arbres. Cinq Poèmes de Baudelaire. Dans le jardin. Fleur des blés. Les Angélus. Mandoline. Nuit d'étoiles. Romance. Trois Mélodies de Verlaine — Le son du cor s'afflige; L'Echelonnement des haies. Trois Poèmes de Stéphane Mallarmé. **Hugues Cuenod** (ten); **Martin Isepp** (pf). Nimbus NI5231 (6/90).

Mélodies — L'âme évaporée. Ariettes oubliées. Beau soir. Les cloches. Fêtes galantes, Sets 1 and 2. Mandoline. Musique. Noël des enfants qui n'ont plus de maison. Nuit d'étoiles. Proses lyriques. **Claudette LeBlanc** (sop); **Valerie Tryon** (pf). Unicorn-Kanchana DKPCD9133 (4/93).

Michel Delalande

French 1657-1726

Delalande. Dies irae, S31. Miserere mei Deus secundum, S27. **Linda Perillo, Patrizia Kwella** (sops); **Howard Crook** (alto); **Herve Lamy** (ten); **Peter Harvey** (bass); **Chorus and Orchestra of La Chapelle Royale/Philippe Herreweghe.** Harmonia Mundi HMC90 1352. Recorded in 1990.

lh 2m DDD 12/91

Grands motets are sacred compositions for solo voices and chorus with instruments which epitomize an aspect of courtly life at Versailles during the reign of Louis XIV, the 'Sun King'. Delalande and his older contemporary Charpentier in their very different ways brought the *grand motet* to an expressive peak. The two works on this disc are especially fine examples of Delalande's skill in this sphere of composition. The *Dies irae* contains some wonderfully descriptive movements from among which we might single out the declamatory "Tuba mirum" whose music breathes the air of the opera house, and the chromatic, tenderly affecting "Lacrimosa". The *Miserere* continues a prevailing C minor tonality and, like the *Dies irae* is a grief-laden utterance. Philippe Herreweghe and the Choir of La Chapelle Royale give fervent performances and there are strong contributions above all from Howard Crook and Linda Perillo. The recording is clear and spacious and the accompanying booklet contains full texts with translations.

Delalande. Te Deum, S32. Super flumina. Confitebor tibi, Domine. **Véronique Gens, Sandrine Piau, Arlette Steyer** (sops); **Jean-Paul Fouchécourt, François Piolino** (tens); **Jérôme Corréas** (bass); **Les Arts Florissants/William Christie.** Harmonia Mundi HMC90 1351. Texts and translations included. Recorded in 1990.

lh 4m DDD 7/91 

Delalande was the greatest court musician of his generation and a gifted composer of *grands motets*, some 64 of which survive. William Christie has chosen three of them for his recording and in varying ways they illustrate Lalande's considerable strengths when working in this medium. These performances are full of affecting gestures, and telling insights to the music and it is all stylishly interpreted though some listeners might take issue over details. Christie's shaping of phrases is eloquent and his articulation crisp though the latter is not always helpfully served by a recording which tends to diffuse the larger sound of singers and instruments rather than focus it. There are some notable solo contributions, outstanding among which is that of the soprano, Sandrine Piau; she is well-matched by another soprano, Véronique Gens though the *haute-contre* or high tenor, Jean-Paul Fouchécourt, sounds a little strained in his uppermost notes. A rewarding disc in spite of a few rough edges in both singing and playing.

Further listening ...

Sinfonies pour les soupers du Roi. **La Symphonie du Marais/Hugo Reyne.** Harmonia Mundi HMC90 1337/40 (4-disc set, reviewed 7/91).

Petits Motets — Miserere a voix seule. Vanum est vobis ante lucem. Miserator et misericors. Cantique quatrième. *Coupled with* ***Lemaire.*** Assumpta est Maria; ***Morin.*** Regina coeli. **Soloists; Les Arts Florissants Chorus and Orchestra/William Christie.** Harmonia Mundi HMC90 1416 (4/93).

Key to Symbols

Gramophone Award winners

Artists of the Year

Leo Delibes

French 1836-1891

Delibes. Sylvia — ballet suite[a]. Coppélia — ballet suite[b].
Gounod. FAUST — ballet music[a]. [a]**Budapest Philharmonic Orchestra/János Sándor;** [b]**Berlin Radio Symphony Orchestra/Heinz Fricke.** LaserLight 15 616. Item marked [b] from 10 073 (12/86).

57m DDD 5/90 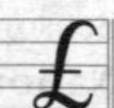

There are some most attractive bargains to be found on various inexpensive CD labels, and this LaserLight collection provides an excellent example. It combines familiar suites from Delibes's two most popular ballet scores with the ballet music that Gounod composed for the Walpurgis Night scene of his opera *Faust*. The music is throughout supremely tuneful, always elegant, and mixing the grace and charm of, say, Delibes's ravishing waltzes with the liveliness of the Csárdás from *Coppélia* and some of the rousing *Faust* items. Whether it be Heinz Fricke and the Berlin Radio Symphony Orchestra in *Coppélia* or János Sándor and the Budapest Philharmonic in *Sylvia* or *Faust*, the interpretations are all finely judged, bringing out all that is natural in the music, without succumbing to the temptation to add extra, artificial excitement. The orchestral playing also is of a higher order of refinement. The recordings are all digital originals and are of splendid clarity, dynamic range and naturalness.

NEW REVIEW

Delibes. Sylvia — ballet[a]. Coppélia — ballet[b]. [a]**London Symphony Orchestra/Anatole Fistoulari;** [b]**Minneapolis Symphony Orchestra/Antál Dorati.** Mercury Living Presence 434 313-2MM3. Items marked [a] from MMA11036/7 (8/59), [b] MMA11000/1 (2/59). Recorded 1957-58.

③ 2h 53m ADD 3/93 

It is really is astonishing that, in recordings some 35 years old, brass and percussion can burst forth with such vividness, or that instrumental detail can be as clear and faithful as they are here — in *Sylvia* especially. Nor, of course, do the attractions of this coupling by any means stop there. These have always been highly regarded performances of two of the most attractively tuneful ballets ever composed. *Coppélia* may be that bit more consistently inventive than its successor, but both repay hearing in full. Moreover, both conductors here had a great deal of experience in, and feeling for, the style of these ballets. As a result, both extract playing that is for the most part gracious and brilliant in turn, only occasionally lacking the final degree of finesse. In such passages as Fistoulari's vigorous "Les Chasseresses" or Dorati's "Musique des Automates" one can scarcely fail to be won over. It is only fair to warn that the recording of *Sylvia* is not absolutely complete, since it lacks the "Pas des esclaves" and "Variation-Valse" from the Act 3 *Divertissement*. On its own terms, though, this coupling represents a most compelling offering.

Additional recommendation ...

Sylvia[a]. ***Massenet.*** *LE CID — ballet music*[b]. [a]**New Philharmonia Orchestra,** [b]**National Philharmonic Orchestra/Richard Bonynge.** Decca Ovation 425 475-2DM2. ② 1h 58m ADD 1/90 £ ▲

Delibes. Coppélia — ballet. **National Philharmonic Orchestra/Richard Bonynge.** Decca 414 502-2DH2. Recorded in 1984.

② 1h 32m DDD 12/86 

Where other conductors may approach ballet recordings with the stage movements in mind, Bonynge sees them very much as an aural experience in their own right. He is ever ready to push the score along and provide all the excitement he can engender. For the armchair listener who may find some of the linking passages a shade tedious this may be just what is required. It may be that such numbers as the celebrated mazurka are approached a shade too aggressively and that the frequent recourse to *fortissimo* climaxes can become a shade wearying and obscure the native charm of a score such as this. On the other hand, orchestral effects such as those in the music of the automata come across with extra vividness, and set numbers such as the Act 2 "Boléro" and the "Valse des heures" achieve a quite thrilling effect. There is beautiful orchestral playing and the digital sound helps a great deal to create an overall effect of undemanding and rewarding listening.

Delibes. LAKME. **Dame Joan Sutherland** (sop) Lakmé; **Alain Vanzo** (ten) Gérald; **Gabriel Bacquier** (bar) Nilakantha; **Jane Berbié** (sop) Mallika; **Claud Calès** (bar) Frederick; **Gwenyth Annear** (sop) Ellen; **Josephte Clément** (sop) Rose; **Monica Sinclair** (contr) Miss Benson; **Emile Belcourt** (ten) Hadji; **Monte-Carlo Opera Chorus; Monte-Carlo National Opera Orchestra/Richard Bonynge.** Decca Grand Opera 425 485-2DM2. Synopsis, text and translation included. From SET387/9 (5/69). Recorded in 1967.

② 2h 18m ADD 12/89 

Like Pinkerton in *Madama Butterfly* (but not a cad like him), the British officer Gérald has succumbed to the exotic charm of the East: in particular, though engaged to a high-born English girl, he has become infatuated with the Brahmin priestess Lakmé, who returns his love, despite the fact that her father is bitterly hostile to the British and is plotting against them. A tragic outcome (with the help of a poisonous plant) is predictable: you might call this a Plain Tale from the Raj. This recording of Delibes's opera, though nearly 25 years old, still sounds fresh and clean. In Alain Vanzo it has a near-ideal lyric tenor hero; Gabriel Bacquier is suitably dark-hued as Lakmé's vengeful father; and in the title-role Joan Sutherland produces strikingly beautiful tone and seemingly effortless precision in florid passages (as in that famous showpiece the "Bell song"). Her words, however, are difficult to make out, owing to her weak consonants — a rare failing of hers, but one which her admirers have learnt to tolerate. In all other respects this is a very recommendable issue (especially at medium price).

Further listening ...

La Source, ou Naila — ballet. *Coupled with* ***Drigo.*** The Magic Flute — ballet. **Orchestra of the Royal Opera House, Covent Garden/Richard Bonynge.** Decca 421 431-2DH2 (9/90).

Frederick Delius

British 1862-1934

Delius. ORCHESTRAL WORKS. [a]**Tasmin Little** (vn), **Welsh National Opera Orchestra/Sir Charles Mackerras.** Argo 433 704-2ZH. Recorded 1990-1991.
Concerto for Violin and Orchestra[a]. Two Aquarelles (arr. Fenby). On hearing the first cuckoo in Spring. Summer Night on the River. Fennimore and Gerda Intermezzo (arr. Fenby). Irmelin Prelude. Dance Rhapsodies — Nos. 1 and 2.

lh 15m DDD 7/92 

This disc of the Violin Concerto should be played to friends who are not committed Delians; it is sure to persuade them that this concerto merits the same devotion as those by Elgar and Walton. Tasmin Little has the edge over Ralph Holmes (but only just) in coping with the work's technical difficulties; and under Mackerras's purposeful guidance, and with greater contrasts of pace between the various sections of its one movement form, the piece behaves more like a conventional concerto. If a certain amount of dream-like atmosphere is shed in the work's opening section in favour of classical rigour and vigour, at the heart of this account is the central accompanied cadenza: a minor miracle of flowing improvisation, with Mackerras and Little more freely rhapsodic than previous partnerships, and as twins in the seamless unfolding of the musical line. Argo's sound is very immediate, with a believable balance between soloist and orchestra, and excellent handling of the (albeit very few) orchestral climaxes. To the many shorter pieces that make up this disc's generous duration, only Beecham has brought a comparable feeling for texture and atmosphere. *Summer Night on the River*, in particular, is remarkable for its Debussian delicacy and the chamber-like intimacy of its sonorities.

Additional recommendations ...

Violin Concerto. Suite. Légende. **Ralph Holmes** (vn); **Royal Philharmonic Orchestra/Vernon Handley.** Unicorn-Kanchana DKPCD9040 — 53m DDD 9/85

Violin Concerto[b]*. Dance Rhapsody No. 1*[a]*. A song of the high hills*[c]*. Paa Vidderne*[d]. [c]**Freda Hart** (sop); [c]**Leslie Jones** (ten); [b]**Jean Pougnet** (vn); [c]**Luton Choral Society; Royal Philharmonic Orchestra/Sir Thomas Beecham.** EMI Beecham Edition mono CDM7 64054-2 — lh 13m ADD 9/92 ▲

NEW REVIEW

Delius. North Country Sketches. Brigg Fair — An English Rhapsody. In a Summer Garden. A Village Romeo and Juliet — The Walk to the Paradise Garden. **Welsh National Opera Orchestra/Sir Charles Mackerras.** Argo 430 202-2ZH. Recorded in 1989.

lh 8m DDD 12/90 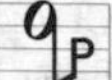

Delius. Florida — suite. North Country Sketches. **Ulster Orchestra/Vernon Handley.** Chandos CHAN8413. From ABRD1150 (7/86). Recorded in 1985.

lh 7m DDD 12/86 

After T*he Walk to the Paradise Garden*, written in 1906, there were for Delius many real gardens of paradise to which Wagner was less readily admitted: *Brigg Fair* (1907), which

Delius called "An English Rhapsody", begins with early morning mists and birdsong leading to variations on the Lincolnshire folk-song of the title. *In a Summer Garden* (1908) incorporates the sensations of Delius's own garden at Grez-sur-Loing outside Paris into perhaps his most intimate, exquisite improvisation; and the *North Country Sketches* (1913-14) paint the seasons and moods of the Yorkshire Moors around his birthplace. These quintessential Delian contemplations require, and here receive, lucidity of texture, a keen response to the moments of quietude, freedom from barlines, and animation for the 'wildlife'. With sound that is generally close and dry, Mackerras's Delius may for some, be wanting in *fin de siècle* opulence and 'impressionist' mist, but the effect is never clinical. This is a Delius disc of striking individuality; one that invites you to listen to music that is so often just heard. *Florida* was Delius's first purely orchestral work and though a frankly derivative score, with scarcely a hint of the mature composer to be, it is skilful and attractive, with plenty of good tunes, including the well-known "La calinda". In a beautifully refined and detailed recording Handley unfolds the music easily and naturally, so that its natural warmth and charm speak to us very directly. The four *North Country Sketches*, by contrast, show the mature Delius at his very finest and is a work of extraordinary power and imagination. Handley is acutely sensitive to the score's numerous fine details and he understands the ebb and flow of the musical argument to perfection. He is particularly successful in achieving a good balance of textures during the climaxes and he is aided both by the refined playing of the Ulster Orchestra and the outstanding quality of recording.

Delius. Paris: The Song of a Great City. Double Concerto[ab]. Cello Concerto[b]. [a]**Tasmin Little** (vn); [b]**Raphael Wallfisch** (vc); **Royal Liverpool Philharmonic Orchestra/Sir Charles Mackerras.** EMI Eminence CD-EMX2185. Recorded in 1991.

lh 4m DDD 3/92 £

Paris is an extravagant nocturnal impression of the city where "Le grand anglais", as Delius was known to his friends (who included Gaugin and Eduard Munch) spent a decade of his life, during which he developed, as Eric Fenby put it, "a painter's sense of orchestral colour". Premièred in 1901, it shows Delius relishing the full palette of his Staussian-sized orchestra to conjure an intoxicating merry-go-round of the city's night-life. Mackerras's performance is very physical, propelling the dancing to wild, whirling climaxes, and his balance engineers place us firmly among the excitement. In the Cello Concerto, a personal favourite of Delius's, Raphael Wallfisch and Mackerras seek out the contrasts inherent in the score, and, for the first time on disc, its pervasive dreaminess is offset by faster decorative passages, and a genuine playfulness. In short, it dances as well as sings. They are joined by Tasmin Little for an account of the Double Concerto that has never before received teamwork of such confidence, security and unanimity of purpose. This Eminence disc is an essential acquisition for all Delians, especially at the modest asking price.

Additional recommendations ...

Paris: The Song of a Great City. Brigg Fair — An English Rhapsody. Florida — suite. **Bournemouth Symphony Orchestra/Richard Hickox.** EMI CDC7 49932-2 — lh 16m DDD 5/91

Paris:. Life's Dance. Dance Rhapsody No. 1. Piano Concerto[a]. [a]**Philip Fowke** (pf); **Royal Philharmonic Orchestra/Norman Del Mar.** Unicorn-Kanchana DKPCD9108 — lh 17m DDD 3/92

Delius. ORCHESTRAL WORKS. **Hallé Orchestra/Vernon Handley.** Classics for Pleasure CD-CFP 4568. Recorded in 1981.

Brigg Fair — An English Rhapsody. In a Summer Garden. Eventyr. A Song of Summer.

56m DDD 8/90 £

Beecham laid a heavy interpretative hand on the scores of Delius, and the composer's approval of the results suggests that such adjustments of orchestral balance are essential to an idiomatic reading of this canon of works. Vernon Handley has latterly adopted Beecham's mantle in this respect, and has taken advantage of modern recording developments to lay down quite a number of the composer's chief works. His readings exalt both the hedonistic delight in life that much of Delius's music displays and intimations of the spiritual dimension that derive from the composer's pantheistic view of the world. This present disc represents remarkable value for money, combining as it does well-known works with some that few would claim to be on intimate terms with, all in a bargain package. The Hallé drive home all the points Handley wishes to make with an intuitive feel for the style and potential of the music. The recording has the fullness and clarity that is so typical of the venue, Manchester's Free Trade Hall, qualities that are normally so difficult to capture on tape. Clean CD transfers of 1981 originals make the disc doubly commendable.

NEW REVIEW

Delius. Sea Drift[a]. Florida — suite. [a]**Thomas Hampson** (bar); **Welsh National Opera** [a]**Chorus and Orchestra/Sir Charles Mackerras.** Argo 430 206-2ZH. Text included. Recorded in 1990.

1h 3m DDD 12/91

Sea Drift is a sublime conjunction of Whitman's poetry and Delius's music describing love, loss and unhappy resignation, with the sea (as Christopher Palmer puts it) as "symbol and agent of parting". Written in 1903-4 (the same years as Debussy's *La mer*), it is surely Delius's masterpiece; right from the swaying opening bars its spell is enduring and hypnotic. The Welsh forces may occasionally lack tonal refinement (the chorus's sopranos are inclined to wobble), but there is no mistaking the passionate commitment as the chorus shoot their voices over the waves of Mackerras's tumultuous orchestra "high and clear" to the absent beloved. It is a performance that has as much direct physical impact as it does well-achieved moments of Delian repose; and Thomas Hampson avoids sentimentality, singing with intelligence and giving musical shape to the meaning of the words. The earlier *Florida Suite* is generous with gorgeous tunes, iridescent orchestration and suffusing warmth, and Mackerras's reading is fresh and clear. The sound throughout, like the rest of this Argo series, is immediate and a little dry, but full and firm with a credible dynamic range.

Delius. THE FENBY LEGACY. **Royal Philharmonic Orchestra/Eric Fenby.** Unicorn-Kanchana DKPCD9008/9. Texts included. From DKP9008/09 (10/81).
Songs of Farewell (with Ambrosian Singers). Idyll (Felicity Lott, sop; Thomas Allen, bar). Fantastic Dance. A Song of Summer. Cynara (Allen). Irmelin Prelude. A Late Lark (Anthony Rolfe Johnson, ten). La calinda (arr. Fenby). Caprice and Elegy (Julian Lloyd Webber, vc). Two Aquarelles (arr. Fenby). Fennimore and Gerda Intermezzo (arr. Fenby. New to UK).

(2) 1h 45m DDD 12/87

It was Fenby's visit to the home of Delius in rural France that re-established the stricken composer's link with the outside world. Fenby became Delius's amanuensis and the tangible results of his French visit are offered here on a pair of CDs which make a perfect supplement to Beecham's EMI set. The *Irmelin* Prelude is the most famous but the most important are the more ambitious and equally evocative *Song of Summer*, and the *Songs of Farewell* set to words from his favourite American poet, Walt Whitman. The characteristically opaque choral textures tend to obscure the words at times, but this is of relatively small importance for Delius was mainly concerned with the sounds and colours of intertwining his ambitious chorus and equally large orchestra. The *Idyll* is an ardent love duet and its erotic element is in no doubt. The other orchestral pieces are characteristically appealing Delian miniatures, played with passionately romantic feeling and a real sense of ecstasy by the RPO; while in the choral music Fenby achieves the richest colours and wonderfully hushed *pianissimos*.

Delius. ORCHESTRAL SONGS. [a]**Felicity Lott** (sop); [b]**Sarah Walker** (mez); [c]**Anthony Rolfe Johnson** (ten); [d]**Ambrosian Singers; Royal Philharmonic Orchestra/Eric Fenby.** Unicorn-Kanchana DKPCD9029. Notes and texts included. From DKP9029 (12/84). Recorded in 1983.

A song of the high hills[d]. Twilight fancies[b]. Wine roses[b]. The bird's story[a]. Let springtime come[a]. Il pleure dans mon coeur[c]. Le ciel est, par dessus le toit[a]. La lune blanche[c]. To Daffodils[b]. I-Brasil[c].

56m DDD 3/85

A song of the high hills is one of Delius's most original masterpieces. Scored for a large orchestra and chorus it evokes with extraordinary power and beauty the grandeur and the spirit of nature. Eight of the nine songs with orchestra were scored by the composer himself, and *To Daffodils* was orchestrated by Eric Fenby. They all reflect in one manner or another Delius's favourite theme of the transience of love. The soloists are admirable, but Sarah Walker's three contributions are particularly perceptive. Fenby and the RPO accompany with total understanding and the recording is superlative.

Additional recommendation ...

Twilight Fancies[bd]. *The Violet*[ad]. *In the Seraglio Garden*[ad]. *Silken Shoes*[cd]. *Autumn*[bd]. *Sweet Venevil*[ad]. *Irmelin Rose*[ad]. *Let Springtime Come*[bd]. *Il pleure dans mon coeur*[cd]. *Le ciel est pardessus le toit*[ad]. *La lune blanche*[cd]. *Chanson d'automne*[bd]. *Avant que tu ne t'en ailles*[ad]. *To Daffodils*[bd]. *So sweet is she*[cd]. *I-Brasil*[cd]. *Three Preludes*[e]. *Zum Carnival — polka*[e]. [a]**Felicity Lott** (sop); [b]**Sarah Walker** (mez); [c]**Anthony Rolfe Johnson** (ten); [d]**Eric Fenby,** [e]**Eric Parkin** (pfs). Unicorn-Kanchana Souvenir UKCD2041 — 5lm DDD 10/91

Delius. A VILLAGE ROMEO AND JULIET. **Arthur Davies** (ten) Sali; **Helen Field** (sop) Vreli; **Thomas Hampson** (bass) The Dark Fiddler; **Barry Mora** (bar) Manz; **Stafford Dean** (bass) Marti; **Samuel Linay** (treb) Sali as a child; **Pamela Mildenhall** (sop) Vreli as a child; **Arnold Schönberg Choir; Austrian Radio Symphony Orchestra/Sir Charles Mackerras.** Argo 430 275-2ZH2. Notes and text included. Recorded in 1989.

② lh 5lm DDD 12/90

This was one of the recordings with which the Argo label was re-launched and very distinguished it proved to be. *A Village Romeo and Juliet* is the Delius opera that has held the stage while his others have appeared from time to time as curiosities. The reasons are twofold: it is dramatically the strongest and musically the most inspired. There have been two previous complete recordings (one conducted by Beecham), but this is incomparably the best, not least because the recording quality itself is so high. It was made in Vienna, with an Austrian orchestra and choir; the latter's English is impeccable. It would be insular to regard this work as English music, for it belongs to the 1900 ambience of Strauss and Mahler and that no doubt is why this cosmopolitan performance is so idiomatic. Sir Charles Mackerras conducts the opera with total authority and understanding. He demonstrates that to inspire orchestral playing as subtle and sensuous as this was not Beecham's Delian prerogative only. As the two young lovers who choose death rather than this world's worldliness, Helen Field and Arthur Davies are ideally cast, the soprano in particular giving a lustrous and moving performance. As The Dark Fiddler, the enigmatic figure whose claim to a disputed strip of land is the lynchpin of the plot, the American baritone Thomas Hampson is first-rate. The final scene of the opera, with the lovers' duet and the distant voices of "the travellers passing by", is magical as music, performance and recording. In the additional Beecham recommendation (below), Alan Sanders in his *Gramophone* review found the main work wanting but concluded his review with the following: "The 'new' *Sea Drift* makes this set an essential acquisition for all Delians, who will also get some satisfaction from listening to the main work."

Additional recommendation ...

A Village Romeo and Juliet. Sea Drift[a]. **Gordon Clinton** (bar); **Soloists; Royal Philharmonic Orchestra/Sir Thomas Beecham.** EMI Beecham Edition mono CMS7 64386-2 — ② 2h 4m ADD 11/92 ▲

Further listening ...

THE COMPLETE STEREO RECORDINGS. Over the Hills and Far Away (ed. Beecham). Sleigh Ride[a]. Irmelin Prelude. Dance Rhapsody No. 2. Summer Evening (ed. and arr. Beecham). Brigg Fair — An English Rhapsody. On hearing the first Cuckoo in Spring. Summer Night on the

River. A Song before Sunrise. Marche Caprice. Florida Suite (ed. and arr. Beecham). Songs of Sunset (with Maureen Forrester, contr; John Cameron, bar; Beecham Choral Society). Fennimore and Gerda — Intermezzo (ed. and arr. Beecham). **Royal Philharmonic Orchestra/Sir Thomas Beecham.** EMI CDS7 47509-8 (6/87).

A Mass of Life[a]. Songs of Sunset[b]. Arabesque[c]. [abc]**Soloists;** [a]**London Philharmonic Choir,** [bc]**Liverpool Philharmonic Choir;** [a]**London Philharmonic Orchestra,** [bc]**Royal Liverpool Philharmonic Orchestra/Sir Charles Groves.** EMI CMS7 64218-2 (2-disc set).

David Del Tredici

American 1937-

Del Tredici. Steps[a] (1990). Haddock's Eyes[b] (1985). [b]**David Tel Tredici** (pf); [b]**Susan Naruki** (sop); [b]**Claire Bloom** (narr); [a]**New York Philharmonic Orchestra;** [b]**New York Philharmonic Ensemble/Zubin Mehta.** New World 80390-2.

54m DDD 

The (extraordinary) music of David Del Tredici has had relatively little exposure on disc so far, which is rather surprising given the approachability and melodiousness of its style. Del Tredici first came to public attention in 1976 when Solti conducted the first performance of *Final Alice* — a large and colourful monodrama scored for amplified soprano and orchestra. The subject matter of *Final Alice* — Lewis Carroll's *Alice in Wonderland* — has become an almost singular preoccupation with Del Tredici since 1968 and has formed the inspiration to nearly all of his compositions since. *Steps* for orchestra is an exception, though even here something of the surreal, dream-like quality of the *Alice* stories permeates this fascinating and richly imaginative score. *Steps* is cast in one movement, divided into four interconnected sections: "Giant Steps", "The Two-Step", "Giant Giant Steps" and "Stepping Down" and has been described by Del Tredici as "a monster — violent, powerful, inexorable ... my most dissonant tonal piece". Mehta and the New York Philharmonic give a stunningly virtuosic performance of this 'jabberwocky' of a piece and make a strong case for Del Tredici as one of America's most imaginative living composers. *Haddock's Eyes*, if the title hasn't already given it away, is one of Del Tredici's many 'Alice'-inspired works, and is a wonderfully affectionate setting of the "White Knight's Song" from *Through the Looking-Glass* scored for soprano, narrator and chamber ensemble. Susan Naruki's performance is a real *tour-de-force* as she spills out Carroll's words and Del Tredici's music in an ever and ever increasing hysterical frenzy. A marvellous introduction to the music of this fascinating American composer.

François Devienne

French 1759-1803

Devienne. OBOE SONATAS. **Peter Bree** (ob); **Roderick Shaw** (fp). Etcetera KTC1106. Recorded in 1991.
G minor, Op. 23 No. 3; C major, Op. 71 No. 3; G major, Op. 71 No. 1; D minor, Op. 71 No. 2.

1h 2m DDD 12/91 

This little-known French composer was a contemporary of Mozart and it is good to make his acquaintance here. He was a wind player, though a flautist rather than an oboist, and wrote a large amount of music (including 12 concertos for flute, four for bassoon and several comic operas) before dying insane at 44. On the evidence of these four oboe sonatas, he was a man of his time who accepted the moods and structures of classicism but was aware of the new feelings coming into music in post-Revolution France and elsewhere: after all, Beethoven's *Moonlight* Sonata was written in his lifetime, though it is unlikely that he knew it. The romantic element is strongest in the slow movements, with their long and richly expressive phrases. These are played by Peter Bree with feeling as well as tonal beauty, and he brings wit and fantasy too to movements such as the *Presto* finales of the D minor and G minor Sonatas and the set of variations that ends the one in C major. Bree comes from Holland, which is also the country to which Roderick Shaw emigrated after studying at Cambridge. They play admirably as a team and both instruments sound right for this music, with the German fortepiano that is used being free of clattery quality. The recording, made in Munich, balances the oboe forwardly, but few will mind that when the playing is so good. The artists contribute an informative booklet note.

David Diamond

American 1915-

NEW REVIEW

Diamond. ORCHESTRAL WORKS. [a]**János Starker** (vc); [b]**New York Chamber Symphony Orchestra,** [c]**Seattle Symphony Orchestra/Gerard Schwarz.** Delos DE3103. Symphony No. 3[c]. Romeo and Juliet[b]. Psalm[c]. Kaddish[ac].

1h 13m DDD 4/93

David Diamond is not a name that immediately springs to mind when thinking of great American symphonists. And yet, as this disc amply demonstrates, his is an individual voice, as deserving of recognition as Walter Piston or Howard Hanson. The pieces on this thoughtfully compiled disc range from *Psalm* (1936) to *Kaddish* (1989), and he's still active today, currently working on his Tenth and Eleventh Symphonies. His early *Psalm* is a remarkably assured work for a 21 year old, bold enough to keep harmonies simple and possessing a defiant energy in the *allegro* section. *Kaddish* (the Jewish prayer for the dead) provides an excellent vehicle for Starker's very special brand of eloquence. But the big work here is the Third Symphony, tightly argued, relentless in the pulsating rhythms of its first movement, lyrical and songful in the *Andante*, with an openness that immediately identifies the nationality of the composer. Prokofiev's work was certainly at the back of Diamond's mind when he wrote his *Romeo and Juliet*. But he shows just the right melodic flair to make it a success — especially in the Balcony Scene. With good sound and an enlightening interview between Diamond and producer Adam Stern in the booklet, this is a highly recommendable issue.

Further listening ...

Symphonies Nos. 2 and 4[a]. Concerto for small orchestra[a]. [a]**Seattle Symphony Orchestra;** [b]**New York Chamber Symphony Orchestra/Gerald Schwarz.** Delos DE3093 (4/91).

Peter Dickinson

British 1934-

Suggested listening ...

Mass of the Apocalypse. Outcry. The Unicorns. **Soloists; London Consort Choir; City of London Sinfonia/Nicholas Cleobury; Solna Brass/Lars-Gunnar Björklund.** Conifer CDCF167 (5/89).

Alphons Diepenbrock

Dutch 1862-1921

Suggested listening ...

The Birds — Overture. Suites — Marsyas; Electra. Hymne for violin and orchestra. **Emmy Verhey** (vn); **The Hague Residentie Orchestra/Hans Vonk.** Chandos CHAN8821 (8/90).

Hymnen an die Nacht No. 2, Muss immer der Morgen wiederkommen. Die Nacht. Im grossen Schweigen. Wenige wissen das Geheimnis der Liebe. **Linda Finnie** (contr); **Christopher Homberger** (ten); **Robert Holl** (bass); **The Hague Residentie Orchestra/Hans Vonk.** Chandos CHAN8878 (4/91).

James Dillon

British 1950-

NEW REVIEW

Dillon. East 11th St NY10003. La femme invisible. Windows and Canopies. **Music Projects London/Richard Bernas.** NMC NMCD004. Recorded in 1991.

57m DDD 9/92

James Dillon obviously has an eclectic taste in titles, but there is nothing equivocal, or non-committal, about the character of his music — one reason why it inspires dedicated contemporary music specialists to give of their best, as Music Projects London does on this exciting and important disc, the first devoted to Dillon's music. *East 11th St NY10003* (1982) is scored solely for percussion, six players charting an itinerary that may well evoke American metropolitan vistas for those who know them, but which can also be enjoyed simply as a brilliantly abstract timbral display. *Windows and Canopies* (1989) sounds a more solemn title but, as with the percussion pieces, the visual image releases a finely-realized musical structure notable for the variety and spontaneity of its ideas. The emotional spectrum ranges from the imposingly dramatic to the divertingly humorous, and even if the style must be classified as 'complex', the music is never in the least ponderous. The same virtues, coupled with an even more richly eventful and expressive musical topography, can be found in *La femme invisible* (1989). Much of Dillon's work deals with the motion between explicit and implicit, open and concealed, and his resourcefulness as a musical colourist alone makes this an exceptionally rewarding disc.

Ernö Dohnányi

Hungarian 1877-1960

Suggested listening ...

Konzertstück for cello and orchestra, Op. 12. *Coupled with* **Dvořák.** Cello Concerto in B minor, B191. **Raphael Wallfisch** (vc); **London Symphony Orchestra/Sir Charles Mackerras.** Chandos CHAN8662 (5/89).

Piano Quintet No. 1 in C minor, Op. 1. String Quartet No. 2 in D flat major, Op. 15. **Wolfgang Manz** (pf); **Gabrieli Quartet.** Chandos CHAN8718 (5/89).

Gaetano Donizetti

Italian 1797-1848

Donizetti. IMELDA DE' LAMBERTAZZI. **Floriana Sovilla** (sop) Imelda; **Andrea Martin** (bar) Bonifacio; **Diego D'Auria** (ten) Lamberto; **Fausto Tenzi** (ten) Orlando; **Gastone Sarti** (bar) Ubaldo; **Chorus and Orchestra of Swiss-Italian Radio and Television/Marc Andreae.** Nuova Era 6778/9. Notes, text and translation included. Recorded in 1989.

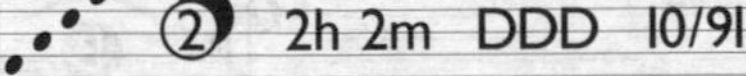

Donizetti's most original opera before *Anna Bolena* in the opinion of William Ashbrook, *Imelda de' Lambertazzi* tells of lovers kept asunder by the wars of the Guelphs and Ghibellines. Nothing particularly original about that perhaps, but it does come as something of a surprise to find that the hero is a baritone. The tenor is Imelda's brother, the bass her father, both implacably opposed to her union with Bonifacio, whose father killed her mother. The final catastrophe occurs when Bonifacio has been poisoned and Imelda tries to suck out the fatal substance. She is duly poisoned too and, rejected by her family, dies what is claimed to be the first death actually to take place on stage. Happily, the music has several points of interest and indeed some touches of inspiration. Particularly fine is the duet for Imelda and her brother in Act 2, and this also has some of the best singing, the general level of which is not that high. Most regrettable is the casting of the baritone role; Andrea Martin appears to have neither the voice nor the style for it. Still, the opportunity to hear this opera is not one to miss. It appeals at various levels, including the unintentionally comic, as when choruses telling of the sorrows of civil war and such matters swing along to a catchy tune which might almost come out of *The Pirates of Penzance*. The performance was given at Lugano "in oratorio form", and the recorded sound is more full-bodied than several in this company's catalogue.

NEW REVIEW

Donizetti. L'ELISIR D'AMORE. **Mariella Devia** (sop) Adina; **Roberto Alagna** (ten) Nemorino; **Pietro Spagnoli** (bar) Belcore; **Bruno Praticò** (bar) Dulcamara; **Francesca Provvisionato** (mez) Giannetta; **Tallis Chamber Choir; English Chamber Orchestra/Marcello Viotti.** Erato 4509-91701-2. Notes, text and translation included.

② 2h 9m DDD 6/93

A modern and completely recommendable set of this delightful piece, country cousin to *Don Pasquale*, was badly needed — and here it is. It is a delight from start to finish, making one fall in love again with this delightful comedy of pastoral life. The plot is a variant of the much used theme of the fake love potion. Here the potion is supplied by the charlatan Doctor Dulcamara to the shy young Nemorino to help him win the love of Adina. Roberto Alagna, disciple of Pavarotti, sings Nemorino with all his mentor's charm and a rather lighter tone appropriate to the role. He also evinces just the right sense of vulnerability and false bravado that lies at the heart of Nemorino's predicament. Here is a tenor with a great future if only he stays with roles within his range. He is partnered by Mariella Devia who has every characteristic needed for the role of Adina. With a fine sense of buoyant rhythm, she sings fleetly and uses the coloratura to enhance her reading. She can spin a long, elegiac line where that is needed, and her pure yet full tone blends well with that of her colleagues. She also suggests all Adina's high spirits and flirtatious nature. The other principals, though not as amusing in their interpretations as some of their more experienced predecessors, enter into the ensemble feeling of the performance. All are helped by the lively but controlled conducting of Viotti and by the ideal recording.

Additional recommendations ...

Soloists; Ambrosian Opera Chorus; English Chamber Orchestra/Richard Bonynge. Decca 414 461-2DH2 — ② 2h 21m ADD 6/86

Soloists; Turin Radio Symphony Chorus and Orchestra/Claudio Scimone. Philips 412 714-2PH2 — ② 2h 7m DDD 6/86

Soloists; Chorus and Orchestra of the Metropolitan Opera, New York/James Levine. DG 429 744-2GH2 — ② 1h 59m DDD 2/91

NEW REVIEW

Donizetti. LUCIA DI LAMMERMOOR. **Cheryl Studer** (sop) Lucia; **Plácido Domingo** (ten) Edgardo; **Juan Pons** (bar) Enrico; **Samuel Ramey** (bass) Raimondo; **Jennifer Larmore** (mez) Alisa; **Fernando de la Mora** (ten) Arturo; **Anthony Laciura** (ten) Normanno; **Ambrosian Opera Chorus; London Symphony Orchestra/Ion Marin.** DG 435 309-2GH2. Notes, text and translation included. Recorded in 1990.

② 2h 18m DDD 4/93

With 12 recordings currently available, *Lucia di Lammermoor*, once regarded as *passé*, appears to be in remarkably good health. Not so long ago it was dismissed as little more than a convenient vehicle for the latest coloratura soprano, who could enjoy a double success, first in the Fountain

Scene where she would be applauded on entry and then able to warm up for the celebrated Mad Scene, which was the real culmination of the evening even to the extent (in Melba's day, for instance) of finishing the opera on Lucia's final high note and eliminating the tenor's big scene which is to follow. Nowadays, while the opera is still a *tour de force* for the soprano, the tenor shares the honours and the whole thing is much more of a company production. Its likely hero is Donizetti himself, whose music has strengths of many kinds, including expert and evocative orchestration. Recordings by Callas and Sutherland are generally respected as permanent classics of the gramophone, but two recent versions deserve consideration, and one of them, with Studer and Domingo in the leading roles, is fit as a whole to stand alongside its eminent predecessors. It does so principally on its comparative merit as an overall performance and recording. The fine deep colours of the orchestra, the sturdy dramatic cohesion and well-wrought climaxes, are well brought out; passages traditionally omitted are in place (and deserve to be). The role of Lucia's confidante is sung with distinction by Jennifer Larmore, and though Juan Pons could do with more bite to his tone and Samuel Ramey with more expressiveness in his vocal acting these have their strengths too. Studer combines beautiful tone, technical accomplishment and touching pathos. Details include an extended cadenza in the Mad Scene, which ends on a not too exposed high E flat (D being the ceiling elsewhere). Domingo triumphantly overcomes the difficulties such a role must pose at this stage of his career: Edgardo di Ravenswood in this recording is as firmly at the centre of the opera as is its eponymous heroine.

Additional recommendations ...

Soloists; Royal Opera House Chorus and Orchestra, Covent Garden/Richard Bonynge. Decca 410 193-2DH3 — ③ 2h 20m ADD 11/85 Ⓑ
Soloists; Maggio Musicale Fiorentino Chorus and Orchestra/Tullio Serafin. EMI mono CMS7 69980-2 — ② 1h 51m ADD 10/89 ▲ Ⓑ
Soloists; Ambrosian Opera Chorus; New Philharmonia Orchestra/Jesús López-Cobos. Philips 426 563-2PM2 — ② 2h 23m ADD 1/91 Ⓑ
Soloists; Chorus of La Scala, Milan; Berlin RIAS Symphony Orchestra/Herbert von Karajan. EMI mono CMS7 63631-2 — ② 1h 59m ADD 2/91 ▲ Ⓑ
Soloists; Ambrosian Singers; London Symphony Orchestra/Richard Bonynge. Teldec 9031-72306-2 — ② 2h 23m DDD 11/92 Ⓑ

Donizetti. GIANNI DI PARIGI. **Giuseppe Morino** (ten) Gianni; **Luciana Serra** (sop) Principessa di Navarra; **Angelo Romero** (bar) Steward; **Elena Zilio** (mez) Oliviero; **Enrico Fissore** (bar) Pedrigo; **Silvana Manga** (sop) Lorezza; **Chorus and Orchestra of RAI, Milan/Carlo Felice Cillario.** Nuova Era 6752/3. Notes, text and translation included. Recorded in 1988.

② 2h 3m DDD 10/91

The title-role in this early comedy of Donizetti's was written for the great tenor Rubini who, it appears, never sang it himself and pocketed the score so that nobody else should do so. It did reappear a couple of times in Donizetti's lifetime but had no success and remained unseen and unheard till the "Donizetti and his Time" Festival at Bergamo in 1988. The story is thin and the characters are pasteboard, but the music sparkles: it is a score full of attractive numbers and more than worth the rediscovery. It concerns a meeting at a country inn of the Princess of Navarre and the amiable Gianni of Paris, introduced as "un onesto borghese" but in reality the son of Philip de Valois. She pretends not to recognize him but likes him all the same, and a good deal of merriment arises out of nothing very much. There are some tuneful choruses with Rossinian crescendoes; an excellent "breakfast" duet for the tenor and buffo-bass enlivens the start of Act 2; and the arias and duets for soprano and tenor are models of grace and charm, provided that these qualities are also present in the singers. The Rubini-role is sung by a tenor who does indeed sometimes remind one of those late nineteenth-century Italian lyric tenors who lived just in time to be recorded: he is Giuseppe Morino, his voice marked by a quick vibrato, his style always sensitive and occasionally exquisite. Luciana Serra as the Princess is reputedly Italy's leading soprano leggiero (not as reassuring a recommendation as it should be). On the whole, the performance goes well and is recorded vividly enough to capture the sense of zest and pleasure in the old score happily new-found.

Donizetti. LA FILLE DU REGIMENT. **Dame Joan Sutherland** (sop) Marie; **Luciano Pavarotti** (ten) Tonio; **Spiro Malas** (bass) Sulpice; **Monica Sinclair** (contr) Marquise of Berkenfield; **Jules Bruyère** (bass) Hortensius; **Eric Garrett** (bar) Corporal; **Edith Coates** (contr) Duchess of Crakentorp; **Alan Jones** (ten) Peasant; **Chorus and Orchestra of the Royal Opera House, Covent Garden/Richard Bonynge.** Decca 414 520-2DH2. Notes, text and translation included. From SET373/4 (11/68).

② 1h 47m ADD 11/86

This is one of those obliging operas which allow you to forget just how many tuneful and charming melodies they contain, thus affording the delight of surprised recognition. On record the good humour comes through without too much underlining, and the *bravura* singing (dazzling flights of scales, staccatos, trills and high notes) puts a brilliant shine on the whole entertainment. Pavarotti has a full share in this: his solo "Ah, mes amis" is one of the most celebrated tenor recordings ever made. As so often with Sutherland one misses a firm singing-line in the simpler melodies, and there is also the depressing pronunciation, where 'fait' sounds like 'feu' and 'coquette' sounds like 'coquutte'. Still, there is much to be marvelled at, much to enjoy; a performance and an opera not to be missed.

Donizetti. DON PASQUALE. **Sesto Bruscantini** (bar) Don Pasquale; **Mirella Freni** (sop) Norina; **Leo Nucci** (bar) Dr Malatesta; **Gösta Winbergh** (ten) Ernesto; **Guido Fabbris** (ten) Notary; **Ambrosian Opera Chorus; Philharmonia Orchestra/Riccardo Muti.** EMI CDS7 47068-2. Notes, text and translation included. From SLS143436 (4/84). Recorded in 1982.

② 2h 3m DDD 8/88

In this delightful opera Donizetti's inspiration is unfaltering, and he manages to combine sentiment and comedy in equal proportions. The somewhat hard-hearted treatment of old Pasquale's weakness for the lovely Norina, and the ruse she and Malatesta play on him are eventually dissolved in the triumph of love over cynicism. Riccardo Muti is a stickler for fidelity to the score, playing it complete and insisting on his cast singing the written notes and nothing else. Donizetti blossoms under such loving treatment. It is a reading, brisk and unvarnished, that demands one's attention throughout, and the playing of the Philharmonia is splendidly vital. As Pasquale, Bruscantini sings with the benefit of long experience in defining line and words. Leo Nucci sings a smiling, resourceful Malatesta, at once Pasquale's friend and the author of the trick played on him. Gösta Winbergh is an accurate and fluent Ernesto, and Mirella Freni, the Norina, delivers her difficult aria with all her old sense of flirtatious fun: but when the joke has gone too far, she finds just the plaintive tone to express Norina's doubts and regret.

Additional recommendation ...

Soloists; Lyon Opera Chorus and Orchestra/Gabriele Ferro. Erato 2292-45487-2 —
② 2h DDD 11/90

Further listening ...

Italian Songs — Canto d'Ugolino. L'amor funesto. Il trovatore in caricatura. Spirito di Dio benefico. Viva il matrimonio. *French Songs* — Le renégat. Noé, scène du Deluge. Le départ pour la chasse. Un coeur pour abri. Le hart (chant diabolique). **Ian Caddy** (bass-bar); **Melvyn Tan** (fp). Meridian CDE84183 (4/90).

UGO, CONTE DI PARIGI. **Soloists; Geoffrey Mitchell Choir; New Philharmonia Orchestra/Alun Francis.** Opera Rara ORC1 (12/90).

EMILIA DI LIVERPOOL. L'EREMITAGGIO DI LIWERPOOL. **Soloists; Geoffrey Mitchell Choir; Philharmonia Orchestra/David Parry.** Opera Rara ORC8 (5/92).

ANNA BOLENA. **Soloists; Chorus and Orchestra of Welsh National Opera/Richard Bonynge.** Decca 421 096-2GH3 (7/88).

LUCREZIA BORGIA. **Soloists; RCA Italiana Opera Chorus and Orchestra/Jonel Perlea.** RCA Victor Gold Seal GD86642 (9/90).

MARIA STUARDA. **Soloists; Bologna Teatro Communale Chorus and Orchestra/Richard Bonynge.** Decca 425 410-2DM2 (9/90).

L'ASSEDIO DI CALAIS. **Soloists; Geoffrey Mitchell Choir; Philharmonia Orchestra/David Parry.** Opera Rara OR9 (7/91).

LA FAVORITA. **Soloists; Slovak Philharmonic Chorus; Italian International Opera Orchestra/Fabio Luisi.** Nuova Era 6823/4 (10/91).

MARIA PADILLA. **Soloists; Geoffrey Mitchell Choir; London Symphony Orchestra/Alun Francis.** Opera Rara ORC6 (2/93).

POLIUTO. **Soloists; Vienna Singakademie Chorus; Vienna Symphony Orchestra/Oleg Caetani.** CBS Masterworks CD44821 (3/90).

John Dowland

British c.1563-1626

Dowland. Lachrimae, or Seaven Teares. **Dowland Consort/Jakob Lindberg** (lte). BIS CD315. From LP315 (10/86).

lh 6m DDD 12/86 

John Dowland was described by a contemporary as "a cheerful person" but the darker side of his nature is evident in many of his works. In *Lachrimae, or Seaven Teares* he constructed seven marvellous pavans based on its opening motif and set for five viols and lute. They are followed by 14 other compositions, some of which bear dance titles whilst others are dedicated to particular persons. The melancholy consequences of technical inadequacy often suffered by viol consorts are entirely absent here and the problem of balancing the lute is solved to perfection in this marvellous recording. If Renaissance music were to be represented by only one disc it should perhaps be this one.

Additional recommendations ...

Hespèrion XX/Jordi Savall. Astrée Auvidis E8701 — lh llm DDD 9/88

The First Booke of Songs — Go Cristall teares; Come heauy sleepe. The Second Booke of Songs — I saw my Lady weepe; Flow my teares; Sorrow sorrow stay. A Pilgrimes Solace — From silent night. A Musicall Banquet — In darkness let me dwell. **Caroline Trevor** (mez); **Jacob Heringman** (lte); **Rose Consort of Viols.** Amon Ra CD-SAR55 — lh 3m DDD 1/93

Dowland. LUTE WORKS. **Ronn McFarlane.** Dorian DOR90148.

Fantasie. P1*a*. Pipers Pavan, P8. Semper Dowland semper dolens, P9. Dr Cases Paven, P12. Lachrimae, P15. Captaine Digorie Piper his Galliard, P10. Dowlands Galliarde, P21. Frogg Galliard, P23*a*. Melancoly Galliard, P25. Doulands Rounde Battele Galliard, P39. Queene Elizabeth, her Galliard, P41. The Earl of Essex, his Galliard, P42*a*. The Lady Cliftons Spirit, P45. Sir John Smith his Almaine, P47. The Lady Laitones Almone, P48*a*. My Lady Hunsdons Puffe, P54. Mistris Winters Jumpe, P55. Mrs Whites Nothing, P56. The Shoemaker's Wife, P58. Tarletones riserrectione, P59. Orlando sleepeth, P61. Fortune, P62. Go from my windowe, P64. My Lord Willobes Wellcome Home, P66. What if a day, P79. Mr Dowland's Midnight, P99. Prelude, P102. A Fancy.

lh 7m DDD 4/92

John Dowland wrote over 100 items for solo lute, covering every type of piece — even, a rarity at that time, a Preludium [*sic*]. Ronn McFarlane's programme includes two each of the magnificent

Fantasies and sets of variations but concentrates on the dance and 'character' pieces, many of them respectfully dedicated to people from whom he may have hoped for favours, though two dedications are enigmatic: Queen Elizabeth was already dead when her rather small-scale Galliard was written, and Digorie Piper was a pirate. The gift of memorable melody which marks his lute songs is no less evident in the lute solos, some of which (for instance, *Lachrimae* and *The Earl of Essex, his Galliard*) exist in both vocal and instrumental forms, and *Tarletones riserrectione* is a positive gem. This music was not meant to be played rigidly to the metronome (even if it had existed at that time!) and McFarlane avails himself of the freedom to use a measure of a rubato that humanizes the music. Dowland was the greatest lutenist of his day and this is reflected in the difficulty of many of the items, but McFarlane has nimble enough fingers to conceal the problems; this is just as well since the close recording would have revealed the slightest lapse. Recommended as a happy cross-section of this remarkable and rewarding repertory.

Additional recommendation ...
Lute Works. **Paul O'Dette.** Astrée Auvids E7715 — ⁘ 55m AAD 11/88

Dowland. The Second Booke of Songs. **The Consort of Musicke/Anthony Rooley** (lte). L'Oiseau-Lyre 425 889-2OH. Texts included. From DSLO528/9 (9/77). Recorded in 1976.

⁘ 1h 10m ADD 8/91

This recording originally appeared in 1977 as part of Florilegium's complete Dowland cycle. The "Second Booke of Songs" dates from 1600 and contains two of Dowland's most famous compositions *Flow my teares* and *I saw my Lady weepe*, though here these are presented unusually (and not entirely convincingly) as vocal duets. In fact there is a surprisingly wide variety of vocal and instrumental combinations throughout the disc, from consort song to four-part vocal to the more familiar sound of solo voice and lute, all of which were suggested as performance possibilities by Dowland himself. It is partly as a result of this that the recording retains its freshness in spite of its age, but it would be wrong to ignore the contribution made by the intelligent and sensitive singing of Emma Kirkby and Martyn Hill, both of whom sound completely in their element.

Further listening ...

The First Booke of Songs — Come againe: sweet loue doth now enuite; Come away, come sweet love; Go Cristall teares. *The Second Booke of Songs* — I saw my Lady weepe; Fine knacks for ladies; A Shepherd in a shade his plaining made. *The Third and Last Booke of Songes* — Weepe you no more, sad fountaines; What if I neuer speede?; Dephne was not so chaste as she was changing. *A Pilgrimes Solace* — Sweete stay a while, why will you? Tell me true Loue. ***R. Dowland.*** *A Musicall Banquet* — In darkness let me dwell. *Lute Solos* — Piper's Pavan, P8; The King of Denmarke, his Galliard, P40; Mistris Winter's Jumpe, P55; Mrs White's Nothing, P56; Mrs Vauxe's Gigge, P57; The Shoemaker's Wife. A Toy, P58. **Andrew Dalton** (alto); **Yasunori Inamura** (lte). Etcetera KTC1030 (7/89).

The First Booke of Songes. **The Consort of Musicke/Anthony Rooley.** L'Oiseau-Lyre 421 653-2OH (10/89).

The Third Booke of Songs. **The Consort of Musicke/Anthony Rooley.** L'Oiseau-Lyre 430 284-2OH (11/91).

The First Booke of Songs — Awake sweet loue thou art returned; Can she excuse my wrongs; All ye whom Loue; Deare if you change. *The Second Booke of Songs* — Sorow sorow stay, lend true repentant teares; Dye not before thy day; Mourne, mourne; Wofull heart; New cease my wandring eyes. *The Third and Last Booke of Songes* — Behold a wonder heare; The lowest trees; Me, me and none but me; Farewell too faire. *A Pilgrimes Solace* — Stay time a while thy flying; Shall I strive with words to move; Thou mighty God. *Instrumental Works* — Semper Dowland semper dolens, P9; Mr Dowland's Midnight, P99; Earle of Darby, his Galliard, P44*a*. Mistris Winters Jumpe, P55. **Emma Kirkby** (sop); **Anthony Rooley** (lute, orpharion). Virgin Classics Veritas VC7 59521-2 (4/90).

Patrick Doyle

British 20th Century

Suggested listening ...

Henry V — *original film soundtrack.* **City of Birmingham Symphony Orchestra/Simon Rattle.** EMI CDC7 49919-2 (2/90).

Riccardo Drigo

Italian 1846-1930

Suggested listening ...

The Magic Flute — ballet. *Coupled with* ***Delibes.*** La Source, ou Naila — ballet. **Orchestra of the Royal Opera House, Covent Garden/Richard Bonynge.** Decca 421 431-2DH2 (9/90).

Guillaume Dufay

French c.1400-1474

Suggested listening ...

Triste plaisir et douleureuse joye — Rondeaux, Ballades and Lamentations. *Coupled with* ***Binchois.*** Rondeaux and Ballades. **Ensemble Gilles Binchois/Dominique Vellard.** Virgin Classics Veritas VC7 59043-2.

Paul Dukas

French 1865-1935

NEW REVIEW

Dukas. La Péri — ballet. L'Apprenti sorcier.
Debussy. La boîte à joujoux — ballet. **Suisse Romande Orchestra/Ernest Ansermet.** Decca 433 714-2DM. Recorded 1957-63.

1h 1m ADD

How strange that the composer of *The sorcerer's apprentice* (1897), a piece that amazes as sheer sound, should later remark, on hearing Richard Strauss's *Salome*, that he realized just how much he had to learn about the orchestra. Learn he did, for it's impossible not to be struck by the resemblance of *La péri*'s central dance to *Salome*'s famous striptease. *La péri*, Dukas's last major work, shares with Ravel's *Daphnis and Chloë* the same sensuality, exoticism and refinement; and both works were written for Diaghilev's Ballets Russes and premièred in Paris in 1912. Its closing pages prompted one French writer to enthuse about their "hazy iridescence, dividing the sounds in the way a rainbow divides light through the droplets of a fountain". Dividing the sounds of a complex orchestral fabric was something for which Ansermet had, and indeed still has, few peers. No one listening to his *Sorcerer* can fail to be amazed by the way figures leap, cascade and dazzle with pinpoint clarity, precision and style (no resort to mere speed for excitement). Qualities that are just as apparent in this classic account of Debussy's ballet for marionettes, *La boîte à joujoux*; Ansermet's affection for this enchanting evocation of the world of toys and childhood speaks from every bar. The sound is a little thin tonally, but as clean as a whistle.

Additional recommendation ...

La Péri — Fanfare and Poème dansé. Symphony in C major. L'Apprenti sorcier. **Netherland Radio Philharmonic Orchestra/Jean Fournet.** Denon CO-75284 — 1h 14m DDD 6/93

Dukas. ARIANE ET BARBE-BLEUE. **Katherine Ciesinski** (sop) Ariane; **Gabriel Bacquier** (bar) Barbe-bleue; **Mariana Paunova** (contr) La Nourrice; **Hanna Schaer** (mez) Sélysette; **Anne-Marie Blanzat** (sop) Ygraine; **Jocelyne Chamonin** (sop) Mélisande; **Michelle Command** (sop) Bellangère; **French Radio Chorus; French Radio New Philharmonic Orchestra/Armin Jordan.** Erato Libretto 2292-45663-2. Notes, text and translation included. From NUM750693 (10/83). Recorded in 1983.

lh 57m DDD 9/91

This is by far the longest of Dukas's works which the highly self-critical composer allowed to survive. Based on Maeterlinck's play, the opera is curiously cast in that the six most important roles are female. Barbe-bleue himself only make a brief appearance as a singer — Gabriel Bacquier nevertheless makes a strong impression in this cameo role — and the other male singers have but a line or two each. The role of Ariane, by contrast, is highly taxing for the singer, for not only is her part very wide-ranging, but she is on the stage for the whole opera. Katherine Ciesinski does not perhaps have the most attractive voice, but she is a highly resourceful artist who brings Ariane to life very vividly. The lesser role of the nurse is competently taken by Hanna Schaer, and the sopranos (Barbe-bleue's previous wives) are all first-rate. Dukas's scoring is very seductive and richly imaginative, and no performance of this opera would be successful in the hands of a lesser conductor. Armin Jordan paces the work superbly, and obtains very fine playing from the Radio France New Philharmonic Orchestra. The recording is tonally very beautiful and highly atmospheric.

Further listening ...

Variations, Interlude and Finale on a theme by Rameau. Prélude élégiaque. La plainte, au loin, du faune. Piano Sonata in E flat minor. **Margaret Fingerhut** (pf). Chandos CHAN8765 (1/90).

Key to Symbols

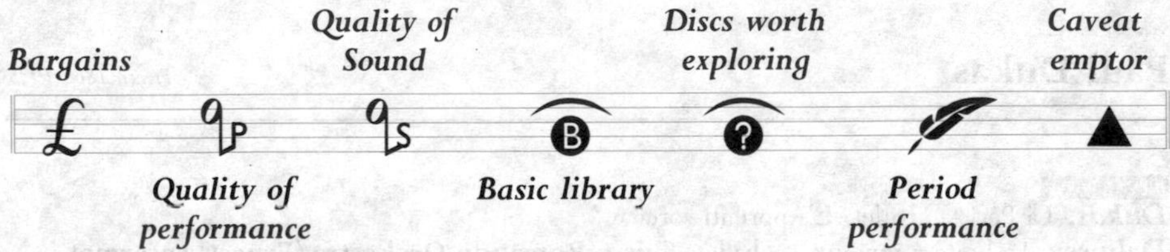

Marie Eugène Duparc

French 1848-1933

Suggested listening ...

Mélodies — L'invitation au voyage. Sérénade florentine. Extase. Chanson triste. Le manoir de Rosemonde. Lamento. Au pays où se fait la guerre. La fuite. La vague et la cloche. Sérénade. Testament. Phidylé. Romance de Mignon. Elégie. Le galop. Soupir. La vie antérieure. **Danielle Borst** (sop); **François Le Roux** (bar); **Jeff Cohen** (pf). REM REM311049 (9/89).

Jacques Duphly

French 1715-1789

Suggested listening ...

Harpsichord Solos La de Redemond. La du Buq. *Coupled with* ***Leclair.*** Violin Sonatas — A minor, Op. 5 No. 7; A major, Op. 9 No. 4. ***Mondonville.*** Violin Sonata in G major, Op. 3

No. 5. ***Guillemain.*** Violin Sonata in A major, Op. 1 No. 4. *Harpsichord Solos* — ***J-B. Forqueray.*** La Morangis ou La Plissay. **Simon Standage** (vn); **Lars Ulrik Mortensen** (hpd). Chandos CHAN0531 (6/93).

Marcel Dupré

French 1886-1971

Suggested listening ...

Prelude and Fugue in A flat major, Op. 36 No. 2. Evocation, Op. 37. Six antiennes pour le temps de Noël, Op. 48. Psalm XVIII, Op. 47. Choral and Fugue, Op. 57. **Jeremy Filsell** (org). Gamut Classics GAMCD530 (5/92).

Dupré. Preludes and Fugues, Op. 7. *Coupled with* ***Alain.*** Intermezzo. Litanies, Op. 79. ***Franck.*** Prélude, fugue et variation in B minor, Op. 18. Fantaisie in A major. ***Tournemire.*** Petite rapsodie improvisée. Cantilène improvisée. Improvisation sur le Te Deum. **Jane Watts** (org). Priory PRCD286 (9/90).

Maurice Duruflé

French 1902-1986

Duruflé. ORGAN WORKS. **John Scott.** Hyperion CDA66368. Played on the organ of St Paul's Cathedral, London.
Prélude sur l'introit de l'Epiphanie. Prélude et fugue sur le nom d'Alain, Op. 7. Suite, Op. 5. Scherzo, Op. 2. Prélude, adagio et choral varié sur le "Veni creator spiritus", Op. 4 (with the men's voices of St Paul's Cathedral Choir). Fugue sur le carillon des heures de la Cathédrale de Soissons, Op. 12.

1h 10m DDD 1/91

The *Requiem* is Duruflé's best-known work. But as an organist it was only natural that the bulk of his music was written for that instrument. While six pieces which comfortably fit on to a single CD may not seem much to show for a lifetime's devotion to the organ, such a meagre output is entirely the result of extreme fastidiousness: Duruflé was almost obsessively self-critical revising his compositions many times over before releasing them for publication. The result is music in which no note is superfluous and where emotional intensity has unusually direct impact. Many characteristics of the *Requiem* will be instantly picked up here by the discerning listener, not least the copious use of plainsong. A singularly beautiful addition to this recording is the use of men's voices to chant verses of *Veni creator spiritus*. But while Duruflé's deeply-felt, sometimes pained expression permeates most of this music, there are flashes of gaiety: in a simply delicious *Siciliano* (from the Suite) and in the bubbly *Scherzo*. John Scott's performances are truly exceptional. Technically he is impressive and he readily bares his sensitive musical soul to release the full beauty of these pieces. Hyperion have made a wonderful job in recording at St Paul's, achieving an ideal blend between clarity and atmosphere. The echo at this venue can have, and does here, a stunning effect: just savour that glorious aftertaste which seems to linger into eternity each time Scott's hands leave the keys.

Duruflé. Requiem, Op. 9[a]. Quatre Motets sur des thèmes grégoriens, Op. 10. [a]**Ann Murray** (mez); [a]**Thomas Allen** (bar); **Corydon Singers;** [a]**English Chamber Orchestra/Matthew Best** with [a]**Thomas Trotter** (org). Hyperion CDA66191. Texts and translations included. From A66191 (5/86).

51m DDD 4/87

The Requiem is adapted from a suite of organ pieces Duruflé based on plainsong from the Mass for the Dead. Although it expresses the same tranquility and optimism as the Fauré Requiem,

Duruflé's language is firmly based in the twentieth century. The Requiem exists in three versions: one uses a full orchestra; another has just cello and organ accompaniment, while the "middle version" of 1961, used here, employs a small orchestra. The performance is admirable in its quiet expressiveness, and Matthew Best conducts with skill and sensitivity. The *Quatre Motets* inhabit a similar world to that of the Requiem and are also based on Gregorian chant. The recording is not ideally clear, but is more than adequate.

Henri Dutilleux

French 1916-

Dutilleux. Violin Concerto, "L'arbre des songes"[a]. ***Maxwell Davies.*** Violin Concerto[b]. **Isaac Stern** (vn); [a]**French National Orchestra/Lorin Maazel;** [b]**Royal Philharmonic Orchestra/André Previn.** CBS Masterworks CD42449.

56m DDD 2/88

This is a unique coupling in many respects, not least among them the fact that both concertos were written for this soloist. The Dutilleux Concerto, unlike the traditional bravura vehicle, is more integrated, more inward looking with the slower passages radiating a distinctive haunting beauty. The Maxwell Davies work also offers comparatively few opportunities for display, although its technical demands are virtuosic indeed, and includes numerous allusions to the dances of the Scottish highlands. Stern gives confident and involving performances of both works, projecting a wide range of colour and conveying an understanding of and confidence in their musical values. The recordings are good.

NEW REVIEW

Dutilleux. Mystère de l'instant[a]. Métaboles[b]. Timbres, Espace, mouvement[b]. [a]**Zurich Collegium Musicum/Paul Sacher;** [b]**French National Orchestra/Mstislav Rostropovich.** Erato MusiFrance 2292-45626-2. Item marked [a] recorded in 1990, [b] 1982.

46m ADD/DDD 8/92

Métaboles was written in 1964 for the fortieth anniversary of the Cleveland Orchestra, and is dedicated to its conductor, George Szell. The work is in five sections, each showing off different sections of the orchestra until the fifth, which alone involves the whole ensemble. Szell had trained the Cleveland Orchestra into a virtuoso instrument, and Dutilleux's score, if structurally somewhat threadbare, reflects the composer's exotic taste for colour and sonority to great effect. If the French National Orchestra is not quite in the Cleveland league it gives a convincing account of the work under Rostropovich's direction. *Timbres, Espace, mouvement* was in fact commissioned by Rostropovich in 1978 for his Washington National Symphony Orchestra. Van Gogh's painting, "The Starry Night" was the source of inspiration, and once more Dutilleux paints his response in vivid sound colours. The work is in two sections, and the unusual scoring is for lower strings only, woodwind, brass and metallic percussion. Rostropovich leads a pungent, brightly lit performance. Paul Sacher commissioned *Mystère de l'instant* in 1989 for his Zurich Collegium Musicum. Once more Dutilleux creates magical sonorities from a smaller ensemble of strings, cymbalum and timbales, but his score, cast in ten short sections which are played continuously, is this time more inward-looking, and has greater substance. Sacher's sensitive, masterly direction gives great pleasure. Recordings throughout the disc are first-rate and it is only to be regretted that the playing time is so short.

Further listening ...

Symphony No. 1. Timbres, espaces, mouvement. **Orchestre National de Lyon/Serge Baudo.** Harmonia Mundi HMC90 5159 (3/87).

Antonin Dvořák

Czechoslovakian 1841-1904

Dvořák. Cello Concerto in B minor, B191.
Tchaikovsky. Variations on a Rococo theme, Op. 33. **Mstislav Rostropovich** (vc); **Berlin Philharmonic Orchestra/Herbert von Karajan.** DG 413 819-2GH. From SLPM139044 (10/69).

1h ADD 3/85 

Dvořák's Cello Concerto dominates the repertoire and above all it needs a larger-than-life soloist and a balancing orchestral partnership. As an interpreter of the work Rostropovich reigns supreme and he has recorded it six times. Undoubtedly the collaboration with Karajan was the most fruitful, with these two great artists striking sparks off one another, resulting in Rostropovich's tendency to romantic indulgence seeming natural and inspirationally spontaneous against the sweep of the background canvas supplied by the Berlin Philharmonic players. It is an admirable performance, helped by a superb, naturally balanced recording. What better coupling than Tchaikovsky's elegant and tuneful *Rococo* Variations, a work displaying the composer's affinity with his beloved Mozart — there never seems to be a note too many. Again, Rostropovich and Karajan are in their element, with the Berlin orchestra providing many inimitable touches, and the result is sheer delight.

Additional recommendations ...

Cello Concerto. ***Schubert.*** *Sonata in A major, D821, "Arpeggione".* **Lynn Harrell** (vc); **London Symphony Orchestra/James Levine.** RCA Papillon GD86531 — 1h 7m ADD 11/87

Cello Concerto[a]. ***Bloch.*** *Schelomo*[b]. ***Bruch.*** *Kol Nidrei, Op. 47*[c]. **Pierre Fournier** (vc); [ab]**Berlin Philharmonic Orchestra/**[a]**George Szell,** [b]**Alfred Wallenstein,** [c]**Jean Martinon.** DG Privilege 429 155-2GR — 1h 11m ADD 5/90 £

Cello Concerto[a]. ***Bruch.*** *Kol Nidrei*[b]. ***Elgar.*** *Cello Concerto in E minor, Op. 85*[c]. **Pablo Casals** (vc); [a]**Czech Philharmonic Orchestra/George Szell;** [b]**London Symphony Orchesta/Sir Landon Ronald;** [c]**BBC Symphony Orchestra/Sir Adrian Boult.** EMI Références mono CDH7 63498-2 — 1h 15m ADD 8/90

Cello Concerto. ***Elgar.*** *Cello Concerto.* **Maria Kliegel** (vc); **Royal Philharmonic Orchestra/Michael Halász.** Naxos 8 550503 — 1h 13m DDD 9/92 £

Cello Concerto (Berlin Philharmonic Orchestra/Lorin Maazel). ***Elgar.*** *Cello Concerto in E minor, Op. 85* (London Symphony Orchestra/André Previn). ***Haydn.*** *Cello Concerto in D major, HobVIIb/2* (English Chamber Orchestra). ***Saint-Saëns.*** *Cello Concerto No. 1 in A minor, Op. 33* (French National Orchestra/Lorin Maazel). ***Schumann.*** *Cello Concerto in A minor, Op. 129* (Bavarian Radio Symphony Orchestra/Sir Colin Davis). **Yo-Yo Ma** (vc). CBS Masterworks CD44562 ② DDD/ADD 2h 20m 5/90 £

Dvořák. Violin Concerto in A minor, B108. Romance in F minor, B39. **Kyung Wha Chung** (vn); **Philadelphia Orchestra/Riccardo Muti.** EMI CDC7 49858-2.

47m DDD 11/89 

Considering the popularity of his Cello Concerto, Dvořák's Violin Concerto has never quite caught on with the general public. But a top class performance can convince us that the neglect is unfair. Kyung Wha Chung plays the concerto with the right blend of simplicity and brilliance, Slavonic warmth and folk-like quality, and the Philadelphia Orchestra under Riccardo Muti give her the right kind of support, unobtrusive enough to make us forget that the orchestral writing is not Dvořák at his most instrumentally imaginative, yet positive enough to provide more than just a discreet background. Ultimately, we probably enjoy the concerto most for its Bohemian lilt, a quality we feel in the violin's very first entry and that is present again in ample measure in the rondo finale — a movement of unfailingly dancing rhythm and considerable charm that here receives a sparkling performance. The delicately scored Romance in F minor that completes the programme is a slightly earlier work than the Violin Concerto and, it has been said, suggests a leisurely walk through the Bohemian countryside with someone who knows it well. The recorded sound is well defined and faithful, capturing Chung's fine tonal palette.

Additional recommendations ...
Violin Concerto[a]. **Sibelius.** *Violin Concerto in D minor, Op. 47*[b]. **Salvatore Accardo** (vn); [a]**Concertgebouw Orchestra,** [b]**London Symphony Orchestra/Sir Colin Davis.** Philips Silver Line 420 895-2PSL — 1h 8m ADD 10/88
Violin Concerto. **Suk.** *Fantasy, Op. 24.* **Josef Suk** (vn); **Czech Philharmonic Orchestra/Karel Ančerl.** Supraphon Crystal Collection 11 0601-2 — 56m ADD 9/89 £

Dvořák. Piano Concerto in G minor, B63[a].
Schumann. Introduction and Allegro appassionato, Op. 92. **András Schiff** (pf); **Vienna Philharmonic Orchestra/Christoph von Dohnányi.** Decca 417 802-2DH. Item marked [a] recorded at a performance in the Musikverein, Vienna during November 1986.

53m DDD 1/89

It seems extraordinary that the Piano Concerto is not all that well known. For a long time it was thought unpianistic, but András Schiff gives a fresh and agile account of what is a delightful score. He is very well partnered by Dohnányi and the Vienna Philharmonic Orchestra, and the playing is singularly sure for a live performance. The music is unmistakably Dvořák's, though in this relatively early work we do not find the consistently Bohemian flavour that is actually stronger in his later music. Schumann wrote his *Introduction* while under the literary influence of Byron's dramatic poem *Manfred* with its tormented hero. Here is another relatively neglected piece, but it has considerable atmosphere and is once again persuasively performed. Clear yet spacious recording in both works.

Dvořák. OVERTURES AND SYMPHONIC POEMS. **Bavarian Radio Symphony Orchestra/Rafael Kubelík.** DG Galleria 435 074-2GGA2. Items marked [a] from 2530 593 (12/75), [b] 2530 785 (2/78), [c] 2530 712 (11/76), [d] 2530 713 (11/76). Recorded 1973-1976.
Overtures and Symphonic Poems — My home, B125*a*[a]. Hussite, B132[b]. In nature's realm, B168[b]. Carnival, B169[b]. Othello, B174[b]. The water goblin, B195[c]. The noon witch, B196[c]. The golden spinning-wheel, B197[d]. The wild dove, B198[d]. Symphonic Variations, B70[c].

② 2h 37m ADD 11/91 £

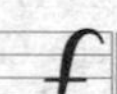

Writing about Richard Strauss's *Don Juan*, Tovey remarked that "programme music ... either coheres as music or it does not". Perhaps Dvořák's symphonic poems have never attained the popularity of those by Richard Strauss because there are a few too many seams in his musical narrative. Equally, the gruesome local folk ballads on which they are based (and which Dvořák gleefully brings to life) afforded him less range for depth of human characterization. But there are lots of good reasons to value them. There's his inimitable stream of heart-easing melody, and alongside the obvious debt to Liszt and Wagner, their harmonic boldness and magical instrumental effects look forward to Suk, Martinů and Janáček. Indeed, in the central section of *The golden spinning-wheel*, where the wheel and assorted paraphernalia are offered to the false queen in return for the various dismembered portions of the heroine's body, the repeated patterns on muted strings sound like pure Janáček. And the exquisite closing pages of *The wild dove* could be the best thing Martinů ever wrote. Also written when Dvořák was at the height of his power (in the 1890s), these two mid-priced discs offer the chance to hear his three concert overtures — *In nature's realm, Carnival* and *Othello* — as he originally conceived them: a thematically linked three movement 'symphonic' work on the theme of nature, life and love. The earlier and no less worthy *Symphonic Variations* and *My home* and *Hussite* overtures complete a set that would be fine value in terms of minutes for your money even if the performances were mediocre. As it is you won't find a finer account at any price. Knowing when to keep this music on the move is the secret of Kubelík's success, but the mobility is always marked by freshness of spirit rather than plain drive. The whole set is informed with his burning belief in the value of the music and his experience is drawing precisely what he wants from his own Bavarian players. DG's mid-seventies recordings project this with clarity and coherence and need fear nothing from more recent digital contenders.

 See below (under Symphonies) for further recommendations.

Dvořák. SLAVONIC DANCES. **Bavarian Radio Symphony Orchestra/Rafael Kubelík.** DG Galleria 419 056-2GGA. Items marked [a] from 2530 466 (11/75), [b] 2530 593 (11/75).
B83[a] — No. 1 in C major; No. 2 in E minor; No. 3 in A flat major; No. 4 in F major; No. 5 in A major; No. 6 in D major; No. 7 in C minor; No. 8 in G major. *B147*[b] — No. 1 in B major; No. 2 in E minor; No. 3 in F major; No. 4 in D flat major; No. 5 in B flat minor; No. 6 in B flat major; No. 7 in C major; No. 8 in A flat major.

1h 10m ADD 8/87 

Dvořák wrote his first set of eight *Slavonic Dances* in 1878 at the request of his publisher. They were originally cast in piano duet form, but the composer almost immediately scored them for orchestra. They achieved a great success and a further set of eight were requested. Dvořák initially doubted his ability to repeat the prescription, and it was not until 1886 that he produced a second set of eight dances. Again they were originally written for piano duet and then orchestrated, and again they proved to be very popular. Kubelík's recording was made at a time when he was head of the Bavarian Radio Symphony Orchestra. As a musician steeped in the romantic traditions of his native Czechoslovakia he managed to persuade his orchestra to play Czech music almost to the manner born. His performances of the dances are brilliant, very vivacious, and highly idiomatic. The recording is very clear but slightly lacking in depth and atmosphere.

Additional recommendations ...
Rheineland-Pfalz State Philharmonic Orchestra/Leif Segerstam. BIS CD425 — 1h 18m DDD 7/89
Carnival — Overture, B169. **Czech Philharmonic Orchestra/Václav Talich.** Music and Arts mono CD-658 — 1h 15m AAD 6/92
Cleveland Orchestra/George Szell. Sony Classical Essential Classics MK48161 — 1h 14m ADD 11/92

Dvořák. Serenades — E major, B52; D minor, B77. **Academy of St Martin in the Fields/Sir Neville Marriner.** Philips 400 020-2PH. From 6514 145 (5/82).

51m DDD 4/83 

These two serenades are works full of melody and good humour, bubbling over with tuneful zest, but always inventive and skilfully scored. The gracefully elegant E major Serenade here receives a wonderfully cultivated reading which never overlooks the subtleties of the part-writing. The D minor is a slightly grittier piece and also benefits from Marriner's attentive guidance. Tempos are finely judged and well related throughout and the fast sections have a lovely zip and panache. The recording is excellent too, the strings having just the right bloom without sacrificing the music's essential intimacy.

NEW REVIEW

Dvořák. Serenade in D minor, B77. Slavonic Dance No. 7 in C major, B147 (arr. Clements).
Krommer. Partita in E flat major, Op. 45[a].
Mysliveček. Octet in E flat major. [a]**Charles Kavalovski,** [a]**Scott Brubaker** (hns); **New York Harmonie Ensemble/Steven Richman.** Music and Arts CD-691. Recorded live in 1990.

59m DDD 8/92 

There's some really high-class wind-playing on this delightful CD; indeed, the performance of the Dvořák Wind *Serenade* is one the finest around, brimful of affectionate vigour and pungent character. This is followed by an idiomatic arrangement of the same composer's C major *Slavonic Dance* (No. 7 from the second set) — again despatched with agreeably earthy panache. Apparently, the members of the Harmonie Ensemble are drawn from the cream of New York's major orchestras, which would account for the technical excellence and first-rate musicianship on show. Two enjoyable Czech rarities comprise the remainder: the E flat Octet by Josef Mysliviček (1737-81) possesses a truly Mozartian grace and delicacy, whilst the Partita of Franz Krommer (1759-1831) (one of three comprising his Op. 45 and first published in 1803) is a concerto for two horns in all but name — bouquets here for the two solo players (Charles Kavalovski and Scott Brubaker) who deal superbly with Krommer's fiendishly demanding writing. Annotations are most helpful, and the recording, made in a New York church during a live concert (though you would never guess it — off-stage noises are virtually non-existent), has ideal warmth and blend, though I would have preferred to hear more of the rasp of double-bass in the Dvořák *Serenade*.

Dvořák. COMPLETE SYMPHONIES AND ORCHESTRAL WORKS. **London Symphony Orchestra/István Kertész.** Decca 430 046-2DC6. Recorded 1963-1966.
Symphonies — No. 1 in C minor, B9, "The Bells of Zlonice" (from SXL6288, 10/67); No. 2 in B flat major, B12 (SXL6289, 9/67); No. 3 in E flat major, B34 (SXL6290, 5/67); No. 4 in D minor, B41 (SXL6257, 4/67); No. 5 in F major, B54 (SXL6273, 3/67); No. 6 in D major, B112 (SXL6253, 11/66); No. 7 in D minor, B141; No. 8 in G major, B163 (SXL6044, 7/63); No. 9 in E minor, B178, "From the New World" (SXL6291, 11/67). Scherzo capriccioso, B131 (SXL6348, 7/63). *Overtures* — In Nature's Realm, B168 (SXL6290, 5/67); Carnival, B169 (SXL6253, 11/66); My Home, B125*a* (SXL6273, 3/67).

⑥ 7h 11m ADD 4/92 £ 9p

István Kertész recorded the Dvořák symphonies during the mid-1960s and his integral cycle was quick to achieve classic status, with his exhilarating and vital account of the Eighth Symphony (the first to be recorded in February 1963) rapidly becoming a special landmark in the catalogue. The original LPs, with their distinctive Breughel reproduction sleeves are now collectors' items in their own right, but these magnificent interpretations are now available once more, in glitteringly refined digitally remastered sound, and it is a tribute to the memory of this tragically short-lived conductor that this cycle continues to set the standard by which all others are judged. Kertész was the first conductor to attract serious collectors to the early Dvořák symphonies which, even today are not performed as often as they should be; and his jubilant advocacy of the unfamiliar First Symphony, composed in the composer's twenty-fourth year, has never been superseded. This work offers surprising insights into the development of Dvořák's mature style, as does the Second Symphony. Kertész shows that Symphonies Nos. 3 and 4 have much more earthy resilience than many commentators might have us believe, insisting that Dvořák's preoccupation with the music of Wagner and Liszt had reached its zenith during this period. The challenging rhetoric of the Fourth has never found a more glorious resolution than here, with Kertész drawing playing of gripping intensity from the London Symphony Orchestra. The Fifth Symphony, and to a still greater extent, its glorious successor, Symphony No. 6, both reveal Dvořák's clear affinity with the music of Brahms. Kertész's superb reading of the Sixth, however, shows just how individual and naturally expressive this under-rated work actually is, whilst the playing in the great climax of the opening movement and the vigorous final peroration remains tremendously exciting, even a quarter of a century after the recording first appeared. In the great final trilogy, Kertész triumphs nobly with the craggy resilience of the Seventh Symphony, and his buoyant ardour brings a dynamic thrust and momentum to the Eighth Symphony, whereas his *New World* is by turns indomitable and searchingly lyrical. The six-disc set also offers assertive and brilliant readings of the Overtures *Carnival, In Nature's Realm* and the rarely heard *My Home*, together with a lucid and heroic account of the *Scherzo capriccioso*. These definitive performances have been skilfully reprocessed, the sound is astonishingly good, even by modern standards, and the playing of the London Symphony Orchestra is often daringly brilliant under the charismatic direction of one of this century's late-lamented masters of the podium.

Additional recommendations ...
Symphonies Nos. 1-9[a]*. Scherzo capriccioso, B131*[b]*. Carnival*[b]*. The Wild Dove, B198*[b]. [a]**Berlin Philharmonic Orchestra;** [b]**Bavrian Radio Symphony Orchestra/Rafael Kubelík.** DG 423 120-2GX6 — ⑥ 7h 5m ADD 10/88
Symphonies Nos. 1-9. Carnival. My Home. Othello, B174. Hussite, B132. **London Symphony Orchestra/Witold Rowicki.** Philips 432 602-2PM6 — ⑥ 7h 9m ADD 4/92
No. 1. The Hero's Song, B199. **Scottish National Orchestra/Neeme Järvi.** Chandos CHAN8597 — 1h 14m DDD 4/89
No. 2. Slavonic Rhapsody in A flat major, B86 No. 3. **Scottish National Orchestra/Neeme Järvi.** Chandos CHAN8589 — 1h 1m DDD 7/88

No. 3. Carnival. Symphonic Variations, B70. **Scottish National Orchestra/Neeme Järvi.** Chandos CHAN8575 — lh 3m DDD 5/88
No. 4. Ten Biblical Songs, B185[a]. [a]**Brian Rayner Cook** (bar); **Scottish National Orchestra/Neeme Järvi.** Chandos CHAN8608 — lh 8m DDD 12/88

Key to Symbols

	② ②	lh 23m	DDD	6/88
Price	*Quantity/ availability*	*Timing*	*Mode*	*Review date*

Dvořák. Symphony No. 5 in F major, B54. Othello, B174. Scherzo capriccioso, B131. **Oslo Philharmonic Orchestra/Mariss Jansons.** EMI CDC7 49995-2. Recorded in 1989.

lh 4m DDD 7/90 P

Of all the romantic composers, it is probably Dvořák who best evokes a sunlit, unspoiled and relatively untroubled picture of nineteenth-century country life. Light and warmth radiate from his Fifth Symphony, composed in just six weeks of the year 1875 when he was in his early thirties. It has been called his "Pastoral Symphony", and it is easy to see why, especially in a performance as fresh and sunny as this one. Mariss Jansons brings out all the expressiveness and heart of the music without exaggerating the good spirits and playful humour that are so characteristic of the composer, and one would single out for praise the fine wind playing of the Oslo Philharmonic Orchestra (and not least its golden toned horns) were it not for the fact that the strings are no less satisfying. The lyrical *Andante con moto* brings out the fine interplay of the instrumental writing, the bouncy *Scherzo* is uninhibited without going over the top and the exciting finale has plenty of momentum. The other two pieces are also nicely done, the *Scherzo capriccioso* having both lilt and vigour and the rarely played *Othello* Overture (a late work) being a suitably dramatic response to Shakespeare's tragedy. The recording is warm and clear.

Additional recommendation ...
No. 5. The water goblin, B195. **Scottish National Orchestra/Neeme Järvi.** Chandos CHAN8552 — lh lm DDD 12/87

Dvořák. Symphony No. 6 in D major, B112.
Janáček. Taras Bulba. **Cleveland Orchestra/Christoph von Dohnányi.** Decca 430 204-2DH. Recorded in 1989.

lh 6m DDD 7/91 P

Dohnányi here turns to a radiant work that until now has been relatively neglected on CD. With its obvious echoes of Brahms's Second Symphony this is a work which, for all its pastoral overtones, gains from refined playing, and quite apart from the imaculate ensemble, the Cleveland violins play ethereally, as in the melody at the start of the slow movement. Dohnányi does not miss the earthy qualities of the writing either, and the impact of the performance is greatly enhanced by the fullness and weight of the recording. This is altogether a superb account of No. 6. There is also the bonus of an unusual makeweight, *Taras Bulba.* The account here is very Viennese in style and warmly expressive against its opulent background. However, if Janáček is your first priority, then Mackerras's version, coupled with the *Sinfonietta* (refer to the Index to Reviews) is the obvious choice, for he characterfully persuades his truly Viennese musicians to sound more like Czechs, playing brilliantly with a sharp attack very apt for the composer's music. But those who want a radiant account of the Dvořák will find comparable joy in the characterful Janáček rhapsody.

Additional recommendation ...
No. 6. The noon witch, B196. **Scottish National Orchestra/Neeme Järvi.** Chandos CHAN8530 — 56m DDD 11/87

NEW REVIEW

Dvořák. Symphonies — No. 7 in D minor, B141; No. 8 in G major, B163. **Oslo Philharmonic Orchestra/Mariss Jansons.** EMI CDC7 54663-2. Recorded in 1992.

1h 14m DDD 6/93

NEW REVIEW

Dvořák. Symphonies — No. 7 in D minor, B141; No. 9 in E minor, B178, "From the New World". **London Philharmonic Orchestra/Sir Charles Mackerras.** EMI Eminence CD-EMX2202. Recorded in 1991.

1h 19m DDD 2/93 £

Mariss Jansons's new EMI CD of this popular pairing proves most agreeable listening. With clean-cut playing from the fine Oslo orchestra and natural, unexaggerated sonics, these are engagingly alive, refreshingly energetic readings, if not quite as warm-hearted or openly affectionate as some Dvořákians might like. Jansons's sophisticated sense of texture impresses throughout, however, and the outer movements of No. 8 in particular emerge with genuinely vivid freshness. True, in terms of irrefutable symphonic strength both these interpretations fall some way short of Sir Colin Davis's magnificent achievement with the Concertgebouw (listed below and now coupled with No. 9 and available on a two-CD set), but Jansons's clean-heeled direction brings with it a certain endearing spontaneity and rhythmic resilience that will undoubtedly give pleasure.

Sir Charles Mackerras's long-standing authority in the Czech repertoire is of course well-known by now, so his thoughts on these two great symphonies are not to be dismissed lightly, especially when, at nearly 80 minutes, they make a terrifically generous pairing. In the tragic Seventh, Mackerras concentrates largely on the more endearingly lyrical side of Dvořák's invention; in this respect both inner movements are particularly memorable in their open-hearted grace and charm. However, those who (rightly) crave a greater degree of intensity and symphonic rigour in the two great flanking outer movements (such as one encounters with rival interpreters like Kubelík, Rowicki, Sir Colin Davis or Dorati, all either listed or reviewed in this section) will perhaps come away not quite so satisfied. Similarly, this *New World* is an affectingly unfussy traversal. The slow movement glows ravishingly at an exceptionally broad tempo, and in the finale Mackerras draws Dvořák's structural threads together with undemonstrative cogency. Overall, this is undoubtedly a fine account, if not quite as winningly spontaneous an experience as Kubelík's famous BPO recording for DG or Barbirolli's inspirational Hallé performance on EMI Phoenixa. With all that, Mackerras's are still warmly affectionate readings, superbly played and resplendently recorded. At mid-price the value is obvious.

Additional recommendations ...

Nos. 7-9. **Royal Concertgebouw Orchestra/Sir Colin Davis.** Philips Duo 438 347-2PM2 — ② ADD 1/89 £

Nos. 7 and 9. **Hallé Orchestra/Sir John Barbirolli.** EMI Phoenixa CDM7 63774-2 — 1h 16m ADD 2/91 £ ▲

Nos. 7 and 8. **Cleveland Orchestra/Christoph von Dohnányi.** Decca Ovation 430 728-2DM — 1h 13m DDD 12/91 £

London Symphony Orchestra/Antál Dorati. Mercury 434 312-2MM — 1h 11m ADD £

No. 8. Scherzo capriccioso. Legends, Op. 59 Nos. 4, 6 and 7. **Hallé Orchestra/Sir John Barbirolli.** EMI Phoenixa CDM7 64193-2 — 1h 1m ADD 6/92 £ ▲

No. 8. The golden spinning-wheel. **Philharmonia Orchestra/Eliahu Inbal.** Teldec 9031-72305-2 — 1h 5m DDD 11/92

No. 8[a]*. Carnival*[b]*. The Wild Dove*[b]. [a]**Berlin Philharmonic Orchestra;** [b]**Bavarian Radio Symphony Orchestra/Rafael Kubelík.** DG 429 518-2GR — 1h 4m ADD £

Dvořák. Symphony No. 9 in E minor, B178, "From the New World"[a]. American Suite[b]. [a]**Vienna Philharmonic Orchestra/Kirill Kondrashin;** [b]**Royal Philharmonic**

Orchestra/Antál Dorati. Decca 430 702-2DM. From [a]SXDL7510 (7/80), [b]410 735-2DH2 (3/85). Recorded 1979-1983.

lh 3m DDD 8/91

Kondrashin's *New World* caused something of a sensation when originally transferred to CD. Here was a supreme example of the clear advantages of the new medium over the old and the metaphor of a veil being drawn back between listener and performers could almost be extended to a curtain: the impact and definition of the sound is quite remarkable and the acoustic of the Sofiensaal in Vienna are presented as quite ideal for this score. The upper strings have brilliance without edginess, the brass — with characteristically bright VPO trumpets — has fine sonority as well as great presence, the bass is firm, full and rich and the ambience brings luminosity and bloom to the woodwind without clouding.

Additional recommendation ...

No. 9. **Cleveland Orchestra/Christoph von Dohnányi.** Decca 414 421-2DH — 41m DDD 1/87

No. 9. Carnival Overture, B169. Scherzo capriccioso. **London Symphony Orchestra/István Kertész.** Decca Ovation 417 724-2DM — lh 5m ADD 12/87 £

No. 9. Symphonic Variations. **London Philharmonic Orchestra/Zdenek Macal.** Classics for Pleasure CD-CFP9006 — lh 6m DDD 9/87 £

Dvořák. String Sextet in A major, B80[a].
Martinů. Serenade No. 2. String Sextet (1932)[a]. **Academy of St Martin in the Fields Chamber Ensemble** (Kenneth Sillito, Malcolm Latchem, vns; Robert Smissen, [a]Stephen Tees, vas; [a]Stephen Orton, [a]Roger Smith, vcs). Chandos CHAN8771. Recorded in 1989.

50m DDD 5/90

There is little which links the music of Dvořák and Martinů except a common Czech background, but the ASMF Chamber Ensemble respond well to both composers' styles and the result is a highly enjoyable, well-contrasted programme. Martinů's smart metropolitan 1930s style is encapsulated in the brief, but rather trifling *Serenade*. The Sextet is a longer and a more substantial work, still written in a busy, neoclassical style and effective in its way. These two works inspire an alert, spick-and-span response in the ASMF players. Their style in the warmly romantic Dvořák work is appropriate, too. In the first movement their tempo variations are quite marked, and the playing is highly expressive. The second movement *Dumka* has effectively strong accents and is followed by a fast, exhilarating third movement *Furiant*. The finale comprises a set of variations, each episode of which is vividly characterized in this performance. The recording was made in a church, but fortunately the acoustic is generous without having unwanted resonances and the balance is good.

Additional recommendation ...

String Sextet. String Quintet in E flat major, B180. **Raphael Ensemble.** Hyperion CDA66308 — lh 5m DDD 8/89

Dvořák. Piano Quintet in A major, B155[a].
Franck. Piano Quintet in F minor[b]. **Sir Clifford Curzon** (pf); **Vienna Philharmonic Quartet** (Willi Boskovsky, Otto Strasser, vns; Rudolf Streng, va; [a]Robert Scheiwein, [b]Emanuel Brabec, vcs). Decca 421 153-2DM. Item marked [a] from SXL6043 (6/63), [b] SXL2278 (9/61). Item marked [a] recorded in 1962, [b] 1960.

lh 9m ADD 4/90 £

These are two self-recommending accounts dating from the 1960s from Clifford Curzon and the Vienna Philharmonic Quartet that long enjoyed classic status. An aristocrat of the keyboard, Curzon gives commanding accounts of both works, and his Viennese partners offer playing of great finesse and subtlety. The Dvořák is among his most endearing and captivating scores, and the Franck belongs to that master's most impassioned utterances. The quintets are separated by barely a decade (the Dvořák comes from 1888, the Franck from 1879), and it would be difficult to improve on these performances. Both are standard classics and belong in every basic collection: together in such fine performances and at such a reasonable price they offer outstanding value. The Decca sound, always very good, is as fresh and powerful as the music itself.

NEW REVIEW

Dvořák. HAUSMUSIK. **Alberni Quartet** (Howard Davis, Peter Pople, vns; Roger Best, [a]vn/[b]va; [c]David Smith, vc); [d]**Virginia Black** (harm). CRD CRD3457. Recorded in 1988. Terzetto in C major, B148[b]. Two Waltzes, B105[bc]. Drobnosti, B149[b]. Gavotte, B164[a]. Bagatelles, B79[cd].

lh DDD 10/92

Since this composer was brought up in the folk fiddle tradition and later held a post for nine years as the principal violist in a Prague orchestra, it is natural that he wrote prolifically and skilfully for stringed instruments and composed no less than 14 string quartets. However, the pieces on the present disc are mostly miscellaneous and not at all well known. The most substantial of them is the *Terzetto* (in other words, Trio) for two violins and viola. This is a four-movement work dating from 1887 that is most attractive when played as well as it is here, and such is Dvořák's skill that we never feel the absence of a bass instrument. The slowish second movement flows along in a characteristically expressive way, and the scherzo is equally effective with its sweetly eloquent middle section. The other pieces are slighter, and the first of the Two Waltzes for string quartet is pretty conventional salon music although good of its kind, while the Gavotte for three violins is just a pleasing curiosity. The four *Drobnosti,* or "Miniatures", are for the same instruments as the *Terzetto* and have more to say, No. 2 having a distinct Bohemian flavour. Likewise, the Bagatelles are no mere trifles, although they were written for amateurs. Pleasing pieces in a folkish idiom, they are scored for two violins, cello, and that now rare instrument the harmonium, which as played by Virginia Black has little in common with the wheezy church instrument that older readers may remember from childhood. All these performances are sympathetic and skilful, and the warm recorded sound matches the glow of the music — not momentous music, admittedly, but very easy pleasant listening.

Dvořák. Piano Quartets — No. 1 in D major, B53; No. 2 in E flat major, B162. **Domus** (Krysia Osostowicz, vn; Timothy Boulton, va; Richard Lester, vc; Susan Tomes, pf). Hyperion CDA66287. Recorded in 1987.

lh 10m DDD 3/89 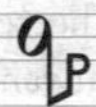

Apart from the so-called *American* Quartet Dvořák's chamber music is too seldom heard. The two piano quartets are delightful works and like so much of his music seem to inhabit a world of apparently limitless melodic invention. The three movements manage to combine a sophistication of form with a folk-song-like simplicity. However, the piano's role is much more inventive in the E flat major Quartet and meets the string players as an equal partner rather than being seen merely as a subservient accompanist. Texture is uppermost in this latter work and Dvořák brings off some delicious instrumental coups. Domus is an uncommonly fine piano quartet and they bring to this music a freshness and unanimity of approach that is hugely rewarding. The recorded sound, too, is very fine.

Additional recommendation ...
Ames Piano Quartet. Dorian DOR-90125 — lh 10m DDD 10/90

NEW REVIEW

Dvořák. String Quintets — G major, B49[a]; E flat major, B180[b]. Intermezzo in B major, B49[c]. **Chilingirian Quartet** (Levon Chilingirian, Mark Butler, vns; Louise Williams, va; Philip De

Groote, vc); [b]**Simon Rowland-Jones** (va); [ac]**Duncan McTier** (db). Chandos CHAN9046. Recorded 1990-91.

1h 9m DDD 11/92

Dating from 1875 (a particularly productive year for the composer), Dvořák's G major String Quintet is a thoroughly engaging affair, winning first prize in a competition for new chamber works organized by the Prague Artistic Circle. Originally in five movements, Dvořák subsequently removed the "Intermezzo" second movement, revising and publishing it separately eight years later as the haunting *Nocturne* for string orchestra. Enterprisingly, this Chandos disc includes that "Intermezzo" in its original string quintet garb. The E flat Quintet from 1893, on the other hand, is a wholly mature masterpiece. Completed in just over two months during Dvořák's American sojourn, it replaces the double-bass of the earlier Quintet with the infinitely more subtle option of a second viola. Brimful of the most delightfully fresh, tuneful invention, the score also shares many melodic and harmonic traits with the popular *American* Quartet — its immediate predecessor. The Chilingirian Quartet, ideally abetted by double-bassist Duncan McTier and violist Simon Rowland-Jones, are enthusiastic, big-hearted proponents of all this lovely material, and the excellent Chandos recording offers both a realistic perspective and beguiling warmth.

Dvořák. String Quartet No. 12 in F major, B179, "American". Cypresses, B152 — Nos. 1, 2, 5, 9 and 11.
Kodály. String Quartet No. 2, Op. 10. **Hagen Quartet** (Lukas Hagen, Annette Bik, vns; Veronika Hagen, va; Clemens Hagen, vc). DG 419 601-2GH.

1h 1m DDD 5/87

Surely no work in the string quartet repertoire expresses so much contentment and joy as Dvořák's *American* Quartet. The very youthful Hagen Quartet penetrate the work's style, with its dance-like rhythms and open-hearted, folksy melodies, very successfully and they produce an attractively full-bodied tone-quality. With Kodály's brief Quartet No. 2 we enter a very different world. As in Dvořák's quartet there is a folk-music influence, but here it is the music of Kodály's native Hungary, which by its very nature is more introspective. The Hagen Quartet again capture the work's nationalistic flavour very adroitly. Dvořák's youthful *Cypresses* were originally voice and piano settings of poems which reflected the composer's love for a singer and are played with an affecting simplicity and warmth. The recording is a little too cavernous, but not so much as to spoil the enjoyment afforded by this excellent disc.

Additional recommendations ...

String Quartets — No. 1 in A major, B8. No. 2 in B flat major, B17. No. 3 in D major, B18. No. 4 in E minor, B19. No. 5 in F minor, B37. No. 6 in A minor, B40. No. 7 in A minor, B45. No. 8 in E major, B57. No. 9 in D minor, B75. No. 10 in E flat major, B92. No. 11 in C major, B121. No. 12 in F major, B179, "American". No. 13 in G major, B192. No. 14 in A flat major, B193. F major, B120 (Fragment). Cypresses, B152. Quartettsatz. Two Waltzes, B105. **Prague Quartet.** DG 429 193-2GCM9 — 9h 49m ADD 8/90 £

String Quartet No. 12. ***Smetana.*** *String Quartet No. 1 in E minor, "From my life".* **Alban Berg Quartet.** EMI CDC7 54215-2 — 54m DDD 3/92

Dvořák. String Quartet No. 12 in F major, B179, "American"[a].
Schubert. String Quartet No. 14 in D minor, D810, "Death and the Maiden"[b].
Borodin. String Quartet No. 2 in D major — Notturno[a]. **Quartetto Italiano** (Paolo Borciani, Elisa Pegreffi, vns; Piero Farulli, va; Franco Rossi, vc). Philips Silver Line 420 876-2PSL. Items marked [a] from SAL3618 (8/67), [b]SAL3708 (5/69). Item marked [a] recorded in 1968, [b] 1965.

1h 15m ADD 3/89 £ 

This is a cherishable coupling of two of the finest quartets in the repertoire. The Quartetto Italiano bring to the Schubert, with its drama and passion so close to the surface, great panache and involvement. The singing theme of the second movement receives a grave intensity that is all too elusive. Similarly Dvořák's *American* Quartet is given exactly the right quality of nostalgia and ease that the work requires. The charming finale, one of Dvořák's most enchanting movements, is given a real folk-like sense of fun. As a bonus the Quartet play the celebrated *Notturno* slow movement from Borodin's Second Quartet; charming though it is it really deserves to be heard in context (refer to the Index to Reviews for a complete recording). The 1960s recordings sound well.

NEW REVIEW

Dvořák. Piano Trios — No. 3 in F minor, B130; No. 4 in E minor, B166, "Dumky". **Barcelona Trio** (Gerard Claret, vn; Lluís Claret, vc; Albert G. Attenelle, pf). Harmonia Mundi HMC90 1404. Recorded in 1991.

lh 10m DDD 11/92

Whereas the current edition of *The Classical Catalogue* (1993, No. 2) lists some 20 different versions of the *Dumky* Trio, there are only eight of its F minor forerunner which dates from nine years earlier. Obviously collectors prefer their Dvořák in national dress. The richly romantic F minor work comes primarily as a reminder of Dvořák's profound admiration for Brahms, who so gallantly championed his cause to the publisher, Simrock, when life was still an uphill struggle. The Barcelona Trio play it with loving care for textural detail while at the same time effortlessly sustaining tension throughout each movement's larger span. The *Dumky* was the last of his piano trios, written in 1891 at the age of 50. Before leaving for America the following year, he and the violinist, Ferdinand Lachner, and the cellist, Hanuš Wihan, undertook a farewell concert tour of some 40 towns in his beloved Bohemia and Moravia with the *Dumky* always their central work. The sharp alternations of melancholy and dance-like gaiety giving this folk-genre its special character are met with splendid intensity and abandon by the Barcelona team. Their own temperament, coupled with the openness of the recorded sound, gives this disc pride of place among recent rivals.

Additional recommendation ...

No. 4. **Schumann.** *Piano Trio No. 1 in D minor, Op. 63.* **Oslo Trio.** Victoria VCD19020 — lh 2m DDD 10/91

Dvořák. Rondo in G minor, B171[a].
Franck (trans. Delsart/Rose). Violin Sonata in A major[b].
Grieg. Cello Sonata in A minor, Op. 36[b]. **Robert Cohen** (vc); **[a]Anthya Rael, [b]Roger Vignoles** (pfs). CRD CRD3391. Item marked [a] from CRD1086/8 (2/81), [b] CRD1091 (8/81). Recorded in 1980.

lh 6m ADD 1/92

César Franck's majestic Violin Sonata in A major has been avidly endorsed by generations of cellists as a major addition to their repertoire, ever since Leonard Rose popularized Delsart's fine cello transcription of the work. In fact, the alterations are minimal, and the sonata emerges with renewed dramatic potency in this glorious performance from Robert Cohen and Roger Vignoles, whose stirring advocacy of the work surely belies its real identity as a violin sonata. The technical finesse and musical cohesion of their playing allow the recurring cyclic themes of this epic work to generate a craggy architectural solidity, which reaches a thrilling climax in the finale. Indeed, the playing here may well convince you that this instrumental combination serves the music more effectively than that for which it was originally intended. Cohen and Vignoles capitalize on the naïve, yet always affecting Nordic sentimentality of the Grieg Cello Sonata, in a reading which is constantly sympathetic to the 'heart on sleeve' languor of its innocuous melodies. They are particularly good in the brief central *Andante*, with its reference to the "Homage March" from Grieg's incidental music to Bjornson's play, *Sigurd Jorsalfar*. This excellent recital disc ends with a dry and skittish account of the Dvořák Rondo in G minor, in which Cohen is partnered by his mother, the pianist Anthya Rael. These fine 1981 performances have superb bloom and presence, and the CD transfers are excellent.

Dvořák. Stabat mater[a]. Psalm 149. [a]**Lívia Aghová** (sop); [a]**Marga Schiml** (contr); [a]**Aldo Baldin** (ten); [a]**Luděk Vele** (bass); [a]**Prague Children's Choir; Prague Philharmonic Choir; Czech Philharmonic Orchestra/Jiří Bělohlávek.** Chandos CHAN8985/6. Notes, texts and translations included.

② 1h 36m DDD 2/92

The *Stabat mater* is a thirteenth-century Christian poem in Latin describing the Virgin Mary standing at the foot of the Cross. It has been set to music by many Catholic composers from Palestrina to Penderecki, and Dvořák's version, first heard in Prague in 1880, soon went on to other countries including Britain, where it had a number of cathedral performances and one in the Royal Albert Hall in London in 1884 that was conducted by the composer himself and used a choir of over 800 singers — "the impression of such a mighty body was indeed enchanting", he wrote. Its ten sections are well laid out for the different vocal and instrumental forces and so avoid the monotony which might seem inherent in a contemplative and deeply sombre text. This performance was recorded by Chandos with Czech forces in Prague Castle, and in it we feel the full dignity and drama of the work, an oratorio in all but name. The four solo singers convey genuine fervour and one feels that their sound, which is quite unlike that of British singers, must be akin to what the composer originally imagined. If they are a touch operatic, that doesn't sound misplaced and they perform well together, as in the second verse quartet "Quis est home". The choral singing is no less impressive, and indeed the whole performance under Bělohlávek gets the balance right between reverent simplicity and intensity of feeling. Psalm 149 is a setting of "Sing unto the Lord a new song" for chorus and orchestra and its celebratory mood provides a fine complement to the other work.

Additional recommendation ...

Stabat Mater. Ten Legends, Op. 59[a]. **Soloists; Bavarian Radio Chorus and Symphony Orchestra, [a]English Chamber Orchestra/Rafael Kubelík.** DG 423 919-2GGA2 — ② 2h 8m ADD 9/90

NEW REVIEW

Dvořák. DIMITRIJ. **Leo Marian Vodička** (ten) Dimitrij Ivanovich; **Drahomíra Drobková** (contr) Marfa Ivanovna; **Magdaléna Hajóssyová** (sop) Marina Mníshkova; **Lívia Aghová** (sop) Xenia Borisnova; **Peter Mikuláš** (bass) Pyotr Fyodorovich Basmanov; **Ivan Kusnjer** (bar) Prince Shuisky; **Luděk Vele** (bass) Iov; **Prague Radio Chorus; Czech Philharmonic Chorus and Orchestra/Gerd Albrecht.** Supraphon 11 1259-2. Notes, text and translation included. Recorded in 1989.

③ 3h 10m DDD 3/93

Only three or four Dvořák operas have been recorded to challenge the generally held view that *Rusalka* is his only successful work in this form. In the early 1980s Supraphon issued an LP of highlights from *Dimitrij*, but this is our first chance to hear the complete opera on record. As such the new set is self-recommending: only an inadequate representation of the score would detract from its obvious value. In fact the performance is eminently satisfactory. The story of the opera more or less takes over from that of Mussorgsky's *Boris Godunov*. The Russian composer's libretto used Pushkin as its source: for his tale of the struggles for the Russian throne in early nineteenth-century Russia Dvořák used a libretto by the Czech writer Marie Cervinková-Riegrová, which derives from the works of Schiller and also her fellow-countryman Ferdinand Mikovec. There are two versions of the work: the original was first performed in 1882, but its failure to be accepted abroad caused Dvořák to re-write the whole opera in 1894, using the same musical material. At the end of his life he sanctioned a production which used a combination of both versions. The new recording restores the original score, using only material written for the first production, plus revisions made shortly afterwards. If none of the singers is outstanding there isn't a weak link anywhere, the choral work is similarly very competent, and Gerd Albrecht conducts a more than serviceable account of an attractive score. It cannot be said, however, that Dvořák's inspiration burned so brightly here as in his orchestral and instrumental works. Some of the invention is distinctive, but there are also passages where the composer is no more than highly efficient. The recording is pleasantly spacious and well-defined.

Dvořák. RUSALKA. **Gabriela Beňačková-Cápová** (sop) Rusalka; **Wieslaw Ochman** (ten) Prince; **Richard Novák** (bass) Watergnome; **Věra Soukupová** (contr) Witch; **Drahomíra Drobková** (mez) Foreign Princess; **Jana Jonášová, Daniela Sounová-Brouková** (sops), **Anna Barová** (contr) Woodsprites; **Jindřich Jindrák** (bar) Gamekeeper; **Jiřina Marková** (sop) Turnspit; **René Tuček** (bar) Hunter; **Prague Philharmonic Chorus; Czech Philharmonic Orchestra/Václav Neumann.** Supraphon 10 13641-2. Notes, text and translation included.

③ 2h 36m DDD 7/86

Dvořák's opera contains some of his most enchanting and haunting music. It tells the tragic story of the water nymph Rusalka who falls in love with a mortal prince. Gabriela Beňková-Cápová's Rusalka is glorious, the voice full, lithe and with a beautiful soaring legato. She sings the famous Moon song quite magically. Richard Novák is a gruff though benign Watergnome, Wieslaw Ochman an ardent prince and Věra Soukupová a splendidly ominous witch. Václav Neumann directs the Czech Philharmonic with a command of the idiom that is totally engaging. The recording is very fine and the dynamic range quite extraordinarily vivid.

Further listening ...

16 Slavonic Dances — piano duet, B78 and B145. **Artur Balsam, Gena Raps** (pf. four hands). Arabesque Z6559 (3/87).

Moravian Duets, B50, B60, B62 and B69. **Kühn Mixed Chorus/Pavel Kühn** with **Stanislav Bogunia** (pf). Supraphon CO-72646 (1/90).

Requiem, B165[a]. *Coupled with* ***Kodály.*** Psalmus Hungaricus, Op. 13[b]. Hymn of Zrinyi[c]. **Soloists; [a]Ambrosian Singers; [b]Wandsworth School Boys' Choir; [bc]Brighton Festival Chorus; [ab]London Symphony Orchestra/István Kertész, [c]László Heltay.** Decca Ovation 421 810-2DM2 (5/89).

Sir George Dyson

British 1883-1964

NEW REVIEW

Dyson. Concerto da camera. Concerto da chiesa. Concerto leggiero[a]. **[a]Eric Parkin** (pf); **City of London Sinfonia/Richard Hickox.** Chandos CHAN9076. Recorded 1991-92.

1h 1m DDD 

This is an admirable première recordings of three forgotten jewels of the English musical renaissance. Yorkshire-born Sir George Dyson studied with Stanford at the Royal College of Music and was later to become Director of that distinguished establishment from 1937 to 1951. All the music on this CD dates from the final two years of that tenureship, and most rewarding and refreshingly 'un-academic' it proves to be. Gorgeously light-textured, the winsome *Concerto leggiero* for piano and string orchestra (with Eric Parkin the ever-sensitive soloist) has something of the poignant melodic appeal of John Ireland's lovely Piano Concerto. Richard Hickox presides over a thoughtful account of this and the two other offerings, the *Concerto da camera* and *Concerto da chiesa* — both for string orchestra, and both sumptuously and expertly laid out. None is an undiscovered masterpiece, but all contain invention of real rustic charm and genuine poetic freshness. Let's leave the last words to this issue's exemplary annotator, Christopher Palmer, who presents the case for Dyson thus: "In the case of a minor composer we are concerned — rightly — that whatever his status as a professional craftsman, the experience he offers us may be second-rate, or no experience at all. Dyson's music is, certainly, beautifully made; but a poetic spirit moves it, imagination lights it and a warm heart inflames it." That's a most eloquent description and this is a most eloquent release.

Dyson. Three Rhapsodies (1905-12).
Howells. String Quartet No. 3, "In Gloucestershire" (1923). **Divertimenti** (Paul Barritt, Rachel Isserlis, vns; Gustav Clarkson, va; Sebastian Comberti, vc). Hyperion CDA66139. From A66139 (6/86). Recorded in 1984.

lh 4m DDD 6/89 

These beautiful rarities are a must for all those with an interest in English music. Herbert Howells is perhaps better known for his choral and organ music, but he also wrote many fine chamber works as well, of which the String Quartet No. 3, subtitled *In Gloucestershire*, is one of the finest. Like many of the pieces of the time (the first version dates from 1916) there are overtones of the Great War, and like Vaughan Williams's *Pastoral* Symphony and Ivor Gurney's songs, the tranquil images of the English countryside (in this instance Howells's beloved Cotswolds) seem at times to be superimposed onto the battle-scarred fields of France. The four movements are simple in design, rhapsodic in feel and poignantly lyrical in expression. The music of George Dyson is even less well known, though recently interest in his music has grown. The *Three Rhapsodies* for string quartet are amongst his earliest compositions. At times the early influences of Parry, Stanford and Richard Strauss can be heard, but on the whole they are notable for their individuality, craftsmanship and more importantly their spontaneity and warmth of writing. The performances are exceptionally fine and sympathetic and the recording creates a pleasantly intimate atmosphere for the listener to discover these little-known gems.

Further listening ...

Choral and Instrumental Works — The Blacksmiths. The Canterbury Pilgrims — suite. To Music. Quo Vadis — Nocturne. Song on May Morning. A Spring Garland. Three Rustic Songs. A Summer Day — suite. **Soloists; Royal College of Music Chamber Choir; Royal Philharmonic Orchestra/Sir David Willcocks.** Unicorn-Kanchana DKPCD9061 (8/88).

Werner Egk

German 1901-1983

Suggested listening ...

La tentation de Saint Antoine[b]. *Coupled with* ***Martin.*** Sechs Monologe aus "Jedermann"[a]. DER STURM[a] — Overture; Mein Ariel!; Hin sind meine Zaubere'in. [b]**Dame Janet Baker** (mez); [a]**Dietrich Fischer-Dieskau** (bar); [b]**Koeckert Quartet** (Rudolf Koeckert, Willi Buchner, vns; Oskar Reidl, va; Josef Merz); [b]strings of **Bavarian Radio Symphony Orchestra/Werner Egk;** [a]**Berlin Philharmonic Orchestra/Frank Martin.** DG 20th Century Classics 429 858-2GC (10/91).

PEER GYNT. **Soloists; Bavarian Radio Chorus; Munich Radio Orchestra/Heinz Wallberg.** Orfeo C005822H (10/89).

Hanns Eisler

German 1898-1962

Suggested listening ...

Lieder and Songs — Spruch 1939. In die Stadte kam ich. An die Uberlebenden. Uber die Dauer des Exils. Zufluchtsstätte. Elegie 1939. An den Schlaf. An den kleinen Radioapparat. In den Weiden. Frühling. Auf der Flucht. Uber den Selbstmord. Gedenktafel für 4000 Soldaten, die im Krieg gegen Norwegen versenkt wurden. Spruch. Hotelzimmer 1942. Die Maske des Bösen. Despite these miseries. The only thing. Die letzte Elegie. unter den grünen Pfefferbäumen. Die Stadt ist nach den Engeln genannt. Jeden Morgen, mein Brot zu verdienen. Diese Stadt hat mich belehrt. In den Hügeln wird Gold gefunden. In der Frühe. Erinnerung an Eichendorff und Schumann. An die Hoffnung. Andenken. Elegie 1943. Die Landschaft des Exils. Verfehlte Liebe. Monolog des Horatio. **Dietrich Fischer-Dieskau** (bar); **Aribert Reimann** (pf). Teldec 2292-43676-2 (7/89).

Edward Elgar

British 1857-1934

Elgar. Cello Concerto in E minor, Op. 85[a]. Sea Pictures, Op. 37[b]. [a]**Jacqueline du Pré** (vc); [b]**Dame Janet Baker** (mez); **London Symphony Orchestra/Sir John Barbirolli.** EMI CMS7 69707-2. From CDC7 47329-2 (5/86). Recorded in 1965.

1h 10m ADD 3/89 

This is a classic recording, offering two performances by soloists at the turning point of their careers. Jacqueline du Pré's performance of the Elgar Concerto is extraordinarily complete: the cello sings, cries almost, with burning force in its upper registers; *pianissimos* barely whisper; pizzicatos ring with muted passion; those moments of palpitating *spiccato* bowing convey more than is almost imaginable. The LSO perform as if inspired; hardly surprising given Barbirolli's magical accompaniment. Dame Janet Baker's *Sea Pictures* are no less masterly. The young voice is gloriously rich but agile, her diction superb whilst some of the exquisite floated high notes simply defy description. The 1965 sound is quite spectacular; its very immediacy and vividness grabs one at the outset and doesn't let go.

Additional recommendations ...

Cello Concerto. ***Bloch.*** *Schelomo.* **Steven Isserlis** (vc); **London Symphony Orchestra/Richard Hickox.** Virgin Classics VC7 59511-2 — 5lm DDD 7/89

Cello Concerto. ***Tchaikovsky.*** *Variations on a Rococo Theme, Op. 33.* **Mischa Maisky** (vc); **Philharmonia Orchestra/Giuseppe Sinopoli.** DG 431 685-2GH — 47m DDD 7/91

Cello Concerto (London Symphony Orchestra/André Previn). ***Dvořák.*** *Cello Concerto in B minor, B191* (Berlin Philharmonic Orchestra/Lorin Maazel). ***Haydn.*** *Cello Concerto in D major, HobVIIb/2* (English Chamber Orchestra). ***Saint-Saëns.*** *Cello Concerto No. 1 in A minor, Op. 33* (French National Orchestra/Lorin Maazel). ***Schumann.*** *Cello Concerto in A minor, Op. 129* (Bavarian Radio Symphony Orchestra/Sir Colin Davis). **Yo-Yo Ma** (vc). CBS Masterworks CD44562 — ② DDD/ADD 2h 20m 5/90 £

Cello Concerto[a]. ***Tchaikovsky.*** *Fantasia on a theme by Thomas Tallis. Fantasia on "Greensleeves" (arr. Greaves).* [a]**Felix Schmidt** (vc); **London Symphony Orchestra/Rafael Frühbeck de Burgos.** Pickwick IMP Classics PCD930 — 49m DDD 1/90 £

Cello Concerto[a]. *Violin Concerto in B minor, Op. 85*[b]. [a]**Beatrice Harrison** (vc); [b]**Sir Yehudi Menuhin** (vn); [a]**New Symphony Orchestra,** [b]**London Symphony Orchestra/Sir Edward Elgar.** EMI Great Recordings of the Century mono CDH7 69786-2 — 1h 15m AAD 11/89

Elgar. Violin Concerto in B minor, Op. 61. **Nigel Kennedy** (vn); **London Philharmonic Orchestra/Vernon Handley.** EMI CD-EMX2058. From EMX412058-1 (12/84). Recorded in 1984.

45m DDD 12/84 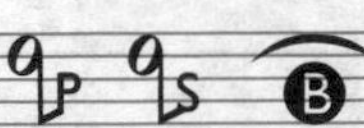

Even after the success of his First Symphony, Elgar's self-doubt persisted and caused his creative instincts to look inward. He could identify with his own instrument, the violin, as his own lonely voice pitted against an orchestra which might represent the forces of the outside world. Usually a concerto consisted of a big first movement, then a lyrical slow movement and a lighter finale: Elgar's finale, which balanced the first movement in weight, was unique, and at first the 45-minute-long work daunted all but the bravest soloists. Nigel Kennedy's technique is such that the work's formidable difficulties hold no terrors for him; his playing is first and foremost immaculate in its execution, and it is complemented by Handley's sensitive accompaniment. But it is more than that. He has a pure silvery tone-quality which is a joy to hear; his response to Elgar's vision is unfailingly sympathetic and understanding, and his projection of it is fresh and stimulating. The natural concert-hall sound is excellent in quality, with important orchestral detail always registering clearly.

Additional recommendations ...
Violin Concerto[a]. **Walton.** *Violin Concerto*[b]. **Jascha Heifetz** (vn); [a]**London Symphony Orchestra/Sir Malcolm Sargent;** [b]**Philharmonia Orchestra/Sir William Walton.** RCA Victor Gold Seal mono GD87966 — ⁚ 1h 10m ADD 3/89
Violin Concerto[a]. *Cello Concerto*[b]. [a]**Sir Yehudi Menuhin** (vn); [b]**Beatrice Harrison** (vc); [a]**London Symphony Orchestra,** [b]**New Symphony Orchestra/Sir Edward Elgar.** EMI Great Recordings of the Century mono CDH7 69786-2 — ⁚ 1h 15m AAD 11/89
Violin Concerto. Cockaigne Overture, Op. 40. **Dong-Suk Kang** (vn); **Polish National Radio Symphony Orchestra/Adrian Leaper.** Naxos 8 550489 — . 1h 1m DDD 4/92 £

Elgar. Variations on an original theme, Op. 36, "Enigma"[a]. Falstaff — Symphonic Study, Op. 68[b]. [a]**Philharmonia Orchestra;** [b]**Hallé Orchestra/Sir John Barbirolli.** EMI Studio CDM7 69185-2. Item marked [a] from ASD548 (11/63), recorded in 1962, [b] ASD610-11 (12/61), recorded in 1964.

⁚ 1h 5m ADD 11/88 

Elgar. Variations on an Original Theme, Op. 36, "Enigma"[a]. Pomp and Circumstance Marches, Op. 39[b]. [a]**London Symphony Orchestra,** [b]**London Philharmonic Orchestra/Sir Adrian Boult.** EMI CDM7 64015-2. Item marked [a] from HMV ASD2750 (11/71), recorded in 1970, [b] ASD3388 (10/77), recorded in 1976.

⁚ 55m ADD 4/92 

The first EMI disc restores to the catalogue at a very reasonable price two key Elgar recordings of works which Sir John Barbirolli made very much his own. Barbirolli brought a flair and ripeness of feeling to the *Enigma* with which Elgar himself would surely have identified. Everything about his performance seems exactly right. The very opening theme is phrased with an appealing combination of warmth and subtlety, and variation after variation has a special kind of individuality, whilst for the finale Barbirolli draws all the threads together most satisfyingly. *Falstaff* is a continuous, closely integrated structure and again Barbirolli's response to the music's scenic characterization is magical while he controls the overall piece, with its many changes of mood, with a naturally understanding flair. The original recordings perhaps sounded more sumptuous but on CD there is more refined detail and greater range and impact to the sound.

As one might expect, Sir Adrian Boult's 1970 recording of the *Enigma* Variations offers similar riches to those of Barbirolli with the additional bonus of a slightly superior recorded sound. Boult's account has authority, freshness and a beautiful sense of spontaneity so that each variation emerges from the preceding one with a natural feeling of flow and progression. There is warmth and affection too coupled with an air of nobility and poise, and at all times the listener is acutely aware that this is a performance by a great conductor who has lived a lifetime with the music. One need only sample the passionate stirrings of Variation One (the composer's wife), the athletic and boisterous "Troyte" variation, or the autumnal, elegiac glow that Boult brings to the famous "Nimrod" variation to realize that this is a very special document indeed. The LSO, on top form, play with superlative skill and poetry and the excellent 1970 recording has been exceptionally well transferred to CD. The *Pomp and Circumstance* Marches, recorded six years later with the London Philharmonic Orchestra, are invigoratingly fresh and direct — indeed the performances are so full of energy and good humour that it is hard to believe that Boult was in his late eighties at the time of recording! A classic.

Additional recommendations ...
"Enigma" Variations. Pomp and Circumstance Marches. **Royal Philharmonic Orchestra/Norman Del Mar.** DG Galleria 429 713-2GGA — ⁚ 58m ADD 9/90
"Enigma" Variations. Serenade for strings in E minor, Op. 20. In the South, Op. 50, "Alassio". **Philharmonia Orchestra/Giuseppe Sinopoli.** DG 423 679-2GH — ⁚ 1h 12m DDD 10/90

"Enigma" Variations. Cockaigne Overture, Op. 40. Serenade for strings. Salut d'amour, Op. 12. **Baltimore Symphony Orchestra/David Zinman.** Telarc CD80192 — lh 2m DDD 10/90

"Enigma" Variations. Cockaigne Overture, Op. 40. Serenade for strings. Introduction and Allegro, Op. 47. **BBC Symphony Orchestra/Andrew Davis.** Teldec British Line 9031-73279-2 — lh 14m DDD 3/92 B

"Enigma" Variations. Froissart, Op. 19. Cello Concerto[a]. [a]**Robert Cohen** (vc); **Royal Philharmonic Orchestra/Sir Charles Mackerras.** Argo 436 545-2ZH — lh 17m DDD 6/93 B

Elgar. The Wand of Youth — Suites Nos. 1 and 2, Opp. 1*a* and 1*b*. Nursery Suite (1931). **Ulster Orchestra/Bryden Thomson.** Chandos CHAN8318. From ABRD1079 (8/83).

lh 3m DDD 10/84

Elgar's music for children remains very special, and in its innocence of atmosphere stands apart from the rest of his output. The two *Wand of Youth* Suites evoke a dream world untainted by adult unreasonableness. Vignettes like the gentle "Serenade", the delicious "Sun dance" with its dainty chattering flutes, and the fragile charm of the delicate "Fairy pipers" are utterly delightful. Orchestral textures are exquisitely radiant while the robust numbers bring elements of direct contrast, as in "Fairies and Giants" or "Wild bears", which have the bright primary colours of toy trains and nursery boisterousness. The origins of this music date from Elgar's own childhood, even though the *Nursery Suite* is quite a late work, and has the haunting nostalgia of the output from the final decade of his life. The wistful charm of "The Serious Doll" and "The Sad Doll" is unforgettable, and the approaching and departing "Wagon" shows a wonderfully sure touch in handling the orchestra. Bryden Thomson has the full measure of the disarming simplicity of Elgar's writing, and the Ulster Orchestra play this music with great affection and finesse. The warm Ulster acoustic is matched by vivid stereo projection and this fairly early digital recording stands the test of time.

Additional recommendation ...

The Wand of Youth Suites. The Starlight Express, Op. 78 — O children, open your arms to me[b]*; There's a fairy that hides*[b]*; I'm everywhere*[a]*; Wake up, you little night winds*[b]*; O stars, shine brightly!*[a]*; We shall meet the morning spiders*[a]*; My old tunes*[b]*; O, think beauty*[a]*; Dustman, Laughter, Tramp and busy Sweep*[ab]*. Dream Children, Op. 43.* [a]**Alison Hagley** (sop); [b]**Bryn Terfel** (bass-bar); **Welsh National Opera Orchestra/Sir Charles Mackerras.** Argo 433 214-2ZZH — lh 14m DDD 10/92

NEW REVIEW

Elgar. Falstaff, Op. 68[a]. Cockaigne Overture, Op. 40[a]. Introduction and Allegro, Op. 47[b]. **London Philharmonic Orchestra/Vernon Handley.** Classics for Pleasure CD-CfP4617. Items marked [a] from CFP403131 (7/79), recorded in 1978, [b] EMI Eminence EMX412011 (8/83), recorded in 1983.

lh 8m ADD 6/93 9P

One of the triumphs of the Classics for Pleasure catalogue, Vernon Handley's magnificent account of *Falstaff* has at last made it onto CD. Superbly played by the LPO and given ripely resonant sound (if now with just a fraction less body than on the original LP), Handley's achievement is considerable, evincing such a hugely impressive alliance of invincible symphonic thrust and warm-hearted characterization as to make his a version worthy of comparison with the very finest on disc. Barbirolli (reviewed elsewhere in this section), Barenboim (CBS Maestro CD46465, 9/91), Solti and most notably Elgar himself (listed under Symphony No. 1) have all given of their best in this masterpiece: Handley now joins their company. To the original vinyl coupling of *Cockaigne* (another swaggering display, incidentally), CfP have added Handley's disciplined, if somewhat less inspired *Introduction and Allegro*: digitally recorded, this sounds rather less beguiling than its analogue companions. No matter, this is an unmissable prospect overall, and a formidable bargain to boot.

Additional recommendations ...

Falstaff[a]*. "Enigma" Variations.*[b]. [a]**Chicago Symphony Orchestra,** [b]**London Philharmonic Orchestra/Sir Georg Solti.** Decca London 425 155-2LM — lh 4m ADD 12/89

Cockaigne Overture. Introduction and Allegro. Serenade for strings in E minor, Op. 20. "Enigma" Variations. **BBC Symphony Orchestra/Andrew Davis.** Teldec British Line 9031-73279-2 — lh 14m DDD 3/92

Elgar. Symphony No. 1 in A flat major, Op. 55. In the South, Op. 50, "Alassio". **London Philharmonic Orchestra/Leonard Slatkin.** RCA Victor Red Seal RD60380.

lh 14m DDD 6/82 

Elgar's First Symphony was one of those rare pieces of music that seemed to attain full stature and admiration from the very first public hearing. At its première in Manchester in 1908 it caused a sensation, and Elgar was received by the audience very much in the same way that the pop stars of today are. The previous successes of the *Enigma* Variations, *Gerontius* and the masterly *Introduction and Allegro* had created high hopes in the public's mind for what they felt would be the first truly great English Symphony, and they were not disappointed. Its popularity has never waned and it still holds a special place in the affections of the public today. Leonard Slatkin is a conductor whose passion for British music has become something of a crusade, and a listener hearing him play Elgar's First Symphony without knowing the artists could well think that this was a performance under a conductor such as Sir Adrian Boult. But good music knows no bounds (after all, you don't have to be Austrian to play Mozart!) and Slatkin's understanding of this composer is abundantly clear throughout. There is no trace of sentimentality in the mighty first movement, for here is real grandeur and not just grandiose utterance while the noble sadness of the coda has especial beauty. The other movements are hardly less fine, for the richly textured *Adagio* is most eloquently done and the finale is thrilling. Elgar's massive though subtle scoring can present problems for engineers; here they are magnificently solved and the sound is rich yet detailed with excellent bass. The Overture *In the South* which begins the disc is brilliantly vivid and dramatic.

Additional recommendations ...

No. 1. Serenade for strings. Chanson de nuit, Op. 15 No. 1. Chanson de matin, Op. 15 No. 2. **London Philharmonic Orchestra/Sir Adrian Boult.** EMI British Composers CDM7 64013-2 — lh 9m ADD

No. 1. **Royal Philharmonic Orchestra/André Previn.** Philips 416 612-2PH — 52m DDD 6/86

No. 1. **London Philharmonic Orchestra/Vernon Handley.** Classics for Pleasure CD-CFP9018 — 52m ADD 8/88

No. 1. Cockaigne Overture. **London Philharmonic Orchestra/Sir Georg Solti.** Decca London 421 387-2LM — lh 3m ADD 8/89

No. 1. Pomp and Circumstance Marches, Op. 39 — No. 1 in D major; No. 3 in C minor; No. 4 in G major. **BBC Symphony Orchestra/Andrew Davis.** Teldec British Line 9031-73278-2 — lh 11m DDD 1/92

Symphonies Nos. 1 and 2[a]*. Falstaff*[a]*. The Dream of Gerontius*[ab] *— excerpts. The Music Makers*[a] *— excerpts. Civic Fanfare*[a]*.* ***Anonymous*** *(arr. Elgar). The National Anthem*[a]*.* [ab]**Soloists;** [a]**London Symphony Orchestra,** [b]**Royal Albert Hall Orchestra/Sir Edward Elgar.** EMI mono CDS7 54560-2 — ③ 3h 31m ADD 6/92

No. 1. Pomp and Circumstance Marches — No. 1; No. 2 in A minor. **Baltimore Symphony Orchestra/David Zinman.** Telarc CD80310 — lh 2m DDD 11/92

No. 1. Cockaigne Overture. **London Symphony Orchestra/Jeffrey Tate.** EMI CDC7 54414-2 — lh 12m DDD 1/93

NEW REVIEW

Elgar. Symphony No. 2 in E flat major, Op. 63. In the South, Op. 50, "Alassio". **BBC Symphony Orchestra/Andrew Davis.** Teldec 9031-74888-2. Recorded in 1992.

lh 10m DDD 11/92 

In what is unquestionably his finest achievement on record to date, Andrew Davis penetrates right to the dark inner core of this great symphony. In the opening *Allegro vivace e nobilmente*, for example, how well he and his acutely responsive players gauge the varying moods of Elgar's glorious inspiration: be it in the exhilarating surge of that leaping introductory paragraph or the spectral, twilight world at the heart of this wonderful movement, no one is found wanting. In fact, Davis's unerring structural sense never once deserts him, and the BBC Symphony Orchestra simply play their hearts out for their music director. Above all, though, it's in the many more reflective moments that Davis proves himself an outstandingly perceptive Elgarian, uncovering a vein of intimate anguish that touches to the very marrow; in this respect, his account of the slow movement is quite heart-rendingly poignant (just listen to those BBC strings at the final climax!) — undoubtedly the finest since Boult's incomparable 1944 performance with this very same orchestra – whilst the radiant sunset of the symphony's coda glows with luminous beauty. Prefaced by an equally idiomatic, stirring *In the South* (and aided throughout by some sumptuously natural engineering), this is an Elgar Second to set beside the very greatest. In every way a treasurable release.

Additional recommendations ...
No. 2. In the South. **London Philharmonic Orchestra/Sir Georg Solti.** Decca 436 150-2DSP — 1h 12m ADD 8/89
London Philharmonic Orchestra/Vernon Handley. Classics for Pleasure CD-CFP4544 — 54m ADD 10/88 £
No. 2. Cockaigne Overture. **London Philharmonic Orchestra/Sir Adrian Boult.** EMI CDM7 64014-2 — 1h 8m ADD
No. 2. Serenade for strings in E minor, Op. 20. **London Philharmonic Orchestra/Leonard Slatkin.** RCA RD60072 — 1h 7m DDD 8/89

Elgar. **MUSIC FOR STRINGS.** [a]**José-Luis Garcia,** [a]**Mary Eade** (vns); [a]**Quentin Ballardie** (va); [a]**Olga Hegedus** (vc); **English Chamber Orchestra/Sir Yehudi Menuhin.** Arabesque Z6563. From ABQ6563 (1/87).

Introduction and Allegro[a]. Chanson de nuit (arr. Fraser). Chanson de matin (arr. Fraser). Three Characteristic Pieces – No. 1, Mazurka. Serenade for strings in E minor. Salut d'amour (arr. Fraser). Elegy.

45m DDD 6/87

Elgar's pieces for string orchestra contain some of his greatest music and certainly the *Introduction and Allegro, Serenade* and *Elegy* included in this delightful programme embody quintessential Elgar. Sir Yehudi Menuhin's readings dig deep into the hearts of these works, drawing out the nostalgia and inner tragedy that underpins even some of the most seemingly high-spirited of Elgar's music. The lighter pieces allow relief from the intensity of the major works, thus making that intensity all the more effective. The English Chamber Orchestra is more than capable of providing first-rate soloists from its own ranks, and the quartet extracted for the *Introduction and Allegro* is suitably virtuosic. Both performers and engineers have produced an ideal integration of this solo group with the main string body, and the generally effervescent sound suits the celebratory nature of the piece.

NEW REVIEW

Elgar. String Quartet in E minor, Op. 83.
Walton. String Quartet in A minor. **Britten Quartet** (Peter Manning, Keith Pascoe, vns; Peter Lale, va; Andrew Shulman, vc). Collins Classics 1280-2. Recorded in 1991.

56m DDD 7/92

Elgar's String Quartet of 1918 is unique in his output, for its shows him reacting to contemporary developments in musical language, and exploring the outer reaches of tonality in a remarkable fashion for a normally conservative 61-year-old composer. The style is still recognizably Elgarian, but much of the work has an ethereal, other-worldly quality. The Britten Quartet capture the disturbing, troubled nature of the work's first movement to perfection. Their playing is superb technically, and in the central slow movement, marked *piacevole* (peacefully), they respond well to both the surface calm and the turbulence which lies beneath.

The work ends with a restless finale, played very strongly and with sharp, uncompromising accents by the four young performers. Walton's only String Quartet was also written at the end of a world war, in this case the second, and like the Elgar it is a deeply felt work. In the first movement spiky astringencies impinge on a basic feeling of romantic warmth, and the duality of the music's nature is brilliantly realized in the performance recorded here. A second movement *presto*, propelled here with a good deal of energy, is followed by an elegiac, even despairing *lento* movement, played with much feeling, and then a finale whose vehement defiance is delivered here with almost savage commitment. These two characterful performances by the Britten Quartet are captured in excellent sound.

Additional recommendation ...

As above. **Gabrieli Quartet.** Chandos CHAN8474 — 56m DDD 10/87

NEW REVIEW

Elgar. Piano Quintet in A minor, Op. 84[a]. String Quartet in E minor, Op. 83. [a]**John Bingham** (pf); **Medici Quartet** (Paul Robertson, Colin Callow, vns; Ivo-Jan van der Werff, va; Anthony Lewis, vc). Medici-Whitehall MQCD7002. Recorded in 1992.

1h 3m DDD 11/92

NEW REVIEW

Wood Magic. The Life or Sir Edward Elgar in Words and Music[a].
Elgar. Violin Sonata in E minor, Op. 82. [a]**Barbara Leigh-Hunt,** [a]**Richard Pasco** (speakers); **Medici Quartet; John Bingham** (pf). Medici-Whitehall MQCD7001. Recorded in 1992.
Includes excerpts from: The Starlight Express, In the South, Salut d'amor, String Quartet and Cello Concerto.

1h 13m DDD 11/92 

The Medici Quartet and the pianist, John Bingham, have returned to Elgar's Piano Quintet and String Quartet to mark the inauguration of Kingston University (formerly Kingston Polytechnic) in England, and the results could hardly be more impressive. Their 1986 Meridian recordings (ECD84082, 6/86) were highly praised, though the Medici's new accounts of these works possess yet more strength and nobility than previously. Elgar composed his Quartet, Quintet, Violin Sonata and Cello Concerto during 1918-9. All are concerned with leave-taking, although Elgar described the Piano Quintet as "full of old times". John Bingham's performance is magnificent; muscular and heroic, and yet by turns deeply resigned, nostalgic and dignified. The Medici Players excel too; their reading of the work has undergone something of a reappraisal since 1986, making this new version unusually fulfilling. The same can be said of their new version of the E minor Quartet; a degree more introspective and regretful perhaps, yet even more masterful, poised and sonorous. A second new release includes a thorough, if occasionally rather economical performance of Elgar's Violin Sonata from the Medici's first violinist, Paul Robertson, accompanied by John Bingham. Richard Pasco and Barbara Leigh-Hunt feature in "Wood Magic", an affectionate account, where possible in Elgar's own words, of the events surrounding the composition of these late masterpieces. This moving and often entertaining piece of theatre is certainly worth hearing, and all Elgarians will want to acquire these glorious new offerings.

Elgar. VIOLIN WORKS. **Nigel Kennedy** (vn); **Peter Pettinger** (pf). Chandos CHAN8380. From ABRD1099 (7/84). Recorded in 1984.
Violin Sonata in E minor, Op. 82. Six Very Easy Melodious Exercises in the First Position, Op. 22. Salut d'amour, Op. 12 (with Steven Isserlis, vc). Mot d'amour, Op. 13. In the South — Canto popolare (In Moonlight). Sospiri, Op. 70. Chanson de nuit, Op. 15 No. 1. Chanson de matin, Op.15 No. 2.

55m DDD 8/85

As a violinist himself, Elgar wrote idiomatically for the instrument, and this music shows the expressive variety that he achieved. The Sonata in E minor was his last work for the instrument and is the centrepiece of the recital. It is the only big work here, a dramatic utterance that the artists play with power and poetry. If the Sonata is a key work to the understanding of this composer, so too in its own way is the lilting piece called *Salut d'amour*, which is among his most popular. The *Chanson de nuit* and *Chanson de matin* are charming miniatures while the *Six Very Easy Melodious Exercises in the First Position* (written for his niece) are tiny pieces which can surely not have received a more elegant performance. A good digital recording catches Kennedy's fine tone and complements an attractive issue.

Elgar. CHORAL MUSIC. **Bristol Cathedral Choir/Malcolm Archer** ([a]org), with **Anthony Pinel** (org). Meridian CDE84168.
The Apostles, Op. 49 — The Spirit of the Lord. Ave verum corpus, Op. 2 No. 1. Drakes Broughton (Hymn Tune). Give unto the Lord, Op. 74. God be merciful unto us (Psalm 67). Great is the Lord, Op. 67 (with Stephen Foulkes, bar; Bristol Cathedral Special Choir). Imperial March, Op. 32 (trans. Martin)[a]. Te Deum and Benedictus, Op. 34.

lh DDD 10/89

When we think of Elgar's choral music we quite rightly remember the great oratorios — *Gerontius, The Apostles, The Kingdom*. The Bristol Cathedral Choir and their former Director of Music, Malcolm Archer, have looked to smaller-scale pieces to fill this delightful CD. Unlike so many English composers Elgar was not brought up in the Anglican church with its strong musical tradition: not for him countless settings of the *Magnificat* and *Nunc Dimittis* or innumerable organ voluntaries. Indeed he wrote only one specifically liturgical piece, the beautifully simple setting of *Ave verum corpus*, and the *Imperial March*, which Archer plays here with such gusto, is a transcription of a fine orchestral piece in the *Pomp and Circumstance* tradition. Other music on this disc includes a pleasant hymn-tune, a run-of-the-mill psalm-chant and items written for major festival occasions, such as *Te Deum and Benedictus* in F and the thrilling choral showpiece *Great is the Lord*. These 'festival' pieces were intended to have orchestral accompaniments, but Anthony Pinel's always imaginative and skilful organ playing is a most satisfactory alternative. The choir have been well trained for these recordings and produce some stirring and innately sensitive performances in the pleasantly warm acoustic of Bristol Cathedral.

Elgar. PART-SONGS.
Vaughan Williams. Festival Te Deum in F major[a]. Mass in minor. [a]**John Birch** (org); **Holst Singers/Hilary Davan Wetton.** Unicorn-Kanchana DKPCD9116. Texts included. Recorded in 1991.
Elgar: My Love Dwelt in a Northern Land, Op. 18 No. 3. Two Choral Songs, Op. 71 — No. 1, The Shower; No. 2, The Fountain. Go, Song of mine, Op. 57. Death on the Hills, Op. 72. Two Choral Songs, Op. 73 — No. 1, Love's Tempest; No. 2, Serenade.

54m DDD 4/92

While these two great British composers are best remembered for their large-scale choral works, given performances as sensitively directed and superbly sung as these, their smaller-scale choral pieces are shown to be real masterpieces in their own right. The one accompanied piece here, Vaughan Williams's *Festival Te Deum* is a ceremonial romp evocative of the occasion for which it was written, the Coronation of George VI, and successfully combining a tangible sense of occasion with great vigour and energy. One view of Vaughan Williams's Mass is that its few moments of inspiration tend to be heavily diluted by much routine note-spinning. Perhaps its the maturity and range of these voices (above all, the Mass is more often sung liturgically by a choir of young boys and men) or Wetton's carefully-moulded approach, but nothing seems superfluous or uninspired here. And while Elgar's delightful part-songs have long been in the repertoire of amateur choirs, here they are elevated to a level of rare musical imagination and emotional scope. Listen to the impassioned appeal of the opening of "Love's Tempest" or the wonderful buoyancy of *My Love Dwelt in a Northern Land* — it seems astonishing that such colour and variety can be achieved purely by unaccompanied human voices. This is a disc of pure delight.

NEW REVIEW

Elgar. The Light of Life, Op. 29, "Lux Christi". **Margaret Marshall** (sop); **Helen Watts** (contr); **Rogin Leggate** (ten); **John Shirley-Quirk** (bar); **Liverpool Philharmonic Choir; Royal Liverpool Philharmonic Orchestra/Sir Charles Groves.** EMI British Composers CDM7 64732-2. Texts included. From HMV ASD3952 (4/81). Recorded in 1980.

lh 4m ADD 5/93

All true Elgarians will surely want to investigate this most welcome reissue. Elgar completed his oratorio *The Light of Life* in 1896. Though no choral masterpiece, it certainly contains more than its fair share of high-quality inspiration, not least the glorious soprano aria "Be not extreme, O Lord" and the relatively familiar orchestral prologue which the composer dubbed "Meditation". Elgar's ever-consummate scoring is heard to excellent advantage in this splendidly warm-toned Liverpool Philharmonic Hall production. Spiritedly as the Liverpool Philharmonic Choir and RLPO perform under Sir Charles Groves's watchful lead, it's the exceptionally eloquent solo team which really takes the palm here, with both Margaret Marshall and John Shirley-Quirk in particular producing consistently rich, noble-toned sounds. Michael Kennedy's lucid accompanying notes, too, are a model of their kind. Altogether a most desirable re-release.

NEW REVIEW

Elgar. Caractacus, Op. 35[a]. Severn Suite, Op. 87*a*. [a]**Judith Howarth** (mez); [a]**Arthur Davies** (ten); [a]**David Wilson-Johnson** (bar); [a]**Stephen Roberts** (bar); [a]**Alistair Miles** (bass); **London Symphony** [a]**Chorus and Orchestra/Richard Hickox.** Chandos CHAN9156/7. Text included. Recorded in 1992.

② 2h DDD 2/93

Dodgy politics (witness the final chorus, where "And ever your dominion from age to age shall grow o'er peoples undiscovered in lands we cannot know" is followed by "Nor shall her might diminish while firm she holds the faith of equal law to all men...") and an even dodgier text ("Shall I meet them — the legions — in the wild Silurian regions?") aside, Elgar's ambitious cantata *Caractacus* makes for enjoyable, if hardly essential listening. Composed for the 1898 Leeds Festival, it relates the story of that ancient British king's last stand in the face of the Roman invaders, subsequent capture and eventual pardon by Emperor Claudius in Rome. Though not one of the composer's strongest creations (parts of the score do outstay their welcome, it's true), there's nevertheless a great deal for all true Elgarians to relish, especially in the radiantly-scored pastoral episodes (indeed, Elgar's remarkable orchestral prowess is evident throughout). Richard Hickox's performance is a splendid one, blessed with choral singing of the highest quality from the London Symphony Chorus and some spirited, committed playing from the LSO. The soloists, too, are uniformly excellent: David Wilson-Johnson makes a commanding, noble Caractacus, a pure-voiced Judith Howard is the chieftain's daughter, Eigen, whilst the part of her minstrel lover, Orbin, is delivered with unflagging fluency and sincerity by tenor Arthur Davies. Recorded in the formidably resonant surroundings of All Saints' Church, Tooting, the Chandos recording is not quite one of this company's finest efforts (one craves a sharper choral focus), though still pretty spectacular for all that! As a most agreeable postscript, Hickox gives a charming account of the relaxed *Severn Suite* — a late work from 1930, originally scored for brass band.

Elgar. Sea Pictures, Op. 37. The Music Makers, Op. 69. **Linda Finnie** (contr); **London Philharmonic** [a]**Choir and Orchestra/Bryden Thomson.** Chandos CHAN9022. Recorded in 1991.

lh 4m DDD 3/92 9P 9S

This was one of the late Bryden Thomson's last recordings and is arguably his finest, reminding us how grievous is the loss to British music. In *Sea Pictures* he receives orchestral playing of great sympathetic richness from veteran Elgarians, the London Philharmonic Orchestra. The second song, "In Haven" ("Capri") is wistfully treated while the accompaniment to "The swimmer" brings an over-whelming dynamic range to Elgar's evocative orchestration. Linda Finnie sings the various texts with just the right colouring of words, intelligent use of vibrato and keenness of articulation.

In *The Music Makers* she identifies closely with the words of verse that is, to say the least, less than inspired and there is light, free singing from the LPO Choir, and pronounced tempo changes between sections. Thomson is equally convincing here too, and his flexible approach suits the work's moody nature, with autobiographical quotations from the *Enigma Variations*, the symphonies and *The Dream of Gerontius*. Chandos's sound quality is superb, with a wonderful bloom on the voices and depth and clarity in the orchestra. Finnie's opera-sized tone easily rides over the orchestra and is natural and comfortably distanced while the sections of *The Music Makers* are individually tracked. There is a poignancy in this posthumous release from Thomson to hear the passage, "Yea, in spite of a dreamer who slumbers, and a singer who sings no more".

Elgar. The Dream of Gerontius, Op. 38[a]. The Music Makers, Op. 69[b]. [b]**Dame Janet Baker** (mez); [a]**Helen Watts** (contr); [a]**Nicolai Gedda** (ten); [a]**Robert Lloyd** (bass); [a]**John Alldis Choir;** [ab]**London Philharmonic Choir,** [a]**New Philharmonia Orchestra;** [b]**London Philharmonic Orchestra/Sir Adrian Boult.** EMI CDS7 47208-8. Notes and texts included. Items marked [a] from SLS987 (5/76), recorded in 1975, [b] ASD2311 (5/67), recorded in 1966.

② 2h 16m ADD 1/87 B

Elgar's best-known oratorio is the nearest he ever came to writing an opera. The story of the anguished Gerontius in his death throes and his momentary vision of Heaven was set by Elgar in the most graphic terms, and the principals are like characters in music-drama. Throughout most of its history Sir Adrian Boult was a renowned interpreter of the work, but it was only late in his life that he came to record it. The results were both worth waiting for and rewarding in their own right, capturing its intensity of emotion while never allowing the structure to weaken through too much affection. Nicolai Gedda may not be the ideal interpreter of the title-role, but Boult persuaded him to catch something of its fervour. Helen Watts's Angel was in the best tradition of singing that sympathetic part — warm but firm — whilst Robert Lloyd is heard to strong effect in both bass roles. The London Philharmonic Choir and the New Philharmonia sing and play to the top of their collective best. The spacious recording is a fine match for the calibre of the reading.

Additional recommendations ...

The Dream of Gerontius[a]. *Sea Pictures, Op. 37*[b]. **Dame Janet Baker** (mez); [a]**Richard Lewis** (ten); [a]**Kim Borg** (bass); [a]**Hallé Choir;** [a]**Sheffield Philharmonic Chorus;** [a]**Ambrosian Singers;** [b]**London Symphony Orchestra,** [a]**Hallé Orchestra/Sir John Barbirolli.** EMI Studio CMS7 63185-2 — ② 2h 2m ADD 12/89 £ B

The Dream of Gerontius[a]. ***Holst.*** *The Hymn of Jesus, Op. 37*[b]. [a]**Yvonne Minton** (mez); [a]**Sir Peter Pears** (ten); [a]**John Shirley-Quirk** (bar); [a]**Choir of King's College, Cambridge;** [a]**London Symphony Chorus and Orchestra/Benjamin Britten;** [b]**BBC Chorus and Symphony Orchestra/Sir Adrian Boult.** Decca London 421 381-2LM2 — ② 1h 53m ADD 5/89 B

NEW REVIEW

Elgar. Coronation Ode, Op. 44[a]. The Spirit of England, Op. 80[b]. [ab]**Teresa Cahill** (sop); [a]**Anne Collins** (contr); [a]**Anthony Rolfe Johnson** (ten); [a]**Gwynne Howell** (bass); **Scottish National Chorus and Orchestra/Sir Alexander Gibson.** Chandos Collect CHAN6574. Recorded in 1976.

1h 7m ADD 11/92

Sir Alexander Gibson can be a fine Elgarian, and this useful coupling (originally made for RCA) enshrines perhaps the two best performances from his 1970s Elgar/SNO series. As the opening of the *Coronation Ode* readily demonstrates, the expansive Paisley Abbey acoustic is just right for this festive music, yet the sound has impressive focus and agreeable bloom, too. Gibson controls his large forces with unassuming authority, and much of the solo singing in particular is first-rate. There's some glorious invention in both these scores. *The Spirit of England* is the lesser-known of the two, a trio of compassionate and deeply-felt settings from 1915-17 of war poems by Lawrence Binyon, of which the last ("For the Fallen") is genuinely inspired and moving — no jingoistic pot-boiler, this. Written in 1902 to celebrate the accession of King Edward VII to the throne, the *Coronation Ode* contains much that is aptly stirring and celebratory, including, of course, the culminatory appearance of the famous Trio melody from the *Pomp and Circumstance* March No. 1, now newly garbed (at the King's personal behest) with A.C. Benson's text of *Land of Hope and Glory*. And yet in some respects its the many more reflective, intimate settings that linger longest in the memory, not least the brief but haunting chorus "Daughter of Ancient Kings" and radiant treatment of "Peace, Gentle Peace". An excellent pairing, then, and an essential supplement to any self-respecting Elgar collection.

Elgar. The Kingdom, Op. 51[a]. ORCHESTRAL TRANSCRIPTIONS. [a]**Yvonne Kenny** (sop); [a]**Alfreda Hodgson** (contr); [a]**Christopher Gillett** (ten); [a]**Benjamin Luxon** (bar); [a]**London Philharmonic Choir; London Philharmonic Orchestra/Leonard Slatkin.** RCA Victor Red Seal RD87862. Notes and text included. Recorded 1987-88.
Orchestral transcriptions — ***Bach*** (trans. Elgar): Fantasia and Fugue in C minor, BWV537. ***Handel*** (trans. Elgar): Overture in D minor.

② lh 56m DDD 3/89

Elgar intended *The Kingdom* to be the second of three oratorios recounting the events which led to the founding of the Christian church. Poor box-office returns from the first performances of *The Apostles* and of *The Kingdom* discouraged him from completing the project. What a shame! Hearing such a powerful performance as this, one is left in no doubt that *The Kingdom* ranks among the finest of all oratorios. Leonard Slatkin measures his performance with a breadth and expansiveness which suits such momentous subject matter. He isn't afraid of slow tempos and it pays off handsomely; the climaxes, when they come, have real impact and the essentially reflective character of the music is all the more convincing. The orchestra and choir respond to his deeply-felt approach with fervour and the recording, made in EMI's Abbey Road studio, is outstanding. The two orchestral transcriptions of Bach and Handel provide slightly disappointing fillers; not because the performances are anything less than first-rate, but simply because these are little more than Elgar fiddling around in a way which today smacks of dubious taste.

Additional recommendation ...
The Kingdom[a]. *Coronation Ode, Op. 44*[b]. **Soloists;** [b]**Cambridge University Musical Society;** [b]**King's College Choir, Cambridge;** [b]**Royal Military School of Music Band, Kneller Hall;** [a]**London Philharmonic Choir and Orchestra/Sir Adrian Boult;** [b]**New Philharmonia Orchestra/Philip Ledger.** EMI CMS7 64209 — ② 2h 10m ADD 5/88

Elgar. The Apostles. **Alison Hargan** (sop); **Alfreda Hodgson** (contr); **David Rendall** (ten); **Bryn Terfel, Stephen Roberts, Robert Lloyd** (basses); **London Symphony Chorus; London Symphony Orchestra/Richard Hickox.** Chandos CHAN8875/6. Text included. Recorded in 1990.

② 2h 7m DDD 12/90

Elgar was concerned that *The Apostles*, and its sequel *The Kingdom*, should seem as music drama rather than oratorio, but there are moments when the biblical texts conspire to defeat this objective; the various soloists appearing to adopt the pious "stand and deliver" manner of the oratorio tradition. It's a problem that Hickox more successfully overcomes with a more theatrical approach to the work than his only predecessor on disc, Sir Adrian Boult. Of the soloists, Hickox's Alison Hargan does not match the radiant singing of Boult's Sheila Armstrong, but his men are preferable. One thinks of Bryn Terfel's magnificently sonorous St Peter, Stephen Roberts's unsanctimonious Jesus, but above all, Robert Lloyd's Judas. Judas's despair at the betrayal of Christ prompted Elgar to touch new heights of sheer human drama, and the moment where he listens with dread to the shouts of "Crucify Him" from within the temple has an impact unequalled in most opera. His final despairing words, as sung here by Lloyd, carry an unbearable tragic intensity. In 1902, the year before he completed *The Apostles*, Elgar spent a week at Bayreuth, and it's perhaps not surprising that the work contains many echoes of *Parsifal*. Chandos's policy of recording in a church really pays dividends here, and there's no denying that its wider dynamic range can cope with the extremes of, say, the rapt *pianissimo* Hickox draws from his 'mystic chorus' in preparation for the final climax, or the astonishing passage in Part One where dawn breaks and the sun rises on the morning prayers in the temple. Who could resist the floor-shaking, full blazing triple *forte* splendour that Hickox and Chandos manage here?

Additional recommendation ...

The Apostles[a]. *The Light of Life — Meditation.* [a]**Sheila Armstrong** (sop); [a]**Helen Watts** (contr); [a]**Robert Tear** (ten); [a]**Benjamin Luxon, John Carol Case** (bars); [a]**Clifford Grant** (bass); [a]**London Philharmonic Choir;** [a]**Downe House School Choir; London Philharmonic Orchestra/Sir Adrian Boult.** EMI CMS7 64206-2 — ② 2h 7m ADD £

Further listening ...

THE ELGAR EDITION, Volume 1. **London Symphony Orchestra, Royal Albert Hall Orchestra/Sir Edward Elgar.** EMI Elgar Edition mono CDS7 54560-2 (6/92).

THE ELGAR EDITION, Volume 2. **Sir Yehudi Menuhin** (vn); **London Symphony Orchestra, Royal Albert Hall Orchestra, New Symphony Orchestra, London Philharmonic Orchestra/Sir Edward Elgar.** EMI Elgar Edition mono CDS7 54564-2 (2/93).

Duke Ellington

American 1899-1974

Suggested listening ...

Mainly Black (Black, brown and beige) — suite. *Coupled with* ***Bartók.*** Sonata for Solo Violin. **Nigel Kennedy** (vn); **Alec Dankworth** (db). EMI CDC7 47621-2 (5/87).

The River — suite. *Coupled with* ***Still.*** Afro-American Symphony. **Detroit Symphony Orchestra/Neeme Järvi.** Chandos CHAN9154 (4/93).

Maurice Emmanuel

French 1862-1938

NEW REVIEW

Emmanuel. Six Sonatines. **Peter Jacobs** (pf). Continuum CCD1048. Recorded in 1987.
No. 1, Sonatine Bourgignone; No. 2, Sonatine Pastorale; No. 3; No. 4, En divers Modes Hindous; No. 5, Alla Francese; No. 6.

1h DDD 10/92 

Here's a real find. The little-known French composer Maurice Emmanuel was a student colleague of Debussy at the Paris Conservatoire and went on to pursue a distinguished academic career, specializing in such diverse areas as the music of Ancient Greece, folk-song, art history and Oriental music. Now the indefatigable Peter Jacobs has unearthed Emmanuel's Six *Sonatines* for piano, which span a period from 1893 to 1926. The composer's chosen idiom possesses something of Fauré's quiet dignity, Chabrier's rhythmic pungency and Debussy's questing harmonic sense; and yet, at the same time, much of this material is highly original and daring for its period, especially the first two *Sonatines* (*Bourgignone* and *Pastorale*). Twenty-three years separate the Second and Third *Sonatines*, the latter strongly Debussian and beautifully crafted. In the Fourth (*En divers Modes Hindous*), Emmanuel follows a strict harmonic scheme derived from two Indian modes, whilst the Fifth (*Alla Francese*) enshrines a modern-day six-movement 'French Suite' rather in the manner of Ravel's *Le Tombeau de Couperin*. Concision and restraint are the keynotes in the Sixth, though its *Presto con fuoco* finale shoots off like a firework display. Jacobs understandably sounds entranced by this wonderful music and his impeccably polished, sensitive (and realistically engineered) advocacy is quite irresistible. Investigate without delay!

Juan del Encina

Spanish 1468-1529

Encina. ROMANCES AND VILLANCICOS. **Hespèrion XX/Jordi Savall.** Astrée Auvidis E8707. Texts and translations included.

Romances — Una sañosa porfia. Qu'es de ti, desconsolado?. Mortal tristura me dieron (instrumental version). Triste España sin ventura. *Villancicos* — Levanta, Pascual, levanta. Amor con fortuna. Fata la parte. Ay triste, que vengo. Cucú, cucú, cucucú. A tal perdida tan triste. Quedate, Carillo, adios (instrumental version). Si abrá en este baldres. El que rigue y el regido. Mas vale trocar. Oy comamos y bebamos. Tragedia — Despierta, despierta tus fuerças, Pegaso (recited).

1h 16m DDD 2/92 

The quest for the rediscovery of Spain's Renaissance musical heritage has yielded considerable treasures on record in recent times and not the least of such treasures is this disc devoted to Encina from the Catalan musician, Jordi Savall. For a quarter of a century he has rescued countless Iberian scores from obscurity and presented them in lively and stimulating performances (seldom without excellent accompanying sleeve-notes and presentation from Auvidis which puts many another record company to shame). The success of this disc, devoted as it is to songs and music from 500 years ago, reflects Encina's important position in Spanish musical history. Born the son of a cobbler in Salamanca, he grew up to become a musician in the pay of the royal family of Aragon. Encina's songs — stirring *romances* and lighter and often more comical and even bawdy *villancicos* (try the lyrics in pieces such as "Cucú, cucú, cucucú" and "Fata la parte" for Encina's earthier side) — are strongly inflected with the nascent Spanish theatrical tradition of which he was a pivotal figure. The musical performances here (there is also a spoken elegy mourning the death of Don Juan, heir to the throne of Castille and Aragon) are all strongly characterized, the soprano Montserrat Figueras and baritone Jordi Ricart being particularly noteworthy. Savall successfully alternates the period instruments (principally early wind and brass instruments as well as violas da gamba, one of which is skilfully played by Savall himself) to match the different moods of the songs. The heights of lyric writing and composition reached half a millenium ago provide us now with a disc to be enjoyed on many levels, not least for its human passion.

George Enescu

Romanian 1881-1955

NEW REVIEW

Enescu. String Octet in C major, Op. 7[a].
Shostakovich. Two Pieces, Op. 11[a].
R. Strauss. Capriccio — Sextet. **Academy of St Martin in the Fields Chamber Ensemble** (Kenneth Sillito, Malcolm Latchem, [a]Josef Frohlich, [a]Robert Heard, vns; Robert Smissen, Stephen Tees, vas; Stephen Orton, Roger Smith, vcs). Chandos CHAN9131. Recorded in 1992.

1h 1m DDD 5/93 

Enescu's Octet was written when the composer was only 19 years old, and shows him attempting to find his feet in a large-scale sonata structure for the first time. Ostensibly the work is written in four contrasting movements, but each is closely related to the next to the extent that the nature of the composition ultimately emerges as a single movement cast in four sections. Enescu's youthfully ambitious intentions do not always come to complete fruition, and there are passages of mere contrapuntal busyness, but there are also many striking features in the work, particularly the haunting first part of the slow third movement. The work is strongly middle-European late romantic in style, and sometimes its highly expressive nature leads to a certain textural density when the eight string players are in full independent flow. The Octet is given marvellous advocacy by the Academy members, who play in a fiery, intense, highly committed fashion, and with great virtuosity. Strauss's calm, masterful sextet from *Capriccio* exists very happily as an independent entity, and its elegant, autumnal atmosphere makes an excellent foil for the Enescu work, as do the Shostakovich pieces. These come from an early phase in the composer's career, and comprise a deeply felt elegy, and a fiercely sardonic scherzo. The players respond brilliantly to the very different demands of Strauss and Shostakovich, and engineering throughout the disc is of a high standard.

Enescu. Violin Sonatas — No. 2 in F minor, Op. 6; No. 3 in A minor, Op. 25, "dans le caractère populaire roumain". Violin Sonata Movement, "Torso". **Adelina Oprean** (vn); **Justin Oprean** (pf). Hyperion CDA66484. Recorded in 1991.

lh 4m DDD 2/92

Enescu's First Violin Sonata, written when he was 16, is said to be immature and derivative: the Second Sonata, composed two years later in 1899, is an impressive achievement for an 18-year-old. It's true that there are still Brahmsian elements, and the work is also clearly influenced by Fauré, who was then Enescu's teacher, but the three movements are well-contrasted, and the quality of invention is high. The *Torso* Sonata dates from 1911, when Enescu's style was in a state of transition. Only one movement of this work survives, and it is a long, somewhat sprawling but impassioned statement. It would seem that Enescu abandoned the composition, but it deserves much more than oblivion. In his fascinating and highly individual Third Sonata Enescu invests the work with a Romanian folk flavour, and the style of country folk-fiddlers is imitated, but all the material is of his own invention. Adelina Oprean is a highly accomplished artist, as is her brother Justin. Together they produce performances which are rich in character and highly idiomatic — both players were born and brought up in Romania, and they understand Enescu's music to perfection. The recordings are excellent.

Additional recommendation ...

No. 3[a]*.* ***Chausson.*** *Poème, Op. 25*[b]*. Also includes works*[a] *by Beethoven, Corelli, D'Ambrosio, Handel, Kreisler, Pugnani and Wagner, recorded 1924-1929.* [a]**Sir Yehudi Menuhin,** [b]**George Enescu** (vns); [a]**Hepzibah Menuhin,** [b]**Sanford Schlüssel** (pfs). Biddulph mono LAB066 — lh 20m ADD ▲

Further listening ...

String Quartets, Op. 22 — No. 1 in E flat major; No. 2 in G major. **Voces Quartet.** Olympia Explorer OCD413 (5/92).

OEDIPE. **Soloists; Les Petits Chanteurs de Monaco; Orféon Donostiarra; Monte-Carlo Philharmonic Orchestra/Lawrence Foster.** EMI CDS7 54011-2 (11/90).

Manuel de Falla

Spanish 1876-1946

NEW REVIEW

Falla. El sombrero de tres picos[a]. Harpsichord Concerto[b]. [a]**Maria Lluisa Muntada** (sop); [b]**Jaime Martin** (fl); [b]**Manuel Angulo** (ob); [b]**Joan-Enric Lluna** (cl); [b]**Santiago Juan** (vn); [b]**Jorge Pozas** (vc); [b]**Tony Millan** (hpd); [a]**Spanish National Youth Orchestra/Edmon Colomer.** Auvidis Valois V4642. Recorded in 1989.

56m DDD 9/92

Falla's *El sombrero de tres picos* ("The three-cornered hat") started life as a 'mimed farce', but Diaghilev then persuaded the composer to revise and enlarge it as a one-act ballet for his company which had its première in London in 1919. Besides the orchestra, it features a soprano solo warning wives to resist temptation and cries of "Olé" from men's voices representing a bullring crowd. Much of the score consists of dances such as the fandango and seguidillas, while the finale is a jota. This performance by Maria Lluisa Muntada and the Spanish National Youth Orchestra, playing under the direction of their founder Edmon Colomer, brings to us all the vivid colours, intense melodies and vigorous rhythms that together evoke that southernmost province of Spain which is Andalusia. These artists clearly love and understand this music and they bring tremendous gusto to the famous "Miller's Dance" (the longest single number) with its chunky chords getting louder and faster. The Harpsichord Concerto, completed in 1926, shows us another side of Falla and was among the first twentieth-century compositions for the instrument. It is less obviously Spanish in style and instead more neo-classical — indeed, Stravinsky was probably the chief model — although we may detect an Iberian element in its directness and even toughness. With just five instruments playing alongside the soloist, it is really a chamber work, but the writing is so powerful that the composer's title is doubtless justified. Here, too, the playing is fine and the recording of both these works is full-blooded and atmospheric.

Additional recommendation ...

El sombrero de tres picos. El amor brujo — ballet[b]. **Colette Boky** (sop); [b]**Huguette Tourangeau** (mez); **Montreal Symphony Orchestra/Charles Dutoit.** Decca 410 008-2DH — ⁘ Ih 2m DDD 8/83

NEW REVIEW

Falla. Noches en los jardins de España[a].
Gerhard. Alegrías.
E. Halffter. Rapsodia portuguesa[a]. [a]**Guillermo Gonzalez** (pf); **Tenerife Symphony Orchestra/Victor Pablo Pérez.** Etcetera KTC1095. Recorded in 1989.

⁘ 57m DDD 7/92

Etcetera have come up with a clever and enterprising programme, Falla's sultry *Noches en los jardins de España* ("Nights in the gardens of Spain") serving very much as the artistic prime mover — especially of Ernesto Halffter's evocative *Portuguese Rhapsody* (written in 1940, revised in 1951). As to the performances, you need only sample Falla's "En el Generalife" on track 1 — say, from 9'27" to the end of the movement — to get the gist of the whole: an enthusiastic body of players that draws together as the music climaxes, and then reduces its pooled tone to an eerie whisper, as per the dictates of the score. The soloist, Guillermo Gonzalez, displays a sensitive touch as well as impressive timing, and the latter quality is crucial for the closing pages of the Falla. The recording itself is relatively close-miked, yet although we remain in closest proximity to the piano, the orchestra is always perfectly clear. The winds have a 'reedy' sound, very characteristic of Spanish orchestras; the strings are sweet but slim (as opposed to thin) in tone, the brass imposing (the horns don just a hint of vibrato) and the piano timbre clean and realistic, especially in the treble. Brass and keyboard emerge with considerable presence in Falla's third movement. Halffter's endearingly atmospheric and aptly-titled *Rhapsody* has considerable charm and a disarming gracefulness that would serve well in the context of an evening concert, either as an appetizer or a dessert; programming it, say, before or after Ravel's complete *Daphnis et Chloé* would set it off to its best advantage. But the real hit of the disc for this writer is Roberto Gerhard's spicy *Alegrías,* premièred in Birmingham in 1943 under Stanford Robinson and jam-paced with humour and irony: if you want to end the day with a smile, then put on the second movement, "Farruca-Jaleo" — eight minutes' worth of Milhaud-style high spirits (and don't be temporarily misled by a mischievous quotation from Chopin's "Funeral March"!).

Falla. El amor brujo — ballet (complete)[a]. Noches en los jardins de España[b].
Rodrigo. Concierto de Aranjuez[c]. [c]**Carlos Bonnell** (gtr); [b]**Alicia de Larrocha** (pf);

[ac]**Montreal Symphony Orchestra/Charles Dutoit;** [b]**London Philharmonic Orchestra/Frühbeck de Burgos.** Decca Ovation 430 703-2DM. Item marked [a] from SXDL7560 (7/83), [b] 410 289-2DH (10/84), [c] SXDL7525 (7/81). Recorded 1980-83.

1h 11m DDD 8/91

This hugely enjoyable disc of Spanish music includes Rodrigo's most famous work, the *Concierto de Aranjuez* which has never lost its popularity since its Barcelona première in 1940 and here Carlos Bonnell imparts a wistful, intimate feeling to the work, aided by a thoughtful accompaniment from Charles Dutoit's stylish Montreal Orchestra. The famous string tune in the *Adagio* enjoys a fulsome rendition. The two Falla items increase the attraction of this CD. Dutoit's beautifully played interpretation of *El amor brujo* captures the wide range of emotions that this fiery, mysterious piece requires and his performance of the famous "Ritual Fire Dance" must be among the best in the catalogue. A cooler mood is captured in *Nights in the gardens of Spain* with Alicia de Larrocha as the distinguished soloist. Her smooth, effortless playing matches the mood of the piece exactly and de Burgos's accompaniment with the London Philharmonic is equally sympathetic, with ripe tone colour and careful dynamics. Those unfamiliar with these great Spanish works will be hard pressed to find a better introduction than this superbly recorded disc.

Falla. SPANISH OPERA ARIAS AND SONGS.
Granados. GOYESCAS — La maja y el ruiseñor[be].
Turína. SPANISH SONGS. **Victoria de los Angeles** (sop); [a]**Gerald Moore** (pf); [b]**Philharmonia Orchestra,** [c]**London Symphony Orchestra/**[d]**Stanford Robinson,** [e]**Anatole Fistoulari,** [f]**Walter Susskind.** EMI Références mono CDH7 64028-2. Item marked [be] from DB21069 (12/50). Recorded 1948-52.
Falla: LA VIDA BREVE[bd] — Vivan los que rien!; Alli está! riyendo (both from HMV DB6702, 6/48). Siete canciones populares españolas[a] (DB9731/2, 2/52). ***Turína:*** Canto a Sevilla[ce] (HMV ALP1185, 11/54). Saeta en forma de Salve[bf]. Poema en forma de canciones— Cantares[bf] (HMV DA1929, 5/50).

1h 18m ADD 4/92 

Victoria de los Angeles performing Spanish music on a mid-price reissue — a self-recommending disc if ever there was one. All the recordings here date from the late 1940s and early 1950s when los Angeles was in her mid-twenties and in great demand by the record companies following her remarkable début in 1944. Her interpretation of the role of Salud in Falla's *La vida breve* is unsurpassed, and this is superbly demonstrated in the two arias recorded here, which were made shortly after her creation of the role for the BBC. Granados's opera *Goyescas* must be one of the only operatic works in history to have been completely constructed from a work originally written for solo piano. The beautiful aria, "La maja y el ruiseñor" ("The maid and the nightingale") from the opera not only provides a rare chance to hear part of the operatic score but also offers an excellent opportunity to sample the extraordinary tonal beauty of los Angeles's voice. Lyricism and tonal beauty are also strong features of her recording of Turína's *Canto a Sevilla*, a mixed cycle of vocal and purely orchestral movements evoking the atmosphere of Seville as a city and arguably Turína's masterpiece, and the two orchestral songs, *Saeta en forma de Salve* and *Cantares* which are vividly coloured and passionately delivered. Less successful, perhaps, are her slightly under-characterized readings of Falla's *Siete canciones populares españolas*. Unfortunately, EMI provide neither texts nor translations. These are, however, rather minor caveats in an otherwise indispensable and generous reissue.

NEW REVIEW

Falla. LA VIDA BREVE. **Teresa Berganza** (mez) Salud; **Paloma Perez Iñigo** (sop) Carmela, First and Third Street Vendors; **Alicia Nafé** (mez) Grandmother, Second Street Vendor; **José Carreras** (ten) Paco; **Juan Pons** (bar) Uncle Salvador; **Manuel Mairena** (bar) Flamenco singer; **Ramon Contreras** (voc) Manuel; **Manuel Cid** (ten) Voice in the smithy, Voice in the distance, Voice of a hawker; **Ambrosian Opera Chorus; London Symphony**

Orchestra/Garcia Navarro. DG 435 851-2GH. Notes, text and translation included. From 2707 108 (11/78). Recorded in 1978.

1h ADD 10/92 

Falla's *La vida breve* marked an auspicious start to a distinguished career. The very day after submitting the work for a competition (March 31st, 1905) Falla was placed first in a piano contest, then learned — some eight months later — that his opera had won the competition! Although not as strikingly original as his much-loved ballet *El amor brujo*, *La vida breve* is none the less one of Falla's most appealing scores. The libretto deals with the betrayal of the main protagonist, Salud (Teresa Berganza), by her lover, Paco (José Carreras), who — unbeknown to her — marries another and then leaves her to die of a broken heart at his wedding ceremony. The music itself alternates between Tchaikovskian pathos (opening), Debussian sensuousness and rhythmic dance music of a strongly national flavour. Readers who are already familiar with the celebrated "Interlude and Dance" (which is frequently included among Spanish orchestral and instrumental anthologies) will be interested to know that here the Dance is accompanied by the fiery stamping of a Flamenco dance and the sexy rattle of castanets. In fact, a good quarter of this "lyrical drama in 2 acts" is either purely orchestral, or scored for chorus and orchestra. The performance here is predominantly lyrical, although Lucero Tena's dancing adds spice and excitement where appropriate. Narciso Yepes plays guitar at the wedding ceremony, and Manuel Mairena portrays a throaty, street-wise balladeer. As to the main cast, it is wholly excellent, with both Berganza and Carreras in marvellous voice; their impassioned love duet is as fine as anything in either singer's discography. Garcia Navarro and the London Symphony Orchestra provide sensitive, cleanly executed support and the recording is clear and immediate. Although only on a single CD, the opera is presented in a box, complete with full libretto, comprehensive notes and translations.

Falla. EL RETABLO DE MAESE PEDRO[a]. **Matthew Best** (bass) Don Quijote; **Adrian Thompson** (ten) Maese Pedro; **Samuel Linay** (treb) El Trujamán; **Maggie Cole** (hpd). ***Milhaud.*** LES MALHEURS D'ORPHEE[b]. **Malcolm Walker** (bar) Orphée; **Anna Steiger** (sop) Eurydice; **Paul Harrhy** (ten) Maréchal, Le sanglier; **Patrick Donnelly** (bass) Le charron; **Matthew Best** (bass) Le vannier, L'ours; **Gaynor Morgan** (sop) Le renard, La soeur Jumelle; **Patricia Bardon** (sop) Le loup, La soeur Ainée; **Susan Bickley** (mez) Le soeur Cadette. ***Stravinsky.*** RENARD[c]. **Hugh Hetherington, Paul Harrhy** (tens); **Patrick Donnelly, Nicolas Cavallier** (basses); **Christopher Bradley** (cimbalom) [abc]**Matrix Ensemble/Robert Ziegler.** ASV CDDCA758. Texts and translations included.

1h 17m DDD 7/91 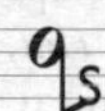

Three complete operas on one disc lasting 77 minutes must be good value, and especially so when they are important works from the first quarter of this century. One thing they have in common is that all were commissioned by the American-born Princess de Polignac, a patroness of music who exercised considerable flair in her choice of gifted artists in a Paris that was then full of them. The performances here by Robert Ziegler and his Matrix Ensemble are full of flair and his chosen singers for the three works (who include the convincingly Spanish boy treble Samuel Linay as El Trujamán in the Falla) sound at home in Spanish, French and Russian in turn. As presented here, Falla's puppet-opera is full of Iberian colour and verve, and although Milhaud's piece on the Orpheus legend is not so striking or dramatic it still has beauty and is elegantly and expressively sung and played. But the best music is still to come in Stravinsky's magnificently earthy and vivid 'barnyard fable' *Renard*, not a long work but a dazzling one, where this performance of great panache simply bursts out of one's loudspeakers to transport us instantly to a farmyard of old Russia. There's excellent cimbalom playing here from Christopher Bradley. The libretto of all three works is usefully provided in the booklet, together with an English translation. The recording is first class, being both immediate and atmospheric.

Further listening ...

Atlántida — scenic cantata[a]. Homenajes. [a]**Montserrat Caballé** (sop); [a]**Heinz Rehfuss** (bar); [a]**Lausanne Youth Choir;** [a]**Suisse Romande Radio Chorus;** [a]**Villamont College Little**

Choir; Orchestre de la Suisse Romande/Ernest Ansermet. Cascavelle OSR Memories mono VEL2005 (11/92).

Giles Farnaby

British c.1563-1640

Suggested listening ...

Keyboard Works — Two Almans, MBXXIV Nos. 22 and 23. Five Fantasias, MBXXIV Nos. 5, 6, 7, 10 and 12. For two virginals (with Elisabeth Joye, hpd). Galiarda. A Gigge. Giles Farnaby — His Dreame. His Humour. The King's Hunt. Lachrymae Pavan. Three Maskes, MBXXIV Nos. 31-33. Meridian Alman. Muscadin. The Old Spagnoletta. Pavana. Pawles Wharfe. Quodling's Delight. Rosseter's Galliard. Spagnoletta. Tell mee Daphne. A Toye. Why aske you. Woody-cock. **Pierre Hantaï** (hpd). Adda 581172 (9/91).

Robert Farnon

Canadian/British 1917-

NEW REVIEW

Farnon. ORCHESTRAL WORKS. **Bratislava Radio Symphony Orchestra/Adrian Leaper.** Marco Polo 8 233401.

Portrait of a Flirt. How Beautiful is Night. Melody Fair. A la Claire Fontaine. Peanut Polka. In a Calm. Gateway to the West. Jumping Bean. Pictures in the Fire. Little Miss Molly. Colditz March. A Star Is Born. Westminster Waltz. Manhattan Playboy. Lake in the Woods. Derby Day. State Occasion.

lh 10m DDD 9/92 

As an arranger for a star-studded array of song stylists from Frank Sinatra to Sarah Vaughan, Robert Farnon has fashioned sensitive orchestral backdrops that complement with effortless grace both the song and the performer; little wonder, then, ol' blue eyes has affectionately dubbed him "the guv'nor". But Farnon's most profound contribution to the world of light music is as a composer of such glamorous and delightfully-crafted musical miniatures as *Peanut Polka, Portrait of a Flirt, Jumping Bean* and *Westminster Waltz*. Heard consistently in cinema newsreels and on radio and television during the 1950s, his captivating melodies played an integral, if subconscious part in many people's musical upbringing. New recordings of Farnon's work have been long overdue but any reservations a prospective buyer may harbour about such cherished and essentially British light music classics being played by a Czech orchestra should be discarded immediately, for this is a collection that will bring endless enjoyment. Listening to the orchestra's nimble and wonderfully idiomatic playing, it is difficult to believe that they are probably performing this music for the first time. Much of the concert's joyful spontaneity is undoubtedly due to the sprightly and warm-hearted approach of conductor Adrian Leaper, who even manages to coax from the string section that vital luxurious sheen that so typifies Farnon's scoring. Apart from the many popular favourites, this generous and well-chosen programme also includes some of Farnon's more serious compositions, most notably the tone-poem *A la Claire Fontaine*, which is handled here with touching eloquence. A bold and well-detailed recording (if perhaps lacking that final degree of sumptuousness) rounds off a truly polished example of light music at its very best.

Further listening ...

Captain Horatio Hornblower RN — Suite. A la Claire Fontaine. State Occasion. Lake in the Woods[a]. A Promise of Spring. Intermezzo for Harp and Strings. Rhapsody for Violin and Orchestra. **Soloists; Royal Philharmonic Orchestra/Robert Farnon, [a]Douglas Gamley.** Reference Recordings RR47CD (9/92).

Gabriel Fauré

French 1845-1924

Fauré. ORCHESTRAL WORKS. [a]**Lorraine Hunt** (sop); [b]**Jules Eskin** (vc); [c]**Tanglewood Festival Chorus; Boston Symphony Orchestra/Seiji Ozawa.** DG 423 089-2GH. Text and translation included where appropriate. Recorded in 1986.
Pelléas et Mélisande (with Chanson de Mélisande — orch. Koechlin)[a]. Après un rêve (arr. Dubenskij)[b]. Pavane[c]. Elégie[b]. Dolly (orch. Rabaud).

56m DDD 1/88 

Fauré's music for Maeterlinck's play *Pelléas et Mélisande* was commissioned by Mrs Patrick Campbell and to the usual four movement suite Ozawa has added the "Chanson de Mélisande", superbly sung here by Lorraine Hunt. Ozawa conducts a sensitive, sympathetic account of the score, and Jules Eskin plays beautifully in both the arrangement of the early song, *Après un rêve* and the *Elégie*, which survived from an abandoned cello sonata. The grave *Pavane* is performed here in the choral version of 1901. *Dolly* began life as a piano duet, but was later orchestrated by the composer and conductor Henri Rabaud. Ozawa gives a pleasing account of this delightful score and the recording is excellent.

Additional recommendation ...
Pelléas et Mélisande. Pavane, Op. 50[a]. ***Chausson.*** *Poème de l'amour et de la mer, Op. 19*[b]*. Poème, Op. 25*[c]. [b]**Linda Finnie** (mez); [a]**Renaissance Singrs; Ulster Orchestra/Paul Tortelier** ([c]vn). Chandos CHAN8952 *(reviewed under Chausson; see the Index to Reviews)* — 1h 9m DDD 12/91

Fauré. Elégie in C minor, Op. 24.
Lalo. Cello Concerto in D minor.
Saint-Saëns. Cello Concerto No. 1 in A minor, Op. 33. **Heinrich Schiff** (vc); **New Philharmonia Orchestra/Sir Charles Mackerras.** DG Privilege 431 166-2GR. From 2530 793 (2/77).

53m ADD 8/91 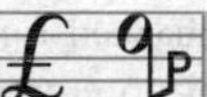

The Saint-Saëns Concerto is concisely put together, and shows the composer in his wittiest and most piquant vein. Schiff responds with appropriately warm and expressive playing, and particularly in the first movement his eager, agile playing is very attractive. In the charming *Allegretto* movement his rich tone is shown off to great advantage, and in the busier sections of the finale his clean, nimble technique is very evident. Fauré's *Elégie* inhabits a vastly different world, but Schiff's noble, emotionally restrained playing captures the mood of the piece perfectly. Lalo's Concerto is not in the same class as the other two compositions, but it has a certain faded charm, and Schiff plays the work with a good deal of energy and commitment. The New Philharmonia play in a spirited and precise fashion throughout the disc under Sir Charles Mackerras's wise and experienced direction, and the late 1970s recording sounds vivid and immediate in this transfer.

Fauré. Piano Quartets — No. 1 in C minor, Op. 15; No. 2 in G minor, Op. 45. **Domus** (Krysia Osostowicz, vn; Robin Ireland, va; Timothy Hugh, vc; Susan Tomes, pf). Hyperion CDA66166. From A66166 (10/86).

1h 2m DDD 10/86 

The First Piano Quartet reveals Fauré's debt to an earlier generation of composers, particularly Mendelssohn. Yet already it has the refined sensuality, the elegance and the craftsmanship which were always to be hallmarks of his style and it is a thoroughly assured, highly enjoyable work which could come from no other composer's pen. The Second Quartet is a more complex, darker work, but much less ready to yield its secrets. The comparatively agitated, quicksilver scherzo impresses at once, however, and repeated hearings of the complete work reveal it to possess considerable poetry and stature. Just occasionally one could wish that the members of Domus had a slightly more aristocratic, commanding approach to these scores, but overall the achievement is highly impressive, for their playing is both idiomatic and technically impeccable. The recording has an appropriately intimate feel to it and is faithful and well-balanced.

Additional recommendations ...
Piano Quartets. Piano Quintets, No. 1 in C minor, Op. 89; No. 2 in D minor, Op. 115. String Quartet in E minor, Op. 121. **Jean-Philippe Collard** (pf); **Augustin Dumay** (vn); **Bruno Pasquier** (va); **Frédéric Lodéon** (vc); **Michel Debost** (fl); **Parrenin Quartet.** EMI Rouge et Noir CMS7 62548-2 — ② 2h 37m ADD 5/89
No. 1[a]. Piano Trio in D minor, Op. 120. **Beaux Arts Trio; [a]Kim Kashkashian** (va). Philips 422 350-2PH — 53m DDD 6/90

Fauré. Violin Sonatas — No. 1 in A major, Op. 13[a]; No. 2 in E minor, Op. 108[a]. ***Franck.*** Violin Sonata in A major[b]. **Arthur Grumiaux** (vn); **[a]Paul Crossley, [b]György Sebok** (pfs). Philips Musica da Camera 426 384-2PC. Items marked [a] from 9500 534 (7/79), recorded in 1977, [b] 9500 568 (10/80), recorded in 1978.

1h 13m ADD 7/90 £

Fauré was only 31, and on the crest of his first great love affair, when writing his radiantly lyrical A major Violin Sonata. But curiously he allowed four decades to elapse before following it up with the E minor Sonata, by which time deafness, no less than the dark background of war, had drawn him into a more recondite world of his own. As portraits of the composer in youth and full artistic maturity the two works make an ideal coupling. But here, as a bonus, we are also given César Franck's one and only Violin Sonata, written when he was 64, bringing the playing time to the very generous total of almost an hour-and-a-quarter. It would be hard to find any two artists closer to Fauré's own heart than the intimately attuned Grumiaux and Crossley. Their original LP was immediately hailed as the best available way back in 1979. And despite fine newcomers in recent years this mellow CD transfer still triumphs over all the catalogue's rivals. An unerring sense of style goes hand in hand with very beautiful, finely nuanced tone and an immediacy of expression suggesting joyous new discovery. Even if Sebok's piano emerges a little more plummy than Crossley's, the Franck Sonata, too, appeals through its warmth of heart.

Additional recommendation ...
Nos. 1 and 2. **Krysia Osostowicz** (vc); **Susan Tomes** (pf). Hyperion CDA66277 — 50m DDD 11/88

Fauré. PIANO WORKS. **Jean-Philippe Collard, [a]Bruno Rigutto** (pfs). EMI Rouge et Noir CZS7 62687-2. Recorded 1970-83.
Barcarolles, Nos. 1-13 (from CDC7 47358-2, 5/87). Impromptus Nos. 1-5 (EMI Pathé-Marconi 2C 069 73058, 9/82). Valses-caprices, No. 1-4. Huit pièces brèves, Op. 84. Mazurka in B flat major, Op. 32. Trois romances sans paroles, Op. 17. Dolly Suite, Op. 56[a]. ***Fauré/ Messager:*** Souvenir de Bayreuth, Op. posth[a].

② 2h 31m ADD 3/92

No composer exemplifies so-called 'English' reserve more than Fauré, a Frenchman, and compared with Beethoven, Verdi or his compatriot Berlioz he can sometimes seem pallid, lacking a strong musical personality. But when his music is really well played, as it is here by Jean-Philippe Collard, one feels its own special kind of poetry and the passion that ebbs and flows beneath its refined surface. Collard does not falsify the natural understatement of these piano works, but rather shapes them on their own terms with a wide yet subtle expressive range, and each of the 13 *Barcarolles*, which in lesser hands can sound too alike, has its own character. (They were not written as a set, but separately over many years.) His command of tone and texture, together with phrasing and pedalling, brings colour and vitality to these pieces, and he knows how to balance grace with strength, lyricism with vigour. He is no less telling in the other solo music, and although these performances are hardly new (the barcarolles were recorded in 1970) they are models of their kind and the sound, while a little enclosed by today's standards, is satisfying. This well-filled mid-price set also brings us two duet works, one being the charmingly melodious *Dolly Suite* and the other the *Souvenir de Bayreuth*, a mischievous pot-pourri of Wagnerian tunes which reminds us that Fauré had a sense of humour.

Additional recommendations ...
Barcarolles Nos. 1-13. **Paul Crossley.** CRD CRD3422 — lh 4m DDD 6/88
Barcarolles Nos. 1, 4, 5 and 6. Impromptus Nos. 1-3. Nocturnes Nos. 1, 4 and 6. Three songs without words. **Kathryn Stott** (pf). Conifer CDCF138 — lh 3m DDD 6/87

Fauré. La bonne chanson, Op. 61[a]. Piano Trio in D minor, Op. 120[b]. [a]**Sarah Walker** (mez); [a]**Nash Ensemble;** [b]**Marcia Crayford** (vn); [b]**Christopher van Kampen** (vc); [b]**Ian Brown** (pf). CRD CRD3389. Text and translation included. From CRD1089 (4/81). Recorded in 1980.

44m ADD 5/90

In *La bonne chanson*, generally considered the finest of Fauré's song-cycles, he perfectly matched the ecstatic moods of Verlaine's love-poems to the young girl who was to become his wife; but though the sentiments expressed are those of a man and the songs were first performed by a baritone, they are more usually sung by a female voice. Sarah Walker, with her warm, voluptuous tone, poetic sensibility, shaping of phrases and, not least, excellent French, makes an admirable interpreter of their passionate lyricism. Fauré's own arrangement of the original piano accompaniment for string quintet and piano is played with tonal finesse by the Nash Ensemble. The final song, "L'hiver a cessé", refers to the music of the previous eight, summing up the atmosphere of radiant devotion that pervades the cycle. The Piano Trio, composed 30 years later when Fauré was 77, was his penultimate work and represents him at his most direct and compact: the artists here are responsive to its subtle harmonic thinking and judge its expressive weight to a nicety, preserving the grace of this essentially elegant, if elusive, work.

Fauré. Requiem, Op. 48 (original 1894 version)[a].
Fauré/Messager. Messe des Pêcheurs de Villerville[b]. [a]**Agnès Mellon** (sop); [a]**Peter Kooy** (bar); [b]**Jean-Philippe Audoli** (vn); [a]**Leo van Doeselaar** (org); **Petits Chanteurs de Saint-Louis; Paris Chapelle Royale Chorus; Musique Oblique Ensemble/Philippe Herreweghe.** Harmonia Mundi HMC90 1292. Texts included.

56m DDD 4/89 B

Fauré's original conception of his Requiem was as a chamber work, but when the work was published it was scored for full orchestra. There is no evidence that Fauré did any more than acquiesce in preparing this 'concert-hall version' of his score. Even accepting that an amplification of the instrumentation is needed when the work is played in large halls, a rediscovery of the score as it existed before publication has long seemed desirable. New and convincing sources have now been discovered by the Fauré authority Jean-Michel Nectoux: a complete set of orchestral parts, apparently prepared for Fauré's use, some of them in his own hand and all corrected by him. The resulting score is as near to authentic Fauré as we shall get and Harmonia Mundi's recording of Nectoux's edition is ideal. It uses boys' voices in the upper parts (as did Fauré himself) and a convincingly boy-like soprano in the *Pie Jesu*. The orchestra is of ideal size and is beautifully balanced in a sympathetic acoustic. As a charming bonus we have another act of Fauréan 'restoration', the original version of what later became the *Messe basse*, with its pretty accompaniment for string quintet, wind trio and harmonium and its two long-suppressed extra movements by Messager. An enchanting record as well as an important document.

Additional recommendations ...
Requiem (original version, ed. Rutter). Motets — Ave verum corpus; Tantum ergo; Ave Maria; Maria, Mater gratiae. Cantique de Jean Racine, Op. 11 (orch. Rutter). Messe basse. **Soloists; Cambridge Singers; City of London Sinfonietta/John Rutter.** Collegium COLCD109 — lh 3m ADD/DDD 1/89 B

Requiem (revised version). Cantique de Jean Racine, Op. 11. Messe basse. **Poulenc.** *Mass in G major Salve Regina.* **Soloists; Academy of St Martin in the Fields; Choir of St John's College, Cambridge/George Guest.** Decca Ovation 430 360-2DM — ⁘ 1h 14m ADD 9/91 £ Ⓑ
Requiem (revised version). Pavane, Op. 50 (orch. version). **Soloists; King's College Choir, Cambridge; New Philharmonia Orchestra/Sir David Willcocks.** EMI CDM7 64715-2 — ⁘ 42m ADD 7/93 Ⓑ

Further listening ...

Nocturnes Nos. 1-7. **Paul Crossley** (pf). CRD CRD3406 (6/88).

Nocturnes Nos. 8-13. 8 Pièces brèves, Op. 84. **Paul Crossley** (pf). CRD CRD3407 (6/88).

Songs: Op. 1 — No. 1, Le papillon et la fleur; No. 2, Mai. *Op. 2* — No. 1, Dans les ruines d'une abbaye; No. 2, Les matelots. *Op. 3* — No. 1, Seule!; No. 2, Sérénade toscane. *Op. 4* — No. 1, La chanson du pêcheur; No. 2, Lydia. *Op. 5* — No. 1, Chant d'automne; No. 2, Rêve d'amour; No. 3, L'absent. *Op. 6* — No. 1, Aubade; No. 2, Tristesse; No. 3, Sylvie. *Op. 7* — No. 1, Après un rêve; No. 2, Hymne; No. 3, Barcarolle. *Op. 8* — No. 1, Au bord de l'eau; No. 2, La rançon; No. 3, Ici-bas!. *Op. 10* — No. 1, Puisqu'ici-bas; No. 2, Tarantelle. *Op. 18* — No. 1, Nell; No. 2, Le voyageur; No. 3, Automne. Poèmes d'un jour, Op. 21. *Op. 23* — No. 1, Les berceaux; No. 2, Notre amour; No. 3, Le secret. *Op. 27* — No. 1, Chanson d'amour; No. 2, La fée aux chansons. *Op. 39* — No. 1, Aurore; No. 2, Fleur jetée; No. 3, Le pays des rêves; No. 4, Les roses d'Ispahan. *Op. 43* — No. 1, Noël; No. 2, Nocturne. *Op. 46* — No. 1, Les présents; No. 2, Clair de lune. *Op. 51* — No. 1, Larmes; No. 2, Au cimetière; No. 3, Spleen; No. 4, La rose. Shylock — Suite. *Op. 57* — No. 1, Chanson; No. 2, Madrigal. Cinq mélodies de Venise, Op. 58. La bonne chanson, Op. 61. Pleurs d'or, Op. 72. *Op. 76* — No. 1, Le parfum impérissable; No. 2, Arpège. *Op. 83* — No. 1, Prison; No. 2, Soir. *Op. 85* — No. 1, Dans la forêt de septembre; No. 2, La fleur qui va sur l'eau; No. 3, Accompagnement. *Op. 87* — No. 1, Le plux doux chemin; No. 2, Le ramier. Le don silencieux, Op. 92. Chanson, Op. 94. La chanson d'Eve, Op. 95. Le jardin clos, Op. 106. Mirages, Op. 113. C'est la paix, Op. 114. L'horizon chimérique, Op. 118. L'aurore, Op. posth. En prière. Sérénade du bourgeois gentilhomme. Pelléas et Mélisande — Suite, Op. 80 No. 5, "Chanson de Mélisande". Vocalise-étude. **Elly Ameling** (sop); **Gérard Souzay** (bar); **Dalton Baldwin** (pf). EMI L'Esprit Français CMS7 64079-2 (4/92).

PENELOPE — *drama lyrique.* **Soloists; Jean Laforge Vocal Ensemble; Monte-Carlo Philharmonic Orchestra/Charles Dutoit.** Erato Libretto 2292-45405-2 (4/92).

Robert Fayrfax

British 1464-1521

Suggested listening ...

Missa Albanus. Aeternae laudis lilium. **The Sixteen/Harry Christophers.** Hyperion CDA66073 (12/89).

Morton Feldman

American 1926-1987

Suggested listening ...

Rothko Chapel[a]. Why Patterns?[b]. **Soloists; [b]California EAR Unit; [a]Berkeley University Chamber Chorus, California/Philip Brett.** New Albion NA039CD (10/92).

Howard Ferguson

British 1908-

Ferguson. Piano Sonata in F minor, Op. 8. Partita for two pianos, Op. 5*b*[a]. **Howard Shelley, [a]Hilary Macnamara** (pfs). Hyperion CDA66130. From A66130 (10/84). Recorded in 1984.

44m DDD 1/91 

Although Howard Ferguson was active as a composer for over 30 years (he laid down his pen in the early 1960s, feeling that he had said all that he had to say as a composer) his published compositions number just 20. His slowness as a composer is almost entirely due to the painstaking care that he devoted to each of his compositions, and this in turn is reflected in the extremely high quality of each work. The Piano Sonata, dating from 1938-40, is dedicated to the memory of his friend and teacher, Harold Samuel, and is arguably the most intensely personal of all Ferguson's works. It is by far his most frequently performed work (though not however on disc), and the astringency of its rhythmic and harmonic writing, coupled with its classical economy and romantic gesture has given rise to Ferguson being labelled a twentieth-century romantic. Howard Shelley is both persuasive and commanding, and is particularly effective in projecting the work's overwhelming sense of despair and loss. The *Partita* for two pianos is another fine example of Ferguson's immaculate craftsmanship and concise economic style, and also underlines his allegiance to both classical and baroque forms. If this gives the impression of a rather dry, academic work, then the reader is urged to sample the seductively undulating and fantastical windswept quality of the second movement or the ebullient, reel-like energy in the outer sections of the finale. An exemplary recording from every point of view.

NEW REVIEW

Ferguson. ORCHESTRAL AND VOCAL WORKS. [a]**Brian Rayner Cook** (bar); [b]**Anne Dawson** (sop); **London Symphony** [ab]**Chorus and Orchestra/Richard Hickox.** Chandos CHAN9082. Texts included. Recorded in 1992.
Overture for an Occasion, Op. 16. Partita, Op. 5a. Two Ballads, Op. 1[a]. The Dream of the Rood, Op. 16[b].

1h 15m DDD 4/93 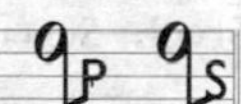

Now in his mid-eighties, Belfast-born Howard Ferguson is at last beginning to receive (on disc at least) the proper attention and acclaim his splendidly crafted art merits. This outstanding new Chandos collection plugs some valuable gaps in the catalogue and contains at least one masterpiece in *The Dream of the Rood*, a large-scale setting for soprano, chorus and orchestra from 1959, which employs as its text the composer's own adaptation of a visionary ninth-century Anglo-Saxon poem. How music of such consummate quality and intrepid scope could have been neglected for so long is quite beyond comprehension: one hopes that Hickox's magnificent advocacy will prompt a revival of this glorious piece, surely a highlight of the British choral tradition. Alas, it proved to be the composer's swan-song (Ferguson has not taken up his pen since then), though elsewhere on this compilation we can also hear his first published work, the Two *Ballads* for baritone and orchestra, the second of which, a setting of the "Lyke-Wake Dirge", he completed as a 20-year-old RCM student. That just leaves the Coronation-inspired *Overture for an Occasion* (a real cut above the average for this kind of festive offering) and hugely endearing *Partita* (presented here in its full-blown orchestral dress). In sum, this is richly communicative, impeccably wrought music of potentially widespread appeal, and it could not be better served than on this CD: Richard Hickox and his LSO forces are simply inspired protagonists throughout (the elderly composer attending the sessions must have been quite delighted) and the Chandos engineers have once more excelled themselves in the range and lustre of the finished product. Don't miss this one!

Further listening ...

Violin Sonata No. 1, Op. 2. *Coupled with* ***Castelnuovo-Tedesco.*** Violin Concerto No. 2, "I profeti"; ***Françaix.*** String Trio in C major; ***K. Khachaturian.*** Violin Sonata in G minor,

Op. 1. **Jascha Heifetz** (vn); **Joseph de Pasquale** (va); **Gregor Piatigorsky** (vc); **Lilian Steuber** (pf); **Los Angeles Philharmonic Orchestra/Alfred Wallenstein.** RCA Victor Gold Seal mono GD87872 (9/90).

Key to Symbols

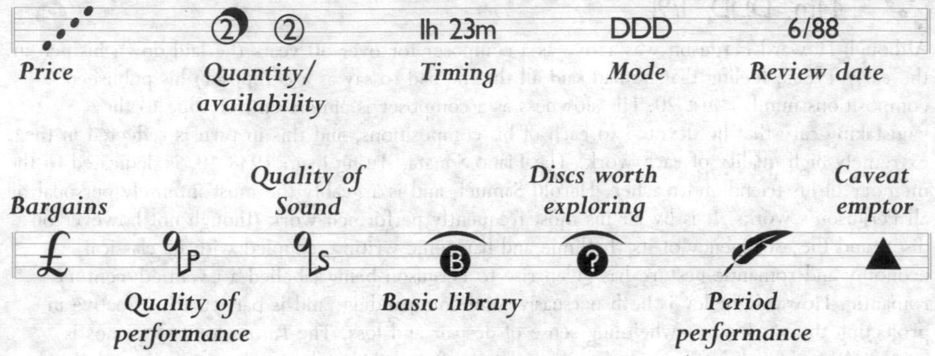

Zdenék Fibich

Bohemian 1850-1900

Suggested listening ...

Symphonies — No. 2 in E flat major, Op. 38; No. 3 in E minor, Op. 53. **Brno State Philharmonic Orchestra/Jiří Bělohlávek.** Supraphon CO-1256 (2/88).

SARKA. **Soloists; Janáček Opera Chorus; Brno State Philharmonic Orchestra/Jan Stych.** Supraphon CO-1746/8 (10/88).

John Field

Irish 1782-1837

Suggested listening ...

Piano Concertos — No. 1 in E flat major, H27; No. 2 in A flat major, H31; No. 3 in E flat major, H32; No. 4 in E flat major, H28; No. 5 in C major, H39, "L'incendie par l'orage"; No. 6 in C major, H49; No. 7 in C minor, H58. **John O'Conor** (pf); **New Irish Chamber Orchestra/Janos Furst.** Onyx ONYX CD101/3 (3-disc set).

Nocturnes — No. 1 in E flat major, H24; No. 2 in C minor, H25; No. 3 in A flat major, H26; No. 4 in A major, H36; No. 5 in B flat major, H37; No. 6 in F major, H40; No. 11 in E flat major, H56*A*; No. 12 in G major, H58*D*; No. 14 in C major, H60. Piano Sonata in E flat major, H8 No. 1. Grand Pastorale, H54*A*. Air russe varié, H10[a]. La danse des ours, H12[a]. Andante, H11[a]. Kamarinskaya, air russe favori varié, H22. Variations in D minor on a Russian song, H41, "My dear bosom friend". **Richard Burnett, [a]Lorna Fulford** (pfs). Amon Ra CD-SAR48 (11/92).

Piano Sonatas — E flat major, H8 No. 1; A major, H8 No. 2; C minor, H8 No. 3; B major, H17. Nocturnes — No. 3 in A flat major, H26; No. 7 in C major, H45; No. 17 in E major, H54*A*. **John O'Conor** (pf). Telarc CD80290 (11/92).

Gerald Finzi

British 1901-1956

Finzi. Cello Concerto, Op. 40.
Leighton. Veris gratia — suite, Op. 9[a]. **Rafael Wallfisch** (vc); [a]**George Caird** (ob); **Royal Liverpool Philharmonic Orchestra/Vernon Handley.** Chandos CHAN8471.

1h 6m DDD 10/86

Finzi wrote his Cello Concerto for the Cheltenham Festival of 1955. At this time he had suffered from leukaemia for four years and he knew that he had not long to live. This knowledge served only to enhance his deep-seated awareness of and preoccupation with questions concerning life's transience, and the result is a work which is large in scale and reflects dark, troubled emotions. Raphael Wallfisch gives a moving and eloquent account of the solo part: he plays with a rich quality of tone, and Vernon Handley provides a sympathetic accompaniment. Kenneth Leighton was still a student when Finzi took an interest in his work. Finzi was conductor of the Newbury String Players, and for this group Leighton wrote his suite *Veris gratia*, a melodious, lyrical work in four movements, inspired by Helen Waddell's translation of *Medieval Latin Lyrics*. The performance is all that could be desired, and is set in a high quality recording.

Finzi. ORCHESTRAL WORKS. [a]**Alan Hacker** (cl); **English String Orchestra/William Boughton.** Nimbus NI5101. Recorded in 1987.
Love's Labour's Lost — Suite, Op. 28. Clarinet Concerto in C minor, Op. 31[a]. Prelude in F minor, Op. 25. Romance in E flat major, Op. 11.

1h 5m DDD 12/88 

There are several other Finzi issues available which include the Clarinet Concerto. Alan Hacker, however, encompasses all his colleagues' virtues, providing special insights and revelling in the brilliant writing. He also adds something extra — an almost mystical realization of the music's poetic vision which is deeply moving. This is in spite of the fact that the string-playing sometimes lacks polish and precision. Finzi wrote incidental music for a BBC production of *Love's Labour's Lost* and expanded it for a later open-air production. It is tuneful, graceful music, but one cannot feel that the stage was Finzi's world. The disc is completed by two interesting early pieces for strings, the *Prelude* and *Romance*, both wholly characteristic of the composer and very well played.

Additional recommendation ...
Clarinet Concerto[a]. *Five bagatelles, Op. 23*[b]. ***Stanford.*** *Clarinet Concerto in A minor, Op. 80*[a]. *Three intermezzos, Op. 13*[b]. **Emma Johnson** (cl); [b]**Malcolm Martineau** (pf); [a]**Royal Philharmonic Orchestra/Sir Charles Groves.** ASV CDDCA787 — 1h 14m DDD 6/92

Finzi. CHORAL WORKS. **Finzi Singers/Paul Spicer** with [a]**Harry Bicket** (org). Chandos CHAN8936. Texts included. Recorded in 1990.
All this night, Op. 33. Let us now praise famous men, Op. 35[a]. Lo, the full, final sacrifice, Op. 26[a]. Magnificat, Op. 36[a]. Seven Part-songs, Op. 17. Though did'st delight my eyes, Op. 32. Three Anthems, Op. 27[a]. Three Short Elegies, Op. 5[a]. White-flowering days, Op. 37.

1h 19m DDD 9/91

Finzi is no composer to look to for the musical counterpart of a quick fix — and how he would have abhorred that expression. To the patient spirit of the listener who seeks music in which the fastidious limitation of its means is itself some guarantee of the depth of its purposes, he will always be rewarding. This is true of all the works collected here. Some, such as the first and last, *God is gone up* and *Lo, the full, final sacrifice*, are relatively well-known, which is not to say that they will necessarily prove the most satisfying. There are some fine shorter pieces including the unaccompanied *Seven Poems of Bridges* and the *Three Drummond Elegies* that delight as word-settings. "White-flowering days", to words by Edmund Blunden, comes from *A Garland for the Queen*, the Coronation gift of ten composers in 1953, none happier than this in catching the fresh hopefulness of the time. Best of all perhaps is the *Magnificat*, which also had its first British performance in that year. It is heard here in its original version with organ, beautifully played on this disc and providing a more spiritual association than is found in the orchestral accompaniment added later. The Finzi Singers are sensitive, assured and accurate; their tone is uniformly good, and they convey a sense of personal involvement in the music. The qualities of recorded sound and presentation are well up to the rest.

Further listening ...

Dies natalis[a]. *Coupled with* **Howells.** Hymnus Paradisi[b]. **[b]Heather Harper** (sop); **[a]Wilfred Brown, [b]Robert Tear** (tens); **[b]Bach Choir; [b]King's College Choir, Cambridge; [a]English Chamber Orchestra/Christopher Finzi; [b]New Philharmonia Orchestra/Sir David Willcocks.** EMI Studio CDM7 63372-2 (5/92).

Gioseffo-Hectore Fiocco

Italian/South Netherlands 1703-1741

G-H. Fiocco. Pièces de clavecin, Op. 1. **Ton Koopman** (hpd). Astrée Auvidis E7731.

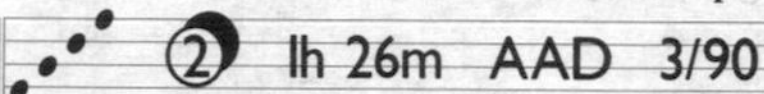

The Belgian-born Gioseffo-Hectore Fiocco was, in spite of his name, at least as francophile as italophile, at least to judge by these two harpsichord suites (published *c.*1730). The suites contain mixtures of French and italianate movements, as well as a few in the more *galant* style of *les goûts réünis*. Couperin's influence is evident in such external details as the titles, ornamentation — although a good proportion of that is the stylish invention of Ton Koopman — and the exquisite melancholy; but Fiocco also mastered the forms, textures and harmonic progressions epitomized by Couperin's music. And while Fiocco never surpassed the sublimity of his model, he did compose powerful and often sombre music worthy of wider circulation. Each suite is a microcosm of contemporary forms. The G major encompasses many contrasts of mood and style (*L'italiene* — surely a parody of Handel — is followed by the Couperinesque *La Françoise*). For all the French movements, Fiocco's first suite ends with a four-movement Italian sonata, in which Vivaldi might have taken pride. The D minor suite is less structured: there are dance movements graced with interesting technical challenges (especially in the Ramellian *Sauterelles*), three *rondeaux* and a lively, stylistically integrated finale (*La Frinqante*). Throughout, Koopman plays masterfully, interestingly and with unimpeachable taste. He has written the extremely informative booklet, revealing much about both the music and his approach to playing. The variety and aptness of his own ornamentation in both French and italianate movements can serve as a valuable guide: this is the crux of his performance which brings the music to life.

Friedrich von Flotow

German 1812-1883

Suggested listening ...

MARTHA. **Soloists; Bavarian Radio Chorus; Munich Radio Orchestra/Heinz Wallberg.** Eurodisc 352 878 (2/89).

Jean-Baptiste-Antoine Forqueray

French 1699-1782

Suggested listening ...

La Morangis ou La Plissay. *Coupled with* **Leclair.** Violin Sonatas — A minor, Op. 5 No. 7; A major, Op. 9 No. 4. *Coupled with* **Mondonville.** Violin Sonata in G major, Op. 3 No. 5.

Guillemain. Violin Sonata in A major, Op. 1 No. 4. *Harpsichord Solos* — ***Duphly.*** La de Redemond. La du Buq. **Simon Standage** (vn); **Lars Ulrik Mortensen** (hpd). Chandos CHAN0531 (6/93).

Antoine Forqueray

French 1671-1745

A. Forqueray. PIECES DE VIOLE. [a]**Jay Bernfield** (va da gamba); **Skip Sempé** (hpd). Deutsche Harmonia Mundi RD77262. Recorded in 1991.
Allemande La Laborde[a]. La Cottin. La Portugaise[a]. La Forqueray. La Régente[a]. La Marella. Sarabande La d'Aubonne. La Ferrand[a]. La Couperin. Chaconne La Buisson[a]. Le Leclair. La Rameau. Jupiter[a].

50m DDD 5/92

Antoine Forqueray was among the most gifted bass viol players at Louis XIV's court. His son, Jean-Baptiste-Antoine assisted him in the editing of his music and, following Antoine's death, brought out an anthology in his father's name. The collection, published in 1747, was presented in two versions, one for bass viol and continuo, the other for solo harpsichord. It is from this anthology that Skip Sempé and Jay Bernfield have compiled their attractive programme which includes pieces both for bass viola and continuo and for solo harpsichord. As with so much French instrumental music of this period the indigenous style is coloured by Italian influences and the resulting subtle interplay and juxtaposition of the two exercise lively play on our imagination. Both players are fluently versed in the particularities of French baroque style and their programme has been constructed in a manner which effectively reveals the varied colours and contrasting gestures of the music. Among the solo harpsichord pieces are delightful tributes to three of Forqueray's greatest contemporaries, Couperin, Rameau and Leclair. Outstanding among the bass viol items, perhaps, is the sensuous *La Régente*.

Additional recommendation ...
La Régente; La Carillon de Passy. ***J-B. Forqueray.*** *La Angrave. La Morangis ou la Plissay.* ***Couperin:*** *Troisième livre de clavecin — La Superbe, ou la Forqueray.* ***Duphly:*** *Pièces de clavecin — La Forqueray.* **Gustav Leonhardt** (hpd). Sony Classical Vivarte SK48080 — lh lm DDD 10/92

John Foulds

British 1880-1939

NEW REVIEW

Foulds. Dynamic Triptych, Op. 88.
Vaughan Williams. Piano Concerto in C major. **Howard Shelley** (pf); **Royal Philharmonic Orchestra/Vernon Handley.** Lyrita SRCD211. From SRCS130 (7/84).

57m DDD 3/93

An outstandingly fine Lyrita issue of two *concertante* masterpieces of twentieth-century English music, of which one is all too rarely heard, and the other — Foulds's *Dynamic Triptych* — is receiving only its second performance in 50 years. The Vaughan Williams Piano Concerto is better known — and more frequently heard — in its 1946 version for two pianos and orchestra, arranged by the composer and Joseph Cooper. Here, however, we are given the opportunity of hearing it in its original glory with the fearsomely difficult solo piano part battling it out with the exceptionally large and colourful orchestral forces. The concerto was much admired by Bartók, perhaps on account of the highly percussive and angular rhythmical features of its outer movements, though these are splendidly contrasted with the rapt and sustained central *Romanza* movement, that was described by its dedicatee, Harriet Cohen, as possessing "ancient and hieratic quality". As such the concerto, with its blend of dynamic vigour and pastoral rhapsody, can be seen as the cement binding the seemingly disparate worlds of the Fourth and Fifth Symphonies. John Foulds's *Dynamic Triptych* shares the boldness of design and unquenchable energy and vitality of the VW concerto, and must surely be reckoned as one of the unsung masterpieces of its period. As one of the more innovative British composers of his generation he was quick to adopt some of the more experimental techniques emerging from Europe, and these, together with his interest in Indian rhythms and harmony, can be heard in the arresting quarter-tone glissandos found in the central movement, and in the dithyrambic rhythmic impetus of the finale. The performances from both Howard Shelley and Vernon Handley are astoundingly fine, and the recording falls firmly into the demonstration bracket.

Jean Françaix

French 1912-

Suggested listening ...

String Trio in C major. *Coupled with* ***Castelnuovo-Tedesco.*** Violin Concerto No. 2, "I profeti"; ***Ferguson.*** Violin Sonata No. 1, Op. 2; ***K. Khachaturian.*** Violin Sonata in G minor, Op. 1. **Jascha Heifetz** (vn); **Joseph de Pasquale** (va); **Gregor Piatigorsky** (vc); **Lilian Steuber** (pf); **Los Angeles Philharmonic Orchestra/Alfred Wallenstein.** RCA Victor Gold Seal GD87872 (9/90).

Alberto Franchetti

Italian 1860-1942

NEW REVIEW

Franchetti. CRISTOFORO COLOMBO. **Renato Bruson** (bar) Cristoforo Colombo; **Roberto Scandiuzzi** (bass) Don Roldano Ximenes; **Rosella Ragatzu** (sop) Isabella, Iguamota; **Marco Berti** (ten) Don Fernan Guevara; **Gisella Pasino** (mez) Anacoana; **Vicente Ombuena** (ten) Matheos; **Andrea Ulbrich** (contr) Yanika; **Enrico Turco** (bass) Bobadilla; **Pierre Lefebre** (ten) Diaz; **Fabio Previati** (bar) Marguerite; **Dalibor Jenis** (bar) Old man; **Hungarian Radio Chorus; Frankfurt Radio Symphony Orchestra/Marcello Viotti.** Koch Schwann 310302. Notes, text and translation included. Recorded in 1991.

③ 2h 39m DDD 7/92 

We owe the opera itself and the present opportunity of hearing it (probably for the first time as far as most of us are concerned) to the taste for centenaries. In 1892 Genoa honoured the memory of its most famous son by commissioning an opera, which duly had its première at the Teatro Carlo Felice and for a while enjoyed considerable success. In 1895, for a performance at La Scala, the original third and fourth Acts were merged, with some abridgement, and this is the version heard in this recording which was timed for the 1992 centenary. Only Act 2 is set in the year of discovery. Act I takes place in Salamanca where five years earlier Columbus gained the Queen's support for his projected voyage. Act 3 covers the finding of gold in 1503 and ends with Columbus's recall to Spain, and the Epilogue has his death at Medina del Campo. Inevitably the construction is episodic; and, as the title-role is written for baritone, a certain ingenuity of contrivance is involved in making work for the tenor and providing the opera with a love-story. Alberto Franchetti was trained in Germany and there is a certain Germanic thoroughness about his score, which could sometimes do with a little more of the native flair for melody. But it has moments of distinction throughout, and Act 2 is genuinely inspired. This happens at sea and comes to a double climax with open mutiny and the sighting of land: its chorus work and ensembles capture the terror of the unknown and eventually the exaltation of deliverance. This alone makes the opera well worth hearing. Renato Bruson as Columbus sings with rich tone, though he is not the most imaginative of artists and his voice is somewhat past its best. The cast forms a reliable company, Viotti conducts a convincing performance and the recorded sound is appropriately ample and generous.

Cesar Franck

Belgian/French 1822-1890

Franck. Symphony in D minor.
d'Indy. Symphonie sur un chant montagnard français, Op. 25[a]. [a]**Jean-Yves Thibaudet** (pf); **Montreal Symphony Orchestra/Charles Dutoit.** Decca 430 278-2DH. Recorded in 1989.

lh 7m DDD 1/92 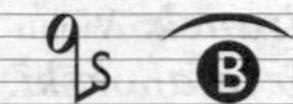

These two French masterpieces of the 1880s complement each other perfectly. The Franck, drawing its inspiration from the other side of the Alps, is very much in the Austro-German symphonic tradition. Its language calls to mind the vaulted splendours and gothic interiors of many a Bruckner Symphony. D'Indy's Symphony, in reality more of a piano concerto, is based on a folk-song he heard whilst holidaying in the Cévennes mountains. Definitely outdoors music this, and far more recognizably French; indeed, with its echoes of Berlioz to its pre-echoes of Debussy and even 'Les Six', it occupies a central position in a century of French music. Dutoit's elegant, flowing way with the Franck (marvellously refined *espressivo* playing from the Montreal violins, and shining, incisive brass) is ideal for those who shy away from the Brucknerian monumentalism of the work; and Jean-Yves Thibaudet's eloquent solo playing in the d'Indy is matched by exquisitely drawn instrumental solos from within the orchestra. Decca's spacious Montreal sound, too, proves just as apt for the organ-like timbres of the Franck, as for the fresh air and wide horizons of the d'Indy.

Additional recommendations ...
Symphony in D minor[a]. ***Berlioz.*** *Béatrice et Bénédict — Overture*[b]. ***d'Indy.*** *Symphonie sur un chant montagnard français*[c]. [c]**Nicole Henriot-Schweitzer** (pf); [bc]**Boston Symphony Orchestra/Charles Munch;** [a]**Chicago Symphony Orchestra/Pierre Monteux.** RCA Victor Papillon GD86805 — lh 12m ADD 3/89 B
Symphony in D minor. Symphonic Variations[a]. [a]**Rudolf Firkušný** (pf); **Royal Philharmonic Orchestra/Claus Peter Flor.** RCA Victor Red Seal RD60146 — lh DDD 8/90 B
Symphony in D minor. ***Lalo.*** Symphony in G minor. **French Radio National Orchestra/Sir Thomas Beecham.** EMI CDM7 63396-2 — lh 6m ADD 9/92 B
Symphony in D minor. Les Eolides. **Concertgebouw Orchestra/Wilhelm van Otterloo.** Pickwick IMP Collectors IMPX9037 — 46m ADD B

Franck. Symphonic Variations, Op. 46[b]
Grieg. Piano Concerto in A minor, Op. 16[a].
Schumann. Piano Concerto in A minor, Op. 54[c]. [ab]**Sir Clifford Curzon,** [c]**Friedrich Gulda** (pfs); [a]**London Symphony Orchestra/Øivin Fjeldstad;** [b]**London Philharmonic Orchestra/Sir Adrian Boult;** [c]**Vienna Philharmonic Orchestra/Volkmar Andreae.** Decca Headline Classics 433 628 2DSP. Item marked [a] from LW5350 (7/59), [b] SXL2173 (1/60), [c] LXT5280 (5/57).

lh 16m ADD 1/92 

Since the advent of the LP the Grieg and Schumann concertos have been ideally paired and here we have Sir Clifford Curzon's classic account of the Grieg from 1959 where he is most sympathetically and idiomatically accompanied by Øivin Fjeldstad and the London Symphony Orchestra. Curzon was at his finest in romantic piano concertos, and his playing achieves an exceptional balance between poetry and strength. This is a performance which clearly stakes a claim for the concerto as a work of genius. These same characteristics are also to the fore in the recording of the Franck *Symphonic Variations*, this time with Sir Adrian Boult conducting. This is probably the finest performance of this popular work on CD: imaginative and romantic with a perfect sense of style, and excellent rapport between conductor and soloist. As if these riches were not enough, and at bargain price, the Decca CD is rounded off with another extremely masterly reading of the Schumann Concerto by Friedrich Gulda, this time dating from 1956 and with Volkmar Andreae leading the Vienna Philharmonic. This reading is absolutely in the centre of the authentic romantic style: it is both extremely personal and authoritative. Decca's recorded sound for all three performances is more than acceptable, with true piano tone throughout. This is probably one of the finest bargain issues currently available.

Additional recommendation …
Symphonic Variations[a]. *Violin Sonata in A major (trans. Delsart)*[b]. *Piano Quintet in F minor*[c]. **Pascal Rogé** (pf); [c]**Richard Friedman, Steven Smith** (vns); [c]**Christopher Wellington** (va); [a]**London Festival Orchestra/Ross Pople** ([bc]vc). ASV CDDCA769 — 1h 19m DDD 11/91 B

Franck. Violin Sonata in A major.
Szymanowski. Mythes, Op. 30. King Roger (trans. Kochański). Kurpian Song (trans. Kochanski). **Kaja Danczowska** (vn); **Krystian Zimerman** (pf). DG Galleria 431 469-2GGA. From 2531 330 (6/81). Recorded in 1980.

58m ADD 8/91

Franck's Sonata, with its yearning romantic nature, makes a good foil for Szymanowski's rather wild, rhapsodic invention. Kaja Danczowska, a pupil of Eugenia Uminska and David Oistrakh, shows a fine technique, a beautiful tone-quality, and plenty of temperament on this very well-recorded disc. In the Franck Zimerman is a mite too reticent, though he plays beautifully and impeccably, but Danczowska captures Franck's changing moods perfectly and brings a not at all inappropriate Polish fervour to the three quicker movements. The third movement, *Recitativo-Fantasia,* is finely characterized, too, with its more thoughtful, inward episodes sympathetically explored. The best known of Szymanowski's three shortish *Mythes* is the first, "La fontaine d'Arethuse", which has often been played on its own. It has an exotic, other worldly beauty which is very well realized by Danczowska, with Zimerman here a more positive, purposeful partner. The second piece, "Narcisse", inhabits a similar world, but "Dryades et Pan" is quite daring for 1915, with its use of quarter-tones. These pieces, and the effective transcriptions, are vividly brought to life by Szymanowski's two compatriots.

Additional recommendation …
Violin Sonata. **Brahms.** *Horn Trio in E flat major, Op. 40*[a]. **Itzhak Perlman** (vn); [a]**Barry Tuckwell** (hn); **Vladimir Ashkenazy** (pf). Decca 414 128-2DH — 56m AAD 4/85

Franck. ORGAN WORKS. **Jean Guillou.** Dorian DOR90135. Played on the organ of St Eustache, Paris.
Cantabile in B major. Chorales — No. 1 in E major; No. 2 in B minor; No. 3 in A minor. Fantaisie in A major. Fantaisie in C major. Final in B flat major. Grande Pièce Symphonique. Pastorale in E major. Pièce Héroïque in B minor. Prélude, Fugue et Variation. Prière in C sharp minor.

2 2h 27m 6/90 

Franck. ORGAN WORKS. **Michael Murray.** Telarc CD80234. Played on the Cavaillé-Coll organ of Saint Sernin Basilica, Toulouse. Recorded in 1989.
Fantaisie in A major. Cantabile in B major. Pièce Héroïque in B minor. Fantaisie in C major. Grande Pièce Symphonique. Prélude, Fugue et variation. Pastorale. Prière in C sharp minor. Final in B flat major. Chorales — No. 1 in E major; No. 2 in B minor; No. 3 in A minor.

2 2h 29m DDD 7/90  

Although Franck wrote a great many small pieces for organ it was with these 12 (the 'masterworks' as the Telarc disc styles them) that he established an organ music tradition which French composers to this day have followed. Jean Guillou is certainly in that tradition. He is a virtuoso organist and gifted improviser (as was Franck) and his own organ music is in the large, colourful, symphonic mould effectively created by Franck. As part of that living tradition Guillou obviously doesn't feel constrained by what Franck actually wrote down. He modifies the original almost to the point of eccentricity: much of what you hear here bears little relation to the published text. But if you are willing to listen with an open mind and don't believe that what the composer wrote has to be considered sacrosanct you will be rewarded with some breathtaking virtuosity and a spectacular recorded sound.

Michael Murray, on the other hand, is entirely respectful of tradition. There is about his performances something akin to reverence. He is completely faithful to the finest detail of the score, and the authenticity of these performances is underlined by being recorded on an instrument contemporaneous (just) with Franck and still in virtually unaltered shape; this was the kind of organ sound that inspired Franck to write these pieces. Authentic and respectful as they are, Murray's performances are beautifully played. Like most American organists he seems to have a natural gift for direct communication; a gift wholeheartedly supported by Telarc's exceptionally fine recording.

Franck. Prélude choral et fugue (1884).
Liszt. PIANO WORKS. **Murray Perahia** (pf). Sony Classical SK47180. Recorded 1990-91. Mephisto Waltz No. 1, S514. Années de pèlerinage, première année, S160, "Suisse"— Aubord d'une source; deuxième année, S161, "Italie" — Sonetto 104 del Petrarca. Two Concert Studies, S145. Rhapsodie espagnole, S254.

1h DDD 10/91

Having surprised many of his admirers by launching the second half of his earlier, much-praised "Aldeburgh Recital" (reviewed in the "Collections" section) with a *Hungarian Rhapsody* by Liszt, Murray Perahia now leaves us in no doubt that his encounter with this composer was no mere passing flirtation in the course of an ever-widening exploration of the romantic repertory. 'Aristocratic' is the adjective that first comes to mind in describing his approach. It is Liszt playing of quite exceptional finesse, ravishing in pellucid sonority, delicately glistening (like frost on every individual blade of grass in early morning winter sunshine) in sleight-of-hand, yet not lacking strength in the bolder climaxes of a bravura piece such as the concluding *Rhapsodie espagnole*. Only in the *Mephisto Waltz* is there just a slight suspicion of caution on the dance-floor and chasteness in the "lascivious, caressing dreams of love". Franck's *Prélude choral et fugue* in its turn has a simplicity and dignity, free of all arrogance or bluster very much Perahia's own. Predictably his unfailing textural clarity is a major asset — not least in the contrapuntal cunning of the fugue. Recorded mainly at The Maltings, Snape, but in part at the Royce Hall in Los Angeles, the sound *per se* is first-class throughout.

Franck. Les Béatitudes. **Diana Montague, Ingeborg Danz** (mezzos); **Cornelia Kallisch** (contr); **Keith Lewis, Scot Weir** (tens); **Gilles Cachemaille** (bar); **John Cheek, Juan Vasle, Reinhard Hagen** (basses); **Stuttgart Gächinger Kantorei and Radio Symphony Orchestra/Helmuth Rilling.** Hänssler 98 964. Text and translation included. Recorded in 1990.

② 2h 11m DDD 7/91 

Without going as far as some of Franck's disciples d'Indy, for example, called *Les Béatitudes* "the greatest work for a long time in the development of the art" — it has to be conceded that sections of the work, such as parts four and five, contain music of great beauty, and that the rich texture and extremely effective orchestration in all of it are impressive. It was intended not as a narrative oratorio in the Handel-Haydn-Mendelssohn tradition but as a series of contemplative devotional studies; and stylistically it shows both an affinity to the Liszt-Wagner school and an anticipation of the Impressionists. The predominantly slow tempos of the Prologue and eight Beatitudes, unenterprising rhythmic invention and the structural uniformity of the sections (each consisting of high-toned but pedestrian moralistic verse followed by the Biblical quotation) flaw the impact of the oratorio as an entity; but this is a case of the parts being greater than the whole. Helmuth Rilling (if over-inclined to exaggerate ritardandos) here delivers a very fine performance, certainly superior to the two current previous recordings, with an excellent chorus and orchestra and some first-rate soloists: radiant singing from Diana Montague and incisively menacing tone from John Cheek as the voice of Satan. Good presentation material and good recording.

Further listening ...

Piano Concerto No. 2 in B minor, Op. 11. Variations brillantes sur la ronde favorite de Gustave III, Op. 8. **Jean-Claude Vanden Eynden** (pf); **RTBF New Symphony Orchestra/Edgar Doneux.** Koch Schwann Musica Mundi 311 111G1 (3/90).

Le Chasseur maudit. Les Eolides. Psyché — symphonic poem. **Basle Symphony Orchestra/Armin Jordan.** Erato 2292-45552-2 (7/86).

Le Chasseur maudit. Rédemption — Morceau symphonique. Nocturne. Coupled with ***Berlioz.*** Roméo et Juliette[a]. [a]**Yvonne Minton, Christa Ludwig** (mezs); [a]**Francisco Araiza** (ten); [a]**Jules Bastin** (bass); [a]**Orchestre de Paris Chorus; Orchestre de Paris/Daniel Barenboim.** DG Galleria 437 244-2GGA2 (1/93).

Hugo Friedhofer

American 1902-1981

Suggested listening ...

The Young Lions; This Earth is Mine — *Original film soundtracks.* Varèse Sarabande VSD2-5403.

Johann Jacob Froberger

German 1616-1667

Suggested listening ...

Harpsichord Suites — I in E minor; II in A minor; III in G minor; IV; V in D major; VI in C major. Lamentation sur la mort sa Majesté Impérial, Ferdinand III for harpsichord. **Kenneth Gilbert** (hpd). Archiv Produktion 437 080-2AT (1/93).

Walter Frye

British fl. c.1450-1475

Suggested listening ...

Missa "Flos Regalis". Trinitatis dies. Salve virgo mater pya. O florens rosa. Ave regina celorum (two settings). Sospitati dedit. Tout a par moy. So ys emprentid. Myn hertis lust. Alas, alas is my chief song. **The Hilliard Ensemble.** ECM New Series 437 684-2 (6/93).

Robert Fuchs

German 1847-1927

NEW REVIEW

Fuchs. Clarinet Quintet in E flat major, Op. 102.
Romberg. Quintet in E flat major, Op. 57[a].
Stanford. Two Fantasy Pieces. **Thea King** (cl); **Britten Quartet** (Peter Manning, vn; Keith Pascoe, vn/[a]va; Peter Lale, va; Andrew Shulman, vc). Hyperion CDA66479. Recorded in 1991.

lh 20m DDD 7/92

Though the clarinet is a beautiful instrument that was admired by several composers from Mozart onwards, its solo repertory is small and we cannot afford to neglect any part of it, particularly as there are many fine players, among whom Thea King stands out as one of the finest. None of these three composers can claim to be among the musical greats, but each wrote sympathetically for the instrument and this sensitively played and well recorded disc makes for pleasing listening. It should win friends for Andreas Romberg (a contemporary of Beethoven and not the Romberg who composed *The Desert Song*), and the turn-of-the-century composers Robert

Fuchs and Sir Charles Villiers Stanford — not least if we also gratefully remember two men for teaching, between them, Mahler, Sibelius, Vaughan Williams and Holst. Romberg's Quintet is fluent and unfailingly agreeable, if not more than that: listening to it, and not least the outer sections of the minuet second movement (the trio is more personal), one is reminded of Mozart in a genial yet elegant mood, and Romberg surely knew that composer's Clarinet Quintet and Concerto. Fuchs's work, written in 1917 when he was 70 and first performed at a concert to mark the occasion, is romantic in an almost Schubertian way although it was composed after the radical works of Stravinsky and Schoenberg had shaken the musical world. But we need not disagree with Brahms, who once said, "Fuchs is a splendid musician: all's so refined, skilled and delightfully inventive that we can always enjoy what we hear". The Two *Fantasy Pieces* by Stanford have similar civilized qualities plus occasional attractive touches of Irishness and complete a valuable and very enjoyable programme.

NEW REVIEW

Fuchs. Cello Sonatas — No. 1 in D minor, Op. 29; No. 2 in E flat minor, Op. 83. Fantasiestücke, Op. 78. **Nancy Green** (vc); **Caroline Palmer** (pf). Biddulph LAW005. Recorded in 1990.

1h 13m DDD 4/93

This is a most important release, as it brings to the CD catalogue music by the little-known Viennese composer and teacher Robert Fuchs. Born in 1847, Fuchs was a close friend of Brahms, and a most distinguished presence at the Vienna Conservatoire. Among his pupils were Wolf, Mahler, Sibelius and Zemlinsky. His stature as a teacher of influence may well have overshadowed his achievements as a composer, and so this disc helps to redress the balance. The two cello sonatas are highly melodic, with plenty of lyrical writing for the cello's tenor register, and with rich but never overwhelming piano accompaniments. Although there is a period of 27 years between the composition of the two (No. 1 was written in 1881, No. 2 in 1908), the style of both is close to the world of Brahms and the late nineteenth century. This fidelity to the best of German nineteenth-century music is even more apparent in the seven fantasy pieces, which look strongly backwards to Schumann. The individual pieces in this set do not carry the emotional weight found in the sonatas, but are still most engaging. The performances of these works by the American cellist Nancy Green and English pianist Caroline Palmer are excellent. Cello tone throughout is rich without being cloying and the important piano parts are played with a fine sense of phrasing and balance. Biddulph's recording is extremely natural, with good balance, confirming this as an important issue for lovers of romantic cello music.

Giovanni Gabrieli

Italian c.1553/6-1612

Suggested listening ...

Canzonas and Sonatas — Sonata pian e forte; Sonata XVIII a 14; Canzon XVII a 12; Sonata XXI con tre violini; Sonata XX a 22; Canzon in echo duodecimi toni a 10. *Motets* — Dulcis Jesu; Jubilate Deo II a 8; O Jesu mi dulcissime II a 8. Hic est filius Dei; Miserere mei, Deus a 4; Gloria Patri a 8; Audite principes. **Taverner Consort, Choir and Players/Andrew Parrott.** EMI Reflexe CDC7 54265-2 (2/92).

Intonatione del noni toni. In ecclesiis. Canzon VIII a 8. Fuga del noni toni. Magnificat a 14. *Coupled with* ***Monteverdi.*** Adoramus te, Christe. Exuta, filia Sion (with Emily Van Evera, sop). Currite populi (Jeffrey Thomas, ten). Christe, adoramus te; ***Grandi.*** O quam tu pulchra es (Jeffrey Thomas); ***Castello.*** Sonata secunda; ***Legrenzi.*** Sonata da chiesa, Op. 8 No. 8, "La Bevilaqua"; ***Lotti.*** Crucifixus a 6. Crucifixus a 10; ***Vivaldi.*** Clarae stellae, RV625 (Randi Stene, contr). **Taverner Consort, Choir and Players/Andrew Parrott.** EMI Reflexe CDC7 54117-2 (8/91).

Niels Gade

Danish 1817-1890

NEW REVIEW

Gade. Elf-shot, Op. 30[a]. Echoes from Ossian, Op. 1[b]. Five Songs, Op. 13[c]. [a]**Eve Johansson** (sop); [a]**Anne Gjevang** (mez); [a]**Poul Elming** (ten); [a]**Danish National Radio Choir;** [c]**Danish National Radio Chamber Choir/Stefan Parkman;** [ab]**Danish National Radio Symphony Orchestra/Dmitri Kitaienko.** Chandos CHAN9075. Texts and translations included. Recorded 1991-92.

1h 17m DDD 11/92

Gade was Denmark's leading nineteenth-century composer and *Elverskud*, variously translated as *The Fairy Spell, The Elf-King's Daughter* or, as on this CD, *Elf-shot* is generally thought to be his finest work. It is much indebted to Mendelssohn's *Die erste Walpurgisnacht* and its text is based on a medieval Danish ballad, the story of Lord Oluf, enticed to his death by the elfins on his wedding night. In *A Short History of Scandinavian Music* (Faber, 1963), John Horton went so far as to say that it "contains some of the most beautiful orchestral writing of the romantic period in any country", and it is difficult not to succumb to its charm and grace, particularly the opening of the second half which evokes the moonlit world of the Fairy Hill. Like Mendelssohn, Gade rarely betrays any hint of tragedy; the symphonies are equally sunny and equable, and the same holds true of *Elf-shot,* which comes from the year after the Fifth Symphony (for piano and orchestra). The soloists are excellent even if Anne Gjevang's vibrato may be just a little too wide for some tastes; the orchestral playing under Dmitri Kitaienko is highly responsive and sympathetic. This CD comes with Gade's very first opus, the overture *Echoes from Ossian* which together with the First Symphony brought him to the attention of Mendelssohn. It has a particularly appealing second subject. The Five Songs, Op. 13, are also delightful. They are beautifully fashioned and there is a pleasing freshness and grace that is absolutely captivating.

Further listening ...

Symphonies — No. 1 in C minor, Op. 5; No. 8 in B minor, Op. 47. **Stockholm Sinfonietta/Neeme Järvi.** BIS CD339 (11/87).

Symphonies — No. 2 in E major, Op. 10; No. 7 in F major, Op. 45. **Stockholm Sinfonietta/Neeme Järvi.** BIS CD355 (12/87).

Symphonies — No. 3 in A minor, Op. 15; No. 4 in B flat major, Op. 20. **Stockholm Sinfonietta/Neeme Järvi.** BIS CD338 (7/87).

Symphonies — No. 5 in D minor, Op. 25[a]; No. 6 in G minor, Op. 32. [a]**Roland Pöntinen** (pf); **Stockholm Sinfonietta/Neeme Järvi.** BIS CD356 (12/87).

Phillipe Gaubert

French 1879-1941

Gaubert. COMPLETE WORKS FOR FLUTE AND PIANO. **Susan Milan** (fl); **Ian Brown** (pf). Chandos CHAN8981/2. Items marked [a] from CHAN8609 (11/88), recorded in 1988, others recorded in 1991.

Sonata. Madrigal. Deux esquisses. Fantaisie[a]. Romance (1908). Flute Sonatas — No. 2; No. 3. Sicilienne. Berceuse. Suite. Nocturne et Allegro scherzando[a]. Romance (1905). Sonatine. Sur l'eau. Ballade.

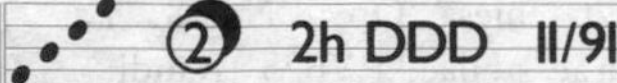

This integral recording of the complete works for flute and piano by Philippe Gaubert commemorates the fiftieth anniversary of the death of one of the seminal figures in the history of modern flute playing. Although still revered as co-author (with Paul Taffanel) of a famous tutorial for the instrument, the majority of Gaubert's enchanting compositions will be largely unfamiliar. Fortunately, his music could hardly find more convincing advocacy than in the hands of Susan Milan and Ian Brown. Listening to these works, one cannot avoid wondering about the remainder of Gaubert's large output, which included operas, ballet scores, a symphony, several concertos, and much chamber music, all of which now seems to be forgotten. Gaubert's three sonatas are lithe, lyrical and affable, although essentially traditional in concept, but the real joys of this set are the various salon miniatures, ranging from the *Madrigal* of 1908 to such delights as *Sur l'eau* and the delectable *Sicilienne* and *Berceuse*. The *Suite* of 1921 is thoughtfully and tastefully cast, with the final "Scherzo-Valse" being particularly memorable. The playing is sparkling and witty, with the mellifluous tone of Susan Milan a lasting pleasure throughout. She is ably supported by the pianist, Ian Brown, and the recordings are beyond criticism. Strongly recommended.

John Gay

British 1685-1732

Suggested listening ...

THE BEGGAR'S OPERA. **Soloists; London Voices; National Philharmonic Orchestra/Richard Bonynge.** Decca 430 066-2DH2 (5/91).

Francesco Geminiani

Italian 1687-1762

NEW REVIEW

Geminiani. Concerti grossi, Op. 2. Concerti grossi after Corelli's Op. 5 — No. 3 in C major; No. 5 in G minor. **Tafelmusik/Jeanne Lamon.** Sony Classical Vivarte SK48043. Recorded in 1990.
Op. 2 — No. 1 in C minor; No. 2 in C minor; No. 3 in D minor; No. 4 in D major; No. 5 in D minor; No. 6 in A major.

59m DDD II/92 

Imagine the scene. The year is 1715 and Francesco Geminiani is playing his violin for King George I, accompanied on the harpsichord by none other than Handel. But Geminiani had not always enjoyed the absolute favour of his colleagues; it is said that in Italy complaints were voiced regarding his excessive use of rubato — a very unexpected phenomenon, especially when seen in the light of our own attitudes to period performance. So, he left his workplace in Naples (where he was concertmaster), came to London — his new 'base', so to speak — and additionally went on to work in Dublin and Paris. The individual works in Geminiani's concerto-style Op. 2 set are forged in the *sonata da chiesa* (slow-fast-slow-fast) format and contain much beautiful music, especially where, in chordal passages, there is an overlapping of string lines. The faster movements set out on dancing feet — an aspect of the music that Tafelmusik indulges with obvious relish — and the slower ones have a mildly sensuous character. Nowhere, however, will you find as much as a hint of the wayward rubato that Geminiani's colleagues complained of! Similar positive qualities apply to the performances of the two Corelli violin sonata transcriptions, the second of which is particularly appealing. The recordings, too, are warm and immediate, with plenty of space around them and impressive definition.

NEW REVIEW

Geminiani. Concerti grossi, Op. 3. **Bern Camerata/Thomas Füri.** Novalis 150 083-2. Recorded in 1991.

No. 1 in D major; No. 2 in G minor; No. 3 in E minor; No. 4 in D minor; No. 5 in B flat major; No. 6 in E minor.

52m DDD 1/93

Geminiani's six Concertos, Op. 3, in Dr Burney's words "established his character, and placed him at the head of all the masters then living" — no small tribute to a composer working at a time when Vivaldi and Handel were still around. The earliest version of Geminiani's Op. 3 appeared in 1733 but between then and 1755 or thereabouts the composer made substantial revisions, and it is the later text which has been chosen by Camerata Bern. This talented ensemble of modern instrumentalists respond stylishly and with infectious enthusiasm to these concertos. Geminiani's art was a versatile one — harmonically bold on occasion, and invariably entertaining; there is an easy blend of virtuosity with simpler gestures which are contained, above all in the many short but beautifully modulating slow movements. A distinctive feature present in all of them is his solo or *concertino* group which, unlike those of Corelli or Handel, for instance, includes a viola in addition to the customary trio of two violins and cello. Strong but sensitive playing throughout which reveals many of the subtleties of Geminiani's music. The recording is clear and ideally resonant.

Key to Symbols

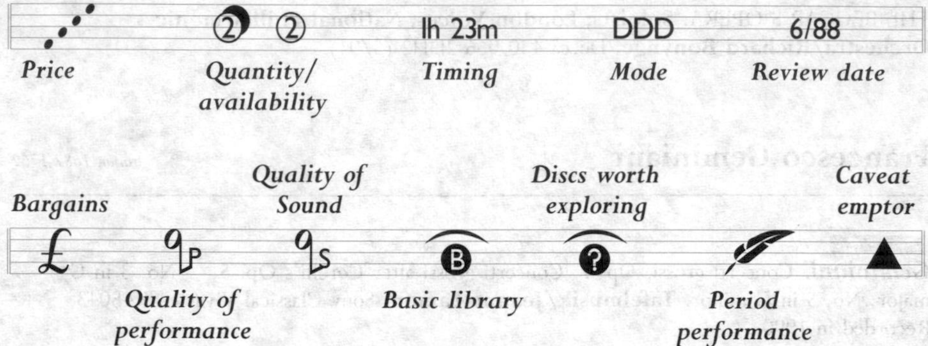

Roberto Gerhard

Spanish/British 1896-1970

NEW REVIEW

Gerhard. Don Quixote. Pedrelliana (En memoria). Albada, Interludi i Dansa. **Tenerife Symphony Orchestra/Victor Pablo Pérez.** Auvidis Valois V4660. Recorded in 1991.

1h 5m DDD 10/92

Roberto Gerhard's music combines the spicy tang of Manuel de Falla with the atmosphere and textural leanness of Jean Sibelius. In fact, Gerhard's powerful homage to the great Catalan composer and musicologist Felipe Pedrell — *Pedrelliana* — sounds, at least in its opening minutes, like a Spanish relation of Sibelius's *Lemminkaïnen*. A familiar nobility is there; the string accompaniments, too, undulate with Sibelian intensity, while Gerhard's woodwind and brass writing has a similar power. The combination of Latin heat and a northern sense of distance is both irresistible and powerful, while the music itself, always beautifully scored and full of fanciful gesture, has a strong thematic profile. *Don Quixote* started life in 1940 as a two-act ballet score; it then re-emerged as an accompaniment for Eric Linklater's radio dramatization of Cervantes's novel, and finally flowered in the version recorded on this superb CD, which was first presented at Covent Garden in 1950 (with Robert Helpmann as Don Quixote and Margot Fonteyn as Dulcinea-Aldonza). It's a marvellous score, full of memorable episodes, including the trance-like cor anglais theme depicting Dulcinea (in track 1) and the music for Lady Belerma and her retinue on track 5 — a catchy dance that, given proper exposure, could easily become immensely popular. The other work on this CD, *Albada, Interludi i Dansa*, was composed in 1937 for a BBC broadcast, reflecting the recent Spanish Civil War. It too is extremely attractive, but *Don Quixote* will surely prove the disc's most durable feature: it is a work that should be admitted to the concert repertory without delay. Performances and recordings are beyond reproach.

Further listening ...

Alegrías. *Coupled with* **Falla.** Noches en los jardins de España[a]; ***E. Halffter.*** Rapsodia portuguesa[a]. [a]**Guillermo Gonzalez** (pf); **Tenerife Symphony Orchestra/Victor Pablo Pérez.** Etcetera KTC1095 (7/92). *Reviewed under Falla; refer to the Index to Reviews.*

Sir Edward German

British 1862-1936

NEW REVIEW

German. ORCHESTRAL WORKS. **Bratislava Radio Symphony Orchestra/Adrian Leaper.** Marco Polo British Light Music 8 223419. Recorded in 1991.
Nell Gwyn — Overture; Country Dance; Pastoral Dance; Merry-maker's Dance; Gipsy Suite. Henry VIII — Shepherds's Dance; Torch Dance; Morris Dance. The Conqueror — Berceuse. Romeo and Juliet — Pavane; Nocturne; Pastorale. Tom Jones — Waltz Song (arr. Tomlinson). Merrie England — Hornpipe; Minuet; Rustic Dance; Jig.

lh 7m DDD 6/93

It seems somewhat shameful that a Hong Kong company and Slovak orchestra should bring us the first significant modern CD collection of music by such a distinctively British composer. Edward German is known as the successor of Sullivan in scores such as *Merrie England* and *Tom Jones*, but also for what have been disparagingly described as his "Olde Englishe Tea Shoppe" orchestral works. Put another way, he wrote some charming and appealing English dances, and the familiar examples from *Nell Gwyn*, *Henry VIII* and *Merrie England* are happily all included here. In addition there is an orchestral arrangement of the swirling waltz song from *Tom Jones*, together with some less familiar items. These include the charming *Gipsy Suite* and the less often heard *Romeo and Juliet* Suite, which is particularly well worth rescuing. The quality of orchestral playing is excellent throughout, with some secure but leisurely playing in the "Pastoral Dance" of the *Nell Gwyn* Suite. On the other hand, the interpretations are just a little inclined to lack that instinctive feel for variations of tempo and dynamics that come naturally to the finest light music conductors, with a tendency to let the tempo flag. Overall, though, we should be thankful for an Edward German collection even half as good as this.

George Gershwin

American 1898-1937

NEW REVIEW

Gershwin. Piano Concerto in F major. Rhapsody in Blue. Second Rhapsody. **Howard Shelley** (pf); **Philharmonia Orchestra/Yan Pascal Tortelier.** Chandos CHAN9092. Recorded in 1992.

lh 4m DDD 3/93 

It is only in recent years that Gershwin's *Second Rhapsody* has emerged from the shadows to take its place beside the vastly successful earlier essay, *Rhapsody in Blue.* With hindsight it is difficult to see how such a likeably attractive, inventive piece should have languished in comparative obscurity for so long. It is probably a better work overall than the Piano Concerto, whose first movement is just a minute or two too long for the basic material used. The combination of a British pianist and orchestra with a French conductor in very American works may seem unpromising, but all concerned enter the fray with great skill and aplomb. It can't be every day that the Philharmonia plays this kind of repertoire, but its players seem to be enjoying themselves immensely, and there is a delicious feeling of spontaneity and exuberance throughout all three performances. Shelley plays with great freedom and brilliance, and with Tortelier in sympathetic support, he gives a particularly sensitive performance of the Piano Concerto's deeply-felt middle *Adagio* movement. The recording quality matches the performances in being fresh, immediate and very attractive to the ear.

Additional recommendations ...
Piano Concerto. Rhapsody in Blue[a]*. An American in Paris. Variations on "I got rhythm".* [a]**Earl Wild** (pf); **Boston Pops Orchestra/Arthur Fiedler.** RCA Papillon GD86519 — lh l0m ADD ll/87 £
Piano Concerto. **Ravel.** *Piano Concerto in G major.* **Bournemouth Symphony Orchestra/Andrew Litton** (pf). Virgin Classics VJ7 59693-2 — 57m DDD 9/90
Piano Concerto[a]*. Rhapsody in Blue. An American in Paris.* [a]**Joanna MacGregor** (pf); **London Symphony Orchestra/Carl Davis.** Collins Classics 1139-2 — lh 5m DDD ll/91

Gershwin. An American in Paris[a]. Rhapsody in Blue[b]. [a]**Columbia Symphony Orchestra;** [b]**New York Philharmonic Orchestra/Leonard Bernstein** (pf[a]). CBS Maestro CD42611. From Philips SABL160 (10/60).

35m ADD ll/90

Bernstein conducted and played the music of Gershwin with the same naturalness as he brought to his own music. Here, *An American in Paris* swings by with an instinctive sense of its origins in popular and film music; no stilted rhythms or four-squareness delay the work's progress, and where ripe schmaltz is wanted, ripe schmaltz is what we get, devoid of all embarrassment. *Rhapsody in Blue* is playful and teasing, constantly daring us to try to categorize its style, and then confounding our conclusions. Although the solo passages from individual players are beautifully taken, both orchestras pull together magnificently to capture the authentic flavour of Gershwin's idiom, and Bernstein pushes them to transcend the printed score. His own playing in the *Rhapsody* is tantalizingly unpredictable. The recording is clear and bright, perhaps a touch hard-edged, and a little of the richness of the original LP issue might have been preferred by some, especially as the editing is now made more obvious. The only major criticism would be of the stingy overall timing of the disc — but with these performances quality compensates.

Gershwin (arr. Russell Bennett). PORGY AND BESS — A Symphonic Picture.
Grofé. Grand Canyon Suite. **Detroit Symphony Orchestra/Antál Dorati**. Decca Ovation 430 712-2DM. From 410 110-2DH (5/84). Recorded in 1982.

lh DDD 8/9l

Antál Dorati was a major European conductor with a great interest in American music, particularly in his last years when he was associated with the Detroit Symphony Orchestra. His performances of Copland's music are richly enjoyable and this disc of works by Gershwin and Grofé is a worthy companion. *Porgy and Bess* is performed here in the well-known arrangement by Robert Russell Bennett. "Bess, you is my woman now" and "I got plenty o' nuthin'" appear in glitzy orchestral colours and Dorati and his orchestra revel in the colour and bring an idiomatic swing to Gershwin's distinctive melodic contours. The companion piece, Grofé's charming *Grand Canyon* Suite is also something of an American tone-poem, complete with clip-clopping mules and evocative dawns and dusks. The concluding cloudburst seems like a transatlantic answer to Richard Strauss's *Alpine* Symphony and Dorati brings a sense of structure and care for detail to the work. The recording is both full and fresh, reaching demonstration quality in the *Grand Canyon*.

Gershwin (arr. Wild). PIANO TRANSCRIPTIONS. **Earl Wild.** Chesky CD32.
Fantasy on "Porgy and Bess". Improvisation in the form of a Theme and Three Variations on

"Someone to watch over me". Seven Virtuoso Etudes: I got rhythm; Lady be good; Liza; Embraceable you; Somebody loves me; Fascinatin' rhythm; The man I love.

59m DDD 10/90

This disc is one of those remarkable contemporary documents of great pianism, to be treasured and brought out for comparison whenever the virtuosos of earlier ages are cited. Earl Wild not only matches many of the giants in technical dexterity and musical insight, but also mirrors the ability of a number to produce enthralling glosses on the music of others in the form of almost ridiculously taxing transcriptions. Here, Gershwin is the subject of Wild's wonderful flights of fancy, a particularly appropriate choice as Gershwin himself produced transcriptions of a number of his own songs, obviously considering them ideal vehicles for jazz-type transformation. Wild magically combines a modern improvisational technique with a Lisztian attention to form, development and unity, producing works that repay repeated listening. The *Porgy and Bess* Fantasy achieves what the best of Liszt's works in the genre do — it conveys the flavour of the opera to those who do not know it, prompting them to hear the original, and gives added insight into the music for those who are already familiar with it. The solid-toned Baldwin piano, captured with effective truthfulness by the recording, is the ideal instrument for such inspirational performances.

NEW REVIEW

Gershwin. FILM MUSIC. [a]**Patti Austin,** [b]**Gregory Hines** (singers); [c]**Wayne Marshall** (pf); **Hollywood Bowl Orchestra/John Mauceri.** Philips 434 274-2PH. Recorded in 1991.
Overture — Gershwin in Hollywood. Delicious — New York Rhapsody[c]. Shall we dance — Walking the dog; I've got beginner's luck[ab]; Slap that bass[b]; They all laughed[a]; Let's call the whole thing off[ab]; Watch your step. A damsel in distress — A foggy day[b]; Nice work if you can get it[b]; An American in London. The Goldwyn follies[a] — Love walked in; Love is here to stay. The shocking Miss Pilgrim — For you, for me, for evermore[ab].

1h 15m DDD 5/92 

What a wonderful disc this is! A glittering celebration of the Gershwins' brief but astonishingly fruitful sojourn in Hollywood that is a joy from beginning to end. Although the brothers would only work on three film scores together (two being composed during George's final year), the melodies they created are clearly some of the most celebrated of their careers. One of the chief delights of this particular selection is hearing the songs played in the arrangements that were made either for the film soundtracks or the commercial recordings of the period, for this immediately infuses the whole enterprise with an authenticity that is totally irresistible. The vocal interpretations of Patti Austin and Gregory Hines may perhaps be rather more contemporary in style, but their slick and relaxed performances blend in with the original orchestrations with beguiling ease; Austin's "They all laughed" and Hines's "Nice work if you can get it" (complete with taps!) are prime examples. The concert is also complemented by several orchestral selections, the two most noteworthy being the "New York Rhapsody" (five minutes shorter and consequently somewhat more pungent than the *Second Rhapsody* it later became) and the complete final ballet from *Shall we dance* (a busy Ravelian pastiche that gradually soars into the sublimely buoyant title song). However, all of this praise would be worthless were it not for the scintillating direction of John Mauceri. His unfailing enthusiasm inspires some gleefully ebullient and idiomatic playing from the Hollywood orchestra and successfully injects the whole disc with a showbiz buzz that is wholly intoxicating. With a warm, intimate recording (made on the old MGM sound stage) and an attractive booklet to crown it all, who could indeed ask for anything more!

KIRI SINGS GERSHWIN. Dame Kiri Te Kanawa (sop); **New Princess Theater Orchestra/John McGlinn.** EMI CDC7 47454-2. Recorded in 1986.
Including — Somebody loves me, Love walked in, Summertime, The man I love, Things are looking up.

46m DDD 10/87 

This recording was made possible by the discovery of a cache of scores, with original orchestrations, in the Warner Brothers warehouse in New Jersey. It is a remarkably successful disc finding Te Kanawa on sparkling form; indeed she sounds more involved here than on many of her more 'classical' recordings. The up-tempo presentation may take a little getting used to (*Love is here to stay* is really rather swift) but the disc has a wonderful verve that is quite intoxicating. *I got rhythm*, complete with its male vocal quartet, is tremendous. John McGlinn directs wholly idiomatically. The recording is a little fierce in the 'pop' style, with a slightly tiring edge lent to this already quite fizzy music. But these are treasurable mementoes of the 1920s and 1930s.

Gershwin. GIRL CRAZY. Cast includes **Lorna Luft, David Carroll, Judy Blazer, Frank Gorshin, David Garrison, Vicki Lewis, chorus and orchestra/John Mauceri.** Elektra Nonesuch 7559-79250-2. Notes and text included. Recorded in Recorded in 1990.

1h 13m DDD 2/91

Girl Crazy is certainly one of the most hit-filled shows the Gershwins ever penned as the rousing Overture alone, with its references to "But not for me", "I got rhythm", "Bidin' my time" and "Embraceable you", immediately and irresistibly confirms. But these are not the only knockout numbers that pepper this terrific score; "Could you use me?", "Sam and Delilah" and "Treat me rough" are equally deserving of the term 'showstopper'. The show's basic setting, a Dude Ranch (where eastern playboys spent their vacation pretending to be western cowboys), may be uniquely American (which could explain why the show did not cross the Atlantic) but any unfamiliarity the overseas listener may have with the plot's finer points will in no way mar enjoyment of this completely captivating recording. One of the chief pleasures to be had from the current crop of Broadway reconstructions is the opportunity of hearing the songs with their original orchestrations, and Robert Russell Bennett's here are no exception. John Mauceri and his hand-picked orchestra respond with infectious gusto to every nuance of Bennett's delightful arrangements and throughout the score they successfully evoke the jazzy atmosphere of 1930s Broadway. Each of the soloists and chorus, too, are all just right, bringing off their respective numbers with tremendous verve and a real feel for the idiom. Packaged with an incredibly lavish and informative booklet (96 pages in all) this issue is an absolute treasure.

Gershwin. PORGY AND BESS. **Willard White** (bass) Porgy; **Cynthia Haymon** (sop) Bess; **Harolyn Blackwell** (sop) Clara; **Cynthia Clarey** (sop) Serena; **Damon Evans** (bar) Sportin' Life; **Marietta Simpson** (mez) Maria; **Gregg Baker** (bar) Crown; **Glyndebourne Chorus; London Philharmonic Orchestra/Simon Rattle.** EMI CDS7 49568-2. Notes and text included. Recorded in 1988.

③ 3h 9m DDD 6/89

The company, orchestra and conductor from the outstanding 1986 Glyndebourne production recreate once more a very real sense of Gershwin's 'Catfish Row' community on EMI's complete recording. Such is the atmosphere and theatricality of this recording, we might easily be back on the Glyndebourne stage; you can positively smell the drama in the key scenes. From the very first bar it's clear just how instinctively attuned Simon Rattle and this orchestra are to every aspect of a multi-faceted score. The cast, too, are so *right*, so much a part of their roles, and so well integrated into the whole, that one almost takes the excellence of their contributions for granted. Here is one beautiful voice after another, beginning in style with Harolyn Blackwell's radiant "Summertime", which at Rattle's gorgeously lazy tempo, is just about as beguiling as one could wish. Willard White conveys both the simple honesty and inner-strength of Porgy without milking the sentiment and Haymon's passionately sung Bess will go wherever a little flattery and encouragement take her. As Sportin' Life, Damon Evans not only relishes the burlesque elements of the role but he really *sings* what's written a lot more than is customary. But the entire cast deliver throughout with all the unstinting fervour of a Sunday revivalist meeting. Sample for yourself the final moments of the piece — "Oh Lawd, I'm on my way" — if that doesn't stir you, nothing will.

Additional recommendations ...

Soloists; Cleveland Chorus and Orchestra/Lorin Maazel. Decca 414 559-2DH3 — ③ DDD

Excerpts. **Soloists; RCA Victor Chorus and Orchestra/Skitch Henderson.** RCA Victor Gold Seal GD85234 — 48m ADD 4/89

Further listening ...

LADY, BE GOOD. **Soloists; chorus and orchestra/Eric Stern.** Elektra Nonesuch 7559-79308-2 (7/93).

STRIKE UP THE BAND. **Soloists; chorus and orchestra/John Mauceri.** Elektra Nonesuch 7559-79273-2 (1/92).

Carlo Gesualdo

Italian c.1561-1613

Gesualdo. MADRIGALS. **Les Arts Florissants Vocal and Instrumental Ensembles/William Christie.** Harmonia Mundi HMC90 1268. Texts and translations included.

Madrigals — Ahi, disperata vita. Sospirava il mio cor. O malnati messaggi. Non t'amo, o voce ingrata. Luci serene e chiare. Sparge la morte al mio Signor nel viso. Arde il mio cor. Occhi del mio cor vita. Mercè grido piangendo. Asciugate i begli ochi. Se la mia morte brami. Io parto. Ardita Zanzaretta. Ardo per te, mio bene. *Instrumental items* — Canzon francese. Io tacerò. Corrente, amanti.

55m DDD 10/88

The music and life of Gesualdo, Prince of Venosa, have become inextricably linked for their controversy and pungency. There is a strange allure to the music of this man who murdered his wife; it drags the vocal art to extremes just as he pushed his own life to the very brink of acceptability. William Christie has gathered together a selection of Gesualdo's five-voice madrigals which ideally trace the composer's development in the realms of expression and distorted beauty. Les Arts Florissants are ever alive to the strangeness of this remarkable music and never smooth out the textures and harmonic excrescences. The clashes of tonalities, used to powerful expressive effect, are relished and the acoustic adds immensely to the fine portrayal of colour and nuance. Christie, somewhat controversially, adds some instrumental parts to the madrigals, historically defensible but stylistically questionable. That said, this is a remarkable and highly enjoyable introduction to one of the great experimenters of Western Music.

Additional recommendation ...

Madrigals, Book 5. **The Consort of Musicke/Anthony Rooley.** L'Oiseau-Lyre 410 128-2OH — 55m DDD 5/84

Gesualdo. Responsoria et alia ad Officium Hebdonadae Sanctae spectantia. Benedictus. Miserere. **The Hilliard Ensemble.** ECM New Series 843 867-2. Texts and translations included. Recorded in 1990.

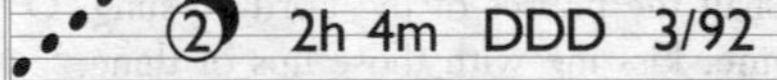

② 2h 4m DDD 3/92

To many, Gesualdo is known above all for the *crime passionnel* which left his wife and her lover impaled on the same sword, but the notion that his highly-charged music is the product of a tortured and unstable mind is, no doubt, over-romanticized. The exaggeratedly chromatic melodies and daring harmonic style of his late music were fully in keeping with the experimental madrigal school of the late sixteenth century. That said, Gesualdo's setting of the Responds for the Tenebrae of Holy Week is surely one of the most intense and disturbing works of the entire period. The complex service of Tenebrae is made up of the two offices, Matins and Lauds. Within Matins come the 27 responsories that were the inspiration for Gesualdo's music, in addition to which he set the "Miserere" and "Benedictus" from Lauds. At the beginning of the service the church is illuminated with candles, but these are extinguished one by one, hence the name *tenebrae* (darkness). It is significant that Gesualdo chose the most dramatic service of the church year, and one that is concerned with betrayal and death. The Hilliard Ensemble has not missed one ounce of the profundity of this music, and their performance is one of those rare artistic achievements that combines a heartfelt emotional response with faultless technical control. Their phrases are perfectly shaped and directed, and while it is virtually impossible to single out one particular contribution, David Beaven's ideally focused bass line should not go unmentioned. The recording is excellent, capturing the resonant acoustic of Douai Abbey, while every detail of the individual voices can be heard. Texts and translations are included, together with an extract from Hildesheimer's *Tynset*, but some explanatory notes would have been helpful.

Additional recommendation ...
Responsoria et alia ad Officium Hebdonadae Sanctae spectantia — excerpts. Marian Motets — Ave, dulcissima Maria; Precibus et meritis beatae Mariae; Ave, regina coelorum; Maria, mater gratiae. **The Tallis Scholars/Peter Phillips.** Gimell CDGIM015 — 52m DDD 12/87

Orlando Gibbons

British 1583-1625

Gibbons. MUSIC FOR PRINCE CHARLES.
Lupo. MUSIC FOR PRINCE CHARLES. **The Parley of Instruments/Peter Holman.** Hyperion CDA66395. Recorded in 1990.
Gibbons: Two Fantasias a 4. 9 Fantasias a 3. Galliard a 3. ***Lupo:*** Fantasy-Airs a 3 — Nos. 16, 17 and 20. Fantasy-Airs a 4 — Nos. 5-7, 11 and 12. Fantasies a 4 — Nos. 4 and 9.

59m DDD 9/91

Don't be put off by the rather forbidding titles: the terms "fantasia" and "fantasy-air" in fact conceal a wonderful mixture of the most varied music — by turns passionate, lively, languid and elegant. Peter Holman and his excellent Parley of Instruments have put together a programme which gives a snap-shot of music at the beginning of the English baroque. The composers represented are two of the most eminent English musicians of the seventeenth century: Orlando Gibbons and Thomas Lupo. Both worked in the service of King Charles I during his years as the Prince of Wales, and this collection represents the type of music the Prince's household musicians wrote for him to play. Charles was a keen patron of the arts and his musical tastes were adventurous: these pieces all include parts for the violin — then a relative newcomer to the English musical scene. Beautifully-judged — and recorded — performances capture the warmth and wit of this music.

Gibbons. CHURCH MUSIC. **King's College Choir, Cambridge/Philip Ledger** with **John Butt** (org) and [a]**London Early Music Group.** ASV Gaudeamus CDGAU123. From DCA514 (6/82).
Canticles — Magnificat; Nunc dimittis, "Short Service"; Magnificat; Nunc dimittis, "Second Service". *Full Anthems* — Almighty and Everlasting God; Lift up your heads; Hosanna to the Son of David. *Verse Anthems*[a] — This is the record of John; See, see, the Word is incarnate; O Thou, the central orb. *Hymnes and Songs of the Church* — Now shall the praises of the Lord be sung; O Lord of Hosts; A song of joy unto the Lord we sing; Come, kiss me with those lips of thine. *Organ works* — Voluntary; Fantasia for double organ; Fantasia.

53m DDD 4/86

Gibbons had close links with King's College, Cambridge, where he himself was a chorister. Little wonder, then, that the choir today frequently performs the music of one of its most illustrious musical sons! This programme is fully representative of Gibbons's output, with the two Services, several hymns, three organ pieces and examples of both his full and his verse anthems. Of these last, *This is the record of John* is particularly delectable. Michael Chance sings the alto solo with remarkable control, to the gentle accompaniment of the five viols, and in alternation with the full choir. His wonderful vocal quality 'makes' this record, but the solo trebles are notable for their poise, professionalism and first-class diction. The three organ pieces, elegantly played by John Butt, are of special interest, because of the place they hold in the development of keyboard music. Gibbons, himself renowned for his playing, was once described by the French Ambassador as "the best finger of that age".

Additional recommendations ...

Second Service (ed. Higginbottom) — Te Deum Laudamus; Jubilate Deo; Magnificat; Nunc dimittis. Full Anthems — O clap your hands; O Lord, in Thy wrath rebuke me not; Verse Anthems — O God, the king of glory; Glorious and powerful God; Sing unto the Lord; See, see, the Word is incarnate. Organ works[a] — Fantasia of four parts; A Fancy in A major; Fantasia for double organ. **New College Choir, Oxford/Edward Higginbottom** with [a]**David Burchell** (org). CRD CRD3451 — lh 6m DDD 12/88

Full Anthems — Hosanna to the Son of David; I am the resurrection; O clap your hands; O Lord, how do my woes increase; O Lord, I lift my heart to thee; O Lord, in thy wrath rebuke me not. Verse Anthems — Lord, we beseech thee, pour thy grace; Praise the Lord, O my soul; See, see, the Word is incarnate; Sing unto the Lord, o ye saints. Hymnes and Songs of the Church — Come, kiss me with those lips of thine; How sad and solitary now; Lord, I will sing to Thee; Lord, thy answer I did hear; Now in the Lord my heart doth pleasure take; Now shall the praises of the Lord; O Lord of Hosts and God of Israel; O my love, how comely now; Sing praises Is'rel to the Lord; Song of joy unto the Lord we sing; The beauty, Israel, is gone; When one among the Twelve there was; Who's this, that leaning on her friend. Preces and Psalm 145. **The Clerkes of Oxenford/David Wulstan.** Calliope CAL9611 — lh 10m ADD 12/89

Alberto Ginastera

Argentinian 1916-1983

NEW REVIEW

Ginastera. Harp Concerto, Op. 25[a].

Glière. Harp Concerto, Op. 74[a]. Concerto for coloratura soprano and orchestra, Op. 82[b]. [b]**Eileen Hulse** (sop); [a]**Rachel Masters** (hp); **City of London Sinfonia/Richard Hickox.** Chandos CHAN9094. Recorded in 1992.

lh 5m DDD 2/93 

Glière was among the comparatively few front-rank Russian composers who stayed on in their homeland after the 1917 Revolution. The music he composed there adopted a middle-of-the-road conservative style which helped him to steer clear of the more viscous controversies of the 1920s and 1930s. The Concertos for harp and coloratura sorano date from 1938 and 1942 respectively and are unashamedly ingratiating, high-grade mood-music, here played and recorded in a manner that those with a sweet tooth should find absolutely irresistible. The Harp Concerto by the Argentinian Alberto Ginastera is made of sterner stuff, but only slightly — it's Bartókian acerbities are tempered by an engaging Latin American swing. Once again the performance is crisp and bouncy, although in this instance the reverberant recording takes something of the edge off the rhythmic bite.

Further listening ...

Harp Concerto, Op. 25[a]. Estancia — ballet suite, Op. 8[a]. Piano Concerto No. 1, Op. 28[b]. [a]**Nancy Allen** (hp); [b]**Oscar Tarrago** (pf); **Mexico City Philharmonic Orchestra/Enrique Bátiz.** ASV CDDCA654 (8/89).

Umberto Giordano

Italian 1867-1948

Giordano. ANDREA CHENIER. **Luciano Pavarotti** (ten) Andrea Chenier; **Leo Nucci** (bar) Gerard; **Montserrat Caballé** (sop) Maddalena; **Kathleen Kuhlmann** (mez) Bersi;

Astrid Varnay (sop) Countess di Coigny; **Christa Ludwig** (mez) Madelon; **Tom Krause** (bar) Roucher; **Hugues Cuénod** (ten) Fleville; **Neil Howlett** (bar) Fouquier-Tinville, Major-domo; **Giorgio Tadeo** (bass) Mathieu; **Piero De Palma** (ten) Incredible; **Florindo Andreolli** (ten) Abate; **Giuseppe Morresi** (bass) Schmidt; **Ralph Hamer** (bass) Dumas; **Welsh National Opera Chorus; National Philharmonic Orchestra/Riccardo Chailly.** Decca 410 117-2DH2. Notes, text and translation included. From 411 117-1DH3 (11/84). Recorded 1982-84.

② Ih 47m DDD 2/85

Andrea Chenier, set at the start of the French Revolution, is a potent blend of the social and the emotional. The three main characters, the aristocratic Maddalena, the idealistic poet Chenier and the fiercely republican Gerard, are caught up in a triangle that pits love against conscience, independence against society. The opera has many well-known set numbers high on any list of favourites must be Chenier's so-called *Improviso* in Act 1 where he bursts out in a spontaneous poem on the power of love, or Maddalena's glorious and moving "La mamma morta" in the Third Act where she describes how her mother gave up her life to save her. Giordano had a real theatrical flair for the 'big moment' and he paces the work masterfully. The tunes seem to flow endlessly from his pen and the characters have real flesh and blood. The cast is strong, with Caballé and Pavarotti making a powerful central pair. Riccardo Chailly conducts the excellent National Philharmonic with flair and feeling and the whole opera is beautifully recorded.

Additional recommendation ...
Soloists; John Alldis Choir; National Philharmonic Orchestra/James Levine. RCA GD82046 — ② Ih 54m ADD 9/89

Giordano. FEDORA[a]. **Magda Olivero** (sop) Fedora; **Mario del Monaco** (ten) Loris; **Tito Gobbi** (bar) de Siriex; **Leonardo Monreale** (bass) Lorek, Nicola; **Lucia Cappellino** (sop) Olga; **Virgilio Carbonari** (bass) Borov; **Silvio Maionica** (bass) Grech; **Piero de Palma** (ten) Rouvel; **Peter Binder** (bar) Kiril; **Dame Kiri Te Kanawa** (sop) Dmitri; **Riccardo Cassinelli** (ten) Desire; **Athos Cesarini** (ten) Sergio; **Pascal Rogé** (pf) Boleslao Lazinski; **Monte-Carlo Opera Chorus and Orchestra/Lamberto Gardelli.**
Zandonai. FRANCESCA DA RIMINI — excerpts[b]. [c]**Magda Oliviero** (sop) Francesca; [d]**Mario del Monaco** (ten) Paolo; [e]**Annamaria Gasparini** (mez) Biancofiore; [f]**Virgilio Carbonari** (bass) Man-at-arms; [g]**Athos Cesarini** (ten) Archer; **Monte-Carlo Opera Orchestra/Nicola Rescigno.** Decca Grand Opera 433 033-2DM2. Notes, texts and translations included. Item marked [a] from SET435/6 (3/70), [b] SET422 (1/70). Recorded in 1969.
Francesca da Rimini: Act 2 — E ancora sgombro il campo del comune? ... Date il segno, Paolo, date ... Un'erba io m'avea, per sanare ... Onta et orrore sopra[cdfg]. Act 3 — No, Smadragedi, no! ... Paolo, datemi pace! ... Ah la parola chi i miei occhi incontrano[cd]. Act 4 — Ora andate ... E così, vada s'è pur mio destino[cde].

② 2h 12m ADD 3/92

Today the name 'Fedora' may suggest a type of hat rather than an opera, but although Giordano was overshadowed by his contemporary Puccini he was a successful composer. *Fedora* is based on a play by Victorien Sardou, the French dramatist whose *La Tosca* provided Puccini with a plot. It is set in the nineteenth century and variously in St Petersburg, Paris and Switzerland, and tells of the tragic love between the Russian Count Loris Ipanov and the Princess Fedora Romazov (Romanov), but to go into further detail of the plot, which disposes of various characters in turn and ends with the heroine herself taking poison, would take up too much space and one admires the booklet writer who has managed to produce a synopsis. *Fedora* has some Trivial Pursuits claim to be the first opera to feature bicycles in the plot! The music is richly textured orchestrally and finely written for the voices, and this recording made in 1969 is notable for the singing of Magda Olivero and Mario del Monaco, who despite being in their mid-fifties bring tremendous verve, vocal resource and dramatic skill to their roles. Tito Gobbi has less to do as the diplomat de Siriex, but gives him character, and another plus is the playing of Pascal Rogé, who performs the non-singing role of the Polish pianist and spy Boleslao Lazinski in Act 2 who, while performing, eavesdrops on a dialogue between Loris and Fedora. This exchange is a marvellous example of verismo writing and singing, and so is their final scene with her death. The set opens with excerpts from another opera, Zandonai's *Francesca da Rimini* with the same two excellent principals. The recordings are as clear and fresh-sounding as they were on the original releases.

Mauro Giuliani

Italian 1781-1829

NEW REVIEW

Giuliani. FLUTE AND GUITAR WORKS. **Mikael Helasvuo** (fl); **Jukka Savijoki** (gtr). BIS CD411 and CD413. Recorded in 1988.
CD411 Duo for flute and guitar. Gran duetto concertante, Op. 52. Grand duo concertant, Op. 85. 12 Ländler samt Coda, Op. 75. Duetinno facile, Op. 77. *CD413* — Grand Pot-pourri, Op. 126. Grand Potpourri, Op. 53. Pièces faciles et agréables, Op. 74. Potpourri tiré de l'Opéra Tancredi, Op. 76. Six Variations, Op. 81.

② lh 14m lh 12m DDD 1/91

Giuliani's success in Vienna was due to his instrumental skill, compositional fluency and, no less, to his awareness of what pleased musical Biedermeier society; its magnitude is shown by the fact that so much of his copious output was published. In maximizing his market he forgot no one, even the humblest amateur, and did not overlook the importance of involving the guitar in chamber works — for both salon-concert and domestic use. His flute/guitar duos (published, for obvious reasons, for flute *or* violin) span the whole range — from genuine partnerships between virtuosos to fodder for aspiring amateurs, from large-scale works (many of them potpourris) to sets of small *Albumblätter*, all designed for those who wanted to be entertained rather than strained — and, happily, there are still many of them! Though not concerned with profundity — and sometimes given to garrulity, Giuliani was a skilful writer of gracious, tuneful and appealing music that can still give as much pleasure to today's listeners as it did to those of his own day. Helasvuo and Savijoki are both Finns — and they use modern instruments, but their performances qualify them as 'honorary Italian' in their enjoyable accounts of the majority of Giuliani's work in this genre.

Giuliani. GUITAR WORKS. **David Starobin.** Bridge BCD9029. Recorded in 1990.
Choix de mes Fleurs chéries, Op. 46 — Le Jasmin; Le Rosmarin; La Rose. Etude in E minor, Op. 100 No. 13. Grande Ouverture, Op. 61. Leçons Progressives, Op. 51 Nos. 3, 7 and 14. Minuetto, Op. 73 No. 9. Preludes, Op. 83 Nos. 5 and 6. Rondeaux Progressives, Op. 14 Nos. 1 and 5. Six Variations, Op. 20. Variazioni sulla Cavatina favorita, "De calma oh ciel", Op. 101.

48m DDD 3/92

Giuliani was born and died in Italy, in between which he lived for many years in Vienna, where he scored great success in salon-music circles with his guitar virtuosity and counted many distinguished musicians amongst his friends and colleagues. He was in a sense the rival of Sor for the guitar's nineteenth-century crown but the two were 'chalk and cheese'. Giuliani the more volatile, ebullient and (as a composer) loquacious — with over 200 works as against Sor's less than 70. Giuliani's incessant desire to please his public (and to make much-needed money in the process) led to the presence of much treadmill dross amongst the gold of his best works, a thing that has contributed to his chronic undervaluation. David Starobin, playing a nineteenth-century guitar, greatly helps to redress the balance in his unfailingly musical and technically fluent playing of a selection of Giuliani's best works. Some testify to Giuliani's contribution to the student literature, the titles of others reflect the salon tastes at which they were aimed; all show that, when he took the trouble, Giuliani could be charming, polished and ingenious, all at the same time. This is a disc to charm the ear without bruising the emotions, in the nicest possible way.

Philip Glass

American 1937-

NEW REVIEW

Glass. AKHNATEN. **Paul Esswood** (alto) Akhnaten; **Milagro Vargas** (mez) Nefertiti; **Melinde Liebermann** (sop) Queen Tye; **Tero Hannula** (bar) Horemhab; **Helmut Holzapfel** (ten) Amon High Priest; **Cornelius Hauptmann** (bass) Aye; **Victoria Schnieder, Lynne Wilhelm-Königer, Maria Koupilová-Ticha** (sops), **Christina Wachtler, Geraldine Rose, Angelika Schwarz** (mezs) Daughters of Akhnaten; **David Warrilow** (narr) Scribe; **Stuttgart State Opera Chorus and Orchestra/Dennis Russell Davies.** CBS Masterworks CD42457. Notes, text and translation included. Recorded in 1987.

② 2h 9m DDD 2/88 

Impressive as they are when staged, Philip Glass's operas also make excellent home listening; for these are statuesque more than dramatic works, expressed through tableaux rather than sustained stage-action. The music of *Akhnaten*, Glass's ancient Egyptian opera, in particular seems calculated to communicate vast spans of time during which cities rise and are destroyed, religions are set up and topple, rulers come to power and are overthrown. So overpowering is the sense of time and space that the characters themselves seem to pass through the score like ghosts, half-hidden in the seamless weft of pulsing chords and arpeggios that make up Glass's minimalist language. A bird's-eye view of the plot is all that is needed before settling down to the marvels of the music itself. Do not be deterred by the fact that much of the singing is in ancient Egyptian, for Glass fills his opera with musical gestures that vividly communicate mood and action. In the Stuttgart State Opera Orchestra and Chorus under Dennis Russell Davies, Glass has interpreters of the highest dedication and distinction.

Further listening ...

"Low" Symphony. **Brooklyn Philharmonic Orchestra/Dennis Russell Davies.** Point Music 438 150-2PTH (5/93).

Metamorphosis. Mad rush. Wichita vortex sutra. **Philip Glass** (pf). CBS CD45576 (3/90).

EINSTEIN ON THE BEACH. **Soloists; Philip Glass Ensemble/Michael Riesman.** CBS CD38875 (9/86).

SATYAGRAHA. **NYC Opera Chorus and Orchestra/Christopher Keene.** CBS CD39672 (9/86).

Alexander Glazunov

Russian 1865-1936

Glazunov. Violin Concerto in A minor, Op. 82[a].
Prokofiev. Violin Concerto No. 2 in G minor, Op. 63[b].
Sibelius. Violin Concerto in D major, Op. 47[c]. **Jascha Heifetz** (vn); **[a]RCA Victor Symphony Orchestra/Walter Hendl; [b]Boston Symphony Orchestra/Charles Münch; [c]Chicago Symphony Orchestra/Walter Hendl.** RCA Red Seal RD87019. Items marked [a] and [b] from GL89833 (9/86), [c] GL89832 (9/86).

1h 9m ADD 10/86 

Here are three great concertos on one CD, all of them classics which have never been equalled, let alone surpassed. Heifetz made the première recording of all three concertos in the 1930s and his interpretations have particular authority. The recordings here were all issued in the early 1960s and in their digital refurbishment sound remarkably good. Heifetz's golden tone shines more brightly than ever and his technical virtuosity and profound musicianship remain dazzling. The performances can only be described as stunning and they remain an indispensable part of any collection.

Additional recommendations ...
Violin Concerto[a]. *The Seasons — ballet, Op. 67.* [a]**Oscar Shumsky** (vn); **Scottish National Orchestra/Neeme Järvi.** Chandos CHAN8596 — 57m DDD 3/89
Violin Concerto[a]. ***Prokofiev.*** *Violin Concerto No. 1 in D major, Op. 19*[a]. ***Shchedrin.*** *Stihira.* [a]**Anne-Sophie Mutter** (vn); **Washington National Symphony Orchestra/Mstislav Rostropovich.** Erato 2292-45343-2 — lh 4m DDD 3/89
Violin Concerto. ***Shostakovich.*** *Violin Concerto No. 1 in A minor, Op. 99.* **Itzhak Perlman** (vn); **Israel Philharmonic Orchestra/Zubin Mehta.** EMI CDC7 49814-2 — 55m DDD 1/90

Glazunov. The seasons — ballet, Op. 67.
Tchaikovsky. The Nutcracker — ballet, Op. 71[a]. [a]**Finchley Children's Music Group; Royal Phiharmonic Orchestra/Vladimir Ashkenazy.** Decca 433 000-2DH2. Recorded 1989-90.

② 2h 11m DDD 4/92

One cannot think of a happier coupling than Glazunov's complete *Seasons* — perhaps his finest and most successful score — with Tchaikovsky's *Nutcracker*. Glazunov's delightful ballet, with even the winter's "Frost", "Hail", "Ice" and "Snow", glamorously presented, and the bitterness of a Russian winter quite forgotten are, like the scenario of the *Nutcracker*, part of a child's fantasy world, for Tchaikovsky too, in Act 2, has a wintry fairy scene and a delectable "Waltz of the snowflakes" (featuring children's wordless chorus). Glazunov's twinklingly dainty scoring of the picturesque snowy characters is contrasted with the glowing summer warmth of the "Waltz of the cornflowers and poppies", and the vigorously thrusting tune (perhaps the most memorable theme he ever wrote) of the Autumn "Bacchanale". Tchaikovsky's ballet opens with a children's Christmas party with the guests arriving, presents distributed and family dancing, in which everyone joins. Ashkenazy captures the atmosphere very engagingly; then night falls, the church clock outside strikes midnight and the magic begins. The drama of the spectacular mock battle between good and evil, the children's journey through the pine forest (to one of Tchaikovsky's most ravishing tunes) and the famous multi-coloured characteristic dances of the Act 2 Divertissement are all beautifully played by the RPO. There is much finesse and sparkle, and the lightest and most graceful rhythmic touch from Ashkenazy: the conductor's affection for the score and his feeling for Tchaikovsky's multi-hued orchestral palette is a constant delight to the ear. Yet the big *Pas de deux* brings a climax of Russian fervour. The recording is properly expansive here; made at Walthamstow, it sets everything within a glowing acoustic ambience. *The seasons* was recorded in Watford Town Hall, and again the ear is seduced by the aural richness and the glowing woodwind detail. The one minor drawback is that in the *Nutcracker* the cueing is not generous and the action not precisely related to the narrative detail. But in every other respect this is marvellous entertainment.

Glazunov. SYMPHONIES. **USSR Ministry of Culture State Symphony Orchestra/Gennadi Rozhdestvensky.** Olympia OCD100/1.
OCD100 — No. 1 in E major, Op. 5, "Slavyanskaya"; No. 7 in F major, Op. 77, "Pastoral'naya". *OCD101* — No. 4 in E flat major, Op. 48; No. 5 in B flat major, Op. 55.

② 1h 10m 1h 10m ADD 8/86

It is always easy to underestimate the Glazunov symphonies. There is no doubt that this set of performances from Rozhdestvensky and the splendid orchestra, give them a 'new look'. There is a sophistication in the playing to match the elegance of Glazunov's often highly engaging wind scoring — especially in the scherzos, always Glazunov's best movements — but there is a commitment and vitality too, which makes all the music spring readily to life. In Rozhdestvensky's hands the fine *Adagio* of No. 1 sounds remarkably mature while the *Andante* movements of Nos. 5 and 7 are romantically expansive in a very appealing way. The Fourth Symphony is a highly inventive piece throughout and held together by a moto theme; and the better-known Fifth does not disappoint when the presentation is so persuasive. On both discs the recording is brightly lit without being too brittle, and has plenty of fullness too. For anyone looking for new nineteenth-century symphonies to explore, this would be a good place to start.

Additional recommendations ...

Nos 1 and 5. **Bavarian Radio Symphony Orchestra/Neeme Järvi.** Orfeo C093101A — lh 6m DDD 9/87

No. 8 in E flat major, Op. 83. Ouverture solennelle, Op. 73. Wedding procession, Op. 21. **Bavarian Radio Symphony Orchestra/Neeme Järvi.** Orfeo C093201A — 56m DDD 1987

No. 2 in F sharp minor, Op. 16. Concert Waltz No. 1 in D major, Op. 47. **Bamberg Symphony Orchestra/Neeme Järvi.** Orfeo C148101A — 50m DDD 11/90

Nos. 4 and 7. **Bamberg Symphony Orchestra/Neeme Järvi.** Orfeo C148201A — lh 6m DDD 11/90

No. 6 in C minor, Op. 58. Lyric Poem, Op. 12. **Bamberg Symphony Orchestra/Neeme Järvi.** Orfeo C157201A — 53m DDD 11/90

No. 3 in D major, Op. 33. Concert Waltz No. 2 in F major, Op. 51. **Bamberg Symphony Orchestra/Neeme Järvi.** Orfeo C157201A — 47m DDD 11/90

Further listening ...

Violin Concerto in A minor, Op. 82[a]. Piano Concerto No. 2 in B major, Op. 100[b]. Saxophone Concerto in E flat major, Op. 109[c]. [a]**Sergei Stadler** (vn); [b]**Dmitri Alexeev** (pf); [c]**Lev Mikhailov** (sax); [a]**Leningrad Philharmonic Orchestra/Vladimir Ponkin;** [b]**USSR Radio Symphony Orchestra/Yuri Nikolaevsky;** [c]**USSR Radio Symphony Orchestra Soloists Ensemble/Alexander Korneiev.** Olympia OCD165 (2/90).

From the middle ages, Op. 79. Scènes de ballet, Op. 52. *Coupled with* ***Liadov.*** A musical snuffbox, Op. 31. **Scottish National Orchestra/Neeme Järvi.** Chandos CHAN8804 (10/90).

Chant du ménestrel, Op. 71. *Coupled with* ***Kabalevsky.*** Cello Concerto No. 2. in C major, Op. 77. ***Khachaturian.*** Cello Concerto. **Raphael Wallfisch** (vc); **London Philharmonic Orchestra/Bryden Thomson.** Chandos CHAN8579 (6/88).

The sea — fantasy, Op. 28. Spring, Op. 34. *Coupled with* ***Kalinnikov.*** Symphony No. 1 in G minor. **Scottish National Orchestra/Neeme Järvi.** Chandos CHAN8611 (10/88).

Piano Sonatas — No. 1 in B flat minor, Op. 74; No. 2 in E flat major, Op. 75. Three Etudes, Op. 31. Grand Waltz Concert in E flat major, Op. 41. **Massimilliano Damerini** (pf). Etcetera KTC1118.

Reyngol'd Glière

Russian 1875-1956

NEW REVIEW

Glière. Symphony No. 2 in C minor, Op. 25. The Zaporozhy Cossacks, Op. 64. **BBC Philharmonic Orchestra/Sir Edward Downes.** Chandos CHAN9071. Recorded in 1991.

lh 4m DDD 7/92 

If the sumptuous Third Symphony (see below) is the one work by Glière that everyone should know, the Second, completed in 1908, makes as good a back-up as anything. It carries no explicit programme, and its four movements are closer in design to the post-Borodin model which had become something of an academic standard in Silver Age Russia (thanks to Glazunov). But the folk-heroic tone is similarly prominent, and Glière's sheer inventive vigour is extraordinarily bracing. After the 1917 Revolution Glière was among those who bent over backwards, at least in terms of musical style, to meet the requirements of the regime. His 1921 tone-poem *The Zaporozhy Cossacks* shows the process of adaptation beginning. The score is attractive enough, but heard after the Symphony it seems drained of its lifeblood. The BBC Philharmonic are on splendid form and Sir Edward Downes brings all the full-blooded conviction to these works that his long-standing commitment to the Russian and Soviet repertoire would lead you to expect. The Chandos engineers manage to enhance the acoustic of BBC Manchester's Studio 7 without undue exaggeration.

Glière. Symphony No. 3 in B minor, Op. 42, "Il'ya Muromets". **Royal Philharmonic Orchestra/Harold Farberman.** Unicorn-Kanchana Souvenir UKCD2014/5. From PCM500-1 (8/79). Recorded in 1978.

What happened to the Russian symphony between Tchaikovsky and Shostakovich? Scriabin and Rachmaninov were active of course, plus the solidly respectable Glazunov. But there was another distinctive voice, one whose interest lay in blending the heroic-saga tone of Borodin with the orchestral opulence of Wagner. This was Reyngol'd Glière, and his Third Symphony of 1912 is his undoubted masterpiece. It is a supremely late-romantic technicolour score, extreme but never uncontrolled in its excess, and always directed towards vividness of narrative rather than self-display. Now usually performed without the once-standard cuts, its four movements are fairly protracted, the more so when taken at exceptional spacious tempos as they are here by Harold Farberman (other more recent uncut recordings have clocked in at single-CD duration). But the spaciousness proves the making of the piece, giving the dimensions a truly epic feel and developing an unstoppable slow momentum. The recording quality no longer quite seems to justify the 'demonstration-class' praise originally accorded it, but it is still impressive enough.

Further listening ...

Symphony No. 1 in E flat major, Op. 8. The Sirens — symphonic poem, Op. 33. **Slovak Philharmonic Orchestra/Stephen Gunzenhauser.** Marco Polo 8 220349 (9/86).

Concerto for Coloratura Soprano, Op. 82[a]. Harp Concerto, Op. 74[b]. *Coupled with* ***Ginastera.*** Harp Concerto, Op. 25[b]. [a]**Eileen Hulse** (sop); [b]**Rachel Masters** (hp); **City of London Sinfonia/Richard Hickox.** Chandos CHAN9094.

Mikhail Ivanovich Glinka

Russian 1804-1857

Suggested listening ...

A LIFE FOR THE TSAR. **Soloists; Sofia National Opera Chorus and Festival Orchestra/Emil Tchakarov.** Sony Classical SK46487 (9/91).

Christoph Gluck

Bohemian 1714-1787

Gluck. ORFEO ED EURIDICE. **Michael Chance** (alto) Orfeo; **Nancy Argenta** (sop) Euridice; **Stefan Beckerbauer** (treb) Amor; **Stuttgart Chamber Choir; Tafelmusik/Frieder Bernius.** Sony Classical Vivarte SK48040. Notes, text and translation included. Recorded in 1991.

Not very long ago, the standard view of Gluck's *Orfeo ed Euridice* was that a compromise text, between the Italian original of 1762 and the French revised version of 1774, was desirable, allowing performers and listeners to have the best of both worlds. But nowadays people are beginning to realize that Gluck may have known what he was doing when he wrote two versions, and that each has its own integrity. This recording also allows us to fully appreciate the beautifully balanced structure of the original version and gives us a good idea of how it might have sounded, through the use of period instruments and the fine countertenor, Michael Chance, in the castrato role. The dramatic drive and integrity are enormous, as are the qualities of both performance and recording. The singing is first class: Chance is a revelation as Orfeo, Nancy Argenta a truly complex Euridice, a real woman rather than just a character from mythology. The performance sets the style and (generally lively) pace of the reading, with Frieder Bernius finding just the right balance of the intriguing tonal qualities to give a special stamp to each number. With all this enhanced by an exceptionally fine recording, full of space and detail, clarity and depth, this is altogether an outstanding issue.

Additional recommendations ...

Orfeo ed Euridice. **Soloists; Glyndebourne Chorus; London Philharmonic Orchestra/Raymond Leppard.** Erato Libretto 2292-45864-2 — ② 2h 7m DDD 5/93

Orfeo ed Euridice. **Soloists; Ghent Collegium Vocale; La Petite Bande/Sigiswald Kuijken.** Accent ACC48223/4D — ② 1h 46m ADD 1/90

Orfeo ed Euridice. Orphée et Eurydice — Air de furies; Ballet des ombres heureuses; Air vif; Menuet; Chaconne. **Soloists; Berlin Radio Chorus; Carl Philipp Emanuel Bach Chamber Orchestra/Hartmut Haenchen.** Capriccio 60 008-2 — ② 1h 54m DDD 1/90

Orphée et Euridice. **Soloists; Monteverdi Choir; Lyon Opéra Orchestra/John Eliot Gardiner.** EMI CDS7 49834-2 — ② 1h 29m DDD 2/90

Orphée et Euridice. **Soloists; Robert Blanchard Vocal Ensemble; Lamoureux Orchestra/Hans Rosbaud.** Philips Opera Collector mono 434 784-2PM2 — ② 1h 55m ADD 5/93

Gluck. IPHIGENIE EN AULIDE. **Lynne Dawson** (sop) Iphigénie; **José van Dam** (bass) Agamemnon; **Anne Sofie von Otter** (mez) Clytemnestre; **John Aler** (ten) Achille; **Bernard Deletré** (bass) Patrocle; **Gilles Cachemaille** (bass) Calchas; **René Schirrer** (bass) Arcas; **Guillemette Laurens** (mez) Diane; **Ann Monoyios** (sop) First Greek woman, Slave; **Isabelle Eschenbrenner** (sop) Second Greek woman; **Monteverdi Choir; Lyon Opéra Orchestra/John Eliot Gardiner.** Erato 2292-45003-2. Notes, text and translation included. Recorded in 1987.

② 2h 12m DDD 6/90

Gluck's first reform opera for Paris has tended to be overshadowed by his other *Iphigénie*, the *Tauride* one. But it does contain some superb things, of which perhaps the finest are the great monologues for Agamemnon. On this recording, José van Dam starts a little coolly; but this only adds force to his big moment at the end of the second act where he tussles with himself over the sacrifice of his daughter and — contemplating her death and the screams of the vengeful Eumenides — decides to flout the gods and face the consequences. To this he rises in noble fashion, fully conveying the agonies Agamemnon suffers. The cast in general is strong. Lynne Dawson brings depth of expressive feeling to all she does and her Iphigénie, marked by a slightly grainy sound and much intensity, is very moving. John Aler's Achille too is very fine, touching off the lover and the hero with equal success, singing both with ardour and vitality. There is great force too in the singing of Anne Sofie von Otter as Clytemnestre, especially in her outburst "Ma fille!" as she imagines her daughter on the sacrificial altar. John Eliot Gardiner's Monteverdi Choir sing with polish, perhaps seeming a little genteel for a crowd of angry Greek soldiers baying for Iphigénie's blood. But Gardiner gives a duly urgent account of the score, pressing it forward eagerly and keeping the tension at a high level even in the dance music. A period-instrument orchestra might have added a certain edge and vitality but this performance wants nothing in authority or drama and can be securely recommended.

Gluck. IPHIGENIE EN TAURIDE. **Diana Montague** (mez) Iphigénie; **John Aler** (ten) Pylade; **Thomas Allen** (bar) Oreste; **Nancy Argenta** (sop); **Sophie Boulton** (mez) First and Second Priestesses; **Colette Alliot-Lugaz** (sop) Diana; **René Massis** (bass-bar) Thoas;

Monteverdi Choir; Lyon Opera Orchestra/John Eliot Gardiner. Philips 416 148-2PH2. Notes, text and translation included.

② 2h 3m DDD 6/86

Many Gluckists reckon *Iphigénie en Tauride* to be the finest of his operas; and although the claims of *Orfeo* are also very strong the breadth and grandeur of this score, the vigour of its declamatory writing, the intensity with which the situations of Iphigénie and Oreste are depicted and the ultimate integration of music and drama produce a uniquely powerful musical realization of classical tragedy. John Eliot Gardiner's sense of dramatic concentration and his intellectual control make him an ideal interpreter; the impassioned accompanied recitatives and the taut, suggestive accompaniments to the arias are particularly impressive, and the dance music is gracefully done. It might, however, have been better if a period orchestra had been used; this one, though efficient and responsive, cannot quite articulate the music as Gluck intended and tends to be string-heavy in the modern manner. Vocally, the set is distinguished above all by Diana Montague's Iphigénie, sung with due nobility and a finely true, clean middle register, and Thomas Allen's noble and passionate Oreste; John Aler's Pylade is warm and flexible and René Massis provides a suitably barbaric Thoas. In all a noble account, the best available on disc, of a remarkable opera.

Further listening ...

LE CINESI — *opera-serenade*. **Kaaren Erickson** (sop) Sivene; **Alexandrina Milcheva** (contr) Lisinga; **Marga Schiml** (contr) Tangia; **Thomas Moser** (ten) Silango; **Munich Radio Orchestra/Lamberto Gardelli.** Orfeo C178891A (1/90).

DON JUAN — *pantomime*. ***Handel.*** ARIODANTE — Overture; Ballet Music. IL PASTOR FIDO — Hunting scene. **Academy of St Martin in the Fields/Sir Neville Marriner.** Decca 433 732-2DM.

ALCESTE. **Soloists; Bavarian Radio Chorus; Bavarian Radio Symphony Orchestra/Serge Baudo.** Orfeo C027823F (6/87).

PARIDE ED ELENA. **Soloists; La Stagione Vocal Ensemble; La Statione/Michael Schneider.** Capriccio 60 027-2 (6/93).

Leopold Godowsky

Polish/American 1870-1938

Godowsky. PIANO TRANSCRIPTIONS. **Rian De Waal.** Hyperion CDA66496.
Godowsky: Passacaglia. Triakontameron — Alt Wien. ***Schubert:*** Die schöne Müllerin, D795 — Das Wandern; Ungeduld. Winterreise, D911 — Gute Nacht. Rosamunde — Ballet Music. Moments musicaux, D780 — No. 3 in F minor. ***Weber:*** Invitation to the dance, J260. ***J. Strauss II:*** Kunstlerleben, Op. 316.

58m DDD 3/92 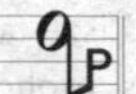

The pianist Leopold Godowsky acquired a legendary stature in his lifetime and remains an idol today. Small, plump and inscrutable, he was nicknamed the Buddha of the instrument and Harold Schonberg's book *The Great Pianists* refers to his possession of "the most perfect pianistic mechanism of the period". He dazzled even his greatest contemporaries, and Vladimir Horowitz, who worked at his *Passacaglia* but never performed it in public, said "it needs six hands to play it". Full marks, therefore, to the young Dutch pianist Rian de Waal, who not only plays it convincingly but also makes it sound pretty effortless; based on the opening theme of Schubert's *Unfinished* Symphony (just 12 notes in B minor), it unfolds magisterially towards a final fugue and is a fine, somewhat Brahmsian composition as well as one of virtuoso pianism. The other compositions are smaller but also worth having, particularly when they're as well played as they are here. The three transcriptions of Schubert songs become remarkable piano pieces, not least

Gute Nacht, which is not a showpiece but a sombre tone poem. There's real charm, too, in de Waal's playing of the Strauss waltz transcription, *An Artist's Life*. There are also pieces which were originally for piano but which Godowsky further reshaped into something personal. His version of Weber's *Invitation to the dance*, here recorded for the first time, has elaborate charm as well as the romantic quality which comes out in Fokine's ballet based on it, *Le spectre de la rose*. The recital ends as it began with an original piece, the leisurely and lilting little waltz called *Old Vienna*.

Further listening ...

Grand Sonata in E minor. **Geoffrey Douglas Madge** (pf). Dante PSG890-7.

3 Studies on Chopin Etudes — Nos. 1-25. **Geoffrey Douglas Madge** (pf). Dante PSG8903/4

53 Studies on Chopin Etudes — Nos. 26-48. **Geoffrey Douglas Madge** (pf). Dante PSG8905/6.

Triakontameron (30 moods and scenes in triple time. **Geoffrey Douglas Madge** (pf). Dante PSG9009.

Alexander Goehr

British 1932-

Suggested listening ...

Metamorphosis/Dance, Op. 36. Romanza, Op. 24[a]. [a]**Moray Welsh** (vc); **Royal Liverpool Philharmonic Orchestra/David Atherton.** Unicorn-Kanchana Souvenir UKCD2039 (7/91).

... a musical offering (J. S. B. 1985) ..., Op. 46. Behold the Sun, Op. 44*a*[a]. Lyric Pieces, Op. 35. Sinfonia, Op. 42. [a]**Jeanine Thames** (sop); [a]**James Holland** (vib); **London Sinfonietta/Oliver Knussen.** Unicorn-Kanchana DKPCD9102 (11/91).

Károly Goldmark

Austrian/Hungarian 1830-1915

Goldmark. Rustic Wedding Symphony, Op. 26. Sakuntula Overture, Op. 13. **Royal Philharmonic Orchestra/Yondani Butt.** ASV CDDCA791.

lh 6m DDD 5/92 

It is good to welcome a major work by Goldmark to the *Guide*. In his lifetime, which was mostly spent in Vienna, he was thought of as the most important Hungarian composer after Liszt, and Brahms admired this work, which dates from 1876. It is something between a symphony and a sequence of symphonic poems and has an idiom not unlike Smetana or in places even Mahler in pastoral mood: tuneful, colourful and occasionally amiably pompous, as in the initial "Wedding March", which at nearly 18 minutes is the longest of the five movements. There's humour, too, as in the central "Serenade", a gentle and genial scherzo. The Royal Philharmonic Orchestra play this music with all one could ask for in the way of zest and charm under a young conductor who was born in Macao but now lives and works in Canada. The recording is rich and a touch too reverberant in climaxes, but detail is mostly clear and the string and wind sound is well captured, not least in the beautifully scored "Serenade" and the dreamy "Garden Scene" that follows. The busy, cheerful finale is a delight. *Sakuntula* was written ten years earlier, and must be among the first western pieces to be inspired by the fifth-century Indian epic called the *Mahabharata*, which Goldmark came across in a German translation; the title is the name of a woodland nymph whose love scene with King Dusjanta is rapturously melodious, and again this is played lovingly as well as skilfully by Butt and the Royal Philharmonic Orchestra.

Additional recommendation ...
Rustic Wedding Symphony. **Utah Symphony Orchestra/Maurice Abravanel.** Vanguard Classics 08.9051.71 — 42m ADD 4/93

Further listening ...

DIE KONIGIN VON SABA. **Soloists; Hungarian State Orchestra/Adám Fischer.** Hungaroton HCD12179/81 (6/86).

Berthold Goldschmidt

German 1903-

NEW REVIEW

Goldschmidt. String Quartet, Op. 8[a]. Piano Sonata, Op. 10[b]. Clarinet Quartet[c]. [c]**Ib Hausmann** (cl); [b]**Kolja Lessing** (pf); [a]**Mandelring Quartet** ([c]Sebastian Schmidt, Nanette Schmidt, vns; [c]Nora Niggeling, va; [c]Bernhard Schmidt, vc). Largo 5117.

55m DDD II/92 

Musical history has witnessed a handful of composers — Jean Sibelius and Igor Markévitch are just two — who, after a creatively industrious youth and maturity, gave their muses the elbow (or vice versa) for late middle age and beyond. However, the eminent composer and conductor Berthold Goldschmidt had *his* muse return after a period of some 60 years! Hard on the heels of Largo's first Goldschmidt success (see below), the second — subtitled "Early" and "Late" — offers compelling evidence of the composer's subtle but telling maturity. The music itself is always beautifully written and highly approachable: sometimes neo-classical in style, and sometimes harbouring a deep-rooted lyricism which contrasts markedly when heard beside other, less accessible contemporary music. The most recent work on this disc is a Clarinet Quartet which, as annotator Michael Struck observes, "is the highly impressive new beginning of an 80-year-old." Busy and absorbing in its outer episodes, the Quartet has a most beautiful middle section, poetic and expressive, and as warmly reflective as any chamber music written during the past 30 or so years. The two earlier works amount to cultivated hives of musical activity; both are somewhat more earnest than the Clarinet Quartet, but hardly less appealing. The String Quartet has distant resonances of Hindemith and Bartók, and yet its taut arguments and clear polyphony are absorbing in themselves, and the central section of the Scherzo is surprisingly songful and brightly-coloured. The Piano Sonata is a drier piece and sounds, initially at least, a little like Stravinsky's only Piano Sonata (written two years earlier); again, it is attractive music and, like everything else on this cleanly recorded CD, is sympathetically performed.

Goldschmidt. CHAMBER AND CHORAL WORKS. [a]**Mandelring Quartet** (Sebastian Schmidt, Nanette Schmidt, vns; Nora Niggeling, va; Bernhard Schmidt, vc); [b]**Jörg Gottschick** (narr); [c]**Alan Marks** (pf); [d]**Berlin Ars Nova Ensemble/Peter Schwarz.** Largo 5115. Text and translation included.
String Quartets[a] — No. 2 (1936); No. 3 (1989). Belsatzar (1985)[d]. Letzte Kapitel[bcd] (1931).

56m DDD II/91 

After decades of neglect, the music of Hamburg-born Berthold Goldschmidt is coming back into favour and a largely forgotten grand old man (resident in the UK since 1935) has begun composing again. Older music lovers may recognize him as one of our earliest Mahler champions: he conducted the première of Deryck Cooke's full performing version of the Tenth Symphony in 1964. Like Shostakovich, whose quartet writing is not altogether dissimilar, Goldschmidt composes tonal music in which Mahler looms larger than Schoenberg, though the dominant influence is probably that of Busoni. The results are hard to describe, but sometimes remind you of Hindemith without the contrapuntal excesses. The present CD, expertly annotated, is designed to show the breadth of Goldschmidt's achievement, ranging from the trenchant, Weill-like expression of *Letzte Kapitel* to the more impressive absolute music of the quartets. Goldschmidt's writing here lacks the striking melodic charge of Shostakovich, but the committed performances and well balanced recordings make them an attractive proposition for the more adventurous collector.

Key to Symbols

•••	② ②	lh 23m	DDD	6/88
Price	*Quantity/ availability*	*Timing*	*Mode*	*Review date*

Jerry Goldsmith

American 1929-

Suggested listening ...

Legend — *original film soundtrack.* **National Philharmonic Orchestra/Jerry Goldsmith.** Silva Screen FILMCD045 (5/93).

Nicolas Gombert

Flanders c.1495-c.1560

NEW REVIEW

Gombert. MUSIC FROM THE COURT OF CHARLES V. **Huelgas Ensemble/Paul van Nevel.** Sony Classical Vivarte SK48249. Texts and translations included. Recorded in 1992. Missa Tempore paschali. Regina caeli. In te Domine speravi. Media vita. Tous les regretz. Je prens congie. Magnificat Secundi toni.

••• lh 16m DDD 4/93

At last the 'forgotten generation' between Josquin and Palestrina is coming to light: composers such as Morales, Manchicourt and Gombert have begun to appear with much greater frequency in concert programmes and recordings. This astonishing disc shows exactly what we have been missing, and together with the anthology of the same composer's works recorded by Ars Nova (listed below) gives a good selection of various genres in which he wrote. Gombert's dark, complex counterpoint and unceasing flow of melodic line — quite unlike Josquin's style — are evident in all these works and most effectively conveyed by the Huelgas Ensemble, who sing with an impressively 'English' precision combined with a choral sound that is not top-heavy in the slightest (a rarer phenomenon than one might think!). In this respect, the most atypical work on the disc is the 12-part *Regina caeli*, whose contrapuntal texture moves regally along without that sense of darkness found in many of Gombert's other motets, such as *Media vita* also recorded here. The *chansons* also maintain the stately, unceasing tread of the motets: indeed, it is a pity that the Huelgas Ensemble did not also record the eight-part motet *Lugebat David Absalon* which is convincingly attributable to Gombert, since its first half is a contrafactum of *Je prens congie*, performed here with an impressive gloominess. More variety of texture may be found in the *Magnificat*, and especially in the *Missa Tempore paschali*, which moves from a six-part *Kyrie* gradually upwards to a 12-part second *Agnus Dei*. The *Credo*, like so many other separate settings of the text by Gombert, is for eight voices. An exceptional recording of exceptional music.

Additional recommendation ...

Magnificats — Primi toni; Octavi toni. Credo. Ave Maria. Si ignoras te o pulchra. Ave salus mundi. **Ars Nova/Bo Holten.** Kontrapunkt 32038 — ••• lh 6m DDD 10/90

Henryk Górecki

Polish 1933-

NEW REVIEW

THE ESSENTIAL GORECKI. Polish National Philharmonic Choir; Polish National Symphony Orchestra, Katowice/Jan Krenz; Polish National Philharmonic Orchestra, Warsaw/Andrzej Markowski. Olympia OCD385. Recorded 1967-70.
Epitafium, Op. 12. Scontri, Op. 17. Genesis II: Canti strumentali, Op. 19 No. 2. Refrain, Op. 21. Old Polish music, Op. 24.

lh l4m AAD 4/93

Górecki's compositional career prior to the Third Symphony is admirably covered on an Olympia disc of archival recordings especially selected by the composer under the title "The Essential Górecki". Covering the period 1958-1969 — in strict chronological order — the disc provides a fascinating insight into Górecki's gradually evolving style form serialist through to avant-garde pioneer and finally, in *Old Polish Music*, to the intimations of the more tonal style that was to eventually find ultimate expression in the Third Symphony. Though heavily indebted to Webern's *Das Augenlicht*, the miniature cantata *Epitafium*, Op. 12 for mixed choir and instrumental ensemble reveals Górecki's early propensity for mixing highly organized serialist techniques, with a freer, more pointillistic and sharply coloured language, and in *Scontri* ("Collisions") the technique is expanded further to allow bolder, larger blocks of sonority (sometimes graphically notated) to collide against each other in an ever increasing frenzy of energy. In *Genesis II* and *Refren* ("Refrain") a process of purification begins to infiltrate Górecki's music, and in the latter we can hear a pre-echo of the arch-like structure of the first movement of the Third Symphony. Finally, the dramatic, almost ritualistic *Old Polish Music* reveals an even leaner, more economical style, which lays the foundation for Górecki's tonal music of the mid 1970s. The recordings show their age a little now, but this is more than compensated for in the commitment and quality of the performances.

NEW REVIEW

Górecki. Symphony No. 3, "Symphony of Sorrowful Songs", Op. 36. **Dawn Upshaw** (sop); **London Sinfonietta/David Zinman.** Elektra Nonesuch 7559-79282-2. Recorded in 1991.

54m DDD 4/93

Górecki's Third Symphony has become legend. Composed over 16 years ago it has always had its champions and admirers within the contemporary music world, but in 1993 it found a new audience of undreamt-of proportions. A few weeks after its release, this Elektra Nonesuch release not only entered the classical top-ten charts, but was also riding high in the UK Pop Album charts. With sales figures exceeding 300,000 it has since become the biggest selling disc of music by a contemporary classical composer. The Symphony, subtitled *Symphony of Sorrowful Songs* was composed during a period when Górecki's musical style was undergoing a radical change from avant-garde serialism to a more accessible style firmly anchored to tonal traditions. The Symphony's three elegiac movements (or 'songs') form a triptych of laments for all the innocent victims of World War Two and are a reflection upon man's inhumanity to man in general, and as such it has become one of the most moving artistic documents of our time. The songs — including a poignant setting of an inscription scratched by a girl prisoner on the wall of her cell in a Gestapo prison — are beautifully and ethereally sung by Dawn Upshaw, and David Zinman and the London Sinfonietta provide an intense and committed performance of the shimmering orchestral writing. The whole venture is supported by an excellent recording.

Additional recommendation ...
No. 3[b]. *Three Pieces in Old Style*[a]. [b]**Stefania Woytowicz** (sop); [a]**Warsaw Chamber Orchestra/Karol Teutsch;** [b]**Berlin Radio Symphony Orchestra/Wlodzimierz Kamirski.** Koch Schwann Musica Mundi 311041 — 55m ADD 4/93

Górecki. String Quartet No. 1, Op. 62, "Already it is Dusk"[a]. Lerchenmusik, Op. 53[b]. [b]**Michael Collins** (cl); [b]**Christopher van Kampen** (vc); [a]**Kronos Quartet** (David

Harrington, John Sherba, vns; Hank Dutt, va; Joan Jeanrenaud, vc); [b]**John Constable** (pf). Elektra Nonesuch 7559-79257-2. Recorded 1989-90.

54m DDD 9/91

The title of Górecki's String Quartet could be read as a synonym for "it's later than you think", and from one angle the work certainly seems to embody a deep resistance to the assumption that music can only progress by being ever more novel and ever more complex. But no composer who finds so much that is new and fresh in traditional tonality can be wholly despairing, and Górecki's work at it best makes a very positive creative statement. The ideas all have intense personal associations for him — he evokes Polish folk music, Catholic chant, and such icons of Western art music as Beethoven's Fourth Piano Concerto, whose opening features in *Lerchenmusik*. The subtitle of this piece, "Recitatives and Ariosos", indicates the two poles of Górecki's style — dramatic declamation and lyric meditation — within both of which he is willing to oppose highly refined delicacy with distinctly primitive aggressiveness. His forms are not entirely non-developmental, but cumulative repetitions and strong contrasts are their principal features. Even if you are left with the suspicion that too much of what music can and should aspire to is being omitted here, Górecki's strong and immediate emotional world is difficult to ignore, and there are no drawbacks to either the performances or the recordings.

Additional recommendation ...

String Quartets — No. 1; No. 2, "Quasi una Fantasia". **Kronos Quartet.** Elektra Nonesuch 7559-79319-2 (*No. 1 is taken from the CD reviewed above*) — 47m DDD 4/93

Further listening ...

Epitafium, Op. 12[ab]. Scontri, Op. 17[b]. Genesis II: Canti strumentali, Op. 19 No. 2[b]. Refrain, Op. 21[b]. Old Polish music, Op. 24[c]. [a]**Polish National Philharmonic Choir;** [b]**Polish National Symphony Orchestra, Katowice/Jan Krenz;** [c]**Polish National Philharmonic Orchestra, Warsaw/Andrzej Markowski.** Olympia OCD385 (4/93).

Old Polish music, Op. 24[a]. Totus tuus, Op. 60[b]. Beatus vir, Op. 38[c]. [c]**Nikita Storojev** (bass); [bc]**Prague Philharmonic Choir;** [ac]**Czech Philharmonic Orchestra/John Nelson.** Argo 436 835-2ZH (4/93).

Louis Moreau Gottschalk

American 1829-1869

Gottschalk. PIANO WORKS. **Philip Martin.** Hyperion CDA66459. Recorded in 1990. Le bananier, RO21. Le banjo, RO22. Canto del gitano, RO35. Columbia, RO61. Danza, RO66. Le mancenillier, RO142. Mazurka in A minor, RO164. Minuit à Seville, RO170. Ojos criollos, RO184. Romance in E flat major, RO270. Sixième ballade, RO14. Souvenir de la Havane, RO246. Souvenir de Porto Rico, RO250. Union, RO269.

1h 11m DDD 9/91 

Pianistic phenomenons of the nineteenth-century European variety are two-a-penny — American ones are as rare as hens' teeth. One such phenomenon however was Louis Moreau Gottschalk. Gottschalk was born in New Orleans in 1829 at a time when America was about as far off the musical map as you could get — to most Europeans America was a place of vast open spaces, wild Indians and white barbarians but certainly not pianistic prodigies. His parents recognized his musical talents at an early age, and at 13 they sent him to Paris where, after considerable difficulty in finding anyone to take him seriously, he eventually found guidance under the tutelage of Charles Hallé and later with Charles Stamaty, who unleashed him onto an unsuspecting Paris audience (among them Chopin and Kalkbrenner) in 1845. Gottschalk's concert career, and his magnetism as a performer (he was a notorious womanizer) paralleled that of Liszt's, and he toured extensively in France, Switzerland and Spain before returning to America in 1853. He was a prolific composer of piano music (well over 100 published works) which vary from Lisztian bravura and Chopinesque musings through to lighter genre pieces of the salon *morceaux* variety. Philip Martin's generous programme presents us with a good cross section; from the immensely popular salon pieces such as *Le banjo, Le bananier* ("The banana tree") and *Columbia* (an exuberant paraphrase on Stephen Foster's *My Old Kentucky Home*) as well as including several examples that reflect Gottschalk's love of Latin American and Creole dance rhythms. Martin concludes the recital with a spirited performance of *Union*; a brilliant concert paraphrase on national airs (including a minor key *Yankee Doodle* and a delicately harmonized *Star Spangled Banner*) where the influence of Liszt (and even Alkan) are very much in evidence. A very enjoyable disc indeed.

Further listening ...

PIANO WORKS, Volumes 1 and 2. [a]**Eugene List,** [b]**Cary Lewis,** [c]**Joseph Werner,** [d]**Reid Nibley** (pfs); [e]**Utah Symphony Orchestra/Maurice Abravanel.** Vanguard Classics 08.4050/1.71 (5/93, recorded 1956-62).
08.4050.71[a] — Le Banjo, RO22. The Dying Poet, RO75. Souvenir de Porto Rico, RO250. Le Bananier, RO21. Ojos Criollos, RO185. Bamboula, RO20. The maiden's blush, RO141. The last hope, RO133. Suis-moi!, RO253. Pasquinade, RO189. La Savane, RO232. Tournament Galop, RO264. *08.4051.71* — La jota aragonesa, RO130[ab]. Souvenir d'Andalousie, RO242[ac]. La gallina, RO100[ac]. Orfa, RO186[ab]. Marche de nuit, RO151[ac]. Printemps d'amour, RO214[ab]. Radieuse, RO217[ac]. Réponds-moi, RO225[ab]. Tremolo, RO265[ab]. L'etincelle, RO80[ac]. Ses yeux, RO234[ac]. The Union, RO269[ab] (arr. Liszt). Grande tarantelle, RO259[de] (arr. Hershykay). Symphony No. 1, RO255, "La nuit des tropiques"[e].

Charles François Gounod

French 1818-1893

Gounod. Symphony No. 1 in D major. Petite symphonie.
Bizet (ed. Hogwood). L'Arlésienne — excerpts. **Saint Paul Chamber Orchestra/ Christopher Hogwood.** Decca 430 231-2DH. Recorded in 1989.
L'Arlésienne — Prélude; Minuetto; Entr'acte; Mélodrame; Pastorale; Carillon.

1h 7m DDD 7/91 

Christopher Hogwood here gives us a delightful recording of works by a pair of French composers who are well matched, for Gounod taught Bizet and spoke tearfully at his funeral. It also reminds us of Gounod's skill outside the opera house, though there is nothing especially French about this symphony that he seems to have written almost as a tribute to Mendelssohn, whom he came to know personally and admired as a musician. In other words, this is the more classical kind of nineteenth-century music and its origin in the romantic era is only revealed in its unashamed charm and elegance — the only way here, perhaps, in which Gounod shows his Gallioc nationality. Hogwood and his expert players of the Saint Paul Chamber Orchestra are perfectly at ease in this work and the performance of the *Petite symphonie* for nine wind instruments is no less stylish. In Bizet's incidental music for Daudet's play *L'Arlésienne*, Hogwood's touch is no less sure. He has gone back to the original theatre scoring rather than playing the better-known orchestral suites that were made later, which means an odd instrumental combination including seven violins but only one viola, a saxophone and a piano, plus the restoration of some original keys. The recording is spacious and detailed, and one only wishes that Decca had provided separate tracks for the six Bizet pieces.

Additional recommendation ...
No. 1; No. 2 in E flat major. **Toulouse Capitole Orchestra/Michel Plasson.** EMI CDM7 63949-2 — 59m DDD 3/92

Gounod. FAUST — ballet music.
Offenbach (arr. Rosenthal). Gaîté parisienne — ballet. **Montreal Symphony Orchestra/Charles Dutoit.** Decca 411 708-2DH. From 411 708-1DH (3/84).

59m DDD 7/84

The very title of Offenbach's *Gaîté parisienne* tells us that this is unashamedly music to delight. However, it is not the composer's own but rather one given to a collection of his music arranged by Ravel's pupil Manuel Rosenthal for Léonide Massine and his Ballets Russes de Monte Carlo in 1938. The ballet is set in a Parisian night club and includes many attractive dance pieces as well as the celebrated Can-can from *Orpheus in the Underworld* and the Barcarolle from *The Tales of Hoffman*. We may forget all about Marlowe's play when we come to the *Faust* ballet, for originally Gounod's opera had no such thing as this elaborate danced section in which the *femmes fatales* of history paraded before Faust. But it seems that the Paris Opéra insisted on it. The music is in different style from Offenbach but still lilting and highly attractive. Dutoit and his excellent Montreal orchestra are admirable in this music, and if there's a trace of brashness in the noisier sections of the Offenbach that is justified by the nature of the music itself.

Gounod. FAUST. **Richard Leech** (ten) Faust; **Cheryl Studer** (sop) Marguerite; **José van Dam** (bass-bar) Méphistophélès; **Thomas Hampson** (bass) Valentin; **Martine Mahé** (mez) Siebel; **Nadine Denize** (sop) Marthe; **Marc Barrard** (bar) Wagner; **French Army Chorus; Toulouse Capitole Choir and Orchestra/Michel Plasson.** EMI CDS7 54228-2. Notes, text and translation included. Recorded in 1991.

③ 3h 24m DDD 12/91 

Here we have a performance that is, at last, worthy of Gounod's concept. Plasson respects and loves the score, lavishing on it infinite care over minutiae. His affection sometimes leads him to very slow speeds but by and large the extra space is used to enhance respect for this epitome of French, nineteenth-century romantic opera. He and his orchestra light the score from within, showing how a perceptive, knowledgeable hand can restore a too-familiar picture. Plasson puts us further in his debt by playing the score complete and, as a bonus, given us, in an appendix, passages cut before the première. Leech is a near-ideal Faust, singing with lyrical, liquid tone, stylish phrasing and evincing idiomatic French. Studer, also at home in the language, produces firm, lovely tone, sensitive phrasing and encompasses every facet of the character. Van Dam is a resolute, implacable Méphistophélès who never indulges in false histrionics and sings with subtlety of accent. Plasson's Toulouse forces are wholly at home in this music and, as an added pleasure, the French Army Chorus are called in to give a touch of authenticity to the Soldiers' Chorus.

Additional recommendations ...
Soloists; Paris Opéra Chorus and Orchestra/Georges Prêtre. EMI CDS7 47493-8 — ③ 3h 10m ADD 4/87 Ⓑ
Soloists; Paris Opéra Chorus and Orchestra/André Cluytens. EMI CMS7 69983-2 — ③ 2h 51m ADD 7/89 ▲ Ⓑ

NEW REVIEW

Gounod. MIREILLE. **Janette Vivalda** (sop) Mireille; **Nicolai Gedda** (ten) Vincent; **Christiane Gayraud** (contr) Taven; **Michel Dens** (bar) Ourrias; **Madeleine Ignal** (sop) Vincenette; **André Vessières** (bass) Ramon; **Christiane Jacquin** (sop) Clemence; **Marcello Cortis** (bar) Ambroise; **Aix-en-Provence Festival Chorus; Paris Conservatoire Orchestra/André Cluytens.** EMI mono CMS7 64382-2. Notes and text included. From Columbia 33CX1299/301 (11/55). Recorded in 1954.

② 2h 14m ADD 12/92 

Unlike *Faust* and *Roméo et Juliette*, Gounod's *Mireille* is a specifically French subject, based on Mistral's epic poem *Mirèio*. It has never really established itself in the international repertory, perhaps partly because of its essentially Provençal atmosphere and story, but also because it went through several revisions in Gounod's lifetime, some of them at the behest of the Parisian prima donnas of the 1860s. The story of the tragic love of Mireille for the peasant boy Vincent, thwarted by her father's intention that she should marry the bully Ourrias, reaches its climax in the scene on the plain of Crau, where Mireille has gone on a pilgrimage to pray for Vincent's recovery after he has been wounded in a duel with Ourrias. This is the big moment for the soprano, much more so than the more famous waltz-song "O légère hirondelle", added as a sop to the divas (and included in this recording as an appendix). It requires a real dramatic force from the singer (Caballé made a marvellous recording of it) and Janette Vivalda rises with quite surprising strength to meet the challenge. Her voice is typically French, on the acid side, but wholly authentic. The very young Gedda is at his honeyed best as Vincent and the veteran Michel Dens superb as Ourrias. The edition used is that made by Henri Busser for the Opéra Comique in the 1930s (the same used on all recordings of *Mireille* to date). This 1955 recording, based on a production staged in the open air at Les Baux as part of the Aix festival, is conducted with aplomb by Cluytens. The sound is a little restricted by modern standards but the performance leaves little to desire.

NEW REVIEW

Gounod. MORS ET VITA. **Barbara Hendricks** (sop); **Nadine Denize** (mez); **John Aler** (ten); **José van Dam** (bass-bar); **Orféon Donostiarra; Toulouse Capitole Orchestra/Michel Plasson.** EMI CDS7 54459-2. Text and translation included.

(2) 2h 36m DDD 2/93

Those who claim to find Verdi's Requiem over-theatrical for a sacred work should hear *Mors et Vita*, an example of high-Victorian lush oratorio. Composed for Birmingham where Gounod's earlier sacred trilogy *La Redemption* had been a big success, *Mors et Vita* was first given there in 1884 and later that year in London for an audience including Queen Victoria, at the Albert Hall, where Gounod had been the first conductor of the Royal Albert Hall Choral Society. It is a large piece requiring the sort of fervent performance that one imagines the Victorians adored. The two main sections, death before life, because according to Gounod "in the order of eternal things death precedes life", are introduced by a Prologue for baritone and choir and linked by a six-part Judgement section which contains what became the most famous passage in the work, *Somnus Mortuorum*, which flummoxed the critics in the 1880s who accused Gounod of composing "a blot, a hideous excrescence, musically unbearable". This is difficult to imagine now, but for those with a taste in higher-flown late nineteenth-century style, this performance could hardly be bettered. The four soloists are all experienced in Gounod's operas (Hendricks was a beautiful Juliette in Paris a few years ago) and the spacious recording gives the work all its spectacular moments — one highlight is the orchestral epilogue to *Mors* in which the main theme is expanded to a swooning crescendo that would have made the balletgoers in the old days at L'Opéra very happy.

Percy Grainger

American/Australian 1882-1961

Grainger. ORCHESTRAL WORKS. **Philip Martin** (pf); [a]**Moray Welsh** (vc); **Bournemouth Sinfonietta/Kenneth Montgomery.** Chandos Collect CHAN6542. From CHAN8377 (8/85). Recorded in 1978.

Youthful Suite — Rustic dance; Eastern intermezzo. Blithe Bells (free ramble on a theme by Bach, "Sheep may safely graze"). Spoon River. My Robin is to the Greenwood Gone. Green Bushes. Country Gardens (orch. Schmid). Mock Morris. Youthful Rapture[a]. Shepherd's Hey. Walking Tune. Molly on the shore. Handel in the Strand (orch. Wood).

55m ADD 2/92

None of the 13 items on this disc is longer than nine minutes, and they are carefully planned to make an attractive sequence for continuous listening. The two items from the *Youthful Suite* were composed when Grainger was but 17 years old and are quite advanced harmonically for 1898-9. *Blithe Bells* is a somewhat florid arrangement of Bach's "Sheep may safely graze", and then we have *Spoon River*, an arrangement of an old American fiddle tune. *My Robin is to the Greenwood Gone, Green Bushes* and the famous *Country Gardens* are all based on English folk-tunes, but the cheerful *Mock Morris* is an original pastiche. *Handel in the Strand* is a set of variations on Handel's *Harmonious Blacksmith* whilst the charming *Walking Tune* for wind quintet came to Grainger's mind when on a walking tour. There's no doubt that Kenneth Montgomery has a strong sympathy for Grainger's music, and he directs lively performances. The recording acoustic is a little reverberant but the sound quality is otherwise good.

Grainger. ORCHESTRAL WORKS. **Melbourne Symphony Orchestra/Geoffrey Simon.** Koch International Classics 37003-2. Recorded in 1989.
The Warriors. Hill-Song No. 1. Irish Tune from County Derry, BFMS20. Hill-Song No. 2. Danish Folk-Music Suite. **Traditional Chinese** (harmonized Yasser, arr. Grainger, orch. Sculthorpe): Beautiful fresh flower.

lh 7m DDD 11/90 

It was Sir Thomas Beecham who first suggested to Percy Grainger the idea of writing a ballet, and though in the event a commission was not forthcoming Grainger went ahead with the work that was to become without doubt one of his largest and most extravagant works — *The Warriors*. Although it has only a relatively short duration — 18 minutes — its demands in every other aspect are gargantuan; in addition to an already large orchestra he calls for six horns, three pianos, a large-tuned percussion section (including wooden and steel marimbas and tubular bells), an off-stage brass section and — if necessary — three conductors! (though in this recording Geoffrey Simon takes on the task single handed), with the musical material deriving from no less than 15 themes and motifs. Grainger described the piece as "an orgy of war-like dances, processions and merry-making broken, or accompanied by amorous interludes" — a sort of "warriors of the world unite". It was described by Delius (the work's dedicatee) as "by far Grainger's greatest thing" and indeed it seems to encapsulate and condense the very essence of Grainger's wild and free-roaming spirit. The two *Hill-Songs* were a response to "the soul-shaking hillscapes" of West Argyllshire after a three-day hike in the Scottish Highlands. Like many of Grainger's compositions they exist in various scorings from the two-piano and solo piano arrangements to the chamber orchestra version of 1923 heard in this recording. Their organic, unbroken flow of melodic ideas and rhythmically complex writing create a bracing, evocative impression of the spirit of the Highlands. The remaining works on the disc consist of the attractive *Danish Folk-Music Suite*, notable for the two haunting ballads "The Power of Love" and "The Nightingale and the Two Sisters" and three short folk-song arrangements from China, Denmark and Ireland. Geoffrey Simon and the Melbourne Symphony Orchestra positively revel in this music, and the excellent recording is clear and spacious. An essential disc for those with an adventurous spirit.

NEW REVIEW

Grainger. PIANO WORKS. **Penelope Thwaites.** Unicorn-Kanchana DKPCD9127. Recorded in 1992.
Danish Folk-Music Suite — The Power of Love; The Nightingale and the two Sisters; Jutish Medley. One More Day, my John. Knight and Shepherd's Daughter. Near Woodstock Town. Country Gardens. Sussex Mummer's Christmas Carol. Shepherd's Hey. To a Nordic Princess. Love at first sight. Over the Hills and far away. Bridal Lullaby. Handel in the Strand. Colonial Song. Paraphrase on the Waltz of the Flowers from Tchaikovsky's "The Nutcracker". ***Fauré*** (arr. Grainger): Nell, Op. 18 No. 1. ***Dowland*** (arr. Grainger): Now, O now, I needs must part.

lh 9m DDD 3/93

Many of Percy Grainger's works exist in as many as half-a-dozen scorings, and deciding which of them is the 'best' version is seldom a simple matter. Sometimes in a later variant he expands or virtually re-writes the original, at other times he strips it to the bone to make it accessible to amateur players. A pretty good general rule, though, is that Grainger is often at his Grainger-est in the versions for solo piano. Sometimes they seem to recapture his own brilliant improvisations, often his most luscious harmonies seem invented at and for the keyboard.

Penelope Thwaites, in this well-recorded recital, has made a shrewd selection from three areas of Grainger's work, the folk-song arrangements, the affectionate tributes to other composers and his original compositions. In the first two categories it was often Grainger's way to swathe the originals with festoons of rich harmony, but Thwaites realizes that in almost every case it was a fine tune that he responded to, and while taking obvious enjoyment in his deep-pile chords she never allows the melody to be obscured. This is an advantage in his own pieces, too; both the seamless melody of *Colonial Song* and the more florid *To a Nordic Princess* (dedicated to Grainger's Swedish wife, and first heard at their wedding before a vast audience in the Hollywood Bowl) can seem a bit too long if they're indulgently played. Thwaites is nimble in *Country Gardens* and agreeably showy in the roof-raising *Flower Waltz* arrangement, but it's the noble melody, lovingly embellished, of *Now, O now, I needs must part* that best typifies her playing.

Grainger. PIANO WORKS, Volume 1. **Martin Jones.** Nimbus NI5220.
Andante con moto. Bridal Lullaby. Children's March. Colonial Song. English Waltz. Handel in the Strand. Harvest Hymn. In a Nutshell — suite. In Dahomey. Mock Morris. Peace. Sailor's Song. Saxon Twi-play. The Immovable Do. To a Nordic Princess. Walking Tune.

1h 12m DDD 4/90 

This is the best of Percy Grainger, and it would be hard to imagine it better played. Most of these pieces are better-known in Grainger's lavish and colourful orchestrations, but they seem to have more pith and urgency to them in their piano versions, even where those were not the originals. The luscious *To a Nordic Princess* has more energy to it in this form, and the slow movement of *In a Nutshell*, far from the lyrical interlude that it can sound in orchestrated form, emerges as a very direct and almost shockingly poignant self-image of Grainger. Even the popular trifles, *Handel in the Strand* and *Mock Morris*, take on added zest at the crisp and airy tempos that Martin Jones chooses; even more importantly the haunting lyricism of *The Immovable Do* and the deep nostalgia of *Colonial Song* are liberated by restoration to Grainger's own instrument. They need something like Grainger's own flamboyantly virtuoso pianism, of course, and one of the reasons that they are far more familiar in their orchestral guise is that they make hair-raising demands of the pianist. Jones is fully equal to them; indeed, he goes well beyond meeting those demands and sounds as though he is positively enjoying himself. A hugely enjoyable collection; the rather disembodied recording is a quirk rather than a real drawback.

Enrique Granados

Spanish 1867-1916

Granados. Danzas españolas, Op. 37. **Alicia de Larrocha** (pf). Decca 414 557-2DH. From SXL6980 (3/82). Recorded in 1980.

56m ADD 10/85 

NEW REVIEW

Granados. Danzas españolas, Op. 37. Seis Escenas románticas. **Jean-François Heisser** (pf). Erato 2292-45803-2. Recorded in 1991.

1h 18m DDD 11/92 

Not long before he drowned, in 1916, when his ship was sunk by a German submarine, Granados had felt that his compositional career was being opened up by the deep vein of genuine Spanish feeling that he was increasingly able to tap in his music. His piano suite, *Goyescas*, and the opera based on it were, perhaps, the most convincing and individual expression of that sentiment, but the numerous shorter pieces for piano that he produced, some of which were collected together in the sets of *Danzas españolas*, also show real sparks of that same nationalism, even though they are still clearly rooted in the common European harmonic and melodic language of the later romantic period. These sparks need to be emphasized in performance by an artist who has an intuitive feel for them, and there is none better suited than Alicia de Larrocha, who has both the technical control and emotional insight to make the most of this music. Her playing, even at moments of highest constraint, has an undercurrent of powerful forces striving to be released; when the constraint is lifted, the effect is tumultuous. Thankfully, the recording can cope. The result is an almost definitive issue of this intriguing collection. However, the French pianist Jean-François Heisser also has much to tell us about this appealing music. His versions of the *Danzas españolas* are crisp, clean-fingered and full of Gallic spirit (try, by way of an example, the famous "Andaluza" on track 5); they suggest that these pieces be brought onto an approximate line of comparison with, say, Smetana's equally colourful — and musically substantial — *Czech Dances*. Furthermore, Heisser adds 25 minutes' worth of *Escenas románticas*, a sequence of six evocative piano tone-poems ranging in style from a simple and affecting "Berceuse" to a large-scale *Allegro appassionato*. Here too Heisser excels, and his Steinway piano is vividly recorded.

Additional recommendation ...
Danzas españolas. **Thomas Rajna** (pf). CRD CRD3321 — 56m ADD 12/90

Granados. Goyescas — suite for piano. **Alicia de Larrocha** (pf). Decca 411 958-2DH. From SXL6785 (12/77). Recorded in 1976.

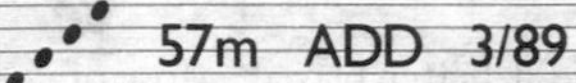

The Granados *Goyescas* are profoundly Spanish in feeling, but the folk influence is more of court music than of the flamenco or *cante hondo* styles which reflect gipsy and Moorish influence. This set of seven pieces was given its first performance by the composer in 1911, and his own exceptional ability as a pianist is evident in its consistently elaborate textures. That performance took place in Barcelona, and as Granados's compatriot and a native of that very city Alicia de Larrocha fully understands this music in its richly varied moods; a fact which tells in interpretations that have a compelling conviction and drive. Thus, she can dance enchantingly in such a piece as "El Fandango de candil", while in the celebrated "Maiden and the nightingale", No. 4 of the set, we listen to a wonderful outpouring of Mediterranean emotion, all the more moving for its avoidance of excessive rubato and over-pedalling. A splendid disc of one of the twentieth century's piano masterpieces, which was atmospherically recorded in the former Decca studios in West Hampstead in 1976 and has transferred well to CD.

Edvard Grieg

Norwegian 1843-1907

Grieg. Piano Concerto in A minor, Op. 16.
Schumann. Piano Concerto in A minor, Op. 54. **Stephen Kovacevich** (pf); **BBC Symphony Orchestra/Sir Colin Davis.** Philips 412 923-2PH. From 6500 166 (3/72).

1h 1m ADD 10/86

Since the advent of the LP the Grieg and Schumann concertos have been ideally paired and the performances on this disc have set the standard by which all other versions are judged. The scale of both is perfectly managed. The Grieg, with its natural charm and freshness, has power too (witness the superb first movement cadenza), but poetry dominates and climaxes must never seem hectoring, as both these artists fully understand. The romanticism of the Schumann Concerto is particularly elusive on record, with its contrasting masculine and feminine elements difficult to set in ideal balance. But here there is no sense of any problem, so naturally does the music flow, the changing moods being seen within the overall perspective. There is refinement and strength, the virtuosity sparkles, the expressive elements are perfectly integrated with the need for bravura. This CD remastering of a very well balanced and felicitous recording gives both performances a new lease of life.

Additional recommendations ...
As above. **Radu Lupu** (pf); **London Symphony Orchestra/André Previn.** Decca Ovation 417 728-2DM — 1h 1m ADD 12/87

As above. **Murray Perahia** (pf); **Bavarian Radio Symphony Orchestra/Sir Colin Davis.** CBS Masterworks CD44899 — lh DDD 5/89

As above. **Pascal Devoyon** (pf); **London Philharmonic Orchestra/Jerzy Maksymiuk.** Classics for Pleasure CD-CFP4574 — lh 3m DDD 2/91 £

As above. **Lars Vogt** (pf); **City of Birmingham Symphony Orchestra/Simon Rattle.** EMI CDC7 54746-2 — lh 2m DDD 1/93

Grieg[a]. *Schumann*[c]. **Franck.** *Symphonic Variations*[b]. [ab]**Sir Clifford Curzon,** [c]**Friedrich Gulda** (pfs); [a]**London Symphony Orchestra/Øivin Fjeldstad;** [b]**London Philharmonic Orchestra/Sir Adrian Boult;** [c]**Vienna Philharmonic Orchestra/Volkmar Andreae.** Decca Headline Classics 433 628-2DSP *(see review under Franck; refer to Index to Reviews)* — lh 16m ADD 1/92 £ ▲

Grieg. Norwegian Dances, Op. 35. Lyric Suite, Op. 54. Symphonic Dances, Op. 64. **Gothenburg Symphony Orchestra/Neeme Järvi.** DG 419 431-2GH.

lh 8m DDD 1/87

Grieg's music has that rare quality of eternal youth: however often one hears it, its complexion retains its bloom, the smile its radiance and the youthful sparkle remains undimmed. Though he is essentially a miniaturist, who absorbed the speech rhythms and inflections of Norwegian folk melody into his bloodstream, Grieg's world is well defined. Both the *Norwegian Dances* and the *Symphonic Dances* were originally piano duets, which Grieg subsequently scored: Järvi conducts both with enthusiasm and sensitivity. In the *Lyric Suite* he restores "Klokkeklang" (Bell-ringing), which Grieg omitted from the final score: it is remarkably atmospheric and evocative, and serves to show how forward-looking Grieg became in his late years. The recording is exceptionally fine and of wide dynamic range; the sound is very natural and the perspective true to life.

Additional recommendation ...

Norwegian Dances. Old Norwegian Romance with Variations, Op. 51. In Autumn, Op. 11. Lyric Pieces, Op. 43 — No. 5, "Erotik". **Svendsen.** *Two Icelandic Melodies.* **Iceland Symphony Orchestra/Petri Sakari.** Chandos CHAN9028 — lh 6m DDD 8/92

Grieg. ORCHESTRAL WORKS. [a]**Ilse Hollweg** (sop); [a]**Beecham Choral Society; Royal Philharmonic Orchestra/Sir Thomas Beecham.** EMI Studio Plus CDM7 64751-2. Items marked [a] from HMV ASD258 (1/59), [b] HMV ASD518 (4/63), [cd] Columbia 22CX1363 (9/56).

Peer Gynt — The Bridal March passes by; Prelude; In the Hall of the Mountain King; Solveig's Song; Prelude; Arab Dance; Anitra's Dance; Prelude; Solveig's Cradle Song[a]. Symphonic Dances, Op. 64 — Allegretto grazioso[b]. In Autumn, Op. 11[c]. Old Norwegian Romance with Variations, Op. 51[d].

lh 16m ADD  

Grieg's incidental music was an important integral part of Ibsen's *Peer Gynt* and from this score Grieg later extracted the two familiar suites. This recording of excerpts from *Peer Gynt* goes back to 1957 but still sounds well and is most stylishly played. He included the best known ("Anitra's Dance" is a delicate gem here) together with "Solveig's Song" and "Solveig's Cradle Song". Sir Thomas uses Ilse Hollweg to advantage, her voice suggesting the innocence of the virtuous and faithful peasant heroine. There is also an effective use of the choral voices which are almost inevitably omitted in ordinary performances of the two well-known orchestral suites: the male chorus of trolls in the "Hall of the Mountain King" are thrilling, and the women in the "Arab Dance" are charming. The other two pieces are well worth having too; *Symphonic Dances* is a later, freshly pastoral work, while the overture *In Autumn* is an orchestral second version of an early piece for piano duet. This reissue is further enhanced by the first release in stereo of the *Old Norwegian Romance*.

Additional recommendations ...

Peer Gynt — complete. Sigurd Jorsalfar — incidental music, Op. 22. **Soloists; Gösta Ohlin's Vocal Ensemble; Pro Musica Chamber Choir; Gothenburg Symphony**

Orchestra/Neeme Järvi. DG 423 079-2GH2 — ② 2h 4m DDD 2/88 Ⓑ
Peer Gynt — excerpts. **Soloists; San Francisco Symphony Chorus and Orchestra/Herbert Blomstedt.** Decca 425 448-2DH — 1h 13m DDD 3/90 Ⓑ

Grieg. String Quartet in G minor, Op. 27.
Schumann. String Quartet No. 1 in A major, Op. 41. **English Quartet** (Diana Cummings, Colin Callow, vns; Luciano Iorio, va; Geoffrey Thomas, vc). Unicorn-Kanchana DKPCD9092. Recorded in 1990.

1h 6m DDD 3/92

Grieg was in his mid-thirties when writing his G minor String Quartet (the only one he ever completed), a work with a phrase from his recently composed Ibsen setting *Spillemaend* ("Fiddlers") as its unifying motto. Frequently criticized for over-thick scoring and moments of laboured invention, it rarely turns up in concert programmes, and for a long time was conspicuous by its absence from the CD catalogue. Now, at last, it has found rescuers on disc, with this vivid performance from the English Quartet most likely to makes its disparagers think again. The music's swift-changing moods and bold dynamic contrasts are in fact caught with a surprisingly un-English intensity of feeling and temperament, not least the first movement's alternations of demonstrative vehemence and seductive lyricism. The players respond with the same imaginative immediacy to the folk-spirit of the Intermezzo's central trio, and find all the bracing brio for the saltarello-inspired finale. As a life-long Schumann devotee, Grieg would no doubt have been delighted to find his own work coupled with Schumann's First in this medium, written in a Mendelssohn-dominated Leipzig at the age of 32. Here, the English Quartet attune themselves to the music's suave lyricism with the same keen sense of style. Apart from a touch of edginess in high-lying climaxes (notably in the Grieg) the tonal reproduction is very acceptable.

Grieg. LYRIC PIECES — excerpts. **Emil Gilels** (pf). DG 419 749-2GH. From 2530 476 (3/75).
Arietta, Op. 12 No. 1. Berceuse, Op. 38 No. 1. Butterfly, Op. 43 No. 1. Solitary Traveller, Op. 43 No. 2. Album-leaf, Op. 47 No. 2. Melody, Op. 47 No. 3. Norwegian Dance, "Halling", Op. 47 No. 4. Nocturne, Op. 54 No. 4. Scherzo, Op. 54 No. 5. Homesickness, Op. 57 No. 6. Brooklet, Op. 62 No. 4. Homeward, Op. 62 No. 6. In ballad vein, Op. 65 No. 5. Grandmother's minuet, Op. 68 No. 2. At your feet, Op. 68 No. 3. Cradlesong, Op. 68 No. 5. Once upon a time, Op. 71 No. 1. Puck, Op. 71 No. 3. Gone, Op. 71 No. 6. Remembrances, Op. 71 No. 7.

56m ADD 10/87 P

This record is something of a gramophone classic. The great Russian pianist Emil Gilels, an artist of staggering technical accomplishment and intellectual power, here turns his attention to Grieg's charming miniatures. He brings the same insight and concentration to these apparent trifles as he did to towering masterpieces of the classic repertoire. The programme proceeds chronologically and one can appreciate the gradual but marked development in Grieg's harmonic and expressive language — from the folk-song inspired early works to the more progressive and adventurous later ones. Gilels's fingerwork is exquisite and the sense of total involvement with the music almost religious in feeling. This is a wonderful recording: pianistic perfection.

Grieg. LYRIC PIECES, Volume 1. **Peter Katin** (pf). Unicorn-Kanchana Souvenir UKCD2033. Recorded in 1989.
Book 1, Op. 12; Book 2, Op. 38; Book 3, Op. 43; Book 4, Op. 47.

1h 3m DDD 9/90

Between 1867 and 1901, Grieg published ten sets of short piano pieces called *Lyric Pieces*, using an adjective which implies something expressive, songlike and on a small scale. Only one of the 29 here lasts more than four minutes and the shortest lasts just 40 seconds, yet they are not mere chips from the composer's work-bench but instead beautifully crafted miniatures in the tradition of Schumann's *Scenes from Childhood*. Although in the past pianists often played them in public, today we hardly ever hear them in the concert hall where, as Peter Katin points out in his booklet note, we usually get "far weightier fare". In fact a recorded performance is all the more welcome in that some of their intimacy is lost in an auditorium and Grieg certainly intended them to be heard in domestic surroundings. Some are 'easy' in the sense that the notes are not hard to play even for learners, but even so we gain immensely from the shaping of tone and rhythm that a fine artist can bring, especially when he so clearly loves the music. It is worth adding that there is plenty of variety here: thus Book 1 ends with a vigorous *National Song* that is very unlike the gentle little *Arietta* with which it begins. There are so many delights that it's hard to list special ones, but we would not go wrong if we lighted on the freshly charming *Butterfly, Little Bird* and *To the Spring* in Book 3, which remind us that Nature was often Grieg's inspiration. Pleasantly clean sound, with a touch of hardness in bigger passages.

NEW REVIEW

Grieg. SONGS. **Anne Sofie von Otter** (mez); **Bengt Forsberg** (pf). DG Grieg Anniversary Edition 437 521-2GH. Texts and translations included. Recorded in 1992.
Haugtussa, Op. 67. Two brown eyes, Op. 5 No. 1. I love but thee, Op. 5 No. 3. A swan, Op. 25 No. 2. With a waterlily, Op. 25 No. 4. Hope, Op. 26 No. 1. Spring, Op. 33 No. 2. Beside the stream, Op. 33 No. 5. From Monte Pincio, Op. 39 No. 1. Six Songs, Op. 48. Spring showers, Op. 49 No. 6. While I wait, Op. 60 No. 3. Farmyard Song, Op. 61 No. 3.

lh 8m DDD 6/93

With performances like this, Grieg in his celebratory year emerged as a first-rank composer in this genre. Anne Sofie von Otter is at the peak of her powers, glorying in this repertoire which she obviously loves and knows intimately. Take the *Haugtussa* cycle, which Grieg considered his greatest achievement in this sphere of writing. Von Otter projects her imagination of the visionary herd-girl with absolute conviction. She is no less successful in the German settings that follow. The sad depths of *One day, my thought* from Six Songs, Op. 48 also set memorably by Wolf in his *Spanish Songbook*, the hopelessness of Goethe's *The time of roses* (Op. 48 No. 5), a setting of great beauty are encompassed with unfettered ease, but so are the lighter pleasures of *Lauf der Welt*. Even the familiar *A dream* (Op. 48 No. 6) emerges as new in von Otter's daringly big-boned reading. Throughout, her readings are immeasurably enhanced by the imaginative playing by Bengt Forsberg. They breathe fresh life into *A swan* and in the almost as familiar *With a waterlily,* another superb Ibsen setting, the questing spirit expressed in the music is marvellously captured by the performers. And there are more pleasures to come. A superb account of *Hope,* a wistful, sweetly voiced and played account of *Spring*, the charming, teasing *While I wait* and a deeply poetic reading of the justly renowned *From Monte Pincio* are just three more definitive interpretations. This should be regarded as a 'must' for any collector of songs, indeed a collector of any kind.

Further listening ...

Funeral March in memory of Rikard Nordraak. In Autumn, Op. 11. Old Norwegian Romance with Variations, Op. 51. Symphony in C minor. **Gothenberg Symphony Orchestra/Neeme Järvi.** DG 427 321-2GH (6/89).

Holberg Suite, Op. 40. *Coupled with* ***Barber.*** Adagio for strings, Op. 11. ***Bloch.*** Concerto grosso No. 1[a]. ***Puccini.*** Crisantemi (arr. string orchestra). [a]**Irit Rob** (pf); **Israel Chamber Orchestra/Yoav Talmi.** Chandos CHAN8593 (8/88).

Lyric Pieces — Book 5, Op. 54; Book 6, Op. 57; Book 7, Op. 62. **Peter Katin** (pf). Unicorn-Kanchana Souvenir UKCD2034 (11/90).

Lyric Pieces — Book 8, Op. 65; Book 9, Op. 68; Book 10, Op. 71. **Peter Katin** (pf). Unicorn-Kanchana Souvenir UKCD2035 (2/91).

Violin Sonatas — No. 1 in F major, Op. 8; No. 2 in G major, Op. 13; No. 3 in C minor, Op. 45. **Rodrigue Milosi** (vn); **Noël Lee** (pf). Adda 581028 (1/90).

6 Songs, Op. 25. 5 Songs, Op. 60. Haugtussa — song cycle, Op. 67. **Ellen Westberg Andersen** (sop); **Jens Harald Bratlie** (pf). Simax PSC1011.

Charles Griffes

American 1884-1920

Suggested listening ...

Songs — Am Kreuzweg wird begraben. An den Wind. Auf geheimem Waldespfade. Auf ihrem Grab. Das ist ein Brausen und Heulen. Das sterbende Kind. Elfe. Meeres Stille. Mein Herz ist wie die dunkle Nacht. Mit schwarzen Segeln. Des Müden Abendlied. Nachtlied. So halt' ich endlich dich umfangen. Der träumende See. Wo ich bin, mich rings umdunkelt. Wohl lag ich einst in Gram und Schmerz. Zwei Könige sassen auf Orkadal. *Coupled with* ***Ives:*** Du bist wie eine Blume. Feldeinsamkeit. Frühlingslied. Gruss. Ich grolle nicht. Ilmenau. Marie. Minnelied. Rosamunde. Rosenzweige. Ton. Weil' auf mir. Widmung. Wiegenlied; ***MacDowell:*** Drei Lieder, Op. 11. Zwei Leider, Op. 12. **Thomas Hampson** (bar); **Armen Guzelimian** (pf). Teldec 9031-72168-2 *(reviewed in Collections section; refer to Index to Reviews).*

Sofia Gubaidulina

Russian 1931-

Gubaidulina. String Quartet No. 2.
Kurtág. String Quartet No. 1, Op. 1. Hommage à Milhály András, Op. 13. Officium breve in memoriam Andreae Szervánzky, Op. 28.
Lutoslawski. String Quartet. **Arditti Quartet** (Irvine Arditti, David Alberman, vns; Levine Andrade, va; Rohan de Saram, vc). Disques Montaigne 789007. Recorded in 1990.

lh 12m DDD 4/92 

Recent political developments ensure that Sofia Gubaidulina's country of birth is given in the notes, not as Russia, but as the Tatar Autonomous People's Republic. Autonomy — the need for a personal tone of voice — is a quality all three of these eastern European composers well understand. Lutoslawski's quartet (1964) came at a crucial time in his development, as the first work to relate his new technique of aleatory counterpoint (in which the pitches but not necessarily the rhythms are prescribed) to a traditional, abstract genre. Compared to the best of his later works the quartet is perhaps too long-drawn-out, but this highly expressive and strongly disciplined performance makes an excellent case for it. Alongside the Lutoslawski the three works by György Kurtág sound remarkably intense and concentrated, yet with a lyricism that prevents their evident austerity from growing merely arid, and which makes the reference to a tonal melody in the *Officium breve* seem natural as well as touching. The world of consonant harmony is also evoked by Gubaidulina, not as an expression of regret for the irretrievable past but as a way of extending her own essentially modern language. There is a special sense of personal certainty and confidence about all the music on this well-recorded disc. It needs no special pleading, but the commanding authority of the Arditti Quartet's performance is still something to marvel at.

Further listening ...

Offertorium[a]. Hommage à T.S. Eliot[b]. [b]**Christine Whittlesey** (sop); [a]**Gidon Kremer,** [b]**Isabelle van Keulen** (vns); [b]**Tabea Zimmermann** (va); [b]**David Geringas** (vc); [b]**Alois Posch** (db); [b]**Eduard Brunner** (cl); [b]**Klaus Thunemann** (bn); [b]**Radovan Vlatkovič** (hn); [a]**Boston Symphony Orchestra/Charles Dutoit.** DG 427 336-2GH (9/89).

Garden of Joys and Sorrows[a]. Seven Last Words[b]. String Trio[c]. [a]**Irena Grafenauer** (fl); [a]**Maria Graf** (hp); [bc]**David Geringas** (vc); [b]**Elsbeth Moser** (accordion); [a]**Vladimir Mendelssohn,** [c]**Isabelle van Keulen,** [c]**Veronica Hagen** (vas); [b]**German Philharmonic Youth Chamber Orchestra/Mario Venzago.** Philips 434 041-2PH.

Louis-Gabriel Guillemain

French 1705-1770

Suggested listening ...

Violin Sonata in A major, Op. 1 No. 4. *Coupled with* **Leclair.** Violin Sonatas — A minor, Op. 5 No. 7; A major, Op. 9 No. 4. ***Mondonville.*** Violin Sonata in G major, Op. 3 No. 5. *Harpsichord Solos* — ***Duphly.*** La de Redemond. La du Buq. ***J-B. Forqueray.*** La Morangis ou La Plissay. **Simon Standage** (vn); **Lars Ulrik Mortensen** (hpd). Chandos CHAN0531 (6/93).

Ivor Gurney

British 1890-1937

Suggested listening ...

Five Preludes — No. 1 in F sharp major; No. 2 in A minor; No. 3 in D flat major; No. 4 in F sharp major. No. 5 in D major. *Preludes* — C major; C minor; D flat major; F sharp major. *Nocturnes* — A flat major; B major. Revery. To E. M. H.: A birthday present from Ivor. A picture. *Coupled with* **Elgar.** Concerto Allegro. Skizze. In Smyrna. Adieu. **Alan Gravill** (pf). Gamut Classics GAMCD516 (3/91).

The Western Playland[b]. Ludlow and Teme[a]. *Coupled with* ***Vaughan Williams.*** On Wenlock Edge[a]. [a]**Adrian Thompson** (ten); [b]**Stephen Varcoe** (bar); **Iain Burnside** (pf); **Delmé Quartet.** Hyperion CDA66385 (9/90).

Reynaldo Hahn

Venezuelan-French 1875-1947

Hahn. Premières Valses. Le rossignol éperdu — excerpts. **Catherine Joly** (pf). Accord 20054-2. Recorded in 1988.

lh 7m DDD 5/90

The very epitome of the suave, exquisite frequenter of fashionable Paris salons, Reynaldo Hahn has until recently been little recognized as a composer except for one or two songs. Moreover, the charming *Ciboulette* (the most successful of his many stage works) and the fact that he enjoyed a reputation as a Mozart conductor and that for the last two years of his life he was music director of the Paris Opéra, prove that he was no mere dilettante. The chain of ten *Premières Valses*, it is true, reflects the atmosphere of the salons, but their wide diversity of moods and their informed passing salutations to Chopin and Schubert betoken a cultivated and inventive mind. More serious are the 25 pieces selected from the later, little-known *Le rossignol éperdu*, which are travel vignettes of a literary provenance (a pity that the introductory quotations are not given here), a kind of musical diary mostly pervaded by a dark nostalgia: in this, as elsewhere in Hahn, melody is paramount. Catherine Joly plays everything here with the utmost subtlety of dynamics, rhythm and coloration. This disc opens up a new storehouse of miniatures — only three last as long as three minutes — which will be appreciated by the discriminating.

Further listening ...

MOZART — *musical comedy.* **Soloists; French Radio Lyric Orchestra/Pierre-Michel Le Conte.** Musidisc 20137-2 (3/92).

George Frederic Handel

German-British 1685-1759

Handel. ORGAN CONCERTOS. **Ton Koopman** (org); **Amsterdam Baroque Orchestra.** Erato Emerald 2292-45613-2.

Op. 4 — No. 2 in B flat major; No. 4 in F major; No. 6 in B flat major. Op 7 — No. 2; No. 4; No. 5.

Ih 18m DDD 11/91 

Handel's highly acclaimed skill as a virtuoso organist was a significant factor in attracting audiences. His organ concertos are rich in catchy tunes, with some of the long *allegros* sailing along with unstoppable momentum. But there are great treasures in the slow movements too — the *Andante* from Op. 4 No. 4 is full of colour and the solo part performs wonders of invention over a simple foundation of chords while the Menuet and Gavotte from Op. 7 No. 5 have great charm and elegance. Handel adapted several of these Concertos from other works — Op. 4 No. 5 comes from a recorder sonata and Op. 4 No. 6 was originally for harp — but the universality of the writing means that everything seems entirely at home in this context, especially given such compelling performances as here. Ton Koopman leads his performances from the organ stool, giving his disc a real feeling of intimacy which makes ideal home listening. He indulges in some thoroughly convincing improvisations at points where Handel too would have given free rein to his skills as a virtuoso organist.

Additional recommendation ...

Op. 4 — No. 1 in G minor; No. 2; No. 3 in G minor; No. 4; No. 5 in F major; No. 6; No. 14 in A major. **Simon Preston** (org); **The English Concert/Trevor Pinnock.** Archiv Produktion 413 465-2AH2 — ② Ih 30m DDD 12/84

Handel. Concerti grossi, Op. 3. **The English Concert/Trevor Pinnock** (hpd). Archiv Produktion 413 727-2AH.

57m DDD 3/85  

The abundant variety of these concertos is in the number and character of their movements, and in the ways in which a comparatively limited palette of instrumental colour is exploited. Collectively they show Handel's enthusiasm for the Italian style and his ability to write the good tunes it required. The recorded performances capture the youthful freshness of Handel's imagination, enhanced by graceful embellishments by the soloists where appropriate. The sound, too, is appropriate, coming from period instruments Handel would recognize, recorded with great clarity and with good balance — the continuo harpsichord is comfortably audible and, played by Pinnock himself, always worth hearing.

Additional recommendations ...

English Baroque Soloists/John Eliot Gardiner. Erato 2292-45981-2 — Ih B

Handel and Haydn Society/Christopher Hogwood. L'Oiseau-Lyre 421 729-2OH — Ih Im DDD 6/89 B

Brandenburg Consort/Roy Goodman. Hyperion CDA66633 — Ih 17m DDD 6/93 B

Tafelmusik/Jeanne Lamon. Sony Classical Vivarte SK52553 — Ih DDD 7/93 B

Handel. Concerti grossi, Op. 6. **The English Concert/Trevor Pinnock.** Archiv Produktion 410 897/9-2AH. From 2742 002 (11/82).

410 897-2AH — No. 1 in G major; No. 2 in F major; No. 3 in E minor; No. 4 in A minor. *410 898-2AH* — No. 5 in D major; No. 6 in G minor; No. 7 in B flat major; No. 8 in C minor. *410 899-2AH* — No. 9 in F major; No. 10 in D minor; No. 11 in A major; No. 12 in B minor.

③ 42m 1h 1m 58m DDD 5/84 6/85 8/85 B

Handel's 12 *Concerti grossi* have from four to six movements and are mostly in *da chiesa* form, i.e. without dance movements. They were written within one month in the autumn of 1739 (an average of two movements per day!) and when a great composer is thus carried on the tide of urgent inspiration it usually shows, as it does here in the flow of felicitous invention and memorable tune-smithing. The range of musical idioms used throughout is impressive and to them all Handel imparts his own indelible and unmistakable stamp. Trevor Pinnock's account contains much that is satisfying: polished ensemble, effectively judged tempos, a natural feeling for phrase, and a buoyancy of spirit which serves Handel's own robust musical language very well. Crisp attack, a judicious application of appoggiaturas and tasteful embellishment further enhance these lively performances. Pinnock varies the continuo colour by using organ and harpsichord and also includes Handel's autograph (though not printed) oboe parts for Concertos Nos. 1, 2, 5 and 6; where they occur a bassoon is sensibly added to fulfil the customary three-part wind texture of the period. Recorded sound is clear and captures the warm sonorities of the instruments.

Additional recommendations ...

Concerti grossi. **Guildhall String Ensemble.** RCA Victor Red Seal. *RD87895 — Nos. 1-4. RD87907 — Nos. 5-8. RD87921 — Nos. 9-12* — ③ 44m 1h 56m DDD 2/90 B

Concerti grossi — Nos. 1-6. **Boston Baroque/Martin Pearlman.** Telarc CD80253 — 1h 16m DDD 10/92 B

Concerti grossi. Concerto grosso in C major, HWV318, "Alexander's Feast". **Collegium Aureum.** Deutsche Harmonia Mundi 05472 77267-2 — ③ 3h 8m ADD 2/93 B

Handel. The Water Music, HWV348-50. **Simon Standage, Elizabeth Wilcock** (vns); **The English Concert/Trevor Pinnock** (hpd). Archiv Produktion 410 525-2AH. From 410 525-1AH (1/84).

54m DDD 2/84 B

The *Water Music* was written for a river journey made by King George I and his retinue in 1717 and is subdivided into three suites, each anchored to its own key and dominated by an instrument of a contrasting timbre: a horn for the Suite in F, a trumpet for the Suite in D and a flute for the G major Suite, the most modestly scored of the three. Some of the tunes such as the hornpipe are now familiar to many people who may not even know where they come from, or who wrote them. The English Concert play the music with a mixture of gaiety, verve and regal pomp, using period instruments and performing practices that enable us to hear it as closely as possible to the way it would have been heard in 1717.

Additional recommendations ...

Consort of London/Robert Haydon Clark. Collins Classics 1015-2 — 1h 3m DDD 6/90 B

Water Music. Music for the Royal Fireworks, HWV351. **Concertgebouw Chamber Orchestra/ Simon Preston.** Decca Ovation 430 717-2DM — 1h 9m DDD 8/91 £ B

English Baroque Soloists/John Eliot Gardiner. Philips 434 122-2PH — 53m DDD 5/93 B

Handel. Music for the Royal Fireworks, HWV351. Concerti a due cori — No. 2 in F major; No. 3 in F major. **The English Concert/Trevor Pinnock.** Archiv Produktion 415 129-2AH.

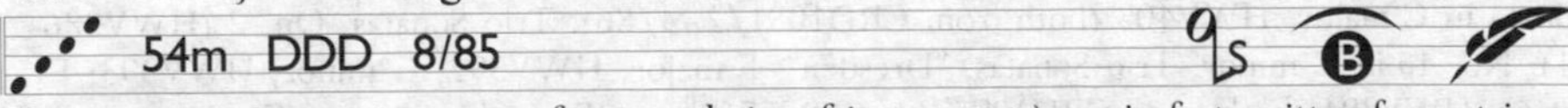

The *Concerti a due cori* (concertos for two choirs of instruments) are in fact written for a string band and two wind bands, each consisting (in the two concertos above) of oboes, horns and

bassoon. The famous *Fireworks* music was written to enliven a firework display in Green Park and although King George III wanted as many warlike instruments as possible, Handel preferred to add a sizeable string band. The quality and balance of the sound are radically affected by the instruments used — period or modern. The English Concert use the former with a skill that makes this a very enjoyable experience. The sound is quite superb.

Additional recommendations ...
Music for the Royal Fireworks. Water Music. **Orpheus Chamber Orchestra/** DG 435 390-2GH — lh 6m DDD 11/92
Music for the Royal Fireworks. Coronation Anthems[a] — *Zadok the priest; The King shall rejoice; My heart is inditing; Let thy hand be strengthened.* [a]**New College Choir, Oxford; King's Consort/ Robert King.** Hyperion CDA66350 — 57m DDD 12/89

NEW REVIEW
Handel. ORCHESTRAL WORKS. **La Stravaganza/Andrew Manze.** Denon Aliare CO-79943. Recorded in 1992.
Music for the Royal Fireworks, HWV351. Solomon — Arrival of the Queen of Sheba. Concerto grosso in C major, "Alexander's Feast". Organ Concerto No. 6 in B flat major, Op. 4. Suite in D major, "Water piece".

58m DDD 3/93

Sixteen years after the publication of Handel's *Water Music*, Walsh published "A Choice Sett of Aires, called Handel's Water Piece" and there is reason to believe that Handel played no direct part in it: the Overture to the Suite in D, preceded by imposing timpani rolls, is followed by four movements arranged from *Partenope*. It isn't what King George heard, but it is a collectable curiosity that deservedly spotlights the trumpeter, Susan Williams. The other items, mostly of Handel in his ceremonial mode, have numerous other recordings, with both period and modern instruments, but no other disc couples them in the same way. La Stravaganza are, despite their names and the presence of a female British trumpeter, a German period-instrument ensemble. Their instrumental skills are beyond reasonable reproach, and the performances are marked by a firm grasp of Handelian style, with well-sprung rhythms in the quicker movements and tender warmth in the slower ones, and the introduction of a little well-judged embellishment. The recording is very well balanced, with a generous but not cavernous acoustic. Whether or not the familiar items are already on your shelves, this is a very desirable disc to have.

NEW REVIEW
Handel. CHAMBER WORKS. **L'Ecole d'Orphée** ([a]Stephen Preston, fl; [b]David Reichenberg, ob; [c]Philip Pickett, [d]Rachel Beckett, recs; [e]John Holloway, [f]Micaela Comberti, [g]Alison Bury, vns; [h]Susan Sheppard, vc; [i]John Toll, [j]Lucy Carolan, [k]Robert Woolley, hpds). CRD CRD3373/8. Recorded 1981-85.
CRD3373[ahij] — Flute Sonatas: E minor, HWV359*b*; G major, HWV363*b*; B minor, HWV367*b*; A minor, HWV374; E minor, HWV375; B minor, HWV376; D major, HWV378; E minor (from CRD1073/4, 3/82). *CRD3374*[behj] — Oboe Sonatas: B flat major, HWV357; F major, HWV363*a*; C minor, HWV366 (CRD1077/8, 1/85). Movements for violin: A minor, HWV408; C minor, HWV412. Violin Sonatas: D minor, HWV359*a*; A major, HWV361; G minor, HWV364*a*; D major, HWV371 (all from CRD1081/2, 4/86). *CRD3375*[acefhik] — Trio Sonatas, Op. 2 (HWV386-91): No. 1 in B minor; No. 4 in F major (CRD1073/4, 3/82); No. 2 in G minor; No. 3 in B flat major; No. 5 in G minor; No. 6 in G minor (CRD1075/6, 9/83). *CRD3376*[efhj] — Trio Sonatas, Op. 5 (HWV396-402): No. 1 in A major; No. 2 in D major; No. 3 in E minor; No. 4 in G major; No. 5 in G minor; No. 6 in F major; No. 7 in B flat major (CRD1079/80, 4/85). *CRD3377*[efghjk] — Sinfonia in B flat major, HWV338. Trio Sonata in C major, HWV403 (both from CRD1081/2, 4/86). Trio Sonatas, Op. 2 (HWV386-91): No. 1*a* in C minor. Trio Sonatas, "Dresden": F major, HWV392; G minor, HWV393; E major, HWV394 (both from CRD1075/6). *CRD3378*[cdhj] — Recorder Sonatas: G minor, HWV360; A minor, HWV362; C major, HWV365; F major, HWV369; B flat major,

HWV377; D minor, HWV367*a*. Trio Sonata in F major, HWV405 (both from CRD1077/8, 1/85). Violin Sonata in G major, HWV358 (CRD1081/2).

⑥ 1h 14m 58m 1h 1m 1h 10m 1h 7m 1h 8m ADD 10/92

These recordings which, taken together represent the most comprehensive survey of Handel's chamber music on disc, were made over a five-year period between 1981 and 1985. The earliest volume contains Handel's sonatas for transverse flute with continuo and sets a standard of ensemble playing unsurpassed by the remaining discs. Stephen Preston brings an effective blend of thoughtfulness, good taste and insight to the music especially where dance rhythms and phrasing are concerned and he is backed up by sympathetic continuo playing. The second volume in the CD edition includes Handel's four authentic violin sonatas and the three genuine oboe sonatas, that in G major (HWV363*a*) being more familiar in its version for flute and continuo. John Holloway gives detailed and lightly articulated performances, if somewhat lacking in the conveyance of broad, noble Handelian gestures such as those which characterize the opening movement of the D major Sonata (HWV371). In the hands of the late oboist David Reichenberg Handel springs to life in playing which is full of character, refinement and good humour. His interpretations along with those of Preston are among the brightest constellations of the series. Volumes 3, 4 and 5 embrace Handel's two sets of Trio Sonatas, Op. 2 and Op. 5 and a group of miscellaneous trios with a Sinfonia in B flat. Performances are stylish and often sympathetic but some mannerisms are, perhaps, projected with too much emphasis and the pitching of notes is not invariably secure. The last volume of the survey includes seven sonatas for treble recorder and a Trio in F major (HWV405) which, in its trio sonata clothes as performed here, is a fairly recent discovery. The soloist is Philip Pickett (treble recorder) who is technically agile and lively in spirit if somewhat perfunctory in approach. But this is, none the less, enjoyable music-making and the survey as a whole provides a valuable account of some comparatively unfamiliar repertory. Recorded sound is exemplary.

Key to Symbols

	② ②	1h 23m	DDD	6/88
Price	***Quantity/ availability***	***Timing***	***Mode***	***Review date***

NEW REVIEW

Handel. TRIO SONATAS. **London Baroque** (Ingrid Seifert, Richard Gwilt, vns; Charles Medlam, vc; Richard Egarr, hpd). Harmonia Mundi HMC90 1379 and 1389. Recorded in 1991. *HMC90 1379* — Op. 2: No. 1 in B minor; No. 2 in G minor; No. 3 in B flat major; No. 4 in F major; No. 5 in G minor; No. 6 in G minor. *HMC90 1389* — Op. 5: No. 1 in A major; No. 2 in D major; No. 3 in E minor; No. 4 in G major; No. 5 in G minor; No. 6 in F major; No. 7 in B flat major.

② 58m 1h 9m DDD 4/93

Handel's publisher, Walsh, printed the six Trio Sonatas, Op. 2 in about 1730, following them up in 1739 with seven further trios which he published as the composer's Op. 5. In each set Handel offered a choice of melody instruments though the writing suggests that he had violins foremost in mind. This is the way in which all 13 sonatas are played on these two separately available discs and the decision is a good one. The performances by London Baroque are poised, well-shaped and susceptible to the subtle nuances of Handel's part-writing. Ingrid Seifert and Richard Gwilt are partners of long standing and their even dialogue, sometimes grave, sometimes lively and at other times playful, serves the music effectively. Tempos are well-judged and phrases are eloquently shaped and articulately spoken. In all this the violinists are sympathetically supported by the continuo players who make their own vital contribution to clear textures and overall balance. Recorded sound is appropriately intimate, serving the sound character of the instruments themselves and evoking a chamber music ambience. The music, it hardly need be said, maintains a high level of craftsmanship and interest which will surely delight listeners.

Handel. KEYBOARD SUITES, HWV426-33. **Colin Tilney**. Archiv Produktion Galleria 427 170-2AGA2. Items marked [a] from 2533 169 (2/75), [b] 2533 168 (2/75). Recorded in 1973. No. 1 in A major[a]; No. 2 in F major[b]; No. 3 in D minor[a]; No. 4 in E minor[b]; No. 5 in E major[b]; No. 5*a* — Air and Variations, "The Harmonious Blacksmith"; No. 6 in F sharp minor[a]; No. 7 in G minor[a]; No. 8 in F minor[b].

② lh 58m ADD 8/91 

Handel published his eight harpsichord suites in 1720 though he had written much of the music earlier in his life. One of the many striking features of these pieces is that of variety. Handel's terms of reference were wide and cosmopolitan and the harpsichord suites contain many contrasting ingredients ranging from well sustained imitative part-writing on the one hand to simpler airs and dances on the other. These two aspects of Handel's art find a happy and celebrated conjunction in the air and variations affectionately known as *The Harmonious Blacksmith*. The music, displaying elements of French, Italian and German styles, reflects Handel's own cosmopolitan nature and tastes. Many readers may be as surprised to find how much of this music is unfamiliar to them as they will be delighted by its ceaseless invention and affecting idiom. Colin Tilney is a persuasive interpreter of this repertory, bringing a muscular strength to Handel's often complex part-writing while never complicating simpler musical ideas with misplaced rhetoric or exaggerated gestures. Preludes with their strongly improvisatory character are given just the right amount of rhythmic freedom even if *The Harmonious Blacksmith* air, though tastefully ornamented, is a shade lacking in conviviality. Tilney plays two especially fine instruments made in Hamburg during the early years of the eighteenth century. The recorded sound is sympathetic.

Additional recommendation ...
Scott Ross. Erato 2292-45452-2 — ② lh 52m DDD 2/90

NEW REVIEW

Handel. Keyboard Suites, HWV426-33 — No. 5 in E major; No. 5*a* — Air and Variations, "The Harmonious Blacksmith"; No. 7 in G minor.
D. Scarlatti. Keyboard Sonatas. **Martin Souter** (hpd). Isis ISISCD001.
Scarlatti: G major, Kk2; D minor, Kk9; C minor, Kk11; G major, Kk14; E minor, Kk15; E major, Kk20; D major, Kk21; D major, Kk23; A major, Kk24.

lh 15m DDD 3/93 

For this attractively devised programme Martin Souter plays a 1772 Kirckman harpsichord belonging to the Ashmolean Museum in Oxford. It is a fine-sounding instrument though the slightly over-resonant acoustic draws attention to its museum status. The music is evenly divided between Handel and Domenico Scarlatti. Handel is represented by two Suites — the E major which includes the celebrated Air and Variations, *The Harmonious Blacksmith*, and G minor with a fine Overture and concluding *Passacaille*. Nine Scarlatti sonatas from the 1738 *Essercizi* make up the remainder of the recital. The recording is very much a performance since, as the accompanying note explains, over 70 minutes of music were put down in under three hours. Inevitably there are a few splashes here and there, but the price is worth paying for spirited and stylish playing which is entirely free from dullness. Few listeners will find themselves unaffected by Souter's spontaneity even if there is a hint of caution — understandable under the circumstances — in his approach to the virtuoso Scarlatti pieces.

Handel. Chandos Anthems, Volume 4 — The Lord is my light, HWV255; Let God arise, HWV256. **Lynne Dawson** (sop); **Ian Partridge** (ten); **The Sixteen Chorus and Orchestra/Harry Christophers.** Chandos Chaconne CHAN0509. Texts included.

49m DDD 7/90 

The Chandos Anthems, which Handel composed during his residence at Canons, Edgware, Middlesex, in the years around 1720, have not had a complete recording before. The Sixteen have now completed their set of these appealing pieces, church music on a modest scale composed for the Duke of Chandos's private worship. Essentially intimate in style, they nevertheless have a touch of the ceremonial about them, echoing Purcell and the English tradition but at the same time reinterpret that tradition in a broad, urbane manner, attuned to the worldliness of the Anglican establishment of the time. Probably they were intended for performance by a very small group, but Harry Christophers's ensemble is well scaled to the music and his chorus sing for the most part with spirit, especially in the quicker music. Ian Partridge sings with his usual impeccable taste and judgement in the tenor solo music; the other soloist here is the soprano Lynne Dawson, whose glowing tone and diamantine passage-work are one of the chief delights of this pleasing disc.

Handel. Dixit Dominus, HWV232[a]. Nisi Dominus, HWV238[b]. Salve Regina, HWV241[c]. [ac]**Arleen Auger,** [a]**Lynne Dawson** (sops); [ab]**Diana Montague** (mez); [a]**Leigh Nixon,** [b]**John Mark Ainsley** (tens); [ab]**Simon Birchall** (bass); **Choir and Orchestra of Westminster Abbey/Simon Preston.** Archiv Produktion 423 594-2AH. Texts and translations included.

56m DDD 2/89

Although *Dixit Dominus* is the earliest surviving large scale work by Handel (he was only 22 at the time of its composition in 1707) it displays a remarkable degree of competence and invention and also looks forward to the mature style to come. The vocal writing for both chorus and soloists is extremely ornate and embellished and requires a considerable amount of expertise and flair in order to do full justice to the music. Fortunately, Simon Preston and his team possess all the necessary requirements — indeed, this is one of the most energetic, exhilarating and purposeful performances of this work ever recorded. One need only single out the rhythmically incisive performances of the opening "Dixit Dominus Domineo meo" or the "Judicabit in nationibus" and the superbly crisp and articulate performances from the Orchestra of Westminster Abbey to realize that it is a very special recording indeed. The well thought out coupling of *Nisi Dominus* and *Salve Regina* are no less impressive, with the latter offering the listener another chance to sample the beautiful solo contributions of Arleen Auger. The recorded sound is also outstandingly fine. A delightful disc.

Additional recommendation ...
Dixit Dominus. Coronation Anthems — Zadok the priest; The King shall rejoice; My heart is inditing; Let thy hand be strengthened. **Soloists; Monteverdi Choir; Monteverdi Orchestra/John Eliot Gardiner.** Erato 2292-45136-2 — ADD

Handel. ITALIAN DUETS. **Gillian Fisher** (sop); **James Bowman** (alto); **The King's Consort/Robert King.** Hyperion CDA66440. Recorded in 1990. Texts and translations included.
A miravi io son intento. Conservate, raddoppiate. Fronda leggiera e mobile. Langue, geme e sospira. Nò, di voi non vuo fidarmi. Se tu non lasci amore. Sono liete, fortunate. Tanti strali al sen. Troppo crudo.

1h 4m DDD 4/91

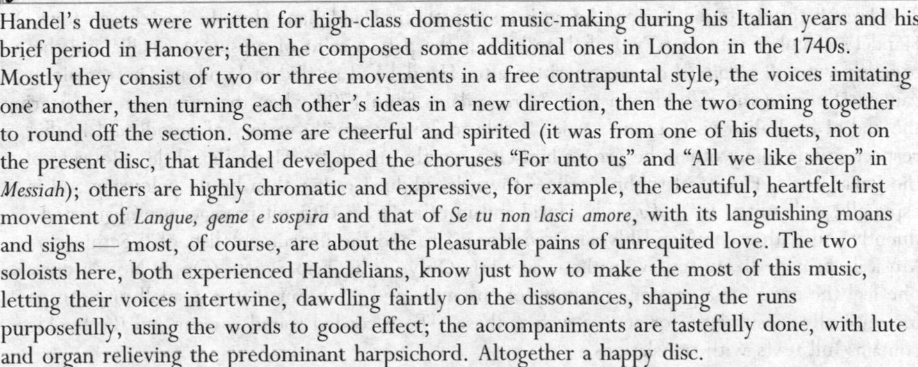

Handel's duets were written for high-class domestic music-making during his Italian years and his brief period in Hanover; then he composed some additional ones in London in the 1740s. Mostly they consist of two or three movements in a free contrapuntal style, the voices imitating one another, then turning each other's ideas in a new direction, then the two coming together to round off the section. Some are cheerful and spirited (it was from one of his duets, not on the present disc, that Handel developed the choruses "For unto us" and "All we like sheep" in *Messiah*); others are highly chromatic and expressive, for example, the beautiful, heartfelt first movement of *Langue, geme e sospira* and that of *Se tu non lasci amore*, with its languishing moans and sighs — most, of course, are about the pleasurable pains of unrequited love. The two soloists here, both experienced Handelians, know just how to make the most of this music, letting their voices intertwine, dawdling faintly on the dissonances, shaping the runs purposefully, using the words to good effect; the accompaniments are tastefully done, with lute and organ relieving the predominant harpsichord. Altogether a happy disc.

Handel. ITALIAN CANTATAS. **Emma Kirkby** (sop); **Michel Piguet** (ob, rec); **Rachel Beckett** (rec); **Charles Medlam** (va da gamba); **Jane Coe** (vc cont); **Academy of Ancient Music/Christopher Hogwood** (hpd). L'Oiseau-Lyre Florilegium 414 473-2OH. Texts and translations included.
Tu fedel? tu costante?; Mi palpita il cor; Alpestre monte; Tra le fiamme.

55m DDD 3/86 

Three of the cantatas in this issue belong to Handel's Italian period whilst the fourth, *Mi palpita il cor* — in its version for soprano, oboe and continuo — probably dates from his first years in England. There is a wealth of fine music to be found in this comparatively neglected area of Handel's output and the composer seldom if ever disappoints us in the subtlety with which he captures a mood or colours an image. The partnership of Emma Kirkby with solo instrumentalists and members of the Academy of Ancient Music is a rewarding one. Her singing is light in texture, fluent and effective in phrasing, and is ideally equipped to bring out the many nuances both of text and music. All concerned contribute towards lively performances under the stylistically informed direction of Christopher Hogwood.

Handel. ITALIAN CANTATAS AND INSTRUMENTAL WORKS. [a]**Julianne Baird** (sop); [b]**John Dornenburg** (va da gamba); [c]**Malcolm Proud** (hpd). Meridian CDE84189. Texts and translations included. Recorded in 1990.
Harpsichord Suite in F minor, HWV433[c]. Occhi mei, che faceste?[abc]. Udite il mio consiglio[abc]. Quel fior che all'alba ride[abc]. Violin Sonata in G minor, HWV364*b*[bc].

lh 9m DDD 12/91 

The chamber cantatas by Handel assembled on this disc are likely to be familiar only to the most ardent Handelians since, until now, they have been largely if not entirely overlooked by recording companies. The programme also includes Handel's Harpsichord Suite in F minor and his Violin Sonata in G minor, but here played on a viola da gamba — the composer seems to have had both instruments in mind at different times. Julianne Baird is one of the leading baroque sopranos but like all interesting artists there is a small element of unpredictability in her singing. In this recital her declamation is excellent and her diction commendably clear but the music, often technically demanding, finds chinks in her armour, so-to-speak. There are hints of strain in her uppermost range and an occasional tightness in the voice but the interpretations are stylish and alluring and Baird's acute ear for the pitching of notes enables her to surmount tricky chromaticisms and teasing intervals with comfortable assurance. The two instrumental pieces are very well executed by Malcolm Proud, joined by John Dornenburg in the sonata. Altogether an attractive programme. Full texts provided.

Handel. CANTATAS FOR COUNTERTENOR[a]. Trio Sonata, Op. 5 No. 4. [a]**Gérard Lesne** (alto); **Il Seminario Musicale.** Virgin Classics VC7 59059-2. Texts and translations included.
Splende l'alba in oriente. La Lucrezia. Mi palpita il cor. Carco sempre di gloria.

lh 10m DDD 12/91 

The French countertenor, Gérard Lesne is a sympathetic Handelian. Here he has chosen four of Handel's chamber cantatas. Two of them honour the patron saint of music, St Cecilia and these together with *Mi palpita il cor* were written after Handel had settled in London. The remaining cantata *O numi eterni*, also known as *La Lucrezia* dates from 1709 when the composer was nearing the end of his Italian visit. Lesne's voice is able to convey a wide variety of moods and in this respect among many others he proves himself a worthy match for Handel's subtle colouring of the Italian texts. His vocal timbre inclines towards subdued rather than bright colouring and is especially well-suited to *La Lucrezia*. Florid and in other ways difficult passages are negotiated fluently and with a commendably sure sense of pitch, and the instrumentalists of Il Seminario Musicale provide lively and sympathetic support. Only in the Trio Sonata (Op. 5 No. 4) does one feel the need for a greater unanimity of ensemble and pitch but that is a small price to pay for musically sensitive performances such as these. The recorded sound is clear and the booklet contains full texts with translations.

Additional recommendation ...

Lungi da me pensier tiranno. Siete rose rugiadose. Udite il mio consiglio. Carco sempre di gloria. Oboe Sonatas — F major, HWV363a; C minor, HWV366. **Derek Lee Ragin** (alto); **Cologne Divitia Ensemble.** Channel Classics CCS0890 — lh lm DDD 2/92

Handel. ARIAS FOR MONTAGNANA. **David Thomas** (bass); **Philharmonia Baroque Orchestra/Nicholas McGegan.** Harmonia Mundi HMU90 7016. Texts and translations included. Recorded in 1989.

Acis and Galatea — Avampo ... Ferito son d'Amore. Athalia — Ah, canst thou but prove me! Deborah — Barak, my son ... Awake the ardour; They ardours warm ... Swift inundation; Tears, such as tender fathers shed. Esther — I'll hear no more ... Pluck root and branch; Turn not, O Queen; How art thou fall'n. Ezio — Perchè tanto tormento? ... Se un bell'ardire; Folle è colui ... Nasce al bosco; Che indegno! ... Già risonar. Orlando — Mira, prendi l'essempio! ... Lascia Amor; Impari ognun da Orlando ... O voi, del mio poter ... Sorge infausta una procella. Sosarme — Addio, principe scrupoloso ... Fra l'ombre e gli orrori; Quanto più Melo ... Sento il core; Tanto s'eseguirà ... Tiene Giove. Tolomeo, re di egitto — Piangi pur.

lh 8m DDD 8/90

Antonio Montagnana was a Venetian who sang bass parts in London in Handel's time: which means that his voice and his capacities gave shape to many of the bass parts Handel composed — it being the custom, in those times, for a composer to write the music to the singer's specific abilities. And Handel's music tells us that Montagnana was a singer quite out of the ordinary, as remarkable, in fact, as his impersonator here, the English bass David Thomas. Some of the arias are big, blustery pieces, suitable for unscrupulous villains or sturdy military men, but others show Montagnana (and Thomas) as what came to be called a *basso cantante* (listen to the eloquent one from *Tolomeo*), and there are sheer virtuoso pieces too (conspicuously those from *Sosarme*). Some of them range from what is practically a tenor compass right down to *basso profondo* regions. Thomas is an astonishing singer, agile to a degree, able to encompass all that Montagnana did and indeed to add apt ornamentation at times; the articulation is precise and energetic, the tone true and even across two-and-a-half octaves, and always there is a touch of wit and spirit behind the singing. Nicholas McGegan's band provides sharp, slightly choppy support.

NEW REVIEW

Handel. Clori, Tirsi e Fileno, HWV96. **Lorraine Hunt, Jill Feldman** (sops); **Drew Minter** (alto); **Paul O'Dette** (archlte); **Philharmonia Baroque Orchestra/Nicholas McGegan.** Harmonia Mundi HMU90 7045. Text and translation included. Recorded in 1990.

lh l6m DDD 2/93

Handel composed this extended cantata (almost a chamber opera) in 1707 whilst staying in Italy as composer-in-residence at the court of the Marquis Ruspoli. It has a charm and freshness of invention unusual for even this particularly fecund period in Handel's career. The story concerns the two-timing shepherdess, Chloris (soprano), and her lovers, shepherds Thyrsis (soprano — possibly originally intended for a castrato) and Philenus (male alto, sung here by countertenor Drew Minter). The shepherds resolve to stay friends, despite their rivalry, and all three finally resign themselves to the pains of love. Despite the misery explored by the plot, the music maintains a brightness that suggests both the joys of adolescent love, and its transience. Each of the three treble voices in this performance has a distinctive quality and an individual stylistic approach that makes both music and drama easy to follow and helps the listener to become involved and to empathise with each character in turn. The ensembles are particularly enhanced by this tactic. Handel himself signposts the twists and turns of the plot not only through changes in musical ideas but by introducing especially delightful variations of scoring, employing both archlute and recorders in an effective manner. Playing by the Philharmonia Baroque Orchestra is first-class throughout. They use a combination of period instruments and modern copies that proves clean-toned yet mellow, and Nicholas McGegan sustains an enthralling rhythmic vitality. The whole is rounded off by a recording in which the individuality of the timbres are crisply retained.

Handel. La Resurrezione, HWV47. **Nancy Argenta, Barbara Schlick** (sops); **Guillemette Laurens** (mez); **Guy de Mey** (ten); **Klaus Mertens** (bass); **Amsterdam Baroque Orchestra/Ton Koopman.** Erato 2292-45617-2. Text and translation included. Recorded in 1990.

② 1h 56m DDD 7/91

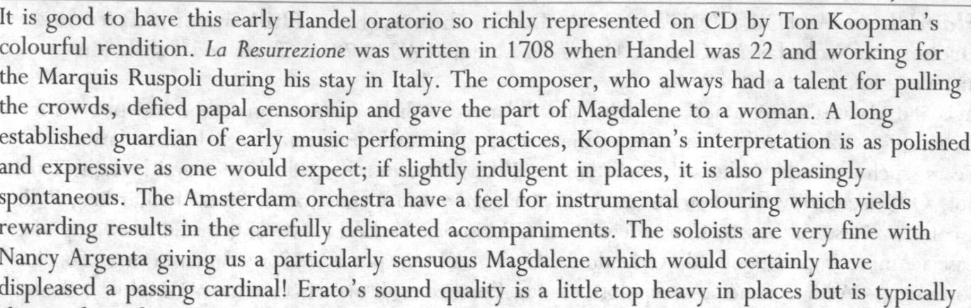

It is good to have this early Handel oratorio so richly represented on CD by Ton Koopman's colourful rendition. *La Resurrezione* was written in 1708 when Handel was 22 and working for the Marquis Ruspoli during his stay in Italy. The composer, who always had a talent for pulling the crowds, defied papal censorship and gave the part of Magdalene to a woman. A long established guardian of early music performing practices, Koopman's interpretation is as polished and expressive as one would expect; if slightly indulgent in places, it is also pleasingly spontaneous. The Amsterdam orchestra have a feel for instrumental colouring which yields rewarding results in the carefully delineated accompaniments. The soloists are very fine with Nancy Argenta giving us a particularly sensuous Magdalene which would certainly have displeased a passing cardinal! Erato's sound quality is a little top heavy in places but is typically clear and vivid.

Handel. Aci, Galatea e Polifemo[a]. Recorder Sonatas[b] — F major, HWV369; C major, HWV365; G major (trans. F major), HWV358. **Emma Kirkby** (sop) Aci; **Carolyn Watkinson** (contr) Galatea; **David Thomas** (bass) Polifemo; [b]**Michel Piquet** (rec); [b]**John Toll** (hpd); **London Baroque/Charles Medlam** ([b]vc). Harmonia Mundi HMC90 1253/4. Notes, text and translation included. Item marked [a] new to UK, [b] from HMC1190/91 (9/86).

② 1h 46m DDD 11/87

Handel's English pastoral *Acis and Galatea* has always been one of his most popular works, but not many of its admirers are aware that he had written a completely different treatment of the same story ten years earlier (when he was 23) for a ducal wedding in Naples. In this version modern ears need to adjust to Acis (a young shepherd lad) being represented by a soprano (originally a castrato), while the nymph Galatea is a contralto. The work is full of invention and instrumental colour, and there are several memorably beautiful items in the score, such as the opening duet (with the lovers' voices intertwining), and above all Acis's dying farewell after the jealous giant Polyphemus has crushed him under a huge rock. To suggest the giant's vast size Handel employed a prodigious vocal range of two-and-a-half octaves, which has proved the chief obstacle to performances of the work, here receiving a very enjoyable first recording. All three singers are excellent and so is the technical quality.

Handel. Acis and Galatea. **Norma Burrowes** (sop) Galatea; **Anthony Rolfe Johnson** (ten) Acis; **Martyn Hill** (ten) Damon; **Willard White** (bass) Polyphemus; **Paul Elliot** (ten); **English Baroque Soloists/John Eliot Gardiner.** Archiv Produktion 423 406-2AH2. Notes, text and translation included. From 2708 038 (9/78). Recorded in 1978.

② 1h 35m ADD 8/88

John Eliot Gardiner made this recording of Handel's masque during the late 1970s when the revival of period instruments was still in a comparatively early stage. Listeners may detect weaknesses both in intonation and in ensemble from time to time but, nevertheless, Gardiner's performance is lively and stylistically assured. He paces the work dramatically revealing nuances both in the text and in the music. The solo team is a strong one and there are especially fine contributions from Norma Burrowes and Anthony Rolfe Johnson. This is an enjoyable performance of an enchanting work.

Additional recommendations ...

Acis and Galatea. Look down, harmonious Saint, "The Praise of Harmony", HWV124. **Soloists; King's Consort/Robert King.** Hyperion CDA66361/2 — ② 1h 46m DDD 6/90

Acis and Galatea (arr. Mozart). **Soloists; Handel and Haydn Society Chorus and Orchestra /Christopher Hogwood.** L'Oiseau-Lyre 430 538-2OH2 — ② 1h 36m DDD 7/92

Handel. Athalia. **Dame Joan Sutherland** (sop) Athalia; **Emma Kirkby** (sop) Josabeth; **Aled Jones** (treb) Joas; **James Bowman** (alto) Joad; **Anthony Rolfe Johnson** (ten) Mathan; **David Thomas** (bass-bar) Abner; **New College Choir, Oxford; Academy of Ancient Music/Christopher Hogwood.** L'Oiseau-Lyre 417 126-2OH2. Notes and text included. From 417 126-1OH2 (11/86). Recorded in 1985.

② 2h 2m DDD 2/87 

Although *Athalia* was a huge success when first performed and has long been recognized as a masterly work, not only is this its first complete recording, but barely a note of it has previously appeared in the catalogues, apart from a couple of excerpts in transcriptions. With lip service constantly paid to Handel, this has been a startling neglect; but fortunately the conspiracy of silence has now been broken with a performance that does justice to this remarkable piece. Handel's treatment of form is exceptionally flexible, his characterization is vivid, and his musical invention is at its most exuberant: the opening Sinfonia (alertly played under Hogwood) immediately whets the appetite. Emma Kirkby delights by the freshness and limpidity of her tone and by the absolute precision and charm of her trills and ornamentation whilst James Bowman sings accurately but is unimaginative in his treatment of words. In the title-role Joan Sutherland makes the most of the apostate queen's vengeful outbursts, and her enunciation is much clearer than usual. There are splendid florid solos for David Thomas and Anthony Rolfe Johnson, and Aled Jones as the boy king sings his one aria with beautifully controlled tone and impeccable intonation. The chorus sings enthusiastically and makes a shattering entry in the brilliant opening of Act 2 — which is certainly the number to sample for anyone wishing to know what this fine work is like.

Handel. Alexander's Feast[a]. Concerto Grosso in C major, HWV318. [a]**Donna Brown** (sop); [a]**Carolyn Watkinson** (contr); [a]**Ashley Stafford** (alto); [a]**Nigel Robson** (ten); [a]**Stephen Varcoe** (bar); [a]**Monteverdi Choir, English Baroque Soloists/John Eliot Gardiner.** Philips 422 053-2PH2. Text included. Recorded at a performance during the 1987 Göttingen Handel Festival, Germany.

② lh 38m DDD ll/88 

Alexander's Feast was the first work Handel had set by a major English poet (Dryden) and it was also the first time he allotted the principal male part to a tenor instead of the castrato heroes of his Italian operas. These two factors, combined with much fine music, scored with great brilliance and imagination, ensured the immediate success of *Alexander's Feast*. It is strange that nowadays it is seldom performed so this recording would have been very welcome even had it not been so full of vitality and so stylishly performed (though perhaps with more sophisticated detail than the eighteenth century would have managed). The Monteverdi Choir and the soloists are all Gardiner regulars, though the pure-voiced Canadian soprano Donna Brown is a fairly recent (and welcome) acquisition; and the English Baroque Soloists have ample opportunities to shine — especially the violins, although the natural horns' lusty entry in the bucolic "Bacchus, ever fair and young" is exhilarating.

Additional recommendation ...

Alexander's Feast. Harp Concerto in B flat major, HWV294. Organ Concerto in G minor/major, HWV289. **Soloists; Tragicomedia; The Sixteen Choir and Orchestra/Harry Christophers.** Collins Classics 7016-2 — ② lh 56m DDD 10/91

Handel. Saul. **Lynne Dawson, Donna Brown** (sops); **Derek Lee Ragin** (alto); **John Mark Ainsley, Neil Mackie, Philip Salmon, Philip Slane** (tens); **Alastair Miles, Richard Savage** (basses); **Monteverdi Choir; English Baroque Soloists/John Eliot Gardiner.** Philips 426 265-2PH3. Recorded at performances in the Stadthalle, Göttingen, Germany, in June 1989.

③ 2h 39m DDD 8/91

Saul is considered by many to be one of the most arresting music dramas in the English language, even though it is officially classed as an oratorio. In it Handel explores in some psychological depth the motivations of his characters, most notably that of the eponymous anti-hero, whose tantrums caused by envy and his searching for supernatural intervention are all vividly delineated; so is the friendship of David and Jonathan and the different characters of Saul's daughters, Merab and Michal. In yet another compelling performance of Handel under his baton, John Eliot Gardiner — in this live recording made at the Göttingen Handel Festival — fulfils every aspect of this varied and adventurous score, eliciting execution of refined and biting calibre from his choir and orchestra. The young British bass Alastair Miles captures Saul in all his moods. John Mark Ainsley and Derek Lee Ragin are both affecting as Jonathan and David; so are Lynne Dawson and Donna Brown as Michal and Merab. There are a few cuts, but they aren't grievous enough to prevent a firm recommendation.

Handel. L'Allegro, il Penseroso ed il Moderato. **Patrizia Kwella, Marie McLaughlin, Jennifer Smith** (sops); **Michael Ginn** (treb); **Maldwyn Davies, Martyn Hill** (tens); **Stephen Varcoe** (bar); **Monteverdi Choir; English Baroque Soloists/John Eliot Gardiner.** Erato 2292 45377-2. Notes, text and translation included. From STU71325 (11/80). Recorded in 1980.

② 1h 55m DDD 7/85 

Handel was the leading opera composer of the age, but when his fortunes in this sphere began to decline he started to develop other dramatic forms, notably those of the English ode and oratorio. Early in 1740 he turned to two great poems of Milton's youth and composed a masterpiece. This was the ode *L'Allegro, il Penseroso ed il Moderato*. Charles Jennens, the librettist, skilfully adjusts and alternates Milton's poems with their strongly contrasting humours to suit the best interests of the music. John Eliot Gardiner has recorded the work almost complete with a small orchestra of period instruments and a first-rate cast of soloists. Patrizia Kwella and Maldwyn Davies are memorable in the beguiling duet, "As steals the morn", one of many arias which reveal Handel's acute sensibility to the natural landscape. The Monteverdi Choir is characteristically well-disciplined in Handel's varied and evocative choruses savouring the colourful images of the poems and responding effectively to Gardiner's stylish direction. The recorded sound is clear and resonant and full texts are provided in English, French and German.

Handel. Israel in Egypt. **Nancy Argenta, Emily Van Evera** (sops); **Timothy Wilson** (alto); **Anthony Rolfe Johnson** (ten); **David Thomas, Jeremy White** (basses); **Taverner Choir and Players/Andrew Parrott.** EMI CDS7 54018-2. Text included. Recorded in 1989.

② 2h 15m DDD 2/91 

If anyone needs to assure themselves as to whether the English choral tradition is alive and well, they need only buy this CD. *Israel in Egypt*, of all Handel's works, is the choral one *par excellence* — so much so, in fact, that it was something of a failure in Handel's own time because solo singing was much preferred to choral by the audiences. Andrew Parrott gives a complete performance of the work, in its original form: that is to say, prefaced by the noble funeral anthem for Queen Caroline, as adapted by Handel to serve as a song of mourning by the captive Israelites. This first part is predominantly slow, grave music, powerfully elegiac; the Taverner Choir show themselves, in what is testing music to sing, firm and clean of line, well focused and strongly sustained. The chorus have their chances to be more energetic in the second part, with the famous and vivid Plague choruses — in which the orchestra too play their part in the pictorial effects, with the fiddles illustrating in turn frogs, flies and hailstones. And last, in the third part, there is a generous supply of the stirring C major music in which Handel has the Israelites give their thanks to God, in some degree symbolizing the English giving thanks for the Hanoverian monarchy and the Protestant succession. Be that as it may, the effect is splendid. The solo work is first-rate, too, with Nancy Argenta radiant in Miriam's music in the final scene and distinguished contributions too from David Thomas and Anthony Rolfe Johnson.

Handel. Messiah. **Judith Nelson, Emma Kirkby** (sops); **Carolyn Watkinson** (contr); **Paul Elliott** (ten); **David Thomas** (bass); **Christ Church Cathedral Choir, Oxford;**

Academy of Ancient Music/Christopher Hogwood. L'Oiseau-Lyre Florilegium 430 488-2OH2. Notes and text included. From D189D3 (4/80). Recorded in 1979.

② 2h 17m ADD 7/84 

Christopher Hogwood's recording of *Messiah* was first issued on LP in 1980. Four years later it was successfully transferred to three CDs. Now, with the advance of technology the three-disc package has been supplanted by this two-disc box retaining the full texts of the original. Hogwood's version of *Messiah* conforms with a Foundling Hospital performance in 1754, directed by the composer himself. A significant difference between this recording and most others is the use of boys' treble voices in the choir as opposed to women's. That is what Handel wanted and it is this feature of the interpretation which, perhaps more than any other makes it appealing. In contrast again with many alternative versions this one dispenses with the solo countertenor, the contralto Carolyn Watkinson singing the music often allotted to the other. She is excellent and a considerable adornment to the set. Only the Academy of Ancient Music is likely to cause occasional disappointment with playing that falls short of ideal in matters of tuning and ensemble. The acoustic is a shade reverberant but the performance comes close to the heart of the music and remains a satisfying interpretation.

Additional recommendations ...

Soloists; Royal Philhrmonic Chorus and Orchestra/Sir Thomas Beecham. RCA Red Seal 09026-61266-2 — ③ 2h 4lm ADD Ⓑ ▲

(Arr. Mozart/Prout/Sargent). **Soloists; Huddersfield Choral Society; Royal Liverpool Philharmonic Orchestra/Sir Malcolm Sargent.** Classics for Pleasure CD-CFPD4718 — ② 2h 24m ADD 5/91 Ⓑ ▲

Soloists; Collegium Musicum 90 Chorus; Collegium Musicum 90/Richard Hickox. Chandos Chaconne CHAN0522/3 — ② 2h 2lm DDD 3/92 Ⓑ

Soloists; The Sixteen; Amsterdam Baroque Orchestra/Ton Koopman. Erato 2292-45960-2 — ② 2h 20m DDD 3/93 Ⓑ

The Scholars Baroque Ensemble/David van Asch (bass). Naxos 8 550667/8 — ② 2h 4lm DDD 4/93 Ⓑ

Handel. Belshazzar. **Arleen Auger** (sop); **Catherine Robbin** (mez); **James Bowman** (alto); **Anthony Rolfe Johnson, Nicholas Robertson** (tens); **David Wilson-Johnson** (bar); **Richard Wistreich** (bass); **The English Concert Choir; The English Concert/Trevor Pinnock.** Archiv Produktion 431 793-2AH3. Notes and text included.

③ 2h 52m DDD 10/91

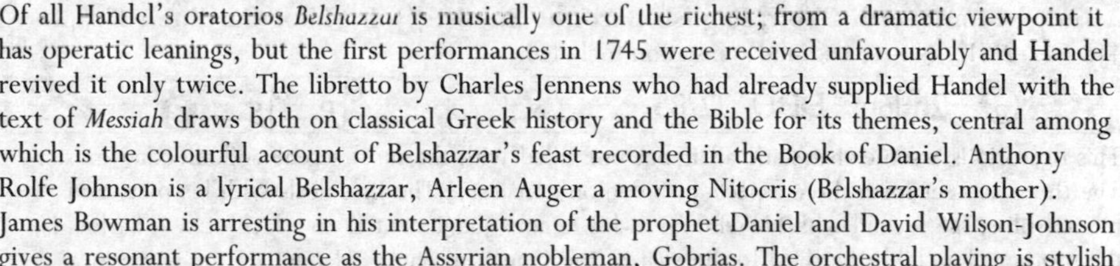

Of all Handel's oratorios *Belshazzar* is musically one of the richest; from a dramatic viewpoint it has operatic leanings, but the first performances in 1745 were received unfavourably and Handel revived it only twice. The libretto by Charles Jennens who had already supplied Handel with the text of *Messiah* draws both on classical Greek history and the Bible for its themes, central among which is the colourful account of Belshazzar's feast recorded in the Book of Daniel. Anthony Rolfe Johnson is a lyrical Belshazzar, Arleen Auger a moving Nitocris (Belshazzar's mother). James Bowman is arresting in his interpretation of the prophet Daniel and David Wilson-Johnson gives a resonant performance as the Assyrian nobleman, Gobrias. The orchestral playing is stylish and the recording is exemplary.

Handel. Hercules. **Jennifer Smith** (sop) Iole; **Sarah Walker** (mez) Dejanira; **Catherine Denley** (mez) Lichas; **Anthony Rolfe Johnson** (ten) Hyllus; **John Tomlinson** (bass) Hercules; **Peter Savidge** (bar) Priest of Jupiter; **Monteverdi Choir; English Baroque Soloists/John Eliot Gardiner.** Archiv Produktion 423 137-2AH3. Notes and text included. From 2742 004 (6/83).

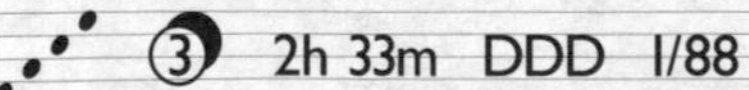

③ 2h 33m DDD 1/88

Handel's *Hercules* is neither opera nor sacred oratorio though it contains elements of both. The story of Dejanira's jealousy of her husband Hercules and of his agonizing death on wearing a poisoned robe which she sends him is brought to life by Handel with typically vivid characterization and in an altogether masterly fashion. Dejanira is sung by Sarah Walker with intensity of feeling, and a fine sense of theatre; Handel capturing the various shades of her character with deep psychological insight and consummate musical genius. Most of the other characters, though skilfully drawn, do not develop to a comparable extent. Jennifer Smith makes an effectively youthful and fresh-sounding princess Iole, and John Tomlinson a resonant and authoritative Hercules. The chorus reflects the varied emotions emerging as a result of the action and respond to Handel's requirements in a lively, articulate fashion. Orchestral playing on period instruments is comparably alert with clean ensemble and several fine obbligato contributions. Clear, resonant recorded sound and exemplary presentation with full text.

Handel. Joshua. **Emma Kirkby** (sop); **Aidan Oliver** (treb); **James Bowman** (alto); **John Mark Ainsley** (ten); **Michael George** (bass); **New College Choir, Oxford; The King's Consort/Robert King.** Hyperion CDA66461/2. Text included. Recorded in 1990.

② 2h 5m DDD 7/91

Typically, Handel composed *Joshua* at great speed in the summer of 1748, completing the work in a single month. It is essentially military in manner (Handel wryly observed that the English "like something they can beat time to"), and was the original setting for "See, the Conqu'ring Hero Comes". As to which of these two performances you prefer, that will depend on how you like your Handel: grand and stately in the best church music tradition, or fleet and eager in a more obviously authentic manner. Robert King's performance is grand and stately in the best church music tradition, with smooth, orchestral playing and a reverberant recording from St Joseph's College in London. His chorus is strictly men only and he has distinctive soloists led by the incomparable Emma Kirkby, who skilfully weaves her ravishing voice with the instrumental texture in the once popular "Oh! Had I Jubal's Lyre". King's Joshua, John Mark Ainsley, portrays proficient musicianship rather than characterization. Overall, however, Handel's vision of battle and brimstone is more than adequately represented.

Additional recommendation ...

Soloists; Palmer Singers; Brewer Chamber Orchestra/Rudolph Palmer. Newport Classics NPD85515 — ② 2h 1m DDD 7/91

Handel. Solomon. **Carolyn Watkinson** (mez) Solomon; **Nancy Argenta** (sop) Solomon's Queen; **Barbara Hendricks** (sop) Queen of Sheba; **Joan Rodgers** (sop) First Harlot; **Della Jones** (mez) Second Harlot; **Anthony Rolfe Johnson** (ten) Zadok; **Stephen Varcoe** (bass) A Levite; **Monteverdi Choir; English Baroque Soloists/John Eliot Gardiner.** Philips 412 612-2PH2. Notes, text and translation included.

③ 2h 16m DDD 12/85 9p 9s B

This oratorio is a somewhat static affair but one filled with the most serene and affecting music. The three acts set forth three aspects of Solomon's majesty. The first deals with his piety and marital bliss, the second with his wisdom in his famous judgement as to which of two harlots is the mother of a child, the third to the visit of the Queen of Sheba. Handel set the scene in a wonderful contrast of pomp and ceremony with the pastoral, his choruses always apt to the mood to be depicted. The scene between the two harlots is brilliantly characterized, the airs for the other principals in Handel's most felicitous vein, while the Sinfonia depicting the Queen of Sheba's entrance is justly famous. The Monteverdi Choir sing with mellifluous tone and precise articulation and the authentic instruments of the English Baroque Soloists play for John Eliot Gardiner with style and virtuosity. The soloists are well chosen with special praise for Nancy Argenta as Solomon's Queen. The recording does full justice to every aspect of the colourful score and it would be hard to imagine a performance that was a better advocate for Handel's cause.

Handel. Susanna. **Lorraine Hunt, Jill Feldman** (sops); **Drew Minter** (alto); **Jeffrey Thomas** (ten); **William Parker** (bar); **David Thomas** (bass); **Chamber Chorus of the**

University of California, Berkeley; Philharmonia Baroque Orchestra/Nicholas McGegan. Harmonia Mundi HMU90 7030/2. Notes and text included.

③ 2h 58m DDD 10/90

Susanna is one of the least often heard of Handel's oratorios. A tale, from the *Apocrypha*, of the betrayal of a beautiful and virtuous woman, in her husband's absence, by two lascivious elders when she rejects their importunities, it gives Handel opportunities for a wide range of music — there are amorous pieces for Susanna and her husband, idyllic rural ones when she is in the garden with her maid, sharply drawn pictures of the elders (one an insinuating tenor, the other a more menacing bass), and several powerful expressions of devoutness, rectitude and faith. It has been called "an opera of village life", and it does contain touches of character and comedy; but in this very fine performance one is never in doubt that it is much more than that, a deeply serious work, whose climaxes come in noble, solemn music such as Susanna's "Bending to the throne of glory" (a B minor aria with rich, five-part strings, grave yet glowing) and the chorus at the end, when she is found to be faultless, in praise of divine justice. Lorraine Hunt sings Susanna's music here with considerable power and focus of tone, rising to the great moments, and also charming and graceful in the lesser ones such as the bathing aria in Part 2. As her husband, the gentle counter-tenor Drew Minter is sensitive and controlled, while the elders are graphically drawn by Jeffrey Thomas and David Thomas. The choral singing by this Californian group, under English direction, is clear and firm in line, direct in rhythm, and Nicholas McGegan's handling of the Baroque orchestra is live and assured, with the tempos and the sense of the music always surely judged.

NEW REVIEW

Handel. Theodora. **Lorraine Hunt** (sop) Theodora; **Jennifer Lane** (mez) Irene; **Drew Minter** (alto) Didymus; **Jeffrey Thomas** (ten) Septimus; **Nigel Rogers** (ten) Messenger; **David Thomas** (bass) Valens; **California University, Berkeley Chamber Chorus; Philharmonia Baroque Orchestra/Nicholas McGegan.** Harmonia Mundi HMU90 7060/2. Text included. Recorded in 1991.

③ 2h 50m DDD 10/92

"The Jews will not come to it … because it is a Christian story, and the ladies will not come to it because it is a virtuous one" wrote Handel somewhat bitterly after the unfavourable reception of his sublime late oratorio, *Theodora*. If contemporary audiences were put off by its theme of martyrdom, we should be grateful that the self-righteous piety of Morell's libretto inspired some of Handel's finest music, complete for the first time on record with the added bonus of both the original and revised versions of "Symphony of Soft Musick". And at last it has a recording which can be wholeheartedly recommended. David Thomas as Valens, the Roman governor, opens the proceedings with a firm and resolute tone and later gives the bloodthirsty "Racks, gibbets, sword and fire" much menace. Lorraine Hunt was an inspired choice for the taxing title-role: the top notes of "Angels ever bright and fair" are celestially floated, while she finds great intensity in "With darkness deep", the emotional centre of the work. Drew Minter gives a mellifluous and characterful account of Didymus, a Roman officer recently converted to Christianity who attempts to save Theodora. Listen to their duet, "To Thee, Thou glorious Son" to hear how winningly they blend their voices. Praise too for Jeffrey Thomas as Septimius, particularly in his elegant ornamentation in the virtuoso aria "Dread the fruits of Christian folly", only occasionally showing strain in the wide leaps in "From virtue springs". Jennifer Lane is also impressive as Irene (described in the libretto simply as "A Christian") — despite being burdened with some of Morell's most trite utterances: "True Happiness is only found, where Grace and Truth and Love Abound, And pure religion feeds the Flame". This is perhaps Nicholas McGegan's best Handel recording yet. He has at his command a highly skilled orchestra, chooses tempos which are unfailingly apt, supporting and giving weight to the vocal lines. Praise too, for the excellent University of California Chamber Chorus, well schooled by their director John Butt. Harmonia Mundi have provided an informative booklet with a full libretto in three languages and an illuminating introductory essay from McGegan himself.

Additional recommendations ...

Soloists; Amor Artis Chorale; English Chamber Orchestra/Johannes Somary. Vanguard Classics 08.4075.72 — 2h 32m ② ADD

Soloists; Vienna Concentus Musicus/Nikolaus Harnoncourt. Teldec 2292-46447-2 — ② 2h 11m DDD 8/91

NEW REVIEW

Handel. OPERA ARIAS. **Nathalie Stutzmann** (contr); **Hanover Band/Roy Goodman.** RCA Victor Red Seal 09026 61205-2. Texts and translations included. Recorded in 1991. ORLANDO — Fammi combattere; Ah stigie larve! ... Già latra Cerbero ... Ma la Furia ... Vaghe pupille. ACI, GALATEA E POLIFEMO — Qui l'augel di pianta. RINALDO — Cara sposa, amante cara. GIULIO CESARE — Va tacito e nascosto; Se in fiorito ameno prato. FLORIDANTE — Bramo te sola; Se dolce m'era già. PARTENOPE — Furibondo spira il vento. RADAMISTO — Ombra cara di mia sposa.

1h 9m DDD 3/93

It is hard to believe from these performances that Nathalie Stutzmann is not yet 30. The richness and variety of her vocal expression, and her deep understanding of music that is all too often performed with a dispassionate reverence, belie her youth. Yet that youth is of use, for the proclamations of love in many of these arias are not conveyed here with matronly recollection but immediate passion. It has to be said that RCA have served her well, for the recording engineers have found that sweet microphone spot for her to enable her qualities to cut through the recording process — and those qualities are many and well worth preserving on disc. The repertoire that makes up this programme, though not ideally documented in the insert-notes, is wide ranging, including a number of items intended for castratos; many items require both a fine bel canto and technical agility. "Ah Stigie larve! ... Vaghe pupille" from Act 2 of *Orlando* is a case in point, and ideally illustrates just how well Stutzmann can cope with both these extreme demands. The Hanover Band give her a spirited accompaniment, packed with fine solo work, more of which should be acknowledged in the notes.

Key to Symbols

Gramophone Award winners

Artists of the Year

Handel. AMADIGI DI GAULA. **Nathalie Stutzmann** (contr) Amadigi; **Jennifer Smith** (sop) Oriana; **Eiddwen Harrhy** (sop) Melissa; **Bernarda Fink** (mez) Dardano; **Pascal Bertin** (alto) Orgando; **Les Musiciens du Louvre/Marc Minkowski.** Erato 2292-45490-2. Notes, text and translation included. Recorded in 1989.

Dating from Handel's early years in London *Amadigi* proved once more his early command in creating drama within the formalities of *opera seria*. It is the second of the composer's magical operas; set in ancient Gaul it describes how the scheming sorceress Melissa tries to entice Amadigi away from the lovely Oriana, who is also hopelessly desired by Dardano, Prince of Thrace. Although the action is dominated by these four characters, all taken by high voices (the hero originally by an alto castrato), Handel entirely avoids monotony through his skill in giving their emotions true expression in a wonderfully varied succession of numbers, every one appropriate to the situation in hand. These are all executed here in an entirely convincing, sensitive and spirited manner by the four singers — Nathalie Stutzmann is a palpitating, eager Amadigi, Bernarda Fink an appropriately earnest, forthright Daradano, Amadigi's friend, Jennifer Smith a soft-grained, plangent Oriana nicely contrasted with Eiddwen Harrhy's fiery, incisive Melissa. Minkowski's direction, lithe, direct, yet ever responsive to the emotional turbulence expressed by the principals, is consistently admirable, sailing a fair course between the Scylla of over-accentuation and the Charybdis of baroque severity, and his period-instrument Les Musiciens du Louvre play with a fluency that sounds absolutely natural.

NEW REVIEW

Handel. FLORIDANTE (abridged). **Catherine Robbin** (mez) Floridante; **Ingrid Attrot** (sop) Timante; **Nancy Argenta** (sop) Rossane; **Linda Maguire** (mez) Elmira; **Mel Braun** (bar) Oronte; **Tafelmusik Baroque Orchestra/Alan Curtis.** CBC Records SMCD5110. Text and translation included.

1h 16m DDD 1/93 

If the first performances of *Floridante* were half as good as this, then it's little wonder it became one of Handel's most successful operas. In many ways its success in the 1720s is responsible for its neglect in the 1990s. Handel revised and rewrote it extensively to accommodate the different voices of various revival casts and it's no easy task to decipher just what his original scheme was. Perhaps, then, such an 'extracts' disc makes good sense: we hear the best of Handel's music without worrying overmuch about the authentic overall shape of the piece. In any case Handel's instinctive genius for writing big set-piece arias for his lead singers is highlighted by this method of presentation. This is an outstanding performance, by any standards, with voices which combine the wonderful purity we have come to expect in such 'authentic' music-making (Ingrid Attrot and Nancy Argenta coo together in the sumptuous duet, "Fuor di periqlio", accompanied by pairs of warm, delicious bassoons and horns) with real dramatic flair and listen to Linda Maguire's seething anger in her aria of hate, "Barbaro! t'odio a morte". Alan Curtis has a gloriously forthright, no-nonsense approach bringing a strong, earthy quality from his robust musicians. If there are any collectors who still have lingering doubts about the strength and tonal variety of these period instruments, this stirring playing should dispel them once and for all. It is enhanced by a fine, full-bodied recording of unusual depth.

NEW REVIEW

Handel. MUZIO SCEVOLA (Act 3).
Bononcini. MUZIO SCEVOLA (Act 2) — Overture[e]; Dolce pensier[a]; E pure in mezzo all'armi[c]; Si, t'ama, o cara[c]; Mutio Scevola — Pupille amate[d]; Come, quando alle mie pene[c]. [a]**John Ostendorf** (bass) Porsenna; **D'Anna Fortunato** (contr) Muzio; [b]**Julianne Baird** (sop) Clelia; [c]**Erie Mills** (sop) Orazio; **Jennifer Lane** (mez) Irene; **Andrea Matthews** (sop) Fidalma; [d]**Frederick Urrey** (ten) Tarquinio; [e]**Brewer Baroque Chamber Orchestra/Rudolph Palmer.** Newport Classic Premier NPD85540. Texts and translations included. Recorded in 1991.

② 1h 56m DDD 3/93

Muzio Scevola was first performed in London in 1721 during the second season of the recently formed Royal Academy of Music. It was, however, a composite work for which Handel was responsible only for the Third Act. Acts 1 and 2 were entrusted to Filippo Amadei and Giovanni Bononcini, respectively. The text was the work of the Academy's Italian secretary, Paolo Rolli. The conductor Rudolph Palmer does not perform the entire opera but does give Handel's contribution more or less complete, as well as some "morceaux favoris" by Bononcini. These are drawn both from the 1721 score and an earlier setting of the opera which Bononcini had made for Vienna in 1710. Reflecting the composite nature of *Muzio Scevola* the three acts, each focusing on a valorous episode in ancient Roman history, are to a great extent autonomous; thus, Handel's contribution, reckoned by his contemporaries to be comfortably superior to the others, stands well on its own. Though singing and playing are not in every respect ideal this recording is, nevertheless a valuable addition to the Handel opera canon on disc. The music, much of which is in the composer's most beguiling manner, is brought to life affectionately and with a good sense of style. The recording, though a shade dry is clear and allows for detail.

Handel. FLAVIO. **Jeffrey Gall** (alto) Flavio; **Derek Lee Ragin** (alto) Guido; **Lena Lootens** (sop) Emilia; **Bernarda Fink** (contr) Teodata; **Christina Högman** (sop) Vitige;

Gianpaolo Fagotto (ten) Ugone; **Ulrich Messthaler** (bass) Lotario; Ensemble 415/René Jacobs. Harmonia Mundi HMC90 1312/3. Notes, text and translation included. Recorded in 1989.

② 2h 36m DDD 7/90

Flavio is one of the most delectable of Handel's operas. Although it comes from his 'heroic' period, it is not at all in the heroic mould but rather an ironic tragedy with a good many comic elements. Does that sound confusing? — well, so it is, for you never know quite where you are when King Flavio of Lombardy starts falling in love with the wrong woman, for although this starts as an amusing idle fancy it develops into something near-tragic, since he imperils everyone else's happiness, ultimately causing the death of one counsellor and the dishonour of another. The delicately drawn amorous feeling is like nothing else in Handel, and in its subtle growth towards real passion and grief is handled with consummate skill. The opera, in short, is full of fine and exceptionally varied music, and it is enhanced here by a performance under René Jacobs that, although it takes a number of modest liberties, catches the moods of the music surely and attractively, with shapely, alert and refined playing from the admirable Ensemble 415. And the cast is strong. The central roles, composed for two of Handel's greatest singers, Cuzzoni and Senesino, are done by Lena Lootens, a delightfully natural and expressive soprano with a firm, clear technique, and the counter-tenor Derek Lee Ragin, who dispatches his brilliant music with aplomb and excels in the final aria, a superb minor-key expression of passion. The singers also include Bernarda Fink as the lightly amorous Teodata and Christina Högman, both fiery and subtle in the music for her lover, and the capable Jeffrey Gall as the wayward monarch. Altogether a highly enjoyable set, not flawless but certainly among the best ever Handel opera recordings.

Handel. GIULIO CESARE. **Jennifer Larmore** (mez) Giulio Cesare; **Barbara Schlick** (sop) Cleopatra; **Bernarda Fink** (mez) Cornelia; **Marianne Rørholm** (mez) Sextus; **Derek Lee Ragin** (alto) Ptolemy; **Furio Zanasi** (bass) Achillas; **Olivier Lallouette** (bar) Curio; **Dominique Visse** (alto) Nirenus; **Concerto Cologne/René Jacobs.** Harmonia Mundi HMC90 1385/7. Notes, text and translation included. Recorded in 1991.

④ 4h 4m DDD 4/92

Handel's greatest heroic opera sports no fewer than eight principal characters and one of the largest orchestras he ever used. Undoubtedly this, and the singing of Francesca Cuzzoni (Cleopatra) and Senesino (Caesar), eighteenth-century operatic superstars, helped to launch *Giulio Cesare* into enduring popularity that it enjoys to this day. But it is primarily the quality of the music, with barely a weak number in four hours of entertainment, that has made it such a favourite choice with musicians and audiences. Surprisingly, this is the only complete performance on period instruments currently available, an immediate advantage in giving extra 'bite' to the many moments of high drama without threatening to drown the singers in *forte* passages. This performance is a particularly fine one with an excellent cast; Caesar, originally sung by a castrato, is here taken by the young mezzo, Jennifer Larmore. She brings weight and a sense of integrity to the role (which surely couldn't be matched by a counter-tenor), seemingly untroubled by the demands of the final triumphant aria, "Qual torrente". Occasionally her vibrato becomes intrusive, particularly near the beginning of the opera, but that is a minor quibble in a performance of this stature. Handel could just as well have called his opera *Cleopatra* as it is she who is the pivotal element in the drama, a role taken here by Barbara Schlick. One of Handel's most vividly developed characters, Schlick represents this many faceted woman with acuity and imagination, ranging from the haunting pathos of "Piangerò", where she occasionally seems stretched on the top notes, to the exuberant virtuosity of "Da tempeste" in the final act. If Cleopatra represents strength in a woman, then Cornelia is surely the tragic figure, at the mercy of events. Her first aria, "Priva son", here taken very slowly, shows Bernarda Fink to be more than equal to the role, admirable in her steady tone and dignity of character. Derek Lee Ragin's treacherous Ptolemy is also memorable, venom and fire injected into his agile voice. A first-rate cast is supported by René Jacobs and Concerto Cologne on fine form, though the continuo line is sometimes less than ideally clear. The excellent recording completes one's pleasure in a momentous issue.

Additional recommendation ...

Sung in English. **Soloists; English National Opera Chorus and Orchestra/Sir Charles Mackerras.** EMI CMS7 69760-2 — ③ 3h 3m DDD 5/89

Handel. ORLANDO. **James Bowman** (alto) Orlando; **Arleen Auger** (sop) Angelica; **Catherine Robbin** (mez) Medoro; **Emma Kirkby** (sop) Dorinda; **David Thomas** (bass) Zoroastro; **Academy of Ancient Music/Christopher Hogwood.** L'Oiseau-Lyre 430 845-2OH3. Notes, text and translation included. Recorded 1989-90.

③ 2h 38m DDD 8/91 

Handel's operas represent the greatest expanse of under-explored musical territory ever to have been written by a major composer. For cherishers of verismo the formalism of Handel's theatrical world no doubt presents a problem or two, but for listeners willing to accept the (not so very restricting) conventions within which the composer worked there are wonderful discoveries to be made. *Orlando* is as good a place as any to start looking. Its pastoral tale of unrequited love and resultant madness is retold by Handel with customary sympathy and psychological insight; and, needless to say, he provides some ravishing music along the way. Christopher Hogwood is not, perhaps, a born opera conductor, but he has assembled a fine cast for this recording, which benefits, too, from being based on a touring production. Thus, though one might feel that there is a slight lack of dramatic weight and pacing in this performance, such faults are redeemed by the polished and confident contributions of its five experienced baroque singers. James Bowman is intelligent and passionate in the title-role, Arleen Auger frequently thrilling as the object of his hopeless love, and the remaining parts are all perfectly suited to the particular strengths of their interpreters. Definitely a Handel recording worth having.

Handel. ALCESTE[a]. COMUS[b]. [a]**Emma Kirkby,** [a]**Judith Nelson,** [b]**Patrizia Kwella,** [a]**Christina Pound** (sops); [ab]**Margaret Cable,** [a]**Catherine Denley** (mezs); [a]**Paul Elliott,** [a]**Rogers Covey-Crump** (tens); [ab]**David Thomas,** [a]**Christopher Keyte** (basses); **Academy of Ancient Music/ Christopher Hogwood.** L'Oiseau-Lyre Florilegium 421 479-2OH. Texts included. Item marked [a] from DSLO581 (12/80), [b] DSLO598 (8/82).

1h 14m ADD 3/89 

The *Alceste* music was written towards the end of Handel's life as masque-like interludes for a production of Tobias Smollett's play. They were never used in that form and were later employed by the composer for *The Choice of Hercules.* The musical numbers Handel created would seem to have provided a kind of musical commentary on the text of the play itself. It consists primarily of arias and choruses with occasional orchestral interludes. One of the highlights is definitely the lovely setting of "Gentle Morpheus, son of night", exquisitely sung here by Emma Kirkby. Paul Elliott, too, sings with great style. The bonus item, *Comus*, consists of three songs linked by choral refrains. They are beautifully done with the AAM playing with great style throughout, and the recordings are finely managed.

Further listening ...

Judas Maccabaeus — *oratorio.* **Soloists; New College Choir, Oxford; The King's Consort/Robert King.** Hyperion CDA66641 (12/92).

Jephtha — *oratorio.* **Soloists; Monteverdi Choir; English Baroque Soloists/John Eliot Gardiner.** Philips 422 351-2PH3 (6/89).

AGRIPPINA. **Soloists; Cappella Savaria/Nicholas McGegan.** Harmonia Mundi HMU90 7063/5 (3/93).

TESEO. **Soloists; Les Musiciens du Louvre/Marc Minkowski.** Erato 2292-45806-2 (3/93).

OTTONE. **Soloists; Freiburg Baroque Orchestra/Nicholas McGegan.** Harmonia Mundi HMU90 7073/5 (3/93).

TAMERLANO. **Soloists; English Baroque Soloist/John Eliot Gardiner.** Erato 2292-45408-2.

RODELINDA. **Soloists; La Stagione/Michael Schneider.** Deutsche Harmonia Mundi RD77192 (1/93).

ALESSANDRO. **Soloists; La Petite Bande/Sigiswald Kuijken.** Deutsche Harmonia Mundi Editio Classica GD77110 (2/91).

PARTENOPE. **Soloists; La Petite Bande/Sigiswald Kuijken.** Deutsche Harmonia Mundi Editio Classica GDD77109 (2/91).

ALCINA. **Soloists; Opera Stage Chorus; City of London Baroque Sinfonia/Richard Hickox.** EMI CDS7 49771-2 (11/88).

ATALANTA. **Soloists; Savaria Vocal Ensemble; Capella Savaria/Nicholas McGegan.** Hungaroton HCD12612/14-2 (3/86).

Key to Symbols

Bargains — *Quality of performance* — *Quality of Sound* — *Basic library* — *Discs worth exploring* — *Period performance* — *Caveat emptor*

Howard Hanson

American 1896-1981

NEW REVIEW

Hanson. Piano Concerto, Op. 36[a]. Symphonies — No. 5, Op. 43, "Sinfonia Sacra"; No. 7, "A Sea Symphony[b]. Mosaics. [a]**Carol Rosenberger** (pf); [b]**Seattle Symphony Chorale and Orchestra/Gerard Schwarz.** Delos DE3130. Recorded in 1992.

lh 8m DDD 3/93

Howard Hanson was once called "the American Sibelius", and not just because he too wrote seven symphonies: there is a rugged grandeur about his music that was considered old-fashioned in his long lifetime, but he did not deviate from the essentials of his art in order to keep up with the times. Now, a dozen years after his death, his music is gaining ground, and Gerard Schwarz and the Seattle Symphony Orchestra have now recorded all the symphonies and several other works, two of which appear on this disc. *Mosaics* reminds us less of Sibelius than of Vaughan Williams in the way that it opens broodingly and then expands into spiritual radiance — and later, it must be said, into a conventional folk-pastoral style (at 5'20"). The consciously spiritual quality in Hanson's music is more convincing: it richly informs the Fifth Symphony, which the composer said was inspired by the story of the Resurrection as described in St John's Gospel. Thus in this work we find echoes of Gregorian chant and chorales: it is in one movement but contains three recognizable sections that culminate in a benediction. Although one hears too much of the Hollywood epic in the rhetorical material and lush scoring, for example in the lead up to a climax just after the 12-minute mark, the sincerity of this music is impressive and the work is admirably structured. In his Seventh Symphony, Hanson again echoed Vaughan

Williams in writing a choral 'sea symphony' that used Walt Whitman's poetry, but Hanson was no VW and this last symphony, written when he was 81, is less sophisticated and memorable than the First Symphony of the Englishman, then in his thirties. The Piano Concerto is the earliest music here and effectively written in a mainly thoughtful idiom rather than a virtuoso one. All these performances are persuasive and remind us that Hanson's "entertaining, big-hearted" music deserves to be better known. It will surely win friends among the many people who find it impossible to come to terms with the twentieth century's more radical composers.

Roy Harris

American 1898-1979

Harris. Symphony No. 3 (1939).
Schuman. Symphony No. 3 (1941). **New York Philharmonic Orchestra/Leonard Bernstein.** DG 419 780 2GH. Recorded at a performance in the Avery Fisher Hall, New York in December 1985.

51m DDD 11/87 

If you already know music by Gershwin and Copland and wish to explore the work of other American composers then these two symphonies provide the ideal opportunity. Harris's short Third Symphony of 1939 is in one continuous movement, which however falls into five sections — Tragic, Lyric, Pastoral, Fugue-Dramatic and Dramatic-Tragic. The style is austere without being in the least forbidding; the musical arguments are terse but easy to follow, the orchestral sound solid but not opaque. When first performed the symphony was an instant critical and popular success, as was Schuman's Third Symphony when premièred two years later. Harris's influence on his slightly younger colleague is apparent, but Schuman has a rather more brilliant orchestral style and the mood of the work, cast in two movements, each of which has two connected sections, is a little more outgoing. The New York Philharmonic has this kind of music in its bones, and it gives superlative performances under its former chief conductor, whose sympathy and insight into the music of his older contemporaries has always been notable. The recordings are superlative.

Further listening ...

American Creed. When Johnny comes marching home. *Couplied with* **Copland:** Fanfare for the Common Man. Lincoln Portrait[a]. Canticle of Freedom[b]. An Outdoor Overture. [a]**James Earl Jones** (spkr); **Seattle** [b]**Chorale and Symphony Orchestra/Gerard Schwarz.** Delos DE3140.
See review under Copland; refer to Index to Reviews.

Lou Harrison

American 1917-

L. Harrison. WORKS FOR GUITAR AND PERCUSSION. **John Schneider** (gtr); [a]**Janice Tipton** (ocarina); [b]**Dave Ross,** [c]**Gene Strimling** (perc); [d]**Cal Arts Percussion Ensemble/John Bergamo.** Etcetera KTC1071. Recorded 1985-89.
Canticle No. 3 (1941)[abd]. Suite No. 1 (1976)[bc]. Plaint and Variations on "Song of Palestine" (1978). Serenado por Gitaro (1952). Serenade (1978)[c]. Waltz for Evelyn Hinrichsen (1977).

50m DDD 9/91 

"The whole round world of music and instruments lives around us. I am interested in a transethnic, a planetary music." Lou Harrison is an eccentric among American composers; however, the popularity of so-called New Age and minimalist music should make us listen afresh to such apparently outmoded precursors as Harrison and his colleagues, John Cage, Harry Partch and Henry Cowell. We might just uncover an eminently approachable avant-garde. Harrison's output, which includes many works in conventional Western forms for conventional Western forces, is particularly unthreatening. Thanks to a preoccupation with oriental modes and instruments, he specializes in delicate attenuated textures which need not preclude tunes. Thus the first piece here, the sensitively percussive *Canticle No. 3* of 1941 is centred on an eerie melodic refrain. The *Suite No. 1* is about as intellectually formidable as the pop-sourced ambient music of Brian Eno. And *Plaint and Variations*, based on instantly medieval material, is not unlike Arvo Pärt for guitar. If some of John Schneider's pitching sounds unconventional — his instrument is equipped with a system of interchangeable fingerboards designed to facilitate the use of various non-standard tuning systems — all is explained in the booklet. The Esperanto-speaking Harrison may yet acquire cult status and this immaculately played and recorded disc should help.

Karl Amadeus Hartmann

German 1905-1963

Suggested listening ...

Symphonies Nos. 1-8. Gesangszene. **Doris Soffel** (contr); **Dietrich Fischer-Dieskau** (bar); **Bavarian Radio Symphony Orchestra/Fritz Rieger, Rafael Kubelík, Ferdinand Leitner, Zdenek Macal.** Wergo WER60187-50 (4-disc set, reviewed 5/90).

Piano Sonata, "27 April1945". Piano Sonatine. Zwei kleine Suiten. Jazz-Toccata und Fuge. **Siegfried Mauser** (pf). Virgin Classics VC7 59017-2 (8/91).

Sir Herbert Hamilton Harty

Irish 1879-1941

Suggested listening ...

Ode to a Nightingale. The Children of Lir. **Heather Harper** (sop); **Ulster Orchestra/Bryden Thomson.** Chandos CHAN8387 (10/87).

Piano Concerto in B minor[a]. In Ireland — Fantasy for flute, harp and orchestra[b]. With the Wild Geese. [a]**Malcolm Binns** (pf); [b]**Claude Fleming** (fte); [b]**Denise Kelly** (hp); **Ulster Orchestra/Bryden Thomson.** Chandos CHAN8321 (4/85).

An Irish Symphony. A Comedy Overture. **Ulster Orchestra/Bryden Thomson.** Chandos CHAN8314 (9/84).

Jonathan Harvey

British 1939-

NEW REVIEW

J. Harvey. From Silence[a]. Natajara[b]. Ritual Melodies[c]. [a]**Karol Bennett** (voc); [b]**Harrie Starreveld** (fl/picc); [a]**Lucy Chapman Stoltzman** (vn); [a]**Michael Thompson** (hn); [a]**Dean Anderson** (perc); [b]**René Eckhardt** (pf); [a]**Kathleen Supove,** [a]**John MacDonald,** [a]**Diana Dabby** (electric keyboards); [ac]**David Atherton** (tape op); [ac]**Brent Koeppel,** [ac]**Ken Malsky,** [ac]**Philip Sohn** (computer/tape ops)/**Barry Vercoe.** Bridge BCD9031.

45m DDD 11/92

This disc offers a useful cross-section of the work of a leading British composer, now in his fifties, who has the rare gift of making complex technology serve strongly expressive ends. *Natajara* is a relatively short piece for flute and piano — no tape, no computer — which enters

Messiaen territory only to transform it into something quite different. It's a dazzlingly virtuosic celebration of the god Shiva, "the four-armed dancer whose movements create and destroy matter throughout eternity", and a particularly salutary corrective for anyone who believes that Harvey writes only quiet, reflective music. *From Silence* is more diverse than *Natajara*, exploring the extremes of aggression and reflection by means of the intriguing interplay between 'live' sounds (including the supremely agile voice of Karol Bennett) and electro-acoustic music. Then, with *Ritual Melodies*, we have a pure computer piece, whose allusions to real instruments, like the shakuhachi, and to chanting voices, serve to underline the fascinating blend of differences and similarities that can exist between live and electro-acoustic worlds. All of Harvey's works are about rituals, all have an overriding spiritual dimension. That this is not a limitation is the message coming loud and clear from this technically excellent disc.

Further listening ...

Cello Concerto[bc]. Curve with Plateaux. Ricercare una melodia[a]. Three Sketches. Philia's Dream[a]. **Frances-Marie Uitti** (vc); [a]**Jonathan Harvey** (electronics); [b]**Emilia Romagna "Toscanini" Symphony Orchestra/José Roman Encinar.** Etcetera KTC1148 (7/93).

Bhakti for chamber ensemble and quadraphonic tape. **Spectrum/Guy Protheroe.** NMC NMCD001 (9/89).

Song Offerings. *Coupled with* ***G. Benjamin.*** Antara. ***Boulez.*** Dérive. Memoriale. **Penelope Walmsley-Clark** (sop); **Sebastian Bell** (fl); **London Sinfonietta/George Benjamin.** Nimbus NI5167 (10/89).
See review under Benjamin; refer to Index to Reviews.

Joseph Haydn

Austrian 1732-1809

Haydn. Cello Concertos — C major, HobVII*b*/1; D major, HobVII*b*/2.
A. Kraft. Cello Concerto in C major, Op. 4. **Anner Bylsma** (bar vc); **Tafelmusik/Jeanne Lamon.** Deutsche Harmonia Mundi RD77757. Recorded in 1989.

1h 7m DDD 9/91 

At best, an 'authentic' performance can only aspire to return to the spirit, rather than the letter of the period it strives to recreate, and yet the fine Dutch cellist Anner Bylsma comes as near as anyone to convincing us that this is indeed the way Haydn might have wished these sunny, yet highly sophisticated concertos to be played. Haydn composed these works for the virtuoso cellist of the Esterházy court orchestra, Anton Kraft, and the bold and adventurous solo writing reflects his fabled technical prowess and musical sensitivity. Bylsma offers a lithe, yet scrupulously classical and poised account of the C major Concerto, with a romantically inflected central *adagio* followed by a dashingly brilliant, yet suitably witty finale. His rapid passagework in higher registers is astonishing, while he reveals the stately dignity of the D major work (long attributed to Kraft) in a cultured and attractively proportioned reading of rich intensity and variety. Bylsma includes his own revisions of period cadenzas, which are never less than apposite, and deftly executed. The real discovery here, though, is the Cello Concerto by Kraft himself, which combines the expected brilliant pyrotechnics with some effective melodic writing, in a work which anticipates the styles developed during the early nineteenth century. In fact, Kraft advised Beethoven on the cello part of his Triple Concerto, and his compositions exercised great influence in the genesis of modern cello technique. Bylsma is superbly supported by the excellent Canadian ensemble, Tafelmusik, and the recording is first rate. A revealing, and often stunningly played collection — highly recommended to all cello enthusiasts.

Additional recommendations ...
Cello Concerto in D major (English Chamber Orchestra). ***Dvořák.*** *Cello Concerto in B minor, B191* (Berlin Philharmonic Orchestra/Lorin Maazel). ***Elgar.*** *Cello Concerto in E minor, Op. 85* (London

Symphony Orchestra/André Previn). ***Saint-Saëns.*** *Cello Concerto No. 1 in A minor, Op. 33* (French National Orchestra/Lorin Maazel). ***Schumann.*** *Cello Concerto in A minor, Op. 129* (Bavarian Radio Symphony Orchestra/Sir Colin Davis). **Yo-Yo Ma** (vc). CBS Masterworks CD44562 — ② 2h 20m DDD/ADD 5/90 £

Haydn. **Truls Mørk** (vc); **Norwegian Chamber Orchestra/Iona Brown.** Simax PSC1078 — 50m DDD 8/92

Haydn. Horn Concerto No. 1 in D major, HobVII*d*/3. Symphony No. 31 in D major, "Hornsignal".
M. Haydn. Horn Concerto in D major. **Anthony Halstead** (natural hn); **Hanover Band/Roy Goodman.** Nimbus NI5190. Recorded in 1989.

1h 1m DDD 11/89

This disc is something of an eulogy to the natural, valveless horn of the eighteenth century. Here it is played with panache by Anthony Halstead whose firm control of a notoriously difficult instrument together with accomplished musicianship ensures performances of assurance and finesse. The two Horn Concertos by the brothers Haydn come over well though they are not, perhaps, especially memorable pieces. Virtuoso horn playing is required and Halstead provides it with brilliant passagework, clearly articulated phrases and a characterful sound. The remaining work on the disc is Haydn's well-known Symphony No. 31, *Hornsignal*; here, the composer requires not one but four horn players who collectively make an imposing phalanx. Haydn's appealing sense of humour caters for various varieties of horn signal loudly barked out or beguilingly *piano* as the case may be. In the lyrical Adagio there is a prominent role allotted the solo violin, whilst in the finale, a set of variations, Haydn gives further solos to cello, flute, horns, violin and violone. The contributions are a little variable here but nevertheless spontaneous and affectionate playing such as this should win friends. Effective recorded sound.

NEW REVIEW

Haydn. Keyboard Concertos — F major, HobXVIII/3; G major, HobXVIII/4; D major, HobXVIII/11. **Franz Liszt Chamber Orchestra/Emanuel Ax** (pf). Sony Classical SK48383.

59m DDD 5/93

Mozart's unique achievement in his 27 piano concertos has tended to overshadow the more modestly scored, less overtly virtuoso works by Haydn and only the D major Concerto is at all well known today. Whilst none of the three works recorded here could claim to add to the development of the form in the way that those of Mozart did, all three possess great charm: take for example the *Largo cantabile* of the early F major work to hear Haydn's melodic gift at its most endearing. The *Presto* finale of the same concerto recalls some of his later piano sonatas in its juxtaposition of knockabout comedy and theatrical minor-key drama. The G major, supposedly written for the blind pianist, composer and singer Maria Theresia von Paradis boasts an extended *Grave* slow movement. But it is the D major with its larger orchestra (horns and oboes added to strings) that works best and the *Rondo all'Ungarese* finale with its myriad key changes and sparkling good humour is predictably the highlight of the disc. Emanuel Ax (directing from the keyboard) gives performances of the utmost finesse and affection: if any performance were to help to restore the fortunes of these works then this is surely it. His playing throughout is deeply felt: graceful in the slow movements and dexterous in the outer ones. In addition, he plays his own charming cadenzas in the F and G major works. Sony's sound is spacious, with the piano forwardly placed and the notes are adequate, though no biographical information is included.

Haydn. Trumpet Concerto in E flat major, HobVII*e*/1[a]. Cello Concerto in D major, HobVII*b*/2[b]. Violin Concerto No. 1 in C major, HobVII[c]. [c]**Cho-Liang Lin** (vn); [b]**Yo-Yo Ma** (vc); [a]**Wynton Marsalis** (tpt); [a]**National Philharmonic Orchestra/Raymond Leppard;**

[b]**English Chamber Orchestra/José Luis Garcia;** [c]**Minnesota Orchestra/Sir Neville Marriner.** CBS Masterworks CD39310. From IM39310 (1/85).

59m DDD 1/86

This compilation of three Haydn concertos has a different soloist and orchestra for each. The young American trumpeter Wynton Marsalis has all the fluency one could wish for and an instrument allowing a full three octaves (E flat — E flat) to be displayed in his own cadenza to the first movement. Although this is an efficient performance, it in no way approaches the class of the next one. The cellist Yo-Yo Ma is very different as a performer: though equally a master of his instrument, and indeed a virtuoso who seems incapable of producing an ugly sound or playing out of tune, one feels a deep emotional involvement in all he does. Also, the recording in this D major Cello Concerto is unusually faithful in blending the cello well into the ensemble without ever covering it. Ma is supported by the excellent English Chamber Orchestra and the qualities of integration and ensemble under their leader's direction are all that one could wish for. In the C major Violin Concerto the skilful Cho-Liang Lin has the benefit of a most sympathetic conductor in Sir Neville Marriner, but he cannot match Ma's subtlety and commitment.

Additional recommendations ...

Trumpet Concerto[a]. *Cello Concerto in C major, HobVIIb/1*[b]. *Horn Concertos*[c] *— No. 1 in D major, HobVIId/3; No. 2 in D major, HobVIId/4.* [a]**Håkan Hardenberger** (tpt); [b]**Heinrich Schiff** (vc); [c]**Hermann Baumann** (hn); **Academy of St Martin in the Fields/**[ab]**Sir Neville Marriner,** [c]**Iona Brown.** Philips Laser Line Classics 432 060-2PM — 1h 10m DDD 2/91

Trumpet Concerto[a]. *Oboe Concerto in C major, HobVIIg/C1*[b]. *Keyboard Concerto in D major, HobXVIII/11*[c]. [a]**Mark Bennett** (tpt); [b]**Paul Goodwin** (ob); **The English Concert/Trevor Pinnock** ([c]hpd). Archiv Produktion 431 678-2AH — 56m DDD 9/92

Haydn. SYMPHONIES. **Philharmonia Hungarica/Antál Dorati.** Decca 430 100-2DM32. Also available as eight four-disc sets. Recorded 1969-73.

425 900-2DM4 (4h 30m) — Nos. 1-16. *425 905-2DM4* (4h 34m) — Nos. 17-33. *425 910-2DM4* (4h 43m) — Nos. 34-47. *425 915-2DM4* (4h 33m) — Nos. 48-59. *425 920-2DM4* (4h 11m) — Nos. 60-71. *425 925-2DM4* (4h 29m) — Nos. 72-83. *425 930-2DM4* (4h 46m) — Nos. 84-95. *425 935-2DM4* (4h 46m) — Nos. 96-104. Symphony "A" in B flat major. Symphony "B" in B flat major. Sinfonia concertante in B flat major, HobI/105.

(3) (2) 36h 31m ADD 6/91 £

Though there are now two period-instrument Haydn cycles underway (from Goodman on Hyperion and Hogwood on L'Oiseau-Lyre), this pioneering modern-instrument cycle recorded by Antál Dorati and his band of Hungarian exiles between 1969 and 1973 is always going to be a hard act to follow. When first issued on LP Dorati's performances won almost universal praise for their style and verve, their eager and imaginative engagement with the music's astonishing, protean inventiveness. And in their very overdue CD incarnation, in eight sets of four discs each, they still have little to fear from most of the competition. Remarkably, in such an extended project, there is hardly a whiff of routine: time and again the orchestra seems to play out of its skin for Dorati, the strings sweet-toned and luminous, the wind deft and resourceful, savouring to the full the wit and whimsy of Hadyn's writing. And though one might have reservations about this or that symphony, Dorati's actual interpretations are often exemplary, combining rhythmic resilience and a splendid overall sweep with an unusual care for detail.

Aficionados of period performances may feel that the strings, especially in the earlier symphonies, are too numerous and too liberal with vibrato. But the buoyancy of Dorati's rhythms and the crispness of the strings' articulation constantly preclude any suggestion of undue opulence. Most of the early symphonies (in which Dorati uses a discreetly balanced harpsichord continuo) are captivatingly done: *Allegros* dance and leap and slow movements are shaped with finesse and affection. Listen, for instance, to the beautiful neo-baroque D minor *Andante* in No. 4, or the grave *siciliano* in No. 12, a particularly appealing, warm-textured work. And in the second box, containing Nos. 17-33, Dorati brings a characteristic breadth and intensity of line to the opening *Adagios* of No. 21 (a notably mature and eloquent movement, this) and No. 22, the so-called *Philosopher*. The famous *Hornsignal*, No. 31, is also irresistibly done, with rollicking, ripe-toned horns; and practically the only disappointment in the first two boxes is the *Lamentatione*, No. 26, where both the tragic first movement and the quizzical final minuet are too smooth and sluggish.

A number of the minuets in the middle-period symphonies (those written between the late 1760s and the early 1780s) are also distinctly leisurely, lacking Dorati's usual rhythmic spring — cases in point are those in Nos. 43, 52 and 49 (the last funereally slow). And one or two of the passionate minor-keyed symphonies, especially Nos. 39 and 52, are, like No. 26, wanting in fire and dramatic thrust. But in many of these works of Haydn's first full maturity (several still virtually unknown) Dorati gives penetrating, shrewdly judged performances. Highlights among the rarer symphonies include No. 41, with its pealing trumpets and high horns (stunningly played), the expansive No. 42, done with real breadth and grandeur, and the subtle, lyrical No. 64, whose sublime *Largo* is sustained at the slowest possible tempo. In one or two works (notably the large-scale D major, No. 61, and the so-called *Laudon*, No. 69), Dorati might seem too frothy and frolicsome. And just occasionally (as in the outrageous six-movement *Il Distratto*, No. 60) he can underplay the earthy, rumbustious side of Haydn's complex musical personality.

Two of the most desirable boxes of all are those containing Symphonies Nos. 72-83 and 84-95 — though some collectors may find it inconvenient that both the "Paris" and the "London" sets are split between boxes. Most of the pre-Paris symphonies are still underrated: but works like Nos. 76, 77 and 81 reveal a new, almost Mozartian suavity of manner and a sophistication of thematic development influenced by the Op. 33 String Quartets, while the two minor-keyed symphonies, Nos. 78 and 80, have notably powerful, concentrated first movements. If Dorati is a shade too comfortable in No. 80 he is superb elsewhere on these discs. Though the competition from rival performances now begins to hot up, he can more than hold his own in the "Paris" set: listen to the mingled grace and strength he brings to Nos. 85 and 87, with their clear, gleaming textures, or his dramatic urgency in the first movement of the misleadingly named *La Poule*, No. 83.

As for the "London" Symphonies, Dorati's readings are as detailed and attentive as any on the market, though at times he can underestimate the music's boldness, grandeur and dangerous wit. This is partly a question of tempos (some distinctly on the slow side) and accent, but also of the variable prominence accorded the brass and timpani — in several works, notably Nos. 94, 96 and, most seriously, the flamboyant, aggressive Nos. 97 and 100, these instruments are too recessed to make their full dramatic effect. Elsewhere, though, the balance is more satisfying: and in symphonies like Nos. 93, 103 and 104 Dorati combines power, incisiveness and symphonic breadth with an unusual sensitivity to the lyrical poignancy which underlies much of Haydn's later music.

The recordings, outstanding in their day, still sound pretty impressive, with a fine spaciousness and bloom, even if the violins can acquire a touch of glare above the stave. All in all, a magnificent, life-enhancing series that has contributed vastly to our deeper understanding of Haydn's genius over the last two decades. Whatever integral cycles may appear in the future, Dorati's will stand as one of the gramophone's grandest achievements.

Haydn. SYMPHONIES. **Hanover Band/Roy Goodman** (hpd). Hyperion CDA66524. Recorded in 1991.
No. 1 in D major. No. 2 in C major. No. 3 in G major. No. 4 in D major. No. 5 in A major.

1h 12m DDD 3/92

These five compact symphonies all date from the period 1757-61 and though there are occasional stretches of arid note-spinning (in the slow movement of No. 2, for example), each of the works here is marked by a formal assurance and a teeming physical energy that sets the young Haydn apart from his contemporaries. All but one are in three movements, though No. 5, following the old *sonata da chiesa* (church sonata) design, begins with a solemn *Adagio*; No. 3, the sole four-movement work here, is the richest of the group, with its lusty, propulsive triple-time opening movement, its rugged canonic minuet and a finale whose four-note subject and free fugal textures anticipate in a modest way the glories of Mozart's *Jupiter*. The Hanover Band's performances have a splendid verve and immediacy with light, buoyant articulation and shrewdly judged tempos. *Allegros*, never unduly precipitate, have a fine earthy exuberance (with an apt touch of majesty in the first movement of No. 2); the *Adagio* opening of No. 5 (which features some spectacular horn writing, immaculately despatched here) nicely balances elegance and gravity, while the lithe, springing *Andantes* of Nos. 1 and 3 find room for expressive shaping in the neo-baroque sequences of suspensions. Textures, as ever in the Hanover Band's cycle, are colourful and transparent, with oboes and horns clearly etched against the strings in the tuttis — the shining sonorities of No. 5, with its high-pitched A major horns, are quite thrilling. Occasionally (as in the finale of No. 1) the violins sound a shade raw; and once or twice, as in the first movement of No. 3, Goodman seems to press the tempo uncomfortably. But for all these trifling reservations, the Hanover Band convey the self-confidence, resource and sheer *élan* of these youthful symphonies more infectiously than any other performance on disc.

Haydn. Symphonies — No. 6 in D major, "Le matin"; No. 7 in C major, "Le midi"; No. 8 in G major, "Le soir". **The English Concert/Trevor Pinnock** (hpd). Archiv Produktion 423 098-2AH.

1h 5m DDD 1/88 

These symphonies represent the times of day; *Le matin* portrays the sunrise, and there is a storm in *Le soir*, but otherwise there is not a lot that could be called programmatic. But Haydn did take the opportunity to give his new colleagues in the princely band something interesting to do, for there are numerous solos here, not only for the wind instruments but for the section leaders — listen especially to the *Adagio* of No. 6, with solo violin and prominent flutes and cello, a delectable piece of writing. Inventively, the music is uneven; the concerto-like style was not wholly harmonious with Haydn's symphonic thinking. But there is plenty of spirited and cheerful music here, and that is well caught in these vivacious performances by Trevor Pinnock and his band, with their brisk tempos and light textures; the playing is duly agile, and the period instruments give a bright edge to the sound.

Additional recommendations ...

Nos. 6-8. **Hanover Band/Roy Goodman.** Hyperion CDA66523 — 1h 9m DDD 12/91

Nos. 6-8; No. 9 in C major; No. 12 in E major; No. 13 in D major; No. 16 in B flat major; No. 40 in F major; No. 72 in D major. **Academy of Ancient Music/Christopher Hogwood.** L'Oiseau-Lyre 433 661-2OH3 — ③ 3h 9m DDD 6/93

Haydn. SYMPHONIES. **Academy of Ancient Music/Christopher Hogwood.** L'Oiseau-Lyre 430 082-2OH3. Recorded 1988-89.

No. 21 in A major; No. 22 in E flat major, "The Philosopher"; No. 23 in G major; No. 24 in D major; No. 28 in A major; No. 29 in E major; No. 30 in C major, "Alleluja"; No. 31 in D major, "Hornsignal"; No. 34 in D minor.

③ 3h 10m DDD 12/90 

As 'the father of the symphony', Haydn had over 100 children! So a complete recorded cycle is a major undertaking for any company, and the one launched with the present issue uses authentic instruments and a slightly lower pitch than modern 'concert' ones. Details of these instruments are listed in the four-language booklet, which has 70 pages including an explanation of the grouping of these works into 15 volumes — the present one, oddly enough, being No. 4 and covering the years 1764-65. The Academy of Ancient Music is usually a small orchestral body, supporting the contention expressed by Joseph Webster that Haydn's orchestra at this time was of about 13 to 16 players and that there was no keyboard continuo. In other words, there is no harpsichord to fill out textures, but although some listeners may miss it initially the playing soon convinces. The music itself cannot be summarized briefly, but as usual with Haydn, even these relatively unfamiliar pieces are inventive and often beautiful. The playing has zest, but however brisk the tempo chosen for quick movements they never degenerate into mere bustle, although other performers may take a less tense view than Christopher Hogwood. There are real discoveries to be made here, beginning with the nervous, dramatic finale to Symphony No. 21, and they also include minuets such as the enigmatic ones to Nos. 28 and 29. Similarly, slow movements have dignity, grace and often a quiet humour too, while phrasing is intelligent and affectionate and textures well balanced. Indeed, Hogwood's wind and string players alike are precise and stylish. Repeats are faithfully observed. Finally, the recording is clear and atmospheric.

Haydn. Symphonies — No. 26 in D minor, "Lamentatione"; No. 52 in C minor; No. 53 in D major, "L'Impériale". **La Petite Bande/Sigiswald Kuijken.** Virgin Classics Veritas VC7 59148-2.

lh 2m DDD 3/89 

This period instrument coupling contains some sprightly and imaginative playing. Symphony No. 26, is sub-titled *Lamentatione* and the nickname alludes to Haydn's use of Gregorian chant in the first two movements. The C minor Symphony No. 52 is a dramatic work, vividly capturing a mood of restless, brooding expectancy. Symphony No. 53, *L'Impériale*, has a glorious confidence and authority to it; the title, scholars suppose, refers to the Empress Maria Theresa. It has an air of sophistication and nobility worthy of Austria's great ruler and receives a vivid and accomplished recording. The sound throughout is warm and ingratiating.

NEW REVIEW

Haydn. Symphonies — No. 30 in C major, "Alleluia"; No. 53 in D major, "Imperial"; No. 69 in C major, "Loudon". **Vienna Concentus Musicus/Nikolaus Harnoncourt.** Teldec Das Alte Werk 9031-76460-2. Recorded in 1990.

lh 7m DDD 6/93 

Three brilliant, extrovert pieces here, with much festive trumpeting and drumming in the two C major symphonies. More, in fact, than Haydn would have expected, since Harnoncourt has added his own trumpet and timpani parts for No. 30 (1765). Whatever the purists might think, the augmented scoring is undeniably effective, enhancing the symphony's celebratory spirit (the nickname, incidentally, comes from the use of the Easter Alleluia plainchant in the first movement); and Harnoncourt and his brilliant period-intrument orchestra give a splendidly vivid, sharp-edged performance. The other symphonies both date from the mid- to late-1770s, and combine ceremonial grandeur with the tuneful, popular manner that Haydn was beginning to cultivate around this time. No. 53, obscurely nicknamed *Imperial* in the early nineteenth century, was among the most spectacular international successes of the composer's career, mainly on account of its *Andante* variations. Harnoncourt is perhaps a touch over-sophisticated here; and the aristocratic minuet is taken at a vehement one-in-a-bar, necessitating a violent deceleration for the trio. But the splendid opening movement is played with verve and flair, while the curious, dullish-looking *Capriccio* which Haydn substituted for the original finale leaps right off the page at Harnoncourt's cracking pace. No. 69, dedicated to the Austrian Field Marshal Laudon (or Loudon), is perhaps one of Haydn's less fetching symphonies, at least until the finale, with its surprisingly violent C minor centrepiece. But Harnoncourt's powerful rhythmic drive and sense of colour (thrilling impact from brass and timpani) make out an unusually strong case for the work. The Teldec recording is spacious and reverberant, but rarely at the expense of clarity.

Haydn. SYMPHONIES. **The English Concert/Trevor Pinnock.** Archiv Produktion 429 756-2AH. Recorded in 1989.
No. 42 in D major; No. 44 in E minor, "Trauer"; No. 46 in B major.

lh 3m DDD 9/90 

These are inspiriting performances of three of Haydn's greatest symphonies from the so-called *Sturm und Drang* years of the early 1770s. Storm and stress is most evident in the *Trauer* ("Mourning"), whose outer movements push the contemporary musical language to new limits of violent intensity; the nickname, incidentally, derives from the sublime *Adagio*, which Haydn is said to have wanted played at his funeral. Symphony No. 46 is probably the only eighteenth-century symphony in the key of B major. And with the outlandish tonality go extremes of expression: the first movement is astonishingly tense and dark-hued for a work of this period in the major key, while the finale is Haydn at his most bizarrely humorous. The other work on the disc, No. 42, is a real rarity, and may well come as a revelation to many. Both the first and second movements have an expansiveness and a harmonic breadth new in Haydn's symphonic music; and the finale is a delightful early example of the racy, popular style which colours so many of his later symphonies. Using an orchestra of around 20 players, as Haydn himself would have done, Pinnock gives vital, characterful readings, with a blend of sophistication and earthiness ideally suited to the composer. The string playing is supple and sweet-toned — no wire-wool associations here — and the expertly played oboes and horns cut through pungently in the tuttis. Outer movements are boldly projected, their often exceptional rhythmic and harmonic tension powerfully controlled. All three slow movements are done with finesse and a beautiful sense of line (none of the exaggerated 'squeezed' phrasing favoured in some authentic performances), though the *Adagio* of No. 44 has a slightly too easy, *grazioso* feel. More controversial are the minuets, taken very smartly indeed, with a loss of dignity and grandeur in Nos. 42 and 46. But these truthfully recorded performances can be recommended to anyone who is not ideologically opposed to period instruments.

Additional recommendations ...

No. 42; No. 43 in E flat major, "Mercury"; No. 44. **Hanover Band/Roy Goodman.** Hyperion CDA66530 — 1h 19m DDD 2/93

No. 41 in C major; Nos. 42-3. **Tafelmusik/Bruno Weil.** Sony Classical Vivarte SK48370 — 1h 6m DDD 4/93

No. 44; No. 51 in B flat major; No. 52 in C minor. **Tafelmusik/Bruno Weil.** Sony Classical Vivarte SK48371 — 1h 2m DDD 4/93

Haydn. Symphony No. 44 in E minor, "Trauer".
Mozart. Symphony No. 40 in G minor, K550. **St John's Smith Square Orchestra/John Lubbock.** Pickwick IMP Red Label PCD820.

55m DDD 8/86 £

Here is a performance of Mozart's No. 40 that looks deeper than the often over-stated surface qualities of charm and grace, resulting in a darker and more sinister account of this highly original work. The elusive opening is skilfully handled, creating a fine air of expectancy. The orchestra's phrasing is always intelligent and well articulated, and in the *Andante* they capture the restlessness of spirit and subtle hesitations. Beautiful phrasing also pervades the *Minuet*, which acts like an impatient upbeat to the finale, emphasized by its vague and abrupt ending. The despairing and impassioned finale has energy and vigour as the dramatic tension builds towards the harmonically daring development section, notable in this performance for some excellent horn playing. Haydn's *Trauer* Symphony receives a fine performance too, if perhaps lacking a little of the sustained vigour and tension found in the Mozart. It is one of Haydn's finest *Sturm und Drang* symphonies, and the first movement is noted for its dramatic strength and dynamic contrast. The *Adagio* is beautifully played in this tender and serene performance; this movement was reputed to be a particular favourite of Haydn's, and he requested it to be played at his funeral (hence the nickname *Trauer*). The finale regains the energy and vigour found in the Mozart, and the clarity of the recording highlights the contrapuntal texture very well indeed. Rewarding performances at a bargain price.

Haydn. Symphonies — No. 45 in F sharp minor, "Farewell"; No. 48 in C major, "Maria Theresia"; No. 102 in B flat major. **Capella Istropolitana/Barry Wordsworth.** Naxos 8 550382. Recorded in 1989.

1h 13m DDD 9/91 

At the rate they're going, Barry Wordsworth and the Bratislava-based Capella Istropolitana look set to become the most recorded team of all time. But, as with their series of Mozart symphonies, their interpretations here are fresh and carefully considered; and if the violins sometimes lack the last degree of refinement, the Capella Istropolitana is a highly proficient chamber-group, with generally excellent intonation and ensemble and tangy, characterful wind — though one wishes they (and the brass in No. 102) had been balanced more forwardly in the otherwise excellent recording. Of the three works here the glittering, ceremonial No. 48 (until recently thought to have been written in honour of the Empress Maria Theresia) is perhaps the most successful. The outer movements and minuet are strong and broadly paced, their texture dominated by the brave pealings of the C alto horns; and the beautiful *Siciliano Adagio* is phrased with real delicacy and affection. The *Farewell* is given an honest, robust reading, a bit cautious in the fast outer movements (rhythms could be more incisive here), though the minuet and the programmatic final *Adagio* are both very neatly managed. At first the performance of No. 102, one of Haydn's boldest, most far-reaching works, might seem rather plain, low in emotional voltage. But for all its deliberate pacing the opening *Vivace* is sturdily built, developing a fine cumulative tension (a thrilling crescendo from the hard-stick timpani at the outset of the recapitulation). And if Wordsworth takes the minuet at a sedate, Beechamesque tempo without quite matching Beecham's rhythmic sleight of hand, his steady approach to the finale reveals the music's robust, pawky humour more readily than the slickly virtuosic performances one sometimes hears. There may be performances of slightly greater polish and penetration in the catalogue; but at super-budget price this disc is an almost ridiculous bargain.

Haydn. Symphony No. 49, "La passione". ***Schubert.*** Symphony No. 5 in B flat major, D485. **St John's Smith Square Orchestra/John Lubbock.** Pickwick IMP Classics PCD819.

53m DDD 1/86 £

Although this reading of Schubert's charming Fifth Symphony will certainly pass muster, with straightforward playing that emphasizes the more naïve aspects of the piece, the gold on this disc is to be found in the coupled performance of Haydn's darkly urgent *La passione* Symphony. Completed in 1768, during Haydn's *Sturm und Drang* period, this work begins with a brooding *Adagio* and is followed by a vigorous, intense *Allegro di molto*. A dour *Menuetto*, with a brighter, oboe and horn dominated Trio for contrast, intervenes before the dramatic, rather brief closing *Presto*, that strangely adumbrates Mendelssohn in places. The total effect is marvellously disturbing, especially so in this involved, purposeful reading from Lubbock and the Smith Square Orchestra. They clearly have the measure of this piece and communicate its burning originality with force. Especially impressive is the way that the spirit of romanticism flourishes here without the just proportion of classicism being split asunder. The enclosed ambience of the recording intensifies the introversion of this Symphony, reflecting the isolation that Haydn welcomed at his employer's palace at Esterhaza, where he composed the work.

Haydn. Symphonies — No. 78 in C minor; No. 102 in B flat major. **Orpheus Chamber Orchestra.** DG 429 218-2GH. Recorded in 1988.

46m DDD 5/90 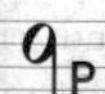

The Orpheus Chamber Orchestra play without a conductor, but their account of these two Haydn symphonies is splendidly precise. The key of C minor was unusual enough when No. 78 was composed in 1782 and Haydn's invention still makes the work a disturbing one, particularly when the first movement and the finale are taken at this spanking pace, surely faster than it would have been in Haydn's time but brought off well here. The quality that comes across strongly here is one of urgent energy, and even in the Adagio the articulation and dynamics keep one from cosily relaxing; but there is nothing wrong with that if the results stand on their own merits as here. We find a vivid energy also in Symphony No. 102, but although the orchestra recognize the brighter mood, sometimes one looks for more playfulness and 'smiling' quality to provide expressive contrast. Nevertheless the playing is highly skilful and though this is not a long CD, collectors wishing to investigate the relatively unfamiliar Symphony No. 78 or an alternative view of No. 102 will be rewarded, not least by the pleasing recorded quality.

NEW REVIEW

Haydn. Symphonies — No. 82 in C major, "L'ours"; No. 83 in G minor, "La poule"; No. 84 in E flat major. **Hanover Band/Roy Goodman** (hpd). Hyperion CDA66527. Recorded in 1991.

1h 19m DDD 10/92 

Written in 1785-6 for the ample forces of the Concert de la Loge Olympique, Haydn's *Paris* symphonies were his grandest and most imposing works in the form to date. The first three in the published order receive bristling, high-voltage performances from Goodman and his period band. No. 82, in particular, is thrillingly done, its magnificent opening movement combining lucidity of detail with a splendid sweep and a sheer brazen brilliance: the C alto horns slash through the texture and the hard-stick timpani crack like gunfire. Goodman's minuet has a fine lordly swagger (and some characteristically delicate, precisely articulated woodwind playing in the trio), while his finale, fast, taut, sharply accented, is full of shrewdly observed instrumental detail. The other two symphonies here are hardly less exhilarating. The outer movements of No. 84, perhaps the least fêted of the *Paris* set, are crisply done, eager, light and transparent of texture, with sharply defined wind detail. The minuet is lusty of gait and accent, while Goodman's briskish tempo imparts an easy sway to the beautiful 6/8 *Andante* Variations. In the vehement opening movement of the misleadingly named *La poule*, No. 83, Goodman's fierce tempo can seem more than a touch hectic; but against this the Hanover Band turn the minuet into an irresistible bucolic waltz and give an unusually piquant, sharply articulated reading of the finale. As usual in this series, Goodman is generous with repeats; and his harpsichord continuo is propulsive and forwardly balanced. The recording is a touch resonant, but never at the expense of clarity. This is by far the most exciting instalment in Hyperion's Haydn Edition and is an essential acquisition for all Haydn lovers.

Additional recommendations ...

Nos. 82 and 83. **Concertgebouw Orchestra/Sir Colin Davis.** Philips 420 688-2PH — 52m DDD 2/88

Nos. 82-84. **Orchestra of the Age of Enlightenment/Sigiswald Kuijken.** Virgin Classics Veritas VC7 59537-2 — 1h 18m DDD 2/90

Nos. 82-86. **Montreal Sinfonietta/Charles Dutoit.** Decca 436 739-2DH2 — ② 2h 26m DDD 6/93

Haydn. Symphonies — No. 85 in B flat major, "La reine"; No. 86 in D major; No. 87 in A major. **Orchestra of the Age of Enlightenment/Sigiswald Kuijken.** Virgin Classics Veritas VC7 59557-2. Recorded in 1989.

1h 19m DDD 5/90

The mention of period instruments can make people fear (with occasional good reason) that they will hear playing less notable for persuasiveness than for bluntness and sometimes roughness of interpretation and execution. If so, this recording should open minds, for the playing is clean yet fully stylish and expressive and there is no question of accepting dull string tone or poor woodwind intonation in the name of the god Authenticity. The period flavour is there all right (listen for example to the clean sound of the oboe and bassoon in Symphony No. 85, and the crisp strings and overall texture) but it convinces. So do the tempos, phrasing, dynamics and articulation, the latter being sharper than with most modern orchestras and making the latter sound heavy by comparison. To this fine playing under young the Belgian conductor you might add that these three symphonies are masterpieces of Haydn's wonderful Indian summer of his sixties, that the 1989 recording in EMI's Abbey Road Studios is atmospheric in the right degree, and that a total length of nearly 80 minutes results in a most attractive CD. The booklet gives useful details of the instruments played in each work, mostly eighteenth-century originals in the case of the strings with modern replicas for wind and nineteenth-century timpani in Symphony No. 86.

Haydn. Symphonies — No. 90 in C major; No. 93 in D major. **Orchestra of the Eighteenth Century/Frans Brüggen.** Philips 422 022-2PH. Recorded in 1987.

51m DDD 5/88

These performances are of a calibre which deserve to be noticed. Amongst the many delights of this recording are the mellow sound and warm textures of the wind instruments and the generally high level of technical expertise with which they are played. Haydn's wind writing is usually interesting, sometimes witty and, especially in the case of the horns, often extremely difficult to play. These fine players surmount most of the difficulties with an admirable degree of self-assurance and Brüggen's direction is always lively. Lovers of Haydn's music should find much that is rewarding in this issue.

Haydn. Symphonies — No. 91 in E flat major; No. 92 in G major, "Oxford". **Concertgebouw Orchestra/Sir Colin Davis.** Philips 410 390-2PH. Recorded in 1983.

5lm DDD 4/85

Symphony No. 91 shows not only the finest degree of craftsmanship of which Haydn was capable but also those hints of other-worldliness that underpin much of his greatest and most mature compositions. Sir Colin Davis and the Concertgebouw play with honesty and simple, unpretentious musicianship; an approach that makes these performances very successful. Although much work must have gone into creating such artless simplicity, it seems as though the music plays itself and the listener has a direct line with the composer's ideas. The timeless *Adagio* of the *Oxford* provides a fine example and Davis produces pure emotions that are very moving. With first-rate, natural sound these recordings demand a place in any collection.

Haydn. LONDON SYMPHONIES. **Concertgebouw Orchestra/Sir Colin Davis.** Philips Silver Line Classics 432 286-2PSL4. Recorded 1975-81.
No. 93 in D major; No. 94 in G major, "The Surprise" (both from 6514 192, 1/83); No. 95 in C minor (6514 074, 1/82); No. 96 in D major, "The Miracle" (6725 010, 6/82); No. 97 in C major (6514 074); No. 98 in B flat major (9500 678, 12/80); No. 99 in E flat major (9500 139, 4/77); No. 100 in G major, "Military" (9500 510, 3/79); No. 101 in D major, "The Clock" (9500 679, 7/81); No. 102 in B flat major (9500 679); No. 103 in E flat major, "Drumroll" (9500 303, 7/78); No. 104 in D major, "London" (9500 510).

4 5h 4m ADD/DDD 7/92

A superb achievement all round — indeed, it's nigh on impossible to imagine better 'big-band' Haydn than one encounters here on these four exceedingly well-filled CDs. Sir Colin Davis's direction has exemplary sparkle (try the superb opening movement of the *Miracle* Symphony) and sensitivity (witness his eloquent moulding of No. 98's great *Adagio*). Minuets are never allowed to plod, outer movements have an ideal combination of infectious zip and real poise, and the humour (a commodity, of course, that is never absent for too long in Haydn's music) is always conveyed with a genial twinkle in the eye. Quite marvellous, wonderfully unanimous playing from the great Amsterdam Orchestra, too (the woodwind contributions are particularly distinguished), with never a trace of routine to betray the six-year recording span of this critically acclaimed project. The Philips engineering, whether analogue or digital, is of the very highest quality throughout, offering a totally natural perspective, gloriously full-bodied tone and consistently sparkling textures within the sumptuous Concertgebouw acoustic. Invest in this set: it will yield enormous rewards for many years to come.

Additional recommendations ...
Nos. 99-104. **Royal Philharmonic Orchestra/Sir Thomas Beecham.** EMI Beecham Edition CMS7 64066-2 — 2 2h 36m ADD 9/92
Nos. 93-104. **London Philhrmonic Orchestra/Sir Georg Solti.** Decca Ovation 436 290-2DM6 — 6 5h 7m DDD 3/93
No. 92 ; No. 104 in D major, "London". **English Sinfonia/Sir Charles Groves.** Pickwick IMP Classics PCD916 — 55m DDD 6/89

NEW REVIEW

Haydn. Symphonies — No. 100 in G major, "Military"; No. 104 in D major, "London". **Orchestra of the Eighteenth Century/Frans Brüggen.** Philips 434 096-2PH. Recorded live in 1990.

54m DDD 6/93

Brüggen and his crack period orchestra give arresting, strongly characterized performances here of two favourite Haydn symphonies. Though the crashing, jangling 'Turkish' instruments (triangle, cymbals and bass drum) in the *Military* are allowed their head, Brüggen's reading consistently stresses the work's drama, boldness and symphonic strength. The Beethovenian development of the first movement, for instance, is built with tremendous power and logic, while the finale's darting wit can scorch and sting, with articulation of virtuoso precision and point from both strings and wind. Brüggen's tempo in the *Allegretto* is on the leisurely side, though this movement gains especially from the distinctive, soft-hued timbres of the period woodwind. The live recording (minimal audience participation) under-balances the timpani and the bass drum, but is otherwise excellent. Curiously, timpani are far better defined in No. 104, where they register with exciting physical impact. After a massive, brooding slow introduction, Brüggen gives plenty of space to the first-movement *Allegro*, phrasing the lyrical music warmly (the slight astringency of the orchestra's violins softened by a touch of vibrato) and bringing an acutely judged cumulative intensity to the development. The minor-keyed eruption in the *Andante* is unusually disquieting, horns and trumpets grinding balefully; and despite the occasional rhythmic vagary, both the minuet and the finale are gloriously incisive and articulate, with Brüggen inspiring the orchestra to playing of incandescent intensity in the finale's closing pages. Even those normally resistant to period instruments should sample these charismatic, superbly executed performances.

Additional recommendations ...

Concertgebouw Orchestra/Sir Colin Davis. Philips 411 449-2PH — 54m ADD 10/84 B

NEW REVIEW

Haydn. STRING QUARTETS, Op. 20. **Salomon Quartet** (Simon Standage, Micaela Comberti, vns; Trevor Jones, va; Jennifer Ward Clarke, vc). Hyperion CDA66621/2. Recorded in 1991.

CDA66621 — No. 1 in E flat major; No. 2 in C major; No. 3 in G minor. *CDA66622* — No. 4 in D major; No. 5 in F minor; No. 6 in A major.

② lh 15m lh 18m DDD 2/93 P

NEW REVIEW

Haydn. STRING QUARTETS, Op. 20. **Mosaïques Quartet** (Erich Höbarth, Andrea Bischof, vns; Anita Mitterer, va; Christophe Coin, vc). Astrée Auvidis E8784 (as a 2-disc set). Recorded in 1990. *Please note that they are also available separately on the numbers given below.*

E8785 — No. 1 in E flat major; No. 5 in F minor; No. 6 in A major. *E8786* — No. 2 in C major; No. 3 in G minor; No. 4 in D major.

② 2h 27m DDD 5/93 P

Haydn was 40 when he completed his set of Op. 20 String Quartets in 1772. They therefore date from the composer's so-called *Sturm und Drang* period, though Haydn's increasingly frequent use of the more dramatic and 'serious' minor mode in these pieces can perhaps be attributed just as much to the fruitful influence of the three operatic projects he had been working on just a few years previously between 1766 and 1769. Moreover, these quartets also reveal a greater preoccupation with counterpoint than any of his music to that date, and the great fugal finales of Nos. 2, 5 and 6 clearly herald the arrival of the consummate craftsman so overwhelmingly displayed in the mature quartets to come. Incidentally, the Op. 20 set's nickname *Sun* derives from the illustration on the handsome title-page of the Hummel edition of this music, at the top of which peers out the sun-god's head. The Salomon Quartet are one of the finest period-instrument groups around at present, and their vibrant, perceptive advocacy of these masterpieces merits the very highest plaudits. What's more, they have been accorded a pleasingly intimate balance by the Hyperion production team, and the resulting sound-picture is a thoroughly lifelike one. Both discs are only available separately, by the way, and, needless to report, both come highly recommended. However, admirable though the Salomon Quartet's readings are, they are if anything surpassed by those of the superb Quatuor Mosaïques on Astrée Auvidis. These wonderfully flexible performances display an altogether breathtaking refinement, sensitivity and illumination. Indeed, in terms of expressive subtlety, imaginative intensity and sheer depth of feeling, the Mosaïques' achievement in these marvellous works is unmatched in the present catalogue and it is difficult to foresee it being surpassed for some considerable time to come. A stunning set in every way, with vividly realistic engineering to match.

Haydn. STRING QUARTETS. **Lindsay Quartet** (Peter Cropper, Ronald Birks, vns; Robin Ireland, va; Bernard Gregor-Smith, vc). ASV CDDCA622. Recorded live in 1987.
Op. 20: No. 2 in C major; Op. 50: No. 1 in B flat major; Op. 76: No. 2 in D minor.

lh 3m DDD 9/88

The second of the *Sun* Quartets (Op. 20) has a gently paced but rich first movement, a dramatic *Capriccio* that gives way to a lyrical *arioso*, flowing into a far from formal Minuet and Trio, and a fugal finale which develops in whispers until vigorous homophony finally prevails. Haydn dedicated his Op. 50 set (the *Prussian* Quartets) to King Friedrich Wilhelm, an amateur cellist, and they are marked by the thematic economy typified in the first movement of No. 1. The finale is another sonata-form movement, likewise sparing with its material, en route to which is a delightful theme, three variations and coda (*Adagio non lento*), and a robust Minuet with a tip-toeing Trio. Count Joseph Erdödy was the dedicatee of the Quartets Op. 76 (1797) and are abundantly nicknamed. The whole work is a torrent of invention, Haydn at his most compelling. These recordings were made live in the Wigmore Hall, a virtual guarantee of a sympathetic acoustic: the presence of an audience can be hazardous, but here it served only to stimulate the Lindsay Quartet to performances so riveting that there isn't so much as a sniffle to be heard — only the richly earned applause at the end of each work.

NEW REVIEW

Haydn. STRING QUARTETS. **Festetics Quartet** (István Kertész, Erika Petöfi, vns; Péter Ligeti, va; Rezsö Pertorini, vc). Quintana QUI90 3002/3. Recorded 1990-91.
Op. 33 — No. 1 in B minor; No. 2 in E flat major, "The Joke"; No. 3 in C major, "The Bird"; No. 4 in B flat major; No. 5 in G major; No. 6 in D major. D minor, Op. 43.

2 2h 20m DDD 8/92 

The so-called 'Russian' quartets of 1781 were, according to the composer, written "in a completely new and special manner". Sales talk, perhaps; but the music does contain various innovations. Most obviously, each of the minuets is marked *scherzo* or *scherzando*, with several foreshadowing the true *scherzi* of Haydn's late years; more significantly, though, the Op. 33 quartets reveal a new sophistication of thematic development and an apparently effortless integration of 'learned' contrapuntal techniques within a tuneful, popular style. And they were the prime influence on the six great quartets which Mozart dedicated to Haydn a few years later. The two nicknamed quartets, *The Joke* and *The Bird* are, inevitably, the best known. But No. 1, in B minor, with its tonally deceptive opening, is a marvellous piece, pungent and acerbic, and though they're perhaps less even in quality, Nos. 4, 5 and 6 are full of subtle and surprising things. The other work on these well-filled discs is the D minor Quartet of 1785, the only survivor from a group of three short, technically simple quartets Haydn wrote in response to a commission from Spain. The Festetics Quartet are a Hungarian period-instrument group intent on a complete Haydn cycle; and if their sonority is slightly dusty, more vibrato-shy than most period-instrument groups, their playing has plenty of colour, dynamic variety and subtlety of detail. The performances of Nos. 3 and 6 are particularly successful — listen, for instance, to their vivid response to the wit and astringency of No. 3's Slavonic finale, and their hushed, devout intensity in the D minor *Andante* of No. 6. Elsewhere the Festetics bring a terrific bite and *élan* to the *Scherzo* of No. 1 (done at a cracking one-in-a-bar), and deliciously milk the *portamenti* that Haydn introduces in the trio of No. 2. One or two movements, such as the finales of Nos. 2 and 4, are a shade under-characterized; and occasionally, as in the *Largo sostenuto* of No. 2, the tuning is uncomfortable. But in the main this is stylish, imaginative playing, well balanced and atmospherically, if over-resonantly, recorded.

Additional recommendations ...

Op. 33: Nos. 1-3. Op. 1: No. 3 in D major. **Weller Quartet.** Decca 433 691-2DM — lh llm ADD 9/92

Op. 33: Nos. 4-6. Op. 103 in D minor (unfinished). **Weller Quartet.** Decca 433 692-2DM — lh l3m ADD 9/92

Haydn. STRING QUARTETS. **Lindsay Quartet** (Peter Cropper, Robin Ireland, vns; Ronald Birks, va; Bernard Gregor-Smith, vc). ASV CDDCA582.
Op. 54: No. 1 in G major; No. 2 in C major; No. 3 in E major.

1h 6m DDD 8/87

All three quartets are in the usual four-movement form but with many surprises: in No. 1, the false recapitulation in the first movement, the dark modulations in the following sonata-form *Allegretto* and the Hungarian-gipsy flavour (anticipated in the Minuet) and mischievousness of the final Rondo. Number 2 has a rhapsodic fiddler in its second movement, a nostalgic Minuet with an extraordinarily anguished Trio, and an *Adagio* finale in which a *Presto* section turns out to be no more than an episode. A notable feature of No. 3 is its tenary-form *Largo cantabile*, the centre of which is more like a mini-concerto for the first violin; 'Scotch snaps' pervade the Minuet, and pedal points the finale. The performances (and the recording) are superb, marked by unanimity, fine tone, suppleness of phrasing, and acute dynamic shaping; in the second movement of No. 1 there are hushed passages whose homogeneity and quality of sound is quite remarkable. Even more remarkable would be the Haydn lover who found this recording resistible.

Haydn. STRING QUARTETS. **Gabrieli Quartet** (Kenneth Sillito, Brendan O'Reilly, vns; Ian Jewel, va; Keith Harvey, vc). Chandos CHAN8531.
Op. 54: No. 2 in C major; Op. 64: No. 5 in D major, "Lark".

39m DDD 11/87 

These are fabulous works, supremely inventive and remarkably innovative, with movements very much integrated into a symphonic-type structure. Few who hear the magical opening of Op. 64 No. 5 can fail to respond to Haydn's arrestingly simple opening. Few, too, could remain unmoved by the depth of emotion conveyed in Haydn's slow movements, by his impassioned melodic lines and astonishing harmonic daring. These are unquestionable masterpieces and are as central to the quartet repertoire as are the greatest essays in the medium from Mozart or Beethoven. The Gabrieli Quartet play very beautifully, demonstrating a deep understanding of both the moment and the movement.

Additional recommendation ...
Op. 54: No. 1 in G major; No. 2; No. 3 in E major. Op. 55: No. 1 in A major; No. 2 in F minor, "Razor"; No. 3 in B flat major. **Amadeus Quartet.** DG 437 134-2GX2 — ② 2h 1m ADD 2/93

Haydn. STRING QUARTETS. **Kodály Quartet** (Attila Falvay, Tamás Szabo, vns; Gábor Fias, va; János Devich, vc). Naxos 8 550394 and 8 550396. Recorded in 1989.
8 550394 — Op. 71: No. 1 in B flat major, No. 2 in D major; No. 3 in E flat major. *8 550396* — Op. 74: No. 1 in C major; No. 2 in F major; No. 3 in G minor, "The Rider".

② 1h 2m 1h 3m DDD 2/91

The enterprising Kodály Quartet are working their way through the middle and late Haydn Quartets and, rightly, taking their time about it. They rehearse together privately, and then every so often turn up at the Hungaroton Studios in Rottenbiller with a new group ready to record. They play with self-evident joy in the music and an easy immaculateness of ensemble, which comes from familiarity with each other's company. There is never a hint of routine and the intercommunication is matched by enormous care for detail and clean ensemble. In short they play as one, and project this wonderful music with enormous dedication. Just sample the elegant *Andante* with variations which form the slow movement of Op. 71 No. 3, or the witty Menuet which follows, or any of the consistently inspired Op. 74 set. The hushed intensity of playing in the *Largo assai* of Op. 74 No. 3 is unforgettable. The recordings are wholly natural and balanced within a well-judged acoustic; the sound is of the highest quality and documentation is excellent. At their modest price this pair of CDs is irresistible.

Additional recommendations ...
Op. 74: Nos. 2 and 3. **Salomon Quartet.** Hyperion CDA66124 — AAD 3/87
Op. 71 No. 3; Op. 74 No. 1. **Salomon Quartet.** Hyperion CDA66098 — 59m AAD 12/87

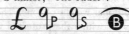

Haydn. STRING QUARTETS. **Takács Quartet** (Gábor Takács-Nagy, Károly Schranz, vns; Gábor Omai, va; András Fejér, vc). Decca 425 467-2DH. Recorded in 1988.
Op. 76: No. 4 in B flat major, "Sunrise"; No. 5 in D major, "Fifths"; No. 6 in E flat major, "Fantasia".

1h 8m DDD 1/90 

In these three quartets from a set of six published in 1797, one can only be delighted by the sheer invention that Haydn showed in his sixties. This youthful Hungarian ensemble bring to this music a freshness that does not inhibit them from the necessary underlining of this or that point. The *Sunrise* Quartet is invigorating in the first movement and lyrically broad in the Adagio, and the syncopated minuet and lilting finale are no less delightful. The D major Quartet starts with an Allegretto suggesting a set of variations but then moves into a section in new keys before ending with a brisk coda. The slow movement's *cantabile e mesto* marking is fully realized, as is the major-minor contrast of the minuet and the playful Presto finale, which begins with an unmistakable joke of six bars that sound more like the end of a movement. The third of these quartets begins with variations that culminate in a fugato; the slow movement (called a fantasia) is another original, and this is followed by a witty scherzo and a finale in which scale fragments participate in a game of dizzy contrapuntal complexity. The recording, made in a London church, is immediate yet atmospheric, although with a touch of glare that tone controls will tame.

Additional recommendation ...
Eder Quartet. Teldec Digital Experience 9031 77602-2 — 1h 2m DDD 12/92 

Haydn. STRING QUARTETS. **Mosaïques Quartet** (Erich Höbarth, Andrea Bischof, vns; Anita Mitterer, va; Christophe Coin, vc). Astrée Auvidis E8799.
Op. 77: No. 1 in G major; No. 2 in F major; Op. 103: D minor (unfinished).

1h 2m DDD 2/90  

Anyone who thinks that period-instrument performance means austerity and coolness should listen to this disc. Here is a group of youngish French players, using instruments of the kind Haydn would have heard, played (as far as we can know) in a style he would have been familiar with: the result is a disc full of expressive warmth and vigour. The opening of Op. 77 No. 1 is done duly gracefully, but with a sturdy underlying rhythm and the Scherzo is as crisp and alive as one could ask for. Then the first movement of the F major work is very beautifully done, with many sensitive details; and the lovely second movement is happily leisurely, so that the players have ample room fof manoeuvre and the leader makes much of his opportunities for delicate playing in the filigree-like high music. The players show a real grasp of the structure and they know when to illuminate the key moments, with a touch of extra deliberation or a little additional weight of tone. These performances, clearly recorded, are competitive ones not merely within the protected world of 'early music' but in the bigger, 'real' world too!

Haydn. DIVERTIMENTOS. **Ricercar Consort** (Claude Maury, Piet Dombrecht, hns; François Fernandez, [a]vn/[b]va; Alda Stuurop, vn; Ryo Terrakado, va; Philippe Pierlot, baryton; Rainer Zipperling, vc; Eric Mathot, db). Ricercar RIC067050. Recorded in 1989.
A minor/major, HobX/3[a]; G major, HobX/5[a]; D major, HobX/10[b]; G major, HobX/12[a].

59m DDD 9/91 

Highly agreeable shavings from Haydn's workshop floor. All four works here feature the baryton, a curious, plangent-toned instrument combining gut strings and synthetic metal strings which was assiduously cultivated by Prince Nikolaus Esterhazy. Haydn satisfied the Prince's passion for this complicated (and quickly obsolete) instrument both in his long series of baryton trios and a group of seven divertimentos "for eight voices" — string quartet, baryton, double bass and two horns. Three of the set are included here. The quicker movements tend to be compact, cheerful and undemanding, though the presence of the baryton in the ensemble makes for some intriguing, dusky-hued textures and there is some quite spectacular writing for the horns, especially in the minuet finale of No. 3. But the real glory of these works lies in their intense, introspective, un-divertimento-like *Adagios*, two of which (in Nos. 3 and 7) are in the minor key, rarely favoured by Haydn for his later slow movements. There is also a noble opening *Adagio* in the fourth work on this disc, a quintet for two horns, baryton, viola and bass, arranged by Haydn from a divertimento for wind band. The playing of the Ricercar Consort, while not always immaculate in intonation, is assured, sympathetic and sensitively balanced. Fast movements are neat and spirited (though the finale of No. 2 is arguably too easygoing for a *Presto*), and the *Adagios* unfold with real breadth. The baryton player, Philippe Pierlot, deserves special praise for his expert negotiation of this excruciatingly difficult instrument; and there is consistently fine playing from the horns, not only in their high-flying virtuoso exploits but also the many places where they add a quiet, subtle gloss to the string texture. The recording is vivid and immediate, with horns and strings well separated. Definitely a disc to consider for late-night listening — though the slow movements may involve you more than you'd bargained for.

NEW REVIEW

Haydn. PIANO TRIOS. **Beaux Arts Trio** (Isidore Cohen, vn; Bernard Greenhouse, vc; Menahem Pressler, pf). Philips 432 061-2PM9. Recorded 1970-79.

G major, HobXV/25; F sharp minor, HobXV/26; C major, HobXV/27 (all from 6500 023, 6/71); E flat major, HobXV/29; E flat major, HobXV/30; E flat major, HobXV/31 (all from 6500 400, 3/73); C major, HobXV/21; D minor, HobXV/23; D major, HobXV/24; E major, HobXV/28 (all from 6500 401, 3/73); A major, HobXV/18; G minor, HobXV/19; E flat major, HobXV/22 (all from 6500 521, 6/74); B flat major, HobXV/20; G major, HobXV/32 (both from 6500 522, 11/73); G minor, HobXV/1; F major, HobXV/37; F major, HobXV/39; G major, HobXV/41; C major, HobXV/C1 (all from 6768 077); A flat major, HobXV/14; G major, HobXV/15 (both from 9500 034, 11/76); C minor, HobXV/13, D major, HobXV/16; F major, HobXV/17 (all from 9500 035, 2/77); G major, HobXIV/6; F major, HobXV/6; B flat major, HobXV/8; G major, XVI/6 (all from 9500 325, 3/78); F major, HobXV/2 (9500 325, 3/78); D major, HobXV/7; A major, HobXV/9; E minor, HobXV/12 (all from 9500 326, 8/77); G major, HobXV/5; E flat major, HobXV/10; E flat major, HobXV/f1 (all from 9500 327, 2/78); F minor, HobXV/11; E flat major, HobXV/36; C major, HobXIV/C1; D major, Hobdeest (all from 9500 472, 7/79); E major, HobXV/34; A major, HobXV/35; B flat major, HobXV/38; F major, HobXV/40 (all from 9500 473, 6/79).

9 6h 34m ADD 7/92 £ P

Far more than Mozart's, Haydn's trios are essentially accompanied keyboard sonatas, with the cello wedded to the keyboard bass almost throughout; this lack of cello independence has deterred many groups from investigating their undoubted musical riches. Not, fortunately, the Beaux Arts, whose acclaimed complete cycle accumulated by stealth during the 1970s (when it was finally completed it received almost universal accolades, including *Gramophone*'s Record of the Year Award) and has now reappeared on nine mid-price discs. A dozen of the works date from the 1760s, or even earlier (which for a late developer like Haydn meant pre-puberty), and offer little more than rococo charm, though the G minor (No. 1 in Hoboken's catalogue), with its neo-baroque severity, is a notable exception. But the majority of the trios date from the 1780s and 1790s and contain some of Haydn's most imaginative, lyrical and harmonically adventurous music. Two outstanding works from the 1780s are the E minor, No. 12, with its passionate, closely worked opening *Allegro*, and No. 14 in A flat, with its exquisitely tender *Adagio* in a remote E major that leads without a break into one of Haydn's most hilariously quixotic finales.

The 14 magnificent trios of the 1790s range from relaxed, intimate pieces like the E flat, No. 29, through the sombre, almost tragic F sharp minor, No. 26, to the C major, No. 27, unsurpassed in the whole series for its intellectual and virtuoso brilliance. Finest of all, perhaps, are the E major, No. 28, with its radiant outer movements (wonderfully fanciful, delicate textures here) and its astonishing central E minor *passacaglia*; and the E flat, No. 30, with its noble, lyrically expansive first movement, its deep-toned, often richly chromatic *Andante* and its glorious German-dance finale. The Beaux Arts's playing throughout is vital, refined, and sharply responsive to the music's teeming richness and variety. The early trios were conceived for harpsichord, though such is the deftness and delicacy of Menahem Pressler's touch here that there is no question of the music being overpowered by the modern Steinway; and among individual delights in the group's performances of these early works mention should be made of their gentle, affectionate way with the central minuets, underlining their dual function as dances and surrogate slow movements. In the later trios they catch beautifully the leisurely, almost improvisatory feel of many of the opening movements, and bring a ruminative intensity, and a wonderful quality of soft playing to the great slow movements, while the finales have immense brio, wit and virtuosity, with ideally clean, crisp articulation from Pressler.

Occasionally in the earlier works the Beaux Arts sound a touch over-sophisticated for this guileless music — the opening violin solo in No. 2 is a case in point. And there are a few disappointments in the later trios — the first movement of the great F sharp minor, No. 26, sounds too lightweight, even skittish while, conversely, in the *passacaglia* of No. 28 they take a surprisingly ponderous view of Haydn's *Allegretto*. But there's a feast of superlative, little-known music here, most of the playing is extraordinarily felicitous, and the recording has Philips's customary warmth and refinement. £70 or so may seem a lot to fork out all at once, but no one is likely to regret the investment — this is a set that will last a lifetime.

NEW REVIEW

Haydn. PIANO TRIOS. **Jaime Laredo** (vn); **Sharon Robinson** (vc); **Joseph Kalichstein** (pf). Dorian DOR90164. Recorded in 1991.
No. 12 in E minor, HobXV. No. 25 in G major, HobXV. No. 27 in C major, HobXV. No. 28 in E major, HobXV.

lh 12m DDD 4/93

Haydn's mature music rarely disappoints, for while doubtless enjoying the mastery that experience gave him, he never lost the inventive boldness that gives his music so much of its attractiveness. These trios were written between 1789 and 1795, during which time he celebrated his sixtieth birthday and saw his fame at its highest point — indeed, the last three of them were composed during his successful second visit to England. Joseph Kalichstein and his two colleagues give assured performances of all this music, and their playing is vital yet refined, reminding us that Haydn was writing for domestic performance and not a large concert-hall. Although the pianist is clearly in charge, Jaime Laredo and Sharon Robinson are not just subordinates and they show fine rapport as well as individual skill and sensitivity, not least in the deeply thoughtful E minor Trio which progresses toward a joyful finale. The finale of the C major Trio is also most enjoyable and should bring a smile to the face of any listener, particularly when it is given the panache and sparkle that the present artists bring to it. Intelligence and wit shine out of this music; indeed, this is true of all four of these trios, which are never merely cheerful despite the essentially sunny nature of Haydn's genius. In fact, each trio has a personality of its own and the one in E major, the last to be written, is quite a striking work with a central *Allegretto* that is far removed from the popular idea of Papa Haydn in its relative bareness and severity. This is a well-filled disc and the recording is as refined as the playing.

Haydn. PIANO WORKS. **Alfred Brendel** (pf). Philips 416 643-2PH4. Booklet included.
Sonatas — C minor, HobXVI/20; E flat major, HobXVI/49 (both from 9500 774, 8/81); E minor, HobXVI/34; B minor, HobXVI/32; D major, Hob XVI/42 (412 228-1PH, 8/85); C major, HobXVI/48; D major, HobXVI/51; C major, Hob XVI/50 (6514 317, 11/83); E flat major, HobXVI/52; G major, HobXVI/40; D major, HobXVI/37 (416 365-1PH, 12/86). Fantasia in C major, HobXVI/4. Adagio in F major, HobXVI/9 (412 228-1PH, 8/85). Andante with variations in F minor, Hob XVI/6 (416 365-1PH, 12/86).

④ 52m 55m 37m lh lm ADD/DDD 3/87 P

The Sonatas collected in this set are some magnificent creations wonderfully well played by Alfred Brendel. Within the order and scale of these works Haydn explores a rich diversity of musical languages, a wit and broadness of expression that quickly repays attentive listening. It is the capriciousness as much as the poetry that Brendel so perfectly attends to; his playing, ever alive to the vitality and subtleties, makes these discs such a delight. The sophistication innate in the simple dance rhythms, the rusticity that emerges, but above all, the sheer *joie de vivre* are gladly embraced. Brendel shows in this music what makes a merely technically accomplished player a truly great one — his continual illumination of the musical ideas through intense study pays huge dividends. The recording quality varies enormously between the various works and though the close acoustic on some of the later discs could be faulted for allowing one to hear too much of the keyboard action, it certainly brings one into vivid contact with the music.

Haydn. PIANO SONATAS. **Emanuel Ax** (pf). CBS Masterworks CD44918. Recorded in 1988.
C minor, HobXVI/20; F major, HobXVI/23; C major, HobXVI/48; C major, HobXVI/50.

lh 4m DDD 12/89

Here is another powerful antidote to the notion of Haydn as a kind of clever comedian — and it seems the point still has to be made. Emanuel Ax avoids romantic overstatement throughout these performances; the interpretation sounds as if it's felt from within the notes, rather than applied to them. Ax can bring out the high seriousness of the great C minor Sonata's first movement without trying to 'Beethovenize' the drama, while in Sonata No. 60 he can pass from childlike humour in the opening theme to taut symphonic argument without a trace of incongruity. Most impressive of all though is his feeling for dramatic shape: the slow first movement of Sonata No. 58 grows steadily to a powerful final climax — as, with very different effect, does the C minor's opening *Moderato*: there's something truly tragic about the final resolution. The slight distant reverberation is a little disconcerting at first — as though Ax were playing to a large deserted auditorium — but it's soon accepted.

Additional recommendations ...
F major, HobXVI/23; G major, HobXVI/27; C major, HobXVI/35; D major, HobXVI/37; E minor, HobXVI/34; G major, HobXVI/40; C major, HobXVI/48; C major, HobXVI/50; E flat major, HobXVI/52. **Michèle Boegner** (pf). Erato 2292-45705-2 — ② 2h 5m DDD 11/92
G minor, HobXVI/44; C minor, HobXVI/20; D major, HobXVI/42. Variations in F minor, HobXVII/6. **Andrew Wilde** (pf). Collins Quest 3017-2— lh 9m DDD 11/92
D major, HobXVI/24; A major, XVI/26; F major, XVI/29; 48 in C major, HobXVI/35; C sharp minor, HobXVI/36. **Julia Cload** (pf). Meridian CDE84210 — lh 17m DDD 3/93

Haydn. Arianna a Naxos. English Canzonettas. **Carolyn Watkinson** (mez); **Glen Wilson** (fp). Virgin Classics Veritas VC7 59033-2. Texts included. Recorded in 1990.
A pastoral song. Despair. Fidelity. The mermaid's song. O tuneful voice. Piercingeyes. Pleasing pain. Sailor's song. She never told her love. The spirit's song. The wanderer.

lh 4m DDD 1/92

This is an absolute must for all lovers of Haydn's music. His delightful songs have been unduly neglected until relatively recently so it's a double pleasure to find such a well presented and sympathetic recording. Carolyn Watkinson's idiomatically plangent and deeply-felt singing merges the elegance of the salon with the passion and strong characterization we associate with Haydn's greatest oratorios. There is certainly a wide range of moods in these pieces, ranging from the theatrical flourishes of *Teseo mio ben!* to the purity of *The spirit's song* (Haydn gave this to Lady Hamilton on her visit to Eisenstadt with Nelson) and the buoyancy of *Sailor's song*. Glen Wilson's accompaniment in the canzonettas is tasteful and idiomatic, although the recording seems more appropriate for an orchestral performance than these essentially intimate works. However, so carefully thought-through is both Watkinson's singing and Wilson's fortepiano playing that the ear adjusts effortlessly. Virgin Classics documentation is both scholarly and entertaining.

Haydn. Mass in D minor, "Nelson"[a]. Te Deum in C major, HobXXIIIc/2. [a]**Felicity Lott** (sop); [a]**Carolyn Watkinson** (contr); [a]**Maldwyn Davies** (ten); [a]**David Wilson-Johnson**

(bar); **The English Concert and Choir/Trevor Pinnock.** Archiv Produktion 423 097-2AH. Texts and translations included.

50m ADD 2/88

The British Admiral had ousted the Napoleonic fleet at the Battle of the Nile just as Haydn was in the middle of writing his *Nelson* Mass. Although the news could not have reached him until after its completion, Haydn's awareness of the international situation was expressed in the work's subtitle, "Missa in Augustiis", or "Mass in times of fear". With its rattle of timpani, its pungent trumpet calls, and its highly-strung harmonic structure, there is no work of Haydn's which cries out so loudly for recording on period instruments; and it is the distinctive sonority and charged tempos of this performance which sets it apart from its competitors. The dry, hard timpani and long trumpets bite into the dissonance of the opening *Kyrie*, and the near vibrato-less string playing is mordant and urgent. The fast-slow-fast triptych of the *Gloria* is set out in nervously contrasted speeds, and the *Credo* bounces with affirmation. Just as the choral singing is meticulously balanced with instrumental inflection, so the soloists have been chosen to highlight the colours in Pinnock's palette. This is an unusually exciting recording.

Additional recommendation ...

Mass in D minor[a]. ***Mozart.*** *Mass in C major, K317*[b]. **Soloists; [a]London Symphony Chorus, [b]Choir of King's College, Cambridge; [a]City of London Sinfonia/Richard Hickox; [b]English Chamber Orchestra/Stephen Cleobury.** Decca Ovation 436 470-2DM —

lh 7m DDD 5/93

Haydn. Stabat mater. **Patricia Rozario** (sop); **Catherine Robbin** (mez); **Anthony Rolfe Johnson** (ten); **Cornelius Hauptmann** (bass); **The English Concert and Choir/Trevor Pinnock.** Archiv Produktion 429 733-2AH. Text and translation included. Recorded in 1989.

lh 9m DDD 9/90

Haydn's deeply expressive *Stabat mater* for soloists, choir and orchestra is all too seldom performed. Composed in 1767 it hints strongly at the *Sturm und Drang* idiom that was to characterize Haydn's music over the next few years. Boldly contrasting juxtapositions, vivid dynamic shading, chromaticism, syncopation and gently sighing gestures all contribute towards an expressive intensity which affectingly complements the celebrated Latin poem. Trevor Pinnock has assembled a fine quartet of soloists whose voices, singly and in varying ensembles are sympathetically partnered by warm-sounding and stylish playing by The English Concert. The choir of The English Concert is effective, too, with well-balanced ensemble and textural clarity. One of the most alluring numbers of the work is the quartet and chorus, "Virgo virginium praeclara" in which all the various components of Haydn's forces join in a fervent, sorrowful prayer of sustained beauty. The recording is ideally resonant yet capturing many details of colour and nuance present in the character of period instruments. The booklet includes the full text of the poem in three languages.

NEW REVIEW

Haydn. The Seven Last Words of Our Saviour on the Cross. **Inge Nielsen, Renate Burtscher** (sops); **Margareta Hintermeier** (contr); **Anthony Rolfe Johnson** (ten); **Robert Holl** (bass); **Arnold Schönberg Choir; Vienna Concentus Musicus/Nikolaus Harnoncourt.** Teldec Das Alte Werk 2292-46458-2. Notes, text and translation included. Recorded in 1990. Recorded in 1990.

lh 2m DDD 5/92

The oratorio version of Haydn's *Seven Last Words* was a favourite with Victorian and Edwardian choral societies, as the yellowing scores in many a second-hand music shop testify. But like the original orchestral score of 1786, it is nowadays eclipsed by the arrangement for string quartet (reviewed above). Though the neglected orchestral original is the most rewarding version, the choral setting, dating from 1795/6, is an essential work for any Haydn lover, above all for the extraordinarily bleak interlude for wind band which the composer inserted between the fourth and fifth *Words*. The D minor instrumental introduction sets the tone of Harnoncourt's performance: lacerating dotted rhythms, stinging *sforzando* accents and violent *fortissimo* eruptions, with the horns glaring through the texture. The cruelty and pity of the scene are palpable. Throughout the seven choral *Words* Harnoncourt's response to the music's chromatic anguish is uncommonly intense and disturbing, while at the other end of the spectrum, he brings a wonderful serenity and breadth of phrase to the vision of Paradise in No. 2. Characteristically, Harnoncourt makes you keenly aware of the subtlety and sheer power of Haydn's orchestral scoring, with the Vienna Concentus Musicus bringing out the full asperity of the wind-band interlude; and the final Earthquake, which can sound like the roaring of a mouse in the quartet version, makes a spectacular effect here. The mixed-voiced Arnold Schönberg Choir, topped by a shining soprano line, are a flexible and superbly responsive body, though like the soloists (who have relatively little to do) they suffer somewhat in the recorded balance. But as a passionate, unflinching performance of Haydn's least-known choral masterpiece this can be recommended to those who might normally resist Harnoncourt's provocative music-making.

NEW REVIEW

Haydn. Die Jahreszeiten. **Barbara Bonney** (sop); **Anthony Rolfe Johnson** (ten); **Andreas Schmidt** (bar); **Monteverdi Choir; English Baroque Soloists/John Eliot Gardiner.** Archiv Produktion 431 818-2AH2. Text and translation included. Recorded in 1990.

② 2h 7m DDD 5/92

The comparative unpopularity of Haydn's *The Seasons* when considered against his other great oratorio *Die Schöpfung* ("The Creation"), is understandable perhaps, but it is not really all that well deserved. Less exalted its subject and libretto may be, but its depiction of the progress of the year amid the scenes and occupations of the Austrian countryside drew from its composer — then in his late sixties — music of unfailing invention, benign warmth and constant musical-pictoral delights. It is charming music written with great affection, and as such it is not only quintessentially Haydnesque, but also virtually guaranteed to raise a smile. As usual, John Eliot Gardiner and his forces turn in disciplined, meticulously professional performances. This is not one of those massive readings currently favoured even by period practitioners for Haydn's oratorios, though the orchestra is slightly larger — and consequently a tiny bit less lucid — than the sort you might nowadays find playing a classical symphony. The choir, however, performs with great clarity and accuracy, and brings, too, an enjoyable sense of characterization to its various corporate roles, be they drunken revellers, improbably noisy hunters, homely fireside spinners, or whatever. The soloists all perform with notable poise and intelligence: Barbara Bonney's voice is pure and even, Anthony Rolfe Johnson sounds entirely at ease with the music, and Andreas Schmidt is gentle-voiced but certainly not lacking in substance. Perhaps in the end this is a performance that just lacks that last inch of necessary warmth to make it unbeatable, but it's a first-rate recommendation none the less.

Additional recommendation ...

Angela Maria Blasi (sop); **Josef Protschka** (ten); **Robert Holl** (bass); **Arnold Schönberg Choir; Vienna Symphony Orchestra/Nikolaus Harnoncourt.** Teldec 2292-42699-2— ② 2h 25m DDD 2/88

Haydn. Die Schöpfung (sung in English). **Emma Kirkby** (sop); **Anthony Rolfe Johnson** (ten); **Michael George** (bass); **Choir of New College, Oxford; Academy of Ancient Music Chorus and Orchestra/Christopher Hogwood.** L'Oiseau-Lyre 430 397-2OH2. Text included. Recorded in 1990.

② lh 39m DDD 3/9l

Haydn. Die Schöpfung. **Gundula Janowitz** (sop); **Fritz Wunderlich, Werner Krenn** (tens); **Dietrich Fischer-Dieskau** (bar); **Walter Berry** (bass); **Christa Ludwig** (alto) **Vienna Singverein; Berlin Philharmonic Orchestra/Herbert von Karajan.** DG

Galleria 435 077-2GGA2. Text and translation included. From 2707 044 (10/69). Recorded 1966-69.

2 1h 49m ADD 12/91

The claims to historical authenticity made on behalf of Hogwood's performance of Haydn's oratorio *Die Schöpfung* ("The Creation"), are diffuse and overstated, but that need not worry the listener overmuch, for what counts is the performance itself. It is the second to have been recorded using period instruments but the first to use Peter Brown's new performing edition based on appropriate sources. The Academy of Ancient Music fields an orchestra expanded to 115 players together with the Choir of New College, Oxford and a strong solo vocal group. The results are mostly satisfying and the performance greatly enhanced by a sympathetic recorded balance which captures the distinctive character of period instruments. When Haydn published the first edition, it included both German and English texts and it would seem probable that he intended one or other to be sung according to the nationality of the audience. This version is sung in English, a feature that many listeners will find illuminating. All in all this is an enterprising project which has largely succeeded in achieving its aim as outlined by the Director of the performance, Christopher Hogwood "to recapture in sound, scale and text the performances conducted by the composer". The booklet contains full texts in four languages and an informative essay.

Herbert von Karajan's 1966 version of *Die Schöpfung* is something of a classic and probably one of the best recordings ever made of this joyous work. In the depiction of the chaos Karajan immediately set the atmosphere with a massive luminous tone quality from the Berlin Philharmonic, sustained fermatas and fortissimos like ocean breakers. The choir's mighty outburst in "and there was light" almost takes the roof off and the elegant accompaniment to the ensuing arias are a continuous delight. But the main glory of this recording are the soloists including Fritz Wunderlich as a brilliantly mercurial Uriel. This performance is a superb monument to the tenor whose tragically premature death occurred before the sessions were completed. Only the recitatives were left unrecorded and Werner Krenn made an excellent substitute. Walter Berry's narration of Haydn's pre-Darwinian evolution is buoyant while Gundula Janowitz's creamy soprano is a pleasure throughout. DG's recording sounds pleasantly fresh and well-balanced.

Additional recommendations ...

(Sung in English). **Soloists; King's College Choir, Cambridge; Academy of St Martin in the Fields/Sir David Willcocks.** EMI Studio CMS7 69894-2 — 2 1h 47m ADD 2/89

(Highlights). **Soloists; Chicago Symphony Chorus and Orchestra/Sir Georg Solti.** Decca Ovation 430 739-2DM — 1h 10m DDD 8/92 £

Further listening ...

Violin Concertos — No. 1 in C major, HobVII*a*/1; No. 3 in A major, HobVII*a*; No. 4 in G major, HobVII*a*. Virgin Classics VC7 59065-2 (11/91).

String Quartets — Op. 1: No. 5 in E flat major; No. 6 in C major. Op. 2: No. 1 in A major; No. 2 in E major. **Kodály Quartet.** Naxos 8 550399.

The Seven Last Words of Our Saviour on the Cross (string quartet version — 1787). String Quartet in D minor, Op. 103 (Unfinished). **Kodály Quartet.** Naxos 8 550346 (2/91).

L'ANIMA DEL FILOSOFO. **Soloists; Netherlands Chamber Choir; La Stagione/Michael Schneider.** Deutsche Harmonia Mundi RD77229 (4/92).

Key to Symbols

Price	Quantity/ availability	Timing	Mode	Review date
	2 2	1h 23m	DDD	6/88

Michael Haydn

Austrian 1737-1806

Suggested listening ...

Violin Concerto in B flat major, P53[a]. Clarinet Concerto in D major, P54[b]. Concerto for harpsichord and viola in C major, P55[c]. **Soloists; [ac]Oradea Philharmonic Orchestra/Ervin Acél; [b]Quodlibet Musicum Chamber Orchestra/Aurelian Octav Popa** (cl). Olympia OCD406 (10/90).

Horn Concerto in D major. Coupled with ***J. Haydn.*** *Horn Concerto No. 1 in D major, HobVIId/3. Symphony No. 31 in D major, "Hornsignal".* **Anthony Halstead** (natural hn); **Hanover Band/Roy Goodman.** Nimbus NI5190 (11/89).
Reviewed above under J. Haydn; refer to Index to Reviews.

Christopher Headington

British 1930-

Headington. Violin Concerto.
R. Strauss. Violin Concerto, Op. 8. **Xue-Wei** (vn); **London Philharmonic Orchestra/Jane Glover.** ASV CDDCA780.

1h 3m DDD 12/91 

Xue-Wei's penetrating and intuitive realization of Christopher Headington's Violin Concerto, written in 1959, is already commanding great admiration for this significant modern concerto, dedicated to the late Ralph Holmes, which in many respects inherits the lyric mantle of the great masterworks for the violin composed earlier in the century by Elgar and Walton. Xue-Wei also reminds the listener of the work's darker aspect, especially during the opening paragraphs of the concerto, where an affinity with the Walton Concerto is apparent. The central *Vivace* movement again has something of Walton's caustic wit, but the Headington concerto is searching and original in concept, without being overtly heroic or virtuosic. The lyrical potential of the solo writing is gloriously revealed by Xue-Wei, whose playing is superb, particularly in the lucid six-variation finale, which leads to a hushed and deeply-felt conclusion. The Violin Concerto by Richard Strauss is very much in the traditionally romantic virtuoso vein of Wieniawski and Vieuxtemps, and although an early work it displays great pointers in the direction of Strauss's mature heroism. Xue-Wei's playing is volatile, affectionate and involving, while his rare tonal finesse has an evocative Heifetzian lustre which is always compelling. He is admirably supported throughout by the London Philharmonic, under Jane Glover, and ASV capture every nuance of the performance in the ample acoustic of London's Henry Wood Hall. The interpretation of the Headington concerto alone could well acquire classic status, and this is a disc which deserves to be heard by all who have an affinity with violin music of the twentieth century.

Further listening ...

Ballade-Image. Cinquanta. *Coupled with* ***Britten.*** Holiday Diary; ***Delius.*** Three Preludes; ***Elgar.*** Adieu. In Smyrna. Serenade; ***Ireland.*** The Island Spell; ***Moeran.*** Summer Valley; ***Patterson.*** A Tunnel of Time, Op. 66. **Christopher Headington** (pf). Kingdom KCLCD2017 (11/90).

Johann David Heinichen

German 1683-1729

NEW REVIEW

Heinichen. DRESDEN CONCERTOS. **Cologne Musica Antiqua/Reinhard Goebel.** Archiv Produktion 437 549-2AH2. Recorded in 1992.

Concertos — C major, S211; G major: S213; S214, "Darmstadt"; S214, "Venezia"; S215; S217; F major: S226; S231; S232; S233; S234; S235. Serenata di Moritzburg in F major, S204. Sonata in A major, S208. Concerto Movement in C minor, S240.

2 2h 17m DDD 5/93

No, not a brand of lager but a late baroque composer whose skill and imagination make us wonder why it has taken so long for him to appear on disc. Reinhard Goebel and his Cologne Musica Antiqua are well-established specialists in music of this period and in this two-CD album they have done Heinichen proud. All the music here was probably written for the Dresden court orchestra which was one of the best in Europe. There are exciting colour combinations at play in these concertos, each of which fields its own distinctive wind group, drawing variously upon recorders, flutes, oboes, bassoons and horns. In addition to these *concertante* instruments is the usual body of strings from which soloists emerge from time to time. In respect of colour and deployment of alternating instrumental 'choirs' Heinichen is the equal of his contemporaries, Telemann and Graupner, as well as Vivaldi who provided German composers of the time with their models. Goebel and his players enable the music to spring to life spontaneously and with an infectious rhythmic suppleness. In short, a refreshing and at times revelatory break from mainstream baroque repertory. Fine recorded sound sets the seal on an outstanding issue.

Heneker, David/John Taylor

British 1906-

Suggested listening ...

CHARLIE GIRL. **Original 1986 London revival cast.** First Night OCRCD9.

George Martin Adolf von Henselt

German 1814-1889

Suggested listening ...

Ballade in B flat major, Op. 31. Grande Valse, Op. 30, "L'aurore boréale". Impromptus — B flat minor, Op. 34; B minor, Op. 37; C minor, Op. 7; F minor, Op. 17. Introduction and Variations on a theme by Donizetti, Op. 1. Pensée fugitive, Op. 8. Rondo serioso. Scherzo in B minor, Op. 9. Toccatina in C minor, Op. 25. Valse mélancolique, Op. 36. **Rudiger Steinfatt** (pf). Koch Schwann 310023.

Hans Werner Henze

German 1926-

Henze. SYMPHONIES. [a]**Berlin Philharmonic Orchestra;** [b]**London Symphony Orchestra/Hans Werner Henze.** DG 20th Century Classics 429 854-2GC2. Items marked [a] from SLPM139203/4 (1/67), recorded in 1965, [b] 2530 261 (11/72), recorded in 1972.
No. 1 (1947, rev. 1963)[a]; No. 2 (1949)[a]; No. 3 (1949-50)[a]; No. 4 (1955)[a]; No. 5 (1962)[a]; No. 6 (1969)[b].

2 2h 30m ADD 12/90

Hans Werner Henze is one of the few remaining composers to continue the German symphonic tradition, which make these authoritative recordings all the more invaluable and welcome. Henze was only 21 when he produced his First Symphony, and though it clearly owes much to Bartók, Stravinsky and Hindemith it is nevertheless a remarkable work for a composer so young. The Second Symphony, completed only two years after the First, is a dark and sombre work, and orchestrated in a style closer to Berg and Schoenberg than any later composer. It is here, also, that his preoccupation with the theatre begins to emerge, until in the Third, Fourth and Fifth Symphonies it becomes integrally part of the structure. The Third dates from the period when he was artistic director of the Wiesbaden Ballet, and its three movements: "Invocation of Apollo", "Dithyramb" and "Conjuring Dance" clearly evoke the spirit of the dance, within the formal structure of its symphonic argument. The Fourth and Fifth Symphonies quote heavily from his operas *König Hirsch* and *Elegy for Young Lovers*, and also begin to reflect his move from Germany to Italy, which brought about a greater feeling of 'arioso' lyricism and poetry to his style. The most radical is the Sixth, which dates from 1969 whilst Henze was living in Cuba, and we find him confronting and re-examining not only his own personal past (and political affiliations), but also the 'bourgeois' new music of the time. A valuable set that repays more and more with repeat hearings.

Further listening …

String Quartets Nos. 1-5. **Arditti Quartet.** Wergo WER60114/5-50 (3/90).

El Cimarrón. **Paul Yoder** (bar); **Michael Faust** (fl); **Reinbert Evers** (gtr); **Mircea Ardeleanu** (perc). Koch Schwann Musica Mundi 314030 (1/92).

BOULEVARD SOLITUDE. **Soloists; Epalinges Children's Chorus; Lausanne Opera Chorus; Orchestre des Rencontres Musicales/Ivan Anguelov.** Cascavelle 1000 Series VEL1006 (12/92).

DIE BASSARIDEN. **Soloists; Berlin Radio Chamber Choir; South German Radio Choir; Berlin Radio Symphony Orchestra/Gerd Albrecht.** Koch Schwann Musica Mundi 314006 (10/91).

THE ENGLISH CAT. **Soloists; Parnassus Orchestra/Markus Stenz.** Wergo WER6204 2 (12/92).

Victor Herbert

American 1859-1924

Herbert. Cello Concertos — No. 1 in D major, Op. 8; No. 2 in E minor, Op. 30. Five Pieces for cello and strings (trans. Dennison). **Lynn Harrell** (vc); **Academy of St Martin in the Fields/Sir Neville Marriner.** Decca 417 672-2DH. Recorded in 1986.
Cello Pieces — Yesterthoughts; Pensée amoureuse; Punchinello; Ghazel; The Mountain Brook.

lh 7m DDD 10/88

Victor Herbert is best known nowadays as the composer of romantic American operettas. However, in his early days he was a cello virtuoso and composed many works for the instrument. The second of his two cello concertos is a powerful piece that is said to have influenced Dvořák to compose his own concerto for the instrument. The First Concerto remained in manuscript until recently and now provides a most rewarding surprise, since it offers the same characteristics of romantic warmth and subtle interplay of soloist and orchestra with even more melodic appeal. The second movement, with a sprightly scherzo section framed by an affecting andante, and ending with the soloist at the very top of the 'cello register, is a real winner. Lynn Harrell brings to the works not only virtuoso technique but an emotional intensity and variety of tone missing in previous recordings of the Second Concerto, and both accompaniment and recording are first class. The inclusion of transcriptions of five of Herbert's short pieces adds up to a very well-filled and immensely rewarding collection.

Jerry Herman

American 1933-

Suggested listening ...

LA CAGE AUX FOLLES. **Original Broadway cast.** RCA Red Seal BD84824 (3/87).

MACK AND MABEL. **Original Broadway cast.** MCA MCLD19089.

Louis Hérold

French 1791-1833

Suggested listening ...

La fille mal gardée — ballet (arr. Lanchbery)[a]. *Coupled with* **Lecocq.** Mam'zelle Angot — ballet[b]. [a]**Orchestra of the Royal Opera House, Covent Garden/John Lanchbery;** [b]**National Philharmonic Orchestra/Richard Bonynge.** Decca Ovation 430 849-2DM2 (12/91).

Bernard Herrmann

American 1911-1975

Suggested listening ...

Symphony No. 1. *Coupled with* **Schuman.** New England Triptych. **Phoenix Symphony Orchestra/James Sedares.** Koch International Classics 37135-2 (9/92).

Film Scores: The Day the Earth Stood Still; Fahrenheit 451; Journey to the Centre of the Earth; The Seventh Voyage of Sinbad. **National Philharmonic Orchestra/Bernard Herrmann.** Decca 421 266-2DA (11/89).

Film Scores: On Dangerous Ground — The death hunt. Citizen Kane — suite[a]. Beneath the 12-Mile Reef — suite. Hangover Square — Concerto macabre[b]. White Witch Doctor — suite. [a]**Dame Kiri Te Kanawa** (sop); [b]**Joaquin Achucarro** (pf); **National Phlharmonic Orchestra/Charles Gerhardt.** RCA Victor GD80707 (11/91).

Vertigo — *Original film soundtrack.* **Sinfonia of London/Muir Mathieson.** Mercury 422 106-2MM (3/90).

WUTHERING HEIGHTS. **Soloists; Elizabethan Singers; Pro Arte Orchestra/Bernard Herrmann.** Unicorn-Kanchana UKCD2050/2.

Hildegard of Bingen

German 1098-1179

Hildegard of Bingen. A FEATHER ON THE BREATH OF GOD. **Gothic Voices/Christopher Page** with **Doreen Muskett** (symphony); **Robert White** (reed drones). Hyperion CDA66039. Texts and translation included. From A66039 (7/82). Columba aspexit. Ave, generosa. O ignis spiritus. O Jerusalem. O Euchari. O viridissima virga. O presul vere civitatis. O Ecclesia.

44m DDD 7/85

Before 1981 Abbess Hildegard of Bingen was little more than a shadowy name in a brief paragraph in the music history text-books. Christopher Page and Gothic Voices have changed all that, revealing her to the world as one of the "greatest creative personalities of the Middle Ages". Hildegard once described herself as a "feather on the breath of God", writing and composing under divine impulsion. Now, with the arrival of this remarkable recording, a selection of her hymns and sequences has had new life breathed into it by these refreshingly unsophisticated performances. The music is all single line monody, freely composed in a modal idiom that owes much to the sort of music Hildegard was singing every day in choir. But these pieces are infused with a lyricism, sometimes even an ecstasy, that are entirely her own, and which seem to have a particular appeal to modern ears. This CD is an outright winner that merits a place in every collection.

Further listening ...

O magne Pater. O aeterne Deus. Ave generosa. O frondens virga. O felix anima. Ave Maria, o auctrix vitae. O quam mirabilis. O virtus sapientiae. O vis aeternitatis. *Coupled with* **Abelard.** Planctus David. O quanta qualia; ***Anonymous.*** Promat chorus hodie. Annus novus in gaudio. Fulget dies celebris. **Augsburg Early Music Ensemble.** Christophorus Musica Practica CHR74584 (3/93).

Ordo Virtutum. **Sequentia Medieval Music Ensemble.** Deutsche Harmonia Mundi Editio Classica GD77051 (1/84).

Paul Hindemith

German 1895-1963

NEW REVIEW

Hindemith. Cello Concerto[a]. The Four Temperaments[b]. [a]**Raphael Wallfisch** (vc); [b]**Howard Shelley** (pf); **BBC Philharmonic Orchestra/Yan Pascal Tortelier.** Chandos CHAN9124. Recorded in 1992.

52m DDD 3/93

These two concertos, both from Hindemith's maturity (1940), make a good pairing. The outwardly conventional Cello Concerto contrasts a relatively small voice (the cello) which carries the work's lyrical message, with a large orchestra used initially for active statements delivered with great power. Hindemith's plan would seem to be to slowly reconcile these apparently contradictory modes of address. *The Four Temperaments* is a concerto for piano and string orchestra, a much more evenly balanced combination, using theme and variations form to integrate and relate the contrasted 'humours'; the old jibe that Hindemith's variations should have been called "Four Equal Temperaments" is not too wide of the mark, and Hindemith's treatment of his material would appear to argue that all temperaments, whatever the dominant disposition, are closely related. His portraiture, in fact, reveals characterization of great depth and dimension. Performances are superbly accomplished, indeed this is the finest of many currently available recordings of *The Four Temperaments*. And Chandos have resisted the temptation, which must be considerable, to move in on the soloist in the Cello Concerto. The sound is open and spacious.

NEW REVIEW

Hindemith. Violin Concerto[a]. Symphonic Metamorphosis on Themes of Carl Maria von Weber[b]. Mathis der Maler — symphony[c]. [a]**David Oistrakh** (vn); [ab]**London Symphony Orchestra/**[a]**Paul Hindemith,** [b]**Claudio Abbado;** [c]**Suisse Romande Orchestra/Paul Kletzki.** Decca Enterprise 433 081-2DM. Item marked [a] from SXL6035 (2/63), recorded in 1962, [b] SXL6398 (5/69), [c] SXL6445 (12/70), both recorded in 1968.

lh 17m ADD 9/92

Hindemithians who can afford to be choosy about the *Mathis der Maler* Symphony and the *Symphonic Metamorphosis* will immediately recognize the superiority of the full-price Blomstedt readings (see below). Consistently spectacular 1960s Decca sound adds allure to the merely proficient performances on offer here. What makes this medium-priced disc indispensable is the 30 minute Violin Concerto with Oistrakh at his legendary best and the composer conducting. The late Deryck Cooke, in his original *Gramophone* review, wrote of Oistrakh as "superbly poised and eloquent ... and as performed here the Concerto shows that behind Hindemith's stony neo-classical facade beats a romantic German heart". Listening to this recording it's hard to understand the Concerto's relative neglect — strange indeed are the tides of fashion — but easy to imagine current star violinists finding Oistrakh's an impossible act to follow. The 1962 sound gives Oistrakh a discreet dominance, and the engineers flatten out the slow movement's central climax, but thankfully no other allowances need be made for this preservation of a classic recording.

Hindemith. ORCHESTRAL WORKS. [b]**Siegfried Mauser** (pf); [a]**Queensland Symphony Orchestra,** [b]**Frankfurt Radio Symphony Orchestra/Werner Andreas Albert.** CPO 999 005-2, 999 006-2, 999 078-2. Recorded in 1989.
999 005-2[a] — Lustige Sinfonietta, Op. 4. Rag Time ("well-tempered"). Symphonische Tänze. *999 006-2*[a] — Das Nusch-Nuschi — dance suite, Op. 20. Konzertmusik for strings and brass, Op. 50. Symphony, "Die Harmonie der Welt". *999 078-2*[b] — Theme and Variations, "The Four Temperaments". Piano Concerto.

③ lh 2m lh 4m lh 2m DDD 12/91

The decline in status of one of this century's most prolific and versatile musical figures is startling (Hindemith was once mentioned in the same breath as Bartók and Stravinsky), and in the last three decades record companies have been loath to put money into new recordings of works other than the established favourites (the *Mathis der Maler* Symphony and the *Symphonic Metamorphosis*). There are now signs of a revival of interest, and we are told that these discs are among the first issues in a series that will include the "complete symphonic repertoire and a collection of concertos". Well over half of these recordings are CD premières, and many of these works haven't been recorded since the 1950s. The earliest work is the *Lustige Sinfonietta*. Written in 1916, it shows the 21-year-old Hindemith, though indebted to Reger and Richard Strauss, using a much smaller orchestra than had been common before the war, and scoring with a freshness and colour not always found in his later works. Sharper-tongued aphoristic wit and hints of Hindemith, the *enfant terrible*, are found in the 1921 *Rag Time*; a modish parodic fragmentation of Bach's C minor fugue, and a fascinating first example of swing J.S. Bach. The same year also produced the "Burmese marionette play", *Das Nusch-Nuschi*, and the three dances recorded here are engagingly daft oriental burlesque, a piece of debunking very much of its period. The gloriously robust 1930 *Konzertmusik for strings and brass*, determinedly contrapuntal and reflecting its destination (it was written for the Boston Symphony Orchestra) in its virtuoso demands and big band allusions, does not receive as idiomatic a reading as Bernstein's (see below), but it is a fine performance none the less. And the work looks forward to *Mathis* as much as the 1937 *Symphonic Dances* were obviously written in its wake, with their use of German folk-song and chorale, even the way some of the movements are constructed. British ears will delight to the frequent echoes of Walton and early Tippett. Of even greater value is the first stereo recording of the Symphony, *Die Harmonie der Welt* (1951). Like the *Mathis* Symphony, it originated in an opera project, this one devoted to the astronomer Kepler and his vision of a harmonic ordering of heavenly bodies; so, not surprisingly, the manner is grand (the scale is Brucknerian), and, equally unsurprisingly, the wide range of modern recordings allows collectors to fully savour that grandeur for the first time.

The last disc offers two concertos from the 1940s: *The Four Temperaments*, a Theme and Variations scored for piano and strings of austere beauty and finely wrought contrasts; and the Piano Concerto, with its variations gradually uncovering the theme, sumptuously scored for full orchestra, and with definite sideways glances to Bartók's night music and the rich string writing found in Prokofiev's Third Piano Concerto. Convincing proof, as are all three discs, of the diversity of Hindemith's vast output. Performances throughout are never less than good, frequently more than that, and CPO's sound is consistently smooth, airy and spacious.

NEW REVIEW

Hindemith. Nobilissima visione — suite. Der Schwanendreher (Concerto after folk-songs)[a]. Konzertmusik for strings and brass, Op. 50. [a]**Geraldine Walther** (va); **San Francisco Symphony Orchestra/Herbert Blomstedt.** Decca 433 809-2DH. Recorded 1989-91.

1h 7m DDD 4/93

This is the second of Blomstedt's Hindemith discs and, like his first of *Mathis der Maler*, in a class of its own. Here are three Hindemith masterpieces which demonstrate the diversity of his output, and mark a progression from his interest in unusual instrumental combinations; the bold and exuberant *Konzertmusik* for strings and brass of 1931, *Der Schwanendreher* of 1935 (literally "The Swanturner", he who turns the swans on the spit), in effect a concerto for viola and small orchestra and the Suite from his 1938 ballet music *Nobilissima visione*, a piece depicting the life of St Francis of Assisi, and inspired by the Giotto frescoes in the church of Santa Croce in Florence. Blomstedt seems to have an instinct for pacing and 'weighting' Hindemith's music, and each piece has its own dimensions and gestures finely considered and realized. No finer performances of any of these works have, or are likely to appear, and Decca's sound is either intimate, or grandly spectacular, as the music demands.

Hindemith. Mathis der Maler — symphony. Trauermusik[a]. Symphonic Metamorphosis on Themes of Carl Maria von Weber. [a]**Geraldine Walther** (va); **San Francisco Symphony Orchestra/Herbert Blomstedt.** Decca 421 523-2DH. Recorded in 1987.

55m DDD 10/88

The charge sometimes levelled against Hindemith of being dry and cerebral utterly collapses in the face of Blomstedt's disc. Masterly craftsmanship and virtuosity there is in plenty; but the powerful emotions of *Mathis der Maler* and the festive high spirits of the *Symphonic Metamorphosis* could not be denied except by those who wilfully close their ears. Each of the three movements of the *Mathis* symphony is based on a panel of Grünewald's great Isenheim altar. The eventual glorious illumination of "The angels" folk-tune, the poignant slow movement and the blazing triumphant Allelujas after the desperate struggle with the demons in the finale have a searing intensity in this performance, which also presents Hindemith's elaborate web of counterpoints with the utmost lucidity. For brilliant and joyously ebullient orchestral writing few works can match that based on Weber's piano duets and his *Turandot* overture: here the San Francisco woodwind and brass have a field day. In addition, this warmly recommended disc contains a heartfelt performance of the touching elegy on the death of King George V which Hindemith wrote overnight in 1936.

Additional recommendations ...

Mathis der Maler. Symphonic Metamorphosis. Konzertmusik for strings and brass, Op. 50. **Israel Philharmonic Orchestra/Leonard Bernstein.** DG 429 404-2GH — 1h 7m DDD 5/91

Symphonic Metamorphosis. Symphony in E flat major. Concerto Music, Op. 50. **New York Philharmonic Orchestra/Leonard Bernstein.** Sony Classical Bernstein Royal Edition SMK47566 — 1h 10m ADD 5/93

NEW REVIEW

Hindemith. KAMMERMUSIK. [c]**Konstanty Kulka** (vn); [d]**Kim Kashkashian** (va); [e]**Norbert Blume** (va d'amore); [b]**Lynn Harrell** (vc); [a]**Ronald Brautigam** (pf); [f]**Leo van Doeselaar** (org); **Royal Concertgebouw Orchestra/Riccardo Chailly.** Decca 433 816-2DH2. Recorded in 1990.

Kammermusik No. 1, Op. 24 No. 1. Kleine Kammermusik No. 1 for wind quintet, Op. 24 No. 2. Kammermusik — No. 2[a]; No. 3, Op. 36 No. 2[b]; No. 4, Op. 36 No. 3[c]; No. 5, Op. 36 No. 4[d]; No. 6, Op. 46 No. 1[e]; No. 7, Op. 46 No. 2[f].

2 2h 18m DDD 11/92

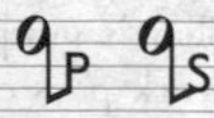

Even were the performances and recordings not outstanding (and they most certainly are) this would be an extremely valuable set. Hindemith's series of *Chamber Music* began in 1921 as an iconoclastic response to the hyper-intense emotionalism of German music over the previous 15 years (somewhat loosely termed Expressionism). It continued until 1927, at which point he began to rationalize both the harmonic and the expressive foundations of his style (and arguably lost as much as he gained). This, then, is neo-classicism with a German accent and as such it was to be a vital force in sweeping away the cobwebs of musty late romanticism; Walton, Prokofiev, Shostakovich and Britten were among those who, however indirectly, would feel the benefit. The music is also immensely enjoyable in its own right. Hindemith cheekily throws together disparate idioms, ideas spiral off with unselfconscious abandon, and sheer force of personality is all that guards against total anarchy. All this is done with more than half an eye on the performers' own enjoyment of recreation, and the fine array of artists assembled by Chailly savour every detail. Recording quality is exemplary.

NEW REVIEW

Hindemith. Organ Sonatas Nos. 1-3.
Reger. Organ Works. **Piet Kee** (org). Chandos CHAN9097. Played on the Müller organ of St Bavo, Haarlem, The Netherlands. Recorded in 1991.
Prelude in D minor, Op. 65 No. 7. Aus tiefer Not schrei ich zu dir, Op. 67 No. 3. Intermezzo in F minor, Op. 129 No. 7. Introduction and Passacaglia in D minor, Op. posth.

1h 8m DDD 12/92

Hindemith wrote solo sonatas for a great many different instruments, although his boast that he could play every one begs the question "how well?". His three for the organ, combining an originality of approach one might expect from a composer not rooted in organ-playing tradition, with an obvious understanding of the instrument which makes them eminently playable, hold a unique and valued place in the instrument's repertory. The Second (with which this disc begins) is a benign, undeniably charming work, the Third is based on old German folk-songs (Hindemith wrote it shortly after escaping to America in 1940) while the First, although substantially longer, is likewise characterized by light textures and clear, uncluttered lines. Piet Kee's performances are immaculately prepared and in choosing to play them on this historic organ he underlines their delicate colours and subtle language. In its weighty, often dauntingly complex language, Reger's music could hardly be more different, but the four pieces included on this disc not only act as the perfect foil for the delicate tracery of Hindemith's sonatas but show the dramatic (*Introduction and Passacaglia*) as well as the charming (*Intermezzo*) faces of Reger without dwelling too much on his more austere and forbidding side. The opulent sound of this wonderful instrument, coupled with a first-rate recording should warm the hearts even of the most ardent anti-Regerite.

Hindemith. When Lilacs Last in the Door-yard Bloom'd (Requiem for those we love). **Jan DeGaetani** (mez); **William Stone** (bar); **Atlanta Symphony Chorus and Orchestra/ Robert Shaw.** Telarc CD80132. Text included.

1h 2m DDD 7/87 9s

Taking as his text Walt Whitman's poem, a work laden with imagery and layers of association, written to mourn the death of President Lincoln, Hindemith adds further layers of meaning to this already intense poem. He was commissioned to compose the work by Robert Shaw for his New York-based Collegiate Chorale so it is appropriate and gratifying to be recommending a recording made some 40 years later by that same Robert Shaw. Hindemith's setting of the poem perfectly moulds itself to Whitman's somewhat sectionalized approach and the virtuosity involved is balanced, if not outweighed, by the sheer power and beauty of the music. Like the lilacs of Whitman's poem the music has a pungency that lingers long after the piece has ended. Shaw's grasp of the subtleties and powerful imagery of the text is total and his experience of the work pays enormous dividends in this moving performance. William Stone is a very sympathetic and sweet-toned baritone matched by Jan DeGaetani's pure mezzo. Shaw's choral and orchestral forces point up every subtlety and the recording is first rate.

Hindemith. CARDILLAC[a]. **Dietrich Fischer-Dieskau** (bar) Cardillac; **Leonore Kirschstein** (sop) Cardillac's daughter; **Donald Grobe** (ten) Officer; **Karl Christian Kohn** (bass) Gold dealer; **Eberhard Katz** (ten) Cavalier; **Elisabeth Söderström** (sop) Lady; **Willi Nett** (bar) Chief of Military Police; **Cologne Radio Chorus and Symphony Orchestra/Joseph Keilberth.**
MATHIS DER MALER[b] — excerpts. **Dietrich Fischer-Dieskau** (bar) Mathis; **Pilar Lorengar** (sop) Regina; **Donald Grobe** (ten) Albrecht; **Berlin Radio Symphony Orchestra/Leopold Ludwig.** DG 20th Century Classics 431 741-2GC2. Item marked [a] from 139435/6 (4/70), recorded in 1968, [b] SLPM138769 (12/62), recorded in 1961.

② 2h 28m ADD 12/91

These discs offer you the two main facets of Paul Hindemith's music at their most convincing. *Cardillac* — the original 1926 version — is fast and furious, fitting the demonic character of the goldsmith who is so obsessed by his own creations that he kills their purchasers in order to regain them. *Mathis der Maler* — Matthias Grünewald, the painter — is introspective and idealistic, as obsessive as Cardillac but finding his way towards an ultimate serenity. Both performances are dominated by Dietrich Fischer-Dieskau, here recorded in his prime, and he is not only able to make Cardillac sound more than a mere monster, but steers clear of exaggeration and mawkishness in Mathis's more lyrical music. Supporting casts are uneven, but never fall below basic acceptability. The medium-price format means that synopses, not librettos, are provided, but given the generous duration of the discs and the (for its age) decent sound, as well as two conductors expert in articulating the tricky rythmic idiom of Hindemith's music, this is a very recommendable issue. (The *Mathis* excerpts are not to be confused with the complete recording Fischer-Dieskau made for EMI in the late 1970s, unfortunately no longer available.)

Alun Hoddinott

British 1929-

Suggested listening ...

Symphony No. 6, Op. 116. Lanterne des morts, Op. 105 No. 2. A contemplation upon flowers, Op. 90[a]. Scena for string orchestra, Op. 119. [a]**Lillian Watson** (sop); **BBC Welsh Symphony Orchestra/Bryden Thomson.** Chandos CHAN8762 (12/89).

Antony Holborne

British fl. 1584-1602

Suggested listening ...

Pavans, Galliards, Almaines and other Short Aeirs — The Choise. The windowes myte. Heres paternus. Muy linda. Infernum. Pardizo. The Sighes. The ngiht watch. As it fell on a holie Eve. Heigh ho holiday. Spero. Last will and testament. Posthuma. The Honie-suckle. The Fairie-round. Almayne. Three Pavans. Seven Galliards. *Solo Pieces* — Almaine. Fantasia. Prelude. Quadro Pavan. Lullaby. The maydens of the Countrey. The Spanish Pavane. A Jyg. **Dowland Consort/Jakob Lindberg.** BIS CD469 (4/92).

Lee Holdridge

American 1944-

Suggested listening ...

El Pueblo del Sol — *Original film soundtrack.* **London Symphony Orchestra/Lee Holdridge.** Bay Cities BCD1031 (10/92).

Vagn Holmboe

Danish 1909-

Suggested listening ...

Symphonies — No. 4, Op. 29, "Sinfonia sacra"[a]; No. 5, Op. 35. [a]**Jutland Opera Choir; Aarhus Symphony Orchestra/Owain Arwel Hughes.** BIS CD572 (6/93).

Symphonies — No. 6, Op. 43; No. 7, Op. 50. **Aarhus Symphony Orchestra/Owain Arwel Hughes.** BIS CD573 (6/93).

Cello Concerto, Op. 120[a]. Benedic Domingo, Op. 59[b]. Triade, Op.123[c]. Quintet, Op. 79[d]. [a]**Erling Bløndal Bengtsson** (vc); [a]**Danish National Radio Symphony Orchestra/János Ferencsik;** [b]**Camerata Chamber Choir/Peter Enevold;** [c]**Edward Tarr** (tbn); [c]**Elisabeth Westenholz** (org); [d]**Swedish Brass Quintet.** BIS CD78 (7/93).

Gustav Holst

British 1874-1934

NEW REVIEW

Holst. ORCHESTRAL WORKS. [c]**William Bennett** (fl); [c]**Peter Graeme** (ob); [b]**Emanuel Hurwitz,** [b]**Kenneth Sillito** (vns); [d]**Cecil Aronowitz** (va); **English Chamber Orchestra/Imogen Holst.** Lyrita SRCD223. Items marked [ab] from SRCS44 (7/70), [cd]SRCS34 (5/67).

Two songs without words, H88[a]. Concerto for Two Violins, H175[b]. The Golden Goose, H163 — Ballet Music[a]. Capriccio for Orchestra, H185[a] (ed. I. Holst). A Fugal Concerto, H152[c]. A Moorside Suite, H173 — Nocturne[c]. Lyric Movement, H191[d]. Brook Green Suite, H190[d].

1h 15m ADD 4/93

Yet more Holstian treasure-trove from Lyrita. With the composer's daughter in charge, here's an unfailingly perceptive and marvellously performed anthology. Both chronologically and stylistically, the selection ranges far and wide: it's certainly a long way from the good-natured, earthy charms of the *Two songs without words* of 1906 (which Holst inscribed to his good friend Vaughan Williams) to the "tender austerity" (in Holst's own description) of the haunting *Lyric Movement* for viola and chamber orchestra (completed in the composer's penultimate year). In addition, we are also served such rarities as *The Golden Goose* (a comparatively slight but effective ballet score from 1926) and the *Capriccio* (both these in reworkings by Imogen Holst herself), the composer's string orchestra transcription of the lovely "Nocturne" from *A Moorside Suite* (originally scored for brass band), as well as the perky, light-textured *Fugal Concerto* and far tougher *Double Concerto*. It's the delightful *Brook Green Suite* — lovingly delivered on this occasion — which will perhaps be the most familiar item here. These vintage late-1960s tapes have been remastered to superb effect and the results remain extraordinarily vivid. For Holst lovers everywhere this will be self-recommending.

NEW REVIEW

Holst. ORCHESTRAL WORKS. [ab]**London Philharmonic Orchestra,** [c]**London Symphony Orchestra/Sir Adrian Boult.** Lyrita SRCD222. Items marked [a] from SRCS56 (5/72), [b] SRCS37 (10/68), [c] SRCS50 (6/71).

Beni Mora, H107[a]. A Fugal Overture, H151[b]. Hammersmith, H178[a]. Japanese Suite, H126[c]. Scherzo, H192[a]. A Somerset Rhapsody, H87[a]

1h 2m ADD 7/92 P

Here's another classic Boult anthology from Lyrita, and unquestionably one of this enterprising company's finest CDs to date. Opening in fine style with a roistering account of the *Fugal Overture*, this indispensable all-Holst concert also includes the haunting *Somerset Rhapsody* (framed by a ravishingly atmospheric oboe d'amore contribution), the riotously colourful "Oriental Suite" entitled *Beni Mora*, the engaging *Japanese Suite*, as well as the very late, bracing *Scherzo* (all that the composer left us of a projected symphony). But the highlight of the collection has to be that utterly magical nocturnal evocation *Hammersmith*: heard here in its full orchestral dress, it's one of Holst's most sublimely personal utterances and an undoubted masterpiece. These uniquely authoritative, radiantly played performances all show Sir Adrian at the height of his considerable powers, and the remastered Lyrita recordings continue to sound, for the most part, quite superb. In a word: unmissable.

Holst. The Planets, H125. Women's voices of the **Montreal Symphony Chorus; Montreal Symphony Orchestra/Charles Dutoit.** Decca 417 553-2DH.
Mars. Venus. Mercury. Jupiter. Saturn. Uranus. Neptune.

53m DDD 4/87 

Holst's brilliantly coloured orchestral suite, *The Planets*, is undoubtedly his most famous work and its success is surely deserved. The musical characterization is as striking as its originality of conception: the association of "Saturn" with old age, for instance, is as unexpected as it is perceptive. Bax introduced Holst to astrology and while he wrote the music he became fascinated with horoscopes, so it is the astrological associations that are paramount, although the linking of "Mars" (with its enormously powerful 5/4 rhythms) and war also reflects the time of composition. Throughout, the work's invention is as memorable as its vivid orchestration is full of infinite detail. No recording can reveal it all but this one comes the closest to doing so. Dutoit's individual performance is in a long line of outstanding recordings.

Additional recommendations ...
The Planets. **Berlin RIAS Chamber Choir; Berlin Philharmonic Orchestra/Herbert von Karajan.** DG 400 028-2GH — 52m DDD 7/83
The Planets[a]. ***Dukas.*** *L'Apprenti sorcier.* ***Gershwin.*** *Rhapsody in Blue*[b]. [a]**Ambrosian Singers; London Symphony Orchestra/André Previn** ([b]pf). EMI CDM7 64441-2 — 1h 17m ADD 10/92
The Planets. **Geoffrey Mitchell Choir; London Philharmonic Orchestra/Sir Adrian Boult.** EMI Studio CDM7 69045-2 — 49m ADD 5/88
The Planets. The Perfect Fool — ballet music. **Royal Liverpool Philharmonic Chorus and Orchestra/Sir Charles Mackerras.** Virgin Classics Virgo VJ7 59645 — 1h DDD 12/91 £
The Planets. **King's College Choir, Cambridge; Royal Philharmonic Orchestra/James Judd.** Denon CO-75076 — 50m DDD 3/93

NEW REVIEW
Holst. Piano Quintet in A minor H11[b]. Wind Quintet in A flat major, H67[a].
Jacob. Sextet, Op. 3[ab]. **Elysian Wind Quintet** ([a]Keith Bragg, fl; Julian Farrell, cl; Christopher O'Neal, ob; Christopher Blake, hn; Richard Skinner, bn); [b]**Anthony Goldstone** (pf). Chandos CHAN9077.

53m DDD 10/92

First, a friendly word of warning: don't expect to hear even the merest whiff of the composer we all know from *The Planets* in these two quintets. Both are early works. The A minor Piano Quintet dates from 1896 when Holst was a 22-year-old student at the Royal College of Music: fluent and amiable, its harmonic world breathes the same air as that of Mendelssohn and early Brahms, with perhaps, here and there, a hint of Dvořák, too. The A flat Wind Quintet was completed some seven years later at a time when Holst was earning his living as a professional trombonist: again, for all the well-meaning craft, there's no evidence of the mature composer's distinctive style. Incidentally, the scores of both works only came to light some years after Holst's death in 1934; he had apparently sent them to potential performers who then never bothered to return them! Gordon Jacob (1895-1984) wrote his Sextet for piano and wind quintet for The Dennis Brain Ensemble in 1962: its five movements contain a wealth of pleasing invention and evince (as one would expect from this respected figure) the most exquisite technical finish. Three most agreeable, if hardly compelling works, then, each most beautifully performed and truthfully recorded.

Holst. CHORAL MUSIC. **Holst Singers and [a]Orchestra/Hilary Davan Wetton.** Hyperion CDA66329. Texts included. Recorded in 1988.
Two psalms, H117[a]. Six choruses, H186[a]. The evening watch, H159. Seven Partsongs, H162[a]. Nunc dimittis, H127.

lh 5m DDD 1/90 

It is incomprehensible that so much of Holst's wonderful music for chorus should still remain comparatively unknown to the general listening public. Hyperion must be particularly commended on the care and attention that have obviously been devoted to the fine recording and production here. Hilary Davan Wetton took on the mantle of Director of Music at St Paul's Girls' School in Hammersmith, the position held by Holst himself from 1905 until his death in 1934, and the spirit of the venue seems to suffuse both the performances and the recording. Featuring a chorus and orchestra dedicated to Holst's music, these readings capture exactly the sonorities that the composer implies in his scores and the spiritual world that the works inhabit. It is perhaps invidious to single out from a programme of such consistent quality a couple of items of particular merit, but the two short unaccompanied pieces for eight-part choir, *The evening watch* and the appropriately concluding *Nunc dimittis* are both outstanding and worthy of special attention.

Holst. The Cloud Messenger, Op. 30[a]. The Hymn of Jesus, Op. 37. [a]**Della Jones** (mez); **London Symphony Chorus and Orchestra/Richard Hickox.** Chandos CHAN8901. Texts included. Recorded in 1990.

lh 6m DDD 5/91

When this CD was first released, the great talking point was *The Cloud Messenger*, a 43-minute work of considerable imaginative power, virtually forgotten since its disastrous première under the baton of Holst himself in 1913. It shows the composer already working on an epic scale — something which casts light on the subsequent eruption of *The Planets*. It is marvellous to have the work on disc, though it is, as you might expect, uneven. Those who admire the ascetic rigour of Holst's later music may share the reservations of Imogen Holst and find the score disappointingly 'backward'. There are certainly echoes of Vaughan Williams's *A Sea Symphony* and several older models. On the other hand, the glittering approach to the sacred city on Mount Kailasa and the stylized orientalism of the climactic dance are new to British music; another world, the world of "Venus", is foreshadowed in the closing pages. The text is Holst's own translation from the Sanskrit. Hickox's expansive account of the familiar *Hymn of Jesus* is more than a mere filler. One of the few incontrovertible masterpieces in Holst's output, it has never received a better performance on disc, although the impressively grand acoustics of London's St Jude's impart a certain warm imprecision — the choral singing itself is splendidly crisp — which can blunt the impact of Holst's acerbic harmonies.

Additional recommendation ...
The Hymn of Jesus[a]. *The Dream of Gerontius*[b]. [b]**Yvonne Minton** (mez); [b]**Sir Peter Pears** (ten); [b]**John Shirley-Quirk** (bar); [b]**Choir of King's College, Cambridge;** [b]**London Symphony Chorus and Orchestra/Benjamin Britten;** [a]**BBC Chorus and Symphony Orchestra/Sir Adrian Boult.** Decca London 421 381-2LM2 — ② lh 53m ADD 5/89

Further listening ...

Beni Mora, H107[a]. St Paul's Suite, H118[b]. Psalm 86, H117/1[c]. Brook Green Suite, H190[d]. Festival Te Deum, H145[e]. The Perfect Fool, H150 — ballet music[f]. Egdon Heath, H172[f]. [c]**Ian Partridge** (ten); [c]**Ralph Downes** (org); [c]**Purcell Singers;** [a]**BBC Symphony Orchestra,** [b]**Royal Philharmonic Orchestra/Sir Malcolm Sargent;** [cd]**English Chamber Orchestra/**[c]**Imogen Holst,** [d]**Steuart Bedford;** [e]**London Symphony Chorus;** [e]**London**

Philharmonic Orchestra/Sir Charles Groves; [f]London Symphony Orchestra/André Previn. EMI CDC7 49784-2 (10/88).

Beni Mora. A Fugal Overture, H151. Hammersmith, H178. Japanese Suite, H126[a]. Scherzo, H192. A Somerset Rhapsody, H87. **London Philharmonic Orchestra, [a]London Symphony Orchestra/Sir Adrian Boult.** Lyrita SRCD222 (7/92).

Key to Symbols

Price	Quantity/ availability	Timing	Mode	Review date
	② ②	lh 23m	DDD	6/88

Simon Holt

British 1958-

NEW REVIEW

Holt. . . . Era madrugada. Canciones[a]. Shadow realm. Sparrow night[b]. **[a]Fiona Kimm** (mez); **[b]Gareth Hulse** (ob); **Nash Ensemble/Lionel Friend.** NMC NMCD008. Recorded in 1991.

lh 3m DDD 5/93

If the generation of British composers born 20 years on from Tippett and Britten — Maxwell Davies and Birtwistle, in particular — has tended to sustain a more radical musical manner into the late twentieth century, the generation which emerged another two decades further on — Simon Holt was born in 1954 — has tended to be more pragmatic and relaxed about matters of progress and experiment. Holt's success undoubtedly has much to do with his flexible and imaginative adaptation of an idiom stemming from the dramatic vigour and ardent lyricism of Birtwistle, in particular. Nevertheless, as these four works from the 1980s make clear, he has progressed well beyond the merely derivative. The compositions have a common theme: all deal with bizarre, sinister states and situations, yet with a brightness of tone-colour and a subtlety of form that steer well clear of over-bearing expressionism. Holt's brilliantly idiomatic writing for clarinet in *Shadow realm* and oboe in *Sparrow night* provides the most obvious and sustained demonstration of a pervasive and persuasive feeling for what instruments can do in the hands of expert performers, and — as Fiona Kimm demonstrates in *Canciones* — his vocal writing has its moments too. The recordings are as rich and spacious as the musical textures demand, and the Nash Ensemble are ideal advocates of music whose strongly-etched lines and newly imagined textures they rightly relish.

Arthur Honegger

French/Swiss 1892-1955

Honegger. ORCHESTRAL WORKS. **Bavarian Radio Symphony Orchestra/Charles Dutoit.** Erato 2292-45242-2. From NUM75254 (4/86).

Symphony No. 1. Pastorale d'été. Three symphonic movements — Pacific 231; Rugby; No. 3.

55m DDD 12/86

Honegger's First Symphony is a highly impressive work, concisely and effectively constructed in what might be generally described as a neoclassical style; and the scoring is attractive and skilful. His evocation of dawn on a summer's day in *Pastorale d'été*, scored for small orchestra with exquisite, quiet beauty, is surely a miniature masterpiece, and both *Pacific 231* (1924) and *Rugby* (1928) are brilliantly contrived essays in imaginative scoring and the use of cross-rhythms. Honegger was distressed by a critical notion that he was trying to imitate the sound of a steam locomotive and specific moves in a game of rugby: he insisted that the two scores conveyed only a general impression of a train journey and the atmosphere of Colombes stadium. So offended was he that he called the third companion piece merely *Mouvement symphonique No. 3*, but it is a little less effective than its two bedfellows. These vigorous performances are excellent.

Honegger. Symphonies — No. 2 for strings and trumpet; No. 3, "Liturgique". **Berlin Philharmonic Orchestra/Herbert von Karajan.** DG 20th Century Classics 423 242-2GC. From 2530 068 (7/73). Recorded in 1969.

59m ADD 6/88 £ 9p

This classic DG recording is unlikely to be surpassed. The Second Symphony is a powerfully atmospheric piece written during the grim years of the German occupation. It is a searching, thoughtful piece, appropriately dark in colouring which eventually breaks into the light with its chorale melody played on the trumpet. The *Liturgique* is a powerhouse of energy and its slow movement is among Honegger's most glorious inspirations. The playing of the Berlin Philharmonic is sumptuous in tone, vibrant with energy and encompasses an enormously wide range of dynamics and colour. One can only marvel at the quality of sound they achieve in both the beautiful slow movements and their virtuosity in the finale of No. 3. Astonishing performances and an indispensable disc for all lovers of modern music.

Additional recommendations ...

No. 2; No. 4, "Deliciae basiliensis". Pastorale d'été. Prélude, arioso et fugue (on BACH). **Lausanne Chamber Orchestra/Jesús López-Cobos.** Virgin Classics VC7 59064-2 — lh 3m DDD 6/92 9p

Nos. 2 and 4. **Bavarian Radio Symphony Orchestra/Charles Dutoit.** Erato 2292-45247-2 — 54m DDD

NEW REVIEW

Honegger. Symphonies[a] — No. 2 for strings and trumpet; No. 5, "di tre re". ***Milhaud.*** Suite Provençale, Op. 152[b]. La création du monde, Op. 81[b]. **Boston Symphony Orchestra/Charles Munch.** RCA GD60685. Items marked [a] recorded in mono in 1952-53, [b] 1960-61.

lh l6m ADD 

No conductor did more than Munch to promote Honegger's music. He gave the first French performance of the Second Symphony in 1942, and the first performance of the Fifth in Boston in 1951. Though Karajan in his DG version of the Second may have cultivated more doom-laden atmosphere at slower tempos, Munch's mono recordings of these Symphonies have an unrivalled expressive urgency and intensity. The Fifth (scored for full orchestra) returns, from the lightness of the Fourth, to the powerful striving of the Third, and takes its name from the fact that each movement ends with a D from the timpani. Munch, in particular, seems to relish Honegger's hugely physical and forceful contrapuntal writing, with sharp and emphatic accenting throughout. The Milhaud items bring welcome relief (and stereo). *Suite Provençale* (1937) is a loving and loveable tribute to Milhaud's musical ancestors and place of birth, and finds Munch in an appropriately mellow mood. And the Boston Symphony's trumpet might have been born and bred in Harlem, such is his mastery of the idiom (and the instrument) in Milhaud's sophisticated evocation of Negro jazz in the ballet *La création du monde* — along with the recent Nagano recording, Munch's remains a top recommendation, and the recording sounds not a whit less elderly.

NEW REVIEW

Honegger. CHAMBER WORKS. Various artists. Timpani 4C1012. Texts and translations included. Recorded in 1991.

Violin Sonatas — D minor (No. 0), H3; No. 1, H17; No. 2, H24. Morceau de concours, H179. Arioso, H214 (all with Dong-Suk Kang, vn; Pascal Devoyon, pf). Solo Violin Sonata, H143 (Kang). Sonatina for Two Violins, H29 (Kang, Jean-Philippe Audoli, vns). Sonatina for

Violin and Cello, H80 (Kang, Raphael Wallfisch, vc). Paduana, H181 (Wallfisch). Cello Sonata, H32 (Wallfisch, Devoyon). Prélude for Double Bass and Piano, H79 (Jean Rossi, db; Devoyon). Viola Sonata, H28 (Pierre-Henri Xuereb, va; Devoyon). Piano Trio in F minor, H6 (Kang; Wallfisch; Devoyon). Sonatina for Clarinet and Piano, H42 (Michel Arrignon, cl; Devoyon). Rapsodie, H13 (Allain Marion, Ashildur Haraldsdottir, fls; Arrignon; Devoyon). Danse de la chèvre, H39 (Marion). Romance, H211 (Marion; Devoyon). Petite Suite, H89 (Marion; Haraldsdottir; Devoyon). Three Contrepoints, H43 (Marion; Christian Moreaux, ob; Kang; Wallfisch). Colloque, H216 (Marion; Devoyon, celesta; Kang; Xuereb). Introduction et Danse, H217 (Marion; Pascale Zanlonghi, hp; Kang; Xuereb; Wallfisch). Intrado, H193 (Thierry Caens, tpt; Devoyon). Hommage du trombono, H59 (Michel Becquet, tbn; Devoyon). Chanson de Ronsard, H54. Trios Chansons de la petite Sirene, H63 (both Fusako Kondo, mez; Haraldsdottir; Ludwig Quartet — Jean-Philippe Audoli, Elenid Owen, vns; Padrig Fauré, va; Anne Copéry, vc). String Quartets — No. 1, H15; No. 2, H103; No. 3, H114. J'avais un fidèle amant, H74 (all Ludwig Quartet). Pacques à New York, H30 (Kondo; Ludwig Quartet).

④ 4h 24m DDD

This four-disc issue of Honegger's chamber music provides a welcome opportunity for a reassessment of the contribution to twentieth-century music made by this composer, who was highly regarded in the inter-war years but then for some while neglected — a situation that his recent centenary did much to repair, although no less than nine of the works played here still remain unpublished. One of them is the Violin Sonata No. 0, a big work that Honegger wrote in 1912 when he was 20: an attractive work with an element of Franckian fervour, it deserves to be played more often than it is and here receives a sympathetic performance by Dong-Suk Kang and that excellent pianist Pascal Devoyon. The other two violin sonatas are also well worth knowing; the composer himself, an accomplished violinist, wrote well for the instrument and indeed performed these pieces with his pianist wife Andrée Vaurabourg. The same instrument also appears in the Sonata for Solo Violin and *Sonatina* for two violins, the former reflecting Honegger's admiration for Bach. Kang plays the unaccompanied work persuasively, but is rather closely recorded and a few passages tend towards roughness: still, that is preferable to a lack of commitment. Another strength of this issue is the participation of Raphael Wallfisch, who, with Devoyon as his partner, is eloquent in the fine Cello Sonata of 1920 and good also with Kang in the duo *Sonatina* for violin and cello. This issue also offers several other big pieces, including three string quartets and a one-movement Piano Trio, along with smaller ones, and although it would be idle to claim that all are masterworks there is nothing here that is unrewarding. The recording of all this music may not always be ideally refined, but it is never less than serviceable.

Honegger. Jeanne d'Arc au bûcher. **Françoise Pollet, Michèle Command** (sops); **Nathalie Stutzman** (contr); **John Aler** (ten); **Marthe Keller, Georges Wilson, Pierre-Marie Escourrou, Paola Lenzi** (narrs); **Chorus and Children's Voices of French Radio; French National Orchestra/Seiji Ozawa.** DG 429 412-2GH. Text and translations included. Recorded live in 1989.

lh 9m DDD 4/91

Honegger described *Joan of Arc at the stake* as a "dramatic oratorio", but it is a work almost impossible to categorize, the two chief characters — Joan and Brother Dominc — being speaking parts, but with a chorus (now commenting on, now involved in, the action), a children's chorus, and a curiously constituted orchestra including saxophones instead of horns, two pianos and, most notably, an ondes martenot which, with its banshee shriek, bloodcurdlingly reinforces the climax as Joan breaks her earthly chains. The action is partly realistic, partly symbolic, unfolding in quasi-cinematic flashbacks. The musical techniques and styles employed by Honegger are extraordinarily varied, with humming and shouting besides singing, and with elements of polyphony, folk-song, baroque dances and jazz rhythms; yet all is fused together in a remarkable way to produce a work of gripping power and, in the final scenes, almost intolerable emotional intensity: the beatific *envoi* "Greater love hath no man ..." is a passage that catches the throat and haunts the mind for long afterwards. Ozawa fully captured the work's dramatic forces in this public performance, which has been skilfully served by the recording engineers; Marthe Keller vividly portrays Joan's bewilderment, fervour and agony,

John Aler makes a swaggering Procus, and Françoise Pollet is radiant-voiced as the Virgin. Even more than *Le roi David*, this is Honegger's masterpiece.

Further listening ...

Les misérables — *film score.* **Bratislava Radio Symphony Orchestra/Adriano.** Marco Polo 8 223181 (3/91).

Alan Hovhaness *American 1911-*

NEW REVIEW

Hovhaness. Symphony No. 2, "Mysterious mountain", Op. 132. Lousadzak, Op. 48[a]. ***L. Harrison.*** Symphony No. 2, "Elegiac". [a]**Keith Jarrett** (pf); **American Composers Orchestra/Dennis Russell Davies.** MusicMasters 7021-2.

lh 7m DDD 5/93 

An exemplary, enterprising pairing. The American composers Alan Hovhaness and Lou Harrison have much in common: both are based on the musically unfashionable West Coast (Hovhaness in Seattle, Harrison in Santa Cruz); both have remained relative outsiders, untouched by contemporary fads; both share a passionate preoccupation with exotic musical cultures — Hovhaness with that of his ancestral Armenia, Harrison with the Indonesian gamelan tradition; and the chosen idioms of both tend to exude an overwhelming sense of meditative ecstasy which seems to be very much in vogue at the present time. Certainly, there's no denying the potent spell of much of the quasi-improvisatory piano writing in Hovhaness's *Lousadzak*; similarly, the trance-like string euphony which dominates the same composer's Second Symphony (*Mysterious mountain*) from 1955 is oddly compelling. Harrison's own Second Symphony (*Elegiac*) is perhaps the most substantial offering of the present trio, though: some three decades in gestation, this is an impressive, five-movement edifice finally completed in 1975 and bearing a dedication to the memory of Serge and Natalie Koussevitzky. Spiritual and serene, this is music of considerable resonance and power, and Harrison's wholly distinctive, often deliciously piquant sound-world draws the listener ineluctably in. Do try and hear this superbly performed and recorded release: given the current interest in the likes of Górecki, Pärt and Tavener, it could well, with proper exposure, become another contemporary cult classic.

Herbert Howells *British 1892-1983*

NEW REVIEW

Howells. Piano Concerto No. 2 in C minor[a]. Three Dances, Op. 7[b]. Concerto for Strings. [a]**Kathryn Stott** (pf); [b]**Malcolm Stewart** (vn); **Royal Liverpool Philharmonic Orchestra/Vernon Handley.** Hyperion CDA66610. Recorded 1991-92.

lh 9m DDD 3/93 

We are used to the old Herbert Howells, the elegiac rhapsodist, the honorary precentor of every cathedral choir in the land. The Second Piano Concerto is the young Howells, wildly exuberant, feverishly inventive, immensely likeable even when you half wish he'd calm down and lower his voice. There are fine tunes in abundance, orchestral writing that manages to be both rich and dazzling, and the calmly lyrical slow movement gives you just enough time to catch breath before Howells's finale catches you by the elbow and rushes you off your feet again. The *Three Dances* are even earlier, still more opulent of colour, but with a more restrained outpouring of gracious melody. In the splendid Concerto for Strings Howells has learned to pace himself more judiciously, to take his time and breathe deeper. It has a much greater range of emotion and incident than the earlier pieces; it also contains the first of his elegies, and one of the most poignant. He had intended the slow movement as a sober monument to Elgar, but the death of his young son turned it into a grief-stricken lament. For the rest of his life his music was affected by that bereavement; to have Howells's first reaction to it set alongside the carefree music of his joyously confident youth makes for a moving coupling as well as a valuable insight into an area of his music that until very recently was practically unknown. The performances are first class, the recording spaciously rich.

Howells. Requiem (1936)[a]. Take him, earth, for cherishing (1963).
Vaughan Williams. Mass in G minor (1922)[b]. Te Deum in G major (1928)[c]. [a]**Mary Seers** (sop); [ab]**Michael Chance** (alto); [ab]**Philip Salmon** (ten); [ab]**Jonathan Best** (bass); **Corydon Singers/Matthew Best** with [c]**Thomas Trotter** (org). Hyperion CDA66076. Texts included. From A66076 (8/83).

lh AAD 10/87

Vaughan Williams's unaccompanied Mass in G minor manages to combine the common manner of Elizabethan liturgical music with those elements of his own folk-music heritage that make his music so distinctive, and in so doing arrives at something quite individual and new. The work falls into five movements and its mood is one of heartfelt, if restrained, rejoicing. Herbert Howells wrote his unaccompanied Requiem in 1936, a year after the death of his only son. The work was not released in his lifetime but was reconstructed and published in 1980 from his manuscripts. It is a most hauntingly beautiful work of an obviously intensely personal nature. *Take him, earth, for cherishing* was composed to commemorate the assassination of President John F. Kennedy. The text is an English translation by Helen Waddell of Prudentius's fourth-century poem, *Hymnus circa Exsequias Defuncti*. Again it demonstrates the great strength of Howells's choral writing, with a clear outline and aptly affecting yet unimposing harmonic twists. The Corydon Singers give marvellous performances of these works and the sound is very fine indeed. An hour of the finest English choral music and not to be missed.

Additional recommendation ...
Requiem. A Sequence for St Michael. The House of the Mind. ***Vaughan Williams.*** *Prayer to the Father of Heaven. A Vision of Aeroplanes. Lord, Thou has been our Refuge.* **Finzi Singers/Paul Spicer** with **Harry Bickett** (org). Chandos CHAN9019 lh 7m DDD 5/92

Howells. SACRED CHORAL AND ORGAN WORKS. [a]**Christopher Dearnley** (org); **St Paul's Cathedral Choir, London/John Scott.** Hyperion CDA66260. Texts included. Recorded in 1987.
Collegium regale — canticles. Six Pieces for organ — No. 3, Master Tallis's Testament[a]. Like as the hart. Behold, O God our defender. Psalm-Preludes, Set 2 — No. 1, De profundis[a]. Take him, earth, for cherishing. St Paul's — canticles.

lh 2m DDD 9/88

This admirable disc is a fine tribute to the memory of Herbert Howells. The choir has used with enormous skill everything St Paul's Cathedral has to offer in the way of acoustical potential: space, resonance — even its echo — a lively response to timbre and volume; all of it justly timed and finally captured in a superb recording. The canticles for Morning Prayer (*Te Deum and Jubilate*) and those for Evensong (*Magnificat* and *Nunc Dimittis*) provide a framework for the organ pieces and the motets, all of them enhanced and enriched by the variety of sonorities obtainable as much from the building itself as from the music. Together, these works epitomize the life and death of this most English of English composers. The choice and planning of the programme is particularly skilful: each piece seems to lead to the next with total inevitability. Behind that lies a measure of expertise and professionalism one rarely encounters; but it passes almost unnoticed simply because the ear is totally satisfied and charmed.

NEW REVIEW
Howells. CHORAL WORKS.
Stevens. Mass for double choir. **Finzi Singers/Paul Spicer.** Chandos CHAN9021. Notes, texts and translations included. Recorded in 1991.

Mass in the Dorian Mode. Salve regina. O salutaris Hostia. Sweetest of sweets. Come, my soul. Let all the world in every corner sing. Nunc dimittis. Regina caeli.

1h 11m DDD 12/92

Both of these Masses are first recordings and fine performances worthy of the distinguished scores. Howells's Mass is surely a masterpiece. An early work dating from 1912, it is far more than an exercise in polyphonic writing: it is a creative act of love on the part of a young man whose soul had been touched by the beauty of the music he heard week after week in Westminster Cathedral, and who now offers the fruits of his devotion, first, to Sir Richard Terry, the man who as Master of the Music was responsible, and then to the whole tradition of church music as represented by the masters of polyphony in England and Italy. Looking at it for the Howells of later years, one may be thwarted (though there are characteristic touches); but the great achievement lies not in any direct expression of personality but in the dedicated work of craftsmanship and imagination. Bernard Stevens's Mass also deserves its preservation, which was primarily due to its discovery in manuscript by the composer's widow many years after its composition in 1939. Its most memorable movement is probably the *Benedictus*, "a series of interlocking duets" as the writer of the accompanying essay describes it. The Finzi Singers bring their finely trained corporate ear to these performances, adding to their already considerable list of highly valued recordings.

NEW REVIEW

Howells. Hymnus Paradisi[a]. An English Mass. [a]**Julie Kennard** (sop); [a]**John Mark Ainsley** (ten); **Royal Liverpool Philharmonic Choir and Orchestra/Vernon Handley.** Hyperion CDA66488. Texts included. Recorded in 1991.

1h 20m DDD 5/92 

It sometimes helps to know a little of the personal circumstances of a composition, and Howells's *Hymnus Paradisi* is a case in point. On first hearing, it is very possible to find its beauty rather too loosely structured: ecstatic but somewhat boneless. Repeated listenings reveal a much more purposeful score, but the discovery of this may be speeded by the knowledge that it was a hard-born work, arising out of the death of Howells's ten-year-old son from polio. He wrote so as to escape from "the crippling numbness of loss". It was 15 years before he felt able to think of making this private expression public, and he showed it to Vaughan Williams. Since its first performance in 1950, *Hymnus Paradisi* has become a favourite work in the choral repertoire but has only had a single recording before this one, in which it is given the alert, detailed kind of attention which repays both performers and listeners. The *English Mass*, written in 1955, is less well-known. A richly-scored work, though modest in its means, it has passages of blazing colour and also of a quietly contemplative mysticism. These are fine performances, with firm, imaginative direction by Vernon Handley. As in many modern recordings, the choir is a degree too recessed, yet the rich texture of both scores is made joyfully clear.

Pelham Humfrey

British 1647-1674

NEW REVIEW

Humfrey. VERSE ANTHEMS. **Donna Deam** (sop); **Drew Minter** (alto); **Rogers Covey-Crump, John Potter** (tens); **David Thomas** (bass); **Clare College Choir, Cambridge; Romanesca/Nicholas McGegan.** Harmonia Mundi HMU90 7053. Texts included. Recorded in 1992.

O give thanks unto the Lord. O Lord my God. Have mercy upon me, O God. By the waters of Babylon. Lift up your heads. Hear, O heav'ns. Hear my prayer, O God. Hear my crying, O God. Like as the hart.

1h 18m DDD 3/93 

Humfrey's cause should be easy to champion. He was arguably the only English composer before Purcell to master foreign styles with enough panache to make the English language truly affecting in Restoration church music. His control of 'modern' vocal idioms makes his confidently written anthems a welcome addition to the catalogue, especially in performances which are as persuasive as these. McGegan's singers and players approach this selection of around half of Humfrey's verse anthems with a sure instinct and empathy for the composer's sustained and stirring passions. So clearly etched are the solo performances that the listener is constantly reminded that his death at only 27 could have been a national catastrophe had Purcell not recovered the initiative of the English baroque. There are many striking works here but none so doleful and intense as *O Lord my God* with its pungent harmony and effortless sense of direction. If the solo singing matches Humfrey's expressive verse writing, this is enhanced by Romanesca's refined and deeply-felt string accompaniments. In the despairing *By the waters of Babylon,* the effect of McGegan's beautifully balanced forces reveals a composer of considerable dramatic skill. An important recording then of some very fine music, rewarded by committed performances.

Johann Hummel

Austrian 1778-1837

Hummel. Piano Concertos — A minor, Op. 85; B minor, Op. 89. **Stephen Hough** (pf); **English Chamber Orchestra/Bryden Thomson.** Chandos CHAN8507.

1h 6m DDD 4/87

This is a staggering disc of Hummel's piano concertos played by Stephen Hough. The most obvious comparison is with the piano concertos of Chopin, but whereas those works rely on the grace and panache of the piano line to redeem an often lacklustre orchestral role, the Hummel works have finely conceived orchestral writing and certainly no shortage of original ideas. The piano part is formidable, combining virtuosity of a very high order indeed with a vigour and athleticism that does much to redress Hummel's somewhat tarnished reputation. The A minor is probably the better known of the two works here, with a thrilling rondo finale, but the B minor is no less inventive with some breathtaking writing in the piano's upper registers. This disc makes strong demands to be heard: inventive and exciting music, a masterly contribution from Stephen Hough, fine orchestral support from the ever sympathetic ECO under Bryden Thomson and, last but not least, a magnificent Chandos recording.

Hummel. Piano Quintet in E flat major, Op. 87.
Schubert. Piano Quintet in A major, D667, "Trout". **Schubert Ensemble of London** (Jacqueline Shave, vn; Roger Tapping, va; Jane Salmon, vc; Peter Buckoke, db; William Howard, pf). Hyperion Helios CDH88010. Recorded in 1988.

1h 1m DDD 6/90

Both works here offer turn-of-the-century Viennese warmth and geniality in full measure, the centuries in question being of course the eighteenth and nineteenth, and Schubert being a native of Vienna while Hummel made his home there. They are also classical in structure, and the Hummel Quintet especially so, which is not surprising since he was a pupil of Mozart and Haydn and a musical conservative compared to Beethoven, with whom he formed a lasting relationship that nevertheless had its ups and downs. The scoring of his Quintet is unusual, with the four strings featuring a double bass instead of being the usual two violins, viola and cello, and evidently this work was known to Schubert when he composed his *Trout* Quintet for the same combination, although it also reflected the instruments played by the music-loving friends in a provincial town for whom it was written. It is this work, with its famous variation-form fourth movement on the theme of the song *Die Forelle*, which begins the programme, and the playing by the Schubert Ensemble of London is vivid yet affectionate, with a recording quality that is on the full side as regards piano tone but still pleasantly natural. They are no less agreeable stylistically in the Hummel, which is more theatrical in its gestures but makes no pretence of offering romantic self-expression or real profundity, and if the first movement seems on the fast side and a touch breathless, they could argue that its marking *Allegro e risoluto assai* justifies this.

NEW REVIEW

Hummel. String Quartets, Op. 30 — No. 1 in C major; No. 2 in G major; No. 3 in E flat major. **Delmé Quartet** (Galina Solodchin, John Trusler, vns; John Underwood, va; Jonathan Williams, vc). Hyperion CDA66568. Recorded in 1991.

1h 18m DDD 9/92

Like Mozart, Hummel was a child prodigy who played both the piano and violin, and he actually studied with Mozart and lived for a while in the Mozart household; however, his life was more prosperous (he died both famous and rich) and considerably longer than that of the greater genius who had been his teacher. His music sometimes suggests a kind of crossover style between Mozart and Beethoven, with the graceful and effortless craftsmanship that he learned from Mozart clothing ideas that belong to the early years of musical romanticism, and these three quartets show him at his very creditable best. The Delmé Quartet are one of Britain's finest quartets as well as among the longest established, and they show an understanding of this gently persuasive music that is apparent throughout the three works here, each of which is in four movements. They bring to the quicker music, as required, elements of drama, vigorous high spirits and wit, while in the gentler music of slow movements their thoughtful playing does full justice to Hummel's tasteful, if somewhat bland, invention. As long as one does not expect this music to offer the radiance and pathos of Mozart or the depth and eloquence of Beethoven, it is very satisfying and the performances are all that one could wish for. Here is music well worth exploring and well played, while the recording is faithful and well balanced.

Further listening ...

Piano Trios — E flat major, Op.12; F major, Op. 22; G major, Op. 35; G major, Op. 65; E major, Op. 83; E flat major, Op. 93; E flat major, Op. 96. **Parnassus Trio.** Dabringhaus und Grimm L3307/08 (2-disc set, reviewed 6/93).

Englebert Humperdinck

German 1854-1921

NEW REVIEW

Humperdinck. FAIRY-TALE MUSIC. **Bamberg Symphony Orchestra/Karl Anton Rickenbacher.** Virgin Classics VC7 59067-2. Recorded in 1990.
DER BLAUE VOGEL — Der Weinachtstraum; Sternenreigen. DORNROSCHEN — Vorspiel; Ballade; Irrfahrten; Dornenschloss; Festklänge. HANSEL UND GRETEL — Overture. KONIGSKINDER — Concert Overture; Hellafest und Kinderreigen; Verdorben-Gestorben ... Spielmanns letzter Gesang.

56m DDD 6/92

Richard Strauss, who conducted the first performance of *Hänsel und Gretel* in 1893, was full of praise for its "heart-warming humour" and "delightfully naïve musical idiom". And the photograph of Humperdinck in the disc's booklet pictures the most benevolent *grossvater* imaginable, with a twinkle in the eye that suggests he is probably the best bedtime story teller ever. Perhaps there is little in the later music quite as uplifting as the "Evening Prayer" from *Hänsel und Gretel*, but the "Minstrel's last song" from *Königskinder* runs it a close second, and concludes with wondrous strange chromatic writing for woodwind and transfiguring E flat major chords for strings; lumps in the throat or at least tingles down the spine are guaranteed. The remainder is catchy tunes and fairy-tale atmosphere from a master craftsman of the art. Rickenbacher seems keen to play down the Wagnerian element, and with generally lively tempos and his violins divided across the stage, his concerns would appear to be clarity of texture and modesty of gesture.

Humperdinck. HANSEL UND GRETEL. **Anne Sofie von Otter** (mez) Hänsel; **Barbara Bonney** (sop) Gretel; **Hanna Schwarz** (mez) Mother; **Andreas Schmidt** (bar) Father;

Barbara Hendricks (sop) Sandman; **Eva Lind** (sop) Dew Fairy; **Marjana Lipovšek** (contr) Witch; **Tölz Boys' Choir; Bavarian Radio Symphony Orchestra/Jeffrey Tate.** EMI CDS7 54022-2. Notes, text and translation included. Recorded in 1989.

② Ih 43m DDD II/90

Humperdinck's delightful and ever popular fairy-tale opera is presented here in an appealing, well paced and unsentimental performance, and though Tate brings out the Wagnerian influence of the work (Humperdinck was greatly admired by Wagner and was musical assistant in preparation for the first performance of *Parsifal*) it is never made to sound heavyweight or protracted. Indeed, Tate's tempos are generally faster than normal and these give the opera a persuasive sense of flow and direction. Though carefully avoiding over-sentimentality (especially in the "Evening Hymn" and "Dream Pantomime") Tate nevertheless brings a natural warmth and charm to the work both in his beautifully crafted phrasing and his subtle and sympathetic approach to the opera. The soloists are particularly well chosen. Anne Sofie von Otter and Barbara Bonney are especially fine in their fresh and youthful portrayal of the young children and Marjana Lipovšek's superb performance as the Witch (avoiding the often melodramatic and histrionic characterization found in other recordings) deserves special mention. The beautiful warm and spacious recording is exceptionally clear and is ideally balanced in terms of voices and orchestra. Destined to become a classic.

Additional recommendations ...

Soloists; Loughton High School for Girls and Bancroft's School Choirs; Philharmonia Orchestra/Herbert von Karajan. EMI mono CMS7 69293-2 — ② Ih 48m ADD 4/88 ▲

Soloists; Cologne Opera Children's Chorus; Cologne Gurzenich Orchestra/Sir John Pritchard. CBS Masterworks CD79217 — ② Ih 48m ADD II/88

Further listening ...

KONIGSKINDER. **Soloists; Tolz Boys' Choir; Bavarian Radio Chorus; Munich Radio Orchestra/Heinz Wallberg.** EMI Studio CMS7 69936-2 (8/89).

William Yeates Hurlstone

British 1876-1906

NEW REVIEW

Hurlstone. Variations on an original theme. The Magic Mirror Suite. Variations on a Hungarian air. **London Philharmonic Orchestra/Nicholas Braithwaite.** Lyrita SRCD208.

56m DDD 4/93

Lyrita have already put us in their debt by releasing a couple of LP compilations showcasing the precocious talents of William Hurlstone, the second of which (a coupling of the Piano Trio and superb Piano Quartet) was especially rewarding. Neither issue has yet to make it to CD, which makes this delightful new concert even more welcome. Anyone with a love of Elgar or Dvořák will go a bundle on the music here. Both sets of variations contain some gorgeous invention, though it's the later, more compact *Variations on a Hungarian air* from 1899 (at some ten minutes or so, half the duration of its supremely enjoyable, rather more garrulous companion) which show Hurlstone's formidable powers of thematic fertility and instrumental resource (Hurlstone's scoring is always impeccably lucid) at their most unassailable — a most exciting discovery, and a work worthy to stand alongside Parry's equally marvellous *Symphonic Variations* from the same period. Touching echoes of Elgar's *Wand of Youth* suites permeate the lovely incidental music to *The Magic Mirror* from 1900. The LPO under Nicholas Braithwaite are not quite at their incomparable best in this latter item, though elsewhere they respond with exemplary sheen and big-hearted enthusiasm to Hurlstone's grateful writing. Suffice to report, Lyrita's warm-toned engineering meets the impeccably high standards one has come to expect from this company over the years. All Anglophiles will want to try this.

Jacques Ibert

French 1890-1962

NEW REVIEW

Ibert. Divertissement.
Milhaud. Le boeuf sur le toit, Op. 58. La création du monde, Op. 81.
Poulenc. Les biches — Suite. **Ulster Orchestra/Yan Pascal Tortelier.** Chandos CHAN9023. Recorded in 1991.

lh 8m DDD 9/92

Here is 1920s French music directed by a conductor who is completely in the spirit of it, and plenty of spirit there is, too. Except for Ibert's *Divertissement*, this is ballet music, and that work too originated in the theatre as incidental music for Eugène Labiche's farce *The Italian Straw Hat*. Poulenc's suite from *Les biches*, written for Diaghilev's ballet company and first heard in Monte Carlo, is unfailingly fresh and bouncy and stylishly played here although Chandos's warm recording, good though it is, takes some edge off the trumpet tone; the genial nature of it all makes us forget that it is a unique mix of eighteenth-century *galanterie*, Tchaikovskian lilt and Poulenc's own inimitable street-Parisian sophistication and charm. As for Ibert's piece, this is uproariously funny in an unbuttoned way, and the gorgeously vulgar trombone in the Waltz and frantic police whistle in the finale are calculated to make you laugh out loud. Milhaud's *Le boeuf sur le toit* also has Parisian chic and was originally a kind of music-hall piece, composed to a scenario by Cocteau. It was while attending a performance of it in London in 1920 that the composer first heard the American jazz orchestra that, together with a later experience of new Orleans jazzmen playing "from the darkest corners of the Negro soul" (as he later expressed it) that prompted him to compose his masterly ballet, *La création du monde*, in which a deep-rooted African voice seems to speak through western instruments. Tortelier and his orchestra understand this strangely powerful music no less than the other pieces. This is a most desirable disc.

Additional recommendation ...

Divertissement. **Ravel.** *Le tombeau de Couperin.* **Debussy.** *Danse sacrée et danse profane*[a]. **Fauré.** *Dolly Suite, Op. 56.* [a]**Osian Ellis** (hp); **Academy of St Martin in the Fields/Sir Neville Marriner.** ASV CDDCA517 — lh ADD 2/85

Further listening ...

Film Suites — Macbeth; Golgotha[b]. Don Quichotte — Chanson de Sancho[a]. Chanson de Don Quichotte[a]. [a]**Henry Kiichli** (bass); [b]**Jacques Tchamkerten** (ondes martenot); **Bratislava Radio Symphony Orchestra/Adriano.** Marco Polo 8 223287 (3/91).

Sigismondo d'India

Italian c.1582-1629

Suggested listening ...

Il Terzo Libro de Madrigali a cinque voci. **Consort of Musicke/Anthony Rooley.** Deutsche Harmonia Mundi RD77119 (11/88).

Le musiche I-V — excerpts. **Nigel Rogers** (ten); **Paul O'Dette** (chitarrone); **Andrew Lawrence-King** (hp, hpd, org). Virgin Classics Veritas VC7 59231-2 (4/93).

Vincent d'Indy

French 1851-1931

d'Indy. Symphonie sur un chant montagnard français in G major, Op. 25[c].
Berlioz. BEATRICE ET BENEDICT – Overture[a].

Franck. Symphony in D minor[b].
[c]**Nicole Henriot-Schweitzer** (pf); [ac]**Boston Symphony Orchestra/Charles Munch;** [b]**Chicago Symphony Orchestra/ Pierre Monteux.** RCA Victor Papillon GD86805. Item marked [a] from SB2125 (10/61), [b] SB6631 (10/65), [c] SB2053 (1/60).

lh 12m ADD 3/89

This exceptionally well-filled disc links three French favourites. Munch directs a fine performance of the Berlioz overture, one which truly relishes the long-breathed string writing. The Boston orchestra play superbly. A similar freshness and idiomatic flair is brought to the rarely heard but delightful d'Indy work, in essence a piano concerto of rhapsodic exuberance. Munch conducts with a great deal of vigour and Gallic verve, and orchestra and soloist join in with high spirits and evident pleasure. The piano tone in this 1958 recording is a trifle clangy but not disagreeably so. Pierre Monteux, surely one of the great conductors of the century, reminds us in his fine reading of the Franck Symphony, that he was quite as adept at controlling the long line and regal architecture of a work that has closer ties to the German symphonic tradition than is sometimes granted, as he was as an equalled colourist in the great French tradition. His performance is never lugubrious but has an appropriate weight and scale whilst always being alive to the work's ardent moments. The 1961 recording still sounds remarkably well for its age.

NEW REVIEW

d'Indy. Symphonie sur un chant montagnard français [a]. Symphony No. 2 in B flat major, Op. 57[b]. [a]**Aldo Ciccolini** (pf); [a]**Paris Orchestra/Serge Baudo;** [b]**Toulouse Capitole Orchestra/Michel Plasson.** EMI CDM7 63952-2. Item marked [a] from ASD3480 (4/78), recorded in 1975 [b] Pathé 2C 069 73100 (1/83), recorded in 1981.

lh llm ADD 3/92

Though still a comparative rarity in the concert-hall, Vincent d'Indy's lovely *Symphony on a French mountain air* has fared well on CD in recent years. Ciccolini and Baudo's partnership from the late 1970s is a sympathetic and stylish one, if no real match either technically or artistically for the wonderfully evocative (and ravishingly well-engineered) Thibaudet/Dutoit account on full-price Decca, coupled with Dutoit's similarly super-refined conception of the Franck Symphony (refer to the Index to Reviews). But the real interest on this mid-price "L'Esprit Français" CD from French EMI comes in the shape of the impressive Second Symphony, a most substantial offering dating from 1903. Conceived along the cyclical lines so beloved of his mentor César Franck, this richly eventful, yet tightly organized 45 minute essay bears an epic countenance to which lovers of, say, the Chausson or Dukas symphonies will readily respond. Michel Plasson conducts with evident conviction, and his Toulouse band, whilst not the last word in richly upholstered tone or orchestral virtuosity, performs with the necessary keen-eyed vigour. The recording, too, is a little pale and cloudy, but these *caveats* should certainly not deter anyone from investigating some fine, thoughtful music.

Further listening ...

String Quartets — No. 1 in D major, Op. 35; No. 2 in E major, Op. 45. **Kodály Quartet.** Marco Polo 8 223140 (10/91).

John Ireland

British 1879-1962

NEW REVIEW

Ireland. Piano Concerto.
Bridge. Phantasm.

Walton. Sinfonia concertante (original version). **Kathryn Stott** (pf); **Royal Philharmonic Orchestra/Vernon Handley.** Conifer CDCF175. Recorded in 1989.

1h 10m DDD 1/90

An excitingly enterprising release, containing three of the very finest British works for piano and orchestra in unimpeachably eloquent interpretations. John Ireland's gorgeous Piano Concerto of 1930 has always remained a favourite — rightly so, considering its glorious fecundity of invention and supremely touching slow movement in particular (ravishingly delivered here, by the way). But how many people will be familiar with another British *concertante* masterpiece from the early 1930s, namely the extraordinary *Phantasm* of Frank Bridge? This nightmarish, darkly introspective vision offers further proof of this underrated figure's genuine stature; certainly, its level of feverish, driven inspiration has few rivals in British music, save perhaps, Sir Arnold Bax's near-contemporaneous *Winter Legends* (also for piano and orchestra). Conifer also give us the opportunity to hear Sir William Walton's colourful *Sinfonia concertante* in its original form — and quite a revelation it proves to be! The fuller orchestration makes a tremendous impact, as does the far more glitteringly assertive piano part (especially in a performance as good as this one). Indeed, Kathryn Stott has committed nothing finer to disc, and her dazzlingly intrepid yet outstandingly sensitive assumption of these three technically demanding and stylistically diverse offerings must be accounted a veritable *tour de force*. What's more, Vernon Handley and an inspired RPO provide absolutely magnificent support, whilst the recording can best be described as stunningly natural. A superb triptych.

Additional recommendation ...

Piano Concerto. Legend. Mai-Dun. **Eric Parkin** (pf); **London Philharmonic Orchestra/Bryden Thomson.** Chandos CHAN8461 — 53m DDD 1/87

NEW REVIEW

Ireland. ORCHESTRAL WORKS. **London Symphony Orchestra/Richard Hickox.** Chandos CHAN8994. Recorded 1990-91.

Scherzo and Cortège (arr. G. Bush). Tritons — symphonic prelude. The Forgotten Rite — Prelude. Satyricon — Overture. The Overlanders — suite from the film (arr. Mackerras).

1h 2m DDD 2/92

Ireland's fluent and approachable orchestral style found its voice in two quite distinct areas, both of which are represented in this recording. The evocative musical imagery of the symphonic prelude *Tritons* typifies Ireland's descriptive essence, sharing the same impressionistic influence of Debussy and Ravel with the *Forgotten Rite* Prelude. Described by the composer as "an evocation of the mystical and occult forces of nature", this is possibly the finest of Ireland's large-scale compositions, and it is splendidly realized here. The concert overture *Satyricon*, Ireland's final orchestral work, juxtaposes brilliant and vigorous material with a reflective central clarinet discourse. These expansive canvases are framed by characteristic examples of Ireland's radio and film scores. Geoffrey Bush, a former student of the composer, has arranged the *Scherzo and Cortège* from surviving sketches for incidental music written for a 1942 BBC production of *Julius Caesar*. The suite from the 1946 Ealing Studios film *The Overlanders* was compiled by Sir Charles Mackerras from original orchestrations by Ernest Irving. This colourful suite is utilitarian, reflecting the obvious needs of the production, but the music is of high quality. Richard Hickox secures forthright and dedicated playing from the LSO, in a rich and characteristically reverberant Chandos recording. As an introduction to John Ireland's orchestral works, this disc can be strongly recommended to all devotees of British music.

NEW REVIEW

Ireland. Cello Sonata in G minor[a].

Bridge. Elegy, H47[a]. Scherzetto, H19[b].

Stanford. Cello Sonata No. 2 in D minor, Op. 39[b]. **Julian Lloyd Webber** (vc); **John**

McCabe (pf). ASV CDDCA807. Items marked [a] from ACA1001 (5/81), recorded in 1979, [b] recorded in 1992.

56m ADD/DDD 2/93

Ireland's Cello Sonata shows the composer in a typically ruminative mood. A feeling of nostalgia pervades the slow movement, the first movement is a restless, disturbed essay, and the vigorous finale shows moments of anger within a prevailing atmosphere of regret and despair. From the early days of his career Julian Lloyd Webber has been a distinguished exponent of this work, and his performance here, with McCabe in full sympathy, leaves absolutely nothing to be desired — every aspect of the Sonata is vividly brought to life. Stanford was always a highly skilled and fluent composer, but he often lacked real inspiration, as is the case here in a work which still, however offers considerable rewards for the listener. The shadow of Brahms hovers strongly over the Sonata, particularly in the way the piano part is laid out, but a lack of individuality is compensated for by vigour and high craftsmanship. Lloyd Webber and McCabe play the work very strongly and with great flair, and it is difficult to think that it could ever receive better advocacy. The two little Bridge pieces give much pleasure, and though the recordings come from sessions which took place 12 years apart there is a consistency both in the nature of the sound and in its high quality.

NEW REVIEW

Ireland. PIANO WORKS, Volume 1. **Eric Parkin.** Chandos CHAN9056. Recorded in 1991. Decorations. The Almond Tree. Four Preludes. Rhapsody. The Towing-Path. Merry Andrew. Summer Evening. Piano Sonata in E minor.

1h 12m DDD 8/92 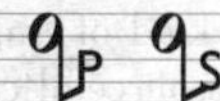

Chandos have laboured mightily in recent years to develop a wider audience for the music of John Ireland. While his orchestral works continue to grow in popularity, Ireland's piano music is now the subject of an ongoing Chandos project featuring the pianist Eric Parkin. This first instalment offers playing of rare insight and compulsion, especially in Parkin's account of the Sonata in E minor which the composer completed in 1920. This challenging work has its share of taxing obstacles (notably in a finale of quasi-orchestral proportions!), but Parkin senses its mystical and spiritual affiliations too, in his fine performance. Ireland's *Rhapsody* of 1915 is the other major work here; the playing is again deeply perceptive, and technically superb. The selection of miniatures are undemanding, yet erudite, essays often clearly rooted in English folk-song. *Summer Evening, The Towing-Path* and *Merry Andrew* find the composer in surprisingly relaxed mood, whilst the impressionistic and improvisatory tendencies of Ireland's piano writing are emphasized in his *Decorations* and *Four Preludes*. Parkin's performances are splendid, and have that sense of vitality and discovery which this unfamiliar music certainly needs. The recorded sound, too, is of the highest quality, and this release is certainly well worth its purchase price.

Heinrich Isaac

Flanders c.1450-1517

Suggested listening ...

Missa de Apostolis a 6. Optime pastor. Regina caeli laetare. Resurexi et adhuc tecum sum. Tota pulchra es. Virgo prudentissima a 6. **The Tallis Scholars/Peter Phillips.** Gimell CDGIM023 (10/91).

Charles Ives

American 1874-1954

Ives. ORCHESTRAL WORKS. **New York Philharmonic Orchestra/Leonard Bernstein.** DG 429 220-2GH. Recorded 1987-88.

Symphony No. 2. The Gong on the Hook and Ladder. Tone Roads — No. 1. A set of 3 Short Pieces — Largo cantabile, Hymn. Hallowe'en. Central Park in the Dark. The Unanswered Question.

1h 8m DDD 8/90

Although Bernstein thought of Ives as a primitive composer, these recordings reveal that he had an undeniably deep affinity for, and understanding of, Ives's music. The Second Symphony (written in 1902 and first performed in 1951) is a gloriously beautiful work, still strongly rooted in the nineteenth century yet showing those clear signs of Ives's individual voice that are largely missing from the charming but lightweight First Symphony. Bernstein brings out all its richness and warmth without wallowing in its romantic elements, and he handles with utter conviction the multi-textures and the allusions to popular tunes and snatches from Bach, Brahms and Dvořák, to name but a few. The standard of playing he exacts from the NYPO, both here and in the disc's series of technically demanding shorter pieces, is remarkably high with the depth of string tone at a premium — and the engineers retain this to a degree unusual in a live recording. Altogether an essential disc for any collection.

Ives. A Symphony: New England Holidays[b]. The Unanswered Question (orig. and rev. versions)[a]. Central Park in the Dark. [a]**Adolph Herseth** (tpt); **Chicago Symphony** [b]**Chorus and Orchestra/Michael Tilson Thomas.** CBS Masterworks CD42381.

1h 3m DDD 10/88

The essential Charles Ives is here and Tilson Thomas proves a most engrossing guide. *Holidays* is a kind of American *Four Seasons* — one tone-poem per National holiday; each a wonderfully resourceful canvas from the ultimate 'American' composer. There can be no mistaking Tilson Thomas's profound affection for these scores: not least the simple home-spun honesty of the quieter reflective paragraphs — sepia memories of times past. The nostalgic winterscape of "Washington's Birthday" is most beautifully realized. So too are the opening pages of "Decoration Day", as the townsfolk of Danbury, Connecticut, gather for their annual procession to the Civil War veterans' graves. As for those rowdy Ivesian collages, the cacophonous *mêlées* of "Washington's Birthday" and, more notoriously, "The Fourth of July", Tilson Thomas and his CBS engineers have worked wonders with their keen ears and some ingenious sleight of hand at the mixing console. You'll catch more of the 'tunes' than you might have thought possible: internal clarity is most impressive, the tonal depth of the recording likewise. So don't be surprised that the Jew's harp more than holds its own during the demented "barn dance" sequence of "Washington's Birthday"! No less impressive is the conductor's concentrated way with the two remaining pieces — classics of their kind.

Ives. Symphonies — Nos. 1 and 4 (including original hymn settings). **Chicago Symphony Orchestra/Michael Tilson Thomas.** Sony Classical SK44939.

1h 17m DDD 2/91

It could be worth asking a musical friend to listen to the start of Ives's First Symphony here and (presuming he or she doesn't already know the work) then to identify the composer. It seems almost impossible that anyone would get the answer right, for this tuneful, vigorous music hardly suggests the wild-eyed 'ornery crittur' and iconoclast represented to many listeners by much of Ives's later music; Dvořák, Mahler and Nielsen all flash through the mind, which is significant because all three drew their deepest inspiration from folk music, as did Ives himself. The explanation is that this is an early work written in 1898 as an exercise for music graduation at Yale; but make no mistake, it shows that this composer in his twenties knew a good deal about symphonic writing and (as the slow second movement, complete with Dvořákian cor anglais, demonstrates) about writing melodies as well. The Fourth Symphony with all its wild and wilful complexities is another matter, for the good tunes (which are sometimes those of hymns and Gospel songs) are interwoven with astonishing boldness into a score of daunting individuality and complexity. This disc also includes some of these hymn tunes in their original form with voices with one, however, *Beulah Land*, being an organ solo played on a modern instrument that sounds splendidly authentic. The conductor Michael Tilson Thomas has a proven affinity with Ives's music, and these authoritative performances have a touching strength, while the recording too does justice to some of the most challenging music ever to come out of America.

Additional recommendation ...
No. 4. **John Alldis Choir; London Philharmonic Orchestra/José Serebrier.** Chandos CHAN8397 — 33m ADD 1/86

Ives. Piano Sonata No. 2, "Concord, Mass., 1840-60".
M. Wright. Piano Sonata (1982). **Marc-André Hamelin** (pf). New World NW378-2. Recorded 1987-88.

58m DDD 9/89

From time to time composers dream of a totally free music, transcending traditional modes of thought, floating on waves of pure untrammelled inspiration. Charles Ives, who seems to have anticipated most European developments by decades, made the dream a remarkable reality. Based on a trial-and-error approach to harmony, notated largely without bar-lines and structured only by the dictates of Ives's inner vision, the *Concord* Sonata attempts to convey the essence of writers associated with the town of Concord, Massachusetts. The music covers a colossal range of mood, from the intrepid philosophical journeys of "Emerson", to the kaleidoscopic variety of "Hawthorne", the homeliness of "the Alcotts" and finally the inner expanses of "Thoreau". Comparison with Beethoven's *Hammerklavier* may seem imprudent, but there is no clearer precedent in the piano repertoire for such a combination of visionary and technical demands. The Canadian pianist, Marc-André Hamelin, is one of the chosen few who can measure up to both aspects and Maurice Wright's Sonata is a by no means negligible fill-up. Both works are excellently recorded. A disc mainly for the adventurous, but the potential rewards of this particular adventure are immense.

Ives. SONGS, Volume 1. **Henry Herford** (bar); **Robin Bowman** (pf). Unicorn-Kanchana DKPCD9111. Texts included. Recorded in 1990.
Ann Street. Berceuse. The Children's Hour. The Circus Band. General William Booth Enters into Heaven. The Housatonic at Stockbridge. Immortality. In Flanders Fields. The Indians. In the Mornin'. Memories, A, Very Pleasant, B, Rather Sad. The New River. Paracelsus. Peaks. Pictures. The See'r. The Side-show. Swimmers. There is a certain garden. They are there! The Things our Fathers Loved. Tom Sails Away. Two Little Flowers. West London. Where the Eagle. The White Gulls. Yellow Leaves.

1h DDD 9/91

For many, the name Charles Ives is synonymous with three things — Ives the innovator and experimentalist, Ives the symphonist and Ives the composer of the kind of fiendishly difficult piano music found in the *Protests* and *Concord* Sonatas. But he was a great miniaturist also, and this is nowhere more evident than in his prolific outpourings of songs. Ives wrote songs like others keep diaries, jotting down ideas as and when they came to him — the inspiration could be great or small, domestic or global but it was always delivered with a considerable amount of care and insight for its subject matter. He also used his songs as sketchbooks for his exploratory techniques, and so one frequently encounters material found in his piano and orchestral works, as is the case in the song *The Housatonic at Stockbridge* which was later to become the third movement (minus voice) of his orchestral work *Three Places in New England*. Subject matters range from meditations and reflections on nature *(Pictures, Yellow Leaves, The White Gulls),* through to the plight of the American Indians and even some comical observations on the expectant buzz of anticipation as an audience awaits curtain rise in the opera house *(Memories A* and *B).* Excellent performances from Henry Herford and Robin Bowman, who have made American vocal music (especially Ives) a particular speciality. Good recording.

Further listening ...

Symphony No. 3, "The camp meeting". Second Orchestral Set. **Royal Concertgebouw Chorus and Orchestra/Michael Tilson Thomas.** CBS Masterworks CDCD46440.

Leos Janáček

Czechoslovakian 1854-1928

Janáček. Sinfonietta, Op. 60[a]. Taras Bulba — rhapsody for orchestra[a]. ***Shostakovich.*** The Age of Gold — suite, Op. 22*a*[b]. [a]**Vienna Philharmonic Orchestra/Sir Charles Mackerras; [b]London Philharmonic Orchestra/Bernard Haitink.** Decca Ovation 430 727-2DM. Item marked [a] from 410 138-2DH (11/83), recorded in 1980, [b] D213D2 (11/80), recorded in 1979.

lh 6m DDD 12/91 £9s

The Janáček items have long been a favourite coupling and in these thoroughly idiomatic performances the effect is spectacular. Of course these are far more than just orchestral showpieces. Both works were fired by patriotic fervour — *Taras Bulba* by Czechoslovakia's struggle towards independence, the *Sinfonietta* by the city of Brno, the composer's adopted home town. Both works display a deep-seated passion for the basic elements of music and yield unprecedented levels of excitement. To get the most out of *Taras Bulba* you really need all its gory programmatic details (of battles, betrayal, torture and murder) to hand. The *Sinfonietta* needs no such props; its impact is as irresistible and physically direct as a massive adrenalin injection. If the listener is to revel in this music a corresponding sense of abandon in the playing is even more important than precision. The Vienna Philharmonic supplies a good measure of both and Sir Charles Mackerras's commitment and understanding are second to none, while the high-level recording captures every detail in vivid close-up. Bernard Haitink's highly disciplined if somewhat straitlaced LPO account of Shostakovich's *Age of Gold* suite is the coupling.

Janáček. String Quartets[a] — No. 1, "Kreutzer Sonata"; No. 2, "Intimate Letters". Along an overgrown path — Suite No. 1[b]. [b]**Radoslav Kvapil** (pf); [a]**Talich Quartet** (Petr Messiereur, Jan Kvapil, vns; Jan Talich, va; Evzen Rattai, vc). Calliope CAL9699. Items marked [a] from CAL1699 (1/86), [b] CAL9206 (8/88).

lh 13m DDD 4/89

Janáček's two string quartets stand with those of Bartók, Debussy and Ravel among the supreme masterpieces of the medium, composed during the first half of this century. Both are relatively late works: the *Kreutzer* Sonata dates from 1923 and was inspired by Tolstoy's tragic short story of the same title, depicting a women's disappointment in love both inside and outside marriage. Janáček translates the emotions of Tolstoy's story into music of intense passion. Even more immediate and personal is the Second Quartet entitled *Intimate Letters*, inspired by Janáček's infatuation at the age of 64 for his young pupil Kamila Slösslova. He poured into this quartet all his feelings for her: doubt, release, joy and despair are all graphically portrayed in Janáček's eliptical music. Inference and statement paradoxically give the quartet a wholeness which eludes other more forthright works. The Talich Quartet portray these two similar psycho-dramas with total commitment and devotion. The immense technical difficulties with which Janáček confronts his performers are set aside by the white heat of emotion clearly felt both by performers and composer. The insight of these readings fortunately even overcomes a recording perhaps too dry for Janáček's highly exposed string writing. As a bonus, Radoslav Kvapil gives an idiomatic reading of the first suite from *Along an overgrown path*, written between 1901 and 1908, and marked by the death of his daughter Olga in 1903. These short piano pieces display in embryo many of the stylistic features which were later to reappear in the two quartets. Again the performance is wholly authentic and committed, allowing Janáček's exceptional creativity to shine through without compromise. Again a rather dry recording.

Additional recommendation ...
Quartets[a]. *Along an overgrown path*[b]. [a]**Talich Quartet; [b]Radoslav Kvapil** (pf). Calliope CAL9699 — lh 13m DDD 4/89

Janáček. PIANO WORKS. **Rudolf Firkušnyý.** DG 20th Century Classics 429 857-2GC. From 2707 055 (6/72). Recorded in 1971.

Piano Sonata 1.X.1905, "From the street". Along an overgrown path. In the mists. Thema con variazioni, "Zdenka".

lh 19m ADD 3/91

Janáček's only piano sonata has a history almost as dramatic as the events which inspired it. Its subtitle, *From the Street* commemorates a student demonstration in which a 20-year-old worker was killed, an event which so outraged Janáček that he wrote a three movement sonata as an expression of his feelings. Before the première in 1906 he burnt the third movement and after a private performance in Prague he threw the remaining movements into a river. It is only thanks to the pianist, Ludmil Tučkova, who had copied out the first two movements, that the work survives. The underlying theme of Firkušný's approach to this work (who may claim historical authenticity as he studied with Janáček) is anger, turning the first movement into a defiant roar of fury whilst the slow movement has an inherent restlessness, bitterness never far below the surface. Much of the same characteristics can be found in the other works — *Along an overgrown path* and the masterly *In the mists* although he occasionally overloads these delicate little pieces with dramatic power. The early Theme and Variations are conventionally romantic but impeccably played. This disc represents playing of the highest class with full notes and tracking details.

Additional recommendations ...

Piano Sonata. Along an overgrown path — Suite No. 1. In the mists. **Josef Páleníček** (pf). Supraphon 10 1481-2 — 54m ADD 3/92

Piano Sonata. Along an overgrown path. In the mists. Reminiscence. Three Moravian Dances. **Mikhail Rudy.** EMI CDC7 54094-2 — lh 19m DDD 3/91

Key to Symbols

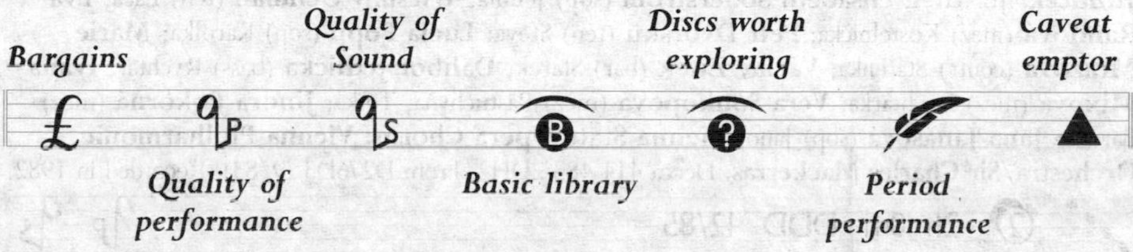

Janáček. The diary of one who disappeared[a]. String Quartet No. 1, "Kreutzer Sonata"[b]. [a]**Clara Wirz** (mez); [a]**Peter Keller** (ten); [a]**Lucerne Singers/Mario Venzago** (pf); [b]**Doležal Quartet** (Bohuslav Matousek, Josef Kekula, vns; Karel Doležal, va; Vladimir Leixner, vc). Accord 22031-2. Item marked [a] recorded in 1979, [b] 1984.

57m AAD 4/90

Both of these works reflect Janáček's innocently ecstatic love for a woman very much younger than himself, but both are also multi-layered. In the quartet the ostensible subject is Tolstoy's novella about a guilty and ultimately fatal love affair, but Janáček also described the piece as a protest against the subjection of women. The *Diary* is fascinatingly ambiguous, too: the poems on which it is based were published as the work of an unlettered peasant, all that he had left behind after abandoning home, family and friends to follow an alluring gipsy girl. There have been suggestions that the supposed authorship of the poems was a hoax, but their very mysterious anonymity makes it possible to hear the cycle both as a gripping drama and as a dream-like metaphor. That dual quality is finely conveyed in this performance of the *Diary* by a combination of directness (the dusky-voiced and intimately insinuating Clara Wirz is the gipsy Zefka to the life; the 'wordless song' at the centre of the cycle — the original poem consisted of nothing more than three suggestive asterisks — is vividly climactic) and mysterious poetry: the off-stage women's chorus both magical and real. Peter Keller has a light but ardent voice, well-suited to conveying the young man's wonder at what is happening to him and his diction is praiseworthily clear (a pity that only French translations of the Czech texts are provided). The quartet, alas, though performed with impetuous urgency and passion, receives a dry, harsh and nasal recording. But this account of the *Diary* will be a recurring pleasure.

NEW REVIEW

Janáček. Sinfonietta, Op. 60[a]. Glagolitic Mass[b]. [b]**Felicity Palmer** (sop); [b]**Ameral Gunson** (mez); [b]**John Mitchinson** (ten); [b]**Malcolm King** (bass); [b]**Jane Parker-Smith** (org); [a]**Philharmonia Orchestra;** [b]**City of Birmingham Chorus and Orchestra/Simon Rattle.** EMI CDC7 47504-2. Text and translation included. Item marked [a] from ASD143522-1 (10/83), recorded in 1982, [b] ASD4066 (5/82), recorded in 1981.

1h 2m DDD 10/88

"I am not an old man, and I am not a believer — until I see for myself." Thus Janáček replied angrily to a critic after the première of his *Glagolitic* Mass. This is a gritty, masterful performance of a jagged, uncomfortable masterpiece. Its unusual title stems from the script of the ancient Slavonic text (Glagol) which Janáček set to music. The recent deletion of two classic recordings — by Mackerras and Ančerl on Supraphon leaves Simon Rattle's version as the clear front runner. It is a full-blooded, urgent view of the work, with particularly fine solo contributions from Felicity Palmer and John Mitchinson. That the language is an unfamiliar one is occasionally evident in the chorus, though they, like the orchestra, give totally committed performances under the inspired leadership of Rattle. Also included on this disc is the *Sinfonietta* (originally entitled "Military Sinfonietta", reflecting in the brass-heavy scoring of the work). It is as much a study in orchestration as form with the melody of the fourth movement appearing unaltered no less than 14 times, changed only in orchestral colour. It is brilliantly played here, with the 12 trumpets coming up gleaming in the final climax. An enticing proposition!

Janáček. JENUFA. **Elisabeth Söderström** (sop) Jenůfa; **Wieslaw Ochman** (ten) Laca; **Eva Randová** (mez) Kostelnička; **Petr Dvorskü** (ten) Steva; **Lucia Popp** (sop) Karolka; **Marie Mrazová** (contr) Stařenka; **Václav Zitek** (bar) Stárek; **Dalibor Jedlička** (bass) Rychtar; **Ivana Mixová** (mez) Rychtarka; **Vera Soukopová** (mez) Pastuchyňa, Tetka; **Jindra Pokorná** (mez) Barena; **Jana Janasová** (sop) Jano; **Vienna State Opera Chorus; Vienna Philharmonic Orchestra/Sir Charles Mackerras.** Decca 414 483-2DH2. From D276D3 (9/83). Recorded in 1982.

2 2h 10m DDD 12/85 

Janáček's first operatic masterpiece is a towering work which blends searing intensity with heart-stopping lyricism. It tells of Jenůfa and the appalling treatment she receives as she is caught between the man she loves and one who eventually comes to love her. But dominating the story is the Kostelnička, a figure of huge strength, pride and inner resource who rules Jenůfa's life and ultimately kills her baby. Eva Randová's characterization of the role of the Kostelnička is frightening in its intensity but also has a very human core. The two men are well cast and act as fine foils to Elisabeth Söderström's deeply impressive Jenůfa. The Vienna Philharmonic play beautifully and Mackerras directs magnificently. The recording is all one could wish for and the booklet is a mine of informed scholarship.

NEW REVIEW

Janáček. KATA KABANOVA[a]. Capriccio[b]. Concertino[b]. **Elisabeth Söderström** (sop) Kátá; **Petr Dvorský** (ten) Boris; **Naděžda Kniplová** (contr) Kabanicha; **Vladimír Krejčík** (ten) Tichon; **Libuše Márová** (mez) Varvara; **Dalibor Jedlička** (bass) Dikoj; **Zdeněk Svehla** (ten) Kudrjáš; **Jaroslav Souček** (bar) Kuligin; **Jitka Pavlová** (sop) Glaša; **Gertrude Jahn** (mez) Fekluša; **Vienna State Opera Chorus; Vienna Philharmonic Orchestra/Sir Charles Mackerras.** [b]**Paul Crossley** (pf); [b]**London Sinfonietta/David Atherton.** Decca 421 852-2DH2. Notes, text and translation included. Item marked [a] from D51D2 (10/77), recorded in 1976, [b] D223D5 (4/81), recorded in 1978.

2 2h 20m ADD 10/89 

With *Kátá Kabanová* in 1919, Janáček embarked on the four operatic masterpieces that would occupy him for the remaining nine years of his life, and Decca in 1976 on their now classic series of Janáček opera recordings with Sir Charles Mackerras. Unlike the other three late operas, *Kátá Kabanová*'s story *is* one you would expect to see on the opera stage: Kátá, a free spirit, is imprisoned by marriage into, and domicile with, a family in a provincial Russian town on the Volga. The family is manipulated by her mother-in-law, a widow whose sole, obsessive concern is her status (familial and social). The only son (Kátá's husband) is understandably spineless, and Kátá looks for escape in love. She finds the love, but true escape only in suicide. Janáček focuses on his heroine, giving her at least two of the most moving scenes in opera: the first where, to music of shimmering, seraphic beauty she describes her childhood imagination given free rein by pillars of sunlight streaming through the dome in church; and the second in the last scene where, after her confession of adultery, she concludes that "not even God's own sunlight" gives her pleasure any more. Söderström has the intelligence and a voice which guarantees *total* credibility (how often can you claim that of an operatic portrayal?); and of the superb all-Czech supporting cast one might only have wished for a slightly younger-sounding sister-in-law. Mackerras persuades from the Vienna Philharmonic their very finest ensemble and tone; and Decca, true to their best operatic traditions, reproduce the whole with clarity, atmosphere, ideal perspectives and discernible stage movement — only a detectable levelling of the score's few extreme *fortissimos* points to the recording's vintage. Decca add the late chamber concertos, both excellently performed and engineered, and equally essential Janáček.

Janáček. THE CUNNING LITTLE VIXEN. The Cunning Little Vixen — orchestral suite (arr. V. Talich)[a]. **Lucia Popp** (sop) Vixen, Young vixen; **Dalibor Jedlička** (bass) Forester; **Eva Randová** (mez) Fox; **Eva Zikmundová** (mez) Forester's wife, Owl; **Vladimir Krejčik** (ten) Schoolmaster, Gnat; **Richard Novák** (ten) Priest, Badger **Václav Zítek** (bar) Harašta; **Beno Blachut** (ten) Pásek; **Ivana Mixová** (mez) Pásek's wife, Woodpecker, Hen; **Libuše Marová** (contr) Dog; **Gertrude Jahn** (mez) Cock, Jay; **Eva Hríbiková** (sop) Frantik; **Zuzana Hudecová** (sop) Pepik; **Peter Saray** (treb) Frog, Grasshopper; **Miriam Ondrášková** (sop) Cricket; **Vienna State Opera Chorus; Bratislava Children's Choir; Vienna Philharmonic Orchestra/Sir Charles Mackerras.** Decca 417 129-2DH2. Notes, text and translation included. From D257D2 (5/82). Item marked [a] new to UK. Recorded in 1981.

② lh 49m DDD 11/86 P S

Janáček used the most unlikely material for his operas. For *The Cunning Little Vixen* his source was a newspaper series of drawings, with accompanying text, about the adventures of a vixen cub and her escape from the gamekeeper who raised her. The music is a fascinating blend of vocal and orchestral sound — at times ludicrously romantic, at others raw and violent. Sir Charles Mackerras's Czech training has given him a rare insight into Janáček's music and he presents a version faithful to the composer's individual requirements. In the title-role, Lucia Popp gives full weight to the text while displaying all the richness and beauty of her voice. There is a well-chosen supporting cast of largely Czech singers, with the Vienna Philharmonic to add the ultimate touch of orchestral refinement. Decca's sound is of demonstration quality, bringing out all the violent detail of Janáček's exciting vocal and orchestral effects.

Additional recommendation ...
The Cunning Little Vixen (sung in English)[a]. *Taras Bulba*[b]. **Soloists; [a]Chorus and Orchestra of the Royal Opera House, Covent Garden, [b]Philharmonic Orchestra/Simon Rattle.** EMI CDS7 54212-2 — ② 2h DDD 3/92

Janáček. THE MAKROPOULOS AFFAIR[a]. Lachian Dances[b]. **Elisabeth Söderström** (sop) Emilia Marty; **Peter Dvorskü** (ten) Albert Gregor; **Vladimir Krejčik** (ten) Vítek; **Anna Czaková** (mez) Kristina; **Václav Zítek** (bar) Jaroslav Prus; **Zdeněk Svehla** (ten) Janek; **Dalibor Jedlička** (bass) Kolenatü; **Jiří Joran** (bass) Stage technician; **Ivana Mixová** (contr) Cleaning woman; **Beno Blachut** (ten) Hauk-Sendorf; **Blanka Vitková** (contr) Chambermaid; **Vienna State Opera Chorus; Vienna Philharmonic Orchestra/Sir Charles Mackerras; [b]London Philharmonic Orchestra/François Huybrechts.** Decca 430 372-2DH2. Notes, text and translation included. Item marked [a] from D144D2 (10/79), recorded in 1978, [b] SXL6507 (10/71), recorded in 1970.

② 1h 58m ADD 10/91 P

Perhaps it was an awareness that old age was overtaking him that prompted the septuagenarian Janáček to base an opera on the subject of immortality. *The Makropoulos Affair* centres around a beautiful opera singer, Emilia Marty, who becomes involved in a prolonged law suit that arose out of an encounter many years earlier. She has managed to hide her age (at 337 she must be the oldest heroine in the history of opera) by changing her name and identity, though always keeping the initials E.M. Though the complexity of the plot makes it a problematic work to stage, *The Makropoulos Affair* works particularly well on record, with a full libretto enabling even those unfamiliar with the work to follow the finer details of the story-line. Elisabeth Söderström gives one of her finest performances as the complex, aloof yet nervous, wary yet calculating, Emilia Marty. Like Janáček's earlier operas, *Jenůfa* and *Katá Kabanová*, the drama centres around a woman but the secondary roles are also very well sung; Václav Zítek gives a forceful account of Prus, the most strongly focused male character in the opera. Special mention must also be made of Beno Blachut, in his sixties when the recording was made, but still in fine voice. His amusing character sketch of the weak Hauk-Sendorf is memorable. Sir Charles Mackerras brings all his experience and love of Janáček's operas to bear, pushing the drama inexorably forward, allowing sharp characterization of the various characters that pass before our eyes (or in this case, ears) without losing the dramatic impetus. The second disc is filled with an account of the *Lachian Dances* played by the London Philharmonic Orchestra under François Huybrechts, satisfactory but rather pedestrian after the brilliance of the opera. Full notes from John Tyrell and translations are included.

Janáček. FROM THE HOUSE OF THE DEAD[a]. Mládí[b]. Nursery rhymes[c]. **Dalibor Jedlička** (bar) Goryanchikov; **Jaroslava Janská** (sop) Alyeya; **Jiří Zahradniček** (ten) Luka (Morosov); **Vladimir Krejčík** (ten) Tall Prisoner; **Richard Novák** (bass) Short Prisoner; **Antonín Svorc** (bass-bar) Commandant; **Beno Blachut** (ten) Old Prisoner; **Ivo Zídek** (ten) Skuratov; **Jaroslav Soušek** (bar) Chekunov, Prisoner acting Don Juan; **Eva Zigmundová** (mez) Whore; **Zdeněk Soušek** (ten) Shapkin, Kedril; **Václav Zítek** (bar) Shishkov; **Zdeněk Svehla** (ten) Cherevin, A Voice; **Vienna State Opera Chorus; Vienna Philharmonic Orchestra/Sir Charles Mackerras; [c]London Sinfonietta Chorus; [bc]London Sinfonietta/David Atherton.** Decca 430 375-2DH2. Notes, texts and translations included. Item marked [a] from D224D2 (11/80), [bc] D223D5 (4/81). Items marked [ac] recorded in 1980, [b] 1978.

② 2h 3m DDD/ADD 10/91 P S

Shortly after completing his *Glagolitic* Mass, which scaled the heights of euphoric joy, Janáček plummeted to the depths of despair with his last opera, *From the House of the Dead*, based on a novel by Dostoyevsky and set in a Siberian prison. At first glance it seems an unlikely choice, charting the day to day misery of nameless prisoners largely identified by size or age. Janáček left the story remarkably unchanged, achieving a static quality in his music with evocative orchestration and recurring folk-tunes. In an opera where male voices predominate (there are only two female roles, one of which, the Whore, is very minor), much depends on the performers; here, surely even the composer himself would have been delighted with the results. Sir Charles Mackerras's *Gramophone* award-winning recording of the original version is now 13 years old, but remains unequalled. From the opening notes of the overture the listener is propelled into the high walled bleakness of prison life, chains rattling ominously. The story inspired Janáček to write some of his finest music; all the features of his earlier operas are here, but pared down to a minimum, laying bare the emotional impact of the drama. Much of the music is intentionally ugly, often with huge gaps between treble and bass, suggesting the emptiness of existence. Unusually for Janáček it is very much an ensemble opera, but the part of Goryanchikov, a political prisoner representing Dostoyevsky's own experiences, stands out: Dalibor Jedlička exudes the right nobility coupled with a pleasing *cantabile* tone. Jaroslava Janská sings the part of Alyeya tenderly and with an endearing straightforwardness. In a recording without weakness it is perhaps unfair to single out individuals but mention must be made of Jiří Zahradníček's fervent characterization of the murderous Luka and Mackerras guides the Vienna

Philharmonic Orchestra and Chorus through a reading of great passion and pathos. As a bonus, there are generous fillers of *Mládi* and the *Nursery rhymes*, excellently played by the London Sinfonietta under David Atherton. Whilst less well-known than *Jenu°fa* and *Vixen*, this is essential listening for all fans of twentieth-century opera. Texts and translations are provided, along with an enlightening essay by Janáček scholar John Tyrrell.

Janáček. OSUD (sung in English). **Helen Field** (sop) Míla Valková; **Philip Langridge** (ten) Zivnü; **Kathryn Harries** (sop) Míla's Mother; **Peter Bronder** (ten) A poet, A student, Hrazda; **Stuart Kale** (ten) Dr Suda; **Welsh National Opera Chorus and Orchestra/Sir Charles Mackerras.** EMI CDC7 49993-2. English text included. Recorded in 1989.

lh 19m DDD 9/90

The story of *Osud* ("Fate") concerns a tragic relationship between a composer (Zivnü) and a girl (Míla) whose mother throws both herself and her daughter to their deaths; the composer has produced an unfinished opera about his life with the girl, and as he finished explaining it to a group of his students he too is felled by a blow of fate. Composed in 1904-6, immediately after *Jenůfa, Osud* had to wait more than 50 years for its first production; and it was not until 1984 and David Pountney's staging for English National Opera that opera-goers in Britain realized they had been missing one of Janáček's most inspired works. Philip Langridge played Zivnü in that production, and his singing here shows complete identification with and mastery of the role. Indeed, given the cast involved, under the guidance of the master-Janáčekian Sir Charles Mackerras, it should not be surprising that the whole performance radiates conviction and a sense of theatre. EMI's recording quality is superb and there are authoritative notes and a full libretto. Anyone who is allergic to opera in English should perhaps think carefully before buying; otherwise this can be confidently recommended, especially to anyone who thinks there is no such thing as a neglected masterpiece.

Clément Janequin

French c.1485-1558

Suggested listening ...

Chansons — Le chant des oiseaux. Toutes les nuictz. J'atens le temps. Il estoit une fillette. Ung jour Colin. O doulx regard, o parler. Or sus vous dormez trop (L'alouette). Quand contrement verras. Hellas mon Dieu, ton ire. Ma peine n'est pas grande. O mal d'aymer. Herbes et fleurs. A ce joly moys. Assouvy suis. Quelqu'un me disoit l'aultre jour. M'y levay par ung matin. M'ayme a eu de Dieu. Le chant du rossignol. Las on peult juger (arr. Morlaye). L'aveuglé dieu qui partout vole (arr. Alberto da Ripa). **Ensemble Clément Janequin.** Harmonia Mundi HMC90 1099 (8/85).

John Jenkins

British 1592-1678

NEW REVIEW

Jenkins. Fantasia-Suites in four parts — F major; C major; E minor; A minor; F major; D major. Airs for lyra consort — C major, "The Six Bells"; G major. **The Parley of Instruments/Peter Holman.** Hyperion CDA66604. Recorded in 1992.

lh DDD 12/92

The four-hundredth anniversary of Jenkins's birth in 1992 has produced two fine recordings which should help to bring greater recognition to his outstanding art. Jordi Savall's multi-voiced consorts reveal the delectable sonority of his early years. Here Peter Holman concentrates on works probably written in the first years of the Restoration, some 30 or 40 years later.

Although Jenkins is often labelled a conservative in an already traditional instrumental climate, the style of these 'late' fantasia suites goes some way to show that within the considered pacing and sober panache of his musical language lies a temperament also quite at home with the mid-baroque styles drawn from continental models. Unmistakably English though these works are in the mellifluous continuity of the melody, the clear textures of the violins and the sprightly rhythms make for some quasi-trio sonatas in the Italian vein. The Parley play with an exceptional feel for the dichotomous nature of this music, responding effortlessly to the varied narrative. Both F major suites reveal a considerable understanding for the logic behind Jenkins's contrasts with the introverted and sprightly sections nicely balanced and argued. If you love Byrd, Gibbons and Purcell, then your appreciation of great English string music is incomplete without Jenkins.

NEW REVIEW

Jenkins. Two Pavans. 11 Fantasias. Two In Nomines. **Hespèrion XX** (Jordi Savall, Eunice Brandao, Sergi Casademunt, Imke David, Laurence Bonnal, Paolo Pandolfo, Lorenz Duftschmid, viols); **Michel Behringer** (org). Astrée Auvidis E8724. Recorded in 1990.

lh 13m DDD 2/92

John Jenkins was, according to many sources of his day, a man whose music and personality were held in the highest esteem. Roger North, his student, describes him as an "accomplisht ingenious person, and so well behaved ... and wheerever he went was always welcome and courted to stay". That his music is arguably the most congenial and classically poised of his day is perhaps no coincidence. These six-part works reveal a master of counterpoint with a rare gift for melodic shape and outstanding pacing. Most of them are almost certainly works of the late Jacobean age, written when Jenkins was supposedly still perfecting his art. Judging by the effervescent and lyrical playing of these fantasias, Jordi Savall and Hespèrion XX treat them as works of an established composer in full flight; and who would doubt them on the evidence of the complete six-part music (one spurious *fantasia* is omitted) with its feast of noble, richly textured and variegated pieces. Understated though Jenkins's language is, Savall is attracted to the idea of impassioned and brooding melody; in this respect a very English type of music is flavoured with continental traits. The sound is dark and full though with the outermost parts illuminated to make a more penetrating and unequal ensemble. This works well in the profoundly-felt chordal sections ("Bell Pavan") but will irritate those who understand this music to be a secret discourse of ideas tossed about in a democratic manner. Savall and his group engage in conversation but light-hearted banter is definitely out of order and Savall himself is clearly the chairman. Approached more openly than English performances of similar music, these magisterial works have been firmly taken out of the parochial closet to smoulder in the hands of foreigners. An indigenous tradition maybe, but cultured playing of this sort makes one wonder whether environment is really the issue.

Joseph Joachim

Austrian/Hungarian 1831-1907

Joachim. Violin Concerto in Hungarian Style, Op. 11[a]. Overtures — Hamlet, Op. 4; Henry IV, Op. 7. [a]**Elmar Oliveira** (vn); **London Philharmonic Orchestra/Leon Botstein.** Pickwick IMP Masters MCD27. Recorded in 1991.

lh 14m DDD 8/91 

Joachim's friendship with Brahms is well known, as is his standing as one of Europe's greatest violinists and teachers. But Joachim, the composer? These days the only compositions to receive a regular airing are his cadenzas to the Beethoven and Brahms Violin Concertos. His meeting with Brahms in 1853 coincided with a determined effort to make his mark as a composer, but after a decade (during which the works on this disc were written) he ceased to compose altogether, feeling that he could not measure up to Brahms. Well, on the evidence of this disc, perhaps not, but his Violin Concerto was hailed by Tovey as "one of the most important documents of the middle of the nineteenth century" and, predictably, it is one of the most fiendishly difficult to play. Oliveira (a gold medal winner at the 1978 Tchaikovsky Competition in Moscow) copes brilliantly with the demands; only occasionally do you feel the concerto is playing him, not the other way around, and Botstein and the LPO provide spirited support. The *Hamlet* and *Henry IV* Overtures are powerfully evocative rather than programmatic and reflect Joachim's change of allegiance from the Liszt camp to Brahms. A touch of glare apart, the sound is rich and full.

John Johnson

British c.1541-c.1594

Robert Johnson II

British c.1583-1633

Suggested listening …

J. Johnson. Walsingham. Passemeasures pavan in F minor. Passemeasures pavan in G minor. Galliard to the Passemeasures pavan. Flat pavan. Galliard to the Flat pavan. Delight pavan. Galliard to Delight pavan. The Carmans Whistle. Johnsons Jewell. The Gathering of Peascods. Galliards — F major; C major. Pavan in F minor. ***R. Johnson.*** Three Dances from Chapman's "Masque of the Middle Temple and Lincoln's Inn". Dances from Ben Johnson's "Masque of Oberon" — Two almans; Fairies' Dance. Almans — "Hit and take it"; "Lady Strang's"; F major; C minor; C major. Galliards — "My Lady Mildemays Delight"; D major. Paavans — F minor; C minor. Fantasia. **Lynda Sayce** (lte). Dervorguilla DRVCD101 (4/93).

R. Johnson: Arm, arm!. As I walked forth. Baboon's Dance. Care-charming sleep. Charon, oh Charon. Dear, do not your fair beauty wrong. The first of the Temple. Full fathom five. Have you seen the bright lily grow?. Mascarada. The noble man's masque tune. Orpheus I am. Satyr's Dance. The third of the Temple. Tis late and cold. Where the bee sucks. *Coupled with* ***Anonymous:*** Cock Lorel. The ape's dance at the Temple. ***Dowland:*** Doulands Rounde Battell Galyard. ***W. Lawes:*** The catts. Come, my Daphne, come away. Gather ye rosebuds while ye may (two versions). Haste you, nimphs. He that will not love. A masque. Royall Consorts — Sett No. 1 in D minor: Fantazy, Aire, Almain, Corranto I and II, Saraband and Ecco; Sett No. 2 in D minor: Aire. To the dews. To pansies. To the sycamore. White though yee be. Wise nature that the dew of sleep prepares. Ye feinds and furies. **Tragicomedia/ Stephen Stubbs.** EMI Reflexe CDC7 54311-2 (2/92).

See also review in the Collections section; refer to Index to Reviews.

Andre Jolivet

French 1905-1974

Suggested listening …

Chant de Linos[a]. Flute Sonata[b]. *Coupled with* ***Koechlin.*** Sonata for piano and flute, Op. 52[c]. Quintet, Op. 156, "Primavera"[ad]. **Philippe Racine** (fl); [ad]**Robert Zimansky** (vn); [ad]**Monika Clemann** (va); [ad]**Curdin Coray** (vc); [ad]**Xenia Schindler** (hp); [bc]**Daniel Cholette** (pf). Claves CD50-9003 (10/90).

Robert Jones

British fl. 1597-1615

R. Jones. THE MUSES GARDIN. **Emma Kirkby** (sop); **Anthony Rooley** (lte). Virgin Classics Veritas VC7 59633-2. Recorded in 1989.

What if I seeke for love of thee. Lie downe poore heart. When love on time. Farewel dear love. Love wing'd my hopes. Now what is love. Love is a bable. Loves god is a boy. When will the fountain. Flye from the world. Happy he. Goe to bed sweete Muze. Ite caldi sospiri. If in this flesh. O Thred of life. When I sit reading. Might I redeeme myne errours.

1h 1m DDD 11/91

Robert Jones was his own worst enemy, jealous of Dowland, at war with many of his contemporaries, and probably fuming posthumously at his undervaluation by the late Edmund Fellowes and in *Grove*. Though his songs neither quite scale the heights nor plumb the emotional depths of Dowland's they contain much of real value. This hand-picked selection from Jones's five songbooks makes it clear that in discarding the bath water we should not allow the baby to accompany it. Whilst it is not impossible, it is unlikely that unworthy material could draw forth such wonderfully expressive and committed performances from a singer whose experience in the field of lute-song is as long and distinguished as Emma Kirkby's; Anthony Rooley provides all the support she needs. The path of musical history is strewn with the sincere but unwise assessments of critics, some of which you may recognize as you enjoy this finely recorded recital.

Joseph Jongen

Belgian 1873-1953

NEW REVIEW

Jongen. Symphonie concertante, Op. 81[a]. Suite, Op. 48[b]. Allegro appassionato, Op. 79[b]. [a]**Hubert Schoonbroodt** (org); [b]**Therese-Marie Gilissen** (va); [a]**Liège Symphony Orchestra/René Defossez;** [b]**RTBF Symphony Orchestra/Brian Priestman.** Koch Schwann 315 012. Recorded 1975-85.

1h 10m DDD 8/92 

Jongen's *Symphonie concertante* is a spectacular showpiece for organ and large orchestra, full of thrilling effects, unforgettable tunes, spine-tingling climaxes and flashes of great beauty. Written in 1926 its rare performances today belie its sheer crowd-pulling potential, so it's very good to have the work readily available on CD. Having said that it should be pointed out that while this is a perfectly acceptable recording, it's neither the only one nor the best (see below for details of the Telarc recording which is very much in the demonstration class). No, what makes this a "Good CD" are the two works for viola and orchestra. The viola is pretty well starved of worthwhile concert repertory yet here is some wonderful music (especially the ravishing "Poème élégiaque" from the *Suite*) which has been allowed to wallow in obscurity for the best part of a century. Hopefully this disc will change all that. Therese-Marie Gilissen puts her all into this music, summoning up a vast array of emotions in the *Suite* and producing the kind of virtuoso playing in the *Allegro appassionato* more usually associated with the violin.

Additional recommendation ...

Symphonie. ***Franck.*** *Fantaisie in A major. Pastorale, Op. 19.* **Michael Murray** (org); **San Francisco Symphony Orchestra/Edo de Waart.** Telarc CD80096 — 56m DDD 3/85

Scott Joplin

American 1868-1917

Joplin. PIANO WORKS. **Dick Hyman** (pf). RCA Victor Gold Seal GD87993. Recorded in 1975.

Maple Leaf Rag. Original Rags. Swipesy. Peacherine Rag. The Easy Winners. Sunflower Slow Drag. The Entertainer. Elite Syncopations. The Strenuous Life. A Breeze from Alabama.

Palm Leaf Rag. Something Doing. Weeping Willow. The Chrysanthemum. The Cascades. The Sycamore.

58m ADD 10/89

The Rag is a simple dance form characterized by the device of syncopation, whereby a strong accent is displaced from its expected place on the first beat of the bar to a subsidiary beat. The effect of this is to give a lift or 'swing' to the rhythm. Traditional Negro folk and popular music provided the basis for this form, which in itself was one of the bases for the development of jazz. Scott Joplin was the most skilled composer of rags, and he wrote over 50 pieces between 1899 and 1904. In 1973 the film, *The Sting*, used Joplin's rag *The Entertainer*, and this was a strong element in a revival of his music. Dick Hyman recorded all of Joplin's rags in 1975, and this disc gives us a selection of 16 items. He manages to invest each piece with its own distinct character, and his buoyant, witty playing in a clear but slightly shallow recording is very attractive.

NEW REVIEW

Joplin. TREEMONISHA. **Carmen Balthrop** (sop) Treemonisha; **Betty Allen** (mez) Monisha; **Curtis Rayam** (ten) Remus; **Willard White** (bass) Ned; **Ben Harney** (bar) Zodzetrick; **Cora Johnson** (sop) Lucy; **Kenneth Hicks** (voc) Andy; **Dorceal Duckens** (voc) Luddud; **Dwight Ransom** (voc) Cephus; **Raymond Bazemore** (voc) Simon; **Edward Pierson** (bar) Parson Alltalk; **Houston Grand Opera Chorus and Orchestra/Gunther Schuller.** DG 435 709-2GX2. Text included. From 2707 083 (7/76). Recorded in 1975.

② 1h 30m ADD 8/92

Despite his successes at the beginning of this century with a succession of remarkable rags for piano, Scott Joplin entertained a burning ambition to achieve renown in the music theatre. His grand opera, *Treemonisha*, with its didactic tale of the value of education to black development, was to suffer the fate of his other efforts in the field, and it still remained unstaged at his death in 1917. The great 1970's revival of his music inspired the reclamation of the opera, most notably in the 1975 production at the Houston Grand Opera, which formed the basis of this recording. For this, Gunther Schuller did a remarkable job in rescoring the work from the 1911 vocal score that Joplin himself paid to have published. The opera has some ragtime elements but is by no means dominated by these. Indeed, there are fully-fledged Italianate arias and some well-written ensembles and choruses; and the orchestra here obviously relish the stylistic diversity with which Joplin and Schuller provide them. With words by Joplin himself, the mix sometimes has the feel of Gilbert and Sullivan about it, though jazzier rhythms soon appear to dispel the Victorian parlour mood. Its general vitality and tunefulness easily compensate for what it may lack in dramatic tension and direction. Although this recording is now beginning to show its age, with some distortion and over-defined miking areas, it still conveys the strong performance with clarity and power. The cast all bring deep involvement to their respective roles and the important contribution of the chorus is particularly effective.

Josquin Desprez

French c.1440-1521

NEW REVIEW

Josquin Desprez. Missa Ave maris stella. MOTETS AND CHANSONS. **Taverner Consort and Choir/Andrew Parrott.** EMI Reflexe CDC7 54659-2. Texts and translations included. Recorded in 1992.

Motets — Illibata Dei virgo nutrix. Gaude virgo, mater Christi. Salve regina. In te Domine speravi (with Andrew Lawrence-King, hp). Plaine de dueil. Que vous madame. Regretz sans fin. Adieu mes amours. Je n'ose plus (both with Andrew Lawrence-King). ***Anonymous:*** Ave maris stella.

1h 17m DDD 5/93

The customary glittering, steely sound of the Taverner Consort and Choir is here altered by the unexpected presence of counter-tenors, in an impressive programme of seldom-heard and seldom-recorded Josquin. The panorama it gives of Josquin's mastery of various techniques is fascinating: nobody could miss the contrast between *Illibata Dei virgo nutrix* and *Gaude virgo, mater Christi*. They are equally impressive, perfect examples of Josquin's contrapuntal and harmonic skill, and yet significantly different in their technical procedures and utterly different in the impression they make. Similarly, the *Missa Ave maris stella*, which stands midway between the earlier Mass settings and later works such as the *Missa Pange lingua*, offers points of comparison and contrast both because of its musical magnificence and because of its relative unfamiliarity. The performances are commensurate with the music, and though it is often a risk for an English group to record French-texted works (especially when experiments in pronunciation are involved), the *chansons* recorded here are also delightful. Altogether a provocative collection.

Key to Symbols

Price	Quantity/ availability	Timing	Mode	Review date
	② ②	lh 23m	DDD	6/88

Josquin Desprez. Missa L'homme armé super voces musicales. Missa L'homme armé sexti toni. ***Anonymous.*** L'homme armé. **The Tallis Scholars/Peter Phillips.** Gimell CDGIM019. Text and translation included.

lh 14m DDD 7/89

Towards the end of the Middle Ages it became customary to use popular secular melodies instead of the usual plainchant themes as the basis for composing polyphonic Masses. One such was the fifteenth-century melody *L'homme armé* ("Beware of the armed man"), a melody that may have originated as a crusader song. These settings would provide endless opportunities for a composer to demonstrate his contrapuntal skills. In the first of Josquin's two settings, *Super voces musicales*, he uses the tune over and over again, beginning each time on successive ascending degrees of the six-note scale *Ut Re Mi Fa Sol La*, so that it rises higher and higher as the Mass progresses. Sometimes the melody appears back to front from half way through the piece on to the end. In the *Sexti toni* Mass the tune is transposed so that F rather than G is the final note. The listener's enjoyment is in no way lessened by all this contrapuntal ingenuity. The music flows along with unsurpassed ease and beauty, displaying that unique quality of seeming inevitability which characterizes all great music. It is well matched by the expertise and enthusiasm of The Tallis Scholars and their first-class recording engineers.

Josquin Desprez. Missa Pange lingua. Missa La sol fa re mi. **The Tallis Scholars/Peter Phillips.** Gimell CDGIM009.

lh 2m DDD 3/87

Throughout his long life Josquin Desprez was held in enormous esteem by his contemporaries and of his 18 surviving Masses the two gathered on this disc come from different periods in his life. The *Missa La sol fa re mi* dates from 1502 and, as its name implies, is based on the notes A,G,F,D,E. From this motif the Mass emerges, a technical feat at which Josquin excelled (and of a kind which he often seemed to set himself as a challenge). The repetition of this theme is carried out with such sophistication that one is hardly aware of its recurrence so many times. The *Missa Pange lingua* is a much later work based on the plainchant written for the feast of Corpus Christi. It has a freedom of invention and harmonic richness that, at times, seem to take us far away from the restraints of a theme-based composition. The eight singers of The Tallis Scholars (who, incidentally, use female voices for the soprano line) make a beautiful sound: rich, integrated but always willing to bring out the melodic subtleties presented to them in this most glorious of renaissance music. The recording matches the excellence of the performance.

Additional recommendations ...

Missa Pange lingua. Vultum tuum deprecabuntur. Planxit autem David. **Westminster Cathedral Choir/James O'Donnell.** Hyperion CDA66614 — 1h 16m DDD 4/93

Missa Pange lingua. **Ensemble Clément Janequin; EnsembleOrganum/Marcel Pérès.** Harmonia Mundi HMC90 1239 — 52m DDD 2/87

Further listening ...

Ave Maria, gratia plena ... Virgo serena a 4. Stabat mater dolorosa a 5. Salve, regina a 4. Ave nobilissima creatura a 6. O bone et dulcissime Jesu a 4. Usquequo, Domine, oblivisceris me a 4. Miserere me, Deus a 5. **La Chapelle Royale Chorus/Philippe Herreweghe.** Harmonia Mundi HMC90 1243 (4/87).

Missa Hercules dux Ferrarie. La déploration de Johannes Ockeghem, "Nymphes des bois". *Coupled with* ***La Rue.*** Missa pro defunctis. **New London Chamber Choir/James Wood.** Amon Ra CDSAR24 (3/87).

Dmitry Kabalevsky

Russian 1904-1987

Suggested listening ...

Cello Concerto No. 1 in G minor, Op. 49. *Coupled with* ***Shostakovich.*** Cello Concerto No. 1 in E flat major, Op. 107. **Yo-Yo Ma** (vc); **Philadelphia Orchestra/Eugene Ormandy.** CBS CD37840 (5/85).

Cello Concerto No. 2. in C major, Op. 77. *Coupled with* ***Glazunov.*** Chant du ménestrel, Op. 71; ***Khachaturian.*** Cello Concerto. **Raphael Wallfisch** (vc); **London Philharmonic Orchestra/Bryden Thomson.** Chandos CHAN8579 (6/88).

Violin Concerto in C major, Op. 48. *Coupled with* ***Khachaturian.*** Violin Concerto in D minor. **Lydia Mordkovitch** (vn); **Royal Scottish National Orchestra/Neeme Järvi.** Chandos CHAN8918 (3/91).

Vaasily Sergeyevich Kalinnikov

Russian 1866-1901

Suggested listening ...

Symphony No. 1 in G minor. *Coupled with* ***Glazunov.*** The sea — fantasy, Op. 28. Spring, Op. 34. **Scottish National Orchestra/Neeme Järvi.** Chandos CHAN8611 (10/88).

Symphony No. 2 in A major. Tsar Boris — Overture. The cedar and the palm. **Scottish National Orchestra/Neeme Järvi.** Chandos CHAN8805 (6/90).

Imre Kalmán

Hungarian/American 1882-1953

Suggseted listening ...

Gräfin Mariza — *operetta: excerpts.* **Soloists; New Sadlers Wells Opera Chorus and Orchestra/Barry Wordsworth.** TER Classics CDTED1007.

Giya Kancheli

Georgian 1935-

Suggested listening ...

Symphonies Nos. 3[a] and 6[b]. [a]**Gamlet Gonashvili** (ten); [b]**Archil Kharadze,** [b]**Giya Chaduneli** (vas); **Georgia State Symphony Orchestra/Dzansug Kakhidze.** Olympia Explorer OCD401 (9/90).

Symphonies — No. 4, "In Commemoration of Michaelangelo" (1975); No. 5 (1976). **Georgia State Symphony Orchestra/Dzansug Kakhidze.** Olympia OCD403 (4/91).

Liturgy for Viola and Orchestra, "Mourned by the Wind"[a]. *Coupled with* **Schnittke.** Viola Concerto[b]. **Kim Kashkashian** (va); [a]**Bonn Beethovenhalle Orchestra,** [b]**Saarbrücken Radio Symphony Orchestra/Dennis Russell Davies.** ECM New Series 437 199-2 (4/93).

Vitěslava Kaprálova

Czechoslovakian 1915-1940

Suggested listening ...

Dubnova Preludia Suite, Op. 13. *Coupled with* **Klein.** Duo. **Schulhoff.** String Quartet No. 1. Concertino. Sonata for Flute and Piano. **Soloists; Hawthorne Quartet.** Northeastern NR248-CD (5/93).

Nikolai Karetnikov

Russian 1930-

NEW REVIEW

Karetnikov. Till Eulenspiegel. **Boris Koudriavtsev** (bar) Tyl; **Ekatérina Mazo** (sop) Nele; **Alexeï Martynov** (ten) Lamme; **Lina Mkrtchian** (contr) Katline, Hostess, Sootkin; **Pyotr Gluboky** (bass) Joost, Charles V, Count Egmont; **Arkady Proujanski** (ten) Count Hoorn, Fishmonger; **Alexeï Motchalov** (bass) Klaas, Admiral; **Chorus; Soviet Cinema Orchestra/Emin Khatchaturian, Valery Poliansky.** CdM Russian Season LDC288 029/30. Notes and translation included. Recorded in 1988.

② 2h 32m DDD 7/92 

A 'representative' Soviet opera from the post-war period would most likely be a tedious experience, given the crippling conditions imposed by Soviet cultural policy; and Karetnikov's *Till Eulenspiegel* is about as determinedly non-conformist as it is possible to be. And yet the circumstances behind it tell us much about the uniquely bizarre world of Soviet culture, and the music itself has much the same mixture of the entertaining and the disconcerting as Shostakovich's *The Nose* and *The Lady Macbeth of Mtsensk District.* Karetnikov's central character derives from a mid-nineteenth century novel by the Belgian writer Charles de Coster, in which Till is embroiled in the conflicts of the sixteenth-century Spanish Netherlands. He is exiled for insulting a monk, his father (Klaas) is burned as a heretic, his mother (Sootkin) is tortured to death, he himself is tried and condemned but saved by the intercession of his fiancée (Nele). Finally he dies, apparently as the result of drinking a magic potion; just as mysteriously he comes to life again and the opera ends in a rather throwaway affirmation and dance. Many more bizarre episodes are interwoven and the whole is set to a bewildering array of pseudo-historical imitative musical styles, each with its own memorable instrumental colouring. Such a manner of realization was hardly likely to earn the blessing of the Composers' Union, never mind the subversive implications of the story. Not surprisingly the work has yet to be staged. But what Karetnikov did, with the help of contacts at the State butchers' shop amongst other things, was to persuade recording engineers and musicians from the Soviet Cinema Orchestra to stay behind after hours and record the work piecemeal over a period of years. The magnetic tape would sometimes come from the cutting-room floor; sometimes bits of the opera would be smuggled into a film score and cut out later on. In other words, this is a *samizdat* (secret publication of banned matter) opera; it is certainly fascinating and unique. That the recording sounds so vivid is already a minor miracle, and the performance is stylish and authoritative.

Jerome Kern

American 1885-1945

Kern. SHOW BOAT. Cast includes **Teresa Stratas, Frederica von Stade, Jerry Hadley, Bruce Hubbard, Karla Burns; Ambrosian Chorus; London Sinfonietta/John McGlinn.** EMI CDS7 49108-2. Notes and text included. Recorded in 1987.

③ 3h 42m DDD 11/88 9P 9S

This three-CD *Show Boat* is a remarkable, inspired achievement that is far from being an example of a musical swamped by the misguided use of operatic voices. *Show Boat* was composed on a large scale for singers of accomplishments far above those we often hear in the theatre today, and here it is given its due. "Make believe", "Ol' man river", "Can't help lovin' dat man", "Why do I love you?" and "You are love" have been sung by countless singers over the years, but in beauty and style the performances here can surely never have been rivalled. The love duets between Frederica von Stade and Jerry Hadley are stunningly beautiful and Bruce Hubbard's firm, honeyed baritone has absolutely nothing to fear from comparisons with Paul Robeson. Teresa Stratas's "Can't help lovin' dat man" is quite ravishing. But the success of this set is due above all to the enthusiasm and dedication of its conductor, John McGlinn. His avowed aim has been to include all the music Kern wrote for the piece over the years for various stage and film productions. Much of this appears in a lengthy and fascinating appendix; but the main text itself includes not only full-length versions of numbers traditionally much shortened but other magnificent items dropped during try-outs and only rediscovered in a Warner Brothers warehouse in 1982. Not least he has restored the original orchestrations of Robert Russell Bennett. The London Sinfonietta clearly revels in them, not least the jazz-flavoured elements of the final Act. The Ambrosian Chorus, too, has a field day in the rousing choral numbers. Bright, spacious recorded sound helps to make this a quite magnificent, quite irresistibly enjoyable achievement.

Further listening ...

KIRI SINGS KERN: High, Wide and Handsome — The folks who live on the hill. You Were Never Lovelier — I'm old fashioned. Swing Time — The way you look tonight; A fine romance. Music in the Air — The song is you. Roberta — Yesterdays; Smoke gets in your eyes. Lady be good. The last time I saw Paris. Very Warm for May — All the things you are. Show Boat — Can't help lovin' dat man; Bill. Cover Girl — Long ago and far away. Centennial Summer — All through the day. Sally — Look for the silver lining. **Dame Kiri Te Kanawa** (sop); **London Sinfonietta/Jonathan Tunick.** EMI CDC7 54527-2 (7/93).

Albert Ketélbey

British 1875-1959

Suggested listening ...

In a Chinese temple garden[c]. In a monastery garden[c]. Sanctuary of the heart. Bank Holiday. Dance of the merry mascots[b]. In a Persian market[c]. In the mystic land of Egypt[ac]. Bells across the meadows. The clock and the Dresden figures[b]. With honour crowned. [a]**Laurence Dale** (ten); [b]**Michael Reeves** (pf); [c]**Ambrosian Chorus; London Promenade Orchestra/Alexander Faris.** Philips 400 011-2PH (4/83).

Aram Khachaturian

Russian 1903-1978

Khachaturian. Spartacus — ballet[a]. Gayaneh — ballet[a].
Prokofiev. Romeo and Juliet — ballet, Op. 64[b]. **[a]Vienna Philharmonic Orchestra/Aram Khachaturian; [b]Cleveland Orchestra/Lorin Maazel.** Decca Ovation 417 737-2DM. Items marked [a] from SXL6000 (1/63), recorded in 1962, [b] SXL6620/22 (9/73), recorded in 1973.
Spartacus — Adagio of Spartacus and Phrygia; Variation of Aegina and Bacchanalia; Scene and dance with Crotala; Dance of Gaditanae and victory of Spartacus. *Gayaneh* — Sabre dance; Aysheh's awakening and dance; Lezghinka; Gayaneh's Adagio; Gopak. *Romeo and Juliet* — Romeo; Juliet as a young girl; Dance of the knights; Balcony scene; Romeo resolves to avenge Mercutio's death; Death of Tybalt; The last farewell.

lh llm ADD 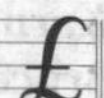

Pulsating rhythms (many high-speed oompahs) and streamers of highly-spiced colours; not forgetting that lush, sweeping and most yearning of string tunes from the *Spartacus* Adagio (which, for more mature collectors, will be impossible to listen to without memories of an aerial camera circling and panning down broadside onto the resplendent white sea-faring craft of BBC TV's "The Onedin Line"), and for which the Vienna Philharmonic strings produced their most sensuous tones, appropriately laden with vibrato and slides. The music could be by no one else. This lovable 1962 Khachaturian coupling has transferred well to CD, with increased clarity of texture and dynamic range, though with a loss of bass richness, and with the close balance and exaggerated stereo separation now more obvious. But the extra sharpness of focus also confirms how much the Vienna Philharmonic must have enjoyed these sessions. Timings are generously extended by the inclusion of the *Romeo and Juliet* excerpts from Maazel's complete Cleveland set (Decca 417 510-2DH2).

Further listening ...

Violin Concerto in D minor. *Coupled with* ***Kabalevsky.*** Violin Concerto in C major, Op. 48. **Lydia Mordkovitch** (vn); **Royal Scottish National Orchestra/Neeme Järvi.** Chandos CHAN8918 (3/91).

Spartacus — Ballet Suite No. 1: Variations of Aegina and Bacchanalia; Dance of the Gaditanian Maidens and Victory of Spartacus; Ballet Suite No. 2: Adagio of Spartacus and Phrygia. Gayaneh — excerpts. Masquerade — incidental music to Lermontov's play. **London Symphony Orchestra/Stanley Black.** Decca Weekend 417 062-2DC (3/90).

Karen Khachaturian

USSR 1920-

Suggested listening ...

Violin Sonata in G minor, Op. 1. *Coupled with* ***Castelnuovo-Tedesco.*** Violin Concerto No. 2, "I profeti". ***Ferguson.*** Violin Sonata No. 1, Op. 2; ***Françaix.*** String Trio in C major. **Jascha Heifetz** (vn); **Joseph de Pasquale** (va); **Gregor Piatigorsky** (vc); **Lilian Steuber** (pf); **Los Angeles Philharmonic Orchestra/Alfred Wallenstein.** RCA Victor Gold Seal GD87872 (9/90).

Gideon Klein

Czechoslovakian 1919-1945

Klein. String Trio. Fantasie a Fuga. Piano Sonata[a]. String Quartet, Op. 2.
Ullmann. String Quartet No. 3, Op. 43. **Hawthorne Quartet** (Roman Lefkowitz, Si Jing

Huang, vns; Mark Ludwig, va; Sato Knudsen, vc); [a]**Virginia Eskin** (pf). Channel Classics CCS1691. Recorded in 1991.

1h 8m DDD 12/91 

This CD is devoted to music by two Jewish musicians incarcerated in the Theresienstadt ghetto camp established by the Nazis in November 1941. On the evidence of the works recorded here, Gideon Klein and Viktor Ullmann were substantial figures whose music needs no special pleading. In stylistic terms, Ullman is perhaps the more predictable of the two. His Third Quartet shows him remaining true to Schoenbergian expressionism within a tonal context. Klein, deported to the camp at the age of 21, was by all accounts an astonishingly accomplished musician. His own music shows unmistakable signs of potential greatness even if the major influences — including Schoenberg, Janáček and Bartók — are not fully assimilated within a definitive creative profile. The bravely invigorating String Trio, completed only nine days before Klein's disappearance, receives a magnificent performance from members of the Hawthorne Quartet, a group drawn from the Boston Symphony Orchestra. Virginia Eskin gives a powerful account of the hard-hitting Piano Sonata, humming along discreetly as she plays. Channel Classics deserve high praise for these ideally balanced recordings which document a form of spiritual resistance we can barely begin to comprehend.

Further listening ...

Duo. *Coupled with* ***Kapralova.*** Dubnova Preludia Suite, Op. 13. ***Schulhoff.*** String Quartet No. 1. Concertino. Sonata for Flute and Piano. **Soloists; Hawthorne Quartet.** Northeastern NR248-CD (5/93).

Oliver Knussen

British 1952-

NEW REVIEW

Knussen. ORCHESTRAL WORKS. [a]**Elaine Barry,** [c]**Linda Hirst** (sops); [c]**Michael Collins,** [c]**Edward Pillinger,** [c]**Ian Mitchell** (clarinets); [d]**Nash Ensemble** (Gareth Hulse, ob; Marcia Crayford, vn; Roger Chase, va; Christopher van Kampen vc); [b]**Philharmonia Orchestra/Michael Tilson Thomas;** [ae]**London Sinfonietta/Oliver Knussen.** Unicorn-Kanchana Souvenir UKCD2010. Items marked [b] from RHD400 (2/82), [acde] DKP9027 (8/84). Recorded 1981-83.

Symphonies — No. 2, Op. 7[a]; No. 3, Op. 18[b]. Trumpets, Op. 12[c]. Coursing, Op. 17[e]. Cantata, Op. 15[d]. Ophelia Dances, Book 1, Op. 18[b].

58m DDD 9/88

An ideal introduction to the art of one of this country's most talented living composers. The finest work here is the Third Symphony from 1979, a one-movement, 15-minute essay of excitingly concentrated power and enormous imagination. Knussen's fastidiously judged orchestration displays genuine mastery, and this score is full of fantastical, ear-tickling sonorities, especially when we enter the hypnotic dream-world which follows the big central climax. Michael Tilson Thomas and the Philharmonia give a meticulously prepared rendering, though one has heard perhaps more sheerly involving accounts 'live' since this 1981 excellently engineered Watford Town Hall production. The composer himself presides over authoritative readings of the remainder, except for the deeply expressive 1977 *Cantata* for oboe and string trio (which is entrusted to a conductor-less Nash Ensemble). For a mere 19-year-old, the Second Symphony from 1970-71 (Knussen wrote and conducted his First Symphony at the age of 16!) represents an astonishingly confident achievement: its settings of verse by Georg Trakl and Sylvia Plath are both haunting and personal, and soprano Elaine Barry makes a superbly assured protagonist. In the resourceful *Trumpets* (1975) for three clarinets and soprano (another Trakl vehicle), it's the turn of the amazingly pure-toned Linda Hirst to shine. That just leaves the exhilarating *Coursing* (1979) and colourful *Ophelia Dances* (1975), both stunningly executed here by the London Sinfonietta. Given such consistently top-notch performance- and production-values, this enterprising mid-price collection deserves the widest exposure.

Further listening ...

WHERE THE WILD THINGS ARE. **Soloists; London Sinfonietta/Oliver Knussen.** Unicorn-Kanchana DKPCD9044 (9/85).

Zoltán Kodály

Hungarian 1882-1967

Kodály. ORCHESTRAL WORKS. **Philharmonia Hungarica/Antál Dorati.** Decca Ovation 425 034-2DM. From SXLM6665-7 (9/74).
Háry János Suite. Dances from Galánta. Variations on a Hungarian folk-song, "The Peacock". Dances from Marosszék.

1h 16m ADD

Four of Kodály's most famous and best loved orchestral works on one mid-priced disc is a rare treat. Dorati conduct an exceptionally vivid and colourful account of the *Háry János* suite, and one that really draws the listener into the hero's elaborate and fantastic story telling. Particularly effective are the *Song* (the orchestral version of the love duet of Háry and Orzse from the opera) and the popular *Intermezzo*, both featuring excellent playing from an uncredited cimbalom player. Like his fellow compatriot, Bartók, Kodály was an avid collector and transcriber of Hungarian folk material and there is hardly a work in his output in which his efforts in this field are not put to some use. The *Dances from Marosszék* and the *Dances from Galánta* together with the colourful and highly enjoyable *Peacock* Variations are perhaps three of the finest examples of his use of folk material, and these can be heard in particularly engaging and affectionate performances from the Philharmonia Hungarica. The superb 1974 recordings still sound exceptionally fresh and have transferred well to CD.

NEW REVIEW

Kodály. CHORAL MUSIC. [a]**Lajos Kozma,** [b]**Ian Caley** (tens); [ab]**Elizabeth Gale,** [b]**Sally Le Sage,** [b]**Hannah Francis** (sops); [b]**Alfreda Hodgson** (contr); [b]**Michael Rippon** (bass); [bc]**Christopher Bowers-Broadbent,** [d]**Gillian Weir** (orgs); [abcd]**Brighton Festival Chorus/László Heltay;** [a]**London Symphony Orchestra/István Kertész.** Decca Enterprise 433 080-2DM. Item marked [a] recorded in 1970, [b] 1975, [c] 1976, [d] 1977.
Psalmus Hungaricus, Op. 13[a]. Missa Brevis[b]. Pange Lingua[c]. Psalm 114[d].

1h 10m ADD 8/92 £ 9p

Kodály composed his stirring and masterly *Psalmus Hungaricus* in response to a commission to celebrate the fiftieth anniversary of the union of Buda, Pest and Obuda to form the city of Budapest. Fellow composer Dohnányi led the hugely successful first performance on November 19th, 1923 (also on the programme that evening was the première of Bartók's wonderful *Dance Suite* — what a concert that must have been!). István Kertész's 1970 account of this choral masterpiece is one of his most fervently inspired achievements on record and the Brighton Festival Chorus (trained by László Heltay) produce a thrillingly idiomatic sonority. Heltay himself takes over at the helm for the remaining items: the wartime *Missa Brevis* is easily the most substantial of these, beautifully conceived for the idiom and framed by an organ-only *Introitus* and a postlude, *Ite, missa est*. *Pange lingua* dates from 1928 (though Kodály added the prelude for organ three years later), and it's a wonderfully heartfelt setting of St Thomas Aquinas's eponymous hymn; and Decca also give us the brief, touchingly direct setting of *Psalm 114*, composed in 1952. Apart from this last offering (set down in Guildford Cathedral), London's Kingsway Hall was the venue for all this material, and its ideal acoustical properties are heard to superb advantage in these recordings: *Psalmus Hungaricus*, in particular, sounds magnificent – the work of that incomparable engineer Kenneth Wilkinson. Given the consistent excellence of this idiomatic music-making (one is reminded that Heltay was a pupil and close friend of the composer), this represents a marvellous mid-price compilation.

Additional recommendation …

Psalmus Hungaricus, Op. 13[a]. *Hymn of Zrinyi*[b]. **Dvořák.** *Requiem, B165*[c]. **Soloists;** [c]**Ambrosian Singers;** [a]**Wandsworth School Boys' Choir;** [ab]**Brighton Festival Chorus;** [ac]**London Symphony Orchestra/István Kertész,** [b]**László Heltay.** Decca Ovation 421 810-2DM2 — ② 2h 17m ADD 5/89

Charles Koechlin

French 1867-1950

Suggested listening …

14 Chants, Op. 157/2[c]. Premier album de Lilian, Op. 139[ac]. Second album de Lilian, Op. 149[c] — Sérénade à l'étoile errante; Swimming; Les jeux du clown; Le voyage chimérique. Morceau de lecture, Op. 218[c]. Sonata for piano and flute, Op. 52[c]. Sonata for two flutes, Op. 75[b]. [a]**Jayne West** (sop); **Fenwick Smith,** [b]**Leone Buyse** (fls); [c]**Martin Amlin** (pf). Hyperion CDA66414 (10/90).

Sonata for piano and flute, Op. 52[c]. Quintet, Op. 156, "Primavera"[nd]. *Coupled with* **Jolivet.** Chant de Linos[a]. Flute Sonata[b]. *Coupled with* **Philippe Racine** (fl); [ad]**Robert Zimansky** (vn); [ad]**Monika Clemann** (va); [ad]**Curdin Coray** (vc); [ad]**Xenia Schindler** (hp); [bc]**Daniel Cholette** (pf). Claves CD50-9003 (10/90).

Joonas Kokkonen

Finnish 1921-

Kokkonen. Cello Concerto[a]. Symphonic Sketches. Symphony No. 4. [a]**Torleif Thedéen** (vc); **Lahti Symphony Orchestra/Osmo Vänskä.** BIS CD468.

1h 2m DDD 12/91

The Finnish composer Joonas Kokkonen belongs to the same generation as Robert Simpson and Peter Racine Fricker in England, and first came to wider attention in the 1960s with his Third Symphony. His style is essentially neoclassical and he has fully assimilated the influences of Hindemith and Bartók without resembling either. His music has an unfailing sense of logic and a finely disciplined craftsmanship to commend it and the three works recorded on this disc form an admirable introduction to his art. The Cello Concerto, composed shortly after the death of his mother, has a strong elegiac element particularly in the slow movement. The *Adagio* is obviously deeply-felt even though its main idea rather overstays its welcome and the emotional effect is weakened. The remarkable young Swedish soloist Torleif Thedéen, still in his twenties at the time of this recording, plays superbly; indeed he must be one of the finest cellists of his generation now before the public. His account has an eloquence, all the more powerful for being understated and restrained. The *Symphonic sketches* (1968), written immediately after the Third Symphony, possess that powerful forward current and logical development that characterize this composer at his best. And the three-movement fourth Symphony also makes a powerful impression. The playing of the Lahti Symphony Orchestra for Osmo Vänskä is alert and responsive, and the BIS recording team certainly do justice to them. The balance is exemplary and there is just the right amount of air around the instruments.

Erich Wolfgang Korngold

Austrian/Hungarian 1897-1957

NEW REVIEW

Korngold. Violin Concerto, Op. 35[a].
Rózsa. Violin Concerto, Op. 24[b]. Tema con variazioni, Op. 29a[c].

Waxman. Fantasy on Bizet's "Carmen"[cd]. **Jascha Heifetz** (vn); [c]**Gregor Piatigorsky** (vc); [c]**Chamber Orchestra,** [a]**Los Angeles Philharmonic Orchestra/Alfred Wallenstein;** [b]**Dallas Symphony Orchestra/Walter Hendl;** [d]**RCA Victor Symphony Orchestra/Donald Voorhees.** RCA Gold Seal [ad]mono/[bc]stereo GD87963. Item marked [a] from HMV ALP1233 (12/55), [b] SB6605 (4/65), [cd] new to UK. Recorded 1946-63.

1h 10m ADD 4/89 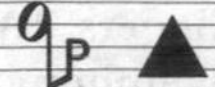

Heifetz's legendary recording of the Korngold Concerto serves a double purpose: as an effective introduction to Korngold's seductive musical style, and as the best possible example of Heifetz's violin artistry. The work itself was written at the suggestion of Bronislaw Huberman, but it was Heifetz who gave the première in 1947. It calls on material that Korngold had also used in three of his film scores (he was at the time composing for Hollywood), although the way he welds the themes into a three-movement structure is masterly enough to suggest that the concerto came to him 'of a piece'. The very opening would be enough to seduce most listeners, unless — that is — they have an aversion to the film music of the period. Miklós Rózsa's Concerto has its roots in the composer's Hungarian soil, and echoes of Bartók are rarely absent. But whereas Korngold's score is taken from movie music, Rózsa's (or parts of it) became a film score — namely, *The Private Life of Sherlock Holmes*. Rózsa's self-possessed, skilfully written "Tema con Variazoni" was taken, in 1962, from a much larger work then in progress, but Heifetz and Piatigorsky play it in a reduced orchestration. As to the *Carmen Fantasy* by Franz Waxman (another notable film composer), its luscious tunes and frightening technical challenges were written with the great violinist very much in mind. It's a stunning piece of playing, and wears its 48 years lightly. The other recordings sound far better, and the Rózsa items are in stereo. Marvellous stuff!

Korngold. Baby Serenade, Op. 24[a]. Cello Concerto, Op. 37[b]. Symphonic Serenade, Op. 39[c]. [b]**Julius Berger** (vc); **North West German Philharmonic Orchestra/Werner Andreas Albert.** CPO 999 077-2. Item marked [a] recorded in 1989, [b] 1991, [c] 1990.

1h 6m DDD/ADD 10/91

Korngold. Symphony in F sharp minor, Op. 40[a]. Theme and Variations, Op. 42[b]. Straussiana[c]. **North West German Philharmonic Orchestra/Werner Andreas Albert.** CPO 999 146-2. Item marked [a] recorded in 1988, [b] 1990, [c] 1987.

1h 8m DDD/ADD 10/91

These are two extremely useful CDs which bring together all of Korngold's post-war music, when he was trying to re-establish himself in Europe and escape his acquired reputation as a master composer of film music. All of Korngold's music to a greater or lesser degree has similar characteristics: virtuoso orchestration which always surprises and delights, memorable lyricism which combines optimism and regret in similar quantities (a quality shared with his beloved Johann Strauss) and rhythmic dynamism which creates tremendous forward motion. The first CD kicks off with the 1928 *Baby Serenade* written to mark the birth of his second son George, who later repaid the compliment by initiating the renaissance of his father's music in the 1960s and 1970s. With a breezy banjo and three vigorous saxophones there is more than a hint of America and jazz in this entertaining piece. The Cello Concerto, which receives a committed performance of the solo part from Julius Berger, is a reworking of the music for a major Bette Davis vehicle of 1946 entitled *Deception*. Like all his film music it is both memorable and atmospheric — indeed a miniature masterpiece of only 16 minutes in length. The Symphonic Serenade was premièred by no less than Wilhelm Furtwängler and the Vienna Philharmonic in December 1950; but despite its similarity in mood to Richard Strauss's *Metamorphosen*, it failed to establish itself in the repertoire. Werner Andreas Albert's well prepared and sympathetic reading makes up for this extraordinary situation.

Like the Serenade, Korngold's greatest post-war work, the Symphony in F sharp was simply out of its time when completed in 1952 — it had to wait for over a decade for its first public performance. In a bizarre way it merges the sound worlds of Mahler and the large-scale Hollywood extravaganza — the tragic *Adagio* rises to several impassioned climaxes using themes from the film *Anthony Adverse*. A great work, which like all of Korngold's music, including the scintillating final orchestral pieces, Theme and Variations and *Straussiana*, should now come into their own as historical taste and influence can be put to one side. All the performances by the North West German Philharmonic Orchestra under Albert are fully up to Korngold's considerable demands, and CPO's recordings are warmly atmospheric with particularly well-judged balance throughout. Highly recommended.

NEW REVIEW

Korngold. DIE TOTE STADT. **René Kollo** (ten) Paul; **Carol Neblett** (sop) Marietta, The apparition of Marie; **Benjamin Luxon** (bar) Frank; **Rose Wagemann** (mez) Brigitta; **Hermann Prey** (bar) Fritz; **Gabriele Fuchs** (sop) Juliette; **Patricia Clark** (sop) Lucienne; **Anton de Ridder** (ten) Gaston, Victorin; **Willi Brokmeier** (ten) Count Albert; **Tolz Boys' Choir; Bavarian Radio Chorus; Munich Radio Orchestra/Erich Leinsdorf.** RCA Opera Series GD87767. Notes, text and translation included. From ARL3 1199 (1/76). Recorded in 1975.

② 2h 17m ADD 11/89 

Korngold's greatest large-scale work is a gripping tale of erotic obsession, draped in music that frequently upstages even Richard Strauss, what with its glittering high percussion, voluptuous, arpeggiating harps, yearning string melodies and frequent climaxes that blossom among exotic flushes of orchestration. Bells and gongs chime *à la Parsifal* and Korngold's decadent sonorities not only recall Strauss (an all-pervading influence) but frequently hark back to Schoenberg's, even Debussy's, *Pelléas*. The story-line concerns a man who has lost his wife, pines for her, becomes elated when he meets a woman who resembles her, and murders the substitute when the chasm between fantasy and reality suddenly dawns. The motto, in Korngold's own words, is "here on earth there can be no reunion with those who have left us, no resurrection". Like Puccini's *Turandot* (composed some years later), *Die tote Stadt* features a multitude of marvellous moments, but just one great single 'number', a duet — "Glück, das mir verblieb", or "Joy, sent from above" — where the wife-substitute entrances her aspiring lover with a haunting air that he heard "in younger and happier days", but that she goes on to frivolously dismiss as a "silly old song". Therein lie the seeds of the tragedy. Many moons ago, Richard Tauber and Lotte Lehmann made a marvellous hit record of the duet, but Carol Neblett and René Kollo are wholly excellent (as are the supporting singers) and Erich Leinsdorf, a seasoned Straussian, keeps Korngold's fulsome waves of sound under control. The recording was made back in 1975 and retains virtually all its impact in an excellent transfer.

NEW REVIEW

Korngold. DAS WUNDER DER HELIANE. **Anna Tomowa-Sintow** (sop) Heliane; **Hartmut Welker** (bar) Ruler; **John David de Haan** (ten) Stranger; **Reinhild Runkel** (contr) Messenger; **René Pape** (bass) Porter; **Nicolai Gedda** (ten) Blind Judge; **Martin Petzold** (ten) Young Man; **Berlin Radio Chorus; Berlin Radio Symphony Orchestra/John Mauceri.** Decca 436 636-2DH3. Notes, text and translation included.

③ 2h 48m DDD 4/93 

This recording — part of Decca's ongoing Entartete Musik series — marks the rediscovery of a major operatic masterpiece of the 1920s, and certainly the rediscovery of one of the most ravishing, opulently orchestrated and complex scores of the period. *Das Wunder der Heliane* was the fourth of Korngold's five magnificent contributions to the genre, and was considered by the composer to be his finest achievement. The plot, based on the play *Die Heilige* by Hans Kaltneker, concerns the strange mystical — non-physical — union between Heliane (wife of the tyrant Ruler) and a character known only as The Stranger who has been imprisoned and condemned to death by Ruler. When their love is discovered, Heliane and The Stranger are put on trial, during which Heliane sings the memorable aria "Ich ging zu ihm" ("I went to him who is to die tomorrow") in her own defence. After an ecstatic duet The Stranger stabs himself. Heliane proves her innocence by miraculously bringing him back to life, but she is stabbed to death by her husband in a fit of jealousy. Heliane is brought to life by The Stranger, and after a tender duet the lovers finally depart this life into the realm of Eternal Love. The opera was premièred in 1927, but despite enjoying a certain success with its audiences it failed to establish itself in the repertoire and disappeared completely after 1930. Reasons for its neglect are numerous and complex (it was labelled 'degenerate' by the Nazis and banned, and it also became embroiled in a musical and artistic battle with Krenek's opera *Jonny spielt auf* which was premièred in the same year) and these are discussed in depth in the excellent booklet-notes. The orchestral writing is lush and harmonically complex (almost bitonal in places) and plays throughout the opera like a vast symphonic poem, and indeed the enormous orchestral and vocal forces required for performance may well have been a contributing factor in its demise. *Das Wunder der Heliane*, however, could not have wished for a more persuasive and triumphant reappraisal than this recording. Anna Tomowa-Sintow is a moving, compassionate Heliane, John David de Haan an ardent and suitably mysterious Stranger, and Hartmut Welker a strong and menacing Ruler. John Mauceri conducts the RSO Berlin with passion, commitment and bravura, and the recording, made in Jesus-Christus-Kirche, Dahlem is excellent. *Heliane* may turn out to be one of the most important and significant opera recordings this decade.

Further listening ...

String Sextet in D major, Op. 10. *Coupled with* **Schoenberg.** Verklärte Nacht. **Raphael Ensemble.** Hyperion CDA66425 (1/91).

The Adventures of Robin Hood — *film score.* **Utah Symphony Orchestra/Varujan Kojian.** That's Entertainment CDTER1066 (3/87).

Cello Concerto in C major, Op. 37[a]. Film Scores : The Private Lives of Elizabeth and Essex — Overture. The Prince and the Pauper — suite. Anthony Adverse — In the forest. The Sea Wolf — suite. Deception. Another Dawn — Night scene. Of Human Bondage — suite. [a]**Francisco Gabarro** (vc); **National Philharmonic Orchestra/Charles Gerhardt.** RCA Victor GD80185 (11/91).

Tomorrow, Op. 33 — tone poem[a]. Film Scores: The Adventures of Robin Hood — Prologue; Duel, Victory and Epilogue. Anthony Adverse — No father, no mother, no name. Between Two Worlds — Main Title; Mother and Son. Captain Blood — Overture. Deception — Overture. Devotion — Death of Emily Brontë. Escape me never — Main Title; Venice; March; Love Scene; Finale. Juarez — Carlotta. Kings Row — Main Title. Of Human Bondage — Nora. The Sea Hawk[b] — Main Title; Reunion; End Title. [a]**Norma Procter** (contr); [ab]**Ambrosian Singers; National Philharmonic Orchestra/Charles Gerhardt.** RCA GD60863.

KING'S ROW — excerpts. **National Philharmonic Orchestra/Charles Gerhardt.** That's Entertainment VCD47203.

VIOLANTA. **Soloists; Bavarian Radio Chorus; Munich Radio Orchestra/Marek Janowski.** CBS CD79229 (9/89).

Leopold Koželuch

Bohemian/Austrian 1747-1818

Suggested listening ...

Clarinet Concerto in E flat major. *Coupled with* ***Crusell.*** Clarinet Concerto No. 1 in E flat major, Op. 1. ***Krommer.*** Clarinet Concerto in E flat major, Op. 36. **Emma Johnson** (cl); **Royal Philharmonic Orchestra/Günther Herbig.** ASV CDDCA763 (9/91).

See review under Crusell; refer to Index to Reviews.

Anton Kraft

Bohemian 1749-1820

Suggested listening ...

Cello Concerto in C major, Op. 4. *Coupled with* ***Haydn.*** Cello Concertos — C major, HobVII*b*/1; D major, HobVII*b*/2. **Anner Bylsma** (bar vc); **Tafelmusik/Jeanne Lamon.** Deutsche Harmonia Mundi RD77757 (9/91).
See review under Haydn; refer to Index to Reviews.

Joseph Martin Kraus

Swedish 1756-1792

NEW REVIEW
Kraus. Symphonies — C minor, "Vienna"; E flat major; D major, "Paris"; C major. **Cologne Concerto.** Capriccio 10 396. Recorded in 1991.

lh 12m DDD 8/92 

Kraus was attracted to the artistically enlightened court of Gustav III in Stockholm during the late 1770s. The four symphonies on this disc have a distinctly cosmopolitan flavour, drawing on fairly wide terms of stylistic reference. Most impressive of them, perhaps, is the C minor Symphony with its four horns, its rhythmic tension and pervasive air of pathos. Listening to this work we can easily understand the high regard in which Kraus was held by Haydn and Gluck, both of whom he met in Vienna. Indeed Kraus dedicated this piece to Haydn who apparently directed its first performance. The remaining symphonies, though perhaps less immediately striking, are hardly of less consequence. The *Larghetto* of the E flat Symphony is a captivating movement with broadly expressive oboe writing foreshadowing the early romantics. The Symphony in C major on the other hand, at least in its opening movement, evokes the *Sturm und Drang* ethos with its dark colours and expressive intensity. Although a debt to Haydn and Gluck is present in these symphonies, Kraus nevertheless speaks with a voice of his own. Performances as lively and as sensitively articulated as these are to be welcomed. Cologne Concerto, one of the finest period instrument ensembles, is on sparkling form.

Johann Krebs

German 1713-1780

Suggested listening ...

Fantasia à giusto Italiano. Fantasia sopra Wer nur den lieben Gott lässt walten. Fugue in B flat major on B-A-C-H. Herr Gott disch loben alle wir. Herzlich lieb hab ich dich, o Herr. Preludes and Fugues — C major; D major. Trios — D minor; E flat major. Wir glauben all an einen Gott. Zeuch ein zu deinen Toren. **Graham Barber** (org). ASV Gaudeamus CDGAU125 (10/91).

Fritz Kreisler

Austrian 1875-1962

Suggested listening ...

Schön Rosmarin. Liebeslied. Liebesfreud. ***Tchaikovsky.*** Méditation, Op. 42 No. 1. Valse-Scherzo, Op. 34. Mélodie, Op. 42 No. 3. ***Dvořák.*** Violin Sonata in G major, B183. ***Schubert.*** Violin Sonatina in G major, B183. **Vera Vaidman** (vn); **Emanuel Krasovsky** (pf). Pickwick CDI PWK1137 (6/90).
See review in the Collections section; refer to Index to Reviews.

Liebesfreud[a]. *Coupled with* ***Mendelssohn:*** Violin Concerto in E minor, Op. 64[b]. ***Bruch:*** Violin Concerto No. 1 in G minor, Op. 26[c]. ***Sarasate:*** Introduction et Tarantelle, Op. 43. **Cho-Liang Lin** (vn); [a]**Sandra Rivers** (pf); [b]**Philharmonia Orchestra/Michael Tilson Thomas;** [c]**Chicago Symphony Orchestra/Leonard Slatkin.** CBS Masterworks CD44902 (3/91).

Ernst Krenek

Austrian/American 1900-1991

NEW REVIEW

Krenek. JONNY SPIELT AUF. **Krister St Hill** (bar) Jonny; **Heinz Kruse** (ten) Max; **Alessandra Marc** (sop) Anita; **Michael Kraus** (bar) Daniello; **Martina Posselt** (sop) Yvonne; **Dieter Scholz** (bass) Manager; **Diter Schwartner** (ten) Hotel Manager; **Martin Petzold** (sngr) Station Announcer, First Policeman; **Matthias Weichert** (sngr) Second Policeman; **Erwin Noack** (sngr) Third Policeman; **Leipzig Opera Chorus; Chinchilla; Leipzig Gewandhaus Orchestra/Lothar Zagrosek.** Decca 436 631-2DH2. Notes, text and translation included. Recorded in 1991.

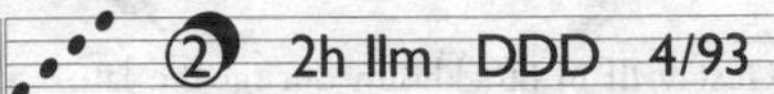

This is the 'jazz opera' that made Krenek's name and fortune, playing to enthusiastic audiences in every opera house in Germany until the rise of Nazism branded it "degenerate music" and cast it into half a century of oblivion. With the appeal of the jazz element in the music went a staging full of sensational effects (a motor-car on stage; a scene in which all the theatre's fire alarms are set off; in another, set halfway up a mountain, music is relayed from the public address system of a hotel in the valley below) and a sort of 'double plot' intended to blow a blast of fresh air from the New World through the stuffy culture of the Old. In one plot Jonny, a black jazz fiddler, steals a valuable violin from a famous virtuoso and ultimately uses it to send the whole cast dancing off to America and freedom. In the other, Max, a composer so obsessed with the icy perfection of his art that he cannot come to terms with the real world (Krenek's own self-portrait?) finds love and the power to control his own destiny. Apart from the excellent cast (Marc, in gorgeous voice as Max's 'muse' Anita, and St Hill as a genially amoral Jonny are especially good) the great quality of this performance is that the subtle and often beautiful lines of Max's music and his duet scenes with Anita are projected with as much flair as the more obviously stage-stealing moments. Jonny's 'theme-song' (a sort of blues), the catchy tango duet and the uproarious final scene, the cheerful incursion into the orchestra of flexatone and swanee whistle — all these are hugely enjoyable, but in the opera's 'other' world a real composer, Krenek himself as much as Max, is finding his own voice, one that's bound to make you wonder why we've heard so little of his 12 subsequent operas.

Franz Krommer

Bohemian 1759-1831

Krommer. WIND OCTETS. **Sabine Meyer Wind Ensemble** (Sabine Meyer, Reiner Wehle, cls; Diethelm Jonas, Thomas Indermühle, obs; Bruno Schneider, Klaus Frisch, hns; George Klütsch, Sergio Azzolini, bns; Klaus Lohrer, cbn). EMI CDC7 54383-2. Recorded in 1990. F major, Op. 57; E flat major, Op. 71; C major, Op. 76; B flat major, Op. 78.

lh 9m DDD 5/92

Born in Czechoslovakia as František Kramář, this composer changed his name to Krommer when he lived in Vienna. Though a contemporary of Mozart, he outlived Beethoven and Schubert and was a major Viennese figure in his time, although to compare him to Haydn (as a contemporary did in 1813) is going too far, for to judge from what we know of his enormous output of music he was a fluent, gifted musician but no genius. The music played here was published under various names, such as partita and Harmonie-musik, which suggest suites for wind players, and although the intended scoring remains unclear the sound of the Sabine Meyer Wind Ensemble is completely convincing. This is the kind of repertory that we hardly ever hear in the concert hall, and we are lucky to have it on record although, to be candid, it earns performance less for its own merit than because it provides a splendid vehicle for fine players. Nevertheless, the performances here will give much satisfaction if you can derive sufficient delight from the artistry of the playing and do not expect too much of the works themselves, and though depth may be lacking in Krommer's music, there is vigour, wit and charm. These qualities are demonstrated most fully in the E flat major and F major Octets which comes third and fourth in this programme. The playing of this fine ensemble is unfailingly stylish, while the recording does justice to its tone and is well balanced.

Further listening ...

Clarinet Concerto in E flat major, Op. 36. *Coupled with* ***Crusell.*** Clarinet Concerto No. 1 in E flat major, Op. 1. ***Koželuch.*** Clarinet Concerto in E flat major. **Emma Johnson** (cl); **Royal Philharmonic Orchestra/Günther Herbig.** ASV CDDCA763 (9/91).
See review under Crusell; refer to Index to Reviews.

Nikolaus von Krufft

Austrian 1779-1818

Suggested listening ...

Sonata for horn and piano in F major. *Coupled with* ***Brahms.*** Horn Trio in E flat major, Op. 40[a]. ***Beethoven.*** Sonata for horn and piano in F major, Op. 17. **Lowell Greer** (hn); [a]**Stephanie Chase** (vn); **Steven Lubin** (pf). Harmonia Mundi HMU90 7037 (9/92).

Daniel Kuhlau

German/Danish 1786-1832

Suggested listening ...

The elf's hill — suite[a]. *Overtures* — Lulu; The triplet brothers from Damascus; The robber's castle; William Shakespeare. **Odense Symphony Orchestra/[a]Othmar Maga, Eduard Serov.** Unicorn-Kanchana DKPCD9132 (5/93).

György Kurtág

Romanian 1926-

Suggested listening ...

Kurtág. String Quartet No. 1, Op. 1. Hommage à Milhály András, Op. 13. Officium breve in memoriam Andreae Szervánzky, Op. 28. *Coupled with* ***Gubaidulina.*** String Quartet No. 2. ***Lutoslawski.*** String Quartet. **Arditti Quartet** . Disques Montaigne 789007 (4/92).
See review under Gubaidulina; refer to Index to Reviews.

Pierre de La Rue

Flanders c.1460-1518

NEW REVIEW

La Rue. Missa cum iocunditate. MOTETS. **Hilliard Ensemble** (David James, Ashley Stafford, altos; Rogers Covey-Crump, John Potter, tens; Paul Hillier, bass). EMI Reflexe CDC7 54082-2. Texts and translations included. Recorded in 1990.

Ave regina celorum. Considera Israel. Delicta juventutis. Gaude virgo. O salutaris Hostia. Plorer, gemier ... Requiem. Vexilla regis ... Passio Domini.

lh 2m DDD 8/92

Pierre de la Rue was one of the most distinguished of the many composers active at the Hapsburg-Burgundian Court at the close of the fifteenth and beginning of the sixteenth centuries: he was extremely prolific, composing more than 30 masses during the course of a lifetime which took him throughout Europe. His works exist in numerous copies, indicating the high repute in which he was held by his contemporaries. The music of La Rue represents a fascinating balance between on the one hand intense expression and on the other complex vocal writing for its own sake, relying on great compositional ingenuity. This CD contains a good cross section of La Rue's work. Its centre is the Mass, *Cum iocunditate,* which contains extreme examples of these two compositional characteristics. In addition, the Hilliard Ensemble include three beautifully crafted motets, which contain much immediately appealing music, and four slightly lesser vocal works. None of these works have been recorded before. The Hilliard Ensemble's performances are efficient without being inspired. The tight recording, made at the Church of Douai Abbey, emphasizes the single voice to a part preferred by the Ensemble; and the sense of ecstatic expansion which characterizes the very finest performances of music of this era is not frequently experienced here. However, in extending our knowledge and experience of this fascinating repertoire, this CD is to be welcomed.

Further listening ...

Missa "L'homme armé". Missa pro defunctis. **Ensemble Clément Janequin** with **Yvon Repérant** (org). Harmonia Mundi HMC90 1296 (9/89).

Missa pro defunctis. *Coupled with* ***Josquin Desprez.*** Missa Hercules dux Ferrarie. La déploration de Johannes Ockeghem, "Nymphes des bois". **New London Chamber Choir/James Wood.** Amon Ra CDSAR24 (3/87).

Edouard Lalo

French 1823-1892

Lalo. Cello Concerto in D minor[a].
Saint-Saëns. Cello Concerto in A minor, Op. 33[b].
Schumann. Cello Concerto No. 1 in A minor, Op. 129[a]. **János Starker** (vc); **London Symphony Orchestra/[a]Stanislaw Skrowaczewski, [b]Antál Dorati.** Mercury 432 010-2MM. Items marked [a] from Philips SAL3482 (3/65), [b] SAL3559 (7/66). Recorded 1962-64.

lh 5m ADD 4/92 £ 9p

János Starker recorded for the Mercury label on several occasions during the 1960s, and the results provide a vivid document of an extraordinary artist heard at the peak of his career. Starker's outward intensity belies a formidable intellectual mastery of Schumann's Cello Concerto, a work whose tangible mood of paranoia and mingled heroism has perplexed generations of players and listeners alike. Interpretations as zealous and charismatic as this are certainly to be treasured, as much for a clarification of the composer's intention, as for the valiant heroism of Starker's playing. He brings a similar clear-sighted gravity of purpose to the Lalo concerto, with a suitably massive opening movement contrasted effectively by a charmingly realized intermezzo and a finale of quicksilver brilliance. The sheer dynamism and drama of this reading has never been bettered, and Starker also succeeds in making Saint-Saëns's First Concerto sound a good deal more substantial than it really is, in a reading of exemplary mastery coupled with scrupulous attention to every requirement of the score. Mercury's original masters traditionally set new standards of fidelity and dynamic range, but in their digitally refurbished form it seems scarcely possible that these classic performances are now almost 30 years old, whilst from a musical standpoint, these individual and occasionally provocative readings remain as enthralling as ever.

Additional recommendation ...

Cello Concerto. **Bruch.** *Kol Nidrei, Op. 47.* **Saint-Saëns.** *Cello Concerto.* **Matt Haimovitz** (vc); **Chicago Symphony Orchestra/James Levine.** DG 427 323-2GH — 59m DDD 6/89

Lalo. Symphonie espagnole, Op. 21.
Saint-Saëns. Introduction and Rondo capriccioso, Op. 28.
Vieuxtemps. Violin Concerto No. 5 in A minor, Op. 37. **Shlomo Mintz** (vn); **Israel Philharmonic Orchestra/Zubin Mehta.** DG 427 676-2GH. Recorded in 1988.

lh DDD 3/92

For violin lovers who want a change from the great concertos of Mendelssohn, Beethoven and Brahms, this captivating collection of lighter, but no less distinctive fare, could be just the thing. Lalo's *Symphonie espagnole* gets the substantial performance it deserves: Shlomo Mintz plays the piece with fine panache, his sweet-toned phrasing always conveying the excitement and sheer enjoyment of this colourful music. Zubin Mehta and the Israel Philharmonic bring keen rhythmic attack to the *Carmen*-like tuttis and pin-point accuracy and tonal balance to the lively orchestration (in the Intermezzo Mehta matches Mintz in his outstanding handling of Lalo's complex cross-rhythms). The Vieuxtemps is no less successful. Composed in 1861, the Fifth Concerto is a comparatively short but rewarding work in the Paganini mould, with a moody, bittersweet aspect which Mintz captures perfectly. Again, there's an almost insolent ease in the way he tackles all these double stops, scales and portamentos. All great virtuosos revel in Saint-Saëns's *Introduction and Rondo capriccioso* and Mintz is no exception. Mehta and the Israel Philharmonic also give Mintz a run for his money in the richly sounded big tuttis. The recording is slightly larger than life with plenty of inner clarity. The overall balance perhaps works best in the Lalo but the general sound quality is very satisfying.

Additional recommendations ...

Symphonie espagnole. **Berlioz.** *Rêverie et caprice, Op. 8.* **Itzhak Perlman** (vn); **Orchestre de Paris/Daniel Barenboim.** DG 400 032-2GH — 41m ADD 3/83

Symphonie espagnole. **Bruch.** *Scottish Fantasy, Op. 46.* **Anne Akiko Meyers** (vn); **Royal Philharmonic Orchestra/Jesús López-Cobos.** RCA Victor Red Seal RD60942 — lh DDD 9/92

Further listening ...

Symphony in G minor. *Coupled with* **Franck.** *Symphony in D minor.* **French Radio National Orchestra/Sir Thomas Beecham.** EMI CDM7 63396-2 (9/92).

Constant Lambert

British 1905-1951

Lambert. Rio Grande[a]. Summer's Last Will and Testament[b]. Aubade héroïque. [a]**Sally Burgess** (mez); [b]**William Shimell** (bar); [a]**Jack Gibbons** (pf); [a]**Opera North Chorus;** [b]**Leeds Festival Chorus; English Northern Philharmonia/ David Lloyd-Jones.** Hyperion CDA66565. Texts included. Recorded in 1991.

lh l5m DDD 6/92 

Constant Lambert was a man of so many talents — conductor, writer, speaker (not merely social but professional, as in the first recording of Walton's *Façade*) — that in his own lifetime it was not always clear how far his greatest gift lay in composition. Even the success of his *Rio Grande* in 1928 hindered him from being taken quite seriously, for, although it was (as the *Musical Times* reported) "the hit of the season", it was also the work of a 22-year-old, brilliant but modish, and considered "a hotch-potch of good and bad" rather than a sound and solid achievement. When *Summer's Last Will and Testament* appeared in 1936 it disappointed those who hoped for another *Rio Grande*, and failed to satisfy the serious ones who wanted something more 'difficult' and 'progressive' in idiom. It became, in Malcolm Arnold's words, "one of the undiscovered treasures of the English choral repertoire" and so remained, for many listeners, until the issue of this excellent recording. What this reveals is a work of varied moods, including the desperate seriousness of black comedy, and of unvarying distinction. It draws its title and text from Thomas Nashe's entertainment written after the plague in 1592, and Lambert incorporates "Spring, the sweet spring" and "Adieu, farewell, earth's bliss", the two best-known lyrics, interposing the *Rondo Burlesca* or "King-Pest", most original of the movements. David Lloyd-Jones conducts a performance which is both powerful and sensitive, and he also gives an additional tautness to the *Rio Grande*, in which Jack Gibbons (a Gershwin specialist) is the outstanding pianist. The third work, *Aubade héroïque*, is an elegiac piece of great beauty, written after Lambert and the Sadlers Wells Ballet Company had been trapped in Holland after the German invasion in 1940. This issue should correct once and for all the notion that Lambert was anything other than an extraordinary and multifarious talent.

NEW REVIEW

Lambert. CONSTANT LAMBERT CONDUCTS LAMBERT. [a]**Gladys Ripley** (contr); [a]**Kyla Greenbaum** (pf); [a]**BBC Chorus;** [b]**Philharmonia Orchestra,** [c]**Liverpool Philharmonic Orchestra,** [d]**Orchestra of the Royal Opera House, Covent Garden/Constant Lambert.** EMI Great Recordings of the Century mono CDH7 63911-2. Text included. Recorded 1945-50.

Lambert: Horoscope — ballet suite: Dance for the followers of Leo[c] (from Columbia DX1196, 7/45); Sarabande for the followers of Virgo[b] (DX1567, 6/49); Valse for the Gemini[c] (DX1196); Bacchanale[b] (DX1568, 6/49); Invocation to the moon and finale[c] (DX1197, 7/45). Rio Grande[ab] (DX1591/2, 9/49). ***Chabrier*** (orch. Lambert): Ballabile[b] (from Cinq pièces posthumes. DX1736, 4/51). ***Liszt/Lambert*** (orch. Jacob): Apparitions[b] — Galop (from Grand Galop Chromatique, S219. DX1568); Cave scene (from Mephisto Waltz No. 3, S216. DX1560, 4/49). ***Rawsthorne:*** Overture — Street Corner[b] (HMV C3502, 8/46). ***Gordon:*** The Rake's Progress — ballet suite[d]: The reception; The faithful girl (both from DX1249, 6/46); The orgy (DX1250, 6/46).

1h 19m ADD 9/92 ▲

In his review (above) of David Lloyd-Jones's Lambert performances on Hyperion the writer touches on the man and his best-known work, *Rio Grande*. The composer recorded this setting of a poem by Sachaverell Sitwell for contralto, chorus, piano and orchestra on two occasions, and it is many years since the later version of 1949 has been made available. Lambert brings out the work's combination of jazzy high spirits and deeply-moving poetry very vividly: he was a most inspiring conductor, and frankly his performance makes that of Lloyd-Jones seem staid by comparison. He composed several ballet scores, and the best-known is *Horoscope*, written for the Vic-Wells ballet in 1937. This story of star-crossed lovers is set to music which is in turn brilliant and poignantly expressive. Lambert arranged a suite from the ballet, and the two sets of excerpts, recorded by him in 1945 and 1949 with two orchestras, make up a very successful, strongly characterized performance of the complete suite. Lambert and Rawsthorne were close friends, and the latter's *Street Corner* Overture receives a very lively, warmly affectionate reading. French music was particularly close to Lambert's heart, too, and his account of the little Chabrier piece is quite delicious. His performances of the Liszt arrangements are also full of vitality, but even he cannot make much of the pallid Gavin Gordon pieces. It's a great pity that one of Lambert's fine recordings of Russian music was not chosen instead, but even apart from the one poor item this very well-filled and excellently engineered disc contains over an hour of sheer delight.

Additional recommendations ...

Horoscope. ***Bliss.*** *Checkmate – suite.* ***Walton.*** *Façade – Suites Nos. 1 and 2.* **English Northern Philharmonia/David Lloyd-Jones.** Hyperion CDA66436 — 1h 14m DDD 3/91

Horoscope. Rio Grande[a]. *Concerto for Piano and nine players*[b]. [a]**Della Jones** (mez); [ab]**Kathryn Stott** (pf); [a]**BBC Singers; BBC Concert Orchestra/Barry Wordsworth.** Argo 436 118-2ZH — 1h 9m DDD 10/92

Rued Langgaard

Danish 1893-1952

NEW REVIEW

Langgaard. Symphonies — No. 4, "Fall of the Leaf"; No. 5, "Steppelands"; No. 6, "Heavens Asunder". **Danish National Radio Symphony Orchestra/Neeme Järvi.** Chandos CHAN9064. Recorded in 1991.

lh 3m DDD 12/92 

This reclusive Dane (pronounced Ruth Langor, should you want to rave about him to your friends) was either a visionary mystic or wildly nutty, depending on your point of view. Unfortunately for Langgaard, the Danes had already embraced Carl Nielsen as their country's answer to Sibelius; and in any case these three Langgaard symphonies seldom display the much valued Scandinavian symphonic virtues of coherence and far-sighted evolution. Indeed Robert Layton, in his original *Gramophone* review, referred to the effect of the Fifth and Sixth as "overwhelmingly episodic". But what astonishing episodes! The Fourth Symphony's "Leaf-fall" is a Danish, foreshortened but distinctly apocalyptic, *Alpine Symphony* with quite as much Wagner along the way as Richard Strauss (it opens with exactly the same brass chord as *Götterdämmerung*); it is thrilling nature music, with moments of wild, flying energy contrasted with episodes of almost Delian contemplation and atmosphere. The Fifth is more ordered and shows that, for all Langgaard's jealousy of Nielsen, in his Rondo theme for the work, he was quite content to powerfully imitate him. And the Sixth's cosmic conflicts recall Bruckner and Charles Ives. That's enough influences to be going on with; you can enjoy spotting many more for yourself. None of them detract from these communications of an extraordinary imagination. As to the performances, suffice it to say that the Danish orchestra sound entirely at home, and Järvi has never been more in his element. And Chandos, even by their own standards, have never produced more spectacular sound.

Orlando Lassus

Franco/Flemish 1532-1594

Lassus. Missa Osculetur me. MOTETS. **The Tallis Scholars/Peter Phillips.** Gimell CDGIM018. Texts and translations included.

Motets — Osculetur me; Hodie completi sunt; Timor et tremor; Alma Redemptoris mater a 8; Salve regina mater a 8; Ave regina caelorum Il a 6; Regina coeli a 7.

49m DDD 7/89 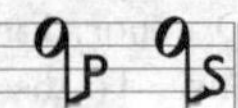

The Tallis Scholars have produced another winner with this recording, performing a fairly recently discovered and relatively unknown masterpiece: the mellifluous *Missa Osculetur me*, built on the composer's own motet of the same title. The Mass, with its two alternating and interlocking choirs and its two solo quartets, presents a fascinating study in the use of vocal textures. Indeed, this is equally true of the motets, variously scored for six, seven and eight voices. The Pentecost motet *Hodie completi sunt*, sung by men's voices, is particularly effective. It bursts into its final "alleluias" after a sustained crescendo of tremendous power. The weirdly chromatic *Timor et tremor* presents a rich, full sound, lightened when the sopranos indulge in lively syncopation towards the end. Such variety is exploited to the full by the Scholars: the listener can hear each strand of the web, and enjoy not only the final blend but also the sheer quality of each and every voice.

Further listening ...

Libro de villanelle, moresche, et altre canzoni — excerpts. Chansons. Chansons (arr. for lute). **Eric Belloq** (lte); **Ensemble Clément Janequin.** Harmonia Mundi HMC90 1391 (2/93).

Lamentationes Hieremiae a 5. **La Chapelle Royale European Ensemble/Philippe Herreweghe.** Harmonia Mundi HMC90 1299 (12/89).

Missa Qual donna attende à gloriosa fama. Tristis est anima mea. Exaltabo te Domine a 4. Psalmi Davidis poenitentiales — De profundis. Missa Venatorum. ***de Rore.*** Qual donna à gloriosa fama. **Christ Church Cathedral Choir, Oxford/Stephen Darlington.** Nimbus NI5150 (4/89).

Antonio Lauro

Venezuelan 1917-1986

Lauro. GUITAR WORKS. **Jesus Castro Balbi** (gtr). Etcetera KTC1110. Recorded in 1990. Suite Venezolana. Carora. El Marabino. Variaciones sobre un Tema Infantil Venezolano. Cuatro Valses Venezolanos. Sonata. Tripitco. Maria Luisa. Angostura.

1h DDD 11/91

Among the ethnic ingredients of South American music it is the Spanish one which predominates in Venezuela, particularly evident in the juxtaposition of 3/4 and 6/8 times (the hemiola), characteristic of many of the renaissance dances taken there by the Spanish conquerors, *c.*1500. The many *valses* of Antonio Lauro owe more to this inheritance than to the Viennese waltz, though their melodies are scarcely less winsome than those of Strauss; several are named after members of Lauro's family or after places in his own country. The *Suite Venezolano* is 'regional' only in its first movement, a depiction of the people from one area who chatter incessantly. A few of his guitar works, here the Sonata and the Variations, are cast in European moulds but their accent is Venezuelan — the slow movement of the Sonata is a *canción* (song), the last a *bolera*. Lauro's music was never more seductively played than by the composer himself but, as he is no longer able to do so, Balbi makes a very satisfying substitute in this clearly recorded selection of polished, charming and tuneful music.

William Lawes

British 1602-1645

Suggested listening ...

The catts. Come, my Daphne, come away. Gather ye rosebuds while ye may (two versions). Haste you, nimphs. He that will not love. A masque. Royall Consorts — Sett No. 1 in D minor: Fantazy, Aire, Almain, Corranto I and II, Saraband and Ecco; Sett No. 2 in D minor: Aire. To the dews. To pansies. To the sycamore. White though yee be. Wise nature that the dew of sleep prepares. Ye feinds and furies. *Coupled with* ***R. Johnson:*** Arm, arm!. As I walked forth. Baboon's Dance. Care-charming sleep. Charon, oh Charon. Dear, do not your fair beauty wrong. The first of the Temple. Full fathom five. Have you seen the bright lily grow?. Mascarada. The noble man's masque tune. Orpheus I am. Satyr's Dance. The third of the Temple. Tis late and cold. Where the bee sucks. *Coupled with* ***Anonymous:*** Cock Lorel. The ape's dance at the Temple. ***Dowland:*** Doulands Rounde Battell Galyard. **Tragicomedia/ Stephen Stubbs.** EMI Reflexe CDC7 54311-2 (2/92).
See review in the Collections section; refer to Index to Reviews.

Claude Le Jeune

French 1528/30-1600

Suggested listening ...

Chansons[ab] — Que je porte d'envie; Je me n'élève icy; Tu ne l'enten pas; Je ne me plain; Susanne un jour (trans. lute); Le chant de l'Alouette; Quelle eau, quel air; Je voulou baiser ma rebelle; Je suis deshéritée; Allons, allons gay; Debat la nostre trill' en May; Mais que es tu, dy moi. Trois Fantasies[b]. [a]**Clément Janequin Ensemble;** [b]**Les Elements Ensembles.** Harmonia Mundi HMC90 1182 (3/87).

Ludwig Lebrun

German 1752-1790

Suggested listening ...

Oboe Concerto No. 1 in D minor. *Coupled with* ***C.P.E. Bach.*** Oboe Concerto in E flat major, H468. ***Mozart.*** Oboe Concerto in C major, K314/285*d*. **Paul Goodwin** (ob); **The English Concert/Trevor Pinnock.** Archiv Produktion 431 821-2AH (7/91).

See review under C.P.E. Bach; refer to Index to Reviews.

Jean-Marie Leclair

French 1697-1764

Leclair. FLUTE SONATAS. **Barthold Kuijken** (fl); **Wieland Kuijken** (va da gamba); **Robert Kohnen** (hpd). Accent ACC58435/6D. From ACC8435/6 (7/85).
ACC58435D — Op. 1: No. 2 in C major. Op. 2: No. 1 in E minor; No. 3 in C major; No. 5 in G major. *ACC58436D* — Op. 1: No. 6 in E minor. Op. 2: No. 8 in D minor; No. 11 in B minor. Op. 9: No. 2 in E minor; No. 7 in G major.

② 50m 59m DDD 2/86

Leclair's Flute Sonatas are technically among the most advanced of their period; only Bach's make comparable demands on the soloist. The music is subtle and much of its charm lies in the successful assimilation and juxtaposition of French and Italian styles. In Leclair's hands the "reunion of tastes" is considerably and brilliantly advanced. Fast movements are outwardly clad in Italian dress, yet French dance measures sometimes lie concealed within. Slow movements are usually of a more overtly French character brought out in ornamentation, gesture and the rhythmic inflexions of courtly dances such as the menuet and gavotte. Kuijken gives fluent and stylistically assured performances, chasing the elusive qualities of the music with unhurried grace and a warm rounded tone. His is a baroque flute and on occasion he is inclined to be smothered by an over-assertive continuo team; but Kuijken's feeling for gesture, his informed use of unequal rhythms and his quietly passionate affair with this great flute literature assures performances that are enduringly satisfying.

Leclair. SCYLLA ET GLAUCUS. **Donna Brown** (sop) Scylla; **Howard Crook** (ten) Glaucus; **Rachel Yakar** (sop) Circé; **Catherine Dubosc** (sop) Dorine, Sicilian girl; **Françoise Golfier** (sop) Cupid; **Agnès Mellon** (sop) Venus; **René Schirrer** (bar) Licas; **Elisabeth Vidal** (sop) Temire; **André Murgatroyd** (ten) Propetide I; **Nicolas Robertson** (ten) Propetide II; **Philip Salmon** (ten) Shepherd; **Elizabeth Priday** (sop) Shepherdess; **Richard Stuart** (bar) Sylvan; **Francis Dudziak** (bar) Hecate, Sylvan; **Monteverdi Choir; English Baroque Soloists/John Eliot Gardiner.** Erato 2292-45277-2. Notes, text and translation included.

③ 2h 50m DDD 4/88

Leclair was foremost an instrumental composer and *Scylla et Glaucus* was his sole contribution to the French operatic stage. There are three principal characters in the drama and they have been strongly cast in Donna Brown (a warmly appealing Scylla), Howard Crook (effortlessly negotiating the highest reaches of his tessitura) and in Rachel Yakar (as Circé). Circé is Leclair's most colourful role and the potency of her magic is vividly captured in the music of Act 4. The Monteverdi Choir and English Baroque Soloists under the informed and lively direction of John Eliot Gardiner set the seal on a splendid achievement. The recorded sound is clear and a full libretto is legibly presented in the accompanying booklet.

Further listening ...

Trio Sonatas, Op. 4 — No. 1 in D minor; No. 2 in B flat major; No. 3 in D minor; No. 4 in F major; No. 5 in G minor; No. 6 in A major. **Purcell Quartet.** Chandos Chaconne CHAN0536 (7/93).

Violin Sonatas — A minor, Op. 5 No. 7; A major, Op. 9 No. 4. *Coupled with* ***Mondonville.*** Violin Sonata in G major, Op. 3 No. 5. ***Guillemain.*** Violin Sonata in A major, Op. 1 No. 4. *Harpsichord Solos —* ***Duphly.*** La de Redemond. La du Buq. ***J-B. Forqueray.*** La Morangis ou La Plissay. **Simon Standage** (vn); **Lars Ulrik Mortensen** (hpd). Chandos Chaconne CHAN0531 (6/93).

Alexandre Charles Lecocq

French 1832-1918

Suggested listening ...

Mam'zelle Angot — ballet[a]. *Coupled with* ***Hérold.*** La fille mal gardée — ballet (arr. Lanchbery)[b]. [a]**National Philharmonic Orchestra/Richard Bonynge;** [b]**Orchestra of the Royal Opera House, Covent Garden/John Lanchbery.** Decca Ovation 430 849-2DM2 (12/91).

Le Jour et la Nuit — *operetta*[a]. Rose Mousse — *musical comedy*[b]. [a]**National Philharmonic Orchestra/Richard Bonynge;** [b]**French Radio Lyric Orchestra/Jean-Claude Hartemann.** Musidic 20136-2 (3/92).

Michel Legrand

French 1932-

Suggested listening ...

MAGIC — THE MUSIC OF MICHEL LEGRAND. *Songs include* His eyes, her eyes; I will say goodbye; magic; The windmills of your eyes; Little boy lost; What are you doing the rest of your life? **Dame Kiri Te Kanawa** (sop); **Ambrosian Singers; London Studio Orchestra/Michel Legrand.** Teldec 9031-73285-2 (11/92).

Franz Lehár

Austrian/Hungarian 1870-1948

Lehár. DIE LUSTIGE WITWE. **Josef Knapp** (bar) Baron Mirko Zeta; **Hanny Steffek** (sop) Valencienne; **Eberhard Waechter** (bar) Graf Danilo Danilowitsch; **Elisabeth Schwarzkopf** (sop) Hanna Glawari; **Nicolai Gedda** (ten) Camille Rosillon; **Kurt Equiluz** (ten) Vicomte Cascada; **Hans Strohbauer** (ten) Raoul de St Brioche; **Franz Böheim** (buffo) Njegus; **Philharmonia Chorus and Orchestra/Lovro von Matačic.** EMI CDS7 47178-8. Notes, text and translation included. From Columbia SAN101/2 (5/63). Recorded in 1962.

② lh 20m AAD 4/86 P B

The Merry Widow contains some marvellous melodies and although versions have come and gone none have ever managed to oust the classic 1962 recording with Elisabeth Schwarzkopf. She is a merry widow without equal, conveying with her rich and alluring voice the ebullience and glamour of the character as in no other recording. EMI's preference for a baritone (rather than tenor) Danilo in successive recordings has not always been successful, but here Eberhard Waechter encompasses the role without difficulty and gives a rousing portrayal of the playboy embassy *attaché*. As the second couple, Nicolai Gedda is in typically radiant voice, whilst Hanny Steffek makes a charming and vibrant Valencienne. Josef Knapp is a spirited ambassador. If von Matačcic's tempos are at times a little on the fast side, this is fully justified by the extra excitement achieved. At the same time there are moments of tenderness, as in the beautifully paced "Vilja" song, which comes off to perfection with Schwarzkopf's beautifully held final note. The contribution of the "Königliche-Pontevedrinische Hof-Tamburrizzakapelle" to provide authentic Balkan atmosphere at Hanna's party is just one of the delightful touches of Walter Legge's production that go to make this a very special recording. The pity is that the score is given less than absolutely complete and that the CD changeover comes in the middle of Act 2. However, the artistry and sheer enjoyment of the recording are unmatched. It is one of those occasions when everything seems to come off perfectly.

Additional recommendations ...

Soloists; BBC Chorus; Philharmonia/Otto Ackermann. EMI mono CDH7 69520-2 — 1h 12m ADD 11/88

Excerpts. **Soloists; Berlin Deutsche Opera Chorus; Berlin Symphony Orchestra/Robert Stolz.** Eurodisc 258 372 — 48m 4/88

Further listening ...

Der Graf von Luxemburg — *operetta: excerpts.* **Soloists; Günther Arndt Choir; Berlin Symphony Orchestra/Robert Stolz.** Eurodisc 258 358 (4/88).

Die Zarewitsch — *operetta: excerpts.* **Berlin Deutsche Opera Chorus; Berlin Symphony Orchestra/Robert Stolz.** Eurodisc 258 357 (4/88).

Paganini — *operetta: excerpts.* **Soloists; Günther Arndt Choir; Berlin Symphony Orchestra/Robert Stolz.** Eurodisc 258 359 (4/88).

Der Land des Lächelns — *operetta.* **Soloists; Günther Arndt Choir; Berlin Symphony Orchestra/Robert Stolz.** Eurodisc 258 373 (4/88).

GIUDITTA — *opera: excerpts.* **Soloists; Günther Arndt Choir; Berlin Symphony Orchestra/Werner Schmidt-Boelcke.** Eurodisc 258 374 (4/88).

Kenneth Leighton

British 1929-1988

NEW REVIEW

Leighton. CHAMBER AND INSTRUMENTAL WORKS. [a]**Janet Hilton** (cl); [ab]**Raphael Wallfisch** (vc); **Peter Wallfisch** (pf). Chandos CHAN9132. Recorded in 1992.
Fantasy on an American Hymn Tune, Op. 70[a]. Alleluia Pascha Nostrum, Op. 85[b]. Variations, Op. 30. Piano Sonata, Op. 64.

1h 10m DDD 5/93

A magnificent showcase for this still grievously under-rated English figure. As all of these pieces readily demonstrate, the art of Kenneth Leighton was a probing, consummately-crafted one. Serial techniques absorbed from studies with the Italian composer Goffredo Petrassi inhabit the impressive early Piano Variations from 1955. The invention both here and in the powerful Piano Sonata of 17 years later is of a very high order indeed; equally, there's no gainsaying the superbly idiomatic quality of Leighton's piano writing (the composer himself was a notably fine pianist). Peter Wallfisch (long a champion of Leighton's music) is a passionate, perceptive interpreter. Wallfisch is then joined by his cellist son, Raphael, and clarinettist Janet Hilton to lend stunning advocacy to the *Fantasy on an American Hymn Tune* — an often inspired free-flowing meditation based on the hymn *The Shining River* which rises to a climax of truly terrifying, virtuosic intensity. Similarly, *Alleluia Pascha Nostrum* for cello and piano from 1981 is another enormously pungent, deeply moving creation; the Wallfisch duo's rapt rendering attains a remarkable level of concentration. In sum, this is fine, thoughtful music which will durably reward the patient listener. Chandos's exemplary production-values add further lustre to what is, quite simply, an outstandingly eloquent release.

NEW REVIEW

Leighton. CATHEDRAL MUSIC. [a]**Neil Mackie** (ten); **St Paul's Cathedral Choir/John Scott** with **Andrew Lucas** (org). Hyperion CDA66489. Texts included. Recorded in 1991.
Te Deum laudamus. Missa brevis, Op. 5. Crucifixus pro nobis, Op. 38[a]. Second Service, Op. 62. An Evening Hymn. Let all the world in every corner sing. ***Traditional*** (arr. Leighton): Lully, lulla (Coventry carol).

1h 14m DDD 12/92

Though church music — the sound of choir and organ, the 'feel' of church as a place for music-making — was part of the air Kenneth Leighton breathed, he was no narrow product or insular exponent of the system. His technical facility as a composer was phenomenal, but 'facile' is one of the last words that could be used of his compositions. They have nothing of the standardized modernism of innocuous discords and brightly quirky rhythms; rather, his work often has a certain bleakness. His structures, like his ideas, are strong, yet quite frequently one feels that "Naught for your comfort" could be the motto. The cantata *Crucifixus pro nobis* is the major work here, to words by the early seventeenth-century poet Patrick Carey, with Phineas Fletcher's *Drop, drop, slow tears* for the final movement. The performance is a fine one, with Neil Mackie as the excellent soloist and with subtle playing of the organ part by Andrew Lucas. The St Paul's choristers, who have made several notable recordings under John Scott, cope expertly throughout, especially in the *Missa brevis* written in 1968 for Liverpool Cathedral. They are also sensitive in their care for words, and the somewhat chilly text of Sir Thomas Browne's *Evening Hymn* comes over with a clarity that also does credit to Hyperion's production team.

Guillaume Lekeu

Belgian 1870-1894

NEW REVIEW

Lekeu. Andromède[a]. Les burgraves — Introduction symphonique. [a]**Dinah Bryant** (sop); [a]**Zeger Vandersteene** (ten); [a]**Philippe Huttenlocher** (bar); [a]**Jules Bastin** (bass); [a]**Namur Symphonic Chorus; Liège Philharmonic Orchestra/Pierre Bartholomée.** Ricercar Secondo RIS099083. Notes, text and translation included. Recorded in 1991.

1h 7m DDD 10/92

Before Lekeu's short life was tragically ended by typhoid fever he produced music of real quality and this recording helps to show what a loss his death was to the musical world. He was only 17, and without much formal tuition in composition (later he studied with Franck and d'Indy), when he started work on what must have been intended as an operatic setting of Victor Hugo's revenge drama *Les burgraves.* But he seems to have abandoned hope of bringing it to completion and what we have here is the solemn, powerful and somewhat Wagnerian "Introduction symphonique", in other words an overture. It is an impressive piece, with atmospheric scoring, that begins slowly and then moves on to a menacing quicker section. After d'Indy suggested that he enter for the Belgian Prix de Rome, Lekeu wrote the regulation cantata on a set subject from antiquity, that of the Ethiopian princess Andromeda who was chained to a rock as a human sacrifice to a sea-monster but was rescued by Perseus. The cantata only won the second prize (in 1891), but the violinist Ysaÿe was so impressed by Lekeu's ability that he commissioned from him the Sonata in G major which remains his best known work. *Andromède* itself is dramatic in tone and well scored. Pierre Bartholomée is a champion of Lekeu's music and the performance under his direction is a stirring one, although the Namur Symphonic Chorus is not a top-rank choir. Much of the vocal weight falls on Dinah Bryant as Andromeda, a skilful singer whose lament as she awaits death chained to her rock is the high point of the work. Perseus is well sung by Zeger Vandersteene, but he does not have much to do, while the experienced Philippe Huttenlocher is a steady narrator.

Further listening ...

Violin Sonata in G major. *Coupled with* ***Debussy.*** Violin Sonata in G minor. ***Ravel.*** Violin Sonata, Op. posth. **Jean-Jacques Kantorow** (vn); **Jacques Rouvier** (pf). Denon CO72718 (8/89).

Ruggero Leoncavallo

Italian 1858-1919

Leoncavallo. PAGLIACCI[a]. **Joan Carlyle** (sop) Nedda; **Carlo Bergonzi** (ten) Canio; **Giuseppe Taddei** (bar) Tonio; **Ugo Benelli** (ten) Beppe; **Rolando Pancrai** (bar) Silvio. ***Mascagni.*** CAVALLERIA RUSTICANA[a]. **Fiorenza Cossotto** (mez) Santuzza; **Adriane Martino** (mez) Lola; **Carlo Bergonzi** (ten) Turiddu; **Giangiacomo Guelfi** (bar) Alfio; **Maria Gracia Allegri** (contr) Lucia; **Chorus and Orchestra of La Scala, Milan/Herbert von Karajan.**
OPERA INTERMEZZOS. **Berlin Philharmonic Orchestra/Herbert von Karajan.** DG 419 257-2GH3. Notes, texts and translations included. Items marked [a] from SLPM139205/07 (10/66), recorded in 1965, [b] SLPM139031 (6/69), recorded in 1965.
Verdi: La traviata — Prelude, Act 3. ***Puccini***: Manon Lescaut — Intermezzo. Suor Angelica — Intermezzo. ***Schmidt***: Notre Dame — Intermezzo. ***Massenet***: Thaïs — Meditátion (with Michel Schwalbé, vn). *Giordano*: Fedora — Intermezzo. ***Cilea***: Adriana Lecouvreur — Intermezzo. ***Wolf-Ferrari:*** I gioiello della Madonna — Intermezzo. ***Mascagni:*** L'amico Fritz — Intermezzo.

③ 3h 18m ADD 10/87 B

Cav and Pag as they are usually known have been bedfellows for many years. Lasting for about 75 minutes each, they have some similarities. Both works concern the passions, jealousies and hatred of two tightly-knit communities — the inhabitants of a Sicilian town and the players in a travelling troupe of actors. *Cavalleria rusticana* ("Rustic chivalry") concerns the triangular relationship of mother, son and his rejected lover. Played against a rich musical tapestry, sumptuously orchestrated, the action is played out during the course of an Easter day. Bergonzi is a stylish, ardent Turiddu whose virile charms glitter in his every phrase and Fiorenza Cossotto makes a thrilling Santuzza motivated and driven by a palpable conviction; her contribution to the well-known Easter hymn scene is gripping. But the real hero of the opera is Karajan, whose direction of this powerful work is magnificent.
Conviction and insight also instil *Pagliacci* with excitement and real drama. A troupe of actors arrive to give a performance of a *commedia dell'arte* play. The illustration of real love, life and hatred is portrayed in the interplay of Tonio, Silvio, Nedda and her husband Canio. As the two rivals, Bergonzi and Taddei are superb. Taddei's sinister, hunchbacked clown, gently forcing the play-within-the-play closer to reality until it finally bursts out violently is a masterly assumption, and Karajan controls the slow build-up of tension with a grasp that few conductors could hope to equal. The Scala forces respond wholeheartedly and the 1965 recording sounds well. The third disc is filled by a selection of very rich, very soft-centred opera intermezzos.

Pagliacci[a]*/Cavalleria*[b]. **Soloists; [a]London Voices; [a]Finchley Children's Music Group; [b]London Opera Chorus; [ab]National Philharmonic Orchestra/[a]Giuseppe Patanè; [b]Gianandrea Gavazzeni.** Decca 414 590-2DH2 — ② 2h 23m ADD 1/89 B
Pagliacci/Cavalleria. **Soloists; Ambrosian Opera Chorus; Philharmonia Orchestra/Riccardo Muti.** EMI CMS7 63650-2 — ② 2h 30m ADD 3/91 B

Anatoli Liadov

Russian 1855-1914

Liadov. ORCHESTRAL WORKS. **Slovak Philharmonic Orchestra/Stephen Gunzenhauser.** Marco Polo 8 220348.

Baba-Yaga, Op. 56. Intermezzo in B flat major, Op. 8 No. 1. Pro starinu — Ballade in D major, Op. 21b. The enchanted lake, Op. 62. Village scene by the inn — Mazurka, Op. 19. Nénie, Op. 67. Polonaise, Op. 49. Polonaise in D major, Op. 55. Kikimora, Op. 63. From the Apocalypse, Op. 66.

58m DDD 10/86 

Liadov was a superb miniaturist and as a professor of composition at the St Petersburg Conservatory he had an interestingly potent influence on the music of his younger contemporaries. His finest works are jewel-like in the depth and luminosity of colour they embody and the finesse with which they are worked. His short tone-poem, *The enchanted lake*, immediately establishes in a few delicate strokes the dank mystery of his subject; *Baba-Yaga* conjures up in only three minutes the menace of the mythical witch in flight; *Kikimora*, so well admired by Stravinsky, summons from out of hushed menace the demon wife of the house spirit, Domovoi. Listening to Liadov's works in succession highlights his problem with more protracted formal structures, but a programme such as this one is worth dipping into for the choice morsel or two. Each of these performances drives straight to the heart of the mood Liadov has in mind and the recording more than adequately captures the sparkle and solidity of the orchestral sound. For anyone interested in Liadov or the flowering of late-romanticism in music, this disc is well worth sampling.

Gyorgy Ligeti

Hungarian 1923-

Ligeti. String Quartet No. 1.
Lutoslawski. String Quartet.
Schnittke. Kanon in memoriam I. Stravinsky. **Hagen Quartet** (Lukas Hagen, Rainer Schmidt, vns; Veronika Hagen, va; Clemens Hagen, vc). DG 431 686-2GH. Recorded in 1990.

54m DDD 9/91  

You won't find Ligeti and Lutoslawski subscribing to the conventional view of the string quartet as requiring four 'symphonic' movements. Ligeti's extended single movement has 17 kaleidoscopically-interacting sub-sections, and Lutoslawski's two main sections are also mosaic-like in form, with a wide variety of different ideas emerging and, on occasion, conflicting. Both quartets — not least because they are superbly imagined for the medium, and finely played on this disc — make fascinating listening, and Ligeti's subtitle ("Nocturnal Metamorphoses") would not be wholly inappropriate for the Lutoslawski as well. There's a dark quality, many rustlings and flickerings, which Ligeti balances against a more fantastic, sardonic tone, and which Lutoslawski leads into both highly dramatic and poignantly lyrical regions. The Ligeti is an early work, beholden to Bartók but bursting with its own very definite ideas about both form and content. The Lutoslawski is more mature, less adventurous, but far from cautious either. With Schnittke's austere, grief-stricken tribute to Stravinsky as a bonus, and with admirably natural yet spacious recorded sound, this is a disc which anyone sceptical about the rewards of modern chamber music can approach with confidence.

Ligeti. LE GRAND MACABRE. **Eirian Davies** (sop) Chief of the Secret Police (Gepopo), Venus; **Penelope Walmsley-Clark** (sop) Amanda; **Olive Fredericks** (mez) Amando; **Kevin Smith** (alto) Prince Go-Go; **Christa Puhlmann-Richter** (mez) Mescalina; **Peter Haage** (ten) Piet the Pot; **Dieter Weller** (bar) Nekrotzar; **Ude Krekow** (bass) Astradamors; **Johann Leutgeb** (bar) Ruffiak; **Ernst Salzer** (bar) Schobiak; **Laszlo Modos** (bar) Schabernack; **Herbert Prikopa** (spkr) White Minister; **Ernst Leopold Strachwitz** (spkr) Black Minister;

Austrian Radio Chorus; Arnold Schönberg Choir; Gumpoldskirchner Spartzen; Austrian Radio Symphony Orchestra/Elgar Howarth. Wergo WER6170-2. Notes, text and translations included. Recorded in 1987.

② 1h 56m ADD 12/91

Contemporary operas can be a risky business for an opera house at the best of times, and even if they do attract sizeable audiences at their first performance, the prospect of future productions is never guaranteed. Ligeti's *Le grand macabre*, however, has been an exception and since its première in Stockholm over 13 years ago it has been produced in well over a dozen different opera houses world-wide. Chronologically it occupies a place between Ligeti's earlier, more experimental works such as the Requiem, *Adventures I & II* and *Clocks and Clouds*, and his more recent compositions which have favoured a superficially more traditional approach. Its intriguing plot is certainly not for those of a prudish disposition: Nekrotzar (the Tsar of Death) visits the dilapidated, imaginary principality of Breughelland in order to announce the imminent destruction of the world. Along the way he encounters various colourful inhabitants: the local inebriate Piet the Pot (whom he enlists as his horse), two star-struck lovers Amando and Amanda (who spend most of their time in mortal love-lock) and the royal astrologer Astradamors and his nymphomaniac wife Mescalina — the latter bestially fulfilled by Nekrotzar. On his arrival at the royal palace of the childish glutton Prince Go-Go he declares the end of the world and ... well, that would be telling, but needless to say, in an opera as bizarre and "Jarryesque" as this anything might happen. Of course a certain amount of visual impact has been lost in its transfer to CD, but then what the eye loses the imagination gains and can run riot with. Excellent performances and a magnificent recording.

Further listening ...

Continuum[a]. Ten Pieces for wind quintet[d]. Artikulation[e]. Glissandi[f]. Two Studies for Organ[b]. Volumina[c]. [a]**Antoinette Vischer** (hpd); [b]**Zsigmond Sathmáry,** [c]**Karl-Erik Welin** (orgs); [d]**South-West German Radio Wind Quintet;** [ef]**Cologne Radio Studio for Electronic Music.** Wergo WER60161-50 (11/89).

Melodien[a]. Concerto for flute and oboe[b]. Chamber Concerto[c]. Ten Pieces for wind quintet[d]. [b]**Aurèle Nicolet** (fl); [b]**Heinz Holliger** (ob); [d]**Vienna Wind Soloists;** [abc]**London Sinfonietta/David Atherton.** Decca Enterprise 425 623-2DM (8/90).

Chamber Concerto[b]. Ramifications (versions for string orchestra[d] and solo strings[c]). Lux aeterna[a]. Atmosphères[d]. [a]**Stuttgart Schola Cantorum/Clytus Gottwald;** [b]**Vienna Die Reihe Ensemble/Friedrich Cerha;** [c]**Saar Radio Chamber Orchestra/Antonio Janigro;** [d]**South West German Radio Symphony Orchestra/Ernest Bour.** Wergo WER60162-50 (10/89).

Thomas Linley

British 1756-1778

NEW REVIEW

T. Linley. Ode on the Spirits of Shakespeare. **Lorna Anderson, Julia Gooding** (sops); **Richard Wistreich** (bass); **The Parley of Instruments Choir; The Parley of Instruments/Paul Nicholson.** Hyperion CDA66613. Text included. Recorded in 1992.

1h DDD 5/93

Like Mozart, who was born in the same year, Thomas Linley was the son of a musician (his father had the same name), and as a boy studying in Florence in 1770 he met and performed with the Austrian genius. His tragic early death in a boating accident robbed English music of what looked like a major talent, and it is good to welcome to the catalogue a work of his in a skilful and stylish performance that should win him friends. This *Ode on the Spirits of Shakespeare,* subtitled "A Lyric Ode on the Fairies, Aerial Beings and

Witches of Shakespeare", was composed under the inspiration of the various presentations of the Bard's works that followed his bicentenary in 1764 and has a text by a literary person with the unlikely name of French Lawrence who was later to become an Oxford Professor. It is eclectic in style, owing something to French and Handelian-English baroque styles but also offering individual and endearing touches of incipient romanticism. The performance under Paul Nicholson is altogether sympathetic and stylish, and the clear-voiced contribution of the soprano Julia Gooding is particularly welcome, although the bass Richard Wistreich could be more dark-toned and sinister at the start of Part 2, where he evokes Macbeth's witches. No doubt this 'lyric ode' composed in 1776 will remain a rarity in the concert-hall, but it is to the credit of Hyperion that we can enjoy it on disc and the recording is clear and atmospheric.

Key to Symbols

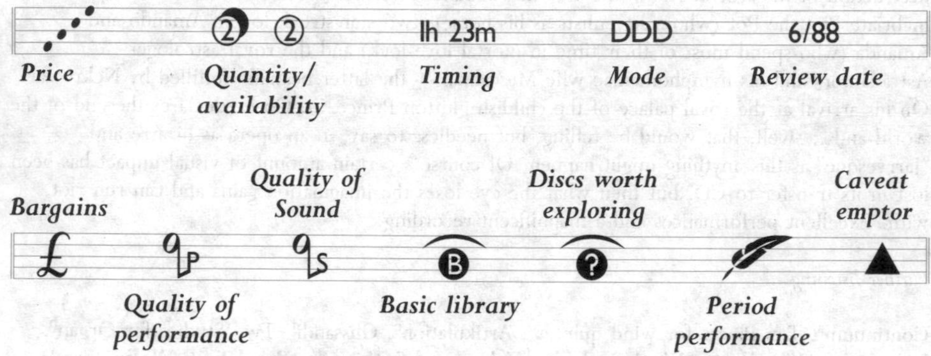

Franz Liszt

Hungarian 1811-1886

NEW REVIEW

Liszt. Piano Concertos — No. 1 in E flat major, S124[b]; No. 2 in A major, S125[b]. ***Beethoven.*** Cello Sonata in G minor, Op. 5 No. 2[a]. **Sviatoslav Richter** (pf); [a]**Mstislav Rostropovich** (vc); [b]**London Symphony Orchestra/Kyrill Kondrashin.** Philips Insignia 434 163-2PM. Item marked [a] from SAL3453/4 (2/64), recorded in 1962, [b] SABL207 (5/62), recorded in 1961.

lh 7m ADD 9/92

At the height of his powers, as he was in the early 1960s shortly after his first appearance in the West, Richter at the piano was an awe-inspiring phenomenon. His recording of the Liszt Concertos was instantly recognized as a classic. Not only was it breathtaking in its pianistic command, it had Kyrill Kondrashin galvanizing the London Symphony Orchestra into something far more vital than mere accompaniment. The opening bars of the E flat Concerto throw down the gauntlet in such a way as to make the soloist's heroics sound motivated as they hardly ever do, and sparks fly between piano and orchestra throughout both works. Admittedly the recording now sounds slightly constricted, but that detracts hardly at all from the cumulative intensity of the performances. And with a rock-solid account of the Beethoven G minor Sonata added for good measure this medium-price issue is clearly one not to be missed.

Additional recommendations ...

Piano Concertos. Totentanz, S126. **Alfred Brendel** (pf); **London Philharmonic Orchestra/Bernard Haitink.** Philips Silverline 426 637-2PSL — 56m ADD 11/90

Piano Concertos. Totentanz. **Krystian Zimerman** (pf); **Boston Symphony Orchestra/Seiji Ozawa.** DG 423 571-2GH — 56m DDD 11/88

Liszt. ORCHESTRAL WORKS. [a]**Shura Cherkassky** (pf); **Berlin Philharmonic Orchestra/Herbert von Karajan.** DG 415 967-2GH2.
Fantasia on Hungarian Folk-themes, S123[a]. Mazeppa, S100 (both from 138 692, 9/61). Les préludes, S97 (139 037, 6/69). Mephisto Waltz No. 2, S111 (2530 244, 10/72). Hungarian Rhapsodies: No. 2 (2530 698, 8/76), No. 4, S359 (135 031, 4/68); No. 5 (2530 698, 8/76). Tasso, lamento e trionfo, S96 (2530 698, 8/76).

2 2h 1m ADD 9/86 

It was Liszt who first used the term "symphonic tone-poem" to describe the orchestral pieces he composed depicting stories and events. This set is a compilation of Liszt recordings made by Karajan over a period of some 15 years, and it is apparent that here is a composer who constantly stimulates the BPO's conductor to his freshest and most imaginative performances. There is a remarkable consistency of style in the playing, which is everywhere fresh, alert and has an abundance of energy and spirit, and the orchestra respond to their director with virtuoso playing of a high order. The *Fantasia* is an ideal vehicle for Cherkassky's brilliant, improvisatory style and although this particular recording was made 32 years ago the piano tone and indeed the orchestral sound are very good. In fact the recordings all sound excellent, despite the difference in their dates of origin.

Liszt. A Faust Symphony, G108. **Kenneth Riegel** (ten); **Tanglewood Festival Chorus; Boston Symphony Orchestra/Leonard Bernstein.** DG Galleria 431 470-2GGA. From 2707 100 (4/78). Recorded in 1976.

1h 17m ADD 8/91 

Goethe's *Faust* provided a source of inspiration for numerous symphonic, operatic, literary and stage works and, indeed, its influence is hardly diminished even in the late twentieth century. With its heroic and undeniably visionary qualities, it is hardly surprising that many romantic composers seized upon Goethe's text and the work offers a huge range of interpretative possibilities. A mystical and philosophical Faust is revealed by Bernstein in his performance with the Boston Symphony Orchestra. He adds the extra dimensions of real musical perception and true dramatic mastery to Liszt's concoction of sinister diablerie. The 1977 DG sound is excellent in its remastered form and has the added attraction of being mid-price.

Additional recommendations ...
Alexander Young (ten); **Beecham Choral Society; Royal Philharmonic Orchestra/Sir Thomas Beecham.** EMI CDM7 63371-2 — 1h 10m ADD 2/88 ▲
Charles Bressler (ten); **New York Choral Art Society; New York Philharmonic Orchestra/Leonard Bernstein.** Sony Clasical Royal Edition SMK47570 — 1h 12m ADD 5/93

Liszt. HUNGARIAN RHAPSODIES, S244 — Nos. 1-19. **Roberto Szidon** (pf). DG Galleria 423 925-2GGA2. From 2720 072 (10/73). Recorded in 1972.
No. 1 in C sharp minor; No. 2 in C sharp minor; No. 3 in B flat major; No. 4 in E flat major; No. 5 in E minor, "Héroïde-Elégiaque"; No. 6 in D flat major; No. 7 in D minor; No. 8 in F sharp minor, "Capriccio"; No. 9 in E flat major, "Carnival in Pest"; No. 10 in E major; No. 11 in A minor; No. 12 in C sharp minor; No. 13 in A minor; No. 14 in F minor; No. 15 in A minor, "Rákóczy"; No. 16 in A minor, "For the Munkascy festivities in Budapest"; No. 17 in D minor; No. 18 in F sharp minor, "On the occasion of the Hungarian Exposition in Budapest"; No. 19 in D minor.

2 2h 23m ADD 3/89 

Liszt's 19 *Hungarian Rhapsodies* contain some formidably difficult music of tremendous flavour and colour. Liszt first encountered gipsy music when he returned to Hungary in 1840 and he was quite entranced with the abandon and ecstasy it seemed capable of inspiring. Although the rhapsodies are perfectly able to stand on their own they can also be seen as an entity, a work with disparate but linked elements. The first 15 pieces (the last four date from the 1880s) therefore form a unified creation. The clash of tempo, tonality and rhythm has a strong place in

Liszt's rhapsodies and the colours and timbres of the gipsy band are beautifully captured by this wizard of the keyboard with almost diabolic accuracy. The last four rhapsodies, in common with his other works from late in his career, have a haunted, introspective quality that makes them sound more abstract than their earlier counterparts. Szidon's recording has always been highly regarded, with a panache and verve that is so vital for the inner life of this music.

Additional recommendation ...

Nos. 2, 3, 8, 13, 15 and 17. Csárdás obstiné. **Alfred Brendel** (pf). Vanguard Classics 08 4024 71 — 46m ADD 2/92 £

Liszt. PIANO WORKS. **Alfred Brendel** (pf). Philips 410 040-2PH. From 6514 147 (11/82).
Piano Sonata in B minor, S178. Légendes, S175 — St François d'Assise: la prédication aux oiseaux; St François de Paule marchant sur les flots. La lugubre gondola Nos. 1 and 2, S200/1-2.

lh 2m DDD 10/83 

Liszt's Piano Sonata is one of the monuments of the romantic period and is the only sonata which the greatest pianist of musical history wrote for his instrument. It is in one long movement that has its component parts contained within a mighty sonata structure.
Unfortunately it is also a work that has often been misunderstood and when treated chiefly as a virtuoso warhorse and vehicle for self-display the Sonata loses its dignity and poise. Alfred Brendel has lived with this music for decades, and his love and understanding of it are evident. Technically it is not flawless, but the blend of the various qualities needed — power, dignity, dexterity, sheer excitement, charm and above all structural cohesion is admirable. The two *St Francis* Legends and the funereal *Gondola* pieces are more than a fill-up and enhance this fine disc, revealing as they do other aspects of the composer.

Additional recommendations ...

Piano Sonata. Piano Concerto No. 1 in E flat major (with orchestra/David Brockman). *Années de pèlerinage, deuxième année, "Italie" — Sonnetto 104 del Petrarca. Rapsodie espagnole. Two Concert Studies — No. 2, Gnomenreigen (two performances). Harmonies poétiques et religieuses — No. 7, Funérailles. Hungarian Rhapsody No. 12 in C sharp minor.* **Gounod** (trans. Liszt): *Faust — Waltz.* **Simon Barere.** APR CDAPR7007 *(reviewed in Collections section; refer to Index to Reviews)* — ② lh 33 ADD 11/89

Piano Sonata. Nuages gris, S199. Unstern: sinistre, disastro, S208. La lugubre gondola No. 1. R. W. — Venezia, S201. **Maurizio Pollini.** DG 427 322-2GH — 46m DDD 7/90

Piano Sonata. Funeral Odes — La notte, S699. Harmonies poétiques et réligieuses, S173 — Funérailles. Nuages gris. La lugubre gondola No. 2. **Krystian Zimerman.** DG 431 780-2GH — lh 6m DDD 10/91

Piano Sonata. ***Schubert.*** *Piano Sonata in B flat major, D960.* **Annie Fischer.** Hungaroton HCD31494 — lh 7m ADD 7/92

Piano Sonata. Two Légendes, S175. Scherzo and March, S177. **Nikolai Demidenko.** Hyperion CDA66616 — lh 7m DDD 2/93

Liszt. PIANO WORKS. **Stephen Hough.** Virgin Classics VC7 59664-2.
Mephisto Waltz No. 1, S514. Venezia e Napoli, S162 — Tarantella. Rhapsodie espagnole, S254. Harmonies poétiques et religieuses, S173 — Bénédiction de Dieu dans la solitude; Pensée des morts. Légendes, S175 — St François d'Assise: la prédication aux oiseaux.

lh 15m DDD 6/88 

The most popular of the virtuoso pieces on this disc is of course the first *Mephisto Waltz,* played here with pronounced contrasts of dazzling diablerie and seductive lyricism. The Italy-inspired *Tarantella* confirms Hough's technical brilliance in breathtakingly fast repetition of single notes, while throughout the dance he preserves an exceptional textural clarity. Characterization in the *Rhapsodie espagnole*'s variations is enhanced by a wide range of tone colour, though just once or twice his scintillating prestidigitation militates against breadth. But there is certainly no lack of that quality in *Pensée des morts*, the fourth and most introspectively searching of the *Harmonies poétiques et religieuses*, whose broodings are sustained with quite exceptional intensity as well as expanding into a magnificently sonorous climax. The simple holiness of *St François d'Assise: la prédication aux oiseaux* is conveyed with pellucid delicacy. Finally comes the deeply consolatory *Bénédiction de Dieu dans la solitude*, where Hough is even able to convince us that its "heavenly lengths" (over 17 minutes) are not a moment too long. The excellent recording artfully contrasts the crispness of the three virtuoso pieces with Hough's more sustained sonority in religious reflection.

Additional recommendation ...

Venezia e Napoli. Années de pèlerinage, Troisième année, S163 — No. 4, Les jeux d'eaux à la Villa d'Este. Harmonies poétiques et religieuses. Ballade No. 2 in B minor, S171. **Jorge Bolet.** Decca 411 803-2DH — 58m DDD 12/85

Liszt. PIANO WORKS, Volume 15 — SONG TRANSCRIPTIONS. **Leslie Howard.** Hyperion CDA66481/2. Recorded in 1990.

Beethoven: Adelaïde, S466. Sechs geistliche Lieder, S467. An die ferne Geliebte, S469. Lieder von Goethe, S468. ***Mendelssohn:*** Lieder, S547. *Dessauer:* Lieder, S485. ***Franz:*** Er ist gekommen in Sturm und Regen, S488. Lieder, S489. ***Rubinstein:*** Two songs, S554. ***Schumann:*** Lieder von Robert und Clara Schumann, S569. Provenzalisches Lied, S570. Two songs, S567. Frühlingsnacht, S568. Widmung, S566.

2 lh 27m DDD 4/92

Few composers have ever shown a more insatiable interest in the music of others than Liszt, or devoted more time to transcribing it for the piano. In this radio-cum-gramophonic age, such activity might even be deemed time wasted. But in Liszt's day it was a godsend for music-lovers and composers alike, and all praise to Leslie Howard for including it in his mammoth pilgrimage through the composer's complete keyboard works. Here, he plays 60 of Liszt's 100 or so song transcriptions, including several by the lesser-known Dessauer, Franz and (as composers) Anton Rubinstein and Clara Schumann, alongside Beethoven, Mendelssohn and Robert Schumann. The selection at once reveals Liszt's variety of approach as a transcriber no less than his unpredictability of choice. Sometimes, as most notably in Beethoven's concert aria, *Adelaïde*, the keyboard virtuoso takes over: he links its two sections with a concerto-like cadenza as well as carrying bravura into an amplified coda. Mendelssohn's *On wings of song* brings imitative subtleties all his own, while the fullness of heart of Schumann's *Dedication* and *Spring Night* is likewise allowed to expand and overflow. But after the dazzling pyrotechnics of many of his operatic arrangements, the surprise here is the self-effacing simplicity of so much included. The five songs from Schumann's *Liederalbum für die Jugend* are literal enough to be played by young children. Even his later (1880) fantasy-type transcriptions of Rubinstein's exotic *The Asra* has the same potent economy of means, characterizing his own original keyboard music in advancing years. Howard responds keenly to mood and atmosphere, and never fails, pianistically, to emphasize the 'singer' in each song — in response to the actual verbal text that Liszt was nearly always conscientious enough to write into his scores. The recording is clean and true.

NEW REVIEW

LISZT AT THE THEATRE. Leslie Howard (pf). Hyperion CDA66575. Recorded in 1991. Capriccio alla turca from "Die Ruinen von Athen", S388. March from "Die Ruinen von Athen", S388*a*. Fantasie über "Die Ruinen von Athen", S389. Wedding March and Dance of the Elves from "A Midsummer Night's Dream", S410. Einsam bin ich, nicht alleine from "La Preciosa", S453. Incidental music to Hebbel's "Nibelungen" and Goethe's "Faust", S496. Symphonisches Zwischensiel zu Calderons schauspiel "Uber allen Zauber Liebe", S497. Pastorale from choruses to Herder's "Prometheus Bound", S508.

lh 18m DDD 3/93

After two volumes of "Liszt at the Opera" in his mammoth cycle, Leslie Howard now introduces us to "Liszt at the Theatre", i.e. as transcriber-paraphraser of incidental music written for various stage productions by Beethoven, Weber, Mendelssohn, Lassen — and even an excerpt from what he himself produced for Herder's *Prometheus Bound*. Best-known, of course, is

Mendelssohn's *Midsummer Night's Dream* inspired "Wedding March" and "Dance of the Elves", miraculously merged in the course of Liszt's transcription. The "Turkish March" from Beethoven's *The Ruins of Athens* is familiar enough too, though it's not every day of the week that we can compare Liszt's first, succinctly piquant transcription with his two extended and elaborated later versions, as Howard allows us to do here. The 'mystery' composer of the five is Liszt's protégé (and ultimately his successor at Weimar), the Danish-born, Belgian-naturalized Eduard Lassen, at his best in his Wagner-influenced music for Hebbel and Calderon, but on this showing no match for Goethe's *Faust*. As always Howard meets diabolical technical challenges with commendable *sang-froid*, and the recording maintains Hyperion's customary fidelity.

Liszt. 12 Transcendental Studies, S139. **Claudio Arrau** (pf). Philips 416 458-2PH. From 6747 412 (2/78).

lh 7m ADD 6/86

Liszt published the *Douze Etudes en Douze Exercices* in 1826, when he was 15. He later expanded all but one to form the basis of his horrendously difficult *Grandes etudes* of 1838 (24 were intended but only 12 completed). Sensitivity to the technical limitations of other virtuosos eventually overcame him, and in 1852 he published a revised, 'easy' version, entitled the *Douze Etudes d'Exécution Transcendante*, which he dedicated to his teacher, Carl Czerny. It is in this (fiendishly difficult) form, with its fanciful titles for ten of the pieces, that the work is usually performed today. Only a very few pianists of each generation can begin to make music of these works in the way Liszt expected. The technique required goes well beyond simple virtuosity and all too often performances sink in a tumultuous sea of the scales and arpeggios that Liszt intended should only provide a background tint. Maintaining speed is the other major problem, for the great melodies must flow and sing as though the myriad of other notes that interpose are hardly there. Arrau has for many years been one of the select band capable of this work and in this stable, well-defined recording from the mid 1970s he gives us this performance against which most others are judged.

Liszt. ORGAN WORKS. **Gunther Kaunzinger.** Novalis 150 069-2. Recorded on the organ of the Stiftsbasilika, Waldsassen, Germany.
Prelude and Fugue on the name B-A-C-H, S260. Evocation à la Chapelle Sixtine, S658. Variations on "Weinen, Klagen, Sorgen, Zagen", S673. Fantasia and Fugue on "Ad nos, ad salutarem undam", S259.

lh 12m DDD 2/91

Liszt's prodigious skill at the piano was legendary. But he was also a most capable organist and in the later years of his life he turned more and more to the organ, making transcriptions and reworkings for it of his own and other composers' music. As for original organ compositions he wrote a mere handful. The *Fantasia and Fugue* on the chorale *Ad nos, ad salutarem undam* (from Meyerbeer's opera *La Prophète*) is a work of considerable stature and virtuosity almost unparalleled in the organ's repertory. Although barely a third the length of the *Fantasia and Fugue*, the *Prelude and Fugue on the name B-A-C-H* is also a virtuoso showpiece paying homage to the composer who Liszt regarded as a supreme master. Homage is also paid to Bach in the Variations on *Weinen, Klagen, Sorgen, Zagen*, a theme Liszt took from Bach's Cantata No. 21. The *Evocation* of the Sistine Chapel combines Allegri's *Miserere* and Mozart's *Ave verum* in a deeply religious work which was, for Liszt, a profound statement of faith. Gunther Kaunzinger gives an outstanding performance of the *Fantasia and Fugue*, and in the other pieces his playing has great authority. He is served by a fine, if rather thick-sounding instrument, and a clean, full-blooded recording.

Liszt. ORGAN WORKS.
Reubke. Sonata on the 94th Psalm. **Thomas Trotter** (org). Argo 430 244-2ZH. Played on the organ of the Münster zur Schönen Unsrer Lieben Frau, Ingolstadt, Germany. Recorded in 1989.

Liszt: Prelude and Fugue on the name B-A-C-H, S260. Gebet, S265 (arr. Gottschalg). Orpheus S98 (arr. Schaab). Prometheus, S99 (trans. Guillou).

1h 13m DDD 2/91

This is a spectacular organ record, made on a big modern instrument in the very resonant acoustic of the Church of Our Lady, at Ingolstadt in Germany, which Thomas Trotter plays with great flair. The music is no less spectacular, belonging as it does to the nineteenth century and a full-blooded romantic tradition. The longest piece is the Reubke Sonata, music by a composer who died at 24 and is virtually unknown except to organists, and even to them by just this one work. It is a mighty one-movement sonata which reflects the influence of his teacher Liszt, to whom he went in 1856 shortly after the older man completed his great Piano Sonata, and was inspired by the powerful text of *Psalm* No. 94, which calls for God's judgement upon the wicked. Liszt himself is represented here by another work of surging strength, the *Prelude and Fugue* on the letters of the name Bach (the notes B flat, A, C, B natural), which make for a tightly chromatic motif yielding great harmonic and contrapuntal possibilities, not least in the fugue. This work begins the recital, and is followed by the same composer's serene tone poem in praise of music which he called *Orpheus*. Then comes the Reubke, and the other Liszt items follow it and thus make a sort of triptych with the longest work (the Sonata) as the centrepiece. Though two of the Liszt pieces are transcriptions rather than original organ works, they are effective in this form.

NEW REVIEW

Liszt. LIEDER. **Brigitte Fassbaender** (mez); **Jean-Yves Thibaudet** (pf). Decca 430 512-2DH. Texts and translations included. Recorded in 1990.

O lieb', so lang du lieben kannst, S298. Freudvoll und leidvoll, S280. Mignons Lied, I, S275. Es war ein König in Thule, I, S278. Uber allen Gipfeln ist Ruh, S306. Der du von dem Himmel bist, S279. Ich möchte hingehn, S296. Und wir dachten der Toten, S338. Lasst mich ruhen, S317. Blume und Duft, S324. Du bist wie eine Blume, S287. Im Rhein, im schönen Strome, S272. Was Liebe sei, S288. Hohe Liebe, S307. Einst, S332. Wieder möcht ich dir begegnen, S322. Ihr Auge, S310. Dei drei Zigeuner, S320.

58m DDD 9/92

The mysteriously widespread idea of Liszt as a piano virtuoso *par excellence* but short on depth is nowhere in his output given the lie more than in his Lieder. These intense, beautiful settings have in many cases been selected by Fassbaender from several different revisions by the composer, and generally she has chosen the pithiest, most emotionally concentrated incarnation. The amount of revision Liszt chose to give the songs may be some suggestion of their significance to him; the operative word, Fassbaender suggests in her loving and illuminating introduction is 'fervour'. Her singing bears this out to its fullest extent: the opening song of the disc, *O lieb', so lang du lieben kannst* (better known in its piano version as the third *Liebestraume*) sets the tone for all that follows including settings of such well-known poems as *Du bist wie eine Blume* and *Im Rhein, im schönen Strome* performed with unshakeable conviction, deep passion and the most glorious tone. Jean-Yves Thibaudet's piano playing glistens and glows around Fassbaender's voice and he sail happily through the most demanding moments such as the disc's final song *Dei drei Zigeuner*. The recorded sound is superb and the interpretations probably as near to definitive as one could hope to find.

NEW REVIEW

Liszt. Missa choralis, S10[a]. Via crucis, S53[b]. [b]**Donna Brown** (sop); [b]**Eliane Tantcheff** (mez); [b]**Marie-Claude Alary** (contr); [b]**Régis Oudot** (ten); [b]**Michel Piquemal** (bar); [ab]**Vocal Audite Nova de Paris Ensemble/Jean Sourisse** with [ab]**Marie-Claire Alain** (org). Erato 2292-45350-2. Recorded in 1986.

1h 7m DDD 10/92

Liszt's late journey into the realms of organized religion witnessed a profound change in his creative character; the older he grew, the deeper, the more simple and — in some respects — the more disturbing his muse became. The *Missa choralis* was composed in the year (1865) he took holy orders, and still retains a suggestion of the life-affirming genius who, just a few years before, had produced some of his most flamboyant piano works. Both its "Gloria" and "Sanctus" open in a mood of healthy exultation, and although undeniably liturgical in tone and occasionally visited by vagrant shadows, the remaining score is full of light and tenderness. How different is the *Via crucis*, written at the Villa d'Este in the mid-to-late 1870s, the period during which Liszt was also occupied with the last and bleakest volume of his *Années de pèlerinage*. The Latin texts (extracted from the Vulgate) commemorate the Stations of the Cross while the music, which oscillates between organ solos, duets and choral pieces, is among the most searching and unsettling that Liszt ever wrote. Chorales are inserted at key points in the score, including Bach's "O Haupt voll Blut und Wunden" from *St Matthew Passion* in the Sixth Station, a placing that approximates, in its powerful effect, Berg's Bach cantata quotation in his Violin Concerto. The central sequence of Stations relates feelings of disorientation and terror, but without the least recourse to rhetoric, sure evidence that Liszt had transcended the limitations of his youthful virtuosity, and entered a new stage of potent, but texturally lean, inspiration. This is great music, but its time is yet to come. All the performers on this CD seem to understand the music's grave import, but special mention should be made of Marie-Claire Alain's unfailingly perceptive solo work. The recordings, too, are excellent and reproduce every detail in both scores — as well as some birds in the rafters!

Further listening ...

Années de pèlerinage, première année, S160, "Suisse". **Jorge Bolet** (pf). Decca 410 160-2DH (12/84).

Années de pèlerinage, deuxième année, S161. **Jorge Bolet** (pf). Decca 410 161-2DH (7/85).

George Lloyd

British 1913-

NEW REVIEW

G. Lloyd. Piano Concerto No. 3. **Kathryn Stott** (pf); **BBC Philharmonic Orchestra/George Lloyd.** Albany TROY019-2. Recorded in 1988.

48m DDD 3/90

All George Lloyd admirers will surely want to investigate this beautifully played and recorded issue of what is undoubtedly a readily approachable and impeccably scored work. Yet it has to be admitted that the large-scale Third Piano Concerto of 1968 is hardly one of this prolific figure's stronger utterances. The outer movements, for all their agreeable fluency and energy, have a tendency to lapse into the all-purpose 'jog-trot' mode which sometimes afflicts this composer, and Lloyd's basic material is not always untouched by banality, either. Easily the finest inspiration is to be found in the central slow movement, a brooding 20-minute *Lento* of haunting introspection and no mean beauty. As one would expect from one of this country's most talented younger virtuosos, Kathryn Stott gives a magnificent rendition of the busy solo part, and the BBC Philharmonic under Lloyd himself provide sterling support. Some momentary (and unexpected) roughness in tuttis apart, the recording is undistractingly natural; certainly, the piano/orchestra balance has been most musically judged on this occasion.

NEW REVIEW

G. Lloyd. Symphonies — No. 6[a]; No. 10, "November Journeys"[b]. John Socman — Overture[a]. [b]**BBC Philharmonic Brass;** [a]**BBC Philharmonic Orchestra/George Lloyd.** Albany TROY015-2. Recorded in 1988.

57m DDD 8/89

Agreeable, unashamedly lightweight listening, but, truth to tell, none of these works finds this approachable composer on truly top form. Both the skipping overture to the 1951 opera *John*

Socman and the Sixth Symphony show Lloyd at his most undemandingly inconsequential, and it's fair to say that some may find the relentless innocuousness of Lloyd's inspiration more than a little frustrating. Indeed, the altogether 'meatier' fare of the Tenth Symphony comes as something of a blessed relief, even though its resolutely tonal idiom, too, is not in the slightest bit challenging. Bearing the subtitle *November Journeys*, this work was inspired by a series of cut-price railway excursions the composer had made that same month in order to visit a number of cathedrals he had never seen before. The scoring, for 13 brass instruments, is always impressively adept, and the *Calma* slow movement in particular exudes a homely, mellow charm. Warm recording and pleasingly polished performances under the composer's lead, although the BBC Philharmonic's playing is not always exactly the last word in dashing commitment. A disc to recommend primarily to Lloyd addicts.

Sir Andrew Lloyd Webber

British 1948-

Suggested listening ...

JESUS CHRIST SUPERSTAR. **Various artists.** First Night Records ENCORECD7 (10/92).

THE PHANTOM OF THE OPERA. **Original London cast.** Polydor 831 273-2 (7/87).

Duarte Lôbo

Portuguese c.1565-1646

NEW REVIEW

D. Lôbo. Missa Pro defunctis a 6. Missa Vox clamantis. **The Tallis Scholars/Peter Phillips.** Gimell CDGIM028. Texts and translations included.

1h 6m DDD 3/93

The Portuguese composer Duarte Lôbo was the leading musician of his country during the first half of the seventeenth century. Heavily influenced by the music of the Spaniard, Victoria, Lôbo's music is an interesting development of the late Renaissance style, to which Lôbo brought both originality and austere expression. The two works on this disc are excellent examples of his music, with the Requiem representing the more creative side of Lôbo's character. Written for six parts this is a sonorous and inventive masterpiece, with a considerable sense of the baroque about it. By contrast the Mass is rather more reserved: written also for six voices it has a noble, restrained character, which still holds the listener's attention throughout. The performances by The Tallis Scholars under Peter Phillips are excellent: intonation is perfect, and Phillips's control of phrasing, tempos and dynamics is masterly throughout. Aided by an excellent ecclesiastical acoustic, the recording is warm without being muddy: both clarity and perspective of sound are exemplary. While Lôbo is unlikely to be a composer whose works command a large following, he was clearly a master in his own right, and this fine recording goes a long way in both establishing and justifying his reputation.

Matthew Locke

British 1621-1677

Suggested listening ...

Sacred Choral Music — Descende caelo cincta sororibus (The Oxford Ode). How doth the city sit solitary. Super flumina Babylonis. O be joyful in the Lord, all ye lands. Audi, Domine, clamantes ad te. Lord let me know mine end. Jesu auctor clementie. Be Thou exalted, Lord.

Choir of New College, Oxford; The Parley of Instruments/Edward Higginbottom with **Peter Holman** (org). Hyperion CDA66373 (9/91).

Frank Loesser

American 1910-1969

Suggested listening ...

GUYS AND DOLLS. **Original 1992 Broadway revival cast.** RCA Victor 09026-61317-2 (10/92).

THE MOST HAPPY FELLA. **Original Broadway cast.** Sony Broadway SK48010 (5/93).

Theo Loevendie

Dutch 1930-

Loevendie. MISCELLANEOUS WORKS. [a]**Rosemary Hardy** (sop); [b]**Jard van Nes** (mez); [c]**John Snijders** (pf); [d]**Nieuw Ensemble/Ed Spanjaard.** Etcetera KTC1097. Recorded in 1990. Venus and Adonis[d]. Strides[c]. Six Turkish Folk Poems[ad]. Music for flute and piano[b]. NAIMA[bd] — A man of life upright; As fast as thou shalt wane. Back Bay Bicinium[d].

1h 5m DDD 12/91 

Theo Loevendie is a Dutch composer who has turned from jazz to more 'serious' composition, with fascinating results. Far from simply juxtaposing two different musical worlds, Loevendie seems to have absorbed the old into the new, so that lightness of touch, flexibility of form and clarity of texture are all prominent features of the works recorded here. In general, the longer, more abstract pieces are the least interesting, although the early *Strides* for solo piano, *Music for flute and piano* and the evocatively titled *Back Bay Bicinium* for seven instruments are all well worth hearing. But Loevendie comes into his own with vocal and theatre music. The two pieces derived from his music for Shakespeare's *Venus and Adonis* grab and sustain the attention, while the two songs to English texts from the opera *Naima* are notable for their fresh and vivid sonorities — there's a hint of the later Stravinsky here. One of the most enjoyable items is the set of *Six Turkish Folk Poems*, brilliantly sung by Rosemary Hardy, and showing Loevendie's ability to allude to ethnic music without resorting to parody. Overall, this disc is technically first rate, and likely to provide pleasures and surprises even for listeners who think they know their way about the contemporary music scene.

Frederick Loewe

German/American 1901-1988

Suggested listening ...

BRIGADOON. **Soloists; Ambrosian Chorus; London Sinfonietta/John McGlinn.** EMI CDC7 54481-2 (1/93).

Albert Lortzing

German 1801-1851

Lortzing. UNDINE. **Monika Krause** (sop) Undine; **Josef Protschka** (ten) Hugo; **Christiane Hampe** (sop) Bertalda; **John Janssen** (bar) Kühleborn; **Klaus Häger** (bass)

Tobias; **Ingeborg Most** (contr) Marthe; **Heinz Kruse** (ten) Veit; **Andreas Schmidt** (bass) Hans; **Günter Wewel** (bass) Heilmann; **Dirk Schortemeier** (spkr) Messenger; **Cologne Radio Chorus and Orchestra/Kurt Eichhorn.** Capriccio 60 017-2. Text and translation included. Recorded 1989-90.

② 2h 37m DDD 3/91

A pity, in a way, that this couldn't have been a video recording, for *Undine*, a curious mixture of the fantastic and the prosaically bourgeois, has one of the most spectacular (though enormously difficult to stage) endings in all opera: the knight Hugo's castle is (in full view) inundated, and he and his living water-nymph Undine (who has been put on earth to find out whether humans, who have souls, are superior to nature-spirits, who have none) are united in a crystal palace at the bottom of the sea. A lot more than he deserved, for having fallen in love with this pretty and ingenuous creature and married her, he had been faithless; but Lortzing allowed himself to be persuaded to give the work a happy ending. His setting of this fable is undemandingly melodious, frequently folk-like, and extremely skilfully scored; and the veteran Kurt Eichhorn secures first-class orchestral playing and choral singing. The sopranos — Undine and the haughty princess who is discovered to be low-born — are less impressive than the men, who are extremely well cast. Protschka as the fickle knight excels in his big 'nightmare' aria in Act 4, Janssen makes a menacing Prince of the Waters, and Kruse is efficient, if sounding over-classy for a mere squire with a weakness for the bottle. Gaps left between the ends of musical numbers and the ensuing dialogues (which are well produced) rather weaken the dramatic flow; but all in all this first complete recording for 25 years of this romantic opera is greatly to be welcomed.

Hermann Løvenskjold

Danish 1815-1870

Suggested listening ...

La Sylphide — ballet. **Royal Danish Orchestra/David Garforth.** Chandos Collect CHAN6546 (4/92)

Nicholas Ludford

British c.1485-1557

NEW REVIEW

Ludford. (ed. Skinner). Missa Videte miraculum. Ave cuius conceptio. **The Cardinall's Musick/Andrew Carwood.** ASV Gaudeamus CDGAU131. Texts and translations included. With Plainsong Propers for the Feast of the Purification.

1h 9m DDD 7/93

A product of singers drawn principally from Oxford and Cambridge college choirs (and steeped in Tudor polyphony), persuasive direction from Andrew Carwood and exemplary research by David Skinner, this disc brings us the music of Nicholas Ludford, about whom we know little beyond his name and approximate dates. Situated chronologically between Robert Fayrfax and John Sheppard, he is a composer of a forgotten generation and little of his music has been performed before, let alone recorded. His Masses, such as that based on *Videte miraculum* performed here (intended for use at the Feast of the Purification of the Virgin Mary) are full of the glorious florid and soaring lines found in the music of the Eton Choirbook – two high soprano lines interweave, yet the overall effect is never aimless as Ludford had a sure sense of structure of the polyphonic Mass form. In the longer sections — the *Gloria* and *Credo* — Ludford never allows the musical ideas to overstay their welcome. His modern interpreters, The Cardinall's Musick (whose name derives from Christ Church in Oxford, founded by Thomas, Cardinal Wolsey) are sure in their intonation and the choir's director wisely varies the dynamics in and between sections of the Mass (and the five-voice antiphon *Ve cuius conceptio*) to allow its musical structure to come over clearly. Judicious use is made by Carwood and his colleague, David Skinner, of the appropriate plainchant music for the Mass's setting, never allowing the ear to tire of undiluted polyphony.

Jean-Baptiste Lully *Italian-French 1632-1687*

Lully. ATYS. *Prologue* — **Bernard Deletré** (bass) Le Temps; **Monique Zanetti** (sop) Flore; **Jean-Paul Fouchécourt** (bass), **Gilles Ragon** (ten) Zephirs; **Arlette Steyer** (sop) Melpomene; **Agnès Mellon** (sop) Iris. *Tragédie-lyrique* — **Guy de Mey** (ten) Atys; **Agnès Mellon** (sop) Sangaride; **Guillemette Laurens** (mez) Cybèle; **Françoise Semellaz** (sop) Doris; **Jacques Bona** (bass) Idas; **Noémi Rime** (sop) Mélisse; **Jean-François Gardeil** (bass) Célénus; **Gilles Ragon** (ten) Le sommeil; **Jean-Paul Fouchécourt** (ten) Morphée, Trio; **Bernard Deletré** (bass) Phobétor, Sangar; **Michel Laplénie** (ten) Phantase; **Stephan Maciejewski** (bass) Un songe funeste; **Isabelle Desrochers** (sop) Trio; **Véronique Gens** (sop) Trio; **Les Arts Florissants Chorus and Orchestra/William Christie.** Harmonia Mundi HMC90 1257/9. Notes, text and translation included.

③ 2h 50m DDD 7/87 

Once upon a time Lully's melodies were the property of the common people. Not so today when, apart from occasional revivals and broadcasts, his operas are largely forgotten. *Atys* is reputed to have been Louis XIV's favourite opera and here William Christie and a fine line-up of soloists bring the work to life in a most compelling way. There are some beautiful choruses and ensembles through-out the opera which should make wide and immediate appeal; but it is in the Third Act where Lully treats his audience to a *sommeil* or sleep scene that much of the most arresting and original music is contained. Recorded sound is effective and the booklet contains the full libretto.

Further listening ...

Divertissements. **Guillemette Laurens** (mez); **Capriccio Stravagante/Skip Sempé.** Deutsche Harmonia Mundi RD77218 (1/91).

Harpsichord Works (trans. d'Anglebert). **Kenneth Gilbert.** Harmonia Mundi HMC90 1267 (4/88).

Le bourgeois gentilhomme — incidental music. *Coupled with* ***Campra.*** L'Europe galante — ballet suite. **Soloists; Tölz Boys' Choir; La Petite Bande/Gustav Leonhardt.** Deutsche Harmonia Mundi Editio Classica GD77059 (2/91).

ALCESTE. **Soloists; Sagittarius Vocal Ensemble; La Grande Ecurie et La Chambre du Roy/Jean-Claude Malgoire.** Disques Montaigne 782012 (4/93).

Thomas Lupo *British c.1598-1628*

Suggested listening ...

Fantasy-Airs a 3 — Nos. 16, 17 and 20. Fantasy-Airs a 4 — Nos. 5-7, 11 and 12. Fantasies a 4 Nos. 4 and 9. *Coupled with* ***Gibbons:*** Two Fantasias a 4. 9 Fantasias a 3. Galliard a 3. **The Parley of Instruments/Peter Holman.** Hyperion CDA66395 (9/91).

Witold Lutoslawski

Polish 1913-

Lutoslawski. ORCHESTRAL WORKS. **[a]Louis Devos** (ten); **[b]Roman Jablónski** (vc); **[b]Katowice Radio Symphony Orchestra; [ad]Warsaw National Philharmonic Orchestra; [cd]Jan Krenz; [ab]Witold Lutoslawski.** Polskie Nagrania Muza PNCD042. Recorded 1964-76. Paroles tissées[a]. Cello Concerto[b] (both from EMI 1C 165 03231/6, 7/79). Postlude I[bc]. Livre pour orchestre[d].

lh 4m ADD 9/90

This volume featuring CD transfers of ageing recordings stands up to today's competition better than most. Although they date from between 1964 and 1976, the recordings still retain much of the clarity and detail of these first-rate performances. Jan Krenz makes a fine job of the intricate textures of that concentrated masterpiece, *Livre pour orchestre* and the somewhat similarly structured Cello Concerto, dedicated to Rostropovich, finds here a committed advocate in Roman Jablónski. These two works date from 1968 and 1970 respectively. *Paroles tissées* predates the first of these by three years and, superficially, seems very different in style with open textures and chamber-music balances. If the tenor here, Louis Devos, lacks the poetry of Sir Peter Pears, for whom the work was written, he nevertheless does the work justice and points its many delights. The first of the three Postludes (1958-63), which opens the disc, shows Lutoslawski's musical antecedents much more clearly than the other works, but it is still a remarkable piece for a composer who, only a few years before, had been producing music that only too well complied with the requirements of a Poland still in the cultural grip of Stalinist dictates.

NEW REVIEW

Lutoslawski. Paganini Variations.
Rachmaninov. Rhapsody on a Theme of Paganini, Op. 43.
Shostakovich. Concerto in C minor for piano, trumpet and strings, Op. 35[a]. **Peter Jablonski** (pf); **[a]Raymond Simmons** (tpt); **Royal Philharmonic Orchestra/Vladimir Ashkenazy.** Decca 436 239-2DH. Recorded in 1991.

55m DDD 12/92 9S

Among Peter Jablonski's credentials are, apparently, having been voted best jazz drummer in Sweden at the age of seven. You can see how such a talent might come in handy for the Shostakovich, as riotous a succession of high and low styles as has ever successfully cohabited in one concerto. Jablonski is in fact a little on the cool side here, but his level-headed approach never misses the idiomatic point, and trumpeter Raymond Simmons is an accomplished partner. Rachmaninov's *Rhapsody* was actually composed one year after the Shostakovich in 1934, and it would not be forcing a point to detect interesting similarities in approach behind their obviously disparate surfaces. Here Jablonski does not quite convince at moments of emotional extreme, though there is certainly nothing in his interpretation to cause offence, and orchestral support from the RPO and Ashkenazy is first-rate. But the gem on this disc is undoubtedly the Lutoslawski. This 1978 arrangement of the familiar 1941 two-piano *Paganini Variations* is masterly in its orchestration and the high jinks of the original are genuinely enhanced by the change of palette, as they are by the panache and verve of the performance. A demonstration quality recording from Decca.

Lutoslawski. Partita for violin, orchestra and obbligato solo piano (1985)[a]. Chain 2 for violin and orchestra (1984)[b].
Stravinsky. Violin Concerto in D[c]. **Anne-Sophie Mutter** (vn); **[a]Phillip Moll** (pf); **[ab]BBC Symphony Orchestra/Witold Lutoslawski; [c]Philharmonia Orchestra/Paul Sacher.** DG 423 696-2GH.

56m DDD 2/89 

This disc contains some spellbinding violin playing in a splendidly lifelike recording, and it's a bonus that the music, while unquestionably 'modern', needs no special pleading: its appeal is instantaneous and long-lasting. Anne-Sophie Mutter demonstrates that she can equal the best in a modern classic — the Stravinsky Concerto — and also act as an ideal, committed advocate for newer works not previously recorded. The Stravinsky is one of his liveliest neoclassical pieces, though to employ that label is, as usual, to underline its rough-and-ready relevance to a style that uses Bach as a springboard for an entirely individual and unambiguously modern idiom. Nor is it all 'sewing-machine' rhythms and pungently orchestrated dissonances. There is lyricism, charm, and above all humour: and no change of mood is too fleeting to escape the razor-sharp responses of this soloist and her alert accompanists, authoritatively guided by the veteran Paul Sacher. Lutoslawski's music has strongly individual qualities that have made him perhaps the most approachable of all contemporary composers. This enthralling collaboration between senior composer and youthful virtuoso is not to be missed.

Further listening ...

Concerto for Orchestra[a]. Funeral Music[b]. Lacrimosa[c]. Symphony No. 1[d]. [c]**Stefania Woytowicz** (sop); [c]**Silesian Philharmonic Choir;** [ab]**Warsaw National Philharmonic Orchestra/Witold Rowicki;** [cd]**Katowice Radio Symphony Orchestra/**[c]**Witold Lutoslawski,** [d]**Jan Krenz.** Polskie Nagrania Muza PNCD040 (9/90).

Concerto for Orchestra. Symphony No. 3. **Chicago Symphony Orchestra/Daniel Barenboim.** Erato 4509-91711-2 (8/83).

Venetian games[a]. Trois poèmes d'Henri Michaux[b]. Symphony No. 2[c]. [b]**Cracow Polish Radio Choir;** [ac]**Warsaw National Philharmonic Orchestra/**[a]**Witold Rowicki,** [c]**Witold Lutoslawski;** [b]**Katowice Radio Symphony Orchestra/Jan Krenz.** Polskie Nagrania Muza PNCD041 (9/90).

Preludes and Fugues for 13 solo strings[a]. Mi-parti[a]. Novelette[b]. [a]**Polish Chamber Orchestra/Witold Lutoslawski;** [b]**Junge Deutsche Philharmonie/Heinz Holliger.** Polskie Nagrania Muza PNCD043 (9/90).

Piano Concerto[a]. Chain 3. Novelette. [a]**Krystian Zimerman** (pf); **BBC Symphony Orchestra/Witold Lutoslawski.** DG 431 664-2GH (4/92).

Sergey Lyapunov

Russian 1859-1924

Suggested listening ...

Lyapunov. TRANSCENDENTAL STUDIES, Op. 11. *Transcendental Studies* — No. 1 in F sharp major, "Berceuse"; No. 2 in D sharp minor, "Rondes des fantômes"; No. 3 in B major, "Carillon"; No. 4 in G sharp minor, "Terek"; No. 5 in E major, "Nuit d'été"; No. 6 in C sharp minor, "Tempête"; No. 7 in A major, "Idylle"; No. 8 in F sharp minor, "Chant épique"; No. 9 in D major, "Harpes éoliennes"; No. 10 in B minor, "Lesghinka"; No. 11 in G major, "Rondes des Sylphes"; No. 12 in E minor, "Elégie en mémoire de François Liszt". **Malcolm Binns** (pf). Pearl SHECD9624 (5/92).

Hamish MacCunn

British 1868-1916

Suggested listening ...

Land of the Mountain and the Flood, Op. 8. *Coupled with* ***Arnold.*** Tam O'Shanter, Op. 51; ***Berlioz.*** Waverley, Op. 2; ***Mendelssohn.*** Hebrides Overture, Op. 26, "Fingal's Cave"; ***Verdi.*** Macbeth — ballet music. Chandos CHAN8379 (9/85).

Edward MacDowell

American 1860-1908

MacDowell. Piano Concerto No. 2 in D minor, Op. 23[a]. Woodland Sketches, Op. 51 — No. 1, To a Wild Rose[b].
Schumann. Piano Concerto in A minor, Op. 54[c]. **Van Cliburn** (pf); **Chicago Symphony Orchestra/[a]Walter Hendl, [c]Fritz Reiner.** RCA Victor Van Cliburn Collection GD60420. Item marked [a] from SB2113 (8/61), recorded in 1960, [b] new to UK, recorded in 1972, [c] SRA6001 (1/62), recorded in 1960.

lh ADD 10/91 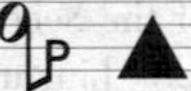

A brilliant pianist himself, MacDowell was still only in his mid-twenties when writing his Second Piano Concerto. Even if lacking an immediately recognizable face of its own, it upholds the grand, later-nineteenth century romantic tradition with enough warmth, verve and virtuosity to explain why the now legendary Van Cliburn could not keep his hands off it. We're told it was the first concerto he ever played professionally with an orchestra (in 1952, when he was 18), and that it was one of the six works with which he toured the Soviet Union in 1960 after winning the first International Tchaikovsky Competition two years before. Also dating from 1960, when he was 26, his recording with Walter Hendl has an irresistible youthful urgency, intensity and élan matching that of the music itself. Though inevitably betraying its age, the sound has been skilfully enough remastered to make the disc something of a collector's piece. The Schumann coupling, recorded early the following year, has a similarly endearing ardour and freshness reminding us that this composer, too, was still then in his prime. Only the slow movement occasionally seems to need phrasing of a more intimately confidential kind.

Guillaume de Machaut

French c.1300-1377

Machaut. Messe de Nostre Dame. Je ne cesse de prier (lai "de la fonteinne"). Ma fin est mon commencement. **Hilliard Ensemble/Paul Hillier.** Hyperion CDA66358. Texts and translations included.

54m DDD 2/90

Machaut's *Messe de Nostre Dame* is the earliest known setting of the Ordinary Mass by a single composer though we cannot be certain either that Machaut wrote it at one time or even that he initially intended to bring its six movements together. Paul Hillier avoids a full reconstruction: his deference to 'authenticity' restricts itself to the usage of fourteenth-century French pronunciation of the Latin. His ensemble sing two to a part, with prominent countertenors. It is arguable whether the group sings the chant at too fast a tempo but they are smooth and flexible and the performance as a whole is fluid and light in texture. Also included are two of Machaut's French compositions. The wonderful *Lai "de la fonteinne"* is admirably sung by three tenors and is pure delight — food for the heart as well as the intellect. The more familiar *Ma fin est mon commencement,* with its retrograde canon, is a final happy addition to this admirable disc.

Additional recommendation ...
Messe de Nostre Dame. **Ensemble Gilles Binchois/Dominique Vellard.** Harmonic Records H/CD8931 — 56m DDD

Further listening ...
Songs — Dame, de qui toute ma joie vient. Foy porter, honneur garder. Dame, je sui cilz/Fins cuers doulz. Tuit mi penser. Dame, mon cuer en vous temaint. Dame a qui m'ottri. Biauté qui toutes autres pere. Je vivroie liement. Rose, liz. Dame, a vous sans retollir. Amours me fait desirer. Douce dame jolie. Felix virgo/Inviolata/Ad te suspiramus. **Gothic Voices/ Christopher Page.** Hyperion CDA66087 (1/84).

Roman Maciejewski

Polish 1910-

Maciejewski. Missa pro defunctis. **Zdzislawa Donat** (sop); **Jadwiga Rappé** (contr); **Jerzy Knetig** (ten); **Janusz Niziolek** (bass); **Warsaw Philharmonic Choir and Orchestra/Tadeusz Strugala.** Polskie Nagrania Muza PNCD039. Recorded in 1989.

② 2h 11m DDD 9/90 

This Requiem was Roman Maciejewski's attempt to come to terms with the catastrophic events of the Second World War and also with his disillusionment with the pre-war avant-garde. It took him until 1959 to finish it, and it had to wait another 16 years for its first performance in Los Angeles — apparently a very emotional event. One of the most extraordinary things about the Requiem though is the way that it anticipates recent developments in music, particularly the rejection of difficult atonalism in favour of sensuous modal harmonies and hypnotic repetitions. Occasionally one may be reminded of the Holst of *Neptune* or the *Rig Veda* hymns — and that's a significant comparison, because whatever else he is, Maciejewski is not a minimalist. In the most beautiful movements — the "Graduale", "Tractus" or "Recordare" for instance — the patterns provide the background to some finely expressive vocal and instrumental writing. It is in these meditative movements rather than in the big apocalyptic numbers that Maciejewski really shows his strength, but he manages to keep the listener hooked right to the end. Performances and recording may lack the final layer of polish, but intense feelings are communicated. A real discovery.

Elizabeth Maconchy

British 1907-

Suggested listening ...

String Quartets Nos. 1-4. **Hanson Quartet.** Unicorn-Kanchana DKPCD9080 (11/89).

String Quartets — Nos. 5-8. **Bingham Quartet.** Unicorn-Kanchana DKPCD9081 (6/90).

String Quartets — Nos. 9-12; No. 13, "Quartetto Corto". **Mistry Quartet.** Unicorn-Kanchana DKPCD9082 (2/91).

Leevi Madetoja

Finnish 1897-1947

NEW REVIEW

Madetoja. Symphonies — No. 1 in F major, Op. 29; No. 2 in E flat major, Op. 35. **Iceland Symphony Orchestra/Petri Sakari.** Chandos CHAN9115. Recorded in 1992.

1h 7m DDD 1/93

Leevi Madetoja briefly studied with Sibelius, though his musical idiom also reflects the influence of Strauss, Reger and the Russian post-nationalists such as Glazunov — and there are strong Gallic touches too. Both symphonies (the Second dates from 1916-8) evince a strong sense of purpose and a feeling for proportion that is striking. As a conductor Madetoja championed such French post-romantic as Vincent d'Indy, with whom he had hoped to study, the impressionist masters and such contemporary masters as Szymanowski and Janáček. His music is conventionally post-nationalist in feeling but is distinguished by a certain rigour and clarity. His debt to Sibelius is considerable and the slow movement of the Second Symphony at one point even anticipates *Tapiola*. Although he is not a composer of the first order, Madetoja is a sensitive and cultured creator with a refined technique and engaging manner. Petri Sakari gets excellent results from the Icelandic orchestra and the recording is completely natural and lifelike.

Albéric Magnard

French 1865-1914

Suggested listening ...

Violin Sonata in G major, Op. 13. Three Piano Pieces, Op. 1. En Dieu mon espérance. Cello Sonata in A major, Op. 20. Promenades, Op. 7. Piano and Wind Quintet in D minor, Op. 8. Piano Trio in F minor, Op. 18. Six poèmes, Op. 3. Quatre poèmes, Op. 15. A Henriette. Suite dans le style ancien in G minor, Op. 2. String Quartet in E minor, Op. 16. **Soloists; Artis Quartet.** Accord 20075-2 (3/90).

Key to Symbols

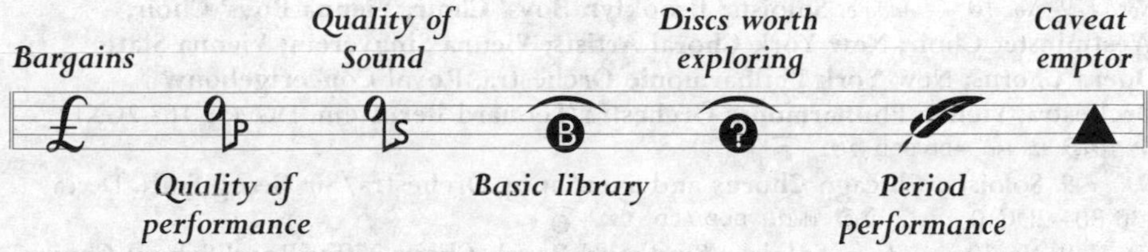

Gustav Mahler

Austrian 1860-1911

Mahler. SYMPHONIES. **Bavarian Radio Symphony Orchestra/Rafael Kubelík.** DG 429 042-2GX10. Recorded 1967-70.

Symphonies — No. 1 (from SLPM139331, 5/68); No. 2, "Resurrection" (Edith Mathis, sop; Norma Procter, contr; Bavarian Radio Chorus 139332/3, 4/70); No. 3 (Marjorie Thomas, contr; Tölz Boys' Choir; Bavarian Rad. Chor. SLPM139337/8, 9/68); No. 4 (Elsie Morison, sop. SLPM139339, 12/68); No. 5 (2720 033, 10/71); No. 6 (139341/2, 11/69); No. 7 (2720 033); No. 8 (Martina Arroyo, Erna Spoorenberg, Mathis, sops; Júlia Hamari, Procter, contrs; Donald Grobe, ten; Dietrich Fischer-Dieskau, bar; Franz Crass, bass; Regensburg Cathedral Boys' Choir; Munich Motet Choir; Bavarian Rad. Chor; North German Radio Chorus; West German Radio Chorus, 2720 033); No. 9 (SLPM139 345/6, 12/67); No. 10 — Adagio (139341/2).

⑩ 10h 51m ADD 5/90

There are hundreds of recordings of Mahler's symphonies listed in the current *Classical Catalogue*, so anyone approaching them for the first time is faced with the daunting problem of which versions to acquire. This reissue may well be something of a solution. Here we have a distinguished and highly commendable cycle of the symphonies at bargain price that provides an excellent opportunity for the newcomer to explore the symphonies at a relatively low cost. Kubelík's cycle is still one of the most completely satisfying on disc. There is a breadth and consistency of vision in these interpretations, that comes only from a conductor who has a deep understanding and a long association with this music. The most successful performances are perhaps Symphonies Nos. 1, 4, 5, 7 and 9. The First, notable for its fresh, youthful account and clearly defined textures, is still one of the finest versions available. The Fourth is equally as impressive, with lively tempos and excellent orchestral playing. There is a strong sense of direction and structural unity in this performance and Elsie Morison's warm and poetic performance in the finale is a real delight. Kubelík's reading of Symphonies Nos. 5 and 7 have not always met with the credit that they deserve. The Fifth is a very individual performance, though certainly not lacking in intensity or power. Kubelík avoids dwelling too much on the tragic elements in the first movement of the Seventh and instead tries to build out of the devastation of the Sixth Symphony's finale. The Ninth is a very strong performance indeed, with great clarity of detail and a strong sense of architecture. It would of course be foolish to suggest that Kubelík's cycle is without flaws — the Second Symphony, although not without intensity, lacks perhaps the drama and spirituality of, say,

Klemperer or Rattle and the same could be said of the Third. The Eighth is a fine performance superbly recorded and with some excellent singing from the soloists, but is ultimately outclassed by the superb award-winning Tennstedt recording (reviewed further on). The recordings are all clear, spacious and naturally balanced and were recorded in the warm and resonant acoustic of the Munich Herkulessaal between 1967 and 1971. A considerable bargain.

Additional recommendations ...

Nos. 1-9. Lieder aus "Des Knaben Wunderhorn". Das klagende Lied — Der Spielmann; Hochzeitstuck. Lieder eines fahrenden Gesellen. Kindertotenlieder. **Soloists; Collegium Musicum Amstelodamense; Amsterdam Toonkunst Choir; Amsterdam Stem des Volks Choir; St Willibrord and Pius X Children's Choir; Netherlands Radio Chorus; St Willibrord's Boys' Choir; Concertgebouw Orchestra/Bernard Haitink.** Philips 434 053-2PM15 — ⑮ 13h 53m ADD/DDD 12/92 Ⓑ

Nos. 1-9. No. 10 — Adagio. **Soloists; Brooklyn Boys' Choir; Vienna Boys' Choir; Westminster Choir; New York Choral Artists; Vienna Singverein; Vienna State Opera Chorus; New York Philharmonic Orchestra, Royal Concertgebouw Orchestra, Vienna Philharmonic Orchestra/Leonard Bernstein.** DG 435 162-2GX13 — ⑬ 12h 44m ADD/DDD 2/92 Ⓑ

Nos. 1-9. **Soloists; Chicago Chorus and Symphony Orchestra/Sir Georg Solti.** Decca 430 804-2DC10 — ⑩ 11h 12m DDD/ADD 4/92 Ⓑ

Nos. 1-9. No. 10 — Adagio. **Soloists; Southend Boys's Choir; Tiffin Boys' School Choir; London Philharmonic Choir and Orchestra/Klaus Tennstedt.** EMI Mahler Edition available as follows:

Nos. 1-4: CMS7 64471-2 — ④ 4h 55m ADD/DDD 4/93 Ⓑ

Nos. 6-8: CMS7 64476-2 — ④ 4h 14m ADD/DDD 4/93 Ⓑ

Nos. 5, 9 and 10 — Adagio: CMS7 64481-2 — ③ 3h 9m ADD/DDD 4/93 Ⓑ

Mahler. Symphony No. 1. **Berlin Philharmonic Orchestra/Claudio Abbado.** DG 431 769-2GH. Recorded live in 1989.

55m DDD 10/91 Ⓑ

While Bernstein's vision of this symphony is intense, with every corner of the work stamped with his personality, Abbado directs a technically immaculate account. Combined with his own particular insight this performance conveys more a sense of Mahler's sound world rather than, as previously, Mahler and Bernstein's. The playing of the BPO combined with the extraordinarily vivid and well balanced recording takes the performance of this work into a new league. Perhaps orchestras are only now fully able to realize Mahler's music in the way that they have been able to with, for instance, Beethoven's for years. There is here a confidence, familiarity and precision that is most unusual and deeply impressive. Added to its technical perfection is Abbado's assured control of tempos, phrasing and dynamics. These define very strongly both the character and atmosphere of each movement which are much more clearly delineated than has usually been the case in the past. The overall result is a major symphonic work at last coming into true focus: both weaknesses, such as its episodic nature, and strengths, its tremendous originality and character, stand fully revealed. Warts and all, this is an outburst of young musical genius fully realized by another, interpretative, genius.

Additional recommendation ...

No. 1. **London Symphony Orchestra/Sir Georg Solti.** Decca 417 701-2DM — DDD Ⓑ

No. 1. **Frankfurt Radio Symphony Orchestra/Eliahu Inbal.** Denon C37-7537 — 55m DDD 12/85 Ⓑ

No. 1. **Berlin Philharmonic Orchestra/Bernard Haitink.** Philips 420 936-2PH — 57m DDD 10/88 Ⓑ

No. 1. **Concertgebouw Orchestra/Leonard Bernstein.** DG 431 036-2GBE — 56m DDD 3/89 Ⓑ

No. 1. **London Symphony Orchestra/Jascha Horenstein.** Unicorn-Kanchana Souvenir UKCD2012 — 57m ADD 4/89 Ⓑ

No. 1. Lieder eines fahrenden Gesellen. **Bavarian Radio Symphony Orchestra/Rafael Kubelík.** DG 3D Classics 429 157-2GR — lh 6m ADD 2/90
No. 1. **Chicago Symphony Orchestra/Klaus Tennstedt.** EMI CDC7 54217-2 — lh lm DDD 11/91

Mahler. Symphony No. 2, "Resurrection". **Arleen Auger** (sop); **Dame Janet Baker** (mez); **City of Birmingham Symphony Chorus and Orchestra/Simon Rattle.** EMI CDS7 47962-8. Text and translation included. From EX270598-3 (10/87).

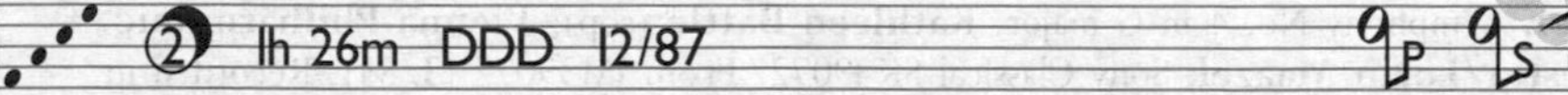

The folk-poems from *Des knaben Wunderhorn*, with their complex mixture of moods and strong ironic edge, formed the basis of Mahler's inspiration for the Second Symphony. It is a work of huge scope, emotionally as well as physically taxing, and here it receives a performance that remarkably rekindles the feeling of a live performance with a quite breathtaking immediacy. The CBSO play magnificently and Rattle's attention to the letter of the score never hinders his overall vision of this masterpiece. The recording is superb.

Additional recommendations …
Gabriela Beňačková (sop); **Eva Randová** (mez); **Czech Philharmonic Chorus and Orchestra/Václav Neumann.** Supraphon Gems 2SUP0020 — lh 15m 12/87 £
Benita Valente (sop); **Maureen Forrester** (mez); **Ardwyn Singers; BBC Welsh Chorus; Cardiff Polyphonic Choir; Dyfed Choir; London Symphony Chorus and Orchestra/Gilbert Kaplan.** Pickwick IMP Classics DPCD910 — 2 lh 23m DDD 1/89
Barbara Hendricks (sop); **Christa Ludwig** (mez); **Westminster Choir; New York Philharmonic Orchestra/Leonard Bernstein.** DG 423 395-2GH2 — 2 lh 34m DDD 7/88
Elisabeth Schwarzkopf (sop); **Hilde Rössl-Majdan** (mez); **Philharmonia Chorus and Orchestra/Otto Klemperer.** EMI Studio CDM7 69662-2 — lh 19m ADD 1/90

Mahler. Symphony No. 3. **Norma Procter** (contr); **Wandsworth School Boys' Choir; Ambrosian Singers; London Symphony Orchestra/Jascha Horenstein.** Unicorn-Kanchana Souvenir UKCD2006/7. Text and translation included. From RHS302/03 (12/70).

2 lh 37m ADD 11/88 £

Every now and again, along comes a Mahler *performance* that no serious collector can afford to be without. Horenstein's interpretation of the Third Symphony is an outstanding example and its reissue on CD at mid-price is a major addition to the Mahler discography. No other conductor has surpassed Horenstein in his total grasp of every facet of the enormous score. Even though the LSO strings of the day were not as powerful as they later became, they play with suppleness and a really tense sound, especially appropriate in the kaleidoscopic first movement, where changes of tempo and mood reflect the ever-changing face of nature. Horenstein gives the posthorn solo to a flügelhorn, a successful experiment. His light touch in the middle movements is admirable, and Norma Procter is a steady soloist in "O Mensch! Gib acht!", with the Wandsworth School Boys' Choir bimm-bamming as if they were all Austrian-born! Then comes the *Adagio* finale, its intensity and ecstasy sustained by Horenstein without dragging the tempo. The recording is not as full and rich in dynamic range as some made recently, but it is still a classic.

Additional recommendations …
No. 3[a]*. Four Rückert Lieder*[b]*. Seven Lieder und Gesänge aus der Jugendzeit*[b]. [a]**Martha Lipton** (mez); [b]**Dietrich Fischer-Dieskau** (bar); [a]women's chorus of the **Schola Cantorum;** [a]**Boys' Choir of the Transfiguration;** [a]**New York Philharmonic Orchestra/Leonard Bernstein** (pf[b]). CBS Masterworks CD42196 — 2h 22m 12/86
No. 3[a]*. Das klagende Lied*[b]. [b]**Heather Harper** (sop); [a]**Maureen Forrester,** [b]**Norma Procter** (contrs); [b]**Werner Hollweg** (ten); [a]**St Willibrord Church Boys' Choir, Amsterdam;** [a]women's voices of the **Netherlands Radio Chorus; Concertgebouw Orchestra/Bernard Haitink.** Philips 420 113-2PH2 — 2 2h 13m ADD 11/88

No. 3. **Jessye Norman** (sop); **Vienna Boys' Choir; Vienna State Opera Concert Choir; Vienna Philharmonic Orchestra/Claudio Abbado.** DG 410 715-2GH2 — ② lh 43m DDD 11/88

No. 3. **Christa Ludwig** (mez); **Brooklyn Boys' Chorus; New York Choral Artists; New York Philharmonic Orchestra/Leonard Bernstein.** DG 427 328-2GH2 (recorded in 1987) — ② lh 46m DDD 6/89

Mahler. Symphony No. 4 in G major. **Kathleen Battle** (sop); **Vienna Philharmonic Orchestra/Lorin Maazel.** Sony Classical SK39072. From IM39072 (3/85). Recorded in 1983.

lh lm DDD 1/86 

"With sincere and serene expression" says Mahler's footnote in the finale — "absolutely without parody!" And that is exactly how Lorin Maazel, Kathleen Battle and the Vienna Philharmonic Orchestra respond to this music: the grotesqueries of the scherzo are nicely underplayed; the darker outbursts of the slow movement are not overloaded with *Angst*; and there is nothing wry or sentimentally nostalgic about "Die himmlischen Freuden". Instead, there is warmth, tenderness and, especially in the closing movement, a kind of heart-easing simplicity, enhanced by the purity and uncloying sweetness of Kathleen Battle's singing. The recording is warm-toned and beautifully balanced and the dynamic range is impressive, though never unrealistic.

Additional recommendations ...

Helmut Wittek (treb); **Concertgebouw Orchestra/Leonard Bernstein.** DG 423 607-2GH — 57m DDD 8/88

Felicity Lott (sop); **London Philharmonic Orchestra/Franz Welser-Möst.** EMI Eminence CD-EMX2139 — lh 3m DDD 12/88 £

Barbara Hendricks (sop); **Los Angeles Philharmonic Orchestra/Esa-Pekka Salonen.** Sony Classical SK48380 — 58m DDD 8/92

Mahler. Symphony No. 5. **Vienna Philharmonic Orchestra/Leonard Bernstein.** DG 423 608-2GH. Recorded live in 1987.

lh 15m DDD 8/88  

Mahler's Fifth begins with a funeral march, in which the military bugle-calls he heard as a boy sound through the textures, leading to a central *scherzo* full of nostalgia for Alpine lakes and pastures, a soulful *Adagietto* for strings which we now know was a love-letter to his future wife and ends with a triumphant, joyous *rondo-finale*. It has been called Mahler's *Eroica* and that is not a far-fetched description. In later years Bernstein tended to go 'over the top' in Mahler, but here he is at his exciting best and the Vienna Philharmonic responds to him as only it can to a conductor with whom it has a special relationship. The recording is exceptionally clear and well-balanced, so that many subtleties of detail in the scoring emerge but are not over highlighted. The symphony again sounds like the daringly orchestrated piece that bewildered its first audiences, only now we realize the genius of it all. Structure, sound and emotion are held in ideal equilibrium by Bernstein in this enthralling performance.

Additional recommendations ...

Czech Philharmonic Orchestra/Václav Neumann. Supraphon Gems 2SUP0021 — lh 10m 12/87 £

New Philharmonia Orchestra/Sir John Barbirolli. EMI CDM7 64749-2 — lh 14m ADD 11/88 £

Cleveland Orchestra/Christoph von Dohnányi. Decca 425 438-2DH — lh 5m DDD 6/89

Mahler. Symphony No. 6. Kindertotenlieder[a]. [a]**Thomas Hampson** (bar); **Vienna Philharmonic Orchestra/Leonard Bernstein.** DG 427 697-2GH2. Recorded live in 1988

② 1h 55m DDD 1/90

Mahler's tragic Sixth Symphony digs more profoundly into the nature of man and Fate than any of his earlier works, closing in desolation, a beat on the bass drum, a coffin lid closing. Bernstein's reading was a live recording at a concert, with all the electricity of such an occasion, and the Vienna Philharmonic Orchestra respond to the conductor's dark vision of Mahler's score with tremendous bravura. Fortunately, the achingly tender slow movement brings some relief, but with the enormous finale lasting over 30 minutes we must witness a resumption of a battle to the death and the final outcome. The coupling is a logical one, for the *Kindertotenlieder* takes up the theme of death yet again. But it is in a totally different, quieter way: these beautiful songs express a parent's grief over the loss of a child, and although some prefer a woman's voice, the sensitive Thomas Hampson makes a good case here for a male singer. The recording of both works is so good that one would not know it was made 'live', particularly as the applause is omitted.

Additional recommendations ...

No. 6. *Five Rückert Lieder*[a]. [a]**Christa Ludwig** (mez); **Berlin Philharmonic Orchestra/Herbert von Karajan.** DG 415 099-2GH2 — ② 1h 42m ADD 4/85

No. 6[a]. *No.* 8[b]. **Soloists; Leeds Festival Chorus; London Symphony Chorus; Orpington Junior Singers; Highgate School Boys' Choir; Finchley Children's Music Group;** [a]**New York Philharmonic Orchestra,** [b]**London Symphony Orchestra/Leonard Bernstein.** CBS CD42199 — ③ 2h 39m DDD 12/86

No. 6. *Five Rückert Lieder*[a]. [a]**Hanna Schwarz** (mez); **Chicago Symphony Orchestra/Claudio Abbado.** DG Galleria 423 928-2GGA2 — ② 1h 44m ADD/DDD 3/89

No. 6. **City of Birmingham Symphony Orchestra/Simon Rattle.** EMI CDS7 54047-2 — ② 1h 26m DDD 11/90

NEW REVIEW

Mahler. Symphony No. 7. **New York Philharmonic Orchestra/Leonard Bernstein.** DG 419 211-2GH2.

This is Mahler's most orchestrally glamorous symphony. After the "roars" of nature in the first movement, there are three night pieces — two full of old world romance that frame a central, almost 'expressionist' nightmare — leading to an emphatically daylight finale; an euphoric, nay, distinctly manic collage where Wagner's *Meistersingers* rub shoulders with Lehar's *Merry Widow*. Arguments will probably rage forever as to whether Bernstein is the only conductor to properly understand and communicate Mahler's language, or whether he hijacked Mahler as the perfect vehicle for his own hyper-emotive brand of music-making. The fact remains that in few other performances of the Seventh do you encounter so complete a realization of Mahler's claim for this Symphony that "with me all the instruments sing, even the brass and kettledrums' (just listen to the woodwind in the fourth bar!); such a wide-ranging mix of the old *and* the new in the central night music (often conducted with too much or too little awareness that, say, Berg's *Wozzeck* was just around the corner); and last but far from least, a conductor that makes long-term sense of the merry-go-round finale. The New York Philharmonic give their all, and DG produce a dry, but very articulate Mahler sound.

Additional recommendations ...

No. 7. **Frankfurt Radio Symphony Orchestra/Eliahu Inbal.** Denon CO-1553/4 — ② 1h 18m 8/87

No. 7. *Kindertotenlieder*[a]. [a]**Jessye Norman** (sop); **Boston Symphony Orchestra/Seiji Ozawa.** Philips 426 249-2PH2 — ② 1h 46m DDD 5/91

No. 7. **City of Birmingham Symphony Orchestra/Simon Rattle.** EMI CDC7 54344-2 — 1h 17m DDD 9/92

Mahler. Symphony No. 8. **Elizabeth Connell, Edith Wiens, Felicity Lott** (sops); **Trudeliese Schmidt, Nadine Denize** (contrs); **Richard Versalle** (ten); **Jorma Hynninen** (bar); **Hans Sotin** (bass); **Tiffin Boys' School Choir; London Philharmonic Choir and Orchestra/Klaus Tennstedt.** EMI CDS7 47625-8. Notes, text and translation included. From EX270474-3 (3/87). Recorded in 1986.

② lh 22m DDD 5/87

Mahler's extravagantly monumental Eighth Symphony, often known as the *Symphony of a Thousand*, is the Mahler symphony that raises doubts in even his most devoted of admirers. Its epic dimensions, staggering vision and sheer profligacy of forces required make it a 'difficult work'. Given a great live performance it will sway even the hardest of hearts; given a performance like Tennstedt's, reproduced with all the advantages of CD, home-listeners, too, can be mightily impressed (and so, given the forces involved, will most of the neighbourhood!) — the sheer volume of sound at the climax is quite overwhelming. The work seeks to parallel the Christian's faith in the power of the Holy Spirit with the redeeming power of love for mankind and Tennstedt's performance leaves no doubt that he believes totally in Mahler's creation. It has a rapt, almost intimate, quality that makes this reading all the more moving. The soloists are excellent and the choruses sing with great conviction.

Additional recommendation ...
Soloists; Vienna State Opera Chorus; Vienna Singverein; Vienna Boys Choir; Chicago Symphony Orchestra/Sir Georg Solti. Decca 414 493-2DH2 — 10/85

Mahler. Symphony No. 9. **Berlin Philharmonic Orchestra/Herbert von Karajan.** DG 410 726-2GH2. Recorded in 1982.

② lh 25m DDD 7/84

Mahler's Ninth is a death-haunted work, but is filled, as Bruno Walter remarked, "with a sanctified feeling of departure". Rarely has this Symphony been shaped with such understanding and played with such selfless virtuosity as it was by Karajan and the Berlin Philharmonic in a legendary series of concerts in 1982. The performance is electric and intense, yet Karajan — ever the enigmatic blend of fire and ice — has the measure of the symphony's spiritual coolness. Karajan had previously made a fine studio recording of the Ninth but this later concert performance is purer, deeper, and even more dauntingly intense. The digital recording has great clarity and a thrilling sense of actuality; no symphony in the repertoire benefits more than this one from the absolute quietness that CD allows. When the history of twentieth-century music-making comes to be written this performance will be seen as one of its proudest landmarks.

Additional recommendations ...
No. 9. No. 10 — Adagio. **Vienna Philharmonic Orchestra/Lorin Maazel.** CBS Masterworks CD39721 — ② lh 51m DDD 10/86
No. 9. No. 10 — Adagio. **Frankfurt Radio Symphony Orchestra/Eliahu Inbal.** Denon CO-1566/7 — ② lh 44m DDD 1/88
No. 9. **Berlin Philharmonic Orchestra/Sir John Barbirolli.** EMI Studio CDM7 63115-2 — lh 18m ADD 11/89 £
No. 9[a]. ***Wagner.*** *Siegfried Idyll*[b]. [a]**New Philharmonia Orchestra;** [b]**Philharmonia Orchestra/Otto Klemperer.** EMI Studio CMS7 63277-2 — ② lh 45m ADD 1/90
No. 9. **Berlin Philharmonic Orchestra/Leonard Bernstein.** DG 435 378-2GH2 — ② lh 22m ADD 5/92

Mahler (ed. Cooke). Symphony No. 10. **Bournemouth Symphony Orchestra/Simon Rattle.** EMI CDC7 54406-2. From HMV SLS5206 (12/80).

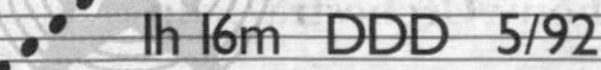

Rattle's superb interpretation of Cooke's performing version of the Tenth Symphony now sweeps the board. His achievement is in a special class, empowering the music with such emotional clout that you forget the scholarly debates. There are in fact several adjustments to Schirmer's published score which Rattle explained in the splendid booklet which accompanied the original LP issue. Unfortunately, this has not been included with this CD reissue. One example of his innovatory approach is his merging of the drum stroke which ends the fourth movement with the one which triggers the fifth; furthermore the opening pages of the finale are truly awesome here. Tempos are unfailingly appropriate and the Bournemouth band is second to none. This is music-making of extraordinary fervour, with excellent sound. It is altogether an essential purchase.

Additional recommendations ...
(Ed. Cooke). ***Schoenberg.*** *Verklärte Nacht, Op. 4.* **Berlin Radio Symphony Orchestra/Riccardo Chailly.** Decca 421 182-2DH2 — ② lh 50m DDD 3/88 B
(Ed. Cooke). **Frankfurt Radio Symphony Orchestra/Eliahu Inbal.** Denon CO-75129 — lh llm DDD 4/93 B

Mahler. LIEDER.
Wolf. LIEDER. **Anne Sofie von Otter** (mez); **Ralf Gothóni** (pf). DG 423 666-2GH. Texts and translations included.
Mahler: Des Knaben Wunderhorn — No. 2, Verlorne Müh; No. 7, Rheinlegendchen; No. 9, Wo die schönen Trompeten blasen; No. 10, Lob des hohen Verstands. Lieder und Gesang — No. 1, Frühlingsmorgen. No. 2, Erinnerung. No. 4, Serenade aus Don Juan. No. 5, Phantasie aus Don Juan No. 7, Ich ging mit Lust durch einen grünen Wald. No. 8, Aus! Aus!. ***Wolf:*** Heiss mich nicht reden (Mignon I). Nur wer die Sehnsucht (Mignon II). So lasst mich scheinen (Mignon III). Kennst du das Land (Mignon). Frühling übers Jahr. Frage nicht. Die Spröde. Der Schäfer. Gesang Weylas.

59m DDD 6/89 P

Anne Sofie von Otter's first record of Lieder proved an outright winner. She obviously owes something of a debt to Christa Ludwig and Brigitte Fassbaender, but she nonetheless establishes a personality and style of her own. Technically she is virtually faultless, and she brings to her performance a nice combination of interpretative insight and emotional involvement. These assets are at once evident in the four settings by Hugo Wolf of Mignon's enigmatic utterances from *Wilhelm Meister*. Each is perceptively characterized by von Otter and her admirable partner Ralf Gothóni, bringing before our eyes the suppressed grief and longing of the sad waif so unerringly portrayed by Wolf. They then find, by contrast, a pleasing simplicity for the next three songs before returning to a more intense manner for the marvellous *Gesang Weylas*. For the Mahler the pair adopt another style and just the right one. Humour and lightness, where relevant, rightly dominate their accounts of the pieces from *Des Knaben Wunderhorn*. Von Otter's singing is playful without ever becoming coy or mannered. In the more serious "Ich ging mit Lust" the singer's melding of line and tone is near-ideal. "Wo die schönen Trompeten blasen" may be taken at a dangerously slow tempo, but this in a way enhances the mesmeric mood of the song. The seldom-heard settings from Molina's *Don Juan*, especially the alluring "Serenade", are precisely tuned to the music in hand. Altogether a delightful disc.

NEW REVIEW
Mahler. Das Lied von der Erde. **Agnes Baltsa** (mez); **Klaus König** (ten); **London Philharmonic Orchestra/Klaus Tennstedt.** EMI CDC7 54603-2. Text and translation included. Recorded 1982-84.

lh 7m DDD 2/93 P B

For some unaccountable reason, this version of Mahler's masterpiece was left to languish in EMI's vaults for almost ten years. Now that it has seen the light of day, it is revealed as by far the most convincing version in recent times, given by one of the most committed Mahler exponents of recent times. Tennstedt penetrates to the heart of every aspect of the soul-searching work. Without any sign of self-indulgence he gives it a searing, emotion-draining performance faithfully supported by the superb work of the London Philharmonic which rivals and, in most cases, surpasses the readings of the work by other great orchestras. Their work would be set at naught were it not for the lifelike and wide-ranging recording (produced by John Willan). Baltsa might seem an unlikely candidate for this piece but her clean line, her nourishing overtones, her direct but eloquent phrasing fulfil almost all its demands. König, a true Heldentenor but one with lightness and sensitivity needed for the middle of his three songs, makes an honest and positive soloist. The alternative recommendations all have much to offer, especially the classic Walter, a truly inspired and dedicated interpretation by one of Mahler's earliest advocates. Walter and Klemperer have, by a small margin, the better soloist but neither is recorded or played with more conviction than the new EMI. At mid-price Fritz Reiner's interpretation presents a fitting alternative and in some ways Barenboim's is the most compelling and spontaneous of recent recordings. Although Meier and Jerusalem give the impression of not having lived quite long enough with this music, the sheer beauty of the sound is outstanding. The première Teldec recording of the composer's own piano version also provides us with a valuable insight into Mahler's creative processes. As the informative booklet-notes point out this is not just a piano transcription of the orchestral score but a valid performing version in its own right. Any doubts one may have about the validity or necessity for such a recording are soon dispelled by the commitment and persuasiveness of the performances by Fassbaender, Moser and Katsaris.

Additional recommendations ...

Kathleen Ferrier (contr); **Julius Patzak** (ten); **Vienna Philharmonic Orchestra/Bruno Walter.** Decca 414 194-2DH — ADD 1/85 ▲
Christa Ludwig (mez); **Fritz Wunderlich** (ten); **Philharmonia Orchestra, New Philharmonia Orchestra/Otto Klemperer.** EMI CDC7 47231-2 — 1h 4m ADD 12/85
Maureen Forrester (contr); **Richard Lewis** (ten); **Chicago Symphony Orchestra/Fritz Reiner.** RCA Victor Gold Seal GD60178 — 1h 3m ADD 10/91
Brigitte Fassbaender (mez); **Thomas Moser** (ten); **Cyprien Katsaris** (pf). Teldec 2292-46276-2 — 1h 1m DDD 6/90
Waltraud Meier (mez); **Siegfried Jerusalem** (ten); **Chicago Symphony Orchestra/Daniel Barenboim.** Erato 2292-45624-2 — 1h DDD 4/92

Mahler. Des Knaben Wunderhorn. **Dame Elisabeth Schwarzkopf** (sop); **Dietrich Fischer-Dieskau** (bar); **London Symphony Orchestra/George Szell.** EMI CDC7 47277-2. From SAN218 (1/69).

48m ADD 11/88

Mahler's reputation rests primarily on his ten symphonies, but running alongside these magnificent works are his great song cycles. The poems of *Des Knaben Wunderhorn* ("The youth's magic horn") are drawn from a collection written in a deliberately 'folk' style. They are often humorous, ironic (as in the military settings), surreal or eerily strange. Mahler's use of the orchestra is delicate and sensitive; he rarely employs its full might but conjures from it a wide variety of colours and sounds. Schwarzkopf and Fischer-Dieskau sing the songs magnificently, drawing from the texts every verbal nuance and subtle shading and Szell's accompaniments, with his distinctive approach to Mahler's unique and evocative sound world, are outstanding. This is a classic.

Additional recommendation ...

Des Knaben Wunderhorn. **Ann Murray** (mez); **Thomas Allen** (bar); **London Philharmonic Orchestra/Sir Charles Mackerras.** Virgin Classics VC7 59037-2 — 51m DDD 11/91

Mahler. Das klagende Lied (complete version including "Waldmärchen"). **Susan Dunn** (sop); **Markus Baur** (alto); **Brigitte Fassbaender** (mez); **Werner Hollweg** (ten); **Andreas Schmidt** (bar); **Städtischer Musikverein Düsseldorf; Berlin Radio Symphony Orchestra/Riccardo Chailly.** Decca 425 719-2DH. Text and translation included. Recorded in 1989.

1h 4m DDD 2/92

Even the musically acute listener would be unlikely to realize that *Das klagende Lied* is the work of a teenager. Mahler's first significant work is as self-assured as anything he was to write in later life. Indeed enthusiastic Mahlerians will recognize here passages which crop up in other works, most notably the Second Symphony. Those same enthusiastic Mahlerians might not recognize much of this recording, however, since only two movements of *Klagende Lied* are usually performed: the 30-minute first movement is considered too rambling. But no one could possibly arrive at that conclusion from this tautly directly, electrifying performance, and it contains some wonderfully imaginative music, including some delightful forest murmurs, which it seems tragic to miss out. For this movement alone this CD is a must for any Mahler fan, but more than that this is a spectacular recording of a one-in-a-million performance. The soloists, choir and orchestra achieve near perfection under Chailly's inspired direction, and the decision to substitute for the marvellous Brigitte Fassbaender a boy alto (Markus Baur) to represent the disembodied voice of the dead brother is a stroke of pure genius. His weird, unnatural voice provide a moment of sheer spine-tingling drama.

Mahler. Kindertotenlieder[a]. Rückert Lieder[b]. Lieder eines fahrenden Gesellen[a]. **Dame Janet Baker** (mez); [a]**Hallé Orchestra;** [b]**New Philharmonia Orchestra/Sir John Barbirolli.** EMI CDC7 47793-2. Texts and translations included. Items marked [a] from ASD2338 (2/68), [b] ASD2518/19 (12/69).

3 1h 5m ADD 12/87 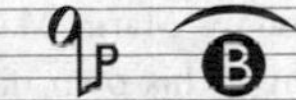

The songs of the *Lieder eines fahrenden Gesellen* ("Songs of a Wayfarer") are directly quoted from Mahler's First Symphony and the same fresh, springtime atmosphere is shared by both works. The orchestration has great textural clarity and lightness of touch. The *Kindertotenlieder*, more chromatically expressive than the earlier work, tap into a darker, more psychologically complex vein in Mahler's spiritual and emotional make-up. The *Rückert Lieder* are not a song cycle as such but gather in their romantic awareness and response to the beauties of the poetry a unity and shape that acts to bind them. Together, Baker and Barbirolli reach a transcendental awareness of Mahler's inner musings. Barbirolli draws from the Hallé playing of great delicacy and precision and establishes a clear case for having this CD in your collection.

Additional recommendations …

Catherine Robbin (mez); **Kitchener-Waterloo Symphony Orchestra/Raffi Armenian.** CBC Records SMCD5098 — 55m DDD 5/92
Andreas Schmidt (bar); **Cincinnati Symphony Orchestra/Jésus López-Cobos.** Telarc CD80269 — 56m DDD 5/93

Gian Francesco Malipiero

Italian 1882-1973

Suggested listening …

String Quartets — No. 1, "Rispetti e strambotti"; No. 2, "Stornelli e ballate"; No. 3, "Cantari alla madrigalesca"; No. 4; No. 5, "dei capricci"; No. 6, "L'arca di Noè"; No. 7; No. 8, "per Elisabetta". **Orpheus Quartet.** ASV CDDCD457 (2/92).

Henry Mancini

American 1924-

Suggested listening …

Film Scores: The Pink Panther; Charade; Hatari!; Breakfast at Tiffany's. **Henry Mancini and His Orchestra.** RCA Victor RD85938.

MANCINI IN SURROUND — *Film Scores:* The White Dawn — Arctic whale hunt. Mommie Dearest. Frenzy. Monster Movie Music Suite. Fear — Casey's theme. The Man Who Loved

Women — Little boys. The Prisoner of Zenda — suite. Nightwing. Without a clue — excerpts. Sunset — suite. **The Mancini Pops Orchestra/Henry Mancini.** RCA Victor RD60471 (5/91).

Marin Marais

French 1656-1728

Marais. ALCYONE. **Jennifer Smith** (sop) Alcyone; **Gilles Ragon** (ten) Ceyx; **Philippe Huttenlocher** (bar) Pélée; **Vincent Le Texier** (bass-bar) Pan, Phorbas; **Sophie Boulin** (sop) Ismène, First Sailor; **Bernard Delétré** (bass) Tmole, High Priest, Neptune; **Jean-Paul Fouchécourt** (alto) Morpheus; **Véronique Gens** (sop) Second Sailor, Priestess; **Les Musiciens du Louvre/Marc Minkowski.** Erato MusiFrance 2292-45522-2. Notes, text and translation included. Recorded in 1990.

② 2h 34m DDD 4/92

Today, Marin Marais is remembered almost entirely for his legacy of music for the bass viol. But in his own day Marais was recognized as a talented opera composer, too. *Alcyone*, first performed in 1706, was his dramatic *chef d'oeuvre* and held the stage at intervals for more than half a century. Though he followed in Lully's footsteps, Marais spoke with a voice of his own and nowhere is this more apparent than in *Alcyone*, which contains in its Fourth Act one of the great moments in French opera literature — a tempest, judged so successful by his contemporaries that not only was it performed as a separate item at court, at the express command of the king, but also found its way into a revival of a Lully opera early in the eighteenth century. The plot centres on the thwarted love of Alcyone for Ceyx, a *tragédie* which moves, however, to a happy ending. Marais's music explores a wide range of emotions. Catchy instrumental pieces — the sailors' dance in Act 3 is especially captivating — supple choruses and touching airs abound, several foreshadowing Rameau in their colourful orchestration. The mainly strong cast is headed by the soprano, Jennifer Smith, in the title role, with lively performances by Sophie Boulin as Ismène, Phorbas's partner in crime, and Gilles Ragon as Ceyx. Minkowski directs with stylish conviction and a good sense of pace. A few rough edges count for little where so much else is enlightened. The vivid recording comes with full texts and translations.

Further listening ...

Pièces en trio — Suites: B flat major; C minor; E minor. *Suite d'un goût étranger* — La rêveuse; Le badinage. **Ensemble Fitzwilliam.** Auvidis Valois V4638 (11/92).

Pièces de viole, troisième livre — Suites: E minor; D major; G major. **Jordi Savall** (va da gamba); **Hopkinson Smith** (theorbo); **Ton Koopman** (hpd). Astrée Auvidis E8761 (12/92).

Pièces de viole, quatrième livre: Suite d'un goût étranger — Marche Tartare; La Tartarine and Double; Les festes champêtre; Le toubillon; Le labyrinthe; L'arabesque; Allemande la superbe; La rêveuse; Marche; Gigue; Le badinage. **Jordi Savall** (va da gamba); **Ton Koopman** (hpd); **Hopkinson Smith** (baroque gtr, theorbo). Astrée Auvidis E7727 (9/88).

Pièces de viole, cinquième livre — Suites: G minor; E minor/major. Le tableau de l'opération de la taille. Le tombeau pour Marais le cadet. **Jordi Savall** (bass viol); **Hopkinson Smith** (theorbo); **Ton Koopman** (hpd) with **Jean-Michael Damian** (spkr). Astrée Auvidis E7708 (2/88).

La gamme et autres morceaux de simphonies — La gamme en forme d'un petit opéra; Sonate à la mariesienne; Saint-Geneviève du Mont. **Boston Musum Trio.** Centaur CRC2129

Pièces en trio — Suites: C major; B flat major; G minor; F major; E minor; G minor. **Quadro Hotteterre.** Teldec 9031-77617-2.

Alessandro Marcello

Italian 1684-1750

Suggested listening ...

Oboe Concerto in D minor. *Coupled with* **Vivaldi.** Trio Sonata in D minor, RV63, "La folia". Flautino Concerto in C major, RV443. Amor hai vinto, RV651. Nulla in mundo pax, RV630. **Soloists; Academy of Ancient Music/Christopher Hogwood.** L'Oiseau-Lyre 421 655-2OH (9/89).

Frank Martin

Swiss 1890-1974

Martin. Cello Concerto[a]. Les quatre éléments[b]. [a]**Jean Decross** (vc); **Concertgebouw Orchestra/Bernard Haitink.** Preludio PRL2147.

43m ADD 10/91

Two works from the 1960s which fill in the picture of the composer after such works as the *Petite symphonie concertante* or the Concerto for seven wind instruments. *The four elements* (1963-64) was designed as an eightieth birthday present for Ernest Ansermet, a lifelong champion of the composer, and the Cello Concerto (1966) was written for the great French cellist Pierre Fournier. (It says much for the swinging, shallow 1960s that their appearance made scarcely any impact at the time.) *The four elements* is a short work of just under 20 minutes but is music of substance and powerful imaginative vision. It was the "world in the original state, without movement" as Martin experienced it in the uppermost part of Northern Norway and Iceland that inspired the first movement, "Earth". "Water" has plenty of movement, and is scored with wonderful delicacy and resource; "Air" is all lightness and transparency and "Fire" is wonderfully evoked. The Cello Concerto is a real discovery, a strong work and vintage Martin. The slow movement has the character of a Sarabande and is particularly haunting. Both in substance and the orchestral presentation, this is inventive and resourceful music. The performances emanate from radio tapes and though the recordings are not perfect, they are very good indeed as one would expect given the Concertgebouw's acoustic, and the balance is excellent. The audience is generally quiet and attentive throughout, and applause is retained at the end of the two works. At under 44 minutes this is open to the charge of short measure even at mid price. But if it is short on quantity, it is long on quality.

Martin. Concerto for seven wind instruments, percussion and string orchestra (1949). Polyptique (1972-3)[a]. Etudes (1955-6). [a]**Marieke Blankestijn** (vn); **Chamber Orchestra of Europe/Thierry Fischer.** DG 435 383-2GH.

1h 6m DDD 6/92

This is a disc of exceptional excellence. These three pieces have all been recorded before but never as well — and they have certainly never been better played! In the concerto the virtuosity and sophistication of the wind of the Chamber Orchestra of Europe is so effortless and their accents far lighter in touch than their rivals. Their playing has real delicacy and clarity of articulation and the slow movement for once really sounds as it is marked, mysterious and yet elegant, while the muted strings have a lightness of sonority and colour which greatly enhances the atmosphere. The artistry of the strings is everywhere in evidence in the Etudes and they quite outclass other performances in their sensitivity of response and range of colour. The *Polyptique* for violin and two string orchestras dates from the last year of Martin's life, when he was 83. It was inspired by a polyptych, a set of very small panels that Martin saw in Sienna representing various episodes in the Passion. The work is inward-looking and powerfully searching, and is played with great beauty and purity of tone, and rapt concentration by Marieke Blankestijn and the Chamber Orchestra of Europe. The recording is one of the best from this (or any other) source. It is completely natural, truthful in timbre and has remarkable clarity and presence. The perspective is very musically judged and both producer and engineer deserve a special mention for the refinement and quality of the sound they have captured.

Additional recommendation ...
Concerto for seven wind instruments. Petite symphonie concertante[a]*. Sechs Monologe aus "Jedermann"*[b]*.* [b]**Gilles Cachemaille** (bar); [a]**Eva Guibentif** (hp); **Christiane Jaccottet** (hpd); [a]**Ursula Riuttimann** (pf); **Suisse Romande Orchestra/Armin Jordan.** Erato 2292-45694-2 —
1h 2m DDD 11/91

Martin. Petite symphonie concertante[a]. Maria-Triptychon[b]. Passacaglia (transc. comp.)[c]. [b]**Irmgaard Seefried** (sop); [b]**Wolfgang Schneiderhan** (vn); [a]**Eva Hunziker** (hp); [a]**Germaine Vaucher-Clerc** (clavecin); [a]**Doris Rossiaud** (pf); [ab]**Suisse Romande Orchestra;** [c]**Berlin Philharmonic Orchestra/Frank Martin.** Jecklin Disco mono JD645-2. Recorded 1963-70.

57m ADD 10/91

Frank Martin's own recording of the *Petite symphonie concertante* comes from a Swiss Radio broadcast in 1970 and confirms the suspicion that most performances and recordings are too fast. He takes the opening at the speed he marked; it is slower and much more concentrated in atmosphere, and the *Adagio* section later on gains from a similar breadth. Two of the soloists, Germaine Vauchet-Clerc and Doris Rossiaud, took part in Ansermet's pioneering recording (Decca mono 430 003-2DM, reviewed in the 1992 edition of this *Guide*). This is a most convincing and atmospheric account of this masterly score. But be warned, the 1970 Swiss Radio recording is mono, which is not in itself worrying, but the sound is less than state-of-the-art even by the standards of the 1960s and 1970s. Nor is the *Maria-Triptychon* very much better. The work was written in the late 1960s in response to a request from Wolfgang Schneiderhan for a work for violin, soprano and orchestra that he could perform with his wife, Irmgaard Seefried. The "Magnificat", which constitutes the middle movement, originally stood on its own, the two outer movements ("Ave Maria" and "Stabat Mater") being added later. There are moments of great vision during the course of the piece but the monochrome recording will undoubtedly limits its appeal somewhat. Martin's refined and imaginative orchestral transcription of the 1944 *Passacaglia* for organ is a rarity: (the 1952 version for string orchestra he made for Karl Münchinger is more commonly encountered). But it is beautifully played under Martin's own direction and readers with a special interest in this remarkable composer should consider investigating this issue for its documentary interest.

NEW REVIEW

Martin. Golgotha[a]. Mass for double chorus[b]. [a]**Wally Staempfli** (sop); [a]**Marie-Lise de Montmollin** (mez); [a]**Eric Tappy** (ten); [a]**Pierre Mollet,** [a]**Philippe Huttenlocher** (bars); [a]**Lausanne University Choir;** [a] **Robert Faller Choir and Symphony Orchestra/Robert Faller** with **André Luy** (org); [b]**Midi Chamber Choir/Denis Martin.** Erato 2292-45779-2. Item marked [a] recorded in 1968, [b] 1990. Texts and translations included.

② 1h 53m ADD/DDD 10/92

Shortly after the war Martin saw *The Three Crosses* of Rembrandt and it was this that triggered the composition of *Golgotha* which occupied him for the following three years, 1945-8. It is one of his major works and can claim the distinction of being the first major *Passion* since Bach. Martin wrote that his intention was to "make the sacred tragedy come to life again before our eyes", and in contradistinction to Bach, the narrative passes freely between the various soloists and the body of the choir. Apart from his debt to Bach and Mussorgsky, his musical language has an affinity at a profound level with the Debussy of *Pelléas*, particularly in the glowing final section, "La Resurrection". *Golgotha* is a work of sustained eloquence, power and dignity, and the conviction of this 1968 performance under Robert Faller communicates effectively and impressively. *Golgotha* is an inspired and inspiring work, very well played and recorded, and this is its only representation in *The Classical Catalogue*. The Mass for unaccompanied double chorus, on the other hand, is a work whose beauties are gaining wider recognition and it is now well represented in the catalogue. This version, however, can hold its own with the best.

Additional recommendation ...

Mass for double chorus. **Poulenc.** *Mass in G major. Quatre petites prières de Saint François d'Assise. Salve regina.* **Christ Church Cathedral Choir, Oxford/Stephen Darlington.** Nimbus NI5197 — 59m DDD 12/89

Further listening ...

Pavane couleur du temps[a]. Piano Quintet[b]. String Trio[c]. Trio sur des mélodies populaires irlandaises[d]. **Zurich Chamber Ensemble** (Brenton Langbein, [ab]Andreas Pfenninger, vns; [a]Cornel Anderes, [bc]Jürg Dähler, vas; Raffaele Altwegg, [a]Luciano Pezzani, vcs); [bd]**Hanni Schmid-Wyss** (pf). Jecklin Disco JD646-2 (10/91).

Requiem. **Elisabeth Speiser** (sop); **Ria Bollen** (contr); **Eric Tappy** (ten); **Peter Lagger** (bass); **Lausanne Women's Chorus; Union Chorale; Ars Laeta Vocal Ensemble; Suisse Romande Orchestra/Frank Martin.** Jecklin Disco JD631-2 (1/90).

Vicente Martín y Soler

Spanish 1754-1806

Suggested listening ...

UNA COSA RARA. **Soloists; La Capella Reial de Catalunya; Le Concert des Nations/Jordi Savall.** Astrée Auvidis E8760 (2/92).

Bohuslav Martinů

Czech 1890-1959

Martinů. Cello Concertos — No. 1; No. 2. Cello Concertino. **Raphael Wallfisch** (vc); **Czech Philharmonic Orchestra/Jiří Bělohlávek.** Chandos CHAN9015. Recorded in 1991.

lh l6m DDD 4/92

Following his centenary year in 1990, Bohuslav Martinů has been returning to favour, although, as the composer of almost 30 concerto-type works, he cannot always escape the charge of flatulent note-spinning that attaches itself to such fertility. On the present disc, his unique imaginative vision is most obvious in the Cello Concerto No. 1. The central slow movement in particular finds Martinů at his best, a deeply moving threnody with a potent nostalgic quality which will be instantly recognizable to admirers of the later symphonies. There is an improvisatory freedom about the Second Concerto which makes it harder to grasp and the thematic material has rather too much in common with other, better scores. The much earlier *Concertino* is in Martinů's playful, more overtly neoclassical vein. You may notice some vamp-until-ready eighteenth-century scrubbing in the concertos, but here the younger composer is preoccupied with the lighter aspects of the style. There's a Stravinskian wit and elegance about the writing and the chamber scoring reflects both the fashionable trends and the economic constraints of life in 1920s Paris. In the First Concerto, Raphael Wallfisch is rather backwardly balanced *vis-à-vis* the Czech Philharmonic, whose regular conductor, Jiří Bělohlávek, is of course totally inside this music. At the same time, the resonant Spanish Hall of Prague Castle provides an agreeable ambient glow which does not mask too much detail. Make no mistake: this is a most attractive proposition for those already familiar with the idiom. Adventurous beginners should perhaps start elsewhere.

NEW REVIEW

Martinů. Double Concerto for two string orchestras, piano and timpani[a]. Sinfonietta giocosa[b]. Rhapsody-Concerto for viola and orchestra[c]. [c]**Rivka Golani** (va); [a]**Jírí Skovajska,** [b]**Dennis Hennig** (pfs); [a]**Brno State Philharmonic Orchestra,** [b]**Australian Chamber Orchestra/Sir Charles Mackerras;** [c]**Berne Symphony Orchestra/Peter Maag.** Conifer CDCF210. Item marked [a] from CDCF202 (3/92), recorded in 1990, [b] CDCF170 (8/89), recorded in 1988, [c] CDCF146 (10/88), recorded in 1986.

1h 13m DDD 9/92

This is as good an entry point into Martinů's world as any. The *Rhapsody-Concerto* (1952) is one of the most lyrical and affecting of his later works and Rivka Golani's account is all the more moving for being completely unaffected and straightforward as, indeed, are Peter Maag and the Berne orchestra whose natural, unforced eloquence are equally persuasive. The *Double Concerto* (1938) was composed as the war-clouds were gathering in Europe, and is a power-house of dark, propulsive energy. Mackerras and the Brno orchestra maintain the right kind of tension and sense of momentum. The lightness and high spirits of the *Sinfonietta giocosa* never fails to amaze, considering the anxious circumstances under which it was composed (Martinů was living in Vichy France and desperately trying to escape from the Nazis). Sir Charles and his pianist, Dennis Hennig, turn in a good performance though by comparison with the *Double Concerto*, the recording is a shade synthetic in perspective with little back-to-front depth. None the less, this provides a well-balanced portrait of a composer who is at long last coming into his own, as evidenced by the number of recordings under review here.

Martinů. ORCHESTRAL WORKS. **Czech Philharmonic Orchestra/Jiří Bělohlávek.** Supraphon 10 4140-2. Recorded in 1987.
The parables. Estampes. Overture. La rhapsodie, "Allegro symphonique".

58m DDD 6/91

Estampes and *The parables* are both descriptive three-movement works written near the end of the composer's life. At this stage Martinů's fertile imagination was quite undiminished, and each piece teems with imaginative, colourful neo-romantic invention and brilliant orchestral effects. The subjects of the three *Parables* are described respectively as a sculpture, a garden and a navire, but it's best simply to enjoy the music as it is without attempting to look further into hidden meanings: the three movements of the *Estampes* are in fact given tempo indications rather than titles. In the busy Overture of 1953 Martinů uses more of a formal neo-classical style to great effect. The *Rhapsodie* dates from 1928, and was written to celebrate ten years of Czech independence. This work has an outgoing, joyful spirit and trumpet and drums are very much to the fore. Jiří Bělohlávek conducts all these works with a great deal of flair and imagination, and the Czech Philharmonic support their chief conductor with highly accomplished, resourceful playing. Supraphon's recording is warm, atmospheric and attentive to detail.

Martinů. SYMPHONIES. **Bamberg Symphony Orchestra/Neeme Järvi.** BIS CD362, BIS CD363 and BIS CD402.
CD362 — No. 1 (1942); No. 2 (1943). *CD363* — No. 3 (1944); No. 4 (1945). *CD402* — No. 5 (1946); No. 6 (1953).

③ 1h 1m 1h 3m 59m DDD 9/87 12/88

Martinů began composing at the age of ten and later studied and lived in Paris, America and Switzerland. Despite his travels he remained a quintessentially Czech composer and his music is imbued with the melodic shapes and rhythms of the folk-music of his native homeland. The six symphonies were written during Martinů's years in America and in all of them he uses a large orchestra with distinctive groupings of instruments which give them a very personal and unmistakable timbre. The rhythmic verve of his highly syncopated fast movements is very infectious, indeed unforgettable, and his slow movements are often deeply expressive, most potently, perhaps, in that of the Third Symphony which is imbued with the tragedy of war. The Bamberg orchestra play marvellously and with great verve for Järvi, whose excellently judged tempos help propel the music forward most effectively. His understanding of the basic thrust of Martinů's structures is very impressive and he projects the music with great clarity. The BIS recordings are beautifully clear, with plenty of ambience surrounding the orchestra, a fine sense of scale and effortless handling of the wide dynamic range Martinů calls for. Enthusiastically recommended.

NEW REVIEW

Martinů. Symphony No. 4. Field Mass[a]. Memorial to Lidice. [a]**Ivan Kusnjer** (bar); **Czech Philharmonic** [a]**Chorus and Orchestra/Jirí Bělohlávek.** Chandos CHAN9138. Text and translation included.

lh 5m DDD 5/93

A powerful wartime Martinů trilogy from Chandos. Jirí Bělohlávek is a sympathetic and lucid guide through this terrain, securing playing of consistently high quality from his great orchestra. In the main work here, the adorable Fourth Symphony (in many ways the most approachable and life-enhancing of the cycle), there's a winning poise and unaffected naturalness about the music-making, though it's perhaps not difficult to imagine a performance of greater fire and temperament. Rival accounts from Järvi (reviewed above) and Bryden Thomson both have considerable strengths of their own, but neither can boast the sheer orchestral splendour of the present version. Bělohlávek directs a most moving rendering of the *Field Mas*, featuring splendidly committed contributions from the men of the Czech Philharmonic Chorus and baritone Ivan Kusnjer. The shattering eight-minute essay entitled *Memorial to Lidice* (written in response to the notorious annihilation by the Nazis of that village in June 1942) makes a powerful curtain-raiser, though, as in the symphony, Bělohlávek's conducting once again lacks that final ounce of intensity one recalls from, say, Karel Ančerl's 1957 recording. Radiantly full Chandos engineering throughout, more helpfully focused than on some previous Prague-based efforts from this source.

Additional recommendations ...

Symphonies Nos. 3 and 4. **Royal Scottish National Orchestra/Bryden Thomson.** Chandos CHAN8917 — lh DDD 6/91

Memorial to Lidice. Symphony No. 5. Les fresques de Piero della Francesca[a]. **Czech Philharmonic Orchestra/Karel Ančerl.** Supraphon Historical mono/[a]stereo 11 1931-2 — lh 17m AAD 3/93 ▲

NEW REVIEW

Martinů. String Sextet. Three Madrigals[a].
Schulhoff. String Sextet. **Raphael Ensemble** ([a]Anthony Marwood, Elizabeth Wexler, vns; [a]Sally Beamish, James Boyd, vas; Andrea Hess, Michael Stirling, vcs). Hyperion CDA66516. Recorded in 1991.

56m DDD 7/92

Ervín Schulhoff and Bohuslav Martinů were both victims of Nazism, but with one significant difference — Martinů survived the regime, while Schulhoff was felled by it. A Jew and communist, the Prague-born Schulhoff was arrested in Russia when the Germans attacked in 1941; he died in Wulzburg concentration camp the following year, and thereafter his considerable output (which included eight symphonies, the last two unfinished) entered a period of almost complete obscurity. But latterly his posthumous fortunes have taken a turn for the better, thanks to the likes of Gidon Kremer (largely through the good offices of his Lockenhaus Festival) and the Raphael Ensemble. Schulhoff's Sextet is as bleak as Sibelius at his most uncompromising, yet its desolation is visited by a wry, unnerving humour (the *Burlesca*) and has a very central-European chromatic core. The opening *Allegro risoluto* is grey and insistent (its rhythmic language isn't too far removed from Martinů's), but the closing *Molto adagio* strikes a note of terror into one's heart, prophetically so, considering that it was written in 1920. Martinů's prize-winning Sextet was submitted for the Elizabeth Sprague Coolidge Medal and triumphed over 144 other entries (at first, Martinů couldn't believe he'd won!). Like the

Schulhoff, it has a serious soul (again, much of the language is deeply chromatic), yet manages to end in a mood of unsullied optimism. But the real joy of the disc — most effectively in such a troubled context — lies in the *Three Madrigals*, written for the brother and sister violin-viola team, Joseph and Lilian Fuchs. A product of Martinů's American sojourn, the *Madrigals* frequently recall the composer's Czech folk roots, and — in the Third, especially — pay more than passing homage to J.S. Bach. This, like its larger and darker companions, is superlatively well played and beautifully recorded.

Martinů. Nonet (1959). Trio in F major (1944). La Rêvue de Cuisine. **The Dartington Ensemble** (William Bennett, fl; Robin Canter, ob; David Campbell, cl; Graham Sheen, bn; Richard Watkins, hn; Barry Collarbone, tpt; Oliver Butterworth, vn; Patrick Ireland, va; Michael Evans, vc; Nigel Amherst, db; John Bryden, pf. Hyperion CDA66084. Recorded in 1982.

50m DDD 

The last few years or so have seen a steadily increasing interest in the music of Martinů. This beautifully balanced programme of chamber music may not be wholly representative of his style, but it's certainly an enjoyable and entertaining disc, and is as good a starting place as any for those approaching his music for the first time. His style has often been described as eclectic; his early works reveal the influence of Debussy and impressionism, and later, in the 1920 and 1930s, jazz and neoclassicism play an increasingly important role in his work. The concert suite from the ballet *La Rêvue de Cuisine* ("The Kitchen Review") dates from 1930 when he lived in Paris. There are plenty of high jinks and comedy in this agreeable and unpretentious work and the sound and influence of the Paris jazz bands are clearly discernible in the dance-inspired movements. The outer movements of the Trio in F major inhabit a similarly bright and cheerful world, and these are contrasted well with the lyrical beauty of the central *Adagio*. The *Nonet*, completed shortly before his death in 1959, is a serene and sunny work, neoclassical in design with its Haydnesque themes and its clarity of texture with a deep nostalgia for his Czech homeland from which he had been separated for so many years. The Dartington Ensemble give fine, committed performances and the recording has warmth and perspective. An essential disc for enthusiasts and toe-dippers alike.

Martinů. The epic of Gilgamesh. **Eva Depoltová** (sop); **Stefan Margita** (ten); **Ivan Kusnjer** (bar); **Ludek Vele** (bass); **Milan Karpíšek** (spkr); **Slovak Philharmonic Choir; Slovak Philharmonic Orchestra/Zdeněk Košler.** Marco Polo 8 223316. Translation included. Recorded in 1989.

56m DDD 4/91  

Gilgamesh is a long Assyrian-Babylonian poem recorded on cuneiform tablets in or before the seventh century BC which predates Homer by at least 1,500 years. Martinů was fascinated not only by the poem, the oldest literature known to mankind, but its universality — "the emotions and issues which move people have not changed ... they are embodied just as much in the oldest literature known to us as in the literature of our own time ... issues of friendship, love and death. It is dramatic; it pursues me in my dreams", he wrote. It certainly inspired in him music of extraordinary vision and intensity as well as enormous atmosphere. The *Epic* tells how Gilgamesh, King of Uruk, hears about the warrior Enkidu, a primitive at home among the works of nature with only animals as friends. He sends him a courtesan to whom he loses his innocence; the King then befriends him but they quarrel and fight before their friendship is really cemented. The second and third parts of the oratorio centre on the themes of death and immortality; the second tells of Enkidu's death and Gilgamesh's grief, his plea to the gods to restore Enkidu and his search for immortality, and the third records his failure to learn its secrets. *Gilgamesh* deals with universal themes and is Martinů at his most profound and inspired. There are no weaknesses in the cast (and the Gilgamesh of Ivan Kusnjer is very impressive indeed), and the chorus and orchestra respond very well to Zdeněk Košler's direction. The recording maintains a generally natural balance between the soloists, narrator, chorus and orchestra, and the somewhat resonant acoustic is used to good advantage.

Those who do not know this extraordinary work of Martinů's last years should investigate it without delay.

NEW REVIEW

Martinů. JULIETTA. **Maria Tauberová** (sop) Julietta; **Ivo Zidek** (ten) Michel; **Antonín Zlesák** (ten) Police Officer, Postman, Forest Warden; **Zdeněk Otava** (bar) Man with the Helmet; **Václav Bednář** (bass) Man in the Window; **Ivana Mixová** (mez) Small Arab; **Vladimír Jedenáctik** (bas) Old Arab; **Jaroslava Procházková** (mez) Bird-Seller; **Ludmila Hanzalíková** (mez) Fishmonger; **Jaroslav Horáček** (bass) Old Man Youth; **Karel Kalaš** (bass) Grandfather; **Milada Cadikovičová** (contr) Grandmother; **Stěpánka Jelinková** (sngr) Old Lady; **Věra Soukupová** (mez) Fortune-Teller; **Jindřich Jindrák** (bar) Souvenir Seller; **Jaroslav Veverka** (bass) Old Sailor; **Zdeněk Svehla** (ten) Young Sailor; **Marcela Lemariová** (mez) Errand-Boy; **Karel Berman** (bass) Beggar; **Dalibor Jedlička** (bass) Convict; **Jaroslav Stříška** (ten) Engine Driver; **Bohumír Lalák** (bass) Night Watchman; **Prague National Theatre Chorus and Orchestra/Jaroslav Krombholc.** Supraphon 10 8176-2. Notes, text and translation included. From SUAST50611/3 (8/73). Recorded in 1964.

③ 2h 25m ADD 6/93

Julietta is Martinů's most magical score, a 'dream book' indeed (the opera's subtitle), set in a land where all the people are amnesiacs, where even imaginary memories are treasured and where falsehood is as real as truth. A young man comes to this country in search of a girl he may once have met there (or did he dream her?). He finds her, but does she really recognize him, or find in him a comforting illusion? He loses her again, and returns to the 'real' world where the only hope of continuing his search for her is to remain in the unreal world of the insane for the rest of his life. But everything in that dream-world is more alluringly real, if also much more surreally strange, than in our reality. The subject immediately appealed to Martinů. As an expatriate and inveterate traveller he identified with the young man. As one whose dearest reality was his magic childhood, suspended above the world in the room at the top of a tower which was his family's home, a childhood around which he had woven a tissue of half-remembered idyll, he felt at home in that land where dreams, reality and imagination can hardly be distinguished. And he knew how to conjure up dreams and half-memories so vividly that we almost recognize them as our own. A fragment of dance-melody, the sound of an accordion, a song that you could swear you have known all your life — and in a flash Martinů's imaginary world (as oddly matter-of-fact and realistic, despite its strangeness, as a painting by Magritte) is there in front of you. It and its inhabitants are so real that a single hearing of this mysteriously poetic opera can haunt you for days. This classic recording could hardly be bettered with Ivo Zidek an ideal exponent of the central role, not a weak link in the rest of the large cast, and Jaroslav Krombholc an outstandingly sensitive conductor. The recording still sounds very good indeed.

Steve Martland

British 1959-

NEW REVIEW

Martland. CROSSING THE BORDER. **Ensemble/Steve Martland.** Factory Classical FACD366.

Crossing the Border. Principia. American Invention. Re-mix. Shoulder to Shoulder.

lh 2m DDD 9/92 

This disc is rather short of printed information, and its title might lead you to expect some kind of marriage between classical and pop. To an extent that's true, in that Martland cultivates a series of eclectic styles which aim at simplicity of form. None of these pieces really develop, but one is aware of a keen, highly imaginative mind at work, and even *Crossing the Border,* which lasts for nearly 24 minutes, commands continual attention through clever variations in instrumental timbre. This work is written for conventional string orchestra, and in a way the form is that of a rondo, whose basic material consists of busy upper strings over slow-moving basses. Sometimes the music sounds like simplified Tippett or occasionally Elgar, but the initial inspiration was apparently Bach's *Chaconne.* Two briefer pieces, *Principia* and *Re-mix,* are scored for a more heterogeneous ensemble, including flügel horn, electric violin, three saxophones, the latter a jolly, upbeat pop-song-like creation. In *American Invention,* for two pianos, string quartet, wind and guitar, Martland has seemingly studied the end of Stravinsky's *Requiem Canticles*, and the work's uneven accents also seem to reflect that composer's style. *Shoulder to Shoulder,* for wind, piano and bass guitar, contains an irregular but intriguing series of stark, slab-like stabs of sound. Performances are highly effective, and the recordings are immediate and faithful.

Giuseppe Martucci

Italian 1856-1909

Suggested listening ...

Piano Concerto No. 2 in B flat minor, Op. 66[a]. Canzonetta, Op. 55 No. 1. Tempo di gavotta, Op. 55 No. 2. Giga, Op. 61 No. 3. Serenata, Op. 57 No. 1. Minuetto, Op. 57 No. 2. Momento musicale, Op. 57 No. 3. [a]**Francesco Caramiello** (pf); **Philharmonia Orchestra/Francesco d'Avalos.** ASV CDDCA691 (7/90).

Symphony No. 1 in D minor, Op. 75. Novelletta, Op. 82 No. 2. Notturno, Op. 70 No. 1. Tarantella, Op. 44 No. 6. **Philharmonia Orchestra/Francesco d'Avalos.** ASV CDDCA675 (12/89).

Symphony No. 2 in F major, Op. 81. Andante in B flat major, Op. 69 No. 2[a]. Colore orientale, Op. 44 No. 3. [a]**George Ives** (vc); **Philharmonia Orchestra/Francesco d'Avalos.** ASV CDDCA689 (5/90).

Pietro Mascagni

Italian 1863-1945

Suggested listening ...

CAVALLERIA RUSTICANA — *See review and listings under Leoncavallo; refer to Index to Reviews.*

IRIS. **Soloists; Bavarian Radio Chorus; Munich Radio Orchestra/Giuseppe Patanè.** CBS Masterworks CD45526 (9/89).

LODOLETTA. **Soloists; Hungarian State Opera Children's Chorus; Hungarian Radio and Television Chorus; Hungarian State Orchestra/Charles Rosekrans.** Hungaroton HCD31307/8 (6/91).

Jules Massenet

French 1842-1912

NEW REVIEW

Massenet. ORCHESTRAL SUITES. **Monte-Carlo Opera Orchestra/John Eliot Gardiner.** Erato 2292-45858/9-2. From STU71208 (1/80).

2292-45858-2: No. 3, "Scènes dramatiques"; No. 6, "Scènes de féerie". La Vierge — Le dernier sommeil de la Vierge. *2292-45859-2:* No. 4, "Scènes pittoresques"; No. 7, "Scènes alsaciennes". Don Quichotte — Interludes.

② 41m 45m ADD 2/93

Massenet is chiefly known today through his operas, but he achieved some success in his lifetime with a series of seven orchestral suites. Of these No. 4, *Scènes pittoresques*, and No. 7, *Scènes alsaciennes*, retain a toehold on the repertoire through their lively rhythms, their appealing melodies and their uncomplicatedly descriptive picture-postcard colour. Suite No. 3, *Scènes dramatiques*, is a more ambitious work, and uses Shakespeare's plays, *The Tempest*, *Othello* and *Macbeth*, as a basis for an evocative triptych. The Sixth Suite, *Scènes de feérie*, is a more straightforward collection of four contrasting ballet-like episodes. *Don Quichotte* was Massenet's last major opera, and its two short interludes show his usual high quality of melodic invention and imaginative use of orchestral textures. The touching and well-known "Dernier sommeil de la Vierge" is an effective make-weight to the first disc, though in each case it will be noted that playing times are short. Monte-Carlo's Opera Orchestra has exactly the right style and timbre for this repertoire: sometimes Eliot Gardiner seems to drive the music a fraction too hard in the faster movements, but in general his performances are very sympathetic. The late-1970s recordings have come up very well in transfer to CD.

NEW REVIEW

Massenet. LE ROI DE LAHORE. **Luis Lima** (ten) Alim; **Dame Joan Sutherland** (sop) Sitâ; **Sherrill Milnes** (bar) Scindia; **Nicolai Ghiaurov** (bass) Indra; **James Morris** (bass) Timour; **Huguette Tourangeau** (mez) Kaled; **London Voices; National Philharmonic Orchestra/Richard Bonynge.** Decca Grand Opera 433 851-2DMO2. Text and translation included. From D210D3 (11/80).

② 2h 26m DDD 2/93

Lashings of exotic flavour were only to be expected from the young Massenet when that doyen of librettists, Louis Gallet, suggested to him a lurid Indian backcloth for this five-act opera. The Paris Opéra audiences of 1877 lapped it up. Typically though, French seasoning still underpins this feast, even extending to the effective use of a saxophone in the scoring. And if now the oriental spicing, after countless products of Hollywood, seems a little tame, then Massenet's liquid melodic lyricism and memorable harmonic twists come into their own; the palate need never become dulled to these. The story, of illicit love, war and religion, is typical of French grand opera of the period and it allows great opportunities for heart-on-the-sleeve displays of passion. The finale to Act 1, especially, gave Massenet the opportunity to develop his skill in large-scale ensemble writing for voices, and the various entr'actes and ballet numbers find him, melodically, at his most charming. The performance here is well worth exploring, even though some of the soloists are not always in best voice. Richard Bonynge holds the disparate elements of plot and musical style loosely together in a way that enables the best qualities of the work to shine. He tightens his grip only in the more ambitious numbers and here ensures intellectual rigour as well as emotional impact. Although the recording does not date from the most auspicious of eras, it serves the performance well, handling the choruses with ease and giving a good sense of presence.

Massenet. WERTHER. **José Carreras** (ten) Werther; **Frederica von Stade** (mez) Charlotte; **Thomas Allen** (bar) Albert; **Isobel Buchanan** (sop) Sophie; **Robert Lloyd** (bass) Bailiff; **Paul Crook** (ten), **Malcolm King** (bass) Bailiff's friends; **Linda Humphries** (sop) Katchen; **Donaldson Ball** (bar) Bruhlmann; **Children's Choir; Royal Opera House Orchestra, Covent Garden/Sir Colin Davis.** Philips 416 654-2PH2. Notes, text and translation included. From 6769 051 (10/81).

② 2h 11m ADD 2/87

Werther is considered by many to be Massenet's outright masterpiece. Here he reaches his zenith in the supple combination of a lyrical and a parlando style. Based faithfully on Goethe's novel, the work exposes movingly the feelings of the lovelorn poet Werther and those of his beloved Charlotte. In Sir Colin Davis's recording the changing seasons, which form a backdrop to Werther's own manic swings between dream and reality, joy and despair, are recreated in exuberant and vibrant detail. The Royal Opera Orchestra play at their very best: the solo detail, in every sentient responsive to Massenet's flickering orchestral palette, operates as if with feverishly heightened awareness. Carreras sees the force of the will to self-destruction in the character as dominating even the passages of brooding lyricism. Charlotte, struggling between the responsibilities of her bourgeois home life and the emotional turmoil in which she sees much of herself reflected in Werther, is sung by Frederica von Stade with winning simplicity and idiomatic French style. Young Sophie, whom Massenet made more important than Goethe did, becomes a true *oiseau d'aurore* in the voice of Isobel Buchanan, while Thomas Allen, characteristically, finds unusual breadth in the role of poor, spurned Albert.

Additional recommendation …

Soloists; Cantoria Children's Choir; Chorus and Orchestra of the Opéra-Comique, Paris/Elie Cohen. EMI Références mono CHS7 63195-2 — ② 2h lm ADD 3/90 ▲

NEW REVIEW

Massenet. CHERUBIN. **Frederica von Stade** (mez) Chérubin; **Samuel Ramey** (bass) Jacoppo; **June Anderson** (sop) L'Ensoleillad; **Dawn Upshaw** (sop) Nina; **Jean-Marc Ivaldi** (bar) Count; **Hélène Garetti** (sop) Countess; **Michel Trempont** (ten) Baron; **Brigitte Balleys** (contr) Baroness; **Michel Sénéchal** (ten) Duke; **Claes Hakon Ahnsjö** (ten) Ricardo; **Armand Arapian** (ten) Innkeeper; **Rainer Scholze** (bass) Officer; **Bavarian State Opera Chorus; Munich Radio Orchestra/Pinchas Steinberg.** RCA Victor Red Seal 09026-60593-2. Notes, text and translation included. Recorded in 1991.

② lh 55m DDD 12/92

Massenet is best known for his operatic heroines, who include Manon and Thaïs, but here, in a late opera which he called a *comédie chantée,* the protagonist is a boy of 17, the Cherubino of Mozart's *The Marriage of Figaro.* But as in Mozart, Cherubino is played by a woman singer, and this gives a special eloquence to the role. A little of the Beaumarchais play that inspired Mozart's opera still survives, in that we are still in Seville and the Count and Countess still live there along with Chérubin himself. But otherwise there is little resemblance and Massenet's opera, based on a later play, makes the flirtatious youth the centre of the action and takes a romanticized view of the emotions with which the story deals. This opera stands or falls by its central character, — Frederica von Stade makes Chérubin as believable as we can hope to expect, and her first entrance (with the words "I'm drunk!" — though only with happiness) has exactly the right ebullience. Both vocally and as an actress, she is equal to the role and evidently enjoys it, and RCA have assembled a supporting cast who are also in sympathy with Massenet's score. Two other roles are those of Nina, who loves Chérubin faithfully and finally wins him, and the dancer L'Ensoleillad: they are well played by Dawn Upshaw and June Anderson. Among the men, Jean-Marc Ivaldi is an imperious Count and Samuel Ramey is suitably weighty in the bass role of the 'philosopher' who is the wayward youth's moral tutor and who finally persuades him to enter a world of adult responsibility. The scene in which this happens, at the end, is movingly written, and the whole opera, without the cuts sometimes made in the theatre, is strongly and sympathetically presented by the singers and orchestra under Pinchas Steinberg. The recording, made in a Munich studio, is clear and spacious.

Massenet. DON QUICHOTTE[a]. Scènes alsaciennes.[b]. **Nicolai Ghiaurov** (bass) Don Quichotte; **Régine Crespin** (sop) Dulcinée; **Gabriel Bacquier** (bar) Sancho Panza; **Michèle Command** (sop) Pedro; **Annick Duterte** (sop) Garcias; **Peyo Garazzi** (ten) Rodriguez; **Jean-Marie Fremeau** (ten) Juan; **Suisse Romande Chorus and Orchestra/Kazimierz Kord;** [b]**National Philharmonic Orchestra/Richard Bonynge.** Decca 430 636-2DM2. Notes, text and translation included. Item marked [a] from D156D3 (11/79), [b] SXL6827 (12/77). Recorded in 1978.

② 2h 13m ADD 4/92 £

Massenet's operas are patchily represented in the catalogue, and this heroic comedy, which was his last big success (in 1910, when he was 67) is most welcome. People who think of him as only a salon composer, lacking the vigour and depth of a Berlioz or a Debussy, should listen to the start of Act 1, set in a Spanish town square at fiesta time; the opening music bursts out of the loudspeakers like that of Verdi's *Otello*, although here the mood is joyous, with tremendous rhythmic verve and gusto. In fact, this opera is closer to Verdi's *Falstaff*, with the same admixture of gentler serious moments amidst the comic bustle and intrigue, and of course, here again the central character is a comic yet lovable figure. The recording, made by a British team in Geneva in 1978, still sounds well although orchestral detail could be clearer. As for the performance by mainly Swiss forces under Kazimierz Kord, and with a Bulgarian bass in the title role (written for Chaliapin), one can only praise it for its idiomatic realization of a 'Spanish' opera by a gifted French composer for the theatre. Though Régine Crespin may be too mature vocally for Dulcinée, the object of the elderly Don Quixote's adoration, she sings splendidly and few will find this a serious weakness. Nicolai Ghiaurov rightly makes Quixote himself a real person, touching and dignified as well as comic, and Gabriel Bacquier gives a rounded portrayal of his servant Sancho Panza, so that Quixote's death scene in the company of his old friend is particularly strong. The booklet provides a synopsis plus the French text and a translation. This is a fine mid-price issue, and the lively and tuneful *Scènes alsaciennes* with a British orchestra under Richard Bonynge make a fine fill-up.

Further listening ...

Piano Concerto in E flat major. Devant la Madonne — Souvenir de la campagne de Rome: Nuit de Noël. Two Impromptus. Musique pour bercer les petits enfants. Deux Pièces. 10 Pièces de genre, Op. 10. Toccata in B flat major. Valse folle. Valse très lente. **Aldo Ciccolini** (pf); **Monte Carlo Philharmonic Orchestra/Sylvain Cambreling.** EMI CDM7 64277-2.

LE CID. **Soloists; Byrne Camp Chorale; New York Opera Orchestra/Eve Queler.** CBS CD79300 (2/90).

THAIS. **Soloists; French Radio Lyric Chorus and Orchestra/Albert Wolff.** Le Chant du Monde LDC278 895/6.

William Mathias

British 1934-1992

NEW REVIEW

Mathias. ORCHESTRAL WORKS. [a]**David Cowley** (ob); **BBC Welsh Symphony Orchestra/Grant Llewellyn.** Nimbus NI5343. Recorded 1991-92.
Helios, Op. 76. Oboe Concerto[a]. Requiescat, Op. 79. Symphony No. 3.

1h 12m DDD 11/92

This distinguished Nimbus issue is a splendid tribute to the late William Mathias, whose Third Symphony forms the focal point of this disc. Composed in 1991, the Symphony has an inner clarity and logic, making it easily the most approachable of his major orchestral works. The BBC Welsh Symphony Orchestra play superbly; the finale in particular affords ample opportunity for every section to demonstrate its prowess, and Grant Llewellyn obviously appreciates the stature of the work. The orchestra's principal oboist, David Cowley, is a compelling exponent of another recent Mathias composition, the Oboe Concerto of 1989. Whilst never debating the weighty issues of the Symphony, this has a neo-classical buoyancy and melodic charm which makes for enjoyable, if essentially undemanding listening. Llewellyn directs an inspirational account of *Helios*, in which Mathias, rather like Nielsen before him, charts the daily course of the sun across the heavens. The disc also includes an equally committed performance of the elegiac *Requiescat*. Orchestral playing and recorded sound are of very high quality, making this issue all the more inviting, even if hitherto the music itself has been unfamiliar. Strongly recommended.

NEW REVIEW

Mathias. ORGAN WORKS. **John Scott** (org). Nimbus NI5367. Played on the organ of St Paul's Cathedral.

Fanfare. Processional. Invocations, Op. 35. Fantasy, Op. 78. Berceuse, Op. 95 No. 3. Jubilate, Op. 67 No. 2. Antiphonies, Op. 88 No. 2. Fenestra. Recessional, Op. 96 No. 4. Chorale.

lh 18m DDD 6/93

Although not an organist himse1f William Mathias's instinctive awareness of what works well on the instrument (and, indeed, what is enjoyable to play) coupled with a fertile musical imagination has resulted in some of the most characteristic and worthwhile music written for the instrument by a British composer in recent times. As a result his relatively small output holds a disproportionately large place in the affections of organists. For the listener encountering Mathias for the first time, *Processional* makes a splendid introduction; a jaunty tongue-in-cheek march with a strong rhythmic momentum and a catchy tune. Then there is *Jubilate*, a true virtuoso display piece, the dark, sometimes chilling *Berceuse* with its dramatic central climax, and the substantial *Antiphonies* making effective use of the medieval French song "L'homme armé" and the plainchant "Vexilla regis". This last piece, written in 1982, was dedicated to John Scott so it seems entirely appropriate that he should have recorded this CD devoted to Mathias's organ music. Scott is meticulous in observing the composer's instructions while at the same time making every note sound fresh and entirely spontaneous. The St Paul's organ makes a spine-tingling noise, although it must be said that this is not the best recording of this magnificent instrument.

Further listening ...

Church, Choral and Organ Works — I will celebrate. O how amiable, Op. 90 No. 3. Rex Gloriae — Four Latin Motets, Op. 83. Missa Aedis Christi, Op. 92. Jesus College Service, Op. 53. A Grace, Op 89 No. 3. Ave Rex, Op. 45. As truly as God is our Father. Let the people praise Thee, O God, Op. 87. Fantasy for organ, Op. 78 — No. 2, Canzonetta. **Simon Lawford** (org); **Christ Church Cathedral Choir/Stephen Darlington.** Nimbus NI5243 (9/90).

Nicola Matteis

Italian/British d. 1707 or later

NEW REVIEW

N. Matteis. AYRES FOR THE VIOLIN. **Arcadian Academy** ([a]Elizabeth Blumenstock, [b]Katherine Kyme, vns; David Bowles, vc; David Tayler, archlte/gtr)/**Nicholas McGegan** (hpd/[c]org). Harmonia Mundi HMU90 7067. Recorded in 1991.

Book 1: Sonata in C minor[bc]. *Book 2:* Suite in G minor[a]. *Book 4:* Suites — A major[ab]; D minor[ab]; E minor[ab]. Sonata in C major[ab].

lh llm DDD 9/92

Nicola Matteis was an Italian violinist and composer who came to England in the early 1670s, became wealthy through his playing, bought a large house in Norfolk and retired there in 1714. Evelyn praised him in his diaries and Roger North reckoned him "to have bin a second to Corelli". The two sonatas and four suites in this recital are drawn from Matteis's four books of *Ayres for the Violin*, published in pairs in 1676 and 1685, respectively. Later Matteis issued second violin parts to the third and fourth books and these feature in four of the works chosen here. The remaining pieces, from Books 1 and 2, are for solo violin. This music is full of character and energy with a strong element of fantasy and a marked predilection for technical display. Sometimes, especially in variation movements like the captivating *Andamento con divisione* of the A major Suite, Matteis approaches the manner of his Bohemian contemporary, Biber. Corelli, on the other hand, springs to mind in the more conventionally dance-oriented movements. But there is a real spark of individuality in most of these pieces which is served well by the imaginative and technically accomplished approach of the two violinists of the Arcadian Academy, Elizabeth Blumenstock and Katherine Kyme. And the continuo group, supplying varied colour from a pool of organ, harpsichord, cello, archlute and guitar, are both stylish and sympathetic. This rarely performed music is well worth investigating.

Nicholas *Maw*

British 1935-

Suggested listening ...

Odyssey. **City of Birmingham Symphony Orchestra/Simon Rattle.** EMI CDS7 54277-2 (9/91).

Life Studies[a]. *Coupled with* **Bennett.** Spells[b]. [b]**Jane Manning** (sop); [a]**Academy of St Martin in the Fields/Sir Neville Marriner;** [b]**Bach Choir;** [b]**Philharmonia Orchestra/Sir David Willcocks.** Continuum CCD1030.

Sir Peter *Maxwell Davies*

British 1934-

Maxwell Davies. Symphony No. 4[a]. Trumpet Concerto[b]. [b]**John Wallace** (tpt); [a]**Scottish Chamber Orchestra/Sir Peter Maxwell Davies.** Collins Classics 1181-2.

1h 13m DDD 6/91 

Sir Peter Maxwell Davies has survived the transition from *enfant terrible* to *éminence grise* with equanimity — perhaps because he was always less 'terrible' than he seemed, and is still far from seriously 'grise'. From his earliest works to his most recent — the Trumpet Concerto and Fourth Symphony date from the late 1980s — he has used his delight in system-building to generate ambitious and complex structures that vibrate with no less complex but utterly uninhibited emotions. The Concerto is the immediately accessible of the two: the nature of the solo instrument, and Maxwell Davies's willingness not to jettison all the conventions of the concerto genre see to that. The work was written for John Wallace, and while it would be wrong to say that he makes light of its difficulties — at times you could swear that only a flautist could get round such florid writing — he succeeds brilliantly in demonstrating that the difficulties serve musical ends. The Symphony has less immediately arresting ideas, but when the music is savoured, returned to, and allowed time to weave its spells, its rewards become progressively more apparent. These recordings capture the composer's own highly-charged readings with commendable fidelity.

Additional recommendation ...

Trumpet Concerto. ***Birtwistle.*** Endless Parade[a]. ***Blake Watkins.*** Trumpet Concerto. **Håkan Hardenberger** (tpt); [a]**Paul Patrick** (vib); **BBC Philharmonic Orchestra/Elgar Howarth.** Philips 432 075-2PH — 1h 19m DDD 6/91

NEW REVIEW

Maxwell Davies. Strathclyde Concertos — No. 3[a]; No. 4[b]. [a]**Randall Cook** (hn); [b]**Lewis Morrison** (cl); [a]**Peter Franks** (tpt); **Scottish Chamber Orchestra/Sir Peter Maxwell Davies.** Collins Classics 1239-2. Recorded in 1991.

1h 1m DDD 10/92

Sir Peter Maxwell Davies's plan to write a sequence of no fewer than ten *Strathclyde* Concertos for the principals of the Scottish Chamber Orchestra is turning into a research project into the nature of the concerto, the relationship between soloist and orchestra. His solo parts are always satisfying, even virtuoso, but the orchestra seldom adopts an accompanying or antagonistic role. In the double concerto for trumpet and horn, for example, the flutes and strings also play a very important part, with material of their own that the soloists hardly touch, but the effect is to emphasize the 'flute-ness' of the flutes and the 'string-ness' of the strings: they become, in effect, co-soloists themselves. Maxwell Davies is also interested of course, in this concerto, in the 'trumpet-ness' and 'horn-ness' of his two principal soloists, and in the beautiful slow movement they dramatize this by eventually exchanging functions, the trumpet becoming lyrical, the horn martial. One of the functions of the clarinet, in its concerto, is to point up the sober beauty, the 'un-clarinet-ness', of the textures against which its cool solo line moves; it has an especially fruitful relationship with that section of the orchestra with which it is in greatest contrast, the low strings. Both works require intent listening; both reward it with readily perceptible formal ingenuity (the way in which the clarinet concerto's main theme is only gradually revealed as a haunting folk-song is especially absorbing) and a fascinating interplay of instrumental character. Both concertos are vividly performed and very cleanly recorded.

NEW REVIEW

Maxwell Davies. Solstice of Light[a]. Five Carols[b]. Hymn to the Word of God[c]. [ac]**Neil Mackie** (ten); [a]**Christopher Hughes** (org); **King's College Choir, Cambridge/Stephen Cleobury.** Argo 436 119-2ZH. Texts included. Recorded in 1991.

59m DDD 2/93

The choristers of King's College, Cambridge may not immediately strike you as the most plausible impersonators of Orkney fishermen and women. But performances of Sir Peter Maxwell Davies's superb choral work *Solstice of Light* depend for success on much more than such superficial plausibility. The singers need the technique and the stamina not only to cope with the composer's considerable technical demands but also to make the musical result dramatically convincing. The fascinating diversity of its various elements — virtuosic organ interludes, elaborate tenor solos, ritualistic choral movements — does not prevent the work from hanging together, and although the King's acoustic precludes close-up clarity of sound the essential atmosphere of this moving portrait of a society struggling to establish itself and to survive is finely caught. Neil Mackie and Christopher Hughes are ideal soloists, and Stephen Cleobury co-ordinates the proceedings with unobtrusive skill. Davies's early set of *Five Carols* is one of his more familiar works, and this recording is definitive in its precision and freshness. The disc is completed by a memorable recent composition to a Greek text, *Hymn to the Word of God*.

Maxwell Davies. Miss Donnithorne's Maggot[a]. Eight Songs for a Mad King[b]. [a]**Mary Thomas** (sop); [b]**Julius Eastman** (bar); **The Fires of London/Sir Peter Maxwell Davies.** Unicorn-Kanchana DKPCD9052. Texts included. Item marked [a] new to UK, [b] from RHS308 (12/71).

Ih 7m ADD/DDD 3/88

King George III in his madness sang the music of his beloved Handel; he also used a miniature mechanical organ in attempts to teach caged birds to sing for him. Eliza Donnithorne, on the other hand, was jilted at the church door and reacted by making the rest of her life an endless wedding-morning. She did not sing, so far as we know, but her crazed monologues are as haunted, in Maxwell Davies's phantasmagoria, by memories of martial music and by overtones of all those Italian opera heroines who went 'mad in white satin' as the King's are by distorted Handel, by folk-songs and the twittering of birds and by grotesque foxtrots. The range of vocal effects required of the two soloists is punishing: howls and screeches and extremes of pitch for the vocalist in *Eight Songs*, burlesque coloratura warblings and swoopings for the soprano in *Miss Donnithorne*. The hysterical intensity of the music is pretty taxing for the listener, too, but he is rewarded in *Eight Songs* by a breathtaking kaleidoscope of vivid allusion, invention and parody, and in *Miss Donnithorne* by a harsh poignancy as well. Both pieces are vehicles for virtuoso performance, from the instrumentalists as well as the singers, and one can scarcely imagine either being done better than it is here. The very immediate recording adds substantially to their uncomfortable impact.

Further listening ...

Cello Concerto[a]. Oboe Concerto[b]. [b]**Robin Miller** (ob); [a]**William Conway** (vc); **Scottish Chamber Orchestra/Sir Peter Maxwell Davies.** Unicorn-Kanchana DKPCD9085 (1/90).

Violin Concerto, "L'arbre des songes"[a]. *Coupled with* **Dutilleux.** Violin Concerto[b]. **Isaac Stern** (vn); [a]**French National Orchestra/Lorin Maazel;** [b]**Royal Philharmonic Orchestra/André Previn.** CBS CD42449 (2/88).

"A Celebration of Scotland". An Orkney Wedding, with Sunrise. Kinloche, his Fantassie[b]. Seven Songs Home[a]. Yesnaby Ground[c]. Dances from "The Two Fiddlers"[b]. Jimmack the Postie[b]. Farewell to Stromness[c]. Lullabye for Lucy[a]. Renaissance Scottish Dances[b]. [a]**St Mary's Music School Choir;** [b]**Scottish Chamber Orchestra/Sir Peter Maxwell Davies** ([c]pf). Unicorn-Kanchana DKPCD9070 (12/88).

Ave maris stella. Image, Reflection, Shadow[a]. Runes from a Holy Island[b]. [a]**Gregory Knowles** (cimbalom); **The Fires of London/**[b]**Sir Peter Maxwell Davies.** Unicorn-Kanchana Souvenir UKCD2038 (3/91).

The Martyrdom of St Magnus. **Soloists; Scottish Chamber Opera Ensemble/Michael Rafferty.** Unicorn-Kanchana DKPCD9100 (3/91).

Billy Mayerl

British 1902-1959

Mayerl. PIANO WORKS. **Eric Parkin.** Chandos CHAN8848.
Four Aces Suite — No. 1, Ace of Clubs; No. 4, Ace of Spades. Mistletoe. Autumn crocus. Hollyhock. White heather. Three Dances in Syncopation, Op. 73. Sweet William. Parade of the Sandwich-Board Men. Hop-O'-My-Thumb. Jill all alone. Aquarium Suite. **Mayerl/Croom-Johnson:** Bats in the Belfry. Green tulips.

50m DDD 11/90 

Billy Mayerl was a Londoner of partly German parentage who became a brilliant pianist and a composer whose piano pieces, immensely popular between the wars, successfully bridge the gap between ragtime and, let's say, Frank Bridge and John Ireland in their lighter piano moods. In this way, he was a middle-of-the-road figure like Eric Coates, and for that reason he later came to be neglected by jazz aficionados and classical buffs alike as representing no pure 'tradition'. Today, it's a delight to return to tuneful music which has such originality, wit, and sparkle as well as being superbly written for the piano. Listen to the very first number (the *Ace of Clubs*), and you at once hear the charm and sharp sophistication of Mayerl's style, which is worthy of his contemporaries Noël Coward and Cole Porter, to say nothing of Gershwin. Though it's a pity we don't have all the 'Aces' of this four-part suite here, that's because Eric Parkin recorded the other two on an earlier CD devoted to this composer on which we also find the famous piece *Marigold* (CHAN8560). Parkin is right inside this music and his playing is stylistically spot on in its tonal warmth, crisp articulation and rhythmic zest. This is a delightful disc. Quite a few classical music lovers, if given a one-way ticket to a desert island and a medium-size suitcase, would gladly sacrifice some Schoenberg for modern music as attractive and well played as this.

Further listening ...

The Legends of King Arthur — Prelude; Merlin the Wizard; Lady of the Lake; The Passing of Arthur. Almond Blossom. April's Fool. The Harp of the Winds. Marigold. Railroad Rhythm. Shallow Waters. From a Spanish Lattice. Song of the Fir Tree. Nimble-Fingered Gentleman. Evening Primrose. Four Aces — Ace of Diamonds; Ace of Hearts. The Joker. **Eric Parkin** (pf). Chandos CHAN8560 (6/88).

Domenico Mazzocchi

Italian 1592-1665

NEW REVIEW

D. Mazzocchi. SACRAE CONCERTATIONES. [a]**Maria Cristina Kiehr,** [b]**Barbara Borden** (sops); [c]**Andreas Scholl** (alto); [d]**Gerd Türk** (ten); [e]**Ulrich Messthaler** (bass); **Netherlands Chamber Choir; Lucia Swarts** (vc); **Karl-Ernst Schröder** (theorbo); **Christophe Rousset** (org/hpd)/**René Jacobs.** Harmonia Mundi HMC90 1357. Texts and translations included. Recorded in 1990.

Misereris omnium, Domine[ac]. Gaudebunt labia mea[ade]. Peccantem me quotidie[abe]. Jesu, dulcis memoria[ade]. Dialogo della Cantica. Vide, Domine, afflictionem nostram. Dialogo di Lazaro. Dialogo della Maddalena. Dialogo dell'Apocalisse. Lamento di David. Concilio de' Farisei.

1h 13m DDD 2/92

The elder of two composing brothers, Domenico Mazzocchi was a reasonably well-off amateur working in Rome during the first half of the seventeenth century. His output was thus not large, but neither did it lack quality or beauties of its own. This disc offers two distinct groups of works, both of which are thought to date from the 1630s. In the first category, motets for solo voices and continuo are sung by a team of five soloists, none of them particularly well-known outside The Netherlands but all of whom demonstrate both accomplishment and sensitivity. In their style of singing (indeed, in some cases even in their actual vocal quality) and in their constant searching for expressiveness they clearly show the influence of their conductor René Jacobs, and this is something which is also in evidence in the performances of the second group of pieces, the Latin *dialogi* or oratorios for soloists and chorus. In these, biblical stories are related in semi-dramatic fashion with some of the soloists actually assuming roles. The Netherlands Chamber Choir takes over here, providing competent soloists from within its own ranks; as a choir they are not so evenly matched as the motet soloists, and their sound is also a little less incisive than some of today's professional choirs, something to which the presence of female altos may well be a contributory factor. But this is beautiful music, and the stylishly characterful way in which it is performed certainly makes this disc a most pleasurable listening experience.

Nikolay Medtner

Russian 1880-1951

Medtner. Piano Concertos — No. 2 in C minor, Op. 50; No. 3 in E minor, Op. 60. **Nikolai Demidenko** (pf); **BBC Scottish Symphony Orchestra/Jerzy Maksymiuk.** Hyperion CDA66580. Recorded in 1991.

1h 14m DDD 4/92 

This is a splendid issue of two piano concertos by a neglected Russian master, with fine recording, good orchestral playing from a Scottish orchestra under a Polish conductor and, above all, truly coruscating and poetic playing from the brilliant young Russian pianist Nikolai Demidenko. It also bids fair to do a splendid rehabilitation job for Nikolay Medtner, a composer who did not feature at all in last year's edition of this *Guide* but who is steadily coming in from the cold after half a century of neglect. He was a contemporary and friend of Rachmaninov who settled in Britain in the 1930s, and like Rachmaninov (to whom the Second Concerto is dedicated and who returned the compliment with his own Fourth) he was an excellent pianist. But while the other composer became immensely popular, Medtner languished in obscurity, regarded (if thought about at all) as an inferior imitation of Rachmaninov who wrote gushing music that was strong on gestures but weak on substance. The fact is that he can be diffuse (not to say long-winded) and grandiose, and memorable tunes are in short supply, so that his music needs to be played well to come off. But when it is there's much to enjoy and the strong Russian flavour of the ornate writing is evident, as is the composer's masterly understanding of the piano.

Further listening ...

Piano Works, Volumes 3 and 4. **Hamish Milne.** CRD CRD3460/1 (3/90). *CRD3460* — Piano Sonatas: G minor, Op. 22; A minor, Op. 30. Romantic Sketches for the Young, Op. 54.

Two Fairy Tales, Op. 8. Three Novelles, Op. 17. *CRD3461* — Piano Sonata in F minor, Op. 5. Second Improvisation (in vartiation form), Op. 47.

Piano Works, Volume 1. Forgotten Melodies, Op. 38 — No. 1, Sonata reminiscenza. Fairy Tales — F minor, Op. 26 No. 3; E minor, Op. 34 No. 2; F minor, Op. 42 No. 1; C major, Op. 48 No. 1; D minor, Op. 51 No. 1; D minor. Romantic Sketches for the Young, Op. 54 — The barrel-organ player. Morceaux, Op. 31 — No. 2, Funeral March; No. 3, Fairy Tale. Piano Sonata in G minor, Op. 22. **Geoffrey Tozer.** Chandos CHAN9050 (11/92).

Felix Mendelssohn

German 1809-1847

Mendelssohn. PIANO CONCERTOS. **Murray Perahia; [a]Academy of St Martin in the Fields/Sir Neville Marriner.** CBS Masterworks CD42401. Items marked [a] from IM76376 (7/75), [b] IM37838 (5/85).

Piano Concertos[a] — No. 1 in G minor, Op. 25; No. 2 in D minor, Op. 40. Prelude and Fugue in E major/minor, Op. 35 No. 1[b]. Variations sérieuses in D minor, Op. 54[b]. Andante and Rondo capriccioso, Op. 14[b].

lh 10m ADD/DDD 11/87 

Though conflict and suffering, the experiences on which Beethovenian music is supposed to feed, were foreign to Mendelssohn's nature, ardour, inspiration, soulfulness and fiery energy he had in abundance. So although both these concertos, products of the composer's twenties, are in minor keys, they have little of the pathos or drama that that might lead one to expect. It is for their consummate ease and naturalness, their ability to make the listener feel as though he is soaring, that they are valued. Not too many pianists are suited by temperament, or indeed equipped by technique, for such music. Murray Perahia undoubtedly is. His dazzling fingerwork and his sensitivity to the direction of harmony are delightful, and he knows just how to step aside to let the more relaxed slow movements make their point. Slight fizziness on the string sound and a less than ideally regulated piano detract but little from one's enjoyment; and CBS have made partial amends by adding 26 minutes from a solo Mendelssohn recital which shows Perahia on top form.

Additional recommendation ...

Nos. 1 and 2[a]. Piano Concerto in A minor[b]. **Cyprien Katsaris** (pf); **[a]Leipzig Gewandhaus Orchestra/Kurt Masur; [b]Liszt Chamber Orchestra/János Rolla.** Teldec Digital Experience 9031 75860-2 — lh 10m DDD 6/92

Mendelssohn. Violin Concertos — E minor, Op. 64; D minor. **Viktoria Mullova** (vn); **Academy of St Martin in the Fields/Sir Neville Marriner.** Philips 432 077-2PH. Recorded in 1990.

50m DDD 5/91 

Since the competition is strong to say the least, new accounts of 'the' Mendelssohn Violin Concerto have to be rather special to make their way in the catalogue, but that of Viktoria Mullova and the ASMF under Sir Neville Marriner falls into the category of distinguished additions. The deliberate mention of the orchestra and conductor here is because this work is emphatically not a show-piece for a soloist in the way that Paganini's or Wieniawski's violin concertos are. Instead it offers a real dialogue with orchestra although there are plenty of opportunities for violin virtuosity as well. Mullova's sweet and somehow youthful tone is beautifully matched here by Marriner and his orchestra, which in turn does not sound so big as to overwhelm the often intimate character of the music. The recording helps, too, with its natural balance between the soloist and the orchestral body. The reference above to this E minor work as 'the' Mendelssohn Violin Concerto is because after his death it was found that as a boy of 13 he also composed the one in D minor which here makes a useful coupling. Of course it shows the influence of classical models, including Mozart, but the slow movement has an attractive warmth and the finale a zest and drive that owes something to gipsy music. Maybe in less than expert hands it could sound ordinary, but not when it is done as stylishly as here.

Additional recommendations ...

E minor. **Bruch.** *Violin Concerto No. 1 in G minor, Op. 26.* **Anne-Sophie Mutter** (vn); **Berlin Philharmonic Orchestra/Herbert von Karajan.** DG 400 031-2GH — 57m DDD 3/83

E minor. **Bruch.** *Violin Concerto.* **Scottish Chamber Orchestra/Jaime Laredo** (vn). Pickwick IMP Red Label PCD829 — 53m DDD 1/87 £

E minor. **Bruch.** *Violin Concerto.* **Schubert.** *Rondo in A major, D438.* **Nigel Kennedy** (vn); **English Chamber Orchestra/Jeffrey Tate.** EMI CDC7 49663-2 — 1h 11m DDD 1/89

D minor. Violin and Piano Concerto in D minor. **Gidon Kremer** (vn); **Martha Argerich** (pf). DG 427 338-2GH — 59m DDD 9/89

Violin Concerto[a]. **Beethoven.** *Violin Concerto in D major, Op. 61*[b]. **Yehudi Menuhin** (vn); [a]**Berlin Philharmonic Orchestra,** [b]**Philharmonia Orchestra/Wilhelm Furtwängler.** EMI Références mono CDH7 69799-2 — 1h 11m ADD 10/89 ▲

E minor[b]. **Bruch.** *Violin Concerto*[c]. **Kreisler.** *Liebesfreud*[a]. **Sarasate.** *Introduction et Tarantelle, Op. 43*[a]. **Cho-Liang Lin** (vn); [a]**Sandra Rivers** (pf); [b]**Philharmonia Orchestra/Michael Tilson Thomas;** [c]**Chicago Symphony Orchestra/Leonard Slatkin.** CBS Masterworks CD44902 — 1h 1m DDD 3/91 £

E minor[a]. **Bruch.** *Violin Concerto*[b]. [a]**Miklós Szenthelý,** [b]**Emmy Verhey** (vns); [a]**Budapest Philharmonic Orchestra/János Sándor;** [b]**Budapest Symphony Orchestra/Arpád Joó.** LaserLight 15 615 — 52m DDD 3/91 £

E minor. **Brahms.** *Violin Concerto in D major, Op. 77.* **Xue-Wei** (vn); **London Philharmonic Orchestra/Ivor Bolton.** ASV CDDCA748 — 1h 7m DDD 4/91

Mendelssohn. STRING SYMPHONIES. **London Festival Orchestra/Ross Pople.**
Hyperion CDA66561/3. Items marked [a] from CDA66196 (6/87), [b] CDA66318 (11/89), others new to UK. Recorded 1985-90.

No. 1 in C major; No. 2 in D major; No. 3 in E minor; No. 4 in C minor; No. 5 in B flat major[b]; No. 6 in E flat major; No. 7 in D minor[b]; No. 8 in D major[b]; No. 9 in C minor[a]; No. 10 in B minor[a]; No. 11 in F major; No. 12 in G minor[a].

③ 3h 23m DDD 12/91

"Mendelssohn — twelve years old — promises much": this prophetic entry made by Beethoven in one of his conversation books, shortly after his first encounter with the young genius, is certainly vindicated in the astonishing cycle of 12 symphonies for string orchestra. These youthful works chart the composer's mastery of symphonic genre and total command of formal classicism over a period of barely two years, and Ross Pople is eager to communicate his own tangible sense of wonderment and deepening incredulity throughout this excellent integral cycle. Whilst Pople himself confirms this ongoing revelation in his performances, Hyperion have ensured that the layout of the discs conform to the chronology of the works themselves. Symphonies Nos. 1 and 2 were evidently compositional studies directed by Mendelssohn's private tutor, Zelter, but they have charm and true melodic interest, whereas No. 3 clearly owes much to the turbulence of Haydn's *Sturm-und-drang-Periode*. The spirit of the high baroque is revealed in the Handelian *Grave* introduction to Symphony No. 4, whilst its successor is evidently something of a fusion of baroque and early classical styles. The central works of the cycle reveal a greater sense of assurance and individuality, but as Pople avidly demonstrates, they have a growing emotional impetus and architectural potency also. Equally, the influence of other composers is diminishing as the later symphonies assume a traditional four-movement form, of increasing complexity and cohesion, and Pople directs a memorably vigorous account of Symphony No. 8, with its astonishing *Scherzo* and ingenious double fugue. If one senses more than ever the forward looking innovation of the last three symphonies, then this is as much a tribute to the sheer excellence of these performances as to the actual resources of the music itself, for Pople conveys all the joy and wonderment of each fresh discovery, and the London Festival Orchestra clearly share in his delight as they unfold the true genius of these extraordinary works. Very highly recommended.

Additional recommendations ...
Nos. 1-6. **English String Orchestra/William Boughton.** Nimbus NI5141 — ⁘ 1h DDD 3/89
Nos. 7, 8 and 10. **English String Orchestra/William Boughton.** Nimbus NI5142 — ⁘ 52m DDD 3/89
Nos. 9, 11 and 12. **English String Orchestra/William Boughton.** Nimbus NI5143 — ⁘ 1h 11m DDD 3/89
Nos. 8, 9 and 10. **Orpheus Chamber Orchestra.** DG 437 528-2GH — ⁘ 58m DDD 8/93

Mendelssohn. SYMPHONIES AND OVERTURES. **London Symphony Orchestra/ Claudio Abbado.** DG 415 353-2GH4.
Symphonies — No. 1 in C minor, Op. 11; No. 2 in B flat major, Op. 52, "Lobgesang" (with Elizabeth Connell, Karita Mattila, sops; Hans-Peter Blochwitz, ten); No. 3 in A minor, Op. 56, "Scottish"; No. 4 in A major, Op. 90, "Italian" (*Nos. 3 and 4 are also available separately — see further on*); No. 5 in D major, Op. 107, "Reformation". Overtures — The Hebrides, Op. 26, "Fingal's Cave"; A Midsummer Night's Dream, Op. 21. The Fair Melusina, Op. 32. Octet in E flat major, Op. 20 — Scherzo.

⁘ ④ 4h 5m DDD 1/86

This is a most valuable collection and Abbado impresses at once in the First Symphony by his serious yet lively account of the score: his approach to the *Lobgesang* is warm and joyful and though he cannot quite rid the work of its Victorian flavour, his performance is fresh and restores the music's charm and innocence. He has a good chorus at his disposal and three dedicated, skilful soloists. In the more familiar *Scottish* Symphony Abbado again invests the work with warmth and stature, never rushing or driving too hard: the familiar *Italian* Symphony, too, gains from his affectionate, respectful yet sparkling approach. Even the *Reformation* Symphony, which can seem even more coloured by Victorian religious sentiment than the *Hymn of Praise*, emerges as a vigorous, uplifting work, with the hymn tunes played in cheerful, direct fashion. Only in the three overtures, where Abbado's tempos and phrasing are strangely idiosyncratic (though never less than interesting), do the performances depart from a very high standard indeed. Throughout the set the LSO respond to Abbado with lean, virile playing. The recordings have a pleasing, natural sound, with a particularly good balance in the choral item.

Additional recommendations ...
Symphonies Nos. 1-5. **New Philharmonia Orchestra/Wolfgang Sawallisch.** Philips 432 598-2PB3 — ⁘ ③ 3h 14m ADD 8/91
Symphonies Nos. 1-5. **Berlin Philharmonic Orchestra/Herbert von Karajan.** DG 429 664-2GSE3 — ⁘ ③ 3h 22m ADD 8/91

NEW REVIEW
Mendelssohn. Symphonies — No. 1 in C minor, Op. 11; No. 5 in D major, Op. 107, "Reformation". **Bamberg Symphony Orchestra/Claus Peter Flor.** RCA Victor Red Seal 09026-60391-2. Recorded in 1990.

⁘ 58m DDD

As a companion CD from RCA of assorted Mendelssohn overtures has already demonstrated (reviewed below), Leipzig-born Claus Peter Flor is an outstandingly sympathetic interpreter of this particular figure. Here, then, is a pair of most enjoyable readings, not as bracingly dynamic as some (Sawallisch, listed above, in his marvellous New Philharmonia account for Philips of the *Reformation* undoubtedly brought more thrust to the opening *Allegro con fuoco*), but always engagingly affectionate. Certainly, Flor's wholly winning presentation of the *Reformation*'s lovely, tripping *Scherzo* is an absolute delight, and here as elsewhere the Bamberg SO's response combines a most agreeably homogeneous tone-production with no little discipline. Warm, if not ideally focused recording to match. For some, this music-making may be a mite *too* relaxed and cosily 'old world'; however, Flor's comparatively laid back manner is easy to enjoy, and his thoughtful interpretations are by no means lacking in guile, character or fresh-faced charm.

Additional recommendations ...
Nos. 1 and 5. **Milton Keynes Chamber Orchestra/Hilary Davan Wetton.** Unicorn-Kanchana DKPCD9117 — 1h 3m DDD 2/93
Nos. 1 and 5. The Hebrides, Op. 26, "Fingal's Cave". **Philharmonia Orchestra/Walter Weller.** Chandos CHAN9099 — 1h 15m DDD 2/93

Mendelssohn. Symphony No. 2 in B flat major, Op. 52, "Hymn of Praise". **Barbara Bonney, Edith Wiens** (sops); **Peter Schreier** (ten); **Leipzig Radio Choir; Leipzig Gewandhaus Orchestra/Kurt Masur.** Teldec 2292-44178-2. Text and translation included. Recorded in 1988.

59m DDD 4/90

In this memorable performance of one of Mendelssohn's lesser-known but highly rewarding symphonies, Kurt Masur carries forward a tradition of music-making of which Mendelssohn was himself a part, through his conducting of the Leipzig Gewandhaus Orchestra. The *Hymn of Praise* stands under the shade of Beethoven's *Choral* Symphony, with its considerable length and choral and solo contributions, both here extremely well delivered, but it does not reach similar heights of sublimity. What it does possess is an unassuming lyricism, vitality and elegance throughout that is highly attractive. Popular with choral societies during the last century, this is an interesting part of Mendelssohn's symphonic canon. Masur's performance is perfectly attuned to the work's character, the orchestral playing is excellent with an assured sense of style, and the recording is spacious. Well worth investigating.

Additional recommendation ...
Cynthia Haymon, Alison Hagley (sops); **Peter Straka** (ten); **Philharmonia Chorus and Orchestra/Walter Weller.** Chandos CHAN8995 — 1h 13m DDD 5/92

NEW REVIEW

Mendelssohn. Symphonies — No. 3 in A minor, Op. 56, "Scottish"[a]; No. 4 in A major, Op. 90, "Italian"[b]. **San Francisco Symphony Orchestra/Herbert Blomstedt.** Decca 433 811-2DH. Item marked [a] recorded in 1989, [b] 1991.

1h 7m DDD 4/93

Recent years have seen a number of competitive releases of this popular coupling, not least a treasurable Teldec CD featuring Nikolaus Harnoncourt at the helm of the remarkably responsive Chamber Orchestra of Europe, full of that conductor's special brand of re-creative insight. Enter Herbert Blomstedt and his splendid San Francisco orchestra, in matters of interpretation more traditionally solid and less daring than that Teldec partnership, perhaps, but with considerable virtues of their own. Blomstedt's *Scottish* impresses most by dint of its joyous vigour (outer movements go with a will), rhythmic bounce (perky, personable winds and razor-sharp strings in the *Scherzo*) and unaffected eloquence (as in his affectionately flowing yet never short-winded conception of the third movement *Adagio*). This new *Italian*, too, is first-rate. Under Blomstedt the opening *Allegro vivace* positively fizzes along, aided by some quite beautifully sprung string playing, whilst the *Saltarello* finale is articulated with real panache. The middle movements are perhaps marginally less memorable, though again the irreproachably stylish orchestral response yields much pleasure. Although the symphonies were actually set down some 17 months apart, Decca's admirably consistent sound-picture possesses the exemplary clarity and sheen we have now come to expect from this particular source. No one can go far wrong with this disc.

Additional recommendations ...
Orchestra of St John's, Smith Square/John Lubbock. ASV Quicksilva QS6004 — 1h 11m ADD 12/87 £
Leipzig Gewandhaus Orchestra/Kurt Masur. Teldec 2292-43463-2 — 1h 7m DDD 11/88
London Symphony Orchestra/Claudio Abbado. DG 3D-Classics 427 810-2GDC 1h 11m DDD 2/90 £

London Classical Players/Roger Norrington. EMI Reflexe CDC7 54000-2 — lh 5m DDD 11/90

Chamber Orchestra of Europe, Nikolaus Harnoncourt. Teldec 9031-72308-2 — lh 9m DDD 5/92

Mendelssohn. Symphony No. 5 in D major, Op. 107, "Reformation"[a]. ***Schumann.*** Symphony No. 3 in E flat major, Op. 97, "Rhenish"[b]. **Berlin Philharmonic Orchestra/Herbert von Karajan.** DG Galleria 419 870-2GGA. Item marked [a] from 2720 068 (12/73), [b] 2720 046 (9/72).

lh 9m ADD 4/88 £

This is just the sort of repertoire at which Karajan excels; his Schumann is strongly characterized, firmly driven and beautifully shaped and his Mendelssohn often achieves a delicacy of touch that belies the size of orchestra employed. Karajan's set of the Schumann symphonies made in 1971 was a notable success and the *Rhenish* speaks for them all. Here the powerful thrust of the work is gorgeously conveyed by the Berlin strings and the spontaneity of the music-making is striking. The Mendelssohn makes an ideal companion, since in scale the *Reformation* embraces wide vistas and far horizons. Laden with references to Protestant worship, Mendelssohn paints a picture of security and solidity achieved over many years and much struggle. Karajan maybe overemphasizes the epic qualities of the work but the playing of the orchestra is superb. The recordings have 'dried-out' a little in the transfer, but still sound well.

Mendelssohn. OVERTURES. **Bamberg Symphony Orchestra/Claus Peter Flor.** RCA Victor Red Seal RD87905. Recorded 1987-88.

Die Hochzeit des Camacho, Op. 10. A Midsummer Night's Dream, Op. 21 (from RD87764, 10/88). Meeresstille und glückliche Fahrt, Op. 27. Ruy Blas, Op. 95. Athalie, Op. 74. The Hebrides, Op. 26, "Fingal's Cave".

59m DDD 1/89

The Marriage of Camacho Overture was written in 1825, two years before the masterly evocation of *A Midsummer Night's Dream*, with its gossamer fairies, robust mortals and pervading romanticism, and already demonstrates the teenage composer's enormous musical facility and organizational skills, together with the high quality of his invention. *Calm sea and prosperous voyage* (1828) anticipates *The Hebrides* of a year later, and celebrates an ocean voyage on a sailing ship. *Ruy Blas* is a jolly, slightly melodramatic, but agreeably tuneful piece and *Athalie* is also attractive in its melodic ideas. *Fingal's Cave* with its beauty and dramatic portrayal of Scottish seascapes matches the Shakespearian overture in its melodic inspiration (the opening phrase is hauntingly unforgettable) and shows comparable skill in its vivid orchestration. Flor directs wonderfully sympathetic and spontaneous performances, with the Bamberg Symphony Orchestra playing gloriously. There is abundant energy and radiant lyrical beauty in the playing and each piece is unerringly paced and shaped. The glowing recording gives a wonderful bloom to the orchestral textures without preventing a realistic definition. There has never been a collection of Mendelssohn's overtures to match this and it will give enormous pleasure in every respect.

Mendelssohn. A Midsummer Night's Dream — incidental music, Opp. 21 and 61. **Edith Wiens** (sop); **Christiane Oertel** (mez); **Friedhelm Eberle** (spkr); **Leipzig Radio Chorus; Leipzig Gewandhaus Orchestra/Kurt Masur.** Teldec 2292-46323-2. Text and translation included. Recorded in 1990.

lh 3m DDD 5/92 

To have a recording of Mendelssohn's incidental music with linking dialogue is an advantage, for the shorter pieces in particular make more of an impact when performed in the appropriate dramatic context. Teldec's recording was made in conjunction with a concert performance. Friedhelm Eberle speaks his lines in German, but no matter, for the insert notes contain Shakespeare's original English text set alongside the German translation. Of more concern is the fact that Eberle takes all the parts, occasionally going into falsetto for female roles. Edith Wiens and Christiane Oertel both sing their brief parts very capably, and in German, and the choral and orchestral contributions are first-rate. Masur's conception of the score is a little more serious and a little tougher than usual, but there is a good deal of personality in his conducting, and plenty of poetic expression. He takes the *Scherzo* a little more slowly than is the norm, but there is still a lightness of touch: the "Wedding March", by contrast, goes at a cheerfully fast pace. Throughout the performance, in fact, textures are kept very clear, and rhythms are appropriately light-footed. The recording quality is fully up to today's best standards.

Additional recommendations ...

Lillian Watson (sop); **Delia Wallis** (mez); **Finchley Children's Music Group; London Symphony Orchestra/André Previn.** EMI CDC7 47163-2 — 58m DDD 9/86 B

Lucia Popp (sop); **Marjana Lipovšek** (mez); **Bamberg Symphony Chorus and Orchestra/Claus Peter Flor.** RCA Victor Red Seal RD87764 — 47m DDD 10/88 B

Edith Wiens (sop); **Sarah Walker** (mez); **London Philharmonic Choir and Orchestra/Andrew Litton.** Classics for Pleasure CD-CFP4593 — 50m DDD 9/92 B

Mendelssohn. Octet in E flat major, Op. 20. String Quintet No. 2 in B flat major, Op. 87. **Academy of St Martin in the Fields Chamber Ensemble.** Philips 420 400-2PH. From 9500 616 (3/80). Recorded in 1978.

1h 3m ADD 11/87 

Mendelssohn was as remarkable a prodigy as Mozart and one can only speculate with sadness what marvels he might have left us had he lived longer. Had death claimed him at 20 we would still have this glorious Octet, a work of unforced lyricism and a seemingly endless stream of melody. The Academy Chamber Ensemble, all fine soloists in their own right, admirably illustrate the benefits of working regularly as an ensemble for they play with uncommon sympathy. The string quintet is a work of greater fervour and passion than the Octet but it is characterized by the same melodiousness and unfettered lyricism with plenty of opportunities for virtuoso playing, which are well taken. The recordings, made in 1978, give a pleasant and warm sheen to the string colour of the ensemble.

Additional recommendation ...

Octet. String Symphonies — No. 6 in E flat major; No. 10 in B minor. **I Solisti Italiani.** Denon CO-73185 — 58m DDD 4/90 B

See also review which follows.

Mendelssohn. String Quintet No. 1 in A major, Op. 18[a]. Octet in E flat major, Op. 20. **Hausmusik** ([a]Monica Huggett, [a]Pavlo Beznosiuk, Paull Boucher, Jolianne von Einem, vns; [a]Roger Chase, [a]Simon Whistler, vas; [a]Anthony Pleeth, Sebastian Comberti, vcs). EMI CDC7 49958-2. Recorded in 1989.

1h 3m DDD 9/90 

Hausmusik is an impressive chamber group, led by Monica Huggett, with Anthony Pleeth the principal cellist. They use original instruments, and create fresh, transparent textures, yet there is no lack of warmth and those horrid bulges on phrases which disfigure some early music performances are mercifully absent. Mendelssohn's miraculous Octet was written in 1825 when the composer was 16 and the almost equally engaging Quintet, with its gently nostalgic *Intermezzo* dates from a year later. The performances here fizz with vitality in outer movements where pacing is brisk and sparkling, yet never sounds rushed. The famous *Scherzo* in the Octet is wonderfully fleet, and articulated with a disarming, feather-light precision, and the *Presto* finale has real exhilaration. Yet the expressive music sings with unforced charm. Excellent, realistic recording, with enough resonance for bloom without clouding. If you arc only familiar with the Octet the Quintet could prove a real bonus.

NEW REVIEW

Mendelssohn. STRING QUARTETS. **Melos Quartet** (Wilhelm Melcher, Gerhard Voss, vns; Hermann Voss, va; Peter Buck, vc). DG 415 883-2GCM3. From 2740 267 (11/82). Recorded 1976-81.

E flat major (1823); No. 1 in E flat major, Op. 12; No. 2 in A minor, Op. 13; No. 3 in D major, Op. 44 No. 1; No. 4 in E minor, Op. 44 No. 2; No. 5 in E flat major, Op. 44 No. 3; No. 6 in F minor, Op. 80. Andante, Scherzo, Capriccio and Fugue, Op. 81 Nos. 1-2.

③ 3h 19m ADD 12/87 

The familiar and misleading cliché of Mendelssohn as the cheerful chappie of early romanticism vanishes at the sound of the F minor Quartet, Op. 80. Here is the intensity, anguish and anger that everyone thought Mendelssohn incapable of. His beloved sister Fanny died in May 1847 (his own death was merely months away), and the ensuing summer saw him leave Berlin for Switzerland, where he began to "write music very industriously". And what remarkable music it is. Right from the opening *Allegro assai* one senses trouble afoot, an unfamiliar restlessness mixed in with the more familiar busyness. Furthermore the second movement is surely the most fervent and punishing that Mendelssohn ever wrote — wild, insistent and unmistakably tragic in tone. This gradual intensification and darkening that occurs throughout Mendelssohn's quartet cycle makes it a most revealing guide to his creative development. But of course much of the earlier music is in fact profoundly 'Mendelssohnian' in the accepted sense of that term: fresh, dynamic, light-textured, beautifully crafted and full of amiable melodic invention. The very early E flat Quartet, Op. posth (composed when Mendelssohn was only 14), although fashioned very much in the style of Haydn and Mozart, points towards imminent developments — a song-like A minor Quartet, already taking its lead from late Beethoven in the same key, the E flat, Op. 12, with its delightful Canzonetta (once popular as a separate 'encore') and the eventful Op. 44 set, three of Mendelssohn's most concentrated full-scale works. And DG also add the four separate pieces, Op. 81, thus treating us to the entire Mendelssohn string quartet canon (the chronology of which, incidentally, is very much at odds with that suggested by the published opus numbers). The Melos Quartet comes up trumps with a really superb set of performances — technically immaculate, transparent in tone and full of enthusiasm. The recordings, too, although analogue, report their playing with great presence and clarity.

Additional recommendations ...

Nos. 1 and 2. **Gabrieli Quartet.** Chandos CHAN8827 — 59m DDD 1/92

Nos. 2 and 6. **Carmina Quartet.** Denon CO-79527 — 53m DDD 3/92

NEW REVIEW

Mendelssohn. Piano Trios — No. 1 in D minor, Op. 49; No. 2 in C minor, Op. 66. **Solomon Trio** (Rodney Friend, vn; Timothy Hugh, vc; Yonty Solomon, pf). Pickwick Masters MCD46.

1h 1m DDD 12/92

Yonty Solomon, insert-note-writer as well as pianist of this group carrying his name, obviously has great respect and affection for Mendelssohn's two piano trios. "An imperishable masterpiece" is his evaluation of the D minor work, adding "its deeply-felt sincerity, emotional intensity and spacious, elegant architectural proportions give the work a perfect balance and timelessness". The C minor work he also hails as a "composition of great stature". Except for the two scherzos, both well up to average timing, the Solomon Trio opt for expansiveness rather than dash in their choice of tempo. Although one wonders if the composer himself might have preferred a little more urgency from time to time, the searching approach adopted by the Trio is so caringly considered that it cannot fail to convince. Only occasionally is Solomon's piano a little stronger than is ideal for Rodney Friend in the softer regions of the violinist's imaginatively varied tonal spectrum, Timothy Hugh's rich cello is delightful and the overall tonal reproduction is mellow and true.

Additional recommendations ...

Fontenay Trio. Teldec 2292-44947-2 — 58m DDD 9/90

Israel Piano Trio. CRD CRD3459 — 1h DDD 5/91

NEW REVIEW

Mendelssohn. WORKS FOR CELLO AND PIANO. **Lynn Harrell** (vc); **Bruno Canino** (pf). Decca 430 198-2DH. Recorded in 1989.
Cello Sonatas — No. 1 in B flat major, Op. 45; No. 2 in D major, Op. 58. Variations concertantes, Op. 17. Songs without words — Op. 19 No. 1; Op. 109.

lh 7m DDD 10/92 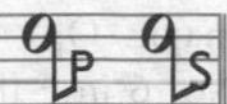

Lynn Harrell's Mendelssohn is bold and hugely compelling; his are full-blooded and overtly dramatic accounts of works which, in the wrong hands, can seem distinctly passive. His partner, Bruno Canino, an accompanist of rare perception, is superb throughout, matching Harell's flair and fantasy with his own specialized musical insight. Mendelssohn wrote his First Sonata in 1838, intending it for his brother Paul, a capable amateur cellist and wealthy financier. Its dignity and breadth impressed Schumann, who considered it to be "a Sonata for the most refined family circle, best enjoyed after some poems by Goethe or Lord Byron". In fact, Mendelssohn's model was the grandest of Beethoven's sonatas, the one in A major, Op. 69; and the similarities of scale and purpose are especially telling in this wonderful performance from Harrell and Canino. The Sonata in D major is more public in utterance, and more assuredly brilliant in form and content. Harrell's playing is nobly ardent, polished, and yet responsive to the structural needs of the music with an insight only rarely encountered. Bruno Canino constantly excels too; the precision and grace of his playing is never more evident than in the chorale episode of the *Adagio*. This is an unsurpassable performance, strong on musical sensitivity as well as sheer dynamism, and certainly very hard to resist! This disc also includes a lucid and enjoyable reading of Mendelssohn's earliest compositions for the medium, the *Variations concertantes*. Predictable economies of scale have been made here, giving the performance a more obviously episodic feel as each section is glowingly characterized. Harrell is evidently in winning mood; his playing has an effortless grace and finesse, also much in evidence in the two *Songs without words*, which complete the disc. With first-class Decca sound and performances of absolute distinction, this is a compulsory purchase.

NEW REVIEW

Mendelssohn. ORGAN WORKS, Volume 1. **Peter Planyavsky.** Motette CD11271. Played on the organ of the Church of St Augustin, Perchtoldsdorf, Germany. Recorded in 1988.
Sonatas, Op. 65 — No. 1 in F minor; No. 2 in C minor. Fugue in D minor. Chorale variations on "Wie gross ist des Allmächt'gen Güte". Andante in D major. Trio in F major. Prelude and Fugue in G major. Andante with variations. Allegro in D minor/major.

lh 9m DDD 10/92

"Mendelssohn is, without doubt, the greatest organist who has ever performed in London." So claimed a *Musical Times* review of 1837. Mendelssohn actually performed more often as an organist in England than he did in his native Germany, and it was for the English market that he wrote his organ music; six great Sonatas, three Preludes and Fugues and a handful of smaller individual works. Peter Planyavsky is making the first-ever comprehensive recordings of Mendelssohn's organ music and it's hard to think of anyone better suited. Planyavsky is himself one of the handful of present-day organists who has a world-wide reputation as a great player and a noted composer and one can't avoid drawing parallels between his career and Mendelssohn's. His playing has the real stamp of authority and, in the nicest possible way, a sense of evangelical zeal. The finale of the First Sonata comes across as a virtuoso *tour de force*, the last two movements of the Second have wonderful majesty and power while the smaller pieces (including a delightful *Andante with variations*) are played with genuine affection. The recording is crisp and well-balanced and the organ suits the music admirably.

Mendelssohn. Violin Sonatas — F minor, Op. 4; F major (1838). **Shlomo Mintz** (vn); **Paul Ostrovsky** (pf). DG 419 244-2GH.

5lm DDD 8/87 

The surprise here is the early F minor Violin Sonata, which is a work of strong character and an amazing achievement for a boy of 14. It is true that the sonata bears the influence of Beethoven and Mozart, but these influences are somehow assimilated and translated in a way that results in the work having its own very distinct personality. Obviously Mintz and Ostrovsky believe strongly in the work, and rightly do not play it down as a piece of juvenilia. Their response to the slow central movement is equally sensitive and beautifully phrased, and the last movement *Allegro agitato* is taut and well-argued. The F major Sonata shows all the elements of Mendelssohn's mature style, and is an altogether more urbane work than its predecessor. Again the soloists deserve high praise for their sympathetic response to the score. The excellent recording does full justice to Mintz's beautiful violin tone.

Mendelssohn. Songs without Words. Kinderstücke, Op. 72. **Daniel Barenboim** (pf). DG 423 931-2GGA2. From 2740 104 (12/74).

② 2h 13m ADD

Mendelssohn's piano music in general, and the *Songs without Words* in particular, are all too often dismissed as 'mere' salon music, not to be mentioned in the same breath as the Octet and the Violin Concerto, works of undoubted genius. Certainly there is engaging intimacy and fine craftsmanship coupled with a fastidious attention to detail that is found in the very finest salon music. But many of the pieces rise to far greater heights, the famous *Duetto* Op. 38 No. 6 beloved of Dame Myra Hess for example, or the hunting song vigour of Op. 19 No. 3. The latter sets of *Songs* become ever more questing in their variety; in Op. 62 we find the gossamer lightness of No. 6 (reminiscent of his *Dream* music) set against No. 2 where clusters of notes demand a sure touch and an agile technique. Daniel Barenboim gives performances combining great sensitivity and musical imagination, the eloquence of his readings allowing the unaffected beauty of these miniatures to shine through. This is equally true of the other works in this two-disc set, particularly *Kinderstücke*, reminiscent of Schumann's *Kinderszenen*, though perhaps less deeply personal. Barenboim also enchants in his seductively sun-drenched *Gondellied*. The remastered sound has just the right degree of resonance and it is difficult to believe that this recording is nearly 21 years old. Useful insert notes including an enlightening essay by Joan Chissell.

Additional recommendations ...

Songs without Words. **Lívia Rév** (pf). Hyperion CDA66221/2 — ② 2h 6m DDD 12/87

Songs without Words. **Luba Edlina** (pf). Chandos CHAN8948/9 — ② 2h 10m DDD 4/92

Mendelssohn. PIANO WORKS. **Murray Perahia** (pf). CBS Masterworks CD37838. From IM37838 (5/85).

Piano Sonata in E major, Op. 6. Prelude and Fugue in E minor/major, Op. 35 No. 1. Variations sérieuses in D minor, Op. 54. Andante and Rondo capriccioso in E minor, Op. 14.

50m DDD

This is a beautifully controlled and very welcome glimpse of a side of Mendelssohn rarely encountered in the concert-hall. Perahia's exquisitely fleet finger-work and finely controlled pianism matches the weight of the music ideally. The four pieces represented here are not of equal stature but there are certainly some fine things. The *Variations sérieuses* is Mendelssohn's best-known work for the piano — as the title might imply there is a darker, maybe even melancholy flavour to the theme and the subsequent variations have real substance. Here and in the other works, particularly the delightful *Rondo capriccioso*, Perahia's performance overlooks nothing in mood or atmosphere.

NEW REVIEW

Mendelssohn. LIEDER. **Barbara Bonney** (sop); **Geoffrey Parsons** (pf). Teldec 2292-44946-2. Texts and translations included. Recorded in 1991.

Op. 8 — No. 8, Andres Maienlied; No. 10, Romanze. *Op. 9* — No. 1, Frage; No. 5, Im Herbst; No. 7, Sehnsucht; No. 8, Frühlingsglaube; No. 9, Ferne; No. 10, Verlust; No. 12, Die Nonne. *Op. 19a* — No. 3, Winterlied; No. 4, Neue Liebe. *Op. 34* — No. 2, Auf Flügeln des

Gesanges; No. 3, Frühlingslied; No. 4, Suleika; No. 5, Sonntagslied. *Op. 47* — No. 3, Frühlingslied; No. 5, Der Blumenstrauss; No. 6, Bei der Wiege. *Op. 57* — No. 3, Suleika. *Op. 71* — No. 2, Frühlingslied; No. 6, Nachtlied. *Op. 86* — No. 3, Die Liebende schreibt; No. 5, Der Mond. *Op. 99* — No. 1, Erster Verlust; No. 5, Wenn sich zwei Herzen Scheiden; No. 6, Es weiss und rät es doch keiner. Pagenlied, Op. posth.

1h DDD 2/93 

The charm of these songs lies in their simple style and almost endless stream of delightful melody. Unlike other Lieder composers Mendelssohn avoided blatant word-painting or vivid characterizations and certainly the most satisfying songs here tend to be settings of texts which do not on the surface of it offer much scope for musical expression. But while this disc may not give us the very best of Mendelssohn, or indeed the finest examples of nineteenth-century Lied, the singing of Barbara Bonney makes this a CD not to be missed. Here is a rare example of a singer caught on record at the very height of her technical and artistic powers, able to exercise seemingly effortless vocal control in portraying the subtle colours and understated moods of each songs. The partnership with that ever-sensitive accompanist Geoffrey Parsons is inspired. Listen to how Bonney seems to float ethereally above the rippling piano figures in that most famous of all Mendelssohn songs, *Auf Flügeln des Gesanges* ("On wings of song") — a performance which can surely never have been bettered on record. An interesting footnote is that three of these songs are by Fanny Mendelssohn but have by convention always been ascribed to her brother.

Mendelssohn. LIEDER. **Nathalie Stutzmann** (contr); **Dalton Baldwin** (pf). Erato 2292-45583-2. Texts and translations included. Recorded in 1989.
Der Blumenstrauss, Op. 47 No. 5. Pagenlied. Des Mädchens Klage. Die Liebende schreibt, Op. 86 No. 3. Suleika, Op. 34 No. 4. Suleika, Op. 57 No. 3. Reiselied, Op. 34 No. 6. Erster Verlust, Op. 99 No. 1. Auf Flügeln des Gesanges, Op. 34 No. 2. Andres Maienlied ("Hexenlied"), Op. 8 No. 8. Der Blumenkranz. Ferne, Op. 9 No. 9. Scheidend, Op. 9 No. 6. Reiselied, Op. 19 No. 6. Herbstlied, Op. 84 No. 2. Venetianisches Gondellied, Op. 57 No. 5. Schlafloser Augen Leuchte. Neue Liebe, Op. 19*a* No. 4. Der Mond, Op. 86 No. 5. An die Entfernte, Op. 71 No. 3. Die Sterne schau'n, Op. 99 No. 2. Frühlingslied, Op. 47 No. 3. Nachtlied, Op. 71 No. 6. Volkslied, Op. 47 No. 4.

59m DDD 5/91 

Nathalie Stutzmann, the young French contralto, has rapidly established herself as one of the most interesting and intelligent Lieder singers of her generation. Here she devotes herself to the songs of Mendelssohn, which have been too long neglected. The composer may not have plumbed the emotional depths of the greatest of his predecessors and successors in his field, but he was unusually faithful to the shape and meaning of the poetry and covered quite a wide range of mood with an unerring sense of the appropriate setting. There are a number of arresting pieces here, such as *Reiselied, Die Liebende schreibt* and *Der Mond*, that are peculiarly Mendelssohnian in style. To these, and to the lighter songs, Stutzmann brings a welcome spontaneity of approach allied to a firm tone and expressive diction that make her singing consistently vital. She is splendidly partnered by the experienced Baldwin.

NEW REVIEW

Mendelssohn. Elijah. **Helen Donath, Kerstin Klein** (sops); **Jard van Nes** (contr); **Donald George** (ten); **Alistair Miles** (bass); **Leipzig Radio Chorus; Israel Philharmonic Orchestra/Kurt Masur.** Teldec 9031-73131-2. Text and translation included. Recorded live in 1991.

② 1h 50m DDD 5/93 

This is a compelling account of a much maligned work. Once the staple of every choral society throughout the land, its popularity declined at the same time as did other things deemed Victorian. Of late it has come back into favour with a number of new recordings of which this is easily the best. Masur has the advantage of the Leipzig Radio Chorus, who are steeped in the work's tradition and sing their varying roles as though their lives depended on it. Masur, with predominantly fast tempos, directs them and the equally vital Israel Philharmonic with unflagging energy, and contrasts the forces of good and evil with operatic ideas about characterization. In consequence the work sounds new-minted. Alastair Miles is by turns a fiery and tormented Elijah, keen with his word-painting and alive to most of the nuances of his part. Jard van Nes intones the alto's famous solos with feeling but rightly avoids sentimentality. Helen Donath defies the years in bringing fresh tone and open-hearted feeling to the soprano role. Only the uningratiating tenor soloist mars an unqualified recommendation for this splendidly prepared and produced recording. It is a worthy successor to the tried and true Sawallisch who employed an antecedent of the same choir. Now that is available on the new Philips mid-price Duo label; though less well recorded than the Teldec, it remains an excellent alternative, a compelling interpretation with soloists just that bit more convincing than Masur's.

Additional recommendations ...

Elly Ameling, Renate Krahmer (sops); **Annelies Burmeister, Gisela Schröter** (contrs); **Peter Schreier, Hans Joachim Rotzsch** (tens); **Theo Adam** (bass-bar); **Hermann Christian Polster** (bass); **Leipzig Radio Chorus; Leipzig Gewandhaus Orchestra/Wolfgang Sawallisch.** Philips Duo 438 368-2PM2 — ② 2h 11m ADD 2/88

(Sung in English). **Jamie Hopkins** (treb); **Yvonne Kenny, Anne Dawson** (sops); **Anne Sofie von Otter, Jean Rigby** (mezs); **Anthony Rolfe Johnson, Kim Begley** (tens); **Thomas Allen** (bar); **John Connell** (bass); **Academy of St Martin in the Fields Chorus and Orchestra/Sir Neville Marriner.** Philips 432 984-2PH2 — ② 2h 7m DDD 10/92

Saverio Mercadante

Italian 1795-1870

Mercadante. Flute Concerto in E minor.
Mozart. Flute Concerto No. 2 in D major, K314/285*d*.
Stamitz. Flute Concerto in G major. **Irena Grafenauer** (fl); **Academy of St Martin in the Fields/Sir Neville Marriner.** Philips 426 318-2PH. Recorded in 1989.

1h DDD 11/91

Given that the flute and the soprano voice share the attributes of flexibility and tonal purity, it is hardly surprising that it should enter the mind of an Italian composer of some 60 operas and a player of the flute, as Mercadante was, to write a few flute concertos; nor is it entirely eyebrow-raising that, despite their classical form, they should sound like winsome, extended showcases for agile divas in libretto less operas. Flautists are beginning to rediscover these works, to their and our benefit. Mozart told his father that he hated the flute but he wrote so wonderfully for it that it is hard to take his statement seriously. Though he was a great composer of operas he was no less prolific in his purely instrumental output; no operatic air hangs over his flute concertos. Neither does it over those of Stamitz, who wrote no opera — and, though he wrote splendidly for it, did not play the flute. Grafenauer is one of the very best young flautists to appear in recent years and she brings freshness (and two of her own cadenzas) to these attractive works; the ASMF are never slow to respond to a good and stimulating soloist, and they make no exception here.

Aarre Merikanto

Finland 1893-1958

Suggested listening ...

Fantasy[a]. Notturno[b]. Pan[a]. Symphonic Study[a]. **Finnish Radio Symphony Orchestra/[a]Leif Segerstam, [b]Jukka-Pekka Saraste.** Finlandia FACD349 (7/88).

Olivier Messiaen

French 1908-1992

Messiaen. Quatuor pour la fin du temps[a]. Le merle noir[b] [b]**Karlheinz Zöller** (fl); [a]**Erich Gruenberg** (vn); [a]**Gervase de Peyer** (cl); [a]**Anthony Pleeth** (vc); [a]**Michel Béroff,** [b]**Aloys Kontarsky** (pfs). EMI CDM7 63947-2. Item marked [a] from ASD2470 (8/69), [b] new to UK. Recorded 1968-71.

51m ADD 3/92 

With its eight sections lasting not far short of 50 minutes, Messiaen's *Quartet for the end of time* is a milestone in twentieth-century chamber music, both for the originality of its language (sometimes complex and sometimes boldly simple) and for a mystical fervour unique in Western music. The other astonishing thing about it is its early date (1941) and the circumstances of its composition, for it was written and first performed by the composer and three friends in the unpromising environment of a German prisoner of war camp called Stalag VIII at Görlitz on the Polish frontier. The score is prefaced by a quotation from the Revelation of St John the Divine describing an angel descending from Heaven to announce that "the mystery of God will be accomplished" and the music as a whole represents Messiaen's response, as a devout Catholic, to what he called "the harmonious silence of the heavens ... the ascent of man towards his God". One might think that this could make for too private a vision, but the invention is so powerful and varied that a sympathetic listener, whether believer or no, can find the work utterly compelling. This was the first recording of the work and it remains among the best, with the four players (who appear more as individuals than in conventional ensemble) bringing to it a rapt intensity. *Le merle noir* ("The blackbird") was written a decade later for a flute competition at the Paris Conservatoire and evokes the birdsong which was a lifelong preoccupation of this composer. This is another fine performance, and both works are well recorded.

Additional recommendations ...

Quatuor. **Tashi.** RCA Victor Gold Seal GD87835 — 47m ADD 4/89

Quatuor. **Eduard Brunner** (cl); **Trio Fontenay.** Teldec 9031-73239-2 — 44m DDD 12/92

Messiaen. Turangalîla-symphonie[a]. Quatuor pour la fin du temps[b]. [b]**Saschko Gawriloff** (vn); [b]**Siegfried Palm** (vc); [b]**Hans Deinzer** (cl); [b]**Aloys Kontarsky,** [a]**Peter Donohoe** (pfs); [a]**Tristan Murail** (ondes martenot); [a]**City of Birmingham Symphony Orchestra/Simon Rattle.** EMI CDS7 47463-8. Item marked [b] from Deutsche Harmonia Mundi 065 99711 (8/79).

② 2h 10m DDD/ADD 12/87

No longer a rarity in the concert-hall, Messiaen's epic hymn to life and love has been lucky on record too, with Rattle's performance staying just ahead of the pack. Messiaen's luxuriant scoring presents a challenge for the engineers as much as the players and the EMI team come through with flying colours. Tristan Murail's ondes martenot is carefully balanced here — evocative and velvety, neither reduced to inaudibility nor over-miked to produce an ear-rending screech. Peter Donohoe's piano obbligato is similarly integrated into the orchestral tapestry yet provides just the right kind of decorative intervention. Rattle is at his best in the work's more robust moments like the jazzy fifth movement and the many rhythmic passages which recall Stravinsky's *Le Sacre*. But those unfamiliar with Messiaen's extraordinary score should perhaps start with the central slow movement, the beautiful *Jardin du sommeil d'amour*, exquisitely done by the Birmingham team. Unlike at least one rival account, this *Turangalîla* spills on to a second CD, which leaves room for a distinguished *Quatuor pour la fin du temps* as a makeweight. The music-making here lacks the youthful spontaneity of the main work, but is notable for an unusually slow and sustained performance of the movement with cello solo.

Additional recommendation ...

Turangalîla-symphonie[a]. ***Lutoslawski.*** *Symphony No. 3*[b]. *Les espaces du sommeil*[c]. [bc]**Soloists;** [a]**Philharmonic Orchestra,** [bc]**Los Angeles Philharmonic Orchestra/Esa-Pekka Salonen.** CBS Masterworks CD42271 — ② 2h 5m DDD 6/87

Messiaen. Des canyons aux étoiles[a]. Oiseaux exotiques. Couleurs de la cité céleste. **Paul Crossley** (pf); [a]**Michael Thompson** (hn); [a]**James Holland** (xylorimba); [a]**David Johnson** (glockenspiel); **London Sinfonietta/Esa-Pekka Salonen.** CBS Masterworks CD44762. Recorded in 1988.

② 2h 2m DDD 2/89

Anyone who has ever responded to Messiaen's *Turangalîla* Symphony should certainly experience its counterpart. *Des canyons aux étoiles* is an awed contemplation of the marvels of the earth and the immensity of space, both seen as metaphors and manifestations of divinity. And yet of the two works it is *Des canyons* that most startlingly conjures up visual, physical images in sound. It is often ravishing music but also often hard-edged and dazzlingly bright. The two shorter works in the collection make interesting points of reference. In *Oiseaux exotiques* Messiaen delights in intensifying birdsong by transposing it to quite un-birdlike instruments: brass, percussion and the piano. And if you imagine that an exclusively religious meditation like *Couleurs de la cité céleste* will be hushed, prayerful and mysterious, watch out. It speaks of rainbows and of trumpets, abysses and measureless spaces, blinding light and jewel-like colour, and the work is scored accordingly for strident clarinets, xylophones, brass and metal percussion: it is one of the loudest scores he has ever written. Both these sound-tributaries flow into *Des canyons aux étoiles*, one of this century's masterpieces of instrumental writing, and it is good to have such a virtuoso performance of it. Paul Crossley produces prodigies of brilliant dexterity throughout all three works and he is worthily backed by Salonen and the Sinfonietta players. The recording is as clear as can be, but not without atmosphere.

Messiaen. Catalogue d'oiseaux — Books 1-3. **Peter Hill** (pf). Unicorn-Kanchana DKPCD9062.

Book 1 — Le Chocard des Alpes; Le Loriot; Le Merle bleu. Book 2 — Le Traquet Stapazin. Book 3 — Le Chouette Hulotte; L'Alouette Lulu.

59m DDD 5/88

Messiaen describes himself as 'ornithologist-musician', but he is a landscape-painter of genius as well. Though each piece in his catalogue bears the name of a single bird, each is really an evocation of a particular place (very often at a particular season and time of day), and most of the pieces contain the carefully transcribed and meticulously labelled songs of many birds. His imagery is naïve but the catalogue's huge range of sonority and gesture, its eloquently visionary intensity and its descriptive power make it one of the peaks of twentieth-century piano literature. It is so long (the complete catalogue plays for about two-and-three-quarters hours) and so difficult that the peak is seldom scaled. The work is fortunate to have found such an interpreter as Peter Hill. He is a complete master of its rhythmic complexity and its finger-breaking defiance of the pianistically possible, but he never loses sight of the fact that the cycle's main objective is to evoke a sense of place, of light and temperature even, and thereby to awake awe in the listener at the majesty and sublimity of creation.

NEW REVIEW

Messiaen. Vingt regards sur l'enfant-Jésus. **Peter Hill** (pf). Unicorn-Kanchana DKPCD9122/3. Recorded in 1991.

② 2h 22m DDD 9/92 

Messiaen's huge 1944 cycle of *20 Contemplations of the Child Jesus* is as much a challenge to the adventurous pianist of the late twentieth century as Liszt's *Transcendental Studies* were to previous generations (and continue to be). And Liszt is parent not only to the fearsome pyrotechnics of the piano writing but to the spiritual aspect of the music as well — compare Messiaen's "Contemplations by the Father" (No. 1) with Liszt's "Bénédiction de Dieu dans la Solitude" from his *Harmonies poétiques et religieuses*. Peter Hill is neither by technique or temperament a card-carrying Lisztian. But he does command an unusual range of subtle colours, and his agility and attention to detail cannot be faulted. So while his performances may not sweep the listener off his feet, they do present the music very much as a set of Contemplations. Similarly the distinctive tone-quality of the Fazioli instrument — a little bland, but capable of the most exquisite quiet shadings — is a perfectly valid alternative to the familiar Steinway sound. Recording quality, as throughout this Unicorn-Kanchana series, is exemplary in its clarity and unobtrusive radiance.

Additional recommendations ...
Vingt regards. **John Ogdon** (pf). Decca Enterprise 430 343-2DM — ② 2h 7m ADD 12/91
Vingt regards. Préludes. **Michel Béroff** (pf). EMI CMS7 69161-2 — ② 2h 26m AAD 3/92

Messiaen. La nativité du Seigneur[a]. Le banquet céleste[b]. **Jennifer Bate** (org). Unicorn-Kanchana DKPCD9005. Played on the organ of Beauvais Cathedral. Item marked [a] from DKP9005 (6/82), [b] DKP9018 (2/83).

1h 2m DDD 2/88 

La nativité du Seigneur comprises nine meditations on themes associated with the birth of the Lord. Messiaen's unique use of registration gives these pieces an extraordinarily wide range of colour and emotional potency and in Jennifer Bate's hands (and feet) it finds one of its most persuasive and capable advocates. Bate is much admired by the composer and is so far the only organist to have recorded his complete works for the instrument. *Le banquet céleste* was Messiaen's first published work for the organ and is a magical, very slow-moving meditation on a verse from St John's Gospel (VI, 56). The very faithful recording captures both the organ and the large acoustic of Beauvais Cathedral to marvellous effect.

Messiaen. Méditations sur le mystère de la Sainte Trinité. **Hans-Ola Ericsson** (org). BIS CD464. Played on the Grönlund organ of Luleå Cathedral, Sweden.

1h 18m DDD 3/92

At the time of his death Messiaen could point to tangible evidence of international stature as a composer of organ music. Several recordings of his organ works were either complete or in the throes of completion including this one from the 35-year-old Swedish organist, Hans-Ola Ericsson. Using the organ of Luleå Cathedral, an instrument which had to be modified in order to be more faithful to Messiaen's score, Ericsson shows a consistently strong command of both the technical and inspirational aspects of this unique body of organ music. Dating from 1969 the principal strands of Messiaen's diverse sources of musical inspiration coalesce in this remarkable work. Precisely annotated birdsong perches happily alongside Greek and Indian rhythms, but the central element throughout is plainsong; Messiaen may have been strongly influenced by exotic elements, but his profound faith and firm Catholic background remained his principal channel of expression. Ericsson's performance is clean, precise and flawless in its technical delivery although, perhaps, Messiaen's mystic vision might seem just a little too sharply focused.

Additional recommendation ...
Méditations. L'Ascension. Messe de la Pentecôte. **Jennifer Bate** (org). Unicorn-Kanchana DKPCD9024/5 — ② 2h 14m DDD 5/89

Messiaen. Livre du Saint Sacrement. **Jennifer Bate** (org). Unicorn-Kanchana DKPCD9067/8. Recorded on the organ of L'Eglise de la Sainte-Trinité, Paris.

② 2h 9m DDD 10/87 

The crowning achievement of Messiaen's unique cycle of music for the organ, the *Livre du Saint Sacrement* is also his largest work for the instrument. It is an intensely personal score based on the cornerstone of Messiaen's Catholic faith, the Blessed Sacrament, and spans a wide range of emotions from hushed, private communion to the truly apocalyptic. Jennifer Bate gave the British première of the work in 1986, following which Messiaen invited her to record it using his own organ at the Trinity Church in Paris. He was on hand throughout the sessions as he so often was. The recording is a model of clarity and it is hard to imagine the complex and often very subtle textures of this music being better conveyed. This is a magnificent achievement and should be heard by all who profess an interest in the music of our time.

Messiaen. ORGAN WORKS, Volume 1. **Hans-Ola Ericsson.** BIS CD409. Played on the Grönlund organ of Luleå Cathedral, Sweden.
L'Ascension. Le banquet céleste. Apparition de l'église éternelle. Diptyque.

lh 4m DDD

This disc contains Messiaen's first organ works written between 1928 and 1934, and they are among his most expressive and attractive pieces. The titles bear testament to his profound Christian faith and his visionary approach to music. His earliest composition, *Le banquet céleste* represents the Holy Communion with long drawn-out manual chords supporting a pedal line which represents the drops of Christ's blood. *Diptyque* is subtitled "essay on earthly life and eternal happiness" and after a bustling, rather sour opening the transformation to the celestial peace is quite unnerving. Most visionary of all, the *Apparition de l'eglise éternelle* portrays the coming into view among swirling clouds of the eternal church and then its subsequent fading away. Incessant hammer blows can be heard from the organ pedals. *L'Ascension* was the first of Messiaen's large-scale cycles for the instrument, and was itself a transcription of an orchestral work. Hans-Ola Ericsson has a richly romantic vein in his soul which he willingly bares here. He produces some lovely playing, especially in the slower pieces, and is supported by a mellow organ tone which is well captured in this fine recording.

Messiaen. Trois petites liturgies de la Présence Divine[a]. Cinq Rechants[b]. O sacrum convivium[c]. [a]**Cynthia Miller** (ondes martenot); [a]**Rolf Hind** (pf); [a]**London Sinfonietta** [a]**Chorus and** [bc]**Voices;** [a]**London Sinfonietta/Terry Edwards.** Virgin Classics VC7 59051-2. Notes, texts and translations included.

lh DDD II/91 9S

Even if, as Messiaen himself insisted, he was pre-eminently a 'theological' composer, dedicated to celebrating the divine presence in his music, that music often seems to embrace the sensuous as wholeheartedly as the spiritual. Indeed, one suspects that anyone listening to the *Trois petites liturgies de la Présence Divine* in ignorance of the content of the text would assume that the chanted phrases and opulent consonances of the all-female chorus, coupled with the swooning tonal quality of the ondes martenot, which is so prominent in the instrumental accompaniment, were hymning an essentially physical union after the manner of Stravinsky's *Les Noces*. In *Cinq Rechants* the secularity is more explicit, though hidden to a degree within Messiaen's own rather surrealistic texts. Here the musical focus is even more directly on the voices, now unaccompanied, and the panache and polish of the London Sinfonietta Chorus are remarkably well sustained. For the ultimate in refined control of a slow moving, quiet choral texture, the short motet *O sacrum convivium* is the ideal foil to the larger, more dramatic compositions, and the recordings are exemplary in ensuring that each vocal strand is clear without any artificial spotlighting.

Messiaen. La nativité du Seigneur[a]. La Transfiguration de Notre Seigneur Jésus-Christ[b]. [b]**Michael Sylvester** (ten); **Paul Aquino** (bar); [b]**Westminster Symphonic Choir;** [b]**Wallace Mann** (fl); [b]**Loren Kitt** (cl); [b]**János Starker** (vc); [b]**Frank Ames** (marimba); [b]**Ronald Barnett** (vibraphone); [b]**John Kane** (xylorimba); [b]**Yvonne Loriod** (pf); [a]**Simon Preston** (org); [b]**Washington National Symphony Orchestra/Antál Dorati.** Decca Enterprise 425 616-2DM2. Notes, text and translation included. Item marked [a] played on the organ of Westminister Abbey and from Argo ZRG5447 (3/66), [b] HEAD1-2 (5/74). Recorded 1965-72.

② 2h 30m ADD 9/90

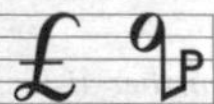

Considering that *La Transfiguration de Notre Seigneur Jésus-Christ* represents one of the most important landmarks in Messiaen's output, it is somewhat surprising that this pioneering account from the 1970s remains the only recording of this work — and even this remained out of circulation for some time. Its neglect undoubtedly has something to do with the work's monumental proportions and equally monumental forces required for performance (it requires an orchestra of over 100 players, a choir of 100 voices as well as a group of seven instrumental soloists). The texts centre around the Gospel narrative of the Transfiguration, interspersed with meditative movements drawn from various biblical and theological texts. Messiaen's fondness for formal symmetry dictates the structure; the work is divided into two groups of seven pieces, which in turn contain internal symmetries and reflections within each part. Stylistically it contains all the ingredients that we have come to associate with Messiaen's music — plainsong, Indian and Greek rhythms and birdsong, in this case a staggering 80 different species. At the time of its composition it represented the summation of Messiaen's art and achievement. Dorati's structural control over this immense work is little short of miraculous, and there are some deeply committed performances from the instrumental soloists too; particularly notable are Yvonne Loriod and János Starker. Not content with giving us just one bargain, Decca have also included as an added bonus Simon Preston's marvellous 1965 recording of *La nativité du Seigneur*. Both works are exceptionally well recorded.

Further listening ...

Cantéyodjayâ[a]. Visions de l'Amen[b]. **Yvonne Loriod, [b]Olivier Messiaen** (pfs). Adès 13233-2 (6/92).

Giacomo Meyerbeer

German 1791-1864

NEW REVIEW

Meyerbeer. SONGS.
Rossini. SONGS. **Thomas Hampson** (bar); **Geoffrey Parsons** (pf). EMI CDC7 54436-2. Texts and translations included. Recorded in 1991.
Meyerbeer: Komm!. Der Garten des Herzens. Lied des venezianischen Gondoliers. Hör' ich das Liedchen klingen. Die Rose, die Lilie, die Taube. Sie und ich. Menschenfeindlich. Chant des moissonneurs vendéens. La barque légère. La chanson de Maître Floh. Sicilienne. La poète mourant. ***Rossini:*** Au chevet d'un mourant. La lazzarone. La chanson du bébé. La gita in gondola. Il rimprovero. Ave Maria. L'ultimo ricordo.

lh l7m DDD 4/92

Neither Meyerbeer nor Rossini are composers whose reputations have yet become fully established beyond the opera house. Therefore this disc of solo songs is all the more welcome, proving that each was indisputably in his element as a sensitive miniaturist. Hopefully this recording will encourage singers to include the best of these works in recitals more frequently. The opportunities afforded to the singer for characterization (and especially humour) are well demonstrated among the Meyerbeer settings by *La chanson de Maître Floh* — a remarkably inventive creation from a flea's point of view — and among the Rossini by *La chanson du bébé*, in which the comedian composer really lets his hair down (the translation is reasonably polite, however). But the variety of the songs ranges from this wicked wit to deep tenderness and glorious melody. The settings are not only of poems in the composers' native tongues — the Meyerbeer songs are both of German and French poetry (including Heine's *Die Rose, die Lilie*, better known from the Schumann *Dichterliebe*), the Rossini of French and Italian. The performance from Thomas Hampson and Geoffrey Parsons is supremely polished and slick. Hampson's voice is smooth and lovely in the lyrical settings. In the more acerbic numbers he never falls into the trap of hamming too much, which, though fun on stage, might have proved difficult to live with on a recording; the character is nevertheless strong and direct throughout. Parsons accompanies with all his usual artistry and sensitivity.

Further listening ...

LES HUGUENOTS. **Soloists; Montpellier Opera Chorus and Orchestra/Cyril Diederich.** Erato 2292-45027-2 (9/90).

Nikolay Miaskovsky

Russian 1881-1950

Miaskovsky. Cello Concerto in C minor, Op. 66.
Shostakovich. The Limpid Stream, Op. 39 — Adagio.
Tchaikovsky. Variations on a Rococo Theme in A minor, Op. 33. Nocturne, Op. 19 No. 4.
Julian Lloyd Webber (vc); **London Symphony Orchestra/Maxim Shostakovich.**
Philips 434 106-2PH.

lh 3m DDD 5/92

Miaskovsky won a Stalin Prize for his Cello Concerto in 1946. It is a beautifully crafted and finely structured piece, scored for an orchestra that Brahms might have used. It shares a certain introspection with the Elgar Cello Concerto, though its autumnal mood is pervaded by an essentially Russian brooding and melancholy; qualities that are drawn out with sensitivity by Lloyd Webber and Shostakovich at slow tempos. Lloyd Webber lingers lovingly over the Tchaikovsky *Rococo* Variations as well, and opts for the original version which restores a cut variation and reverts to the composer's first thoughts on how the Variations should be ordered. His smooth, rich tone and sense of line are a joy to hear, though one could possibly wish for a little more virtuosic projection in, say, the final variation and coda. The *Limpid Stream* Adagio, too, is an original, and preferable version (and a world première recording) of a seven minute piece that turns up with bolstered orchestration in Shostakovich's Ballet Suite No. 2. Philips supply spacious sound, with a very full bass; and the soloist is placed within the orchestra, though slightly left of centre in the Miaskovsky. A valuable and rewarding disc.

Further listening ...

Violin Concerto in D minor, Op. 44[a]. Symphony No. 22 in B minor, Op. 54[b]. [a]**Grigori Feigin** (vn); [a]**USSR Radio Symphony Orchestra/Alexander Dmitriev;** [b]**USSR Symphony Orchestra/Yevgeni Svetlanov.** Olympia OCD134 (2/88).

Piano Sonatas — No. 1 in D minor, Op. 6; No. 2 in F sharp minor, Op. 13; No. 3 in C minor, Op. 19; No. 6 in A flat major, Op. 64 No. 2. **Murray McLachlan** (pf). Olympia OCD214 (12/88).

Piano Sonatas — No. 4 in C minor, Op. 27; No. 5 in B major, Op. 64 No. 1. Sonatine in E minor, Op. 57. Prelude, Op. 58. **Murray McLachlan** (pf). Olympia OCD217 (3/89).

Luis de Milán

Spanish c.1500-c.1561

Suggested listening ...

Libro de musica de vihuela de mano, "El maestro" — excerpts. **Hopkinson Smith** (vihuela). Astrée Auvidis E7748 (5/91).

Darius Milhaud

French 1892-1974

NEW REVIEW

Milhaud. Harp Concerto, Op. 323[a]. Le boeuf sur le toit, Op. 58. La création du monde, Op. 81. [a]**Frédérique Cambreling** (hp); **Lyon Opéra Orchestra/Kent Nagano.** Erato MusiFrance 2292-45820-2. Recorded in 1992.

59m DDD 2/93

Here is music to delight, with performances to match. Milhaud's ballet *Le boeuf sur le toit* was written for Jean Cocteau in 1919 and is set in an American bar during the Prohibition period (forbidding the manufacture and sale of alcohol) that was then just beginning. Some performances of this vivid French score lay the humour on too thick, but this one under Kent Nagano has more Gallic taste and sophistication and the playing is above all musicianly, while the more uproarious moments come over all the more effectively for this very reason. The playing by the accomplished Lyon orchestra is excellent, not least the wind players who have plenty to do. Written four years later, *La création du monde* was one of the first works by a European composer to take its inspiration from African folklore and the raw black jazz that Milhaud heard in New Orleans. This ballet on the creation myth ends with a mating dance and the whole work is powerfully and darkly sensual. Nagano and his French orchestra bring out all the character of this music and take the jazz fugue in Scene 1 more urgently than usual, to excellent effect. The Harp Concerto dates from 1953, three decades further on into Milhaud's career, and inevitably it has a brighter character, though here, too, there is some jazz influence, though of a far gentler kind. Frédérique Cambreling is a fine player and the radiant good spirits that emerge by the finale are typical of this uneven but nearly always fascinating composer who composed no less than 25 concertos in all.

Additional recommendation ...

Le boeuf sur le toit. La création du monde[b]*. Scaramouche, Op. 165b*[a]*. Saudades do Brasil, Op. 67. Suite provençale, Op. 152b.* **Marcelle Meyer** (pf); **Concerts Arts Orchestra; Champs Elysées Theatre Orchestra/Darius Milhaud**[a]. EMI Composers in Person [a]mono CDC7 54604-2 — ∴ lh 17m ADD 4/93 ▲

Key to Symbols

∴	② ②	lh 23m	DDD	6/88
Price	**Quantity/ availability**	**Timing**	**Mode**	**Review date**

NEW REVIEW

Milhaud. ORCHESTRAL WORKS. [a]**Jack Gibbons** (pf); **New London Orchestra/Ronald Corp.** Hyperion CDA66594. Recorded in 1992.

Le carnaval d'Aix, Op. 83*b*[a]. Le boeuf sur le toit, Op. 58. Le carnaval de Londres, Op. 172. L'Apothéose de Molière, Op. 286.

∴ lh 17m DDD 12/92

The centenary of Milhaud's birth prompted a number of valuable issues of his music, among which we would certainly include this disc. Not every work here is of equal quality, for it was in the very nature of the composer's uninhibited musical impulse that he occasionally gave us something less than gold along with the real thing. Thus *L'Apothéose de Molière* offers neo-classical pastiche of a kind that we may think was better done by Ravel and Stravinsky, not least because their scoring is transparent while Milhaud's tends to be thick, while Britten was defter at handling the *Beggar's Opera* themes that feature in the 26 short numbers making up *Le carnaval de Londres.* Even so, the occasional awkwardness of this music is part of Milhaud's likeable personality, and everything here is played with a panache and conviction that should dispel doubts. But this disc contains much that is vintage Milhaud, and the episodic and balletic fantasy, *Le carnaval d'Aix* is performed as stylishly and captivatingly as the composer surely intended. Ronald Corp and his fellow musicians are at home in this repertory and have been well served by an expert recording team headed by the admirable musician and scholar Christopher Palmer, who wrote the article on Milhaud in the *New Grove* and whose championship of this composer is based on a deep knowledge, judgement and insight. For many people who buy this disc, the plum in the programme will surely be *Le boeuf sur le toit,* with its Gallic verve and delightful impertinence (using two keys at once was one of Milhaud's specialities), but one suspects that they will go on to enjoy other things nearly as much. The recording is on the rich side, but that suits the music, and in general detail is clear.

NEW REVIEW

Milhaud. LITTLE SYMPHONIES AND LITTLE OPERAS. **Capella Cracoviensis/Karl Anton Rickenbacher.** Koch Schwann 311392. Recorded 1990-91.

Symphonies — No. 1, Op. 43, "Le printemps"; No. 2, Op. 49, "Pastorale"; No. 3, Op. 71, "Serenade"; No. 4, Op. 74, "Dixtuour"; No. 5, Op. 75; No. 6, Op. 79. L'enlèvement d'Europe. L'abandon d'Ariane. La deliverance de Thésée.

59m DDD 5/93

Six symphonies on one disc, and three operas as well? It sounds like madness, but here is the proof, thanks to Milhaud's enjoyment of writing 'large' works on a miniature scale. His "little symphonies" , as he called them, are really chamber works for various combinations; thus No. 4 is for ten strings and No. 5 for ten wind, while No. 6 is uniquely written for a wordless vocal quartet, oboe and cello. They date from the years around 1920 and reflect the young composer's work at that time as a diplomat in Brazil, not least his love of the teeming rain forest that has a parallel in his busy and often multi-keyed textures. The invention here is considerable, and so is the wit, and the performances by Rickenbacher and his Polish artists are both intelligent and affectionate, indeed a model of style. Milhaud's three *opéras-minutes* are based on Greek myth and one of them, *L'abandon d'Ariane,* has a story that has been used by other composers including Monteverdi and Richard Strauss. This is the longest of these miniature operas, but even so its five scenes only last around ten minutes. These stage pieces are somewhat tougher than the "little symphonies", but they are still rewarding and once again the performances have commitment and authority. The only drawback to this imaginative and well recorded issue is that the booklet provides no texts for the vocal pieces.

Ernest Moeran

British 1894-1950

Moeran. Symphony in G minor. Overture to a Masque. **Ulster Orchestra/Vernon Handley.** Chandos CHAN8577. Recorded in 1987.

56m DDD 4/88

It has been suggested that Moeran's Symphony is "among the five or six most original [symphonies] to appear between the two world wars". Original? The Anglo-Irish Moeran all too obviously knew and loved his Sibelius, and the stylistic imprints of just about every major British composer from and including Elgar onwards are here too. So why does the symphony exert such a powerful spell? The bracing *allegros* of the outer movement frame and punctuate some of the most sublime land and seascape imagery ever composed. Folk melody is richly and unashamedly deployed (never mind the derivations, what a supreme melodist Moeran was!) yielding legendary echoes, and a yearning lyricism. The orchestration throughout, even when undercurrents erupt into moments of violence, has lucidity of texture, a light-as-air quality. Perhaps the marvel of this symphony is that Moeran has fused his derivations into something completely personal. It is a disturbing work, disquiet lingering in the memory long after its final chords, which, though commanding, resolve nothing. Handley, the Ulster Orchestra and Chandos have done so much for music from these shores. Never have they made a better disc.

Additional recommendation ...

Symphony. ***Ireland.*** *Piano Concerto in E flat major*[a]. [a]**Eileen Joyce** (pf); **Hallé Orchestra/ Leslie Heward.** Dutton Laboratories mono CDAX8001 — lh 7m ADD 5/93 ▲

Further listening ...

Cello Concerto. Sinfonietta. **Bournemouth Sinfonietta/Norman Del Mar.** Chandos CHAN8456 (9/87).

Violin Concerto[a]. Lonely Waters. Whythorne's Shadow. [a]**Lydia Mordkovitch** (vn); **Ulster Orchestra/Vernon Handley.** Chandos CHAN8807 (9/90).

Johann Molter
German 1696-1765

Suggested listening ...

Trumpet Concertos in D major Nos. 1-3. Concertos for two trumpets Nos. 1, 2, 4 and 5. **Guy Touvron, Guy Messler** (tpts); **Württemberg Chamber Orchestra/Jörg Faerber.** RCA Victor Red Seal 09026 61200-2 (5/93).

Federico Mompou
Spanish 1893-1987

NEW REVIEW

Mompou. PIANO WORKS. [a]**Gonzalo Soriano,** [b]**Carmen Bravo** (pfs). EMI CDM7 64470-2. Recorded in 1958.

Canciones y danzas[a]. Suburbis[b]. Escenas de niños[b]. Fiestas lejanas[b]. Pessebres[b]. Paisajes[b].

1h 16m ADD 12/92 ▲

Federico Mompou sought, like Erik Satie before him, to achieve maximum musical effect through the simplest means: his piano music has something of Satie's freshness, but with an additional harmonic dimension beyond which resides very different worlds, modern jazz being one of them. This particular collection includes what are probably Mompou's finest solo piano works, his exceptionally beautiful *Canciones y danzas*, eight miniature tone-poems that invariably alternate sultry, even melancholy outer sections with livelier dance episodes. The fifth was made famous by the great Michelangeli, but the others are just as attractive. Gonzalo Soriano plays them with immense style and obvious affection; his touch is both warm and assured, and the 1958 recording captures it with considerable presence. The rest of the CD is taken up with miscellaneous works in recordings by Carmen Bravo who, again, shows obvious sympathy for the music, if not attaining quite the distinction of Soriano. With titles translated as "Slums", "Children scenes", "Faraway feasts" and "Nativity Scenes", the picture-postcard element is obvious, but Mompou was a natural impressionist and these little vignettes are well worth hearing. Bravo's instrument (it sounds like a fair-quality upright) isn't as well recorded as Soriano's, but remains perfectly adequate.

Jean-Joseph de Mondonville
French 1711-1772

Suggested listening ...

Violin Sonata in G major, Op. 3 No. 5. *Coupled with* ***Leclair.*** Violin Sonatas — A minor, Op. 5 No. 7; A major, Op. 9 No. 4. ***Guillemain.*** Violin Sonata in A major, Op. 1 No. 4. *Harpsichord Solos* — ***Duphly.*** La de Redemond. La du Buq. ***J-B. Forqueray.*** La Morangis ou La Plissay. **Simon Standage** (vn); **Lars Ulrik Mortensen** (hpd). Chandos CHAN0531 (6/93).

TITON ET L'AURORE. **Soloists; Françoise Herr Vocal Ensemble; Les Musiciens du Louvre/Marc Minkowski.** Erato MusiFrance 2292-45715-2 (10/92).

Michel Pignolet de Montéclair
French 1667-1737

NEW REVIEW

Montéclair. Jephté. **Jacques Bona** (bass-bar) Jephté; **Sophic Daneman** (sop) Iphise; **Claire Brua** (sop) Almaise, Vénus; **Nicolas Rivenq** (bass) Phinée, Apollon; **Mark Padmore** (ten)

Ammon; **Bernard Loonen** (ten) Abdon; **Jean-Claude Sarragosse** (bass) Abner; **Sylviane Pitour** (sop) Polhymnie, Israelite; **Sylvie Colas** (sop) Terpsichore; **Mary Saint-Palais** (sop) Woman of Maspha, Shepherdess, Truth. **François Bazola** (bass) Man of Maspha; **Patrick Foucher** (ten) A Hebrew; **Anne Pichard** (sop) Elise; **Les Arts Florissants Chorus and Orchestra/William Christie.** Harmonia Mundi HMC90 1424/5. Notes, text and translation included. Recorded in 1992.

② 2h 30m DDD 1/93

Growing acquaintance with the operas of Lully, Charpentier and Rameau has led to an increasing curiosity about the works of fellow compatriots: composers whom we have long suspected might have something more to say than we have been led to believe. It is clear from the opening bars of *Jephté* that Montéclair's dramatic instincts are embedded in the finest French traditions of opera. Writing at a time when the 'giants' were either dead or yet to influence the stage (Rameau's *Hippolyte et Aricie* was performed a year after *Jephté,* in 1733), Montéclair has been historically judged as an operatic footnote between Lully and Rameau. On the evidence of this fine *tragédie lyrique* opinions of French opera in the early eighteenth century need to be seriously revised. *Jephté* is a full-scale work which deservedly had a considerable following in its day. The plot is an entertaining conflation of a fiery, action-packed Old Testament story with a tale of romance running simultaneously. Jephté returns from exile to defend Israel from Ammon, vowing that he will not permit himself to see his wife or daughter until he has defeated him, and that he will sacrifice the first person he sees after conquering the enemy. Ammon is spared but falls in love with Iphisa, Jephté's daughter. Iphisa is the unfortunate soul whom her father first notices, her grief compounded by the guilt of loving Jephté's enemy. A thunderbolt removes Ammon permanently and Iphisa's life is spared. Far-fetched certainly, but like Handel, Montéclair has the resource to elevate standard emotions in a convincing and inventive manner. William Christie is as alert to the possibilities of colour as the composer himself, pacing the narrative with momentum and extreme sensitivity to nuance. All the singers, without exception, are well-groomed for the delicacies of the style and vocally they make a pleasantly contrasting team. The choir are not as exact as the outstanding instrumental group but they are exciting and always alive to theatricality. Many moments to savour then: try Iphisa's haunting and sensual scene at the beginning of Act 4 evoking memories of Charpentier's *Médée* (and Christie's recording too) or instrumental vignettes, such as the enchanting *Air* in Act 2, which anticipates Rameau. Every effort should be made to get acquainted with this spellbinding masterpiece.

Claudio Monteverdi

Italian 1567-1643

Monteverdi (ed Parrott/Keyte). Vespro della Beata Vergine. **Taverner Consort; Taverner Choir; Taverner Players/Andrew Parrott.** EMI CDS7 47078-8. From EX270129-3 (5/85).

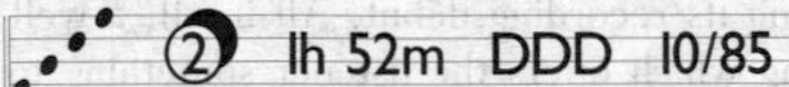

For a generation, performances have revelled in the colossal aspect of this work: huge choirs, generously-sized orchestras of modern instruments and lavish interpretations, all of which go hand in hand with a such a view of the music. Without question, splendour was part of Monteverdi's conception, but it was the splendour of ritual that he had in mind. It is this ritualistic aspect that Andrew Parrott restores in this special recording. Plainchant and instrumental sonatas mix authentically with Monteverdi's music; changes are made to the printed order of items to conform to the requirements of the *Vespers* service; several movements are transposed downwards to make them easier on the voice. If the result undermines the conventional view of the *Vespers* as an unbroken chain of glorious concert pieces, culminating in the huge, high-pitched Magnificat, then it does so to the advantage of Monteverdi's original intentions. Parrott brings together the cream of today's early-music specialists and both the playing (entirely on period instruments) and the singing are of the highest order. Few liturgical reconstructions on record have worked so well as this one does. It is a noble and moving experience.

Additional recommendations ...

Vespro della Beata Vergine. **Soloists; Collegium Vocale; Les Saqueboutiers de Toulouse; La Chapelle Royale Chorus and Orchestra/Philippe Herreweghe.** Harmonia Mundi HMC90 1247/8 — ② lh 30m DDD 2/88

Vespro della Beata Vergine. Dixit Dominus. Confitebor tibi, Domine a 3. Beatus vir a 5. Laudate pueri a 5. Laudate Dominum omnes gentes a 9. Ut queant laxis. Magnificat a 8. Laudate Dominum in sanctis eius. **G. Gabrieli.** *Two Toccatas*[a]. **Grandi.** *Hic est praecursor dilectus.* **Castello.** *Sonate concertante — No. 5 in C major; No. 9 in C major.* **Bazzino.** *Angelus Gabriel descendit. Plainsong chant fot the feast day of St John the Baptist.* [a]**Bob van Asperen** (org); **Soloists; Netherlands Chamber Choir; Chorus Viennensis/Hubert Dopf; Amsterdam Monteverdi Ensemble/Gustav Leonhart.** Philips 422 074-2PH — lh 11m DDD 4/89

Vespro della Beata Vergine. **Soloists; New London Consort/Philip Pickett.** L'Oiseau-Lyre 425 823-2OH2 — ② lh 32m DDD 3/91

NEW REVIEW

Monteverdi. BALLETS AND DRAMATIC MADRIGALS. **Red Byrd** (Catherine Pierard[a], Mary Seers, sops; Susan Bickley, mez; John Potter[b], Mark Padmore[c], tens; Richard Wistreich, bass). **The Parley of Instruments/Peter Holman.** Hyperion CDA66475. Texts and translations included. Recorded in 1991.

Altri canti d'amor. Il Combattimento di Tancredi e Clorinda[abc]. Volgendo il ciel. Il Ballo delle ingrate.

lh 9m DDD 9/92 

All four fine works on this disc come from Monteverdi's eighth and last book of madrigals, his *Madrigali guerrieri et amorosi* ("Madrigals of Love and War"), and are essentially dramatic in concept: the extraordinary Tasso setting *Il Combattimento di Tancredi e Clorinda* still makes its way into opera houses today; *Il Ballo delle ingrate* — a teasing, all-singing all-dancing admonishment to ladies in the audience too 'ungrateful' to yield to love — is unequivocally theatrical; while the other two pieces are certainly easy to envisage on stage. Accordingly, Red Byrd and The Parley of Instruments work hard to bring out the theatrical nature of the music, without ever being in danger of going over the top. *Il Combattimento* progresses effectively through its prancing horses and belligerent fight scenes to a moving conclusion, and in all the performances strongly marked contrasts are combined with determined efforts to suggest something of the sensuousness and passion of the Italian texts (these last two being most clearly demonstrated in the first track, *Altri canti d'amor*). The singing is characterized by intelligence of interpretation rather than sheer beauty of sound, with John Potter as the narrator of *Il Combattimento* and Susan Bickley and Richard Wistreich in *Il Ballo* making particularly notable contributions. Soundwise, there is much to enjoy in some happy choices of continuo instrumentation and the bright, fresh tones of the Parley of Instruments's band of renaissance (as opposed to baroque) violins, here making its recording début. All in all, a well considered, enjoyable, professionally executed recording which offers the listener something to think about.

Additional recommendations ...

Il combattimento. Il ballo delle ingrate. Tempro lacetra. Tirsi e Clori. **Tragicomedia/Stephen Stubbs.** Teldec Das Alte Werk 4509-90798-2 — lh 16m DDD

Il combattimento. Lamento d'Arianna. **Capriccio Stravagante/Skip Sempé.** Deutsche Harmonia Mundi 05472 77190-2 — lh DDD

NEW REVIEW

Monteverdi. Madrigali guerrieri et amorosi. **Taverner Consort and Players/Andrew Parrott.** EMI Reflexe CDC7 54333-2. Texts and translations included. Recorded in 1991.

Altri canti d'amor. Gira il nemico insidioso. Hor ch'el ciel e la terra. Altri canti di marte. Chi vol haver felice. Lamento della Ninfa. Su su su pastorelli vezzosi. Vago augelletto, che cantando vai. Volgendo il ciel.

57m DDD 12/92

This attractive selection also comes from Monteverdi's "Madrigals of Love and War" of 1638, offering familiar masterpieces such as the *Lamento della Ninfa, Hor ch'el ciel e la terra* and the symbolically complementary pair *Altri canti d'amor* and *Altri canti di marte*, alongside some of the lesser-known pieces from the set. They are performed with an ear more for the sensuous beauty of the music and its harmonies than its directly dramatic qualities, and it means that it is expansiveness rather than urgency (or for that matter overt virtuosity) that characterizes the singing here, helped by the ability of the Taverner Consort to blend in superb style. It's an approach that is slightly against the prevailing fashion in this repertoire, and it certainly brings affecting and occasionally spine-tingling results (though there are times when a little more excitement might have been welcome). Another way in which these performances ignore current lavish trends is in the continuo department, which is here kept to comparatively small dimensions, never using more than three players (indeed in one case being reduced — most effectively — to just a single guitar). All the instrumental playing is in fact extremely cultured and this, together with an excellent recording, contributes to a disc full of beauties; one that is liable to give little else but pleasure.

NEW REVIEW

Monteverdi. L'ORFEO. **John Mark Ainsley** (ten) Orfeo; **Julia Gooding** (sop) Euridice; **Catherine Bott** (sop) Music, Messenger, Proserpina; **Tessa Bonner** (sop) Nymph; **Christopher Robson** (alto) Hope, Shepherd II; **Andrew King** (ten) Shepherd I, Spirit I, Echo, Apollo; **Michael George** (bass) Plutone, Shepherd IV; **Simon Grant** (bass) Caronte, Spirit III; **Robert Evans** (bass) Shepherd III, Spirit II; **New London Consort/Philip Pickett.** L'Oiseau-Lyre 433 545-2OH2. Notes, text and translation included. Recorded in 1991.

② lh 48m DDD 2/93

However one defines the term 'opera' *Orfeo* is arguably the first work which capitalizes on the sort of features which today draw thousands to box offices around the world: a cohesive and well-paced drama and a stage for emotionally-charged vocalizing where contemporary fantasy can be expressed through a magical blend of artistic mediums and musical forms. Monteverdi left few clear instructions on how this, strictly speaking, "Favola in Musica" of 1607 should be performed. Pickett, however, is a master of visualizing and imagining the essence of the work he is investigating. Although he has assembled a number of singers with a natural dramatic disposition, it is Pickett's attention to detail and feeling for instrumental colour which tend to define Striggio's text rather more than an emotional response to affecting lines and individual virtuosity. As a result *Orfeo* is possibly a little under-explored in the traditional sense, especially when it comes to instinctive characterization, but equally Pickett's sense of considered effect is a persuasive alternative. John Mark Ainsley responds to this rationally-conceived approach with an accomplished sensitivity to tonal colour and a warmth which never detracts from the overall resonance of Pickett's ideal. This is by far the most acutely-observed recording of *Orfeo* at present but even Catherine Bott's magnificent contribution in the triple-casted prologue left me wanting to 'feel' more for these unfortunate lovers; self indulgence, no doubt.

Additional recommendation ...

Soloists; Munich Capella Antiqua; Vienna Concentus Musicus/Nikolaus Harnoncourt. Teldec Das Alte Werk 2292-42494-2 — ② lh 48m ADD 7/85

NEW REVIEW

Monteverdi. IL RITORNO D'ULISSE IN PATRIA. **Christoph Prégardien** (ten) Ulisse; **Bernarda Fink** (contr) Penelope; **Christina Högmann** (sop) Telemaco, Siren; **Martyn Hill** (ten) Eumete; **Jocelyne Taillon** (mez) Ericlea; **Dominique Visse** (alto) Pisandro, Human Fragility; **Mark Tucker** (ten) Anfinomo; **David Thomas** (bass) Antinoo; **Guy de Mey** (ten) Iro; **Faridah Subrata** (mez) Melanto; **Jörg Dürmüller** (ten) Eurimaco; **Lorraine Hunt**

(sop) Minerva, Fortune; **Michael Schopper** (bass) Nettuno, Time; **Olivier Lallouette** (bass) Giove; **Claron McFadden** (sop) Giunone; **Martina Bovet** (sop) Siren, Love; **Concerto Vocale/René Jacobs.** Harmonia Mundi HMC90 1427/9. Notes, text and translation included. Recorded in 1992.

③ 2h 59m DDD 3/93 9p 

The only surviving manuscript score of this major musical drama, preserved in Vienna, presents an incomplete version of three acts. For this recording, René Jacobs has, within the spirit of seventeeth-century music-making, added more music by Monteverdi and others to expand the work to a satisfying five-act structure suggested by some surviving librettos. He has also considerably expanded the scoring, very much enlivening the instrumental palette that Monteverdi would have had available to him for his original production in Vienna in 1641. For some, this will rule this recording out of consideration. However, the result, even though weakly argued for in the insert-notes, is so powerful and effective that it is to be hoped that most would not be prey to such reservations. The extensive cast, led by Christoph Prégardien in the title role, is excellently chosen, not only for vocal quality but also for a convincing awareness of Monteverdi's idiom. Without that, the performance could have seemed tame, and that is nowhere better exemplified than in Act 1, Scene 7 where Ulysses awakes, wondering where he is and what is to happen to him. Prégardien here manages to convey as much depth of feeling as a Pagliaccio yet stays clearly within the bounds of Monteverdi's expressive style. The result is a *tour de force*, one of the many within this production. The adept instrumental contribution certainly helps to maintain variety throughout the work, and an accompaniment suited to the sentiments expressed by the vocalists is always possible with these resources. Ultimately, this production is very much one for our time. It presents a practical solution to the problems of performing music of another age — this realization was, in fact, for a 1992 Montpellier production — and one that turns out to be inspired, moving and totally compelling.

Soloists; Vienna Concentus Musicus/Nikolaus Harnoncourt. Teldec Das Alte Werk 2292-42496-2 — ③ 3h 13m ADD

Further listening ...

Madrigals, Book 4. **Consort of Musicke/Anthony Rooley.** L'Oiseau-Lyre 414 148-2OH (2/87)

Madrigals, Book 5. **Consort of Musicke/Anthony Rooley.** L'Oiseau-Lyre 410 291-2OH (11/89).

Madrigals, Book 6. **Concerto Italiano Vocal Ensemble/Rinaldo Alessandrini.** Arcana A66 (7/93).

Motets — Dixit Dominus a 8; Confitebor tibi, Domine a 3; Beatus vir a 6; Laudate pueri a 5; Laudate Dominum a 5; Deus tuorum militum a 3; Magnificat a 8 (ed. Parrott); Jubilet tota civitas a 1; Salve Regina a 3. **Soloists; Taverner Consort, Choir and Players/Andrew Parrott.** EMI CDC7 47016-2 (3/85).

Motets — Gloria in excelsis Deo a 7; Chi vol che m'innamori; O ciechi il tanto affaticar; Confitebor tibi, Domine a 5; E questa vita un lampo; Beatus vir a 6; Adoramus te, Christe a 6; Confitebor tibi, Domine a 1; Laudate Dominum a 1. **Les Arts Florissants Vocal and Instrumental Ensemble/William Christie.** Harmonia Mundi HMC90 1250 (7/87).

Motets — Dixit Dominus. Laetanie della beata vergine. Laetatus sum. Lauda, Jerusalem. Laudate pueri, Dominum. Nisi Dominus. Beatus vir. Memento et omnis mansuetudinis. Adoramus te, Christe. Christe, adoramus te. Cantate Domino. Domine, ne in furore. **Trinity College Choir, Cambridge/Richard Marlow.** Conifer CDCF212 (11/92).

Mass of Thanksgiving. Ab aeterno ordinata sum. Salve Regina a 2. *Coupled with* **Fantini.** Intrada, Toccata e Sonata Imperiale I. Sonata Imperiale II e Intrada. ***Scarani.*** Sonata a 3.

Rovetta. Credo a 7 (Et in spiritum sanctum). ***Usper.*** Sonata a 8. ***Marini.*** Canzon quarta. Plainsong chant for the Feast of S. Maria della salute. **Soloists; Taverner Consort, Choir and Players/Andrew Parrott.** EMI Reflexe CDS7 49876-2 (11/89).

L'INCORONAZIONE DI POPPEA. **Soloists; Vienna Concentus Musicus/Nikolaus Harnoncourt.** Teldec Das Alte Werk 2292-42547-2 (9/86).

Cristóbal de Morales

Spanish c.1500-1553

NEW REVIEW

Morales. Missa Pro defunctis a 5. Officium defunctorum a 5. **La Capella Reial de Catalunya; Hespèrion XX/Jordi Savall.** Astrée Auvidis E8765. Texts and translations included.

lh 12m DDD

Two little known choral masterpieces from mid-sixteenth century Spain are presented here by Jordi Savall in one of the more successful releases in his *Siglo de Oro* series. Cristóbal de Morales was famous in his day (and for a long time after, since much of his prodigious, almost exclusively sacred output was published widely) and the two groups of works on this recording are some of his more important pieces. Both the Requiem Mass and the six polyphonic motets forming the *Officium defunctorum* (intended for use in the Liturgy of the Dead) were probably performed at services for the deceased Holy Roman Emperor Charles V and his wife, Isabel of Portugal. Savall uses an all-male choir discreetly matched by an ensemble of mainly lower-voiced stringed instruments (plus sackbuts, a cornet and a bassoon) and he captures perfectly the restraint and solemnity of the music. Morales's personal musical style is rich and austere, dignified but impassioned, characteristics which are also found in the music of the later and more influential Iberian composer, Victoria.

Robert Moran

American 1937-

NEW REVIEW

Moran. DESERT OF ROSES — Arias, Interludes and Inventions (Movement 1; I can go? I can go to my father?; Movement 3; Look into my eyes; Movement 5[a]). Open Veins[b]. Ten Miles high over Albania[c]. [a]**Jayne West** (sop); [b]**Alexander Balanescu** (vn); [c]**Mario Falco** (hp); [ab]**Piano Circus/**[a]**Craig Smith;** [bc]**Robert Moran.** Argo 436 128-2ZH. Text included. Recorded in 1991.

lh 6m DDD 8/92

While this unclassifiable but irresistible disc has been described as New Age Eric Coates, it is probably more helpful to locate it in the crossover Eden somewhere between the minimalism of Steve Reich and the TV music of Geoffrey Burgon! An American musician of eccentric inclinations, Moran won fame as stager of 1960s performance art 'happenings' à la Yoko Ono. And yet the Stravinskian clarity and precision of his scoring here reminds us that he also studied with Darius Milhaud. True, the musical content is not exactly hard-hitting. To enjoy *Open Veins*, scored for eight harps (or one harp multi-tracked seven times as on this occasion), you really do need a sweet tooth. And *Ten Miles high* ... is no more than a mildly diverting jam session. The main work, an extended suite from the Sondheimish opera which lends Argo's collection its name, is another matter. Moran gives a post-modern, post-pop gloss on that curious vein of American innocence we find in the music of Samuel Barber and the films of Walt Disney. "Disgracefully pretty" as it all is (the composer's own words), there is none the less a sense of pace and harmonic tension here not always detectable in the more familiar music of, say, Philip Glass. The playing is generally excellent and the brilliant, closely-focused sound projects it to great advantage.

Thomas Morley

British 1557-1602

Morley. JOYNE HANDS. **Red Byrd; Musicians of Swanne Alley/Paul O'Dette; Lyle Nordstrom.** Virgin Classics Veritas VC7 59032-2. Texts included.

Morley: Joyne hands. A lieta vita. O griefe, even on the bud. Our bonny bootes could toote it. Pavan (arr. Cutting). Galliard. Sleepe slumbr'ring eyes. Thirsis and Milla Sacred End Pavin (arr. Rosseter). Galliard to Sacred End (arr. Baxter). Pavin and Galliard. A painted tale. Faire in a morne. Sayd I that Amarillis. Now is the gentle season. Harke; Alleluia cheerely. Hard by a cristall fountaine. Now is the month of maying (arr. Rosseter). ***P. Philips:*** Philips Paven and Galliard. *Conversi:* Sola soletta (arr.? Morley). ***Strogers:*** In Nomine Pavin and Galliard. ***Anonymous:*** O mistresse mine (vocal and consort versions). La Coranto (all arr.? Morley). Monsieurs Almaine. My Lord of Oxenfordes March.

1h 12m DDD 1/92 

Thomas Morley was a central figure in English renaissance music, a composer of the first rank, an arranger of his own and other people's music, and a publisher who greatly helped to spread the gospel of Italian style on these shores. His major contribution to instrumental music was his two books (1599 and 1611) of "Lessons" for that most English of bands, the 'broken consort', an ingenious and flexible combination of blown, bowed and plucked instruments (here the Musicians of Swanne Alley) which grew out of the Elizabethan theatre. The music of the "Lessons" was of both instrumental and vocal origin and included only one arrangement known to be by Morley, that which gives this album its title. His books of vocal music (again mostly by others) were numerous and it is in these that his helping hand to Italian music was strongest. The traffic was two-way: Morley's music, including some of the lute solos in this recording, was also arranged and published by others. When the Musicians of Swanne Alley play in concert you can see that they are enjoying themselves; on record you can *hear* it just as easily, and this recording is no exception. Very little of the music is to be had in any other recording, and hearing it you may well wonder why. These magnificent performances are a worthy tribute to the multi-faceted work of a man of no small importance.

Jerome Moross

American 1913-1983

Suggested listening ...

The Big Country — *film score.* **Philharmonia Orchestra/Tony Bremner.** Silva Screen FILMCD030 (5/89).

Moritz Moszkowski

German 1854-1925

Moszkowski. Piano Concerto in E major, Op. 59.
Paderewski. Piano Concerto in A minor, Op. 17. **Piers Lane** (pf); **BBC Scottish Symphony Orchestra/Jerzy Maksymiuk.** Hyperion CDA66452. Recorded in 1991.

1h 12m DDD 2/92 

How the music-loving public suffer at the hands and whims of the musical literati. Twenty years ago the concertos on this disc were enjoying something of a revival thanks to the sterling efforts of such pianists as Earl Wild and Michael Ponti and enterprising record companies like Vox, Candide and Genesis. Then came the 1980s when once again such works found themselves very much out of favour. However, with the launch of a new series from Hyperion entitled "The Romantic Piano Concerto" we now seem set to enjoy an exciting new revival. These concertos may not be masterpieces in the accepted sense (though they're certainly masterpieces of their genre) but do all pieces of music have to be earth-shatteringly great to be appreciated? Listening to these wonderfully exhilarating and tuneful works the answer has to be a resounding no! Both the Moszkowski and Paderewski concertos take the listener back to a time when pianist-composers weren't afraid of wearing their hearts on their sleeves, but let no one try to convince you that these are empty vessels. The slow movements of both are beautifully constructed and contain some of the most gorgeous melodies to be encountered anywhere and the outer movements are full of sunny optimism and brilliance. To add icing to an already very tasty cake Piers Lane gives performances of exceptional poetry and virtuosity and the recording is first class. Strongly recommended.

Jean-Joseph Mouret

French 1682-1738

NEW REVIEW

Mouret. LES AMOURS DE RAGONDE. **Michel Verschaeve** (ten) Ragonde; **Jean-Paul Fouchécourt** (ten) Colin; **Sophie Marin-Degor** (sop) Colette; **Jean-Louis Bindi** (bass) Lucas; **Noémi Rime** (sop) Mathurine; **Gilles Ragon** (ten) Thibault; **Jean-Louis Serre** (bar) Blaise; **Les Musiciens du Louvre/Marc Minkowski.** Erato MusiFrance 2292-45823-2. Notes, text and translation included. Recorded in 1991.

56m DDD 12/92 

Jean-Joseph Mouret was one of a handful of notably gifted but, until comparatively recently, under-rated composers who bridged the period of French stage music between Lully and Rameau. *Les Amours de Ragonde* is a *comédie-lyrique* and perhaps the earliest of its kind, though it must be acknowledged that the version performed here is a revision of Mouret's original, now lost, undertaken for the Paris Opéra in 1742, four years after the composer's death. The story is slight but entertaining and it afforded Mouret an opportunity for witty caricature. Ragonde is an elderly, toothless widow who has set her sights on Colin, a young village lad. Colin prefers her daughter Colette, but Ragonde will have none of that nonsense. Either he marries Ragonde herself or else he will be haunted by the frightening nocturnal demons whom he has already briefly encountered. Ragonde gets her way and a double wedding of mother and daughter (Colette pairs off with Lucas, another village boy) is celebrated with an elaborate divertissement and a very rowdy charivaria. Mouret's music is delightful — not for nothing was he dubbed "musicien des graces" — and it is performed with humour and affection by all concerned. The tenor Michel Verschaeve gives a deliciously mischievous performance as Ragonde and the little drama is tautly directed by Marc Minkowski. Recorded sound is first-rate.

Leopold Mozart

German/Austrian 1719-1787

Suggested listening ...

Trumpet Concerto in D major. *Coupled with* ***Hummel.*** Trumpet Concerto in E major. ***M. Haydn.*** Concertos for Trumpet and Strings — C major; D major. ***J. Haydn.*** Trumpet Concerto in E flat major, HobVII*e*/1. **Reinhold Friedrich** (tpt); **Academy of St Martin in the Fields/Sir Neville Marriner.** Capriccio 10 436 (6/93).

Wolfgang Amadeus Mozart

Austrian 1756-1791

NEW REVIEW

Mozart. Sinfonia concertante in E flat major, K364/320*d*[a]. Concertone in C major for two violins, oboe, cello and orchestra, K190/186*E*[b]. **Cho-Liang Lin** (vn); **Jaime Laredo**

([b]vn/[a]va); **English Chamber Orchestra/Raymond Leppard.** Sony Classical SK47693. Recorded in 1991.

lh DDD 6/92

Cho-Liang Lin's Mozart concerto cycle has been quite the best to have appeared in the last few years: he possesses great beauty of tone and purity of style. His accounts of the *Sinfonia concertante* in E flat and the *Concertone* in C, with Jaime Laredo and the English Chamber Orchestra under Raymond Leppard are performances of great quality. They possess all the spontaneity and warmth of live music-making with the perfection of the studio. Both Lin and Laredo bring to this music an aristocratic finesse and a magic that put the listener wholly under their spell. The slow movement of the *Sinfonia concertante* shows a marvellous interplay between these distinguished artists and has both depth and eloquence. Excellent, well-balanced recordings too.

Additional recommendations ...

As Sony. **Itzhak Perlman** (vn); **Pinchas Zukerman** (va, vn); **Chaim Jouval** (ob); **Marcel Bergman** (vc); **Israel Philharmonic Orchestra/Zubin Mehta.** DG 415 486-2GH — lh DDD 12/85

Sinfonias concertante — K364/320d; E flat major, KAnh9/C14.01/297b[a]. **Todd Phillips** (vn); **Maureen Gallagher** (va); [a]**Stephen Taylor** (ob); [a]**David Singer** (cl); [a]**Steven Dibner** (bn); [a]**William Purvis** (hn); **Orpheus Chamber Orchestra.** DG 429 784-2GH — lh 3m DDD 4/91

Further recommendations for the Sinfonia concertante appear elsewhere in this section.

Mozart. Clarinet Concerto in A major, K622[a]. Clarinet Quintet in A major, K581[b]. **Thea King** (basset cl); [b]**Gabrieli String Quartet** (Kenneth Sillito, Brendan O'Reilly, vns; Ian Jewel, va; Keith Harvey, vc); [a]**English Chamber Orchestra/Jeffrey Tate.** Hyperion CDA66199. From A66199 (3/86).

lh 4m DDD 9/86 

The two works on this disc are representative of Mozart's clarinet writing at its most inspired; however, the instrument for which they were written differed in several respects from the modern clarinet, the most important being its extended bass range. Modern editions of both the Concerto and the Quintet have adjusted the solo part to suit today's clarinets, but Thea King reverts as far as possible to the original texts, and her playing is both sensitive and intelligent. Jeffrey Tate and the ECO accompany with subtlety and discretion in the Concerto, and the Gabrielli Quartet achieve a fine sense of rapport with King in the Quintet. Both recordings are clear and naturally balanced, with just enough distance between soloist and listener.

Additional recommendations ...

Clarinet Concerto[a]. *Flute and Harp Concerto in C major, K299/297c*[b]. [a]**Emma Johnson** (cl); [b]**William Bennett** (fl); [b]**Osian Ellis** (hp); **English Chamber Orchestra/Raymond Leppard.** ASV CDDCA532 — 54m DDD

Clarinet Concerto. Oboe Concerto in C major, K314/285. **Antony Pay** (basset cl); **Michael Piguet** (ob); **Academy of Ancient Music/Christopher Hogwood** (fp, hpd). L'Oiseau-Lyre 414 339-2OH — 47m DDD 5/86

Clarinet Concerto. Oboe Concerto. **Jack Brymer** (cl); **Neil Black** (ob); **Academy of St Martin in the Fields/Sir Neville Marriner.** Philips 416 483-2PH — 50m ADD 10/88

Clarinet Quintet. Oboe Quartet in F major, K370/368b. Horn Quintet in E flat major, K407/386c. **Antony Pay** (basset cl); **Stephen Hammer** (ob); **Michael Thompson** (hn); **Academy of Ancient of Music Chamber Ensemble.** L'Oiseau-Lyre Florilegium 421 429-2OH — lh 14m DDD 12/88

Clarinet Quintet. Oboe Quartet. Horn Quintet. **Anthony Pay** (cl); **Neil Black** (ob); **Timothy Brown** (hn); **Academy of St Martin in the Fields Chamber Ensemble.** Philips Musica da Camera 422 833-2PC — lh 9m ADD 10/89

Clarinet Concerto. Bassoon Concerto in B flat major, K191/186e. Sonata in B flat major for bassoon and cello, K292. **Karl Leister** (cl); **Klaus Thunemann** (bn); **Stephen Orton** (vc);

Academy of St Martin in the Fields/Sir Neville Marriner. Philips 422 390-2PH — 55m DDD 3/90

Clarinet Concerto[a]. *Oboe Concerto*[b]. *Bassoon Concerto*[d]. [a]**Jacques Lancelot** (cl); [b]**Pierre Pierlot** (ob); [c]**Paul Hongne** (bn); [a]**English Chamber Orchestra/Jean-Pierre Rampal;** [b]**Jean-François Paillard Chamber Orchestra/Jean-François Paillard;** [c]**Bamberg Symphony Orchestra/Theodore Guschlbauer.** Erato Bonsai 2292-45937-2 — lh 7m ADD 6/93

Clarinet Concerto[a]. ***Spohr.*** *Clarinet Concerto No. 1 in C minor, Op. 26*[b]. ***Weber.*** *Clarinet Concerto No. 2 in E flat major, J118*[b]. **Gervase de Peyer** (cl); **London Symphony Orchestra/**[a]**Peter Maag,** [b] **Sir Colin Davis.** Decca Serenata 433 727-2DM — lh 12m ADD 7/93

Mozart. Flute Concerto No. 1 in G major, K313/285*c*. Andante in C major, K315/285*e*. Flute and Harp Concerto in C major, K299/297*c*[a]. **Susan Palma** (fl); [a]**Nancy Allen** (hp); **Orpheus Chamber Orchestra.** DG 427 677-2GH. Recorded in 1988.

58m DDD 3/90

Mozart described the flute as “an instrument I cannot bear” in 1778 before composing his G major Flute Concerto for the Dutch amateur Ferdinand DeJean. However, he was incapable of writing poor music and this is a work of much charm and some depth that comes up with admirable freshness in this performance by Susan Palma. She is a remarkably gifted player and a member of the no less skilled Orpheus Chamber Orchestra, a conductorless ensemble of 24 players who shape the music with unfailing skill and unanimity so that everything is alert, lithe and yet sensitive. Palma’s tone is liquid and bright, and she offers fine tonal nuances too, while her cadenzas are no less well imagined. The Concerto for Flute and Harp, written for another amateur player (the Count de Guines) to play with his harpist daughter, combines these two beautiful instruments to celestial effect; again the soloists are highly skilled and beyond that, they are perfectly matched. Palma is as delightful as in the other work and the spacious *Andante* in C major that separates the two concertos, while Nancy Allen makes an exquisite sound and also articulates more clearly than many other harpists in this work. The balance between the soloists and the orchestra is natural and the recording from New York’s State University has a very pleasing sound.

Additional recommendations ...

As DG. Bassoon Concerto in B flat major, K191/186a. **Soloists; Academy of Ancient Music/Christopher Hogwood.** L’Oiseau-Lyre 417 622-2OH — lh 14m DDD 5/88

Flute Concertos — No. 1; No. 2 in D major, K314/285d. Flute and Harp Concerto. Andante. Rondo in D major for flute and orchestra, K373 (arr. Galway). Divertimento in D major, K334 — Menuetto (arr. Galway). Serenade in G major, K525, “Eine kleine Nachtmusik”. **Marisa Robles** (hp); **Chamber Orchestra of Europe/James Galway** (fl). RCA Red Seal RD87861 — ② lh 49m DDD 7/89

As DG. **Irena Grafenauer** (fl); **Maria Graf** (hp); **Academy of St Martin in the Fields/Sir Neville Marriner.** Philips 422 339-2PH — 58m DDD 7/89

NEW REVIEW

Mozart. HORN CONCERTOS. **Barry Tuckwell** (hn); **Academy of St Martin in the Fields/Sir Neville Marriner.** EMI Studio CDM7 69569-2. From ASD2780 (4/72).

No. 1 in D major, K412/386*b*; No. 2 in E flat major, K417; No. 3 in E flat major, K447; No. 4 in E flat major K495. Fragment in E flat major, K494*a*. Rondo in E flat major, K371 (cpted Tuckwell).

lh ADD 1/89 

It is almost impossible to suggest a clear choice for Mozart’s horn concertos as this and all of those listed below are guaranteed to give great pleasure and satisfaction. Barry Tuckwell’s name appears no less than eight times in this repertoire in the current *Classical Catalogue* (No. 2, 1993). This one has characteristically elegant and graceful playing from Tuckwell, Sir Neville and his ASMF. The Romanze of No. 3 and the *Andante* of No. 4 both have a glorious lyrical flow, Tuckwell’s timbre is rich and yet the rondos are delectably pointed and spontaneous. The

Academy strings sound very fresh and dance beautifully in the *allegros.* This re-issue also has the advantage of including the *Concerto Rondo,* K371 and the Fragment, K494*a*, which ends in mid-air, as it were. Strongly recommended on all counts.

Additional recommendations ...
Horn Concertos. **English Chamber Orchestra/Barry Tuckwell** (hn). Decca 410 284-2DH — 52m DDD 9/85
Horn Concertos. **Dennis Brain** (hn); **Philharmonia Orchestra/Herbert von Karajan.** EMI Références mono CDH7 61013-2 — 55m ADD 2/88 £ ▲
Horn Concertos. Fragment. **Anthony Halstead** (natural hn); **Hanover Band/Roy Goodman.** Nimbus NI5104 — 55m DDD 8/88
Horn Concertos. **Alan Civil** (hn); **Royal Philharmonic Orchestra/Rudolf Kempe.** EMI Eminence CD-EMX2004 — 59m ADD 1/89
Horn Concertos. Rondos — E flat major, K371 (cptd Greer); D major, K514 (cptd Jeurissen). **Lowell Greer** (natural hn); **Philharmonia Baroque Orchestra/Nicholas McGegan.** Harmonia Mundi HMU90 7012 — 1h 2m AAD 3/89

Mozart. Oboe Concerto in C major, K314/285.
R. Strauss. Oboe Concerto in D major. **Douglas Boyd** (ob); **Chamber Orchestra of Europe/Paavo Berglund.** ASV CDCOE808. From COE808 (7/87).

44m DDD 11/87

This coupling links two of the most delightful oboe concertos ever written. Mozart's sprightly and buoyant work invests the instrument with a chirpy, bird-like fleetness encouraging the interplay of lively rhythm and elegant poise. Boyd's reading of this evergreen work captures its freshness and spontaneity beautifully. If the Mozart portrays the sprightly side of the instrument's make-up the Strauss illustrates its languorous ease and tonal voluptuousness. Again Boyd allows himself the freedom and breadth he needs for his glowing interpretation; he handles the arching melodies of the opening movement and the witty staccato of the last with equal skill. Nicely recorded.

Additional recommendations ...
Oboe Concerto. Clarinet Concerto in A major, K622. **Michael Piguet** (ob); **Antony Pay** (basset cl); **Academy of Ancient Music/Christopher Hogwood** (fp, hpd). L'Oiseau-Lyre 414 339-2OH — DDD 5/86
Oboe Concerto. Clarinet Concerto. **Neil Black** (ob); **Jack Brymer** (cl); **Academy of St Martin in the Fields/Sir Neville Marriner.** Philips 416 483-2PH — 50m ADD 10/88

Mozart. PIANO CONCERTOS. **English Chamber Orchestra/Daniel Barenboim** (pf). EMI CZS7 62825-2. Recorded 1967-74.
No. 1 in F major, K37; No. 2 in B flat major, K39; No. 3 in D major, K40; No. 4 in G major, K41 (all from SLS5031, 1/76); No. 5 in D major, K175 (ASD2484, 11/69); No. 6 in B flat major, K238 (ASD3032, 11/74); No. 8 in C major, K246 (ASD3033, 1/75); No. 9 in E flat major, K271, "Jeunehomme" (ASD2484); No. 11 in F major, K413/387*a* (ASD2999, 9/74); No. 12 in A major, K414/385*p* (ASD2956, 2/74); No. 13 in C major, K415/387*b* (ASD2357, 4/68); No. 14 in E flat major, K449; No. 15 in B flat major, K450 (both ASD2434, 11/68); No. 16 in D major, K451 (ASD2999); No. 17 in G major, K453 (ASD2357); No. 18 in B flat major, K456 (ASD2887, 7/73); No. 19 in F major, K459 (ASD2956); No. 20 in D minor, K466 (ASD2318, 7/67); No. 21 in C major, K467 (ASD2465, 2/69); No. 22 in E flat major, K482 (ASD2838, 11/72); No. 23 in A major, K488 (ASD2318); No. 24 in C minor, K491 (ASD2887); No. 25 in C major, K503 (ASD3033); No. 26 in D major, K537, "Coronation" (ASD3032); No. 27 in B flat major, K595 (ASD2465). Rondo in D major, K382 (ASD2838).

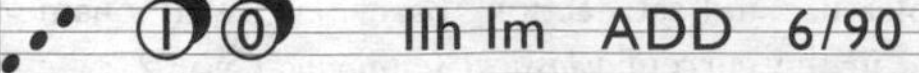

Here are all 27 of Mozart's piano concertos plus the D major Rondo, K382, on ten medium-priced discs giving a total of 11 hours' listening. The skills of Daniel Barenboim and the English Chamber Orchestra in this repertory are well proven, and his account of these concertos, directed from the keyboard, is spacious and satisfying. This artist has always been a master of clean exposition and structure, and from the early Concertos to the late masterpieces such as Nos. 21, 24 and 27 he is a sure guide with a full awareness of Mozart's inventive and expressive range. Sometimes one may feel that he allows a rather romantic self-indulgence to creep in, and in the more dramatic music (e.g. in the D minor and C minor concertos) he may be thought to be too powerfully Beethovenian and, incidentally, he uses a Beethoven cadenza, as arranged by Edwin Fischer, in the first movement of the first of these. Ideally, too, we might prefer a smaller body of strings than was used in these performances from the late 1960s and early 1970s. But these are only small reservations, given the high overall standard, and certainly this is a major achievement. The recordings sound well, with mellow piano tone and good balance.

Additional recommendations ...

Nos. 1-27. Rondos — D major, K382; A major, K386. Three Concertos after J.C. Bach, K107 — D major; G major; E flat major. **Schröter**. *Concerto in C major, Op. 3 No. 3.* **English Chamber Orchestra/Murray Perahia** (pf). CBS Masterworks CD42055 — ⑬ ADD 4/86

Nos. 5-27. Double Piano Concertos — F major, K242, "Lodron"; E flat major, K365/316a. Rondos — D major, K382; A major, K386. **Alfred Brendel** (pf); **Academy of St Martin in the Fields/Sir Neville Marriner.** Philips 412 856-2PH10 — ⑩ ADD/DDD 4/86

Nos. 1-27. **Salzburg Mozarteum Orchestra/Géza Anda** (pf). DG 429 001-2GX10 — ⑩ 10h 10m ADD 6/90

Nos. 1-27. Concerto in F major for three pianos, K242. Double Piano Concerto in E flat major, K365/316a. **Philharmonia Orchestra/Vladimir Ashkenazy** (pf). Decca430 641-2DM12 — ⑫ 11h 48m ADD/DDD 6/90

Nos. 1-27. Concertos after J.C. Bach, K107 — D major; G major; E flat major. Double Piano Concertos — F major, K242, "Lodron"; E flat major, K365/316a. Concerto in F major for three pianos, K242, "Lodron". Rondos — D major, K382; A major, K386. **Alfred Brendel, Imogen Cooper, Katia** and **Marielle Labèque** (pfs); **Ingrid Haebler** (fp); **Academy of St Martin in the Fields/Sir Neville Marriner; Berlin Philharmonic Orchestra/Semyon Bychkov** (pf); **Vienna Capella Academica/Eduard Melkus; Amsterdam Baroque Orchestra/Ton Koopman** (hpd). Philips Mozart Edition 422 507-2PME12 — ⑫ 12h 35m ADD/DDD 5/91

Nos. 5 and 8. Rondos — D major, K382; A major, K386. **Malcolm Bilson** (fp); **English Baroque Soloists/John Eliot Gardiner.** Archiv Produktion 415 990 2AH 1h DDD 6/87

Nos. 11, 12 and 14. **English Chamber Orchestra/Murray Perahia** (pf). CBS Masterworks CD42243 (*see review further on*) — 1h 10m DDD 9/87

Nos. 12 and 14. **Louis Lortie** (pf); **I Musici de Monteal/Yuli Turovsky.** Chandos CHAN8455 — 48m DDD 1/87

Nos. 12 and 15. **Mozartian Players/Steven Lubin** (fp). Arabesque Z6552 — 48m DDD 3/87

Nos. 16 and 17. **Malcolm Bilson** (fp); **English Baroque Soloists; John Eliot Gardiner.** Archiv Produktion 415 525-2AH — 54m DDD 2/87

Nos. 18 and 19. **Malcolm Bilson** (fp); **English Baroque Soloists; John Eliot Gardiner.** Archiv Produktion 415 111-2AH — DDD 6/86

NEW REVIEW

Mozart. Piano Concertos — No. 9 in E flat major, K271; No. 17 in G major, K453. **London Mozart Players/Howard Shelley** (pf). Chandos CHAN9068. Recorded in 1991.

1h 1m DDD 11/92

Howard Shelley has already proved himself to be an excellent performer in the Mozart piano concertos, and the present disc only reinforces that view. The performance of the E flat major Concerto, in which the piano unconventionally enters very near the start instead of waiting throughout a lengthy orchestral exposition, is warm, gentle and vigorous as the music requires. As for the partnership between the soloist and the orchestra, it is ideal: Shelley has often worked as a soloist-cum-director with this fine body of players, and their rapport is evident. Perhaps most important of all in Mozart's music, the pianist achieves distinction without mannerism; the music sounds above all natural and unforced, not least in the beautiful central *Andantino* in C minor and the buoyant finale, which is unconventional in incorporating a Watteau-like rococo minuet. The G major Concerto also demonstrates the skill and sensitivity of these artists. Chandos's recording also deserves praise: it was made in a London church and manages to be both clear and atmospheric, with the piano tone (a modern piano but played in scale with the music) perfectly caught with a good overall balance. Indeed, the disc is so pleasing as a whole that one is aware that the musicians, the producer Ralph Couzens and the sound engineers have to be a happy team with the kind of mutual respect and trust that make for good teamwork.

Additional recommendations ...
No. 9. No. 13 in C major, K415. **András Schiff** (pf); **Salzburg Mozarteum Camerata Academica/Sándor Végh.** Decca 425 466-2DH — 59m DDD 7/90
No. 9. No. 27 in B flat major, K595. **Jenö Jandó** (pf); **Concentus Hungaricus/András Ligeti.** Naxos 8 550203 — 58m DDD 10/90
No. 17. No. 18 in B flat major, K456. **Jenö Jandó** (pf); **Concentus Hungaricus/Mátyás Antal.** Naxos 8 550205 — 57m DDD 10/90
No. 8 in C major, K246; No. 9. **Mitsuko Uchida** (pf); **English Chamber Orchestra/Jeffrey Tate.** Philips 432 086-2PH — 55m DDD 7/92
Nos. 9 and 17. **Berlin Philharmonic Orchestra/Daniel Barenboim** (pf). Teldec 9031-73128-2 — 1h 3m DDD 11/92

NEW REVIEW

Mozart. Piano Concertos — No. 15 in B flat major, K450; No. 16 in D major, K451. **András Schiff** (pf); **Salzburg Mozarteum Camerata Academica/Sándor Végh.** Decca 433 374-2DH. Recorded in 1990.

48m DDD 10/92

This is another valuable disc in the Mozart piano concerto series which András Schiff and Sándor Végh have been recording, unhurriedly, for Decca. Their B flat major Concerto is glowing and graceful, with Végh and his Salzburg orchestra providing Schiff with a characterful yet always attentive partnership. Maybe the pianist makes the first movement a touch winsome, with mannered little gusts of sound in places, but his interpretation is all of a piece and convincing, even if one would not necessarily always want to hear the music played this way. As always, too, one must admire the way in which he can use a Bösendorfer to produce tone, articulation and phrasing which suit this music conceived for an earlier and less powerful keyboard instrument. In the gentle middle movement, it sounds as if he is using the soft pedal, which may be wrong stylistically but has its own kind of beauty; this movement is sensitively played (also by the flautist Irena Grafenhauer and the oboist Heinz Holliger) and the hunting-type finale has both high spirits and delicacy. The Concerto in D major is a more virile piece, with trumpets and timpani (not used in K450) giving the first movement a touch of the military (or mock-military). The artists bring this out without overdoing it, so that we get elegance as well as energy. The slow movement and good-natured rondo finale also go well, although Schiff's normally impeccable articulation is momentarily less than clear at one point early in the latter. But that is just one tiny passage in a performance that is assured and satisfying. The recording of both concertos has fine presence.

Additional recommendations ...
English Chamber Orchestra/Murray Perahia (pf). CBS Masterworks CD37824 — 50m DDD
No. 14 in E flat major, K449. Nos. 15 and 16. **English Chamber Orchestra/Daniel Barenboim** (pf). EMI Studio CDM7 69124-2 — 1h 14m ADD 12/88

Mozart. Piano Concertos — No. 19 in F major, K459; No. 27 in B flat major, K595. **András Schiff** (pf); **Salzburg Mozarteum Camerata Academica/Sándor Végh.** Decca 421 259-2DH.

59m DDD 3/89

Listening to this disc one is immediately struck by a quality rarely encountered in so much music-making today. It is civilized, urbane, 'old fashioned' even, but always alive to the inner vitality of the music. It is also pleasant to encounter music-making where both soloist and conductor evidently enjoy playing together and achieve an almost chamber-music intimacy. Sándor Végh conducts with sympathy, panache and an evident love of the music. His hand-picked orchestra are quite outstanding with some remarkable wind playing. András Schiff responds with equal amounts of sympathy, giving razor-sharp articulation to the music. It is subtle pianism, performed with taste. The recording is generous, initially slightly disconcerting (reverberance somewhat diminishing the piano's impact) but one soon adjusts, aided by perceptive musicianship at its very best.

Additional recommendations ...

Nos. 23 and 27. **Alfred Brendel** (pf); **Academy of St Martin in the Fields/Sir Neville Marriner.** Philips Silver Line 420 487-2PM — 55m ADD 6/87 B

Nos. 19 and 27. **Pavel Stěpán** (pf); **Musici de Praga/Libor Hlaváček.** Supraphon Gems 2SUP0029 — 59m AAD 12/88 B

Mozart. PIANO CONCERTOS. **English Chamber Orchestra/Murray Perahia** (pf). CBS Masterworks CD42241 and CD42243. Items marked [a] from 76651 (4/78), [b] 76731 (5/80), [c] 76481 (5/76).

CD42241 — No. 20 in D minor, K466[a]; No. 27 in B flat major, K595[b]. *CD42243* — No. 11 in F major, K413[a]; No. 12 in A major, K414/385*p*[b]; No. 14 in E flat major, K449[c].

② 2h 3m 1h 10m ADD/DDD 9/87 B

These discs happily epitomise some of the best qualities of the complete Perahia/ECO set. Always intelligent, always sensitive to both the overt and less obvious nuances of this music, Perahia is firstly a true pianist, never forcing the instrument beyond its limits in order to express the ideas, always maintaining a well-projected singing touch. The superb ECO reflect his integrity and empathy without having to follow slavishly every detail of his articulation or phrasing. K414 and K413 are charming and typically novel for their time, but do not break new ground in quite the way that K449 does. Here, Mozart's success in the theatre may have suggested a more dramatic presentation and working of ideas for this instrumental genre. K595 is a work pervaded by a serenity of acceptance that underlies its wistfulness. Mozart had less than a year to live, and the mounting depression of his life had already worn him down, yet there is still a sort of quiet joy in this music. The vast range of styles, emotions, and forms that these few works encompass are evocatively celebrated in these performances, and admirably captured in civilized recordings.

Additional recommendations ...

No. 12. No. 21 in C major, K467. ***Beethoven.*** *32 Variations in C minor, WoO80.* **Radu Lupu** (pf). **English Chamber Orchestra/Uri Segal.** Decca Ovation 417 773-2DM — 1h 4m ADD 1/89 B

No. 13 in C major, K415. No. 20. **Jenö Jandó** (pf); **Concentus Hungaricus/András Ligeti.** Naxos 8 550117 — 56m DDD 10/90

Nos. 12 and 14. No. 21. **Jenö Jandó** (pf); **Concentus Hungaricus/András Ligeti.** Naxos 8 550202 — 1h 11m DDD 10/90

No. 8 in C major, K246; No. 11. Rondo in A major, K386. **András Schiff** (pf); **Salzburgh Mozarteum Camerata Academica/Sándor Vegh.** Decca 433 042-2DH — 55m DDD 5/93

Mozart. Piano Concertos — No. 20 in D minor, K466; No. 27 in B flat major, K595. **Sir Clifford Curzon** (pf); **English Chamber Orchestra/Benjamin Britten.** Decca 417 288-2DH. From SXL7007 (2/83). Recorded in 1970.

1h 5m ADD 10/86 B

Sir Clifford Curzon's playing is extraordinarily alert and concentrated: shaping and shading of even the minutest details is superbly subtle, while each movement as a whole has a sense of grand inevitability. This ability to focus intently upon foreground detail without losing the sense of the overall shape is one of the hallmarks of Curzon's genius, and one could be thankful that he was able to find such an understanding and sympathetic accompanist as Benjamin Britten. Their partnership in this music radiates a sense of shared joy in music-making. There is a quick fade-in at the start of K595, slightly blunting the effect of the opening tutti, but otherwise the transfers are excellent.

Additional recommendations ...
No. 20. No. 21 in C major, K467. **Mitsuko Uchida** (pf); **English Chamber Orchestra/Jeffrey Tate.** Philips 416 381-2PH — lh 2m DDD 7/86
Nos. 20 and 21. **Malcolm Bilson** (fp); **English Baroque Soloists/John Eliot Gardiner.** Archiv Produktion 419 609-2AH — 58m DDD 1/88
Nos. 20 and 21. **Berlin Philharmonic Orchestra/Daniel Barenboim** (pf). Teldec 9031-75710-2 — lh lm DDD 11/92
No. 12 in A major, K414/385p. No. 20. Rondo in D major, K382. **Evgeni Kissin** (pf); **Moscow Virtuosi/Vladimir Spivakov.** RCA Victor Red Seal 09026 60400-2 — lh 7m DDD 2/93

Key to Symbols

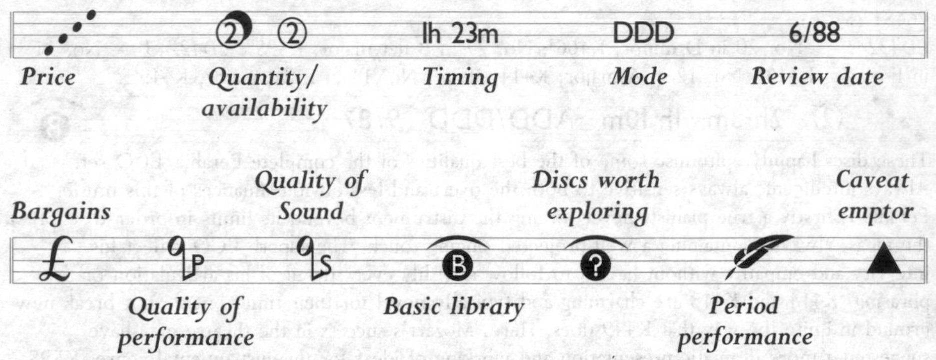

Mozart. PIANO CONCERTOS. **Robert Casadesus, [a]Gaby Casadesus** (pfs); **[b]Cleveland Orchestra, Columbia Symphony Orchestra/George Szell; [a]Philadelphia Orchestra/Eugene Ormandy.** Sony Legendary Interpretations MK46519. Recorded 1959-69. No. 21 in C major, K467[b] (from SBRG72234, 7/65); No. 22 in E flat major, K482; No. 23 in A major, K488 (both 61021); No. 24 in C minor, K491[b] (SBRG72234, 7/65); No. 26 in D major, K537, "Coronation"; No. 27 in B flat major, K595 (both SBRG72107, 4/63). Concerto for two pianos in E flat major, K365[a] (SBRG72008, 5/62).

3h 15m ADD 9/92

It's good to welcome back to the catalogue these refreshingly direct, unfussy performances of a selection of Mozart concertos by Robert Casadesus. Despite their age, these successfully remastered early 1960s recordings have come up well. There is a clear, cool logic in Casadesus's pianism, which harbours an unhurried, old-world charm all its own. He has a superb foil in George Szell and the Cleveland Orchestra, whose accompaniments blaze with an operatic intensity Mozart might well have enjoyed. In the popular Concerto No. 21 Casadesus is deft and elegant, with clear passagework and an engaging simplicity. He imparts a Bachian severity to the F sharp minor *Adagio* of No. 23 and his playing of No. 24 is both powerful and profound. Szell's conducting throughout is lively and polished. The odd one out here is Casadesus's Concerto for two pianos where he is joined by his wife, Gaby. Here, their sympathetic playing gets rather stolid support from Ormandy and the Philadelphia Orchestra. Despite consistent background hiss, the recordings are full-bodied, beautifully balanced and surprisingly detailed. At mid-price this three-CD set is certainly worth investigating and could be a fine introduction to these timeless masterpieces.

Additional recommendations ...
Nos. 21 and 23. **Rudolf Serkin** (pf); **London Symphony Orchestra/Claudio Abbado.** DG 410 068-2GH — DDD 9/83

No. 17 in G major, K453; No. 21. **Philharmonia Orchestra/Vladimir Ashkenazy** (pf). Decca 411 947-2DH — lh lm DDD 12/85 B
Nos. 21 and 24. **City of London Sinfonia/Howard Shelley.** Pickwick IMP Red Label PCD832 — lh DDD 1/87 B
Nos. 9 and 21. **English Chamber Orchestra/Murray Perahia** (pf). CBS Masterworks CD34562 — 59m DDD 6/87 B
Nos. 26 and 27. **Mitsuko Uchida** (pf); **English Chamber Orchestra/Jeffrey Tate.** Philips 420 951-2PH — lh 5m DDD 11/88 B
Nos. 21 and 24. **Robert Casadesus** (pf); **Cleveland Orchestra/George Szell.** CD42594 *(part of the 3-CD set reviewed above)* — 57m ADD 2/90 B

NEW REVIEW

Mozart. Piano Concertos — No. 20 in D minor, K466; No. 23 in A major, K488. **Melvyn Tan** (fp); **London Classical Players/Roger Norrington.** EMI CDC7 54366-2. Recorded in 1991.

54m DDD 11/92 

This A major Concerto is among the most popular of all Mozart's piano concertos, perhaps because its predominantly sunny mood is effectively contrasted with the hauntingly beautiful minor-key slow movement. Collectors who already have more than one version may see no need for another, but such is the persuasiveness of this performance on period instruments by Tan and Norrington that their disc is tempting. As always in Mozart, one must balance energy and sweetness, and this is well achieved in the flowing first movement, first by Norrington's orchestra and then by the fortepianist with his first entry, quieter than one expects but with adequate authority. If Tan's instrument sounds small against the orchestra, we may remember that Mozart's did, too, and no significant detail of the piano part is covered although in places one wonders if it will be. The fortepiano sound may also convert people who dislike honkytonk varieties: this is a sweet, clear sound whose expressive range fits and serves the music. Tan's view of the *Adagio* is quite purposeful, with an unselfconscious expressiveness and his playing here (with a few tasteful extra ornaments) has rightly been called "fluent and fragrant". The D minor Piano Concerto offers an example of *Sturm und Drang*, particularly in the outer movements. Tan's fortepiano is arguably less appropriate here and one may wish at first for the fuller sound of a modern piano. But one is soon convinced, for after all, Mozart didn't write for a modern grand and the power of the solo instrument is not just a matter of decibels. Tan's own cadenza for the first movement is another plus, suiting the music better than the one by Beethoven that we often hear.

Mozart. Piano Concertos — No. 21 in C major, K467; No. 25 in C major, K503. **Stephen Kovacevich** (pf); **London Symphony Orchestra/Sir Colin Davis.** Philips Concert Classics 426 077-2PC. From 6500 431 (4/74). Recorded in 1972.

59m ADD 2/90 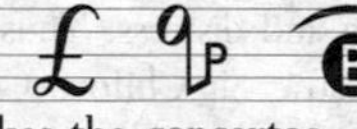

This disc may contain fairly standard readings but Stephen Kovacevich makes the concertos sparkle with crystalline tone, perfectly even, though shapely passagework, and a total dedication to conveying the music's directness of expression. In the *Andante*s, his absorption with the sheer perfection of the sound ideally transmits the inner light of the work, and in the faster movements he delights in their fluidity and rhythmic vitality. Sir Colin Davis seems well in tune with the soloist's intentions but, though the LSO generally provides a pleasingly coherent accompaniment, the whole is let down on occasions by obtrusive width of vibrato and moments of sour chording from the woodwind. That aside, there is little here that is other than delightful. The recording sets the soloist fairly far forward and provides plenty of orchestral detail, so any anomalies are particularly obvious: Kovacevich's playing blooms under these conditions, his avoidance of overstatement made all the more pertinent.

Additional recommendations ...
No. 25. No. 26 in D major, K537, "Coronation". **Malcolm Bilson** (fp); **English Baroque Soloists/John Eliot Gardiner.** Archiv Produktion 423 119-2AH — lh lm DDD 7/88

No. 21. ***Tchaikovsky.*** *Piano Concerto No. 2 in G major, Op. 44.* **Emil Gilels** (pf); **USSR Symphony Orchestra/Kyrill Kondrashin.** Mezhdunarodnaya Kniga MK417106 — lh 3m AAD 5/93

Mozart. Piano Concertos — No. 22 in E flat major, K482[a]; No. 23 in A major, K488[b]. **English Chamber Orchestra/Daniel Barenboim** (pf). EMI CDM7 69122-2. Item marked [a] from ASD2838 (11/72), recorded in 1971, [b] ASD2318 (7/67), recorded in 1967.

lh 2m ADD 6/88 

These two concertos make a good coupling, especially in these affecting, elegant readings from Barenboim and the ECO. What Barenboim may have lacked in authenticity of instruments or style when recording these concertos, he more than made up for in authenticity of spirit and musicianship. Both the slow movements of these works are especially fine, poised, shapely, and heartfelt: Barenboim employs both great subtlety and great simplicity, keeping the listener on the edge of his seat waiting for even the slightest of gestures that can open the way to new meanings. The faster, outer movements are ideally paced and although dexterity obviously plays a part in their successful realization, it never intrudes. We have here two performances of the highest calibre from a soloist and orchestra of the front rank. They will bear much repetition, and the close yet well-spaced recordings lend an easy, genial feel to the proceedings.

Additional recommendations ...

Nos. 22 and 23. **Mitsuko Uchida** (pf); **English Chamber Orchestra/Jeffrey Tate.** Philips 420 187-2PH — lh 2m DDD 8/87

No. 22[a]. *Concerto in E flat major for two pianos, K365/316a*[b]. [a]**Philharmonia Orchestra/Vladimir Ashkenazy** ([ab]pf); [b]**English Chamber Orchestra/Daniel Barenboim** ([b]pf). Decca 421 036-2DH — lh 2m ADD 1/89

Nos. 22 and 23. **Malcolm Bilson** (fp); **English Baroque Soloists/John Eliot Gardiner.** Archiv Produktion 423 595-2AH — lh DDD 3/89

Nos. 22 and 23. **Berlin Philharmonic Orchestra/Daniel Barenboim** (pf). Teldec 9031-75711-2 — lh 3m DDD 11/92

Mozart. Piano Concertos[a] — No. 23 in A major, K488; No. 24 in C minor, K491. ***Schubert.*** Impromptus[b] — G flat major, D899; A flat major, D899. **Sir Clifford Curzon** (pf); **London Symphony Orchestra/István Kertész.** Decca 430 497-2DWO. Items marked [a] from SXL6354 (11/68), recorded in 1968, [b] SXL6135 (11/64), recorded in 1964.

lh 9m ADD 10/91 

These two piano concertos succeed one another in Mozart's catalogue but could hardly be more different, the A major being a sunny work (at least in its outer movements) and the C minor one of storm and distress. Thus the coupling is attractive. Attentively partnered by his conductor and orchestra, Sir Clifford Curzon takes a serene, unusually spacious view of the first movement of the A major which allows every detail to tell and yet does not lose sight of the whole. The lovely *Adagio* (in F sharp minor, the only instance of Mozart using this key) is not beautified tonally but its slight understatement makes it all the more poignant, and the bustling finale is all of a piece with the rest of the interpretation in being distinctly unhurried. The performance of the C minor Concerto is again typical of this fine pianist in that nothing is exaggerated and no 'effects' are sought: what we have instead is quietly artistic and sensitive playing, much less urgent and dramatic than some other performances but equally satisfying in its own way; predictably, the oasis of calm that is the slow movement has a quiet simplicity. The two Schubert impromptus make an unusual fill-up, but receive attractive performances, though the sound has a good deal of background hiss. In the concertos, the piano sound could have more brilliance and the orchestral violins are somewhat whiskery; but this need not be a major consideration when the performances are of this quality.

Additional recommendations ...

No. 22 in E flat major, K482; No. 24. **English Chamber Orchestra/Murray Perahia.** CBS Masterworks CD42242 — lh 7m 8/87

Nos. 23 and 24. **Wilhelm Kempff** (pf); **Bamberg Symphony Orchestra/Ferdinand Leitner.** DG Galleria 423 885-2GGA — 56m ADD 12/88

Nos. 23 and 24. **Jenö Jandó** (pf); **Concentus Hungaricus/Mátyás Antal.** Naxos 8 550204 — 1h 3m DDD 10/90

No. 24. No. 27 in B flat major, K595. **Malcolm Bilson** (fp); **English Baroque Soloists/John Eliot Gardiner.** Archiv Produktion 427 652-2AH — 1h 3m DDD 2/90

Mozart. Double Piano Concertos[a] — E flat major, K365/316*a*; F major, K242, "Lodron". Andante and Variations in G major, K501. Fantasia in F minor, K608 (arr. Busoni). **Murray Perahia, Radu Lupu** (pfs); [a]**English Chamber Orchestra.** Sony Classical SK44915. Recorded 1988-90.

1h 2m DDD 10/91

Since each of the pianists on this disc is a fine Mozartian, it will attract many collectors, who should not be disappointed despite a couple of reservations listed below. The recording of the two concertos derives from a packed-out concert at The Maltings, Snape, during the 1988 Aldeburgh Festival and has a live immediacy, but the microphone placing does not allow a spacious sound. The playing itself is also immediate, and in the famous Concerto for two pianos there is a consistent feeling of energy in the outer movements. Less expectedly, we note it also in the central *Adagio*, which could have been more restfully done, particularly as the piano tone is close and full throughout. But there it is, the performance is all of a piece and its vigour certainly does not exclude grace, while the English Chamber Orchestra play with its customary skill. The less memorable *Lodron* Concerto was originally a triple piano concerto written for Countess Lodron and her two daughters and is here done in the composer's own duo transcription. The other two pieces on the disc were recorded a year later in London's Abbey Road Studio No. 1 and are skilfully done, but the beautiful and dramatic F minor *Fantasia* for mechanical organ loses much in Busoni's tubby arrangement for two pianos, particularly as Perahia and Lupu choose a deliberate tempo for the outer sections. However, the G major *Andante and Variations* for piano duet, presented here in a somewhat restrained performance, are both graceful and attractive.

Additional recommendations ...

Concerto in E flat major for two pianos, K365/316a[a]. *Piano Concerto No. 22 in E flat major, K482*[b]. [b]**Philharmonia Orchestra/Vladimir Ashkenazy** ([ab]pf); [a]**English Chamber Orchestra/Daniel Barenboim** ([b]pf). Decca 421 036-2DH — 1h 2m ADD 1/89

NEW REVIEW

Mozart. VIOLIN CONCERTOS. [a]**Richard Morgan** (ob); [b]**Henryk Szeryng,** [c]**Gérard Poulet** (vns); [d]**Nobuko Imai** (va); [e]**Norman Jones,** [f]**Stephen Orton** (vcs); [g]**Howard Shelley** (pf); [b]**New Philharmonia/Sir Alexander Gibson;** [h]**Academy of St Martin in the Fields/Iona Brown** (vn). Philips Mozart Edition 422 508-2PME4. Recorded 1966-70. *Violin Concertos*[b] — No. 1 in B flat major, K207; No. 2 in D major, K211; No. 3 in G major, K216; No. 4 in D major, K218 (all from 6706 011-1/4, 10/70); No. 5 in A major, K219; D major, K271*a*/271*i* (both from SAL3588, 2/67). *Rondos*[b] — B flat major, K269/261*a*; C major, K373 (6707 011-1/4). Concertone in C major, K190/186*E* (6707 011-1/4)[abce]. Adagio in E major, K261 (6500 036, 1/72)[b]. Sinfonia concertante in E flat major, K364/320*d*[dh]. Keyboard and Violin Concerto in D major, KAnh56/315*f*[gh]. Sinfonia concertante in A major, KAnh104/320*e*[dfh] (all new to UK).

④ 4h 25m ADD/DDD 6/91 £

Leaving aside works of doubtful authenticity, there are five Mozart violin concertos. They belong to his late teenage years in Salzburg and were composed in 1775. They have always been overshadowed by the piano concertos which, of course, are not only five times as numerous but also span the composer's whole career and include many mature masterpieces. While this is understandable, it would be a pity to miss out on these violin works which are surprisingly refreshing, youthful works of great charm. They agreeably reflect their creator's love and understanding of an instrument which he himself played more than capably. It is believed that his father Leopold, who was an authority on violin playing as well as a performer, may have encouraged him to compose them and then play them himself. It seems likely that Mozart did play them, at least for his own pleasure. The concertos have much in common with Mozart's cassations, divertimentos and serenades, which also highlight the solo violin and have other concerto-like elements in them. But their lightweight means of expression in no way diminishes their long-term appeal, for Mozart filled them to the brim with wonderful ideas. Henryk Szeryng has a relaxed way with these works and the orchestral contribution from the New Philharmonia under Sir Alexander Gibson is alert yet sensitive. Szeryng's tone is unfailingly beautiful with a sweetness that is greatly appealing. His evident affection for these works makes for pleasing listening and the vivid and witty 'Turkish' episode in the finale of No. 5 has great spirit. This disc also includes the 'doubtful' but agreeable solo Concerto in D major, K271*a*, together with a rather laid-back account of the *Sinfonia concertante* with Iona Brown and Nobuko Imai as the soloists (beautifully matched and blending). In addition we have the reconstructions of the incomplete projected Concerto for keyboard and violin and the single-movement *Sinfonia concertante* in A major for string trio and orchestra. The quality of the recordings is quite satisfying and at mid-price this compilation is very good value indeed.

Additional recommendations ...

Nos. 1-5. Adagio in E major, K261. Rondos — C major, K373; B flat major, K261a/269. **Itzhak Perlman** (vn); **Vienna Philharmonic Orchestra/James Levine.** DG 419 184-2GH3 — ③ 2h 18m DDD 12/86 Ⓑ

Nos. 1 and 2. Rondo in B flat major, K269/261e. **Jean-Jacques Kantorow** (vn); **Netherlands Chamber Orchestra/Leopold Hager.** Denon C37-7506 — 47m DDD 12/86 Ⓑ

Nos. 3 and 5. Adagio in E major, K261. **Cho-Liang Lin** (vn); **English Chamber Orchestra/Raymond Leppard.** CBS Masterworks CD42364 — 1h 2m DDD 12/87 Ⓑ

Concertos Nos. 3, 4 and 5. **Christian Altenburger** (vn); **German Bach Soloists/Helmut Winscherman.** LaserLight 15 525 — 1h 15m DDD 5/90 £ Ⓑ

No. 1. Adagio in E major, K261. Sinfonia concertante in E flat major, K364/320d[a]. **Anne-Sophie Mutter** (vn); [a]**Bruno Giuranna** (va); **Academy of St Martin in the Fields/Sir Neville Marriner.** EMI CDC7 54302-2 — 59m DDD 1/92 Ⓑ

Concertos Nos. 1-5. Adagio in E major, R261. Rondos — B flat major, K269/261a; C major, K373. **Simon Standage** (vn); **Academy of Ancient Music/Christopher Hogwood.** L'Oiseau-Lyre 433 045-2OH2 — ② 2h 8m DDD 4/92 Ⓑ

Nos. 1-5. **Andrea Cappelletti** (vn); **European Community Chamber Orchestra/Eivind Aaland.** Koch Schwann Musica Mundi 311164 — ② 2h 3m DDD 5/92 Ⓑ

Nos. 2 and 4. Sinfonia concertante in E flat major, K364/320d[a]. [a]**Josef Suk** (vn); **Academy of St Martin in the Fields/Iona Brown** (vn). Argo 433 171-2DM — 1h 14m ADD/DDD 5/92 £ Ⓑ

Nos. 1, 3 and 5. **Academy of St Martin in the Fields/Iona Brown** (vn). Argo 433 170-2DM — 1h 10m ADD/DDD 5/92 £ Ⓑ

Nos. 2, 3 and 5. **Moscow Vituosi/Vladimir Spivakov** (vn). RCA Victor Red Seal RD60152 — 1h 15m DDD 9/92 Ⓑ

Nos. 3 and 5. **Frank Peter Zimmermann** (vn); **Württemberg Chamber Orchestra/Jörg Faerber.** EMI CDD7 64288-2 — 1h 19m DDD 9/92 Ⓑ

NEW REVIEW

Mozart. Serenade No. 7 in D major, K250/248*b*, "Haffner". March in D major, K249, "Haffner". **Orchestra of the Eighteenth Century/Frans Brüggen.** Philips 432 997-2PH. Recorded in 1991.

55m DDD 3/93

Mozart's *Haffner* Serenade could rightly be considered all things to all men. It has the breadth of a fully-fledged symphony, the soloistic charisma of a violin concerto, the intimacy of chamber music and the celebratory ring of a work written for a specific occasion — which was, in this particular case, the wedding of Elisabeth Haffner, daughter of a wealthy banker and Burgomaster of Salzburg, to Franz Xaver Späth. The so-called *Haffner* Symphony — which Mozart pared down to symphonic proportions from a six-movement serenade — was written for another personage of the same name, and is not musically related to K250. The haughty March in D serves as a splendid overture and sets the tone for the main work's varied eight movements, the fourth of which, a *concertante* Rondo, was transcribed and popularized as a violin solo by Fritz Kreisler (who made a memorable recording of it). Frans Brüggen's recording on period instruments is pure joy. With keenly inflected phrasing, swift tempos, a relatively warm sonority and an abundance of enthusiasm from the players, it leaps into action and maintains a feeling of spontaneity from start to finish. Lucy van Dael (the Orchestra of the Eighteenth Century's concert master) despatches her solos with great agility, and the recording, made at the Anton Philipzaal, The Hague, is splendidly alive. There's a fascinating footnote to the production, too: Frans Brüggen dispenses with cellos and fills the gap between viola and bass with horns. The reasons? In Mozart's time, it was customary to play open-air music (which this is) standing up; furthermore, it was considered ill-mannered to stay seated if higher-ranking persons were standing. So the exchange of horns for cellos is both historically acceptable and aesthetically pleasing.

Additional recommendations ...

Serenade. **Josef Suk** (vn); **Prague Chamber Orchestra/Libor Hlaváček.** Supraphon Gems 2SUP0006 — 54m AAD 12/87 £

Serenade. March. **Pavlo Beznosiuk** (vn); **Amsterdam Baroque/Ton Koopman.** Erato 2292-45436-2 — 1h 4m DDD 2/90

Complete Edition, Volume 3 — Serenades, Marches and Cassations for Orchestra. Serenades: No. 3 in D major, K185/167*a*; No. 4 in D major, K203/189*b*; No. 5 in D major, K204/231*a*; No. 6 in D major, K239, "Serenata notturna"; No. 7 in D major, K250/248*b*, "Haffner"; No. 9 in D major, K320, "Posthorn"; No. 13 in G major, K525, "Eine kleine Nachtmusik". *Marches:* D major, K62; D major, K189/167*b*; D major, K215/213*b*; D major, K237/189*c*; D major, K249; D major, K335/320*a* No. 1; D major, K335/320*a* No. 2. *Cassations:* G major, K63; B flat major, K99/63*a*; D major, K100/62*a*. Divertimento in D major, K131. Notturno in D major, K286/269*a*. Galimathias musicum, K32. **Soloists; Academy of St Martin in the Fields/Sir Neville Marriner.** Philips Mozart Edition 422 503-2PME7 — ⑦ 6h 44m DDD 12/90

NEW REVIEW

Mozart. Serenade No. 10 in B flat major for 13 wind instruments, K361/370*a*, "Gran Partita". **Amadeus Winds/Christopher Hogwood.** L'Oiseau-Lyre 421 437-2OH. Recorded in 1987.

47m DDD 4/89 B

The Amadeus Winds are no relation to the Amadeus Quartet, but there is no copyright on Mozart's second Christian name and these are fine American players whose skilful performance of the so-called *Gran Partita* (the title was not Mozart's) certainly earns them the right to use it. The work is in fact a serenade on a large scale, with seven movements lasting just short of 50 minutes, which seems to have been composed for the wind ensemble led by the clarinettist Anton Stadler, who played it at a benefit concert in 1784. The 12 wind players are pairs of oboes, clarinets, basset horns (a kind of clarinet) and bassoons plus four horns, and they are joined fairly unobtrusively by a double-bass to provide a firmer underpinning of the harmony. In the present performance the players use period instruments or modern replicas playing a little below today's normal concert pitch, and the sound is convincingly authentic. The performance under Christopher Hogwood is no less stylish, although on this occasion he is working with American players and recording in Massachusetts. All flows smoothly and naturally, and as the music unfolds one sees why one scholar has claimed that this work with all its elegance and wit has proved to be "the most influential piece of wind music ever composed" — Richard Strauss was not the only later composer to use it as a model for works for wind ensemble of his own, one of which he even dedicated "to the godlike spirit of Mozart". The recording is pleasing, although a touch bland, as if the engineers were anxious to remove any rawness from the sound of the period instruments.

Additional recommendations ...

Serenade. **Chamber Orchestra of Europe Wind Soloists/Alexander Schneider.** ASV CDCOE804 — 52m DDD 4/87 B

Serenade. **Academy of St Martin in the Fields Wind Ensemble/Sir Neville Marriner.** Philips 412 726-2PH — 49m DDD 5/87
Orpheus Chamber Orchestra. DG 423 061-2GH — 51m DDD 1/88
Serenade. Divertimento in F major, K213. **Scottish National Orchestra Wind Ensemble/Paavo Järvi.** Chandos CHAN8553 — 59m DDD 5/88
Serenade. **Orchestra of the Eighteenth Century/Frans Brüggen.** Philips 422 338-2PH — 51m DDD 4/89
Serenade. **Hungarian State Opera Wind Ensemble/Ervin Lukács.** Hungaroton White Label HRC076 — 51m ADD 10/90 £
Serenade. **Sabine Meyer Wind Ensemble.** EMI CDC7 54457-2 — 47m DDD 7/93

Mozart. Serenades — No. 11 in E flat major, K375; No. 12 in C minor, K388/384*a*. **Orpheus Chamber Orchestra.** DG 431 683-2GH. Recorded in 1990.

48m DDD 9/91

These two big pieces for wind instruments are well-contrasted although they share the same title. Indeed, the use of a minor key for the four-movement K388 tells us at once that it is no ordinary serenade and certainly not just music for casual entertainment — in fact it is quite stormy in character, and the DG booklet notes go so far as to call it "dramatic and sombre". Why Mozart called it a serenade we do not know: but at any rate it has a tense first movement and a terse finale in variation form, and in between them a minuet with some ingenious counterpoint for oboes and bassoon. As for the E flat major Serenade, K373, this has delicacy as well as expressive qualities (the *Adagio* is notably eloquent), and the finale really dances. Few artists or orchestral bodies who regularly contribute to the record catalogue can claim an unbroken record of success, but the Orpheus is among them. The oboes, clarinets, bassoons and horns of this fine ensemble blend together so well that one's only regret may be the feeling that Mozart himself can never have heard such sensitive playing of this music, and the recording in a New York location is no less worthy of it.

Additional recommendation ...
Wind soloists of the **Chamber Orchestra of Europe/Alexander Schneider.** ASV CDCOE802 — 47m DDD 5/88

NEW REVIEW

Mozart. Serenade No. 13 in G major, "Eine kleine Nachtmusik". Divertimentos — E flat major, K252/240*a*; D major, K131. **Orpheus Chamber Orchestra.** DG 419 192-2GH.

1h 4m DDD 12/86

There are many worthy recorded performances of Mozart's most famous Serenade, the one that is now universally called *Eine kleine Nachtmusik,* but this one by the string section of a conductorless American chamber orchestra has qualities of refinement and alertness, even enthusiasm, that make it rather special. These players clearly enjoy the music, but bring to it a delightful precision as well as the necessary *joie de vivre* and spontaneity, and each of the four movements is beautifully shaped and characterized, so that this very familiar music comes up as fresh as anyone could wish for. The two early divertimentos which accompany the serenade provide a pleasing complement and contrast. Each has a different instrumentation, the one in D (written when Mozart was 16, but sounding more mature) being for flute, oboe, bassoon, four horns and strings while the one in E flat is for just six instruments, these being pairs of oboes, bassoons and horns. Here, too, the Orpheus players are of the highest calibre both technically and artistically and their sound is well captured, as is that of the strings in *Eine kleine Nachtmusik.*

Additional recommendations ...
Eine kleine Nacthmusik. Serenade No. 6 in D major, "Serenata notturna", K239. ***Elgar.*** *Serenade for Strings in E minor, Op. 20.* ***Grieg.*** *Holberg Suite, Op. 40.* **Serenata of London.** Pickwick IMP Classics PCD861 — 1h 5m DDD 11/87 £

Eine kleine Nachtmusik. Serenata notturna. Notturno in D major, K286/269a. Ein musikalischer Spass, K522. **Vienna Mozart Ensemble/Willi Boskovsky.** Decca Serenata 430 259-2DM — lh 9m ADD 7/91

Eine kleine Nachtmusik. Serenata notturno. Divertimentos for Strings (Salzburg Symphonies) — No. 1 in D major, K136/125a; No. 2 in B flat major, K137/125b; No. 3 in F major, K138/125c. **I Musici.** Philips Laser Line Classics 432 055-2PM — lh 4m DDD 2/91

Eine kleine Nachtmusik. Divertimentos — K252/240a; K131. **Berlin Philharmonic Orchestra/Herbert von Karajan.** DG Mozart Masterpieces 429 805-2GMM — lh lm ADD 8/90 £

Eine kleine Nachtmusik. ***Tchaikovsky.*** *Symphony No. 5 in E minor, Op. 64.* **Vienna Philharmonic Orchestra/David Oistrakh.** Orfeo C302921B — lh 7m ADD 6/93

Mozart. Divertimentos — B flat major, K287/271*h*; D major, K205/167*a*. **Salzburg Mozarteum Camerata Academica/Sándor Végh.** Capriccio 10 271.

59m DDD 11/89

Mozart's Divertimento, K287 is a six-movement work cast on quite a large scale, and is scored for two violins, viola, two horns and bass, a combination which presents some difficulties of balance. One solution is to use a full orchestral string section, as did Toscanini and Karajan in their recordings, but this can bring its own problems, for Mozart demands playing of virtuoso standard in this score, and anything less than this is ruthlessly exposed. Sandor Végh's smallish string band is of high quality, and has a pleasantly rounded tone quality. The engineers have managed to contrive a satisfactory balance which sounds not at all unnatural, and the sound quality itself is very good. Végh directs an attractive, neatly-pointed performance of the work, one which steers a middle course between objective classicism and expressive warmth. The Divertimento, K205, has five movements, but none lasts longer than five minutes, and the work is much shorter and more modest than K287. Scoring in this case is for violin, viola, two horns, bassoon and bass, to provide another difficult but well resolved problem for the engineers. Végh directs another characterful, delightful performance, to round off a very desirable disc.

Additional recommendations ...

K287. F major, K247. **Berne Camerata.** Novalis 150 040-2 — lh 5m DDD 3/90

Complete Edition, Volume 4 — Divertimentos and Marches. Divertimentos: E flat major, K113; D major, K136/125*a*; B flat major, K137/125*b*; F major, K138/125*c*; D major, K205/167*a*; F major, K247; D major, K251; B flat major, K287/271h; D major, K334/320*b*. *Marches:* F major, K248; D major, K290/167*ab;* D major, K445/320*c*. Serenade in G major, K525, "Eine kleine Nachtmusik". Ein musikalischer Spass, K522. **Academy of St Martin in the Fields/Sir Neville Marriner.** Philips Mozart Edition 422 504-2PME5 — 5 4h 31m DDD 12/90

Mozart. Divertimentos — D major, K205/167*a*[a]; D major, K334/320*b*[b]. March in D major, K290/167*ab*[a]. **Franz Liszt Chamber Orchestra/[a]János Rolla, [b]Frigyes Sándor.** Hungaroton White Label HRC080.

lh 7m ADD 5/90 

The Franz Liszt Chamber Orchestra of Budapest is a fine ensemble, and here they play two of Mozart's divertimentos with a crisp, lithe style and pleasant and well varied tone. The bigger work here is the first, K334, which has a Theme (in D minor) and Variations as its second movement and a well known Minuet as its third. The earlier Divertimento, also in D major, is preceded by the little March, K290, which was also evidently played at its first performance at a garden party in 1773. Neither work is deep music, as the title tells us, but each entertains delightfully and the minuets, of which there are four in all, dance with both gravity and grace. Excellent recording in a resonant acoustic that does not obscure detail and of course the price is another attraction, while there is an informative booklet note provided too.

NEW REVIEW

Mozart. Cassations — G major, K63, "Final-Musik"; B flat major, K99/63*a*; D major, K100/62*a*. **Salzburg Chamber Orchestra/Harald Nerat.** Naxos 8 550609. Recorded in 1992.

lh 7m DDD 4/93 £

Look at the Köchel numbers here and you will rightly guess that these pieces all represent the boy Mozart. Indeed, all of them date from the summer of 1769, when he was iust 13 years old. But unlike some of his early music, these pieces are more than just the fluent doodling of a boy wonder and so this disc is well worth investigating. Thus the *Allegro* second movement of the Cassation in G major has genuinely buoyant invention and attractive textures in which two horns stand out, and this attractive movement is followed by a charming little *Andante* in which a plucked-string accompaniment complements a graceful and witty tune. One's praise for this Cassation (the word implies outdoor entertainment music) is matched by enjoyment of the performance. Harald Nerat is a viola player in the famous Salzburg Mozarteum Orchestra, and his experience is evident in the playing of the Chamber Orchestra of the city that was Mozart's birthplace. It has qualities of poise, affection and vitality in the right proportions, and deserves to make friends for this orchestra and conductor. We also hear stylish solo violin playing from Georg Hölscher in the slow fifth movement. The other two cassations are also good value, and although the one in B flat major is less striking than the one discussed above, the one in D major is splendidly vivid. Here we have trumpets and flutes as well as the oboes, horns and strings of the other cassations, and there are attractive wind solos. The recording is excellent, with a pleasing bloom on the string sound, and altogether this is a fine issue which at super-bargain price should not be missed by collectors looking for some different Mozart.

Additional recommendation ...

K63. K99/63a. Adagio and Fugue in C minor, K546. **Salzburg Camerata/Sándor Végh.** Capriccio 10 192 — 51m DDD 3/88

Mozart. ORCHESTRAL WORKS. [a]**Arvid Engegard** (vn); **Salzburg Mozarteum Camerata Academica/Sándor Végh.** Capriccio 10 302. Recorded 1988-89.

Serenade No. 3 in D major, K185/167*a*[a]. March in D major, K189/167*b*. Five Contretanze, K609. Notturno in D major, K286/269*a*.

lh 6m DDD 10/91 

The main work here is the big Serenade, K185, commissioned by the Antretter family of Salzburg and first performed in August 1773 to celebrate the end of the university year. Like other works of its kind it incorporates a miniature two-movement violin concerto within a loose symphonic framework: an *Andante* designed to display the instrument's powers of cantilena, and a brisk *contredanse* with plenty of opportunities for ear-catching virtuosity. There is also a violin solo in the glum D minor trio of the second minuet. But perhaps the finest movements are the sensuous A major *Andante grazioso*, with its *concertante* writing for flutes and horns, and the rollicking 6/8 finale, preceded by an unexpectedly searching *Adagio* introduction. The performance by Végh and his hand-picked Salzburg players is affectionate, rhythmically alive and beautifully detailed, with an imaginative, subtly coloured solo violin contribution from Arvid Engegard. The tempo and specific character of each movement is shrewdly judged: the two minuets, for example, are vividly differentiated, the first properly swaggering, with a nice lilt in the trio, the second spruce and quick-witted. Only in the finale is Végh arguably too leisurely, though here too the style and rhythmic lift of the playing are infectious. Végh follows the serenade with deft, colourful readings of five contredanses from Mozart's last year and a beguiling performance of the *Notturno* for four orchestras, exquisitely imagined open-air music, with its multiple echoes fading into the summer night. All in all a delectable disc, offering a varied concert of Mozart's lighter music performed with exceptional flair and finesse. The recording, too, is outstandingly vivid, with the spatial effects in the *Notturno* beautifully managed.

Mozart. ORCHESTRAL WORKS. **Orpheus Chamber Orchestra.** DG 429 783-2GH. Recorded in 1989.

Ein musikalischer Spass, K522. *Contredanses* — C major, K587, "Der Sieg vom Helden Koburg"; D major, K534, "Das Donnerwetter"; C major, K535, "La Bataille"; G major, K610, "Les filles malicieuses"; E flat major, K607/605*a*, "Il trionfo delle donne". Gallimathias musicum, K32. *German Dances* — K567; K605; C major, K611, "Die Leyerer". March in D major, K335 No. 1.

1h 9m DDD 4/91

After all the Mozart with which we were bombarded during his bicentenary year, it is a mark of his greatness that an issue such as this comes up with an incomparably engaging freshness. The celebrated *Musikalischer Spass* ("Musical Joke") which begins the disc is never so crudely funny that it wears thin, but make no mistake, the jokes are there in just about every passage, whether they are parodying third-rate music or wobbly playing, and oddly enough sound still more amusing when the performance is as stylishly flexible as this one by the conductorless Orpheus Chamber Orchestra. One of the tunes here (that of the finale on track four) is that of the BBC's *Horse of the Year* programme — and what a good tune it is, even at the umpteenth repetition as the hapless composer finds himself unable to stop. The rest of this programme is no less delightful and includes miniature pieces supposedly describing a thunderstorm, a battle, a hurdy-gurdy man and a sleigh-ride (with piccolo and sleigh-bells). There is also a *Gallimathias musicum*, a ballet suite of dainty little dances averaging less than a minute in length, which Mozart is supposed to have written at the age of ten. Whatever the case this CD, subtitled "A Little Light Music", provides proof of his genius, though differently from his acknowledged masterpieces. The recording is as refined as anyone could wish yet has plenty of impact.

Mozart. DANCES, MARCHES AND OVERTURES. [a]**Staatskapelle Dresden/Hans Vonk;** [d]**Salzburg Mozarteum Orchestra/Hans Graf.** Capriccio 10 809. Items marked [a] from 10 070, [b] new to UK, [c] 10 253 (11/89).

Five Minuets, K461/448*a*[bd]. *Contredanses*[bd] — Six, K462/448*b*; D major, K534, "Das Donnerwetter"; C major, K535, "La Bataille"; C major, K587, "Der Sieg vom Helden Koburg"; Two, K603. Two Minuets with Contredanses (Quadrilles), K463[bd]. *German Dances*[bd] — Six, K509; Six, K600; Three, K605. *Marches*[cd] — D major, K52; D major, K189/167*b*; C major, K214; D major, K215/213*b*; D major, K237/189*c*; F major, K248; D major, K249; Two in D major, K335/320*a*; C major, K408 No. 1/383*e*; D major, K408 No. 2/385*a*; C major, K408 No. 3/383*F*; D major, K445/320*c*. *Overtures*[a] — Die Zauberflöte; Le nozze di Figaro; Ascanio in Alba; Idomeneo; Der Schauspieldirektor; Così fan tutte; Die Entführung aus dem Serail; La finta giardiniera; Lucio Silla; La clemenza di Tito; Don Giovanni. Idomeneo — Marches[cd]: Nos. 8, 14 and 25. Le nozze di Figaro: March[cd]: No. 23.

③ 3h 2m DDD 10/91

The first of these discs offers 11 operatic overtures and a convenient means of surveying Mozart's contribution to this form, ranging from the bustle of *Le nozze di Figaro* ("The marriage of Figaro") to the profundities of *Die Zauberflöte* ("The Magic Flute") — although that too has its elements of vivacity, befitting music which was always intended to capture the attention of an audience before the stage action began. Hans Vonk and his Dresden orchestra play these overtures with a light touch, and the recording in the Dresden Lukaskirche is clear yet atmospheric. The second disc, with different forces recorded in the composer's native city of Salzburg, has no less than 17 marches, but some of them, like the one on track two, have such a spring in their step that they are more akin to dance music than to military drill; it is thanks not only to Mozart's invention but also to the neat, alert playing of the Salzburg Mozarteum Orchestra under Hans Graf that monotony and boredom are never allowed to set in here. The same artists bring equal stylishness to the dances and minuets on the third disc, some of which have earthy peasant rhythms and humour, while the programmatic *Contredanses* are no less enjoyable. One is called *The Thunderstorm* and anticipates Beethoven's similar movement in his Sixth Symphony by including a piccolo. There's also a *Battle* and the disc ends thoughtfully with a *German Dance* called *The Sleighride* which features two posthorns, drums and tambourines. The Salzburg recording of all these pieces is satisfying if rather reverberant.

Mozart. OVERTURES. Serenade No. 13 in G major, K525, "Eine kleine Nachtmusik". **Tafelmusik/Bruno Weil.** Sony Classical Vivarte SK46695. Recorded in 1991.

Overtures — Idomeneo; Die Entführung aus dem Serail; Der Schauspieldirektor; Le nozze di Figaro; Don Giovanni; Così fan tutte; La clemenza di Tito; Die Zauberflöte.

1h DDD 5/92

These exhilarating accounts of the overtures to eight of Mozart's greatest stage works come from the Canadian ensemble Tafelmusik, conducted by Bruno Weil. The fresh vigour and *élan* of these period-instrument performances reveal these works in an altogether grander light than some and Bruno Weil's dynamic interpretations never fail to generate a powerful impression of what would follow in complete productions of the operas. The challenging gravity and intimidating momentum of the overture to *Don Giovanni* leaves little unsaid, whilst the masonic pomp which opens *Die Zauberflöte* could not be more telling. Weil's relaxed tempo for *Le nozze di Figaro* may not generate the impetus and galvanism of those conductors who dash through this overture in barely three-and-a-half minutes, but the chance to luxuriate in the genius of Mozart's scoring is all the more welcome when all the parts are clearly audible and well balanced. In the remaining overtures, too, the advantages of period instruments are constantly brought to the fore, as fresh instrumental details leap from these scores with renewed clarity and emphasis, whilst the antiphonal division of first and second violins allows each contrapuntal surprise to register powerfully. The disc also includes an articulate rendition of the ever-popular G major Serenade, *Eine kleine Nachtmusik*; again superbly played by the Tafelmusik strings, and with a total lack of contrived artifice. These performances combine thrilling and dramatic musicianship with refined period sensibilities in a recording of the highest technical quality, and this excellent disc will fascinate and challenge the preconceptions of any Mozart enthusiast.

NEW REVIEW

Mozart. SYMPHONIES AFTER SERENADES. **Tafelmusik/Bruno Weil.** Sony Classical SK47260. Recorded in 1991.

D major — K100/62*a*; K185/167*a*; K203/198*b*; K204/213*a*; K250/248*b*; K320.

2 2h 31m DDD 12/92

Even Mozart ran out of time to compose sometimes. At least five of his 50 or so symphonies he produced simply by extracting a suitable sequence of movements from one of his large-scale orchestral serenades, in which symphonic movements were originally mixed with marches and whole violin concertos. This two-disc set offers all five of these symphonies, and takes the not-very-great liberty of adopting the same procedure with another Serenade (K185) to provide a sixth 'new' work. The result is a sparkling batch of early Mozart symphonies which, far from being in any way inferior to the custom-built ones, actually tend to be both larger in scale and a little more progressive in outlook. Above all, this is music in which Mozart revels in the fluency and promise of his own youthful talent as well as in the splendid sounds of the modern classical orchestra. It's not deep stuff, but it is fresh and uplifting, and right now it's hard to think of an ensemble better equipped to make the most of such refined brilliance than the Toronto-based Tafelmusik, who are quite simply one of the most polished and disciplined period orchestras around. Here they are invigoratingly conducted by Bruno Weil, a Mozart specialist who likes his tempos brisk but who doesn't let that sweep away any of the music's charm. At moments, too, where these serenade-symphonies take a darker turn (admittedly rare, though there is a sombre minor-key slow movement to K320, and the *Allegro maestoso* introduction to K250 is more searching than most), he is able to respond effectively yet still without seriously compromising the music's overall amiability of mood. Pure pleasure from beginning to end then, and an excellent recording too.

Mozart. SYMPHONIES. **Prague Chamber Orchestra/Sir Charles Mackerras.** Telarc CD80256, CD80272/3. Recorded in 1991.

CD80256 — No. 1 in E flat major, K16; F major, K19*a*; No. 4 in D major, K19; No. 5 in B flat major, K22; No. 6 in F major, K43; B flat major, KAhn214/45*b*; No. 7 in D major, K45. *CD80272* — No. 8 in D major, K48; No. 9 in C major, K73/75*a*; D major, K731/81; D major, K73*m*/97; D major, K75*n*/95; D major, K73*n*/95; D major, K73*q*/84. *CD80273* — No.

10 in G major, K74/73*p*; C major, K111*b*/96; F major, K75; G major, K75*b*/110; No. 13 in F major, K112.

③ 1h 13m 1h 1m 58m DDD 11/91

These three discs present the earliest, least-known of Mozart's symphonic works. The numbers are useful for identification only, as the symphonies were not written in the numbered order and several (not included in these CDs) have been established as the works of others. The value of resuscitating composers' juvenalia is often called into question. After all, when he composed the earliest of these works (in London, during a period when his father was ill and required him not to practise the piano) Mozart had reached the grand old age of eight; these discs follow his symphonic music up to the age of 16. But Mozart is, as usual, a case apart, and in listening to these symphonies one can learn not only a great deal about the context from which his mature masterpieces were to develop but also discover many movements which are enchanting in their own right. Inevitably, the music is patchy — some is extremely repetitive — but take the tender *Andantino* third movement of No. 42, or the spirited second movement *Allegro* of No. 10 and it becomes clear that there is much to enjoy here, and music which seems little short of miraculous for a composer of such tender years. There are also some surprises for those unfamiliar with these little-known works, most notably in the very first symphony. The second movement presents, over a gentle triplet accompaniment, a four-note theme on the horns which seems uncomfortably familiar. It is academic whether Mozart remembered it consciously, unconsciously or not at all when he trotted it out again as the basis of the last movement of *Jupiter* (No. 41). Throughout the recordings Sir Charles Mackerras and the Prague Chamber Orchestra give affectionate performances which are full of sparkle and precision. Devotees of period performance will not find original instruments here, but the Prague orchestra combines the best of both worlds, reduced vibrato and lively tempos, without the tendency towards scrawny tone of some period performances, giving a clear-cut, lean quality which brings to life even the music's less imaginative moments. First and second violins are positioned on opposite sides, to left and right, which enhances antiphonal effects, and the harpsichord continuo is kept in the background where it provides unobtrusive crispness. The recorded sound is resonant, but beneficially so, complementing the orchestra's admirable clarity.

Additional recommendations ...

Complete Edition, Volume 1 — Early Symphonies: No. 1 in E flat major, K16; No. 4 in D major, K19; F major, KAnh223/19*a*; No. 5 in B flat major, K22; No. 6 in F major, K43; No. 7 in D major, K45; G major, Kdeest, "Neue Lambacher" (attrib. L. Mozart); No. 7*a* in G major, KAnh221/45*a*, "Alte Lambacher"; (No. 55) in B flat major, KAnh214/45b; No. 8 in D major, K48; No. 9 in C major, K73; No. 10 in G major, K74; (No. 42) in F major, K75; (No. 43) in F major, K76/42*a*; (No. 44) in D major, K81/73*l*; No. 11 in D major, K84/73*q*; (No. 45) in D major, K95/73*n*; (No. 46) in C major, K96/111*b*; (No. 47) in D major, K97/73*m*; No. 12 in G major, K110/75*b*; No. 13 in F major, K112; No. 14 in A major, K114 (with additional alternative minuet); No. 15 in G major, K124; No. 16 in C major, K128; No. 17 in G major, K129; No. 18 in F major, K130; No. 19 in E flat major, K132 (with additional alternative slow movement); No. 20 in D major, K133; (No. 50) in D major, K141*a* (K161 and K163); (No. 48) in D major, K111*a* (K111 and K120); (No. 51) in D major, K207*a* (K196 and K121); (No. 52) in C major, K213*c* (K208 and K102). Minuet in A major, K61*g* No. 1. **Academy of St Martin in the Fields/Sir Neville Marriner.** Philips Mozart Edition 422 501-2PME6 — ⑥ 6h 39m ADD/DDD 12/90

Complete Edition, Volume 2 — Middle and Late Symphonies: No. 21 in A major, K134; No. 22 in C major, K162; No. 23 in D major, K181/162*b*; No. 24 in B flat major, K182/173*dA*; No. 25 in G minor, K183/173*dB*; No. 26 in E flat major, K184/161*a*; No. 27 in G major, K199/161*b*; No. 28 in C major, K200/189*k*; No. 29 in A major, K201/186*a*; No. 30 in D major, K202/186*b*; No. 31 in D major, K297/300*a*, "Paris" (with additional alternative slow movement); No. 32 in G major, K318; No. 33 in B flat major, K319; No. 34 in C major, K338; No. 35 in D major, K385, "Haffner"; No. 36 in C major, K425, "Linz"; No. 38 in D major, K504, "Prague"; No. 39 in E flat major, K453; No. 40 in G minor, K550; No. 41 in C major, K551, "Jupiter". Minuet in C major, K409/383*f*. Adagio maestoso in G major, K444/425*a*. **Academy of St Martin in the Fields/Sir Neville Marriner.** Philips Mozart Edition 422 502-2PME6 — ⑥ 6h 42m ADD 12/90

Early Symphonies — No. 1; No. 4; No. 5; No. 10; No. 11; No. 13; (Nos. 44-48); K32, "Gallimathias musicum"; K87; KAnh223. **Academy of Ancient Music/Jaap Schröder** with **Christopher Hogwood** (hpd). L'Oiseau-Lyre 417 140-2OH — ② 2h 20m DDD 2/87

Various Symphonies (composed between 1767-88) — No. 6; No. 7; No. 7a; No. 8; (No. 37) in G major, K425a (K444); No. 40 (second version); (No. 43); (No. 55) in B flat major, K45b (KAnh214); A minor, K16a, "Odense"; G major, Kdeest, "Neue Lambacher"; D major, K46a (K51), "La finta semplice"; B flat major, K74g (KAnh216/C11.03). **Academy of Ancient Music/Jaap Schröder** with **Christopher Hogwood** (hpd). L'Oiseau-Lyre 421 135-2OH3 — ③ 3h 16m DDD 9/88

NEW REVIEW

Mozart. SYMPHONIES. **Amsterdam Baroque Orchestra/Ton Koopman.** Erato 2292-45714-2. Recorded 1990-91.
No. 17 in G major, K129; No. 18 in F major, K130; No. 19 in E flat major, K132; No. 22 in C major, K162; No. 32 in G major, K318.

lh 9m DDD 8/92 

Except for No. 32, all the works here date from 1772-3, Mozart's most prolific period as a symphonist. Symphonies K129 and K162 are in three movements only, the former a bustling, lightly scored piece, elegantly and wittily developed, the latter a more brilliant, ceremonial C major work. Symphonies K130 and K132 both include a minuet (both trios, curiously, haven an archaic, quasi-modal flavour) and feature a quartet of horns. Incidentally, Mozart composed alternative slow movements for K132, both recorded here so you can programme your own version; the original *Andante* opens with a Gregorian plainsong melody, and later quotes a medieval German carol — some private joke may be intended here. With his brilliant period-instrument band, Koopman gives readings of immense flair and verve. Faster movements are fiery and inspiriting, with sharp dynamic contrasts, yet always allow space for telling expressive detail and the lithe, springing bass lines ensure that the minuets and the jig finales truly dance. Slow movements tend to be more leisurely than in most period performances, and are shaped with finesse and a keen ear for Mozart's subtleties of texture. But the most arresting feature of these performances are the pungent, colourful sonorities Koopman draws from his Amsterdam players: in both K130 and K132 the four horns, superlatively played, cut through the texture with thrilling effect, while the raw, rasping horns and trumpets and the incisive, crisply articulated strings lift the apparently conventional outer movements of K162 right off the page. Here and there Koopman's phrasing can sound a bit precious; and some may feel that the string section is too slender for K318, with its rich scoring and Mannheim-inspired orchestral effects. But these are uncommonly stylish, physically exciting performances, spaciously and transparently recorded; and they could well come as a revelation to those who still resist period instruments.

Additional recommendation ...
No. 18. No. 19. No. 20 in D major, K133; No. 21 in A major, K134; No. 22; No. 23 in D major, K181/162b; No. 24 in B flat major, K182/173dA; D major, K135; (No. 50) in D major, K141a/161-3; No. 26 in E flat major, K161a/184; No. 27 in G major, K199/161b. **Academy of Ancient Music/Jaap Schröder** (vn) with **Christopher Hogwood** (hpd). L'Oiseau-Lyre 417 592-2OH3 — ③ 2h 56m DDD 10/87

Mozart. SYMPHONIES. **The English Concert/Trevor Pinnock** (hpd). Archiv Produktion 431 679-2AH. Recorded in 1990.
No. 25 in G minor, K183/173*dB*; No. 26 in E flat major, K184/161*a*; No. 29 in A major, K201/186*a*.

53m DDD 7/91 

The bicentenary year brought so many Mozart issues (and reissues) that there is a danger that with its passing some of them may quickly be forgotten. However, this one has enough personality to keep its place in the catalogue, and that quality comes across instantly at the start of Symphony No. 26, which is played first. Admittedly the marking is *molto presto*, but even so the listener may be startled by the brisk pace and the near-aggressive vigour of this sound. This is a performance with period instruments (note the veiled string tone in quiet passages), yet there is also something modern about the spotless efficiency of it all and one wonders whether Mozart heard or intended performances like this and if Trevor Pinnock's penchant for pace and sheer energy is sometimes excessive. Set aside that doubt, however, and one must admire the polish and ensemble of this playing, and make no mistake, there is sensitivity too, as the *Andante* shows. This miniature symphony lasts less than nine minutes and its three movements are played without a break. Predictably, Pinnock brings out all the "storm and stress" drama of the G minor Symphony, but there is mystery too in the strangely gliding slow movement and the quiet start of the finale. The elegantly genial A major is nicely shaped, too, and only in the finale might one wish for more space for the music to sound. A vivid and well balanced recording complements this expert playing.

Additional recommendation ...
No. 24 in B flat major, K182/173dA. No. 26. No. 27 in G major, K199/161b. No. 30 in D major, K202/186b. **Prague Chamber Orchestra/Sir Charles Mackerras.** Telarc CD80186 — ∴
58m DDD 8/89

Mozart. SYMPHONIES. **Capella Istropolitana/Barry Wordsworth.** Naxos 8 550113, 8 550119, 8 550164, 8 550186, 8 550264 and 8 550299. Recorded in 1988.
8 550113 (65 minutes): No. 25 in G minor, K183/173*dB*; No. 32 in G major, K318; No. 41 in C major, K551, "Jupiter". *8 550119* (69 minutes): No. 29 in A major, K201/186*a*; No. 30 in D major, K202/186*b*; No. 38 in D major, K504, "Prague". *8 550164* (61 minutes): No. 28 in C major, K200/189*k*; No. 31 in D major, K297/300*a*, "Paris"; No. 40 in G minor, K550. *8 550186* (62 minutes): No. 34 in C major, K338; No. 35 in D major, K385, "Haffner"; No. 39 in E flat major, K543. *8 550264* (65 minutes): No. 27 in G major, K199/161*b*; No. 33 in B flat major, K319; No. 36 in C major, K425, "Linz". *8 550299* (62 minutes): No. 40 in G minor, K550; No. 41 in C major, K551, "Jupiter".

⑥ 6h 24m DDD 4/91 £ B

Collectors who complain about the price of CDs will find their prayers answered in this marvellous Naxos set of the 15 greatest symphonies of Mozart, digitally recorded, yet offered at super-bargain price. Moreover, for those who do not need them all, Naxos have combined the two greatest, No. 40 in G minor and the *Jupiter* on a single disc, which at its modest price should surely find a place in every collection, for it is exceptionally satisfying in every respect. The Capella Istropolitana was founded in 1983, drawing for its players on members of the Slovak Philharmonic Orchestra. The orchestra has already recorded a wide range of baroque music for Naxos and through these discs is gaining a reputation for freshness of musical presentation and polish of ensemble that recalls the early days of the Academy of St Martin in the Fields. Like the first series of Argo ASMF recordings, the impression is that the players really care about the music; there is not a whiff of routine about the music-making. And, as observed in the original *Gramophone* review, "there is an inescapable feeling of fine players enjoying themselves". They are fortunate to have a musical director as sensitive in matters of style and phrasing as Barry Wordsworth, a British conductor, who began his conducting career with the Royal Ballet. His star is ascending very quickly into the firmament, and these discs represent his finest achievement so far. His gift of spontaneity in the recording studio is of course helped by the natural response of his orchestra, which is surely exactly the right size for Mozart. One of his greatest gifts is his sense of pacing, which seems unerring. One has only to turn to the two most famous works (Nos. 40 and 41) to find that tempos are perfectly interrelated. Yet one can go back to the delightful early G minor Symphony (No. 25) and find the *Allegro con brio*, exactly that, and the following *Andante* bringing balm to the senses, with a warmly relaxed *espressivo*. Yet there is never a feeling that the momentum is flagging, for a gently sustained tension beneath the surface of the music keeps it flowing onwards. This is even more striking in the poignant elegy of the *Andante* of No. 29, with its exquisitely gentle cantilena in the violins, while the gracious melodies of the *Andantes* of the *Haffner* (No. 35) and the *Prague* (No. 38) are shaped with disarming beauty. The Introduction of the first movement of the *Prague* is particularly imposing (clearly Mozart wanted to make a strong impression at its first performance): then follows a bright, alert *Allegro*, here full of the spirited momentum one also finds in the finale of No. 29 and the brightly, vivacious outer movements of No. 28. This is an early masterpiece that has only recently been receiving its full due from the general public. Symphony No. 39, a great favourite of many, has another portentous introduction, made the more impressive here by the hard-sticks used on the timpani. Its merry finale (comparable with the genial *Allegro molto* of No. 34) almost anticipates Mendelssohn in its sparkle, and the bright colours from the woodwind. The key of A major means that in the *Allegros* of No. 29 the horns are pitched high, and how wonderfully they shine out over the strings in the finale. Indeed, another aspect of these discs is their excellent balance, with the orchestra believably set out in front of the listener in a natural concert hall acoustic that is warm, yet not too resonant for clarity. Barry Wordsworth is wholly sensible in the matter of repeats, observing them in the expositions of first movements (where they are needed so that the main themes register firmly with the listener, before the argument of their development begins), and in the finales only where they are necessary to establish the appropriate character of the work. As in the *Jupiter*, where the repeat emphasizes the power and breadth of the closing movement, with its great culminating fugal denouement. In all this is a superb set, among the very finest new offerings made during the Mozart bicentennial. To quote further from the original *Gramophone* review, "In every way these are worthy rivals to the best full-price versions". Unless you insist on original instruments they will give very great satisfaction. There are adequate notes (only the disc with Nos. 28, 31 and 40 is deficient in this respect) and they currently cost around £22 for the six discs, which provide around five-and-a-half hours of the greatest music ever written.

Mozart. Symphonies — No. 25 in G minor, K183/173*dB*; No. 28 in C major, K200/189*k*; No. 29 in A major, K201/186*a*. **Prague Chamber Orchestra/Sir Charles Mackerras.** Telarc CD80165.

lh 18m DDD 9/88

Here are three symphonies from Mozart's late teens, written in his native Salzburg, in crisply articulated performances. The first of them is a *Sturm und Drang* piece in a key that the composer reserved for moods of agitation. Mackerras takes the orchestra through the big opening *Allegro con brio* of No. 25 with drive and passion, although it is unlikely that Mozart would have expected a Salzburg orchestra in the 1770s to play as fast as this skilful body of Czech players. The gentle *Andante* comes therefore as a relief, though here too Mackerras keeps a firm rhythmic grasp on the music, and indeed a taut metrical aspect is a feature of all three symphonies as played here, so that minuets dance briskly and purposefully and finales bustle. However, the sunlit warmth of the beautiful A major Symphony, No. 29, comes through and the bracing view of the other two symphonies is a legitimate one, though giving little or nothing in the direction of expressive lingering, much less towards sentimental indulgence. The Prague Chamber Orchestra is an expert ensemble, not over-large for this style of music and the recording is admirably clear although a little reverberant. A well-filled disc.

Additional recommendation ...
Nos. 28 and 29. No. 35. **Berlin Philharmonic Orchestra/Claudio Abbado.** Sony Classical SK48063 — lh 14m DDD 3/92

Mozart. Symphonies — No. 27 in G major, K199/161*b*; No. 28 in C major, K200/189*k*; No. 34 in C major, K338. **English Sinfonia/Sir Charles Groves.** Pickwick IMP Classics PCD933. Recorded in 1989.

lh 3m DDD 3/90

Most music lovers are familiar with half a dozen or so of the Mozart symphonies, but there are others worth exploring too, and this account of three of them is most agreeably done. In the quicker movements, Sir Charles Groves and the English Sinfonia are deft yet alert, but they also respond to nuance, while in the slow movements the playing is quietly expressive. There is an unforced quality about the interpretation overall that is attractive, though some listeners might feel that individual works need fuller characterization. Nevertheless, the playing is always stylish and faithful, and No. 34 (which uses Beecham's performing edition where the woodwind textures are finely realized) is well projected here in its sturdy utterance. One curious fault, at least on the copy reviewed here, is that the track for the bustling finale of this latter symphony (Track 10) begins too early and takes in the last phrase of the *Andante di molto*; however, this will not be noticed if the two are played consecutively, as that phrase, ending with a perfect cadence in F major, is followed by an appropriate small pause. The recording has a natural balance and reverberation.

Additional recommendation ...
No. 21 in A major, K134. No. 23 in D major, K181/162b. No. 24 in B flat major, K182/173dA. No. 27. **Amsterdam Baroque Orchestra/Ton Koopman.** Erato 2292-45544-2 — 53m DDD 2/91

Mozart. Symphonies — No. 29 in A major, K201/186*a*; No. 33 in B flat major, K319. **English Baroque Soloists/John Eliot Gardiner.** Philips 412 736-2PH. From 412 736-1PH (4/86).

44m DDD 8/86

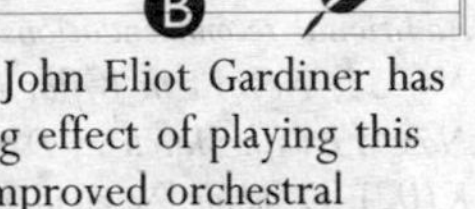

These performances on period instruments sound entirely idiomatic and John Eliot Gardiner has taken pains to avoid anything anachronistic. But perhaps the most striking effect of playing this music on 'authentic' instruments is the gain in textural clarity and the improved orchestral balance: the woodwind stand out distinctly without microphonic assistance and it is no longer necessary to subdue the horns. Performances are marvellously fresh and vital, and the attentive and sympathetic recordings ensure that nothing is lost. Both works are highly inventive and rich in melodic interest, although it is the earlier symphony, No. 29, which impresses most — an astonishing achievement for an 18 year old!

Additional recommendations ...
No. 29. No. 35 in D major, K385, "Haffner". No. 40 in G minor, K550. **Academy of St Martin in the Fields/Sir Neville Marriner.** Philips Silver Line 420 486-2PM — 1h 10m DDD 6/87
No. 29. No. 32 in G major, K318; No. 33. **English Sinfonia/Sir Charles Groves.** Pickwick IMP Classics PCD922 — 1h 1m DDD 11/91

Mozart. Symphonies — No. 31 in D major, K297, "Paris"; No. 38 in D major, K504, "Prague". **English Sinfonia/Sir Charles Groves.** Pickwick IMP Classics PCD892.

55m DDD 9/88

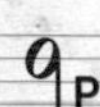

Groves's no-nonsense approach to music of the classical era pays dividends with these two masterworks. He loves this music but, rather than harbouring too precious an infatuation, he greets it with the warm embrace of long acquaintance, letting his natural sense of style control any romantic excess that might otherwise ensue. He brings to these performances the poise of a great performer, unhurried even in the fastest sections, palpably delighting in the fact that repeats provide the opportunity to hear more of this wonderful music. The three movements of both these symphonies require careful balancing if they are not to seem too lightweight and too close to the operatic-overture beginnings of the genre. Sir Charles achieves this by bringing out the warmth of the slow movements, with their elegant phrasing, and avoiding an overdriven and frenetic feel to the finales, by the use of well-judged tempos. The recording, agreeable in most respects, lacks impact in the loudest sections but the overall result is still a happy example of music-making at its best.

Additional recommendation ...
No. 31. No. 33 in B flat major, K319; No. 34. **Prague Chamber Orchestra/Sir Charles Mackerras.** Telarc CD80190 — 1h 5m DDD 3/90

Mozart. Symphonies — No. 35 in D major, K385, "Haffner"[a]; No. 36 in C major, K425, "Linz"[a]. Rondo for violin and orchestra in B flat major, K269[b]. **[a]Bavarian Radio Symphony**

Orchestra/Rafael Kubelík; [b]Saint Paul Chamber Orchestra/Pinchas Zukerman (vn). CBS Masterworks CD44647.

57m DDD 9/89 

These are very satisfying accounts of the *Linz* and *Haffner* Symphonies. Kubelík's ability to project a strong sense of architecture and formal balance is remarkable, and this is reflected on the small scale too, with melodic phrases beautifully shaped and refined. The outer movements of both works are consistently well paced with plenty of rhythmic drive, vitality and drama, with Kubelík never allowing his grip on the symphonic argument to falter or slacken. His unfussy approach in the *Andante* of the *Haffner* allows the pastoral freshness of this movement to surface with ease, and in the *Menuetto* much is made of the contrast between loud and soft, emphasizing the Haydnesque qualities of this movement. The Bavarian orchestra respond well to Kubelík's approach with playing that is warm, full-toned and very assured. The disc also contains an extra bonus in the shape of the *Rondo* in B flat, originally written as an alternative finale to the Violin Concerto No. 1, K207, and is played here in a very attractive performance. The recorded sound has warmth and presence.

Additional recommendations ...

No. 32; No. 33 in B flat major, K319; D major ("Posthorn Serenade"), K320; No. 34 in C major, K338. Nos. 35 with March in D major, K385a (K408 No. 2) and 36. (No. 52) in C major, K213c (K208 and K102); D major (Serenade), K248b (K250); **Academy of Ancient Music/Jaap Schröder** (vn) with **Christopher Hogwood** (hpd). L'Oiseau-Lyre 421 104-2OH3 — ③ 3h 6m ADD 4/88

No. 32 in G major, K318; Nos. 35 and 36. **Scottish Chamber Orchestra/Jukka-Pekka Saraste.** Virgin Classics VJ7 59679-2 — 1h 9m DDD 6/88

Nos. 34 and 35. No. 39 in E flat major, K453. **London Mozart Players/Jane Glover.** ASV CDDCA615 — 1h 14m DDD 7/88

Nos. 32; Nos. 35 and 36. **English Baroque Soloists/John Eliot Gardiner.** Philips 422 419-2PH — 1h 13m DDD 9/89

Nos. 35 and 36, No. 38 in D major, K504, "Prague". No. 39. No. 40 in G minor, K550. No. 41 in C major, K551, "Jupiter". **Columbia Symphony Orchestra/Bruno Walter.** CBS Maestro CD45676 — ② 2h 34m ADD 7/90

Mozart. Symphonies — No. 36 in C major, K425, "Linz"; No. 38 in D major, K504, "Prague". **Prague Chamber Orchestra/Sir Charles Mackerras.** Telarc CD80148.

1h 6m DDD 10/87  

Mozart wrote his *Linz* Symphony in great haste (five days to be precise), but needless to say there is little evidence of haste in the music itself, except perhaps that the first movement has all the exuberance of a composer writing on the wing of inspiration. The slow movement with its siciliano rhythm certainly has no lack of serenity, although it has drama too. The *Prague* Symphony was written only three years later, yet Mozart's symphonic style had matured and the work is altogether more ambitious and substantial. A glorious spaciousness surrounds Sir Charles's performances. The recording venue is reverberant, yet there is no loss of detail, and the fullness of the sound helps to add weight to climaxes without going beyond the bounds of volume that Mozart might have expected. Sir Charles captures the joy and high spirits that these symphonies embody without in any way undermining their greatness. This vivacity is emphasized by the east-European sound of the Prague Chamber Orchestra, with the out-of-doors timbre of its winds which provides a pleasing contrast both with those of the standard British and Germanic orchestras and specialist, authentic ensembles. Mackerras does, however, adopt some aspects of the modern approach to Mozart performance: he includes harpsichord continuo, his minuets are taken trippingly, one-to-a-bar, and he prefers bowing that is crisper, more detached, and pointed. Phrasing and articulation are taken with a natural grace and without overemphasis, dynamics being graded to provide drama at the right moments. The very rightness of the result is recommendation enough.

Additional recommendations ...

No. 38. Le Nozze di Figaro — Overture. **Orchestra of the Eighteenth Century/Franz Brüggen.** Philips 426 231-2PH — 42m DDD 2/90

No. 38. No. 39 in E flat major, K543. **Bavarian Radio Symphony Orchestra/Rafael Kubelík.** CBS CD44648 — 56m DDD 2/90

Nos. 38 and 39. **English Baroque Soloists/John Eliot Gardiner.** Philips 426 283-2PH — 1h 6m DDD 2/91

No. 38. No. 40 in G minor, K550. **London Classical Players/Roger Norrington.** EMI CDC7 54336-2 — 1h 10m DDD 11/92

No. 31 in D major, K300a, "Paris" (first and second versions). No. 35 in D major, K385, "Haffner" (second version). No. 38. No. 39. No. 40 (first version). No. 41 in C major, K551, "Jupiter". **Academy of Ancient Music/Jaap Schröder** (vn) with **Christopher Hogwood** (hpd). L'Oiseau-Lyre 421 085-2OH3 — ③ 3h 11m DDD 9/88

No. 39. **Beethoven.** *Symphony No. 2 in D major, Op. 36.* **Orchestra of the Eighteenth Century/Frans Brüggen.** Philips 422 389-2PH — 1h 3m DDD 6/89

No. 38 in D major, K504, "Prague". No. 39. **Sinfonia Varsovia/Sir Yehudi Menuhin.** Virgin Classics VC7 59561-2 — 56m DDD 3/90

Key to Symbols

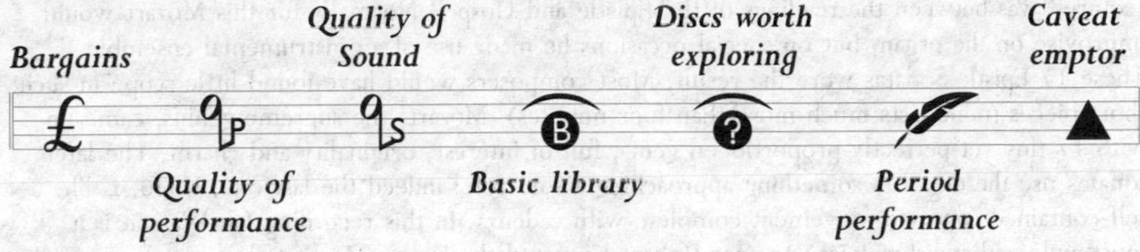

Mozart. Symphonies — No. 40 in G minor, K550; No. 41 in C major, K551, "Jupiter". **English Chamber Orchestra/Jeffrey Tate.** EMI CDC7 47147-2. From EL270154-1 (2/85).

1h 4m DDD 7/85

Jeffrey Tate's approach to both these works is fresh and vigorous and, while he has obviously laboured long and hard over these scores, there isn't the faintest suggestion of contrivance or self-conscious novelty-seeking. His lucid articulation and attention to detail give the music a distinctive textural clarity. There is a monumental quality about these interpretations but this by no means precludes expressive intimacy, for human interest is there too. Just listening to this sportive, yet exultant performance of the finale of the *Jupiter*, with its dazzling contrapuntal devices, the listener is prompted to recall that Mozart's greatness lay so much in his ability to rise above his personal misery to create music that, whilst profoundly meaningful, could still retain a strong element of childlike playfulness.The playing of the English Chamber Orchestra is a constant delight, and the recording is admirably clear and realistically balanced.

Additional recommendations ...

No. 40. **Beethoven.** *Symphony No. 1 in C major, Op. 21.* **Orchestra of the Eighteenth Century/Frans Brüggen.** Philips 416 329-2PH — DDD 7/86

No. 40. **Haydn.** *No. 44 in E minor, "Trauer".* **St John's Smith Square Orchestra/John Lubbock.** Pickwick IMP Red Label PCD820 — DDD 8/86

Nos. 40 and 41. **Prague Chamber Orchestra/Sir Charles Mackerras.** Telarc CD80139 — 1h 11m DDD 5/87

No. 41. **Beethoven.** *Symphony No. 2 in D major, Op. 36.* **Royal Philharmonic Orchestra/Sir Thomas Beecham.** EMI Studio CDM7 69811-2 — 1h 2m ADD 2/89

Nos. 40 and 41. **Bavarian Radio Symphony Orchestra/Rafael Kubelík.** CBS Masterworks CD44649 — 58m DDD 9/89 £

No. 40 and 41. **Sinfonia Varsovia/Sir Yehudi Menuhin.** Virgin Classics VC7 59564-2 — 58m DDD 3/90

Nos. 40 and 41. **Cleveland Orchestra/George Szell.** CBS Maestro CD42538 — 53m ADD 5/90 ▲

No. 40. Eine kleine Nachtmusik. **Haydn.** *Cello Concerto in D major.* **Lynn Harrell** (vc);

Academy of St Martin in the Fields/Sir Neville Marriner. EMI CDM7 64448-2 — lh 5m ADD 10/92

Nos. 40 and 41. **English Baroque Soloists/John Eliot Gardiner.** Philips 426 315-2PH — lh 15m DDD 11/92

No. 28 in C major, K200/189k; No. 29 in A major, K201/186a; No. 30 in D major, K202/186b; Nos. 40 and 41. **Academy of St Martin in the Fields/Sir Neville Marriner.** EMI Digital Twins CZS7 67564-2 — ② 2h 7m DDD 6/93

Mozart. 17 Church Sonatas. **Ian Watson** (org); **Classical Orchestra of the King's Consort/Robert King** (org). Hyperion CDA66377. Recorded in 1990.

lh DDD 11/90

At the age of 16 Mozart was appointed Konzertmeister to the Prince-Archbishop of Salzburg. Opportunities for composing large-scale church music in this post were rather restricted since the Archbishop had ruled that music for the Mass had to be kept to an absolute minimum: the whole service could not exceed 45 minutes. One area where a brief musical interlude was required was between the readings of the Epistle and Gospel. Normally for this Mozart would improvise on the organ, but on special occasions he made use of an instrumental ensemble. These 17 Epistle Sonatas were the result. Most composers would have found little scope in such short pieces (none lasts much more than four minutes). Mozart, the supreme genius, came up with 17 tiny yet perfectly-proportioned gems, full of interest, originality and charm. The later sonatas use the organ in something approaching a solo role; indeed the last one, K336, is like a self-contained concerto movement complete with cadenza. In this recording Ian Watson is a most agile and stylish soloist. As ever Robert King and the King's Consort show total involvement in the music and play with refreshing enthusiasm.

Additional recommendations ...
János Sebestyén (org); **Ferenc Erkel Chamber Orchestra.** Naxos 8 550512 — lh 5m DDD 3/93

Mozart. COMPLETE EDITION, Volume 14 — PIANO QUINTET, QUARTETS, TRIOS, etc. [a]**Aurèle Nicolet** (fl); [ac]**Heinz Holliger** (ob); [a]**Eduard Brunner,** [b]**Jack Brymer** (cls); [a]**Hermann Baumann** (hn); [a]**Klaus Thunemann** (bn); [cd]**Bruno Hoffmann** (glass harmonica); [b]**Patrick Ireland,** [c]**Karl Schouten,** [e]**Bruno Giuranna** (vas); [c]**Jean Decroos** (vc); [ef]**Beaux Arts Trio** (Isidore Cohen, vn; Bernard Greenhouse, vc; Menahem Pressler, pf); [a]**Alfred Brendel,** [b]**Stephen Kovacevich** (pfs). Philips Mozart Edition 422 514-2PME5. Quintet in E flat major for piano and wind, K452[a] (from 420 182-2PH, 8/87). Clarinet Trio in E flat major, K498, "Kegelstatt"[b] (6500 073, 2/71). Adagio and Rondo in C minor, K617[c] (9500 397, 5/78). Adagio in C major, K356/617*a*[d]. Piano Quartets[e] — No. 1 in G minor, K478; No. 2 in E flat major, K493 (both from 410 391-1PH, 10/84). Piano Trios[f] — B flat major, K254; D minor, K442 (cpted. Stadler and Marguerre); G major, K496; B flat major, K502; E major, K542; C major, K548; G major, K564 (all from 422 079-2PH3, 11/88).

⑤ 4h 34m ADD/DDD 9/91

These recordings come from different locations and dates, ranging from 1969 to 1987. Four discs out of the five offer the two piano quartets and seven piano trios, played by the Beaux Arts Trio who are joined in the quartets by the viola player Bruno Giuranna; these are clearly the centrepiece of the issue and the playing of this fine ensemble is strongly characterful yet thoughtful. These are alert, direct and yet refined performances and earn only praise, although the recording in Philips's favoured Swiss location of La-Chaux-de-Fonds could have placed a little more distance between the players and the listener (we also hear the odd intake of breath). But otherwise this clear sound suits the music, and Menahem Pressler's piano tone is well captured. The D minor Trio which ends the series is not wholly authentic, being mainly Maximilian Stadler's compilation from existing material found by Mozart's widow Constanze after his death. Before we come to the piano quartets and piano trios, the first disc also has important works in fine performances in which Alfred Brendel and Heinz Holliger are just two of the artists involved (the Quintet for piano and wind was among the composer's favourite works). The first disc also offers two pieces featuring the ravishing sound of the glass harmonica (musical glasses), which is played by its leading exponent, Bruno Hoffmann, and the solo *Adagio* in C major is quite ethereally beautiful if rather closely recorded. This unique instrument is usefully described and illustrated in the booklet.

Additional recommendations ...
Piano Quartets Nos. 1 and 2. **Malcolm Bilson** (fp); **Elizabeth Wilcock** (vn); **Jan Schlapp** (va); **Timothy Mason** (vc). Archiv Produktion 423 404-2AH — ⁂ 1h 1m DDD 3/89
Piano Quartets Nos. 1 and 2. **Mozartean Players.** Harmonia Mundi HMU90 7018 — ⁂ 1h 4m DDD 3/91
Piano Trios — K496; K502; K542; K548; K564. Divertimento in B flat major, K254. **Trio Fontenay.** Teldec 2292-46439-2 — ⁂ ② 2h 9m DDD 11/91

Mozart. COMPLETE EDITION, Volume 11 — STRING QUINTETS. **Arthur Grumiaux, Arpad Gérecz** (vns); **Georges Janzer, Max Lesueur** (vas); **Eva Czako** (vc). Philips Mozart Edition 422 511-2PME3. From 6747 107 (1/76). Recorded in 1973.
B flat major, K174; C minor, K406/516*b*; C major, K515; G minor, K516; D major, K593; E flat major, K614.

⁂ ③ 2h 50m ADD 9/91

Of the six works which comprise Mozart's complete *oeuvre* for string quintet, that in B flat major, K174, is an early composition, written at the age of 17. It is a well-made, enjoyable work, but not a great deal more than that. The C minor work, K406, is an arrangement by Mozart of his Serenade for six wind instruments, K398. It is difficult not to feel that the original is more effective, since the music seems to sit a little uncomfortably on string instruments. But the remaining four works, written in the last four years of Mozart's life, are a different matter. The last string quintets from Mozart's pen were extraordinary works, and the addition of the second viola seems to have encouraged him to still greater heights. It has been suggested that Mozart wrote K515 and K516 to show King Friedrich Wilhelm II of Prussia that he was a better composer of string quintets than Boccherini, whom the King had retained as chamber music composer to his court. There was no response, so he offered these two quintets for sale with the K406 arrangement to make up the usual set of three. K593 and K614 were written in the last year of his life. Arthur Grumiaux and his colleagues recorded their survey in 1973. Refinement is perhaps the word that first comes to mind in discussing these performances, which are affectionate yet controlled by a cool, intelligent sensitivity. The recordings have been well transferred, the quality is warm and expansive and Grumiaux's tone, in particular, is a delight to the ear but all the playing is alert and stylish. In all, this Philips release is one to earn a strong recommendation, offering as it does Mozart playing of fine quality allied to very decent sound.

Additional recommendations ...
K515. K593. **Simon Whistler** (va); **Salomon Quartet.** Hyperion CDA66431 — ⁂ 1h 6m DDD 11/91
K516. K614. **Simon Whistler** (va); **Salomon Quartet.** Hyperion CDA66432 — ⁂ 1h 4m DDD 11/91
K515. K516. **Hausmusik.** EMI CDC7 54482-2 — ⁂ 1h 12m DDD 3/93

Mozart. COMPLETE EDITION, Volume 12 — STRING QUARTETS. **Quartetto Italiano** (Paolo Borciani, Elisa Pegreffi, vns; Piero Farulli, va; Franco Rossi, vc). Philips Mozart Edition 422 512-2PME8. Recorded 1966-73.
G major, K80/73*f*; D major, K155/134*a*; G major, K156/134*b* (with additional original Adagio); C major, K157 (all from 6500 142, 12/71); F major, K158; B flat major, K159; E flat major, K160/159*a*; F major, K168 (6500 172, 12/72); A major, K169; C major, K170; E flat major, K171; B flat major, K172; D minor, K173 (6747 097, 9/74); G major, K387; D minor, K421/417*b* (SAL3632, 10/67); E flat major, K428/421*b*; B flat major, K458, "Hunt"

(SAL3633, 10/67); A major, K464; C major, K465, "Dissonance" (SAL3634, 10/67); D major, K499; D major, K575 (6500 241, 7/72); B flat major, K589; F major, K590 (6500 225, 7/73).

⑧ 7h 54m ADD 8/91 9p

These are classic performances which have won praise ever since they began to appear back in 1967. Admittedly, a little allowance has to be made for the sound since the recordings date from between 1966 and 1973. For example, it is a touch heavy and close in the 1966 recording of the D minor Quartet that is one of the wonderful set of six that Mozart dedicated to Haydn. In a way, this accords to some extent with the playing of the Quartetto Italiano, which is at times rather earnest — and in the first movement of this work, rather deliberate in its pace. But these are really the only criticisms of a generally splendid issue, and the innate seriousness of these fine Italian artists is almost always a plus feature: indeed, they bring an overall intelligence, refinement and, above all, range of interpretative values to this often superb and always attractive music. As for quality of ensemble, they are impeccable. This is undeniably still the best general survey of Mozart's string quartets available, and at mid-price the eight discs represent a safe investment that should yield many years of pleasure.

Additional recommendation ...
String Quartets — K80/73f; K155/134a; K156/134b; K157; K158; K159; K160/159*a; K168; K169; K170; K171; K172; K173. Divertimentos — D major, K136/125a; B flat major, K137/125b; F major, K138/125c.* **Hagen Quartet.** DG 431 645-2GH3 — ③ 3h 36m DDD 6/91

Mozart. String Quartets — D major, K575; F major, K590. **Salomon Quartet** (Simon Standage, Micaela Comberti, vns; Trevor Jones, va; Jennifer Ward Clarke, vc). Hyperion CDA66355. Recorded in 1990.

1h 1m DDD 4/91 

It is not always that the sound of a string quartet is as easy on the ear as here, and although the recording has fine clarity and bloom it really seems as if this is thanks to the unusually sensitive playing of the four artists using modern replicas of fine period instruments. The result sounds authentic, in the best sense of that much-misused word, and an attractive warmth is imparted to the music. Along with that the members of the Salomon Quartet phrase thoughtfully and affectionately, articulate springily and exercise good judgement in their choice of tempos, not least that of the opening *Allegretto* of the D major Quartet, an unusual pace for a Mozart first movement. Just here and there one might wish for the greater humour, vigour and momentum that other ensembles find, say in the finale of the same work, but the playing is still highly enjoyable and it is a further plus that repeats are faithfully observed. The quartets themselves are the first and third of his three *Prussian* quartets written in 1789-90 for the cello-playing King Friedrich Wilhelm of Prussia — hence their sometimes prominent cello writing and also, probably, the not excessive technical demands placed upon the players. The recording has already been praised and it remains only to add that although it is a little close, lacking really soft dynamics, the intimacy of the playing style still pleases and the instruments are well balanced.

Additional recommendations ...
D major, K499. K575. **Chilingirian Quartet.** CRD CRD3427 — 53m DDD 2/87
B flat major, K598. K590. **Hagen Quartet.** DG 423 108-2GH — 51m DDD 10/87

Mozart. String Quartets — D minor K421/417*b*; C major, K465, "Dissonance". **Salomon Quartet** (Simon Standage, Micaela Comberti, vns; Trevor Jones, va; Jennifer Ward-Clarke, vc). Hyperion CDA66170. From A66170 (12/85).

1h 3m DAD 4/87

Although the string quintet is usually cited as the chamber-music medium into which Mozart poured his most profound thoughts, his canon of some 23 string quartets contains so much that is typical of his genius that to write those works off as being of lesser interest would be to mistake their importance and stature. The thoughtful, warm yet often incisive playing (the violin tone altogether lacks gloss) here, with period instruments, leads to performances that are finely shaped and beautifully clear in detail. The minuets tend to be quickish by modern standards, which is in line with the latest thinking about how they were done in Haydn and Mozart's time, and makes good musical sense. These performances may not represent the ultimate word on the music but they have real integrity and are very satisfying.

Additional recommendation ...

K421/417b. G major, K387. **Bartók Quartet.** Hungaroton White Label HRC129 — 59m ADD 10/89 £

Mozart. STRING QUARTETS. **Chilingirian Quartet** (Levon Chilingirian, Mark Butler, vns; Nicholas Logie, va; Philip de Groote, vc). CRD CRD3362/4. From CRD1062/4 (12/80). Recorded in 1979.

CRD3362 — G major, K387; D minor, K421/417*b*. *CRD3363* — E flat major, K428/421*b*, B flat major, K458, "Hunt". *CRD3364* — A major, K464; C major, K465, "Dissonance".

③ 59m 56m 1h 8m ADD 9/90

NEW REVIEW

Mozart. STRING QUARTETS. **Mosaïques Quartet** (Erich Höbarth, Andrea Bischof, vns; Anita Mitterer, va; Christophe Coin, vc). Astrée Auvidis E8748. Recorded in 1991.

A major, K464; C major, K465, "Dissonance".

1h 16m DDD 8/92

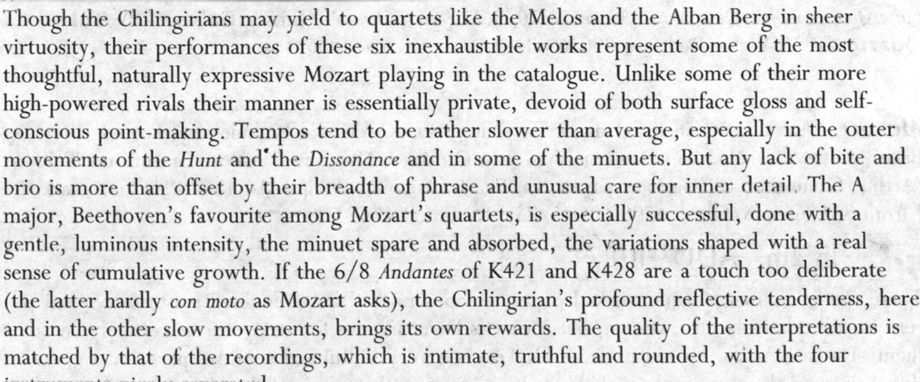

Though the Chilingirians may yield to quartets like the Melos and the Alban Berg in sheer virtuosity, their performances of these six inexhaustible works represent some of the most thoughtful, naturally expressive Mozart playing in the catalogue. Unlike some of their more high-powered rivals their manner is essentially private, devoid of both surface gloss and self-conscious point-making. Tempos tend to be rather slower than average, especially in the outer movements of the *Hunt* and the *Dissonance* and in some of the minuets. But any lack of bite and brio is more than offset by their breadth of phrase and unusual care for inner detail. The A major, Beethoven's favourite among Mozart's quartets, is especially successful, done with a gentle, luminous intensity, the minuet spare and absorbed, the variations shaped with a real sense of cumulative growth. If the 6/8 *Andantes* of K421 and K428 are a touch too deliberate (the latter hardly *con moto* as Mozart asks), the Chilingirian's profound reflective tenderness, here and in the other slow movements, brings its own rewards. The quality of the interpretations is matched by that of the recordings, which is intimate, truthful and rounded, with the four instruments nicely separated.

Using period instruments, the Mosaïques offer searching, richly imagined interpretations of the final two "Haydn" quartets. The first movement of the A major, the most chromatic, elusive and densely argued of Mozart's quartets, is done with grace and a subtle rhythmic fluidity; but the Mosaïques's reading has an underlying urgency: *fortes* are robustly physical, climaxes powerfully clinched, the development's counterpoint and cross-rhythms sharply etched. Their minuet is taut and disquieting, and they bring a real cumulative intensity to the *Andante* variations, with the cello's faintly ominous drumbeat towards the close building to a disturbing climax. The Mosaïques are equally compelling in the more worldly, sociable atmosphere of the C major. The outer movements have a fine sweep and an athletic, unaggressive brilliance, with a marvellous clarity and detail of articulation from Erich Höbarth in rapid semiquaver passages. And in the *Andante* the Mosaïques's breadth and tenderness of line, their discreet, telling use of vibrato and their care for the fine details of Mozart's part-writing make for an exceptional performance, as moving as any of the more overtly expressive readings on modern instruments. The recording gives a vivid immediacy to each of the instruments, not least to Christophe Coin's rich, gutty cello.

Additional recommendations ...

K458. K465. **Alban Berg Quartet.** Teldec 2292-43037-2 — 57m ADD 7/86

As CRD. **Melos Quartet.** DG 415 870-2GCM3 — ③ 2h 51m ADD 6/87

Mozart. FLUTE QUARTETS. **William Bennett** (fl); **Grumiaux Trio** (Arthur Grumiaux, vn; Georges Janzer, va; Eva Czako, vc). Philips Musica da Camera 422 835-2PC. From 6500 034 (6/71). Recorded in 1969.
D major, K285; G major, K285*a*; C major, KAnh171/285*b*; A major, K298.

49m ADD 10/89

Though he confessed that he did not much like the flute, Mozart was incapable of writing dull or poorly constructed music, and as it happens we know that he gave especial attention to the D major Flute Quartet, rewriting part of its finale, while its *Adagio* with its pizzicato accompaniment has a liquid beauty that utterly suits the instrument. This is all attractive music, and the four pieces played here include two charming sets of variations. The playing is of a high order, for William Bennett is an agile and sensitive flautist with a sure sense of the Mozart style, while the Grumiaux Trio, always reliable in this composer, blend beautifully with him tonally. Tempos are well judged also, always a good test of the understanding of the music. The recording dates from 1969, but nothing in the sound suggests this save perhaps a lack of real *pianissimo,* while the instruments are nicely balanced by the Philips engineers in a slightly (but not excessively) reverberant acoustic.

Additional recommendations ...
Flute Quartets[a]. *Clarinet trio in E flat major, "Kegelstatt", K498*[b]. [a]**János Szebenyi** (fl); [b]**Béla Kovács** (cl); [a]**András Kiss** (vn); [a]**László Bársony,** [b]**Géza Németh** (vas); [a]**Károly Botvay** (vc); [b]**Ferenc Rados** (pf). Hungaroton White Label HRC128 — 1h 10m ADD 10/89 £
Flute Quartets. Oboe Quartet in F major, K370/368b[a]. *Clarinet Quintet in A major, K581*[b]. *Horn Quintet in E flat major, K407/386c*[c]. [a]**Lothar Koch** (ob); [b]**Gervase de Peyer** (cl); [c]**Gerd Seifert** (hn); **Amadeus Quartet.** DG 437 137-2GCM2 — ② 1h 55m ADD 2/93
Flute Quartets. Oboe Quartet in F major, K370/368b (arr. Galway)[a]. [a]**James Galway** (fl); **Tokyo Quartet.** RCA Victor Red Seal 09026 60442-2 — 1h 9m DDD 6/93

Mozart. Divertimento in E flat major for string trio, K563[a]. Six Preludes and Fugues (after Bach), K404*a*[b] — No. 1 in D minor; No. 2 in G minor; No. 3 in F major. **Grumiaux Trio** (Arthur Grumiaux, vn; Georges Janzer, va; Eva Czako, vc). Philips 416 485-2PH. Item marked [a] from SAL3664 (8/68), [b] 6500 605 (5/75). Recorded 1967-73.

1h 2m ADD 11/87

There cannot be many major works by great composers that are undoubted masterpieces and yet remain still relatively little known, but Mozart's Divertimento for string trio is certainly one of them. The late Arthur Grumiaux leads his Trio in a very skilful and sensitive performance, and they bring out the tragic power of the *Andante* in a way that cannot fail to impress and move a sympathetic listener. This is a work that all who love Mozart should know, and this performance is persuasive and very well recorded, so that one would not guess that the date of the sessions was 1967. The three Preludes followed by Fugues in three contrapuntal parts were recorded in 1973 and while not personal in the obvious sense they have a special interest of their own for students of this composer.

Additional recommendations ...
Divertimento. Duos for violin and viola — G major, K423; B flat major, K424. **Dénes Kovács** (vn); **Géza Németh** (va); **Ede Banda** (vc). Hungaroton White Label HRC072 — 1h 13m ADD 5/90 £
Divertimento. Six Preludes and Fugues (after Bach), K404a — No. 1 in D minor; No. 2 in G minor; No. 3 in F major; No. 6 in F minor. **L'Archibudelli Trio.** Sony Classical Vivarte MK46497 — 1h 3m DDD £

Mozart. COMPLETE EDITION, Volume 18 — PIANO VARIATIONS, RONDOS, etc. [a]**Ingrid Haebler,** [b]**Mitsuko Uchida** (pfs); [c]**Ton Koopman** (hpd). Philips Mozart Edition 422 518-2PME5.
Variations — G major, K24[a]; D major, K25[a]; C major, K179/189*a*[a]; G major, K180/173*c*[a]; C major, K264/315*d*[a]; C major, K265/300*e*[a]; F major, K352/374[ca]; E flat major, K353/300*f*[a]; E

flat major, K354/299*a*[a]; F major, K398/416*e*[a]; G major, K455[a] (all from 6747 380, 6/79); A major, K460/454*a*[c] (new to UK); B flat major, K500[a]; D major, K573[a]; F major, K613[a] (6747 380). *Minuets* — F major, K1*d*[c]; G major/C major, K1/1*e*/1*f*[c]; F major, K2[c]; F major, K4[c]; F major, K5[c]; D major, K94/73*h*[c]; D major, K355/576*b*[b] (all new to UK). Fantasia in D minor, K397/385*g*[b] (412 123-1PH, 7/84). *Rondos* — D major, K485[b] (420 185-2PH, 7/87); A minor, K511[b] (412 122-1PH, 11/84). Adagio in B minor, K540[b]. Gigue in G major, K574[b] (both from 412 616-1PH, 4/85). Klavierstück in F major, K33*B*[c]. Capriccio in C major, K395/300*g*[c]. March No. 1 in C major, K408/383*e*[c]. Prelude and Fugue in C major, K394/383*a*[c]. *Allegros* — C major, K1*b*[c]; F major, K1*c*[c]; B flat major, K3[c]; C major, K5*a*[c]; G minor, K312/590*d*[c]; B flat major, K400/372*a* (cpted Stadler)[c]. Suite in C major, K399/385*i*[c]. Kleine Trauermarsch in C minor, K453*a*[c]. Andante in C major, K1*a*[c]. Fugue in G minor, K401/375*e*[c] (with Tini Mathot, hpd. All new to UK).

⑤ 4h 34m ADD/DDD 10/91

These five mid-price discs offer music of fine and often superb quality in a convenient format. The piano was Mozart's own instrument (though he also played the violin) and he composed much music for it besides the sonatas and concertos. Of the three artists here, two are generally fine and satisfying, though the third is more controversial. Ingrid Haebler was recorded back in 1975, but the piano sound is good and little tape background remains, and her performances of the variation sets, which take up the first three discs, are delicate without cuteness, effortlessly encompassing the music's wide range of moods. Mitsuko Uchida, on the fourth disc, performs individual pieces including the two rondos and the beautiful *Adagio* in B minor (the only piece Mozart wrote in this key) in a highly refined manner, a touch over-sophisticated perhaps but still beautiful and expressive and taking full, unashamed advantage of the sound of a modern grand. By contrast, Ton Koopman's disc of minuets and other miscellaneous things is played on a harpsichord at a semitone below modern concert pitch and offers a recording of such immediacy that some listeners will regard it as too bright. Koopman puts gusto into everything he does, but not always to good effect. However, even if grace is in short supply in his performances, they undeniably offer ample personality and such reservations as one may have about his playing should not affect the desirability of the set as a whole.

Mozart. SONATAS FOR KEYBOARD AND VIOLIN. **Szymon Goldberg** (vn); **Radu Lupu** (pf). Decca 430 306-2DM4. From 13BB 207/12 (11/75).

C major, K296; G major, K301/293*a*; E flat major, K302/293*b*; C major, K303/293*c*; E minor, K304/300*c*; A major, K305/293*d*; D major, K306/300*l*; F major, K376/374*d*; F major, K377/374*e*; B flat major, K378/317*d*; G major, K379/373*a*; E flat major, K380/374*f*; B flat major, K454; E flat major, K481; A major, K526; F major, K547.

④ 4h 42m ADD 9/91 £

This set of Mozart's violin sonatas has acquired something like classic status since it was released on six vinyl discs in 1975. Now on four mid-price CDs, it represents fine value: Szymon Goldberg and Radu Lupu make an excellent partnership, for the inherent vigour of the violinist's playing is tempered by the innate warmth of the pianist in such a way that their various qualities appear to advantage according to the nature of each sonata as well as individual movements. In other words, Lupu is still there as a personality in his own right, which is as it should be when one remembers that, strictly speaking, these are sonatas designated as "for piano and violin" but he is never over-assertive. There's much to enjoy here, such as the agreeable quiet charm with which the artists handle the finale of the two-movement Sonata in G major, K301, and the elegance of the finale in the late A major Sonata, K526, one of the finest of all as well as the most challengingly difficult. But similar examples of their empathy abound in the 42 movements (and 16 sonatas) that are played, and even if some collectors may feel that the minuets in K303 and K377 are a touch too dreamy, this is a most desirable set, clearly yet warmly recorded in London's Kingsway Hall.

Additional recommendation ...

K481, K526 and K547. **Szymon Goldberg** (vn); **Radu Lupu** (pf). Decca 425 420-2DM *(part of the 4-disc set reviewed above)* — 1h 2m ADD 10/89

NEW REVIEW

Mozart. SONATAS AND VARIATIONS FOR KEYBOARD AND VIOLIN. **Yuuko Shiokawa** (vn); **András Schiff** (fp). Decca 436 547-2DH. Recorded in 1992.
Sonatas — E minor, K304/300*c*; G major, K379/373*a*; C major, K403/385*c*; B flat major, K454. Variations in G minor on "Hélas, j'ai perdu mon amant", K360/374*b*.

1h 11m DDD 3/93

What immediately makes this record special is the instruments used. The violin that Yuuko Shiokawa plays once belonged to Mozart's sister Nannerl and is currently on display in the house in Salzburg where the composer was born. As for the fortepiano, which is also in the Mozart Museum, according to tradition it was the composer's own and was played by him in the last years of his life. Finally, the recording has been made in the actual room where he was born. Given these facts, it is easy to feel that that the sounds we hear are as close as we are likely to get to the ones that Mozart himself imagined and listened to two centuries ago. And beyond this, there is a warmth about the playing of the two artists that surely reflects circumstances which must have made them feel privileged and excited. The three sonatas have been well chosen, for the G major and E minor (the only one of the violin sonatas that is in a minor key) in different ways suggest the imaginative vigour and occasional stressfulness of the young musician whose Salzburg background first inspired and then frustrated him while the B flat Sonata, although composed when he was still under 30, comes from his noble maturity and sounds like it. The Variations in G minor, on a French folksong, are less familiar, but attractively wistful and played with elegance. Overall, these performances have both energy and subtlety. For an example of the latter, witness Schiff's quiet, silvery introduction to the *Minuet* second movement of the E minor Sonata. It must be admitted, however, that after this Shiokawa enters rather too boldly, and if one has a reservation about the playing it is that the violin is often a little loud relative to the keyboard, a matter partly of recording but not entirely so. The two instruments are tuned about a semitone below normal concert pitch.

Mozart. Double Piano Sonata in D major, K448/375*a*.
Schubert. Fantasia in F minor, D940. **Murray Perahia, Radu Lupu** (pfs). CBS Masterworks CD39511. From IM39511 (3/86). Recorded in 1984.

42m ADD 10/86

One of the highlights of concert-going at Snape in the 1980s was to hear Lupu and Perahia, two of the greatest pianists of our era, performing together as one, and yet retaining their own, very individual identities. This disc is a happy reminder of that experience; it was recorded live at The Maltings and it captures exactly that peculiarly characterful, wayward acoustic that has been the bane of so many recording engineers. Having an audience present makes the job infinitely simpler, yet the task is still not an easy one. The performances that are so admirably conveyed here are not of the conventional block-buster type. Neither of these pianists has made tickets to their recitals as difficult to grasp as the Grail by producing virtuosic histrionics. Perfect tone control, total dedication to the inner life of the music, satisfying originality of vision, and a beguiling spontaneity have made their solo performances special; together they show themselves to be selfless chamber musicians of the highest order, capable of lifting already great music to a higher plain. Despite the warm tone of the instruments and ambience, their Mozart is totally classical in ethos, their Schubert divinely other-worldly. One of the desert island's life-sustaining Eight.

Additional recommendations ...
Double Piano Sonatas — K448/375a; C major, K19d; D major, K381/123a; B flat major, K358/186c; G major, K357/497a; F major, K497. C major, K521. Andante and Variations in G major, K501. Adagio and Allegro in F minor, K594. Fantasia in F minor, K608. Fugues — C minor, K426; G minor, K401. **Güher** and **Süher Pekinel.** Teldec 2292-46014-2 — ③ 2h 5lm DDD 6/92
K448/375a. Andante and Variations in G major, K501. **Schubert.** *Fantasie in F minor, D940.* **Louis Lortie, Hélène Mercier** (pfs). Chandos CHAN9162 — 50m DDD 7/93

NEW REVIEW

Mozart. KEYBOARD WORKS. [a]**Bernard Foccroulle** (org); [b]**Luc Devos** (pf); [c]**Dennis James** (glass harmonica); **Guy Penson** ([d]hpd/[e]clav/[f]tangent pf). Ricercar RIC105081. Recorded in 1991.

Andante in B flat major, K15*ii*[a]. Piano Piece in F major, K33*b*[a]. Allegro in G major, K72*a*[a]. Andante in C major, K1*a*[e]. *Allegros* — C major, K1*b*[e]; F major, K1*c*[e]. *Minuets* — F major, K1*d*[e]; G major, K1/1*e*[e]; C major, K1*f*[e]; F major, K2[d]. Allegro in B flat major, K3[d]. *Minuets* — F major, K4[d]; F major, K5[d]; C major, K9*a*[d]. Londoner Notenskizzenbuch — K15*a*, K15*m*[e]. *Minuets* — C major, K61*g*/*ii*[d]; D major, K94/73*h*[d]. Eight Minuets, K315*a*[f]. Allegro in G minor, K312/590*d*[d]. Capriccio in C major, K395/300*g*[f]. Fugue in G minor, K401/375*e*[a]. Prelude and Fugue in C major, K394/383*a*[b]. March in C major, K408/1[b]. *Fantasias* — C minor, K396/385*f*[b]; D minor, K397/385*g*[b]. Suite in the style of Handel in C major, K399/385*i*[d]. Allegro in B flat major, K400/372*a*[b]. Kleiner Traurermarsch in C minor, K453*a*[b]. Fantasia in C minor, K475[b]. Rondo in D major, K485[b]. Six German Dances, K509[b]. Rondo in A minor, K511[b]. Adagio in B minor, K540[b]. Allegro and Allegretto in F major, KAnh135/547*a*[b]. Minuet in D major, K355/567*b*[b]. Andantino (theme with variations) in E flat major, K236[b]. Gigue in G major, K574[a]. Andante fur eine Walze in eine kleine Orgel in F major, K616[a]. Adagio and Rondo in C minor, K617[c].

3 2h 55m DDD 12/92

Here are the odds-and-ends of Mozart's vast output for keyboard — the pieces which don't easily fit on to CDs devoted to more significant works (like the piano sonatas and sets of variations). Ricercar have taken the "lump them all together" approach and the result is not only immensely fascinating but this whole three-CD package makes a thoroughly rewarding listening experience in spite of its somewhat piecemeal appearance. There are six different keyboard instruments involved including the peculiar glass harmonica, which isn't strictly speaking a keyboard instrument at all but basically a set of tuned wine-glasses carefully recreated by Dennis James from contemporary accounts of the instrument for which Mozart wrote the *Allegro and Rondo* in C minor. But Mozart didn't always specify which instrument a piece was intended to be played on and a certain amount of guesswork has been involved in distributing music to instrument for these recordings. However, even if the *Allegro* in G (K72*a*) seems more likely to have been written for clavichord, and the Minuets of K315*a* were probably intended to be orchestrated at some later date, their performance here on a charming sweet-toned Dutch organ and the *Tantgentenflügel* (a tangent piano) respectively works well. Each disc is designed to give a varied selection both of pieces and instruments, and the playing and recordings are exemplary. For the most part the music is simple, charming but unexceptional, the real joy of these discs being to hear it played on instruments which would have been entirely familiar to Mozart's ears.

Mozart. PIANO WORKS. **András Schiff.** Decca 421 369-2DH.

Variations on "Ah, vous dirai-je, maman", K265/300*e*. Andante in F major, K616. Rondo in A minor, K511. Adagio in C major, K356/617*a*. Minuet in D major, K355/576*b*. Gigue in G major, K574. Adagio in B minor, K540. Variations on "Unser dummer Pöbel meint", K455.

1h 12m DDD 10/88 P

This young Hungarian can boast fingers second to none when dazzling prestidigitation is the order of the day. Here, however, we meet him not as a virtuoso but as a musician. Nothing in the recital makes heavy technical demands, but since everything dates from Mozart's last decade, each note in a sense is laden. And Schiff brings this home with a rare understanding of the eloquence of simplicity. The Variations themselves testify to Mozart's ever-burgeoning ingenuity of invention as time ran on — and out. In the field of the so-called miniature, surely no composer has ever written anything more profound than the A minor *Rondo* and B minor *Adagio*, both beautifully timed and shaded here. The harmonically audacious *Minuet* in D and the teasing G major *Gigue* in their turn bring just the right contrast from the *Andante* in F for Mechanical Organ and the *Adagio* in C for Glass Harmonica, which in their Elysian purity touch the heart just that much more for having both grown from Mozart's very last spring. In sum, a disc to be treasured.

Mozart. COMPLETE EDITION, Volume 17 — COMPLETE PIANO SONATAS. **Mitsuko Uchida** (pf). Philips Mozart Edition 422 517-2PME5.
C major, K279/189*d* (from 412 617-1PH, 1/86); F major, K280/189*e*; B flat major, K281/189*f*; E flat major, K282/189*g*; G major, K283/189*h* (all from 420 186-2PH, 4/88); D major, K284/205*b* (420 185-1PH, 7/87); C major, K309/284*b*; A minor, K310/300*d*; D major, K311/284*c* (412 174-1PH, 4/86); C major, K330/300*h* (412 616-1PH, 4/85); A major, K331/300*i*; F major, K332/300*k* (412 123-1PH, 7/84); B flat major, K333/315*c* (412 616-1PH); C minor, K457 (412 617-1PH); F major, K533/494; C major, K545 (412 122-1PH, 11/84); B flat major, K570 (420 185-1PH); D major, K576 (420 617-1PH). Fantasia in C minor, K475 (412 617-1PH).

⑤ 5h 25m DDD 9/91 

By common consent, Mitsuko Uchida is among the leading Mozart pianists of today, and her recorded series of the piano sonatas won critical acclaim as it appeared and finally *Gramophone* Awards in 1989 and 1991. Here are all the sonatas, plus the Fantasia in C minor, K475, which is in some ways a companion piece to the sonata in the same key, K457. This is unfailingly clean, crisp and elegant playing, that avoids anything like a romanticized view of the early sonatas such as the delightfully fresh G major, K283. On the other hand, Uchida responds with the necessary passion to the forceful, not to say *Angst*-ridden, A minor Sonata, K310. Indeed, her complete series is a remarkably fine achievement, comparable with her account of the piano concertos. The recordings were produced by Erik Smith in the Henry Wood Hall in London and offer excellent piano sound; thus an unqualified recommendation is in order for what must be one of the most valuable volumes in Philips's Complete Mozart Edition. Do not be put off by critics who suggest that these sonatas are less interesting than some other Mozart compositions, for they are fine pieces written for an instrument that he himself played and loved.

Additional recommendations ...

K280/189e. K281/189f. K282/189g. K283/189h. **Mitsuko Uchida.** Philips 420 186-1PH *(part of the 5-disc set reviewed above)* — 54m DDD 4/88 Ⓑ

K280/189e. K281/189f. K283/189h. K311/284c. K330/300h. K331/300i. **Malcolm Bilson** (fp). Hungaroton HCD31009/10 — ② 1h 56m DDD 12/89 Ⓑ

Complete Sonatas. Fantasia, K475. **Maria João Pires.** DG 431 760-2GH6 — ⑥ 6h 37m DDD 2/92 Ⓑ

Complete Sonatas. Fantasia, K475. **András Schiff.** Decca 430 333-2DM5 — ⑤ 5h 21m ADD 2/92 Ⓑ

Complete Sonatas. Fantasias — D minor, K397/385g; K475. **Lili Kraus.** Sony Classical SM4K47222 — ④ 5h 2m ADD Ⓑ

K310/300d. K331/300i. K533/494. **Murray Perahia** (pf). Sony Classical SK48233 — 1h 4m DDD 12/92 Ⓑ

K281/189f. K282/189g. K533/494. **Maria-João Pires** (pf). DG 437 546-2GH — 1h 2m DDD 7/93 Ⓑ

Mozart. MASONIC MUSIC. [a]**Werner Krenn** (ten); [b]**Tom Krause** (bar); [c]**Edinburgh Festival Chorus; György Fischer** ([d]org/[e]pf); [f]**London Symphony Orchestra/István Kertész.** Decca Serenata 425 722-2DM. Texts and translations included. From SXL6409 (10/69).
Lobegesang auf die feierliche Johannisloge, K148[ae]. Dir, Seele des Weltalls, K429/K468*a*[acf]. Lied zur Gesellenreise, K468[ae]. Die Maurerfreude, K471[acf]. Maurerische Trauermusik, K477[f]. Zerfliesset heut', geliebte Brüder, K483[acd]. Ihr unsre neuen Leiter, K484[acd]. Die ihr des unermesslichen Weltalls, K619[ae]. Laut verkünde unsre Freude, K623[abcf]. Lasst uns mit geschlungnen Händen, K623*a*[cd].

53m ADD 11/90

In the late eighteenth century, the Freemasons' belief in a human brotherhood and mutual responsibility that was independent of birth or wealth was a force for social change which proved so strong and influential that Masonry was banned in Austria not long after Mozart's death. Since he, Haydn and Beethoven were all Masons, it is clear that this secretive society meant much to several major artists, and in Mozart's case this is reflected in the many Masonic works he composed, of which the opera *Die Zauberflöte* is the most celebrated. This disc offers a number of other Masonic pieces, mostly little known, some of which were actually used in Viennese Lodges. They begin with a simple tenor hymn in praise of brotherhood, and include several other vocal pieces, some honouring God the 'Great Architect'; there is also the powerful *Masonic Funeral Music* of 1785, written for an unusual orchestral body (including a double-bassoon) just 11 months after the composer was admitted to the Viennese Lodge 'Beneficence', with its name implying the doing of good works. These performances sound dedicated as well as being skilful, with the tenor soloist Werner Krenn sounding particularly suited to the music with its touch of solemn earnestness. The recording does not show its age and balances the various vocal and instrumental forces well.

Mozart (ed. Maunder). Mass in C minor, K427/417*a*. **Arleen Auger, Lynne Dawson** (sops); **John Mark Ainsley** (ten); **David Thomas** (bass); **Winchester Cathedral Choir; Winchester College Quiristers; Academy of Ancient Music/Christopher Hogwood.** L'Oiseau-Lyre Florilegium 425 528-2OH. Text and translation included. Recorded in 1988.

51m DDD 7/90

Mozart left unfinished the work that ought to have been the choral masterpiece of his early Viennese years but there is enough of it to make up nearly an hour's music — music that is sometimes sombre, sometimes florid, sometimes jubilant. Christopher Hogwood avoids any charge of emotional detachment in his steady and powerful opening *Kyrie*, monumental in feeling, dark in tone; and he brings ample energy to the big, bustling choruses of the *Gloria* — and its long closing fugue is finely sustained. The clarity and ring of the boys' voices serve him well in these numbers. There is a strong solo team, headed by the late Arleen Auger in radiant, glowing voice and, as usual, singing with refined taste; Lynne Dawson joins her in the duets, John Mark Ainsley too in the trio. But this is essentially a "soprano mass" — Mozart wrote it, after all, with the voice of his new wife (and perhaps thoughts of the much superior one of her sister Aloysia) in his mind — and Auger, her voice happily stealing in for the first time in the lovely "Christe", excels in the florid and expressive music of the "Et incarnatus" (where Richard Maunder has supplied fuller string parts than usual, perhaps fuller than Mozart would have done had he finished the work). Hogwood directs with his usual spirit and clarity.

Additional recommendations ...
Mass in C minor. **Soloists; Monteverdi Choir; English Baroque Soloists/John Eliot Gardiner.** Philips 420 210-2PH — 54m DDD 5/88
Mass in C minor. ***Beethoven.*** *Missa solemnis.* **Soloists; Atlanta Symphony Chorus and Orchestra/Robert Shaw.** Telarc CD80150 — ② 2h 19m DDD 11/88
Mass in C minor. **Soloists; Berlin Radio Chorus; Berlin Philharmonic Orchestra/Claudio Abbado.** Sony Classical SK46671 — 53m DDD 10/91

Mozart (cptd Süssmayr). Mass in D minor, K626, "Requiem". **Sylvia McNair** (sop); **Carolyn Watkinson** (contr); **Francisco Araiza** (ten); **Robert Lloyd** (bass); **Chorus and Academy of St Martin in the Fields/Sir Neville Marriner.** Philips 432 087-2PH. Text and translation included. Recorded in 1990.

50m DDD 12/91

Alongside those old musical teasers, "Who wrote Haydn's *Toy* Symphony?" (Leopold Mozart) and "Who wrote Purcell's Trumpet Voluntary?" (Jeremiah Clarke) can be added "Who wrote Mozart's Requiem?". Mozart's pupil Süssmayr was responsible for much of the work as most modern audiences would recognize it, but exactly how much was Mozart's, how much Süssmayr's, and how much anybody else's is anyone's guess. But performers don't seem unduly perturbed by this masterpiece's less than certain provenance, and there is no shortage of first-rate CD versions. Sir Neville Marriner's interpretation stands out as one of towering authority with a nobility and emotional impact few performances outside the concert-hall could expect to muster. From the stately opening "Requiem aeternam" to the Requiem's emotional climax, the "Agnus Dei", Marriner's musicians produce superlative performances. The chorus is remarkably well disciplined (just listen to the beautifully incisive singing with its dramatic dynamic contrasts in the "Domine Jesu"), and from the soloists Robert Lloyd's resonant "Tuba mirum" is a stunning contribution to a disc of exceptional quality.

Additional recommendations ...

Requiem. Kyrie in D minor K341. **Soloists; Monteverdi Choir; English Baroque Soloists/John Eliot Gardiner.** Philips 420 197-2PH — 54m DDD 11/87

Requiem. **Soloists; St John's College Choir, Cambridge; English Chamber Orchestra/George Guest.** Chandos CHAN8574 — 54m DDD 2/88

Requiem. **Soloists; John Alldis Choir; BBC Symphony Orchestra/Sir Colin Davis.** Philips Silver Line 420 353-2PM — 54m ADD 2/88

Requiem. **Soloists; Northern Sinfonia and Chorus/Richard Hickox.** Virgin Classics Virgo VJ7 59648-2 — 47m DDD 12/91 £

Requiem (ed. Druce). Ave verum corpus, K618. Maurerische Trauermusik, K477/479. **Soloists** including **John Mark Ainsley** (ten); **Schütz Choir of London; Schütz Consort; London Classical Players/Roger Norrington.** EMI CDC7 54525-2 — 58m DDD 11/92

NEW REVIEW

Mozart. LIEDER. **Peter Schreier** (ten); **András Schiff** (pf). Decca 430 514-2DH. Texts and translations included. Recorded in 1990.

Dans un bois solitaire, K308/295*b*. Die Zufriedenheit, K349. Komm, liebe Zither, K351/367*b*. Ich würd'auf meinem Pfad, K390/340*c*. Lied zur Gesellenreise, K468. Der Zauberer, K472. Die Zufriedenheit, K473. Die betrogene Welt, K474. Das veilchen, K476. Lied der Freiheit, K506. Die Alte, K517. Der Verschweigung, K518. Das Lied der Trennung, K519. Als Luise die Breife, K520. Abendempfindung, K523. An Chloe, K524. Das Traumbild, K530. Das kleine Spinnerin, K531. Sehnsucht nach dem Frühling, K596. Frühlingsanfang, K597. Eine kleine deutsche Kantate, K619.

1h 10m DDD 8/92 

Two songs in this collection bear the title *Die Zufriedenheit* ("Contentment") and that word virtually sums up this disc of 21 songs. It is wholly satisfying in every way, not something that can be said of any recordings but the very best. The Lieder range from the popular and often-heard songs such as *An Chloe* ("To Chloe") and *Abendempfindung* ("Thoughts at eventide") to the devoutness of the masonic-like Cantata, K619, *Die ihr des unermesslichen Weltalls Schopfer ehrt* ("You who honour the Creator of the infinite Universe"). Peter Schreier and András Schiff offer a range of expression which swings effortlessly between the calm, profound qualities of the Masonic settings and the charm and subtlety of the narrative or allegorical songs. Throughout, the performers tenderly convey Mozart's lightness of touch, keeping the emotions balanced on the fine thread between longing, objectivity, irony and the deep, childlike directness of *Sehnsucht nach dem Frühling* ("Longing for Spring") — on which the last movement of Mozart's last piano concerto is based. Schreier and Schiff are an equal partnership from start to finish. Schreier's full, deep tenor can characterize *Die Alte* ("The old woman") with a nasal nastiness or infuse some of the other songs with real anguish. Schiff's playing is glorious, embodying emotional essences within the simplest accompaniment figuration or dazzling with the lightness and vividness of his touch in the quasi-pizzicato in *Komm, liebe Zither* ("Come, my dear Zither").

Mozart. ARIAS. **Cecilia Bartoli** (mez); [a]**András Schiff** (pf); **Peter Schmidtl** ([b]basset cl and [c]basset hn); **Vienna Chamber Orchestra/György Fischer.** Decca 430 513-2DH. Texts and translations included. Recorded 1989-90.

LE NOZZE DI FIGARO — Non so più; Voi che sapete; Giunse alfin il momento ... Deh vieni. COSI FAN TUTTE — E'amore un ladroncello. DON GIOVANNI — Vedrai, carino. LA CLEMENZA DI TITO — Parto, parto[b]; Deh, per questo; Ecco il punto, o Vitellia ... Non piu di fiori[c]. Concert Arias — Chi sa, chi sa, qual sia, K582; Alma grande e nobil core, K578; Ch'io mi scordi di te?, K505[a].

58m DDD 12/91

Mozart wrote some of his most appealing music for the mezzo-soprano voice with the roles of Cherubino and Susanna in *Le nozze di Figaro*, Dorabella in *Così fan tutte* and Zerlina in *Don Giovanni* each boasting at least one memorable aria. Alongside these this disc includes a handful of concert arias including *Ch'io mi scordi di te?* which was written for the farewell performance of the great mezzo Nancy Storace with Mozart himself playing the concertante piano role. Here with as innate an interpreter of Mozart's piano writing as András Schiff and a voice so remarkably self-assured as Cecilia Bartoli's the electricity of that first, historic performance seems almost to be recreated. And, here as elsewhere, György Fischer directs the splendid Vienna Chamber Orchestra with disarming sensitivity while the recording is wonderfully warm and vibrant. Cecilia Bartoli boasts a voice of quite extraordinary charm and unassuming virtuosity: her vocal characterizations would be the envy of the finest actresses and her intuitive singing is in itself a sheer delight. But she also brings to these arias a conviction and understanding of the subtleties of the language which only a native Italian could. Listen to the subtle nuances of "Voi che sapete", the depth of understanding behind Dorabella's seemingly frivolous "E'amore un ladroncello"; these are not mere performances, but interpretations which penetrate to the very soul of the music. No Mozart lover should be without this CD.

Additional recommendation ...

COSI FAN TUTTE — Temerari! ... Come scoglio. LA CLEMENZA DI TITO — Non più di fiori. DON GIOVANNI — In quali eccessi ... Mi tradì quell'alma ingrata. DIE ENTFUHRUNG AUS DEM SERAIL — Marten aller Arten. IDOMENEO — Oh smanie! ... D'Oreste e d'Aiace. LE NOZZE DI FIGARO — E Susanna non vien! ... Dove sono i bei momenti; Porgi, amor. DIE ZAUBERFLOTE — O zittre nicht ... Zum Leiden bin ich auserkoren; Der Hölle Rache; Ach, ich fühl's. **Cheryl Studer** (sop); **Academy of St Martin the Fields/Sir Neville Marriner.** Philips 426 721-2PH — 55m DDD 5/91

Mozart. LE NOZZE DI FIGARO. **Sesto Bruscantini** (bar) Figaro; **Graziella Sciutti** (sop) Susanna; **Franco Calabrese** (bass) Count Almaviva; **Sena Jurinac** (sop) Countess Almaviva; **Risë Stevens** (mez) Cherubino; **Monica Sinclair** (contr) Marcellina; **Ian Wallace** (bass) Bartolo; **Hugues Cuénod** (ten) Don Basilio; **Daniel McCoshan** (ten) Don Curzio; **Gwyn Griffiths** (bar) Antonio; **Jeanette Sinclair** (sop) Barbarina; **Glyndebourne Festival Chorus and Orchestra/Vittorio Gui.** Classics for Pleasure CD-CFPD4724. From HMV ALP1312/15 (1/56). Recorded in 1955.

(2) 2h 38m ADD 9/91 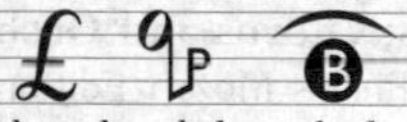

Le nozze di Figaro ("The marriage of Figaro") is comically inventive (though subtly spiked with irony), musically fleet and theatrically well-nigh perfect. The plot revolves around the domestic arrangements of the Count and Countess and their servants Figaro and Susanna, and more specifically around the male/female struggle in the household. Plots involving disguise and much hiding lead effortlessly through this most enchanting of operas to a rousing chorus when, in true Mozartian style, the world is restored to rights and everyone is just that bit chastened and a little wiser. This set is an outright bargain. Although the performance hasn't quite the dramatic drive or vocal glamour of the others listed below it has a lively, intimate ambience deriving from performances at Glyndebourne and boasts the loveliest of all Countesses in Jurinac and a vitally idiomatic Figaro in Bruscantini. The recording is more than adequate. The impecunious newcomer should hurry to catch this set while it's available — such reissues have the habit of not lasting long in the catalogue.

Additional recommendations ...

Soloists; Glyndebourne Chorus; London Philharmonic Orchestra/Bernard Haitink with **Martin Isepp** (hpd). EMI CDS7 49753-2 — (3) 2h 58 DDD 7/88

Soloists; Chorus and Orchestra of the Drottningholm Court Theatre/Arnold Ostman with **Mark Tatlow** (hpd cont). L'Oiseau-Lyre 421 333-2OH3 — (3) 3h 6m DDD 12/88

Soloists; Philharmonia Chorus and Orchestra/Carlo Maria Giulini. EMI CMS7 63266-2 — ② 2h 33m ADD 1/90
Soloists; Vienna State Opera Chorus; Vienna Philharmonic Orchestra/Erich Kleiber. Decca Grand Opera Series 417 315-2DM3 — ③ 2h 52m ADD 2/90

Mozart. DON GIOVANNI. **Eberhard Waechter** (bar) Don Giovanni; **Dame Joan Sutherland** (sop) Donna Anna; **Dame Elisabeth Schwarzkopf** (sop) Donna Elvira; **Graziella Sciutti** (sop) Zerlina; **Luigi Alva** (ten) Don Ottavio; **Giuseppe Taddei** (bar) Leporello; **Piero Cappuccilli** (bar) Masetto; **Gottlob Frick** (bass) Commendatore; **Philharmonia Chorus and Orchestra/Carlo Maria Giulini.** EMI CDS7 47260-8. Notes, texts and translation included. From Columbia SAX2369/72 (2/61).

③ 2h 42m ADD 12/87

Although this set is more than 30 years old, none of its successors is as skilled in capturing the piece's drama so unerringly. It has always been most recommendable and he captures all the work's most dramatic characteristics, faithfully supported by the superb Philharmonia forces of that time. At this stage of Giulini's career, he was a direct, lithe conductor, alert to every turn in the story and he projects the nervous tension of the piece ideally while never forcing the pace, as can so easily happen. Then he had one of the most apt casts ever assembled for the piece. Waechter's Giovanni combines the demonic with the seductive in just the right proportions, Taddei is a high-profile Leporello, who relishes the text and sings with lots of 'face'. Elvira was always one of Schwarzkopf's most successful roles: here she delivers the role with tremendous intensity. Sutherland's Anna isn't quite so full of character but it is magnificently sung. Alva is a graceful Ottavio. Sciutti's charming Zerlina, Cappuccilli's strong and Italianate Masetto and Frick's granite Commendatore are all very much in the picture. The recording still sounds well.

Additional recommendations ...
Soloists; Glyndebourne Festival Chorus; London Philharmonic Orchestra/ Bernard Haitink. EMI CDS7 47037-8 — ③ 2h 52m DDD 12/84
Soloists; Glyndebourne Festival Chorus and Orchestra/Fritz Busch. EMI Références mono CHS7 61030-2 — ③ 2h 52m ADD 3/89
Soloists; Drottningholm Theatre Chorus and Orchestra/Arnold Ostman. L'Oiseau-Lyre 425 943-2OH3 — ③ 2h 51m DDD 12/90
Soloists; Vienna State Opera Chorus; Vienna Philharmonic Orchestra/Wilhelm Furtwängler. EMI Références mono CHS7 63860-2 — ③ 3h 2m ADD 7/91
Soloists; Chorus and Orchestra of the Royal Opera House, Covent Garden/Sir Colin Davis. Philips Mozart Edition 422 541-2PME3 — ③ 2h 44m ADD 1/92 £

Mozart. COSI FAN TUTTE. **Dame Elisabeth Schwarzkopf** (sop) Fiordiligi; **Christa Ludwig** (mez) Dorabella; **Hanny Steffek** (sop) Despina; **Alfredo Kraus** (ten) Ferrando; **Giuseppe Taddei** (bar) Guglielmo; **Walter Berry** (bass) Don Alfonso; **Philharmonia Chorus and Orchestra/Karl Böhm.** EMI CMS7 69330-2. Notes, text and translation included. From SAN103/6 (5/63). Recorded in 1962.

③ 2h 45m ADD 11/88 £

Così fan tutte is the most balanced and probing of all Mozart's operas, formally faultless, musically inspired from start to finish, emotinally a matter of endless fascination and, in the second act, profoundly moving. It has been very lucky on disc, and besides this delightful set there have been several other memorable recordings. However, Böhm's cast could hardly be bettered, even in one's dreams. The two sisters are gloriously sung — Schwarzkopf and Ludwig bring their immeasurable talents as Lieder singers to this sparkling score and overlay them with a rare comic touch. Add to that the stylish singing of Alfredo Kraus and Giuseppe Taddei and the central quartet is unimpeachable. Walter Berry's Don Alfonso is characterful and Hanny Steffek is quite superb as Despina. The pacing of this endlessly intriguing work is immaculate. The emotional control of the characterization is masterly and Böhm's totally idiomatic response to the music is without peer. It is as close as you could wish to get to ideal Mozart, and its mid price only serves to makes this a truly desirable issue.

Additional recommendations ...

Soloists; Chorus and Orchestra of the Drottningholm Court Theatre/Arnold Ostman. L'Oiseau-Lyre 414 316-2OH3 — ③ ADD 7/86

Soloists; Glyndebourne Chorus; London Philharmonic Orchestra/Bernard Haitink with **Martin Isepp** (hpd). EMI CDS7 47727-2 — ③ 3h 6m DDD 7/87

Soloists; Ambrosian Opera Chorus; Academy of St Martin in the Fields/Sir Neville Marriner. Philips 422 381-2PH3 — ③ 3h 11m DDD 11/90

Soloists; Royal Concertgebouw Orchestra/Nikolaus Harnoncourt. Teldec 9031-71381-2 — ③ 3h 17m DDD 11/91

Mozart. APOLLO ET HYACINTHUS — COMPLETE EDITION, Volume 26. **Cornelia Wulkopf** (mez) Apollo; **Edith Mathis** (sop) Hyacinthus; **Anthony Rolfe Johnson** (ten) Oebalus; **Arleen Auger** (sop) Melia; **Hanna Schwarz** (mez) Zephyrus; **Salzburg Chamber Choir; Salzburg Mozarteum Orchestra/Leopold Hager.** Philips Mozart Edition 422 526-2PME2. Notes, text and translation included. From DG 2707 129 (3/82).

② 1h 22m AAD 11/91

Mozart was 11 when this first of his stage works had its première at Salzburg University. It is a 'comedy intermezzo' lasting around 80 minutes, to a text written by a Benedictine monk and teacher called Dom Rufinus Widl, which modifies a Greek legend into an improving tale, not least because the original singers were choirboys. It is far from dull, for it shows a born operatic composer discovering himself and his excitement comes across. There are fine soloists here in Arleen Auger, Edith Mathis and Anthony Rolfe Johnson but neither Cornelia Wulkopf nor Hanna Schwarz, playing Apollo and Zephryus sound masculine, and in this respect the alternative listed below is more satisfying. We must remember that the boy Mozart was writing for boys' voices and accept Pavane Prestige's claim that theirs is the recording première of the original version. Those seeking fine singing above all should go to Philips, but for an extra freshness you can choose Pavane Prestige — where the death of the boy Hyacinthus is all the more moving for being sweetly sung by the treble Sébastien Pratschke.

Additional recommendation ...

Soloists; Nice Baroque Ensemble/Gerhard Schmidt-Gaden. Pavane Prestige ADW7236/7 — ② 1h 21m DDD 11/91

Mozart. LA FINTA SEMPLICE — COMPLETE EDITION. **Barbara Hendricks** (sop) Rosina; **Siegfried Lorenz** (bar) Don Cassandro; **Douglas Johnson** (sngr) Don Polidoro; **Ann Murray (mez)** Giacinta; **Eva Lind** (sop) Ninetta; **Hans-Peter Blochwitz** (ten) Fracasso; **Andreas Schmidt** (bar) Simone; **C.P.E. Bach Chamber Orchestra/Peter Schreier.** Philips Mozart Edition 422 528-2PME2. Notes, text and translation included. Recorded in 1988.

② 2h 27m DDD 11/91

The "finta semplice" or "feigned simpleton" is a clever woman who, so as to smooth the path of the young lovers, hoodwinks the objectionable people who stand in their way. These are two brothers, one a bully, the other a nitwit, and they provide the main touch of originality in a story that could be considered both silly and heartless (despite deriving from a comedy by Goldoni). The point in its favour is that it provides good situations for musical numbers, including the kind of sustained finale which was to be a special feature of Mozart's mature masterpieces. Not that there is anything notably immature about the finales of Acts 1 and 2 in the work of the 12-year-old on exhibition here. It was his first *opera buffa*, written in 1768, a massive achievement in terms of length alone, yet eventually put aside without performance. This is not its first recording, but it does in almost every respect improve on its predecessor, not least in shortening the recitatives and reducing the number of discs from three to two. The quartet of lovers are fresh-voiced and sprightly, and the title-role is well sung by Barbara

Hendricks. Siegfried Lorenz hardly succeeds in turning the bully-brother into a genuine comic character, but Douglas Johnson is good as the nincompoop and sings well when he has the chance. Peter Schreier encourages a lively sense of rhythm and attention to detail in his players. The recorded sound is clear and well balanced. But above all else is the miracle of composition. Not simply the degree of technical mastery but the depth of feeling attained by the 12-year-old genius, working in a comic genre too, becomes more astounding every time one listens.

Mozart. IDOMENEO. **Anthony Rolfe Johnson** (ten) Idomeneo; **Anne Sofie von Otter** (mez) Idamante; **Sylvia McNair** (sop) Ilia; **Hillevi Martinpelto** (sop) Elettra; **Nigel Robson** (ten) Arbace; **Glenn Winslade** (ten) High Priest; **Cornelius Hauptmann** (bass) Oracle; **Monteverdi Choir; English Baroque Soloists/John Eliot Gardiner.** Archiv Produktion 431 674-2AH3. Notes, text and translation included. Recorded in 1990.

③ 3h 3lm DDD 6/91 

This is unquestionably the most vital and authentic account of the opera to date on disc. We have here what was given at the work's first performance in Munich plus, in appendices, what Mozart wanted, or was forced, to cut before that première and the alternative versions of certain passages, so that various combinations of the piece can be programmed by the listener. Gardiner's direct, dramatic conducting catches ideally the agony of Idomeneo's terrible predicament — forced to sacrifice his son because of an unwise row. This torment of the soul is also entirely conveyed by Anthony Rolfe Johnson in the title role to which Anne Sofie von Otter's moving Idamante is an apt foil. Sylvia McNair is a diaphanous, pure-voiced Ilia, Hillevi Martinpelto a properly fiery, sharp-edged Elettra. With dedicated support from his own choir and orchestra, who have obviously benefited from a long period of preparation, Gardiner matches the stature of this noble *opera seria*. The recording catches the excitement which all who heard the live performances will recall.

Additional recommendations ...

Soloists; Zurich Opera House Chorus and Mozart Orchestra/Nikolaus Harnoncourt. Teldec 2292-42600-2 — ③ ADD 3/86

Soloists; Leipzig Radio Choir; Staatskapelle Dresden/Karl Böhm. DG 429 864-2GX3 — 2h 50m ADD 12/90

Soloists; Bavarian Radio Chorus and Orchestra/Sir Colin Davis. Philips Mozart Edition 422 537-2PME3 ③ 4h 2m DDD 12/91

Mozart. DIE ENTFUHRUNG AUS DEM SERAIL. **Lynne Dawson** (sop) Konstanze; **Marianne Hirsti** (sop) Blonde; **Uwe Heilmann** (ten) Belmonte; **Wilfrid Gahmlich** (ten) Pedrillo; **Gunther von Kannen** (bass) Osmin; **Wolfgang Hinze** (spkr) Bassa Selim; **Academy of Ancient Music Chorus and Orchestra/Christopher Hogwood.** L'Oiseau-Lyre 430 339-2OH2. Notes, text and translation included. Recorded in 1990.

② 2h 24m DDD 11/91

This is the first recording of Mozart's delectable harem *Singspiel* to use period instruments, and very persuasive it is too. Hogwood's direction is fresh and unfussy, high on comic energy but always allowing his cast ample room for manoeuvre. If the string sound is sparer and dustier than with some other period groups, Mozart's wonderful, sometimes exotic scoring for wind in this opera has never been more tellingly realized, from the piping, piercing piccolo in the overture and the 'Turkish' numbers to the rasping brass in the Act One finale and the dark, nutty basset-horns in Konstanze's sorrowful *Traurigkeit.* Hogwood uses a fortepiano continuo, following the composer's own practice; and his musical text is absolutely complete, restoring the optional cuts Mozart made in several arias, and including for good measure a little march in Act One that has only recently come to light. Though other recordings have fielded starrier casts, Hogwood's singers are aptly and appealingly youthful, and characterize their roles with flair. Pride of place goes to Uwe Heilmann's elegant, ardent Belmonte, a Mozartian of real distinction, with plenty of sap in the voice and a honeyed *mezza voce*. His Konstanze is Lynne Dawson, less grand and impassioned than some exponents of the role but singing with grace, warmth and all the agility Mozart demands; and she and Heilmann bring a rare poignancy to their final duet. Marianne Hirsti makes a delicious, quick-witted Blonde, Wilfrid Gahmlich a likeable Pedrillo, though his intonation falters in the romance, "Im Mohrenland". And though others have brought a juicier, more rotund bass to the plum role of Osmin, Gunther von Kannen has ample weight for Mozart's subterranean writing, articulates vividly and relishes the gleeful malice of "Ach, wie will ich triumphieren". The dialogue is delivered naturally by the singers themselves (many other recordings bus in actors for this, thereby causing a frequent sense of culture shock), while Wolfgang Hinze brings nobility and some pathos to the spoken role of the Bassa Selim. Altogether a fetching, colourful and involving reading of this most lovable of Mozart's operas, captured in a clear, crisp, if slightly dry, recording.

Additional recommendations ...

Soloists; Zurich Opera House Chorus and Orchestra/Nikolaus Harnoncourt. Teldec 2292-42643-2 — ③ 2h 15m DDD 5/88

Soloists; Leipzig Radio Choir; Staatskapellle Dresden/Karl Böhm. DG 429 868-2GX2 — ② 2h 11m ADD 12/90

Soloists; Vienna State Opera Chorus; Vienna Symphony Orchestra/Bruno Weil. Sony Classical SK48053 — ② 2h 3m DDD 5/92

Mozart. LA CLEMENZA DI TITO. **Anthony Rolfe Johnson** (ten) Tito; **Julia Varady** (sop) Vitellia; **Anne Sofie von Otter** (mez) Sesto; **Catherine Robbin** (mez) Annio; **Sylvia McNair** (sop) Servilia; **Cornelius Hauptmann** (bass) Publio; **Monteverdi Choir; English Baroque Soloists/John Eliot Gardiner.** Archiv Produktion 431 806-2AH2. Notes, text and translation included. Recorded in June 1991.

② 1h 58m DDD 12/91

This matches the twin recording of the *Gramophone* award-winning *Idomeneo* as an almost ideal interpretation of *opera seria*. There is nothing marmoreal or static about Gardiner's reading which suggests a taut and vivid drama unfolding before the listener, enhanced by a sense of an occasion and of an ensemble dedicated to the work in hand. Tempos are keenly judged and related unerringly to each other. The playing of the period instruments is disciplined, phrasing keen and well pointed. Rolfe Johnson makes a convincingly sensitive, clement Emperor who dispatches his runs with imperial finesse. Beside him, von Otter is superb in her taxing arias, using her runs to expressive purpose. Their rapport is heartening. Varady makes a bitingly vengeful and jealous Vitellia, also sensual and eventually remorseful. Sylvia McNair is a sweet-voiced, slightly bland Servilia, Catherine Robbin a stylistically and vocally secure Annio. The recitatives (by Süssmayr) are substantially cut, probably an advantage in a recording.

Additional recommendations ...

Soloists; Leipzig Radio Choir; Staatskapelle Dresden/Karl Böhm. DG 429 878-2GX2 — ② 2h 20m ADD 12/90

Soloists; Chorus and Orchestra of the Royal Opera House, Covent Garden/Sir Colin Davis. Philips Mozart Edition 422 544-2PME2 — ② 2h 8m ADD 4/92

Mozart. DIE ZAUBERFLOTE. **Ruth Ziesak** (sop) Pamina; **Sumi Jo** (sop) Queen of Night; **Uwe Heilmann** (ten) Tamino; **Michael Kraus** (bar) Papageno; **Kurt Moll** (bass) Sarastro; **Andreas Schmidt** (bar) Speaker; **Heinz Zednik** (ten) Monostatos; **Lotte Leitner** (sop) Papagena; **Adrianne Pieczonka** (sop), **Annette Kuettenbaum, Jard van Nes** (mezs) First, Second and Third Ladies; **Max Emanuel Cencic, Michael Rausch, Markus Leitner** (trebs) First, Second and Third Boys; **Wolfgang Schmidt** (ten), **Hans Franzen** (bass) Two Armed Men; **Clemens Bieber** (ten), **Hans Joachim Porcher** (bar) Two Priests; **Vienna Boys' Choir; Vienna State Opera Concert Choir; Vienna Philharmonic Orchestra/Sir Georg Solti.** Decca 433 210-2DH2. Notes, text and translations included. Recorded in 1990.

② 2h 32m DDD 10/91

Sir Georg Solti's *Flute* is a lively enticement, with the promise of fun and adventure. He showed this very well in his first recording, in 1969, but the new version has still more spring in its step, and probably a better cast of singers too. The high and low of it, Sumi Jo as the Queen of Night, Kurt Moll as Sarastro, have spirit to match Solti's as well as the vocal and technical qualities necessary for the mastery of their daunting roles. Ruth Ziesak, the Pamina, may not suit all tastes (hers is a brighter voice than generally heard), but beauty and intelligence distinguish much of her singing, and the Tamino (Uwe Heilmann) and Papagena (Michael Kraus) are excellent. If Andreas Schmidt makes a somewhat youthful-sounding Speaker of the Temple, that is in keeping with the performance as a whole, where the spirit of youth prevails: in the players, the ever-youthful veteran conductor, and indeed in Sarastro himself, whose exposition of the 'holy halls' is less the usual solemn recitation than a genial and sensible provider of useful information.

Additional recommendations ...

Soloists; Bavarian Radio Chorus and Symphony Orchestra/Bernard Haitink. EMI CDS7 47951-8 — ③ 2h 39m DDD 3/88 B

Soloists; Favres Solisten Vereinigung; Berlin Philharmonic Orchestra/Sir Thomas Beecham. Pearl mono GEMMCDS9371 — ② 2h 10m AAD 3/90 B ▲

Soloists; Schütz Choir of London; London Classical Players/Roger Norrington. EMI Reflexe CDS7 54287-2 — ② 2h 19m DDD 11/91 B

Soloists; Scottish Chamber Chorus and Orchestra/Sir Charles Mackerras. Telarc CD80302 — ② 2h 33m DDD 12/91 B

Soloists; Dresden Kreuzchor; Leipzig Radio Chorus; Staatskapelle Dresden/Sir Colin Davis. Philips Mozart Edition 422 543-2PME3 — ③ 2h 42m DDD 4/92 B

Further listening ...

Mass in C major, K317, "Coronation". Vesperae solennes de confessor in C major, K339. Epistle Sonata in C major, K278/271*e*. **Soloists; Winchester Cathedral Choir; Winchester Quiristers; Academy of Ancient Music/Christopher Hogwood** with **Alastair Ross** (org). L'Oiseau-Lyre 436 585-2OH (4/93).

MITRIDATE — *opera seria*. **Soloists; Salzburg Mozarteum Orchestra/Leopold Hager.** Philips Mozart Edition 422 529-2PME3 (2/92).

LUCIO SILLA — *opera seria*. **Soloists; Arnold Schönberg Choir; Vienna Concentus Musicus/Nikolaus Harnoncourt.** Teldec 2292-44928 (3/91).

LA FINTA GIARDINIERA — *opera buffa*. **Soloists; Salzburg Mozarteum Orchestra/Leopold Hager.** Philips Mozart Edition 422 533-2PME3 (5/92).
IL RE PASTORE — *serenata*. **Soloists; London Symphony Orchestra/Sir Colin Davis.** Philips Mozart Edition 422 535-2PME2 (4/92).

Modest Mussorgsky

Russian 1839-1881

Mussorgsky. Pictures at an Exhibition (orch. Ravel). A night on the Bare Mountain (arr. Rimsky-Korsakov).
Ravel. Valses nobles et sentimentales. **New York Philharmonic Orchestra/Giuseppe Sinopoli.** DG 429 785-2GH.

1h 7m DDD 5/91 B

Sinopoli's recording of *Pictures at an Exhibition* has great panache and is full of subtle detail and sharply characterized performances. Of course none of this would be possible without the marvellous virtuosity of the New York Philharmonic, whose brass section play with a wonderful larger-than-life sonority (just what's needed in this colourful extravaganza) and whose woodwind section produce playing of considerable delicacy and finesse, as for example in "Tuileries" and the "Ballet of the Unhatched Chicks". Sinopoli clearly revels in the drama of this work and this is nowhere more noticeable than in his sinister readings of "Catacombs" and

"Baba-Yaga". *A night on the Bare Mountain* is no less impressive, where again the flair and dazzling virtuosity of the NYPO have an almost overwhelming impact. Less successful are Ravel's *Valses nobles et sentimentales* which are perhaps a little too idiosyncratic for an individual recommendation despite some superb performances and moments of great beauty. The sound is beautifully balanced and engineered.

Additional recommendations ...

Pictures at an Exhibition. A night on the Bare Mountain. **Cleveland Orchestra/Lorin Maazel.** Telarc CD80042 — 41m DDD 11/84

Pictures at an Exhibition. ***Stravinsky.*** *Petrushka*[a]. [a]**Leslie Howard** (pf); **London Symphony Orchestra/Claudio Abbado.** DG 423 901-2GH — 1h 8m DDD 3/89

Pictures at an Exhibition. A night on the Bare Mountain. Khovanshchina — Prelude. **Oslo Philharmonic Orchestra/Mariss Jansons.** EMI CDC7 49797-2 — 49m DDD 1/90

Pictures at an Exhibition (arr. Howarth)[a]. ***Saint-Saëns.*** *Le carnaval des animaux (arr. Reeve)*[b]. **Philip Jones Brass Ensemble/**[a]**Elgar Howarth,** [b]**Philip Jones.** Decca Ovation 425 022-2DM — 58m ADD/DDD 6/91

Pictures at an Exhibition (arr. Howarth). A night on the Bare Mountain (arr. Wiltshire). ***Khachaturian.*** *Spartacus — Adagio of Spartacus and Phrygia (arr. Wiltshire).* **Wallace Collection/John Wallace.** Collins Classics 1227-2 — 53m DDD 6/91

Pictures at an Exhibition. A night on the Bare Mountain. ***Borodin.*** *In central Asia. Prince Igor — Polovtsian Dances.* **Slovak Philharmonic Orchestra/Daniel Nazareth.** Naxos 8 550051 — 1h 8m DDD 7/91

Pictures at an Exhibition. Khovanshchina — symhonic excerpts. **Rotterdam Philharmonic Orchestra/James Conlon.** Erato 2292-45596-2 — 49m DDD 8/91

Pictures at an Exhibition. A night on the Bare Mountain. Khovanshchina — Prelude. **Atlanta Symphony Orchestra/Yoel Levi.** Telarc CD80296 — 50m DDD 4/92

Mussorgsky. Pictures at an Exhibition — original piano version.
Tchaikovsky (arr. Pletnev). The Sleeping Beauty, Op. 66 — excerpts. **Mikhail Pletnev** (pf). Virgin Classics VC7 59611-2.
The Sleeping Beauty — Introduction; Danse des pages; Vision d'Aurore; Andante; La feéargent; Le chat botté et la chatte blanche; Gavotte; Le canari qui chante; Chaperon rouge et la loup; Adagio; Finale.

1h 4m DDD 4/91

Mikhail Pletnev brings a strong personality to whatever he does, and his *Pictures* are no exception, with subtlety and intensity in such quieter pieces as "The Old Castle" and a tremendous urgency and sense of space in the really big numbers like "Baba Yaga" and of course the monumental final "Great Gate of Kiev". In both these latter pieces, and most obviously the "Gate", the pianist adds some notes of his own which sound musically convincing; although purists with an eye on Mussorgsky's score will shake their heads and say that he has gone over the top, others will forgive him for being, as it seems, simply carried away by the sheer dynamic sweep of performance. Pletnev's mastery of atmosphere is also well illustrated by the conversation of the two Jews, Goldenberg and Schmuyle, and his evocation of the black "Catacombs". All this is enhanced by a wonderfully vivid recording. The Tchaikovsky ballet transcriptions made by Pletnev himself are much more than a fill-up. They are splendidly conceived in piano terms and his playing here is so stylish as to be in a class quite of its own.

Additional recommendations ...

Pictures at an Exhibition[a]. *Pictures at an Exhibition (orch. Ashkenazy).*[b] [b]**Philharmonia Orchestra/Vladimir Ashkenazy** ([a]pf). Decca 414 386-2DH. — 1h 7m DDD 5/86

Pictures at an Exhibition. Gopaks. Souvenirs d'enfance — No. 2. First punishment (Nurse shuts me in a dark room). Intermezzo in modo classico. Ein Kinderscherz. Une larme. Au village. **Mario Papadopoulos** (pf). Helicon CDHLR143-2 — 59m DDD 1/89

Pictures at an Exhibition. ***Stravinsky.*** *Three movements from "Petrushka".* ***Tchaikovsky.*** *Dumka: Russian rustic scene in C minor, Op. 59.* **Yefim Bronfman** (pf). Sony Classical SK46481 — 56m DDD 1/92

Mussorgsky. SONGS. **Boris Christoff** (bass); [a]**Alexandre Labinsky,** [b]**Gerald Moore** (pfs); **French Radio National Orchestra/**[a]**Georges Tzipine.** EMI Références mono CHS7 63025-2. [a] from ALP1652/5 (1/59), [b] DB21383 (2/52). Notes, texts and translations included. Recorded 1951-57.
Sadly rustled the leaves; Where art thou, little star; Hour of Jollity; Tell me why; I have many palaces and gardens; What are words of love to you?; King Saul; Old man's song; But if I could meet thee again; Wild wind blows; Night; Kalistratushka; Salammbô — Balearic Song; Prayer; Outcast; Lullaby; Dear one, why are thine eyes?; From my tears; Gopak; Darling Savishna; Seminarist; Hebrew Song; Magpie; Gathering mushrooms; Feast; Ragamuffin; He-Goat; Garden by the Don; Classicist; Orphan; Child's song; Nursery; Eremushka's lullaby; Peepshow; Evening song; Forgotten; Sunless; Songs and Dances of Death; Epitaph; Sphinx; Not like thunder; Softly the spirit flew; Is spinning man's work; It scatters and breaks; Vision; Pride; Wanderer; On the Dnieper; Song of the flea.

③ 3h 11m ADD 8/89 

This set is undoubtedly one of the all-time glories. Unavailable on LP for many years, its welcome reappearance on CD should make it a 'must' for any worthwhile collection on account of both its content and execution. Listening through the set without interruption gives one a wonderful idea of the range and variety of Mussorgsky's writing and leaves one amazed at the virtuosity of Christoff's singing. This is unquestionably the famous bass's most importance legacy to music simply because one cannot imagine another singer attempting so many of these songs so successfully. The composer's range of characterization is veritably Dostoyevskian. Even on the first disc, in the earlier and slightly less remarkable songs, he offers a range of personalities and emotions until then unexplored in Russian song. In their interpretation, Christoff brings before us a whole cast of characters portrayed with an amazing palette of sound-colours, everything from the utterly ferocious to the gentlest whisper. The second disc brings many of the better-known songs, all arrestingly interpreted, and the *Nursery* cycle, in which Christoff manages to adapt his dark tone miraculously to a convincing impersonation of a small boy. On the final disc, we hear predictably penetrating performances of the other two cycles. Christoff catches the bleak gloom of *Sunless* and the histrionic force of *Songs and Dances of Death* (though unfortunately a corrupt orchestration is used), some lesser songs and finally a rollicking *Song of the Flea*. Labinsky is a vivid, imaginative pianist. All in all, a set to treasure.

Mussorgsky. KHOVANSHCHINA. **Aage Haugland** (bass) Ivan Khovansky; **Vladimir Atlantov** (ten) Andrey Khovansky; **Vladimir Popov** (ten) Golitsin; **Anatolij Kotscherga** (bar) Shaklovity; **Paata Burchuladze** (bass) Dosifey; **Marjana Lipovšek** (contr) Marfa; **Brigitte Poschner-Klebel** (sop) Susanna; **Heinz Zednik** (ten) Scribe; **Joanna Borowska** (sop) Emma; **Wilfried Gahmlich** (ten) Kouzka; **Vienna Boys' Choir; Slovak Philharmonic Choir; Vienna State Opera Chorus and Orchestra/Claudio Abbado.** DG 429 758-2GH3. Recorded in 1989. Notes, text and translation included.

③ 2h 51m DDD 11/90 

The booklet essay with this issue suggests that, like Dostoevsky's novels, Mussorgsky's music constantly poses a question to his Russian compatriots: "What are the causes of our country's continuing calamities, and why does the state crush all that is good?". Anyone who follows today's news from Russia and then experiences this opera will understand what is meant, and while we observe with sympathy we seem no nearer than the citizens of that great, tormented country to finding solutions for its endemic problems. However, Mussorgsky was not the least of those Russian musicians who found lasting beauty in her history and he expressed it in a powerfully dramatic idiom that drew on folk-music and had both epic qualities and deep humanity as well as an occasional gentleness. There is also an element here of Russian church music, since *Khovanshchina* has a political and religious theme and is set in the 1680s at the time of Peter the Great's accession. Since the work was unfinished when Mussorgsky died, performances always involve conjectural work, and the version here — which works convincingly — is mostly that of Shostakovich with the choral ending that Stravinsky devised using Mussorgsky's music. The cast in this live recording is not one of star opera singers, but they are fully inside the drama and the music, as is the chorus and the orchestra under Abbado, and the result is deeply and compellingly atmospheric. The booklet has the Russian text and a translation as well as informative essays on the music.

Additional recommendations ...

Soloists; Kirov Theatre Chorus and Orchestra/Valery Gergiev. Philips 432 147-2PH3 — ③ 3h 16m DDD 6/92

Khovanshchina — Prelude; Galitsin's journey (Introduction, Act 4). Joshua[ab]. *Salammbô — Chorus of priestesses*[b]. *Scherzo in B flat major. The destruction of Sennacherib*[b]. *St John's Night on the Bare Mountain. Oedipus in Athens — Chorus of people in the temple*[b]. *Triumphal march, "The capture of Kars".* [a]**Zehava Gal** (contr); **London Symphony** [b]**Chorus and Orchestra/Claudio Abbado.** RCA Gold Seal Master Series 09026 61354-2 — 54m ADD 6/93

Mussorgsky. BORIS GODUNOV. **Alexander Vedernikov** (bass) Boris Godunov; **Vladislav Piavko** (ten) False Dmitri; **Irina Arkhipova** (mez) Marina; **Vladimir Matorin** (bass) Pimen; **Artur Eizen** (bass) Varlaam; **Andrei Sokolov** (ten) Prince Shuisky; **Anatoli Mishutin** (ten) Missail; **Yuri Mazurok** (bar) Rangoni; **Glafira Koroleva** (mez) Feodor; **Elena Shkolnikova** (sop) Xenia; **Nina Grigorieva** (mez) Nurse; **Ludmila Simonova** (mez) Hostess; **Janis Sporgis** (ten) Simpleton; **Alexander Voroshilo** (bar) Shchelkalov; **Yuri Elnikov** (ten) Lavitsky, Khrushchov, Boyar; **Vladimir Silaev** (bar) Chernikovsky; **Spring Studio Children's Chorus; USSR TV and Radio Large Chorus and Symphony Orchestra/Vladimir Fedoseyev.** Philips 412 281-2PH3. Notes, text and translation included. From 412 281-1PH4 (12/84).

③ 3h 18m ADD 3/85

Boris is often regarded as the quintessential Russian opera as it embodies in a highly-charged dramatic scheme the best of Russian folk idioms and word setting. After the composer's death, Rimsky-Korsakov extensively reworked the opera and it is in various versions of his revised score that the work is best known today. But although he did a great service in keeping the opera in the repertoire, many would regard Mussorgsky's original version to be superior. To have an all-Russian production for this opera has not always been of such benefit as one might expect, with the delight in watery vocal tone and wide vibrato sometimes obscuring the music's direction, but on this recording the overall dedication and empathy of the performers produces a vital and soul-searching interpretation that easily compensates for lack of the stage's visual drama. Much of the opera's success lies with the strength of the title-role and here Alexander Vedernikov scores with a psychologically penetrating account of the great Tsar's mental, spiritual, and physical decline. Fedoseyev conducts with complete understanding of the essence of each scene, and draws excellent singing and playing from the chorus and orchestra. Though the wide-spread recording sessions have not been fully integrated, the overall effect is appropriate to the sequence of events and in no way distracts from this moving production.

Josef Mysliveček

Bohemian 1737-1781

Suggested listening ...

IL BELLEROFONTE. **Soloists; Czech Philharmonic Chorus; Prague Chamber Orchestra/Zoltán Peskó.** Supraphon 11 0006-2 (3/92).

Conlon Nancarrow

Mexican 1912-

Studies for Player Piano — Nos. 42, 45*a*, 45*b*, 45*c*, 48*a*, 48*b*, 48*c*, 49*a*, 49*b*, 49*c*. Wergo 60165-50 (8/89).

Ernesto Nazareth

Brazilian 1863-1934

Suggested listening ...

Apanhei-tecavaquinho. Cavaquinho. Vitorioso. Odeon. Nove de Julho. Labirinto. Guerreiro. Plangente. Cubanos. Fon-Fon! *Coupled with* **Scott.** Evergreen Rag. Modesty Rag. Peace and Plenty Rag. Troubadour Rag. ***Lamb.*** Ragtime Nightingale. American Beauty Rag. Bohemia Rag. Topliner Rag. **Joshua Rifkin** (pf). Decca 425 225-2DH (4/92).

See also review in the Collections section; refer to Index to Reviews.

Alfred Newman

American 1900-1970

Suggested listening ...

Film Scores: 20th Century-Fox fanfare. Street scene. Captain from Castile — Pedro and Catana. Conquest[a]. Wuthering Heights — Cathy. Down to the Sea in Ships — Hornpipe. The Song of Bernadette — Prelude; The vision[b]. The Bravados — main title. Anastasia — main title. Airport — main title. The Robe — suite[ab]. [a]**Grenadier Guards Band;** [b]**Ambrosian Singers; National Philharmonic Orchestra/Charles Gerhardt.** RCA Victor GD80184 (10/90).

Carl Nielsen

Danish 1865-1931

Nielsen. Violin Concerto, FS61[a].
Sibelius. Violin Concerto in D minor, Op. 47[b]. **Cho-Liang Lin** (vn); [a]**Swedish Radio Symphony Orchestra,** [b]**Philharmonia Orchestra/Esa-Pekka Salonen.** CBS Masterworks CD44548. Recorded 1987-88.

1h 9m DDD 1/89 

Nielsen. Violin Concerto, FS61[a]. Flute Concerto, FS119[b]. Clarinet Concerto, FS129[c]. [d]**Toke Lund Christiansen** (fl); **Niels Thomsen** (cl); [a]**Kim Sjøgren** (vn); **Danish National Radio Symphony Orchestra/Michael Schønwandt.** Chandos CHAN8894. Recorded in 1990.

1h 20m DDD 4/91 

Oddly enough no one has previously recorded the two greatest Nordic violin concertos on one disc and the result on the CBS disc is a triumphant success. This is the best recording of the Sibelius Concerto to have appeared for more than a decade and probably the best ever of the Nielsen. Cho-Liang Lin brings an apparently effortless virtuosity to both concertos. He produces a wonderfully clean and silvery sonority and there is no lack of aristocratic finesse. Only half-a-dozen years separate the two concertos, yet they breathe a totally different air. Lin's perfect intonation and tonal purity excite admiration and throughout them both there is a strong sense of line from beginning to end. Esa-Pekka Salonen gets excellent playing from the Philharmonia Orchestra in the Sibelius and almost equally good results from the Swedish Radio Symphony Orchestra. This should take its place among the classic concerto recordings of the century. The well-filled Chandos CD brings all three concertos together: the Violin Concerto comes from the period of the Third Symphony and the two wind concertos were written after the Sixth during the last years of his life. Nielsen planned to write five concertos, one for each member of the Copenhagen Wind Quintet. Kim Sjøgren may not command the purity of tone of Cho-Liang Lin but he has the inestimable advantage of totally idiomatic orchestral support: Michael Schønwandt has an instinctive feeling for this music — and this shows throughout the whole disc. The perspective between soloist and orchestra is well-judged (Sjøgren is never larger than life) and so is the internal balance. In the Flute Concerto, which veers from Gallic wit to moments of great poetic feeling, Toke Lund Christiansen is an excellent soloist. He has no want of brilliance or authority and his performance also has plenty of character. Niels Thomsen's account of the Clarinet Concerto is one of the very finest now before the public. If there is any music from another planet, this is it! There is no attempt to beautify the score nor to overstate it: every dynamic nuance and expressive marking is observed by both the soloist and conductor. Thomsen plays as if his very being is at stake and Michael Schønwandt secures playing of great imaginative intensity from the Danish Radio Orchestra.

Additional recommendations ...
Flute Concerto[a]. *Clarinet Concerto*[b]. *Violin Concerto*[c]. [a]**Patrick Gallois** (fl); [b]**Olle Schill** (cl); [c]**Dong-Suk Kang** (vn); **Gothenburg Symphony Orchestra/Myung-Whun Chung.** BIS CD616 — lh 19m DDD 7/93
Flute Concerto[a]. *Clarinet Concerto*[b]. ***Hindemith.*** *Violin Concerto*[c]. [a]**Julius Baker** (fl); [b]**Stanley Drucker** (cl); [c]**Isaac Stern** (vn); **New York Philharmonic Orchestra/Leonard Bernstein.** Sony Classical Bernstein Royal Edition SMK47599 — lh 13m ADD 7/93

Nielsen. Symphonies — No. 1 in G minor, FS16; No. 6, "Sinfonia semplice", FS116. **San Francisco Symphony Orchestra/Herbert Blomstedt.** Decca 425 607-2DH. Recorded in 1989.

lh 7m DDD 8/90 

Nielsen always nurtured a special affection for his First Symphony — and rightly so, for its language is natural and unaffected. It has great spontaneity of feeling and a Dvořákian warmth and freshness. Blomstedt's recording is one of the best to have appeared for some years. It is vital, beautifully shaped and generally faithful to both the spirit and the letter of the score. The recording, too, is very fine: the sound has plenty of room to expand, there is a very good relationship between the various sections of the orchestra and a realistic perspective. Blomstedt gives a powerful account of the Sixth, too, with plenty of intensity and an appreciation of its extraordinary vision. It is by far the most challenging of the cycle and inhabits a very different world from early Nielsen. The intervening years had seen the cataclysmic events of the First World War and Nielsen himself was suffering increasingly from ill health. Blomstedt and the fine San Fransisco orchestra convey the powerful nervous tension of the first movement and the depth of the third, the *Proposta seria*. He is splendidly served by Decca's recording team.

Additional recommendation ...
No. 1. Flute Concerto[a]. *An imaginary trip to the Faroe Islands — rhapsody overture, FS123.* [a]**Patrick Gallois** (fl); **Gothenburg Symphony Orchestra/Myung-Whun Chung.** BIS CD454 — lh 3m DDD 8/90

Nielsen. Symphonies — No. 2, FS29, "The Four Temperaments"; No. 3, FS60, "Sinfonia espansiva"[a]. [a]**Nancy Wait Fromm** (sop); [a]**Kevin McMillan** (bar); **San Francisco Symphony Orchestra/Herbert Blomstedt.** Decca 430 280-2DH.

lh 7m DDD 8/90 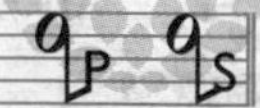

This disc couples two of Nielsen's most genial symphonies, both of which come from the earliest part of the century, in performances of the very first order. The Second (1902), inspired by the portrayal of *The Four Temperaments* (Choleric, Phlegmatic, Melancholic, Sanguine) that he had seen in a country inn, has splendid concentration and fire and, as always, from the right pace stems the right character. Moreover the orchestra sounds as if it is fired at having encountered this music, for there is a genuine excitement about their playing. Indeed Blomstedt's accounts are by far the most satisfying to have appeared for some time. The Third *Espansiva*, is even more personal in utterance than *The Four Temperaments*, for during the intervening years Nielsen had come much further along the road of self-discovery. His melodic lines are bolder, the musical paragraphs longer and his handling of form more assured. It is a glorious and richly inventive score whose pastoral slow movement includes a part for two wordless voices. Blomstedt gives us an affirmative, powerful reading and in the slow movement, the soprano produces the required ethereal effect. The Decca sound is very detailed and full-bodied, and in the best traditions of the company. Blomstedt's *Espansiva* has greater depth than most rival accounts; the actual sound has that glowing radiance that characterizes Nielsen, and the tempo, the underlying current on which this music is borne, is expertly judged — and nowhere better than in the finale. Blomstedt is an experienced guide in this repertoire and this shows, while his orchestra play with refreshing enthusiasm.

Additional recommendation ...

No. 2. Aladdin — suite for orchestra, Op. 34. **Gothenburg Symphony Orchestra/Myung-Whun Chung.** BIS CD247 — 56m DDD 5/84

NEW REVIEW

Nielsen. Symphonies — No. 3, FS60, "Sinfonia espansiva"[a]; No. 5, FS97. [a]**Catherine Bott** (sop); [a]**Stephen Roberts** (bar); **Royal Scottish Orchestra/Bryden Thomson.** Chandos CHAN9067. Recorded in 1991.

1h 11m DDD 2/93 

The late Bryden Thomson and the Royal Scottish Orchestra give fresh and direct readings of the *Espansiva* and the Fifth which are eminently satisfying. At no point are we aware of the conductor interposing himself between composer and listener, and one can sense an evident enthusiasm on the part of the players. This is Nielsen plain and unadorned without any frills. Thomson has a very good feeling for Nielsen's tempos and his account of the finale feels just right. All in all, a splendidly sane performance with good singing from the fine soloists in the slow movement. The Fifth Symphony is another unaffected and straightforward performance that has a great deal going for it — not least the beautiful clarinet playing in the coda, and the thoroughly committed second movement. One is, perhaps, more aware of the beat in the first movement than in Blomstedt's Decca account (reviewed below) and it rarely seems to float or sound disembodied as it does with him. However, Thomson gets very spirited playing from all departments of the orchestra and the recordings are very good and present, even if the sound lacks the transparency Decca achieved for Blomstedt. These are eminently enjoyable, ardent performances that can hold their head high amongst any competition.

Additional recommendations ...

No. 3. Clarinet Concerto, FS129[a]. *Maskarade — Overture.* **Pia Raanoja** (sop); **Knut Skram** (bar); [a]**Olle Schill** (cl); **Gothenburg Symphony Orchestra/Myung-Whun Chung.** BIS CD321 — 1h 8m DDD 8/86

Nos. 3 and 5. **New York Philharmonic Orchestra/Leonard Bernstein.** Sony Classical Bernstein Royal Edition SMK47958 — 1h 11m ADD 7/93

Nielsen. Symphonies — No. 4, FS76, "Inextinguishable"; No. 5, FS97. **San Francisco Symphony Orchestra/Herbert Blomstedt.** Decca 421 524-2DH.

1h 12m DDD 10/88 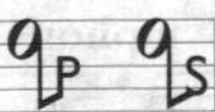

NEW REVIEW

Nielsen. Symphonies — No. 4, FS76, "Inextinguishable"; No. 6, FS116, Sinfonia semplice". **Royal Scottish National Orchestra/Bryden Thomson.** Chandos CHAN9047. Recorded in 1991.

1h 10m DDD 3/93 

The Decca recording presents two of Nielsen's most popular and deeply characteristic symphonies on one CD. Both are good performances that can hold their own with any in the current catalogue, and as recordings they surpass the competition. The Fourth Symphony occupied Nielsen between 1914 and early 1916 and reveals a level of violence new to his art. The landscape is harsher; the melodic lines soar in a more anguished and intense fashion (in the case of the remarkable slow movement, "like the eagle riding on the wind", to use the composer's own graphic simile). The title *Inextinguishable* tries to express in a single word what only the music alone has the power to fully express: "the element will to life". Blomstedt's opening has splendid fire: this must sound as if galaxies are forming; he is not frightened of letting things rip. The finale with its exhilarating dialogue between the two timpanists comes off splendidly. The Fifth Symphony of 1922 is impressive, too: it starts perfectly and has just the right glacial atmosphere. The climax and the desolate clarinet peroration into which it dissolves are well handled. The recording balance could not be improved upon: the woodwind are decently recessed (though clarinet keys are audible at times), there is an almost ideal relationship between the various sections of the orchestra and a thoroughly realistic overall perspective. Blomstedt has a good rapport with his players who sound in excellent shape and respond to these scores as to the manner born.

Bryden Thomson's accounts of the Fourth and Sixth calls to mind the ardent intensity of the pioneering Danish recordings (no longer available) by Launy Gróndahl and Thomas Jensen such are their fire. The orchestra play as if their lives depend on it and the underlying violence of No. 4 makes a powerful impact, both at the opening and in the finale. But his Sixth is arguably the very finest version of the work on disc, notwithstanding the cultured and splendidly recorded account by Herbert Blomstedt reviewed above. Thomson strikes exactly the right tempo for the first movement nor has the problematic "Humoreske" ever made better sense. He takes it at a steadier pace than most rival conductors, so that its questioning spirit registers. The third movement, the "Proposta seria", is both eloquent and searching. Even in a strongly competitive field this splendidly recorded Chandos account brings one closer to this extraordinary work than any other.

Additional recommendations ...

Nos. 4 and 5. Maskarade — Overture. **BBC Symphony Orchestra/Andrew Davis.** Virgin Classics VC7 59618-2 ∴ lh 14m DDD 4/91 Ⓑ

Nos. 3 and 6. **Royal Danish Orchestra/Paavo Berglund.** RCA Victor Red Seal RD60427 — ∴ lh 8m DDD 4/92 Ⓑ

Nielsen. CHAMBER MUSIC. [a]**Bergen Wind Quintet** (Gro Sandvik, fl[fgh], rec[i]; [c]Steinar Hannevold, ob; [be]Lars Kristian Holm Brynildsen, cl; [de]Vidar Olsen, hn; Per Hannevold, bn[e], rec[i]); [f]**Turid Kniejski** (hp); [h]**Lars Anders Tomter** (va); [e]**Sally Guenther** (vc); [e]**Torbjorn Eide** (db); [bcd]**Lief Ove Andsnes** (pf). BIS CD428.

Wind Quintet, FS100[a]. Fantasy Piece for clarinet and piano, FS3h[b]. Fantasy Pieces for oboe and piano, FS8[c]. Canto serioso for horn and piano, FS132[d]. Serenata in vano, FS68[e]. The Mother, FS94 — The fog is lifting[f]; The children are playing[g]; Faith and Hope are playing[h]. Allegretto for two recorders, FS157[i].

∴ 56m DDD 9/89 ꟼs

The Wind Quintet was one of the first works to spread Nielsen's fame outside Denmark on 78s in the classic account by its dedicatees, the Wind Quintet of the Royal Orchestra, Copenhagen whose Mozart playing had so delighted Nielsen in the early 1920s. Before the vogue for his music of the 1950s got under way, it remained Nielsen's visiting card in the record catalogues together with the Second Symphony. It is still generously represented in the catalogue but there are few versions of it that are so logically coupled as this BIS account by the Bergen Wind Quintet or, for that matter, better recorded. The Norwegian players are all principals of the Bergin Philharmonic and are completely at home in this repertoire. Their collection also offers the remainder of Nielsen's chamber music for wind. There is a delightful account of the slight but charming *Serenata in vano* for clarinet, bassoon, horn, cello and double bass and the Op. 2 *Fantasy Pieces* as well as an earlier *Fantasy Piece* for clarinet and piano, written when he was 16 years old.

Nielsen. SAUL AND DAVID. **Aage Haugland** (bass) Saul; **Peter Lindroos** (ten) David; **Tina Kiberg** (sop) Mikal; **Kurt Westi** (ten) Jonathan; **Anne Gjevang** (contr) Witch of Endor; **Christian Christiansen** (bass) Samuel; **Jørgen Klint** (bass) Abner; **Danish National**

Radio Choir and Symphony Orchestra/Neeme Järvi. Chandos CHAN8911/12. Notes, text and translation included. Recorded in 1990.

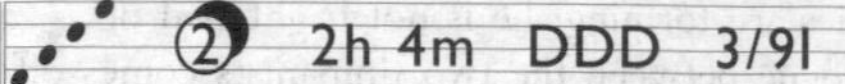

Although Scandinavia has produced a number of great dramatists and an abundance of world-famous singers, scarcely a handful of operas have reached the international repertoire. *Saul and David* is one of them. It comes from the period immediately preceding the Second Symphony and inhabits much the same world. Nielsen served in the Orchestra of the Royal Theatre for many years and became its conductor when Svendsen retired, and so knew the operatic repertoire from the inside. Before he began work on Saul he wrote, "The plot must be the 'pole' that goes through a dramatic work; the plot is the trunk; words and sentences are fruits and leaves, but if the trunk is not strong and healthy, it is no use that the fruits look beautiful". His librettist, Einar Christiansen certainly provided a strong 'pole', and in this splendid Chandos version sung in the original Danish we are at last able to hear it as both author and composer intended. However intelligent and sensitive a translation may be, something valuable is lost when the original language is abandoned (as it is when Mussorgsky, Janáček or Debussy are sung in translation). It is on Saul that the opera really focuses: his is the classic tragedy of the downfall of a great man through some flaw of character and it is for him that Nielsen (and the splendid Aage Haugland) mobilizes our sympathy. Haugland's portrayal is thoroughly full-blooded and three-dimensional, and he builds up the character with impressive conviction. The remainder of the cast is also good and the Danish Radio Choir does justice to the powerful choral writing, some of it strongly polyphonic, which distinguishes the score. The action is borne along effortlessly on the essentially symphonic current of Nielsen's musical thought. What is, of course, so striking about this piece is the sheer quality and freshness of its invention, its unfailing sense of line and purpose! No attempt is made at stage production but thanks to the committed performers under Neeme Järvi, the music fully carries the drama on its flow. The conductor paces the work to admirable effect and the Chandos recording made in collaboration with the Danish Radio is well-balanced and vivid.

Further listening …

ALADDIN. **Soloists; Danish National Radio Chamber Choir; Danish National Radio Symphony Orchestra/Gennadi Rozhdestvensky.** Chandos CHAN9135 (5/93).

Arne Nordheim

Norwegian 1931-

NEW REVIEW

Nordheim. Tenebrae[a]. Magma. [a]**Truls Mørk** (vc); **Oslo Philharmonic Orchestra/Yoav Talmi.** Aurora ACD4966. Recorded in 1991.

47m DDD 12/92 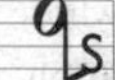

Arne Nordheim uses very much the musical language of today, and clearly he relishes the challenge of composing large-scale structures. Both works on this disc are in single movement form and each lasts for well over 20 minutes. *Tenebrae*, for cello and orchestra, was written in 1982 for Mstislav Rostropovich. The first part of the composition is dominated by a ruminative soloist, with the large orchestra playing very much an accompanying role. Then, halfway through the piece, the orchestra takes the limelight in a march-like episode, and from then on cello and orchestra engage in a more equal dialogue. It was perhaps inevitable that in a wide-ranging recording the cello soloist should be forwardly balanced. Fortunately Truls Mørk is equal to the situation — he plays with great virtuosity and total commitment. *Magma* also explores the resources of a large orchestra, and to brilliant effect. The work was written in 1988 for the one hundredth anniversary of the Concertgebouw Orchestra, and here Nordheim identifies with the stark, somewhat menacing nature of the elements at work amid the fjørds and mountains of Norway. Though the piece is very dark and turbulent, with sharp and imaginatively created contrasts in orchestral timbre and dynamics, it is not at all a difficult work to assimilate, even over such a long span. The Oslo Philharmonic play with total conviction and great virtuosity in both items under Yoav Talmo, and the recordings are spectacular.

Vítězslav Novák

Bohemian 1870-1949

Suggested listening ...

Pan — tone-poem, Op. 43. **Slovak Philharmonic Orchestra/Zdenek Bílek.** Marco Polo 8 223325 (10/91).

Eternal Longing, Op. 33[a]. In the Tatra Mountains, Op. 26[a]. Slovak Suite, Op. 32[b]. **[a]Czech Philharmonic Orchestra, [b]Brno State Philharmonic Orchestra/Karel Sejna.** Supraphon Crystal Collection 11 0682-2 (6/93).

Michael Nyman

British 1944-

Suggested listening ...

String Quartets Nos. 1-3. **Balanescu Quartet.** Argo 433 093-2ZH (8/91).
Prospero's Books (music from the film by Peter Greenaway). **Sarah Leonard, Ute Lemper, Marie Angel** (sops); **Deborah Conway** (sngr); **Michael Nyman Band/Michael Nyman.** Decca 425 224-2DH (11/91).

THE MAN WHO MISTOOK HIS WIFE FOR A HAT. **Soloists; Nyman Band/Michael Nyman** (pf). CBS CD44669 (11/88).

Knut Nystedt

Norwegian 1915-

Suggested listening ...

Chamber and Vocal Works — Lucis creator optime, Op. 58[a]. Pia memoria, Op. 65[b]. Rhapsody in Green, Op. 82[c]. 19 Motets[d]. **[a]Erna Skaug** (sop); **[a]Olav Eriksen** (bar); **[c]Norwegian Brass Quintet; [d]Bergen Cathedral Choir/Magnar Mangersnes; [a]Norwegian Soloists Choir; [a]Oslo Philharmonic Orchestra, [b]Brass Ensemble/[ab]Knut Nystedt** with **[d]Tor Grønn** (org). Aurora ACD4971 (5/93).

Johannes Ockeghem

Flanders c.1410-1497

NEW REVIEW

Ockeghem. COMPLETE SECULAR MUSIC. **The Medieval Ensemble of London/Peter Davies, Timothy Davies.** L'Oiseau-Lyre 436 194-2OH2. From D254D3 (10/82). Texts and translations included. Recorded in 1981.
Ma bouche rit. La despourveue. D'un autre amer. Quant ce viendra. Il ne m'en chault plus. Presque trainsi. Ma maistresse. Les desleaux. Mort tu as navre. Quant de vous. Au travail suis. Prenez sur moi. Fors seulement l'actente. L'autre d'antan. S'elle m'amera. O rosa bella. Tant fuz gentement. Je n'ay dueil. Malheur me bat. Se vostre cuer. Qu'es mi vida. Qu'es mi vida

(original version by Johannes Cornago). Je n'ay dueil. Ce n'est pas jeu. Resjois toy. Departez vous. Ung aultre l'a. Autre Venus. Baissiez moi. Fors seulement contre ce.

② 2h 11m DDD

If it is an exaggeration to claim Ockeghem as the Schubert of the fifteenth century, it can only be because there were so many other excellent song writers working at the same time. The collection of the complete secular music sounds as fresh as it did when it first appeared in 1982. While Ockeghem's melodic gifts are evident in every piece, songs such as *Ce n'est pas jeu* and *Fors seulement contre ce* are simply extraordinarily beautiful. In addition to this, the handling of the various forms of song is itself fascinating, and Peter Davies's insert-note helps to elucidate this and many other aspects of the repertoire in exemplary fashion. The performances themselves show their age remarkably little (it is extraordinary how a performance of this kind of repertoire can date after a mere ten years), and are in general all that one could wish. A greater variety of colour would occasionally be welcome, but the vocal and instrumental blend (*Ung aultre l'a* provides a very good example) remains very impressive in its clarity and convincing linear sense. This collection really demands repeated listening; the more one listens the more one becomes aware of the subtlety of Ockeghem's melodic writing and harmonic movement and the more one becomes aware of the way in which these features — as, in fact, with Schubert — combine to make a whole with the poetry.

Further listening ...

Missa Pro defunctis. *Coupled with* **Josquin Desprez.** *Missa l'homme armé super voces musicales.* **Pro Cantione Antiqua/Bruno Turner.** Archiv Produktion 415 293-2AH (4/86).
Missa Prolationum. *Coupled with* **Lupi.** Ergone conticuit. **Capella Nova/Richard Taruskin.** ASV Gaudeamus CDGAU103 (2/87).

Jacques Offenbach

German/French 1819-1880

NEW REVIEW

Offenbach. CHRISTOPHER COLUMBUS. **Maurice Arthur** (ten) Christopher Columbus; **Joy Roberts** (sop) Beatriz; **Johanna Peters** (mez) Rosa Columbus; **Lissa Gray** (sop) Fleurette Columbus; **Marilyn Hill Smith** (sop) Gretel Columbus; **Christian du Plessis** (bar) Luis de Torres; **Alan Opie** (bar) Chief of Police; **Anna Dawson** (sop) Queen Isabella; **Alec Bregonzi** (ten) King Ferdinand; **Clive Harré** (bar) Tourist; **John Duxbury** (ten) Waiter; **Rosemary Ashe** (sop) Princess Minnehaha Columbus, Esperanza; **Celia Kite** (sop) Carmelita; **Kathleen Smales** (mez) Manuela; **Amilia Dixey** (mez) Valencia; **Geoffrey Mitchell Choir; London Mozart Players/Alun Francis.** Opera Rara ORC2. Notes and text included. From OR2 (8/78). Recorded in 1977.

② 2h 4m ADD 4/93 P

You will look in vain for *Christopher Columbus* in lists of Offenbach's works. It was put together by Opera Rara for the 1976 American bicentenary celebrations, using a totally new book allied to music from a variety of Offenbach works. But not without reason has it been described as "the best Offenbach opera Offenbach never wrote". It is an absolutely hilarious piece, right from the opening chorus, in which the young ladies of Córdoba express their boredom at having nothing to do but snap their castanets and shout "Olé!" through to the marvellously inventive conclusion. The lyrics are quite brilliant, and the racy melodies, whose sources are all listed in the accompanying libretto, are all the better for being generally unfamiliar. If the whole doesn't sound quite like an authentic Offenbach piece, it is only for the very good reason that it largely forswears dialogue and the lead-ins to numbers in favour of the big juicy tunes. One should not look to a performance of a work such as this for mere purity of vocal sound, so much as for ability to put a number across. In this respect, with singers and singing actors of the quality of Marilyn Hill Smith, Johanna Peters, Anna Dawson and Alec Bregonzi supporting Maurice Arthur in the title-role, it would be difficult to imagine the piece performed with greater skill or relish. If you want a CD set for sheer uninhibited enjoyment, this should be it.

Offenbach. LA PERICHOLE. **Régine Crespin** (sop) La Périchole; **Alain Vanzo** (ten) Piquillo; **Jules Bastin** (bass) Don Andrès; **Gérard Friedmann** (ten) Miguel de Panatellas; **Jacques Trigeau** (bar) Don Pedro; **Aimé Besançon, Paul Guigue** (tens) First and Second Notaries; **Rebecca Roberts** (sop) Guadalena, Manuelita; **Eva Saurova** (sop) Berginella, Ninetta; **Geneviève Baudoz** (mez) Mastrilla, Frasquinella; **Ine Meister** (mez) Bramdilla; **Rhine Opera Chorus; Strasbourg Philharmonic Orchestra/Alain Lombard.** Erato Libretto 2292-45686-2. Notes, text and translation included. Recorded in 1976.

② 1h 26m ADD 5/92 

Of all Offenbach's operetta scores, *La Périchole* is perhaps the one that oozes the greatest charm. The satirical touch is there, to be sure, but the edge is less sharp. One detects a vein of genuine feeling for the fate of the Peruvian street-singer forced to marry a man she only later discovers is her own true love, that one never does with Eurydice, Helen, or the Grand-Duchess of Gerolstein. The splendid songs Offenbach composed for her (the "Letter Song", "Ah! quel dîner", "Ah! que les hommes sont bêtes" and "Je t'adore, brigand" head up a richly melodic score. Régine Crespin is a somewhat matronly Périchole, but she knows how to tease the best out of the textual and melodic phrases. Her Piquillo, Alain Vanzo, is the ideal Offenbach tenor, gliding lightly over the score, while Jules Bastin brings experience to the role of the Viceroy, if perhaps not quite capturing all its comic possibilities. Alain Lombard directs sympathetically. The absence of spoken dialogue to provide atmosphere is unfortunate, but Erato have generously provided a full libretto, which also includes a linking narration by Alain Decaux that featured in the original LP recording but has been edited out of the CD reissue. This is a fine opportunity to fall under the spell of this captivating score.

Offenbach. LES CONTES D'HOFFMANN. **Plácido Domingo** (ten) Hoffmann; **Dame Joan Sutherland** (sop) Olympia, Giulietta, Antonia, Stella; **Gabriel Bacquier** (bar) Lindorf, Coppélius, Dapertutto, Dr Miracle; **Huguette Tourangeau** (mez) La Muse, Nicklausse; **Jacques Charon** (ten) Spalanzani; **Hugues Cuénod** (ten) Andres, Cochenille, Pitichinaccio, Frantz; **André Neury** (bar) Schlemil; **Paul Plishka** (bass) Crespel; **Margarita Lilowa** (mez) Voice of Antonia's Mother; **Roland Jacques** (bar) Luther; **Lausanne Pro Arte Chorus; Du Brassus Chorus; Suisse Romande Chorus and Orchestra/Richard Bonynge.** Decca 417 363-2DH2. Notes, text and translation included. From SET545/7 (11/72).

② 2h 23m ADD 11/86 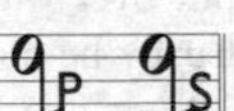

Offenbach died after finishing the piano score of *The Tales of Hoffmann* plus the orchestration of the First Act and a summary of the scoring of the rest, which was then completed by Ernest Guiraud. The work became an instant popular success, but not exactly as the composer conceived it. Bonynge's recording returns to Offenbach's original conception as far as seems practicable, but includes certain desirable extra numbers such as the inserted arias for Dapertutto and Coppélius — both of which would be sorely missed — and restores a fine missing quartet to climax the Epilogue. It is essential that the four main soprano roles are taken by one singer, here Dame Joan Sutherland in superb form, and the four faces of villainy (Lindorf, Coppélius, Dapertutto and Dr Miracle) must also be given to a single artist, here the magnificent Gabriel Bacquier. Plácido Domingo is outstanding as Hoffmann (and it is not easy to be convincing in a role that demands ingenuous amorous liaisons with first a clockwork doll, then a courtesan and finally an opera star, determined to sing herself to death). He sings with optimistic fervour throughout all his disappointments, while Huguette Tourangeau is most appealing as his companion and confidante, Nicklausse. Bonynge directs with splendid vitality and romantic feeling and finds the right lightness of touch for the doll scene. The whole performance goes with a swing and Decca's recording, vividly atmospheric, is fully worthy of it.

Additional recommendation ...

Soloists; Leipzig Radio Chorus; Staatskapelle Dresden/Jeffrey Tate. Philips 422 374-2PH3 — ③ 2h 55m DDD 11/92

Further listening ...

Gaîté parisienne — ballet. *Coupled with* **Gounod.** Faust — ballet music. **Montreal Symphony Orchestra/Charles Dutoit.** Decca Ovation 430 718-2DM (8/91).

LA BELLE HELENE. **Soloists; Toulouse Capitol Chorus and Orchestra/Michel Plasson.** EMI CDS7 47157-8 (9/86).

LES BRIGANDS. **Soloists; Chorus and Orchestra of the Lyon Opéra/John Eliot Gardiner.** EMI CDS7 49830-2 (2/90).

ORPHEE AUX ENFERS — *operetta.* **Soloists; Les Petits Chanteurs à la Croix Potencée; Toulouse Capitole Chorus and Orchestra/Michel Plasson.** EMI CDS7 49647-2 (1/89).

Carl Orff

German 1895-1982

Orff. Carmina burana. **Sheila Armstrong** (sop); **Gerald English** (ten); **Thomas Allen** (bar); **St Clement Danes Grammar School Boys' Choir; London Symphony Chorus and Orchestra/André Previn.** EMI CDC7 47411-2. Text and translation included. From ASD3117 (10/75). Recorded in 1974.

1h 3m DDD 12/86 

There are at least 20 digital recordings of Orff's flamboyant and inspired cantata, using Latin texts taken from a thirteenth-century manuscript, and it is a work that particularly benefits from the range and clarity of digital techniques. Nevertheless, Previn's 1975 version sweeps the board. Not only has the performance a unique bite and exuberance, plus at times an infectious joy, but the three soloists are outstanding and the recording has been most effectively remastered to seem fresher than ever. For once all three soloists are splendid. If Thomas Allen especially catches the attention, the tenor, Gerald English, is excellent too and the soprano, Sheila Armstrong, is suitably ravishing in her love songs, with words explicitly conveying that they are about physical lovemaking. The boys, too, obviously relish the meaning of the lyrics, which they put over with much gusto. Indeed, this pantheistic celebration of life's earthy pleasures could hardly be more vividly projected: the recording is a triumph.

Additional recommendations ...

Soloists; Southend Boys' Choir; Philharmonia Chorus and Orchestra/Riccardo Muti. EMI CDC7 47100-2 — ADD 4/85
Soloists; Schöneberger Boys' Choir; Deutsche Oper Chorus and Orchestra, Berlin/Eugen Jochum. DG Galleria 423 886-2GGA — 56m ADD 11/88
Soloists; Shinyukai Choir; Berlin Cathedral Boys' Choir; Berlin Philharmonic Orchestra/Seiji Ozawa. Philips 422 363-2PH — 1h DDD 7/89
Soloists; San Francisco Girls' Chorus; San Francisco Boys' Chorus; San Francisco Symphony Chorus and Orchestra/Herbert Blomstedt. Decca 430 509-2DH — 59m DDD 12/91

Further listening ...

Catulli carmina. *Coupled with* **Stravinsky.** Les noces. **Soloists/Wolfgang Schäfer.** Koch Schwann Musica Mundi 314021 (7/91).
De temporum fine comoedia — symbolic drama. **Soloists; Cologne Radio Chorus; Tölz Boys' Choir; Berlin RIAS Chamber Chorus; Cologne Radio Symphony Orchestra/Herbert von Karajan.** DG Twentieth Century Classics 429 859-2GC.

Die Kluge; Der Mond — operas. **Soloists; Rudolf Kiermeyer Children's Choir; Bavarian Radio Chorus; Munich Radio Orchestra/Kurt Eichhorn.** Eurodisc GD69069 (3/91).

Johann Pachelbel

German 1653-1706

Suggested listening ...

Suite in G major. Musicalische Ergotzung — Suite No. 4 in E minor. Aria con variazoni in A major. Canon and Gigue in D major. *Coupled with* ***Buxtehude.*** *Trio Sonatas* — C major, BuxWV266; G major, BuxWV271; B flat major, BuxWV273. **Cologne Musica Antiqua/Reinhard Goebel.** Archiv Produktion Galleria 427 118-2AGA (6/89).
See review in the Collections section; refer to the Index to Reviews.

Ignacy Paderewski

Polish 1860-1941

Suggested listening ...

Piano Concerto in A minor, Op. 17. *Coupled with* ***Moszkowski.*** Piano Concerto in E major, Op. 59. **Piers Lane** (pf); **BBC Scottish Symphony Orchestra/Jerzy Maksymiuk.** Hyperion CDA66452 (2/92).
See review under Moszkowski; refer to the Index to Reviews.

Niccolo Paganini

Italian 1782-1840

Paganini. Violin Concertos — No. 1 in D major, Op. 6; No. 2 in B minor, Op. 7, "La campanella". **Salvatore Accardo** (vn); **London Philharmonic Orchestra/Charles Dutoit.** DG 415 378-2GH. From 2740 121 (11/75).

lh 9m ADD 2/87 

Paganini's violin music was at one time thought quite inaccessible to lesser mortals among the violin-playing fraternity, but as standards of technique have improved master technicians are now able to do justice to such works as these concertos. Salvatore Accardo is certainly among them, and we can judge his skill as early as the opening violin solo of the First Concerto. This is typical of the style, with its authoritative and rhetorical gestures and use of the whole instrumental compass, but so is the second theme which in its refinement and songlike nature demands (and here receives) another kind of virtuosity expressed through a command of tone, texture and articulation. Dutoit and the London Philharmonic Orchestra have a mainly subordinate role, certainly when the soloist is playing, but they fulfil it well and follow Accardo through the kind of rhythmic flexibilities which are accepted performing style in this music and which for all we know were used by the virtuoso performer-composer himself. The 1975 recording is faithful and does justice to the all-important soloist.

Additional recommendations ...

No. 1. ***Wieniawski.*** *Violin Concerto No. 2 in D minor, Op. 22.* **Mark Kaplan** (vn); **London Symphony Orchestra/Mitch Miller.** Arabesque Z6597 — 57m DDD 7/89 B

No. 1. ***Vieuxtemps.*** *Violin Concerto No. 5 in A minor, Op. 37.* **Viktoria Mullova** (vn); **Academy of St Martin in the Fields/Sir Neville Marriner.** Philips 422 332-2PH — 55m 10/89 B

No. 1. ***Saint-Saëns.*** Violin Concerto No. 3 in B minor, Op. 61[a]. **Zino Francescatti** (vn); **Philadelphia Orchestra/Eugene Ormandy;** *Nos. 1 and 2.* **[a]New York Philharmonic Orchestra/Dimitri Mitropoulos.** CBS Masterworks Portrait mono CD46728 — 51m ADD 12/91 B ▲

Nos. 1 and 2. **Auvergne Orchestra/Jean-Jacques Kantorow** (vn). Denon CO-77611 — lh DDD 4/92 B

Paganini. 24 Caprices, Op. 1. **Itzhak Perlman** (vn). EMI CDC7 47171-2. From SLS832 (6/72).

lh 12m ADD 7/88

This electrifying music with its dare-devil virtuosity has long remained the pinnacle of violin technique, and they encapsulate the essence of the composer's style. For a long time it was considered virtually unthinkable that a violinist should be able to play the complete set; even in recent years only a handful have produced truly successful results. Itzhak Perlman has one strength in this music that is all-important, other than a sovereign technique — he is incapable of playing with an ugly tone. He has such variety in his bowing that the timbre of the instrument is never monotonous. The notes of the music are despatched with a forthright confidence and fearless abandon that are ideal. The frequent double-stopping passages hold no fear for him. Listen to the fire of No. 5 in A minor and the way in which Perlman copes with the extremely difficult turns in No. 14 in E flat; this is a master at work. The set rounds off with the famous A minor Caprice, which inspired Liszt, Brahms and Rachmaninov, amongst others, to adapt it in various guises for the piano.

Additional recommendation ...
Midori (vn). CBS Masterworks CD44944 — lh 17m DDD 3/90

Key to Symbols

Price	Quantity/availability	Timing	Mode	Review date
	② ②	lh 23m	DDD	6/88

Giovanni Palestrina

Italian c.1525/6-1594

Palestrina: Missa Papae Marcelli. Tu es Petrus. ITALIAN SACRED CHORAL WORKS. **Westminster Abbey Choir/Simon Preston.** Archiv Produktion 415 517-2AH. Texts and translations included.
Allegri: Miserere. ***Anerio:*** Venite ad me omnes. ***Nanino:*** Haec dies. ***Giovannelli:*** Jubilate Deo.

59m DDD 5/86

Palestrina. Missa Papae Marcelli.
Allegri. Miserere[a].
W. Mundy. Vox patris caelestis. [a]**Alison Stamp** (sop); **The Tallis Scholars/Peter Phillips.** Gimell CDGIM339. From Classics for Pleasure CFP40339 (10/80).

lh 9m ADD 7/86

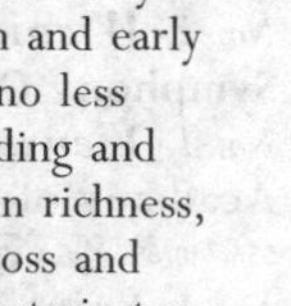

To listen to Simon Preston's disc is to enjoy a feast of sacred choral music composed by members of the well-known school of eminent Roman musicians of the sixteenth and early seventeenth centuries. Palestrina heads the list with his *Missa Papae Marcelli*, but no less famous is the Allegri *Miserere,* which is performed here with a musical understanding and penetration that is comparatively rare. The alternating *falsobordone* verses excel in richness, and those of the semi-chorus, admirably distanced from the main choir, float across and upwards with an ethereal quality of amazing beauty and magic. The Choir of Westminster Abbey find plenty of scope to display their varied musical skills in the Mass itself, the psalm, and the four motets, and particularly enjoyable is the precision and crispness of the rhythm in Giovannelli's *Jubilate*, and also the careful balance and fullness of the sound in Anerio's *Venite ad me*. The highlight of the Gimell disc is Allegri's *Miserere*. Peter Phillips has used the natural acoustics of Merton College Chapel, adding a note of variety which relieves the repetitious nature of the long penitential psalm: what a simple idea it was to space the singers so that those with the low-lying verses were near the microphone and the others half-way down the chapel, with Alison Stamp's high C rising pure and clear above distant hushed voices! *Vox patris caelestis* is an imaginative and cleverly-designed motet for the Assumption of the Virgin, dating from the mid-sixteenth-century Catholic revival and based on texts from the *Song of Songs*. The music rises to an ecstatic climax at the words "Veni, veni ...", with two high trebles at the top of their range crowning the rich harmonies of the lower voices. In marked contrast to such exuberance, the *Missa Papae Marcelli*, dating from the same period, represents a sober, lapidary style. The declamatory speech-rhythms are admirably rendered and the performance is notable for its moments of intense, if restrained, emotion. Highly recommended.

Additional recommendations ...
Missa Papae Marcelli. Missa Aeterna Christi munera. **Oxford Camerata/Jeremy Summerly.** Naxos Early Music 8 550573 — 56m DDD 12/92
Missa Aeterna Christi munera. Sicut cervus; Super flumina Babylonis a 4; Vidi turbam magnam; Quae est ista; Duo ubera tua; Nigra sum, sed formosa; Surge, amica mea; Magnificat Primi Toni. **Anonymous.** Aeterna *Christi munera.* **Westminster Cathedral Choir/James O'Donnell.** Hyperion CDA66490 — lh 7m DDD

Palestrina. SACRED CHORAL WORKS. **Christ Church Cathedral Choir, Oxford/Stephen Darlington.** Nimbus NI5100. Texts and translations included. Recorded in 1987.
Missa Dum complerentur. *Motets* — Super flumina Babylonis; Exsultate Deo; Sicut cervus; O bone Jesu, exaudi me a 8; Dum complerentur a 6.

55m DDD 11/88

The full potential of this choir gradually unfolds as they sing through the movements of Palestrina's parody mass *Dum complerentur dies pentecostes* — one of the 22 masses the composer based on one of his own earlier motets. The choir's approach to the Pentecost mass is generally restrained and they find greater scope in the five motets, ending with a brilliant performance of *Dum complerentur* upon which the Mass is built. They clearly revel in its cascading descending phrases in all six voices, which they pour forth jubilantly. Darker, more sombre colours are displayed in *Super flumina Babylonis*, whilst rejoicing and exuberance characterize *Exsultate Deo*, with its crisp treble lead. Anyone coming fresh to this type of music will benefit by following the excellent notes.

Palestrina. SACRED CHORAL WORKS. **Westminster Cathedral Choir/James O'Donnell.** Hyperion CDA66316. Texts and translations included. Recorded in 1988.
Masses — Viri Galilaei; O Rex gloriae. *Motets* — Viri Galilaei; O Rex gloriae.

lh 8m DDD 1/90

This is music in which Westminster Cathedral Choir excel: their response to the richly reverberant acoustic is warm and generous; they perform with the ease and freedom of kinship — a far cry from the studied perfection of many other choirs. Each motet is heard before its reworking as a Mass. The six-part scoring of *Viri Galilaei* (two trebles, alto, two tenors and bass) invites a variety of combinations and textures, culminating in the joyful cascading Alleluias at the end of Part I and the jubilant ascending series in Part II. In the Mass the mood changes from triumph to quiet pleading — a change partly due to revised scoring: the two alto parts beneath the single treble produce a more subdued sound. The Choir clearly relishes this exploration of the deeper sonorities: in the *Creed* one entire section is entrusted to the four lowest voices. The four-part motet *O Rex gloriae* is lithe and fast-moving. The corresponding Mass, largely syllabic in style, gives the Choir the chance to demonstrate their superb command of phrasing and accentuation: the Latin comes over with intelligibility and subtlety. Listen, also, to the wonderful solo boys' trio in the "Crucifixus", and for the carefully crafted canons in the *Benedictus* and the *Agnus Dei*.

Suggested listening ...

Masses — Assumpta est Maria; Sicut lilium inter spinas. *Motets* — Assumpta est Maria a 6; Sicut lilium inter spinas I. *Coupled with* **Plainchant.** Assumpta est Maria. **The Tallis Scholars/Peter Phillips.** Gimell CDGIM020 (9/90).

Selim Palmgren

Finland 1878-1951

Suggested listening ...

Piano Concertos — No. 2, Op. 33; No. 3, Op. 41; No. 5 in A major, Op. 99. **Soloists; Turku Philharmonic Orchestra/Jacques Mercier.** Finlandia FACD379.

Sir Andrzej Panufnik

Polish/British 1914-1991

Panufnik. Sinfonia sacra[a]. Arbor cosmica[b]. **[a]Royal Concertgebouw Orchestra; [b]New York Chamber Symphony/Sir Andrzej Panufnik.** Elektra Nonesuch 7559-79228-2. Recorded in 1988.

59m DDD 5/91 

Panufnik's *Sinfonia sacra* of 1963 is a tribute to his native Poland. The work is cast in two movements, the first of which divides into "Three visions". Four trumpets provide an opening fanfare; then a contemplative atmosphere is provided in a section for strings alone. Finally the full orchestra combines to evoke a mood of agitation and war. The second movement is based on an old Polish hymn called the *Bogurodzica*. This work very much needs a virtuoso orchestra to make its full effect, and Panufnik, an experienced conductor who studied with Felix Weingartner, gets very disciplined, high quality playing from the Concertgebouw. *Arbor cosmica*, written in 1983 for string orchestra, reflects Panufnik's lifelong affinity with trees, and in 12 sections depicts contrasted moods and feelings experienced by the composer when in contact with the phenomenon of photosynthesis. Each section is brief, but each also clearly poses very difficult problems for the string players. The New York Orchestra rise to the occasion brilliantly. *Sinfonia sacra* enjoys a very clear, spacious 1987 recording; the other 1988 New York recording has an appropriately closer acoustic.

Additional recommendation ...

Concerto festivo[a]. *Landscape*[a]. *Katyn epitaph*[a]. *Concertino for timpani, percussion and strings*[a]. *Sinfonia sacra*[b]. **[b]Soloists; [a]London Symphony Orchestra, [b]Monte-Carlo Opera Orchestra/Sir Andrzej Panufnik.** Unicorn-Kanchana Souvenir UKCD2020 — lh 9m DDD 8/89

Further listening ...

Autumn Music. Nocturne. Tragic Overture. Heroic Overture. Sinfonia rustica[a]. **London Symphony Orchestra/Jascha Horenstein; [a]Monte-Carlo Opera Orchestra/Sir Andrzej Panufnik.** Unicorn-Kanchana Souvenir UKCD2016 (4/89).

Concerto festivo. Landscape. Katyn epitaph. Concertino for timpani, percussion and strings. Sinfonia sacra[a]. **London Symphony Orchestra, [a]Monte-Carlo Opera Orchestra/Sir Andrzej Panufnik.** Unicorn-Kanchana Souvenir UKCD2020 (8/89).

Symphony No. 8, "Sinfonia Votiva". *Coupled with* **Sessions.** Concerto for Orchestra. **Boston Symphony Orchestra/Seiji Ozawa.** Hyperion CDA66050 (7/89).

Symphony No. 9, "Sinfonia della Speranza". Piano Concerto[a]. [a]**Ewa Poblocka** (pf); **London Symphony Orchestra/Sir Andrzej Panufnik.** Conifer CDCF206 (5/92).

Sir Hubert Parry

British 1848-1918

NEW REVIEW

Parry. Symphony No. 1 in G minor. Concertstück in G minor. **London Philharmonic Orchestra/Matthias Bamert.** Chandos CHAN9062. Recorded 1991-92.

53m DDD 7/92

Written in its composer's thirty-second year, Parry's First Symphony witnessed the realization of several decades of aspiration and dedication toward this grandest of musical objectives. Despite its obvious Germanic, and more specifically Brahmsian affiliations, the symphony reflects much of the comfortable optimism of the Victorian era. Even so, there's little in the way of Gothic excess, and not a trace of inflated jingoism here. The symphony is ably constructed and tastefully orchestrated, with several of its most powerful statements returning in the finale. Matthias Bamert's performance is assured and totally committed, as he makes out the strongest possible case for the work from its very opening bars. The important cyclic elements are highlighted, so that their reappearance later seems all the more logical and inevitable. Bamert and the LPO never overlook the more introspective aspects of the work, in an eloquently sustained *Andante*, featuring superb playing from the first horn as the movement gets under way. Fine wind details register clearly during the *Scherzo*: equally the result of Bamert's expert judgement, and the superb Chandos engineering. The finale is brilliantly executed, and the avoidance of empty rhetoric during the closing pages is ample testimony to the Swiss conductor's compelling belief in this work. Bamert also includes an ardently reasoned account of Parry's *Concertstück* in G minor, hardly music of the calibre of the Symphony, but worth hearing, none the less. This is a revelatory issue, and with the complete cycle of Parry's symphonies now available from Chandos, it's difficult to imagine Mathias Bamert's triumphant offerings being superseded for a very long time to come.

Parry. Symphony No. 2 in F major, "Cambridge". Symphonic Variations (1897). **London Philharmonic Orchestra/Matthias Bamert.** Chandos CHAN8961. Recorded in 1991.

52m DDD 10/91

Matthias Bamert and the London Philharmonic score another important first here with these fine recordings of the *Cambridge* Symphony and the *Symphonic Variations* by Parry. Like its predecessors in the splendid Chandos/Parry series, this disc also offers some surprises, for its seems incredible that this music has remained virtually unknown for the best part of a century! The Second Symphony has no particular link with Cambridge, save for the fact that it received its première there in 1883. Bamert and the London Philharmonic offer a revelatory performance here in which the real qualities of the music are allowed to shine through any reverential backward glances at the works of Brahms, Dvořák and Schumann. Parry was enthusiastic, however, about Dvořák's *Symphonic Variations* and Brahms's *Haydn* Variations, and followed the example of both in his own set for orchestra. It is also fascinating to speculate about the impact made upon Parry by Wagner, whom he met in 1877, for much of the music here has a broad conception and often employs sumptuous orchestration with much emphasis upon grand gestures. The London Philharmonic are captured here on vibrant form and the Chandos sound is especially full-bodied and resonant. Matthias Bamert directs these performances with energy and vision and like his other Parry discs this deserves the strongest recommendation.

Parry. Symphonies — No. 3 in C major, "English"; No. 4 in E minor. **London Philharmonic Orchestra/Matthias Bamert.** Chandos CHAN8896. Recorded in 1990.

1h 16m DDD 1/91

It has been encouraging to find the Swiss conductor, Matthias Bamert, championing Parry's music in the Chandos cycle of the symphonies and some choral works of which this was the first issue. He is clearly a convinced enthusiast and brings to the music a probing passion that eluded Boult in his last years when he recorded some Parry with the same orchestra. The discovery here is the Fourth Symphony, first performed (conducted by Hans Richter) in 1889, revised in 1910, performed twice in its new version and then forgotten for nearly 80 years. It is a deeply personal work, almost confessional in its repressed passion. The first movement (16 minutes) is on an immense scale, covering an emotional range comparable with Elgar's Second (which it preceded). The Third Symphony is more conventional, an English equivalent of Schumann's *Rhenish*. Its sunny exuberance and the lightness of the scoring make it highly attractive. Performance and recording are both admirable. Highly recommended.

Parry. Symphony No. 5 in B minor, "Symphonic Fantasia 1912". From Death to Life (1914). Elegy for Brahms (1897). **London Philharmonic Orchestra/Matthias Bamert.** Chandos CHAN8955. Recorded in 1991.

57m DDD 9/91

Parry's Fifth Symphony dates from 1912 and like so much of his output this substantial work reveals the composer's enduring devotion to the music of Brahms. However, Parry was fascinated by the idea of writing a programmatic symphony, in the Lisztian mould, and thus each of the four linked movements have titles which relate strongly to his personal ethical outlook. The finale, entitled "Now" culminates with an expansive review of material from earlier in the work, and here it is clearly a sense of confidence and affirmation, expressed in grandiose Edwardian musical rhetoric, which concludes Parry's symphonic cycle. The remaining movements, "Stress", "Love" and "Play" also serve to remind us of the clear romantic origins of this splendid and inexplicably neglected British symphony. Also included on this disc are two shorter, although no less weighty Parry rarities, and the Symphonic Poem *From Death to Life* shares much common ground with the Fifth Symphony, at least in terms of its general subject matter. The orchestral parts have been reconstructed only recently, and the work receives its first modern performance on this disc. Both the Symphony and the *Elegy for Brahms* were recorded by Sir Adrian Boult, a great champion of Parry's music, in 1978. By then Sir Adrian was nearing the end of a long career of course, and it was left to Matthias Bamert to take up the cause, which he has done with notable distinction. Bamert reveals the true fire and dignity which colours the music of this remarkable composer and the London Philharmonic respond with tremendous conviction and brilliance.

Further listening ...

Parry (ed J. Dibble). Nonet in B flat major. *Coupled with* ***Stanford.*** Serenade (Nonet) in F major, Op. 95. **Capricorn.** Hyperion CDA66291 (9/89).

Parry. Violin Sonata in D major. 12 Short Pieces. Fantasie-sonata in B minor . **Erich Gruenberg** (vn); **Roger Vignoles** (pf). Hyperion CDA66157 (9/91).

Parry. The Soul's Ransom — sinfonia sacra[a]. Choric song from Tennyson's "The Lotos Eaters". **Della Jones** (mez); [a]**David Wilson-Johnson** (bar); **London Philharmonic Choir and Orchestra/Matthias Bamert.** Chandos CHAN8990 (1/92).

Blest pair of sirens. I was glad (orch. Jacob). Jerusalem (orch. Elgar). Judith — Long since in Egypt's plenteous land. *Coupled with* ***Bairstow.*** Blessed city, heavenly Salem. ***Elgar.*** Give unto the Lord, Op. 74. Great is the Lord, Op. 67. O hearken Thou. ***Hadley.*** My beloved spake. ***Stanford.*** Evening Service in B flat major, Op. 10. Te Deum in B flat major. **Winchester Cathedral Choir; Waynflete Singers; Bournemouth Symphony Orchestra/David Hill** with **Timothy Byram-Wigfield** (org). Argo 430 836-2ZH (4/92).

Arvo Pärt

Estonian 1935-

Pärt. TABULA RASA. [ad]**Gidon Kremer,** [d]**Tatjana Grindenko** (vns); [a]**Keith Jarrett** (pf); [d]**Alfred Schnittke** (prepared pf); [b]**Stuttgart State Orchestra/Dennis Russell Davies;** [c]cellists of the **Berlin Philharmonic Orchestra;** [d]**Lithuanian Chamber Orchestra/Saulus Sondeckis.** ECM New Series 817 764-2. Item marked [d] recorded at a live performance in Bonn in 1977.

Fratres[a]. Cantus in memory of Benjamin Britten[b]. Fratres for 12 cellos[c]. Tabula rasa[d].

55m ADD/DDD 

If Reich, Adams and Glass represent the so-called composers of minimalist music there is a strong case to be made for the Estonian-born Arvo Pärt as a composer who has blended the most alluring elements of that 'school' with his own individual musical voice and a definite message. His strongly held religious beliefs find frequent expression in his music; indeed, a discernible relationship can be made between his 'works of suffering' and the society that emerged under the former Soviet régime. These four works were composed between 1974 and 1976. *Fratres* appears twice: once in a version for piano and violin and again in a version for 12 cellos. They both comprise variations on a theme which formed the original version. The piece is constructed in strict metrical and mathematically conceived units but none the less possesses a freedom of utterance that is totally beguiling. The *Cantus* is no less bewitching, spinning a long cantilena with enormous simplicity. *Tabula rasa* is the most substantial piece on the disc, some 26 minutes long, employing two violins, prepared piano and chamber orchestra. Across a great chasm the lower registers of the piano seem to cry out to the upper harmonics of the violins. The effect is quite extraordinary. Gidon Kremer, who was deeply involved in the work's creation, clearly inspired his colleagues to give their utmost to produce a performance of great luminosity and intensity. The recording is well balanced and offers a fascinating picture of a composer whose language is direct, profound and hauntingly beautiful.

Further listening ...

Cello Concerto, "Pro et contra"[a]. Perpetuum mobile, Op. 10. Symphonies — No. 1, "Polyphonic"; No. 2; No. 3. [a]**Frans Helmerson** (vc); **Bamberg Symphony Orchestra/Neeme Järvi.** BIS CD434 (9/89).

Passio Domini nostri Jesu Christi secundum Johannem. **Michael George** (bass); **John Potter** (ten; **Hilliard Ensemble; Western Wind Chamber Choir/Paul Hillier.** ECM New Series 837 109-2 (2/89).

Pärt. Miserere[a]. Festina lente[b]. Sarah was ninety years old[c]. [a]**Western Wind Choir;** [ac]**Hilliard Ensemble/Paul Hillier;** [b]**Bonn Beethovenhalle Orchestra/Dennis Russell Davies.** ECM New Series 847 539-2 (1/92).

Francisco de Peñalosa

Spanish c.1470-1528

Suggested listening ...

Motets — Inter vestibulum et altare. Tribularer, si nescirem. Ne reminiscaris, Domine. Versa est in luctum. Domine, secundum actum meum. Adore te, Domine Jesus Christe. Ave, verum corpus natum. Nigra sum, sed formosa. Sancta Maria. Unica est colomba mea. Ave, vera caro Christi. Ave, vere sanguis Domini. In passione positus. Precor te, Domine Jesu Christe. Pater noster. Ave Regina caelorum. Sancta Mater, istud agas. O Domina sanctissima. Emendemus in melius. Deus, qui manus tuas. Domine Iesu Christe, qui neminem. Transeunte Domino Jesu. **Pro Cantione Antiqua/Bruno Turner.** Hyperion CDA66574 (7/92).

Krzysztof Penderecki

Polish 1933-

Suggested listening ...

Violin Concerto[a]. Symphony No. 2, "Christmas Symphony"[b]. [a]**Konstanty Andrzej Kulka** (vn); **Polish National Radio Orchestra/**[a]**Krzysztof Penderecki,** [b]**Jacek Kaspszyk.** Polskie Nagrania PNCD019 (6/90).

St Luke Passion (Passio et mors Domini nostri Jesu Christi secundum Lucam). **Soloists; Cracow Boys' Choir; Warsaw National Philharmonic Chorus; Polish Radio National Symphony Orchestra/Krzysztof Penderecki.** Argo 430 328-2ZH (3/91).

Polish Requiem. **Soloists; North German Radio Chorus; Bavarian Radio Chorus; North German Radio Symphony Orchestra/Penderecki.** DG 429 720-2GH2 (3/91).

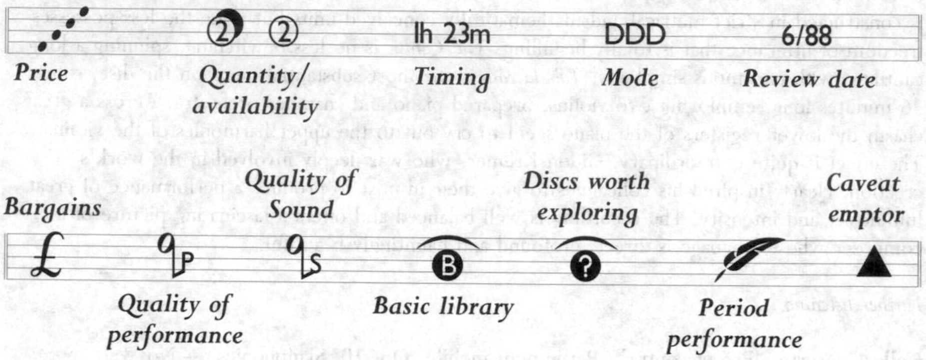

Ernst Pepping

German 1901-1981

Suggested listening ...

Concerto No. 2. Four Fugues. Partita No. 1, "Ach wie flüchtig". Wie schön leuchtet der Morgenstern. **Wolfgang Stockmeier** (org). CPO CPO999 039-2 (7/91).

Giovanni Pergolesi

Italian 1710-1736

Pergolesi. Stabat mater[a]. Salve regina in C minor. **Emma Kirkby** (sop); [a]**James Bowman** (alto); **Academy of Ancient Music/Christopher Hogwood.** L'Oiseau-Lyre Florilegium 425 692-2OH. Texts and translations included.

Pergolesi's *Stabat mater*, written in the last few months of his brief life, enjoyed a huge popularity throughout the eighteenth century. But modern performances often misrepresent its nature, either through over-romanticizing it or by transforming it into a choral work. None of the its qualities is overlooked in this affecting performance, for Emma Kirkby and James Bowman are well-versed in the stylistic conventions of baroque and early classical music — and their voices afford a pleasing partnership. Both revel in Pergolesi's sensuous vocal writing, phrasing the music effectively and executing the ornaments with an easy grace. Singers and instrumentalists alike attach importance to sonority, discovering a wealth of beguiling effects in Pergolesi's part writing. In the *Salve regina* in C minor, the better known of two settings by Pergolesi, Emma Kirkby gives a compelling performance, pure in tone, expressive and poignant, and she is sympathetically supported by the string ensemble. The recording is pleasantly resonant and does justice to Pergolesi's translucent textures. Full texts are included.

Additional recommendation ...
Stabat mater[ab]. *Salve regina*[a]. *In coelestibus regnis*[b]. [a]**Gillian Fisher** (sop); [b]**Michael Chance** (alto); **King's Consort/Robert King.** Hyperion CDA66294 — 54m DDD 11/88

NEW REVIEW

Pergolesi. LA SERVA PADRONA. **Maddalena Bonifaccio** (sop) Serpina; **Siegmund Nimsgern** (bass-bar) Uberto; **Collegium Aureum/Franzjosef Maier** (vn). Deutsche Harmonia Mundi RD77184. Text included. From 1C 065 99749 (3/80). Recorded in 1969.

49m ADD 9/92

It was a performance in Paris in 1752 of Pergolesi's celebrated intermezzo *La serva padrona* which sparked off that celebrated pamphleteer squabble, the "Querelle des Bouffons". It was a confrontation between supporters of Italian music and supporters of the French, in which the king and queen took opposing sides. Convincing performances of Pergolesi's comic domestic 'contretemps' are few and far between but this version, recorded in the late 1960s, is certainly one of them. Maddalena Bonifaccio as the scheming servant-girl Serpina and Siegmund Nimsgern as her vain, foolish and elderly employer play their roles to the hilt, but thankfully not beyond it as many others have done. The leader and director of the Collegium Aureum, Franzjosef Maier sets mostly ideal tempos for the arias and, of even greater importance to the drama, keeps the recitative moving at a brisk pace and in a lively conversational way. Listeners, though, may be irritated by the absence of any translation of the Italian libretto, though a clearly argued synopsis *is* provided in translation. The mid- to late-1960s and early 1970s were the heyday of the Collegium Aureum and many of their recordings dating from this period are withstanding the passage of time well. Recorded sound is of a comparably high level.

George Perle

American 1915-

Suggested listening ...

Wind Quintets — No. 1, Op. 37; No. 2, Op. 41; Nos. 3 and 4. **Dorian Quintet; Julie Landsman** (hn). New World NW359-2 (10/88).

Pérotin

French c.1160-c.1225

Suggested listening ...

Viderunt omnes. Alleluia, Posui adiutorium. Dum sigillum summi Patris. Alleluia, Nativitas. Beata viscera. Sederunt principes. *Coupled with* ***Anonymous Twelfth Century:*** Veni creator spiritus. O Maria virginei. Isias cecinit. **Hilliard Ensemble/Paul Hillier** (bar). ECM New Series 837 751-2 (2/90).

Vincent Persichetti
American 1915-1987

Suggested listening ...

Piano Sonata No. 3. *Coupled with* ***Barber.*** Piano Sonata. ***Corigliano.*** Fantasia on an ostinato. ***Pozdro.*** Four Preludes. ***Copland.*** Variations. **David Allen Wehr** (pf). Chandos CHAN8761 (11/89).

Hans Pfitzner
German 1869-1949

Suggested listening ...

Piano Concerto in E flat major, Op. 31. **Volker Banfield** (pf); **Munich Philharmonic Orchestra/Werner Andras Albert.** CPO CPO999 045-2.

Violin Concerto in B minor, Op. 34. Duo for violin cello and orchsetra, Op. 43. Scherzo in C minor. **Saschko Gawriloff** (vn); **Julius Berger** (vc); **Bamberg Symphony Orchestra/Werner Andreas Albert.** CPO CPO999 079-2 (5/91).

Das Fest auf Solhaug — three preludes. Kleine Symphonie in G major, Op. 44. Symphony in C major, Op. 46. **Bamberg Symphony Orchestra/Werner Andreas Albert.** CPO CPO999 080-2 (5/91).

PALESTRINA. **Soloists; Tölz Boys' Choir; Bavarian Radio Chorus and Symphony Orchestra/Rafael Kubelík.** DG 20th Century Classics 427 417-2GC3 (7/91).

Philippe the Chancellor
French c.1160-1236

NEW REVIEW

Philippe the Chancellor. SACRED AND SECULAR WORKS. **Sequentia/Benjamin Bagby, Barbara Thornton.** Deutsche Harmonia Mundi RD77035. Texts and translations included.

Luto carens et latere — a 3; a 1. Sol oritur in sydere. Clavis pungens acumine. Si vis vera frui luce. Gedeonis area. Dic, Christi veritas. Veritas equitas. ***Anonymous 13th-Century French:*** Lai des pucelles.

lh 3m ADD 11/90

Scanty indeed as regards musical information, Peter Dronke's illuminating insert-note for this recording provides the key to Sequentia's approach in its concentration upon the extraordinary texts by Philippe, one of the great poets of his age. The poetry is as daring and brilliant as Philippe himself was. He is a crucial figure in many ways, not least because of his part in the transmission of elements of the Aristotelian philosophy then so hotly disputed and which would have such wide-reaching consequences for European culture. The poetry sung on this recording — a selection from a group of a possible 90 works that Dronke feels able to attribute to Philippe — is exclusively religious or moral in character. The voices and instruments of Sequentia avoiding any artificial sense of variety for its own sake, subtly underline the texts, always clearly enunciated, as was surely the composer's original intention: poetry of this complexity requires clarity in its presentation. It is not known whether any of the music was written by Philippe himself, though he was certainly both a composer and performer according to contemporary evidence, but it is hypnotically impressive, and often very beautiful. An important addition to the medieval discography.

Peter Philips

British 1560/1-1628

Suggested listening ...

Consort Music — Pavan and Galliard Pavan. Paget Pavan and Galliard. Aria del Gran Duca. Galliard. Bassano Galliard. Morley Pavan and Galliard. Bassano Pavan and Galliard. Dolorosa Pavan and Galliard. Alman Tregian. Balla d'Amore. Pavan and Galliard in F major. Aria. Passamezzo Pavan. **The Parley of Instruments.** Hyperion CDA66240 (1/89).

Astor Piazzolla

Argentinian 1921-1992

Suggested listening ...

Five Tango Sensations for String Quartet and bandoneon. **Astor Piazzolla** (bandoneon); **Kronos Quartet.** Elektra Nonesuch 7559-79254-2.

Histoire du Tango[ab]. Five Pieces[b]. Six Etudes tanguistiques[a]. [a]**Mikael Helasvuo** (fl); [b]**Jukka Savijoki** (gtr). Ondine ODE781-2 (12/92).

Walter Piston

USA 1894-1976

Piston. Symphony No. 2 (1943)[a].
Ruggles. Sun-treader (1926-31)[b].
Schuman. Violin Concerto (1959)[c]. [c]**Paul Zukofsky** (vn); **Boston Symphony Orchestra/Michael Tilson Thomas.** DG 20th Century Classics 429 860-2GC. Items marked [a] and [c] from 2530 103 (7/71), [b] 2530 048 (4/71).

1h 15m ADD 1/91

Though British collectors know their Gershwin, Copland, Bernstein, and maybe some Ives, Carter, Glass or Adams, there are still unfamiliar areas of American music and the composers here are major figures. The most radical is Ruggles, whose music is as uncompromising as Ives's though without that composer's folksy quality; not surprisingly, he was long neglected and *Sun-treader* waited 35 years for its American première at the time of his ninetieth birthday. This tough, big-scale piece is played first, and with considerable expressive force, under Michael Tilson Thomas, who was in his twenties when these recordings were made but had already made a name as a conductor willing to explore unfamiliar repertory, and the sound needs no apology for its age, being detailed and satisfying. Schuman and Piston are later figures than Ruggles, and both were distinguished teachers though in no way academic in their composing styles. The Schuman Concerto has violin writing that is lively as well as sometimes calmly lyrical (although the orchestration tends to be heavy), and Paul Zukofsky is a strong soloist. But Piston's Second Symphony, though a shorter work, has more to offer with its melodic sweep and well varied textures (the *Adagio* second movement has climaxes worthy of Shostakovich) and an element of lightness and even tunefulness that the Schuman lacks, while the structure convinces, too, as being well thought out. An important and well filled issue, and one that is especially desirable at medium price.

Additional recommendation ...
Nos. 2 and 6. Sinfonietta[a]. **Seattle Symphony Orchestra,** [a]**New York Chamber Symphony Orchestra/Gerard Schwarz.** Delos DE3074 — 1h 7m DDD 9/90

NEW REVIEW

Piston. Symphony No. 6. The Incredible Flutist — suite. Three New England Sketches. **St Louis Symphony Orchestra/Leonard Slatkin.** RCA Victor Red Seal RD60798. Recorded 1989-90.

57m DDD 1/92

The Incredible Flutist is by far Piston's best-known work. The title is perhaps misleading, for there is no solo flute part, and in fact the score consists of a series of short, attractive dance movements. The original music was written for a 1938 ballet: two years later Piston used about half the material for a concert suite which soon became quite popular. The *Three New England Sketches* date from 1959. They comprise "Seaside", a mostly peaceful, evocative essay, "Summer Evening", a wispy, delicate scherzo and "Mountains", whose very grand, portentous outer sections surround a central episode of busy counterpoint. Piston's Sixth Symphony is generally regarded as his best. Written in 1955, it is typically direct in expression, and has no programme. The first movement is very American in its suggestion of wide-open space and in its rhythmic irregularities. A quicksilver scherzo forms the second movement, and then a serene *Adagio* is followed by a cheerful finale, with strident brass, rushing strings, and bubbling woodwind. Leonard Slatkin always conducts music of his own country with great sympathy and insight, as he does here. His orchestra has exactly the right timbre, which is important in American repertoire of this kind, and the engineering is very good.

John Playford I

British 1623-1686

Suggested listening ...

The English Dancing Master — country dance collection. Musick's Delight on the Cithren, Restored and Refined — collection for the cithren. Musick's Recreation on the Lyra viol. **Broadside Band/Jeremy Barlow.** Amon Ra CD-SAR28 (3/88).

Manuel Ponce

Mexican 1882-1948

Suggested listening ...

Sonatina meridional. Thème varié et finale. Sonata III. Variations and Fugue on "La Folia de España". **Timo Korhonen** (gtr). Ondine ODE770-2 (7/92).

Amilcare Ponchielli

Italian 1834-1886

Ponchielli. LA GIOCONDA. **Maria Callas** (sop) La Gioconda; **Fiorenza Cossotto** (mez) Laure Adorno; **Pier Miranda Ferraro** (ten) Enzo Grimaldo; **Piero Cappuccilli** (bar) Barnaba; **Ivo Vinco** (bass) Alvise Badoero; **Irene Companeez** (contr) La Cieca; **Leonardo Monreale** (bass) Zuane; **Carlo Forte** (bass) A Singer, Pilot; **Renato Ercolani** (ten) Isepo, First Distant Voice; **Aldo Biffi** (bass) Second Distant Voice; **Bonaldo Giaiotti** (bass) Barnabotto; **Chorus and Orchestra of La Scala, Milan/Antonio Votto.** EMI mono CDS7 49518-2. Notes, text and translation included. From Columbia SAX2359/61 (11/60). Recorded in 1959.

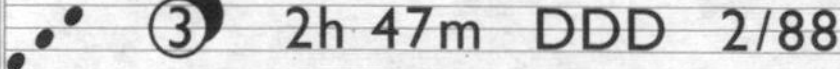

Ponchielli's old warhorse has had a bad press in recent times, which seems strange in view of its melodic profusion, his unerring adumbration of Gioconda's unhappy predicament and of the sensual relationship between Enzo and Laura. But it does need large-scale and involved singing — just what it receives here on this now historic set. Nobody could fail to be caught up in its conviction. Callas was in good and fearless voice when it was made, with the role's emotions perhaps enhanced by the traumas of her own life at the time. Here her strengths in declaiming recitative, her moulding of line, her response to the text are all at their most arresting. Indeed she turns what can be a maudlin act into true tragedy. Ferraro's stentorian ebullience is most welcome. Cossotto is a vital, seductive Laura. Cappuccilli gives the odious spy and lecher Barnaba a threatening, sinister profile, whilst Vinco is a suitably implacable Alvise. Votto did nothing better than this set, bringing out the subtlety of the Verdi-inspired scoring and the charm of the "Dance of the Hours" ballet. The recording sounds excellent for its age.

Additional recommendations ...

Soloists; London Opera Chorus; Finchley Children's Music Group; National Philharmonic Orchestra/Bruno Bartoletti. Decca 414 349-2DH3 — ③ lh lm ADD 7/85

Soloists; Chorus and Orchestra of the Accademia di Santa Cecilia, Rome/Lamberto Gardelli. Decca Grand Opera 430 042-2DM3 — ③ 2h 35m ADD

Cole Porter

American 1891-1964

Suggested listening ...

ANYTHING GOES. **Soloists; Ambrosian Chorus; London Symphony Orchestra/John McGlinn.** EMI CDC7 49848-2 (12/89).

KISS ME KATE. **Soloists; Ambrosian Chorus; London Sinfonietta/John McGlinn.** EMI CDS7 54033-2 (12/90).

Cipriani Potter

British 1792-1871

Suggseted listening ...

Symphonies — No. 8 in E flat major; No. 10 in G minor. **Milton Keynes Chamber Orchestra/Hilary Davan Wetton.** Unicorn-Kanchana DKPCD9091 (3/90).

Francis Poulenc

French 1899-1963

NEW REVIEW

Poulenc. CONCERTOS AND ORCHESTRAL WORKS. [e]**Aimée van de Wiele** (hpd); [f]**Francis Poulenc,** [f]**Jacques Février** (pfs); [a]**Ambrosian Singers;** [ab]**Philharmonia Orchestra,** [c]**Orchestre de Paris,** [d]**Paris Conservatoire Orchestra/Georges Prêtre.** EMI Rouge et Noir CZS7 62690-2. Recorded 1962-80.

Les Biches[a]. Bucolique[b]. Pastourelle[b]. Matelote provençale[b] (all from ASD4067, 9/81). Les Mariés de la Tour Eiffel[c] — Discours; La baigneuse de Trouville. Suite française, d'après Claude Gervaise[c] (all from ASD2450, 6/69). Les animaux modèles[d] (ASD2316, 7/67). Sinfonietta[c]. Marches et un intermède[c] (both from ASD2450, 6/69). Concert champêtre[de]. Concerto for two pianos in E minor[df] (both from ASD517, 4/63).

② 2h 36m ADD/DDD 3/92

Now here's a bargain not to be missed. There are over two-and-a-half hours of the inimitably frothy art of Francis Poulenc crammed onto just two CDs for this compilation. The highlight has to be Georges Prêtre's marvellous 1980 recording of the complete *Les Biches* ballet music: with the Philharmonia on sparkling form and a suitably lusty contribution from the Ambrosian Singers, it makes for deliciously inconsequential entertainment. This item, as well as a trio of shorter purely orchestral offerings (the graceful *Pastourelle*, cheeky *Matelote provençale* and sublimely haunting *Bucolique: Hommage à Marguerite Long*), are captured here in a stunningly vivid Abbey Road recording — unquestionably one of EMI's very finest early digital efforts. In fact, Prêtre directs proceedings with no little flair throughout, though the robust response of the two Paris-based groups may come as something of a shock after the silky refinement of our own Philharmonia. Vintage accounts of the winsomely skittish *Concert champêtre* (with harpsichordist Aimée van de Wiele) and elegant Concerto for two pianos (featuring Jacques Février and the composer himself) are joined by lively readings of the engagingly anachronistic *Suite française*, *Sinfonietta* and the rarely-heard wartime ballet *Les Animaux modèles*. This last item suffers most from orchestral imprecision (and is rather dully engineered into the bargain), though Poulenc's actual music is well worthy of further investigation: both outer tableaux ("Le petit jour" and "Le repos de midi") are supremely touching in their wistful nobility. In sum, an irresistible package — and it's at mid-price, too!

Poulenc. Concerto in D minor for two pianos and orchestra[a]. Piano Concerto. Aubade. **François-René Duchable, [a]Jean-Philippe Collard** (pfs); **Rotterdam Philharmonic Orchestra/James Conlon.** Erato 2292-45232-2. From NUM75023 (2/86).

59m DDD 9/88

The *Aubade* is a most delicious ballet score, with clear-cut rhythms, aggressive Stravinskian harmonic clashes, and an abundance of good melodies, some jolly, some sentimental. Duchable and Conlon give a good account of the score, though they are sometimes a little too straightfaced. The Concerto for two pianos is another brilliant *divertissement*. The first movement has a superficially neoclassical style, but pert little tunes crop up to dispel any temporary seriousness. There follows a *Larghetto* which possesses genuine elegance and melodic beauty, and then there is a final energetic romp. The shortish Piano Concerto is another *jeu d'esprit* in three movements, but the style is noticeably that of the later Poulenc. Though the recording tends to favour the soloists it is otherwise very satisfactory.

Additional recommendation ...

Concerto for two pianos[a]. Sonata for piano duet. Capriccio. L'embarquement pour Cythère. Elégie. ***Milhaud.*** *Scaramouche.* **Katia and Marielle Labèque** (pfs); **[a]Boston Symphony Orchestra/Seiji Ozawa.** Philips 426 284-2PH — 50m DDD 8/91

Poulenc. Organ Concerto in G minor[a]. Concert champêtre[b]. Piano Concerto[c]. **[a]Gillian Weir** (org); **[b]Maggie Cole** (hpd); **[c]Jean-Bernard Pommier** (pf); **City of London Sinfonia/Richard Hickox.** Virgin Classics VC7 59540-2. Recorded in 1988.

1h 10m DDD 4/90

From the concerto's first, huge organ chord (thundering here from London's Royal Festival Hall as dramatically as one could wish for) you might get the impression that Poulenc's Organ Concerto is a work of almost Gothic pretensions. But even in his darkest hour Poulenc could never remain serious for long, and moments of simple pathos and disarming humour constantly bubble to the surface. Gillian Weir reflects these ever-changing moods admirably in her superbly controlled performance, entering into a dialogue with Richard Hickox and the City of London Sinfonia which bounces along with remarkable agility. The *Concert champêtre* sets the spindly harpsichord against a surprisingly large orchestra, but a careful balance has been achieved by the Virgin team, and Maggie Cole's deft fingerwork, scuttling along like an energetic spider, is always perfectly audible. Poulenc wrote this concerto for the famous harpsichordist Wanda Landowska who was renowned for her volatile personality, by turns playful and aggressive, and this is mirrored in his music. On the other hand the Piano Concerto is pure fun. Written for an American audience Poulenc attempted to charm them with the inclusion, in the finale, of the song *Swanee River*. The joke fell rather flat among the Boston audience in 1949, but this sprightly performance (slightly muffled by a boomy acoustic) is sure to lift anyone's spirits.

Additional recommendations ...
Organ Concerto[a]. **Saint-Saëns.** *Symphony No. 3 in C minor, Op. 78, "Organ"*[b]. **George Malcolm,** [b]**Anita Priest** (orgs); [a]**Academy of St Martin in the Fields/Iona Brown;** [b]**Los Angeles Philharmonic Orchestra/Zubin Mehta.** Decca Ovation 417 725-2DM — 56m ADD 12/87
Organ Concerto[a]. *Concert champêtre*[b]. *Gloria*[c]. **George Malcolm** ([a]org/[b]hpd); [ab]**Academy of St Martin in the Fields/Iona Brown;** [c]**Sylvia Greenberg** (sop); [c]**Lausanne Pro Arte Chorus;** [c]**Suisse Romande Chorus and Orchestra/Jesús López-Cobos.** Decca Enterprise 425 627-2DM — lh 13m ADD/DDD 7/90

NEW REVIEW

Poulenc. CHAMBER MUSIC. **Ozi Wind Trio** ([ce]Claude Villevielle, ob; [abd]Lucien Aubert, cl; [bc]Alexandre Ouzounoff, bn); [d]**Jacques Di Donato** (cl); [ace]**Kun Woo Paik** (pf). Adda 590042. Recorded in 1990.
Sonata for clarinet and piano[a]. Sonata for clarinet and bassoon[b]. Trio for oboe, bassoon and piano[c]. Sonata for two clarinets[d]. Sonata for oboe and piano[c].

56m DDD 9/92

The last two chamber works that Poulenc wrote here flank three others from 1918-26. The Clarinet Sonata and Oboe Sonata both pay tribute to a dead composer friend, the one to Honegger and the other to Prokofiev, and although the clarinet work begins perkily the first movement has the unusual marking of *Allegro tristamente* and lives up to it in its disquieting writing, while the *Romanza* that follows is touching in its quasi-Schubertian simplicity and pathos. Lucien Aubert is entirely inside this idiom, and so is the Korean pianist Kun Woo Paik; the same is true of Claude Villevielle and his pianist colleague in the no less touching Oboe Sonata, music that ends with a moving slow finale subtitled "Déploration". The Sonata for clarinet and bassoon and Sonata for two clarinets are short pieces lasting less than eight minutes each and are delightfully lightweight in character. These too come across extremely well, thanks to the idiomatic playing, and these artists balance the many mock-serious passages that occur with the extrovert comedy and even farce. The slow introduction to the Trio for oboe, bassoon and piano offers an example of this kind of mock-serious passage, with which Poulenc likes to tease his listener before launching into music of uninhibited high spirits. The crisp recording captures every detail of this stylish playing. Unfortunately the booklet essay in 'English' is not so stylish and looks like a bad translation from French as well as being peppered with spelling mistakes, but that should deter no one from acquiring this delightful disc.

Additional recommendation ...
Sextet for piano and wind quintet[ac]. *Cello Sonata*[b]. *Clarinet Sonata*[b]. *Elégie for horn and piano*[b]. *Flute Sonata*[b]. *Oboe Sonata*[b]. *Sonata for two clarinets*[b]. *Sonata for clarinet and bassoon*[b]. *Sonata for horn, trumpet and trombone*[b]. *Violin Sonata*[b]. *Trio for oboe, bassoon and piano*[c]. [a]**Paris Wind Quintet.** [b]**Sir Yehudi Menuhin** (vn); [abc]**Jacques Février** (pf); [b]**Pierre Fournier** (vc); [c]**Robert Casier** (ob); [c]**Gérard Faisandier** (bn); [b]**Michel Debost** (fl); [b]**Maurice Bourgue** (ob); [b]**Michel Portal** (cl); [b]**Alan Civil** (hn); [b]**Maurice Gabai** (cl); [b]**Amaury Wallez** (bn); [b]**John Wilbraham** (tpt); [b]**John Iveson** (trbn). EMI CZS7 62736-2 — ② 2h 25m ADD 12/89 £

Poulenc. PIANO WORKS. **Pascal Rogé.** Decca 417 438-2DH. Recorded in 1986.
Les soirées de Nazelles. Deux novelettes — No. 1 in C major; No. 2 in B flat minor. Novelette "sur un thème de M de Falla". Pastourelle (arr. pf). Trois mouvements perpétuels. Valse. 15 Improvisations — No. 1 in B minor; No. 2 in A flat major; No. 3 in B minor; No. 6 in B flat major; No. 7 in C major; No. 8 in A minor; No. 12 in E flat major, "Hommage à Schubert"; No. 13 in A minor; No. 15 in C minor, "Hommage à Edith Piaf". Trois Pièces.

lh 7m DDD 7/87

Poulenc. PIANO WORKS. **Pascal Rogé.** Decca 425 862-2DH. Recorded in 1989.
Humoresque. Nocturnes. Suite in C. Thème varié. 15 Improvisations — No. 4 in A flat major; No. 5 in A minor; No. 9 in D major; No. 10 in F major, "Eloge des gammes"; No. 11 in G

minor; No. 14 in D flat major. Two Intermezzos. Intermezzo in A flat major. Villageoises. Presto in B flat major.

1h 3m DDD 4/91

These beautifully recorded and generously filled discs offer a rich diversity of Poulenc's output. On the first disc, the masterly *Soirées de Nazelles* were improvised during the early 1930s at a country house in Nazelles as a memento of convivial evenings spent together with friends. It paints a series of charming portraits — elegant, witty and refined. The *Trois mouvements perpétuels* are, like so many of the works represented here, lighthearted and brief, improvisatory in flavour and executed with a rippling vitality. The *Improvisations* constantly offer up echoes of the piano concertos with their infectious rhythmic drive — the "Hommage à Schubert" is a tartly classical miniature in three-time played with just the right amount of nonchalant ease by Pascal Rogé. The "Hommage à Edith Piaf" is a lyrical and touching tribute — obviously deeply felt.

The *Humoresque* which opens the second recital is open-air and open-hearted in style, yet songlike too in its melodic richness. The simplicity of this music is deceptive, as is that of the warmly caressing C major Nocturne that follows, for both pieces need subtle phrasing, rubato and the kind of textures only obtainable through the most refined use of the sustaining pedal. Rogé has these skills, and he is also fortunate in having an excellent piano at his disposal as well as a location (the Salle Wagram in Paris) that gives the sound the right amount of reverberation. There are many delights in this music and the way it is played here: to mention just one, listen to the masterly way that the composer and pianist together gradually bring around the flowing freshness of the C major Nocturne towards the deeply poignant feeling of the close. Both discs hold the listener's attention effortlessly from one piece to the next, and though suitable for any time of day they make perfect late-night listening. They should especially delight, and to some extent reassure, anyone who deplores the absence of charm and sheer romantic feeling in much of our century's music.

Additional recommendations ...

Suite in C. Les biches — Adagietto. Trois mouvements perpétuels. Les soirées de Nazelles. Intermezzo No. 3 in A flat major. Valse-improvisation sur le nom de Bach. Trois pièces. Badinage. Napoli. **Eric Parkin** (pf). Chandos CHAN8637 — 59m DDD 10/88

Humoresque. Deux novelettes. Novelette "sur un thème de M de Falla". Villageoises. 15 Improvisations. Intermezzos — No. 1 in C major; No. 2 in D flat major. Suite française. Presto. Mélancolie. Thème varié. **Eric Parkin** (pf). Chandos CHAN8847 — 1h 12m DDD 12/90

NEW REVIEW

Poulenc. CHORAL WORKS. **Trinity College Choir, Cambridge/Richard Marlow.** Conifer CDCF151. Texts and translations included.

Mass in G major. Quatre motets pour le temps de Noël. Quatre petites prières de Saint François d'Assise. Quatre motets pour un temps de pénitence. Laudes de Saint Antoine de Padoue. Salve regina. Ave verum corpus. Exultate Deo.

1h 10m DDD 10/88 

The lusciously chromatic harmony of the Mass in G major can easily cloy but the bright, radiant textures of the singing of the Trinity College Choir avoids this entirely. Readers unfamiliar with this work will be surprised how potent it is. The *Ave verum corpus* for high high voices is quite exquisite and in the St Francis *Prières* Marlow is assured and musically aware. The choir does, however, produce occasional curious French pronunication, with some very odd mute "e"s. An interesting personal sidelight on these graceful and expressive pieces for male voices is revealed by the dedication to Frère Jérome of Champfleury "in memory of his grandfather, my uncle Camille Poulenc". The interpretation of the Penitential Motets is very dramatic and the short motet *Salve regina* is graceful and serene. Caution needs to be taken not to listen to too many of these works — virtually entirely homophonic, and nearly all characterized by Poulenc's special brand of tartly sweet harmonies — one after the other. The performances, with fine balance, expressive dynamic shadings, pure intonation, intelligent phrasing and excellent enunication, are very impressive. Marlow, of course, is operating on home ground, in the almost ideal acoustics of Trinity College Chapel in Cambridge. The accompanying notes are interesting and informative.

Additional recommendations ...
Gloria[ab]. *Salve regina. Ave verum corpus. Exultate Deo. Litanies à la Vierge Noire*[b]. *Quatre motets pour un temps de pénitence*[c]. *Quatre motets pour le temps de Noël.* [a]**Donna Deam,** [c]**Mary Seers** (sops); **Cambridge Singers;** [b]**City of London Sinfonia/John Rutter.** Collegium COLCD108 — lh 7m DDD 10/88
Mass. Quatre petites prières. Salve regina. ***Martin.*** *Mass for double chorus.* **Christ Church Cathedral Choir, Oxford/Stephen Darlington.** Nimbus NI5197 — 59m DDD 12/89
Mass[a]. *Quatre motets pour le temps de Noël. Quatre motets pour un temps de pénitence. Quatre petites prières de Saint François d'Assise*[b]. [a]**Donna Carter** (sop); [b]**Christopher Cock** (ten); **Robert Shaw Festival Singers/Robert Shaw.** Telarc CD80236 — 52m DDD 10/90
Mass[d]. *Salve Regina.* ***Fauré.*** *Requiem (revised version)*[a]. *Cantique de Jean Racine, Op. 11*[b]. *Messe basse*[c]. [ad]**Jonathon Bond** (treb); [c]**Andrew Brunt** (treb); [a]**Benjamin Luxon** (bar); [abc]**Stephen Cleobury** (org); [a]**Academy of St Martin in the Fields; Choir of St John's College, Cambridge/George Guest.** Decca Ovation 430 360-2DM — lh 14m ADD 9/91 £

Poulenc. Gloria[a]. Piano Concerto[b]. Les biches — ballet suite[c]. [a]**Norma Burrowes** (sop); [b]**Cristina Ortiz** (pf); **City of Birmingham Symphony Orchestra and** [a]**Chorus/Louis Frémaux.** EMI CDM7 69644-2. Items marked [ab] from SQ ASD3299 (12/76), [c]ASD2989 (5/74). Recorded 1973-76.

lh 2m ADD 1/89

Poulenc is a difficult figure to classify, and the frivolities and Gallic charm of his music go hand in hand with a deep if unorthodox religious feeling and an occasional sadness. His admiration for light music and for classical figures as different as Schubert and middle-period Stravinsky are reflected in the melodic richness and rhythmic bounce of his music, so that a movement such as the "Laudamus te" of his *Gloria* sounds at first as if Stravinsky's *Symphony of Psalms* had been rewritten by a twentieth-century Offenbach, while the soprano solo "Dominus Deus" that follows has a Franckian fervour. But like Stravinsky, Poulenc made everything he borrowed delightfully his own. The Piano Concerto and the ballet suite *Les biches* are no less delightful and touching. This is music to give pleasure, not to be intellectualized or analysed. Good performances and satisfying digital transfer from 1970s originals.

Additional recommendation ...
Gloria[a]. *Stabat mater*[a]. *Litanies à la Vierge noire.* [a]**Catherine Dubosc** (sop); **Westminster Singers; City of London Sinfonia/Richard Hickox.** Virgin Classics VC7 59286-2 — lh 8m DDD 2/93

Further listening ...

Banalities[b] — Chansons d'Orkenise; Hôtel. La courte paille[b] — Le carafon; La reine de coeur. Chansons villageoises[b] — Les gars qui vont à la fête. Deux poèmes de Louis Aragon[b]. *Coupled with* ***Berlioz.*** Les nuits d'été[a]. ***Ravel.*** Shéhérazade[a]. ***Debussy.*** Trois chansons de Bilitis[b]. **Régine Crespin** (sop); [b]**John Wustman** (pf); [a]**Suisse Romande Orchestra/Ernest Ansermet.** Decca 417 813-2DH (11/88).
LES DIALOGUES DES CARMELITES. **Soloists; Lyon Opera Chorus and Orchestra/Kent Nagano.** Virgin Classics VCD7 59227-2 (9/92).

LA VOIX HUMAINE. **Julia Migenes** (sop); **French National Orchestra/Georges Prêtre.** Erato 2292-45651-2 (9/91).

John Walter Pozdro

American 1923-

Suggested listening ...

Four Preludes. *Coupled with* ***Barber.*** Piano Sonata. ***Corigliano.*** Fantasia on an ostinato. ***Copland.*** Variations. ***Persichetti.*** Piano Sonata No. 3. **David Allen Wehr** (pf). Chandos CHAN8761 (11/89).

Michael Praetorius

German 1571-1621

Praetorius. Terpsichore — excerpts. **New London Consort/Philip Pickett.** L'Oiseau-Lyre Florilegium 414 633-2OH.

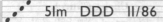

5lm DDD 11/86 

For the full range of late Renaissance instruments, impressively played and brimming over with good humour, this is unquestionably the finest disc in the catalogue. Schryari, racketts, crumhorns, sorduns, theorboes, archlutes, viols, regal: all these and lots more, played by some of Britain's finest exponents and recorded with dazzling clarity. Moreover, should you be at all unsure about the difference between the sound of a shawm and a rauschpfeife, for example, you will find all the instruments used carefully itemized for each of the 31 different dances presented here. And the insert reproduces the pictures of these instruments that Praetorius himself published in his massive *Syntagma musicum*. The dances themselves are chosen from over 300 that Praetorius published in his *Terpsichore* of 1612. They are the perfect vehicle for this array of machinery. Pickett and his musicians go to work on them with considerable verve and the result fairly fizzles.

Further listening ...

Magnificat per omnes versus. Aus tiefer Not à 4. Der Tag vertreibt die finster Nacht. Venite exultemus Domino. Maria Magdalena. Peccavi fateor. Psalm 116. **Huelgas Ensemble/Paul van Nevel.** Sony Classical Vivarte SK48039.

Sergey Prokofiev

Russian 1891-1953

Prokofiev. PIANO CONCERTOS. **Vladimir Ashkenazy** (pf); **London Symphony Orchestra/André Previn.** Decca 425 570-2DM2. From 15BB 218 (10/75). Recorded 1974-75.

No. 1 in D flat major, Op. 10. No. 2 in G minor, Op. 16. No. 3 in C major, Op. 26. No. 4 in B flat major, Op. 53, "for the left hand". No. 5 in G major, Op. 55.

② 2h 6m ADD 3/90 £ B

While it's true that the Prokofiev piano concertos are an uneven body of work, there's enough imaginative fire and pianistic brilliance to hold the attention even in the weakest of them, while the best by common consent Nos. 1, 3 and 4 have stood the test of time very well. As indeed have these Decca recordings. The set first appeared in 1975, but the sound is fresher than many contemporary digital issues, and Ashkenazy has rarely played better. Other pianists have matched his brilliance and energy in, say, the Third Concerto, but few very few have kept up such a sure balance of fire and poetry. The astonishingly inflated bravura of the Second Concerto's opening movement is kept shapely and purposeful even the out-of-tune piano doesn't spoil the effect too much. And the youthful First has the insouciance and zest its 22-year-old composer plainly intended. Newcomers to the concertos should start with No. 3: so many facets of Prokofiev's genius (including that wonderfully piquant lyricism) are here, and Ashkenazy shows how they all take their place as part of a kind of fantastic story. But there are rewards everywhere, and the effort involved in finding them is small. Why hesitate?

Additional recommendations ...

Nos. 1-5. Overture on Hebrew themes, Op. 34[a]. *Visions fugitives, Op. 22.* **Michel Béroff** (pf); [a]**Michel Portal** (cl); [a]**Parrenin Quartet; Leipzig Gewandhaus Orchestra/Kurt Masur.** EMI CMS7 62542-2 — ② 2h 28m ADD 7/89 B

Nos. 1-5. **Kun Woo Paik** (pf); **Polish National Radio Symphony Orchestra/Antoni Wit.** Naxos 8 550565 (*Nos. 2 and 5*); 8 550566 (*Nos. 1, 3 and 4*) — ② 57m lh 12m DDD 11/92 £ B

Nos. 1-5. **Vladimir Krainev** (pf); **Frankfurt Radio Symphony Orchestra/Dmitri Kitaienko.** Teldec 9031-73257-2 — ② 2h 3m DDD 7/93
Nos. 1, 4 and 5. **Boris Berman** (pf); **Royal Concertgebouw Orchestra/Neeme Järvi.** Chandos CHAN8791 — lh 4m DDD 10/90
Nos. 1 and 3. Piano Sonata No. 7 in B flat major, Op. 83. **Mari Kodama** (pf); **Philharmonia Orchestra/Kent Nagano.** ASV CDDCA786 — lh 4m DDD 4/92

Prokofiev. Piano Concerto No. 3 in C major, Op. 26[a].
Tchaikovsky. Piano Concerto No. 1 in B flat major, Op. 23[b]. **Martha Argerich** (pf); [a]**Berlin Philharmonic Orchestra/Claudio Abbado;** [b]**Royal Philharmonic Orchestra/Charles Dutoit.** DG 415 062-2GH. Item marked [a] from 138349 (2/68), [b] 2530 112 (10/71).

lh 3m ADD 5/85 

By general consensus Martha Argerich's 1971 recording of Tchaikovsky's B flat minor Piano Concerto is still among the best of the currently available recordings. The opening of the first movement sets the mood of spaciousness and weight, with the lovely secondary material bringing poetic contrast. The *Andantino* has an appealing delicacy, with the centrepiece dazzling in its light-fingered virtuosity to match the exhilaration of the last movement. The admirably balanced recording has plenty of spectacle, the strings are full and firm and the piano image is strikingly real and tangible. The unexpected but inspirational coupling was one of Argerich's début recordings, and for those less familiar with Tchaikovsky's twentieth-century compatriot, the music itself will come as a refreshing surprise. The apparent initial spikiness soon dissolves with familiarity and Prokofiev's concerto reveals itself as very much in the romantic tradition. Its harmonies are more pungent than those of Tchaikovsky, but the melodic appeal is striking and the sheer vitality of the outer movements is irresistible as projected by Martha Argerich's nimble fingers.

Prokofiev. Piano Concerto No. 4 in B flat major, Op. 53[a].
Reger. Piano Concerto in F minor, Op. 114[b]. **Rudolf Serkin** (pf); **Philadelphia Orchestra/Eugene Ormandy.** CBS Masterworks Portrait CD46452. Item marked [a] from SBRG72109 (5/63), [b] SBRG72399 (6/66). Recorded 1958-59.

lh 2m ADD 12/91

Prokofiev's Fourth Piano Concerto was written for the Austrian pianist, Paul Wittgenstein, after he lost his right arm; his other commissions included similar works from Ravel and Britten — quite a formidable array! In this pioneering recording, which dates from 1958, Rudolf Serkin gives a most captivating performance; he expertly balances Prokofiev's staccato style of piano writing with beautiful legato playing of his long-limbed romantic melodies. The recorded sound is very good for its age: rich and atmospheric. The pairing of the Prokofiev with Reger's rarely heard Piano Concerto is an unusual decision which pays off handsomely. Although the work itself is not one of Reger's best — it has a rather four-square character and the level of musical invention does not hold one's attention throughout, Serkin gives a most valiant performance, making light of Reger's handfuls of notes. The accompaniments by Eugene Ormandy and the Philadelphia Orchestra in both recordings are highly expert. Not only is Ormandy extraordinarily punctilious, he also draws from his orchestra stylistically varied and appropriate playing in both concertos. This is a CD which, especially at medium price, is well worth investigation.

Prokofiev. Piano Concerto No. 5 in G major, Op. 55[a].
Rachmaninov. Piano Concerto No. 2 in C minor, Op. 18[b]. **Sviatoslav Richter** (pf); **Warsaw Philharmonic Orchestra/**[a]**Witold Rowicki,** [b]**Stanislaw Wislocki.** DG 415 119-2GH. Item marked [a] from 138075 (3/60), [b] 138076 (1/60).

58m ADD 6/85 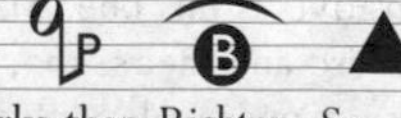

Prokofiev was to find no more dedicated an advocate for his keyboard works than Richter. So how good that this artist's now legendary account of the Fifth Piano Concerto has been granted a new lease of life on CD. Although it has never enjoyed the popularity of Prokofiev's Nos. 1 and 3, here, however, attention is riveted from first note to last. Richter delights in the music's rhythmic vitality and bite, its melodic and harmonic unpredictability. Both piano and orchestra are so clearly and vividly reproduced that it is difficult to believe the original recording dates back to 1959. Though betraying its age slightly more, notably in the sound of the keyboard itself, Rachmaninov's No. 2 is no less gripping. Not all of Richter's tempos conform to the score's suggested metronome markings, but his intensity is rivalled only by his breathtaking virtuosity. Never could the work's opening theme sound more laden, more deeply and darkly Russian.

Prokofiev. Violin Concertos — No. 1 in D major, Op. 19[a]; No. 2 in G minor, Op. 63[a]. ***Stravinsky.*** Violin Concerto in D major. **Kyung-Wha Chung** (vn); **London Symphony Orchestra/André Previn.** Decca Ovation 425 003-2DM. Items marked [a] from SXL6773 (3/77), [b] SXL6601 (5/73). Recorded 1972-75.

lh 12m ADD 7/90 

This is Chung at her most compelling, never deliberately attention seeking, yet riveting attention from the first bar. Her deft mastery of the solo sword-play in the First Concerto's *Scherzo* defies criticism, yet it is the contemplative moments one remembers most of all: the very start of the First Concerto, for example, with tone of extraordinary delicacy and finesse; and the withdrawn, initially almost whispered delivery of the opening melody of the Second Concerto's slow movement. The LSO were audibly inspired by the example and by the time the Prokofiev concertos were made, Previn was already a proven Prokofievian and Chung's most frequent partner on disc. The Stravinsky was an earlier collaboration. The concerto is in Stravinsky's most diamond-edged neoclassical manner. It finds Chung at her most incisive and high spirited, and Previn relishing the sonorities and the syncopations.

Additional recommendations ...
Nos. 1 and 2. **Shlomo Mintz** (vn); **Chicago Symphony Orchestra/Claudio Abbado.** DG 410 524-2GH — DDD 4/84 B
Nos. 1 and 2. **Itzhak Perlman** (vn); **BBC Symphony Orchestra/Gennadi Rozhdestvensky.** EMI CDC7 47025-2 — DDD 9/84 B
No. 2[a]. ***Glazunov.*** *Violin Concerto in A minor, Op. 82*[b]. ***Sibelius.*** *Violin Concerto in D major, Op. 47*[c]. **Jascha Heifetz** (vn); [b]**RCA Victor Symphony Orchestra/Walter Hendl;** [a]**Boston Symphony Orchestra/Charles Münch;** [c]**Chicago Symphony Orchestra/Walter Hendl.** RCA Red Seal RD87019 — lh 9m ADD 10/86 B ▲
No. 2. ***Shostakovich.*** *Violin Concerto No. 1 in A minor, Op. 99.* **Viktoria Mullova** (vn); **Royal Philharmonic Orchestra/André Previn.** Philips 422 364-2PH — lh DDD 6/89 B

NEW REVIEW
Prokofiev. Symphony-Concerto for cello and orchestra, Op. 125.
Tchaikovsky. Variations on a Rococo theme for cello and orchestra, Op. 33. Andante cantabile for cello and strings. **Yo-Yo Ma** (vc); **Pittsburgh Symphony Orchestra/Lorin Maazel.** Sony Classical SK48382. Recorded in 1991.

lh 8m DDD 11/92 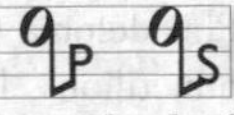

The *Symphony-Concerto* or *Sinfonia Concertante* as it is called on this disc, is Prokofiev's overhaul of his earlier Cello Concerto, made in the last two years of his life in collaboration with Rostropovich. The balance of the work was radically changed: he expanded the role of the orchestra (hence the new title), reorganized the themes and even wrote some new ones. Compared to the rather rambling Cello Concerto, dominated by the soloist, this piece is both more effectively structured, and it tells stories — times were grim for the composer in his last years and it's hard not to feel this colouring the entire revision, particularly in a performance as sensitive as this one. Ma and Maazel find more variety of expression than any other partnership on disc and theirs, too, is the only recording amongst recent competition that has the solo cello on a proper scale with the orchestra — a crucial consideration: not only does Ma not obscure any detail in the orchestra, but he often comes across as a lone small voice playing with, or at the mercy of something far more powerful. A rare elegance informs the Tchaikovsky *Rococo Variations* (standard version); there is a dreamlike beauty in the *Andante cantabile* that is quite hypnotic — even the silences soothe. Both recordings boast state of the art sound.

Additional recommendations ...
Symphony-Concerto. **Shostakovich.** *Cello Concerto No. 1 in E flat major, Op. 107.* **Mstislav Rostropovich** (vc); **London Symphony Orchestra/Seiji Ozawa.** Erato 2292-45332-2 — lh 3m DDD 1/89

Prokofiev. ORCHESTRAL WORKS. [a]**Sting** (narr); [b]**Stefan Vladar** (pf); **Chamber Orchestra of Europe/Claudio Abbado.** DG 429 396-2GH. Recorded 1986-90.
Peter and the wolf, Op. 67[a]. Symphony No. 1 in D major, Op. 25, "Classical". March in B flat minor, Op. 99. Overture on Hebrew Themes, Op. 34*bis*[b].

50m DDD 4/91 

Abbado and the multi-talented Sting offer a lively and beautifully crafted account of Prokofiev's ever popular *Peter and the wolf*. The choice of Sting as narrator is clearly aimed at a younger audience who would otherwise never give this delightful work a second glance. Any fears that the original freshness of Prokofiev's creation may be lost in favour of a less formal approach are soon dispelled — Sting is an effective and intelligent storyteller capable of capturing the imagination of adults and children alike, and there is never a feeling of contrivance or mere gimmickry. The orchestral playing is a real delight too; sharply characterized and performed with great affection. The *Overture on Hebrew Themes* is more commonly heard in its drier, more acerbic version for clarinet, piano and string quartet, but makes a welcome and refreshing appearance on this disc in Prokofiev's own arrangement for small orchestra. Abbado's elegant and graceful reading of the *Classical* Symphony is one of the finest in the catalogue, and is particularly notable for its beautifully shaped phrasing, clarity of inner detail and crisp articulation.

Additional recommendations ...
Peter and the Wolf[a]. **Britten.** *The Young Person's Guide to the Orchestra, Op. 34. GLORIANA — Courtly dances.* **Royal Philharmonic Orchestra/André Previn** ([a]narr). Telarc CD80126 — 55m DDD 10/87 B
Peter and the Wolf[a]. **Saint-Saëns.** *Le carnaval des animaux*[b]. **Mozart.** *Serenade No. 13 in G major, "Eine kleine Nachtmusik".* [a]**Sir John Gielgud** (narr); [b]**Anton Nel, Keith Snell** (pfs); **Academy of London/Richard Stamp.** Virgin Classics VC7 59533-2 — lh 7m DDD 9/89 B
Peter and the Wolf[a]. *Symphony No. 1 in D major, Op. 25, "Classical"*[b]. *Lieutenant Kijé Suite, Op. 60*[c]. *The Love for Three Oranges — Suite*[d] [a]**Sir Ralph Richardson** (narr); [b]**London Symphony Orchestra/Sir Malcolm Sargent;** [c]**Paris Conservatoire Orchestra/Sir Adrian Boult;** [d]**London Philharmonic Orchestra/Walter Weller** Decca Headline Classics 433 612-2DSP — lh 16m ADD 1/92 £ B

NEW REVIEW

Prokofiev. Cantata for the 20th Anniversary of the October Revolution, Op. 74[a]. The tale of the stone flower — excerpts. [a]**Gennadi Rozhdestvensky** (spkr); **Philharmonia** [a]**Chorus and Orchestra/Neeme Järvi.** Chandos CHAN9095. Texts and translations included. Recorded in 1992.

lh 15m DDD 3/93

Every ten years until 1987 (when there were passionate anti-Communist demonstrations) the October Revolution was 'celebrated' in style; and composers were expected to play their part to the full. Prokofiev, having only just returned to full-time residence in Moscow, saw in the 1937 festivities a chance to confirm his citizen's credentials. But despite setting speeches by Lenin and Stalin, and despite putting in an extraordinary agglomeration of forces, including military band, accordion band, bells and siren, plus a "Voice of Lenin" declaiming through a megaphone, plus a good quota of high-quality music, he did not even succeed in getting the piece passed for performance. In the context of the ongoing Great Terror and of Stalin's ultra-conservative musical text that may have been just as well. This is the first recording of the unexpurgated version, and a rousing experience it is; chilling, too, if you allow yourself to think of the social context in which the work was originally conceived. Towards the end of his life a sadder and wiser Prokofiev adopted a compromise style in order to compose music which had some chance of being performed. His last ballet, *The tale of the stone flower*, on which he was still working at the time of his death in March 1953, contains some distinctive and attractive movements, most of which are gathered into the Suite Järvi records here. Both works are energetically and stylishly played, and Chandos supply their customary full-blooded recording; the only drawback is that the chorus in the Cantata has some trouble with the Russian words and even more trouble making itself heard above the hubbub elsewhere.

NEW REVIEW

Prokofiev. War and Peace — Symphonic Suite (arr. Palmer). Summer night, Op. 123. Russian Overture, Op. 72. **Philharmonia Orchestra/Neeme Järvi.** Chandos CHAN9096. Recorded in 1991.

lh 4m DDD 3/93 9s

This issue comes to us thanks not only to Chandos, Neeme Järvi and the Philharmonia but also to that intelligent and selfless musician Christopher Palmer, who in providing us with a symphonic suite from the opera *War and Peace* does Prokofiev the same kind of service as he has already performed in the case of his *Ivan the Terrible* film music, also recorded for Chandos by the same conductor and orchestra. The music taken here from *War and Peace* is vintage Prokofiev, unmistakable in its personal language — direct yet never conventional — and its sheer individuality of orchestral sound. Here is the epic power that is proper to his treatment of Tolstoy's great novel, as well as a lighter dance music style that shows him as the compatriot of Tchaikovsky and the fine ballet composer that he was. The finale of this immensely colourful triptych portrays the retreat from Moscow of Napoleon's defeated French troops in all its agony (from their point of view) and triumph (from that of the Russian forces who harry them unmercifully). *Summer night is* Prokofiev's own concert suite from another opera called *Betrothal in a Monastery,* a love story which perhaps had its parallel in the composer's own life, since at the time of writing it he was about to leave his wife for another woman whom he later married. This is no longer epic music, but it is no less Russian in its quiet yet rich sensuality, and most of all in the movement called "Dreams". The *Russian Overture* is earlier, written shortly after the composer's return to the Soviet Union after his years of self-imposed exile following the Revolution. The original version of 1936 had an enormous orchestra with quadruple woodwind; Prokofiev reduced this in his revision of the following year which is played here, but even as it stands the score is demandingly brilliant and powerful, abounding in vitality and the quirky humour that is unique to this composer. Järvi and the Philharmonia play this music with tremendous panache and Chandos's recording is outstanding.

NEW REVIEW

Prokofiev. Cinderella, Op. 87 — ballet suite: excerpts[a]. Romeo and Juliet, Op. 64 — ballet: excerpts[b]. [a]**Royal Philharmonic Orchestra/Robert Irving;** [b]**Philharmonia Orchestra/Efrem Kurtz.** EMI Eminence CD-EMX2194. Items marked [a] recorded in 1957, [b] 1963.

lh 4m ADD 12/92 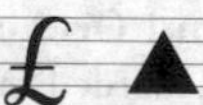

Although Prokofiev's two greatest ballets share certain stylistic characteristics, they inhabit very different worlds. As well as being musically the more substantial, *Romeo and Juliet* (1936) has the ambitious sweep of a major symphony, whereas *Cinderella* (1941) constitutes — as is appropriate to its subject matter — more a succession of colourful, fantasy-filled miniatures. Of the two, it is also the one that perhaps gains more in concert from being trimmed down into a sequence of carefully chosen excerpts. On this excellent reissue, *Romeo* is represented by seven items, most of them very well known ("Montagues and Capulets" especially); these excellently refurbished 1963 Philharmonia recordings under Efrem Kurtz are delicately pointed, if just a little lacking in drama — especially in the predominantly propulsive "Death of Tybalt".

Cinderella, however, is played with more imagination than is often the case on disc, and has the added advantage of superb instrumental solos from Sir Thomas Beecham's Royal Philharmonic Orchestra. Robert Irving phrases with sensitivity and a vivid sense of theatre: rarely has "Midnight" (which is slightly cut in this recording) sounded so musical, its doleful, descending brass motives registering as *melody*, which they rarely do elsewhere. Again, the sound is excellent; in fact, these 1957 Kingsway Hall sessions sound, if anything, even cleaner and more realistic than their 1963 Abbey Road coupling. A real delight.

Additional recommendation ...
Cinderella — Suite (arr. Slatkin). **St Louis Symphony Orchestra/Leonard Slatkin.** RCA Red Seal RD85321 — DDD 3/86

Prokofiev. Romeo and Juliet, Op. 64 — Ballet Suites Nos. 1-3: excerpts. Chout, Op. 21 — ballet suite. **London Symphony Orchestra/Claudio Abbado.** Decca Ovation 425 027-2DM. From SXL6286 (5/67).

54m ADD 6/91 

It was an excellent idea to couple nine items from the familiar *Romeo and Juliet* ballet score with a similar sequence from the unjustly neglected *Chout* — the blackly comic tale of a village trickster, the Buffoon of the alternative title. *Romeo and Juliet* is more popular than ever these days, but Abbado's mid-sixties selection — less predictable than most — retains its freshness and appeal; only his sluggish *Dance of the girls with lilies* lacks something in charm. The sound is pretty good, the brass very immediate. While *Chout* has that rather sadistic plot — and the audiences of 1921 had ultra-modern cubist sets, costumes and choreography to object to — its neglect seems unaccountable today, given the quality of the music. Here, Prokofiev was clearly inspired by Stravinsky's *Petrushka*. Even if there remains some loosely-written connective tissue, there is also a fund of melodic invention that could only have come from the younger man. The orchestration glitters throughout, sharp-edged and totally distinctive. Decca's analogue recording remains impressive with the scintillating textures clearly defined.

Additional recommendations ...
Romeo and Juliet — Suites Nos. 1 and 2: excerpts. **Cleveland Orchestra/Yoel Levi.** Telarc CD80089 — 50m DDD 2/87
Romeo and Juliet — Suites Nos. 1 and 2. **Oslo Philharmonic Orchestra/Mariss Jansons.** EMI CDC7 49289-2 — 59m DDD 5/89
Romeo and Juliet — Suites Nos.1-3[a]. ***Mussorgsky.*** *A night on the Bare Mountain*[b]. [a]**Minneapolis Symphony Orchestra/Stanislav Skrowaczewski;** [b]**London Symphony Orchestra/Antal Dorati.** Mercury Living Presence 432 004 2MM Ih 7m ADD 3/91
Romeo and Juliet — Suites Nos.1-3. **Royal Scottish National Orchestra/Neeme Järvi.** Chandos CHAN8940 — Ih 18m DDD 9/91
Romeo and Juliet — Suites Nos.1-3: excerpts. **Czecho-Slovak State Philharmonic Orchestra, Košice/Andrew Mogrelia.** Naxos 8 550380 — 55m DDD 9/91
Romeo and Juliet — Suites Nos.1-3. **Suisse Romande Orchestra/Armin Jordan.** Erato 2292-45817-2 — Ih 16m DDD 7/93

Prokofiev. Romeo and Juliet, Op. 64 — ballet: excerpts. **Montreal Symphony Orchestra/Charles Dutoit.** Decca 430 279-2DH. Recorded in 1989.
Introduction; Romeo; The street awakens; Morning Dance; The Quarrel; The Fight; The Prince gives his order; Juliet, as a young girl; Arrival of the guests; Mask; Dance of the Knights; Romeo and Juliet; Folk Dance; Friar Laurence; Dance; Tybalt and Mercutio fight; Mercutio dies; Romeo decides to avenge Mercutio's death; Romeo fights Tybalt; Introduction to Act 3; The last farewell; Dance of the girls with the lilies; Juliet's funeral; Death of Juliet.

Ih 15m DDD 9/91 

Prokofiev's *Romeo and Juliet* is one of the greatest of all Russian ballets and a masterly successor to Tchaikovsky's works. The melodic invention, always consistently inspired, the harmonic flavour, often pungent, and the individual and brilliantly colourful orchestration bring the ear constant diversity and stimulation. Charles Dutoit's 1991 recording is extremely attractive: by judicious selection he compresses the epic span of the ballet into 24 separate items from the original score. The playing of the Montreal Symphony Orchestra is spectacular with very fleet strings and brass playing of imposing weight and tragic pungency. Dutoit's interpretation is highly theatrical: the lighter excerpts from the score are pointed and witty, while the more romantic elements are given full expression and the variety of Shakespeare's and Prokofiev's dramatic vision is most expertly recreated by Dutoit. The recording is top class, not only expertly balanced but capturing the wide dynamic range and finesse of the splendidly virtuoso Montreal orchestra.

Additional recommendations ...

Complete ballet. **Cleveland Orchestra/Lorin Maazel.** Decca 417 510-2DH2 — ⠊ ② 2h 21m ADD 2/87

Excerpts. **Berlin Philharmonic Orchestra/Esa-Pekka Salonen.** CBS Masterworks CD42662 — ⠊ 56m DDD 8/88 (B)

Key to Symbols

⠊	② ②	1h 23m	DDD	6/88
Price	*Quantity/ availability*	*Timing*	*Mode*	*Review date*

NEW REVIEW

Prokofiev. COMPLETE SYMPHONIES. **Royal Scottish National Orchestra/Neeme Järvi.** Chandos CHAN8931/4.

No. 1 in D major, Op. 25, "Classical" (from CHAN8400, 3/86); No. 2 in D minor, Op. 40 (CHAN8368, 10/85); No. 3 in C minor, Op. 44; No. 4 in C major, Op. 47 (original 1930 version, both from CHAN8401, 5/86); No. 4 in C major, Op. 112 (revised 1947 version, from CHAN8400, 3/86); No. 5 in B flat major, Op. 100 (CHAN8450, 7/86); No. 6 in E flat minor, Op. 111 (CHAN8359, 7/85); No. 7 in C sharp minor, Op. 131 (CHAN8442, 7/86).

⠊ ④ 4h 20m DDD 𝄢P

Prokofiev was not a natural symphoniest. Albeit successful in emulating Haydn in the *Classical* Symphony, the Sixth Symphony is his only undisputed integrated symphonic structure (and an epic-tragic utterance as intense as any by Shostakovich). It has been suggested that his symphonies all have a sense of some unstaged scenario, and the Third and Fourth (and to a lesser extent, the Seventh) Symphonies actually rework material from his music for the stage. The Fourth (in both versions) in particular fails to convince as a symphony owing to the profusion and individuality of its often strikingly beautiful thematic ideas — it's a real patchwork quilt of a piece. Enter Neeme Järvi, nothing if not a man of the theatre, to give maximum dramatic intensity and character to all Prokofiev's ideas, whether they add up symphonically or not; capable of overawing his Scottish forces into playing of aerial lightness and easeful lyricism in the *Classical* Symphony, and pulling no punches where Prokofiev's inspiration (as in the Second and Third Symphonies) is at is most strident, violent and hysterical. Make no mistake, though, these are also readings of real stature: where there is symphonic 'line', Järvi unerringly finds it. Drawbacks? Some may feel the need for a deeper pile of string sound, particularly in the Fifth Symphony; and these typically spacious Chandos productions do not always ensure adequate projection for the woodwind (e.g. some of the quiet, lyrical woodwind lines in the Fourth Symphony), but more often than not one is impressed by the coherence and co-ordination, both musically and technically, of some of this century's most fabulous and fraught orchestral essays. As a cycle, this is unlikely to be challenged for some time.

Prokofiev. Symphonies[a] — No. 1 in D major, Op. 25, "Classical"; No. 7 in C sharp minor, Op. 131. The Love for Three Oranges — Suite, Op. 33*a*[b]. **Philharmonia**

Orchestra/Nicolai Malko. Classics for Pleasure CD-CFP4523. Items marked [a] from HMV CLP1044 (6/55), [b] CLP1060 (11/55). Recorded in 1955.

57m ADD

NEW REVIEW

Prokofiev. Symphonies — No. 1 in D major, Op. 25, "Classical"[a]; No. 3 in C minor, Op. 44[b]. **Philadelphia Orchestra/Riccardo Muti.** Philips 432 992-2PH. Item marked [a] recorded in 1990, [b] 1991.

49m DDD 2/93

Few twentieth-century symphonies have quite the immediate melodic appeal of Prokofiev's *Classical* Symphony. It is so familiar that its perfect proportions, its effervescent high spirits and its striking originality tend to be taken for granted. Malko's readings of Prokofiev's most charming symphonies have an assured place in gramophone history. These were in fact EMI's first stereo recordings, made in London's Kingsway Hall in February 1955 and very good they sound too via Christopher Parker's balancing, only fractionally thin on top, superbly balanced within an attractively resonant acoustic space. Malko's view of No. 7 is warm and obliging, superbly played by the Philharmonia but not over-characterized. It may disappoint those who look for darker currents even in this most wistful of symphonies, but perhaps we should not look for a political statement in every nook and cranny of Soviet symphonism. Prokofiev, gravely ill and under pressure from Stalin's regime, wrote the work with an audience of children in mind. Malko, himself a Soviet *émigré*, was responsible for its British première. The *Classical* Symphony goes similarly well (at a fairly moderate pace), and the bonus items from *The Love for Three Oranges* demonstrate Malko's legendary care for clarity and balance of sonority. This is music that can easily sound raucous and facile. Not so here: the famous March is irresistible, the love scene genuinely moving. All in all, this disc is a remarkable bargain.

Muti's account of the *Classical* Symphony will appeal to those who prefer a rather more easy-going performance, with a Gavotte which is taken at a distinctly slow tempo. The Third Symphony was a reworking of material from Prokofiev's opera *The Fiery Angel*, a task undertaken because there was no prospect that this stage work would be produced. If the Symphony seems to work very well in its revised form this is because the composer had conceived its thematic material symphonically long before he had started work on the opera. Muti gets magnificent playing from his orchestra, and he also has the advantage of a superlative recording. He is especially skilful in balancing the forceful and lyrical aspects of the music: these contrasting elements are a particular feature in the opening movement and in the finale. Muti conducts the second movement *Andante* with the most affecting tenderness, and the troubled, quicksilver *Scherzo* is brilliantly brought to live.

Additional recommendations ...

No. 1. No. 4 in C major, Op. 112 (revised 1947 version). **Scottish National Orchestra/Neeme Järvi.** Chandos CHAN8400 52m DDD 3/86

No. 3. No. 4 (original 1930 version). **Scottish National Orchestra/Neeme Järvi.** Chandos CHAN8401 — 59m DDD 5/86

No. 1. No. 5 in B flat major, Op. 100. **Los Angeles Philharmonic Orchestra/André Previn.** Philips 420 172-2PH — 58m DDD 11/87

No. 1. ***Bizet.*** *Symphony in C major.* ***Britten.*** *Simple Symphony, Op. 4.* **Orpheus Chamber Orchestra.** DG 423 624-2GH — 1h 4m DDD 1/89

Nos. 1 and 5. **Berlin Philharmonic Orchestra/Herbert von Karajan.** DG Galleria 437 253-2GGA — 1h 11m ADD 1/93

No. 1[a]. No. 5[b]. **[a]London Philharmonic Orchestra, [b]Saint Louis Symphony Orchestra/Leonard Slatkin** RCA Masters Collection 09026 61350-2 — 57m DDD 3/93

Prokofiev. Symphony No. 2 in D minor, Op. 40. Romeo and Juliet, Op. 64 — Suite No. 1. **Scottish National Orchestra/Neeme Järvi.** Chandos CHAN8368. From ABRD1134 (9/85). Recorded in 1984.

1h 1m DDD 10/85

Prokofiev's Second Symphony very much reflects the iconoclastic temper of the early twenties, and the violence and dissonance of its first movement betrays his avowed intention of writing a work "made of iron and steel". It is obvious that he was keen to compete with Mossolov's Steel Foundry from the *Symphony of Machines* or the Honegger of *Horace Victorieux* or *Pacific 231* in orchestral violence. In its formal layout (but in no other respect) the symphony resembles Beethoven's Op. 111 Sonata in being in two movements, the second of which is a set of variations. It is the latter that more than compensates for the high decibel quotient of its companion. It is rich in fantasy and some of the variations are wonderfully atmospheric — indeed Nos. 2 and 3 are altogether magical. In this it almost recalls the "Night" movement from the *Scythian Suite*. Neeme Järvi has a real flair for the music of this composer and produces altogether excellent results from the Scottish Orchestra. Moreover the Chandos recording has admirable detail, presence and body, and is a clear first choice. The *Romeo and Juliet* suite comes off well, too, and the Scottish Orchestra play with as much character here as in the companion work.

Prokofiev. Symphony No. 6 in E flat minor, Op. 111. Waltz Suite, Op. 110 — Nos. 1, 5 and 6. **Scottish National Orchestra/Neeme Järvi.** Chandos CHAN8359. From ABRD1122 (5/85).

57m DDD 7/85 P S

Although it appeared after the end of the war, the Sixth Symphony reflects much of the anguish and pain of those years, and it certainly strikes a deeper vein of feeling than any of its companions. It begins in a way that leaves no doubt that it is made of sterner stuff, the brass and lower strings spitting out a few notes that are so striking and bitter that the relatively gentle main theme comes as a surprise. Järvi has an intuitive understanding of this symphony, and indeed the whole Prokofiev idiom, and he shapes the details as skilfully as he does its architecture. The various climaxes are expertly built and the whole structure is held together in a masterly fashion. As a fill-up there are three movements from the *Waltz Suite*, in which Prokofiev draws from the ballet, *Cinderella*, and the opera, *War and Peace*. The recording is remarkably vivid and well detailed with a particularly rich bass.

Prokofiev. Symphony No. 7 in C sharp minor, Op. 131. Sinfonietta in A major, Op. 48. **Scottish National Orchestra/Neeme Järvi.** Chandos CHAN8442. From ABRD1154 (4/86). Recorded in 1985.

51m DDD 7/86

The two pieces on this disc come from the opposite extremes of Prokofiev's career, the *Sinfonietta* from the beginning and the Symphony from the end. Both have that blend of wit and fantasy that Prokofiev so made his own. The Seventh Symphony is a relaxed and genial composition, some of whose ideas recall the fairy-tale atmosphere of *Cinderella*. The *Sinfonietta* is a tuneful, delightful piece that ought to be as popular as the *Classical* Symphony or *Peter and the Wolf*. Järvi is totally inside this music and the Scottish National Orchestra play splendidly for him. The recording has great range and depth, effectively conveying the impression of a concert hall experience.

Prokofiev. String Quartets — No. 1 in B minor, Op. 50; No. 2 in F major, Op. 92. **American Quartet** (Mitchell Stern, Laurie Carney, vns; Daniel Avshalomov, va; David Geber, vc). Olympia OCD340. Recorded in 1982.

50m ADD 2/90

Prokofiev's wider popularity has never extended to his chamber music. Of his two quartets, the Second is by far the better-known and comes from the war years when Prokofiev was evacuated to the Caucasus, where he made a study of the musical folklore of Kabarda — indeed, it is sometimes known as the "Kabardinian" Quartet. Although the material is folk-derived, it is completely absorbed into Prokofiev's own melodic bloodstream and doesn't sound in the least bit 'folksy'. The second movement quotes a Kabardinian love song of great lyrical beauty, and at one point in the slow movement, the accompaniment imitates a Caucasian stringed instrument, the kamancha. It is a work of real quality which has the astringent flavouring and poetic flair that characterizes Prokofiev at his best. Although the First Quartet, written at the behest of the Library of Congress in 1930, is not so immediately appealing it, too, is a work of substance which grows on the listener. Prokofiev's friend and colleague, Nikolay Miaskovsky, who composed 13 string quartets and more than twice as many symphonies, particularly admired the last movement, and encouraged Prokofiev to score it for full strings. The American Quartet communicate conviction and belief in this music: theirs is a persuasive account, sensitive and yet full-blooded, and they are very well recorded.

Additional recommendation ...
Nos. 1 and 2. Overture on Hebrew Themes in C minor, Op. 34[a]. **Coull Quartet; [a]Angela Malsbury** (cl); **[a]David Petitt** (pf). Hyperion CDA66573 — 57m DDD 9/92

Prokofiev. Violin Sonatas — No. 1 in F minor, Op. 80; No. 2 in D major, Op. 94*a*. **Shlomo Mintz** (vn); **Yefim Bronfman** (pf). DG 423 575-2GH. Recorded in 1987.

56m DDD 2/89

Both Prokofiev sonatas are wartime pieces; both follow the classical four-movement plan and both must be numbered among Prokofiev's very finest achievements. There the similarities end, for the First is declamatory, agonized and predominantly introspective, whereas the Second, originally for flute and piano, is untroubled, intimate and consoling. This essential difference in character presents a challenge which not all duos have risen to. Mintz and Bronfman have got right to the heart of the matter, however, and if their First Sonata is still marginally the finer that is only because it is on a truly rare level of insight. Both players deploy a wide range of colour and accent, superbly captured in a bright but not over-reverberant acoustic, and they are united in their nuanced response to Prokofiev's lyricism and motoric drive. In the extraordinary first movement coda of the First Sonata, they create an atmosphere of almost hypnotic numbness, and it is a pity that one terrible edit breaks the spell here (the violin tone changes abruptly in mid-bar). But that is the only serious defect in what is a truly outstanding recital.

Additional recommendation ...
Violin Sonata No. 2. ***Ravel.*** *Violin Sonata (1927).* ***Stravinsky.*** *Divertimento.* **Viktoria Mullova** (vn); **Bruno Canino** (pf). Philips 426 254-2PH — lh lm DDD 8/90

Prokofiev. PIANO SONATAS, Volume 1. **Murray McLachlan.** Olympia OCD255.
Piano Sonatas — No. 1 in F minor, Op. 1; No. 4 in C minor, Op. 29; No. 5 in C major (revised version), Op. 135; No. 9 in C major, Op. 103; No. 10 in E minor, Op. 137.

lh l0m DDD 3/90

The first volume of Murray McLachlan's complete survey of the Prokofiev Piano Sonatas contains some very fine performances indeed. A suitably bold and youthfully exuberant account of the romantic First Sonata Op. 1 is followed by a particularly thoughtful and probing reading of the introverted and less frequently heard Fourth Sonata — the slow movement is especially intense and poetic. Indeed, one of McLachlan's strengths, both here and in the other sonatas on this disc, is his ability to bring out the poetry and lyricism of these pieces that so often get overlooked by pianists in favour of the more abrasive and dissonant aspects. The Fifth Sonata (again most persuasively handled) is heard here in its revised version of 1953, which used to be the accepted version among pianists but which is now taking something of a back seat in favour of the original 1938 version. However, the real gem of the disc lies in McLachlan's performance of the much underrated Ninth Sonata. Richter (to whom it was dedicated) described it as "intimately chamber in character, concealing riches which are not immediately obvious to the eye". Performed as it is here, with a great deal of poetry and insight, the concealed riches become more readily apparent and one is left wondering why the sonata has remained neglected for so long. The disc concludes with the tiny fragment (a mere 27 bars) that would have become the Tenth Sonata had Prokofiev's death not intervened. Excellent sleeve notes from Murray McLachlan.

Additional recommendations ...
No. 1. Gavotte No. 4 from "Hamlet", Op. 77bis. Three Pieces, Op. 96. Sonatinas, Op. 54 — No. 1 in E minor; No. 2 in G major. Four Pieces, Op. 4. **Buxtehude** *(arr. Prokofiev). Organ Prelude and Fugue in D minor.* **Boris Berman.** Chandos CHAN9017 — 57m DDD 11/92
Piano Sonata No. 3 in A minor, Op. 28. Three Pensées, Op. 62. Three Pieces from "Cinderella", Op. 95. Ten Pieces, Op. 12. **Boris Berman.** Chandos 9069 — 56m DDD 11/92

Prokofiev. PIANO WORKS. **Barry Douglas.** RCA Victor Red Seal RD60779. Recorded in 1991.
Piano Sonatas — No. 2 in D minor, Op. 14; No. 7 in B flat major, Op. 83. The Love for three oranges, Op. 33*ter* — March. Ten Pieces from "Cinderella", Op. 97 — No. 10, Waltz. Six Pieces from "Cinderella", Op. 102 — No. 4, Amoroso. Three Pieces, Op. 96 — No. 1, Waltz from "War and Peace".

56m DDD 3/92

NEW REVIEW

Prokofiev. PIANO WORKS. **Tedd Joselson.** Olympia OCD453. Recorded in 1991.
Ten Pieces from "Romeo and Juliet", Op. 75. Ten Pieces from "Cinderella", Op. 97. The Love for three oranges, Op. 33*ter* — March; Scherzo.

1h 2m DDD 10/92

There has often been a tendency with Prokofiev's piano music for pianists to overplay the percussive, steely qualities of the piano writing at the expense of the lyrical aspects. Barry Douglas, however, attains the perfect blend — muscular and athletic where power and agility are called for, but ever alert to the lyricism which lies beneath the surface. The Second Sonata is a prime example. Douglas has the full measure of this youthful, energetic masterpiece, and one feels that he has fully assimilated this piece before committing it to disc. The first movement with its restless oscillation between expressive melody and ruminative figuration is thoughtfully fashioned, and the knockabout scherzo and fleet-footed energetic finale are delivered with much vigour and flair. The Seventh Sonata (the central work of Prokofiev's "War Trilogy") is impressive too, with Douglas fully in command of its bristling difficulties. As for the rest of the disc, Douglas offers some of the less frequently heard piano transcriptions, of which the delirious 'love' Waltz from *Cinderella* and the March from *The Love for three oranges* crave particular attention. The recording is beautifully engineered and balanced.

Crisp, clean finger-work and a fine sense of rhythmic buoyancy can also be found on a very recommendable Olympia disc featuring the American pianist Tedd Joselson. Joselson made a considerable impact in 1976 with his recording of Prokofiev's Sonatas Nos. 2 and 8 (no longer available), and his special empathy with this composer can be heard further in his readings of Prokofiev's own transcriptions from the ballets *Cinderella* and *Romeo and Juliet*. Both collections contain some of the composer's most delightful and engaging numbers: from the charming character portrait "Juliet as a young girl" (brilliantly characterized here by Joselson) and the famous "Montagues and "Capulets" found in *Romeo and Juliet*, to the capricious "Grasshoppers and Dragonflies" and miniature "Four Seasons" suite from *Cinderella*. Joselson displays a keen talent for story-telling and atmosphere throughout, and has been exceptionally well served with a clear and vivid recording.

Additional recommendations ...
Piano Sonata No. 7. **Boulez.** *Piano Sonata No. 2.* **Stravinsky.** *Three movements from "Petrushka".* **Webern.** *Variations for piano, Op. 27.* **Maurizio Pollini.** DG 419 202-2GH — 1h 9m ADD 11/86
Piano Sonata No. 7. Toccata, Op. 11. **Poulenc:** *Presto in B flat major.* **Barber:** *Piano Sonata, Op. 26.* **Kabalevsky:** *Piano Sonata No. 3, Op. 46.* **Fauré:** *Nocturne No. 13 in B minor, Op. 119*[a]. **Vladimir Horowitz.** RCA Gold Seal mono/[a]stereo GD60377 *(reviwed in the Collections section; refer to Index to Reviews)* — 1h 5m ADD 6/92 £ ▲
Piano Sonata No. 7. Visions fugitives, Op. 22 — Nos. 3, 6 and 9. **Debussy.** *Estampes. Préludes, Book 1 — Voiles; Le vent dans la plaine; Les collines d'Anacapri.* **Scriabin.** *Piano Sonata No. 5 in F sharp major, Op. 53.* **Sviatoslav Richter.** DG Dokumente 423 573-2GDO *(reviwed in the Collections section; refer to Index to Reviews)* — 1h 7m ADD 9/88

Piano Sonatas Nos. 2 and 7. Visions fugitives. **Laurent Cabasso.** Auvidis Valois V4655 — 58m DDD 11/92

Prokofiev. Piano Sonata No. 6 in A major, Op. 82.
Ravel. Gaspard de la nuit. **Ivo Pogorelich** (pf). DG 413 363-2GH. From 2532 093 (6/83).

52m DDD 11/84 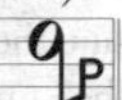

Although Prokofiev's Sixth Sonata is less well known than its successors, it is every bit as brilliant and if anything more inventive. Ivo Pogorelich has remarkable technical address, as is evident from these performances, and he plays with a mixture of abandon and discipline that is enormously exhilarating. Ravel's evocations of Aloysius Bertrand's prose poems in *Gaspard de la nuit* is a *tour de force*, one of the most totally pianistic works in the whole keyboard repertoire. Pogorelich produces a remarkable range of keyboard colour and the recording does justice to his dynamic range. His account of "Le gibet" is particularly imaginative and chilling.

Additional recommendation ...
Etude in C minor, Op. 2 No. 3. Piano Sonata No. 6 in A major, Op. 82. **Chopin:** *Waltz in C sharp minor, Op. 64 No. 2.* **Liszt:** *Etude d'exécution transcendante in F minor, S139 No. 10, "Appassionata". Liebestraum No. 3, S541. Rhapsodie espagnole, S254.* **Schumann:** *Etudes symphoniques, Op. 13. Theme and Variations on the name "Abegg", Op. 1.* **Schumann/Liszt:** *Widmung, S566.* **Evgeni Kissin.** RCA Victor Red Seal RD60443 *(reviwed in the Collections section; refer to Index to Reviews)* — ② 1h 13m DDD 3/91

Prokofiev. Visions fugitives, Op. 22.
Scriabin. PIANO WORKS. **Nikolai Demidenko** (pf). Conifer CDCF204. Recorded 1989-90.
Scriabin: Piano Sonatas — No. 2 in G sharp minor, Op. 19, "Sonata-fantasy"; No. 9 in F major, Op. 68, "Messe noire". Etudes — F sharp minor, Op. 8 No. 2; B major, Op. 8 No. 4; E major, Op. 8 No. 5; F sharp major, Op. 42 No. 3; F sharp major, Op. 42 No. 4; F minor, Op. 42 No. 7. Four Pieces, Op. 51. Vers la flamme, Op. 72.

1h 13m DDD 8/91 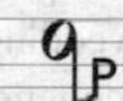

The remarkable talent of Nikolai Demidenko is heard here to its full advantage. The Scriabin items not only display the breadth of Demidenko's expressive powers, but also serve to illustrate Scriabin's astonishing transition from post-romantic to the visionary modernist. The early *Sonata-fantasy* of 1892-7 (surely one of his most beautiful and sensuous pieces) is played here with much poetry and affection, and the final movement (an exhilarating *Presto* in 3/4 time) is a fine example of Demidenko's precision, clarity and immaculate pedal control. With the six etudes and the *Four Pieces*, Op. 51 that follow the listener is taken on a fascinating journey that culminates in the volatile sound-worlds of the Ninth Sonata and *Vers la flamme*. These nebulous, shadowy works are delivered with an extraordinary degree of intensity and perception. His account of Prokofiev's *Visions fugitive* is in a class of its own. Each tiny miniature is jewelled to perfection, and his acute sense of colour and tonal variation make this one of the finest performances on disc. A remarkable début recording in every respect.

Prokofiev. Alexander Nevsky — cantata, Op. 78[a]. Scythian Suite, Op. 20. [a]**Linda Finnie** (contr); **Scottish National** [a]**Chorus and Orchestra/Neeme Järvi.** Chandos CHAN8584. Text and translation included.

1h DDD 5/88 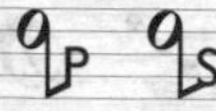

Järvi's disc must earn the top recommendation amongst all the currently available recordings of *Alexander Nevsky*. As recorded sound, it is stunning. The ample acoustics of Caird Hall, Dundee add extra atmosphere for the wide icy expanses and chill of the Russian winter and the huge dynamic range allows an overwhelming force in the "Battle on the Ice". On first hearing, the chorus's frenzied war cries could well induce heart failure. The only small blot on the landscape is the slightly inflated prominence given to Linda Finnie's already rich contralto in the "Field of the Dead". All this would amount to naught were not Järvi and his Scottish forces to give the performance of a lifetime (surely, both singers and players must have some slavic blood coursing their veins?). Järvi, never afraid to intensify the drama with a few ideas of his own, does just that at the start of the "Battle of the Ice" with a gradual acceleration for the advancing forces. It's not in the score, but it is a master-stroke. The earlier *Scythian Suite*, with its more complex textures and spicier harmonies to suit the blood-drinking, pagan god worshipping Scythians, makes an ideal coupling. Try the end — the sun-god appearing to a crescendo of metal and searing, stratospheric woodwind — at a realistic volume setting, and deafness is almost guaranteed. Järvi, teeth bared and nostrils flared, probably gets closer than anyone to the core of this brutal, but mesmerizing score.

Additional recommendation ...

Alexander Nevsky[a]. ***Rachmaninov.*** *The Bells, Op. 35*[b]. [b]**Sheila Armstrong** (sop); [a]**Anna Reynolds** (mez); [b]**Robert Tear** (ten); [b]**John Shirley-Quirk** (bar); **London Symphony Chorus and Orchestra/André Previn.** EMI Studio CDM7 63114-2 — 1h 18m ADD 10/89 £ 9p

Alexander Nevsky[a]. *Lieutenant Kijé Suite, Op. 60.* ***Glinka.*** *Russlan and Ludmilla — Overture.* **Chicago** [a]**Chorus and Symphony Orchestra/Fritz Reiner.** RCA GD60176 — 1h 8m ADD 1/90 9p ▲

Prokofiev (ed. Palmer). Ivan the Terrible — concert scenario. **Linda Finnie** (contr); **Nikita Storojev** (bass-bar); **Philharmonia Chorus and Orchestra/Neeme Järvi.** Chandos CHAN8977. Recorded in 1991.

59m DDD 11/91

Christopher Palmer is a scholar, stylish writer, and above all a skilful and enthusiastic musician, and he has done a major service to Prokofiev by arranging this performing concert scenario from his music to Sergei Eisenstein's epic 1940s film *Ivan the Terrible* with its view of an episode in Russia's turbulent history. When the director began work on it in 1941, he had recently produced Wagner's *Die Walküre* at the Bolshoi Theatre in Moscow, and he brought to it a spectacular operatic treatment. In turn, Prokofiev's music heightened the drama to fever pitch and provided plenty of big set pieces such as arias and choruses, Russian liturgical music, a wedding scene and a lullaby. From all this music, Palmer has created a satisfying musical sequence of 13 sections which also follows the drama. The performance under Neeme Järvi is immensely atmospheric, and while his male solo singer Nikita Storojev is predictably idiomatic, the fine contralto Linda Finnie sounds no less Russian. Though the Philharmonia Chorus cannot quite match them in this respect, they sing strongly and expressively throughout. This is inspired music which sweeps the listener along irresistibly, and Chandos's recording is worthy of it, capturing the full-blooded primitivism and primary colours of Prokofiev's score with its powerful writing for voices and its bold instrumentation. The booklet has a translation of the text as well as an informative essay by Palmer himself.

Prokofiev. THE LOVE FOR THREE ORANGES (sung in French). **Gabriel Bacquier** (bar) King of Clubs; **Jean-Luc Viala** (ten) Prince; **Hélène Perraguin** (mez) Princess Clarissa; **Vincent Le Texier** (bass-bar) Leandro; **Georges Gautier** (ten) Truffaldino; **Didier Henry** (bar) Pantaloon, Farfarello, Master of Ceremonies; **Gregory Reinhart** (bass) Tchelio; **Michèle Lagrange** (sop) Fata Morgana; **Consuelo Caroli** (mez) Linetta; **Brigitte Fournier** (sop) Nicoletta; **Catherine Dubosc** (sop) Ninetta; **Jules Bastin** (bass) Cook; **Béatrice Uria Monzon** (mez) Smeraldina; **Chorus and Orchestra of Lyon Opéra/Kent Nagano.** Virgin Classics VCD7 59566-2. Notes, text and translation included.

② 1h 42m DDD 12/89 9p 9s

This is a wonderfully zany story about a prince whose hypochondriac melancholy is lifted only at the sight of a malevolent witch tumbling over, in revenge for which she casts on him a love-spell for three oranges: in the ensuing complications he encounters an ogre's gigantic cook who goes all gooey at the sight of a pretty ribbon, princesses inside two of the oranges die of oppressive desert heat, and the third is saved only by the intervention of various groups of 'spectators' who argue with each other on the stage. The music's brittle vivacity matches that of the plot, and though there are no set-pieces for the singers and there is practically no thematic development — the famous orchestral March and Scherzo are the only passages that reappear — the effervescent score is most engaging. The performance, conducted by the musical director of the Lyon Opéra, is full of zest, with lively orchestral playing and a cast that contains several outstanding members and not a single weak one; and the recording is extremely good. Those desirous of so doing can delve into the work's symbolism and identify the objects of its satire — principally Stanislavsky's naturalistic Moscow Arts Theatre: others can simply accept this as a thoroughly enjoyable romp.

NEW REVIEW

Prokofiev. WAR AND PEACE. **Lajos Miller** (bar) Prince Andrei Bolkonsky; **Galina Vishnevskaya** (sop) Natasha Rostova; **Katherine Ciesinski** (mez) Sonya; **Maria Paunova** (mez) Maria Akhrosimova; **Dimiter Petkov** (bass) Count Ilya Rostov; **Wieslaw Ochman** (ten) Count Pytor Bezukhov; **Stefania Toczyska** (mez) Helena Bezukhova; **Nicolai Gedda** (ten) Anatol Kuragin; **Vladimir de Kanel** (bass-bar) Dolokhov; **Mira Zakai** (contr); Princess Maria Bolkonsky; **Malcolm Smith** (bass) Colonel Vasska Denisov; **Nicola Ghiuselev** (bass) Marshal Mikhail Kutuzov; **Eduard Tumagian** (bar) Napoleon Bonaparte; **Radio France Chorus; French National Orchestra/Mstislav Rostropovich.** Erato Libretto 2292-45331-2. Notes, text and translation included. From ECD75480 (1/89). Recorded in 1986.

④ 4h 7m DDD 4/92

Over four hours long, 72 characters, 13 scene changes: is it any wonder that Prokofiev's *War and Peace*, adapted from Tolstoy's famously epic novel, has had few performances and even fewer forays into the recording studio? At the front of the booklet Rostropovich recalls how, as Prokofiev lay dying, he reiterated one wish, that Rostropovich should make this opera known to the world. It comes as no surprise, then, to find a deeply committed performance from both soloists (only 45 of them due to some adroit doubling), chorus and orchestra. Prokofiev adapted the novel into seven 'peace' and six 'war' tableaux, thus sustaining drama through contrast throughout its Wagnerian length. With few exceptions the multinational cast sing in good Russian and among them Lajos Miller is particularly affecting as Prince Andrei, pleasingly ardent in his opening moonlit aria. The central female role of Natasha is taken by Galina Vishnevskaya. She sang the role in the 1959 première and inevitably no longer sounds like an innocent 16 year old. Unfortunately, problems are compounded by a hardness in her tone and a lack of attention to detail in some of the quieter sections — particularly in her exchanges with Helena where the asides sound like part of the normal conversation. Stefania Toczyska as the treacherous Helena makes a great impression, as does Katherine Ciesinski as Natasha's confidante, Sonya. Of the men, Nicolai Gedda as Prince Anatol sings with character and great style and Eduard Tumagian is a suitably heroic and steadfast Napoleon. An added attraction of the recording are the sound effects, particularly in the war scenes, convincing but never overly obtrusive. Good translations are provided in three languages, crowning a laudable achievement.

Further listening ...

Flute Sonata in D major, Op. 94. *Coupled with* ***Poulenc.*** Flute Sonata. ***E. Burton.*** Flute Sonatina. ***Fauré.*** Morceau de lecture. ***Martinů.*** Flute Sonata No. 1. **Jennifer Stinton** (fl); **Scott Mitchell** (pf). Collins Classics 1103-2 (12/91).
THE FIERY ANGEL. **Soloists; Ohlin Vocal Ensemble; Gothenburg Pro Musica Chamber Choir; Gothenburg Symphony Orchestra/Neeme Järvi.** DG 431 669-2GH2 (7/91).

Giacomo Puccini

Italian 1858-1924

Puccini. OPERA ARIAS. **Leontyne Price** (sop); **New Philharmonia Orchestra/Sir Edward Downes.** RCA RD85999. Texts and translations included. Items marked [a] from SER5674 (12/73), [b] ARL1 0840 (4/76), [c] SER5589 (1/71), [d] new to UK.

LA BOHEME[a] — Sì, mi chiamano Mimì; Donde lieta uscì; Quando me'n vo'soletta. EDGAR[a] — Addio, mio dolce amor. LA RONDINE[a] — Ore dolce e divine. TOSCA[a] — Vissi d'arte. MANON LESCAUT[a] — In quelle trine morbide; Sola, perduta, abbandonata. LE VILLI[a] — Se come voi. MADAMA BUTTERFLY — Bimba, bimba, non piangere (with Elizabeth Bainbridge, mez; Plácido Domingo, ten; New Philh/Nello Santi)[b]; Un bel dì, vedremo[a]. LA FANCIULLA DEL WEST[a] — Laggiù nel Soledad. GIANNI SCHICCHI[c] — O mio babbino caro (London Symphony Orchestra/Downes). TURANDOT[d] — In questa reggia (Daniele Barioni, ten; Ambrosian Opera Chorus; New Philh/Santi).

1h 11m ADD 2/88

Puccini. OPERA ARIAS. **Montserrat Caballé** (sop); **London Symphony Orchestra/Sir Charles Mackerras.** EMI CDC7 47841-2. Texts and translation included. From ASD2632 (2/71).

TURANDOT — Signore, ascolta; Tu che di gel sie cinta. MADAMA BUTTERFLY — Un bel dì vedremo; Tu, tu, piccolo iddio. MANON LESCAUT — In quelle trine morbide; Sola, perduta, abbandonata. GIANNI SCHICCHI — O mio babbino caro. TOSCA — Vissi d'arte. LA BOHEME — Sì, mi chiamano Mimì; Donde lieta uscì. LE VILLI — Se come voi. LA RONDINE — Chi il bel sogno di Doretta.

44m ADD 10/87

These two immensely cherishable discs show off a couple of the most beautiful voices of recent decades. Leontyne Price's smokey soprano is gloriously displayed and even in roles one would not expect of her, such as Turandot, her artistry and feeling for line reaps rich rewards. The rarely heard aria from *Edgar* proves a fine vehicle for Price's fluidly-produced legato line and her sure-footed building of climax. Montserrat Caballé's lighter voice is also used to ravishing effect in a similarly wide-ranging programme. She focuses primarily on Puccini's 'little women', singing the role of Liù rather than Turandot, capturing her vulnerability as well as her resolve. She offers the *Rondine* aria that Price passes over and sings it for all it is worth. Her phrasing is quite superb and always used to illuminate the characterization. Mackerras, sensitively aided by the London Symphony Orchestra, accompanies with feeling.

Puccini. MANON LESCAUT. **Maria Callas** (sop) Manon Lescaut; **Giuseppe di Stefano** (ten) Des Grieux; **Giulio Fioravanti** (bar) Lescaut; **Franco Calabrese** (bass) Geronte; **Dino Formichini** (ten) Edmondo; **Fiorenza Cossotto** (mez) Singer; **Carlo Forti** (bass) Innkeeper; **Vito Tatone** (ten) Dancing-master; **Giuseppe Maresi** (bass) Sergeant; **Franco Ricciardi** (ten) Lamplighter; **Franco Ventrigilia** (bass) Captain; **Chorus and Orchestra of La Scala, Milan/Tullio Serafin.** EMI mono CDS7 47393-8. Notes, text and translation included. From EX290041 (3/86). Recorded in 1957.

② 2h ADD 9/86 P ▲

Manon Lescaut is not by any means the most lucidly constructed of Puccini's works, but the youthful ardour of it all combined with his already evident skill as an orchestrator make it an attractive work to encounter both in the theatre and on disc. Manon herself needs a touch of the capriciousness of a spoilt child in her portrayal and only Maria Callas has really encompassed all its needs; she is the character to the life, her verbal pointing subtle as always. As Des Grieux, Giuseppe di Stefano is her ardent partner, and their duets are as impassioned and desperate as they should be. Serafin's conducting is attuned to the needs of Puccini's score. His pacing is exemplary, serving the cause of the work's overall shape and the intricate detail of the scoring, drawing authentic sounds from the forces of La Scala. The sound may leave something to be desired but that hardly seems important bearing in mind the arresting nature of the performance.

Additional recommendations ...

Soloists; Chorus of the Royal Opera House, Covent Garden; Philharmonia Orchestra/Giuseppe Sinopoli. DG 413 893-2GH2 — ② DDD 3/85

Soloists; Jack Gregoor Choir; Belgian Radio and TV Philharmonic Chorus and Orchestra/Alexander Rahbari. Naxos 8 660019/20 — ② 2h 6m DDD 12/92 £

Puccini. LA BOHEME. **Jussi Björling** (ten) Rodolfo; **Victoria de los Angeles** (sop) Mimì; **Robert Merrill** (bar) Marcello; **Lucine Amara** (sop) Musetta; **John Reardon** (bar) Schaunard; **Giorgio Tozzi** (bass) Colline; **Fernando Corena** (bass) Benoit, Alcindoro; **William Nahr** (ten) Parpignol; **Thomas Powell** (bar) Customs Official; **George del Monte** (bar) Sergeant; **Columbus Boychoir; RCA Victor Chorus and Orchestra/Sir Thomas Beecham.** EMI mono CDS7 47235-8. Notes, text and translation included. From ALP1409/10 (1/57).

② lh 48m ADD 6/87

To recommend a 37-year-old mono recording of *La bohème* over all the more glamorously star-studded and sumptuously recorded versions that have appeared since may seem perverse, but the Beecham version is a true classic which has never been surpassed. This intimate opera is not about two superstars showing off how loudly they can sing their top Cs, but about a poverty-stricken poet's love for a mortally-ill seamstress. De los Angeles's infinitely-touching Mimì and Björling's poetic, ardent Rodolfo are backed by consistently fine and characterful ensemble work making this the most realistic version ever recorded. The recording of course shows its age, but this is scarcely noticeable as page after page of the score come freshly alive again: not a *tour de force* of vocalism, not a sequence of famous arias with bits of dialogue between but a lyric tragedy of wrenching pathos and truth.

Additional recommendations ...

Soloists; Chorus and Orchestra of La Scala, Milan/Antonino Votto. EMI mono CDS7 47475-2 — ② lh 46m ADD 11/87

Soloists; Schöneberger Boys' Choir; Berlin German Opera Chorus; Berlin Philharmonic Orchestra/Herbert von Karajan. Decca 421 049-2DH2 — ② lh 50m ADD 11/87

Soloists; Rome Opera Chorus and Orchestra/Thomas Schippers. EMI CMS7 69657-2 — ② lh 43m ADD 4/92

Puccini. TOSCA. **Maria Callas** (sop) Floria Tosca; **Giuseppe di Stefano** (ten) Mario Cavaradossi; **Tito Gobbi** (bar) Baron Scarpia; **Franco Calabrese** (bass) Cesare Angelotti; **Angelo Mercuriali** (ten) Spoletta; **Melchiorre Luise** (bass) Sacristan; **Dario Caselli** (bass) Sciarrone, Gaoler; **Alvaro Cordova** (treb) Shepherd Boy; **Chorus and Orchestra of La Scala, Milan/Victor de Sabata.** EMI mono CDS7 47175-8. Notes, text and translation included. From Columbia 33CX1094/5 (12/53). Recorded in 1953.

② lh 48m ADD 9/85

In the course of *Tosca*'s history there have been many notable interpreters, but few have been able to encompass so unerringly the love, jealousy and eventual courage of Tosca as well as Maria Callas. Her resinous, sensuous tone, her wonderful diction, and her inborn passion filled every phrase of the score with special and individual meaning. In 1953 she was in her early prime, the tone seldom prey to those uneasy moments on high that marred her later recordings, and with the vital, vivid conducting of Victor de Sabata, her performance has rightly attained classic status. Giuseppe di Stefano is the ardent Cavaradossi, his tone forward and vibrant in that way peculiar to Italians. Tito Gobbi's cynical, snarling Scarpia, aristocratic in manner, vicious in meaning, remains unique in that part on record. The mono recording stands up well to the test of time.

Additional recommendations ...

Soloists; Vienna State Opera Chorus; Vienna Philharmonic Orchestra/Herbert von Karajan. Decca Grand Opera 421 670-2DM2 — ② lh 54m ADD 1/89

Soloists; Slovak Philharmonic Chorus; Czecho-Slovak Radio Symphony Orchestra, Bratislava/Alexander Rahbari. Naxos 8 660001/2 — ② lh 56m DDD 10/91 £

Puccini. MADAMA BUTTERFLY. **Renata Scotto** (sop) Madama Butterfly; **Carlo Bergonzi** (ten) Pinkerton; **Rolando Panerai** (bar) Sharpless; **Anna di Stasio** (mez) Suzuki; **Piero De Palma** (ten) Goro; **Giuseppe Morresi** (ten) Prince Yamadori; **Silvana Padoan** (mez) Kate

Pinkerton; **Paolo Montarsolo** (bass) The Bonze; **Mario Rinaudo** (bass) Commissioner; **Rome Opera House Chorus and Orchestra/Sir John Barbirolli.** EMI CMS7 69654-2. Notes, text and translation included. From SAN184/6 (9/67). Recorded in 1966.

② 2h 22m ADD 5/89

This is not quite the best sung *Butterfly* available but Barbirolli ensures that it is the most richly and enjoyably Italianate. Italian opera was in his blood and as a cellist at Covent Garden, playing under Puccini's direction, and as a conductor whose formative years were spent in the theatre (his Covent Garden début was in this very opera), Barbirolli's pleasure in returning to the world of opera is audible throughout this recording. The rapport between him and the Italian orchestra is close and affectionate; it is a heartwarming performance, subtle and supple in the pacing of the love duet, urgently passionate in the great outbursts. Scotto is a touching Butterfly, with all the tiny and crucial details of characterization delicately moulded. There have been more dashing Pinkertons than Bergonzi, but not many who have so effectively combined suavity of sound with neatness of phrasing and good taste. Panerai is a first-class Sharpless and di Stasio a sympathetic Suzuki; there are no weak links elsewhere, and the recording is decent enough for its date, if a bit narrow in perspective and with the singers rather forwardly placed. Barbirolli's *Butterfly* has several distinguished rivals on CD, but for a performance that will remind you of the first time you fell in love with this opera it has permanent value and great eloquence.

Additional recommendations ...

Soloists; Vienna State Opera Chorus; Vienna Philharmonic Orchestra/Herbert von Karajan. Decca 417 577-2DH3 — ③ 2h 25m ADD 6/87

Soloists; Chorus and Orchestra of La Scala, Milan/Herbert von Karajan. EMI mono CDS7 47959-8 — ② 2h 19 ADD 10/87 ▲

Soloists; Rome Opera Chorus and Orchestra/Gabriele Santini. EMI Studio CMS7 63634-2 — ② 2h 17m ADD 3/91

Soloists; Slovak Philharmonic Chorus; Czecho-Slovak Radio Symphony Orchestra, Bratislava/Alexander Rahbari. Naxos 8 660015/6 — 2h 21m DDD 5/92 £

Puccini. LA FANCIULLA DEL WEST. **Carol Neblett** (sop) Minnie; **Plácido Domingo** (ten) Dick Johnson; **Sherrill Milnes** (bar) Jack Rance; **Francis Egerton** (ten) Nick; **Robert Lloyd** (bass) Ashby; **Gwynne Howell** (bass) Jake Wallace; **Paul Hudson** (bass) Billy Jackrabbit; **Anne Wilkens** (sop) Wowkle; **Chorus and Orchestra of the Royal Opera House, Covent Garden/Zubin Mehta.** DG 419 640-2GH2. Notes, text and translation included. From 2709 078 (9/78). Recorded in 1977.

② 2h 10m ADD 11/87

This opera depicts the triangular relationship between Minnie, the saloon owner and 'mother' to the entire town of gold miners, Jack Rance, the sheriff and Dick Johnson (alias Ramerrez), a bandit leader. The music is highly developed in Puccini's seamless lyrical style, the arias for the main characters emerge from the texture and return to it effortlessly. The vocal colours are strongly polarized with the cast being all male except for one travesti role and Minnie herself. The score bristles with robust melody as well as delicate scoring, betraying a masterly hand at work. On the DG recording Carol Neblett is a strong Minnie, vocally distinctive and well characterized, whilst Plácido Domingo and Sherrill Milnes make a good pair of suitors for the spunky little lady. Zubin Mehta conducts with real sympathy for the idiom and the orchestra respond well.

Additional recommendation ...

Soloists; Santa Cecilia Academy Chorus and Orchestra, Rome/Franco Capuana. Decca Grand Opera 421 595-2DM2 — ② 2h 13m ADD 1/89 £ ▲

Puccini. SUOR ANGELICA. **Ilona Tokody** (sop) Suor Angelica; **Eszter Póka** (mez) Princess; **Zsuzsa Barlay** (mez) Mother Superior, Lay Sister II; **Maria Teresa Uribe** (mez) Sister Superior; **Tamara Takács** (mez) Mistress of the Novices, Sister of the Infirmary; **Katalin Pitti**

(sop) Suor Genovieffa; **Magda Pulveri** (sop) Suor Osmina; **Zsuzsa Misura** (sop) Suor Dolcina, Lay Sister I; **Janka Békás** (sop) First Nursing Sister; **Margit Keszthelyi** (sop) Second Nursing Sister; **Ildikó Szönyi** (sop) Novice; **Hungarian State Opera Chorus and Orchestra/Lamberto Gardelli.** Hungaroton HCD12490-2. Notes, text and translation included.

52m DDD

Suor Angelica risks sentimentality, telling of a young nun confined to a convent tò atone for the scandal of having given birth to a child out of wedlock. She is visited by her aunt, the frosty Princess, who tells Angelica of the death of her son. Angelica resolves on suicide and as her life ebbs away sees a vision of the Holy Virgin. The orchestration is lush and the texture can become monotonous with its preponderance of female voices. The lament "Senza mamma" is the opera's 'hit', and when sung in so winning a way as here by Ilona Tokody, achieves a moving sense of the young girl's spiritual innocence and nobility of purpose. The other parts are sung competently and the choral passages are nicely balanced. Gardelli directs a highly sympathetic performance, never overlooking the score's felicitous detail. The recording is clear if a little generous of acoustic.

Puccini. TURANDOT. **Dame Joan Sutherland** (sop) Princess Turandot; **Luciano Pavarotti** (ten) Calaf; **Montserrat Caballé** (sop) Liù; **Tom Krause** (bar) Ping; **Pier Francesco Poli** (ten) Pang, Prince of Persia; **Piero De Palma** (ten) Pong; **Sir Peter Pears** (ten) Emperor Altoum; **Nicolai Ghiaurov** (bass) Timur; **Sabin Markov** (bar) Mandarin; **Wandsworth School Boys' Choir; John Alldis Choir; London Philharmonic Orchestra/Zubin Mehta.** Decca 414 274-2DH2. From SET561 (9/73). Notes, text and translation included.

② 1h 57m ADD 5/85 P B

Turandot is a psychologically complex work fusing appalling sadism with self-sacrificing devotion. The icy Princess of China has agreed to marry any man of royal blood who can solve three riddles she has posed. If he fails his head will roll. Calaf, the son of the exiled Tartar king Timur, answers all the questions easily and when Turandot hesitates to accept him, magnanimously offers her a riddle in return — "What is his name?". Liù, Calaf's faithful slave-girl, is tortured but rather than reveal his identity kills herself. Turandot finally capitulates, announcing that his name is Love. Dame Joan Sutherland's assumption of the title role is statuesque, combining regal poise with a more human warmth, whilst Montserrat Caballé is a touchingly sympathetic Liù, skilfully steering the character away from any hint of the mawkish. Pavarotti's Calaf is a heroic figure in splendid voice and the chorus is handled with great power, baying for blood at one minute, enraptured with Liù's nobility at the next. Mehta conducts with great passion and a natural feel for Puccini's wonderfully tempestuous drama. Well recorded.

Additional recommendations ...

Soloists; Chorus and Orchestra of La Scala, Milan/Tullio Serafin. EMI CDS7 47971-2 — ② 1h 58m ADD 11/87 B ▲

Soloists; Rome Opera Chorus and Orchestra/Francesco Molinari-Pradelli. EMI CMS7 69327-2 — ② 1h 52m ADD P B

Further listening ...

Messe di Gloria in A flat major[a]. *Coupled with* ***Mozart.*** Vesperae solennes de confessore — Laudate Dominum[b]. [a]**Soloists;** [b]**Dame Kiri Te Kanawa** (sop); [a]**West German Radio Chorus;** [b]**London Symphony Chorus;** [a]**Frankfurt Radio Symphony Orchestra/Eliahu Inbal;** [b]**London Symphony Orchestra/Sir Colin Davis.** Philips 434 170-2PM (1/93).

LE VILLI. **Soloists; Ambrosian Opera Chorus; National Philharmonic Orchestra/Lorin Maazel.** CBS Masterworks CD768890 (5/88).

EDGAR. **Soloists; New York Schola Cantorum; New York City Opera Children's Chorus; New York Opera Orchestra/Eve Queler.** CBS CD79213 (10/89).

LA RONDINE. **Soloists; Ambrosian Opera Chorus; London Symphony Orchestra/Lorin Maazel.** CBS CD37852 (10/85).

IL TRITTICO — IL TABARRO[a], SUOR ANGELICA[b]. GIANNI SCHICCHI[c]. **Soloists; Rome Opera Chorus and Orchestra/[a]Vincenzo Bellezza, [b]Tullio Serafin, [c]Gabriele Santini.** EMI mono/[c]stereo CMS7 64165-2 (6/93).

Maximo Diego Pujol

Argentinian 1957-

Suggested listening ...

Tristango en vos. Preludio tristón. Candombe en mi. *Coupled with* ***Tippett:*** The blue guitar. ***Villa-Lobos:*** Five Preludes. ***Delerue:*** Mosaïque. ***Giorginakis:*** Four Greek images. ***Fampas:*** Greek Dances Nos. 1 and 3. **Eleftheria Kotzia** (gt). Pearl SHECD9609 (6/89).
See review in the Collections section; refer to the Index to Reviews.

Henry Purcell

British 1659-1695

NEW REVIEW

Purcell. INSTRUMENTAL MUSIC. **Freiburg Baroque Orchestra/Thomas Hengelbrock.** Deutsche Harmonia Mundi RD77231. Recorded in 1991.
The Fairy Queen. Dido and Aeneas. King Arthur. Abdelazer. Chaconne in G minor, Z730.

lh 16m DDD 3/92 

Even in Purcell's day, it was common practice to take instrumental numbers from his stage works and perform them as independent suites to be enjoyed for their own sake. It was not considered necessary then for them to reflect the dramas from whence they came, and in putting together these four suites today the Freiburg Baroque Orchestra have not felt the need to pay attention to any consideration other than how well they go together. It means there are a few surprises — including the occasional vocal line rendered on instruments and a little harpsichord cadenza that leads us straight from the "Witches' Dance" from *Dido and Aeneas* into the well-known (and, as far as is known, entirely untheatrical) Chaconne in G minor — but the result is a highly entertaining hour-and-a-quarter in the company of some of Purcell's most wonderful tunes, all exhilaratingly played by this brilliant young German period-instrument orchestra. The sheer energy and vigorous commitment with which the group attacks this music, at the same time never allowing things to degenerate into ugly aggressiveness, is refreshing in its excitement and utterly infectious in its youthful *joie de vivre*.

Purcell. SONATAS, Volume 3. **Purcell Quartet** ([a]Catherine Mackintosh, Elizabeth Wallfisch, vns; Richard Boothby, va da gamba; [b]Robert Woolley, org). Chandos CHAN8763.
Ten Sonatas in Four Parts, Z802-11 — No. 3 in A minor; No. 4 in D minor; No. 5 in G minor; No. 6 in G minor; No. 7 in G major; No. 8 in G minor (with two variant movements); No. 9 in F major; No. 10 in D major. Organ Voluntaries, Z717-20[b] — No. 2 in D minor; No. 4 in G major. Prelude for Solo Violin in G minor, ZN773[a].

lh 3m DDD 12/89 

For Purcell lovers this recording promises an hour of sheer delight. The performers play upon instruments of choice, one violin (Jan Bouwmeester, 1669) being contemporary with the composer, the other a fine-toned eighteenth-century Italian instrument. Both gamba and chamber organ are modern reconstructions based on seventeenth-century English models. The acoustics of Orford Church where the recording took place ensure warmth and clarity and even give you the extraordinary feeling that the players are actually present in your sittingroom, with the strings close beside you and the organ only a step away. Many listeners will be familiar with Purcell's *Sonatas in Four Parts*: generations of young fiddlers have been brought up on pieces like the *Golden* Sonata (No. 9) or the famous Chaconne (No. 6). This performance, with its sensitivity, ease and wit should therefore arouse happy memories. It all seems so simple, yet what perfection of detail! — small points, such as the choice of the order in which the sonatas are played, ensuring smooth transitions and apt contrasts; the adoption of appropriately graded tempos; the delicacy, grace and elegance of the music, but also the mysteriously expressive chromaticism and certain moments of unexpected exploratory harmony.

Additional recommendations ...

Ten Sonatas in Four Parts — No. 1 in B minor; No. 2 in E flat major. 12 Sonnatas of Three Parts, Z790-801 — No. 8 in G major; No. 9 in C minor; No. 10 in A minor; No. 11 in F minor; No. 12 in D major. Fantasia upon a Ground in D major/F major/Z731 (with Risa Browder, vn). *Pavans — A major, Z748; G minor, Z751. Chaconne in G minor, Z730* (with Risa Browder, va). **Purcell Quartet.** Chandos CHAN8663 — 53m DDD 10/89

Ten Sonatas in Four Parts. **Catherine Mackintosh, Monica Huggett** (vns); **Christophe Coin** (va da gamba); **Christopher Hogwood** (spinet/org). L'Oiseau-Lyre 433 190-2OH — 1h 2m ADD 3/93

Purcell. AYRES FOR THE THEATRE. **The Parley of Instruments/Peter Holman.** Hyperion CDA66212. Recorded in 1986.

Abdelazer, Z570 — suite. Timon of Athens, Z632 — No. 1, Overture; No. 20, Curtain tune. The Gordion Knot Unty'd, Z597 — suite. Bonduca, Z574 — suite. The Virtuous Wife, Z611 — suite. Chaconne in G minor, Z730.

57m DDD 9/87 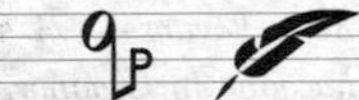

This well recorded disc gathers some of Purcell's most delightful incidental music for the many theatrical productions his music graced. Listeners familiar with Britten's *The Young Person's Guide to the Orchestra* will recognize the theme plucked from *Abdelazer* and here given a very sprightly gait. There is some outstanding instrumental playing — with some virtuoso natural trumpet playing from Crispian Steele-Perkins — and tempos are consistently crisper and more alert than normal. The collection also includes Purcell's well-known *Chaconne* in a brisk performance — it may have originated in the theatre anyway and so makes a logical addition. This delightful disc is far more generously cued than the sleeve would have one believe, and makes for pleasing listening in an intimate recording acoustic.

Purcell. THEATRE MUSIC. **Joy Roberts, Judith Nelson, Emma Kirkby, Elizabeth Lane, Prudence Lloyd** (sops); **James Bowman** (alto); **Martyn Hill, Paul Elliott, Alan Byers, Peter Bamber, Rogers Covey-Crump, Julian Pike** (tens); **David Thomas, Christopher Keyte, Geoffrey Shaw, Michael George** (basses); **Taverner Choir; Academy of Ancient Music/Christopher Hogwood** (hpd). L'Oiseau-Lyre 425 893-2OM6. Texts included.

Abdelazar, Z570. Distressed Innocence, Z577. The Married Beau, Z603. The Gordian Knot Unty'd, Z597 (all from DSLO504, 6/76). Sir Anthony Love, Z588. Bonduca, Z574. Circe, Z575 (DSLO527, 2/78). The Virtuous Wife, Z611. The Old Bachelor, Z607. Overture in G minor, Z770. Amphitryon, Z572 (DSLO55Q, 12/79). The Comical History of Don Quixote, Z578 (DSLO534, 11/78). The Double Dealer, Z592. The Richmond Heiress, Z608. The Rival Sisters, Z609. Henry the Second, King of England Z580. Tyrannic Love, Z613 (DSLO561, 4/81). Overture in G minor, Z772. Theodosius, Z606. The Libertine, Z600. The Massacre of Paris, Z604. Oedipus, Z583 (DSLO590, 3/82). Overture in D minor, Z771. The History of King Richard II, Z581. Sir Barnaby Whigg, Z589. Sophonisba, Z590. The English Lawyer, Z594. A Fool's Preferement, Z571. The Indian Emperor, Z598. The Knight of Malta, Z599. Why, my Daphne, why complaining?, Z525. The Wifes' Excuse, Z612. Cleomenes, Z576. Regulus, Z586. The Marriage-hater Match'd, Z602 (414 173-1OH, 7/85). Love Triumphant, Z582. Rule a Wife and have a Wife, Z587. The Female Virtuosos, Z596. Epsom Wells, Z579.

The Maid's Last Prayer, Z601. Aureng-Zebe, Z573. The Canterbury Guests, Z591. The Fatal Marriage, Z595. The Spanish Friar, Z610. Pausanias, Z585. The Mock Marriage, Z605. Oroonoko, Z584 (414 174-1OH, 9/85). Pavans — A major, Z748; A minor, Z749; B flat major, Z750; G minor, Z751; G minor, Z752. Trio Sonata for violin, bass viol and organ, Z780. Chaconne in G minor, Z730 (DSLO514, 10/77).

⑥ 6h 54m ADD/DDD 4/91 

This six-CD anthology of vocal and instrumental music by Purcell is as rich and rewarding in its variety as it is indispensable to our picture of this English genius. Although Restoration England continued to take an interest in theatre music from abroad towards the end of the seventeenth century she began to develop staged musical entertainments along hybrid lines of her own. Most of the music contained here dates from the last six years of Purcell's life when plays, from Shakespeare to Shadwell were seldom staged without songs, instrumental interludes and dances. Purcell's legacy to the Restoration stage contains jewels of almost priceless worth and these are lovingly burnished by Christopher Hogwood, the Academy of Ancient Music and an excellent group of vocalists; choruses are imaginatively sung by the Taverner Choir under Andrew Parrott's direction. It would be difficult to isolate any particular songs and dances from such a vast treasure-trove but few may be able to resist Emma Kirkby's saucy "Lads and Lasses, blithe and gay" (*Don Quixote*), Martyn Hill's "Thus to a ripe, consenting maid" (*The Old Bachelor*), the ravishing trio "With this sacred charming wand" (*Don Quixote*) or the "Scotch tune" from *Amphitryon*. Performances are lively and stylish if not always polished but that, one suspects, is as authentic a touch as anything else here. The booklet contains texts of all the songs and the discs are pleasantly recorded.

Additional recommendation ...

Fantasia upon a Ground in D major/F major/Z731. Ten Sonnatas in Four Parts — No. 6 in G minor, Z801. Pavans — A major, Z748; A minor, Z749; B flat major, Z750; G minor, Z751; G minor, Z752. Chaconne in G minor, Z730. Sonnatas of Three Parts — E minor, Z796; D major, Z801. Overtures — D minor, Z771; G minor, Z772. Swiftere Isis, swifter flow, Z336 — Overture in G major. Suite in G major, Z770. **London Baroque.** Harmonia Mundi HMC90 1327 — 1h 4m DDD 10/90

NEW REVIEW

Purcell. AYRES AND SONGS FROM ORPHEUS BRITANNICUS. **Jill Feldman** (sop); **Nigel North** (lte); **Sarah Cunningham** (va da gamba). Arcana A2. Texts included. Recorded in 1992.

Dido and Aeneas — Ah! Belinda I am prest. The Comical History of Don Quixote — From rosy bow'rs. Oedipus — Music for a while. Fly swift, ye hours, Z369. Come ye sons of art, away, Z323 — Strike the viol. Pausanias — Sweeter than roses. The Indian Queen — I attempt from love's sickness. From silent shades, Z370. The Spanish Friar — Whilst I with grief. What a sad fate is mine, Z428. Tyrannic Love — Ah! how sweet it is to love. The History of Dioclesian — Since from my dear Astrea's sight. The Fairy Queen — Thrice happy lovers; Hark! Hark! How all things; Ye gentle spirits. Hail, Bright Cecilia, Z328 — 'Tis Nature's voice. King Arthur — Fairest Isle. The Tempest — Dear pretty youth. Bonduca — O lead me to some peaceful gloom. Timon of Athens — The cares of lovers. If music be the food of love, Z379/3.

1h 10m DDD 1/93 

NEW REVIEW

Purcell. SONGS. **Drew Minter** (alto); [a]**Paul O'Dette** (lte); **Mitzi Meyerson** ([b]hpd/[c]org); [d]**Mary Springfels** (va da gamba). Harmonia Mundi HMU90 7035. Texts included. Recorded in 1990.

O Solitude! my sweetest choice, Z406[cd]. Hail, Bright Cecilia, Z328 — 'Tis Nature's voice[ac]. The Rival Sisters — Celia has a thousand charms[ad]. The Indian Queen — I attempt from love's sickness[b]. If music be the food of love, Z379/3[ad]. Not all my torments can your pity move, Z400[ad]. From silent shades, Z370[ad]. Oedipus — Music for a while[a]. Pausanias — Sweeter than roses[ad]. Celebrate this Festival, Z321 — Crown the altar, deck the shrine[c]. Lord, what is man?, Z192[acd]. Sleep, Adam, sleep and take thy rest, Z195[a]. Now that the sun hath veiled his light,

Z193[acd]. The Fatal hour comes on apace, Z421[cd]. Welcome to all the pleasures, Z339 — Here the deities approve[b]. Fly, bold rebellion, Z324 — Be welcome then, great Sir[acd]. The Fairy Queen — Thrice happy lovers[b]; Hark! Hark! How all things[bd]; Hark! the echoing air[bd].

1h 2m DDD 1/93

Both these selections of songs contain some of Purcell's most freely-expressed creations. Convincing results from two such different approaches as Jill Feldman's and Drew Minter's make one realize just how much leeway Purcell allows the performer in this repertoire, not to mention the extent of the composer's extraordinary musical imagination. Comparison of the eight songs common to each proves the point, though the potential buyer may well find this an irrelevance if he or she has already decided that only one of the voice-types, soprano or countertenor, is for them. Feldman's songs are all taken from "Orpheus Britannicus", a posthumous publication of songs whose initial offerings appeared in 1698 and helped to ensure that Purcell's music remained in the public domain after his death. Theatre songs are the order of the day here and Feldman's mellow tone is well-suited to running legato lines which she executes with considerable *élan*. Smooth it may be but as *Sweeter than roses* shows, her pure sound has a habit of emphasizing intonation lapses and a restricted vocal colour. Drew Minter is less hooty (a curious comparison in favour of a male alto) and despite an unconvincing opening to the same song he tends to bring the text alive with greater variety of articulation and sound. As well as drawing his selection from theatre genres, Minter's offerings also straddle the world of the devotional song; pieces such as *An Evening Hymn* seem particularly to suit his unassuming and ruminative vocal quality. Despite a few reservations then, there are many songs from each of these selections to be enjoyed and some of them certainly rank amongst the finest on record so far.

NEW REVIEW

Purcell. ODES AND WELCOME SONGS, Volumes 6-8. **Gillian Fisher, Mary Seers, Susan Hamilton, Tessa Bonner** (sops); **James Bowman, Nigel Short, Michael Chance** (altos); **Mark Padmore, Andrew Tusa, Rogers Covey-Crump, Charles Daniels, John Mark Ainsley** (tens); **Michael George, Robert Evans** (basses); **New College Choir, Oxford; King's Consort/Robert King.** Hyperion CDA66494, CDA66587 and CDA66598. Texts included. Recorded in 1991.

CDA66494 — Love's goddess sure was blind, Z331. Raise, raise the voice, Z334. Laudate Ceciliam, Z329. From those serene and rapturous joys, Z326. *CDA66587* — Of old, when heroes thought it base, Z333. Swifter, Isis, swifter flow, Z336. What, what shall be done on behalf of the man?, Z341. *CDA66598* — Come ye sons of art, away, Z323. Welcome, viceregent of the mighty king, Z340. Why, why are all the Muses mute?, Z343.

③ 1h 8m 1h 6m 1h 8m DDD 3/93

These three CDs represent the final instalments in Hyperion's complete recording of Purcell's Odes and Welcome Songs. Purcell composed a number of these celebratory works between 1680 and 1695, and 24 survive. They were written for a considerable range of events: most of them for royal birthdays, of King James II and Queen Mary, but also for a royal wedding, educational celebrations, and the 'Yorkshire Feast' of 1689. Up until now this cornucopia of wonderful music has largely been ignored, and Hyperion's edition is to be warmly welcomed, not only for bringing to the catalogue such magnificent music, but also for the extremely sympathetic and musical performances by the King's Consort under the direction of Robert King. Of all the works on these discs, probably the most well-known is *Come ye sons of art, away* written for Queen Mary in 1694 (Volume 8). This joyous work contains some of Purcell's most ebullient music, typified by the duet for two counter-tenors, "Sound the trumpet". Like all of the works in the set this is surrounded by a well contrasted group of solos and duets for individual voices, instrumental interludes, and the occasional chorus. Less famous, but equally full of Restoration pomp and ceremony is the Yorkshire Feast song (Volume 7). Like many of the odes, the text for this is second-rate, ostensibly telling the story of York from the Roman occupation to the seventeenth century. However this is merely the pretext for a splendidly varied set of vocal and instrumental items, the climax of which might be more fitting for a coronation than for a dinner of Yorkshire worthies! Volume 6 contains four of the least well-known if no less rich and varied odes, two of which are dedicated to the patron saint of music, St Cecilia. While composed for slightly smaller forces than the more ceremonial odes, these contain music which is equally jaunty and exhilarating. Throughout all three volumes the most striking fact is Purcell's extraordinary inventiveness, and his incredible facility at word setting: even the most lame texts come alive in his hands, and the variety of expression throughout is astonishing. That such fine music should have lain unrecognized and unplayed for so long is cause for some amazement, but no less rejoicing that at last it has been restored in such understanding performances. Robert King's direction is always sensitive to both the broad span and individual nuances of Purcell's kaleidoscopic writing for voice and instruments. The King's Consort play with great understanding throughout and has clearly wholly absorbed the often elusive style of this music, in which many influences, most notably those from France, are combined. The vocal soloists are uniformly excellent, but special mention must be made of the ravishing soprano Gillian Fisher, and the versatile counter-tenor James Bowman. Hyperion's recordings throughout are without fault, achieving both excellent internal balance and appropriate atmosphere and perspective.

Purcell. CHORAL WORKS. **Taverner Choir; Taverner Players/Andrew Parrott.** EMI Reflexe CDC7 49635-2. Texts included.
Ode for St Cecilia's Day, 1683 — Welcome to all the pleasures, Z339 (with John Mark Ainsley, Charles Daniels, tens). Funeral Sentences — Man that is born of a woman, Z27; In the midst of life, Z17*a*; Thou know'st, Lord, Z58*b*. Ode for Queen Mary's Birthday, 1694 — Come ye sons of art, away, Z323 (Emily Van Evera, sop; Timothy Wilson, alto; Ainsley, Daniels; David Thomas, bass). Funeral Music for Queen Mary — March and Canzona, Z860. Thou know'st, Lord, Z58*c*.

55m DDD 2/90

This is a satisfying anthology of vocal music by Purcell which includes the masterly and memorable *Come ye sons of art, away*. Andrew Parrott, as so often, has some surprises in store for the unsuspecting listener; here he performs the famous duet "Sound the trumpet" not with two countertenors but with two voices of contrasting timbres and registers: a countertenor and a tenor, albeit a high one. This has been achieved by a choice of low pitch for the entire work and the results are convincing. Likewise, the air "Sound the viol", traditionally countertenor's property, has been allotted to a high tenor. Parrott brings this beautiful work to life with insight, affection and rigorous attention to all aspects of style. Much else on the disc is comparably successful and, if the music does not always maintain the dizzy heights of *Come ye sons of art* it is never far below. Outstanding from a musical and interpretative standpoint are the profoundly affecting *Funeral Sentences* and *Funeral Music for Queen Mary* both of which are notably well served by EMI in its sympathetic recording.

Purcell. Hail, bright Cecilia, Z328. **Emma Kirkby** (sop); **Michael Chance, Kevin Smith** (altos); **Rogers Covey-Crump, Charles Daniels, Paul Elliott, Neil Jenkins, Andrew King** (tens); **Michael George, Simon Grant, David Thomas, Richard Wistreich** (basses); **Robert Woolley** (org); **Taverner Choir and Players/Andrew Parrott.** EMI Reflexe CDC7 47490-2. Text included. Recorded in 1985.

57m DDD 1/87 

Purcell's Ode in praise of the patroness of music is but one of a whole series of such works written by various composers between 1683 and 1703 for festivities held at the Stationer's Hall in London. Purcell had written the first ode for these gatherings and was later asked to make a setting of words by the Royal Chaplain Nicholas Brady. Throughout its 13 sections poet and composer hymn the praises of the various instruments of music. Purcell's limpid music beautifully and tastefully adorns this most gracious of poetry and vividly observes both its vigour and sublimity. The Taverner Consort, Choir and Players comprise some of the finest musicians in the early-music field and with such fresh and versatile voices as Emma Kirkby's, Rogers Covey-Crump's and Michael Chance's, to single out but three, singing the praises of music, who could complain? The recording is clear, spacious and natural-sounding.

Additional recommendations ...
Soloists; Monteverdi Choir; English Baroque Soloists/John Eliot Gardiner. Erato 2292-45187-2 — DDD 12/84
Soloists; Tiffin Choir; Ambrosian Singers; English Chamber Orchestra/Sir Charles Mackerras. Archiv Produktion Galleria 427 159-2AGA — 55m DDD 5/91

Purcell. DIDO AND AENEAS. **Dame Janet Baker** (sop) Dido; **Patricia Clark** (sop) Belinda; **Eileen Poulter** (sop) Second Woman; **Raimund Herincx** (bass) Aeneas; **Monica Sinclair** (contr) Sorceress; **Rhianon James** (mez) First Witch; **Catherine Wilson** (mez) Second Witch; **John Mitchinson** (ten) Sailor; **Dorothy Dorow** (sop) Spirit; **St Anthony Singers; English Chamber Orchestra/Anthony Lewis.** Decca Serenata 425 720-2DM. From L'Oiseau-Lyre 1961 SOL60047 (3/62). Recorded in 1961.

53m ADD 12/90 

This now historic recording has never really been surpassed in excellence. It is arguably the best performance of Purcell's tightly-constructed opera — better even than Flagstad's and Schwarzkopf's rendering in the 1950s and certainly equal to more recent recordings. It is a collector's item, with Janet Baker, in the role of Dido, rising to the height of her vocal powers. Her first aria, "Ah! Belinda I am prest", is full of tender foreboding and her final lament powerfully grief-stricken. She is well supported by Patricia Clark, Dido's light-hearted confidante. Monica Sinclair reveals herself as a truly sinister, though somewhat unevenly-voiced Sorceress. The hero's role in the opera is minimal, but Raimund Herincx matches up well to the heroine in their famous final duet. The St Anthony Singers give ample proof of their versatility producing, as required by the score, cackling witches, boozy sailors and rabble or merely a crowd of gently gossiping English courtiers running for shelters from the elements. The strings of the English Chamber Orchestra are supported by Thurston Dart on the harpsichord continuo — a definite plus, this, and a reminder of the tragically early death of a brilliant performer who combines, here as always, both discretion and inspired imagination.

Additional recommendation ...
Soloists; The English Concert and Choir/Trevor Pinnock. Archiv Produktion 427 624-2AH — 54m DDD 10/89
Soloists; English Chamber Choir and Orchestra/Raymond Leppard. Erato Libretto 2292-45263-2 — 56m ADD 11/91
Soloists; Taverner Choir and Players/Andrew Parrott. Chandos Chaconne CHAN0521 — 56m DDD 11/91

NEW REVIEW

Purcell. THE FAIRY QUEEN. **Gillian Fisher, Lorna Anderson** (sops); **Ann Murray** (mez); **Michael Chance** (alto); **John Mark Ainsley, Ian Partridge** (tens); **Richard Suart, Michael George** (basses); **The Sixteen Choir and Orchestra/Harry Christophers.** Collins Classics 7013-2. Text included. Recorded in 1990.

② 2h 13m DDD 4/92 

As the Purcell tercentenary approaches, it seems more and more likely that it will be his stage works — in particular his four semi-operas in which extended musical set-pieces or masques are mixed with substantial dialogue — that will emerge most strongly from the inevitable reassessments of the true masterpieces that they are. And of these, it is perhaps *The Fairy Queen* that stands the best chance of catching the public's imagination, not only because of its superb music but also on account of its foundation in such a well-loved part of England's literary heritage as *A Midsummer Night's Dream*. Much has been made of the liberties taken by Purcell's anonymous librettist for this work, but no one who has heard the music could deny that the composer conjures just as truthfully as Shakespeare the pains and pleasures of love, the interludes of low comedy, and the magical atmosphere of the fairy wood. Harry Christophers has assembled a strong cast for this recording. With singers like Gillian Fisher, Michael Chance, John Mark Ainsley and Ian Partridge aboard, things are hardly likely to go far astray, while the contribution of the always excellent Sixteen Choir means, too, that this is a performance without any serious weakness. The orchestra, it's true, could sound more committed at times, while Ann Murray seems a little out of place in this particular company (though there's certainly nothing wrong with her singing as such); but in general there is a refreshing lightness, an authentic Englishness, to this recording that serves the music well. Perhaps the highlight is the gentle Second Act Masque which lulls the eponymous Titania to sleep, but also highly enjoyable are the comic scenes, such as the one in which a drunken poet suffers an uncomfortable encounter with some fairies. This is not a recording which has everything — it lacks sheer splendour for one thing — but of those available it perhaps comes closest to the ideal.

Additional recommendations ...

Soloists; Monteverdi Choir; English Baroque Soloists/John Eliot Gardiner. Archiv Produktion 419 221-2AH2 — ② 2h 18m DDD 8/87

Soloists; Les Arts Florissants/William Christie. Harmonia Mundi HMC90 1308/9 — ② 2h 8m DDD 1/90

Soloists; Ambrosian Opera Chorus; English Chamber Orchestra/Benjamin Britten. Decca Serenata 433 163-2DM2 — ② 1h 36m ADD 5/92

Further listening ...

KING ARTHUR — *semi-opera.* **Soloists; Monteverdi Choir; English Baroque Soloists/John Eliot Gardiner.** Erato 2292-45211-2 (7/86).

THE INDIAN QUEEN — *semi-opera.* **Soloists; Deller Choir; The King's Music/Alfred Deller.** Harmonia Mundi HMC90 243 (8/87).

Key to Symbols

Gramophone Award winners

Artists of the Year

Johann Quantz

German 1697-1773

Suggested listening ...

Flute Concertos — C major; D major, "pour Potsdam"; G major; G minor. **James Galway** (fl); **Württemberg Chamber Orchestra/Jörg Faerber.** RCA Victor Red Seal RD60247 (11/91).

Roger Quilter

British 1877-1953

Suggested listening ...

Songs — Three Songs, Op. 3 — No. 1, Love's Philosophy; No. 2, Now Sleeps the Crimson Petal. At Close of Day. Three Shakespeare Songs, Op. 6. To Julia, Op. 8. Four Songs, Op. 14. Seven Elizabethan Lyrics, Op. 12. Three Songs of William Blake, Op. 20. Go, Lovely Rose,

Op. 24 No. 3. Arab Love Song, Op. 25 No. 4. Music, When Soft Voices Die, Op. 25 No. 5. In the Bud of the Morning-o, Op. 25 No. 6. I Arise from Dreams of Thee, Op. 29. **Benjamin Luxon** (bar); **David Willison** (pf). Chandos CHAN8782 (3/90).

Sergey Rachmaninov

Russian/American 1873-1943

Rachmaninov. Piano Concerto No. 1 in F sharp minor, Op. 1[a]. Rhapsody on a Theme of Paganini, Op. 43[b]. **Vladimir Ashkenazy** (pf); [a]**Concertgebouw Orchestra,** [b]**Philharmonia Orchestra/Bernard Haitink.** Decca 417 613-2DH.

52m DDD 12/87

Showpiece that it is, with its lush romantic harmonies and contrasting vigorous panache, the First Concerto has much to commend it in purely musical terms and although its debts are clear enough (most notably perhaps to Rimsky-Korsakov), it stands on its own two feet as far as invention, overall design and musical construction are concerned. The *Paganini* Rhapsody is one of the composer's finest works and arguably the most purely inventive set of variations to be based on Paganini's catchy tune ever written. The wealth of musical invention it suggested to Rachmaninov is truly bewildering and his control over what can in lesser hands become a rather laboured formal scheme is masterly indeed. Ashkenazy gives superb performances of both works and the Concertgebouw and the Philharmonia are in every way the perfect foils under Bernard Haitink's sympathetic direction. There is weight, delicacy, colour, energy and repose in equal measure here and it is all conveyed by a full-bodied and detailed recording.

Additional recommendations ...

No. 1. No. 2 in C minor, Op. 18. No. 3 in D minor, Op. 30. No. 4 in G minor, Op. 40. Rhapsody on a Theme of Paganini. **Earl Wild** (pf); **Royal Philharmonic Orchestra/Jascha Horenstein.** Chandos CHAN8521/2 — 2 2h 14m ADD 9/87

No. 4 in G minor, Op. 40. ***Ravel.*** *Piano Concerto in G major.* **Arturo Benedetti Michelangeli** (pf); **Philharmonia Orchestra/Ettore Gracis.** EMI CDC7 49326-2 — 47m ADD 9/88

Nos. 1-4. **Vladimir Ashkenazy** (pf); **Concertgebouw Orchestra/Bernard Haitink.** Decca 421 590-2DH2 — 2 2h 14m DDD 4/89

Nos. 1-4. **Vladimir Ashkenazy** (pf); **London Symphony Orchestra/André Previn.** Decca 425 576-2DM2 — 2 2h 15m ADD 3/90 £

Nos. 1 and 4. **Vladimir Ashkenazy** (pf); **London Symphony Orchestra/André Previn.** Decca 425 004-2DM — 55m ADD 7/90

Nos. 1-4. Rhapsody on a Theme of Paganini. **Howard Shelley** (pf); **Royal Scottish National Orchestra/Bryden Thomson.** Chandos CHAN8882/3 — 2 2h 34m DDD 4/91

Rachmaninov. Piano Concerto No. 2 in C minor, Op. 18. Rhapsody on a Theme of Paganini, Op. 43. **Vladimir Ashkenazy** (pf); **London Symphony Orchestra/André Previn.** Decca Ovation 417 702-2DH. From SXLF6565/7 (9/72).

58m ADD 7/87 £ B

Rachmaninov. Piano Concerto No. 3 in D minor, Op. 30[a]. PRELUDES[b]. **Vladimir Ashkenazy** (pf); [a]**London Symphony Orchestra/André Previn.** Decca Ovation 417 764-2DM. Item marked [a] from SXLF6565/7 (9/72), recorded in 1971, [b] 5BB 221/2 (2/76), recorded 1974-75.

24 Preludes — C sharp minor, Op. 3 No. 2; B flat major, Op. 23 No. 2; G minor, Op. 23 No. 5; B minor, Op. 32 No. 10; D flat major, Op. 32 No. 13.

1h 10m ADD 10/88 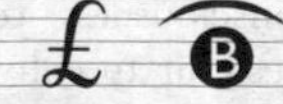

The C minor Concerto of Rachmaninov symbolizes romanticism at its ripest. Its combination of poetry and sensuous warmth with languorously memorable melodic lines balanced by exhilarating pianistic brilliance happily avoids any suggestion of sentimentality. The simple chordal introduction from the soloist ushers in one of the composer's most luscious tunes, yet the slow movement develops even greater ardour in its melodic contour, and the composer holds back a further haunting expressive idea to bring lyrical contrast to the scintillating finale. Ashkenazy's 1972 performance with Previn is a superb mid-price bargain, coupled with an exhilarating performance of the *Rhapsody on a theme of Paganini*, where the famous Variation No. 18 blossoms with passionate fervour. The Concerto is no less involving, the first movement building to an engulfing climax, the *Adagio* radiantly beautiful, perhaps the finest on disc. The recording represents Decca vintage analogue sound at its best and the remastering is extremely successful, rich, well balanced and vivid. Ashkenazy's recording of the Third Concerto complements the composer's own (listed below). It is more conspicuously expressive, more heroic and more yielding by turns; it is uncut, includes the more massive of the first movement cadenzas, and it enjoys a full-blooded modern recording. There is a tendency to bang away when the chords are coming thick and fast and to overdo expressive lingerings; also, Previn's accompaniment is fine but not outstandingly idiomatic. But these points do not outweigh the advantages of what, especially at mid-price, is one of the top recommendations for this concerto. A selection of five of Rachmaninov's most popular Preludes enhances the attractions of the disc.

Additional recommendations ...

No. 2[a]. ***Prokofiev.*** *Piano Concerto No. 5 in G major, Op. 55*[b]. **Sviatoslav Richter** (pf); **Warsaw Philharmonic Orchestra/**[a]**Stanislaw Wislocki;** [b]**Witold Rowicki.** DG 415 119-2GH *(reviewed under Prokofiev; refer to the Index to Reviews)* — 58m ADD 6/85

No. 2. Rhapsody on a Theme of Paganini. **Philip Fowke** (pf); **Royal Philharmonic Orchestra/Yuri Temirkanov.** EMI Eminence CD-EMX9509 — 59m DDD 10/87

Nos. 2[a] *and 3*[b]. **Sergei Rachmaninov** (pf); **Philadelphia Orchestra/**[a]**Leopold Stokowski;** [b]**Eugene Ormandy.** RCA Red Seal mono RD85997 — 1h 6m ADD 10/88

Nos. 2 and 3. **Earl Wild** (pf); **Royal Philharmonic Orchestra/Jascha Horenstein.** Chandos Collect CHAN6507 — 1h 6m ADD 2/91

No. 2. Rhapsody on a Theme of Paganini. **Jenö Jandó** (pf); **Budapest Symphony Orchestra/György Lehel.** Naxos 8 550117 — 58m DDD 10/90 £

NEW REVIEW

Rachmaninov. SYMPHONIES. ORCHESTRAL WORKS. **London Symphony Orchestra/André Previn.** EMI CMS7 64530-2. Items marked [a] from ASD3259 (9/76), [b] ASD3284 (12/76), [c] ASD3369 (8/77). Recorded 1974-76.

Symphonies — No. 1 in D minor, Op. 13; No. 2 in E minor, Op. 27; No. 3 in A minor, Op. 44[c]. Symphonic Dances, Op. 45[a]. The isle of the dead, Op. 29[a]. Vocalise, Op. 34 No. 14[b] (arr. composer). Aleko[c] — Intermezzo; Gipsy Girls' Dance.

③ 3h 47m ADD £

Rachmaninov's three symphonies reflect three very different phases in his creative development: the first (1895) is a stormy synthesis of contemporary trends in Russian symphonic music, the Second (1906-7), an epic study in Tchaikovskian opulence, and the third (1935-6) a seemingly unstoppable stream of original ideas and impressions. The Second was the first to gain wide acceptance, and for good reason. It shares both the key and general mood of Tchaikovsky's Fifth. Cast in E minor, its initial gloom ultimately turns to triumph, and the Symphony includes enough glorious melodies to keep Hollywood happy for decades. The First Symphony had a difficult birth, largely through the incompetent musical midwifery of Alexander Glazunov whose conducting of the work's première apparently left much to be desired. It is, however, an immensely promising piece and although undeniably the product of its times, prophetic not only of the mature Rachmaninov, but of other Northern voices, including — occasionally— the mature Sibelius. Both the Third Symphony and its near-contemporary, the *Symphonic Dances* find Rachmaninov indulging a fruitful stream of musical consciousness, recalling motives and ideas from earlier compositions, yet allowing gusts of fresh air to enliven and rejuvenate his style. Both works have yet to receive their full due in the concert-hall, although the strongly evocative *Isle of the dead* is more securely embedded in the repertory. What with these and a trio of warming shorter pieces, André Previn's mid-1970s LSO package makes for an excellent mid-price bargain package. The performances are entirely sympathetic, avoiding familiar interpretative extremes such as slickness, bombast and emotional indulgence. Previn shows particular understanding of the Third Symphony, the *Symphonic Dances* and *The isle of the dead,* works that represent Rachmaninov at his most innovative and assured. The Second Symphony is played without cuts (not invariably the case, even today) and Christopher Bishop's recordings are generous in tone and revealing of detail, especially among the woodwinds.

Additional recommendations ...
Nos. 1-3. Youth Symphony. **Concertgebouw Orchestra/Vladimir Ashkenazy.** Decca 421 065-2DM3 — ③ 2h 30m DDD 12/87
Symphonic Dances. The isle of the dead. **Concertgebouw Orchestra/Vladimir Ashkenazy.** Decca Ovation 430 733-2DM — 55m DDD 8/91
No. 1. The isle of the dead. **Royal Philharmonic Orchestra/Andrew Litton.** Virgin Classics VC7 59547-2 — 1h 7m DDD 5/90

Rachmaninov. Symphony No. 2 in E minor, Op. 27. **Orchestre de Paris/Semyon Bychkov.** Philips 432 101-2PH.

58m DDD 9/91 

Semyon Bychkov's account of the Second Symphony on Philips may be rather ungenerous regarding value (no couplings), but what it lacks in length it more than makes up for in quality. Indeed, apart from Previn's classic account, Bychkov's reading may well lay strong claims to being the finest version on disc. His is an account that is both full-blooded and romantic, never overindulgent, and refreshingly direct. The *Adagio* is given a very dignified, almost stoical reading which never lapses into maudlin sentimentality as it sometimes can, and from which Bychkov coaxes from his players some extremely telling and subtle performances. Unlike Litton, Bychkov omits the exposition repeat in the first movement, but makes none of the other cuts that have sometimes plagued this score. Stunningly recorded.

Additional recommendations ...
No. 2. **Concertgebouw Orchestra/Vladimir Ashkenazy.** Decca 400 081-2DH — 55m 3/83 DDD
No. 2. Vocalise, Op. 34 No. 14. **Royal Philharmonic Orchestra/Andrew Litton.** Virgin Classics VC7 59548-2 — 1h 10m DDD 5/90
No. 2. Vocalise[a]. [a]**Sylvia McNair** (sop); **Baltimore Symphony Orchestra/David Zinman.** Telarc CD80312 — 1h 8m DDD 10/92
No. 2. Vocalise. **BBC Welsh Symphony Orchestra/Tadaaki Otaka.** Nimbus NI5322 — 1h 6m DDD 5/92

Rachmaninov. Symphony No. 3 in A minor, Op. 44[a].
Shostakovich. Symphony No. 6 in B minor, Op. 54[b]. **London Symphony Orchestra/André Previn.** EMI Studio CDM7 69564-2. Item marked [a] from ASD3369 (8/77), recorded in 1976, [b] ASD3029 (12/74), recorded 1973-74.

1h 15m ADD 12/88 

Previn's highly praised recording of Rachmaninov's Third Symphony came at the peak of a very successful period in the EMI studios, the Shostakovich, hardly less fine, was done three years earlier. They make a splendid and distinguished mid-price coupling showing the symbiosis Previn had with the LSO at that time. The string section play Rachmaninov's lyrical themes with a rapturous romantic sweep and the nervous intensity of the reading is immensely gripping. The first movement of the Shostakovich Sixth is an expansive *Largo*, longer than the other two movements put together, especially when Previn's treatment is so eloquently spacious; the scherzo which follows is full of wit, and the ebullient finale seems optimistic, but maybe things are not what they seem. Previn is clearly deeply involved in this powerful score and so are his players and the remastered recording is full and clear without too much loss of ambience in the clarification process.

Additional recommendations ...

No. 3. Symphonic Dances, Op. 45. **Royal Philharmonic Orchestra/Andrew Litton.** Virgin Classics VC7 59549-2 — lh 18m DDD 5/90

No. 3. The isle of the dead, Op. 29. Vocalise, Op. 34 No. 14 (arr. composer). **Philadelphia Orchestra/Sergey Rachmaninov.** Pearl GEMMCD9414 — 59m AAD ▲

No. 3. The isle of the dead. **BBC Welsh Symphony Orchestra/Tadaaki Otaka.** Nimbus NI5344 — lh 4m DDD 4/93

Rachmaninov. PIANO MUSIC FOR FOUR AND SIX HANDS. **Brigitte Engerer, Oleg Maisenberg.** Harmonia Mundi HMC90 1301/2.

Russian Rhapsody in E minor. Suites — No. 1, Op. 5, "Fantaisie-tableaux"; No. 2, Op. 17. Polka italienne. Romance in G major. Six Duets, Op. 11. Two pieces for six hands (with Elena Bachkirova). Symphonic Dances, Op. 45*a*.

② 2h llm DDD 3/90

Rachmaninov's four- and six-hand piano music covers his whole composing career, from the *Russian Rhapsody* of 1891 to the *Symphonic Dances* of nearly 50 years later (the latter being better known in Rachmaninov's orchestral version). It is a rewarding repertoire, even if it is only with the *Symphonic Dances* that it is appropriate to speak of a masterpiece. One reason why these works get so much less exposure than the solo piano music is the inherent problem of the two-piano or duet medium — the need to synchronize the instantaneous attacks of two pianists can easily stifle their expressive freedom (and to leave attacks unsynchronized can sound terribly amateurish). Engerer and Maisenberg have a shared understanding of the idiom which helps them around this problem, and their performances are fluent, warmly expressive and cleanly recorded. Recording quality gourmets should note that not all the pieces were recorded on the same occasion or with the same set-up of instruments — in the second movement of the First Suite the two pianos even appear to swap channels. It should also be said that the Second Suite, a favourite with students and adventurous amateurs, is a little less exciting as a performance than the rest of the programme. Apart from those things, this is an exceptionally fine issue.

Additional recommendation ...

Russian Rhapsody. Suites Nos. 1 and 2. Polka italienne. Romance. Romance in G major. Six Morceaux, Op. 11. Waltz. Symphonic Dances. Prelude in C sharp minor, Op. 3. **Ingryd Thorson, Julian Thurber, David Gardiner.** Paula PACD46 — ② 2h 6m AAD 10/88

Rachmaninov. Piano Sonatas — No. 1 in D minor, Op. 28; No. 2 in B flat minor, Op. 36 (original version). **Gordon Fergus-Thompson** (pf). Kingdom KCLCD2007. Recorded in 1987.

lh 13m DDD 6/89

Familiar though Rachmaninov is as a composer of piano concertos, his two Piano Sonatas have not attained anything like the same level of popularity. But here is a recording that couples them together in performances that are both persuasive and masterly. Gordon Fergus-Thompson has the technique and the temperament to do full justice to this music. In his later life, Rachmaninov made considerable cuts in his Second Sonata, but today the tendency is to return to his original, which is what Fergus-Thompson does here to good advantage. In this form the Sonata lasts some 28 minutes, but it does not outstay its welcome; and as a matter of fact the First Sonata is longer at nearly three-quarters of an hour. Both sonatas contain thrilling and highly personal music, and they have been well recorded.

Additional recommendations ...

Piano Sonata No. 2. Morceau de fantaisie in G minor. Song without words in D minor. Pièce in D minor. Fughetta in F major. Fragments in A flat major. Oriental Sketch in B flat major. Three Nocturnes — No. 1 in F sharp minor; No. 2 in F major; No. 3 in C minor. Quatre Pièces — Romance in F sharp minor;

Prélude in E flat minor; Mélodie in E major; Gavotte in D major. **Howard Shelley** (pf). Hyperion CDA66198 — 59m DDD 9/87

Piano Sonata No. 2. Five morceaux de fantaisie, Op. 3. Four Pieces. Lilacs, Op. 21 No. 5. **Beate Berthold** (pf). EMI CDC7 54458-2 — 1h DDD 2/93

Rachmaninov. 24 Préludes[a], Op. 23 and Op. 32. Piano Sonata No. 2 in B flat minor, Op. 36[b]. **Vladimir Ashkenazy** (pf). Decca 414 417-2DH2. Item marked [a] from 5BB 221/2 (2/76), [b] SXL6996 (9/82).

2 1h 46m ADD 11/85

These recordings were outstanding on LP and they sound even better in CD format. Ashkenazy gets as close as possible to making the C sharp minor *Prelude* sound fresh, and one might also note the becalmed melancholy of Op. 23 No. 1, the exquisite management of the different threads in the texture of Op. 23 No. 4, the supple flow of Op. 23 No. 6. Superficially the two sets of *Preludes* are similar, yet in reality they are a lot different. Closely linked to the quality of Ashkenazy's interpretations is the fact that he brings to this music a technique perfectly adapted to Rachmaninov's way of writing for the piano in these works, a good illustration being Op. 23 No. 9, which is an *étude* rather than a prelude. The Sonata also receives a magnificent performance, though one whose recorded sound is less sumptuous than that of the *Preludes*. These two CDs of Ashkenazy's are unlikely to be surpassed in terms of sheer mastery of this composer's music.

Additional recommendations ...

24 Preludes — B flat major, Op. 23 No. 2; G minor, Op. 23 No. 5; C minor, Op. 23 No. 7; C major, Op. 32 No. 1; B flat minor, Op. 32 No. 2. ***Tchaikovsky.*** *Piano Concerto No. 1 in B flat minor.* **Sviatoslav Richter** (pf); **Vienna Symphony Orchestra/Herbert von Karajan.** DG Galleria 419 068-2GGA — 50m ADD 8/87

24 Preludes. **Peter Katin** (pf). Olympia OCD110 — 2 1h 20m ADD 10/87

24 Preludes — C sharp minor, Op. 3 No. 2; B flat major, Op. 23 No. 2; G minor, Op. 23 No. 5; B minor, Op. 32 No. 10; D flat major, Op. 32 No. 13. Piano Concerto No. 3 in D minor, Op. 30. **Vladimir Ashkenazy** (pf); **London Symphony Orchestra/André Previn.** Decca Ovation 417 764-2DM — 1h 10m ADD 10/88 £

Rachmaninov. The bells, Op. 35[a]. Vocalise, Op. 34 No. 14[b]. ***Tchaikovsky.*** Romeo and Juliet (orch. Taneyev) — duet[ac]. Festival Coronation March in D major. [abc]**Suzanne Murphy** (sop); [ab]**Keith Lewis** (ten); [a]**David Wilson-Johnson** (bar); **Scottish National** [a]**Chorus and Orchestra/Neeme Järvi.** Chandos CHAN8476. Notes and English texts included.

1h 3m DDD 2/87

Rachmaninov had grown up in a land where different kinds of church bells were often heard, and their sound evoked in him vivid childhood memories. Edgar Allan Poe's evocation of four human states and their bell connotations seemed to Rachmaninov an ideal basis for a four-part choral symphony. This is well realized by Järvi, though perhaps the urgency of the "Loud Alarum Bells" could be expressed more vehemently. The soloists are not ideal, but a rich, atmospheric recording provides a suitable vehicle for some lusty though well-disciplined choral singing. *Vocalise* is reasonably well sung, as is the Tchaikovsky *Romeo and Juliet* duet. After Tchaikovsky's death Taneyev discovered and then put together sketches for the operatic duet recorded here: no doubt he was aided by the fact that the duet re-uses material from the Fantasy overture. *The Festival Coronation March* was written to celebrate the 1883 crowning of Tsar Alexander III.

Additional recommendation ...

The bells[a]. ***Prokofiev.*** *Alexander Nevsky[b].* [a]**Sheila Armstrong** (sop); [a]**Anna Reynolds** (mez); [a]**Robert Tear** (ten); [a]**John Shirley-Quirk** (bar); **London Symphony Chorus and Orchestra/André Previn.** EMI Studio CDM7 63114-2 — 1h 18m ADD 10/89 £

Rachmaninov. Vespers, Op. 37. **Corydon Singers/Matthew Best.** Hyperion CDA66460. Text and translation included. Recorded in 1990.

lh 6m DDD 7/91

Rachmaninov's piano concertos and solo pieces are among the most popular of classical works, but he covered a wider range than this and his setting of the Vespers (or to use his own title, *All-night vigil*) has long been admired by the few outside Russia who knew it. It uses a liturgical text of the Russian Church for the services of Vespers (starting at sunset), Matins and The First Hour (Prime), and is deeply religious in feeling, for although the composer did not always adhere to the faith of his childhood he was married in church and thought much about the beliefs of his forefathers. After he wrote this work in a mere two weeks of 1915, one of his friends said that basses who could sing a low C, to say nothing of the B flat at the end of the fifth section, "were as rare as asparagus at Christmas" and that was in Russia, famous for its low basses! Nevertheless, Matthew Best and his Corydon Singers rise (or rather fall) splendidly to this occasion, and overall their style, tonal quality and pronunciation are alike convincingly authentic, with fine alto and tenor soloists; indeed, hearing John Bowen in the *Nyne Otpushchaeshi* ("Nunc dimittis") one could imagine oneself at a real Orthodox service, especially as the recording was made in a church. There's an excellent booklet note and the text is given in a transliteration from the original Cyrillic script into our own Roman alphabet, with an English translation. This is music of spiritual beauty that fully embodies the Russian Orthodox saying that "the mind should enter the heart".

Additional recommendation ...

St Petersburg Cappella/Vladislav Chernushenko. CdM Russian Season LDC288 050 — lh 2m DDD 5/93

Further listening ...

THE COMPLETE RECORDINGS. [a]**Fritz Kreisler** (vn); [b]**Sergey Rachmaninov** (pf); **Philadelphia Orchestra/**[c]**Leopold Stokowski,** [d]**Eugene Ormandy,** [e]**Sergey Rachmaninov.** RCA Victor Gold Seal mono 09026 61265-2 (10-CD set reissued from recordings dating from 1919-42, 3/93).

Rachmaninov. Piano Concertos[b] — No. 1 in F sharp minor, Op. 1[d]; No. 2 in C minor, Op. 18[c]; No. 3 in D minor, Op. 30[d]; No. 4 in G minor, Op. 40[d]. Rhapsody on a Theme of Paganini, Op. 43[bc]. The isle of the dead, Op. 29[e]. Vocalise, Op. 34 No. 14[e]. Symphony No. 3 in A minor, Op. 44[e]. *Solo piano works*[b] — Daisies. 9 Etudes-tableaux, Op. 33 — No. 2 in C major; No. 7 in E flat major. 9 Etudes-tableaux, Op. 39 — No. 6 in A minor. Lilacs (two versions, recorded in 1923 and 1942). 6 Moments musicaux, Op. 16 — Allegretto. 5 Morceaux de fantaisie, Op. 3 — No. 5, Sérénade in B flat minor. 7 Morceaux de salon, Op. 10 — No. 5, Humoresque in G major. Oriental Sketch in B flat major. Polka de W.R. (three versions, recorded in 1919, 1921 and 1928). *24 Preludes* — C sharp minor, Op. 3 No. 2 (three versions, recorded in 1919, 1921 and 1928); G minor, Op. 23 No. 5; G flat major, Op. 23 No. 10; E major, Op. 32 No. 3; G major, Op. 32 No. 5; F minor, Op. 32 No. 6; G sharp minor, Op. 32 No. 12. *Coupled with* ***Beethoven.*** Sonata for Violin and Piano No. 8 in G major, Op. 30 No. 3[ab]. 32 Variations on an original theme in C minor, WoO80[b]. ***Schubert.*** Sonata for Violin and Piano in A major (Duo), D574[ab]. ***Grieg.*** Sonata for Violin and Piano No. 3 in C minor, Op. 45[ab]. ***Schumann.*** Carnaval, Op. 9[b]. ***Chopin.*** Piano Sonata No. 2 in B flat minor, Op. 35[b]. *Also includes solo piano works by* ***Bach, Beethoven, Bizet, Borodin, Chopin, Daquin, Debussy, Dohnányi, Gluck, Grieg, Handel, Henselt, Kreisler, Liszt, Mendelssohn, Moszkowski, Mozart, Mussorgsky, Paderewski, Rimsky-Korsakov, Saint-Saëns, D. Scarlatti, Schubert, Schumann, Scriabin, J. Strauss II and Tchaikovsky.***

Six Songs, Op. 4 — No. 1, Oh no, I beg you, forsake me not; No. 3, In the silence of the secret night; No. 4, Sing not to me, beautiful maiden. *Six Songs, Op. 8* — No. 5, The dream. *12 Songs, Op. 14* — No. 9, She is as lovely as the noon. *12 Songs, Op. 21* —No. 6, Fragment from Musset. *15 Songs, Op. 26* — No. 2, He took all from me; No. 6, Christ is risen; No. 13, When yesterday we met. *Coupled with* ***Tchaikovsky.*** *Six Songs, Op. 6* — No. 4, A tear trembles; No. 6, None but the lonely heart. *Six Songs, Op. 25* — No. 1, Reconciliation. *Six Songs, Op. 28* — No. 6, The fearful minute. *Six Songs, Op. 38* — No. 1, Don Juan's Serenade. *12 Songs, Op. 60*

— No. 4, The nightingale; No. 11, Exploit. *Six Songs, Op. 63* — No. 2, I opened the window. *Six Songs, Op. 73* — No. 6, Again, as before, alone. **Dmitri Hvorostovsky** (bar); **Oleg Boshniakovich** (pf). Philips 432 119-2PH (10/91).

Joseph Raff

Swiss/German 1822-1882

Suggested listening ...

Symphonies — No. 3 in F major, Op. 153, "Im Walde". Overtures to Shakespeare's plays — Romeo and Juliet (ed. MacDowell). Abends-Rhapsodie, Op. 163*b*. **Philharmonia Orchestra/Francesco D'Avalos.** ASV CDDCA793 (10/92).

Symphonies — No. 8 in A major, Op. 205, "Frühlingsklänge"; No. 9 in E minor, Op. 208, "Im Sommer". **Košice State Philharmonic Orchestra/Urs Schneider.** Marco Polo 8 223362 (11/92).

Priaulx Rainier

South African 1903-1986

NEW REVIEW

Rainier. String Quartet[a]. Quanta[b]. String Trio[b]. Ploërmel[c]. [a]**Edinburgh Quartet** (Miles Baster, Peter Markham, vns; Michael Beeston, va; Mark Bailey, vc); [b]**Redcliffe Ensemble** (Robert Canter, ob; Nicholas Ward, vn; Richard Muncey, va; Gillian Thoday, vc); [c]**Royal Northern College of Music Wind Ensemble/Timothy Reynish.** Redcliffe Recordings RR007. Recorded in 1991.

1h DDD 11/92 

Priaulx Rainier was a composer of great gifts and original vision who never received the recognition she deserved. She was a late developer, in her earlier years not very prolific (because she had to work for her living), she followed no 'ism' and was a member of no school; much of her music is difficult to perform. The fact that she was a woman, at a time when women composers were an exotic and suspicious rarity, can't have helped. Even her name and nationality (she was born on the borders of Natal and Zululand) may have told against her. You could hardly choose a better work than *Ploërmel* to discover her quality. It's a vivid, clamorous piece for wind and percussion, suggested by the bells and the stained-glass of a church in Brittany, but there's a sense of dazzling sunlight, too, bringing with it perhaps recollections of Africa, as well as a solemn, chorale-like refrain that evokes antiquity and maybe the presence in the background of the sea. But it isn't an 'impressionist' piece; it's hard-edged, brightly coloured, gripping both as argument and as sound. The much earlier String Quartet is already assured in its command of a highly original language, which is refined and developed in the other two chamber pieces. Lyricism is stripped to the bone; every note works for its living; elegantly bare lines and subtle harmonic tensions build a powerful sense of movement and cumulation. The music is austere but passionate and exhilarating. An important rediscovery, all the more valuable for the excellence of these performances and the clarity of the recording.

Stěpán Rak

Czechoslovakian 1945-

Suggested listening ...

Guitar Works — First Love. Hiroshima. Danza Mauretana. Cry of the guitar. Hora/Czardas. Remembering Prague. The Czech Chorale. Pavanne. **Stěpán Rak** (gtr). Chandos CHAN8622 (9/88).

David Raksin

American 1912-

Suggested listening ...

Film Scores — Laura. Forever Amber — Suite. The Bad and the Beautiful — suite. **New Philharmonia Orchestra/David Raksin.** RCA Victor GD81490 (6/90).

Jean-Philippe Rameau

French 1683-1764

NEW REVIEW

Rameau. LES PALADINS — Suite. **Orchestra of the Age of Enlightenment/Gustav Leonhardt.** Philips 432 968-2PH. Recorded in 1991.

lh 4m DDD 9/92

Les Paladins was Rameau's last opera to be presented by the Paris Académie Royale de Musique. First staged in 1760 it ran for only 15 performances after which, as far as we know, the work was not seen again until a revival in Lyon in 1967. The Suite on this disc includes virtually all the purely instrumental numbers from the opera and these are played with panache by the Orchestra of the Age of Enlightenment under Gustav Leonhardt's direction. There are 24 items in all but not for a moment does the ear tire of Rameau's distinctive and subtle instrumental palette. Indeed, his wonderful sense of orchestral colour makes one regret that he never harnessed his genius to the emerging early classical symphony. It is a pity with programmes of this kind, however, that the dances are not punctuated by a handful of vocal airs. Such 'concerts', in which airs and dances from a particular work were intermingled were much favoured in Rameau's lifetime and those of *Les Paladins* are of a high order. The lucid textures, understanding of idiom and technical fluency are but three virtues of this performance; and, as always, we are left wondering at Rameau's deft handling of piccolo and bassoon parts, a beautiful example of which occurs in the wistful "Menuets en Rondeau".

NEW REVIEW

Rameau. Pièces de clavecin en concerts. **Ryo Terakado** (vn); **Kaori Uemura** (va da gamba); **Christophe Rousset** (hpd). Harmonia Mundi HMC90 1418. Recorded in 1992.

lh 14m DDD 4/93

Although Rameau went to some pains to demonstrate that his *Pièces de clavecin en concerts* could be played as harpsichord solos they are nevertheless ensemble pieces *par excellence.* There are five suites, each movement of which contains a fully written out harpsichord part with additional parts for violin or flute, bass viol or second violin. These performances have throughout favoured two violins, bass viol and, of course, harpsichord. Any initial disappointment concerning the absence of a flute, which does indeed express the mood of this music uncommonly well, is soon dispelled by the sheer excellence of the string playing. It is agile, warm in sound and expressive and the artists, furthermore, listen carefully to what the harpsichord is doing, taking their cue from this most important part of the texture. Christophe Rousset himself is impressive, making those subtle and discreet gestures so much a characteristic of French baroque style. Unlike any rival recording of these pieces, Rousset also plays the versions for solo harpsichord which Rameau included in the 1741 publication in addition to those *en concerts*. These artists, in short, are up to all the tricks of the French baroque trade, so-to-speak, and the results are immensely enjoyable. Fine recorded sound.

Additional recommendation ...

Masahiro Arita (fl); **Natsumi Wakamatsu** (vn); **Wieland Kuijken** (va da gamba); **Chiyoko Arita** (hpd). Denon Aliare CO-79045 — lh 8m DDD 10/92

Rameau. HARPSICHORD WORKS. **Christophe Rousset** (hpd). L'Oiseau-Lyre 425 886-2OH2. Recorded in 1989.
Premier livre de pièces de clavecin. Pièces de clavecin en concerts. Nouvelles suites de pièces de clavecin. Les petits marteaux de M Rameau. La Dauphine.

② 2h 9m DDD 12/91 

Christophe Rousset's recording of Rameau's solo harpsichord music outdistances the competitors currently available on CD in the UK. Rousset does not include everything that Rameau wrote for the instrument but he does play all the music contained in the principal collections of 1706, 1724 and *c.*1728 as well as *La Dauphine*. Rousset's phrasing is graceful and clearly articulated, the inflexions gently spoken and the rhythmic pulse all that one might wish for. Tempos are, for the most part, well-judged and the playing admirably attentive to detail and delightfully animated. Only occasionally does Rousset perhaps just miss the mark with speeds that are uncomfortably brisk and lacking that choreographic poise which is such a vital ingredient in French baroque music. But Rousset at his strongest is irresistible and this is how we find him in "Les niais de Sologne" and its variations, the reflective "L'entretien des Muses", the animated "Les cyclopes", "La poule", "L'enharmonique" and the dazzling A minor Gavotte and variations. In these and in many other of the pieces, too, Rousset's impeccable taste and seemingly effortless virtuosity provide the listener with constant and intense delight. The quality of the recording is ideal as are the two instruments which Rousset has chosen to play.

Additional recommendations ...
Nouvelles suites de pièces de clavecin — A minor. Pièces de clavècin — Suite in E minor. **Trevor Pinnock.** CRD3310 — 52m ADD 8/88
Premier livre de pièces de clavecin — Suite in A minor. La Dauphine. Cinq pièces pour clavecin seull. Pièces de clavecin en concerts. La pantomime. **Trevor Pinnock.** CRD3320 — 43m ADD 8/88
Pièces de clavecin — Suite in D minor/major. Nouvelles suites de pièces de clavecin — G major/minor. **Trevor Pinnock.** CRD3330 — 52m ADD 8/88

Rameau. LES INDES GALANTES — *Prologue:* **Claron McFadden** (sop) Hébé; **Jérôme Corréas** (bar) Bellone; **Isabelle Poulenard** (sop) L'Amour. *Le Turc généreux:* **Nicolas Rivenq** (bass) Osman; **Miriam Ruggieri** (sop) Emilie; **Howard Crook** (ten) Valère. *Les Incas du Pérou:* **Bernard Delétré** (bass) Huascar; **Poulenard** (Phanie); **Jean-Paul Fouchécourt** (ten) Carlos. *Les fleurs:* **Fouchécourt** (Tacmas); **Corréas** (Ali); **Sandrine Piau** (sop) Zaïre; **Noémi Rime** (sop) Fatime. *Les sauvages:* **Rivenq** (Adario); **Crook** (Damon); **Delétré** (Don Alvar); **McFadden** (Zima); **Les Arts Florissants/William Christie.** Harmonia Mundi HMC90 1367/9. Notes, text and translation included.

③ 3h 23m DDD 2/91

Les Indes galantes was Rameau's first *opéra-ballet*. He completed it in 1735 when it was performed at the Académie Royale in Paris. *Opéra-ballet* usually consisted of a prologue and anything between three and five entrées or acts. There was no continuously developing plot but instead various sections might be linked by a general theme, often hinted at in the title. Such is the case with *Les indes galantes* whose linking themes derives from a contemporary taste for the exotic and the unknown. Following a prologue come four entrées, "Le Turc généreux", "Les Incas du Pérou", "Les fleurs" and "Les sauvages". William Christie and Les Arts Florissants give a characteristically warm-blooded performance of one of Rameau's most approachable and endearing stage works. Christie's control of diverse forces — his orchestra consists of some 46 players — his dramatic pacing of the music, his recognition of Rameau's uniquely distinctive instrumental palette and his feeling for gesture and rhythm contribute towards making this a lively and satisfying performance. The choir is alert and well-disciplined and the orchestra a worthy partner in respect of clear textures and technical finesse; this can be readily appreciated in the splendid, spaciously laid out and tautly constructed orchestral Chaconne which concludes the work. The booklet contains full texts in French, English and German and the music is recorded in a sympathetic acoustic.

Rameau. PLATEE. **Gilles Ragon** (ten) Platée; **Jennifer Smith** (sop) La Folie, Thalie; **Guy de Mey** (ten) Thespis, Mercure; **Vincent le Texier** (bass-bar) Jupiter, A satyr; **Guillemette Laurens** (mez) Junon; **Bernard Deletré** (bass) Cithéron, Momus; **Véronique Gens** (sop) L'Amour, Clarine; **Michel Verschaeve** (bass) Momus; **Françoise Herr Vocal Ensemble; Musiciens du Louvre/Marc Minkowski.** Erato MusiFrance 2292-45028-2. Notes, text and translation included. Recorded in 1988.

② 2h 15m DDD 9/90

The *comédie-lyrique, Platée* is one of Rameau's masterpieces. It dates from 1745 when it was performed at Versailles as part of the celebrations for the Dauphin's marriage to the Infanta Maria-Theresa of Spain. The story concerns Platée, a nymph of unprepossessing appearance who is the butt of a cruel joke which leads her to believe that she will be the bride of Jupiter, no less. The theme may appear heartless but the music most certainly is not, and the charades, disguises and comic figures, evoking Carnival spirit, provides Rameau with almost unparalleled opportunities to display his unique genius as an orchestrator. There is hardly a weak moment in the score and anyone hitherto intimidated by this giant of the French baroque will find in *Platée* an enchanting introduction to Rameau's music. The performance under Marc Minkowski's direction is full of life and mischievous little insights. The solo cast is strong with Gilles Ragon in the high tenor travesti role of Platée and Jennifer Smith dazzlingly virtuosic and high-spirited as La Folie. This is, in short, a robust and well-paced account of a captivating work. The score is presented without cuts and with only a very few repeats omitted. The recorded sound is bright and effective and the accompanying booklet contains full texts in French, English and German.

NEW REVIEW

Rameau. PYGMALION. **Howard Crook** (ten) Pygmalion; **Agnès Mellon** (sop) Céphise; **Donatienne Michel-Dansac** (sop) Statue; **Sandrine Piau** (sop) Amour.
Rameau. NELEE ET MYRTHIS. **Agnès Mellon** (sop) Myrthis; **Jérôme Corréas** (bass) Nélée; **Françoise Semellaz** (sop) Corinne; **Donatienne Michel-Dansac, Caroline Pelon** (sops) Argive Maidens; **Les Arts Florissants Chorus and Orchestra/William Christie.** Harmonia Mundi HMC90 1381. Notes, texts and translations included. Recorded in 1991.

1h 18m DDD 7/92

Pygmalion is a self-contained *acte de ballet* and is perhaps Rameau's most alluring piece in this form. It was written during the late 1740s when the composer's creative powers were at a peak. The high tenor role of Pygmalion himself is a demanding one which few singers can perform without a hint of vocal strain. Howard Crook succeeds admirably, sounding comfortable in the highest reaches of his tessitura, and conveying his passionate responses to the statue, which he has brought to life, with finely controlled, touching declamation. He is supported by an equally strong cast of soloists with Agnès Mellon as the disenchanted Céphise and Sandrine Piau as an alluring Amour. The other work on the disc, *Nélée et Myrthis* is also an *acte de ballet* which here receives its first performance on disc. This is another love story but this time set at the Argive Games. The two sopranos, Agnès Mellon and Françoise Semellaz are well contrasted, allowing for plenty of character definition; and the *sportif* Nélée is agilely sung by Jérôme Corréas. The instrumentalists of Les Arts Florissants are on splendid form, bringing Rameau's colourful orchestration to life with vivacity and an informed sense of style under William Christie's assured direction. This issue is a considerable success and lovers of Rameau's music will be delighted to add a new title to their shelves.

Additional recommendation ...
Pygmalion. **Soloists; Paris Chapelle Royale Chorus; La Petite Bande/Gustav Leonhardt.** Deutsche Harmonia Mundi Editio Classica GD77143 — 47m ADD 7/90

Rameau. ZOROASTRE. **John Elwes** (ten) Zoroastre; **Greta de Reyghere** (sop) Amélite; **Mieke van der Sluis** (sop) Erinice; **Agnès Mellon** (sop) Céphie; **Gregory Reinhart** (bass) Abramane; **Jacques Bona** (bar) Oramasés, Voice from the Underworld; **Michel Verschaeve** (bass) Zopire; **François Fauché** (bass) Narbanor; **Philippe Cantor** (ten) God of Revenge;

Ghent Collegium Vocale; La Petite Bande/Sigiswald Kuijken. Deutsche Harmonia Mundi Editio Classica GD77144. Notes, text and translation included. From HM1999813 (5/84). Recorded in 1983.

③ 3h 4m ADD 7/90 

Zoroastre was first performed in Paris in 1749 and was Rameau's penultimate serious opera or *tragédie en musique*. It was fairly well received but not without criticism concerning, above all, the librettist, Cahusac's text. When the work was revived in 1756 shifts of emphasis were made within the plot and it is this later version which is performed here. The story deals with the conflict between Light (Good) and Darkness (Evil) central to Zoroastrianism. Rameau brings to life the chief protagonists Zoroastre and Abramane with consummate skill and his characteristic feeling for colour is seldom absent from the many fine choruses, airs and instrumental dances. John Elwes (tenor) sings the title role with a firm grasp of the French baroque idiom, while Gregory Reinhart (bass) makes a formidable opponent in the person of Abramane with clear diction and a commanding vocal presence. The three principal female roles are sung with equal assurance though their voices are perhaps insufficiently distinctive from one another to make the strong contrasts implicit in their characters. Agnès Mellon as the innocent Céphie is, nonetheless, a particularly happy piece of casting. Sigiswald Kuijken directs the performance with insight into and affection for Rameau's subtle art and the recording comes with an informative booklet in French, English and German.

Further listening ...

Hippolyte et Aricie — orchestral suite. **La Petite Bande/Sigiswald Kuijken.** Deutsche Harmonia Mundi Editio Classica GD77009 (7/90).

Abaris (Les Boréades) — *tragédie lyrique:* Orchestral Suite. Dardanus — *tragédie en musique.* **Eighteenth Century Orchestra/Frans Brüggen.** Philips 420 240-2PH (11/87).

Castor et Pollux — *tragédie en musique.* **Soloists; Les Arts Florissants Chorus and Orchestra/William Christie.** Harmonia Mundi HMC90 1435/7.

Maurice Ravel

French 1875-1937

NEW REVIEW

Ravel. PIANO CONCERTOS AND ORCHESTRAL WORKS. [a]**Pascal Rogé** (pf); **Montreal Symphony Chorus and Orchestra/Charles Dutoit.** Decca Ovation 421 458-2DM4. Boléro. Alborada del gracioso. Rapsodie espagnole. La valse (all from SXDL7559, 9/82). Ma mère l'oye — ballet. Pavane pour une infante défunte. Le tombeau de Couperin. Valses nobles et sentimentales (all from 410 254-1DH, 8/84). Piano Concerto in G major[a]. Piano Concerto for the left hand[a]. Menuet antique. Une barque sur l'océan. Fanfare from "L'Eventail de Jeanne" (all from SXDL7592, 8/83). Daphnis et Chloé — ballet (from SXDL7526, 6/81).

④ 3h 50m DDD 

Ravel's orchestral music, during the eight-year span of this *Guide*, has had more than its fair share of claimants for an entry. Yet in every edition, three of these four discs have consistently remained top recommendations (the fourth disc was, and still is, equally worthy of inclusion, and is newly reviewed below), and Decca have conveniently gathered together their four discs (in their original format) into this mid-price box. The survey turns out to be not absolutely complete, as Dutoit omitted the early *Shéhérazade* Overture (not a serious loss) and the violin work *Tzigane*, but there is, to date, no comparably comprehensive set of Ravel's orchestral music. It is, of course, possible to build a satisfying Ravel library from different sources, but that would bring unavoidable duplication of repertoire. Yet collections like this one, however convenient and financially attractive, are rarely consistent in quality. This is that rare case: not one of these recordings is seriously outclassed, either interpretatively or sonically. Dutoit and his

Montreal orchestra are superb stylists; Ravel was just as much of a musical magpie as Stravinsky, with few historical, contemporary, or popular styles remaining exempt from a sophisticated Ravelian transformation (in some works they rub shoulders, for example, the *Valses nobles et sentimentales*). Dutoit ensures that the styles register, but without labouring the point — the result is always pure Ravel. There is also a consistent elegance, both of execution and expression, though Dutoit has a cunning (or sixth sense) in knowing when to let the players off the leash, and by how much (the G major Piano Concerto abounds in examples). A balletic stance goes hand in hand with rare departures from Ravel's suggestions of pace; for example, the languorous *Rapsodie espagnole* "Prélude" is kept on its toes (even this atmospheric nocturne is a slow dance), and the virtuosity of his orchestra allows him to take the mercurial "Prélude" to *Le tombeau de Couperin* at Ravel's marking, without loss of composure. One radical departure from the score is his slow tempo for the strings' melody as we enter the "Jardin féerique" in *Ma mère l'oye*, but even the most fastidious Ravelian will surely succumb to the rapt beauty of the result. Ravel, the time traveller, from the childhood, fairy-tale world of *Ma mère l'oye* to *Le tombeau de Couperin*'s homage to the French Baroque, also benefits from an acoustic setting where space can add an extra dimension, a depth for, say, the horn fanfares at the "once upon a time" start of *Ma mère l'oye* or the last post resonances that the trumpet imparts in the Trio of *Le tombeau*'s Minuet. St Eustache in Montreal has just such an acoustic, and nowhere is it put to better use than in *Daphnis*, where the perspective laid out by the different planes draws you in and envelops you. Unlike so many recordings made in churches these days, there's no blurring of detail, or ungainly weight in *fortissimos*; and microphone placement gives a discreet presence to all that glitters. The only possible causes for concern may be the gremlin in the machine that brings some momentary (and hardly serious) distortion near the end of *Boléro*; and there is a general, prudent tailoring of extreme *fortissimos* (compared to Rattle's recent recordings, for example), but many will regard that as an attribute. No, after almost ten years, Dutoit's Ravel firmly remains *the* reference.

Additional recommendations ...

Piano Concerto in G major. **Rachmaninov.** *Piano Concerto No. 4 in G minor, Op. 40.* **Arturo Benedetti Michelangeli** (pf); **Philharmonia Orchestra/Ettore Gracis.** EMI CDC7 49326-2 — 47m ADD 9/88 ▲

Piano Concerto in G major. Gaspard de la nuit. Sonatine. **Martha Argerich** (pf); **Berlin Philharmonic Orchestra/Claudio Abbado.** DG Galleria 419 062-2GGA — 54m ADD 12/87

Piano Concerto in G major. Piano Concerto for the left hand. **Louis Lortie** (pf); **London Symphony Orchestra/Rafael Frühbeck de Burgos.** Chandos CHAN8773 — 57m DDD 1/90

Piano Concerto in G major. **Gershwin.** *Piano Concerto* in F major. **Bournemouth Symphony Orchestra/Andrew Litton** (pf). Virgin Classics VJ7 59693-2 — 57m DDD 9/90

NEW REVIEW

Ravel. PIANO CONCERTOS AND ORCHESTRAL WORKS. [a]**Pascal Rogé** (pf); **Montreal Symphony Orchestra/Charles Dutoit.** Decca 410 230-2DH. From SXDL7592 (8/83). Recorded in 1982.

Piano Concerto in G major[a]. Piano Concerto for the left hand[a]. Menuet antique. Une barque sur l'océan. Fanfare from "L'éventail de Jeanne".

57m DDD 3/84

Given Ravel's early mastery of the piano, it's surprising that he waited until he was in his late fifties before writing a piano concerto; and then, starting in 1929, he wrote two, in tandem! The year before, Ravel had toured America, where jazz from the likes of King Oliver and Paul Whiteman was rampant, and both concertos reflect the encounter. The diverting G major Concerto often echoes Gershwin in its 'cool' first movement third theme and clarinet shrieks in the finale (surrounding a genuinely cool, limpid slow movement, as far removed as possible from the world of jazz). There's a 'cake-walk' *allegro* section two-thirds of the way through the Left-hand Concerto, but this is more nightmare than night club (eventually, the whole passage struts menacingly towards you); indeed, this Concerto is a much darker, deeper work altogether, full of Lisztian grandiloquence and expressionist threat. Rogé's freewheeling manner is ideal for the seemingly improvised passages of both concertos. And there's flamboyance and pianistic thunder aplenty for the Left-hand Concerto's grander gestures; a good sense of line, too, in the pacing and linking of this single-movement work's various sections, for which Dutoit deserves equal credit. As ever, he and his orchestra manage powerful expression with refinement; and the Decca engineers, clarity with atmosphere.

Ravel. VOCAL AND ORCHESTRAL WORKS. [a]**Maria Ewing** (mez); **City of Birmingham Symphony Orchestra/Simon Rattle.** EMI CDC7 54204-2. Text and translation included. Recorded in 1989.
Fanfare pour "L'éventail de Jeanne". Shéhérazade[a]. Alborada del gracioso. Miroirs — La vallée des cloches (arr. Grainger). Ma mère l'oye. La valse.

1h 15m DDD 8/91

A paean of British critical praise greets almost every new issue from this team with monotonous regularity, so it is gratifying, in this instance, to note *Diapason*'s (the French contemporary to *Gramophone*) reviewer finding Rattle's *Ma mère l'oye* of a "striking delicacy" and "releasing an indescribable emotion" (apologies to Rémy Louis for a wholly inadequate translation). In the past there have been instances of Rattle's intensive preparation for setting down a much loved masterpiece precluding spontaneity in the end result. Not here. Along with the customary refinement and revelation of texture, there is a sense of Rattle gauging the very individual fantasy worlds of this varied programme with uncanny precision: an aptly childlike wonder for *Ma mère l'oye*'s fairy tale illustrations; the decadence and decay that drive *La valse* to its inevitable doom; and the sensual allure of the Orient in *Shéhérazade* providing a vibrant backdrop for soprano Maria Ewing's intimate confessions. Space does not permit enthusing about the three shorter items that make up this indispensable (and generously filled) disc, recorded with stunning realism. Try it for yourself and marvel at the astonishing range of Ravel's imagination.

Additional recommendation ...
Shéhérazade[a]*. Vocalise en forme de habanera (orch. Hoerée)*[a]*. Alborada del gracioso. Boléro. La valse. Pavane pour une infante défunte.* [a]**Arleen Auger** (sop); **Philharmonia Orchestra/Libor Pešek.** Virgin Classics VC7 59235-2 — 1h 4m DDD 3/93

Ravel. ORCHESTRAL WORKS. **Montreal Symphony Orchestra/Charles Dutoit.** Decca 410 254-2DH. From 410 254-1DH (8/84).
Ma mère l'oye — ballet. Pavane pour une infante défunte. Le tombeau de Couperin. Valses nobles et sentimentales.

1h 7m DDD 11/84

There is no more magical score than Ravel's *Ma mère l'oye* ("Mother Goose"). It has the elegance and perfection of Mozart, yet the translucence of the scoring is a Ravelian hallmark. *Le tombeau de Couperin* also shows the composer at his most elegant. This neoclassical evocation again demonstrates an affinity with a different age from Ravel's own, yet the delicious orchestral colour essentially belongs to the twentieth century. The *Valses nobles et sentimentales*, more melodically diffuse, have comparable subtlety. This is a very different work from *La valse* and much more characteristic of the essence of the composer. The Montreal orchestra show a natural rapport with these scores and their playing is warmly sympathetic yet not indulgent, so that the delicacy of texture is never over-laden. It is difficult to think of many other discs where everything comes together so perfectly to serve the composer's inspiration.

Additional recommendations ...
Ma mère l'oye. ***Debussy.*** *La boîte à joujoux — ballet.* **Ulster Orchestra/Yan Pascal Tortelier.** Chandos CHAN8711 — 57m DDD 9/89
Ma mère l'oye. ***Bizet.*** *Symphony in C major.* **Scottish Chamber Orchestra/Jukka-Pekka Saraste.** Virgin Classics Virgo VJ7 59657-2 — 1h 4m DDD 12/91 £

Ravel. Daphnis et Chloé — ballet[a]. Rapsodie espagnole[b]. Pavane pour une infante défunte[b]. [a]**Chorus of the Royal Opera House, Covent Garden; London Symphony Orchestra/Pierre Monteux.** Decca Historic 425 956-2DM. Item marked [a] from SXL2164 (12/59), recorded in 1959, [b] SXL2312 (7/62), recorded in 1961.

lh 14m ADD 5/90

Diaghilev's ballet *Daphnis et Chloé*, based on a pastoral romance by the ancient Greek poet Longus, was first produced in June 1912, with Nijinsky and Karsavina in the title roles and choreography by Mikhail Fokine. Pierre Monteux conducted the first performance, and 47 years later he recorded his peerless interpretation for Decca. Though the Second Suite from the ballet is familiar to concert-goers and makes an effective piece in its own right, the full score, with wordless chorus, conveys still greater atmosphere and magic. No work of more sheer sensual beauty exists in the entire orchestral repertoire, and Monteux was its perfect interpreter. He conducts with a wonderful sense of clarity and balance: every important detail tells, and there is refinement of expression, yet inner strength too. The LSO play with superlative poetry and skill, and the chorus is magnificent in its tonal blend and colour. The *Rapsodie espagnole* and *Pavane* are also given ideal performances, and the recordings show off Decca's exceedingly high standards during the late 1950s and early 1960s.

Additional recommendations ...

Daphnis et Chloé. **Montreal Symphony Chorus and Orchestra/Charles Dutoit.** Decca 400 055-2DH — 56m DDD 3/83

Daphnis et Chloé — Suite No. Boléro. **Debussy.** *La mer. Prélude à l'après-midi d'un faune.* **Berlin Philharmonic Orchestra/Herbert von Karajan.** DG Galleria 427 250-2GGA — lh 4m ADD 7/89

Daphnis et Chloé[a]. **Roussel.** *Bacchus et Ariane — Ballet Suite No. 2*[b]. [a]**New England Conservatory Chorus;** [a]**Alumni Chorus; Boston Symphony Orchestra/Charles Munch.** RCA Victor Gold Seal [a]stereo/[b]mono GD60469 — lh llm ADD 12/91

Daphnis et Chloé. Boléro. **City of Birmingham Symphony Orchestra/Simon Rattle.** EMI CDC7 54303-2 — lh 14m DDD 6/92

Daphnis et Chloé. Rapsodie espagnole. Alborada del gracioso. Pavane pour une infante défunte. Le tombeau de Couperin. Valses nobles et sentimentales. Ma mère l'oye. **Geneva Motet Choir; Suisse Romande Orchestra/Ernest Ansermet.** Decca 425 997-2DM2 — 2h 16m ADD 9/92

Daphnis et Chloé. **London Symphony Chorus and Orchestra/Kent Nagano.** Erato 4509-91712-2 — 58m DDD 7/93

NEW REVIEW

Ravel. ORCHESTRAL WORKS. **Chicago Symphony Orchestra/Daniel Barenboim.** Erato 2292-45766-2. Recorded in 1991.

Daphnis et Chloé — Suite No. 2. Rapsodie espagnole. Pavane pour une infante défunte. Alborada del gracioso. Boléro.

lh 3m DDD 12/92 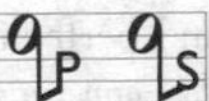

Some are undoubtedly going to find Barenboim's Ravel too (at times, self-consciously) beautiful. But make no mistake, this is a real showcase disc for Chicago and its new director. The flute solo in the "Pantomime" from *Daphnis* must be the slowest on disc, but this is unmistakably "un air mélancholique" as the drama demands; and the sustaining of the alto flute at the end of the solo, though unmarked, is sheer sorcery. Flutes are prominent in the Erato balance throughout *Daphnis*, as is the entire woodwind section as they reel and squeal in the final "Danse générale". Barenboim has grouped the remaining four items into "a kind of Spanish symphony", and sees to it that the many guitar-like effects (plucked strings) of these scores are picked out. Fritz Reiner, a famous predecessor in Chicago, is recalled in the very slow and atmospheric "Prélude" from the *Rapsodie espagnole*, though Reiner wouldn't have allowed the single lapse of ensemble in its last movement "Feria" (at 3'42") to pass. Elsewhere there is brilliance and precision aplenty, and the selective miking favoured by the engineers rarely impedes a rendering of the full orchestra with a natural spread and good depth.

Ravel. Alborada del gracioso. Rapsodie espagnole. La valse. Boléro. **Montreal Symphony Orchestra/Charles Dutoit.** Decca 410 010-2DH. From SXDL7559 (9/82). Recorded in 1982.

5lm DDD 8/83

Ravel's *Boléro* is now so popular and universally familiar that it is easy to forget its originality. Dutoit plays it magnetically as a steady, remorseless crescendo and its power and marvellous command of orchestral colour are freshly revealed. The glittering *Alborada del gracioso* and the sensuous and exciting *Rapsodie espagnole* readily demonstrate the special feeling French composers had for the Spanish idiom, with diaphanous textures to capture the sultry quality of the Mediterranean evening and offset the sparkle of the Flamenco dance rhythms. *La valse* begins in the mists and expands to a breathtaking climax with a vision of countless dancing couples whirling round in an intoxicating infinity of space; then cruelly and abruptly the imagery disintegrates into silence. This CD is a model of its kind while the music-making combines a feeling for spectacle with the utmost refinement of detail.

Additional recommendations ...

Alborada del gracioso. Rapsodie espagnole. Valses nobles et sentimentales. Pavane pour une infante défunte. **Debussy.** *Images.* **Chicago Symphony Orchestra/Fritz Reiner.** RCA GD60179 — lh 8m ADD 1/90

Alborada del gracioso. Rapsodie espagnole. La valse. Pavane pour une infante défunte. Le tombeau de Couperin. ***Ibert.*** *Escales.* **Detroit Symphony Orchestra/Paul Paray.** Mercury Living Presence 432 003-2MM — lh 7m ADD 4/91

Alborada del gracioso. Boléro. La valse. **Debussy.** *La mer. Prélude à l'après-midi d'un faune.* **Orchestre de Paris/Herbert von Karajan.** EMI CDM7 64357-2 — lh 15m ADD 11/92 £

Ravel. String Quartet in F major.
Vaughan Williams. On Wenlock Edge[ab]. String Quartet No. 1 in G minor. [a]**Philip Langridge** (ten); [b]**Howard Shelley** (pf); **Britten Quartet** (Peter Manning, Keith Pascoe, vns; Peter Lale, va; Andrew Shulman, vc). EMI CDC7 54346-2. Recorded 1990-91.

lh 18m DDD 2/92

This outstanding disc from the Britten Quartet brings together several works which share far more in common than one might at first imagine. Vaughan Williams spent a short study vacation in Paris during 1908 hoping, on his own admission, to acquire "a little French polish" from Ravel, who himself took part in the French première of his student's song cycle, *On Wenlock Edge*. Ravel's String Quartet receives a provocative, and yet totally convincing reading from the Britten Quartet, who choose to dwell upon the polarization of tonal and melodic content in this work to a greater degree than any of their rivals on disc, all of whom offer the more usual coupling in the shape of the Debussy Quartet. *On Wenlock Edge*, a setting of six poems selected from A.E. Housman's set of 63 poems, *A Shropshire Lad*, is heard here in a quite exceptional performance from the tenor, Philip Langridge, joined by pianist Howard Shelley and the Britten Quartet. Langridge recognizes the irony and understatement of Housman's verse, whilst exploiting its more sinister undertones with searching skill, as he does in the uncanny dialogue between the living and the dead, in "Is my team ploughing", bringing chilly pallor to his delivery of the opening stanza in particular. It would be difficult to match the communicative power of this performance even in the concert-hall. The Brittens also excel in a crystalline and devoted account of Vaughan Williams's underrated G minor Quartet, which sounds more than usually weighty and musically coherent in this fluid and sharply perceived reading. The technical aspects of the playing are second to none, while its added sensitivity contributes to an involving and frequently moving musical experience. The recorded sound is brilliant and immediate, and this disc is a clear triumph from every conceivable viewpoint!

Additional recommendations ...

String Quartet. **Debussy.** *String Quartet in G minor, Op. 10.* **Melos Quartet.** DG 419 750-2GH — 53m DDD 10/87

String Quartet. **Debussy.** *String Quartet.* **Quartetto Italiano.** Philips Silver Line 420 894-2PSL — 57m ADD 10/88

String Quartet. **Debussy.** *String Quartet.* **Dvořák.** *String Quartet No. 12 in F major, Op. 96, "American".* **Bartók Quartet.** Hungaroton White Label HRC122 — 1h 14m ADD 1/90 £
String Quartet. **Debussy.** *String Quartet.* **La Salle Quartet.** DG Galleria 435 589-2GGA — 52m ADD 9/92

NEW REVIEW

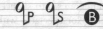

Ravel. COMPLETE PIANO WORKS. **Jean-Yves Thibaudet.** Decca 433 515-2DH2. Recorded in 1991.

Sérénade grotesque. Menuet antique. Pavane pour une infante défunte. Jeux d'eau. Sonatine. Miroirs. Gaspard de la nuit. Menuet sur le nom de Haydn. Valses nobles et sentimentales. Prélude. A la manière de Borodine. A la manière de Chabrier. Le tombeau de Couperin.

② 2h 10m DDD 11/92

Jean-Yves Thibaudet could hardly have chosen better for his first Decca solo album. Blessed with an innate musical elegance and quick-silver technique he compels one to reassess Ravel's elusive genius at every point; his sophisticated mix of archaism and modernity, of *tendresse* and malevolence. Few pianists have played "Scarbo" from *Gaspard de la nuit* with such immaculate dexterity or evoked his will-o'-the-wisp antics — now you see him, now you don't — with such luminous tone or pianistic cunning. His poetic delicacy is no less remarkable in Ravel's more amiable creations, in, for example, "La Vallée des cloches" from *Miroirs* or in the dawn freshness of the "Prélude" from *Le tombeau de Couperin.* And if you want a sense of his range, his capacity to capture Ravel's idiom in all its multi-faceted glory, then follow the *Sérénade grotesque* (an early example of Ravel's Hispanism) with the A minor *Prélude*, written for a Paris Conservatoire sight-reading test yet characterized by rare subtlety and transparency. Above all Thibaudet is sensitive to writing as fastidiously wrought as the finest jewellery. The recordings are of demonstration quality and so this two-disc set is a treasurable addition to the catalogue. All those listed below, together with this one, represent the *crème de la crème.*

Additional recommendations ...

Miroirs. Jeux. Pavane. Gaspard. **Vlado Perlemuter.** Nimbus NIM5005 — 59m AAD 1/84
Gaspard. **Prokofiev.** *Piano Sonata No. 6 in A major, Op. 82.* **Ivo Pogorelich.** DG 413 363-2GH *(See review under Prokofiev; refer to the Index to Reviews)* — 52m DDD 11/84
Gaspard. Pavane. Valses nobles. **Vladimir Ashkenazy.** Decca 410 255-2DH — ADD 6/85
Gaspard. Sonatine. Piano Concerto in G major[a]. **Martha Argerich;** [a]**Berlin Philharmonic Orchestra/Claudio Abbado.** DG Galleria 419 062-2GGA — 54m ADD 12/87
Le tombeau — Toccata. Coupled with works by **Debussy, Liszt** and **Scriabin. Emil Gilels.** Olympia mono OCD166 — 1h 12m AAD 12/88 ▲
Pavane. Le tombeau. Sérénade. Jeux. Valses nobles. La valse. **Louis Lortie.** Chandos CHAN8620 — 1h 6m DDD 5/89
Gaspard. Menuet antique. Menuet sur le nom de Haydn. A la manière de Borodine. A la manière de Chabrier. Prélude. Miroirs. Sonatine. **Louis Lortie.** Chandos CHAN8647 — 1h 14m DDD 10/89

Ravel. MUSIC FOR TWO PIANOS. **Louis Lortie, Hélène Mercier** (pfs). Chandos CHAN8905. Recorded in 1990.

Boléro. Introduction and Allegro. La valse. Ma mère l'oye. Rapsodie espagnole.

1h 5m DDD 3/91 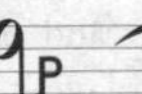

Ravel. MUSIC FOR TWO PIANOS. **Stephen Coombs, Christopher Scott** (pfs). Gamut Classics GAMCD517.

Frontispice. Introduction and Allegro. La valse. Rapsodie espagnole. Sites auriculaires — Entre cloches. Shéhérazade — Ouverture de féerie.

56m DDD 2/91

Louis Lortie is an excellent Ravel pianist and he and his fellow Canadian Hélène Mercier have played as a duo since their student days in Montreal. Their performance of *Ma mère l'oye* is as delicate and tender as befits a piece written for children, but it also has the passion which is also part of a child's world, not least in the deep sense of joyful wonder of the final movement called "The Fairy Garden", which opens up to our inner vision the kind of childhood paradise that for all but the rarest mortals is forever lost, like innocence, as we reach adulthood. The *Rapsodie espagnole* is also done with great refinement, and although some collectors might like it more overtly sensual this is a performance to place beside the more familiar orchestral version of the same music. So is the *Boléro* in Ravel's own two-piano transcription, for although the piece might seem to depend wholly on orchestral colour it comes off well when played as excitingly as this at a fairly taut tempo. Again, the *Introduction and Allegro* may seem to depend on the sound of a chamber ensemble including harp, but this keyboard transcription made by the composer is beautiful. The programme ends with an account of *La valse* which offers playing that can only be described in superlatives or in terms of Dionysiac frenzy; this is a glowing, sumptuous dream-turning-to-nightmare that should not be missed by anyone who cares about Ravel's music and yet again reveals what an extraordinarily unsettling masterpiece this is. The recording made in the Snape Maltings is outstanding, detailed yet atmospheric.

Stephen Coombs and Christopher Scott formed a duo in 1985 and their outstanding début recording of Debussy will be found elsewhere in the *Guide* (refer to the Index to Reviews). Here they turn their attention to Ravel, and the result is equally satisfying. They play with such style and sensitivity that the works in the composer's own piano transcriptions have more than documentary interest, while *Entre cloches* and *Frontispice* are original works for two pianos. One notes, however, that *Ma mère l'oye* is not here, and nor is *Boléro*; the latter work was recorded and edited, but finally the artists and producer decided that it did not succeed in keyboard form, which one may regret since other duos, like Lortie and Mercier, have recorded it successfully. The richly atmospheric yet delicate recording is another plus for this attractive disc.

NEW REVIEW

Ravel. Shéhérazade[a]. Deux mélodies hébraïques[a]. Trois poèmes de Stéphane Mallarmé[a]. **Berlioz.** Les nuits d'été, Op. 7[b]. **Suzanne Danco** (sop); [a]**Suisse Romande Orchestra/Ernest Ansermet;** [b]**Cincinnati Symphony Orchestra/Thor Johnson.** Decca 425 988-2DH. Notes, text and translation included. Items marked [a] from LXT5031 (7/55), recorded in 1954, [b] LXT2605 (10/51), recorded in 1951.

lh ADD

Though the *Guide* lists recommendations of more modern recordings of the Berlioz *Nuits d'été* and the Ravel *Shéhérazade* songs, space had to be found for this disc. Suzanne Danco not only possessed a soprano voice of unique shining purity, but every song bears witness to the beauty and clarity of diction, her natural ease with the language; and, above all, as the booklet writer remarks, to "her striving for the correct style and appropriate expression". Arguably the *Shéhérazade* songs respond to her innocent enthusiasm and sensitive colouring rather more than to Maria Ewing's overtly voluptuous relish (reviewed elsewhere in this section); and it's hard to believe that the Mallarmé settings, with their obscure but tantalizing imagery, are so difficult to perform, such is Danco's complete surety of pitch and line. The sound, from the early 1950s (stereo, excepting the Mallarmé settings and Berlioz songs), is orchestrally thin, but with a good dynamic range. Crucially, the voice itself is reproduced with full tone, a lovely bloom and crystalline clarity.

Additional recommendations ...

Shéhérazade[a]. **Berlioz:** *Les nuits d'été.* **Debussy:** *Trois chansons de Bilitis*[b]. **Poulenc:** *Banalities*[b] *— Chansons d'Orkenise; Hôtel. La courte paille*[b] *— Le carafon; La reine de coeur. Chansons villageoises*[b] *— Les gars qui vont à la fête. Deux poèmes de Louis Aragon*[b]. **Régine Crespin** (sop); [b]**John Wustman** (pf); [a]**Suisse Romande Orchestra/Ernest Ansermet.** Decca 417 813-2DH *(reviewed in the Collections section; refer to the Index to Reviews)* — lh 8m ADD 11/88
Shéhérazade. Deux mélodies hébraïques. Cinq mélodies populaires grecques. Vocalise en forme de Habanera. **Duparc.** *L'invitation au voyage. Au pays où se fait la guerre. La vie antérieure. Le manoir de Rosemonde. Phidylé. Chanson triste.* **Barbara Hendricks** (sop); **Lyon Opéra Orchestra/John Eliot Gardiner.** EMI CDC7 49689-2 — 56m DDD 4/89

Ravel. L'HEURE ESPAGNOLE. **Jane Berbié** (sop) Concepción; **Jean Giraudeau** (ten) Torquemada; **Gabriel Bacquier** (bar) Ramiro; **José van Dam** (bass-bar) Don Inigo Gomez; **Michel Sénéchal** (ten) Gonzalve; **French Radio National Orchestra/Lorin Maazel.** DG 423 719-2GH. Notes, text and translation included. From SLPM138 970 (10/65). Recorded in 1965.

46m ADD 3/89 

For genuinely witty operas *L'heure espagnole* is in a class of its own; and to do it justice it needs a conductor with an alert ear for all Ravel's minutely judged and ingeniously scored jests (the automata in the shop, the story of the toreador's watch, the jangling of the pendulum as the grandfather clock is hoisted on to the muleteer's brawny shoulder) and no conductor is more mentally alert than Maazel. It also requires a cast which relishes the verbal nuances and adopts the *quasi-parlando* style that the composer asked for; and these desiderata are met in this classic, and unequalled, 1965 performance. All the singers give excellent characterizations — Berbié as the frustrated and exasperated young wife, Bacquier as the simple, somewhat bemused muleteer who is happy to oblige, Sénéchal as the poet whose head is too far in the clouds to attend to practicalities, van Dam as the fatuous portly banker, and Giraudeau as the doddery old watchmaker who at the end shows an unexpectedly astute business sense. A delicious work, in a performance to savour.

Ravel. L'ENFANT ET LES SORTILEGES. **Françoise Ogéas** (sop) Child; **Jeanine Collard** (contr) Mother, Chinese cup, Dragonfly; **Jane Berbié** (sop) Sofa, She Cat, Squirrel, Shepherd; **Sylvaine Gilma** (sop) Fire, Princess, Nightingale; **Colette Herzog** (sop) Bat, Little Owl, Shepherdess; **Heinz Rehfuss** (bar) Armchair, Tree; **Camille Maurane** (bar) Grandfather Clock, Tom Cat; **Michel Sénéchal** (ten) Teapot, Little Old Man (Mr Arithmetic), Frog; **Chorus and Children's Voices of French Radio; French Radio National Orchestra/Lorin Maazel.** DG 423 719-2GH. Notes, text and translation included. From SLPM138675 (6/61). Recorded in 1960.

43m ADD 3/89 

This is a Desert Island Disc if ever there was one. Every musical and verbal point in Ravel's brilliantly ingenious, deliciously witty and entirely enchanting score is brought out by a well-nigh perfect cast, backed by orchestral playing of the first class; and the recording is as vivid as anyone could wish. The story is that of a petulant brat who breaks the china, pulls the cat's tail, pricks the pet squirrel with a pen-nib, puts the fire out by upsetting the kettle on it, tears the wallpaper and his books and snaps off the pendulum of the grandfather clock — only to find that all these come to life and turn on him. Their anger is appeased only when he tends the squirrel's paw; and finally the naughty child, having seen the error of his ways, falls tearfully into his mother's arms. Everyone will have their own favourite passages but the last pages of the opera, in particular, are hauntingly beautiful. An absolute gem of a disc.

Further listening ...

Violin Sonata. *Coupled with* ***Prokofiev.*** Violin Sonata No. 2 in D major, Op. 94a. ***Stravinsky.*** Divertimento. **Viktoria Mullova** (vn); **Bruno Canino** (pf). Philips 426 254-2PH (8/90).

Piano Trio. *Coupled with* ***Debussy.*** Premier Trio in G major. ***Fauré.*** Piano Trio in D minor, Op. 120. **Solomon Trio.** Pickwick IMP Masters MCD41 (7/92).

Thomas Ravenscroft

British c.1582-c.1635

Ravenscroft. THERE WERE THREE RAVENS. **Consort of Musicke/Anthony Rooley.** Virgin Classics Veritas VC7 59035-2. Texts included.

A Round of three Country dances in one. A wooing Song of a Yeoman of Kents Sonne. Browning Madame. The crowning of Belphebe. The Cryers Song of Cheape-Side. Laboravi in gemitu meo. The Marriage of the Frogge and the Mouse. Martin said to his man. Musing mine owne selfe all alone. Ne laeteris inimica mea. Of all the birds that ever I see. There were three ravens. Three blinde Mice. To morrow the Fox will come to towne. Wee be Souldiers three. The wooing of Hodge and Malkyn. Yonder comes a courteous knight. Instrumental works — Fancy No. 1. Fantasia No. 4. Viol Fancy a 5.

1h 1m DDD 8/91 

Thomas Ravenscroft was a learned musician (even a pedant in some respects) who is perhaps best known for his 1621 collection of psalms; and to illustrate that side of him this disc contains two deeply expressive Latin motets and some attractive and skilfully written fantasias for viols. However, as a likeable and lively-minded person, he also delighted in writing music for entertainment, "mirth and jocund melody", and in 1609 printed the first known collection in England of catches and rounds, under the title *Pammelia*. From this and two similar subsequent volumes the Consort of Musicke have made a selection which they themselves obviously thoroughly enjoyed performing and whose enjoyment is infectious. (The assumption of a variety of accents, from Cockney for a Cheapside crier's song to a Somerset-dialect wooing dialogue for once does not seem an irritating gimmick.) Anthony Rooley has skilfully arranged the programme to present a diversity of types, pace and scoring; but among the highlights here are the melancholy *Musing mine owne selfe all alone* and *There were three ravens* and the merry *The Marriage of the Frogge and the Mouse* and the saucy *Yonder comes a courteous knight*.

Key to Symbols

Bargains · *Quality of Sound* · *Discs worth exploring* · *Caveat emptor*

Quality of performance · *Basic library* · *Period performance*

Alan Rawsthorne

British 1905-1971

NEW REVIEW

Rawsthorne. Piano Concerto No. 2. Concerto for piano, strings and percussion No. 1. Concerto for Two Pianos[a]. **Geoffrey Tozer, [a]Tamara-Anna Cislowski** (pfs); **London Philharmonic Orchestra/Matthias Bamert.** Chandos CHAN9125. Recorded in 1992.

1h 3m DDD 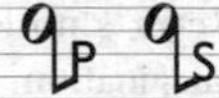

Since his death in 1971, the music of Alan Rawsthorne has largely disappeared from our concert-hall life, though there have been a handful of useful recordings, most notably a superb Lyrita coupling from 1977 (no longer available) of the marvellous *Symphonic Studies* (surely this underrated composer's masterpiece) and the First Symphony with the LPO under Sir John Pritchard which must make it to CD before too long. In the meantime, Chandos have stepped in with this outstanding new collection which contains at least one work of potentially widespread popular appeal, namely the Second Piano Concerto. Dedicated to Sir Clifford Curzon (who premièred the piece at the 1951 Festival of Britain), this is an impressively resourceful, impeccably crafted affair, containing more than its fair share of genuinely memorable tunes, not least in the hugely catchy finale. Its predecessor, from 1939, is similarly distinguished by first-rate craftsmanship: the toccata-like ebullience of its outer movements contrasts most satisfyingly with the grave beauty of the central *Chaconne*. Only the Concerto for Two Pianos proves an altogether tougher nut to crack: the concentration and restraint of the writing certainly command respect, if not immediate affection. Rawsthorne's music is superbly well served here. Geoffrey Tozer deserves the highest plaudits for his dazzling contribution throughout, and he is most sensitively partnered by Tamara-Anna Cislowski in the Double Concerto. Under Mathias Bamert a beautifully prepared LPO respond with palpable enthusiasm, whilst the Chandos engineers have excelled themselves once again — this immaculately balanced, ideally airy production is demonstration-worthy in every way. Do try this disc; you won't regret it!

Max Reger

German 1873-1916

Reger. Variations and Fugue on a Theme of J.A. Hiller, Op. 100. Eine Ballettsuite, Op. 130. **Bavarian Radio Symphony Orchestra/Sir Colin Davis.** Orfeo CO90841A. From SO90841A (2/85).

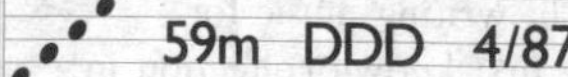

NEW REVIEW

Reger. Four Symphonic Poems after Arnold Böcklin, Op. 128. Variations and Fugue on a Theme of J.A. Hiller, Op. 100. **Royal Concertgebouw Orchestra/Neeme Järvi.** Chandos CHAN8794. Recorded in 1989.

1h 7m DDD 3/90 

Mention of Reger's name in 'informed' circles is likely to produce a conditioned reflex: "Fugue!". In his day he was the central figure of the 'Back to Bach' movement, but he was also a romantic who relished all the expressive potential of the enormous post-Wagnerian orchestra. Then came the slender acerbities of the next generation of neo-classicists, and Reger's backward glances were deemed inflated and in shocking taste. Until recently he has proved largely unexportable from his native Germany. Times are changing though, and collectors who respond to the musical ingenuity of Elgar's *Enigma* Variations should give Reger's *Hiller* Variations a try. As in his excellent disc of Reger's *Mozart* Variations reviewed below, Sir Colin Davis ensures sufficient contrast between the ravishingly scored slower variations and the bouncing contrapuntal energy and interplay of the faster ones. And the engineers avoid the danger of over-egging the pudding: the textures here are light, airy and transparent. In *Eine Ballettsuite* Reger wished "to write something infinitely graceful, subtle in tone, dainty musically and cobweb-fine". That he succeeded is a tribute, in no small measure, to the love and dedication (felt in every bar) of these Bavarian players.

Chandos, not surprisingly, exploit the open spaces of the Amsterdam Concertgebouw, forsaking some of the healthy transparency of the Orfeo disc for an extra spatial dimension; a more sumptuous glow. With Järvi's instinct for pacing in late romantic music, and his great orchestra's evident delight in the copious riches of the discovery, for the *Hiller* Variations, this disc is a tempting alternative; and the coupling is more generous. Anyone who warms to Vaughan Williams's *Tallis Fantasia* will immediately respond to the "Hermit playing the violin", the first of the four *Böcklin* tone-poems; Debussy's "Jeux de vagues" from *La mer* was obviously in Reger's mind for the second poem "At play in the waves"; and the "Isle of the dead" is Reger's no less doom- and gloom-laden response to the painting that so captured Rachmaninov's imagination. The final painting, "Bacchanal", was described as a Munich beer festival in Roman costume — an entirely fitting description for Reger's setting of it!

Additional recommendation ...

Variations and Fugue on a Theme of J.A. Hiller. ***Zemlinsky.*** *Gesänge nach Maeterlinck, Op. 13*[a]. [a]**Hedwig Fassbender** (mez); **Czech Philharmonic Orchestra/Václav Neumann.** Supraphon 11 1811-2 — lh DDD 7/93

Reger. Variations and Fugue on a Theme of Mozart, Op. 132.
Hindemith. Symphonic Metamorphosis on Themes of Carl Maria von Weber. **Bavarian Radio Symphony Orchestra/Sir Colin Davis.** Philips 422 347-2PH. Recorded in 1989.

55m DDD 9/90 

Debussy once dismissed variation technique as "an easy way of making a lot out of a little". It is certainly astonishing what Reger manages to make out of Mozart's little theme (one of those tunes you know, even if you didn't know that you knew it) and the long journey to the inevitable king-sized fugue is full of late romantic nostalgia, fantasy and an enlivening lightness of touch. If, to quote Wilfred Mellers, Reger's "chromatic elaboration did not follow Tristan into a transfigured night", his writing for strings is surely as sensuous as in Schoenberg's early masterpiece. The flavour of Davis's performance of Hindemith's *Symphonic Metamorphosis* is more Anglo-Bavarian than American but, as in the Reger, the playing is superb and the sound very natural.

NEW REVIEW

Reger. Violin Sonatas — No. 6 in E minor, Op. 122; No. 7 in C minor, Op. 139. **Hansheinz Schneeberger** (vn); **Jean-Jacques Dünki** (pf). Jecklin Disco JD649-2. Recorded in 1991.

lh 13m DDD 5/93

For some people, Reger's name and vast output stands for all that is ponderous and humourless in German music, and there are pieces that make one understand why, so that one may be deterred from investigating further. Which is a pity, for there is good music here even if few would use the word 'great' of this contemporary of Rachmaninov. These violin sonatas (his Sixth and Seventh) are late works of 1911 and 1915 and the sympathetic performances by the Swiss artists Hansheinz Schneeberger and Jean-Jacques Dünki do much to persuade us that they deserve to be played and heard; we remember, too, that the composer himself thought the C minor Sonata "without doubt the best chamber music I have written". Like Rachmaninov, Reger was a conservative and the chief affinity here is with Brahms, whom he greatly admired — no bad model in chamber music, as some British composers of his generation also recognized. This is most immediately evident in music such as the hushed openings of the *Adagio* in the E minor Sonata and the corresponding *Largo* in the C minor work. But he never shared Brahms's characteristic economy, his clean textures and his melodic strength: rather, he too often luxuriates at somewhat shapeless length. For all this, there is something about this quirky music that wins respect and performances such as these should win it friends. The recording is satisfying, if a little reverberant.

Further listening ...

Piano Concerto, Op. 114. **Gerhard Oppitz** (pf); **Bamberg Symphony Orchestra/Horst Stein.** Koch Schwann 311058.

Variations and Fugue on a Theme by Telemann, Op. 134. *Coupled with* **Brahms.** Variations and Fugue. **Jorge Bolet** (pf). Decca Ovation 417 791-2DM (2/90).

Latin Requiem, Op. 145*a*. Requiem, Op. 144*b*. **Soloists; North German Radio Chorus and Symphony Orchestra/Roland Bader.** Koch Schwann 313004.

Steve Reich

American 1936-

Reich. Different Trains (1988)[a]. Electric Counterpoint (1987)[b]. [a]**Kronos Quartet** (David Harrington, John Sherba, vns; Hank Dutt, va; Joan Jeanrenaud, vc); [b]**Pat Metheny** (gtr). Elektra Nonesuch 7559-79176-2.

42m DDD 6/89

The name 'minimalist' clings to Steve Reich, but in fact there's little that can be called minimal in works of the richness and comparative complexity of *Octet* or *The Desert Music*, where all that's left of his earlier style is a taste for pulsating rhythms, short-term circular repetitions and a sonorous harmoniousness. *Different Trains* also combines strong ideas with superb craftsmanship, and it is carried out with total confidence. The programme is autobiographical: Reich evokes his long childhood train journeys across America in the aftermath of the Second World War, and ponders on the parallel but enforced train journeys undertaken by Jewish refugees in Europe. A tinge of melancholy darkens the otherwise excited mood of music, which draws most of its imagery from the driving motor-rhythms of steam trains, constantly punctuated by the evocative sound of whistles, and scraps of recorded interviews. *Different Trains* is given an exemplary reading by the Kronos Quartet, and it is nicely complemented by Pat Metheny's performance of the short *Electric Counterpoint* for live and multi-tracked acoustic guitars.

NEW REVIEW

Reich. The desert music. **Brooklyn Philharmonic Chorus and Orchestra/Michael Tilson Thomas** with **Steve Reich.** Elektra Nonesuch 7559-79101-2.

50m DDD 6/86 

The idea of the desert symbolizes many different things for Steve Reich: the deserts of the biblical Jews in exile, of Jesus confronting his temptations, of Mojave in California (where Reich himself suffered the effects of dehydration) and of the White Sands and Alamagordo in New Mexico, "where weapons of the most intense and sophisticated sort are constantly being developed and tested". This last is the pivot of *The desert music*, a work that draws on fragments of poetry (chosen by Reich himself) taken from a collection so-named by the American poet William Carlos Williams. At the time of composition (1982-4), *The desert music* marked a radical stylistic departure for Reich who, although having previously produced Psalm-settings and tape pieces based on the spoken word, had not composed choral music on this scale. Reich does not tailor his music to 'reflect' the meaning of Williams's poetry; rather, he sets a pulse at the beginning and, through different rhythmic patterns (some of them intriguingly ambiguous), builds a sort of musical arch in seven interlinking movements: fast, moderate, slow — moderate (the 'centre' of the arch) — slow, moderate, fast. The result is a sensually appealing but fairly intense synthesis of words and music (as opposed to a 'setting', which is something quite different), with many of Williams's words serving not only to warn and edify, but to reflect the general tenor of Reich's music. For example, "It is a principle of music/to repeat the theme. Repeat/and repeat again ...". And anyone who knows Reich's work of old, will also know that Reich takes Williams at his word! *The desert music* is a fine and important piece, and one that offers a useful corrective for those who think that so-called minimalism is simply an opiate for people in search of a musical drug. Reich himself recommends listening 'blind' to start with, then studying the text the more involved you become with the music itself. It seems a sensible recipe, and one that's particularly easy to follow given the superlatively high standards of this première performance and recording.

Further listening ...

Drumming. Six Pianos. Music for Mallet Instruments, Voices and Organs. **Steve Reich and Musicians.** DG 20th Century Classics 427 428-2GC2 (9/89).

The Four Sections[a]. Music for Mallet Instruments, Voices and Organ[b]. [b]**Steve Reich and Musicians;** [a]**London Symphony Orchestra/Michael Tilson Thomas.** Elektra Nonesuch 7559-79220-2 (6/91).

Tehillim (Psalms) for women's voices and instruments. **Vocal Ensemble, Instrumental Ensemble George/Manahan.** ECM New Series 827 411-2.

Antoine-Joseph Reicha

Bohemian/French 1770-1836

Suggested listening ...

Wind Quintets — F major, Op. 88 No. 6; D major, Op. 91 No. 3; E flat major, Op. 100 No. 3. **Albert Schweitzer Quintet.** CPO999 026-2 (3/91).

Wind Quintets — C major, Op. 91 No. 1; G major, Op. 99 No. 6; A minor, Op. 100 No. 5. **Albert Schweitzer Quintet.** CPO999 027-2 (3/91).

Wind Quintets — C minor, Op. 91 No. 6; B flat major, Op. 100 No. 6. Andante in E flat major. **Albert Schweitzer Quintet.** CPO999 029-2 (3/91).

Franz Reizenstein

German/British 1911-1968

Reizenstein. Piano Quintet in D major, Op. 23[a]. Sonata for Violin and Piano, Op. 20[b]. Sonatina for Oboe and Piano, Op. 11[c]. [a]**Melos Ensemble** (Emanuel Hurwitz, Ivor McMahon, vns; Cecil Aronowitz, va; Terence Weil, vc; Lamar Crowson, pf). [b]**Erich Gruenberg** (vn); [b]**David Wilde** (pf); **Janet Craxton** (ob); [c]**Lamar Crowson** (pf). Continuum CCD1024. From L'Oiseau-Lyre SOL344 (7/75).

lh llm ADD 11/91 

Franz Reizenstein's uproarious contributions to the ever popular Hoffnung concerts quickly achieved a degree of notoriety which overshadowed virtually all of his remaining output, and this excellent Continuum disc offers pioneering recordings of several of his finest chamber works, fittingly played by some of his closest associates. The Melos Ensemble, with the pianist Lamar Crowson, are heard in a definitive reading of Reizenstein's Piano Quintet in D major, a finely structured and readily approachable work which deserves renewed attention today. This expansive composition is finely presented by the Melos players, all of whom excel in the irascible *moto perpetuo* Scherzo; the highlight of an obscure and neglected work which will not disappoint the adventurous listener. Reizenstein's mildly ironic style is evident, too, in the central movement of his Violin Sonata which is engagingly realized by Erich Gruenberg and David Wilde. The constant melodic interest and harmonic coloration makes the sonata sound refreshingly inventive, in a performance of great authority from two of the composer's staunchest advocates. The final work here is the delightful Oboe Sonatina, heard in a reading which is by turns witty and plangent, from the late Janet Craxton, who is joined at the piano by Lamar Crowson. The recordings sound a touch brittle and a little dated, but given the excellence of these authoritative and affectionate performances, there is much to enjoy here.

Ottorino Respighi

Italian 1879-1936

NEW REVIEW

Respighi. Symphonic Poems — Pines of Rome; Fountains of Rome; Roman Festivals. **Royal Philharmonic Orchestra/Enrique Bátiz.** Naxos 8 550539. Recorded in 1991.

lh lm DDD 8/92 

In gathering together Respighi's colourful Roman triptych onto one super-budget CD, Naxos have pulled off something of a commercial coup. Most accomplished renderings they are, too: under the Mexican conductor Enrique Bátiz the RPO respond to the cinematographic spectacle of Respighi's masterly scoring with palpable enthusiasm, and Brian B. Culverhouse's typically vivid production shows commendably little sign of strain throughout (though for a real sonic treat Decca's full-price disc remains unsurpassable). OK, if we're being really honest, Bátiz's conducting doesn't always show quite the same degree of affection or remarkable feeling for atmosphere one hears on Toscanini's legendary mono recordings; nor does the orchestral playing possess quite the breathtaking refinement and assurance one encounters in some of the other versions. That said, there's still much to savour: in *Pines*, witness the ravishing string textures during the gorgeous "Pines of the Janiculum", which leads us to the all-engulfing tread of the legions marching along "The Pines of the Appian Way"; next, try *Fountains* and the riveting central climax of "The Fountains of Trevi at midday", with resplendent brass and organ. This disc would be recommendable at full price; at this ridiculously low price it is unbeatable. Remember, though, for a couple of pounds more István Kertész's classic LSO accounts of *Fountains*, *Pines* and *The Birds* on Decca Weekend offers possibly even greater musical satisfaction.

Additional recommendations ...
Pines of Rome. Fountains of Rome. **Mussorgsky.** *Pictures at an Exhibition.* **Fritz Reiner.** RCA 09026 61401-2 — lh 10m ADD 8/93
Pines of Rome. Fountains of Rome. Roman Festivals. **Montreal Symphony Orchestra/Charles Dutoit.** Decca 410 145-2DH — lh DDD 11/83
Pines of Rome. Fountains of Rome. The birds (Gli uccelli). **London Symphony Orchestra/István Kertész.** Decca Weekend 425 507-2DC — 56m ADD 4/90 £
Pines of Rome. Fountains of Rome. Roman Festivals. **NBC Symphony Orchestra/Arturo Toscanini.** RCA Gold Seal mono GD60262 — lh ADD 1/91
Pines of Rome. Fountains of Rome. Roman Festivals. **Philadelphia Orchestra/Eugene Ormandy.** RCA Silver Seal VD60486 — lh 2m ADD 2/91 £
Pines of Rome. Fountains of Rome. Roman Festivals. **Academy of St Martin in the Fields/Sir Neville Marriner.** Philips 432 133-2PH — lh 4m DDD 4/92

Respighi. WORKS FOR VIOLIN AND ORCHESTRA. **Ingolf Turban** (vn); [a]**Neil Black** (ob); [a]**Graham Ashton** (tpt); [a]**Stephen Williams** (db); [a]**Ian Watson** (pf); [b]**English Chamber Orchestra/Marcello Viotti.** Claves CD50-9017. Recorded in 1990.
Chaconne (after Vitali)[b]. Pastorale in C major (after Tartini)[b]. Concerto all'antica[b]. Concerto a cinque[a].

lh 19m DDD 10/91

An enterprising disc — both concertos are world première recordings — and one which offers further examples of Respighi's desire to relate the best of bygone eras to modern ears. Or, to be more precise, to modern ears if you happened to be listening in the first three decades of this century. Even then you might have been surprised at the warmth of the most neoclassical works here, the 1933 *Concerto a cinque* (a sort of Corellian *concerto grosso*), given the astringency that is generally associated with neoclassicism. The *Concerto all'antica* is a much earlier work, a beautifully crafted, highly engaging mish-mash of styles from Bruch and Mendelssohn back to the baroque, with hardly an identifiably Respighian fingerprint in earshot. But with music as lucid and graceful as this, few will complain. Inevitably, given the music's unfamiliarity, there are a few tentative moments in the playing. Though one craves, say, a Heifetz in the Vitali transcription, Turban is an accomplished violinist and corporate commitment is rarely in doubt. The sound, ideally distanced, has bloom and warmth.

NEW REVIEW

Respighi. Ancient airs and dances for lute. **Philharmonia Hungarica/Antal Dorati.** Philips Mercury 434 304-2MM. From 416 496-2PH (1/87). Recorded in 1960.

55m ADD

This is the second appearance on CD of Dorati's vintage recording of the *Ancient Airs*. It has retained its vivid open-air freshness remarkably well and although a small amount of tape hiss can be heard in the quieter sections it in no ways spoils the enjoyment of the music. Respighi's skill as a transcriber of other men's music is once again evident here and although these are rather straightforward as transcriptions, there is much charming invention. The performances are notable for their refinement, elegance and well balanced textures; strings and woodwind blend particularly well in Suites Nos. 1 and 2 (Suite No. 3 is for strings alone), emphasizing Respighi's skilful and translucent scoring. The Philharmonia Hungarica's playing has sparkle and vitality, and the dance rhythms are always incisive and strongly projected. A very enjoyable issue.

Additional recommendation ...
The birds (Gli uccelli). Antiche danze ed arie per liuto — Suites Nos. 1 and 3. Trittico botticelliano. **Orpheus Chamber Orchestra.** DG 437 533-2GH — lh 9m DDD 7/93

Respighi. The birds (Gli uccelli). Il tramonto[a]. Adagio con variazioni[b]. Trittico botticelliano. [a]**Linda Finnie** (contr); [b]**Raphael Wallfisch** (vc); **Bournemouth Sinfonietta/Tamás Vásáry.** Chandos CHAN8913. Recorded in 1990.

1h 5m DDD 3/92

Respighi's arrangements for small orchestra are unashamedly picturesque and romantic, and Tamás Vásáry secures alert, affectionate playing from the Bournemouth Sinfonietta. Three Botticelli paintings housed in a Florence gallery inspired Respighi to write his *Trittico botticelliano* ("Three Botticelli Pictures"). The music is again richly colourful in tone paintings depicting "The Spring", "The Adoration of the Magi", and "The Birth of Venus", and once more Vásáry conducts in a spirited, characterful fashion. *Il tramonto*, for voice and string orchestra (or string quartet), is a vivid setting of Shelley's poem *The sunset*, in an Italian translation. Linda Finnie sings beautifully, even if her Italian pronunciation is a little Anglicized. The *Adagio con variazioni* was originally written for cello and piano, and later orchestrated by the composer. This pleasant, well-ordered work is sensitively played by Raphael Wallfisch. The four works on offer here make up a nicely contrasted programme, and Chandos have provided an attractively rich sound quality.

Respighi. Violin Sonata in B minor.
R. Strauss. Violin Sonata in E flat major, Op. 18. **Kyung-Wha Chung** (vn); **Krystian Zimerman** (pf). DG 427 617-2GH. Recorded in 1988.

52m DDD 2/90

This is wonderful violin playing, as richly romantic as both works often demand, but with a wide range of colour to underline the subtleties and the varying tones of voice that both employ. To add to the coupling's appeal, Kyung-Wha Chung's pianist is a musician of exceptional subtlety who is clearly as intent as she is to demonstrate that both sonatas deserve a position much closer to the centre of the repertory than they have so far been given. In the Strauss in particular they succeed eloquently. It is often described as the last work of his apprentice years, but in this performance the mature Strauss steps out from the shadow of Brahms so often and so proudly that its stature as his 'real' Op. 1 seems confirmed. The Respighi is a lesser piece, no doubt, but its melodies and its rhapsodic manner are attractive, and Chung's warm response to Respighi's idiomatic way with the instrument (he was a violinist himself) is infectious. Good and natural-sounding balance between violin and piano is not easy to achieve, but the recording here, significantly helped by Zimerman's combination of poetry and alert responsiveness, is outstandingly successful.

Additional recommendation ...
Violin Sonata. ***Franck.*** *Violin Sonata.* ***Poulenc.*** *Violin Sonata.* **Josef Suk** (vn); **Josef Hála** (pf). Supraphon 11 0710-2 1h 10m ADD 5/90

NEW REVIEW

Respighi. VOCAL AND ORCHESTRAL WORKS. [b]**Patricia Rozario** (sop); [a]**Dame Janet Baker,** [b]**Louise Winter** (mezs); [b]**Lynton Atkinson** (ten); [b]**Richard Hickox Singers; City of London Sinfonia/Richard Hickox.** Collins Classics 1349-2. Texts and translations included. Recorded in 1991.
Aretusa[a]. Il tramonto[a]. Lauda per la natività del Signore[b]. Trittico botticelliano.

1h 12m DDD 9/92 

Attention is probably attracted towards this disc in the first place by Dame Janet Baker's presence on it, especially if the listener has previously heard the earlier recording on which she sang *La sensitiva*, Respighi's setting of Shelley's *The Sensitive Plant* (Virgin Classics VC7 91164-2, 6/91 — unfortunately, the Berlioz half of this programme is not particularly recommendable). *Aretusa* and *Il tramonto* are also set to translations of poems by Shelley: colourful works with a wide range of expression, stimulating just that kind of boldness and generosity of utterance in which Dame Janet is expert. She is in fine voice here, and at the end of *Il tramonto* ("the tomb of the dead self") her tone is stern, strong and dark, intensely personal. Even so, going to the disc initially for these tone-poems for solo voice and orchestra, one may still eventually be most glad of the purchase for its introduction to the choral *Lauda per la natività del Signore*. This was written in the late 1920s and is a most lovely work. It has solo parts for Mary, the Angel and a shepherd (all well taken), but the great joy lies in the choral and orchestral writing, rich and imaginative, its medievalism shot through with delight in the idiom. The better-known *Trittico botticelliano* (elaborated upon above) is highly enjoyable too, and all are fine in performance and recorded sound.

NEW REVIEW

Respighi. LA FIAMMA. **Klára Takács** (mez) Eudossia; **Sándor Sólyom-Nagy** (bar) Basilio; **Péter Kelen** (ten) Donello; **Ilona Tokody** (sop) Silvana; **Tamara Takács** (mez) Agnese; **Katalin Pitti** (sop) Monica; **Mária Takács** (sop) Agata; **Zsuzsa Barlay** (mez) Lucilla; **Eszter Póka** (mez) Sabina; **Anna Bogdány** (mez) Zoe; **Kolos Kováts** (bass) The Bishop; **József Gregor** (bass) The Exorcist; **Mária Temesi** (sop) Mother; **István Basky** (ten) A Voice; **Hungarian Radio and Television Chorus; Hungarian State Orchestra/Lamberto Gardelli.** Hungaroton HCD12591/3. Notes, text and translation included.

 12/85 

La Fiamma ("The Flame") has the sort of setting (the Byzantine magnificence of seventh century Ravenna) that Respighi excelled at evoking, and a scenario filled with spectacular crowd scenes, ritual, black magic and doomed forbidden love. Just up his street, you might think, but what seems to have drawn him even more strongly to this subject were the opportunities it offered to conjure up the remote past. His interest in antiquity is obvious in his popular Roman scenes ("Pines", "Fountains" and "Festivals"), but he also came from a generation of Italian composers who were concerned to rediscover the roots of Italian music in the pure but poignantly expressive lines of Monteverdi and his contemporaries. These two preoccupations fuse in *La Fiamma*, and most of its finest moments are those in which strong emotion is conveyed in simple, even chaste melody rendered haunting by an elusive archaism. Tellingly enough almost the only moment of conventionally operatic passion, a duet almost in Puccini's manner, is intended to evoke false love: Silvana, the opera's central character, learning that she has inherited the 'flame' of black magic from her mother, uses sorcery to arouse the love of her own step-son. But almost all the other scenes of high emotion have the quality of a music that taps deep historic roots. Silvana's reply to her step-son's instinctive revulsion, at the very height of their duet, has a strangely moving gravity to it; so does her chastely happy memory of the first time she saw him, as a child; so does her sinister, pitiful mother's salute to Byzantium, the golden city of her birth that she will never see again. Even Silvana's unloved and betrayed husband is touched by this quality; it gives dignity, even nobility, to his admission of hopeless love for her. Respighi's attempt to forge a new operatic language with power drawn from an ancient source is halting: there are pages, whole scenes, which simply refuse to catch fire. But when the spell does work the opera's sheer theatricality and its exciting Italianate lyricism are electrifying, especially in a cast headed by two such vivid singing actresses as Ilona Tokody and Klára Takács. The other singers are of a high standard, Gardelli communicates his enthusiasm for the score infectiously and the recording, a rather recessed chorus apart, is first-class.

Further listening ...

Brazilian Impressions. Church Windows. **Philharmonia Orchestra/Geoffrey Simon.** Chandos CHAN8317 (8/84).

Belkis, Queen of Sheba — Orchestral Suite. Metamorphosen modi XII. **Philharmonia Orchestra/Geoffrey Simon.** Chandos CHAN8405 (5/86).

BELFAGOR. **Soloists; Hungarian Radio and Television Chorus; Hungarian State Orchestra/Lamberto Gardelli.** Hungaroton HCD12850/51 (1/90).

Silvestre Revueltas

Mexican 1899-1940

Suggested listening ...

Caminos[b]. Musica para charlar[b]. Ventanas[b]. *Coupled with* **Chávez.** Sinfonia de Antigona[a]. Symphony No. 4, "Sinfonia romantica"[a]. [a]**Royal Philharmonic Orchestra,** [b]**Mexican State Philharmonic Orchestra/Enrique Bátiz.** ASV CDDCA653 (8/89).

Emil Nikolaus von Rezniček

Austrian 1860-1945

Suggested listening ...

Symphonies — No. 3 in D major; No. 4 in F minor. **Philharmonia Hungarica/Gordon Wright.** Koch Schwann 312032.

Joseph Rheinberger

German 1839-1901

Suggested listening ...

Organ Concertos — No. 1 in F major, Op. 137; No. 2 in G minor, Op. 177. **Andreas Juffinger** (org); **Berlin Radio Symphony Orchestra/Hartmut Haenchen.** Capriccio 10336.

Nicolay Rimsky-Korsakov

Russian 1844-1908

Rimsky-Korsakov. Scheherazade, Op. 35. Capriccio espagnol, Op. 34. **London Symphony Orchestra/Sir Charles Mackerras.** Telarc CD80208. Recorded in 1990.

1h DDD 10/90

Sir Charles Mackerras throws himself into this music with expressive abandon, but allies it to control so that every effect is realized and the London Symphony Orchestra play this familiar music as if they were discovering it afresh. Together they produce performances that are both vivid and thoughtful, while the solo violin in *Scheherazade*, who represents the young queen whose storytelling skills prolong and finally save her life in the court of the cruel Sultan Shahriar (portrayed by powerful brass), is seductively and elegantly played by Kees Hulsmann, not least at the wonderfully peaceful end to the whole work. The finale featuring a storm and shipwreck is superbly done, the wind and brass bringing one to the edge of one's seat and reminding us that Rimsky-Korsakov served in the Russian Navy and well knew the beauty and danger of the sea. This sensuous and thrilling work needs spectacular yet detailed sound, and that is what it gets here, the 1990 recording in Walthamstow Town Hall being highly successful and giving us a CD that many collectors will choose to use as a demonstration disc to impress their friends. The performance and recording of the *Capriccio espagnol* is no less of a success, and this issue is worth every penny of its price.

Additional recommendations ...

Scheherazade[a]. *Sadko, Op. 5*[b]. *May Night — Overture*[b]. [a]**London Symphony Orchestra/Pierre Monteux;** [b]**Suisse Romande Orchestra/Ernest Ansermet.** Decca Weekend 421 400-2DC — 59m ADD

Scheherazade. **Debussy.** *La mer.* **Chicago Symphony Orchestra/Fritz Reiner.** RCA GD60875 — 1h 9m ADD B ▲

Scheherazade. **Tchaikovsky.** *Capriccio italien.* **Philharmonia Orchestra/Paul Kletzki.** Classics for Pleasure CD-CFP4341 — 1h m ADD B

Scheherazade. **Herman Krebbers** (vn); **Royal Concertgebouw Orchestra/Kirill Kondrashin.** Philips 400 021-2PH — 44m ADD 3/83 B

Scheherazade. **Borodin.** *Prince Igor — Polovtsian Dances*[a]. [a]**Beecham Choral Society; Royal Philharmonic Orchestra/Sir Thomas Beecham.** EMI CDC7 47717-2. — 58m ADD 9/87 B ▲

Scheherazade[a]. **Mussorgsky.** *A night on the Bare Mountain (orig. version)*[b]. [b]**Rodney Friend** (vn); **London Philharmonic Orchestra/**[a]**David Lloyd-Jones,** [b]**Bernard Haitink.** Philips Silverline 420 898-2PSL — 1h ADD 3/90 B

Scheherazade. **Ravel.** *Boléro.* **London Philharmonic Orchestra/Andrew Litton.** Virgin Classics Virgo VJ7 91470 — 1h 4m DDD 12/91 £ B

Rimsky-Korsakov. SYMPHONIES AND ORCHESTRAL WORKS. **Gothenburg Symphony Orchestra/Neeme Järvi.** DG 423 604-2GH2.

Symphonies — No. 1 in E minor, Op. 1; No. 2 (Symphonic Suite), Op. 9, "Antar"; No. 3 in C major, Op. 32. Russian Easter Festival Overture, Op. 36. Capriccio espagnol, Op. 34.

② 2h 5m DDD 2/89

No one is going to claim Rimsky's First and Third Symphonies to be neglected masterpieces. He came to refer to his First (partly written whilst the young naval officer was on duty!) as a "disgraceful composition", and along with the other two symphonies, it was subjected to extensive revision by the later learned master of musical technique. As the equally learned, entertaining and informative essay accompanying this set points out, the opening of the symphony could have been a trial run for the opening of Schumann's Fourth (and a very fine one, too!). It's the beautifully lyrical second theme which reminds us that Rimsky was reared in the country and had the early advantage of a good soaking in folk-song. Though the debt to Glinka is obvious, to our ears classical concerns seem uppermost throughout, and the music is free from anything that could be called exoticism. Not so the Second. Rimsky was a member of the 'Mighty Five', a group of composers (including Mussorgsky, Balakirev and Borodin) sworn to the nationalist cause, professing horror at anything tinged with German academicism and ever searching for subjects on which they could lavish a preference for orchestral colour above form. Rimsky's *Antar* combined these ideals, and more. Our hero of the title is allocated a Berliozian *idée fixe*, an oriental location (the desert of Sham) and the joys of vengeance, power and love from the grateful fairy Gul-Nazar as a gift for saving her from a winged monster. It is, in every way, an antecedent of *Sheherazade* and, after hearing Järvi's rich and eloquently descriptive account, one wonders why it has never attained anything like the same popularity. His Third Symphony reverts to a more academic manner. In 1871 he was invited to join the theory and composition faculty at the St Petersburg Conservatory and, in Tchaikovsky's words, "from contempt of schooling he had turned all at once to the cult of musical technique". Despite a paucity of truly memorable ideas, it is a symphony to admire for its construction and light-as-air orchestration. The set is completed with urgent, vibrant accounts of the *Capriccio espagnol* and the *Russian Easter Festival Overture*, quite the most colourful and exciting versions on disc, and they confirm that the less familiar symphonies could not be in better hands. DG's engineers resist the temptation to glamorize the music and offer a lucid and spacious panorama of sound.

NEW REVIEW

Rimsky-Korsakov. Orchestral Suites — The Golden Cockerel; The Tale of Tsar Saltan; Christmas Eve. **Armenian Philharmonic Orchestra/Loris Tjeknavorian.** ASV CDDCA772.

1h 16m DDD 9/92

There's plenty here to satisfy the most heady of orchestral palettes. What a master painter Rimsky was! Of the three intoxicating suites recorded here, both *The Golden Cockerel* and *The*

Tale of Tsar Saltan (the latter appended by a winsome outing for "Flight of the Bumble Bee") are reasonably well-known by now, but how many people will be familiar with the gorgeous orchestral suite from the 1895 opera *Christmas Eve*? Pure enchantment from start to finish, it opens with a wonderful evocation of snow and stars on the night before Christmas, progressing by way of a Witches' Sabbath and terrific polonaise (worthy of Tchaikovsky at his most inspired) to a bell-laden apotheosis. Throughout, Loris Tjeknavorian draws an enthusiastic response from his own Armenian Philharmonic Orchestra: intonation is not always spot-on, nor is ensemble entirely immaculate (its strings, too, aren't exactly in the luxury class), but the vigour and spontaneity of the playing offers ample compensation. The sound could ideally be richer though otherwise it lacks nothing in spectacle or sheer brilliance.

Additional recommendation ...
May Night — Overture. Orchestral Suites: Golden Cockerel; Tale of Tsar Saltan; Christmas Eve; The Snow Maiden; Mlada; The Invisible City of Kitezh. **Scottish National Orchestra/Neeme Järvi.** Chandos CHAN8327/9 — ③ 2h 28m DDD

Richard Rodgers

American 1902-1979

Suggested listening ...

Overtures — Oklahoma!. Allegro. South Pacific. The King and I. Me and Juliet. Pipe Dream. Cinderella. Flower Drum Song. Carousel — waltz. State Fair — suite. The Sound of Music — entr'acte. **Hollywood Bowl Orchestra/John Mauceri.** Philips 434 127-2PH (9/92).

Carousel — *original film soundtrack.* EMI Angel ZDM7 64692-2.

Oklahoma! — *original film soundtrack.* EMI Angel ZDM7 64691-2.

South Pacific — *original film soundtrack.* RCA ND83681 (12/89).

THE RODGERS AND HAMMERSTEIN SONGBOOK. *Selections* — Oklahoma!. Carousel. South Pacific. The King and I. Cinderella. Flower Drum Song. The Sound of Music. **Original Broadway casts, etc.** Sony Broadway CD53331.

THE BOYS FROM SYRACUSE. **Soloists; orchestra/Lehman Engel.** Sony Broadway CD53329.

THE KING AND I. **Soloists; Hollywood Bowl Orchestra/John Mauceri.** Philips 438 007-2PH (10/92).

ON YOUR TOES. **Original 1983 Broadway revival cast.** That's Entertainment CDTER1063 (10/83).

Joaquin Rodrigo

Spanish 1901-

Rodrigo. Concierto de Aranjuez. Fantasía para un gentilhombre. **John Williams** (gtr); **Philharmonia Orchestra/Louis Frémaux.** CBS Masterworks CD37848. From IM37848 (7/84).

53m DDD 7/85 B

The *Concierto de Aranjuez* is a romantic work whose success remains unparalleled. Rodrigo's recipe for both works on this recording is to express his reverence for past traditions in terms of his own, neoclassical musical language — lush tunes and harmonies, some courtly formality and a soupçon of mischievous spikiness. The *Fantasía* (the *Gentilhombre* is Segovia) pays its respects also to a great guitarist of the seventeenth century, Gaspar Sanz, some of whose themes are winsomely reworked by Rodrigo. Both works call for a high degree of virtuosity but difficulties present no problem to John Williams, who brings to both pieces the proper blend of expressiveness and poise. To describe a recording as 'vivid' has become a cliché but in this case it is inevitable.

Additional recommendations ...

Concierto de Aranjuez. Fantasía para un gentilhombre. ***Villa-Lobos.*** *Guitar Concerto.* **Göran Söllscher** (gtr); **Orpheus Chamber Orchestra.** DG 429 232-2GH — Ih 5m DDD 6/90 B

Concierto de Aranjuez. Fantasía para un gentilhombre. ***Vivaldi.*** *Guitar Concerto in D major, RV93.* **Lausanne Chamber Orchestra/Lawrence Foster.** Virgin Classics VC7 91192-2 — 58m DDD 11/91 B

NEW REVIEW

Rodrigo. Concierto pastoral.
Khachaturian (arr. Gallois). Flute Concerto in D minor. **Patrick Gallois** (fl); **Philharmonia Orchestra/Ion Marin.** DG 435 767-2GH. Recorded in 1991.

Ih Im DDD 10/92

Rodrigo composed his *Concierto pastoral* in 1978, at the request of the flautist James Galway. Even if its title suggests a relaxed exploration of rural byways, or perhaps a folk-inspired anthology of undemanding melodic interest, this is a virtuoso concerto in a very real sense. Rodrigo's probing investigation of every bravura technique which falls even remotely within the feasible possibilities of the flute calls for playing of the highest order; and that's just about the best description of this account from Patrick Gallois. Of course, the work has its introspective side too (and one could hardly expect otherwise from the composer of the *Concierto de Aranjuez*), revolving around an elegiac B minor slow movement, ravishingly played here by Gallois. He is articulate and elegant, with a fine-spun liquidity of tone and no lack of brilliance when the occasion demands. Khachaturian's so-called Flute Concerto, also in D minor, is in fact a reworking of his Violin Concerto, written in 1940 for David Oistrakh. Purists would be largely correct to suggest that the work fares best in its intended form, but it is nevertheless very convincing in this version (arranged by Gallois), based on an earlier flute transcription by Jean-Pierre Rampal. The performance is tremendously exciting, and with the vibrant support of the Philharmonia it's easy to forget that this is a second generation concerto from an unrelated source. The recordings of both works are breathtaking; clear and unusually detailed, yet with totally natural balanced perspectives. Definitely a disc to consider then, and especially recommended to collectors whose appetite for the flute might perhaps be a little jaded.

NEW REVIEW

Rodrigo. PIANO WORKS. **Gregory Allen, [a]Anton Nel** (pfs). Bridge BCD9027. Recorded 1989-91.

Suite. Preludio al gallo mañanero. Zarabanda lejana. Pastorale. Bagatela. Serenata española. Sonada de adiós (Hommage à Paul Dukas). Tres Danzas de España. Danza de la Amapola. Tres Evocaciones. Preludio de Añoranza. Cinco Sonatas de Castilla con Toccata a modo de pregón. Berceuse de printemps. Berceuse d'automne. Air de Ballet sur le nom d'une Jeune Fille. El Album de Cecilia (Seis Piezas para manos pequeñas). A l'ombre de Torre Bermeja. Cuatro Piezas. Cuatro Estampas andaluzas. Cinco Piezas infantiles[a]. Sonatiuna para dos Munecas[a]. Gran Marcha de los Subsecretarios[a]. Atardecer[a].

② 2h 33m DDD 7/92

It is ironic that Rodrigo, a virtuoso pianist, should be world-famous for the music he has written for the guitar and other instruments he does not play, rather than for his considerable number of solo and duo piano works, none of which were in the current catalogue before this integral recording. Rodrigo's musical life has been devoted to portraying the scenes, customs and the folk-

and art-musical heritage of his country in a manner befitting the last of the great Spanish Romantics. He does this with affection and wry humour, often paying tribute to the external influences that helped to shape his personal style — French composers and Stravinsky. The foregoing applies to Rodrigo's piano music no less than to his compositional output as a whole. The piano works, spanning the years 1923-1987, form a *curriculum vitae* of a composer who has lived and written down his musical dreams, sometimes with childlike simplicity; they form part of an aural guide to Spain, past and present. If you like the *Concierto de Aranjuez* (and you *must* have heard it!) you will enjoy dipping into this collection of superbly played and recorded piano music.

Further listening ...

Concierto serenata[a]. Concierto de Aranjuez[b]. *Coupled with* **Casteldnuovo-Tedesco.** Guitar Concerto No. 1[c]. [a]**Nicanor Zabaleta** (hp); [bc]**S. Behrend** (gtr); [a]**Berlin Radio Symphony Orchestra/Ernst Märzendorfer;** [bc]**Berlin Philharmonic Orchestra/Reinhard Peters.** DG 427 214-2GR.

Johan Helmich Roman

Swedish 1694-1758

NEW REVIEW

Roman. Suites — D major, "Lilla Drottningholmsmusiquen"; G minor, "Sjukmans musiquen". Piante amiche[a]. [a]**Pia-Maria Nilsson** (sop); **Stockholm Nationalmuseum Chamber Orchestra/Claude Génetay.** Musica Sveciae MSCD417. Recorded in 1991.

lh 3m DDD 1/93

Johann Helmich Roman, the "Father of Swedish Music" was a contemporary of Bach and Handel. He lived most of his life in Stockholm but also travelled and, in 1714, arrived in London where he met Handel. It is the latter composer's music which perhaps most readily springs to mind when encountering Roman's style. The *Drottningholmsmusiquen* ("Royal Wedding Music") is an extended orchestral suite composed for the royal wedding in 1744 of the Swedish Crown Prince Adolf Frederick to the Prussian princess, Lovsa Ulrika, sister of Frederick the Great. This disc features a shorter suite which Roman wrote for the same occasion, and which contains no duplicated material. In addition, the programme includes the *Sjukmans musiquen* ("Invalid Music"), whose somewhat puzzling title may refer to the opening of a hospital in the late 1720s, and a cantata *Piante amiche* of doubtful authenticity. All the music here is immediately attractive and imaginatively played by an orchestra of modern instruments. The soprano, Pia-Maria Nilsson has a pleasing voice and the performances are affectionately directed by Claude Génetay, a champion of Roman's music.

Sigmund Romberg

Hungarian/American 1887-1951

THE STUDENT PRINCE (Romberg/Donelly). Cast includes **Marilyn Hill Smith, Rosemary Ashe** (sops); **Diana Montague** (mez); **David Rendall, Bonaventura Bottone, Neil Jenkins** (tens); **Jason Howard, Norman Bailey** (bars); **Donald Maxwell** (bass); **Ambrosian Chorus; Philharmonia Orchestra/John Owen Edwards.** TER Classics CDTER2 1172. Recorded in 1989.

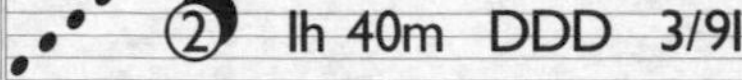

Although we think of the 1920s as a period of great success for the musical comedies of the Gershwins and Rodgers and Hart it was, too, a glorious decade for Sigmund Romberg, who scored three personal triumphs with his operettas *The Student Prince*, *The Desert Song* and *New Moon*. Each of these scores exudes an air of confidence both in the sweep of their melodic lines, and the vigorous choral writing that has stood the test of time rather better than the flimsy story lines that support them. In order to include as much of Romberg's score as feasible, it has been necessary to include some rather embarrassing cues that certainly defeats one of the more senior members of the cast, which in the main is the same team that was assembled by TER for their outstanding recording of *Kismet*, with John Owen Edwards once again drawing assured playing from the Philharmonia. In addition to David Rendall sporting boyish good humour in the title role, there are distinctive contributions from Bonaventura Bottone leading the Drinking song, Norman Bailey in "Golden days" and a lovely version of the Lehár-like duet, "Just we two" from Diana Montague and Steven Page. The one slight disappointment in this line-up is Marilyn Hill Smith who on this occasion can't escape a charge of blandness, and a touch of shrillness on the high Cs of "Come boys, let's be gay boys". That apart, there is no hesitation in extending a warm welcome to this much-needed new recording which surprises more than once by the charm of its lesser known numbers: the Act 2 gavotte, for instance, and the sophistication of Romberg's handling of the score's big duet, "Deep in my heart" and the humorous chorus, "Student life".

Ned Rorem

American 1923-

NEW REVIEW

Rorem. Winter pages[a]. Bright music[b]. [b]**Marya Martin** (fl); [a]**Todd Palmer** (cl); [a]**Frank Morelli** (bn); **Ida** and [b]**Ani Kavafian** (vns); **Fred Sherry** (vc); [a]**Charles Wadsworth,** [b]**André-Michel Schub** (pfs). New World 80416-2. Recorded 1989-91.

51m DDD 10/92

Ned Rorem has a name that sticks in the mind, but while many people know that he is an American composer, his music is not widely known. That's partly because its communicative style was way out of fashion in the 'radical' 1960s and 1970s, and maybe also partly because he has spread his talents — indeed, *New Grove* calls him a "composer, diarist and essayist". The music here is alert, intelligent and fun and should make him better known. One writer has likened Rorem to Poulenc, and although one wouldn't actually mistake these pieces for that French composer, one sees what is meant: his is a musical personality unafraid of directness, wit and charm (but, thank Heavens, averse to intellectual pomposities) and possesses an enchanting ability to indulge. These do seem like French qualities and, in fact, he lived in Paris in the 1950s and studied with Honegger. Listen to the fourth number of *Winter pages*, a waltz for clarinet and piano called "Paris then", and you will be transported back to that time in music of Poulencian gamin charm. The final "Still life" also recalls Poulenc in its elegant sadness. True, alongside these numbers there are others with arguments and clashes that Poulenc would not have written. For example, Rorem is more elliptical in the one called "Hesitations", but this piece for piano, violin and cello (another waltz, as it happens), in which each instrument seems to go its own way, has its own quiet appeal. Appeal is Rorem's strong suit: but his intelligent, inventive and sensitive music is quite unlike that of minimalists who rely on the repetition of simple figures. Space forbids detailed discussion of *Bright music*; suffice it to say that it is witty, melodious and finely written for the five players — and that it is difficult to relate its finale, entitled "Chopin", to that composer! The playing of both works is expert and the recording clear and atmospheric.

Hilding Rosenberg

Swedish 1892-1985

Suggested listening ...

Symphony No. 4, "The Revelation of St John". **Håkan Hagegård** (bar); **Swedish Radio Choir; Pro Musica Choir; Rilke Ensembe; Gothenburg Symphony Orchestra/Sixten Ehrling.** Caprice CAP21429 (5/93).

Orpheus in Town. Sinfonia concertante. Violin Concerto No. 1, Op. 22. Suite in D major, Op. 13 — Pastorale. Symphonies — No. 3; No. 4, "The Revelation of St John": fragments; No. 5, "Ortågardsmästern". The Holy Night. **Soloists; Swedish Radio Choir, Stockholm Chamber Choir, Radiojänst Symphony Orchestra, Stockholm Concert Society Orchestra, Radiotjänst Entertainment Orchestra, Swedish Radio Orchestra/Hilding Rosenberg.** Caprice Collector's Classics mono CAP21510 (3-CD set, recorded from broadcast performances between 1940-49, 5/93).

Antonio Rosetti

Bohemian c.1750-1792

Rosetti. Horn Concertos — E major, K3:42; E major, K3:44; E flat major, K3:39. **English Chamber Orchestra/Barry Tuckwell** (hn). Classics for Pleasure CD-CFP4578. Recorded in 1986.

53m DDD 8/91 

Although Rosetti's contemporaries ranked him with Haydn and Mozart, posterity has been less kind. Born near Prague in 1750, he was christened Franz Anton Rössler, but preferred the Italianized form of his name, Rosetti ("little roses"), for professional use. He was a prolific composer, mostly of orchestral and chamber music, but is remembered for his wind concertos. His idiomatic writing for horn, in particular, greatly contributed to the development of a melodic style for the instrument. This disc is something of a labour of love. All three of the concertos were edited by John Humphries, from the printed parts in the possession of various libraries, especially for the recording. To be honest, the concertos are not in the same league as Mozart's, though they should be snapped up by all horn *aficionados* and explorers of musical byways. Not only is the asking price very modest, but their challenge brings some stunning playing from one of the world's greatest horn virtuosos. The English Chamber Orchestra react well to him and the recording has exactly the right mix of intimacy and space with plenty of headroom for Tuckwell's most forthright bursts of tone.

Luigi Rossi

Italian c.1597-1653

Rossi. ORFEO. **Agnès Mellon** (sop) Orfeo; **Monique Zanetti** (sop) Euridice; **Dominique Favat** (mez) Nutrice, Bacco; **Sandrine Piau** (sop) Aristeo; **Nicholas Isherwood** (bass) Satiro; **Caroline Pelon** (sop) Amore; **Noémi Rime** (sop) Venere, Vittoria; **Jean-Paul Fouchécourt** (ten) Vecchia, Giove; **Jérôme Corréas** (bar) Endimione; **Marie Boyer** (mez) Giunone; **Cécile Eloir** (mez) Gelosia; **Bernard Deletré** (bass) Augure, Plutone; **Benoît Thivel** (alto) Apollo, Mercurio; **Jean-Marc Salzmann** (bar) Caronte, Momo; **Donatienne Michel-Dansac** (sop) Proserpina; **Beatrice Malleret** (sop) Himeneo; **Les Arts Florissants/William Christie.** Harmonia Mundi HMC90 1358/60. Notes, text and translation included. Recorded in 1990.

(3) 3h 39m DDD 3/92 

Luigi Rossi spent most of his career in Rome, but in 1646 he was invited by Cardinal Mazarin to the Parisian Court. Shortly after he arrived, and while he was working on his second opera *Orfeo*, he received the tragic news of his wife's death in Italy. Small wonder, then, that he produced such profound and affecting music for the subject of this opera. Francesco Buti's libretto consists of three acts, with a prologue and postlude in praise of Louis XIV — dramatically, quite inapposite. Buti supplemented the mythological characters with a host of minor roles, many of them comic figures to lighten the mood. With these resources, Rossi was able to intersperse the recitatives and arias with ensembles, choruses, and dance music, no doubt to appeal to French taste. This recording is most welcome, not just because it is the only one available, but more because it is so impeccably performed. William Christie achieves the finest musical precision as well as giving a powerful dramatic thrust to the whole. He has a crack orchestra, with some admirably fleet cornetts and very polished continuo playing. Of the soloists, Agnès Mellon handles the title role beautifully, and her interpretation of "Lagrime, dove sete?", which Orfeo sings on hearing of Euridice's death, is particularly moving. What emotive and perfectly crafted music this is; and how deeply Rossi must have felt it. Monique Zanetti is appropriately sweet-toned as Euridice — very poised in her death scene; and Sandrine Piau's interpretation of the complex character of Aristeo is particularly admirable. One or two of the minor roles are not so strong, and Buti's interpolations do tend to interrupt the dramatic thread, but these are insignificant quibbles. It is an absolutely first-rate recording of a work which deserves to be better known.

Further listening ...

Cantatas — Oratorio per la Settimana Santa. Un peccator pentito. **Les Arts Florissants Vocal and Instrumental Ensembles/William Christie.** Harmonia Mundi HMC90 1297 (10/89).

Gioachino Rossini

Italian 1792-1868

NEW REVIEW

Rossini. OVERTURES. **Chicago Symphony Orchestra/Fritz Reiner.** RCA GD60387. From SB2075 (7/60). Recorded in 1958.
Guillaume Tell; La scala di seta; Il Signor Bruschino; Il barbiere di Siviglia. La gazza ladra; La Cenerentola.

47m ADD 9/90 

This is one of the most famous of all collections featuring this sparkling repertoire. By the time of this recording, Fritz Reiner had built the Chicago Symphony into one of the world's greatest ensembles, and its swaggering yet supremely flexible virtuosity is heard to superb effect on this survey. Not that these accounts are in any sense over-driven or that Rossini's music is used merely as an excuse for high-powered orchestral display; far from it: Reiner's direction possesses elegance, genial high-spirits and (at times) an almost Beechamesque wit — sample, say, the pointed woodwind dialogue in the scintillating reading of *La Cenerentola* to hear this. In fact, the only regret one could possibly have about this simply marvellous music-making is that, with a total duration of just under 47 minutes there isn't more of it! Despite some (inevitable) residual hiss, the RCA transfer engineers have worked wonders with these elderly tapes, producing a far more full-blooded, transparent sound-picture than one would have thought possible. At mid-price, this is unmissable. Buy it!

Additional recommendations ...

Tancredi. L'italiana in Algeri. L'inganno felice. La scala di seta. Il barbiere di Siviglia. Il Signor Bruschino. La cambiale di matrimonio. Il turco in Italia. **Orpheus Chamber Orchestra.** DG 415 363-2GH — 52m DDD 10/85

La scala di seta. Il Signor Bruschino. L'italiana in Algeri. Il barbiere di Siviglia. La gazza ladra. Semiramide. Guillaume Tell. **London Classical Players/Roger Norrington.** EMI Reflexe CDC7 54091-2 — 1h DDD 4/91

Complete Overtures — La cambriale di matrimonio. La scala di seta. Il barbiere di Siviglia. Tancredi. L'italiana in Algeri. Il Signor Bruschino. Il turco in Italia. L'inganno felice. Guillaume Tell. Semiramide. Le siège de Corinthe. La Cenerentola. La gazza ladra. Il viaggio a Reims. Maometto II. Ricciardo e Zoriade. Otello. Armida. Ermione. Torvaldo e Dorliska. Bianca e Falliero. Demetrio e Polibio. Eudardo e Cristina. Edipo a Colono. Sinfonia al Conventello. Sinfonia di Bologna. **Academy of St Martin in the Fields/Sir Neville Marriner.** Philips 434 016-2PM3 — 3h 29m ADD 10/92

Rossini. SONATE A QUATTRO. **Serenata of London** (Barry Wilde, Clive Lander, vns; Roger Smith, vc; Michael Brittain, db). ASV CDDCA767.

No. 1 in G major; No. 2 in A major; No. 3 in C major; No. 4 in B flat major; No. 5 in E flat major; No. 6 in D major.

1h 18m DDD 10/91

Rossini's six string sonatas are usually heard performed by a string orchestra, although they were in fact composed for a quartet of two violins, cello and double bass. This issue, which gives us for the first time on CD the original instrumentation, is therefore most welcome. The sonatas, which display amazing musical dexterity and assurance may date from 1804, when Rossini was only 12. The world of eighteenth-century opera is never far away, with the first violin frequently taking the role of soprano soloists, particularly in the slow movements. Written for Rossini's friend Agostino Triosso, who was a keen double bass player, the sonata's bass parts are full of wit and suavity. The performances by the Serenata of London are full of elegance and polish. Rossini's youthful high spirits are always to the fore and some of the fearsome string writing clearly holds no terrors for the members of this group. ASV's resonant recording adds the final touch of satisfaction to a most welcome recording.

Additional recommendations ...

Nos. 1-6. **Academy of St Martin in the Fields/Sir Neville Marriner.** Decca 430 563-2DM2 — ② 1h 52m ADD

Nos. 1-6. **Elizabeth Wallfisch, Marshall Marcus** (vns); **Richard Tunnicliffe** (vc); **Chi-Chi Nwanoku** (db). Hyperion CDA66595 — 1h 20m DDD 10/92

Nos. 1, 3 and 6. Variations in C major[a]. *Variazoni a più instrumenti obbligati in F major*[a]. *Serenata in E flat major.* [a]**Dmitri Ashkenazy** (cl); **Bologna Teatro Communale Orchestra/Riccardo Chailly.** Decca 433 701-2DH — 1h 13m DDD 2/93

Key to Symbols

	② ②	1h 23m	DDD	6/88
Price	*Quantity/ availability*	*Timing*	*Mode*	*Review date*

NEW REVIEW

Rossini. Messa di gloria. **Sumi Jo** (sop); **Ann Murray** (mez); **Raúl Giménez, Francisco Araiza** (tens); **Samuel Ramey** (bass); **Academy of St Martin in the Fields Chorus and Orchestra/Sir Neville Marriner.** Philips 434 132-2PH. Text and translation included. Recorded in 1992.

59m DDD 12/92

Though it is not perhaps one of his best known pieces, no Rossini enthusiast should be without this recording of the *Messa di gloria* (the only recording at the time of publication) and this version, with its splendid line-up of soloists and dedicated reading from Marriner with his St Martin in the Fields forces, brings out the music's finest qualities. Of course, the work is gloriously operatic: although some critics have carped over the seeming trivialization of religious sentiments, as they did with Verdi's Requiem, the audiences of Rossini's time seemed to be happy with the composer praising his God in the way he knew best and, at the first performance in 1820 given in the church of San Ferdinando in Naples, the *Gloria* was soundly applauded. Rossini was in his prime at the time of writing this work, and it shows — ensembles, such as the remarkably delicate trio of the "Domine Deus", are poised and astutely scored for the voices, the solo arias virtuosic and memorable, the choruses full-blooded, and the whole is scored throughout with Rossini's keen sense of colour and balance. It is worth noting that the fugal finale, "Cum sancto spiritu", is probably not by Rossini, who lacked confidence in his own contrapuntal skills, but commissioned from expert Pietro Raimondo. This performance is first-rate throughout and, although one might wish for greater drive in the *Kyrie* and the "Cum sancto spiritu", the overall pacing seems ideal, with Marriner allowing his excellent soloists, both vocal and instrumental, the space to let the music fully flower. Though the recorded sound seems to lack the complete lucidity that some other recordings made at St John's, Smith Square in London have been able to achieve, in all other respects this is an exemplary issue and should quickly make this one of Rossini's most widely prized works.

Rossini. Stabat mater. **Helen Field** (sop); **Della Jones** (mez); **Arthur Davies** (ten); **Roderick Earle** (bass); **London Symphony Chorus; City of London Sinfonia/Richard Hickox.** Chandos CHAN8780. Text and translation included. Recorded in 1989.

59m DDD 3/90

This used to be a ripe nineteenth-century favourite, and many a proudly bound vocal score at present languishing in a pile of second-hand music would testify to a time when its owner felt enabled, with its help, to combine the pleasure of church-going with the duty of attendance at the opera. The words are those of Jacapone da Todi's sacred poem, but Rossini's music is dramatic, exciting and sometimes almost indecently tuneful. Certainly the soloists have to be recruited from the opera company; the soprano who launches out into the "Inflammatus" must be generously supplied with high Cs as well as the power to shoot them over the heads of full choir and orchestra, while the tenor at one alarming moment is asked for a top D flat and has to ring out the melody of his "Cujus animam" with tone to match the trumpets which introduce it. In all four soloists, grace and technical accomplishment are as important as range and power; they must also have the taste and discipline to work harmoniously as a quartet. In this recording they certainly do that, and neither are they lacking in range or technique; if there is a limitation it is rather in richness of tone and in the heroic quality which the solos mentioned above ideally need. Even so, individually and collectively, they compare well with most of their competitors on record, and the choral and orchestral work under Hickox is outstanding.

Additional recommendations ...

Soloists; Philharmonia Chorus and Orchestra/Carlo Maria Giulini. DG 410 034-2GH — 1h 5m DDD 9/83

Soloists; London Symphony Chorus and Orchestra/István Kertész. Decca Ovation 417 766-2DM — 54m ADD 7/89

Soloists; Bavarian Radio Chorus and Symphony Orchestra/Semyon Bychkov. Philips 426 312-2Ph — 1h 5m DDD 3/91

Rossini. Petite messe solennelle. **Helen Field** (sop); **Anne-Marie Owens** (mez); **Edmund Barham** (ten); **John Tomlinson** (bass); **David Nettle, Richard Markham** (pfs); **Peter King** (harmonium); **City of Birmingham Symphony Orchestra Chorus/Simon Halsey.** Conifer CDCF184. Text and translation included. Recorded in 1989.

1h 18m DDD 10/90

Of Rossini's later works, none has won such affection from the general listening public as the *Petite messe solennelle*. He called it "the final sin of my old age" and, as with the other of his *pêches de vieillesse*, he declined to have it published. Editions issued in 1869, the year after his death, failed to retain his original scoring and contained numerous inaccuracies, yet these have been the basis of most subsequent recordings of the work. This disc presents the mass in a revelatory new Oxford University Press edition by Nancy Fleming, using two pianos in addition to a fine, French harmonium. That alone would mark it out for prime consideration, even if the reading were only passable, but here we have the bonus of dedicated, heartfelt performances from all involved. Above all, the scale of the work is finely captured — it was intended for chamber performance and both writing and scoring reflect the intimacy of Rossini's ideas. Much praise must go to Simon Halsey for so clearly establishing the parameters for this performance, and to the recording engineers for making it all seem so convincing. The whole issue establishes a new benchmark for assessing recordings of this work.

Rossini. HEROINES. **Cecilia Bartoli** (mez); [a]**Chorus and Orchestra of the Teatro La Fenice, Venice/Ion Martin.** Decca 436 075-2DH. Recorded in 1991. Texts and translations included.

ZELMIRA — Riedi al soglio[a]. Le nozze di Teti e di Peleo — Ah, non potrian reistere. MAOMETTO II — Ah! che invan su questo ciglio; Giusto ciel, in tal periglio[a]. LA DONNA DEL LAGO — Tanti affetti in tal momento[a]. ELISABETTA, REGINA D'INGHILTERRA — Quant' è grato all'alma mia[a]; Fellon, la penna avrai[a]. SEMIRAMIDE — Serenai vaghirai ... Bel raggio lusinghier[a].

59m DDD 2/92

This sparkling disc brings together a collection of arias composed by Rossini for one of the great prima donnas of the nineteenth century, who was also his wife, Isabella Colbran. It is tempting to wonder whether even she had a voice to match that of Cecilia Bartoli, one of the newest, luscious, most exciting voices in opera. All those dazzling chromatic runs, leaps, cadenzas and cascading coloraturas are handled with consummate ease. Throughout, Bartoli sounds as if she's enjoying the music; there is always an engaging smile in the voice, although she is properly imperious in the extracts from *Elisabetta* and disarmingly simple in the prayerful "Giusto ciel, in tal periglio" ("Righteous heaven in such danger") from *Maometto II*. The orchestral and choral forces bring a delightful intimacy to the proceedings, with some cheeky woodwind solos and fruity brass passages. The recording, produced at the Teatro La Fenice by Decca veteran Christopher Raeburn, favours the voices but gives it just enough distance to accommodate high Cs and astounding A flats at the bottom of the range. The orchestral perspective is changeable but satisfactory. For Rossini and Bartoli fans alike, this disc is a must.

Rossini. OPERA ARIAS. **Della Jones** (mez); **[a]Richard Hickox Singers; City of London Sinfonia/Richard Hickox.** Chandos CHAN8865. Texts and translations included. Recorded in 1990.

L'ITALIANA IN ALGERI — Quanta roba! ... Cruda sorte! Amor tiranno![a]. LA DONNA DEL LAGO — Mura felici ... O quante lacrime finor versai. IL SIGNOR BRUSCHINO — Ah, voi condur volete ... Ah, donate i caro sposo. ADELAIDE DI BORGOGNA — Soffri la tua sventura; Salve, Italia, un dì regnante[a]. OTELLO — Assisa apiè d'un salice (with Carol Smith, sop). IL BARBIERE DI SIVIGLIA — Una voce poco fà. BIANCA E FALLIERO — Tu non sai qual colpo atroce. LA CENERENTOLA — Nacqui all'affanno ... Non più mesta[a] (Smith; Katherine Steffan, mez; Harry Nicholl, Gerard Finley, tens; Simon Birchall, bass).

1h 18m DDD 2/91 

In the court of the mezzo-soprano, Rossini would be composer-laureate. He wrote for the mezzo voice most extensively and excitingly, providing opportunities for comedy and pathos, for a pure, even melodic line and for brilliant displays of virtuosity. He exploited the whole vocal range, two octaves or more, yet was considerate in keeping the 'lie' or *tessitura* of the notes within the comfortable middle of the voice, avoiding strain at either extreme. Above all, he put the mezzo-soprano into the centre of the stage: for once, she, and not the full, high soprano, would be the star. Over the last 30 or 40 years many famous singers have been associated with these roles. Marilyn Horne and Teresa Berganza perhaps come to mind first, while most recently added to the line has been Cecilia Bartolli. None has coped more ably with the technical demands than Della Jones. She is fluent and precise, and exercises an easy mastery over the most difficult passage-work. She can express tenderness and concern (as in *La cenerentola*), but most of all these are *spirited* performances, some of them, too, in little-known music such as the arias from *Adelaide di Borgogna* and *Bianca e Falliero*. The acoustic may be a trifle too reverberant, but both the singing and the playing are so well defined that any loss of clarity is minimal.

NEW REVIEW

Rossini. L'OCCASIONE FA IL LADRO. **Maria Bayo** (sop) Berenice; **Natale De Carolis** (bass-bar) Don Parmenione; **Iorio Zennaro** (ten) Count Alberto; **Francesca Provvisionato** (mez) Ernestina; **Fabio Previati** (bar) Martino; **Fulvio Massa** (ten) Don Eusebio; **English Chamber Orchestra/Marcello Viotti.** Claves CD50-9208/9. Notes and texts included. Recorded in 1992.

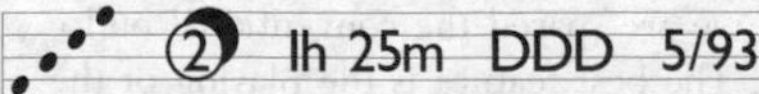

As the only currently available version of this sprightly one-acter, at the time of publication, this would be a self-recommending issue on those terms alone, but in addition there are at least two first-rate performances to lap up here: Maria Bayo is entrancing in her portrayal of Berenice, and Natale De Carolis, as Don Parmenione, enlivens the whole proceedings with his razor-sharp re-creation of the deceitful nobleman. Although Iorio Zennaro find himself a little stretched by Count Alberto's popular aria, "D'ogni più sacro impegno", he compensates with some sympathetic characterization. The whole production is skilfully handled by Marcello Viotti, who has a knack for finding the right speeds for his performers and pulls all the elements together convincingly. His style is to let the music make its own impact, and with early Rossini the unforced charm of the work can only benefit from that. The recorded orchestral sound is lively and the vocal soloists are well placed on the sound stage, with a vivid atmosphere enhancing the whole. A limitation, though, is the lack of an English translation of the libretto in the insert-notes. If you can live with that, then this issue fills an important gap in the recorded canon of Rossini's works with some aplomb.

NEW REVIEW

Rossini. LA PIETRA DEL PARAGONE. **José Carreras** (ten) Giocondo; **Beverly Wolff** (mez) Clarice; **Elaine Bonazzi** (mez) Aspasia; **Anne Elgar** (sop) Fulvia; **John Reardon** (bar) Asdrubale; **Andrew Foldi** (bass-bar) Macrobio; **Justino Diaz** (bass) Pacuvio; **Raymond Murcell** (bar) Fabrizio; **New York Clarion Concerts Chorus and Orchestra/Newell Jenkins.** Vanguard Classics 08903173. Notes, text and translation included. Recorded in 1972.

③ 2h 46m ADD 12/92

A glance through the surrounding entries in this *Guide* will quickly reveal Rossini's amazing profligacy: his tally, when he effectively retired from operatic composition at the age of 37, was approaching 40. *La Pietra del paragone* was his seventh opera and ran for an astonishing 53 performances, earning Rossini instant fame and fortune as well as exemption from military service. Its comic libretto is enriched by some superbly crafted character portraits which would certainly have appealed to the Milan audiences of 1812 but which still ring true today. As ever Rossini was writing tailor-made roles for specific singers — including one for his prima donna who, anxious to show off her legs, is brought into the final scene dressed as a Captain of the Hussars. Beverly Wolff takes on this classic mezzo-soprano role here and while her legs must be left to the imagination, the power and hypnotic appeal of her voice are unquestionable. Other fine performances are turned in by Justino Diaz as the poet Pacuvio and Anne Elgar as Donna Fulvia but the name which will immediately attract notice is José Carreras, recorded here at the start of his distinguished career. He makes his mark as the poet, Giocondo, in an exquisite forest scene at the start of Act 2. The Clarion Concerts Orchestra and Chorus under the intelligent direction of Newell Jenkins provide the mix of enthusiasm and stylistic awareness which makes this performance not only enjoyable to listen to but truly authoritative.

Rossini. IL SIGNOR BRUSCHINO. **Bruno Praticò** (bar) Gaudenzio; **Natale di Carolis** (bass-bar) Bruschino padre; **Patrizia Orciani** (sop) Sofia; **Luca Canonici** (ten) Florville; **Pietro Spangnoli** (bar) Filiberto; **Katia Lytting** (mez) Marianna; **Fulvio Massa** (ten) Bruschino figlio, Commissario; **Turin Philharmonic Orchestra/Marcello Viotti.** Claves CD50-8904/5. Text included. Recorded in 1988.

② 1h 24m DDD 10/89

It may take a wise father to know his own son, but even a fool can recognize a complete impostor: that, roughly, is the upshot of this little comedy in which the young Rossini tried out several ideas that were going to come in handy later on, and which is still revived from time to time to act as a pleasant part of a double-bill or a curtain-raiser. It is a pity that this recording could not have run in harness, for 84 minutes on two discs hardly constitutes good value these days. Still, the performance is likeable and at present has no competitor on CD. The singers are young and fresh-voiced; they miss a few tricks which their elders might have brought to the catch-phrases and the supposedly unexpected turn of events, but we are spared the conventional buffo clowning, with its exaggerated diction and falsetto squeaks. The best feature is the playing of the accomplished Turin orchestra under Marcello Viotti. The score is delightfully melodious and inventive, and the delicacy of orchestral texture as well as the spring of its rhythms can be well appreciated here, starting, of course, with the Overture and its famous raps of the second violins' bows on their music-stands which brought the musicians out on strike at the première in 1813.

NEW REVIEW

Rossini. IL TURCO IN ITALIA. **Simone Alaimo** (bar) Selim; **Sumi Jo** (sop) Fiorilla; **Enrico Fissore** (bar) Geronio; **Raúl Giménez** (ten) Narciso; **Susanne Mentzer** (mez) Zaida; **Peter Bronder** (ten) Albazar; **Alessandro Corbelli** (bar) Prosdocimo; **Ambrosian Opera Chorus; Academy of St Martin in the Fields/Sir Neville Marriner.** Philips 434 128-2PH2. Notes, text and translation included. Recorded in 1991.

② 2h 34m DDD 12/92

The audience at the première of *Il turco in Italia*, given in 1814 at La Scala in Milan, presumed (wrongly) that Rossini was recycling material for what was essentially *L'italiana in Algeri* in another guise. The notion has stuck with the opera, and its reputation has not been helped by the fact that Rossini delegated much of the work on the *secco* recitative and arias. In fact, and in contrast to *L'italiana*, *Il turco* is a surprisingly searching piece of psychological drama, given the seemingly trivial and prejudiced nature of its subject matter, and it very much benefits from the insight that repeated listening on CD, with commentary and translation, can supply. It depends for its effect on ensembles, rather than finding its dramatic and emotional heart in the solo arias and so, inevitably, the chief star of this performance must be Sir Neville Marriner, as the skilful development of the drama rests chiefly in his hands. The soloists are generally first rate. Although Sumi Jo is not perhaps as forceful or acerbic a Fiorilla as Caballé or Callas in their recordings of this work, she is nevertheless a highly skilled performer who makes her entrance with delicate phrasing and sweet tone. Alaimo, Corbelli and Fissore bring a particularly distinguished solidity to the casting. Captured in a clean, unfussy recording, the result is enthralling. Typically for a Rossini opera, recording *Il turco* has not been without its problems of deciding which version of the text to use. This issue scores heavily because it finds a happy balance of theatrical necessity and authenticity. The opera's music that is not by Rossini has been pruned and the result added to in order to develop the dramatic pacing. But in the end it is the overall quality of this performance that carries the day.

Additional recommendations ...

Soloists; Chorus and Orchestra of La Scala, Milan/Gianandrea Gavazzeni. EMI mono CDS7 49344-8 — ② 1h 53m ADD 12/87 £ ▲

Soloists; Ambrosian Opera Chorus; National Philharmonia Orchestra/Riccardo Chailly. CBS Masterworks CD37859 — ② 2h 26m DDD 9/89

Rossini. IL BARBIERE DI SIVIGLIA. **Thomas Allen** (bar) Figaro; **Agnes Baltsa** (mez) Rosina; **Domenico Trimarchi** (bar) Dr Bartolo; **Robert Lloyd** (bass) Don Basilio; **Francisco Araiza** (ten) Count Almaviva; **Matthew Best** (bass) Fiorello; **Sally Burgess** (mez) Berta; **John Noble** (bar) Official; **Ambrosian Opera Chorus; Academy of St Martin in the Fields/Sir Neville Marriner** with **Nicholas Kraemer** (fp). Philips 411 058-2PH3. Notes, text and translation included. From 6769 100 (6/83).

③ 2h 27m DDD 4/84  

The Overture gives the clue: this is to be a real *Barbiere* on the boards. Incisive, sprung rhythms, cheeky, rather than seductive, woodwind and a sense of fun as much as of intrigue characterize this performance from start to finish. It has a lot to do with Marriner's phrasing and rollicking sense of Rossinian style, to which the orchestra of the Academy respond so readily. But the barometer of this performance is its recitatives, and with Nicholas Kraemer's astute playing of a sweet-toned fortepiano in place of a spidery harpsichord, the voltage of the Rosina/Figaro encounters and the comic timing of Bartolo and Basilio is excitingly high. It keeps the soloists on their toes, too; and they are a strong team. The outstanding recommendation of this *Barbiere,* though, is its Rosina. From the first bars of "Una voce poco fa", Agnes Baltsa shows that this "dolce amorosa" can turn to the sting of a viper, too: the dark recesses of her chest voice and the brilliance of her high register flash in turn to follow every volatile mood of the role in a searching performance of superb dramatic timing.

Additional recommendations ...

Soloists; Philharmonia Chorus and Orchestra/Alceo Galliera. EMI CDS7 47634-8 — ② 2h 10m ADD 6/87

Soloists; Chorus and Orchestra of the Teatro Communale, Bologna/Giuseppe Patanè. Decca 425 520-2DH3 — ③ 2h 41m DDD 9/89

Soloists; Glyndebourne Festival Chorus; Royal Philharmonic Orchestra/Vittorio Gui. EMI Rossini Edition CMS7 64162-2 — ② 2h 21m ADD 5/92

Rossini. L'ITALIANA IN ALGERI. **Marilyn Horne** (mez) Isabella; **Ernesto Palacio** (ten) Lindoro; **Domenico Trimarchi** (bar) Taddeo; **Samuel Ramey** (bass) Mustafà; **Kathleen Battle** (sop) Elvira; **Clara Foti** (mez) Zulma; **Nicola Zaccaria** (bass) Haly; **Prague Philharmonic Chorus; I Solisti Veneti/Claudio Scimone.** Erato Libretto 2292-45404-2. Notes and text included. From STU7 1394 (3/81). Recorded in 1980.

② 2h 20m ADD 1/92 £

Written within the space of a month during the spring of 1813, and with help from another anonymous hand, Rossini's *L'italiana in Algeri* was an early success, and one which went on to receive many performances during the nineteenth century, with an increasingly corrupt text. A complete reconstruction was undertaken by Azio Corghi and published in 1981; this recording uses this new edition which corresponds most closely to what was actually performed in Venice in 1813. *L'italiana* is one of Rossini's wittiest operas, featuring as did a number of his most successful works a bewitching central character, in this case Isabella, who makes fun of her various suitors, with the opera ending with a happy escape with her beloved, Lindoro, a typical *tenorino* role. This fine recording on Erato has plenty of vocal polish. Scimone's biggest asset is Marilyn Horne as Isabella: possibly the finest Rossini singer of her generation and a veteran in this particular role, she sings Rossini's demanding music with great virtuosity and polish. Her liquid tone and artful phrasing ensure that she is a continuous pleasure to listen to. She is strongly supported by the rest of the cast: Kathleen Battle, making an early (1981) operatic appearance, is a beguiling Elvira, Domenico Trimarchi a most humorous Taddeo, and Samuel Ramey a sonorous Bey of Algiers — Isabella's opponent and pursuer. Ernesto Palacio's Lindoro, however, has patches of white tone and is correct rather than inspiring. Scimone's conducting is likewise efficient if at times slightly lacking in sparkle. It is, however, guaranteed to give considerable pleasure.

Additional recommendation ...

Soloists; Cologne West German Radio Male Chorus; Cappella Coloniensis/Gabriele Ferro. CBS Masterworks CD39048 — ② 2h 26m ADD 8/88

Rossini. ARMIDA. **Cecilia Gasdia** (sop) Armida; **William Matteuzzi** (ten) Goffredo, Carlo; **Bruce Ford** (ten) Ubaldo, Gernando; **Chris Merritt** (ten) Rinaldo; **Charles Workman** (bar) Eustazio; **Ferruccio Furlanetto** (bass) Idraote, Astarotte; **Ambrosian Opera Chorus; I Solisti Veneti/Claudio Scimone.** Europea Musica 350211. Notes and Italian text included.

② 2h 33m DDD 12/91

The story of Armida the sorceress must be one of the most popular in the history of opera. Monteverdi tackled it in the seventeenth century, Handel, Haydn and Glück in the eighteenth, and here in the nineteenth Rossini gives it full-blown Italianate treatment, complete with crescendos, ballet music and virtuoso vocal lines. It provides one of the few opportunities in Rossini for the soprano to head the cast; and considering the demands of this role and the scenario's opportunities for spectacle (descending clouds for example) it is perhaps surprising that it is not more frequently performed. There are fewer memorable melodies than, for instance, in the *Barber of Seville*, but nevertheless some of the music is appropriately enchanting, with particularly luscious orchestration, as in the Act 2 nymphs' chorus, and a glorious duet for Armida and Rinaldo in the same act, with obbligato cello. Armida is admirably sung with command, clarity and stunningly articulated consonants by Cecilia Gasdia. Her Rinaldo, Chris

Merritt, is an excellent match, and there is much fine singing from the supporting cast which includes Ferruccio Furlanetto, Bruce Ford and Charles Workman, though William Matteuzzi sounds a little strained when contending with the full orchestra, not aided by the resonant acoustic. The Ambrosian Opera Chorus, directed by John McCarthy, is superbly mellifluous, and from I Solisti Veneti and the conductor Claudio Scimone comes enthusiastic and wonderfully fresh playing with fine soloists for the obbligatos. The whole performance has much warmth, tenderness and spirit. The one quibble concerns the booklet. No English translation is provided, and no full synopsis; and it would have been better to insert track numbers beside the Italian text instead of identical black boxes at the start of each track, which do not help you to keep your place.

Rossini. LA CENERENTOLA. **Teresa Berganza** (mez) Angelina; **Luigi Alva** (ten) Don Ramiro; **Renato Capecchi** (bar) Dandini; **Paolo Montarsolo** (bar) Don Magnifico; **Margherita Guglielmi** (sop) Clorinda; **Laura Zannini** (contr) Tisbe; **Ugo Trama** (bass) Alidoro, **Scottish Opera Chorus; London Symphony Orchestra/Claudio Abbado.** DG 423 861-2GH2. Notes, text and translation included. From 2709 039 (6/72) and 415 698-2GH3 (9/86). Recorded in 1971.

② 2h 24m ADD 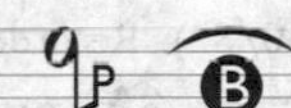

Rossini's Cinderella is a fairy-tale without a fairy, but no less bewitching for the absence of a magic wand. In fact the replacement of the winged godmother with the philanthropic Alidoro, a close friend and adviser of our prince, Don Ramiro, plus the lack of any glass slippers and the presence of a particularly unsympathetic father character, makes the whole story more plausible. *La Cenerentola*, Angelina, is more spunky than the average pantomime Cinders, not too meek to complain about her treatment or to beg to be allowed to go to the ball. She herself gives Don Ramiro one of her pair of bracelets, charging him to find the owner of the matching ornament and thus taking in hand the control of her own destiny. Along the way, Don Ramiro and his valet Dandini change places, leading to plenty of satisfyingly operatic confusion and difficult situations. This recording, when originally transferred to CD, was spread across three discs, but it has now been comfortably fitted into two. It gives a sparkling rendition of the score with a lovely light touch and well-judged tempos from Abbado and the London Symphony Orchestra and virtuoso vocal requirements are fully met by the cast. The chief delight is Teresa Berganza's Angelina, gloriously creamy in tone and as warm as she is precise. The supporting cast is full of character, with Luigi Alva a princely Don Ramiro, Margherita Guglielmi and Laura Zannini an affected and fussy pair of sisters, and Renato Capecchi as Dandini, gleeful and mischievous as he takes on being prince for a day. Although the recording was made in 1972 it has survived its technological transfers more than usually well.

Additional recommendations ...

Soloists; West German Radio Choir; Cappella Coloniensis/Gabriele Ferro. Sony Classical S2K46433 — ② 2h 28m ADD 6/91

Soloists; Glyndebourne Festival Chorus and Orchestra/Vittorio Gui. EMI Rossini Edition mono CMS7 64183-2 — ② 1h 57m ADD 5/92 ▲

Soloists; Chorus and Orchestra of the Maggio Musicale, Florence/Oliviero de Fabritiis. Decca Grand Opera 433 030-2DM2 — ② 2h 25m ADD 5/92

Rossini. LA GAZZA LADRA. **Katia Ricciarelli** (sop) Ninetta; **William Matteuzzi** (ten) Giannetto; **Samuel Ramey** (bass) Gottardo; **Bernadette Manca di Nissa** (contr) Pippo; **Luciana d'Intinto** (mez) Lucia; **Ferruccio Furlanetto** (bar) Fernando Villabella; **Roberto Coviello** (bass) Fabrizio Vingradito; **Oslavio di Credico** (ten) Isacco; **Pierre Lefebre** (ten) Antonio; **Francesco Musinu** (bass) Giorgio; **Marcello Lippi** (bass) Ernesto; **Prague Philharmonic Choir; Turin Radio Symphony Orchestra/Gianluigi Gelmetti.** Sony Classical MK45850. Notes, text and translation included. Recorded live in 1989.

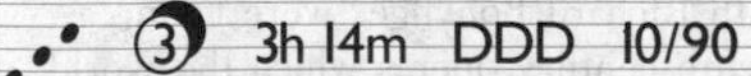

Recorded live during the 1989 Rossini Opera Festival in Pesaro, and suffused with the atmosphere of the venue, this performance sports a first-class line-up of soloists, a strong chorus and an enthusiastic orchestra. Ricciarelli, though perhaps a little rich-toned for the role of a country girl, stylishly ornaments her part and brings great authority and conviction to the role. Similarly, Samuel Ramey, as the Mayor, is particularly telling; but even the smallest parts are effectively done. The score employed here is unusually close to that used when this "Melodrama in due atti" first saw the light of day at La Scala in 1817, and as such gives us a good idea of Rossini's intentions for the work, unencumbered by the 'improvements' of later hands; the sentiments of the original play by d'Aubigny and Caigniez, that so moved Parisian audiences of 1815 and 1816, are once again made vital and relevant. Most importantly, the conductor, Gianluigi Gelmetti, must be commended for pacing the opera so astutely: Act 1 seems relatively low-key at first hearing, but emotion steadily builds in the long Act 2 to culminate in a stunning finale.

NEW REVIEW

Rossini. MOSE IN EGITTO. **Ruggero Raimondi** (bass) Mosè; **June Anderson** (sop) Elcia; **Zehava Gal** (contr) Amaltea; **Sandra Browne** (mez) Amenosi; **Salvatore Fisichella** (ten) Aronne; **Ernesto Palacio** (ten) Osiride; **Keith Lewis** (ten) Mambre; **Siegmund Nimsgern** (bass-bar) Faraone; **Ambrosian Opera Chorus; Philharmonia Orchestra/Claudio Scimone.** Philips 420 109-2PM2. Notes, text and translation included. From 6769 081 (10/82). Recorded in 1981.

② 2h 26m ADD 12/92

Mosè in Egitto integrates the biblical story of the Israelites in Egypt with a tragic tale of the love between Elcia, a Hebrew girl, and the Egyptian prince, Osiride. The love story is chiefly important in the Second Act, but Acts 1 and 3 are devoted to the completion of Mosè's mission. This balance in favour of the political situation lends strength to the opera, and the result is arguably one of Rossini's finest works, but its popularity has been sustained in its chubby French version of 1827, *Moïse et Pharaon*. The Italian version was first produced in Naples in 1818 and although this recording uses the first revision of 1819, it still retains much of the leaner power of the more integrated drama that Rossini first conceived. Nearly all of the important features of the Italian version have been retained in *Moïse*, but the majority of Rossini *aficionados* will find sufficient difference between them to warrant the expense of having both in their collection, and if only one were to be afforded, the tautness of this performance, with Scimone at his most persuasive, could well tip the balance. As if the power of Scimone's vision of the work were not alone sufficient, Ruggero Raimondi, as Mosè, gives one of his finest recorded performances here, digging deep into the essence of this role, yet retaining a clear-voiced, floated tone quality that ideally marries music and drama. When he enters the action, he dominates, and it takes a marvellously committed June Anderson, as Elcia, to sustain audience involvement during Act 2. With so much to commend here, the recording quality might be overlooked, but Philips have produced sound that is redolent of the theatre but which captures detail cleanly and maintains a balance between the performing forces.

Rossini. SEMIRAMIDE. **Dame Joan Sutherland** (sop) Semiramide; **Marilyn Horne** (mez) Arsace; **Joseph Rouleau** (bass) Assur; **John Serge** (ten) Idreno; **Patricia Clark** (sop) Azema; **Spiro Malas** (bass) Oroe; **Michael Langdon** (bass) Ghost of Nino; **Leslie Fryson** (ten) Mitrane; **Ambrosian Opera Chorus; London Symphony Orchestra/Richard Bonynge.** Decca 425 481-2DM3. Notes, text and translation included. From SET317/19 (10/66). Recorded in 1966.

③ 2h 48m ADD 2/90 £ 9p

Wagner thought it represented all that was bad about Italian opera and Kobbe's *Complete Opera Book* proclaimed that it had had its day — but then added what looked like second thoughts, saying that "were a soprano and contralto to appear in conjunction in the firmament the opera might be successfully revived". That was exactly what happened in the 1960s, when both Sutherland and Horne were in superlative voice and, with Richard Bonynge, were taking a prominent part in the reintroduction of so many nineteenth-century operas which the world thought it had outgrown. This recording brought a good deal of enlightenment in its time. For one thing, here was vocal music of such 'impossible' difficulty being sung with brilliance by the two principal women and with considerable skill by the men, less well-known as they were. Then it brought to many listeners the discovery that, so far from being a mere show-piece, the opera contained ensembles that possessed quite compelling dramatic intensity. People who had heard of the duet "Giorno d'orroré" (invariably encored in Victorian times) were surprised to find it remarkably unshowy and even expressive of the ambiguous feelings of mother and son in their extraordinary predicament. It will probably be a long time before this recording is superseded, admirably vivid as it is in sound, finely conducted and magnificently sung.

Rossini. IL VIAGGIO A REIMS. **Cecilia Gasdia** (sop) Corinna; **Katia Ricciarelli** (sop) Madama Cortese; **Lella Cuberli** (sop) Contessa di Folleville; **Lucia Valentini Terrani** (mez) Marchesa Melibea; **Edoardo Gimenez** (ten) Cavalier Belfiore; **Francisco Araiza** (ten) Conte di Libenskof; **Samuel Ramey** (bass) Lord Sidney; **Ruggero Raimondi** (bass) Don Profondo; **Enzo Dara** (bar) Barone di Trombonok; **Leo Nucci** (bar) Don Alvaro; **Prague Philharmonic Chorus; Chamber Orchestra of Europe/Claudio Abbado.** DG 415 498-2GH2. Notes, text and translation included. Recorded at performances at the 1984 Rossini Opera Festival, Pesaro, Italy.

③ 2h 16m DDD 1/86 

Composed as an elaborate and sophisticated entertainment for the coronation of Charles X, *Il viaggio a Reims* marked Rossini's début in Paris as the international superstar which his dazzling and innovative Italian career had justly made him. Musically it is bewitching: an intoxicant that gives sustained sensuous pleasure quite independent of the libretto. The rediscovery and assembly of the complete score, which Rossini partially dismantled and expertly reallocated to *Le Comte Ory,* is the brilliant scholarly achievement of Janet Johnson and Philip Gosset. The set is also a triumph for Claudio Abbado, the finest Rossini conductor of our day, and for DG whose munificence helped make possible the assembly of that dazzling array of vocal talent which the piece needs. The recording is a miracle of clarity and brilliance, with the kind of electricity in the atmosphere which is virtually impossible to reproduce in studio conditions.

Rossini. LE COMTE ORY. **John Aler** (ten) Comte Ory; **Sumi Jo** (sop) Adèle; **Gille Cachemaille** (bar) La Gouverneur; **Diana Montague** (mez) Isolier; **Gino Quilico** (bar) Raimbaud; **Raquel Pierotti** (mez) Ragonde; **Maryse Castets** (sop) Alice; **Francis Dudziac** (ten) First Chevalier; **Nicholas Rivenq** (bar) Second Chevalier; **Chorus and Orchestra of Lyon Opera/John Eliot Gardiner.** Philips 422 406-2PH2. Notes, text and translation included. Recorded in 1988.

② 2h 12m DDD 10/89 

Rossini's last comedy had its première in 1828 and for English audiences it came delightfully to new life at Glyndebourne in 1955. More than most, it is an opera that needs to be seen, especially the part where Ory and his men disguised as nuns are solicitously cared for by the ladies whom they hope to vanquish in the few hours remaining before their husbands return from the Crusades. Still, all is played vividly, and the ear catches the infection of laughter much as sight does in the theatre. Gardiner's direction has pace and point, and his young-sounding cast have a natural grace and lightness of touch. Outstanding among them is the Korean-born soprano Sumi Jo, charming in tone and style, highly accomplished in the rapid scale-work and high coloratura abounding in her part. Her duet with Ory in Act 2 is one of the high-spots; one among many, it has to be added, for all of the principal singers add something distinctive and delightful when their turn comes. Best of all perhaps is the concerted work of the whole company in the finale of Act 1: the very essence of Rossinian comedy is here, and one can hardly imagine a performance more happily combining refinement and exhilaration.

Additional recommendation ...

Soloists; Glyndebourne Festival Chorus and Orchestra/Vittorio Gui. EMI Rossini Edition mono CMS7 64180-2 — ② 1h 53m ADD 5/92 ▲

Rossini. GUILLAUME TELL. **Gabriel Bacquier** (bar) Guillaume Tell; **Montserrat Caballé** (sop) Mathilde; **Nicolai Gedda** (ten) Arnold; **Kolos Kovacs** (bass) Walter Furst; **Gwynne Howell** (bass) Melcthal; **Mady Mesplé** (sop) Jemmy; **Jocelyne Taillon** (mez) Hedwige; **Louis Hendrikx** (bass) Gessler; **Charles Burles** (ten) Fisherman; **Ricardo Cassinelli** (ten) Rudolph; **Nicholas Christou** (bar) Leuthold; **Ambrosian Opera Chorus; Royal Philharmonic Orchestra/Lamberto Gardelli.** EMI CMS7 69951-2. Notes and text included. From SLS970 (11/73). Recorded in 1972.

4 3h 58m ADD 3/89

Rossini's last opera was not only his grandest but also the very epitome of operatic grandeur. In length alone it involves a formidable commitment, but more fundamental are the span of the scenes, the amplitude of the forces employed and the range of mood and feeling from simple rustic happiness to a passionate affirmation of liberty hard-won in the face of cruelty and personal loss. Near the end of the whole epic work, as the sky clears, literally and figuratively, there comes a passage of inspired sublimity, with an effect worthy of *Fidelio*; it also is built with Rossini's favourite device of the crescendo, but having its excitement now transfigured and ennobled, so that even if Rossini had composed more operas one feels he could hardly have gone beyond this. Though frequently given in Italian, it was written to a French text and the language gives a strong initial advantage to this recording over its notable rivals. Among the principals Bacquier is a dignified, elderly-sounding Tell, Caballé a tender yet patrician Mathilde, Gedda a lyrical Arnold who fortifies his voice manfully for the heroic passages. Gardelli conducts with control and flexibility; the orchestral playing and chorus work are alike admirable, as are the clarity and sense of presence in the recorded sound.

Further listening ...

Piano Works — Danse sibérienne. Péchés de vieillesse, Book 5 — Thème naïf et variations idem. Péchés de vieillesse, Book 6 — Une caresse à ma femme; Barcarolle in E flat major; Un petit train de plaisir. Péchés de vieillesse, Book 7 — Petite valse, "L'huile de Ricin". Péchés de vieillesse, Book 9 — Marche et réminiscences pour mon dernier voyage. Péchés de vieillesse, Book 10 — Petit caprice (style Offenbach). Petite promenade de Passy à Courbevoie. **Helge Antoni** (pf). Etcetera KTC1107 (11/91).

Giovanna d'Arco. *Songs* — Ariette à l'ancienne. Beltà crudele. Canzonetta spagnuola. Il risentimento. Il trovatore. L'âme délaissée. L'Orpheline du Tyrol. La Grande Coquette. La légende de Marguerite. La pastorella. La regate veneziana. Mi lagnerò. Nizza. **Cecilia Bartoli** (mez); **Charles Spencer** (pf). Decca 430 518-2DH (4/91).

LA DONNA DEL LAGO. **Soloists; Prague Philharmonic Chorus; Chamber Orchestra of Europe/Maurizio Pollini.** CBS Masterworks CD39311 (8/88).

OTELLO. **Soloists; Ambrosian Opera Chorus; Philharmonia Orchestra/Jesús López-Cobos.** Philips 432 456-2PM2 (12/92).

Key to Symbols

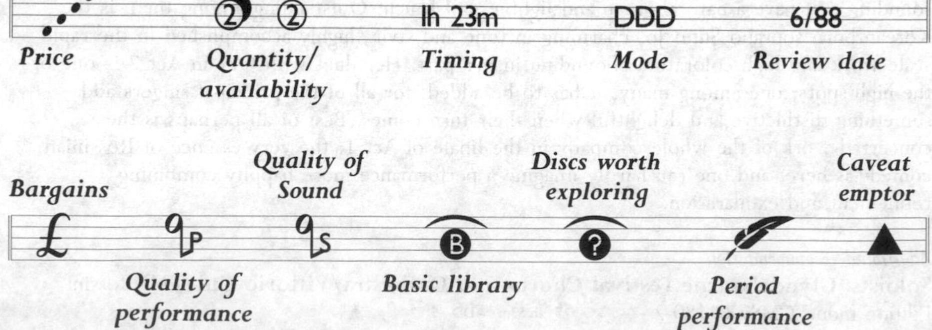

Nino Rota

Italian 1911-1979

Suggested listening ...

Film Scores — Il Gattopardo. La Strada. War and Peace. Waterloo. **Monte Carlo Philharmonic Orchestra/Gianluigi Gelmetti.** EMI CDC7 54528-2 (3/93).

Hans Rott

Austrian 1858-1884

NEW REVIEW

Rott (ed. Banks). Symphony in E major. **Cincinnati Philharmonic Orchestra/Gerhard Samuel.** Hyperion CDA66366. Recorded in 1989.

58m DDD 12/89 

It is October 1880. Picture the scene: 22-year-old Hans Rott, one-time fellow student with Mahler at the Vienna Conservatory, has failed to establish himself as a composer in Vienna, and is travelling by train to take up a provincial choirmaster's post elsewhere. The final rejection had come from Brahms: in the month before his journey he had played the completed Symphony to Brahms, but despite the finale's big tune resembling the one in the finale of Brahms's own First Symphony, the Symphony had paid just as many 'homages' to Wagner. On the train journey a fellow traveller tries to light a cigar, and ... Rott suddenly draws a revolver to restrain him, insisting that Brahms has dynamited the train! Hallucinatory insanity and persecution mania were diagnosed, and Rott died in a mental hospital three years later. It is a cliché to observe that genius and insanity are two sides of the same coin, but Rott's *Scherzo*, even without hindsight, seems disturbingly close to the edge; almost incapable of stopping. And here is a Symphony of astonishing daring that, for all its derivations (including Bruckner, from whose organ class Rott graduated in 1877), is most remarkable for its apparent influence on Mahler: to cite but one example, the *Scherzo*'s opening could be a draft for the one in Mahler's First. It is, in short, essential listening for anyone interested in the development of the Austro-German symphonic tradition. The recording has natural perspectives and a wide range, and if the players from the University of Cincinnati lack the last degree of finesse, or stamina for parts of the finale, they are obviously inspired by the enterprise.

Albert Roussel

French 1869-1937

Roussel. Symphonies — No. 1 in D minor, Op. 7, "Le poème de la forêt"; No. 3 in G minor, Op. 42. **French National Orchestra/Charles Dutoit.** Erato 2292-45254-2. From NUM75283 (2/87).

59m DDD 6/87 

Roussel's First Symphony is not a symphony in the usual sense at all, but more a cycle of four tone-poems. When the first of these, "Soir d'été", was performed Roussel did not envisage any further seasonal depictions of nature, but after "Renouveau" was written it was quickly followed by "Forêt d'hiver" and "Faunes et Dryades" — this last piece having autumnal connotations to complete Roussel's own 'Four Seasons'. The completed Symphony was Roussel's first major orchestral work, and although it is more romantic than his later works it already has characteristic fingerprints in his use of the orchestra. The Third Symphony is a very outgoing work in conventional four movement form, with characteristic 'motor' rhythms, and breezy, rather terse melodies — except in the *Scherzo*, which almost has the air of a jaunty popular song. Dutoit's performances are quite admirable in their clarity and understanding of Roussel's contrasted styles. The orchestra have just the right timbre and the recording is superb.

Roussel. Symphonies — No. 2 in B flat major, Op. 23; No. 4 in A major, Op. 53. **French National Orchestra/Charles Dutoit.** Erato 2292-45253-2.

1h DDD 6/87 — 9p 9s

This disc couples one of Roussel's most often-played symphonies with one of his least. The Fourth Symphony is a late work written only a few years before his death, and is a delightful score, the product of a richly-stocked imagination. It has a dark and powerful slow movement, a most infectiously engaging scherzo and a captivating finale. The Second Symphony is a rarity. It is abundantly resourceful and full of colour, and the scoring is refined and opulent. Dutoit gets playing of great vitality from this great French orchestra, dynamic markings are scrupulously observed but it is not just the letter but the spirit of the score that is well served. The Erato engineers do full justice to the dark and richly-detailed orchestral textures and the sound is particularly imposing in the definition of the bottom end of the register. Not to be missed.

NEW REVIEW

Roussel. La Festin de l'arraigneé — ballet[a]. Symphonies[b] — No. 3 in G minor, Op. 42; No. 4 in A major, Op. 53. **Suisse Romande Orchestra/Ernest Ansermet.** Decca Ovation 433 719-2DM. From LXT5234 (1/57). Item marked [a] recorded in 1954, [b] 1956.

1h 15m ADD 

NEW REVIEW

Roussel. Symphonies — No. 3 in G minor, Op. 42; No. 4 in A major, Op. 53. **Lamoureux Concerts/Charles Munch.** Erato 2292-45687-2. From ERA9515 (7/78). Recorded in 1965.

48m ADD

Nobody would choose these recordings for glamorous orchestral tone or state of the art sound. But the narrow frequency range of the Erato recording in no way detracts from the power and sweep of Charles Munch's readings of Roussel's two finest symphonies. Both works date from the 1930s and under Munch their almost irreconcilable moods of mechanistic power, dark disquiet, brief oases of calm and cheerful indifference are fully explored and yet add up to a convincing whole. Ernest Ansermet wrote of Roussel that "his melodies pass from one instrument to another, crossing a variety of orchestral textures, where they risk being lost". In Ansermet's recordings of the symphonies, which date from 1956, he ensures that nothing is lost. The textual clarity and rhythmic precision, enduring hallmarks of his best recordings, are invaluable for getting to grips with Roussel's methods and from there to his message. Hallmarks that are just as vital for the minimal detailing and delicacy of Roussel's earlier (1913) ballet *La Festin de l'arraigneé* ("The Spider's Banquet"), a generous addition to Ansermet's disc.

Further listening ...

Bacchus et Ariane — ballet. **Orchestre de Paris/Charles Dutoit.** Erato 2292-45278-2 (9/88).

Bacchus et Ariane — Ballet Suite No. 2[b]. *Coupled with* ***Ravel.*** Daphnis et Chloé[a]. **[a]New England Conservatory Chorus; [a]Alumni Chorus; Boston Symphony Orchestra/Charles Munch.** RCA Victor Gold Seal [a]stereo/[b]mono GD60469 (12/91).

Miklós Rózsa

Hungarian/American 1907-

Suggested listening ...

Film Scores — The Red House — suite[a]. The Thief of Bagdad — The love of the princess. The Lost Weekend — suite. The Four Feathers — Sunstroke/River journey. Double Indemnity — Mrs Dietrichson/The conspiracy. Knights of the Round Table — Hawks in flight. The Jungle

Book — Song of the jungle[a]. Spellbound — The dream sequence; The mountain lodge. Ivanhoe — Overture. [a]**Ambrosian Singers; National Philharmonic Orchestra/Charles Gerhardt.** RCA Victor GD80911 (5/91).

Lust for Life — suite. Background to Violence — suite. **Frankenland State Symphony Orchestra/Miklós Rózsa.** Varèse Sarabande VSD5405.
See also under Korngold.

Edmund Rubbra

British 1901-1986

Rubbra. ORCHESTRAL WORKS. **Philharmonia Orchestra/Norman Del Mar.** Lyrita SRCD202.
Symphonies — No. 3, Op. 49, No. 4, Op. 53. A Tribute, Op. 56. Resurgam — overture, Op. 149.

1h 13m DDD 11/90 

These are the only recordings of either symphony after half-a-century of indifference and neglect! Yet the opening of the Fourth Symphony is one of the most beautiful things not just in Rubbra but in all present-day English music. It is often said that Rubbra's music is "not of our time but could not have been written at any other", to which one might add that it could not have been composed anywhere other than England. It is predominantly pastoral in feeling but there is little sense of what Constant Lambert called the 'cow-pat' school. It is obvious from the first bars of each work that this music possesses eloquence and nobility and clearly tells of deep and serious things. The opening pages of the Fourth Symphony are free from any kind of artifice and their serenity and quietude resonate long in the memory. The overture, *Resurgam*, is a late work, also of great beauty, written in response to a commission from the Plymouth Orchestra, and another first recording. It commemorates the rebuilding of the Church of St Andrew, destroyed by Nazi bombers in 1941. Only its tower remained intact on whose north door of its tower stood one word, *Resurgam* ("I will rise again"). The performances by the Philharmonia Orchestra under Norman Del Mar are dedicated and the recorded sound offers superb clarity and presence with transparent well-defined textures. An important and rewarding issue.

NEW REVIEW

Rubbra. Symphonies — No. 2 in D major, Op. 45[a]; No. 7 in C major, Op. 88[b]. Festival Overture, Op. 62[c]. [ac]**New Philharmonia Orchestra/Vernon Handley;** [b]**London Philharmonic Orchestra/Sir Adrian Boult.** Lyrita SRCD235. Items marked [ac] from SRCS96 (5/75), [b] SRCS41 (4/70).

1h 18m ADD 12/92 

Although he revered Vaughan Williams and also possessed a keen sense of nature's power, which you can feel in the opening pages of the Seventh Symphony, there is little of the overtly pastoral in Rubbra's music. Nor does his music possess surface appeal: for him matter and not manner is of the essence. The Second Symphony comes from 1937 and was dedicated to Sir Adrian Boult. However, the orchestration worried him and he revised it in 1950, reducing the scoring from triple to double woodwind, making a cut in the middle of the first movement and so on. The emphasis on linear growth is evident from the start and as with many of his other symphonies, his musical processes are deeply organic. The heart of the work is its slow movement, a searching meditation on three ideas — first, a melody on the violas heard right at the beginning; secondly, a dotted theme that grows out of it and lastly an idea in thirds in contrary motion. The Seventh Symphony, written to a commission from the City of Birmingham Symphony Orchestra comes from 1957 and its opening is one of the most beautiful things he ever wrote. The recordings made in the 1970s were superb in their day and have been digitally remastered to striking effect.

NEW REVIEW

Rubbra. Symphonies — No. 6, Op. 80[a]; No. 8, Op. 132, "Hommage à Teilhard de Chardin". Soliloquy, Op. 57[b]. [b]**Rohan de Saram** (vc); [b]**London Symphony Orchestra/Vernon Handley;** [a]**Philharmonia Orchestra/Norman Del Mar.** Lyrita SRCD234. Items marked [a] from SRCS127 (5/82), [b] SRCS119 (1/80).

1h 13m ADD 10/92 

The Sixth Symphony comes from the early 1950s, when Rubbra enjoyed something of a vogue. All the movements in one way or another derive their material from the four notes heard on the cor anglais at the beginning of the finale. When he began work on the symphony he had intended the finale as the first movement and it was only when the work was well under way that he realized its true place in the overall scheme. The first is a sonata design in which the whole argument is borne along by a strong sense of linear continuity: the burden of the melodic line remains virtually unbroken. The emotional and spiritual centre of gravity is the "Canto", a wonderfully serene and deeply-felt movement. Rubbra possessed a deeply religious nature which shines through both here and in the Eighth Symphony, an act of homage to the Catholic theorist and philosopher, Teilhard de Chardin, for in the late 1940s, he became a Catholic. The Eighth takes as its starting point an interval generated by the opening chord. But the intervals get progressively smaller, which prompted Rubbra to write of the "intensity generated by the progressive contraction of intervals, as comparable to the energy engendered by the astronomical phenomenon of star contraction". There is a strong sense of vision in this music. An added inducement for collectors is Rohan de Saram's fervent account of another fine Rubbra score, the *Soliloquy* he wrote for William Pleeth (the cellist of the Rubbra-Gruenberg-Pleeth Trio). All three works sounded excellent on LP and a comparison is very much to the advantage of the CD. A superb issue.

Further listening ...

Violin Concerto, Op. 103[a]. [a]**Carl Pini** (vn); [b]**Geoffrey Tozer** (pf); **Melbourne Symphony Orchestra/David Measham.** *Coupled with* ***Ireland.*** Piano Concerto in E flat major[b]. Unicorn-Kanchana DKPCD9056 (1/87).

Anton Rubinstein

Russian 1829-1894

Suggested listening ...

Piano Concertos — No. 1 in E major, Op. 25; No. 2 in F major, Op. 35. **Joseph Banowetz** (pf); **Košice State Philharmonic Orchestra/Alfred Walter.** Marco Polo 8 223456.

Piano Concertos — No. 3 in G major, Op. 45; No. 4 in D minor, Op. 70. **Joseph Banowetz** (pf); **Košice State Philharmonic Orchestra/Robert Stankovsky.** Marco Polo 8 223382.

Violin Concerto in G major, Op. 46[a]. Don Quixote — musical picture after Cervantes, Op. 46. [a]**Takako Nishizaki** (vn); **Slovak Philharmonic Orchestra/Michael Halász.** Marco Polo 8 220359.

Symphony No. 2 in C major, Op. 42, "Ocean". **Slovak Philharmonic Orchestra/Stephen Gunzenhauser.** Marco Polo 8 220449 (11/87).

Poul Ruders

Danish 1949-

Ruders. Violin Concerto No. 1[a]. Concerto for clarinet and twin orchestra[b]. Drama-Trilogy — Cello Concerto, "Polydrama"[c]. [a]**Rebecca Hirsch** (vn); [b]**Niels Thomsen** (cl); [c]**Morten**

Zeuthen (vc); **Odense Symphony Orchestra/Tamás Vetö.** Unicorn-Kanchana DKPCD9114. Recorded in 1990.

lh DDD 4/92

In recent years Poul Ruders has emerged as one of the leading and most imaginative younger Danish composers of our time. This CD collects three of his works, all of them concertos, from the 1980s. He has an excellent feeling for colour and his textures even at their most complex, are never thick or cluttered. The most powerful and atmospheric of the three is the Clarinet Concerto (1985) written for Niels Thomsen (who has, incidentally, made an impressive recording of the Nielsen concerto). It is a short one-movement work in which (to quote the composer), the soloist is a Pierrot-like figure "in a vice of orchestral onslaught"; the overall effect is of conflict and turbulence. The effect, both here and in the Cello Concerto, at times is almost surrealistic. The Concerto No. 1 for violin, harp and harpsichord (1981) was inspired by a visit to Amalfi and has warmth and colour; it is an appealing piece, simpler in style than its companions, with brief echoes of Vivaldi's *Primavera*. It is perhaps best described as a blend of neoclassicism and minimalism. The performances by the Odense Orchestra are both expert and dedicated and the recordings are very good too.

NEW REVIEW

Ruders. Psalmodies[a]. Vox in Rama[b]. Nightshade[c]. [a]**David Starobin** (gtr); [a]**Speculum Musicae/David Palma;** [bc]**Capricorn/**[c]**Oliver Knussen.** Bridge BCD9037. Recorded in 1992.

47m DDD 5/93

The titles of these instrumental works, all composed during the 1980s, might lead you to expect music in deadly earnest, sombre and solemn. But Ruders is no Pärt or Gorecki. His main concern is not to suppress the potentially rich flowerings of his often quite simple musical ideas, but to direct them positively, allowing his ear for innovative instrumental sonorities and his feeling for comprehensible yet never monotonous formal design to provide the necessary controls. In *Vox in Rama*, which Ruders calls a scherzo, material evoking uninhibited lament develops in a dance-like way without the least incongruity, and the postponement of strong contrast until near the end is no less effective. *Nightshade* might be accused of occasionally pandering to the kind of mood music suggested by the title, but its unobtrusive exploration of a wide range of instrumental colours, coupled with an expressive restraint that works especially well when heard immediately after *Vox in Rama*, makes this a very satisfying piece. With its 11 short movements, *Psalmodies* is less subtle, but as a sequence of brief dialogues between guitar and ensemble it steers refreshingly clear of cliché. All the performances are highly polished yet sound natural and spontaneous: the recordings are no less convincing.

Further listening ...

String Quartets — No. 2; No. 3, "Motet". *Coupled with* ***Abrahamsen.*** String Quartets Nos. 1 and 2. **Kontra Quartet.** Marco Polo DCCD9006.

Corpus Cum Figuris[a]. Manhattan Abstraction[b]. Thus Saw Saint John[c]. [a]**Ensemble Intercontemporain/Peter Eötvös;** [bc]**Danish Radio Symphony Orchestra/**[b]**Michael Schønwandt;** [c]**Oliver Knussen.** Point Music PCD5084.

Carl Ruggles

American 1876-1971

Ruggles. Sun-treader[b]. *Coupled with* ***Piston.*** Symphony No. 2[a]. ***Schuman.*** Violin Concerto[c]. [c]**Paul Zukofsky** (vn); **Boston Symphony Orchestra/Michael Tilson Thomas.** DG 20th Century Classics 429 860-2GC (1/91).

See review under Piston; refer to the Index to Reviews.

John Rutter

British 1945-

NEW REVIEW

Rutter. FANCIES. [b]**Duke Dobing** (fl); [b]**Wayne Marshall** (hpd); [ac]**Cambridge Singers;** [ab]**City of London Sinfonia/John Rutter.** Collegium COLCD117. Texts included. Recorded in 1991.

Fancies[a]. Suite antique[b]. Five Childhood Lyrics[c]. When icicles hang[a].

1h 5m DDD 3/93

John Rutter writes music that is designed to give pleasure to performers as well as listeners. He knows exactly how to bring the best out of a body of singers and players, especially at that level where amateur and professional can meet and share. These four works, each of 15 to 20 minutes" duration, are charming in their freshness of ideas, unabashed appeal through melody and relatively comfortable harmonic idiom, and the avoidance of clichés and over-emphasis. One, the *Suite antique*, is for orchestra alone, using the same combination of instruments as Bach's Fifth Brandenburg Concerto, played in the concert for which this was commissioned. The *Childhood Lyrics* are for unaccompanied choir; *When icicles hang* uses a full orchestra; and *Fancies* has a chamber group. Each of the poems generates its characteristic musical idea, and the Cambridge Singers, who are Rutter's own choir, have the quick intelligence and the youth in their voices to give precisely the right kind of performance. In the orchestral suite, the City of London Sinfonia catches the lilt and grace of the music, and there is some particularly delightful playing by the flautist. This is light music, but not empty-headed and the disc is among the happiest discoveries of the year.

Further listening ...

Gloria for chorus and orchestra. *Anthems* — All things bright and beautiful; The Lord bless you and keep you; The Lord is my shepherd; O clap your hands; Open thou mine eyes; Praise ye the Lord; A Prayer of St Patrick. **Cambridge Singers; Philip Jones Brass Ensemble/John Rutter.** Collegium COLCD100 (6/87).

Requiem. I will lift up mine eyes — Psalm 121. **Caroline Ashton, Donna Deam** (sops); **Cambridge Singers; City of London Sinfonia/John Rutter.** Collegium COLCD103 (11/86).

Camille Saint-Saëns

French 1835-1921

NEW REVIEW

Saint-Saëns. Cello Concerto No. 1 in A minor, Op. 33[a]. Violin Concerto No. 3 in B minor, Op. 61[b]. Piano Concerto No. 2 in G minor, Op. 22[c]. [a]**Yo-Yo Ma** (vc); [b]**Cho-Liang Lin** (vn); [c]**Cécile Licad** (pf); [a]**Orchestre National de France/Lorin Maazel;** [b]**Philharmonia Orchestra/Michael Tilson Thomas;** [c]**London Philharmonic Orchestra/André Previn.** CBS Digital Masters CD46506. Item marked [a] from 35949 (5/81), [b] 35007 (6/84), [c] IM39153 (1/85). Recorded 1980-83.

1h 12m DDD 7/91

The concertos of Saint-Saëns are expert vehicles for subtle virtuosity, and the First Cello Concerto — which the composer completed in 1872 — is possibly the most fluent of them all. However, Saint-Saëns found the technical means of the instrument so restrictive that he vowed never to write another one, a vow he failed to keep. With an ardent, swirling *Allegro non troppo* as a prelude, a delicate *Allegretto* at its core and the cyclic return of important first movement material (supplemented by one of Saint-Saëns's most heartfelt melodies), the First Cello Concerto is a pleasing, symmetrical design, full of engaging music. The G minor Piano Concerto — the second of five — was written in 1868 in just over a fortnight; it starts out with overtly grand designs before settling to relative urbanity, while its sunny central *Scherzo* is delectably light and frothy. Incidentally, this appealing pattern of grave, commanding introductions followed by comparatively light-hearted argument is a formula that Francis Poulenc went on to develop with consummate artistry. The warmly melodic Third Violin Concerto is the longest piece in the programme, though its tunes and textures are no less appealing. A passionate and outgoing piece, it was written in 1880 for Sarasate and is full of engaging, colourfully contrasted music. Of the performances gathered here, the Lin/Tilson Thomas recording of the Violin Concerto is the most distinctive, with superb solo playing and a buoyant, balletic orchestral accompaniment under Tilson Thomas. Yo-Yo Ma offers a highly personable reading of the Cello Concerto, strongly supported by Maazel, and if Cécile Licad lacks the aristocratic poise of, say, Rubinstein or Ciccolini, both of whose performances are available at mid-price (listed below), her playing is never less than vital, and Previn offers her excellent support. A generous, well played collection, admirably recorded.

Additional recommendations ...
Piano Concerto No. 2.[a]. **Falla.** *Nights in the gardens of Spain*[a]. *El amor brujo. Ritual Fire Dance (arr. Rubinstein).* **Franck.** *Symphonic Variations, Op. 46*[b]. **Prokofiev.** *The Love for Three Oranges — March.* **Artur Rubinstein** (pf); [a]**Philadelphia Orchestra/Eugene Ormandy;** [b]**Symphony Orchestra of the Air/Alfred Wallenstein.** RCA Red Seal RD85666 — ⁘ 1h 3m ADD 10/87
Cello Concerto No. 1. **Bruch.** *Kol Nidrei, Op. 47.* **Lalo.** *Cello Concerto in D minor.* **Maat Haimovitz** (vc); **Chicago Symphony Orchestra/James Levine.** DG 427 323-2GH — ⁘ 59m DDD 6/89

Saint-Saëns. PIANO CONCERTOS. **Pascal Rogé** (pf); [a]**Philharmonia Orchestra,** [b]**Royal Philharmonic Orchestra,** [c]**London Philharmonic Orchestra/Charles Dutoit.** Decca 417 351-2DH2. From D244D3 (10/81).
No. 1 in D major, Op. 17[a]; No. 2 in G minor, Op. 22[b]; No. 3 in E flat major, Op. 29[c]; No. 4 in C minor, Op. 44[a]; No. 5 in F major, Op. 103, "Egyptian"[b]

⁘ 2h 21m ADD 12/86

Saint-Saëns's First Concerto was written when the composer was 23 years old, and it is a sunny, youthful, happy work conventionally cast in the traditional three-movement form. A decade later he wrote the Second Concerto in a period of only three weeks. This concerto begins in a mood of high seriousness rather in the style of a Bach organ prelude; then this stern mood gives way to a jolly fleet-footed scherzo and a *presto* finale: it is an uneven work, though the most popular of the five concertos. The Third Concerto is perhaps the least interesting work, whilst the Fourth is the best of the five. It is in effect a one-movement work cast in three ingeniously crafted sections. Saint-Saëns wrote his last, the *Egyptian*, in 1896 to mark his 50 years as a concert artist. Mirroring the sights and sounds of a country he loved, this is another brilliant work. Pascal Rogé has a very secure, exuberant sense of rhythm, which is vital in these works, as is his immaculate, pearly technique. Dutoit is a particularly sensitive accompanist and persuades all three orchestras to play with that lean brilliance which the concertos demand. The recordings are true and well-balanced.

Additional recommendations ...
Nos. 1-5. **Aldo Ciccolini** (pf); **Orchestre de Paris/Serge Baudo.** EMI Rouge et Noir CMS7 69443-2 — ⁘ ② 2h 18m ADD 3/92 £
Nos. 2 and 4. **Jean-Philippe Collard** (pf); **Royal Philharmonic Orchestra/André Previn.** EMI CDC7 47816-2 — ⁘ 50m DDD 10/87
Nos. 2 and 4. **Idil Biret** (pf); **Philharmonia Orchestra/James Loughran.** Naxos 8 550334 — ⁘ 55m DDD 12/90

NEW REVIEW
Saint-Saëns. Violin Concerto No. 3 in B minor, Op. 61.
Wieniawski. Violin Concerto No. 2 in D minor, Op. 22. **Julian Rachlin** (vn); **Israel Philharmonic Orchestra/Zubin Mehta.** Sony Classical SK48373. Recorded in 1991.

⁘ 52m DDD 12/92

Saint-Saëns's expansive Third Violin Concerto has the rare distinction of providing a showcase for virtuosos without compromising purely musical values. In terms of thematic material and orchestration, it has all the gracefulness and restraint of a classical concerto (as well it might, given its composer's admiration for Beethoven), but, additionally, it manages to find space for passion (first movement) and tenderness (second), as well as encourage a highly musical brand of technical display (third). Written for Sarasate in the early 1880s, the Concerto has long attracted the attention of leading players, yet has still to achieve the popularity of Saint-Saëns's more celebrated shorter works for violin and orchestra, his *Havanaise* and *Introduction and Rondo capriccioso*. Tchaikovsky was much taken with Henryk Wieniawski's Second Concerto (1862), a less ambitious piece than the Saint-Saëns but one that, over the years, has proved more popular. A great violinist himself, Wieniawski knew how to challenge his interpreters with devilishly difficult passage-work and gorgeous melodies (such as we encounter at the heart of this D minor Concerto), and it is a pleasure to encounter a young player who so fully understands its idiom. Lithuanian-born Julian Rachlin has a smooth, velvety tone and a lightning left hand; his playing has something of the cultured refinement of the late Nathan Milstein, yet it has its own personality and on this particular CD enjoys the added advantage of superb accompaniments, beautifully recorded. Incidentally, in the Wieniawski, the orchestral tutti passages are played complete — a bonus that you won't find on either of Jascha Heifetz's classic recordings!

Additional recommendations ...

Violin Concerto No. 3. **Lalo.** *Symphonie espagnole, Op. 21.* **Itzhak Perlman** (vn); **Paris Orchestra/Daniel Barenboim.** DG 429 977-2GDC — ADD 3/84

Violin Concerto No. 3. **Wieniawski.** *Violin Concerto No. 2.* **Bruch.** *Violin Concerto No. 2 in D minor, Op. 44.* **Conus.** *Violin Concerto in E minor.* **Tchaikovsky.** *Sérénade mélancolique in B minor, Op. 26*[a]. **Jascha Heifetz** (vn); **RCA Victor Symphony Orchestra/Izler Solomon;** [a]**Los Angeles Philharmonic Orchestra/Alfred Wallenstein.** RCA Victor Gold Seal mono GD60927 — lh 6m ADD 11/92

NEW REVIEW

Saint-Saëns. ORCHESTRAL WORKS. [a]**Kyung-Wha Chung** (vn); [a]**Royal Philharmonic Orchestra, Philharmonia Orchestra/Charles Dutoit.** Decca 425 021-2DM.

Danse macabre in G minor, Op. 40. Phaéton in C major, Op. 39. Le Rouet d'Omphale in A major, Op. 31. La Jeunesse d'Hercule in E flat major, Op. 50. Marche héroïque in E flat major, Op. 34. Introduction and Rondo capriccioso in A minor, Op. 28[a]. Havanaise in E major, Op. 3[a].

lh 6m ADD

It's enough to make you weep — at the age of three, Saint-Saëns wrote his first tune, analysed Mozart's *Don Giovanni* from the full score when he was five, and at ten claimed he could play all of Beethoven's 32 piano sonatas from memory. There is some consolation in the fact that, according to a contemporary, physically "he strangely resembled a parrot", and perhaps even his early brilliance was a curse rather than a blessing, as he regressed from being a bold innovator to becoming a dusty reactionary. In his thirties (in the 1870s) he was at the forefront of the Lisztian avant-garde. To Liszt's invention, the 'symphonic poem' (Saint-Saëns was the first Frenchman to attempt the genre, with César Franck hard on his heels), he brought a typically French concision, elegance and grace. Charles Dutoit currently has few peers in this kind of music; here is playing of dramatic flair and classical refinement that exactly matches Saint-Saëns intention and invention. Decca's sound has depth, brilliance and richness.

Additional recommendation ...

Introduction and Rondo capriccioso. Havanaise. **Paganini.** *Violin Concerto No. 1 in D major, Op. 6.* **Waxman.** *Carmen Fantasy.* **Maxim Vengerov** (vn); **Israel Philharmonic Orchestra/Zubin Mehta.** Teldec 9031-73266-2 — lh 3m DDD 5/92

Saint-Saëns. SYMPHONIES. [a]**Bernard Gavoty** (org); **Orchestre National de l'ORTF/Jean Martinon.** EMI CZS7 62643-2. Recorded 1972-75.

A major; F major, "Urbs Roma"; No. 1 in E flat major, Op. 2; No. 2 in A minor, Op. 55; No. 3 in C minor, Op. 78, "Organ"[a].

.• ② 2h 36m ADD 5/91 £

Saint-Saëns's four early symphonies have rather tended to be eclipsed by the popularity of his much later *Organ* Symphony. It's easy to see why the latter, with its rich invention, its colour and its immediate melodic appeal has managed to cast an enduring spell over its audiences, but there is much to be enjoyed in the earlier symphonies too. The A major dates from 1850 when Saint-Saëns was just 15 years old and is a particularly attractive and charming work despite its debt to Mendelssohn and Mozart. The Symphony in F major of 1856 was the winning entry in a competition organized by the Societé Sainte-Cécile of Bordeaux but was immediately suppressed by the composer after its second performance. The pressures of writing for a competition no doubt contribute to its more mannered style but it nevertheless contains some impressive moments, not least the enjoyable set of variations that form the final movement. The Symphony No. 1 proper was in fact written three years before the *Urbs Roma* and shares the same youthful freshness of the A major, only here the influences are closer to Schumann and Berlioz. The Second Symphony reveals the fully mature voice of Saint-Saëns and in recent years has achieved a certain amount of popularity which is almost certainly due in part to this particularly fine recording. Inevitably we arrive at the *Organ* Symphony, and if you don't already have a recording then you could do a lot worse than this marvellously colourful and flamboyant performance. Indeed, the performances throughout this generous set are persuasive and exemplary. A real bargain and well worth investigating.

NEW REVIEW

Saint-Saëns. Symphony No. 3 in C minor, Op. 78, "Organ"[a]. Le Carnaval des animaux[b]. [a]**Peter Hurford** (org); [b]**Pascal Rogé,** [b]**Christina Ortiz** (pfs); [a]**Montreal Symphony Orchestra,** [b]**London Sinfonietta/Charles Dutoit.** Decca Ovation 430 720-2DM.

.• 58m DDD 12/91 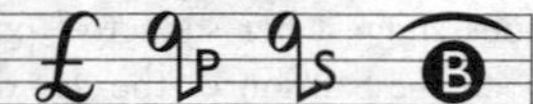

Let's face it, 'motto' themes and their transformations rarely produce good singable tunes. This Symphony uses a unifying motto theme, but it is fertile enough to produce two unforgettable melodies: the sensuous, arching string cantilena in the slow movement, and the grandly striding theme of the finale (so singable it was even borrowed for a pop chart-topping hit in the 1970s). In 1886 Saint-Saëns poured his considerable experience as an unequalled virtuoso of the organ, piano and practitioner of Lisztian unifying techniques into his *Organ* Symphony; it instantly put the French Symphony on the map, and provided a model for Franck and many others. With its capacity for grand spectacle (aside from the organ and a large orchestra, its scoring includes two pianos) it has suffered inflationary tendencies from both conductors and recording engineers. Dutoit's (and Decca's) achievement is the restoration of its energy and vitality. The private and affectionate portraits in the 'zoological fantasy', *The Carnival of the animals,* benefit from more intimate though no less spectacular sound, and a direct approach that avoids obvious clowning.

Additional recommendations ...

No. 3. **Daniel Chorzempa** (org); **Berne Symphony Orchestra/Peter Maag.** Pickwick IMP Red Label PCD847 — .• 37m DDD 4/87 Ⓑ

No. 3[a]*. Samson et Dalila — Bacchanale*[b]*. Le déluge — Prélude*[b]*. Danse macabre*[b]. [a]**Gaston Litaize** (org); [a]**Chicago Symphony Orchestra,** [b]**Orchestre de Paris/Daniel Barenboim.** DG Galleria 415 847-2GGA — .• 56m DDD 4/87 9p Ⓑ

No. 3. ***Dukas.*** *L'apprenti sorcier.* **Simon Preston** (org); **Berlin Philharmonic Orchestra/James Levine.** DG 419 617-2GH — .• 47m DDD 8/87 9p Ⓑ

No. 3[a]*.* ***Poulenc.*** *Organ Concerto*[b]. [a]**George Malcolm,** [b]**Anita Priest** (orgs); [a]**Academy of St Martin in the Fields/Iona Brown;** [b]**Los Angeles Philharmonic Orchestra/Zubin Mehta.** Decca Ovation 417 725-2DM — .• 56m ADD 12/87 Ⓑ

No. 3[a]*.* ***Poulenc.*** *Organ Concerto*[a]*.* ***Franck.*** *Le Chasseur Maudit.* [a]**Berj Zamkochian** (org); **Boston Symphony Orchestra/Charles Munch.** RCA Red Seal RD85720 — .• 1h 11m ADD 2/88 Ⓑ

Le carnaval des animaux[a]*.* ***Bizet.*** *Jeux d'enfants.* ***Ravel.*** *Ma mère l'oye.* [a]**Julian Jacobson,** [a]**Nigel Hutchinson** (pfs); members of **London Symphony Orchestra/Barry Wordsworth.** Pickwick IMP Classics PCD932 — .• 1h 3m DDD 4/90 Ⓑ

Le carnaval des animaux (arr. Reeve)[a]. ***Mussorgsky.*** *Pictures at an Exhibition (arr. Howarth)*[b]. **Philip Jones Brass Ensemble/**[a]**Philip Jones,** [b]**Elgar Howarth.** Decca Ovation 425 022-2DM — 58m ADD/DDD 6/91 B

No. 3[a]. *Phaeton, Op. 39.* [a]**Michael Murray** (org); **Royal Philharmonic Orchestra/Christian Badea.** Telarc CD80274 — 46m DDD 12/91 9s B

NEW REVIEW

Saint-Saëns. SAMSON ET DALILA. **Plácido Domingo** (ten) Samson; **Waltraud Meier** (mez) Dalila; **Alain Fondary** (bar) Priest; **Jean-Philippe Courtis** (bass) Abimelech; **Samuel Ramey** (bass) Old Hebrew; **Christian Papis** (ten) Messenger; **Daniel Galvez-Vallejo** (ten), **François Harismendy** (bass) First and Second Philistines; **Chorus and Orchestra of the Bastille Opera, Paris/Myung-Whun Chung.** EMI CDS7 54470-2. Notes, text and translation included.

② 2h 4m DDD 2/93 9p

Surviving the shafts of Bernard Shaw, bans by the Lord Chamberlain, and cries of "oratorio" from New York pundits, this impressive, subtly composed work continues to hold the attention of the opera-going public whenever and wherever it is performed, mainly because of its discreet combination of the pagan and the religious, the exotic and the erotic. Within a framework of the struggle between the Jews and Philistines, Delilah's overpowering sexuality and her dark soul are magnificently portrayed as are the proud, sensual and eventually tragic sides of Samson, while the High Priest is a vengeful, preening, frustrated figure. Their well-defined characters are depicted against a background of splendidly written choruses for Jews and Philistines. Here, at last, we have a modern version worthy of the piece, largely owing to Chung's understanding of tempo relationships, the refinement of the composer's orchestration and the energy of the pagan sections. Meier may not have the ideally voluptuous tone called for by Delilah's music but she does suggest her seductive powers and equivocal nature, singing in good French. Domingo has been *the* Samson of the day delivering Samson's defiance and love with equal aplomb if without the particular insights of great French tenors of the past. Being French and a splendid baritone, Fondary is an ideal High Priest. The recording is exemplary.

Additional recommendations ...

Soloists; Bavarian Radio Symphony Chorus and Orchestra/Sir Colin Davis. Philips 426 243-2PH2 — ② 2h 3m DDD 1/91

Soloists; Chorus and Orchestra de Paris/Daniel Barenboim. DG 413 297-2GX2 — ② 2h 6m ADD 11/91

Antonio Salieri

Italian 1750-1825

Suggested listening ...

AXUR, RE D'ORMUS. **Soloists; Guido d'Arezzo Choir; Russian Philharmonic Orchestra/René Clemencic.** Nuova Era 6852/4 (12/90).

Aulis Sallinen

Finnish 1935-

NEW REVIEW

Sallinen. Shadows, Op. 52. Cello Concerto, Op. 44[a]. Symphony No. 4, Op. 49. [a]**Arto Noras** (vc); **Helsinki Philharmonic Orchestra/Okko Kamu.** Finlandia FACD346.

1h DDD 6/86

Although he is one of the leading forces behind the revival of opera in Finland, Sallinen has an impressive amount of orchestral and chamber music to his credit including six symphonies.

Shadows (1982) is a highly atmospheric and effective prelude for orchestra, related both thematically and in its atmosphere, to his opera, *The King Goes Forth to France*. Hardly surprising, since Sallinen composed it immediately after finishing the Second Act. Although it is an independent work, it reflects or 'shadows' the content of the opera. The Fourth Symphony (1979) was a commission from the city of Turku and is a three-movement work, though it was composed, as it were, backwards: the first movement on which Sallinen began work eventually becoming the finale. The middle movement is marked *Dona nobis pacem* and throughout the finale bells colour the texture, as is often the case in his orchestral writing. In fact, the familiar fingerprints are to be found all over the score, and it is not long before the listener succumbs to it. The two-movement Cello Concerto (1977) is oddly proportioned, its long, expansive first movement taking almost 20 minutes and its companion just over five. Yet the first, which is based on variation, never seems discursive and Sallinen's ideas and his sound-world long resonate in the mind. Arto Noras has its measure and plays with a masterly eloquence. The performances under Okko Kamu are very impressive and the recording is exemplary.

Further listening ...

THE HORSEMAN. **Soloists; Savonlinna Opera Festival Chorus and Orchestra/Ulf Söderblom.** Finlandia FACD101 (12/91).

THE RED LINE. **Soloists; Finnish National Chorus and Orchestra/Okko Kamu.** Finlandia FACD102 (12/91).

Pablo Sarasate

Spanish 1844-1908

Sarasate. Zigeunerweisen, Op. 20.
Wieniawski. Violin Concertos — No. 1 in F sharp minor, Op. 14; No. 2 in D minor, Op. 22. Légende, Op. 17. **Gil Shaham** (vn); **London Symphony Orchestra/Lawrence Foster.** DG 431 815-2GH. Recorded in 1990.

lh 8m DDD 12/91

Sarasate's *Zigeunerweisen* brings forth one of those voluptuous gipsy tunes that insist on gorgeous tone, a temperamental warmth of feeling and a naturally seductive line. Then comes the fireworks, fizzling and effervescing; here the soloist needs to be enormously dashing and exuberant, yet at the same time relaxed, so that the listener senses no real effort. Gil Shaham takes naturally to all the demands made on his technique and musicianship, entrancing the listener with his provocative phrasing, and easy panache. Wieniawski's *Légende* has another melting violinistic melody and a livelier central section before the more gentle reprise of the main theme. Again Shaham is completely at home, the melodic line flowing ravishingly. But these pieces are merely encores for the two Wieniawski Violin Concertos of which the First is much less often played than the Second. Yet the lyrical theme of the first movement has a touch of magic on Shaham's bow and he is no less bewitching in the slow movement *Preghiera*, while the Paganinian pyrotechnics and the finale's dance rhythms are hardly less enticing. Lawrence Foster and the LSO, who until now have been simply providing a faultless backcloth for their young soloist, now come into their own in their imposing introduction for the Second Concerto, and Shaham's contribution is hardly less winning than in the earlier work, especially in the comparative innocence of the Romance. Another volatile zigeuner finale is thrown off with entertaining panache by all concerned. Excellent DG sound throughout.

Additional recommendation ...
Zigeunerweisen. ***Saint-Saëns:*** *Introduction and Rondo capriccioso, Op. 28.* ***Massenet:*** *THAIS — Méditation.* ***Chausson:*** *Poème, Op. 25.* ***Ysaÿe:*** *Caprice d'après l'etude en forme de valse de Saint-Saëns.* ***Ravel:*** *Tzigane.* **Joshua Bell** (vn); **Royal Philharmonic Orchestra/Andrew Litton.** Decca 433 519-2DH *(See review in the Collections section; refer to the Index to Reviews)* — lh DDD 1/92

Further listening ...

Introduction et Tarantelle, Op. 43[a]. *Coupled with* ***Mendelssohn:*** Violin Concerto in E minor, Op. 64[b]. ***Bruch:*** Violin Concerto No. 1 in G minor, Op. 26[c]. ***Kreisler:*** Liebesfreud[a]. **Cho-Liang Lin** (vn); [a]**Sandra Rivers** (pf); [b]**Philharmonia Orchestra/Michael Tilson Thomas;** [c]**Chicago Symphony Orchestra/Leonard Slatkin.** CBS Masterworks CD44902 (3/91).

See review in the Collections section; refer to the Index to Reviews.

Danzas españolas, Op. 22 No. 1 (Romanze andaluza). *Coupled with* ***Glazunov:*** Violin Concerto in A minor, Op. 82. ***Tchaikovsky*** (arr. Glazunov): Souvenir d'un lieu cher, Op. 42. ***Chausson:*** Poème, Op. 25. ***Saint-Saëns*** (trans. Ysaÿe): Caprice en forme de valse, Op. 52. **Hideko Udagawa** (vn); **London Philharmonic Orchestra/Kenneth Klein.** Pickwick IMP Classics PCD966 (3/92).

See review in the Collections section; refer to the Index to Reviews.

Erik Satie

French 1866-1925

NEW REVIEW

Satie. BALLET AND ORCHESTRAL TRANSCRIPTIONS. **New London Orchestra/Ronald Corp.** Hyperion CDA66365. Recorded in 1989.

Parade. Gymnopédies — Nos. 1 and 3 (orch. Debussy); No. 2 (orch. Corp). Mercure. Three Gnossiennes (orch. Corp). Relâche.

1h 6m DDD 2/90 

In 1918, the year after Diaghilev's Russian Ballet staged Satie's *Parade* in Paris, Poulenc wrote that "to me, Satie's *Parade* is to Paris what *Petrushka* is to St Petersburg" (André Gide, however, commented on its poverty-stricken pretentiousness). Satie was thenceforth adopted as the spiritual father of "Les Six", whose ideal was the marriage of serious music with jazz, vaudeville, and the circus. Those who only know Satie from his early *Gymnopédies* and *Gnossiennes* — take heed: *Parade* shuffles along its apparently aimless, deadpan and wicked way with interjections from typewriters, lottery wheels, pistols and sirens. What does it all mean? Ronald Corp could be accused of retaining a slightly stiff upper lip, but there may well be a seriousness of purpose behind Satie's balletic miniatures. Certainly, there is little here of the uproarious debunking of some of "Les Six". His orchestrations of the *Gnossiennes* and the remaining *Gymnopédie* are idiomatic, and his performances of all six have the requisite cool beauty. Hyperion's sound is spacious and natural.

Satie. PIANO WORKS. **Anne Queffélec.** Virgin Classics VC7 90754-2.

Six Gnossiennes. Véritables préludes flasques (pour un chien). Vieux séquins et vieilles cuirasses. Chapitres tournés en tous sens. Trois Gymnopédies. Embryons desséchés. Je te veux valse. Sonatine bureaucratique. Heures séculaires et instantanées. Le Picadilly. Avant-dernières pensées. Sports et divertissements.

1h 16m DDD 5/89 

Satie. PIANO WORKS. **Pascal Rogé** (pf). Decca 410 220-2DH. From 410 220-1DH (6/84). Recorded in 1983.

Trois Gymnopédies. Je te veux valse. Quatre préludes flasques. Prélude en tapisserie. Nocturne No. 4. Vieux séquins et vieilles cuirasses. Embryons desséchés. Six Gnossiennes. Sonatine bureaucratique. Le Picadilly.

1h 1m DDD 5/89 

Satie. PIANO WORKS. **Peter Dickinson.** Conifer CDCF512.

Chapitres tournés en tous sens. Croquis et agaceries d'un gros bonhomme en bois. Je te veux valse. Le Picadilly. Pièces froides. Le piège de Méduse. Poudre d'or. Trois préludes du fils des étoiles. Prélude en tapisserie. Sonatine bureaucratique. Sports et divertissements. Trois Gymnopédies. Véritables préludes flasques (pour un chien). Vexations. From CDCF183 (12/90).

lh 17m DDD 5/93 

Satie is a composer who defies description. His piano music has the same quirky originality as his life and his love of flying in the face of convention are crystallized in these fascinating miniatures. Anne Queffélec has made an excellent selection of Satie piano music starting with the famous and well-loved *Gnossiennes* and also including the *Gymnopédies*, works of a chaste almost ritualistic stillness. Also included are the wicked *Véritables préludes flasques (pour un chien)* containing his celebrated parody of Chopin's funeral march, credited typically à la Satie as a quotation "from the famous mazurka by Schubert". The programme ends with the whimsical and charming *Sports et divertissements* played with just the right air of mock seriousness. The recorded quality is good. It is a hard-hearted and humourless listener who cannot respond to the often childlike charm and evident warm and guileless heart of this very individual composer. Pascal Rogé plays these short pieces with the right kind of (again one must use the word) childlike gravity and sensuousness and the 1983 recording made in London's Kingsway Hall is excellent.

Peter Dickinson also succeeds admirably in his selection; the gravity and/or humour of these pieces is perfectly caught and conveyed, and as regards the latter quality the slightly understated playing in, say, *Le piège de Méduse* is right for this enigmatic composer. The three *Gymnopédies* provide a good test of Satie performance as well as being his most popular work, and Peter Dickinson is dead on target in his blend of gravity, sadness and tenderness — one almost writes "suppressed tenderness", given that their rarely understood titles evokes ceremonial dances of ancient Sparta performed by naked boys. There's also charm in plenty in the *café-concert* waltzes called *Poudre d'or* and *Je te veux*, and though not distinguished as music they have a fetching Gallic variety of schmaltz, while the Rosicrucian music of *Le fils des étoiles* is impressively serious. The recording has piano sound that is immediate yet well textured.

Additional recommendation ...

Six Gnossiennes. Avant-dernières pensées. Premiére pensée Rose + Croix. Trois préludes du fils des étoiles. Chapitres tournés en tous sens. Trois Gymnopédies. Le Piège de Méduse. Rêverie du pauvre. Je te veux valse. Prélude de la Porte héroïque du ciel. **John Lenehan.** Earthsounds CDEEASM003 — lh 3m DDD 5/93

Further listening ...

Vocal Works — Socrate: drame syphonique. Trois mélodies (1887). Trois mélodies (1916). Trois autres mélodies (1887). Quatres petites mélodies. Ludlions. **Music Projects London; instrumenalists/Richard Bernas.** Factory Classical FACD356 (10/91).

Robert Saxton

British 1953-

Suggested listening ...

Concerto for Orchestra[a]. The Sentinel of the Rainbow[b]. The Ring of Eternity[a]. Chamber Symphony: The Circles of Light[b]. **[a]BBC Symphony Orchestra, [b]London Sinfonietta/Oliver Knussen.** EMI CDC7 49915-2 (4/90).

Violin Concerto[a]. I will awake the dawn[b]. In the beginning[c]. **[a]Tasmin Little** (vn); **[b]BBC Singers/John Poole; [ac]BBC Symphony Orchestra/Matthias Bamert.** Collins Classics 1283-2 (4/92).

Alessandro Scarlatti

Italian 1660-1725

A. Scarlatti. Venere e Adone: Il giardino d'amore. **Catherine Gayer** (sop); **Brigitte Fassbaender** (mez); **Munich Chamber Orchestra/Hans Stadlmair.** Archiv Produktion

Galleria 431 122-2AGA. Text and translation included. From SAPM198344 (8/65). Recorded in 1964.

59m ADD 10/91 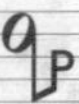

This performance of Scarlatti's engaging Serenata based on the legend of Venus and Adonis was recorded during the mid 1960s. Many aspects of baroque interpretation have changed since then but a musically enlightened and imaginative approach such as that captured on this disc has an enduring appeal. And deservedly so since both singing and playing are first rate. Catherine Gayer makes a spirited, ardent-sounding Adonis while Brigitte Fassbaender is wonderfully alluring and passionate throughout. Her "Augelletti, si cantate" is irresistible and her radiant duet with Adonis at the conclusion of the work something to treasure. The instrumental accompaniment reflects much that was best in baroque performance during the 1950s and 1960s with fine contributions from Hans-Martin Linde (sopranino recorder). In short this is music making of a kind which brings Scarlatti's score — and what a ravishing score it is — to life affectionately and convincingly. The recorded sound is almost all that one could wish for and full texts with translations are included.

A. Scarlatti. Variations on "La folia"[a]. Cantatas[b] — Correa nel seno amato; Già lusingato appieno. [b]**Lynne Dawson** (sop); **Purcell Quartet** (Catherine Mackintosh, Elizabeth Wallfisch, vns; Richard Boothby, va da gamba; [a]Robert Woolley, hpd). Hyperion CDA66254. Texts and translations included.

52m DDD 3/90 

To their series devoted to *La folia* variations, the Purcell Quartet have added this CD of music by Alessandro Scarlatti, who set the familiar tune in startlingly original harpsichord couplets. Robert Woolley plays 30 of them — many with striking touches of chromaticism — in glorious fashion; it is hard to imagine a performance that could match his wonderfully disciplined yet witty virtuoso one, which culminates in arpeggiated harp effects. Most of this disc, however, is devoted to two 'unfoliated' cantatas in which the Purcell Quartet is joined by the bewitching voice of Lynne Dawson. *Correa nel seno amato* is a pastoral cantata, the natural imagery of the text beautifully reflected in the music. The opening sinfonia and lyrical opening recitative are characterful and sensitively paced. Both singer and quartet capitalize on the chromatic inflexions and echoes in "Idolo amato". "Già lusingato appieno" is unusual for its textual references to an 'English hero' — possibly James II — bidding farewell to his family as he goes into exile. Among the highlights are the movements of collaboration between voice and strings, as in "Cara sposa" with its concertante violins, and "Sento l'aura", in which slow trills and echoes are made to sound like "whispering breezes". Just as in "Correa nel seno amato", Dawson commands the listener's attention from the very first notes of recitative with her beautifully weighted projection of the text. Both cantatas end with magical epilogues cast in recitative.

Further listening ...

Cain overo Il Primo Omicidio — *oratorio*. **Concerto Italiano; L'Europa Galante/Fabio Biondi.** Opus 111 OPS30-75/6.

Domenico Scarlatti

Italian 1685-1757

NEW REVIEW

D. Scarlatti. KEYBOARD SONATAS, Volume 2. **Andreas Staier** (hpd). Deutsche Harmonia Mundi 05472-77274-2. Recorded in 1991.

D minor, Kk64; B minor, Kk87; D major, Kk96; C major, Kk132; C major, Kk133; A minor, Kk175; B flat major, Kk202; D minor, Kk213; D major, Kk214; E minor, Kk263; E major,

Kk264; D major, Kk277; D major, Kk278; C major, Kk420; C major, Kk421; C major, Kk460; C major, Kk461.

lh llm DDD 3/93

D. Scarlatti. KEYBOARD SONATAS. **Ivo Pogorelich** (pf). DG 435 855-2GH.
D minor, Kk1; G minor, Kk8; D minor, Kk9; C minor, Kk11; G major, Kk13; E major, Kk20; B minor, Kk87; E minor, Kk98; D major, Kk119; E major, Kk135; C major, Kk159; E major, Kk380; G minor, Kk450; C major, Kk487; B flat major, Kk529.

lh DDD 1/93

These two first-rate issues epitomize the two extremes of approach to recording Scarlatti sonatas shown in the recommended list below. Though both are brilliantly and sympathetically recorded, the resulting sounds could not be more different. Staier uses a modern harpsichord, constructed according to traditional principles, that is mild-mannered and deliciously expressive, and his playing reflects this with supple articulation and well-chosen ornament — though he also injects an invigorating degree of sparkle and zest into a number of the pieces. His programme of mainly not-so-well-known sonatas (with over 550 of these single-movement works to choose from, such a choice is not problematic) provides insight into the more intimate aspects of Scarlatti's art, through works in which the composer is less intent on novelty and show for their own sakes though, for our delight, he never completely avoids these qualities. Pogorelich has gone for much better-known sonatas and, of course, uses a modern grand piano, but makes his effect time and again through restraint: dynamics are within eighteenth-century bounds, textures are kept crisply open, and speeds are consistently on the slow side; expression, though deeply felt and effective, is achieved through suggestion. But he also allows the fine tonal gradation and dynamic shading of the modern piano to add to the expressive range of this music. Staier is revolutionary in his 'authentic' approach, Pogorelich 'conservative' in his less authentic choice of instrument, yet both succeed in revealing the true voice of the composer through the sheer quality of their playing.

Additional recommendations ...

A major, Kk113; E major, Kk380; E major, Kk381; D minor, Kk213; D major, Kk119; D minor, Kk120; C major, Kk501; C major, Kk502; F minor, Kk466; G major, Kk146; F sharp major, Kk318; F sharp major, Kk319; A major, Kk24. **Virginia Black** (hpd). CRD CRD3442 — lh DDD 6/87

G major, Kk124; C minor, Kk99; G major, Kk201; B minor, Kk87; E major, Kk46; C major, Kk95; F minor/major, Kk204a; D major, Kk490; D major, Kk491; D major, Kk492; G major, Kk520; G major, Kk521; C major, Kk513. **Trevor Pinnock** (hpd). CRD CRD3368 — lh lm ADD 12/86

D minor, Kk9; E major, Kk46; E minor, Kk98; C minor, Kk129; A major, Kk208; A major, Kk209; B flat major, Kk360; B flat major, Kk361; G major, Kk454; G major, Kk455; C major, Kk514; C major, Kk515. **Gilbert Rowland** (hpd). Keyboard Records KGR1025CD — 51m DAD 10/89

D major, Kk33; A major, Kk39; A minor, Kk54; G major, Kk55; D major, Kk96; G major, Kk146; E major, Kk162; E minor, Kk198; A major, Kk322; E major, kk380; G major, Kk455; F minor, Kk466; E flat major, Kk474; F minor, Kk481; D major, Kk491; F major, Kk525; E major, Kk531. **Vladimir Horowitz** (pf). CBS Masterworks CD42410 — lh lm AAD 5/89 -

D minor, Kk52; A major, Kk211; A major, Kk212; B flat major, Kk248; B flat major, Kk249; B major, Kk261; B major, Kk262; E minor, Kk263; E major, Kk264; F sharp major, Kk318; F sharp major, Kk319; G minor, Kk347; G major, Kk348; D major, Kk416; D minor, kk417; D major, kk490; D major, Kk491; D major, Kk492. **Elaine Thornburgh** (hpd). Koch International Classics 37014-2 — lh 12m DDD 10/91

G minor, Kk108; D major, Kk118; D major, Kk119; D minor, Kk141; E minor, Kk198; E minor, Kk203; G major, Kk454; G major, Kk455; D major, Kk490; D major, Kk491; D major, Kk492; C major, Kk501; C major, Kk502; D minor, Kk516; D minor, Kk517; F major, Kk518; F minor, Kk519. **Andreas Staier** (hpd). Deutsche Harmonia Mundi RD77224 — lh 10m DDD 2/92

Further listening ...

Stabat mater[a]. *Coupled with* ***Esteves.*** Mass for eight voices. [a]**Elisabeth Hermans** (sop); [a]**Jan Van Elsaker** (ten); **Currende Vocal Ensemble/Erik Van Nevel** with **Jacques Van Der Meer** (va da gamba); **Lidewij Scheifes** (vc); **Herman Stinders** (org). Accent ACC9069D (5/92).

Cantatas — Scritte con falso inganno. Tinte a note di sangue. O qual meco Nice cangiata. Dir vorrei. **Kate Eckersley** (sop); **Fiori Musicali/Penelope Rapson** (hpd). Unicorn-Kanchana DKPCD9119 (5/92).

Giacinto Scelsi

Italian 1905-1988

NEW REVIEW

Scelsi. Trilogia. Ko-Tha. **Frances-Marie Uitti** (vc). Etcetera KTC1136. Recorded in 1978-79.

Anyone who has encountered Scelsi's music before will find this present disc a satisfying supplement, and well worth investigating, despite the fact that it contains a relatively small amount of music. That music is in part a collaboration between composer and performer. *Ko-Tha* was written with a special six-string cello of Frances-Marie Uitti's own design in mind, and she plays it with a combination of emotional commitment and technical brilliance that disarms any potential criticism. *Trilogia* is the larger of the two works, and Uitti's notes in the booklet are invaluable in explaining the various mutings and retunings that give the music its special sound. Compositions with subtitles like *Trilogia*'s "The three ages of man" will rightly be approached with some caution in case they lead to terminal pretentiousness. But Scelsi's unique amalgam of intensity and serenity renders such caution redundant. This may not be a music for all seasons, but its spiritual and intellectual integrity is rare indeed. The recording keeps the cello in close-up without losing the sense of space vital to such rarefied music.

Further listening ...

Aion. Pfhat[a]. Konx-Om-Pax[a]. **Cracow Radio and Television [a]Chorus and Symphony Orchestra/Jürg Wyttenbach.** Accord 20040-2 (8/90).

Chukrum. Hurqualia. Hymnos. **Cracow Radio and Television Orchestra/Wyttenbach.** Accord 20111-2.

String Quartets Nos. 1-5. String Trio. Khoom[a]. **[a]Michiko Hirayama** (sop); **[a]Frank Lloyd** (hn); **[a]Maurizio Ben Omar** (perc); **Arditti Quartet/[a]Aldo Brizzi.** Salabert Actuels SCD8904/05 (9/90).

Piano Suites — No. 8, "Bot-Ba" (Tibet); No. 9, "Ttai" (Paix). **Werner Bärtschi** (pf). Accord 20080-2.

Franx Xaver Scharwenka

Polish 1850-1924

Suggested listening ...

Piano Concerto No. 1 in B flat minor, Op. 32. *Coupled with* **Chopin.** Piano Concerto No. 1 in E minor, Op. 11. **Seta Tanyel** (pf); **Philharmonia Orchestra/Yuri Simonov.** Collins Classics 1263-2.

Five Polish Dances, Op. 3. Piano Sonata No. 1 in C sharp minor, Op. 6. First Polonaise, Op. 12. Impromptu, Op. 17. Valse-Caprice, Op. 31. Polonaise, Op. 42. Eglantine Waltz, Op. 84. **Seta Tanyel** (pf). Collins Classics 1325-2 (9/92).

Johann Hermann Schein

German 1586-1630

Suggested listening ...

Vocal Works — O Amarilli zart. Aurora schön mit ihrem Haar. Frischauf, ihr Klosterbrüder mein. Ringstum mich schwebet Trauerigkeit. Als Filli schön und fromm. In Filli schönen Augelein. O Scheiden, o bitter Scheiden. Unlängst dem blinden Gröttelein. Wie kommst's, o zarte Filli mein. Kickehihi, kakakanei. Cupido blind, das Venuskind. Wenn Filli ihre Liebesstrahl. O Amarilli, schönste Zier. Heulen und schmerzlichs Weinen. All wilden Tier im grünen Wald. O Venus und Cupido blind. Amor, das liebe Räuberlein. O seidene Härelein. Ihr Brüder, lieben Brüder mein. Mirtillo hat ein Schäfelein. Die Vöglein singen. Mein Schifflein lief im wilden Meer. **Cantus Cölln/Konrad Junghänel.** Deutsche Harmonia Mundi RD77088 (10/90).

Johann Heinrich Schmelzer

Austrian c.1620/23-1680

Suggested listening ...

Trumpet music — Sonata con arie zu der kaiserlichen Serenada. Sonata à 7 flauti. Balletto di spiritelli. Sonata I à 8. Balletto di centauri, ninfe e salvatici. *Coupled with* ***Biber:*** Trumpet music — Sonata à 7. Sonata pro tabula. Sonata VII à 5. Sonata à 3. Sonata à 6. Sonata I à 8. Sonata Sancti Polycarpi à 9. **New London Consort/Philip Pickett.** L'Oiseau-Lyre 425 834-2OH (9/91).

Balletto in G major, "Fechtschule". Polonische Sackpfeiffen in G major. *Coupled with* ***Biber.*** Sonata in B flat major, "Die Bauern-Kirchfartt genandt". Battalia in D major. Serenade in C major, "Nightwatchman's Call". Sonata in A major, "La Pastorella". Sonata jucunda in D major (attrib). Sonata in G major, "Campanarum" (attrib). ***J.J. Walther.*** Sonata in G major, "Imitatione del Cucu". **Cologne Musica Antiqua/Reinhard Goebel.** Archiv Produktion 429 230-2AH (1/91).
See review in the Collections section; refer to the Index to Reviews.

Sonatas — Lamento sopra la morte Ferdinandi III; Sonata a tre violini. Sonata a tre; Sonata a tre "Lanterly"; Duodena selectarum sonatarum — No. 9. *Coupled with* ***Muffat.*** Sonata for violin and basso continuo. Armonico tributo — Five Sonatas: No. 5. **London Baroque/Charles Medlam.** Harmonia Mundi HMC90 1220 (11/87).

Franz Schmidt

Austrian 1874-1939

Schmidt. Symphony No. 3 in A major.
Hindemith. Concerto for Orchestra, Op. 38. **Chicago Symphony Orchestra/Neeme Järvi.** Chandos CHAN9000. Recorded at performances in Orchestra Hall, Chicago on January 30th and February 3rd, 1991.

55m DDD 3/92

A cold shower followed by a warm bath. Hindemith's brisk 1925 Concerto is in his defiantly anti-romantic, neo-classical vein. The composer often seems to delight in demanding quite impossible feats of virtuosity from the violins, as much as giving soloists and instrumental groups a fighting chance to show off. But the real virtuosity is the composer's own. Who but Hindemith could have written a "Basso ostinato" finale with 47 statements of its six-note theme in two minutes and 20 seconds? Schmidt's Third Symphony, written three years later for a competition for the best new symphony "in the spirit of Schubert", nostalgically harks back to a bygone era through a haze of harmonic complexity. Schmidt often tantalizes the listener with a dizzying journey of departures from his chosen key, though wherever the undercurrents take you, the music's firm tonal foundation is never in doubt. Of all Schmidt's Austrian antecedents, the composer most vividly recalled is Bruckner, particularly in the last two movements and in the organ-like sonorities of the orchestration. Forgivably fallible strings in the Hindemith apart, the Chicago Orchestra and Järvi are on top form, and these live recordings preserve the concert-hall experience.

NEW REVIEW

Schmidt. Symphony No. 2 in E flat major. **Chicago Symphony Orchestra/Neeme Järvi.** Chandos CHAN8779. Recorded in 1989.

47m DDD 3/90

Franz Schmidt, a Czech-born Viennese, was a cellist in the Vienna Philharmonic under Mahler, and an exact contemporary of Schoenberg, but you'd be hard put in his four symphonies to find any evidence of Mahler's world-embracing concept of the late romantic symphony, or of Schoenberg's negation of it. The Second Symphony was completed in 1913 and, as one biographer put it, "on the eve of the international war, in which the Danube monarchy was defeated, Schmidt erected to that monarchy a monument in music". It's not difficult to hear the Danube itself in the Symphony's flowing opening pages, but on the whole this is absolute music in the symphonic tradition of Brahms and Bruckner, with Czech woodwind colourings and a Straussian opulence. Järvi restores a cut sometimes made in the reprise of the *Scherzo*, and keeps the music moving purposefully forward. The Chandos engineers take a little while to find the correct levels for this live taping, made in Orchestra Hall, Chicago, but as with the Third Symphony (listed below), once you have found the right replay level, the sound is satisfyingly full, bright and airy.

Further listening ...

Symphonies Nos. 1-4. **Bratislava Radio Symphony Orchestra/L'udovít Rajter.** Opus 9350 1851/4 (four-disc set, also available separately, 2/88).

NOTRE DAME. **Soloists; Choir of St Hedwig's Cathedral, Berlin; Berlin RIAS Chamber Choir; Berlin Radio Symphony Orchestra/Christof Perick.** Capriccio 10 248/9 (5/89).

Florent Schmitt

French 1870-1958

Suggested listening ...

Pièces romantiques, Op. 42. Trios valses nocturnes, Op. 31. Mirages, Op. 70. **Pascal Le Corre** (pf). Cybelia CY809 (3/87).

Artur Schnabel

German 1882-1951

NEW REVIEW

Schnabel. Symphony No. 2. **Royal Philharmonic Orchestra/Paul Zukofsky.** Musical Observations CP2104. Recorded in 1988.

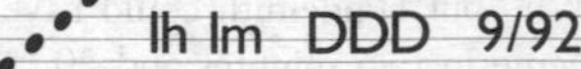

This disc is one of the more remarkable fruits of a recent vogue for exploring the compositions of prominent musicians better known for their skills as executants. Unlike such colleagues as

Wilhelm Furtwängler, Artur Schnabel composed in a peculiarly 'advanced' idiom and preferred not to compromise his efforts on behalf of, say, the Schubert piano sonatas by baffling audiences with his own experimental scores. Schnabel's major musical influences included Busoni, Schoenberg and Krenek and, though he was also impressed by Hindemith and the prodigal Korngold, there's neither rhythmic zest nor melodic charm in the huge, grey, brooding edifice of this symphony. The writing is occasionally reminiscent of the Berg of *Wozzeck* but parallels have also been drawn with a subsequent generation of modernists. Spiritually if not technically, the mood comes closer to the wintry desolation of Shostakovich, especially in the quasi-passacaglia that launches the slow movement. Under the direction of Paul Zukofsky, an ardent champion of Schnabel's music, the Royal Philharmonic manages much more than a standard run-through and the recording is very effective. Schnabel himself felt that "every music student should be obliged to write music, whether or not he is gifted for it or attracted by it.". Only then could his own imaginative world find its fullest expression in revivifying the music of others. In fact, Schnabel seems to have enjoyed his own composing more than either playing or teaching.

Alfred Schnittke

Russian 1934-

NEW REVIEW

Schnittke. Cello Concerto No. 1.
Schumann. Cello Concerto in A minor, Op. 129. **Natalia Gutman** (vc); **London Philharmonic Orchestra/Kurt Masur.** EMI CDC7 54443-2. Recorded in 1991.

lh 5m DDD 8/92

One suspects that no composer since Mahler has been more predisposed to translate personal crises into music than Alfred Schnittke, and the concerto provides him with an ideal medium for the synthesis of feeling and thought, the triumph of the individual over potentially tragic circumstances. This composition seems to gain a stronger identity and greater conviction as it proceeds, and the remarkable final movement, written after one of Schnittke's bouts of serious illness in 1985, carries the work into a visionary world where ideas representative of vulnerability and victory engage in a battle royal. Without a recording as carefully and cleanly balanced as this one the music could sound incoherent and congested: without a performance as skilfully placed and sensitively projected as this, the work could come across as self-indulgent and even hysterical. Given that the concerto was written for Natalia Gutman you might expect her account to emphasize emotional involvement. Fortunately, she is also able to stand back and convey its sense of formal stability without over-indulging the expressive details, and she receives admirable support from Masur and the LPO. The Schumann is a worthwhile coupling in that it reminds us that romanticism has a gentler, less barnstorming side to it.

NEW REVIEW

Schnittke. Minnesang. Choir Concerto. **Danish National Radio Choir/Stefan Parkman.** Chandos CHAN9126. Texts and translations included. Recorded in 1992.

59m DDD 2/93

To observe that the music on this disc does not actually sound like Schnittke is to fall into the trap of regarding a perceived consistency of style as basic in the modern composer's world. What we have here is a relatively new, relatively under-exploited aspect of Schnittke, but only a composer with his voracious enthusiasm for adapting his musical personality to what he feels to be right for the medium in question could have produced two such work as these. *Minnesang* is a reasonably concise, generally light-hearted setting of thirteenth-century secular texts — a display of lively counterpoint that preserves the essentially romantic feeling of the words. The *Choir Concerto* is quite a contrast: the texts, by a tenth-century Armenian poet, are devotional, the musical style richly chordal and expansive in a manner evocative of the Russian choral tradition and its culmination in the grand rhetoric of Tchaikovsky and Rachmaninov. Both works take a little getting to know, and may after all prove to be the result of Schnittke in disguise rather than of Schnittke extending his range, but they are masterly of their kind. In particular, the beautifully serene ending of the Concerto is one of his most haunting inspirations. The Danish performances are beyond praise, and the recording excellent in clarity and atmosphere.

Schnittke. Concerto Grosso No. 1[a]. Quasi una sonata[b]. Moz-Art à la Haydn[c]. [ac]**Tatiana Grindenko** (vn); **Yuri Smirnov** ([a]hpd/[a]prep pf/[b]pf); **Chamber Orchestra of Europe/[a]Heinrich Schiff, [bc]Gidon Kremer** ([a]vn). DG 429 413-2GH. Recorded live in 1988.

lh 2m DDD 9/90 

For a single representative of Alfred Schnittke's work you could choose nothing better than the first *Concerto Grosso* of 1977. Here are the psychedelic mélanges of baroque and modern, the drastic juxtapositions of pseudo-Vivaldi with pseudo-Berg, producing an effect at once aurally exciting and spiritually disturbing. The piece has been recorded several times over, but never with the panache of Gidon Kremer and friends and never with the vivid immediacy of this live DG recording (in fact the solo violins are rather too closely miked for comfort, but that's only a tiny drawback). *Quasi una sonata* was originally composed in 1968 for violin and piano and it was something of a breakthrough piece for Schnittke as he emerged from what he called "the puberty rites of serialism", letting his imagination run riot for the first time. No-one could call it a disciplined piece, but if that worries you, you should leave Schnittke alone anyway. The transcription for solo violin and string orchestra is an ingenious one and Kremer again supplies all the requisite agonized intensity. *Moz-Art à la Haydn* is a very slight piece of work, and it really depends on visual theatricality to make its effect. Still, it complements the other two pieces well enough, and the disc as a whole makes an excellent introduction to a composer currently enjoying an enormous vogue.

Schnittke. Concerti grossi — No. 3; No. 4/Symphony No. 5. **Royal Concertgebouw Orchestra/Riccardo Chailly.** Decca 430 698-2DH. Recorded 1989-90.

59m DDD 2/92

Although the Concertgebouw and Chailly gave the 1988 première of Schnittke's *Concerto grosso* No. 4/Symphony No. 5 they were pre-empted in the recording world by the Gothenburg Symphony and Neeme Järvi. That BIS recording (listed below) was strongly recommended in the 1992 *Guide*: but this new Decca version is even finer. As more and more of Schnittke's music appears on CD it becomes clear that this work is a synthesis of his achievements, just as the title itself suggests a synthesis of his main preoccupations as a composer. The idea is to start in the world of the neo-baroque *concerto grosso* (with barely concealed references to Stravinsky and Prokofiev) and to end up as a full-blown tragic Mahlerian symphony. Each stage on this musical journey is riveting, and the performance is wholly authoritative. The earlier *Concerto grosso* leaves more room for doubt, though it too offers the wary listener plenty of familiar jumping-off points. Recording quality is in the very best Decca/Concertgebouw tradition.

No. 4/Symphony No. 5. Pianissimo. **Gothenburg Symphony Orchestra/Neeme Järvi.** BIS CD427 — 49m DDD 8/90

Schnittke. Viola Concerto[a]. Trio Sonata (arr. Bashmet)[b]. [a]**London Symphony Orchestra/Mstislav Rostropovich;** [b]**Moscow Soloists/Yuri Bashmet** ([a]va). RCA Victor Red Seal RD60446. Recorded 1988-90.

lh 2m DDD 2/92 

Just like Shostakovich, to whom he is in many ways the natural successor, Schnittke has been inspired by the cream of Russia's string virtuosos. The Viola Concerto was written in 1985 for Yuri Bashmet, a charismatic musician who himself can claim to be carrying on where Oistrakh left off. Its three movements are characteristically extreme in their emotional intensity, alternately brooding and explosive, and there is an especially memorable episode when the fast central movement gives way to bleak images of past innocence — that should strike a chord with anyone who enjoys Russian art films. Bashmet and Rostropovich interpret the music to the manner born. The coupling is both apt and poignant — Bashmet's arrangement of the String Trio is his expression of thanks for the Concerto and at the same time a get-well present after the composer's near-fatal stroke. It too is magnificently played, and both works are superbly recorded.

Additional recommendation ...
Viola Concerto[a]. ***Kanchelli.*** *Liturgy for Viola and Orchestra, "Mourned by the Wind*[b]. **Kim Kashkashian** (va); [a]**Saarbrücken Radio Symphony Orchestra,** [b]**Bonn Beethovenhalle Orchestra/Dennis Russell Davies.** ECM New Series 437 199-2 — lh 8m DDD 4/93

NEW REVIEW

Schnittke. String Quartet No. 3. Piano Quintet[a].
Mahler/Schnittke. Piano Quartet[a]. **Borodin Quartet** (Mikhail Kopelman, Andrei Abramenkov, vns; Dmitri Shebalin, va; Valentin Berlinsky, vc); [a]**Ludmilla Berlinsky** (pf).
Virgin Classics VC7 59040-2. Recorded in 1990.

lh 6m DDD 12/91

Schnittke's chamber music does not have the high public profile of some of his symphonies and concertos, but in many ways it is more fastidiously composed and it certainly makes for equally rewarding listening at home. The Piano Quintet is the outstanding feature of this disc. Predominantly slow and mournful (it is dedicated to the memory of the composer's mother) and with a haunting waltz on the notes of the BACH monogram, it is here played with compelling intensity, especially by the pianist Ludmilla Berlinsky, daughter of the Borodin Quartet's cellist. The Piano Quartet is a conflation of the 16-year-old Mahler's first movement with his incomplete second movement in Schnittke's own paraphrase — another haunting experience, beautifully played and recorded. Less satisfying as a performance, because slightly glossed over, is the Third Quartet; but this is perhaps the finest and undoubtedly the most often performed of Schnittke's chamber works, and as a whole the disc can be warmly recommended to those looking for a representative sample of Schnittke rather than a comprehensive library.

Additional recommendation ...
String Quartets Nos. 1-3. **Tale Quartet.** BIS CD467 — lh 2m DDD 7/90

Schnittke. Piano Sonata (1987).
Stravinsky. Piano Sonata (1924). Serenade in A (1925). Piano-rag-music (1919). **Boris Berman** (pf). Chandos CHAN8962. Recorded 1989-90.

55m DDD 10/91

This is a disc to encourage thoughts about what might have been. In particular: if Stravinsky had launched his great neoclassical initiative from within the Soviet Union in the 1920s, and if that regime had continued to encourage free artistic expression, would the kind of reborn Russian late romanticism we associate with Shostakovich, and now with Schnittke, ever have come about? These are futile questions, of course. Yet what is clear from this strongly projected, cleanly recorded recital is that a positive conjunction between a high degree of self-consciousness (the constant hints of other composers' music) and an instinctive, strongly personal expressive impulse, is present in and crucial to both Schnittke and Stravinsky. Berman probes Stravinsky's piano works for their innate eloquence, to a degree which not all listeners will accept. Certainly, if you like your Stravinsky objectively light and airy you will need to look elsewhere. But the effect here is to build a bridge to Schnittke's large-scale, wide-ranging sonata design, in which simple beginnings usually escalate to imposingly intense climaxes: and while Schnittke would not be Schnittke without a touch of melodrama, Berman moulds the potentially wayward outpourings with convincing and never merely coercive control.

Johann Schobert

Silesian c.1735-1767

Suggested listening ...

Sonates en quatuor, Op. 7 — No. 2 in F minor[ab]. Piano Trios, Op. 16 — No. 1 in B flat major[b]; No. 4 in F major[b]. Sonatas, Op. 14 — No. 1 in E flat major[ab]; No. 4 in D minor; No. 5 in A major. **Luciano Sgrizzi** (pf); **Chiara Banchini, [a]Véronique Méjean** (vns); **[b]Philipp Bosbach** (vc). Harmonia Mundi HMC90 1294 (12/89).

Othmar Schoeck

Swiss 1886-1957

NEW REVIEW

Schoeck. Concerto quasi una fantasia, Op. 21[a]. PENTHESILEA — Suite (arr. Delfs). **[a]Bettina Boller** (vn); **Swiss Youth Symphony Orchestra/Andras Delfs.** Claves CD50-9201. Recorded in 1991.

1h 1m DDD 2/93 

Othmar Schoeck is best known for his songs — he is the greatest Lieder composer after Wolf. Anyone listening to Schoeck's Violin Concerto will be amazed that a work of such extraordinary rich warmth and lyrical ardour has languished so long in neglect. It was inspired by Stefi Geyer for whom Bartók wrote his First Violin Concerto, and a few years later Schoeck fell under her spell. (She actually recorded this concerto towards the end of her career.) The idiom is very much that of Brahms and Strauss though in the slow movement there is a foretaste of that autumnal melancholy one finds in Elgar. None of the earlier versions shows anywhere near the understanding of and love for this piece as does Bettina Boller. The quality of both interpretation and the playing of the Swiss Youth Orchestra reflects great credit on the conductor, Andreas Delfs. It is beautifully phrased and spacious; the orchestra sounds completely inside this music, and conveys the remarkable atmosphere Schoeck evokes to compelling effect. Boller also plays with depth of feeling and sensitivity, and although the recording engineer does not do full justice to her tone, which sounds hard and wiry above the stave, the performance has enormous dedication. Delfs's arrangement of the Suite from the opera, *Penthesilea,* gives an excellent idea of Schoeck's highly inventive and imaginative score, which offers an occasional reminder of the Strauss of *Elektra* but occupies a totally original sound-world.

Arnold Schoenberg

Austrian/Hungarian 1874-1951

Schoenberg. Verklärte Nacht, Op. 4. Variations for Orchestra, Op. 31. **Berlin Philharmonic Orchestra/Herbert von Karajan.** DG 415 326-2GH. From 2711 014 (3/75).

52m ADD 3/86 

NEW REVIEW

Schoenberg. Verklärte Nacht, Op. 4.
R. Strauss. Metamorphosen for 23 solo strings, AV142.
Wagner. Siegfried Idyll. **Sinfonia Varsovia/Emmanuel Krivine.** Denon CO-79442. Recorded in 1990.

1h 14m DDD 10/92 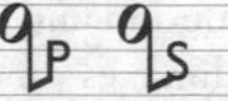 

The decadence of German culture in the 1920s and 1930s is already very apparent in the saturated romanticism of *Verklärte Nacht* (1899), the most lusciously sentient work ever conceived for a string group. By comparison the *Variations for Orchestra* comes at the peak of the composer's atonal period and is perhaps the most impressive and imaginative demonstration of the possibilities of this compositional method. Thus the two works on this CD are pivotal in Schoenberg's career and Karajan and the Berlin Philharmonic make the very best case for both works. It is impossible not to respond to the sensuality of *Verklärte Nacht* in their hands, while the challenging *Variations* also make a profound impression. The recording matches the intensity of the playing brilliantly.

The stimulating Denon issue embraces three works which are as ideally matched as one could wish for. The performances verge on the miraculous; Krivine's visionary direction summons up playing of exultant intensity from the Polish orchestra. *Verklärte Nacht* has seldom sounded so moving; with Krivine, the transformation from aspiration to absolution is magical. His nobly compelling *Metamorphosen* charges each strand of Strauss's valedictory essay with tangible dismay and regret, as quotations from *Tristan* and Beethoven's *Eroica* lament the passing of a once great culture. An ardent yet naturally paced account of Wagner's *Siegfried Idyll* recalls that sense of sanctified joy which filled the Villa Triebschen on Christmas morning in 1870, as this musical birthday offering was heard for the first time. Krivine's spiritual empathy with these works combined with the outstanding orchestral playing and exemplary recorded sound make this a disc to covet.

Additional recommendations ...

Verklärte Nacht. **Mahler.** *Symphony No. 10.* **Berlin Radio Symphony Orchestra/Riccardo Chailly.** Decca 421 182-2DH — ② 1h 50m DDD 3/88

Verklärte Nacht. Variations for Orchestra. Pelleas und Melisande, Op. 5 — symphonic poem. **Berg.** *Three Pieces for string orchestra.* **Webern.** *Passacaglia, Op. 1. Five Movements, Op. 5. Six Pieces for Orchestra, Op. 6. Symphony, Op. 21.* **Berlin Philharmonic Orchestra/Herbert von Karajan.** DG 427 424-2GC3 *(the Webern pieces are reviewed under Webern; refer to the Index to Reviews)* — ③ 3h 1m ADD 9/89 B

Verklärte Nacht. **R. Strauss.** *Metamorphosen.* **Webern.** *Five Movements, Op. 5.* **Academy of St Martin in the Fields/Sir Neville Marriner.** Decca Enterprise 430 002-2DM — 1h 7m ADD 11/90 B

Variations for Orchestra. Cello Concerto in D major. Five Orchestral Pieces, Op. 16. Modern Psalm. **Soloists/Bratislava Philharmonic Choir; South-West German Radio Symphony Orchestra/Michael Gielen.** Wergo WER60185-50 — 1h DDD 10/90

NEW REVIEW

Schoenberg. Variations for Orchestra, Op. 31. Pelleas und Melisande, Op. 5. **Chicago Symphony Orchestra/Pierre Boulez.** Erato 2292-45827-2. Recorded in 1991.

1h 2m DDD 4/93

The two faces of Schoenberg could scarcely be more starkly juxtaposed than they are on this superbly performed and magnificently recorded disc — Boulez and the CSO at their formidable best. *Pelleas und Melisande* can be taken not only as Schoenberg's 'answer' to Debussy's opera (also based on Maeterlinck's play) but as his challenge to Richard Strauss's supremacy as a composer of symphonic poems. It is indeed an intensely symphonic score in Schoenberg's early, late-romantic vein, with an elaborate single-movement structure and a subtle network of thematic cross-references. Yet none of this is an end in itself, and the music is as gripping and immediate a representation of a tragic love story as anything in the German romantic tradition. To move from this to the abstraction of the 12-note Variations, Op. 31 may threaten extreme anticlimax. Yet from the delicate introduction of the work's shapely theme to the turbulent good-humour of the extended finale Schoenberg proves that his new compositional method did not drain his musical language of expressive vitality. The elaborate counterpoint may not make for easy listening, but the combination of exuberance and emotion is irresistible — at least in a performance like this.

Additional recommendation ...

Pelleas und Melisande. **Webern.** *Passacaglia for Orchestra, Op. 1.* **Scottish National Orchestra/Matthias Bamert.** Chandos CHAN8619 — 54m DDD 10/88

Schoenberg. Chamber Symphonies — No. 1, Op. 9; No. 2, Op. 38. Verklärte Nacht, Op. 4 (arr. string orch). **Orpheus Chamber Orchestra.** DG 429 233-2GH. Recorded in 1989.

1h 9m DDD 7/90

In the late twentieth century there's increasing evidence that the early twentieth century's most radical music is becoming so easy to perform that it may at last be losing its terrors for listeners as well as players. This can only be welcomed, provided that performances do not become bland and mechanical, and the unconducted Orpheus Chamber Orchestra triumphantly demonstrate how to combine fluency with intensity. If you like your Schoenberg effortful — to feel that the players are conquering almost insuperable odds — these recordings may not be for you. But if you like spontaneity of expression that is never an end in itself, and communicates Schoenberg's powerfully coherent forms and textures as well as his abundant emotionalism, you should not hesitate. The DG disc is the first to place Schoenberg's two Chamber Symphonies alongside *Verklärte Nacht*, whose original version for string quartet was the prime mover of so many later developments, in Schoenberg and others. Here, in *Verklärte Nacht*, is Schoenberg the late-romantic tone poet, the equal of Richard Strauss: the First Chamber Symphony shows Schoenberg transforming himself from late-romantic into expressionist, while in the Second the recent American immigrant, in the 1930s, looks back to his romantic roots and forges a new, almost classical style. With superb sound, this is a landmark in recordings of twentieth-century music.

Additional recommendations ...
Symphony No. 1. Serenade, Op. 24[a]. [a]**Thomas Paul** (bass); **Marlboro Festival Chamber Ensemble/**[a]**Leon Kirchner.** Sony Classical MK45894 — 56m ADD 6/91
Symphony No. 1. Pierrot lunaire, Op. 21[a]. [a]**Marianne Pousseur** (sop); **Musique Oblique Ensemble/Philippe Herreweghe.** Harmonia Mundi HMC90 1390 — 58m DDD 8/92

Schoenberg. PIANO MUSIC. **Maurizio Pollini.** DG 20th Century Classics 423 249-2GC. From 2530 531 (5/75). Recorded in 1974.
Three Piano Pieces, Op. 11. Six Little Piano Pieces, Op. 19. Five Piano Pieces, Op. 23. Piano Suite, Op. 25. Piano Pieces, Opp. 33*a* and 33*b*.

50m ADD 6/88 £

When Pollini claims these as probably the most important piano pieces of the twentieth century he does so with good reason. For example, the Op. 11 pieces are generally reckoned to be the first wholly atonal work and the Prelude of Op. 25 was Schoenberg's first 12-note piece. Not surprisingly they are tough going for the uninitiated. Schoenberg expects the listener to come all the way to meet him, however uninviting the journey may appear; and getting to the sense behind the notes has defeated plenty of would-be exponents, for it tolerates no weakness of technical or musical equipment. Fortunately, Pollini is just about the ideal guide across Schoenberg's bleak ridges and past his sudden avalanches, and for combined intellectual and pianistic mastery he stands unchallenged. DG's recording is clear and lifelike and at mid-price this CD is superb value.

Schoenberg. Gurrelieder. **Susan Dunn** (sop); **Brigitte Fassbaender** (mez); **Siegfried Jerusalem, Peter Haage** (tens); **Hermann Becht** (bass); **Hans Hotter** (narr); **St Hedwig's Cathedral Choir, Berlin; Dusseldorf Musikverin Chorus; Berlin Radio Symphony Orchestra/Riccardo Chailly.** Decca 430 321-2DH2. Text and translation included. Recorded in 1985.

2 1h 41m DDD 3/91

"Every morning after sunrise, King Waldemar would have a realization of the renewing power of nature, and would feel the love of Tove within the outward beauty of Nature's colour and form" (thus said Leopold Stokowski, who made the first-ever recording of *Gurrelieder*). This vast cantata, here more than ever experienced as a direct descendant of Wagnerian music-drama, was for the turn-of-the-century musical scene in general, more the ultimate gorgeous sunset. Schoenberg started work on it in 1899, the same year as his *Verklärte Nacht* (see above), but delayed its completion for over a decade, by which time some of his more innovatory masterpieces were already behind him. But there is little here to upset those who shy away from the forbidding father of the atonal 12-note technique. Indeed nothing could be more tonal than the shining C major to which the final chorus ascends with the words "behold the sun", and there are few moments in music of such cumulative power and radiance. Schoenberg's forces are, to put it mildly, extravagant. As well as the six soloists and two choruses, the orchestra sports such luxuries as four piccolos, ten horns and a percussion battery that includes iron chains; and so complex are some of the textures that, to achieve a satisfactory balance, a near miracle is required of conductor and recording engineers. Decca have never been mean with miracles where large scale forces are concerned: one thinks immediately of Solti's *Götterdämmerung*, and this set is no exception. In fact much of the black majesty of the "gathering of the vassals" scene from Act 2 of the latter is recalled here, both musically and sonically, in Waldemar's nocturnal hunt with his male chorus of 'un-dead' warriors. It is but one of many highlights in Chailly's and Decca's superbly theatrical presentation of the score. The casting of the soloists is near ideal. Susan Dunn's Tove has youth, freshness and purity on her side. So exquisitely does she float her lines that you readily sympathize with King Waldemar's rage at her demise. Siegfried Jerusalem has the occasional rough moment but few previous Waldemars on disc have possessed his heroic ringing tones and range of expression. And Decca make sure that their trump card, the inimitable Hans Hotter as the speaker in "The wild hunt of the summer wind", is so tangibly projected that we miss not one single vowel or consonant of his increasing animation and excitement at that final approaching sunrise.

Additional recommendation ...

Soloists; Tanglewood Festival Chorus; Boston Symphony Orchestra/Seiji Ozawa. Philips 412 511-2PH2 — ⁘ ② lh 5lm ADD 3/85

Further listening ...

Piano Concerto, Op. 42. *Coupled with* ***Schumann.*** Piano Concerto in A minor, Op. 54. **Maurizio Pollini** (pf); **Berlin Philharmonic Orchestra/Claudio Abbado.** DG 427 771-2GH (7/90).

Choral Works — Friede auf Erden, Op. 13. Kol nidre, Op. 39. Drei Volkslieder, Op. 49. Zwei Kanons — Wenn der schwer Gedrückte klagt; O dass der Sinnen doch so viele sind!. Drei Volkslieder — Es gingen zwei Gespielen gut; Herzlieblich Lieb, durch Scheiden; Schein uns, du liebe Sonne. Vier Stücke, Op. 27. Drei Satiren, Op. 28. Sechs Stücke, Op. 35. Dreimal tausen Jahre, Op. 50*a*. De profundis (Psalm 130), Op. 50*b*. Modern Psalm (Der erste Psalm), Op. 50*c*. A Survivor from Warsaw, Op. 46. **John Shirley-Quirk, Günter Reich** (narrs); **BBC Singers; BBC Chorus and Symphony Orchestra; London Sinfonietta/Pierre Boulez.** Sony Classical S2K44571 (8/90).

Pierrot lunaire, Op. 21[a]. *Coupled with* ***Webern.*** Concerto, Op. 24. [a]**Jane Manning** (sop); **Nash Ensemble/Simon Rattle.** Chandos Collect CHAN6534 (8/92).

Claude-Michel Schönberg

French 20th century

Suggested listening ...

LES MISERABLES. **Original London cast.** First Night ENCORECD1 (3/87).

Franz Schreker

Austrian 1878-1934

Schreker. DIE GEZEICHNETEN. **Charles van Tassel** (bass) Adorno/Capitaneo di Giustizia; **Sigmund Cowan** (bar) Count Tamare; **Wout Oosterkamp** (bass) Podestá; **Marilyn**

Schmiege (mez) Carlotta; **William Cochran** (ten) Alviano; **Hein Meens** (ten) Guidobald; **Frieder Lang** (ten) Menaldo; **Ernst Daniel Smid** (bar) Michelotto; **Math Dirks** (bar) Gonsalvo; **Emile Godding** (bass) Julian; **Lieuwe Visser** (bass) Paolo; **Ellen Bollongino** (sop) Ginevra/A maiden; **Michael Austin** (ten) A youth; **Alex Vermeulen** (ten) First Senator; **Hans van Heiningen** (bar) Second Senator; **Traian Aga** (bass) Third Senator; **Dutch Radio Philharmonic Chorus and Orchestra/Edo de Waart.** Marco Polo 8 223328/30. Notes, text and translation included. Recorded in 1990.

③ 2h 27m DDD 12/91 

A contemporary of Richard Strauss who earned the respect of Schoenberg and Berg, Schreker is far less well-known although his operas were performed in Austria and Germany until they were suppressed by the Nazis as decadent (he was also Jewish). His music owes much to the German tradition and sometimes recalls Strauss, but in his sumptuous orchestral writing and tendency towards hothouse operatic subjects he most resembles the Polish composer Szymanowski. The title of this opera, written to his own libretto in 1913-15, means something like *The Branded Ones* and tells of a sixteenth-century Genoese prince of great ugliness who makes a private island called Elysium into an erotic paradise for his friends, where abducted young girls are debauched and sometimes die before the tormented Prince Alviano himself goes mad. The music suits this melodramatic and improbable tale, and is at its most lurid in Act 3, set in the pagan 'paradise garden' of Elysium with its fauns and fountains, where the vocal forces and large orchestra depict a powerfully sensuous scene. This Dutch performance recorded in the Amsterdam Concertgebouw is a strong one, and if William Cochran's Alviano is too heavily declamatory and wobbly to be attractive that may be acceptable in this role and his lengthy mad scene is effective. The other soloists, chorus and orchestra under Edo de Waart are clearly in sympathy with the style, and only purists need mind that some cuts have been made in Act 3. The booklet has the libretto in German and English.

Further listening ...

Chamber Symphony[a]. Prelude to a Drama[a]. Valse lente[b]. Die Ferne Klang — Night Interlude[b]. **Berlin Radio Symphony Orchestra/[a]Michael Gielen, [b]Karl Anton Rickenbacher.** Koch Schwann 311078 (11/88).

DER FERNE KLANG. **Soloists; Berlin RIAS Chamber Chorus; Berlin Radio Chorus and Symphony Orchestra/Gerd Albrecht.** Capriccio 60 024-2 (12/91).

Franz Schubert

Austrian 1797-1828

Schubert. SYMPHONIES. **Chamber Orchestra of Europe/Claudio Abbado.** DG 423 651-2GH5.

Symphonies — No. 1 in D major, D82; No. 2 in B flat major, D125; No. 3 in D major, D200; No. 4 in C minor, D417, "Tragic"; No. 5 in B flat major, D485; No. 6 in C major, D589; No. 8 in B minor, D759, "Unfinished"; No. 9 in C major, D944, "Great". Grand Duo in C major, D812 (orch. J. Joachim). Rosamunde, D644 — Overture, "Die Zauberharfe".

⑤ 5h 20m DDD 2/89 

For this covetable box-set Abbado has had original sources researched in order to restore bars and details that have been missed out by later editors and to expurgate those added by some, Brahms included, who felt Schubert's originals did not quite balance! For those who know these Symphonies in the later, corrupted versions, these performances can be startling at times, and real eye-openers. The balance of the first movement of the Fourth Symphony, for example, where eight bars added by Brahms to the exposition have been cut, is so radically altered that the effect persists throughout the work, and changes its meaning. Such dedication to Schubert's intentions must be applauded, and the more so because Abbado also draws from his small orchestra of brilliant young performers playing of the utmost sympathy and commitment. The whole set sounds like a labour of love. It has the occasional weaker point but, as a whole, it sustains a remarkably high standard, and the admirably-detailed recordings permit an unstrained appreciation of the finer qualities of the playing.

Additional recommendations ...
Nos. 1-6. No. 7 in E major, D729. Nos-8 and 9. No. 10 in D major, D936A (realized Newbould). Symphonic fragments — D major, D615 (orch. Newbould); D major, D708A (completed and orch. Newbould). **Academy of St Martin in the Fields/Sir Neville Marriner.** Philips 412 176-2PH6 — ⑥ DDD 3/85
Nos. 1-6, 8 and 9. Rosamunde — incidental music, D797: Entr'acte No. 3 in B flat major; Ballet Music No. 1 in B minor; Ballet Music No. 2 in G major. **Cologne Radio Symphony Orchestra/Günter Wand.** RCA GD60096 — ⑤ 4h 27m ADD/DDD 2/89
Nos. 1-6, 8 and 9. **Hanover Band/Roy Goodman.** Nimbus NI5270 — ④ 4h 20m DDD 3/91

Schubert. Symphonies — No. 1 in D major, D82; No. 5 in B flat major, D485. Overtures — D major, D590, "In the Italian Style"; "Des Teufels Lustschloss", D84. **English Sinfonia/Sir Charles Groves.** Pickwick IMP Classics PCD944. Recorded in 1990.

1h 18m DDD 11/91

Young master Schubert had not yet turned 16 when he penned his First Symphony (1813); he then embarked immediately on an opera called *Des Teufels Lustschloss* ("The Devil's Pleasure Castle"). What matters is not that the models are obvious (Haydn, Mozart and Beethoven in the symphony) but the music's mix of confidence and daring experimentation: the symphony's majestic writing for woodwind and brass in the highest registers; and the high drama of the overture (complete with threatening timpani crescendos and a strange central *Largo* for trombones). Two years on Schubert gave us his sunny Fifth Symphony, "a pearl of great price" as Tovey put it, banishing the percussion and most of the brass; and the following year saw one of Schubert's reactions to the Rossini mania that was sweeping through Vienna at the time with his *Overture in the Italian Style*. Sir Charles Groves, like Abbado (reviewed above), uses a small orchestra of modern instruments to obtain the textural clarity of period performances without what some feel as the rawness of authentic instruments. He may not have as polished an ensemble of players as Abbado, but freshness of spirit makes up for any lack of elegance of execution. The sound is excellent, the duration generous — a fine bargain.

Additional recommendations ...
Nos. 1 and 2. **Chamber Orchestra of Europe/Claudio Abbado.** DG 423 652-2GH *(taken from the Award-winning five-disc set reviewed above)* — 59m DDD 9/89
Nos. 1 and 4. **Hanover Band/Roy Goodman.** Nimbus NI5198 59m DDD 7/90

NEW REVIEW

Schubert. Symphonies — No. 3 in D major, D200; No. 8 in B minor, D759, "Unfinished". **Vienna Philharmonic Orchestra/Carlos Kleiber.** DG 415 601-2GH. From 2531124 (11/79). Recorded in 1979.

46m ADD 12/85

Kleiber's Schubert furrowed more than a few critical brows when it first appeared in 1979. The main objections centred on a perceived temperament too restless for Schubert, and some swift tempos, in particular that of the Third Symphony's *Allegretto* slow movement. Those last three words are, of course, a contradiction in terms. Who said Schubert called it a slow movement? He did, however, leave us the marking *Allegretto*, and Kleiber is perfectly justified in taking the movement at a proper 'allegretto' pace. In any case, all this is to ignore his Third Symphony's general attributes: athleticism, balletic grace, wit, immensely sophisticated use of *rubato*, and, for its time, peerless orchestral balance; in short, its sheer *style*. In the *Unfinished*, Kleiber's dramatization, with its extremes of dynamics and variation of pace, might just arguably threaten the longer line. But normal standards seem irrelevant here. Kleiber's temperament is indeed a questing, impulsive and explosive one; and one which galvanizes the Vienna Philharmonic into playing of alternately blazing intensity and a truly elevated beauty and tenderness. Tempos are closer than all other 'traditional' performances to 'authentic' practice, so this is not an *Unfinished* for those who like their Schubertian lyricism imbued with a homely charm. It is, however, for those that want the two movements presented, as John Reed observes, as "born rather than made, bar succeeding bar with an inevitable logic". The sound is superb.

Additional recommendations ...
Nos. 3 and 8. **London Sinfonia/Richard Hickox.** Pickwick IMP Red Label PCD848 — 49m DDD 4/87 £ Ⓑ
Nos. 3 and 5. **Hanover Band/Roy Goodman.** Nimbus NI5172 — 58m DDD 7/89 Ⓑ
Nos. 3 and 4. **Chamber Orchestra of Europe/Claudio Abbado.** DG 423 653-2GH *(taken from the Award-winning five-disc set reviewed above)* — 58m DDD 9/89
Nos. 3, 5 and 6. **Royal Philharmonic Orchestra/Sir Thomas Beecham.** EMI Studio CDM7 69750-2 — 1h 18m ADD 8/90 Ⓑ ▲
Nos. 5 and 8. Rosamunde, D797 — Entr'acte in B minor; Ballet Music No. 2 in G major. **Orchestra of the Age of Enlightenment/Sir Charles Mackerras.** Virgin Classics Veritas VC7 59273-2 — 1h 14m DDD 12/92 Ⓑ
Nos. 3 and 5. Overture in the Italian style in C major, D591. **Northern Sinfonia/Heinrich Schiff.** Chandos CHAN9136 — 59m DDD 6/93 Ⓑ

Schubert. Symphonies — No. 4 in C minor, D417, "Tragic"; No. 6 in C major, D589. **London Classical Players/Roger Norrington.** EMI Reflexe CDC7 54210-2. Recorded in 1990.

1h DDD 5/92

It makes sense that the private, or semi-private music-making for which Schubert's first six symphonies were destined, should be performed by a small orchestra of instruments of the period, rather than given the full blown modern symphony orchestra treatment. The subtitle of the Fourth, *Tragic*, and its minor key, have led many an interpreter, encouraged by the extra weight of modern instruments, to invest it with a profundity (tragedy to triumph on a Beethovenian scale) it manifestly does not possess. Norrington's tempos are expertly judged to give natural expression to its passion and melancholy; its theatrical, rather than genuinely tragic concerns. And the swing into the major at the end of the finale here is a memorable *coup de théâtre*; only period brass and timpani can respond with this degree of enthusiasm without masking the rest of the orchestra. Again, in the *Scherzo* of the Sixth (with its unmistakable echoes of the one in Beethoven's Seventh), the reduced density of period instruments allows sharp accenting without the threat of over-emphasis. Its springing vitality is as irresistible as are the period woodwind colours for the rest of the Symphony's Rossinian charm, humour and high spirits. With lucid sound, there will be little here to offend, and plenty to enchant even the most die-hard traditionalist.

Additional recommendation ...
Nos. 4 and 6. **Orchestra of St John's Smith Square/Oliver Gilmour.** Pickwick IMP Classics PCD936 — 1h 5m DDD 5/90

Schubert. Symphonies — No. 5 in B flat major, D485; No. 8 in B minor, D759, "Unfinished". **London Classical Players/Roger Norrington.** EMI Reflexe CDC7 49968-2. Recorded in 1989.

49m DDD 12/90 Ⓑ

This recommendation may seem rather perverse, particularly as Norrington's urgency in Schubert's "charming symphony in B flat major" puts a noticeable strain on his players in the first movement. The romantic warmth of the sunny Schubert Five that we have always known and loved, and which remains intact in other period instrument performances of the work, is here replaced with a restless, almost *Sturm und Drang*, seriousness. After one has recovered from the initial shock of such a presentation, it remains a thoroughly plausible view, and a consistently stimulating one. Which is why it merits a recommendation. The Eighth was discovered and became popular long after its period, and interpreters throughout the ages have been tempted to compensate for its "unfinished" state by investing its two existing movements with a weight and breadth that was probably not originally envisaged. They can, of course, withstand this. But a less expansive view, such as Norrington's, does not diminish their stature. Indeed, the resulting concentration of Schubert's symphonic argument, with classical proportions and a true 'sense of line' restored, is very compelling. Together with the very determined pointing of accents, and a magically withdrawn pianississimo in the second movement, this is an *Unfinished* that, based on fidelity to the score, realizes a great deal more of the music's expressive potential than many a modern instruments version. The sound is firm and superbly focused.

Additional recommendations ...

Nos. 5[a] *and 8*[b]. [a]**Columbia Symphony Orchestra,** [b]**New York Philharmonic Orchestra/Bruno Walter.** CBS Masterworks CD42048 — 53m ADD 9/86

Nos. 5 and 6. Overture in D major in the Italian style, D591. **Stockholm Sinfonietta/Neeme Järvi.** BIS CD387 lh 12m DDD 9/88

Nos. 5 and 6. **Chamber Orchestra of Europe/Claudio Abbado.** DG 423 654-2GH *(taken from the Award-winning five-disc set reviewed above)* — lh lm DDD 9/89

Nos. 5 and 8. **Royal Concertgebouw Orchestra/Leonard Bernstein.** DG 427 645-2GH — 57m DDD 1/90

Nos. 5 and 8. **Vienna Philharmonic Orchestra/Sir Georg Solti.** Decca 430 439-2DM — 59m DDD 5/91

No. 5. ***Mendelssohn.*** *Symphony No. 4 in A major, Op. 90, "Italian".* **Orchestra of the Eighteenth Century/Frans Brüggen.** Philips 432 123-2PH — 56m DDD 12/91

Key to Symbols

Price	Quantity/ availability	Timing	Mode	Review date
	② ②	lh 23m	DDD	6/88

Schubert. Symphony No. 8 in B minor, D759, "Unfinished".
Schumann. Symphony No. 4 in D minor, Op. 120. **North German Radio Symphony Orchestra/Günter Wand.** RCA Victor Red Seal RD60826. Recorded live in 1991.

57m DDD 5/92

Wand's is a traditionally unhurried unfolding of Schubert's *Unfinished*, and one which does not exploit its troubled lyrical expanses, bar by bar, for the utmost drama. Perceptible deviations from his well maintained pulse give heightened expressiveness to crucial moments in the 'symphonic' drama, such as the fearful start of the first movement's development section, and the second movement's haunting central transition. But the quality here that is most easy to recognize, and just as impossible to analyse, is its spirituality. The live origins may help to explain this, as they do a few trifling imprecisions in the playing. His Schumann Fourth has impressive cumulative power; something the composer obviously intended with all four movements linked and sharing common themes. Wand's purposeful manner does not preclude many individual touches early in the work (the *Romanze* is darkly coloured and beautifully phrased), but as Schumann's thematic unity in continuity becomes more established, so Wand tightens his grip: the finale's introductory "darkness to dawn", for example, is here no interpolated episode, but an amassing of energies already in the air. The sound is full, deep and natural.

Additional recommendations ...

No. 8. ***Schumann.*** *Symphony No. 3 in E flat major, Op. 97, "Rhenish".* **Concertgebouw Orchestra/Leonard Bernstein.** DG 431 042-2GBE — DDD

No. 8. ***Mendelssohn.*** *Symphony No. 4 in A major, Op. 90, "Italian".* **Giuseppe Sinopoli.** DG 410 862-2GH — DDD 4/84

No. 8[a]. ***Schumann.*** *Symphony No. 3*[b]. [a]**Philharmonia Orchestra/Giuseppe Sinopoli;** [b]**Los Angeles Philharmonic Orchestra/Carlo Maria Giulini.** DG 3D Classics 427 818-2GDC — lh 3m DDD 4/90

Schubert. Symphony No. 9 in C major, D944, "Great". **London Classical Player/Roger Norrington.** EMI Reflexe CDC7 49949-2.

58m DDD 4/90 

We now know that Schubert's *Great* C major was not a farewell offering from the last year of his life (1828), but written two or three years earlier, shortly after the *Unfinished*, at white heat, and with a new found confidence and maturity. "Forget all that 'Schubert with one foot in the grave' rubbish — the thing's so *alive*!" remarked Roger Norrington in a *Gramophone* interview. And so it proves in Norrington's extraordinary disc, which admirably bears out the validity of his dictum "it's only by being a bit purist to begin with, that you can allow later freedom". The freedoms are here, for example, in the relaxing of tempo for the awestruck response to the slow movement's central crisis, and in many dynamic inflexions throughout, but they will pass by those who crave the kind of distortions of tempo perpetrated on poor Schubert by revered podium luminaries from the past as the *sine qua non* for enjoyment of this symphony. And if the propulsive energy generated by Norrington's speeds, and say, the gentle pianissimo for the slow movement's second theme, or the precisely registered (and hugely effective) pianississimo at the start of the finale's momentous coda, are example of purism, then long may it reign in this work. The disc also offers convincing proof that period instruments do help to realize Schubert's intentions: Tovey remarked that the woodwind melody of the Trio needed a double wind band to be heard, or the string accompaniment damped down till it lost its energy of character. Here you can have both; a gloriously full and detailed woodwind sound and a splendidly energetic accompaniment. The balance, in fact, offers textural revelations in virtually every bar.

Additional recommendations ...

No. 9. **Vienna Philharmonic Orchestra/Sir Georg Solti.** Decca 430 747-2DM — 55m DDD 3/83

No. 9. **Staatskapelle Dresden/Karl Böhm.** DG Galleria 419 484-2GA — 50m DDD 12/87

No. 9. **Orchestra of the Age of Enlightenment/Sir Charles Mackerras.** Virgin Classics VC7 59669-2 — lh DDD 6/88

No. 9. **North German Radio Symphony Orchestra/Günter Wand.** RCA Victor Red Seal RD60978 — 53m DDD 1/92

No. 9. **Royal Concertgebouw Orchestra/Leonard Bernstein.** DG 427 646-2GH — 50m DDD 1/90

No. 9. ***Mendelssohn.*** *No. 4 in A major, Op. 90, "Italian".* **Berlin Philharmonic Orchestra/Klaus Tennstedt.** EMI CDD7 64085-2 — lh 17m DDD 1/92 £

Schubert. Octet in F major, D803. **Academy of St Martin in the Fields Chamber Ensemble** (Kenneth Sillito, Malcolm Latchem, vns; Stephen Shingles, va; Denis Vigay, vc; Raymund Koster, chbr bass; Andrew Marriner, cl; Timothy Brown, hn; Graham Sheen, bn). Chandos CHAN8585. Recorded in 1987.

lh DDD 8/88 

Schubert used material from previous years in composing this work which ostensibly has a serenade-like character, but shows a great depth of feeling, almost pathos at times. Schubert was already afflicted with the illness which was to dog the rest of his short life, and in the six-movement Octet he looked back nostalgically to happier days. It is one of his great masterpieces. The ASMF Chamber Ensemble have recorded the Octet on two occasions, but this Chandos version is considerably the better of the two. The engineers have succeeded in resolving problems of balance posed by the unequal power of solo strings and wind with great skill, and the sound itself is superlatively fine. The players respond eagerly to the Octet's song-like spontaneity, and they manage to capture its relaxed, Viennese flavour in a very authentic style, but they also understand and express with rare eloquence the work's underlying profundity of expression.

Additional recommendations ...

Octet. **Academy of Ancient Music Chamber Ensemble.** L'Oiseau-Lyre Florilegium 425 519-2OH — lh DDD 5/90

Octet. **Gaudier Ensemble.** ASV CDDCA694 — lh 4m DDD 5/90

Octet. Minuet and Finale in F major, D72[a]. **Vienna Octet; [a]Vienna Wind Soloists.** Decca 430 516-2DH — lh 12m DDD 2/93

NEW REVIEW

Schubert. String Quintet in C, D956. **Mstislav Rostropovich** (vc); **Emerson Quartet** (Eugene Drucker, Philip Setzer, vns; Lawrence Dutton, va; David Finckel, vc) DG 431 792-2GH. Recorded live in 1990.

53m DDD 9/92 

Arguably the finest of Schubert's late chamber works, the String Quintet, like the *Unfinished* and *Great* C major symphonies, had to wait some years after his death for its first performance. Many consider it to be the finest of his late works, with its virtually perfect fusion of compositional technique and artistic balance, its natural marriage of rhythmic and harmonic subtlety. Unlike Mozart, who added a second viola to give the basic string quartet texture a more mellow centre, Schubert employs the extra weight of a second cello, though he gives it free rein to explore its exceptionally wide compass. The Emerson Quartet are joined in this performance by none other than Mstislav Rostropovich, a partnership of persuasive integrity, steeped in the kind of mutual understanding that one would expect of such a meeting of minds; this is a marvellously well structured performance, conceived very much as a whole across its long, 53-minute span. The recording serves well enough; it is very clear and well laid out across the sound stage, but perhaps a little too closely focused and, as a result, a shade over-bright.

Additional recommendations ...

String Quintet. **Heinrich Schiff** (vc); **Alban Berg Quartet.** EMI CDC7 47018-2 — DDD 8/84

String Quintet. **Douglas Cummings** (vc); **Lindsay Quartet.** ASV CDDCA537 — DDD 9/85

String Quintet. **Yo-Yo Ma** (vc); **Cleveland Quartet.** CBS Masterworks CD39134 — 54m DDD 8/86

String Quintet. **Bruno Schrecker** (vc); **Aeolian Quartet.** Saga Classics SCD9011 — 54m ADD 4/92

String Quintet[a]*. String Quartet No. 12 in C minor, D703, "Quartettsatz".* **Takács Quartet; [a]Miklos Perényi** (vc). Decca 436 324-2DH — lh 4m DDD 6/93

String Quintet. **Wenn-Sinn Yang** (vc); **Brandis Quartet.** Nimbus NI5313 — 54m DDD 6/93

Schubert. Piano Quintet in A major, D667, "Trout"[a]. String Quartet No. 14 in D minor, D810, "Death and the Maiden"[b]. **[a]Sir Clifford Curzon** (pf); [a]members of the **Vienna Octet** (Willi Boskovsky, vn; Gunther Breitenbach, va; Nikolaus Hübner, vc; Johann Krump, db); [b]**Vienna Philharmonic Quartet** (Willi Boskovsky, Otto Strasser, vns; Rudolf Streng, va; Robert Scheiwein, vc). Decca 417 459-2DM. Item marked [a] from SXL2110 (6/59), recorded in 1957, [b] SXL6092 (5/64), recorded in 1963.

lh llm ADD 6/88 

Schubert composed the *Trout* Quintet in his early twenties for a group of amateur musicians in the town of Steyr in Upper Austria, which lies upon the River Enns which was then noted for its fine fishing and keen fishermen. The Quintet was certainly tailored for special circumstances, but like all great occasional music it stands as strongly as ever today, with its freshly bubbling invention and sunny melodiousness. Willi Boskovsky's gentle and cultured mind is very much responsible for the success of these performances of Schubert's two best-known chamber works. In the delectable *Trout* Quintet there is real unanimity of vision between the players, as well as an immaculate attention to the details of the scoring. Clifford Curzon's part in the performance is memorable especially for his quiet playing — the atmosphere is magical in such moments. Everywhere there is a great awareness of the delicacy and refinement of Schubert's inventiveness. The *Death and the Maiden* Quartet is no less successful. Schubert's strikingly powerful harmonies, together with a sustained feeling of intensity, all go to heighten the urgency of the first movement. Despite this, string textures are generally kept light and feathery. In the *Andante* all is subtly understated and although a mood of tragedy is always lurking in the background, never is it thrown at the listener. Boskovsky's understanding of the music is very acute and the performance cannot fail to satisfy even the most demanding. These are two vintage recordings and in the quartet the quality of sound is quite remarkable.

Additional recommendations ...

Piano Quintet. **Alfred Brendel** (pf); **James van Denmark** (db); **Cleveland Quartet.** Philips 400 078-2PH — ADD 3/83

Piano Quintet. **Clemens Hagen** (vn); **Veronika Hagen** (va); **Lukas Hagen** (vc); **Alois Posch** (db); **András Schiff** (pf). Decca 411 975-2DH — 44m DDD 4/85

Piano Quintet. Der Hirt auf dem Felsen, D965[b]. [b]**Felicity Lott** (sop); **Nash Ensemble.** Pickwick IMP Classics PCD868 — 57m DDD 12/87

Piano Quintet[a]. **Beethoven.** *Piano Trio No. 5 in D major, Op. 70 No. 1, "Ghost"*[b]. **Beaux Arts Trio;** [a]**Georg Hörtnagel** (db); [b]**Samuel Rhodes** (va). Philips Silver Line Classics 420 716-2PSL — 1h 2m ADD 6/88

Piano Quintet. String Trios[a] *— B flat major, D471; B flat major, D581.* **Ingrid Haebler** (pf); **Jacques Cazauran** (db); [a]**Grumiaux Trio.** Philips Musica da Camera 422 838-2PC — 1h 3m ADD 10/89

Piano Quintet. **Hummel.** *Piano Quintet in E flat major, Op. 87.* **Schubert Ensemble of London.** Hyperion Helios CDH88010 *(reviewed under Hummel; refer to the Index to Reviews)* — 1h 1m DDD 6/90

Piano Quintet[a]. *Adagio and Rondo concertante in F major, D487.* **Jenö Jandó** (pf); **Kodály Quartet;** [a]**István Tóth** (db). Naxos 8 550658 — 53m DDD 4/93

NEW REVIEW

Schubert. THE LAST QUARTETS. **Melos Quartet** (Wilhelm Melcher, Gerhard Voss, vns; Hermann Voss, va; Peter Buck, vc). Harmonia Mundi HMC90 1408/9.

String Quartets — No. 12 in C minor, D703, "Quartettsatz"[b]; No. 13 in A minor, D804[a]; No. 14 in D minor, D810, "Death and the Maiden"[a]; No. 15 in G major, D887[b]. Items marked [a] recorded 1989, [b] 1991.

② 2h 14m DDD 12/92

These quartets belong to the years 1820-26 and thus the last decade of Schubert's short life. As the violent *fortissimo* attack of the D minor reminds us right away, they don't make for comfortable listening: there's plenty of passion and tension here, and even an occaional alarming outburst such as occurs in the *Andante un poco moto* of the G major Quartet. Yet since this is still Schubert's music, there's also melodic richness. In fact one often senses a dramatic contrast between Viennese *Gemütlichkeit* and something like terror or pain, maybe even the thought of approaching death which we know haunted the already ill composer. The Melos Quartet have played this music in public over a period of years and bring authority as well as insight to the performance of the three late quartets and the earlier but no less compelling *Quartettsatz* in C minor. Thus, the big first movement of *Death and the Maiden* has both vigour in the fiery first subject and gentleness in the lilting second, while the coda smoulders impressively before bursting into flames. There is a hushed beauty in the famous slow movement, based on the song which gave its name to the work, while the final *Presto* has all the urgency of an Erl King-like pursuit. The Melos are equally at home in the radiantly melodious yet sorrowful A minor Quartet and the dramatic and enigmatic G major Quartet. These are performances of distinction, and the recording is truthful, with a natural degree of resonance.

Additional recommendations ...

No. 14. **Beethoven.** *String Quartet in E flat major, Op. 74, "Harp".* **Brodsky Quartet.** Pickwick IMP Red Label PCD831 — lh 10m DDD 1/87

Nos. 12 and 14. **Lindsay Quartet.** ASV CDDCA560 — 52m DDD 3/87

Nos. 14 and 15. **Busch Quartet.** EMI Références mono CDH7 69795-2 — lh 13m ADD 5/89

No. 13 (trans. Mahler). No. 14 (trans. Liszt CO). **Franz Liszt Chamber Orchestra/János Rolla.** Quintana QUI90 3025 — 56m DDD 3/92

No. 2 in C major, D32. No. 14. **Artis Quartet.** Sony Classical SK52582 — 59m DDD 6/93

Schubert. Piano Trios — B flat major, D28 (Sonata in one movement); No. 1 in B flat major, D898. Notturno in E flat major, D897. **Trio Zingara** (Elizabeth Layton, vn; Felix Schmidt, vc; Annette Cole, pf). Collins Classics 1215-2.

lh lm DDD 10/91

Schubert was a mere schoolboy of 15 when writing his Sonata Movement in B flat, D28, in 1812. Yet curiously he allowed some 14 years to elapse before producing his two full-scale masterpieces in this medium, likewise the independent *Adagio* in E flat, posthumously published under the title *Notturno*. Here, we're given three of the four in performances as mellow in feeling as in actual sound — not for nothing was the chosen recording venue The Maltings at Snape. So hopefully it will not be too long before this musicianly young team goes back there to complete its cycle with the big E flat major Trio. The occasionally audible intakes of breath betray the extent of their involvement. Yet there is no self-conscious attempt to hold any listener captive. The predominant impression left by their playing is of complete naturalness, of total absence of special pleading, just as if they were in the relaxed atmosphere of Joseph von Spaun's drawingroom on 28th January 1828, when the B flat Trio is thought to have had its first performance in the presence of the composer himself.

Additional recommendations ...

No. 1. **Borodin Trio.** Chandos CHAN8308 — 43m DDD 3/84

No. 2 in E flat major, D929. **Borodin Trio.** Chandos CHAN8324 — DDD 11/84

NEW REVIEW

Schubert. Violin Sonatas — D major, D384; A minor, D385; G minor, D408; A major (Duo), D574. **Raphaël Oleg** (vn); **Théodore Paraskivesco** (pf). Denon CO-75027. Recorded in 1991.

lh 11m DDD 3/93

Though Schubert was a violinist himself and wrote beautifully for the instrument, his Violin Sonatas have never quite made it into the concert repertory, perhaps because the first three of them were written when he was only 19 but not published after his death, and then with the diminishing title of "sonatinas" that was bestowed on them by their publisher. Yet these sonatas are not all that lightweight or short, and although the D major is brief and undemanding, those in A minor and G minor are in four movements and emerge as substantial works which sometimes offer quite an intense emotional experience. The same is true of the later *Duo* (again this was the publisher's name) in A major that Schubert composed a year later: this has an even better claim to be thought of as a fully fledged classical sonata, in the mould that was established by Mozart and Beethoven, since its piano part has plenty of character and does not merely follow the violin. Raphaël Oleg and Théodore Paraskivesco are a well-matched duo who judge tempos well and play sensitively, while not weighing the music down with excessive point-making. Their recording, made in a German church, is as clean and pleasing as their playing, even if the sound would benefit from still more space and depth. This is a well-filled disc, with good performances of worthwhile music.

Additional recommendation ...

D384. D385. D408; A major (Duo), D574. **Gidon Kremer** (vn); **Oleg Maisenberg** (pf). DG 437 092-2GH — lh 2m DDD 4/93

Schubert. Violin Sonata in A major (Duo), D574. Rondo brillant in B minor, D895. Fantasy in C major, D934. **Gidon Kremer** (vn); **Valery Afanassiev** (pf). DG 431 654-2GH. Recorded in 1990.

1h 7m DDD 3/92

Few indeed are the recital discs which can offer the listener such unalloyed pleasure as this gloriously played and generously conceived Schubert recording from Gidon Kremer and Valery Afanassiev. Rarer yet by far, though, are releases capable of generating the kind of communicative ambience more normally revealed by the intimacy of live music making. The very opening bars of Afanassiev's piano introduction at the start of the *Duo* in A major, D574, with its restrained yet expectant dignity of utterance would mesmerize the heart of the sternest critic, whilst Kremer exhibits charm, wit, understatement and sheer delight in this work. The B minor Rondo and the magnificent Fantasy in C major were written a decade after the *Duo* and were both intended to display the talents of the composer's friend, the Czech violinist, Josef Slavic, who had settled in Vienna during 1826. Neither work found favour at the time, and quite possibly the dark premonitions of the Rondo, whose emotional sympathies recalled those of the *Unfinished* Symphony, were inappropriate for Viennese popular tastes. However, although Kremer's approach avoids mere rhetoric here, this superb recording is surely crowned by a magisterial performance of the C major Fantasy. This account combines bravura, elegance and a deep affinity with the Schubertian genre, captured with splendid realism by a recording which is technically beyond criticism.

Schubert: Sonata in A minor, D821, "Arpeggione". WORKS FOR VIOLA AND PIANO. **Yuri Bashmet** (va); **Mikhail Muntian** (pf). RCA Victor Red Seal RD60112. Recorded in 1989. ***Schumann:*** Märchen-bilder, Op. 113. Adagio and Allegro, Op. 70. ***Bruch:*** Kol nidrei, Op. 47. ***Enescu:*** Konzertstück.

1h 13m DDD 12/90

The booklet tells us that Yuri Bashmet, aged 38 at the time of this recording, had already 30 new works for the viola dedicated to him. Perhaps thanks should go to this Russian artist, with his glorious tone, and his closely attuned pianist, Mikhail Muntian, for enriching the CD catalogue with Georges Enescu's rarely heard *Konzertstück*, written in Paris in the composer's impressionable early twenties, and played here with intuitive understanding of its fantasy and lyrical rapture. Like that work, the four miniatures of Schumann's *Märchenbilder* of 1851 were also inspired by the viola itself, whereas Schumann's *Adagio and Allegro*, Bruch's *Kol nidrei* (based on one of the oldest and best-known synagogue melodies) and Schubert's charming A minor Sonata were originally written for valve-horn, cello and the now obsolete arpeggione respectively. But with his wide range of colour and his "speaking" phrasing Bashmet makes them all entirely his own, only causing the occasional raised eyebrow with slower tempo for slow numbers (such as Schumann's lullaby-like Op. 113, No. 4 and the *Adagio* of Schubert's Sonata) than could be enjoyed from players without his own fine-spun, intimately nuanced line. Strongly recommended.

Additional recommendations ...

Sonata. ***Debussy.*** *Cello Sonata.* ***Schumann.*** *Fünf Stücke im Volkston, Op. 102.* **Mstislav Rostropovich** (vc); **Benjamin Britten** (pf). Decca 417 833-2DH *(reviewed under Debussy; refer to the Index to Reviews)* — 59m ADD 9/87

(All trans. Stallman). Sonata. Violin Sonatina in G minor, D408. Fantasy in C major, D934. **Robert Stallman** (fl); **Erika Nickrenz** (pf). ASV CDDCA742 — 1h 9m DDD 4/92

Sonata. ***Schumann.*** *Fantasiestücke, Op. 73. Fünf Stücke im Volkston. Adagio and Allegro in A flat major, Op. 70.* ***Mendelssohn.*** *Variations concertantes, Op. 17. Song without words in D major, Op. 109.* **Friedrich-Jürgen Sellheim** (vc); **Eckart Sellheim** (pf). Sony Classical Essential Classics MK48171 — 1h 12m ADD 10/92

Schubert. Impromptus — D899; D935. **Murray Perahia** (pf). CBS Masterworks CD37291. From 37291 (1/84).

1h 3m 4/85

NEW REVIEW

Schubert. Impromptus — D899; D935. **Lambert Orkis** (fp). Virgin Classics Veritas VC7 59600-2. Recorded in 1989.

1h 3m DDD 9/92 

Though an able pianist, Schubert was not a concert-giving virtuoso out to conquer an international public with largescale bravura works. The music-making he most enjoyed was at informal parties (they came to be known as Schubertiads) in the homes of music-loving friends, hence the very large number of miniatures — with the *Impromptus* among them — that flowed unceasingly from his pen. Whereas so much of what he wrote was never published in his lifetime, he had the satisfaction of seeing all eight *Impromptus* in print the year before he died. And their popularity has never waned, as the quickest glance at any catalogue at once makes clear. Inevitably Murray Perahia has strong rivals all equally deserving of a place in this *Guide*. His own version nevertheless constantly enchants with its pellucid tone and spontaneous spring-like freshness. Note the rippling lightness of the triplets in No. 2 in E flat and the pinpoint clarity of his semiquaver articulation in No. 4 in A flat in the first set, likewise the dancing lilt he brings to the variations of No. 3 in B flat and his respect for the *scherzando* expressively qualifying the *allegro* in No. 4 in F minor in the second set. None are 'overloaded'. The recording is no less pleasing. Those who prefer to hear the *Impromptus* on an instrument of Schubert's own day are excellently served by the American, Lambert Orkis, who plays a finely restored 1826 Graf fortepiano now housed in Antwerp's sixteenth-century Vleeshuis Museum where this recording was made. He admits to having been immediately captivated by its "beautiful singing treble range" and its "light and smooth action". As is already so clear from his other performances with the Castle Trio, he again proves himself a musician of inexhaustible imaginative vitality, bringing up all eight judiciously-timed pieces as if newly minted. The sound is excellent.

Additional recommendations ...

D899. D935. **Alfred Brendel** (pf). Philips 420 840-2PM — 1h 2m DDD 4/84 (B)
D899. D935. **Radu Lupu** (pf). Decca 411 711-2DH — DDD 10/84 (B)
D899. D935. **Alfred Brendel** (pf). Philips 422 237-2PH — 1h 1m DDD 10/89 (B)
D899. D935. **Krystian Zimerman** (pf). DG 423 612-2GH — 1h 5m DDD 5/91 (B)
D899. Six Moments musicaux, D780. Ungarische Melodie in B minor, D817. Six Deutsche Tänze, D820. Grazer Galopp, D925. **András Schiff** (pf). Decca 430 425-2DH — 1h 11m DDD 11/92 (B)
D899. D935. **Edwin Fischer** (pf). Dante Historical Piano Collection mono HPC006 — 53m ADD 5/93 (B) ▲

Schubert. PIANO WORKS. **András Schiff.** Decca 425 638-2DH. Recorded in 1988.
Allegretto in C minor, D915. Impromptus — D935; D946. 12 Ländler, D790.

1h 14m DDD 7/90

Throughout his life Schubert was as irresistibly drawn to the keyboard miniature as he was to the realm of song. On this disc András Schiff assembles a choice assortment of these shorter pieces, playing them with the youthful freshness and charm with which Schubert himself must so often have delighted his friends. Most familiar, of course, are the last four *Impromptus*, dating from the year before he died but inexplicably left unpublished for the next 12 years. For these Schiff favours fleeter tempos than we often hear (notably for the Second in A flat), giving each piece an effortless lyrical flow. The three *Klavierstücke* of his last year, with their strong internal contrasts, are richly characterized, yet again Schiff resists all temptation to over-interpret or emotionally inflate. The minor/major bittersweetness of the C minor *Allegretto*, written for Schubert's "dear friend", Ferdinand Walcher, on his departure from Vienna in April 1827, is brought home with the same disarming simplicity. Lighter relief comes in the 12 *Ländler* of 1823 (always so dear to Brahms, who owned the manuscript and eventually arranged for their publication), where Schiff prefers imaginative vitality to *schmalz*. The recording (made in Vienna's Konzerthaus) respects his light-fingered textural clarity.

Schubert. Fantasy in C major, D760, "Wanderer".
Schumann. Fantasia in C major, Op. 17. **Murray Perahia** (pf). CBS Masterworks CD42124.

52m DDD 12/86

The *Wanderer* Fantasy is a work in four linked movements using a motto theme that is variously transformed as the work proceeds, a technique that we find later in such works as Liszt's Piano Concertos and Franck's Symphony. It is a vigorous piece and in some ways somewhat classical and symphonic in utterance, strong in rhetoric as well as poetry. On the other hand, Schumann's *Fantasia*, written some 16 years later around 1837, is more obviously pianistic (of the two composers it was he who was the better pianist) and inspired more clearly by the romantic spirit that had already developed in music during Schubert's lifetime. Both works are major landmarks of the piano repertory, and Murray Perahia plays them with an unerring sense of their different styles as well as impeccable technical command. He is unfailingly exciting and uplifting in the quicker music, but it is probably in the slower and more expressive sections that his nobly personal eloquence is most strikingly revealed. Two different American locations were used for these performances, but the second of them (for the Schumann) allows a richer and more atmospheric piano sound.

Additional recommendation ...

Fantasy. Piano Sonata in A minor, D845. **Maurizio Pollini** (pf). DG 419 672-2GH — 58m DDD 8/87

NEW REVIEW

Schubert. PIANO SONATAS. **Sviatoslav Richter** (pf). Olympia OCD286/8. Recorded live in 1979.
OCD286 — Piano Sonatas: B major, D575; F minor, D625. Six Moments musicaux, D780 — No. 1 in C major; No. 3 in F minor; No. 6 in A flat major. *OCD288* — Piano Sonatas: A major, D664; A minor, D784. Impromptus, D899 — No. 2 in E flat major; No. 4 in A flat major. *OCD287* — ***Chopin:*** Preludes, Op. 28 — No. 2 in A minor; No. 4 in E minor; No. 5 in D major; No. 6 in B minor; No. 7 in A major; No. 8 in F sharp minor; No. 9 in E major; No. 10 in C sharp minor; No. 11 in B major; No. 13 in F sharp major; No. 19 in E flat major; No. 21 in B flat major; No. 23 in F major. ***Schumann:*** Novelletten, Op. 21 — No. 2 in D major; No. 4 in D major; No. 8 in F sharp minor. Fantasiestücke, Op. 12 — In der Nacht; Traumes-Wirren.

③ lh 5m lh 3m 50m DDD 10/92

Richter's dislike for studio recording can be frustrating — some of his most stupendous performances can only be heard on unofficial tapes of almost unlistenable quality; and when in the mid-1980s the record companies finally started recording his concerts in a big way something of the edge had already gone off his formerly unassailable mastery. But these 1979 Tokyo performances have the best of most worlds. The sound is drier and closer than usual. That suits the monumentality of the playing, which itself marks the beginning of Richter's ultra-austere late manner without betraying the least technical discomfort. The Chopin Preludes are perhaps uninvitingly plain, for all their consummate pianism. But the Schumann *Novelettes* on the same disc are uncannily insightful, and "Traumes-Wirren" is quite breathtaking. Both Schubert compilations demonstrate a philosophical approach to this composer which some listeners may find an acquired taste. Richter shuns surface beauty and charm and instead follows the music to elevated realms of reflection. Slow movements are profoundly inward and meditative, fast ones crackle with energy, and the rapt attention of the audience tells you as much about the atmosphere generated as the wild applause and raucous bravos which conclude one of the finest piano recordings this writer has ever had the privilege of reviewing.

Additional recommendation ...

Piano Sonatas — D664; C minor, D958; A major, D959; B flat major, D960. Impromptus, D899. Allegretto in C minor, D915. **Claudio Arrau** (pf). Philips Arrau Edition 432 307-2PM3 — ③ 3h 3m ADD 5/92

Schubert. Piano Sonata in B flat major, D960. Fantasy in C major, D760, "Wanderer". **Alfred Brendel** (pf). Philips 422 062-2PH.

58m DDD 1/90

Brendel meets Schubert on his own ground, exulting in the *con fuoco* panache of the earlier work, and just as keenly revealing the 'other-worldliness' of Schubert's farewell. For immediacy of response, it would be hard to name any player more aware of Schubert's own impressionability — the impressionability of a composer who died young enough to have known only "the poignancy and rapture of first sensations". Some might feel that Brendel's reaction to the mood of the moment at times results in over-elasticity of pulse, as in his drastic slowings-down for the lyrical second subject in the *Wanderer*'s first movement. But never mind. Whatever he does is done with enough conviction to make you feel, at the moment of listening, that there could be no other way. The recording is both rich and clear.

Additional recommendations ...

Piano Sonata. **Stephen Kovacevich.** Hyperion CDA66004 — 42m DDD 4/87

Piano Sonata. Fantasy. **Alfred Brendel** (pf). Philips Silver Line 420 644-2PM — 57m ADD 8/87

Piano Sonata. Impromptu in A flat major, D935 No. 2. Six Moments musicaux, D780. **Sir Clifford Curzon** (pf). Decca 417 642-2DH — 1h 10m ADD 8/87

Piano Sonata. Allegretto in C minor, D915. Impromptus, D946. **Maurizio Pollini.** DG 427 326-2GH — 1h 11m DDD 5/89

Piano Sonatas — D960; A major, D959. **Melvyn Tan** (fp). EMI Reflexe CDC7 49631-2 — 1h 7m DDD 9/89

Piano Sonatas — D959; A minor, D537. **Laurent Cabasso** (pf). Auvidis Valois V4630 — 1h 4m DDD 4/91

Schubert. Piano Sonata in C minor, D958. Impromptus, D899. Deutsche Tänze, D783. **Imogen Cooper** (pf). Ottavo OTRC78923. Recorded in 1989.

1h 10m DDD 2/92

This is in fact the last of Imogen Cooper's six-disc cycle of the piano music of Schubert's last six years, a cycle launched in 1988 hard on the heels of similar cycles given on the concert platform in both London and Amsterdam. Like its predecessors, it confirms her as a Schubert player of exceptional style and finesse. Intuitively perceptive phrasing and a willingness to let the music sing within a wholly Schubertian sound-world are prime virtues. And though (like her erstwhile mentor, Alfred Brendel) she is no slave to the metronome when contrasting first and second subjects in sonata expositions, she still makes the music her own without the self-consciously mannered kind of interpretation heard from one or two more recent rivals in this strongly competitive field. Her urgent yet poised performance of the late C minor Sonata certainly confirms her admission (in a 1988 *Gramophone* interview) that the comparatively clinical atmosphere of an audience-less recording venue worries her not at all. In London's Henry Wood Hall her Yamaha is as clearly and truthfully reproduced (save for a slight suspicion of pedal-haze in the sonata's demonically driven finale) as most else in the series. The Impromptus reveal an acutely sensitive response to Schubert's dynamic subtleties and surprises of key, while the 16 *German Dances* tell their own simple Viennese tale without any suggestion of applied make-up.

D958. D960. **Jenö Jandó** (pf). Naxos 8 550475 — 1h 9m DDD

Schubert. Piano Sonata in A minor, D845. Impromptus, D946. **Alfred Brendel** (pf). Philips 422 075-2PH.

1h 1m DDD 10/89

Schubert. Piano Sonatas — A minor, D845[a]; G major, D894[b]. **Radu Lupu** (pf). Decca 417 640-2DH. Item marked [a] from SXL6931 (12/79), [b] SXL6741 (5/76).

lh 14m ADD 6/87 

The coupling of Brendel and Schubert inspires confidence. Though love of the music alone, as pianists know, is not enough to master these pieces, it is essential, and in this big A minor Sonata (a key that was somehow especially important to Schubert) Brendel presents us with a drama that is no less tense for being predominantly expressed in terms of shapely melody. There is a flexibility in this playing that reminds us of the pianist's own comment that in such music "we feel not masters but victims of the situation": he allows us plenty of time to savour detail without ever losing sight of the overall shape of the music, and the long first movement and finale carry us compellingly forwards, as does the scherzo with its urgent energy, while the *Andante* second movement, too, has the right kind of spaciousness. In the *Impromptus* which date from the composer's last months, Brendel is no less responsive and imaginative. Richly sonorous digital recording in a German location complements the distinction of the playing on this fine Schubert disc.

Radu Lupu also understands Schubert's style as do few others and the way in which he is able to project this essentially private world is outstanding. His tone is unfailingly clear, and this adds substantially to the lucidity of the readings. The simplicity of the opening themes of the A minor Sonata is a marvel of eloquence and when it is reset in the development section of the first movement one is amazed to hear Lupu transforming it into something far more urgent and full of pathos. The G major Sonata again fires Lupu's imagination and in the Minuet third movement he uses a considerable amount of rubato for the dance; its solid rhythmic pulse is an ideal foil to offset the extraordinary transitions of the finale that follows. The recorded sound does full justice to the colour of the pianist's tone.

Additional recommendations ...

Piano Sonatas — D845; G major, D894. **Radu Lupu** (pf). Decca 417 640-2DH — lh 14m ADD 6/87

Piano Sonatas — D845; E major, D157. Valses sentimentales, D779 — No. 1 in C major; No. 3 in G major; No. 5 in B flat major; No. 7 in G minor; No. 13 in A major; No. 14 in D major; No. 19 in A flat major; No. 21 in E flat major; No. 24 in G minor; No. 28 in E flat major; No. 30 in C major; No. 34 in A flat major. Waltz in A flat major, D978. **Michel Dalberto** (pf). Denon CO-73787 — lh 7m DDD 4/90

Piano Sonatas — D894; A minor, D784. 12 Waltzes, D145. **Vladimir Ashkenazy** (pf). Decca Ovation 425 017-2DM — lh 14m ADD 8/90

Piano Sonata, D894. ***Haydn.*** *Piano Sonata in C major, HobXVI/50.* ***Brahms.*** *Four Piano Pieces, Op. 119.* ***Lachenmann.*** *Five Variations on a theme of Franz Schubert.* **Lars Vogt** (pf). EMI CDC7 54446-2 — lh 14m DDD 5/92

Schubert. Piano Sonatas — D major, D850; A minor, D784. **Alfred Brendel** (pf). Philips 422 063-2PH.

lh 3m DDD 11/88

There is an extraordinary amount of highly experimental writing in Schubert's piano sonatas. The essence of their structure is the contrasting of big heroic ideas with tender and inner thoughts; the first impresses the listener, the second woos him. The two works on this CD are in some ways on a varying scale. The D major lasts for 40 minutes, the A minor for around 23. However, it is the latter that contains the most symphonically inspired writing — it sounds as if it could easily be transposed for orchestra. Alfred Brendel presents the composer not so much as the master of lieder-writing, but more as a man thinking in large forms. Although there are wonderful quiet moments when intimate asides are conveyed with an imaginative sensitivity one remembers more the urgency and the power behind the notes. The A minor, with its frequently recurring themes, is almost obsessive in character whilst the big D major Sonata is rather lighter in mood, especially in the outer movements. The recorded sound is very faithful to the pianist's tone, whilst generally avoiding that insistent quality that can mar his loudest playing.

Additional recommendations ...
Piano Sonata — D784. Six Moments musicaux, D780. Scherzos, D593. **Maria João Pires** (pf). DG 427 769-2GH — ⁄ ⁄ lh 3m DDD 2/90
Piano Sonatas — D784; A minor, D845; Gmajor, D894; A major, D959. **Trudelies Leonhardt** (fp). Jecklin J4420/1-2 — ⁄ ⁄ ② 2h 21m ADD 11/91
D784. D157 in E major. D959 in A major. **Radu Lupu** (pf). Decca Ovation 425 033-2DM — ⁄ ⁄ lh 13m ADD 2/92

NEW REVIEW

Schubert. LIEDER, Volumes 1-3. **Dietrich Fischer-Dieskau** (bar); **Gerald Moore** (pf). DG 437 214-2GX21. Volumes also available separately, as detailed below. Recorded 1966-72. *437 215-2GX9* (Volume 1: nine discs: 6h 44m): 234 Lieder, written between 1811 and 1817 (from 2720 022, 12/70). *437 225-2GX9* (Volume 2: nine discs: 6h 35m): 171 Lieder, written between 1817 and 1828 (from 643547/58, 1/70). *437 235-2GX3* (Volume 3: three discs: 3h 4m): Die schöne Müllerin, D795. Winterreise, D911. Schwanengesang, D957 (2720 059, 1/73).

②① 24h 23m ADD 3/93 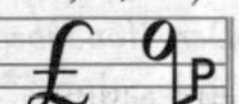

Twenty-one discs at under £100 bringing together two of this century's greatest Lieder interpreters — it sounds like a recipe for success, as indeed it is, fulfilling the highest expectations. The recordings were made when Dietrich Fischer-Dieskau was at his peak and Gerald Moore could draw on a lifetime's experience and love of this repertoire. Though the set makes no claims to completeness (in the way that Graham Johnson's Schubert series on Hyperion does), most of the songs for male voice are included here. The use of a single singer and pianist gives the set a unity that allows the listener to gasp anew at the composer's wide-ranging inspiration and imagination. Fischer-Dieskau brings a unique understanding, an elegant line and a diction that renders the text clear without resort to the written texts. If occasionally he imparts an unnecessary weightiness to the lighter songs, this quibble is as nothing when his historic achievement is taken as a whole. And though he made many recordings of the song cycles these are perhaps the finest, with Moore the ideal partner. Try for example, the bleakness of "Ihr Bild" from *Schwanengesang* or the hallucinatory happiness of "Der Lindenbaum" from *Winterreise*. The songs themselves are basically in chronological order (but with the three song cycles collected together in the final box). It is unfortunate there is no index — trying to find individual songs can be frustrating. It should also be added that the translations are distinctly quirky in places; better to use Richard Wigmore's excellent book *Schubert: The Complete Song Texts* (Gollancz: 1988) if you have a copy to hand. This is undoubtedly one of the greatest bargains in the *Guide*. Buy, without fear of disappointment.

NEW REVIEW

Schubert. LIEDER, Volume 15. **Dame Margaret Price** (sop); **Graham Johnson** (pf). Hyperion CDJ33015. Texts and translations included. Recorded in 1991.
An die untergehende Sonne, D457. Der Mondabend, D141. Klage an den Mond, D436. Die Mainacht, D194. Der Unglückliche, D713. An die Sonne, D270. Der Morgenkuss, D264. Kolmas Klage, D217. Ins stille Land, D403. Gondelfahrer, D808. Der Winterabend, D938. Der Wanderer an den Mond, D870. Im Freien, D880. Am Fenster, D878. Der blinde Knabe, D833. Die junge Nonne, D828.

lh 12m DDD 2/93 

Schubert. LIEDER, Volume 16. **Thomas Allen** (bar); **Graham Johnson** (pf). Hyperion CDJ33016. Texts and translations included.
Leichenfantasie, D7. Laura am Klavier, D388. Die Entzückung an Laura — first version, D390, second version (completed van Hoorickx), D577. An die Freude, D189. An Emma, D113. Das Mädchen aus der Fremde, D117. Das Geheimnis, D793. Die Bürgschaft, D246. Der Jüngling am Bache, D638. Die vier Weltalter, D391. Sehnsucht, D52. Der Pilgrim, D794.

lh 18m DDD 3/93 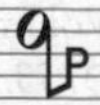

The accompanist Graham Johnson's labour of love, recording Schubert's complete output of solo (and ensemble) songs for Hyperion with some of the world's greatest singers, is at the time of publication halfway through, with another 18 Volumes anticipated. Two of the most recent additions come from Thomas Allen and Dame Margaret Price, both in finest voice; interestingly the abiding impression is of Johnson himself, not only at the piano where he approaches each song with utter commitment, but also in the accompanying booklet where he often devotes several pages of commentary to one song. If the performances were not so beautiful it would be easy to say the discs were worth buying for the notes alone. Allen's disc consists entirely of Schiller settings, opening with the gloomy *Leichenfantasie*, ("Funereal Fantasy") telling of a son's emotions at his father's funeral. "Inside every fat man is a thin one desperately trying to escape", and inside the Lieder-writing Schubert there was a composer of operas frantically aiming to air his declamatory gifts, which certainly emerge in lengthy, romantic and sometimes rambling settings such as this and *Die Bürgschaft*. Their effectiveness is food for speculation, but it is interesting to view the more concise Lieder, such as the three *Laura* songs, *An die Freude* and *An Emma*, with the perspective of the ambitious romantic displayed in the extended ballads. Allen's dramatic capabilities suit this selection superbly. Dame Margaret Price approaches her 17 songs with an astounding purity of tone, applying vibrato sparingly and selectively, which proves ideal in such songs as *An die untergehende Sonne, Der Mondabend* and the masterpiece *Der Winterabend*, focusing attention on their mingled peace and sadness. Here there are both well-known and neglected Lieder, the linking thread being the themes of evening and night, longing, restlessness versus peace. The disc culminates with the celebrated *Die junge Nonne*, which perhaps shows Price's artistry at its most characteristic — sombre, flexible and profound.

Additional recommendations ...

Volume 1. *Der Jüngling am Bache, D30. Thekla, D73. Schäfers Klagelied, D121 (first version). Nähe des Geliebten, D162 (second version). Meerestille, D216. Amalia, D195. Die Erwartung, D159 (second version). Wandrers Nachtlied, D224. Der Fischer, D225 (second version). Erster Verlust, D226. Wonne der Wehmut, D260. An den Mond, D296. Das Geheimnis, D250. Lied, D284. Der Flüchtling, D402. An den Frühling, D587 (second version). Der Alpenjäger, D588 (second version). Der Pilgrim, D794. Sehnsucht, D636 (second version).* **Dame Janet Baker** (mez); **Graham Johnson.** Hyperion CDJ33001 — ⁘ 1h 10m DDD 10/88 ℗

Volume 6. *Die Nacht, D534 (completed by Anton Diabelli). Jagdlied, D521 (with chorus). Abendstern, D806. Abends unter der Linde, D235. Abends unter der Linde, D237. Der Knabe in der Wiege, D579. Abendlied für die Entfernte, D856. Willkommen und Abschied, D767. Vor meiner Wiege, D927. Der Vater mit dem Kind, D906. Des Fischers Liebesglück, D933. Die Sterne, D939. Alinde, D904. An die Laute, D905. Zur guten Nacht, D903 (chorus).* **Anthony Rolfe Johnson** (ten); **Graham Johnson.** Hyperion CDJ33006 — ⁘ 1h 13m DDD 6/90 ℗

Volume 7. *Minona, D152. Der Jüngling am Bache, D192. Stimme der Liebe, D187. Naturgenuss, D188. Des Mädchens Klage, D191. Die Sterbende, D186. An den Mond, D193. An die Nachtigall, D196. Die Liebe (Klärchens Lied), D210. Meeresstille, D215a. Idens Nachtgesang, D227. Von Ida, D228. Das Sehnen, D231. Die Spinnerin, D247. Wer kauft Liebesgötter?, D261. An den Frühling, D283. Das Rosenband, D280. Liane, D298. Idens Schwanenlied, D317. Luisens Antwort, D319. Mein Gruss an den Mai, D305. Mignon, D321. Sehnsucht, D310 (two versions).* **Elly Ameling** (sop); **Graham Johnson.** Hyperion CDJ33007 — ⁘ 1h 11m DDD 8/90 ℗

Volume 8. *An den Mond, D259. Romanze, D114. Stimme der Liebe, D418. Die Sommernacht, D289. Die frühen Gräber, D290. Die Mondnacht, D238. An den Mond in einer Herbstnacht, D614. Die Nonne, D208. An Chloen, D462. Hochzeit-Lied, D463. In der Mitternacht, D464. Trauer der Liebe, D465. Die Perle, D466. Abendlied der Fürstin, D495. Wiegenlied, D498. Ständchen, D920 (with chorus). Bertas Lied in der Nacht, D653. Der Erlkönig, D328.* **Sarah Walker** (mez); **Graham Johnson.** Hyperion CDJ33008 — ⁘ 1h 12m DDD 10/90 ℗

Volume 10. *Der Sänger, D149. Auf einen Kirchhof, D151. Am Flusse, D160. An Mignon, D161. Vergebliche Liebe, D177. An die Apfelbäume, wo ich Julien erblickte, D197. Seufzer, D198. Auf den Tod einer Nachtigall, D201. Der Liebende, D207. Adelwold und Emma, D211. Der Traum, D213. Die Laube, D214. Der Weiberfreund, D271. Labetrank der Liebe, D302. An die Geliebte, D303. Harfenspieler I, D325.* **Martyn Hill** (ten); **Graham Johnson.** Hyperion CDJ33010 — ⁘ 1h 14m DDD 5/91 ℗

Volume 11. *An den Tod, D518. Auf dem Wasser zu singen, D774. Auflösung, D807. Aus Heliopolis I, D753. Aus Heliopolis II, D754. Dithyrambe, D801. Elysium, D584. Der Geistertanz, D116. Der König in Thule, D367. Lied des Orpheus, D474. Nachtstück, D672. Schwanengesang, D744. Seligkeit, D433. So lasst mich scheinen, D727. Thekla, D595. Der Tod und das Mädchen, D531. Verklärung, D59.*

Vollendung, D989. Das Zügenglöcklein, D871. **Brigitte Fassbaender** (mez); **Graham Johnson.** Hyperion CDJ33011 — ⁘ lh 5m DDD 8/91 ℗

Volume 14. *An die Leier, D737. Amphiaraos, D166. Gruppe aus dem Tartarus, D396. Gruppe aus dem Tartarus, D583. Hippolits Lied, D890. Memnon, D541. Fragment aus dem Aeschylus, D450. Philoktet, D540. Uraniens Flucht, D554. Hektors Abschied, D312. Antigone und Oedip, D542 (both with Marie McLaughlin, sop). Lied eines Schiffers an die Dioskuren, D360. Orest auf Tauris, D548. Der entsühnte Orest, D699. Der zürnenden Diana, D707. Freiwilliges Versinken, D700. Die Götter Griechenlands, D677.* **Thomas Hampson** (bar); **Graham Johnson.** Hyperion CDJ33014 — ⁘ lh 20m DDD 4/92 ℗

Volume 17. *Lied (Mutter geht durch ihre kammern), D373. Lodas Gespenst, D150. Klage, D371. Lorma, D376. Der Herbstabend, D405. Die Einsiedelei, D393. Der Herbstnacht, D404. Lied in der Abwesenheit, D416. Frühlingslied, D398. Winterlied, D401. Minnelied, D429. Aus Diego Manazares (Ilmerine), D458. Pflicht und Liebe, D467. An den Mond, D468. Litanei auf das Fest aller Seelen, D343. Geheimnis (An Franz Schubert), D491. Am Grabe Anselmos, D504. An die Nachtigall, D497. Klage um Ali Bey, D496a. Phidile, D500. Herbstlied, D502. Lebenslied, D508. Lieden der Trennung, D509. An mein Klavier, D342.* **Lucia Popp** (sop); **Graham Johnson** (pf). Hyperion CDJ33017 — ⁘ lh 11m DDD 6/93

Volume 18. *Das Finden, D219. Die Nacht, D358. An den Schlaf, D477. Blumenlied, D431. Auf den Tod einer Nachtigall, D399. Erntelied, D434. An die Harmonie, D394. Das Heimweh, D456. Abendlied, D499. An die Entfernte, D765. Drang in die Ferne, D770. Das Heimweh, D851. Auf der Bruck, D853. Um Mitternacht, D862. Die Blume und der Quell, D874 (cpted R. Van Hoorickx). Der liebliche Sterns, D861. Tiefes Lied (Im Jänner 1817), D876. Im Walde, D834. Im Frühling, D882. Lebensmut, D883. Uber Wildemann, D884. Am mein Herz, D860.* **Peter Schreier** (ten); **Graham Johnson** (pf). Hyperion CDJ33018 — ⁘ lh 16m DDD 7/93 ℗

NEW REVIEW

Schubert. LIEDER. **Edith Wiens** (sop); [a]**Joaquin Valdepeñas** (cl); **Rudolf Jansen** (pf). CBC Records Musica Viva MVCD1053. Texts and translations included.

Seligkeit, D433. Frühlingsglaube, D686. Das Lied im Grunen, D917. Lachen und Weinen, D777. Der Jüngling an der Quelle, D300. Auf dem Wasser zu singen, D774. Die junge Nonne, D828. Die Verschworenen (Der hausliche Krieg) — Ich schleiche bang und still[a]. Claudine von Villa Bella — Liebe schwarmt auf allen Wegen. Der Einsame, D800. Nacht und Träume, D827. Die Mutter Erde, D788. Der Hirt auf dem Felsen, D965[a]. Fischerweise, D881. Heidenröslein, D257. An Silvia, D891. Liebhaber in allen Gestalten, D558. An die Musik, D547.

⁘ lh 6m DDD 5/93

The high, 'white' voice of Edith Wiens may not be the first timbre that one might think suitable for Schubert Lieder. However, in this disc which encompasses some of the most popular and often-performed songs, she proves that inner feeling can deliver the most rewarding of interpretations. Her voice is, in fact, superbly malleable, transforming its quality almost to a mezzo for *Der Jüngling an der Quelle*. Her sense of Schubertian longing — the virtually untranslatable "Sehnsucht" comes through beautifully in *Seligkeit*, the disc's first song, and *Lachen und Weinen*, while the total stillness of *Nacht und Träume* is deeply moving. Rudolf Jansen is a sensitive accompanist — well illustrated by *Auf dem Wasser zu singen*, in which what at first sounds like a slightly mannered lingering note at the start of each bar turns out to be an aid to the singer for the upward sixth leap that begins each chain of quick, raindrop-like descending notes. The only small bone of contention is over the ordering of some of the songs. Two settings — "Romanze" from *Die Verschworenen* and *Der Hirt auf dem Felsen* — include a clarinet, here melifluously played by Joaquin Valdepeñas. But rather than opening or closing the disc with the rather longer, varied and more serious *Der Hirt*, each clarinet song is placed in the middle of the disc, separately and apparently at random. But this is a small quibble in what is a very beautiful recording overall.

Schubert. LIEDER. **Felicity Lott** (sop); **Graham Johnson** (pf). Pickwick IMP Classics PCD898. Recorded in 1988.

Die Forelle, D550. An Sylvia, D891. Heidenröslein, D257. Du bist die Ruh, D776. Der Musensohn, D764. An die Musik, D547. Auf dem Wasser zu singen, D774. Sei mir gegrüsst,

D741. Litanei, D343. Die junge Nonne, D828. Ave Maria, D839. Im Frühling, D882. Gretchen am Spinnrade, D118. Nacht und Traüme, D827. Ganymed, D544. Mignon und der Harfner, D877. Seligkeit, D433.

1h 5m DDD 10/88 

This mid-price disc of Schubert Lieder presents many of his best-loved songs in attractive, fresh performances. Felicity Lott shows her complete command of the genre. Secure tone, confident phrasing, exemplary control of breathing, combined with an understanding of the idiom are evident throughout. They help to make songs such as *Du bist die Ruh, Nacht und Träume* and *Ganymed* a pleasure from start to finish. Throughout she cleverly varies her tone and style: for instance, light for *Ganymed*, smiling for *Seligkeit*, sombre for *Litanei*. The more dramatic songs are dealt with strongly and in *Die junge Nonne*, she creates the right sense of unease conquered by serenity. In everything she is superbly supported by Graham Johnson's pertinent and perceptive playing, which recalls that of his mentor Gerald Moore in its softness of touch and clarity of detail.

Additional recommendation ...

Heimliches Lieben, D922. Minnelied, D429. Die abgeblühte Linde, D514. Der Musensohn, D764. **Schumann:** *Frauenliebe und -leben, Op. 42.* **Brahms:** *Die Mainacht, Op. 43 No. 2. Das Mädchen spricht, Op. 107 No. 3. Nachtigall, Op. 97 No. 1. Von ewiger Liebe, Op. 43 No.* **Dame Janet Baker** (mez); **Martin Isepp** (pf). Saga Classics SCD9001 *(reviewed in the Collections section; refer to the Index to Reviews)* — 47m AAD 3/92 £

Schubert. LIEDER. **Cheryl Studer** (sop); **Irwin Gage** (pf). DG 431 773-2GH. Texts and translations included. Recorded in 1990.

Am See, D746. Auf dem Wasser zu singen, D774. Auflösung, D807. Der Fluss, D693. Die Forelle, D550. Ganymed, D544. Die Gebüsche, D646. Im Abendrot, D799. Im Frühling, D882. Klage der Ceres, D323. Das Lied im Grünen, D917. Nacht und Träume, D827. Die Rose, D745. Die Vögel, D691. Wehmut, D772.

1h 5m DDD 10/91 

We know that it is not necessary to have one of the best voices in the world to sing Schubert, but it helps. Here the sheer beauty of sound is one of the recital's principal assets in a highly competitive field. Cheryl Studer comes to Lieder on record after making her name in the world's leading opera houses, but she is no novice: her teachers included two of the most honoured Lieder singers of an earlier generation (Hans Hotter and Irmgard Seefried) and she was a prizewinner of the Schubert Institute in Vienna. She is also working with one of the most interesting and insightful of accompanists, and Irwin Gage's touch in these songs always helps to add distinction. There are limits too: a kind of formality inhabits the sense of a smiling presence in songs such as *Auf dem Wasser zu singen*, and *Nacht und Träume* sounds like what it is — a song which puts the technique to a very severe test. But there are lovely things. *Das Lied im Grünen* has an infectious enthusiasm; *Auflösung* gains much from the ability of this voice to soar; *Die Gebüsche* is given a most lovely performance, with great sensitivity on the part of both artists and a ravishing quality of tone in the voice. The programme itself is thoughtfully arranged, its theme a Wordsworthian one of nature and emotions, its contents an enjoyable mixture of the famous and the less familiar.

Schubert. LIEDER[a].
Schumann. LIEDER[b]. **Elly Ameling** (sop); **Jörg Demus** (fp). Deutsche Harmonia Mundi Editio Classica GD77085. Texts and translations included. Items marked [a] from BASF BAC3088 (2/75), [b] Deutsche Harmonia Mundi 1C 065 99631 (11/78). Recorded 1965-67.

Schubert: Der Hirt auf dem Felsen, D965 (with Hans Deinzer, cl). Seligkeit, D433. Gretchen am Spinnrad, D118. Du liebst mich nicht, D756. Heimliches Lieben, D922. Im Frühling, D882. Die Vögel, D691. Der Jüngling an der Quelle, D300. Der Musensohn, D764. ***Schumann:*** Myrthen, Op. 25 Widmung; Der Nussbaum. Aufträge, Op. 77 No. 5. Sehnsucht, Op. 51 No. 1. Frage, Op. 35 No. 9. Mein schöner Stern, Op. 101 No. 4. Lieder Album für die Jugend, Op. 79 — Schmetterling; Käuzlein; Der Sandmann; Marienwürmchen; Er ists's;

Schneeglöckchen. Erstes Grün, Op. 35 No. 4. Die Sennin, Op. 90 No. 4. Sehnsucht nach der Waldgegend, Op. 35 No. 5. Jasminenstrauch, Op. 27 No. 4. Liederkreis, Op. 39 — Waldesgespräch. Loreley, Op. 53 No. 2. Die Meerfee, Op. 125 No. 1.

1h 9m ADD 5/90

This recital has been compiled from two LPs dating from the mid 1960s when the soprano, Elly Ameling was at the height of her career. The older and perhaps more beautiful of the two is the Schubert recital in which Elly Ameling is accompanied on a fortepiano by Jörg Demus. It was an early gesture towards 'authenticity' and this is reflected both in the choice of piano and in the early clarinet played by Hans Deinzer in the most celebrated of the songs *Der Hirt auf dem Felsen*. But whatever the merits of the approach, and they are in this instance considerable, it is the superlative singing of Elly Ameling that sets the seal of distinction on this beautiful recital. *Gretchen am Spinnrad* is exquisitely felt, *Im Frühling* fervent, wistful and perhaps unrivalled in its freshness of tone and warmth of sentiment. This is a performance to treasure for a lifetime, leaving an indelible mark upon the sensibilities. There is not one disappointment here and the atmosphere one imagines to have suffused a Schubertiad is at times almost unbearably strong. The Schumann songs are no less well sung but, with a more up-to-date sounding piano the atmosphere is somewhat less heady. But these are affecting performances and no-one with a love of the repertory could fail to be enchanted by them. Full texts are provided in German and English and the sound, capturing much that was most attractive in recording techniques of the period, is appealing. An outstanding achievement.

NEW REVIEW

Schubert. LIEDER. **Per Vollestad** (bar); **Sigmund Hjelset** (pf). Simax PSC1071. Texts and translations included.

Der Einsame, D800. Der Kreuzzug, D932. Der Pilgrim, D794. Abendstern, D806. Der Wanderer an den Mond, D870. Sei mir gegrüsst, D741. Im Frühling, D882. Der Blumenbrief, D622. Wie Ulfru fischt, D525. Fischerweise, D881. Des Fischers Liebesglück, D933. Im Walde, D834. Das Weinen, D926. Du bist die Ruh, D776. An den Mond, D193. An die Laute, D905. Hoffnung, D637. Wiedersehen, D855. Lied des gefangenen Jägers, D843. Normans Gesang, D846.

1h 11m DDD 9/92

There is no doubt about it: the young Norwegian, Per Vollestad, is certainly a singer to watch. His baritone is rich and warm, occasionally reminiscent of Fischer-Dieskau, and as this is just his second CD it will be fascinating to see where he goes from here. This selection of Schubert Lieder is perhaps on balance rather sombre, with *Im Frühling* and *An die Laute* providing some limited sunny moments; and the approach taken by Vollestad and the sensitive accompaniment of Sigmund Hjelset is generally serious in the extreme. While the singing and playing is always deeply felt and beautiful in tone, occasionally the coloration seems limited; it would be nice to hear more of the understated, flowing Schubertian *innigkeit* in place of this mostly extrovert approach, through which *Du bist die Ruh* in particular falls prey to far too much rubato. This is more about musical imagination than anything else; for example, the imagery of *Des Fischers Liebesglück* offers far more scope for expressive variety and vision than this rather matter-of-fact interpretation suggests. Nevertheless, interpretations can only deepen with age and experience and there are many moments of both beauty and tenderness here: in *Hoffnung* and *An den Mond*, to name but two. *Sei mir gegrüsst* is particularly heartfelt, from both singer and pianist. Even if you're collecting the Hyperion set don't overlook this very rewarding achievement from an artist still at the start of his career.

Schubert. LIEDER. **Elisabeth Speiser** (sop); **John Buttrick** (pf). Jecklin Disco JD630-2. Texts and translations included. Recorded in 1988.

Abendbilder, D650. Abschied, D475. Am Grabe Anselmos, D504. An mein Herz, D860. Beim Winde, D669. Frühlingsglaube, D686. Ganymed, D544. Strophe aus Die Götter Griechenlands, D677. Gretchen am Spinnrade, D118. Heimliches Lieben, D922. Im Abendrot, D799. Der Knabe, D692. Lachen und Weinen, D777. Lied der Anne Lyle, D830. Nachtstück, D672. Die

Rose, D745. Schlaflied, D527. Sehnsucht, D879. Der Wanderer an den Mond, D870. Wanderers Nachtlied, D224. Der Winterabend, D938.

1h 15m ADD 2/91

Sometimes it is a less well-known artist who yields more gratifying insights into a composer's music than a more familiar one. That is the case here where Elisabeth Speiser, a soprano who has been unassumingly on the scene for some time now, calls on her experience to look into the heart of a group of Schubert songs, familiar and unfamiliar, on a very well-filled CD. Time and again she goes to the heart of the matter through the thoughtfulness of her phrasing and the acuity of her verbal emphases. That would be of little avail if it were not for the sheer beauty of Speiser's singing. Though she recalls at times Irmgard Seefried and Margaret Price, she has a plaintive quality in her tone very much her own. All this makes her ideally fitted to the programme she has chosen, which has the sub-title *Schöne Welt, wo bist du ...?* ("Beautiful world, where are you ...?"). She and her admirable pianist John Buttrick have chosen well from Schubert's many songs dealing with the search for a peace and happiness mostly just beyond reach. For instance, the grief of *Am Grabe Anselmos*, the longing of *Der Wanderer an den Mond*, the unease amidst happy surroundings of *Frühlingsglaube* are moods all caught and held, with speeds ideal, line clear and accents precisely placed. These are typical of the whole.

Schubert. LIEDER. **Peter Schreier** (ten); **András Schiff** (pf). Decca 425 612-2DH. Texts and translations included. Recorded in 1989.
Schwanengesang, D957. Herbst, D945. Der Wanderer an den Mond, D870. Am Fenster, D878. Bei dir allein, D866 No. 2.

1h 3m DDD 6/90

Schubert. LIEDER. **Brigitte Fassbaender** (mez); **Aribert Reimann** (pf). DG 429 766-2GH. Texts and translations included. Recorded 1989-91.
Schwanengesang, D957. Sehnsucht, D879. Der Wanderer an den Mond, D870. Wiegenlied, D867. Am Fenster, D878. Herbst, D945.

1h 8m DDD 6/92 

Though *Schwanengesang* is not a song-cycle but a collection of Schubert's last (or 'swan') songs by their first publisher, it is generally felt to form a satisfying sequence, with a unity of style if not of theme or mood. This is certainly not weakened by the addition on the Decca disc of the four last songs which were originally omitted, all of them settings of poems by Johann Seidl. Seidl is one of the three poets whose work Schubert used in these frequently sombre songs and it is strange to think that all concerned in their creation were young men, none of the poets being older than Schubert. The listener can scarcely be unaware of a shadow or sometimes an almost unearthly radiance over even the happiest (such as "Die Taubenpost", the last of all) and that is particularly true when the performers themselves have such sensitive awareness as here. Peter Schreier is responsive to every shade of meaning in music and text; graceful and charming in "Das Fischermädchen", flawlessly lyrical in "Am Meer", he will sometimes risk an almost frightening raw-boned cry as in the anguish of "Der Atlas" and "Der Doppelgänger". András Schiff's playing is a miracle of combined strength and delicacy, specific insight and general rightness. One of the great Lieder recordings, and not merely of recent years.

Fassbaender and Reimann offer something equally compelling but rather different in their account of *Schwanengesang*. Fassbaender's interpretation, idiosyncratic in every respect, pierces to the heart of the bleak songs with performances as daring and challenging as the playing of her partner. More than anyone, these two artists catch the fleeting moods of these mini-dramas, and their searing originality of concept. Even the lighter songs have a special individuality of utterance. This is a starkly immediate interpretation that leaves the listener shattered. The extra Seidl settings, rarely performed, are all worth hearing. The true lover of Lieder will need to have both these notable partnerships, superb in their own, searching ways.

Additional recommendations ...
Schwanengesang. **Bryn Terfel** (bass-bar); **Malcolm Martineau** (pf). Sain SCDC4035 —
57m DDD 5/92

Schwanengesang. Die schöne Müllerin, D795. Winterreise, D911. **Dietrich Fischer-Dieskau** (bar); **Gerald Moore** (pf). DG 437 235-2GX3 *(reviewed above)* — ③ 3h 4m ADD 3/93 £

Schubert. Die schöne Müllerin, D795. **Peter Schreier** (ten); **András Schiff** (pf). Decca 430 414-2DH. Texts and translations included. Recorded in 1989.

1h 3m DDD 5/91

NEW REVIEW

Schubert. Die schöne Müllerin, D795. **Christoph Prégardien** (ten); **Andreas Staier** (fp). Deutsche Harmonia Mundi 05472 77273-2. Texts and translations included.

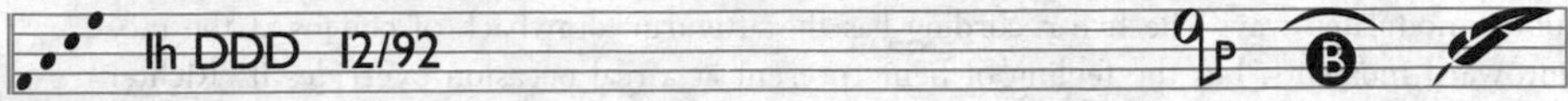

NEW REVIEW

Schubert. Die schöne Müllerin, D795. **Wolfgang Holzmair** (bar); **Jörg Demus** (pf). Preiser 93337. Recorded in 1984.

1h 8m ADD 3/89

The 20 songs of *Die schöne Müllerin* portray a Wordsworthian world of heightened emotion in the pantheistic riverside setting of the miller. The poet, Wilhelm Müller, tells of solitary longings, jealousies, fears and hopes as the river rushes by, driving the mill-wheel and refreshing the natural world. Schreier's partnership with a notable Schubert pianist, András Schiff, surpasses all its predecessors and should be part of any worthwhile collection of Lieder. With his plangent tone, now more disciplined than ever, allied to his poignant and finely accented treatment of the text, Schreier gives moving expression to the youth's love and loss, nowhere more so than in his colloquy with the stream, "Der Müller und der Bach". Everything in his reading has been carefully thought through yet the result sounds wholly spontaneous and natural. To his role Schiff brings an inquiring mind, deft and pliant fingers and an innate feeling for Schubertian phraseology. He probes as deep into the music's meaning, perhaps deeper than any before him yet without giving the accompaniment undue prominence or calling attention to the piano. More than anything, it is as a unified concept that this reading achieves its greatness. It is recorded with an ideal balance between voice and piano, in a sympathetic acoustic.

It is possible to approach the cycle in a simpler way than Schreier's, emphasizing the youthful, ingenuous character of the sad protagonist. This is the way adopted by Prégardien in his finely shaped, understated version. It is a reading that is instinctively shaped and felt, the tenor suggesting the boy's vulnerability to perfection. It is neither as broadly conceived nor as romantic as the Schreier, and the straightforward character is emphasized by strict tempos and a fortepiano accompanist, the instrument finely and sympathetically played by Staier. If you prefer a baritone in the cycle, the recommendation must be for Holzmair's 1984 performance which first revealed this singer's gifts as a Lieder singer of sensitivity and one, who like Prégardien, catches the youth's joy and inner suffering through a natural feeling for word and phrase. His light tone and instinctive way with the text are immediately appealing and with Demus as a faultless partner, this version never fails to make its mark.

Additional recommendations ...

Die schöne Müllerin. **Dietrich Fischer-Dieskau** (bar); **Gerald Moore** (pf). DG 415 186-2GH — 1h 2m ADD 9/85

Die schöne Müllerin. **Josef Protschka** (ten); **Helmut Deutsch** (pf). Capriccio 10 082 — 1h 6m DDD 6/87

Die schöne Müllerin. **Olaf Bär** (bar); **Geoffrey Parsons** (pf). EMI CDC7 47947-2 — 1h 5m DDD 8/87

Die schöne Müllerin. **Siegfried Lorenz** (bar); **Norman Shetler** (pf). Capriccio 10 220 — 1h 8m DDD 5/90

Die schöne Müllerin. **Beethoven.** *An die ferne Geliebte, Op. 98.* **Gerhard Hüsch** (bar); **Hanns Udo Müller** (pf). Preiser Lebendige Vergangenheit mono 89202 — ② 2h 17m AAD 12/92

Schubert. Winterreise, D911[a]. Piano Sonata in C major, D840, "Reliquie"[b]. **Peter Schreier** (ten); **Sviatoslav Richter** (pf). Philips 416 289-2PH2. Text and translation included. Item marked [a] recorded live in 1985, [b] 1979.

② 2h 3m ADD/DDD 3/86

Winterreise can lay claim to be the greatest song cycle ever written. It chronicles the sad, numbing journey of a forsaken lover, recalling past happiness, anguishing over his present plight, commenting on how the snow-clad scenery reflects or enhances his mood. Although the songs were written for a tenor, very often in recent years they have been sung by lower voices, which made the appearance of Peter Schreier's recording all the more welcome, particularly as he was partnered by Sviatoslav Richter. Schreier's plangent tenor and finely moulded phrasing are supported by almost limitless breath control. Richter's playing is communicative in a refined and subtly modulated way. The live recording has the attendant drawback of coughs at the most untoward moments, but the feeling of being present at a real occasion overrides it. Richter offers Schubert's *Reliquie* Sonata as a substantial filler in a mesmeric performance.

Additional recommendations ...

Winterreise. **Dietrich Fischer-Dieskau** (bar); **Alfred Brendel** (pf). Philips 411 463-2PH — 1h 10m DDD 12/86

Winterreise. **Robert Holl** (bass-bar); **Konrad Richter** (pf). Preiser 93317 — 1h 12m ADD 8/89

Winterreise. **Olaf Bär** (bar); **Geoffrey Parsons** (pf). EMI CDC7 49334-2 — 1h 15m DDD 11/89

Winterreise. **Brigitte Fassbaender** (mez); **Aribert Reimann** (pf). EMI CDC7 49846-2 — 1h 10m DDD 7/90

Winterreise. **Sir Peter Pears** (ten); **Benjamin Britten** (pf). Decca 417 473-2DM — 1h 13m ADD 10/91 £

Winterreise. **Andreas Schmidt** (bar); **Rudolf Jansen** (pf). DG 435 384-2DG — 1h 12m DDD 3/92

Winterreise. **Max van Egmond** (bar); **Jos van Immerseel** (fp). Channel Classics CCS0190 — 1h 7m DDD 3/92

Winterreise. **Victor Braun** (bar); **Antonín Kubalek** (pf). Dorian DOR90145 — 1h 16m DDD 8/92

Schubert. Masses — G major, D167[a]; E flat major, D950[b]. [a]**Dawn Upshaw,** [b]**Benita Valente** (sops); [b]**Marietta Simpson** (mez); [a]**David Gordon,** [b]**Jon Humphrey,** [b]**Glenn Siebert** (tens); [a]**William Stone** [b]**Myron Myers** (bars); **Atlanta Symphony Chamber Chorus; Atlanta Symphony Chorus and Orchestra/Robert Shaw.** Telarc CD80212. Text and translation included. Recorded 1988-89.

1h 18m DDD 9/90

Schubert's second Mass, D167, was written in six days during 1815 when he was 18. This small-scale, tuneful work, given only a light accompaniment of strings and organ, conformed closely with what was expected of Schubert by his teacher, Salieri, and has many moments of simple charm, expressive of a simple faith. The Mass in E flat was completed, along with *Tantum Ergo* and the *Offertorium*, in the autumn of 1828, the year of Schubert's death, and is clearly the work of a composer at the height of his powers, intent on extending the boundaries of expression whilst still having to retain some of the conventions of formal liturgical structure. The accompaniment here is for the full orchestra of the time, minus flutes, and the dramatic impact of these resources is exploited to the full. Yet more than this, it is the revolutionary harmonic ideas that single this Mass out for special note, orchestral colours emphasizing the drastic shifts and subtle slides. The composer's faith had, by this time, become more individual, less conformist, and there are hints in this work of that reassessment. Robert Shaw and his Atlanta forces set the two works in stark contrast, underlining the individual qualities of each. The choral singing is of a high order and there is an underlying detachment in their approach that fits well with the intended use of this music; operatic emotion would hardly have been in keeping.

Additional recommendations ...
D167. Salve regina in A major, D676. ***Haydn.*** *Missa brevis Sancti Joannis de Deo, "Kleine Orgelmesse". Flute-clock pieces, HobXIX — Nos. 6, 9, 15, 20 and 32.* **Soloists; Haydn Society Chorus and Orchestra/Denis McCaldin.** Meridian Duo DUOCD89003 — .⋰ 55m AAD 2/90
D950. **Soloists; Vienna State Opera Concerto Choir; Vienna Philharmonic Orchestra/Claudio Abbado.** DG 423 088-2GH — .⋰ 57m DDD 8/88
D950. **Soloists; Suisse Romande Chamber Choir; Lausanne Pro Arte Choir; Suisse Romande Orchestra/Armin Jordan.** Erato 2292-45300-2 — .⋰ 54m DDD 8/88

Schubert. FIERRABRAS. **Josef Protschka** (ten) Fierrabras; **Karita Mattila** (sop) Emma; **Robert Holl** (bass) Charlemagne; **Thomas Hampson** (bar) Roland; **Robert Gambill** (ten) Eginhard; **László Polgár** (bass) Boland; **Cheryl Studer** (sop) Florinda; **Brigitte Balleys** (contr) Maragond; **Hartmut Welker** (bar) Brutamonte; **Arnold Schönberg Choir; Chamber Orchestra of Europe/Claudio Abbado.** DG 427 341-2GH2. Notes, text and translation included. Recorded in 1988.

.⋰ ② 2h 24m DDD 10/90 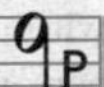

The pathetic comment that Schubert "wrote more beautiful music than the world has time to know" is gradually being corrected as more of his almost completely neglected works are being brought to light. This opera was commissioned in 1823 in Vienna but, because of the Rossini craze, the departure of several German singers and a consequent managerial upheaval, not produced, and Schubert received no payment for it, either: it remained in limbo until it was published almost 60 years after his death. The 1988 performances in Vienna, from which this recording was taken, revealed the riches of his score, which — especially in Act 2, contains an astonishing sequence from a lovely duet for two girls and a forceful quintet to an unaccompanied chorus and a moving recognition scene — are overwhelming. The plot, a complicated web of medieval chivalry, love, honour and war at the courts of Charlemagne and a defeated but vengeful Moorish prince (whose daughter is secretly in love with the Frankish knight Roland, and his son Fierrabras with Charlemagne's daughter who, however, has been dallying with the knight Eginhard), would have been enough to defeat an experienced operatic composer; and Schubert, without a hand to guide him, allowed his matchless lyrical invention to swamp dramatic pace, though there *is* drama too, in the rescue by the Moorish princess of Roland and his fellow ambassadors for peace from the prison in which they have basely been thrown. The orchestral writing is splendid and very characteristic, and Abbado misses no opportunity to underline its strength — perhaps a trifle at the expense of the voices, who are not always ideally balanced in ensembles: the choruses are brilliantly handled. The well-integrated cast is very satisfactory: chief honours go to Karita Mattila as Charlemagne's daughter, to Josef Protschka as the noble Moorish prince ready to sacrifice himself to shield her, and to Robert Gambill as the guilt-ridden Eginhard. The spoken dialogue is omitted but printed in full in the admirably produced booklet.

Ervin Schulhoff

Bohemian 1894-1942

Further listening ...

String Quartet No. 1. Concertino. Sonata for Flute and Piano. *Coupled with* ***Kaprálova.*** Dubnova Preludia Suite, Op. 13. ***Klein.*** Duo. **Soloists; Hawthorne Quartet.** Northeastern NR248-CD (5/93).

William Schuman

American 1910-1992

NEW REVIEW

Schuman. American Festival Overture. New England Triptych. Symphony No. 10, "American Muse".

Ives (orch. Schuman). Variations on "America". **St Louis Symphony Orchestra/Leonard Slatkin.** RCA Victor Red Seal 09026 61282-2. Recorded 1991-92.

lh 7m DDD 5/93

The *American Festival Overture* of 1939 was one of William Schuman's early successes, and it is easy to see why, for it is an engagingly attractive, outgoing piece, and very traditionally American in its style and sentiment. Qualities of openness and directness, and a kind of rugged honestly shine through all the works here. *New England Triptych*, composed in 1956, is based on hymn tunes by William Billings: here a tranquil central movement, "When Jesus wept" is flanked by the vigorous "Be glad then, America," and the forthright "Chester". A similar three-movement format comprises Schuman's tenth and last symphony of 1975. This work is subtitled *American Muse*, and has a pervading spirit of affirmation, especially in the finale, with its pungently vivid scoring and superabundance of energy. The first movement is also a strong, confident piece of writing, with the central *Larghissimo* movement making an effective contrast. Schuman was attracted by the irreverent wit of Ives's *Variations*, written for organ, and his realization more than preserves the good humour of the original. Once more Leonard Slatkin shows that he is without superior in this kind of repertoire (he was a friend of the composer), and his performances have great insight and mastery. No praise can be too high for the playing of the St Louis Symphony Orchestra, and Schuman's brilliant orchestral writing is well-captured by an excellently balanced, spacious recording.

New England Triptych. Symphony for Strings (Symphony No. 5). Judith. ***Ives*** *(orch. Schuman). Variations on "America".* **Seattle Symphony Orchestra/Gerard Schwarz.** Delos DE3115 — lh 4m DDD 7/93

Further listening ...

Symphony No. 3. *Coupled with* ***Harris.*** Symphony No. 3. **New York Philharmonic Orchestra/Leonard Bernstein.** DG 419 780-2GH (11/87).
See review under Harris; refer to the Index to Reviews.

Clara Schumann

German 1819-1896

NEW REVIEW

C. Schumann. PIANO WORKS. **Josef de Beenhouwer.** Partridge PART9293-2. Recorded in 1991.

Sonata in G minor. Romance in B minor. Impromptu in E major. Romance in A minor. Scherzo in D minor, Op. 10 Deuxième Scherzo in C minor, Op. 14. Präludium in F minor. Soirées musicales, Op. 6. Etude in A flat major. Geburtstagmarsch in E flat major. Three Preludes and Fugues, Op. 19. Variations on a theme of Robert Schumann Op. 20. Three Romances, Op. 11. Nine Caprices en forme de valse, Op. 2. Souvenir de Vienne, Op. 9. Valses romantiques, Op. 4. Variations de concert sur la cavatine du Pirate de Bellini, Op. 8. Four Polonaises, Op. 1. Four Pièces caracteristiques, Op. 5. Four Pièces fugitives, Op. 15. Three Fugues on Themes of Bach. Three Romances, Op. 21.

③ 3h 40m DDD 1/93

Except for a *Geburtstagmarsch* in E flat, written within sight of her sixtieth birthday for the golden wedding of two old friends, Clara Schumann, with seven children to support, had no time for composition after Robert's death. But in earlier days all was different: so often whatever he wrote sparked off something in similar vein of her own. Collectors now owe the Dutch pianist, Josef de Beenhouwer, a tremendous debt of gratitude for giving us this three-disc assemblage of Clara's complete works for solo piano — including a handful of unpublished miniatures (amongst them *Three Fugues* on themes from Book 2 of Bach's *48*) only very recently brought to light. With influences like Robert Schumann, Mendelssohn and even Chopin omnipresent, it was not easy to find a voice all her own. Yet once juvenilia were despatched, already the four *Pièces caracteristiques* and the six *Soirées musicales* of her mid-teens reveal her immediate response to the century's new spirit of romance — so eloquently reaffirmed in the last work written before her marriage, the *Trois Romances*, Op. 11. Of the earlier works, however, nothing testifies better to her sterling craftsmanship than the *Bellini Variations*, Op. 8, of 1837, with its happy compromise between the keyboard bravura then expected from every pianist-composer and the poetic dictates of her own maturing heart. Of the post-marital works, the two most ambitious are the Op. 20 *Variations on a theme of Robert Schumann* (No. 4 of the *Bunte Blätter*), written for his forty-third birthday in June, 1853, and the concisely crafted G minor Piano Sonata begun in 1841 as an intended Christmas present for her husband though in fact not completed for another 13 months — the latter, incidentally, now destined for a new lease of life thanks to its welcome recent Breitkopf publication edited by Dr Gerd Nauhaus, of the Robert-Schumann-Haus in Zwickau. Even if perhaps not the world's greatest keyboard wizard, Josef de Beenhouwer wins the day with the sincerity and warmth of his dedication, while any small quibbles about tonal reproduction fade into insignificance alongside the inestimable value of this issue as an enrichment to the library of any keyboard enthusiast.

Robert Schumann

German 1810-1856

NEW REVIEW

Schumann. WORKS FOR CELLO. **Heinrich Schiff** (vc); [b]**Gerhard Oppitz** (pf); [a]**Berlin Philharmonic Orchestra/Bernard Haitink.** Philips 422 414-2PH. Item marked [a] recorded in 1988, [b] arranged Grützmacher, recorded in 1991.

Cello Concerto in A minor, Op. 129[a]. Adagio and Allegro in A flat major, Op. 70[b]. Fantasiestücke, Op. 73[b]. Funf Stücke im Volkston, Op. 102[b].

lh DDD 6/93 

Schumann's Cello Concerto is a fairly dark, troubled work, and sometimes cellists are tempted to adopt a somewhat overwrought approach when playing it. In fact, it responds best to a more balanced approach, as exemplified in this performance by Heinrich Schiff. His playing is very eloquent, and quite strong, but there is also a feeling of dignity and refinement in his response to the music. Everything is perfectly in scale, and the work's essential nobility is allowed to emerge in a most moving fashion. Schiff's technique is faultless, and his tonal quality is very beautiful. Haitink and the BPO seem totally in sympathy with the soloist, and the recording is warm and well-detailed. The three items with piano accompaniment comprise a series of short pieces which are for the most part sunnier in outlook than the Concerto, and they make an effective contrast to the larger-scale work. Again Schiff's playing is expressive, but his phrasing is full of subtlety and poetry, and Oppitz is a highly responsive partner.

Additional recommendations ...

Fünf Stücke im Volkston, Op. 102. **Debussy.** *Cello Sonata.* **Schubert.** *Sonata in A minor, D821, "Arpeggione".* **Mstislav Rostropovich** (vc); **Benjamin Britten** (pf). Decca 417 833-2DH *(see review under Debussy; refer to the Index to Reviews)* — 59m ADD 9/87

Cello Concerto. Fantasiestücke. Fünf Stücke im Volkston. Adagio and Allegro. **Yo-Yo Ma** (vc); **Emanuel Ax** (pf); **Bavarian Radio Symphony Orchestra/Sir Colin Davis.** CBS Masterworks CD42663 — lh 11m DDD 10/88

Cello Concerto. Fantasiestücke. Fünf Stücke im Volkston. Adagio and Allegro. **Lluis Claret** (vc); **Rose-Marie Cabestany** (pf); **English Chamber Orchestra/Edmon Colomer.** Harmonia Mundi HMC90 1306 — lh 3m DDD 5/90

Cello Concerto[a]. **Lalo.** *Cello Concerto in D minor*[a]. **Saint-Saëns.** *Cello Concerto in A minor, Op. 33*[b]. **János Starker** (vc); **London Symphony Orchestra/**[a]**Stanislaw Skrowaczewski,** [b]**Antál Dorati.** Mercury 432 010-2MM *(see review under Lalo; refer to the Index to Reviews)* — lh 5m ADD 4/92 £

Cello Concerto. **Schnittke.** *Cello Concerto No. 1.* **Natalia Gutman** (vc); **London Philharmonic Orchestra/Kurt Masur.** EMI CDC7 54443-2 *(see review under Schnittke; refer to the Index to Reviews)* — lh 5m DDD 8/92

Fantasiestücke. Fünf Stücke im Volkston. Adagio and Allegro. **Schubert.** *Sonata in A minor, D821, "Arpeggione".* **Mendelssohn.** *Variations concertantes, Op. 17. Song without words in D major, Op. 109.* **Friedrich-Jürgen Sellheim** (vc); **Eckart Sellheim** (pf). Sony Classical, Essential Classics MK48171 — lh 12m ADD 10/92

Cello Concerto[a]. *Piano Concerto in A minor, Op. 54*[b]. *Introduction and Allegro appassionato, Op. 92*[c]. [a]**Jacqueline du Pré** (vc); [a]**New Philharmonia Orchestra/Daniel Barenboim** ([b]pf); [bc]**London Philharmonic Orchestra/Dietrich Fischer-Dieskau.** EMI CDM7 64626-2 — lh 14m ADD 3/93

NEW REVIEW

Schumann. Piano Concerto in A minor, Op. 54[b]. Piano Quintet in E flat major, Op. 44[a]. **Alicia de Larrocha** (pf); [a]**Tokyo Quartet** (Peter Oundjian, Kikuei Ikeda, vns; Kazuhide Isomura, va; Sadao Harada, vc); [b]**London Symphony Orchestra/Sir Colin Davis.** Victor Red Seal 09026 61279-2. Recorded in 1991.

lh 4m DDD 5/93 

One hopes it is not ungallant to note that Alicia de Larrocha was 70 last year, for this recording of Schumann's best known chamber work and concerto demonstrates the best qualities of age. Indeed, affection and experience are here allied to an untarnished technical command. The Piano Quintet, recorded in New York, moves along in a relaxed yet glowing way, with the pianist taking the overall lead but never in a dominating manner, while her colleagues of the Toyko Quartet clearly enjoy the first movement's friendly exchanges with her and each other. This is not to say that these artists miss the more dramatic aspects of the work, however, and thus the strangely march-like second movement has plenty of atmosphere, as has its resolution into more peaceful music towards the end. The *Scherzo* is rightly both forceful and dancelike, and the finale has melodiousness as well as momentum. Though this pianist must have played Schumann's Concerto hundreds of times, it has clearly not diminished her sympathy with this most loveable work, in which buoyancy of invention goes hand in hand with tenderness. Her playing here has been called both "mature" and "contented", and one can see what was meant: nothing is exaggerated, though no point is missed either, and instead the music is simply allowed to unfold in a spacious yet alert way, with a notably unhurried finale. "Ripeness is all", we feel: Shakespeare's words are an altogether suitable description for this performance, in which the London Symphony Orchestra under Sir Colin Davis are the most attentive of partners. This recording was made in EMI's Abbey Road Studios and the sound is rich yet natural.

Additional recommendations ...

Piano Concerto. **Grieg.** *Piano Concerto in A minor, Op. 16.* **Stephen Kovacevich** (pf); **BBC Symphony Orchestra/Sir Colin Davis.** Philips 412 923-2PH — lh lm ADD 10/86

Piano Concerto. **Grieg.** *Piano Concerto.* **Radu Lupu** (pf); **London Symphony Orchestra/André Previn.** Decca Ovation 417 728-2DM — lh lm ADD 12/87

Piano Concerto[a]. *Davidsbündlertänze, Op. 6. Kinderszenen, Op. 15.* **Fanny Davies** (pf); [a]**Royal Philharmonic Society Orchestra/Ernest Ansermet.** Pearl mono GEMM CD9291 — lh 5m ADD 5/88 ▲

Piano Concerto. **Grieg.** *Piano Concerto.* **Murray Perahia** (pf); **Bavarian Radio Symphony Orchestra/Sir Colin Davis.** CBS CD44899 — lh DDD 5/89

Piano Concerto. **Schoenberg.** *Piano Concerto, Op. 42.* **Maurizio Pollini** (pf); **Berlin Philharmonic Orchestra/Claudio Abbado.** DG 427 771-2GH — 5lm DDD 7/90

Piano Concerto. **Grieg.** *Piano Concerto.* **Pascal Devoyon** (pf); **London Philharmonic Orchestra/Jerzy Maksymiuk.** Classics for Pleasure CD-CFP4574 — lh 3m DDD 2/91

Piano Concerto[a]. **MacDowell.** *Piano Concerto No. 2 in D minor, Op. 23*[b]. *Woodland Sketches, Op. 51 — No. 1, To a Wild Rose*[b]. **Van Cliburn** (pf); **Chicago Symphony Orchestra/**[a]**Fritz Reiner,** [b]**Walter Hendl.** RCA Victor Van Cliburn Collection GD60420 *(see review under MacDowell; refer to the Index to Reviews)* — lh ADD 10/91 ▲

Piano Concerto[a]. **Franck.** *Symphonic Variations, Op. 46*[b]. **Grieg.** *Piano Concerto in A minor, Op. 16*[c]. [a]**Friedrich Gulda,** [bc]**Clifford Curzon** (pfs); [a]**Vienna Philharmonic Orchestra/Volkmar Andreae;** [b]**London Philharmonic Orchestra/Sir Adrian Boult;** [c]**London Symphony Orchestra/Øivin Fjeldstad.** Decca Headline Classics 433 628-2DSP *(see review under Franck; refer to the Index to Reviews)* — ⁘ 1h 16m ADD 1/92 £

Piano Concerto. ***Grieg.*** *Piano Concerto.* **Lars Vogt** (pf); **City of Birmingham Symphony Orchestra/Simon Rattle.** EMI CDC7 54746-2 — ⁘ 1h 2m DDD 1/93

Schumann. Violin Concerto in D minor, Op. posth. Fantasie in C major, Op. 131. **Thomas Zehetmair** (vn); **Philharmonia Orchestra/Christoph Eschenbach.** Teldec 2292-44190-2. Recorded in 1988.

⁘ 45m DDD 4/90

Schumann had barely six months of normal working life left to him when writing his only two works for violin and orchestra in the autumn of 1853. Both were inspired by the 22-year-old Joachim, who though immediately taking the *Fantasie* into his repertory, subsequently decreed that the Concerto was unworthy of its composer and should be suppressed. However, his great-niece, Jelly d'Aranyi, secured its publication and performance in 1938 and we now know that any shortcomings in the finale are more than redeemed by the quality of the first two movements, particularly the nostalgically beautiful *Langsam*. For Thomas Zehetmair's rapt playing of that movement alone, the disc would be invaluable. Though questionably deliberate in tempo in the finale, the performance as a whole emerges as a labour of love from soloist, orchestra and conductor alike, very sumptuously recorded. All musicians were grateful for the Concerto's coupling with the *Fantasie*, a work which until the appearance of this recording, had been unobtainable on CD. Here the disposition of the solo part and its interplay with the orchestra suggest that Joachim himself may have proffered a few helpful performing suggestions. Though not wholly seamless, the sonata-form argument is memorable for its recall of the inspired introductory theme in both the development section and coda. With their close attunement and fine balance, the warmly lyrical Zehetmair and Eschenbach certainly explain Joachim's own enthusiasm for this now unjustly neglected work.

Schumann. SYMPHONIES. **Staatskapelle Dresden/Wolfgang Sawallisch.** EMI Studio CMS7 64815-2. From CDM7 69471/2-2 (11/88, 5/89). Recorded in 1972.
No. 1 in B flat major, Op. 38, "Spring"; No. 2 in C major, Op. 61; No. 3 in E flat major, Op. 97, "Rhenish"; No. 4 in D minor, Op. 120. Overture, Scherzo and Finale, Op. 52.

⁘ ② 2h 28m ADD 

Schumann's symphonies come in for a lot of criticism because of his supposed cloudy textures and unsubtle scoring, but in the hands of a conductor who is both skilful and sympathetic they are most engaging works. These two mid-price CDs, brightly transferred, provide us with a much admired set. Sawallisch's style, fresh and unforced, is not as high powered as some other conductors but it is sensible, alert and very pleasing. He achieves great lightness in the First and Fourth Symphonies — there's always a sense of classical poise and control but never at the expense of the overall architecture of the pieces. The Second and Third Symphonies, larger and more far-reaching in their scope, again benefit from Sawallisch's approach. The playing of the Staatskapelle Dresden is superlative in every department, with a lovely veiled string sound and a real sense of ensemble. These are real bargains and with the *Overture, Scherzo and Finale* thrown in for good measure, definitely not to be missed.

Additional recommendations ...

Nos. 1-4. Cello Concerto in A minor, Op. 129[a]. *Piano Concerto in A minor, Op. 54*[b]. [a]**Justus Franz** (pf); [b]**Mischa Maisky** (vc); **Vienna Philharmonic Orchestra/Leonard Bernstein.** DG 423 009-2GH3 — ⁘ ③ 3h 18m DDD 3/88

Nos. 1-4. **Berlin Philharmonic Orchestra/Herbert von Karajan.** DG Symphony Edition 429 672-2GSE2 — ⁘ ② 2h 12m ADD 7/90

Nos. 1-4. **Suisse Romande Orchestra/Armin Jordan.** Erato 2292-45496-2 — ⁘ ② 2h 11m DDD 12/90

Nos. 2 and 3. **Baltimore Symphony Orchestra/David Zinman.** Telarc CD80182 — ⁘ 1h 10m DDD 6/91

Nos. 1 and 2. **Bavarian Radio Symphony Orchestra/Rafael Kubelík.** Sony Classical Essential Classics SBK48269 — ⁘ 1h 14m ADD 7/93 £

Nos. 3 and 4. Manfred, Op. 115 — Overture. **Bavarian Radio Symphony Orchestra/Rafael Kubelík.** Sony Classical Essential Classics SBK48270 — lh 16m ADD 7/93 £ B

Schumann. Symphonies — No. 1 in B flat major, Op. 38, "Spring"; No. 4 in D minor, Op. 120. **Royal Concertgebouw Orchestra/Riccardo Chailly.** Decca 425 608-2DH. Recorded in 1988.

lh 3m DDD 12/90 

Recent recordings of Schumann Symphonies have sought to bring new insights often at the expense of beauty of tone, or the composer's perceived romanticism. Here is one which triumphantly proves that Schumann, played on modern instruments without radical interpretative standpoints, need not be a stale or bloated experience. Listening to this disc, one wonders why critics used to constantly berate poor Schumann for his inept orchestration. The lean, but wonderfully expressive, Concertgebouw strings are equal partners with the fresh and characterful woodwind (rarely, if ever, has this balance been so well managed); Chailly's direction is warm, precise, both taut and yielding in all the right places. Sawallisch's indispensable set of the 1970s on EMI (reviewed above) offers playing of more energy and determination in the Fourth, but the recording lacks the detail and transparent textures of this newcomer. Indeed the pristine clarity and three dimensional depth of Decca's sound is one of this disc's principal joys.

Additional recommendations ...

No 1. Manfred, Op. 115 — Overture. Overture, Scherzo and Finale, Op. 52. **Stuttgart Radio Symphony Orchestra/Sir Neville Marriner.** Capriccio CD10 063 — DDD 6/86 B

No. 4. Manfred Overture. ***Haydn.*** *Symphony No. 88 in G major, "Letter V".* **Berlin Philharmonic Orchestra/Wilhelm Furtwängler.** DG mono 427 404-2GDO — lh 6m AAD 6/86 B ▲

Schumann. Symphonies – No. 3 in E flat major, Op. 97, "Rhenish"; No. 4 in D minor, Op. 120. **London Classical Players/Roger Norrington.** EMI CDC7 54025-2.

57m DDD 3/91 

Spearheading the authentic brigade's excursion into romantic repertoire, it's surprising how euphonious Roger Norrington's ensemble sounds here. Gone is the braying brass obscuring fragile strings that was often a feature of period performance. As in his recent Schubert discs, Norrington controls his forces with an acute ear and intelligence for what is germane to the music, and the brass only 'open up' where structure demands it, or where the overall balance would be unaffected. The strength of purpose, separated violin desks and close balance are often reminiscent of the best of Klemperer's work for EMI in the sixties. There is too a similar lack of concern for mere beauty of sound. Textural revelations aside (they are too numerous to mention), the most striking feature of these accounts is their strict adherence to Schumann's explicit indications of tempo: the middle movements of both symphonies are much faster than usual. Some collectors may initially feel short changed on graceful singing lines and variety of moods but compensation lies in the revitalization of the music's rhythms, and its sense of direction. The Fourth Symphony, in particular, is experienced in one single sweep. It's a pity, here, in music that should be continuous, that the CD contains breaks between the first three movements.

Additional recommendations ...

No. 3. ***Schubert.*** *No. 8 in B minor, D759, "Unfinished".* **Concertgebouw Orchestra/Leonard Bernstein.** DG 431 042-2GBE — DDD B

No. 3. ***Mendelssohn.*** *Symphony No. 5 in D major, Op. 107, "Reformation".* **Berlin Philharmonic Orchestra/Herbert von Karajan.** DG Galleria 419 870-2GGA — lh 9m ADD 4/88 B

Symphony No. 3 in E flat major, Op. 97, "Rhenish[a]". ***Schubert.*** *No. 8 in B minor, D759, "Unfinished"[b].* [a]**Los Angeles Philharmonic Orchestra/Carlo Maria Giulini;** [b]**Philharmonia Orchestra/Giuseppe Sinopoli.** DG 3D Classics 427 818 2GDC — lh 3m DDD 4/90 B

NEW REVIEW

Schumann. Piano Quartets — E flat major, Op. 47; C minor. **Young Uck Kim** (vn); **Heiichiro Ohyama** (va); **Gary Hoffman** (vc); **André Previn** (pf). RCA Victor Red Seal 09026 61384-2. Recorded in 1991.

47m DDD 5/93

Schumann lovers the world over owe a great debt of gratitude to André Previn and his colleagues for giving us the "world première recording" of Schumann's C minor Piano Quartet, written when he was still a law student of only 18. Though favourably impressing several Leipzig musical friends at an informal try-out in 1829, the work remained unpublished for 150 years until a performing edition was prepared by that dedicated Schumann scholar, Wolfgang Boetticher. The nimble *Minuetto* and tenderly spun *Andante* are its gems: Schumann himself subsequently described the trio of the *Minuetto* (containing a phrase destined to reappear in the fourth of his Op. 4 *Intermezzos* for solo piano) as the moment he knew he belonged to a new world of romance. Though the more classically inspired flanking movements need (and in this splendidly vivid performance receive) a few discreet cuts, both have irrepressible buoyance of spirit. His familiar second and last Quartet in E flat followed towards the end of 1842, a year almost exclusively devoted to chamber music, by which time he had an eminently distinguished pianist wife to help promote it. With his clear texture and rhythmic crispness, Previn ensures that the important keyboard part never dominates. And even though just now and again (notably in the meltingly heartfelt *Andante cantabile*) the sensitive cellist lacks the warmest and richest tonal glow, the playing, no less than the recording, holds its own with all the catalogue's rivals.

Additional recommendations ...
Quartet, Op. 47[a]. *Piano Quintet in E flat major, Op. 44*[b]. **Beaux Arts Trio;** [b]**Dorf Bettelheim** (vn); [ab]**Samuel Rhodes** (va). Philips 420 791-2PH — 58m ADD 2/88
As Philips. **Jiří Panocha** (vn); **Miroslav Sehnoutka** (va); **Jaroslav Kulhan** (vc); **Jan Panenka** (pf); **Smetana Quartet.** Supraphon 11 0367-2 — 57m DDD 10/91

Schumann. Violin Sonatas — No. 1 in A minor, Op. 105; No. 2 in D minor, Op. 121. **Gidon Kremer** (vn); **Martha Argerich** (pf). DG 419 235-2GH.

49m DDD 1/87

The rapidity of composition of the two violin sonatas (four and six days respectively) is nowhere evident except perhaps in the vigour and enthusiasm of the music. Argerich and Kremer, both mercurial and emotionally charged performers, subtly balance the ardent Florestan and dreamily melancholic Eusebius elements of Schumann's creativity. This is even more striking in the Second Sonata, a greater work than its twin, thematically vigorous with a richness and scope that make it at once a striking as well as ideally structured work. Kremer and Argerich have established a close and exciting duo partnership and this fine recording shows what like minds can achieve in music so profoundly expressive as this.

Schumann. Piano Sonata No. 1 in F sharp minor, Op. 11. Fantasie in C major, Op. 17. **Maurizio Pollini** (pf). DG 423 134-2GH. From 2530 379 (5/74).

lh 3m ADD 5/88 B

These works grew from Schumann's love and longing for his future wife Clara. Both performances are superb, not least because they are so truthful to the letter of the score. By eschewing all unspecified rubato in the *Fantasie*, Pollini reminds us that the young Schumann never wrote a more finely proportioned large-scale work; this feeling for structure, coupled with exceptional emotional intensity, confirms it as one of the greatest love-poems ever written for the piano. His richly characterized account of the Sonata is refreshingly unmannered. Certainly the familiar charges of protracted patterning in the faster flanking movements are at once dispelled by his rhythmic *élan*, his crystalline texture and his ear for colour. The sound re-emerges with all its original clarity on CD.

Additional recommendation ...
No. 1. Waldszenen, Op. 82. Kinderszenen, Op. 15. **Vladimir Ashkenazy** (pf). Decca 421 290-2DH — ⋰ 1h 14m DDD 2/89

Schumann. Kinderszenen, Op. 15[a]. Faschingsschwank aus Wien, Op. 26[b]. Carnaval, Op. 9[b]. **Daniel Barenboim** (pf) DG Privilege 431 167-2GR. Item marked [a] from 2531 079 (6/79), [b] 2531 089 (7/79).

• 1h 13m ADD 8/91 £

The extremely fine DG budget price CD recital of three of Schumann's finest works finds Daniel Barenboim at the peak of his pianistic power. Recorded in 1979, Barenboim achieves both the virtuosity and interpretative prowess necessary to fully realize the brilliant miniatures within each work. Above all it is the strong sense of character which he imparts to Schumann's individual sound world that makes the disc as a whole so successful. The *Kinderszenen* ("Scenes from Childhood") contain some of Schumann's most eloquent and intimate piano writing and Barenboim brings a wonderful delicacy and wistfulness to this music. The more robust *Faschingsschwank aus Wien* ("Carnival Jest from Vienna") is given a performance of great vitality, more than sufficient to hide the work's occasional weaknesses. The crowning glory of the disc as a whole is a splendidly vibrant and intense performance of *Carnaval* which perfectly captures the extrovert intentions of Florestan, while equally successfully portraying the poetic side of Eusebius. The climax, with Schumann triumphing against the Philistines, is extraordinarily exhilarating. DG's sound is fully worthy of this magnificent example of romantic interpretation.

Additional recommendations ...
Kinderszenen. Kreisleriana, Op. 16. **Martha Argerich** (pf). DG 410 653-2GH — ⋰ 52m DDD 5/84
Kreisleriana. Fantasia in C major, Op. 17. **Artur Rubinstein** (pf). RCA Gold Seal 09026 61264-2 — ⋰ 1h 6m ADD 2/93

NEW REVIEW

Schumann. Davidsbündlertänze, Op. 6. Waldszenen, Op. 82. Fantasiestücke, Op. 111. **Andreas Haefliger** (pf). Sony Classical CD48036. Recorded in 1991.

⋰ 1h 5m DDD 10/92

NEW REVIEW

Schumann. Davidsbündlertänze, Op. 6. Fantasiestücke, Op. 12. **Benjamin Frith** (pf). Naxos 8 550493. Recorded in 1991.

• 1h 3m DDD 3/93

Although by 1851 Schumann had dropped overt references to that Laurel and Hardy of his creative imagination, Florestan and Eusebius (referring, more or less, to the *yin,* and *yang* — masculine and feminine, assertive and reflective — characters of individual pieces), frequent and telling changes of mood remained an essential ingredient of his mature style. *Davidsbündlertänze*, or "Dances of the League of David" exemplify this trend most vividly: two books, each containing nine separate pieces, alternating fast with slow, humorous with serious and invariably maintaining an element of surprise. There are two 'versions' of the *Davidsbündlertänze*, one from 1837, the other from 1851 and Andreas Haefliger achieves a felicitous musical balance by combining elements of both. His is an intelligent and thoughtful brand of pianism, sensitive to modulation and wonderfully warm in tone; this writer was often reminded of the similarly perceptive art of our own much-loved (and much missed) master pianist, Solomon. What is most striking about the *Davidsbündlertänze* is the way Schumann plots key changes from one miniature to the next, effecting many magical contrasts, especially in the second book. Furthermore, the actual level of invention is always high, and the closing sequence utilizes some of Schumann's most bewitching invention: try, by way of example, the final pair — "Wie aus der Ferne" and "Nicht schnell" (tracks 17 and 18). *Waldszenen* is less a sweeping inspiration than a series of lonely vignettes; "The Prophet Bird" (track 25), a frequently performed 'encore' in its own right, is possibly the most atmospheric evocation of tree-top bird song pre-Messiaen, an eerie, questioning *morceau* that twists and turns with the unpredictability of its natural model. If *Waldszenen* takes us deep into the woods, the late *Fantasiestücke* take us further still; here loneliness transforms to disorientation (second movement), and youthful passion becomes defiant grandeur (third). Haefliger charts both this and the disc's companion pieces with sure intuition, and he is most beautifully recorded. The young prize-winning British pianist Benjamin Frith indulges the *Davidsbündlertänze*'s caprice, highlighting the contrasts between fast and slower pieces, and summoning his excellent technique for some exciting pianism. But then contrast lies at the very heart of Schumann's inspiration. Frith is quite unlike Haefliger in that he favours impulse over refinement, and isn't afraid to throw caution to the winds, if the mood dictates. His *Fantasiestücke*, too, are forthright and outspoken, although "Des Abends", "Warum" and "Ende vom Lied" each contain plenty of poetry. Naxos's recording is excellent. Certainly recommended, not only for the budget-conscious collector, but for those who enjoy youthful pianistic exuberance.

Additional recommendation ...
Papillons, Op. 2. Davidsbündlertänze. Carnaval, Op. 9. Fantasie in C major, Op. 17. Etudes Symphoniques, Op. 13. Kreisleriana, Op. 16. Kinderszenen, Op. 15. Piano Sonata No. 2 in G minor, Op. 22. Arabeske, Op. 18. Bunte Blätter, Op. 99 Novellette. Drei Romanzen, Op. 28. Humoreske, Op. 20. Waldszene. Nachtstücke, Op. 23. **Wilhelm Kempff** (pf). DG 435 045-2GX4 — ④ 4h 57m ADD 5/92

Schumann. Dichterliebe, Op. 48. Liederkreis, Op. 39. **Olaf Bär** (bar); **Geoffrey Parsons** (pf). EMI CDC7 47397-2. Texts and translations included. From EL270364-1 (6/86).

54m DDD 9/86 B

The 16 songs of *Dichterliebe* ("A poet's love") form not so much a cycle as a sequence of *tableaux* charting the many emotions of the lover, from the wonder at the beauties of nature to the stoic resignation at love's fickleness. This is young man's music — ardent, vigorous and heartfelt. From Olaf Bär we have a young man's response — virile, firm of tone and warmly beautiful, never hectoring or over-insistent. This is mature singing of surpassing elegance. In the softer, dusky contours of the *Liederkreis* Bär demonstrates his fine legato and again impresses with his varied expressive range, capturing both the sense of mystery and the bitter-sweet quality of such songs as "Zwielicht" or "Wehmut". Geoffrey Parsons offers sensitive accompaniments and the recording assists Bär's immaculate diction, though never at the piano's expense.

Additional recommendations ...
Dichterliebe. Liederkreis. **Josef Protschka** (ten); **Helmut Deutsch** (pf). Capriccio 10 215 1h 2m DDD 12/88 B
Dichterliebe, Op. 48. Der Nussbaum, Op. 25 No. 3. ***Brahms:*** *Deutsche Volkslieder — No. 1, Sagt mire, o schönste Schäf'rin; No. 4, Guten Abend, mein tausiger Schatz; No. 15, Schwesterlein, Schwesterlein; No. 34, Wie komm'ich denn zur Tür herein? Wiegenlied, Op. 49 No. 4.* ***Prokofiev:*** *Three Children's Songs, Op. 68. The Ugly Duckling, Op. 18 (all sung in German).* **Peter Schreier** (ten); **Wolfgang Sawallisch** (pf). Philips 426 237-2PH *(see review in the Collections section; refer to the Index to Reviews)* — 1h 12m DDD 4/90 B
Hans Peter Blochwitz (ten); **Rudolf Jansen** (pf). EMI CDC7 54042-2 — 50m DDD 12/90 B

Schumann. LIEDER. **Peter Schreier** (ten); **Christoph Eschenbach** (pf). Teldec 2292-46154-2. Texts and translations included. Recorded in 1988.
Liederkreis, Op. 24. Liederkreis, Op. 39. Dichterliebe, Op. 48. Myrthen, Op. 25 — No. 1, Widmung; No. 2, Freisinn; No. 3, Der Nussbaum; No. 7, Die Lotosblume; No. 15, Aus den hebräischen Gesängen; No. 21, Was will die einsame Träne?; No. 24, Du bist wie eine Blume; No. 25, Aus den östlichen Rosen; No. 26, Zum Schluss, Lieder-Album für die Jugend, Op. 79 — No. 4, Frühlingsgruss; No. 7, Zigeunerliedchen; No. 13, Marienwürmchen; No. 26, Schneeglöckchen. Zwölf Gedichte, Op. 35 — No. 3, Wanderlied; No. 4, Erstes Grün; No. 8,

Stille Liebe; No. 11, Wer machte dich so krank?; No. 12, Alte Laute. Liebesfrühling, Op. 37 — No. 1, Der Himmel hat eine Träne geweint; No. 5, Ich hab in mich gesogen; No. 9, Rose, Meer und Sonne. Fünf Lieder, Op. 40. Mein schöner Stern!, Op. 101 No. 4. Nur ein lächelnder Blick, Op. 27 No. 5. Geständnis, Op. 74 No. 7. Aufträge, Op. 77 No. 5. Meine Rose, Op. 90 No. 2. Kommen und Schneiden, Op. 90 No. 3. Lieder und Gesange, Op. 51 — No. 1, Sehnsucht; No. 3, Ich wandre nicht. An den Mond, Op. 95 No. 2. Dein Angesicht, Op. 127 No. 2. Lehn deine Wang, Op. 142 No. 2. Der arme Peter, Op. 53 No. 3.

③ 2h 45m DDD 6/91

This is a very fair conspectus of Schumann's genius as a Lieder composer and all the offerings are authoritatively performed. They include recommendable accounts of the three cycles appropriate for a male singer to tackle. Schreier with Eschenbach, who has made a special study of the composer, make the most of *Dichterliebe* and the two *Liederkreise*, identifying themselves with the various moods and characters depicted within. Schreier's idiomatic and pointed diction and accents allied to Eschenbach's exploratory and imaginative way with Schumann's highly individual writing for piano would be hard to better. The remainder of these three well-filled CDs is given over to single songs and to discerning choices from groups other than the cycles. Here are the most telling pieces from *Myrthen* and from the 12 Kerner settings, Op. 35. Late Schumann is acknowledged to be a more doubtful quantity, but he could still write great songs such as the poignant *Meine Rose* and the lovely Heine setting, *Dein Angesicht*. To these, as to the delightful *Zigeunerliedchen*, and much else, this pair of superb performers bring their unfailing artistry, always seeking and finding the heart of the matter. The well-balanced recording is an unobtrusive support.

Schumann. LIEDER. **Eberhard Waechter** (bar); **Alfred Brendel** (pf). Decca 425 949-2DM. Texts and translations included. From SXL2310 (6/62). Recorded in 1961.
Dichterliebe, Op. 48. Liederkreis, Op. 24 — Schöne Wiege meiner Leiden; Mit Myrten und Rosen. Lehn deine Wang an meine Wang, Op. 142 No. 2. Mein Wagen rollet langsam, Op. 142 No. 4.

41m ADD 6/91 

This recording of *Dichterliebe*, 31 years old and somewhat overlooked when first issued, is one of the most satisfying ever made of the cycle, by virtue of Waechter's total identification with the jilted man's sorrow expressed in warm, vibrant, wholehearted, never self-conscious singing. Here the romantic thoughts, melancholy, anger, torment, resignation, so memorably achieved in Schumann's setting of Heine, receives an answering identification on Waechter's part. Nowhere else in Schumann's output are the voice and piano so closely entwined as if in a single outpouring of inspiration. Here that achievement is fully realized through Brendel's discerning, probing execution. Always achieving rapport with his partner, Brendel is here caught before he became the famous pianist he is today. Anybody listening to his marvellously perceptive accounts of Schumann's ingenious postludes would hear what a masterly pianist he already was. The extra songs are given with just as much illumination on both sides.

Schumann. LIEDER. **Brigitte Fassbaender** (mez); **Irwin Gage** (pf). DG 415 519-2GH. Recorded in 1984. Texts and translations included.
Frauenliebe und -leben, Op. 42. Tragödie, Op. 64 No. 3. Liederkreis, Op. 24. Abends am Strand, Op. 45 No. 3. Lehn' deine Wang, Op. 142 No. 2. Mein Wagen rollet langsam, Op. 142 No. 2.

57m DDD 2/86

Schumann's cycle, *Frauenliebe und -leben*, depicting a woman's adoring relationship with her perfect man, who marries her, gives her a child, then dies prematurely can seem a trifle sentimental in the wrong hands — or voice. Fassbaender wholly avoids any pitfall in her typically intense and individual reading, one that projects all the subjective ardour and infatuation of the early songs, catches the contented centre of the middle ones and the inner tragedy and emptiness of the finale after the husband's death. She is ably supported by Gage, who also is perceptive in the Op. 24 *Liederkreis*. This isn't a true cycle but a collection of settings of Heine texts. Fassbaender is equally at home here in the dramatic and reflective songs, once more going to the heart of the matter through her probing approach to note and text. The three late Schumann songs are welcome bonuses on this well-filled and excellently recorded disc.

Schumann. Das Paradies und die Peri, Op. 50. **Edith Wiens, Sylvia Herman** (sops); **Anne Gjevang** (contr); **Robert Gambill, Christoph Prégardien** (tens); **Hans-Peter Scheidegger** (bar) **Lausanne Pro Arte Choir; Suisse Romande Chamber Choir and Orchestra/Armin Jordan.** Erato 2292-45456-2. Text and translation included. Recorded in 1988.

(2) 1h 36m DDD 4/90 

"An oratorio — not for an oratory but for bright, happy people" was how Schumann once described *Das Paradies und die Peri*, his first venture into the choral field at the age of 33. The text (taken from Thomas Moore's *Lalla Rookh*) in fact appealed to him not only for its moral message but just as strongly for its eastern exoticism as the Peri (a fallen angel) journeys to India, Egypt and Syria in search of the "gift most dear to heaven". Neither the blood of a hero slain in freedom's cause, nor the last sigh of a maiden choosing to die alongside her plague-stricken lover, suffice. Not until she returns with the tear of a sinner moved to repentance by the sight of a child at prayer do the gates of Paradise reopen to let her in. With its stirring battle music and seductive choruses of Egyptian genii of the Nile and Syrian houris as well as such treasures as "Schlaf' nun und ruhe" for soprano and choir (which if he had written nothing else would still have made Schumann one of the immortals) the work won an immediate success before virtually disappearing from the concert repertory in the early years of this century. Now no less than three fine performances are currently available on CD. That of Armin Jordan and his Swiss forces (first to reach the catalogue and winner of the 1990 *Gramophone* Choral Award) still heads the list for its judiciously chosen tempos, its effortless continuity and its well-judged balance of voices and orchestra. Jordan, eminently stylish, never over-dramatizes or over-sentimentalizes this heartfelt music and his collaborators (with a caring cast of soloists headed by Edith Wiens in the title role) do not let him down.

Schumann. Szenen aus Goethes Faust. **Elizabeth Harwood, Jenny Hill, Jennifer Vyvyan, Felicity Palmer** (sops); **Meriel Dickinson, Margaret Cable, Pauline Stevens** (mezs); **Alfreda Hodgson** (contr); **Sir Peter Pears, John Elwes, Neil Jenkins** (tens); **John Noble, Dietrich Fischer-Dieskau, John Shirley-Quirk** (bars); **Robert Lloyd** (bass); **Wandsworth School Choir; Aldeburgh Festival Singers; English Chamber Orchestra/Benjamin Britten.** Decca 425 705-2DM2. Notes, text and translation included. From SET567/8 (12/73). Recorded in 1972.

(2) 1h 58m ADD 7/90 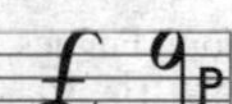

It was with Goethe's mystical closing scene, never approached by any composer before, that Schumann began his *Scenes from Faust* in 1844, when around the age of 34. The impending Goethe centenary celebrations sufficiently rekindled his life-long enthusiasm for the subject for three Gretchen-inspired scenes to follow in the summer of 1849, and three more Faust-inspired scenes the next year. But it was not until 1853 that he finally added the overture, and the work was never performed in its entirety until six years after his death. Even today it remains enough of a rarity for Benjamin Britten's revelatory revival in June 1972, to stand out as one of the most memorable of all his Aldeburgh Festival's many glories. So hats off to Decca for this CD reissue of the LP recording made at The Maltings in Snape shortly afterwards, with some, if not all, of the festival cast — incidentally a recording happily timed for first release on Britten's sixtieth birthday in November 1973. Whereas in Goethe's closing scene (Part 3) we are reminded of the lyrical Schumann, the great surprise of the work is the drama of the subsequently composed Parts 1 and 2. Not for nothing had Schumann by this time moved from a Mendelssohn-dominated Leipzig to a Wagner-stirred Dresden. The late and still sorely lamented Elizabeth Harwood is a touchingly vulnerable, pure toned Gretchen, while Fischer-Dieskau responds with quite exceptional immediacy and intensity to Faust's blinding, visionary dreams and moment of death. As Mephistopheles and Ariel, John Shirley-

Quirk and Sir Peter Pears are equally outstanding for their sensitive tonal shading and shapely line. Under Britten's inspired direction all soloists are splendidly upheld by the ECO, and last but not least, by the Aldeburgh Festival Singers and Wandsworth School Choir who sing with as much flexibility and character in their various guises as anyone on the platform. The CD reproduction is excellent.

Schumann (arr. Beecham). Manfred — incidental music, Op. 115. **Gertrud Holt** (sop); **Claire Duchesneau** (mez); **Glyndwr Davies, Ian Billington** (tens); **Niven Miller** (bar); **Laidman Browne, Jill Balcon, Raf de la Torre, David Enders** (spkrs); **BBC Chorus; Royal Philharmonic Orchestra/Sir Thomas Beecham.** Sir Thomas Beecham Trust mono BEECHAM4. From Fontana CFL1026/7 (2/59). Recorded 1954-56.

1h 18m ADD 9/91 

Schumann was haunted by Byron's autobiographically-inspired dramatic poem, *Manfred*, from a very early age. When eventually writing his incidental music for it (15 numbers and an overture) in 1848-9 he confessed to never having devoted himself to any composition before "with such lavish love and power". No one in this country has ever done more for it than Sir Thomas Beecham, who even staged it at the Theatre Royal, Drury Lane, London, way back in 1918, some 36 years before reviving it for the BBC and at the Festival Hall in performances leading to this now legendary recording. Score-followers will at once note Beecham's appropriation and scoring of two of the composer's roughly contemporaneous keyboard miniatures as additional background music for the guilt-wracked, soliloquizing Manfred. But their choice and placing is so apt that even Schumann himself might have been grateful. By present-day standards Laidman Browne might be thought a shade too overtly emotional in the title-role. But speakers (including a splendidly awesome Witch of the Alps and rustic chamois-hunter), like singers, orchestra and the magnetic Sir Thomas himself, are all at one in vividness of atmospheric evocation. Splendid remastering also plays its part in making this medium-priced disc a collector's piece.

Further listening ...

Works for Piano Trio — Piano Trios: No. 1 in D minor, Op. 63; No. 2 in F major, Op. 80; No. 3 in G minor. Fantasiestücke, Op. 88. **Borodin Trio.** Chandos CHAN8832/3 (11/90).

Piano Sonata No. 2. Kreisleriana, Op. 16. Novellette in F sharp minor, Op. 21 No. 8. **Vladimir Ashkenazy** (pf). Decca 425 940-2DH (4/92).

Four Fugues, Op. 72. Marches, Op. 76 — No. 2 in G minor. Toccata, Op. 7. Blumenstück, Op. 19. Vier Nachtstücke, Op. 23. **Sviatoslav Richter** (pf). Decca 436 456-2DH (3/93).

Heinrich Schütz

German 1585-1672

NEW REVIEW

Schütz. MOTETS. **Tölz Boys' Choir/Gerhard Schmidt-Gaden** with **Roman Summereder** (org). Capriccio 10 388. Texts and translations included. Recorded 1989-90. Ich hab mein Sach Gott heimgestellt, SWV305. Ich will dem Herren loben allezeit, SWV306. Was hast du verwirket, SWV307. O Jesu, nomen dulce, SWV308. O misericordissime Jesu, SWV309. Ich leige und schlafe, SWV310. Habe deine Lust an dem Herren, SWV311. Herr, ich hoffe darauf, SWV312. Bone Jesu, verbum Patris, SWV313. Verbum caro factum est, SWV314. Hodie Christus natus est, SWV315. Wann unsre Augen schlafen ein, SWV316. Meister, wir haben die ganze Nacht gearbeitet, SWV317. Die Furcht des Herren, SWV318. Ich beuge meine Knie, SWV319. Ich bin jung gewesen, SWV320. Herr, wann ich nur dich habe, SWV321.

Rorate coeli desuper, SWV322. Joseph, du Sohn David, SWV323. Ich bin die Auferstehung, SWV324.

1h 17m DDD 4/93 

Getting music published evidently encountered economic difficulties during the Thirty Years' War, for Heinrich Schütz had to issue his *Kleine Geistliche Konzerte* ("Little Sacred Concertos") — short motets for vocal soloists and continuo — in two parts in, respectively, 1636 and 1639. No. 24 from Part I and Nos. 1-19 from Part II comprise the programme for this second volume from soloists of the Tölz Boys' Choir and although, at first sight, this may seem too regimented an approach to produce satisfying listening for the whole disc, Schütz himself structured the items so that there is a progression throughout the set, not only in increased numbers of soloists but also in intensity and intellectual scope. The voices of the soloists here are typically very individual and characterful, and all are remarkably adroit and stylish, so the personal witness that is so pronounced in the text is particularly well portrayed. These are performers well used to the subtleties of baroque word setting and they highlight all the ingenuity that Schütz lavished on these seemingly simple texts. There is an evident delight in the way the composer deployed his limited resources, constantly ringing the changes on traditional formulas to produce a richness of ideas that it took a Bach or Handel to emulate. The rather close recording allows all these intricacies to emerge undiminished and although the resonance of the acoustic seems restrained, this is no bad thing for music that, despite its title, has the feel of chamber music.

Schütz. SACRED CHORAL WORKS. **Monteverdi Choir; English Baroque Soloists; His Majesties Sagbutts and Cornetts/John Eliot Gardiner.** Archiv Produktion 423 405-2AH. Texts and translations included.
Freue dich des Weibes deiner Jugend, SWV453 (with Frieder Lang, ten). Ist nicht Ephraim mein teuer Sohn, SWV40. Saul, Saul, was verfolgst du mich, SWV415. Auf dem Gebirge, SWV396 (Ashley Stafford, Michael Chance, altos). Musicalische Exequien, SWV279-81 (Lang).

51m DDD 11/88

Unlike so much of Schütz's huge output, made up largely of short motet-like settings, the *Musicalische Exequien* is a work of ample proportions; the opening "concerto in the form of a burial Mass" alone runs to more than 20 minutes of music. But it is not mere size that makes this work so striking. It is also a work of impressive solemnity. For all the exuberance trained into him through early contact with Venice in the age of the Gabrielis, in his mature works Schütz's distinguishing quality is his sobriety and austere nobility. Without question the climax of the *Musicalische Exequien* comes in the concluding "Nunc dimittis", an extraordinary setting in which a semi-chorus, half-heard from the dark recesses of the church, punctuates the main text with its own exquisite words, "Blessed are the dead which die in the Lord". Both here and in the selection of four short motets, the Monteverdi Choir sing with authority and great beauty, revealing in the process the true colours of music which in the wrong hands all too often is made to seem grey.

Arthur Schwartz

American 1900-1984

Suggested listening ...

A TREE GROWS IN BROOKLYN. **Original Broadway cast.** Sony Broadway CD48014.

Cyril Scott

British 1879-1970

Suggested listening ...

Two Pieces, Op. 47. Two Pierrot Pieces, Op. 35. Pierrette. Poems. Trois Danses tristes, Op. 74. Sonata, Op. 66. **Dennis Hennig** (pf). Etcetera KTC1132 (10/92).

James Scott

American 1885-1938

Suggested listening ...

Scott: Evergreen Rag. Modesty Rag. Peace and Plenty Rag. Troubadour Rag. *Coupled with* ***Nazareth:*** Apanhei-tecavaquinho. Cavaquinho. Vitorioso. Odeon. Nove de Julho. Labirinto. Guerreiro. Plangente. Cubanos. Fon-Fon! ***Lamb:*** Ragtime Nightingale. American Beauty Rag. Bohemia Rag. Topliner Rag. **Joshua Rifkin** (pf). Decca 425 225-2DH (4/92).

Alexander Scriabin

Russian 1872-1915

Scriabin. Piano Concerto in F sharp minor, Op. 20[a]. Prometheus, Op. 60[b]. Le poème de l'extase, Op. 54[c]. [ab]**Vladimir Ashkenazy** (pf); [b]**Ambrosian Singers;** [ab]**London Philharmonic Orchestra,** [c]**Cleveland Orchestra/Lorin Maazel.** Decca 417 252-2DH. Items marked [a] and [b] from SXL6527 (1/72), recorded in 1971, [c] SXL6905 (9/79), recorded in 1978.

lh 6m ADD 4/89

This CD gives us the essential Scriabin. The Piano Concerto has great pianistic refinement and melodic grace as well as a restraint not encountered in his later music. With *Le poème de l'extase* and *Prometheus* we are in the world of *art nouveau* and Scriabin in the grip of the mysticism (and megalomania) that consumed his later years. They are both single-movement symphonies for a huge orchestra: *Prometheus* ("The Poem of Fire") calls for quadruple wind, eight horns, five trumpets, strings, organ and chorus as well as an important part for solo piano in which Ashkenazy shines. The sensuous, luminous textures are beautifully conveyed in these performances by the LPO and the Decca engineers produce a most natural perspective and transparency of detail, as well as an appropriately overheated sound in the sensuous world of *Le poème de l'extase*.

Additional recommendation ...

Piano Concerto[a]. *Le poème de l'extase.* [a]**Garrick Ohlsson** (pf); **Czech Philharmonic Orchestra/Libor Pešek.** Supraphon CO2047 — 53m DDD 11/89

Piano Concerto[a]. *Symphony No. 3.* [a]**Roland Pöntinen** (pf); **Stockholm Philharmonic Orchestra/Leif Segerstam.** BIS CD475 — lh 17m DDD 1/91

Scriabin. ORCHESTRAL WORKS. **Philadelphia Orchestra/Riccardo Muti.** EMI CDS7 54251-2. Text and translation included.

Symphonies — No. 1 in E major, Op. 26 (with Stefania Toczyska, mez; Michael Myers, ten; Westminster Choir. From EL270270-1, 3/86); No. 2 in C minor, Op. 29 (CDC7 49859-2, 11/90); No. 3 in C minor, Op. 43, "Le divin poème" (CDC7 49115-2, 4/89). Le poème de l'extase, Op. 54 (Frank Kaderabek, tpt. CDC7 54061-2). Prometheus, Op. 60, "Le poème du feu" (Dmitri Alexeev, pf; Philadelphia Choral Arts Society, CDC7 54112-2).

③ 3h 8m DDD 7/91

Harken all hedonists! Herein are contained all Scriabin's symphonies — the *Poem of Ecstasy* and *Prometheus* couldn't possibly be referred to by anything as mundane as mere symphonic numbers — at last in performances that mingle dramatic fervour with an ability to float all those gorgeous *cantabiles*; and achieve climaxes that radiate enlightenment and, yea, cause the very earth to move. The first two Symphonies find the budding luminary still bound by the fetters of tradition (such stars in the firmament as Liszt, Tchaikovsky and Wagner exerting a strong gravitational pull). *The Divine Poem* (No. 3) shows Scriabin's universe magnificently broadening, using an enormous orchestra (to match the expanded mission), whilst the single movement *Poem of Ecstasy* and *Prometheus* represent the full flowering of his genius, and manage some startling musical innovations in the process. High Priest Riccardo Muti has at his command an orchestra whose opulent tones are here at their legendary best and a group of technical acolytes who see to it that the mystical waves of sound are aptly tidal.

Scriabin. Symphony No. 3 in C minor, Op. 43, "Le divin poème". Le poème de l'extase, Op. 54. **New York Philharmonic Orchestra/Giuseppe Sinopoli.** DG 427 324-2GH.

1h 10m DDD 6/89

Scriabin's "Divine Poem" is a gorgeous tapestry of shot colours and sinuous arabesques, portraying languorous and ecstatic emotions, visionary states and scarcely communicable ecstasies, but it is also a piece of music with a beginning, a middle and an end. What makes Sinopoli's account so special is his refined care for balance, both of texture and of tempo, and his choice of the *Poem of Ecstasy* as the obvious coupling. There is a fine sense, in both works, that you really are hearing every note that Scriabin wrote, and that foreground and background are both audible but never confused with each other. The secret seems to be a very precise control of the subtle slackenings and hastenings of tempo that are essential to Scriabin's idiom, and after one has relished all the impossible richnesses of this music it is an absorbing experience to go back for a repeat hearing to work out how Sinopoli does it. He couldn't have done it, of course, without orchestral playing of great subtlety and responsiveness and a recording that combines richness with exceptional clarity. Here he has both, and the result is both sumptuous and vital.

Additional recommendations ...

No. 3. ***Arensky.*** *Silhouettes (Suite No. 2), Op. 23.* **Danish National Radio Symphony Orchestra/Neeme Järvi.** Chandos CHAN8898. — 1h 6m DDD 10/91

No. 3. Le poème de l'extase. **Berlin Radio Symphony Orchestra/Vladimir Ashkenazy.** Decca 430 843-2DH — 1h 10m DDD 11/91

NEW REVIEW

Scriabin. PIANO WORKS. **Roger Woodward.** Etcetera KTC1126. Recorded in 1991. Piano Sonatas — No. 6, Op. 62; No. 10, Op. 70. Three Etudes, Op. 65. Two Dances, Op. 73. Five Preludes, Op. 74. Poèmes, Opp. 63, 67, 69 and 71. Poème-Nocturne, Op. 61. Vers la flamme, Op. 72

1h 15m DDD 10/92 

Although Roger Woodward is primarily known for his unflagging championship of contemporary avant-garde music, his repertoire in the concert-hall (though not necessarily apparent on disc) ranges from Beethoven through to the late-romantics. This recording of late Scriabin piano music is therefore a welcome addition to his discography. The shorter pieces on the disc are what William Blake would have described as "worlds in a grain of sand", and it is Woodward's ability to project this, together with the feeling that these are minor satellites inextricably linked by gravity to the larger bodies of the sonatas, that most impress. Good examples of this can be heard in the *Two Dances,* Op. 73, the two tiny Preludes, Op. 67 (the second of which comes over as a veritable cosmic-shimmer in the hands of Woodward) and the three spellbinding and demonically taxing *Etudes,* Op. 65. As for the Sixth and Tenth Sonatas, these are certainly amongst the most structurally convincing and logical accounts on disc at present. The Tenth exemplifies Woodward's linear approach to the music, with Scriabin's vaporescent material gradually opening out into wider and ever more expansive vistas, and in the spine-tingling Sixth Sonata we are privy to some exceptionally intense and concentrated playing. Woodward's tonal and dynamic range is extremely wide and this has been faithfully captured in the clear and atmospheric recording. Generous measure and a stunning addition to Scriabin's music on disc.

Additional recommendation ...

Fantaisie in B minor, Op. 28. Piano Sonatas — No. 1 in F minor, Op. 6; No. 2 in G sharp minor, Op. 19, "Sonata-fantasy"; No. 3 in F sharp minor, Op. 23; No. 4 in F sharp major, Op. 30; No. 5, Op. 53; No. 6, Op. 62; No. 7, Op. 64, "White Mass"; No. 8, Op. 66; No. 9, Op. 68, "Black Mass"; No. 10, Op. 70. Sonata in E flat minor. Sonate-fantaisie in G sharp minor. **Roberto Szidon.** DG 20th Century Classics 431 747-2GC3 — 3h ADD 4/92 £

Scriabin. PIANO WORKS. **Graham Scott.** Gamut Classics CD520.
Piano Sonatas — No. 3 in F sharp minor, Op. 23; No. 9 in F, Op. 68, "Black Mass". Three Pieces, Op. 2 — No. 1, Etude in C sharp minor; No. 2, Prelude in B major. Five Preludes, Op. 16. Four Preludes, Op. 22. Two Preludes, Op. 27. Four Preludes, Op. 31. Four Preludes, Op. 33. Five Preludes, Op. 74.

1h 7m DDD 10/91

This is an exceptionally well played and carefully thought-out recital of Scriabin's piano music. The first half of the disc is devoted to a selective survey of Scriabin's Preludes which, when heard in chronological order as they are here, provide an excellent opportunity for the listener to experience the astonishing trajectory of Scriabin's musical development; from the early Chopinesque musings of Opp. 2 and 16, and the more rhythmically complex and harmonically adventurous Preludes of Opp. 31 and 33, through to the theosophical and quasi-atonal utterances of the Five Preludes, Op. 74. Scriabin was a master of economy, and some of these Preludes are tiny in the extreme ("as short as a Sparrow's beak" as Tolstoy once remarked), yet contained within their diminutive frames there lies a wealth of emotion and experience. Scott brings to them an outstanding degree of intensity and concentration and his delicacy of touch and beautifully singing *cantabile* are much to be admired. There are several fine performances of the Ninth Sonata *Black Mass* in the catalogue at present, but Scott's impressive and exhilarating account bears comparison with the finest; the build up of tension before the desolation of the closing bars is delivered with considerable *frisson*, and Scott reveals an instinctive feel for Scriabin's complex layering of individual strands. The final item brings us full circle to the stormily romantic Scriabin of 1897 and an impassioned and beautifully crafted account of the Third Sonata. The sound is well balanced and engineered.

NEW REVIEW

Scriabin. COMPLETE ETUDES. **Piers Lane** (pf). Hyperion CDA66607. Recorded in 1992.
Etude in C sharp minor, Op. 2 No. 1. Twelve Etudes, Op. 8. Eight Etudes, Op. 42. Etude in E flat major, Op. 49 No. 1. Etude, Op. 56 No. 4. Three Etudes, Op. 65.

56m DDD 12/92

Although Scriabin's *études* do not fall into two neatly packaged sets in the same way as Chopin's celebrated contributions, there is nevertheless a strong feeling of continuity and development running throughout the 26 examples produced between the years 1887 and 1912. This is admirably demonstrated in this excellent issue from Hyperion, which, far from being an indigestible anthology proves to be an intriguing and pleasurable hour's worth of listening charting Scriabin's progression from late-romantic adolescence, to harmonically advanced mystical poet. Indeed, although these studies can be counted as amongst the most digitally taxing and hazardous of their kind, Scriabin also saw them as important sketches and studies for his larger works, and as experiments in his gradually evolving harmonic language and mystical vision. Piers Lane attains the perfect balance between virtuoso display and poetic interpretation. Expressive detail and subtle nuance are finely brought out, and he is more than receptive to Scriabin's sometimes highly idiosyncratic sound-world; rarely, for instance, has the famous "Mosquito" *Etude* (Op. 42 No. 3) been captured with such delicate fragility as here, and in No. 1 of the three fiendishly difficult *Etudes,* Op. 65 (fifths, sevenths and ninths!) the tremulous, ghostly flutterings are tellingly delivered with a gossamer-light touch and an appropriate sense of eerie mystery. The clear, spacious recording is exemplary.

Peter Sculthorpe

Australian 1929-

Sculthorpe. PIANO WORKS.
W. Stanley (ed. Sculthorpe). Rose Bay Quadrilles. **Max Cooke, Darryl Coote, Linda Kouvaras, Robert Chamberlain, Gudrun Beilharz, Alex Furman, Michael Hannan, Peter Sculthorpe** (pfs). Move MD3031.

Four Little Pieces — Morning song; Sea chant; Little serenade; Left Bank waltz (1979). Callabonna. Night Pieces — Snow; Moon; Flowers; Night; Stars. Mountains. Djilile. Nocturnal. Sonatina. Koto I. Koto II. Landscape. Sea chant (trans pf.) Left Bank waltz (1958).

lh 15m ADD/DDD 3/92

Peter Sculthorpe, now in his early sixties, is Australia's leading composer. His music gives expression to aspects of Australia's landscape and history and in many ways it feels as different from that of European composers as many American composers do. There's a continental sense of space, an awareness of aboriginal culture and myth and a commitment to preserving the environment. This collection of piano pieces is an enjoyable source-book drawn from four decades of the composer's life, starting when he was a student at Melbourne University. It includes Sculthorpe's own playing of his charming *Left Bank waltz* plus a team of seven other pianists to cope with the rest, including piano duets. Two pieces called *Koto* emphasize the oriental component in Sculthorpe — Japan is much closer than Europe — and his use of the piano played directly on the strings is poetic and sensitive. There's a strong atmosphere, too, in each of the *Night Pieces.* Sculthorpe's arrangement of the *Rose Bay Quadrilles* by the mid-nineteenth century composer William Stanley adds zest to the collection. Overall the recorded quality is variable but this Sculthorpe retrospective is an ideal introduction to his personality and his larger works now on CD.

José Serebrier

Uruguain 1938-

Suggested listening ...

Poema elegíaco. Momento psicológico. *Coupled with* **Bloch.** Violin Concerto. Baal Shem. **Michael Gutman** (vn); **Royal Philharmonic Orchestra/José Serebrier.** ASV CDDCA785 (5/92).

Claudin de Sermisy

French c.1490-1562

Suggested listening ...

Chansons. *Coupled with* **Janequin.** Chansons. **Ensemble Clément Janequin.** Harmonia Mundi HMC90 1271.

Roger Sessions

American 1896-1985

Suggested listening ...

Piano Sonatas Nos. 1-3. Pages from a Diary. Five Pieces. Waltz. **Barry David Salwen** (pf). Koch International Classics 37106-2 (12/92).

Rodion Shchedrin

Russian 1932-

Suggested listening ...

Stihira. *Coupled with* **Glazunov.** Violin Concerto in A minor, Op. 82[a]; ***Prokofiev.*** Violin Concerto No. 1 in D major, Op. 19[a]. [a]**Anne-Sophie Mutter** (vn); **Washington National Symphony Orchestra/Mstislav Rostropovich.** Erato 2292-45343-2 (3/89).

Bright Sheng
Chinese-American 1955-

NEW REVIEW

Sheng. H'un (Lacerations): In memoriam 1966-76[a]. The stream flows[b]. Three Chinese Love Songs[c]. My song[d]. [c]**Lisa Saffer** (sop); [b]**Lucia Lin** (vn); [c]**Paul Neubauer** (va); [c]**Bright Sheng,** [d]**Peter Serkin** (pfs); [a]**New York Chamber Symphony Orchestra/Gerard Schwarz.** New World 80407-2. Texts and translations included. Recorded 1990-91.

49m DDD 9/92 

Here are four authoritative interpretations, sensitively recorded and expertly packaged to present a comprehensive portrait of a young Chinese-American composer already making his mark. In the shorter vocal and instrumental works, Sheng shows the eclectic, tonal face you might expect of a Bernstein protégé. It was Bernstein who advised him that Western music could incorporate Eastern culture, that all music — whether Haydn or Mahler was "fusion". Thus *The stream flows* weaves oriental melodies into a Bartókian framework, the ravishing *Chinese Love Songs* seem to emulate Ravel and *My song* responds in a more predictable way to what will work pianistically without deserting the legacy of the East. *H'un (Lacerations)* is an altogether tougher proposition, a searing, emotive response to the composer's first-hand experience of the horrors of the Cultural Revolution. Varèse, Penderecki and Shostakovich have all been cited as influences but Sheng sounds very much his own man, not least through the deployment of Chinese percussion instruments. Be warned though: there are no tunes here. "Melodies are beautiful, and when I think of the Cultural Revolution, I cannot think of anything beautiful". *H'un* grinds away like a juggernaut before dying away in despair. It sounds unappealing but perhaps it had to be, and its obvious sincerity and emotional directness have been winning it an increasing number of performances.

John Sheppard
British c.1515-1559-60

Suggested listening ...

Mass — "Be not afraide" (with plainsong Propers). *Sacred Choral Works* — Steven firste after Christ. Sancte Dei pretiose. Impetum fecerunt unanimes. Gaudete caelicole omnes. *Coupled with* **Sampson.** Psallite felices. **The Cardinall's Musick/Andrew Carwood.** Meridian CDE84220 (12/92).

Sacred Choral Works — In manus tuas Domine II. Gaude virgo Christiphera. Reges Tharsis et insulae. Libera nos, salva nos I. Libera nos, salva nos II. *Coupled with* **Tye.** Missa Euge Bone. Peccavimus Patribus nostris. **Clerkes of Oxenford/David Wulstan.** Proudsound PROUCD126 (5/90).

Church Music — Jesu salvator seculi, verbum. Deus tuorum militum II. Ave maris stella. Jesu salvator seculi, redemptis Missa "Cantate". Salvator mundi Domine. **The Sixteen/Harry Christophers.** Hyperion CDA66418 (12/92).

Church Music — Gaude gaude gaude Maria virgo. Dum transisset Sabbatum I. Spiritus Sanctus procedens II. In manus tuas II. Audivi vocem de caelo. Libera nos, salva nos II. Beata nobis gaudia. Impetum fecerunt unanimes. Sancte Dei pretiose. Sacris solemniis iuncta sint gaudia. **The Sixteen/Harry Christophers.** Hyperion CDA66570 (12/92).

Richard M. Sherman/Robert B. Sherman
American 1928-; 1925-

Suggested listening ...

Mary Poppins — *original film soundtrack.* Pickwick/Disney DSMCD459.

Dmitry Shostakovich

Russian 1906-1975

Shostakovich. Cello Concertos — No. 1 in E flat major, Op. 107; No. 2, Op. 126. **Heinrich Schiff** (vc); **Bavarian Radio Symphony Orchestra/Maxim Shostakovich.** Philips 412 526-2PH. From 412 526-1PH (8/85).

1h 1m DDD 10/85 

These two concertos make an obvious and useful 'coupling' for they are both vintage Shostakovich. Indeed, the First occupies a commanding position in the post-war repertory and is probably the most often-heard modern cello concerto. If the Second Concerto has not established itself in the repertory to anywhere near the same extent, the reason may be that it offers fewer overt opportunities for display. It is a work of grave beauty, inward in feeling and spare in its textures. It is pensive, intimate and withdrawn and on first encounter its ideas seem fugitive and shadowy, though the sonorities have a characteristic asperity. The recording's balance is generally excellent: very natural yet very clear, and there is quite outstanding definition and realism.

Additional recommendations ...

No. 1[a]. *Piano Concertos No. 2 in F major, Op. 102. Piano Concerto in C minor for piano, trumpet and strings, Op. 35.* [a]**Mstislav Rostropovich** (vc); [a]**Philadelphia Orchestra/Eugene Ormandy; New York Philharmonic Orchestra/Leonard Bernstein** (pf). CBS Maestro CD44840 — 1h 9m ADD 11/89

Nos. 1 and 2. **Natalia Gutman** (vc); **Royal Philharmonic Orchestra/Yuri Temirkanov.** RCA Victor Red Seal RD87918 — 1h 6m DDD 1/91

NEW REVIEW

Shostakovich. PIANO CONCERTOS AND PIANO WORKS. **Dmitri Shostakovich** (pf); [a]**Ludovic Vaillant** (tpt); [b]**French Radio National Orchestra/André Cluytens.** EMI Composers in Person mono CDC7 54606-2. Recorded 1958-59.

Piano Concertos — No. 1 in C minor, Op 35[ab]; No. 2 in F major, Op. 102[b]. Three Fantastic Dances, Op. 5 (all from French Columbia FCX769, 10/61). 24 Preludes and Fugues, Op. 87 — No. 1 in C major; No. 4 in E minor; No. 5 in D major; No. 23 in F major (FCX771); No. 24 in D minor (Parlophone PMC1056, 7/58).

1h 16m ADD 4/93 

Before devoting himself entirely to composition Shostakovich pursued a successful parallel career as a concert pianist, playing mostly romantic repertoire. These recordings were made at a time when he still played his own works in public, and they show him to have been a highly skilled player. His performances of both concertos are quite brilliant, and have a particularly vivacious, outgoing quality. In the First Concerto Ludovic Vaillant plays the trumpet part with character and great virtuosity, and the orchestral playing under Cluytens matches that of the composer in its joyous high spirits. The three little *Fantastic Dances* are wittily brought to life. A different, far more serious and academic world is evoked by Shostakovich in his Preludes and Fugues. Here the composer shapes his own long contrapuntal lines with great skill, and these are very compelling, highly concentrated performances. The mono recordings are all very acceptable, save that of the last Prelude and Fugue, where a certain rustiness creeps into the sound. All these items have obvious historical importance, but they also offer many rewards to the listener who is primarily interested in the music.

Shostakovich. Concerto in C minor for piano, trumpet and strings, Op. 35[a]. Piano Concerto No. 2 in F major, Op. 102. The Unforgettable Year 1919, Op. 89 — The assault on beautiful Gorky. **Dmitri Alexeev** (pf); [a]**Philip Jones** (tpt); **English Chamber Orchestra/Jerzy Maksymiuk.** Classics for Pleasure CD-CFP4547. From CFP414416-1 (11/83).

48m DDD 1/89 

Shostakovich's Piano Concertos were written under very different circumstances, yet together they contain some of the composer's most cheerful and enlivening music. The First, with its wealth of perky, memorable tunes, has the addition of a brilliantly-conceived solo trumpet part (delightfully done here by Philip Jones) that also contributes to the work's characteristic stamp. The Second Concerto was written not long after Shostakovich had released a number of the intense works he had concealed during the depths of the Stalin era. It came as a sharp contrast, reflecting as it did the optimism and sense of freedom that followed the death of the Russian dictator. The beauty of the slow movement is ideally balanced by the vigour of the first, and the madcap high spirits of the last. The poignant movement for piano and orchestra from the Suite from the 1951 film *The Unforgettable Year 1919*, "The assault on beautiful Gorky", provides an excellent addition to this disc of perceptive and zestful performances by Alexeev. He is most capably supported by the ECO under Maksymiuk, and the engineers have done them proud with a recording of great clarity and finesse. A joyous issue.

Additional recommendation ...
Concerto for piano, trumpet and strings. **Lutoslawski.** *Paganini Variations.* **Rachmaninov.** *Rhapsody on a Theme of Paganini, Op. 43.* **Peter Jablonski** (pf); **Raymond Simmons** (tpt); **Royal Philharmonic Orchestra/Vladimir Ashkenazy.** Decca 436 239-2DH — 55m DDD 12/92

Shostakovich. Violin Concertos — No. 1 in A minor, Op. 99; No. 2 in C sharp minor, Op. 129. **Lydia Mordkovitch** (vn); **Scottish National Orchestra/Neeme Järvi.** Chandos CHAN8820. Recorded in 1989.

1h 9m DDD 4/90 

These two heartfelt violin concertos are fine examples of Shostakovich's genius. It is the First, composed in 1948 for David Oistrakh, that is the better known and some people think it the finer work; but the Second was written for the same violinist two decades later and Lydia Mordkovitch, who studied with him in Moscow, reveals its sparer lines no less successfully than the big romantic gestures of No. 1. Her tone has a dark warmth that suits the soliloquizing lyrical music of these pieces admirably, but she is also not afraid to be uncompromisingly rough and tough (more so than Oistrakh himself) in the delivery of the scherzo and finale of the First Concerto as well as its great cadenza. Neeme Järvi is himself a committed performer of the Shostakovich symphonies who well understands the composer's style, and the Scottish National Orchestra sounds as Russian as anyone could wish, even to the tone of its brass section, which has the fine principal horn that both concertos require. The recording of the solo violin is closer than one would hear in the concert hall — Glasgow's City Hall in this case — and at times (for example, the cadenza of the First Concerto) positively tactile and percussive in effect, but with playing such as this few will complain. The orchestral sound is rich in the Chandos tradition and if it occasionally almost overwhelms the ear that is maybe what the composer intended. An exciting disc.

Additional recommendation ...
Nos. 1 and 2. **Dmitry Sitkovetsky** (vn); **BBC Symphony Orchestra/Andrew Davis.** Virgin Classics VC7 59601-2 — 1h 7m DDD 9/90

NEW REVIEW

Shostakovich (trans. Barshai). Symphony, Op. 73*a*. Chamber Symphony, Op. 83*a*. **Chamber Orchestra of Europe/Rudolf Barshai.** DG 435 386-2GH.

1h DDD 8/92 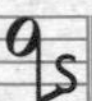

No, these are not rarely heard original compositions, but orchestrations by Barshai of Shostakovich's String Quartets Nos. 3 and 4. The conductor was originally a viola player who performed Shostakovich chamber works with the composer when the latter still played the piano in public, and thus his knowledge of the man and his style is authoritative. Some purists will question the validity or even the point of having unauthorized transcriptions such as the ones here, but many listeners will find Shostakovich's style more immediately assimilable in orchestral form. Then, having got to know the music, they may even go on to explore the leaner textures of the originals. Barshai has undoubtedly made a convincing case for his orchestrations. In the case of Op. 73*a* he has scored the work for strings and woodwind; for Op. 83*a* he has added two horns, trumpet and percussion. The earlier work is cast in five movements — a pert *Allegretto* is followed by a more astringent *Moderato* movement, then a spiky *Allegro non troppo* and an elegiac *Adagio.* This leads directly into an anguished *Moderato,* which has a distinctly unquiet ending. The original work dates from the dark Soviet days of 1946. The later quartet was originally written in 1949, and is in four movements; a warmly expressive *Allegretto,* then a romantically expressive *Andantino,* followed by a brief mysterious episode which is then linked to a final, somewhat agitated quicker movement. Barshai secures virtuoso playing from the Chamber Orchestra of Europe and the recording quality is superlative.

NEW REVIEW

Shostakovich. Chamber Symphony, Op. 110*a*. Symphony for Strings in A flat major, Op. 118*a*. String Quartet No. 15 in E flat minor, Op. 144 (arr. Rachlevsky). **Kremlin Chamber Orchestra/Misha Rachlevsky.** Claves CD50-9115.

lh 20m DDD 3/93

Shostakovich was not immune to flattery, and although he did not himself choose to arrange any of his 15 String Quartets for full string band he was happy to give such arrangements by others his blessing. A number of commentators have regretted that he did so — the gain in power in such versions tends to be offset by a loss of concentrated energy. But here is a recording which sweeps away any doubts. The Kremlin Chamber Orchestra was founded in September 1991. Not only does it sound as virtuosic as any of the specialist groups Russia has produced in recent years, but it also directs that virtuosity into subtler, less attention-seeking regions of characterization. Misha Rachlevsky encourages his players to achieve intensity as much through restraint as through abandon, and often with the barest minimum of vibrato. The sense of identity with the composer's message is almost tangible. Moreover, Rachlevsky has produced his own extremely convincing version of the funereal Fifteenth Quartet and contrived to fit all three performances onto a single, excellently recorded CD.

Additional recommendation ...

Chamber Symphony. Two Pieces, Op. 11 — Scherzo. ***Bartók.*** *Romanian folkdances, Sz68. Divertimento, Sz113.* **Zagreb Soloists/Tonko Ninic.** Pickwick PCD1000 — lh lm DDD II/92

Shostakovich (arr. Atovm'yan). The gadfly — suite, Op. 97*a*. **USSR Cinema Symphony Orchestra/Emin Khachaturian.** Classics for Pleasure CD-CFP4463. From EMI ASD3309 (2/77).

42m ADD 4/89

This film score belongs to the 1950s, a period when the composer produced some of his finest and most characteristic work, and if this is hardly profound or very personal Shostakovich it is still often striking, usually charming and unmistakably his. In a way the bargain price goes with the music: this is emphatically not top-drawer Shostakovich but it is worth having and the 1962 Melodiya recording has come up well in the present digital remastering. Sample No. 6 in the Suite, the entertaining "Galop", to see how the composer could be absolutely simple yet effective; sample the following "Introduction into the Dance" to hear how he could turn conventional phrases into something genuinely touching. The Suite shows how much music from the film was worth preserving and it has been well arranged by Lev Atovm'yan from the original score. The USSR Cinema Symphony Orchestra plays it as to the manner born.

NEW REVIEW

Shostakovich. Symphonies — No. 1 in F minor, Op. 10; No. 6 in B minor, Op. 54. **Scottish National Orchestra/Neeme Järvi.** Chandos CHAN8411. Recorded 1984-85.

lh 4m DDD 6/86

The First Symphony, the 19-year-old composer's graduation piece from the then Leningrad Conservatory in 1925, may be indebted to Stravinsky, Prokofiev, Tchaikovsky and even

Scriabin. But it rarely sounds like anything other than pure Shostakovich. The sophisticated mask of its first movement is drawn aside for a slow movement of Slav melancholy and foreboding, and the finale brilliantly stage-manages a way out. The Sixth (1939) takes the familiar Shostakovichian extremes of explosive activity and uneasy contemplation (that the composer reconciles in the finale of the First) and separates them into individual movements. Two swift movements (a mercurial but menacing *Scherzo*, and a real knees-up of a finale) follow on from an opening *Largo* whose slow lyrical declamations eventually all but freeze into immobility. Järvi has a will (and Chandos, the engineering) to explore the extremes of pace, mood and dynamics of both symphonies; his account of the First Symphony convinces precisely because those extremes intensify as the work progresses. Some may crave a fuller, firmer string sound, but the passionate intensity of the playing (in all departments) is never in doubt.

Additional recommendations ...

Nos. 1 and 3. **London Philharmonic Orchestra/Bernard Haitink.** Decca Ovation 425 063-2DM — lh 5m ADD

Nos. 1 and 6. **Royal Philharmonic Orchestra/Vladimir Ashkenazy.** Decca 425 609-2DH — lh 4m DDD 6/90

Nos. 6 and 12. **Royal Concertgebouw Orchestra/Bernard Haitink.** Decca Ovation 425 067-2DM — lh 14m DDD

Shostakovich. Symphonies — No. 2 in B major, Op. 14, "To October"[a]; No. 10 in in E minor, Op. 93[b]. **London Philharmonic [a]Choir and Orchestra/Bernard Haitink.** Decca Ovation 425 064-2DM. Texts and translations included. Items marked [a] from SXDL7535 (7/82), [b] SXL6838 (10/77).

lh 16m DDD

Slamming the door noisily on the First Symphony, which he quickly came to regard as too traditional, Shostakovich, in his early twenties, embarked on two symphonies (Nos. 2 and 3) which married "abstract experimentalism" (his own term) with choral finales whose revolutionary poems demanded simple and direct settings (the two styles distinctly unhappy bedfellows). But those looking for symphonic continuity and coherence need read no further. For this is music that daringly turns conventions upside down and inside out. His innate lyricism occasionally allows us to come up for air in between the wildly over the top gestural rhetoric. So why include this disc in the *Guide*? Simply because the untamed creative energy is more often exhilarating than exhausting and much of the language of the later symphonies is explicitly foreshadowed. Haitink's version of No. 10, whilst not ultimately so compelling as Karajan's (reviewed further on), is nonetheless generally a perfectably acceptable performance. Decca's admirable recording belies its years.

Shostakovich. Symphony No. 4 in C minor, Op. 43. **Scottish National Orchestra/Neeme Järvi.** Chandos CHAN8640.

lh lm DDD 12/89 9s

Shostakovich withdrew the Fourth Symphony before its first performance and one can readily see why: Stalin would have loathed it. It is a work of extraordinary bitterness and anger, curdled with dissonance, raucous derision and eerie unease, the very model of what a Soviet symphony should not be, but at the same time the teeming cauldron from which much of the troubling ambiguity of Shostakovich's later style was cast. It needs a performance that takes risks, not least of setting the listener's teeth on edge and of terrifying him out of his wits. Järvi is prepared to allow his orchestra to yell at times to allow the occasional ugly, poisoned sound in a work that boils with discontent but also with sheer unreleased creative energy. No one who admires the Fifth Symphony should be without a recording of the Fourth that presents its towering frustration and disquiet at full strength. Järvi does so more successfully than any other conductor. Both his orchestra and the recording engineers hang on like grim death. The effect can only be described as magnificently appalling.

Additional recommendations ...
No. 4. **London Philharmonic Orchestra/Bernard Haitink.** Decca Ovation 425 065-2DM — lh 8m DDD
No. 4. Suite No. 1 for Jazz Band. **soloists ensemble; USSR Ministry of Culture State Symphony Orchestra/Gennadi Rozhdestvensky.** Olympia OCD156 — lh 15m DDD/AAD 5/89
National Symphony Orchestra/Mstislav Rostropovich. Teldec 9031 76261-1 — lh 5m DDD 11/92

Shostakovich. Symphony No. 5 in D minor, Op. 47. Ballet Suite No. 5, Op. 27*a*. **Scottish National Orchestra/Neeme Järvi.** Chandos CHAN8650. Recorded in 1988.

lh 16m DDD 4/90 

There are more Shostakovich Fifths than you can shake a stick at in the CD catalogue at present, and several of them are very good. Järvi's makes perhaps the safest recommendation of them all: it has a generous coupling (which cannot be said of many of its rivals), it has no drawbacks (save, for some tastes, a slight touch of heart-on-sleeve in the slow movement) and a number of distinct advantages. A profound seriousness, for one thing, and an absolute sureness about the nature of the finale, which many conductors feel the need to exaggerate, either as brassy optimism or as bitter irony. Järvi takes it perfectly straight, denying neither option, and the progression from slow movement (the overtness of its emotion finely justified) to finale seems more natural, less of a jolt than usual. The SNO cannot rival the sheer massiveness of sound of some of the continental orchestras who have recorded this work, but while listening one hardly notices the lack, so urgent and polished is their playing. A very natural and wide-ranging recording, too, and the lengthy Suite (eight movements from Shostakovich's early ballet *The Bolt*, forming an exuberantly entertaining essay on the various modes that his sense of humour could take) makes much more than a mere fill-up.

Additional recommendations ...
No. 5. Five Fragments, Op. 42. **Royal Philharmonic Orchestra/Vladimir Ashkenazy.** Decca 421 120-2DH — 56m DDD 6/88 B
No. 5. **Hallé Orchestra/Stanislav Skrowaczewski.** Pickwick IMP Classics PCD940 — 48m DDD 8/91 B
No. 5[a]. *Cello Concerto No. 1 in E flat major, Op. 107*[b]. [a]**New York Philharmonic Orchestra/Leonard Bernstein;** [b]**Yo-Yo Ma** (vc); [b]**Philadelphia Orchestra/Eugene Ormandy.** CBS Maestro CD44903 — lh 17m DDD 4/90 £ B
Nos. 5 and 9. **Atlanta Symphony Orchestra/Yoel Levi.** Telarc CD80215 — lh 18m DDD 6/90 B
No. 5. Novorossisk Chimes. October — symphonic poem, Op. 131. Overture on Russian and Kirghiz Folk Themes, Op. 115. **Royal Philharmonic Orchestra/Enrique Bátiz.** ASV CDDCA707 — lh 16m DDD 9/90 B
No. 5. Festival Overture, Op. 96. **London Symphony Orchestra/Maxim Shostakovich.** Collins Classics 1108-2 — 59m DDD 9/90 B

Shostakovich. Symphonies — No. 7 in C major, Op. 60, "Leningrad". No. 1 in F minor, Op. 10. **Chicago Symphony Orchestra/Leonard Bernstein.** DG 427 632-2GH2. Recorded in 1988.

② 2h DDD 1/90

The *Leningrad* Symphony was composed in haste as the Nazis sieged and bombarded the city (in 1941). It caused an immediate sensation, but posterity has been less enthusiastic. What business has the first movement's unrelated long central 'invasion' episode doing in a symphonic movement? Is the material of the finale really distinctive enough for its protracted treatment? Michael Oliver, in his original *Gramophone* review wrote that in this performance "the Symphony sounds most convincingly like a symphony, and one needing no programme to justify it". Added to which, and no disrespect is intended by this observation, the work's epic and cinematic manner has surely never been more powerfully realized. These are live recordings, with occasional noise from the audience (and the conductor), but the Chicago Orchestra has rarely sounded more polished or committed under any conditions. The strings are superb in the First Symphony, full and weightily present, and Bernstein's manner in this Symphony is comparably bold and theatrical of gesture. A word of caution: set your volume control carefully for the *Leningrad* Symphony's start; it is scored for six of both trumpets and trombones, and in the above mentioned 'invasion' episode, no other recording has reproduced them so clearly, and to such devastating effect.

Shostakovich. Symphony No. 8 in C minor, Op. 65. **Leningrad Philharmonic Orchestra/Evgeni Mravinsky.** Philips 422 442-2PH. Recorded at a performance in Leningrad in February 1982.

1h ADD 6/89

Dedicated to Mravinsky, the Eighth Symphony, written in 1943, two years after the *Leningrad*, offers a wiser, more bitterly disillusioned Shostakovich. The heroic peroration of the Seventh's finale is here replaced by numbed whimsy and eventual uneasy calm. Whether the grim visions that the journey there depicts are wartime or peacetime ones, rarely can a performance have presented them with more lacerating force. The solo cor anglais, after the first movement's central climax, plays as if his very life depended on his lament being heard at the other side of the world. Speeds are generally faster than we are used to from western interpreters, and the standard of playing, given the risks taken, and that this is a one-off live performance, defies criticism. If you're cursed with perfect pitch you will notice that the whole Symphony is a semitone sharper than it should be; for the rest of us, only a restricted dynamic range mars an excellent piece of engineering. The Leningrad audience, clearly immobilized, maintain an awed silence.

Additional recommendations ...
No. 8. **Concertgebouw Orchestra/Bernard Haitink.** Decca Ovation 425 071-2DM — 1h 2m DDD
No. 8. **Washington National Symphony Orchestra/Mstislav Rostropovich.** Teldec 9031-74719-2 — 1h 1m DDD 10/92

Shostakovich. Symphonies — No. 9 in E flat major, Op. 70; No. 5 in D minor, Op. 47. **USSR Ministry of Culture State Symphony Orchestra/Gennadi Rozhdestvensky.** Olympia OCD113.

1h 13m DDD 5/89

Some of Rozhdestvensky's interpretations in his Shostakovich cycle on Olympia are quirky in the extreme. In the Fifth Symphony he is at his most restrained, and the result is one of the finest accounts on CD of this much-recorded work. Listening to it you wonder why so many conductors fail to achieve a natural flow, and why those who do achieve it often sound bland. Rozhdestvensky gives us just about the best of both worlds, as he does in the Ninth Symphony — a kind of not-the-Ninth-Symphony, written in 1945 in a spirit of deliberate non-celerbation and full of black humour and evasiveness. Neither playing nor recording are in the highest class, but the communicative instincts are in the right place throughout and the coupling is a generous one.

Additional recommendation ...
No. 9. No. 15 in A major, Op. 141. **Royal Philharmonic Orchestra/Vladimir Ashkenazy.** Decca 430 227-2DH — 1h 5m DDD 10/92

Shostakovich. Symphony No. 10 in E minor, Op. 93. **Berlin Philharmonic Orchestra/Herbert von Karajan.** DG Galleria 429 716-2GGA. From SLPM139020 (1/69). Recorded in 1966.

51m ADD 8/90  

Stalin died on 5 March 1953, the same day as Prokofiev. In the summer of that year Shostakovich produced a symphony which can be taken as his own return to life after the dark night of dictatorship — the last two movements included, for the first time in his output, his personal DSCH signature (the notes D, E flat, C, B natural, in the German spelling). In the West the Tenth Symphony is now widely regarded as the finest of the cycle of 15, not just for its sheer depth of personal feeling, but because it finds the purest and subtlest musical representation of that feeling. Perhaps this is why it is less dependent than some of Shostakovich's major works on a conductor steeped in the Russian idiom. Karajan's profound grasp of the overall drama unites with a superb instinct for atmosphere and mood to put the earlier of his two recordings into a class of its own. It is a performance of compelling integrity and sweep, with an almost palpable sense of what is at stake emotionally. The recording sounds a little bass-heavy in this digital remastering but is still far more realistic than Karajan's 1982 remake.

Additional recommendations ...
No. 10. Hamlet — Suite, Op. 32: excerpts[a]. **USSR Ministry of Culture State Symphony Orchestra/Gennadi Rozhdestvensky; [a]Leningrad Chamber Orchestra/Eduard Serov.** Olympia OCD131 — lh 9 DDD/ADD 5/89 B
No. 10. **Hallé Orchestra/Stanislaw Skrowaczewski.** Pickwick IMP Classics PCD955 — 52m DDD 10/91 B
No. 10. ***Lutoslawski.*** *Funeral music.* **Cleveland Orchestra/Christoph von Dohnányi.** Decca 430 844-2DH — lh 5m DDD 9/92 B

Shostakovich. Symphony No. 11 in G minor, Op. 103, "The year 1905". **Concertgebouw Orchestra/Bernard Haitink.** Decca Ovation 425 072-2DM. From 411 939-2DH2 (8/85). Recorded in 1982.

lh lm DDD

Shostakovich's Eleventh Symphony is a real challenge to the interpreter. The work makes extensive use of a sequence of bold, poster-like images of the abortive 1905 uprising in Russia, using a number of tunes that are not Shostakovich's own (revolutionary songs of the period, mostly) and are not wholly suited to a symphonic structure on such a scale. The orchestral playing throughout is of the utmost splendour: the sheer power and attack of the strings especially is rendered with precision as well as weight. The recording is very clean, natural and spacious.

Shostakovich. Symphony No. 13, "Babi Yar". **Marius Rintzler** (bass); male voices of the **Concertgebouw Orchestra Choir; Concertgebouw Orchestra/Bernard Haitink.** Decca Ovation 425 073-2DM. From 417 261-2DH (5/86). Notes, texts and translations included.

lh 4m DDD

In 1962 Shostakovich, setting Yevtushenko's poetry, made a bold public statement about concerns close to his heart. One of his most unambiguous works, the symphony's five movements are powerful, impassioned statements on anti-semitism, the indestructible power of humour, Russian women "who have endured everything", fears of the informer, and finally, artistic integrity. With its direct and simple (though never plain) appeal, and the texts divided between a solo bass and a unison male chorus, it is Shostakovich at his most Mussorgskian. It is a pity that Marius Rintzler isn't as passionate in manner as he is sonorous of tone, but worries that the Dutch chorus may lack the range and richness of Russian men, or that the woodwinds' humour may not be sharp-edged enough are confounded in Haitink's vividly characterized account. Decca, superseding their own previous triumphs in the Concertgebouw, produce spectacularly ample and spacious sound; full and firm in the bass (so many of the themes are for cellos and basses) and able to resolve the massive tuttis as clearly and coherently as the work's frequent chamber-like textures.

Shostakovich. Symphony No. 14[a]. Six Poems of Marina Tsvetayeva[b]. [a]**Julia Varády** (sop); [b]**Ortrun Wenkel** (contr); [a]**Dietrich Fischer-Dieskau** (bar); **Concertgebouw**

Orchestra/Bernard Haitink. Decca Ovation 425 074-2DM. Texts and translations included. From 417 514-2DH (3/87).

lh 13m DDD 3/87

"I'll follow my career in such a way that I'm not following it" sings the soloist at the end of the Thirteenth Symphony, followed by the exquisitely private sound of solo violin and viola. And so it was to be. There were no more public statements. The Fourteenth is not a symphony at all, but a song cycle on the theme of Death, for a soprano and bass with a small complement of strings and light percussion; and the Fifteenth is a series of unresolved riddles. This is a unique and logical coupling: the poems of the symphony are sung here in the original languages (a version which had the composer's approval); and both the Symphony and the Tsvetayeva cycle are essentially private expressions. The expressions, though, of scorn, bitterness and, in the symphony, violence, are as potent as ever, the more so for their needle-sharp presentation by a small ensemble. There are one or two moments in the symphony where Haitink does not live dangerously enough and, arguably, the recording over-projects Fischer-Dieskau and Varády, but this is the most consistently satisfying version currently available. As ever, the Concertgebouw acoustic supplies atmosphere in abundance without ever impeding clarity.

Shostakovich. Symphony No. 15 in A major[a]. From Jewish Poetry, Op. 79[b]. [b]**Elisabeth Söderström** (sop); [b]**Ortrun Wenkel** (contr); [b]**Ryszard Karcykowski** (ten); [a]**London Philharmonic Orchestra,** [b]**Concertgebouw Orchestra/Bernard Haitink.** Decca Ovation 425 069-2DM. Notes, text and translation included. From 417 581-2DH (4/87).

lh 13m AAD 4/87

By the end of the 1960s Shostakovich was an ill and troubled man and it seemed that his death-haunted Fourteenth Symphony of 1969 would be his last. Instead, in 1971 he produced this surprising successor, with a definite key of A major but also enigmatic quotations from Rossini's *William Tell* Overture and Wagner's *Ring* cycle besides several from his own music and his favourite DSCH (D, E flat, C, B) motto. The Rossini was bouncy, and the Wagner profoundly gloomy — but what did it all mean? Later the composer offered some clues, for example saying that the first movement represents a toyshop at night with the toys coming to life, but the suspicion remains that the work has other darker secrets. Bernard Haitink understands this Russian world in which the childishly playful and the grimly grotesque co-exist, and his orchestra play the music as to the manner born, with fine work from the important percussion section of 12 instruments besides timpani which include vibraphone and bells. The other work is earlier: it was written in 1948 after Shostakovich found a book of Jewish poetry and felt that a vocal cycle could help combat the increasing anti-Semitism that he saw around him. It was not, in fact, performed until 1955, during the cultural thaw that came after Stalin's death, and was orchestrated later. "Jews were tormented for so long that they express despair in dance music", said the composer, but though this big cycle hardly makes for cosy listening it has a fine semitic character and the performance and recording are splendid.

Shostakovich. String Quartets — No. 1 in C major, Op. 49; No. 3 in F major, Op. 73; No. 4 in D major, Op. 83. **Brodsky Quartet** (Michael Thomas, Ian Belton, vns; Paul Cassidy, va; Jacqueline Thomas, vc). Teldec 2292-46009-2. Recorded in 1989.

lh 12m DDD 6/90

The young Brodsky Quartet are in the course of issuing a complete cycle of Shostakovich's string quartets and on this evidence it should be well worth collecting. The First, Third and Fourth Quartets make a particularly absorbing coupling, with hinted depths and plans for further exploration clearly audible beneath the acknowledgements to quartet tradition in the First (which also has a touch of very likeable open-eyed naïvety to it), an enormous step forward to the grandeur of the Third's impassioned slow movement and a path forward firmly indicated by the troubled ambiguities and poignancies of the Fourth. The Brodsky will have the range for the complete cycle, there seems no doubt of that; already there is a fine balance between bigness of gesture and an expressive but strong lyricism. They are especially good at pacing and concentration over a long span, too, and they leap the technical hurdles with ease. A very clean and direct but rather close recording; but the sense of being amidst such responsive players, almost watching their intentness, has its own rewards.

Additional recommendation ...

No. 1. No. 2 in A major, Op. 68. Nos. 3 and 4. No. 5 in B flat major, Op. 92. No. 6 in G major, Op. 101. No. 7 in F sharp minor, Op. 108. No. 8 in C minor, Op. 110. No. 9 in E flat major, Op. 117. No. 10 in A flat major, Op. 118. No. 11 in F minor, Op. 122. No. 12 in D flat major, Op. 133. No. 13 in B flat minor, Op. 138. No. 14 in F sharp minor. No. 15 in E flat minor, Op. 144. **Fitzwilliam Quartet.** Decca Enterprise 433 078-2DM6 — ⑥ 6h 17m ADD 6/92

Shostakovich. String Quartet No. 8 in C minor, Op. 110.
Tippett. String Quartet No. 3. **Duke Quartet** (Louise Fuller, Martin Smith, vns; John Metcalfe, va; Ivan McCready, vc). Factory Classical FACD246.

51m DDD 1/90 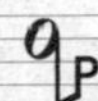

Shostakovich's Eighth is his most 'public' quartet, a sustained and bitter outcry at oppression and inhumanity. Its official dedication is "in memory of the victims of fascism and war"; but its copious self-quotations and its incessant use of the composer's musical monogram DSCH (D, E flat, C, B in German notation) makes it clear that the work is 'about' far more than the aftermath of the Second World War. Tippett's Third, by contrast, is in a sense his most private quartet, a prolonged and at times visionary wrestling with the shade of Beethoven, containing audacious formal experiments. By choosing for their recording début two of the most technically and expressively demanding works in the repertory, the young Duke Quartet certainly nailed their colours to the mast. They are powerfully communicative players, with what seems like a burning desire to convey the protesting grief of the Shostakovich and the sometimes inward, sometimes ecstatic musings of the Tippett. They have the virtuoso technique and the ample tone to achieve this. No less important, they have a very firm sense of the music's impulse; whether the movement is fast or slow, there is a strong feeling of forward impetus and clearly perceived destination. The recording, appropriately enough, brings these passionately urgent readings very close to the listener.

Additional recommendation ...

No. 8. 24 Preludes and Fugues (arr. Dubrinsky) — No. 1 in C major; No. 15 in E flat major.
Tchaikovsky. *String Quartet No. 1 in D major, Op. 11.* **Lafayette Quartet.** Dorian DOR90163 — 1h 8m DDD 7/92

Shostakovich. Piano Quintet in G minor, Op. 57[a]. String Quartets — No. 7 in F sharp minor, Op. 108; No. 8 in C minor, Op. 110. [a]**Sviatoslav Richter** (pf); **Borodin Quartet** (Mikhail Kopelman, Andrei Abramenkov, vns; Dmitri Shebalin, va; Valentin Berlinsky, vc). EMI CDC7 47507-2. From EL270338-1 (11/85).

1h 10m ADD 10/87 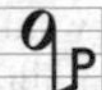

The Seventh and Eighth Quartets are separated by only one opus number and both works inhabit a dark and sombre sound world. The Seventh is dedicated to the memory of his first wife, Nina, who died in 1954 and is one of his shortest and most concentrated quartets. The Eighth Quartet provides a perfect introduction to Shostakovich's music. It is very much an autobiographical work. The Piano Quintet is almost symphonic in its proportions, lasting some 35 minutes and has been popular with audiences ever since its first performance in 1940. Much of its popularity stems from Shostakovich's highly memorable material, particularly in the boisterous and genial Scherzo and finale movements. The Borodin Quartet play with great authority and conviction and in the Seventh Quartet there is a fine sense of poetry and intimacy. Richter's performance of the Piano Quintet matches the grandeur of the work, with playing that has tremendous power and strength. The recording, taken from a live performance, is rather dry with a slightly hard piano sound, but this does little to distract from so commanding a performance as this. The earlier studio recordings of the string quartets are well recorded. An excellent introduction to the chamber music of Shostakovich.

NEW REVIEW

Shostakovich. Violin Sonata, Op. 134. Viola Sonata, Op. 147. **Shlomo Mintz** (vn, va); **Victoria Postnikova** (pf). Erato 2292-45804-2. Recorded in 1991.

lh 9m DDD 11/92

These are two of the most unremittingly bleak works in the entire chamber repertoire — Shostakovich in his last decade was more or less free to choose whatever musical means would suit his message, and that message drains the cup of sorrow to its bitterest dregs. What strange force compels us then to listen? Perhaps it is simply our responsibility to commemorate even the darkest aspects of life in the twentieth century; perhaps it is also the sense that such experiences can be survived and transfigured through the creative will. Certainly performances as intense, yet subtle, as Mintz's and Postnikova's leave you awe-struck rather than simply despairing. Erato's recording could perhaps have been a little more immediate, and Mintz's viola sound is not as individual as some. But his grasp of the idiom is extraordinary, and Postnikova is an ideal partner. It is a joy to welcome playing which gets so consistently to the emotional core.

Shostakovich. 24 Preludes and Fugues, Op. 87. **Tatyana Nikolaieva** (pf). Hyperion CDA66441/3. Recorded in 1990.

2h 46m DDD 3/91

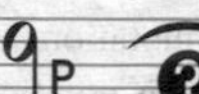

Even if you didn't know that Shostakovich had written his 24 Preludes and Fugues specially for Tatyana Nikolaieva it would be difficult not to sense the unique authority. The playing isn't without the odd small blemish here and there (memory lapses?) and the reverberant acoustic adds a sustaining pedal effect of its own in one or two places, but for playing of such strength, character and insight one would willingly put up with far worse. Inevitably, particular pieces linger in the memory — the impassioned F sharp minor Fugue, the dancing A major Prelude or the haunted stillness of the B flat minor Fugue — but the most impressive aspect of Nikolaieva's interpretation is the way she communicates her belief that these 24 small pieces add up to a complete musical experience — after this it's very difficult to disagree: the monumental D minor Fugue really does feel like the final stage in a long and fascinatingly varied process. If you still think that Shostakovich's contribution to piano literature is relatively insignificant, try this.

NEW REVIEW

Shostakovich. Suite on Verses of Michelangelo Buonarroti, Op. 145*a*[a]. Four Verses of Captain Lebyadkin, Op.146*a*. **Dietrich Fischer-Dieskau** (bar); **Radio-Symphonie-Orchester Berlin/Vladimir Ashkenazy** ([a]pf). Decca 433 319-2DH. Recorded in 1991.

5lm DDD

"You have believed, lord, in untrue fables and tittle-tattlers are rewarded by you; I am your good servant: my labours are devoted to you, like the rays of the sun; but you are not pleased with all I want to do, and my efforts are all in vain." Michelangelo's words set to Shostakovich's music, an alliance that's hardly surprising given the constraints of censorship and the pain of disapproval that Shostakovich suffered throughout his career. But the "Michelangelo Verses" (as Op. 145*a* is sometimes referred to) is no mere reaction against Soviet Russia's one-time ruling powers; rather, it amounts to a deeply expressive, searching, even sensual parting gesture, a profound late utterance by a man who knew that death was close to hand. The music itself alternates between finely-honed reflection ("Morning", "Love", "Separation"), violent outbursts ("Anger", "Creativity") and child-like simplicity ("Immortality"); it is economically (though imaginatively) scored, yet leaves an extremely powerful impression. The coupling provides an apposite, if somewhat jarring contrast: a brief song-cycle (composed at about the same time as the *Michelangelo* Suite), to texts by Dostoevsky, a vivid and disturbing study in parody, and shot through with political metaphor. It's a bit like Mussorgsky, but more ranting in tone and coarser-grained. Both performances are beautifully considered, although Fischer-Dieskau's consummate artistry isn't always matched by parallel vocal refinement, at least not where the music calls for declamation. Still, there's much beautiful singing on offer (especially in the predominantly lyrical *Michelangelo* Suite) and Ashkenazy's supportive accompaniments — both solo and orchestral — are admirable.

Further listening ...

Cello Sonata in D minor, Op. 40. Moderato for cello and piano. *Coupled with* **Prokofiev.** Cello Sonata in C major, Op. 119. **Lynn Harrell** (vc); **Vladimir Ashkenazy** (pf). Decca 421 774-2DH (3/90).

Piano Trio No. 2 in E minor, Op. 67. *Coupled with* **Ravel.** Piano Trio in A minor. **Trio Zingara.** Collins Classics 1040-2 (3/90).

LADY MACBETH OF THE MTSENSK DISTRICT. **Soloists; Ambrosian Opera Chorus; London Philharmonic Orchestra/Mstislav Rostropovich.** EMI CDS7 49955-2 (5/90).

Jean Sibelius

Finnish 1865-1957

Sibelius. Violin Concerto in D major, Op. 47 (original 1903-04 version and final 1905 version). **Leonidas Kavakos** (vn); **Lahti Symphony Orchestra/Osmo Vänskä.** BIS CD500.

1h 15m DDD 4/91

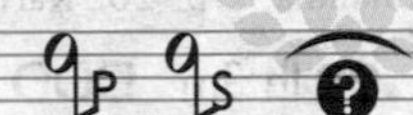

In the 1950s the BBC Third Programme regularly broadcast a series called "Birth of an opera" which traced the evolution of an operatic masterpiece from gestation to first performance. This disc could almost be called "Birth of a Concerto", for it offers Sibelius's first thoughts alongside the final version of the Violin Concerto. After its unsuccessful first performance in Helsinki in 1904, the composer decided to overhaul it and putting the two versions alongside each other is an absorbing experience. One is first brought up with a start by an incisive figure just over a minute into the proceedings after which the orchestra does all sorts of 'unexpected' things! In the unaccompanied cadenza 21 bars later there is some rhythmic support while to the next idea on cellos and bassoon (figure 2), the soloist contributes decoration. And then at seven bars before figure 3 a delightful new idea appears which almost looks forward to the light colourings of the later *Humoresques*. Although it is a great pity that it had to go, there is no doubt that the structural coherence of the movement gains by its loss both here and on its reappearance. It is the ability to sacrifice good ideas in the interest of structural coherence that is the hallmark of a good composer. The fewest changes are in the slow movement which remains at the same length. As in the case of the Fifth Symphony where the revision is far more extensive than it is here the finished work tells us a great deal about the quality of Sibelius's artistic judgment, and that, of course, is what makes him such a great composer. This disc offers an invaluable insight into the workings of his mind, and even in its own right, the 1904 version has many incidental beauties to delight us. Leonidas Kavakos and the Lahti Orchestra play splendidly throughout and the familiar concerto which was struggling to get out of the 1903-04 version emerges equally safely in their hands.

Additional recommendations ...

Violin Concerto[a]. **Glazunov.** *Violin Concerto in A minor, Op. 82*[b]. **Prokofiev.** *Violin Concerto No. 2 in G minor, Op. 63*[c]. **Jascha Heifetz** (vn); [a]**Chicago Symphony Orchestra/Walter Hendl;** [b]**RCA Victor Symphony Orchestra/Walter Hendl;** [c]**Boston Symphony Orchestra/Charles Münch;** RCA Red Seal RD87019 — 1h 9m ADD 10/86 ▲

Violin Concerto[a]. **Brahms.** *Violin Concerto in D major, Op. 77*[b]. **Ginette Neveu** (vn); **Philharmonia Orchestra/**[a]**Walter Susskind,** [b]**Issay Dobrowen.** EMI Références mono CDH7 61011-2 — 1h 10m ADD 3/88 ▲

Violin Concerto. Symphony No. 5 in E flat major, Op. 82. **Nigel Kennedy** (vn); **City of Birmingham Symphony Orchestra/Simon Rattle.** EMI CDC7 49717-2 — 1h 2m DDD 9/88

Violin Concerto. **Bruch.** *Violin Concerto in G minor, Op. 26.* **Shizuka Ishikawa** (vn); **Brno State Philharmonic Orchestra/Jirí Bělohlávek.** Supraphon Gems 2SUP 0002 — 56m AAD 9/88 £

Violin Concerto[a]. **Dvořák.** *Violin Concerto in A minor, B108*[b]. **Salvatore Accardo** (vn); [a]**Concertgebouw Orchestra,** [b]**London Symphony Orchestra/Sir Colin Davis.** Philips Silver Line 420 895-2PSL — 1h 8m ADD 10/88
Violin Concerto[a]. *Overture in A minor. Menuetto. In Memoriam, Op. 59.* [a]**Silvia Marcovici** (vn); **Gothenburg Symphony Orchestra/Neeme Järvi.** BIS CD372 — 54m DDD 1/89
Violin Concerto[a]. **Prokofiev.** *Violin Concerto No. 2 in G minor, Op. 63*[a]. **R. Strauss.** *Violin Sonata in E flat major, Op. 18*[c]. **Jascha Heifetz** (vn); [c]**Arpád Sándor** (pf); [a]**London Philharmonic Orchestra/Sir Thomas Beecham;** [b]**Boston Symphony Orchestra/Serge Koussevitzky.** Biddulph mono LAB018 — 1h 18m ADD 1/91 ▲
Violin Concerto. Six Humoresques, Opp. 87 and 89a. Two Humoresques, Op. 69. Two Serenades, Op. 69. **Joseph Swensen** (vn); **Finnish Radio Symphony Orchestra/Jukka-Pekka Saraste.** RCA Victor Red Seal 09026 60444-2 — 1h 6m DDD 1/93
Violin Concerto. **Brahms.** *Violin Concerto.* **Tasmin Little** (vn); **Royal Liverpool Philharmonic Orchestra/Vernon Handley.** EMI Eminence CD-EMX2203 *(see review under Brahms; refer to the Index to Reviews)* — 1h 12m DDD 2/93 £

Sibelius. ORCHESTRAL WORKS. **Philharmonia Orchestra/Vladimir Ashkenazy.**
Decca Ovation 417 762-2DM. From 417 378-1DM5. Recorded 1980-85.
Finlandia, Op. 26. Karelia Suite, Op. 11. Tapiola, Op. 112. En Saga, Op. 9.

1h 3m DDD 12/88 £

More than 30 years separate *En Saga* and *Tapiola*, yet both works are quintessential Sibelius. The latter is often praised for the way Sibelius avoided 'exotic' instruments, preferring instead to draw new and inhuman sounds from the more standard ones; and the former is, in many ways, just as striking in the way Sibelius's orchestration evokes wind, strange lights, vast expanses and solitude. Both works suggest some dream-like journey; *En Saga* non-specific though derived from Nordic legend; *Tapiola* more of an airborne nightmare in, above and around the mighty giants of the Northern forests inhabited by the Green Man of the Kalevala, the forest god Tapio (the final amen of slow, bright major chords brings a blessed release!). Ashkenazy's judgement of long term pacing is very acute; the silences and shadows are as potent here as the wildest hurricane. And Decca's sound allows you to visualize both the wood and the trees: every detail of Sibelius's sound world is caught with uncanny presence, yet the overall orchestral image is coherent and natural. In addition, his *Finlandia* boasts some of the most vibrant and powerful brass sounds on disc.

Additional recommendation ...
Finlandia. Legends, Op. 22 — No. 2, The swan of Tuonela. Kuolema, Op. 44 — Valse triste. Tapiola. **Berlin Philharmonic Orchestra/Herbert von Karajan.** DG 413 755-2GH — 44m DDD 1/85

Sibelius. ORCHESTRAL WORKS. **Gothenburg Symphony Orchestra/Neeme Järvi.** BIS CD312.
Pohjola's daughter, Op. 49. Rakastava, Op. 14. Tapiola, Op. 112. Andante lirico.

56m DDD 6/87

This disc offers two of Sibelius's most powerful and concentrated symphonic poems together with one of his most affecting works, *Rakastava* for strings, timpani and triangle. *Tapiola* is his last major work, a terrifying evocation of the vast forests of the North and the spirits that dwell within them. *Pohjola's daughter* is one of the greatest examples of the genre, having all the narrative power of a Strauss tone poem and yet the concentration and organic cohesion of a symphonic movement. *Rakastava* began life as a work for unaccompanied male voices in 1894 but Sibelius reworked it at about the time of the Fourth Symphony (1911) to striking effect. The *Andante lirico*, alternatively known as the Impromptu for string orchestra, is a rarity from 1893 (the year after the *Kullervo* Symphony and before *The Swan of Tuonela*), which draw for its material on the last two of the Impromptus, Op. 5. Persuasive and splendidly recorded performances by the Gothenburg Orchestra under Neeme Järvi.

Sibelius. ORCHESTRAL WORKS. **Royal Philharmonic Orchestra/Sir Thomas Beecham.** EMI Beecham Edition CDM7 63400-2. Recorded in 1955.
Pelléas et Mélisande — incidental music, Op. 46. The Oceanides, Op. 73. Symphony No. 7 in C major, Op. 105 (all from HMV ASD468, 7/62). Tapiola, Op. 112 (ASD518, 4/63).

1h 16m ADD 7/90 £ 9p ▲

Sibelius. ORCHESTRAL WORKS. [a]**Royal Philharmonic Orchestra;** [b]**BBC Symphony Orchestra;** [c]**London Philharmonic Orchestra/Sir Thomas Beecham.** EMI Beecham Edition mono CDM7 63397-2. Recorded 1938-1955.
The Tempest — incidental music, Op. 109 (from Philips ABR4045, 12/55)[a]. Scènes historiques: Op. 25 — No. 3, Festivo; Op. 66 (both from Columbia 33C1018, 11/53)[a]. Karelia Suite, Op. 11 — No. 1, Intermezzo; No. 3, Alla marcia (HMV DB6248. Recorded 1945)[b]. Finlandia, Op. 26 (Columbia LX704, 4/38)[c].

1h 13m ADD 7/90 £ 9p ▲

Sibelius. ORCHESTRAL WORKS. [a]**London Philharmonic Orchestra,** [b]**Royal Philharmonic Orchestra/Sir Thomas Beecham.** EMI Beecham edition mono CDM7 64027-2. Recorded 1937-47.
Symphonies — No. 4 in A minor, Op. 63[a] (from HMV DB3351/5, 3/38); No. 6 in D minor, Op. 104[b] (DB6640/42, 6/50). The Tempest — incidental music, Op. 109: Prelude[a] (DB3894, 12/39). Legends, Op. 22 — Lemminkäinen's Homeward Journey[a] (DB3355/6, 3/38). The bard, Op. 64[a] (DB3891, 12/39).

1h 19m ADD 3/92 £ 9p ▲

One of the special things about Beecham's Sibelius was its sheer sonority: there was a fresh, vernal sheen on the strings quite different from the opulence of Koussevitzky or Karajan but with all their flexibility and plasticity of phrasing, and a magic that is easier to discern than define. Suffice it to say that his feeling for atmosphere in Sibelius was always matched by a strong grip on the architecture. The first CD collects together some of his greatest performances from the early days of stereo — *Pelleas, Tapiola* and *The Oceanides*, the latter recorded specifically at Sibelius's request. They are unsurpassed in atmosphere and poetic feeling. His 1956 recording of the two suites from *The Tempest* enjoys legendary status and is pure magic. The 1952 performances of four of the *Scènes historiques* have that similar ring of authenticity that transcend any sonic limitations. Beecham's stark account of the Fourth Symphony carries special authority since it was done after a long correspondence with the composer; and the 1947 RPO performance of the Sixth enjoyed Sibelius's imprimatur. The Prelude to *The Tempest* is as chillingly realistic as *Lemminkainen's Homeward Journey* is exciting.

Additional recommendation ...
Pelleas and Melisande. Swanwhite, Op. 54 — excerpts. King Christian II — incidental music, Op. 27[a]. [a]**Sauli Tiilikainen** (bar); **Iceland Symphony Orchestra/Petri Sakari.** Chandos CHAN9158 — 1h 19m DDD 7/93 9p

Sibelius. Four Legends, Op. 22. **Gothenburg Symphony Orchestra/Neeme Järvi.** BIS CD294.

49m DDD 6/86 9p 9s

In later life Sibelius spoke of the Op. 22 *Legends* as "a kind of Kalevala symphony", though the four tone poems do not have the organic cohesion of the four movements of the First and Second symphonies. He revised them twice, once in 1897 and then again in 1900, though only *The Swan of Tuonela* and *Lemminkäinen's Homeward Journey* entered the repertoire. (The other two remained tucked away in a drawer until the 1930s: indeed, the whole work was not performed in its entirety until after the Second World War.) The very opening of the first one, *Lemminkäinen and the maidens of the island* establishes an entirely new voice in music as, for that matter does *The Swan*, which was originally the Prelude to a projected opera, *The Building of the Boat*. Neeme Järvi gives a passionate and atmospheric account of this lovely movement and his performance of *The Swan* is altogether magical. He takes a broader view of *Lemminkäinen in Tuonela* than many of his rivals and builds up an appropriately black and powerful atmosphere, showing the Gothenburg brass to excellent advantage. The recording quality is impressive with splendid range and presence — and it is good to hear the two solo violins towards the end of the first *Legend* sounding so naturally life-size — and not larger than life! All four pieces are very well played and the complete naturalness of the recorded balance is admirable. This Gothenburg version can hold its head high in the company of all the performances recorded in the last decade or so.

Additional recommendation ...
Legends. Luonnotar, Op. 70[a]*. The bard, Op. 64.* [a]**Phyllis Bryn-Julson** (sop); **Scottish National Orchestra/Sir Alexander Gibson.** Chandos Collect CHAN6586 — lh 2m ADD 11/92

Sibelius. Scaramouche — incidental music, Op. 71. The Language of the Birds — wedding march. **Gothenburg Symphony Orchestra/Neeme Järvi.** BIS CD502.

lh 8m DDD 4/92

Scaramouche is Sibelius's longest uninterrupted orchestral work and this is its first complete recording — and something of a discovery. In all it runs to some 65 minutes of music and though there are some passages deficient in inspiration, the score contains much music that is touched by both distinction and vision. Indeed, the first Act is quite captivating. He composed it in 1913 with much reluctance on a commission from the Danish publisher, Wilhelm Hansen, thinking that it would not involve the composition of more than a few dance numbers. However the idea of the Danish writer, Poul Knudsen was a dance pantomime and Sibelius was furious with himself when it suddenly dawned on him that he had bound himself to compose a full-length ballet! Some of its music recalls the lighter Sibelius of the *Suites mignonne* and *Champêtre* but if the music is occasionally thin (particularly the Second Act) there are some moments of great poetic feeling, almost evoking the luminous colouring of the world of the *Humoresques* for violin and orchestra that were to follow in 1917. (We also glimpse ideas that were forming in his mind for use in *The Oceanides* the following year and, in the music where solo viola and cello depict Scaramouche's hypnotic viola playing, a figure that was to emerge in the Seventh Symphony.) The wistful gentle sadness of the first Act casts a strong spell, and its charms grow stronger on each hearing. *The Language of the Birds* was a play by Adolf Paul for whose *King Christian II* Sibelius had provided the music, but he never thought well enough of the Wedding March to publish it. It is quite an attractive piece and like *Scaramouche* itself is given very persuasively and affectionately by Neeme Järvi and the Gothenburg Symphony Orchestra and splendidly recorded.

Sibelius. SYMPHONIES. **Philharmonia Orchestra/Vladimir Ashkenazy.** Decca 421 069-2DM4.
Symphonies — No. 1 in E minor, Op. 39 (from 414 534-1DH, 5/86); No. 2 in D major, Op. 43 (SXDL7513, 11/80); No. 3 in C major, Op. 52 (414 267-1DH, 8/85); No. 4 in A minor, Op. 63 (SXDL7517, 5/81); No. 5 in E flat major, Op. 82 (SXDL7541, 1/82); No. 6 in D minor, Op. 104 (414 267-1DH, 2/85); No. 7 in C major, Op. 105 (SXDL7580, 8/83).

4 3h 52m ADD/DDD 12/87 

Of all the cycles of Sibelius's symphonies recorded during recent years this is one of the most consistently successful. Ashkenazy so well understands the thought processes that lie behind Sibelius's symphonic composition just as he is aware, and makes us aware, of the development between the Second and Third Symphonies. His attention to tempo is particularly acute and invariably he strikes just the right balance between romantic languor and urgency. The Philharmonia play for all they are worth and possess a fine body of sound. The recordings are remarkably consistent in quality and well complement the composer's original sound-world.

Additional recommendations ...
Nos. 1-7. The oceanides, Op. 73. Kuolema, Op. 44 — scene with cranes. Night ride and sunrise, Op. 55. **City of Birmingham Symphony Orchestra; Philharmonia Orchestra/Simon Rattle.** EMI CMS7 64118-2 — 4 4h 27m 2/92 DDD

Nos. 1-7. **Vienna Philharmonic Orchestra/Lorin Maazel.** Decca 430 778-2DC3 — ③ 3h 32m ADD 2/92

Nos. 1 and 2[b]*. Nos. 3 and 5*[a]*. Belshazzar's Feast — incidentla music, Op. 51*[a]*. Pohjola's daughter, Op. 49*[a]*. Karelia Suite, Op. 11*[b] *— Intermezzo; Alla marcia. Tapiola*[a]. [a]**London Symphony Orchestra,** [b]**Symphony Orchestra/Robert Kajanus.** Finlandia mono FACD81234 — ③ 3h 7m ADD 2/92

NEW REVIEW

Sibelius. Symphony No. 1 in E minor, Op. 39. Karelia Suite, Op. 11. Finlandia, Op. 26. **Oslo Philharmonic Orchestra/Mariss Jansons.** EMI CDC7 54273-2. Recorded in 1990.

lh 2m DDD 1/92

Jansons's account of the First Symphony is quite the most thrilling version to have appeared for some years. It has all the excitement and brilliance of the Vienna Philharmonic version under Bernstein without its exaggerations. Tempos throughout are just right, the phrasing breathes naturally and the sonority is excellently focused. Jansons never presses on too quickly but allows each phrase, each musical sentence to register so that the listener feels borne along on a natural currrent. Moreover, excitement is not whipped up but arises naturally from the music's forward momentum. The Oslo Philharmonic is a highly responsive orchestra of no mean virtuosity and they play with a splendid intensity and fire not only in the symphony but also the *Karelia Suite* and *Finlandia* which sound very fresh. All the artistic decisions in this reading seem to be right and the orchestral playing further enhances the high renown this ensemble now enjoys. Very good recording too.

Additional recommendations ...

Nos. 1 and 4. **Vienna Philharmonic Orchestra/Lorin Mazel.** Decca Ovation 417 789-2DM — ADD

No. 1. Karelia Suite. **Philharmonia Orchestra/Vladimir Ashkenazy.** Decca 414 534-2DH — 57m DDD 5/86

No. 1. Karelia Suite. **Berlin Philharmonic Orchestra/Herbert von Karajan.** EMI Studio CDM7 69028-2 — 55m DDD 9/87

Nos. 1 and 6. **Berlin Philharmonic Orchestra/Herbert von Karajan.** EMI CDD7 63896-2 — lh 9m DDD 7/91

No. 1. **Vienna Philharmonic Orchestra/Leonard Bernstein.** DG 435 351-2GH — 41m DDD 4/92

Sibelius. Symphony No. 2 in D major, Op. 43. Romance in C major, Op. 42. **Gothenburg Symphony Orchestra/Neeme Järvi.** BIS CD252.

48m DDD 10/84 

The Second Symphony possesses a combination of Italianate warmth and Nordic intensity that has ensured its wide popular appeal. None of Sibelius's other symphonies has enjoyed such immediate and enduring success. If it inhabits much the same world as the First, it views it through more subtle and refined lenses. As in the First Symphony, it is the opening movement that makes the most profound impression. Its very air of relaxation and effortlessness serves to mask its inner strength. Järvi's version has sinew and fire and the Gothenburg orchestra are splendidly responsive and well disciplined. There is an unerring sense of purpose and direction: the momentum never slackens and yet nothing seems over-driven. The performance is concentrated in feeling and has freshness and honesty. The short but charming *Romance* in C for strings, written at about the same time, is an excellent fill-up.

Additional recommendations ...

No. 2. Finlandia. Valse triste, Op. 44 No. 1. The Swan of Tuonela, Op. 22 No. 2. **Boston Symphony Orchestra/Sir Colin Davis.** Philips Silver Line 420 490-2PM — lh 9m ADD 6/87

No. 2. **Royal Philharmonic Orchestra/Sir John Barbirolli.** Chesky CD-3 — 44m ADD 6/91 ▲

Nos. 2, 5 and 7. Swanwhite, Op. 54 — The Maidens with roses. Tapiola. Pohjola's daughter, Op. 49. **Boston Symphony Orchestra; BBC Symphony Orchestra/Serge Koussevitzky.** Pearl mono GEMMCDS9408 — ② 2h 5m AAD 7/90 ▲

No. 2. ***Dvořák.*** *Symphony No. 8 in G major, Op. 88.* **BBC Symphony Orchestra, Royal Philharmonic Orchestra/Sir Thomas Beecham.** EMI Beecham Edition mono CDM7 63399-2 — 1h 17m ADD 7/90

No. 2. Finlandia. Karelia Suite, Op. 11. **Philharmonia Orchestra/Vladimir Ashkenazy.** Decca Headline 430 737-2DM — 1h 12m DDD 8/92

No. 2. Tapiola. Valse Triste. **San Francesco Symphony Orchestra/Herbert Blomstedt.** Decca 433 810-2DH — 1h 9m DDD 3/93

No. 2. The Swan of Tuonela. Valse triste. Andante festivo for strings. **Oslo Philharmonic Orchestra/Mariss Jansons.** EMI CDC7 54804-2 — 1h 1m DDD 7/93

Sibelius. Symphonies — No. 3 in C major, Op. 52[a]; No. 2 in D major, Op. 43[b]. **City of Birmingham Symphony Orchestra/Simon Rattle.** EMI CDM7 64120-2. Item marked [a] from EL270496-1 (4/87), [b] EL270160-1 (1/85).

51m DDD 2/92

Sibelius's Third Symphony is a striking advance on his first two; whilst they speak the same language as the music of Tchaikovsky and Grieg, the Third strikes us because of its spareness of texture and concentration of ideas. The weight of string tone associated with Sibelius is here apparent and carries tremendous expressive power. The finale, in particular, is a remarkable movement possessing a power and inevitability that evolve from the Symphony's unusual structure. In the Second Symphony, Rattle's first movement is, perhaps, on the slow side. In general, though, both performance and recording are very fine.

Sibelius. Symphonies — No. 4 in A minor, Op. 63[a]; No. 6 in D minor, Op. 104[b]. **Berlin Philharmonic Orchestra/Herbert von Karajan.** DG 415 107-2GH. Item marked [a] from SLPM138974 (6/66), [b] SLPM139032 (10/68).

1h 3m ADD 6/85

Both of these symphonies are dark almost sombre pieces, lacking the harmonic colouring and textural richness of many of the other compositions from this period. The Fourth is cast in greys and silvers rarely employing the orchestral resources at their most opulent, preferring instead a sparer, more restrained weave. Sibelius employs a motto theme which, like so many works that seem to lie under a shadow cast by Fate, adds to its powerful sense of internal unity. The Sixth Symphony, too, is a work of restraint and sombre colour. Again the composer eschews vibrant surface life to dig deep in the soul and the music receives a strong sense of unity through the use of motifs but here they have a rich modal flavour that place the work apart as a product of the carefree 1920s. Karajan was long a champion of Sibelius's music and the icy depths of the Berlin strings, their peerless winds and dark, baying brass add a powerful sense of inevitability to these two scores. The mid 1960s recording are very good.

Additional recommendations ...

Nos. 4 and 5. **San Francisco Symphony Orchestra/Herbert Blomstedt.** Decca 425 858-2DH — 1h 8m DDD 7/91

No. 4. The Tempest, Op. 109 — Suite No. 1. **Danish National Radio Symphony Orchestra/Leif Segerstam.** Chandos CHAN8943 — 1h 5m DDD 8/91

Nos. 4 and 6. **City of Birmingham Symphony Orchestra/Simon Rattle.** EMI CDM7 64121-2 — 1h 7m DDD 2/92

Nos. 4 and 6[a]. The Tempest — incidental music, Op. 109: Prelude. Legends, Op. 22 — Lemminkaïnen's return. The bard, Op. 64. **London Philharmonic Orchestra, [a]Royal Philharmonic Orchestra/Sir Thomas Beecham.** EMI mono CDM7 64027-2 — 1h 19m ADD 3/92 ▲

Sibelius. Symphonies — No. 5 in E flat major, Op. 82[a]; No. 7 in C major, Op. 105[b]. **Berlin Philharmonic Orchestra/Herbert von Karajan.** DG 415 108-2GH. Item marked [a] from SLPM138973 (9/65), [b] SLPM139032 (10/68).

55m ADD 6/85 

The Fifth Symphony, like the Seventh, is epic and heroic in character, and the finale has a tremendous feeling of momentum as well as an awe-inspiring sense of the majesty of nature. The one-movement Seventh is the most extraordinary of his symphonies and the most sophisticated in its approach to form. Karajan has recorded the Fifth no fewer than four times and the best is undoubtedly this DG version made in 1965. It has grandeur and nobility and, it goes without saying, superlative orchestral playing. The transfer to CD is so successful that it would be difficult to guess its age. This is a classic account of the Fifth.

Additional recommendation ...

Nos. 5 and 7. Kuolema, Op. 44 — Scene with cranes. Night ride and sunrise, Op. 55[a]. **City of Birmingham Symphony Orchestra, [a]Philharmonia Orchestra/Simon Rattle.** EMI CDM7 69122-2 — DDD 2/92

Sibelius. Piano Quintet in G minor (1890)[a]. String Quartet in D minor, Op. 56, "Voces intimae". **Gabrieli Quartet** (John Georgiadis, Brendan O'Kelly, vns; Ian Jewel, va; Keith Harvey, vc) with [a]**Anthony Goldstone** (pf). Chandos CHAN8742. Recorded in 1989.

lh l4m DDD 2/90 

Only a few months after its composition in 1890, Sibelius dismissed his Piano Quintet as "absolute rubbish". It is far from that, though Busoni's description of it as "wunderschön" is rather overdoing things. The first movement is probably the finest though the *Andante,* too, has a lot of good music in it, if let down by a rather lame, march-like second theme. The scherzo is attractive and very neatly played. To maximize contrast, these artists reverse the order of the scherzo and the *Andante* so that the two slow movements are separated. Although the finale is less satisfactory in terms of structure, it has a good deal of spirit and some memorable ideas. Anthony Goldstone is consistently imaginative and intelligent throughout and the Gabrielis play with conviction. The *Voces intimae* Quartet comes from Sibelius's maturity — between the Third and Fourth symphonies. It is a masterly score and is selflessly played. The fourth movement certainly needs more bite and forward movement; yet the scherzo could not be done with greater delicacy and finesse — and no one comes closer than they to the spirit of this music in the closing bars of the slow movement or the celebrated bars that Sibelius marked "voces intimae".

NEW REVIEW

Sibelius. COMPLETE STRING QUARTETS. **Sibelius Academy Quartet** (Seppo Tukiainen, Erkki Kantola, vns; Veikko Kosonen, va; Arto Noras, vc). Finlandia FACD209. Items marked [a] from FACD375 (7/90), [b] FACD345 (7/86), [c] new to UK. Recorded 1980-88.
E flat major[a]; A minor[b]; B flat major, Op. 4[b]; D minor, Op. 56, "Voces intimae"[c].

(2) lh 47m ADD/DDD 8/92

Not so long ago the only Sibelius quartet on disc was *Voces intimae*. Yet before the *Kullervo* Symphony, Sibelius had hardly composed anything other than chamber music. After his breakthrough as an orchestral composer he continued to write music for domestic use but into none of it did he pour ideas of any real significance or inspiration with the sole exception of *Voces intimae*. This box collects all his early quartets together with the *Voces intimae* and must be of prime interest to Sibelians. True, the E flat Quartet of 1885 is purely derivative and modelled on the Viennese classics, a well-schooled exercise and little more. The A minor composed in 1889, his last year as a student in Helsinki, and the B flat, Op. 4, composed the following year are a completely different matter. It is clear from the title-page of the Op. 4, which he calls Quartet No. 2, that he thought of the A minor as his first. Indeed the A minor long remained listed as Op. 2 before being removed from his opus list. For long it was thought lost, but a complete set of parts was discovered during the 1980s in his brother's library. Erik Tawaststjerna rightly speaks of its “fragile Nordic melancholy linked stylistically to Grieg”. It has something of the freshness of Dvořák and the innocence of Schubert. Sibelius obviously had ambivalent feelings towards the fine B flat Quartet since he never published it and actively discouraged its performance. The playing of the Sibelius Academy Quartet is strongly characterized and the recordings good.

Sibelius. SONGS. **Anne Sofie von Otter** (mez); **Bengt Forsberg** (pf). BIS CD457. Texts and translations included.

Arioso, Op. 3. Seven Songs, Op. 17. Row, row duck. Six Songs, Op. 36. Five Songs, Op. 37. Pelleas and Melisande, Op. 46 — The three blind sisters. Six Songs, Op. 88. Narcissus.

57m DDD 6/90 

In all, Sibelius composed about 100 songs, mostly to Swedish texts but his achievement in this field has, naturally enough, been overshadowed by the symphonies. Most music-lovers know only a handful like “Black roses”, Op. 36 No. 1, and “The Tryst” and the most popular are not always the best. Sibelius's output for the voice has much greater range, diversity and depth than many people suppose. For collectors used to hearing them sung by a baritone, the idea of a soprano will seem strange but many of them were written for the soprano Ida Ekman. Anne Sofie von Otter not only makes a beautiful sound and has a feeling for line, but also brings many interpretative insights to this repertoire. The very first song from the Op. 17 set is a marvellous Runeberg setting, “Since then I have questioned no further” and it was this that Ida Ekman sang for Brahms. Von Otter captures its mood perfectly and has the measure of its companions too. Her account of “Black roses” is particularly thrilling and she is very persuasive in the weaker Op. 88 set. She sings throughout with great feeling for character and her account of “Astray”, Op. 17 No. 6, has great lightness of touch and charm. The Opp. 36 and 37 sets are among the finest lyrical collections in the whole of Sibelius's song output, and they completely engage this artist's sensibilties. These are performances of elegance and finesse; Bengt Forsberg proves an expert and stylish partner and both artists are well recorded.

NEW REVIEW

Sibelius. The Tempest — complete incidental music, Op. 109. **Kirsi Tiihonen** (sop); **Lilli Paasikivi** (mez); **Anssi Hirvonen, Paavo Kerola** (tens); **Heikki Keinonen** (bar); **Lahti Opera Chorus and Symphony Orchestra/Osmo Vänskä.** BIS CD581. Text and translation included. Recorded in 1992.

lh 8m DDD 2/93

A first recording of the full score! Sibelius's music for *The Tempest,* his last and greatest work in its genre, was the result of a commission for a particularly lavish production at the Royal Theatre, Copenhagen in 1926. The score is far more extensive than the two suites and consists of 34 musical numbers for soloists, mixed choir, harmonium and large orchestra. Readers will be brought up with a start by the music for the “Berceuse”, the second item, which uses a harmonium rather than the strings with which we are familiar from the two suites and although it is still more magical in the familiar orchestral suite, the original has an other-worldly quality all its own. The music is played in the order in which it was used in the 1927 production of the play and there are ample and excellent explanatory notes. The “Chorus of the Winds” is also different but no less magical in effect. Of course, taken out of the theatrical context, not everything comes off — but even if the invention is not consistent in quality, at its best it is quite wonderful. The singers and chorus all rise to the occasion and Osmo Vänskä succeeds in casting a powerful spell in the “Intermezzo”, which opens Act 4. The recording is marvellously atmospheric though it needs to be played at a higher than usual level setting as it is a little recessed. For Sibelians this is a self-recommending issue.

Further listening ...

Kullervo, Op. 7. **Marianne Rørholm** (contr); **Jorma Hynninen** (bar); **Helsinki University Chorus; Los Angeles Philharmonic Orchestra/Esa-Pekka Salonen.** Sony Classical SK52563 (7/93).

THE MAIDEN IN THE TOWER. Karelia Suite, Op. 11. **Soloists; Gothenburg Concert Hall Chorus and Symphony Orchestra/Neeme Järvi.** BIS CD250 (3/85).

Robert Simpson

British 1921-

NEW REVIEW

Simpson. Symphonies — No. 2; No. 4. **Bournemouth Symphony Orchestra/Vernon Handley.** Hyperion CDA66505. Recorded 1991-92.

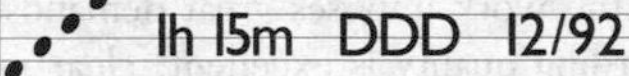
lh 15m DDD 12/92

Why oh why, as the tabloids might say, have these two symphonies had to wait so long for their first recordings? Admittedly their commitment to the more abstract aspects of the Beethovenian legacy — energy, momentum, inner exploration — has had difficulty making its presence felt over the clamour of more catchy slogans. Admittedly the Second Symphony had a stroke of bad luck when a recording project foundered — it was written for the same forces as Beethoven's Seventh and was to have appeared with it on LP. But the ebullience and wit of the outer movements of the Second, and the sheer audacity of the *Scherzo* of the Fourth (a paraphrase of the corresponding movement from Beethoven's Ninth), not to mention the gently restorative poetry of the slow movements, should have won both symphonies instant recognition. No matter, here they are now, in first-rate performances and exemplary recordings. For anyone interested in the continuing power of the symphonic genre, Simpson's cycle is essential listening; and there is no better starting-point than these two excellently contrasted works.

Simpson. Symphony No. 3[a]. Clarinet Quintet[b]. [b]**Bernard Walton** (cl); [b]**Aeolian Quartet** (Sydney Humphreys, Raymond Keenlyside, vns; Margaret Major, va; Derek Simpson, vc); [a]**London Symphony Orchestra/Jascha Horenstein.** Unicorn-Kanchana Souvenir UKCD2028. Item marked [a] from UNS225 (9/70), [b] UNS234 (8/71). Recorded in 1970.

lh 6m ADD 6/90

The British have been accused of chauvinism, but by no way of thinking can this be said to apply to British opinion of native composers, which has often been disparaging, as both Elgar and Britten found to their cost until the pendulum swung the other way, and it is disgraceful that Robert Simpson has only recently been recognized as the major figure that he is although he has been a symphonist for 40 years and not long ago wrote his Tenth Symphony. This is not the place to apportion blame, but rather to say that many of us are doing some belated catching up with this composer who proves that one doesn't have to be a serialist or minimalist to write music that is personal and worth hearing. His Third Symphony (1962) is not easy listening, though, for it offers an uncompromising argument forcefully scored, but it also reveals real purpose and repays the close acquaintance that a recording allows. The sound here is from 1970 and has a rather cramped acoustic quality, but it is still acceptable and the performance by the LSO under Horenstein, an early Simpson champion, brings out the strength of the writing, not least in the big second movement (there are only two) which the composer calls "Nature music, in a sense" and which, after a hushed start on violins, steadily grows in pace and excitement though ending quietly. The Clarinet Quintet (1968) is in five connected sections, and though it has some dourness it is finely written and well played here, so that careful listening brings rewards. Both works were recorded under the composer's supervision.

NEW REVIEW

Simpson. String Quartet No. 12. String Quintet[a]. **Coull Quartet** (Roger Coull, Philip Gallaway, vns; David Curtis, va; John Todd, vc); [a]**Roger Bigley** (va). Hyperion CDA66503. Recorded in 1991.

lh 7m DDD 7/92

A tautly-argued, single-movement work for five string players lasting 34 minutes presents a formidable challenge in performance, even in the recording studio, where retakes and patches can be undertaken. The Coull Quartet and their visiting viola player maintain a high sense of concentration over the Quintet's long span, and convey the work's complex argument and structure very skilfully. In essence the movement is cast in a slow basic tempo, with a central scherzo, but scherzo elements appear in the outer sections, and there are elements of a slow pulse in the scherzo. These ambiguities of tempo are cleverly conveyed by the performers. Technically their playing is on a high level, with just the odd slip to suggest that the producer has rightly aimed at maintaining tension and momentum rather than ensuring absolute perfection of execution. The Coull Quartet gave the first performance not only of Quartet No. 12, but also of the two previous ones. Their experience and expertise in Simpson's music is very evident in the Twelfth Quartet. This is in a two-movement form, with a long, concentrated, meditative *Adagio* followed by a powerful, highly rhythmic scherzo. Again, the work imposes great demands on the players, and the players respond magnificently. The recording quality is excellent, clear in detail but set in a comfortable acoustic.

Futher listening ...

Symphonies Nos. 6 and 7. **Royal Liverpool Philharmonic Orchestra/Vernon Handley.** Hyperion CDA66280 (6/88)

Symphony No. 9. **Bournemouth Symphony Orchestra/Vernon Handley.** Hyperion CDA66299 (12/88).

Music for Brass Band: Energy — symphonic study. The Four Temperaments. Introduction and Allegro on a Bass by Max Reger. Volcano — symphonic study. Vortex. **Desford Colliery Caterpillar Band/James Watson.** Hyperion CDA66449 (1/91).

String Quartets Nos. 3 and 6. String Trio (Prelude, Adagio and Fugue). **Delmé Quartet.** Hyperion CDA66376 (7/90).

String Quartets Nos. 7 and 8. **Delmé Quartet.** Hyperion CDA66117 (2/90).

String Quartet No. 9. **Delmé Quartet.** Hyperion CDA66127 (2/90).

Howard Skempton

British 1947-

Suggested listening ...

Lento. **BBC Symphony Orchestra/Mark Wigglesworth.** NMC NMCD005 (6/93).

Henry Smart

British 1813-1879

NEW REVIEW

Smart. ORGAN WORKS. **Anne Marsden-Thomas.** Priory PRCD368. Played on the organ of St Giles, Cripplegate, London. Recorded in 1991.

Postlude in D major. Air and Variations and Finale Fugato. Three Andantes — G major; A major; E minor. Minuet in C major. Grand Solemn March in E flat major.

lh 4m DDD 9/92

English organ music hit an all-time low during the middle years of the nineteenth century. The tendency is, though, to tar every composer of the period with the same brush; which would be grossly unfair since there were several whose music deserves serious attention. One such was Henry Smart who was born into a noted musical family. Until fairly recently his music, always well crafted, but also adventurous and innovative in a way few of his contemporaries could match, had fallen into virtual oblivion. Hopefully with this disc Anne Marsden-Thomas will help to re-establish his reputation. Certainly anyone who enjoys a good tune and who likes the sound of fine, accessible organ music played by a most talented player will not be disappointed by anything here. Ranging from a stirring Postlude, the kind of piece played after morning service every Sunday, to a charming neo-classical Minuet, Smart's undoubted qualities as a composer are clearly in evidence. An interesting historic footnote to this disc is that the organ used was moved to its present home from nearby St Luke's, Old Street, where for 20 years Smart had been organist.

Bedrich Smetana

Bohemian *1824-1884*

NEW REVIEW

Smetana. Symphonic Poems — Richard III, Op. 11; Wallensteins Camp, Op. 14; Hakon Jarl, Op. 16. Prague Carnival.
Janáček. Sinfonietta. **Bavarian Radio Symhony Orchestra/Rafael Kubelík.** DG Galleria 437 254-2GGA. Recorded in 1971.

1h 11m ADD 1/93 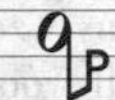

Here is music from the first and the last great Czech nationalists. Smetana was also the first composer to follow Liszt in writing symphonic poems — in his twenties, he sided with the patriots in the abortive 1848 uprising, but finding himself on the official blacklist thereafter, he moved to Sweden for six years where the three early symphonic poems were written. The source for *Hakon Jarl* is Norwegian history, but *Richard III* and *Wallenstein's Camp* are based on the Shakespeare and Schiller plays (the later, being set in Bohemia, offered Smetana as much opportunity as *Má vlast* for native folk culture derivations). All these works are vividly communicative and well constructed, if occasionally bombastic. Occasional bombast of a more elemental, even oriental kind frames the Janáček *Sinfonietta*, his largest purely orchestral work, but never before or since has Czech national pride been fanfared with such bizarre instrumental combinations, hypnotic repetitions and peasant hues; alongside it most twentieth-century music sounds impotent. DG's early 1970s sound may lack today's expected transparency, sheen and range, a matter of little consequence given Kubelík's passionate, urgent advocacy.

Smetana. Má vlast. **Czech Philharmonic Orchestra/Rafael Kubelík.** Supraphon 11 1208-2. Recorded at a performance in the Smetana Hall, Prague in May 1990.

1h 18m DDD 9/91 

Smetana's great cycle of six tone-poems, *Má vlast*, celebrates the countryside and legendary heroes and heroines of Bohemia. It is a work of immense national significance encapsulating many of the ideals and hopes of that country. What a triumphant occasion it was when Rafael Kubelík returned to his native Czechoslovakia and to his old orchestra after an absence of 42 years and conducted *Má vlast* at the 1990 Prague Spring Festival. Supraphon's disc captures that live performance — not perfectly, since the sound is efficient rather than opulent — but well enough to show off what is arguably the finest performance on record since Talich's early LP set. You would never imagine that Kubelík had emerged from five years of retirement and a recent serious illness, such is the power and eloquence of his conducting. Typically he takes a lyrical rather than a dramatic view of the cycle, and if there is strength enough in more heroic sections there is also a refreshing lack of bombast. Kubelík's intimate knowledge of the score (this is his fifth recording of it) shows time and time again in the most subtle touches. Even the weakest parts of the score are most artfully brought to life, and seem of much greater stature than is usually the case. "Vltava" flows beautifully, with the most imaginative flecks of detail, and in "From Bohemia's Woods and Fields" there are vivid visions of wide, open spaces. The orchestra, no doubt inspired by the occasion, reward their former director with superlative playing.

Additional recommendations ...

Royal Liverpool Philharmonic Orchestra/Libor Pešek. Virgin Classics VC7 59576-2 — lh 16m DDD 7/90

Czech Philharmonic Orchestra/Václav Talich. Koch International Legacy mono 37032-2 — lh 19m ADD 2/91

Israel Philharmonic Orchestra/Walter Weller. Decca Headline Classics — lh 14m 1/92 £

Smetana. THE BARTERED BRIDE. **Gabriela Beňačková** (sop) Mařenka; **Peter Dvorský** (ten) Jeník; **Miroslav Kopp** (ten) Vašek; **Richard Novák** (bass) Kecal; **Jindřich Jindrák** (bar) Krušina; **Marie Mrázová** (contr) Háta; **Jaroslav Horáček** (bass) Mícha; **Marie Veselá** (sop) Ludmila; **Jana Jonášová** (sop) Esmeralda; **Alfréd Hampel** (ten) Circus master; **Karel Hanuš** (bass) Indian; **Czech Philharmonic Chorus and Orchestra/Zdeněk Košler.** Supraphon 10 3511-2. Notes, text and translation included. From 1116 3511 (7/82).

3 2h 17m DDD 10/91 

There is something special about a Czech performance of *The bartered bride* and this one is no exception. The hint of melancholy which runs through the work is wonderfully evoked, as well as its marvellous gaiety. Zdeněk Košler has the rhythm and lilt of the music in his bones, like any Czech conductor worth his salt. The Czech Philharmonic has long had one of the finest of all woodwind sections, and especially in this music they play with a sense of their instruments' folk background, with phrasing that springs from deep in Czech folk-music. This sets the musical scene for some moving performances. The warm, lyrical quality of Gabriela Bennačková's voice can lighten easily to encompass her character's tenderness in the first duet, "Věrné milováni", or "Faithful love", the considerable show of spirit she makes when Jeník appears to have gone off the rails. Her Act 1 lament is most beautifully song. Peter Dvorský as Jeník plays lightly with the score, as he should, or the character's maintaining of the deception can come to seem merely cruel. Even old Kecal comes to new life, not as the conventional village bumbler, but as a human character in his own right as Richard Novák portrays him — quite put out, the old boy is, to find his plans gone astray. In fact, all of the soloists are excellent. The chorus enjoy themselves hugely, never more so than in the Beer chorus. Altogether a delightful, touching and warming performance.

Further listening ...

THE TWO WIDOWS. **Soloists; Prague Radio Chorus and Symphony Orchestra/Jaroslav Krombholc.** Praga PR250 022/3 (6/93).

Dame Ethel Smyth

British 1858-1944

Smyth. Mass in D major[a]. THE BOATSWAIN'S MATE — Suppose you mean to do a given thing. March of the Women[b]. **Eiddwen Harrhy** (sop); [a]**Janis Hardy** (contr); [a]**Dan Dressen** (ten); [a]**James Bohn** (bass); **Plymouth Festival** [ab]**Chorus and Orchestra/Philip Brunelle.** Virgin Classics VC7 59022-2. Texts and translation included.

lh 15m DDD 8/91 

Dame Ethel Smyth's Mass was performed by the Royal Choral Society under Sir Joseph Barnby in 1893, when *Musical Opinion* found in it "many pages of supreme beauty, for which parallels must be sought in the masterpieces of the great choral writers". *The Musical Times* detected royal patronage, which "explained all, prevented the action of the committee from being assailed, and revealed Miss Smyth in the character of a very fortunate person". Whatever the cause, her good fortune then deserted her, for the Mass was not heard again till 1924, when *The Musical Times* decided after all that "its genuine character and its vehemence make it intrinsically worth hearing". Now in 1991 it gains its first recording, not from London or

Birmingham (where the second performance took place) but Minnesota. Time, certainly, has done nothing to weaken its effects. "Parallels ... in the masterpieces of the great choral writers" do indeed come to mind, most notably the Beethoven of the *Missa solemnis*, but what impresses now is the individuality and scale of the achievement. The *Kyrie*, for instance, may start like a text-book fugue with echoes of Bach's B minor Mass, but it soon develops along its own lines, and the declamatory use of the choir, the quickening pace, growing intensity and unforeseen turns of form and style are expressions of an almost fiercely independent spirit at work. Each movement has its special strength, and the *Gloria*, transposed from its normal place in the Mass, provides a joyfully rumbustious finale. The attractive solo from *The Boatswain's Mate* makes one wish to hear the rest of the opera (and the other five), while the *March of the Women* or *Suffragettes' Battle Hymn* recalls another part of that contentious and vigorous life. The performances carry conviction; recorded sound is adequate except that, as usual, one would like the choir to be more forward.

Antonio Soler

Spanish 1729-1783

NEW REVIEW

Soler. CONCERTOS FOR TWO ORGANS. **Tini Mathot, Ton Koopman** (orgs). Erato 2292-45741-2. Played on the Nacchini and Callido organs of the church of Maria S.S. Misericordia, San Elpidio a Mare, Italy. Recorded in 1990.

No. 1 in C major; No. 2 in A minor; No. 3 in G major; No. 4 in F major; No. 5 in A major; No. 6 in D major.

lh DDD 7/92 

NEW REVIEW

Soler. CONCERTOS FOR TWO ORGANS. **Peter Hurford, Thomas Trotter** (orgs). Decca 436 115-2DH. Played on the Epistle and Gospel organs of Salamanca Cathedral, Spain. Recorded in 1991.

No. 1 in C major; No. 2 in A minor; No. 3 in G major; No. 4 in F major; No. 5 in A major; No. 6 in D major.

lh 4m DDD 

Many Spanish churches boast two organs and it is probable that Antonio Soler wrote these concertos for performance either in one such church or the opera theatre in the El Escorial Palace (where he had been appointed organist at the age of 23). Certainly he wrote them for himself to play alongside his talented pupil Don Gabriel de Borbon (Carlos III's son). A great deal of fun they must have had with them, too, for these are immensely enjoyable works from both the players' and the listener's point of view. With the exception of the Second Concerto (the only one in a minor key), all consist of two movements ending with a sprightly Minuet. Clearly the husband and wife team of Ton Koopman and Tini Mathot thoroughly enjoyed themselves during the recording sessions, for in addition to the musicality and stylishness one has come to expect from any project involving Koopman, there is a real sense of *joie de vivre* and a tangible rapport between the players which leaps out of every bar. The charming pair of eighteenth-century Italian organs they use make the kind of rattling, wheezing sounds (with some comically buzzing reed stops) which increase rather than detract from the enjoyment of these effervescent performances. In Peter Hurford and Thomas Trotter the teacher/pupil relationship is recreated and in their choice of the two organs in Salamanca Cathedral theirs is a recording which probably gets closer to the spirit of Soler's original intentions. They possess a somewhat tighter ensemble and cleaner rhythmic control than the Koopmans and while there isn't quite the same sense of fun in their playing, the precision and authority of these performances, some immaculately selected registrations (including, in No. 6, a thrilling *en chamade* [horizontal] trumpet stop) all aided by a top-notch recording, makes this CD a most attractive buy.

Soler. KEYBOARD SONATAS. **Maggie Cole** ([a]fp/[b]hpd). Virgin Classics Veritas VC7 59624-2. No. 18 in C minor[a]; No. 19 in C minor[a]; No. 41 in E flat major[a]; No. 72 in F minor[a]; No. 78

in F sharp minor[a]; No. 84 in D major[b]; No. 85 in F sharp minor[b]; No. 86 in D major[b]; No. 87 in G minor[a]; No. 88 in D flat major[b]; No. 90 in F sharp major[b]. Fandango.

1h 11m DDD 5/91

If Soler's name is not widely known, that is doubtless because this eighteenth-century Spanish monk devoted much of his creative time to writing 120 keyboard sonatas which have been overshadowed by those of his predecessor Domenico Scarlatti — who was also his teacher. But they have a character of their own and are longer and more elaborate than Scarlatti's. Maggie Cole takes into account the fact that Soler knew both the fortepiano and harpsichord and sensibly divides the 12 here into two parts, playing the first six on the former and the second on the older instrument. The overriding character of the music is energy, and pieces such as Sonatas Nos. 84 and 88 (played on a three-manual Goble harpsichord after a Hamburg instrument of 1740) fairly burst out of the loudspeakers in a recording that will be too closely-miked for some tastes but is undeniably realistic. Still, there's enough variety in the invention for listening in sequence — though nothing is especially Spanish-sounding save for the *Fandango* on track 7. The fortepiano (by Derek Adlam and based on a Viennese instrument) is more expressive than many, as the gravely melancholy Sonata No. 18 demonstrates. This piece is one of the longest at nearly ten minutes, and is nicely complemented by the shorter and bouncier No. 19 that follows. Maggie Cole's playing is wonderfully crisp and clean, and by using discreet rhythmic flexibility (and tonal shading in the fortepiano pieces) she never allows busy passagework to become merely mechanical.

Additional recommendations ...

Sonatas — No. 1 in A major; No. 3 in B flat major; No. 24 in D minor; No. 25 in D minor; No. 28 in C major; No. 29 in C major; No. 30 in G major; No. 31 in G major; No. 96 in E flat major; No. 118 in A minor. Prelude No. 1 in D minor. **Bon van Asperen** (hpd). Astrée Auvidis E8768 — 1h 11m DDD 7/92

Sonatas — No. 7 in C major; No. 8 in C major; No. 9 in C major; No. 20 in C sharp minor; No. 21 in C sharp minor; No. 34 in E major; No. 95 in A major. Prelude No. 3 in C major. **Bon van Asperen** (hpd). Astrée Auvidis E8769 — 1h 8m DDD 7/92

Sonatas — No. 10 in B minor; No. 11 in B major; No. 12 in G major, "de la Cordorniz"; No. 13 in G major; No. 14 in G major; No. 52 in E minor; No. 73 in D major; No. 74 in D major; No. 92 in D major, "Sonata de clarines"; No. 106 in E minor. Prelude No. 6 in G major. **Bon van Asperen** (hpd). Astrée Auvidis E8780 — 1h 9m DDD 7/92

Sonatas — No. 37 in D major; No. 46 in C major; No. 56 in F major; No. 98 in B flat major; No. 100 in C minor; No. 103 in C minor; No. 108 in C major, "del Gallo"; No. 109 in F major; No. 112 in C major. Fandango. Prelude No. 5 in D major. **Bon van Asperen** (hpd). Astrée Auvidis E8771 — 1h 17m DDD 7/92

Sonatas — No. 15 in D minor; No. 22 in D flat major; No. 23 in D flat major; No. 54 in D minor; No. 61 in C major; No. 75 in F major; No. 76 in F major; No. 80 in G minor; No. 81 in G minor; No. 84 in D major; No. 86 in D major. **Bon van Asperen** (hpd). Astrée Auvidis E8772 — 1h 10m DDD 7/92

Sonatas — No. 18 in C minor; No. 19 in C minor; No. 26 in E minor; No. 27 in E minor; No. 36 in C minor; No. 85 in F sharp minor; No. 90 in F sharp minor; No. 91 in C major. No. 94 in G major. **Bon van Asperen** (hpd). Astrée Auvidis E8773 — 1h 15m DDD 7/92

Stephen Sondheim

American 1930-

Suggested listening ...

FOLLIES. **Original Broadway cast.** EMI Angel ZDM7 64666-2

INTO THE WOODS. **Original London cast.** RCA Victor RD60752 (9/91).

SUNDAY IN THE PARK WITH GEORGE. **Original Broadway cast.** RCA Victor RD85042 (7/90).

PACIFIC OVERTURES. **English National Opera.** That's Entertainment CDTER21152 (8/88).

Fernando Sor

Spanish 1778-1839

Sor. GUITAR WORKS. **Lex Eisenhardt.** Etcetera KTC1025. From ETC1025 (11/85). Variations on the Scottish Air, "Ye banks and braes", Op. 40. Six Airs from Mozart's "Die Zauberflöte", Op. 19. Le calme — caprice, Op. 50. Sonata in C minor, Op. 25.

49m DDD 1/89

In May 1819 *Die Zauberflöte* was performed in London and it may have been there that Sor heard it — and was stimulated to write his famous Variations (Op. 9) on *Das klinget so herrlich*, published in 1821; two years later, when he was living in Russia, he made simple, charming settings of six more airs from the opera which he sent to his publisher in Paris. Variations were in the salon-musical air that Sor regularly breathed and those on *Ye banks and braes* may have resulted from his hearing the tune in London, or perhaps, reflected the contemporary continental taste for Scottish melodies, shared by Beethoven, Haydn and (in London) J.C. Bach. By 1832 Sor had returned to Paris, where he dedicated the elegant little Caprice *Le calme* to one of his lady students. Of the few guitar composers of the time who ventured to write full-scale sonatas, Sor was the most lyrical, adventurous in departing from the guitar's most grateful keys, and fastidious in his craftsmanship; the Sonata Op. 25 is the finest of his works in this genre. Lex Eisenhardt plays all this music most persuasively and is clearly recorded in a generous acoustic.

Sor. GUITAR WORKS **Eduardo Fernández.** Decca 425 821-2DH. Recorded in 1989. Grand solo, Op. 14. Fantasia élégiaque, Op. 59. Sonatas — C major, Op. 15 No. 2; C minor, Op. 25. Etudes — Op. 6 Nos. 4, 6 and 8; Op. 29 No. 25; Op. 35 Nos. 16 and 17; Op. 21. "Les adieux".

1h 9m DDD 11/91

Although best known for his guitar music Sor wrote much for other mediums; it was through his ballet music that he visited Russia. Stylistically, his music sits between that of Mozart and Beethoven, and little of it shows any trace of his Hispanic origins. Of his several sonata-form works, Op. 25 is the most developed of its time for the guitar, and the *Grand solo* is in effect one sonata-form movement. The *Fantasia élégiaque* is a lament on the death of his friend Charlotte Beslay above the final bars is written "Charlotte! Adieu" and it is arguably the most moving piece written for the guitar before this century. Sor also wrote numerous pieces for didactic purposes (which they serve without sacrifice of musical appeal), including 97 studies under five opus numbers, of which there is a selection in this recording. Though the quest after authenticity has marched beyond the date of Sor's death, no recording of this music on a nineteenth-century guitar and played with period technique is yet available; Fernández's clean performances complement Eisenhardt's and both provide an excellent introduction to Sor's music as it is perceived by today's guitarists.

Kaikhosru Shapurji Sorabji

British 1892-1988

Sorabji. Piano Sonata No. 1. **Marc-André Hamelin.** Altarus AIR-CD-9050.

22m DDD 5/91

Imagine the perfumed mysticism of Scriabin combined with the mind-bending jazz arabesques of Art Tatum, and you have some idea of the character of this music. Son of a Parsi father and a Spanish-Sicilian mother, Kaikhosru Shapurji Sorabji lived for many years as a recluse in England, deliberately discouraging performance of his own music. In 1919 Sorabji played his First Sonata to his idol Busoni, who aptly summed it up as being "like a tropical forest" (although by the standards of his later works it is restrained in both its musical language and its dimensions — his most famous piano extravaganza, *Opus Clavicembalisticum,* fills some four and a half hours!). Marc-André Hamelin describes the sonata as "a thrilling magic-carpet ride, hurtling from splendour to splendour". That's well put, and the young Canadian's playing fully lives up to his description. It is a pianistic *tour de force* which should appeal to anyone with adventurous tastes. Recording quality is beautifully clean. Even the duration of the disc seems quite appropriate to the unusual density of the music.

Further listening ...

Organ Symphony No. 1. **Kevin Bowyer** (org). Continuum CCD1001/2 (5/89).

Le jardin parfumé — poem for piano. Prelude, Interlude and Fugue. Nocturne. Djâmî. Pastiche on Rimsky-Korsakov's Hindu Merchant Song. Pastiche on Chopin's Waltz, Op. 64 No. 1. **Michael Habermann** (pf). ASV Musicmasters CDAMM159 (5/89).

Opus clavicembalisticum. **John Ogdon** (pf). Altarus AIR-CD-9075 (9/89).

Key to Symbols

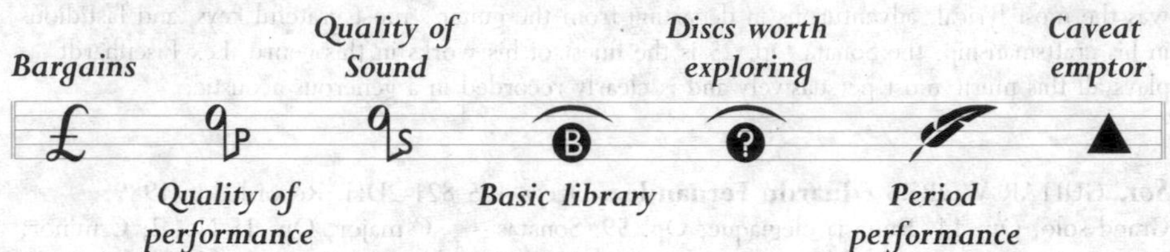

John Sousa

American 1854-1932

Suggested listening ...

GREAT AMERICAN MARCHES, Volume 1 — King Cotton. Hands across the sea. Solid Men to the Front. Gladiator. The Royal Welch Fusiliers. Marquette University March. Semper Fidelis. The Legionnaires. The Northern Pines. The Belle of Chicago. The Daughters of Texas. The Gallant Seventh. Nobles of the Mystic Shrine. The Invincible Eagle. Golden Jubilee. New York Hippodrome. **Royal Marines Band/Lt-Col. G.A.C. Hoskins.** EMI Great American Series CDM7 64671-2.

GREAT AMERICAN MARCHES, Volume 2 — El Capitan. Hail to the Spirit of Liberty. The Charlatan. The Washington Post. From Maine to Oregon. The Lambs' March. The Beau Ideal. The Crusader. The Diplomat. The National Game. The Black Horse Troop. Powhatan's Daughter. On the Campus. The Kansas Wildcats. La Flor de Sevilla. The Fairest of the Fair. Sound Off. Jack Tar. The High School Cadets. The Thunderer. The Glory of the Yankee Navy. The Stars and Stripes Forever. **Royal Marines Band/Lt-Col. G.A.C. Hoskins.** EMI Great American Series CDM7 64672-2.

FENNELL CONDUCTS SOUSA. Sound Off. Nobles of the Mystic Shrine. Sabre and Spurs. The Picadore. Our Flirtation. The High School Cadets. The Invincible Eagle. Bullets and Bayonets. The Liberty Bell. Riders for the Flag. Solid Men to the Front. The Gallant Seventh. The Rifle Regiment. The Pride of the Wolverines. Golden Jubilee. The Gridiron Club. New Mexico. Sesqui-Centennial Exposition. The Black Horse Troop. The Kansas Wildcats. Manhattan beach.

Ancient and Honorable Artillery Company (of Boston). The National Game. The Glory of the Yankee Navy. **Eastman Wind Ensemble/Frederick Fennell.** Mercury Living Presence 434 300-2MM.

Louis Spohr

German 1784-1859

NEW REVIEW

Spohr. Symphonies — No. 1 in E flat major, Op. 20; No. 5 in C minor, Op. 102. **Košice State Philharmonic Orchestra/Alfred Walter.** Marco Polo 8 223363. Recorded in 1990.

lh 5m DDD 12/92

In his day Spohr was held in high esteem by his contemporaries: E.T.A. Hoffman spoke as highly of his First Symphony as Schumann did of his Fifth and this fine new disc from Alfred Walter and the Košice State Philharmonic Orchestra restores both works to the catalogue. Spohr wrote nine symphonies and 25 years separate the two recorded here. The First owes something in style to Mozart, though its dark chromaticism puts it firmly into the nineteenth century. Walter is attentive to the pacing of this symphony, careful to bring out subtleties of Spohr's orchestral writing, particularly that of the wind instruments. It is perhaps the first movement which is the most remarkable with its grandiloquent *Adagio* opening leading into a self-confident *Allegro*; the second is hidebound by the chugging rhythm whilst the *Scherzo*, lasting only two minutes less than the finale, outstays its welcome. The lightweight fourth movement harks back to the eighteenth century and Walter displays an ideal lightness of touch.The Fifth Symphony, in C minor like Beethoven's, exists in a different world and Spohr was by this time writing in a much more overtly Romantic idiom. Its drama is supported by a substantial brass section (including four horns and three trombones) and the orchestral writing is far more daring, with Spohr's favourite clarinet hogging the best solos. This trait is also evident in the mellow slow movement and a *Scherzo* which gains much from its compactness. Both symphonies are performed with bravura and committment by the Košice orchestra in a clear acoustic, allowing the felicities of Spohr's scoring to shine through. Warmly recommended.

Spohr. JESSONDA. **Julia Varady** (sop) Jessonda; **Renate Behle** (sop) Amazili; **Kurt Moll** (bass) Dandau; **Thomas Moser** (ten) Nadori; **Dietrich Fischer-Dieskau** (bar) Tristan d'Acunha; **Peter Haage** (ten) Pedro Lopes; **Hamburg State Opera Chorus; Hamburg Philharmonic Orchestra/Gerd Albrecht.** Orfeo C240912H. Notes, text and translations included. Recorded in 1990.

② 2h 7m DDD 11/91

Spohr is generally association with the pieties of *The Last Judgement* and the prettiness of a few songs and chamber pieces, but his opera set among the Brahmins and bayadères enjoyed considerable success in its time (it appeared in 1823, the same years as Weber's *Euryanthe*) and it generally receives respectful, if brief, mention in the history books. This is its first recording. The music is mild in its orientalism, as in most things else. Mourning for the late Rajah quickly cheers up along the lines of "He's gone to Heaven", with a jolly chorus in compound time suggestive of later times of Gilbert and Sullivan. The natives take part in a war-dance, which is as decorous as a gavotte, and when the hero and heroine have their love duet there is nothing remotely erotic about it. Even so, the music is graceful, unfailingly workmanlike and notably well-orchestrated. At a rather late stage in the drama, which poses the familiar love-or-duty dilemma and ends with a last-minute rescue by the gallant Portuguese just as the heroine is about to be sacrificed to Brahma, some real inspiration arises and Jessonda's final aria achieves something not far short of sublimity. In the recording it is helped by the exquisite singing of Julia Varady, who brings distinction to everything she touches. As much can usually be said of Kurt Moll also, but on this occasion, though the depth and quality of his voice are impressive as ever, he makes little pretence of thinking this a dramatic as well as a musical entertainment. Renate Behle sings well and Fischer-Dieskau does nothing by half-measures. Thomas Moser, playing Nandori, a Brahmin with liberal tendencies, makes the most of his opportunities. Gerd Albrecht conducts a spirited performance, bringing one more near-forgotten work down from the shelves and giving it a new chance of survival as living sound.

Further listening ...

Spohr. Clarinet Concerto No. 1 in C minor, Op. 26[a]. *Coupled with* ***Mozart.*** Clarinet Concerto[b]. ***Weber.*** Clarinet Concerto No. 2 in E flat major, J118[a]. **Gervase de Peyer** (cl); **London Symphony Orchestra/[a]Sir Colin Davis, [b]Peter Maag.** Decca Serenata 433 727-2DM (7/93).

Sir John Stainer

British 1840-1901

Suggested listening ...

The Crucifixion — *oratorio.* Come, Thou long-expected Jesus — *hymn.* I saw the Lord — *anthem.* **Richard Lewis** (ten); **Owen Brannigan** (bass); **St John's College Choir, Cambridge/George Guest.** Decca Headline 436 146-2DSP.

Carl Philipp Stamitz

German 1745-1801

Suggested listening ...

Flute Concerto in C major. *Coupled with* ***Mercadante.*** Flute Concerto in E minor. ***Mozart.*** Flute Concerto No. 2 in D major, K314/285*d.* **Irena Grafenauer** (fl); **Academy of St Martin in the Fields/Sir Neville Marriner.** Philips 426 318-2PH (11/91).
See review under Mercadante; refer to the Index to Reviews.

Charles Villiers Stanford

Irish/British 1852-1924

NEW REVIEW

Stanford. Piano Concerto No. 2 in C minor, Op. 126[a]. Irish Rhapsody No. 4 in A minor, Op. 141[b]. Becket, Op. 48 — Funeral Music[c]. [a]**Malcolm Binns** (pf); **London Symphony Orchestra/Nicholas Braithwaite;** [c]**London Philharmonic Orchestra/Sir Adrian Boult.** Lyrita SRCD219. Item marked [a] from SRCS102 (8/85), [b] SRCS71 (4/78), [c] SRCS123 (8/85).

1h 3m ADD 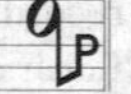

Another welcome compilation garnered from Lyrita's outstanding back-catalogue, most notable for a breathtakingly evocative performance of what is probably Stanford's finest single work, the Fourth *Irish Rhapsody*. Basking in the wondrous subtitle of "The Fisherman of Lough Neagh and what he saw", this is a stirring, colourfully orchestrated tone-poem dating from 1913. Nicholas Braithwaite and the LPO deliver a magnificent, utterly routine-free rendition (just listen to those strings swoop in the passionate coda!) and the 1978 recording is stunning even by this company's exalted standards. Sir Adrian Boult then takes over at the helm of the same group for a noble account of the impressive Funeral March from Stanford's 1892 incidental music for Tennyson's tragedy *Becket*. But by far the most ambitious offering here is the large-scale Second Piano Concerto of 1911: distinguished by fine craft and pleasing invention, it makes a thoroughly diverting impression (especially in the hands of so nimble-fingered and affectionate a soloist as Malcolm Binns), even if, in all honesty, there's precious little stubbornly memorable material on show. No matter: Braithwaite and the LSO offer alert, sympathetic backing and the Lyrita engineers have certainly secured a pleasingly natural balance.

NEW REVIEW

Stanford. Symphony No. 1 in B flat major. Irish Rhapsody No. 2 in F minor, Op. 84, "Lament for the son of Ossian". **Ulster Orchestra/Vernon Handley.** Chandos CHAN9049. Recorded in 1991.

1h 2 DDD 10/92 9S

Vernon Handley's highly successful Stanford symphony cycle is brought to a satisfying conclusion with this issue of the First Symphony. The work was written in 1876, just after the Irish-born composer had completed a period of study in Germany, and it won second prize in a British symphony competition organized by the owners of the Alexandra Place concert-hall in London. After just one performance the work lay completely forgotten until it was rescued for this recording. At the age of 23 Stanford was already a skilled orchestrator, and his use of form is very assured. An attractive, vigorous and fresh work, it is only flawed by a lack of individuality in the thematic material. The style unsurprisingly shows a marked degree of Austro-German influence, but a slight Irish flavour is also present. In 1902 Stanford responded to a commission from the Dutch conductor Willem Mengelberg with his *Irish Rhapsody* No. 2. This depicts a legend which tells of the events surrounding the violent death of Oscar, the son of the Irish hero Ossian. Here the music has a darker and more dramatic nature than in the Symphony, and it also possesses a more obviously Irish flavour since it uses traditional melodies from that country. Handley conducts highly sympathetic performances of both works. The playing is first-rate, and the recording is beautifully clear and sonorous.

Stanford. Symphony No. 2 in D minor, "Elegiac". Clarinet Concerto in A minor, Op. 80[a]. [a]**Janet Hilton** (cl); **Ulster Orchestra/Vernon Handley.** Chandos CHAN8991. Recorded in 1991.

55m DDD 1/92

Though Stanford is best known as the teacher of Vaughan Williams, Holst, Bliss and Ireland, this Irish composer is an important figure in his own right. Trained at Cambridge and then in Germany, where he became a lifelong admirer of Brahms, Stanford was essentially conservative, but that does not mean a lack of quality and in listening to the Second Symphony one immediately detects links with Elgar, though he lacks Elgar's passion and pathos. Perhaps it is only in Britain that a work as good as this should have lain unperformed for over a century — that is, between 1883 and 1990, when it was revived by the Ulster Orchestra. Their performance here under the sympathetic direction of Vernon Handley (who has now recorded all of Stanford's seven symphonies) brings out the warmth of the music, which is melodious, shapely and finely scored. The subtitle refers to the lines from Tennyson's *In Memoriam* with which the composer prefaced the score, but the prevailing mood is more positive than sombre and the slow second movement is satisfyingly serene. The vigorous scherzo has been likened to the music of Beethoven, but it is Dvořák who comes more readily to mind, while the spacious finale may recall Brahms — but even if there is no special individuality or innovation, this is fine music. So is the Clarinet Concerto, which is better known since players are glad to have this well written piece in a smallish concerto repertory. It is in three linked movements, played fluently and persuasively by Janet Hilton, whose rich tone is a delight, not least in the central *Andante con moto*. The recording of both these works is unspectacular but pleasing.

Additional recommendation ...

Clarinet Concerto[a]. *Three intermezzos, Op. 13*[b]. **Finzi.** *Clarinet Concerto*[a]. *Five bagatelles, Op. 23*[b]. **Emma Johnson** (cl); [b]**Malcolm Martineau** (pf); [a]**Royal Philharmonic Orchestra/Sir Charles Groves.** ASV CDDCA787 — 1h 14m DDD 6/92

Stanford. Symphony No. 3 in F minor, Op. 28, "Irish". Irish Rhapsody No. 5 in G minor, Op. 147. **Ulster Orchestra/Vernon Handley.** Chandos CHAN8545. Recorded in 1986.

56m DDD 1/88

The Third Symphony is marvellously well written and incorporates traditional Irish folk melodies in a rich palette of ideas, presenting these ingredients in a Brahmsian orchestral environment which nevertheless retains a perfectly individual voice. Few can resist the deft jig-scherzo of its second movement or can remain unmoved by the beautiful slow movement. The coupling is the *Irish Rhapsody* No. 5. Written some 30 years after the symphony it again draws heavily on Irish tunes and inflexions, with vigorous outer sections and a seamlessly beautiful, nostalgic central episode. The Ulster Orchestra play magnificently, giving a performance that would be hard to match let alone surpass, and the recording is a truly magnificent example of the art.

Stanford. Symphony No. 4 in F major, Op. 31. Irish Rhapsody No. 6, Op. 191[a]. Oedipus tyrannus, Op. 29 — Prelude. **[a]Lydia Mordkovitch** (vn); **Ulster Orchestra/Vernon Handley.** Chandos CHAN8884. Recorded 1989-90

1h 5m DDD 3/91 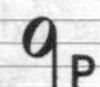

Chandos's exploration of the wilder — or, at any rate, unfamiliar — shores of British music has led them to record all the Stanford symphonies in excellent sound. The Fourth Symphony was commissioned by Berlin, where it was first performed in 1889. Its first audience would no doubt have recognized the twin influences of Brahms and Dvořák, but if they had any sense would have put them to the back of their minds as they enjoyed the light and luminous orchestration. Although the finale is the weakest moment, it is melodically enchanting. The Sixth *Irish Rhapsody* is a rarity, dating from 1922, two years before the composer's death when he was out of fashion and knew it. Perhaps this accounts for the sense of isolation in this haunting piece for violin and orchestra, played most eloquently by Lydia Mordkovitch and conducted with rare understanding by Vernon Handley. The Ulster Orchestra's playing of all the music on the disc is admirable.

Further listening ...

Morning Services — A major, Op. 12; C major, Op. 115. Evening Service in B flat major. *Coupled with* ***Bairstow.*** The Lamentation. ***F. Jackson.*** Benedicite in G major. ***Noble.*** Magnificat in A minor. **Ely Cathedral Choir/Paul Trepte** with **Jeremy Filsell** (org). Gamut Classics GAMCD527 (2/92).
See review in the Collections Section; refer to the Index to Reviews.

Three motets, Op. 38 — Justorum animae; Coelos ascendit hodie; Beati quorum via. *Coupled with* ***Martin.*** Mass for double chorus. ***Duruflé.*** Four motets sur des thèmes grégoriens, Op. 10 — Ubi caritas; Tota pulchra es; Tu es Petrus; Tantum ergo. ***Górecki.*** Totus tuus, Op. 60. ***Byron.*** Verba. **[a]Rebecca Outram** (sop); **Schola Cantorum, Oxford/Jeremy Summerly.** Proudsound PROUCD129 (4/92).
See review in the Collections Section; refer to the Index to Reviews.

John Stanley

British 1712-1786

NEW REVIEW

Stanley. Organ Concertos, Op. 10. **Northern Sinfonia/Gerald Gifford** (org). CRD CRD3365. From CRD1065 (3/80). Played on the organ of Hexham Abbey.
No. 1 in E major; No. 2 in D major; No. 3 in B flat major; No. 4 in C minor; No. 5 in A major; No. 6 in C major.

54m ADD 10/92

When he was only two years old John Stanley was blinded by a domestic accident, so as a diversion he was encouraged to study music. He didn't get on very well with his first teacher, but when he subsequently went for lessons with Maurice Greene, then organist at St Paul's Cathedral in London, he developed so quickly that, at the tender age of 12, he was appointed organist at All Hallows Church in nearby Bread Street. Five years later he became the youngest person ever to gain a B.Mus. degree from Oxford University, and from then on his reputation as a leading figure in the musical life of eighteenth-century England was assured. At the height of his powers musicians (including Handel) flocked to hear him play and his organ voluntaries remain mainstays of the repertoire to this day. The six Organ Concertos (Op. 10) show clearly the influence of Handel but also look forward towards the more modern style then being introduced into London musical life by J.C. Bach and later Haydn. There is immense charm and elegance about these concertos which Gerald Gifford, who directs stylish performances from the organ stool, brings out superbly. These are first-rate performances, nicely-moulded and intelligently played. The recording itself is of the very highest order, and if at times Hexam Abbey's most generous acoustic tends to create a slightly overblown effect, this never obscures the impressive precision of both the Northern Sinfonia and Gifford's own playing.

Max Steiner

Austrian/American 1888-1971

Suggested listening ...

Film Scores: Now, Voyager — excerpts. King Kong — suite. Saratoga Trunk — As long as I live. The Charge of the Light Brigade — Forward the Light Brigade. Four Wives — Symphonie moderne[a]. The Big Sleep — suite. Johnny Belinda — suite. Since You Went Away — main title. The Informer — excerpts[b]. The Fountainhead — suite. [a]**Earl Wild** (pf); [b]**Ambrosian Singers; National Philharmonic Orchestra/Charles Gerhardt.** RCA Victor GD80136 (10/90).

Wilhelm Stenhammar

Swedish 1871-1927

NEW REVIEW

Stenhammar. Piano Concerto No. 1 in B flat minor, Op. 1[a]. Symphony No. 3 — fragment. [a]**Mats Widlund** (pf); **Stockholm Philharmonic Orchestra/Gennadi Rozhdestvensky.** Chandos CHAN9074. Recorded in 1992.

51m DDD 10/92

NEW REVIEW

Stenhammar. Piano Concerto No. 1 in B flat minor, Op. 1[a]. Two Sentimental Romances, Op. 28[b]. Florez och Blanzeflor, Op. 3[c]. [a]**Love Derwinger** (pf); [b]**Ulf Wallin** (vn); [c]**Peter Mattei** (bar); **Malmö Symphony Orchestra/Paavo Järvi.** BIS CD550. Text and translation included. Recorded in 1992.

1h 8m DDD 10/92

The First Piano Concerto comes from 1893, when Stenhammar was 22, and such was its success during the 1890s that he was invited to play it with the Berlin Philharmonic under Richard Strauss. In time, however, he grew tired of it and became careless as to its fate. Both the autograph and the orchestral parts were destroyed when Breslau was bombed during the Second World War. But recently a copy probably made for the American première came to light in the Library of Congress. Now two recordings appear at the same time, both of them so good that one is hard put to choose between them. Chandos offer a short fragment from the Symphony No. 3 in C, on which Stenhammar embarked in 1918-9 while BIS give us a more substantial offering in the form of the *Two Sentimental Romances*, Op. 28, and *Florez och Blanzeflor*. In a sense since both CDs are so well played and recorded, the BIS might make the better choice for those who have relatively little Stenhammar in their collections. Ulf Wallin gives very good performances of the charming *Romances* and in the Tristanesque *Florez och Blanzeflor* has excellent timbre and much tonal beauty. Järvi *fils*, making his début on CD, conducts with great sympathy and sensitivity. The Symphony has an exhilarating and sturdy opening, and some characteristic touches elsewhere, but as a whole it does not add up to much. The First Concerto, at not much under 50 minutes is perhaps overlong, but still has much charm, and Widlund and Rozhdestvensky make a most persuasive case for it. The Chandos recording has slightly greater depth and warmth (not that the BIS is anything other than excellent), the strings of the Stockholm Orchestra have greater richness of sonority — and Mats Widlund brings just that little bit more colour and subtlety to the solo part. That said, however, no one investing in Love Derwinger's splendid account will be in the least disappointed.

Stenhammar. Serenade in F major, Op. 31 (with the "Reverenza" movement). **Gothenburg Symphony Orchestra/Neeme Järvi.** BIS CD310.

44m DDD 2/87

The Serenade for Orchestra is without doubt Stenhammar's masterpiece, an imaginative and magical work, full of memorable ideas and delicate orchestral colours. But it was not an immediate success and after the appearance of his Second Symphony Stenhammar returned to the Serenade, removing one of the movements and revising the outer ones. The jettisoned *Reverenza* survives in the Swedish Royal Academy Archives and Järvi has chosen to restore the movement to its original place. The *Reverenza* has some of the melancholy charm of Elgar and its refined texture enriches this wholly enchanting piece. The performance here is eloquent and committed. Glorious music, sensitively played and finely recorded, this CD is strongly recommended.

Stenhammar. SONGS. [a]**Anne Sofie von Otter** (mez); [b]**Håkan Hagegård** (bar); [a]**Bengt Forsberg,** [b]**Thomas Schuback** (pfs). Musica Sveciae MSCD623. Texts included.
In the forest[a]. Ingalill[b]. Fylgia[a]. My ancestor had a great goblet[b]. I was dear to you[b]. The girl came from meeting her lover[a]. The girl tying on Midsummer's Eve[a]. A fir tree stand alone[a]. The ballad of Emperor Charles[b]. Leaning against the fence[a]. The girl to her aged mother[a]. To a rose[a]. Under the maple tree at dusk[b]. Were I a small child[b]. A barrel-organ ballad[b]. Melody[a]. Star eye[a]. At the window[a]. Old dutchman[b]. Moonlight[a]. Adagio[a]. The Wanderer[b]. The Star[b]. Mistress Blond and Mistress Brunett[b]. A ship is sailing[b]. When through the room[b]. Why so swift to retire?[b]. Voyage to the happy country[b]. Prince Aladdin of the lamp[b]. Love song[b].

lh 14m DDD 7/90

Alongside his many accomplishments as composer and conductor Stenhammar was a pianist of some renown. He played with most of the major conductors of his day including Hans Richter and Richard Strauss, and was a noted interpreter of the Brahms concertos as well as his own. His late Beethoven was also much admired, as was his chamber music playing. What is less well-known is that he was much in demand as an accompanist, and toured extensively in that capacity. At home in his childhood, the family could muster a vocal quartet, for which he composed a number of small pieces though most of his youthful output was for solo voice, for which he wrote throughout his life. This CD brings no fewer than 30 songs into the catalogue and is the most comprehensive survey yet to appear. They cover his whole career from *In the forest*, written when he was only 16, through to his very last work, a love song from 1924. The bulk come from the 1890s and 1900s including *The girl came from meeting her lover* (or "The Tryst") made famous by Sibelius's slightly later setting. (In this instance Stenhammar's is the more subtle setting.) Some of the earlier songs are a bit conventional but they never fall below a certain level of distinction, and some are captivating. They can be original and forward-looking as in *Prince Aladdin of the lamp*, or have an unaffected naturalness and charm as in *A barrel-organ ballad*, both of which are good tracks to sample. But they are all beautifully fashioned with not a note out of place and the product of a man of fastidious taste and poetic feeling. The majority are allotted to Håkan Hagegård and Thomas Schuback, who accompanies superbly. Anne Sofie von Otter is a joy throughout. The original texts are all given with detailed summaries in English, and there is an authoritative and scholarly essay, which is a model of its kind.

Rudi Stephan

German 1887-1915

Suggested listening ...

Music for Orchestra. Music for Violin and Orchestra[a]. Liebeszauber[b]. [a]**Hans Maile** (vn); [b]**Dietrich Fischer-Dieskau** (bar); **Berlin Radio Symphony Orchestra/Hans Zender.** Koch Schwann 011623 (7/86).

Sir William Sterndale Bennett

British 1816-1875

Suggested listening ...

Piano Concertos — No. 1 in D minor, Op. 1; No. 3 in C minor, Op. 9. Caprice in E major, Op. 22. **Malcolm Binns** (pf); **London Philharmonic Orchestra/Nicholas Braithwaite.** Lyrita SRCD204 (11/90).

Piano Concertos — No. 2 in E flat major, Op. 4; No. 5 in F minor. Adagio. **Malcolm Binns** (pf); **Philharmonia Orchestra/Nicholas Braithwaite.** Lyrita SRCD205 (11/90).

William Grant Still

American 1895-1978

Suggested listening ...

Afro-American Symphony. *Coupled with* **Ellington.** The River — suite. **Detroit Symphony Orchestra/Neeme Järvi.** Chandos CHAN9154 (4/93).

Karlheinz Stockhausen

German 1928-

NEW REVIEW

Stockhausen. Michaels Reise um die Erde. **Markus Stockhausen** (tpt); **Suzanne Stephens** (basset-hn); **Kathinka Pasveer** (alto fl); **Ian Stuart** (cl); **Lesley Schatzberger** (cl/basset-hn); **Michael Svoboda** (tbn/bar hn); **Andreas Boettger, Isao Nakamura** (perc); **Michael Obst, Simon Stockhausen** (synths); **Karlheinz Stockhausen** (sound projection). ECM New Series 437 188-2. Recorded in 1989.

49m DDD 3/93

Stockhausen originally wrote "Michael's Journey round the Earth" in 1978 for trumpet and orchestra, where it comprised the second act of his opera *Donnerstag*. This "tour-version" for trumpet, plus ensemble of nine players and sound projectionist, was made in 1984. Both versions were written for Stockhausen's trumpeter son Markus, and he portrays in his playing the character of Michael, who is one of the three central figures in the opera. The other players represent "the world". After an introduction the work describes Michael's journey through seven centres, including Germany, New York, Japan and Bali. It's rather a pity that the whole work, which is played without a break, has only one CD track, since it would be helpful and interesting to be able to identify the separate episodes. It's not a difficult piece to listen to, however, since Stockhausen creates continually stimulating sonorities and patterns. Electronic synthesis is kept to a minimum, the playing is very brilliant and the recording has extraordinary vividness and presence.

Stockhausen. Mantra. **Yvar Mikashoff, Rosalind Bevan** (pfs); **Ole Orsted** (electronics). New Albion NA025CD.

1h 10m DDD 1/91

A mantra is "a sacred text used as an incantation"; but although the two pianists in Stockhausen's fascinating composition do occasionally call out to one another the work is predominantly a sustained and highly original exploration of instrumental sonority, which confirms the richness of Stockhausen's aural imagination in the late 1960s, before he embarked on the grandiose operatic project that continues to absorb all his compositional energies today. *Mantra* offers you a gripping musical argument, but not in terms of normal piano sound. The consistent use of ring modulation either distorts or enriches that sound, depending on your point of view. Stockhausen's attitude is that only through the use of such weird and wonderful technological advances can the innate spirituality of music be enhanced, and he has consistently sought to escape the mundane and embrace the transcendental in his compositions. *Mantra* is typical of his work in that its spiritual ambitions make enormous demands on the performers, and the composer's earthly messengers, in the form of Yvar Mikashoff and Rosalind Bevan, realize his intentions with both brilliance and dedication. Beyond the spirituality, there is enormous excitement in the way the music builds to its dazzling concluding toccata, and the recording does the whole enterprise full justice.

Stockhausen. Stimmung. **Singcircle/Gregory Rose.** Hyperion CDA66115. Text and translation included. From A66115 (10/84).

1h 10m DDD 2/87

Stimmung relies totally on vocal harmonics formed from six notes centred around various words. The six voices work closely together following a leading singer into sympathetic treatments of tempo, rhythm and dynamic. When the voices have achieved an 'identity' another singer leads into the next section. Of the 51 sections of the work (all individually cued on this CD) 29 employ a 'magic name' drawn from a diversity of cultures, others employ erotic poetry written by the composer himself. The variety of timbres created by the quite extraordinarily virtuosic group Singcircle is astonishing — the mesmerizing web of sounds at times seems to reject any association with the human voice. This is a very acquired taste but really does deserve to be heard. Fascinating!

Further listening ...

Klavierstück XII-XIV. **Bernhard Wambach** (pf). Koch Schwann 310015 (5/90).

Aus den sieben Tagen — Setz die Segel sur Sonne verbindung. **Ensemble Musique Vivante/Diego Masson** with **Karlheinz Stockhausen** (filters/potentionmeters). Harmonia Mundi HMA190 795 (9/89).

Alessandro Stradella

Italian 1644-1682

NEW REVIEW

Stradella. San Giovanni Battista. **Catherine Bott, Christine Batty** (sops); **Gérard Lesne** (alto); **Richard Edgar-Wilson** (ten); **Philippe Huttenlocher** (bar); **Les Musiciens du Louvre/Marc Minkowski.** Erato 2292-45739-2. Notes, text and translation included. Recorded in 1991.

1h 1m DDD 10/92

Corelli's older contemporary, Alessandro Stradella, was regarded in his own lifetime foremost as a composer for the theatre. It was his great gifts in this direction which enabled him to treat the New Testament story of the imprisonment and murder of John the Baptist with such dramatic force. Stradella's oratorio, *San Giovanni Battista*, was first performed in Rome in 1657 and is in two parts with an opening sinfonia. Part One deals with John's departure from the countryside, his arrival at Herod's court and his confrontation with the king during the royal birthday celebrations. Part Two recounts events leading to the beheading of John and concludes with a masterly duet in which the contrasting emotions of Herod and Salome are skilfully contrasted. The conductor, Marc Minkowski, has assembled a strong team of soloists with Gérard Lesne in the title-role, the sopranos Catherine Bott and Christine Batty as Salome and Herodias, respectively, and Philippe Huttenlocher as Herod. The drama is well-paced and for the most part very well sung. Salome's "Sù, coronatemi" in which the callousness and cruelty of her character are underlined is marvellously done and is one of the performance's high spots. Minkowski realizes not only the fertile invention of Stradella's craft but also the sheer beauty of the music. Full texts are provided in the booklet.

Eduard Strauss *Austrian 1835-1916*

Johann Strauss I *Austrian 1804-1849*

Johann Strauss II *Austrian 1825-1899*

Johann Strauss III *Austrian 1866-1939*

Suggested listening ...

JOHANN STRAUSS AND FAMILY IN LONDON — ***J. Strauss I.*** Huldigung der Königin Victoria von Grossbritannien–Waltz, Op. 103. Frederica–Polka, Op. 259. March of the Royal Horse Guards. Alice–Polka, Op. 238. Almacks–Quadrille, Op. 243. Exeter–Polka, Op. 249. ***J. Strauss II.*** Erinnerung an Covent-Garden–Walzer nach Englischen Volksmelodien, Op. 329. Poppourri–Quadrille. ***J. Strauss III.*** Krönungs–Walzer, Op. 40. ***E. Strauss.*** Old England for ever!–Polka, Op. 239. Greeting Waltz on English airs. **London Symphony Orchestra/John Georgiadis.** Chandos CHAN8739 (11/89).

Josef Strauss *Austrian 1827-1870*

NEW YEAR'S DAY CONCERT IN VIENNA, 1987. [a]**Kathleen Battle** (sop); **Vienna Philharmonic Orchestra/Herbert von Karajan.** DG 419 616-2GH. Recorded live in 1987. ***J. Strauss I:*** Beliebte Annen–Polka, Op. 137. Radetzky March, Op. 228. ***J. Strauss II:*** DIE FLEDERMAUS — Overture. Annen–Polka, Op. 117. Vergnügungszug–Polka, Op. 281. Unter Donner und Blitz–Polka, Op. 324. Frühlingsstimmen–Waltz, Op. 410[a]. An die schönen blauen Donau–Waltz, Op. 314. ***J. Strauss II/Josef Strauss:*** Pizzicato Polka. ***Josef Strauss:*** Sphärenklänge–Waltz, Op. 235. Delirien–Waltz, Op. 212. Ohne Sorgen–Polka, Op. 271.

Ih 9m DDD II/87

This has claims to being the finest Johann Strauss compilation ever recorded. It was the first time Karajan had conducted a New Year concert in Vienna and before he did so he prepared himself by returning to the scores for a period of intensive study. In the famous *Radetzky March* the audience was allowed to join in with the traditional hand-claps, but Karajan had only to glance over his shoulder and the sound was almost instantaneously quelled, so that the lyrical strains of the piece were not drowned. Throughout, the performances have the spontaneity of the most memorable live occasion. The Waltzes, *Delirien* and *Sphärenklänge*, are superb and in *Frühlingsstimmen* Kathleen Battle's deliciously radiant roulades are wonderfully scintillating, yet lyrically relaxed. The polkas, too, have irrepressible flair and high spirits. But it is at the arrival of the great *Blue Danube* that the magic of magic arrives. The horns steal out of the silence with their famous arpeggio theme and the strings take it up with an almost voluptuous richness. The rhythmic lilt has a special feeling unique to the VPO and at the end one is left quite overwhelmed by the experience, as if hearing the piece for the very first time. The recording is quite superb, with the acoustic of the Musikverein adding bloom and richness without robbing the definition of its natural clarity; few live occasions have been caught on the wing like this. An indispensable disc.

NEW YEAR'S DAY CONCERT IN VIENNA, 1989. Vienna Philharmonic Orchestra/Carlos Kleiber. Sony Classical SK45938. Recorded live in 1989. From CBS CD45564 (7/89).

Johann Strauss I: Radetzky March, Op. 228. ***J. Strauss II:*** Accelerationen–Waltz, Op. 234. Bauern–Polka, Op. 276. DIE FLEDERMAUS — Overture. Künstlerleben–Waltz, Op. 316. Eljen a Magyar!–Polka, Op. 322. Im Krapfenwald'l–Polka française, Op. 336. Frühlingsstimmen–Waltz, Op. 410. RITTER PASMAN — Csárdás. An die schönen blauen Donau–Waltz, Op. 314. ***J. Strauss II/Josef Strauss:*** Pizzicato Polka. ***Josef Strauss:*** Die Libelle–Polka Mazur, Op. 204. Moulinet–Polka française, Op. 57. Plappermäulchen–Polka schnell, Op. 245. Jockey–Polka schnell, Op. 278.

1h 16m DDD 2/91

The special ingredient added in 1989 to Vienna's usual New Year's Day confection of waltzes and polkas from the Strauss family was Carlos Kleiber. He brought a depth of flavour to the expected spice and froth without making the mixture too heavy, and the result delighted even the most particular gourmets. Captured on disc, the concert retains much of the sparkle of the occasion and some of Kleiber's individual contribution to Strauss interpretation, but the issue as a whole is perhaps best heard as a record of a special event that incidentally meets a demand that most of the standard, run-of-the-mill collections of Strauss waltzes only half-heartedly fulfil. The Sony recording is surprisingly good considering the problems of recording live in this venue and whilst the sound does not equal the best of some studio recordings of this repertoire, it does sizzle with authenticity.

NEW REVIEW

NEW YEAR'S DAY CONCERT IN VIENNA, 1992. Vienna Philharmonic Orchestra/Carlos Kleiber. Sony Classical SK48376. Recorded at a performance in the Grosser Saal, Musikverein, Vienna on January 1st 1992.

J. Strauss I: Radetzky March, Op. 228. ***J. Strauss II:*** Stadt und Land, Op. 332. Vergnügungszug, Op. 281. DER ZIGEUNERBARON — Overture. Eine Tausend und eine Nacht, Op. 346. Neue Pizzicato Polka. Persischer Marsch, Op. 289. Tritsch–Tratsch Polka, Op. 214. Unter Donner und Blitz–Polka, Op. 324. An die schönen blauen Donau–Waltz, Op. 314. ***Josef Strauss:*** Dorfschwalben aus Oesterreich, Op. 164. Sphärenklänge, Op. 235. ***Nicolai:*** DIE LUSTIGEN WEIBER VON WINDSOR — Overture.

1h 17m DDD 4/92 

In every respect, this is superb, a 'must'. Carlos Kleiber's second New Year's Day Concert, celebrating the arrival of 1992, was a delightful occasion in every way. Here is proof positive of its musical enchantments. Kleiber combined in a single baton his father Erich's discipline, Clemens Krauss's innate sense of rhythm, Karajan's elegance and Krips's insinuating charm. It's a formidable brew. Anyone who saw and heard the concert on television will know just how delightfully Kleiber, with his unorthodox, seemingly effortless methods, achieves his aims and how willingly his compliant orchestra responds to his peculiar gifts. Among the outright winners here is the champagne effervescence of *Eine Tausend und eine Nacht*, the ethereal beauty of *Sphärenklänge*, the irresistible verve of the *Pizzicato Polka* and the panache of *Unter Donner und*

Blitz. To crown one's pleasure, the recording is faultless: it has presence, warmth, depth, and captures ideally a sense of the occasion. It is not merely a wonderful souvenir of a special event but a thing of joy forever.

J. Strauss I. Radetzky March, Op. 228.
J. Strauss II. WALTZES AND POLKAS. **Vienna Philharmonic Orchestra/Willi Boskovsky** (vn). Decca Ovation 417 747-2DM. Recorded 1958-73.
J. Strauss II: DIE FLEDERMAUS — Overture. Perpetuum mobile, Op. 257. Accelerationen–Waltz, Op. 234. Unter Donner und Blitz–Polka, Op. 324. Morgenblätter–Waltz, Op. 279. Persischer Marsch, Op. 289. Explosionen–Polka, Op. 43. Wiener Blut–Waltz, Op. 354. Egyptischer Marsch, Op. 335. Künstl erleben–Waltz, Op. 316. Tritsch-Tratsch Polka, Op. 214. ***J. Strauss II/Josef Strauss:*** Pizzicato Polka.

1h 5m ADD 

There have been no finer recordings of Johann Strauss than those by Boskovsky and the Vienna Philharmonic. The velvety sheen and elegance of the orchestra's sound, combined with the unique lilt that comes so naturally to Viennese players, produced magical results. For this compilation Decca have sensibly mixed seven of the most famous waltzes and polkas from those sessions with other popular Strauss compositions in various rhythms, from the celebrated *Die Fledermaus* Overture, through popular polkas and novelty pieces (for *Perpetuum mobile* Boskovsky himself can be heard explaining that it has no ending) to the ever-popular *Radetzky March*. The recorded sound is not up to the most modern digital standards, but reprocessing has produced a remarkably homogeneous sound for recordings originating over a 15-year period.

J. Strauss II. WALTZES AND OVERTURES. **London Philharmonic Orchestra/Franz Welser-Möst.** EMI CDC7 54089-2. Recorded in 1990.
Künstlerleben–Waltz, Op. 316. Rosen aus dem Süden–Waltz, Op. 388. DER ZIGEUNERBARON — Overture. G'schichten aus dem Wienerwald–Waltz, Op. 325. Kaiser–Waltz, Op. 437. DIE FLEDERMAUS — Overture. An die schönen, blauen Donau-Waltz, Op. 314.

1h 6m DDD 12/91 

This Johann Strauss collection offers five of the most popular waltzes and the two most popular operetta overtures in interpretations in the best symphonic style. That is to say the performances make the very most of the miniature tone poems that Strauss provided as introductory sections to his waltzes, with the actual waltz sections themselves full of the hesitations, inflexions and tempo changes that would make the music impossible to dance to, but make it so much more effective in the concert-hall. What matters most is that all the rubato and dynamic changes evolve utterly naturally and with a delightful lilt. As the accompanying notes suggest, Welser-Möst's Austrian background gives him an advantage in evoking the special colour, gaiety and melancholy of Strauss's music, and in addition the LPO rise superbly to the lead he sets. There is a sparkle to the playing, and the instrumental solos are expertly and delicately played. All these virtues are well shown in the opening sections of *Rosen aus dem Süden* (for older music lovers always associated with radio's sometime "Grand Hotel" programme), though the fourth waltz section is somewhat rushed. Some potential buyers may regret the lack of rustic authenticity created by the absence of a zither in *G'schichten aus dem Wienerwald*, but the string alternative is beautifully played.

NEW REVIEW

J. Strauss II. COMPLETE EDITION, Volume 17. **Bratislava Radio Symphony Orchestra/Alfred Eschwé.** Marco Polo 8 223217. Recorded in 1989.
Freiheits–Leider, Op. 52. Armenball, Op. 176. Melodien–Quadrille (on themes by Verdi), Op. 112. Windsor–Klänge, Op. 104. 's gibt nur a Kaiserstadt!, 's gibt nur a Wien, Op. 291.

Bürgersinn, Op. 295. Liebchen, schwing dich, Op. 394. Feenmärchen, Op. 312. Fest–Polonaise, Op. 352. Adelen–Walzer, Op. 424. Violetta, Op. 404. Kaiser Franz Joseph Marsch, Op. 67.

1h 14m DDD 10/92

NEW REVIEW

J. Strauss II. COMPLETE EDITION, Volume 27. **Austrian Radio Symphony Orchestra, Vienna/Peter Guth.** Marco Polo 8 223227. Recorded in 1991.
Künstler–Quadrille, Op. 71. Drollerie–Polka, Op. 231. Aeolstöne–Walzer, Op. 68. Express–Polka schnell, Op. 311. Gruss an Wien–Polka française, Op. 225. Souvenir de Nizza–Walzer, Op. 200. Spanischer Marsch, Op. 433. Annina–Polka Mazurka, Op. 415. Wein, Weib und Gesang–Walzer, Op. 333. Sans-Souci–Quadrille, Op. 63. Durchs Telephon–Polka, Op. 439. Frühlingsstimmen–Walzer, Op. 410.

1h 9m DDD 8/92 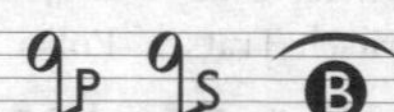

Balancing the familiar and unfamiliar, individual volumes of Marco Polo's complete Johann Strauss Edition have inevitably varied in their appeal. However, the freshness of impact that comes from unfamiliarity often outweighs any lesser invention. What is far more striking about the series has been the variation in approach and grasp of idiom of the conductors. The two here, both Viennese-trained but with slightly different approaches, come out very much at the top of the range. Alfred Eschwé's style is essentially a relaxed one, though he understands the crucial importance of differentiating one dance tempo from another. Having done so, he encourages the music to speak for itself, allowing the waltzes to breathe and flow with a lilt too often missing from conductors who seek to impose themselves on the music. For all their unfamiliar titles, the contents too are a delight. The *Windsor-Klänge* waltzes, composed for a ball at the British Embassy in Vienna, are splendid, and the quick polka *'s gibt nur a Kaiserstadt!* can seldom have been so excitingly played. Perhaps even better, though, is the collection by the Austrian Radio Symphony Orchestra under its leader Peter Guth. In quality of contents, sensitivity of conducting, sprightliness of playing and clarity of recorded sound alike this is outstanding. One marvels anew at how Vienna orchestras seem to have this music in their blood. Under Guth they manage not merely extra lilt, but extra lift. Even in the more familiar items such as *Frühlingsstimmen* and, above all, *Wein, Weib und Gesang* Guth has little to fear from comparisons. In the latter waltz he brings out details that are usually unheard and he makes more of its long introduction than perhaps any previous recording. Among the less familiar items, the waltzes *Aeolstöne* and *Souvenir de Nizza* and the polkas *Gruss an Wien* and *Express* (familiar for its use in the ballet *Graduation Ball*) are outstandingly enjoyable.

J. Strauss II. DIE FLEDERMAUS. **Dame Elisabeth Schwarzkopf** (sop) Rosalinde; **Rita Streich** (sop) Adele; **Nicolai Gedda** (ten) Eisenstein; **Helmut Krebs** (ten) Alfred; **Erich Kunz** (bar) Doctor Falke; **Rudolf Christ** (ten) Orlovsky; **Karl Dönch** (bar) Frank; **Erich Majkut** (ten) Blind; **Luise Martini** (sop) Ida; **Franz Böheim** (bar) Frosch; **Philharmonia Chorus and Orchestra/Herbert von Karajan.** EMI CHS7 69531-2. From Columbia 33CX1309-10 (11/55). Recorded in 1955.

② 1h 50m ADD 11/88 

Anyone less concerned with modernity of sound than with enjoying a well-proven, classic interpretation of Strauss's operetta masterpiece can readily be recommended to EMI's 1955 recording. Herbert von Karajan, whose preference for slow tempos and beauty of sound above all else was then still in the future, here directs with affection and *élan*. Amongst the principals Elisabeth Schwarzkopf leads the cast majestically and ravishingly. Notably in the *Csárdás*, her firm lower notes swell gloriously into a marvellously rich and individual register. As her maid, Adele, Rita Streich is an agile-voiced, utterly charming foil, launching her "Laughing Song" with deliciously credible indignation. Nicolai Gedda also enters into the fun with supreme effect. Throughout he sings with youthful ardour and freshness, but he also has a high old time impersonating the stammering Blind in the Act 3 trio. Erich Kunz's rich, characterful baritone is also heard here to good effect as Doctor Falke, the character who arranges the 'bat's revenge' which forms the story of *Die Fledermaus*. Unconventionally, the young Prince is played by a tenor rather than the mezzo-soprano for whom the role was written. Purists may object, but the result is dramatically convincing, and musically could hardly be bettered when the singer is the sweet-toned Rudolf Christ. Altogether this set can still rival any later one in theatrical effectiveness and EMI have done a good job in refurbishing it, with the disc-break sensibly placed between Acts 1 and 2.

Additional recommendations ...

Die Fledermaus. **Soloists; Bavarian State Opera Chorus and Orchestra/Carlos Kleiber.** DG 415 646-2GH2 — ② 1h 47m ADD 12/86

Die Fledermaus (with Gala Sequence). **Soloists; Vienna State Opera Chorus and Orchestra/Herbert von Karajan.** Decca 421 046-2DH2 — 2h 23m ADD 12/87 ▲

Die Fledermaus. **Vienna State Opera Chorus; Vienna Philharmonic Orchestra/André Previn.** Philips 432 157-2PH2 — ② 1h 52m DDD 9/91

Die Fledermaus[a]. *New Year's Day Concert in Vienna, 1951*[b] — **J. Strauss II:** *G'schichten aus dem Wienerwald–Waltz, Op. 325. Im Krapfenwald'l–Polka française, Op. 336. Eljen a Magyar!–Polka, Op. 332. Egyptischer Marsch, Op. 335. Vergnügungszug–Polka Galop, Op. 281.* **J. Strauss II/Josef Strauss:** *Pizzicato Polka.* **Josef Strauss:** *Mein Lebenslauf ist Lieb und Lust–Waltz, Op. 263. Die Libelle–Polka mazur, Op. 204. Jockey–Polka schnell, Op. 278.* **Soloists; Vienna State Opera Chorus; Vienna Philharmonic Orchestra/Clemens Krauss.** Decca Historic Series mono 425 990 2DM2 ② 2h 17m ADD 10/92 ▲

Richard Strauss

German 1864-1949

NEW REVIEW

R. Strauss. ORCHESTRAL WORKS, Volume 1. [ab]**Peter Damm** (hn); [c]**Manfred Clement** (ob); [d]**Manfred Weise** (cl); [d]**Wolfgang Liebscher** (bn); [e]**Malcolm Frager** (pf); [fg]**Peter Rösel** (pf); **Staatskapelle Dresden/Rudolf Kempe.** EMI CMS7 64342-2. Items marked [abcdefg] from HMV SLS5067 (10/76), [h] SLS894 (3/75), [i]SLS861 (10/73), [j]SLS880 (6/74).

Horn Concertos — No. 1 in E flat major, Op. 11[a]; No. 2 in E flat major, AV132[b]. Oboe Concerto, AV144[c]. Duet Concertino, AV147[d]. Burleske in D minor, AV85[e]. Parergon, Op. 73[f]. Panathenäenzug symphonic study in the form of a passacaglia, Op. 74[g]. Till Eulenspiegels lustige Streiche, Op. 28[h]. Don Juan, Op. 20[i]. Ein Heldenleben, Op. 40[j].

③ 3h 44m ADD 12/92

NEW REVIEW

R. Strauss. ORCHESTRAL WORKS, Volume 2. [a]**Ulf Hoelscher** (vn); **Staatskapelle Dresden/Rudolf Kempe.** EMI CMS7 64346-2. Items marked [a] from HMV SLS5067 (10/76), [bfi]SLS894 (3/75), [cgh]SLS861 (10/73), [de]SLS880 (6/74).

Violin Concerto in D minor, Op. 8[a]. Sinfonia domestica, Op. 53[b]. Also sprach Zarathustra, Op. 30[c]. Tod und Verklärung, Op. 24[d]. Der Rosenkavalier — Waltzes[e]. Salome — Dance of the Seven Veils[f]. Le bourgeois gentilhomme — Suite, Op. 60[g]. Schlagobers — Waltz[h]. Josephslegende — Suite[i].

③ 3h 42m ADD 12/92

NEW REVIEW

R. Strauss. ORCHESTRAL WORKS, Volume 3. [e]**Paul Tortelier** (vc); [e]**Max Rostal** (va); **Staatskapelle Dresden/Rudolf Kempe.** EMI CMS7 64350-2. Items marked [abd] from HMV SLS861 (10/73), [c] SLS894 (3/75), [ef] SLS880 (6/74).

Metamorphosen for 23 solo strings, AV142[a]. Eine Alpensinfonie, Op. 64[b]. Aus Italien, Op. 16[c]. Macbeth, Op. 23[d]. Don Quixote, Op. 35[e]. Dance Suite on keyboard pieces by François Couperin, AV107[f].

③ 3h 28m ADD 12/92

"From the store of glorious memories of my artistic career, the tones of this master orchestra ever evoke feelings of deepest gratitude and admiration" (thus spoke Richard Strauss when greeting the Dresden Orchestra in 1948 on its 400th Anniversary). You get the feeling that this orchestra is justifiably proud of its tones, and its Straussian associations; it takes only a few minutes of the wind concertos disc (the first CD in Volume 1), with the principals as soloists, to be aware of those tones, and to detect a special radiance that probably derives from that pride. Kempe, it seems, was the man to draw it out, and give it purpose; after his *Till Eulenspiegel*, for example, virtually all others either affect character, or are characterless. Some may find Kempe an occasionally circumspect Straussian, one who preferred decorum to decibels in the protracted cacophony that concludes the *Sinfonia domestica*, and who ensures that the famous "2001" opening to *Also sprach Zarathustra* isn't so awesome that the rest of the piece is an anti-climax. Neither did he have at his disposal the saturated sonorities of the Berlin Philharmonic that supported Karajan's breadth and power. It is difficult, though, to think of many other Straussians with the imagination and understanding to bring these scores to life from within. To catalogue Kempe's Straussian credentials would take up half this *Guide*; suffice it to say that, like Fritz Reiner, clarity of texture and a natural flexibility of pacing were prerequisites for the characterful animation and interaction of orchestral soloists or instrumental groups, but never at the expense of the long-term direction of the music. His technique, too, ensured the kind of feats of ensemble and precision that you might have expected from the Chicago Symphony Orchestra under Reiner, but Kempe's orchestra, of course, retains its warmer and cherishably Old World tones.

There are many self-evidently great Strauss performances here. A lithe, demon-driven *Don Juan*; perhaps the most vital and communicative *Don Quixote* ever recorded (greatly ennobled by Tortelier's presence); and *Ein Heldenleben* whose hero is drawn with humanity, even vulnerability and self-doubt (the reaction to the critics is unbearably sad; the scene with the hero's wife, properly reactive) and the ideal choice for those who find the work's egotism unpalatable. EMI have mixed the familiar with the unfamiliar in each box, and dedicated Straussians will find the by-ways explored with comparable commitment and skill. The recordings, made between 1970 and 1975 (the year before Kempe's premature death), vary in perspective from an ideally distanced, natural layout (*Till* and *Aus Italien*), to the closer and slightly 'contained' (*Eine Alpensinfonie* and *Ein Heldenleben*), and the vividly present (*Le bourgeois gentilhomme* and *Metamorphosen*). Clear, light-toned timpani with very little bass resonance further enhance Kempe's precise rhythmic control (even though they sound like tom-toms at the start of *Also sprach Zarathustra*), and soloists are invariably up-front, but rarely at the expense of orchestral detail. The whole invaluable enterprise benefits from the warm acoustics of the Lukaskirche in Dresden.

Additional recommendations ...

Horn Concertos. **Weber.** *Concertino for horn and orchestra in E minor, J188.* **Hermann Bauman** (hn); **Leipzig Gewandhaus Orchestra/Kurt Masur.** Philips 412 237-2PH — ∴ DDD 6/85 ℗

Horn Concertos[a]. ***Hindemith.*** *Horn Concerto*[b]. **Dennis Brain** (hn); **Philharmonia Orchestra/**[a]**Wolfgang Sawallisch**; [b]**Paul Hindemith.** EMI CDC7 47834-2 — ∴ 49m ADD 10/87 ℗ ▲

R. Strauss. Don Juan, Op. 20[a]. Tod und Verklärung, Op. 24[b]. Also sprach Zarathustra, Op. 30[c]. **Vienna Philharmonic Orchestra/Herbert von Karajan.** Decca Ovation 417 720-2DM. Item marked [a] from SXL2269 (5/61), [b] SXL2261 (4/61), [c] SXL2154 (8/59). Recorded 1959-60.

∴ 1h 15m ADD 12/87 

The orchestral playing here is magnificent — the sheer ecstatic fervour of the violins brings out all the sexuality of the glorious *Don Juan* love-music, while at the end the feeling of the desolate ebbing away of all feeling is marvellously conveyed. *Also sprach Zarathustra* is full of subtle detail, and the CD background quiet brings the most potent atmospheric feeling, as is immediately instanced by the hushed string entry of "The dwellers in the world beyond". The punch of the brass and again the soaring violins in "Of joys and passions" compensates for any lack of amplitude while the "Dance Song" has a special rhythmic lilt from an orchestra famous for their feeling for the dance idiom. The transfiguration theme of *Tod und Verklärung* is another instance where the leonine timbre of the VPO brings a new dimension. All in all, this is a splendid triptych, confirming Karajan as a great and indeed uniquely perceptive Straussian.

Additional recommendations ...

Don Juan. Tod und Verklärung. Till Eulenspiegel. **London Philharmonic Orchestra/Karl Rickenbacher.** Classics for Pleasure CD-CFP4592 — 55m DDD £

Also sprach Zarathustra. Ein Heldenleben, Op. 40. **Chicago Symphony Orchestra/Fritz Reiner.** RCA 09026 61494-2 — lh 16m ADD 4/93

R. Strauss. Metamorphosen for 23 solo strings, AV142. Tod und Verklärung, Op. 24. **Berlin Philharmonic Orchestra/Herbert von Karajan.** DG 410 892-2GH. From 2532 074 (5/83).

52m DDD 2/84

In his handling of *Metamorphosen* Karajan holds his power in reserve until the climactic C major eruption just before the coda, with thrilling effect — everything, one feels, has been in some way a preparation for this moment, and the final turn to the minor acquires greater poignancy and dramatic force as a result. The playing of the Berlin Philharmonic strings is magnificent, and the recording manages to be both spacious and intimate. After this, the prospect of another long stretch of C minor may seem a little daunting, but *Tod und Verklärung* provides a strong contrast to the much later *Metamorphosen*, and once again Karajan's superbly controlled and intense reading ensures a gripping musical experience.

Additional recommendation ...

Metamorphosen for 23 solo strings. Tod und Verklärung, Op. 24. Drei Hymnen, Op. 71[a]. [a]**Felicity Lott** (sop); **Scottish National Orchestra/Neeme Järvi.** Chandos CHAN8734 — lh 12m DDD 3/90

R. Strauss. Don Juan, Op. 20. Don Quixote, Op. 35[a]. [a]**Franz Bartolomey** (vc); [a]**Heinrich Koll** (va); **Vienna Philharmonic Orchestra/André Previn.** Telarc CD80262. Recorded in 1990.

lh DDD 10/91

Strauss's two Dons make an obvious coupling. There are versions of *Don Juan* where "youth's fiery pulses race" like a tornado sweeping through the entire orchestra. Previn's isn't one of them. Control is the keynote here, a certain nobility and dignity, with the Vienna strings lending their own inimitable brand of sweetness and vibrancy to the love music. Similarly, there are versions of *Don Quixote* which place the principal characters (cello and viola) emphatically down at the footlights. Previn and Telarc respect the composer's original intentions and use the principals of the orchestra who are quite clearly balanced within the orchestra. It's a patient and considered reading full of warmth and humanity that does not yield all its treasures on first hearing but will only initially disappoint if you have become used to the piece being recorded as a double concerto. There have also been recordings that render the sound of the Vienna Philharmonic with more richness and gloss, but momentary suspicions of the woodwind in *Don Juan*, to borrow Debussy's phrase, "sending out distress signals from the back of the orchestra" are the only blot on a superbly natural, ideally distanced sound from Telarc.

Additional recommendation ...

Don Quixote. Salome — Dance of the Seven Veils. **Miklos Perényi** (vc); **László Bársony** (va); **Hungarian State Orchestra/János Ferencsik.** Hungaroton White Label HRC081 — 49m ADD £

R. Strauss. Don Quixote, Op. 35[a]. Le bourgeois gentilhomme — suite, Op. 60[b]. [a]**Leonard Rubens** (va); [a]**Paul Tortelier** (vc); **Royal Philharmonic Orchestra/Sir Thomas Beecham.** EMI Great Recordings of the Century mono CDH7 63106-2. Item marked [a] from HMV DB6796/800 (4/49), [b] DB6643, DB6646/8 (11/49). Recorded 1947-48.

lh 6m ADD 9/89 

Although *Don Quixote* has been well served on record, this recording must be chosen for its special qualities of insight. It combines the youthful freshness of the young soloist at the beginning of his career, who only a few years earlier had played the work under Strauss himself, with the wisdom and maturity of a lifelong advocate of the composer. Moreover, the composer was present not only during the recording of *Don Quixote* but also during some of the movements from *Le bourgeois gentilhomme*, which are given with such sparkle here. Beecham was one of the few conductors to bring a rare kind of delicacy and lightness to Strauss's scores, nowhere more so than in *Le bourgeois gentilhomme*. Tortelier brings to *Don Quixote* nobility and great poetic insight and no reader of whatever generation is likely to be disappointed by the quality of the orchestral playing. Indeed it is pretty electrifying, with the newly-formed RPO on their best form.

NEW REVIEW

R. Strauss. Divertimento, Op. 86. Le bourgeois gentilhomme — suite, Op. 60. **Orpheus Chamber Orchestra.** DG 435 871-2GH. Recorded in 1991.

1h 8m DDD 3/93

This coupling should give much pleasure to those prepared to take a little New World zest and stringency with their Strauss; despite the absence of a conductor, there is nothing remotely bland or mechanical about the playing. The little-known *Divertimento* is often confused with the similar-sounding *Dance Suite* of 1923, also based on Couperin originals. The *Divertimento* came together as late as 1943 and has never established a firm place in the repertoire. Until now: the Orpheus Chamber Orchestra is mightily impressive here, eclipsing previous exponents by restoring something of the freshness of Couperin's *Pièces de clavecin* to Strauss's outrageous realizations. Behind the inauthentic, chocolate-box sonorities lurks an affecting undercurrent of nostalgia and there are obvious links with *Capriccio*'s pastiche of Passepied, Gigue and Gavotte. *Le bourgeois gentilhomme* is of course the stronger score and this stylish account of the suite is absolutely complete, unlike some famous versions of the past. Again, the players are on world-beating form, lacking perhaps the very last ounce of charm and flexibility but compensating with a dazzling display of technique. Sensitive microphone placement minimizes the problems of an over-resonant venue. This is modern music-making at its best.

R. Strauss. Aus Italien, Op. 16. Don Juan, Op. 20. **Berlin Philharmonic Orchestra/Riccardo Muti.** Philips 422 399-2PH. Recorded in 1989.

1h 1m DDD 9/90 

Muti's interpretation of *Aus Italien*, Strauss's early 'symphonic fantasy', composed after a holiday in Italy, glows and glistens with Southern warmth and colour. The Berlin Philharmonic revels in the masterly scoring and its rich sound is fully captured by the Philips recording. Muti achieves a splendid balance and one can almost feel the heat of the sun as the young Strauss glories in his first experience of the land that has inspired so many composers. The performance of *Don Juan* is also extremely good, but Muti's interpretation favours excessively slow tempos in the romantic episodes.

R. Strauss. Eine Alpensinfonie, Op. 64. Don Juan, Op. 20. **San Francisco Symphony Orchestra/Herbert Blomstedt.** Decca 421 815-2DH. Recorded in 1988.

1h 10m DDD 6/90 

The *Alpine* Symphony is the last of Richard Strauss's great tone-poems and is in many ways the most spectacular. The score is an evocation of the changing moods of an alpine landscape and the huge orchestral apparatus of over 150 players encompasses quadruple wind, 20 horns, organ, wind machine, cowbells, thunder machine, two harps and enhanced string forces. Its pictorialism may be all too graphic but what virtuosity and inspiration Strauss commands. Herbert Blomstedt's reading penetrates beyond the pictorialism into the work's deeper elements. It emerges as a gigantic hymn to nature on a Mahlerian scale. Tempos are slower, but these are justified by the noble expansiveness of the final pages, towards which the whole performance moves with impressive inevitability. The San Francisco Symphony's playing is magnificent, with subtle use of vibrato by the strings and superb performances, individual and corporate, by the wind sections. The recording is on a spacious scale to match the performance, the big climaxes really thrilling and the whole well balanced. The *Don Juan* performance is fine too.

Additional recommendations ...
Eine Alpensinfonie. **Concertgebouw Orchestra/Bernard Haitink.** Philips 416 156-2PH — 50m DDD 7/86
Eine Alpensinfonie. Der Rosenkavalier — suite[a]. [a]**Augmented Tivoli Orchestra, Bavarian State Orchestra/Richard Strauss.** Koch Legacy mono 37132-2 — 1h 12m ADD 1/93 ▲
Eine Alpensinfonie[a]. *Songs*[b] — *Freundliche Vision, Op. 48 No. 1; Meinem Kinde, Op. 37 No. 3; Das Bächlein, Op. 88 No. 1; Morgen!, Op. 27 No. 4.* [a]**Felicity Lott** (sop); [b]**Edwin Paling** (pf); **Scottish National Orchestra/Neeme Järvi.** Chandos CHAN8557 — 1h 1m DDD 12/87 £

NEW REVIEW

R. Strauss. Ein Heldenleben, Op. 40. **Berlin Philharmonic Orchestra/Herbert von Karajan.** DG 415 508-2GH.

47m DDD 4/86 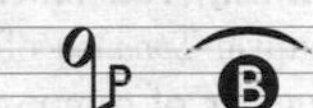

Karajan brings a particular wealth of experience to Strauss's exuberant account of a hero's life. The hero is of course Strauss himself and the heroine, his wife, but this is no Nietzschean superman; in Karajan's third stereo recording the characterization of the carping critics is as sharp as ever and the legendary Pauline provokes as well as consoles (with close-miked soloist Leon Spierer playing it deliberately straight). Perhaps the hero's exploits on the battlefield lack the last ounce of vigour and athleticism, but then this is an older man's view and there is surely ample compensation in the Berliners' rich yet detailed sonorities. Even here, after a slow start, the excitement builds in masterly fashion and there is a tremendous climax. Throughout the piece, Karajan's control of line never falters; phrases are long and immaculately tailored. There is never any danger of this life collapsing into a series of minutely characterized but disparate incidents. DG's recording brings an inconsistent, rather close focus at times and playing time is less than generous. Nevertheless, the magnificent overall sweep and glorious orchestral response make this a very special issue for admirers of an opulent brand of music-making which it has become fashionable to deprecate as heartless or insincere. Although no true Straussian will be without other versions, Karajan is still the major claimant for supremacy.

Additional recommendations ...
Ein Heldenleben. Don Juan. **Berlin Philharmonic Orchestra/Herbert von Karajan.** DG Galleria 429 717 2GGA ADD ▲
Ein Heldenleben. **Staatskapelle Dresden/Herbert Blomstedt.** Denon C37-7561 — 46m DDD 12/84
Ein Heldenleben. Macbeth, Op. 23. **Staatskapelle Dresden/Rudolf Kempe.** EMI Studio CDM7 69171-2 — 1h 4m ADD 5/88
Ein Heldenleben. Don Juan. **Vienna Philharmonic Orchestra/Clemens Krauss.** Decca Historic mono 425 993-2DM — 59m ADD 9/92 ▲

R. Strauss. Till Eulenspiegels lustige Streiche, Op. 28. Ein Heldenleben, Op. 40. **Chicago Symphony Orchestra/Daniel Barenboim.** Erato 2292-45621-2.

1h 3m DDD 8/91 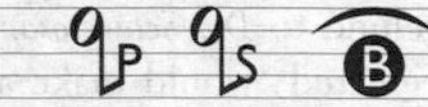

This disc kicks off with Barenboim's suave reading of *Till Eulenspiegel*. The performance is brilliant, combining tenderness (as in the introduction) with exuberance. His pacing and judging of the tricky corners is exemplary and his approach shows an awareness that this above all is a young man's music. For sheer splendour and opulence it is quite staggering. Barenboim's hero in *Ein Heldenleben* is impetuous and romantic and he gives the Chicago Symphony Orchestra a free rein to bring their customary flair and virtuosity to the work. The battle sequence is properly exciting while Samuel Magad's violin solo is sweet and seductive. This reading is a major claimant for supremacy. Erato have given Barenboim a big full sound, eminently suited to the music. The entire recording is very fine, with plenty of inner detail and for sheer opulence and splendour it surpasses other versions.

Additional recommendations ...

Till Eulenspiegels lustige Streiche. Ein Heldenleben. **London Symphony Orchestra/Michael Tilson Thomas.** CBS CD44817 — 1h 3m DDD 5/89 qp qs B

Ein Heldenleben[a]. *Don Juan, Op. 20*[b]. *Till Eulenspiegels lustige Streiche*[c]. [a]**Philadelphia Orchestra/Eugene Ormandy;** [bc]**Cleveland Orchestra/George Szell.** Sony Classical Essential Classics MK48272 — 1h 15m ADD 5/93 qp B

NEW REVIEW

R. Strauss. Suite in B flat major, Op. 4. Sonatina No. 1 in F major, "Aus der Werkstatt eines Invaliden", AV135. **Norwegian Wind Ensemble/Gerard Oskamp.** Victoria VCD19045.

1h 2m DDD 8/92

The Norwegian Wind Ensemble's ongoing survey of the complete Strauss wind music can be cordially recommended to those eager to explore the byways of this composer's art. The more familiar *Sonatina* of 1943 is a characteristically fluent, not to say garrulous piece, which shares a number of compositional traits with *Metamorphosen* while operating on a rather different level. The much earlier Suite is an intriguing makeweight. It's no masterpiece, but it displays a degree of musical imagination and technical resource remarkable for a student composer: having a distinguished horn player for a father must have helped. It is sometimes difficult to believe that the two works are separated by some 60 years. Gerard Oskamp's ensemble makes an impressive showing throughout — the musicians are drawn from the Oslo Philharmonic and Opera orchestras — and the recording is very naturally balanced. Viennese performances of this repertoire can be more subtly inflected, more exquisitely refined, but there is a naturalness of utterance here which is very satisfying.

NEW REVIEW

R. Strauss. ORCHESTRAL MUSIC. **Rotterdam Philharmonic Orchestra/Jeffrey Tate.** EMI CDC7 54581-2. Recorded 1991-92.

Intermezzo — Four Symphonic interludes. Capriccio — Sextet. Die Schweigsame Frau — Potpourri. Guntram — Prelude. Die Frau ohne Schatten — Symphonic fantasy.

1h 15m DDD 4/93

These are Strauss's own concert arrangements of music that he hoped might have an independent existence outside the opera house. The interludes from *Intermezzo*, a thinly disguised account of one of the Strauss's marital tiffs, were an obvious candidate for arranging, since the opera's many scene-changes mean that it contains a great deal of purely orchestral music, including an obvious and loving portrait of Strauss's wife, and a charmingly unassuming one of himself contentedly playing cards with his cronies. There's an element of self-portraiture in the freely re-composed "Symphonic fantasy" on themes from *Die Frau ohne Schatten*, too, since it concentrates very largely on scenes involving the noble-hearted but sorely-tried husband Barak, as well as the sonorous magnificence of the opera's conclusion. The Prelude to the early *Guntram* (savaged by the critics and soon forgotten — by all save Strauss, who erected a gravestone to the opera in his garden) becomes, with the addition of a brief concert ending, a 'new' Strauss tone-poem, and a nobly passionate one. The lovely string sextet that acts as prelude to *Capriccio* is an exquisite example of Strauss's later style at its most serenely lyrical, while the bustling prelude to *Die Schweigsame Frau* (another opera that Strauss, with some reason, thought unduly neglected) would make an effective beginning to any concert. They span a whole lifetime and a world of different subject-matter, these pot-pourris (to borrow Strauss's own title for the *Schweigsame Frau* prelude), and Tate's performances take full account of this, the orchestral colour of each being judged most beautifully. Fine playing and an admirable recording.

R. Strauss. LIEDER. OPERA EXCERPTS. **Lisa della Casa** (sop); **Vienna Philharmonic Orchestra/**[a]**Karl Böhm;** [b]**Rudolf Moralt,** [c]**Heinrich Hollreiser.** Decca Historic mono 425

959-2DM. Texts and translations included. Recorded 1953-54.
Four Last Songs, AV150 (from LW5056, 12/53)[a]. ARABELLA — Er ist der Richtige nicht (with Hilde Gueden, sop. LW5029, 10/53)[b]; Der Richtige so hab ich stets zu mir gesagt (Paul Schoeffler, bass-bar. LXT5017, 4/55)[c]; Das war sehr gut, Mandryka (Alfred Poell, bar. LW5029)[b]. ARIADNE AUF NAXOS — Es gibt ein Reich[c]. CAPRICCIO — Closing scene (Franz Bierbach, bass. Both LXT5017)[c].

1h 7m ADD 4/90 

Strauss's *Four Last Songs* are a perfect summation of the composer's lifelong love-affair with the soprano voice deriving from the fact that he married a soprano, Pauline Ahna. They are also an appropriate and deeply moving farewell to his career as a composer and to the whole romantic tradition and they have inspired many glorious performances. In recent times there has been a tendency to linger unnecessarily over what are already eloquent enough pieces. Lisa Della Casa, in her naturally and lovingly sung performance under Karl Böhm (the first-ever studio recording of the pieces back in 1953) makes no such mistake. In this new incarnation this is a wonderful offering at medium price backed by other invaluable Strauss interpretations from the Swiss diva. Her particular gift is to sing the pieces in a natural, unforced manner with gloriously unfettered tone. Her and Böhm's tempos tend to be faster than those employed by most of her successors.

Additional recommendations ...
Four Last Songs[a]. *CAPRICCIO — Morgen mittag um Elf*[a]. *ARABELLA*[b] *— Ich danke, Fräulein ... Aber der Richtige; Mein Elemer; Sie wollen mich heiraten; Das war sehr gut* (all with Anny Felbermayer, sop; Josef Metternich, bar). Dame Elisabeth Schwarzkopf (sop); Philharmonia Orchestra/[a]Otto Ackermann, [b]Lovro von Matačic. EMI Références mono CDH7 61001-2 — 1h 8m ADD 4/88
Four Last Songs. **Bach:** *Cantata No. 199, "Mein Herze schwimmt im Blut"* (Schwarzkopf; Philharmonia/Thurston Dart). *Mass in B minor, BWV232 — Christe eleison; Laudamus te; Et in unum Dominum* (Schwarzkopf, Kathleen Ferrier, contr; Vienna Philharmonic Orchestra/Karajan). ***Mozart:*** *Nehmt meinen Dank, K383* (Schwarzkopf; Philharmonia/Alceo Galliera). ***Gieseking:*** *Kinderlieder* (Schwarzkopf/Walter Gieseking, pf). Dame Elisabeth Schwarzkopf (sop); Philharmonia Orchestra/Herbert von Karajan. EMI CDM7 63655-2 — 1h 19m ADD 12/90
Four Last Songs, AV150[a]. *All' mein Gedanken, Op. 21 No. 1*[b]. *Allerseelen, Op. 10 No. 8*[b]. *Begegnung, AV72*[b]. *Cäcilie, Op. 27 No. 2*[b]. *Hat gesagt, Op. 36 No. 3*[b]. *Madrigal, Op. 15 No. 1*[b]. *Malven, Op. posth*[b]. *Morgen, Op. 27 No. 4*[b]. *Muttertändelei, Op. 43 No. 2*[b]. *Die Nacht, Op. 10 No. 3*[b]. *Schlechtes Wetter, Op. 69 No. 5*[b]. *Ständchen, Op. 17 No. 2*[b]. *Zueignung, Op. 10 No. 1*[b]. Dame Kiri Te Kanawa (sop); [a]Vienna Philharmonic Orchestra/Sir Georg Solti ([b]pf). Decca 430 511-2DH — 50m DDD 9/91
Four Last Songs, AV150[a]. *Tod und Verklärung, Op. 24*[b].
Wagner. *GOTTERDAMMERUNG*[c] *— Dawn and Siegfried's Rhine Journey; Siegfried's Death and Funeral Music.* [a]Lucia Popp (sop); [ab]London Philharmonic Orchestra; [c]Berlin Philharmonic Orchestra/Klaus Tennstedt. EMI Digital CDD7 64290-2 — 1h 10m DDD 8/92

R. Strauss. LIEDER[a]. Metamorphosen for 23 solo strings. [a]**Gundula Janowitz** (sop); **Academy of London/Richard Stamp.** Virgin Classics VC7 59538-2. Texts and translations included.
Lieder — Ruhe, meine Seele, Op. 27 No. 1; Waldseligkeit, Op. 49 No. 1; Freundliche Vision, Op. 48 No. 1; Morgen!, Op. 27 No. 4; Befreit, Op. 39 No. 4; Meinem Kinde, Op. 37 No. 3; Winterweihe, Op. 48 No. 4; Wiegenlied, Op. 41 No. 1; Die heiligen drei Könige aus Morgenland, Op. 56 No. 6.

1h DDD 2/91 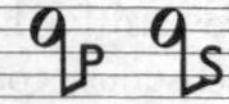

Gundula Janowitz has given some of the most beautiful performances of the music of Richard Strauss in the last three decades. Why no one asked her to record more songs during her heyday is a great mystery, but here is a quite lovely collection that shows her musicality and fine feeling for the Strauss idiom at its best. Obviously, given the passing of the years, she is happiest in the gentler, more legato numbers where her quite exquisite breath control and beauty of tone reap rich rewards — the floated line in *Wiegenlied* is absolutely ravishing and her feeling for words has, if anything, deepened over the years. She instils appropriate drama into the ecstatic *Die heiligen drei Könige aus Morgenland*, a lovely song. Throughout the disc the Academy of London play with great feeling and a good regard for the sound-world that Richard Strauss's music demands. As a very substantial fill-up. Richard Stamp and his orchestra offer a sensitive reading of Strauss's heartrending *Metamorphosen*, that threnody for the great opera-houses of Germany destroyed by Allied bombing during the Second World War. The complex lines are interwoven with care and sensitivity, and the work's true character emerges powerfully in this passionate performance. The recording is rich and clear. A delightful disc.

R. Strauss. LIEDER.
Wolf. LIEDER. **Barbara Bonney** (sop); **Geoffrey Parsons** (pf). DG 429 406-2GH. Texts and translations included. Recorded in 1989.
R. Strauss: Du meines Herzens Krönelein, Op. 21 No. 2; Meinem Kinde, Op. 37 No. 3; Ich schwebe wie auf Engelsschwingen, Op. 48 No. 2; Die Nacht, Op. 10 No. 3; Morgen, Op. 27 No. 4; Allerseelen, Op. 10 No. 8; Mein Auge, Op. 37 No. 4; Schön sind, doch kalt die Himmelssterne, Op. 19 No. 3; Ich wollt' ein Sträusslein binden, Op. 68 No. 2; Ständchen, Op. 17 No. 2. ***Wolf***: Mörike Lieder — Der Knabe und das Immlein; Er ist's; Das verlassene Mägdlein; Begegnung; Nimmersatte Liebe; Verborgenheit. Eichendorff Lieder — Verschwiegene Liebe. Italienisches Liederbuch — Auch kleine Dinge. Spanisches Liederbuch — In dem Schatten meiner Locken. Bescheidene Liebe.

55m DDD 8/90 

Bonney's clear, bell-like tone and faultless technique are heard at their most appealing here. Adding to her purely vocal accomplishments is the imagination behind the singing. Cannily choosing some of Wolf's most approachable songs, she proceeds to interpret them with unaffected, stylish singing. She finds truth in simplicity, avoiding the need for any over-detailed word painting; at the same time she unerringly finds the right mood and timbre for each piece. *Das verlassene Mägdlein* is properly empty and weary, *Begegnung* smiling and playful, *Nimmersatte Liebe* sensuous, *Verschwiegene Liebe* easily playful. Her Strauss might sometimes benefit from more flowing tempos, but the phrasing is as inevitable and natural as it is in the Wolf. Most attractive here is the conjuring up of unnamed threats in *Die Nacht* and the proper rapture in *Ständchen*. Parsons is at his most free-ranging and keen. Both artists are well supported by an open, forward recording. Anyone wanting a representative choice of these composers' songs need look no further.

R. Strauss. SALOME. **Cheryl Studer** (sop) Salome; **Bryn Terfel** (bar) Jokanaan; **Horst Hiestermann** (ten) Herod; **Leonie Rysanek** (sop) Herodias; **Clemens Bieber** (ten) Narraboth; **Marianne Rørholm** (contr) Page; **Friedrich Molsberger** (bass) First Nazarene; **Ralf Lukas** (bass) Second Nazarene; **William Murray** (bass) First Soldier; **Bengt Rundgren** (bass) Second Soldier; **Klaus Lang** (bar) Cappadocian; **Orchestra of the Deutsche Oper, Berlin/Giuseppe Sinopoli.** DG 431 810-2GH2. Notes, text and translation included. Recorded in 1990.

② 1h 42m DDD 9/91 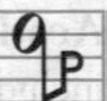

Strauss's setting of a German translation of Oscar Wilde's play is original and erotically explicit. It caused a sensation in its day and even now stimulates controversy. This recording is a magnificent achievement, mainly because of Cheryl Studer's representation of the spoilt Princess who demands and eventually gets the head of Jokanaan (John the Baptist) on a platter as a reward for her striptease ("Dance of the Seven Veils"). Studer, her voice fresh, vibrant and sensuous, conveys exactly Salome's growing fascination, infatuation and eventual obsession with Jokanaan, ending in the arresting necrophilia of the final scene. She expresses Salome's wheedling, spoilt nature, strong will and ecstasy in tones apt for every aspect of the strenuous role. She is supported to the hilt by Sinopoli's incandescent conducting and by Bryn Terfel's convincing Jokanaan, unflaggingly delivered, by Hiestermann's neurotic Herod, who makes a suitably fevered, unhinged sound as the near-crazed Herod, and Rysanek's wilful Herodias. The playing is excellent and the recording has breadth and warmth. This is eminently recommendable. For a newcomer to the work, Studer's superb portrayal just tips the balance in favour of Sir Georg Solti's famous version in which Birgit Nilsson offers a gloriously sung Salome and the playing of the Vienna Philharmonia is ravishingly beautiful..

Additional recommendation ...

Soloists; Vienna Philharmonic Orchestra/Sir Georg Solti. Decca 414 414-2DH2 — ② lh 39m ADD 7/85

R. Strauss. ELEKTRA. **Birgit Nilsson** (sop) Elektra; **Regina Resnik** (mez) Klytemnestra; **Marie Collier** (sop) Chrysothemis; **Tom Krause** (bar) Orestes; **Gerhard Stolze** (ten) Aegisthus; **Pauline Tinsley** (sop) Overseer; **Helen Watts** (contr), **Maureen Lehane, Yvonne Minton** (mezs), **Jane Cook, Felicia Weathers** (sops) First, Second, Third, Fourth and Fifth Maids; **Tugomir Franc** (Tutor); **Vienna Philharmonic Orchestra/Sir Georg Solti.** Decca 417 345 2DH2. Notes, text and translation included. From SET354/5 (11/67).

② lh 48m 12/86

Elektra is the most consistently inspired of all Strauss's operas and derives from Greek mythology, with the ghost of Agamamenon, so unerringly delineated in the opening bars, hovering over the whole work. The invention and the intensity of mood are sustained throughout the opera's one-act length, and the characterization is both subtle and pointed. It is a work peculiarly well-suited to Solti's gifts and he has done nothing better in his long career in the studios. He successfully maintains the nervous tension throughout the unbroken drama and conveys all the power and tension in Strauss's enormously complex score which is, for once, given complete. The recording captures the excellent singers and the Vienna Philharmonic in a warm, spacious acoustic marred only by some questionable electronic effects.

Additional recommendations ...

Soloists; Bavarian Radio Chorus and Symphony Orchestra/Wolfgang Sawallisch. EMI CDS7 54067-2 — ② lh 42m DDD 12/90

Soloists; Dresden State Opera Chorus; Staatskapelle Dresden/Karl Böhm. DG 431 737-2GX2 — ② lh 40m ADD 8/91 ▲

NEW REVIEW

R. Strauss. ELEKTRA[a] — Allein! Weh, ganz allein; Was willst du, fremder Mensch?; Elektra; Schwester! SALOME — Dance of the seven veils[b]; Ach, du wolltest mich nicht deinen Mund küssen lassen[c]. [ac]**Inge Borkh** (sop) Elektra, Salome; [a]**Paul Schoeffler** (bass bar) Orestes; [a]**Frances Yeend** (sop) Chrysothemis; [a]**Chicago Lyric Opera Chorus; Chicago Symphony Orchestra/Fritz Reiner.** RCA Gold Seal GD60874. Texts and translations included. Item marked [a] from VICS2009 (3/82), [b] HMV ALP1214 (11/55), [c] new to UK. Recorded 1954-56.

lh 7m ADD 5/93 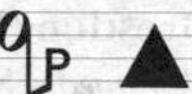

If there's only room for a single Richard Strauss disc in your collection, let it be this one. It's one of the tragedies of gramophone history that so little of Reiner 'in the pit' has been preserved on disc. After hearing this disc, you will probably want to curse RCA for lack of foresight in not setting up complete recordings of *Salome* and *Elektra* with Reiner, but in truth, in the early 1950s, complete opera recording was not the well-oiled and funded machine it is nowadays, and assembling suitable casts for recording was fraught with difficulties, one of which was record company covetousness of their artists' contracts. In 1914 Reiner was appointed principal conductor of the Dresden Royal Opera, where he worked (and became friends) with Strauss. Later on in the States, his Strauss opera performances became overnight legend: Virgil Thomson hailed Reiner's 1949 Metropolitan Opera début with *Salome* as "one of the great musico-dramatic performances of our century". These Chicago tapings, though only tantalizing samples, vividly uphold that claim. Where, on disc, is there such consistent clarification and dramatization of Strauss's hyperactive orchestration?

Where such tenacious pursuit of the operas' themes of obsession and cruelty? Where such contrast between the silkiest of caressing string tone and the force, either devastating or liberating, of the full brass (the moment Elektra recognizes her brother here simply defies description)? Fortunately Reiner had, in Inge Borkh, a soprano equal to the technical and temperamental demands of both roles, an orchestra with an already impressive Straussian pedigree that are audibly outreaching themselves for their recently appointed Music Director; and engineers realizing the new potential of stereo with an opulence and spectacle that still thrill today. Indeed, invite a few audiophile friends around, arm them with stiff Bloody Marys, play them the "Dance of the seven veils" and watch their jaws drop as you tell them the recording was made 40 years ago.

R. Strauss. DER ROSENKAVALIER. **Dame Elisabeth Schwarzkopf** (sop) Die Feldmarschallin; **Christa Ludwig** (mez) Octavian; **Otto Edelmann** (bass) Baron Ochs; **Teresa Stich-Randall** (sop) Sophie; **Eberhard Waechter** (bar) Faninal; **Nicolai Gedda** (ten) Italian Tenor; **Kerstin Meyer** (contr) Annina; **Paul Kuen** (ten) Valzacchi; **Ljuba Welitsch** (sop) Duenna; **Anny Felbermayer** (sop) Milliner; **Harald Pröghlöf** (bar) Notary; **Franz Bierbach** (bass) Police Commissioner; **Erich Majkut** (ten) Marschallin's Majordomo; **Gerhard Unger** (ten) Faninal's Majordomo, Animal Seller; **Karl Friedrich** (ten) Landlord; **Loughton high School for Girls and Bancroft's School Choirs; Philharmonia Chorus and Orchestra/Herbert von Karajan.** EMI CDS7 49354-2. Notes, text and translation included. From Columbia SAX2269/72 (11/59). Recorded in 1956.

③ 3h 11m ADD 1/88

Der Rosenkavalier concerns the transferring of love of the young headstrong aristocrat Octavian from the older Marschallin (with whom he is having an affair) to the young Sophie, a girl of *nouveau riche* origins who is of his generation. The portrayal of the different levels of passion is masterly and the Marschallin's resigned surrender of her ardent young lover gives opera one of its most cherishable scenes. The comic side of the plot concerns the vulgar machinations of the rustic Baron Ochs and his attempts to seduce the disguised Octavian (girl playing boy playing girl!). The musical richness of the score is almost indescribable with stream after stream of endless melody, and the final trio which brings the three soprano roles together is the crowning glory of a masterpiece of our century. This magnificent 1956 recording, conducted with genius by Karajan and with a cast such as dreams are made of, has a status unparalleled and is unlikely to be challenged for many a year. The Philharmonia play like angels and Elisabeth Schwarzkopf as the Marschallin gives one of her greatest performances. The recording, lovingly remastered, is outstanding.

Additional recommendations ...

Soloists; Vienna State Opera Chorus; Vienna Philharmonic Orchestra/Sir Georg Solti. Decca 417 493-2DH3 — ③ 3h 20m ADD 3/87

Soloists; Dresden Kreuzchor; Dresden State Opera Chorus; Staatskapelle Dresden/Bernard Haitink. EMI CDS7 54259-2 — ③ 3h 43m DDD 9/91

(Abridged). **Soloists; Vienna State Opera Chorus; Vienna Philharmonic Orchestra/Robert Heger.** *Coupled with DIE AEGPTISCHE HELENA — Helen's awakening; Funeral march; Bei jener Nacht; Zweite Brautnacht, Zaubernacht!;* **Rose Pauly** (sop); **Berlin State Opera Orchestra/Fritz Busch.** *Breit über mein Haupt, Op. 19 No. 2. Morgen, Op. 27 No. 4.* **Robert Hutt** (ten); **Richard Strauss** (pf). Pearl mono GEMMCDS9365 — ② 1h 55m ADD 3/90

NEW REVIEW

R. Strauss. ARIADNE AUF NAXOS. **Gundula Janowitz** (sop) Ariadne; **Teresa Zylis-Gara** (sop) Composer; **Sylvia Geszty** (sop) Zerbinetta; **James King** (ten) Bacchus; **Theo Adam** (bass-bar) Music Master; **Hermann Prey** (bar) Harlequin; **Siegfried Vogel** (bass) Truffaldino; **Hans Joachim Rotzsch** (ten) Brighella; **Peter Schreier** (ten) Scaramuchio, Dancing Master; **Erika Wustmann** (sop) Naiad; **Annelies Burmeister** (mez) Dryad; **Adele**

Stolte (sop) Echo; **Erich-Alexander Winds** (spkr) Major-Domo; **Staatskapelle Dresden/Rudolf Kempe.** EMI Opera CMS7 64159-2. Notes, text and translation included. From HMV SAN215/7 (11/68).

② 1h 58m ADD 11/92 £

This classic set has made a welcome reappearance. At mid-price it cannot be recommended too highly. Nobody knew more about how to pace Strauss's operas than Kempe and he was at his best when working with the Dresden Staatskapelle, a group of players who have Strauss in their veins. This reading brings out all the sentiment and high spirits of this delightful work, and the results are beautifully recorded. Janowitz's golden tones were ideal for the title role, which she sings with poise and inner feeling, though she makes little of the text. Zylis-Gara is a suitably impetuous Composer in the engaging Prologue where 'he' meets and has a gently erotic encounter with the charming but flighty Zerbinetta, a role here taken with brilliant accomplishment by Sylvia Geszty, who made it her own in the 1960s. James King is a forthright though none too flexible Bacchus. The smaller parts are also well taken. The piece has fared well on disc, and some may prefer the elegant Karajan version in mono on EMI with Elisabeth Schwarzkopf's highly detailed, silver-voiced Ariadne, Rita Streich's appealing Zerbinetta, Irmgard Seefried as the most impulsive of all Composers and Rudolf Schock as an ardent Bacchus, but Karajan's reading lacks the heart of Kempe's. The more recent Masur version, with the admirable Leipzig Gewandhaus, has Jessye Norman as a stately Ariadne, Julia Varady as a fiery Composer, Edita Gruberová as a bright-eyed, dexterous Zerbinetta, Paul Frey as an anonymous Bacchus. Masur, like Kempe, is steeped in the work's performing tradition and is the best of modern sets.

Additional recommendations ...

Soloists; Philharmonia Orchestra/Herbert von Karajan. EMI mono CMS7 69296-2 ② 2h 8m ADD 4/88 ▲

Soloists; Leipzig Gewandhaus Orchestra/Kurt Masur. Philips 422 084-2PH2 — ② 1h 58m DDD 11/88

Soloists; London Philharmonic Orchestra/Sir Georg Solti. Decca Grand Opera 430 384-2DM2 — ② 2h 1m ADD 5/92

R. Strauss. DIE FRAU OHNE SCHATTEN. **Julia Varady** (sop) Empress; **Plácido Domingo** (ten) Emperor; **Hildegard Behrens** (sop) Dyer's Wife; **José van Dam** (bar) Barak the Dyer; **Reinhild Runkel** (contr) Nurse; **Albert Dohmen** (bar) Spirit-Messenger; **Sumi Jo** (sop) Voice of the Falcon; **Robert Gambill** (ten) Apparition of a Young Man; **Elzbieta Ardam** (mez) Voice from above; **Eva Lind** (sop) Guardian of the Threshold; **Gottfried Hornik** (bar) One-eyed Brother; **Hans Franzen** (bass) One-armed Brother; **Wilfried Gahmlich** (ten) Hunchback Brother; **Vienna Boys' Choir; Vienna State Opera Chorus; Vienna Philharmonic Orchestra/Sir Georg Solti.** Decca 436 243-2DH3. Notes, text and translation included. Recorded 1989-91.

③ 3h 15m DDD 5/92

This was the most ambitious project on which Strauss and his librettist Hugo von Hofmannthal collaborated. It is both fairy tale and allegory with a score that is Wagnerian in its scale and breadth. The Solti version presents the score absolutely complete in an opulent recording that encompasses every detail of the work's multi-faceted orchestration. Nothing escapes his keen eye and ear or that of the Decca engineers. The cast boasts splendid exponents of the two soprano roles. Behrens's vocal acting suggests complete identification with the unsatisfied plight of the Dyer's Wife and her singing has a depth of character to compensate for some tonal wear. Varady gives an intense, poignant account of the Empress's taxing music. The others, though never less than adequate, leave something to be desired. Domingo sings the Emperor with customary vigour and strength but evinces little sense of the music's idiom. José van Dam is likewise a vocally impeccable Barak but never penetrates the Dyer's soul. Runkel is a mean, malign Nurse as she should be though she could be a little more interesting in this part. It benefits from glorious, dedicated playing by the Vienna Philharmonic Orchestra.

Additional recommendations ...
Soloists; Tölz Boys' Choir; Bavarian Radio Chorus and Symphony Orchestra/Wolfgang Sawallisch. EMI CDS7 49074-2 — ③ 3h 11m DDD 9/88
Soloists; Vienna State Opera Chorus; Vienna Philharmonic Orchestra/Karl Böhm. Decca Historic 425 981-2DM3 — ③ 3h 16m ADD 10/91 ▲

R. Strauss. CAPRICCIO. **Dame Elisabeth Schwarzkopf** (sop) The Countess; **Eberhard Waechter** (bar) The Count; **Nicolai Gedda** (ten) Flamand; **Dietrich Fischer-Dieskau** (bar) Olivier; **Hans Hotter** (bass-bar) La Roche; **Christa Ludwig** (mez) Clairon; **Rudolf Christ** (ten) Monsieur Taupe; **Anna Moffo** (sop) Italian Soprano; **Dermot Troy** (ten) Italian Tenor; **Karl Schmitt-Walter** (bar) Major-domo; **Philharmonia Orchestra/Wolfgang Sawallisch.** EMI mono CDS7 49014-8. Notes, text and translation included. From Columbia 33CX1600/02 (3/59). Recorded 1957-58.

② 2h 15m ADD 9/87 ▲

The plot of *Capriccio* centres on the Countess and her two suitors, a poet and a composer. Both are in love with the lovely Countess Madeleine who cannot choose between them. The opera moves as surefootedly as one would expect of this master, to its closing scene, one of Strauss's most magical, in which the Countess speculates on her predicament. We are left in the air not knowing which of them has won her heart. This work, though never by its nature likely to be popular in the wider sense, has always had a dedicated following. Right from the opening notes of this classic performance, where the string sextet evokes the mood so delicately, one can sense that this is a recording that will never be equalled. There is not a weak link in the chain and the cast couldn't be more perfectly matched. Though the recording is in mono it sounds quite magnificent.

Additional recommendation ...
CAPRICCIO. DAPHNE. **Soloists; Vienna State Opera Chorus; Vienna Symphony Orchestra/Karl Böhm.** DG 423 579-2GH2 — ② 1h 35m ADD 10/88

Further listening ...

ARABELLA. **Soloists; Bavarian State Opera Chorus and Orchestra/Wolfgang Sawallisch.** Orfeo C169882H (1/89).

Igor Stravinsky

Russian/French/American 1882-1971

Stravinsky. Orpheus. Jeu de cartes. **Royal Concertgebouw Orchestra/Neeme Järvi.** Chandos CHAN9014. Recorded in 1991.

53m DDD 3/92

Here are two well contrasted neoclassical ballets, both collaborations with the choreographer Balanchine. *Jeu de cartes* (1937) has the dancers as cards in a game of poker which is perpetually disturbed by the entry of the joker. And the jokes in Stravinsky's score come as he looks back with humour and raids the scores of past masters for affectionate parodies. From Stravinsky's love of Greek mythology came *Orpheus* (1948), less well known as not everyone responds to its remoteness, its "mimed song" (Stravinsky's own words); and the fact that in half an hour's duration, the music only rises above mezzo-forte for a matter of seconds. The music's timeless, other-worldly stillness, and gentle spirit are beautifully evoked in this performance (helped by the Concertgebouw's wide open acoustic) though some may prefer the composer's own sharper focus for his characteristic motor rhythms (reviewed as part of the Stravinsky Edition). There are no worries on that account in Järvi's *Jeu de cartes*, a reading of grace, humour and high contrasts; and in the final 'deal', at a faster pace than either Abbado or the composer (see below), tremendous agility. The acoustic adds an unfamiliar but welcome richness to Stravinsky's timbres, particularly the tuba and spectacular bass drum, without blurring essential rhythmic definition.

Stravinsky. The Rite of Spring. Apollo. **City of Birmingham Symphony Orchestra/Simon Rattle.** EMI CDC7 49636-2.

1h 5m DDD 11/89

Recordings of *The Rite of Spring* are legion, but it is rare to find Stravinsky's most explosive ballet score coupled with *Apollo*, his most serene. The result is a lesson in creative versatility, confirming that Stravinsky could be equally convincing as expressionist and neoclassicist. Yet talk of lessons might suggest that sheer enjoyment is of lesser importance, and it is perfectly possible to relish this disc simply for that personal blend of the authoritative and the enlivening that Simon Rattle's CBSO recordings for EMI so consistently achieve. Rattle never rushes things, and the apparent deliberation of *The Rite*'s concluding "Sacrificial Dance" may initially surprise, but in this context it proves an entirely appropriate, absolutely convincing conclusion. Rattle sees the work as a whole, without striving for a spurious symphonic integration, and there is never for a moment any hint of a routine reading of what is by now a classic of the modern orchestral repertoire. The account of *Apollo* has comparable depth, with elegance transformed into eloquence and the CBSO strings confirming that they have nothing to fear from comparison with the best in Europe or America. The recordings are faithful to the intensity and expressiveness of Rattle's Stravinsky, interpretations fit to set beside those of the composer himself.

Additional recommendations ...

The Rite of Spring. Four Etudes. **Orchestre National de France/Pierre Boulez.** Adès 13222 — 42m AAD

The Rite of Spring. ***Mussorgsky.*** *Pictures at an Exhibition.* **Concertgebouw Orchestra/Riccardo Chailly.** Decca Ovation 430 709-2DM — 1h 6m DDD 8/91

The Rite of Spring. Fireworks, Op. 4. Circus Polka. Greeting Prelude, "Happy birthday to you". **London Philharmonic Orchestra/Sir Charles Mackerras.** EMI Eminence CD-EMX2188 — 42m DDD 8/92

The Rite of Spring. Petrushka. **London Philharmonic Orchestra/Bernard Haitink.** Philips Insignia 434 147-2PM — 1h 9m ADD 8/92

NEW REVIEW

Stravinsky. Le baiser de la fée — ballet.
Tchaikovsky (arr. Stravinsky). The Sleeping Beauty — Bluebird pas de deux. **Scottish National Orchestra/Neeme Järvi.** Chandos CHAN8360. Recorded in 1984.

51m DDD 7/85 

Le baiser de la fée ("The Fairy's Kiss") was Stravinsky's 1928 "compatriotic homage" to Tchaikovsky, using the latter's songs and piano music, and imitating parts of *The Sleeping Beauty*. The scenario is based on Andersen's tale *The Ice Maiden*, as according to Stravinsky "it suggested an allegory of Tchaikovsky himself. The fairy's kiss on the heel of the child is also the music marking Tchaikovsky at his birth, though the muse did not claim Tchaikovsky at his wedding, as she did the young man in the ballet, but at the height of his powers." What this hauntingly beautiful performance proves is that the work has never really had the recognition it deserves because, until this one, no recording has done it full justice. Stravinsky's own 1965 account is, by comparison, dutiful and has a very restricted dynamic range. There are fine accounts available of the *Divertimento*: a suite that Stravinsky later extracted from the ballet, but the complete work is a must, not least for the penultimate scene where the Fairy lures the young man from his wedding: after a passionate but strangely troubled *crescendo*, the Fairy throws off her veil of disguise to a *subito piano* dissonance (track three at 19'32") that chills you to the marrow. The coupling is apt, and great fun.

Stravinsky. The Firebird — ballet. Scherzo à la russe (versions for jazz ensemble and orchestra). Quatre études (1952 version). **City of Birmingham Symphony Orchestra/Simon Rattle.** EMI CDC7 49178-2.

1h 5m DDD 4/89 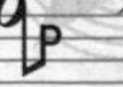 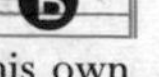

Diaghilev chose *The Firebird* as the subject of the first ballet which he himself created for his own company. Lyadov's tardiness in delivering the musical score caused the great impresario to take a risk in transferring his commission to a young and inexperienced composer, but Stravinsky seized his first important opportunity to great effect, and the result was an early masterpiece. Simon Rattle emphasizes the work's romantic influences rather than those elements which suggest a composer who would soon take a radically new path. We are reminded that Rimsky-Korsakov was Stravinsky's teacher, and that he was influenced at the time by Scriabin and Glinka. On its own terms it is a very fine, illuminating performance, brilliantly colourful and superbly played by the Birmingham orchestra. The four *Etudes*, completed in 1929, are neoclassical in style and Rattle delivers these pithy, pungent little pieces with wit and clarity. It's interesting to hear both the original orchestral version of *Scherzo à la russe*, written in 1944, and the composer's own arrangement of this poker-faced piece for Paul Whiteman's band, made later the same year. Both seem equally effective in their different ways. The recording is very good indeed to match a high-quality, highly sympathetic performance.

Additional recommendations ...

The Firebird. Le chant de rossignol — symphonic poem. Fireworks, Op. 4. Scherzo à la russe. Tango. **London Symphony Orchestra/Antál Dorati.** Mercury 432 012-2MM — lh 14m ADD 11/91

The Firebird. Apollon musagète. **Detroit Symphony Orchestra/Antál Dorati.** Decca Headline 430 740-2DM — lh 14m DDD 8/92

The Firebird. Le chant de rossignol. **Danish National Radio Symphony Orchestra/Dmitri Kitaienko.** Chandos CHAN8967 — lh 17m DDD 9/92

Stravinsky. Petrushka (1947 version)[a]. Symphony in Three Movements. [a]**Peter Donohoe** (pf); **City of Birmingham Symphony Orchestra/Simon Rattle.** EMI CDC7 49053-2.

57m DDD 5/88

Stravinsky's second great ballet score has been well served on disc from the earliest days of LP. He recorded it himself (rather indifferently) but there is in any event a good case for preferring the brilliance and clarity of digital sound in this of all works. Should this be your priority, Bernard Haitink's stunning (if synthetically recorded) Berlin Philharmonic version (listed below) makes a plausible choice. Simon Rattle's performance is most notable for its fresh look at details of scoring and balance, with pianist Peter Donohoe making a strong impression. The results are robust and persuasive, though one sometimes has the impression that the characters are being left to fend for themselves. The atmospheric sound with its generous middle and bass is certainly more natural than Philips's for Haitink. The symphony too is eminently recommendable, sounding more grateful and high spirited than it sometimes has, with Rattle particularly relishing the jazzy bits.

Additional recommendation ...

Petrushka (1911 version)[a]. *Scènes de ballet.* [a]**Philip Moll** (pf); **Berlin Philharmonic Orchestra/Bernard Haitink.** Philips 422 415-2PH — 52m DDD 10/91

NEW REVIEW

Stravinsky. WORKS FOR TWO PIANOS. **Vladimir Ashkenazy, Andrei Gavrilov** (pfs). Decca 433 829-2DH. Recorded 1990-91.

Scherzo à la russe. Sonata for two pianos. Concerto for two solo pianos. The Rite of Spring.

lh 8m DDD 2/93

Scant attention has been paid to Stravinsky's two-piano output on disc to date, so it is especially pleasurable to welcome a CD that brings together his two original works for the medium, together with the rarely heard 'piano-duet' version (arranged by the composer) of the *Rite of Spring* and the two piano version of the *Scherzo à la russe*. The latter, more often heard in either its orchestral or jazz ensemble versions, is an invigorating breath of Russian fresh air, which, although written in 1944 looks back to the folk inspired sound-world of *Petrushka*. The Sonata and Concerto, dating from 1931 and 1943 respectively, are much more astringent and classical in tone, but their spiky, contrapuntal textures and acute contrasts are splendidly projected here by Ashkenazy and Gavrilov, who lift what can often sound like two of Stravinsky's more academic essays into much more attractive and approachable works. Stravinsky once said, "All my life I have tried out my music as I have composed it, orchestral as well as any other kind, four hands at one piano". *The Rite of Spring* was no exception, and the initial piano-duet version of the work (heard on this disc in an arrangement for two pianos) was actually published in 1913, the year of *The Rite*'s tumultuous orchestral première. Ashkenazy and Gavrilov's account is one of the most exciting and galvanizing renditions of this version on disc; no pale imitation, but a rhythmically incisive reading with every minute gear change, and every nuance of this complex and thrilling score finely judged and delivered. Excellent recording — a must!

Stravinsky. The Rite of Spring. Perséphone[a]. [a]**Anthony Rolfe Johnson** (ten); [a]**Anne Fournet** (narr); [a]**Tiffin Boys' Choir; London Philharmonic** [a]**Choir and Orchestra/Kent Nagano.** Virgin Classics Duo VCK7 59077. Notes, text and translation included.

② lh 23m DDD 6/92 

The American composer Elliott Carter described *Perséphone* as "a humanist *Rite of Spring*", so this makes a logical and thought-provoking coupling (timings are not generous on the two CDs but they do come at mid-price). Although 20 years separate both works they could not be more different. The primal energy of the earlier *Rite of Spring*'s very naturalistic setting of scenes from pagan Russia is almost wholly absent from the cool, hieratic beauty of *Perséphone*'s ritual, and predominantly lyrical mode of address. The latter fuses elements of melodrama (literally, speech with music), oratorio and ballet, is set in classical Greece and has a text that is spoken and sung in French. Nagano's recording is the first to have appeared since Stravinsky's own 1966 account (part of the Stravinsky Edition but not one of the items to be made available separately) and is, in many ways, finer. A modern dynamic range predictably benefits the thrilling theatre of the choral invocation for Perséphone's return from the underworld in the third part of the work (culminating in a triple *forte* cry of "Printemps" as powerful as anything in the *Rite*); and both Anne Fournet in the spoken role of Perséphone, and Anthony Rolfe Johnson as the priest of the Eleusinian mysteries are preferable to their predecessors. Nagano's tempos are swifter than Stravinsky's which, in music that is predominantly slow moving, will be welcomed by many. Nagano's *Rite* is balletic and sharply emphatic; closely miked in a way often reminiscent of Stravinsky's own, with strongly projected woodwind and a crisp, forceful, though never heavy presence for the percussion. Other versions may remind us more powerfully of the work's extremism, but Nagano is often strikingly individual — one thinks of the almost reptilian coiling of clarinets at the end of the "Ritual of the Ancestors" — with more expressive phrasing and pacing than usual in the work's mysterious moments.

Stravinsky. Pulcinella — ballet (rev. 1947)[a]. Jeu de cartes. [a]**Teresa Berganza** (mez); [a]**Ryland Davies** (ten); [a]**John Shirley-Quirk** (bar); **London Symphony Orchestra/Claudio Abbado.** DG Galleria 423 889-2GGA. Text and translation included. Item marked [a] from 2531 087 (6/79), [b] 2530 537 (8/57).

lh 2m ADD 1/89 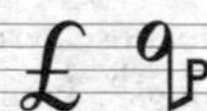

Claudio Abbado's 1970s recordings of these two so-called neoclassical ballet scores are very tempting at mid-price. "So called" because *Jeu de cartes* ("Game of cards"), one of Stravinsky's wittiest concoctions, contains a dash of Beethoven, Rossini, Johann Strauss, Ravel and even Stravinsky himself. Leaving pedantry aside, not even the composer himself achieved Abbado's combination of rapier-like pointing of accents (the snap in those rhythmic displacements), of humour in the instrumental interplay and of grace in the singing lines. Remastering has revealed slightly edgy violin tone in *Jeu de cartes*, but the bright sound is wholly suitable for the diamond edged profile of Stravinsky's orchestration.

Additional recommendation ...

Pulcinella[a]. *Le chant du rossignol*[d]. [a]**Ann Murray** (mez); [a]**Anthony Rolfe Johnson** (ten); [a]**Simon Estes** (bass); [a]**Ensemble Intercontemporain;** [b]**French Naitonal Orchestra/Pierre Boulez.** Erato 2292-45382-2 — ADD 5/86

Key to Symbols

Gramophone Award winners **Artists of the Year**

Stravinsky. Concerto in E flat major, "Dumbarton Oaks". Pulcinella[a] — ballet (with original inspirations). [a]**Bernadette Manca di Nissa** (mez); [a]**David Gordon** (ten); [a]**John Ostendorf** (bass); **St Paul Chamber Orchestra/Christopher Hogwood.** Decca 425 614-2DH. Recorded in 1989.

Inspirations — ***Gallo*:** Trio Sonatas — No. 1 in G major: Moderato; No. 2 in B flat major: Presto, Presto; No. 7 in G minor: Allegro (Romuald Tecco, Thomas Kornacker, vns; Peter Howard, vc; Hogwood, hpd). ***Pergolesi*:** Cello sinfonia (Howard, Joshua Koestenbaum, vcs; Hogwood).

lh 6m DDD 6/90 

Both *Dumbarton Oaks* and *Pulcinella* are deeply involved with the eighteenth century and the benefit of involving an eighteenth-century specialist in performing them is, firstly, that he will adopt a scholarly attitude to both pieces (Hogwood has sorted out one or two textual problems in *Dumbarton Oaks* by going back to the sources, just as if Stravinsky were an obscure composer of concerti grossi) and secondly that he will be likely to try out some of what he knows of period performing practice on these products of Stravinsky's kleptomaniac (his own word) forays into the eighteenth century. So, we have on the whole non-legato, eighteenth-century style bowing among the strings (expressive slurs and slides only where Stravinsky asks for them), an implicit assumption that if a note appears in the score it is intended to be heard and a feeling, in both works, of an inherently vocal, Italianate grace to the sustained lines. Together with clean, crisp rhythms (this music dances more often than it pounds) and a deft pointing of accents it makes for great freshness and zest and a clear demonstration of Stravinsky's deep love for and understanding of the past and of the wholly twentieth-century creative response it awoke in him. The fragments of eighteenth-century music that Stravinsky used as a basis for *Pulcinella* make an entertaining supplement, but how one misses his inspired 'distortions' while listening to them. Admirable playing throughout, acceptable soloists and a first-class recording.

Stravinsky. SONGS. [a]**Phyllis Bryn-Julson** (sop); [b]**Ann Murray** (mez); [c]**Robert Tear** (ten); [d]**John Shirley-Quirk** (bar); **Ensemble Intercontemporain/Pierre Boulez.** DG 20th Century Classics 431 751-2GC. Texts and translations included. From 2531 377 (7/82). Recorded in 1980.

Pastorale[a]. Deux poèmes de Paul Verlaine[d]. Two poems of Konstantin Bal'mont[a]. Three Japanese lyrics[a]. Three little songs, "Recollections of my childhood"[a]. Pribaoutki[d]. Cat's Cradle Songs[b]. Four Songs[a]. MAVRA — Chanson de Paracha[a]. Three Songs from William Shakespeare[b]. In memoriam Dylan Thomas[c]. Elegy for J.F.K.[d]. Two Sacred Songs (after Wolf)[c].

58m ADD 2/92

It may be true that this disc lacks the focus of a single major work, but it is also much more than a random compilation of unrelated miniatures. Principally, it offers an aurally fascinating contrast between two groups of pieces: Stravinsky's relatively early Russian settings, as he worked through his own brand of nationalism, reaching from the salon style of *Pastorale* to the folk-like vigour of a work like *Pribaoutki*; then the late serial compositions, written in America, which prove that the rhythmic vitality and melodic distinctiveness of the early works survived undimmed into his final years. Stravinsky may have regarded texts as collections of sounds whose natural rhythms had no role to play in their musical setting, but the essential meaning still comes through unerringly, whether it is that of the plaintive Paracha's song from the opera *Mavra* or the sombre *Elegy for J.F.K.* (to an Auden text). The disc is rounded off by the very late Wolf arrangements, and whilst one might quibble here and there about Boulez's choice of tempo, or the balance of voice and instruments, the disc as a whole is immensely satisfying as a comprehensive survey of an important repertory.

Stravinsky. SACRED CHORAL WORKS. [a]**John Mark Ainsley** (ten); [b]**Stephen Roberts** (bar); **Westminster Cathedral Choir;** [c]**City of London Sinfonia/James O'Donnell.** Hyperion CDA66437. Texts and translations included. Recorded in 1990.
Symphony of Psalms[c]. Pater noster. Credo. Ave Maria. Mass[c]. Canticum sacrum[abc].

lh 8m DDD 9/91

It is no ordinary cathedral choir that can cope with the music of Stravinsky. The relatively traditional style of the *Symphony of Psalms* and the Mass provide plenty of challenges, especially in the pitching of those dissonant yet still tonal chords, while the *Canticum sacrum* offers even fewer familiar landmarks for singers who spend most of their time with the euphonious polyphony of Palestrina or Victoria. Yet the Westminster Cathedral Choir is remarkably assured throughout this disc. There is no sense of strain, rather a genuine sense of style, reinforcing the rightness of the composer's instincts in arguing the case for all-male singers in these works. Just occasionally, indeed, one might welcome a more wholehearted response to the weight and urgency of the music. Overall, nevertheless, there is a clarity and poise which underline Stravinsky's concern with the timeless rituals of religious observation, and the sense that sacred music is above all a celebration of belief. There is admirable support from the soloists and the City of London Sinfonia, and the recording avoids the excessive resonance that often afflicts the cathedral environment. The conductor James O'Donnell merits particular praise for the disciplined flexibility of the performances.

Stravinsky. Les noces[a]. Mass[b]. [a]**Anny Mory** (sop); [a]**Patricia Parker** (mez); [a]**John Mitchinson** (ten); [a]**Paul Hudson** (bass); **English Bach Festival Chorus;** [b]**Trinity Boys' Choir;** [a]**Martha Argerich,** [a]**Krystian Zimerman,** [a]**Cyprien Katsaris,** [a]**Homero Francesch** (pfs); [a]**English Bach Festival Percussion Ensemble;** [b]members of the **English Bach Festival Orchestra/Leonard Bernstein.** DG 20th Century Classics 423 251-2GC. Texts and translations included. From 2530 880 (2/78).

44m ADD 6/88 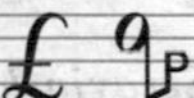

Like *Les noces*, the *Mass* presents a fundamental ritual experience, here the sacrament of worship rather than marriage. It does so in a similar depersonalized way but with the emphasis on stillness and awe rather than driving rhythmic energy. In its austerity the *Mass* is the gateway to the later serial Stravinsky of the 1950s and 1960s. The English Bach Festival Chorus, joined by the Trinity Boys' Choir in the *Mass*, carry the burden of the all-important choral parts, and do so triumphantly. The glamorous line-up of pianists (Argerich, Zimerman, Katsaris, Francesch) supplies the expected panache in *Les noces* and the vocal soloists are first-rate. Bernstein co-ordinates the ensemble superbly and ensures that the sense of wonder underlying both works is fully conveyed. In DG's digital remastering the original analogue recording sounds in mint condition.

The reviews which follow comprise part of "The Complete Edition" (Sony Classical S22K46290, medium price, 22 CDs, ADD, 7/91). The items reviewed here were subsequently issued as separate sets.

NEW REVIEW

Stravinsky. THE COMPLETE EDITION. **Various artists/Igor Stravinsky.** Sony Classical SM3K46291 (Volume 1). Recorded 1959-62.
The Firebird (Columbia Symphony Orchestra. From CBS 72046, 9/62). Scherzo à la russe (Columbia Symphony Orchestra). Scherzo fantastique (CBC Symphony Orchestra). Fireworks (Columbia Symphony Orchestra. All from CBS GM31, 2/82). Petrushka (Columbia Symphony Orchestra. Philips SABL175, 4/61). The Rite of Spring (Columbia Symphony Orchestra. SABL174, 4/61). Les noces (Mildred Allen, sop; Regina Sarfaty, mez; Loren Driscoll, ten; Richard Oliver, bass; Samuel Barber, Aaron Copland, Lukas Foss, Roger Sessions, pfs; American

Concert Choir; Columbia Percussion Ensemble). Renard (George Shirley, Loren Driscoll, tens; William Murphy, bar; Donald Gramm, bass; Toni Koves, cimbalom; Columbia Chamber Ensemble. Both from CBS SBRG72071, 12/62). L'histoire du soldat — suite (Columbia Chamber Ensemble. SBRG72007, 6/62).

③ 3h 14m ADD 8/92

Inspiration for this collection of mainly stage music came from Stravinsky's native folk-song, folk-dance, folk-tale and folk ritual; and the set contains virtually all the music from Stravinsky's 'Russian' period, including the three great ballets. It is fascinating to chart his development from the 1908 *Scherzo fantastique* with its orchestral colours scintillating in the best Rimsky-Korsakovian manner, to the wholly original language of *Les noces* with its almost exclusively metrical patterns and monochrome scoring (soloists, chorus, pianos and percussion) begun only six years later. The links are there: witness the Rimskian bumble-bee that flies through the *Scherzo* to find its winged counterpart two years on in *The Firebird*; and the primitive rhythmic force of Kastchei's "Infernal dance" in *The Firebird* finding its fullest expression, another three years later, in *The Rite of Spring*; and so on. Each work is a logical, if time-lapse progression from the previous one. The set concludes with the 15-minute long animal rites of the farmyard opera-cum-burlesque *Renard* (1916); and *L'histoire du soldat* (1918), a morality play designed for a small touring theatre company (the Suite included here omits the speaking roles); both, like *Les noces*, leaving behind the lavish orchestra of *The Rite* for small and unusual instrumental and vocal combinations.

To have the composer at the helm, and a consistent approach to the way the music is recorded, ensures that those links are clearly established. And the orchestra that takes the lion's share of the task, the Columbia Symphony, was assembled by CBS to include many of the finest players in America. It is possible to criticize the recordings (made between 1959 and 1963) for close balances and spotlighting, but many modern contenders, more distantly recorded, will more often than not deprive you of adequate articulation of the music's linear and rhythmic ingenuity. The dynamic range and contours of *The Rite of Spring* do seem momentarily reduced and disturbed by the techniques, otherwise all these recordings reproduce with good tone, range, openness and presence. As to Stravinsky the conductor, only *Les noces* finds him at less than his usual rhythmically incisive self. This *Petrushka* is more representative: it pulsates with inner life and vitality — incidentally, Stravinsky uses his leaner, clearer 1947 revision, not the original 1911 score as the booklet claims.

Stravinsky. THE COMPLETE EDITION. **Various artists/Igor Stravinsky.** Sony Classical SM3K46292 (Volume 2).

Apollo (Columbia Symphony Orchestra). From SBRG72355, (11/65). Agon (Los Angeles Festival Symphony Orchestra. SBRG72438, 8/66). Jeu de cartes (Cleveland Orchestra). Scènes de ballet (CBC Symphony Orchestra). Bluebird — Pas de deux (Columbia Symphony Orchestra. All from SBRG72270, 5/65). Le baiser de la fée (Columbia Symphony Orchestra. SBRG72407, 5/66). Pulcinella (Irene Jordan, sop; George Shirley, ten; Donald Gramm, bass; Columbia Symphony Orchestra. SBRG72452, 7/66). Orpheus (Chicago Symphony Orchestra. SBRG72355).

③ 3h 30m 8/92

Volume 2 of Sony's Stravinsky Edition comprises ballets written between 1919 and 1957. *Pulcinella* was based on music originally thought to have been written by Pergolesi, but now known to be the work of various eighteenth-century composers. In 1919 Stravinsky had not long embraced neoclassical style, but here was a brilliant example of old wine in new bottles, with the melodies sounding as if they come from the pen of Stravinsky himself. The composer conducts a lively, sharply-accented account of the score. 1928 saw the production of two Stravinsky ballets. *Appolo*, a mainly quiet, contemplative score, written for string orchestra, has many passages of great beauty. Stravinsky the conductor does not linger over these, but allows the work's cool classical elegance to speak for itself. In *Le baiser de la fée* Stravinsky used themes by Tchaikovsky as the basis for his score. Once again, the music seems quite transformed, and the result is a most captivating work. Stravinsky's watchful, affectionate performance is perfectly proportioned. His arrangement of the "Pas de deux" from Tchaikovsky's *Sleeping Beauty* is no more than a reduction for small pit orchestra, however, and a mere curiosity.

In *Jeu de cartes*, which dates from 1936, Stravinsky used music by Rossini and others, but here the references are only fleeting, and merely enhance the humour of this robust, outgoing score. His performance brings out all the work's vigour and personality very effectively, but here and there rhythms become slightly unstuck, and a slightly hectic quality manifests itself. *Scènes de ballet* was written in 1944, and possesses a slightly terse quality in the main, though there are some more lyrical passages. Stravinsky does nothing to soften the work's edges in his performance, and it emerges as a strong, highly impressive piece. *Orpheus* was completed in 1947, and shows Stravinsky's neoclassical style at its most highly developed. Much of the music is quiet, after the manner of *Apollo*, but then the orchestra suddenly erupts into a passage of quite savage violence. Stravinsky conducts this passage with amazing energy for a man in his eighties, and elsewhere his performance has characteristic clarity and a very direct means of expression typical of a composer performance. Finally *Agon*, written in 1957, attracts the listener with its colourful opening fanfares, and then pursues an increasingly complex serial path in such a brilliant and highly rhythmical fashion that one is hardly aware that the technique is being used. This work, brilliantly conducted by Stravinsky, is an ideal introduction to his late style, and to the serial technique itself. Remastering has been carried out with the greatest skill, and all the recordings in this set sound very well indeed for their age.

Stravinsky. THE COMPLETE EDITION. **Various artists/Igor Stravinsky.** Sony Classical SM2K46294 (Volume 4).
Symphonies — No. 1 in E flat major (Columbia Symphony Orchestra SBRG72569, 11/67). Stravinsky in rehearsal. Stravinsky in his own words (GM31). Symphony in Three Movements (Columbia Symphony Orchestra. SBRG72038, 9/62). Symphony in C (CBC Symphony Orchestra). Symphony of Psalms (Toronto Festival Singers, CBC Symphony Orchestra. SBRG72181, 8/64).

(2) 2h 23m 8/92

The word 'symphony' appears in the title of each work on these two discs, but this term covers some very diverse material. Stravinsky was in his mid-twenties when he wrote his Symphony in E flat, and the score is very much in the style of his teacher Rimsky-Korsakov. It has genuine colour and flair, however, and the octogenarian conductor brings paternalistic affection and a good deal of vigour to his performance. The *Symphony in C* dates from 1940, when Stravinsky was in his neoclassical phase. The work has many beautiful pages, as well as much pungent wit. In this performance Stravinsky drives the music much harder than he did in his 1952 mono recording with the Cleveland Orchestra, and although there are some exciting moments the music does tend to lose its elements of grace and charm. The performance of the *Symphony in Three Movements* is also characterized by the use of fastish tempos. But this violent work, written in 1945, and inspired by events in the Second World War, responds more readily to a strongly driven interpretation. Stravinsky wrote his *Symphony of Psalms* in 1930, and this composition reflects his deep religious convictions in varied settings from the Book of Psalms. His use of a chorus is interestingly combined with an orchestra which lacks upper strings. Stravinsky conducts a fervent, serious, beautifully balanced performance. All the 1960s recordings in this set sound very well in their new CD transfers. In some quarters the elderly Stravinsky has been wrongly portrayed as a frail, inadequate figure who only took over performances when works had been thoroughly rehearsed for him. Nothing could prove more clearly that this was not true than the rehearsal excerpts in this set, which show a vigorous, alert octogenarian very much in control of proceedings, and rehearsing passages in some detail.

NEW REVIEW

Stravinsky. OEDIPUS REX[a]. Symphony of Psalms[b]. **Ivo Zídek** (ten); Oedipus; **Věra Soukupová** (mez) Jocasta; **Karel Berman** (bass) Créon; **Eduard Haken** (bass); Tiresias; **Antonin Zlesák** (ten) Shepherd; **Zdeněk Kroupa** (bar) Messenger; **Jean Desailly** (narr); **Czech Philharmonic Chorus and Orchestra/Karel Ančerl.** Supraphon Historical 11 1947-2. Item marked [a] from SUAST50678 (1/68), [b] SUAST50778 (8/68). Recorded 1964-66.

1h 13m AAD 3/93

Oedipus Rex is one of Stravinsky's most compelling theatre pieces, a powerful drama that re-enacts the full force of a glorious highspot in ancient culture. The text is by Jean Cocteau, who once said, pertaining to his work on *Oedipus,* that "any serious work, be it of poetry or music, of theatre or of film, demands a ceremonial, lengthy calculation, an architecture in which the slightest mistake would unbalance the pyramid" (quoted from *Diary of an Unknown*, pub. Paragon House). The fusion of words and music in *Oedipus,* indeed its very 'architecture' is masterly and arrests the attention consistently, from the animated severity of the opening narration, through the cunningly calculated tension of its musical argument, to the tragic restraint of its closing pages. Stravinsky has nearly always been well served by Czech musicians, and the late Karel Ančerl was one of his most committed exponents. This particular recording of *Oedipus Rex* was taped in the Dvořák Hall of the House of Artists, Prague, and earned itself at least three major gramophone awards. Ančerl traces and intensifies salient points in the tragedy yet maintains a precise, sensitive touch; his vocal collaborators include the noble Karel Berman (Créon) who, like Ančerl himself, suffered considerably during the Nazi occupation of Czechoslovakia; then there's a fine Jocasta in Věra Soukupová and the convincing but occasionally unsteady Ivo Zídek singing the part of Oedipus. Both here and in the *Symphony of Psalms* — one of the most serenely perceptive performances of the work ever recorded — the Czech Philharmonic Chorus excels, while Supraphon's 1960s engineering (not, alas, the DDD suggested on the box) has an appealing brightness .

Stravinsky. THE RAKE'S PROGRESS (THE COMPLETE EDITION). **Alexander Young** (ten) Tom Rakewell; **Judith Raskin** (sop) Anne Truelove; **John Reardon** (bar) Nick Shadow; **Regina Sarfaty** (mez) Baba the Turk; **Kevin Miller** (ten) Auctioneer; **Jean Manning** (mez) Mother Goose; **Don Garrard** (bass) Truelove; **Peter Tracey** (bar) Keeper of the Mad House; **Sadler's Wells Opera Chorus; Royal Philharmonic Orchestra/Igor Stravinsky.** Sony Classical SM2K46299 (Volume 9).

② 2h 20 8/92

Stravinsky's only full-length opera was inspired by a viewing of Hogarth's *Rake's Progress* paintings in 1947. The composer asked W.H. Auden to supply an English text in verse form, and with the librettist he evolved a series of scenes depicting the feckless Tom Rakewell's meeting with the Devil in the form of Nick Shadow, his journey to London in pursuit of promised fortune, separation from his faithful fiancée Anne Truelove in favour of the dubious Baba the Turk, his financial failure, and his demise in Bedlam. The music is cast in classical forms, and was in fact Stravinsky's last important composition in neoclassical style. The composer directs a strong, dramatic, sharply-accented performance, with excellent playing from the RPO, and good singing from the Sadler's Wells Chorus. Alexander Young brings out Tom's blustering weakness and subsequent bewilderment very tellingly in a finely sung, strongly characterized performance. John Reardon plays the part of Nick Shadow in an appropriately ingratiating, wheedling manner, and Judith Raskin's performance as the rejected but single-minded Anne Truelove is very touching. The other parts are all more than adequately taken, and the well-balanced 1964 recording has come out very vividly on CD.

Further listening ...

Violin Concerto in D major. *Coupled with* ***Mozart.*** Violin Concerto in B flat major, K207. **David Oistrakh** (vn); **Orchestre des Concerts Lamoureux/Bernard Haitink.** Philips Collector 434 167-2PM (1/93).

Works for String Orchestra — Concerto in D major for string orchestra. Double Canon, "Raoul Dufy in memoriam". Three Pieces. Apollon musagète. **Guildhall String Ensemble/Robert Salter.** RCA RD60156 (10/90).

Works for Chamber Orchestra — Divertimento (arr. from "La baiser de la fée"). Suites Nos. 1 and 2. Octet. Suite from "L'histoire du soldat". **London Sinfonietta/Riccardo Chailly.** Decca Enterprise 433 079-2DM (5/92).

MISCELLANEOUS WORKS. **Various artists.** EMI Composers in Person mono CDS7 54607-2 (5/93). Recorded 1928-34.

Les noces (sung in English. Kate Winter, sop; Linda Seymour, contr; Parry Jones, ten; Roy Henderson, bar; Berkeley Mason, Leslie Heward, Ernest Lush, Edwin Benbow, pfs; BBC Chorus; percussion ensemble/Igor Stravinsky. *Octet* (Marcel Moyse, fl; Emile Godeau, cl; Gustave Dhérin, Marius Piard, bns; Eugène Foveau, Pierre Vignal, tpts; André Lafosse, Raphaël Delbos, tbns/Stravinsky). *Capriccio* (Stravinsky, pf; Walther Straram Concerts Orchestra/Ernest Ansermet). *Symphony of Psalms* (Alexis Vlassov Choir; Straram Orchestra/Stravinsky). *Pastorale* (Louis Gromer, ob; Georges Durand, cor ang; André Vacellier, cl; Gabriel Grandmaison, bn; Samuel Dushkin, vn/Stravinsky). *Petrushka — Danse russe. The Firebird — Scherzo; Berceuse. Le chant du rossignol — Airs du rossignol; Marche chinoise* (all with Dushkin, vn; Stravinsky, pf). *Ragtime* (Lucien Lavaillotte, fl; Godeau, cl; Jean Devemy, hn; Foveau, tpt; Roger Tudesq, tbn; Roland Charmy, Henri Volant, vns; Etienne Ginot, va; Louis Juste, db; Aladar Racz, cimbalom; Jean Morel, perc/Stravinsky). *Pian-rag-music* (Stravinsky). *Suite italienne — Serenata; Scherzino. Duo concertant* (Dushkin; Stravinsky). *Serenade in A major* (Stravinsky). *Concerto for Two Pianos* (Soulima and Stravinsky, pfs).

Capriccio. Concerto for piano and wind instruments. Movements for Piano and Orchestra. Symphonies of wind instruments. **Paul Crossley** (pf); **London Sinfonietta/Esa-Pekka Salonen.** Sony Classical SK45797 (10/90).

Barbara Strozzi

Italian 1619-1664 or later

Suggested listening ...

Gite, o giorni dolenti. Questa è la nuova. Non mi dite. Soccorrete, luci avare. Amor, non dormir più. Voglio morire. Perle care. Amore è trandito. Rissolvetevi pensieri. *Coupled with* ***Granata.*** Toccata. ***Piccinini.*** Toccata. **Glenda Simpson** (mez); **Camerata of London.** Hyperion CDA66303 (10/89).

Jule Styne

American 1905-

Suggested listening ...

FUNNY GIRL. **Original Broadway cast.** EMI Angel ZDM7 64661-2.

GYPSY. **Original 1990 Broadway revival cast.** Elektra Nonesuch7559 79239-2.

Josef Suk

Bohemian 1874-1935

NEW REVIEW

Suk. Fairy Tale, Op. 16, "Pohádka". Serenade for strings in E flat major, Op. 6. **Czech Philharmonic Orchestra/Jiří Bělohlávek.** Chandos CHAN9063.

1h DDD 3/93

These two works were completed in the period before Suk's most moving achievement, *Asrael*, and they inhabit another world, one in which uninhibited joy and beauty were still possible. The *Fairy Tale* was developed from incidental music he had composed for Julius Zeyer's play, *Radúz a Mahulena*, in 1898. To make best use of this, he integrated elements of it into this magical four-movement suite, completed in 1890 and first performed in 1901. The radiant *Serenade for strings* was finished in 1892, the same year as Elgar's. It was begun as an exercise set by his teacher and father-in-law, Dvořák, to eschew his habitual minor-mode approach to tonality and to move into the light of a major key. Of course, there are reminiscences of the older composer's E major *Serenade* in the work of the 18-year-old, but it is fascinating to hear just how original, and skilful, this youngster could be. Both Dvořák and Brahms commended the work, though, later in life, Suk made some amendments to it. These are deeply moving performances from the Czech Philharmonic and Bělohlávek, going well beyond technical assurance, as idiomatic as you would expect but also filled with a profound inner life; and the vivid recording develops a rich patina that is a delight in itself.

Additional recommendation ...
Serenade. ***Martinů.*** *Sinfonietta giocosa*[a]. [a]**Dennis Hennig** (pf); **Australian Chamber Orchestra/Sir Charles Mackerras.** Conifer CDCF170 — 59m DDD 8/89

Suk. Asrael — Symphony, Op. 27. **Royal Liverpool Philharmonic Orchestra/Libor Pešek.** Virgin Classics VC7 59638-2.

lh 2m DDD 9/91 

To use large scale symphonic form for the purging of deep personal grief carries the danger that the result will seriously lack discipline. In 1904-5 Suk's world was shattered by two visits from *Asrael* (the Angel of Death in Muslim mythology): he lost his father-in-law (and revered teacher) Dvořák, and his beloved wife, Otylka. Forgivably, Suk does perhaps linger a little too long in the fourth movement's gentle, mainly lyrical portrait of Otylka, but elsewhere the progress is as satisfying psychologically as it is symphonically. Much of the music has a concentrated dream-like quality; at the extremes, spectral nightmare visions merge with compensatory surges of lyrical ardour. It would be easy to cite the presence of Mahler in the former and Richard Strauss in the latter, but Suk's language remains identifiably Czech, not least in the woodwind colouring, the moments of consolation in nature. To define the symphony as employing a very sophisticated use of the Lisztian cyclic principle of construction is to deaden with dusty analysis a work whose every bar communicates experiences worth communicating with an intensity that Mahler would certainly have envied. It's not just an eloquent funeral oration. It was, for the composer, a piece that had to be written ("I was saved by music") and is the perfect example of music taking over where mere words are inadequate — and universalizing the experience. Pešek and his Liverpool musicians deserve our gratitude for their faith and commitment, Virgin Classics for supporting the enterprise with a wide-ranging recording that does Suk's sound world full justice.

Czech Philharmonic Orchestra/Václav Neumann. Supraphon 11 0715-2 — 58m DDD 9/91

NEW REVIEW

Suk. PIANO WORKS. **Margaret Fingerhut.** Chandos CHAN9026/7. Recorded in 1990. Six Pieces, Op. 7 — Love Song; Humoreske; Dumka; Idyll No. 2. Spring, Op. 22*a*. Summer moods, Op. 22*b*. About Mother, Op. 28. Things lived and dreamt, Op. 30. Lullabies, Op. 33.

2 2h 8m DDD 4/93

Most of the best Czech romantic piano music is a fusion of autobiography, folk-dance and exquisite tone poetry. One thinks, in particular, of Smetana, Janáček, Martinů, some Dvořák (the *Poetic tone pictures*) and, especially, Josef Suk. Suk's piano output, a fair sampling of which is presented here by Margaret Fingerhut, boasts a profusion of dream images and reflective gestures, all couched in terms of a deeply sensuous harmonic language. It starts with the overt romanticism of the Op. 7 Piano Pieces of 1893 (which number among their ranks Suk's most famous — and most frequently arranged — melody, his "Love Songs"), then proceeds to the more ambitious *Spring* (1902) through *Summer moods* (1902), *About Mother* (1907), *Things lived and dreamt* and *Lullabies*. Places to sample are legion, but special mention should be made of *Spring*'s last movement, "Longing" and the last of *Summer moods*, "Evening Mood", written at a time when Suk was infatuated with his future bride, Otilka Dvořák — the composer's daughter — and which quotes from Dvořák's *Requiem*. As it happened, the reference was terrifyingly prophetic:

within the space of just three years, Suk was to lose both his young wife and his father-in-law. Another high-spot is "About Mother", where Suk recalls Smetana and anticipates Shostakovich by musically tabulating the effects of a medical condition, but only within the context of the most profound musical poetry. The harmonic language of *Things lived and dreamt* (1909) is very much of the twentieth century, yet poetic intensity remains and troubling dissonances are few and far between. Both these and the *Lullabies* of (1910-12) repay close scrutiny and, like everything else in this collection, receive sympathetic, beautifully recorded performances.

Arthur Sullivan

British 1842-1900

NEW REVIEW

Sullivan. OVERTURES. **New Sadler's Wells Opera Orchestra; D'Oyly Carte Opera Orchestra/John Pryce-Jones, Simon Phipps, John Owen Edwards.** TER CDVIR8316. Recorded 1987-92.

HMS Pinafore. The Pirates of Penzance. Patience. Iolanthe. Princess Ida. The Mikado. The Gondoliers. The Yeomen of the Guard. Di ballo. Ruddigore.

lh 16m DDD 5/93

This collection of overtures has been assembled largely from TER complete recordings made in recent years. Despite the varied origins and different conductors, there is homogeneity about the performances, with an undoubted theatricality and a consistently high level of musicality. The selection covers all the overtures that one might reasonably expect in a Gilbert and Sullivan collection, plus the sparkling concert overture *Di Ballo*. It is a generously filled CD, which permits one to accept some idiosyncrasies in the content. In the first place, the version of *Di Ballo* played follows the original, fuller-length text, with some extra repeats. Then, in addition to the familiar *Ruddigore* overture, put together for the 1921 revival, TER also include the original 1887 version. Also, some may regret that the version of *The Gondoliers* is that in the original score, omitting the *cachucha* usually added for concert performances. Altogether, though, there is a great deal to enjoy here, whether in the well-tried melodies or the finely-shaped performances.

Sullivan. THE PIRATES OF PENZANCE. **Eric Roberts** (bar) Major-General Stanley; **Malcolm Rivers** (bar) Pirate King; **Gareth Jones** (bar) Samuel; **Philip Creasy** (ten) Frederic; **Simon Masterton-Smith** (bass) Sargeant of Police; **Marilyn Hill Smith** (sop) Mabel; **Patricia Cameron** (sop) Edith; **Pauline Birchall** (mez) Kate; **Susan Gorton** (contr) Ruth; **D'Oyly Carte Opera Chorus and Orchestra/John Pryce-Jones.** TER CDTER2 1177. Recorded in 1990.

② lh 25m DDD 9/90

The revival of the D'Oyly Carte Opera Company has produced the first digital recordings of complete Gilbert and Sullivan scores, and this TER set is a very happy example. Philip Creasy is an engaging and vocally secure Frederic, and Marilyn Hill Smith trips through "Poor wandering one" with a delectable display of vocal ability and agility. The couple's interplay with the chorus in "How beautifully blue the sky" is quite enchanting, and their exchanges in "Stay, Frederic, stay" splendidly convincing. Eric Roberts makes the Major-General a thoroughly engaging personality, and the dotty exchanges between Simon Masterton-Smith's Sargeant of Police and his police force are sheer joy. Even such details as the girls' screams at the appearance of the pirates in Act 1 have a rare effectiveness. John Pryce-Jones keeps the score dancing along. Those who want the dialogue as well as the music must look elsewhere, but this version is certainly to be recommended for its musical and acting values as well as its fine modern sound.

Sullivan. THE MIKADO. **Donald Adams** (bass) The Mikado; **Anthony Rolfe Johnson** (ten) Nanki-Poo; **Richard Suart** (bar) Ko-Ko; **Richard Van Allan** (bass) Pooh-Bah;

Nicholas Folwell (bar) Pish-Tush; **Marie McLaughlin** (sop) Yum-Yum; **Anne Howells** (mez) Pitti-Sing; **Janice Watson** (sop) Peep-Bo; **Felicity Palmer** (mez) Katisha; **Welsh National Opera Chorus and Orchestra/Sir Charles Mackerras.** Telarc CD80284. Notes and text included. Recorded in 1991.

lh 19m DDD 5/92

It is generosity indeed to be offered *The Mikado* complete on a single CD, and with full libretto, even if we have to do without spoken dialogue and the overture, whose purpose in the home is obviously less significant than in the theatre, and which anyway was put together by one of Sullivan's assistants. What is more, the performance is an outstanding one of a work that has not always fared too well in recordings. Sullivan has been among the diverse specialities of Sir Charles Mackerras ever since he arranged *Pineapple Poll* over 40 years ago, but this is the first time he has committed any of the comic operas to disc. That we have waited far too long is soon evident from he way he brings out not only the familiar delicacies of Sullivan's score but also very many points of fine detail — the "short, sharp shock" in "I am so proud" for instance, and a chilling shriek in "The criminal cried". His tempos are generally on the quicker side, except for Richard Suart's Ko-Ko, who is here somewhat lacking in character though agreeably musical. Anthony Rolfe Johnson is a delicious Nanki-Poo, shading his voice to delightful effect, and Felicity Palmer is an absolutely magnificent Katisha. Marie McLaughlin is a good Yum-Yum, and Anne Howells a ravishing Pitti-Sing. Donald Adams has here recorded the title role for the second time — no less than 33 years after the first — and generally the years seem to have stood still.

Additional recommendation ...

Soloists; D'Oyly Carte Chorus; Royal Philharmonic Orchestra/Royston Nash. Decca 425 190-2LM2 — ② lh 30m ADD 1/90

NEW REVIEW

Sullivan. THE YEOMEN OF THE GUARD. **Donald Maxwell** (bass) Sir Richard Cholmondeley; **David Fieldsend** (ten) Colonel Fairfax; **Terence Sharpe** (bar) Sergeant Meryll; **Julian Jenson** (ten) Leonard Meryll; **Fenton Grey** (bar) Jack Point; **Gary Montaine** (bass) Shadbolt; **Lesley Echo Ross** (sop) Elsie; **Janine Roebuck** (mez) Phoebe; **Jill Pert** (contr) Dame Carruthers; **Carol Lesley-Green** (sop) Kate; **D'Oyly Carte Opera Chorus and Orchestra/John Owen Edwards.** TER CDTER2 1195. Recorded in 1992.

② lh 55m DDD 5/93

This impressive new recordings of *The Yeomen of the Guard* has a tremendous freshness and naturalness, theatricality and musicality about it. It is splendidly paced by the conductor, John Owen Edwards, who produces impressive solemnity in the more serious moments (including a really haunting Funeral March) but deliciously imparts life into lighthearted numbers such as "Here's a man of jollity" and "Rapture, Rapture". Among the cast, there is real pleasure in the singing of Lesley Echo Ross, who was Phyllis in TER's *Iolanthe* and is here a refreshingly clear, youthful Elsie Maynard, her voice soaring beautifully in the ensembles. Likewise Jill Pert, as Dame Carruthers, repeats the favourable impression she created in *The Gondoliers* and *Iolanthe*. Fenton Grey is a first-rate light baritone Jack Point, too, enunciating his words with considerable clarity. But why, in "O, a private buffoon", does he suddenly display a cockney accent that is totally missing elsewhere in his singing. Perhaps Janine Roebuck's imposing mezzo-soprano creates a somewhat mature-sounding Phoebe, but she and the other principals all contribute to a strong cast. The theatricality of the venture is nowhere better demonstrated than in the inclusion of the dialogue over the music that precedes "I have a song to sing, O!". This uniquely complete version also includes some extra, usually omitted verses and, in an appendix, an alternative version of "Is life a boon?" and two other discarded numbers.

Additional recommendation ...

THE YEOMEN OF THE GUARD[a]. *TRIAL BY JURY*[b]. **Soloists; D'Oyly Carte Opera Chorus,** [a]**Royal Philharmonic Orchestra/Sir Malcolm Sargent;** [b]**Orchestra of the Royal Opera House, Covent Garden/Isidore Godfrey.** Decca 417 358-2LM2 — ② 2h 5m ADD 1/90 £

Sullivan. THE GONDOLIERS. Overture di Ballo (1870 version). **Richard Suart** (bar) Duke of Plaza-Toro; **Philip Creasey** (ten) Luiz; **John Rath** (bass) Don Alhambra; **David Fieldsend** (ten) Marco; **Alan Oke** (bar) Giuseppe; **Tim Morgan** (bar) Antonio; **David Cavendish** (ten) Francesco; **Toby Barrett** (bass) Giorgio; **Jill Pert** (contr) Duchess of Plaza-Toro; **Elizabeth Woollett** (sop) Casilda; **Lesley Echo Ross** (sop) Gianetta; **Regina Hanley** (mez) Tessa; **Yvonne Patrick** (sop) Fiametta; **Pamela Baxter** (mez) Vittoria; **Elizabeth Elliott** (sop) Giulia; **Claire Kelly** (contr) Inez; **D'Oyly Carte Opera Chorus and Orchestra/John Pryce-Jones.** TER CDTER2 1187. Recorded in 1991.

② lh 49m DDD 5/92

This is one of a new series of recordings by the new D'Oyly Carte Opera Company that offers a vastly better quality of sound than any of its ageing competitors. Orchestral detail is the most immediate beneficiary, and the overture serves to demonstrate John Pryce-Jones's lively tempos and lightness of touch. Outstanding among the singers are perhaps John Rath, who gives Don Alhambra's "I stole the prince" and "There lived a king" real presence, and Jill Pert, a formidable Duchess of Plaza-Toro. Richard Suart not only provides the leading comedy roles with exceptionally clear articulation and musicality, but also adds considerable character to his portrayals; his "I am a courtier grave and serious" is a sure winner. David Fieldsend and Alan Oke provide attractive portrayals of the two gondoliers, and Lesley Echo Ross and Regina Hanley are also most agreeable. Seasoned listeners may note numerous changes of detail as a result of the purging of the performance material of changes made to the parts around the time of the 1920s Savoy Theatre revivals. There is no dialogue, but added value is provided by Sullivan's sunniest comic opera score being accompanied by the sparkling *Overture di Ballo*, played in its original version with some traditional cuts opened up.

Further listening ...

Songs — Let me dream again. Mary Morison. The Marquis de Mincepie. The moon in silent brightness. Five Shakespeare Songs — O mistress mine; Orpheus with his Lute; The Willow Song. The lost chord. Sweethearts. St Agnes's Eve. The Dove Song. Gone! Winter. What does little birdie say? The Absent-minded Beggar. **Jeanne Ommerle** (sop); **Sanford Sylvan** (bar); **Gary Wedow** (pf). Conifer CDCFC156 (9/87).

HMS PINAFORE — *comic opera.* **Soloists; D'Oyly Carte Opera Chorus; New Symphony Orchestra/Isidore Godfrey.** Decca 414 283-2LM2 (1/90).

IOLANTHE — *comic operetta.* **Glyndebourne Festival Chorus/Pro Arte Orchestra/Sir Malcolm Sargent.** EMI CMS7 64400-2.

RUDDIGORE — *operetta.* THE PIRATES OF PENZANCE — *operetta.* **Soloists; Glyndebourne Festival Chorus/Pro Arte Orchestra/Sir Malcolm Sargent.** EMI CMS7 64412-2.

Franz von Suppé

Austrian 1819-1895

Suppé. OVERTURES. **Academy of St Martin in the Fields/Sir Neville Marriner.** EMI CDC7 54056-2. Recorded in 1989.

Leichte Kavallerie. Tantalusqualen. Die Irrfahrt um's Glück. Die Frau Meisterin. Ein Morgen, ein Mittag, ein Abend in Wien. Pique-Dame. Wiener Jubel. Dichter und Bauer.

lh lm DDD 10/90 9P 9S

Suppé. OVERTURES. **Royal Philharmonic Orchestra/Gustav Kuhn.** Eurodisc RD69226. Recorded in 1990.

Die Irrfahrt um's Glück. Donna Juanita. Fatinitza. Das Modell. Der Gascogner. Wiener Jubel. Die Frau Meisterin.

57m DDD 11/91

Suppé's overtures are delightful creations brimming with melodic invention, and Marriner brings out all their warmth and infectious vitality in his highly successful interpretations. The orchestra respond to their conductor's obvious enthusiasm for this music with great aplomb, their expressive playing breathing new life into the more familiar items, like *Leichte Kavallerie* ("Light Cavalry") and *Dichter und Bauer* ("Poet and Peasant"). But what makes this winning collection so valuable is the inclusion of four Suppé rarities, *Tantalusqualen*, *Die Irrfahrt um's Glück*, *Wiener Jubel* and *Die Frau Meisterin*, all of which are constructed with great skill and deserve to be more widely known. Sparkling, crisp recorded sound provides the final icing on the cake.

Kuhn offers a refreshingly individual approach to Suppé's overtures, with particularly spacious slower sections building up to glorious climaxes. Not everything comes off altogether convincingly, and some sections seem altogether too slow. However, the beauties of the playing and the shaping of the themes are readily evident in, for example, the jaunty build-up and rousing conclusion of the familiar *Fatinitza*. Elsewhere, an attraction of this CD, as on the Marriner, is that the contents are anything but oft-played. The overture to *Die Irrfahrt um's Glück* is a fine early Suppé overture, while that to *Das Modell* was evidently one of the last things Suppé composed, the operetta being left unfinished at his death. The *Wiener Jubel* overture is a particularly marvellous discovery, with one theme especially that darts irresistibly hither and thither. *Donna Juanita* is a longer and generally more subdued overture, with a beautiful violin solo and delightfully intertwining woodwind, and Kuhn's command over the music is nowhere shown to better effect than in the major theme towards the end, which he alternately holds back and then moves on to captivating effect. This is not a collection to be acquired in preference to that by Marriner, but one that admirably complements it.

Additional recommendation ...

Leichte Kavallerie. Fatinitza. Ein Morgen, ein Mittag, ein Abend in Wien. Pique-Dame. Banditenstreiche. Die schöne Galathee. Dichter und Bauer. **Montreal Symphony Orchestra/Charles Dutoit.** Decca 414 408-2DH — 57m DDD 2/86

Further listening ...

Requiem. **Soloists; Franco-German Choir, Lyon; Bonn Youth Symphony Orchestra/Wolfgang Badun.** BNL BNL112774 (1/92).

Johann Svendsen

Norwegian 1840-1911

Svendsen. Symphonies — No. 1 in D major, Op. 4; No. 2 in B flat major, Op. 15. Two Swedish folk-melodies, Op. 27. **Gothenburg Symphony Orchestra/Neeme Järvi.** BIS CD347.

1h 11m DDD 11/87 

The justified popularity of Grieg's music has perversely obscured that of his contemporary Svendsen, for no impression of Norwegian music of Grieg's time can be complete without experiencing the freshness and joyous exuberance of Svendsen's rich invention. Where Grieg concentrated mainly on miniature forms, it was Svendsen who explored larger structures. His two symphonies have justifiably been described as being, together with Berwald's, the finest to appear in Scandinavia before Sibelius. The first is a youthful work, but one of remarkable freshness and assurance, its *scherzo* a gloriously infectious piece, deliciously orchestrated. Everything there finds a worthy counterpart in the mature Second Symphony, which builds up to a sparkling finale. These captivating works are here given first-class, sensitive and lively performances, with excellent digital sound. As if to reassert the affinity with Grieg, the CD offers a fill-up of string arrangements of two Swedish folk-tunes, the second of which became the Swedish National Anthem.

Jan Pieterszoon Sweelinck

Dutch 1562-1621

NEW REVIEW

Sweelinck. PSEAUMES DE DAVID. **Trinity College Choir, Cambridge/Richard Marlow.** Conifer CDFC205. Texts and translations included.

Or soit loué l'Etérnal. Mon Dieu, j'ay en toy esperance. Qui au conseil des malins. Vous tous qui la terr' habitez. Revenge moy, pren la querelle. Mon am'en Dieu taut seulement. Les cieux en chacun lieu. Du Seigneur les bontez. Ne sois fasché. Or sus serviteurs de Seigneur. Jamais ne cesseray. Vouloir m'est pris. Le Toutpuissant à mon Seigneur. D'ou vient, Seigneur. Vous tous les habitans.

1h 17m DDD 8/92

The Dutchman Jan Pieterszoon Sweelinck has always been best known for his influential keyboard music, but surprisingly it was only his vocal works that made it into print in his own day. His output in this department included *a cappella* settings in French for four to eight voices of the entire Psalter, published in four books between 1604 and 1621, and it's from the third of these books of *Psalms of David* (1614) that the 15 works on this disc are taken. This is highly attractive music, full of variety and compositional resourcefulness and containing some charming touches of wordpainting (including a delightful vocal impersonation of a tabour and an imposing representation of the creatures of the deep). The Choir of Trinity College, Cambridge, is a mixed voice ensemble with female altos, not as sharply focused as some ensembles around today perhaps, but pleasing to the ear nevertheless. Furthermore, they are intelligently and imaginatively directed at all times by Richard Marlow, whose careful elucidation of the ever-changing choral textures and attention to niceties of pacing and declamation ensure that there is never any danger of monotony. There are not many recordings around at the moment of vocal music by the man usually reckoned to be The Netherlands's last great composer, a fact which makes this fine release a doubly valuable one.

Karol Szymanowski

Polish 1882-1937

Szymanowski. String Quartets — No. 1 in C major, Op. 37; No. 2, Op. 56. ***Webern.*** Slow Movement (1905). **Carmina Quartet** (Matthias Enderle, Susanne Frank, vns; Wendy Champney, va; Stephan Goerner, vc). Denon CO-79462-2.

45m DDD 3/92

Szymanowski's sound world is totally distinctive: there is an exotic luxuriance, a sense of ecstasy and longing, a heightened awareness of colour and glowing, almost luminous textures. The two quartets are separated by a decade: the First, whose sense of ecstasy and longing permeates its opening, is a subtle and deeply-felt performance and much the same can be said of No. 2. Again heady perfumes and exotic landscapes are in evidence, though with his increasing interest in folk-music, the finale has slight overtones of Bartók. The Swiss-based Carmina Quartet play both Szymanowski works with great understanding and emotional involvement, and technically they are quite brilliant. If we associate Webern with brief, highly compressed atonal and serial works, the Slow Movement for String Quartet shows the composer in his early twenties still writing in a late-romantic style, appropriately enough for a piece which reflects for Webern the pleasures of a walk through Austrian woods with his future wife. The Movement sprawls a little, but is very pleasingly written. The Carmina Quartet give a sympathetic, warm-hearted performance of this piece, and the sound obtained by Denon's largely Japanese team throughout the disc is very detailed, but also has a very attractive bloom.

Additional recommendation ...

String Quartets. ***Lutoslawski.*** *String Quartet.* ***Penderecki.*** *String Quartet No. 2.* **Varsovia Quartet.** Olympia OCD328 — 1h 8m AAD 6/89

Szymanowski. PIANO WORKS. **Dennis Lee.** Hyperion CDA66409. Recorded in 1990. Four Etudes, Op. 4. Metopes, Op. 29. Fantasy, Op. 14. Masques, Op. 34.

lh 4m DDD 7/91

Szymanowski is to Polish music what Bartók was to Hungarian, in that he revived his country's musical creativity and enriched its repertory in the early part of this century. Like Bartók, too, he was attracted to Richard Strauss's harmonic and instrumental opulence, and sometimes drew upon his native folk-music and allowed it to influence his works. But here the resemblance ends, for this Pole was a hothouse romantic more akin to Scriabin, and his piano music resembles his in being characteristically luxuriant and decadent in a *fin de siècle* way. Like Scriabin's, his earlier pieces owe much to Chopin, as we hear at once in the Four Studies. Dennis Lee plays them persuasively, and these studies (of which the melodiously poignant third was a favourite of Paderewski) have charm as well as brilliance. But already in No. 4 we find the more chromatic style to which Szymanowski's music was soon to adhere and into which we are immediately plunged in "Isle of the Sirens", the first of the *Metopes* of 1915: their title suggests scenes depicted in antique Greek friezes. Here are what someone has called "swarms of notes", and this lushness is characteristic of the other works too, but though the constant runs and trills and the shifting harmony may cloy some palates, in certain moods this music can carry one away into a world of mystery, especially when it is played with this quiet authority. A valuable Szymanowski anthology, with piano sound that is pleasing though not in the demonstration class.

Additional recommendation ...

Four Etudes. 12 Etudes, Op. 33. Two Mazurkas, Op. 62. Masques — No. 1, "Sheherazade". Variations on a Polish folk theme, Op. 10. **Arielle Vernède** (pf). Channel Classics Canal Grande CG9110 — lh 7m DDD 10/92

Szymanowski. Harnasie, Op. 55[a]. Mandragora, Op. 43[b]. **[a]Jozef Stepien, [b]Paulus Raptis** (tens); **Polish National Opera [a]Chorus and Orchestra/Robert Satanowski.** Koch Schwann Musica Mundi 311064.

lh 2m DDD 12/91 

After the First World War Szymanowski's musical language underwent a striking change: the heavy exoticism of the First Violin Concerto and Third Symphony was enriched by his encounter with the folk-music of the Polish highlands (or Tatras). Its accents inform the melodic character of the Mazurkas for piano, Op. 50, which have an extraordinary refinement and melancholy and are all pervasive in his choral ballet, *Harnasie*. The exotic luxuriance, the familiar sense of ecstasy and longing, the glowing colours and luminous textures are still strongly in evidence but they are tempered by an altogether earthier melodic language. Szymanowski worked on *Harnasie* for the best part of a decade (1923-32). It calls for enormous forces, including a large orchestra and chorus, and lasts only 35 minutes. Small wonder that few ballet companies outside Poland can afford to put it on. It is set in the High Tatras and the colourful plot centres on a bridal abduction by a band of highland brigands, the Harnasie, who take their name from their leader, Harnas, a kind of Robin Hood about whom there were many folk legends. It is all heady, intoxicating stuff and no one who enjoys the rich luxuriant textures in which Szymanowski's scores abound, should miss it. While Szymanowski laboured over *Harnasie*, he polished off *Mandragora* in ten days. By contrast this harlequinade is for chamber forces and designed for a performance of Molière's *Le Bourgeois Gentilhomme*. It is far less characteristic and sounds rather more like Prokofiev than Szymanowski. The performances have plenty of colour and spirit and the recording is naturally balanced with plenty of detail and presence.

Further listening ...

Violin Concertos — No. 1, Op. 35[a]; No. 2, Op. 61[b]. Nocturne and Tarantella, Op. 28[a]. **[a]Konstanty Kulka, [b]Roman Lascocki** (vns); **Polish State Philharmonic Orchestra, Katowice/Karol Stryja.** Marco Polo 8 223291 (4/91).

Songs with orchestra — Love-songs of Hafiz, Op. 26; Songs of the infatuated muezzin, Op. 42; Songs of a fairytale princess, Op. 31. KING ROGER — Roxana's Song. Three Fragments from

Poems by Jan Kasprowicz, Op. 5. **Soloists; Polish State Philharmonic Orchestra, Katowice/Karol Stryja.** Marco Polo 8 223294 (4/92).

KING ROGER[a]. Harnasie — suite, Op. 55[b]. **Soloists; Warsaw National Opera Chorus and Orchestra/Mieczyslaw Mierzejewski, [b]Bohdan Wodiczko.** Olympia OCD303 (5/89).

Toru Takemitsu

Japanese 1930-

NEW REVIEW

Takemitsu. November Steps[a]. Eclipse[b]. Viola Concerto, "A String around Autumn"[c]. **[ab]Katsuya Yokoyama** (shakuhachi); **[ab]Kinshi Tsuruta** (biwa); **[c]Nobuko Imai** (va); **[ac]Saito Kinen Orchestra/Seiji Ozawa.** Philips 432 176-2PH. Recorded 1989-90.

46m DDD 8/92

Not a particularly generous disc in terms of playing time by any means, but what this disc lacks in value per minute it more than compensates for in committed performances and quality of music. Stylistically the three works presented on this disc represent the two extremes of Takemitsu's output, from the post-war avant-garde techniques of *November Steps* and *Eclipse* to the lush, opulent textures of the Viola Concerto of 1989. However, despite their stylistic differences all three works share Takemitsu's hallmark for delicately detailed texture and sonority, and his desire to write music reflecting the harmony of nature and the seasons. This acute sensitivity for capturing the mood and spirit of nature can be heard to great effect in the *concertante* work *November Steps,* for orchestra with shakuhachi and biwa, that combines certain Western avant-garde techniques with a strong flavour of Japanese (meditative) aesthetics. The more recent, extremely attractive, Viola Concerto (subtitled *A String around Autumn*) is perhaps an even stronger evocation of Autumn than its predecessor, and is wholly characteristic of Takemitsu's recent work in that the music unfolds in a series of beautifully proportioned waves of sound. Heady and intoxicating, this is music for the senses rather than the analytical mind, which asks only that the listener allow themselves to be drawn into what the composer describes as "an imaginary landscape". And when your travelling partner happens to be the exquisite playing of Nobuko Imai this is very hard to resist indeed. A thoroughly recommendable disc, despite its relatively short playing time.

Takemitsu. ORCHESTRAL, CHAMBER AND INSTRUMENTAL WORKS. **John Williams** (gtr); **[a]Sebastian Bell** (alto fl); **[b]Gareth Hulse** (ob d'amore); **[c]London Sinfonietta/Esa-Pekka Salonen.** Sony Classical SK46720.
To the Edge of Dream[c]. Folios — I, II and III. Toward the Sea[a]. Here, There and Everywhere. What a Friend. Amours Perdues. Summertime. Vers, l'Arc-en-ciel, Palma[bc].

lh DDD l/92

Toru Takemitsu is an original, refined composer and something of a latter-day impressionist, as titles like *To the Edge of Dream* suggest. It may therefore come as a surprise to find him arranging songs by Lennon and McCartney, Gershwin and others, for solo guitar. Yet these prove to have attractive touches of the subtlety found in Takemitsu's own compositions, and they also provide useful contrast to the more substantial works on this beguiling disc. *Folios*, the earliest composition included, already reveal Takemitsu's musical catholicity in its reference to a Bach chorale. *Toward the Sea* and *Vers, l'Arc-en-ciel, Palma* are both more expansive mood pieces, the former (for guitar and alto flute) almost too reticent and hesitant beside the richer textures of the latter, which is enhanced by the additional solo role given to the oboe d'amore as well as its beautifully laid out orchestral accompaniment. *To the Edge of Dream* is in effect a guitar concerto, with a wider range of mood and an even more developed role for the orchestra than *Vers, l'Arc-en-ciel, Palma*. It provides a particularly satisfying focus for a sensitively performed and well recorded disc. Even if we hear rather more of the guitar relative to the orchestra than we would in the concert-hall, there is nothing unreasonably artificial about the result.

Further listening ...

Rain Coming. Rain Spell. riverrun [a]. Tree Line. Water-ways. [a]**Paul Crossley** (pf); **London Sinfonietta/Oliver Knussen.** Virgin Classics VC7 59020-2 (9/91).

Corona. The Crossing. Far Away. Les yeux clos. Litany. Pause uninterrupted. Piano Distance. Rain Tree Sketch. **Roger Woodward** (pf). Etcetera KTC1103 (6/91).

Thomas Tallis

British c.1505-1585

NEW REVIEW

Tallis. Lamentations of Jeremiah. MOTETS. **The Tallis Scholars/Peter Phillips.** Gimell CDGIM025. Texts and translations included.
Motets — Absterge Domine. Derelinquat impius. Mihi autem nimis. O sacrum convivium. In jejunio et fletu. O salutaris hostia. In manus tuas. O nata lux de lumine. Salve intemerata virgo.

lh 8m DDD 5/92

This, the third volume of the survey by The Tallis Scholars of the music of the Tudor composer, Thomas Tallis, contains the well-known *Lamentations,* eight motets, and the extended motet *Salve intemerata virgo.* The *Lamentations* and motets are typical of the style of late Renaissance English composers. The overall mood is one of considerable austerity and their simplicity is indicative of the probability of their having been written for the private use of loyal Catholics rather than for formal ritual. *Salve intemerata virgo,* on the other hand, looks back to the glories of the late fifteenth century. In particular Tallis's use of the phrygian mode gives the work as a whole a strong sense of the medieval. Despite this disparity of styles the Tallis Scholars acquit themselves, as always, with great distinction. In the *Lamentations* and motets they achieve an appropriate sense of intimacy, while in *Salve intermerata virgo* they rise fully to the challenges of one of the more extended and demanding examples of Tudor choral composition. In addition the formidable challenges which this latter work sets for the conductor, such as the sense of pace, variation of dynamics, and overall architecture of the work, are all extremely well handled by Peter Phillips. Like much music of this era, the compositions of Thomas Tallis repay repeated listenings, and in these distinguished readings, aided by Gimell's fine recording, Tallis's genius is fully revealed.

Additional recommendation ...
Lamentations of Jeremiah. Salvator mundi II a 5. O sacrum convivium. Mass a 4. Absterge Domine. **The Hilliard Ensemble/Paul Hiller.** ECM New Series 833 308-2 — DDD 4/88

Tallis. SACRED CHORAL WORKS. **The Hilliard Ensemble/Paul Hillier.** ECM New Series 833 308-2. From 833 308-1 (4/88).
Lamentations of Jeremiah the Prophet a 5. Salvator mundi II a 5. O sacrum convivium a 5. Mass a 4. Absterge Domini a 5.

54m DDD

The Hilliard Ensemble appear here in sombre mood. They sing with restraint and gravity a programme of quite uncommon beauty, in the main austere and penitential. Apart from the Mass for Four Voices, most of these pieces would have been written during the reign of Elizabeth I, when Latin had ceased, in England, to be the official language of liturgy. *Salvator mundi* and *O sacrum convivium* are short five-part antiphons from the feasts of the Exaltation of the Cross and Corpus Christi respectively. The singers respond to both with perfect objectivity, appearing to have greater affinity with the final piece, *Absterge Domine,* which is forward-looking in its delicate sensitivity to the words. The whole performance is distinguished by the careful shaping of every musical phrase and the impressive vocal quality — a glorious richness devoid of any vibrato.

Tallis. SACRED CHORAL WORKS. [a]**Taverner Consort;** [b]**Taverner Choir/Andrew Parrott.** EMI Reflexe CDC7 49555-2, CDC7 49563-2. Texts and translations included. *CDC7 49555-2* — Videte miraculum[b]. Homo quidam[b]. Audivi vocem[a]. Candidi facti sunt Nazarei[b]. Dum transisset Sabbatum[b]. Honor, virtus et potestas[b]. Hodie nobis[a]. Loquebantur variis linguis[b]. In pace, in idipsum[a]. Spem in alium (with Wim Becu, bass sackbut; Paul Nicholson, Alan Wilson, orgs)[ab]. *CDC7 49563-2* — Gaude gloriosa Dei mater[ab]. Te lucis ante terminum … Procul recedant somnia I[a]. Miserere nostri[a]. Salvator mundi I[a]. Salvator mundi[b]. Lamentations of Jeremiah[a]. O sacrum convivium[b]. Suscipe, quaeso Domine[b]. O nata lux[b]. In jejunio et fletu[a].

② 1h 2m 1h 8m DDD 5/89 

Tallis, one of the greatest composers of sacred music, has been sympathetically and generously acknowledged by Andrew Parrott and the Taverner Choir with two separately available discs of Latin church music. They include 12 pieces from the Cantiones Sacrae of 1575, the two *Lamentations of Jeremiah*, and the masterly 40-part responsary *Spem in alium* written, it would seem, in reply to a similarly ambitious one by Tallis's Italian contemporary, Alessandro Striggio. The performances are characterized by translucent textures, a wonderful feeling for structure and a fluent understanding of the composer's contrapuntal ingenuity. Certainly there are occasional hints of vocal strain in the uppermost reaches of the part writing but they do little to spoil an affectionate, technically assured account of thrilling music. Among many impressive features to be found in these discs is the performance of the *Gaude gloriosa Dei mater*, spacious in dimension, rich in counterpoint and concluding with an extended "Amen". Parrott illuminates the music with his own deep understanding of it, but above all with the skilful deployment of vocal talent that he has at his command.

Additional recommendation …

O salutaris hostia. In jejunio et fletu. Salvator mundi I. Salvator mundi II. In manuas tuas, Domine. Lamentations of Jeremiah. O sacrum convivium. O nata lux de lumine. Te lucis ante terminum. Spem in alium (with Winchester College Quiristers; Vocal Arts; Timothy Byram-Wifield, org). **Winchester Cathedral Choir/David Hill.** Hyperion CDA66400 — 59m DDD 5/90

Tallis. MOTETS. **The Tallis Scholars/Peter Phillips.** Gimell CDGIM006. Spem in alium. Salvator mundi (I, II). Sancte Deus, sancte fortis. Gaude gloriosa Dei mater. Miserere nostri. Loquebantur variis linguis.

43m DDD 3/86 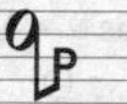  

In Thomas Tallis's celebrated *Spem in alium* the Roman Catholic composer pleads to his queen for tolerance of his faith in the language he knows best, the tongues of collected voices. The result is humbling, overwhelming and quite lovely. The Tallis Scholars directed by Peter Phillips offer this monumental work in their glorious Tallis programme. The blend of voices, capped by a penetrating soprano line, makes a versatile and tremendously powerful instrument. *Gaude gloriosa* deploys the choir with a richness of texture and gradual accumulation of voices that are used to hymn Queen Mary for being "the means of salvation", the restorer of the faith. The recording, made in Merton College Chapel, Oxford, is beautifully handled. The space and shape of the building virtually appear before one's ears and eyes as the music unfolds.

Tallis. Missa Salve intemerata virgo.
Taverner. Mass a 4, "Western Wynde". Song, "Western Wynde". **St John's College Choir, Cambridge/George Guest.** EMI Eminence CD-EMX2155.

58m DDD 2/90

The St John's College Choir, Cambridge under its now retired Director, George Guest here gives fervent and firmly structured performances of Masses by two great masters of English sixteenth-century sacred vocal music. Taverner, the earlier composer of the two was innovative in his use of a secular cantus firmus, the tune of *Western Wynde* throughout the Mass. In the present performance, a solo tenor introduces the listener to this famous and beautiful sixteenth century song which in the Mass is treated to 36 variations. Tallis's five-part Mass *Salve intemerata virgo* is based on his own motet of that name. Its masterly counterpoint is lucidly sustained and is balanced in such a way as to highlight details in vocal character and texture. Nowhere, perhaps, is this more movingly demonstrated than in the second *Agnus Dei* where the four lower voices pursue a course of vocalization on the syllable 'O' of "nobis". This and the re-entry of the trebles for the final invocation is affectingly realized by Guest and his accomplished choir. The recording is sympathetic but the booklet omits the Latin texts.

Key to Symbols

	② ②	lh 23m	DDD	6/88
Price	*Quantity/ availability*	*Timing*	*Mode*	*Review date*

Sergey Ivanovich Taneyev

Russian 1856-1915

Suggested listening …

Symphony No. 4 in C minor, Op. 12. THE ORESTEIA — Overture. **Philharmonia Orchestra/Neeme Järvi.** Chandos CHAN8953 (4/92).

THE ORESTEIA. **Soloists; Chorus and Orchestra of the Belorussian State Opera and Ballet Theatre/Tatyana Kolomyzeva.** Olympia OCD195 (9/88).

Alexandre Tansman

Polish/French 1897-1986

Suggested listening …

Le Jardin du Paradis — Danse de la sorcière[abcde]. *Coupled with* ***Saint-Saëns:*** Caprice sur des airs danois et russes, Op. 79[abc]. ***d'Indy:*** Sarabande et menuet, Op. 72[abcde]. ***Roussel:*** Divertissement, Op. 6[abcde]. ***Françaix:*** L'heure du berger[abce]. ***Poulenc:*** Elégie[e]. ***Milhaud:*** Sonata for flute, oboe, clarinet and piano, Op. 47[abc]. [a]**Catherine Cantin** (fl); [b]**Maurice Bourgue** (ob); [c]**Michel Portal** (cl); [d]**Amaury Wallez** (bn); [e]**André Cazalet** (hn); **Pascal Rogé** (pf). Decca 425 861-2DH (5/91).
See review in the Collections Section; refer to the Index to Reviews.

String Quartets Nos. 2-8. Triptyque. **Silesian Quartet.** Etcetera KTC2017 (8/92).

Francisco Tárrega

Spanish 1852-1909

Suggested listening …

Mazurka in G major. Study in A major. Marietta. Capricho árabe. Prelude in A minor. Recuerdos de la Alhambra. *Coupled with* ***Malats*** (arr. Tárrega). Serenata española. ***Pujol.*** Tango espagnol. Guajira. ***Llobet.*** Popular Catalan folksongs. **Julian Bream** (gtr). RCA Victor Red Seal RD60429 (7/92).
See review in the Collections Section; refer to the Index to Reviews.

Giuseppe Tartini

Italian 1692-1770

Tartini. Violin Concertos — E minor, D56; A major, D96; A minor, D113. **Uto Ughi** (vn); **I Solisti Veneti/Claudio Scimone.** Erato Emerald 2292-45380-2.

53m DDD 11/91 

Tartini used to be known to the musical public at large as the composer of the *Devil's Trill* Sonata (echoes of Paganini). His output is surprisingly underexplored on record, but this is music surely due for a revival. This highly rewarding triptych demonstrates its quality. None of these violin concertos contains routine gestures and Uto Ughi makes a real case for their return to the repertoire. Outer movements have genuine vitality and all three slow movements are expressively appealing. The A major Concerto even offers an alternative, a particularly lovely *Andante*. I Solisti Veneti give persuasively polished accompaniments and the whole atmosphere of the collection is of cultivated music-making and enjoyment. This disc is a real find: all three concertos are beautifully played and the sound is excellent — sweet and full. A lovely disc for the late evening.

NEW REVIEW

Tartini. VIOLIN SONATAS. **Locatelli Trio** (Elizabeth Wallfisch, vn; Richard Tunnicliffe, vc; Paul Nicholson, hpd). Hyperion CDA66430. Recorded in 1990.
Sonate e una pastorale — No. 2 in F major; No. 8 in C minor; No. 10 in G minor, "Didone abbandonata"; No. 12 in F major. Pastorale in A major. Sonata in G minor, "Le trille du diable".

1h 13m DDD 4/92 

The members of the Locatelli Trio have an impressive pedigree as performers of baroque music. Here they bring their wealth of experience most fruitfully to bear upon six of about 42 authenticated violin sonatas by Giuseppe Tartini, the violin virtuoso and pedagogue who established such an influential school of playing in Padua in the second quarter of the eighteenth century. These sonatas are well selected to illustrate the range of Tartini's style and to produce a balanced, developing programme. Two important and better known works — nicknamed *Didone abbandonata* and *Le trille du diable* — frame others that are equally rich in graceful melody, dazzling passagework and innovative scoring but which perhaps lack a distinctive selling point. The three-movement *Pastorale* in A major is a particularly effective work, worthy of much wider dissemination in recital programmes. The multi-sectioned final movement is a triumph of novel ideas and balanced structure. This performance is especially affecting, with the lightness of approach nevertheless conveying a depth of feeling not always to the fore elsewhere on this disc. In general, warmth and invention abound in this playing, yet the galant style is never transgressed, the emotions never pushed to romantic proportions. Elizabeth Wallfisch's baroque violin has a full, rounded tone and she plays with admirable security of technique, even in the most demanding sections. The resonance of the ensemble is delightfully reflected in the spacious acoustic of the recording, further helping the cause of such fine music that has for too long been neglected.

NEW REVIEW

Tartini. VIOLIN SONATAS, Volume 2. **Locatelli Trio** (Elizabeth Wallfisch, vn; Richard Tunnicliffe, vc; Paul Nicholson, hpd). Hyperion CDA66485. Recorded in 1991.
D major, BD19; B flat major, BB1; A major, BA4, "sopra lo stile che suona il Prette dalla Chitarra Portoghese"; B flat major, BB5 (Op. 5 No. 6).

1h 7m DDD 11/92 

The four works here are unfailingly inventive, ranging in style from the militaristic first *Allegro* of the D major Sonata to the delicate *Largo* of the B flat work. Each sonata here receives performances of the highest calibre from the Locatelli Trio, richly detailed and compelling in tone. Listen to the extraordinary Sonata, BA4 "In the style of the priest who plays the Portuguese guitar". The second movement *Andante* sets biting double-stopped dissonances of the violin against limpid pizzicato cello in such a manner as to sound almost improvised. Tempos are unfailingly apt — in the B flat Sonata, Op. 5 No. 6, the opening *Affetuoso* is given ample space before launching into the breezy *Allegro*, with Elizabeth Wallfisch throwing off the intricate figurations with effortless grace and impeccable tuning, even in the top-most registers, of which Tartini was inordinately fond. Unless the very thought of original instruments brings you out in a rash, there is much to delight here, both in the pieces and the performances. The immediate recording brings the players right into the room with the listener and the scholarly yet readable notes from Peter Holman set the works in their proper context.

John Tavener

British 1944-

Tavener. The Protecting Veil[a]. Thrinos.
Britten. Solo Cello Suite No. 3, Op. 87. **Steven Isserlis** (vc); [a]**London Symphony Orchestra/Gennadi Rozhdestvensky.** Virgin Classics VC7 59052-2.

1h 14m DDD 3/92 

The Protecting Veil is one of the feasts of the Mother of God, according to the ritual of the Orthodox Church. John Tavener's ability to transfer such a concept into a concert work of wide appeal and proven impact is indeed remarkable, even if its success has more to do with the simple, direct emotionalism of the music than with its specific religious connotations. Direct emotionalism, certainly — but the music's predominantly slow pace and sustained lyricism, offset by occasional, striking dramatic gestures of sorrow and lamentation, make huge demands on the stamina and technique of the performers. Both Steven Isserlis and Gennadi Rozhdestvensky, not normally one of the more self-effacing of conductors, deserve high praise for the way they sink themselves into the music's contemplative but far from monotonous ethos, and refugees from the battering of more complex contemporary music need look no further for solace and consolation. The brief lament of the unaccompanied cello piece *Thrinos* is no less affecting, while the Britten suite provides valuable contrast through music from which the intense and unshakeable religious faith of Tavener's work is conspicuous by its absence. Even by modern standards, the recording quality is outstandingly good.

Tavener. Ikon of Light (1984)[a]. Funeral Ikos[b]. Carol — The Lamb[c]. [a]Members of the **Chilingirian Quartet** (Mark Butler, vn; Csaba Erdelyi, va; Philip de Groote, vc); **The Tallis Scholars/**[ab]**Peter Phillips,** [c]**John Tavener.** Gimell CDGIM005. Texts and translations included. From 1585-05 (12/84).

55m DDD 6/91 

John Tavener first met with critical acclaim in 1968 with his dramatic cantata on biblical (and not so biblical) texts — *The Whale*. There followed a series of works (*Ultimos Ritos, Celtic Requiem* and the opera *Therese* to name but three) in which he seemed to be re-examining and questioning the very nature of his faith and his relationship with his creator, and this culminated in his being received, in 1977, into the Russian Orthodox Church. Since then many of his works have been inspired by Russian Orthodox texts and the quietly omnipotent image of the ikon. One such work, and arguably an important turning point in his approach to composition, is the *Ikon of Light*. This penetrating and visionary work is a setting of the "Mystic Prayer to the Holy Spirit" by mystical poet St Simeon, the New Theologian. To describe the opening as luminous would be an understatement. Five repetitions of the word *Phos* ("Light"), each proportionally longer than the previous, are interspersed by the sound of a distant string trio (representing the Soul's yearning for God) before dissolving into the radiantly polyphonic music of the second movement "Dhoxa" ("Glory"). As an expression of faith in contemporary art it is without doubt one of the most important works of the last 20 years, and deserves to win many friends and renewed recognition for this often undervalued and extraordinarily gifted composer. The austere and simple, yet equally moving *Funeral Ikos* — a setting of the Greek funeral sentences for the burial of priests — and the gentle stillness of the now popular carol *The Lamb* complete this richly rewarding disc. Beautifully performed and vividly recorded.

Further listening ...

Eonia. God is with us — Christmas proclamation. Hymn for the Dormition of the Mother of God. Hymn to the Mother of God. Little Lamb, who made thee? Love bade me welcome. Magnificat. Nunc dimittis. Ode of St Andrew of Crete. The Tiger. Today the Virgin. The Uncreated Eros. **St George's Chapel Choir/Christopher Robinson.** Hyperion CDA66464.

We shall see Him as He is. **Soloists; Britten Singers; Chester Festival Chorus; BBC Welsh Symphony Chorus and Orchestra/Richard Hickox.** Chandos CHAN9128 (1/93).

The Whale — dramatic cantata. **Soloists; London Sinfonietta Chorus; London Sinfonietta/David Atherton.** EMI CDSAPCOR15.

John Taverner

British c.1490-1545

Taverner. Missa Gloria tibi Trinitas. Kyrie a 4, "Leroy". Dum transisset Sabbatum. **The Tallis Scholars/Peter Phillips.** Gimell CDGIM004. From 1585-04 (12/84).

47m DDD 7/86

Taverner's Mass *Gloria tibi Trinitas* is a gloriously rich work showing a strong awareness of continental styles that was a hallmark of the cultural life encouraged by Henry VIII until he broke with Rome. Taverner was appointed the first choir-master of Cardinal College, Oxford (now Christ Church) and it seems almost certain that the Mass was composed for that choir. Musicians today accept the work's superiority and though there are several excellent recordings currently in the catalogue, Peter Phillips's recording with The Tallis Scholars is perhaps the most exciting, splendidly recorded in the chapel of Merton College, Oxford.

NEW REVIEW

Taverner. Missa Sancti Wilhelmi. MOTETS. **The Sixteen/Harry Christophers.** Hyperion CDA66427. Texts and translations included.
Motets — O Wilhelme, pastor bone. Dum transisset Sabbatum. Ex eius tumba.

52m DDD 4/92

The *Missa Sancti Wilhelmi* is not one of Taverner's best known works, but there is no reason why this should be the case. Though it does not have the sometimes rather wild melodic beauty of the six-voice Masses, it is nevertheless an impressive work in a more modern imitative style, in keeping with its model *O Wilhelme, pastor bone*. The Sixteen perform with their customary clarity and precision, and convey enthusiasm even in the somewhat syllabic *Gloria* and *Credo* movements of the Mass, something which is not always easy to do. While both the 'Wilhelm' works and *Dum transisset Sabbatum* are among Taverner's later works, there is no doubt at all that *Ex eius tumba* is one of the earliest. It is firmly late medieval in style, and the intricate tracery of its construction, so well captured here by The Sixteen, makes a thought-provoking contrast to the pieces in a more 'continental' imitative style. At 15 minutes this is a substantial composition, and one can only be surprised that it is so little-known: perhaps the large amount of chant which forms an integral part of the work has discouraged performers. *Dum transisset Sabbatum* is, however, the high point of the disc, and if The Sixteen do not quite attain the ecstatic heights achieved in the recording by The Tallis Scholars (reviewed above), neither do they fail to rise to Taverner's inspiration.

Further listening ...

Missa Corona spinea. *Motets* — Gaude plurimum; In pace in idipsum. **The Sixteen/Harry Christophers.** Hyperion CDA66360 (1/90).

Mass a 4, "Western Wynde". Mater Christi. *Coupled with* **Tallis.** *Motets* — Sancte Deus. Audivi vocem de caelo. Honor, virtus et potestas. O sacrum convivium. Salvator mundi I a 5. **New College Choir, Oxford/Edward Higginbottom.** CRD CRD3372 (4/89).

Missa Mater Christi. O Wilhelme, pastor bone. Mater Christi sanctissima. **Christ Church Cathedral Choir, Oxford/Stephen Darlington.** Nimbus NI5218 (4/90).

Pyotr Ill'yich Tchaikovsky

Russian 1840-1893

Tchaikovsky. Piano Concerto No. 1 in B flat minor, Op. 23[a]. Violin Concerto in D major, Op. 35[b]. [a]**Emil Gilels** (pf); [a]**New York Philharmonic Orchestra/Zubin Mehta;** [b]**Pinchas Zukerman** (vn); [b]**Israel Philharmonic Orchestra/Zubin Mehta.** CBS Masterworks CD44643. Item marked [a] from 36660 (5/81), [b] IM39563 (10/85).

lh 9m DDD 9/89 

The factor of cost which sometimes worries people buying CDs is put into perspective here, with a mid-price disc lasting nearly 70 minutes and containing Tchaikovsky's two most popular concertos, works which we would in the past normally have bought on separate LPs, and played by top-class artists who for all their virtuosity put expression first and foremost and bring considerable charm to the music. The Piano Concerto No. 1 is a 1979 live performance from New York, and has all the excitement which that implies, a kind of urgency that keeps you at the edge of your seat. Emil Gilels is in his best form, which is saying something, and the New York Philharmonic under Zubin Mehta are caught up in this fine music-making. The recording does not bring the piano as close as we are accustomed to, perhaps, but that is no bad thing, and though there are some noticeable audience noises, few people will consider this too high a price to pay for being present, as it were, on a memorable occasion. In the Violin Concerto, Pinchas Zukerman joined the same conductor in Tel Aviv in 1984 and here, too, we have a thrilling live performance of one of the great violin concertos by a soloist and conductor entirely in sympathy with the music. Applause follows both performances, but sensibly it is faded fairly quickly.

Additional recommendations ...

Piano Concerto. ***Grieg.*** *Piano Concerto in A minor, Op. 16*[a]. **Artur Rubinstein** (pf); **Boston Symphony Orchestra/Erich Leinsdorf;** [a]**Orchestra/Alfred Wallenstein.** RCA Gold Seal 09026-61262-2 — lh 3m ADD

Piano Concerto. ***Rachmaninov.*** *Piano Concerto No. 2 in C minor, Op. 18.* **Alexei Sultanov** (pf); **London Symphony Orchestra/Maxim Shostakovich.** Teldec Digital Experience 9031-77601-2 — lh 10m DDD

Piano Concerto[a]. ***Prokofiev.*** *Piano Concerto No. 3 in C major, Op. 26*[b]. **Martha Argerich** (pf); [a]**Royal Philharmonic Orchestra/Charles Dutoit;** [b]**Berlin Philharmonic Orchestra/Claudio Abbado.** DG 415 062-2GH *(see review under Prokofiev; refer to the Index to Reviews)* — lh 3m ADD 5/85

Piano Concerto. ***Dohnányi.*** *Variations on a Nursery Song.* **András Schiff** (pf); **Chicago Symphony Orchestra/Sir Georg Solti.** Decca 417 294-2DH — 59m DDD 12/86

Piano Concerto[a]. ***Chopin.*** *Piano Concerto No. 2 in F minor, Op. 21*[b]. **Vladimir Ashkenazy** (pf); **London Symphony Orchestra/**[a]**Lorin Maazel;** [b]**David Zinman.** Decca Ovation 417 750-2DM — lh 6m ADD 1/89

Piano Concertos — No. 1; No. 3 in E flat major, Op. 73. **Emil Gilels** (pf); **New Philharmonia Orchestra/Lorin Maazel.** EMI Eminence CD-EMX2001 — 52m ADD 8/90

Piano Concerto. Concert Fantasia, Op. 56. **Mikhail Pletnev** (pf); **Philharmonia Orchestra/Vladimir Fedoseyev.** Virgin Classics VC7 59612-2 — lh 4m DDD 4/91

Violin Concerto. ***Brahms.*** *Violin Concerto in D major, Op. 77.* **Jascha Heifetz** (vn); **Chicago Symphony Orchestra/Fritz Reiner.** RCA Living Stereo 09026 61495-2 — lh 4m ADD 4/93

Violin Concerto. Sérénade mélancolique in B minor, Op. 26. Valse-scherzo in C major, Op. 34. **Pierre Amoyal** (vn); **Philharmonia Orchestra/Charles Dutoit.** Erato Libretto 2292-45971-2 — 51m ADD 5/93 9p B

Tchaikovsky. Violin Concerto in D major, Op. 35[a]. WORKS FOR VIOLIN AND PIANO[b]. **Itzhak Perlman** (vn); [b]**Janet Goodman Guggenheim** (pf); [a]**Israel Philharmonic Orchestra/Zubin Mehta.** EMI CDC7 54108-2. Recorded live in 1990.

Bazzini: La ronde des lutins, Op. 25. ***Bloch:*** Baal shem — Nigun. ***Kreisler:*** Liebeslied. ***Prokofiev*** (arr. Heifetz): The Love for Three Oranges — March. ***Tartini:*** Violin Sonata in G minor, "The devil's trill". ***Tchaikovsky*** (arr. Kreisler): String Quartet No. 1 in D major, Op. 11 — Andante. ***Wieniawski*** (arr. Kreisler): Caprice in A minor.

1h 12m DDD 2/91 

Tchaikovsky. WORKS FOR VIOLIN AND ORCHESTRA. **Xue-Wei** (vn); **Philharmonia Orchestra/Salvatore Accardo.** ASV CDDCA713.

Violin Concerto in D major, Op. 35. Sérénade mélancolique in B minor, Op. 26. Souvenir d'un lieu cher, Op. 42 — No. 3, Mélodie (orch. Glazunov). Valse-scherzo in C major, Op. 34.

54m DDD 9/90 B

EMI's recording has a special interest in that it provides a memento of Itzhak Perlman's first visit to the Soviet Union in 1990, which happens also to have been the first visit of the Israel Philharmonic Orchestra and the conductor Zubin Mehta. There is a sense of immediacy that belongs to a live performance before an audience, and for this most collectors will accept the debit side, which frankly includes a fair amount of audience noise including applause not only at the end of pieces — note that in Russia, the slow handclap is a mark of special enthusiasm! but, for example, when the violinist announces some of the pieces he played at his Moscow concert with piano (this occupies the seven tracks after the three that are taken up with the Tchaikovsky Concerto, played in Leningrad). Judging by the odd murmurs, rustles and bumps, Soviet concert audiences who are obviously enjoying themselves are none too silent either while the music is actually happening, and if you think this could matter a lot to you, try to listen to the slow movement of the concerto before purchasing this CD. Otherwise, there's little to fear and much to delight, for the violin playing is masterly in its vibrant eloquence and bravura, and Mehta and the orchestra accompany most attentively in the concerto although the recording (excellent of Perlman) could ideally have captured more detail of their contribution. The wonders of violin virtuosity in the final piece with piano by Bazzini draw gasps of delighted amazement from the Moscow audience, as well they might!

If the audience noise in Perlman's live performance of the Tchaikovsky Concerto on EMI distracts you, then all is quiet in the studio version featuring Xue-Wei as soloist. In fact, the recording quality is conspicuously good, with an unusually sensible balance struck between soloist and orchestra. This disc is also notable for the Philharmonia's particularly expressive and sensitive playing under Salvatore Accardo, whose knowledge of these works as a soloist must have been a great boon to his fellow violinist. Xue-Wei plays the first movement of the concerto with plenty of feeling, generosity of phrase and a beautiful quality of tone. The *Canzonetta* is notable for a high degree of concentration and expressive warmth on the part of the soloist, and a particularly close rapport between him and his conductor: in the finale virtuosity and high spirits are apt partners. The three shorter pieces make appropriate pendants to the concertos — two charming, melodious sweetmeats flanking the lively *Valse-scherzo*. Playing and conducting in these fill-ups are as winning as in the main work.

Tchaikovsky. 1812 — Overture, Op. 49. Capriccio italien, Op. 45. MAZEPPA — Cossack Dance. **Cincinnati Symphony Orchestra/Erich Kunzel.** Telarc CD80041. From DG10041 (4/80).

35m DDD 12/83 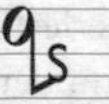 

Kunzel's recording of the *1812* is an unashamed hi-fi spectacular, so much so that purchasers are warned that the cannon at the end can damage loudspeakers with their extreme volume. At the time of the recording it is claimed that windows nearby were shattered. In the *Capriccio italien* too, another colourful popular favourite, this version uses the full range of high-fidelity digital sound with the bass drum very prominent and astonishingly vivid in its exploitation of the lowest register. The forwardness of such effects may detract from the purely musical qualities of the performances, which are strong and energetic without being so perceptive or so exciting as some, though very well played. Particularly enjoyable is the third item, the vigorous and colourful "Cossack Dance".

Additional recommendation ...
Overture. Romeo and Juliet. Hamlet, Op. 67a. **London Philharmonic Orchestra/Sir Alexander Gibson.** Collins Quest 3048-2 — 5lm DDD

Tchaikovsky. Serenade in C major, Op. 48. Souvenir de Florence, Op. 70. **Vienna Chamber Orchestra/Philippe Entremont.** Naxos 8 550404. Recorded in 1990.

lh 5m DDD 10/91 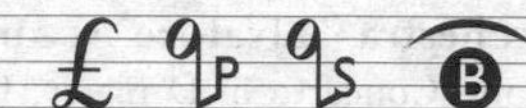

This is one of the many CDs now on the market that dispel the myth once and for all that only full-price recordings contain really outstanding performances. The Naxos label is just about as 'bargain' as you will get, and here they have given us superlative performances of two of Tchaikovsky's most endearing works. The Serenade in C contains a wealth of memorable and haunting music, beautifully and inventively scored and guaranteed to bring immense pleasure and delight to those dipping their toes in to the world of classical music for the first time. Philippe Entremont and the Vienna Chamber Orchestra give a marvellously polished and finely poised performance full of warmth, affection and high spirits, and the famous second movement Waltz in particular is played with much elegance and grace. The *Souvenir de Florence*, originally written for string sextet, makes a welcome appearance here in Tchaikovsky's own arrangement for string orchestra. This is a delightfully sunny performance, full of suavity, exuberance and romantic dash, but always alert to the many subtleties of Tchaikovsky's skilful and intricate part-writing. The *Adagio cantabile* is particularly notable for some extremely fine and poetic solo playing from the violin and cello principals of the VPO. The beautifully spacious recording does ample justice to the performances. A magnificent bargain.

Additional recommendations ...
Serenade. Suite No. 4 in G major, Op. 61, "Mozartiana". Elegy in G major in honour of Ivan Samarin. String Quartet No. 1 in D major, Op. 11 — Andante cantabile (orch. Serebrier). The Sleeping Beauty (orch. Stravinsky) — Variations de la Fée de lilas; Entr'acte. **Scottish Chamber Orchestra/José Serebrier.** ASV CDDCA719 — lh 17m DDD 3/91
Serenade. ***Grieg.*** *Holberg Suite, Op. 40. Two Norwegian Melodies, Op. 63.* **Moscow Soloists/Yuri Bashmet.** RCA Victor Red Seal RD60368 — lh lm DDD 3/91
Serenade. Souvenir de Florence. **Auvergne Orchestra/Jean-Jacques Kantorow.** Denon CO-75026 — lh 2m DDD 3/93

Tchaikovsky. Romeo and Juliet — Fantasy Overture. The Nutcracker — ballet suite, Op. 71a. **Berlin Philharmonic Orchestra/Herbert von Karajan.** DG 410 873-2GH. From 410 873-1GH (2/84).

44m DDD 4/84 

It might be argued that *Romeo and Juliet* is the most successful symphonic poem in the repertoire, economically structured, wonderfully inspired in its melodies and with the narrative and final tragedy depicted with imaginative vividness. Karajan brings out all the intensity of the composer's inspiration and the playing of the Berlin Philharmonic creates much excitement. *The Nutcracker* shows the other side of the composer's personality, the most wonderfully crafted light music, and the suite is utter perfection. Each of the *danses caractéristiques* is a miracle of melody and orchestration and their charm never cloys, especially when they are played so winningly and with such polish. The recording is admirably clear and well balanced and though a little more warmth would have made the upper strings sweeter in the ballet music, this remains a very recommendable disc.

Additional recommendations ...
Romeo and Juliet. Capriccio italien, Op. 45. Francesca da Rimini, Op. 32. Elegy in honour of Ivan Samarin. **Royal Philharmonic Orchestra/Vladimir Ashkenazy.** Decca 421 715-2DH — lh 6m DDD 8/89 B
The Nutcracker — ballet suite. The Sleeping Beauty — excerpts. Swan Lake — excerpts. **Berlin Philharmonic Orchestra/Mstislav Rostropovich.** DG Galleria 429 097-2GGA — lh 9m ADD 4/90 B
The Nutcracker — ballet suite[a]*. The Sleeping Beauty — excerpts. Swan Lake — excerpts.* [a]**Ambrosian Singers; London Symphony Orchestra/André Previn.** EMI CZS7 62816-2 — ② 2h 28m ADD 3/92 B

Tchaikovsky. ORCHESTRAL WORKS. **Royal Liverpool Philharmonic Orchestra/Sian Edwards.** EMI Eminence CD-EMX2152.
1812 — Overture, Op. 49. Romeo and Juliet — Fantasy Overture. Marche slave, Op. 31. Francesca da Rimini, Op. 32.

lh 6m DDD 12/89 

It is an extraordinary achievement that the young British conductor, Sian Edwards, should have made her recording début with a Tchaikovsky programme of such distinction. She immediately achieves a splendid artistic partnership with the Royal Liverpool Philharmonic Orchestra, whose playing is so full of vitality, and whether in *1812* with its vigour and flair, its cluster of lyrical folk melodies, and a spectacular finale with thundering canon, or in *Marche slave*, resplendently patriotic, in a uniquely Russian way, together they bring the music tingling to life in every bar. *Romeo and Juliet*, on the other hand, needs a finely judged balance between the ardour and moonlight of the love music, the vibrant conflict of the battle, and the tragedy of the final denouement, which is uncannily well managed. Most intractable interpretatively is *Francesca da Rimini*, with its spectacularly horrifying picture of Dante's inferno which the composer uses to frame the central sequence depicting the lovers, Francesca and Paolo, and the doom-laden atmosphere which surrounds their intense mutual passion. Edwards's grip on this powerfully evocative sequence of events is unerringly sure, and she takes the orchestra through the narrative as only an instinctive Tchaikovskian could. The work opens with an unforgettable sense of nemesis and ends with a truly thrilling picture of the whirlwinds of Hell, into which the lovers are cast, still in their final passionate embrace. All in all this is one of the best Tchaikovsky discs in the mid-price catalogue and the fine EMI Eminence recording combines weight and sonority with brilliance, and brings a most attractive ambient effect.

Additional recommendations ...
Francesca da Rimini. Hamlet — fantasy overture, Op. 67. **New York Stadium Orchestra/Leopold Stikowski.** dell'Arte CDDA9006 — ADD 4/88 B
Romeo and Juliet. Capriccio italien, Op. 45. Francesca da Rimini. Elegy in honour of Ivan Samarin. **Royal Philharmonic Orchestra/Vladimir Ashkenazy.** Decca 421 715-2DH — lh 6m DDD 8/89 B
Romeo and Juliet. Francesca da Rimini. Mazeppa — Cossack Dance. Festival Coronation March in D major. **Leipzig Gewandhaus Orchestra/Kurt Masur.** Teldec 9031-76456-2 — 53m DDD 5/93 B

Tchaikovsky. ORCHESTRAL WORKS. [a]**Carl Pini,** [b]**Pinchas Zukerman** (vns); [a]**Philharmonia Orchestra/Michael Tilson Thomas;** [b]**Israel Philharmonic Orchestra/Zubin Mehta.** CBS Digital Masters CD46503.
Orchestral Suites[a] — No. 2 in C major, Op. 53; No. 4 in G major, Op. 61, "Mozartiana". Sérénade mélancolique in B minor, Op. 26[b]. Mélodie in E flat major, Op. 42 No. 3[b].

lh 12m DDD 8/91

The musical 'marriage' of Tchaikovsky and Mozart might seem odd in that it allies a full-blooded romantic composer with one of an incomparable classical poise. But when one remembers that the Russian composer's ballet music has an equally admirable grace and elegance, and that he adored Mozart, it is less surprising that he succeeded when he chose three of Mozart's piano pieces (a gigue, a minuet and a theme with variations) and his choral *Ave verum* as the basis of the Fourth Orchestral Suite. *Mozartiana* is enjoyable music, and represents what Tchaikovsky called "the past revisited in a contemporary work". However, the effect is lush because of the orchestration, which includes a solo violin, harp and cymbals, and that is emphasized by Michael Tilson Thomas's slowish tempos (at least until the finale) and the rich recording — indeed, it's surprising how romantic Mozart's virtually unaltered classical notes become. The Second Suite is all Tchaikovsky and even more delightful, with characteristically fine scoring and a wealth of tunes; it has an eloquence and drama more reminiscent of the composer's ballets than of his symphonies — indeed, the second movement is a waltz, while the fourth is called "A Child's Dream" and could have come from *The Nutcracker*. Tilson Thomas brings charm and zest to this music, and Zubin Mehta, with a different orchestra, is no less successful in the other two pieces, in which the superbly polished violin playing of Pinchas Zukerman is a considerable bonus.

NEW REVIEW

Tchaikovsky. Orchestral Suite No. 3 in G major, Op. 55. Festival Coronation March. **USSR Ministry of Culture Symphony Orchestra/Gennadi Rozhdestvensky.** Erato 2292 45970-2. Recorded in 1991.

46m DDD

He wanted a symphony and ended up with a suite, but "what's in a name" Tchaikovsky added. This, his most famous Suite, was written in 1884 between the Fourth and Fifth Symphonies, and it shares their breadth, but has no comparable psychological programme. No matter. Where in all Tchaikovsky's output is there a melody quite as gorgeous as the one that eventually becomes airborne at the end of the first movement "Elégie"? The Suite's crowning glory, however, is its final Theme and Variations, hailed in 1906 by the English music critic Edwin Evans as standing "in sheer plastic beauty above any modern set for orchestra, Elgar's *Enigma Variations* alone excepted". Rozdestvensky is in his element: melody is broadly sung and founded on a strong bass line, details are lovingly attended to, and the rich variety of Russian woodwind hues really make their mark. How marvellous, too, to hear this orchestra decently recorded for once (brass penetrate without dominating), with intelligent use of the ambience of Moscow Conservatory's Great Hall. Quality not quantity, then. And for an encore, the *Festival Coronation March* — Russian pomp and circumstance at its best.

NEW REVIEW

Tchaikovsky. Swan Lake, Op. 20 — ballet. **Montreal Symphony Orchestra/Charles Dutoit.** Decca 436 212-2DH2. Recorded in 1991.

② 2h 34m DDD 2/93 B

No one wrote more beautiful and danceable ballet music than Tchaikovsky, and this account of *Swan Lake* is a delight throughout. This is not only because of the quality of the music, which is here played absolutely complete including additions the composer made after the première, but also thanks to the richly idiomatic playing of Charles Dutoit and his Montreal orchestra in the superb and celebrated location of St Eustache's Church in that city. Maybe some conductors have made the music even more earthily Russian, but it is worth remembering that the Russian ballet tradition in Tchaikovsky's time was chiefly French and that the most influential early production of this ballet, in 1895, was choreographed by the Frenchman Marius Petipa. Indeed, the symbiosis of French and Russian elements in this music (and story) is one of its great strengths, the refinement of the one being superbly allied to the vigour of the other, notably in such music as the "Russian Dance" with its expressive violin solo. This is a profoundly romantic reading of the score, and the great set pieces such as the Waltz in Act 1 and the marvellous scene of the swans on a moonlit lake that opens Act 2 are wonderfully evocative; yet they do not for that reason overshadow the other music, which supports and strengthens them as gentler hills and valleys might surround and enhance magnificent, awe-inspiring peaks, the one being indispensable to the other. You do not have to be a ballet aficionado to fall under the spell of this wonderful music, which here receives a performance that combines romantic passion with an aristocratic refinement and is glowingly recorded.

Additional recommendations ...
Swan Lake. **Royal Opera House Orchestra, Covent Garden/Mark Ermler.** Royal Opera House Records ROH301/03 — ③ 2h 33m DDD 12/89
Swan Lake. **Philharmonia Orchestra/John Lanchbery.** Classics for Pleasure CD-CFPD 4727 — ② 2h 34m DDD 9/89 £
Swan Lake — excerpts. The Nutcracker — ballet suite. Romeo and Juliet. **Chicago Symphony Orchestra/Sir Georg Solti.** Decca Ovation 430 707-2DM — 1h 10m DDD 8/91
Swan Lake. **Slovak Radio Symphony Orchestra, Bratislava/Ondrej Lenárd.** Naxos 8 550246/7 — ② 2h 20m DDD 12/91 £
Swan Lake. **London Symphony Orchestra/Michael Tilson Thomas.** Sony Classical SK46592 — ② 2h 29m DDD 4/92

NEW REVIEW

Tchaikovsky. The Sleeping Beauty, Op. 66 — ballet. **Philharmonia Orchestra/John Lanchbery.** EMI CDS7 49216-2. Recorded in 1982.

Many authorities regard this as Tchaikovsky's finest ballet score and, indeed, one of the greatest ballet scores of all time. It has many wonderful things: the Waltz from Act One includes some wonderfully arching phrasing that soars with tremendous passion, while the "Panorama" of Act 2 is one of the composer's finest melodic ideas. The "Pas de six" of Act 1 and the contrasted Fairy dances of Act 3 bring the same almost Mozartian grace (combined with Tchaikovsky's own very special feeling for orchestral colour) that he displays in the *Nutcracker* characteristic dances, which turn simple ballet vignettes into great art. Lanchbery's reading has great zest and vitality, combining a marvellous sense of drama without any loss of classical grace. The recording is not so opulent as more recent versions but it still sounds splendid and unlike many of the alternatives listed below, it fits on two CDs.

Additional recommendations ...
Sleeping Beauty (incomplete). **Philharmonia Orchestra/George Weldon.** Classics for Pleasure CD-CFPD4458 — ② 1h 57m ADD 1/89 ▲
Sleeping Beauty. **Royal Opera House Orchestra, Covent Garden/Mark Ermler.** Royal Opera House Records ROHCD306/8 — ③ 2h 53m DDD 5/90
Sleeping Beauty — excerpts. **Royal Opera House Orchestra, Covent Garden/Mark Ermler.** Royal Opera House Records ROHCD003 — 1h 12m DDD 5/90
Sleeping Beauty. **Czecho-Slovak State Philharmonic Orchestra/Andrew Mogrelia.** Naxos 8 550490-2 — ③ 2h 53m DDD 4/93

Tchaikovsky. The Nutcracker, Op. 71 — ballet[a]. QUEEN OF SPADES — Duet of Daphnis and Chloë[b]. [b]**Cathryn Pope** (sop); [b]**Sarah Walker** (mez); [a]**Tiffin Boys' School Choir; London Symphony Orchestra/Sir Charles Mackerras.** Telarc CD80137. Recorded in 1986.

② 1h 28m DDD 5/87

The *Nutcracker* ballet shows Tchaikovsky's inspiration at its most memorable and the orchestration creates a unique symbiosis with the music. The ballet is based on a grotesque tale by E.T.A. Hoffmann, but in the ballet it becomes more of a fairy story, with only the eccentric Drosselmeyer who provides the heroine, Clara, with the Nutcracker at a Christmas party, reflecting anything of the mood of the original narrative. Tchaikovsky's music, a stream of wonderful tunes, radiantly, piquantly or glitteringly scored, as the character of each demands, contains much that enchants the listener which is not included in the famous Suite, notably the "Waltz of the Snowflakes" (with its wordless chorus) and the glorious climbing melody that accompanies the journey through the pine forest to the Magic Castle. Under Mackerras the music glows with colour and has superb vitality; the stunningly rich Telarc recording helps too. This is a wonderful entertainment from the first bar to the last and the documentation is admirable. As a bonus we are offered a charming duet from the *Queen of Spades*.

Additional recommendations ...
The Nutcracker. **Ambrosian Singers; Philharmonia Orchestra/Michael Tilson Thomas.** CBS CD42173 — ② DDD 3/87
The Nutcracker. Serenade in C major, Op. 48[a]. **London Symphony Orchestra, [a]Philharmonia Hungarica/Antál Dorati.** Mercury 432 750-2MM2 — ② 1h 9m ADD 9/92

NEW REVIEW

Tchaikovsky. SYMPHONIES. **London Symphony Orchestra/Igor Markevitch.** Philips 426 848-2PB4. Recorded 1962-66.
No. 1 in G minor, Op. 13, "Winter Daydreams"[a]; No. 2 in C minor, Op. 17, "Little Russian"[b]; No. 3 in D major, Op. 29, "Polish"[c]; No. 4 in F minor, Op. 36[d]; No. 5 in E minor, Op. 64[e]; No. 6 in B minor, Op. 74, "Pathétique"[f]. Item marked [a] from SAL3578 (10/66), [b] SAL3601 (3/67), [c] SAL3549 (2/66), [d] SAL3481 (2/65), [e] SAL3579 (12/66), [f] 835126AY (10/62).

④ 4h 16m ADD 3/91 £

If you want to avoid routine in standard repertoire, then entrust its interpretation to a composer-performer. It's a formula that doesn't always work, but when it does the results are usually illuminating beyond belief. Igor Markevitch started life as a composer; in fact, before the Second World War he was considered one of Nadia Boulanger's most promising protégées, and his compositions were held in high esteem (a renaissance of interest in them is currently under way). Markevitch's approach to Tchaikovsky is refreshing, spontaneous and insightful; no wonder Stravinsky (another Markevitch speciality) felt such a deep love for this music, with its piquant scoring, acute sense of harmonic development and dramatic impact. Markevitch avoids a blanket approach to the six symphonies. He doesn't merely select and indulge those aspects of the music that appeal to him; rather, he treats each separate work as a unique phase in an ongoing symphonic journey. His are more recreations than interpretations; and although attentive to structure, he's quite willing to underline small details, varying the pulse to expressive ends — as he does in the first movements of the Fourth and Sixth Symphonies — and guiding us through musical events that we might otherwise have missed. But where a lesser conductor might turn selective observation into tiresome point-making, Markevitch always retains a sense of structural proportion. His handling of the Third Symphony's introduction is masterly, with the transition into the main *Allegro* as effective as it is cunning. He brings both expressive weight and balletic sensibility to the early symphonies, and although Bernard Haitink's versions are not displaced (see below), Markevitch's are especially supple, with the LSO strings and woodwinds excelling themselves in keenness of attack and clarity of articulation. The Fifth, too, is supremely alive and eager to yield its secrets, with a first movement that forges forwards and resists the temptation to linger over the big tunes. Musical punctuation can be a problem in Tchaikovsky, but Markevitch understands how to make this music breathe; and with clean, open recordings (just a little short on lustre), his work is borne to us much as it sounded on the day.

Additional recommendations ...
Nos. 1-4. **Bournemouth Symphony Orchestra/Andrew Litton.** Virgin VMT7 59699-2 — ③ 3h 43m DDD
Nos. 1-6. Capriccio italien, Op. 45. Manfred Symphony, Op. 58. **Oslo Philharmonic Orchestra/Mariss Jansons.** Chandos CHAN8672/8 — ⑦ 5h 19m DDD 1/89
Nos. 4-6. Manfred Symphony, Op. 58[a]. **Philharmonia Orchestra, [a]New Philharmonia Orchestra/Vladimir Ashkenazy.** Decca 425 586-2DM3 — ③ 3h 12m ADD 3/90 £
No. 1[a]*; Nos. 2-6*[b]*. Romeo and Juliet — fantasy overture*[b]. **[a]New Philharmonia Orchestra, [b]Philharmonia Orchestra/Riccardo Muti.** EMI CZS7 67314-2 — ④ 4h 32m ADD 9/91 £
Nos. 1-6. Romeo and Juliet. **Vienna Philharmonic Orchestra/Lorin Maazel.** Decca 430 787 2DC4 — ④ 4h 27m ADD 4/92

NEW REVIEW

Tchaikovsky. Symphony No. 1 in G minor, Op. 13, "Winter daydreams". **Oslo Philharmonic Orchestra/Mariss Jansons.** Chandos CHAN8402.

44m DDD 2/86

NEW REVIEW

Tchaikovsky. Symphony No. 2 in C minor, Op. 17, "Little Russian". Capriccio italien, Op. 45. **Oslo Philharmonic Orchestra/Mariss Jansons.** Chandos CHAN8460.

48m DDD 11/87

The composer himself gave the work the title *Winter daydreams*, and also gave descriptive titles to the first two movements. The opening *Allegro tranquillo* he subtitled "Dreams of a winter journey", while the *Adagio* bears the inscription "Land of desolation, Land of mists". A *Scherzo* and finale round off a conventional four-movement symphonic structure. In the slow movement Jansons inspires a performance of expressive warmth and tenderness, while the *Scherzo* is managed with great delicacy and sensitivity. Both the opening movement and the finale are invested with vigour and passion, and everywhere the orchestral playing is marvellously confident and disciplined. The recording has not only impact and immediacy but also warmth and refinement. Jansons also has the full measure of Tchaikovsky's Second Symphony. It is a direct performance — the first movement allegro is relatively steady, but never sounds too slow, because of crisp rhythmic pointing — and the second movement goes for charm and felicity of colour. The finale is properly exuberant, with the secondary theme full of character, and there is a fine surge of adrenalin at the end. The *Capriccio italien,* a holiday piece in which the composer set out to be entertaining, is also played with great flair and the hint of vulgarity in the Neapolitan tune is not shirked. Again the closing pages produce a sudden spurt of excitement which is particularly satisfying. The recording here is just short of Chandos's finest — the massed violins could be sweeter on top, but the hall resonance is right for this music and there is a proper feeling of spectacle.

Additional recommendations ...

No. 1. Variations on a Rococo Theme in A major, Op. 33[a]. [a]**Mstislav Rostropovich** (vc); **Berlin Philharmonic Orchestra/Herbert von Karajan.** DG Galleria 431 606-2GCE — 1h 4m ADD 8/91

No. 2 (original version). **London Symphony Orchestra/Geoffrey Simon.** Chandos CHAN8304 — 39m DDD 1/84

NEW REVIEW

Tchaikovsky. Symphony No. 3 in D major, Op. 29, "Polish". Capriccio italien, Op. 45. **St Louis Symphony Orchestra/Leonard Slatkin.** RCA Victor Red Seal RD60433. Recorded 1988-89.

1h 3m DDD 8/92

Leonard Slatkin and the St Louis Symphony Orchestra rise memorably to each successive challenge in this most intractable of symphonies. Although the Third has its undoubted structural flaws, it responds well to assertive yet unsentimental conducting, and Slatkin's ably considered reading keeps its more obvious ambiguities firmly in check. Each of the five movements has its own particular obstacles; Slatkin's handling of the difficult transition into the main section of the opening movement is totally convincing, whilst no finer reading of the over-inflated development section exists on disc. Slatkin's unusually fast tempos for the *Alla Tedesca* and of course the penultimate *Scherzo* hold no terrors for the St Louis players, whose corporate virtuosity and refinement astound and delight the ear in equal measure. There is warmth and ardent, dark-hued tenderness from every section in the *Andante,* so often delegated to the role of inconsequential musical backwater in this symphony. The finale, a glittering orchestral *Polonaise* (from which the work takes its subtitle Polish), offers playing of enthralling brilliance. Slatkin draws resplendent, virile playing from his orchestra, and yet manages to avoid any suggestion of brazen swagger during the anthem-like peroration which brings the symphony to a thrilling conclusion. The disc also includes a refreshingly audacious performance of that perennial holiday journal, the *Capriccio italien*. Definitely the disc to have then, if you've previously harboured doubts about the Third, and easily the best version recorded to date.

Additional recommendations ...

No. 3. **Oslo Philharmonic Orchestra/Mariss Jansons.** Chandos CHAN8463 — 45m DDD 7/86

No. 3. **Berlin Philharmonic Orchestra/Herbert von Karajan.** DG 419 178-2GH — 1h 4m 12/86

No. 3. Serenade in C major, Op. 48. **Berlin Philharmonic Orchestra/Herbert Von Karajan.** DG Galleria 431 605-2GCE — 1h 16m ADD/DDD 8/91

Tchaikovsky. Symphony No. 4 in F minor, Op. 36. **Oslo Philharmonic Orchestra/Mariss Jansons.** Chandos CHAN8361. From ABRD1124 (7/85).

42m DDD 9/86 

A high emotional charge runs through Jansons's performance of the Fourth, yet this rarely seems to be an end in itself. There is always a balancing concern for the superb craftsmanship of Tchaikovsky's writing: the shapeliness of the phrasing; the superb orchestration, scintillating and subtle by turns; and most of all Tchaikovsky's marvellous sense of dramatic pace. Rarely has the first movement possessed such a strong sense of tragic inevitability, or the return of the 'fate' theme in the finale sounded so logical, so necessary. The playing of the Oslo Philharmonic Orchestra is first rate: there are some gorgeous woodwind solos and the brass manage to achieve a truly Tchaikovskian intensity. Recordings are excellent: at once spacious and clearly focused, with a wide though by no means implausible dynamic range.

Additional recommendations ...

No. 4. No. 5 in E minor, Op. 64; No. 6 in B minor, Op. 74, "Pathétique". **Leningrad Philharmonic Orchestra/Evgeny Mravinsky.** DG 419 745-2GH2 — ② 2h 9m ADD 8/87

No. 4. Marche slave, Op. 31. **London Symphony Orchestra/Gennadi Rozhdestvensky.** Pickwick IMP Classics PCD867 — 53m DDD 12/87

No. 4[a]*.* ***Beethoven.*** *Egmont, Op. 84 — incidental music*[b]*.* [b]**Pilar Lorengar** (sop); [a]**London Symphony Orchestra,** [b]**Vienna Philharmonic Orchestra/George Szell.** Decca Historica 425 972-2DM — 1h 4m ADD 4/91

Nos. 2 and 4. **New Philharmonia Orchestra/Claudio Abbado.** DG Galleria 431 604-2GCE *(this is also available on DG Privilege at bargain price: 429 527-2GR)* — 1h 15m ADD 8/91

Nos. 2 and 4. **Polish National Radio Symphony Orchestra/Adrian Leaper.** Naxos 8 550488 — 1h 19m DDD 5/93 £

Tchaikovsky. Symphony No. 5 in E minor, Op. 64. **Oslo Philharmonic Orchestra/Mariss Jansons.** Chandos CHAN8351.

43m DDD 3/85  

Many of the remarks made about Mariss Jansons's performance of the Fourth Symphony also apply here, though it should be stressed that there isn't the vaguest hint of sameness about his interpretations. One's impressions in the Fifth are very different: the rich dark tones of the clarinets in the first movement's introduction, the beautiful tone and elegant phrasing of the horn in the *Andante cantabile*, the ardent, sweeping intensity of the strings at climaxes and, above all, Jansons's extraordinarily coherent vision of the Symphony as a complete utterance. This is a most recommendable version of the Fifth, despite the lack of a fill-up.

Additional recommendations ...

No. 5. Sérénade mélancolique[a]*.* [a]**Shizuka Ishikawa** (vn); **Czech Philharmonic Orchestra/Lovro von Matačic,** [a]**Zdenek Kosler.** Supraphon Crystal Collection 11 0656-2 — 52m ADD

No. 5. EUGENE ONEGIN — Tatiana's letter scene[a]. [a]**Eilene Hannan** (sop); **London Philharmonic Orchestra/Sian Edwards.** EMI Eminence CD-EMX2187 — 59m DDD 1/92 £ B

NEW REVIEW

Tchaikovsky. Symphony No. 6 in B minor, Op. 74, "Pathétique". **Leningrad Philharmonic Orchestra/Evgeny Mravinsky.** Erato 2292-45756-2. Recorded live in 1982.

45m DDD 6/92 P B

NEW REVIEW

Tchaikovsky. Symphony No. 6 in B minor, Op. 74, "Pathétique". Romeo and Juliet — fantasy overture. **Bournemouth Symphony Orchestra/Andrew Litton.** Virgin Classics VC7 59239-2.

lh 7m DDD 5/93 P B

There are some interpretations that penetrate the heart of the matter with such certainty, such rock-solid intuitive perception, that rivals tend never to totally displace them. Evgeny Mravinsky's reading of the *Pathétique* Symphony is very much in that class, and the fact that its supremacy is based not just on one recording, but four, underlines the sureness of its vision. Although Mravinsky had already set down the symphony in Russia when LP was still wet behind the ears, the majority of us first heard his reading in the mid-1950s when DG issued a recording made when the Leningrad Philharmonic visited Vienna. That LP was immediately acclaimed as a classic; its tension, vividness, virtuosity (never for its own sake, only to musical ends) and refinement setting new standards in Tchaikovsky interpretation. When Mravinsky rerecorded the Symphony in London a few years later, some critics, although bowled over by the precision of the playing, wondered whether his approach wasn't just a little too hard-driven. But posterity has stolen an earlier lead than usual, and the later performance is nowadays considered as fine and compelling as its two predecessors. The Erato recording was made over 20 years later and shows that by then, Mravinsky had broadened his vision even further. The drama is still there, the attack — although by now a little ragged around the edges — still red-blooded, and the climaxes moved up a notch from overwhelming to devastating. The first movement's development has a breathless urgency that fully reflects the passion of its material, and the final charge screams in alarming desperation, with loudly braying brass and crashing timpani. The *Allegro con grazia* is subdued but beautifully phrased, the March-scherzo thrilling, the finale heartrending in its candid emotional response. The recording, made live at the Leningrad Philharmonic Large Hall, is occasionally raucous, but reports a profoundly moving musical event, one that all lovers of this great work should share.

Of more modern recordings, two stand out, both remarkably from the same company: the Pletnev (listed below) and the very different, but equally convincing Litton recording. The Bournemouth Symphony Orchestra may not be one of the giants of the orchestral world, but under the inspired leadership of Andrew Litton they reach great heights and plumb profound depths in their new recording. Their experience in the other symphonies is brought to fruition here, with beautifully moulded lines in the yearning *Adagio* section of the first movement, exploding into the dramatic, brass-heavy *Allegro*, urgent without ever losing rhythmic definition. Also notable is Litton's control of the third movement—tempo for once held steady so that the march theme emerges naturally and with due weight. The finale is exactly the dragging, aching lament that one imagines inspired the work's nickname. The playing throughout is without reproach and an added benefit over the Mravinsky and Pletnev versions is the addition of the *Romeo and Juliet fantasy overture*, a beautifully measured, expertly characterized reading. Two enduring masterpieces, magnificently recorded—this disc should be in the possession of any self-respecting record collector.

Additional recommendations ...

No. 6. **Oslo Philharmonic Orchestra/Mariss Jansons.** Chandos CHAN8446 — 44m DDD 5/87 P B

No. 6. Marche slave, Op. 31. **Russia National Orchestra/Mikhail Pletnev.** Virgin Classics VC7 59661-2 — 53m DDD 1/92 P S B

Tchaikovsky. Manfred Symphony, Op. 58. **Oslo Philharmonic Orchestra/Mariss Jansons.** Chandos CHAN8535.

53m DDD 5/88

This Symphony "in Four Scenes" was inspired by a reading of Byron's dramatic poem. Tchaikovsky seems to have felt great affection for the work but was unsure of its structural validity. It has proved difficult to bring off successfully in performance, despite the straightforward appeal of much of its melodic invention. In this performance, Jansons selects rather fast tempos for the most part and manages to bring out the warmth of the melodic writing whilst holding the whole work together most convincingly. The Oslo Philharmonic responds with adroit vivacity. Spectacularly open sound complements all the best qualities of this performance, securing here what is likely to be a prime recommendation for quite some time to come.

Additional recommendation ...

Bournemouth Symphony Orchestra/Andrew Litton. Virgin Classics VC7 59230-2 — 57m DDD 3/93

Tchaikovsky. String Quartets — No. 1 in D major, Op. 11; No. 2 in F major, Op. 22; No. 3 in E flat minor, Op. 30. Souvenir de Florence, Op. 70[a]. **Borodin Quartet** (Mikhail Kopelman, Andrei Abramenkov, vns; Dmitri Shebalin, va; Valentin Berlinsky, vc) with [a]**Yuri Bashmet** (va); [a]**Natalia Gutman** (vc). EMI CDS7 49775-2. Recorded 1978-80.

② 2h 20m ADD 8/88

Tchaikovsky's writing for string quartet shows considerable mastery, and all three works have an open-hearted fluency and a high quality of invention. There are no hints of constraint, and it seems that Tchaikovsky enjoyed the task of writing for a gentler medium. The Third Quartet has an elegiac quality throughout, with a particularly deeply-felt slow movement. The First Quartet, with the famous *Andante cantabile* slow movement, has a delightfully spring-like, outgoing lyrical character, and is the most popular of the three: the Second Quartet has a slightly greater range of expression, and the movements are more contrasted in mood. The Borodin Quartet play these works with a fine sense of style, and their readings are totally free of mannerisms and interpretative quirks. They are particularly impressive in the way that they float the long melodies in Tchaikovsky's slow movements, though they can play with plenty of brilliance when required. In *Souvenir de Florence* the two extra players combine happily with the Quartet. The recordings have plenty of presence and warmth.

NEW REVIEW

Tchaikovsky. SONGS. **Joan Rodgers** (sop); **Roger Vignoles** (pf). Hyperion CDA66617. Texts and translations included. Recorded in 1992.

Op. 6 — No. 1, Do not believe; my friend; No. 2, Not a word, o my friend; No. 5, Why?; No. 6, None but the lonely heart. Cradle song, Op. 16 No. 1. The canary, Op. 25 No. 4. *Op. 28* — No. 3, Why did I dream of you?; No. 6, The fearful minute. *Op. 38* — No. 2, It was in the early spring; No. 3, At the ball. *Op. 47* — No. 1, If only I had known; No. 6, Does the day reign?; No. 7, Was I not a little blade of grass?. *Op. 54* — No. 8, The cuckoo; No. 9, Spring song; No. 10, Lullaby in a storm. *Op. 60* — No. 1, Last night; No. 4, The nightingale; No. 10, Behind the window in the shadow. *Op. 63* — Serenade: O child beneath thy window. To forget so soon.

1h 5m DDD 2/93

The features which make Tchaikovsky's great orchestral showpieces so universally popular — the profoundly human emotions, the unforgettable melodies — are also much in evidence in these songs. Indeed, condensed into this miniature form and shorn of opulent orchestral colour Tchaikovsky's outpourings have an even more direct appeal. *None but the lonely heart* is justly famous for its aching sense of loneliness, but others speak with equal intensity. *The nightingale*'s sorrowful mood is given greater poignancy by the echoes of its solitary song in the piano while *Was I not a little blade of grass?* tugs at the very heart-strings as the singer recounts the misery of an arranged marriage. But if this seems to suggest a CD full of unrelieved gloom, that's certainly not the case. Melancholia may be the dominant mood but this cleverly balanced programme includes songs of simple joy (*Cradle song* — written in celebration of the Rimsky-Korsakovs's first child) and at least one genuinely funny moment as an eponymous cuckoo reiterates her familiar call *ad nauseam*. Joan Rodgers does not give big, dramatic performances but her subtle, understated characterizations suit these songs admirably — the Russian texts may be incomprehensible to most readers (English translations are included), but no one can fail to understand their spirit from these appealing performances. As her partner (and the piano is no mere accompaniment to the voice) Roger Vignoles is ever sensitive, displaying by turn discretion and flair and adding real authority to these distinguished and delightful songs.

Additional recommendations ...
Six Songs, Op. 6 — No. 4, A tear trembles; No. 6, None but the lonely heart. *Six Songs, Op. 25* — No. 1, Reconciliation. *Six Songs, Op. 28* — No. 6, The fearful minute. *Six Songs, Op. 38* — No. 1, Don Juan's Serenade. *12 Songs, Op. 60* — No. 4, The nightingale; No. 11, Exploit. *Six Songs, Op. 63* — No. 2, I opened the window. *Six Songs, Op. 73* — No. 6, Again, as before, alone. ***Rachmaninov.*** *Six Songs, Op. 4* — No. 1, Oh no, I beg you, forsake me not; No. 3, In the silence of the secret night; No. 4, Sing not to me, beautiful maiden. *Six Songs, Op. 8* — No. 5, The dream. *12 Songs, Op. 14* — No. 9, She is as lovely as the noon. *12 Songs, Op. 21* —No. 6, Fragment from Musset. *15 Songs, Op. 26* — No. 2, He took all from me; No. 6, Christ is risen; No. 13, When yesterday we met. **Dmitri Hvorostovsky** (bar); **Oleg Boshniakovich** (pf). Philips 432 119-2PH — 52m DDD 10/91

Tchaikovsky. EUGENE ONEGIN. **Bernd Weikl** (bar) Onegin; **Teresa Kubiak** (sop) Tatyana; **Stuart Burrows** (ten) Lensky; **Júlia Hamari** (mez) Olga; **Nicolai Ghiaurov** (bass) Gremin; **Anna Reynolds** (mez) Larina; **Enid Hartle** (mez) Filippyevna; **Michel Sénéchal** (ten) Triquet; **Richard Van Allan** (bass) Zaretsky; **William Mason** (bass) Captain; **John Alldis Choir; Orchestra of the Royal Opera House, Covent Garden/Sir Georg Solti.** Decca 417 413-2DH2. Notes, text and translation included. From SET596/8 (6/75). Recorded in 1974.

② 2h 23m ADD 8/87

In *Eugene Onegin* the young, sensitive Tatyana falls in love with the blasé dandy Onegin only to be bluntly rejected. Onegin's emotional insensitivity leads to the death of his friend Lensky in a duel, but he realizes his mistake and confronts his true feelings for Tatyana. The seven scenes of *Onegin* do not follow the usual narrative progression of a Mozart or Verdi opera, but rather present a series of situations like cartoon pictures, concentrated and emotionally precise. Tchaikovsky's intense sympathy with Tatyana's unrequited love is evident and in the famous Letter scene he gives her some of his most exquisite music, highlighting every emotional twist and turn she encounters. This recording is well conceived and sounds very good in this transfer.

Additional recommendations ...
Soloists; Chorus and Orchestra of the Bolshoi Theatre, Moscow/Boris Khaikin. Legato Classics LCD163-2 — ② 2h 21m ADD 10/90 ▲
Soloists; Sofia National Opera Chorus; Sofia Festival Orchestra/Emil Tchakarov. Sony Classical S2K45539 — ② 2h 23m DDD 3/91

Tchaikovsky. THE QUEEN OF SPADES. **Wieslaw Ochman** (ten) Hermann; **Stefka Evstatieva** (sop) Lisa; **Penka Dilova** (mez) Countess; **Ivan Konsulov** (bar) Count Tomsky; **Yuri Mazurok** (bar) Prince Yeletsky; **Stefania Toczyska** (mez) Paulina; **Angel Petkov** (ten) Chekalinsky; **Peter Petrov** (bass) Surin; **Mincho Popov** (ten) Chaplitsky, Major-domo; **Stoil Georgiev** (bass) Narumov; **Wesselina Katsarova** (mez) Governess; **Rumyana Bareva** (sop) Masha; **Elena Stoyanova** (sop) Prilepa; **Gouslarche Boys' Choir; Svetoslav Obretenov**

National Chorus; Sofia Festival Orchestra/Emil Tchakarov. Sony Classical S3K45720. Notes, text and translation included. Recorded in 1988.

③ 2h 39m DDD 12/90

Recordings of what many consider to be Tchaikovsky's greatest opera have been few and far between, and none too satisfactory so that this excellent performance is a most welcome addition to the catalogue. It is one of a series of Russian operas issued by Sony and conducted by Tchakarov, who rises magnificently to the challenge of this work's astonishing originality of concept and structure. He is splendidly supported by his Bulgarian forces, his Bulgarian chorus and orchestra singing and playing with vigour tempered by sensitivity. The set has been carefully cast. Ochman's anguished, intensely subjective, slightly crazed Hermann could hardly be bettered in either interpretation or singing. Evstatieva makes a vibrant, highly strung Lisa, just right. Mazurok's authoritative Yeletsky and Konsulov's properly gruff Tomsky are other assets. Dilova's old Countess may not be as characterful as some but the part is well sung, as are the smaller roles, including Toczyska's Paulina. The recording is full of the right, haunted atmosphere in the private scenes, big scale in the public ones.

Additional recommendation ...

Soloists; American Boychoir; Tanglewood Festival Chorus; Boston Symphony Orchestra/Seiji Ozawa. RCA Victor Red Seal 09026-60992-2 — ③ 2h 36m DDD 11/92

Further listening ...

Variations on a Rococo Theme in A minor, Op. 33. Nocturne in C sharp minor, Op. 19 No. 4. ***Miaskovsky.*** Cello Concerto in C minor, Op. 66. *Coupled with* ***Shostakovich.*** The Limpid Stream, Op. 39 — Adagio. **Julian Lloyd Webber** (vc); **London Symphony Orchestra/Maxim Shostakovich.** Philips 434 106-2PH (5/92).
See review under Miaskovsky; refer to the Index to Reviews.

Symphony No. 7 in E flat major (cpted Bogatryryev). Piano Concerto No. 3 in E flat major, Op. 73[a]. [a]**Geoffrey Tozer** (pf); **London Philharmonic Orchestra/Neeme Järvi.** Chandos CHAN9130 (4/93).

Suite No. 3 in G major, Op. 55 — Theme and Variations. **Hungarian National Philharmonic Orchestra/Tibor Ferenc.** Pickwick IMP Classics PCD1016 (6/93).

Piano Trio in A minor, Op. 50. **Pierra Amoyal** (vn); **Pascal Rogé** (pf); **Frédéric Lodéon** (vc). Erato Libretto 2292-45972-2 (5/93).

Souvenir d'un lieu cher, Op. 42 — No. 1, Méditation in D minor. Valse-scherzo, Op. 34. *Coupled with* ***Bartók.*** Sonata for solo violin, Sz117. ***Brahms.*** Hungarian Dance No. 1 in G minor. ***Chaminade*** (arr. Kreisler). Sérénade espagnole. ***Falla*** (trans. Kochanski). Suite populaire espagnole. **Kyoko Takezawa** (vn); **Philip Moll** (pf). RCA Victor Red Seal 09026 60704-2 (2/93).
See review in the Collections Section; refer to the Index to Reviews.

Three Morceaux, Op. 9 — Rêverie. *Two Morceaux, Op. 10* — Nocturne in F major; Humoresque in E minor. *Six Morceaux, Op. 19* — Rêrverie du soir in G minor; Capriccioso in B flat major. *12 Morceaux* — Mazurka in C major; Danse russe in A minor. *Six Morceaux* — Polka peu dansante in B minor; Romance in F major. *18 Morceaux* — Tendres reproches in C sharp minor; Polacca de concert in E flat major; Dialogue in B major; L'espiègle in E major. *Three Souvenirs de Hapsal* — Scherzo. **Ilona Prunyi** (pf). Naxos 8 550504.

Key to Symbols

	② ②	1h 23m	DDD	6/88
Price	*Quantity/ availability*	*Timing*	*Mode*	*Review date*

Alexander Tcherepnin

Russian/French/American 1899-1977

Suggested listening ...

Symphony No. 4, Op. 91. Suite, Op. 87. Russian Dances. Romantic Overture, Op. 67. **Košice State Philharmonic Orchestra/Win-Sie Yip.** Marco Polo 8 223380 (10/92).

Georg Philipp Telemann

German 1681-1767

NEW REVIEW

Telemann. CONCERTOS, Volumes 1 and 2. **Collegium Musicum 90/Simon Standage** (vn). Chandos CHAN0519 and CHAN0512. Recorded 1990-91.
CHAN0519: Concertos — A minor for violin; E minor for flute and violin (Rachel Brown, fl); G major for four unaccompanied violins; A major for four violins (Micaela Comberti, Miles Golding, Andrew Manze, vns); E major for violin. Orchestral Suite in G minor, "La Changeante". *CHAN0512:* Concertos — G major for violin; D major for two flutes, violin and cello (Brown, Siu Peasgood, fls; Jane Coe, vc); F sharp minor for violin; G major for two violins (Comberti). Orchestral Suite in B flat major, "Ouverture burlesque".

② lh 3m lh 4m DDD 4/92

It is difficult to mention Telemann without referring to the prolific and eclectic nature of his output, both of which are reflected in his very numerous concertos, and in these recordings the two works that are *not* concertos — *La Changeante* and *Ouverture burlesque*, both of which evoke the spirit of the *commedia dell'arte*. What changes in *La Changeante* is not only the moods of the movements but also their keys; only the first and last of the eight are in the home key of G minor, the others are in a variety of different ones, a most unusual feature at that time. The ouverture-suites are predominantly French in style but the concertos represent Telemann's highly individual variant of Venetian models. Whilst Vivaldi's concertos are predominantly in three movements (quick-slow-quick), Telemann's are usually in four or five, with no set pattern of pace, and they take both *da chiesa* and *da camera* forms. Telemann's muse seems rarely to have slept, likewise his acute sense of instrumental colour. When Playford wrote of "Sprightly and cheerful musick" he was referring to that of the cittern; had he lived a little longer he might have felt the same about that of Telemann, not least if he had heard it played so expertly by Collegium Musicum 90, who are brought into your home by most faithful recorded sound.

Telemann. ORCHESTRAL WORKS. **Stephen Preston** (fl); **John Turner** (rec); **Clare Shanks** (ob d'amore); **Friedmann Immer, Michael Laird, Iain Wilson** (tpts); **Monica Huggett** (va d'amore); **Academy of Ancient Music/Christopher Hogwood** (hpd). L'Oiseau-Lyre Florilegium 411 949-2OH. From DSDL701 (1/83). Recorded in 1981.
Concerto in D major for three trumpets, strings and continuo. Quadro in B flat major. Concerto in E minor for recorder and flute. Concerto polonois. Concerto in E major for flute, oboe d'amore, viola d'amore, strings and continuo.

54m DDD 8/84

Telemann's distinctive eclecticism, uniting Italian energy and brilliance with French delicacy of expression, is often irresistibly appealing. Sometimes, too, his music is seasoned with Polish folk rhythms, melodies which had always fascinated the composer. Telemann claimed to have found difficulty in writing concertos but he nevertheless composed well over a hundred of them. This modest selection contains two of his finest works in the form, the Concertos in E major and E minor. The delicately blended textures of the first provide a wonderful example of Telemann's instrumental writing in which the solo parts are clearly outlined in registers that emphasize their individual character. In the second, the partnership of flute and recorder creates an engagingly subtle tonal palette, especially in the slow movements while the finale is a swirling dance in

Telemann's best Polish manner. The performances capture the spirit of the music delightfully with Christopher Hogwood providing stylish direction.

Telemann. ORCHESTRAL WORKS. **Cologne Musica Antiqua/Reinhard Goebel.** Archiv Produktion 413 788-2AH.
Suite in C major. Concertos — B flat major; F major; A minor.

49m DDD 3/85

Telemann's love for the French overture suite is in little doubt, if only because he wrote so many of them. A notably fine example of his skill in this medium exists in the Suite in C major. The programmatic element is a strong one and most of its movements have titles relating to figures from classical myth. Reinhard Goebel and Cologne Musica Antiqua vividly evoke the aquatic fun and games of Aeolus, Thetis, Neptune, Zephyr, Tritons, Naiads and the like in a varied sequence of French dance movements. These are prefaced by a splendid Overture in the French manner. The remainder of the disc is given over to three of Telemann's concertos for pairs of treble recorder and oboes, with bassoon and strings. They are attractive pieces, two of them having not been previously recorded and the crisp woodwind playing makes the most of this graceful, unassuming repertoire. Clear recorded sound and informative presentation.

Telemann. RECORDER WORKS. **Peter Holtslag** (rec); **The Parley of Instruments/Peter Holman, [a]Roy Goodman.** Hyperion CDA66413. Recorded in 1989.
Overture Suite in A minor[a]. Concertos — F major; C major. Sinfonia in F major[a].

1h 6m DDD 10/91

Telemann professed a working knowledge of most of the standard instruments of his day and consequently wrote rewardingly for them. This is especially true in his treatment of woodwind instruments for which he has left a generous legacy. This disc, as well as containing two concertos, includes a suite and a sinfonia. The Suite in A minor is Telemann's best-known work for treble recorder; indeed, it is to recorder players what Bach's B minor Orchestral Suite is to flautists. The soloist, Peter Holtslag, is an accomplished player whose sensibilities exert a favourable influence over matters of texture, articulation and phrasing. He is a good judge of tempos and, almost alone among his competitors on disc, hits on an effective pace for the beautifully constructed French overture with which the Suite begins. The concertos are attractive pieces, too, that in F major concluding with an engaging pair of menuets. The Sinfonia, unusually scored for recorder, viola da gamba, cornett, three trombones, strings and continuo with organ introduces a distinctive splash of colour. The recording is most sympathetic.

Additional recommendation ...
Overture Suite. Concerto in C major. Concerto for recorder, viola da gamba and strings in A minor[a]. [a]**Mark Levy** (va da gamba); **New London Consort/Philip Pickett** (rec). L'Oiseau-Lyre 433 043-2OH — 1h 8m DDD 11/92

Telemann. Musique de table — Productions I-III. **Vienna Concentus Musicus/Nikolaus Harnoncourt.** Teldec Das Alte Werk 2292-44688-2.

4 4h 21m DDD 10/89

Telemann. Musique de table — Productions I-III. **Cologne Musica Antiqua/Reinhard Goebel.** Archiv Produktion 427 619-2AH4. Recorded in 1988.

4 4h 14m DDD 10/89

By some curious quirk of fate Archiv Produktion and Teldec have managed not once but twice simultaneously to issue complete recordings of Telemann's three-part orchestral and instrumental anthology *Musique de table*. Notwithstanding what must have seemed commercially bad timing we should be grateful to both companies for instigating performances which, though uneven in places are by and large outstandingly successful. Both Nikolaus Harnoncourt and Reinhard

Goebel direct ensembles of period instruments but what each does with them is in striking contrast with the other. In matters of instrumental finesse Goebel's Musica Antiqua Cologne has the edge on the Vienna Concentus Musicus and listeners will hardly fail to recognize disciplined and lively playing of a high order throughout this set. Nevertheless rigorous precision of this kind is sometimes at the cost of spontaneity and lyricism and it is in these respects that Harnoncourt's performances may well strike a more sympathetic chord in the listener.

Nowhere are the two approaches more divergent, perhaps, than in the beautiful G major Quartet of the First Production of the *Musique de table*. There Harnoncourt captures the gently sighing, *galant* gestures of the opening movement with sympathy and insight while Goebel is rhythmically stiff, and self-consciously mannered. But the positions are frequently reversed especially at such times when Harnoncourt's group sounds comparatively rough in ensemble or when occasionally it makes heavy weather over rhythmic patterns. To conclude on a positive note, neither version of Telemann's *magnum opus* is likely to cause disappointment. Ultimately it must be a question of taste and temperament. It may well be some while before such performances as these are equalled let alone bettered. Fine recorded sound and helpful documentation are features of both issues.

Telemann. Fourth Book of Quartets. **American Baroque** (Stephen Schultz, fl; Elizabeth Blumenstock, vn; Roland Kato, va; Roy Whelden, va da gamba; Cheryl Ann Fulton, hp; Charles Sherman, hpd). Koch International Classics 37031-2. Recorded in 1989.
No. 1 in D major; No. 2 in F major; No. 3 in A major; No. 4 in C major; No. 5 in G major; No. 6 in D minor.

54m DDD 1/92 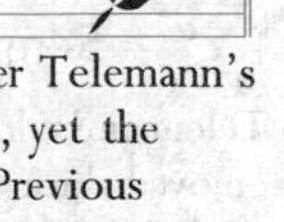

The six quartets in this recording were published as *Quatrième Livre du Quatuors* under Telemann's name in Paris, probably in 1752. There is some doubt concerning their authenticity, yet the likelihood is that they are early exercises in quartet writing from Telemann's pen. Previous publications of his quartets had gone down well in Paris and it is possible that Telemann sanctioned the publication of these owing to popular demand. Be that as it may, the music is performed with imagination and sensibility by American Baroque. The pieces are scored for flute, violin, viola and bass but, rather than use a harpsichord continuo throughout, a triple harp is sometimes substituted. There is no precedence for this yet the resulting colours are undeniably attractive and it is hard to believe that Telemann himself would have other than approved. The group's ensemble and intonation is excellent throughout and the individual players respond affectionately to the composer's finely wrought textures and delicate tracery. Telemann or no the programme is an attractive one not least for the many engaging slow movements. The recorded sound is clear, complementing the chamber character of the music.

Telemann. 12 Fantaisies for transverse flute. **Barthold Kuijken** (transverse fl). Accent ACC57803D.

48m DDD 9/85 

Telemann's music reached full maturity during the 1730s and in the flute *Fantaisies* we find pieces of sustained concentration, varied invention and easy grace. As so often with this composer the idiom is frequently forward-looking, hinting not only at the incipient 'galant' style but also at the acutely sensitive style (*emfindsamer Stil*) later developed above all in the keyboard music of Telemann's godson and successor at Hamburg, C.P.E. Bach. Barthold Kuijken plays a baroque flute which is strikingly different in sound from a present day instrument. His technique is secure, his articulation clear and communicative, and his phrasing pleasingly shaped. He is able to feel beyond what is written on the printed page and this pays off handsomely in movements such as the *Largo* of the B minor *Fantaisie*. Set in contrast with 'affective' pieces such as these are captivating little dances like the pastoral finale of the *Fantaisie* No. 5. Recorded sound is first-rate.

NEW REVIEW

Telemann. VOCAL WORKS. **René Jacobs** (alto); **Berlin Academy for Ancient Music.** Capriccio 10 338. Texts and translations included. Recorded in 1989.

Cantatas — Tirsis am Scheidewege; Nach Finsternis und Todesschatten; Meines Bleibens ist nicht hier. Das Frauenzimmer verstimmt sich immer. Vergiss dich selbst, mein schönster Engel. An der Schlaf. Die Einsamkeit. Concerto grosso in E minor — Adagio.

lh DDD 11/92

Telemann lovers will find some rarities among the items chosen by the countertenor, René Jacobs, for his solo recital. By far the most extensive and consistently interesting of them is the cantata *In einem Tal, umringt von hohen Eichen* or *Tirsis am Scheidewege* as it is called in its modern performing edition. It comes from a collection of "Moral Cantatas" published in Hamburg in 1731. But do not be put off by such a collective title for the music is unfailingly entertaining and is engagingly sung by Jacobs with a small group of period instruments played by the Berlin Academy for Ancient Music. The remainder of the programme consists of two airs which Telemann included in his pioneering musical journal "Der getreue Music-Meister", a sacred cantata from his collection of "Harmonischer Gottes-Dienst", two songs and a further sacred cantata *Meines Bleibens ist nicht hier*. There is much here to please the listener and Jacobs's sensibility both to text and music brings the programme to life with style and charm. One purely instrumental item, an *Adagio* for strings from a *Concerto grosso*, acts as an overture to the programme. Full texts with translations are included.

Telemann. Ino[a]. Overture-Suite in D major. [a]**Barbara Schlick** (sop); **Cologne Musica Antiqua/Reinhard Goebel.** Archiv Produktion 429 772-2AH. Text and translation included. Recorded in 1989.

54m DDD 4/91

Telemann's dramatic cantata, *Ino,* is the product of an Indian summer which the composer enjoyed during the decade 1755-1765. He was, in fact, 84 when he composed *Ino* but we could easily be forgiven for believing it to be the work of a composer half his age. The Enlightenment poet Ramler's text is based on one of Ovid's *Metamorphoses* and concerns Ino, daughter of Cadmus and Hermione. She married Athamos who went mad, murdered one of their sons and attempted murder on the other. Ino, with husband in hot pursuit hurls herself into the sea clutching her child. Neptune comes to her aid, transforms her into the goddess Leukothea and her son into the god Palaemon. Telemann, with music wonderfully fresh in spirit, brings the tale to life in a manner hardly equalled and never surpassed by any of his earlier dramatic works. Barbara Schlick sounds cool in the face of such adversity as Ovid and Ramler place in her path, but there is an underlying passion in her interpretation and the result is musically satisfying. That is also true of Cologne Musica Antiqua under the informed and enthusiastic direction of Reinhard Goebel. This stylish ensemble comes into its own in a performance of another product of Telemann's Indian summer, the Overture-Suite in D major. A feast for lovers of this composer's music and one which offers delights that no baroque music enthusiast should overlook. Outstanding.

Telemann. Missa brevis[a]. Deus judicium tuum[b]. Alles redet jetzt und singet[c]. [bc]**Barbara Schlick,** [b]**Martina Lins** (sops); [b]**Silke Weisheit** (contr); [a]**David Cordier** (alto); [b]**Christoph Prégardien** (ten); [bc]**Stephen Varcoe** (bar); [b]**Hans-Georg Wimmer** (bass); [b]**Rheinische Kantorei; Das kleine Konzert/Hermann Max.** Capriccio 10 315. Texts and translations included. Recorded 1982-89.

lh 3m DDD 11/91

This programme contains three strongly contrasting vocal works dating from different periods in the composer's long life. Earliest by far is the Lutheran Mass — in B minor, as it happens — which Telemann may have composed even as early as his student days at Leipzig during the early years of the eighteenth century. The cantata *Alles redet jetzt und singet* is a setting of the spring song from an enormously long poem by the Hamburg poet and senator, Barthold Heinrich Brockes, who was also the author of a Passion text set by Handel, Telemann and others. This piece belongs to Telemann's Frankfurt period (1712-1721) while the remaining work, the motet *Deus judicium tuum* was a product of the composer's visit to Paris in 1737-38. Musically this is the most consistently satisfying of the three compositions. Telemann modelled it on the French *grand motet* with chorus, vocal ensembles and instruments, doubtless in deference to his hosts. They seem to have liked it since it was twice heard at the Paris Concert Spirituel. The performances are engaging and affectionate with notably strong contributions from the vocal soloists. Both the chorus and the orchestra respond in a lively manner to Hermann Max's direction and the recorded sound is clear and pleasingly resonant.

Telemann. PIMPINONE. **John Ostendorf** (bass) Pimpinone; **Julianne Baird** (sop) Vespetta; **St Luke's Baroque Orchestra/Rudolph Palmer.** Newport Classics NCD60117. Notes, text and translation included.

lh 7m DDD 1/92

Telemann's comic intermezzo, *Pimpinone* was probably first performed between the acts of Handel's *Tamerlano* in Hamburg in 1725. Pimpinone, an elderly bachelor, is looking for a maid. He engages Vespetta who persuades him to marry her, only to play fast and loose with his affections and his cash. This recording of *Pimpinone* is stylish and fluently sung. The soprano Julianne Baird is well cast in the role of Vespetta which she enlivens with appropriately coquettish and waspish singing. Her intonation is not always secure but her vivacious characterization and pleasing vocal timbre are a constant delight. The bass John Ostendorf turns in an endearing performance, eager, lustful but, as the story unfolds, increasingly irritable and not without self-pity. A weaker element is provided by the St Luke's Baroque Orchestra for whom period instruments pose problems still to be overcome. The interpretative ideas are good but ensemble is sometimes untidy and the string sound lustreless and weakly projected. But this is a largely successful enterprise and the animated exchanges which take place between the two vocal protagonists are well sustained. The text, partly in German, partly in Italian, is printed in full with English translations.

Further listening ...

Paris Quartets — Concerto No. 1 in G major; Sonata No. 1 in A major. Nouveaux Quatuors — No. 2 in A minor; No. 6 in E minor. **Wilbert Hazelzet** (fl); **Trio Sonnerie.** Virgin Classics Veritas VC7 59049-2 (3/92).

Overture Suites — C major, TWV55: C6; D major, TWV55: D19; B flat major, TTWV55: B10. **The English Concert/Trevor Pinnock.** Archv Produktion 437 558-2AH (6/93).

Charles Thomas

French 1811-1896

Suggested listening ...

RAYMOND — Overture. *Coupled with* ***Chabrier:*** Joyeuse marche. España. ***Dukas:*** L'apprenti sorcier. ***Satie*** (orch. Debussy): Gymnopédies — Nos. 1 and 3. ***Saint-Saëns:*** SAMSON ET DALILA — Bacchanale. ***Bizet:*** Jeux d'enfants. ***Ibert:*** Divertissement. **Montreal Symphony Orchestra/Charles Dutoit.** Decca 421 527-2DH (6/89).
See review in the Collections section; refer to the Index to Reviews.

HAMLET — A vos jeux, mes amis; O vin, disippe la tristesse. MIGNON — Adieu, Mignon; Elle ne croyait pas. LE CAID — Enfant chéri ... Le tambour-major.
The works listed above feature in separate reviews in the Collections Section.

Virgil Thomson

American 1896-1989

Suggested listening ...

Symphony on a Hymn Tune[b]. Symphony No. 2[b]. LORD BYRON[ac] — Alas! the love of woman!; A wanderer from the British world of fashion; Sweet Lady; I'd sooner burn in hell;

Fare thee well thus disunited. Shipwreck and Love Scene from Byron's Don Juan[ac]. A Solemn Music[c]. A Joyful Fugue[c]. [a]**Martyn Hill** (ten); [b]**Monadnock Festival Orchestra;** [c]**Budapest Symphony Orchestra/James Bolle.** Albany TROY017-2 (4/90).

Dimitri Tiomkin

Russian/American 1894-1979

Suggested listening ...

Film Scores: Lost Horizon — suite[a]. The Guns of Navarone — Prelude. The Big Sky — suite. The Fourposter — Overture. Friendly Persuasion — Love scene in the barn. Search for Paradise — finale[a]. [a]**John Alldis Choir; National Philharmonic Orchestra/Charles Gerhardt.** RCA Victor GD81669 (5/91).

Michael Tippett

British 1905-

Tippett. ORCHESTRAL WORKS. [c]**Heather Harper** (sop); [abc]**London Symphony Orchestra/Sir Colin Davis;** [d]**Chicago Symphony Orchestra/Sir Georg Solti.** Decca London 425 646-2LM3. Item marked [a] recorded in 1975, [b] 1967, [c] 1973, [d] 1979-81. Symphonies — No. 1[a] (from Philips 9500 107, 10/76); No. 2[b] (Argo ZRG535, 1/68); No. 3[c] (Philips 6500 662, 1/75); No. 4[d], Suite in D for the Birthday of Prince Charles[d] (both from Decca SXDL7546, 8/81).

③ 2h 5lm ADD/DDD 7/90

These four symphonies comprise one of the most considerable contributions to the genre by a British composer this century. Numbers 1 and 2 are examples of Tippett's earlier, still relatively traditional language, while Nos. 3 and 4 are more radical. Bounding energy is the predominant quality of Nos. 1 and 2, an energy whose individual attributes are by no means diminished by association with Stravinsky. But Tippett's more personal, magical lyricism is also prominent, especially in the marvellous slow movement of No. 2, and this lyricism forms a clear link to the more reflective passages of No. 3. This glorious, 55-minute work evolves from purely instrumental arguments about active and reflective states of mind into a series of songs (for soprano) that confront some of the most urgent social issues of our time. Though arguing the need to counter violence and repression with tolerance and love, the music offers its own irreconcilable confrontation between allusions to Beethoven's Ninth and Bessie Smith-style blues, swept up into a stark coda as uncompromising in its modernism as anything in Tippett's output. After this the Fourth Symphony is less hectic, though no less diverse in its materials, a half-hour single movement of dazzling colours and vivid emotions. Although the performances occasionally remind us of the difficulties Tippett presents to his interpreters, and the recordings are not, on the whole, of the latest digital vintage, this is — thanks mainly to the commitment and persuasiveness of Sir Colin Davis — a set of considerable distinction.

NEW REVIEW

Tippett. Byzantium[a]. Symphony No. 4[b]. [a]**Faye Robinson** (sop); **Chicago Symphony Orchestra/Sir Georg Solti.** Decca 433 668-2DH. Text included. Item marked [a] recorded in 1991, [b] from SXDL7546 (8/81) and recorded live in 1979.

58m DDD 4/93

Tippett's works seems to have what one can only call an incubation period. You hear them, you react favourably or otherwise and then, months or even years later they knock you over, you succumb. That has already happened with his "birth to death piece", the Fourth Symphony, discussion of which for a while centred almost entirely on whether its use of breathing sounds as a musical resource really worked and on its at first perplexingly abrupt cross-cuttings between strongly contrasting blocks of material. Now all this seems irrelevant beside its sustained intensity, its many beauties and its cumulative power. It is a masterpiece, surely, and one immensely fortunate in this, its virtuoso first recording. *Byzantium*'s incubation period may be shorter. Dazzling and bewitching images pursue each other even more pell-mell than in the symphony, in an intense response to W.B. Yeats's poem about the teeming cauldron of an artist's imagination. Tippett's images are as rich and strange as Yeats's own, and they have something very like the same dream logic to them. The exquisite portrayal of "a starlit or a moonlit dome", the bright jangle of the jewelled mechanical bird, the mysterious flame that both dances and is still, "that dolphin-torn, that gong-tormented sea" — there is an over-arching imaginitive unity to this succession, and repeated hearing confirms it. Its intensity taxes the soprano's virtuosity to the utmost. Faye Robinson negotiates the huge leaps and spectacular hocketings and ululations with amazing aplomb, and the orchestral playing is again vivid. Both pieces are splendidly recorded.

Tippett. CHORAL WORKS. **Christ Church Cathedral Choir/Stephen Darlington.** Nimbus NI5266. Texts included. Recorded in 1990.
Dance, Clarion Air. The Weeping Babe. Plebs angelica. Bonny at Morn (with Michael Copley, Maurice Hodges, Evelyn Nallen, recs). Crown of the Year (Medici Quartet — Paul Robertson, David Matthews, vns; Ivo-Jan van der Werff, va; Anthony Lewis, vc; Copley, Hodges, Nallen; John Anderson, ob; Colin Lawson, cl; Graham Ashton, tpt; Peter Hamburger, Martin Westlake, Jeremy Cornes, perc; Martin Jones, pf). Music (Jones, pf). A Child of Our Time — Five Negro Spirituals.

51m DDD 1/91 P

Here is choral singing of the very highest order sumptuously recorded in the mellow surrounds of the Abbey at Dorchester-on-Thames. Under Stephen Darlington the men and boys of Christ Church Cathedral Choir sing with precision, immaculate control and great sensitivity. They achieve an almost perfect blend: no voice stands out in isolation, there are no rough edges and the whole effect is of a single, immensely versatile musical instrument. Of course there is a price to be paid: any individuality or character in the voices has had to be subjugated. So it's probably something of a mistake to project singers from the choir as soloists in the four Spirituals from *A Child of Our Time*. There are no reservations about anything else on this lovely disc. The principal work, *Crown of the Year*, was written in 1958 for a children's choir supported by very economical instrumental resources, Surprisingly this hasn't been recorded before; yet as this performance demonstrates most vividly, it is a colourful and vibrant work full of joy and vigour and incorporating such familiar tunes as "For he's a jolly good fellow". With the exception of the captivating *Bonny at Morn*, which uses a trio of fluttering recorders as a descant to a beautifully sung unison line, the other pieces on this CD are unaccompanied. The music is Tippett in his most simple and magical vein. Performed and recorded with such excellence the whole thing is a delight to the ear.

Tippett. A Child of Our Time. **Jessye Norman** (sop); **Dame Janet Baker** (mez); **Richard Cassilly** (ten); **John Shirley-Quirk** (bar); **BBC Singers; BBC Choral Society; BBC Symphony Orchestra/Sir Colin Davis.** Philips 420 075-2PH. Text included. From 6500 985 (11/75). Recorded in 1975.

1h 4m ADD 11/87 

A Child of Our Time takes as its narrative kernel the shooting in 1938 of a minor German diplomat by a 17-year-old Jew, Herschel Grynspan, and so causing one of the most savage anti-Jewish pogroms seen in Nazi Germany. But the universality of the dilemma of an individual caught up in something he cannot control gives it a much broader relevance. Just as Bach used the Lutheran hymns for the chorale sections within his Passions, so Tippett uses the negro spiritual to tap a similarly universal vein. The soloists provide the narrative thread against the more reflective role of the chorus but they come together forcefully in the spirituals. Sir Colin Davis directs a powerful and atmospheric performance and his soloists are very fine. The 1975 recording sounds well.

Additional recommendations ...
Soloists; City of Birmingham Symphony Chorus and Orchestra/Sir Michael Tippett. Collins Classics 1339-2 — 1h 9m DDD 9/92 B
Soloists; London Symphony Chorus and Orchestra/Richard Hickox. Chandos CHAN9123 — 1h 13m DDD 2/93 B

Tippett. The Mask of Time. **Faye Robinson** (sop); **Sarah Walker** (mez); **Robert Tear** (ten); **John Cheek** (bass); **BBC Singers; BBC Symphony Chorus and Orchestra/Andrew Davis.** EMI CDS7 47705-8. From EX270567-3 (5/87). Recorded live in 1986.

② 1h 32m DDD 10/87

A huge work in two parts, each lasting some 45 minutes, *The Mask of Time* comprises ten 'scenes', the five in Part One more obviously mythological in character and moving from the 'creation' of the cosmos to the emergence of civilization and an earthly paradise, and those in Part Two more to do with the individual in history. The work calls for four soloists, chorus and large symphony orchestra and presents all manner of difficulties in performance and recording with its contrasting of full-blown episodes (with typically thrilling brass and percussion writing) and intimate chamber-like ensembles. There are many unforgettable moments in this deeply felt and thought-provoking score, and none more moving than Tippett's post-Hiroshima threnody for "those who have never had a life". This performance is superb, Andrew Davis demonstrating a fine grasp of the overall structure as well as the fine detail of this complex work. The live recording, too, is first-rate. This is by no means an easy work to assimilate, but those prepared to give it open-minded consideration will find themselves richly rewarded.

Tippett. KING PRIAM. **Norman Bailey** (bar) Priam; **Heather Harper** (sop) Hecuba; **Thomas Allen** (bar) Hector; **Felicity Palmer** (sop) Andromache; **Philip Langridge** (ten) Paris; **Yvonne Minton** (mez) Helen; **Robert Tear** (ten) Achilles; **Stephen Roberts** (bar) Patroclus; **Ann Murray** (mez) Nurse; **David Wilson-Johnson** (bar) Old man; **Peter Hall** (ten) Young guard; **Kenneth Bowen** (ten) Hermes; **Julian Saipe** (treb) Paris, as a boy; **Linda Hirst** (sop) Serving woman; **London Sinfonietta Chorus; London Sinfonietta/David Atherton.** Decca London 414 241-2LH2. Notes and text included. From D246D3 (11/81). Recorded in 1980.

② 2h 8m DDD 1/90 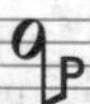

King Priam is the exception among Tippett's five operas in taking its plot from existing literature. But the text itself is Tippett's own, and the dramatic themes — the horrors of war, the torments of families whose destinies and choices create only tragedy — reverberate in various ways in many of his other works, though never again with the stark immediacy and sense of despair embodied here. It is astonishing how so uncompromising an opera can leave the listener more exhilarated than depressed: it must be something to do with witnessing human creativity asserting its power so convincingly. And Tippett's power here extends well beyond the blood and gore of the Trojan War. Even more moving and compelling is the mutual compassion of those who share bereavement, and the tortured hope of the one character (Achilles) who imagines what life might be like "after the war" — though he too will die in battle. No praise can be too high for this performance, in which a fine cast and the matchless London Sinfonietta are galvanized by David Atherton into an account which achieves maximum expressive fidelity while also affirming the opera's great structural strength. The recording does not seek to reproduce a theatrical ambience, but it is totally convincing in its own terms.

Tippett. THE ICE BREAK. **David Wilson-Johnson** (bar) Lev; **Heather Harper** (sop) Nadia; **Sanford Sylvan** (bar) Yuri; **Carolann Page** (sop) Gayle; **Cynthia Clarey** (mez) Hannah; **Thomas Randle** (ten) Olympion; **Bonaventura Bottone** (ten) Luke; **Donald Maxwell** (bar) Lieutenant; **Christopher Robson** (alto) and **Sarah Walker** (mez) Astron;

London Sinfonietta Chorus; London Sinfonietta/David Atherton. Virgin Classics VC7 59048-2. Notes and text included.

lh 14m DDD 2/92

When *The Ice Break* was first performed in 1977, it was widely regarded as too modern for its own good. The story of a Solzhenitsyn-like writer exiled to a New York-like urban jungle where his son is almost killed in race riots but is finally, miraculously reborn, could indeed have been an all-too-simplistic piece of musical reportage, not least because the libretto is so liberally spiced with slang and colloquialisms, jostling against more poetic passages. Nevertheless, now that time has brought some distance to both story and music, the deeper resonances implicit in the opera's title, which refers both to the writer's memories of the beginning of the Russian spring as well as to the need to rebuild relationships in a new world, can be properly appreciated. That the music — and the drama — supports and strengthens these deeper resonances is abundantly clear from this exemplary performance, guided by David Atherton with a compelling blend of energy and restraint. The recording ensures that the vivid instrumental detail (and occasional, essential sound effects) do not submerge the voices. So, even if *The Ice Break* remains a problem in the theatre, this recording makes the best possible case for it as music drama.

Further listening ...

Concerto for double string orchestra. Fantasia concertante on a Theme of Corelli. Little Music for strings. **Academy of St Martin in the Fields/Sir Neville Marriner.** Decca London 421 389-2LM (8/89)

Thomas Tomkins

British 1572-1656

Suggested listening ...

Third Service — Magnificat and Nunc dimittis. *Cathedral Music* — O sing unto the Lord a new song. Then David mourned. My beloved spake unto me. Above the stars my saviour dwells. Glory be to God on high. Almighty God, the fountain of all wisdom. When David heard. My shepherd is the living Lord. Sing unto God. Behold, the hour cometh. O God, the proud are risen against me. **St George's Chapel Choir, Windsor/Christopher Robinson** with **Roger Judd** (org). Hyperion CDA66345 (3/90).

Third or Great Service. *Anthems* — Almighty God, the fountain of all wisdom; Be strong and of good courage; O God, the proud are risen against me; O sing unto the Lord; Then David mourned; When David heard; Woe is me. **The Tallis Scholars/Peter Phillips.** Gimell CDGIM024 (3/92).

Ernest Tomlinson

British 1927-

Suggested listening ...

Little Serenade. An English Overture. The Story of Cinderella — Fairy Coach; Cinderella Waltz. Kielder Water. Silverthorne Suite. Second Suite of English Folk-Dances. Lyrical Suite — Nocturne. Pastoral Dances — Hornpipe. Gaelic Sketches — Gaelic Lullaby. Nautical Interlude. Sweet and Dainty. **Bratislava Radio Symphony Orchestra/Ernest Tomlinson.** Marco Polo 8 223413 (12/92).

Michael Torke

American 1961-

NEW REVIEW

Torke. COLOR MUSIC. **Baltimore Symphony Orchestra/David Zinman.** Argo 433 071-2ZH. Green. Purple. Ecstatic Orange. Ash. Bright Blue Music.

54m DDD 2/92

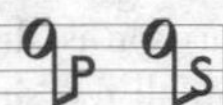

The proverb says: "a wonder lasts nine days, and then the puppy's eyes are open". In an age when the eyes of the young are opened to the harsh realities and darker sides of life at an ever increasing early age it's more than refreshing to come across a young composer who, whilst certainly not naïve, has managed to hold on to a certain innocence and whose music is powerfully optimistic and positive in its outlook. Imagine, if you will, the excitement and thrill of a dazzling roller-coaster ride through an ever changing terrain of harmony and colour, of an almost Disneyesque flight of imagination fused with the power and energy of a Beethoven scherzo, and you'll have some idea of the experience that is *Green.* As the colour and title might suggest *Purple is* altogether more sophisticated in harmonic language — silky-smooth and lyrical, with an occasional touch of dissonance for added spice and spiky, syncopated rhythms that reveal an interest in jazz and dance music. The relentless energy and drive of *Ecstatic Orange* (amazingly Torke's first attempt at orchestral music) draws much of its zest and essence from the pop culture of Torke's own generation, whilst the remaining two works — *Ash* and *Bright Blue Music* — reveal a classical influence infiltrating Torke's music that is respectively confrontational and positively joyous. Superb performances from Zinman and the Baltimore Symphony Orchestra and an immaculate and beautifully produced recording. A disc guaranteed to raise the lowest of spirits.

Further listening ...

The Yellow Pages[e]. Slate[abcd]. Adjustable Wrench[d]. Vanada[d]. Rust[e]. **Michael Torke** (pf); [a]**Edmund Niemann, Nurit Tilles** (pf, four hands); [b]**James Pugliese** (xylophone); [c]**Gary Schall** (marimba); **London Sinfonietta/**[d]**Kent Nagano,** [e]**David Miller.** Argo 430 209-2ZH (12/90).

Veljo Tormis

Estonian 1930-

Suggested listening ...

Livonian Heritage. Votic Wedding Songs. Izhorian Epic. Ingrian Evenings. Vespian Paths. Karelian Destiny. **Estonian Philharmonic Chamber Choir/Tonu Kaljuste.** ECM New Series 434 275-2 (10/92).

Charles Tournemire

French 1870-1939

Tournemire. Suite Evocatrice, Op. 74.
Vierne. Symphony No. 3, Op. 28.
Widor. Symphonie Gothique, Op. 70. **Jeremy Filsell** (org). Herald HAVPCD145. Played on the Harrison and Harrison organ of Ely Cathedral. Recorded in 1991.

1h 11m DDD 3/92

Compared with, say, the symphonies of Tchaikovsky or Sibelius the organ symphonies of Widor and his pupil Vierne are not particularly long. But in terms of organ music they are among the longest single works in the repertory. Within their five-movement form the composers set out to exploit the full expressive range of the organ and it was no coincidence that the organ symphony developed in turn of the century France. The great French organ builder Aristide Cavaillé-Coll was then producing instruments capable of hitherto undreamt-of colour and expression. Both Widor (at St Sulpice) and Vierne (at Notre Dame) had at their disposal the finest instruments in Paris and they indulged themselves fully in their symphonies. The subtitle of Widor's Ninth (*Gothic*) says it all. The structure is vast, intricately detailed, and almost forbidding in its grandness. Vierne's Third also presents an awesome spectacle, full of complex music and technically demanding writing, while Tournemire's neoclassical Suite provides a moment almost of light relief in such heavyweight company. Jeremy Filsell is an outstanding virtuoso player with a gift for musical communication and, in the Ely Cathedral organ, an instrument which produces the range of the great French instruments, but within an altogether clearer acoustic. These are performances of exceptional quality captured in a recording of rare excellence from the small independent company, Herald.

Eduard Tubin

Estonian-Swedish 1905-1982

Tubin. Symphony No. 3; Symphony No. 8. **Swedish Radio Symphony Orchestra/Neeme Järvi.** BIS CD342. Recorded in association with the Estonian Church Foundation, Vancouver.

lh 3m DDD 9/88

Tubin's Third Symphony comes from 1940, six months after Stalin had "incorporated" Estonia into the Soviet Union. Not surprisingly, it is strongly nationalist in feeling, reflecting the mood of a nation that had just lost its independence. The first two movements are full of imaginative and individual touches, the listener borne along on a current of movement. The finale is not wholly free from rhetoric and bombast, but all the same it is a strong piece and those who have the Second and Fourth Symphonies will find familiar resonances. The Eighth Symphony, however, is possibly his masterpiece: it is the darkest in colouring and most intense in feeling of all his symphonies. It comes from 1966 and the opening movement has a sense of vision and mystery whose atmosphere stays with you long afterwards. There is an astringency and a sense of the tragic that leaves a strong impression. Järvi's tireless championship of Tubin puts us much in his debt and the playing of the Swedish Radio Symphony Orchestra displays real commitment. The recording has quite exceptional body, clarity and definition.

Tubin. Symphonies No. 4, "Sinfonia lirica"[a]; No. 9[b]. Toccata[b]. [a]**Bergen Symphony Orchestra,** [b]**Gothenburg Symphony Orchestra/Neeme Järvi.** BIS CD227. Item marked [a] from LP227 (12/83), [b] LP264 (3/85).

lh 4m AAD l0/86

The atmosphere of the Fourth Symphony is predominantly pastoral, a mixture of the Slavonic and the Nordic, with a strongly Sibelian feel to much of it. It is immediately accessible music, with real imaginative vitality and a strong feeling for structure. A quarter of a century separates it from the Ninth Symphony, where the mood is elegiac and the gently restrained melancholy of the slower sections makes a strong emotional impact. The fluid harmonies are quite haunting but as always Tubin's musical language is direct, tonal and, in its way, quite personal. Though there is an overriding sadness and resignation about this music, there is not a trace of self-pity. The exuberant and inventive *Toccata* for orchestra is also an enjoyable piece. The orchestral playing is first-class and the recorded sound splendidly firm and rich.

Further listening ...

Six Preludes. Piano Sonatas Nos. 1 and 2. Lullaby. Album Leaf. Three Pieces for Children. A little March, for Rana. Three Estonian Folk-dances. Prelude No. 1. Variations on an Estonian Folk Tune. Ballad on a Theme by Mart Saar. Four Folk-songs from my country. Sonatina in D minor. Seven Preludes. Suite on Estonian Shepherd Melodies. **Vardo Rumessen** (pf). BIS CD414/16 (3-CD set, 3/89).

Joaquín Turína

Spanish 1882-1949

NEW REVIEW

Turína. ORCHESTRAL WORKS. **Bamberg Symphony Orchestra/Antonio de Almeida.** RCA Victor Red Seal RD60895.

Danzas fantásticas, Op. 22. La procesión del Rocio, Op. 9. Sinfonía sevillana, Op. 23. Ritmos, Op. 43.

lh 3m DDD 7/92 — 9P 9S

An hour's worth of musical sunshine, with the occasional cloud drifting by just for tonal contrast. Turína was a magnificent orchestrator and although he was — as Antonio de Almeida points out in his useful booklet annotations — a "quintessential Sevillian", he was also acutely aware of musical trends beyond his own locality. His style approximates the youthful opulence of early Debussy (whose sensuous *Printemps* frequently comes to mind), yet the piquant instrumentation that graces, say, "Exaltación" from the *Danzas fantásticas*, or the whole of *La procesión del Rocio* is refreshingly individual — beautifully aired and crafted, with the sum of its gleaming parts amounting to an appealing tonal blend. Were it not for the give-away nature of specifically Spanish melodies, Dvořák (of the *Slavonic Dances*) would as likely come to mind as Falla — particularly in the *Danzas*. *La procesión* (1912) predates the other pieces on the disc, while *Ritmos* was composed as late as 1928. It was premièred by Casals, but here more than anywhere else on the disc, one is reminded of Almeida's great mentor, Sir Thomas Beecham. Just listen to the way he points *Ritmos*'s atmospheric "Danza lenta", or sample the excitement he generates in the "Danza exótica" from he same work; then turn back to "Fiesta en San Juan de Aznalfarache" from *Sinfonía sevillana* — awash with colour from the first bar to the last — and witness how the Bamberg players exploit Turína's varied tonal palette. As for the recording (a co-production between BMG Classics and Bavarian Radio), it's truly demonstration-worthy; a fair sampling point is the "Valse trágico" from *Ritmos*, which features a spectacular mushrooming tam-tam. But then Turína is the answer to a recording engineer's dream: his use of winds, brass and percussion, in particular, is as judicious as it is impressive, and he never overcrowds his orchestral climaxes. Quite simply, this disc is unalloyed delight from start to finish — *Fantásticas* in name *and* nature!

Further listening ...

Piano Trios — No. 1, Op. 35; No. 2, Op. 76. Circulo, Op. 91. **Munich Piano Trio.** Calig CAL50 902.

La oración del torero. *Coupled with* ***Wagner:*** Siegfried Idyll. ***Wolf:*** Italian Serenade. ***Puccini:*** Crisantemi. ***Berlioz:*** Rêverie et caprice, Op. 8[a]. ***Sibelius:*** Valse triste, Op. 44. ***Dvořák:*** Nocturne in B major, B47. [a]**Guillermo Figueroa** (vn); **Orpheus Chamber Orchestra.** DG 431 680-2GH (10/91).

See review in the Collections Section; refer to the Index to Reviews.

Poeme en forma de canciones. *Coupled with* ***Padilla:*** Valencia. ***Grever:*** Jurame. ***F. Alonso:*** Maitechu mia. ***Lara:*** Granada. ***Vives:*** Doña Francisquita — Por el humo. ***Soutullo:*** Ultimo romantico — Noche de amor. ***Serrano:*** Alma da Dios — Canción húngara. ***Falla:*** Canciones populares españolas. ***Mompou:*** Combat del somni. ***Obradors:*** Canciones clásicas españolas — Del cabello más sutil. Corazón porqué pasais. **José Carreras** (ten); **Martin Katz** (pf); **English Chamber Orchestra/Robin Stapleton, Roberto Benzi, Antoni Ros Marbá.** Philips 432 825-2PM (7/92).

See review in the Collections Section; refer to the Index to Reviews.

Mark-Antony Turnage

British 1960-

NEW REVIEW

Turnage. Three Screaming Popes. **City of Birmingham Symphony Orchestra/Simon Rattle.** EMI TSP204681-2. Recorded in 1992.

16m DDD 9/92

The paintings of Francis Bacon, from which Mark-Anthony Turnage takes his title, are among the twentieth century's most enduring visual images, with the pope a figure of supreme authority apparently reduced to abject terror. Bacon's obsessive extremism is not something to which many British composers would wish to aspire, and Turnage does not seek to outdo the ultra-expressionism of Peter Maxwell Davies in the 1960s, but responds rather to the tension in Bacon's work between intense feeling and textural discipline. *Three Screaming Popes* is never blatantly programmatic and its cogent design carries material of immediate appeal which is neither crude nor overly complex. To sum it up as a blend of Stravinsky and Birtwistle only hints at the strengths of Turnage's own musical personality, and he receives high-class advocacy from Simon Rattle and the CBSO in a recording tingling with life.

Christopher Tye

British c.1505-1572

Suggested listening ...

Consort Music — Complete Instrumental Works. **Hespèrion XX/Jordi Savall.** Astrée Auvidis E8708 (11/89).

Sacred Choral Works — Kyrie, "Orbis factor". Mass, "Euge bone". Quaesumus omnipotens. Miserere mei, Deus. Omnes gentes, plaudite. Peccavimus cum patribus. **Winchester Cathedral Choir/David Hill.** Hyperion CDA66424 (1/91).

Viktor Ullmann

Austrian/Hungarian 1898-1944

Suggested listening ...

String Quartet No. 3, Op. 43. *Coupled with* **Klein.** String Trio. Fantasie a Fuga. Piano Sonata[a]. String Quartet, Op. 2. **Hawthorne Quartet; [a]Virginia Eskin** (pf). Channel Classics CCS1691 (12/91).

See review under Klein; refer to the Index to Reviews.

Edgard Varèse

French/American 1883-1965

Varèse. VARIOUS WORKS. **[a]Rachel Yakar** (sop); **[b]Lawrence Beauregard** (fl); **[c]New York Philharmonic Orchestra; [d]Ensemble Intercontemporain /[e]Pierre Boulez.** Sony Classical MK45844. Texts and translations included.

Ionisation (1929-31)[ce]. Amériques (1921)[ce]. Arcana (1925-7. All from CBS 76520, 6/78)[ce]. Density 21.5 (1936)[b]. Offrandes (1921)[ade]. Octandre (1923)[de]. Intégrales (1924-5. All from IM39053, 3/85)[de].

1h 17m ADD/DDD 10/90

These classic recordings make a welcome return to the catalogue, especially since the music of Varèse has been so poorly represented on disc and in the concert hall in recent years. Quite why so important a figure in twentieth-century music should be neglected like this is hard to say, and even more difficult to comprehend when one samples the quality of the music presented here. Varèse was a pioneer, a quester and above all a liberator. Music for him was a form of twentieth-century alchemy — the transmutation of the ordinary into the extraordinary, an alchemical wedding of intellectual thought with intuitive imagination. Indeed, it was the writings of the fourteenth century cosmologist and alchemist Paracelsus that formed the inspiration behind his orchestral work *Arcana*, a vast canvas of sound built entirely out of one melodic motive. Discernible are echoes of Stravinsky and others, but the totality of *Arcana* is pure Varèse. The same is true of *Amériques*, a title that Varèse emphasized was not to be taken as "purely geographical but as symbolic of discoveries — new worlds on earth, in the sky or in the minds of men". Here romanticism and modernism seem to coexist side by side, where allusions from works such as *La mer* and *The Firebird* seem like racial memories carried into his brave new world. The remaining items consist of smaller chamber works which display Varèse's most radical, though equally rewarding, styles. Boulez and his players give committed, virtuosic performances of these challenging and intriguing works. Well worth exploring.

Ralph Vaughan Williams

British 1872-1958

Vaughan Williams. Job — a masque for dancing. **David Nolan** (vn); **London Philharmonic Orchestra/Vernon Handley.** Classics for Pleasure CD-CFP4603. From CD-EMX9506 (10/87).

• 48m DDD 3/93 

The work of William Blake was close to the heart of Vaughan Williams, and from Blake's *21 Illustrations to the Book of Job*, he produced a ballet score that came to represent a watershed in his career, looking backwards to the pastoral, folk-song idiom of his Third Symphony and forwards to the violence and vigour of the Fourth. *Job* requires an orchestra that is particularly flexible, with full and poignantly-toned soloists and a string body that can produced a rounded, consistent timbre with great depth. The London Philharmonic display all those qualities here, and a good deal more besides, and all is captured in a spacious, characterful acoustic and in a full-bodied recording that can handle equally well the hushed opening of the work and the enormities of the sixth scene. This highly persuasive performance is a particularly good bargain.

Additional recommendations ...

Job. ***Holst.*** *The Perfect Fool, H150 — ballet music.* **Philharmonia Orchestra/Barry Wordsworth.** Collins Classics 1124-2 — ⁘ 57m DDD 5/90

Job. Variations for orchestra (orch. Jacob). **Bournemouth Symphony Orchestra/Richard Hickox.** EMI British Composers CDC7 54421-2 — ⁘ lh 2m DDD 7/92

Vaughan Williams. Symphony No. 1, "A Sea Symphony". **Felicity Lott** (sop); **Jonathan Summers** (bar); **Cantilena; London Philharmonic Choir and Orchestra/Bernard Haitink.** EMI CDC7 49911-2. Text included. Recorded in 1989.

⁘ lh llm DDD l/90 

A firm hand on the tiller is needed to steer a safe course through this, Vaughan Williams's first and most formally diffuse symphony, completed in 1909. Haitink is clearly an ideal choice of helmsman and he is helped by a remarkably lucid recording that resolves details that would rarely be revealed in live performance. What might be more unexpected here is the obvious affinity he shows for this music: whilst never transgressing the bounds of Vaughan Williams's characteristically English idiom, he manages to place the work in the European mainstream, revealing a whole range of resonances, from Bruckner and Mahler to the Impressionists. Not all the glory should go to the conductor, of course. Both soloists are particularly fine, the vulnerability behind the spine-tingling power of Felicity Lott's voice providing excellent contrast to the staunch solidity of Jonathan Summers. The LPO Chorus, aided by Cantilena, are on top form and the whole enterprise is underpinned by the London Philharmonic's total commitment and expertise. Here is the recording of this glorious work for which the catalogue was waiting.

Additional recommendations ...

Margaret Marshall (sop); **Stephen Roberts** (bar); **London Symphony Chorus; Philharmonia Orchestra/Richard Hickox.** Virgin Classics VJ7 59687-2 — lh 4m DDD

Yvonne Kenny (sop); **Brian Rayner Cook** (bar); **London Symphony Chorus; London Symphony Orchestra/Bryden Thomson.** Chandos CHAN8764 — lh 6m DDD 2/90

Vaughan Williams. Symphony No. 2, "A London Symphony". Concerto Grosso. **London Symphony Orchestra/Bryden Thomson.** Chandos CHAN8629. Recorded in 1988.

lh 5m DDD 10/89 

A London Symphony presents a vision of the capital far removed from the busy cosmopolitan metropolis it has become today. The London Vaughan Williams knew then was more elegant and less hectic though, alas, its Edwardian charm would soon be changed for ever by the First World War. At the beginning of the work, slow Westminster chimes signal the beginning of the day; the main section of the first movement then evokes London's hustle and bustle. In the second *Lento* movement we explore some quieter byways, while the *Scherzo-Nocturne* third movement depicts the city at night. The finale looks at several city scenes and its epilogue portrays the River Thames as evening draws in. The clear layout of the Chandos performance, so finely aimed at the climax of the final movement and then sustained into the magical Epilogue, carries all before it. The succulent recording admirably reflects Thomson's delight in the sheer beauty of sound that Vaughan Williams can summon, and it is agreeably wide-ranging for the coupled *Concerto Grosso* of 1950, performed with an equal empathy for its idiom.

Additional recommendations ...

No. 2. Fantasia on a Theme by Thomas Tallis. **London Philharmonic Orchestra/Bernard Haitink.** EMI CDC7 49394-2 — lh 6m DDD 7/88

No. 2. Concerto Accademico[a]*. The Wasps — Overture.* [a]**James Oliver Buswell IV** (vn); **London Symphony Orchestra/André Previn.** RCA Gold Seal GD90501 — lh 11m ADD 3/91

No. 2. Fantasia on a Theme by Thomas Tallis. **London Philharmonic Orchestra/Sir Adrian Boult.** EMI CDM7 64017-2 — lh ADD 5/92

No. 2. No. 8 in D minor. **Hallé Orchestra/Sir John Barbirolli.** EMI CDM7 64197-2 — lh 14m ADD 6/92

Nos. 2 and 8. **Royal Liverpool Philharmonic Orchestra/Vernon Handley.** EMI Eminence CD-EMX2209 — lh 12m DDD 8/93

NEW REVIEW

Vaughan Williams. Symphonies — No. 3, "A Pastoral Symphony"[a]; No. 4 in F minor. [a]**Alison Barlow** (sop); **Royal Liverpool Philharmonic Orchestra/Vernon Handley.** EMI Eminence CD-EMX2192. Recorded in 1991.

lh 7m DDD 11/92 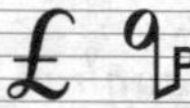

Vaughan Williams composed his Third Symphony, *A Pastoral,* between 1916 and 1921, and since its first performance in 1922 its title has frequently led to misconceptions concerning the underlying inspiration behind the music. The music itself almost seems to encourage the idea of an idyllic English landscape complete with gently rolling hills and frolicking lambs, but as Vaughan Williams once explained to a friend: "It's really war-time music", and went on to describe how a great deal of it originated during his time as an ambulance driver in the battle fields of Ecoivres in the First World War. When heard with this in mind one can hear the uneasy tension that constantly permeates the score, and the predominantly quiet and contemplative music begins to reveal itself as the poignant elegy that it truly is — a requiem for the young men who sacrificed lives in this pastoral landscape. Ironically the Fourth Symphony has suffered the opposite fate to its predecessor in that images of war, and in particular the growing rise of Fascism at the time of its composition (1931-34), have frequently been aligned to the score's somewhat angry, dissonant mood. Vaughan Williams, however, vigorously denied any such programmatic undercurrent, and was adamant that the work was no more than just a description of a typical modern symphony. Today the symphony is viewed as such — a superb essay in symphonic argument and musical invention. Vernon Handley's accounts of both works are of the highest calibre; the Third glows with an aura of mystery, and features a very fine account of the wordless soprano lament by Alison Barlow, and the Fourth is given a reading that is every bit as compelling and electrifying as the composer's own recording. At mid-price this is a bargain not to be missed.

Additional recommendations ...

Nos. 3 and 4. **Heather Harper** (sop); **London Symphony Orchestra/André Previn.** RCA Gold Seal GD90503 — lh 13m ADD 3/91

No. 3. Oboe Concerto in A minor[a]. **Yvonne Kenny** (sop); [a]**David Theodore** (ob); **London Symphony Orchestra/Bryden Thomson.** Chandos CHAN8594 — 56m DDD 8/88

NEW REVIEW

Vaughan Williams. Symphony No. 4 in F minor[a].
Holst. The Planets, H125[b]. [a]**BBC Symphony Orchestra/Ralph Vaughan Williams;** [b]**London Symphony Orchestra/Gustav Holst.** Koch International Classics mono 37018-2. Item marked [a] from HMV DB3367/70 (1/38, recorded in 1937), [b] recorded and issued by Columbia in 1926.

lh 9m ADD 4/91

During a rehearsal for the sessions that preceded this recording of his Fourth Symphony, Vaughan Williams is reported to have put down his baton and said "Gentlemen, if that's modern music, you can have it!". Well, here is VW letting us have it, with a determination that no other recording has since matched (though Handley comes close). His priority would seem to be to give expression to what Hugh Ottaway has called the Symphony's "constructive drive": for once, the second movement goes at a proper *Andante*, and no concessions are made to the human frailty of his players in the *Allegro molto* finale (none are needed). Holst's 1926 recording of *The Planets* is arguably less successful than his pre-electric recording made two years previously, though it has incomparably finer sound. Again tempos are swift (this "Jupiter" is no Falstaffian "Bringer of Jollity") and the entire recording bears out Imogen Holst's observation that, for her father, rhythm was the most important thing in life. Both recordings sound their age — the Vaughan Williams is emphatically not a comfortable listening experience — though textural clarity is good in these transfers.

Additional recommendations ...

No. 4. Violin Concerto in D minor, "Concerto accademico"[a]. [a]**Kenneth Sillito** (vn); **London Symphony Orchestra/Bryden Thomson.** Chandos CHAN8633 — 50m DDD 1/89

Nos. 4 and 6. **New Philharmonia Orchestra/Sir Adrian Boult.** EMI CDM7 64019-2 — lh 9m ADD 5/92

Vaughan Williams. Symphony No. 5 in D major. Flos campi — suite[a]. [a]**Christopher Balmer** (va); [a]**Liverpool Philharmonic Choir; Royal Liverpool Philharmonic Orchestra/Vernon Handley.** EMI Eminence CD-EMX9512. From EMX2112 (8/87). Recorded in 1986.

lh 2m DDD 3/88  

This disc is a bargain, both artistically and economically. The recording is full-toned and carefully balanced, preserving the luminous qualities of two of Vaughan Williams's most visionary and subtly devised scores; and the RLPO's playing under Vernon Handley is totally in sympathy with the music. The performance of *Flos campi* is outstandingly good. This work is deeply influenced by Ravel and has marvellous use of a wordless choir to intensify the erotic and sensuous longing of the music inspired by the *Song of Solomon*. The viola's impassioned and lyrical outpouring is beautifully played by Christopher Balmer, with excellent woodwind soloists in support, and the Liverpool Philharmonic Choir sings with secure intonation and flexible dynamic range. Handley's interpretation of the Fifth Symphony emphasizes the strength and passion in this music. His control of the architectural splendour of the first movement is masterly and he allows the ecstasy of the slow movement to unfold most naturally.

Key to Symbols

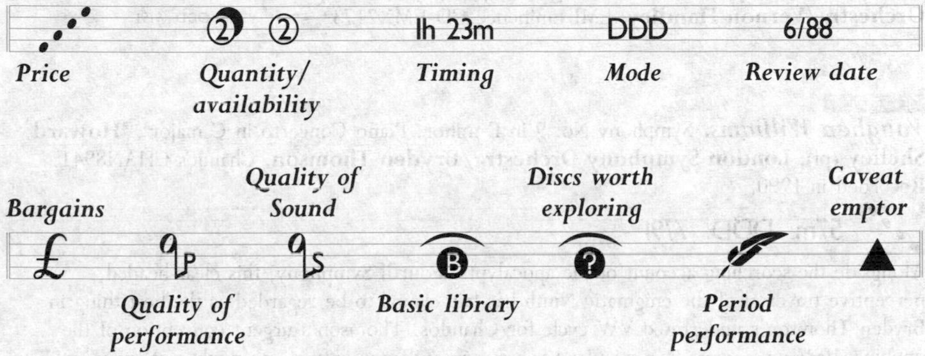

Vaughan Williams. Symphony No. 6 in E minor. Fantasia on a Theme by Thomas Tallis. The Lark Ascending[a]. [a]**Tasmin Little** (vn); **BBC Symphony Orchestra/Andrew Davis.** Teldec British Line 9031-73127-2. Recorded in 1990.

1h 2m DDD 8/91

Andrew Davis has clearly thought long and hard before committing this enigmatic and tragic symphony to disc, and the result is one of the most spontaneous and electrifying accounts of the Sixth Symphony available. The urgency and vigour of the first and third movements is astonishing, leaving one with the impression that the work might have been recorded in one take. His treatment of the second subject's reprise in the closing pages of the first movement is more underplayed and remote than the beautifully sheened approach of some recordings, but is arguably more nostalgic for being so. The feverish, nightmare world of the *Scherzo* is a real *tour de force* in the hands of an inspired BBC Symphony Orchestra, and the desolate wasteland of the eerie final movement has rarely achieved such quiescence and nadir as here. Davis's searchingly intense *Tallis Fantasia* is finely poised with a beautifully spacious acoustic. The disc concludes on a quietly elevated note with Tasmin Little's serene and gently introspective reading of *The Lark Ascending*. The recording is excellent.

Additional recommendation ...
Fantasia on a Theme by Thomas Tallis. Partita for Double String Orchestra. Oboe Concerto[a]. *English Folk-Song Suite (orch. Jacob). Fantasia on "Greensleeves" (arr. Greaves).* [a]**Jonathan Small** (ob); **Royal Liverpool Philharmonic Orchestra/Vernon Handley.** EMI Eminence CD-EMX2179 — 1h 8m DDD 12/91

Vaughan Williams. Symphony No. 7, "Sinfonia antartica". **Sheila Armstrong** (sop); **London Philharmonic Choir and Orchestra/Bernard Haitink.** EMI CDC7 47516-2. From EL270318-1 (10/85). Recorded in 1984.

Scored for wordless soprano solo and chorus plus a large orchestra, this Seventh Symphony was based on the composer's music for the film *Scott of the Antarctic*. It comprises five movements; the Prelude, which conveys mankind's struggle in overcoming hostile natural forces; a *Scherzo*, which depicts the whales and penguins in their natural habitat; "Landscape", which portrays vast frozen wastes; Intermezzo, a reflection of the actions and thoughts of two members of the party;

and "Epilogue", describing the final tragic assault on the South Pole. Bernard Haitink's conducting is highly imaginative, very concentrated and very committed and the LPO respond to him with some wonderfully atmospheric playing, full of personality and colour. Sheila Armstrong's eerie disembodied soprano voice and the remote chorus heighten the atmosphere, so that the score emerges as a powerful, coherent essay in symphonic form. Every detail has been captured by a magnificently sonorous and spacious recording.

Additional recommendation ...
No. 7[a]. *Serenade to Music.* [a]**Alison Hargan** (sop); **Royal Liverpool Chöir and Orchestra/Vernon Handley.** EMI Eminence CD-EMX2173 — 57m DDD 9/91

NEW REVIEW

Vaughan Williams. Symphony No. 9 in E minor. Piano Concerto in C major[a]. [a]**Howard Shelley** (pf); **London Symphony Orchestra/Bryden Thomson.** Chandos CHAN8941. Recorded in 1990.

57m DDD 7/91

Alongside the scorching account of the apocalyptic Fourth Symphony, this clear-headed, perceptive traversal of the enigmatic Ninth has fair claims to be regarded as the best thing in Bryden Thomson's underrated VW cycle for Chandos. Thomson's urgent conception of the opening *Moderato maestoso* in particular has a sweep and momentum one might not have previously associated with this movement, yet the gain in terms of sheer concentration and symphonic stature is irrefutable. Granted, some may find the outer sections of the succeeding *Andante sostenuto* just a little too lacking in evocative magic, but there's no gainsaying the effectiveness of gallumphing woodwind in the oafish scherzo; certainly, the LSO's saxophone trio seem to be enjoying their day out hugely. In the finale, too, Thomson's approach is more boldly assertive than usual — not the way one would always want to hear this music, perhaps, but a thoroughly valid and convincing performance all the same. The coupling, Howard Shelley's distinguished remake of the same composer's craggily elusive Piano Concerto, is both imaginative and desirable. All in all, a highly recommendable disc: the LSO are in fine fettle throughout, whilst Chandos's glowing sonics come close to the ideal.

NEW REVIEW

Vaughan Williams. ORCHESTRAL AND CHORAL WORKS. [ab]**Frederick Riddle** (va); [a]**Bournemouth Sinfonietta Chorus; Bournemouth Sinfonietta/**[ab]**Norman Del Mar,** [c]**George Hurst.** Chandos Collect CHAN6545. Items marked [ab] from RCA RL25137 (4/78), [c] Polydor 2383 359 (4/76). Recorded in 1977.
Flos Campi — Suite[a]. Viola Suite[b]. Two Hymn-Tune Preludes[c]. The Poisoned Kiss — Overture[c]. The Running Set[c].

1h 6m ADD 11/92

Still all-too-seldom heard, Vaughan Williams's masterpiece *Flos campi* (truly one of his most sublime creations) was inspired by a biblical source, namely the erotic outpourings of *The Song of Solomon*. Scored for solo viola, small wordless chorus and chamber orchestra, it's an intensely evocative, personal utterance — VW at his visionary best, in fact. This is a lovely performance: the contribution of that experienced violist Frederick Riddle is sensitive and quietly idiomatic, and Norman Del Mar directs his excellent Bournemouth forces with all the natural fluency and profound sympathy one has come to expect from him in such repertoire. Indeed, VW rarities abound on this enterprising CD, for we are also offered the little-known Suite for Viola and Orchestra (written for Lionel Tertis in 1934), with Riddle, again, on excellent form — in the words of Michael Kennedy: "It has no pretension to be other than enjoyable, light music". Then it's the turn of George Hurst to preside over reliable (if hardly the most imaginative) renderings of the engaging overture to VW's 1929 'Romantic Extravaganza' in three acts, *The Poisoned Kiss*, *The Running Set* (a frothy folk-song fantasia from 1933) and the two contemplative *Hymn-tune Preludes* of 1936. These remastered recordings from the mid-1970s (originally made for RCA) have all come up exceedingly well, though it's a pity Chandos didn't use this opportunity to band the six linked sections of *Flos campi*.

Vaughan Williams. String Quartets — No. 1 in G minor; No. 2 in A minor. Phantasy Quintet[a]. **English Quartet** (Diana Cummings, Colin Callow, vns; Luciano Iorio, va; Geoffrey Thomas, vc) with [a]**Norbert Blume** (va). Unicorn-Kanchana DKPCD9076. Recorded in 1988.

1h 1m DDD 9/89

See the word 'Phantasy' or its like in the title of some British chamber work of the early years of this century, and you would rarely lose money betting that it was produced for the wealthy patron, Walter W. Cobbett, who was fascinated by the Elizabethan form. He commissioned Vaughan Williams's Quintet through the Worshipful Company of Musicians in 1912, and received a short piece in four sections, played without break. The scoring is highly effective and the players here lose no opportunity to bring out the music's richly evocative atmosphere, perceptively varying tone-colour and vibrato to add an extra dimension to the notes of the score. They capture the contrasting moods of the First and Second String Quartets, of 1908 and 1944 respectively, with a very keen awareness of the different backgrounds to these pieces. Quartet No. 1, with its overtones of Ravel (with whom Vaughan Williams had been studying), is the most lighthearted of these three works, whilst No. 2 has a flavour of wartime darkness, emphasized by the dominance of the viola — it was dedicated to the violist of the Menges Quartet, Jean Stewart. These front-ranking performances are set in a pleasing, resonant acoustic that lends a genial ease to the proceedings.

Vaughan Williams. VOCAL WORKS. [a]**Elizabeth Connell,** [a]**Linda Kitchen,** [a]**Anne Dawson,** [a]**Amanda Roocroft** (sops); [a]**Sarah Walker,** [a]**Jean Rigby,** [a]**Diana Montague** (mezs); [a]**Catherine Wyn-Rogers** (contr); [a]**John Mark Ainsley,** [a]**Martyn Hill,** [a]**Arthur Davies,** [a]**Maldwyn Davies** (tens); [acd]**Thomas Allen,** [a]**Alan Opie** (bars); [a]**Gwynne Howell,** [a]**John Connell** (basses); [b]**Nobuko Imai** (va); [bcd]**Corydon Singers; English Chamber Orchestra/Matthew Best.** Hyperion CDA66420. Texts included.
Serenade to Music[a]. Flos campi[b]. Five mystical songs[c]. Fantasia on Christmas carols[d]. Recorded in 1990.

1h 8m DDD 8/90 

In 1938 Sir Henry Wood celebrated his 50 years as a professional conductor with a concert. Vaughan Williams composed a work for the occasion, the *Serenade to Music*, in which he set words by Shakespeare from Act 5 of *The Merchant of Venice*. Sixteen star vocalists of the age were gathered together for the performance and Vaughan Williams customized the vocal parts to show off the best qualities of the singers. The work turned out to be one of the composer's most sybaritic creations, turning each of its subsequent performances into a special event. Hyperion have gathered stars of our own age for this outstanding issue and Matthew Best has perceptively managed to give each their head whilst melding them into a cohesive ensemble. A mellow, spacious recording has allowed the work to emerge on disc with a veracity never achieved before. The coupled vocal pieces are given to equal effect and the disc is substantially completed by Nobuko Imai's tautly poignant account of *Flos campi*, in which the disturbing tension between viola solo and wordless chorus heighten the work's crypticism. Altogether, an imaginative issue that is a must for any collection.

NEW REVIEW

Vaughan Williams. VOCAL WORKS. [a]**Sir John Gielgud** (narr); [a]**Lynne Dawson,** [d]**Linda Kitchen** (sops); [c]**Catherine Wyn-Rogers** (contr); [d]**John Mark Ainsley,** [b]**John Bowen,** [d]**Adrian Thompson** (tens); [d]**Alan Opie** (bar); [d]**Bryn Terfel** (bass-bar); [d]**Jonathan Best** (bass); [a]**John Scott,** [bce]**Roger Judd** (orgs); [a]**London Oratory Junior Choir; Corydon Singers; City of London Sinfonia/Matthew Best.** Hyperion CDA66569. Texts included. Recorded 1990-91.
A Song of Thanksgiving[a]. Three Choral Hymns[b]. Magnificat[c]. The Shepherds of the Delectable Mountains[d]. The Old Hundredth Psalm Tune[e].

1h 13m DDD 8/92

Welcome for many reasons, this is in the first place a timely filler-in of gaps. The *Magnificat* of 1930, for instance, is rarely heard, and so, more surprisingly perhaps, is *The Shepherds of the*

Delectable Mountains. Both are works of great beauty, the *Magnificat* being set in a particularly imaginative way with solo flute and women's voices for the Angels of the Annunciation, while the three choral hymns from *Pilgrim's Progress,* relatively spare in texture and restrained in expression, reminds us of the composer's lifelong affection for Bunyan's allegory. There are various shorter pieces, including VW's splendid arrangement of the *Old Hundredth* psalm-tune as used in the 1953 Coronation. Then the other major work, *A Song of Thanksgiving* (or *Thanksgiving for Victory* as it was originally called in 1945), is a richly-scored work, rejoicing from a full heart and without taint of vainglory, national or otherwise. Sir John Gielgud as speaker confers further dignity and restraint, his voice no longer the sonorous instrument of earlier years but still beautiful in quality and usage. Distinguished among the other solo contributions are those of Bryn Terfel in *The Shepherds* and the flautist Duke Dobing in the *Magnificat*. The impressively massed forces of choir and orchestra are finely directed by Matthew Best, and the recorded sound has both clarity and spaciousness.

NEW REVIEW

Vaughan Williams. VOCAL WORKS.
Walton. VOCAL WORKS. [b]**Lynda Russell** (sop); [a]**Peter Williams,** [c]**Timothy Moule** (trebs); [c]**William Kendall** (ten); **Waynfelte Singers; Winchester Cathedral Choir; Bournemouth Symphony Orchestra/David Hill.** Argo 436 120-2ZH. Texts included. Recorded in 1991.
Vaughan Williams: The Old Hundreth Psalm. Toward the Unknown Region. O taste and see[a]. O clap your hands. Let us now praise famous men. Benedicite[b]. ***Walton:*** Orb and Sceptre. Set me as a seal upon thine heart[c]. Jubilate Deo. A Litany. Coronation Te Deum.

1h 10m DDD 9P 9S

Vaughan Williams's setting of Walt Whitman's *Toward the Unknown Region* is probably the most beautiful thing he ever composed. With its rich tapestry of orchestral colour and wealth of flowing lines for the voices, reaching a stunning climax with the verse "Then we burst forth", it is every bit as much a joy to perform as it is to listen to. Clearly David Hill and his musicians relish every moment in this enthralling performance. Vaughan Williams could also find inspiration in the slightest of texts, and his tiny setting of the psalm verse *O taste and see* has been a firm favourite of church choirs ever since it was performed during the coronation of Queen Elizabeth II in 1953. Music performed at that service provides the mainstay of this glittering CD — including Walton's tremendously exuberant coronation march *Orb and Sceptre* and his scintillating *Coronation Te Deum*. The mood is set with an electrifying performance of Vaughan Williams's setting of that most famous of all hymn-tunes *The Old Hundredth Psalm* ("All people that on earth do dwell"). Here is what English composers do best of all — writing ceremonial music for big state occasions. This outstanding recording made in the opulent splendour of Winchester Cathedral (if played at full volume the rumbling organ pedals and the powerful brass and percussion will prove fertile testing grounds both for your audio equipment and neighbourly relations) recreates vividly the sound and atmosphere of such an occasion.

Giuseppe Verdi

Italian 1813-1901

Verdi. OVERTURES AND PRELUDES. **Berlin Philharmonic Orchestra/Herbert von Karajan.** DG 419 622-2GH. From 413 544-1GX2 (2/86). Recorded in 1975.
Nabucco; Ernani; I Masnadieri; Macbeth; Il Corsaro; La Battaglia di Legnano; Luisa Miller; Rigoletto; La Traviata; I Vespri Siciliani; Un Ballo in maschera; La Forza del Destino; Aida.

1h 13m ADD 10/87 

Karajan was one of the most adaptable and sensitive of dramatic conductors. His repertoire in the theatre is extraordinarily wide being at home equally in Verdi, Wagner, Richard Strauss and Puccini. In this selection from his celebrated 1976 collection of all of Verdi's overtures, he gives us some fine insights into the composer's skill as an orchestrator, dramatist and poet. Though

Karajan had only recorded *Aida* complete his dramatic instincts bring some fine performances of the lesser known preludes. The earliest, *Nabucco* from 1842 (the collection is arranged chronologically), already shows a mastercraftsman at work, with a slow introduction promising much. *La Traviata* shows a quite different skill — the delcate creation of a sensitive poet working in filigree. The final four preludes are great works fully worthy of this individual presentation. Even the lesser known Preludes are enhanced by Karajan's dramatic instincts. Good recordings, though less than outstanding.

Verdi. Messa da Requiem[a]. OPERA CHORUSES. [a]**Susan Dunn** (sop); [a]**Diane Curry** (mez); [a]**Jerry Hadley** (ten); [a]**Paul Plishka** (bass); **Atlanta Symphony Chorus and Orchestra/Robert Shaw.** Telarc CD80152. Texts and translations included.
Opera choruses: DON CARLOS — Spuntato ecco il dì. MACBETH — Patria oppressa. OTELLO — Fuoco di gioia. NABUCCO — Va, pensiero, sull'ali dorate. AIDA — Gloria all'Egitto.

② 1h 53m DDD 3/88 B

Of all nineteenth-century choral works, Verdi's setting of the Requiem Mass seems to be the most approachable. The choral writing is of the utmost splendour and conviction, and is a very personal statement of belief although written by an unbeliever. In many sections soloists and chorus are intermingled in a masterly fashion, and the writing for the orchestra is always appropriate to the text. Robert Shaw directs a performance that avoids histrionics and display and impresses by sheer musicianship. Tempos are well judged and for once rarely depart from the composer's markings. The team of soloists are well blended. The chorus are well drilled and full bodied and contribute lustily to the operatic choruses included as a bonus. The recording is very fine, spacious yet clear.

Additional recommendations ...
Messa da Requiem. Quattro pezzi sacri[a]. **Soloists;** [a]**Berlin RIAS Chamber Choir; St Hedwig's Cathedral Choir, Berlin; Berlin Radio Symphony Orchestra/Ferenc Fricsay.** DG Dokumente mono 429 076-2GDO2 — ② 2h 12m ADD B ▲
Messa da Requiem. Quattro pezzi sacri. **Soloists; Philharmonia Chorus and Orchestra/Carlo Maria Giulini.** EMI CDS7 47257-2 — ② 2h 9m ADD 4/87 B

Verdi. OPERA CHORUSES. **Chicago Symphony Chorus and Orchestra/Sir Georg Solti.** Decca 430 226-2DH. Texts and translations included. Recorded in 1989.
NABUCCO — Gli arredi festivi giù cadano infranti; Va, pensiero, sull'ali dorate. I LOMBARDI — Gerusalem!; O Signore, dal tetto natio. MACBETH — Tre volte miagola; Patria oppressa. I MASNADIERI — Le rube, gli stupri. RIGOLETTO — Zitti zitti. IL TROVATORE — Vedi! le fosche notturne spoglic; Squilli, echeggi la tromba guerriera. LA TRAVIATA — Noi siamo zingarelle ... Di Madride nio siam mattadori (with Marsha Waxman, mez; David Huneryager, Richard Cohn, basses). UN BALLO IN MASCHERA — Posa in pace. DON CARLOS — Spuntato ecco il dí. AIDA — Gloria all'Egitto. OTELLO — Fuoco di gioia. REQUIEM — Sanctus.

1h 10m DDD 4/91 gp gs B

Verdi's choruses occupy a special place in his operas. They are invariably red-blooded and usually make a simple dramatic statement with great impact. Such is their immediacy and communicative force that they have sometimes produced an influence on listeners, over and above that pertinent to the plot, especially where the audience has already been primed with patriotic nationalistic feeling by local events outside the theatre. The arresting "Chorus of the Hebrew Slaves" ("Va, pensiero") from *Nabucco* is a prime example. Probably the best-known and most popular chorus in the entire operatic repertoire, it immediately tugs at the heart-strings with its gentle opening cantilena, soon swelling out to a great climax. Solti, in this splendidly vibrant Decca collection, with the Chicago Symphony Chorus, shows just how to shape the noble melodic line which soars with firm control, yet retaining the urgency and electricity in every bar. He is equally good in "Gli arredi festivi", from the same opera, not only in the bold opening statement, shared between singers and the resplendent sonority of the Chicago brass, but also later when the mood lightens, and women's voices are heard floating over seductive harp roulades. The dramatic contrasts at the opening of "Gerusalem!" from *I Lombardi* are equally powerfully projected, and the brass again makes a riveting effect in "Patria oppressa" from *Macbeth*. But, of course, not all Verdi choruses offer blood and thunder: the volatile "Fire chorus" from *Otello* flickers with an almost visual fantasy, while the wicked robbers in *I Masnadieri* celebrate their excesses (plunder, rape, arson and murder) gleefully, and with such rhythmic jauntiness that one cannot quite take them seriously. The "Gypsies chorus" from *La Traviata* has a nice touch of elegance, and the scherzo-like "Sanctus", from the *Requiem*, which ends the concert, is full of joy. But it is the impact of the dramatic moments which is most memorable, not least the big triumphal scene from *Aida*, complete with the ballet music, to provide a diverse interlude in the middle. Throughout we have demonstration-worthy sound from the Decca engineers in the suitably resonant acoustic of Chicago's Orchestra Hall, and the back-up documentation includes full translations.

Additional recommendations ...
NABUCCO — Gli arredi festivi giù cadano infranti; Va, pensiero, sull'ali dorate. MACBETH — Patria oppressa. IL TROVATORE — Vedi! le fosche notturne spoglie; Ora co'dadi, ma fra poco. LA TRAVIATA — Noi siamo zingarelle; Si ridesta in ciel (with Alena Cokova, mez; Stanislav Vrabel, bass). *DON CARLOS — Spuntato ecco il dì d'esultanza. AIDA — Gloria all'Egitto. OTELLO — Fuoco di gioia. LA BATTAGLIA DI LEGNANO — Deus meus, pone illos ut rotam* (Eva Jenisova, sop; Cokova); *Giuramento* (L'udovit Ludha, ten). *ERNANI — Si rideste il Leon di Castiglia. LA FORZA DEL DESTINO — Rataplan! rataplan!* (Ida Kirilová, mez). **Slovak Philharmonic Choir; Slovak Radio Symphony Orchestra/Oliver Dohnányi.** Naxos 8 550241 — . 56m DDD 4/91 £ ℘ Ⓑ
NABUCCO — Gli arredi festivi giù cadano infranti; Va, pensiero, sull'ali dorate. MACBETH — Tre volte miagola; Patria oppressa. LA BATTAGLIA DI LEGNANO — Giuriam d'Italia. I LOMBARDI — Gerusalem!; O Signore, del tetto nation. IL TROVATORE — Vedi! le fosche notturne spoglie. DON CARLOS — Spuntato ecco il dì d'esultanza. OTELLO — Fuoco di gioia. AIDA — Gloria all'Egitto. **Santa Cecilia Academy Chorus and Orchestra, Rome/Carlo Rizzi.** Teldec 4509-90267-2 — .·' lh lm DDD 8/93 ℘ Ⓑ

Verdi. I DUE FOSCARI. **Piero Cappuccilli** (bar) Francesco Foscari; **José Carreras** (ten) Jacopo Foscari; **Katia Ricciarelli** (sop) Lucrezia; **Samuel Ramey** (bass) Jacopo Loredano; **Vincenzo Bello** (ten) Barbarigo; **Elizabeth Connell** (sop) Pisana; **Mieczyslaw Antoniak** (ten) Officer; **Franz Handlos** (bass) Doge's servant; **Austrian Radio Chorus and Symphony Orchestra/Lamberto Gardelli.** Philips 422 426-2PM2. Notes, text and translation included. From 6700 105 (4/78). Recorded in 1976.

.·' ② lh 44m ADD 12/89 ℘

This is one of the most impressive of Verdi's early scores, a dark, dour drama of a dynastic and family drama played out on a historic plane. The performance is worthy of the piece. Gardelli has always been a loving exponent of Verdi's 'galley-years' opera and here his conducting brings out the colour and character of the piece unfussily yet with innate eloquence. Tempos, dynamics and rhythmic emphasis are all ideally adumbrated; so is the depth of feeling in the score. He is blessed with a near-ideal cast, all three principals being at the peak of their achievement in 1978 when the set was made. Cappuccilli is absolutely in his element as the gloomy old Doge and father, a portrait to set alongside his superb Boccanegra. His breath control and line in his first aria, "O vecchio cor", is a classic of Verdian singing. Carreras, as the condemned Jacopo, sings with the right feeling of sincerity and desperation in his Prison scene. Ricciarelli offers the role of Lucrezia with lustrous tone and unflinching attack, one of her best performances on disc. She and Cappuccilli make the most of their wonderful duet in the last act. The recording is true and well balanced.

Verdi. ATTILA. **Samuel Ramey** (bass) Attila; **Cheryl Studer** (sop) Odabella; **Giorgio Zancanaro** (bar) Ezio; **Neil Shicoff** (ten) Foresto; **Ernesto Gavazzi** (ten) Uldino; **Giorgio**

Surian (bass) Leone; **Chorus and Orchestra of La Scala, Milan/Riccardo Muti.** EMI CDS7 49952-2. Notes, text and translation included.

② lh 49m DDD 5/90

This is one of the most successful of the collaborations between Muti and the La Scala forces. The raw vigour of Verdi's early triumph is splendidly captured by Muti's fiery yet sensitive direction, with his forces fired to great things. Tenor excepted, this cast couldn't be bettered anywhere today. Samuel Ramey is an incisive, dark-hued Attila, singing with accuracy and confidence. His main adversary is the indomitable Odabella, here taken with spirit, vital attack and well-fashioned phrasing by Cheryl Studer, who might now give us the Norma for which we have all been waiting. Giorgio Zancanaro can be rough as Ezio but he is dramatically well in the picture, and Neil Shicoff is never less than honourable in tone and line. The recording, though not ideal in every respect, gives the voices their rightful prominence.

Additional recommendation ...

Soloists; Chorus and Orchestra of La Scala, Milan/Riccardo Muti. EMI CDS7 49952 2 — ② lh 49m DDD 5/90

Verdi. STIFFELIO. **José Carreras** (ten) Stiffelio; **Sylvia Sass** (sop) Lina; **Matteo Manuguerra** (bar) Stankar; **Wladimiro Ganzarolli** (bass) Jorg; **Ezio di Cesare** (ten) Raffaele; **Maria Venuti** (mez) Dorotea; **Thomas Moser** (ten) Federico; **Austrian Radio Chorus and Symphony Orchestra/Lamberto Gardelli.** Philips 422 432-2PM2. Notes, text and translation included. From 6769 039 (10/80). Recorded in 1979.

② lh 49m ADD 3/90

This work is gradually gaining the reputation it deserves as companies and audiences realize its quality (it gains its first performance at Covent Garden in the 1992-3 season). It tells of Stiffelio, a Protestant clergyman, in a Catholic country, whose wife Linda has committed adultery and finds it in his heart, after her father has killed her lover, to forgive her. The work has elements that pre-echo *Otello* and is yet another example of Verdi finding the specific music for a specific predicament. This performance, firmly conducted by Gardelli, has an involved, involving assumption of the title-role by Carreras. This role is a gift for an accomplished tenor and he catches the moral fervour and uncertainties of the part with his open-hearted, spontaneous performance. Sylvia Sass also offers a rewarding, strongly emotional performance as Lina.

Verdi. MACBETH. **Piero Cappuccilli** (bar) Macbeth; **Shirley Verrett** (mez) Lady Macbeth; **Nicolai Ghiaurov** (bass) Banquo; **Plácido Domingo** (ten) Macduff; **Antonio Savastano** (ten) Malcolm; **Carlo Zardo** (bass) Doctor; **Giovanni Foiani** (bass) Servant; **Sergio Fontana** (bass) Herald; **Alfredo Mariotti** (bass) Assassin; **Stefania Malagú** (mez) Lady-in-waiting; **Chorus and Orchestra of La Scala, Milan/Claudio Abbado.** DG 415 688-2GH3. Notes, text and translation included. From 2709 062 (10/76). Recorded in 1976.

③ 2h 34m ADD 9/86

Verdi's lifelong admiration for Shakespeare resulted in only two operas based on his plays. *Macbeth*, the first, originally written in 1847, was extensively revised in 1865. Without losing the direct force of the original, Verdi added greater depth to his first ideas. Once derided as being un-Shakespearian, it is now recognized as a masterpiece for its psychological penetration as much as for its subtle melodic inspiration. Abbado captures perfectly the atmosphere of dark deeds and personal ambition leading to tragedy, projected by Verdi, and his reading holds the opera's disparate elements in the score under firm control, catching its interior tensions. He is well supported by his Scala forces. Shirley Verrett may not be ideally incisive or Italianate in accent as Lady Macbeth, but she peers into the character's soul most convincingly. As ever, truly inspired by Abbado, Cappuccilli is a suitably haunted and introverted Macbeth who sings a secure and unwavering legato. Domingo's upright Macduff and Ghiaurov's doom-laden Banquo are both admirable in their respective roles.

Additional recommendations ...
Soloists; Berlin Deutsche Opera Chorus and Orchestra/Giuseppe Sinopoli. Philips 412 133-2PH3 — ③ 2h 15m DDD 2/85
Soloists; Metropolitan Opera Chorus and Orchestra/Erich Leinsdorf. RCA Victor GD84516 — ② 2h 10m ADD 9/88
Soloists; Chorus and Orchestra of the Santa Cecilia Academy, Rome/Thomas Schippers. Decca Grand Opera 433 039-2DM2 — ② 2h 1m ADD 5/92
Soloists; Ambrosian Opera Chorus; New Philharmonia Orchestra/Riccardo Muti. EMI CMS7 64339-2 — ② ADD 2/93

NEW REVIEW

Verdi. LUISA MILLER. **Montserrat Caballé** (sop) Luisa; **Luciano Pavarotti** (ten) Rodolfo; **Sherrill Milnes** (bar) Miller; **Bonaldo Gaiotti** (bass) Count Walter; **Anna Reynolds** (mez) Federica; **Richard Van Allan** (bass) Wurm; **Annette Céline** (mez) Laura; **Fernando Pavarotti** (ten) Peasant; **London Opera Chorus; National Philharmonic Orchestra/Peter Maag.** Decca 417 420-2DH2. Notes, text and translation included. From SET606/08 (5/76).

② 2h 24m ADD 10/88

This transitional work shows Verdi enhancing his skills at presenting characters in the round and refining his musical style so as to characterize the put-upon Luisa, a notable forerunner of Gilda and Violetta. The plot, based on a Schiller drama, involves the tragedy and death of Luisa and her beloved Rodolfo brought about by the evil Wurm, apt predecessor of Verdi's Iago. The title-role could not find a more appealing interpreter than Caballé, who spins a fine line and is highly responsive to Luisa's sad situation. She is partnered by Pavarotti at the height of his powers as Rodolfo. He excels in "Quando le sere al polacido", the work's most famous aria. As Luisa's equivocal father, Miller, Milnes gives one of his best performances on disc and Van Allan is a properly snarling Wurm. Maag, an underrated conductor, directs a strong, well-proportioned performance. He gives the impression of being in love with this opera and he goes right to the heart of the score, finding its seriousness as well as its fire. The last act is specially fine, containing what should be regarded as among the gramophone classics, the two duets of Luisa, first with her father, then with Rodolfo. The production by Ray Minshull is unobtrusively effective in creation of atmosphere and is spaciously recorded.

Additional recommendation ...
Soloists; Chorus and Orchestra of the Royal Opera House, Covent Garden/Lorin Maazel. DG 423 144-2GH2 — ② 2h 13m ADD 5/88

Verdi. RIGOLETTO. **Tito Gobbi** (bar) Rigoletto; **Giuseppe di Stefano** (ten) Duke; **Maria Callas** (sop) Gilda; **Nicola Zaccaria** (bass) Sparafucile; **Adriana Lazzarini** (mez) Maddalena; **Giuse Gerbino** (mez) Giovanna; **Plinio Clabassi** (bass) Monterone; **William Dickie** (bar) Marullo; **Renato Ercolani** (ten) Borsa; **Carlo Forti** (bar) Count Ceprano; **Elvira Galassi** (sop) Countess Ceprano; **Chorus and Orchestra of La Scala, Milan/Tullio Serafin.** EMI mono CDS7 47469-8. Notes, text and translation included. From Columbia 33CXS1324, 33CX1325/6 (2/56). Recorded in 1955.

② 1h 58m ADD 2/87 

The story of the hunchbacked jester Rigoletto at the court of a licentious Duke who seduces the Fool's daughter Gilda by masquerading as a poor student, and the consequent attempts at revenge on the part of Rigoletto, produced from Verdi one of the most telling of his mid-period triumphs. His identification with each of the characters and the sheer energy and sensuous ardour of the score is quite remarkable. Nowhere else on record have these characterizations been delineated with such intelligence and commitment as by Gobbi, Callas and di Stefano on this 37 year old set. Over all Serafin presides with an unerring grasp of Verdian timing.

Additional recommendations ...
Soloists; Chorus and Orchestra of La Scala, Milan/Rafael Kubelík. DG 435 050-2GH2 — ② 2h 3m ADD

Soloists; Vienna State Opera Chorus; Vienna Philharmonic Orchestra/Carlo Maria Giulini. DG 415 288-2GH2 — ② DDD 11/85

Soloists; Slovak Philharmonic Chorus; Czecho-Slovak Radio Symphony Orchestra/Alexander Rahbari. Naxos 8 660013/4 — ② 1h 55m DDD 3/92 £

Verdi. LA TRAVIATA. **Maria Callas** (sop) Violetta Valéry; **Alfredo Kraus** (ten) Alfredo Germont; **Mario Sereni** (bar) Giorgio Germont; **Laura Zanini** (mez) Flora Bervoix; **Maria Cristina de Castro** (sop) Annina; **Piero De Palma** (ten) Gaston; **Alvero Malta** (bar) Baron Douphol; **Vito Susca** (bass) Marquis D'Obigny; **Alessandro Maddalena** (bass) Doctor Grenvil; **Manuel Leitao** (ten) Messenger; **Chorus and Orchestra of the Teatro Nacional de San Carlos, Lisbon/Franco Ghione.** EMI mono CDS7 49187-8. Notes, text and translation included. Recorded at a performance in the Teatro Nacional de San Carlos, Lisbon on March 27th, 1958. From RLS757 (10/80).

② 2h 3m ADD 11/87 

Most sopranos in the part of Violetta (forced to give up her true love for the sake of convention) make you cry in the last act; Callas also made you cry in the second. A fullness of heart and voice informs everything she does in the long colloquy with the elder Germont. The sorrow and emptiness that enters her tone when she realizes she will have to give up her beloved Alfredo is overwhelmingly eloquent. Then the final scene is almost unbearable in its poignancy of expression: the reading of the letter so natural in its suggestion of emptiness. However, the sense of sheer hollowness at "Ma se tornando ..." proves the most moving moment of all as Violetta knows nothing can save her life. All that and so much else suggests that Callas more than anyone understood what the role is about. To add to one's pleasure the young Kraus is as appealing as any tenor on disc as Alfredo. His Schipa-like tone, his refinement of phrase, especially in his duets with Callas, and his elegant yet ardent manner are exactly right for the part. Mario Sereni may not be in his colleagues' class, but his elder Germont is securely, sincerely and often perceptively sung. Franco Ghione is a prompt and alert conductor and the mono recording has plenty of theatrical presence.

Additional recommendations ...
Soloists; Rome Opera Chorus and Orchestra/Fernando Previtali. RCA Gold Seal GD84144 — ② 1h 53m ADD

Soloists; Bavarian State Opera Chorus and Orchestra/Carlos Kleiber. DG 415 132-2GH2 ② 3/86

Soloists; Ambrosian Opera Chorus; Band of HM Royal Marines; Philharmonia Orchestra/Riccardo Muti. EMI CDS7 47538-8 ② 2h 9m DDD 11/87

Soloists; RCA Italiana Opera Chorus and Orchestra/Georges Prêtre. RCA Red Seal RD86180 — ② 2h 5m ADD 9/88

(Sung in English). **Soloists; English National Opera Chorus and Orchestra/Sir Charles Mackerras.** EMI CMS7 63072-2 — ② 1h 58m ADD 10/89

Soloists; Metropolitan Opera Chorus and Orchestra/James Levine. DG 435 797-2GH2 — ② 2h 2m DDD 11/92

Verdi. IL TROVATORE. **Maria Callas** (sop) Leonora; **Giuseppe di Stefano** (ten) Manrico; **Rolando Panerai** (bar) Count di Luna; **Fedora Barbieri** (mez) Azucena; **Nicola Zaccaria** (bass) Ferrando; **Luisa Villa** (mez) Ines; **Renato Ercolani** (ten) Ruiz, Messenger; **Giulio Mauri** (bass) Old Gipsy; **Chorus and Orchestra of La Scala, Milan/Herbert von Karajan.** EMI mono CDS7 49347-2. Notes, text and translation included. From Columbia 33CXS1483, 33CX1484/5 (11/57).

② 2h 9m ADD 12/87 

Written in between *Rigoletto* and *La traviata, Il trovatore* has its own distinct identity. Pictorially, the nightscape of its action is penetrated by the watchman's torch, the gipsy's campfire and the cruel flame of the witch's stake. Dramatically, the passions of the present flare up among the shadows of a death-ridden past. Musically, the melodies surge to the background of an uneasy chromaticism, with taut rhythms and a predominantly minor tonality. A great performance can be exhilarating, but an indifferent one will often appear depressingly shabby. This recording finds Callas in fine voice and liable at any moment to bring a special thrill of conviction and individuality. As so often when one returns to reissues of her recordings, it is to find her quite remarkably restrained for most of the time: then a moment of rapt lyricism or fierce declamation produces a tingling effect with its feeling of spontaneous intensity and personal involvement. Her collaboration with Karajan is also among the most distinguished on record, and it often seems that his more calculated procedure with its care for the dignity of the score acts as both a foil and a balance to her impulsively emotional approach. Among the other singers, the most impressive is Fedora Barbieri, giving here her most inspired performance on record and Rolando Panerai, whose dark vibrancy suits the character of the Count di Luna. If di Stefano has neither the requisite steel in his voice nor the nobility of style, he is best in the full-voiced passion of the final scene.

Additional recommendations …

Soloists; Saint Cecilia Academy Chorus and Orchestra/Carlo Maria Giulini. DG 423 858-2GH2 — ② 2h 20m 2/85 ℗ Ⓑ

Soloists; Ambrosian Opera Chorus; New Philharmonia Orchestra/Zubin Mehta. RCA Red Seal RD86194 — ② 2h 17m ADD 8/88 ℗ Ⓑ

Soloists; Robert Shaw Chorale; RCA Victor Orchestra/Renato Cellini. RCA Victor mono GD86643 — ② 1h 57m ADD 8/88 ℗ Ⓑ

Verdi. I VESPRI SICILIANI. **Cheryl Studer** (sop) Elena; **Chris Merritt** (ten) Arrigo; **Giorgio Zancanaro** (bar) Montforte; **Ferruccio Furlanetto** (bass) Procida; **Gloria Banditelli** (contr) Ninetta; **Enzo Capuano** (bass) De Béthune; **Francesco Musinu** (bass) Vaudemont; **Ernesto Gavazzi** (ten) Danieli; **Paolo Barbacini** (ten) Tebaldo; **Marco Chingari** (bass) Roberto; **Ferrero Poggi** (ten) Manfredo; **Chorus and Orchestra of La Scala, Milan/Riccardo Muti.** EMI CDS7 54043-2. Notes, text and translation included. Recorded 1989-90.

③ 3h 19m DDD 1/91

Verdi's French opera, here given in its more familiar Italian guise, is a difficult work to bring off. Verdi felt he had to try to accommodate Parisian taste for the grand and theatrically exciting while at the same time showing his own preferences for the interplay of characters. It's to the credit of this performance, taken live from La Scala, that both aspects are thrillingly encompassed by virtue of Muti's vivid and acute conducting that never allows the score to sag yet allows for its many and varied moods. Although he plays it at full length, EMI have nonetheless managed to contain it on three discs. The singers, with one serious exception, are equal to their roles, none more than Studer as an Elena of positive character and vocal security. Chris Merritt turns in his best performance on disc to date as the hero Arrigo. Even better is Zancanaro as the tyrant Montforte, who yet has an anguished soul. Furlanetto is frankly overparted by the demands of the role of Procida, leader of the Sicilian rebellion, but that drawback shouldn't prevent anyone from enjoying the *frisson* of hearing La Scala, on a good night, performing comparatively rare Verdi with such zest.

Additional recommendation …

Soloists; James Alldis Choir; New Philharmonia Orchestra/James Levine. RCA Red Seal RD80370 — ③ 3h 7m ADD 9/88

Verdi. SIMON BOCCANEGRA. **Piero Cappuccilli** (bar) Simon Boccanegra; **Katia Ricciarelli** (sop) Amelia; **Plácido Domingo** (ten) Gabriele; **Ruggero Raimondi** (bass) Fiesco; **Gian Piero Mastromei** (bar) Paolo; **Maurizio Mazzieri** (bass) Pietro; **Piero de Palma** (ten) Captain; **Ornella Jachetti** (sop) Maid; **RCA Chorus and**

Orchestra/Gianandrea Gavazzeni. RCA Red Seal RD70729. Notes, text and translation included. From SER5696 (2/74).

② 2h 5m ADD 9/87

This opera has the most complex of plots, difficult to unravel in the opera house but more easily understood with the libretto in front of you at home. It mainly concerns the struggle between the nobility and the populace, represented respectively by Fiesco and Boccanegra and complicated by the fact that the seafaring Simon has seduced the noble's daughter Maria, who has borne his daughter, Amelia. It is lovingly conducted here by Gianandrea Gavazzeni with that easy yet unassuming command of Verdian structure which is not always achieved by his successors. His cast is an excellent one headed by the warm, sympathetic Boccanegra of Cappuccilli and the youthful, attractive Amelia of Ricciarelli. The recording is spacious and clear in detail.

Additional recommendations ...

Soloists; Chorus and Orchestra of La Scala, Milan/Claudio Abbado. DG 415 692-2GH2 — ② DDD 9/86

Soloists; Chorus and Orchestra of the Rome Opera House/Gabriele Santini. EMI mono CMS7 63513-2 — ② 1h 59m ADD 9/90 ▲

Key to Symbols

Gramophone Award winners

Artists of the Year

Verdi. UN BALLO IN MASCHERA. **Giuseppi di Stefano** (ten) Riccardo; **Tito Gobbi** (bar) Renato; **Maria Callas** (sop) Amelia; **Fedora Barbieri** (mez) Ulrica; **Eugenia Ratti** (sop) Oscar; **Ezio Giordano** (bass) Silvano; **Silvio Maionica** (bass) Samuel; **Nicola Zaccaria** (bass) Tom; **Renato Ercolani** (bar) Judge; **Chorus and Orchestra of La Scala, Milan/Antonino Votto.** EMI mono CDS7 47498-8. Notes, text and translation included. From Columbia 33CX1472/4 (10/57).

② 2h 10m ADD 9/87 

Ballo manages to encompass a vein of lighthearted frivolity (represented by the page, Oscar) within the confines of a serious drama of love, infidelity, noble and ignoble sentiments. No more modern recording has quite caught the opera's true spirit so truly as this one under Votto's unerring direction. Callas has not been surpassed in delineating Amelia's conflict of feelings and loyalties, nor has di Stefano been equalled in the sheer ardour of his singing as Riccardo. Add to that no less a singer than Tito Gobbi as Renato, at first eloquent in his friendship to his ruler, then implacable in his revenge when he thinks Riccardo has stolen his wife. Fedora Barbieri is full of character as the soothsayer Ulrica, Eugenia Ratti a sparky Oscar. It is an unbeatable line-up.

Additional recommendations ...

Soloists; Chorus and Orchestra of La Scala, Milan/Claudio Abbado. DG 415 685-2GH2 — ② DDD 9/86

Soloists; Haberdashers' Aske's School Girls' Choir; Medici Quartet; Royal Opera House Chorus, Covent Garden; New Philharmonia Orchestra/Riccardo Muti. EMI CMS7 69576-2 — ② 2h 7m ADD 11/88

Soloists; RCA Italiana Opera Chorus and Orchestra/Erich Leinsdorf. RCA Gold Seal GD86645 — ② 2h 8m ADD 11/88 9P

NEW REVIEW

Verdi. LA FORZA DEL DESTINO. **Martina Arroyo** (sop) Leonora; **Carlo Bergonzi** (ten) Don Alvaro; **Piero Cappuccilli** (bar) Don Carlos; **Ruggero Raimondo** (bass) Padre Guardiano; **Biancamaria Casoni** (mez) Preziosilla; **Sir Geraint Evans** (bar) Melitone; **Antonio Zerbini** (bass) Marchese; **Florindo Andreolli** (ten) Trabuco; **Mila Cova** (mez) Curra; **Virgilio Carbonari** (ten) Mayor; **Derek Hammond-Stroud** (bar) Surgeon; **Ambrosian Opera Chorus; Royal Philharmonic Orchestra/Lamberto Gardelli.** EMI Opera CMS7 64646-2. Notes, text and translation included. From HMV SLS948 (3/70).

③ 2h 48m ADD 6/93

This wonderfully multifarious opera demands an array of principal singers who need to be skilled in an unusually wide range of vocal and dramatic skills. It is a 'chase' opera in which Carlos pursues Alvaro and Leonora through two countries, through cloister and convent, through scenes popular and martial, all treated on the most expansive scale. It is dominated by its series of magnificent duets that are composed so that the music marches with the development of situation and character. This reissue is an excellent and completely satisfying mid-price buy. It features Bergonzi, that prince among Verdi tenors, as an exemplary and appealing Alvaro, the best in any complete set, and Piero Cappuccilli — like Bergonzi at the peak of his powers in 1969 when this set was made — as a full-blooded and Italianate Carlos. In the three all-important duets, their voices blend ideally. Leonora was the most successful of Arroyo's recorded roles, and she sings here with a feeling and urgency appropriate to Leonora's desperate situation. Casoni's vital Preziosilla, Raimondi's grave but over-lugubrious Padre Guardiano and Sir Geraint's keenly characterized Melitone complete a well-chosen cast. Over all presides Gardelli, a Verdi conductor with an instinctive feeling for the ebb and flow of his music, always attending to the needs of the music, never calling attention to himself. All of the versions listed here have much to commend them. The Levine is more opulently but not so stylishily sung and perhaps a little too hectically conducted. The *Gramophone* Award-winning Sinopoli is the stuff of which great music drama is made, especially in the opera's closing pages. It is wonderfully enacted by Paata Burchuladze (Padre Guardiano), Rosalind Plowright (Leonora) and José Carreras (Alvaro), with subtle changes of pace and perspective from Sinopoli and glorious string playing. The Serafin boasts the irreplaceable Callas and conducting on the Gardelli level but has some indifferent singing, significant excisions and a mono recording.

Additional recommendations ...

Soloists; Ambrosian Opera Chorus; Philharmonia Orchestra/Giuseppe Sinopoli. DG 419 203-2GH3 — ③ 2h 58m DDD 5/87

Soloists; Chorus and Orchestra of La Scala, Milan/Riccardo Muti. EMI CDS7 47485-8 — ③ 2h 44m 5/87

Soloists; Chorus and Orchestra of La Scala, Milan/Tullio Serafin. EMI mono CDS7 47581-8 — ③ 2h 44m ADD 10/87 ▲

Soloists; John Alldis Choir; London Symphony Orchestra/James Levine. RCA RD81864 — ③ 2h 51m ADD 10/87

Verdi. DON CARLO. **Plácido Domingo** (ten) Don Carlos; **Montserrat Caballé** (sop) Elisabetta; **Shirley Verrett** (mez) Princess Eboli; **Sherrill Milnes** (bar) Rodrigo; **Ruggero Raimondi** (bass) Philip II; **Giovanni Foiani** (bass) Grand Inquisitor; **Delia Wallis** (mez) Thibault; **Ryland Davies** (ten) Count of Lerma; **Simon Estes** (bass) A Monk; **John Noble** (bar) Herald; **Ambrosian Opera Chorus; Royal Opera House Orchestra, Covent Garden/Carlo Maria Giulini.** EMI CDS7 47701-8. Notes, text and translation included. From SLS956 (7/71).

③ 3h 28m ADD 7/87

In no other Verdi opera, except perhaps *Aida*, are public and private matters so closely intermingled, so searchingly described as in this large-scale, panoramic work, in which the political intrigues and troubles of Philip II's Spain are counterpointed with his personal agony and the lives and loves of those at his court. This vast canvas inspired Verdi to one of his most varied and glorious scores. Giulini, more than any other conductor, searches out the inner soul of the piece and his cast is admirable. The young Plácido Domingo makes a vivid and exciting Carlos, whilst Montserrat Caballé spins glorious tone and phrases in encompassing Elisabeth's difficult music. Shirley Verrett is a vital, suitably tense Eboli, Sherrill Milnes an upright, warm Rodrigo and Ruggero Raimondi a sombre Philip. Throughout, the Covent Garden forces sing and play with fervour and understanding for their distinguished conductor.

Additional recommendation ...
(Includes appendix). **Soloists; Chorus and Orchestra of La Scala, Milan/Claudio Abbado.** DG 415 316-2GH4 — ④ DDD 12/85

Verdi. AIDA. **Maria Callas** (sop) Aida; **Richard Tucker** (ten) Radames; **Fedora Barbieri** (mez) Amneris; **Tito Gobbi** (bar) Amonasro; **Giuseppe Modesti** (bass) Ramfis; **Nicola Zaccaria** (bass) King of Egypt; **Elvira Galassi** (sop) Priestess; **Franco Ricciardi** (ten) Messenger; **Chorus and Orchestra of La Scala, Milan/Tullio Serafin.** EMI mono CDS7 49030-8. Notes, text and translation included. From Columbia 33CX1318/20 (1/56). Recorded in 1955.

③ 2h 24m AAD 11/87 

Aida, the daughter of the Ethiopian king, is a prisoner at the Egyptian court where she falls in love with Radames, an Egyptian captain of the guard; Amneris, the Egyptian princess, also loves him. The tensions between these characters are rivetingly portrayed and explored and the gradual build-up to Aida's and Radames's union in death is paced with the sureness of a master composer. Callas's Aida is an assumption of total understanding and conviction; the growth from a slave-girl torn between love for her homeland and Radames, to a woman whose feelings transcend life itself represents one of the greatest operatic undertakings ever committed to disc. Alongside her is Fedora Barbieri, an Amneris palpable in her agonized mixture of love and jealousy — proud yet human. Tucker's Radames is powerful and Gobbi's Amonasro quite superb — a portrayal of comparable understanding to stand alongside Callas's Aida. Tullio Serafin is quite simply ideal and though the recording may not be perfect by current standards, nowhere can it dim the brilliance of the creations conjured up by this classic cast.

Additional recommendations ...
Soloists; Chorus of the Royal Opera House, Covent Garden; Trumpeters of the Royal Military School of Music, Kneller Hall; New Philharmonia Orchestra/Riccardo Muti. EMI CDS7 47271-8 — ③ 2h 28m 1/87 B
Soloists; Rome Opera House Chorus and Orchestra/Sir Georg Solti. Decca 417 416-2DH3 — ③ 2h 32m ADD 9/87 B
Soloists; Rome Opera House Chorus and Orchestra/Jonel Perlea. RCA Victor mono GD86652 — ③ 2h 29m ADD 8/88 B ▲

Verdi. OTELLO. **Jon Vickers** (ten) Otello; **Leonie Rysanek** (sop) Desdemona; **Tito Gobbi** (bar) Iago; **Florindo Andreolli** (ten) Cassio; **Mario Carlin** (ten) Roderigo; **Miriam Pirazzini** (mez) Emilia; **Ferrucio Mazzoli** (bass) Lodovico; **Franco Calabrese** (bass) Montano; **Robert Kerns** (bar) Herald; **Rome Opera Chorus and Orchestra/Tullio Serafin.** RCA Victor GD81969. Text and translation included. From LDS6155 (1/61). Recorded in 1960.

② 2h 24m ADD 11/88 

The role of Otello is notoriously demanding and there are few voices that one would say were 'made for it'. Jon Vickers's is certainly one of them. Simply as singing his is a magnificent performance: the voice is at its most beautiful and the breadth of his tone in the upper notes is astonishing. Stylistically, too, he is quite remarkably scrupulous, allowing himself no effect that is not authorized in the score, and always exact in his observations of *piano* markings. Giving this recording a unique distinction is Tito Gobbi as Iago, justly the most famous singer of the role in post-war years and the Desdemona too is clearly a great artist. Serafin conducts in a way that allows everything to be clearly heard, forfeiting some excitement but never cheapening by exaggeration or sentimentality. He secures clean, spirited playing from the Rome orchestra and keeps a control that is firm without being inflexible. This is a well-produced set that has scarcely aged over the years.

Additional recommendations ...

Soloists; Chorus and Orchestra of La Scala, Milan/Lorin Maazel. EMI CDS7 47450-8 — ② 2h 22m DDD 1/86

Soloists; Metropolitan Opera Children's Chorus; Chicago Symphony Chorus and Orchestra/Sir Georg Solti. Decca 433 669-2DH2 — ② 2h 9m DDD 11/91

Soloists; NBC Chorus and Symphony Orchestra/Arturo Toscanini. RCA Victor Gold Seal mono GD60302 — ② 2h 5m ADD 3/92 £ ▲

Soloists; Metropolitan Opera Chorus and Orchestra/Ettore Panizza. Music and Arts mono CD645 — ② 2h 19m AAD 9/91 £ ▲

Verdi. FALSTAFF. **Tito Gobbi** (bar) Falstaff; **Rolando Panerai** (bar) Ford; **Luigi Alva** (ten) Fenton; **Elisabeth Schwarzkopf** (sop) Alice; **Anna Moffo** (sop) Nannetta; **Fedora Barbieri** (mez) Quickly; **Renato Ercolani** (ten) Bardolfo; **Nicola Zaccaria** (bass) Pistola; **Tomaso Spatoro** (ten) Dr Caius; **Nan Merriman** (mez) Meg Page; **Philharmonia Chorus and Orchestra/Herbert von Karajan.** EMI CDS7 49668-2. Notes, text and translation included. From SAX2254/6 (7/61). Recorded in 1956.

② 2h ADD 9/88 

Verdi's *Falstaff* is one of those works that sum up a career with perfection, yet though it was his last opera it was also his first comic opera. The classic EMI recording enshrines one of the finest Falstaffs to have graced the stage in post-war years, Tito Gobbi. His assumption of the role is magnificent, and the completeness with which he embraces the part tends to overshadow his many successors. Assembled around this larger-than-life character is a near ideal cast, sprightly of gait, sparklingly comic and above all, beautifully sung. Karajan's conducting is always deeply cherishable as he leads the Philharmonia Orchestra surefootedly through the score and the recording has come up sounding as fresh as the day it was set down.

Additional recommendation ...

FALSTAFF. AIDA. Quattro pezzi sacri — Te Deum. Requiem. NABUCCO — Va, pensiero. LUISA MILLER — Quando le sere al placido. Inno delle Nazioni. **Soloists; Robert Shaw Chorale; NBC Symphony Orchestra/Arturo Toscanini.** RCA Gold Seal mono GD60326 — ⑦ 6h 13m ADD 5/90 ▲

Tomas Luis de Victoria

Spanish 1548-1611

Victoria (ed. Turner). Responsories for Tenebrae. **Westminster Cathedral Choir/David Hill.** Hyperion CDA66304. Texts and translations included.

1h 15m DDD 7/89

Westminster Cathedral is probably one of the few places where compositions of such noble inspiration may still be heard during the last three days of Holy Week. Such a living link with tradition goes to explain the inner understanding, the tremendous pathos of a superbly tragic and musically satisfying performance. The carefully chosen texts tell of the betrayal and arrest of Jesus, his passion and burial. The music expresses with anguish the suffering and sorrow of those days. Certain passages in the recording are particularly memorable: a gentle treble lead at the opening of "Una hora", the dramatic juxtaposition of the evil vigil of Judas and the naïvety of the disciples' sleep. Variations of tempo, especially that for the plotting of Jeremiah's enemies and the exact dovetailing, as in "Seniores", combine to heighten the dramatic effect. These pieces, of tragic magnificence, are performed with intensity and integrity, so that a great recording will now ensure that an incomparable treasure of Christian music will be safely preserved for future generations.

Additional recommendation ...

Responsories for Tenebrae. **The Sixteen/Harry Christophers.** Virgin Classics Veritas VC7 59042-2 — ⁘ lh l0m DDD 7/92

Victoria. Missa O quam gloriosum. Motet — O quam gloriosum. Missa Ave maris stella. **Westminster Cathedral Choir/David Hill.** Hyperion CDA66114. Texts and translations included. From A66114 (10/84).

⁘ 57m DDD 6/86

The *Missa O quam gloriosum* is not a work of enormous technical complexity but rather seeks for its effect in measure and poise. The long soaring treble lines have a serenity and restrained intensity that have made it Victoria's most often performed Mass. The Westminster Cathedral Choir sing with a fervour and passion that puts their Anglican colleagues in the shade in this repertoire. The *Missa Ave maris stella* is a more elaborate work with a plainchant melody and the highlight of this rarely performed work must be the beautiful second *Agnus dei*, with divided tenors — gloriously performed by the choir. Recording is first rate.

Further listening ...

Missa O magnum mysterium. Missa Ascendens Christus in altum. *Motets* — O magnum mysterium. Ascendens Christus. **Westminster Cathedral Choir/David Hill.** Hyperion CDA66190 (9/87).

Officium defunctorum. **Westminster Cathedral Choir/David Hill.** Hyperion CDA66250 (9/87).

Officium defunctorum. *Coupled with* ***Lôbo.*** Versa est in luctum. **The Tallis Scholars/Peter Phillips.** Gimell CDGIM012 (9/87).

Louis Vierne

French 1870-1937

Vierne. Triptyque, Op. 58. Pièces en style libre, Op. 31. **Colin Walsh** (org). Priory PRCD319. Played on the organ of Lincoln Minster. Recorded in 1990.

⁘ ② 2h DDD 3/92

Vierne wrote his 24 pieces "in free style" for a specific purpose; to fill the space occupied by the Offertory in the Mass. Of necessity, then, these had to be brief and, as not every church boasted a large pipe organ, they were designed to be played on a harmonium with just a single keyboard. But if this sounds like a menu of aimless miniatures lacking any real interest to the ardent listener, then this two-CD set will come as a bit of a shock. For not only does Vierne respond to these limitations with remarkable creative imagination, but Colin Walsh, always a perceptive and committed interpreter of the French romantic repertoire, brings the full weight of his performing skills to bear, lifting these short pieces way above the level of mere musical fillers and into the realms of true musical poetry. It helps, of course, that he has at his disposal the superb instrument in Lincoln Cathedral which, as the resident organist there, he knows well. He can can find exactly the right sound for each piece, giving a convincing portrayal of its individual character while providing an all-embracing tour around the undeniable charms of this famous Willis organ. Highlights include a sparkling "Carillon", a bustling "Divertissement", a beautifully lyrical "Lied" and, or course, the delightfully innocent "Berceuse" which Vierne dedicated to his young daughter.

Vierne. PIECES DE FANTAISIE — Première Suite, Op. 51; Deuxième Suite, Op. 53; Troisième Suite, Op. 54; Quatrième Suite, Op. 55. **Susan Landale** (org). Adda 581246. Played on the organ of the Abbey Church of Saint Ouen in Rouen.

1h 15m DDD 3/92

Vierne's 24 *pièces de fantaisie* contain some of the most colourful music ever written for the organ. Some, like the atmospheric "Cathédrales", paint vivid musical pictures while others are dazzling showpieces; the best-known being the thrilling "Carillon" based on the Westminster chimes, but there is also an invigorating "Toccata" and a mischievously impish "Impromptu". In a more impressionistic vein there is the haunting "Feux Follets". In all these pieces Vierne takes the organ to new descriptive heights and any successful performance demands a large, resourceful instrument and an organist of exceptional virtuosity. Both have undoubtedly been found here. The Rouen organ is one of the greatest masterpieces of the work of Aristide Cavaillé-Coll while Susan Landale, although Scottish by birth, is now an established figure in Parisian musical life and plays with all the Gallic fervour of a true native. To keep her programme on a single disc (albeit an exceptionally generous 75 minutes long) she plays only 14 of the pieces, but she has chosen with care to provide the perfect balance between pieces of differing moods and character. Adda's atmospheric recording rounds off a most invigorating disc.

Henry Vieuxtemps

Belgian 1820-1881

Suggested listening ...

Violin Concerto No. 5 in A minor, Op. 37. *Coupled with* ***Paganini.*** Violin Concerto No. 1 in D major, Op. 6. **Viktoria Mullova** (vn); **Academy of St Martin in the Fields/Sir Neville Marriner.** Philips 422 332-2PH (10/89).

Heitor Villa-Lobos

Brazilian 1887-1959

Villa-Lobos. Guitar Concerto[a]. Five Preludes[b]. 12 Etudes[c]. **Julian Bream** (gtr); **London Symphony Orchestra/André Previn.** RCA Red Seal RD89813. Items marked [a] and [b] from SB6852 (2/72), [c] RL12499 (12/78).

1h 9m ADD 2/87

This disc illustrates Villa-Lobos's interest in writing for the guitar. Two sets of solo works flank the concerto, a brief (18 minute) and attractive work of spiky syncopation and fleet-fingered solo writing. The piece retains a 'chamber' feel and Villa-Lobos never unleashes the full might of the orchestra, so one rarely feels the naturalness of the balaηce to be strenuously or artificially achieved. Bream's warm tone is nicely caught by the recording. The 12 *Etudes* employ a technical range of quite remarkable variety; the *glissandos* are striking and perfectly executed by Julian Bream. The Preludes are bigger works and seek to portray the variety of Brazilian life in a number of moods.

Additional recommendation ...

Guitar Concerto. ***Rodrigo.*** *Concierto de Aranjuez. Fantasia para un gentilhombre.* **Göran Söllscher** (gtr); **Orpheus Chamber Orchestra.** DG 429 232-2GH — 1h 5m DDD 6/90

Villa-Lobos. Piano Concertos Nos. 1-5. **Cristina Ortiz** (pf); **Royal Philharmonic Orchestra/Miguel Gómez-Martínez.** Decca 430 628-2DH2. Recorded 1989-90.

② 2h 19m DDD 5/92 P S

Villa-Lobos's five piano concertos have been unjustly neglected both in the concert-hall and on disc, but these exceptionally committed performance more than make up for any past oversights.

The Brazilian pianist Cristina Ortiz makes a most convincing case for these most remarkable and unorthodox concertos, with her colourful and exuberantly rhythmic playing catching every ounce of detail and kaleidoscopic nuance. The best way to approach these sometimes unwieldy concertos is to bear in mind Villa-Lobos's somewhat maverick approach to composition in general and simply go with the flow; melodies are frequently long and spun-out and the orchestral accompaniments are often as dense and as complex as Villa-Lobos's beloved Brazilian forests, but for those of an adventurous spirit there are rich rewards to be had from these highly inventive and uniquely beautiful scores. A critic at the first performance of No. 1 remarked that it "appeared to us too complex to judge and understand at one hearing", but of course the luxury of a recording enables the listener to return at leisure and after only a few hearings memorable landmarks begin to emerge, such as the haunting, almost Rachmaninov-like second subject of the first movement. With the exception of the Fifth, which is shorter and more tightly constructed than the rest, the remaining concertos follow broadly similar lines, with the Fourth and Fifth being perhaps the best places to begin an exploration. Miguel Gómez-Martínez and the Royal Philharmonic Orchestra provide excellent support and make light work of the sometimes horrendously difficult orchestral writing. Stunningly recorded — a must for fans of the exotic.

Villa-Lobos. ORCHESTRAL WORKS. **Czecho-Slovak Radio Symphony Orchestra, Bratislava/Roberto Duarte.** Marco Polo 8 223357. Recorded in 1990.
Gênesis — ballet. Erosño (Origem do rio Amazonas). Amazonas — symphonic poem. Dawn in a tropical forest.

lh 2m DDD 3/92

Do not be deterred by the thought of an Eastern European orchestra playing unfamiliar Villa-Lobos. The Czecho-Slovak Radio Orchestra is clearly a very skilled and flexible body, and the conductor Roberto Duarte, a Brazilian authority on Villa-Lobos, has instilled South American colour and rhythmic vitality into his players quite brilliantly. The best of the four works is probably the earliest, *Amazonas*, which was written in 1917. Here, at the age of 30, Villa-Lobos's imagination was extraordinarily fertile, and this early evocation of Brazilian folklore, with its use of unusual instruments and strange orchestral timbres, is remarkably advanced for its date. The short tone poem *Dawn in a tropical forest* is a late work dating from 1953, and this has a more lyrical, more classical style. The remaining two works also come from the last phase in Villa-Lobos's career, and have similar themes. *Gênesis*, written in 1954, is a large-scale symphonic poem and ballet which depicts its enormous subject with all the extravagant colour and use of complex rhythms which were the composer's trademark. *Erosño*, or *The origin of the Amazon*, composed in 1950, is another ambitiously complex work. All four items are captured in faithful, wide-ranging sound.

Villa-Lobos. CHAMBER WORKS. **William Bennett** (fl); [ae]**Neil Black** (ob); [a]**Janice Knight** (cor ang); [aef]**Thea King** (cl); [acf]**Robin O'Neill** (bn); [d]**Charles Tunnell** (vc); [b]**Simon Weinberg** (gtr). Hyperion CDA66295.
Quinteto em forma de chôros[a]. Modinha[b]. Bachianas brasileiras No. 6[c]. Distribuçiño de flôres[b]. Assobio a jato[d]. Chôros No. 2[e]. Cançño do amor[b]. Trio for oboe, clarinet and bassoon[f].

lh lm DDD 9/89 qp

If there is one consistent feature in Villa-Lobos's enormous and diverse output, it is his unpredictability. His restless, supercharged mind never tired of experimenting with new sonorities, and he never felt inhibited, in the course of a work, from following unrelated new impulses. This has the effect of making his music at the same time attractive and disconcerting. The multi-sectional Quintet, the most significant item here, is highly complex but extremely entertaining in its quirky way; and it is played with marvellous neatness, finely judged tonal nuances and high spirits. The rarely heard Trio, the earliest work here, is a particularly spiky atonal piece, typical of its period (1921), depending almost entirely on exuberantly thrusting and counter-thrusting rhythm: it calls for virtuosity, and gets it. The sixth of the *Bachianas brasileiras* (easily the best available recorded performance) is most sensitively shaped, and the second

Chôros, which makes great demands on the two players both individually and in mutual responsiveness, is outstandingly polished. A disc of outstanding artistry.

NEW REVIEW

Villa-Lobos. STRING QUARTETS. **Danubius Quartet** (Judit Tóth, Adél Miklós, vns; Cecilia Bodolai, va; Ilona Wibli, vc). Marco Polo 8 223389/90.
8 223389 — No. 1; No. 8; No. 13. *8 223390* — No. 11; No. 16; No. 17. *8 223391* — No. 4; No. 6; No. 14.

③ lh 4m lh 6m lh 4m DDD 11/92

It's quite astonishing that a musical legacy as rich and varied as Villa-Lobos's 17 string quartets should for so long have been overshadowed. Like the quartets of Beethoven, Bartók and Shostakovich, those of Villa-Lobos span their composer's entire creative career, falling into three distinct categories (again a rough parallel with Beethoven springs to mind): 'early' (Quartets Nos. 1-4), 'middle' (Quartets Nos. 5-6, composed after a gap of some 14 years) and 'middle-late' (Quartets Nos. 7-17). They are ceaselessly inventive in their rhythms, textures, thematic variety and overall design, ranging in structure from the multi-movement 'suite' (Quartet No. 1) to the profound economy of the four-movement Seventeenth Quartet. Throughout the cycle, one is constantly amazed by the sheer beauty of the writing, most especially in the slow movements: the Eighth, for example, features a ravishing *Lento*; the Eleventh, too has at its core the most moving and soulful *Adagio*, music that, once heard, immediately commits itself to memory. And there was certainly no falling off in Villa-Lobos's creative capabilities; his capacity for potent lyrical invention was as marked in 1957 (two years before his death) as it was in 1915, the year in which the First Quartet was composed.

That the quartets incorporate plentiful echoes of Brazilian folk music (most particularly in the faster movements of the later works) is hardly surprising, and there is a frequent and predictable focus on the cello — the composer's own instrument. Villa-Lobos also indulges in a fair amount of busy contrapuntal writing, but it's the sort of terse argument that engages rather than exhausts the imagination, and is in any case offset by a wide-ranging tonal palette. Of the three Marco Polo "Latin-American Classics" volumes so far issued (there will be four in all), the coupling of Quartets Nos. 11, 16 and 17, is perhaps a good place to start. But whichever disc you happen to invest in first is likely to yield immense musical pleasure; after all, it was Villa-Lobos himself who said, "I love to write quartets. One could say that this is a mania." And the superb Danubius Quartet, who are beautifully recorded, translate that mania into music that is both meaningful and memorable.

Villa-Lobos. PIANO WORKS. **Cristina Ortiz.** Decca 417 650-2DH.
Bachianas brasileiras No. 4 (pf version). Guia prático. Poema singélo. Caixinha de música quebrada. Saudades das selvas brasileiras No. 2. As tres Marias. Valsa da dor. Cirandas — No. 4, O cravo brigou com a rosa; No. 14, A canôa virou. Ciclo brasileiro.

lh 7m DDD 12/87

Cristina Ortiz has chosen a programme which sensitively evokes Brazilian life — children's songs, folk-songs, affectionate pictures in music of favourite places, all add up to a rounded musical portrait. The *Bachianas brasileiras* No. 4 is performed complete and Ortiz reveals her Brazilian nationality in the vivid depiction of the araponga, a bird with a call like a hammer on an anvil. The charming *Caixinha de música quebrada* ("The broken little musical box") has a "Ravelian" flavour, and Ortiz plays it with corresponding attention to detail and delicacy of touch. The recording is very fine indeed and provides an excellent introduction to an all too-rarely heard repertoire.

Villa-Lobos. WORKS FOR STRINGS AND VOICE. [a]**Pleeth Cello Octet;** [b]**Jill Gomez** (sop); [c]**Peter Manning** (vn). Hyperion CDA66257. Texts and translations included where appropriate. Recorded in 1987.
 Bachianas brasileiras — No. 1[a]; No. 5[ab]. Suite for voice and violin (1923)[bc]. ***Bach*** (trans. Villa-

Lobos): The Well-tempered Clavier[a] — Prelude in D minor (BWV853); Fugue in B flat major (BWV846); Prelude in G minor (BWV867); Fugue in D major (BWV874).

54m DDD 12/87

Sandwiched between two of the composer's best-known works, the First and Fifth of the *Bachianas brasileiras*, are the Suite for voice and violin and four pieces arranged from Bach's *48*. In the Suite Villa-Lobos allows soprano voice and violin to chase, cavort and imitate with great fluidity and freedom. It is just the sort of piece at which Jill Gomez excels, her feeling for mood and rhythm are ideal and Peter Manning is a spirited partner. The other pieces on the disc employ massed cellos and the Pleeth Cello Octet play with uncommon sympathy. The two *Bachianas* capture a real sense of the music's flavour and the Bach arrangements are fascinating studies in the fusion of identities — a fusion developed and perfected in the *Bachianas* where the forms and ideals of Bach are melded with the wholly Brazilian idioms of Villa-Lobos. A well recorded and most intelligently constructed programme.

Philippe de Vitry

French 1291-1361

Vitry. CHANSONS AND MOTETS. **Sequentia/Benjamin Bagby** (singer, hp) and **Barbara Thornton** (singer). Deutsche Harmonia Mundi RD77095. Notes, texts and translations included. Recorded in 1988.

1h 8m ADD 1/92

This disc is made up of 14 of the motets which modern scholarship has attributed to Vitry, plus five chansons from the famous *Roman de Fauvel* manuscript and two organ intabulations which may also be by the fourteenth-century theorist. It is a fascinating repertoire, and the academic nature of the motets is offset by the more improvisatory style of the chansons. Sequentia appear undaunted by the rhythmic comlexity of this music; but despite the technical prowess the performances are occasionally a touch too fast: it is good to have a sense of the intricate musical phrases as a whole, but sometimes the dissonant sonorities are passed over too quickly and the words swallowed as a result. Still, in the motets they certainly capture the vehement tone of these profound political arguments. By way of contrast, the chansons all deal with the traditional and more accessible theme of courtly love. These link Vitry and his circle with the troubadours; and Patricia Neely's evocative accompaniments suggest an even earlier, Arab-Andalusian influence. Barbara Thornton's voice is well-suited to the song, although her sense of direction and conviction are not always maintained in the long and elaborate *Talant j'ai*. None the less, it is an intelligent and thoughtful collection, and a welcome contribution to this little-known repertoire.

Further listening ...

De Vitry and the Ars Nova. **The Orlando Consort.** Amon Ra CD-SAR49 (10/91).

Antonio Vivaldi

Italian 1678-1741

Vivaldi. CELLO CONCERTOS AND SONATAS. **Christophe Coin** (vc); **Academy of Ancient Music/Christopher Hogwood** (hpd). L'Oiseau-Lyre 433 052-2OH. Recorded in 1990.

Concertos — D minor, RV406; C minor, RV402; G major, RV414. *Sonatas* — A minor, RV44; E flat major, RV39; G minor, RV42.

1h 7m DDD 1/92

With this disc Christophe Coin completes his recording of Vivaldi's nine cello sonatas as well as including three of the composer's cello concertos. Vivaldi wrote rewardingly for the cello as the music on this issue demonstrates. Coin's feeling for dance rhythms, his clear articulation and musical phrasing and his sharp ear for detail bring the pieces alive in an infectious way. He is both firmly and imaginatively supported in the sonatas by a fine continuo group, and in the concertos by the strings of the Academy of Ancient Music. In the sonatas Christopher Hogwood varies the colour of the accompaniments by moving between harpsichord and organ while cello and baroque guitar add further variety and support. In the concertos fast movements are characterized by vigorous, idiomatic passagework for the solo instrument punctuated by pulsating Vivaldian rhythms in the tuttis. In the slow movements, richly endowed with lyricism, the expressive intensity of the music is, on occasion, almost startling, revealing Vivaldi as a composer capable of far greater affective gestures than he is often given credit for. This music was intended to move the spirit, to appeal to the senses, and it seldom, if ever, fails to do so.

Additional recommendations ...

Cello Concertos — B minor, RV424; G minor, RV416; A minor, RV418; F major, RV412; C minor, RV401; G major, RV413. **Christophe Coin** (vc); **Academy of Ancient Music/Christopher Hogwood.** L'Oiseau-Lyre 421 732-2OH — 58m DDD 8/89

Cello Concertos — C minor, RV402; D major, RV403; D minor, RV406; F major, RV412; G major, RV414; A minor, RV422; B minor, RV424. **Ofra Harnoy** (vc); **Toronto Chamber Orchestra/Paul Robinson.** RCA Victor Red Sea RD60155 — lh 13m DDD 4/90

Cello Sonatas — E flat major, RV39; E minor, RV40; F major, RV41; G minor, RV42; A minor, RV43; A minor, RV44; B flat major, RV45-RV47. **Anthony Pleeth, Suki Towb** (vcs); **Robert Woolley.** (hpd/org). ASV Gaudeamus CDGAD201 — ② 2h 3m DDD 11/91

NEW REVIEW

Vivaldi. CONCERTOS. [a]**Stephen Marvin,** [b]**Chantal Rémillard,** [c]**Cynthia Roberts** (vns); [d]**Anner Bylsma,** [e]**Christina Mahler** (vcs); **Tafelmusik/Jeanne Lamon** ([f]vn). Sony Vivarte SK48044. Recorded in 1990.

Concertos for cello and strings[d] — G major, RV413; A minor, RV418. Concerto for violin, cello and strings in B flat major, RV547[df]. Concerto for two violins, two cellos and strings in G major, RV575[adef]. Concerto for four violins and strings in D minor, RV549[abcf]. Concertos for strings — C major, RV117; E minor, RV134; F minor, RV143; A major, RV159.

lh 6m DDD 9/92 

The Canadian period-instrument group Tafelmusik has been building up an impressive discography of music ranging from Corelli to Mozart. Here the players address themselves to Vivaldi in a first-rate recording of concertos for various combinations of strings. Though Vivaldi himself was a violinist he wrote for almost every other instrument of his day with informed skill. One of those to benefit was the cello which features as a solo instrument to a greater or lesser extent in five of the concertos in this programme. The soloist is the Dutch virtuoso Anner Bylsma whose animated playing generates a feeling of excitement and spontaneity by no means easily captured on disc. If he has a fault then it is that he is too often attracted by breakneck tempos and it is that which detracts from the opening movement of the G major Concerto (RV413). Apart from that one minor criticism the disc is one to be treasured not only for the excellence of the playing but also for the judicious choice of repertory. The Concerto in G major for two violins, two cellos and strings (RV575) is a beautifully crafted work with notably expressive writing for the solo instruments. The four concertos for ripieno strings, in which Vivaldi foreshadows the early classical symphonists, provide a rewarding contrast with the remaining programme and are played here with accomplishment and affection.

Vivaldi. FLUTE CONCERTOS. **Orchestra of the Eighteenth Century/Frans Brüggen** (fl/rec). RCA Red Seal Seon RD70951. From RL30392 (4/82).

Flute Concertos — G major, RV435; F major, RV442. *Chamber Concertos* — F major, RV98, "La tempesta di mare"; G minor, RV104, "La notte"; D major, RV90, "Il gardellino"; G major, RV101.

53m DDD 2/87 

Frans Brüggen is well known as a virtuoso recorder player and appears as both soloist and director in these notably imaginative performances of Vivaldi's music. He listens to every nuance of inflexion and unfailingly capitalizes on the rich sonorities provided by Vivaldi's carefully chosen instrumental combinations. What too often sounds routine in the composer's tuttis is here transformed into elegant and bold gestures, with a lively feeling for caricature. Brüggen's own playing reaches a pinnacle in the set of variations which conclude the Sixth Concerto and which he dispatches with dazzling virtuosity. The recording is admirably clear, picking up every detail of baroque bassoon mechanism!

NEW REVIEW

Vivaldi. OBOE CONCERTOS. **Douglas Boyd** (ob); [a]**Marieke Blankestijn** (vn); **Chamber Orchestra of Europe.** DG 435 873-2GH. Recorded in 1991.

Oboe Concertos — C major, RV447; C major, RV450; D major, RV453; A minor, RV461; A minor, RV463. Concerto for Violin and Oboe in B flat major, RV548.

59m DDD 5/93

As well as being an inspired composer for his own instrument — the violin — Vivaldi could equally turn his hand to concertos for a great many other instruments. One of the principal beneficiaries of his skill was the oboe, for which he wrote 17 solo concertos, three for two oboes and another for oboe and violin. In this virtuoso programme the oboist, Douglas Boyd, has chosen five of the solo oboe concertos together with the more modestly conceived but no less captivating Concerto in B flat for oboe and violin. The oboe concertos have been selected discerningly, not only for their musical interest but also, it would seem, with an eye to their rarity value on the concert platform. Boyd, playing a modern oboe, gives fluent, sensitively shaped performances and is supported in a lively manner by the strings of the Chamber Orchestra of Europe. Boyd is expressive in slow movements — they almost invariably possess considerable lyrical appeal — and athletic in faster ones; and he needs to be, for Vivaldi seldom showed mercy on his soloists. From among the many beautiful movements here the *Larghetto* of the Concerto in A minor (RV461) stands out and may be ranked among Vivaldi's happiest creations for the oboe. Fine recorded sound.

Vivaldi. 12 Violin Concertos, Op. 4, "La stravaganza". **Monica Huggett** (vn); **Academy of Ancient Music/Christopher Hogwood.** L'Oiseau-Lyre Florilegium 417 502-2OH2.

② lh 4lm DDD 3/87

In *La stravaganza* Vivaldi makes a further decisive step towards the virtuoso solo violin concerto and though the quality of the music is a little uneven, the set nevertheless contains several movements of outstanding beauty. From among them we might single out the *Grave* of the Concerto No. 4 in A minor whose suspensions, chromaticisms and lyrical solo violin part cast a spell of almost fairy-tale enchantment, and the *Largo* of the Concerto No. 12 in G major with its ostinato bass above which a simple but haunting melody is treated to a series of variations. Monica Huggett gives a lively, inspired account of the music. Her warm tone, well-nigh impeccable intonation, sensitive dynamic shading and sheer virtuosity lead us to the heart of these pieces in a seemingly effortless fashion. There is a rich vein of fantasy coursing through *La stravaganza* and this is vividly realized in her communicative playing. The small string forces provide sympathetic support and Christopher Hogwood generates an enthusiastic atmosphere with well-judged tempos and tautly sustained rhythms.

Additional recommendation ...

Felix Ayo (vn); I Musici. Philips 426 935-2PM2 — ADD 7/91

Academy of St Martin in the Fields/Sir Neville Marriner. Decca Serenata 430 566-2DM2 — ② lh 50m ADD 2/92

Vivaldi. Violin Concertos, Op. 8 Nos. 1-4, "The Four Seasons" (Manchester version). Concerto for Violin in C major, RV171. Concerto in B flat major for strings, RV163, "Conca". **L'Europa Galante/Fabio Biondi** (vn). Opus 111 OPS56-9120. Recorded in 1991.

54m DDD 4/92 

Although, understandably, almost all recordings of Vivaldi's *Four Seasons* follow modern editions based on that published in the composer's lifetime, a set of parts preserved in Manchester

Central Library provides us with a more faithful account of Vivaldi's intentions. These manuscript parts apparently once belonged to Corelli's influential patron, Cardinal Ottoboni, and probably predate the printed version (1725). This lively performance by L'Europa Galante follows the Manchester version. The soloist/director, Fabio Biondi is an accomplished violinist well able to cope with Vivaldi's supple and athletic writing. He has an intuitive feeling for affective ornamentation and his supportive ensemble complement his engagingly impressionistic view of the music with a highly developed sense of fantasy. Collectors already plentifully supplied with these perennial favourites should be attracted by two further concertos in the programme which are far less often heard. One of them, in C major (RV171), dedicated to the Hapsburg Emperor Charles V, probably appears for the first time on disc. The other (RV163) is intriguingly subtitled *Conca*, a reference it would seem to a primitive instrument made from a conch shell.

Additional recommendations ...

Op. 8 Nos. 1-12. Concerto for Flute in D major, RV429. Concerto for Cello in B minor, RV424. **Stephen Preston** (fl); **Simon Standage** (vn); **Anthony Pleeth** (vc); **The English Concert/Trevor Pinnock.** CRD CRD3348/9 — ② 2h 34m ADD 8/88 Ⓑ

Op. 8 Nos. 1-12. **Felix Ayo** (vn); **I Musici.** Philips 426 943-2PM2 — ② ADD 7/91 Ⓑ

NEW REVIEW

Vivaldi. 12 Violin Concertos, Op. 9,"La cetra". **Simon Standage** (vn); **Academy of Ancient Music/Christopher Hogwood** (hpd). L'Oiseau-Lyre 421 366-2OH2. Recorded in 1987.

② lh 50m DDD 4/89

La cetra ("The lyre"), published in 1727, was Vivaldi's last great set of printed concertos. All but one of the 12 concertos are for solo violin, the odd one out being the ninth in the set which is scored for two violins; in this work Simon Standage, the soloist in each of the remaining concertos of the set, is partnered by Catherine Mackintosh. Two others, in A major (RV348) and B minor (RV391) require 'scordatura' or retuning of the solo violin. These are satisfying concertos, less obviously innovative than some of those in Vivaldi's earlier sets, but none the less containing a rich diversity of ideas and collectively representative of the composer's mature style. Christopher Hogwood has a refreshingly robust approach to the music, evident not only in his choice of lively tempos, but in the crisp, brightly articulated sound of the Academy of Ancient Music and in the imaginatively realized continuo, this last a feature of almost all Hogwood's recordings. Standage's tone quality matches that of the ripieno strings and his playing has something of that demonic virtuosity which we might imagine Vivaldi himself to have possessed. There is an infectious vitality in this playing which is very exciting. Intonation is not always impeccable nor is the playing invariably as refined as one would like. But the virtues easily outweigh the shortcomings and few will be other than captivated by the sort of performance qualities present in the finale of the Sixth Concerto (RV348), for instance. There is, in short, nothing of the routine or the world-weary in this recording.

Additional recommendations ...

Felix Ayo (vn); **I Musici.** Philips 426 946-2PM2 — ② ADD 7/91

I Solisti Italiani. Denon CO-79475/6 — ② lh 56m DDD 9/92

Vivaldi. L'estro Armonico, Op. 3. **Academy of Ancient Music/ Christopher Hogwood.** L'Oiseau-Lyre Florilegium 414 554-2OH2. From D245D2 (12/81).

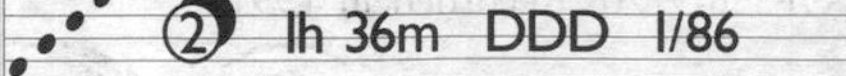

This set of Concertos is arranged as a display of variety, and ordered in a kaleidoscopic way that would maintain interest were it to be played in its entirety. These works are often played with an inflated body of *ripieno* (orchestral) strings, but in this recording they are played as Vivaldi intended them; only four violins are used. The contrast does not come from antiphony or weight of numbers but is provided through the *tutti* versus episodic passages. One could not assemble a more distinguished 'cast' than that of the AAM in this recording, showing clearly just why this music is best played on period instruments, by specialists in baroque style, who are not afraid to add a little embellishment here and there. Neither the enchanting performances nor the quality of their recording could be better; this is required listening.

Additional recommendations ...
Roberto Michelucci (vn); **I Musici.** Philips 426 932-2PM2 — ② ADD 7/91
Solisti Italiani. Denon CO-72719/20 — ② 1h 49m DDD 8/89
Academy of St Martin in the Fields/Sir Neville Marriner. Decca Serenata 430 557-2DM2 — ② 1h 42m ADD 2/92 £

NEW REVIEW

Vivaldi. DOUBLE CONCERTOS. **Collegium Musicum 90/Simon Standage** (vn). Chandos Chaconne CHAN0528. Recorded in 1991.
Concertos for two violins and strings — C major, RV505; D major, RV511; A minor, RV523 (Micaela Comberti, vn). Concerto for two cellos and strings in G minor, RV531 (Jane Coe, David Watkin, vcs). Concerto for two oboes and strings in D minor, RV535 (Anthony Robson, Catherine Latham, obs). Concerto for two violins, oboe and strings in C major, RV554.

1h 5m DDD 3/93

It was natural, with so many talented young ladies available at the Pietà, that Vivaldi should have written a large number of concertos with two or more soloists. More than two dozen are for two violins and most remain unrecorded; RV505 and 511 are both mature works, the former leaning toward *galant* style and the latter 'unified' by elements that are common to its outer movements. RV554, originally a triple concerto for violin, oboe and organ, was rewritten by Vivaldi for oboe and two violins, in which latter form it is given in this recording. The Concerto for two oboes, RV535, is 'Corellian' in its four-movement *da chiesa* form and in its 'conversations' between the soloists and the *ripieno* strings — a Vivaldian rarity. If Vivaldi wrote a more eloquently pathetic melody than that of the *Largo* of the Double Cello Concerto, RV531, it is hard to bring it to mind; it is an early work — why did he never return to that most rewarding of media? Collegium Musicum 90 field a modest string band, which adds leanness of sound to their other virtues of stylishness and crispness of ensemble. Excellent oboe soloists contribute to the allure of this recording.

Vivaldi. CONCERTOS — ALLA RUSTICA. **The English Concert/Trevor Pinnock.** Archiv Produktion 415 674-2AH.
G major, RV151, "Alla rustica"; B flat major for violin and oboe, RV548 (with Simon Standage, vn; David Reichenberg, ob); G major for two violins, RV516 (Standage, Elizabeth Wilcock, vns); A minor for oboe, RV461 (Reichenberg); G major for two mandolins, RV532 (James Tyler, Robin Jeffrey, mndls); C major, RV558 (Standage, Micaela Comberti, vns "in tromba"; Philip Pickett, Rachel Beckett, recs; Colin Lawson, Carlos Reoira, chalumeaux; Tyler, Jeffrey, mndls; Nigel North, Jakob Lindberg, theorbos; Anthony Pleeth, vc).

53m DDD 9/86

The *Concerto con molti stromenti*, RV558, calls for a plethora of exotic instruments and Vivaldi's inventiveness, everywhere apparent, seems to know no bounds. The vigorous melodies have splendid verve whilst the slow movements are no less exciting. The concertos, which employ plucked instruments, are particularly entrancing to the ear — here is virtuosity indeed, with Pinnock sensibly opting for an organ continuo to emphasize the difference between the plucked strings and the bowed. The Double Mandolin Concerto, RV532, is beautifully played with a real build-up of tension in the tuttis. The playing of The English Concert is affectionate and rhythmically precise and the recording is good with the gentler sounding instruments well brought out of the fuller textures.

Vivaldi. STRING CONCERTOS. **I Musici.** Philips 422 212-2PH. Recorded 1986-87.
D major for two violins and two cellos, RV564; G minor for two cellos, RV531; C major for violin and two cellos, RV561; F major for three violins, RV551; F major for violin and cello, RV544; F major for violin and organ, RV542.

lh lm DDD 5/89

Many of Vivaldi's concertos deploy two or more string soloists and there are some very attractive examples of them in this recording. To his endlessly resourceful treatment of *ritornello* form in the quicker movements, Vivaldi adds further variety by ringing the changes on his solo forces — the number of violins and/or cellos, which may converse with one another or play in concert. In RV542 the solo honours are shared between violin and organ and some delightful sonorities result, whilst RV531, the only two-cello concerto in Vivaldi's *oeuvre*, contains a lovely *Adagio* in which the soloists speak to one another tenderly. I Musici are renowned for their enthusiasm and love of tonal opulence and this recording is also a fine example of the proper use of modern instruments. Clarity of texture is a *sine qua non* and it is provided by both players and recordists in this very fine issue.

Vivaldi. STRING CONCERTOS. [a]**Adrian Chamorro** (vn); [b]**Maurizio Naddeo** (vc); **L'Europa Galante/Fabio Biondi** (vn). Opus 3 OPS309004. Recorded in 1990.
C minor, RV761; D minor, RV129, "Concerto madrigalesco"; G minor, RV517[a]; B flat major, RV547[b]; C minor, RV202; E flat major, RV130, "Sonata al santo sepolcro". Sinfonia in B minor, RV169, "Sinfonia al santo sepolcro".

52m DDD 9/91 

This invigorating programme contains well-known and less well-known concertos by Vivaldi. The performances sparkle with life and possess an irresistible spontaneity. The Concertos for one and two violins (RV761 and RV202) are comparative rarities and are played with agility and insight by the soloist director Fabio Biondi and his alert and responsive ensemble. Biondi himself is capable of light and articulate bowing and has a natural feeling for graceful turns of phrase. Vivaldi's virtuoso writing occasionally finds chinks in his armour but with enlightened music-making of this order it matters little. Everywhere Vivaldi's infectious rhythms are tautly controlled and the music interpreted with character and conviction. Perhaps the highlight of the disc is the Concerto in B flat for violin and cello. Outer movements are crisply articulated and played with almost startling energy while the poignant lyricism of the *Andante* is touchingly captured. A refreshing and illuminating disc whose imaginative and passionate interpretations have few rivals in the catalogue. The recorded sound is clear and ideally resonant.

Vivaldi. CELLO SONATAS. **Anner Bylsma** (vc); **Jacques Ogg** (hpd); **Hideimi Suzuki** (cont). Deutsche Harmonia Mundi RD77909.
E flat major, RV39; E minor, RV40; F major, RV41; G minor, RV42; A minor, RV43; A minor, RV44.

lh 2m DDD 6/90 

Nine cello sonatas by Vivaldi have survived and in this virtuoso recital Anner Bylsma plays six of them. Vivaldi wrote as expressively for the cello as for his own instrument, the violin, and Bylsma's interpretations are variously endowed with fire and melancholy. He brings gesture to the music, sometimes in the manner of a caricaturist, at others with nobler, grander statements. Tempos are occasionally a little hard driven and technically demanding passages consquently accident prone, but at all times Bylsma sounds passionately involved in the music, giving performances which seem refreshingly far away from the specialized disciplines of the recording studio. Bylsma's choice of sonatas is attractive, though, since none of the nine works are in any sense of the word dull, sacrifices have had to be made. It is regrettable perhaps that neither of the B flat Sonatas is included, but the best known and perhaps finest of all, in E minor, is played with lyricism and a fine sense of poetry. Here and in the G minor Sonata Vivaldi reached considerable expressive heights and if only for these two works Bylsma's performances are to be treasured. Fine recorded sound but the documentation, especially where catalogue numbers are concerned, is slipshod and unhelpful.

NEW REVIEW

Vivaldi. VIOLIN SONATAS. **Fabio Biondi** (vn); **Maurizio Naddeo** (vc); **Paolo Pandolfo** (db); **Rolf Lislevand** (theorbo/bar gtr); **Rinaldo Alessandrini** (hpd). Arcana A4/5. Recorded in 1991.

No. 1 in C major, RV3; No. 2 in D minor, RV12; No. 3 in G minor, RV757; No. 4 in D major, RV755; No. 5 in B flat major, RV759; No. 6 in A major, RV758; No. 7 in C minor, RV6; No. 8 in G major, RV22; No. 9 in E minor, RV17*a*; No. 10 in B minor, RV760; No. 11 in E flat major, RV756; No. 12 in C major, RV754.

② 2h 37m DDD 11/92

Vivaldi is so well-known for his concertos that we are apt to overlook his admittedly much smaller output of sonatas. This set of 12 for violin and continuo was discovered in Manchester's Central Music Library during the 1970s though five of them exist in versions which have been known for much longer. It is probable that all of them date from the early- to mid-1720s when Vivaldi assembled them to present to Cardinal Ottoboni on the occasion of his visit to Venice, the city of his birth, in 1726. The soloist, Fabio Biondi, is a sensitive interpreter of Vivaldi's music with a lively feeling for its poetry and expressive potential. Lapses of good intonation are small and infrequent enough to matter little when so much else is maintained at such an imaginative level of executancy. Biondi is furthermore supported by an excellent continuo team whose variety of instrumental colour greatly enhances performances which are both stylish and affectionate. This is, in other words, no stuffy exercise in "getting it right" but eloquent, passionate playing full of Latin temperament. Only the recorded sound fails to please with its hollow, boxy acoustic. But the ear soon adjusts to it and that is just as well, for the performances and the music are well worth becoming acquainted with.

NEW REVIEW

Vivaldi. CONCERTOS AND CANTATAS. [a]**Catherine Bott** (sop); **Tom Finucane** ([b]mand/[c]lte); **New London Consort/Philip Pickett** ([d]rec). L'Oiseau-Lyre 433 198-2OH. Texts and translations included. Recorded 1989-90.

All'ombra di sospetto, RV678[a]. Lungi dal vago volto, RV680[a]. Vengo a voi, luci adorate, RV682[a]. Concerto for two mandolins and strings in G major, RV532[b]. Chamber Concerto for lute, two violins and continuo in D major, RV93[c]. Chamber Concerto for recorder, two violins and continuo in A minor, RV108[d]. Concertos, Op. 10 — No. 3 in G minor, RV439, "La notte".

1h 13m DDD 1/93

This disc is a welcome incursion to one of the least explored areas of Vivaldi's music — the chamber cantata. As well as three cantatas the programme includes four well contrasted concertos by Vivaldi who was, of course, one of the greatest masters of the form. Catherine Bott gives sparkling performances. Her clear, well-focused voice and secure technique are a constant pleasure as is the intelligence with which she draws together text and music. This is indeed singing to enchant the ear and beguile the senses and all the more so when it is supported by sympathetic and stylish accompaniments. Continuo lines are imaginatively realized and there are attractive obbligatos for both recorder and violin. The concertos with which the cantatas are interspersed are among Vivaldi's more modestly conceived. Two of them feature plucked string instruments, a lute (RV93) and two mandolins (RV532). Thanks to the wonders of modern recording Tom Finucane takes both mandolin parts, playing with sprightly zeal and an ear for detail; and he gives an affecting performance of the wistfully alluring *Largo* of the Lute Concerto. Philip Pickett is the solo recorder player in the remaining concertos, giving performances which are fluent and full of vitality.

Vivaldi. VOCAL AND ORCHESTRAL WORKS. [a]**Emma Kirkby,** [b]**Suzette Leblanc,** [b]**Danièle Forget** (sops); [b]**Richard Cunningham** (alto); [a]**Henry Ingram** (ten); **Tafelmusik** [a]**Chamber Choir and Baroque Orchestra/Jean Lamon** ([c]vn). Hyperion CDA66247. Texts and translations included where appropriate.

In turbato mare irato, RV627[a]. Concertos — D minor, "Concerto madrigalesco", RV129; G minor, RV157; G major, "Concerto alla rustica", RV151. Lungi dal vago volto, RV680[ac]. Magnificat, RV610[ab].

57m DDD 12/87 

This thoughtfully and effectively chosen programme deserves the attention of all baroque music enthusiasts. The approach of the Tafelmusik Baroque Orchestra, playing period instruments, is both stylish and sympathetic. They are joined by Emma Kirkby who sings two of Vivaldi's little-known chamber cantatas with precision, warmth of sentiment and dazzling virtuosity. These performances are the high spots of the programme but few listeners will be disappointed with the lively account of three of Vivaldi's little concertos for strings; one of them, the *Concerto alla rustica*, is particularly enchanting. The remaining item, the Magnificat, is an effective work scored for divided choir with an orchestra of strings and oboes, although sadly the oboes have been omitted. The choral singing is firm and the disc as a whole is appealing and well recorded.

Vivaldi. SACRED CHORAL WORKS, Volume 1. [abcd]**Margaret Marshall,** [d]**Felicity Lott** (sops); [bc]**Anne Collins** (mez); [b]**Birgit Finnilä** (contr); **John Alldis Choir; English Chamber Orchestra/Vittorio Negri.** Philips 420 648-2PH. Texts and translations included. Items marked [a], [b] and [e] from 6769 032 (12/79), [c] 6768 016 (12/78), [d] 6768 149 (9/80). Recorded 1976-79.

Introduzione al Gloria — Ostro picta in D major, RV642[a] (ed. Giegling). Gloria in D major, RV589[b] (ed. Negri). Lauda Jerusalem in E minor, RV609[c]. Laudate pueri Dominum in A major, RV602[d] (ed. Giegling). Laudate Dominum in D minor, RV606[e] (ed. Giegling).

lh 6m ADD 5/88

Vivaldi. SACRED CHORAL WORKS, Volume 2. **Margaret Marshall,** [cd]**Felicity Lott,** [c]**Sally Burgess** (sops); [b]**Ann Murray,** [d]**Susan Daniel** (mezs); [c]**Linda Finnie,** [bc]**Anne Collins** (contrs); [b]**Anthony Rolfe Johnson** (ten); [b]**Robert Holl** (bass); [bcd]**John Alldis Choir; English Chamber Orchestra/Vittorio Negri.** Philips 420 649-2PM. Texts and translations included. Items marked [a] and [b] from 6768 016 (12/78), [c] and [d] 6769 046 (12/80). Recorded 1976-79.

Introduzione al Dixit, RV636. Dixit Dominus, RV594. Magnificat, RV611. Beatus vir, RV598.

lh 7m ADD 2/89

A lively performance of the better-known of Vivaldi's two settings of the *Gloria* as well as several other less familiar items are included in these two volumes. One of the most captivating works is a setting for double choir and soloist of the psalm, *Laudate pueri*, RV602. No lover of Vivaldi's music should overlook this radiant piece which is beautifully sung and vividly recorded. Negri's direction is lively and his evident affection for Vivaldi's music seems to have fired the enthusiasm of all concerned, prompting firm and responsive support from both choir and orchestra. Margaret Marshall, who is outstanding in her solos, and Felicity Lott are well matched in their duets and the timbre of their voices is suited both to the repertoire and to the style of the performances. Recorded sound is excellent and full Latin texts with translations are included in the booklet.

NEW REVIEW

Vivaldi. Domine ad adiuvandum me festiana, RV593. Beatus vir, RV597. Stabat mater, RV621. Magnificat, RV610. **Ex Cathedra Chamber Choir and Baroque Orchestra/Jeffrey Skidmore.** Ecce EXCCD001. Texts and translations included. Recorded in 1991.

lh 10m DDD 12/92

This is an interesting and mainly successful attempt to place a handful of Vivaldi's sacred pieces in a liturgical context. The well-known work here is the *Stabat mater* for alto voice and strings, but the others deserve to be heard more often than they are. Ex Cathedra Chamber Choir is a well-disciplined, youthful sounding ensemble whose contribution to the recording is first-rate.

And it is from the choir that solo voices emerge as required, giving the performances an homogeneity of sound and intent. The instrumentalists, too, make a strong contribution and together with the voices project interpretations which are full of vitality. There are, of course, rival versions on disc of all the music sung here (see below and other reviews in this section) but, on the strength of the thoughtful way it has been presented by the director of Ex Cathedra, Geoffrey Skidmore, this is perhaps the most affecting of them. Few will be disappointed, for example, by the gently inflected, poignant account of the *Stabat mater* by the male alto Nigel Short. Hardly a detail has been overlooked, even to the extent of allowing the listener to hear a distant bell during the opening Versicle. In short, only the painfully and unnecessarily small typeface of the accompanying texts fails to please.

Additional recommendations ...

Vestro Principi divino, RV633. Stabat mater. Filiae mestae, RV638. Nisi Dominus, RV608. **Gérard Lesne** (alto); **Il Seminario Musicale Ensemble.** Harmonic H/CD8720 — ⁘ 58m DDD 3/91

Laudate pueri Dominum, RV600[a]*. Stabat mater*[b]*. Deus tuorum militum, RV612*[c]*. Sanctorum meritis, RV620*[d]. [ad]**Margaret Marshall** (sop); [bc]**Jochen Kowalski** (alto); [ad]**Jacques Ogg** (org); **Concertgebouw Chamber Orchestra/Vittorio Negri.** Philips 432 091-2PH — ⁘ 49m DDD 2/92

Vivaldi. Juditha Triumphans, RV645. **Elly Ameling** (sop); **Birgit Finnilä, Annelies Burmeister, Ingeborg Springer** (mezs); **Júlia Hamari** (contr); **Berlin Radio Ensemble; Berlin Chamber Orchestra/Vittorio Negri.** Philips 426 955-2PM2. Text and translations included. From 6747 173 (10/75). Recorded in 1974.

⁘ ② 2h 33m ADD 4/92

This recording of Vivaldi's only surviving oratorio, *Juditha Triumphans,* was made in 1974 and though various new recordings have appeared since then none have surpassed it. Vittorio Negri fields an orchestra of modern instruments, and a very good one it is too. The obbligato playing is first-rate although an over-ornate harpsichord continuo gives the performance a dated aspect. The soloists are excellent for the most part with Birgit Finnilä in the title role. Her "Quanto magis generosa" with viola d'amore, and the memorable "Veni, veni, me sequere fide" with an obbligato chalumeau are particularly affecting. Júlia Hamari brings a lively sense of theatre to her portrayal of the warrior, Holofernes, and his servant Vagaus is agilely sung by the soprano, Elly Ameling. Judith's servant, Abra, is portrayed with clarity and conviction by Ingeborg Springer. No male voice soloists here, since Vivaldi wrote the oratorio for the musically gifted girls of the Pietà orphanage in Venice where he worked on and off for most of his life. Negri brings as much drama to the piece as music and text will allow and the results are by-and-large rewarding. Full texts are included and the recorded sound is excellent.

Additional recommendation ...

Soloists; Savaria Vocal Ensemble; Capella Savaria/Nicholas McGegan. Hungaroton HCD31063/4 — ⁘ ② 2h 4m DDD 4/91

Further listening ...

CONCERTI DA CAMERA, Volumes 2-4:

C major, RV87; C major, RV88; D major, RV95, "La pastorella"; F major, RV100; G minor, RV103. Trio Sonata in D minor, RV63. **Il Giardino Armonico.** Teldec Das Alte Werk 9031-73268-2.

D major, RV91; D major, RV93; D major, RV94; F major, RV97; G minor, RV106. Trio Sonata in A minor, RV86. **Il Giardino Armonico.** Teldec Das Alte Werk 9031-73269-2.

D major, RV92; F major, RV99; A minor, RV108; G minor, RV105; G minor, RV107. Sonata for Oboe and Continuo in C minor, RV53. **Il Giardino Armonico.** Teldec Das Alte Werk 9031-74727-2.

Kevin Volans

South African 1949-

Volans. White man sleeps (1982[d] and 1986[a] versions). Mbira[b]. She who sleeps with a small blanket[c]. [bd]**Kevin Volans,** [b]**Deborah James,** [d]**Robert Hill** (hpds); [d]**Margriet Tindemans** (va da gamba); [bcd]**Robyn Schulkowsky** (perc); [a]**Smith Quartet** (Steven Smith, Clive Hughes, vns; Nic Pendelebury, va; Sophie Harris, vc). Landor Barcelona CTLCD111. Item marked [c] recorded at a performance in Belfast in April 1989.

lh 12m AAD 10/91 

There's a distinct whiff here of the Third World. Keith Volans is South African by origin, and his scores pay homage to black musical culture in a manner that is fresh and wholly unpatronizing. In *Mbira* and the original version of *White man sleeps*, for example, instruments are tuned to intervals variously wider or narrower than those of normal Western scales, and their slippery rhythms obliquely evoke dance and ceremonial ritual. The music has an evasive tunefulness about it: not tunes that you can actually hum, but rather ones that tread and retread familiar ground, never quite going anywhere or settling into a final cadence. Comparisons with American minimalism soon break down. True, Volans's music relies on harmoniousness and regular rhythmic patter, but there's nothing here of the endless cellular repetitiveness of a Philip Glass or a Steve Reich. Above all this is a supremely happy disc, and the performances are wholly in sympathy with the spirit of the music. Altogether a stunning CD, and warmly recommended.

Johann Wagenaar

Dutch 1862-1941

Suggested listening ...

Overtures — The Taming of the Shrew, Op. 25; Twelfth Night, Op. 36; Le Cid, Op. 27; Amphitrion, Op. 45; Cyrano de Bergerac, Op. 23. Saul and David — symphonic poem, Op. 24. Wiener Dreivierteltakt — waltz cycle, Op. 38. **Royal Concertgebouw Orchestra/Riccard Chailly.** Decca 425 833-2DH (6/91).

Richard Wagner

German 1813-1883

Wagner. ORCHESTRAL WORKS. **Philharmonia Orchestra/Yuri Simonov.** Collins Classics 1207-2.
GOTTERDAMMERUNG — Siegfried's Rhine Journey; Siegfried's Funeral March. PARSIFAL — Prelude, Act 1. SIEGFRIED — Forest Murmurs. TRISTAN UND ISOLDE — Prelude and Liebestod. DIE WALKURE — Ride of the Valkyries.

lh 8m DDD 10/91 

"The old poisoner" Debussy called him. Be it the dragon's blood, a love potion or sacrament from the Holy Grail, for those who prefer it administered in short, concentrated doses, this disc is an obvious choice. If there exists a more forceful paean of brass and timpani as Siegfried and Brünnhilde emerge to greet daybreak before the Rhine journey, it has yet to be heard. Yet this is no mere sonic spectacular: every phrase is lovingly turned and shaded, and the expression in each extract is finely attuned to its dramatic context: The brass intone the "Faith" motive from *Parsifal* with dignity and restraint, and while the playing at the climax of Isolde's Liebestod lacks nothing in passion, Simonov shows respect for Wagner's single *forte* marking. This is also one of the most coherent Wagner sounds on disc, offering separation of textures, a telling projection of the lower orchestral voices, and a real sense of space. You hear the pedal notes that evoke the stillness of the forest, you feel its depths, you rejoice with Siegfried at its natural wonders, and you understand why Debussy (despite his protestations) could never entirely cleanse himself of Wagner's influence.

Wagner. TANNHAUSER — Overture. Siegfried Idyll. TRISTAN UND ISOLDE — Prelude and Liebestod[a]. [a]**Jessye Norman** (sop); **Vienna Philharmonic Orchestra/Herbert von Karajan.** DG 423 613-2GH. Text and translation included. Recorded live in 1987.

54m DDD 8/88 

For the Wagner specialist who has a complete *Tannhäuser* and *Tristan* on the shelves, this disc involves some duplication. Even so, it is not hard to make room for such performances as are heard here. For the non-specialist, the programme provides a good opportunity for a meeting halfway, the common ground between Master and general music-lover being the *Siegfried Idyll*. This offers 20 minutes of delight in the play of musical ideas, structured and yet impulsive, within a sustained mood of gentle affection. The orchestration is something of a miracle, and it can rarely have been heard to better advantage than in this recording, where the ever-changing textures are so clearly displayed and where from every section of the orchestra the sound is of such great loveliness. It comes as a welcome contrast to the *Tannhäuser* Overture, with its big tunes and *fortissimos*, the whole orchestra surging in a frank simulation of physical passion. A further contrast is to follow in the *Tristan* Prelude, where again Karajan and his players are at their best in their feeling for texture and their control of pulse. Jessye Norman, singing the *Liebestod* with tenderness and vibrant opulence of tone, brings the recital to an end. There is scarcely a single reminder that it was recorded live.

Additional recommendations ...

Siegfried Idyll. ***Bruckner.*** *Symphony No. 8 in C minor.* **Royal Concertgebouw Orchestra/Bernard Haitink.** Philips 412 465-2PH2 — ② 1h 44m DDD 7/86 B

Siegfried Idyll. LOHENGRIN — Prelude, Act 1; Prelude, Act 3. DIE MEISTERSINGER VON NURNBERG — Prelude, Act 1. DIE WALKURE — Ride of the Valkyries; Wotan's Farewell and Magic Fire Music[a]. [a]**John Tomlinson** (bass); **Philharmonia Orchestra/Francesco d'Avalos.** ASV CDDCA666 — 1h 4m DDD 3/90 B

Siegfried Idyll. ***Dvořák.*** *Serenade for strings in E major, B52. Romance in F minor, B39*[a]. **Scottish Chamber Orchestra/Jaime Laredo** ([a]vn). Pickwick IMP Classics PCD928 — 1h 4m DDD 4/90 £ B

DER FLIEGENDE HOLLANDER — Overture. LOHENGRIN — Prelude, Act 1. DIE MEISTERSINGER VON NURNBERG — Prelude, Act 1. TANNHAUSER — Overture and Venusberg Music. TRISTAN UND ISOLDE — Prelude und Liebestod. **Berlin Philharmonic Orchestra/Seiji Ozawa.** Philips 426 271-2PH — 1h 6m DDD 4/91 B

Wagner. OPERA CHORUSES. **Bayreuth Festival Chorus and Orchestra/Wilhelm Pitz.** DG Privilege 429 169-2GR. From SLPM136006 (5/59).
Der fliegende Holländer. Tannhäuser. Lohengrin. Die Meistersinger von Nürnberg. Götterdämmerung. Parsifal.

53m ADD 4/90 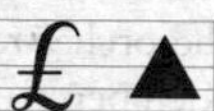

Most of the favourites are here: Spinning Chorus, Wedding Chorus, pilgrims, sailors, vassals, the good folk of Nuremberg, knights of the Grail and boys up in the cupola. There is nothing from *Tristan und Isolde* but one might have expected the hearty Communion chorus from *Parsifal*. As it is, there is much to enjoy as a way of renewing appetite for the operas themselves, and perhaps in some instances serving as an introduction. If the operas are new to any intending purchaser it is as well to note that beyond the German text of the first line no information is supplied. Moreover some of the other printed material is wrong (the mezzo sings in *Der fliegende Holländer* not *Tannhäuser*, and Josef Greindl is in the *Götterdämmerung* excerpt not *Parsifal*). Tracks 5 and 6 (*Tannhäuser*) and 10 and 11 (*Meistersinger*) run without a break, so that the list of items could prove misleading. As to the performances, the choral work is excellent when the men are singing, somewhat tremulous when the sopranos are involved. Recording varies from vivid (as in *Lohengrin* and *Götterdämmerung*) to misty (*Meistersinger*). The bargain price and fond memories of Wilhelm Pitz are the principal incentives here.

Wagner. RIENZI. **René Kollo** (ten) Cola Rienzi; **Siv Wennberg** (sop) Irene; **Janis Martin** (sop) Adriano; **Theo Adam** (bass) Paolo Orsini; **Nikolaus Hillebrand** (bass) Steffano Colonna; **Siegfried Vogel** (bass) Raimondo; **Peter Schreier** (ten) Baroncelli; **Günther Leib** (bass) Cecco del Vecchio; **Ingeborg Springer** (sop) Messenger of Peace; **Leipzig Radio Chorus; Dresden State Opera Chorus; Staatskapelle Dresden/Heinrich Hollreiser.** EMI CMS7 63980-2. Notes, text and translation included. From SLS990 (11/76). Recorded 1974-76.

③ 3h 45m ADD 2/92

Rienzi is grand opera with a vengeance. Political imperatives count for more than mere human feelings, and politics means ceremony as well as warfare: marches, ballet music and extended choruses are much in evidence, while even the solo arias often have the rhetorical punch of political harangues. It could all be an enormous bore. Yet the young Wagner, basing his work on Bulwer Lytton's story of the tragic Roman tribune, did manage to move beyond mere tub-thumping into a degree of intensity that — for those with ears to hear — prefigures the mature genius to come. In the end, Rienzi himself is more than just a political animal, and the existential anguish of Tannhäuser, Tristan and even Amfortas glimmers in the distance. It would be idle to pretend that this performance is ideal in every respect, either musically, or as a recording. But its virtues outweigh its weaknesses by a considerable margin. Siv Wennberg was not in best voice at the time, but the other principals, notably René Kollo and Janis Martin, bring commendable stamina and conviction to their demanding roles. Above all the conductor Heinrich Hollreiser prevents the more routine material from sounding merely mechanical, and ensures that the whole work has a truly Wagnerian sweep and fervour. Moreover, it is the only complete recording in the current edition of *The Classical Catalogue*.

Wagner. DER FLIEGENDE HOLLANDER. **Theo Adam** (bar) Holländer; **Anja Silja** (sop) Senta; **Martti Talvela** (bass) Daland; **Ernst Kozub** (ten) Erik; **Annelies Burmeister** (mez) Mary; **Gerhard Unger** (ten) Steersman; **BBC Chorus; New Philharmonia Orchestra/Otto Klemperer.** EMI Studio CMS7 63344-2. Notes, text and translation included. From SAN207/9 (12/68). Recorded in 1968.

③ 2h 32m ADD 2/90 9P

The young Wagner, sailing across the North Sea for the first time to England, went through a violent storm, and the experience left so vivid an impression that it prompted him to go ahead with a project he had already conceived, to turn the legend of the Flying Dutchman, condemned to sail the seas for ever until absolved by love, into an opera. The very opening of the Overture recaptures the violence of that storm at sea, and it leads to a work in which for the first time the full individuality of the would-be revolutionary can be appreciated. Klemperer's magisterial interpretation treats the opera symphonically. As ever he justifies moderate speeds by virtue of the way he sustains line and emphasizes detail. At the same time the reading has a blazing intensity quite surprising from an older conductor. The storm and sea music in the Overture and thereafter has a stunning power and the Dutchman's torture and unrequited passion is graphically evoked in the orchestra. Indeed, the playing of the Philharmonia is a bonus throughout. As well as anyone Klemperer catches the elemental power of the work, its adumbration of surging emotions against a sea-saturated background. Theo Adam conveys all the anguish of the Dutchman's character contained within a secure line. His is a profoundly moving interpretation, most intelligently sung. As Senta, Anja Silja is the very epitome of trust and love unto death, the performance of a great singing-actress, sung in an all-in, occasionally piercing manner. Talvela is a bluff, burly Daland, Ernst Kozub a sympathetic Erik and Unger offers a clearly articulated, ardent Steersman.

Additional recommendation ...

Soloists; Bayreuth Festival Chorus and Orchestra/Woldemar Nelsson. Philips 434 599-2PH2 — ② 2h 14m DDD 10/92 9P

Wagner. TANNHAUSER. **Wolfgang Windgassen** (ten) Tannhäuser; **Anja Silja** (sop) Elisabeth; **Eberhard Waechter** (bar) Wolfram; **Grace Bumbry** (mez) Venus; **Josef Greindl**

(bass) Hermann; **Gerhard Stolze** (ten) Walther; **Franz Crass** (bass) Biterolf; **Georg Paskuda** (ten) Heinrich; **Gerd Nienstedt** (bass) Reinmar; **Else-Margrete Gardelli** (sop) Shepherd; **Bayreuth Festival Chorus and Orchestra/Wolfgang Sawallisch.** Philips 434 599-2PH2. Notes, text and translation included. From 420 122-2PH3 (8/87). Recorded live in 1962.

③ 2h 50m ADD 8/87 £

Wagner's opera about the medieval minstrel-knight of the title who wavers between the erotic charms of Venus and the pure love of Elisabeth is hard to bring off in the opera house and in the recording studio. Its structure is diffuse and its demands on the singers, Tannhäuser in particular, inordinate. The opera calls for a dedication and dramatic intensity such as it received in Wieland Wagner's staging at Bayreuth in 1962. Sawallisch directs an account that catches the fervour of the protagonist from the start and goes on to relate the torture in his soul as he is cast out from society and refused forgiveness by the Pope. The title part itself is sung with tense feeling, keen tone and immaculate diction by Wolfgang Windgassen – the famous Rome Narration has seldom sounded so anguished. Anja Silja's clear, evocative voice and youthful eagerness inform all aspects of Elisabeth's role and as Venus, Grace Bumbry caused something of a sensation through her glamorous appearance and rich tones. Eberhard Waechter sings the part of the sympathetic Wolfram with glowing tone and sensitive phrasing. Together, cast and conductor make the inspired Third Act a fitting conclusion to this inspired reading.

Additional recommendations ...

Soloists; Vienna Boys' Choir; Vienna State Opera Chorus; Vienna Philharmonic Orchestra/Sir Georg Solti. Decca 414 581-2DH3 — ③ DDD 2/86

Soloists; Chorus of the Royal Opera House, Covent Garden; Philharmonia Orchestra/Giuseppe Sinopoli. DG 427 625-2GH3 — ③ 2h 56m DDD 9/89

Wagner. LOHENGRIN. **Jess Thomas** (ten) Lohengrin; **Elisabeth Grümmer** (sop) Elsa of Brabant; **Christa Ludwig** (mez) Ortrud; **Dietrich Fischer-Dieskau** (bar) Telramund; **Gottlob Frick** (bass) King Henry; **Otto Wiener** (bass) Herald; **Vienna State Opera Chorus; Vienna Philharmonic Orchestra/Rudolf Kempe.** EMI CDS7 49017-8. Notes, text and translation included. From SAN121/5 (2/64). Recorded 1962-63.

③ 3h 29m ADD 2/88

This is a *Lohengrin* of considerable historical interest, a finely judged studio recording with a superb cast under a conductor whose ability to shape and control the music's long paragraphs, in the most natural and unobtrusive way, will not be underestimated by listeners who have endured more mannered, less well-integrated performances. To find so much restraint and understatement in Wagner is no mean feat. Among the singers, pride of place must go to Jess Thomas and his persuasive account of the title role. Fischer-Dieskau's Telramund is the perfect adversary; there's a genuine anguish in this interpretation that gives the character rare substance. A comparable contrast exists between Elisabeth Grümmer's Else and Christa Ludwig's Ortrud: Grümmer moving from somanambulistic naïvety to uncomprehending despair, Ludwig from bitterness to malevolent triumph. With Gottlob Frick and Otto Weiner providing strong support, this is a cast with no weak links. Nor should the fine contribution of the Vienna chorus and orchestra be overlooked. Kempe was a musician's conductor, as the uniformly excellent response of all involved in this enterprise amply confirms.

Additional recommendation ...

Soloists; Bayreuth Festival Chorus and Orchestra/Peter Schneider. Philips 434 602-2PH4 — ④ 3h 22m DDD 10/92

Wagner. TRISTAN UND ISOLDE. **Wolfgang Windgassen** (ten) Tristan; **Birgit Nilsson** (sop) Isolde; **Christa Ludwig** (mez) Brangäne; **Eberhard Waechter** (bar) Kurwenal; **Martti Talvela** (bass) King Marke; **Claude Heater** (ten) Melot; **Peter Schreier** (ten) Sailor; **Erwin Wohlfahrt** (ten) Shepherd; **Gerd Nienstedt** (bass) Helmsman; **Bayreuth Festival Chorus**

and Orchestra/Karl Böhm. Philips 434 425-2PH3. From DG 419 889-2GH3 (7/88). Notes, text and translation included. Recorded in 1966.

③ 3h 39m ADD 10/91

Böhm's recording is a live Bayreuth performance of distinction, for on stage are the most admired Tristan and Isolde of their time, and in the pit the 72-year-old conductor directs a performance which is unflagging in its passion and energy. Böhm has a striking way in the Prelude and *Liebestod* of making the swell of passion seem like the movement of a great sea, sometimes with gentle motion, sometimes with the breaking of the mightiest of waves. Nilsson characterizes strongly and her voice with its marvellous cleaving-power can also soften quite beautifully. Windgassen's heroic performance in the Third Act is in some ways the crown of his achievements on record, even though the voice has dried and aged a little. Christa Ludwig is the ideal Brangäene, Waechter a suitably-forthright Kurwenal, and Talvela an expressive, noble-voiced Marke. Orchestra and chorus are at their finest.

Additional recommendations ...

Soloists; Bavarian Radio Chorus and Symphony Orchestra/Leonard Bernstein. Philips 438 241-2PH4 — ④ 4h 26m DDD

Soloists; Chorus of the Royal Opera House, Covent Garden; Philharmonia Orchestra/Wilhelm Furtwängler. EMI mono CDS7 47322-8 — ④ 3h 56m ADD 5/86 ▲

Soloists; Chorus of the Royal Opera House, Covent Garden; London Philharmonic Orchestra/Fritz Reiner, Sir Thomas Beecham. EMI Références mono CHS7 64037-2 — ③ 3h 32m ADD 1/92 ▲

Wagner. DIE MEISTERSINGER VON NURNBERG. **Theo Adam** (bass-bar) Hans Sachs; **Helen Donath** (sop) Eva; **René Kollo** (ten) Walther von Stolzing; **Sir Geraint Evans** (bass-bar) Beckmesser; **Peter Schreier** (ten) David; **Karl Ridderbusch** (bass) Veit Pogner; **Eberhard Büchner** (ten) Vogelgesang; **Ruth Hesse** (mez) Magdalene; **Horst Lunow** (bass) Nachtigall; **Zoltán Kélémen** (bass) Kothner; **Hans-Joachim Rotzsch** (ten) Zorn; **Peter Bindszus** (ten) Eisslinger; **Horst Hiestermann** (ten) Moser; **Hermann Christian Polster** (bass) Ortel; **Heinz Reeh** (bass) Schwarz; **Siegfried Vogel** (bass) Foltz; **Kurt Moll** (bass) Nightwatchman; **Leipzig Radio Chorus; Dresden State Opera Chorus; Staatskapelle, Dresden/Herbert von Karajan.** EMI CDS7 49683-2. Notes, text and translation included. From SLS957 (10/71). Recorded in 1970.

④ 4h 26m ADD 7/88 

Joyfully celebrating youth and midsummer, altruism and civic pride, Wagner is here the unstinting giver. It's a cornucopia of an opera, generous with the tunes, the colour, the sheer glory of sound as well as the desires and disappointments of the normal human heart. It is also essentially a company-opera, a vast collaborative enterprise which certainly benefits from the presence of a few great singers in the leading roles. In this recording, greatness is found not so much in the cast as in the man at the centre. Karajan directs an inspired, expansive performance, catching all the splendour and lyrical warmth of the writing. The singers are excellent in ensemble, and the whole company is alert in the disciplined chaos at the end of Act 2. Kollo's tone has power and clarity, Helen Donath's Eva is fresh and pretty and Theo Adam's Sachs is genial and authoritative. But the best singing comes from the two basses, Karl Ridderbusch (an unusually warm-hearted Pogner) and Kurt Moll. In a class of its own is Sir Geraint Evans's Beckmesser, his sly, nervously-calculating absurdity wonderfully preserved in this vivid recording.

Additional recommendations ...

Soloists; Bayreuth Festival Chorus and Orchestra/Herbert von Karajan. EMI Références mono CHS7 63500-2 — ④ 4h 27m ADD 9/90 ▲

Soloists; St Hedwig's Cathedral Choir, Berlin; Chorus of the Deutsche Oper, Berlin; Berlin State Opera Chorus; Berlin Philharmonic Orchestra/Rudolf Kempe. EMI mono CMS7 64154-2 — ④ 4h 20m ADD 2/93

Wagner. DER RING DES NIBELUNGEN.
DAS RHEINGOLD. **Theo Adam** (bass-bar) Wotan; **Annelies Burmeister** (mez) Fricka; **Wolfgang Windgassen** (ten) Loge; **Erwin Wohlfahrt** (ten) Mime; **Gustav Neidlinger** (bass) Alberich; **Anja Silja** (sop) Freia; **Hermin Esser** (ten) Froh; **Gerd Nienstedt** (bass) Donner; **Vera Soukupova** (mez) Erda; **Martti Talvela** (bass) Fasolt; **Kurt Boehme** (bass) Fafner; **Dorothea Siebert** (sop) Woglinde; **Helga Dernesch** (sop) Wellgunde; **Ruth Hesse** (mez) Flosshilde; **Bayreuth Festival Chorus and Orchestra/Karl Böhm.** Philips 412 475-2PH2. Notes, text and translation included. Recorded at a performance in the Festpielhaus, Bayreuth in 1967. From 6747 037 (9/73). Recorded in 1967.

.·' ② 2h 17m ADD 7/85 

DIE WALKURE. **James King** (ten) Siegmund; **Leonie Rysanek** (sop) Sieglinde; **Birgit Nilsson** (sop) Brünnhilde; **Theo Adam** (bass) Wotan; **Annelies Burmeister** (mez) Fricka, Siegrune; **Gerd Nienstedt** (bass) Hunding; **Danica Mastilovic** (sop) Gerhilde; **Liane Synek** (sop) Helmwige; **Helga Dernesch** (sop) Ortlinde; **Gertraud Hopf** (mez) Waltraute; **Sona Cervená** (mez) Rossweisse; **Elisabeth Schärtel** (contr) Grimgerde; **Sieglinde Wagner** (contr) Schwertleite; **Bayreuth Festival Chorus and Orchestra/Karl Böhm.** Philips 412 478-2PH4. Notes, text and translation included. Recorded live in 1967. From 6747 037 (9/73).

.·' ④ 3h 30m ADD 2/85 

SIEGFRIED. **Wolfgang Windgassen** (ten) Siegfried; **Theo Adam** (bass) Wanderer; **Birgit Nilsson** (sop) Brünnhilde; **Erwin Wohlfahrt** (ten) Mime; **Gustav Neidlinger** (bass) Alberich; **Vera Soukupova** (mez) Erda; **Kurt Boehme** (bass) Fafner; **Erika Köth** (sop) Woodbird; **Bayreuth Festival Orchestra/Karl Böhm.** Philips 412 483-2PH4. Notes, text and translation included. Recorded live in 1967. From 6747 037 (9/73).

.·' ④ 3h 43m ADD 8/85 

GOTTERDAMMERUNG. **Birgit Nilsson** (sop) Brünnhilde; **Wolfgang Windgassen** (ten) Siegfried; **Josef Greindl** (bass) Hagen; **Gustav Neidlinger** (bass-bar) Alberich; **Thomas Stewart** (bar) Gunther; **Ludmila Dvořáková** (sop) Gutrune; **Martha Mödl** (mez) Waltraute; **Dorothea Siebert** (sop) Woglinde; **Helga Dernesch** (sop) Wellgunde; **Sieglinde Wagner** (contr) Flosshilde; **Marga Höffgen** (contr) First Norn; **Annelies Burmeister** (mez) Second Norn; **Anja Silja** (sop) Third Norn; **Bayreuth Festival Chorus and Orchestra/Karl Böhm.** Philips 412 488-2PH4. Notes, text and translation included. Recorded live in 1967. From 6747 037 (9/73).

.·' ④ 4h 9m ADD 5/85 

Wagner's *Der Ring des Nibelungen* is the greatest music-drama ever penned. It deals with the eternal questions of power, love, personal responsibility and moral behaviour, and has always been open to numerous interpretations, both dramatic and musical. For every generation, it presents a new challenge, yet certain musical performances have undoubtedly stood the test of time. One would recommend the recording made at Bayreuth in 1967 because, above all others, it represents a true and living account of a huge work as it was performed in the opera house for which it was largely conceived. Every artist who appears at Bayreuth seems to find an extra dedication in their comportment there, and on this occasion many of the singers and the conductor surpassed what they achieved elsewhere. Böhm's reading is notable for its dramatic drive and inner tension. For the most part he also encompasses the metaphysical aspects of the score as well, and he procures playing of warmth and depth from the Bayreuth orchestra. Birgit Nilsson heads the cast as an unsurpassed Brünnhilde, wonderfully vivid in her characterization and enunciation, tireless and gleaming in voice. Wolfgang Windgassen is equally committed and alert as her Siegfried and Theo Adam is an experienced, worldly-wise Wotan. No *Ring* recording is perfect or could possibly tell the whole story but this faithfully recorded, straightforward version conveys the strength and force of the epic's meaning.

Additional recommendations ...
DAS RHEINGOLD. **Soloists; Bayreuth Festival Orchestra/Clemens Krauss.** Foyer mono 3-CF2007 — .·' ③ 2h 25m ADD 6/88 qp B ▲

DIE WALKURE. **Soloists; Bayreuth Festival Orchestra/Clemens Krauss.** Foyer mono 4-CF2008 — ④ 3h 32m ADD 6/88 ▲
SIEGFRIED. **Soloists; Bayreuth Festival Orchestra/Clemens Krauss.** Foyer mono 4-CF2009 — ④ 3h 57m ADD 6/88 ▲
GOTTERDAMMERUNG. **Soloists; Bayreuth Festival Orchestra/Clemens Krauss.** Foyer mono 4-CF2010 — ④ 4h 20m ADD 6/88 ▲
DER RING DES NIBELUNGEN. **Vienna State Opera Chorus; Vienna Philharmonic Orchestra/Sir Georg Solti.** Decca 414 100-2DM15 — ⑮ 14h 37m ADD 3/89 £ ▲
DER RING DES NIBELUNGEN. **Soloists; Chorus and Orchestra of RAI, Rome/Wilhelm Furtwängler.** EMI mono CZS7 67123-2 — ⑬ 15h 2m ADD 2/91 ▲

Wagner. GOTTERDAMMERUNG. **Hildegard Behrens** (sop) Brünnhilde; **Reiner Goldberg** (ten) Siegfried; **Matti Salminen** (bass) Hagen; **Ekkehard Wlaschiha** (bar) Alberich; **Bernd Weikl** (bar) Gunther; **Cheryl Studer** (sop) Gutrune; **Hanna Schwarz** (mez) Waltraute; **Hei-Kyung Hong** (sop) Woglinde; **Diane Kesling** (mez) Wellgunde; **Meredith Parsons** (contr) Flosshilde; **Helga Dernesch** (mez) First Norn; **Tatiana Troyanos** (mez) Second Norn; **Andrea Gruber** (sop) Third Norn; **Metropolitan Opera Chorus and Orchestra/James Levine.** DG 429 385-2GH4. Notes, text and translation included. Recorded in 1989.

④ 4h 30m DDD 8/91 

This performance of the climax of the *Ring* cycle is of a stature to match the inspired nature of the opera. Levine encompasses every aspect, heroic and tragic, of the vast work, finding the right tempos for each section and welding them together as imperceptibly as the composer into a consistent and inspired whole. He is magnificently supported by his own Metropolitan Opera Orchestra who play and are recorded with remarkable fidelity and virtuosity. Levine's cast, the one with whom he has performed the work at the Met and on television, is as about as excellent as could be assembled today, headed by Hildegard Behrens's all-consuming Brünnhilde, responsive to every aspect of the role's many-faceted character. Reiner Goldberg isn't quite her equal as an interpreter but, as Siegfried, he sings with unfailing musicality and with a firm line. Evil is convincingly represented by Salminen's implacable, black-voiced Hagen. Hanna Schwarz is a deeply eloquent Waltraute, who makes the very most of her long narration. Cheryl Studer's lyrical Gutrune and Bernd Weikl's sound Gunther are further assets, as are the splendid Norns and Rhinemaidens.

Additional recommendation ...
(Sung in English). **Soloists; English National Opera Chorus and Orchestra/Sir Reginald Goodall.** EMI CMS7 64244-2 — ⑤ ADD 11/92

Wagner. SIEGFRIED (sung in English). **Alberto Remedios** (ten) Siegfried; **Norman Bailey** (bar) Wanderer; **Rita Hunter** (sop) Brünnhilde; **Gregory Dempsey** (ten) Mime; **Derek Hammond-Stroud** (bar) Alberich; **Anne Collins** (contr) Erda; **Clifford Grant** (bass) Fafner; **Maurine London** (sop) Woodbird; **Sadler's Wells Opera Orchestra/Sir Reginald Goodall.** EMI CMS7 63595-2. Notes and English text included. From HMV SLS875 (4/74). Recorded in 1973.

④ 4h 38m ADD 3/91 

The Goodall recording of the *Ring* has over the years gained an almost legendary reputation. Now that the first work that was committed to disc has appeared on CD, that reputation proves to have been well justified. The breadth and cogency of Goodall's reading, its epic quality, once more stand out as a magnificent achievement. Even more remarkable is Goodall's unerring sense of transition, as important in this opera as it is in any of the cycle's components. For this cycle Goodall had assembled a group of specially prepared singers; every part was carefully cast and sung with a sense of characterization and articulacy of enunciation (in Andrew Porter's excellent translation) that will surely gain the performance new friends. The team is headed by Alberto Remedios's youthful-sounding and forthright Siegfried, a performance that nicely combines lyrical ardour with heroic timbre. Around him in the various colloquia of which this work is largely comprised are Gregory Dempsey's characterful but seldom exaggerated Mime, Norman Bailey's authoritative, worldly-wise Wanderer and eventually, on the mountain-top, Rita Hunter's gleaming Brünnhilde. To these fine performances can be added Derek Hammond-Stroud's menacing Alberich and Anne Collins's grave, imposing Erda. The live recording has stood the test of time. This is a performance worthy to be placed among any in the original language.

Wagner. PARSIFAL. **Jess Thomas** (ten) Parsifal; **George London** (bass-bar) Amfortas; **Hans Hotter** (bass) Gurnemanz; **Irene Dalis** (mez) Kundry; **Gustav Neidlinger** (bass) Klingsor; **Martti Talvela** (bass) Titurel; **Niels Möller** (ten) First Knight; **Gerd Neinstedt** (bass) Second Knight; **Sona Cervená** (mez), **Ursula Boese** (contr), **Gerhard Stolze, Georg Paskuda** (tens) Squires; **Gundula Janowitz, Anja Silja, Else-Margrete Gardelli, Dorothea Siebert, Rita Bartos** (sops), **Sona Cervená** (mez) Flower Maidens; **Bayreuth Festival Chorus and Orchestra/Hans Knappertsbusch.** Philips 416 390-2PH4. Notes, text and translation included. Recorded at the 1962 Bayreuth Festival. From SAL3475 (11/64).

④ 4h 10m ADD 6/86

There have been many fine recordings of this great Eastertide opera, but none have so magnificently captured the power, the spiritual grandeur, the human frailty and the almost unbearable beauty of the work as Hans Knappertsbusch. This live recording has a cast that has few equals. Hotter is superb, fleshing out Gurnemanz with a depth of insight that has never been surpassed. London's Amfortas captures the frightening sense of impotence and anguish with painful directness whilst Thomas's Parsifal grows as the performance progresses and is no mean achievement. Dalis may lack that final degree of sensuousness but gives a fine interpretation. Throughout Knappertsbusch exercises a quite unequalled control over the proceedings; it is a fine testament to a great conductor. The Bayreuth acoustic is well reproduced and all in all it is a profound and moving experience.

Additional recommendations ...

Soloists; Berlin State Opera Chorus; Berlin Philharmonic Orchestra/Daniel Barenboim. Teldec 9031-74448-2 — ④ 4h 16m DDD 10/91

Soloists; Bayreuth Festival Chorus and Orchestra/Hans Knappertsbusch. Teldec Historic Series mono 9031-76047-2 — ④ 4h 32m ADD 8/93 ▲

Charles Waldteufel

French 1837-1915

Suggested listening ...

Waltzes — España. Les patineurs. Estudiantina. Acclamations. *Coupled with* ***Offenbach.*** Gaîteé parisienne[a] — complete. **Monte-Carlo Philharmonic Orchestra/[a]Manuel Rosenthal, Willy Boskovsky.** EMI Studio CDM7 63136-2 (12/89).

Johann Gottfried Walther

German 1684-1748

NEW REVIEW

Walther. ORGAN WORKS. **Stephen Farr.** Meridian CDE84213. Played on the organ of Clare College Chapel, Cambridge.

Concertos — del Signor Torelli; del Signor Taglietti; del Signor Telemann in G major and C minor; del Signor Meck. *Chorale Preludes* — Herr Jesu Christ, ich weiss gar wohl; Es ist das Heil uns kommen her; Hilf mir Gott, dass mir's gelinge; Herr Gott, nun schleuss der Himmel auf; Schmücke dich, o liebe Seele. *Partita* — Jesu meine Freude.

lh 17m DDD 8/92

So towering a figure in baroque organ music was J.S. Bach that we are inclined to overlook his contemporaries. One whose music would surely be better known today had it not been for Bach's all-pervading shadow was Johann Gottfried Walther who was not only an almost exact contemporary of Bach, but also his cousin and close friend. Indeed for a time both men were in the employ of Duke Wilhelm Ernst in Weimar. Living and working within the same musical and social circles inevitably led to parallels between their music — one of the most obvious being the organ transcriptions both made of Italian string concertos. Bach wrote five, Walther rather more, including those recorded here. Walther's transcriptions remain close to the original (Bach tended to be a little more inventive) but, as you can hear, they do make excellent organ music, requiring a performer who is both technically proficient and has a well-informed understanding of the style and characteristics of the baroque concerto. In Stephen Farr, both criteria are met in full measure. He imbues all his playing with a great sense of fun — these may be academically sound performances, but they are also immensely enjoyable, and few listeners will remain unaffected by the exuberant *Taglietti* Concerto. The Clare College Chapel organ makes a lovely sound and is well recorded.

William Walton

British 1902-1983

Walton. Violin Concerto. Viola Concerto. **Nigel Kennedy** (vn, va); **Royal Philharmonic Orchestra/André Previn.** EMI CDC7 49628-2. From EL749628-1 (1/88).

57m DDD 4/88

These Concertos are among the most beautiful written this century. Walton was in his late twenties when he composed the viola work and in it he achieved a depth of emotion, a range of ideas and a technical assurance beyond anything he had so far written. Lacking in the brilliance of the violin, the viola has an inherently contemplative tonal quality and Walton matches this to perfection in his score, complementing it rather than trying to compensate as other composers have done. There is a larger element of virtuosity in the Violin Concerto, but it is never allowed to dominate the musical argument. Sir Yehudi Menuhin recorded both works and now Nigel Kennedy has equalled, and in some respects surpassed his achievement, giving wonderfully warm and characterful performances which are likely to stand unchallenged as a coupling for a long time. He produces a beautiful tone quality on both of his instruments, which penetrates to the heart of the aching melancholy of Walton's slow music, and he combines it with an innate, highly developed and spontaneous-sounding sense of rhythmic drive and bounce which propels the quick movements forward with great panache. Previn has long been a persuasive Waltonian and the RPO respond marvellously, with crisp and alert playing throughout. The recordings are very clear and naturally balanced with the solo instrument set in a believable perspective.

Additional recommendation ...
Violin Concerto. Sonata for violin and piano. Two Pieces. **Lydia Mordkovitch** (vn); **London Philharmonic Orchestra/Jan Latham-Koenig.** Chandos CHAN9073 — lh 9m DDD 10/92

Walton. ORCHESTRAL WORKS. **London Philharmonic Orchestra/Bryden Thomson.** Chandos CHAN8968.
Overtures — Johannesburg Festival; Portsmouth Point; Scapino. Capriccio burlesco. The First Shoot (orch. Palmer). Granada Prelude. Prologo e Fantasia. Music for Children. Galop final (orch. Palmer).

lh 10m DDD 11/91

While enthusiasts for Walton's music may justifiably complain that there is not enough of it, they usually concede that what there is is readily available in good recorded performances.

However, thanks to the dedicated and skilful work of Christopher Palmer, still more of it is now coming to light. How many people, one wonders, have ever heard *The First Shoot*, a miniature ballet written for a C.B. Cochran show in 1935, the *Granada Prelude* devised for that television company in the 1960s, or the *Prologo e Fantasia* which was the composer's last work, written for Rostropovich and his National Symphony Orchestra of Washington. Such fresh and welcome goodies as these appear along with familiar material such as the splendidly open-air, nautical overture *Portsmouth Point* that Walton wrote nearly 40 years earlier at the very start of his career. The Cochran piece, as orchestrated by Palmer, has five little sections that are delightfully jazzy in a way that recalls *Façade* and one's only regret is that there's not more of it. All this music is in the excellent hands of the late Bryden Thomson and the LPO, and Palmer's booklet essay is a model of stylish, informative writing. The recording is richly toned in the successful Chandos style, which takes some edge off the composer's characteristically sharp scoring but is still most enjoyable.

Walton. The Quest — ballet (ed. Palmer). The Wise Virgins — ballet suite. **London Philharmonic Orchestra/Bryden Thomson.** Chandos CHAN8871. Recorded in 1990.

1h 2m DDD 4/91 qp qs

These two strongly-coloured Walton ballets make an especially effective coupling in such brilliantly played, attractively recorded performances. And one, *The Quest*, based on Spenser's *Faerie Queen*, is recorded here in its entirety for the first time. The work was a rushed, wartime enterprise, "written more or less as one writes for the films", as the composer commented in a letter to John Warrack. It was first performed in April 1943 by the Sadler's Wells Ballet company and was not afterwards revived; the score was lost until 1958 and even then only a four-movement suite — arranged by Vilem Tausky, and approved and later recorded by Walton — saw the light of day. In reviving the work, Christopher Palmer has added the extra instruments used in the suite, knowing that Walton had been inhibited by the small size of the band available to him for the work's première. *The Wise Virgins*, based on music by J.S. Bach, is perennially popular and, like *The Quest*, receives a typically full-blooded, totally committed reading from Bryden Thomson, who stirs the London Philharmonic to great heights of power and dexterity. The recording venue's liberal acoustic has not prevented Chandos from letting us hear all that Walton intended.

Walton (arr. Palmer). Henry V — a Shakespeare scenario. **Christopher Plummer** (narr); **Westminster Abbey Choristers; Chorus and Academy of St Martin in the Fields/Sir Neville Marriner.** Chandos CHAN8892. Texts included. Recorded in 1990.

1h 7m DDD 4/91

A mercurial young actor and a palely reticent young composer, Laurence Olivier and William Walton, met for the first time on a film set in 1935. It was an auspicious day for the British cinema, and long afterwards, in 1982, the great actor paid tribute to his collaborator on three Shakespeare films by saying that Walton's music had a "heart-quickening feeling ... something to do with sex, but a lot more to do with love". *Henry V* (1944) was the first of this celebrated trilogy and Walton's musical score contributed greatly to its scenes of fifteenth-century England, whether in Shakespeare's Globe Theatre, the London inn called The Boar's Head, an army's embarkation at Southampton, at the French court, or — most memorably of all — depicting the Battle of Agincourt in 1415. This disc triumphantly shows us that Walton's music stands up on its own and has beauty as well as tremendous atmosphere. It is thanks to the dedication and skill of Christopher Palmer (whose booklet notes are a model of information and readability) that we now have not just the few extracts from it that were made long ago for concert use, but about 90 per cent of the whole. It is presented in eight sections that follow the order of screen action and make a superb sequence. The performance of all this music under Sir Neville Marriner, which includes the finest of the King's speeches magnificently spoken by Christopher Plummer, is no less than inspired, and Chandos's richly textured recording made in a London church is equally fine. This glorious disc ends with three period pieces that Walton used in his music.

NEW REVIEW

Walton. Symphony No. 1 in B flat minor. Cello Concerto[a]. [a]**Lynn Harrell** (vc); **City of Birmingham Symphony Orchestra/Simon Rattle.** EMI British Composers CDC7 54572-2. Recorded 1990-91.

1h 14m DDD 12/92

Simon Rattle's version of Walton's First Symphony is as intelligent and dynamic a traversal as one would expect from this talented figure. Texturally speaking, the inner workings of Walton's score are laid bare as never before, aided by what sounds like a meticulously prepared CBSO. Some may find a touch of contrivance about Rattle's control of dynamics in the scorching first movement, but there's absolutely no gainsaying the underlying tension or cumulative power of the whole. Under Rattle the *Scherzo* darts menacingly (the most convincing account of this music since the classic 1966 Previn account), whilst the slow movement is an unusually nervy, anxious affair. Certainly, the finale is superbly athletic and lithe, though by now one is beginning to register that EMI's sonics are, for all their transparency and natural perspective, perhaps a little lightweight for such enormously red-blooded inspiration. Overall, though, Rattle's is a very strong account – indisputably one of the finest we've had in recent years – and his disc's claims are enhanced by the coupling, a wholly admirable performance of the same composer's luxuriant Cello Concerto. Here Rattle and Lynn Harrell form an inspired partnership, totally dedicated and achieving utter concentration throughout — no mean feat in this of all works, whose predominantly slow-moving progress demands so much from both performers and listeners.

Additional recommendations ...

Symphonies — No. 1[a]*; No. 2*[b]. [a]**London Philharmonic Orchestra,** [b]**London Symphony Orchestra/Sir Charles Mackerras.** EMI Eminence CD-EMX2206 — 1h 14m DDD 12/89 £

No. 1. ***Vaughan Williams.*** *The Wasps — Overture.* **London Symphony Orchestra/André Previn.** RCA Victor Gold Seal GD87830 — 52m ADD 2/89 £

NEW REVIEW

Walton. Symphonies — No. 1 in B flat minor; No. 2. **Royal Philharmonic Orchestra/Vladimir Ashkenazy.** Decca 433 703-2DH. Recorded in 1991.

1h 12m DDD 4/93 

Even in the face of intense competition from the similarly coupled EMI Eminence issue with Sir Charles Mackerras, Ashkenazy's new pairing has a lot going for it. Although not quite as glowingly rich as some of this company's previous efforts from Walthamstow Assembly Hall, Decca's production is a splendidly analytical affair, and the ear revels in the thrilling amount of detail captured by the engineers in these superbly orchestrated scores. The RPO, too, respond with no little dash or commitment; certainly, the *Scherzo* of the First Symphony is delivered with impressive poise and rhythmic (indeed almost balletic) flair, and if one might crave a rather larger, more refulgent body of string tone on occasion (as in the gorgeous Mediterranean seascape which comprises the Second Symphony's slow movement), the brass playing has exemplary thrust and flashing brilliance throughout. Ashkenazy's conception of the First is laudably clear-sighted and undisruptive. What's missing, however, is simply that last ounce of crackling tension one finds on rival readings from the likes of Slatkin, Rattle, Mackerras and, above all, Previn (see above). Indeed, the last-mentioned's blistering 1966 LSO account remains pre-eminent, and in the Second, too, many will understandably prefer the greater emotional pungency of Mackerras and sheer orchestral spectacle of George Szell's famous Cleveland recording from 1961 (listed below). Still, the present coupling is a generous one, and no-one will be disappointed with either Ashkenazy's achievement here nor the impact of the Decca engineering.

Additional recommendation ...

No. 2. Partita. Variations on a Theme by Hindemith. **Cleveland Orchestra/George Szell.** CBS Masterworks CD46732 — 1h 5m ADD 12/91

Walton. FILM MUSIC, Volume 2. **Academy of St Martin in the Fields/Sir Neville Marriner.** Chandos CHAN8870. Recorded in 1990.
Spitfire Prelude and Fugue. A Wartime Sketchbook (arr. Palmer). Escape Me Never — suite (arr. Palmer). The Three Sisters (ed. Palmer). The Battle of Britain — suite.

1h 5m DDD 12/90

Walton's film work reveals a remarkably fluent appreciation of the important role music plays in the medium and his magnificent scores for Olivier's Shakespeare trilogy (*Henry V*, *Hamlet* and *Richard III*) have quite rightly crossed over into the concert repertoire. But it is a little unfortunate that their popularity has somewhat overshadowed Walton's other achievements in this area for, as this collection proves, much more of his film music merits similar recognition. The emphasis here is on the composer's music for the war film and the familiar *Spitfire Prelude and Fugue*, with its stirring and characteristically solid march theme, provides a strong opening. *A Wartime Sketchbook* is an adroit arrangement by Christopher Palmer of contrasting segments from *Went the Day Well?*, *Next of Kin*, *The Foreman went to France* and *Battle of Britain* which lives up to its title most successfully (Walton's own authentic foxtrots, put over with delightful ease by the Academy, are particularly evocative), whilst the 11-minute selection from *Battle of Britain* serves to emphasize once again the idiocy of the nameless studio executive who decreed that the entire score should be scrapped (the stunning "Battle in the air" did remain in the film, however). Away from the battlefield, the programme also includes *Escape Me Never*, a heady and warmly romantic score complete with a strikingly rhythmic ballet, and *The Three Sisters*, Walton's final film score which perhaps overplays its references to the Russian national anthem but compensates with a lovely waltz in the "Dream Sequence". Sir Neville has just the right approach to this music and the orchestra's sturdy performances have been captured in a bright and well-detailed recording.

Walton. String Quartets — No. 1 (1919-22)[a]; A minor (1945-7)[b]. **Gabrieli Quartet** ([a]John Georgiadis, [b]Kenneth Sillito, Brendan O'Reilly, vns; Ian Jewel, va; Keith Harvey, vc). Chandos CHAN8944. Item marked [a] new to UK, [b] from CHAN8474 (10/87). Recorded 1986-90.

1h 5m DDD 10/91

Here is a disc that offers the kind of fascinating musical experience to be encountered only very rarely in the concert-hall. Walton's A minor string quartet is the familiar, late romantic Walton, from a time when the abrasiveness of *Façade* and the swagger of *Belshazzar's Feast* were well in the past, and the relatively relaxed lyricism of the viola and violin concertos was the determining element of his style. The music is nostalgic, neatly crafted and, while undemanding, attractive and distinctive. The early quartet, by contrast, is a product of youthful uncertainty and extravagance which Walton soon discarded but never destroyed. It is the sort of young man's music which leaves you conscious that such a gifted composer could have developed quite differently. Its particular point of reference is the music of Bartók, in the first quartet even more markedly than the second, though whether this was a matter of natural affinity or conscious imitation is difficult to say. While the effect is more that of an instinctive outpouring than a disciplined discourse, the sheer musicality and abundant imagination of the quartet disarm criticism. This is a well-engineered recording of performances in which the Gabrielis demonstrate the range and character of Walton's musical world with a special authority.

Walton. Piano Quartet[a]. Violin Sonata. **Kenneth Sillito** (vn); [a]**Robert Smissen** (va); [a]**Stephen Orton** (vc); **Hamish Milne** (pf). Chandos CHAN8999. Recorded in 1991.

56m DDD 3/92

Compared with Britten and Tippett, Walton did not leave a large legacy of music, and there is not so much of it that we can afford to neglect the two works here, neither of which is particularly well known. The Piano Quartet was his first major work, started when he was 16 and a very young Oxford undergraduate, though he revised it in later years. It's pretty well the sort of music that one might expect of the young composer who had come to Oxford from unsophisticated Northern England as a chorister and was now quickly absorbing all kinds of new influences: if we want to, we can trace here everything from richly textured Brahms via Vaughan Williams to the brilliant rhythms of Stravinsky's *Petrushka*. But there's also a lyricism that is very much Walton's own, and the writing for the piano and strings is skilful and idiomatic. He also could already write in a fugal style (in the scherzo and finale) that was alive rather than academic. Altogether the work comes over very effectively in this strong yet sensitive performance by four fine British artists, and the slow and romantic third movement, for all its echoes of Vaughan Williams and Ravel, is particularly beautiful, despite what sounds like the accidental plucking of the violin's open A string at 7'18". Walton composed his Violin Sonata soon after the War, partly because he needed the 2,000 Swiss francs which Yehudi Menuhin paid him as a commissioning fee. It is in just two movements, the second being a set of variations, and although it's not the easiest work to hold together in performance (Walton later admitted that it was written sporadically over two years and added, "it's surprising that the piece has any continuity at all!"), it has a bitter-sweet elegance that is attractive. Kenneth Sillito and Hamish Milne bring it off to fine effect, and Chandos's full-toned recording is excellent.

WALTON CONDUCTS WALTON. [a]Dennis Noble (bar); **[a]Huddersfield Choral Society; [a]Liverpool Philharmonic Orchestra, [b]Philharmonia Orchestra, [c]London Philharmonic Orchestra, [d]Hallé Orchestra/Sir William Walton.** EMI Great Recordings of the Century mono CDH7 63381-2. Text included.
Belshazzar's Feast[a] (from HMV C3330/34, 3/43). Henry V[b] — Death of Falstaff; Touch her soft lips and part (both from C3480, 1/46). Scapino — comedy overture[b] (HMV DB21499, 8/52). Façade[c] — Suites Nos. 1 and 2 (C2836/7, 5/36 and C3042, 1/39). Spitfire Prelude and Fugue[d] (C3359, 8/43). Siesta[c] (C3042).

lh 19m ADD 4/92

In his younger days Walton was an exciting conductor of his own music, far more so than in his comfortable middle and old age. So although EMI re-recorded the composer in most of the items listed above during the LP era, they have been right to go back to the original versions. The major work here, *Belshazzar's Feast*, was recorded under the auspices of the British Council, and was an amazing venture in time of war. There is certainly the atmosphere of a special occasion in the performance, with everybody singing and playing their hearts out, and Walton driving his forces with enormous energy. Dennis Noble was the soloist at the work's first performance: he sings in a highly dramatic fashion, and with perfect diction. The recording sounds dated of course, but the transfer has been well-made. Ensemble is not always perfect in the *Façade* Suites, but the LPO play with tremendous zest and high spirits. Here the recording does sound a little confined. *Scapino* was recorded some years later, in rather better sound, and Walton gets magnificently vital playing from the superb Philharmonia Orchestra. The four remaining shorter pieces all receive excellent performances, and the sound is never less than acceptable. This is a desirable reissue and a must for all who enjoy Walton's music.

Walton. Belshazzar's Feast[a]. Coronation Te Deum. Gloria[b]. **[b]Ameral Gunson** (contr); **[b]Neil Mackie** (ten); **[a]Gwynne Howell, [b]Stephen Roberts** (bars); **Bach Choir; Philharmonia Orchestra/Sir David Willcocks.** Chandos CHAN8760. Texts included. Recorded in 1989.

lh 2m DDD 1/90

With Sir David Willcocks in charge of the choir which he has directed since 1960, one need have no fears that the composer's many near-impossible demands of the chorus in all three of these masterpieces will be met with elegance and poise. There is as well, in *Belshazzar*, a predictably fine balance of the forces to ensure that as much detail as possible is heard from both chorus and orchestra, even when Walton is bombarding us from all corners of the universe with extra brass bands and all manner of clamorous percussion in praise of pagan gods. Such supremely musical concerns bring their own rewards in a work that can often seem vulgar. The revelation here is the sustained degree of dramatic thrust, exhilaration and what Herbert Howells called "animal joy" in the proceedings. How marvellous, too, to hear the work paced and scaled to avoid the impression of reduced voltage after the big moments. Gwynne Howell is the magnificently steady, firm and dark toned baritone. The *Gloria* and *Coronation Te Deum* are informed with the same concerns: accuracy and professional polish are rarely allowed to hinder these vital contributions to the British choral tradition. The recording's cathedral-like acoustic is as ideal for the *Te Deum*'s ethereal antiphonal effects, as it is for *Belshazzar*'s glorious spectacle; and Chandos match Willcocks's care for balance, bar by bar.

Walton. Façade[a]. Overtures — Portsmouth Point; Scapino[b]. Siesta[b]. ***Arnold.*** English Dances, Op. 33[c]. **[a]Dame Edith Sitwell; [a]Sir Peter Pears** (spkrs); **[a]English Opera Group Ensemble/Anthony Collins; [bc]London Philharmonic Orchestra/Sir Adrian Boult.** Decca London mono 425 661-2LM. Items marked [a] from LXT2977 (11/54), [b] LXT5028 (6/55), [c] LW5166 (6/55).

1h 14m DDD

This is the classic and authoritative reading of the fully approved selection of *Façade* settings. Dame Edith herself reads two-thirds of the numbers, Sir Peter the remaining third. The poetess herself reads them with such *joie de vivre*, such a natural feeling for her own verses and inflections that nobody could be expected to rival her. Her timing is perfect, her delivery deliciously idiosyncratic, the intonations obviously what she and presumably Walton wanted. Sir Peter isn't far behind her in ability to relish the writing and the instrumental ensemble plays with refinement allied to virtuosity. The 1950s mono recording stands the test of time remarkably well.

Additional recommendations ...

Façade[a]. ***Sitwell.*** *Poems: Two Kitchen Songs. Five Songs — Daphne; The Peach Tree; The Strawberry; The Greengage Tree; The Nectarine Tree. On the Vanity of Human Aspirations. Two Poems from "Facade" — The Drum; Clowns' Houses. The Wind's Bastinado. The Dark Song. Colonel Fantock. Most Lovely Shade. Heart and Mind.* **Prunella Scales, Timothy West** (spkrs); [a]members of **London Mozart Players/Jane Glover.** ASV CDDCA679 — 1h 4m DDD/ADD 4/90

Façade – Suites Nos. 1 and 2. ***Bliss.*** *Checkmate – suite.* ***Lambert.*** *Horoscope – suite.* **English Northern Philharmonia/David Lloyd-Jones.** Hyperion CDA66436 — 1h 14m DDD 3/91

Key to Symbols

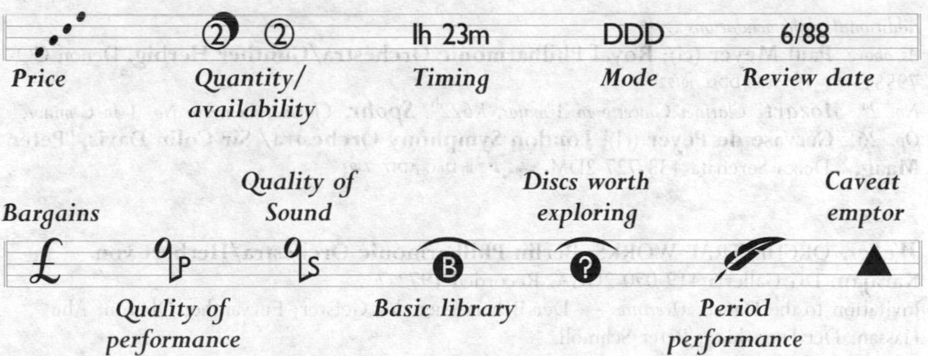

Peter Warlock

British 1894-1930

Suggested listening ...

The Curlew — song cycle. The Water Lily. Mourn no Moe. Chopcherry. My gostly fader. Five Nursery Jingles — How many miles to Babylon?; O my kitten; Little Jack Horner; Suky you shall be my wife; Jenny Gray. The Birds. Sleep. The fairest May. **James Griffett** (ten); **Mary Ryan** (fl); **Mary Murdoch** (cor ang); **Haffner Quartet.** Pearl SHECD9510 (12/87).

Franz Waxman

German/American 1906-1967

Suggested listening ...

Film Scores: Prince Valiant — suite. A Place in the Sun — suite. The Bride of Frankenstein — Creation of the female monster. Sunset Boulevard — suite. Rebecca — suite. The Philadelphia Story. Old Acquaintance — Elegy for strings. Taras Bulba — Ride to Dubno. **National Philharmonic Orchestra/Charles Gerhardt.** RCA Victor GD80708 (11/91).

Rebecca — *film score.* **Bratislava Radio Symphony Orchestra/Adriano.** Marco Polo 8 223399 (10/92).

Carl Maria von Weber

German 1786-1826

Weber. Clarinet Concertos — No. 1 in F minor, J114; No. 2 in E flat major, J118. Clarinet Concertino in E flat major, J109. **Orchestra of the Age of Enlightenment/Antony Pay** (cl). Virgin Classics VC7 59002-2.

52m DDD 10/88 

Among the major composers, it was Weber who most of all enriched the solo repertory of the clarinet. He was inspired by his acquaintance with a fine player, in this case Heinrich Bärmann, and for this recording Antony Pay has used a modern copy of a seven-keyed instrument of around 1800, to which two extra keys have been added to come nearer to the ten-keyed instrument that Bärmann played. The orchestra also uses period instruments and in several passages, such as the hymnlike one with horns in the slow movement of the F minor Concerto, one hears this in their subtly different tone. The music itself is consistently fluent and elegant, witty and attractive and is stylishly played, with lovely clarinet tone in all registers.

Additional recommendations ...

As above. **Paul Meyer** (cl); **Royal Philharmonic Orchestra/Günther Herbig.** Denon CO-79551 — 50m DDD 10/92

No. 2[a]. ***Mozart.*** *Clarinet Concerto in A major, K622*[b]. ***Spohr.*** *Clarinet Concerto No. 1 in C minor, Op. 26*[a]. **Gervase de Peyer** (cl); **London Symphony Orchestra/**[a]**Sir Colin Davis,** [b]**Peter Maag,** . Decca Serenata 433 727-2DM — 1h 12m ADD 7/93

Weber. ORCHESTRAL WORKS. **Berlin Philharmonic Orchestra/Herbert von Karajan.** DG Galleria 419 070-2GGA. Recorded 1972-73.

Invitation to the Dance. *Overtures* — Der Beherrscher der Geister; Euryanthe; Oberon; Abu Hassan; Der Freischütz; Peter Schmoll.

56m ADD 6/88 

Often rich in atmosphere and melodically inspired, Weber's operas invariably have an overture at which, as this mid-price disc illustrates, he excelled. The distillation of the mood and thematic significance achieved in these brief introductions invariably reached great concentration. A slow prelude, often mystical and veiled in character, leads into a faster *Vivace* section which presents the primary thematic material for the forthcoming opera. The overtures to *Oberon*, *Der Freischütz* and *Peter Schmoll* work in this way, whilst *Abu Hassan*, *Euryanthe* and *Der Beherrscher der Geister* literally burst in with unchecked verve and excitement — the first having a Turkish flavour with its use of percussion, the last having a tremendous timpani call set at its centre. Karajan and the Berlin Philharmonic Orchestra play these skilful works for all they are worth and they sound even better for it.

NEW REVIEW

Weber. Piano Sonatas — No. 1 in C major, J138; No. 2 in A flat major, J199. Rondo brillante in E flat major, J252, "La gaité". Invitation to the dance, J260. **Hamish Milne** (pf). CRD CRD3485. Recorded in 1991.

1h 16m DDD 9/92

Weber's piano music, once played by most pianists, has since suffered neglect and even the famous *Invitation to the dance* is now more often heard in its orchestral form. Since he was a renowned pianist as well as a major composer, the neglect seems odd, particularly when other pianist composers such as Chopin and Liszt are at the centre of the concert repertory; but part of the trouble may lie in the difficulty of the music, reflecting his own huge hands and his tendency to write what the booklet essay calls "chords unplayable by others". Hamish Milnes makes out a real case for this music, and his playing of the two sonatas is idiomatic and resourceful, even if one cannot banish the feeling that Weber all too readily used the melodic and harmonic formulae of eighteenth-century *galanterie* and simply dressed them up in nineteenth century salon virtuosity. From this point of view, a comparison with Chopin's mature sonatas or Liszt's magnificent single essay in the form reveals Weber as a lightweight. A hearing of the first movement in the First Sonata will quickly tell you if this is how you may react, while in its *Presto* finale you may praise a Mendelssohnian lightness but also note a pomposity foreign to that composer. Leaving aside the musical quality of these sonatas, this is stylish playing which should win them friends. The *Rondo brillante* and *Invitation to the dance* make no claim to be other than scintillating salon music, and are captivating in Milne's shapely and skilful performances. The recording is truthful and satisfying.

Additional recommendations ...

No. 2. ***Brahms.*** *Four Ballades, Op. 10.* **Alfred Brendel** (pf). Philips 426 439-2PH — 53m DDD 6/91

Nos. 1 and 2. **Martin Jones** (pf). Pianissimo PP20792 — 58m DDD 9/92

Weber. DER FREISCHUTZ. **Peter Schreier** (ten) Max (Hans Jörn Weber); **Gundula Janowitz** (sop) Agathe (Regina Jeske); **Edith Mathis** (sop) Aennchen (Ingrid Hille); **Theo Adam** (bass) Caspar (Gerhard Paul); **Bernd Weikl** (bar) Ottokar (Otto Mellies); **Siegfried Vogel** (bass) Cuno (Gerd Biewer); **Franz Crass** (bass) Hermit; **Gerhard Paul** (spkr) Samiel; **Günther Leib** (bar) Kilian (Peter Hölzel); **Leipzig Radio Chorus; Staatskapelle Dresden/Carlos Kleiber.** DG 415 432-2GH2. Notes, text and translation included. From 2720 071 (11/73).

② 2h 10m ADD 11/86

This opera tells of a forester Max and his pact with the forces of darkness to give him the ability to shoot without missing. Carlos Kleiber's recordings are always fascinating and for this one he went back to the manuscript seeking out details rarely heard in the standard opera house text. His direction is imaginative and where controversial (his tempos do tend to extremes) one feels he presents a strong case. His cast is very fine too: Schreier's Max is more thoughtful than some, though always ready to spring back after his hellish encounters. Janowitz is a lovely Agathe and Mathis a perky Aennchen, whilst Adam's Caspar is suitably diabolic. The use of actors to speak the dialogue does take a little getting used to, but the recording is good and the Dresden orchestra play magnificently.

Additional recommendation ...

Soloists; Chorus of the Deutsche Oper, Berlin; Berlin Philharmonic Orchestra/Joseph Keilberth. EMI CMS7 69342-2 — ② 2h 14m ADD 9/89

Weber. OBERON. **Donald Grobe** (ten) Oberon (Martin Benrath); **Birgit Nilsson** (sop) Rezia (Katharina Matz); **Plácido Domingo** (ten) Huon (Gerhard Friedrich); **Hermann Prey** (bar) Scherasmin (Hans Putz); **Júlia Hamari** (contr) Fatime; (Ingrid Andree) **Marga Schiml** (sop) Puck (Doris Masjos); **Arleen Auger** (sop) Mermaid; **Bavarian Radio Chorus and**

Symphony Orchestra/Rafael Kubelík. DG 419 038-2GX2. Notes, text and translation included. From 2709 035 (7/72). Recorded in 1970.

② 2h 19m ADD 12/91

Though its characters include Oberon, Titania and Puck, Weber's last opera, to an English libretto and written for Covent Garden, has little to do with Shakespeare's *A Midsummer Night's Dream*. It has been variously called a pantomime and, more rudely, a dramatic shambles, but that is unkind to this story of chivalry and magic telling of the love of Sir Huon of Bordeaux for the daughter of the Sultan Haroun al Rashid and set in varied locations including Tunis and Baghdad. The other characters include Sir Huon's squire Scherasmin and Rezia's attendant Fatime, a pair of mermaids, elves and slaves. Today it is a rarity in the opera house, though the delicately scored overture (beginning with a horn call from fairyland) is well known, as is Rezia's big Act 2 scene, "Ocean, thou mighty monster". This performance uses a German translation and there is a linking narration in that language as well as much spoken dialogue, rather hammily spoken at that — in fact, the roles of Haroun and three other minor characters are not singing ones at all. Furthermore, when Huon and Rezia speak, Domingo and Nilsson are replaced by actors and the two voices of Huon do not resemble each other, while even the Berlin-born baritone Hermann Prey as Scherasmin is not allotted his spoken lines. Still, the speech can be skipped or followed in the translation provided in the booklet which, however, lacks an English synopsis. It's rather for the singers and the music that collectors will enjoy this mid-price set which doesn't show its age of 23 years. The young Plácido Domingo, entering exultantly on track 11 of the first disc, is in turn heroic and gentle, and the celebrated Wagnerian soprano Birgit Nilsson, who is predictably in her element addressing the ocean after the lovers' shipwreck, can also be more intimate as the music demands. The rest of the cast is strong, and the orchestra under Rafael Kubelík play sensitively and, in the storm, excitingly.

Further listening ...

Grand duo concertant, J204. *Coupled with* **Brahms.** Clarinet Sonatas, Op. 120 — No. 1 in F minor; No. 2 in E flat major. **Paul Meyer** (cl); **François-René Duchable** (pf). Erato 2292-45480-2 (9/90).

Anton Webern

Austrian 1883-1945

Webern. Passacaglia for Orchestra, Op. 1. Five Movements, Op. 5. Six Pieces, Op. 6. Symphony, Op. 21. **Berlin Philharmonic Orchestra/Herbert von Karajan.** DG 20th Century Classics 423 254-2GC. From 2711 014 (3/75). Recorded 1973-74.

46m ADD 7/88 

This mid-price disc, with good, digitally remastered sound, provides an excellent introduction to one of modern music's most important and influential masters. All three phases of Webern's development are represented. In the *Passacaglia* the youthful late-romantic is ready to shake off the shackles of Brahms and Strauss, and Karajan brings particular intensity to the work's moments of crisis and upheaval. In Op. 5 and Op. 6 the process of miniaturization is well under way, and together they provide powerful evidence of the fact that concentration and economy brought no loss of emotional power. Even in the less extravagant orchestration of the 1928 version, the funeral march movement from Op. 6 is as stark and volcanic an experience of raw grief and despair as any Mahler Adagio. After this the ten-minute, two-movement Symphony, with its coolly symmetrical serial canons, may sound like a retreat from reality. It is certainly more classical in concept than the earlier works, but that means a more equal balance of restraint and expressiveness, not a rejection of either. As an outstanding exponent of late-romantic symphonies, Karajan is especially sensitive to the lyricism, as well as the refinement, of the music.

NEW REVIEW

Webern. Passacaglia, Op. 1. Six Pieces, Op. 6. Five Pieces, Op. 10. Variations, Op. 30.
Bach (arr. Webern). Musikalisches Opfer, BWV1079 — Ricercar a 6.
Schoenberg. A Survivor from Warsaw, Op. 46[a]. [a]**Gottfried Hornik** (narr); [a]**Vienna State Opera Chorus; Vienna Philharmonic Orchestra/Claudio Abbado.** DG 431 774-2GH. Text and translation included. Recorded 1989-92.

50m DDD 5/93

Claudio Abbado has recorded rather more in the way of progressive twentieth-century music over the years than many other star conductors. It would be good to have much more. Meanwhile, we must be grateful for these recordings of Webern, including a fine reading of the rarely-heard and forcefully dramatic Variations, Op. 30. Abbado and the VPO are predictably responsive to the romantic intensity of the early Passacaglia, with nothing routine in their performance, and the sets of expressionist miniatures are even more convincing in their blend of delicacy and power. The fourth piece from Op. 6, the closest Webern ever came to concentrating the essence of a Mahlerian funeral march, and ending with an ear-splitting percussion crescendo, is all the more effective for Abbado's refusal to set a self-indulgently slow tempo. Technically, these recordings outshine the competition, though both Boulez and Karajan remain memorable as interpreters — Boulez especially in Op. 30, Karajan most notably in Op. 6. Given the evident rapport between Webern and Abbado it seems odd that the disc doesn't include more of Webern's music — for example, the Symphony, Op. 21. The Bach arrangement is nevertheless an ear-opening exercise in passing baroque counterpoint through a kaleidoscope of expressionist tone-colours, and Schoenberg's *A Survivor from Warsaw* retains its special power to move and disturb.

Webern. COMPLETE WORKS, Opp. 1-31. **Various artists.** Sony Classical M3K45845. Notes, texts and translations included. From 79204 (12/78). Recorded 1967-72.
Passacaglia, Op. 1 (London Symphony Orchestra/Pierre Boulez). Entflieht auf leichten Kähnen, Op. 2 (John Alldis Choir/Boulez). Five Songs from "Der siebente Ring", Op. 3. Five Songs, Op. 4 (Heather Harper, sop; Charles Rosen, pf). Five Movements, Op. 5 (Juilliard Quartet). Six Pieces, Op. 6 (LSO/Boulez). Four Pieces, Op. 7 (Isaac Stern, vn; Rosen, pf). Two Songs, Op. 8 (Harper, sop; chamber ensemble/Boulez). Six Bagatelles, Op. 9 (Juilliard Qt). Five Pieces, Op. 10 (LSO/Boulez). Three Little Pieces, Op. 11 (Gregor Piatigorsky, vc; Rosen, pf). Four Songs, Op. 12 (Harper, sop; Rosen, pf). Four Songs, Op. 13. Six Songs, Op. 14 (Harper, sop; chbr ens/Boulez). Five Sacred Songs, Op. 15. Five Canons on Latin Texts, Op. 16 (Halina Lukomska, sop; chbr ens/Boulez). Three Songs, Op. 18 (Lukomska, sop; John Williams, gtr; Colin Bradbury, cl/Boulez). Two Songs, Op. 19 (John Alldis Ch, mbrs LSO/Boulez). String Trio, Op. 20 (mbrs Juilliard Qt). Symphony, Op. 21 (LSO/Boulez). Quartet, Op. 22 (Robert Marcellus, cl; Abraham Weinstein, sax; Daniel Majeske, vn; Rosen, pf/Boulez). Three Songs from "Viae inviae", Op. 23 (Lukomska, sop; Rosen, pf). Concerto, Op. 24 (mbrs LSO/Boulez). Three Songs, Op. 25 (Lukomska, sop; Rosen, pf). Das Augenlicht, Op. 26 (John Alldis Ch, LSO/Boulez). Piano Variations, Op. 27 (Rosen, pf). String Quartet, Op. 28 (Juilliard Qt). Cantata No. 1, Op. 29 (Lukomska, sop; John Alldis Ch; LSO/Boulez). Variations, Op. 30 (LSO/Boulez). Cantata No. 2, Op. 31 (Lukomska, sop; Barry McDaniel, bar; John Alldis Ch; LSO/Boulez). Five Movements, Op. 5 — orchestral version (LSO/Boulez). *Bach* (orch. Webern): Musikalischen Opfer, BWV1079 — Fuga (Ricercata) No. 2 (LSO/Boulez). *Schubert* (orch. Webern): Deutsche Tänze, D820 (Frankfurt Radio Orchestra/Anton Webern. Recorded at a performance in the studios of Radio Frankfurt on December 29th, 1932).

③ 3h 43m ADD 6/91 £

Webern is as 'classic' to Pierre Boulez as Mozart or Brahms are to most other conductors, and when he is able to persuade performers to share his view the results can be remarkable — lucid in texture, responsive in expression. Despite his well-nigh exclusive concern with miniature forms, there are many sides to Webern, and although this set is not equally successful in realizing all of them, it leaves the listener in no doubt about the music's sheer variety, as well as its emotional power, whether the piece in question is an ingenious canon-by-inversion or a simple, folk-like *Lied*. From a long list of performers one could single out Heather Harper and the Juilliard Quartet for special commendation; and the smooth confidence of the John Alldis Choir is also notable. The recordings were made over a five-year period (1968-72) and have the typical CBS dryness of that time. Even so, in the finest performances which Boulez himself directs — the *Orchestral Variations*, Op. 30 is perhaps the high point — that remarkable radiance of spirit so special to Webern is vividly conveyed. It is a fascinating bonus to hear Webern himself conducting his Schubert arrangements — music from another world, yet with an economy and emotional poise that Webern in his own way sought to emulate.

Webern. WORKS FOR STRING TRIO AND QUARTET. **Arditti Quartet** (Irvine Arditti, David Alberman, vns; Levine Andrade, va; Rohan de Saram, vc). Disques Montaigne 789008. Recorded in 1990.
Five Movements, Op. 5. Six Bagatelles, Op. 9. String Quartet, Op. 28. Trio, Op. 20. Movement (1925). String Quartet (1905). Slow Movement (1905). Rondo (*c.* 1906).

1h 6m DDD 12/91

Webern's music, like that of his revered master Schoenberg, is vulnerable in performance. So much of it is so difficult to play at all that its expressive core is easily overlooked, all the more so because of the legend of saintly modernism slapped on it by the post-war avant-garde. The Arditti Quartet are among the select few who can get beyond the surface complexity and play the music like music; they also benefit from exceptional clarity of recording quality. And the works for quartet and trio are in any case particularly encouraging to the non-specialist listener, in that they lead step by step from the warm, Straussian romanticism of Webern's apprentice years, through the highly-charged expressionist masterpieces of his first maturity (Op. 5 and Op. 9) to the apparently forbidding later 12-note works. There's no use pretending that the Trio and the Op. 28 Quartet will ever be easy listening, but at least this disc comes with the guarantee that it's not the players' or the recording's fault if you don't respond.

Additional recommendation ...
Movement. String Quartet (1905). Five Movements. Six Bagatelles. String Quartet, Op. 28. **Quartetto Italiano.** Philips 420 796-2PH — 53m ADD 4/88

Matthias Weckmann

German c.1616-1674

NEW REVIEW
Weckmann. CANTATAS. **Greta de Reyghere, [a]Jill Feldman** (sops); **James Bowman** (alto); **Ian Honeyman, [a]Guy de Mey** (tens); **Max van Egmond** (bass); **[a]Capella Sancti Michaelis/Erik van Nevel; Ricercar Consort.** Ricercar RIC109097/8. Texts and translations included. Recorded in 1992.
Weine nicht, es hat über wunde. Zion sprecht, der Herr hat mich verlassen. Herr, wenn ich nur dich habe. Wie liegt die Stadt so wüste. Dialogo von Tobias und Raguel. Kommet her zu mir alle. Wenn der Herr die Gefangen zu Zion erlösen wird. Angelicus coeli chorus. Gegrüsset seist du, Holdselige. Rex virtutum. Der Tod ist verschlungen. Es erhub sich ein Streit[a].

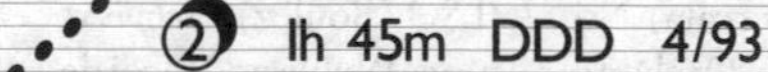

This is the ninth volume in Ricercar's excellent survey of German sacred music before and including Bach and Telemann. This two-CD set contains the complete cantatas of Schütz's pupil, Matthias Weckmann. Weckmann was born in about 1616 and after periods in Dresden and Denmark was appointed organist of the Jacobikirche in Hamburg which housed one of the finest organs in Germany. Weckmann's cantatas follow in the tradition of concerted music for solo voices, choir and instruments established in Germany by Schütz. The younger composer's debt to Schütz is often evident in these cantatas, but Weckmann nevertheless speaks with a voice of his own in which both vocal and instrumental parts are charged with emotion. Each of the pieces reveals Weckmann's sensitivity to texts which he colours with acute, sometimes searing intensity. The performances are given by a very strong cast of singers, joined in one work only — the triple-choir *Es erhub sich ein Streit* ("And there was war in heaven") by the Capella Sancti Michaelis directed by Erik van Nevel. The Ricercar Consort of period instruments also makes an effective contribution with a commendably strong violin section. There is neither a dull work nor a weak performance here, and pieces like *Zion sprecht* and *Wenn der Herr die Gefangen zu Zion* are highly imaginative and thrilling to the senses. First-rate sound and useful documentation with full texts merely add to the pleasure afforded by this music-making.

Thomas Weelkes

British 1576-1623

Suggested listening ...

Cathedral Music — Alleluia, I heard a voice. All laud and praise. Laboravi in gemitu meo. Give the king thy judgements. O Lord, arise. If King Manasses. When David heard. O how amiable are they dwellings. Gloria in excelsis Deo (Sing my soul to God). O Jonathan, woe is me. Hosanna to the Son of David. Pavane[a]. Evening Service for Trebles — Magnificat; Nunc dimittis. Voluntaries I and II[a]. **Winchester Cathedral Choir/David Hill** with [a]**Timothy Byram-Wigfield** (org). Hyperion CDA66477 (10/92).

Cathedral Music — Alleluia, I heard a voice. Give ear, O Lord. Hosanna to the Son of David. When David heard. O Lord, grant the King a long life. Give the King thy judgements. Gloria in excelsis Deo (Sing my soul to God). Evening Service a 5. Ninth Service. **Christ Church Cathedral Choir, Oxford/Stephen Darlington.** Nimbus NI5125 (3/89).

Kurt Weill

German/American 1900-1950

Weill. Concerto for violin and wind orchestra, Op. 12[a]. Kiddush[b]. Kleine Dreigroschenmusik. [a]**Yuval Waldman** (vn); [b]**Grayson Hirst** (ten); [b]**Ray Pellerin** (org); [b]**Amor Artis Chamber Choir and Orchestra/Johannes Somary.** Newport Classics NCD60098.

55m DDD 12/91

Kurt Weill's posthumous reputation as a composer for the stage, and the universal popularity of his most famous collaboration with Berthold Brecht, *Die Dreigroschenoper* ("The Threepenny Opera"), still tends to divert attention away from his achievements elsewhere, and this disc presents three works which could scarcely offer greater contrasts of style and content. The Concerto for violin and wind orchestra, for example, reveals Weill's close sympathies with the Second Viennese School, and like his two symphonies, this arresting work owes much to the combined influence of Hindemith, Busoni and even Mahler. The idea of setting the solo violin against the pungent background of the wind group is particularly fascinating, and Yuval Waldman's rich tone makes him an ideal exponent of the concerto. He is excellently supported by Johannes Somary and the Amor Artis Orchestra. Weill's setting of the *Kiddush*, in which the incantations of the cantor are set against blues-inspired choral responses underpinned by a discreet organ part, recall the composer's Jewish heritage, and especially his family associations with the synagogue at Dessau. The tenor, Grayson Hirst, sings here with eloquent gravity, and his diction in the Hebrew text is exemplary. Of course, no Weill compilation would be complete without at least some music from *Die Dreigroschenoper* and Johannes Somary's performance of the popular concert suite would be hard to beat. This maudlin assemblage of tawdry dance tunes set in a period idiom includes "Mack the knife" and "Ballad of the easy life", both of which recall Weill's experience of the decadent years, and his admiration for Brecht's acrimonious text, with all the tragicomic, caustic sarcasm of a George Gross cartoon. The performances are first class and the recording could hardly be bettered — strongly recommended.

Weill. Symphonies — No. 1; No. 2. Kleine Dreigroschenmusik. **Lisbon Gulbenkian Foundation Orchestra/Michel Swierczewski.** Nimbus NI5283.

lh 14m DDD 

The *Kleine Dreigroschenmusik*, a transcription of the jazz-band flavoured numbers from *The Threepenny Opera*, is here given an admirably jaunty performance and serves well as a sweetener to tempt the hesitant to less well-known Weill. The two symphonies couldn't be more different: the First is a student work, never performed in the composer's lifetime. It is full of experimentation, with one eye on Schoenberg, written for large orchestra, and yet with passages of sparse, austere chamber writing; the uninitiated would do well to identify the composer. The Second is a mature composition from the time of Weill's departure from Germany via Paris. Right from the start it is recognizably the Weill of *Mahagonny* or *The Seven Deadly Sins* — a composer speaking with his natural voice. The symphonic Weill, though, has nothing to do with 1920s dance rhythms. These are works in the symphonic line of Mahler, Strauss, Schoenberg, Hindemith and Shostakovich, and it it as such that they should be approached and appreciated. The Second Symphony, especially, is a work crying out for a place in the symphonic repertory — a powerful work with a haunting slow movement. Swierczewski's interpretations are full of assurance, the tempos aptly chosen to bring out all the contrasts of grandeur and introspection in the music.

Weill. SONGS. **Ute Lemper** (sop); **Berlin Radio Ensemble/John Mauceri.** Decca New Line 425 204-2DNL. Texts and translations included.

Der Silbersee — Ich bin eine arme Verwandte (Fennimores-Lied); Rom war eine Stadt (Cäsars Tod); Lied des Lotterieagenten. Die Dreigroschenoper — Die Moritat von Mackie Messer; Salomon-Song; Die Ballade von der sexuellen Hörigkeit. Das Berliner Requiem — Zu Potsdam unter den Eichen (arr. Hazell). Nannas-Lied. Aufstieg und Fall der Stadt Mahagonny — Alabama Song; Wie man sich bettet. Je ne t'aime pas. One Touch of Venus — I'm a stranger here myself; Westwind; Speak low.

50m DDD 3/89 

The songs in this collection are mostly from the major works Weill composed between 1928 and 1933, but also included are one from his years in France and three items from the 1943 Broadway musical *One Touch of Venus*. The collection introduces a most exciting talent in the person of Ute Lemper. By comparison with the husky, growling delivery often accorded Weill's songs in the manner of his widow Lotte Lenya, we here have a voice of appealing clarity and warmth. What distinguishes her singing, though, is the way in which these attributes of vocal purity are allied to a quite irresistible dramatic intensity. Her "Song of the Lottery Agent" is an absolute *tour de force*, apt to leave the listener emotionally drained, and her *Je ne t'aime pas* is almost equally overwhelming. Not least in the three numbers from *One Touch of Venus*, sung in perfect English, she displays a commanding musical theatre presence. With John Mauceri on hand to provide authentic musical accompaniments, this is, one feels, how Weill's songs were meant to be heard.

Weill. DIE DREIGROSCHENOPER. **Lotte Lenya,** Jenny; **Erich Schellow,** Macheath; **Willy Trenk-Trebitsch,** Mr Peachum; **Trude Hesterburg,** Mrs Peachum; **Johanna von Kóczián,** Polly Peachum; **Wolfgang Grunert,** Tiger Brown; **Inge Wolffberg,** Lucy; **Wolfgang Neuss,** Streetsinger; **Günther-Arndt Choir;** members of the Dance Orchestra of **Radio Free Berlin/Wilhelm Brückner-Rüggeberg.** CBS Masterworks CD42637. Notes, text and translation included. From 77268 (12/72). Recorded in 1958.

lh 18m ADD 3/89 

In *Die Dreigroschenoper* ("The Threepenny Opera") Kurt Weill sought to match the satire of Bertolt Brecht's updating of John Gay's *The Beggar's Opera* with numbers in the dance rhythms and jazz-tinged orchestrations of the time. The number that later became famous as "Mack the Knife" is merely the best known of the many catchy numbers in a score that none the less bears the hallmark of a cultivated musician. This 1958 reading has eclipsed all others. It has the distinction of featuring the composer's widow, Lotte Lenya, in the role of Jenny that she had created back in 1928. The recording carries about it an undeniable feeling of authenticity in the pungency of its satire and the catchiness of its score. Johanna von Kóczian is a charming Polly, Erich Schellow a winning Macheath, and Trude Hesterberg a formidable Frau Peachum, while Wilhelm Brückner-Rüggeberg has just the right feel for Weill's dance rhythms. This is an absolutely complete recording of the score, including the once expurgated "Ballad of Sexual Dependency" and the usually omitted "Jealousy Song". Despite its age, the recorded sound remains good, and the whole is a compelling experience.

Additional recommendation ...
Soloists; Berlin RIAS Chamber Choir and Sinfonietta/John Mauceri. Decca 430 075-2DH — lh 14m DDD 3/90

Weill. DIE SIEBEN TODSUNDEN. MAHAGONNY SONGSPIEL[a]. **Ute Lemper** (sop); [a]**Susanne Tremper** (sngr); **Helmut Wildhaber, Peter Haage** (tens); **Thomas Mohr** (bar); **Manfred Jungwirth** (bass); **Berlin RIAS Sinfonietta/John Mauceri.** Decca 430 168-2DH. Notes, text and translation included. Recorded in 1989.

lh 6m DDD 4/91

In these two works, Brecht and Weill used much the same musical style as in *The Threepenny Opera. The Seven Deadly Sins* is a vocal ballet, with sections representing each sin, while the *Mahagonny Songspiel* is a concert piece that summarizes the political thrust and music of the opera *Rise and Fall of the City of Mahagonny*. Superficially it seems a shame that Ute Lemper should adopt an unauthentic downward transposition of *The Seven Deadly Sins* (mostly by a fourth) that was prepared by Wilhelm Brückner-Rüggeberg for the composer's widow Lotte Lenya. Yet there are strong plus points in favour of it as recorded here. In the first place, Weill's original orchestration is fully followed. In the second place, the lower vocal line undoubtedly suits Lemper. And to hear her singing Weill in a register that suits her is joy indeed! She has just the right youthfulness, the musicality and expressiveness, and a control of both music and text that confirm her as a musical theatre singer of rare talent. The intensity that pours forth from singer and orchestra in, say, "Lust", sets this recording apart from earlier versions. In the *Mahagonny Songspiel*, with its irresistible songs, Lemper again seems completely the part.

Additional recommendation ...
DIE SIEBEN TODSUNDEN. KLEINE DREIGROSCHENMUSIK. **Soloists; London Symphony Orchestra/Michael Tilson Thomas.** CBS Masterworks CD44529 — 55m DDD 3/89

Weill. DER SILBERSEE. **Wolfgang Schmidt** (ten) Severin; **Hildegard Heichele** (sop) Fennimore; **Hans Korte** (bar) Olim; **Eva Tamassy** (mez) Frau von Luber; **Udo Holdorf** (ten) Baron Laur; **Frederic Mayer** (ten) Lottery Agent; **Cologne Pro Musica; Cologne Radio Symphony Orchestra/Jan Latham-König.** Capriccio 60 011-2. Notes, text and translation included. Recorded in 1989.

② lh 47m DDD 8/90

The sub-title of *Der Silbersee*, "A winter's tale", is to be interpreted both literally and metaphorically, for this is a remarkable parable of the dark night of the soul of a Germany about to be plunged into Nazi oppression: the infamous Reichstag fire took place only a matter of days after its première. The symbolism is patent in this tale of poverty, famine, avarice, unscrupulous trickery and turbulent emotions, and a final escape over a bleak lake to an uncharted future: cultured theatre-goers at the time would in any case have remembered that the same sub-title was affixed to Heine's satirical verse epic *Deutschland*. Apart, however, from the punch of Georg Kaiser's social and political message, Weill's music is impressively powerful and moving, both in his 'serious' vein (as in the voices of the policeman Olim's conscience after he has shot Severin, escaping after raiding a food store, or the lovely orchestral passage while snow is falling on the lake) and in his 'popular' (the lottery agent's tango or the foxtrot at a celebratory meal). It should perhaps be emphasized that this is a play with music rather than a 'proper opera'; but the skilful reduction here of the spoken dialogue (very well handled by the actors) throws the music into greater relief. It includes several big set-pieces, such as the girl Fennimore's ballad about Caesar's death (small wonder the Nazis banned the work!), Severin's savage cry for revenge, and the "Fools' paradise" song of the wicked schemers Frau von Lubin and Baron Laub. It is vital however that these should be heard in their rightful context; and the strength of this performance — something of a triumph for Jan Latham-König, his producer and the cast — lies in its tremendous dramatic grip.

Weill. STREET SCENE. **Kristine Ciesinski** (sop) Anna Maurrant; **Richard Van Allan** (bass) Frank Maurrant; **Janis Kelly** (sop) Rose Maurrant; **Bonaventura Bottone** (ten) Sam Kaplan; **Terry Jenkins** (ten) Abraham Kaplan; **Meriel Dickinson** (mez) Emma Jones; **Angela Hickey** (mez) Olga Olsen; **Claire Daniels** (sop) Jennie Hildebrand; **Fiametta Doria** (sop) First Nursemaid; **Judith Douglas** (mez) Second Nursemaid; **English National Opera Chorus and Orchestra/Carl Davis.** TER Classics CDTER21185. Recorded in 1989.

② 2h 26m DDD 11/91

Street Scene is the most ambitious product of Weill's American years. It's something of a *Porgy and Bess* transferred from Catfish Row to the slum tenements of New York. Where *Porgy and Bess* is through-composed with recitatives, though, *Street Scene* offers a mixture of set musical numbers, straight dialogue, and dialogue over musical underscoring. The musical numbers themselves range from operatic arias and ensembles to rousing 1940s dance numbers. This complete recording is one of two resulting from a joint Scottish Opera/English National Opera production of 1989. This one offers the cast and conductor of the ENO production, with just a couple of relatively minor substitutions. Of the two recordings this is probably the more consistently well sung, particularly where style is concerned. Weill described the work as a "Broadway opera", and it demands a vernacular rather than a classical operatic singing style. This it duly gets from Kristine Ciesinski as Anna Maurrant, while Janis Kelly's beautifully clear but natural enunciation and her sense of emotional involvement make daughter Rose's "What good would the moon be?" a performance of real beauty. Praiseworthy too is Richard Van Allan as the murderous husband, his "Let things be like they always was" creating a suitably sinister effect. Among the subsidiary attractions is the appearance of Catherine Zeta Jones, of ITV's *The Darling Buds of May*, performing the swinging dance number "Moon-faced, starry-eyed".

Additional recommendation ...

Soloists; Scottish Opera Chorus and Orchestra/John Mauceri. Decca 433 371-2DH2 — ② 2h 28m DDD

Samuel Wesley

British 1766-1837

S. Wesley. SYMPHONIES. **Milton Keynes Chamber Orchestra/Hilary Davan Wetton.** Unicorn-Kanchana DKPCD9098. Recorded in 1990.
No. 3 in A major; No. 4 in D major; No. 5 in E flat major; No. 6 in B flat major.

1h 4m DDD 10/91 

Son of Charles the hymn-writer and father of Samuel Sebastian, Samuel Wesley was a wunderkind ("an English Mozart" was Boyce's description) who never quite realized his potential, partly, perhaps, because a serious fall in 1787 damaged his skull and left him prone to frequent bouts of irritability and depression. But the four symphonies recorded here — three from 1784 and the fourth from 1802 — are a delightful find, revealing a marvellously fresh and fluent melodic gift allied to a penchant for the quirky turn of phrase. The opening movement of the A major Symphony, for instance, has a grace of demeanour and warmth of sonority characteristic of J.C. Bach (and, for that matter, of Mozart in the same key); but there is an ear-catching individuality both in the themes themselves and in the way the initial idea is augmented and expanded to form the second subject. And the finale, a lusty countrified gavotte, has an unmistakably English flavour. Beguiling as the three teenage symphonies are, the B flat is an altogether more colourful and sophisticated work, and a tantalizing suggestion of what he might have achieved in the form if his health and inclination had allowed. Wesley obviously knew Haydn's "London" symphonies well; but the music has a genial, unfettered quality of melodic invention and an attractive waywardness that are entirely individual. If they lack Haydn's sheer dynamism, both outer movements are purposefully developed, drawing on Wesley's lightly worn contrapuntal skill; and the nonchalant, throw away ending of the opening *Allegro* is one of many characteristic moments in the work where Wesley slyly foils the listener's expectations. The performances are first-rate: polished, poised, vital of rhythm and fully alive to the warmth of Wesley's lines and textures. The woodwind relish their prominent roles in the B flat symphony, and there's a discreetly balanced harpsichord continuo. The recording is exemplary in its clarity and spaciousness. Highly recommended to any Haydn or Mozart lover with a streak of musical adventure.

Samuel Sebastian Wesley

British 1810-1876

S.S. Wesley. ANTHEMS AND ORGAN WORKS. **New College Choir, Oxford/Edward Higginbottom** (org). CRD CRD3463. Texts included. Recorded 1987-90.
Anthems — Ascribe unto the Lord. Blessed be the God and Father. Cast me not away. Thou wilt keep him in perfect peace. Wash me throughly. The wilderness and the solitary place. *Organ works* — Andante in E minor. Choral song and fugue. Larghetto in F minor.

1h 7m DDD 10/91

At some time in the last half-century somebody in church-music circles must have compiled a list of anthems comprising what today would be called the "Top Ten". If so, S.S. Wesley would surely be prominent among the composers. *Blessed be the God and Father*, with its famous treble solo, "Love one another", might indeed emerge as the outright favourite. *Thou wilt keep him in perfect peace* is certainly one of the most beautiful, its arching phrases, strong melody and well-judged admixture of polyphony being firmly bound in a well-designed architecture. From the large-scale anthem, *Ascribe unto the Lord*, the final section, "The Lord hath been mindful of us", often serves as an anthem in its own right, and this too has the great merit of tunefulness, with ample opportunity for all voices, including the oft-neglected altos. Then there is *The wilderness and the solitary place*, a cathedral Sunday anthem, 15 minutes long, with one of the supreme challenges to the self-respecting head-choirboy: the clean 'take' of those exposed top As in "and sorrow and sighing". The New College trebles, individually and collectively, are well up to all the demands, and the men's voices (some fine soloists among them too) also sound well. The style of performance, as opposed to the quality of sound, may be more questionable: the slow tempo of the last chorus in *Blessed be the God and Father*, for instance, has a ponderous effect, and the punctuation is frequently too self-conscious. Even so, this is a good disc for representing Wesley in one's collection, especially as it also has two of the finest anthems (*Cast me not away* and *Wash me throughly* that surely come in direct line from Purcell, with the additional pleasure of three organ solos.

Charles Marie Widor

French 1844-1937

NEW REVIEW

Widor. ORGAN WORKS. **Thomas Trotter.** Argo 433 152-2ZH. Played on the Cavaillé-Coll organ of Saint François-de-Sales, Lyon, France. Recorded in 1990.
Symphonies, Op. 42: No. 5 in F minor — Adagio; Toccata. No. 6 in C minor — Allegro. No. 7 — Moderato cantabile; Allegro. Symphonie gothique in C minor, Op. 70. Trois nouvelles pièces, Op. 87.

1h 14m DDD 10/92

Two pieces of organ music stand head and shoulders above anything else in sheer popularity. After Bach's Toccata and Fugue in D minor, Widor's Toccata has justifiably attracted admiration from generations of music-lovers. Any church organist will tell you that it's requested as frequently for weddings as any music, and in performance it displays not only the player's virtuosity but also the power and glory of the instrument itself. But to assess Widor's qualities as a composer on the strength of this one piece is to do him a major disservice. Let's say straight away that Thomas Trotter's sturdy performance is the equal of any, and this full-throated French organ makes a simply wondrous noise. The Toccata comes from one of ten full-scale symphonies Widor wrote for the organ attempting to recreate in scope and range on one instrument what other symphonists achieve through the medium of a large orchestra. These organ symphonies exploit a vast array of colours and effects and in addition to a complete symphony (the aptly named *Gothic*) Trotter has selected a number of individual movements — the majestic opening of the Sixth, the lyrical *moderato cantabile* from the Eighth and not only the Toccata but the reflective *adagio* which precedes it in the Fifth (and without which no performance of the Toccata should be considered complete). Argo have captured these splendid performances in a most atmospheric recording which will hopefully inspire the inquisitive listener to delve beyond the flamboyant Toccata.

Further listening ...

Sinfonia sacra, Op. 81[a]. Symphony No. 3, Op. 69[b]. **Paul Wisskirchen** (org); [a]**Cologne Gurzenich Orchestra,** [b]**Philharmonia Hungarica/Volker Hempfling.** Motette CD40071.

John Williams

American 1932-

Suggested listening ...

Flute Concerto[a]. Violin Concerto[b]. [a]**Peter Lloyd** (fl); [b]**Mark Peskanov** (vn); **London Symphony Orchestra/Leonard Slatkin.** Varèse Sarabande VSD5345.

Dracula — *original film soundtrack.* Varèse Sarabande VSD5250.

E.T.: The Extra-Terrestrial — *original film soundtrack.* MCA DMCL1878.

Hook — *original film soundtrack.* Epic 469 349-2.

Film scores — Close Encounters of the Third Kind; Star Wars. **National Philharmonic Orchestra/Charles Gerhardt.** RCA Victor GD82698.

Henryk Wieniawski

Polish 1835-1880

Suggested listening ...

Violin Concerto No. 2 in D minor, Op. 22. *Coupled with* **Paganini.** Violin Concerto No. 1 in D major, Op. 6. **Mark Kaplan** (vn); **London Symphony Orchestra/Mitch Miller.** Arabesque Z6597 (7/89).

Meredith Willson

American 1902-1984

Suggested listening ...

THE MUSIC MAN. **Original Broadway cast.** EMI Angel ZDM7 64663-2.

Key to Symbols

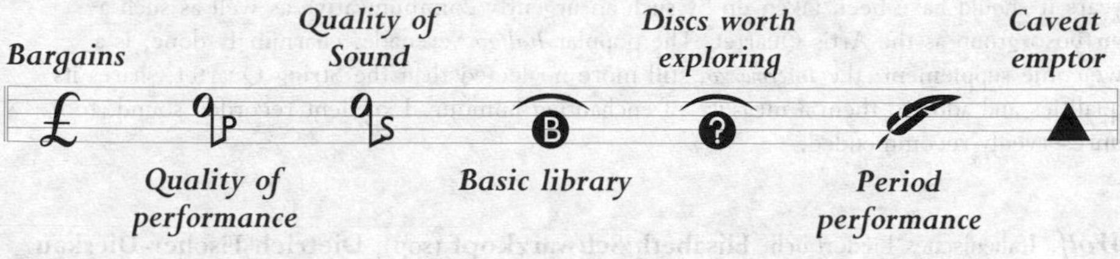

Sandy Wilson

Suggested listening ...

THE BOY FRIEND. **Original 1984 London revival cast.** That's Entertainment CDTER1095 (3/87).

Hugo Wolf

Austrian 1860-1903

Wolf. ORCHESTRAL WORKS. **Orchestre de Paris/Daniel Barenboim.** Erato 2292-45416-2. Recorded in 1988.
Penthesilea[a]. DER CORREGIDOR — Prelude; Intermezzo. Italian Serenade[a]. Scherzo and Finale.

57m DDD 4/90

Daniel Barenboim has done Wolf's admirers a great service by not only giving *Penthesilea* its first recording for many years, but by adding all of Wolf's other purely orchestral music. We can now speculate about what manner of symphonist he might have become: an assured and masterly one if the so-called scherzo and finale are anything to go by. They date from his teens, and the scherzo in particular is both finely made and ingeniously imagined. The joyously exuberant finale is almost light music, and good company for the two little operatic entr'actes and the already popular *Italian* Serenade. *Penthesilea* prompts similar questions about how Wolf might have developed as an operatic composer if he had followed up the wayward but entrancing *Der Corregidor* with something on a mythic subject and a grander scale. It is gorgeously coloured music, wildly inventive and hugely urgent; a bit undisciplined at times, and occasionally over-scored (Wolf knew that; he was struggling to revise the piece in the last months before his mind broke down) but with unobtrusively firm control from the conductor and superfine playing (both provided here) it becomes possible to suspect that the next stage of Wolf's creativity might have been to rival Strauss as Wagner's operatic successor. The recording, made at a public concert, has a moment or two of congestion but is otherwise both rich and brilliant.

Wolf. Intermezzo. Italian Serenade. String Quartet in D minor. **Artis Quartet** (Peter Schumayer, Johannes Meissl, vns; Herbert Kefer, va; Othmar Muller, vc). Accord 22080-2. Recorded in 1987.

57m DDD 6/90

Wolf's astonishing String Quartet suggests that his early death and the discouragingly contemptuous treatment his larger works received during his lifetime, robbed us of a great composer of chamber music. The Quartet is without the slightest shadow of doubt a masterpiece. For a composer not yet 20 to have had such a mastery of large-scale structure, such skilled command of complex thematic working and such confidence in handling big and dramatic ideas is nothing short of breathtaking. But these profoundly serious qualities are combined with a youthful prodigality of invention and an exuberance of spirit that are winning as well as awesome. Only the work's huge difficulty in performance can have kept it on the furthest fringes of the repertory for so long. How fortunate that for its first recording in many years it should have been taken up by such an urgently communicative as well as such a virtuoso group as the Artis Quartet. The popular *Italian* Serenade, charmingly done, is a welcome supplement; the *Intermezzo*, still more neglected than the String Quartet, shares its qualities and adds to them a measure of enchanting humour. Excellent recorded sound, too: unreservedly recommended.

Wolf. Italienisches Liederbuch. **Elisabeth Schwarzkopf** (sop); **Dietrich Fischer-Dieskau** (bar); **Gerald Moore** (pf). EMI CDM7 63732-2. Text and translation included. From SAN210/1 (2/69). Recorded 1965-67.

1h 19m ADD 12/90 £ 9p

Even today the songs of Hugo Wolf are underrated, and do not always draw an audience or sell on disc. If anything can change that situation it ought to be this reissue of a classic account of Wolf's most delightful Songbook, in which the blessings and cares and amusements of love are charmingly retailed. Walter Legge, the century's greatest Wolf advocate after Ernest Newman, was the knowledgeable producer behind this offering, which was joyfully greeted in its LP form some 20 years ago. Its transfer to CD is greatly to be welcomed. Between them Schwarzkopf and Fischer-Dieskau have just about every attribute, vocal and interpretative, to sing these pieces with total devotion and understanding. The many characters portrayed so subtly and unerringly by the composer are all brought to life by the wit and wisdom of his interpreters without whom the songs would lie forgotten on the page. As their partner the veteran Gerald Moore plays with all his old skill and perception. All one needs to add is that the recording is unforced and natural. This is a 'must' for all lovers of Lieder.

Additional recommendation ...

Irmgard Seefried (sop); **Dietrich Fischer-Dieskau** (bar); **Erik Werba, Jörg Demus** (pfs). DG Dokumente 435 752-2GDO — 1h 15m ADD 11/92 £ 9p

NEW REVIEW

Wolf. LIEDER. **Thomas Allen** (bar); **Geoffrey Parsons** (pf). Virgin Classics VC7 59221-2. Texts and translations included.

Mörike Lieder — Jägerlied; Der Tambour; Er ist's; Nimmersatte Liebe; Fussreise; An eine Aeolsharfe; Verborgenheit; Elfenlied; Der Gärtner; Gesang Weylas; An die Geliebte; Gebet; Auf ein altes Bild; Heimweh; An eine Aeolsharfe; Bei einer Trauung; Abschied. Goethe Lieder — Erschaffen un Beleben; Harfenspieler I-III; Spottlied aus "Wilhelm Meister"; Der Rattenfänger; Blumengruss; Gleich und Gleich; Anakreons Grab; Phänomen; Ob der Koran von Ewigkeit sei?; Trunken müssen wir alle sein!; So lang man nüchten ist; Sie haben wegen der Trunkheit; Was in der Schenke waren heute.

1h 16m DDD 10/92

Hugo Wolf shared a fair number of characteristics with Robert Schumann — not only his particular gift for creating perfectly crafted miniatures but also, less fortunately, the syphilis which led him finally to total mental disintegration. Wolf's case was in fact the more extreme: apparently manic-depressive and suffering from extremes of mood from wild creativity to depression and exhaustion. The powerful contrast between the inward tenderness of *Verborgenheit* and the group of songs concerning drunkenness which are positively violent in character is perhaps an indication of Wolf's own state of mind; in which case this disc offers a panorama of a composer's psyche in all its depth and darkness. Not least striking, in the brighter areas of depth, is Wolf's unfailing melodic conviction, shown most strongly in the first song, *Fussreise*, the delightful lightness of *Der Gärtner*, and the *élan* of *Er ist's*. Thomas Allen's readings are delivered with maturity, a great emotional awareness and deep, beautifully varied tone, for instance, in *An eine Aeolsharfe*, an extraordinary sense of wonder and tenderness. Geoffrey Parsons proves an ideal accompanist, characterizing the complex settings with great sensitivity. The sound quality is excellent.

Ermanno Wolf-Ferrari

Italian 1876-1948

NEW REVIEW

Wolf-Ferrari. ORCHESTRAL MUSIC. **Academy of St Martin in the Fields/Sir Neville Marriner.** EMI CDC7 54585-2. Recorded in 1991.

IL SEGRETO DI SUSANNA — Overture; Intermezzo. I QUATTRO RUSTEGHI — Overture; Intermezzo. LA DAMA BOBA — Overture. IL CAMPIELLO — Intermezzo; Ritornello. L'AMORE MEDICO — Overture; Intermezzo. I GIOIELLI DELLA MADONNA — Festa popolare; Intermezzo; Serenata; Danza napoletana.

54m DDD 3/93

Wolf Ferrari initially followed his German father into painting, but later turned to composing lightweight comic operas (the verismo *The Jewels of the Madonna* is atypical of his general style). He was a protégé of Boito and a pupil of Rheinberger and, although he achieved his greatest successes in Germany with operas to Italian librettos later translated into German, he was director of the conservatory in Venice for ten years. Such contradictions abounded in his life, yet his music, as illustrated by the works astutely programmed for this disc, is singularly consistent. Melodic charm, an easygoing harmonic style, and an admirable facility in effective scoring are typical. Sir Neville Marriner has a great way with all of these and although this disc will not unduly tax the intellect, it should provide a warm feeling of relaxation and well-being. The well-known Intermezzo to *I quattro rusteghi* ("The Four Boors") is a perfect example of what is best about Wolf-Ferrari's idiom — a delicate pizzicato accompaniment introduces a gentle, shapely tune (already heard in the opera sung by Marina, the hero's aunt) that sleepily runs its course with some rescoring but very little interruption. The result is a miniature of gem-like purity and delight. The EMI sound is fine-grained enough to capture all the small details of these performances, and the ASMF play with their usual dash and warmth, obviously finding pleasure in the softly-spoken qualities of this elusive composer.

Stefan Wolpe

German/American 1902-1972

NEW REVIEW

Wolpe. CHAMBER AND VOCAL WORKS. [a]**Joyce Castle** (mez); [b]**Raymond Mase** (tpt); [c]**Parnassus/Anthony Korf.** Koch International Classics 37141-2. Notes, text and translations included. Recorded 1987-91.

In Two Parts[c]. Three Lieder[ac]. Quartet[c]. Hamlet[c]. Piece for Two Instrumental Units[c]. To the Dancemaster[ac]. Solo Piece for Trumpet[b]. Piece for trumpet and seven instruments[bc].

1h 2m DDD 12/92

Stefan Wolpe was taught by Busoni in his native Berlin. When the Nazis came to power he moved to Vienna, where he studied with Webern. Finally he settled in New York. His music shows stylistic differences which are no doubt caused by the contrasting personal and environmental influences of his background. *In Two Parts*, written for a sextet of diverse instruments, and *Piece for Two Instrumental Units*, scored for nine players, both date from 1962 and show the influence of Webern. Serial techniques are used, but Wolpe creates works which are easier to assimilate than those by the older composer. Joyce Castle gives a vigorous performance of the three songs written in 1943 to texts by Bertolt Brecht. Here the writing is pungently expressive, recalling the work of Weill and to some extent Wolf. The influence of modern jazz permeates the Quartet of 1950, for trumpet, tenor saxophone, percussion and piano. *To the Dancemanster*, written in 1938 to an Israeli text, has a Jewish folk-song flavour: *Hamlet* is a spiky, atonal piece from 1929, written for flute, clarinet and cello to accompany a scene from Shakespeare's play. The two late pieces featuring Raymond Mase's trumpet explore the instrument's resources in brilliant fashion. On this evidence Wolpe was a gifted rather than a great composer. His works are given first-class advocacy by the New York-based Parnassus ensemble plus the two soloists, and the engineering is excellent.

Charles Wood

Irish 1866-1926

NEW REVIEW

C. Wood. St Mark Passion[a].
Holloway. Since I believe in God the Father Almighty. [a]**William Kendall** (ten); [a]**Paul Robinson,** [a]**Kwame Ryan** (bars); [a]**Peter Harvey** (bass); **Gonville and Caius College Choir, Cambridge/Geoffrey Webber** with **Richard Hill** (org). ASV CDDCA854. Notes and texts included.

lh 3m DDD 5/93

Charles Wood's *St Mark Passion* is a work which will certainly prove interesting to church music enthusiasts and scholars of late nineteenth-century English music. It has never been recorded before and is here treated with care and respect by the choir of Gonville and Caius College, Cambridge, under Geoffrey Webber. Wood's setting stands out from contemporary Passion settings through its biblical text and its imaginative idiom and handling of the chorus's role, which occasionally takes over the Evangelist's narrative at key dramatic moments. Musically the work has some surprises in store, switching between rather bland, austere polyphony and some astonishing chromaticism at times of high tension, here and there proving a Wagnerian influence. The disc notes suggest that the work has not held much currency because of the lack of congregational participation — most of the hymns are arranged for choir only. Wood was lecturer in harmony and counterpoint and also organist of Gonville and Caius College, so the performance here is probably as 'authentic' as one could wish, sung in the most pure Cambridge choir tradition. William Kendall as the Evangelist and Peter Harvey as Christ have true, clear voices and there is a glorious boy soprano lurking in a descant role in the hymn "My God I love Thee". The singing style generally is short on variety and contrast but strong on text declamation and tone quality, which is probably appropriate to this largely serious and meditative writing. The filler provides a chance to hear a lovely short work, *Since I believe in God the Father Almighty,* by Gonville and Caius's present music Fellow, Robin Holloway.

Haydn Wood

British 1882-1959

NEW REVIEW

Haydn Wood. ORCHESTRAL WORKS. **Bratislava Radio Symphony Orchestra/Adrian Leaper.** Marco Polo 8 223402. Recorded in 1991.
Sketch of a dandy. Serenade to Youth. Mannin veen. Three London cameos — suite. Mylecharane. Moods Suite No. 6, "Joyousness". A brown bird singing. Apollo. The seafarer.

lh 9m DDD 8/92

Haydn Wood obtained his unusual first name from parents inspired by a performance of *The Creation.* Best remembered nowadays for the First World War ballad *Roses of Picardy,* he also composed a great deal of light orchestral music in the style of his close contemporary, Eric Coates. If Wood's orchestral music never achieved the huge popularity of Coates's, the evidence presented in this collection suggests that he was unlucky. The programme contents vary between the reflective, the rhapsodic and the romantic, but are consistently tuneful. If the two pieces inspired by Wood's Manx childhood perhaps slightly outstay their welcome, there are rich delights in the sentimental *Serenade to Youth,* the sparkling *Sketch of a dandy,* the swirling waltz "Joyousness" and the rhapsody on sea songs, *The seafarer.* Perhaps most impressive of all is the *London cameos* suite, from which "Ball at Buckingham Palace" has often been played on BBC Radio 2's "Melodies for You". Considering that the Slovak players can hardly have heard of Wood or his music before making the recording, Adrian Leaper has done an astonishing job to produce such authentic playing. This excellently recorded collection cannot be recommended too highly to anyone who is interested in British light music.

William Wordsworth

British 1908-1988

Wordsworth. Symphonies — No. 2 in D major, Op. 34; No. 3 in D major, Op. 48. **London Philharmonic Orchestra/Nicholas Braithwaite.** Lyrita SRCD207.

1h 11m DDD 11/90

This composer is a descendant of the poet whose name he shares, and a contemporary of another William W. who did honour to British music. But while Walton won early fame, Wordsworth languished in obscurity, respected by the few who came across his work but unknown to the musical public. The BBC did little to promote his music and actually rejected his Second Symphony of 1948, a scandalously high-handed treatment of a fine creator which may have partly stifled his development. At any rate, this work went on to win an Edinburgh Festival competition two years later and is a forceful, serious statement by a natural symphonist which deserves to be heard and provides some compelling listening. Admittedly, memorable melody and easy charm are in short supply, but there are other rewards, for a strong intellect and imagination are at work. Admirers of the symphonies of Bax and Vaughan Williams (whose Fourth Symphony comes to mind in the brooding slow movement) will find much to satisfy them here, particularly in this committed and well recorded performance. The Third Symphony is shorter but arguably still finer, having just three movements and being lighter in texture and spirit. But once again a powerful imagination is at work, and there is a quirky Shostakovich-like invention, for example in the writing for celesta in the slow movement (the longest of the three). Whatever the case, this disc reminds us of the injustice the British musical establishment did to a composer who died in his eightieth year, two years before its release.

Robert Wright

American 1914-

KISMET (Wright/Forrest, after Borodin). Cast includes **Valerie Masterson, Donald Maxwell, David Rendall, Richard Van Allan, Judy Kaye; Ambrosian Chorus; Philharmonia Orchestra/John Owen Edwards.** TER Classics CDTER2 1170. Includes five songs from "Timbuktu".

② 1h 37m DDD 7/90

There have been a number of expensively mounted star-led studio recordings of the big musicals in recent years, most of them flawed somewhere along the line in their casting of the principal roles. How good then to be able to welcome a faultlessly performed, superbly played and thrillingly recorded account of Wright and Forrest's musical extravaganza which was subtitled in the original programme *A Musical Arabian Night*. This venerable team would probably be the first to acknowledge their debt to Borodin whose music, from the opera *Prince Igor* to a Little Serenade for Piano, they've reworked so convincingly in their tale of a poet (Donald Maxwell) in ancient Baghdad whose daughter Marsinah (Valerie Masterson) he plans to marry to a handsome Caliph (David Rendall) after drowning her husband, the wicked Wazir (Richard Van Allan) in a fountain! The score reads like a hit parade of the 1950s, "Stranger in Paradise", "Night of My Nights", "And This is my Beloved" and "Baubles, Bangles and Beads" which has become a favourite with jazzers over the years. Even those readers who might shy away from operetta or thumb their noses at the reworking of the classics will acknowledge the wholehearted conviction with which *Kismet* is executed by this nearly all British cast, under John Owen Edwards's idiomatic direction. The one import in this line-up is Broadway's Judy Kaye who delivers a gutsy rendition of "Not Since Ninevah", the score's one homage to syncopation and the glitter of neon light. Several years after *Kismet*, Wright and Forrest rewrote their old favourite for Eartha Kitt and an all black cast as *Timbuktu* and it is with several songs from that score that this pair of CDs is filled out.

Iannis Xenakis

Romanian/French 1922-

Xenakis. Palimpsest. Dikhthas[a]. Epeï. Akanthos[b]. [a]**Irvine Arditti** (vn); [a]**Claude Helffer** (pf); [b]**Penelope Walmsley-Clark** (sop); **Spectrum/Guy Protheroe.** Wergo WER6178-2. Recorded in 1986.

44m DDD 

Contemporary music has often come under attack for being unapproachable, élitist and intellectual. True, many of the techniques used by contemporary composers are often heavily indebted to mathematical procedures, but does the listener need to have a full understanding of these to appreciate the music? After all, how many music lovers fully understand the working techniques of Mozart or Beethoven? An over-simplification perhaps, but often the best way to begin exploring contemporary music is to drop any preconceived ideas and approach the music on a 'sensational' rather than intellectual level. The music of Iannis Xenakis, for example, often uses techniques that would seem more at home on an architect's or mathematician's drawing board, but the resulting music, far from being arid or intellectual, often has a physical, tactile effect upon the listener — Xenakis is a true alchemist. In *Palimpsest* a simple idea of non-repeating scale patterns becomes an exhilarating, roller-coaster ride for the listener as the instruments jostle for prominence. By contrast, *Epeï* ("since") is introverted and pensive, a musical ripple emanating from a central musical point in time. *Dikhthas* (violin and piano) means double or duel, and here Xenakis explores the two very different qualities of the instruments — sometimes placing the violin and piano in conflict with each other, sometimes merging them together as one. *Akanthos* is a marvellous evocation of the twisting, convoluted patterns produced by the ornamental leaves of the Acanthus plant, with the miasmatic meanderings of the instruments and solo soprano voice producing some unusual and striking melodic ideas. The performances by the ensemble, Spectrum, under the direction of Guy Protheroe, are of an exceptionally high quality, and the recorded sound is excellent. A tough but very rewarding disc.

Further listening ...

Jalons[a]. Phlegra[b]. Thalleïn[b]. Keren[c]. Nomos Alpha[d]. [c]**Benny Sluchin** (trombone); [d]**Pierre Strauch** (vc); **Ensemble Intercontemporain/**[a]**Pierre Boulez,** [b]**Michel Tabachnik.** Erato 2292-45770-2.

Naama[b]. A l'Ile de Gorée[bc]. Khoaï[b]. Komboï[ab]. [a]**Sylvio Gualda** (perc); [b]**Elisabeth Chojnacka** (hpd); [c]**Xenakis Ensemble/Huub Kerstens.** Erato MusiFrance 2292-45030-2 (10/90).

Metastasis. Pithoprakta. Eonta[a]. **French Radio National Orchestra/François Le Roux;** [a]**Paris Contemporary Music Instrumental Ensemble/Konstantin Simonovic.** Le Chant du Monde LCD278 368.

ORESTIA. **Strasbourg University Music Department; Colmar Women's Voices; Anjou Vocal Ensemble; Basse-Normandie Ensemble/Dominique Debart.** Salabert Actuels SCD8906 (9/90).

Eugène Ysaÿe

Belgian 1858-1931

NEW REVIEW

Ysaÿe. SOLO VIOLIN SONATAS, Op. 27. **Lydia Mordkovitch** (vn). Chandos CHAN8599. Recorded in 1986.

No. 1 in G minor; No. 2 in A minor; No. 3 in D minor, "Ballade"; No. 4 in E minor; No. 5 in G major; No. 6 in E major.

1h 12m DDD 5/88

Best known as perhaps the most dazzlingly gifted violinist of his generation, the Belgian Eugène Ysaÿe composed his Six Sonatas for Solo Violin in 1923. Each was conceived with a specific virtuoso in mind — No. 1 for Joseph Szigeti, No. 2 for Jacques Thibaud, No. 3 for Georges Enesco, No. 4 for Fritz Kreisler, and so forth — and indeed the set as a whole encompasses an entertainingly diverse number of styles whilst at the same time always evincing a stunningly idiomatic and often genuinely intrepid violinistic language. To be honest, this is by no means the easiest repertoire to bring off, demanding unswerving concentration from listener and interpreter alike, but it must be said straight away that Lydia Mordkovitch's passionately vibrant advocacy is hard to resist. Generally speaking, she makes commendably light work of the formidable difficulties these pieces present, and her playing throughout possesses both considerable character and intelligence. The admirably natural recording was made in the ideal surroundings of The Maltings, Snape. Heartily recommended.

Further listening ...

Caprice d'après l'etude en forme de valse de Saint-Saëns. *Coupled with* ***Saint-Saëns:*** Introduction and Rondo capriccioso, Op. 28. ***Massenet:*** THAIS — Méditation. ***Sarasate:*** Zigeunerweisen, Op. 20. ***Chausson:*** Poème, Op. 25. ***Ravel:*** Tzigane. **Joshua Bell** (vn); **Royal Philharmonic Orchestra/Andrew Litton.** Decca 433 519-2DH (1/92).

Jan Dismas Zelenka

Bohemian 1679-1745

Zelenka. ORCHESTRAL WORKS. **Berne Camerata/Alexander van Wijnkoop.** Archiv Produktion 423 703-2AX3. From 2710 026 (11/78).

Capriccios — No. 1 in D major; No. 2 in G major; No. 3 in F major; No. 4 in A major; No. 5 in G major. Concerto a 8 in G major. Sinfonia a 8 in A minor. Hipocondrie a 7 in A major. Overture a 7 in F major.

③ 2h 44m ADD 1/89 

This three-CD album contains all Zelenka's surviving orchestral music. Most of it is anything but commonplace and some of it has a quirky individuality which baroque enthusiasts will find intriguing. The most readily conspicuous feature of the five *Capriccios* is that of the horn writing whose virtuosity exceeds that of almost all his contemporaries; but he shares with Telemann a predilection for rhythms and melodies deriving from central European folk tradition. Barry Tuckwell and Robert Routch turn in dazzling performances on modern horns and are effectively matched by the crisp and invigorating playing of the Berne Camerata. The remaining pieces are formally varied and though sometimes Zelenka just fails to maintain a high level of interest, for the most part his music is full of charm and, at its best, is quite irresistible. The Berne Camerata present a colourful picture of Zelenka's music in this fascinating anthology and their performances are well recorded and thoroughly documented.

Zelenka. The Lamentations of Jeremiah. **Michael Chance** (alto); **John Mark Ainsley** (ten); **Michael George** (bass); **Chandos Baroque Players.** Hyperion CDA66426. Texts and translations included. Recorded in 1990.

1h 13m DDD 7/91 

Between the incomparable settings by Thomas Tallis and the extremely austere one by Stravinsky (which he called *Threni*) the "Lamentations of Jeremiah" have attracted surprisingly few composers. Perhaps the predominantly sombre tone, without even the dramatic opportunities presented by the *Dies irae* in a Requiem, is off-putting. Be that as it may, Zelenka showed remarkable resourcefulness in his 1722 setting for the electoral chapel at Dresden, where he was Kapellmeister. His musical language is in many ways similar to that of J.S. Bach — they even shared the indignity of being thought old-fashioned for the apparent severity and complexity of their styles — but there are also daring turns of phrase which are entirely personal. The six *Lamentations* feature each singer twice; this performance is intimate, even mystical, slightly spacious in tempo and with a resonant acoustic.

Additional recommendation ...
Soloists; Amsterdam Bregynhof Academy/Roderick Shaw. Globe GLO5050 — ·∴ 1h 4m DDD 12/91

Alexander Zemlinsky

Austrian 1871-1942

Zemlinsky. Lyrische Symphonie, Op. 18. **Julia Varady** (sop); **Dietrich Fischer-Dieskau** (bar); **Berlin Philharmonic Orchestra/Lorin Maazel.** DG 419 261-2GH. Texts and translations included. From 2532 021 (3/82).

·∴ 44m DDD 6/87

Zemlinsky's powerful symphonic song cycle for soprano and baritone employs the vast forces of the late-romantic orchestra at its most opulent. The poems by the composer gradually build up, if not to a narrative, then to a series of symbolist portrayals of the spirit of love. The male singer contributes a more abstract, more idealized yearning after the "dweller in my endless dreams", the soprano a more down-to-earth evocation of emotional longing. Dietrich Fischer-Dieskau and his wife Julia Varady cope well with the tormented legato phrasing and tortured harmonies as the vision of an idealized love shimmers before their eyes just beyond their reach. The Berlin Philharmonic play this unfamiliar score with great virtuosity, strongly conducted by Lorin Maazel and have been recorded in a wonderfully mellow acoustic.

Zemlinsky. EINE FLORENTINISCHE TRAGODIE, Op. 16. **Doris Soffel** (mez) Bianca; **Kenneth Riegel** (ten) Guido Bardi; **Guilermo Sarabia** (bass) Simone. **Berlin Radio Symphony Orchestra/Gerd Albrecht.** Koch Schwann CD11625. From VMS1625 (9/85).

·∴ 53m DDD 12/85

Zemlinsky's *A Florentine Tragedy* is an opulent work entwining adultery, murder and sexual desire in a powerful union. Bianca, the wife of a wealthy Florentine merchant Simone, is having an adulterous liaison with Guido. Simone returns to find the two lovers together; he gradually grasps the situation and after a cat-and-mouse game with Guido challenges him to a duel and kills him. The story is based on a play by Oscar Wilde and, typically, has a verbal lushness powerfully matched by Zemlinsky's potent score. The cast of three is strong with some electric moments as the tension increases. Gerd Albrecht directs sympathetically and the orchestra play this rich score well. Nicely recorded.

Zemlinsky. DER KREIDERKREIS. **Renate Behle** (sop) Tschang-Haitang; **Gabriele Schreckenbach** (mez) Mrs Tschang; **Roland Hermann** (bar) Ma; **Siegfried Lorenz** (bar) Tschao; **Reiner Goldberg** (ten) Emperor Pao; **Uwe Peter** (ten) Tong; **Hans Helm** (bar) Tschang-Ling; **Gertrud Ottenthal** (sop) Mrs Ma; **Kaja Borris** (mez) Midwife; **Gidon Saks** (bar) Soldier; **Celina Lindsley** (sop) A girl; **Berlin Radio Symphony Orchestra/Stefan Soltesz.** Capriccio 60016-2. Notes, text and translation included. Recorded in 1990.

·∴ ② 2h 4m DDD 1/92

This is Zemlinsky's seventh and last opera, composed in 1931-32 and one of the last of its kind to be staged in Germany before the clamp-down of Nazi cultural policy. The story is Klabund's reworking of a Chinese morality play, made more famous in the setting by Brecht, in which a dispute over a child is solved when the true mother refuses to compete for it in a tug-of-war. But where Brecht in 1955 stressed the social message, Klabund in 1923 was equally interested in the exotic and sensual aspects. His version of the story enabled Zemlinsky to blend his late-romantic instincts with a tangy orientalism and elements of the detached matter-of-factness which had come into fashion in the 1920s. It makes for an intriguing mixture, something like Ravel crossed with Weill, and if the drama ultimately lacks a strong centre, the score is still wonderfully seductive in its own right. Strong performances and a warm, realistic recording.

Further listening ...

Die Seejungfrau. Psalm 13, Op. 24[a]. [a]**Ernst Senff Chamber Chorus; Berlin Radio Symphony Orchestra/Riccardo Chailly.** Decca 417 450-2DH (6/87).

Gesänge nach Maeterlinck, Op. 13[a]. *Coupled with* **Reger.** Variations and Fugue on a Theme of J.A. Hiller. [a]**Hedwig Fassbender** (mez); **Czech Philharmonic Orchestra/Václav Neumann.** Supraphon 11 1811-2 (7/93).

Collections

Orchestral

NEW REVIEW

AMERICAN MUSIC. Boston Symphony Orchestra/Serge Koussevitzky. Pearl mono GEMMCD9492.
Foote: Suite in E minor, Op. 63 (from RCA Victor 11-8571/2. Recorded in 1940). ***McDonald:*** San Juan Capistrano (RCA Victor 17729. 1939). ***Copland:*** El salón México (HMV DB3812/13, 10/40). ***Harris:*** Symphonies — No. 1 (American Columbia 68183/6. 1934); No. 3 (DB6137/8, 12/42).

1h 19m AAD 12/91

Music lovers with a romantic hankering for the American desert and the Great Outdoors may well know Roy Harris's high, wide and handsome Third Symphony already, but the chances of having heard Serge Koussevitzky's 1939 recording of it are somewhat more remote. If you can accept and enjoy the sound-tracks of classic westerns, then you'll have no trouble with this CD: the playing of the Boston Symphony burns through a veil of surface hiss with the ease and accuracy of a blow-torch, and Koussevitzky's conducting tends to confirm the judgement of many, that this is indeed the greatest American symphony. It's a tremendous experience, and although the work is barely 17 minutes long, it none the less constitutes an epic journey. Koussevitzky was a great musical pioneer, and his recordings of Copland's saucy *El salón México* and Arthur Foote's delightful Suite (easily as appealing as, say, Grieg's *Holberg* Suite) are rightly regarded as classics. Add Harris's First Symphony — a poorer recording, but a fascinating prophecy of greater work to come — and Harl McDonald's colourful essays, and you have the basis of an absorbing concert, one that you're likely to replay many times.

BALLET GALA. English Concert Orchestra/Richard Bonynge. Decca 421 818-2DH2.
Minkus (arr. March): Paquita. Don Quixote. ***Pugni*** (arr. March): Pas de quatre. ***Offenbach***: Le papillon. ***Drigo*** (arr. Lanchbery): Le corsaire — Pas de deux. ***Auber***: Pas classique. Les rendez-vous (arr. Lambert). ***Drigo*** (arr. March): Diane et Actéon. ***D. Scarlatti*** (arr. Tommasini): The good-humoured Ladies. ***Thomas***: Françoise de Rimini.

② 2h 6m DDD 11/90 

This is a delightful selection of largely unfamiliar ballet music from the nineteenth century, which makes a pleasant change from the usual collection of oft-recorded Tchaikovsky favourites. Although many of the excerpts here are heard in arrangements by more recent hands, the essential flavour of the original works has been retained. Little of the music is particularly striking but it is all nonetheless wonderfully tuneful, animated and very easy on the ear. However, the two sprightly Minkus excerpts, Drigo's exciting *Pas de deux* from *Le corsaire* and highlights from Offenbach's only full-length ballet *Le papillon* are probably the pieces most likely to afford prolonged enjoyment. Richard Bonynge is a trusty interpreter of this sort of repertoire and with the help of equally dedicated playing from the ECO he makes each work shine to its best advantage. The excellent recording is a further bonus, bringing out all the colourful orchestral details with notable clarity. This set is a treat not only for ballet lovers but anyone who appreciates attractive, well-crafted melodies.

BAROQUE CLASSICS. Taverner Players/Andrew Parrott. EMI Reflexe CDM7 69853-2.
Handel: Solomon — Arrival of the Queen of Sheba. Harp Concerto in B flat major, Op. 4 No. 6 (with Andrew Lawrence-King, hp). ***Purcell:*** Three Parts upon a Ground. A Suite of Theatre Music: The Indian Queen — Trumpet Overture, Symphony, Dance. Abdelazer — Rondeau; The Gordion Knot Unty'd — Chaconne. ***Pachelbel:*** Canon and Gigue. ***Bach:*** "Wir danken dir, Gott, wir danken dir", BWV29 — Sinfonia. "Ich steh mit einem Fuss im Grabe",

BWV156 — Sinfonia. "Der Himmel lacht! die Erde jubiliert", BWV31 — Sonata. "Ich liebe den Höchsten von ganzem Gemüte", BWV174 — Sinfonia. Christmas Oratorio, BWV248 — Sinfonia. "Gottes Zeit ist die allerbeste Zeit", BWV106 — Sonatina. "Herz und Mund und Tat und Leben", BWV147 — Chorale, "Jesus bleibet meine Freude" ("Jesu, joy of man's desiring") (with Taverner Consort).

lh DDD 12/88 

If you have ever felt the desire to hear 'baroque classics' as the composer might have heard them, but have been deterred by the unfriendly sounds and deadpan renditions offered by some early-instrument groups, you may do the former without suffering the latter by adding this disc to your collection. Though the performances have every benefit of stylistic scholarship and early-instrumental mastery they are in no way 'dry', nor are there any chalk-on-blackboard sounds to set the teeth on edge; on the contrary, the late David Reichenberg's oboe playing is likely to be a delightful revelation. Like other baroque composers, Bach was wont to rework some of his music for other media: thus you may recognize the Sinfonias from Cantatas 29, 156 and 31 as being related to the *Preludium* of the Third Violin Partita (BWV1006), the *Largo* of the F minor Harpsichord Concerto (BWV1056) and the first movement of the Third Brandenburg Concerto (BWV1048). This represents a doorway to the appreciation of baroque music in authentic performance, through which you may enter with as much enthusiasm as do the Taverner Players.

BAROQUE FAVOURITES. [a]Academy of St Martin in the Fields/Sir Neville Marriner; [b]Bath Festival (Chamber) Orchestra/Sir Yehudi Menuhin. Classics for Pleasure CD-CFP4557.

Pachelbel: Canon in D major[a]. ***Purcell:*** Chacony in G minor, Z730[a]. ***Vivaldi:*** Concerto in B minor, Op. 10 No. 3[b] (with Sir Yehudi Menuhin, Robert Masters, Eli Goren and Sydney Humphreys, vns). ***Corelli:*** Concerto Grosso in F major, Op. 6 No. 2[b] (Menuhin, Masters, vns; Derek Simpson, vc). ***Gluck:*** ORFEO ED EURIDICE — Dance of the Blessed Spirits[a]. ***Monteverdi*** (ed. Leppard): Se vittorie si belle. O sia tranquillo (Gerald English, Hugues Cuenod, tens; Bath Festival Ensemble/Raymond Leppard). ***Handel:*** Concerto grosso in A major, Op. 6 No. 11[b].

lh 6m ADD 11/89 

What qualifications are required, one wonders, for a piece of music to be eligible for consideration as a "baroque favourite"? The exclusion of Albinoni's *Adagio* — a sickly confection with which Albinoni had nothing whatsoever to do — merits a strong recommendation for this anthology. Some of the pieces, such as Gluck's *Dance of the Blessed Spirits* and Pachelbel's *Canon* are indeed standard favourites but others like the Monteverdi madrigals and the Corelli Concerto Grosso may strike listeners as much less familiar. The performances are lively though somewhat variable in their degree of finesse. The programme is somewhat arbitrarily chosen and the absence of Bach from the menu a surprising omission. Never mind, the disc offers variety and entertainment and if it leads the curious to explore further the rich legacy of these and other baroque composers, then its arbitrariness will not have been in vain.

CONCERTANTE CELLO WORKS. Steven Isserlis (vc); **Chamber Orchestra of Europe/John Eliot Gardiner.** Virgin Classics VC7 59595-2.

Tchaikovsky: Variations on a Rococo Theme, Op. 33. Pezzo capriccioso, Op. 62. Nocturne, Op. 19 No. 4. Andante cantabile, Op. 11. ***Glazunov:*** Two Pieces, Op. 20. Chant du menestrel, Op. 71. ***Rimsky-Korsakov:*** Serenade, Op. 37. ***Cui:*** Deux morceaux, Op. 36 — Scherzando; Cantabile.

lh 4m DDD 10/90 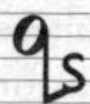

This delicious collection of Russian concertante works for cello offers the immediate advantage of a version of Tchaikovsky's *Rococo* Variations that aligns closely with the composer's original intentions for the work — many other recordings use heavily edited and reordered versions. Its second advantage is the considered, clean-toned playing of Steven Isserlis, one of a mighty handful of first-rate cello soloists that the UK can now boast. His style is not as demonstrative as that of some, though he is quite capable of opening the emotional floodgates when it is appropriate, and his delicacy and stylish phrasing bring out the best in this programme. Whether the music is lyrical, introspective, or playful, his restraint lends it another level of meaning that illuminates its inner life. Praise must also go to John Eliot Gardiner and the Chamber Orchestra of Europe. Accompanying of this sort is never easy, as expert control is demanded for long periods with few attendant moments in the spotlight. Gardiner and the engineers have attained an ideal balance between soloist and orchestra and the players demonstrate an intuitive feel for the late nineteenth-century idiom of the music.

CONCERTOS FOR TWO FLUTES. Shigenori Kudo (fl); **Salzburg Mozarteum Orchestra/Jean-Pierre Rampal** (fl). Sony Classical SK45930.
Mozart: Concertone in C major, K190/186*E*. ***Cimarosa***: Concerto in G major. ***Vivaldi:*** Concerto in C major, RV533. ***A. Stamitz:*** Concerto in G major.

lh 8m DDD 2/92

Two flutes make such amiable companions that it is remarkable to find so few major works — and what is more 'major' than a concerto — for them. Anton Stamitz, the son of Johann of Mannheim fame, wrote one concerto for one flute and one (*Symphonie concertante*) for two, and it is happily strange that Cimarosa, who wrote little instrumental music, gave one of his only two concertos to a pair of flutes. Mozart's two concertos for solo flute, an instrument he claimed not to like, were written in response to a commission, and his generosity did not extend to a double concerto. Two violins are the soloists in the *Concertone*, a precursor of the famous *Sinfonia concertante* for violin and viola but it is no less comfortably playable on two flutes. Vivaldi, another enthusiast of the genre, wrote only one concerto for two flutes. Stamitz, Cimarosa and Mozart all stand under the same stylistic umbrella, and Vivaldi is linked to them by the ritornello form of the first movement of the Mozart concerto — but there is really no need to justify the make-up of such a pleasing programme. Rampal and Kudo, impeccable French-school flautists, make perfectly matched conversation, attentively supported by the Salzburg Mozarteum and vividly recorded.

NEW REVIEW

CONCERTOS FOR FOUR VIOLINS. Cologne Musica Antiqua/Reinhard Goebel. Archiv Produktion 435 393-2AH.
Torelli: Concerto in E minor for four violins and strings. ***Mossi:*** Concertos, Op. 4 — No. 12 in G minor. ***Valentini:*** Concerti grossi, Op. 7 — No. 11 in A minor. ***Locatelli:*** Introduttioni teatrali and concerti, Op. 4 — No. 12 in F major. ***Leo:*** Concerto in D major for four violins and strings.

lh 6m DDD 9/92

Even the most assiduous collectors and discerning connoisseurs of baroque concertos are likely to find novelties in this 'off the beaten track' programme from Cologne Musica Antiqua. Mossi, Valentini and Locatelli belong to the Roman school, though the latter shows marked Venetian leanings, while the remaining two composers are products of Bologna (Torelli) and Naples (Leo). Whatever doubts there may be concerning the intrinsic merit of these works they nevertheless provide a fascinating and valuable glimpse of what composers other than Corelli (Rome) on the one hand or Vivaldi (Venice) on the other were up to. Reinhard Goebel who, alas, was unable to lead his group from the violin in his usual manner, following an injury to his arm, directs effectively. The textures in these concertos are rich and contrasting and the players draw subtle resonances from them. The opening *Largo* and ensuing fugue of the Valentini work affords striking examples of Musica Antiqua's skill in pointing up the variety of string sound inherent in this repertory. This is a fascinating programme performed with Musica Antiqua's customary *élan* and precision.

CONTEMPORARY WORKS FOR ORCHESTRA. [a]**Istvan Matuz** (fl); **Ensemble Intercontemporain/**[b]**Pierre Boulez;** [c]**Peter Eötvös.** Erato 2292-45409-2.
Dufourt. Antiphysis for flute and chamber orchestra[ab]. ***Ferneyhough.*** Funérailles — versions

I and II for strings and harp[b]. ***Harvey.*** Mortuos Plango, Vivos Voco — concrete sounds processed by computer[c]. ***Höller.*** Arcus for 17 instruments and tape[c].

1h 12m AAD

Not easy listening granted, but for those interested in exploring what the outer limits of contemporary music have to offer then the rewards are great indeed. Jonathan Harvey's *Mortuos Plango, Vivos Voco* is arguably one of the most successful pieces of tape montage to have emerged in recent years. The title and text are taken from the inscription on the great tenor bell at Winchester Cathedral: "I count the hours which fly past, I weep for the dead and I call the living to prayer". From this, and the electronic manipulation of a boy's voice and the great tenor bell itself, Harvey constructs a colourful and chilling atmosphere in which he says: "One must imagine the walls of the concert-hall enclosing the [listener] like the side of the bell around which the soul of the young boy flies freely". The hyper complexities of Ferneyhough's *Funérailles* I and II for harp and strings are less easily assimilated but no less fascinating, and subsequent hearings yield up more of its inner secrets and labyrinthine workings. Ferneyhough calls them: "Rite[s] taking place behind a curtain, or in the far distance". Dufourt's *Antiphysis* for flute and chamber orchestra, and Höller's *Arcus* for 17 instruments and tape, both date from 1978, and in their own utterly different ways, reflect the extraordinary virtuosity and artistry of the Ensemble Intercontemporain, for whom they were written, and who play with such stunning conviction on this disc. Exceedingly well recorded.

THE ENGLISH CONNECTION. Academy of St Martin in the Fields/Sir Neville Marriner. ASV CDDCA518. From DCA518 (5/83).
Vaughan Williams: The Lark Ascending (Iona Brown, vn). Fantasia on a Theme by Thomas Tallis. ***Elgar:*** Serenade in E minor, Op. 20. ***Tippett:*** Fantasia concertante on a Theme of Corelli.

1h 2m DDD 2/85 

It is difficult to imagine a more 'English' work than *The Lark Ascending*. Written in the last days of pre-First World War peace, it evokes the tranquillity of a rural England which would never be quite the same again. Iona Brown's solo violin soars effortlessly above the orchestra: she and Marriner contrive a performance which is admirable in every way. This is coupled with the *Tallis* Fantasia, written for the spacious acoustic of Gloucester Cathedral, and Elgar's *Serenade*, an early work but entirely characteristic of the great composer's skill in writing music which pretends no great profundity yet charms and moves the spirit. Tippett's *Fantasia concertante* is a slightly harder piece to assimilate: its busy counterpoint again has a very English quality despite an aura of the Italian *concerto grosso*. There is a slight edge to the string sound on this disc, but it is not enough to affect enjoyment of a very attractive programme.

ENGLISH MINIATURES. Northern Sinfonia/Richard Hickox. EMI CDC7 49933-2.
Gardiner: Overture to a Comedy. ***Quilter:*** Three English Dances, Op. 11. Where the Rainbow Ends — suite. ***Walton:*** Siesta. ***Goossens:*** By the Tarn, Op. 15, No. 1. ***Bax:*** Mediterranean. ***Warlock:*** An old song. ***German:*** Henry VIII — three dances.

1h 1m DDD 9/91 

Here's a collection of lollipops worthy of Sir Thomas Beecham. Richard Hickox and the Northern Sinfonia rise to the occasion with buoyancy and style, revelling in the bright and breezy sounds of Balfour Gardiner's *Overture to a Comedy* and imparting a Purcellian elegance to Quilter's *Three English Dances*. The clear, spacious recording captures the numerous melodic turns and orchestral trimmings which abound in this collection, with wind and strings carefully balanced. More subdued pieces like Walton's curiously chromatic *Siesta* and Warlock's haunting *An old song* are lovingly phrased by the Northern Sinfonia, while Hickox secures a delightful rhythmic lilt in *Where the Rainbow Ends*, a charming suite by Quilter which accompanied the once popular Mills and Owen play. The fine recording assimilates the exotic percussive effects of Bax's *Mediterranean* and the busy orchestral textures of German's *Henry VIII* dances. This disc is a delightful portrait of these lesser-known English masters and captures the gentle benevolence of kinder, simpler times.

ENGLISH MUSIC FOR STRINGS. Guildhall String Ensemble/Robert Salter. RCA Red Seal RD87846.
Britten: Simple Symphony, Op. 4. ***Tippett:*** Little Music. ***Walton:*** Sonata.
Oldham/Tippett/L. Berkeley/Britten/Searle/Walton: Variations on an Elizabethan theme, "Sellinger's Round".

lh 9m DDD 5/89

ENGLISH MUSIC FOR STRINGS. Guildhall String Ensemble/Robert Salter (vn). RCA Victor Red Seal RD87761.
Holst: St Paul's Suite, H118. ***Delius*** (orch. Fenby): Two Aquarelles. ***Ireland:*** A Downland Suite — Minuet. ***Finzi:*** Prelude, Op. 25. Romance, Op. 11. ***Walton:*** Henry V — Passacaglia (Death of Falstaff); Touch her soft lips and part. ***Elgar*** (ed. Young): The Spanish Lady — suite. ***Warlock:*** Capriol Suite.

lh lm DDD 9/88

The Guildhall String Ensemble are a most skilful, professional band and these enterprising collections show them off to great advantage. Britten's early *Simple Symphony*, a slight but accomplished work, is given a suitably playful reading as is Tippett's charming *Little Music*, though here they nicely capture the slightly mysterious quality of the piece. The two substantial works on the disc are also authoritatively despatched. The *Variations on an Elizabethan theme* was composed by five different composers for the 1953 Aldeburgh Festival and these undemanding variations on an old English dance tune make enjoyable listening, especially when performed so well. The Walton Sonata is a 1972 reworking on his 1947 String Quartet. The transformation from solo strings to a more substantial body works well and takes on a new, and for some, more accessible nature. The unusual item in the second collection is the group of five short pieces rescued from a late, unfinished opera by Elgar — not vintage Elgar by any means but attractive nevertheless. Holst's much better-known suite has a simple but robust cheerfulness. Ireland's elegant little *Minuet* began life as a test piece for military band and the two Delius pieces are effective transcriptions by Eric Fenby of two wordless part-songs. Warlock used old French dance tunes in a suite which also conveys his own lively personality; Finzi's two pieces have a typical, wistful nostalgia, and Walton's grave little fragments from his music for Olivier's film are effective in their own right. The recordings are beautifully spacious and capture well the ensemble's fine string tone.

FETE A LA FRANCAISE. Montreal Symphony Orchestra/Charles Dutoit. Decca 421 527-2DH.
Chabrier: Joyeuse marche. España. ***Dukas:*** L'apprenti sorcier. ***Satie*** (orch. Debussy): Gymnopédies — Nos. 1 and 3. ***Saint-Saëns:*** SAMSON ET DALILA — Bacchanale. ***Bizet:*** Jeux d'enfants. ***Thomas:*** RAYMOND — Overture. ***Ibert:*** Divertissement.

lh l0m DDD 6/89 P S B

With great style and huge amounts of panache Charles Dutoit presides over a highly enjoyable collection of French 'lollipops'. Moving forward from Chabrier's *Joyeuse marche*, this *fête* includes such favourites as *The sorcerer's apprentice*, deliciously pointed and coloured, Chabrier's tribute to Spain, *España*, and Saint-Saëns's steamy Bacchanale from *Samson et Dalila*. A cool, limpid interlude is provided by two Satie *Gymnopédies*, here in orchestrations by Debussy. The whole programme is rounded off with tremendous fun by Ibert's outrageous *Divertissement* in a truly winning performance. The Montreal Symphony Orchestra are, without doubt, a first-rate orchestra and their grasp of French repertoire is certainly not equalled by any native band. Add to that a recording of quite breathtaking brilliance and you have a disc to treasure and delight.

NEW REVIEW

FRENCH FAVOURITES. [a]Royal Philharmonic Orchestra, [b]French Radio National Orchestra, [c]London Philharmonic Orchestra/Sir Thomas Beecham. EMI Beecham Edition mono CDM7 63401-2.

Chabrier: GWENDOLINE — Overture[b] (from HMV ALP1843, 6/61). España[c] (Columbia LX880, 5/40). ***Gounod:*** FAUST — Ballet Music[a]. ***Massenet:*** CENDRILLON — Valse[a] (both from ALP1656, 4/59). La Vierge — Le dernier sommeil de la Vierge[a] (HMV DB6645. Recorded 1947). ***Bizet:*** Roma — Carnaval[a] (ALP1656). Patrie — Overture, Op. 19[a] (ALP1497, 10/57). ***Grétry*** (arr. Beecham): ZEMIRE ET AZOR — Ballet Music[a] (ALP1656).

1h 16m ADD 9/92

If you think that the *Faust* Ballet Music is merely a faded relic from Victorian days when tastes were not very sophisticated, then listen to the way Sir Thomas brings the score vividly to life with infinite care, grace and affection. To make lesser scores seem for the moment like masterpieces was part of Beecham's genius. In the case of the *Patrie* Overture even he could not make this rambling piece seem anything other than what it is, but the last movement from *Roma* has plenty of cheerful swagger, and the music from *Zemire et Azor,* arranged in somewhat romantic garb, is very charming and elegant. Chabrier's Wagnerian *Gwendoline* Overture is given a marvellously uplifting, thunderous performance; the open-hearted good humour of *España* is brilliantly realized, and the Massenet items are played in an appealingly delicate, gently expressive fashion. Two of the items have been transferred very well from 78s; the remainder were recorded rather later but on mono tapes only. The sound is everywhere more than good enough to capture the unique, legendary flavour of Beecham's performances.

FRENCH ORCHESTRAL WORKS. [a]French Radio National Orchestra; [b]Royal Philharmonic Orchestra/Sir Thomas Beecham. EMI Beecham Edition CDM7 63379-2.
Bizet: Carmen — Suite No. 1 (from HMV HQS1108, 12/67)[a]. ***Fauré:*** Pavane, Op. 50 (HMV ASD518, 4/63)[a]. Dolly Suite, Op. 56 (orch. Rabaud. HQS1136, 5/68)[a]. ***Debussy:*** Prélude à l'après-midi d'un faune (ASD259, 6/59)[b]. ***Saint-Saëns:*** Le rouet d'Omphale, Op. 31 (ASD259)[b]. ***Delibes:*** Le Roi s'amuse — ballet music (HQS1136)[b].

1h 8m ADD 7/90 

Even to those who never heard him in the flesh there is no mistaking Beecham's relish in, and flair for, the French repertoire. His combination of mischievous high spirits, almost dandyish elegance, cool outer classicism masking passionate emotion, swagger, refined nuance and delicate charm was perhaps unique — not matched even by such committed Francophiles as Constant Lambert. *Elan* is at once in evidence here in the *Carmen* prelude, and subtle dynamic gradations in the entr'actes to Acts 2 and 4; there is lightness, vivacity and tenderness in Fauré's *Dolly* suite and a true Gallic reserve in his *Pavane*; and he enters with prim finesse into Delibes's pastiche dances. Debussy's erotic study, on repeated hearings of this performance, becomes the more Grecian and effective for its conscious understatement; and only the Saint-Saëns symphonic poem, for all the RPO's delicacy, seems to hang fire. But four or five bull's eyes out of six is a pretty good score, and at medium price not to be missed.

GERMAN CONSORT MUSIC, 1660-1710. The Parley of Instruments/Roy Goodman, Peter Holman. Hyperion CDA66074. From A66074 (8/83).
Böhm (reconstr. Holman): Ouverture in D major. ***Fischer:*** Le journal du printems — Suite No. 7. ***Rosenmüller:*** Sonata da camera No. 2 in D major. ***Schmelzer:*** Sacro-profanus concentus musicus — Sonata No. 8 in G major. ***Telemann:*** Ouverture in C major.

46m DDD 9/91 

This entertaining and varied programme of German consort music is mainly orientated around composers of the pre-Bach generation. Here we have an early flowering of the mixed influences of France and Italy which were to characterize German music of the late baroque period. As with gardens, architecture and painting so too was music of the French court at Versailles the envy, and thus the model for many an aspiring princely or ducal establishment elsewhere in Europe. Fischer's Suite No. 7 from *Le journal du printems* provides an exemplary instance of the skill with which German composers digested the Lullian overture and dance idioms. In contrast with this piece the Rosenmüller Sonata reveals more strongly Italianate disciplines while the Telemann Ouverture looks further forward though casting a backward glance as well. The playing of the Parley of Instruments is stylish and invigorating but sometimes lacks finesse in ensemble and tuning. The character of period instruments is vividly realized in a recording which furthermore illuminates the rich textures of the music.

HOMMAGE A SIBELIUS. Helsinki Philharmonic Orchestra/Sergiu Comissiona. Ondine ODE767-2.
Sibelius: En saga, Op. 9. ***T. Musgrave:*** Song of the enchanter. ***Englund:*** Ciacona. ***J. Yuasa:*** The midnight sun. ***E-S. Tüür:*** Searching for roots. ***T. Picker:*** Séance. ***W. Josephs:*** In the north. ***M. Constant:*** Hämeenlinna. ***P. Ruders:*** Tundra.

lh 6m DDD 4/92

Apart from *En saga* all the music recorded here was commissioned by the conductor, Sergiu Commissiona, to mark the 125th anniversary of Sibelius's birth. Though they are generously represented, not all are Nordic composers: Marius Constant, Thea Musgrave and the gifted Japanese composer, Joji Yuasa who has as yet made little impact outside specialist circles. Many of the pieces make allusions to Sibelius and the disc is obviously a valuable memento of the Helsinki concert season in which these novelties were presented. Some of the pieces here are more successful than others. The disc starts with a lively — and presumably authentic — account of Sibelius's *En saga*. This music must surely be surging through the veins of all Finnish musicians. The pieces by Musgrave and Constant are quite striking and well worth having on disc. The Helsinki Orchestra play as if they believe in every note and the recordings are well detailed. Although this is a commemorative disc which will be a must for Sibelius admirers, it will also be of interest to those with a taste for the less demanding byways of new music.

ITALIAN BAROQUE MUSIC. English Chamber Orchestra/Raymond Leppard. Classics for Pleasure CD-CFP4371. From HQS1232 (10/70).
Albinoni: Sonatas a cinque, Op. 2 — No. 3 in A major; No. 6 in G minor. ***Corelli:*** Concerto Grosso in F major, Op. 6 No. 9. ***Vivaldi:*** Concertos — D major, RV121; E flat major, RV130, "Al Santo Sepolcro"; G minor, RV156.

44m ADD 11/89 £

This well-chosen anthology of late baroque Italian concertos was recorded in 1970. Ideas about how to perform eighteenth-century music have changed considerably since then but in no way does that diminish interpretations as tasteful and animated as these. A disc such as this contains much that was most stylish in baroque performance 20 years ago and many a supposedly 'authentic' approach to the same repertory has subsequently fallen far short of what Raymond Leppard and the English Chamber Orchestra achieve here. The two Albinoni works are, perhaps, especially appealing for their tender slow movements which Leppard treats with affecting warmth; but there is little or nothing here to disappoint listeners. The programme is pleasingly contrasted, well played and well recorded.

ITALIAN FLUTE CONCERTOS. Jean-Pierre Rampal (fl); **I Solisti Veneti/Claudio Scimone.** Sony Classical SK47228.
Romano: Concerto in G major. ***Cecere:*** Concerto in A major. ***Alberti:*** Concerto in F major, "Con sordini". ***Sammartini:*** Concerto in G major.

52m DDD 2/92

Italy was slower than most other countries to favour the transverse flute over its fipple relative, as Vivaldi's well known concertos testify, but there were composers who responded to the flute's siren song, possibly persuaded by approaches from Margrave Carl Friedrich, a player and enthusiast thereof, in whose large collection of music (housed in Karlsruhe) there are numerous flute works. Some of these composers were Italian and four of their flute concertos, unpublished and otherwise unrecorded, form the programme of this recording; indeed, only the name of Sammartini was to be found in *The Classical Catalogue* prior to this recording, and of Romano and Cecere it may be said that "little is known of their lives". Alberti's Concerto is high baroque and, time and taste having marched on, Sammartini's is both 'high-transitional' and virtuosic; the others inhabit the middle ground. What they all have in common is clean-cut, melody-rich charm, persuasively displayed by Rampal, the most seductive of flautists, with the spruce support of I Solisti Veneti in a pristine recording. It isn't for instrumental purists but it is certainly for anyone who enjoys happy, uncomplicated and unfamiliar music, played with a smile.

NEW REVIEW

ORCHESTRAL WORKS. [a]**Anton Kontra** (vn); **Malmö Symphony Orchestra/James DePreist.** BIS CD570.

Rosenberg: The Marionettes — Overture. ***Bizet:*** Carmen Suite No. 1. ***Larsson:*** The Hours of the Day. ***Glinka:*** Ruslan and Ludmilla — Overture. ***Satie*** (orch. Debussy): Gymnopédies — No. 1, Lent et douloureux; No. 3, Lent et grave. ***Shostakovich:*** Festive Overture in A major, Op. 96. ***Svendsen:*** Romance in G major, Op. 26[z]. ***Alfvén:*** The Mountain King, Op. 37 — Herdsmaiden's dance.

lh 18m DDD 1/93

Here is a somewhat curious collection of familiar and very out of the way works. The Swedish composer Lars-Erik Larsson wrote the six episodes which comprise his *Hours of the Day* Suite in 1938 to accompany a series of recited poems. Three of the movements later formed what became one of his best-known works, the *Pastoral* Suite. Here the original six-movement work is given its first complete recording: the style is neo-romantic and the material quite colourful and varied in mood. Hilding Rosenberg, another Swedish composer, wrote his jolly, bustling *Marionettes* Overture in 1926 as part of incidental music for a play by Jacinto Benaventes. Svendsen's *Romance* for violin and orchestra, written in 1881, is a charming piece, and it is beautifully played by the Malmö orchestra's leader, Anton Kontra. Apart from Hugo Alfvén's cheerful little dance all the rest of the programme is familiar. The Satie pieces are straightforwardly played, to their benefit, and the Glinka overture is for once taken at a good steady tempo. Shostakovich's somewhat pert *Festival Overture* is given a neat, lively performance while Bizet's Suite is efficiently played, but rather lacks atmosphere and temperament. The Malmö Symphony Orchestra is an accomplished body, and in the Scandinavian repertoire DePreist conducts diligent performances which sometimes lack the last ounce of imagination and rhythmic finesse. The recording is up to the usual high BIS standard.

ORCHESTRAL WORKS. [a]**Guillermo Figueroa** (vn); **Orpheus Chamber Orchestra.** DG 431 680-2GH.

Wagner: Siegfried Idyll. ***Turína:*** La oración del torero. ***Wolf:*** Italian Serenade. ***Puccini:*** Crisantemi. ***Berlioz:*** Rêverie et caprice, Op. 8[a]. ***Sibelius:*** Valse triste, Op. 44. ***Dvořák:*** Nocturne in B major, B47.

lh 2m DDD 10/91

The Orpheus Chamber Orchestra, of some 25 instrumentalists who play without a conductor, are an American group founded in the 1980s who have achieved success with every one of their discs — and this collection of seven pieces from seven European countries (if we count Wolf's sprightly, single movement *Italian Serenade* as Italian) is another winner. Wagner wrote his *Siegfried Idyll* as a birthday present for his wife, and it was first played in their home to waken her on that day in 1870 (which happened also to be Christmas Day); it is unusually tender music and one of his most immediately attractive works which here receives a loving performance. At 19 minutes this is the longest piece in the programme; the others last under nine, but each of them still comes across strongly. Another example of instrumental music from an opera composer is Puccini's *Crisantemi* ("Chrysanthemums"), an elegiac piece, originally for string quartet, that he wrote in memory of Duke Amadeo of Savoy but which later provided material for his opera *Manon Lescaut*. Like the Puccini, Wolf's *Serenade* was originally for just four players but sounds well when played by larger forces. Guillermo Figueroa is a persuasive soloist in Berlioz's *Rêverie et caprice*, which is suavely passionate and very Gallic. Indeed, everything in this well chosen programme — a European musical tour — is worth hearing and even the familiar *Valse triste* (Sibelius in waltz time, but mysteriously so) comes up freshly and strongly. The recording is richly atmospheric.

ORCHESTRAL WORKS. Cristina Ortiz (pf); **Royal Philharmonic Orchestra/Moshe Atzmon.** Decca 414 348-2DH. From 414 348-1DH (5/86).
Rachmaninov. Piano Concerto No. 2 in C minor, Op. 18. ***Addinsell:*** Warsaw Concerto. ***Litolff:*** Concerto symphonique No. 4 in D minor, Op. 102 — Scherzo. ***Gottschalk*** (orch. Hazell): Grande fantaisie triomphale sur l'hymne national brésilien, RO108.

58m DDD 9/86

The C minor Concerto of Rachmaninov symbolizes romanticism at its ripest. Its combination of poetry and sensuous warmth with languorously memorable melodic lines balanced by exhilarating pianistic brilliance happily avoids any suggestion of sentimentality. The simple chordal introduction from the soloist ushers in one of the composer's most luscious tunes, yet the slow movement develops even greater ardour in its melodic contour, and the composer holds back a further haunting expressive idea to bring lyrical contrast to the scintillating finale. The couplings here are most apt. The genuinely inspired pastiche *Warsaw Concerto* by Richard Addinsell has a principal theme worthy to stand alongside those of Rachmaninov and its layout shows satisfying craftsmanship. Ortiz plays this main theme with great affection and she is equally beguiling in the delicious Litolff *Scherzo*. The effect here is of elegance rather than extrovert brilliance: this is reserved for the Gottschalk *Grande fantaisie triomphale*, which is played with a splendid panache that almost covers its inherent vulgarity and certainly emphasizes its ingenuous charm. Throughout the recording balance is realistic and the reverberation adds the most attractive bloom.

ORCHESTRAL WORKS. Polish Chamber Orchestra/Jan Stanienda ([a]vn). Linn Records CKD001. Recorded at a performance in the City Halls, Glasgow on May 24th, 1990.
Bach: Violin Concerto in A minor, BWV1041[a]. ***Bartók:*** Divertimento, Sz113.
Elgar: Introduction and Allegro, Op. 47. ***Mozart:*** Divertimento in F major, K138/125*c*.
Vivaldi: 12 Concertos, Op. 3, "L'estro armonico" — No. 10 in B minor.

1h 10m DDD 12/91

Under its long-standing conductor, Jerzy Maksymiuk, the Polish Chamber Orchestra developed a world-wide reputation during the early 1980s for its polished virtuosity and clarity of articulation. Maksymiuk now has close links with the BBC Scottish Symphony Orchestra, and it seems fitting that this association enabled his Polish colleagues to take part in the Glasgow 1990 Mayfest when this attractive programme, directed by the Polish Chamber Orchestra's concert-master, Jan Stanienda, was recorded live. The orchestral and solo playing is masterly, and the recording superb, resulting in a wholly credible and enjoyable listening experience. The effervescent Mozart Divertimento reveals the stylish and refined orchestra to be as fine as ever, with some impressively clear violin articulation in rapid passagework. Stanienda is joined by soloists from the orchestra in Vivaldi's Concerto for four violins from the *L'estro armonico* set, and this performance, like his own reading of the A minor Bach Concerto, is dramatic and large-scale in concept. Meanwhile, the convulsive energy and latent remorse of Bartók's *Divertimento* receives a highly charged reading, characterized by an added sense of immediacy only really attainable in the concert-hall. The supremely disciplined Polish players revel in Bartók's taxing score, making this the highlight of their programme. They also offer a noble and committed version of Elgar's masterpiece for strings, the *Introduction and Allegro*, played with great breadth and appropriate gravity, especially in the response of the solo quartet. This enjoyable disc recreates all the excitement and sense of occasion of a public event, while the recorded sound is vivid and spacious.

POPULAR ORCHESTRAL MUSIC. Dallas Symphony Orchestra/Eduardo Mata. RCA VD87727. From RCD14439 (6/83).
Dukas: L'Apprenti Sorcier, ***Enescu:*** Roumanian Rhapsody No. 1 in A major, Op. 11.
Mussorgsky: A Night on the Bare Mountain. ***Tchaikovsky:*** Capriccio Italien, Op. 45.

51m DDD 9/89 £

This disc is something of a showcase for Eduardo Mata and the Dallas Symphony Orchestra, with a recorded sound that is in the demonstration bracket. All four works receive excellent performances, but the Tchaikovsky and Enescu items are in a class of their own, and can be counted as amongst the finest in the catalogue. The *Capriccio Italien* is a truly riveting performance, with the opening brass fanfares sounding so realistic that you are transported to the best seat in the concert hall. This is a very Italianate reading, which glows with a sumptuous and full-bodied string sound, and the coda has a marvellous feeling of joy and abandonment, whilst still maintaining an air of elegance. Mussorgsky's *A Night on the Bare Mountain* is given a very fine performance technically, with excellent articulation in the strings and powerful playing from the brass section, but somehow misses the terror of the piece. Much the same can be said of their account of Dukas's ever popular *The Sorcerer's Apprentice*, which is a very smooth and polished reading, but lacking perhaps that last ounce of malfeasance required to really make the spine tingle in the climax. Enescu's kaleidoscopic *Roumanian* Rhapsody No. 1 provides the perfect ending to this superb disc (a real encore item if ever there was one). The Dallas Symphony Orchestra play with unflagging energy here, with the woodwind section positively sparkling. At mid-price this disc is an absolute must.

THE ROMANTIC CLARINET. Emma Johnson (cl); **English Chamber Orchestra/ Gerard Schwarz.** ASV CDDCA659.
Weber: Clarinet Concerto No. 2 in E flat major, Op. 64. ***Spohr:*** Clarinet Concerto No. 1 in C minor, Op. 26. ***Crusell:*** Clarinet Concerto No. 3 in B flat major, Op. 11.

1h 10m DDD

This nicely balanced and beautifully played recital couples three concertos of great charm from around the turn of the last century. All three works were written with specific clarinet virtuosos in mind. Weber's prowess as an operatic composer finds an exciting outlet in his charming Concerto which treats the clarinet very much in the role of soloistic diva. The Spohr Concerto is gentler in texture, searching out the more plangent qualities of the solo instrument. Crusell's three concertos are works of great charm and melodiousness and are rightly enjoying a just revival in recent years — no doubt due to Emma Johnson's characterful advocacy. She plays beautifully and with great taste throughout this disc. The English Chamber Orchestra accompany with great panache and Gerard Schwarz presides sympathetically. The recording is good with a pleasantly immediate presentation of the soloist.

SAXOPHONE CONCERTOS. John Harle (sax); **Academy of St Martin in the Fields/Sir Neville Marriner.** EMI CDC7 54301-2.
Debussy (ed. Harle): Rapsodie. ***Glazunov:*** Saxophone Concerto in E flat, Op. 109. Out of the Cool. ***Ibert:*** Concertino da camera. ***R.R. Bennett:*** Saxophone Concerto.
Villa-Lobos: Fantasia.

1h 11m DDD 1/92 9p

As the issue of a mixed marriage the saxophone has had problems in gaining general acceptance in 'respectable' (musical) society. Sigurd Rascher did wonders for it in the pre-war years, but overall its image has remained what it has been throughout this century, that of an instrument which rose to fame in houses of ill repute and smoky dens in which jazz developed — and from which came the players with the most fluent techniques. At the same time the saxophone's potential as a solo instrument was recognized by a number of notable composers, among them Glazunov and Ibert in the 1930s, Villa-Lobos in 1958 and, some decades later, by Bennett and Heath — the last a composer with a jazz pedigree. Debussy preceded all these but, writing for a lady of his acquaintance who had breathing problems, didn't really have his heart in it; his *Rapsodie* is here presented with worthier orchestration by John Harle. Harle is the virtuoso for whom the saxophone may have long been waiting; the selected works show his splendid musicianship and spectacular technical command to good advantage. If you have any prejudice against the saxophone that is less than incurable, this outstanding disc could easily change your mind — as well as introducing you to some unfamiliar and attactive music.

SCANDINAVIAN SUITES. Guildhall String Ensemble/Robert Salter. RCA Victor Red Seal RD60439.

Nielsen: Little Suite in A minor, FS6. ***Grieg:*** Holberg Suite, Op. 40. Two Elegiac Melodies, Op. 34. Two Melodies, Op. 53. ***Sibelius:*** Romance in C major, Op. 42. ***Wirén:*** Serenade for strings, Op. 11.

1h 10m DDD 3/92

All of these, with the possible exception of the Sibelius *Romance*, are popular repertoire pieces, and are eminently well served by the excellent Guildhall String Ensemble and Robert Salter. *The Classical Catalogue* lists few alternatives of the Nielsen and the Wirén that are finer; and although the Grieg pieces are far more generously represented on disc the Guildhall Strings can more than hold their own. Indeed these performances are touched with distinction. Tempos are sensibly judged and their phrasing and blend are admirable. Yet while they are attentive to every detail of dynamic nuance and tonal finesse, there is no trace of self-consciousness. The second of the Grieg *Melodies*, Op. 53, is particularly affecting in their hands. The recording, made at Forde Abbey, Chard in Somerset, is spectacularly good, having altogether excellent range, body and presence.

SCHERZOS FROM SEVENTEENTH CENTURY GERMANY. Cologne Musica Antiqua/Reinhard Goebel. Archiv Produktion 429 230-2AH.

J.H. Schmelzer: Balletto in G major, "Fechtschule". Polonische Sackpfeiffen in G major. ***Biber:*** Sonata in B flat major, "Die Bauern-Kirchfartt genandt". Battalia in D major. Serenade in C major, "Nightwatchman's Call". Sonata in A major, "La Pastorella". Sonata jucunda in D major (attrib). Sonata in G major, "Campanarum" (attrib). ***J.J. Walther:*** Sonata in G major, "Imitatione del Cuccu".

1h 6m DDD 1/91

This entertaining disc is not without its zany moments; do not, for instance, be unduly deterred at the outset by hearing the band cross a spacious hallway or saloon before tuning up, for what follows is a highly imaginative sequence of largely unfamiliar pieces of a mildly programmatic character. Most of the music hails from the Austrian south of Germany and contains that rewarding blend of fantasy and virtuosity which Reinhard Goebel and his Musica Antiqua Köln understand so well. They play with rhythmic clarity and a feeling for gesture and Goebel, furthermore, overlooks neither the humour nor the charming eccentricities present in some of these fascinating pieces. His own solo violin playing in Sonatas by Biber (*La Pastorella*) and Walther (*Imitatione del Cuccu*) is detailed, incisive and passionate and he demands both these and other estimable qualities from his ensemble. Unusual sonorities and startling harmonies are inherent in this music and Goebel savours every one of them. Biber's *Battalia* is vividly interpreted, at times with ferocious but entirely appropriate zeal and the delightful *Nightwatchman's Call* is played with warmth and sensibility. Goebel's accompanying essay and Arcimboldo's illustration provide a pleasing complement to an entertaining programme.

SYMPHONIC SPECTACULAR. Cincinnati Pops Orchestra/Erich Kunzel. Telarc CD80170.

Shostakovich: Festival Overture, Op. 96. ***Wagner:*** DIE WALKURE — Ride of the Valkyries. ***Falla:*** El amor brujo — Ritual fire dance. ***Bizet:*** L'Arlésienne — Suite No. 2: Farandole. ***Järnefelt:*** Praeludium. ***Chabrier:*** España. ***Tchaikovsky:*** Marche slave, Op. 31. ***Halvorsen:*** Entry of the Boyars. ***Enescu:*** Roumanian Rhapsody No. 1 in A major, Op. 11. ***Khachaturian:*** Gayaneh — Sabre dance.

54m DDD 10/89

From this disc's title you might suppose that it provides a diet of music that is loud, fast, and luridly orchestrated — and you wouldn't be far wrong in that assessment. Yet there must be some leavening to make this palatable and the Cincinnati Pops provide this in those unguarded moments that most of these works contain, when more reposeful ideas allow the players to bring gentle solos and quiet dialogues to the fore. The opening of the first of Enescu's *Roumanian Rhapsodies*, some episodes in Chabrier's *España*, and much of Järnefelt's *Praeludium* are such instances, and the playing here is particularly refined and atmospheric. When the heat is on, the orchestra reveals its familiarity with this music and lets rip with invigorating zest. The recording copes unobtrusively with all this, without complaint or artificial highlighting, and the orchestra is genially set in its moderately resonant acoustic. Tchaikovsky's *Marche slave* is ideally treated by this ambience and Erich Kunzel can maintain a fair pace throughout without the chords producing too lengthy a delay. If a collection of lollipops is what you are looking for, you could do a lot worse than opting for this nicely balanced selection.

NEW REVIEW

THE TOSCANINI COLLECTION. New York Philharmonic Orchestra/Arturo Toscanini. RCA Gold Seal mono GD60318.
Gluck: Orfeo ed Euridice — Ballet in D minor (from HMV D1784, 7/30). ***Rossini:*** Il barbiere di Siviglia — Overture (D1835, 10/30). L'italiana in Algeri — Overture (HMV DB2943, 10/36). Semiramide — Overture (DB3079/80, 3/37). ***Verdi:*** La traviata — Preludes, Acts 1 and 3 (D1672, 6/30). ***Wagner:*** Götterdämmerung — Dawn and Siegfried's Rhine Journey (DB2860/61, 7/36). Lohengrin — Preludes: Act 1 (DB2904, 9/36); Act 3 (DB2861).

ADD 1h 4m 11/92

RCA's Toscanini Collection contains many very desirable reissues, but this disc has a particular quality in that it shows very clearly several outstanding but differing aspects of the great conductor's genius. The recordings, made in 1929 and 1936, have been made to yield a quality of sound which most listeners will find perfectly acceptable, and they date from a period when, as chief conductor of the New York Philharmonic Orchestra, Toscanini was in his artistic prime. Those who still imagine him always to be a hard, relentless interpreter should hear the exquisitely poised Gluck ballet music, or the tender, extraordinarily eloquent *Traviata* preludes. The Rossini Overtures are certainly propelled with a good deal of energy, but there's plenty of air in the rhythms, and some elegant phrasing amid the virtuoso playing of the magnificent New York Philharmonic. Wagner was particularly near to Toscanini's heart: the *Lohengrin* Act 1 Prelude has a wonderfully luminous quality, and "Siegfried's Rhine Journey" is played with tremendous strength and majesty.

TRUMPET CONCERTOS. Håkan Hardenberger (tpt); **Academy of St Martin in the Fields/Sir Neville Marriner.** Philips 420 203-2PH.
Hummel: Trumpet Concerto in E major. ***Hertel:*** Trumpet Concerto in D major.
J. Stamitz (realized Boustead): Trumpet Concerto in D major. ***Haydn:*** Trumpet Concerto in E flat major, HobVII*e*/1.

59m 12/87 

This recording made such a remarkable impression when it first appeared in 1987 that it created overnight a new star in the firmament of trumpeters. The two finest concertos for the trumpet are undoubtedly those of Haydn and Hummel and Hardenberger plays them here with a combination of sparkling bravura and stylish elegance that are altogether irresistible. Marriner and his Academy accompany with characteristic finesse and warmth, with the lilting dotted rhythms of the first movement of the Hummel, seductively jaunty. The lovely *Andante* of the Haydn is no less beguiling and both finales display a high spirited exuberance and an easy bravura which make the listener smile with pleasure. He is no less distinctive in the lesser concerto of Johann Hertel and the other D major work attributed to Johann Stamitz but probably written by someone with the unlikely name of J.B. Holzbogen. This takes the soloist up into the stratosphere of his range and provides him also with some awkward leaps. The Hertel work also taxes the soloist's technique to the extremities but Hardenberger essays all these difficulties with an enviably easy aplomb and remains fluently entertaining throughout. The recording gives him the most vivid realism and presence but it is a pity that the orchestral backcloth is so reverberant; otherwise the sound is very natural.

TRUMPET CONCERTOS. [a]**Hannes Läubin,** [b]**Wolfgang Läubin,** [c]**Bernhard Läubin** (tpts); **English Chamber Orchestra/Simon Preston** (hpd, org). DG 431 817-2GH.

Telemann: Concerto in D major for three trumpets, timpani, two oboes, strings and continuo[abc]. Concerto in D major for three trumpets, timpani, strings and continuo[abc]. ***Rathgeber:*** Concerto in E flat major for two trumpets, two violins and continuo, Op. 6 No. 15[ac]. ***Franceschini:*** Sonata in D major for two trumpets, strings and continuo[ab]. ***Albinoni:*** Concerto in B flat major for trumpet and orchestra[a]. ***Vivaldi:*** Concerto in C major for two trumpets, strings and continuo, RV537[ab].

46m DDD 12/91

This is a disc of trumpet concertos with a difference. All the works included here except one (the Albinoni B flat major Concerto, originally written for oboe) involve two or more of the very gifted Laubin family of virtuosos. The first piece by Telemann calls not only for three trumpets, but a pair of oboes, too, and the wind and brass instruments sing along together with the most colourful interplay of ideas. There are five movements and the composer's invention is inexhaustibly diverse. The Double Concerto by Rathgeber is hardly less winning, with glittering bravura in the two outer movements while the relaxed central *Adagio* makes a captivating contrast of expressive repose. The Double Concerto by Vivaldi is better known and does not disappoint here while the Franceschini Sonata has four sections, none of which outstay their welcome. Telemann's second Triple Concerto is perhaps less memorable than the work with oboes, but still enjoyable when presented with such assurance. The vital solo playing is matched throughout by spiritedly polished accompaniments from the ECO and Simon Preston, who also provides the organ continuo. What a good case this beautifully recorded concerto makes for playing these baroque works on modern instruments!

TWENTIETH-CENTURY FLUTE CONCERTOS. Jennifer Stinton (fl); [a]**Geoffrey Browne** (cor ang); **Scottish Chamber Orchestra/Steuart Bedford.** Collins Classics 1210-2. ***Honegger***: Concerto da camera[a]. ***Ibert***: Flute Concerto (1934). ***Nielsen***: Flute Concerto, FS119. ***Poulenc*** (orch. L. Berkeley): Flute Sonata.

1h 6m DDD 8/91

This is basically a vehicle for the artistry of the flautist Jennifer Stinton who presents two flute concertos (by Nielsen and Ibert) plus a transcription of the Poulenc Flute Sonata and a duo concertante by Honegger for flute, cor anglais and strings dating from the period of the Fourth Symphony. The Honegger in which Jennifer Stinton is joined by Geoffrey Browne will come as a surprise to those music-lovers who have not encountered it before; it is pastoral in character and has enormous charm and these artists play with great sympathy for the idiom. Gallic charm is a feature of the Ibert Concerto which also comes off very well. Stinton gives thoroughly expert performances both of this lollipop and Sir Lennox Berkeley's arrangement of the no-less delightful Poulenc. The note reminds us that Honegger was present at the first performance of the Nielsen Concerto (which took place in Paris in 1926), which as the only Scandinavian piece is the 'odd-man-out' here. Though it is less brilliant than the Gallois performance, it is well played and the recording is very good in respect to balance, naturalness and presence.

TWENTIETH CENTURY PLUS. [f]**Andrew Marriner** (cl); [ace]**BBC Sympony Orchestra/**[a]**Peter Eötvös,** [c]**Matthias Bamert,** [e]**Lothar Zagrosek;** [b]**BBC Philharmonic Orchestra/Sir Peter Maxwell Davies;** [f]**London Symphony Orchestra/Michael Tilson Thomas;** [d]**English Chamber Orchestra/Steuart Bedford.** Collins Classics 2001/5-2. Items marked [a] recorded at a performance in the Royal Albert Hall, London on August 30th, 1990, [b] Cheltenham Town Hall, July 12th, 1990, [c], [d] and [e] recorded in association with the Arts Council. *2001-2:* ***Birtwistle:*** Earth Dances[a]. *2002-2:* ***Maxwell Davies:*** Caroline Mathilde — Concert Suite from Act One[b]. *2003-2:* ***Saxton:*** In the beginning[c]. Music to celebrate the resurrection of Christ[d]. *2004-2:* ***Mason:*** Lighthouses of England and Wales[e]. *2005-2:* ***Tavener:*** The Repentant Thief[f].

5 37m 25m 30m 16m 20m DDD 3/92 

No, not a five-CD set, but five separately available CD singles, each featuring the music of a contemporary British composer. At first sight the overall title "Twentieth Century Plus" may seem a contradiction in terms (the longest CD has a duration of only 37 minute) but when one considers that the price of each CD is considerably less than that of a full-price issue and that both performances and recordings are of exceptionally high quality then these are bargains indeed. The most important (and long awaited) issue here is perhaps Birtwistle's large and impressive orchestral work — *Earth Dances*. Though massively complex in its construction and organization of material, *Earth Dances* can be a richly rewarding experience for the listener. Its title relates both to the 'geological' strata-like layers of the music, and often violent surface energy that almost makes the earth dance. Tavener's *The Repentant Thief* for clarinet and orchestra is built around a rondo-like structure made up of 10 segments — five "Refrains", three "Dances" and two "Laments", and its title refers to the thief who was crucified with Jesus on Golgotha. It was composed shortly after Tavener had finished work on two large scale works (*Resurrection* and the opera *Mary of Egypt*) and is described by the composer as "a shorter, simple and rather primitive piece". Its simplicity, clear cut formal scheme and tunefulness make it an immediately accessible and absorbing experience, and this is all the more enhanced by a magical performance of the solo clarinet part by Andrew Marriner. Like the *Eight Songs for a Mad King* before it, the Concert Suite from Act 1 of the ballet *Caroline Mathilde* by Maxwell Davies explores the subject of madness — Caroline Mathilde was the wife of the unbalanced King Christian VII of Denmark. The ballet traces the King's gradual mental deterioration, and his wife's subsequent love affair with the King's physician (Dr Struensee) through a series of short tableaux that mix Maxwell Davies's musical parody style with his more acerbic and intricate methods of composing. The remaining discs feature music by the younger composers Benedict Mason and Robert Saxton. The highly original, if somewhat unusual *Lighthouses of England and Wales* reveals Mason to be a composer of a striking individuality, not to mention an extremely gifted orchestrator, and Saxton's richly colourful pieces — *In the beginning* and *Music to celebrate the resurrection of Christ* — continue the composer's interest in the religious theme of darkness into light.

VICTORIAN CONCERT OVERTURES. English Northern Philharmonia/David Lloyd-Jones. Hyperion CDA66515.
Macfarren: Chevy Chace. ***Pierson:*** Romeo and Juliet. ***Sullivan:*** Macbeth. ***Corder:*** Prospero. ***Elgar:*** Froissart, Op. 19. ***Parry:*** Overture to an Unwritten Tragedy. ***Mackenzie:*** Britannia, Op. 52.

lh 7m DDD 1/92

With the exception of Elgar's *Froissart*, none of the concert overtures featured on this valuable Hyperion disc have remained in the repertory, and indeed, this release stands as a fitting tribute to the unwarranted neglect of some splendid music. Through no particular fault of their own, the works of many composers prominent in British musical life a century or so ago have fallen into virtual, if not total oblivion, and David Lloyd-Jones and the English Northern Philharmonia make the best possible case for a timely revival of interest in this unique area. The lively rhythmic energy and genuine melodic worth of George Macfarren's *Chevy Chace* Overture makes it an ideal curtain-raiser for any orchestral concert, and the work found willing advocates in Wagner and Mendelssohn, both of whom included it in public concerts. Even though Macfarren, a blind stalwart of the mid-Victorian musical establishment, does not hide his admiration for Beethoven's Seventh Symphony, this engaging work will be a revelation to many listeners, as will Sullivan's superbly dramatic *Macbeth* Overture, intended for Sir Henry Irving's 1888 Lyceum season. The influence of the new German school looms large in Frederick Corder's idiomatic *Prospero*, and the sonorous Wagnerian gestures are convincing, even if any Shakespearian connections are rather vague, as is the case with Hugo Pierson's competent *Romeo and Juliet* overture, a work in which the enmity of bitter family rivalry is subordinate to expressive piquancy and grace. Elgar scored his first real orchestral triumph with *Froissart*, a depiction of knightly renown of noble utterance; the Parry work which follows it is the least memorable work here, whilst Mackenzie makes good use of Dr Arne's famous tune, in his nautical overture, *Britannia*. The performances are consistently alert and spontaneous and much of the music, although unfamiliar, will fascinate adventurous devotees of British music.

NEW REVIEW

VIENNA PREMIERE, Volume 3. **Viennese Orchestra of London/Jack Rothstein.** Chandos CHAN9127.

E. Strauss: Blauäuglein, Op. 254 — Polka française. Osterreichs Völker-Treue Marsch, Op. 211. Schleier und Krone — Walzer, Op. 200. ***P. Fahrbach II:*** Storchschnäbel — Galopp, Op. 149. ***J. Strauss I:*** Der Carneval in Paris — Galopp, Op. 100. Freiheits-Marsch, Op. 226. ***J. Strauss II:*** Nur nicht mucken! — Polka française, Op. 472. ***J. Strauss III:*** Unter den Linden — Walzer, Op. 30. ***Josef Strauss:*** Pauline — Polka-Mazur (second version), Op. 190*b*. Wallonen-Marsch, Op. 41. Zeit-Bilder — Walzer, Op. 51. ***Millöcker:*** Klopf' an! — Polka française. ***Ziehrer:*** Casimir-Walzer, Op. 511. Die Lustigmacherin — Schnell-Polka, Op. 4.

lh lm DDD 5/93

Like its two predecessors, this "Vienna Première" volume is devoted to Viennese dances and marches not previously recorded commercially on LP or CD. Johann Strauss the Waltz King is little in evidence, but the other composers represented ensure no significant loss of quality. Johann III, for instance, is generally reckoned to be the least inventive composer of the family, and yet his *Unter den Linde*n waltz is blessed with one absolutely heavenly waltz section. Not the least of the delights come from the two Ziehrer contributions, of which the *Casimir-Walzer* opens with a surprise in quoting *Yankee Doodle* in its introduction (the waltz is based on an operetta with an American setting) before developing into a gorgeous sequence of rousing waltzes. Welcome, too, is Philipp Fahrbach's *Storchschnäbel* ("Storks' Bills") galop (with appropriate stork effects) and two Eduard Strauss contributions — the rousing *Osterreichs Völker-Treue* March and above all the utterly charming *Blauäuglein* ("Little Blue Eyes"). There is no attempt here to find undue emotional depths in the music. Rather, Jack Rothstein's tempos are onward-going, concentrating on bringing out the sheer joy in the music. The result is consistently elating, with refined playing and first-class sound completing a splendid collection.

NEW REVIEW

A VIENNA SOUVENIR. Ensemble Wien (Paul Guggenberger, Günter Seifert, vns; Peter Götzel, va/vn; Josef Pitzek, db). Sony Classical SK47187.

A. Lanner: D'ersten Gedanken, Op. 1. Amalien-Polka, Op. 14. ***J. Lanner:*** Die Schmetterlinge, Op. 65. Dampf-Walzer, Op. 94. Die Bestürmung von Constantine, Op. 127. ***J. Strauss I:*** Chinese Galop, Op. 20. Die vier Temperamente, Op. 59. ***J. Strauss II:*** Rasch in der That, Op. 409. DIE FLEDERMAUS — Overture. ***Schubert:*** Grazer Galopp in C major, D925.

58m DDD 9/92

When the Viennese waltz was young, dances were commonly published in reductions for two violins, viola and double-bass, which serve admirably to bring out the dances' lyrical lines. The Ensemble Wien, comprising four instrumentalists from the Vienna Philharmonic and the Austrian Radio Symphony Orchestras, has done a splendid job not only in producing such beautifully elegant playing but in selecting seldom- or never-recorded pieces. Joseph Lanner's *Die Schmetterlinge* has been recorded before, but his *Storming of Constantine* and father Strauss's *Four Temperaments*, with its contrasted sections (sanguine, melancholic, choleric, phlegmatic), are real rarities. Perhaps the greatest interest attend the inclusion of two pieces by Josef Lanner's son August — both of them well worth hearing. Though it may be difficult to imagine the sparkling overture to *Die Fledermaus* reduced for string quartet, doubts are swept aside when the playing is as stylish as here. Apart from a low volume level in father Strauss's *Chinese Galop,* the recording is beautifully engineered. This should appeal to anyone interested in exploring the byways of Viennese dance music or simply seeking tuneful, relaxing listening.

WIEN MODERN. [a]Vienna Jeunesse Choir; Vienna Philharmonic Orchestra/Claudio Abbado. DG 429 260-2GH. Texts and translations included. Recorded at performances in the Musikverein, Vienna in October 1988.

Boulez: Notations I-IV (1945/78). ***Ligeti:*** Atmosphères (1961). Lontano (1967). ***Nono:*** Liebeslied (1954)[a]. ***Rihm:*** Départ (1988)[a].

46m DDD 4/90

Live recordings of contemporary music concerts are, understandably, rare. Too much can go wrong: in particular, the playing, however well-rehearsed, can develop the rough edges of anxiety and even hostility which make for dispiriting listening, especially when repeated. All the more reason, then, to celebrate the fact that *Wien Modern* is something of a triumph. Even without the crowning glory heard at the actual event, Berg's great set of *Three Orchestral Pieces*, Op. 6, the programme has the strong central focus of two of Ligeti's hypnotic orchestral soundscapes, played with brilliant precision under Abbado's strong yet never overbearing control. The Boulez miniatures — reworkings of early piano pieces — are no less riveting. The rarity, Nono's early exercise in 12-note lyricism, and the novelty, Wolfgang Rihm's specially-composed Rimbaud setting, are not on the same high level of inspiration, but in these secure, confident performances, with an electric, live concert atmosphere conveyed in a first-class recording, they contribute substantially to what was, unmistakably, a very special musical occasion.

NEW REVIEW

THE WOMEN'S PHILHARMONIC. [a]**Angela Cheng** (pf); [b]**Gillian Benet** (hp); **Women's Philharmonic Orchestra/JoAnn Falletta.** Koch International Classics 37169-2.
Mendelssohn-Hensel: Overture in C major. ***C. Schumann:*** Piano Concerto in A minor, Op. 7[a]. ***Tailleferre:*** Concertino for Harp and Orchestra[b]. ***Boulanger:*** D'un soir triste. D'un matin du printemps.

lh 5m DDD 2/93

Collectors should know that this all-female orchestra from San Francisco won an award enabling them to record a two-disc anthology of works by women composers, of which the first was devoted to five from the eighteenth century. Shared by discerningly paired nineteenth-century German and twentieth-century French ladies, this second disc opens with a neatly crafted, classically orientated Overture by Mendelssohn's elder sister, Fanny, of whom the musical world would surely have heard more but for her family's insistence that a woman's place was in the home. In that respect Clara Wieck was luckier: her fame-seeking father fought only to prevent her marriage to the impulsively romantic Robert Schumann, the guiding star behind her three-movement Concerto, which she herself introduced at the Leipzig Gewandhaus when still a mere 16-year-old. The maturest music nevertheless comes from France, with a Ravel-glancing as well as racy *Concertino* for harp written by the 36-year-old Germaine Tailleferre in 1928 to explain how she held her own alongside the five male members of Les Six. Finally, two poignant reminders, and especially the longer and more darkly searching *D'un soir triste*, of all that we might have been given by Lili Boulanger had she not died in 1918 when still only 24. The playing throughout, like the reproduction, helps to make the disc a very worthwhile investment, the more so since only Clara's Concerto is otherwise obtainable.

NEW REVIEW

WORKS FOR HORN AND ORCHESTRA. Hermann Baumann (hn); **Leipzig Gewandhaus Orchestra/Kurt Masur.** Philips 416 380-2PH. Recorded in 1985.
Glière: Horn Concerto in B flat major, Op. 91. ***Saint-Saëns:*** Morceau de concert in F minor, Op. 94. ***Chabrier:*** Larghetto. ***Dukas.*** Villanelle (orch. Bujanowski).

47m DDD 5/93

The combination of the virtuoso horn player Hermann Baumann, the conductor Kurt Masur and the great Leipzig Gewandhaus Orchestra in an unbeatable recording presents current German music-making at its finest. And the extraordinary bonus about this recording, quite apart from the superlative performances, is the imaginative and interesting repertoire. The music of the Russian composer Reinhold Glière has existed in a kind of twilight, overshadowed by the more familiar names of Tchaikovsky, Rachmaninov, and Prokofiev. Yet his works are shot through with a lush late romanticism which exerts a strong fascination. The Horn Concerto is a highly typical work: wide arching lyric themes; brilliantly orchestrated, and unsparing in its demands upon the soloist. With many backward glances to Tchaikovsky, this is a most welcome addition to the romantic concerto repertoire for the horn. The three shorter pieces which complete this CD are all by French composers of the late nineteenth century. None of these works is of the calibre of the Glière concerto, but each one is both an effective display piece for the horn and a composition of some musical imagination. Hermann Baumann's playing is beyond reproach and he sails through all the trials of each work effortlessly and with burnished tone. Masur's direction of the Gewandhaus is impassioned as well as disciplined, and the recorded sound is suitably rich and excellently balanced.

WORKS FOR OBOE AND ORCHESTRA. John de Lancie (ob); **[a]London Symphony Orchestra/André Previn; [b]chamber orchestra/Max Wilcox.** RCA Victor Gold Seal GD87989. Items marked [a] from SB6721, 11/67, [b] Recorded in 1987 and new to UK.
Françaix. L'horloge de flore[a]. ***Ibert.*** Symphonie concertante[a]. ***Satie*** (orch. Debussy). Gymnopédie No. 1[a]. ***R. Strauss.*** Oboe Concerto[b].

lh 12m ADD/DDD 12/91

This delightful collection focuses on the career and talent of the American oboist John de Lancie. De Lancie was the American soldier who in 1945 asked Strauss to write him a few bars of music for the oboe — the result, no less, was the delightfully sunny Oboe Concerto. De Lancie's return to the United States prevented him from attending the première, but a few years later Strauss granted him permission to give the work its American première. Bureaucracy and protocol intervened however, and in the event the solo part was entrusted to Mitchell Miller. This 1987 recording (and a very fine one it is too) therefore closes the circle that began over 45 years ago in the Bavarian Alps. It was de Lancie too, who commissioned Françaix's gorgeous suite for oboe and orchestra, *L'horloge de flore* ("The flower clock"). Each of its seven movements represent a flower (and the time of day that the bloom opens), in the Flower Clock developed by the Swedish botanist Carl von Linne. Quite why this charming and melodious work should not be more well known and indeed performed is a complete mystery — it would certainly be a winner with any audience. Inexplicable, too, is the apparent neglect in the catalogue at present of Ibert's *Symphonie concertante* for oboe and strings. This substantial work is a fine example of Ibert's natural gift for seamless melodic invention and exquisite string writing; if you know and love the Flute Concerto then this work should be next on your list of acquisitions. The Françaix and Ibert items were recorded in 1966 but are remarkably fresh and clear, with Previn and the LSO providing most sympathetic accompaniments.

WORKS FOR TWO AND FOUR HORNS AND ORCHESTRA. Israel Philharmonic Orchestra/Meir Rimon (hn). Pickwick IMP Masters MCD31.
Handel (arr. Rimon): Double Concerto in F major. ***Barsanti:*** Concerto Grosso for two horns in D major, Op. 3 No. 4. ***Haensel:*** Double Concerto in F major, Op. 80. ***O. Franz:*** Concert Piece for two horns in F major, Op. 4. ***Hübler:*** Concerto for four horns in F major. ***Schumann:*** Konzertstück for two horns in F major, Op. 86.

lh 7m DDD 2/92 £

Meir Rimon was born in 1946 and, sadly, died just after completing this recording. It demonstrates that he was not only a skilful horn player but also a versatile and positively hyperactive one, for he plays all the solo parts himself — 16 in six works — conducts the orchestra, and arranged some of the music. The playing and conducting obviously involved multitracking, and you may feel that a double concerto goes better with two different artists and instruments, just as a quadruple one is better with four. But the result here is satisfying, and at least Rimon gives us a unified view of each piece. Handel's Concerto exists as two quick outer movements and Rimon has placed another Handel piece between them as a slow one to make up the usual three. The cheerful finale is familiar, being identical to a hornpipe in the *Water Music*; Francesco Barsanti, A. Haensel, Oscar Franz and Heinrich Hübler are little known figures (we don't even know Haensel's first name), and the musical quality here is more patchy. But the Barsanti *Concerto grosso* has a richly Italianate slow movement and Franz's *Concert Piece* conveys the "happy mood" that the composer asks for. Hübler's Concerto for four horns is a pleasingly warm romantic work, written in 1854 and owing something to the example set shortly before by Schumann with his strikingly vigorous and telling *Concert Piece* (in three movements and a concerto in all but name) for the same combination. While there's a lot of F major in this programme, it is attractive and well recorded and features this golden-toned instrument in the hands of a master performer.

WORKS FOR VIOLIN. Cho-Liang Lin (vn); [a]**Sandra Rivers** (pf); [b]**Philharmonia Orchestra/Michael Tilson Thomas;** [c]**Chicago Symphony Orchestra/Leonard Slatkin.** CBS Masterworks CD44902. Items marked [a] from IM39133 (2/85); [b] 39007 (6/84), [c] 42315 (3/87).
Mendelssohn: Violin Concerto in E minor, Op. 64[b]. ***Bruch:*** Violin Concerto No. 1 in G minor, Op. 26[c]. ***Sarasate:*** Introduction et Tarantelle, Op. 43[a]. ***Kreisler:*** Liebesfreud[a].

lh lm DDD 3/91 £ B

The current catalogue is not short of good recordings of the Mendelssohn Violin Concerto and Bruch's First Concerto, and the two certainly make a good pair on a CD, particularly when the 50 odd minutes that they take are complemented, as here, with two short pieces (though only with piano) by virtuoso violinists who not surprisingly wrote superbly for their instrument. At medium price, this is a desirable disc, for Cho-Liang Lin plays with passion and tenderness, bringing out the various, but always romantic, moods of the two main works and the graceful *salon* charm of the others. He has an unfailingly expressive tone quality, and can shape an individual phrase with elegance while keeping in perspective the longer term issues of paragraphs and indeed whole movements. Maybe some other players have found a more sensuous beauty in the melody of the slow movement in the Mendelssohn, and let themselves go more as regards tempo in the finale, but Lin's slight restraint pays dividends with its own kind of aristocratic eloquence and his refinement is also a positive feature in the Bruch. The recordings are not especially new and come from different locations, which in three cases are American ones: the oldest is that of the Mendelssohn, which was recorded in London and dates from 1982. But the sound is well enough matched and fully digital as well as offering both clarity and atmosphere.

WORKS FOR VIOLIN AND ORCHESTRA. Joshua Bell (vn); **Royal Philharmonic Orchestra/Andrew Litton.** Decca 433 519-2DH.
Saint-Saëns: Introduction and Rondo capriccioso, Op. 28. ***Massenet:*** THAIS — Méditation. ***Sarasate:*** Zigeunerweisen, Op. 20. ***Chausson:*** Poème, Op. 25. ***Ysaÿe:*** Caprice d'après l'etude en forme de valse de Saint Saëns. ***Ravel:*** Tzigane.

lh DDD 1/92 P

The Spaniard, Pablo de Sarasate, and the great Belgian virtuoso, Eugene Ysaÿe, both travelled to study in Paris during the second half of the last century, and although both were celebrated as distinguished exponents of violin technique, their collective influence upon the composers active in France at much the same time proved to be far more significant, as this brilliant selection of virtuoso showpieces will readily confirm. The young American violinist, Joshua Bell, himself a grand-pupil of Ysaÿe via his teacher, Joseph Gingold, is heard to superb advantage here in commanding performances of music which will captivate as much as it will astonish. Bell captures the heady bravura of Saint-Saëns *Introduction and Rondo capriccioso* with breathtaking ease, and his spiccato playing in the coda is little short of phenomenal. Sarasate's perennial favourite *Zigeunerweisen* will also astound, with Bell's mastery of the whole panoply of technical effects, including multiple-stopping and left hand pizzicato, contributing to an authentic gypsy-style performance. No recording of this kind would be complete without the celebrated "Méditation" from Massenet's *Thaïs*, made especially compelling here, in Bell's affectionately rich-toned account. The same tonal refinement and sensitivity characterize his elegiac reading of the *Poème* by Chausson, ably supported by the Royal Philharmonic Orchestra under Andrew Litton. Ysaÿe's *Caprice d'après l'etude* is another, although rather less familiar *tour de force*, affording every possibility for virtuosic display, although it does not challenge Ravel's devilish *Tzigane* in terms of pure technical difficulty. This truly hair-raising rendition of the *Tzigane* would bring any concert audience to its feet, and Bell is wholly at ease with its Bartókian gypsy style. This thrilling playing crowns a hugely enjoyable collection from this dazzling young virtuoso. The clear and incisive Decca sound ensures that the forces are balanced effectively, and the natural ambience of Watford Town Hall lends a realistic dramatic weight to full orchestral climaxes, without undue spotlighting of the soloist. An admirable and meticulous release, then, whose appeal will gain Joshua Bell many new admirers.

WORKS FOR VIOLIN AND ORCHESTRA. Hideko Udagawa (vn); **London Philharmonic Orchestra/Kenneth Klein.** Pickwick IMP Classics PCD966.
Glazunov: Violin Concerto in A minor, Op. 82. ***Tchaikovsky*** (arr. Glazunov): Souvenir d'un lieu cher, Op. 42. ***Chausson:*** Poème, Op. 25. ***Sarasate:*** Danzas españolas, Op. 22 No. 1 (Romanze andaluza). ***Saint-Saëns*** (trans. Ysaÿe): Caprice en forme de valse, Op. 52.

lh 4m DDD 3/92

Although it begins with a full-scale concerto, this disc is essentially a collection of what Sir Thomas Beecham used to call lollipops, in other words romantic works intended to fall sweetly on the ear, which in this case are for violin and orchestra. The Glazunov Concerto was written in the early twentieth century but is a romantic Russian work in the tradition of Tchaikovsky although certainly none the worse for that. Indeed, for people who wish there were more such concertos in the repertory this one may confidently be recommended, particularly as Hideko Udagawa plays it with full-blooded, passionate commitment. Thereafter the programme is of shorter pieces, each one a fine example of its kind, with the Tchaikovsky triptych, *Souvenir d'un lieu cher* (which was actually orchestrated by Glazunov) being particularly winning, with the final "Mélodie" as the most glowing gem of all. However, Chausson's eloquent and ardent *Poème* for violin and orchestra is also a masterpiece and, like the Saint-Saëns *Caprice en forme de valse*, which was orchestrated by the violinist Eugène Ysaÿe, reminds us how lovingly and idiomatically French composers, too, wrote for the violin. The solo instrument is placed fairly close in this richly-toned recording, but few will mind that in this repertory and the orchestral playing of the LPO under Kenneth Klein matches Udagawa's own warmly expressive and strongly projected style.

Chamber

NEW REVIEW

BALANESCU QUARTET. Balanescu Quartet (Alexander Balanescu, Clare Connors, vns; Bill Hawkes, va; Caroline Dale, vc). Argo 436 565-2ZH.
Byrne: High Life. ***Moran:*** Music from the Towers of the Moon. ***Lurie:*** Stranger than Paradise. ***Torke:*** Chalk.

52m DDD 3/93

All four of the American composers represented here write in easily approachable styles. Each work is excellently served by highly dedicated, expert performances from the Balanescu Quartet, and by a faithful, well-defined recording. David Byrne's *High Life* is the shortest piece on the disc, and consists of syncopated, repeated patterns over which apparently random, free-floating ideas come into being and then dissolve away. Robert Moran's contribution uses material from his opera *From the Towers of the Moon* and is in four short sections. His style is readily enjoyable, with fresh and energetic ideas, and attractive melodic invention. John Lurie's *Stranger than Paradise* is based on music written for a film of the same name: six descriptive episodes form a pleasantly evocative work which is influenced by blues and minimalist styles. *Chalk* is Michael Torke's word for the resinous residue formed by the action of a bow drawn strongly across a stringed instrument. The basic pulse of his piece is constant, in the style of the minimalists, and indeed there is plenty of vigorous, even hectic writing for the four instruments. Torke's insert-notes indicate that he much admires the Balanescu players, and they certainly play their hearts out for him.

CONTEMPORARY WORKS FOR STRING QUARTET. Kronos Quartet (David Harringon, John Sherba, vns; Hank Dutt, va; Joan Jeanrenaud, vc). Elektra Nonesuch 7559-79111-2. From 979 111-1 (7/87).
P. Sculthorpe: String Quartet No. 8. ***Sallinen:*** String Quartet No. 3. ***Glass:*** Company. ***C. Nancarrow:*** String Quartet. ***J. Hendrix*** (arr. Rifkin): Purple Haze.

49m DDD 2/89

Of all string quartets currently active none has done more than the Kronos to change the image of the medium. Snappy dressing and theatrical presentation are part of it, so are rock arrangements like the Jimi Hendrix *Purple Haze* on this CD. But there is nothing trendy about their choice of repertoire and the technical finish of their playing can stand the closest scrutiny — it's just that they have an added rhythmic bounce and colouristic flair which are the envy of many another ensemble. The stylistic and geographical spread of this programme is impressive. There is Sculthorpe, an Australian responding to the music of Bali, Sallinen, a Finn responding hauntingly to his own country's folk-music and Nancarrow, an American now resident in Mexico and best known for his zany series of Studies for pianola. This selection should win over any listener wary of anything more modern than Bartók. And you could not wish for more full-blooded advocacy or more vivid recording quality.

NEW REVIEW

DEBUT. Sarah Chang (vn); **Sandra Rivers** (pf). EMI CDC7 54352-2.
Sarasate: Concert Fantasy on "Carmen", Op. 25. ***Elgar:*** Salut d'amour, Op. 12. La Capricieuse, Op. 17. ***Khachaturian:*** Gayaneh — Sabre Dance. ***Kreisler:*** Tempo di Menuetto in the style of Pugnani. ***Paganini:*** Caprices, Op. 1 — No. 1 in E major; No. 15 in E minor. ***Chopin*** (arr. Milstein): Nocturne in C sharp minor, Op. posth. ***Shostakovich*** (arr. Zyganow): Preludes, Op. 34 — No. 10 in C sharp minor; No. 15 in D major. ***Gershwin*** (trans. Heifetz): Porgy and Bess — It ain't necessarily so. ***Liszt*** (arr. Milstein): Consolations, S172 — Lento placido. ***Tchaikovsky:*** Souvenir d'un lieu cher, Op. 42 — Mélodie in E flat major. ***Prokofiev*** (arr. Heifetz): The Love for Three Oranges — March.

51m DDD 1/93

This astonishing disc heralds the recording début of another much-vaunted violinistic phenomenon, the 11-year-old Sarah Chang. A student of the acclaimed pedagogue Dorothy DeLay, Chang actually made this recording at the age of nine, playing a quarter-sized violin. With an impressive catalogue of major orchestral engagements to her credit, she is now continuing her studies at the Juilliard School in New York. Her taxing programme opens with an impeccable account of Sarasate's *Carmen* Fantasy, in an edition prepared by Zino Francescatti; dazzling playing, even if that last *frisson* of excitement is held in check. The two Elgar favourites are charming, even if slightly mannered, but Chang's bristling performances of Khachaturian's "Sabre Dance" and the famous Heifetz transcription of the March from Prokofiev's *The Love for Three Oranges* are both sensational. Her Paganini, too, is electrifying — she despatches the First and Fifteenth *Caprices* with the confident *élan* of a seasoned virtuoso. The same technical assurance is evident in two Preludes by Shostakovich, but undemonstrative offerings are marginally less convincing perhaps, at this very early stage, with some inflexibility in the Tchaikovsky and Kreisler works. She is a shade unyielding in her approach to Nathan Milstein's winning Chopin and Liszt arrangements, but her natural spontaneity works to greater advantage in "It ain't necessarily so", from *Porgy and Bess*, in the famous Heifetz version. "Sarah Chang is the most ideal violinist I have ever heard" was Sir Yehudi Menuhin's verdict on this monumentally gifted young virtuoso. Her recording début will enthral and captivate in equal measure — hear it as a matter of priority!

JACQUELINE DU PRE — HER EARLY BBC RECORDINGS. Jacqueline du Pré, [f]**William Pleeth** (vcs); [deg]**Ernest Lush,** [c]**Stephen Kovacevich** (pfs). EMI Studio mono

CDM7 63165/6-2. Recorded at broadcast performances on [a]January 7th, 1962, [b]January 26th, 1962, [c]February 25th, 1965, [dg]March 22nd, 1961, [e]September 3rd, 1962, [f]March 17th, 1963. *CDM7 63165-2* — ***Bach:*** Solo Cello Suites — No. 1 in G major, BWV1007[a]; No. 2 in D minor, BWV1008[b]. ***Britten:*** Cello Sonata in C major, Op. 65 — Scherzo and March[c]. ***Falla*** (arr. Maréchal): Suite populaire espagnole[d]. *CDM7 63166-2* — ***Brahms:*** Cello Sonata No. 2 in F major, Op. 99[e]. ***F. Couperin:*** Nouveaux Concerts — Treizième Concert[f]. ***Handel*** (arr. Slatter): Oboe Concerto in G minor, HWV287[g].

② lh 52m ADD 9/89 £ 9p ▲

We owe the BBC and EMI a debt of gratitude for making these valuable recordings available on disc. The performances date from her mid- to late- teens, and reveal a maturity and passion that is rare in so young a performer. This, together with her wonderful gift of communication, make these performances very special indeed. The two Bach Cello Suites have a magical, intimate poetry that transfixes the attention from the very first note and her beautifully phrased and lyrical readings more than compensate for any slight imperfections of articulation. Sadly we have only the Scherzo and March movements from the Britten Cello Sonata, and judging by the quality of these, a complete performance would surely have been a recording to treasure. These are sparkling performances, full of wit and good humour, reflecting the obvious rapport between the two young artists. The recording of Falla's *Suite populaire espagnole* dates from 1961 when du Pré was only 16 but is no less assured or technically accomplished. The performance is full of life and rhythmic vitality, with some very tender and expressive playing, as in the cantabile melodies of the "Nana" and "Cancion" movements. The mono recordings are not of the highest quality (the Bach Suites are taken from transcription discs, so there are traces of surface noise and clicks) but this is of little relevance when we are presented with playing as beautiful and captivating as this.

FRENCH CHAMBER MUSIC. [a]**Catherine Cantin** (fl); [b]**Maurice Bourgue** (ob); [c]**Michel Portal** (cl); [d]**Amaury Wallez** (bn); [e]**André Cazalet** (hn); **Pascal Rogé** (pf). Decca 425 861-2DH.
Saint-Saëns: Caprice sur des airs danois et russes, Op. 79[abc]. ***d'Indy:*** Sarabande et menuet, Op. 72[abcde]. ***Roussel:*** Divertissement, Op. 6[abcde]. ***Tansman:*** Le Jardin du Paradis — Danse de la sorcière[abcde]. ***Françaix:*** L'heure du berger[abce]. ***Poulenc:*** Elégie[e]. ***Milhaud:*** Sonata for flute, oboe, clarinet and piano, Op. 47[abc].

lh 7m DDD 5/91

French composers are noted for their special fondness for writing for wind instruments, but their wide diversity of styles is illustrated by this attractive disc, which is notable for superbly clean and sensitive playing by musicians in complete accord with each other and in instinctive sympathy with the music. Of the three works here for wind quintet and piano, the Roussel *Divertissement* is a particular delight, in turn sprightly and seductive; the d'Indy movements (transcribed from an earlier suite for the curious combination of trumpet, two flutes and string quartet) are an expressively contrapuntal sarabande and an oddly chirpy minuet; and the pungent Tansman dance is from an unfinished ballet. Jean Françaix's habitual spirit of *gaminerie* reigns in his three portraits for wind quartet and piano, written with his usual consummate craftsmanship. The works for wind trio and piano could scarcely be more unlike: Saint-Saëns's suave confection on (reputedly bogus) Danish and Russian airs, with a brilliant piano part, and Milhaud's often abrasive sonata (despite a pastoral opening), which ends with a dirge for victims of a Spanish influenza epidemic. And there's Poulenc's elegy for Dennis Brain, its broad lament tinged with just a touch of the humour that Dennis himself would have enjoyed.

NEW REVIEW

FRENCH PIANO WORKS. Robert Casadesus, Gaby Casadesus (pfs, four hands). Sony Classical Masterworks Portrait [c]mono/[ab]stereo SK52527. Items marked [a] from CBS SBRG72050 (10/62), [b] SBRG72233 (6/65), [c] new to UK).

Debussy: Petite suite[a]. En blanc et noir[b]. ***Fauré:*** Dolly Suite, Op. 56[a]. ***R. Casadesus:*** Trois danses Méditerranéennes, Op. 36[c]. ***Satie:*** Trois morceaux en forme de poire[a].

lh 6m ADD 4/93

The husband-and-wife team Robert and Gaby Casadesus constituted a real meeting of musical minds; their expert traversal of the two-piano and piano-duet repertories lead to many a gramophone classic, and this CD provides a first-rate sampling of their considerable art. French keyboard works were of course central to the Casadesus's repertoire, and their sculpted, poised performances of, in particular, the Debussy items, make for a pleasurable listening experience. *En blanc et noir* (a late and forward-looking masterpiece) has genuine grandeur, while the charming *Petite suite* (which includes, "En bateau", one of the composer's most beguiling melodies) is played here with grace and no mean virtuosity. The opening Berceuse of Fauré's aromatic *Dolly* Suite will be familiar to many as the theme music to "Listen with Mother"; here again, there is charm a-plenty, while Satie's mischievously-titled *Trois morceaux en forme de poire* ("Three Pieces in the Form of a Pear") are anything but trite or superficial. Robert Casadesus recorded a number of his own works over the years, and his catchy *Trois danses Méditerranéennes* fill out this well-planned and reasonably well-recorded collection in a pleasing and unexpected fashion. A gentle, life-affirming programme.

GERMAN CHAMBER MUSIC. Barthold Kuijken (fl); **Sigiswald Kuijken** (vn, va da gamba); **Wieland Kuijken** (vc, va da gamba); **Robert Kohnen** (hpd). Accent ACC58019D. From ACC8019 (8/81).

J.S. Bach: Trio Sonata No. 1 in E flat major, BWV525 (trans. for flute, violin and continuo in G major). ***C. P. E. Bach:*** Trio Sonata in A major for flute, violin and continuo, Wq146. ***Telemann:*** Sonata in G major for flute, two violas da gamba and harpsichord. Suite in D minor for flute, violin and continuo.

57m DDD 3/86 

A recital of carefully chosen pieces, sensitively played and extremely well recorded, makes this baroque anthology very appealing. The interpretative skills of these musicians are impressive, both on account of their thoughtfulness and for their unerring sense of an appropriate style. The repertoire consists mainly of rarely performed pieces of more than passing interest. The J.S. Bach 'Sonata in G major' is an arrangement for transverse flute, violin and continuo of the E flat Sonata for two manuals and pedal, whilst the two Telemann pieces show off the composer's chamber style at its most original and engaging. The C.P.E. Bach Trio Sonata, though marginally less interesting, perhaps, is a long way from being either dull or routine. Documentation is sketchy but is hardly required when the music speaks for itself as eloquently as this.

NEW REVIEW

THE LINDSAYS: 25 YEARS. Lindsay Quartet (Peter Cropper, Ronald Birks, vns; [a]Robin Ireland, [b]Roger Bigley, vas; Bernard Gregor-Smith, vc). ASV CDDCA825. Taken from BBC broadcast performances.

Wirén: String Quartet No. 3 in D minor, Op. 18 (recorded in 1987)[a]. ***A. Tchaikovsky:*** String Quartet No. 2 in C major, Op. 5 (1978)[b]. ***Hugh Wood:*** String Quartet No. 3, Op. 20 (1980)[b]. ***Barber:*** String Quartet, Op. 11 (1988)[a].

lh l7m ADD 1/93

As its name suggests, this issue celebrates the Lindsay String Quartet's twenty-fifth anniversary, with all but the present violist Robin Ireland chalking up over 20 years membership. The quartet has played works ranging from the classics to the less familiar modern ones by André Tchaikovsky and Hugh Wood that feature here. Indeed, what we have here is in no way central twentieth-century repertory: no 'great' composer at all, some will say, and regret it. Furthermore, these are recordings of BBC concert performances from 1978-88, and inevitably there are a few rustles that would otherwise have been edited out and applause after each work except the Tchaikovsky. However, such is the vitality of the playing that one can overlook these matters, and the overall quality of the sound is good. Dag Wirén is a Swedish composer known mainly for just one work, a Serenade for Strings, but his Third Quartet has plenty of personality although in a conservative idiom. André Tchaikovsky was Polish-born but spent much of his life in England before dying by his own hand at the age of 46; a fine pianist as well as a composer, he had a prickly personality that is strongly reflected in his Second Quartet, written for the Lindsays and first played by them in this BBC performance of January 1978. Hugh Wood's Third Quartet, which the Lindsays premièred, is also a tough piece, and relies heavily on Second Viennese School gesturings that now sound very dated, but the Lindsays play it with commitment. Finally, Samuel Barber's Quartet is maybe the best music here. Its celebrated central *Adagio* sounds strikingly fresh played in context on four instruments instead of alone in the usual version for string orchestra. It is a pleasure to salute the Lindsays and to welcome this excellent tribute disc.

MUSIC FOR WIND ENSEMBLE. Aulos Quintet ([a]Peter Rijkx, fl; [a]Diethelm Jonas, ob; [a]Karl-Theo Adler, cl; [a]Ralph Sabow, bn; Dietmar Ullrich, hn). Koch Schwann Musica Mundi 310087.

Briccialdi: Wind Quintet, Op. 124. ***Lefébure:*** Suite, Op. 57. ***Rossini:*** Wind Quartet No. 6[a]. ***Taffanel:*** Wind Quintet.

59m DDD 10/91

The image of wind music for some people is of something faintly comic, even perhaps of piping, burping and blasting, according to whether the instruments are high or low and playing softly or loudly — certainly not music offering the expressive sophistication that we associate with piano or strings. Nevertheless, in the hands of first-class players these instruments are as refined and subtle as any others. It's a pity that some of the great composers — Mozart is a notable exception — gave us little music for wind alone, though they often wrote splendidly for these instruments in orchestral music. Still, Rossini is a great figure, and even if the others represented in this nineteenth-century programme are not, they make up for lack of depth by writing superbly for the players. The members of the Aulos Wind Quintet are totally equal to this music and the performances are a delight — but then, so is the music itself, mainly on the lighter side and presented here with tremendous panache as well as affection. Each work here has its own kind of charm, and each player brings both skill and refinement to a satisfyingly well-blended whole; the second movement of Rossini's Quartet is particularly good at showing them off individually in a series of variations. The recording is clear, atmospheric and well balanced. This is a disc to give much delight.

ROMANTIC MUSIC FOR VIOLIN AND PIANO. Vera Vaidman (vn); **Emanuel Krasovsky** (pf). CDI/Pickwick PWK1137.

Tchaikovsky: Méditation, Op. 42 No. 1. Valse-Scherzo, Op. 34. Mélodie, Op. 42 No. 3. ***Dvořák:*** Violin Sonatina in G major, B183. ***Schubert:*** Violin Sonata in A minor, D385. ***Kreisler:*** Schön Rosmarin. Liebeslied. Liebesfreud.

1h 11m DDD 6/90 9p 9s

Here is a splendid collection of inspired music for violin and piano, marvellously played and given a digital recording of great realism and immediacy. The Dvořák *Sonatina* was written in New York at around the same time that the great Czech composer created his most popular work, the *New World* Symphony, and it deserves to be equally well known. All four movements are brimming over with the same kind of memorable melody that makes the symphony such a favourite with the public. The first movement makes an impression of great vigour and impulse, the *Larghetto* sings beguilingly, the *Scherzo* dances vivaciously and the finale sparkles and introduces another quite lovely lyrical folksy melody which is instantly memorable and stays in the mind long after the work has concluded. Vera Vaidman's performance has great sympathy and spontaneity and her partner, Emanuel Krasovsky gives all the support she could ask for, though it is she who dominates — for that is the way the music is written. The programme opens with an engaging Tchaikovsky triptych, each miniature strikingly characterful and the third, *Mélodie*, having that bittersweet Russian melancholy for which the composer is famous. The Schubert *Sonata* which follows the Dvořák has a disarming, simple lyricism. Like the Dvořák it is in four movements: the *andante* is gently eloquent, and the finale flows with captivating innocence. The programme ends with three Kreisler lollipops, dashingly played, to end the recital exuberantly. This disc is in the bargain price range and the recording is in the demonstration class: on a minor label, with an Israeli source, it could be so easily passed by, but it should be sought out, for its rewards are very considerable.

NEW REVIEW

SOUTH AMERICAN FLUTE MUSIC. Anna Noakes (fl); [b]**Marios Argiros** (ob); [d]**Leslie Craven** (cl); [a]**Mark Denman** (vn); [a]**Richard Friedman** (vn); [a]**Kate Musker** (va); [c]**Sebastian New** (bn); [fg]**James Woodrow** (gtr); [ac]**Justin Pearson** (vc). Kingdom KCLCD2027.

Ginastera: Impresiones de la Puna[a]. Duo, Op. 13[b]. ***Villa-Lobos:*** Bachianas brasileiras No. 6[c]. Chôros No. 2[d]. Assobio a jato[e]. Distribuição de flores[f]. ***Piazzola:*** Histoire du Tango[g].

lh 5m DDD 12/92

Anyone who think flute music began with Fauré's *Fantaisie* and ended with Debussy's *Syrinx* should hear this disc. From the dulcet tones of the first of Ginastera's *Impresiones de la Puna* to the jaunty rhythms of the third, "Danza", Anna Noakes's mellifluous tone beguiles the ear. The intertwining counterpoint of his *Duo* (with sensitive oboe playing from Marios Argiros) culminating in a foot-tapping Fuge is also skilfully handled. Neither of these works are in the standard repertoire, yet both are worthy of more regular performances. Villa Lobos's *Bachianas brasileiras* have fared better and in No. 6, an extended duet for flute and bassoon, the long-breathed lines of the Aria contrast with the energy of the Fantasia present a challenge energetically fulfilled by Noakes and bassoonist Sebastian New, eagerly contrasting with the acrobatic cavortings of flute and clarinet in *Chôros* No. 2. Combine flute with strings, as the last two works in this programme do, and the flute suddenly becomes the singer. Quite why Villa-Lobos whould have called such a graceful and airy work "The Jet Whistle" remains unclear; even in the final movement *Vivo,* grace and poise rule over the experimental harmonies. Piazzolla's *Histoire du Tango*, at over 20 minutes is the longest piece on the disc. Despite playing that is unfailingly capricious and characterful from Noakes and guitarist James Woodrow, it rather outstays its welcome and the insert-notes to the disc leave something much to be desired in their command of the English language. But this disc is well worth hearing for its expert performances of out-of-the-way repertoire.

TRANSCRIPTIONS FOR GUITAR AND HARPSICHORD. Norbert Kraft (gtr); **Bonnie Silver** (hpd). Chandos CHAN8937. All works transcribed by Kraft and Silver.

Vivaldi: Lute Concerto, RV93. ***Haydn:*** Divertimenti a quattro, Op. 2 — No. 2 in D major. ***Boccherini:*** Guitar Quintet No. 4 in D major, G448. ***Rodrigo:*** Fantasia para un gentilhombre.

54m DDD 11/91

The guitar and harpsichord are both plucked-string instruments and thus are natural bedfellows, so too were the lute and harpsichord or virginal, yet there is very little original repertory for either combination. The guitar in its present form sprang to life in the early 1800s, when the harpsichord had fallen on hard times, but in this century it has revived and the advent of numerous playing partnerships has stimulated composers to write for them. This said, all the music in this recording has been arranged by the performers from other sources, the harpsichord gracefully wearing an 'orchestral' or 'chamber-strings' mantle and, in the Vivaldi and Haydn, with the guitar reading the lute's lines. The husband-and-wife duo of Kraft and Silver represents the marriage of two fine musicians and outstandingly capable performers, and is here responsible for the variety of beguiling sounds in which the light but good-quality music is dressed — and which are faithfully preserved in the recording. As a pleasingly new musical experience this would be hard to beat.

TWENTIETH-CENTURY CHAMBER WORKS. Jascha Heifetz (vn); [a]**Gregor Piatigorsky** (vc); [b]**Emanuel Bay,** [c]**Artur Rubinstein** (pfs). RCA Victor Gold Seal GD87871.

Debussy[b]: Violin Sonata in G minor. Préludes — Book 1, No. 8, La fille aux cheveux de lin (arr. Hartmann. Both mono and new to UK). ***Respighi:*** Violin Sonata in B minor[b] (new to UK). ***Ravel*** (arr. Roques): Sonatine in F sharp minor — Menuet[b] (from RB16243, 6/61). Piano Trio in A minor[ac] (HMV mono DB9620/22, 6/51). ***Martinů:*** Duo[a] (SB6661, 7/66).

1h 13m ADD 9/90

Though the twentieth century has produced many fine violinists, the name of Jascha Heifetz still inspires a special awe, not least among fellow musicians, for his playing had exceptional eloquence and personality alongside a technical command that he displayed not only in dexterity but more often than not by imparting a subtle, inimitable colour to his tone when shaping a phrase. The works here are of the violinist's own time, for he had already made his début aged five a decade before Debussy wrote his Violin Sonata towards the end of the First World War. He recorded that Sonata with Emanuel Bay in 1950, but we would not know it when hearing the sound as successfully remastered here, and this is playing of real distinction, even if the elusive middle movement is arguably over-forceful. Heifetz and his celebrated colleagues are also impressive in the Ravel Trio recorded in the same year, also a wartime work but of a different kind, having great power and feeling, though the gentle little Minuet from the piano Sonatine is taken too briskly. The Respighi and Martinů pieces are perhaps less striking at first, but here too we are fully held by the authority of the playing. As already suggested, little apology need be made for the sound in the major works despite the age of the recordings, though there is 78-type needle hiss in *La fille aux cheveux de lin* and one misses really quiet tone in the Ravel Trio. This disc is for everyone, not just for connoisseurs of fine violin playing.

TWENTIETH CENTURY OBOE MUSIC. Robin Williams (ob); [a]**Julian Kelly** (pf). Factory Classical FACD236.

Poulenc: Oboe Sonata[a]. ***Britten:*** Six Metamorphoses after Ovid, Op. 49. ***Hindemith:*** Oboe Sonata[a]. ***Lalliet:*** Prelude and Variations[a].

49m DDD 1/90

A very enjoyable recital of twentieth-century oboe music. The Poulenc Sonata was written in 1962, and was one of his last compositions. It is largely elegiac in character and this is finely captured in this elegant and sensitive performance. The gently flowing tempo in the opening Elegie is just right, and Williams's carefully shaped phrasing has much beauty and symmetry. The spirit of Prokofiev (whose memory the work is dedicated to) seems to hover over the energetic Scherzo with its spiky rhythms and angular melodic line, and the sadness of the "Deploration" has great plangency. The highlight of the disc is Williams's performance of Britten's *Six Metamorphoses after Ovid*; this highly inventive piece for solo oboe is a set of six character studies after Greek mythological beings: Pan, Bacchus, Phaeton et al. Williams's musicality really shines through, coupling subtle dynamic shading (Pan and Niobe) with great dexterity (Arethusa). Rhythmic vitality is strongly projected by both players in the jaunty opening movement of Hindemith's two movement Sonata (1938), and this is well contrasted with the more introspective *Sehr langsam* movement. A first-rate performance of Lalliet's *Prelude and Variations* rounds off the disc nicely. The recorded sound is fine, if a little close.

NEW REVIEW

VIOLIN RECITAL. Kyoko Takezawa (vn); **Philip Moll** (pf). RCA Victor Red Seal 09026 60704-2.

Bartók: Sonata for solo violin, Sz117. ***Brahms:*** Hungarian Dance No. 1 in G minor. ***Chaminade*** (arr. Kreisler): Sérénade espagnole. ***Falla*** (trans. Kochanski): Suite populaire espagnole. ***Tchaikovsky:*** Souvenir d'un lieu cher, Op. 42 — No. 1, Méditation in D minor. Valse-scherzo, Op. 34.

1h 5m DDD 2/93 

Brave indeed is the violinist who elects to open a début recital disc with the Bartók solo sonata! Kyoko Takezawa's fearless performance is outstandingly good; her playing has idiomatic refinement and formidable virtuosity, sufficient to guarantee success in this most taxing of works for unaccompanied violin. For the remainder of her programme, this 1986 Gold Medal winner at the 1986 Indianapolis Violin Competition, and former student of Dorothy DeLay at the Juilliard School is joined at the piano by Philip Moll. Their Tchaikovsky performances are particularly memorable; affecting and nostalgic in the "Méditation" in D minor, and appropriately zestful in the case of the "Valse-scherzo". Takezawa's dazzling account of de Falla's *Suite populaire espagnole* (Paul Kochanski's arrangement) has an intuitive flair and individuality, also much in evidence in the other Spanish-flavoured offering here, Chaminade's *Sérénade espagnole*, once a regular Kreisler encore piece, but seldom heard these days. Takezawa shows her true mettle in a spirited rendition of the *Hungarian Dance* No. 1 by Brahms, which concludes the programme. This is an outstanding release, a brilliantly played and perceptively chosen programme crowned by a stunning version of the Bartók Sonata. A must for all lovers of the violin.

NEW REVIEW

WORKS FOR CELLO AND PIANO. Maria Kliegel (vc); **Raimund Havenith** (pf). Marco Polo 8 223403.

Cassadó: Dance of the Green Devil. ***Popper:*** Fantasy on Little Russian songs, Op. 43. Serenade, Op. 54 No. 2. ***Bach*** (trans. Rose): Suite in D major, BWV1068 — Air. ***Schubert:*** Schwanengesang, D957 — Ständchen. ***F. Schubert II:*** Bagatelle, Op. 13 No. 9. Die Biene. ***Granados:*** Goyescas — Intermezzo. ***Shostakovich:*** The gadfly, Op. 97 —Tarantella. ***Ravel:*** Sites auriculaires — Habanera. ***Debussy:*** Préludes, Book 1 — La fille aux cheveux de lin. ***Senaillé:*** Violin Sonata No. 5 in D minor — Allegro spirituoso. ***Vieuxtemps:*** 36 Etudes, Op. 48 — No. 21, Cantilena. ***Barchet:*** Images de Menton — Boulevard de Garavan. ***Offenbach:*** Danse bohémienne, Op. 28. ***Rachmaninov:*** Vocalise, Op. 34 No. 14. ***Gershwin:*** Short Story.

lh 15m DDD 9/92

With just over 75 minutes of superb playing, and a programme of rewarding variety and scope, this recital disc from German-born Maria Kliegel and Raimund Havenith ranks with the finest now available. A casual glance at the repertoire reveals quite a few surprises; the selections are fascinating, striking an ideal balance between the adventurous and the reassuringly familiar, all heard in performances of spectacular quality. Gaspar Cassadó's *Dance of the Green Devil* (Falla's influence is obvious!) is incisively played, and Kliegel is especially fine in two works by the "Paganini of the cello", David Popper. The Bach Air and "Ständchen" from Schubert's *Schwanengesang* will be familiar, as will "La fille aux cheveux de lin", transcribed from Book 1 of Debussy's *Préludes*. As transcriptions, all are remarkably effective, but Kliegel's virtuosity comes very much to the fore in the Intermezzo from *Goyescas* and the Ravel "Habanera", whilst her account of Shostakovich's witty "Tarantella", from orchestrations for the 1955 film *The Gadfly*, has flair and brilliance. An introspective reading of the familiar Rachmaninov *Vocalise* could have benefited from a degree of extra flexibility perhaps, but Kliegel gives a fascinating performance of Barchet's pizzicato study of vaguely flamenco idioms, "Boulevard de Garavan". Gershwin's *Short Story* offers a total contrast to the remaining items by Vieuxtemps and Offenbach, completing an unusually distinguished recital, vividly played and glowingly recorded. Definitely worth investigating.

NEW REVIEW

WORKS FOR CLARINET AND PIANO. Nicholas Carpenter (cl); **David McArthur** (pf). Herald HAVPCD152.

Arnold: Sonatina for clarinet and piano, Op. 29. ***Dunhill:*** Phantasy Suite, Op. 91. ***Finzi:*** Five Bagatelles, Op. 23. ***M. Henry:*** Jazz Song. ***Ireland:*** Fantasy-Sonata in E flat major. ***McCabe:*** Three Pieces.

lh 6m DDD 10/92

Here is clarinet music by five British composers, doubtless reflecting the tradition of interest in this instrument that John Ireland inherited from his teacher Stanford — who, in his turn, surely knew and admired the clarinet works by his idol Brahms. Ireland's *Fantasy-Sonata* is a strong piece, sensitive yet impassioned in a way that is typical of this still underestimated composer.

Nicholas Carpenter and David McArthur play it eloquently even if at times they let the emotional temperature fall lower than it should. Thomas Dunhill was also Stanford's pupil, but remains far less known than Ireland. His *Phantasy Suite* is less of a personal statement than Ireland's piece, but he was a good craftsman and his music is well written and not without charm. One may say much the same about Gerald Finzi's five *Bagatelles*: he has his staunch admirers, but these fluent pieces, all too familiar to thousands of student clarinettists and long-suffering music examiners, are pleasant but unremarkable — though it is good to hear them played as elegantly and sympathetically as they are here. The pleasingly tonal *Jazz Song* by the young composer Mike Henry is shapely and attractive, and John McCabe's *Three Pieces* are typically characteristic of this composer in being both thoughtful and entertaining. But the real star of this well chosen programme is Sir Malcolm Arnold's *Sonatina:* it offers gutsy invention, incisiveness, tenderness and charm of a kind that is deplorably rare in the 'serious' music of the twentieth century. The recording of all this music is vivid although not very refined.

NEW REVIEW

WORKS FOR CLARINET AND PIANO. Michael Collins (cl); **Kathryn Stott** (pf). EMI Virtuosi CDC7 54419-2.

Schumann: Fantasiestücke, Op. 73. ***Debussy:*** Première rapsodie. ***Poulenc:*** Clarinet Sonata. ***Lovreglio:*** Fantasia on Verdi's "La traviata", Op. 45. ***Weber:*** Grand duo concertant, J204. ***Messager:*** Solo de concours.

lh 7m DDD 9/92

NEW REVIEW

WORKS FOR CLARINET AND PIANO. Victoria Soames (cl); **Julius Drake** (pf). Clarinet Classics CC0001.

Copland: Clarinet Sonata. ***Tailleferre:*** Arabesque. Sonata for solo clarinet. ***Honegger:*** Sonatine. ***Poulenc:*** Clarinet Sonata. ***Milhaud:*** Sonatine, Op. 100. Duo concertant, Op. 351.

lh 8m DDD 9/92

One wishes that more music existed for the clarinet as a solo instrument, and it seems unfair that an instrument loved by Mozart, Weber and Brahms (to name but three composers) has such a small solo repertory. But there it is, and besides music by the men just mentioned there are other works of importance such as Schumann's *Fantasy Pieces,* Debussy's *Rapsodie* and the Poulenc Sonata which appears on both these British discs. Michael Collins is one of the finest clarinettists playing today, and certainly earns the title of virtuoso with the performances on the EMI disc. Messager's "competition solo" demands and receives great agility and panache, and Debussy's later piece is no less well served by this artist's refinement and subtlety. Weber's *Grand duo concertant* is a sonata in all but name, with fine melodies in its central *Andante* and a theatrical finale, and here Kathryn Stott matches Collins in her handling of the challenging piano part. The recording is excellent.

On the Clarinet Classics disc, Copland's Clarinet Sonata nominally dates from the very end of his life but proves to be an expert reworking of the Violin Sonata which he composed four decades earlier in 1943. This was a vintage period for him and he described the work as mainly lyrical, with little virtuosity. In fact there is an American purity of flavour here that is uniquely his and which we also find in other works of this time such as the ballet, *Appalachian Spring.* Victoria Soames and Julius Drake give this Sonata guts as well as quiet poetry, and they are no less good in Poulenc's, which has the same blend of energy and tenderness, although Collins and Stott bring even more brilliance to its finale. The music by four members of Les Six is not all of the same stature, and although Milhaud's two pieces (separated by some three decades) are good value in their quirky way, the Honegger is not so interesting until its vivid finale. But it is good to have all these works together and the performances by Soames and Drake are unfailingly stylish, while the recording is well balanced and faithful.

NEW REVIEW

WORKS FOR FLUTE AND PIANO. Peter Lloyd (fl); [a]**Rebecca Holt** (pf). Pickwick IMP Classics PCD991.

Gaubert: Flute Sonata No. 1[a]. ***Caplet:*** Rêverie et petite valse[a]. ***Fauré:*** Fantaisie, Op. 79[a].

Saint-Saëns: Romance in D flat major, Op. 37[a]. ***Busser:*** Prélude et scherzo[a]. ***Poulenc:*** Flute Sonata[a]. ***Roussel:*** Andante and scherzo, Op. 51[a]. ***Ferroud:*** Trois pièces.

1h 6m DDD 9/92

Poulenc's Flute Sonata forms the focal point of this superb recital from Peter Lloyd, accompanied at the piano by Rebecca Holt. The recording was made in Henry Wood Hall, London, whose warm acoustic ambience imparts a sensuous glow to the flute sound, and gives the piano a degree of natural transparency and weight without too much technical intervention. Lloyd's Poulenc is particularly satisfying; effortlessly played, and yet perceptive enough to reveal the sinister undercurrents concealed behind the obvious melodic appeal of the music. Gaubert's First Flute Sonata is possibly less stimulating; its language is certainly less demonstrative, but it is hardly less enjoyable for all that. Lloyd's account is effective and the sensitivity of his playing more than compensates for any passing deficiencies in the music itself. Henri Busser's *Prélude et scherzo* and the *Rêverie et petite valse* by Caplet are undemanding, yet undeniably charming, and like the *Trois pièces* by Ferroud, they typify their genre with a certain romantic innocence. Much the same could be said of the Fauré and Saint-Saëns items too, but the performances are consistently excellent and raise the musical worth of these slender offerings to an altogether higher level. The duo also include Albert Roussel's *Andante and scherzo*, in an ideally balanced performance which makes the most of the languorous and outwardly virtuosic possibilities of this unfamiliar work. An enjoyable disc then, offering first rate recorded sound and performances of great distinction.

Instrumental

THE ALDEBURGH RECITAL. Murray Perahia (pf). Sony Classical SK46437.
Beethoven: 32 Variations in C minor on an Original Theme, WoO80. ***Schumann:*** Faschingsschwank aus Wien, Op. 26. ***Liszt:*** Hungarian Rhapsody No. 12, S244. Consolation No. 3 in D flat major, S172. ***Rachmaninov:*** Etudes-tableaux, Op. 33 — No. 2 in C major. Etudes-tableaux, Op. 39 — No. 5 in E flat minor; No. 6 in A minor; No. 9 in D major.

59m DDD 4/91 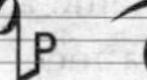 

Murray Perahia's attachment to Beethoven and Schubert has always been close. What may surprise some of his followers is to find the second half of this recital given over to such overtly demonstrative romantics as Liszt and Rachmaninov. It was a programme he had recently played at London's Festival Hall before recording it in 1989 at the Maltings in Snape — though not as part of that year's Aldeburgh Festival, as the title might suggest. Collectors can rest assured that no extraneous audience noise disturbs these 59 minutes. The piano is faithfully and sympathetically reproduced, with only an occasional touch of edginess in some of Rachmaninov's bigger climaxes. The playing itself is a joy. Potent contrasts of character allied with an inevitable-sounding continuity give Beethoven's C minor Variations (allegedly disowned by their composer) a maturity commensurate with his 36 years of age. Schumann's *Faschingsschwank aus Wien* in its turn gains a new youthful spontaneity and sparkle from his delectable lightness of touch and rhythmic *élan*. Even if rubato could have been more teasing in Liszt's twelfth *Rhapsody*, its virtuoso demands are brilliantly met, and surely not even Liszt himself could have floated the melody of the D flat *Consolation* with more assuaging beauty of tone and line. In the concluding Rachmaninov group Perahia throws his cap to the winds with the best of them while at the same time preserving his own unmistakably crystalline sound-world.

AMERICAN PIANO SONATAS, Volume 1. **Peter Lawson.** Virgin Classics VC7 59008-2.
Copland: Piano Sonata. ***Ives*** (ed. Cowell): Three-page Sonata. ***Carter:*** Piano Sonata. ***Barber:*** Piano Sonata, Op. 26.

1h 16m DDD 5/91

This disc offers four relatively unfamiliar but highly characterful American piano works in authoritative performances by a British-born pianist who clearly has their idiom at his fingertips

— as well as their pretty challenging notes. As played here, the Copland Piano Sonata of 1941 has softness as well as strength, and for all its powerful utterance there is a strangely compelling lyricism at work too; one can see why the young Leonard Bernstein adored the work and played it. The recording matches the music, being on the close side but extremely lifelike as piano sound. Ives's *Three-page Sonata*, which at over seven minutes is longer than the miniature that its title suggests, is a gnomic utterance, but as always with this composer we feel that he has something to say that could be said in no other way. Carter's Piano Sonata is an early work of 1946, which the composer revised much later in 1982; its debt to Copland is evident, but there is also a personal voice and the scope and sweep of the music is deeply impressive. Barber's Sonata (1949), which was written for Horowitz, is less radical in idiom than the other works played and thus more immediately approachable if by no means conventional, being a work of considerable power and eloquence, very well written for the piano.

NEW REVIEW

SIMON BARERE AT CARNEGIE HALL. Simon Barere (pf). APR mono CDAPR7007/08 (two double CD sets). Recorded 1946-9.
CDAPR7007 — ***Liszt:*** Piano Concerto No. 1 in E flat major (with orchestra/David Brockman). Années de pèlerinage, deuxième année, "Italie" — Sonnetto 104 del Petrarca. Piano Sonata in B minor. Rapsodie espagnole. Two Concert Studies — No. 2, Gnomenreigen (two performances). Harmonies poétiques et religieuses — No. 7, Funérailles. Hungarian Rhapsody No. 12 in C sharp minor. ***Gounod*** (trans. Liszt): Faust — Waltz. *CDAPR7008* — ***Bach:*** Chromatic Fantasia and Fugue in D minor. ***Schumann:*** Toccata in C major, Op. 7. Fantasiestücke, Op. 12 — No. 7, "Traumes Wirren". ***Weber:*** Piano Sonata No. 1 in C major — Presto . ***Godowsky:*** Renaissance — No. 6, Tambourin; No. 8, Pastorale; No. 12, Gigue. ***Blumenfeld:*** Etude for the left hand. ***Glazunov:*** Etude in C major, Op. 31 No. 1. ***Scriabin:*** Etudes, Op. 8 — No. 10 in D flat major; No. 12 in D sharp minor. ***Rachmaninov:*** Piano Concerto No. 2 in C minor, Op. 18 (orch). Preludes — G minor, Op. 23 No. 5; G sharp minor, Op. 32 No. 12. Polka de W.R. ***Balakirev:*** Islamey.

② lh 33m lh 37m ADD 11/89

He became an esoteric legend, one that only pianists knew about; yet even now, Simon Barere is but a mere name to many — he doesn't even have an entry in the *Grove Dictionary of Music*. Barere was a pupil of Blumenfeld (who also taught Horowitz) and a technician without peer; he made a few 78s before the war, but his post-war recordings and broadcasts reached only a select public. In fact, it wasn't until APR reinstated his name to *The Classical Catalogue* (this is the first of four volumes) that Barere's art was finally heard again in the UK. These are of course old recordings, and — for ears not accustomed to 'historic' reissues — they sound it. But I doubt that any reader who ventures beyond the opening pages of the Liszt Sonata will be able to stop there: this is simply the grandest, most brilliantly executed and exciting (as opposed to note-perfect) performance of the work in the current catalogue. Barere knows just when to assert his massive tone, when to attack the keyboard, or retract for a most beautiful *pianissimo*. His is also a fairly consistent overview of the piece, and no mere sequence of pianistic thrills. The rest of APR's set is hardly less striking (the solo items, especially), yet the Sonata remains its crowning glory and is essential listening for anyone who cares about what is unquestionably the greatest piano sonata in the entire romantic repertory.

SIMON BARERE. THE COMPLETE HMV RECORDINGS, 1934-6. **Simon Barere** (pf). APR mono CDAPR7001.
Liszt: Etudes de concert, S144 — La leggierezza (from HMV DB2166, 7/34). Années de pèlerinage, Deuxième année, S161, "Italie" — Sonetto 104 del Petrarca. Etudes de concert, S145 — Gnomenreigen (both from DB2167, 9/34). Réminiscences de Don Juan, S418 (two versions. DB2749/50. Recorded 1934 and 1936). Valse oubliée, S215 No. 1. Rhapsodie espagnole, S254 (DB2375/6, 6/35). ***Chopin:*** Scherzo No. 3 in C sharp minor, Op. 39 (APR7001, 12/85. 1935). Mazurka in F sharp minor, Op. 59 No. 3 (two versions — DB2674, 1/37; second previously unpublished. 1935-6). Waltz in A flat major, Op. 42 (DB2166).
Balakirev: Islamey — Oriental Fantasy (two versions. DB2675,

4/36). ***Blumenfeld:*** Etude for the left hand. ***Glazunov:*** Etude in C major, Op. 31 No. 1 (DB2645, 12/35). ***Scriabin:*** Etudes — C sharp minor, Op. 2 No. 1 (1934); D sharp minor, Op. 8 No. 12 (two versions. 1934-5). ***Lully*** (arr. Godowsky): Gigue in E major. ***Rameau*** (arr. Godowsky): Tambourin in E minor (both 1934. All from APR7001). ***Schumann:*** Toccata in C major, Op. 7 (three versions — two on DB2674, 1/37; third previously unpublished. 1935-6).

② 2h 6m ADD 5/91

For many years following his death in 1951 Simon Barere was simply a legendary name to conjure with, whose phenomenal pianism appeared to have been lost to future generations of music lovers. Then in the late 1980s a small specialist company, Appian Recordings, began to reissue his recordings — all extremely rare — in a series of three volumes. This, the first, contains all of the recordings (including rejected takes) which Barere made for HMV between 1934 and 1936, following his emigration from Russia and then Germany to the USA where his reputation was firmly, if briefly, established. Barere was part of the generation of super-pianists, including Horowitz, who succeeded the first wave of Russian virtuosos such as Rachmaninov and Lhévinne. For musicians such as these the normal peaks of the piano literature became mere starting points for complete and thorough investigations of the musical and technical capabilities of the instrument itself. The HMV sessions included such monumental tests of virtuosity as Balakirev's fantasy *Islamey*, Liszt's *Réminiscences de Don Juan*, and "Gnomenreigen", together with a whole range of shorter but equally testing pieces by Schumann, Chopin, Scriabin, Godowsky and Barere's final teacher, Blumenfield. To all of this music Barere brought a technique which knew no difficulties and a sense of musical taste which kept vulgar display firmly at bay. The results are frankly benchmarks of performance by which all aspiring virtuosos must be tested and which few will ever equal. Simon Barere's playing is simply breathtaking in its unrestrained vigour and superb technical control, both laid at the feet of a unique and powerful musical insight. This two-CD set is an essential memorial to one of the greatest, if unsung, heroes of the piano this century. The production by Bryan Crimp is faultless, with full and highly faithful transfers from the original 78s, and completely comprehensive accompanying documentation. No lover of truly great piano playing can afford to be without this issue.

BAROQUE ORGAN MUSIC. Peter Hurford (org). Argo 414 496-2ZH. Played on the Blank organ of the Bethlehemkerk, Papendrecht, The Netherlands.
G. Böhm: Prelude and Fugue in C major. Vater unser im Himmelreich. Auf meinen lieben Gott. Von Himmel hoch da komm'ich her. ***L. Couperin:*** Branle de basque. Fantaisie in G minor. ***J. K. Kerll:*** Capriccio sopra il cucu. ***Buxtehude:*** Mensch, willt du leben seliglich. Wir danken dir, Herr Jesu Christ. Vater, unser im Himmelreich. ***Walond:*** Voluntary No. 5 in G major. ***G. B. Pescetti:*** Sonata in C minor. ***Pachelbel:*** Ciaccona in D minor. ***Sweelinck:*** Unter der Linden grüne. ***Stanley:*** Voluntary in C major, Op. 5 No. 1.

1h 11m DDD 10/87

At first glance we may be a little dismayed to find an anthology called "Baroque Organ Music" which omits a single note of Bach. More careful scrutiny of the contents, however, may well persuade us that it is for our own good since Peter Hurford has chosen a programme of all too seldom-heard music by composers who were also noted organists of their day. The outstanding figures here are Jan Pieterszoon Sweelinck, Georg Böhm, Dietrich Buxtehude, Johann Pachelbel and Louis Couperin and although these works form the main body of the recital, listeners are unlikely to be disappointed by the several smaller, lighter-textured pieces with which Hurford makes discerning contrast, as well as showing off the appealing character of the organ.

BEST LOVED PIANO CLASSICS, Volume 1. **Moura Lympany** (pf). EMI Laser CDZ7 62523-2.
Chopin: Fantaisie-Impromptu in C sharp minor, Op. 66. Etudes, Op. 10 — C sharp minor, No. 4; G flat major, No. 5, "Black Keys". ***Brahms:*** Waltz in A flat major, Op. 39 No. 15. ***Mozart:*** Piano Sonata in A major, K331 — Rondo alla turca. ***Beethoven:*** Minuet in G major. Bagatelle No. 25, "Für Elise". ***Schumann:*** Kinderszenen, Op. 15 No. 7, Träumerei.

Liszt: Concert Studies, S144 — Un sospiro. ***Dvorák:*** Humoresque, Op. 101 No. 7. ***MacDowell:*** Woodland Sketches, Op. 51 No. 1, "To a Wild Rose". ***Chaminade:*** Automne, Op. 35 No. 2. ***Debussy:*** Suite Bergamasque No. 3, "Claire de lune". Children's Corner — Suite No. 6, "Golliwog's Cakewalk". ***Rachmaninov:*** Prelude in C sharp minor, Op. 3. No. 2. ***Rubinstein:*** Melody in F major, Op. 3 No. 1. ***Granados:*** Goyescas — No. 4, "The Maiden and the Nightingale". ***Falla:*** El amor brujo: Ritual Fire Dance. ***Albéniz/Godowsky:*** España, Op. 165 — Tango.

1h 11m DDD 1/89

This is not a reissue but a new recital digitally recorded in January 1988, and the consistently excellent Moura Lympany shows no sign of her 71 years. Indeed her technique is as sure as ever, as she demonstrates at the start in the tricky *Fantasie- Impromptu*, while she shows her musical sensitivity no less emphatically in the celebrated central section of the same piece, the melody of which was once made into a popular song called "I'm always chasing rainbows". Lympany mixes virtuoso pieces with more intimate, gentler ones, so that elaborate numbers like Liszt's concert study, *Un sospiro* ("A sigh") and Granados's "The Maiden and the Nightingale" contrast beautifully with Brahms's Waltz in A flat major and Schumann's *Träumerei* ("Dreaming"), from *Kinderszenen* ("Scenes of childhood"). Altogether, this is an admirably chosen sequence of piano classics from Mozart to Godowsky, and Lympany shows sympathy with every piece that she performs. Not only is it finely played, it is excellently recorded and the disc is a remarkable bargain and a quite splendid example of the art of a pianist whose skills seem only enhanced by the passing years. It would make a perfect present for someone new to classical piano music, yet will have no less appeal for a sophisticated and discriminating connoisseur.

BLACK ANGELS. Kronos Quartet (David Harrington, John Sherba, vns; Hank Dutt, va; Joan Jeanrenaud, vc). Elektra Nonesuch 7559-79242-2.
Crumb: Black Angels. ***Tallis*** (arr. Kronos Qt): Spem in alium. ***Marta:*** Doom. A sigh. ***Ives*** (arr. Kronos Qt/Geist): They are there! ***Shostakovich:*** String Quartet No. 8 in C minor, Op. 110.

1h 2m DDD 4/91 

This is very much the sort of imaginative programming we've come to expect from this talented young American quartet. With an overall theme of war and persecution the disc opens with George Crumb's *Black Angels*, for electric string quartet. This work was inspired by the Vietnam War and bears two inscriptions to that effect — *in tempore belli* (in time of war) and "Finished on Friday the Thirteenth of March, 1970", and it's described by Crumb as "a kind of parable on our troubled contemporary world". The work is divided into three sections which represent the three stages of the voyage of the soul — fall from grace, spiritual annihilation and redemption. As with most of his works he calls on his instrumentalists to perform on a variety of instruments other than their own — here that ranges from gongs, maracas and crystal glasses to vocal sounds such as whistling, chanting and whispering. *Doom. A sigh* is the young Hungarian composer István Marta's disturbing portrait of a Roumanian village as they desperately fight to retain their sense of identity in the face of dictatorship and persecution. Marta's atmospheric blend of electronic sound, string quartet and recorded folk-songs leave one with a powerful and moving impression. At first sight Tallis's *Spem in alium* may seem oddly out of place considering the overall theme of this disc, but as the sleeve-notes point out the text was probably taken from the story of Judith, in which King Nebuchadnezzar's general Holofernes besieged the Jewish fortress of Bethulia. Kronos's own arrangement of this 40-part motet (involving some multi-tracking) certainly makes a fascinating alternative to the original. A particularly fine account of Shostakovich's Eighth String Quartet (dedicated to the victims of fascism and war) brings this thought-provoking and imaginative recital to a close. Performances throughout are outstanding, and the recording first class.

THE BRITTEN CONNECTION. Anthony Goldstone (pf). Gamut Classics GAMCD526.
Bridge: Dramatic Fantasia, H66. Gargoyle, H177. ***Ireland:*** Ballade of London Nights.

Britten: Five Waltzes. Night Piece. ***L. Berkeley:*** Six Preludes, Op. 23. ***R. Stevenson:*** Sonatina Serenissima. ***C. Matthews:*** Five Studies.

lh 9m DDD 3/92

Britten never taught composition, but his contacts with other composers extended from his own years as a pupil (of Frank Bridge and John Ireland) to the final period of ill-health when he needed assistants like the young Colin Matthews. Otherwise, 'the Britten connection' was through friendship (Lennox Berkeley) or homage (Ronald Stevenson). As is well known, Britten was a fine pianist who wrote little solo music for the instrument. Yet one cannot imagine slight compositions like the *Waltzes* and *Night Piece* being better done than they are here by Anthony Goldstone. The whole programme, even though the music is of variable quality, is performed with the kind of poise and unobtrusive technical skill which stands out even in an era of wall-to-wall virtuosity. The weakest pieces are the Ireland and the early *Dramatic Fantasia* by Bridge. Bridge's *Gargoyle* is a different matter, written in 1928, and with precisely the kind of tough-minded features that the young Britten was to seize on as the basis for his own style. The Berkeley Preludes and the Matthews Studies are attractive, economical display pieces, while Stevenson's *Sonatina Serenissima*, deriving from Britten's *Death in Venice*, complements the opera by moving into a quite different musical world. A fascinating compilation, then, with admirably natural recorded sound.

SHURA CHERKASSKY LIVE. PIANO RECITAL, Volume 1. **Shura Cherkassky.** Decca 433 653-2DH. Items marked [a] from L'Oiseau-Lyre DSL015 (11/76), [b] DSL024 (6/78).
Albéniz (arr. Godowsky): España, Op. 165 — Tango[a]. ***Chopin:*** Ballade No. 3 in A flat major, Op. 47[a]. Etudes[a] — C sharp minor, Op. 10 No. 4; C sharp minor, Op. 25 No. 7; B minor, Op. 25 No. 10. Preludes, Op. 28[b] — No. 4 in E minor; No. 6 in D minor; No. 7 in A major; No. 10 in C sharp minor; No. 13 in F sharp minor; No. 17 in A flat major; No. 20 in C minor; No. 23 in F major. Nocturne in F minor, Op. 55 No. 1[b]. ***Rachmaninov:*** Polka de V.R.[b]. ***Rubinstein:*** Melody in F, Op. 3 No. 1[b]. ***Schubert:*** Piano Sonata in A major, D664[b]. Moment musical in F minor, D780 No. 3[a] (arr. Godowsky). ***Scriabin:*** Prelude in D major, Op. 11 No. 5[b].

lh 12m ADD 10/91

Shura Cherkassky has always been one of the most mercurial pianists of the day, a throwback — if you like — to the great virtuosos of bygone days — brilliant, unpredictable, wholly spontaneous. This disc is as fair a representation of his extraordinary abilities as any. You can hear here his delightful if idiosyncratic Chopin, wilful maybe but surely in the spirit of the composer's genius. Schubert's A major Sonata has long been a favourite of his, featuring in many of his recitals; he seems to warm to its slightly elusive, elegiac nature, and in the *Moment musical* (in Godowsky's arrangement), Cherkassky is at his most tellingly teasing. The pieces by Albéniz, Rachmaninov and Rubinstein have always been favourite encores of this pianist, and here they receive performances of amazing lightness and dexterity.

COLSTON HALL ORGAN CLASSICS. Malcolm Archer (org). Priory PRCD305. Played on the organ of The Colston Hall, Bristol.
W. Faulkes: Grand Choeur. ***Mascagni*** (arr. Lloyd Webber): Cavalleria rusticana — Intermezzo. ***Wagner*** (arr. Archer): Parsifal — Fanfares from Good Friday Music. ***Saint-Saëns*** (arr. Guilmant): The Carnival of the Animals — The Swan. ***Salomé:*** Grand Choeur. ***Pierné:*** Trois Pièces — Prelude; Cantilene; Scherzando. ***H. Smart:*** Festive March. ***F. Rickman:*** Mélodie Lyrique. ***W.T. Best:*** Concert Fantasia on an Old Welsh March. ***J. Strauss II:*** Tritsch, Tratsch Polka (arr. Lowry); Radetsky March (arr. Archer). ***Holzmann:*** Blaze Away.

lh 9m DDD 8/91 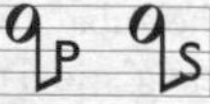

Malcolm Archer's career has taken him through cathedral organ lofts at Norwich and Bristol but in addition to these impeccable credentials in the British organ establishment he is also well known and admired by aficionados of the theatre organ and its music. The reason is not hard to discern from these ebullient performances which simply erupt with sparkling wit and infectious fun. Underlying it all, though, is the security of technique and musical sensitivity which can only come from a thorough grounding in the more serious side of musical performance. The programme harks back to the days when organ recitals could fill provincial town halls and civic theatres with audiences thirsty for spectacular displays of virtuosity from organist and organ alike. Transcriptions of orchestral and operatic items were a popular feature. These not only proved the technical virility of the recitalist but gave plenty of opportunity to display the lavish pseudo-orchestral effects which no self-respecting concert or theatre organ would be without. This marvellous recording of a splendid virtuoso player on a magnificent concert instrument recreates vividly the flavour of those spectacular organ concerts. Transcriptions of Saint-Saëns, Mascagni, Wagner and Johann Strauss sit happily alongside original organ pieces (including W.T. Best's scintillating *Fantasia on "Men of Harlech"*) and this immensely enjoyable disc ends with that all-time theatre organ favourite, *Blaze Away*.

NEW REVIEW

EIGHTIETH BIRTHDAY RECITAL, Volume 2. **Shura Cherkassky** (pf). Decca 433 654-2DH. Recorded at a performance in Carnegie Hall, New York in December 1991.
Bach (arr. Busoni): Partita in D minor, BWV1004 — Chaconne. ***Schumann:*** Etudes Symphoniques, Op. 13. ***Chopin:*** Nocturne in F minor, Op. 55 No. 1. Tarantelle in A flat major, Op. 43. ***Ives:*** Three-page Sonata, Op. 14. ***Hofmann:*** Kaleidoskop, Op. 40. ***Pabst:*** Concert Paraphrase from Tchaikovsky's "Eugene Onegin", Op. 81. ***M. Gould:*** Boogie Woogie Etude.

1h 18m DDD 1/93

Shura Cherkassky has long enjoyed the slightly dubious reputation of being a pianist's pianist. Capable of transforming familiar masterpieces into delectable kaleidoscopes of nuance and voicing he can be enchanting or infuriating according to taste. But when he is really on form it is difficult for even the hardest-hearted listener to resist. Big occasions tend to bring the best out of him, and they don't come much bigger than an eightieth-birthday concert at Carnegie Hall. That recital is here complete save for three items scheduled to appear on a future disc; a patching session took place the following day but was apparently not used for the CD. Spontaneous enjoyment is here in abundance. The extraordinary freedom in the repeated sections of the Schumann is one obvious proof of that; and the relishing of the last three lightweight pieces is another. But more deeply rewarding virtues are to be found too — in the dramatic pacing of the Bach/Busoni *Chaconne*, in the breathtaking poetry of the Chopin pieces, and not least in the full-blooded assault on Ives's craggy *Three-Page Sonata* which Cherkassky learned especially for the occasion. Here, and after each of the encores, the Carnegie Hall audience goes into justifiable raptures. Decca's recording has been done with exemplary care for balance and perspective.

NEW REVIEW

ENGLISH ORGAN MUSIC. Gareth Green. Naxos 8 550582. Played on the organ of Chesterfield Parish Church.
C.S. Lang: Tuba tune. ***Howells:*** Three Psalm-Preludes (Set 1), Op. 32. ***Elgar:*** Organ Sonata No. 1 in G major, Op. 28. ***Vaughan Williams:*** Three Preludes on Welsh Hymn Tunes — Rhosymedre. ***Whitlock:*** Hymn Preludes — on Darwall's 148th; on Song 13. ***Cocker:*** Tuba tune.

1h 4m DDD 3/93

Most large English church and cathedral organs boast at least one tuba stop — making a huge, fat, trumpet-like noise so powerful it can overwhelm every other stop on the organ. The *Tuba tune*, of which there are two classic examples on this CD, is a uniquely English creation in which the tuba stop is pitted against the rest of the instruments in a light-hearted, tuneful battle. C.S. Lang's jovial romp with its instantly-singable tune is certainly the most famous tuba tunes of all while Norman Cocker's slightly more demanding one runs it a close second. The Chesterfield organ possesses a fine tuba which brings these two pieces thrillingly to life in this thoroughly enjoyable CD. The remainder of the programme represents the very best of early twentieth-century English organ music with a handful of characteristic pieces; memorable for their fine melodies and stirring qualities. Gareth Green has an instinctive feel for this music and plays it all with great aplomb and this organ suits it to a tee — although Naxos's recording might have been a little clearer.

THE ESSENTIAL HARPSICHORD. Virginia Black. Collins Classics 5024-2.
Arne: Keyboard Sonata No. 3 in G major. ***D. Scarlatti:*** Keyboard Sonatas — C major, Kk159; G major, Kk337; E major, Kk380. ***J.S. Bach:*** Italian Concerto, BWV971. ***Balbastre:*** Pièces de clavecin I — La Suzanne. ***Daquin:*** Pièces de clavecin I — Le coucou. ***Duphly:*** Pièces de clavecin III — Le Forqueray. ***F. Couperin:*** Livre de clavecin II — Les baricades mistérieuses; Le dodo; Le tic-toc-choc. ***Handel:*** Keyboard Suites — No. 5 in E major, "Harmonious Blacksmith"; No. 7 in G minor — Passacaille. ***Mozart:*** Piano Sonata in A major, K331/300*i* — Rondo alla turca. ***Paradies:*** Toccata in A major. ***Rameau:*** Les cyclopes. ***W.F. Bach:*** Polonaise in E minor.

lh l4m DDD 5/9l

Virginia Black has assembled a delightful programme of music which should conquer all ears not yet won over by the sound of a harpsichord. She is a communicative player, spontaneous in transferring her thoughts to the keyboard and with a lively sense of poetry. These qualities and others too may be sensed in her interpretation of Bach's *Italian Concerto*. This is the most substantial piece in her recital and it comes over well with clearly articulated phrases, rhythmic elasticity and well-chosen tempos. There are occasions when Miss Black pushes the music along just a little harder than is good for it — listeners may sense that in the concluding Variations of Handel's famous so-called *Harmonious Blacksmith* theme — but her liveliness of temperament ensures her performances against any accusations of stuffy convention or dullness. Only the W.F. Bach Polonaise seems perhaps not to speak from the heart. A recital, in short, which deserves to win friends. Few are likely to be disappointed either by her choice of music or her colourfully imaginative treatment of it.

A EUROPEAN ORGAN TOUR. Priory PRCD903.
Reger: Symphonic Fantasia and Fugue, Op. 57, "Inferno" (Graham Barber/St Mary Magdalene, Bonn). ***Bowen:*** Fantasia, Op. 136 (Marc Rochester/St David's Hall, Cardiff). ***Dupré:*** Variations sur un Nöel, Op. 20 (Kimberly Marshall/St Sernin, Toulouse). ***Karg-Elert:*** Cathedral Windows (John Scott Whiteley/York Minster). ***Bach:*** Fantasia in C major, BWV573 (Scott Whiteley/St Bavo, Haarlem).

lh l0m DDD

From the comfort of your armchair, you can enjoy a real taste of Europe. Here on a single, generously-filled disc are the authentic voices of some of the finest organ builders (Muller, Cavaillé-Coll, Klais, Walker and Peter Collins) from Europe's leading organ building nations (Holland, France, Germany and Britain). There is also an interesting programme of music, with only one of the pieces available elsewhere. That is Dupré's Op. 20 Variations. He wrote it with a Cavaillé-Coll organ in mind, and the example in St Sernin, Toulouse is certainly one of the best-preserved. Not only that, in Kimberly Marshall this music finds a most sensitive and eloquent advocate. It is good to hear Bach played on an instrument built in his lifetime too. But this Fantasia in C is unusual: only the first page exists in Bach's manuscript and the version played here was completed this century by Wolfgang Stockmeier. John Scott Whiteley gives it a compelling performance as he does Karg-Elert's beautifully evocative and richly colourful suite. York Bowen's only published organ work is the Fantasia written for the Festival of Britain in 1951. That was a time of radical thinking and fundamental changes in British organ design and it is entirely appropriate that it should be played on the brand new Peter Collins instrument in Cardiff's magnificent concert hall.

NEW REVIEW

FRENCH ORGAN WORKS. Simon Lindley. Naxos 8 550581. Played on the organ of Leeds Parish Church, UK.

Guilmant: Grand Choeur in D major, "alla Handel". Cantilene pastorale, Op. 19. ***Vierne:*** 24 Pièces en stile libre, Op. 31 — Epitaphe; Berceuse. Stele pour un enfant défunte. ***M-A. Charpentier:*** Te Deum, H146 — Prelude. ***Langlais:*** Trois méditations (1962). ***Bonnet:*** Romance sans paroles. ***de Maleingreau:*** Suite mariale. ***Boëllmann:*** Suite gothique, Op. 25. ***Widor:*** Symphony No. 5 in F minor, Op. 42 No. 1 — Toccata.

lh 14m DDD 3/93 £

Two of the most popular organ showpieces are here — Widor's Toccata and the Toccata which comes as the last movement of Boëllmann's *Suite gothique*. In addition there is the majestic *Te Deum* Prelude by Charpentier (familiar to a wide audience as the Eurovision signature tune) and the gentle *Berceuse* which Vierne wrote for his baby daughter. Alongside these evergreens, mainstays of any organ-lover's CD collection, are some more unusual but no less enjoyable pieces: Guilmant's glorious *Grand Choeur "alla Handel"*, Bonnet's delightful *Romance sans paroles* and Paul de Maleingreau's *Suite mariale*. In short, a real feast of some of the best French organ music. Simon Lindley, organist at the musically-renowned Leeds Parish Church, gives fine, no-nonsense performances which should appeal especially to those exploring this music for the first time. The organ makes a super noise, and the Naxos recording is highly commendable. It may not be an instrument which the *cognoscenti* of French organ music would immediately approve of, but there is enough sensitivity and interpretative insight in Lindley's performances to make this a worthwhile buy for casual listener and specialist alike.

FROM STANLEY TO WESLEY, Volume 6. **Jennifer Bate** (org). Unicorn-Kanchana DKPCD9106. Played on the organs of Adlington Hall, Cheshire; The Dolmetsch Collection, Haslemere, Surrey; The Chapel of St Michael's Mount, Cornwall; The Iveagh Bequeast, Kenwood, London; Killerton House, Broadclyst, Exeter, Devon and The Chapel of Our Lady and St Everilda, Everingham, Yorkshire.
Boyce: Voluntary in D major. ***Handel:*** Fugue in G major. Voluntary in C major. ***Heron:*** Voluntary in G major. ***Hook:*** Voluntary in C minor. ***Russell:*** Voluntary in F major. ***Stanley:*** Voluntaries — A minor, Op. 6 No. 2; D minor, Op. 7 No. 4; G major, Op. 7 No. 9. ***Stubley:*** Voluntary in C major. ***S. Wesley:*** Voluntaries — E flat major, Op. 6 No. 7; B flat major.

lh 5m DDD 11/91

Whilst most people would regard Bach and his North German contemporaries as synonymous with all that is best in eighteenth-century organ music there was also a significant school of organist-composers thriving in England. Chief amongst these was John Stanley whose music was greatly admired at the time, in particular by a recent immigrant from Germany, one George Frederic Handel (two fine examples of his own organ music are to be found on this CD). But while the German composers were writing for their great, majestic organs, their English counterparts were faced with something far humbler in scope and more delicate and intimate in character. To hear this music played on such an instrument is to have its true beauty revealed: here it is played not just on one authentic contemporaneous instrument, but the Unicorn-Kanchana team have scoured the length and breadth of England, from Cornwall to Yorkshire, to unearth six classic, and virtually unaltered examples. Jennifer Bate's immense musical and technical powers and her innate, native sense of style, imbues this disc with compelling musical authority which, added to the captivating sound of these six delightful organs, makes it an intriguing historical document — real 'living history', if you like. This CD is the sixth in a series and while each is a valuable addition to the recorded legacy of English music, this one in particular gives the less specialist collector a representative and varied selection of this wonderful, yet woefully overlooked area of our musical heritage.

NEW REVIEW

PERCY GRAINGER RECITAL. Percy Grainger (pf). Biddulph mono LHW008.
Schumann: Piano Sonata No. 2 in G minor, Op. 22 (from American Columbia 67509/10D. Recorded in 1927). Etudes symphoniques, Op. 13 (67506/08D. 1928). ***Brahms:*** Piano Sonata

No. 3 in F minor, Op. 5 (Columbia L1954/7, 12/27). Also includes other works by ***Schumann*** and ***Brahms***, recorded between 1924 and 1928.

lh 15m ADD 4/93

Imagine a virtuoso pianist-composer spontaneously strolling over to the keyboard to entertain a few close friends with his personal visions of the classics, and you'll know roughly what to expect from Percy Grainger's records. Grainger gave recitals for most of his professional career and was hailed as among the most intuitive and perceptive of pianists. These recordings capture something of the sweep and lyricism that characterized his style: the Brahms F minor Sonata is all youthful ardour; a grand, energetic and warmly expressive performance, well recorded for the period, whereas Schumann's *Etudes symphoniques* and G minor Sonata are thought-provoking and rough-hewn, and boast a multitude of insights not normally encountered. Grainger was of course a hugely talented composer, and his considerable creative insights are apparent throughout this programme. Odd technical mishaps — a few of them crop up from time to time — hardly matter at all, and the benefit of hearing pianism that is musically sincere and oblivious to trivial surface perfection is substantial indeed. The smaller pieces (Brahms's A minor Waltz and Schumann's "Warum") are equally memorable, while Biddulph's transfers successfully report the relative clarity of Columbia's 78rpm originals.

NEW REVIEW

GREAT EUROPEAN ORGANS, Volume 26. **Keith John** (org). Priory PRCD370. Played on the organ of Gloucester Cathedral, UK.
Stanford: Fantasia and Toccata in D minor, Op. 57. ***Reger:*** Five Easy Preludes and Fugues, Op. 56 — No. 1 in E major. ***Shostakovich:*** Lady Macbeth of the Mtsensk district — Passacaglia. ***Schmidt:*** Chaconne in C sharp minor. ***Ravanello:*** Theme and Variations in B minor.

lh 13m DDD 11/92 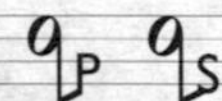

On the face of it this CD might look as if its appeal is purely for those with a specialist taste in large-scale post-romantic organ music. Certainly Schmidt's gargantuan *Chaconne* represents a daunting prospect both to player and listener, while Shostakovich's only organ solo begins with the kind of chilling dissonance which would certainly scare off those of a delicate disposition. Similarly neither Stanford nor Reger usually attract a crowd when their organ music played — and who has ever heard of Ravanello? But if ever a recording was made to shatter preconceptions, this is it. For a start the Gloucester organ makes a wondrous sound and Priory's recording is in a class of its own; in terms of sound alone this surely ranks as one of the best ever organ CDs. Then Keith John quite literally pulls out all the stops to produce an unparalleled display of virtuosity and musicianship. His technical prowess turns the Schmidt into a thrilling *tour de force* while few could question, after hearing his performances, that the Stanford is one of the best organ works ever written by a British composer or that Ravanello's music doesn't deserve the neglect it currently suffers. An essential disc in anyone's CD collection — what more is there to say?

GUITAR RECITAL. Eleftheria Kotzia (gt). Pearl SHECD9609.
Tippett: The blue guitar. ***Pujol:*** Tristango en vos. Preludio tristón. Candombe en mi. ***Villa-Lobos:*** Five Preludes. ***Delerue:*** Mosaïque. ***Giorginakis:*** Four Greek images. ***Fampas:*** Greek Dances Nos. 1 and 3.

lh 7m DAD 6/89

Many guitar recitals have a familiar appearance, but Ms Kotzia is not given to stale cloning in her choice of repertory. Here she assembles a nicely varied programme of music by six composers, none of whom is Spanish. The Five Preludes of Villa-Lobos, vignettes of Brazil and its life, have been recorded many times but this clear and firm account is, if not the best, good enough to live with. The most substantial is Tippett's only solo-guitar work, *The blue guitar*. Georges Delerue is briefer but no less purposeful in putting together his 'mosaic' of textures. The rest speak with distinctly regional accents: Pujol's Preludes celebrate Argentinian folk idioms in present-day popular terms, whilst Giorginakis's *Images* and Fampas's arrangements of traditional dances are as Greek as Ms Kotzia herself. Her freshness, spontaneity and positiveness are mirrored in this squeaky-clean and admirable recording. She clearly enjoys herself and transmits her pleasure to the listener.

NEW REVIEW

LA GUITARRA ROMANTICA. Julian Bream (gtr). RCA Victor Red Seal RD60429.
Tárrega: Mazurka in G major. Study in A major. Marietta. Capricho árabe. Prelude in A minor. Recuerdos de la Alhambra. ***Malats*** (arr. Tárrega): Serenata española. ***Pujol:*** Tango espagnol. Guajira. ***Llobet:*** Popular Catalan folk-songs.

48m DDD 7/92

It was in Spain that the guitar's revival began after the instrument's mid-nineteenth century eclipse. The prime mover was Francisco Tárrega, a concert virtuoso, teacher and composer, who also laid the foundations on which modern playing technique has been built. Tárrega's compositions were for the most part charming miniatures, some of which paid tribute to Spain's Moorish past; the *Capricho árabe* and *Recuerdos de la Alhambra* (his most famous and evocative piece) are two of these. It was also Tárrega who developed the art of arranging 'other' music for the guitar, a means by which its repertory has been greatly enlarged since then; it is principally through his arrangements that Malats's *Serenata* and Alard's Study in A major are now remembered. His Catalonian pupils, Miguel Llobet and Emilio Pujol were concert performers and also attractive composers in a similar romantic vein; Llobet died at the age of 50, whilst Pujol eventually found his true calling to be that of a teacher and musicologist. Llobet is represented by his delightful settings of folk-songs from his native land, Pujol by two transatlantic glances (to Argentina and Cuba). This music could not have a more eloquent advocate than Julian Bream in a very vivid recording.

HARP RECITAL. Maria Graf. Philips 432 103-2PH.
Caplet: Divertissements. ***Debussy:*** Deux arabesques. ***Fauré:*** Une châtelaine en sa tour, Op. 110. Impromptu, Op. 86. ***Ravel:*** Pavane pour une infante défunte. ***Roussel:*** Impromptu, Op. 21. ***Tailleferre:*** Harp Sonata. ***Tournier:*** Au matin.

54m DDD 11/91

The harp is a very idiosyncratic instrument and the composers who have made the most skilful use of its resources have been those who, like Tournier, played it. Prominent amongst those who were/are not harpists have been those of French birth, as were all the others represented in Maria Graf's recording — and as the modern harp itself was. The works by Caplet, Fauré, Roussel and Tailleferre were written specifically for the harp; those of Debussy and Ravel were originally for the piano, though both used the harp in their chamber music. However, all five composers has as instinctive an understanding of the harp's essence as Spanish composers have had of that of the guitar; even the items by Debussy and Ravel sound like original harp music. Performer/composers have often relied overly on the seductive effects the harp can produce, and much harp music by others is little more than pleasantly soporific; the music in this recording is neither 'tricksy', trivial nor anodyne. Maria Graf, one of the very best harpists to have emerged during the last few years, is a fine player, with a touch that is responsive to every nuance and, irrespective of instrument, a first-class musician. The recording is vivid enough to have picked up any extraneous mechanical noise such as harpists are wont to produce, but there is none.

NEW REVIEW

THE HARPSICHORD, 1689-1789. John Henry (hpd). Victoria VCD19013.
Handel: Keyboard Suites, Set 2 — No. 1 in B flat major; HWV434. ***Purcell:*** Suite No. 5 in C major, Z666. ***Bach:*** English Suite No. 3 in G minor, BWV808. ***F. Couperin:*** Livres de
 clavecin — Book 2: La Visionnaire; Book 4: Les Baricades Mistérieuses. ***D. Scarlatti:*** Sonata

in A minor, Kk175. ***D'Anglebert:*** Suite No. 2 in G minor. ***Duphly:*** Pièces de clavecin, Book 1 — Chaconne; Les Grâces. ***Balbastre:*** Air gay.

lh 10m DDD 10/92

In this programme we are taken on a veritable musical grand tour with suites by Purcell and Handel, Bach's *English Suite* in G minor (BWV808), a sonata by Domenico Scarlatti and pieces by D'Anglebert, Couperin, Duphly and Balbastre. The absence of Rameau in this context is conspicuous and regrettable but, having said that, there is little else in John Henry's recital that is other than stimulating and immensely enjoyable. Perhaps the D'Anglebert suite is driven too hard and lacking in "gentillesse" but much else here is first-rate. Henry launches into the Handel B flat Suite with infectious energy, giving a virtuoso account of the concluding Aria with variations. The Purcell Suite is full of vitality, too, but occasionally in the Bach *English Suite* there is a feeling that Henry's warm rapport with the music and his imaginative treatment of it are running ahead of detail. The Couperin and Scarlatti pieces came over convincingly with bold dashes of colour which show off the fine-sounding instrument effectively. The Duphly pieces are executed with that sensibility which seemed lacking in the D'Anglebert and the Balbastre provides a dazzling conclusion to Henry's entertaining recital. Recorded sound is excellent and the accompanying notes informative.

VLADIMIR HOROWITZ. PIANO WORKS. RCA Gold Seal mono/[a]stereo GD60377.
Prokofiev: Piano Sonata No. 7 in B flat major, Op. 83 (from RB6555, 12/63. Recorded 1945). Toccata, Op. 11. ***Poulenc:*** Presto in B flat major (both from HMV DB6971, 1947). ***Barber:*** Piano Sonata, Op. 26 (RB6555. 1950). ***Kabalevsky:*** Piano Sonata No. 3, Op. 46 (new to UK. 1947). ***Fauré:*** Nocturne No. 13 in B minor, Op. 119[a] (RL12548, 2/78. Recorded at a performance in May 1977).

lh 5m ADD 6/92 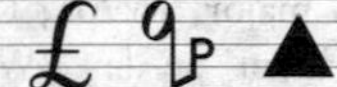

Even today, when there is a six-deep queue of virtuosos that, laid end to end, would stretch halfway round the world, Vladimir Horowitz's playing is something to make the listener gasp and sit up. He has been called, with justification, "the greatest pianist alive or dead". Horowitz was associated with all three of these sonatas from their very beginnings. Prokofiev wrote his Seventh Sonata in 1942, and Horowitz gave the first American performance less than two years later. He sent a copy of this 1945 recording to the composer, and Prokofiev sent him an autographed copy of the score in return, inscribed "to the miraculous pianist from the composer". The performance is indeed superlative, with playing of extraordinary virtuosity, and Horowitz responds with equal flair to the sonata's 'barbaric' and lyrical elements. Kabalevsky's Third Sonata dates from 1946, and Horowitz gave the American première in February 1948, two months after he made this recording. The work is of lesser stature than the Prokofiev, but its three well-contrasted movements make up an effective enough sonata. Again, Horowitz plays brilliantly and very sympathetically throughout the work. The world première of Barber's Piano Sonata was given by Horowitz in 1949. This piece is brilliantly written and technically very difficult to play — a perfect vehicle, in fact, for Horowitz the virtuoso. The great pianist brings great flair to the shorter Poulenc and Prokofiev items: the Fauré was recorded at a later stage of his career, and is played in a more deliberate, though perfectly idiomatic fashion. Four of the items have been transferred from 78s in good sound. The Barber and Fauré come from tape sources and sound well — the latter is even in stereo. This is a disc all pianists and piano enthusiasts should have — and it's mid-price too!

VLADIMIR HOROWITZ. THE LAST RECORDING. **Vladimir Horowitz** (pf). Sony Classical SK45818.
Haydn: Keyboard Sonata in E flat major, HobXVI/49. ***Chopin:*** Mazurka in C minor, Op. 56 No. 3. Nocturnes — E flat, Op. 55 No. 2; B major, Op. 62 No. 1. Fantaisie-impromptu in C sharp minor, Op. 66. Etudes — A flat major, Op. 25 No. 1; E minor, Op. 25 No. 5.

Liszt: "Weinen, Klagen, Sorgen, Zagen", Präludium, S179. ***Wagner/Liszt:*** Paraphrase on Isolden's Liebestod from "Tristan und Isolde", S447.

58m DDD 8/90

More than any other pianist of his generation, Vladimir Horowitz was a legend in his lifetime, not only for his staggering technique but also for the personality and authority of his playing. Other pianists such as Rubinstein and Arrau may have been finer all-rounders (there were gaps in his repertory even in the classical and romantic field), but none has left so many performances distinguished by a special individuality that is covered, though hardly explained, by the word magic. As Murray Perahia has written, from the point of view of a pianist over 40 years his junior, "he was a man who gave himself completely through his music and who confided his deepest emotions through his playing". The performances in this last of his recordings, made in New York in 1989 and with superlative piano sound, are wonderfully crystalline and beautifully articulated, yet there is warmth too in the Haydn sonata that begins his programme and nothing whatever to suggest that octogenarian fingers were feeling their age or that his fine ear had lost its judgement. The rest of the disc is devoted to Chopin and Liszt, two great romantic composers with whom he was always associated, the last piece being Liszt's mighty transcription of Wagner's *Liebestod*, in which the piano becomes a whole operatic orchestra topped by a soprano voice singing out her love for the last time. Apparently this was the last music Horowitz ever played, and no more suitable ending can be imagined for a great pianistic career informed by a consuming love of music that was expressed in playing of genius. A uniquely valuable record.

NEW REVIEW

VLADIMIR HOROWITZ. THE LOST RECORDINGS. **Vladimir Horowitz** (pf). Sony Classical SK48093. All items new to UK and recorded between 1962 and 1972.
D. Scarlatti: Keyboard Sonatas — F sharp minor, Kk25; D minor, Kk52; B minor, Kk197; G major, Kk201; C minor, Kk303; G major, Kk547. ***Bach*** (arr. Busoni): Chorale Prelude — Ich ruf' zu dir, BWV639. ***Clementi:*** Keyboard Sonatas — E flat major, Op. 12 No. 2 — Rondo; B flat major, Op. 25 No. 3 — Rondo; A minor, Op. 50 No. 1 — Adagio. Gradus ad Parnassum, Op. 44 — Book 1: No. 14 — Adagio sostenuto in F major. ***Chopin:*** Etudes — A flat major, Op. posth; E flat minor, Op. 10 No. 6. Prelude in D flat major, Op. 28 No. 15, "Raindrop". ***Medtner:*** Fairy Tales, Op. 51 — No. 3 in A major. ***Scriabin:*** Feuillet d'album, Op. 58. Three Etudes, Op. 65. ***Liszt:*** Consolation in E major, S172 No. 2.

1h 7m ADD 11/92 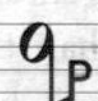

Every record by the late Vladimir Horowitz is beyond price, particularly in those areas of the repertoire closest to his heart. Scarlatti, Clementi, Chopin, Scriabin and Liszt were always among his favourites while Bach-Busoni (a romantic hyphenation he characteristically preferred to Bach pure and simple) figured in many of his recitals. Medtner, now enjoying a timely renaissance, appeared less frequently, but his ultra-Russian sensibility greatly appealed to Horowitz who played much of his music privately. Recorded between 1962 and 1972 all these performances were spin-offs from recording sessions, put aside for further consideration and possible future release, yet almost without exception they are vintage Horowitz. What pin-point diamond brilliance he brings to his Scarlatti, and how he revels in the fearless drama and dissonance of Clementi's remarkable A minor *Adagio*! The Medtner, too, makes one long to hear him in more extended examples of that composer's genius; in the Sonatas, *Dithyramb*, etc., while at the same time leaving one intensely grateful for this single and magical offering. Satanic, later Scriabin, with its obsessive whirling round minute cell-like motifs, was always to Horowitz's taste, and the Chopin items, like everything else on this invaluable disc, display to perfection Horowitz's unique sonority, his colour and fire. Lovers of pianistic sorcery need look no further.

EVGENI KISSIN CARNEGIE HALL DEBUT CONCERT. Evgeni Kissin (pf). RCA Victor Red Seal RD60443. Recorded at a performance in Carnegie Hall on September 30th, 1990.
Chopin: Waltz in C sharp minor, Op. 64 No. 2. ***Liszt:*** Etude d'exécution transcendante in F minor, S139 No. 10, "Appassionata". Liebestraum No. 3, S541. Rhapsodie espagnole, S254. ***Prokofiev:*** Etude in C minor, Op. 2 No. 3. Piano Sonata No. 6 in A major, Op. 82.

Schumann: Etudes symphoniques, Op. 13. Theme and Variations on the name "Abegg", Op. 1. ***Schumann/Liszt:*** Widmung, S566.

② lh 43m DDD 3/91

A Carnegie Hall début is a rite of passage for any pianist on the way to international stardom. To make that début ten days before your nineteenth birthday and with top recording engineers present is really something. Evgeni Kissin's reputation preceded him, as anyone will realize who has heard his phenomenal Tokyo recital (reviewed below) and recorded three years earlier; he did not disappoint. Starting with a beguiling account of Schumann's Op. 13 and finishing with a mind-boggling display of dexterity in Prokofiev's Etude, this is one recital which lived up to all its hype. In between, Kissin occasionally seems determined to prove his worth rather than just revelling in the music — the Prokofiev Sonata, for example, is more finished, but less electrifying than in Tokyo. But as a rule his youthful virtuosity and almost preternatural maturity of temperament have you on the edge of your seat. The recording is bright and close, with some loss of atmosphere but with the bonus of minimal audience noise; and playing like this sounds marvellous in close up.

EVGENI KISSIN IN TOKYO. Evgeni Kissin (pf). Sony Classical SK45931. Recorded at a performance in Suntory Hall, Tokyo on May 12th, 1987.
Rachmaninov: Lilacs, Op. 21 No. 5. Etudes tableaux, Op. 39 — No. 1 in C minor; No. 5 in E flat minor. ***Prokofiev:*** Piano Sonata No. 6 in A major, Op. 82. ***Liszt:*** Concert Studies, S144 — La leggierezza; Waldestauschen. ***Chopin:*** Nocturne in A flat major, Op. 32 No. 2. Polonaise in F sharp minor, Op. 44. ***Scriabin:*** Mazurka in E minor, Op. 25 No. 3. Etude in C sharp minor, Op. 42 No. 5. ***Anonymous*** (arr. Saegusa): Natu — Wa Kinu. Todai — Mori. Usagi.

lh 13m DDD 11/90 

One reason for buying this CD is that it contains dazzling piano playing by a 15-year-old Russian set fair for a career of the highest distinction. A better reason is that the recital contains as full a revelation of the genius of Prokofiev as any recording ever made in any medium. The Sixth Sonata is the first of a trilogy which sums up the appalling sufferings of Russia under Stalin in a way only otherwise found in Shostakovich's 'middle' symphonies. Kissin plays it with all the colour and force of a full orchestra and all the drama and structural integrity of a symphony, plus a kind of daredevilry that even he may find difficult to recapture. As for the rest of the recital only the Rachmaninov pieces are as memorable as the Prokofiev, though everything else is immensely impressive (the Japanese encore-pieces are trivial in the extreme, however). Microphone placing is very close, presumably in order to minimize audience noise; but the playing can take it, indeed it may even be said to benefit from it.

LATE ROMANTIC MASTERWORKS. Andrew Fletcher (org). Mirabilis MRCD903. Played on the organ of St Mary's Collegiate Church, Warwick.
Andriessen: Thema met variaties. ***Bridge:*** Three Organ Pieces, H63 — Adagio in E major. ***Dupré:*** Cortège et litanie, Op. 19 No. 2. ***Howells:*** Siciliano for a High Ceremony. ***Pach:*** Introduction and Fugue. ***Peeters:*** Aria, Op. 51. Variations on an Original Theme, Op. 58. ***Reger:*** Benedictus, Op. 59 No. 9. ***Schmidt:*** Prelude and Fugue in D major, "Hallelujah". ***Willan:*** Introduction, Passacaglia and Fugue.

lh 21m DDD 11/91 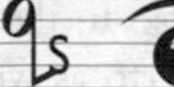

St Mary's Church, Warwick, boasts an extraordinary organ. In fact it is two quite separate organs housed at opposite ends of the church but playable from just one console. Listening to this disc using an UHJ Ambisonic decoder the spatial effect is most vividly recreated: Mirabilis's 'surround-sound' recording places the West End organ through the front pair of speakers while the Transept organ speaks from the rear speakers. The effect is aurally astonishing, but it could be a recipe for musical disaster. As it is, Andrew Fletcher knows better than almost anyone what its strengths and weaknesses are — what works and what doesn't; he was responsible for its present design and in this thoroughly enjoyable recital guides us expertly through its manifest glories. Fletcher not only shows the organ off to best effect, he also plays this entire programme with impressive fluency. Most of these pieces are old favourites to church organists but neither the music nor, in many cases, the names of the composers will be familiar to those outside the intimate world of organ aficionados. But don't be put off, everything here from Flor Peeter's appealing *Aria* to Healey Willan's dramatic *Introduction, Passacaglia and Fugue* is well worth exploring, and you can rest assured that Fletcher's stirring playing, the organ's wonderful wealth of sounds and Mirabilis's top-notch recording provides an exceptionally generous programme of real delights.

NEW REVIEW

THE LAST RECITAL FOR ISRAEL. Artur Rubinstein (pf). RCA Victor Red Seal 09026 61160-2. Recorded in 1975.
Beethoven: Piano Sonata No. 23 in F minor, Op. 57, "Appassionata".
Schumann: Fantasiestücke, Op. 12. ***Debussy:*** La plus que lente. Pour le piano — Prélude.
Chopin: Etudes — C sharp minor, Op. 10 No. 4; E minor, Op. 25 No. 5. Nocturne in F sharp major, Op. 15 No. 2. Polonaise in A flat major, Op. 53.

lh 15m ADD 3/93 

Ever a supporter of youth in music, Artur Rubinstein gave a special concert in January 1975 at Ambassador College (California) for the benefit of the International Cultural Centre for Youth in Jerusalem; it was merely days before his eighty-eighth birthday. The event was sponsored entirely by contributions, and Rubinstein played to a packed house, which of course was no great surprise. However, what does truly amaze is the vitality and concentration of the performances. It might seem something of a cliché to say that Rubinstein plays the *Appassionata* like a man half his age, but it also happens to be the truth: the sheer energy and panache of the first movement so far exceeds expectations that one finds oneself checking the recording date to make sure that this isn't a reissue of an earlier Rubinstein recording. And in truth, the recording — taken from a video sound-track — tends, unlike the playing, to sound older than it is. In addition to barnstorming Beethoven and endearingly warm-hearted Schumann, Rubinstein plays two Chopin *Etudes* that, believe it or not, he never recorded commercially: Op. 25 No. 5 and Op. 10 No. 4. Both are remarkable, as is a battle-scarred but riveting A Flat Polonaise (a Rubinstein speciality). But best of all is the famous E flat Nocturne, Op. 15 No. 2 — an intimate, beautifully phrased performance, so typical of the man and the best possible way to remember him. A simultaneously-released RCA video contains the entire programme, but the best items are on this CD. A life-affirming experience.

LIGHT IN DARKNESS. PERCUSSION WORKS. **Evelyn Glennie.** RCA Victor Red Seal RD60557.
Rosauro: Eldorado. ***Abe:*** Dream of the cherry blossoms. ***McLeod:*** The Song of Dionysius (with Philip Smith, pf). ***Edwards:*** Marimba Dances. ***Miki:*** Marimba Spiritual (with Steve Henderson, Gregory Knowles, Gary Kettel, perc). ***Glennie:*** Light in darkness. ***Tanaka:*** Two Movements for Marimba.

59m DDD 1/92 

Evelyn Glennie has transformed her chosen instrument (in this case a whole kitchen cabinet of percussion) into a real solo one and has opened up fresh vistas not only to the musical public but also to the composers who have written for her. One is John McLeod, with his Percussion Concerto as well as the longish piece played here, *The Song of Dionysius*. This was inspired by the ancient world, for Dionysius I was a ruler of Syracuse (*c*.430-367 BC) who, suspicious of all around him, devised a listening chamber so as to hear every whisper in his palace. Hence the mysterious, hollowly echoing murmurs and tappings on which the piece is based. It uses a wide variety of instruments, including the marimba which has tuned wooden bars and produces notes of definite pitch, and there's also a piano part played by Philip Smith which seems rather a modern intruder. Glennie also plays the marimba with three percussionist colleagues in Miki's vivid *Marimba Spiritual* (which has shouting as well!), and then solo in her teacher Keiko Abe's gentler but no less oriental-sounding *Dream of the cherry blossoms* and other pieces including her own *Light in darkness*, which she says expresses religious feeling and relaxation. Relaxation is the keynote of much of this music, which is inspired by Brazilian, Australian and Japanese styles among others and is atmospheric though not always substantial. The sound is immediate and spacious, with a large dynamic range, but one would have welcomed pictures and perhaps descriptions of the instruments used, which include "stones" and "small bits".

NEW REVIEW

LUTE WORKS. Nigel North. Linn Records CKD006.
Weiss: Sonata in A minor, "L'infidèle". Prelude, Fantasia and Fugue in C major. Tombeau sur la mort de M. Comte de Logy. ***Vivaldi*** (trans. North, after Bach): Concerto in D major, RV230. ***Bach*** (trans. North): Partita in D minor, BWV1004 — Chaconne.

lh lm DDD 12/92

Bach was a friend, admirer and almost exact contemporary of Sylvius Leopold Weiss, the greatest lutenist of his time and famed for his skill as an improviser. The tale of the unsuccessful attempt by a jealous violinist to bite off Weiss's thumb has often been told. Most of his 600-plus works for the baroque lute are preserved in manuscripts held in London and Dresden, the rest are spread around various (often surprising) places. The title of the Sonata *L'infidèle* reflects the current interest in Turkish music as fashionable exotica, the *Tombeau sur la mort de M. Comte de Logy*, marking the death of another famous lutenist, is a poignant elegy that can hold its own in any company; the other three pieces fit well together, though not so coupled by Weiss. In adapting the famous *Chaconne* of Bach to a plucked-string instrument, North is not the first in the field, but he is among the most successful. Vivaldi's RV230, a violin concerto, was arranged for solo harpsichord by Bach. North has rearranged Bach's version for the lute — and why not, when it is so well done ? North, one of today's best lutenists, adds comely embellishments where fitting, preserving some of Weiss's improvisatory spirit, in one of the finest and best-recorded discs of lute music on the market.

ORGAN FIREWORKS, Volume 3. **Christopher Herrick.** Hyperion CDA66457. Played on the organ of St Eustache, Paris.
Batiste: Offertoire in D minor. ***Bossi:*** Pièce héroïque in D minor, Op. 128. Scherzo in D minor, Op. 49 No. 2. ***Dubois:*** Grand choeur in B flat major. ***Dupré:*** Cortège et Litanie, Op. 19 No. 2. ***Jolivet:*** Hymne à l'Univers. ***Lefébure-Wély:*** Marche in F major, Op. 122 No. 4. ***Lemare:*** Concert fantasy on "Hanover", Op. 4. Marche héroïque in D major, Op. 74. ***Saint-Saëns:*** Allegro giocoso in A minor, Op. 150 No. 7.

lh llm DDD 9/91 9p 9s

Here is something truly spectacular. The brand new organ in St Eustache's Church, Paris was designed by the organist Jean Guillou who made sure it was an instrument fit for the finest of players and the greatest of music. In addition to a large array of stops, manuals and pipes it also boasts such extravagances as two consoles and a playback facility which enables the organ to play unattended. For this disc Christopher Herrick took advantage of this latter facility so that performances made during the day could be recorded in the small hours when extraneous noise was at a minimum. But the organ itself makes such a tremendously powerful, not to say, awesome noise, that one would have thought such a precaution unnecessary. Hyperion's vivid recording of this magnificent instrument stands out as one of the best recordings of an organ currently available on CD. Herrick's programme shows both the instrument and his own amazing virtuosity off to brilliant effect. There is great fun to be had from these pieces, none of which can really be said to be well-known. This is a disc of pure, unadulterated pleasure.

NEW REVIEW

ORGAN FIREWORKS, Volume 4. **Christopher Herrick.** Hyperion CDA66605. Played on the Aeolian-Skinner organ of St Bartholemew's Church, New York City.
D. Johnson: Trumpet Tune in A major. ***Lemare:*** Toccata di Concerto, Op. 59.
Buck: Variations on "The Star-Spangled Banner", Op. 23. ***Guilmant:*** Paraphrase on a chorus

from Handel's "Judas Maccabaeus", Op. 90 No. 16. ***Whitlock:*** Pieces for organ — Paean. ***Bourgeois:*** Variations on a Theme of Herbert Howells, Op. 87. ***Vierne:*** 24 Pièces en style libre, Op. 31 — Divertissement. ***Batiste:*** Grand Offertoire in D major. ***Shostakovich:*** Lady Macbeth of the Mtsensk district — Passacaglia. ***Bonnet:*** Pièces nouvelles, Op. 7 — Etude de Concert. ***Widor:*** Symphony No. 6 in C minor, Op. 42 No. 2 — Allegro. ***Lefébure-Wély:*** Sortie in E flat major.

1h 15m DDD 10/92 — 9P 9S

For the fourth of his spectacular "Organ Fireworks" CDs Christopher Herrick has crossed the Atlantic to a New York monster organ. It's a typically no-expense-spared American beast — huge, extravagant and able to produce a range of sounds beyond any organist's wildest dreams. The only drawback is, as with so many other large American organs, the acoustics of the building in which it is housed are not quite spacious enough to comfortably accommodate its vastness. Nevertheless the Hyperion engineers have done their customary magnificent job and few lovers of organ sound will be disappointed with the result. Of course Herrick's performances need no recommendation to those already acquainted with his dazzling skills. He plays with extrovert enthusiasm — the virtuoso showpieces of Widor, Bonnet and Lemare leave us breathless in admiration — while his mischievous sense of humour is given full rein in Buck's tongue-in-cheek variations on America's national anthem and Derek Bourgeois's unashamedly English piece combining a genteel melody by Herbert Howells with the famous refrain "For he's a jolly good fellow". Bourgeois intended this as a musical vote of thanks to Howells; we could justifiably alter these words to "for it's a jolly good disc!".

PIANO RECITAL. Sviatoslav Richter. DG Dokumente 423 573-2GDO.
Scriabin: Piano Sonata No. 5 in F sharp major, Op. 53. ***Debussy:*** Estampes (both from SLPM138849, 4/63. Recorded at performances in Italy during November 1963). Préludes, Book 1 — Voiles; Le vent dans la plaine; Les collines d'Anacapri. ***Prokofiev:*** Piano Sonata No. 7 in B flat major, Op. 84. Visions fugitives, Op. 22 — Nos. 3, 6 and 9 (all from SLPM138950, 8/65).

1h 7m ADD 9/88 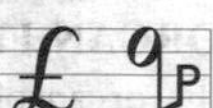

Richter has long been acclaimed as one of the most dedicated champions of Prokofiev's keyboard music, with the Eighth Sonata always particularly close to his heart. It would certainly be hard to imagine a more profoundly and intensely experienced performance than the one we get here, or one of greater keyboard mastery. After the yearning introspection of the temperamental opening movement and the *Andante*'s evocation of a more gracious past, the rhythmic tension and sheer might of sonority he conjures in the finale make it easy to understand why the composer's biographer, I.V. Nestyev, suspected some underlying programme culminating in "heroic troops resolutely marching ahead, ready to crush anything in their path". In the uniquely Prokofievian fantasy of the three brief *Visions fugitives* he is wholly bewitching. As for the Fifth Sonata of Scriabin, his impetuous start at once reveals his understanding of its manic extremities of mood. For just these Russian performances alone, this excellently refurbished disc can be hailed as a collector's piece. And as a bonus there is Debussy too, with infinite subtleties of tonal shading to heighten atmospheric evocation.

PIANO TRANSCRIPTIONS. Louis Lortie. Chandos CHAN8733. Items marked [a] from CHAN8620 (5/89), remainder new to UK.
Stravinsky: Three movements from "Petrushka"[a]. ***Prokofiev:*** Ten pieces from "Romeo and Juliet", Op. 75 — Juliet as a young girl; Montagues and Capulets; Romeo and Juliet before parting. ***Ravel:*** La valse[a]. ***Gershwin:*** Rhapsody in Blue.

57m DDD 9/89 — 9P 9S

In Liszt's day the piano transcription could be a valuable means for the wider dissemination of orchestral music, as well as a vehicle for dazzling individual virtuosity. Since the advent of the recording the educational function has ceased to apply, but the potential for audience-dazzlement remains. With all four composers in Louis Lortie's recital it is also true to say that orchestral inventiveness draws an important part of its inspiration from pianistic idioms and *vice versa*. The three *Petrushka* movements are notorious for their pyrotechnic demands — none of which floor Lortie, whose playing is quite breathtaking in its finesse. His Prokofiev and Ravel are no less outstanding, with an almost uncanny ear for atmospheric texture (beautifully captured by Chandos in as fine a piano recording as you are likely to hear). The Gershwin *Rhapsody* is less happy — its individual touches seem more forced than idiomatic. But that's a minor blemish on an otherwise magnificent recital.

PIANO WORKS. Maurizio Pollini. DG 419 202-2GH. Items marked [a] from 2530 225 (6/72), [b] 2530 893 (7/78).
Stravinsky: Three movements from "Petrushka"[a]. ***Prokofiev:*** Piano Sonata No. 7 in B flat major[a]. ***Webern:*** Variations for piano, Op. 27[b]. ***Boulez:*** Piano Sonata No. 2 (1948)[b].

lh 9m ADD 11/86

The capacity to stupefy is not the only measure of greatness in a performer; but it is an important factor, and in very few piano recordings is it embodied to the extent of this one. It is there from the very first bar of the first *Petrushka* movement — few pianists have ever attempted the tempo Pollini takes. Similarly, the Boulez Second Sonata has never been recorded with anything approaching this accuracy, glinting articulation and incandescent vigour. The bitterness at the heart of Prokofiev's slow movement with its remorseless tolling of bells is starkly revealed, and Pollini responds no less acutely to the distilled poetry behind the apparently arid surface of Webern's *Variations.* Clearly the Russian works are the more likely to grab the first-time listener; the Webern and Boulez may leave you utterly cold, or else touch regions of your psyche you did not know you had. With Pollini as exponent and with exemplary DG recording, the second possibility should not be ruled out. Intellectually, dramatically, lyrically, virtuosically, whichever way you look at it, this is a superlative disc.

RAGS AND TANGOS. Joshua Rifkin (pf). Decca 425 225-2DH.
Nazareth: Apanhei-tecavaquinho. Cavaquinho. Vitorioso. Odeon. Nove de Julho. Labirinto. Guerreiro. Plangente. Cubanos. Fon-Fon! ***Scott:*** Evergreen Rag. Modesty Rag. Peace and Plenty Rag. Troubadour Rag. ***Lamb:*** Ragtime Nightingale. American Beauty Rag. Bohemia Rag. Topliner Rag.

lh 4m DDD 4/92

Though he made his name as a scholar of renaissance and baroque music, Joshua Rifkin is also a pianist who has popularized the piano rags of Scott Joplin. Here, however, he turns his attention to three other composers from the same continent and period. Of these, James Scott from Missouri seems the nearest to Joplin and his *Evergreen Rag* only differs from him in having less memorable tunes than Joplin at his best. Still, he is well worth hearing, and Joseph F. Lamb even more so because his music has a different feel to it, more introspective as if a pianist is playing not to entertain but just for himself. Lamb spent nearly all his life in New York, but there's nothing urban about his style unless its intimacy suggests the loneliness that can affect those who live in a huge city. Ernesto Nazareth was also a lifelong city-dweller, but in Rio de Janeiro, where he became the 'demo pianist' of a music publisher; later he became insane and escaped from an asylum into a forest where he was found dead "with his arms outstretched, as if he was playing an invisible piano". His music, too, has an inward-looking quality and also a dreamy delicacy that shows his love of Chopin: try *Nove de Julho* or *Plangente* to hear this. But there is also a Latin quality here and most of the nine pieces by him which Rifkin plays are tangos (sometimes labelled as Argentine or Brazilian) rather than rags, although the one called *Apanhei-tecavaquinho*, is neither and makes unusual play with the top register of the keyboard. Villa-Lobos and Milhaud admired Nazareth and the latter said that hearing him play the piano gave him a "deeper insight into the Brazilian soul". Improbably, this sensitively and affectionately played recital was recorded in the UK in a Bristol church (St George's, Brandon Hill) that is regularly used for BBC concerts; but the piano sounds very natural and is rightly placed at a correct distance.

SPIRIT OF THE GUITAR. MUSIC OF THE AMERICAS. **John Williams** (gtr). CBS Masterworks CD44898.

York: Sunburst. Lullaby. ***Mangoré:*** Aconquija. La ultima canción. ***Piazzolla:*** Verano porteño. Cueca. ***Ponce:*** Scherzino mexicano. ***Lauro:*** Natalia. El niño. Maria Luisa. ***Brouwer:*** Berceuse. Danza carateristica. ***C. Byrd:*** Three blues (for classic guitar). ***Villa-Lobos:*** Chôros No. 1. ***Sagreras:*** El colibri. ***Crespo:*** Norteña.

54m ADD 8/89

Early forms of the classic guitar were among the instruments introduced into South America by the Spanish *conquistadores* in the sixteenth century; there they survived and prospered. Together with various other related plucked-string instruments, the present-day 'classic' guitar now flourishes in the multi-racial climate of that continent and its music has acquired a concomitant diversity of styles, characterized by tunefulness and rhythmic vitality. John Williams has assembled an immediately attractive programme of pieces by composers (some of whom play or played the guitar) from Paraguay, Argentina, Mexico, Venezuela, Brazil and Cuba. In time, the guitar spread through North America and, in this century, learned to speak jazz; items in Williams's programme by two guitarist-composers from the USA mark this further spread, those by Charlie Byrd are benignly jazz-based. The disc as a whole, played with Williams's precision-engineered perfection and finely recorded, celebrates the guitar's transatlantic transposition of a wholly light-musical level.

TWENTIETH CENTURY PIANO WORKS. Rolf Hind. Factory Classical FACD256.

Ligeti: Six Etudes, Book 1. ***Martland:*** Kgakala. ***Messiaen:*** Catalogue d'oiseaux — Le courlis cendré. ***Carter:*** Piano Sonata.

Ih 6m DDD I/90

Even if you would need a lot of persuading to attend an all-twentieth century piano recital in the concert hall, you might well find Rolf Hind's programme well-chosen and well-balanced enough to listen to as if it were a short, continuous concert. Hind is a powerful player who needs good reason (that is, unambiguous instructions in the score) before he takes refuge in restraint. This means that his reading of Ligeti's second study is less gentle that it might be, but this is a rare miscalculation, and he crowns the set with an overwhelming realization of the complex textures of the sixth study, which seems to express a very direct and intense anguish. Martland's *Kgakala* — an African word meaning 'distance' — is the shortest item, but earns its place alongside Carter and Messiaen at their grandest. Carter's Sonata, from the days before he set tonality aside, and Messiaen's hypnotic evocation of the curlew's piercing melancholy are both, in their utterly different ways, major works, as well as intensely personal statements. Rolf Hind penetrates to the personalities behind the structures, and a close but undistorted recording helps to make sure that the listener is involved from first note to last.

NEW REVIEW

THE VIRTUOSO PIANO. Earl Wild. Vanguard Classics 08.4033.71. From VSL11038 (11/68).

Herz: Variations on "Non più mesta" from Rossini's "La Cenerentola". ***Godowsky:*** Symphonic Metamorphosis on themes from Johann Strauss II's "Kunstlerleben". ***A. Rubinstein:*** Etude, Op. 23 No. 2, "Staccato". ***Thalberg:*** Don Pasquale Fantasy, Op. 67. ***Hummel:*** Rondo in E flat major, Op. 11. ***Paderewski:*** Theme and Variations, Op. 16 No. 3.

55m ADD 8/92 P

During the 1960s Earl Wild recorded three recitals, one for RCA (Scharwenka, Balakirev, Medtner and d'Albert) and the other two for Vanguard (Liszt — 08.4035.71, 2/92) and the above. There were, of course, many others, but these three discs — the first shamefully still not on CD — quickly became collectors' items, leaving one in no doubt of Wild's place among the super-virtuosos. Here, the most formidable acrobatics (cascades of repeated notes, *glissandos* in thirds and so on) are tossed aside not only with fearless abandon, without even a hint of studio caution or a safety net, but with a coruscating wit and stylistic aplomb. And whether in

Godowsky's surreal polyphony or Thalberg's three-handed effects you will hear a technique of an evenness and glitter that even the most legendary pianists might envy (Horowitz was always among Wild's greatest admirers). Such heart-stopping virtuosity, nonchalantly deployed, lies at the very core of such repertoire. And although the sound, with its curious acoustical bloom or haze around each note, is hardly the most natural, the actual playing always ensures that a golden rather than tinsel age of the keyboard is evoked.

Early Music

Medieval – Early Renaissance 12th–15th centuries

NEW REVIEW

PROENSA. SONGS OF THE TROUBADOURS. **Paul Hillier** (bass); **Stephen Stubbs** (lte, psaltery); **Andrew Lawrence-King** (medieval hp, psaltery); **Erin Headley** (vielle). ECM New Series 837 360-2. Texts and translations included.
Guillaume IX: Farai un vers de dreit nien. ***Giraut de Bornelh:*** Reis glorios. ***Raimon de Miraval:*** Aissi cum es genser pascors. ***Marcabru:*** L'autrier jost' una sebissa. ***Bernart de Ventadorn:*** Be m'an perdut lai enves Ventadorn. Quan vei la lauzeta mover. ***Peire Vidal:*** Pos tornatz sui en Proensa. ***Riquier:*** Be'm degra de chantar tener.

lh l0m DDD 7/89

Among the few records of troubadour songs available, this is one of the most interesting and unusual. The stark black-and-white cover photograph gives a clue to the intensity of these performances, which rely much more than is customary simply on the musical content of the melodies themselves. There are no excessive instrumental contributions — variations, improvisations, etc. — rather the harp, psaltery, and vielle serve to underline Paul Hillier's singing (and, in the case of Guillaume IX's *Farai un vers de dreit nien* and Guirault Riquier's *Be'm degra de chantar tener*, speaking). If it might be argued that more variety is in fact necessary to such a programme, it must also be said that Hillier's measured, dramatic performances bring something quite new to this repertoire. It is the kind of recording that one should perhaps listen to in a dark room with a candle burning: the revelation that it offers is a very satisfying one.

MUSIC FOR THE LION-HEARTED KING. Gothic Voices/Christopher Page. Hyperion CDA66336. Texts and translations included.
Anonymous Twelfth Century: Mundus vergens. Novus miles sequitur. Sol sub nube latuit. Hac in anni ianua. Anglia, planctus itera. Etras auri reditur. Vetus abit littera. In occasu sideris. Purgator criminum. Pange melos lacrimosum. Ver pacis apperit. Latex silice. ***Gace Brulé:*** A la doucour de la bele seson. ***Blondel de Nesle:*** L'amours dont sui espris. Ma joie me semont. ***Gui IV, "Li chastelain de Couci":*** Li nouviauz tanz.

lh DDD l0/89

Christopher Page has a remarkable gift for creating enthralling programmes of early music bound together by a brilliantly-chosen central theme, or appellation. This new collection is no less distinguished and every bit as fascinating, musically and historically. Whether or not Richard himself ever actually listened to any of these pieces is beside the question: they are all representative of the period of his lifetime and are gathered together here in his name for the 800th anniversary of his coronation (1189). Two types of twelfth-century vocal music are represented: the *conductus* — which can be written for one, two, three or even four voices and the *chanson*, or noble, courtly love song. The singers cannot be applauded too highly for performances marked by an extraordinary insight into how this music should be tackled, that is, with a fair degree of restraint as well as know-how, given the sort of audience it might have had in Richard's day: the royal court or the household of some high-ranking ecclesiastic.

NEW REVIEW

THE COURTS OF LOVE. MUSIC FROM THE TIME OF ELEANOR OF AQUITAINE. **Sinfonye** (Mara Kiek, voc; Andrew Lawrence-King, medieval hp; Jim Denley, perc)/**Stevie Wishart.** Hyperion CDA66367. Texts and translations included.
Gui d'Ussel: Si be'm partetz, mala domna, de vos. ***Raimbaut de Vaqeiras:*** Calenda maya (vocal and instrumental versions). ***Anonymous 12th Century:*** L'on qui dit q'amors est dolce chose. ***Bernart de Ventadorn:*** Ara'm conseillatz seignor. Conartz, ara sai au be. Quan vei la lauzeta mover. ***Cadenet:*** S'anc fuy belha ni prezada (vocal and instrumental versions). ***Giraut de Bornelh:*** S'ie'us queir conseil, bel' amig' Alamanda. ***Gace Brulé:*** Quant je voi la noif remise. Quant voi le tens bel et cler. Quant flours et glais et verdues s'esloigne. Quant li tens reverdoie.

lh 4m DDD 8/90

This recital consists of songs and instrumental pieces dating from the end of the twelfth century and derived from the "courts of love" of Aquitaine, Champagne, Flanders and elsewhere. The courts of love, created around aristocratic figures such as Marie of Champagne and Eleanor of Aquitaine, were essentially a charade of the medieval law courts, to which lovers could bring their complaints. Thus the texts of the songs are concerned with the dilemmas of infidelity, betrayal and unrequited love. All that survives of this music is melodies for singing: these have been sensitively arranged by Stevie Wishart for a small selection of medieval instruments, including the symphony, a sort of hurdy-gurdy, medieval fiddles, lutes and percussion. All the players of Sinfonye are both expert and relaxed, projecting the music with great character. Six of the pieces are sung by Mara Kiek with considerable feeling: her unusual voice production and tone help to give a sense of 'distance' to the performances, and throughout strike a suitably plaintive note. Hyperion's recording catches all the vocal and instrumental inflexions with great fidelity and a most natural sense of balance. All in all, a fascinating glimpse of music and manners from a remote if influential corner of medieval civilization.

NEW REVIEW

BELLA DOMNA. THE MEDIEVAL WOMAN: LOVER, POET, PATRONESS AND SAINT. **Sinfonye** (Mara Kiek, voc; Andrew Lawrence-King, medieval hp; Jim Denley, perc)/**Stevie Wishart** (medieval fiddle, symphony). Hyperion CDA66283. Texts and translations included.
Martin Codax: Cantigas de Amigo. ***Anonymous 13th Century:*** Domna, pos vos ay chausida. Estampies Royals — No. 3; No. 4; No. 6. Danse Royale. ***de Fournival:*** Onques n'amai tant que jou fui amee. ***La Comtesse de Die:*** A chantar m'er de so qu'ieu non volria. ***Anonymous 14th Century:*** Lasse, pour quoi refusai.

lh DDD 6/88

This intriguing CD collection of medieval songs joined together by the themes of woman as lover, poet, patroness and saint was originally released in 1988 and represented the début of Stevie Wishart's group Sinfonye. The performances of this elusive music have all the freshness and excitement of first encounter. The musical centre stage is held predominantly by the extraordinary vocalist Mara Kiek, whose plaintive as well as idiosyncratic tone ideally matches the distance of the music between its composition and the present day: this is genuinely music from another time and place, with hardly any relationship to the present day at all. Stevie Wishart's playing of the medieval fiddle, used predominantly as a drone instrument and the symphony, a kind of hurdy-gurdy, well matches in its freedom and espressivity Kiek's singing, as does the supportive percussion playing of Jim Denley on two types of medieval drum. The fourth and final member of the group is the harpist Andrew Lawrence-King, whose playing adds tremendous colour to these intriguing recreations of the medieval woman's expression of emotions such as betrayal and violation. The harshness as well as vigour of the medieval era is powerfully recreated in these performances. Hyperion's recording is appropriately neutral, catching at times some of the claustrophobia of the emotions expressed in the music. An extremely interesting recital of music unlikely to be encountered elsewhere.

MUSIC OF THE GOTHIC ERA. Early Music Consort of London/ David Munrow. Archiv Produktion 415 292-2AH. From 2723 045 (11/76).

Léonin: Viderunt omnes. ***Pérotin:*** Viderunt omnes. ***Anonymous thirteenth century French*** (Montpelier Codex): Alle, psallite cum luya. Amor potes. S'on me regarde. In mari miserie. O mitissima. ***Petrus de Cruce:*** Aucun ont trouvé. ***Adam de la Halle:*** De ma dame vient. J'os bien a m'amie parler. ***Anonymous fourteenth century French*** (Roman de Fauvel): La mesnie fauveline. ***Philippe de Vitry:*** Impudentur circumivi. Cum statua. ***Anonymous thirteenth/fourteenth centuries French*** (Ivrea Codex): Clap, clap, par un matin. Febus mundo oriens. ***Machaut:*** Qui es promesses. Lasse! comment oublieray. Hoquetus David. ***Anonymous fourteenth century French*** (Chantilly Codex): Inter densas deserti meditans.

lh lm ADD 8/85 

There is still no better all-round introduction to the marvels of medieval music than this exquisite anthology, a selection from the last and arguably the most enduring project undertaken by the late David Munrow. Much of this music had never been performed in modern times before and the singing and playing exude unusual freshness and vitality, inspired no doubt by the sheer excitement of discovery. The most indispensable performances here are without question those of music by Léonin and Pérotin, the earliest named European composers of polyphony. Their audacious and ambitious settings of *Viderunt omnes*, written for the newly built Cathedral of Notre Dame in Paris during the second half of the twelfth century, rank among the most thrilling and taxing music ever devised for the human voice, and Munrow's interpretations remain unsurpassed. Following them comes a survey of the early history of the motet which in its chronological layout and comprehensiveness is no less an education than an entertainment. The only real regret is that the contents of the original three-LP boxed set have been pared down to an hour's worth of highlights..

NEW REVIEW

THE PILGRIMAGE TO SANTIAGO. New London Consort/Philip Pickett. L'Oiseau-Lyre 433 148-2OH2. Texts and translations included.

Including Cantigas de Santa María (collected/composed by Alfonso el Sabio), the seven Cantigas de Amigo by Martin Codax and other medieval vocal and instrumental works from the Codices Las Huelgas and Calixtinus.

② 2h 6m DDD 7/92 

In recent years a far higher standard of performance together with more rigorous scholarship has come to be expected from those who choose to perform this kind of repertoire. Philip Pickett has been in the forefront of this impressive rise in confidence (as much about what is not known as is definitely known) as this two-disc set amply demonstrates. What may perhaps be surprising to some is the quality of the music itself. The Cantigas remain some of the most enticing melodies ever written, and the New London Consort do them full justice with an array of instrumentalists and singers who are, however, used with discretion. Similarly the moving *Cantigas de Amigo* of Martin Codax are beautifully sung with a restraint that pays expressive dividends, though they do not have quite the transcendent quality of Maria Kiek's recording with Sinfonye (Bella Domna; refer to the Index to Reviews). The polyphonic music from the Las Huelgas and Calixtinus manuscripts completes, with a flourish, the survey tied together by the "Santiago" label. If there is early polyphony that sounds fresher than the four-part *Belial vocatur*, for example, it has yet to be recorded. In addition to polyphonic works of various genres, Pickett has also chosen to record the four *planctus* settings from the Las Huelgas Codex: moving music in themselves, they are valuable also for their historical associations, as is explained in the comprehensive notes to the set.

NEW REVIEW

VOX IBERICA I. SONS OF THUNDER. **Sequentia/Benjamin Bagby, Barbara Thornton.** Deutsche Harmonia Mundi RD77199. Texts and translations included.

Codex Calixtinus — Ad superni regis decus. Alleluia: Vocavit Ihesus Iacobum. Annua gaudia, Iacobe debita. Benedicamus Domino. Congaudeant catholici. Cum vidissent autem. Cunctipotens genitor deus. Dum pater familias. Dum esset. Exultet celi curia. Gratulantes celebremus festum.

Huic Iacobo. Iacobe sancte tuum repettio. Iacobi virginei. In hac die laudes cum gaudio. Jocundetur et letetur. Misit Herodes. Nostra phalans. O adiutor. Regi perhennis glorie. Rex immense, pater pie. Vox nostra resonet.

1h 14m DDD 12/92

NEW REVIEW

VOX IBERICA II. CODEX LAS HUELGAS. **Sequentia/Benjamin Bagby, Barbara Thornton.** Deutsche Harmonia Mundi 05472-77238-2. Texts and translations included.

Codex Las Huelgas — Audi, pontus. Ave Maria, gracia plena. Benedicamus Domino cum cantico. Benedicamus: Hic est enim precursor. Benedicamus virgini matri. Casta catholica. Catholicorum concio. Ex illustri. Fa fa mi fa/ut re mi ut. In hoc festo gratissimo. Maria, virgo virginum. Mater patris et filia. Mundi dolens de iactura. O gloriosa Dei genitrix. O, plangant nostri prelati. O plena gracia. Psallat chorus in novo carmina. Qui nos fecit ex nichilo. Resurgentis Domini. Salve regina glorie. Stabat iuxta Christi crucem. Verbum patris hodie. Virgo sidus aureum. Four Planctus — Plange Castella misera; Quis dabit meo aquam; Rex obiit et labitur Castelle gloria; O monialis concio Burgensis.

1h 15m DDD 12/92 

NEW REVIEW

VOX IBERICA III. CANTIGAS DE SANTA MARIA. **Sequentia/Benjamin Bagby, Barbara Thornton.** Deutsche Harmonia Mundi 05472-77173-2. Texts and translations included.

Alfonso el Sabio: Por nos, Virgen Madre. Como o nome da Virgen. Sobelos fondos do mar. Nenbre-sse-e, Madre de. Dized', ai trobadores. Maldito seja quen non loara. Quantos me creveren loaran. Quen bõa dona querrá. Pero que seja a gente. Santa Maria, strela do dia. Pois que Deus quis da Virgen. Macar poucos cantares acabei e con son. En todo logar á poder. ***Riquier:*** Humils, forfaitz, repres e penedens. ***Anonymous 13th Century:*** *Kharajas* — Que faray, mamma?; Meu sidi Ibrahim; Gar si yes devina; Gardi vos ay yermanellas.

1h 18m DDD 12/92 

These three generously-filled discs provide a fascinating insight into Spain between the twelfth and fourteenth centuries. The country's history and culture as encompassed in the texts and music of the three repertories recorded is brought to life by Sequentia with all the immediacy of an illuminated miniature in a mediaeval manuscript. The music comes from three famous Spanish mediaeval manuscripts — the Las Huelgas manuscript, the Codex Calixtinus, and the collection of Cantigas de Santa María compiled at the court of King Alfonso "El Sabio" of Castille. What strikes one immediately is the freshness and imagination of virtually every piece here recorded. Sequentia's performances are commensurate with these qualities — listen, for example, to the magical textures of the women's choir singing *Sobelos fondos do mar* from the Cantigas collection, or the robust, steely harmony projected by the men in the organa from the Calixtinus manuscript. Surely one of the most remarkable pieces of the Middle Ages is the enormous *Virgo sidus aureum*, a prosa *"de Sancta Maria"* lasting over 14 minutes, whose text is a radiant mystical contemplation of the Mother of God. Liturgico-poetic parallels for it may well be sought in the East rather than the West — the Greek *Akathist* hymn from several centuries earlier, for example — but if Hildegard of Bingen, the "feather on the breath of God" is brought to mind, that would also be no surprise. It must be said that the poetic quality of all three of these collections is so high that the music could hardly fail to be of the same level of inspiration. This astonishing piece is given a splendid, coherent rendition (no easy task with a monophonic work of this length) by two soloists, female choir and symphonia, and one only has to listen to it after one of the rather shorter three-part conductus, such as *Mundi dolens de iactura*, or one of the powerful *organa* for St James, the "Son of thunder", from the Calixtinus collection, to gain some idea of the impact and the extent of the variety to be found on these discs. The Cantigas collection convincingly conveys the accomplishments of the court of the king who "while he was pondering the heavens and looking at the stars...lost the earth and his kingdom", and places the Cantiga repertory in the context not only of the troubadours (in particular Guirault Riquier) but also the Mozarabic *kharjas* (or *jarchas*), whose music has been reconstructed, with some success, by Benjamin Bagby. This testament to the richness of musical life in mediaeval Spain should not be missed: it has lost none of its power over the centuries.

NEW REVIEW

THE MARRIAGE OF HEAVEN AND HELL. THIRTEENTH-CENTURY FRENCH MOTETS AND SONGS. **Gothic Voices/Christopher Page.** Hyperion CDA66423. Texts and translations included.

Anonymous: Je ne chant pas. Talens m'est pris. Trois sereurs/Trois sereurs/Trois sereurs. Plus bele que flors/Quant revient/L'autrier jouer. Par un martinet/Hé, sire!/Hé, bergier! De la virge Katerine/Quant froidure/Agmina milicie. Ave parens/Ad gratie. Super te Jerusalem/Sed fulsit virginitas. A vous douce debonnaire. Mout souvent/Mout ai esté en doulour. Quant voi l'aloete/Dieux! je ne m'en partiré ja. En non Dieu/Quant voi la rose. Je m'en vois/Tels a mout. Festa januaria. ***Blondel de Nesle:*** En tous tans que vente bise. ***Colin Muset:*** Trop volontiers chanteroie. ***Bernart de Ventadorn:*** Can vei la lauzeta mover. ***Gautier de Dargies:*** Autre que je ne seuill fas.

46m DDD 12/90

The reasons for the dazzling success of Gothic Voices both in the recording studio and in the concert-hall are once again evident in this collection. It is both an entertaining and well-planned recital and, if one chooses to take it that way, reading Christopher Page's insert-notes while listening, a detailed lecture-recital. The music, all French and dating from the thirteenth century, is that seemingly impenetrable repertoire of polytextual motets, unexpectedly compared and contrasted with monophonic trouvère songs. The comparison is illuminating, and the performances of both genres of music are up to Gothic Voices' usual standards: intonation is perfect, textures are finely balanced, the performances are always conceived just as much melodically as harmonically, and the greatest respect is always paid to the words (even when there are three texts at the same time, as is often the case here!). The clever juxtaposition of the trouvère Bernart de Ventadorn's *Can vei la lauzeta mover* with the triple-texted motet *Quant voi l'aloete/Dieux! je ne m'en partiré ja/NEUMA* encapsulates the thinking behind this recording: a compelling musical experience and a provocative intellectual one.

THE SERVICE OF VENUS AND MARS. [a]**Andrew Lawrence-King** (medieval hp); **Gothic Voices/Christopher Page.** Hyperion CDA66238.
Texts and translations included where appropriate.

Philippe de Vitry: Gratissima virginis/Vos qui admiramini/Gaude gloriosa/Contratenor. ***P. des Molins:*** De ce que fol pense. ***Pycard:*** Gloria. ***L. Power:*** Sanctus. ***F. Lebertoul:*** Las, que me demanderoye. ***J. Pyamour:*** Quam pulchra es. ***Dunstable:*** Speciosa facta es. ***Soursby:*** Sanctus. ***R. Loqueville:*** Je vous pri que j'aye un baysier[a]. ***Anonymous fourteenth century:*** Singularis laudis digna. De ce fol pense (after des Molins)[a]. Lullay, lullay. ***Anonymous fourteenth or fifteenth centuries:*** There is no rose of swych virtu. Le gay playsir[a]. Le grant pleyser[a]. The Agincourt Carol.

50m DDD 11/87 

This collection is of music loosely associated with the Order of the Garter, founded by Edward III in the middle years of the fourteenth century. It includes some wonderful English works from the years 1340-1440, including the motet *Singularis laudis digna*, a wonderful canonic Gloria by Pycard, works by composers of the school of Dunstable (who influenced continental composers as no English composer has done since), and finally the famous carol celebrating Henry V's victory at Agincourt. Gothic Voices have in the last few years set new standards in the performance of this kind of music and their attention to inner detail produces some beautiful results. Hyperion's characteristically informative and persuasive notes are also considerably helpful in bringing this music to life.

NEW REVIEW

IL SOLAZZO. The Newberry Consort/Mary Springfels. Harmonia Mundi HMU90 7038. Texts and translation included.

Anonymous Fourteenth Century Italian: La Badessa. Bel fiore danza. Nova stella. Cominciamento di gioia. Trotto. Principe di virtu. ***Jacopo da Bologna:*** Non al suo amante. ***Landini:*** La bionda treccia. Dolcie signorie. Donna, s'i, t'o fallito. El gran disio. ***Ciconia:*** O rosa bella. Ligiadra donna. ***Zacharo de Teramo:*** Rosetta. Un fior gentil. ***Bartolino da Padova:*** Alba columba.

lh 2m DDD 7/93

If medieval Italian music pales somewhat in comparison to the glories of opera from the nineteenth century onwards, there are still riches to be discovered in this collection of *trecento* vocal and instrumental works. The Chicago-based ensemble, The Newberry Consort, use a mere five performers to provide over an hour of entertainment. This was the era of writers such as Dante, Petrarch, Boccaccio, but also of Simone Prodenzani — the author of a cycle of sonnets entitled *Il Solazzo*, many of which were later set to music. Whilst some of the *Solazzo* texts are presented here in musical form (the scurrilous *La Badessa* is one), Italian ballata from leading composers of the time are also represented — Ciconia's *O rosa bella* and Landini's *La bionda treccia*, for example. The vocal numbers are all taken by mezzo Judith Malafronte and counter-tenor Drew Minter who clear the hurdles of tricky pronunciation and flamboyantly complex vocal lines to give a thoroughly communicative performance of this wonderful music. Mary Springfels provides elegant and musical direction as well as that essential ingredient to a disc such as this — the informative booklet. If the prospect of an hour of early Italian song sounds daunting, fear not, for the instrumental dances on the disc (especially the anonymous *Cominciamento di gioia*) are played with a vitality that will make you want to jump up and join in! Explorers of the riches from Italian times long gone by need have no qualms when sampling from this lively, superbly performed disc.

NEW REVIEW

THE MEDIEVAL ROMANTICS. FRENCH SONGS AND MOTETS, 1340-1440. **Gothic Voices/Christopher Page.** Hyperion CDA66463. Texts and translations included.
Solage: Joieux de cuer en seumellant estoye. ***De Porta:*** Alma polis religio/Axe poli cum artica. ***Machaut:*** C'est force, faire le weil. Tant doucement me sens emprisones. Comment qu'a moy lonteinne. ***Tenorista:*** Sofrir m'estuet et plus non puis durer. ***De Senleches:*** En ce gracieux tamps joli. ***Dufay:*** Je requier a tous amoureux. Las, que feray? Ne que je devenray? ***G. Velut:*** Je voel servir plus c'onques mais. ***De Lymburgia:*** Tota pulcra es, amica mea. ***Anonymous:*** Various works.

56m DDD 3/92 

A revelatory disc, this. As with Gothic Voices' previous recordings, a large and almost completely unknown selection of medieval repertoire is presented with cordon bleu elegance and panache. Christopher Page's excellent insert-notes provide the rationale behind this particular anthology, and if the ravishing sound of the ensemble does not convince you that this music is of the highest quality, then nothing will. The connections between pieces by composers such as Solage and Senleches with later music by Dufay are brought into sharp relief in this well-planned collection. Page's enlightening dissection of Solage's extraordinary *Joieux de cuer en seumellant estoye* in the commentary is the focal point of a wider discussion of the way in which composers of the fifteenth century reacted to the accomplishments of the fourteenth; and the concrete result of these speculations is the delightful programme here recorded. Listen to the Johannes de Lymburgia's smoothly consonant *Tota pulchra es* immediately after the eccentric harmonies of the Solage song and ask yourself whether music history was ever so absorbing.

LANCASTER AND VALOIS. Gothic Voices (Margaret Philpot, contr. Rogers Covey-Crump, Andrew Tusa, Charles Daniels, Leigh Nixon, tens; Stephen Charlesworth, Donald Grieg, bars; Andrew Lawrence-King, hp)/**Christopher Page** (lte). Hyperion CDA66588. Texts and translations included.
Machaut: Donnez, signeurs. Quand je ne voy ma dame. Riches d'amour et mendians. Pas de tor en thies pais. ***Solage:*** Tres gentil cuer. ***Cesaris:*** Se vous scaviez, ma tres douce maistresse. Mon seul voloir/Certes m'amour. ***Cordier:*** Ce jur de l'an. ***Pycard:*** Credo. ***Sturgeon:*** Salve mater domini/Salve templum domini. ***Fonteyns:*** Regali ex progenie.

Anonymous: Puis qu'autrement ne puis avoir. Soit tart, tempre, main ou soir. Le ior. Avrai je ja de ma dame confort? Sanctus. Je vueil vivre au plaisir d'amours.

59m DDD 9/92

This is the tenth recording to come from Christopher Page's Gothic Voices and, the considerable success of their previous recordings notwithstanding, this is perhaps their best yet. In the space of 11 years, Page and his group have reinvented performance practice in medieval and fifteenth century music, as powerful and popularizing an influence as David Munrow and his Early Music Consort of London in the 1970s. "Lancaster and Valois" takes its name from the chosen repertoire: French secular songs of the late fourteenth and early fifteenth centuries juxtaposed with sacred English pieces from around 1400. Much thought has been given to the ordering of the pieces and the grouping of the voices, resulting in the greatest possible diversity. In *Tres gentil cuer* by Solage, Page sets an ideally lilting tempo, with the text finely enunciated by Margaret Philpot, the tenors (in this instance Charles Daniels and Leigh Nixon) adding definition but never threatening to engulf. This is followed by a *Credo* by the English composer Pycard, the longest and most stately piece on the disc, exploiting the richer timbres of tenors and baritones. With excellent sound and entertaining and scholarly notes by Christopher Page, this is an irresistible disc.

THE GARDEN OF ZEPHIRUS. FIFTEENTH-CENTURY COURTLY SONGS. **Gothic Voices/Christopher Page** with **Imogen Barford** (medieval hp). Hyperion CDA66144. Texts and translations included. From A66144.

Dufay: J'attendray tant qu'il vous playra. Adieu ces bons vins de Lannoys. Mon cuer me fait tous dis penser. ***Briquet:*** Ma seul amour et ma belle maistresse. ***Anthonello de Caserta:*** Amour m'a le cuer mis. ***Landini:*** Neesun ponga speranza. Giunta vaga biltà. ***Reyneau:*** Va t'en, mon cuer, avent mes yeux. ***Matheus de Sancto Johanne:*** Fortune, faulce, parverse. ***Francus de Insula:*** Amours n'ont cure de tristesse. ***Brollo:*** Qui le sien vuelt bien maintenir. ***Anonymous:*** N'a pas long temps que trouvay Zephirus. Je la remire, la belle.

50m DAD 12/86 

Springtime, as Chaucer and almost all medieval poets remind us, stirs the gentle heart from sleep. But it was Zephyr, the West Wind, who inspired the humble lover to seek his lady. As often as not she was unattainable but it was an ennobling aspiration, nonetheless. This aspect of refined or courtly society is engagingly captured by Gothic Voices under Christopher Page in a selection of French and Italian chansons, ballades and rondeaux dating from the early to mid fifteenth century. The wealth of vivid images, warm sentiments and formal variety contained in the poems is highlighted both by the musical settings themselves and by polished, communicative performances. The rondeaux of Dufay are perhaps especially affecting — ardent lovers of France and followers of Bacchus will be refreshed by a fragrant tribute to the wines of the Laon district in his *Adieu ces bons vins de Lannoys* — but Landini's ballate, sounding a more objective note, are hardly less so. Full texts with translations are provided and the recorded sound is excellent.

LE BANQUET DU VOEU 1454. Gilles Binchois Ensemble/Dominique Vellard. Virgin Classics Veritas VC7 59043-2. Notes, text and translations included.

First entertainment — ***Vide:*** Et c'est asses. ***Anonymous:*** Adieu ma tres belle maistress. Une foys avant que morir. ***Legrant:*** Wilhelmus Legrant. ***Dufay:*** Ave regina celorum. *Second entertainment:* ***Anonymous:*** Au chant de l'alowette. ***Binchois:*** Je ne vis oncques le pareille. Vostre tres doulx regart plaisant. Gloria, laus et honour. ***Frye:*** Ave regina celorum. *Third entertainment* — ***Grenon:*** Je ne requier de ma dame. ***Dufay:*** Je me complains pitieusement. ***Anonymous:*** Ellend du hast. ***Binchois:*** Chanson. ***Fontaine:*** Pur vous tenir. *Fourth entertainment:* ***Anonymous:*** Du cuer je suopire. Venise. Preambulum super re. ***Binchois:*** Seule esgarée. Deo gracias. ***Vide:*** Il m'est si grief.

Ih DDD 3/92  

When Philip the Good of Burgundy was invited by the Pope to lead a new crusade against the Turks, who had taken Constantinople in May 1453, it was public confirmation of his power and influence. Philip acknowledged this, and kicked off his campaign for support with an extravagant, and now famous, banquet, known in English as the Feast of the Pheasant. A pie with 28 minstrels inside, and a model church — complete with bells and organ, and containing four singers — provided the musical entertainment, along with 'loud' minstrels in the hall. Jousting, dancing, mimes telling the story of Jason, speeches, and the taking of vows also contributed to the festivities. Although the crusade itself never came to anything, the structure of four groups of entertainments to be performed between the courses of the feast has survived, and pieces that might have been performed have been put together for this disc. These are subtle, elegant readings which, though they may lack the boisterous *bonhomie* that was probably in attendance at the original feast, are particularly suited to repeated listening on disc. The performances of the a cappella pieces clearly maintain the independence of the voices, rather than aiming for a smooth meld, and the instrumentation of the other works has been sensitively chosen. Playing is well articulated and not without virtuosity. The spacious acoustic lends an agreeably authentic ambience to the whole.

NEW REVIEW

THE BRIGHTEST HEAVEN OF INVENTION. New London Chamber Choir/James Wood. Amon Ra CD-SAR56. Texts and translations included.
Regis: O admirabile commercium. ***Obrecht:*** Factor orbis. Salve crux. ***Josquin Desprez:*** Praeter rerum seriem. ***Brumel:*** Nato canunt omnia. ***Busnois:*** In hydraulis. Anthoni usque limina. ***Dufay:*** Ave regina celorum.

lh DDD 3/93

The motets on this disc are linked by much more than their Flemish origin and the period of their composition (about 1450-1525). First, there is their sheer originality: even from the outset, with *O admirabile commercium* by Johannes Regis, we are in the world of unconventionality and innovation. Secondly, riddles and cryptic references enliven the task of realizing these scores — even to the extent, in Busnois's *Anthoni usque limina*, that we are still unsure as to how the cryptograph for the tenor part is to be interpreted! Thirdly, many of these composers obviously knew and respected each other: Antoine Brumel's *Nato canunt omnia* is a parody work based on the Regis motet. Above all, these motets are connected by a general attitude of approach, based on the development from a secure tradition for a discerning audience that would be able to follow the new paths to be trod. The New London Chamber Choir performs on a semi-professional basis and offers urgently committed performances that do not always display subtleness of balance or dynamic shading, and have their moments of rawness, but which ultimately convince by the strength of their imagination. A lucid recording, set in a lively-enough ambience, complements the whole.

THE ROSE AND THE OSTRICH FEATHER. Music from the Eton Choirbook, Volume 1. **The Sixteen/Harry Christophers.** Collins Classics 1314-2. Notes and texts included.
Fayrfax: Magnificat ("Regale"). ***Hygons:*** Salve regina. ***Turges:*** From stormy wyndis. Stabat iuxta Christi crucem. ***Anonymous:*** This day day dawes. ***Cornysh:*** Salve regina.

lh 3m DDD 4/92 9P 9S

The sacred music of early Tudor England (the end of the fifteenth century) has been unjustly neglected on CD and the welcome extended to this Collins release is further enhanced by the fact that Harry Christophers and his ensemble have since added two further volumes to this series dedicated to music from the Eton Choirbook. The destruction of great swathes of manuscript in the sixteenth century has left us with only isolated jewels such as this to remind us in sound what the eye can behold in the Perpendicular style of the architecture of the cathedrals of Canterbury, Worcester, Winchester and the Minster at York. Both architecture and music present soaring vaulted vistas and an attention to florid and ornate tracery. The Rose and the Ostrich Feather? These were both potent symbolic emblems of members of the royal house of Tudor and the words are incorporated into the two secular songs with English texts. The white rose was also an image closely associated with the Virgin Mary and most of the scores in the Choirbook are dedicated to her. Sadly, the disc is without translations of the Latin works but there is a fascinating essay by John Milsom. This music finds The Sixteen at their best, especially attentive to the severe tuning demands placed on the singers, for whom there is no instrumental accompaniment. Particularly notable is the control that Christophers exerts over the sound of his singers in this very taxing music (four of the performances on the disc last for over ten minutes). The recorded sound expertly captures and balances the expressive singing. Whether used as an aural accompaniment to a great architectural style or enjoyed purely for its sharply-defined reflection of one of the greatest periods of English music (existing within the choral traditions which continues to this day), this disc is altogether outstanding and should not be missed.

SACRED AND SECULAR MUSIC FROM SIX CENTURIES. Hilliard Ensemble.
Hyperion CDA66370. Texts and translations included.
Anonymous: Dezi, flor resplandeciente. Nuevas, nuevas Por tu fe!. ***Byrd:*** Ne irascaris Domine. ***Dufay:*** Gloria ad modem tubae. Vergene bella. ***Fayrfax:*** Most clere of colour. ***Flecha:*** El jubilate. ***Hermannus Contractus:*** Salve regina. ***Godefroy de St Victoire:*** Planctus ante nescia. ***Goudimel:*** Bonjour mon coeur. ***Isaac:*** Tota pulchra es. ***Janequin:*** Le chant des oiseaux. ***Machaut:*** Quant je sui mis au retour. ***Peñalosa:*** Sancta mater. ***Tallis:*** O nata lux.

lh 2m DDD 6/91

The title of this disc might lead you to expect a selection of pieces progressing gently from the renaissance to the present day. But in fact the *latest* item recorded here dates from the sixteenth century; the earliest is by a Benedictine monk born in 1013 – a reminder of the way in which, these days, the boundaries of vocal repertoire are being pushed further and further back into the mists of musical history. As always with the Hilliards, though, this is far from being just a dry, academic survey: the primary consideration is the music – and on this recording they have included many of their own favourite pieces. Not surprisingly, then, it is a selection that shows the group at its best – from the restrained devotion of the eleventh-century antiphon to the Virgin which begins the programme, through the extrovert hocketing of Dufay's *Gloria ad modem tubae* (which ends in a blaze of what can only be described as vocal ping-pong), through to the concluding item: Janequin's famous musical representation of French bird-life. En route, there are many other delights, both familiar and unusual – and although some faintly audible traffic noise provides an occasional reminder of the twentieth century it doesn't detract from these highly polished – and highly enjoyable performances.

Late Renaissance *16th–17th centuries*

NEW REVIEW

TUDOR CHURCH MUSIC. Worcester Cathedral Choir/Donald Hunt with **Raymond Johnston** (org). Abbey 'Alpha CDCA943. Texts included.
Weelkes. Hosanna to the Son of David. Gloria in exelsis Deo. When David heard. ***Byrd.*** Teach me, O Lord. Cantate Domino. Ave verum corpus. Sing joyfully unto God our strength. ***Tomkins.*** When David heard. Almighty God, the fountain of all wisdom. ***Tallis.*** Salvator mundi, salva nos I. If ye love me. Hear the voice and prayer. ***Gibbons.*** O Lord, in thy wrath rebuke me not. This is the record of John. Hosanna to the Son of David.

5lm DDD 5/93

Its church music was one of the glories of Tudor England, and the standard as represented by relatively minor composers was as high as the output was generous. But here we have the masters, "the big five", all heard in some of their finest and most famous works, so that the recital presents a small but useful anthology, ideal for adding to collections which otherwise have nothing of this sort in them. The Choir of Worcester Cathedral have many recordings to their credit but probably none better than this. They are a fine example of the Cathedral tradition in England; and one does not have to have just finished reading Joanna Trollope's *The Choir* to feel strongly convinced of the need for its preservation. The first sound of Weelkes's *Hosanna to the Son of*

David itself tells of a rich culture, especially when the luxury of a choice in settings arrives later with the version by Orlando Gibbons. There are also two settings of the lament *When David heard*, both of them superbly 'built' by the singers as well as the two composers, Weelkes and Tomkins. Some of the anthems have organ accompaniment and soloist; most are sung *a cappella*, in recorded sound that does not (as is frequently the case) place the choir in too distant a perspective.

IN NOMINE. Fretwork (Richard Campbell, treb viols; Julia Hodgson, Richard Boothby, ten and bass viols; Elizabeth Liddle, treb and ten viols; William Hunt, treb, ten and great bass viols) with [a]**Christopher Wilson** (lte). Amon Ra CDSAR29.
Tallis: In Nomines — à 4 Nos. 1 and 2. ***Tallis*** (attrib.): Solfaing Song à 5[a]. Fantasia à 5 (reconstr. Milsom). Libera nos, salva nos à 5. ***Tye:*** In Nomines — à 5, "Crye"; "Trust". ***Cornyshe:*** Fa la sol à 3. ***Baldwin:*** In Nomine à 4. ***Bull:*** In Nomine à 5[a]. ***Byrd:*** In Nomine à 4 No. 2. Fantasia à 3 No. 3[a]. ***Taverner:*** In Nomines — for lute[a]; à 4. ***Preston:*** O lux beata Trinitas à 3[a]. ***R. Johnson***: In Nomine à 4. ***Parsons:*** In Nomine à 5. Ut re mi fa sol la à 4. ***Ferrabosco I:*** In Nomine à 5[a]. Lute Fantasia No. 5[a]. Fantasia à 4[a].

lh DDD 3/88

For the wary, *In Nomines* are instrumental chamber works popular in England during the sixteenth and seventeenth centuries, in which counterpoints are woven around a pre-existing tune from the Sarum antiphon *Gloria tibi Trinitas*. Fretwork is an ensemble of young viol players who are rapidly revitalizing the English repertory. Many of the composers will be familiar; others — such as Tye, Cornyshe, Baldwin, Preston, Johnson and Parsons — will be known only to the initiated. Nevertheless, together they represent the core of a rich tradition of music for accomplished amateurs, music which kings and commoners alike enjoyed playing up until the Restoration. This is a very attractive and well recorded programme of undemanding music.

AWAKE, SWEET LOVE ... [a]**James Bowman** (alto); [b]**David Miller** (lte); [c]**King's Consort of Viols** ([d]Wendy Gillespie, Richard Boothby, William Hunt, [e]Mark Caudle). Hyperion CDA66447. Notes and texts included.
Dowland: Can she excuse my wrongs[abc]. Flow my teares[abe]. A fancy, P5[b]. Sorrow stay[abe]. Queene Elizabeth, her Galliard[b]. Goe nightly cares[abde]. Now, O now I needs must part[ab]. Preludium[b]. A Fantasie, P1[b]. Say love if ever thou didst finde[ab]. Frogg Galliard[b]. Awake sweet love, thou art returned[ab]. Tell me, true Love[abc]. ***Campion:*** Author of light[abe]. Oft have I sigh'd[abe]. ***Ford:*** Since first I saw your face[ab]. ***Johnson:*** Eliza is the fairest queen[ac]. ***Ferrabosco:*** Pavin[b]. ***Danyel:*** Eyes, look no more[abe]. Thou pretty bird how do I see[abe]. I doe whenas I do not see[ab]. ***Hunnis:*** In terrors trapp'd[ac]. ***Anonymous:*** Come, tread the paths[ac].

lh 12m DDD 10/91

Domestic music-making flourished in the times of Good Queen Bess, when many households boasted the odd lute, maybe a chest of viols, and citizens whose singing voices could be heard (not only at bathtime); many were those who rewarded the publishers of music for their use and delight. This situation is mirrored in the programme of songs (with lute or consort) and lute solos, by James Bowman and the King's Consort. The music of Dowland lies naturally at the heart of the matter and here it frames that of some of his distinguished contemporaries. The inclusion of the viol part specified in some of the lute songs restores a dimension of beauty that is often sacrificed in present-day performances. In keeping with the album title, many of the songs deal with aspects of love — even the lute-solo *Frogg Galliard* pokes fun at the unrequited love of Mounsier le Duc d'Alençon for the Queen herself. James Bowman brings more than two decades of experience and devotion to bear in these memorable performances, and he is most sympathetically supported by the King's Consort, amongst whom David Miller should be singled out for special mention for his clear and intelligent playing of the lute solos. Happy the family that spent its leisure hours with this music, and happy the owner of this disc.

ORPHEUS I AM. Tragicomedia/Stephen Stubbs. EMI Reflexe CDC7 54311-2. Texts and translations included.

Anonymous: Cock Lorel. The ape's dance at the Temple. ***Dowland:*** Doulands Rounde Battell Galyard. ***W. Lawes:*** The catts. Come, my Daphne, come away. Gather ye rosebuds while ye may (two versions). Haste you, nimphs. He that will not love. A masque. Royall Consorts – Sett No. 1 in D minor: Fantazy, Aire, Almain, Corranto I and II, Saraband and Ecco; Sett No. 2 in D minor: Aire. To the dews. To pansies. To the sycamore. White though yee be. Wise nature that the dew of sleep prepares. Ye feinds and furies. ***R. Johnson:*** Arm, arm!. As I walked forth. Baboon's Dance. Care-charming sleep. Charon, oh Charon. Dear, do not your fair beauty wrong. The first of the Temple. Full fathom five. Have you seen the bright lily grow?. Mascarada. The noble man's masque tune. Orpheus I am. Satyr's Dance. The third of the Temple. Tis late and cold. Where the bee sucks.

1h 19m DDD 2/92 

The Jacobean masque was an extremely popular form of entertainment at the Stuart court, one in which all the arts, visual and aural, were brought to the service of fantasy, fun and, sometimes, the making of political points. It was staged at the end of a spoken play, preceded by the antimasque in which various kinds of professional entertainer appeared, and ending in general revelry with audience participation. Despite all this only one masque (by William Lawes) and fragments of a few others have survived in detail. Tragicomedia have used surviving fragments of masques and theatre music of the time to reconstruct a notional masque, together with a musical synopsis of the preceding – equally notional play. The result is an adroit juxtaposition of vocal and instrumental music, and a kaleidoscope of changing moods that is punctuated at appropriate moments by the appearance of various grotesques and an early version of *Cats* – Lawes got there long before Lloyd Webber. In its conception, execution (both vocal and instrumental) and quality of recording and balance, this disc is a touchstone by which others might be measured. It is also first-class entertainment.

WATKINS ALE. MUSIC OF THE ENGLISH RENAISSANCE. **Baltimore Consort.** Dorian DOR90142. Texts included.

J. d'Estrée: The Buffens. ***J. Johnson:*** Green garters. Greensleeves. ***Ravenscroft:*** There were three ravens. ***R. Alison:*** Goe from my window. The Quadro Pavin. De la tromba pavin. ***Morley:*** La sampogna. Joyne hands. ***Byrd:*** The carmans whistle, BK36. ***Dowland:*** Can she excuse, P42. Lachrimae, P15. ***R. Nicolson:*** Jewes daunce. ***Anonymous:*** Nuttmigs and ginger. Howells delight. Unto the prophet Jonas I read. Singers Jig. Grimstock. Pavane Quadro and Galliard. Watkins ale.

1h 8m DDD 4/92  

In early times the boundary between popular and art music was less clearly marked than it is now; they spoke recognizable variants of the same musical languages and composers based sets of variations on popular tunes with no air of patronization. The "garde" was not so "avant". In England a more or less standardized band of instruments evolved — the 'mixed' or 'broken' consort, since it included instruments of different types — wind and strings, both plucked and bowed; to this The Baltimore Consort add a singer and a keyboard instrument (a virginal). There is splendid vitality in both the selected music and the way it is played in this recording, a happy view of the English musical scene of those times, consort and solo instrumental items and songs, one of which, *Watkins ale*, is robustly salacious. Song texts and helpful notes are provided. The pleasures enjoyed by our ancestors (and here by our transatlantic 'cousins') may and should be shared through this splendid disc.

SIXTEENTH- AND SEVENTEENTH-CENTURY CHORAL WORKS. King's College Choir, Cambridge/Stephen Cleobury with [a]**David Briggs** (org). EMI CDC7 47065-2. From EL270095-1 (12/84).

Allegri: Miserere mei, Deus (with Timothy Beasley-Murray, treb). ***Nanino:*** Adoramus te Christe a 5. ***Marenzio:*** Magnificat a 8[a]. ***Frescobaldi:*** Messa sopra l'aria della Monica. ***Ugolini:*** Beata es Virgo Maria a 12[a].

45m DDD 5/85

The central work on this disc, Allegri's setting of the penitential Psalm 51, *Have mercy upon me, O God*, is by far the simplest in construction, alternating a single strand of plainsong with straightforward harmonic passages for five-part choir and verses for a quartet of solo voices. Yet it speaks to the heart nowadays as clearly as it did in the early seventeenth century when it was written. There is a special frisson each time the treble soloist soars effortlessly to his top C. All the composers represented here worked in Rome, and this anthology seeks to illustrate the variety of musical styles current in Roman church music at this time. The choir sing all this ageless music with that understated confidence for which they are famous. Their voices are as cool as the spreading fan vault high above their heads. The recording embraces the stillness of this great space but with a balance which loses no detail.

NEW REVIEW

MUSICA DOLCE. Julianne Baird (sop); [a]**Colin Tilney** (hpd). Dorian DOR90123. Texts and translations included.

Monteverdi: Ohimè ch'io cado. Voglio di vita uscir. Exulta, filia Sion. Selva morale e spirituale — Jubilet tota civitas. Scherzi musicali — Quel sguardo sdegnosetto. ***Cavalli:*** Gli amori d'Apollo e di Dafne — Musica dolce. ***Caccini:*** Le nuove musiche — Ardi, cor mio; Dolcissimo sospiro. ***Rossi:*** Orfeo — Mio ben. La Gelosia. ***India:*** Mentre che'l chor. ***B. Strozzi:*** Di-porti di Euterpe, Op. 7 — Lagrime mie. ***B. Storace:*** Passamezzo[a]. ***Cima:*** La Novella[a]. ***G. Strozzi:*** Toccata de Passacagli[a].

lh 10m DDD 12/92

The doctrine of the affect was first propounded by German musicologists (the *Affekt)* but adopted enthusiastically by Italians (the *affetto),* who knew very well how to exploit it. So too does Julianne Baird here, with unforced *mese di voce,* filigree *fiorature* and expressive shading of tone. She is particularly affecting in Barbara Strozzi's "Lagrime mie" and "Musica dolce" by Cavalli (Strozzi's teacher), which, like three other items in the programme, have rarely, if ever, been recorded before. Hers is one of the most beautiful voices in the present early-music field. In order to match the ebb and flow of such performances one needs an alertly sensitive accompanist — which Julianne Baird has in the person of Colin Tilney. He faithfully follows her every move and, to add variety, adds three solo items, one by Giulio Strozzi, whose adopted daughter Barbara became — there are wheels within the wheels of this programme! Caccini said, that in a small room one can hear the words better; if, sitting at home, you do not always find this entirely true in this recording you will find ample compensation in the *'bel*-ness' of Baird's *canto;* and the unfamiliarity of much of the repertory.

NEW REVIEW

LA DOLCE VITA. [a]**The King's Singers;** [b]**Tragicomedia/Stephen Stubbs.** EMI CDC7 54191-2. Notes, texts and translations included.

Agostini: Non t'aricordi. ***Anonymous:*** L'amanza mia. Catalina, Catalina![a]. Chi passa per'st strada. Corten espadas afiladas. Pavana d'España[b]. ***Cornet:*** Parmi di star. ***Giramo:*** Festa, riso. ***Lambardi:*** Toccata e gagliarda[b]. ***Macque:*** Gagliarda seconda[b]. ***Mudarra:*** Fantasia que contrahaze la harpa en la maniera de Luduvico[b]. ***Nola:*** Chi la gagliarda. Tre ciechi siamo[a]. ***D. Ortiz:*** Ricercarda quarta[b]. ***Piccinini:*** Colascione[b]. ***Willaert:*** Ave virgo sponsa Dei[a]. O dolce vita mia (two versions). Qual dolcezza giamai[a]. Vecchie letrose.

lh 10m DDD 9/92

Whether or not the phrase "See Naples and die" perhaps had less minacious overtones in renaissance times than today, you can hear it in complete safety through this artfully compiled montage of music that probably echoed through its streets and rooms at that time. Music was then an important part of *la dolce vita* in its broadest sense: the chosen items express not only love, lust, laughter and protests against petty offences but also piety, and they are presented in an order that gives variety through both Italianate swings of mood and vocal versus instrumental contrast. Naples was for a long time viceregally governed from Spain, which accounts for the appropriate inclusion of popular instrumental pieces by Mudarra and Ortiz, whilst the magnetic effect of Italian music on northerners is marked by the presence of the arch-madrigalist Willaert, whose *O dolce vita mia,* given in both vocal and instrumental versions, provides the album with its title. The King's Singers blend beautifully, with irreproachable intonation and, in the jollier songs, zest and well-honed diction — but without the coarseness that Bruno Turner once described as that of "pickled Bulgarian peasants". Tragicomedia put their polished versatility to telling effect, constantly varying both tone-colour and texture, and presenting some old wines in new instrumental bottles. These attributes, together with those of first-class recording quality and annotation, make this an indispensable addition to any collection.

ITALIAN RECORDER MUSIC. Amsterdam Loeki Stardust Quartet (Daniel Brüggen, Bertho Driever, Paul Leenhouts, Karel van Steenhoven, recs). L'Oiseau-Lyre 430 246-2OH. ***Battiferri:*** Ricercare secundo. ***Cima:*** Canzon la Capriccio. ***Conforti:*** Ricercar del quarto tono. ***Frescobaldi:*** Capriccio sopra la Spagnoletta. Canzon decima detta la Paulini. Ricercare terzo. Capriccio V sopra la Bassa Fiamenga. ***Guami:*** Canzons — La Bastina; La Brillantina; La Gentile. ***Merula:*** Canzons — La Ghirardella; La Merula. Dum Illuscescente Beati. Iste est Joannes. O Glorioso Domina. ***Palestrina:*** Lamentationes Hieremiae. ***Trabaci:*** Canto fermo primo del primo Tono. Canzona franzesa quinta sopra dunque credete ch'io. Canzona franzesa terza.

lh 2m DDD 2/92

None of the music in this programme was written for recorders but this is not important: it dates from a time when the boundaries between instrumental and vocal music were far less clear than they later became, and in which the music was very often more important than the identity of the instruments on which it was played. What mattered most was that the interwoven lines should be heard clearly and in proper balance. Italy was the Alma Mater of such music and it was also the country in which the recorder resisted the onslaught of the transverse flute for the longest. Few sounds are more depressing than that of an ensemble of mediocre recorder players, but few are more suited to presenting music of the above kind with the clarity and (thanks to the recording engineers) precise balance, and without a variety of tone-colours to seduce the ear in the direction of one line or another, than a recorder consort of the impeccable quality of the Amsterdam Loeki Stardust Quartet. For those who delight in hearing contrapuntal lines, mellifluously and ingeniously spun, this disc is custom-made.

THE HARP OF LUDOVICO. Andrew Lawrence-King (hpd). Hyperion CDA66518. ***A. Mudarra:*** Fantasia que contrahaze la harpa en la maniera de Ludovico. Divisions on Spagnoletta. ***L. Milan:*** El Maestro — Fantasia de consonancias y redobles. Divisions on the Spanish Pavan. ***D. Ortiz:*** Trattado de glosas — Fantasia; Divisions on Paradetas. Tutte le vecchie. ***G. de Macque:*** Prima stravaganza. Gagliarda prima. Toccata a modo di trombetta. ***O. Michi:*** Arie Spirituali — Su duro tronco; I diletti di mundo; Quel signor. ***Frescobaldi:*** Il primo libro di Toccate — Toccata quinta; Toccata Nona; Toccata Decima; Ciacona. Il secondo libro di Toccate — Arie detta Balletto; Arie detta la Frescobalda. ***Monteverdi:*** Vespro della Beata Vergine — Nigra sum.

lh llm DDD 6/92

The earliest harps had a single row of strings, tuned only to the notes of the prevailing key; today's harp also has one row of strings but their pitches can be varied chromatically by means of pedals. Before this happy state of affairs was reached the harp was made 'chromatic' during baroque times by having two (or even three) rows of strings, one for the white notes and the other for the black. The two rows of the Spanish *arpa doblada* crossed one another, whilst those of the Italian *arpa doppia* were parallel — which made life a lot easier for the player; in his recording Lawrence-King uses both types. Though the music he plays was not specifically written for it, the harp was a common and valid optional instrument — the 'wrong-note' Fantasia by Mudarra was written for the vihuela but in the style of Ludovico, a popular harpist of the time. It was also usual for players to improvise their own variations on grounds and dance-form pieces, and Lawrence-King exercises this licence with the greatest of skill and enthusiasm. Much of this music has no other recording — and none of it on the harp, and Lawrence-King plays it with rare sensitivity and conviction. In every respect this is a marvellous disc, with none of the barbiturate effect that some harp music can have. If you doze off before this one ends you should consult your doctor. Vivid, stimulating and highly recommended — you should treat yourself to it, even if it means pawning something you can live without.

NEW REVIEW

THE LUTE IN DANCE AND DREAM. Lutz Kirchhoff (lte). Sony Classical Vivarte SK48068.

Anonymous: Italiana. Galliarda. Passamezzo moderno. Sarabande. La Cardinalle. ***Milano:*** Fantasia di M. Francesco Milanese. ***Mudarra:*** Fantasia que contrahaze la harpa en la manera de Ludovico. ***R. Godard:*** Ce mois de May. ***Reis:*** Courante. ***Hassler:*** Canzon. ***Mertel:*** So wünsch ich ihr eine gute Nacht. ***Dowland:*** A dream, P75. The shoemaker's wife, A toy, P58. ***Ballard:*** Branles de village. ***Mouton:*** Menuet. Prelude. ***Dubut:*** Chaconne. ***D. Gaultier:*** Gigue. ***Durante:*** Carillon. ***E. Gaultier:*** Chaconne. ***Falkenhagen:*** Variations on "Wer nur den lieben Gott lässt walten". ***Weiss:*** Tombeau sur la mort de M. Comte de Logy. ***Kapsperger:*** Libro I d'intavolatura di lauto — Gagliarda la. Libro I d'intavolatura di chitarrone — Aria di Fiorenze; Corrente 2*a*.

1h DDD 11/92

This disc should be of particular interest to those who may excusably have formed the impression that the world of lute music is overly concerned with solemnity and academicism — and no less to those who have not. Kirchhoff, a strong and stylish player, has assembled a programme of European music for both the renaissance and baroque lutes — Mudarra's *Fantasia* was written for the vihuela, not the lute, but it suits the latter just as well and its uniqueness entitles it to an honorary 'boarding pass'. Dances were a staple of early instrumental music and there are plenty in this programme, albeit mostly of renaissance genres; Weiss's *Tombeau sur la mort de M. Comte de Logy* is in the form of an allemande. The programme lives up to the promise of its name: songs appear as intabulations or as the subject for variations. The 'dream' element is that of the composer's fancy, the 'abstract' fantasias and the like, and Dowland's miniature that lends its name to the album as a whole. The lute repertory represents a microcosmic overview of the music of its times, and this well chosen selection of it, played with sensitivity and vitality (and pristinely recorded), does it full justice.

VIHUELA MUSIC OF THE SPANISH RENAISSANCE. Christopher Wilson. Virgin Classics Veritas VC7 91136-2.

Milán: Libro de musica de vihuela de mano, "El Maestro", Book 1 — Fantasias I, VIII, XI and XII; Pavanas IV and VI. ***Narváez:*** Los seys libros del Delfin — Guardame las vacas (two versions); Milles regres; Fantasia; Baxa de contrapunto. ***Mudarra:*** Tres libros de música en cifra para vihuela — Romanesca: O guardame las vacas; Pavana de Alexandre; Gallarda; conde claros; Fantasia que contrahaze la harpa en la manera de Ludovico. ***Valderrábano:*** Silva de Sirenas — Fantasia; Soneto lombardo a manera de dança; Soneto. ***Fuenllana:*** Orphenica Lyra — Duo de Fuenllana; Tant que vivray; Fantasia de redobles; De Antequera sale el moro. ***López:*** Fantasia. ***Pisador:*** Libro de Musica de Vihuela — Dezilde al cavallero que; Madona mala vostra; Pavana muy llana para tañer. ***Mendoza:*** Diferencias de folías. ***Daza:*** El Parnasso — Quien te hizo Juan pastor; Fantasia. ***Anonymous sixteenth century:*** La morda.

59m DDD 4/91 9s

This generously filled disc reflects virtually the entire vihuela repertory from Luis Milán (1536) to the much less familiar Esteban Daza (1572). The vihuela is a member of the viol family but whose strings, typically arranged in six or seven courses, each paired in unison, are plucked rather than bowed. Christopher Wilson, better known to us as a lutenist, has chosen his programme well though the quality of the music is, almost inevitably, uneven. The most impressive pieces belong to the earliest of the composers represented here — Milán, Mudarra and Narváez. Between them they produced music rich in fantasy and varied both in colour and form. Wilson brings their compositions to life imaginatively, rhythmically and with a fluent technique that should win many friends. The recording itself is admirable, capturing the wide range of colours of which both instrument and performer are capable.

A VENETIAN CORONATION, 1595. Gabrieli [a]Consort and Players/Paul McCreesh. Virgin Classics Veritas VC7 59006-2. Texts and translations included.

G. Gabrieli: Intonazioni — ottavo tono; terzo e quarto toni; quinto tono alla quarta bassa (James O'Donnell, org solo). Canzonas — XIII a 12; XVI a 15; IX a 10. Sonata VI a 8 pian e forte. Deus qui beatum Marcum a 10[a]. Omnes gentes a 16[a]. ***A. Gabrieli***: Intonazioni — primo tono (O'Donnell); settimo tono (Timothy Roberts, org). Mass Movements[a] — Kyrie a 5-12; Gloria a 16; Sanctus a 12; Benedictus a 12. O sacrum convivium a 5[a]. Benedictus Dominus Deus sabbaoth (arr. Roberts. O'Donnell; Roberts). ***Bendinelli***: Sonata CCC-XXXIII. Sarasinetta. ***M. Thomsen***: Toccata I.

Ih IIm DDD 5/90 

The coronation of a new Doge of Venice was always a special occasion, and never more than when Marino Grimani (1532-1605) was elected to that office. We do not know what music was played then, but the whole ceremony is notionally and credibly reconstructed in this recording by Paul McCreesh and his cohorts. The recording was made in Brinkburn Priory, a church whose acoustic (aided by some deft manipulation of the recording controls) is spacious enough to evoke that of the Basilica of St Mark, the site of the original event. Space *per se* is vital to the music of the Gabrielis, who excelled in using it by placing instrumental and vocal groups in different parts of the building — which thereby became an integral part of the music. A fine selection of music that *could* have been played then is enhanced by the opening tolling of a bell, a crescendo marking the leisurely approach of the ducal procession, and the impression of architectural space created by changing stereo focus. It would be difficult to speak too highly of the performances, supplemented by first-class annotation, in this memorable recording. A trip to Venice would cost a lot more than this disc but, though you could visit the real St Mark's, it would not buy you this superb musical experience.

VENICE PRESERV'D. [a]Emma Kirkby, [b]Judith Nelson (sops); **[c]Nigel Rogers** (ten); **[d]Academy of Ancient Music/Christopher Hogwood** ([e]org). L'Oiseau-Lyre 425 891-2OH. Texts and translations included. From FS1007/08 (6/81).

A. Gabrieli: Intonatione del primo tono[e]. ***Cavalli:*** Canzon a 3[d]. ***Cima:*** Canzona, La Novella[d]. ***G. Gabrieli:*** Fuga del nono tono[e]. Intonatione del primo tono[e]. Sonata con tre violini[d]. ***Grandi:*** O intemerata (1621)[cd]. ***Legrenzi:*** Trio Sonata, Op. 4 No. 6, "La pezzoli"[d]. ***Marini:*** Sonata a tre, Op. 22[d]. ***Monteverdi:*** Exulta, filia Sion[abd]. Laudate Dominum[cd]. Salve, O regina[cd]. Salve regina (1640)[cd]. Sancta Maria, succurre miseris[abd]. ***Spiridion:*** Toccatina I[e].

52m ADD 8/91 

Monteverdi aside, early seventeenth-century Venetian music has been sadly neglected on CD. This recording was made over ten years ago using authentic instruments, and it is still one of the few commercially available sources for much of this fascinating repertoire. The performances stand up well; and the 15 short pieces are thoughtfully arranged so that vocal music contrasts with instrumental solos and chamber works, while a logical progression of keys and considered pacing between items gives a coherent flow to the disc as a whole. Nigel Rogers floats through his virtuoso solos with admirable agility and ease, while the voices of Emma Kirkby and Judith Nelson are sweet-toned and perfectly matched in their duets. Organ intonations by Andrea and Giovanni Gabrieli serve as introductions to the vocal pieces, and Christopher Hogwood gives them an appropriate improvisatory feel. There are some miniature gems for chamber ensemble by Cavalli, Marini and Legrenzi, whose sonatas paved the way for Corelli. The sound is well balanced — resonant and spacious to suggest the famous acoustic of St Mark's where virtually all of these composers worked. The only slight reservation is that at times the performances are just a touch too cool; but this is a fine disc and essential listening for anyone interested in this rewarding repertoire.

NEW REVIEW

VENETIAN VESPERS. Gabrieli Consort and Players/Paul McCreesh with **[a]Timothy Roberts** (org). Archiv Produktion 437 552-2AH2. Texts and translations included.

Sacristy bell. ***Gabrieli*** (ed. Roberts): Intonazione[a]. *Versicle and response:* Deus in adiutorium; Domine ad adiuvandum. ***Rigatti:*** Dixit Dominus. ***Grandi:*** O intemerata. *Antiphon:*Beata es Maria. ***Monteverdi:*** Laudate pueri. ***Banchieri:*** Suonata prima[a]. *Antiphon:* Beatam me dicent.

Monteverdi: Laetatus sum. ***Finetti:*** O Maria, quae rapis corda hominum. *Antiphon:* Haec est quae nescavit. ***Rigatti:*** Nisi Dominus. ***Banchieri:*** Dialogo secondo[a]. *Antiphon:* Ante thronum. ***Cavalli:*** Lauda Jerusalem. ***Grandi:*** O quam tu pulchra es. ***Anonymous:*** Praeambulum[a]. *Chapter:* Ecce virgo. ***Monteverdi:*** Deus qui mundum crimine iacentem. *Versicle and response.* Ave maria; Dominus tecum. *Antiphon.* Spiritus Sanctus. ***Rigatti:*** Magnificat. ***Marini:*** Sonata con tre violini in eco. *Collect:* Dominus vobiscum — Deus, qui de beatae Mariae. *Dismissal:* Dominus vobiscum — Benedicamus Domino. ***Monteverdi:*** Laudate Dominum. ***Fasolo*** (ed. Roberts): Intonazione — excerpts[a]. ***Rigatti:*** Salve regina.

② lh 36m DDD 4/93

Paul McCreesh's sense of adventure made quite an impact with his reconstruction of Doge Grimani's Coronation in 1595. This follow-up takes as its starting point a Vespers service "as it might have been celebrated in St Mark's, Venice 1643", and it is no less striking a speculation. McCreesh is wisely not attempting to re-create a historical event but to provide a rejuvenating context for some more wonderful Venetian church music. There can be little doubt that listening to psalm settings within a liturgical framework illuminates the theatricality and significance of the works in a unique way, barely possible in an ordinary format where one work simply follows another. Yet the quality of the music is what really counts and this is where McCreesh deserves the greatest praise. He has skilfully blended a range of diverse concerted works with equally innovative and expressive solo motets, each one offset by ornate organ interludes and home-spun plainchant. Monteverdi is well represented, as one would expect, but by introducing resident composers (who were regularly employed by the great basilica) a strong Venetian sensibility prevails in all these works despite the many contrasting styles of the new baroque age. The little-known Rigatti is arguably the sensation of this release with his highly dramatic and richly extravagant sonorities. The settings of *Dixit Dominus* and *Magnificat* are almost operatic at times though they maintain the spatial elements inspired by St Mark's. The Gabrieli Consort and Players are a group with an extraordinary homogeneity of sound and focused energy: Monteverdi's *Laetatus sum* is one of the many examples where they reach new heights in early seventeenth-century performance. The solo performances are deliciously executed too, particularly those involving the falsettists. The purity and control in Finetti's *O Maria, quae rapis* knows no bounds. This CD is an achievement of the very highest possible order.

LAMENTO D'ARIANNA. VARIOUS SETTINGS. **The Consort of Musicke/Anthony Rooley.** Deutsche Harmonia Mundi Editio Classica GD77115. Texts and translations included. From 1C 165 169504-3 (2/85).

Monteverdi: Lamento d'Arianna a voce sola. Lamento d'Arianna a 5. Pianto della Madonna voce sola. ***Bonini:*** Lamento d'Arianna in stile recitavo. ***Pari:*** Il lamento d'Arianna. ***Costa:*** Pianto d'Arianna a voce sola. ***Il Verso:*** Lasciatemi morire a 5. ***Roscarini:*** Reciproco amore a 3.

② lh 48m ADD 12/90 £

This is an historic recording and it recalls a moment of particular significance in the history of music. Monteverdi's *Arianna* first saw the light of day in Mantua in 1608. None of it survives except for Arianna's great dramatic lament after she has been abandoned by Teseo. The lament, which had apparently moved the Mantuan audience to tears, was central to the whole opera and it became extremely popular in its own right. Other composers imitated it and a new style of dramatic composition for solo voice was born as a result. In 1984 Anthony Rooley had the splendid idea of searching out some of these other seventeenth-century compositions and bringing them all together in a single programme. The two resulting LPs are now reissued as CDs and we can enjoy, first and foremost, Monteverdi's own original version, ably sung with profound understanding by Emma Kirkby, with accompaniment for chitarrone; and also the composer's well-known five-part madrigal using the same material (1614), as well as his much later (1640) reworking of this music, transformed into a somewhat sentimental meditation, for solo voice and organ, a religious lament placed in the mouth of the Madonna at the foot of the Cross. The five lesser-known compositions have each something new to offer: Bonini's dramatic setting may well come closest to the action of the original opera; Pari's contribution is a series of 12 madrigals analysing the successive emotions of the heroine. Costa's solo lament (Emma Kirkby again) is totally restrained and dignified. Antonio il Verso's madrigalian version, for all its extravagance, is clearly derived from Monteverdi's model. Roscarini, the latest of the six (1695), pushes extravagance to its limits. All of this is delightfully performed. This is a recording that throws much fascinating light on the way music changed course during the seventeenth century, but it is no less enjoyable for fulfilling such a useful purpose.

Choral and Song

NEW REVIEW

ARIE ANTICHE. Cecilia Bartoli (mez); **György Fischer** (pf). Decca 436 267-2DH. Texts and translations included.

A. Scarlatti: Già il sole dal Gange. Son tutta duolo. Se Florindo è fedele. O cessate di piagarmi. Spesso vibra per suo gioco. ***Giordani:*** Caro mio ben. ***Lotti:*** Pur dicesti, o bocca bella. ***Cesti:*** Intorno all'idol mio. ***Paisiello:*** Nel cor più non mi sento. Il mio ben quando verrà. Chi vuol la zingarella. ***Anonymous:*** O leggiadri occhi belli. ***Marcello:*** Quella fiamma che m'accende. ***Caldara:*** Selve amiche. Sebben, crudele. ***Caccini:*** Tu ch'hai le penne, amore. Amarilli. ***Parisotti:*** Se tu m'ami. ***Cavalli:*** Delizie contente. ***Vivaldi:*** Sposa son disprezzata. ***Carissimi:*** Vittoria, vittoria!

1h 6m DDD 12/92

With Scarlatti and Vivaldi among the composers, these *arie antiche* are not necessarily very old. Italian singers have long been accustomed to lumping together all songs earlier than Mozart (or perhaps Haydn) under this heading, piously including them at the start of a recital so as to establish a classical tone and give them time to try out their voices before entering on the more strenuous and popular part of their programme. Bartoli here devotes a whole disc to them, as things delightful in themselves, varied in mood and style, and calling in turn on almost all the essential arts of a good singer. No one can come away with a feeling of having been short-changed at the end of this. Her voice is ideal, both silken and chaste, finely controlled, cleanly produced. With a simple, direct song such as the famous *Caro mio ben* she will never fuss or show off; with Vivaldi's *Sposa son disprezzata* she exploits the most deliciously languishing tone and sometimes one more frankly passionate and 'operatic'. Most of the items are gems, and to all of them György Fischer brings the touch of the expert jeweller, knowing exactly how best to set off the beauties of voice and melody.

NEW REVIEW

BAROQUE DUET. Kathleen Battle (sop); **[a]Wynton Marsalis** (tpt); **St Luke's Orchestra/John Nelson.** Sony Classical SK46672. Texts and translations included.

Handel: Samson, HWV57 — Let the bright Seraphim. Ode for the birthday of Queen Anne, HWV74 — Eternal source of light divine. O come chiare e bella, HWV143 — Alle voci del bronzo guerriero. ***A. Scarlatti:*** Su le sponde del Tebro. Si suoni la tromba. Con voce festiva. Rompe sprezza con un sospir. Mio tesoro, per te moro. ***Bach:*** Cantata No. 21, Ich hatte viel Bekümmernis — Seufzer, Tränen, Kummer, Not. Cantata No. 51, Jauchzet Gott in allen Landen! — Jauchzet Gott; Sei Lob und Preis. ***Predieri:*** ZENOBIA — Pace una volta. ***Stradella:*** Sinfonia alla Serenata Il barcheggio — Part One[a].

1h 5m DDD 8/92

Here is music of some splendour performed with skill, enthusiasm and panache. Kathleen Battle's agile and elegant soprano is paired with dazzling playing from Wynton Marsalis, a trumpeter of remarkable gifts as one hears at once in the opening number, Handel's "Let the bright Seraphim". Whether Handel would have recognized this instrument and performance as corresponding to what he intended is more debatable, for nobility is sacrificed to brilliance and, for some ears, the trumpet's skating up to a high E (at 4'27") will jar stylistically. But however one feels about the taste of this playing, its skill is undeniable and many listeners will find it exhilarating and infectious even though for others it might be over the top. The rest of the programme provides some contrast, and not all the music is loud and fast. But much of it is, and the recording matches the briskness and slight brashness of the two soloists in being sharp-edged and very stimulating. Most of the pieces here were written for an audience that obviously wanted to be astonished — as we are now — but there is music too that is touchingly lyrical. The whole effect is American, and 1990s American at that, rather than richly and seriously rounded in the way that we may think appropriate to European music from this period. All is efficient and glitteringly gold-plated, even if at times we may wish that there had been less 'glister' and more of the quiet lustre of real gold. The presentation of the disc is of a piece with the rest, with playful, slightly twee photos of the two soloists, and although the booklet with its essay in four languages, texts and translations meet scholarly requirements, the packaging is awkward, with the jewel-case and thick booklet of over 50 pages being placed together in a sleeve from which they do not easily emerge. An overwhelming *tour de force* then but not, perhaps, to be listened to all at once.

CABARET CLASSICS. Jill Gomez (sop); **John Constable** (pf). Unicorn-Kanchana DKPCD9055. Texts and translations included.
Weill: Marie Galante — Les filles de Bordeaux; Le grand Lustucru; Le Roi d'Aquitaine; J'attends un navire. Lady in the Dark — My ship. Street Scene — Lonely house. Knickerbocker Holiday — It never was you. ***Zemlinsky:*** Songs, Op. 27 — Harlem Tänzerin; Elend; Afrikanischer Tanz. ***Schoenberg:*** Arie aus dem Spiegel von Arcadien. Gigerlette. Der genügsame Liebhaber. Mahnung. ***Satie:*** La diva de l'Empire. Allons-y, Chochotte. Je te veux.

57m DDD 6/88

Schoenberg writing cabaret songs with a popular touch? Yes, and quite catchy ones too, as can be heard particularly in *Gigerlette* — prompting the intriguing speculation of what might have been had he not concentrated on *Gurrelieder*. On the other hand, his *Der genügsame Liebhaber* and Zemlinsky's three songs would have been most unlikely to go down with cabaret audiences, however intellectual. At the other end of the spectrum are Satie's café-concert songs (the sentimental waltz *Je te veux* is languidly attractive) and the Weill items, which were not written for cabaret but are drawn from a 1934 Paris play and post-war Broadway musicals. That all these songs do not require a gin-sodden voice or raucous delivery is demonstrated with the utmost artistry by Jill Gomez, in turn seductive, pathetic, sly, sweet, swaggering, passionate, salacious — or simply singing beautifully. Her performance of Weill's *Lonely house* (one of his best) remains hauntingly in the mind.

CANTICLES FROM ELY. Ely Cathedral Choir/Paul Trepte with **Jeremy Filsell** (org). Gamut Classics GAMCD527.
Bairstow: The Lamentation. ***F. Jackson:*** Benedicite in G major. ***Noble:*** Magnificat in A minor. ***Stanford:*** Morning Services — A major, Op. 12; C major, Op. 115. Evening Service in B flat major.

52m DDD 2/92

For Matins the *Te Deum*, with *Benedicite* or *Jubilate* for a somewhat rare change, for Evensong *Magnificat* and *Nunc Dimittis*: these were the canticles sung or recited at Church of England services throughout the centuries, and in most cathedrals they are so still. Setting them to music has also been a preoccupation of British composers through the ages. In late Victorian times and the early part of the twentieth century it was almost a national industry, with Sir Charles Villiers Stanford as its High Master. He wrote ten services altogether, the one in B flat being the most popular, that in C probably the most admired among musicians. A notable feature in their time was the independence of the organ parts, but to modern listeners it is the richness of sound, the unfailing tunefulness and the sure professionalism of craftsmanship that are likely to be most striking. The Morning Service in A, written in 1880, is also remarkable for boldness of invention with some fine modulations and a particularly inspired breadth at the end of the *Jubilate*. In between the three Stanford services heard here come others by three organists of York Minster: Tertius Noble (represented by a less well-known and on the whole less successful setting than his B minor service), Sir Edward Bairstow, and Francis Jackson (a colourful, and in this company distinctly modern, setting of the *Benedicite*). The *Lamentations* of Jeremiah are designed for alternative use in Lent but, while Bairstow's music is resourceful, it is probably not sufficiently so to justify the length of the piece on musical grounds alone. The Choir of Ely Cathedral sing with fine tone and precision, the organ accompaniments are distinguished by imaginative registration and a strong rhythmic sense, and the disc is well produced.

CHORAL WORKS. [a]**Michael Pearce,** [c]**Leo Hussain** (trebs); [a]**Peter Winn** (alto); [b]**Ameral Gunson** (mez); [a]**John Bowley,** [c]**Simon Williams** (tens); [a]**Daniel Sladden** (bass) [a]**Rachel Masters** (hp); [ac]**David Corkhill;** [c]**Michael Skinner,** [c]**Stephen Whittaker,** [c]**Nigel Bates** (perc); **Choir of King's College, Cambridge/Stephen Cleobury** with [ac]**Peter Barley** (org). EMI CDC7 54188-2. Texts and translation included.

Bernstein: Chichester Psalms[a]. ***Copland:*** In the Beginning[b]. ***Ives:*** Psalm 90[c]. ***Larsen:*** How it thrills us. ***Schuman:*** Carols of Death.

1h DDD 10/91 

Bernstein's familiar *Chichester Psalms* were composed to a commission from our own Southern Cathedrals Festival in 1965 and this unusual programme gives us a chance to place them in the context of the English choral tradition. There are some problems of co-ordination in the resonant cavern of King's College Chapel, but it is fascinating to hear again the reduced scoring for organ, harp and percussion. In his cruelly exposed solo, young Michael Pearce has nothing to fear from his rivals. The rest of this accessible all-American collection is no less appealing. Copland's *In the Beginning* is one of his best pieces, and William Schuman's Holstian *Carols* suit the King's acoustic and performance style particularly well. Libby Larsen wrote *How it thrills us* specifically for King's. Only in Ives's extraordinary *Psalm 90* is there perhaps some lack of transcendental magic — that English reserve again? EMI provide unusual, provocative notes from David Nichols and full texts.

NEW REVIEW

THE CHRISTMAS ALBUM. FESTIVE MUSIC FROM EUROPE AND AMERICA. **Taverner Consort, Choir and Players/Andrew Parrott.** EMI Reflexe CD46672. Texts and translations included.

Billings: Methinks I see an heaven'ly host. A virgin unspotted. ***J. Foster:*** While shepherds watched their flocks. ***Cererols:*** Serafin, que con dulce harmonia. ***Vidales:*** Los que fueren de buen gusto. ***M. Praetorius:*** Magnificat super "Angeles ad pastores". ***Charpentier:*** In nativitatem Domini Nostri Jesu Christi canticum, H414. ***Pascha:*** Christmas Mass — Gloria. Arr. ***Greatorex:*** Adestes, fideles.

1h 3m DDD 12/92 

Here is a Christmas record for all the year round. It also takes a good round trip to countries far and near, beginning and ending in New England, where William Billings, a one-legged, one-eyed tanner and "arguably the first American composer with a truly individual voice", provides carols of spirited simplicity and uninhibited gusto. Also from the New World comes a religious pop-song, a *jàcara*, from 1702 performed originally by the nuns of the convent at Pueblo, a charming poem set to a catchy tune with syncopations and knocks on the guitar. Europe, after that, seems a little tame. Lower Saxony offers a *Magnificat* on the carol *Angelus ad pastores* by Praetorius, based on a motet by Lassus, France a courtly musical shepherds-play by Charpentier, and Slovakia a kind of miniature Christmas oratorio, with shepherd-pipes and alphorn. The English contribution comprises early versions of *While shepherds watched their flocks* in Haydnesque scoring by John Foster of Sheffield, and *Adeste, fideles* as it was heard in London in the spring of 1797. Most delightful, perhaps, is the piece from Catalonia, gracefully sung by Emily Van Ethera and Timothy Wilson. Andrew Parrott's singers and players give pleasure throughout, and the disc owes much to the work of Clifford Bartlett as musical editor and writer of the informative notes.

CHRISTMAS MUSIC. [bd]**Gavin Williams** (org); [a]**Pro Arte Orchestra,** [b]**Guildford Cathedral Choir/Barry Rose;** [c]**Light Music Orchestra/Sir Vivian Dunn.** EMI Classics CDM7 64131-2. From CSD3580.

Hely-Hutchinson: Carol Symphony[a]. ***Vaughan Williams:*** Fantasia on Christmas Carols[bd] (John Barrow, bar). ***Warlock:*** Bethlehem Down[b] (words Blunt); Adam lay y-bounden[bd] (Robert Hammersley, ten). ***Quilter:*** Children's Overture, Op. 17[c]. ***E. Tomlinson:*** Suite of English Folk Dances[c]. And all in the morning[bd] (trad. Derbyshire arr. Vaughan Williams). Wassail Song[bd] (trad. Yorkshire arr. Vaughan Williams with Clifford Mould, ten).

1h 12m ADD 12/91

Few people in the musical world can point to such success as Barry Rose who, appointed as Guildford Cathedral's first choirmaster, built up (literally from nothing) a choir which was generally considered the best of its day. It is a testament to the quality of his choir that many of the records it made in the 1960s have now been reissued on CD. The sensitivity of Rose's direction and the musical commitment he inspires from his choristers is most obvious in four unusual Christmas carols. Peter Warlock's have a depth and sincerity one doesn't usually associate with this genre while the innocent beauty of two traditional carols is perfectly captured in a recording which doesn't begin to show its age. Vaughan Williams's *Fantasia* is altogether better known, but here again this performance is imbued with a rare feeling for the essential spirit of the music and the poetry of the words. The real gem on this disc, though, is the remarkably vivid account of Hely-Hutchinson's ingenious *Carol Symphony*, an orchestral suite based on several well-known carols. Again Rose directs an outstanding performance which underlines magnificently the inventiveness and near-genius of Hely-Hutchinson's music. The disc is rounded off with two justly popular examples of British light orchestral music at its best.

DRAW ON SWEET NIGHT. Hilliard Ensemble/Paul Hillier. EMI Reflexe CDC7 49197-2. Texts included.
Morley: O greefe even on the bud. When loe, by breake of morning. Aprill is in my mistris face. Sweet nimphe, come to thy lover. Miraculous love's wounding. Fyer and lightning. In nets of golden wyers. ***Weelkes:*** Thule, the period of cosmographie. O care thou wilt dispatch mee. Since Robin Hood. Strike it up tabor. ***Wilbye:*** Sweet hony sucking bees. Adew, sweet Amarillis. Draw on sweet night. ***J. Bennet:*** Weepe O mine eyes. ***Gibbons:*** The silver swanne. ***Tomkins:*** See, see, the shepheard's Queene. ***Ward:*** Come sable night. ***Vautor:*** Sweet Suffolke owle.

55m DDD 2/89

This refreshingly attractive and well-presented anthology of English madrigals promises to be a delight for the specialist and non-specialist alike. The programme is nicely balanced: the more richly textured, *Sweet hony sucking bees*, are interspersed with a number of the little two- and three-part Morley canzonets, either charmingly phrased and dovetailed by two well-matched sopranos (*Sweet nimphe, come to thy lover*), or sung with boundless energy by two tenors, or two tenors and a bass (the tautly drummed *Strike it up tabor*). The order in which the pieces occur is planned to reflect the changing moods of a single day and variety of mood and emotion is perhaps the chief characteristic of this choice collection. Another unusual feature is the adoption of what is claimed to have been Elizabethan pronunciation of English. This gives the sound of the music a rather special flavour, with the style, the tuning, the lively diction and the wit all contributing to the general excellence and immediacy of this performance.

NEW REVIEW
ENGLISH CHURCH MUSIC, Volume 1. **Queen's College Choir, Oxford/Matthew Owens** with **[a]David Went** (org). ASV CDDCA851. Texts included.
Howells: Chichester Service[a]. A Hymn for St Cecilia[a]. Salve regina. O salutaris hostia. My eyes for beauty pine[a]. Like as the hart[a]. ***Leighton.*** Second Service, Op. 62[a]. Give me wings of faith[a]. O sacrum convivium. Solus ad victimam[a]. Crucifixus pro nobis, Op. 38[a].

1h 14m DDD 5/93

Herbert Howells was at Queen's College, Oxford, in 1916, and Kenneth Leighton read Classics there in 1947, so it is appropriate that they should be brought together by their college choir. A quality they had in common was their sure instinct for choral sound, and at the take-over point in this recital (the opening of Leighton's *Second Evening Service*) the succession is felt to be a very close and natural one. Both are well represented. A lot of Howells's choral work has been recorded recently, but the selection here overlaps very little with other desirable records: *Like as the hart* is the principal exception, and as this is a particularly lovely performance the duplication is easily justified. The Chichester Service has its first recording: a fine work, rising in characteristic ecstasy. Leighton's Service is also impressive, the *Magnificat*'s "Gloria" swaying slowly, while that of the *Nunc Dimittis* ends in subdued fashion, beautiful in its quietness. The other major work, the *Crucifixus pro nobis*, is probably better served by a tenor soloist, but this is a fine, urgent performance with excellent work by the choir, as indeed there is throughout the recital.

FRENCH SONGS AND DUETS. [a]**Ann Murray** (mez); [b]**Philip Langridge** (ten); **Roger Vignoles** (pf). Virgin Classics VC7 91179-2. Texts and translations included.
Chausson: La caravane, Op. 14[b]. Sept mélodies, Op. 2 — No. 3, Les papillons[a]; No. 5, Sérénade italienne[b]; No. 7, Le colibri[a]. Two duos, Op. 11 — No. 2, Le réveil. ***Fauré:*** Arpège, Op. 76 No. 2[b]. Pleurs d'or, Op. 72. Puisqu'ici bas, Op. 10 No. 1. Soir, Op. 83 No. 2[a]. ***Gounod:*** Barcarola. Boire à l'ombre[b]. Ce que je suis sans toi[a]. Le premier jour de mai[a]. Sérénade[b]. ***Messiaen:*** La mort du nombre (with Andrew Watkinson, vn). ***Saint-Saëns:*** Aimons-nous[b]. L'attente[a]. La cloche[a]. Danse macabre. Viens!

1h 7m DDD 6/91

This enterprising collection includes some little-known works, thanks for their rescue being due to this intelligent husband-and-wife team, backed by an excellent and sympathetic pianist. Chausson's sombre *La caravane*, for example (admirably sung by Langridge), can fairly be called an unjustly neglected masterpiece. The most substantial work here, of particular interest in view of the composer's later development, is the 22-year-old Messiaen's *La mort du nombre*, a dialogue between a soul in purgatory and his beloved who has attained spiritual peace: it calls forth feelings of intense torment by Langridge and rapt serenity from Murray, with a first-class contribution from Vignoles (plus a small but significant violin obbligato). Fauré's warmly sensuous *Pleurs d'or* is perhaps the most outstanding other duet here, but there is charm, also, in Gounod's *Barcarola* (sung in the French translation of the Italian original) and satiric humour in Saint-Saëns's *Danse macabre* (later expanded into the popular symphonic poem). In the solos, *La cloche* (with Murray at her best) belies its composer's reputation for only superficial facility, and Langridge shows a striking range from the easy lyricism of Gounod's *Sérénade* to the passion of Saint-Saëns's *Aimons-nous*.

GERMAN CHURCH MUSIC. Exon Singers/Christopher Tolley. Priory PRCD243.
H.L. Hassler: Motets — Deus noster refugium; Verbum caro factum est; O admirabile commercium; Cantate Domino Jubilate Deo; O Domine Jesu Christe; O sacrum convivium. ***Bruckner:*** Tantum ergo in A flat major. ***Liszt:*** O salutaris hostia, S43. ***Cornelius:*** Three Choral Songs, Op. 18.

53m DDD 7/89

The Exon Singers began as a group of students from Exeter University who gathered during vacations to sing the services in various cathedrals. Here they explore an unjustifiably neglected area of the repertoire. Hassler studied with Gabrieli in Venice and became a master of the Venetian Polyphonic style. The motet, "O admirabile commercium", is one of his best examples, bearing comparison with anything by Palestrina. Bruckner was a devout Catholic and composed some of his most personal and deeply-felt music for liturgical use. This is one of no less than eight settings he made of the *Tantum ergo* and its simple, direct style will come as a surprise to those who know Bruckner only through the symphonies. Peter Cornelius's songs for unaccompanied eight part choir are richly colourful and the Exon Singers produce some sumptuous singing here. Christopher Tolley is a thorough and sympathetic musician who inspires his singers to some magnificent performances. Their beautifully blended and perfectly balanced tone, caught in a splendidly warm and full-bodied recording, is a model of unaccompanied choral singing. This is a disc to treasure.

GERMAN SONGS BY AMERICAN COMPOSERS. Thomas Hampson (bar); **Armen Guzelimian** (pf). Teldec 9031-72168-2. Notes, texts and translations included.
Griffes: Am Kreuzweg wird begraben. An den Wind. Auf geheimem Waldespfade. Auf ihrem Grab. Das ist ein Brausen und Heulen. Das sterbende Kind. Elfe. Meeres Stille. Mein Herz ist wie die dunkle Nacht. Mit schwarzen Segeln. Des Müden Abendlied. Nachtlied. So halt' ich endlich dich umfangen. Der träumende See. Wo ich bin, mich rings umdunkelt. Wohl lag ich einst in Gram und Schmerz. Zwei Könige sassen auf Orkadal. ***Ives:*** Du bist wie eine Blume. Feldeinsamkeit. Frühlingslied. Gruss. Ich grolle nicht. Ilmenau. Marie. Minnelied. Rosamunde. Rosenzweige. Ton. Weil' auf mir. Widmung. Wiegenlied. ***MacDowell:*** Drei Lieder, Op. 11. Zwei Leider, Op. 12.

1h 12m DDD 4/92 

This is a most rewarding American collection which will appeal to lovers of Lieder who can trace some of the same poems, mostly by Heine, set by German composers. Followers of American music will also be intrigued by the early works of Ives, MacDowell and Griffes which, in performances like these, come close to the impact of their German models. It is particularly fascinating to see what Ives does with these romantic poems made famous by the great Lieder composers. He originally set them in German, when he was a student at Yale, and then adapted them to various English texts of a quite different purport. Familiar Ives songs such as *The World's Wanderers* (Shelley) and *I travelled among unknown Men* (Wordsworth) started life as settings of Heine. Ives's ravishing *Wiegenlied* started life in partnership with a poem from *Des Knaben Wunderhorn*. Then, compare his *Ich grolle nicht* with Schumann and no apologies need to be made. These unexpected and little-known connections between the old and the new worlds provide endless richness and the same goes for the MacDowell and the Griffes, if not to quite the same extent. MacDowell, with his gift for miniatures, is adept both at near-salon melody and eloquent piano parts. These may not be the best songs of Griffes, or even the other two composers, but since they were all under 30 at the time and the songs get such revelatory performances from the distinguished team of Thomas Hampson and Armen Guzelimian, it hardly matters. Well recorded too.

HAIL, GLADDENING LIGHT. Cambridge Singers/John Rutter. Collegium COLCD113. Texts and translations included.
Anonymous: Rejoice in the Lord. ***Purcell:*** Remember not, Lord, our offences, Z50. ***J. Amner:*** Come, let's rejoice. ***Tomkins:*** When David heard. ***Bairstow:*** I sat down under his shadow. ***J. Goss:*** These are they that follow the lamb. ***Taverner:*** Christe Jesu, pastor bone. ***Philips:*** O beatum et sacrosanctum diem. ***Howells:*** Nunc dimittis. ***Vaughan Williams:*** O vos omnes. ***Dering:*** Factum est silentium. ***Stanford:*** Justorum animae, Op. 38 No. 1. ***C. Wood:*** Hail, gladdening light. ***Tavener:*** A hymn to the mother of God. Hymn for the dormition of the mother of God. ***Elgar:*** They are at rest. ***Walton:*** A litany. ***Morley:*** Nolo mortem peccatoris. ***Tallis*** O nata lux. ***Rutter:*** Loving shepherd of Thy sheep. ***R. Stone:*** The Lord's Prayer. ***J. Sheppard:*** In manus tuas. ***W.H. Harris:*** Bring us, O Lord God.

1h 12m DDD 4/92

This has the subtitle "Music of the English Church" and it is arranged under four main headings: anthems and introits (these count as one), Latin motets, settings of hymns and other poetry, and prayer-settings. Each of them is well represented in a programme that varies delightfully in period and style, and in performances which are remarkably consistent in quality. Some of the items will come as discoveries to most listeners: for example, the anthem *Come, let's rejoice*, a splendid, madrigal-like piece written by John Amner, organist from 1610 to 1641 at Ely Cathedral where these recordings were made. Others are equally impressive in their present performance: a deep quietness attends the opening of Richard Dering's *Factum est silentium*, which ends with rhythmic Alleluias set dancing with subdued excitement. Among the hymn-settings is one by a 16-year-old called William Walton. Included in the prayers is the choirmaster's own setting, characteristically made for pleasure, of *Loving shepherd of Thy sheep*. All are unaccompanied, and thus very exactingly test the choir's blend of voices, its precision, articulation and feeling for rhythm. In all respects they do exceptionally well; the tone is fresh, the attack unanimous, the expression clear and sensitive, the rhythm on its toes. These are young and gifted singers, formed with disciplined enthusiasm into a choir with a distinctive style — and, incidentally, recorded with admirable results by a family firm which operates from a studio built at the bottom of the garden.

HEAR MY PRAYER. [a]**Jeremy Budd** (treb); **St Paul's Cathedral Choir/John Scott** with [b]**Andrew Lucas** (org). Hyperion CDA66439. Texts and translations included.
Allegri: Miserere (with Nicholas Thompson, treb; Wilfred Swansborough, alto; Timothy Jones, bass)[a]. ***B. Rose:*** Feast Song for St Cecilia (Simon Hill, alto; Alan Green, ten)[a]. ***Brahms:*** Ein deutsches Requiem — Ich hab nun Traurigkeit (sung in English)[ab]. ***Britten:*** Festival Te Deum, Op. 32[ab]. ***Harvey:*** Come, Holy Ghost (Andrew Burden, ten; Nigel Beaven, bass)[a]. ***Mendelssohn:*** Hear my prayer[ab]. ***Stanford:*** Evening Canticles in G major (Jones)[ab]. ***Tavener:*** I will lift up mine eyes. ***Wise:*** The ways of Zion do mourn (Charles Gibbs, bass)[ab].

1h 16m DDD 10/91

The special distinction of this disc is the work of the treble soloist, Jeremy Budd. He sings in a programme which is very much the choirboy's equivalent of an operatic soprano's "Casta diva" and more of that sort (come to think of it, Master Budd could probably have sung a splendid "Casta diva" into the bargain). As it is, he crowns the Allegri *Miserere* with its five top Cs, spot-on, each of them (rather like Melba singing "Amor" at the end of Act 1 in *La bohème* five times over). He commands the breath, the long line and the purity of tone needful for the solo in Brahms's Requiem. He follows in the Ernest Lough tradition in Mendelssohn (who, with his 78rpm recording of *Hear my prayer*, now transferred to CD — EMI CDH7 63827-2 — became one of the most famous singers in the world) and copes with the difficult modern idiom of Jonathan Harvey's *Come, Holy Ghost* with an apparent ease that to an older generation may well seem uncanny. Other modern works are included. John Tavener's *I will lift up mine eyes*, written for St Paul's in 1990, has its characteristic compound of richness and austerity; and in this, the words penetrate the mist of echoes more successfully than do those of the *Feast Song for St Cecilia*, written by Gregory Rose and set to some very beautiful music by his father Bernard. It is good, as ever, to hear Stanford's Evening Service in G, with its almost Fauré-like accompaniment finely played by the excellent Andrew Lucas; and for a morning canticle there is Britten's *Te Deum* with its effective build-up to "Lord God of Sabaoth" and its faint pre-echo of *The Turn of the Screw* at "O Lord, save Thy people". There is also a melancholy anthem by Michael Wise, whose fate it was to be knocked on the head and killed by the watchman to whom he was cheeky one night in 1687.

INTERMEDIOS DEL BARROCO HISPANICO. [a]**Montserrat Figueras** (sop); **Hespèrion XX/Jordi Savall** (va da gamba). Astrée Auvidis E8729.
M. Romero: Caiase de un espino[a]. ***Aguilera de Héredia:*** Tiento de Batalla. Ensalada. ***Lope de Vega/Anonymous:*** De pechos sobre una torre[a]. Como retumban los remos[a]. ***F. Guerrero:*** Si tus penas[a]. ***J. Cabanilles:*** Pasacalles V. Tiento lleno. Corrente italiana. ***J.K. Kerll:*** Batalla Imperial. ***M. Machado:*** Afuera, afuera que sale[a]. ***Correa de Arauxo:*** Batalla des Morales. ***J. Blas de Castro:*** Desde las torres del alma[a]. Entre dos Alamos verdes[a]. ***J. Marin:*** Ojos, que me desdenais[a]. ***Anonymous:*** No hay que decirle el primor[a].

1h 11m DDD 2/92

A heady Hispanic baroque cocktail. All the vocal numbers here are settings of texts by the colourful and astonishingly prolific Spanish poet and dramatist Lope de Vega (1562-1635), described by Cervantes as "a monster of nature". They range from blithe, folkish pieces through the powerful *De pechos sobre una torre*, in whch a woman laments her lover who has sailed for England with the Armada, to Guerrero's haunting prayer to Jesus, declaimed over a bare string bass and culminating in an extraordinary spoken climax. The instrumental items interspersed with the vocal settings include several rousing battle pieces — a popular seventeenth-century genre — and, for contrast, three beautiful polyphonic numbers by one of the greatest figures of the Spanish Baroque, Joan Cabanilles. If Jordi Savall has touched up the scoring of some of the pieces, no matter: the performances are exciting, sensual, dramatic, with kaleidoscopically varied instrumental colouring, from the entertaining percussion effects of Machado's *Afuera, afuera que sale* to the grave viol consort of Cabanilles's *Pasacalles V* (strong Purcellian associations here). And Savall's wife, Montserrat Figueras, with her distinctive, plangent tone, makes a subtle, stylish, richly imaginative soloist. An irresistible disc, and an ideal introduction to the largely unexplored treasures of the Spanish Baroque.

LIEDER RECITAL. Dame Janet Baker (mez); **Martin Isepp** (pf). Saga Classics SCD9001. Texts and translation included. From STXID5277 (4/66).
Schumann: Frauenliebe und -leben, Op. 42. ***Brahms:*** Die Mainacht, Op. 43 No. 2. Das Mädchen spricht, Op. 107 No. 3. Nachtigall, Op. 97 No. 1. Von ewiger Liebe, Op. 43 No. 1. ***Schubert:*** Heimliches Lieben, D922. Minnelied, D429. Die abgeblühte Linde, D514. Der Musensohn, D764.

47m AAD 3/92 £

AN ANTHOLOGY OF ENGLISH SONG. Dame Janet Baker (mez) **Martin Isepp** (pf). Saga Classics SCD9012. From STXID5213 (8/66).
Vaughan Williams: Five mystical songs — The call. Songs of travel — Youth and love. ***Ireland:*** A Thanksgiving. Her song. ***Head:*** A piper. ***Armstrong-Gibbs:*** This is a sacred city. Love is a sickness. ***Dunhill:*** The cloths of heaven. To the Queen of heaven. ***Warlock:*** Balulalow. Youth. ***Howells:*** King David. Come, sing and dance. ***Gurney:*** Sleep. I will go with my father a-ploughing. ***Finzi:*** Let us garlands bring, Op. 18 — Come away, death; It was a lover and his lass.

45m AAD 3/92 

These recordings were rapturously reviewed in *Gramophone* when they first appeared, and there was no doubt that a singer of great achievement and still greater promise had arrived in our midst. Over the next many years, the name of Janet Baker (Dame-to-be) graced the monthly lists of new recordings and unfailingly brought distinction with it. Her interpretative powers were to mature, and she was certainly to be better recorded, but it is quite likely that nothing brought greater pleasure in the sheer sound of the voice than these early recitals, one of English song, one of Lieder. Her *Frauenliebe und -leben* here has the mark of a great interpreter upon it particularly in the song of happy motherhood, "An meinem Herzen"; but earlier, the conviction of her singing irradiates the performance, and in the last song the fine dark tone and change of expression on the 'face' of the voice are both eloquent and moving. In the Schubert group, her *Musensohn* has a joyous unselfconsciousness, and in the Brahms her *Von ewiger Liebe* still ranks among the finest of all. The selection of English songs is a joy in itself, with Howells's *King David* and *Come, sing and dance* as perhaps the most memorable of all. And nothing could be lovelier than Finzi's setting of *Come away, death* or this performance of it. Some listeners may be deterred by the level of tape-hiss; regrettable too are the short playing times of both discs and the failure of the presenters to give the dates of the original recordings. These are small matters, however, and there is nothing small about such singing.

LIEDER AND SONG RECITAL. Peter Schreier (ten); **Wolfgang Sawallisch** (pf). Philips 426 237-2PH. Texts and translations included. Recorded at a performance in Munich on 6th February 1984.
Brahms: Deutsche Volkslieder — No. 1, Sagt mire, o schönste Schäf'rin; No. 4, Guten Abend, mein tausiger Schatz; No. 15, Schwesterlein, Schwesterlein; No. 34, Wie komm'ich denn zur Tür herein? Wiegenlied, Op. 49 No. 4. ***Prokofiev:*** Three Children's Songs, Op. 68. The Ugly Duckling, Op. 18 (all sung in German). ***Schumann:*** Dichterliebe, Op. 48. Der Nussbaum, Op. 25 No. 3.

lh 12m DDD 4/90

This live recital caught Schreier and his pianist, Sawallisch, at the top of their form as a partnership. Their account of *Dichterliebe* encompasses every facet of the cycle, holding the attention from start to finish through the intensity of its utterance and flights of imagination. The grief, so poetically and movingly expressed by Heine and Schumann, is here delineated with raw immediacy yet no sense of exaggeration. The troubled, abandoned lover sings, in Schreier's plangent tones, with a poignant, tearful feeling that goes to the heart of things and Sawallisch's playing is fully supportive of the tenor's reading. As compared with Bär (refer to the Index to Reviews), Schreier sings in the original keys throughout: his is a more overtly emotional reading, but both deserve recommendation. In the Brahms, Schreier and Sawallisch rightly adopt a lighter, yet equally pointed style. The Prokofiev group shows Schreier equally adept in a very different idiom. Here, instead of attempting phonetic Russian, he very sensibly uses his own German translations and thus makes the most of the text. The audience noises, applause apart, are minimal and the recording conveys the sense of a real occasion.

MASTERS OF TWENTIETH CENTURY A CAPPELLA. [a]**Susse Lillesoe** (sop); [b]**Karl-Gustav Andersson** (ten); **Danish National Radio Chamber Choir/Stefan Parkman.** Chandos CHAN8963. Texts and translations included.
I. Lidholm: ... a riveder le stelle (1971-73)[a]. ***Henze:*** Orpheus behind the wire (1981-83)[b]. ***Schoenberg:*** Friede auf Erden, Op. 13. ***Nørgård:*** Wie ein Kind (1979-80). ***Poulenc:*** Figure humaine (1943).

1h 17m DDD 12/91 

This is one of the most impressive displays of unaccompanied choral singing you are likely to hear for a very long time. The Danish National Radio Chamber Choir have mastered the fiendish technical demands of these pieces with breathtaking success. Schoenberg's *Friede auf Erden* was considered so difficult that in 1911 the composer was obliged to add an accompaniment for it, but here it is sung in its original version with total authority, while the awesome technical obstacles thrown up by the other composers (sliding tonality from Ingvar Lidholm, distorted vocalizations from Per Nørgård, dense chromatic harmonies from Henze) are overcome with an ease which seems almost condescending. It is the emphasis placed on the musical and emotional aspects of the pieces that is the most impressive quality in Stefan Parkman's direction. It would be easy to leave the listener aghast at the sheer virtuosity of it all, but Parkman has gone beyond that and shows, by means of meticulously prepared performances just what truly beautiful music there is to be found in these uncompromising twentieth-century scores. For the uninitiated, 77 minutes of modern unaccompanied choral music might seem rather an over-indulgence, but few could fail to be captivated by Per Nørgård's delightful setting of nonsense verses, while the emotional power of Poulenc's *Figure humaine* (written during the Nazi occupation of France this became something of an unofficial anthem for the Resistance organization) culminating in the wonderfully hypnotic *Liberté* is beyond adequate description especially given such a powerfully committed performance as this one.

MELODIES SUR DES POEMES DE BAUDELAIRE. Felicity Lott (sop); **Graham Johnson** (pf). Harmonia Mundi Musique d'abord HMA90 1219. Texts included.
Duparc: L'invitation au voyage. La vie antérieure. ***Fauré:*** Chant d'automne. La rançon. Hymne. ***Bréville:*** Harmonie du soir. ***Sauguet:*** Le chat. ***Capdevielle:*** Je n'ai pas oublié, voisine de la ville. ***Chabrier:*** L'invitation au voyage. ***Debussy:*** La balcon. Harmonie du soir. Le jet d'eau. Recueillement. La mort des amants. ***Séverac:*** Les hiboux.

1h 5m DDD 4/88 

This is an outstandingly creative and ingenious piece of programme-planning. The recital begins with Duparc's two masterly Baudelaire songs, demonstrating that with the right temperament and approach the writer is by no means unsettable. The Fauré, Chabrier and Debussy settings are in a sense uncharacteristic. In another sense, though, how very characteristic of Fauré that the most successful of his three songs (the charming *Hymne*) should set a poem that is hardly characteristic of Baudelaire, and how thoroughly typical that Chabrier should have lavished on *L'invitation au voyage* a virtual prospectus of his later musical style, and that he should then have withdrawn the song in modest acknowledgement of Duparc's supremacy. It is a striking piece, sung here with all the panache that its bold gestures need. The Debussy here is the enraptured young Wagnerite, matching Baudelaire's imagery with his own rich, saturated colours and brocaded textures: heady, sumptuous and impulsive. The four 'minor' composers each contribute a more than minor song that makes one eager to hear more of their work: a finely spun line rising to genuine passion from de Bréville, a delicately pretty miniature from de Séverac, Capdevielle's amply curving melody and, best of all, Sauguet's haunting evocation of a cat. Felicity Lott has the subtlety and the intelligence for these pieces and her pianist is no less resourceful. The recording is good and though texts are provided, translations are not.

NEW REVIEW

ON WINGS OF SONG. SONGS AND DUETS. [a]**Felicity Lott** (sop); [b]**Ann Murray** (mez); **Graham Johnson** (pf). EMI CDC7 54411-2. Texts and translations included.
Purcell (arr. Britten): Come ye sons of art, away, Z323 — Sound the trumpet[ab]. The Indian Queen — I attempt from love's sickness[b]. Lost is my quiet for ever, Z502[ab]. King Arthur — Fairest Isle[a]. What can we poor females do, Z518[ab]. ***Mendelssohn:*** Wasserfahrt[ab]. Duets, Op. 63[ab] — No. 5, Volkslied; No. 6, Maiglöckchen und die Blümelein. Auf Flügeln des Gesanges, Op. 34 No. 2[b]. Neue Liebe, Op. 19*a* No. 4[ab]. Abendlied[ab]. ***Rossini:*** Soirées musicales — No. 1, La promessa[a]; No. 10, La pesca[ab]. Péchés de vieillesse, Book 1 — Anzoletta co passa la regata[b]. Duetto buffo di due gatti[ab]. ***Gounod:*** La siesta[ab]. ***Delibes:*** Les trois oiseaux[ab]. ***Massenet:*** Rêvons, c'est l'heure[ab]. Joie![ab]. ***Paladilhe:*** Au bord de l'eau[ab]. ***Aubert:*** Cache-cache[ab]. ***Balfe:*** Trust her not[ab]. ***Sullivan:*** Coming home[ab]. ***Quilter:*** It was a lover and his lass, Op. 23 No. 3[ab]. ***Britten:*** Mother comfort[ab]. Underneath the abject willow[ab].

1h 16m DDD 7/92

These expert duettists (fellow contributors to the Songmakers's Almanac, Marschallin and Octavian in many a *Rosenkavalier*, and recently back from a European tour at the time of publication) have already one highly successfully disc (Sweet Power of Song — reviewed further on) to their joint credit, and now achieve what often proves the more difficult task of providing an equally good sequel. But of course this is not really a double-act but a trio, and Graham Johnson is, as ever, more than accompanist. When he arranges a programme, delight follows as sure as night follows day. Here the delight lies partly in discovery (for instance, there is a charmer of Gounod's, in Spanish style, the voices in dreamy thirds, the ending softly delicate). Then there is the range of mood, from Purcell's assured, outward-going "Sound the trumpet" at the start to the desolation that burrows within Britten's haunting *Mother comfort* near the end. Solos are deftly chosen to bring out the best in each singer, as in the clean style and unostentatious manner of Felicity Lott's "Fairest Isle" and Ann Murray's finely phrased, evenly sustained *Auf Flügeln des Gesanges*. Then there are the charming oddities: Sullivan's "Coming home" turns out to be a duet from *Cox and Box* (but with different words), and 'Rossini's' cat-duet is now attributed to that singularly unpredictable minor genius, Robert Pearsall. The recording is exemplary.

NEW REVIEW

A PROGRAM OF SONG. Leontyne Price (sop); **David Garvey** (pf). RCA Living Stereo 09026 61499-2. Texts and translations included. Recorded in 1959. New to UK.
Fauré: Clair de lune, Op. 46 No. 2. Notre amour, Op. 23 No. 2. Au cimetière, Op. 51 No. 2. Au bord de l'eau, Op. 8 No. 1. Mandoline, Op. 58 No. 1. ***Poulenc:*** Main dominée par le coeur. Miroirs brûlants. Ce doux petit visage. ***R. Strauss:*** Allerseelen, Op. 10 No. 8. Schlagende Herzen, Op. 29 No. 2. Freundliche Vision, Op. 48 No. 1. Wie sollten wir geheim, Op. 19 No. 4. ***Wolf:*** Mörike Lieder — Der Gärtner; Lebe wohl. Lieder für eine Frauenstimme — Morgentau. Spanisches Liederbuch — Geh' Geliebter, geh' jetz.

40m ADD 5/93

There can be few recordings which so vividly resemble the sound of singer and pianist performing live in one's own home. This forward, warts-and-all 1959 RCA recording has a disconcerting immediacy, but it's not just the recorded sound which creates this sense of close intimacy. Leontyne Price sings with a captivating directness which belongs more to the domestic room than the concert-hall — or even the opera house, for it was here that her reputation was made, becoming revered as one of the foremost Verdi sopranos. Her recorded legacy encompasses major roles from Mozart through Berlioz and Puccini to Gershwin and Samuel

Barber, but this CD is special. This was her recording début made in the Town Hall, New York City, and shows her in repertoire with which she has not generally been associated. Yet she sings it with an intuition and sensitivity which would be the envy of singers whose lifetimes' work has been in *Lieder* and *chanson*. The French and German accents have an unmistakable American twang, but it's not the words which matter so much as the sense of involvement she brings to each and every one of these beautiful and memorable songs. A CD of great historic and artistic value.

SACRED CHORAL WORKS. Various artists. Classics for Pleasure CD-CFP4532. From EMI recordings made between 1957-81.
Arias from Sacred Choral Works by: ***Bach, Handel, Mozart, Haydn, Rossini, Mendelssohn, Fauré*** and ***Verdi.***

lh 5m ADD 8/89 £

Here is a good collection of popular arias, which includes some interesting contributions from singers of the recent past. Elsie Morison's clear soprano tone and unfussy musicianship can be admired in "I know that my Redeemer liveth" from Handel's *Messiah*, from which oratorio Richard Lewis also sings "Comfort ye" and "Ev'ry valley" in fine style. Lewis's acount of "Sound an alarm" from Handel's *Judas Maccabeus* is also very accomplished, as is the young Kiri Te Kanawa's rendering of "Laudamus te" from Mozart's Mass in C minor, K427. Janet Baker's "O rest in the Lord" from Mendelssohn's *Elijah* was also recorded at a fairly early stage in her career, when her gorgeous voice still had a contralto characteristic and Lucia Popp's singing of the "Alleluja" from Mozart's *Exsultate, jubilate*, K165, also has an appealing freshness. Victoria de los Angeles is not quite at her best in the "Pie Jesu" from Fauré's Requiem and Robert Gambill's comparatively recent recording of "Cujus animan" from Rossini's *Stabat mater* is fairly ordinary, but items from Joan Sutherland, John Shirley-Quirk, Dietrich Fischer-Dieskau and Nicolai Gedda all have some distinction. The recordings are mostly over 20 years old, but all bear their years lightly.

SONG RECITAL. Anne-Lise Berntsen (sop); **Einar Henning Smebye** (pf). Victoria VCD19012. Texts and translations included.
Mussorgsky: Songs and Dances of Death. ***Sibelius:*** The dream, Op. 13 No. 5. And I questioned them no further, Op. 17 No. 1. Black roses, Op. 36 No. 1. But my bird, Op. 36 No. 2. ***Wagner:*** Wesendonk Lieder.

56m DDD 11/91

SONG RECITAL. Anne-Lise Berntsen (sop); [a]**Terje Tønnesen** (vn); [a]**Aage Kvalbein** (vc); **Einar Henning Smebye** (pf). Victoria VCD19017. Texts and translations included.
Berg: Four Songs, Op. 2. ***Kvandal:*** Norwegian folk-songs, Op. 40. ***Shostakovich:*** Seven Romances, Op. 127[a].

57m DDD 11/91

Here is an interesting singer with interesting programmes. In the first disc the *Songs and Dances of Death* live an intensely imaginative life, the voice ranging widely with at first a hollow, other-worldly tone in the "Lullaby", then a silvery quality to set the starlit scene in the "Serenade", with a ringing power in Death's rapacious call at the end. In the third song, the famous "Trepak", the story-telling has a ghostly eeriness, and there is apt command in the voice of the "Commander-in-Chief". These are grimly compassionate songs, contrasting with the warmer romanticism of Sibelius (even when a folk-idiom is present), and still more with Wagner's five songs dedicated to his beloved Mathilde Wesendonk who herself wrote the poems. Anne-Marie Berntsen is less well-suited in these, yet here too (and particularly in "Im Treibhaus") her mastery of mood is very evident. This remains impressive throughout the second recital. Berg's *Four Songs* again have an element of ghostliness about them, mirrored in the singer's tone. The folk-songs of John Kvandal, published in 1970, bring the voice out into the happier world of nature, and it is good to find a smile in the singing. There are 12 songs, all attractive in words and melody, arranged in a well-disciplined style that has individuality and some sophistication but does not impose. Shostakovich's songs of 1967 add violin and cello to the voice and piano, though only the last, "Music", brings all of them together. Emotions here may be fierce one moment, tender another, and all are beautifully caught by the string players as they are by the singer and her excellent accompanist.

SONGS BY FINZI AND HIS FRIENDS. [a]**Ian Partridge** (ten); [b]**Stephen Roberts** (bar); **Clifford Benson** (pf). Hyperion CDA66015. Texts included.
Finzi: To a Poet, Op. 13*a*[b]. Oh fair to see, Op. 13*b*[a]. ***Milford***[a]: If it's ever spring again. The colour. So sweet love seemed. ***Farrar:*** O mistress mine![a]. ***Gurney***[b]: Sleep. Down by the salley gardens. Hawk and Buckle. ***Gill:*** In Memoriam[b].

51m ADD 9/91

This is a record that drew from its original reviewer, Trevor Harvey, high and unstinting praise when it appeared in 1981 as part of the commemoration of Finzi 25 years after his death. Finzi was never an avant-garde composer and during his lifetime received quiet and grateful acknowledgement from kindred spirits rather than anything more spectacular. In the last 20 years or so, appreciation has deepened and become more widespread. His songs, particularly, have a depth of feeling that is not always apparent at first hearing, and their idiom is that of a writer to whom overstatement or any other kind of cheapening would have been abhorrent. In this selection most of the chosen poems are affectionate and gentle, but F.L. Lucas's *June on Castle Hill* contains "whispers of wars to come", and George Barker's "Ode on the Rejection of St Cecilia" is a strong and sombre utterance that evokes an uncommonly hard-hitting style in the composer. His friend, Robin Milford, sets Hardy and Bridges with comparable sensitivity, and Ernest Farrar (killed in 1918) is remembered by his charmingly nonchalant "O mistress mine!". Stephen Roberts is an admirable singer of the songs by Ivor Gurney, and Ian Partridge gives a lovely account of Finzi's Op. 13*b* songs. Clifford Benson is the excellent accompanist throughout and recording and presentation are first-rate.

NEW REVIEW

THE SPLENDOUR OF SPAIN. José Carreras (ten); **Martin Katz** (pf); **English Chamber Orchestra/Robin Stapleton, Roberto Benzi, Antoni Ros Marbá.** Philips 432 825-2PM. Recorded 1978-85.
Padilla: Valencia. ***Grever:*** Jurame. ***F. Alonso:*** Maitechu mia. ***Lara:*** Granada. ***Vives:*** Doña Francisquita — Por el humo. ***Soutullo:*** Ultimo romantico — Noche de amor. ***Serrano:*** Alma da Dios — Canción húngara. ***Falla:*** Canciones populares españolas. ***Mompou:*** Combat del somni. ***Obradors:*** Canciones clásicas españolas — Del cabello más sutil. Corazón porqué pasais. ***Turína:*** Poeme en forma de canciones.

1h 4m ADD/DDD 7/92

To celebrate "The Splendour of Spain" Philips have plundered their archives to come up with a series of discs each reflecting a different facet of Spanish music. This CD, devoted to song, has that greatest of all Spanish voices, José Carreras, beginning in classic Carreras fashion with big, crowd-pulling displays of vocal power and emotional extravagance. Never can Augustin Lara's classic *Granada* have packed quite such a punch, with opulent orchestral accompaniment (including that archetypically Spanish instrument, the guitar) and Carreras giving it his all, while the semi-operatic *Alma da Dios* positively oozes Eastern magic casting a spell few could resist. But the real highlights of this CD are a group of more intimate and subtle art songs by Falla, Mompou, Obradors and Turína. Here the true measure of Carreras's artistry is to be found. He sings with warmth, sensitivity and remarkable control. Martin Katz's piano accompaniments, especially in Mompou's three songs *Combat del somni* are in a class of their own. Only a singer of the calibre of Carreras could bring off such a diverse programme with such utter conviction and he has been served well by consistently high quality recordings.

SWEET POWER OF SONG. Felicity Lott (sop); **Ann Murray** (mez); **Graham Johnson** (pf) with [a]**Galina Solodchin** (vn) and [a]**Jonathan Williams** (va). EMI CDC7 49930-2. Texts and translations included.

Beethoven[a]: 25 Irish Songs, WoO152 — Sweet power of song; English Bulls. 12 Irish Songs, WoO154 — The Elfin Fairies; Oh! would I were but that sweet linnet. ***Berlioz:*** Pleure, pauvre Colette. Le trébuchet, Op. 13 No. 3. ***Brahms:*** Vier Duette, Op. 61. ***Chausson:*** Two duos, Op. 11. ***Fauré:*** Pleurs d'or, Op. 72. Tarantelle, Op. 10 No. 2. ***Gounod:*** D'un coeur qui t'aime. L'Arithmétique. ***Saint-Saëns:*** Pastorale. El desdichado. ***Schumann:*** Liederalbum für die Jugend, Op. 79 — No. 15, Das Glück; No. 19, Frühlings Ankunft; No. 23, Er ist's; No. 26, Schneeglöckchen.

lh 2m DDD 11/90

This is a delightful presentation of an entertaining programme. The singers' careers have run concurrently with growing success on the international scene yet faithful to Graham Johnson as founding members of the Songmakers' Almanac. Here they recall many evenings of happy duetting at that group's recitals. They sing together with an instinctive rapport that is most gratifying. Johnson has devised a programme for them that provides an ingenious variety of mood and style. Beethoven's Irish Songs may not be great music but they are given vivid advocacy here. So are the more attractive and deeper duets by Schumann and Brahms. The Berlioz pieces, nicely contrasted, are well done; so are the Gounod, Fauré and Chausson items, even if a shade more accenting of words would have been welcome here. The real winner among the French items — surely a collector's item of the future — is Gounod's *L'Arithmétique*, an amusing lesson in Victorian thrift delivered in both French and English. Johnson supplies appropriate accompaniments and interesting notes. The recording naturally balances voices and piano.

NEW REVIEW

TRADITIONAL CATALAN SONGS. Victoria de los Angeles (sop); **Geoffrey Parsons** (pf). Collins Classics 1318-2. Texts and translations included.
El cant dels ocells. Muntanyes regalades. El mariner. El mestre. Mariagneta. Muntanyes del Canigó. El rossinyol. El bon caçador. La filla del marxant. L'hereu Riera. Els estudiantes de Tolosa. La ploma de perdiu. Els fadrins de Sant Boi. Caterina d'Alió. La Margarideta. La Mare de Déu. Josep i Maria. El Noi de la Mare. El desembre congelat. La dama d'Aragó. El testament d'Amèlia. La muller del gavatxot. La filadora. La presó de Lleida. Cançó del lladre. Els pobres traginers. La filla del Carmesí. Els tres tambors. Els segadors.

57m DDD 7/92

Born in Barcelona, Victoria de los Angeles is the ideal singer for these Catalan songs and she brings out fully their lilt, vivacity, seductiveness and pathos. The booklet reminds us that Catalonia once existed as a country in its own right and that since it became a mere province of Spain the Catalonians have, as they see it, suffered social and political misfortunes. Hence we should not be surprised at the frequent minor keys and the touch of melancholy that informs some of these melodies, although there are lighter ones too. In any case, this experienced and sensitive singer has devised a programme that allows no sense of monotony. She was born in 1923 and was therefore in her late sixties when she recorded these songs at London's Abbey Road Studios in 1991, but her voice with its rich maturity is still a fine instrument and her artistry has remained unimpaired by the passing years. One might single out songs such as the bold *El mariner*, the sad love song *Mariagneta*, the cheerful *L'hereu Riera* and the quietly lilting *Caterina d'Alió* as being especially fetching, but every purchaser of this disc will have his or her own favourites and nothing here lacks quality or appeal. The piano accompaniments by Manuel Garcia Morante are simple and tasteful, while Geoffrey Parsons is an admirable pianist. Altogether, this is a valuable and well recorded recital that brings into the catalogue a number of fine if mostly unfamiliar folk-songs, and the booklet provides full texts and translations.

NEW REVIEW

TWENTIETH CENTURY SACRED MUSIC. [a]**Rebecca Outram** (sop); **Schola Cantorum, Oxford/Jeremy Summerly.** Proudsound PROUCD129. Texts and translations included.
Martin: Mass for double chorus. ***Duruflé:*** Four motets sur des thèmes grégoriens, Op. 10 — Ubi caritas; Tota pulchra es; Tu es Petrus; Tantum ergo. ***Stanford:*** Three motets, Op. 38

— Justorum animae; Coelos ascendit hodie; Beati quorum via. ***Górecki:*** Totus tuus, Op. 60. ***Byron:*** Verba.

lh 3m DDD 4/92

The fresh, young, thoroughly musical voices of the Schola Cantorum of Oxford are certainly put through their paces in this programme of often complex, always emotionally demanding and unfailingly beautiful music. Drawing from the wealth of unaccompanied liturgical music their programme starts with one of the finest of all twentieth-century settings of the Mass, that by the Swiss composer Frank Martin. Martin was such a deeply committed Christian that he felt his music wasn't worthy to be associated with so profound a statement of faith as the Mass and held this marvellous work back from publication until 1962, some 40 years after its composition. It is deeply-felt and intense, designed to be both accessible to the listener and demanding for the performers — such important words deserve the finest music. Here it receives as sincere and musically rewarding a performance as one could wish for: Jeremy Summerly has thought out his interpretation with painstaking care, and his singers are eager to fulfil his wishes. Other highlights are a gloriously effervescent performance of Stanford's Ascensiontide motet "Coelos ascendit hodie", written in 1905, and Rebecca Outram's delightful solo singing in John Byron's *Verba*, the most modern piece (1989) on this warmly recommended CD.

VOCAL RECITAL. Régine Crespin (sop); [b]**John Wustman** (pf); [a]**Suisse Romande Orchestra/Ernest Ansermet.** Decca 417 813-2DH. Texts and translations included. Items marked [a] from SXL6081 (3/64), [b]SXL6333 (6/68).
Berlioz: Les nuits d'été. ***Ravel:*** Shéhérazade[a]. ***Debussy:*** Trois chansons de Bilitis[b]. ***Poulenc:*** Banalities[b] — Chansons d'Orkenise; Hôtel. La courte paille[b] — Le carafon; La reine de coeur. Chansons villageoises[b] — Les gars qui vont à la fête. Deux poèmes de Louis Aragon[b].

lh 8m ADD 11/88

Some recordings withstand the test of time and become acknowledged classics. This is one of them. Crespin's voluptuous tone, her naturally accented French and her feeling for the inner meaning of the songs in both these cycles are everywhere evident. Better than most single interpreters of the Berlioz, she manages to fulfil the demands of the very different songs, always alive to verbal nuances. In the Ravel, she is gorgeously sensuous, not to say sensual, with the right timbre for Ravel's enigmatic writing. The other songs on this CD enhance its worth. Crespin offers a highly evocative, perfumed account of the Debussy pieces and is ideally suited to her choice of Poulenc, of which her interpretation of "Hôtel" is a classic. Ansermet and his orchestra, though not quite note perfect, are — like the singer — right in timbre and colour for both these rewarding cycles. The sound is reasonable given the age of the recording. This is a most desirable acquisition.

NEW REVIEW

WHERE THE MUSIC COMES FROM. AMERICAN SONGS. **Cynthia Haymon** (sop); **Warren Jones** (pf). Argo 436 117-2ZH. Texts included.
Hoiby: Where the music comes from. Always it's Spring. ***Rorem:*** See how they love me. Early in the morning. O you whom I often and silently come. ***Burleigh:*** Among the fuchsias. Till I wake. Worth while. The prayer. ***Barber:*** O boundless, boundless evening. Sleep now. ***Nordoff:*** Embroidery for a faithless friend. ***Farwell:*** Wild nights! Wild nights! ***Beck:*** Songs of devotion. ***Logan:*** Marrow of my bone. ***Hundley:*** Strings in the earth and air. Come ready and see me. ***Dougherty:*** Love in the dictionary. ***Griffes:*** In a myrtle shade. ***Lekberg:*** The spring and the fall.

54m DDD 12/92

Seeing a CD devoted to American songs most people would probably think of Gershwin, Bernstein and the big numbers from smash-hit Broadway musicals. In presenting her own very personal selection portraying the 'many shades of love', Cynthia Haymon is displaying an altogether different side of twentieth-century American music. All 20 of these songs show a simplicity and gentleness which seems worlds away from the brashness of the Broadway stage, yet there is still something uniquely American in their openness and unashamed romanticism. Haymon, whose reputation largely rests on her operatic and stage roles (most recently as Bess in *Porgy and Bess* and Coretta King in the recording of the musical *King*) seems here to be baring her true self. She sings with a directness and unpretentiousness which seems like a mere extension of a sensitive yet exuberant personality and which suits this gentle programme perfectly. Accompanied by the ever-astute Warren Jones, she passes easily from the turn-of-the-century salon style of Burleigh's *Among the fuchsias* to Ned Rorem's somewhat austere *See how they love me*, always singing with absolute conviction and sincerity. An all-too brief CD of intimate moments to soothe the heart and refresh the soul.

MARY WIEGOLD'S SONGBOOK. Mary Wiegold (sop); [a]**Composers Ensemble/Dominic Muldowney.** NMC NMCD003. Texts included.
Dowland (arr. J. Woolrich)[a]: Complaint, P63. Galliard to Lachrimae, P46. Lachrimae, P15. ***J. Weir:*** The Romance of Count Arnaldos. ***C. Matthews:*** Cantata on the death of Antony. Strugnell's Haiku. ***S. Bainbridge:*** A song from Michelangelo. ***H. Skempton:*** How slow the wind. ***Birtwistle:*** White and Light. ***P. Wilby:*** Easter Wings. ***K. Tippett:*** Sun — The Living Son. ***J. Woolrich:*** The Turkish Mouse. ***Muldowney:*** On Suicide. ***S. Beamish:*** Tuscan Lullaby. ***B. Northcott:*** "The maidens came ...". ***D. Bedford:*** Even Now. ***Nyman:*** Polish Song.

55m DDD 4/92 

If this disc serves one particularly useful purpose, it is as a sampler for a wide range of living British composers. It reflects current fashions in playing down the more complex, modernist manner (no Ferneyhough, no Maxwell Davies) in favour of compositions which display varying degrees of closeness to the 'romantic' past. Yet there is nothing predictable or uniform about the selection of songs, which takes in the sweet simplicity of Howard Skempton and the folk-like vigour of Michael Nyman as well as the terse expressionism of Colin Matthews and the chilly eloquence of Sir Harrison Birtwistle. The enterprise is all the more valuable for introducing relatively unfamiliar composers — Sally Beamish, Bayan Northcott, John Woolrich — and for providing the further perspective and contrast of Woolrich's three Dowland arrangements for the instrumental ensemble (two clarinets with saxophone, viola, cello and double bass). Mary Wiegold is a leading advocate of contemporary music, and the Songbook is a tribute to her dedication and technical skill. One or two of the pieces strain her resources to the limit, but everything is musical, the words clearly articulated, the melodies sensitively phrased in a warm but never over-bright recording. Further instalments of "Mary Wiegold's Songbook" are to be anticipated with pleasure.

NEW REVIEW

WORKS FOR TENOR AND GUITAR. [a]**Ian Partridge** (ten); **Jukka Savijoki** (gtr). Ondine ODE779-2. Texts included.
L. Berkeley: Theme and Variations, Op. 77. Sonatina, Op. 52 No. 1. Songs of the half-light, Op. 65[a]. ***Britten:*** Six Chinese Songs, Op. 58[a]. Nocturnal after John Dowland, Op. 70. Folk-song arrangements[a] — I will give my love an apple; Sailor-boy; Master Kilby; Bonny at morn; The soldier and the sailor; The shooting of his dear.

1h 9m DDD 1/93

This disc is all the more welcome in that Lennox Berkeley's music is currently neglected, although his eldest son Michael is well known, both as composer and television personality. In fact, Michael Berkeley was Britten's godson, reflecting his father's close friendship from the mid-1930s with the younger composer, whom he recognized from the start as the genius that he was. Anyone making the acquaintance of Berkeley's music through this recital will find that his is a civilized and highly intelligent voice, and that his music is by no means overshadowed by Britten's in its qualities of taste, charm and craftsmanship. This programme has been chosen with a perceptiveness worthy of the composers themselves. Even the Britten pieces are not very well known, and those by Berkeley are even less familiar. Yet unlike so many rarities that get dragged into an undeserved prominence, these are pieces which one responds to at once and wants to hear again, especially since Ian Partridge and Jukka Savijoki are fine artists in an excellent partnership and seem totally at home in this repertory. Both men also produce sounds of considerable beauty and subtlety. Add to these qualities the fact that the recording, made in Helsinki, is wonderfully clear yet atmospheric, and this issue is a real winner.

Operatic highlights and recitals

THE ART OF THE PRIMA DONNA. Dame Joan Sutherland (sop); **Chorus and Orchestra of the Royal Opera House, Covent Garden/Francesco Molinari-Pradelli.** Decca 425 493-2DM2. Texts and translations included. From SXL2556/7 (12/60).
Arne: ARTAXERXES — The soldier tir'd. ***Bellini:*** LA SONNAMBULA — Care compagne ... Come per me sereno ... Sopra il sen. NORMA — Sediziose voci ... Casta diva ... Ah! bello a me ritorna. I PURITANI — Son vergin vezzosa; O rendetemi la speme ... Qui la voce ... Vien, diletto. ***Delibes:*** LAKME — Ah! Où va la jeune Indoue. ***Gounod:*** FAUST — O Dieu! que de bijoux ... Ah! je ris. ROMEO ET JULIETTE — Je veux vivre. ***Handel:*** SAMSON — Let the bright Seraphim. ***Meyerbeer:*** LES HUGUENOTS — O beau pays de la Touraine! ***Mozart:*** DIE ENTFUHRUNG AUS DEM SERAIL — Martern aller Arten. ***Rossini:*** SEMIRAMIDE — Bel raggio lusinghier. ***Thomas:*** HAMLET — A vos jeux, mes amis. ***Verdi:*** OTELLO — Mia madre aveva una povera ancella ... Piangea cantando. LA TRAVIATA — E strano ... Ah fors' è lui ... Sempre libera. RIGOLETTO — Gualtier Maldè ... Caro nome.

② lh 49m ADD 1/90 P ▲

Those who have not heard Dame Joan until recent times can only speculate on the full beauty of her voice in its prime. This album, from 1960, preserves the real Sutherland quality as well as any of her records have done and it is a delight from start to finish. Sutherland and her husband, Richard Bonynge, have long been interested in the history of opera and particularly of its singers, so *The Art of the Prima Donna* was arranged to relate each of the solos to a famous soprano of the past. Arne's *Artaxerxes* recalls Mrs Billington, and the final items are associated with more recent artists such as Tetrazzini and Galli-Curci. It presents a brilliant conspectus, with Sutherland mastering the most fearsome of technical demands and showing a wonderfully complete command of the required skills. She was then fresh from the triumph at Covent Garden in *Lucia di Lammermoor* which brought her international fame in 1959. Her voice was at its purest, and her style had not developed the characteristics which later partly limited the pleasure of her singing. What the record may not quite convey is the sheer house-filling volume of her voice. Even so, nobody who hears these recordings can be in any doubt about her mastery or about the aptness of the title, bestowed on her by the Italians, of "la stupenda".

NEW REVIEW

MARIA CALLAS. RARITIES. **Maria Callas** (sop); [a]**Paris Conservatoire Orchestra/Nicola Rescigno;** [b]**Maggio Musicale Fiorentino Orchestra/Tullio Serafin;** [c]**Rome RAI Orchestra/Alfredo Simonetto;** [d]**Philharmonia Orchestra/Antonio Tonini;** [e]**Paris Opera Orchestra/Georges Prêtre.** EMI CDC7 54437-2. Texts and translations included. Items marked [c] recorded at a concert in San Remo, Italy in 1954.
Beethoven: Ah! perfido, Op. 65[a] (from Columbia SAX2540, 8/64). ***Mozart:*** Don Giovanni — Non mi dir[b] (CMS7 63750-2, 11/91. Recorded in 1953). Die Entführung aus dem Serail — Martern aller Arten[c] (sung in Italian. New to UK). ***Weber:*** Oberon — Ozean du Ungeheuer![d] (English. Previously unpublished. 1962). ***Rossini:*** Armida — D'amore al dolce impero[c] (EX769741-1, 4/89). ***Donizetti:*** Lucrezia Borgia — Tranquillo ei posa ... Com'è bello![d] (1961). ***Verdi:*** Don Carlos — O don fatale[d] (1961). I vespri siciliani — Arrigo! ah, parli[d] (1960). Il trovatore — Vanne ... lasciami ... D'amor sull'ali rosee[a]. I lombardi — Te, Vergin santa[a] (all previously unpublished). Both recorded in

1964/5). Aida — Pur' ti riveggo ... Fuggiam gli ardor[e] (with Franco Corelli, ten. New to UK. 1964).

lh 18m ADD 2/93 ▲

'Rarity' is one of those tricky words which, being really only quantitative, seems to imply something about quality as well. So the reader may well look doubtfully at the title: the "Callas Rarities" may indeed be rarities for the best of reasons, that of inferiority to versions and recordings that are less rare. In this instance, though, they are genuinely well worth having. For example, here is the Nile Duet from *Aida* with Franco Corelli, sole survivor of a projected album of duets to be recorded in 1964. Corelli provides the vocal thrills, sometimes even responding in kind to the dramatic intensity which characterizes Callas's performance from the start. Her voice is sometimes raw, and the soft B flat on "fuggiam" only just arrives and stays put. But always there is something distinctive: here it is the nostalgia, "Là tra foreste" being sung as a wistful, private vision of the homeland. Then there are the two incredibly brilliant solos from a concert at San Remo in 1954 ("Martern aller Arten" and "D'amore al dolce impero"); also previously unpublished versions, not alternative 'takes' but different performances, products of a different session. Usually one can see why they were not issued at the time, but here it is easier to see why they deserve to see the light of this later day.

NEW REVIEW

COLORATURA ARIAS. Dilbèr (sop); **Estonia Opera Orchestra/Eri Klas.** Ondine ODE768-2. Texts and translations included.

Bellini: I PURITANI — Son vergin vezzosa. LA SONNAMBULA — Care compagne ... A te, diletta ... Come per me sereno. ***Verdi:*** RIGOLETTO — Caro nome. ***Meyerbeer:*** DINORAH — Ombre légère. ***Delibes:*** LAKME — Où va la jeune indoue. ***Donizetti:*** LUCIA DI LAMMERMOOR — Il dolce suono ... Ardon gl'incensi. ***R. Strauss:*** ARIADNE AUF NAXOS — Grossmächtige Prinzessin. ***J. Strauss II:*** Frühlingsstimmen, Op. 410.

lh 9m DDD 9/92

Dilbèr is a Chinese coloratura soprano, a principal of the Beijing Opera and more recently at Helsinki. She has a beautifully clear voice with extensive upward range and firm definition in the lower and middle registers. Her technique enables her to sing this succession of test-pieces (and more than just that, of course) with a high degree of assurance and accomplishment. Moreover, her manner has a charm and delicacy appropriate to most of this repertoire, with an affectionate expression at command for *La sonnambula*, a smile for the Polonaise in *I puritani*, and a haunted tone which gives way to serenity in poor Lucia's Mad scene. So the performances are not unfeeling; yet it is in this respect that the admirable singer's art shows most limitation. That she *has* also powers of characterization and of expressiveness through the words of her music is proved in the long solo of Zerbinetta in *Ariadne auf Naxos*. Here there is a live responsiveness and sense of authority: she gives an excellent account of what may well be the most demanding solo of all for this type of voice. The recital is happily concluded with a Strauss waltz, sung with a brilliance that is none the less agreeable for having a well-mannered gentleness about it.

NEW REVIEW

COVENT GARDEN ON RECORD, Volumes 1-4. 143 singers with various accompaniments. Pearl mono GEMMCDS9923/6 (four 3-disc sets: only available separately).

3h 33m 3h 25m 3h 47m 3h 42m AAD 7/92 

An Aladdin's cave, where whatever the torch lights upon is treasure. At the entrance: Adelina Patti, well past her prime to be sure, but in that *Ah, non credea mirarti* what heartfelt pathos when she comes to the lines "Mi ravivar l'amore il pianto mio non puèo", what delicacy in the soft tones and the trill, and, after all, what a miracle that we should be able to hear as clearly as this, from the 63-year-old woman in retirement at her Welsh castle in 1906, the beauty remaining to the most world-renowned voice of her century. Further in among the treasures, the first Otello, the first Falstaff; near to them, a baritone, one Mario Ancona of 1904, almost forgotten today but truly superb in his Donizetti, as, by his side, is the bass Marcel Journet, sonorous and with a funny old chorus to support him in a passage from that epitome of nineteenth-century grand opera, *Les Huguenots*. Into the next chamber, and a voice arises celebrating the fickleness of womankind — the voice of the god of tenors, Enrico Caruso. His Irish friend McCormack, his business-partner Melba, his Neapolitan *amico* Scotti: all are there. Deeper in, and we have come through the First World War, to where British singers — Walter Widdop, Heddle Nash and Joan Cross among them — mingle freely and quite rightly with tip-top company such as Lotte Lehmann, Elisabeth Rethberg and Friedrich Schorr. At the end of the journey we reach the ominous date 1939: for the chambers of this Aladdin's cave of records have also been the years of the Covent Garden Opera House, with singers heard there, in the present theatre, as early as 1871, up to the end of the international seasons and the outbreak of World War Two. The singers are heard in the roles they sang, and are sometimes recorded 'live' from the stage, as with Chaliapin in 1928 and Gigli in 1939. Many of the recordings are of extreme rarity, and thanks to the expertise of Keith Hardwick, who compiled the programme and effected the transfers, a sizeable proportion of them are heard to greater advantage than ever before on CD or LP. Not everything is perfect, either in the singers themselves (they don't always do what we want them to), or the selections (nothing of some famous Covent Garden roles such as Caruso's Canio and Turner's Turandot) or even the transfers (a certain harshness in some of the later recordings). But the four albums, three CDs to a volume and each volume available separately, comprise one of the best of anthologies. They also document a fascinating period in the history of a great opera house: an extraordinary concentration of enterprise, historical time, musical talent and in some instances genius, all within the compass of these 12 small discs.

NEW REVIEW

FAVOURITE SOPRANO ARIAS. Luba Orgonasova (sop); **Bratislava Radio Symphony Orchestra/Will Humburg.** Naxos 8 550605.

Bellini: I PURITANI — Qui la voce. I CAPULEI ED I MONTECCHI — Oh! quante volte. LA SONNAMBULA — Come per me sereno. ***Donizetti:*** LINDA DI CHAMOUNIX — O luce di quest'anima. Lucia di Lammermoor — Il dolce suono; Ardon gl'incensi; Alfin son tua; Spargi d'amaro pianot. ***Puccini:*** TURANDOT — Signore, ascolta!; Tu, che di gel sei cinta. GIANNI SCHICCHI — O mio babbino caro. LA RONDINE — Chi il bel sogno di Doretta. ***Verdi:*** RIGOLETTO — Tutte le feste.

58m DDD 2/93 £

Here is a young and excellent singer in the fresh prime of her voice and with her artistry developed quite far enough to make her an effective communicator. She comes (like Edita Gruberová before her) from Bratislava and has enjoyed considerable success at Salzburg. Her voice is deliciously clear, and though in the category of light soprano she nevertheless has a certain depth and richness of tone which impart a warmer humanity to her singing than is often found among singers in this repertory. Limitations are felt from time to time: a musical one, for instance, when she gives a push to the final B flat in Liù's "Signore, ascolta!", and a dramatic one when she seems not to feel the pathos of Gilda's narrative in "Tutte le feste". Yet the solos from *Lucia di Lammermoor* and the Bellini operas are touching in their emotional warmth as well as being sung with a charming sweetness and remarkable technical skill. She is sympathetically accompanied and well recorded: in sum, one of the most enjoyable recitals by a relative newcomer, and especially good value at its super-bargain price.

NEW REVIEW

OPERA ARIAS. Nazzareno De Angelis (bass); **orchestra/Lorenzo Molajoli.** Preiser Lebendige Vergangenheit mono 89042. All items sung in Italian.

Rossini: MOSE IN EGITTO — Eterno, immenso, incomprensibil Dio!; Dal tuo stellato soglio (with Elena Cheni, sop; Ida Mannarini, mez; Emilio Venturini, ten. Both from Italian Columbia GQX18070. Recorded 1929). IL BARBIERE DI SIVIGLIA — La calunnia. ***Weber:*** DER FREISCHUTZ — Hier im ird'schen Jammerthal (Columbia L2073, 6/28). ***Meyerbeer:*** ROBERT LE DIABLE — Nonnes, qui reposez. ***Halévy:*** LA JUIVE — Vous qui du Dieu vivant (Italian Columbia D18058). ***Verdi:*** NABUCCO — Sperate, o figli!; Tu sul labbro dei veggenti (GQX10196. All 1928). DON CARLOS — Ella giammai m'amò ... Dormirò sol (L2071, 6/28). ***Wagner:*** DIE WALKURE — Leb' wohl (GQX10208. 1929). ***Gounod:*** FAUST — Vous qui faites l'endormie (L2247, 4/29); Seigneur, daignez permettre (Gina Cigna, sop. Columbia LX233, 5/33). ***Boito:*** MEFISTOFELE — Ave, Signor!; Son lo spirito (L2072, 6/28); Popoli, e scettro e clamide (D18077. 1929); Ecco il mondo (L2247).

lh 9m AAD 7/92

On the whole, we consider ourselves at the present time to be fairly well provided with basses, but we do not have, and probably never have had in the second half of the century, any Italian bass to match this singer. De Angelis was born in 1881, made his début in 1903 and was in his prime during the 1920s when these records were made. In Italy he was probably the most admired of all, though partly because of his absence from Covent Garden and the Metropolitan Opera, and partly because of the great international popularity of Ezio Pinza (his junior by ten years) he remained relatively little-known here and in the States. His voice was magnificent in its sonority and firmness, a thoroughly committed bass too, with no compromising baritonal tinge. Though not always as smooth as might be wished in legato, *cantabile* passages, he nevertheless had many graces, including a well-spun trill, that are rare in singers of his type. An outstanding example of his art is found in the Prayer from Rossini's *Mosè in Egitto*, which is as impressive in the eloquence of its emotion as it is beautiful in the sheer nobility of tone. Wotan's Farewell and the solo from *Der Freischütz* add their reminder that Italians in those days regularly undertook roles outside the repertoire normally associated with them, frequently bringing the gifts of the lyricism and resonance for which their country's singers have been traditionally famed. The selection is a good one, and the transfers are excellent.

NEW REVIEW

OPERA ARIAS AND DUETS. Giovanni Martinelli (ten); [a]**Metropolitan Opera Chorus and Orchestra/Giulio Setti;** [b]**Josef Pasternack,** [c]**Rosario Bourdon.** Preiser Lebendige Vergangenheit mono 89062. Recorded 1926-7

Verdi: RIGOLETTO — La donna è mobile. Il trovatore — Quale d'armi fragor ... Di quella pira[a] (with Grace Anthony, sop). LA FORZA DEL DESTINO — Oh, tu che in seno; Invano Alvaro ... Le minacciei fieri accenti (with Giuseppe de Luca, bar). AIDA — Se quel guerrier io fossi ... Celeste Aida[b]; Nume, custode e vindici (with Ezio Pinza, bass). ***Giordano:*** ANDREA CHENIER — Un dì all'azzurro spazio[b]; Come un bel dì di maggio[c]. FEDORA[b] — Amor ti vieta; Mia madre, la mia vecchia madre. ***Mascagni:*** CAVALLERIA RUSTICANA[c] — O Lola; Mamma, quel vino è generoso. ***Leoncavallo:*** PAGLIACCI — Recitar! ... Vesti la giubba[c]; Per la morte! smettiamo ... No, Pagliaccio non son[a] (with Grace Anthony). ZAZA — E un riso gentil[c]. ***Puccini:*** LA BOHEME — Che gelida manina[b]. TOSCA — E lucevan le stelle[b].

lh 8m AAD 3/93 

Here is one of the most fascinating of singers. He can also be one of the most thrilling, his voice having at its best a beauty unlike any other, his art noble in breadth of phrase and concentration of tone. It also has to be said that his records hardly make easy or restful listening, but what at first may even repel soon becomes compulsive, the intensity of expression and individuality of timbre impressing themselves upon the memory with extraordinary vividness. Martinelli's career was centred on the Metropolitan, New York, where he sang first at the height of the Caruso era, inheriting Caruso's more dramatic roles in 1921. This selection makes an unrepresentative start with "La donna è mobile", but the excerpts from *Il trovatore* and *La forza del destino* have the very essence of the man, masterly in his shaping and shading of recitative, or in the long curves of his melodic line and the tension of his utterance. There are also superb performances of solos from *Andrea Chénier* and *Pagliacci*, the involvement of his "No, Pagliaccio non son" unequalled before or since. These are recordings from 1926 and 1927, the period in which his vocal and artistic qualities were probably best matched. The transfers are fine apart from the song from Leoncavallo's *Zazà* which plays below pitch.

OPERA ARIAS AND DUETS. Richard Tauber (ten) with various artists. EMI Références mono CDH7 64029-2. All items sung in German except that marked [a].

Mozart: DON GIOVANNI — Dalla sua pace (from Odeon O-8227. Recorded 1922); Il mo tesoro[a] (Parlophone R20444, 7/39). DIE ZAUBERFLOTE — Dies Bildnis ist bezaubernd schön (O-8226. 1922). ***Méhul:*** JOSEPH — Champs paternels (R20543, 12/45). ***Offenbach:*** LES CONTES D'HOFFMANN — Il était une fois; O Dieu! de quelle ivresse (R20089, 10/29). ***Thomas:*** MIGNON — Adieu, Mignon; Elle ne croyait pas (both from O-8229). ***Tchaikovsky:*** EUGENE ONEGIN — Faint echo of my youth (O-8224. All 1923). ***Smetana:*** THE BARTERED BRIDE — Faithful love cannot be marred (with Elisabeth Rethberg, sop); How could they believe (O-8027. 1919). ***Wagner:*** DIE MEISTERSINGER VON NURNBERG — Am stillen Herd; Morgenlich leuchtend (Odeon 123506. 1927). ***Puccini:*** MADAMA BUTTERFLY — Quest'obi pomposa di scioglier mi tarda (Rethberg. O-8055. 1922). TURANDOT — Non piangere, Liù; Nessun dorma (O-8401. 1926). ***Korngold:*** DIE TOTE STADT — Glück das mir verblieb (Lotte Lehmann, sop); O Freund, ich werde sie nicht wiedersehen (O-9507. 1924).

lh 12m ADD 3/92

This is a must for anyone interested in the history of singing on disc. Richard Tauber had a voice of irresistible charm and individuality that was instantly recognizable. This issue includes some of his most desirable recordings, if not necessarily his most popular. From Mozart to Wagner he shows a sovereign style and tone allied to that uniquely ardent manner of his: a heady combination. Everything is sung from the heart and goes to it. The disc also demonstrates the breadth of his repertory when he was in his prime and before he became the star of operetta. In a couple of duets he is joined by his soprano colleagues of his time — the lovely Elisabeth Rethberg and the impulsive Lotte Lehmann. Tauber's voice rings out full and true on these transfers, though a few are troubled by extraneous noises. A treasure of glorious singing.

NEW REVIEW

OPERA ARIAS AND SONGS. Beniamino Gigli (ten) with various artists. Memoir Classics mono CDMOIR417. From HMV originals. Recorded 1921-39.
Arias from — L'AFRICAINE; ANDREA CHENIER; LA BOHEME; CAVALLERIA RUSTICANA; L'ELISIR D'AMORE; LA FORZA DEL DESTINO; MARTHA; MEFISTOFELE; LES PECHEURS DE PERLES; RIGOLETTO. *Songs by* ***Bixio, Cottrau, De Curtis, Denza, Di Chiara and Toselli.***

lh 5m AAD 6/93

Of all the famous Italian tenors, Gigli was the one whose voice seemed most to embody the sweets of nature — the sunshine, the fruit filled "with ripeness to the core" and so forth. He sang as though for the love of it, though of course collecting a substantial fee too (and in fact rather than submit to the indignity of a reduction in salary he quit the Metropolitan in their financial crisis of 1932). The records included here come from the years either side of that date and show him in his magnificent prime, the leading lyric-dramatic tenor of the world. The programme begins with his "Che gelida manina" of 1931, one of the top best-sellers in the HMV catalogues for many a year. His appeal lies not only in the sweetness, the easy power and ring of his well-rounded voice, but also in a personality that is almost winsomely human: a chubby chuckle, a boyish pleading, lightens up the 'face' of his singing. There is fervour in his *Andrea Chénier*, good humour in his "La donna è mobile", and appropriate bad temper in his *Cavalleria rusticana* duet with the formidable Dusolina Giannini. Then, in a selection of shamelessly tuneful Italian songs, he woos beguilingly, sometimes in the honeyed half-voice, ultimately with the thrilling vibrancy of his *fortissimo*. Two of the items (from *Mefistofele* and *La forza del destino*) are reproduced a semitone too high, but in general the quality of transfers is fine and the selection excellent. A superb performance.

NEW REVIEW

OPERA ARIAS AND SONGS. Maria Ivogün (sop); [a]**Michael Raucheisen** (pf); [b]**orchestra;** [c]**Berlin State Opera Orchestra/Leo Blech.** Nimbus Prima Voce NI7832.
Bishop: Lo, here the gentle lark[b] (from Brunswick 10174, 11/25). ***Handel:*** L'allegro, il penseroso ed il moderato, HWV55 — Sweet bird[b] (Polydor 85313, recorded 1925).

Donizetti: DON PASQUALE — Ah! un foco insolito[b] (85302, recorded 1924). LUCIA DI LAMMERMOOR — Ardon gl'incensi[b] (Odeon 76977, recorded 1917). ***Rossini:*** Il BARBIERE DI SIVIGLIA — Una voce poco fa[b] (85309, recorded 1925). ***Verdi:*** LA TRAVIATA — E strano ... Ah, fors'è lui ... Sempre libera[b] (sung in German. 76982/3, recorded 1916). ***Chopin:*** Nocturne in E flat major, Op. 9 No. 2[b] (arr. sop/orch. 76975). ***Meyerbeer:*** LES HUGUENOTS — Une dame noble et sage[b] (German. 76997). ***Nicolai:*** DIE LUSTIGEN WEIBER VON WINDSOR — Nun eilt herbei[b] (76811. All recorded 1917). ***Schubert:*** Ständchen (Horch! Horch! die Lerch), D899[b]. Winterreise, D911 — Die Post[b] (both from Brunswick 15075, 9/24). ***J. Strauss II:*** Frühlingsstimmen, Op. 410[b] (85313, recorded 1924). G'schichten aus dem Wienerwald, Op. 325[b] (10174). An die schönen, blauen Donau, Op. 314[c]. DIE FLEDERMAUS — Klänge der Heimat[c] (HMV DB4412, 6/34). ***Kreisler:*** Liebesfreud[b] (Brunswick 50050, 12/24). ***Anonymous:*** O du liebs Angeli[a]. Z'Lauterbach han i'mein Strumpf verlor'n[a]. Gsätzli. Maria auf dem Berge[a] (all from HMV DA4402, 6/33).

1h 18m ADD 8/92

Somewhere or other, after much searching of the memory, ransacking of the catalogues and phoning around among connoisseurs, it might be possible to discover a more delightful example of the coloratura's art than that of Maria Ivogün as displayed in her recording of Kreisler's *Liebesfreud*, made in 1924: if so, one such does not spring to mind now. With the most pure and delicate of tones, nothing shrill or piercing about them, she sings way above a normal mortal's reach, ease and accuracy in the purely technical feats going along with a lilt and feeling for the idiomatic give-and-take of waltz rhythm that are a joy musically. Turn to Handel, with the solo from *Il penseroso*, and the same art is put to lovely use in a different idiom. Her *Traviata* aria has warmth and spontaneity; her Frau Fluth in *Die lustigen Weiber von Windsor* is a woman of charm and energy; and the 1934 recording of the Czardas in *Die Fledermaus* shines as bright in spirit as in clarity of timbre. From the same period comes the set of four songs, Swiss and German, that show most touchingly her command of the art to be simple. This is an admirable introduction to a most lovely singer, and it represents the Prima Voce series at its best.

NEW REVIEW

OPERA ARIAS AND SONGS. Oscar Natzke (bass); [a]**Hubert Greenslade** (pf); **Orchestra/**[b]**Henry Geehl,** [c]**Warwick Braithwaite.** Ode New Zealand Heritage Series mono CDODE1365.

Handel: SAMSON — Honour and arms[b]. ***W.H. Weiss:*** The village blacksmith[b] (both from Parlophone E11402, 4/39). ***Mozart:*** DIE ZAUBERFLOTE — O, Isis und Osiris[b] (E11423, 10/39); In diesen heil'gen Hallen[c] (sung in English. Australian Parlophone A4544. Recorded in 1940). DON GIOVANNI — Madamina, il catalogo (not definitely known, either A7362, 1940 or Columbia DB2291, 4/47). ***Rossini:*** IL BARBIERE DI SIVIGLIA — La calunnia[b] (E11423). ***Mussorgsky:*** Song of the flea (English. A7250, 1940 or DB2363, 2/48). ***Ketèlbey:*** Sanctuary of the heart[c]. In a monastery garden[c] (E11439, 3/40). ***Beethoven:*** Die Ehre Gottes aus der Natur, Op. 48 No. 4[a]. Zärtliche Liebe, WoO123[a] (DB2460, 11/48). ***Schumann:*** Die beiden Grenadiere, Op. 49 No. 1[a] (A7250). ***Tchaikovsky:*** I bless you, forests, Op. 47 No. 5[a] (all English). ***Lehmann:*** In a Persian garden — Myself when young[a] (E11397, 3/39). ***Malashkin:*** Oh could I but express in song[a] (English. DB2363). ***Hewitt:*** Out where the big ships go (DB2177, 7/45). ***L. Fischer:*** DER KRITIKASTER UND DER TRINKER — In kühlen Kellar sitz[a] (English). ***M. Phillips:*** Wimmen oh Wimmen[a] (A7277, 1940). ***Traditional:*** Shenandoah. Blow the man down. Hullaballo balay (all from DB2167, 4/45). The Drunken Sailor. Rio Grande. Billy boy (DB2177).

1h 9m ADD 12/92

The Gramophone of May 1940 included an article by W.S. Meadmore who had been impressed by a new bass in a recording session at the Wigmore Hall. Oscar Natzke, from New Zealand, was not then entirely new as he had sung at Covent Garden in 1938 and been highly praised in such inconspicuous roles as Wagner in *Faust* and De Fulke in George Lloyd's *The Serf*. What should have alerted wider interest was the fact that he had the backing of Walter Legge, who even then was known as a shrewd judge of singers. The war came and Natzke made records for Parlophone and Columbia, but then left for the States where he joined the New York City

Opera, dying in 1951 after suffering a stroke on stage during a performance of *Die Meistersinger*. The beauty of his voice and the excellence of his technique are well attested by these records, which show him to have been potentially of the first rank. Handel and Mozart reveal his abilities best, and the runs of "Honour and arms", like the legato phrases and wide range of Sarastro's arias in *Die Zauberflöte*, find in him a singer in the best traditions of Dawson, Plançon or whoever sets the appropriate standards. He was not at this time so skilled in vocal characterization, so that Leporello and Basilio fail to emerge very vividly in their respective 'catalogue' and 'slander' arias. But the songs and shanties are superb: it is a magnificent voice caught in its prime, and the reproduction is excellent throughout.

NEW REVIEW

OPERA ARIAS AND SONGS. Adelina Patti (sop); various artists. Nimbus Prima Voce mono NI7840/1. Recorded 1902-28.

Mario Ancona, Mattia Battistini, Emma Calvé, Fernando De Lucia, Edouard de Reszke, Emma Eames, Lucien Fugère, Wilhelm Hesch, Lilli Lehmann, Félia Litvinne, Francesco Marconi, Victor Maurel, Dame Nellie Melba, Lillian Nordica, Adelina Patti, Pol Plançon, Maurice Renaud, Sir Charlles Santley, Marcella Sembrich, Francesco Tamagno and Francesco Viñas.

② 2h ADD 7/93 ▲

This is a 'historical' issue for straightforward enjoyment. Although the originals were made in the very earliest years of recording, they are reproduced here with a vividness that calls for very little in the way of 'creative listening', making allowances and so forth. It starts in party mood with the first Falstaff of all, Victor Maurel, singing to a bunch of cronies in the studio of 1907 the "Quand'ero paggio" which he sang at La Scala in the première of 1893. They cheer and call for an encore, which he gives them, then again (and best of all) this time in French. The record has been transferred many times to LP and CD, but never has it been so easy for the listener to 'see' it and feel part of it. The magnificent bass Pol Plançon follows with King Philip's solo from *Don Carlos*, beautifully even in production and deeply absorbed in the character and his emotions. The hauntingly pure, well-rounded soprano of Emma Eames in Tosti's *Dopo* (a real passion there despite its restraint), and then the miraculously spry and elegant 80-year-old Lucien Fugère lead to the first of the Patti records: the one her husband thought unladylike and asked to be withdrawn from the catalogue, *La calesera*, and the most joyous she ever made. Tamagno, Melba, Nordica, Renaud: they are all here, and on thrillingly good form. The copies of these rarities have been selected with great care, and, while other transfers have, technically, got more "off" the record, none has captured the beauty of the voices more convincingly.

NEW REVIEW

OPERA ARIAS AND SONGS. Ezio Pinza (bass) with various artists. RCA Victor Gold Seal Vocal Series mono 09026 61245-2. From Victor and RCA Victor originals. Recorded 1927-52.

Arias from L'amor contrastato, L'Arianna, Armida e Rinaldo, Il barbiere di Siviglia, La bohème, Boris Godunov, Le caïd, Don Giovanni, Ernani, Eteocle e Polinice, Faust, Il flavio, Floridante, L'incoronazione di Poppea, Norma, Messa da Requiem (Verdi), Simon Boccanegra, Il trionfo di Camilla, Il trovatore, Die Zauberflöte. Songs by Cavalli, Falconierei, Giordani, Torelli, Tosti and Weill.

lh l4m ADD ▲

The voice that, in the late 1940s, warmed America with the promise of "Some Enchanted Evening" (*South Pacific*) was also one of the great operatic voices of the 1920s, 1930s and 1940s. The inimitable Ezio Pinza was the possessor of a dark, sonorous but above all lyrical bass which emerges regally in RCA's generous anthology of some of his greatest recordings. The period covered is from 1927, the time of Pinza's early prime (and represented here by Tosti, Puccini and Thomas) through the 1930s to 1940 — a superb series of "Ancient Airs" — and the early 1950s, with a gripping performance of Mussorgsky's "Death of Boris" conducted by the Hollywood composer Alfred Newman. Perhaps best of all is the classic Bellini-Verdi-Mozart sequence on tracks 6-10 (especially "Che mai vegg'io Infelice!", from Verdi's *Ernani* — track 7) which reports a voice of immense range and substance in repertory that could have been tailor-made for its unique qualities. The last track on the CD is a touching performance of Kurt

Weill's haunting "September Song", and some selections included are issued here for the very first time.

OPERA CHORUSES. Chorus and Orchestra of the Royal Opera House, Covent Garden/Bernard Haitink. EMI CDC7 49849-2. Texts and translations included.
Beethoven: FIDELIO — O welche Lust (with John Mark Ainsley, ten; Alistair Miles, bar). ***Berlioz:*** LES TROYENS — Royal Hunt and Storm. ***Bizet:*** CARMEN — Les voici! voici la quadrille! (Haberdashers' Aske's School Boys' Choir). ***Donizetti:*** LUCIA DI LAMMERMOOR — Per te d'immenso giubilo; D'immenso giubilo. ***Giordano:*** ANDREA CHENIER — O pastorelle, addio. ***Mascagni:*** CAVALLERIA RUSTICANA — Easter Hymn (Helen Field, sop). ***Verdi:*** AIDA — Gloria all'Egitto. NABUCCO — Va, pensiero. OTELLO — Fuoco di gioia. IL TROVATORE — Vedi! le fosche notturne spoglie. ***Wagner:*** LOHENGRIN — Treulich geführt. ***Weber:*** DER FREISCHUTZ — Was gleicht wohl auf Erden dem Jägervergnügen.

lh lm DDD 12/89

After an evening at the opera it is usually the arias and soloists that come in for remark and discussion, but quite often what actually brings the greatest enjoyment and remains in the memory as most vivid and colourful is a chorus or a passage of ensemble. Composers tend to reserve their broadest tunes for the chorus, and in this selection we have the Easter Hymn, Anvil Chorus, Wedding March and Chorus of Hebrews, all among the world's best. Less obvious, and a delight in context (both here and in the opera), is the Pastoral from *Andrea Chenier*. Altogether deeper in feeling, and most moving of all, is the Prisoners' Chorus from *Fidelio*. In each of the excerpts, the Covent Garden Chorus (so often overlooked in reviews) show themselves fully worthy of the attention bestowed on them. Haitink, never insensitive, sometimes misses the full effect of a climax, but the Orchestra are in fine form and give a particularly good account of the "Royal Hunt and Storm" from *The Trojans*. For the general listener it is a disc that will give pleasure in itself and in stirring up a determination to go and see the operas again; for the Covent Garden *habitué* it will bring back memories, almost as if one were turning the pages of a picture-book, as the scenes and evenings return vividly to mind.

OPERA RECITAL. Ezio Pinza (bass) with various artists. Pearl mono GEMMCD9306.
Verdi: AIDA — Mortal diletto ai Numi (Metropolitan Opera Orchestra, New York/Giulio Setti); Nume custode vindici (Giovanni Martinelli, ten; Metropolitan Opera Chorus and Orchestra. Both from Victor 8111). ERNANI — Che mai vegg'io ... Infelice! (orchestra/Rosario Bourdon. HMV DB1750). DON CARLOS — Dormiro sol nel manto mio regal (orchestra/Bourdon. DB1087, 3/28). I VESPRI SICILIANI — O patria ... O tu Palermo (orchestra/Bourdon. DB1087). Messa da Requiem — Confutatis maledictis (orchestra/Bourdon. HMV AGSB103). SIMON BOCCANEGRA — A te l'estremo addio ... Il lacerato spirito (chorus and orchestra/Carlo Sabajno. DB699, 6/24). IL TROVATORE — Di due figli ... Abbietta zingara (chorus and orchestra/Sabajno. DB828). ***Mozart:*** DON GIOVANNI — Finch'han dal vino; Deh vieni alla finestra (orchestra/Bourdon. HMV DA1134, 10/31). DIE ZAUBERFLOTE — O Isis und Osiris (sung in Italian. Orchestra/Bourdon. DB1088, 3/28). ***Meyerbeer:*** ROBERT LE DIABLE — Nonnes, qui reposez (sung in Italian. Orchestra/Bourdon. DB1088). ***Thomas:*** LE CAID — Enfant chéri ... Le tambour-major (orchestra/Bourdon. DB1086, 3/28). ***Gounod:*** FAUST — Le veau d'or (Metropolitan Opera Chorus and Orchestra/Setti. DA1108, 9/38). ***Bellini:*** NORMA — Ah del tebro (Chorus and orchestra/Sabajno. DA566, 5/25). I PURITANI — Cinta de fiori (Orchestra/Sabajno. HMV VB70, 6/52). ***Donizetti:*** LA FAVORITA — Splendon più belle (orchestra. DA708). LUCIA DI LAMMERMOOR — Dalle stanze (chorus and orchestra/Sabajno. VB70). ***Boito:*** MEFISTOFELE — Ave Signor (orchestra. DB829); Son lo spirito (orchestra/Sabajno. DA567). ***Halévy:*** LA JUIVE — Si la rigeur (sung in Italian. Orchestra/Sabajno. DB698, 11/24); Vous qui du Dieu vivant (sung in Italian. Orchestra. DB829).

lh 16m AAD 2/89

The first half of the century brought forth three fine Italian basses: Nazzareno de Angelis, Tancredi Pasero and Ezio Pinza. Of these it was Pinza who gained the greatest international fame, partly through the beauty of his voice and partly through the strength and vividness of his personality.

Eventually it was the musical *South Pacific* that made him a household name, but his success here owed much in turn to the fact that he came to the Broadway show from the Metropolitan Opera House where he was leading bass from his house début in 1926 until 1948. Before coming to America he had sung at La Scala under Toscanini, his repertoire then ranging from the role of Pimen in *Boris Godunov* (he was later to sing Boris himself) to King Mark in *Tristan und Isolde*. At the Metropolitan he sang mostly in the Italian and French operas, with an increasing interest in Mozart, whose Don Giovanni became his most famous role, which he sung also at Salzburg and Covent Garden. This is represented in the present selection (called "The Golden Years") by two short solos, which may well be found to be the least satisfying of the performances. Sarastro's "O Isis und Osiris", on the other hand, sung in Italian as "Possenti numi" is magnificent in the sonority of tone and dignity of style. There is also some superb Verdi, above all the aria from *Ernani*, sung with deep feeling and subtlety of shading, and the "Confutatis" from the *Requiem*, ideally smooth, resonant and authoritative. In these and the earlier pre-electrical recordings Pinza shows clearly why he is so widely regarded as having been the supreme *basso cantate* of the century.

NEW REVIEW

OPERA RECITAL. Titta Ruffo (bar); **Orchestra/[a]Carlo Sabajno, [b]Walter B. Rogers, [c]Joseph Pasternack.** Nimbus Prima Voce NI7810.
Thomas: HAMLET — O vin, disippe la tristesse[a] (sung in Italian. From HMV 052188. Recorded in 1907). ***Verdi:*** LA TRAVIATA — Di Provenza il mar[a] (HMV 2-52529. 1907). OTELLO — Credo in un Dio crudel[b] (2-052090. 1914); Era la notte (2-052181. 1920). Sì, pel ciel![b] (with Enrico Caruso, ten. 2-054049. 1914). NABUCCO — Che tenti? ... Oh trema insano! ... Tremin gl'insani[b] (HMV 7-52063. 1914). UN BALLO IN MASCHERA — Eri tu, che macchiavi[b] (2-052170. 1915). RIGOLETTO — Pari siamo[c] (2-052185. 1920). FALSTAFF — Quand'ero paggio[c] (7-52224. 1922). ***Ponchielli:*** LA GIOCONDA — Enzo Grimaldo, Principe di Santafior[c] (Beniamino Gigli, ten. HMV HQM1194, 6/69. 1926). O monumento[a] (052376. 1912); Pescator affonda l'esca (052378. 1912). ***Leoncavallo:*** PAGLIACCI — Si può?[a] (052381, 052379. 1912). ZAZA — Buono Zazà! (7-52035. 1912); Zazà, piccola zingara (7-52031. 1912). ***Ferradini:*** Non penso a lei (7-52040. 1912). ***Donizetti:*** LA FAVORITA — Vien, Leonora, a piedi tuoi[a] (2-052075. 1912). ***Massenet:*** THAIS — Voilà donc la terrible cité[b] (Sung in Italian. 7-52050. 1914). ***Meyerbeer:*** L'AFRICAINE — Hola! Matelots[b] (Italian. 7-52072. 1915). ***Puccini:*** TOSCA — Già, mi dicon venal[b] (7-52143. 1915). ***Rossini:*** IL BARBIERE DI SIVIGLIA — Largo al factotum[c] (2-052184. 1920).

1h 16m ADD 11/90

Ruffo was the lion among baritones. Looking back on his career not long before his death in 1953 he himself said so, and he was quite right. His contemporary, De Luca, who survived to sing well, and well into old age, was the mouse, while Ruffo, who was more or less sung-out by the age of 50 or thereabouts, was the lion: "and the lion can roar no more". He was also an interesting man, one of the few Italian singers who stood against Mussolini, his brother-in-law Matteotti having been found dead in a ditch, dumped by the Fascists who killed him. He despised many of his contemporaries but acknowledged Caruso, who in turn respected him, the only singer (it was said) with whom he was nervous of singing. On records they sang together in the Oath Duet from *Otello*, included in this recital: a noble and mighty performance. With Gigli he sings on less equal terms. Gigli, a lyric tenor of unsurpassed beauty, was here in his prime; Ruffo, heroic and dramatic, was past his. The result is an unbalanced recording, yet there are marvels here too. In his solos, Ruffo has such resonance and sheer volume that his subtler qualities are sometimes overlooked. Yet few have sung Rigoletto's monologue more expressively, and his is the classic version of Iago's Creed. He was also a master of the veiled tone, and in the song *Non penso a lei* he laughs! Much more than simply the attributes of the roaring lion lay within the compass of his marvellous art.

NEW REVIEW

TEN TOP TENORS. OPERA ARIAS AND SONGS. Various artists. Continuum mono SBT1005.
Enrico Caruso — ***Leoncavallo:*** PAGLIACCI — Recitar! ... Vesti la giubba (from G&T 052159. Recorded in 1907). ***Cardillo:*** Core 'ngrato (HMV 2-052060. 1911). **Helge**

Roswaenge — *Adam:* LE POSTILLON DE LONJUMEAU — Mes amis, écoutez l'histoire. ***Auber:*** FRA DIAVOLO — Pour toujours, disaitelle (both sung in German. Both from HMV DA4414. 1936). **Beniamino Gigli — *Gounod:*** FAUST — Quel trouble inconnu ... Salut! demeure chaste et pure (sung in Italian. HMV DB1538. 12/31). ***Puccini:*** TOSCA — E lucevan le stelle (DA1372. 6/34). **Richard Tauber — *Korngold:*** DIE TOTE STADT — O Freund, ich werde sie nicht wiedersehen (Odeon LXX80946). ***J. Strauss II:*** DIE ZIGEUNERBARON — Als flotter Geist (Odeon RXX80239. Both 1924. **Georges Thill — *Bizet:*** CARMEN — La fleur que tu m'avais jetée (Columbia L1985, 9/27). ***Massenet:*** WERTHER — Je ne sais si je veille ... O nature pleine de grâce (L2064, 6/28). **John McCormack — *Donizetti:*** L'ELISIR D'AMORE — Una furtiva lagrima (2-052022. 1910). ***Rachmaninov:*** To the children, Op. 26 No. 7 (DA680, 5/25). **Jussi Björling — *Ponchielli:*** LA GIOCONDA — Cielo e mar! (DB3302, 1/38). ***Verdi:*** RIGOLETTO — La donna è mobile (DA1548, 3/37). **Lauritz Melchior — *Wagner:*** LOHENGRIN — Mein lieber Schwann (DB3664. 1938). DIE MEISTERSINGER VON NURNBERG — Am stillen Herd (DA1227, 8/32). **Giovanni Martinelli — *Verdi:*** IL TROVATORE — Ah sì, ben mio (2-052102, 1915). ***Mario:*** La leggenda del Piave (DB935, 1926). **Tito Schipa — *Donizetti:*** LA FAVORITA — Una vergine, un angel di Dio (DA1016. 1928). ***Tosti:*** 'A vucchella (DA974, 10/31).

1h 12m ADD 10/92 ▲

In days when talk about tenors tends to focus upon 'the three', a disc which reminds its listeners that there have been others may be both welcome and timely. Certainly any one of these ten merits as much attention as the members of our modern trinity. Melchior in Wagner, Thill in Massenet, Tauber in Johann Strauss: there are three for a start who in such areas will probably stand as supreme when the first 100 years of recording eventually become due for survey. Gigli's sweetness, Schipa's grace, Martinelli's intensity — and of course the unmistakable personality of each — also present themselves to posterity, and they are well represented here. McCormack shows his versatility as a near-perfect exponent of *bel canto* and as a richly communicative singer of songs. A more surprising inclusion may be that of the Dane, Helge Roswaenge, but any initial surprise of this kind will vanish when the robust tone is heard, capped with a ringing high D. Then there is Björling, at his youthful best in "Cielo e mar!", and perhaps closest among all of these (many people thought so) in succession to the King — who comes first, but really ought to be last so that everybody can see just why. Transfers by Keith Hardwick include some specially good ones of Tauber and Martinelli.

VIVA ROSSINI. OPERA AND ORATORIO ARIAS. Various artists. Testament mono SBT1008. IL BARBIERE DI SIVIGLIA — Largo al factotum (Titta Ruffo, bar. From HMV 2-052184. Recorded 1920); Se il mio nome (Dino Borgioli, ten. Columbia L2054, 5/28); O meglio mi scordavo ... Numero quindici (John McCormack, ten; Mario Sammarco, bar. 2-054021), Una voce poco fa (Luisa Tetrazzini, sop. 2-053046. Both 1911); La calunnia (Adam Didur, bass. Fonotipia 74119. 1908); Dunque io son (Maria Barrientos, sop; Riccardo Stracciari, bar. Columbia 71003D. 1919); Ah! qual colpo (Giuseppina Huguet, sop; Fernando De Lucia, ten; Antonio Pini-Corsi, bar. G&T 054083. 1906). LA CENERENTOLA — Miei rampoli (Arcangelo Rossi, bass. Victor 4406. 1905); Nacqui all'affanno ... Non più mesta (Conchita Supervia, mez. Parlophone R20140, 5/31). GUILLAUME TELL — Sombre forêt (Lina Pagliughi, sop. R30004, 3/50); Ses jours qu'ils ont osé proscrire (Giovanni Martinelli, ten; Giuseppe de Luca, bar; José Mardones, bass. 2-054130. 1923); A sa voix ... Sois immobile (Alexander Sved, bar. All sung in Italian. HMV DB5366. 1940); Asile héréditaire (André d'Arkor, ten. French Columbia RFX22. 1930); Amis, amis, secondez ma vengeance (Francesco Tamagno, ten. Italian. G&T 52683. 1903). MOSE IN EGITTO — Dal tuo stellato soglio (Anna Turchetti, sop; Ezio Pinza, bass; chorus. DB698, 11/24). SEMIRAMIDE — Ah! quel giorno (Ebe Stignani, mez. R30023, 10/50); Bel raggio lusinghier (Celestina Boninsegna, sop. Columbia 30539. 1910). Stabat mater — Cuius animam (Enrico Caruso, ten. 2-052086. 1913); Inflammatus (Florence Austral, sop; Chorus of the Royal Opera House, Covent Garden. HMV D1506, 1/29).

1h 16m ADD 9p ▲

This disc came out in 1992 to mark the bicentenary of Rossini's birth. It demonstrates the skills of Rossini singers from the dawn of recording through to the end of the 78rpm era. It offers a vocal panorama of changing styles in the execution of Rossini's music, and includes such famous pieces as Tetrazzini's coruscating "Una voce poco fa", Titta Ruffo's unsurpassed "Largo al factotum", Martinelli's sovereign "O muto asil" from *William Tell,* Austral's glorious singing of the "Inflammatus" from the *Stabat mater*, Supervia's irresistible "Non più mesta" from *La cenerentola* and other items not so well-known but equally interesting. Technically today's singers may be superior; in terms of character their predecessors carry off the honours. Excellent transfers.

NEW REVIEW

HAROLD WAYNE COLLECTION, Volume 8. **Suzanne Adams, Emma Calvé** (sops)); **Antonio Scotti, Maurice Renaud** (bars); **Anton van Rooy** (bass-bar); **Pol Plançon** (bass); **Sir Landon Ronald** (pf). Symposium mono 1100. From G&T originals. Recorded in 1902 with piano accompaniment.

Suzanne Adams — excerpts from Faust and Roméo et Juliette; songs by Stern, Vidal and Bishop. **Emma Calvé** — Carmen and Cavalleria rusticana. **Scotti** — Méssaline, Don Giovanni, Faust, Carmen and Falstaff; songs by Rotoli and Tosti. **Maurice Renaud** — Tannhäuser; song by Holmès. **Anton Van Rooy** — Die Walküre, Die Meistersinger von Nürnberg, Tannhäuser and Das Rheingold. **Pol Plançon** — Philémon et Baucis, Roméo et Juliette, Le caïd and Les huguenots; songs by J-B. Faure and Godard.

lh 19m AAD 3/93 ▲

Though this is the eighth volume of a remarkable series, it is probably the first that can be recommended with assurance to a wider public than those listeners who have a specialized interest in the singers recorded during the early years of the gramophone. Those on the present disc were all made in London in 1902: they were the 'London Reds', beloved of collectors and now worth a small fortune. The first likely surprise for a newcomer is how vividly the voices come through. The great French bass Pol Plançon is heard in the opening tracks, and the immediacy and naturalness of reproduction are often astonishing. So too is the singing, with sonority and refinement, superb fluency of scales and triplets, a brilliantly articulated trill, the well-bound evenness of cello tone, and a lively sense of fun. Not all are as satisfyingly caught as Plançon: the famous Carmen of the time, Emma Calvé, proves more elusive, though her little asides and exclamations are entertaining. Harold Wayne is the owner of one of the world's finest private collections, and his generosity has allowed these rarities to become public property. It is an opportunity to gain a privileged glimpse of another age and of singers who are far too special, both as voices and artists, to be merely forgotten.

Films and Show Music

Suggested listening ...

BIG WAR THEMES. ***Jarre:*** Lawrence of Arabia. Is Paris Burning?. ***Tiomkin:*** The Guns of Navarone. ***Goodwin:*** Battle of Britain. Where Eagles Dare. 633 Squadron. ***Coates:*** The Dam Busters — march. Eighth Army march. ***Anka:*** The Longest Day. ***E. Bernstein:*** The Great Escape. ***Rózsa:*** The Green Berets. ***Myers:*** The Deer Hunter — Cavatina. ***Cobert:*** The Winds of War. ***Farnon:*** Colditz. ***Parker:*** Sink the Bismark. ***Rodgers:*** Victory at Sea — excerpts. ***King:*** We'll Meet Again. ***Addison:*** Reach for the Sky. **Geoff Love and His Orchestra.** Compacts for Pleasure CC211.

CAPTAIN BLOOD: CLASSIC FILM SCORES FOR ERROL FLYNN. ***Steiner:*** The Adventures of Don Juan — suite. They Died With Their Boots On — suite. Dodge City — suite. ***Korngold:*** The Sea Hawk — suite[a]. Captain Blood — Ship in the night. The Adventures of Robin Hood — suite. ***Waxman:*** Objective, Burma! — Parachute drop. ***Friedhofer:*** The Sun Also Rises — Prologue; The lights of Paris. [a]**Ambrosian Singers; National Philharmonic Orchestra/Charles Gerhardt.** RCA Victor GD80912 (11/91).

CASABLANCA: CLASSIC FILM SCORES FOR HUMPHREY BOGART. ***Steiner:*** Casablanca — suite. Passage to Marseille — Rescue at sea. The Treasure of the Sierra Madre — suite. The Big Sleep — love themes. The Caine Mutiny — march. Virginia City — Stagecoach; Love scene. Key Largo — suite. ***Waxman:*** To Have and Have Not — main title. The Two Mrs Carrolls — suite. ***Hollander:*** Sabrina — main title. ***Young:*** The Left Hand of God — love theme. ***Rózsa:*** Sahara — main title. **National Philharmonic Orchestra/Charles Gerhardt.** RCA Victor GD80422 (10/90).

CLASSIC BRITISH FILM MUSIC. ***Vaughan Williams:*** Coastal Command — suite. ***Easdale:*** The Red Shoes — ballet. ***Schurmann:*** Attack and celebration. ***Bliss:*** Conquest of the Air — suite. **Philharmonia Orchestra/Kenneth Alwyn.** Silva Screen FILMCD713.

CLASSIC FILM SCORES FOR BETTE DAVIS. ***Steiner:*** Now, Voyager — It can't be wrong. Dark Victory — excerpts. A Stolen Life — main title. In This Our Life — suite. Jezebel — waltz. Beyond the Forest — suite. The Letter — main title. All This and Heaven Too — suite. ***Korngold:*** The Private Lives of Elizabeth and Essex Elizabeth. Juarez Carlotta. ***Waxman.*** Mr Skeffington — Forsaken. ***Newman:*** All About Eve — main title. **National Philharmonic Orchestra/Charles Gerhardt.** RCA Victor GD80183 (3/90).

GREAT WESTERN THEMES. ***Moross:*** The Big Country. Wagon Train. ***Morricone:*** A Fistful of Dollars. For a Few Dollars More. The Good, the Bad and the Ugly. Once Upon a Time in the West. ***Young:*** Shane — The call of the faraway hills. ***Newman:*** How the West Was Won. ***Tiomkin:*** The Alamo — The green leaves of summer. Gunfight at the OK Corral. High Noon. Rawhide. ***E. Bernstein:*** The Magnificent Seven. True Grit. ***Fielding:*** The Wild Bunch. ***Livingston:*** Cat Ballou. ***Faith:*** The Virginian. ***Buttolph:*** Maverick. ***Darby/Gertz:*** The Legend of Jesse James. ***Bacharach:*** The Man who Shot Liberty Valance. ***Rose:*** Hombre. ***Duning:*** The Big Valley. ***Mockridge:*** Laramie. ***Spencer:*** Gunsmoke. **Geoff Love and His Orchestra.** Compacts for Pleasure CC204.

HOLLYWOOD DREAMS. ***Schoenberg:*** Fanfare for the Hollywood Bowl. ***Rodgers:*** Carousel — waltz. ***Steiner:*** Gone with the Wind — main title. ***Stravinsky:*** The Firebird — Lullaby; Finale. ***Newman:*** 20th Century-Fox fanfare. Street scene. ***Waxman:*** A Place in the Sun — suite. ***Bernstein:*** On the Waterfront — love theme. ***Arlen/Stothart:*** The Wizard of Oz — suite. ***Prokofiev:*** Semyon Kotko — Southern night. ***Korngold:*** The Adventures of Robin Hood — excerpts. ***Gore:*** Defending Your Life — finale. ***Barry:*** Dances with Wolves — theme. ***Williams:*** ET — Flying. **Hollywood Bowl Orchestra/John Mauceri.** Philips 432 109-2PH.

Information

Gramophone Blue Riband Dealers

The *Gramophone Blue Riband Dealer Scheme* is designed to identify record dealers throughout the UK who can be relied upon to provide a certain level of classical record availability and service to customers.

The dealers listed below are all *Gramophone Blue Riband Dealers* and are identified as follows:
Ⓑ ***Gramophone Blue Riband Dealers.*** A fundamental requirement is that the dealer carries a stock of classical recordings and provides a good standard of service. Although the level of commitment to classical recordings may be modest, a desire and ability to order recordings not stocked is obligatory.
Ⓒ ***Gramophone Blue Riband Classical Dealers*** will carrry a worthwhile stock of classical recordings together with additional items such as publications, videos, accessories, etc. Staff expertise should be considerable, complementing an overall specific commitment to classical recordings.
Ⓢ ***Gramophone Blue Riband Specialist Dealers*** will be those recognized as having extensive product and specialist musical knowledge. They will offer a superior service and a true depth and comprehensiveness of stock. Many such dealers will be identified by record companies and distributors and endorsed by *Gramophone* readers as being qualified for this category.

Gramophone Blue Riband Mail Order Dealers (appearing as a group at the end of this list) will be able to offer customers an extensive and efficient service by post. A number of dealers will fall into the above categories but will also offer a mail order service. Once again, the skill and standing of this type of dealer will be recognized by the classical record industry as a whole.

LONDON

Ⓒ LES ALDRICH MUSIC SHOP
98 Fortis Green Road, Muswell Hill, London N10 3BH (081-883 5631)

Ⓢ ARCADE MUSIC
13-14 Grand Arcade, Tally-Ho Corner, Finchley, London N12 0EH (081-445 6369)

Ⓑ BUSH BOOKS & RECORDS
113 Shepherds Bush Centre, Shepherds Bush, London W14 9HP (081-740 5342)

Ⓢ CARUSO & CO
10 Charlotte Place, London W1P 1AP (071-636 6622)

Ⓢ COVENT GARDEN RECORDS
84 Charing Cross Road, London WC2H 0JA (071-379 7427)

Ⓢ DILLONS THE BOOKSTORE
82 Gower Street, London WC1E 6EQ (071-636 1577)

Ⓢ FARRINGDONS RECORDS
64-72 Leadenhall Market, London EC3V 1LT (071-623 9605)

Ⓢ FARRINGDONS RECORDS
Royal Festival Hall, South Bank Centre, London SE1 8XX (071-620 0198)

Ⓑ GRAHAMS HI-FI
Canonbury Yard, 190a New North Road, London N1 7BS (071-226 5500)

Ⓒ THOMAS HEINITZ LTD, MUSIC IN THE HOME
35 Moscow Road, Bayswater, London W2 4AH (071-229 2077)

Ⓑ HERGA MUSIC
2a High Street, Wealdstone, Harrow, Middlesex HA3 7AA (081-861 1590)

Ⓒ HMV
2 Waterglade Centre, Ealing Broadway, London W5 2ND (081-566 2590)

Ⓢ HMV
150 Oxford Street, London W1N 0DJ (071-631 3423)

Ⓢ HMV
363 Oxford Street, London W1R 2BJ (071-629 1240)

Ⓒ HMV
70 George Street, Richmond, Surrey TW9 1HE (081-940 9880)

Ⓑ HMV
Trocadero, 18 Coventry Street, London WC1 (071-439 0447)

Ⓢ HAROLD MOORES RECORDS
2 Great Marlborough Street, London W1V 1DE (071-437 1576 / 439 9206)

Ⓢ MUSIC DISCOUNT CENTRE
46 Thurloe Street, South Kensington, London SW7 2LT (071-584 3338)

Ⓢ MUSIC DISCOUNT CENTRE
1 Creed Lane, St Pauls, London EC4V 5BR (071-489 8077)
Mail order (071-236 0060)

Ⓢ MUSIC DISCOUNT CENTRE
29 Rathbone Place, London W1P 1AD (071-637 4700)

Ⓢ MUSIC DISCOUNT CENTRE AT ENO
31 St Martin's Lane, London WC2N 4ER (071-240 0270)

Ⓢ MUSIC DISCOUNT CENTRE
437 The Strand, London WC2R 0RN (071-240 2157)

Ⓢ ORCHESOGRAPHY
15 Cecil Court, Leicester Square, London WC2N 4EZ (071-240 1950)

Ⓢ ROYAL OPERA HOUSE SHOP
7 James Street, Covent Garden, London WC2E 9DD (071-240 1200 ext. 343)
Mail Order (071-240 1200 ext. 217)

Ⓒ SIMPLY CLASSICS
23 Old Brompton Road, Kensington, London SW7 3HZ (071-225 2111)

Ⓒ WH SMITH LTD
Brent Cross Shopping Centre, Brent Cross, London NW4 3FB (081-202 4226)

Ⓢ TEMPLAR RECORDS
Leicester Square Bookstore Ltd, 9A Irving Street, London WC2H 7AT (071-930 3579)

Ⓢ TOWER RECORDS
62-64 Kensington High Street, Kensington, London W8 4PL (071-938 3511)

Ⓢ TOWER RECORDS
1 Piccadilly Circus, London W1R 8TR (071-439 2500)

Ⓢ TOWER RECORDS
Unit 001B Whiteleys of Bayswater, Queensway, London W2 4YR (071-229 4550)

Ⓑ TURNTABLE
40 Station Road, North Chingford, London E4 6DX (081-524 3917)

Ⓒ VIRGIN RETAIL
527 Oxford Street, London W1R 1DD (071-491 8582)

Ⓢ VIRGIN MEGASTORE
14-16 Oxford Street, London W1R 7DD (071-580 5822/071-631 1234)

Ⓒ WANDA'S CLASSICS
82a High Street, Wimbledon Village, London SW19 5EG (081-946 3556)

SOUTH EAST

Ⓒ BASTOW'S CLASSICS
50a North Street, Chichester, West Sussex PO19 1MQ (0243 533264)

S BLUMLEIN'S
9a Dragon Street, Petersfield, Hampshire GU31 4JN
(0730 266605)
S BRENTWOOD HI FIDELITY LTD
2 Ingrave Road, Brentwood, Essex CM15 8AT (0277 221210)
B BRITTENS MUSIC LTD
3 Station Approach, West Byfleet, Surrey KT14 6NG
(0932 351165)
S CAMDEN CLASSICS
5 Grosvenor Road, Tunbridge Wells, Kent TN1 2AH
(0892 515705)
C CARUSO'S
3 Upper Brook Street, Winchester, Hampshire (0962 842383)
B THE CD SHOP
206 Field End Road, Eastcote, Pinner, Middlesex HA5 1RD
(081-866 0017)
C CHEW & OSBORNE
148 High Street, Epping, Essex CM16 4AG (0992 574242)
S CLASSICAL LONGPLAYER
31 Duke Street, Brighton, East Sussex BN1 1AG
(0273 329534)
S CLASSICAL LONGPLAYER
6 St Peter's Street, Canterbury, Kent CT1 2AT (0227 768888)
B CLASSICAL ROCK
10 Station Road, Harpenden, Hertfordshire (0582 764475)
S H & R CLOAKE LTD
29 High Street, Croydon, Surrey CR0 1QB (081-681 3965
(Classical) / 081-686 1336 (Pop/Jazz))
B CRANNAGE BROS
93 High Street, Uckfield, East Sussex TN22 1RJ
(0825 765422)
B DAVID'S MUSIC
12 Eastcheap, Letchworth, Hertfordshire SG6 3DE
(0462 483459)
C DILLONS THE BOOKSTORE
The Bentall Centre, Unit 59, Kingston, Surrey KT1 1TR
(081-974 6811)
B DISQUES
64 High Street, Heathfield, East Sussex TN21 8JS
(0435 866920)
B EARFRIEND
8 Broad Street, Teddington, Middlesex TW11 8RF
(081-977 0348)
C FINE RECORDS
32 George Street, Hove, East Sussex BN3 3YB (0273 723345)
B FIVES
22 Broadway, Leigh-on-Sea, Essex SS9 1NN (0702 711629)
B GRAMMAR SCHOOL RECORDS
The Old Grammar School, High Street, Rye, East Sussex
TM31 7JF (0797 222752)
C HMV
61-62 Western Road, Brighton, East Sussex BN1 2HA
(0273 747221)
C HMV
90-92 High Street, Bromley, Kent BR1 1EY (081-313 0727)
C HMV
137 North End, Croydon, Surrey CR0 1TN (081-686 5557)
C RECORD HOUSE
84 Sycamore Road, Amersham, Buckinghamshire HP6 5DR
(0494 433311)
C HMV
Units 11/12, 1st Floor, Bentalls Centre, Clarence Street,
Kingston, Surrey KT1 1TR (081-974 8037)
S JUST CLASSICS
Unit 8, Royal Star Arcade, Maidstone, Kent (0622 693670)
B LANGLEY'S RECORDS
466 Walton Road, West Moseley, Surrey KT8 2JG
(081-979 3648)
S MICHAEL'S CLASSICAL RECORD SHOP
183 Montague Street, Worthing, West Sussex BN11 3DA
(0903 207478)
C THE MUSIC CENTRE
Grove Hill Road, Tunbridge Wells, Kent TN1 1RZ
(0892 526659)
B NOVA
9 Surrey Street, Littlehampton, West Sussex BN17 5AZ
(0903 713716)
B OCTAVE RECORDED MUSIC SPECIALIST
18 High Street, Lewes, East Sussex BN7 2LN (0273 473611)
S ORPHEUS
27 Marmion Road, Southsea, Hampshire PO5 2AT
(0705 812397)
C RECORD CORNER
Pound Lane, Godalming, Surrey GU7 1BX (0483 422006)
B RICEMANS
Canterbury, Kent CT1 2TB (0227 766866)
S SEAFORD MUSIC
24 Pevensey Road, Eastbourne, East Sussex BN21 3HP
(0323 732553)
B SECOND SPIN
14 Sackville Road, Bexhill on Sea, East Sussex TN34 3JL
(0424 210894)
B SHOWELLS
94 High Street, West Wickham, Kent BR4 0NF
(081-777 5255)
B SLOUGH RECORD CENTRE
243 Farnham Road, Slough, Berkshire SL2 1DE (0753 528194)
C WH SMITH LTD
The Bentalls Centre, Woods Street, Kingston, Surrey KT1 1TR
(081-549 7631)
C WH SMITH LTD
54 The Harlequin, Watford, Hertfordshire WD1 2TF
(0923 211388)
S SOUND BARRIER
24 Tunsgate, Guildford, Surrey GU1 3QS (0483 300947)
S TOWER RECORDS
17 Fife Road, Kingston, Surrey KT1 1SB (081-541 2500)
C TRANSITIONS
19 The Centre, Walton-on-Thames, Surrey KT12 1QJ
(0932 253554)
B TRUMPS RECORDS AND TAPES LTD
28 Station Lane, Hornchurch, Essex RM12 6NJ (0708 446810)
B TRUMPS
257 High Road, Loughton, Essex IG10 1AD (081-508 4565)
B THE TURNTABLE
1 Corner House Parade, Ewell, Surrey KT17 1NX
(081-393 1881)
C VIRGIN RETAIL
157-161 Western Road, Brighton, East Sussex BN1 2BB
(0273 323216)
C WHITWAMS LTD
70 High Street, Winchester, Hampshire SO23 9DE
(0962 865253)
C THE WOODS
12 The Arcade, Bognor Regis, West Sussex PO21 1LH
(0243 827712)

SOUTH WEST
S AMADEUS CLASSICAL RECORDS
7 Frankfort Gate, Plymouth, Devon PL1 1QA (0752 671992)
S AUDIOSONIC (GLOUCESTER) LTD
6 College Street, Gloucester, Gloucestershire GL1 2NE
(0452 302280)
S BATH COMPACT DISCS
11 Broad Street, Bath, Avon BA1 5LJ (0225 464766)
B BECKETTS MUSIC SHOP
56 Commercial Road, Southampton, Hampshire SO1 0GD
(0703 224827)
B BRIDPORT RECORD CENTRE
33a South Street, Bridport, Dorset DT6 3NY (0308 25707)
S BRISTOL CLASSICAL DISCS
59 Broad Street, Bristol, Avon BS1 2EJ (0272 276536)
C CANTABILE
4 Dove Lane, Sidmouth, Devon EX10 8AN (0395 578517)
S CLASSICS
Devon Square Gallery, 81 Queen Street, Newton Abbot,
Devon TQ12 2AU (0626 55099)
S THE COLLECTORS ROOM
Suttons Music Centre, 3 Endless Street, Salisbury, Wiltshire
SP1 1DL (0722 326153)
S COMPACT CLASSICS
7-8 Criterion Arcade, Old Christchurch Road, Bournemouth,
Dorset BH1 1BU (0202 558407)

C COMPACT DISC CENTRE
5 The Old Pannier Mall, High Street, Honiton, Devon EX14 8LS (0404 45693)
B COMPACT RECORDS & TAPES
31 High Street, Falmouth, Cornwall TR11 2AD (0326 311936)
B THE CRY OF THE GULLS
4 Fore Street, Fowey, Cornwall PL23 1AQ (0726 833838)
C DILLONS THE BOOKSTORE
Units 23-24, Marlands Shopping Centre, Civil Centre Road, Southampton, Hampshire SO1 0SJ (0703 329325)
B DORCHESTER MUSIC
15 High West Street, Dorchester, Dorset DT1 1JP (0305 264977)
C THE DORSET MUSIC HOUSE
The Green, Sherborne, Dorset DT9 3HX (0935 812914)
C DUCK, SON & PINKER
59 Bridge Street, Swindon, Wiltshire SN1 1BT (0793 522220)
C DUCK, SON & PINKER
51 Oxford Street, Weston-Super-Mare, Avon BS23 1TL (0934 621174)
C GILLIAN GREIG MUSIC
164a Kingston Road, Taunton, Somerset TA2 7ST (0823 333317)
S HANCOCK & MONKS MUSIC EMPORIUM
65 Westbury Hill, Westbury-on-Tryn, Bristol, Avon BS9 3AD (0272 623251)
C HICKIES
153 Friar Street, Reading, Berkshire RG1 1HG (0734 575771)
C HMV
13-15 Stall Street, Bath, Avon BA1 1QE (0225 466681)
S HMV
138-141 Friar Street, Reading, Berkshire RG1 1EY (0734 560086)
B HMV
16-17 Regents Street, Swindon, Wiltshire SN1 1JQ (0793 420963)
S C MILSOM AND SON
12 Northgate, Bath, Avon BA1 5AS (0225 465975 ext 136)
C MUSIC MASTERS
28 Fore Street, Lostwithiel, Cornwall PL22 0BL (0208 873525)
B JOHN OLIVER
33 Fore Street, Redruth, Cornwall TR15 2AE (0209 216494)
S OPUS
The Gallery, Guildhall Centre, Exeter, Devon EX4 3HW (0392 214044)
C OPUS MUSIC
21 Pydar Street, Truro, Cornwall TR1 2AY (0872 223327)
C OTTAKAR'S
15 Eastgate Street, Gloucester, Gloucestershire GL1 1NS (0452 422464)
C OTTAKERS
9 New Canal, Salisbury, Wiltshire SP1 2AA (0722 414060)
B THE RECORD SHOP
99 High Street, Crediton, Devon EX17 3LF (0363 774299)
B RECORD SELECT
Polmorla Road, Wadebridge, Cornwall PL27 7NB (0208 812625)
C SOLO MUSIC LTD
22a Market Arcade, Guildhall Shopping Centre, Exeter, Devon EX4 3HW (0392 496564)
S SOUNDS GOOD
26 Clarence Street, Cheltenham, Gloucestershire GL50 3NU (0242 234604)
B SQUARE RECORDS
14 High Street, Wimborne, Dorset BH21 1HU (0202 883203)
B TRADING POST
23 Nelson Street, Stroud, Gloucestershire GL5 2HH (0453 759116)
C TRAX MUSIC
59 High Street, Christchurch, Dorset BH23 1AS (0202 499629)
C VIRGIN RETAIL
140 Armada Way, Plymouth, Devon PL1 1JB (0752 254400)
C VIRGIN RETAIL
1-5 Oxford Road, Reading, Berkshire RG1 7QG (0734 575222)
B WATERSIDE MUSIC
1 Waterside House, The Plains, Totnes, Devon TQ9 5DW (0803 867947)
B WISEMANS
13 The Broadway, Portswood Road, Southampton, Hampshire SO2 1WE (0703 557705)

CHANNEL ISLANDS

C SOUND ENGINEERING LTD
6 Columberie, St Helier, Jersey, Channel Islands JE2 4QA (0534 21735)
B SOUNDTRACK
Church Square, St Peter Port, Guernsey, Channel Islands (0481 722178)
B TELESKILL LTD
3-4 Market Street, St Peter Port, Guernsey, Channel Islands (0481 722323)

EAST ANGLIA

C AMBERSTONE BOOKSHOP
49 Upper Orwell Street, Ipswich, Suffolk IP4 1HP (0473 250675)
B ANDY'S RECORDS
90 St Johns Street, Bury St Edmonds, Suffolk IP33 1TZ (0284 767502)
B ANDY'S RECORDS
31-33 Fitzroy Street, Cambridge, Cambridgeshire B1 1ER (0223 61038)
B ANDY'S RECORDS
53-54 High Street, Chelmsford, Essex CM1 1DH (0245 344800)
B ANDY'S RECORDS
4 Longwyre Street, Colchester, Essex CO1 1LH (0206 44334)
B ANDY'S RECORDS
8 Buttermarket Centre, St Stephen's Lane, Ipswich, Suffolk IP1 1DT (0473 258933)
B ANDY'S RECORDS
14-16 Lower Goat Lane, Norwich, Norfolk NR2 1EL (0603 617047)
S CAMULOS CLASSICS
49 Crouch Street, Colchester, Essex CO3 3EN (0206 369310)
C CHEW & OSBORNE
70 South Street, Bishop's Stortford, Hertfordshire CM23 3AZ (0279 656401)
C CHEW & OSBORNE
26 King Street, Saffron Walden, Essex CB10 1ES (0799 523728)
S CMS RECORDS
1A All Saints' Passage, Cambridge, Cambridgeshire CB2 3LT (0223 460818)
S THE COMPACT DISCOUNT CENTRE
5 Headgate Buildings, Sir Isaacs Walk, Colchester, Essex CO1 1JJ (0206 762422)
C JAMES DACE & SON LTD
33 Moulsham Street, Chelmsford, Essex CM2 0HX (0245 352133)
S EUROPADISC
89-91 North Street, Sudbury, Suffolk CO10 0AR (0787 375743)
C GALLEON MUSIC
High Street, Aldeburgh, Suffolk IP15 5AX (0728 453298)
C GARON RECORDS
70 King Street, Cambridge, Cambridgeshire CB1 1LN
S HEFFERS SOUND
19 Trinity Street, Cambridge, Cambridgeshire CB2 3NG
B HMV
23 Market Street, Cambridge, Cambridgeshire CB2 3NZ (0223 322 521)
S MILLERS MUSIC CENTRE
12 Sussex Street, Cambridge, Cambridgeshire CB1 1PW (0223 354452)
C NICHOLLS BROS LTD
82 High Street, Braintree, Essex CM7 7JP (0376 326694)
S PRELUDE RECORDS
25b St Giles Street, Norwich, Norfolk NR2 1JN (0603 628319)

C VIRGIN RETAIL
Castle Mall, Castle Meadow, Norwich, Norfolk NR1 8DD
(0603 767376)

MIDLANDS

C RUSSELL ACOTT
124 High Street, Oxford, Oxfordshire OX1 4DE
(0865 241195)

B ANDY'S RECORDS
37 Bridge Street, Peterborough, Oxfordshire PE1 1HA
(0733 345252)

B ANDYS RECORDS LTD
Unit 38, Waterside Centre, High Street, Lincoln, Lincolnshire
LN2 1AP (0522 568476)

B ASTLEYS
3 Market Place, Wallingford, Oxfordshire OX10 0EG
(0491 834349)

B BAKEWELL MUSIC SHOP
Water Street, Bakewell, Derbyshire DE45 1EW (0629 812584)

C JAMES BEATTIE PLC
71-80 Victoria Street, Wolverhampton, West Midlands
WV1 3PQ (0902 22311)

S BLACKWELLS MUSIC SHOP
38 Holywell Street, Oxford, Oxfordshire OX1 3SW
(0865 792792)

B THE BOOK CASTLE
12 Church Street, Dunstable, Bedfordshire LU5 4RU
(0582 605670)

B CHAPPELL OF BOND STREET
21 Silbury Arcade, Central Milton Keynes, Buckinghamshire
MK9 3AG (0908 663366)

C CLASSIC MUSIC
7 Lime Street, Bedford, Bedfordshire MK40 1LD
(0234 357221)

S CLASSIC TRACKS
21 East Bond Street, Leicester, Leicestershire LE1 4SX
(0533 537700)

S CLASSICAL CD
27 Heathcote Street, Nottingham, Nottinghamshire NG1 3AG
(0602 483832)

C COLLECTORS RECORD CENTRE
6 Duckworth Square, Derby, Derbyshire DE1 1JZ
(0332 45957)

C COMPLETE DISCERY
Wallace House, Oat Street, Evesham, Worcestershire
WR11 4PJ (0386 442899)

C I M E COUNTERPOINT
1a Clarburgh House, 32 Church Street, Malvern,
Worcestershire (0684 561860)

S DILLONS THE BOOKSTORE
128 New Street, Birmingham, West Midlands B2 4DB
(021-631 4333)

C DILLONS THE BOOKSTORE
25 Wheeler Gate, Nottingham, Nottinghamshire NG1 2NF
(0602 473531)

B DISCUS MUSIC
14 Bridge Street, Bishops Stortford, Hertfordshire CM23 2UU
(0279 755861)

C DURRANT RECORDS
84 Wyle Cop, Shrewsbury, Shropshire SY1 1UT
(0743 351008)

B EASY LISTENING LTD
1135 Warwick Road, Acocks Green, Birmingham B27 6RA
(021-707 1620)

B EASY LISTENING LTD
224 Stratford Road, Shirley, Solihull, West Midlands B27 6RA
(021-744 1524)

C FORSYTH BROS LTD
6 The Midway, Newcastle-Under-Lyme, Staffordshire ST5 1QG
(0782 616177)

HMV
38 High Street, Birmingham, West Midlands B4 7SL
(021-643 0177)

B HMV
212 The Potteries Shopping Centre, Market Square, Hanley,
Staffordshire ST1 1PS (0782 283232)

S HMV
44-46 Cornmarket Street, Oxford, Oxfordshire OX1 3HA
(0865 728190)

B HMV
9-17 High Street, Leicester, Leicestershire LE1 4FP
(0533 539638)

B MUSIC BOX
5 Kings Walk, Guildhall Street, Grantham, Lincolnshire
NG31 6NL (0476 72151)

B NOT JUST BOOKS
7a Market Place, Uppingham, Rutland LE15 9QH
(0572 821306)

C OTTAKAR'S
16 High Street, Banbury, Oxfordshire OX16 8EE
(0295 270498)

C THE OUTBACK
16 Church Street, Hereford, Herfordshire HR1 2LR
(0432 275063)

C PRESTO MUSIC
23 Portland Street, Leamington Spa, Warwickshire CV32 5EZ
(0926 334834)

C RECORD HOUSE
36 High Street, Aylesbury, Buckinghamshire HP20 1SF
(0296 20770)

C WH SMITH LTD
29 Union Street, Birmingham, West Midlands B2 4LR
(021-631 3303)

C WH SMITH LTD
14-16 Listergate, Nottingham, Nottinghamshire NG1 7DD
(0602 582919)

C SOUNDS EXPENSIVE
12 Regent Street, Rugby, Warwickshire, CV21 2QF
(0788 540772)

B SPINADISC RECORDS
83-87 Lower Precinct
Coventry, West Midlands CV1 1DS (0203 632004/5)

B SPINADISC RECORDS
75a Abington Street, Northampton, Northamptonshire
NN1 2BH (0604 31144)

C STAMFORD MUSIC SHOP
11 St Mary's Hill, Stamford, Lincolnshire PE9 2DP
(0780 51275)

S ST MARTINS RECORDS
23 Hotel Street, Leicester, Leicestershire LE1 5AW
(0533 539292)

B BRIAN SUNDERLAND (MUSIC)
62 Earlsdon Street, Coventry, West Midlands CN5 6EJ
(0203 714272)

C TOWER SOUNDS
9 Market Place, Cirencester, Gloucestershire Gl7 2NX
(0285 654283)

S VIRGIN RETAIL
98 Corporation Street, Birmingham, West Midlands B4 6SX
(021-236 2523)

S VIRGIN RETAIL
6-8 Wheelergate, Nottingham, Nottinghamshire NG1 2NB
(0602 476126)

NORTH EAST

C ADAGIO CLASSICAL RECORDS
Westminster Arcade, Harrogate, North Yorkshire HG1 2RN
(0423 506507)

S BANKS & SON (MUSIC) LTD
18 Lendal, York, North Yorkshire YO1 2AU (0904 658836)

C BERRY'S MUSIC
23 Bridge Place, Worksop, Nottinghamshire S80 1PT
(0909 473532)

S CALM & CLASSICAL
144 West Street, Sheffield, South Yorkshire S1 4ES
(0742 755795)

B CHARTBOX MUSIC LTD
5 Wells Road, Ilkley, West Yorkshire LS29 9JB (0943 816733)

S THE CLASSICAL RECORD SHOP
2 Merrion Centre, Leeds, West Yorkshire LS2 8NG
(0532 452059)

C BERNARD DEAN
10-12 St Thomas Street, Scarborough, North Yorkshire
YO11 1DR (0723 372573)

Ⓑ THE DEN
38 Cavendish Street, Keighley, West Yorkshire BD21 3RG
(0535 606086)
Ⓒ FORSYTH BROS LTD
St George House, 40 Great George Street, Leeds, West Yorkshire LS1 3DL (0532 444494)
Ⓑ GRAPEVINE
4 King's Parade, King Street, Cottingham, North Humberside HU16 5QQ (0482 849191)
Ⓑ HMV
1:13 Schofields Centre, Leeds, West Yorkshire LS1 6JB
(0532 442992)
Ⓒ HMV
46-48 Northumberland Street, Newcastle-upon-Tyne, Tyne & Wear NE1 7TT (091-232 7470)
Ⓒ HMV
121-123 Pinstone Street, Sheffield, South Yorkshire S1 2HL
(0742 751445)
Ⓒ HMV
10a Coney Street, York, North Yorkshire YO1 1NA
(0904 640218)
Ⓒ J & K RECORDS
39 Ladygate, Beverley, North Humberside HU17 8BH
(0482 868033)
Ⓒ METRO MUSIC
12 Victoria Road, Scarborough, North Yorkshire YO11 1SD
(0723 379471)
Ⓒ PLAYBACK
122-124 Linthorpe Road, Middlesborough, Cleveland TS1 2JR
(0642 219133 (Classical CDs), 250060)
Ⓒ RECORD COLLECTOR
233-235 Fulwood Road, Broomhill, Sheffield, South Yorkshire S10 3BA (0742 668493)
Ⓢ SERENADE TO MUSIC
16 Bradford Row, Doncaster, South Yorkshire DN1 3NF
(0302 432235)
Ⓒ TIME & TUNE
Grove Bookshop, 10 The Grove, Ilkley, West Yorkshire
LS29 9EG (0943 817301)
Ⓑ VIRGIN RETAIL
94-96 The Briggate, Leeds, West Yorkshire LS1 6BR
(0532 443681)
Ⓒ VIRGIN RETAIL
Monument Mall, 15-21 Northumberland Street, Newcastle-upon-Tyne, Tyne & Wear NE1 7AE (091-230 5959)
Ⓢ VIRGIN RETAIL
Orchard Square, Fargate, Sheffield, South Yorkshire S1 2HD
(0742 731175)
Ⓒ WESTSIDE MUSIC
959 Ecclesall Road, Sheffield, South YorkshireS11 8TN
(0742 670718)
Ⓢ J G WINDOWS LTD
1-7 Central Arcade, Newcastle upon Tyne, Tyne & Wear
NE1 5BP (091 232 1356)
Ⓒ J WOOD & SONS LTD
38 Manningham Lane, Bradford, West Yorkshire BD1 3AE
(0274 307636)

NORTH WEST & ISLE OF MAN
Ⓑ ANDY'S RECORDS
2 Marble Place, Southport, Merseyside PR8 1DF
(0704 549222)
Ⓑ ANDY'S RECORDS
27-29 Victoria Square, Bolton, Lancashire BL1 1RJ
(0204 373388)
Ⓑ ASTON AUDIO
4 West Street, Alderley Edge, Cheshire SK9 7EG
(0625 582704)
Ⓒ BLACKWELL'S ACADEMIC BOOKSHOP
149-153 Oxford Road, Manchester, Greater Manchester
M13 9RU (061 274 3331)
Ⓒ BLUEBELL BOOKSHOP & MUSIC
Angel Square, Penrith, Cumbria CA11 7BP (0768 66660)
Ⓒ BOOKCASE
17 Castle Street, Carlisle, Cumbria CA3 8TP (0228 44560)
Ⓒ CHESTER COMPACT DISC CENTRE
18 Paddock Row, Grosvenor Precinct, Chester, Cheshire
CH1 1ED (0244 311991)

Ⓢ CIRCLE RECORDS
33 Victoria Street, Liverpool, Merseyside L1 6BG
(051-236 1000)
Ⓢ CONCERT CORNER
94b-96b Lord Street, Southport, Merseyside PR8 1JR
(0704 533883)
Ⓒ DILLONS THE BOOKSTORE
2-4 St Anne's Square
Manchester, Greater Manchester M2 7HH (061-832 0424)
Ⓢ FORSYTH BROTHERS LIMITED
126 Deansgate, Manchester, Greater Manchester M3 2GR
(061-834 3281)
Ⓒ KENNETH GARDNER LTD
28 New Street, Lancaster, Lancashire LA1 1EG
(0524 64328 ext. 215)
Ⓢ GIBBS BOOKSHOP LTD
10 Charlotte Street, Manchester, Greater Manchester M1 4FL
(061-236 7179)
Ⓒ HMV
48-50 Foregate Street, Chester, Cheshire CH1 1HA
(0244 310307)
Ⓢ HMV
22-36 Church Street, Liverpool, Merseyside L1 3AW
(051-709 1088)
Ⓢ HMV
90-100 Market Street, Manchester, Greater Manchester
M1 1PD (061-834 8550)
Ⓑ HMV
51-53 Merseyway, Stockport, Greater Manchester SK1 1PW
(061-460 0548)
Ⓒ KELLY'S MUSIC SHOP
2-4 The Mall, Dalton Road, Barrow-in-Furness, Cumbria
WA14 1HL (0229 822973)
Ⓑ JOE KOCZUR LTD
185 Yorkshire Street, Rochdale, Lancashire OL12 0DR
(0706 42107)
Ⓒ KOVARY'S OPUS III
44 Market Place, Cockermouth, Cumbria CA13 9NG
(0900 822314)
Ⓑ MARGIN MUSIC
3 Market Place, Macclesfield, Cheshire SK10 1EB
(0625 619013)
Ⓑ MARPLE RECORDS
22 Market Street, Marple, Stockport, Cheshire SK6 7AD
(061-427 3234)
Ⓑ MARY'S MUSIC
44-46 Whalley Road, Accrington, Lancashire BB5 1AR
(0254 253060)
Ⓑ MOORGATE MUSIC
Unit 35, Indoor Market Hall, Moorgate, Ormskirk, Lancashire
L39 2RY (0695 571007)
Ⓑ KEN PALK LTD
Shopping Centre, Bramhall, Stockport, Cheshire SK7 1AW
(061 439 8479)
Ⓢ RARE RECORDS
13 Bank Square, Wilmslow, Cheshire SK9 1AN (0625 522017)
Ⓒ REIDY'S HOME OF MUSIC
9-13 Penny Street, Blackburn, Lancashire BB1 6HJ
(0254 265303)
Ⓒ RUSHWORTHS MUSIC LIMITED
31a Bridge Street, Chester, Cheshire CH1 1NG (0244 325252)
Ⓒ RUSHWORTHS MUSIC HOUSE LTD
42-46 Whitechapel, Liverpool, Merseyside L1 6EF
(051-709 9071)
Ⓒ WH SMITH LTD
11 Foregate Street, Chester, Cheshire CH1 1HH
(0244 321106)
Ⓒ WH SMITH LTD
10-16 Church Street, Liverpool, Merseyside L1 3EG
(051-709 1435)
Ⓑ SMITHS OF WIGAN
41 Mesnes Street, Wigan, Lancashire WN1 1QY
(0942 42810/46270)
Ⓑ SMYTH'S RECORDS
123-125 Highgate, Kendal, Cumbria LA9 4EN (0539 729595)
Ⓢ VIRGIN RETAIL
52-56 Market Street, Manchester, Greater Manchester
M1 1QA (061-833 1111/2)

B VOLUMES
88 London Road, Stockton Heath, Warrington, Cheshire WA4 6LE (0925 601424)

ISLE OF MAN
C ISLAND COMPACT DISC CENTRE
80 Parliament Street, Ramsey, Isle of Man (0622 815521)

SCOTLAND
S BAUERMEISTER BOOKSELLERS
15-16 George IV Bridge, Edinburgh EH1 1EH (031-226 5561)
C BRUCE MILLERS
363 Union Street, Aberdeen AB9 1EN (0224 592211)
B CASA CASSETTES LTD
325 Sauchiehall Street, Glasgow G2 3HW (041-332 1127)
B CONCORDE
15 Scott Street, Perth PH1 5EJ (0738 21818)
C JOHN M HAY (STIRLING) LTD
Friars Gait, 29-31 Friars Street, Stirling FK8 1HE (0786 473573)
B HMV
247-251 Union Street, Aberdeen AB1 2BQ (0224 575323)
C HMV
Unit 6, Lewis's Centre, Argyle Street, Glasgow G2 8AD (041-204 4787)
C HMV
154-160 Sauchiehall Street, Glasgow G2 3DH (041-332 6631)
C HMV
129 Princes Street, Edinburgh, EH2 4AH (031-226 3466)
S MCALISTER MATHESON MUSIC LTD
1 Grindlay Street, Edinburgh EH3 9AT (031-228 3827)
B MUSICMATTERS
42-44 East Church Street, Buckie, Banffshire AB56 1AB (0542 832020)
C THE MUSICMONGERS
151 South Street, St Andrews, Fife KY16 9UN (0334 78625)
C JAMES THIN LTD
53-59 Southbridge, Edinburgh EH10 4QR (031-556 6743)
C TOP NOTE
123 Crown Street, Aberdeen AB1 2HN (0224 210259)
S TOWER RECORDS
217-221 Argyle Street, Glasgow G2 8DL (041-204 2500)
S VIRGIN RETAIL
133 Union Street, Aberdeen AB1 2BH (0224 213050)
S VIRGIN RETAIL
131 Princes Street, Edinburgh EH2 4AH (031-225 4583)
C VIRGIN RETAIL
28-32 Union Street, Glasgow G1 3QX (041-221 0103)
C VIRGIN RETAIL
Unit 4, Lewis' Building, Argyle Street, Glasgow G1 2AQ (041-221 2606)

WALES
C ABERGAVENNY MUSIC
23 Cross Street, Abergavenny, Gwent NP7 5EW (0873 853394)
C CERDD YSTWYTH MUSIC
7 Upper Portland Street, Aberystwyth, Dyfed SY23 2DT (0970 623382/617626)
S CITY RADIO
27a Morgan Arcade, Cardiff, South Glamorgan CF1 2AF (0222 228169)
S CITY RADIO
24 Charles Street, Newport, Gwent NP9 1JT (0633 840728)
B CLWYD BOOKS
Harmony House, St George's Place, Llandudno, Gwynedd (0492 877510)
B HMV
51 Queen Street, Cardiff, South Glamorgan CF1 4AS (0222 227147)
B MARJAN MUSIC
190 High Street, Prestatyn, Clwyd LL19 8SR (0745 853160)
C THE MUSE
43 Holyhead Road, Bangor, Gwynedd LL57 2UE (0248 362072)
C SWALES MUSIC CENTRE LTD
2-6 High Street, Haverfordwest, Pembrokeshire, SA61 2DJ (0437 762059/763261)
B VIDEOVENTURE HOME ENTERTAINMENTS
4 St Mary Street, Cardigan, Dyfed SA43 1HA (0239 615036)
S VIRGIN RETAIL
Units 7-9, Capitol Arcade, The Capitol, Queens Street, Cardiff, South Glamorgan CF1 4HQ (0222 388273)

NORTHERN IRELAND
S CLASSICAL TRACKS
15a Castle Arcade, Belfast BT1 5DG (0232 333868)
S KOINONIA
6 Pottinger's Entry, High Street, Belfast BT1 2JZ (0232 247873)
C VIRGIN RETAIL
Unit 1C, Castlecourt, Royal Avenue, Belfast BT1 1DD (0232 236623)

MAIL ORDER
CDX CLASSICAL
The Olde Coach House, Windsor Crescent, Radyr, South Glamorgan CF4 8AE (0222 844443/843890)
CLUB 50/50 MUSIC & VIDEO
PO Box 1277, Chippenham, Wiltshire SN15 3YZ (0249 445400)
COMPACT CLASSICS LTD
87 Portland Road, London W11 4LN (071-221 1735)
CROTCHET & COMPANY
Church Stretton, Shropshire. (0694 722982)
EDEN COMPACT DISCS
41 Hever Road, Edenbridge, Kent TN8 5DH (0732 863392)
MDT CLASSICS LTD
6 Old Blacksmiths Yard, Sadler Gate, Derby, Derbyshire DE1 3PD (0332 368251)
MUSIC ESTABLISHED LTD
25 Newgate Street, Morpeth, Northumberland NE61 1AW (0670 511744)
THE MUSIC GROUP
West Haddon, Northamptonshire NN6 7AA (0788 510693)
OPUS 1 MUSIC
19 Brunswick Road, Bangor, County Down BT20 3DY (0247 457775)
OSCAR 'C'
127a East Barnet Road, New Barnet, Hertfordshire EN4 8RF (081 441 0134)
RECORDS-BY-POST
28 Barton Heys Road, Formby, Merseyside L37 2EY
SILVER SERVICE CD
24 Touch Wards, Dunfermline, Fife KY12 7TG (0383 738159)
SPECTRUM MUSIC
York House, Tylers Court, Cranleigh, Surrey GU6 8SS (0483 274903)
SQUIRES GATE MUSIC CENTRE
Squires Gate Station Approach, Blackpool, Lancashire FY8 2SP (0253 44360)
TANDY'S RECORDS LIMITED
24 Islington Row, Birmingham, West Midlands B15 1LJ (021-455 8866)
WINGS MAIL ORDER
32 Witham Bank West, Boston, Lincolnshire PE21 8PT (0205 358134)
WORLDWIDE MUSIC/BOOK SERVICES
4 Kendall Avenue, Sanderstead, Surrey CR2 0NH (081-660 4940)

SECOND HAND SPECIALISTS
BARGAIN CLASSICAL RECORDS
9 The Arcade, High Street, Eltham, London SE9 1BE (081-859 5836)
GARON RECORDS
65-66 The Covered Market, Oxford, Oxfordshire OX1 3DX (0865 246887)
MICHAEL G THOMAS
5a Norfolk Place, Paddington, London W2 1QN (071-723 4935)

Manufacturers and Distributors

Entries are listed as follows: MANUFACTURER or LABEL—UK Distributor *(Series)*

ABBEY—Gamut
ACCENT—Gamut
ACCORD (Musidisc)—Discovery Records
ADDA—Gamut
ADES—Discovery Records
ALBANY—Albany
ALTARUS—New Note
AMON RA (Saydisc)—Gamut/Harmonia Mundi
APR—Harmonia Mundi
ARABESQUE—Albany
ARCANA—New Note
ARCHIV PRODUKTION—PolyGram Record Operations *(Archiv Produktion, Archiv Produktion Galleria)*
ARGO—PolyGram Record Operations
ARION—Discovery Records
ASV—ASV/Koch International *(ASV, Gaudeamus)*
AUVIDIS—Koch International *(Astrée, Valois)*
AURORA—Gamut
BAYER—Koch International
BEECHAM TRUST—Sir Thomas Beecham Trust
BIDDULPH—Koch International
BIS—Conifer
BNL—Koch International
BRIDGE—Albany
CALA—Complete Record Co.
CALLIOPE—Harmonia Mundi
CAPRICCIO—Target
CAPRICE—Complete Record Co.
CASCAVELLE—Scott Butler
CBC RECORDS—Albany
CBS—Sony Music Entertainment *(Masterworks, Masterworks Portrait, Digital Masters)*
CDM RUSSIAN SEASON—Harmonia Mundi
CENTAUR—Harmonia Mundi
CHANDOS—Chandos *(Chandos, Chaconne, Collect)*
CHANNEL CLASSICS—Complete Record Co.
CHESKY—New Note
CHRISTOPHORUS—Select
CLARINET CLASSICS—New Note
CLASSICS FOR PLEASURE—Music for Pleasure
CLAVES—Complete Record Co.
COLLEGIUM—Gamut/Koch International
COLLINS CLASSICS—Conifer *(Collins Classics, Quest)*
CONIFER—Conifer
CONTINUUM—Complete Record Co/Priory
CPO—Priory
CRD—Chandos
CYBELIA—Rare Records
DABRINGHAUS UND GRIMM—Priory
DANTE—Scott Butler
DECCA—PolyGram Record Operations *(Decca, New Line, London, Ovation, Enterprise, Grand Opera, Headline, Historic, Serenata, Weekend)*
DELL'ARTE—Harmonia Mundi
DELOS—New Note
DENON—Conifer *(Denon, Aliare)*
DERVORGUILLA RECORDS—New Note
DEUTSCHE HARMONIA MUNDI—BMG UK *(Deutsche Harmonia Mundi, Editio Classica)*
DG—PolyGram Record Operations *(DG, DG Galleria, 3-D Classics, 20th Century Classics, Compact Classics, Dokumente, Karajan Symphony Edition, Privilege)*
DISQUES MONTAIGNE—New Note
DORIAN—Conifer
DUTTON LABORATORIES—Dutton Laboratories
EARTHSOUNDS—Scott Butler
EBS—Complete Record Co.
ECM NEW SERIES—New Note
ELEKTRA NONESUCH—Warner Classics
EMI EMINENCE—Music for Pleasure
EMI LASER—Music for Pleasure
EMI—EMI *(EMI, Reflexe, Studio, Beecham Edition, British Composers, Great Recordings of the Century, Melodiya, Phoenixa, Références, Rossini Edition, Rouge et Noir)*
ERATO—Warner Classics *(Erato, MusiFrance, Libretto, Emerald)*
ETCETERA—Scott Butler
EURODISC—BMG UK
EUROPA MUSIC—Koch International
FACTORY CLASSICAL—New Note
FINLANDIA—Conifer
FIRST NIGHT RECORDS—Pinnacle
GAMUT CLASSICS—Gamut
GIMELL—Gamut/Pickwick
HÄNSSLER—Koch International
HARMONIA MUNDI—Harmonia Mundi *(Harmonia Mundi, Musique d'abord)*
HARMONIC RECORDS—Complete Record Co.
HERALD—Gamut
HUNGAROTON—Conifer *(Hungaroton, Antiqua, White Label)*
HYPERION—Complete Record Co./Gamut *(Hyperion, Helios)*
ISIS RECORDS—Priory
JECKLIN DISCO—Scott Butler
KEYBOARD RECORDS—Scott Butler
KINGDOM RECORDS—Kingdom
KOCH INTERNATIONAL CLASSICS—Koch International
KOCH SCHWANN—Koch International
LANDOR BARCELONA—New Note
LARGO—New Note
LASERLIGHT (Capriccio)—Target
LE CHANT DU MONDE—Harmonia Mundi

LEGATO CLASSICS—Complete Record Co.
LINN RECORDS—PolyGram Record Operations
LYRITA—Conifer
L'OISEAU-LYRE—PolyGram Record Operations
MARCO POLO—Select
MEDICI-WHITEHALL—Complete Record Co.
MELODIYA—Koch International
MEMOIR CLASSICS—BMG UK
MERCURY—PolyGram Record Operations
MERIDIAN—Gamut
MIRABILIS—Priory
MOTETTE—Priory
MUSIC AND ARTS—Harmonia Mundi
MUSICA SVECIAE—Gamut
MUSICAL OBSERVATIONS—Albany
MUSIDISC—Discovery Records
MUSICMASTERS—Nimbus
NAXOS—Select
NEW ALBION—Harmonia Mundi
NEW WORLD—Harmonia Mundi
NEWPORT CLASSIC—Rare Records *(Newport Classics, Premier)*
NIMBUS—Nimbus
NMC—New Note
NORTHEASTERN—Albany
NOVALIS—Complete Record Co.
NUOVA ERA—Complete Record Co.
ODE—Discovery Records
OLYMPIA—Complete Record Co.—*(Olympia, Explorer)*
ONDINE—Koch International
ONYX—Scott Butler
OPERA RARA—Complete Record Co./Scott Butler
OPUS—Rare Records
OPUS 3—Quantum Audio
OPUS III—Conifer
ORFEO—Koch International
OTTAVO—Priory
PARTRIDGE—Albany
PAULA—Gamut
PAVANE—Kingdom
PEARL (Pavilion)—Harmonia Mundi
PHILIPS—PolyGram Record Operations *(Philips, Silver Line, Legendary Classics, Mozart Edition, Musica da Camara, Concert Classics)*
PIANISSIMO—Albany
PICKWICK—Pickwick/Gamut *(IMP Masters, IMP Classics, IMP Red Label)*
POINT MUSIC—PolyGram Record Operations
POLSKIE NAGRANIA—Complete Record Co.
POLYDOR—PolyGram Record Operations
PRAGA—Harmonia Mundi
PREISER—Harmonia Mundi
PRELUDIO—Scott Butler
PRIORY—Priory
PROUDSOUND—Gamut
PYRAMID RECORDS—Priory
QUINTANA—Harmonia Mundi
RCA—BMG UK *(RCA Victor, Red Seal, Gold Seal, Papillon, Seon, Victrola)*
REDCLIFFE RECORDINGS—Complete Record Co.
REFERENCE RECORDINGS—Quantum Audio
REM EDITIONS—Priory
RICERCAR—Gamut
ROYAL OPERA HOUSE RECORDS—Conifer
SAGA CLASSICS—Complete Record Co.
SAIN—Target
SALABERT ACTUELS—Harmonia Mundi
SIGNUM—Chord
SILVA SCREEN—Conifer
SIMAX—Gamut
SONY CLASSICAL—Sony Music Entertainment *(Sony Classical, Vivarte, Essential Classics)*
SUPRAPHON—Koch International
TELARC—Conifer
TELDEC—Warner Classics *(Teldec Classics, British Line, Das Alte Werk, Das Alte Werk Reference)*
TER CLASSICS—Conifer
TESTAMENT—Gamut
TIMPANI—New Note
TRITTICO—Trittico Distributor
UNICORN-KANCHANA—Harmonia Mundi *(Unicorn-Kanchana, Souvenir)*
VANGUARD CLASSICS—Complete Record Co.—*(Vanguard Classics, Omega)*
VARESE SARABANDE—Pinnacle
VICTORIA—Gamut
VIRGIN CLASSICS—EMI *(Virgin Classics, Veritas, Virgo, Venture)*
WERGO—Harmonia Mundi

For additional information on Manufacturers and Distributors, refer to *The Classical Catalogue* (published by General Gramophone Publications).

Record Company Names and Addresses

Unless otherwise indicated all the companies listed below are based in the UK; addresses for record companies from outside the UK are given, where available.

ABBEY RECORDING CO – 1 Abbey Street, Eynsham, Oxford OX8 1HS (0865 880240)

ACCENT RECORDS – Eikstraat 31, 1673 Beert, *BELGIUM* (322 356 1878)

ACCORD – 3-5 Rue Albert de Vatimsnil, 92305 Levallois, *FRANCE* (4758 1290)

ADDA – 8 Rue Jules Verne, 93400 Saint-Ouen, *FRANCE* (1 4012 6030)

ADES – 54, Rue Saint Lazare, 75009 Paris, *FRANCE* (1 4874 8530)

ALBANY RECORDS UK – PO Box 12, Carnforth, Lancashire LA5 9PD (0524 735873); US – Box 5011, Albany NY12205, *USA* (518 453 2203)

ALTARUS RECORDS – 17 Knole Road, Sevenoaks, Kent TN13 3XH (0732 455972)

APPIAN PUBLICATIONS AND RECORDINGS (APR) – PO Box 1, Wark, Hexham, Northumberland NE48 3EW (0434 220627)

ARABESQUE RECORDINGS – 60 East 42nd Street, New York NY10165, *USA* (212 983 1414)

ARCHIV PRODUKTION – 1 Sussex Place, Hammersmith, London W6 9XS (081-846 8515)

ARGO – 1 Sussex Place, Hammersmith, London W6 9XS (081-846 8515)

ARION – 36, Avenue Hoche, 75008 Paris, *FRANCE* (1 4563 7670)

ASV – Martin House, 179-181 North End Road, London W14 9NL (071-381 8747)

AUVIDIS – 12 Avenue Maurice Thorey, 94200 Ivry-sur-Seine, *FRANCE* (1 4672 3939)

SIR THOMAS BEECHAM TRUST – Denton House, Denton, Harleston, Norfolk IP20 0AA (098686 780)

GRAMMOFON AB BIS – Bragevägen 2, 18264 Djursholm, *SWEDEN* (8 755 4100)

BAYER – Dept. Ku-m/1-m, Building E60, 5090 Leverkusen, *GERMANY* (21430 8507)

BIDDULPH RECORDINGS – 35 St George Street, London W1R 9FA (071-491 8621)

BMG CLASSICS – Bedford House, 69-79 Fulham High Street, London SW6 3JW (071-973 0011)

BMG UK – Lyng Lane, West Bromwich, West Midlands B70 7ST (061-525 3000)

BNL PRODUCTIONS – 28 Rue Louis Nouveau, 06400 Cannes, *FRANCE* (9292 2584)

BRIDGE RECORDS – GPO Box 1864, New York, NY10116, *USA* (516 487 1662)

SCOTT BUTLER DISC AND TAPE FACTORS – Unit 2, Lansdowne Mews, Charlton Lane, London SE7 8AZ (081-858 9190)

CALA RECORDS – 17 Shakespeare Gardens, London N2 9LJ (081-883 7306)

CALLIOPE – 14 Rue de la Justice, Boîte Postale 166, 60204 Compiègne Cedex, *FRANCE* (4423 2765)

CAPRICCIO – Zur Mühle 2, 50226 Frechen, *GERMANY* (02234 60060)

CAPRICE RECORDS – Box 1225, 111 82 Stockholm, *SWEDEN* (8 791 4692)

CASCAVELLE – 23 Ch Bellefontaine, CH-1223 Cologny, Geneve, *SWITZERLAND* (22 735 7862)

CBC RECORDS – PO Box 500, Station A, Toronto, Ontario M5W 1E6, *CANADA* (416 975 3501)

CBS RECORDS – *see* SONY MUSIC ENTERTAINMENT

CENTAUR RECORDS INC – 8867 Highland Road, Suite 206, Baton Rouge, LA 70808, *USA* (504 336 4877)

CHANDOS RECORDS – Chandos House, Commerce Way, Colchester, Essex CO2 8HQ (0206 794000)

CHANNEL CLASSICS RECORDS – Jacob van Lennepkade 334 e, 1053 NJ Amsterdam *THE NETHERLANDS* (20 6161775)

CHESKY RECORDS – 311 West 43rd Street, Suite 702, New York, NY10036, *USA* (212 586 7799)

CHORD RECORDS AND DISTRIBUTION – PO Box 1, South Street, Axminster, Devon EX13 7UQ (0404 45693)

CLARINET CLASSICS – 77 St Alban's Avenue London E6 4HH (081-472 2057)

CLASSICS FOR PLEASURE – 1-3 Uxbridge Road, Hayes, Middlesex UB4 0SY (081-561 8722)

CLAVES RECORDS – Trüelweg 14, 3600 Thun, *SWITZERLAND* (0 3323 1649)

COLLEGIUM RECORDS – PO Box 172, Whittlesford, Cambridge CB2 4QZ (0223 832474)

COLLINS CLASSICS – Electron House, Cray Avenue, St Mary Cray, Orpington, Kent BR5 3PN (06898 98711)

THE COMPLETE RECORD CO. – 12 Pepys Court, 84 The Chase, London SW4 0NF (071-498 9666)

CONIFER RECORDS – Horton Road, West Drayton, Middlesex UB7 8JL (0895 447707)

CONTINUUM CDs – 26 Highgate High Street, London N6 5JG (081-348 0466)

CPO – Ackerstraße 59, 4500 Osnabruck, *GERMANY* (54157 1087)

CRD – PO Box 26, Stanmore, Middlesex HA7 4XB (081-958 7695)

DANTE – 208, Rue Marcadet, 75018 Paris, *FRANCE* (1 4252 7677)

DECCA CLASSICS – 1 Sussex Place, Hammersmith, London W6 9XS (081-846 8515)

DELL'ARTE RECORDS – PO Box 26, Hampton, Middlesex TW12 2NL (081-979 2479)

DELOS INTERNATIONAL – Hollywood and Vine Plaza, 1645 North Vine Street, Suite 340, Hollywood, California CA90028, *USA* (213 962 2626)

DENON/NIPPON COLUMBIA – 14-14, Akasaka 4-Chome, Minatu-Ku, Tokyo 107-11, *JAPAN* (03 3584 8271)

DEUTSCHE GRAMMOPHON CLASSICS – 1 Sussex Place, Hammersmith, London W6 9XS (081-846 8515)

DISCOVERY RECORDS – The Old Church Mission Room, King's Corner, Pewsey, Wilts SN9 5BS (0672 63931)

DISQUES MONTAIGNE – 15 Avenue Montaigne, 75008 Paris, *FRANCE* (1 4231 6540)

DORIAN RECORDINGS – 17 State Street, Suite 2E, Troy, NY12180, *USA* (518 274 5475)

DUTTON LABORATORIES – PO Box 576, Harrow, Middlesex HA3 6YW (081-421 1117)

EARTHSOUNDS – PO Box 1, Richmond, North Yorkshire DL10 5GB (0748 825 959)

EBS RECORDS – Pforzheimer Straße 30, 74321 Bietigheim-Bissingen, *GERMANY* (7142 45505)

ECM – Gleichmanstraße 10, 8000 München 60, *GERMANY* (08985 1048)

ELEKTRA NONESUCH: *US* – 75 Rockefeller Plaza, New York NY10019, *USA* (212 484 7200); UK – 46 Kensington Court, London W8 5DP (071-938 5542)

EMI RECORDS – Customer Services Dept, 20 Manchester Square, London W1A 1ES (071-487 4442)

EMI CLASSICS – 30 Gloucester Place, London W1A 1ES (071-486 6022)

EMI – Sales & Distribution Centre, Hermes Close, Tachbrook Park, Leamington Spa, Warwickshire CV34 6RP (0926 888888)

ERATO: FRANCE – 50 Rue des Tournelles, 75003 Paris, *FRANCE* (1 4027 7000); *UK* – 46 Kensington Court, London W8 5DP (071-938 5542)

ETCETERA – Keizersgracht 518, 107 EK Amsterdam, *THE NETHERLANDS* (020 23 48 05)

FINLANDIA RECORDS – PO Box 169, 02101 Espoo, *FINLAND* (358 0 435011)

FIRST NIGHT RECORDS – 2/3 Fitzroy Mews, London W1P 5DQ (071-387 7767)

GAMUT DISTRIBUTION – Gamut House, Lancaster Way, Ely, Cambridgeshire CB6 3NP (0353 662366)

GIMELL RECORDS – 4 Newtec Place, Magdalen Road, Oxford OX4 1RE (0865 244557)

BRIAN GRIFFIN DISTRIBUTION – Storey House, White Cross, South Road, Lancaster LA1 4XQ (0524 846446)

HÄNSSLER CLASSIC – Postfach 12 20, 73762 Neuhausen, *GERMANY* (7158 1770)

HARMONIA MUNDI: *UK* – 19-21 Nile Street, London N1 7LR (071-253 0863); *FRANCE* – Mas de Vert, 13200 Arles, (9049 9049); *USA* – 3364 S. Robertson Boulevard, Los Angeles, California CA90034, (310 559 0802)

HARMONIC RECORDS – Parc de Montigny, Maxilly-sur-Léman, 74500 Evian-les-Bains, *FRANCE* (5075 6900)

HERALD AUDIOVISUAL PUBLICATIONS – The Studio, Alfred Road, Farnham, Surrey GU9 8ND (0252 725349)

HUNGAROTON – Vörösmarty tér 1, 1051 Budapest, *HUNGARY* (361 1187 193)

HYPERION RECORDS – PO Box 25, Eltham, London SE9 1AX (081-294 1166)

ISIS RECORDS – 2 Henley Street, Oxford, OX4 1ER (0865 726553)

JECKLIN & CO – Rämistraße 42, 8024 Zürich, *SWITZERLAND* (01 261 7774)

KEYBOARD RECORDS – 418 Brockley Road, London, SE4 2DH (081-699 2549)

KINGDOM RECORDS – 61 Collier Street, London N1 9BE (071-713 7788)

KOCH INTERNATIONAL: *UK* – 23 Warple Way, London W3 0RX (081-749 7177); *USA* – 177, Cantiague Rock Road, Westbury, NY11590, *USA* (516 938 8080)

KOCH SCHWANN – PO Box 7640, AM Wehrahn 1000, 4000 Düsseldorf 1, *GERMANY*

LARGO RECORDS – Mommsenstr. 61, 50935 Köln, *GERMANY* (0221 431313)

LE CHANT DU MONDE – 108 Rue Vieille-du-Temple, 75003 Paris, *FRANCE* (1 4276 0997)

LEGATO CLASSICS – Lyric Distribution, 18 Madison Avenue, Hicksville, NY 1180,1 *USA* (516 932 5503)

LINN RECORDS – Floors Road, Waterfoot, Eaglesham, Glasgow G76 0EP (041-634 5111)

L'OISEAU-LYRE – 1 Sussex Place, Hammersmith, London W6 9XS (081-846 8515)

LYRITA – 99 Green Lane, Burnham, Slough, Bucks SL1 8EG (0628 604208)

MARCO POLO – 58 Pak Tai Street, 8th Floor, Kai It Bldg, Tokwawan, Kowloon, *HONG KONG* (852 760 7818)

MEMOIR CLASSICS – 15 Burwood Avenue, Eastcote, Pinner, Middlesex HA5 2RY

MERCURY – 1 Sussex Place, Hammersmith, London W6 9XS (081-846 8515)

MERIDIAN RECORDS – PO Box 317, Eltham, London SE9 4SF (081-857 3213)
MIRABILIS RECORDS – 5 King's Croft Gardens, Leeds LS17 6PB (0532 685123)
MOTETTE-URSINA – Neusser Weg 63a, 40474 Düsseldorf, *GERMANY* (211 434864)
MUSIC AND ARTS PROGRAMS OF AMERICA – PO Box 771, Berkeley, Claifornia CA94701, *USA* (415 525 4583)
MUSIC FOR PLEASURE – 1-3 Uxbridge Road, Hayes, Middlesex UB4 0SY (081-561 8722)
MUSICMASTERS – 1710 Highway 35, Ocean, NJ 07712-2910, *USA* (908 531 3375)
MUSICA SVECIAE – Knugl, Musikalaiska Akadamien, Blasieholmstorg 8, 111 Stockholm, *SWEDEN* (468 611 1870)
MUSIDISC (UK) – 32 Queensdale Road, London W11 4SB (071-602 1124)
NAXOS – 58 Pak Tai Street, 8th Floor, Kai It Bldg, Tokwawan, Kowloon, *HONG KONG* (852 760 7818)
NEW ALBION RECORDS – 584 Castro Street, Suite 515, San Francisco, CA94114, *USA* (415 621 5757)
NEW NOTE – Unit 2, Orpington Trading Estate, Sevenoaks Way, St Mary Cray, Orpington, Kent BR5 3SR (06898 77884)
NEW WORLD RECORDS – 701 Seventh Avenue, 7th Floor, New York, NY10036, *USA* (212 302 0460)
NEWPORT CLASSIC – 106, Putnam Street, Providence, Rhode Island RI02909, *USA* (401 421 8143)
NIMBUS RECORDS – Wyastone Leys, Monmouth, Gwent NP5 3SR (0600 890682)
NMC – Francis House, Francis Street, London SW1P 1DE (071-828 3432)
NORTHEASTERN RECORDS – PO Box 3589, Saxonville, MA 01701-0605, *USA* (508 820 4440)
NUOVA ERA RECORDS – Via Vincenzo Monti 38, 22060 Carugo (Como), *ITALY* (031 763 838)
ODE RECORD CO – 19 Earle Street, Parnell, Box 37-331, Auckland, *NEW ZEALAND* (9 790007)
OLYMPIA COMPACT DISCS – 31 Warple Way, London W3 0RX (081-743 6767)
ONDINE – Fredrikinkatu 77 A 2, 00100 Helsinki, *FINLAND* (0493 913)
OPERA RARA – 25 Compton Terrace, London N1 2UN (071-359 1777)
OPUS 111 – 37 Rue Blomet, 75015 Paris, *FRANCE* (1 4567 3344)
ORFEO INTERNATIONAL MUSIC – Augustenstraße 79, 80333 München, *GERMANY* (089 522031)
OTTAVO RECORDINGS – Nassau Dillenburgstraat 1, 2596 AB Den Haag, *THE NETHERLANDS* (7032 47557)
PARTRIGE RECORDINGS – Wassenaarseweg 135, 2596 CN Den Haag – *THE NETHERLANDS* (70 328 4144)
PAVANE RECORDS – 17 Rue Ravenstein, 1000 Bruxelles, *BELGIUM* (02 513 0965)
PAVILION RECORDS – Sparrows Green, Wadhurst, East Sussex TN5 6SJ (0892 783591)
PHILIPS CLASSICS – 1 Sussex Place, Hammersmith, London W6 9XS (081-846 8515)
PIANISSIMO – Ridgeway Road, Pyrford, Woking, Surrey GU22 8PR (0932 345371)
PICKWICK GROUP – The Waterfront, Elstree Road, Elstree, Hertfordshire WD6 3BE (081-207 6207)
PINNACLE – Electron House, Cray Avenue, St Mary Cray, Orpington, Kent BR5 3PN (06898 70622)
POLYGRAM CLASSICS AND JAZZ – 1 Sussex Place, Hammersmith, London W6 9XS (081-846 8515)
POLYGRAM RECORD OPERATIONS – PO Box 36, Clyde Works, Grove Road, Romford, Essex RM6 4QR (081-590 6044)
POLSKIE NAGRANIA – 6, Goleszowska Street, 01249 Warsaw, *POLAND* (373794)
PRIORY RECORDS – Unit 9b, Upper Wingbury Courtyard, Wingrave, Nr. Aylesbury, Bucks HP22 4LW (0296 682255)
PROUDSOUND – 61 Iffley Road, Oxford OX4 1EB (0865 723764)
QUANTUM AUDIO – PO Box 26, Kilmarnock, Ayrshire KA1 1BA (0563 71122)
RARE RECORDS – 13 Bank Square, Wilmslow, Cheshire SK9 1AN (0625 522017)
RCA – Bedford House, 69-79 Fulham High Street, London SW6 3JW (071-973 0011)
REFERENCE RECORDINGS – Box 7725X, San Francisco, California CA94107, *USA* (415 355 1892)
REM EDITIONS – 4 Rue Sainte Marie des Terreaux, 69001 Lyon, *FRANCE* (7830 0571)
RICERCAR – Burnaumont 73, G912 Anloy, Liban, *BELGIUM*
ROYAL OPERA HOUSE RECORDS – *see* Conifer Records
SAIN – Llandwrog, Caernarfon, Gwynedd LL54 5TG (0286 831111)
SAYDISC – Chipping Manor, The Chipping, Wotton-under-Edge, Glos GL12 7AD (0453 845036)
SELECT MUSIC AND VIDEO DISTRIBUTORS – 34a Holmethorpe Avenue, Holmethorpe Estate, Redhill, Surrey (0737 760020)
SILVA SCREEN – 261 Royal College Street, London NW1 9LU (071-284 0525)
SIMAX – Sandakerveien 76, PO Box 4379, Torshov, 0402 Oslo 4, *NORWAY* (271 0140)
SONY MUSIC ENTERTAINMENT – 1 Red Place, London W1Y 3RE (071-629 5555)

SONY MUSIC OPERATIONS – Rabans Lane, Aylesbury, Buckinghamshire HP19 3RT (0296 395151)

SUPRAPHON – Palackého 1, 11299 Praha 1, *CZECH REPUBLIC* (268141)

TARGET RECORDS – 23 Gardner Industrial Estate, Kent House Lane, Beckenham, Kent BR3 1QZ (081-778 4040)

TELARC INTERNATIONAL – 23307 Commerce Park Road, Cleveland, Ohio 44122, *USA* (216 464 2313)

TELDEC CLASSICS – 46 Kensington Court, London W8 5DP (071-938 5542)

TER CLASSICS – 107 Kentish Town Road, London NW1 8PB (071-485 9593)

TESTAMENT – 14 Tootswood Road, Bromley, Kent BR2 0PD (081-464 5947)

TIMPANI – 10 Rue Saint Marc, 75002 Paris, *FRANCE* (1 4039 9379)

TRIM RECORDS – 10 Dane Lane, Wilstead, Bedford MK45 3HT (0234 741152)

TRITTICO – 45 Argylle Road, London W8 7DA (071-937 2869)

TUXEDO MUSIC – Avenue des Baumettes 15, 1020 Renens, *SWITZERLAND* (021 635 9091)

UNICORN-KANCHANA RECORDS – PO Box 339, London W8 7TJ (071-727 3881)

VANGUARD CLASSICS – 27, West 72nd Street, New York, NY10023, *USA* (212 769 0360)

VICTORIA – Sandakerveien 76, PO Box 4379, Torshov, 0402 Oslo 4, *NORWAY* (271 0140)

VIRGIN CLASSICS – *see* EMI Records

WARNER CLASSICS (UK) – 46 Kensington Court, London W8 5DP (071-938 5542)

WERGO – Postfach 3640, 55026 Mainz, *GERMANY* (06131 246891)

Index

Index to Reviews

Collections

Films and Show Music